# THE OXFORD
## DICTIONARY
### OF THE
# WORLD

# THE OXFORD
# DICTIONARY
## OF THE
# WORLD

David Munro

OXFORD UNIVERSITY PRESS · 1995

Oxford University Press, Walton Street, Oxford OX2 6DP

Oxford New York

Athens Auckland Bangkok Bombay
Calcutta Cape Town Dar es Salaam Delhi
Florence Hong Kong Istanbul Karachi
Kuala Lumpur Madras Madrid Melbourne
Mexico City Nairobi Paris Singapore
Taipei Tokyo Toronto

and associated companies in
Berlin Ibadan

Oxford is a trade mark of Oxford University Press

Published in the United States by
Oxford University Press Inc., New York

British Library Cataloguing in Publication Data
Data available

Library of Congress Cataloging in Publication Data
The Oxford dictionary of the world / [edited by] David Munro.
p.    cm.
ISBN 0–19–866184–3 (alk. paper)
1. Gazetteers.    I. Munro, David.
G103.5.094    1995
910.3—dc20       95–22546 CIP
ISBN 0–19–866184–3

1  3  5  7  9  10  8  6  4  2

Typeset by Alliance, Pondicherry, India

Printed in Great Britain
on acid-free paper by
The Bath Press, Avon

# CONTENTS

# PREFACE

In his preface to *The Imperial Gazetteer,* first published in 1855, the Scottish publisher W. G. Blackie suggested that 'next to a good dictionary, the most generally useful book is a good gazetteer'. Nearly a century and a half later that assertion still holds true. Day by day the modern world is changing and the need for such a descriptive gazetteer or topographical dictionary is just as great as it was during the golden age of exploration. In recent years we have seen both history and geography turned on its head. The disintegration of the Soviet Union, the collapse of communism in Eastern Europe, the reunification of Germany and, in the five years between the end of 1988 and the beginning of 1994, an increase in the total number of member states of the United Nations from 159 to 184. Following hard on the heels of these momentous events place-names have changed, new styles of government have emerged, and old grievances have surfaced to create new flashpoints across the face of the globe.

This dictionary captures many of the changes that have taken place throughout the world in recent years. In a simple A to Z format it comprises topographical descriptions of places in every country of the world, descriptions of peoples, languages, and religions, and definitions of selected geographical and environmental terms. A core text of 3,000 entries was drawn from *The Oxford English Reference Dictionary*, each entry being amended, updated, and expanded where appropriate. The text was further supplemented by the addition of 7,000 new entries and reference data relating to some 5,000 locations in tables and appendices. Topographical descriptions and definitions are presented in a straightforward readable style with the minimum of symbols and abbreviations, and a number of maps are included as an aid to spatial reference. The appendices offer useful information that is more easily presented in a tabulated form, listing, for example, member states of the United Nations, abbreviations for international organizations, and major rivers, lakes, mountains, islands, deserts, and urban areas of the world.

While every effort has been made to ensure the accuracy of the information contained in this volume the reader should appreciate the dependence on a wide range of sources and the inevitable difficulty in obtaining reliable data from certain parts of the world. Wherever possible, information has been drawn from up-to-date sources throughout the world in the form of statistical abstracts, official yearbooks, trade directories, guide books, and tourist literature.

Deciding which words and places to include in a reference work of this kind is never easy. Above and beyond the essential description of countries, capitals, leading cities, and major physical features of the world there is inevitably a degree of subjectivity in making the selection. Even deciding what constitutes a major city is not straightforward. The final list is shaped not just by the size of the book, but also by the sources of information available to the editor, trends in current affairs, the global pattern of population distribution, and the geographical distribution of those who are likely to use this title as a reference. For example, it is not possible to include every city in the world over a certain population. While cities in the United States with more than 50,000 inhabitants all have entries, that population cut-off point applied worldwide would lead to the inclusion of only twenty-one urban centres in Australia which, in addition to places of special interest, is in fact represented in this volume by some seventy-five towns and cities with a population greater than 13,800 in the 1991 Census. The same book compiled in five or ten years time might, therefore, include a completely different list of entries.

Throughout the work the aim has been to present as much information as possible in a clear, concise, and balanced style so as to offer the maximum help and interest to the reader.

D.M.

*April 1995*

# GUIDE TO USE OF THE DICTIONARY

## 1. *Use of Conventions*

1.1 A great deal of the information given in the dictionary entries is self explanatory but with respect to place-names a number of conventions has been used.

1.1.1 The names of countries are given in the conventional English short form recommended for use by the UK Diplomatic Service and are designed to reflect current English usage. Burma, Ivory Coast, and Burkina are therefore used in preference to Myanmar, Côte d'Ivoire, and Burkina Faso. Variant names and long-form official names are also provided in the main entry for each country.

1.1.2 Except where there is a widely recognized and conventional English form, the names of other topographical features are given in a form generally recommended by the US Board on Geographic Names or the Permanent Committee on Geographical Names for British Official Use. The most commonly used variant forms are cross-referenced. Cologne, Florence, and Lisbon are therefore used as headwords in preference to Firenze, Köln, and Lisboa, which are cross-referenced.

1.1.3 The Pin-yin system of romanization is used in the spelling of Chinese names.

1.1.4 Where a place-name incorporates a definite article or a generic term, the specific part usually comes first in the headword, i.e. Everglades, the and Everest, Mount. Exceptions to this include place-names where the definite article or generic term are in a language other than English and where the definite article preceding the specific part is a more widely recognizable form, i.e. Los Angeles, El Alamein.

## 2. *Headwords*

2.1 The headword is printed in bold roman type.

2.2 Pronunciation and variant forms are given between the headword and the description or definition. Pronunciation of variants is given where it is sufficiently different from the headword.

2.3 Headwords with the same name are usually listed in the alphabetical order of the country in which they are located, i.e. Victoria, Australia, precedes Victoria, Canada.

2.4 Place-names with identical spelling within the same country or words that are different but spelt the same way (homographs) are distinguished by superior numerals.

2.5 Derivatives are to be found in italics at the end of entries.

## 3. *Pronunciation*

3.1 Guidance on pronunciation follows the system of the International Phonetic Alphabet (IPA).

3.2 The symbols used, with their values, are as follows:

3.2.1 *Consonants*:

*b, d, f, h, k, l, m, n, p, r, s, t, v, w*, and *z* have their usual English values. Other symbols are used as follows:

| | | | |
|---|---|---|---|
| g | get | θ | *thin* |
| tʃ | *chip* | ð | *this* |
| dʒ | *jar* | ʃ | *she* |
| x | lo*ch* | ʒ | de*cision* |
| ŋ | ri*ng* | j | *yes* |

3.2.2 *Vowels*:

| | | | |
|---|---|---|---|
| æ | *cat* | aɪ | *my* |
| ɑː | *arm* | ɒ | *hot* |
| eɪ | *day* | ɔː | *saw* |
| eə | *hair* | ɔɪ | *boy* |
| e | *bed* | əʊ | *no* |
| ə | *ago* | ʌ | *run* |
| əː | *her* | ʊ | *put* |
| iː | *see* | uː | *too* |
| ɪə | *near* | ʊə | *poor* |
| ɪ | *sit* | aʊ | *how* |

3.2.3.1 ə signifies the indeterminate sound as in gard*e*n, carn*a*l, and rhyth*m*.

3.2.3.2 r at the end of a word indicates an *r* that is sounded when a word beginning with a vowel follows, as in *clutter up* and *an acre of land*.

3.2.4 The mark ~ indicates a nasalized sound, as in the following sounds:

| | |
|---|---|
| ɛ̃ | t*i*mbre |
| ɑ̃ | *é*lan |
| ɔ̃ | gar*ç*on |
| œ̃ | *feu* (French) |

3.2.5 The main or primary stress of the word is shown by ' preceding the relevant syllable; any secondary stress in words of three or more syllables is shown by , preceding the relevant syllable.

# ABBREVIATIONS

| | |
|---|---|
| abbr. | abbreviation |
| adj. | adjective |
| b. | born |
| c. | century |
| *c.* | *circa* |
| d. | died |
| ft. | feet |
| km. | kilometres |
| m. | metres |
| Mt. | Mount |
| n. | noun |
| pl. | plural |
| pop. | population |
| R. | River |
| sq. km. | square kilometres |
| sq. miles | square miles |
| UK | United Kingdom |
| US or USA | United States of America |

# THE OXFORD
# DICTIONARY
# OF THE
# WORLD

# A*a*

**Aa** /ɑː/ **1.** a river of northern France that rises in the Artois Hills of Pas-de-Calais, flows north-east, then turns north-west following the Franco-Belgian frontier to the North Sea **2.** a small river that rises north of the Mittelland Canal in the German state of Lower Saxony and flows west towards the Ems. **3.** a river that flows westwards across the German state of North Rhine-Westphalia before meeting the River Oude on the German-Dutch frontier. **4.** the Aa of Weerys, a river in Brabant that rises north-east of the Belgian city of Antwerp and flows north into the Netherlands where it is joined by the Turfvaart on the outskirts of Breda. **5.** several rivers in Switzerland including one in Schwyz canton which flows into Lake Zurich (Zürichsee), a tributary of the Aar in Aargau canton, the Sarner Aa and the Engeberger Aa, the last two of which flow into Lake Lucerne (Vierwaldstätter See).

**Aabenraa** /ˈɔːbənˌrɔː/ (also **Åbenrå**) a port and resort town in south-east Jutland, Denmark; pop. (1990) 21,460. Situated at the head of the Aabenraa Fjord, which is an inlet of the Little Belt strait, Aabenraa is the capital of Sønderjylland district. The town has a mercantile history that dates back to 1335, the year it first received trading rights. From 1864 to 1920 it was held by Prussia.

**Aachen** /ˈɑːxən/ (French **Aix-la-Chapelle** /ˌeɪkslæʃæˈpel/) an industrial city and spa in the state of North Rhine-Westphalia, western Germany. Close to the Belgian and Dutch borders, it is the most westerly city in Germany; pop. (1991) 244,440. The Springs of Grannus (Latin *Aquae Granni*) were named after the Celtic god of healing and later used by the Romans as public baths. The cathedral was built by Charlemagne who was born and buried in Aachen. From 946 (Otto I) to 1531 (Ferdinand I) monarchs of the Holy Roman Empire were crowned in Aachen which came to be known as the 'watering-place of kings'.

**Aalborg** /ˈɔːlbɔːg/ (also **Ålborg**) an industrial city and port in north Jutland, Denmark; pop. (1990) 155,000. Situated on the Limfjord, which links the Kattegat with the North Sea, Aalborg is the capital of Nordjylland district and the country's leading centre of trade with Greenland. Shipbuilding and the production of aquavit are important industries.

**Aalen** /ˈɑːlən/ an industrial city on the River Kocher, in the northern foothills of the Swabian Alps, Baden-Württemberg, Germany; pop. (1983) 62,800. Noted for its 16th–18th c. half-timbered houses and a museum featuring the occupation of Germany by the Romans, Aalen was united with the municipality of Wasseralfingen in 1975. The city gives its name to the Aalen Stage, a period of geological time during the Middle Jurassic System.

**Aalesund** /ˈɔːləˌsʊn/ (also **Ålesund**) a commercial seaport and fishing town situated on several islands in Møre og Romsdal county, west Norway; pop. (1991) 35,900. Established in 1848, the town was destroyed by fire in 1904 but quickly rebuilt in an architectural style that blended Art Nouveau with Norwegian National Romanticism. The 8-km.-long tunnels that link offshore islands with Aalesund are the longest submarine tunnels in Scandinavia.

**Aalsmeer** /ˈɑːlsmiːr/ a town in North Holland province, west-central Netherlands, on the Westeinder Plassen lake, south-west of Amsterdam; pop. (1991) 22,200. Aalsmeer has the largest flower-auction market in the world and many nurseries.

**Aalst** /ˈɑːlst/ (French **Alost** /æˈlɒst/) a commercial and industrial city on the River Dender in East Flanders, Belgium, 22 km. (14 miles) north-west of Brussels; pop. (1991) 76,380. Each year before Lent, Carnival is celebrated with the traditional 'throwing of the onions' from the belfry of the former town hall which is the oldest of its kind in Belgium. A monument in front of the town hall commemorates Belgium's first printer, Dirk Martens, born here in 1450. Its industries include textiles and clothing.

**Äänekoski** /ˌɑːnəˈkɒskɪ/ a town in Keski-Suomi province, south-central Finland; pop. (1990) 11,850. Founded in 1932, the town is a centre for the manufacture of paper, chemicals, and timber products.

**Aarau** /ˈɑːraʊ/ the capital of the canton of Aargau in north Switzerland; situated on the River Aare and at the foot of the Jura Mts., 37 km. (23 miles) west of Zurich; pop. (1990) 15,880.

**Aare** /ˈɑːrə/ (French **Aar** /ˈɑːr/) a tributary of the Rhine forming the largest river entirely within Switzerland. Rising in the Bernese Alps, the upper Aare passes through Lake Grimsel and flows generally north and west for a distance of 295 km. (184 miles) before meeting the Rhine opposite the German town of Waldshut.

**Aargau** /ˈɑːrgaʊ/ (French **Argovie** /ˌɑːrgəˈviː/) a German-speaking canton of north Switzerland which joined the Swiss Confederation in 1803; area 1,405 sq. km. (543 sq. miles); pop. (1990) 490,410; capital, Aarau. It is one of the most fertile agricultural regions of Switzerland.

**Aarhus** /'ɔːrhuːs/ (also **Århus**) the capital of Århus county, east Jutland, Denmark, on Aarhus Bay, an arm of the Kattegat; pop. (1990) 261,440. Aarhus is the second-largest city in Denmark. It is a cultural centre with a cathedral, museums, a concert hall, and a university founded in 1934. Its industries include clothing, paper, and foodstuffs.

**Aarlen** see ARLON.

**Aba** /ɑːˈbɑː/ an industrial city in Imo state, southern Nigeria, north-east of Port Harcourt, developed as an administrative centre by the British in the early 20th c.; pop. (1983) 216,000. The Imo River gas field lies to the south of the city. Soap, oil palm, textiles, and beer are produced.

**Abaco Islands** /'æbəˌkəʊ/, **the** (also **Abacos**) a boomerang-shaped chain of islands and coral cays stretching over 210 km. (130 miles) of the Little Bahama Bank in the northern Bahamas; area 1,681 sq. km. (649 sq. miles); pop. (1990) 10,060. The islands are noted for their native pine trees and the building of Abaco pine boats.
**Abaconian** *adj. & n.*

**Abadan** /ˌæbəˈdɑːn/ a city on an island of the same name on the Shatt al-Arab waterway in western Iran; pop. (1986) 308,000. It developed from a small village after the discovery of oil in 1908 and is today a major port and oil-refining centre with petrochemical industries.

**Abakan** /ˌæbəˈkɑːn/ the capital of the autonomous Russian republic of Khakassia in west Siberia; pop. (1989) 154,000. An industrial centre at the confluence of the Abakan and Yenisey rivers, Abakan was known as Ustabakanskoye until 1931. It has been the western terminus of the southern Siberian railway since 1960. It has numerous light industries.

**Abancay** /ˌæbənˈkaɪ/ the capital of Apurimac department in the Andes of southern Peru, on the east bank of the Marino River, 480 km. (300 miles) south-east of Lima; pop. (1990) 29,200.

**Abbasid** /əˈbæsɪd/ a dynasty of caliphs ruling in Baghdad 750–1258, claiming descent from Abbas, uncle of the prophet Muhammad. Some were outstanding patrons of culture such as Mamun (813–33). Their power ended with the fall of Baghdad to the Tartars in 1258.

**Abbé** /æˈbeɪ/, **Lake** a lake in the Afar Depression, straddling the frontier between Ethiopia and Djibouti. It is noted for its large populations of flamingos, ibises, and pelicans.

**Abbeville** /'æbvɪl/ an industrial and commercial town in Picardy, northern France; pop. (1990) 24,590. Situated in the Somme valley to the north-east of Amiens, Abbeville was an important British Army headquarters during World War I. The town

gives its name to the earliest lower palaeolithic flint hand-axe industries in Europe which date from c. 500,000 BC. Its industries include sugar refining, brewing, and textiles.
**Abbevillian** *adj. & n.*

**Abbey Craig** /'æbɪ kreɪg/ a small hill to the east of Stirling in central Scotland, crowned by the 67-m. (220-ft.) high Wallace Monument which was built in 1869 to commemorate the Scottish patriot Sir William Wallace (c. 1274–1305).

**Abbey Theatre** a theatre in Abbey Street, Dublin, first opened in 1904, staging chiefly Irish plays. W. B. Yeats was associated with its foundation. In 1925 it became the first state-subsidized theatre in the English-speaking world.

**Abbotsford** /'æbətsˌfərd/ a gothic-style mansion-house on the south bank of the River Tweed near Melrose in the Borders Region of Scotland, built by the novelist Sir Walter Scott who lived there from 1812 until his death in 1832. Originally known as Clartyhole, the property was renamed by Scott.

**Abbot's Langley** a small town to the south-west of St. Alban's in Hertfordshire, England. Bedmond, on the outskirts of the town, was the birthplace of Nicholas Breakspear, the only Englishman to become a Pope (Adrian IV, 1154–9).

**Abbottabad** /'æbətæˌbæd/ a city in the North-West Frontier province of Pakistan, situated 56 km. (35 miles) north of Islamabad at an altitude of 1,255 m. (4,117 ft.) in the foothills of the Himalayas; pop. (1981) 66,000. Named after a British Army officer, Abbottabad became a popular hill resort after it was founded in 1853.

**ABC Islands** an acronym for the Dutch islands of Aruba, Bonaire, and Curaçao which lie in the Caribbean Sea near the northern coast of Venezuela.

**ABCD Cities** the collective name given to the industrial cities of Santo André, São Bernardo do Campo, São Caetano, and Diadema which surround São Paulo in southern Brazil.

**Abéché** /ˌæbeɪˈʃeɪ/ (also **Abeshr**) the capital city of Ouaddaï préfecture, eastern Chad; pop. (1993) 187,760. Situated on the south-western edge of the Massif Maraoné in semidesert, Abéché was the capital of the Muslim Ouaddaï empire and a centre of the Sahelian slave-trade from the 17th century until the arrival of the French in 1911. Frequented by nomad caravans, its craftsmen produce camel-hair blankets.

**Åbenrå** see AABENRAA.

**Abeokuta** /ˌæbiːˈəʊkətə/ the capital of Ogun State, south-west Nigeria, founded in the 1830s as a refuge of the Egba people (remnants of the Oyo empire), from slave-traders, and from Dahomey raiders in search of oil-palm; pop. (1983) 308,800. Coming under British protection in 1895, Abeokuta was the capital of the Egba until the colony of Nigeria was established in 1914. Once a defensive location, the Olumo Rock is now an important local shrine. Citrus fruit, bananas, and cacao are produced locally.

**Aberbrothock** /ˌæbəˈbrɒθək/ an early form of ARBROATH, a seaport on the east coast of Scotland.

**Aberconwy** /ˌæbəˈkɒnwɪ/ a district of Gwynedd, north-west Wales, extending from the Penmaenmawr headland southwards along the River Conwy to Lake Conwy; area 606 sq. km. (234 sq. miles); pop. (1991) 54,100.

**Aberdare** /ˌæbəˈdeə(r)/ an industrial town in Mid Glamorgan, south Wales; pop. (1981) 31,680.

**Aberdare Mountains** /ˌæbəˈdeə(r)/ a range of mountains forming a national park to the north of Nairobi, west Kenya. Rising to 3,994 m. (13,104 ft.), the highest peak is Lesatima.

**Aberdeen** /ˌæbəˈdiːn/ the principal seaport of north-east Scotland, situated between the rivers Dee (south) and Don (north); pop. (1991) 201,100. Known to the Romans as Devena, or the 'town of the two waters', it is the third-largest city in Scotland, a cultural centre, fishing port, and a centre of the offshore North Sea oil industry. In modern times Aberdeen has been named the 'Granite City' after its fine grey granite buildings. The city received its charter from William the Lion in 1179. In 1860 King's College (founded in 1494) united with Marischal College (founded by the Earl Marischal of Scotland in 1593) to form the modern University of Aberdeen. The Robert Gordon University (formerly the Robert Gordon Institute of Technology) was established in 1992. Historic buildings also include St. Machar's Cathedral, Robert Gordon's College, Provost Skene's House (the oldest domestic dwelling house in Aberdeen). In the 14th century the poet and historian John Barbour was Archdeacon of Aberdeen and in the early 16th century Hector Boece the Scottish historian was the first principal of King's College. The first ten years of the poet Byron's life were spent in the city.
**Aberdonian** adj. & n.

**Aberdeenshire** /ˌæbəˈdiːnʃɪə(r)/ a former county of north-east Scotland, from 1975 to 1996 part of the larger Grampian Region.

**Aberfan** /ˌæbəˈvæn/ a village in Mid Glamorgan, south Wales, on the River Taff near Merthyr Tydfil, where, in 1966, a slag-heap collapsed and mining waste overwhelmed houses and a school, killing 28 adults and 116 children.

**Aberfoyle** /ˌæbəˈfɔɪl/ a resort village in the Trossachs area of central Scotland, immortalized by Sir Walter Scott in his novel *Rob Roy*.

**Abergavenny** /ˌæbəgəˈvenɪ/ (Welsh **Y Fenni**, anc. **Gobannium**) a town in Gwent, south-east Wales, at the confluence of the Usk and Gavenny rivers; pop. (1981) 14,400. The site of a Roman fortress and a Norman castle.

**Abergele** /ˌæbəˈgelɪ/ a resort town on the coast of Clwyd, north-east Wales; pop. (1981) 12,600. There are memorials to the victims of the *Ocean Monarch* shipwreck (1848) and the Irish mail-train disaster (1868).

**Aberystwyth** /ˌæbəˈrɪstwɪθ/ a resort town on Cardigan Bay, Dyfed, west Wales, at the mouth of the Ystwyth and Rheidol rivers; pop. (1981) 11,170. The town, which was built around a fortress of Edward I, is home to a University College (founded in 1872) and the National Library of Wales.

**Abha** /ˈæbhə/ the capital of the Southern Province of south-west Saudi Arabia; pop. (est. 1986) 155,400. Built at the junction of caravan routes, it is the centre of an agricultural region growing wheat, sorghum, rice, and dates.

**Abia** /æbˈiːə/ a state in south-eastern Nigeria, created in 1991 from part of the state of Imo; pop. (1991) 2,297,980; capital, Umuahia.

**Abidjan** /ˌæbɪˈdʒɑːn/ the former capital, commercial centre, and chief port of the Ivory Coast, on the Ebrié Lagoon; pop. (1986) 2,534,000. It is the largest port in West Africa and the principal transit point for goods to and from the West African Sahel. Settled by the French at the end of the 19th century, Abidjan first owed its development to the building of the Ocean–Niger railway line (begun in 1903). In the 1920s the city became a seaport with the opening of the Vridi Canal that links the Ebrié Lagoon to the Gulf of Guinea, and in 1935 Abidjan became the administrative centre of the French Ivory Coast. It has many light industries including sawmilling, textiles, and food processing.

**Abilene** /ˈæbəliːn/ **1.** a farming town on the Smoky Hill River, east-central Kansas, founded in the 1860s as a cattle transportation railhead; pop. (1990) 6,240. 'Wild Bill' Hickok (1837–76) was marshal of Abilene and President Eisenhower (1890–1969), who lived in Abilene as a boy, is buried there. **2.** a city in central Texas at the end of the Old Chisholm Trail; pop. (1990) 106,650. Founded in 1881 as a major cattle-shipping centre and named after Abilene in Kansas, the city's economy is based on petroleum and agriculture. Abilene is home to the Abilene Christian University, Hardin-Simmons University, and McMurry College.

**Abingdon** /ˈæbɪŋˌdən/ a market town on the River Thames, Oxfordshire, south-central England. There are the remains of a Benedictine abbey founded in the 7th c. and other historic buildings; pop. (1981) 22,690.

**Abitibi** /ˌæbəˈtɪbiː/, **Lake** a lake straddling the border between the Canadian provinces of Ontario and Quebec; area 906 sq. km. (350 sq. miles). The Abitibi River flows north from the lake to meet the Moose River near James Bay.

**Abkhazia** /æbˈkɑːzɪə/ a territory on the Black Sea coast of the Republic of Georgia; area 8,600 sq. km. (3,320 sq. miles); pop. (1990) 537,500. Its capital is the resort of Sukhumi. Identified with the ancient province of Colchis, the region was captured by the Romans, Byzantines, Arabs, and Ottoman Turks before coming under Russian protection in 1810. Under Russian occupation, large numbers of Muslim Abkhazis moved to Turkish territory. In 1921 the region was constituted as the Abkhazian Autonomous Soviet Socialist Republic and in 1992, following the breakup of the former Soviet Union, the local parliament unilaterally declared itself an independent state, launching the region into armed conflict with the government of Georgia. In 1993 Abkhazian forces expelled the Georgian National Army from the self-declared republic of Abkhazia and took the city of Sukhumi. Tobacco, tea, and fruit are the chief crops grown between the coast and the thickly forested mountains.
**Abkhazian** or **Abkhazi** adj. & n.

**Abnaki** /æbˈnɑkɪ/ (also **Abneki** or **Wabunaki**) a North American Algonquian Indian tribe of New England which retreated into Canada after encounters with the British in 1724–5 but had returned to settle in Maine by 1890. In 1985 the Maine reservation population was 2,918.

**Åbo** /ˈəʊbuː/ the Swedish name for the city of TURKU in Finland.

**Abomey** /æbəˈmeɪ, æˈbəʊmiː/ a trading town in the province of Zou, southern Benin; pop. (1982) 54,420. Abomey was the capital of the former kingdom of Dahomey which became a French protectorate in 1892. The town was rebuilt by the French and linked by rail with the coast in 1905. The restored palaces of King Ghezo and King Glele house artefacts from the old Dahomey kingdom.

**aborigine** /ˌæbəˈrɪdʒɪnɪ/ a member of a race of people or a natural phenomenon inhabiting or existing in a land from the earliest times or from before the arrival of colonists.
**aboriginal** adj. & n.

**Aborigines** the aboriginal inhabitants of Australia comprising several physically distinct groups of dark-skinned hunter-gatherers who arrived in prehistoric times and brought with them the dingo. Before the arrival of Europeans they were scattered through the whole continent, including Tasmania. In 1788 the population was estimated to stand at around 250,000–300,000 Aborigines who were divided into more than 500 linguistic groups. Today nearly 1.5 per cent of the people of Australia are Aborigine, the population (1986) totalling 227,645. Although over 65 per cent now live in towns and cities, the cultural heritage of the Aborigines has been protected in recent years by changes in Australian federal and state laws that have established land rights, community development programmes, and educational assistance.

**Aboukir Bay** /ˌæbuːˈkɪr/ (also **Abukir** or **Abu Qir**) a bay on the Mediterranean coast of Egypt, lying between Alexandria and the Rosetta mouth of the Nile. Nelson defeated the French fleet under Brueys at the Battle of the Nile which was fought in the bay on 1–2 August 1798. Sir Ralph Abercromby's expedition landed near the village of Aboukir and defeated the French in 1801.

**Abraham, Plains of** SEE PLAINS OF ABRAHAM.

**Abruzzi** /əˈbrʊtsɪ/ a mountainous region on the Adriatic coast of east-central Italy, between the Tronto and Trigno rivers; area 10,795 sq. km. (4,168 sq. miles); pop. (1990) 1,272,390; capital, L'Aquila. The Abruzzi Apennines include the highest peaks in the Italian peninsula: Gran Sasso d'Italia (2,912 m., 9,553 ft.), the Maiella (2,793 m., 9,163 ft.), and Mt. Laga (2,458 m., 8,064 ft.). Abruzzi National Park, which extends over 400 sq. km. (155 sq. miles) in the Upper Sangro Valley, was established in 1922 to protect beech forests which are home to the wolf, bear, chamois, and otter.

**Abu Dhabi** /ˌæbuː ˈdɑːbɪ/ **1.** the largest of the seven member-states of the United Arab Emirates, lying to the south of Dubai, between the Sultanate of Oman and the Gulf coast; area 67,600 sq. km. (26,101 sq. miles); pop. (1985) 670,125. Although most of the emirate comprises desert or *sabkhah* salt flats, it has two main centres of population at Abu Dhabi on the coast and Al Ain on the frontier with Oman. The economy is largely based on the production of oil and on petrochemical industries which are located on Das Island and at the Ruwais industrial area west of the city of Abu Dhabi. The international airport is an important stopping-off point on long-haul air flights from Europe to Australia and the Far East. Port Zayed is the emirate's leading container port. The sheikdom of Abu Dhabi became a British Protectorate in 1892 and joined the federation of the United Arab Emirates in 1971. Oil was discovered in the early 1960s. **2.** its capital city (pop. 242,975), which is also the federal capital of the United Arab Emirates. It is one of the region's most modern cities with little left of its old town.

**Abuja** /əˈbuːdʒə/ a newly built city at the geographical centre of Nigeria, designated in 1982 to replace Lagos as the national capital; pop. (1991) 378,670. Designed by Kenzo Tange, the city is modelled on Milton Keynes in England. In 1991 a treaty establishing the African Economic Community was signed in Abuja.

**Abu** /ˈæbuː/, **Mount 1.** a mountain rising to a height of 1,722 m. (5,650 ft.) in the state of Rajasthan, north-west India, near the frontier with Gujarat. Mt. Abu is a celebrated place of pilgrimage for Jains. **2.** a hill station on the same mountain at an altitude of 1,200 m. (3,937 ft.), offering a retreat from the plains during the hot season. The five Dilwara temples at Mt. Abu, built in the 11th and 12th centuries, are described as the finest examples of Jain architecture in India.

**Abukir Bay** SEE ABOUKIR BAY.

**Abu Musa** /ˌæbuː ˈmuːsə/ a small island in the Persian Gulf formerly held by the Emirate of Sharjah but occupied by Iranian troops since November 1971, two days prior to the inauguration of the United Arab Emirates. Iran's claim over Abu Musa is based on its former occupation of the island until ejected by the British at the end of the 19th c. In the 1960s, prior to British withdrawal from the region, the disputed status of Abu Musa and the Tunb Islands complicated negotiations over the demarcation of the continental shelf boundary between Iran and the Sheikdoms.

**Abu Simbel** /ˌæbuː ˈsɪmb(ə)l/ (also **Ipsambul**) a former village in southern Egypt, site of two rock-cut temples built by Rameses II (13th c. BC), a monument to the greatest of the pharaohs and a constant reminder to possibly restive Nubian tribes of Egypt's might. The great temple, with its façade (31 m., 103 ft., high) bearing four colossal seated statues of Rameses, faces due east, and is dedicated to Amun-Ra and other principal state gods of the period; the small temple is dedicated to Hathor and Nefertiti, first wife of Rameses. In 1963 an archaeological salvage operation was begun, comparable in scale to the original construction of the temples, in which engineers sawed up the monument and carried it up the hillside to be rebuilt, with its original orientation, well above the rising waters of Lake Nasser, whose level was affected by the building of the High Dam at Aswan.

**Abydos** /əˈbaɪdəs/ **1.** a town of ancient Mysia in Asia Minor, situated on a hill overlooking the Dardanelles, north-east of the modern Turkish city of Çanakkale. Abydos was the scene of the story of Hero and Leander and the place where the Persian King Xerxes constructed his bridge of boats over the Hellespont on his expedition against the Greeks in 480 BC. The poet Byron repeated Leander's epic swim from Abydos across the strait to Sestos in 1810. **2.** a town in ancient Egypt and burial place of the first pharaohs, situated on the left bank of the Nile near modern El Balyana. In mythology, it was here that the head of Osiris was buried after he was murdered by his brother Seth. Ruins of ancient temples on the site include the Temple of Osiris, the Temples of Rameses I and II, and the Cenotaph Temple of Set I.

**abyssal zone** /əˈbɪs(ə)l/ the deepest region of the oceans, generally considered to fall below depths of 1,000 m. (3,300 ft.) or, in geological terms, an area of igneous rock which has consolidated at a great depth.

**Abyssinia** /ˌæbɪˈsɪnɪə/ a former name of ETHIOPIA.
**Abyssinian** adj. & n.

**Acadia** /əˈkeɪdɪə/ (French **Acadie** /ˈækədiː/) a name given to Nova Scotia in Canada prior to the establishment of the first French settlement there in 1604. The name, from which the term Cajun derives, was later applied to the territory between the St. Lawrence River and the Atlantic Ocean that now forms the south-east part of Quebec, east Maine, New Brunswick, Nova Scotia, and Prince Edward Island. Encroached upon by British colonists, much of Acadia was ceded to Britain by the Treaty of Utrecht in 1713. Some of its French inhabitants withdrew to French territory in the following year, and during the French Indian War (1754–63) three-quarters of the remaining population of 10,000 French settlers, who were considered to be a threat to the British position, were forcibly resettled in other parts of North America as far apart as Maine and Louisiana. In 1764, a year after all of Acadia was ceded to Britain, Acadians were once more given the right to own land in Nova Scotia, New Brunswick, and Prince Edward Island. The present-day Acadian proportion of the population in these Canadian provinces is 10.2, 32, and 13.7 per cent respectively. The distinctiveness of the Acadian or Cajun culture is emphasized by the existence of institutions such as the Centre d'Études Acadiennes at the Université de Moncton in New Brunswick.
**Acadian** adj. & n.

**Acadian Coast** a region of south Louisiana to the west of the lower Mississippi River, settled by French farmers deported from Acadia in the 1750s.

**Acajutla** /ˌɑːkəˈhuːtlə/ an industrial seaport on the coast of Sonsonate department, western El Salvador. Rebuilt to accommodate enlarged dock facilities in the late 1960s, Acajutla is El Salvador's leading Pacific port, exporting coffee and sugar.

**Acapulco** /ˌækəˈpʊlkəʊ/ (fully **Acapulco de Juárez**) a port and holiday resort in the south of Mexico, on the Pacific coast; pop. (1990) 592,290. Established in 1530, Acapulco was the only Mexican port authorized to receive Spanish trading galleons from the Orient. When Mexico severed its trade links with Spain in 1821 Acapulco declined as a port city and remained isolated until linked to Mexico City by a road built in 1927.

**Acarnania** /ˌækərˈneɪmɪːə/ (also **Akarnania**) **1.** a region of ancient Greece lying between the Achelous River and the Ionian Sea. **2.** an area of modern Greece now united with Aetolia to form a department in the region of Central Greece and Euboea; area 5,461 sq. km. (2,109 sq. miles); pop. (1991) 230,690; capital, Missolonghi.

**Acatenango** /ˌækətəˈnæŋgəʊ/ a volcanic peak in the highlands of Guatemala, rising to 3,960 m. (12,992 ft.) south-west of Guatemala City. It is the highest active volcano in Central America.

**Accra** /əˈkrɑː/ the capital of Ghana, a port on the Gulf of Guinea; pop. (1984) 867,450. Greater Accra, which extends over an area of 2,030 sq. km. (784 sq miles), has a population of 1,431,100. Originally the capital of the Ga kingdom, the city developed around three trading posts at Jamestown, Crèvecœur, and Christianborg established respectively by Britain, France, and Denmark in the 17th century. In 1850 and 1871 the French and Danish posts were ceded to Britain and in 1875 it became the capital of the Gold Coast Colony. Accra grew more rapidly after the building of a railway to Kumasi at the centre of the wealthy Ashanti region in 1923. It is an administrative, commercial, and cultural centre with numerous light industries including timber and plywood, textiles, and chemicals.

**Accrington** /'ækrɪŋtən/ a textile-manufacturing and brick-making town in Lancashire, northwest England; pop. (1981) 36,500. It was the birthplace of the composer Harrison Birtwhistle.

**acculturation** the process of adapting to or adopting a different culture.

**Aceh** /'ɑːtʃeɪ/ (also **Atjeh** or **Achin** /ɑːˈtʃiːn/) a special region of Indonesia, comprising the northern tip of the island of Sumatra; area 55,392 sq. km. (21,395 sq. miles); pop. (1980) 2,611,270; capital, Banda Aceh. A former Islamic sultanate penetrated by the Dutch and British East India companies between 1599 and 1602, Aceh lost its independence in 1873 but was never fully pacified by either country. The fiercely independent Acehnese (of whom there are about 2 million) comprise the Galos and Alas hill people of early Malayan stock as well as lowland coastal ethnic groups. Having struggled for nearly half a century to gain autonomy from Dutch colonial rule, Aceh is now treated as a politically sensitive special region of Indonesia where Islamic law functions. Since independence there have been sporadic uprisings by separatist movements against the central government.
**Acehnese** or **Achinese** adj. & n.

**Achaea** /əˈkiːə/ (also **Achaia**, Greek **Akhaïa**) **1.** a region of ancient Greece on the north coast of the Peloponnese, first achieving political unity with the formation of the Achaean League of 12 cities which allied itself with Athens against Sparta. Powerful after the death of Alexander the Great, the League was eventually dissolved by the Romans who occupied Achaea as an imperial province between 146 BC and the 4th century AD. **2.** a department of the Peloponnese region of south-west Greece; area 3,271 sq. km. (1,263 sq. miles); pop. (1991) 297,320; capital, Patras.
**Achaean** adj. & n.

**Achagua** /æˈtʃɑːgwə/ a tribe of South American Indians occupying the tropical forests of Venezuela and eastern Colombia and speaking the language of the Maipurean Arawakan ethnolinguistic group.

**Achelous** /ˌækəˈluəs/ (Greek **Akhelóos**, anc. **Aspropotamos**) the second-longest river in Greece. Rising in the Pindus Mountains, it flows south for 219 km. (137 miles) to meet the Ionian

Sea near the entrance to the Gulf of Patras, west of Missolonghi. At 150 m. (490 ft.), the Kremasta hydro-electric dam is the highest earth-filled dam in Europe. In 1994 the Greek government decided to proceed with the Achelous Project, a scheme to divert water from the river to irrigate rice, cotton, and tobacco fields in the Plain of Thessaly.

**Achen** /'ɑːxən/, **Lake** (German **Achensee**) a lake in western Austria, north-east of Innsbruck. It is the largest lake in the Tyrolean Alps.

**Acheron** /'ækərɒn/ **1.** In Greek mythology, a river flowing in Hades. **2.** the name of several rivers in Greece, including one in Threspotía, Epirus. Passing through dark gorges, caves and underground tunnels, it has been imagined that these 'rivers of woe' go to Hades.

**Acheulian** /əˈtʃuːlɪən/ a culture of the lower palaeolithic named after an archaeological site at Saint-Acheul near Amiens in the department of Somme, northern France, where small hand-axes, flat oval implements, and other tools have been found.

**Achill Island** /'ækəl/ (also **Eagle Island**) an island in County Mayo, the largest of the islands lying off the west coast of Ireland; area 148 sq. km. (57 sq. miles). Achill Sound is the largest settlement and the highest peak is Slievemore 672 m. (2,204 ft.). Rising to 668 m. (2,192 ft.) above the sea at Croaghan, the cliffs on the north coast of Achill Island are the highest in north-west Europe. The island is a traditional centre of the Irish shark-fishing industry.

**Achiltibuie** /ˌæxəltɪˈbuːɪ/ a village on the northwest coast of Ross and Cromarty, Highland Region, Scotland. Situated on the shore of Loch Broom overlooking the Summer Isles, 21 km. (13 miles) north-west of Ullapool.

**Achin** an alternative form of ACEH in Sumatra.

**Achinsk** /əˈtʃɪnsk/ a town in west Siberian Russia, on the Chulym River west of Krasnoyarsk; pop. (1990) 122,000.

**Acholi** /æˈkəʊliː/ (also **Acoli**, **Gang**, or **Shuli**) a distinct ethnolinguistic group of northern Uganda and southern Sudan.

**Achumawi** /ˌætʃəˈmɒwɪ/ (also **Achomawi**) a North American Indian tribe of the Hokan-Shasta linguistic group, often called Pit River Indians after their homeland in the foothills of the Sierra Nevada, north-east California.

**acid rain** a term used to describe the deposition of chemical pollutants either as dry particles or as acidified rain, hail, snow, or fog. Motor vehicles, industrial processes, and the burning of fossil fuels in power-stations create pollution, chiefly in the form of sulphur dioxide, nitrogen oxide, and hydrocarbons all of which react with water and sunlight to form dilute sulphuric acid, nitric acid, ammonium salts, and other mineral acids. These fall to earth, often long distances from their source, causing corrosion, health risks, tree death, and the detrimental acidification of water and soil. The degree of acidity is usually measured on the pH scale, a logarithmic measure of the concentration of hydrogen ions present. Values range from 0 (maximum acidity) to 14 (maximum alkalinity), with clean water registering an average pH of 5.6.

**Acklins Island** /'æklənz/ an island in the Bahamas, 480 km. (300 miles) south-east of Nassau; area 497 sq. km. (192 sq. miles); pop. (1990) 428; The island produces aloe vera for use in skin preparations and cascarilla bark which is used in the production of Campari.

**Acoma Rock** /'ækə‚mɔː/ a mesa rock in Valencia county, central New Mexico, USA, 96 km. (60 miles) north-west of Albuquerque. Discovered in 1540 by the Spanish conquistador Coronado, the Acoma Indian pueblo on top of the steep-sided sandstone mesa is considered to be the oldest continuously inhabited settlement in the United States.

**Aconcagua** /‚ækɒn'kɑːgwə/ **1.** a snow-capped extinct volcano rising to a height of 6,960 m. (22,834 ft.) in the Andes of South America, on the frontier between Chile and Argentina. First climbed by Edward A. Fitzgerald's expedition in 1897, it is the highest mountain in the Western Hemisphere. **2.** a river rising at the north-west foot of Mt. Aconcagua, central Chile. It flows 193 km. (120 miles) west, entering the Pacific Ocean north of Valparaiso.

**Acor Mountains** /æ'kɒr/ (Portuguese **Serra de Acor**) a western extension of the Serra da Estrela mountain range in central Portugal, rising to a height of 1,340 m. (4,396 ft.).

**ACP States** countries in Africa, the Caribbean, and the Pacific which signed the Lomé Conventions establishing co-operation with the European Community in trade and industrial development.

**Acre** /'aːkrə/ a state in north-west Brazil on the frontier with Peru and Bolivia; area 152,589 sq. km. (58,937 sq. miles); pop. (1991) 417,165; capital, Rio Branco. Lying in the tropical Amazon basin, Acre is drained by the Tauaraca, Acre, Purus, and Juruá rivers. Until 1903 it was part of Bolivia.

**Acre** /'aːkər/ (also **'Akko** /'aːkəʊ/, French **Saint-Jean-d'Acre**) an industrial seaport of Israel, on the Bay of Haifa; pop. (1982) 39,100. Known to the Phoenicians as Ptolemaïs, Acre was taken by the Arabs in AD 683 and used as a supply port for Damascus. Captured by the Crusaders in the 12th century, it became part of the Kingdom of Jerusalem and later a residence of the Knights of St. John. It fell into Muslim hands again in 1291 and was eventually taken by the Ottoman Turks in 1517. Captured by British forces in 1918, Acre was assigned to the Arabs in the proposed 1948

partition of Palestine but was subsequently absorbed into the new State of Israel.

**Acropolis** /ə'krɒpəlɪs/, **the,** the ancient citadel of Athens, containing the Parthenon, Erechtheion, temple of Athena Nike, and other notable buildings, some of which date from the 5th c. BC. It stands on a limestone cliff that rises 158 m. (512 ft.) above the surrounding plain. The term acropolis is generally applied to the citadel or upper fortified part of an ancient Greek city.

**Actium** /'æktɪʌm/ a promontory on the northwest coast of Acarnania in western Greece, the scene of a battle in 31 BC at which Octavian defeated Mark Antony to become ruler of Rome.

**Adamawa** /‚ædə'mɑːwə/ (French **Adamaoua**) **1.** a large plateau (Adamawa Massif) in northcentral Cameroon and eastern Nigeria occupying an area of c. 67,000 sq. km. (25,880 sq. miles). **2.** a former Fulani emirate in eastern Nigeria founded by Modibbo Adama, a soldier and scholar who initiated a holy war in 1809. In 1901 Adamawa was partitioned between British Northern Nigeria and German Cameroon. **3.** a state of eastern Nigeria created in 1991 out of part of northern Gongola; pop. (1991) 2,124,000; capital, Yola. **4.** a province of central Cameroon; area 63,691 sq. km. (24,600 sq. miles); pop. (1976) 359,230; capital, Ngaoundéré.

**Adam's Bridge** a line of shoals lying between north-west Sri Lanka and the south-eastern coast of Tamil Nadu, India, and separating the Palk Strait from the Gulf of Mannar. Muslim legend has it that Adam crossed here on his way to Adam's Peak, while Hindu tradition links it with Rama, hero of the *Ramayana*, who allegedly created this passage into Sri Lanka in order to rescue his wife, Sita.

**Adam's Peak** (Sinh. **Samanala** /'səmənə‚lə/) a mountain peak rising to 2,243 m. (7,360 ft.) in south-central Sri Lanka, sacred to Buddhists, Hindus, and Muslims. At its summit a large hollow resembling a footprint is believed by Buddhists to be the Sri Pada, or sacred footprint, left by Buddha on leaving Sri Lanka. One Muslim tradition has it that Adam stood here on one foot for 1,000 years as an act of penance after his expulsion from Paradise.

**Adamstown** the only settlement on the Pacific island of Pitcairn; pop. (1990) 59. It serves as a port on the shipping route midway between Panama and New Zealand.

**Adana** /'aːdənə/ (also **Seyhan** /seɪ'hɑːn/) **1.** a province in southern Turkey, stretching from the Taurus Mts. down to the Mediterranean through a fertile cotton-growing plain that is watered by the Seyhan and Ceyhan rivers; area 17,253 sq. km. (6,664 sq. miles); pop. (1990) 1,725,940. **2.** the capital of Adana province and fourth-largest city in Turkey, on the Seyhan River, to the south of the Cilician Gates; pop. (1990) 916,150. It has many ancient buildings and is the commercial centre of the province and has agricultural machinery and food-processing industries.

**Adangme** /əˈdɑːŋmɪ/ an ethnic group speaking a variant of the Kwa branch of the Niger-Congo family of languages and occupying the coastal area of Ghana and the valley of the River Volta.

**Adapazari** /ˌɑːdəˈpɑːzəˈriː/ (also **Sakarya**) a market city in north-west Turkey, on the Sakarya River, between Ankara and Istanbul; pop. (1990) 171,225. It is capital of Sakarya province and has sugar-refining, agricultural machinery, and textile industries.

**Adda** /ˈɑːdə/ a river in Lombardy, northern Italy. Rising in the Rhaetian Alps, it flows south and west for a distance of 313 km. (194 miles) before entering Lake Como. The river irrigates the Lombardy Plain and provides hydroelectric power.

**Ad Dakhla** see DAKHLA.

**Addis Ababa** /ˌædɪs ˈæbəbə/ (also **Adis Abeba**) the capital city of Ethiopia, situated at an altitude of c. 2,440 m. (8,000 ft.) in the highlands of Shewa province; pop. (est. 1990) 1,913,000. Founded by King Menelik II in 1887, Addis Ababa replaced Intotto as capital of Abyssinia two years later. In 1917 an 800-km. (500-mile) rail link with the port of Djibouti was completed. It is the head-quarters of the Organization of African Unity and the United Nations Economic Commission for Africa and the trade centre for coffee, Ethiopia's chief export. It has numerous light industries.

**Addo** /ˈɑːdəʊ/ a national park extending over an area of evergreen scrub in Eastern Cape, South Africa, in the Sundays River valley, north of Port Elizabeth; area 69 sq. km. (26.5 sq. miles). Estab-lished in 1931, the park protects wild animals that include the rare Cape buffalo, black rhino, and the remnants of a once-large herd of elephants.

**Adelaide** /ˈædəˌleɪd/ the capital and chief port of South Australia, at the mouth of the Torrens River, between the Mount Lofty Ranges and the Gulf of St. Vincent; pop. (1991) 957,480. Founded in 1836, Adelaide was named after the wife of William IV. It is the oldest city in the state and was in 1840 the first Australian settlement to be incorporated into a municipal government. Adelaide is a Formula One Grand Prix city of Australia and since 1960 there has been a biennial Festival of the Arts. Its historic buildings include its Town Hall, Government House, and Parliament House. Its principal industries are vehicle as-sembly, railway workshops, and electrical and household appliances.

**Adélie Land** /æˈdeɪlɪ/ (also **Adélie Coast**, French **Terre Adélie**) a section of the Antarctic continent lying south of the 60th parallel, between Wilkes Land and King George V Land. Placed under French sovereignty in 1938, the Adélie Coast was discovered in 1840 by the naval explorer Dumont d'Urville who named it after his wife.

**Adelphi** /əˈdelfɪ/, **the** a terrace of neo-classical style houses in London, built as a speculative venture by Robert and James Adam during the period 1768–74. Refurbished in the 1930s, the Adelphi lies between the Strand and the Victoria Embankment gardens. The actor-manager David Garrick (1717–79) and George Bernard Shaw (1856–1950) lived in Adelphi Terrace.

**Aden** /ˈeɪd(ə)n/ a port commanding the entrance to the Red Sea, the commercial capital of the Republic of Yemen and former capital of South Yemen 1967–90; pop. (1987) 417,370. A trading centre since Roman times, it was formerly under British rule, first as part of British India (from 1839), then from 1935 as a Crown Colony. It has an oil refinery and building materials industries.

**Aden, Gulf of** an arm of the Arabian Sea lying between the south coast of Yemen and the Horn of Africa. In the west it is linked to the Red Sea via the narrow strait of Bab al Mandeb. In the east it stretches as far as the limit of the continental shelf.

**Adena Culture** /æˈdeɪnə/ an ancient North American Indian culture flourishing in Ohio from c. 500 BC to 100 AD. The culture takes its name from the home of an Ohio governor close to which Adena Indian mounds were first discovered.

**adiabatic lapse rate** the rate at which rising or falling air cools or warms up as it expands or contracts. Unsaturated rising air cools at a rate of about one degree centigrade per hundred metres. If rising air is saturated, it condenses and gives out heat, thus reducing the rate of adiabatic cooling to 0.5–0.6° per hundred metres.

**Adige** /ˈɑːdɪˌdʒeɪ/ (German **Etsch** /etʃ/) a river in north-east Italy, which rises in the Rhaetian Alps and flows 408 km. (255 miles) southwards to meet the Adriatic Sea between Venice and the mouth of the River Po. The Adige, which supplies hydro-electric power in its upper reaches and irrigation water to the lowlands of Venetia, is Italy's second-longest river.

**Adirondack Mountains** /ˌædɪˈrɒndæk/ (also **Adirondacks**) a range of mountains in New York State, north-eastern USA, source of the Hudson and Mohawk rivers. The highest peak is Mt. Marcy (1,629 m., 5,344 ft.). Ancient glaciers have left rugged gorges, lakes, and waterfalls, and the region, with its forests, is now one of great scenic beauty.

**Adiyaman** /ˌɑːdiːəˈmɑːn/ **1.** a province in south-east Turkey; area 7,614 sq. km. (2,941 sq. miles); pop. (1990) 513,130. **2.** the capital city of Adiyaman province; pop. (1990) 100,045.

**Adjaria** see ADZHARIA.

**Admiralty Islands** an island group of Papua New Guinea in the western Pacific Ocean. In 1884 the islands became a German protectorate, but after 1920 they were administered as an Australian mandate. Lorengau on Manus Island is the chief settlement.

**Admiralty Range** a range of mountains in Antarctica, forming the northern part of the Transantarctic Mountains and lying to the west of the Ross Sea. The dramatic peaks, which rise abruptly from the sea to heights of 3,000 m. (10,000 ft.), were first seen and named by Sir James Ross in 1841.

**Ado-Ekiti** /ˌeɪdəʊ əˈkɪtɪ/ a city in Ondo State, south-western Nigeria, in the Yoruba Hills; pop. (1983) 265,800. Founded by the Ekiti people in *c.*15th c., it later developed as a light industrial centre.

**Adoni** /ˈædəʊniː/ a cotton-marketing town in western Andhra Pradesh, southern India; pop. (1991) 135,720.

**Adour** /əˈdʊər/ a river of south-west France, which rises in the central Pyrenees and flows 288 km. (180 miles) north-westwards to meet the Atlantic near Bayonne.

**adrar** /ɑːˈdrɑːr/ a Berber word for a mountain.

**Adrar** /ɑːˈdrɑːr/ **1.** a department of Saharan west-central Algeria; pop. (1982) 151,400. **2.** the chief oasis of the department of Adrar and largest of the Touat palm-grove oasis settlements of Algeria, situated on the main trans-Saharan route-way linking Oran with Timbuktu. The town is also known as Timmi; pop. (1982) 57,440.

**Adrar des Iforas** /deɪˌziːfʊˈrɑː/ a massif region in the central Sahara, north-east of Timbuktu, on the frontier between Mali and Algeria.

**Adria** /ˈɑːdriːə/ a town in Venetia, north-east Italy, between the Po and Adige rivers; pop. (1990) 21,250. It was formerly situated on the coast but now lies several miles inland. The ancient settlement of Hadria, occupied as a trading port by Greeks, Etruscans, and Romans in succession, gave its name to the Adriatic Sea.

**Adrianopole** (also **Adrianopolis**) the former name for the Turkish city of EDIRNE.

**Adriatic Sea** /ˈeɪdrɪˈætɪk/ an arm of the Mediterranean Sea between the Balkans and the Italian peninsula. Extending a distance of 720 km. (450 miles) from the Gulf of Otranto in the south to the coast of Istria in the north, the Adriatic has an area of some 135,200 sq. km. (52,220 sq. miles). The Adige and the Po are the two principal rivers flowing into the Adriatic.

**Aduwa** /ˈɑːdəwə/ (also **Adua**, **Adowa**, or **Adoa**) a town in northern Ethiopia, a former capital of Tigré province; pop. (1984) 20,000. In 1896 the Italians were heavily defeated by the Abyssinians at Aduwa.

**advection fog** /ædˈvekʃ(ə)n/ a type of fog that is formed when warm air passes horizontally over cold land or sea, generally occurring in mid-latitudes during winter.

**Adygea** /ˌɑːdəˈgeɪ/ (also **Adygey**) **1.** a republic of the Russian Federation lying between the Caucasus and the Kuban River; area 7,600 sq. km. (2,934 sq. miles); pop. (1989) 432,000; capital, Maikop. Peopled by Circassians who were converted to Islam in the 17th century, Adygea was established as an autonomous region of the USSR in 1922. It was given the status of a republic in 1992 after the breakup of the Soviet Union. It produces timber and cattle. **2.** a language spoken in the northern Caucasus region.

**Adzharia** /əˈdʒɑːriːə/ (also **Adjaria** or **Adzharistan**) an autonomous republic on the Black Sea coast of the Republic of Georgia populated by Muslim Georgians; area 3,000 sq. km. (1,160 sq. miles); pop. (1990) 382,000; capital, Batumi. Formerly held by the Ottoman Turks, the agricultural and predominantly Muslim Adzharia region became an autonomous republic of the Soviet Union in 1921.
**Adzhar** *adj. & n.*

**Aegean Islands** /ɪˈdʒiːən/ a group of islands in the Aegean Sea forming a region of Greece; pop. (1991) 460,760. The principal islands of the group are Chios, Samos, Lesbos, the Cyclades, and the Dodecanese.

**Aegean Sea** that part of the Mediterranean Sea lying between Greece and Turkey, bounded to the south by the islands of Crete and Rhodes. It is linked to the Black Sea by the Dardanelles, the Sea of Marmara, and the Bosporus and takes its name from the legendary Aegeus who drowned himself in the belief that his son Theseus had been killed by the minotaur. The prehistoric Aegean civilization flourished in this region *c.*3,000–1,000 BC.

**Aegina** /iːˈdʒaɪnə/ (Greek **Aíyina** /ˈæjɪnɑː/) a resort island in the Saronic Gulf, south-west of Athens; area 83 sq. km. (33 sq. miles); pop. (1981) 11,127. It was an important early centre of trade until the island's economic power was broken by Athens. The first coins in Europe were minted here in 650 BC.

**aeolian** /iːˈəʊlɪən/ a term applied to the action of wind in relation to the land surface, as in aeolian erosion or aeolian deposits.

**Aeolian Islands** /iːˈəʊlɪən/ the ancient name for the Italian LIPARI ISLANDS.

**Aeolic** /iːˈəʊlɪk/ the dialect of the ancient Aeolian Greeks.

**Aeolis** /iːˈəʊlɪs/ (also **Aeolia**) an ancient Greek colony in north-west Asia Minor occupied by Aeolians driven from east-central Greece by the Dorians during the 12th c. BC.

**Aetolia** /iːˈtəʊlɪə/ **1.** a region of ancient Greece lying to the east of the Achelous River. **2.** an area of modern Greece now united with Acarnania to form a department (Aetolia and Acarnania) in the region of Central Greece and Euboea; area 5,461 sq. km. (2,109 sq. miles); pop. (1991) 230,690; capital, Missolonghi.

**Afar Depression** /ˈɑːfɑːr/ (also **Afar Triangle**) a hot desert trough in Ethiopia and Djibouti, at the junction of the Red Sea, the Gulf of Aden, and Africa's Great Rift Valley. It is thought to be the collapsed dome of a thermal plume rising from a hot spot deep in the earth's interior.

**Afars and Issas** /ˈɑːfɑːrz, iːˈsɑːz/, **French Territory of the** the former name of DJIBOUTI between 1946 and 1977.

**affluent** any tributary stream that flows into another stream.

**Afghanistan** /æfˈgænɪˌstæn/ official name **The Islamic State of Afghanistan** a mountainous, landlocked country in central Asia bordered by Iran to the west, Pakistan to the south and east, and the republics of Turkmenistan, Uzbekistan, and Tajikistan to the north; area 647,697 sq. km. (250,173 sq. miles); pop. (est. 1991) 16,600,000; official languages, Pashto and a form of Persian (Dari); capital, Kabul. The mountains of the Hindu Kush dominate more than three-quarters of the country, with peaks rising to heights of over 6,400 m. (21,000 ft.). Between the central highlands and the Amu Darya (Oxus) River on the northern frontier lies a fertile plain, while in the south-west there is desert and semi-desert. The climate of Afghanistan is generally dry with cold winters and hot summers. Rainfall, which mostly occurs between October and April, rarely exceeds 38 cm. (15 inches). The principal products are cotton, carpets, rugs, natural gas, fruit, and vegetables. Conquered in the 4th c. BC by Alexander the Great, Afghanistan fell under Arab domination in the 7th c. AD, before being conquered by the Mongols. Part of the Indian Mughal empire, Afghanistan became independent in the mid-18th c. under Ahmen Khan, and in the 19th and early 20th c. became the focal point for conflicting Russian and British interests on the North-west Frontier, the British fighting three wars against the Afghans between 1839 and 1919. A constitutional monarchy since 1930, Afghanistan became progressively politically unstable in the 1970s. A puppet regime was set up in Kabul in 1979 with the support of the Soviet Union, but large parts of the country remained disaffected; the occupying Soviet forces were subjected to continuing attacks by Afghan guerrillas, while 5 million people left as refugees. After the Soviet withdrawal in 1988–9 the regime, which had remained strongly pro-Soviet, was finally toppled by mujaheddin guerrillas in April 1992 and an Islamic State was proclaimed.

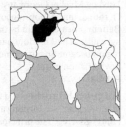

The overthrow of the Communist regime, however, failed to bring peace to Afghanistan where mujaheddin groups remained deeply divided along ethnic, tribal, and sectarian lines.
**Afghan** adj. & n

Afghanistan is divided into 29 provinces:

| Province | Area | Pop. (sq. km.) | Capital (est. 1984) |
|---|---|---|---|
| Badakhshan | 540,280 | 47,403 | Feyzabad |
| Badghis | 227,437 | 21,858 | Qal'eh-ye Now |
| Baghlan | 536,783 | 17,109 | Baghlan |
| Balkh | 635,332 | 12,593 | Mazar-e Sharif |
| Bamian | 291,476 | 17,414 | Bamian |
| Farah | 254,820 | 47,788 | Farah |
| Faryab | 588,452 | 22,279 | Meymaneh |
| Ghazni | 702,054 | 23,378 | Ghazni |
| Ghowr | 366,823 | 38,666 | Chagcharan |
| Helmand | 562,043 | 61,828 | Lashkargah |
| Herat | 868,564 | 61,315 | Herat |
| Jowzjan | 683,870 | 25,553 | Sheberghan |
| Kabul | 1,659,377 | 4,585 | Kabul |
| Kandahar | 625,101 | 47,676 | Kandahar |
| Kapisa | 271,915 | 1,871 | Mahmud-e 'Eraqi |
| Konar | 271,470 | 10,479 | Asadabad |
| Konduz | 606,211 | 7,827 | Konduz |
| Laghman | 337,274 | 7,210 | Mehtarlam |
| Lowgar | 234,789 | 4,652 | Pol-e 'Alam |
| Nangarhar | 812,466 | 7,616 | Jalalabad |
| Nimruz | 112,536 | 41,356 | Zaranj |
| Oruzgan | 482,091 | 29,295 | Tarin Kowt |
| Paktia | 525,389 | 9,581 | Gardeyz |
| Paktika | 266,139 | 19,336 | Zareh Sharan |
| Parvan | 548,000 | 9,400 | Charikar |
| Samangan | 284,351 | 15,465 | Aybak (Samangan) |
| Takhar | 564,545 | 12,376 | Taloqan |
| Vardak | 312,135 | 9,023 | Kowt-e Ashrow |
| Zabol | 194,710 | 17,293 | Qalat |

**Africa** /ˈæfrɪkə/ the second-largest of the world's continents, a southward projection of the land mass which constitutes the Old World, surrounded by sea except where the isthmus of Suez joins it to Asia; area c. 30,097,000 sq. km. (11,620,451 sq. miles); pop. (est. 1990) 642 million. Divided almost exactly in two by the equator, the northern half is dominated by the Sahara Desert, while southern Africa is dominated by a central plateau comprising a southern tableland with a mean altitude of 1,070 m. (3,000 ft.) that falls northwards to a lower plain at c. 400 m. (1,300 ft.). The highest peak is Mt. Kilimanjaro (5,895 m., 19,340 ft.) and the lowest point is Lake Assal in the Afar Depression of Djibouti (−153 m., −502 ft.). Principal physical features include the Great Rift Valley in the east, the Atlas Mountains in the north-west, the Kalahari, Namib, and Karoo deserts in the south and the Nile, Congo (Zaïre), Niger, Zambezi, Limpopo, Volta, and Orange rivers. On either side of the equator a belt of dry savanna known as the Sahel stretches across the entire continent. Africa extends from Ras Ben Sekka on the coast of Tunisia to Cape Agulhas at the southern tip of Cape

Province, South Africa, and from Cape Han in the east to Cape Alamadies in the west. Over 30 per cent of the world's minerals, including more than 50 per cent of the world's diamonds and 47 per cent of its gold, are mined in Africa. With a growth rate of 3 per cent (ten times greater than Europe) Africa's population has more than doubled since 1960 when it stood at 278 million. Food shortages in Africa, especially in the 1980s, have been the direct result of war, drought, and population growth. Cities with a population of more than one million include Cairo, Alexandria, Kinshasa, Casablanca, Abidjan, Johannesburg, Algiers, Giza, Cape Town, Addis Ababa, Nairobi, Luanda, Lagos, Dar es Salaam, Ibadan, Douala, and Mogadishu. Over 1,000 languages are spoken, the principal linguistic groups being the Niger-Kordofanian languages that are spoken over half of Africa, from Mauritania to South Africa (Yoruba, Bemba, Kwa, Lingala, Mandinke); the Nilo-Saharan languages spoken in central Africa (Dinka, Masai, Nuer, Shilluk); Afroasiatic languages spoken in the north and north-east (Arabic, Berber, Ethiopian Amharic); and Khoisan languages with 'click' consonants spoken in south-west Africa by Bushmen, Hottentots, and the Nama of Namibia. Egypt in the north-east was one of the world's earliest centres of civilization, and the Mediterranean coast has been subject to European influence since classical times, but much of the continent remained unknown to the outside world until voyages of discovery along the coast between the 15th and 17th centuries. The continent was explored and partitioned by European nations in the second half of the 19th c., Liberia and Ethiopia alone remaining under African rule. Since World War II most of the former colonies have secured their independence, but decolonization has left a legacy of instability which in many areas has yet to be satisfactorily resolved.

**Afrikaans** /ˌæfrɪˈkɑːns/ a language that since 1925 has been one of the two official languages of the Republic of South Africa (the other being English). It is a development of 17th-c. Dutch brought to South Africa by settlers from Holland, and its subsequent isolation gave rise to various differences so that it is now considered to be a separate language. It is spoken by 4 million people—2 million White Afrikaners and about 2 million people of mixed race.

**Afton** /ˈæftən/ a tributary of the River Nith in the Scottish Borders near New Cumnock, immortalized by the poet Robert Burns in the song *Afton Water*.

**Afyon** /ɑːfˈjəʊn/ (also **Afyon Karahisar** /ˌkɑːrəhɪsˈɑːr/) **1.** a province of Anatolia in western Turkey; area 14,230 sq. km. (5,496 sq. miles); pop. (1990) 739,220. **2.** the capital of Afyon province; pop. (1990) 95,640. A traditional source of opium which grows in the area and gives both city and province their name (= opium black castle).

**Agadez** /ˌæɡəˈdez/ an ancient Saharan caravan town, once the capital of a Tuareg kingdom but now the administrative centre of Agadez department, central Niger; pop. (1983) 27,000.

**Agadir** /ˌɑːɡəˈdiːr/ a southern seaport and resort town on the Atlantic coast of Morocco; pop. (1982) 110,480. The city was rebuilt and developed as a tourist resort after a devastating earthquake in 1960. In 1911 Franco-German relations were strained by the 'Agadir Crisis' after the arrival on the Moroccan coast of the German gunboat *Panther*. An arts festival is held in July.

**Agaña** /əˈɡɑːnjə/ the seat of government of Guam in the North Pacific Ocean, 12 km. (8 miles) from Apra Harbour; pop. (1980) 3,000. Captured by the Japanese in 1941, the town was largely destroyed when it was retaken by the Americans in 1944.

**Agartala** /ˌəɡərtəˈlɑː/ the capital of the state of Tripura in north-east India; pop. (1991) 157,640. Rice, tea, cotton, and mustard are produced locally.

**Agassiz** /ˈæɡəsiː/, **Lake** an enormous glacial lake that once existed in North America. In the post-glacial period it drained into the Mississippi basin leaving Lakes Winnipeg and Manitoba as residual lakes. It was named after the Swiss-American naturalist and geologist Louis Agassiz (1807–73).

**Agau** /ˈæɡaʊ/ a Cushtic dialect spoken by the Agau people of northern Ethiopia.

**Agen** /ɑːˈʒɑ̃/ the capital of the department of Lot-et-Garonne in Aquitaine, south-west France, on the Garonne River; pop. (1990) 32,220. It was the the birthplace of the scholar Joseph Scaliger (1540–1609) and the Provençal barber-poet Jasmin (1798–1864).
**Agenais** or **Agenois** *adj. & n.*

**Agenais** /ˈæʒəneɪ/ a region of France centred on the town of Agen in Aquitaine and more or less coextensive with the department of Lot-et-Garonne.

**Aghios Nikolaos** /ˈaɪɒs ˌnɪkɒˈlaɪɒs/ (Greek **Ayios Nikólaos**) a holiday resort in the department of Lasithi, on the north coast of Crete; situated on the Bay of Mirabello, east of Heraklion; pop. (1981) 8,100. Named after a Byzantine church, the modern town was established in 1869. An archaeological museum displays exhibits from sites in eastern Crete.

**Aghlabid** /ˈɑːɡləˌbɪd/ a dynasty of Arab emirs ruling in north Africa AD 800–909. The Aghlabid capital was Kairouan in modern Tunisia.

**Agilkia** /əˈɡɪlkɪə/ an island in Lake Nasser, near Aswan, Egypt, site of the reconstruction in the 1970s of the ancient Temples of Philae. Following the construction of the Aswan High Dam rising water threatened to engulf the island of Philae. Over 45,000 stones were transported to higher ground on the nearby island of Agilkia.

**Agincourt** /'ædʒɪnˌkɔːt/ (French **Azincourt** /ˌæzæ̃'kʊə(r)/) a village in the department of Pas-de-Calais, northern France, scene of Henry V's famous victory over a much larger French army in 1415. The victory allowed Henry to occupy Normandy and consolidate his claim to the French throne.

**Agra** /'ɑːɡrə/ a city on the River Jumna in Uttar Pradesh state, northern India; pop. (1991) 899,195. Founded by Akbar in 1566, Agra was capital of the Mogul empire until 1658. Its most famous building is the Taj Mahal, a white marble mausoleum built by the Emperor Shah Jahan for his favourite wife who died in 1629. The city is noted for its shoes, glass, and handicrafts.

**Agri** /ɑː'ɡriː/ **1.** a mountainous province in eastern Turkey, on the border with Iran; area 11,376 sq. km. (4,394 sq. miles); pop. (1990) 437,090. **2.** the capital of Agri province in Turkey, 100 km. (63 miles) west of Mt. Ararat (Agri Dagi). It is also known as Karaköse; pop. (1990) 58,040.

**Agri Dagi** the Turkish name for Mount Ararat. see ARARAT, MOUNT.

**Agrigento** /ˌɑːɡrɪ'dʒentəʊ/ the capital of the Italian province of Agrigento on the south coast of the island of Sicily and a market and tourist centre; pop. (1990) 56,660. Described by the Greek poet Pindar as 'loveliest of mortal cities', Agrigento was the birthplace of the Italian novelist and dramatist Luigi Pirandello (1867–1936). The town is noted for its classical monuments, the oldest of which date back to the 7th c. BC.

**Agrinion** /ɑː'ɡriːnjɔːn/ the largest town in the department of Aetolia-Acarnania, western Greece; pop. (1981) 45,087. On the north shore of Lake Trikhonis, 27 km. (17 miles) to the east, is the sanctuary of Apollo built in the early 7th c. BC. Agrinion is a centre for the local tobacco trade.

**Aguaruna** /ˌæɡwæ'ruːnə/ a South American Amerindian tribe found on the frontier between Ecuador and Peru. The Aguarana speak a Jívaroan branch of the Equatorial language group.

**Aguascalientes** /ˌɑːɡwəskæl'jenteɪz/ **1.** a state of central Mexico that takes its name from the numerous hot springs that exist; area 5,471 sq. km. (2,217 sq. miles); pop. (1990) 719,650. The economy of the state is largely based on its ranches, vineyards, and orchards. **2.** its capital, a health resort in the Sierra Madre Occidental north-east of Guadalajara; pop. (1990) 506,380. The town is noted for its catacombs which were built before the arrival of the Spanish in 1522.

**Agulhas Current** /æ'ɡʌləs/ (also **Mozambique Current**) a warm ocean current that flows southward along the coast of East Africa.

**Ahaggar Mountains** see HOGGAR MOUNTAINS.

**Ahlen** /'ɑːlən/ an industrial city in North Rhine-Westphalia, western Germany, 27 km. (17 miles) south of Münster; pop. (est. 1984) 52,600.

**Ahmadabad** /'ɑːmədəˌbɑːd/ (also **Ahmedabad**) an industrial city in the state of Gujarat in western India, on the Sabarmati River; pop. (1991) 2,873,000. Founded in 1411 by Ahmed Shah, Ahmadabad has developed into one of the leading industrial cities of India, specializing in textiles. In 1930 Gandhi set out from his *ashram* here on his 320-km. (200-mile) march to the sea in defiance of the government's Salt Law.

**Ahmadnagar** /ˌɑːməd'nɑːɡər/ (also **Ahmednagar**) a commercial and industrial city in Maharashtra state, west-central India, on the Sina river, between Pune and Aurangabad; pop. (1991) 221,700.

**Ahr** /'ɑːr/ a river in North Rhine-Westphalia, western Germany, a tributary of the Rhine. The Ahr valley is the northernmost vine-growing area of Europe.

**Ahuachapán** /ˌɑːwətʃə'pɑːn/ **1.** a coffee-growing department in western El Salvador, on the frontier with Guatemala; area 1,281 sq. km. (495 sq. miles); pop. (1985) 257,900. **2.** its capital and market centre in the Sierra Apaneca y Lamatepeque, south-west of Santa Ana; pop. (1985) 71,850. The ausoles (geysers) in the area are a source of geothermal power.

**Ahvaz** /ɑː'vɑːz/ (also **Ahwaz**) the capital of the oil-producing province of Khuzestan in western Iran, on the River Karun, with petrochemical and textile industries; pop. (1991) 725,000. Ahvaz was badly damaged between 1985 and 1988 during the phase of the Iran–Iraq war known as the 'war of the cities'.

**Ahvenanmaa Islands** the Finnish name for the ÅLAND ISLANDS in the Gulf of Bothnia.

**Aigues-Mortes** /eɡ'mɔːrt/ a town in the department of Gard, south-east France, in the Rhône delta; pop. (1982) 4,106. Its name is derived from the Latin *aquae mortuae* (= dead waters), referring to the saline marshland which surrounds it. The site was chosen by St. Louis (Louis IX) to serve as the military base and embarkation port for his two Crusades (1248 and 1270). He began to construct fortifications and his son Philip the Bold (1245–85) completed the vast rectangle of battlemented walls strengthened by 15 towers. The harbour has long been silted up.

**aiguille** /eɪ'ɡwiː/ a sharp peak of rock usually above the snowline and formed by the action of frost. The term is commonly used in place-names, especially in the Alps, as in **Aiguille du Midi** (3,842 m., 12,605 ft.), a peak in the Mont Blanc massif and the highest point in the Alps reached by Téléphérique.

**Aihole** /'aɪhəʊl/ a village in the central Deccan, Karnataka, south-west India, the site of over 70

Hindu temples built between the 4th and 7th centuries AD when Aihole was capital of the Chalukyan empire.

**Ailsa Craig** /ˌeɪlsə ˈkreɪg/ a small rocky island in the Firth of Clyde, opposite the town of Girvan in south-west Scotland. Its granite rock has been used to make curling stones.

**ain** /iːn/ an Arabic word for a spring, as in the town of Ain Beni Mathar in north-east Morocco.

**Ain** /æ̃/ **1.** a department in the Rhône-Alpes Region of east France, between the rivers Rhône and Saône; area 5,762 sq. km. (2,226 sq. miles); pop. (1990) 471,020; capital, Bourge-en-Bresse. **2.** a river that rises in the Jura Mountains of eastern France and flows 194 km. (120 miles) southwards to meet the Rhône above Lyon.

**Aintab** /aɪŋˈtæb/ the former name (until 1922) of the city of GAZIANTEP in southern Turkey.

**Aintree** /ˈeɪntriː/ a suburb of Liverpool, in Merseyside, site of a racecourse over which the Grand National steeplechase has been run since 1839.

**Ainu** /ˈaɪnʊ/ a non-Mongoloid people inhabiting the Japanese archipelago whose physical characteristics (light skin colour, round eyes, and exceptionally thick, wavy hair) set them apart dramatically from the majority population of the islands and have stimulated much speculation as to their possible Caucasoid origin, although recent studies suggest close relations with some of the neighbouring Tungusic, Altaic, and Uralic populations of Siberia. Archaeological evidence suggests that the Ainu were resident in the area as early as 5,000 BC, thereby predating the great Mongoloid migrations. Forced by Japanese expansion to retreat to the northernmost islands (i.e. Hokkaido, Sakhalin, and the Kurile Islands) the Ainu are on the verge of cultural extinction and now number c. 25,000. Of these, only about 10 per cent are 'pure' Ainu. Assimilation has resulted in a shift from hunting and gathering to sedentary agriculture, and the Japanese language has all but replaced the unique Ainu tongue which is unrelated to any known form of speech and remains unwritten. Traditional practices such as female tattooing and the i-omante (bear sacrifice) have also declined as a result of Japanese cultural influence. (Ainu = Man in the Ainu language of Hokkaido.)

**Aïr Highlands** /ɑːˈɪ(ə)r/ (also **Azbine** /æzˈbiːn/ or **Asben** /æsˈben/) a mountainous region rising to 1,524 m. (5,000 ft.) in central Niger, once the centre of the African kingdom of Asben.

**Airdrie** /ˈeɪrdrɪ/ an industrial town in central Scotland, 18 km. (11 miles) east of Glasgow; pop. (1981) 45,750.

**Airedale** /ˈeɪrdeɪl/ the upper valley of the River Aire which rises in the West Yorkshire Pennines, northern England, and flows 123 km. (70 miles)

south-eastwards through Leeds to meet the River Ouse near Goole.

**Aisén** /aɪˈsen/ (also **Aysen** or fully **Región Aisén del General Carlos Ibañez del Campo**) a region of southern Chile dominated by ravines, river valleys, glaciers, and lakes; area 108,997 sq. km. (4,210 sq. miles); pop. (est. 1984) 70,600; capital, Coihaique.

**Aisne** /ˈeɪn/ **1.** a department of Picardy in northern France; area 7,369 sq. km. (2,846 sq. miles); pop. (1990) 537,260; capital, Laon. **2.** a river that rises in the Argonne area of north-east France and flows 240 km. (150 miles) west and north-west to meet the River Oise near Compiègne.

**Aix-en-Provence** /ˌeɪksɑ̃prɒˈvɑ̃s/ an ancient cultural and commercial city of Provence in southern France, 30 km. (19 miles) north of Marseille; pop. (1990) 126,850. Founded in 123 BC by the Roman Consul Caius Sextius, the city has long been famous for its thermal springs. A major centre of Provençal culture, it has many 17th- and 18th-c. buildings, an 11th-c. cathedral and a university founded in 1409. Aix-en-Provence was the home of the painter Paul Cezanne (1839–1906). Its industries include food processing, wine-making and electrical equipment, and tourism.

**Aix-la-Chapelle** the French name for the German town of AACHEN.

**Aix-les-Bains** /ˌeɪkslɛɪˈbæ̃/ a spa town in the Savoy, south-east France, situated on the south-east shore of Lake Bourget; pop. (1990) 24,830.

**Aizawl** /ˈaɪdʒ(ə)l/ (also **Aijal**) the capital of the state of Mizoram in north-east India, in the Lushai Hills; pop. (1991) 154,000.

**Ajaccio** /æˈjætʃɪˌəʊ/ a seaport on the west coast of Corsica, overlooking the Bay of Ajaccio; the capital of Corse-du-Sud department; pop. (1990) 59,320. Napoleon I was born here on 15 August 1769.

**Ajanta Caves** /əˈdʒʌntə/ a series of 29 caves in the state of Maharashtra, south-central India, containing Buddhist frescoes and sculptures of the 1st c. BC–7th c. AD, with the finest examples belonging to the Gupta period (5th–6th c. AD). The caves are cut into the steep rock-face of a gorge on a bend of the Waghore River.

**Ajka** /ˈɔɪkə/ an industrial town in the Trans-Danubian Highlands of west Hungary, on the Torna River in Veszprém county; pop. (1984) 31,000. Brown coal, manganese, and bauxite are mined nearby.

**Ajman** /ædʒˈmaːn/ the smallest of the seven emirates of the United Arab Emirates; area 250 sq. km. (96 sq. miles); pop. (1985) 64,320; capital, Ajman. Ajman comprises territory on the south-west coast of the Persian Gulf and exclaves at Masfut, in the Hajar Mts. to the south-east, and Manama, east of Ajman town. Fishing, pearling, and dhow building are traditional industries that survive alongside oilfield service industries such as engineering and ship repair.

**Ajmer** /ʌdʒ'miːr/ an industrial city in the state of Rajasthan, north-west India; situated by Ana Sagar, an artificial lake created by the damming of the River Luni in the 12th c.; pop. (1991) 402,000. Ajmer was the capital of the former state of the same name which was merged with Rajasthan in 1956. The Dargah tomb, burial place of a Sufi saint who came to Ajmer in 1192, is an important place of Muslim pilgrimage. It has large railway workshops and many light industries.

**AK** *abbr.* US Alaska (in official postal use).

**Akan** /æ'kɑːn/ a people of southern and central Ghana and south-east Ivory Coast speaking a language of the Kwa linguistic group. The Ashanti emerged as the most powerful of the Akan people during the 18th c.

**Akarnania** see ACARNANIA.

**Akashi** /ɑːˈkɑːʃi/ a city in Hyogo prefecture, Japan, on the south-west coast of Honshu Island, 20 km. (12 miles) west of Kobe; pop. (1990) 270,730. Linked by ferry to Awaji Island, the meridian at Akashi is the standard time meridian for Japan. It is a fishing port with electrical machinery industries.

**Akeman Street** /ˈeɪkmən/ a Roman road in south-central England, running from Cirencester to St. Albans.

**Akershus** /ˈɑːkərsˌhʊs/ a county to the east of Oslo in east Norway; area 4,916 sq. km. (1,900 sq. miles); pop. (1991) 418,110. Asker, Skedsmo, and the engineering community of Bærum are the largest municipalities.

**Akhaïa** the Greek name for ACHAEA.

**Akharnai** /ˌɑːkərˈneɪ/ (also **Acharnae** /əˈkɑːrniː/) a town in the department of Attica, central Greece, 10 km. (6 miles) north of Athens; pop. (1981) 40,185. Occupied since Mycenaean times, Akharnai was the setting of the *Acharnians* by the comic poet and playwright Aristophanes.

**Akhetaten** see AMARNA, TELL EL-.

**Akita** /ɑːˈkiːtə/ a port and industrial city in Tohoku region, Japan, on the north coast of Honshu Island, at the mouth of the Omono River; pop. (1990) 302,360. The Kanto autumn harvest festival takes place in August each year. A procession of lanterns, known as Kanto takes place during the Tanoboto festival in August each year. Its industries include woodworking and food products.

**Akjoujt** /æk'ʒuːʒʊt/ a copper-mining town in the Inchiri region of west-central Mauritania, between Nouakchott and Atar; pop.(est.) 3,000.

**Akkad** /ˈɑːkɑːd/ a city on the Euphrates (as yet undiscovered) which gave its name to an ancient northern Semitic kingdom, traditionally founded by Sargon (2334–2279 BC) in north-central Mesopotamia (modern Iraq). Its power extended over Babylonia, Assyria, and Syria, and even penetrated into Asia Minor, until it was overwhelmed by invading tribes from the east *c.* 2150 BC. The Akkadian language, used in Mesopotamia from about 3,000 BC and known from cuneiform inscriptions, is the oldest recorded Hamito-Semitic language. Two dialects of Akkadian, Assyrian and Babylonian, were spoken in the Middle East for the next 2,000 years before they gave way to Aramaic. **Akkadian** *adj. & n.*

**Akko** see ACRE.

**Akmola** see AQMOLA.

**Akola** /əˈkəʊlə/ a cotton-manufacturing city in the state of Maharashtra, central India; pop. (1991) 327,900. It is also a major grain-trading centre.

**Akranes** /ˌækrəˈnes/ a fishing port in the Vesturland region of western Iceland, on Faxa Bay, opposite Reykjavik; pop. (1990) 5,230. Cement is manufactured from local sea shells and volcanic rhyolite.

**Akron** /ˈækrən/ the county seat of Summit county, north-eastern Ohio, USA, on the Little Cuyahoga River; pop. (1990) 223,000. Once described as the 'rubber capital of the world', Akron was for many years a major centre of the rubber and tyre industry after the opening of the first factory in 1870; it now has numerous light industries.

**Akrotiri** /ˌɑːkrəˈtɪriː/ **1.** a bay on the south coast of Cyprus. Its chief settlement is the port of Limassol. **2.** a peninsula in southern Cyprus separating Akrotiri Bay from Episkopi Bay. **3.** a small village on the Akrotiri Peninsula; pop. (est. 1985) 700. **4.** a sovereign base-area held by the British after the independence of Cyprus in 1960.

**Aksai Chin** /ˌæksaɪ ˈtʃɪn/ a region of the Himalayas adjacent to Kashmir, forming a strategic link between the Chinese provinces of Tibet and Xinjiang; area *c.* 36,000 sq. km. (13,900 sq. miles). Occupied by China since 1950, it is claimed by India as part of Kashmir.

**Aksu** /ˈɑːksuː/ (formerly **Wensu**) a city in Xinjiang autonomous region, western China, situated on the Aksu River in the southern foothills of the Tien Shan range; pop. (1986) 341,000. It was a Mongol capital during the 14th c.

**Aksum** /ˈɑːksəm/ (also **Axum**) a town in the province of Tigré in northern Ethiopia. It was a religious centre and the capital of a powerful kingdom during the 1st–6th centuries AD. According to ancient Aksumite tradition their kings were descended from Menelik (legendary son of Solomon and Sheba) who brought to the country the Ark of the Covenant containing the original Tablets of the Law given to Moses. **Aksumite** *adj. & n.*

**Aktau** see AQTAU.

**Aktyubinsk** /ɑːkˈtjʊbɪnsk/ (the former name of AQTÖBE in Kazakhstan.

**Akureyri** /ˈɑːkəˌreɪri:/ a fishing port in Nordurland region, Iceland, at the head of Eyja Fjord; pop. (1990) 14,170. Founded in the late 1700s by a Danish trader, Akureyri is now the largest settlement in northern Iceland. Its shipyard is the largest in the country. The Icelandic poet laureate and dramatist Matthías Jochumsson (1835–1920), author of Iceland's national anthem, lived in Akureyri.

**Akwa Ibom** /ˌækwə ˈiːbʌm/ a state in southern Nigeria; area 7,081 sq. km. (2,735 sq. miles); pop. (1991) 2,359,736; capital, Uyo. Akwa Ibo state was created from the western part of the state of Cross River in 1987.

**Akyab** see SITTWE.

**AL** abbr. US Alabama (in official postal use).

**Alabama** /ˌæləˈbæmə/ a state in the south-eastern US bordering on the Gulf of Mexico; area 133,915 sq. km. (51,705 sq. miles); pop. (1990) 4,040,587; capital, Montgomery. The largest cities are Birmingham, Mobile, Montgomery, and Huntsville. Alabama is also known as the Yellowhammer State, the Heart of Dixie, and the Camellia State. Visited by Spanish explorers in the mid-16th c., and later settled by the French, it passed to Britain in 1763 and to the US in 1783, becoming the 22nd state of the US in 1819. Its chief products are lumber, pulp, paper, electronics, chemicals, textiles, motor tyres, fabricated metals, cement, and processed food. Alabama is divided into 67 counties:

| County | Area (sq. km.) | Pop. (1990) | County Seat |
| --- | --- | --- | --- |
| Autauga | 1,546 | 34,220 | Prattville |
| Baldwin | 4,114 | 98,280 | Bay Minette |
| Barbour | 2,289 | 25,420 | Clayton |
| Bibb | 1,618 | 16,580 | Centreville |
| Blount | 1,665 | 39,250 | Oneonta |
| Bullock | 1,618 | 11,040 | Union Springs |
| Butler | 2,017 | 21,890 | Greenville |
| Calhoun | 1,582 | 116,030 | Anniston |
| Chambers | 1,543 | 36,880 | Lafayette |
| Cherokee | 1,432 | 19,540 | Centre |
| Chilton | 1,799 | 32,460 | Clanton |
| Choctaw | 2,353 | 16,020 | Butler |
| Clarke | 3,184 | 27,240 | Grove Hill |
| Clay | 1,566 | 13,252 | Ashland |
| Cleburne | 1,452 | 12,730 | Heflin |
| Coffee | 1,760 | 40,240 | Elba |
| Colbert | 1,525 | 51,670 | Tuscumbia |
| Conecuh | 2,211 | 14,050 | Evergreen |
| Coosa | 1,701 | 11,050 | Rockford |
| Covington | 2,687 | 36,480 | Andalusia |
| Crenshaw | 1,582 | 16,635 | Luverne |
| Cullman | 1,911 | 67,610 | Cullman |
| Dale | 1,452 | 49,630 | Ozark |
| Dallas | 2,524 | 48,130 | Selma |
| De Kalb | 2,014 | 54,650 | Fort Payne |
| Elmore | 1,610 | 49,210 | Wetumpka |
| Escambia | 2,462 | 35,520 | Brewton |
| Etowah | 1,403 | 99,840 | Gadsden |
| Fayette | 1,631 | 17,960 | Fayette |
| Franklin | 1,665 | 27,810 | Russellville |
| Geneva | 1,496 | 23,650 | Geneva |
| Greene | 1,624 | 10,150 | Eutaw |
| Hale | 1,711 | 15,500 | Greensboro |
| Henry | 1,442 | 15,370 | Abbeville |
| Houston | 1,494 | 81,330 | Dothan |
| Jackson | 2,770 | 47,800 | Scottsboro |
| Jefferson | 2,897 | 651,520 | Birmingham |
| Lamar | 1,566 | 15,715 | Vernon |
| Lauderdale | 1,711 | 79,660 | Florence |
| Lawrence | 1,794 | 31,510 | Moulton |
| Lee | 1,577 | 87,150 | Opelika |
| Limestone | 1,447 | 46,005 | Athens |
| Lowndes | 1,848 | 12,660 | Hayneville |
| Macon | 1,590 | 24,930 | Tuskegee |
| Madison | 2,087 | 238,910 | Huntsville |
| Marengo | 2,542 | 23,080 | Linden |
| Marion | 1,924 | 29,830 | Hamilton |
| Marshall | 1,468 | 70,830 | Guntersville |
| Mobile | 3,205 | 378,640 | Mobile |
| Monroe | 2,638 | 23,970 | Monroeville |
| Montgomery | 2,053 | 209,085 | Montgomery |
| Morgan | 1,489 | 100,040 | Decatur |
| Perry | 1,859 | 12,760 | Marion |
| Pickens | 2,304 | 20,700 | Carrollton |
| Pike | 1,740 | 27,595 | Troy |
| Randolph | 1,512 | 19,980 | Wedowee |
| Russell | 1,641 | 46,860 | Phenix City |
| St Clair | 1,672 | 49,810 | Ashville & Pell City |
| Shelby | 2,071 | 99,360 | Columbiana |
| Sumter | 2,348 | 16,170 | Livingston |
| Talladega | 1,949 | 74,110 | Talladega |
| Tallapoosa | 1,815 | 38,830 | Dadeville |
| Tuscaloosa | 3,459 | 150,520 | Tuscaloosa |
| Walker | 2,081 | 67,670 | Jasper |
| Washington | 2,799 | 16,690 | Chatom |
| Wilcox | 2,286 | 13,570 | Camden |
| Winston | 1,587 | 22,050 | Double Springs |

**Alabama** a river in the USA formed by the junction of the Coosa and Talapoosa rivers just north of Montgomery, Alabama. It flows nearly 500 km. (312 miles) in a south-westerly direction before joining the Tombigbee River to become the Mobile River 70 km. (44 miles) north of Mobile.

**Alabama** an Algonquian Indian tribe of southeast USA.

**Alagoas** /ˌæləˈgəʊəs/ a small coastal state in east Brazil; area 27,731 sq. km. (10,711 sq. miles); pop. (1991) 2,512,990; capital, Macaeió. Oil, textiles, sugar, fish, and cattle are its main products.

**Alagón** /ˌɑːləˈgɒn/ a river in western Spain that rises in Castilla-León and flows 200 km. (125 miles) south-west to meet the River Tagus near Alcantara.

**Alajuela** /ˌɑːləˈhweɪlə/ **1.** a province in the tropical lowlands of northern Costa Rica; area 9,753 sq. km. (3,767 sq. miles); pop. (1984) 427,960. It is watered by the Culcaracha, Platanares, Frio, and San Carlos rivers, tributaries of the San Juan River which flows from Lake Nicaragua eastwards along the Costa Rica–Nicaragua frontier to the Caribbean. There are mountain ranges in the west and south with several active volcanoes. The chief agricultural products are coffee, maize, rice, beans, pineapples, sugar-cane, and livestock. **2.** its capital town, on the Inter-American Highway, 20 km. (12 miles) north-west of San José; pop. (1984) 34,550. Alajuela, which produces soap and textiles, was capital of Costa Rica during the 1830s.

**Alameda** /ˌæləˈmiːdə/ an island city on San Francisco Bay, California, USA; pop. (1990) 76,460. Once an important commercial aviation centre, it now has a naval air station and several yachting marinas.

**Alamein** see EL ALAMEIN.

**Alamo** /ˈæləməʊ/, **the** a Franciscan mission in San Antonio, Texas, USA, founded c. 1718 and later turned into a fortress. It was the site of a siege in 1836 by Mexican forces during the Texan struggle for independence from Mexico. It was defended by a handful of volunteers (including Davy Crockett), all of whom were killed.

**Åland Islands** /ˈəʊlɑːnd/ (Finnish **Ahvenanmaa** /ˈɑːvənɑːnˌmɑː/) a group of islands in the Gulf of Bothnia forming an autonomous region of Finland; area 1,552 sq. km. (600 sq. miles); pop. (1990) 24,600. The group includes more than 6,500 islands and rocky islets of which only 80 are inhabited. The only town is the capital, Mariehamn (Maarianhamina). Swedish is the main language. In 1809 the islands became part of Russia, eventually becoming a demilitarized zone under the Treaty that ended the Crimean War. In 1921 they were assigned to Finland by the League of Nations with special privileges that included the right to veto decisions of the Finnish parliament affecting their status. Shipping, tourism, and agriculture are the chief industries.

**Alania** /əˈlæniə/ the name adopted in 1994 by the Caucasian Republic of North Ossetia in Russia. See OSSETIA.

**Alaska** /əˈlæskə/ the largest state of the US, in the extreme north-west of North America, with coasts in the Arctic Ocean, Bering Sea, and North Pacific; area 1,530,700 sq. km. (591,004 sq. miles); pop. (1990) 550,000; capital, Juneau. The largest settlements are Anchorage, Kenai, and Fairbanks. About one-third of Alaska lies within the Arctic Circle. It was discovered by Russian explorers (under Vitus Bering) in 1741, and further explored by Cook, Vancouver, and others during the last quarter of the 18th c. The territory was purchased from Russia in 1867 for the sum of $7.2 million and in 1896 the famous Gold Rush began. Alaska became the 49th state of the US in 1959. Oil, gas, timber,

fishing, and tourism are the principal industries. The state is divided into 25 census divisions:

| Census Division | Area (sq. km.) | Pop. (1990) |
| --- | --- | --- |
| Aleutian East Borough | 18,013 | 2,460 |
| Aleutians West Census Area | 9,948 | 9,480 |
| Anchorage Borough | 4,484 | 226,370 |
| Bethel | 93,473 | 13,660 |
| Bristol Bay Borough | 1,375 | 1,410 |
| Dillingham | 119,203 | 4,010 |
| Fairbanks North Star Borough | 19,169 | 77,720 |
| Haines Borough | 6,146 | 2,120 |
| Juneau Borough | 6,799 | 26,750 |
| Kenai Peninsula Borough | 41,569 | 40,800 |
| Ketchikan Gateway Borough | 3,215 | 13,830 |
| Kodiak Island Borough | 12,416 | 13,310 |
| Lake and Peninsula Borough | 1,670 | |
| Matanuska-Susitna Borough | 63,436 | 39,680 |
| Nome | 61,802 | 8,290 |
| North Slope Borough | 235,482 | 5,980 |
| Northwest Arctic Borough | 6,110 | |
| Prince of Wales-Outer Ketchikan | 19,832 | 6,280 |
| Sitka Borough | 7,606 | 8,590 |
| Skagway-Yakutat-Angoon | 31,687 | 4,385 |
| Southeast Fairbanks | 62,573 | 5,910 |
| Valdez-Cordova | 101,564 | 9,950 |
| Wade Hampton | 46,126 | 5,790 |
| Wrangell-Petersburg | 15,443 | 7,040 |
| Yukon-Koyukuk | 411,907 | 8,480 |

**Alaska Current** a warm current that flows northwards then westwards in the Gulf of Alaska.

**Alaska, Gulf of** the north-eastern part of the North Pacific Ocean lying to the south of the US state of Alaska, between the Alaska Peninsula and the Alexander Archipelago. The Trans-Alaskan oil pipeline terminates at Valdez on the northern shore of the Gulf of Alaska.

**Alaska Highway** originally known as the Alcan Highway (ALaska–CANada), the Alaska Highway links the Canadian town of Dawson Creek in British Columbia with Fairbanks, Alaska, passing through Fort St. John, Fort Nelson, and Whitehorse. Built as a military supply route by US Army engineers in 1942, the highway was later improved and realigned with a total length of 2,450 km. (1,523 miles).

**Alaska Range** the largest mountain chain in Alaska, USA, including Mt. McKinley which is North America's highest peak.

**Alava** /ˈɑːləvə/ the largest of the three Basque provinces of northern Spain; area 3,047 sq. km. (1,177 sq. miles); pop. (1991) 272,450; capital, Vitoria. The province occupies a large cereal-growing plateau (Llanada Alavesa) to the north of the River Ebro.

**Alawites** /ˈɑːləˌwaɪts/ (also **Alawi** or **Nusairis**) an offshoot of the Shiite Islamic faith with beliefs that include elements of Christianity and ancient eastern cults. In Syria, where they took power in 1966, Alawites account for an estimated 8–9 per cent of the population.

**Alba** /ˈɑːlbə/ a county to the north of the Transylvanian Alps, central Romania; area 6,231 sq. km. (2,407 sq. miles); pop. (1989) 428,250; capital, Alba Iulia. Grain, fruit, and wine are produced.

**Albacete** /ˌælvəˈθeɪtiː/ **1.** a province in the Castilla-La Mancha region, south-east Spain, on the fertile La Mancha plain; area 14,858 sq. km. (5,739 sq. miles); pop. (1991) 342,680. **2.** its capital city, an agricultural centre once noted for the manufacture of knives; pop. (1991) 134,584.

**Alba Iulia** /ˌælbə ˈjuːljə/ a marketing city in west-central Romania, to the north of the Transylvanian Alps; pop. (1989) 72,330. Founded by the Romans in the 2nd c. AD, it was the capital of Transylvania and for a short time (1599–1601) capital of the united principalities of Transylvania, Moldavia, and Walachia. Transylvania's union with Romania was proclaimed from Alba Iulia in 1918. It is the centre for a wine-making region.

### Albania

/ælˈbeɪnɪə/ official name **The Republic of Albania** a small country in south-east Europe, bordering on the Adriatic Sea; area 28,748 sq. km. (11,104 sq. miles); pop. (est. 1991)  3,300,000; Albanian, the official language, has two distinct dialects, Tosk in the north and Gheg in the south; capital, Tiranë (Tirana). Much of the land is mountainous and there are extensive forests, but the coastal areas are fertile. Major cities are located on the coast or in the larger upland valleys. While the coast has mild, wet winters and dry, hot summers, the interior uplands are generally cooler and wetter. Until World War II more than 90 per cent of Albanians worked on the land. Under Communist rule industrial development took place in the post-war period, reducing the number engaged in agriculture to 50 per cent of the total population by the mid-1980s. The chief agricultural products are tobacco, cotton, grain, potatoes, and sugar-beets. Industrial products include chemicals, textiles, coal, and processed minerals such as chromium, copper, and iron. Although Albania was part of the Byzantine empire from the 6th c. and part of the Turkish empire from the 15th c., its mountain tribes always remained fiercely independent and central rule was never completely effective. It became an independent state as a result of the Balkan Wars in 1912, and after a brief period as a republic became a rather unstable monarchy under King Zog in 1928. Invaded by Italy in 1939, it became a Communist state under Enver Hoxha after World War II, and although under the influence of the USSR until

1960 and later that of China, it has generally remained isolationist in policy and outlook. The country's first legal opposition party was formed in 1990 but in its first multi-party elections held in 1991 the Communist Party retained a majority. **Albanian** *adj. & n.*

There are 26 administrative districts:

| District | Area (sq. km.) | Pop. (1990) | Capital |
|---|---|---|---|
| Berat | 1,026 | 180,490 | Berat |
| Dibrë | 1,569 | 153,775 | Peshkopi |
| Durrës | 859 | 251,030 | Durrës |
| Elbasan | 1,466 | 248,670 | Elbasan |
| Fier | 1,191 | 251,115 | Fier |
| Gjirokastër | 1,137 | 67,390 | Gjirokastër |
| Gramsh | 695 | 44,790 | Gramsh |
| Kolonjë | 805 | 25,290 | Ersekë |
| Korçë | 2,181 | 218,220 | Korçë |
| Krujë | 607 | 109,880 | Krujë |
| Kukës | 1,564 | 104,730 | Kukës |
| Lezhë | 479 | 63,500 | Lezhë |
| Librazhd | 1,013 | 73,870 | Librazhd |
| Lushnjë | 712 | 137,830 | Lushnjë |
| Mat | 1,028 | 78,750 | Burrel |
| Mirditë | 698 | 51,700 | Rrëshen |
| Përmet | 930 | 40,420 | Përmet |
| Pogradec | 725 | 73,330 | Pogradec |
| Pukë | 969 | 50,290 | Pukë |
| Sarandë | 1,097 | 89,460 | Sarandë |
| Shkodër | 2,528 | 241,550 | Shkodër |
| Skrapar | 775 | 47,605 | Çorovodë |
| Tepelenë | 817 | 51,020 | Tepelenë |
| Tiranë | 1,222 | 374,480 | Tiranë |
| Tropojë | 1,043 | 45,965 | Bajram Curri |
| Vlorë | 1,609 | 180,725 | Vlorë |

**Albany** /ˈɒlbənɪ/ an ancient name for that part of Scotland lying north of the Firth of Forth and the Firth of Clyde.

**Albany** a seaport and resort on the south coast of the state of Western Australia, on the Ataturk Entrance of King George Sound; pop. (1991) 18,830. Originally named Frederickstown after the Duke of York and Albany, it was founded as a penal colony in 1826.

**Albany 1.** an industrial town and capital of Dougherty county, south-west Georgia, USA, on the River Flint; pop. (1990) 78,120. It is the centre of pecan and peanut processing. It also has aircraft and agricultural machinery industries. **2.** the capital of New York State, on the Hudson River; pop. (1990) 101,080. Combined with Shenectady and Troy it forms a metropolitan area with a population of 874,300. It was settled by the Dutch in 1614 and surrendered to the British in 1664. The city grew with the development of the Champlain and Erie canals in the 1820s. Today it is an administrative and cultural centre with many old buildings. It is also an important river port and trans-shipment centre with oil tanks, machine shops, foundries, breweries, and numerous light industries. **3.** the capital of Linn county, west Oregon, on the Williamette River; pop. (1990) 29,460. It is a metallurgical and lumbering centre.

**Albany Doctor** a cool afternoon sea-breeze that blows far inland from the Southern Ocean across the south coast of Western Australia.

**Albarracin** /ˌɑːlvɑːrɑːˈθiːn/ a picturesque walled town in the Sierra de Albarracín, north-east Spain, 40 km. (25 miles) from Teruel; pop. (1981) 1,127. Situated at an altitude of 1,182 m. (3,838 ft.), Albarracin is protected as a national monument. South of the town there are caves with prehistoric paintings.

**albedo** the proportion of light or radiation reflected by a surface. Generally, white objects reflect more than dark ones. The mean albedo or reflectivity of the earth's surface is 40 per cent, varying from 80 per cent on fresh clean snow to 10 per cent on dark peaty soil.

**Albena** /ælˈbiːnə/ a resort town in Bulgaria, on the coast of the Black Sea. Developed as a modern resort from 1968, it was named after a character created by the Bulgarian playwright Yordan Yokov.

**Albert** /ˈælbət/, **Lake** (also **Albert Nyanza**) a lake on the Zaire–Uganda frontier in the Rift Valley of east-central Africa, named after the Prince Consort by the English explorer Samuel Baker, who was the first European to sight it (1864); area 5,346 sq. km. (2,064 sq. miles). In 1973 Zaire renamed the lake after its president, Mobutu Sese Seko.

**Alberta** /ælˈbɜːtə/ the westernmost of the three prairie provinces of Canada, bounded on the south by the US and on the west by the Rocky Mountains; area 661,190 sq. km. (255,287 sq. miles); pop. (1991) 2,545,550; capital, Edmonton. Largest cities, Edmonton, Calgary, Lethbridge, Red Deer, Medicine Hat. Highest peak, Mount Columbia (3,747 m., 12,293 ft.). Southern Alberta was once the domain of the Blackfoot nation, settlement by people of European descent taking place largely between 1896 and 1914. Named after the fourth daughter of Queen Victoria, it became a province of Canada in 1905. Coal, oil, gas, timber, grain, and livestock are the chief products, Alberta's greatest period of growth following the development of the petroleum industry after 1947. Amongst the province's leading tourist attractions are the Calgary Stampede and Banff and Jasper national parks.

**Alberta lows** a name given to the climatic depressions that develop east of the northern Rockies, chiefly in Alberta and the Mackenzie valley.

**Albert Canal** a canal in north-east Belgium linking the Meuse and Scheldt rivers, connecting the industrial city of Liège with the port of Antwerp. Built in the 1930s and named after King Albert I, the canal is 128 km. (80 miles) long.

**Albert Nile** that part of the River Nile flowing through north-western Uganda between Lake Albert and Sudan.

**Albertville** /ˈælbətviːl/ a resort town in the Savoy region of south-east France, at the entrance to the Val d'Arly; pop. (1982) 17,500. The town was built in 1845 by King Charles Albert (1798–1849) to replace the old military town of Conflans on the opposite side of the River Arly. It was the venue for the 1992 Winter Olympics.

**Albi** /ælˈbiː/ an industrial town in the Midi-Pyrénées region of southern France, on the River Tarn; pop. (1990) 48,700. Its huge Gothic cathedral is famous for its many paintings, and an annual summer pageant recalls the 13th c. suppression of the Albigensian heretics. The artist Henri de Toulouse-Lautrec (1864–1901) was born in Albi. Agribusiness and the manufacture of glass, chemicals, and textiles, and tourism are the chief industries. **Albigeois** or **Albigensian** adj. & n.

**Albion** /ˈælbɪən/ an ancient name for Great Britain often used in literature as in Shakespeare's Henry V, III. v.—'that nook-shotten isle of Albion'.

**Ålborg** /ˈɔːlbɔːr/ an industrial, transportation and cultural centre on the Lim Fjord, north Jutland, Denmark; pop. (1990) 155,000. The city, which is capital of Nordjylland county, is linked by bridge and tunnel to Nørresundby on the north side of the Lim Fjord, and has many historic buildings and a world-famous art gallery. It has large cement plants and distilleries.

**Albufeira** /ˌælbəˈfeɪrə/ a resort and fishing town on the coast of the Algarve region of southern Portugal; pop. (1991) 6,260.

**Albula Alps** /ælˈbʊlə/ a range of the Rhaetian Alps in south-east Switzerland, to the north of St. Moritz. Rising to heights in excess of 2,000 m. (6,500 ft.), the Albula Alps are traversed by road over the Albula Pass and by rail through the Albula Tunnel.

**Albuquerque** /ˈælbəˌkɜːkɪ/ the largest city in the state of New Mexico, USA; pop. (1990) 384,620. Founded in 1706 by the governor of New Mexico, the original settlement or 'Old Town' was named after the Duke of Alburquerque, Viceroy of New Spain. After 1880 the 'New Town' of Albuquerque developed further east alongside the Santa Fe Railroad. The University of New Mexico (1889), the Bataan Lovelace Medical Center, and the Sandia nuclear and solar research laboratories are located in the city which is a centre for the livestock trade and the production of electronics.

**Albury** /ˈælbərɪ/ a market town on the north bank of the Murray River, New South Wales, Australia; pop. (1991) 63,610 (with Wodonga). Wine, wool, and food-processing are the chief industries.

**Alcalá de Guadaira** /ælkəˈlɑː ðeɪ gwæˈðiːrə/ a city in Andalusia, south-west Spain, on the right bank of the Guadaira River, 12 km. (8 miles) south-east of Seville; pop. (1991) 49,200.

**Alcalá de Henares** /eɪˈnɑːreɪz/ a picturesque city in central Spain, on the River Henares, 25 km. (15 miles) north-east of Madrid; pop. (1991) 162,780. Known to the Romans as Complutum, Alcalá de Henares was the seat of a university (1508) that was moved to Madrid in 1836. The city was the birthplace of Ferdinand I, Catherine of Aragon, and Miguel de Cervantes (1547–1616), author of *Don Quixote*. It has light industries.

**Alcan Highway** see ALASKA HIGHWAY.

**Alcarria** /ˌælkəˈriːə/ a rural district to the east of Guadaljara in central Spain, featured in the books of Camilo José Cela. It includes the Entrepenas Reservoir and the towns of Budia, La Puerta, Pareja, Casana, Cifuentes, Sacedon, Valfermoso, and Trillo.

**Alcatraz** /ˌælkəˈtræz/ a rocky island in San Francisco Bay, California, named after its pelicans (Spanish *álcatraces*). It was the site of a top-security federal prison (1933–63). Since 1972, the island has been part of the Golden Gate National Recreation Area.

**Alcázar de San Juan** /ælˈkæðər ðeɪ sæn hwæn/ a town on the La Mancha plain, in the Castilla-La Mancha region of south-central Spain; pop. (1991) 25,679.

**Alcira** /ælˈθiːrə/ (also **Alzira**) an agricultural centre in the province of Valencia, south-east Spain, on the River Júcar; pop. (1991) 38,300.

**Alcobaça** /ˌælkəˈbɑːsə/ a small town in the district of Leiria, west-central Portugal, in a fruit- and vine-growing region between the Alcoa and Baça rivers; pop. (1991) 5,160. A Cistercian abbey founded in the 12th c. is the burial place of King Pedro I of Portugal.

**Alcobendas** /ælkəˈvendəs/ an industrial town in central Spain, north-east of Madrid; pop. (1991) 79,000.

**Alcorcón** /ælkɒrˈθəʊn/ a south-western outer suburb of Madrid, central Spain; pop. (1991) 140,140.

**Alcoy** /ælˈkɔɪ/ an industrial town in the Valencia region of east Spain, at the centre of an olive- and vine-growing area at the foot of the Sierra de Montcabrer; pop. (1991) 64,580. An annual spring fiesta commemorates the struggle between Christians and Moors. Its industries include paper, textiles, and matches.

**Aldabra** /ælˈdæbrə/ a coral-island group in the Indian Ocean, north-west of Madagascar, comprising the island of Aldabra and the smaller atolls of Assomption, Astove, and Cosmoledo. From 1963 to 1976 it was part of the British Indian Ocean Territory. Noted for its giant land tortoises, it has been administered as a nature reserve since

1976, when it became an outlying dependency of the Seychelles.

**Aldan** /ælˈdæn/ a river in the Yakut (Sakha) region of east Siberia. It flows a distance of 2,240 km. (1,400 miles) north and east from the Stanovoy Khrebet mountains to meet the River Lena east of Yakutsk.

**Aldeburgh** /ˈɔːldəbərə/ a resort town on the coast of Suffolk, England, home of the composer Benjamin Britten who died there in 1976; pop. (est. 1981) 3,000. The annual Aldeburgh Music Festival is held at Snape Maltings near the head of the Alde estuary to the west of the town. The pioneer lady physician Elizabeth Garrett Anderson (1836–1917) who lived at Alde House was the first woman mayor in England (1908).

**Aldermaston** /ˈɔːldərˌmæstən/ a village in Berkshire, England, site of an atomic weapons research establishment. The Campaign for Nuclear Disarmament (CND) held an anti-nuclear protest march (the Aldermaston March) from London to Aldermaston and back each year at Easter from 1958 to 1963.

**Alderney** /ˈɔːldənɪ/ the third-largest and north-ernmost of the Channel Islands; area 8 sq. km. (3 sq. miles); pop. (1986) 2,130. The chief town is St. Anne's. The island gives its name to a breed of cattle that is more generally known as the Guernsey.

**Aldershot** /ˈɔːldəʃɒt/ a town in the county of Hampshire, southern England, site of a military training centre established in 1854; pop. (1981) 54,360.

**Aldwinkle** /ˈɔːldwɪŋkl/ a village in Northamptonshire, England, 8 km. (5 miles) south-west of Oundle. The poet John Dryden (1631–1700) was born in the Old Rectory opposite the church of Aldwinkle All Saints.

**Aleksandrovsk-Sakhalinskiy** /ˌælɪkˈsɑːndrefsk-ˌsakəˈlɪnski/ a seaport on the Russian island of Sakhalin, on the Tatar Strait. Founded in 1881 as a place of exile, the city developed as a local centre for the coal, timber, and fishing industries.

**Aleksinac** /æˈleksiːnæts/ a mining town and agricultural centre in the Republic of Serbia, situated to the north of the River Morava; pop. (1981) 67,290.

**Alençon** /ɑːlɑ̃ˈsɔ̃/ the capital of the department of Orne in the Basse-Normandie region of north-west France; pop. (1990) 31,140. The town, which lies on a bend of the River Sarthe, produces lace and household appliances. Alençon was the birthplace of Thérèse Martin (1873–97) who was canonized St. Thérèse in 1927.

**Alentejo** /ælemˈteɪʒʊ/ a region of south-east Portugal extending over the arid agricultural districts of Beja, Evora, and Portalegre. Its name is derived from an Arabic phrase meaning 'beyond the Tagus' and it was the site of numerous battles in the Middle Ages against both the Moors and the Spaniards. Evora is the main town of Upper or Alto Alentejo, to the north, and Beja the chief centre of Lower or Baixo Alentejo, to the south. Geologically a continuation of the Castillian meseta of central Spain, the natural vegetation includes the commercially important cork oak. Nearly one-tenth of the people of Portugal live in the sparsely populated Alentejo which covers one-quarter of the whole area of the country. The Alter Real breed of horse has been reared in the region since the 18th c.

**Aleppo** /æ'lepəʊ/ (Arabic **Halab** /ha:'la:b/) an ancient city in north-west Syria, the second-largest in the country; pop. (1990) 1,355,000. Occupied by the Hittites, Assyrians, Persians, and Seleucids, Aleppo developed as a commercial centre on the caravan route between the Mediterranean and the countries of the East, particularly after the fall of Palmyra in AD 273, but declined in importance after the advent of sea-trade with the Far East in the late 19th c. The city prospered again after 1921 under French control and continued to develop after Syrian independence in 1941. Grain, fruit, and cotton are grown in the surrounding semidesert region.

**Alessandria** /a:le'sa:ndri:ə/ a city on the River Tanaro in the Piedmont region of north-west Italy, capital of the province of Alessandria; pop. (1990) 93,350. The city is named after the warrior-pope Alexander III who led the local people against the Emperor Frederick Barbarossa in the 12th c. During the 19th c. Alessandria was an important military stronghold. It is now a market and industrial centre with light industries including clothing, furniture, and machinery.

**Ålesund** see AALESUND.

**Aletschhorn** /'a:letʃ,hɔ:n/ a mountain in the Bernese Alps, Switzerland, rising to a height of 4,195 m. (13,763 ft.). The Aletsch glacier is amongst the largest in Europe.

**Aleut** /ə'lju:t/ a native of the Aleutian Islands, Alaska, USA. Closely related to the Inuit, the Aleuts comprise two linguistic subgroups, the Unalaskans of the Alaskan Peninsula and the eastern Aleutian Islands, and the Atkans of the western Aleutians.

**Aleutian Islands** /ə'lju:ʃ(ə)n/ (also **Aleutians**) a chain of virtually treeless volcanic islands in US possession, extending c. 1,930 km. (1,200 miles) west-south-west from the tip of the Alaska Peninsula. Separating the Bering Sea from the Pacific Ocean, the Aleutians comprise five main groups: Fox Islands, Islands of the Four Mountains, Andreanof Islands, Rat Islands, and Near Islands. The main settlement is the town of Dutch Harbor on Unalaska Island. There are several active volcanoes, the highest of which (Shishaldin)

rises to 2,856 m. (9,370 ft.) on Unimak. The islands with their indigenous population of Aleuts were discovered by the Danish explorer Vitus Bering in 1741. Exploited by Russian trappers and fur traders, the Aleutians were later incorporated into the USA following the Alaska purchase of 1867. Their proximity to the Soviet Union gave them a strategic significance during the Cold War.

**Aleutian low** a sub-arctic belt of low pressure that stretches across the North Pacific and is centred over the Aleutian Islands. It is separated by an area of relatively high pressure over the North Pole from a similar North Atlantic low pressure belt centred over Iceland. The Aleutian lows are most intense during mid-winter.

**Aleutian Range** a range of mountains extending c. 965 km. (600 miles) south-westwards along the Alaska Peninsula from Anchorage. Rising to 2,047 m. (6,715 ft.) at Mt. Katmai and 2,537 m. (8,225 ft.) at Veniaminof Volcano, it continues into the North Pacific as the Aleutian Islands.

**Aleutian Trench** a deep ocean trench in the North Pacific that runs west of and parallel to the Aleutian Islands, falling to depths below 7,000 m. (22,700 ft.).

**Alexander Archipelago** /,ælɪg'za:ndə(r)/ a group of c. 1,100 US islands in the Gulf of Alaska, forming the remnants of a submerged mountain system. Rugged and densely forested, the largest islands are Baranof, Chichagof, Prince of Wales, Admiralty, Kuiu, Kupreanof, and Revillagigedo. Sitka, Hoonah, Petersburg, and Ketchikan are the chief settlements.

**Alexander Bay** a bay at the mouth of the Orange River on the frontier between Namibia and South Africa.

**Alexandretta** /,ælɪgza:n'dretə/ **1.** a former administrative district on the east Mediterranean coast of Turkey that gained the status of a semi-autonomous region of Syria after World War I. A constant source of tension between Syria and Turkey, the so-called Sanjak of Alexandretta voted in 1938 to become an autonomous state known as the Republic of Hatay, but a year later it was once more incorporated into Turkey. **2.** the former name of the Turkish Mediterranean port of ISKENDERUN.

**Alexandria** /,ælɪg'za:ndrɪə/ (Arabic **El Iskandarîya**) the chief port and second-largest city of Egypt, on the Mediterranean coast, north-west of Cairo; pop. (1991) 3,295,000. Founded in 332 BC by Alexander the Great, after whom it is named, it became a major centre of Hellenistic and Jewish culture, with renowned libraries, and was the capital city until the Arab invasions c. AD 641. On an island off the coast was the Pharos lighthouse (3rd c. BC), often considered one of the Seven Wonders of the World. It is a modern industrial city with tanneries, oil refinery, chemical plants, and vehicle-assembly plants. Its deep-water docks handle three-quarters of Egypt's overseas trade. **Alexandrian** *adj. & n.*

**Alexandria 1.** a US city in central Louisiana, on the Red River; pop. (1990) 49,190. The city is a service centre for tourism, agriculture, and forestry. **2.** a deep-water port and residential suburb of Washington on the Potomac River, north-east Virginia, USA; pop. (1990) 111,180. George Washington, who helped plan the street layout in 1749, lived at nearby Mount Vernon. Its varied industries include fertilizers, chemicals, and farm equipment.

**Alexandroupolis** /ˌælɪgzɑːnˈdruːpələs/ an Aegean seaport of Thrace in north-eastern Greece, capital of the district of Evros; pop. (1981) 34,535. Annexed by Bulgaria during World War I, the city was returned to Greece in 1919.

**Alföld** see GREAT ALFÖLD and LITTLE ALFÖLD.

**Alfortville** /ˈælfɔːviːl/ a town in the Val-de-Marne department of northern France, immediately south-east of Paris; pop. (1990) 36,240.

**Al Fujayrah** see FUJAIRAH.

**Algarve** /ælˈgɑːv/, **the** (also **Faro**) the southernmost region of Portugal, on the Atlantic coast, stretching from Cape St. Vincent in the west to the River Guadiana on the Spanish frontier; area 5,072 sq. km. (1,959 sq. miles); pop. (1989) 344,900; capital, Faro. The hilly Upper Algarve (Alto Algarve) is sparsely populated while the scenic, rocky coastline of the Lower Algarve (Baixo Algarve) has attracted tourism development. Coextensive with the administrative district of Faro, the irrigated plantations of the Algarve produce almonds, olives, figs, oranges, sugar-cane, cotton, and rice. (Arabic *al* the + *gharb* west).

**Algeciras** /ˌældʒɪˈsɪərəs/ a city in the province of Cadiz, southern Spain, a ferry port and resort on the Bay of Algeciras, opposite Gibraltar; pop. (1991) 101,365.

**Algeria** (French **L'Algérie**) official name **The Democratic and Popular Republic of Algeria** a North African country that lies between Morocco, to the west, and Libya, to the east, and  stretches from the heart of the Sahara Desert northwards to the Mediterranean coast; area 2,318,741 sq. km. (919,595 sq. miles); pop. (est. 1991) 26,000,000; official language, Arabic; capital, Algiers. The second-largest state in Africa, Algeria has a narrow fertile coastal plain that is separated from the Sahara Desert by the Tellian and Saharan Atlas mountain ranges. In the northern 12 per cent of the country, where 91 per cent of the people live, summers are hot with little rainfall. Winter rain

begins in October, with frost and snow occurring only on the highest slopes of the Atlas mountains. The people are mainly Muslim and of Arab and Berber stock; about 1.5 million are nomads or semi-settled Bedouin. Largely under state control, the economy is dependent on the export of crude oil, liquefied natural gas, and their derivatives. While about 30 per cent of Algerians are dependent on the land, agriculture contributes less than 12 per cent of the country's GDP. Main agricultural products are wheat and dates. Algeria came under nominal Turkish rule in the 16th c., but the indigenous peoples always retained a high degree of independence, dominating the Barbary coast until colonized by France in the mid-19th c. Heavily settled by French immigrants, Algeria was closely integrated with metropolitan France, but the refusal of the European settlers to grant equal rights to the Arab and Berber populations led to increasing political instability and civil war in the 1950s. In 1962 the country was granted independence as a result of a referendum and became a republic. The departure of the French caused grave damage to the previously prosperous Algerian economy, with the result that the next two decades were characterized by slow economic recovery and limited external contacts. Following independence, the country was governed with military backing by the National Liberation Front (FLN) which maintained a one-party system until 1989. Growing support for the Islamic Salvation Front (FIS), which advocated the creation of an Islamic state, led to the cancellation of democratic elections in 1992 and renewed political instability.
**Algerian** *adj. & n.*

**Algiers** /ælˈdʒɪəz/ (French **Alger** /ælˈʒeɪ/, Arabic **El Djezair** /dʒeˈzeə(r)/) the capital of Algeria and one of the leading Mediterranean ports of North Africa, on the Bay of Algiers; pop. (1989) 1,722,000. Founded by the Phoenicians, the city was later known as Icosium by the Romans. It was re-established by the Arabs in the 10th c. and later captured by the Turks in 1511. Thereafter it became a base for the Barbary pirates who preyed upon European shipping until French forces captured the port in 1830. During World War II Algiers was the headquarters of the French provisional government and of the Allied Forces. One of the oldest buildings in the city, the Sidi Abderrahman Mosque is a major centre of Muslim pilgrimage and there are many other fine mosques and museums. Wine, citrus fruit, iron ore, and cork are major exports and industries include oil refining, metallurgy, chemicals, engineering, and consumer goods.

**Algoa Bay** /ælˈgəʊə/ a bay on the south-east coast of Cape Province, South Africa. Port Elizabeth is the principal seaport. Diaz landed here after rounding the Cape in 1488.

**Algonquian** /ælˈgɒŋkwɪən/ (also **Algonkian**) **1.** a large group of North American Indian tribes speaking related languages, pushed northward and westward by colonial expansion in the 18th and 19th c. **2.** any of their languages or dialects, forming one of the largest groups of American Indian languages and including Ojibwa, Cree, Blackfoot, Cheyenne, Fox, and Delaware, which are spoken mainly in the north Middle West of the US, Montana, and south-central Canada. Many English and American words have been adopted from this group, e.g. *moccasin, moose, pow-wow, squaw, toboggan.*

**Alhambra** /æl'hæmbrə/ a fortified Moorish palace, the last stronghold of the Muslim kings of Granada, built between 1248 and 1354 in the Andalusian city of Granada, southern Spain. It is an outstanding example of Moorish architecture with its marble courts and fountains, delicate columns and archways, and wall decorations of carved and painted stucco. (Arabic = red castle.)

**Alhambra** a city in the Los Angeles conurbation, southern California, USA, forming a residential and industrial suburb to the north-east of Los Angeles and to the south of Pasadena; pop. (1990) 82,100. Electronic and electrical goods are manufactured.

**Al-Hudayda** see HODEIDA.

**Aliákmon** /æl'jɑːkmɒn/ (also **Haliacmon** or **Vistritsa**) the longest river in Greece. Rising near Lake Prespa in Macedonia, it flows *c.* 320 km. (200 miles) south-east then north-east towards the Gulf of Salonika.

**Alicante** /ˌælɪˈkænteɪ/ **1.** a province of Valencia, south-east Spain; area 5,863 sq. km. (2,264 sq. miles); pop. (1991) 1,292,560. **2.** the seaport capital of Alicante province, on the Mediterranean coast of south-east Spain; pop. (1991) 270,951. Known to the Romans as Lucentum and the Moors as Al-Lucant, Alicante is now an important centre for the shipping of wine, fruit, raisins, almonds, oil, esparto grass, and vegetables.

**Alice Springs** /'ælɪs/ a railway terminus and supply centre, serving the outback of Northern Territory; pop. (1991) 20,450. European discovery was by William Whitfield Mills while surveying a route for the Overland Telegraph Line in 1871, the site was named after the wife of the South Australian Superintendent of Telegraphs. The Royal Flying Doctor Service is based in Alice Springs.

**alidade** /'ælɪdeɪd/ a surveying instrument for determining directions or measuring angles.

**Aligarh** /ˌæliːˈɡɑːr/ a city in the state of Uttar Pradesh, north-central India; pop. (1991) 480,000. Comprising the ancient fort of Aligarh and the former city of Koil, Aligarh is a centre of agricultural trade and cotton milling. Its Muslim university (1921) was opened in 1875 as the Anglo-Oriental College.

**Al Jizah** the Arabic name for EL GIZA.

**Alkmaar** /'ælkmɑː(r)/ a city and tourist centre in the province of North Holland, north-west Netherlands; pop. (1991) 90,780. Founded in the 10th c., it received its charter in 1254. The city is noted for its Edam cheese market, and has light industries.

**Allahabad** /'ɑːləhəˌbɑːd/ a city in the state of Uttar Pradesh, north-central India; pop. (1991) 806,000. Situated at the confluence of the sacred Jumna and Ganges rivers, Allahabad is a place of Hindu pilgrimage. The Ashoka Pillar dating from 232 BC stands inside the Moghul fort built by Akbar in 1583. It was here that the East India Company handed over control of India to the British government in 1858. There is a Great Mosque and a university founded in 1887. Anand Bhawan was the family home of the Nehru dynasty of political leaders which included Jawaharlal Nehru, Indira Gandhi, and Rajiv Gandhi. The main industries are textiles and foodstuffs.

**Allegheny Mountains** /ˌæləˈɡemɪ/ (also **Alleghenies**) a mountain range of the Appalachian system in the eastern USA. Rising to heights between 610 m. (2,000 ft.) and 1,463 m. (4,800 ft.) and extending *c.* 805 km. (500 miles) from Pennsylvania southwards to Virginia and West Virginia, the Alleghenies are rich in coal, iron ore, hydrocarbons, and timber. Its eastern face is sometimes known as the Allegheny Front.

**Allentown** an industrial and commercial city in east Pennsylvania, USA, on the River Lehigh; pop. (1990) 105,090. Laid out in 1752, Allentown was originally incorporated as Northamptontown. The city, which lies at the heart of Pennsylvania Dutch country, later took the name of its founder, Chief Justice William Allen. There are vehicle, cement, clothing, machinery, and many light industries.

**Alleppey** /əˈlepiː/ (also **Alappuzha**) a port on the Malabar coast of Kerala state, south India; pop. (1991) 264,900. Copra, coir, spices, and coffee are the chief products of this trading centre which is noted for its canals and its annual snake-boat race.

**Allerød** /'ælɜːrɒd/ the name given to a warm climatic epoch that occured during the late glacial period *c.* 10,000–9,000 BC.

**Allgau Alps** /'ɔːlɡɔɪ/ (German **Allgäuer Alpen**) a range of the European Alps separating Bavaria from the Tyrol of Austria. The highest peak is Madelegabel (2,645 m., 8,678 ft.)

**Allier** /'ælɪˌeɪ/ **1.** a department in the Auvergne region of central France, comprising the watersheds of the Allier, Loire, and Cher rivers; area 7,340 sq. km. (2,835 sq. miles); pop. (1990) 357,710; capital, Moulins. **2.** a river of central France which rises in the Cévennes and flows 410 km. (258 miles) north-west to meet the Loire near Nevers.

**Alloa** /'æləʊə/ Clackmannan, a town in central Scotland, on the River Forth; pop. (1981) 26,430.

Textiles, brewing, distilling, and engineering are the chief industries.

**Alloway** /'æləweɪ/ a small village just south of Ayr in south-west Scotland, birthplace of the poet Robert Burns (1759–96).

**alluvium** /ə'lu:vɪəm/ a deposit of sand, silt, or gravel laid down by rivers, especially when in flood. An alluvial fan is formed when a river opens out into a valley after following a constricted course.

**Alma-Ata** /ˌælmə 'ɑ:tə/ see ALMATY.

**Almadén** /ˌælmə'den/ a town in the province of Ciudad Real, south-central Spain, in the Sierra Morena Mountains; pop. (1981) 15,000. Mercury has been mined locally since ancient times. The nearby mercury mines were rented by the Fugger family of Augsburg (1525–1645) and by the Rothschilds in the 19th c.

**Almanzora** /ˌælmən'θɔ:rə/ a river in the province of Almeria, southern Spain. Rising in the Sierra de los Filabres, it flows 130 km. (81 miles) east and south-east to meet the Mediterranean near the town of Vera, not far from which are the **Cuevas de Almanzora** cave dwellings.

**Almaty** /æl'mɑ:tɪ/ (formerly **Alma-Ata**) the capital of Kazakhstan in Central Asia; pop. (1991) 1,515,300. Founded in 1854 as a military town and trading centre, and known as Verny until 1921, Almaty developed into an industrial and commercial city after becoming a terminus of the Turkestan–Siberia railroad. Following the breakup of the USSR, representatives of 11 former Soviet republics established the Commonwealth of Independent States at an historic meeting held in Almaty in December 1991 (Alma-Ata Declaration). In 1993 the government changed the city's name from Alma-Ata to Almaty, a closer transliteration of the Kazakh name long rendered in the Russian form. It trades in local agricultural products and manufactures machinery, railway equipment, leather, and timber.

**Almelo** /æl'mələʊ/ a textile-manufacturing city in the province of Overijssel, east Netherlands; pop. (1991) 62,668.

**Almeria** /ˌælmeɪˈri:ə/ **1.** a mountainous province in Andalusia, southern Spain; area 8,774 sq. km. (3,389 sq. miles); pop.(1991) 455,500. Iron, copper, mercury, silver, and lead are mined. **2.** the seaport capital of Almeria province; pop. (1991) 157,760. It exports grapes, esparto grass, and iron ore. It has refineries and processing plants.

**Almetyevsk** /ˌælmɪt'jefsk/ an oil-refining town in the autonomous Russian republic of Tatarstan, south-east of Kazan; pop. (1990) 130,000.

**Almirante Brown** /ˌælmə'rɑ:nti:/ a city in the province of Buenos Aires, eastern Argentina; pop. (1991) 449,105. It was first settled in 1873 by residents of Buenos Aires fleeing from a yellow fever epidemic.

**Almohad** /'ælmə‚hæd/ an Islamic dynasty that ruled in Morocco and Spain during the 12th and 13th centuries. The Almohads built many of the defensive monasteries or *ribats* of North Africa. They were defeated by the Portuguese and Spanish on the Iberian peninsula in 1228 and superseded by the Merenid dynasty in Morocco in 1269.

**Almoravid** /ˌælmər'eɪvɪd/ an Islamic dynasty that ruled in Morocco and Spain in the 11th and 12th centuries until overthrown by the Almohads in 1147. They founded the city of Marrakesh.

**almwind** /'ɑ:mwɪnd/ a warm wind that blows over the Tatra Mountains into southern Poland.

**Alnwick** /'ænɪk/ a market town in Northumberland, north-east England, on the River Aln; pop. (est. 1981) 7,500. Alnwick Castle has been the historic seat of the Percy family, Dukes of Northumberland since 1310. Malcolm Canmore, King of Scotland, was murdered here in 1093.

**Alor Setar** /ˌælɒr sə'tɑ:r/ the capital of the Malaysian state of Kedah, at the confluence of the Kedah and Padang Terap rivers, central Malay Peninsula; pop. (1980) 71,682. It is a centre for trading in rice and rubber.

**Alost** /æ'lɒst/ the French name for the city of AALST in Belgium.

**alp** /ælp/ a high summer pasture in Switzerland.

**Alpe Adria** /ælp 'eɪdrɪə/ an international association of eleven neighbouring regions in Austria, Germany, Italy, Croatia, and Slovenia set up in 1978 to promote cultural and economic links.

**Alpes-de-Haute-Provence** /ælp də əʊt prɒ'vãs/ a mountainous department at the southern end of the Alps, in the region of Provence-Alpes-Côtes d'Azur, south-east France; area 6,925 sq. km. (2,675 sq. miles); pop. (1990) 130,880; capital, Digne. The department was known as Basses-Alpes until 1970.

**Alpes Maritimes** /ˌælp mærɪ'ti:m/ a department in the region of Provence-Alpes-Côtes d'Azur, south-east France, on the Italian frontier and at the southern end of the French Maritime Alps; area 4,299 sq. km. (1,660 sq. miles); pop.(1990) 871,830; capital, Nice.

**Alpheeus** /æl'fi:əs/ (Greek **Alfiós** /ɑ:l'fjɒs/) a river of southern Greece that rises in the Taygetus Mts. and flows 112 km. (70 miles) north-westwards across the Peloponnese peninsula to the Ionian Sea near Pyrgos.

**Alphen aan den Rijn** /'ɑ:lfən ɑ:n den ‚raɪn/ an industrial city in the province of South Holland, west Netherlands, on the Rhine, north-east of Rotterdam; pop. (1991) 62,400.

**Alps** /ælps/ one of the principal mountain systems of Europe extending through a series of ranges for a distance of 800 km. (500 miles) in a wide curve from the Mediterranean coast of south-east France, through northern Italy, Switzerland, Liechtenstein, southern Germany, Austria, Slovenia, and Croatia. The principal ranges are divided into three groups: (1) the Western Alps (Ligurian, Maritime, Cottian, Dauphiné, Graian); (2) the Middle Alps (Pennine, Bernese, Glarner, Lepontine, Albula, Otztaler, Ortler, Trientine, Rhaetian, Silvretta); and (3) the Eastern Alps (Zillertaler, Kitzbühler, Noric, Carnic, Julian). The Mont Blanc Group (with 25 peaks over 4,000 m., 13,000 ft.) rises to a height of 4,807 m. (15,771 ft.) at Mont Blanc which is the highest mountain in the Alps. There are numerous glaciers, amongst the largest of which is the Aletsch glacier in the Bernese Alps. While the railway across the Semmerling Pass was in 1854 the first to cross the main range of the Alps, the Bernina Pass railway is the highest Alpine through-line at 2,257 m. (7,405 ft.). A rack railway to the saddle between the Jungfrau and the Mönch (completed in 1912) is the highest railway in Europe at 3,454 m. (11,332 ft.). The Alps are the source of many of Europe's greatest rivers including the Rhine, Rhône, Po, and Drava.

**Al Qahira** the Arabic name for CAIRO.

**Als** /æls/ (German **Alsen**) a Baltic island lying off the east coast of Jutland, Denmark, from which it is separated by the Alsen Sound (Alsensund); area 321 sq. km. (125 sq. miles). Sønderborg is the chief town. The island, which is now a popular tourist resort, belonged to Germany between 1864 and 1920.
**Alpine** *adj. & n.*

**Alsace** /æl'sæs/ a region of north-east France between the Vosges Mts. and the Rhine; area 8,280 sq. km. (3,198 sq. miles); pop. (1990) 1,624,370; capital, Strasbourg. Mulhouse is the chief centre of industry. The region comprises the departments of Bas-Rhin and Haut-Rhin. It was annexed with part of Lorraine (the annexed territory was known as Alsace-Lorraine) after the Franco-Prussian war of 1870, and restored to France after World War I. Its architecture and traditions reflect both German and French influence. It is a major industrial region with hydroelectric power from the Rhine and specializing in textiles and wine-making.
**Alsatian** *adj. & n.*

**Alta** /'æltə/ (Norwegian **Altaelv**) a river in northern Norway that rises near the Finnish frontier and flows northwards through Finnmark county to meet the Alta Fjord at the town of Alta. Prehistoric rock carvings of the Komsa culture were discovered at Hjemmeluft near Alta in 1925.

**Altai** /'æltaɪ/ (also **Altay**) a territory (*kray*) of Russia in south-west Siberia; area 261,590 sq. km. (101,000 sq. miles); pop. (1990) 2,835,000; capital, Barnaul.

**Altai Mountains** (also **Altai Shan**) a mountain system of central Asia that extends eastwards from Kazakhstan into west Mongolia and

northern China with an average height between 2,000 and 3,000 m. (6,500–10,000 ft.) above sea-level. The Irtysh and Ob rivers rise in the Altai.

**Altaic** /æl'taɪk/ a family of central Asian languages comprising the Turkic, Mongolian, and Tungusic groups, whose common features include vowel harmony, with all the vowels of a word belonging to the same class (i.e. either front or back).

**Altamira** /ˌæltə'miːrə/ a town in the state of Pará, north-east Brazil; pop. (1990) 157,880. Altamira attracted world attention in 1989 when it was the venue of a major rally of Amerindians and environmentalists who gathered to protest against the devastation of the Amazonian rain forest.

**Altamira** the site of a cave with palaeolithic rock paintings, south of Santander in north-east Spain, discovered in 1879. The paintings are boldly executed polychrome figures of animals, including deer, wild boar, aurochs, and especially bison, depicted with a sure realism; they are dated to the upper Magdalenian period.

**Altamura** /ˌæltə'muːrə/ a market and commercial town in Apulia (Puglia), south-east Italy that takes its name from the high wall built around it in the 13th c. by Frederick II as a defence against the Moors; pop. (1990) 57,270.

**Altay** see ALTAI.

**Altay** /'æltaɪ/ a town in Xinjiang autonomous region, north-west China, situated in the southern foothills of the Altai Mountains, close to the Mongolian frontier; pop. (1986) 169,000.

**Altay** the capital of Gobi-Altai county, south-west Mongolia, situated in the Altai Mountains to the north of the Gobi Desert.

**Altdorf** /'æltdɔːf/ the capital of the canton of Uri in central Switzerland, on the south-east shore of Lake Urner; pop. (1980) 8,200. There is a statue of William Tell on the site where he is alleged to have shot the apple on his son's head. Dating from 1581, the Capuchin monastery is the oldest in Switzerland.

**Altenburg** /'ɑːltənbʊəg/ an industrial town in the German state of Saxony, on the River Pleisse; pop. (1981) 55,830. From 1826 to 1918 it was capital of the Duchy of Saxe-Altenburg. Its light industries include sewing machines and machine tools.

**altiplano** /ˌæltɪ'plɑːnəʊ/ a high-altitude plateau or plain, especially that in the Andes in western Bolivia and southern Peru.

**Alto Adige** /ˌæltəʊ 'ɑːdɪˌdʒeɪ/ (also **South Tyrol**, German **Südtirol**) a largely German-speaking region of north-eastern Italy that became an autonomous region in 1992. It comprises the northern part of the former Trentino-Alto Adige region.

**altocumulus** /ˌæltəʊˈkjuːmjʊləs/ a cloud formation at medium altitude consisting of rounded masses with a level base.

**Alton** /ˈɔːltən/ a market town in east Hampshire, southern England, near Basingstoke; pop. (1981) 14,370. Alton was the home of the 16th-c. English poet Edmund Spenser and the novelist Jane Austen who lived here from 1809 to 1817. The town was also the 'Galton' of Sir Compton Mackenzie's novels.

**Alton** a commercial and industrial city in south-west Illinois, USA, on the Mississippi River near its junction with the Missouri; pop. (1990) 32,900. The city, which was laid out in 1817, was a major supply centre for the Union armies during the Civil War. It has oil refineries, machine shops, and a large bottle-making industry. Alton was the home of Robert Wadlow who was alleged to be the tallest man in history with a height of 9 ft.

**Alton Towers** a pleasure ground at the former seat of the Earls of Shrewsbury, near Ashbourne in Staffordshire, central England. Alton Towers features as 'Muriel Towers' in Disraeli's novel *Lothair* published in 1870.

**Altoona** /ælˈtuːnə/ an industrial city and railway centre in Pennsylvania, USA, on the eastern slopes of the Allegheny Mts.; pop. (1990) 51,881. First settled in 1769 the city was laid out in 1849 by the Pennsylvania Railroad as a switching point for trains about to negotiate the famous 'Horseshoe Bend' on the line crossing the Alleghenies from Pittsburgh to Philadelphia. It has large railway construction and repair shops, and many light industries.

**altostratus** /ˌæltəʊˈstrɑːtəs/ a continuous and uniformly flat cloud formation at medium altitude.

**Altötting** /æltˈɜːtɪŋ/ a town in Bavaria, southern Germany, in the valley of the River Inn east of Munich, a place of pilgrimage since a local miracle took place in 1489; pop. (1991) 11,000. Its Holy Chapel houses a 'Black Madonna' and in the Stiftskirche is a richly endowed treasury which includes among its collection the late-Gothic Golden Horse.

**Altrincham** /ˈɔːltrɪŋəm/ a market town in the borough of Trafford, Greater Manchester, England; pop. (1981) 39,641. Engineering and market gardening are important.

**Altun Ha** /ˈæltʊn hɑː/ the remains of an ancient Mayan ceremonial centre to the north of Belize City, Belize, Central America.

**Altun Mountains** /ˈɑːltʊn/ (Chinese **Altun Shan**) a range of mountains at the northern edge of the Tibetan plateau, in the Chinese province of Xinjiang. The Altun Mts. are an offshoot of the Kunlun range, separating the Tarim and Qaidam basins.

**Alturas Mountains** /ælˈtuːrəs/ a mountain range in north-east Portugal rising to 1,279 m. (4,196 ft.) at Cabreira in the district of Braga.

**Älvsborg** /ˈælfsbɒr/ (also **Elfsborg**) a county of south-west Sweden on the Norwegian frontier; area 11,394 sq. km. (4,401 sq. miles); pop. (1990) 441,390; capital, Vänersborg.

**Alwar** /ˈælwər/ a city in Rajasthan state, north-central India; pop. (1991) 211,000. Noted for its huge fort and palaces, Alwar was capital of a state of the same name that merged with Rajasthan in 1949. Cotton, grain, oilseed, and marble are traded.

**Amagasaki** /ˌæməɡəˈsɑːkɪ/ an industrial city to the west of Osaka in the Kinki region of Honshu Island, Japan; pop. (1990) 499,000. It has iron and steel, chemical, and textile industries.

**Amalfi** /əˈmɑːlfɪ/ a small resort town and ferry port on the coast of Campania, southern Italy, on the Gulf of Sorrento, 40 km. (25 miles) south-east of Naples; pop. (1990) 5,900. During the 9th c. Amalfi became the focal point of a tiny but wealthy maritime republic, but fell into decline in the 12th c. after being sacked by Normans and Pisans. In 1343 a storm destroyed the greater part of the town which survived thereafter as a fishing settlement.

**Amalfi Coast** that part of the coastline of Campania in southern Italy stretching from Positano to Cetara and centred on the town of Amalfi. Noted for its fishing villages and vineyards, the Amalfi Coast largely comprises the territory of the former maritime republic.

**Amapá** /æməˈpɑː/ a federal administrative territory in northern Brazil, to the north of the Amazon delta; area 140,276 sq. km. (54,181 sq. miles); pop. (1991) 288,690; capital, Macapá. Largely covered by tropical rainforest, Amapá has a fast-growing population attracted by the timber, rubber, and mining industries.

**Amaravati** /əməˈrɑːvətiː/ a ruined city in Andhra Pradesh, eastern India, on the Krishna River. It was a Mahayana Buddhist centre and later, capital of the medieval Reddi kings of Andhra.

**Amarillo** /æməˈrɪləʊ/ a city in the panhandle of north-west Texas; pop. (1990) 157,615. Originally known as Ragtown when it was settled in 1887, it was later renamed Amarillo after the colour of a creek bank (Spanish = yellow). The 'Yellow Rose of Texas' is a symbol of the city which lies at the centre of one of the world's largest cattle-producing areas. In addition to copper, oil and natural gas, nearly all of the world's supply of helium gas comes from within a 150-mile radius of Amarillo. It is also a centre of the nuclear-weapons industry.

**Amarna** /əˈmɑːnə/, **Tell el-** the modern name of Akhetaten (= the horizon of the Aten), the short-lived capital of ancient Egypt, founded by Akhenaten in the fifth year of his reign 450 km.

(280 miles) north of Thebes and dismantled by his successors. It is particularly famous for its lively and expressionistic art, which shows a conscious divergence from the old artistic conventions, and for the cuneiform tablets known as the Amarna Letters, discovered in 1887. These texts contain letters written by Assyrian and Mitannian kings, and by native chiefs and Egyptian governors in Syria and Palestine, providing valuable insight into Near Eastern diplomacy of the 14th c. BC.

**Amasya** /ə'mɑːsjə/ (also **Amasia**) **1.** a province of northern Turkey; area 5,520 sq. km. (2,132 sq. miles); pop. (1990) 357,190. **2.** its capital, situated just north of the ancient caravan route from Smyrna (Izmir) to Persia; pop. (1990) 162,544. It is a marketing centre for the surrounding fertile region. Formerly the seat of the kings of Cappadocia, Amasya was the birthplace of the Greek geographer and historian Strabo c. 60 BC.

**Amazon** /'æməz(ə)n/ a member of a mythical race of female warriors in Scythia and Asia Minor. Their name was explained by the ancient Greeks as meaning 'without a breast', in connection with the fable that they destroyed the right breast so as not to interfere with the use of the bow, but this is probably the popular etymology of an unknown word. They caught the Greek imagination and appear in many legends. Amazons appear as allies of the Trojans in the Trojan war, and their queen, Penthesilea, was killed by Achilles. One of the labours of Hercules was to obtain the girdle of Hippolyta, queen of the Amazons. According to Athenian legend, Attica once suffered an invasion of Amazons, which Theseus repelled. In later years the name has been applied to groups of female warriors such as the Amazons of South America and the royal bodyguard of the former kings of Dahomey in Africa.

**Amazon** (Spanish **Río de las Amazonas**, Portuguese **Rio Amazonas**) a great river in South America, 6,570 km. (4,080 miles) long, flowing through Peru, Colombia, and Brazil into the Atlantic Ocean on the north coast of Brazil. Its two principal headstreams in the Andes are the Marañon and Ucayali rivers. After the Nile, it is the second-longest river in the world. It drains two-fifths of the continent (7 million sq. km., 2.8 million sq. miles) and in terms of water-flow it is the largest river in the world with a mean annual discharge of 95,000 cu. m. of water per second. Northern tributaries, which include the Napo, Japurá, Negro, and Jari rivers, flood in June while southern tributaries, such as the Purus, Madeira, Tapajos, and Xingu rivers, flood in March. At its mouth, alluvial deposits and land submergence have created a large delta with many islands, the largest of which is Marajó. The Amazon bore various names after its discovery by Vincente Pinzón in 1500 and was finally named because of a tribe of female warriors believed to live somewhere on its banks. In 1541 the Spanish explorer Francisco de Orellana was the first man to travel the greater part of its full

length from the Andes to the Atlantic. Ships with a draft of 4.3 m. (14 ft.) can reach as far upstream as Iquitos in Peru, c. 3,700 km. (2,300 miles) from the Atlantic.
**Amazonian** adj. & n.

**Amazonas** /æmə'zəunəs/ the largest of the federal states of Brazil, occupying the north-west corner of the country and traversed by the River Amazon; area 1,564,445 sq. km. (604,266 sq. miles); pop. (1991) 2,102,900; capital, Manaus.

**Amazonas** an administrative territory in south-east Colombia with a southern boundary along the River Amazon; area 109,665 sq. km. (42,358 sq. miles); pop. (1985) 13,210; capital, Leticia.

**Amazonas** a department of northern Peru through which flows the River Marañon, the shorter of the two headstreams of the River Amazon; area 41,297 sq. km. (15,951 sq. miles); pop. (est. 1990) 335,300; capital, Chachapoyas.

**Amazonas** a federal territory of southern Venezuela, between the Orinoco and Negro rivers; area 170,500 sq. km. (65,857 sq. miles); pop. (1980) 45,600; capital, Puerto Ayacucho.

**Amazonia** /æmə'zəunɪə/ **1.** a general name for the territory surrounding the Amazon river in South America, principally in Brazil, Peru, Colombia, Venezuela, and Bolivia. Crossed by the equator in the north, this region comprises about one-third of the world's remaining tropical rainforest. The building of the Trans-Amazonian Highway, linking the overpopulated cities of the east coast to the interior, has resulted in a rapid increase in the immigrant population of Brazilian states such as Amazonas and Pará. The alarming rate of forest clearance and its impact on the environment, coupled with the scale of proposed mining and hydroelectric developments and the fate of indigenous Amerindian people brought Amazonia to the attention of the wider world during the 1980s. **2.** a national park protecting 10,000 sq. km. (3,850 sq. miles) of tropical rainforest in the state of Pará, northern Brazil.

**Ambala** /əm'bɑːlə/ (also **Umballa**) an industrial city and railway junction in the state of Haryana, north-central India; pop. (1991) 120,000. It is a centre of the wheat trade, and a military station, with numerous light industries including vehicle parts, pharmaceuticals, and scientific instruments. Nearby is the Ambala Sadar, a cantonment laid out by the British in a grid pattern.

**Ambato** /æm'bɑːtəu/ the capital of the Andean province of Tungurahua, central Ecuador, on the River Ambato; pop. (1990) 229,190. Known as the 'garden city' of Ecuador, the picturesque market town of Ambato was devastated by a volcano in 1698 and an earthquake in 1949. It has a colourful weekly market and an annual fruit and flower festival in February.

**Amber Coast** /'æmbə(r)/ the name given to the northern Atlantic coastline of the Dominican Republic. Its chief town is Puerto Plata, behind which are mountains that contain the world's richest deposits of amber.

**Amberg** /'ɑ:mbɜ:g/ a city in Bavaria, southern Germany, in the valley of the Vils east of Nuremberg; pop. (1991) 43,150. Formerly the capital of the Upper Palatinate, it is a centre of the iron industry.

**Ambergris Cay** /'æmbə,gri:s/ a southern extension of the Yucatán Peninsula forming a long island lying to the east of Chetumal Bay which separates it from the coast of mainland Belize, Central America. The chief town is the Belizean resort of San Pedro.

**Ambleside** /'æmb(ə)lsaɪd/ a small town in the Lake District of north-west England, in Cumbria region, north of Lake Windermere; pop. (1981) 3,188. Ambleside has literary associations with Matthew Arnold who lived here for a time, and with William and Dorothy Wordsworth who lived in nearby Grasmere.

**Ambon** /æm'bɔ:n/ (also **Amboina** or **Amboyna**) **1.** a mountainous island in the Banda Sea just to the south-west of Seram in the Moluccas, east Indonesia; area c. 1,000 sq. km. (386 sq. miles). Discovered by Portuguese explorers in 1512, Ambon was taken by the Dutch in 1605. It was held for short periods (1796–1802, 1810–14) by the British. Its principal exports are copra and spices. The island gives its name to the decorative wood known as amboyna which is derived from the tree *Pterocarpus indicus*. The Ambonese are one of Indonesia's few Christian communities. **2.** its chief port and town, also capital of Maluku province (the Moluccas); pop. (1980) 79,640. Maintained by the Dutch as a naval base until its capture by the Japanese in 1942, Ambon was, in 1950, the focal point of a revolt against the Indonesian government in an attempt to establish a South Moluccan Republic.

**Ambrym** /'æmbrɪm/ (also **Ambrim**) a Pacific island in the Vanuatu archipelago, dominated by the twin volcanic peaks of Mt. Marum and Mt. Benbow; area 682 sq. km. (263 sq. miles); pop. (est. 1988) 8,000. The island has also been called the Black Island because of the volcanic ash that dominates the landscape. Major volcanic eruptions occured in 1913, 1929, and 1950. Ambrym is noted for its sorcery and its sand drawings.

**Ameland** /'ɑ:mələ:nt/ a Dutch island in the West Frisian group, separated from the mainland of the Netherlands by the Waddenzee; area 57 sq. km. (22 sq. miles). Nes is the principal settlement of the island which is noted for its horses. There is a ferry link with Holwerd.

**America** (also **the Americas**) a name sometimes applied specifically to the United States of America but more generally used to describe a continent of the New World or Western Hemisphere, consisting of two great land masses, North and South America, joined by the narrow isthmus of Central America. Human beings first arrived in the Americas c. 30,000 BC; by 8,000 BC they had settled the whole continent. North America was probably visited by Norse seamen in the 8th or 9th c., but its European discovery is credited to Christopher Columbus, who reached the West Indies in 1492 and the South American mainland in 1498. America derives its name from *Americus Vespucius*, the Latin form of the name of the Italian navigator Amerigo Vespucci (1441–1512) who travelled along the coast of South America in search of a sea route to the Orient in 1501 and concluded that this was not a part of Asia. The name was first used by the German geographer Martin Waldseemüller in 1507 in an account of Vespucci's travels in the New World and again in 1538 by Mercator.

**American Indian** a member of a group of indigenous peoples of North and South America and the Caribbean Islands, called Indians by the error of Columbus and other Europeans in the 15th–16th c., who thought they had reached part of India by a new route. They are characterized by certain blood-type features which are markedly different from those of the Mongoloid peoples whom they otherwise resemble and with whom they were formerly classified. The Amerindian population of North America is c. 2 million compared with a South American total of c. 8 million.
**Amerindian** or **Amerind** adj. & n.

**American Samoa** /sə'məʊə/ an unincorporated overseas territory of the USA comprising a group of five volcanic islands and two coral atolls in the South Pacific Ocean, to the east of Western Samoa; area 197 sq. km. (76.2 sq. miles); pop. (1990) 46,770; capital, Fagatogo. The principal inhabited islands are Aunu'u, Ofu, Olosega, Ta'u, and Tutuila. Rose Island is uninhabited and Swain's Island, with a population of 29 (1980), lies 334 km. (210 miles) to the north-west. The largely Polynesian people of American Samoa mostly work for the US government or in the tuna fish canning industry. In 1899 the USA acquired rights to the islands by agreement with Germany and Britain, and in April 1900 the High Chiefs of Tutuila ceded the islands of Tutuila and Aunu'u to the USA. In 1904 the islands of the Manu'a group (Ofu, Olosega, Ta'u, and Rose) were handed over and in 1925 Swain's Island was added to the territory. American Samoa was administered by the US Department of Navy until 1951 when administrative responsibility was transferred to the Department of the Interior.

**Amersfoort** /'ɑːməs‚fɔːt/ a commercial and industrial city in the province of Utrecht, central
Netherlands, 20 km. (13 miles) north-east of the
city of Utrecht; pop. (1991) 101,970. After receiving its charter in 1279, it developed in association
with brewing and the textile industry. Engineering,
food processing, and the manufacture of chemicals
are now important industries.

**Amersham** /'æmərʃ(ə)m/ a residential town on
the southern edge of the Chiltern Hills,
Buckinghamshire, England; pop. (1981) 21,490.
The town has associations with the composer Eric
Coates and was the birthplace of Tim Rice,
librettist of the musicals *Jesus Christ Superstar* and
*Evita*.

**Ames** /eɪmz/ a town in central Iowa, USA, on
the Skunk river north of Des Moines; pop. (1990)
47,200. The town is named after Oakes Ames, a
congressman who helped fund a local railway. Iowa
State University of Science and Technology (1858)
is located here.

**Amesbury** /'eɪmzbərɪ/ a small town in Wiltshire, southern England, associated with Joseph
Addison (1672–1719) who went to school here;
John Gay wrote *The Beggar's Opera* (1728) at
Amesbury Abbey which was the home of the Duke
of Queensberry. Nearby is the WOODHENGE prehistoric circle.

**Amharic** /æm'hærɪk/ the official and commercial language of Ethiopia, spoken by about
one-third of the population in the area of the capital, Addis Ababa, and the region to the north of it.
It belongs to the Semitic language group but within
the Ethiopic branch of this group it is directly
descended from the ancient Classical Ethiopian or
Ge'ez tongue.

**Amiens** /'æmjæ/ the capital of Picardy
(Picardie) in northern France, on the River
Somme; pop. (1990) 136,230. A market town and
textile centre since the Middle Ages, Amiens has
been famous for its velvet since the 16th c. and
today has textile, clothing, tyres, and chemical
industries. Its 13th-c. Gothic cathedral is the largest
in France.

**Amindivi Islands** /‚əmən'diːviː/ (also
**Amindivis**) the northernmost group of islands in
the Indian territory of Lakshadweep in the Indian
Ocean.

**Amirante Islands** /'æmɪ‚rænt/ a group of
coral islands in the Indian Ocean, forming part of
the Seychelles.

**Amish** /'eɪmɪʃ/ a strict US Mennonite sect that
shuns most modern technical appliances. Centred
in rural Pennsylvania, thousands of Amish moved
to the Midwest during the mid-19th c. The sect is
divided into 'Church Amish' or 'Amish Mennonites' and 'House Amish' or 'Old Order' who worship in their own homes.

**Amityville** /'æməti‚vɪl/ a resort town on the
southern shore of Long Island, New York, USA;
pop. (1990) 9,080.

**Amman** /ə'mɑːn/ the capital of Jordan, on the
Zarqa River; pop. (est. 1986) 1,160,000. Noted for
its coloured marble, Amman produces leather, textiles, tobacco, and tiles. Occupied since ancient
times, the city lay on the desert highway linking
Egypt with the Levant and Tigris-Euphrates
basins. Described as Rabbath-Ammon in the Old
Testament, Amman was known as Philadelphia
throughout the Roman and Byzantine periods. It
declined after the Arab conquest of AD 635 but was
made capital of Trans-Jordan in 1921. After 1945
the city expanded rapidly, absorbing refugees from
Palestine. There are remains of a Roman amphitheatre.

**Ammer** /'ɑːmə(r)/, **Lake** (German **Ammersee**
/'ɑːmər‚zeɪ/) a glacial lake in the German state of
Bavaria, 35 km. (22 miles) south-west of Munich;
area 47 sq. km. (18 sq. miles). The River Ammer,
which rises in the Tyrol, flows through Lake
Ammer to join the Isar River near Moosburg.

**Amol** /æ'məʊl/ a market city in the province of
Mazandaran, northern Iran, in the northern
foothills of the Elbruz Mountains near the Caspian
Sea; pop. (1991) 140,000.

**Amorgos** /ə'mɔːrgəs/ the most easterly of the
islands of the Greek Cyclades in the Aegean Sea, to
the south-east of Naxos; area 121 sq. km. (47 sq.
miles). Amorgos (Khora) is the chief settlement.
North-east of the town is the Convent of the
Presentation of the Virgin which contains an ikon
of the Virgin Mary 'miraculously' transported
there from Cyprus. Amorgos was the birthplace of
the 7th-c. poet Semonides.

**Amorites** /'æmə‚raɪts/ a group of semi-nomadic
tribes, bearing Semitic personal names, from the
east Syrian steppe and desert region. In the late 3rd
and early 2nd millenium BC they founded a number
of states and dynasties, including Mari on the
Euphrates and the First Dynasty of Babylon,
associated with Hammurabi I (d. 1750 BC).

**Amoy** /ɑː'mɔɪ/ the local dialect name for the city
and island of XIAMEN in south China.

**Amravati** /əm'rævəti:/ (formerly **Amraoti**
/əm'raʊti:/) a city in the state of Maharashtra, central India; pop. (1991) 434,000. It has the largest
cotton market in India and a 2nd-c. Stupa of the
Andhra dynasty.

**Amritsar** /æm'rɪtsə(r)/ a city in the state of
Punjab, north-west India; pop. (1991) 709,000.
Founded in 1577 by Ram Das, fourth guru of the
Sikhs, it became the centre of the Sikh faith and the
site of its holiest temple, the Golden Temple. It was
the scene of a riot in 1919 when British troops
killed 400 people and in 1984 a Sikh leader was
killed there during fighting between Sikh militants
and the Indian Army. The city is famous for its
crafts, particularly carpets and woollen cloths.

**Amroha** /ɑːmˈrəʊhɑː/ a town in Uttar Pradesh, northern India, situated east of Delhi; pop. (1991) 136,890. It is a Muslim centre of pilgrimage.

**Amstelveen** /ˈɑːmstəlˌveɪn/ an industrial southern suburb of Amsterdam in the province of North Holland, west Netherlands; pop. (1991) 70,340. Engineering, shipbuilding, and food-processing are important industries.

**Amsterdam** /ˌæmstəˈdæm/ the capital and largest city of the Netherlands, one of the major ports and commercial centres of Europe, built on c. 100 islands separated by the canals for which it is noted; pop. (1991) 702,440. Founded in the 13th c., its prosperity increased in the 16th c. during the Dutch Wars of Independence after the destruction of Ghent and the decline of Antwerp. Its chief landmarks are the Royal Palace, Anne Frank House, Rembrandt House, and the Rijksmuseum which features famous works by Dutch artists such as Rembrandt, Vermeer, and Frans Hals. Its many industries include engineering, shipbuilding, oil refining, brewing, diamond cutting, tourism, and the manufacture of petrochemicals, steel, textiles, and vehicles.

**Amstetten** /ˈæmʃtet(ə)n/ a town in the state of Lower Austria, northern Austria, situated on the Ybbs River to the east of Linz; pop. (1991) 22,110.

**Amu Darya** /ˌɑːmuː ˈdɑːrɪə/ a great river of central Asia, c. 2,541 km. (1,578 miles) long, formed by the confluence of the Pyandzh and Vaksh headstreams which rise in the Pamirs. Flowing west for 270 km. (170 miles) along the northern frontier of Afghanistan it turns north-west across the deserts of central Asia before entering the Aral Sea. In classical times it was known as the Oxus.

**Amundsen Sea** /ˈɑːmʊns(ə)n/ an arm of the South Pacific Ocean in the seas of Antarctica, off the coast of Marie Byrd Land. It was explored and named by a Norwegian, Nils Larsen, in 1929.

**Amur** /əˈmʊə(r)/ (Chinese **Hei Ho** or **Heilung Jiang**) a river of north-east Asia, forming for the greater part of its length the boundary between Russia and China before entering the Sea of Okhotsk via the Tatar Strait. Its length is 2,824 km. (1,777 miles), but including its northern head-stream, the Shilka River, its total length is 4,416 km. (2,744 miles).

**Amzirght** /ˈæmziːrt/ the language of the Berber people of North Africa.

**anabatic wind** /ˌænəˈbætɪk/ a meteorological term used to describe a wind caused by air that is drawn upwards by convection currents on mountain slopes.

**Anaconda** /ˌænəˈkɔːndə/ a town in south-west Montana, USA; pop. (1990) 10,278. Originally named Copperopolis, the town was founded in 1884 by Marcus Daly as the site of a major copper-smelting plant.

**Anadarko** /ˌænəˈdɑːrkəʊ/ a town in west-central Oklahoma, USA, on the Washita River; pop. (1990) 6,500. It was founded as the Wichita Indian Agency after eastern American Indian tribes were relocated here in 1859.

**Anadolu** /ɑːnədəʊˈluː/ the Turkish name for ANATOLIA.

**Anadyr** /ˌənəˈdɪər/, **Gulf of** (also **Anadir**) an inlet of the Bering Sea just south of the Arctic Circle and the Chukostski Peninsula of north-east Siberian Russia. The fishing and lignite mining town of Anadyr lies at the mouth of the Anadyr River which flows into the Gulf from its source in the Anadyr or Chukot Range.

**Anaheim** /ˈænəhaɪəm/ a city in Orange County, south-west California, USA, a part of the greater Los Angeles conurbation to the east of Long Beach; pop. (1990) 266,400. Founded by German settlers in 1857, Anaheim developed into an industrial centre, producing electronics, aircraft parts, and canned fruit. It is the site of the Disneyland amusement park which was opened in 1955.

**Anáhuac** /əˈnɑːwɑːk/ a large plateau in central Mexico situated between the Sierra Madre Occidental and Sierra Madre Oriental ranges at an elevation of 1,500–2,750 m. (5,000–9,000 ft.). Mexico City lies at the heart of the Anáhuac plateau.

**Anambra** /əˈnæmbrə/ a state in southern Nigeria; pop. (1991) 2,767,900; capital, Awka.

**Anantapur** /əˈnʌntəˌpʊə(r)/ a town in Andhra Pradesh, eastern India; pop. (1991) 174,790.

**Anápolis** /əˈnæpələs/ a city in the state of Goiás, central Brazil; pop. (1991) 226,170. It is a commercial centre trading in rice, maize, coffee, and cattle.

**Anasazi** /ˌænəˈsɑːzɪ/ an ancient culture of the south-western US from which the Pueblo culture (which continues to the present) developed. Its earliest phases are known as the Basket Maker period.

**Anatolia** /ˌænəˈtəʊlɪə/ (Turkish **Anadolu**, in history called **Asia Minor**) a name generally applied to the western peninsula of Asia that now forms the greater part of Turkey, bounded by the Black Sea and the Aegean and Mediterranean Seas. Most of it consists of a high plateau; the mountain ranges in the east include Mt. Ararat.
**Anatolian** adj. & n.

**Anchorage** /ˈæŋkərɪdʒ/ the largest city in the state of Alaska, USA, at the head of the Cook Inlet; pop. (1990) 226,340. Founded as a railway town in 1915, Anchorage developed into an important port, transportation hub, and centre of the oil, fishing, and gold-mining industries. The city was badly damaged during an earthquake in 1964.

**Ancona** /æŋˈkəʊnə/ an Adriatic port and capital of the Marche region of central Italy; pop. (1990) 103,270. Founded near a sharp bend in the coast

(Greek *ankon* elbow) by Greeks from Syracuse *c.*390 BC, it was named Dorica Ancon. Later as a Roman colony it was developed as a naval base by Caesar and Trajan. In the 9th c. Ancona became a semi-independent maritime state which was in 1532 incorporated as part of the Papal States. There is a large naval and commercial port with ferry services to Greece and the Balkans. Industries include fishing, ship repairing, sugar refining, and the making of musical instruments.

**Ancyra** the ancient name for ANKARA.

**Anda** /'ændə/ a city in Heilongjiang province, north-east China, situated between Daqing and Harbin; pop. (1986) 423,000.

**Andalusia** /ˌændə'luːsɪə/ (Spanish **Andalucia** /ˌɑːndəluːˈθiːə/) the southernmost and largest of the regions of Spain, bordering on the Atlantic Ocean and the Mediterranean Sea; area 87,268 sq. km. (33,707 sq. miles); pop.(1991) 6,940,520. It comprises the provinces of Almeria, Cadiz, Córdoba, Granada, Huelva, Jaén, Malaga, and Sevilla and includes the tourist resorts of the Costa del Sol and Spain's highest mountain, Mulhacén (3,482 m., 11,424 ft.). The Guadalquivir River flows westwards through Andalusia to the Gulf of Cadiz. It is rich in minerals and grows olives, grapes, and citrus fruits. From 711 to 1492 the region was under Moorish rule.

**Andaman and Nicobar Islands** /'ændəmən, 'nɪkə,baː(r)/ a Union Territory of India consisting of two groups of tropical islands in the Bay of Bengal; area 8,293 sq. km. (3,203 sq. miles); pop. (1991) 279,110; capital, Port Blair. The 19 small islands of the Nicobar group lie to the south of the Andamans which comprise the Great Andamans and Little Andaman. Peopled by Negrito aborigines, the islands export timber, coffee, fruit, and coconuts. They have served as a penal colony since the mid-19th c.

**Andaman Sea** an arm of the Bay of Bengal lying between the Andaman and Nicobar Islands and the Malay peninsula.

**Anderlecht** /'aːndə,lext/ an industrial suburb to the north of Brussels in the province of Brabant, Belgium, situated on the River Senne; pop. (1991) 87,880. Erasmus lived here from 1517 to 1522.

**Anderson** /'ændərsən/ **1.** a city in east-central Indiana, USA, on the White River; pop. (1990) 59,460. Originally the site of a Delaware Indian village, Anderson was named after a chief of the Delawares named Kikthawenund or Captain Anderson. The city developed after the discovery of natural gas in 1886. **2.** a city in north-west South Carolina; pop. (1990) 26,180. It is named after General Robert Anderson who fought in the War of Independence, the city is now a centre for high-tech research, and the production of textiles and fibreglass.

**Andes** /'ændiːz/ a major mountain system running the length of the Pacific coast of South America, a distance of some 8,000 km. (5,000 miles). It is the world's longest range of mountains with a continuous height of more than 3,000 m. (10,000 ft.). The mountains are of varying age, with ancient remnants dating back to the Palaeozoic. More recent uplift during the Tertiary period raised former coastlines to more than 1,000 m. (3,000 ft.) above present sea-levels. Tectonic activity continues throughout the length of the Andes occasionally causing damage through earthquakes, hot ash, and mudslides. Aconcagua, the highest peak in the Western Hemisphere reaches a height of 6,960 m. (22,834 ft.) on the border between Argentina and Chile, and Guallatiri in Chile (6,060 m., 19,882 ft.) is the highest active volcano in the world. Throughout its length the Andes system breaks up into three or more parallel lines of mountain ranges (cordilleras) that are separated by high fertile basins. The largest of these intermontane basins is the altiplano of Peru and Bolivia. The headwaters of the Amazon River rise in the northern Andes and on the Chilean side of the southern Andes, low temperatures and heavy precipitation result in the presence of a discontinuous ice-cap of more than 10,000 sq. km. (3,850 sq. miles). The Andes gives its name to a fine-grained brown or greyish volcanic rock called andesite.

**Andean** *adj.*

**Andhra Pradesh** /ˌɑːndrə prə'deʃ/ a state in south-east India, on the Bay of Bengal; area 276,814 sq. km. (106,919 sq. miles); pop. (1991) 66,304,850; capital, Hyderabad. The principal language is Telugu. Andhra state was formed in 1953 out of territory separated from Madras. In 1956 and 1960 its boundaries were further altered to form the present-day state of Andhra Pradesh which produces forest-products, tobacco, textiles, paper, chemicals, and ships.

**Andijon** /ændɪ'ʒɑːn/ a city in the Fergana Valley at the eastern extremity of Uzbekistan; pop. (1990) 296,000. Known as Andizhan until the dissolution of the Soviet Union in 1991, it is an industrial centre producing cotton and silk.

**Andizhan** the former name of ANDIJON.

**Andorra** /æn'dɒrə/ official name **Principality of Andorra** a small autonomous principality in the southern Pyrenees, between France and Spain; area 468 sq. km. (181 sq. miles); pop. (est.  1991) 60,000 (59% Spanish, 6% French, 27% Andorran, 8% other); capital, Andorra la Vella. Andorra comprises the seven parishes of Canillo, Encamp, Ordino, La Massana, Andorra la Vella, Sant Julià de Lòria, and Escaldes-Engordany. The languages are Catalan (official), Spanish, and French. The principal resources are mineral water,

hydroelectric power, tobacco, cattle, and sheep. Tourism and commerce are also important. Its independence dates from the late 8th c. when Charlemagne is said to have granted the Andorrans self-government for their help in defeating the Moors. This right was eventually handed over to the Spanish Counts of Urgell who donated most of the land to the Bishops of Urgell. Under the protection of the House of Caboet, Andorra found itself in the hands of the French Count of Foix during the 12th c. Hostility between the Counts of Foix and the Bishops of Urgell came to an end in 1287 with the signing of an agreement whereby each became a co-prince of the Andorran valleys. Their present-day successors are the Bishop of Urgell and the President of France. In March 1993 Andorra's first constitution as a parliamentary co-principality was approved following a referendum that voted to give the Andorran government full legislative and executive powers. The country is governed by a legislative General Council of the Valleys with the Spanish and French co-princes as heads of state.
**Andorran** *adj. & n.*

**Andorra la Vella** /-'veljə/ (Spanish **Andorra la Vieja**, French **Andorre le Vielle**) the capital of the Principality of Andorra, situated on the eastern slopes of the Pic d'Enclar at an altitude of just over 1,000 m. (3,000 ft.); pop. (1990) 20,000.

**Andover** /'ændəʊvə(r)/ a market town in Hampshire, southern England, on the River Anton; pop. (1981) 30,900. The organist and composer George Bennet (1863–1930) was born here.

**Andover** a town in north-east Massachusetts, USA; pop. (1990) 29,150. Noted for its silk production in the 19th c., it now produces electronic parts as well as woollen and rubber goods. Phillips Academy, founded by Samuel Phillips in 1776, is the oldest incorporated school in the USA. The American novelist Harriet Beecher Stowe (1811–96), author of *Uncle Tom's Cabin*, once lived in Andover.

**Andros** /'ɑːndrəs/ the largest island in the Bahamas; area 5,955 sq. km. (2,300 sq. miles); pop. (1990) 8,155. A mile to the east the sea floor drops into an Ocean Trench that falls to 1,830 m. (6,000 ft.). Over 222 km. (140 miles) in length, its Great Barrier Reef is the third-largest underwater coral reef in the world

**Andros** (Greek **Andhros**) the northernmost island of the Greek Cyclades in the Aegean Sea between Euboea (Evvoia) and Tínos; area 380 sq. km. (147 sq. miles); pop. (1991) 9,020; capital, Andros. The island produces, figs, oranges, lemons, wine, and silk. The ancient Greeks dedicated the island to the god Dionysius.

**Andújar** /æn'duːhɑːr/ a town in the province of Jaén, southern Spain, on the River Guadalquivir; pop. (1991) 34,370. Soap, textiles, and porous water jars called *alcarrazas* are produced.

**Aného** /æ'neɪhəʊ/ a town on the coast of Togo, on the Bight of Benin, east of Lomé; pop. (1977) 13,300. It was a slave-trading town and capital of Togo under German and French rule.

**Angara** /æŋə'rɑː/ a river in south-east Siberia. It flows from the south-west end of Lake Baikal north-westwards then westwards for a distance of 1,779 km. (1,039 miles) before meeting the Yenisei River just south of Yeniseysk. It is a major source of hydroelectric power.

**Angarsk** /əŋ'ærsk/ an industrial city in East Siberia in the Russian Federation, 50 km. (31 miles) north-west of Irkutsk, at the junction of the Angara and Kitoi rivers; pop. (1990) 267,000. Founded in 1949, it is a centre for the production of petrochemicals, clothing, and building materials on the Trans-Siberian Railway.

**Angel Falls** a waterfall in the Guiana Highlands of south-east Venezuela. With an uninterrupted fall of 978 m. (3,210 ft.) it is the highest waterfall in the world. The falls were discovered in 1935 by the American aviator and prospector James Angel, after whom they are named.

**Ångerman** /'ɒŋərmɑːn/ (Swedish **Ångermanälven**) a river which rises in the mountains of northern Sweden near the Norwegian frontier and flows c. 450 km. (280 miles) southeastwards through lakes to meet the Gulf of Bothnia at Härnösand.

**Angers** /'ɑ̃ʒeɪ/ a city in the Pays de la Loire region of western France, on the River Maine (Mayenne); pop. (1990) 146,160. Capital of the former province of Anjou, it is the present-day capital of Maine-et-Loire department and a centre for the production of wine and Cointreau liqueur.

**Angevin** /'ændʒɪvɪn/ a native or inhabitant of Anjou in France.

**Angkor** /'æŋkɔː(r)/ the capital of the ancient Khmer kingdom in north-west Cambodia, famous for its temples, especially Angkor Wat (early 12th c.), decorated with relief sculptures. Abandoned in 1443, the site was overgrown with jungle when it was rediscovered in 1860.

**Anglesey** /'æŋgəlsɪ/ (Welsh **Yns Môn**) an island of north-west Wales, separated from the mainland by the Menai Strait; area 715 sq. km. (276 sq. miles); pop. (1991) 67,800. Holyhead and Beaumaris are the chief towns.

**Anglo-Saxon** /ˌæŋgləʊ'sæks(ə)n/ a person or language of the English Saxons, distinct from the Old Saxons and the Angles, a group of Germanic peoples who invaded and settled in Britain between the 5th and 7th centuries.

**Angmagssalik** /ɑː'mɑːsəlɪk/ a trading settlement on an island of the same name on the east coast of Greenland, just south of the Arctic Circle. Established in 1894, its radio-meteorological station (1925) is the oldest on Greenland.

## Angola

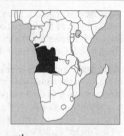

/ˌæŋˈɡəʊlə/ official name **The Republic of Angola** a country on the west coast of Africa, bounded by the South Atlantic to the west, Namibia to the south, Zambia to the east, and Congo and Zaire to the north; area 1,245,790 sq. km. (481,186 sq. miles); pop. (est. 1991) 8,500,000; official language, Portuguese; capital, Luanda. The centre of Angola is dominated by a plateau with a mean elevation of 1,200 m. (4,000 ft.) that gradually falls to a narrow coastal plain in the west and the valleys of the Congo and Zambezi rivers in the north and east. The exclave of Cabinda lies to the north of the mouth of the Congo (Zaire) River. Temperature and rainfall on the coast are reduced by the Benguela Current which flows northwards from the Southern Ocean, but the climate is generally tropical with a dry season extending from April to September. Timber, coffee, tobacco, diamonds, and oil are the chief exports. Discovered by the Portuguese at the end of the 15th c., the area was colonized by them a century later, and remained in Portuguese possession until it achieved independence in 1975 after a bitter anti-colonial war. After the collapse of the first civil government the Marxist Popular Movement for the Liberation of Angola (MPLA) seized control of the capital, banishing supporters of the National Union for the Total Independence of Angola (UNITA) to the countryside. There followed years of civil war, during which South Africa supported UNITA and a 50,000-strong force was sent from Cuba to help the MPLA. Although a peace agreement was signed in Lisbon in 1991 and democratic multiparty elections were held in 1992, bitter fighting continued, making this one of the world's longest and most devastating civil conflicts in modern times. **Angolan** *adj. & n.*

Angola is divided into the following 17 provinces:

| Province | Capital |
| --- | --- |
| Zaire | Mbanza Congo |
| Uige | Uige |
| Bengo | Caxito |
| Cuanza Norte | N'Dalatando |
| Cuanza Sul | Sumbe |
| Malanje | Malanje |
| Lunda Norte | Lucapa |
| Lunda Sul | Saurimo |
| Luanda | Luanda |
| Bié | Cuito |
| Huambo | Huambo |
| Moxico | Luena |
| Benguela | Benguela |
| Huila | Lubango |
| Namibe | Namibe |
| Cunene | N'Giva |
| Cuando-Cubango | Menongue |

**Angora** /æŋˈɡɔːrə/ the former name (until 1930) of ANKARA, capital of Turkey. Angora wool, a mixture of sheep's wool and rabbit hair takes its name from Angora.

**Angostura** /ˌæŋɡəˈstjʊərə/ the former name (1824–49) of the city of CIUDAD BOLIVAR in south-east Venezuela. The tonic known as Angostura Bitters was first made there by a physician in 1824.

**Angoulême** /ãɡuːˈlem/ a commercial and industrial town in Poitou-Charentes region, west France, on the River Charente; pop. (1990) 46,190. Once a river port, it is now a major transport centre and capital of Charente department. Its paper industry dates from the 15th c. Known to the Romans as Iculisma, the fortified town of Angoulême was capital of the former province of Angoumois.

**Angoumois** /ˌãɡuːˈmwɑː/ a former province of western France extending over parts of present day Dordogne and Charente departments.

**Angra do Heroismo** /ˈɑːŋɡrə duː ˌeruːˈiːʒmuː/ a port on Terceira Island in the Azores; pop. (1991) 11,670. Capital of the Azores until 1832, it is now capital of a Portuguese district of the same name. Founded in 1464, its name (which means 'Bay of Heroism') commemorates 19th-c. resistance against Spanish rule.

**Anguilla** /æŋˈɡwɪlə/ the most northerly of the Leeward Islands in the West Indies; area 155 sq. km. (60 sq. miles); pop. (est. 1989) 7,020; official language, English; capital, Valley. Anguilla is a flat tropical coral island dependent on tourism, fishing, agriculture, and salt production. The territory also includes Sombrero Island and a number of small offshore islets. Colonized in 1650 by English settlers from St. Kitts, Anguilla was eventually incorporated into the British colony of St. Kitts-Nevis-Anguilla from which it was separated in 1980. It is now a self-governing dependency of the UK.

**Angus** /ˈæŋɡəs/ a district of eastern Scotland, situated between the Sidlaw Hills and the Grampian Mountains; area 2,022 sq. km. (780 sq. miles); pop. (1991) 92,880; administrative centre, Forfar.

**Anhalt** /ˈɑːnhɑːlt/ a former duchy and state of central Germany named after the Castle of Anhalt and now (since 1990) forming part of the federal state of Saxony-Anhalt. It was subdivided and reunited continuously by branches of the ducal family until reconstituted as a duchy by Leopold IV in 1863. After World War I it lost its status as a duchy and became a constituent republic of Germany until 1945.

**Anhui** /ˈɑːnhweɪ/ (also **Anhwei**) a province in eastern China in the middle and lower valleys of the Yangtze and Huai rivers; area 139,900 sq. km. (54,036 sq. miles); pop. (1990) 56,181,000; capital, Hefei (Hofei). It was named after the first letters of the two cities of Anqing and Huizhou. The province is divided into three distinct regions by its leading rivers, namely, Huaibei, to the north of the

Huai River, Huainan between the Huai and Yangtze Rivers, and Wannan to the south of the Yangtze. Rich in mineral and agricultural resources, including coal, iron ore, rice, tea, bamboo, and timber, Anhui is noted for its paper, brushes, and ink sticks which are sought after by Chinese calligraphers and artists.

**Aniene** /ɑːˈnjeɪneɪ/ (Italian **Teverone** /teɪvəˈrəʊneɪ/) a tributary of the River Tiber in central Italy, which rises in the Apennines and flows generally westwards through the Tivoli cascades to meet the Tiber near Rome.

**Anjou** /ɑ̃ˈʒuː/ a former province of western France, on the Loire, now part of the department of Main-et-Loire. Henry II of England, as a Plantagenet, was Count of Anjou, but it was lost to the English Crown by King John in 1204. Its capital was the town of Angers.
**Angevin** adj. & n.

**Ankara** /ˈæŋkərə/ (formerly **Angora**) an inland city of Asia Minor, the capital of Turkey since 1923; pop. (1990) 2,559,470. Known to the Hittites as Ankuwash and to the Romans as Ankyra, it prospered at the junction of east–west and north–south trade routes. Under Ottoman rule it later dwindled to insignificance until chosen by Kemal Atatürk in 1920 as his seat of government. Modern Ankara is a planned city with long, wide boulevards. Industries include the manufacture of cement, textiles, and leather products.

**Annaba** /ˈænəbə/ (formerly **Bône**) a seaport on the Mediterranean coast of Algeria; pop. (1989) 348,000. The former city of Hippo or Hippo Regius, whose ruins lie to the south of Annaba, was the home and bishopric of St. Augustine from 396 to 430. Destroyed by Vandals in the 5th c., Annaba was rebuilt by the Arabs and later occupied by Italians, Spaniards, and Genoese before being taken by the French in 1832. Its industries include chemicals and iron and steel. Iron ore, phosphates, cork, and wine are exported.

**An Nafud** /ˌænəˈfuːd/ a desert region of northern Saudi Arabia, between the Syrian Desert to the north and the Empty Quarter (Rub' al Khali) to the south.

**An Najaf** /æn ˈnædʒæf/ a regional capital in central Iraq, on a lake near the Euphrates River between Baghdad and Basra; pop. (1985) 242,600. The burial place of the Prophet Muhammad's son-in-law Ali is a holy shrine of the Shia Muslims.

**Annam** /æˈnɑːm/ a former kingdom on the east coast of Indochina now lying largely in Vietnam. After driving out the Chinese in AD 939, the Annamese maintained an independence that lasted until 1883 when the French established a protectorate. Its last ruler was deposed in 1955.

**Annan** /ˈænən/ a river in southern Scotland that rises near Hartfell Mt. and flows southwards for 78 km. (49 miles) to join the Solway Firth near the market town of Annan.

**Annapolis** /əˈnæpəˌlɪs/ the capital of the state of Maryland, USA, on the Severn River near its mouth on Chesapeake Bay; pop. (1990) 33,180. Settled in 1649 by Puritans from Virginia who named it Providence, the town later changed its name to Anne Arundel Town. In 1695 when it was planned and laid out as the state capital of Maryland it was renamed Annapolis in honour of Princess (later Queen) Anne. It is the home of the United States Naval Academy which was founded by George Bancroft in 1845. The Scottish-born American sailor John Paul Jones (1747–92) is buried in Annapolis.

**Annapolis Royal** a small settlement in Nova Scotia, Canada, on the Bay of Fundy. Founded in 1605 by Sieur de Monts and named Habitation Port-Royal, it is the oldest permanent French settlement in Canada and was the first capital of Nova Scotia. It was held alternately by France and Britain until finally captured by the British in 1710. Its chief landmarks are the historic Fort Anne and a tidal power-station which was established in 1985. The fertile **Annapolis Valley** stretches northwards from Annapolis Royal, running parallel to the coastline of the Bay of Fundy.

**Annapurna** /ˌænəˈpɜːnə/ a ridge of the central Himalayas, in north-central Nepal. Its highest peak, rising to 8,078 m. (26,503 ft.), was first climbed in 1950 by a French expedition under Maurice Herzog.

**Ann Arbor** /æn ˈɑːrbə(r)/ a city in the state of Michigan, USA, 50 km. (32 miles) west of Detroit; pop. (1990) 109,600. First settled in 1823, the University of Michigan was moved here from Detroit in 1837. It is a centre of research and high technology.

**Annecy** /ˌænəˈsiː/ the capital of the department of Haute-Savoie, in the Rhône-Alpes region of south-east France, at the north-west end of Lake Annecy; pop. (1990) 51,140. In addition to producing paper, textiles, and precision instruments, the town is a popular tourist resort. There is a nuclear-research centre.

**Anniston** /ˈænɪstən/ an industrial town in north-east Alabama, USA; pop. (1990) 26,620. The city was founded as a company town in 1872 by Samuel Noble and Daniel Tyler who established textile mills and iron foundries which were designed to regenerate industry after the Civil War. The settlement was named Annie's Town after Mrs Anne Scott Taylor, the wife of one of the local iron magnates.

**Annobón** /ˌænəˈbɔːn/ a small island of Equatorial Guinea, in the Gulf of Guinea; area 17 sq. km. (7 sq. miles); pop. (est. 1984) 3,000. From 1778 to 1968 it was a Spanish possession and between 1973 and 1979 it was called Pagalu.

**Anqing** /ɑːnˈkɪŋ/ a city in Anhui province, eastern China, on the Yangtze River south-west of Nanjing; pop. (1986) 441,000.

**Ansbach** /'ɑːnzbɑːx/ an industrial town in Bavaria, south-west Germany, 42 km. (26 miles) south-west of Nuremberg; pop. (1991) 38,380. The town grew up around a Benedictine monastery founded by St. Gumbertus in the 8th c. and was the residence of the Margraves of Brandenburg-Ansbach who extended the town and built baroque mansions in the 18th c. Ansbach passed to Prussia in 1791. It produces machine tools and electrical products.

**Anshan** /ˌɑːnˈʃɑːn/ a city in the province of Liaoning, north-east China; pop. (1986) 2,517,000. Situated close to iron ore deposits, Anshan has developed as one of China's largest integrated iron and steel complexes. Other industries include chemicals, tractors, and machinery.

**Anshun** /ˌɑːnˈʃʊn/ a city in Guizhou province, southern China, situated 100 km. (63 miles) south-west of Guiyang; pop. (1986) 216,000. It is known for its green tea and sugar refining.

**Antakya** /ˌæntəˈkjɑː/ (also **Hatay**, English **Antioch**) the capital of Hatay province, southern Turkey, and a marketing centre at the foot of Mount Habib Neccar in the alluvial plain of the River Asi (Orontes); pop. (1990) 123,871. Part of Syria until 1939, it was the ancient capital of the Seleucid kings of Syria who founded the city c. 300 BC. It was a noted centre of commerce and culture in Hellenistic times and an early stronghold of Christianity. Its museum has an outstanding collection of Roman mosaics. After its destruction by the Mamelukes in 1266 it fell into decline and its harbour silted up. The city was devastated by earthquakes in 525 and 1872.

**Antalya** /ˌænt(ə)lˈjɑː/ **1.** a province of southwest Turkey; area 20,591 sq. km. (7,953 sq. miles); pop. (1990) 602,190. **2.** its capital, a Mediterranean seaport and resort on the Gulf of Antalya on the south coast of Turkey; pop. (1990) 378,200. The city is named after Attalus II, king of Pergamum who founded Antalya c. 150 BC. Its industries are timber, food processing, and tourism.

**Antananarivo** /ˌæntəˌnænəˈriːvəʊ/ the capital of Madagascar and its chief industrial centre, situated at an altitude of 1,200–1,500 m. (4,000–5,000 ft.) above sea-level overlooking the eastern coastal plains of the island; pop. (1990) 802,390. Until 1975 the city was known as Tananarive. It produces tobacco, processed foods, textiles, and leather goods.

**Antarctica**

/ænt'ɑːktɪkə/ a continent centred on the South Pole, situated mainly within the Antarctic Circle and almost entirely covered by an ice sheet that has an average thickness of 1,880 m.

(6,170 ft.) but in places reaches depths of 5,000 m. (16,000 ft.). With an area of 13.9 million sq. km. (5.4 million sq. miles), the Antarctic continent occupies 10 per cent of the world's surface and contains 90 per cent of the world's ice and 70 per cent of its fresh water. It is divided by the Transantarctic Mountains into West Antarctica or Lesser Antarctica, which includes the mountainous Antarctic Peninsula, Palmer Land, and Ellsworth Land, and East Antarctica or Greater Antarctica, which includes Terre Adélie, Queen Maud Land, and Wilkes Land. Only a few patches of moss and lichen grow—too few to support land animals, but there is abundant life in the sea, including whales, seals, penguins, and other sea birds. Exploration at first concentrated on establishing the existence of a continent. Bransfield, Biscoe, Foster, Wilkes, Ross, and Dumont D'Urville all explored the coastline of Antarctica between 1820 and 1840. Later explorers concentrated on reaching the South Pole. Scott pioneered the way in 1902, followed by Shackelton in 1908; in 1911 Amundsen was the first to reach the Pole, and Scott reached it a month later. The American aviator Richard Byrd flew over the South Pole in 1929. Although there is no permanent human habitation Norway, Australia, France, New Zealand, and the UK claim sectors of the continent (Argentina and Chile claim parts of the British sector); its exploration and exploitation are governed by an international treaty (Antarctic Treaty) of 1959 renewed in 1991.

**Antarctic Circle** an imaginary line on the earth's surface 23° 30' north of the South Pole (latitude 66° 30' S) marking the southernmost point at which the sun is visible during the midsummer solstice and the northernmost point of the south polar region at which the midnight sun can be seen.

**Antarctic convergence** the process by which nutrient-laden cold water flowing from Antarctica meets and descends below the warmer waters of the South Atlantic and South Pacific oceans. Such areas are rich in phytoplankton, fish, and marine animals.

**Antarctic Peninsula** a mountainous peninsula extending northwards for a distance of c. 1,900 km. (1,200 miles) from west Antarctica. Explored by the British navigator Edward Bransfield in 1820 it was not confirmed to be a continuous part of the Antarctic continent until the British Graham Land Expedition of 1934–7 was able to show that the peninsula was not intersected by ice-filled straits. The northern tip of the peninsula is known as Graham Land

**Antequera** /ˌɑːnteɪˈkerə/ a town in the Andalusian province of Málaga, south Spain, in the valley of the River Guadalhorce; pop. (1991) 38,310. There are megalithic tombs and standing stones nearby at Menga, Vera, and El Romeral.

**anthropology** /ˌænθrəˈpɒlədʒɪ/ the study of mankind especially of its societies and customs.

Interest in the activities of other cultures is as old as written records, and anthropology traces its antecedents to the Greek travellers Xenophanes (6th c. BC) and Herodotus. Travellers' reports (e.g. Marco Polo) continued to be a popular form of proto-anthropology in the Middle Ages and Renaissance. The philosophical debates on the nature of man during the Enlightenment stimulated further interest in other cultures, but it was not until the advances of Saint-Simon and Comte that the foundation for a 'science of man' was laid. Modern academic anthropology traces its origin to the evolutionary theories of Darwin, which stimulated European interest in the 'primitive' peoples of the world who were seen to provide a living laboratory to test theories of cultural evolution and diffusion. The second half of the 19th c. saw an expansion of scholarly attention in and the quest for reliable information about the isolated and technologically less-developed peoples of the world. Initially ambitious comparative studies were undertaken on diverse topics including kinship systems, law, magic and religion, and culture, by a generation of library-bound scholars. At the beginning of the 20th c. advances by Durkheim saw a retreat from these evolutionary beginnings and a shift to the study of the ways in which societies maintain themselves. The functionalist revolution occasioned by Malinowski and Radcliffe-Brown in Britain and Boas in the US saw an increasing emphasis on ethnographic fieldwork studies utilizing the technique of participant observation that has since become the single most important feature distinguishing anthropolgy from its sister discipline sociology.

**Antibes** /ɑ̃'tiːb/ a fishing port on the French Riviera, in the Alpes-Martimes department of Provence-Alpes-Côte d'Azur, south-east France; pop. (1990) 70,690. It exports dried fruit, olives, tobacco, perfume, and wine. The town was established by the Greeks as a colony in the 4th c. BC. Napoleon landed here on his return from Elba in 1815. Nearby is the fashionable resort of Cap d'Antibes.

**anticline** /'æntɪˌklaɪn/ a ridge or fold of stratified rock in which the strata slope down from the crest. The opposite is a syncline.

**Anticosti Island** /ˌæntəˈkɒstiː/ a tree-covered island in the Gulf of St. Lawrence, part of Quebec in eastern Canada; area 7,941 sq. km. (3,066 sq. miles). The island is noted for its dangerous offshore reefs and its white-tailed deer which were introduced in 1896. Its population of c. 300 are all French-speaking.

**anticyclone** /ˌæntɪˈsaɪkləʊn/ a system of winds rotating outwards from an area of high barometric pressure, clockwise in the northern hemisphere and anticlockwise in the southern hemisphere. Anticyclones are usually associated with dry, cold, and sometimes foggy weather in the winter and fine

weather in the summer. At the centre of an anticyclone the weather is usually calm and settled. **anticyclonic** *adj.*

**Antigonish** /ˌæntɪɡəˈnɪʃ/ a town in north Nova Scotia, Canada; pop. (1991) 5,360. It was founded in 1784 by Scotsmen disbanded from the Nova Scotia regiment. The St. Francis Xavier University was established in 1853.

**Antigua** /ænˈtiːgwə/ (also **Antigua Guatemala**) a town in the Central Highlands of Guatemala; pop. (1988) 26,630. Founded in 1543 to replace Ciudad Real as capital of Spanish Guatemala, Antigua flourished until destroyed by an earthquake in 1773. In 1776 a new capital was established at Guatemala City. Antigua is now capital of Sacatépequez department and lies at the centre of a rich coffee-growing area. Its many fine Spanish colonial buildings make it one of the country's leading tourist centres.

**Antigua and Barbuda**
/ænˈtiːgə, bɑːˈbjuːdə/
an independent
Caribbean state
forming a tropical
island group in the
Leeward Islands of
the West Indies. It
comprises the islands

of Antigua (280 sq. km., 108 sq. miles), Barbuda (161 sq. km., 62 sq. miles), and Redonda (1 sq. km., 0.4 sq. miles); total area 442 sq. km. (171 sq. miles); pop. (1991) 65,960; official language, English; capital, St. John's (on Antigua). Codrington is the only settlement on Barbuda. Discovered in 1493 by Columbus and settled by the English in 1632, Antigua became a British colony with Barbuda as its dependency; the islands gained full independence as a state of the Commonwealth in 1981. The economy, once dependent on sugar, is now much more diversified and contains a large element of tourism.

**Anti-Lebanon** /ˌæntɪˈlebənən/ (Arab. **Jebel esh Sharqi**) a range of mountains running north to south along the frontier between Lebanon and Syria, east of the Lebanon range from which it is separated by the Beqa'a Valley. The highest point is Mount Hermon (2,814 m., 9,232 ft.).

**Antilles** /ænˈtɪliːz/ a group of islands forming the greater part of the West Indies. The **Greater Antilles**, extending roughly east to west, comprise Cuba, Jamaica, Hispaniola (Haiti and the Dominican Republic), and Puerto Rico; the **Lesser Antilles**, to the south-east, include the Virgin Islands, Leeward Islands, Windward Islands, and various small islands to the north of Venezuela, including the NETHERLANDS ANTILLES.

**Antioch** /'æntɪˌɒk/ **1.** an alternative name for the city of ANTAKYA, southern Turkey. **2.** the site of an ancient town of Pisidia in Asia Minor, located in present-day Isparta province, western Turkey, 127 km. (80 miles) west of Konya.

**antipodes** /æn'tɪpə,diːz/ any two places on diametrically opposite sides of the globe. The **Antipodes Islands** in the South Pacific are so named because they are diametrically opposite Greenwich in England.

**Antisana** /,ɑːntə'sɑːnɑː/ an active snow-capped volcano rising to a height of 5,704 m. (18,714 ft.) south-east of Quito in the Andes of north-central Ecuador.

**anti-trade winds** westerly winds in the atmosphere (above 2,000 m., 6,600 ft.) blowing in the opposite direction to middle latitude surface winds known as trade winds.

**Antofagasta** /,æntəʊfə'gæstə/ a port on the Pacific coast of northern Chile; pop. (1991) 218,750. Founded in 1870 as an outlet for copper and nitrates from the Atacama Desert, it is capital of Antofagasta province. It has large ore refineries and foundries.

**Antonine Wall** /'æntənaɪn/ a defensive fortification about 59 km. (37 miles) long, built across the narrowest part of central Scotland between the Firth of Forth and the Firth of Clyde c. AD 140, in the time of Antoninus Pius. It was intended to mark the frontier of the Roman province of Britain, and consisted of a turf wall with a broad ditch in front and a counterscarp bank on the outer edge, with 29 small forts linked by a military road. The Romans, however, were unable to consolidate their position and in c. 181 the wall was breached and the northern tribes forced a retreat from the Forth–Clyde frontier, eventually to that established earlier at Hadrian's Wall.

**Antony** /æntə'niː/ a town in the Hauts-de-Seine department of northern France, immediately south of Paris; pop. (1990) 57,920.

**Antrim** /'æntrɪm/ **1.** a county of Northern Ireland; area 2,831 sq. km. (1,093 sq. miles); pop. (1981) 642,250; capital, Belfast. **2.** a market town in County Antrim, Northern Ireland, on the north-east shore of Lough Neagh; pop. (1981) 22,340.

**Antseranana** /,ɑːntsə'rɑːnənə/ (also **Antsirane**, formerly **Diégo Suarez**) an Indian Ocean seaport at the northern tip of Madagascar; pop. (1990) 54,420.

**Antsirabe** /,ɑːntsə'rɑːbeɪ/ a resort town with thermal springs in the Ankaratra Mountains of central Madagascar, 169 km. (106 miles) south of Antananarivo; pop. (1982) 90,800. The town was founded by Norwegian missionaries in 1869.

**Antung** see DANDONG.

**Antwerp** /'æntwɜːp/ (French **Anvers** /'ãveə(r)/, Flemish **Antwerpen** /'ɑːntveərpən/) a commercial and industrial seaport in Belgium, on the River Scheldt; pop. (1991) 467,520. It is capital of a province of the same name and was designated European City of Culture 1993. Founded as a small

trading centre in the 8th c., Antwerp became a seat of the Counts of Flanders. By the 16th c. it had eclipsed Bruges and Ghent to become one of Europe's leading commercial and financial centres and was a distribution centre for spices from the East Indies. Still one of Europe's busiest entrepôts, its 19th c. links with southern Africa have resulted in Antwerp becoming a major centre of diamond cutting for both jewellery and industry. It was the birthplace of Anthony Van Dyke and the home of Paul Peter Rubens.

**Anuradhapura** /,ənuərədə'puərə/ the ancient capital of the Sinhalese kings of Sri Lanka from the 4th c. BC to the 11th c. AD when it was abandoned in the face of invading Hindu Tamils. The modern city is the capital of a district of the same name in north-central Sri Lanka; pop. (1981) 36,000. Because the Sinhalese ruler Mahinda was converted to Buddhism here in the 3rd c. BC it is a centre of pilgrimage to Buddhists. The sacred Bo-tree brought as a sapling from the Buddha's original tree in Bodh Gaya in India over 2,000 years ago is alleged to be the oldest living tree in the world.

**Anvers** the French name for the Belgian city of ANTWERP.

**Anyang** /ɑːn'jɑːŋ/ **1.** a city in the province of Henan, central China; pop. (1990) 480,670. Once known as Yin it was the last capital (1300–1066 BC) of the Shang (or Yin) dynasty and one of China's earliest centres of civilization. Ruins of the ancient city lie to the north-west of Anyang on the banks of the Huan or Anyang River which is a tributary of the Yellow River. The *I Ching Book of Changes* was compiled here during the Zhou Dynasty (1122–221 BC). Modern Anyang is an industrial city manufacturing iron and steel, textiles, and light industry products. **2.** a city in the province of Kyonggi, north-west Korea; pop. (1990) 480,670.

**Anzhero-Sudzhensk** /ɑːn,ʒerəsuː'djensk/ a coal-mining town in the Kuznetsk basin of Siberian Russia, 80 km. (50 miles) east of Tomsk, on the Trans-Siberian Railway; pop. (1990) 108,000. It manufactures mining equipment, chemicals, and pharmaceuticals.

**Anzio** /'ænziː,əʊ/ a fishing port and resort on the coast of Latium, central Italy, situated on the Tyrrhenian Sea, 57 km. (36 miles) south of Rome; pop. (1990) 34,680. It was the birthplace of the Emperor Nero. During World War II Allied troops landed on the beaches of Anzio (Jan. 1944).

**Anzus** /'ænzəs/ (also **ANZUS**) an acronym for Australia, New Zealand, and the US, as an alliance for the Pacific area. Signed in 1951 and known as the Pacific Security Treaty, it recognized the common danger of an armed attack on any of these countries and declared its readiness to act to meet this. After New Zealand's declaration of an anti-nuclear policy (1985), which included the banning of nuclear-armed ships from its ports, the US suspended its security obligations to New Zealand (1986).

**Aomori** /'aʊməˌriː/ a port at the northern tip of Honshu Island, Japan, on Musu Bay; pop. (1990) 287,810. It is the leading port of north Japan, capital of a prefecture of the same name, and a centre of high-technology and biochemical industries, and the site of the Nebuto Festival held in early August each year.

**Aorangi** /aʊˈræŋi/ the Maori name for MT. COOK, New Zealand's highest mountain.

**Aosta** /ɑːˈɔːstə/ an industrial and tourist city, the capital of the region of Valle d'Aosta, north-west Italy, 76 km. (48 miles) north-west of Turin, in the valley of the Dora Baltea River; pop. (1990) 36,095. Founded in 25 BC by the Romans who named it Augusta Praetoria, it developed as a junction for transalpine traffic. Its many surviving Roman remains have earned it the title of 'Rome of the Alps'. It was the birthplace of St. Anselm (1033–1109) who became Archbishop of Canterbury. It has iron and steel, aluminium, and chemical industries.

**Aotearoa** /ˌaʊtɪəˈrəʊə/ the Maori name for New Zealand, meaning 'land of the long, white cloud'.

**Aozou Strip** /'aʊzuː/ a narrow corridor of disputed desert land in north Chad, stretching the full length of the frontier separating Chad and Libya.

**Apache** /əˈpætʃi/ an Athapaskan-speaking American Indian tribe which migrated from Canada to what are now the south-western states of the USA (primarily to Arizona and New Mexico with smaller numbers in Utah, Colorado and Texas) over 1,000 years ago. The arid ecological conditions inhibited colonial expansion in the region with the result that the indigenous groups of the south-west (e.g. Apache, Navajo, and the various *pueblo* cultures) suffered less cultural disruption than most Amerindian groups. When contact finally came the Apache put up fierce resistance to colonial expansion and were, in the late 19th c., the last American Indian group to be conquered by the US cavalry, which has had a considerable effect on the popular imagination. Forcibly concentrated on reservations after 1887 and deprived of the freedom necessary to continue their traditional hunting and gathering by the policies of the US Bureau of Indian Affairs, Apache society has undergone profound restructuring in the 20th c. They now number *c.* 50,000.

**apartheid** /əˈpɑːrteɪt/ an Afrikaans word meaning 'apartness', applied to a policy or system of segregation or discrimination on grounds of race practised especially in South Africa in respect of Europeans and non-Europeans. Adopted by the successful Afrikaner National Party as a slogan in the 1948 election, apartheid intensified and institutionalized existing racial segregation guaranteeing the dominance of the White minority. In the early 1960s domestic and international opposition to

apartheid began to intensify, but despite rioting and terrorism at home and isolation abroad, the White regime maintained the apartheid system intact until liberal alterations were made in the early 1990s.

**Apeldoorn** /'æpəlˌdɔːn/ a town in the province of Gelderland, east-central Netherlands, 27 km. (17 miles) north of Arnhem; pop. (1991) 148,200. The Het Loo Palace here has been a summer residence of the Dutch royal family since 1685. It is a light industrial and tourist centre.

**Apennines** /'æpɪˌnaɪnz/ (Italian **Appennino**) a mountain range running the length of Italy from the north-west to the southern tip of the peninsula, a distance of some 1,400 km. (880 miles). The highest point is Mt. Corno in the Gran Sasso d'Italia (2,914 m., 9,560 ft.).

**Aphrodisias** /ˌæfrəˈdɪsɪəs/ a ruined city in western Turkey, with a temple dedicated to Aphrodite. It is situated 80 km. (50 miles) south-east of Aydin.

**Apia** /'ɑːpɪə/ the capital of Western Samoa in the central Pacific, situated on the north coast of the island of Upolu; pop. (1986) 32,200. It was the home of Robert Louis Stevenson from 1888 until his death in 1894.

**Apo** /'ɑːpəʊ/, **Mount** an active volcano rising to 2,954 m. (9,692 ft.) on Mindanao Island in the Philippines, south-west of Davao. It is the highest peak in the Philippines.

**apogean tide** /ˌæpəˈdʒɪən/ a tidal condition that exists when the moon is at its apogee or farthest distance from the earth in its orbit. The moon's gravitational pull is reduced resulting in lower high tides and higher low tides.

**Apollonia** /æpəˈləʊnɪə/ the site of an ancient city of Illyria, situated near present-day Fier in Albania. Founded by Corinthians in the 7th c. BC., its importance as a trading centre was later superseded by Vlorë.

**Appalachian Mountains** /ˌæpəˈleɪʃ(ə)n/ (also **Appalachians**) a mountain system of eastern North America which confined early European settlers to the eastern coastal belt. Stretching from the Gulf of St. Lawrence to central Alabama it comprises a series of parallel ridges separated by wide valleys. The highest peak is Mt. Mitchell (2,037 m., 6,684 ft.) in the Black Mts. of North Carolina.

**Appalachian Trail** a 3,200-km. (2,000-mile) footpath through the Appalachians from Mount Katahdin in Maine to Springer Mountain in Georgia. Completed in 1937 and passing through 14 states, it is the longest continuous hiking path in the world.

**Appenzell** /'ɑːpəntsel/ the capital of the demi-canton of Appenzell Inner Rhoden in north-east Switzerland, in the valley of the River Sitter, south of St. Gallen; pop. (1980) 4,900.

**Appenzell Ausser Rhoden** (French **Appenzell Rhodes Extérieures**) a demi-canton in north-east Switzerland; area 243 sq. km. (94 sq. miles); pop. (1990) 51,470; capital, Herisau.

**Appenzell Inner Rhoden** (French **Appenzell Rhodes Intérieures**) a demi-canton in north-east Switzerland; area 172 sq. km. (66 sq. miles); pop. (1990) 13,500; capital, Appenzell.

**Appian Way** /'æpɪən/ (Latin **Via Appia**) the principal southward road from Rome in classical times, named after the censor Appius Claudius Caecus who in 312 BC built the section to Capua (c.210 km., 132 miles). The southern terminus of the Appian Way is Brindisi in Apulia.

**Appleton** /'æpəlt(ə)n/ a paper-making city in east Wisconsin, USA, on the Fox River; pop. (1990) 65,700. It is the seat of Lawrence University (1847). The escapologist Erich Weiss (stage name Harry Houdini) was born here in 1874.

**Appleton Layer** a layer of ionized gases in the upper atmosphere from which short-wave radio waves are reflected back to Earth. It is named after the physicist Sir Edward Appleton (1892–1965) whose work assisted the development of long-range radio transmission and radar.

**Apulia** /ə'pju:lɪə/ (Italian **Puglia** /'pu:ljə/) a region forming the south-eastern 'heel' of Italy and comprising the provinces of Bari, Brindisi, Foggia, Lecce, and Taranto; area 19,345 sq. km. (7,472 sq. miles); pop. (1990) 4,081,540; capital, Bari. In medieval times the region was divided into the northern Capitanata covering the forested Gargano peninsula and the Tavoliere plain, the central Terra di Bari which consists of a series of plateaus, and the Terra di Otranto extending over the hilly southern peninsula of Salento. The Tremite Islands in the Adriatic are part of Apulia.

**Apuré** /ɑː'pʊəreɪ/ a South American river rising in the Andes of Colombia and flowing c.800 km. (500 miles) eastwards across west-central Venezuela to meet the Orinoco River.

**Apurímac** /ˌɑːpʊ'ri:mæk/ a South American river rising in the Andes of Peru and flowing north-westwards for a distance of 880 km. (550 miles) to meet the Urubamba where it forms the Ucayali River, one of the main headwaters of the Amazon.

**Aqaba** /'ækəbə/ a port and popular resort at the northern end of the Gulf of Aqaba, southern Jordan; pop. (est. 1983) 40,000. Developed after the Arab–Israeli war of 1948, it is Jordan's only seaport.

**Aqaba, Gulf of** an arm of the Red Sea extending northwards for 190 km. (118 miles) between the Sinai and Arabian peninsulas. It is entered through the Straits of Tiran.

**Aqmola** /æk'məulə/ (also **Akmola**) a city in the steppeland of north-central Kazakhstan, on the Ishim (Esil) River; pop. (1990) 281,400. It is capital of the so-called Virgin Lands, a major wheat-producing region brought under the plough in 1954–63. Its industries are agriculturally based. Formerly named Akmolinsk, the city was known

as Tselinograd from 1961 to 1993. It is designated to be the new capital of Kazakhstan from the year 2000.

**Aqtau** /'æktaʊ/ (also **Aktau**) a city in western Kazakhstan, on the eastern shore of the Caspian Sea; pop. (1989) 159,000. The city was known as Shevchenko from 1934 to 1993.

**Aqtöbe** /æk'tju:bɪ/. an industrial city in Kazakhstan, in the southern foothills of the Urals, on the River Ilek; pop. (1990) 261,000. Founded in 1869 it developed after the building of the Trans-Caspian railway in 1905. Before the breakup of the Soviet Union it was known as Aktyubinsk. Industries include heavy engineering, oil, and the manufacture of textiles.

**aquiclude** /'ækwɪˌklu:d/ a porous rock such as shale which becomes impermeable after its pores are saturated by water.

**aquifer** /'ækwɪfə(r)/ a layer of rock or soil able to hold or transmit water.

**Aquila** /ɑː'kwi:lə/ (Italian **L'Aquila**) the chief city of the Abruzzi region in east-central Italy, on the Aterno River; pop. (1990) 67,820. Founded in the 13th c., it was a century later the second city of southern Italy after Naples.

**Aquitaine** /ˌækwɪ'teɪn/ **1.** an ancient province of south-west France, comprising at some periods the whole country from the Loire to the Pyrenees. By the marriage of Eleanor of Aquitaine to Henry II in 1152 it became one of the English possessions in France. It was held by the English Crown until 1453 when Charles VII took Bordeaux and united the region with France as the province of Aquitaine. **2.** a region of modern France comprising the departments of Dordogne, Gironde, Landes, Lot-et-Garonne, and Pyrénées-Atlantiques; area 41,308 sq. km. (15,955 sq. miles); pop. (1990) 2,795,830; capital, Bordeaux.

**AR** *abbr.* US Arkansas (in official postal use).

**Arab** /'ærəb/ a Semitic people inhabiting originally the Arabian Peninsula and neighbouring countries, now also parts of the Middle East and North Africa. The Arabic language, with a script that is written from right to left, has spread as far east as Malaysia, Indonesia, and the Philippines, and as far west as Morocco. It is the language of some 120 million people and is the language of the Koran. Arabic numerals, which probably originated in India, were adopted by the people of Europe in the Middle Ages in place of Roman numerals.

**Arab Co-operation Council** an economic, cultural and mutual defence union established in 1989 by the governments of Egypt, Jordan, Iraq, and North Yemen.

**Arabia** the original homeland of the Arabs on the Arabian Peninsula of south-west Asia. Lying between the Red Sea and the Persian Gulf and bounded to the north by Jordan and Iraq, modern Arabia comprises the states of Saudi Arabia,

Yemen, Oman, Bahrain, Kuwait, Qatar, and the United Arab Emirates. Mainly desert (An Nafud Desert in the north and the Empty Quarter in the south), it forms a large plateau of ancient crystalline rock covered by sedimentary sandstone and limestone. With an area of some 3,250,000 sq. km. (1,250,000 sq. miles), Arabia is the largest peninsula in the world. During the 18th and 19th centuries Arabia was explored by European travellers including Burckhardt, Burton, Palgrave, Doughty, and the Blunts. During the 20th c. travellers such as Lawrence, Philby, Thomas, Shakespear, and Thesiger have explored Arabia in the wake of the discovery of oil in the region.

**Arabian Desert** an alternative name for the EASTERN ÐESERT.

**Arabian Gulf** an alternative name for the PERSIAN GULF.

**Arabian Sea** the north-western part of the Indian Ocean, between Arabia and India.

**Arabistan** /ˌærəbɪsˈtɑːn/ an Arab name for the province of KHUZESTAN in western Iran which is occupied by over 2 million Sunni Muslim Arabs.

**Arab League** an alternative name for the LEAGUE OF ARAB STATES.

**Arab Maghreb Union** an economic, cultural, and mutual defence union in North Africa, established in 1989 by the governments of Morocco, Mauritania, Algeria, Tunisia, and Libya.

**Aracajú** /ˌærəkəˈʒuː/ a port in north-east Brazil, on the Sergipe River, capital of the state of Sergipe; pop. (1990) 404,830. Chosen as the new state capital (replacing São Cristóvão) in 1855, Aracajú was Brazil's first planned city. Sugar refining and cotton milling are the two chief industries.

**Arad** a commercial and industrial city in Transylvania, western Romania, on the River Mures; pop. (1989) 191,430. It is the capital of Arad county and a railway junction linking lines to Budapest, Bucharest, and Belgrade. It has a citadel built by the Empress Maria Theresa in the 18th c. Its industries include sawmilling, textiles, distilling, machine tools, and electrical goods.

**Arafura Sea** /ˌærəˈfʊərə/ a shallow sea lying between northern Australia and the islands of east Indonesia. It is linked to the Indian Ocean by the Timor Sea and the Pacific Ocean by the Coral Sea.

**Aragon** /ˈærəgən/ (Spanish **Aragón**) **1.** a former kingdom of north-east Spain, conquered by the Visigoths in the 5th c. and then the Moors in the 8th c. but later united with Catalonia (1137) and Castile (1479). **2.** an autonomous region of modern Spain, bounded on the north by the Pyrenees and on the east by Catalonia and Valencia; area 47,669 sq. km. (18,412 sq. miles); pop. (1991) 1,188,820; capital, Saragossa (Zaragoza). It comprises the provinces of Huesca, Teruel, and Zaragoza.

**Araguaía** /ˌærəˈgwaɪə/ a river rising in south-central Brazil on the frontier between Mato Grosso and Goiás. It flows a distance of c. 2,100 km. (1,300 miles) northwards to meet the Tocantins River west of Imperatriz. The island of Bananal which separates the river into two arms is one of the largest freshwater islands in the world.

**Arak** a market city and route junction in Markazi province, central Iran, situated in the Zagros Mountains south-west of Tehran; pop. (1991) 331,000. It is famous for its rugs and carpets.

**Arakan** /ˈɑːrəˈkɑːn/ (also **Rakhine**) a state of western Burma facing onto the Bay of Bengal; pop. (1983) 2,045,900; capital, Sittwe. It is separated from the inland states of Chin, Magwe, Pegu, and Irrawaddy by the Arakan Yoma mountain range which also forms a natural boundary between India and Burma. Arakan has a short border with Bangladesh to the north.

**Araks** /əˈrɑːks/ (anc. **Araxes**, Turkish **Aras** /əˈrɑːs/) a river of eastern Turkey which rises in the Bingöl Dagi mountains of Armenia and flows c. 900 km. (566 miles) eastwards to the Caspian Sea. For part of its course it follows the frontier between Turkey and Iran in the south and the republics of Armenia and Azerbaijan to the north. The fertile Araks valley is claimed in legend to be the 'Garden of Eden'.

**Aral Sea** /ˈær(ə)l/ (Russian **Aral'skoye More**) an inland sea in the Central Asian states of Kazakhstan and Uzbekistan. Fed by the Amu Darya (Oxus) in the south and the Syr Darya in the north-east, it was at its full extent the fourth-largest inland lake in the world. The diversion for irrigation of water flowing into the Aral Sea led to water-level falling by 13 m. (43 ft.) and the area of the sea being reduced to two-thirds of its original size of 64,501 sq. km. (24,904 sq. miles) between 1960 and 1990.

**Aramaic** /ˌærəˈmeɪk/ a Semitic language of ancient Syria (whose Biblical name was Aram) which was used as the lingua franca in the Near East from the 6th c. BC and gradually replaced Hebrew as the language of the Jews in those parts. It was supplanted by Arabic in the 7th c. AD. A modern form of Aramaic is still spoken in small communities in Syria and Turkey. One of its most important descendants is Syriac; Aramaic was written in the Hebrew alphabet from which the various Syriac scripts developed.

**Aranda** /əˈrændə/ (also **Aranta** or **Arunta**) an Aboriginal people of central Australia, noted for their complex system of kinship reckoning and their distinctive language.

**Aran Islands** /ˈærən/ (Irish **Oileain Arann**) a group of three rugged and barren islands (Inishmore, Inishmaan, and Inisheer) in Galway Bay, off the west coast of the Republic of Ireland; pop. (1981) 1,381. Its chief settlement is Kilronan. The islands were immortalized by the playwright J. M. Synge.

**Aranjuez** /ˌɑːrɑːŋˈhweɪθ/ a horticultural market town and former royal summer residence on the River Tagus, in the province of Madrid, central Spain; pop. (1991) 35,870.

**Arapaho** /əˈræpəhəʊ/ an Uto-Aztecan-speaking American Indian tribe of the Great Plains and prairies of eastern North Dakota and western Minnesota. In 1870 with the founding of the Arapaho Agency most settled on a reservation in Oklahoma.

**Ararat** /ˈærəˌræt/ a former gold-mining town in west-central Victoria, Australia, south-east of the Grampians; pop. (1986) 8,000. It grew up during a brief gold-rush in 1854–8 and later survived as a market town dependent on wool, wine, and grain.

**Ararat, Mount** (Turkish **Agri Dagi**) either of two volcanic peaks of the Armenian plateau in eastern Turkey, near the frontiers of Iran and Armenia, of which the higher (**Great Ararat**, 5,122 m., 16,804 ft.) last erupted in 1840. **Little Ararat** to the south-east rises to a height of 3,896 m. (12,782 ft.). A site to the south is the traditional resting place of Noah's ark after the Flood (Genesis 8: 4).

**Araucanía** /ˌærɔːˈkeɪnɪə/ a region of southern Chile, south of the Bío-Bío River; area 31,946 sq. km. (12,339 sq. miles); pop. (1982) 692,920; capital, Temuco. A Frenchman (who is buried in Tortoirac, France), Orllie Antoine, declared himself King of Araucania and Patagonia in 1860.

**Araucanian Indian** a South American Indian people who were the original inhabitants of central Chile and parts of Argentina. They resisted both Spanish and Chilean rule until the late 19th c., their last revolt ending in a treaty signed in 1881.

**Aravalli Range** /əˈrɑːvəliː/ a mountain range in the centre and south of the state of Rajasthan, north-west India. About 560 km. (350 miles) in length, the highest peak is Mount Abu (1,722 m., 5,650 ft.)

**Arawak** /ˈærəˌwæk/ an indigenous American people of the Greater Antilles and northern and western South America, speaking languages of the same linguistic family. They were forced out of the Antilles by the more warlike Carib Indians shortly before Spanish expansion in the Caribbean.
**Arawakan** *adj. & n.*

**Arbil** /ærˈbiːl/ (also **Irbil**) **1.** a Kurdish province in northern Iraq; area 14,428 sq. km. (5,573 sq. miles); pop. (est. 1985) 742,700. In 1974 it joined with the provinces of Dohuk and Suleimaniya to form a Kurdish Autonomous Region. **2.** the capital of the province of Arbil, 80 km. (50 miles) east of Mosul; pop. (est. 1985) 333,900. Alexander the Great defeated the Persians under Darius III near here in 331 BC.

**Arbroath** /ɑːrˈbrəʊθ/ (formerly **Aberbrothock**) a North Sea-fishing port on the Angus coast of east Scotland; pop. (1981) 24,100. At Arbroath Abbey (built in 1178) the Declaration of Arbroath asserting Scotland's independence from England was signed in 1320 by King Robert I.

**Arcadia** /ɑːˈkeɪdɪə/ (Greek **Arkhadia**) a mountainous district in the Peleponnese of southern Greece; pop. (1991) 103,840; area 4,419 sq. km. (1,706 sq. miles); capital, Tripolis. In ancient times Arcadia was the home of the god Pan and a noted centre of song and music. In poetic fantasy Arcadia is a rustic paradise, the idyllic pastoral home of song-loving shepherds.
**Arcadian** *adj. & n.*

**Archaean** /ɑːˈkiːən/ (also **Archean**) a geological period of time relating to the earlier part of the Precambrian era.

**Archangel** /ˈɑːkˌeɪndʒ(ə)l/ (Russian **Arkhangelsk**) a port of north-west European Russia, near the mouth of the North Dvina River where it meets the White Sea (Beloye More); pop. (1990) 419,000. Established in 1584 as Novo-Kholmogory, the port was renamed in 1613 after the monastery of the Archangel Michael. It was Russia's leading seaport until the building of St. Petersburg in 1703, but regained its importance as a supply route with the completion of a rail link to Moscow in 1898. From December to April the port is usually icebound. Its principal exports are timber and timber products. Its factories produce pulp and paper, turpentine, resin, cellulose, and building materials. Fishing and shipbuilding are also important.

**archipelago** /ˌɑːkɪˈpeləˌgəʊ/ a group of islands or a sea with many islands, as in the MALAY ARCHIPELAGO.

**Archipiélago de Colón** the official name in Spanish for the GALAPAGOS ISLANDS.

**Arctic** /ˈɑːktɪk/ the region of the world surrounding the North Pole, largely comprising the Arctic Ocean but also including the northern reaches of Canada, Alaska, Russia, and Norway as well as Iceland, Greenland, and Svalbard. Pack ice, which reaches a maximum extent in February and a minimum in August, occupies almost the entire region from the North Pole to the coasts of North America and Eurasia. In spring the pack ice begins to break up into ice floes which are carried southwards to the Atlantic Ocean. The plants of the Arctic tundra (including lichens, mosses, grasses, shrubs, and perennial plants) spring into life for two months of the summer. Animals include polar bear, musk ox, reindeer, caribou, fox, hare, lemming, seal, and walrus.

Exploration of Arctic regions began in the 16th c. when northern European nations tried to find a way to the rich trade of China and the East Indies by way of a north-east or north-west passage across the Arctic Ocean at a time when the longer but easier routes round Africa and South America were secured by Portugal and Spain. John Davis, William Barents, Henry Hudson, and Vitus Bering searched for these routes in the period 1585–1740 and during the relatively ice-free years of the early 19th c. John Ross, William Parry, David Buchan, John Franklin, and James Clark Ross renewed British interest in finding a north-west passage. The north-east passage was first navigated in 1878–9 by Nils Nordenskjöld in the *Vega*. In the late 19th c. attention turned to reaching the North Pole over the floating sea-ice with the explorations of Frederic Nansen, Otto Sverdrup, and Roald Amundsen. In 1909 the American explorer R. E. Peary claimed to be the first man to reach the Pole and the aviator Richard Byrd claimed to have flown over the North Pole in 1926. The charting of Arctic regions by Vilhjalmur Stefansson, Rudolph Anderson, and Gino Watkins pioneered the way for the 'Great Circle' air routes over polar ice and in 1958–9 the US submarine *Nautilus* made the first crossing of the Arctic Ocean under the polar ice-cap, a distance of 1,600 km. (1,000 miles) from the Pacific to the Atlantic. In 1969 Wally Herbert led the first surface crossing of the Arctic Ocean.

**Arctic Circle** an imaginary line on the surface of the globe 23° 30' south of the North Pole (latitude 66° 30' N), marking the northern most point at which the sun is visible during the midwinter solstice and the southernmost point at which the midnight sun can be seen during northern midsummer.

**Arctic front** a relatively inactive climatic zone in the northern hemisphere between latitudes 50°N and 60°N in which cold air from the Arctic meets less cold air.

**Arctic Ocean** an ocean that surrounds the North Pole, entirely within the Arctic Circle. It is the world's smallest ocean with an area of 14 million sq. km. (5.4 million sq. miles), but the ocean with the world's widest continental shelf. The Arctic Ocean, which deepens to 2,000 fathoms at its centre, is largely covered with pack ice 2–4.3 m. (6–14 ft.) thick. It reaches a maximum depth of 5,450 m. (17,880 ft.) in an abyssal plain to the north of the Chukchi Sea. Connected to the Pacific Ocean by the Bering Sea, its chief link with the Atlantic Ocean is the Greenland Sea.

**Arctic sea smoke** a dense fog that occurs over water in high latitudes during winter when icy cold, dry air from the land or from an expanse of pack ice passes over warmer moister air lying over open water.

**Ardabil** /'ɑːrdə͵biːl/ (also **Ardebil**) a city in the province of East Azerbaijan, north-west Iran; pop. (1991) 311,000. Noted for its carpets and rugs, it was capital of Azerbaijan in the 10th c.

**Ardèche** /ɑːrˈdeʃ/ **1.** a department in the Rhône-Alpes region of eastern France, bounded by the River Rhône in the east and the Cévennes Hills in the west; area 5,529 sq. km. (2,136 sq. miles); pop. (1990) 277,580; capital, Privas. **2.** a river of eastern France that rises in the Cévennes and flows south-east for 120 km. (75 miles) to meet the River Rhône near Pont-St.-Esprit.

**Arden** /'ɑːdən/, **Forest of** an area of Warwickshire, central England, that was formerly part of an extensive forest that stretched across the Midlands. It was possibly the setting of Shakespeare's *As You Like It*.

**Ardennes** /ɑːrˈden/ **1.** a forested upland region of north-west Europe, rising to heights above 610 m. (2,000 ft.) and extending over parts of south-east Belgium, north-east France, and Luxembourg. It was the scene of the last great German offensive of World War II. **2.** a department in the Champagne-Ardenne region of north-east France; area 5,229 sq. km. (2,020 sq. miles); pop. (1990) 296,360; capital, Charleville-Mézières.

**Ardersier** /͵ærdərˈsiːr/ a former fishing village on the Moray Firth, 16 km. (10 miles) north-east of Inverness, Scotland, developed in the late 1970s as a site for the fabrication of large oil-production platforms. It is a dormitory for Nairn and Inverness.

**Ardnamurchan** /͵ɑːdnəˈmɜːxən/ an exposed peninsula on the deeply indented west coast of Lochaber in Highland Region, Scotland. Ardnamurchan Point is the most westerly point on the British mainland.

**Ardrossan** /ɑːrˈdrɒs(ə)n/ a port on the Firth of Clyde coast of North Ayrshire, south-west Scotland; pop. (1981) 11,420. There is a ferry link with the island of Arran.

**Arecibo** /͵ærerˈsiːbəʊ/ a port and old colonial city on the north coast of the Caribbean island of Puerto Rico, 65 km. (40 miles) west of San Juan; pop. (1990) 93,385. Its principal industry is rum distilling.

**Arendal** /'ɑːrən͵dɑːl/ a seaport in south Norway, on the Skagerrak; pop. (1991) 12,480. It is the capital of Aust-Agder county and has maintained a sizeable fishing fleet since the 1880s.

**Arequipa** /͵ærerˈkiːpə/ the capital of the department of Arequipa in southern Peru, and an oasis city that stands at an altitude of c. 2,325 m. (7,628 ft.) in the western Andes; pop. (1990) 634,500. It lies in a valley at the foot of the dormant volcano El Misti. The second-largest city in Peru, Arequipa was built by the Spanish in 1540 on the site of an earlier Inca settlement. It was restored after the disastrous earthquake of 1868 and has textiles, leather goods, and foodstuffs industries.

**arête** /æ'ret/ a sharp, steep-sided narrow mountain ridge. In the US it is also known as a comb ridge.

**Arezzo** /ɑːˈretsəʊ/ a city in Tuscany, north-central Italy, at the junction of the Arno and

Chiana rivers, capital of the province of Arezzo; pop. (1990) 91,620. It was the birthplace of the Italian poets Francesco Petrarch (1304–74) and Pietro Aretino (1492–1557). The city is noted for its trade in antiques and olive oil.

**Argenteuil** /ˌɑːʒɑ̃ˈtɜːɪ/ an industrial north-western suburb of Paris in the department of Val-d'Oise, on the River Seine; pop. (1990) 94,160. The Seamless Tunic, said to have been worn by Christ and given by the Emperor Charlemagne to the former convent, is now in the Saint-Denis Basilica which was built in 1866. Its market gardens are noted for their asparagus and grapes. Textiles, vehicle parts, and electrical equipment are manu-factured. The French painter Georges Braques (1882–1963) was born in Argenteuil; Monet lived there from 1871 to 1878 and painted some of his most famous works, as did other Impressionist painters.

## Argentina

/ˌɑːdʒənˈtiːnə/ official name **The Argen-tine Republic** a country occupying much of the southern part of South Amer-ica, bounded to the west by Chile, to the north by Bolivia and Paraguay, and to the north-east and east by Brazil, Uruguay, and the Atlantic Ocean; area 2,780,092 sq. km. (1,073,809 sq. miles); pop. (1991) 32,606,200; languages, Spanish (official), English, French, German, and Italian; capital, Buenos Aires. Between the Atlantic coast and the foothills of the Andes lies a treeless semi-arid plain known as the *pampa*. The northern plains are drained by the Paraguay, Uruguay, and Paraná rivers which join to form the wide estuary of the River Plate and in the south many rivers flow down to the Atlantic from the Andes. Argentina is one of the leading agricultural and industrial nations of South Amer-ica, depending on exports of grain and meat for the greater part of its income. In recent years oil and gas have been expoited off the coast of Patagonia and a wide variety of minerals (including copper, iron ore, silver, tungsten, and manganese) have been extracted. Colonized by the Spanish in the 16th c., Argentina declared its independence in 1816 and played a crucial role in the overthrow of European rule in the rest of South America. After a period of semi-dictatorial rule, the country emerged as a democratic republic in the mid-19th c., but has since had recurrent problems with political and economic instability, periodically falling under military rule, most notably at the time of Juan Peron. In 1982 the Argentine claim to the Falkland Islands led to an unsuccessful war with Britain. Some 85 per cent of the people of Argentina are of European origin; most are Roman Catholic. Argentina is governed by an executive president

and a bicameral legislature comprising a Senate and a Chamber of Deputies.
**Argentine** *adj. & n.*
Argentina is divided into a federal district and 23 departments:

| Federal District | Area (sq. km.) | Pop. (1991) | Capital |
|---|---|---|---|
| Buenos Aires | 200 | 2,960,976 | |
| Department | Area (sq. km.) | Pop. (1991) | Capital |
| Buenos Aires | 307,804 | 12,582,321 | |
| Catamarca | 99,818 | 265,571 | Catamarca |
| Córdoba | 168,766 | 2,764,176 | Córdoba |
| Corrientes | 88,189 | 795,021 | Corrientes |
| Chaco | 99,633 | 838,303 | Resistencia |
| Chubut | 224,686 | 356,587 | Rawson |
| Entre Ríos | 76,216 | 1,020,377 | Paraná |
| Formosa | 72,066 | 404,367 | Formosa |
| Jujuy | 53,219 | 513,992 | Jujuy |
| La Pampa | 143,440 | 260,034 | Santa Rosa |
| La Rioja | 92,331 | 220,729 | La Rioja |
| Mendoza | 150,839 | 1,414,858 | Mendoza |
| Misiones | 29,801 | 789,677 | Posadas |
| Neuquén | 94,078 | 388,934 | Neuquén |
| Río Negro | 203,013 | 506,796 | Viedma |
| Salta | 154,775 | 866,771 | Salta |
| San Juan | 86,137 | 529,920 | San Juan |
| San Luis | 76,748 | 286,334 | San Luis |
| Santa Cruz | 243,943 | 159,964 | Gallegos |
| Santa Fe | 133,007 | 2,797,293 | Santa Fe |
| Santiago del Estero | 135,254 | 672,301 | Santiago del Estero |
| Tierra del Fuego | 21,263 | 69,450 | Ushuaia |
| Tucumán | 22,524 | 1,142,247 | San Miguel deTucumán |

**Arges** /ˈɑːrdʒeʃ/ **1.** a county in south-central Romania to the north-west of Bucharest; area 6,801 sq. km. (2,626 sq. miles); pop. (1989) 676,730; capital, Pitesti. **2.** a river in southern Romania that rises in the Transylvanian Alps and flows southwards to meet the Danube south-east of Bucharest.

**Argolis** /ˈɑːɡələs/ (Greek **Argolida**) a depart-ment in the Peleponnese region of Greece; area 2,154 sq. km. (832 sq. miles); pop. (1991) 97,250; capital, Nauplia. In ancient times it was dominated by the powerful city of Argos.

**Argos** /ˈɑːɡɒs/ a city in the north-east Peleponnese of Greece; pop. (1981) 20,700. One of the oldest cities of ancient Greece, it was in the 7th c. the dominant city of the Peloponnese and the western Aegean.
**Argive** *adj. & n.*

**Argyll and Bute** /ɑːˈɡaɪəl, bjuːt/ an adminis-trative district of western Scotland; area 6,497 sq. km (2,509 sq. miles); pop. (1991) 66,990; capital, Lochgilphead. The district includes the island of Bute whose chief town is Rothesay.

**Argyllshire** /ɑːˈɡaɪəlʃə(r)/ a former county on the west coast of Scotland. It was divided between Strathclyde and Highland regions in 1975.

**Argyrocastro** see GJIROKASTËR.

**Arhangay** /'ɑːrxæn,gaɪ/ (also **Arkhanga**, **Arakhangai**, and **Tsetserleg**) the capital of a livestock-rearing county of the same name in central Mongolia; pop. (1990) 22,200.

**Århus** see AARHUS.

**Ariana** /,æriːˈɑːnə/ a name given to the eastern provinces of the ancient Persian empire lying to the south of the Oxus River (Amu Darya).

**Arica** /ɑːˈriːkɑː/ a Pacific port in the Tarapacá region of northern Chile, situated close to the border with Peru and north of the Atacama Desert; pop. (1991) 195,000. Formerly (until 1929) part of Peru, it is linked by rail to La Paz in Bolivia. Over 50 per cent of Bolivia's foreign trade passes through Arica.

**Ariège** /ɑːrˈjeʒ/ **1.** a department on the northern slopes of the Pyrenees, in the Midi-Pyrénées region of southern France; area 4,890 sq. km. (1,888 sq. miles); pop. (1990) 136,455; capital, Foix. **2.** a river in southern France that rises in the Pyrenees and flows north-west for *c.* 160 km. (100 miles) to meet the Garonne near Toulouse.

**Arizona** /,ærɪˈzəʊnə/ a state in south-west USA, on the Mexican frontier, between California and New Mexico; area 295,260 sq. km. (114,000 sq. miles); pop. (1990) 3,665,230; capital, Phoenix. The largest cities are Phoenix, Tucson, and Mesa. Arizona is also known as the Grand Canyon State. It was acquired from Mexico in 1848 and 1853 (Gadsden Purchase) and became the 48th state of the US in 1912. The chief products of the state are copper, electrical equipment, aeronautical parts, and agricultural produce. Major tourist attractions include the Grand Canyon, Petrified Forest, Hoover Dam, Fort Apache, and the reconstructed London Bridge at Lake Havasu City. Arizona has the largest Indian population in the US, with more than 14 tribes represented on 19 reservations. The state is divided into 15 counties:

| County | Area (sq. km.) | Pop. (1990) | County Seat |
| --- | --- | --- | --- |
| Apache | 29,149 | 61,590 | Saint Johns |
| Cochise | 16,167 | 97,620 | Bisbee |
| Coconino | 48,381 | 96,590 | Flagstaff |
| Gila | 12,355 | 40,220 | Globe |
| Graham | 12,038 | 26,550 | Safford |
| Greenlee | 4,776 | 8,010 | Clifton |
| La Paz | 11,469 | 13,840 | Parker |
| Maricopa | 23,730 | 2,122,100 | Phoenix |
| Mohave | 34,541 | 93,500 | Kingman |
| Navajo | 25,883 | 77,670 | Holbrook |
| Pima | 23,886 | 666,960 | Tucson |
| Pinal | 13,892 | 116,380 | Florence |
| Santa Cruz | 3,219 | 29,680 | Nogales |
| Yavapai | 21,120 | 107,710 | Prescott |
| Yuma | 25,984 | 106,895 | Yuma |

**Arkansas** /'ɑːkən,sɔː/ a state in south-central USA, bounded by the Mississippi River on the east

and Oklahoma to the west; area 137,754 sq. km. (53,187 sq. miles); pop. (1990) 2,350,725; capital, Little Rock. The largest cities are Little Rock, Fort Smith, North Little Rock, and Pine Bluff. Arkansas is also known as the 'Land of Opportunity'. In 1803 it was acquired by the US as part of the Louisiana purchase and became the 25th state in 1836. Arkansas is a major producer of bauxite and agricultural produce such as cotton, rice, and soybeans. Major attractions include the radioactive mineral waters of Hot Springs National Park and the Buffalo National River in the Ozarks. The state is divided into 75 counties:

| County | Area (sq. km.) | Pop. (1990) | County Seat |
| --- | --- | --- | --- |
| Arkansas | 2,616 | 21,650 | DeWitt and Stuttgart |
| Ashley | 2,428 | 24,320 | Hamburg |
| Baxter | 1,420 | 31,190 | Mountain Home |
| Benton | 2,192 | 97,500 | Bentonville |
| Boone | 1,518 | 28,300 | Harrison |
| Bradley | 1,700 | 11,790 | Warren |
| Calhoun | 1,633 | 5,830 | Hampton |
| Carroll | 1,648 | 18,650 | Berryville and EurekaSprings |
| Chicot | 1,687 | 15,710 | Lake Village |
| Clark | 2,254 | 21,440 | Arkadelphia |
| Clay | 1,667 | 18,110 | Corning and Piggott |
| Cleburne | 1,433 | 19,410 | Heber Springs |
| Cleveland | 1,557 | 7,780 | Rison |
| Columbia | 1,994 | 25,690 | Magnolia |
| Conway | 1,451 | 19,150 | Morrilton |
| Craighead | 1,854 | 68,960 | Jonesboro and Lake City |
| Crawford | 1,544 | 42,490 | Van Buren |
| Crittenden | 1,557 | 49,940 | Marion |
| Cross | 1,617 | 19,225 | Wynne |
| Dallas | 1,737 | 9,610 | Fordyce |
| Desha | 1,940 | 16,800 | Arkansas City |
| Drew | 2,161 | 17,370 | Monticello |
| Faulkner | 1,677 | 60,010 | Conway |
| Franklin | 1,583 | 14,900 | Charleston and Ozark |
| Fulton | 1,602 | 10,040 | Salem |
| Garland | 1,708 | 73,400 | Hot Springs |
| Grant | 1,646 | 13,950 | Sheridan |
| Greene | 1,505 | 31,800 | Paragould |
| Hempstead | 1,885 | 21,620 | Hope |
| Hot Spring | 1,599 | 26,115 | Malvern |
| Howard | 1,492 | 13,570 | Nashville |
| Independence | 1,984 | 31,190 | Batesville |
| Izard | 1,511 | 11,360 | Melbourne |
| Jackson | 1,646 | 18,940 | Newport |
| Jefferson | 2,293 | 85,490 | Pine Bluff |
| Johnson | 1,758 | 18,220 | Clarksville |
| Lafayette | 1,347 | 9,640 | Lewisville |
| Lawrence | 1,531 | 17,455 | Walnut Ridge |
| Lee | 1,565 | 13,050 | Marianna |
| Lincoln | 1,461 | 13,690 | Star City |
| Little River | 1,342 | 13,970 | Ashdown |
| Logan | 1,864 | 20,560 | Booneville and Paris |

(cont.)

| County | Area (sq. km.) | Pop. (1990) | County Seat |
|---|---|---|---|
| Lonoke | 2,036 | 39,270 | Lonoke |
| Madison | 2,176 | 11,620 | Huntsville |
| Marion | 1,526 | 12,000 | Yellville |
| Miller | 1,609 | 38,470 | Texarkana |
| Mississippi | 2,330 | 57,525 | Blytheville and Osceola |
| Monroe | 1,583 | 11,330 | Clarendon |
| Montgomery | 2,012 | 7,840 | Mount Ida |
| Nevada | 1,612 | 10,100 | Prescott |
| Newton | 2,140 | 7,670 | Jasper |
| Ouachita | 1,916 | 30,570 | Camden |
| Perry | 1,430 | 7,970 | Perryville |
| Phillips | 1,781 | 28,840 | Helena |
| Pike | 1,555 | 10,090 | Murfreesboro |
| Poinsett | 1,981 | 24,660 | Harrisburg |
| Polk | 2,236 | 17,350 | Mena |
| Pope | 2,132 | 45,880 | Russellville |
| Prairie | 1,706 | 9,520 | Des Arc and De Valls Bluff |
| Pulaski | 1,994 | 349,570 | Little Rock |
| Randolph | 1,706 | 16,560 | Pocahontas |
| St. Francis | 1,659 | 28,500 | Forrest City |
| Saline | 1,885 | 64,180 | Benton |
| Scott | 2,330 | 10,205 | Waldron |
| Searcy | 1,737 | 7,840 | Marshall |
| Sebastian | 1,391 | 99,590 | Fort Smith and Greenwood |
| Sevier | 1,456 | 13,640 | De Queen |
| Sharp | 1,659 | 14,110 | Ash Flat |
| Stone | 1,576 | 9,775 | Mountain View |
| Union | 2,738 | 46,720 | El Dorado |
| Van Buren | 1,843 | 14,010 | Clinton |
| Washington | 2,473 | 113,410 | Fayetville |
| White | 2,704 | 54,680 | Searcy |
| Woodruff | 1,539 | 9,520 | Augusta |
| Yell | 2,418 | 17,760 | Danville and Dardanelle |

**Arkansas** a river that rises in the Rocky Mountains of central Colorado, USA, and flows 2,333 km. (1,450 miles) south-east across the Great Plains of Colorado, Kansas, Oklahoma, and Arkansas before it joins the Mississippi south of Memphis.

**Arkhangelsk** /ɑːˈxæŋgelsk/ the Russian name for the port of ARCHANGEL.

**Arklow** /ˈɑːrkləʊ/ a port in County Wicklow on the Irish Sea coast of Leinster in the Republic of Ireland; pop. (1991) 8,388. It is one of Ireland's leading east-coast resorts. Gypsy Moth IV, the yacht in which Sir Francis Chichester made his solo voyage around the world in 1966–7, was built in an Arklow shipyard.

**Arlberg** /ˈɑːlbə(r)g/ an alpine pass on the frontier between the west Austrian states of Tyrol and Vorarlberg (= the land beyond the Arlberg). A high-altitude tunnel links Bludenz to Landeck and Innsbruck.

**Arles** /ɑːl/ **1.** a medieval kingdom of France created in the 10th c. by the union of the kingdoms of Burgundy and Provence. A century later it was annexed by the Holy Roman Empire which held it until the Emperor Charles IV ceded it to the dauphin of France in 1378. **2.** a marketing and tourist city in the Bouche-du-Rhône department of Provence-Alpes-Côte d'Azur region in south-east France, at the head of the Camargue delta on the River Rhône; pop. (1990) 52,590. It was capital of Provence and the medieval kingdom of Arles and has been an important centre of communication since Roman times. Constantine I convoked a synod at Arles in AD 314 in order to condemn the revolutionary Donatist Christian movement in North Africa. It has a large Roman arena (now used for bullfighting), a Roman theatre, and a Provençal museum. Arles has attracted many artists including Gaugin and Van Gogh who spent his last and most productive years (1888–90) in the city.

**Arlington** /ˈɑːlɪŋt(ə)n/ **1.** a county in north Virginia, USA, forming a residential suburb of Washington on the opposite side of the Potomac River; pop. (1990) 170,936. The Pentagon, which is one of the largest office buildings in the world, and the Arlington National Cemetery (1864) are located here. **2.** an industrial city in northern Texas, between Dallas and Fort Worth; pop. (1990) 261,720. The Six Flags Over Texas amusement park is located here. It has a vast industrial estate and produces iron and steel, vehicle and aircraft parts, oilfield and electronic equipment, and many light industrial products.

**Arlington Heights** a residential and industrial town in north-east Illinois, USA, 40 km. (25 miles) north-west of Chicago; pop. (1990) 75,460. The Arlington International Racecourse is the site of the annual Arlington Million thoroughbred horse-racing event. Its industries include electronic components, and domestic and office equipment and supplies.

**Arlon** /ɑːlɔ̃/ (Flemish **Aarlen**) the chief town of the province of Luxembourg in south-east Belgium; pop. (1991) 23,420.

**Armageddon** /ˌɑːməˈged(ə)n/ (also **Megiddo** /mɪˈgɪdəʊ/) an archaeological site in Israel on the plain of Esdraelon to the south of Haifa. (Hebrew *har megiddon* = hill of Megiddo.) It was an important fortress in ancient times and in the New Testament Armageddon is the name given to the last battle between good and evil before the Day of Judgement (Revelations 16:16).

**Armagh** /ɑːrˈmɑː/ **1.** a county in Northern Ireland, lying to the south of Lough Neagh; area 1,254 sq. km. (484 sq. miles); pop. (1981) 118,820. **2.** its county town; pop. (1981) 12,700. Armagh, which was the seat of the kings of Ulster from c. 400 BC to AD 333, became the religious centre of Ireland in AD 445 when St. Patrick was made archbishop.

**Armagnac** /ˈɑːmənˌjæk/ an area of Aquitaine in south-west France noted for its brandy and its attractive fortified towns (Bastides). It now forms the greater part of the department of Gers. During the 10th c. the counts of Armagnac emerged as vassals of the dukes of Gascony. The last of their line married the king of Navarre whose grandson, Henry IV of France, added Armagnac to his kingdom in 1607.

**Armavir** /ˌɑːməˈvɪr/ an industrial city and transportation centre in the northern foothills of the Caucasus, south-central Russia, situated on the Kuban River, 160 km. (100 miles) east of Krasnodar; pop. (1990) 162,000. It lies in a rich agricultural area near the Maykop oil fields. It has machine and tool plants.

**Armenia** /ɑːˈmiːnɪə/ the country of the Armenians, a former kingdom in the Anatolian plains of western Asia, which first gained autonomy in the 9th c. AD but was by the end of the 16th c. under Turkish rule. It is now divided between Turkey, Iran, and the former Soviet Republic of Armenia. In the early 19th c. the Russians advanced into the crumbling Ottoman empire, and in 1828 the Sultan was obliged to surrender part of the Armenian homeland. In 1915 the Turks, at war with Russia, suspected their Armenian subjects of sympathizing with kinsmen across the border and with the Western forces who had embarked on the Dardanelles campaign, and decided on mass deportation of an estimated 1,750,000 Armenians to the deserts of Syria and Mesopotamia. This, coupled with alleged persecution during the 1890s, resulted in deep and lasting Armenian hatred towards the Turks. The language of Armenia constitutes a separate branch of the Indo-European language group although its vocabulary has been substantially influenced by Iranian languages. Its characteristic alphabet contains 38 letters and was invented in AD 400 by missionaries. There are some 4 million speakers of the modern language of whom about 3 million live in the Republic of Armenia. The independent Armenian Apostolic Church has been the national church of the Armenians since Armenia, in the 4th c. AD, became the first kingdom to be converted to Christianity.

**Armenia** official name **Republic of Armenia** an independent state in the southern Caucasus of western Asia, bounded to the north by Georgia, to the south by Iran, to the west by Turkey and  to the east by Azerbaijan; area 29,800 sq. km. (11,510 sq. miles); pop. (est. 1991) 3,360,000; official language, Armenian; capital, Yerevan. Its chief products are cotton, rice, fruit, and tobacco. Ceded to Russia by Turkey in 1828, this part of the Armenian homeland joined with Turkish Armenia

in 1920 to gain a brief period of independence as Greater Armenia. In the same year, Communists took control of Russian Armenia, proclaiming the region a constituent republic of the Soviet Union. In 1991, with the break-up of the Soviet Union, Armenia declared its independence as a member of the Commonwealth of Independent States.

**Armentières** an industrial town in the Nord department of north-west France, to the west of Lille on the River Lys; pop. (1990) 26,240. It has foundries, breweries, and textile factories, but is best known through the World War I song *Mademoiselle from Armentières*.

**Armidale** /ˈɑːmɪdeɪl/ a city in New South Wales, south-east Australia, situated between Sydney and Brisbane at the centre of a rich agricultural region in the New England plateau; pop. (1991) 21,605. The University of New England (1954) lies northwest of the city.

**Armorica** /ɑːˈmɔːrɪkə/ an early name for the north-west corner of France between the Seine and Loire rivers. The name is applied to periods of mountain building from the Carboniferous to the Permian geological eras.
**Armorican** *adj. & n.*

**Arnhem** /ˈɑːnəm/ the capital of the province of Gelderland, in the east Netherlands, situated on the Rhine near its junction with the IJssel; pop. (1991) 131,700. Founded in the 13th c., it prospered in the Middle Ages as a river trading port. In September 1944 British airborne troops made a famous landing on the nearby Veluwe moorland but were overwhelmed by superior German forces.

**Arnhem Land** a peninsula in Northern Territory, Australia, situated to the west of the Gulf of Carpentaria and inhabited by Aborigines for over 40,000 years; area *c.* 80,776 sq. km. (31,200 sq. miles); pop. (est. 1985) 96,000. The chief town is Nhulunbuy. In 1976 Arnhem Land was declared Aboriginal Land.

**Arno** /ˈɑːrnəʊ/ a river of northern Italy, which rises on Monte Falterona in the Apennines and flows 240 km. (150 miles) north-westwards through Florence to meet the Ligurian Sea near Pisa.

**Arnsberg** /ˈɑːnzbɜːg/ an industrial city in North Rhine-Westphalia, Germany, on the River Ruhr, south-east of Münster; pop. (1983) 76,100. It was the capital of the medieval region of Westphalia which later became a province of Prussia.

**Arrah** /ˈɑːrə/ a town in the state of Bihar, north-eastern India, on a branch of the Son irrigation canals; pop. (1991) 156,870.

**Arran** /ˈærən/ an island in the Firth of Clyde, Scotland, situated between the Mull of Kintyre and the Ayrshire coast; area 430 sq. km. (166 sq. miles). It chief town is the port of Brodick. A popular tourist island, its attractions include Goat Fell

(874 m., 2,867 ft), the Machrie Moor stone circles, and Brodick Castle. In 1787 the geologist James Hutton found evidence to support his 'Theory of the Earth' when he discovered an unconformity in the rock formations near Lochranza.

**Arras** /'ærəs/ the capital of Pas-de-Calais department in north-west France, between Lille and Amiens; pop. (1990) 42,715. Known as Nemetocenna in Gallo-Roman times, the town became an important trading and commercial centre during the Middle Ages, but was devastated during a war between France and Burgundy which ended in 1435 with the signing of the Treaty of Arras. Noted for its Flemish architecture which has been restored after further devastation in World War I, Arras gives its name to a fabric used to make a rich tapestry.

**Arrecife** /ˌɑːrəˈsiːfeɪ/ (also **Puerto Arrecife** or **Arrecife de Lanzarote**) a port on the south coast of the island of Lanzarote in the Spanish Canary Islands; pop. (1991) 33,560.

**Arta** /'ɑːrtə/ **1.** a department in Epirus, western Greece; area 1,662 sq. km. (642 sq. miles); pop. (1991) 78,880. **2.** its capital, on the Arta (Arakhthos) River; pop. (1981) 18,280. It was known as Ambracia to the Corinthians who founded the city in the 7th c. BC. Pyrrhus, king of Epirus made his capital here in 295 BC and much later in Byzantine times a new town named Arta was established.

**Arthur's Pass** /'ɑːθːə(r)z/ a mountain pass through the Otira Gorge in the Southern Alps of central South Island, New Zealand. Opened in 1866, the 17-km. (10.7-mile) highway through the pass links the townships of Otira and Arthur's Pass. Beneath the pass runs the 8.5-km. (5.3-mile) Otira Rail Tunnel which was completed in 1923 and is the only rail link across South Island.

**Arthur's Seat** the remains of a volcanic plug that forms a prominent hill overlooking the city of Edinburgh in central Scotland. Rising to a height of 250 m. (823 ft.) it stands in the middle of a royal park.

**Artigas** /ær'tiːɡəs/ a town in north-west Uruguay, on the River Cuareim; pop. (1985) 34,150. It is a trading centre for cattle, grain, fruit, and wool and is the capital of a department of the same name on the frontier with Brazil.

**Artois** /ɑːˈtwæ/ a former province in north-west France between Picardy and Flanders. Known in Roman times as Artesium, the area gave its name to the artesian well which was first sunk here in the 12th c.

**Artvin** /'ærtvən/ **1.** a mountainous province in the Anatolian plateau of north-east Turkey; area 7,436 sq. km. (2,872 sq. miles); pop. (1990) 212,830. **2.** its capital, on the River Coruh; pop. (1990) 20,300.

**Aruba** /əˈruːbə/ a Dutch island in the Caribbean Sea 24 km. (15 miles) north of the Venezuelan coast. Formerly part of the Netherlands Antilles, it separated from that group in 1986 in advance of

gaining full independence; area 193 sq. km. (74 sq. miles); pop. (est. 1991) 60,000; chief town, Oranjestad. The economy is based on the refining of crude oil imported from Venezuela.

**Aru Islands** /'ɑːruː/ (also **Aroe Islands**) a group of 95 low-lying islands in the Arafura Sea, forming part of the Moluccas group of eastern Indonesia; area 8,562 sq. km. (3,306 sq. miles). Pearl and mother-of-pearl are its main products. At the end of a long journey, the naturalist Alfred Russell Wallace stayed on these islands prior to announcing his theory of evolution in 1858.

**Arunachal Pradesh** /ɑːrəˈnɑːtʃ(ə)l prəˈdeʃ/ a mountainous state of north-east India, bounded to the north by Tibet, to the east by Burma and to the west by Bhutan; area 83,578 sq. km. (32,282 sq. miles); pop. (1991) 858,350; capital, Itanagar. Formerly the North East Frontier Agency of Assam in British India, Arunachal Pradesh became the 24th state of India in 1986. Nearly two-thirds of the state is under forest, the chief products being coffee, rice, rubber, fruits, and spices. There are over 80 tribal groups speaking 50 different dialects.

**Arundel** /'ærənd(ə)l/ a market town in the county of West Sussex, southern England, on the River Arun; pop. (1981) 2,500. Nearby is the 12th-c. Arundel Castle, seat of the dukes of Norfolk.

**Arusha** /əˈruːʃə/ an industrial town in north-east Tanzania, to the north of the Masai Steppe, at the southern foot of Mount Meru; pop. (1984) 69,000. Situated at the centre of a coffee-growing area, it is the capital of a province of the same name and the main safari base for the northern park areas. Nearby are Mt. Kilimanjaro and the Ngorongoro crater.

**Arvand** /'ɑːvənd/ the Iranian name for the SHATT AL-ARAB waterway between Iraq and Iran.

**Aryan** /'eərɪən/ a member of the peoples (not to be regarded as a race) speaking any of the languages of the Indo-European (esp. Indo-Iranian) family. The idea current in the 19th c. of an Aryan race corresponding to a definite Aryan language was taken up by nationalistic, historical, and romantic writers. It was given especial currency by M. A. de Gobineau, who linked it with the theory of the essential inferiority of certain races. The term 'Aryan race' was later revived and used for purposes of political propaganda in Nazi Germany.

**Arzamas** /ˌɑːrzə'mɑːs/ a town and railway junction in western Russia, 95 km. (60 miles) south of Nizhniy Novgorod; pop. (1990) 111,000. It has diverse light industries.

**Asahikawa** /ˌæsəhi'kɑːwə/ a city in Hokkaido prefecture at the centre of Hokkaido Island, northern Japan; pop. (1990) 359,070. Manufactures include textiles, furniture, paper, and the Japanese drink saké. The Ainu people live nearby.

**Asama** /ə'sɑːmə/ (Japanese **Asamayama**) a volcano rising to a height of 2,542 m. (8,340 ft.) at the centre of Honshu Island, Japan. It is one of the largest active volcanoes in Japan. The last major eruption took place in 1783.

**Asamankese** /ˌæsəmən'keɪzɪ/ a town in the Eastern Region of Ghana, to the north-west of Accra; pop. (1970) 101,140.

**Asansol** /əsən'sɔːl/ an industrial city in West Bengal, India, 192 km. (120 miles) north-west of Calcutta and in a coal-mining region; pop. (1991) 262,000. Railway engineering and the production of iron, steel, and chemicals are the chief industries.

**Asante** see ASHANTI.

**Ascalon** see ASHQUELON.

**Ascension Island** /ə'senʃ(ə)n/ a small island in the South Atlantic, incorporated with St. Helena with which it is a dependency of the UK; area 88 sq. km. (34 sq. miles); pop. (1988) 1,007. It was discovered by the Portuguese, traditionally on Ascension Day in 1501, but remained uninhabited until a small British garrison was stationed there on the arrival of Napoleon for imprisonment on St. Helena in 1815. It is now a British telecommunications centre and a US air base. The island has been strategically important during (and since) the military operations in the Falkland Islands in 1982, serving as a base for British forces and a landing-point for aircraft travelling between Britain and the South Atlantic.

**Aschaffenburg** /ə'ʃæfənbʊək/ a city in the German state of Bavaria, on the River Main, south-east of Frankfurt; pop. (1991) 64,470. Its river port is a major outlet for coal, timber, textiles, wine, and scientific equipment. It manufactures precision and optical instruments and machinery.

**Aschersleben** /ɑːʃərsˌleɪbən/ an industrial city in the German state of Saxony-Anhalt, west of Dessau; pop. (1984) 59,600. There are potash, lignite, and salt mines nearby. Its industries include iron and steel, machine tools, and chemicals.

**Ascoli Piceno** /ˌɑːskəʊli piː'tʃeɪnəʊ/ a tourist resort and the capital of a province of the same name in the Marche region of east-central Italy, 25 km. (16 miles) from the Adriatic coast at the junction of the Tronto and Castellano rivers; pop. (1990) 52,625. The original Roman town was built on a salt-trading route.

**Ascot** /'æskət/ a racecourse near Windsor in Berkshire, England. It is the scene of an annual race-meeting in June (Ascot Week), founded by Queen Anne in 1711.

**ASEAN** /'æsɪən/ an abbreviation for the Association of South East Asian Nations, a regional organization formed by Indonesia, Malaysia, the Philippines, Singapore, and Thailand through the Bangkok Declaration of 1967. Brunei joined the organization in 1984; area 3,069,690 sq. km. (1,185,213 sq. miles); pop. (1989) 321,200,000. Although ASEAN has aimed to accelerate economic growth, its main success has been in the promotion of regional security, diplomatic collaboration, the exchange of cultural resources, and co-operation in transport and communication.

**Asgard** /'æzgɑːd/ in Scandinavian mythology, a region at the centre of the universe inhabited by the gods.

**Ashanti** /ə'ʃæntɪ/ (Also **Asante**) a region of central Ghana inhabited by the Ashanti, one of Ghana's principal ethnic groups; area 25,123 sq. km. (9,700 sq. miles); pop. (1984) 2,089,700. The regional capital, Kumasi, was the capital of the former Ashanti confederation, a tribal union (covering a wider area) that was forged in the 17th c. After a series of wars the area was formally annexed by Britain on 1 January 1902 and became part of the British colony of the Gold Coast. The Ashanti people speak a dialect of the Kwa group within the Niger-Kordofanian family of African languages.

**Ashburton** /'æʃbɜːt(ə)n/ a river in Western Australia, which rises 240 km. (150 miles) south of Nullagine and flows north-west for 480 km (300 miles) before it meets the Indian Ocean near Onslow.

**Ashby-de-la-Zouch** /'æʃbɪ də læ zuːʃ/ a town and former spa in Leicestershire, central England, 24 km. (15 miles) north-west of Leicester; Mary Queen of Scots was imprisoned in the castle in 1569. Nearby is the Tournament Field that features in Sir Walter Scott's novel *Ivanhoe*.

**Ashdod** /'æʃdɒd/ a deep-water seaport and industrial centre on the Mediterranean coast of southern Israel, to the south of Tel Aviv; pop. (est. 1982) 62,000. It manufactures synthetic fibres, wool, and knitted goods.

**Ashdown Forest** /'æʃdaʊn/ a region of heath and woodland in Sussex, south-east England. It is the remaining portion of the once extensive Wealden Forest.

**Asheville** /'æʃvɪl/ a commercial and industrial city in west North Carolina, USA, on the French Broad River in the Blue Ridge Mountains; pop. (1990) 61,600. It is the seat of Buncome County. The writers Thomas Wolfe and O. Henry (William Sydney Porter) are buried in the Riverside Cemetery. The University of North Carolina at Asheville was established in 1927. Local industries include electronics, textiles and clothing, glass, and tourism.

**Ashford** /'æʃfə(r)d/ a market town in Kent, south-east England, on the Great Stour River; pop. (1981) 45,962. It is the site of a terminus of the Channel Tunnel.

**Ashgabat** /'ɑːʃgəbæt/ (formerly **Ashkhabad**) the capital of the central Asian republic of Turkmenistan between the Kopet Dagh mountains and the Kara-Kum desert; pop. (1990) 407,200. Established in 1881 as a Russian fort, it was known as Poltoratsk from 1919 to 1927 and Ashkhabad until 1992. The city, which lies 40 km. (25 miles) from the Iranian border, was rebuilt following an earthquake in 1948. It has numerous light industries including textiles, carpets, brewing, and food processing.

**Ashington** /'æʃɪŋtən/ a former coal-mining town in Northumberland, north-east England, to the north of Newcastle upon Tyne; pop. (est. 1985) 27,790.

**Ashkelon** see ASHQUELON.

**Ashkenazi** /ˌæʃkə'nɑːzɪ/ (pl. **Ashkenazim** /- zɪm/) an East European Jew or a Jew of East European ancestry.
**Ashkenazic** adj.

**Ashkhabad** /'ɑːʃkəbæd/ see ASHGABAT.

**Ashmolean Museum** /æʃ'məʊlɪən/ a museum of art and antiquities in Oxford, England, founded by the English antiquary Elias Ashmole (1617–92) in 1683.

**Ashmore and Cartier Islands** /'æʃmɔː(r), 'kɑːtɪə/ an external territory of Australia in the Indian Ocean, comprising the uninhabited Ashmore Reef and Cartier Islands; area c. 3 sq. km. (1 sq. mile). Part of Australia since 1931, the islands were administered by Northern Territory from 1938 to 1978. A national nature reserve was established in 1983.

**Ashquelon** /'æʃkələn/ a resort on the Mediterranean coast of Israel, about 56 km. (35 miles) south of Tel Aviv. It is the site of an ancient Philistine city (called Ashkelon in the Bible) which has given its name to a kind of onion.

**Ashton-in-Makerfield** /'æʃtən, 'meɪkərfiːld/ a suburb of Tameside borough in Greater Manchester, north-west England; pop. (1981) 28,400.

**Ashton-under-Lyne** /-laɪn/ an industrial suburb of Tameside borough in Greater Manchester, north-west England, on the Tame River.

**Asi** /'æsi:/ the modern name for the ORONTES River which flows through Lebanon, Syria, and Turkey before entering the Mediterranean Sea.

**Asia** /'eɪʃə/ the largest of the world's continents, constituting nearly one-third of the land mass, lying in the eastern hemisphere, entirely north of the equator except for some south-east Asian islands. It stretches from Cape Chelyubinsk on the Arctic coast to Cape Piai at the southern tip of the Malay peninsula, and from Cape Baba in western Turkey through more than 165° of longitude to Cape Dezhnev in north-east Siberia. The world's highest mountain (Mount Everest), lowest elevation (the Dead Sea), greatest area of coniferous forest (the taiga of Siberian Russia), and largest inland sea (Caspian) are all located in Asia. The continent is connected to Africa by the Isthmus of Suez, and generally divided from Europe (which forms part of the same land mass) by a line running through the Ural Mountains and the Caspian Sea; area 44 million sq. km. (17 million sq. miles); pop. (est. 1990) 3,113 million. The principal cities are Tokyo, Shanghai, Beijing, Seoul, Calcutta, Bombay, Jakarta, Tehran, Delhi, Bangkok, Tianjin, and Karachi. Major rivers include the Yangtze, Yellow River, Ob-Irtysh, Amur, Lena, Mekong, Yenisei, Indus, Ganges, Brahmaputra, Tigris, Euphrates, Amu Darya, and Irrawaddy. Extensive areas of desert include the Gobi, Takla Makan, Kara-Kum, Syrian Desert, Arabian Desert, and the Negev. Over 90 per cent of the world's rice, rubber, jute, flax, cotton, and tobacco comes from Asia. It is also the world's leading source of tropical timber.
**Asian** or **Asiatic** adj. & n.

**Asia Minor** the westernmost part of Asia now comprising Asiatic Turkey. The first major civilization established there was that of the Hittites in the 2nd millenium BC. The Greeks colonized the western coast, while the kingdoms of Lydia and Phrygia developed independently. The land was subjugated by various invaders, including Cyrus of Persia (546 BC) and Alexander the Great (333 BC). It was subsequently the Roman province of Asia and then part of the Byzantine empire. Conquered by the Turks, it became part of the Ottoman empire from the end of the 13th c. until the establishment of modern Turkey after World War I.

**asif** /æ'si:f/ a Berber word for a river.

**Asir Mountains** /ə'sɪə(r)/ a range of mountains in the south-west of Saudi Arabia, running parallel to the coast of the Red Sea. It rises to 3,133 m. (10,279 ft.) at Jebel Abha which is the highest peak in Saudi Arabia.

**Asmara** /æs'mɑːrə/ (also **Asmera**) the capital of Eritrea in East Africa, situated at an altitude of 2,350 m. (7,710 ft.) on the Hamasen plateau; pop. (1991) 367,300. In 1900 Asmara became the capital of the Italian colony of Eritrea and in the 1930s it was developed as an Italian base from which the invasion of Ethiopia was launched in 1935. The US built a large military communications centre here in the 1950s. Today it has numerous light industries but was severely affected by famines and droughts in the 1970s and 1980s.

**Asnam** /æs'nɑːm/, **El** see ECH CHLEF.

**Asnières-sur-Seine** /ɑːn'jer sʊr sen/ an industrial suburb of north-west Paris in the department of Hauts-de-Seine, northern France, situated on the River Seine; pop. (1990) 72,250. Vehicles, machine tools, aircraft parts, and perfume are the chief products.

**Aso** /'ɑːsəʊ/ (Japanese **Asosan**) a volcano with five peaks on the island of Kyushu, southern Japan, 40 km. (25 miles) east of Kumamoto. Rising to a height of 1,592 m. (5,222 ft.) its crater is one of the largest in the world with a diameter of 16–24 km. (10–15 miles).

**Aspen** /'æspən/ a popular resort town in south-central Colorado, on the Roaring Fork River; pop. (1990) 6,850. From a booming silver-mining camp with a population of 15,000 in 1887 Aspen nearly became a ghost town after the collapse of silver prices in the 1890s, but with the help of a Chicago industrialist, Walter P. Paepcke, it became a thriving recreational and cultural centre. During winter Aspen Mountain attracts large numbers of skiers.

**Aspropotamus** /ˌæsprəʊpə'teɪməs/ the an-cient name for the ACHELOUS River in Greece.

**Assab** /'ɑːsəb/ (also **Aseb**) a seaport on the Red Sea coast of Eritrea; pop. (est. 1984) 21,000. It was a major port of entry for food aid into Eritrea and the Ethiopian province of Tigré during the famine and civil war of the 1980s. Ethiopia negotiated a right to use the port in 1993.

**Assal** /æ'sɑːl/, **Lake** (also **Asal**, French **Lac Assal**) a salt lake in Djibouti, East Africa which, at 153 m. (502 ft.) below sea-level is the lowest eleva-tion in Africa.

**Assam** /æ'sæm/ a state in north-east India; area 88,438 sq. km. (30,673 sq. miles); pop. (1991) 22,294,560; capital, Dispur. Oil, coal, textiles, tea, rice, jute, and oilseed are exported. It became a British protectorate in 1826 but after partition in 1947 territory was lost to Pakistan and Bhutan. In 1972 Meghalaya state was created from part of Assam. Since the 1960s the Bodo minority (with a population of some 4 million) has fought for the right to create its own state on the northern banks of the Brahmaputra River.

**Assen** /'ɑːsən/ the capital of the province of Drenthe in the Netherlands; pop. (1991) 50,357. Linked by canal with Groningen and the Wadden Zee, it is a market town and an important junction for Dutch inland shipping. There are large pre-historic megaliths in the vicinity.

**Assiniboin** /ə'sɪnəˌbɔɪn/ a Siouan tribe of North American Indians originally occupying the plains of western Saskatchewan but later resettled in Alberta and in Montana where they number over 2,500.

**Assiniboine** /ə'sɪnəˌbɔɪn/ a river in southern Canada that rises in south-eastern Saskatchewan and flows 1,070 km. (673 miles) south-east then east through Manitoba to meet the Red River of the North at Winnipeg. Its chief headstreams are the Souris and the Qu'Appelle. The valley of the

Assiniboine was the route to the plains followed by colonists from the Red River valley.

**Assisi** /ə'siːsɪ/ an historic medieval town of Umbria in central Italy, situated in the Apennines in the province of Perugia; pop. (1990) 24,790. St. Francis of Assisi (1182–1226) who lived and died there founded an order in Assisi that bears his name. The saint's tomb is located beneath two churches which form the Basilica of St. Francis.

**Association of Caribbean States** an association of 25 Caribbean basin countries formed in 1994 for the purpose of promoting regional integration, economic co-operation, and a common approach to regional political problems.

**Assumption Island** /ə'sʌmʃən/ an island in the Indian Ocean in the Aldabra group adminis-tered by the Seychelles.

**Assynt** /'æsɪnt/ an area of the rugged north-west coast of Scotland to the north of Loch Broom and Ullapool. Mountain peaks rising up from flat boggy moorland include Suilven, Quinag, Canisp, Stac Polly, and Ben More Assynt. Lochinver and Achiltibuie are the chief settlements.

**Assyria** /ə'sɪrɪə/ an ancient country in what is now northern Iraq. It was originally centred on Ashur, a city-state on the west bank of the Tigris, which first became prominent and expanded its borders in the 14th c. BC. From the 8th to the late 7th c. BC Assyria was the dominant Near Eastern power and created an empire which stretched from the Persian Gulf to Egypt. Its capital city was Nineveh near modern Mosul, Iraq. The state fell in 612 BC, defeated by a coalition of Medes and Chaldeans.
**Assyrian** *adj. & n.*

**asthenosphere** /əs'θenəˌsfiːr/ a zone of hot molten rock underneath the earth's hard crust (lithosphere). Horizontal currents in this layer are associated with continental-plate movements.

**Asti** /'æstɪ/ (anc. **Asta Pompaeia** or **Asta Colonia**) the capital of Asti province in the Piedmont region of north-west Italy, at the junction of the Borbore and Tanaro rivers; pop. (1990) 74,500. It has several medieval monuments and is noted for its sparkling wine.

**Astrakhan** /ˌæstrə'kɑːn/ a market city and port in southern Russia at the head of the Volga River delta near the Caspian Sea; pop. (1990) 510,000. It was capital of a Tatar khanate before being taken by Ivan IV for Russia in the 16th c. The Astrakhan fur which comes from further east in Turkistan takes its name from the city which was a major trading post on the route between Central Asia and European Russia. Its industries include fishing, shipbuilding, cotton, and the processing of lamb-skins.

**astrolabe** /'æstrɒˌleɪb/ an instrument usually consisting of a disc and pointer, formerly used to make astronomical measurements, especially of the altitudes of celestial bodies, and as an aid in navigation. Its form and structure varied with the progress of astronomy and the purpose for which it was intended. In its earliest form (which dates from classical times) it consisted of a disc with the degrees of the circle marked round its edge, and a pivoted pointer along which a heavenly body could be sighted. From late medieval times it was used by mariners for calculating latitude, until replaced by the sextant.

**Asturias** /æsˈtjʊərɪəs/ an autonomous region and former principality of north-west Spain, co-extensive with the province of Oviedo; area 10,565 sq. km. (4,080 sq. miles); pop. (1991) 1,093,940; capital, Oviedo. Prince of Asturias is the title of the eldest son of the king of Spain. Coal, zince, fluorspar, and iron are mined in the region.

**Asunción** /əˌsʌnsɪˈɒn/ the capital and chief port of Paraguay, on the River Paraguay near its junction with the Pilcomayo; pop. (est. 1990) 729,300. Founded in 1538 by the Spanish, it was the first permanent European settlement in the La Plata region of South America. It is Paraguay's only large city and has textile and agricultural processing industries, especially meat packing.

**Aswan** /æsˈwɑːn/ a city in southern Egypt on the right bank of the Nile, 16 km. (10 miles) north of Lake Nasser; pop. (1991) 215,000. It is situated close to two dams across the Nile. The first was built in 1898–1902 to regulate the flooding of the Nile and control the supply of water for irrigation and other purposes. It is now superseded by the high dam, built in 1960–70 with Soviet aid, about 3.6 km. (2.25 miles) long and 111 m. (364 ft.) high. The controlled release of water from Lake Nasser behind it produces the greater part of Egypt's electricity. Aswan has long been a winter resort and commercial centre. It has steel and textile industries.

**Asyut** /ˌæsiːˈuːt/ (anc. **Lycopolis**) a commercial city on the west bank of the Nile, 380 km. (240 miles) south of Cairo; pop. (1991) 313,000. It is the largest city in Upper Egypt. Carpets, camels, cotton, and grain are its chief trading commodities. It was once the head of the great caravan route to the Western Desert and across the Sahara. The Asyut Barrage was built across the Nile in the late 19th c. in order to regulate the flow of water into the Ibrahimya Canal and provide irrigation water.

**Atacama Desert** /ˌætəˈkɑːmə/ the most arid region of South America, extending for a distance of some 965 km. (600 miles) southwards into Chile from the Peruvian border. Nitrate, iodine, and borax are extracted from salt basins.

**Athabasca** /ˌæθəˈbæskə/, **Lake** the fourth-largest lake in Canada, situated in north-east Alberta and north-west Saskatchewan; area c. 7,935 sq. km. (3,064 sq. miles).

**Athabasca** a river that rises in the Rocky Mountains of west-northern Alberta and Saskatchewan Canada and flows 1,231 km. (775 miles) northwards into Lake Athabasca. It was an important fur and grain trading route and the source of rich deposits of crude oil and oil-sands.

**Athens** /ˈæθɪnz/ (Greek **Athínai** /æˈθiːneɪ/) the capital city of Greece, lying 6 km. (nearly 4 miles) from its port Piraeus; pop. (1991) 784,110. It was a flourishing city-state from early times in ancient Greece, and by the mid-5th c. BC was established as leader of a league of Greek states from whom it exacted tribute. Under Pericles it became a cultural centre, and many of its best-known buildings (e.g. the Parthenon and Erechtheum) date from the extensive rebuilding that he commissioned. Athens recovered only slowly from defeat in the Peloponnesian War (404 BC). In 146 BC it became subject to Rome, but in the early Roman Empire it enjoyed imperial favour and was still the cultural centre of the Greek world. Gothic invaders captured and sacked Athens in AD 267, and its importance declined as power and wealth were transferred to Constantinople. After its capture by the Turks in 1456 it declined to the status of a village until chosen as the capital of a newly independent Greece in 1834 after the successful revolt against Turkish rule. Today the traffic of its noisy busy streets creates pollution problems for humans and ancient monuments alike. It is the main commercial and communications centre of Greece. Greater Athen (pop. 3,096,775), which includes the port of PIRAEUS, has industries ranging from steel, ship-building, and chemicals to the manufacture of consumer goods of all kinds. Tourism is a major earner of foreign currency.

**Atherton Tableland** /ˈæθət(ə)n/ a plateau in the Great Dividing Range in north-east Queensland, Australia. The highest point is Mt. Bartle Frere (1,612 m., 5,287 ft.).

**Athínai** the Greek name for the city of ATHENS.

**Athlone** /æθˈləʊn/ a town in County Westmeath, Leinster, in the centre of the Irish Republic, on the River Shannon; pop. (1991) 8,815. It is a marketing and distribution centre at a rail junction and on Ireland's inland navigation system.

**Athos** /ˈæθɒs/, **Mount** (Greek **Pangaíon Oros**) a mountainous peninsula projecting into the Aegean Sea from the coast of Macedonia, an autonomous district of Greece since 1927; area 336 sq. km. (130 sq. miles); pop. (1991) 1,557. It is inhabited by monks of the Eastern Orthodox Church in twenty monasteries; the earliest monastic settlement dates from 962. A curious rule of the monks forbids women, or even female animals, to set foot on the peninsula.
**Athonite** adj. & n.

**Atitlán** /ˌɑːtɪtˈlɑːn/ a volcano in central Guatemala rising to a height of 3,546 m. (11,633 ft.) south-west of Guatemala City. **Lake Atitlán** occupies a crater to the north of the volcano.

**Atlanta** /ət'læntə/ the capital and largest city of the state of Georgia, USA; pop. (1990) 394,000. Founded at the end of a railroad line in 1837, the city was originally called Terminus; in 1843 it was incorporated as Marthasville, and in 1845 its name was finally changed to Atlanta. Vehicles, aircraft parts, and soft drinks (it is the headquarters of the Coca-Cola company) are produced. The city is the venue of the 1996 summer Olympics.

**Atlantic City** /ət'læntɪk/ a beach-resort town on the Atlantic coast of south-east New Jersey, USA, on a sand bar at Absecon Beach; pop. (1990) 37,986. It is known for its conventions, gambling casinos, and its 60-foot-wide boardwalk which extends along 8 km. (5 miles) of beaches. The board game Monopoly was originally based on Atlantic City and the Miss America pageant has been held here annually since 1921.

**Atlantic Ocean** (also **the Atlantic**) the ocean lying between Europe and Africa to the east and North and South America to the west. The Atlantic is divided by the equator into the North Atlantic and South Atlantic oceans; area 82.4 million sq. km. (31.5 million sq. miles). It has an average depth of 3 km. (2 miles), falling to 9,220 m. (30,249 ft.) in the Milwaukee Depth in the Puerto Rico Trench. A submarine ridge known as the Mid-Atlantic Ridge runs down the centre from north to south. On either side lie deep basins which include the North American, Guyana, Brazil, and Argentina basins to the west and the North-east Atlantic, Canary, Cape Verde, Guinea, Angola, and Cape basins to the east.

**Atlantic Provinces** a general term used to describe the eastern Canadian provinces of Newfoundland, Nova Scotia, New Brunswick, and Prince Edward Island.

**Atlantis** /ət'læntɪs/ a legendary island said to have been submerged following an earthquake nearly 12,000 years ago.

**atlas** /'ætləs/ a term describing a book of maps or charts first used by Gerhard Kremer (Mercator) whose collection of maps was published between 1585 and 1595 under the title *Atlas, or cosmographical meditations upon the creation of the universe, and the universe as created*. His introductory text outlined the ancestry of Atlas, the mythological character who led the giant Titans in their war against the god Jupiter, and as a punishment was condemned to support the heavens on his shoulders. The legend describes how he asked Perseus to turn him into stone and was transformed with the aid of Medusa's head into the Atlas Mountains.

**Atlas Mountains** a range of mountains in North Africa extending from Morocco to Tunisia in a series of folded mountain chains which include the Anti-Atlas, High Atlas, Middle Atlas, Rif Mountains, Tell Atlas, and Sahara Atlas. The highest peak in the Atlas Mountains and in North

Africa is Djebel Toubkal which rises to 4,166 m. (13,664 ft.) in the High Atlas south of Marrakech.

**atmosphere** /'ætməs,fɪər/ the envelope of air surrounding the earth. In its lowest layer (the troposphere) it comprises oxygen (21%), nitrogen (78%), carbon dioxide, water vapour, and other gases. It is in this layer that most weather phenomena are generated. The upper layers of the atmosphere include the ionosphere which enables radio waves to be reflected back to the earth's surface over long distances, a hot layer known as the thermosphere, and an ozone layer that shields the earth's surface from lethal doses of ultra-violet radiation.

**atoll** /'ætɒl/ a ring-shaped coral reef that appears above the surface of the water enclosing a lagoon. The word is derived from the Maldivian 'atolu' or atoll, of which there are 26 in the Maldives. The central Pacific island of Kwajalein in the Marshall Islands is the world's largest atoll.

**Atrato** /ɑ:'trɑ:təʊ/ a South American river that rises in the Cordillera Occidental of western Colombia and flows north for c. 600 km. (375 miles) to enter the Gulf of Uraba, an inlet of the Caribbean Sea to the north of the Isthmus of Panama. Gold and platinum are mined near its headwaters.

**Attairo** /ə'taɪrəʊ/ (Greek **Atáviros** /ə'tɑ:vɪ,rəs/) the highest mountain on the Greek island of Rhodes (1,387 m., 3,986 ft.).

**Attica** /'ætɪkə/ (Greek **Attikí**) a triangular promontory, constituting the easternmost part of central Greece which, with the Saronic Gulf islands, forms a department of Greece; area 3,381 sq. km. (1,306 sq. miles); pop. (1991) 426,000 (excluding Athens).
**Attic** *adj. & n.*

**Attila Line** /'ætɪlə/ (also **Sahin Line**) a name given to the frontier line dividing Greek from Turkish Cyprus following the Turkish invasion of 1974. The invasion, which was likened to the action of Attila the Hun, put into effect Turkey's scheme for the partition of Cyprus (the Attila Plan). It stretches from Morphou Bay in the west to Famagusta in the east.

**Atter** /'ætə(r)/, **Lake** (German **Attersee**, also **Lake Kammer**) a lake to the east of Salzburg in Upper Austria, the largest Alpine lake in Austria.

**Attleboro** /'æt(ə)l,bərə/ a city in south-east Massachusetts, USA, near the border with Rhode Island; pop. (1990) 38,380. In addition to producing electronics and scientific equipment it is noted for its silverware and jewellery business.

**Aube** /əʊb/ **1.** a department in the Champagne-Ardenne region of north-east France; area 6,004 sq. km. (2,319 sq. miles); pop. (1990) 289,200; capital, Troyes. It is the centre of the Champagne wine-producing area. **2.** a river of north-east France that rises in the Langres plateau, Haute-Marne department, and flows 248 km. (154 miles) north-westwards to meet the River Seine near Romilly-sur-Seine.

**Aubervilliers** /ˌəʊbər'viːljə/ an industrial town in Seine-Saint Denis department, northern France, to the north-east of Paris; pop. (1990) 67,840. It produces perfume, paint, and varnish.

**Auburn** /'ɔːbən/ **1.** an industrial city in south-west Maine, USA, on the Androscoggin River, 48 km. (30 miles) north of Portland; pop. (1990) 24,310. A centre for the manufacture of shoes since 1836. **2.** the largest city in the Finger Lakes region of upstate New York, USA, on Lake Owasco; pop. (1990) 31,260. It was the home of Senator William Seward who was instrumental in buying Alaska from Russia in 1867.

**Auch** /əʊʃ/ (anc. **Elimberrum** or **Augusta Auscorum**) the capital of the department of Gers in Gascony, south-west France, on the Gers River; pop. (1990) 24,730. It was capital of Gascony in the 17th c. and Armagnac during the 10th c.

**Auchterarder** /ˌɒxtə'rɑːdə(r)/ a burgh town in Perthshire, central Scotland. Opposition to the minister presented to the parish in 1834 resulted in a struggle that led to the formation of the Free Church in 1843.

**Auchtermuchty** /ˌɒxtə'mʌxtɪ/ a royal burgh town in north-east Fife, eastern Scotland.

**Auckland** /'ɔːklənd/ **1.** a local government region at the northern end of North Island, New Zealand created in 1989 and comprising the cities of Auckland, North Shore, Waitakere, and Manukau, and districts of Rodney, Papakura, and part of Franklin; pop. (1991) 953,980. **2.** the largest city and chief seaport of New Zealand, at the northern end of North Island; pop. (1991) 315,670. The port, which was established in 1840 on land purchased from the Maoris, handles 60 per cent of the country's trade. Its industries include engineering, vehicle assembly, metals, textiles, chemicals, and food processing. Founded by Captain William Hobson, Lieutenant-Governor of New Zealand, it was named after the 1st Earl of Auckland who, as First Lord of the Admiralty, had given Hobson the command of the ship that brought him to New Zealand in 1837. The first immigrants from Scotland arrived in 1842 and in 1854 the first parliament of New Zealand was opened in Auckland. The capital was transferred to a more central location at Wellington in 1865.

**Aude** /əʊd/ **1.** a department in the Languedoc-Roussillon region of southern France; area 6,139 sq. km. (2,371 sq. miles); pop. (1990) 298,710; capital, Carcassonne. **2.** a river of southern France that rises in the Pyrenees and flows northwards to Carcassonne then east into the Mediterranean near Narbonne.

**Audenarde** the French name for OUDENARDE.

**Augrabies Falls** /ɔː'græbiːz/ a series of dramatic waterfalls on the Orange River in Northern Cape, South Africa, pouring water into one of the world's longest granite gorges. Their name is de-rived from a Hottentot word meaning 'the place of the great noise'.

**Augsburg** /'aʊgzbɜːg/ a city in south Bavaria, Germany, at the junction of the Lech and Wertach rivers; pop. (1991) 259,880. In 15 BC the Emperor Augustus founded a Roman colony known as Augusta Vindelicorum. During the Middle Ages Augsburg was a prosperous centre of commerce on the trade route to Italy and in the Reformation the Augsburg Confession was a statement of the Lutheran position approved by Luther before being presented to Charles V at Augsburg on 25 June 1535. The Peace of Augsburg in 1555 allowed princes of the Holy Roman Empire to impose a religion on their subjects. Augsburg was the birth-place of the artist Hans Holbein (1497–1543), the engineer Rudolf Diesel (1858–1913), Willy Messerschmitt (1898–1978), and Bertolt Brecht (1898–1956). The city's cathedral dates from the 9th c. and has the world's oldest stained glass. Augsburg has an old-established textile industry now superseded by engineering.

**Augusta** /aʊ'gʌstə/ a name given to many important towns in the Roman empire, usually in honour of the Emperor Augustus (63 BC–AD 14).

**Augusta** (anc. **Agosta**) an industrial port on the east coast of the Italian island of Sicily, north of Syracuse; pop. (1990) 39,980. The town, which was founded in 1232 by Frederick II, is built on an island linked to the mainland by a series of bridges.

**Augusta** **1.** a resort town in east Georgia, USA, at the head of navigation on the Savannah River; pop. (1990) 44,640. A former tobacco town and river trading post, Augusta was named by James Oglethorpe in 1735 after the mother of George III. It now produces fertilizers, cotton goods, and kaolin bricks and tiles. Nearby is the Fort Gordon military base and training school. The annual Masters golf tournament is played at Augusta. **2.** the state capital of Maine, USA, on the River Kennebec; pop. (1990) 21,325. It was founded as a trading post in 1628 by settlers from Plymouth. Manufactures include textiles, steel, and processed food.

**Aunis** /əʊ'niːs/ an ancient district of western France, co-extensive with the modern departments of Charente-Maritime and Deux-Sèvres. Its capital was La Rochelle.

**Aurangabad** /aʊ'rəŋgɑːˌbɑːd/ a textile industry town in the state of Maharashtra, west India; pop. (1991) 592,000. Once known as Khadke, it became the 17th-c. capital of the Mogul emperor Aurangzeb during his attempt to pacify the southern Muslim states. A copy of the Taj Mahal was erected as a mausoleum for his wife in 1679.

**Aurès Mountains** a mountain massif in the Sahara Atlas of north-eastern Algeria rising to 2,329 m. (7,641 ft.) at Djebel Chélia. Mountain villages are largely peopled by the Kabyle Berbers.

**Aurignac** /ɔːriːˈnjɑːk/ a village in the Haute-Garonne department of Midi-Pyrénées region, southern France, in the northern foothills of the Pyrenees. Nearby caves excavated in 1860 revealed archaeological evidence of prehistoric people of the upper palaeolithic Aurignacian Period which takes its name from this site.
**Aurignacian** *adj. & n.*

**Aurillac** /ɔːriːˈjɑːk/ the capital of the department of Cantal in the Auvergne region of south-central France, on the River Jordanne; pop. (1990) 32,650. It is an agricultural market town with an important livestock trade. Aurillac was the home of Gerbert, a monk of St. Géraud, who became the first French Pope (as Sylvester II) in 999.

**aurora** /ɔːˈrɔːrə/ a luminous phenomenon caused by solar radiation interacting with the upper atmosphere, seen as streamers of light in the sky above the northern (aurora borealis) or southern (aurora australis) magnetic pole.

**Aurora** /ɔːˈrɔːrə/ an industrial city in north-east Illinois, USA, on the Fox River west of Chicago; pop. (1990) 99,580. It is the site of a high-energy particle-accelerator laboratory, and has varied industries including steel products and electric tools. It was the first city to use electricity for street lighting (1881).

**Auschwitz** /ˈaʊʃvɪts/ (Polish **Oswieecim**) a town near Cracow in southern Poland that was the site of one of the largest Nazi concentration camps of World War II.

**Aust-Agder** /aʊstˈɑːɡdə/ a county in southern Norway, on the Skaggerak; area 9,212 sq. km. (3,558 sq. miles); pop. (1991) 97,310; capital, Arendal.

**Austerlitz** /ˈaʊstəlɪts/ (Czech **Slavkov u Brna**) a town in the Czech Republic, to the east of Brno. It was the scene in 1805 of Napoleon's defeat of the Austrians and Russians.

**Austin** /ˈɔːstɪn/ **1.** a city in south-east Minnesota, USA, on the Cedar River; pop. (1990) 21,910. Named after a pioneer settler, Austin is a trading and processing centre for livestock, grain, and vegetables from the surrounding farm land. **2.** the state capital of Texas, USA, on the Colorado River; pop. (1990) 465,620. The first settlement of 1839 was named after Stephen F. Austin, son of Moses Austin, leader of the first Texas colony. The University of Texas at Austin was founded in 1883. Seven hydroelectric dams across the nearby Colorado River create a series of reservoirs known as the Highland Lakes. It is the market for a major agricultural region and a convention, education, and manufacturing centre. Many electronic research firms are located here.

**Australasia** /ˌɒstrəˈleɪzɪə/ a term occasionally used to refer to the region that comprises Australia, New Zealand, New Guinea, and the neighbouring islands of the Pacific.
**Australasian** *adj. & n.*

**Australia**

/ɒsˈtreɪlɪə/ a country of two main islands with the larger forming a continent of the southern hemisphere, bounded on the west by the Indian Ocean, the east by the South Pacific, the south by the Southern Ocean, and the north by the Timor and Arafura seas which separate Australia from the islands of Indonesia and New Guinea; area 7,682,300 sq. km. (2,966,253 sq. miles); pop. (est. 1991) 17,500,000; official language, English; capital, Canberra; chief cities, Sydney, Melbourne, Brisbane, Perth, and Adelaide. Much of the continent has a hot dry climate and a large part of the central area is desert or semidesert; the most fertile areas are the eastern coastal plains and the south-western corner of Western Australia. Australia's climate is mainly continental, and ranges from tropical in the north to temperate in the south. Because it is such a flat continent and because of the moderating influences of the surrounding oceans Australia does not experience great climatic extremes. The north is influenced by mild dry south-east trade winds and the south experiences cool moist westerly winds. Australia's fauna is remarkable for the presence of many unique animals and the absence of many orders known in other continents. Nearly half the 230 species of mammals present are marsupials such as the kangaroo, koala bear, wombat, and platypus. Agriculture has always been of vital importance to the economy, with cereal crops grown over wide areas and livestock producing wool (the world's greatest producer), meat, and dairy products for export. There are significant mineral resources (including bauxite, coal, copper, iron, lead, uranium, and zinc), and oilfields produce nearly 70 per cent of the country's energy requirements. The people are mainly of European descent but there are Aborigines (*c.* 1.5 per cent of the population) and immigrants from Europe, Indochina, the Middle East, and Latin America. About 15 per cent of the population live in rural areas. Human habitation in Australia dates from prehistoric times (See ABORIGINES). The existence of an unknown southern land (*terra australis*) was postulated in ancient Greek geographical writings and the idea was passed on in medieval writings and maps. Pre-17th c. European sightings of Australia are claimed but not firmly attested. From 1606 onwards its western coast was explored by the Dutch, and in 1642 Abel Tasman proved that it was an island; it was visited by an Englishman, William Dampier, in 1688 and 1699. In 1770 Captain James Cook landed at Botany Bay on the eastern side of the continent and formally took possession of New South Wales. British colonization began in 1788. The interior was gradually explored and opened up in the 19th c. by men such

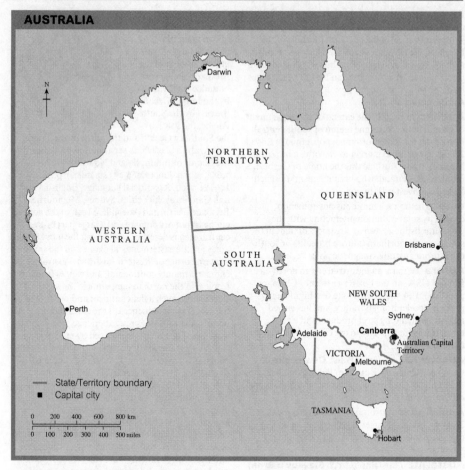

**AUSTRALIA**

- State/Territory boundary
- ■ Capital city

```
0    200   400   600   800 km
0   100  200  300  400  500 miles
```

as Edward Eyre, Peter Warburton, Augustus and Frank Gregory, John McDouall Stuart, and Charles Sturt. Robert Burke and William Wills were the first to complete the north–south crossing of Australia in 1860–1 and John Forrest the first to make a west–east crossing in 1874. Political consolidation resulted in the declaration of a Commonwealth in 1901, when the six colonies (New South Wales, Victoria, Queensland, South Australia, Western Australia, and Tasmania) federated as sovereign states. In 1911 an Australian Capital Territory was established in New South Wales and Northern Territory (formerly governed by South Australia) was transferred to Federal Government control. In 1978 Northern Territory eventually achieved self-government. Australia supported Great Britain heavily in each of the two World Wars, being threatened herself by Japanese invasion during the second, but although still maintaining ties with the former mother country has more and more pursued her own interests both domestically and internationally, the latter with particular reference to south-east Asia and the South Pacific. Governed by a bicameral parliament comprising a Senate and House of Representatives, Australia is divided into six states and two territories, each of the states having its own legislature:

| State | Area (sq. km.) | Pop. | Capital (1991) |
|---|---|---|---|
| New South Wales | 801,428 | 5,940,800 | Sydney |
| Victoria | 227,600 | 4,439,400 | Melbourne |
| Queensland | 1,727,200 | 2,999,900 | Brisbane |
| Western Australia | 2,525,500 | 1,650,600 | Perth |
| South Australia | 984,000 | 1,454,000 | Adelaide |
| Tasmania | 67,800 | 469,200 | Hobart |
| **Territory** | | | |
| Australian Capital Territory | 2,400 | 292,700 | Canberra |
| Northern Territory | 1,346,200 | 167,800 | Darwin |

**Australian Alps** the south-eastern and highest section of the Great Dividing Range of eastern Australia in the states of Victoria and New South Wales. It includes the highest peak in Australia, Mt. Kosciusko (2,228 m., 7,310 ft.).

**Australian Antarctic Territory** territory in Antarctica claimed by Australia and lying between 142°E and 136°E; land area 6,043,852 sq. km. (2,334,435 sq. miles). Scientific stations were established at Mawson in Macrobertson Land (1954), Davis in the Vestfold Hills (1957), and Casey (1961).

**Australian Capital Territory** federal territory of Australia forming (since 1911) an enclave in New South Wales; area 2,400 sq. km. (927 sq. miles); pop. (1991) 292,700. Created in 1901, it includes the national capital, Canberra. From 1915 to 1988 it also included Jervis Bay on the coast of New South Wales.

**Austral Islands** /'ɒstrəl/ see TUBUAI ISLANDS.

**Austria** /'ɒstrɪə/ (German **Österreich** /'ɜːstə‚raɪk/) official name **Republic of Austria** a country in central Europe, much of it mountainous, with the River Danube flowing through the north-

east; area 83,854 sq. km. (32,389 sq. miles); pop. (est. 1991) 7,700,000; official language, German; capital, Vienna; largest cities, Graz, Linz, Salzburg, Innsbruck, and Klagenfurt. Agriculture, largely based in the region to the north of the Alps and in the Danube valley, produces the greater part of Austria's food requirements. Forests which cover nearly 45 per cent of Austria are a major source of income. Austria's highly developed industries depend on hydroelectric power, local supplies of oil and gas, and a wide range of mineral resources which include iron ore, lead, zinc, graphite, talc, and kaolin. The Celtic tribes settled in the area were conquered by the Romans in 15–9 BC and it

remained part of the Roman empire, with the Danube as its frontier, until overrun by Germanic peoples in the 5th c. AD. Dominated from the early Middle Ages by the Habsburg family, Austria became the centre of a massive Central European empire which held sway over the area until World War I. The collapse of the Habsburg empire in 1918 left Austria a weak and unstable country which was easily incorporated within the Nazi Reich in 1938. After World War II the country remained under Allied military occupation until 1955. Since regaining her sovereignty Austria has emerged as a prosperous and stable democratic republic. Declaring itself a neutral state, Austria has been a haven for refugees from many countries in Eastern Europe. It joined the European Union in 1995. Under a federal constitution, Austria is divided into nine states:

| State | Area (sq. km.) | Pop. (1991) | Capital |
| --- | --- | --- | --- |
| Burgenland | 3,970 | 273,540 | Eisenstadt |
| Carinthia | 9,533 | 552,420 | Klagenfurt |
| Lower Austria | 19,172 | 1,480,930 | St. Pölten |
| Upper Austria | 11,980 | 1,340,080 | Linz |
| Salzburg | 7,154 | 483,880 | Salzburg |
| Styria | 16,387 | 1,184,600 | Graz |
| Tyrol | 12,647 | 630,360 | Innsbruck |
| Vorarlberg | 2,601 | 333,130 | Bregenz |
| Vienna | 415 | 1,533,180 | Vienna |

**Austria-Hungary** (also called the **Austro-Hungarian Empire**) the 'Dual Monarchy', established by the Austrian emperor Francis Joseph after Austria's defeat by Prussia in 1866 in which Austria and Hungary became autonomous states under a common sovereign. The dualist system came under increasing pressure from the other subject nations, including Croatians, Serbs, Slovaks, Romanians, and Czechs, and failure to resolve

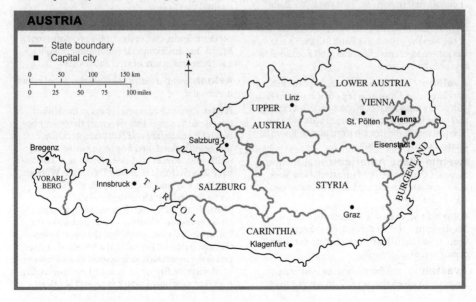

AUSTRIA

these nationalistic aspirations was one of the causes of World War I. After their victory the Allies gave support to the emergent nations, and the Austro-Hungarian Empire was dissolved by the Versailles peace settlement (1919).

**Auvergne** /əʊˈvɜːn/ **1.** an ancient province of south-central France, that takes its name from the Averni, a Celtic tribe living there in Roman times. **2.** a region of modern France comprising the departments of Allier, Cantal, Haute-Loire, and Puy-de-Dôme; area 26,013 sq. km. (10,047 sq. miles); pop. (1990) 1,321,210; capital, Clermont-Ferrand. The region is traversed by the Allier River.

**Auxerre** /əʊˈseə(r)/ the capital of Yonne department in the Burgundy region of north-central France, on the Yonne River and a commercial and industrial centre particularly concerned with Chablis wine; pop. (1990) 40,600.

**Avalon** /ˈævələn/ in Arthurian legend the place to which Arthur was conveyed after his death. In Welsh mythology it is the kingdom of the dead. It was alleged in medieval times that the Benedictine abbey of Glastonbury, one of England's oldest religious houses, was founded on the site of Avalon by Joseph of Arimathea.

**Avar** /ˈɑːvə(r)/ a Turkic people prominent in south-east Europe in the 6th–9th c. In the 7th c. their kingdom extended from the Black Sea to the Adriatic. They were finally subdued by Charlemagne (791–9).

**Avebury** /ˈeɪvbərɪ/ a village in Wiltshire, southern England, on the site of one of Britain's most impressive henge monuments of the late neolithic period (3rd millenium BC).

**Aveiro** /əˈveɪrəʊ/ **1.** a district on the Atlantic coast of north-west Portugal; area 2,708 sq. km. (1,046 sq. miles); pop.(est. 1989) 674,400. **2.** its capital on the Aveiro lagoon to the south of Oporto; pop. (1991) 35,250. A former fishing port of the Newfoundland cod-bank fishers, Aveiro now has salt-pans, ceramic factories, and a seaweed fishing industry.

**Avellino** /ˌɑːvəˈliːnəʊ/ the capital of Avellino province in the Campania region of southern Italy, 56 km. (22 miles) east of Naples and a marketing and manufacturing centre; pop.(1990) 556,830. The remains of the Roman town of Abellinum lie on the eastern edge of town.

**Avenue of the Americas** an alternative name for 6th Avenue in Manhattan, New York, USA, given to honour the Latin American countries in the 1940s.

**Avernus** /əˈvɜːnəs/ (also **Averno**) a lake near Naples in Italy, filling the crater of an extinct volcano. It was regarded by the ancients as the entrance to the underworld.

**Avestan** /əˈvest(ə)n/ the ancient east-Iranian language in which the sacred Zoroastrian Avesta

scriptures are written (often incorrectly called Zend), closely related to Vedic Sanskrit.

**Aveyron** /ˌæveɪˈrɔ̃/ **1.** a department in the Midi-Pyrénées region of southern France, at the southern edge of the Massif Central; area 8,735 sq. km. (3,374 sq. miles); pop. (1990) 270,140; capital, Rodez. **2.** a river in southern France that rises in the limestone Causse de Sauveterre and flows 250 km. (157 miles) westwards to meet the River Tarn near Montauban.

**Aviemore** /ˌævɪˈmʊər/ a resort town in Strathspey, northern Scotland, close to the Cairngorm Mountains and surrounded by extensive areas of pine and birch forest; pop. (1981) 2,426. It was largely developed after 1966 as a winter sports resort.

**Avignon** /ˌæviːˈnjɔ̃/ the capital of the department of Vaucluse in the Provence-Alpes-Côte d'Azur region of south-east France; on the River Rhône; pop. (1990) 89,440. From 1309 until 1377 it was the residence of the popes during their exile from Rome, and became papal property by purchase in 1348. After the papal court had returned to Rome two antipopes re-established a papal court in Avignon. The second of these was expelled in 1408, but the city remained in papal hands until the French Revolution and the Palace of the Popes still stands. Today it is a centre of commerce and tourism with varied manufactures. John Stuart Mill is buried in the city's cemetery.

**Avila** /ˈævɪlə/ **1.** a province in the Castilla-León region of north-central Spain; area 8,048 sq. km. (3,108 sq. miles); pop. (1991) 174,380. **2.** its capital (also **Avila de los Caballeros**), an ancient walled city of Old Castile at the foot of the Sierra de Guadarrama; pop. (1991) 49,870. It was the birthplace of St. Teresa (1515–82) and Queen Isabella of Castile (1451–1504).

**Avilés** /ˈævɪləs/ a port in the Asturias region of northern Spain, on the Bay of Biscay; pop. (1991) 84,088. Industries include fishing, shipbuilding, and the manufacture of steel and textiles.

**Avlona** an alternative name for the city of VLORË in Albania.

**Avon** the name of several rivers in the United Kingdom: **1.** a river that rises near the border between Leicestershire and Northamptonshire, southern England, and flows 154 km. (96 miles) south-west to meet the Severn River near Tewkesbury. **2.** a river that rises near Devizes in Wiltshire, southern England, and flows 77 km. (48 miles) across Salisbury Plain to the English Channel at Christchurch in Dorset. **3.** a river that rises on the Gloucestershire-Wiltshire border and flows 121 km. (75 miles) east, south, and then north-west through Bath and Bristol to the Severn. **4.** a river that flows from Dartmoor in south-west England southwards to Bigbury Bay near Thurlestone. **5.** a river that rises near Falkirk in central Scotland, then flows past Linlithgow to the Firth of Forth near Bo'ness. **6.** a river that rises in the Cairngorm Mountains of northern Scotland, and flows east then north to join the River Spey at Ballindalloch.

**Avon** /ˈeɪvən/ a county of south-west England; area 1,346 sq. km. (520 sq. miles); pop. (1991) 919,800; county town, Bristol. The county comprises six districts:

| District | Area (sq. km.) | Pop.(1991) |
| --- | --- | --- |
| Bath | 29 | 79,900 |
| Bristol | 109 | 370,300 |
| Kingswood | 48 | 87,100 |
| Northavon | 463 | 129,600 |
| Wansdyke | 323 | 78,700 |
| Woodspring | 374 | 174,300 |

**Avranches** /ɑːˈvrɑːnʃ/ a town in the Manche department of Basse-Normandie region, north-west France, on the English Channel; pop. (1982) 10,420. The rocky island of Mont-Saint-Michel lies nearby, and the town has a busy tourist trade.

**Awash** /ˈɑːwɑːʃ/ a river that rises near Addis Ababa in the central Highlands of Ethiopia and flows north-eastwards into the Danakil Desert where it meets Lake Abbé on the Djibouti frontier. Somalis consider the Awash to mark the true eastern limit of Ethiopian sovereignty.

**Awe** /ɔː/ a loch in Argyll and Bute, west Scotland; length, 40.5 km. (25.5 miles). It is the longest freshwater loch in Scotland. Its water is used to generate power on the slopes of Ben Cruachan.

**Axel Heiberg** /ˌæks(ə)l ˈhaɪbɜːg/ an island in the Canadian Arctic, in the Queen Elizabeth Islands west of Ellesmere Island; area 43,178 sq. km. (16,670 sq. miles). It is dominated by the Princess Margaret Range which rises to 2,211 m. (7,254 ft.). The island was visited in 1899 by a Norwegian expedition led by Otto Sverdrup who named it after the Norwegian consul.

**Axholme** /ˈækshəum/, **Isle of** a low-lying area of Lincolnshire in east England, to the west of the River Trent. It was drained and settled by Dutch and Flemish immigrants in the early 17th c. The evangelist brothers Charles and John Wesley were born at Epworth.

**Axminster** /ˈæksˌmɪnstə(r)/ a town in Devon, south-west England, on the River Axe, famous in the 18th and 19th c. for its carpets.

**Axum** see AKSUM.

**Ayacucho** /æjəˈkuːtʃəʊ/ a city in the Andes, capital of the department of Ayacucho in Peru; pop. (1990) 101,600. The modern city was founded by Pizarro in 1539. The last great battle in the war of independence against Spain was fought here in 1824. The Shining Path guerrilla movement first emerged in this part of Peru in 1980. The city is the commercial centre of a rich mining region; tourism is also important.

**Ayala** a strong warm wind that blows in the Massif Central of France.

**Aydin** /ˈaɪdən/ **1.** a province of western Turkey on the Aegean Sea; area 8,007 sq. km. (3,093 sq. miles); pop. (1990) 824,820. Drained by the Menderes (Meander) and Akcay rivers, Aydin has a wide range of mineral deposits including iron, copper, magnesite, antimony, and emery. **2.** its capital, on the River Menderes, to the south-east of Izmir (Smyrna); pop. (1990) 107,000. Formerly known as Tralles, it was an important trading centre of ancient Lydia.

**Aylesbury** /ˈeɪlzbərɪ/ the county town of Buckinghamshire in southern England, to the north of the Chiltern Hills; pop. (est. 1985) 50,000. The town gives its name to a breed of large white domestic ducks. Printing is an important local industry.

**Aylesford** /ˈeɪlzf(ə)rd/ an industrial town in Kent, south-east England, on the Medway, 5 km. (2 miles) north-east of Maidstone; pop. (1981) 8,000. It has paper-making industries.

**Ayers Rock** /eəz/ (Aborigine **Uluru**) a red rock-mass in Northern Territory, Australia, 450 km. (283 miles) south-west of Alice Springs. The largest monolith in the world, it is 348 m. (1,143 ft.) high and about 9 km. (6 miles) in circumference, rising in impressive isolation from the surrounding plain. Ayers Rock is the tip of a huge bed of coarse sandstone laid down on the floor of an inland sea some 600 million years ago during the Cambrian period. On its surface there are paintings and carvings made thousands of years ago by the Loritja and Pitjanjatjara Aborigines who believed the rock to be a sacred place. It is named after Sir Henry Ayers, Premier of South Australia in 1872–3 when the rock was first recorded.

**Ayeyarwady** /ˌaɪəˈwædɪ/ the Burmese name for the IRRAWADDY RIVER.

**Ayia Napa** /ˈaɪə ˈnæpə/ a resort and fishing village to the south of Famagusta in south-east Cyprus; pop. (1981) 850. With nearby Paralimni, it has developed into one of the major resort areas of Cyprus. There is a 16th-c. Venetian monastery.

**Aymara** /ˈaɪməˌrɑː/ an indigenous American Indian people mainly inhabiting the plateau lands of Bolivia and Peru near Lake Titicaca.

**Ayot St. Lawrence** /ˈeɪət sənt ˈlɒrəns/ a village in Hertfordshire, southern England, near Welwyn Garden City, the home of George Bernard Shaw from 1906 until the end of his life.

**Ayr** /eə(r)/ a resort town and fishing port on the south-west coast of Scotland, at the mouth of the River Ayr where it meets the Firth of Clyde; pop. (1981) 49,500. Its well-known racecourse lies to the east of the town.

**Ayrshire** /ˈeəʃə(r)/ a former Scottish county in south-west Scotland, on the Firth of Clyde. It became part of Strathclyde Region in 1975.

**Ayutthaya** /'ɑːjuː,taɪə/ a market and tourist town, the capital of a province of the same name in south-central Thailand, on the Chao Phraya River, noted for its early Siamese royal palace, temples, and pagodas; pop. (1990) 61,185. Built on the site of a Khmer settlement, Ayutthaya became the capital of a Thai kingdom in the mid-14th c. It was destroyed by the Burmese in 1559, rebuilt by the Siamese and later laid waste again by the Burmese in 1767.

**AZ** *abbr.* US Arizona (in official postal use).

**Azania** /ə'zeɪnɪə/ the alternative African name for South Africa.

**Azerbaijan** /,æzɜːbaɪ'ʒɑːn/ a region of north-western Iran forming the southern part of the historic Transcaucasian region of Azerbaijan. It is divided into the two provinces of East and West Azerbaijan; area 105,952 sq. km. (40,924 sq. miles); pop. (1986) 6,085,760. The provincial capitals are Tabriz and Orumiyeh. Iranian Azerbaijan is separated from the former Soviet Republic of Azerbaijan by the River Araks.

**Azeri** or **Azerbaijani** *adj. & n.*

**Azerbaijan** official name **The Azerbaijani Republic** an independent state of western Asia lying between the Black and Caspian seas in the southern Caucasus, with Iran to the south, Russia to  the north, and Armenia to the west; area 86,600 sq. km. (33,450 sq. miles); pop. (est. 1991) 7,219,000; capital, Baku; chief towns, Gyandzha and Sumgait. Azerbaijan includes the predominantly Armenian autonomous region of Nagorno-Karabakh and the Azeri autonomous republic of Nakhichevan which forms an exclave within the Republic of Armenia. The Greater Caucasus in the north are separated from the Lesser Caucasus in the south by the valley of the River Kura which flows into the Caspian Sea. Rich in agricultural products such as cotton, grain, rice, fruit, and vegetables, Azerbaijan is one of the world's oldest centres of oil production (from the Baku oilfields). Lying in the northern part of the Transcaucasian region of Azerbaijan, the area to the north of the River Araks that now forms the Republic of Azerbaijan was ceded to Russia by Persia through the treaties of Gulistan (1813) and Turkamanchai (1828). In 1917 it joined with Armenia and Georgia to form a short-lived anti-Bolshevik union known as the Transcaucasian Federation, but declared itself independent in 1918. Two years later it was absorbed into the Soviet Union as a Soviet Republic. Between 1922 and 1936 it formed part of the Transcaucasian Soviet Federal Republic and in 1991 it gained full independence with the breakup of the Soviet Union.

**Azilian** /ə'zɪlɪən/ an early mesolithic industry in Europe, named after the type-site, a cave at Mas d'Azil in the French Pyrenees, succeeding the Magdalenian and dated to 10,000–8,000 BC. It is characterized by flat-bore harpoons, painted pebbles, and microliths.

**azimuth** /'æzɪməθ/ **1.** the angular distance from a north or south point of the horizon to the intersection with the horizon of a vertical circle passing through a given celestial body. **2.** the horizontal angle or direction of a compass bearing.

**azimuthal equidistant projection** a map projection constructed around a central point with a scale that expands along parallels of latitude but is constant along the radii from the central point. It allows accurate measures of distance from a point on a small-scale map.

**Azores** /ə'zɔːz/ (Portuguese **Ilhas dos Açores**) a group of volcanic islands in the North Atlantic, 1,287 km. (800 miles) west of Portugal, in Portuguese possession, but partially autonomous; pop. (1991) 241,590; chief port and capital, Ponta Delgada (on São Miguel). The nine largest islands lie in three distinct groups, Santa Maria and São Miguel to the south-east, Corvo and Flores to the north-west, and Faial, Pico, Graciosa, Terceira, and São Jorge in the middle. Portugal's highest mountain rises to 2,351 m. (7,714ft.) on the island of Pico. Known to the Phoenicians and the Norse, the islands were not settled until they were rediscovered by the Portuguese during the early 15th c. Used as a port of call by navigators on voyages of exploration, the islands were developed as strategic naval and air bases during both world wars. In summer the islands are exposed to the trade winds blowing from the north-east and in winter strong winds blow in from the south-west.

**Azores High** an area of almost stationary subtropical high pressure that appears over the Atlantic between the Azores and Bermuda, the centre lying a little further north in summer than in winter.

**Azov** /'æzɒf/, **Sea of** (Russian **Azovskoye More**) a shallow inland sea between the Russian Federation and the Ukraine, separated from the Black Sea by the Crimea and communicating with it by a narrow strait; area 37,555 sq. km. (14,500 sq. miles). It is fed by the Don and Kuban rivers and is an important source of fish. Zhdanov, Taganrog, and Kerch are the chief ports.

**Aztec** /'æztek/ the indigenous people dominant in Mexico before the Spanish conquest of the 16th c. (also called *Mexica* or *Tenochca*) who arrived in the central valley of Mexico after the collapse of the Toltec civilization in the 12th c. By the early 15th c. they had risen to dominance of the area, and a century later commanded a territory that covered most of the central and southern part of present-day Mexico, exacting tribute from their subjects. They were a warring people who slew captives as human sacrifices to their chief god, but their life-style was comfortable and (for the rulers) luxurious, and the Spaniards under Cortés arrived to find a rich and elaborate civilization centred on the city of Tenochtitlán, which boasted vast pyramids, temples, and palaces.

**Azua** /ˈɑːswə/ (fully **Azua de Compostella**) the capital of a province of the same name near the south coast of the Dominican Republic, at the southern end of the Sierra de Ocoa; pop. (1986) 71,800.

# B *b*

**Baabda** /'bɑːbdə/ a town in the Lebanon Mountains of west Lebanon, to the south of Beirut. It is the capital of the province of Mount Lebanon (Jebel Lubnan) and seat of the Lebanese presidential palace.

**Baalbek** /'bɑːlbek/ a town in eastern Lebanon at the foot of the Anti-Lebanon Mountains, site of the ancient city of Heliopolis (Greek = city of the sun) associated in Phoenician times with the worship of the sun-god Baal, its principal surviving monuments date from the Roman period, and include the Corinthian temples of Jupiter and Bacchus, and private houses with important mosaics.

**bab** /bæb/ an Arabic word for a strait, as in Bab el Mandeb.

**Baba Burnu** /bɑːˈbɑː bərˈnuː/ the Turkish name for Cape Baba on the west coast of Turkey, the most westerly point of Asia.

**Babahoyo** /bæbəˈhɔɪəʊ/ a town in the western lowlands of Ecuador, on the Babahoyo River north-east of Guayaquil; pop. (1990) 106,330. It is capital of the province of Los Ríos.

**Bab al-Zakak** /ˌbæb ˌæzəˈkɑːk/ the Arabic name for the Strait of Gibraltar between Spain and Africa.

**Babar Islands** /bɑːˈbɑː(r)/ a group of islands lying to the south of the Banda Sea in the south Moluccas, eastern Indonesia. Situated between the island of Timor and the Tanimbar group, it comprises the island of Babar and five small islets.

**Babel** /'beɪb(ə)l/ the Biblical name for the site of a tower allegedly built on the plain of Shinar in Mesopotamia in an attempt to reach heaven, which God frustrated by confusing the languages of its builders (Genesis 11: 1–9). The story was probably inspired by the Babylonian ziggurat, a staged temple about 100 m. high, such as the unfinished ziggurat at the ancient Akkadian city of Borsippa whose ruins lie to the south of Hilla in Iraq.

**Bab el Mandeb** /bæb el 'mændeb/ a narrow strait 27 km. (17 miles) wide, linking the Red Sea with the Indian Ocean via the Gulf of Aden and separating the Arabian Peninsula from the east coast of Africa.

**Babol** /bɑːˈbəʊl/ (also **Babul**) a commercial city in northern Iran just south of the Caspian Sea in the province of Mazandaran; pop. (1983) 96,000. It has textiles and food-processing industries. Babol was founded during the 16th c. on the site of the

ancient city of Mamter. Its port on the Caspian Sea is Babol Sar.

**Babruysk** /bəˈbruːəsk/ (formerly **Bobruysk** or **Bobruisk**) a river port and railway junction in Belorussia, on the Benezina River, 136 km (85 miles) south-east of Minsk; pop. (1990) 222,900. The making of tyres is an important industry

**Babuyan Islands** /ˌbɑːbʊˈjɑːn/ a group of 24 volcanic islands lying to the north of Luzon Island in the northern Philippines. **Babuyan Claro** is an active volcano rising to 1,088 m. (3,569 ft.) on Babuyan Island.

**Babylon** /'bæbɪlən/ an ancient city in Mesopotamia, first prominent under Hammurabi who made it capital of the kingdom of Babylonia. The city (now in ruins) lay on the Euphrates 88 km. (55 miles) south of present-day Baghdad and was noted for its luxury, its fortifications, and particularly for the 'Hanging Gardens' which were one of the Seven Wonders of the World.

**Babylonia** /ˌbæbɪˈləʊnɪə/ the ancient name for southern Mesopotamia (earlier called Sumer), which first became a political entity when an Amorite dynasty united Sumer and Akkad in the first half of the 2nd millenium BC. At this period its power ascended over Assyria and part of Syria. After *c.* 1530 BC first the Hittites then other invaders, the Kassites, dominated the land, and it became part of the Assyrian empire. With the latter's decline Babylonia again became prominent under the Chaldeans 625–538 BC, only to fall to Cyrus the Great, whose entry into Babylon ended its power for ever.
**Babylonian** *adj. & n.*

**Bacau** /bæˈkɑːuː/ the capital town of Bacau county in north-east Romania, situated in the foothills of the Carpathians on the River Bistriţa near its junction with the Siret; pop. (1989) 193,270. Its industries include wood-processing and the manufacture of pulp, paper, leather goods, textiles, clothing, processed food, and equipment for mining and the oil industry.

**Baccarat** /'bækərɑː/ a town on the western edge of the Vosges mountains, Meurthe-et-Moselle department, north-east France; pop. (1982) 5,437. It is noted for its crystalworks established in 1764.

**Backs** /bæks/, **the** a name given to the lawns and gardens that slope down to the River Cam behind the colleges of Cambridge, England.

**backveld** /'bækvelt/ a term used in South Africa to describe remote districts, especially those where people are strongly conservative.

**Bacolod** /bɑ:'kəʊlɒd/ the chief city on the island of Negros in the central Philippines; pop. (1990) 364,180. Situated on the north-west coast of the island, it is a major port and processing centre for sugar-cane. The city, which is capital of Negros Occidental province, is also a leading producer of ceramics.

**Bactria** /'bæktrɪə/ the ancient name for a country that included the northern part of modern Afghanistan and parts of the central Asian republics. Its capital was Bactra (present-day Balkh in northern Afghanistan). Traditionally the home of Zoroaster and the Zend-Avesta, it was the seat of a powerful Indo-Greek kingdom in the 3rd and 2nd c. BC. It gives its name to the Bactrian camel (*Camelus bactrianus*) which has two humps and is native to central Asia.
**Bactrian** adj. & n.

**Badacsóny** /'bɔ:də,tʃəʊnjə/ a district to the north-west of Lake Balaton in Hungary noted for its white wine.

**Badajoz** /bæðæ'hɔ:θ/ **1.** a province in the Extremadura region of western Spain; area 21,657 sq. km. (8,365 sq. miles); pop. (1991) 650,390. It is the largest Spanish province. **2.** its capital on the River Guadiana; pop. (1991) 129,737. Known to the Romans as Colonia Pacensis, the Aftasside Moors made it the capital of a small kingdom that was eventually captured by Alfonso IX of León in 1229. It was the birthplace of the Spanish artist Luis de Morales (1509–86), and the site of a bloody action in the Peninsular War (1812). It is the marketing centre of a fertile region and has food-processing industries.

**Badalona** /bæðə'ləʊnə/ a Mediterranean port and suburb of north-east Barcelona, Catalonia, north-east Spain; pop. (1991) 206,120. It is a centre of shipbuilding and textile and chemical industries.

**Bad Ems** /bæd 'emz/ (also **Ems**) a resort town in the German state of Rhineland-Palatinate, on the River Lahn. It was the scene of an encounter between the King of Prussia and the French Ambassador on 13 July 1870 which resulted in the sending of the famous Ems dispatch prior to the outbreak of the Franco-Prussian War of 1870–1.

**Baden** /'bɑ:d(ə)n/ Austria's most famous spa town situated 30 km. (19 miles) south of Vienna in the province of Lower Austria; pop. (1991) 24,000. Known to the Romans as Thermae Pannonicae, it became a royal summer retreat and fashionable resort in the 19th c.

**Baden** a former Grand Duchy (created in 1806) that became a constituent republic of Germany in 1918. It was partitioned in 1945 into the states of Württemberg-Baden in the north and Baden in the south. In 1952 these states were reunited and joined with Württemberg-Hohenzollern to form the state of Baden-Württemberg.

**Baden** a spa town in the Aargau canton of northern Switzerland, on the Limmat River; pop. (1990) 14,780. Known to the Romans as Thermae Helveticae, its hot sulphurous springs have attracted visitors since ancient times. In 1714 a treaty between France and the Habsburg empire was signed in Baden during the War of Spanish Succession.

**Baden-Baden** a spa town with hot mineral springs in the state of Baden-Württemberg, south-west Germany, in the Black Forest; pop. (1991) 52,520. Known to the Romans as Aquae Aureliae, Baden-Baden became a fashionable watering place in the 19th c. The town has literary associations with Dostoevsky, Gogol, Turgeniev, Balzac, and Mark Twain.

**Badenoch and Strathspey** /'beɪdənɒx, stræθ'speɪ/ a district in the Highland Region of northern Scotland from 1975 to 1996, situated between the Cairngorm and Monadhliath mountains and extending over part of the upper valley of the River Spey; area 2,325 sq. km. (898 sq. miles); pop. (1991) 12,941. Kingussie is its chief town and Aviemore its principal resort.

**Baden-Württemberg** /,bɑ:dən'vʊətəm,berk/ a state of south-west Germany; area 35,751 sq. km. (13,809 sq. miles); pop. (est. 1990) 9,619,000; capital, Stuttgart.

**Bad Homburg** /bæd 'hɒmbɜ:g/ (also **Homburg** or in full **Bad Homburg vor der Höhe**) a spa town at the foot of the Taunus Mts. in the German state of Hesse, to the north-east of Wiesbaden; pop. (1983) 50,600. The first Homburg felt hats for men were made here. To the north-west of the town is a Roman fort restored during the reign of Kaiser Wilhelm II.

**Bad Ischl** /bæd 'ɪʃ(ə)l/ (also **Ischl**) a spa town in the Salzkammergut region of the Austrian state of Upper Austria, on the River Traun; pop. (1991) 13,929. During the 19th c. it was the summer residence of the Austrian imperial family.

**badlands** /'bædlændz/ extensive uncultivable eroded tracts in arid areas, especially the striking eroded areas of the USA, characterized by sharp-crested ridges and pinnacles. Such topography is found where, owing to an arid climate or overgrazing, there is little vegetation to protect the land surface from erosion, so that streams and rivers have incised it with numerous gullies and ravines. The name was originally applied to parts of South Dakota and Nebraska, which the French trappers (applying the Indian name) found 'bad lands to cross'. Exposure of the rock layers has resulted in substantial finds of fossil vertebrates. A 98,617-hectare (243,500-acre) **Badlands National Park** was established in South Dakota in 1978.

**Badminton** /'bædmɪnt(ə)n/ two villages (Great and Little Badminton) in Avon, south-west

England, east of Chipping Sodbury. Badminton House, seat of the Duke of Beaufort, gave its name to the game of badminton which was first played there in the 19th c. During the 1870s badminton was a popular game with army officers in India and in 1893 the Badminton Association was founded in England.

**Badon Hill** /ˈbeɪd(ə)n/ according to some sources, the site of a successful defensive battle fought by King Arthur's forces against the Saxons in AD 516. Another source implies that the battle was fought c. 500 but does not connect it with Arthur. The location of the site is uncertain.

**Badrinath** /ˌbədrɪˈnɑːt/ a mountain peak in the Garwhal Himalayas of Uttar Pradesh, northern India. It is one of four important Hindu holy sites (Yamunotri, Gangotri, and Kedarnath are the others) near the sources of the great rivers that flow down from the mountains.

**Badulla** /bəˈdələ/ the capital town of Badulla district in Uva province, southern Sri Lanka, situated at an altitude of 680 m. (2,200 ft.); pop. (1981) 33,000.

**Baedeker** /ˈbeɪdɪkə(r)/ any of various travel guidebooks published by the firm founded by the German Karl Baedeker (1801–59).

**Baeza** /bɑːˈeɪzə/ a medieval town in the province of Jaén, southern Spain, in the foothills of the Loma de Ubeda at an altitude of 760 m. (2,500 ft.); pop. (1981) 18,000.

**Baffin Bay** /ˈbæfɪn/ the strait between Baffin Island and Greenland, linked to the North Atlantic Ocean by the Davis Strait and to the Arctic Ocean by the Nares Strait and the Lancaster and Jones sounds. Baffin Bay is largely ice-bound in winter and in summer navigation is made more dangerous by the presence of icebergs brought down by the Labrador current. The bay is named after William Baffin (c. 1584–1622) who explored the area in 1616 with Robert Bylot.

**Baffin Island** the largest island in the Canadian Arctic, and the fifth-largest island in the world, situated at the mouth of Hudson Bay; area 507,451 sq. km. (195,928 sq. miles). The west coast is covered largely by tundra vegetation while the east is dominated by snow-covered mountains with extensive glaciers and snow-fields. Coastal fishing stations include Frobisher Bay, Cape Dyer, and Cape Dorset.

**Bafoussam** /bəˈfuːsəm/ the chief town of West province, western Cameroon; pop. (est. 1984) 88,000. It is the centre of a major coffee-producing area.

**Baghdad** /bægˈdæd/ the capital of Iraq, on the River Tigris; pop. (est. 1985) 4,648,600. Under Caliph Harun-al-Rashid (d. 809) it became one of the greatest cities of Islam until its destruction at the hands of the Mongols in 1258, Tamerlane in 1400, and the Persians in 1524. During the Gulf War of 1991 the city was badly damaged by bombing. The rich brocade known as baldachin derives its name from Baldacco, the Italian name for Baghdad. The city is rich in ancient walls, gates, and bazaars, as well as having a 13th-c. university and 14th-c. *khan* or inn. It is a commercial and industrial centre with mainly light industries including carpets and textiles.

**Baghlan** /bægˈlɑːn/ (also **Baghlan Jadid**) a town in north-east Afghanistan on the main routeway across the Hindu Kush linking Kabul with the northern frontier of Afghanistan; pop. (est. 1984) 43,000. It is capital of the province of Baghlan.

**Baguio** /bæˈgiːəʊ/ a mountain resort and summer capital of the Philippines, on the island of Luzon; pop. (1990) 183,140. First settled by the Spanish, the modern city was laid out by the Americans in 1909. The city lends its name to the tropical storms that occur in the Philippines during July–November.

**Baha'i** /bəˈhɑːɪ/ a monotheistic religion founded in Persia in the 19th c. by Baha-ullah (1817–92) and his son Abdul Baha (1844–1921). The seat of its governing body, the Universal House of Justice, is in Haifa, Israel, adjacent to the golden-domed shrine of the Bab where his bones were buried in 1909 after freedom was granted to religious minorities in the Ottoman empire.

**Bahamas** /bəˈhɑːməz/ official name **The Commonwealth of the Bahamas** a country consisting of an archipelago of some 700 islands lying off the south-east coast of Florida, USA,  where it forms part of the West Indies; area 13,939 sq. km. (5,380 sq. miles); pop. (1991) 254,685; official language, English; capital and largest city, Nassau. It was here that Columbus made his first landfall in the New World (12 Oct. 1492). The islands were depopulated in the 16th c. as the Spaniards carried off most of the inhabitants to slavery. In 1648 a group of English Puritans settled there, and the islands were administered as a British colony from the 18th c. until they gained independence in 1973. The subtropical climate and extensive beaches make tourism the main industry, but banking, fishing, the manufacture of pharmaceuticals, and the refining of petrol are also important.

**Baharampur** /bəˈhɑːrəmˌpʊ(ə)r/ a town in West Bengal, north-east India, near the border with Bangladesh and south of the Ganges; pop. (1991) 126,300.

**Bahasa Indonesia** /bɑːˌhɑːsə ˌɪndəˈniːsɪə/ the official language of Indonesia. Bahasa Malaysia is a variant of Bahasa Indonesia.

**Bahawalpur** /bəˈhɑːwəlˌpʊə(r)/ a city in the Punjab province of central Pakistan, on the Sutlej River; pop. (1981) 178,000. It was formerly the capital of the princely state of Bahawalpur.

**Bahía** /bəˈhiːə/ a state of north-eastern Brazil; area 561,026 sq. km. (216,696 sq. miles); pop. (1991) 11,855,160; capital, Salvador.

**Bahía Blanca** /bəˈhiːə ˈblæŋkə/ a commercial centre and port at the head of an inlet of the Atlantic Ocean in Buenos Aires province, south-east Argentina; pop. (1991) 271,470. It is the principal port serving the southern pampas of Argentina and ships grain and fruit.

**Bahraich** /bəˈraɪk/ a town in Uttar Pradesh, northern India, north-east of Lucknow; pop. (1991) 135,350.

**Bahrain** /bɑːˈreɪn/ a sheikdom consisting of a group of flat islands in the Persian Gulf, off the coast of Saudi Arabia; area 691 sq. km. (255 sq. miles); pop. (1991) 518,250; languages, Arabic (official),  English, Farsi, and Urdu; capital, Manama. The islands, famous in ancient times for their pearls, were ruled by the Portuguese in the 16th c. and the Persians in the 17th c. They became a British protectorate in 1861 under a treaty by which the sheikh pledged himself to refrain from 'the prosecution of war, piracy, or slavery', and independent in 1971. Bahrain's economy is almost wholly dependent on the refining and export of oil, chiefly that coming by pipeline from Saudi Arabia. The climate is hot and humid in summer; temperate in winter.
**Bahraini** adj. & n.

**Bai** /baɪ/ a minority nationality of southern China, mostly found in Yunnan where the Bai people number c. 1.1 million.

**Baia Mare** /ˌbaːjə ˈmaːrɪ/ (Hungarian **Nagybánya** /ˌnaːdʒˈbaːnjɒ/) the capital town of Maramureş county in north-west Romania; pop. (1989) 150,460. Founded by Saxon immigrants in the 12th c., it was originally known as Neustadt. It is situated in a region where lead, zinc, and copper are mined, and has food-processing, machine-building, and chemical industries.

**Baicheng** /baɪˈtʃɛŋ/ a city in the province of Jilin, north-east China; pop. (1986) 286,000.

**Baikal** /baɪˈkɑːl/, **Lake** (Russian **Ozero Baykal**) a large lake in southern Siberia, the largest freshwater lake in Asia and the deepest lake in the world; area 31,494 sq. km. (12,160 sq. miles); max. depth 1,743 m. (5,714 ft.). Fed by the Barguzin and Selenga rivers, its only outlet is the Angara River.

**Baikonur** /ˈbaɪkənʊə(r)/ a coal-mining town in Kazakhstan, north-east of the Aral Sea. Nearby is the Baikonur Cosmodrome from which the world's first satellite (1957) and first manned space flight (1961) were launched. A major centre of Russia's space programme, it continued in use as a space centre after the breakup of the Soviet Union, Russia agreeing in 1994 to rent the site for 20 years.

**Bairisch** /baɪˈrɪʃ/ a form of German similar to Austrian and spoken in Bavaria, southern Germany.

**Bairrada** /baɪˈrɑːdə/ a wine-producing region of Portugal, in the coastal province of Beira Litoral.

**Bai-U** /ˈbaɪuː/ the Japanese name for the rains that occur during the transition from the winter to summer monsoon.

**Baiyin** /baɪˈjɪn/ a town in Sichuan province, central China, north-east of Lanzhou; pop. (1986) 325,000.

**Baja California** /ˈbæxə/ **1.** (also **Lower California**) an arid mountainous peninsula in northwest Mexico that separates the Gulf of California from the Pacific Ocean. It stretches c. 1,225 km. (760 miles) southwards from the US state of California. Tourism is developing along its Pacific coastlands.**2.** (also **North Baja**) a state of northwest Mexico comprising that part of the Baja California (Lower California) peninsula lying to the north of the 28th parallel; area 69,921 sq. km. (27,007 sq. miles); pop. (1990) 1,657,930; capital, Mexicali. It was formerly known as Baja California Norte.

**Baja California Sur** (also **South Baja**) a state of north-west Mexico comprising that part of the Baja California (Lower California) peninsula to the south of the 28th parallel; area 73,475 sq. km. (28,380 sq. miles); pop. (1990) 317,330; capital, La Paz.

**Bajram Curri** /ˌbiːrəm ˈkərɪ/ a town in northern Albania, on the River Drin. It is capital of Tropojë province and a winter sports centre for nearby Mt. Jezercë (2,693 m., 8,835 ft.)

**Baker Island** an uninhabited island in the North Pacific, just north of the equator, 2,575 km. (1,620 miles) south-west of Hawaii; area 1.5 sq. km. (1 sq. mile). An unincorporated territory of the USA, it was last occupied by the US military during World War II.

**Bakersfield** /ˈbeɪkərzˌfiːld/ a mining city and agricultural centre at the southern end of the San Joaquin valley in central California, USA; pop. (1990) 174,820. The city developed after the discovery of gold in 1855 and oil in 1899.

**Bakewell** /ˈbeɪkwel/ a market town in Derbyshire, central England, on the River Wye 16 km. (25 miles) north-west of Derby, noted for its finely carved Saxon cross and as the home of the Bakewell tart.

**Bakhchisarai** /ˌbæxtʃiːsəˈraɪ/ a town on the Crimean peninsula of southern Ukraine, southwest of Simferopol. It was the capital of a Tartar khanate from the 15th to the 18th century. The palace of the khans, built in 1519 and destroyed in 1736, was restored by Field Marshall Potemkin in 1787 four years after he had annexed Crimea and become its governor.

**Bakhtaran** see KERMANSHAH.

**Bakony Mountains** /bɔːˈkəʊnjə/ a forested range of mountains to the north of Lake Balaton in the Transdanubian Highlands of western Hungary. Mt. Köris (702 m., 2,303 ft.) is the highest peak.

**Baku** /bæˈkuː/ the capital of Azerbaijan, on the Caspian Sea; pop. (1990) 1,779,500. It is an industrial port and has been a major centre of the oil industry since 1872 with oil refineries, oilfield equipment manufacturing, chemicals, and shipbuilding. It was the birthplace in 1927 of the cellist and composer Mstislav Rostropovich.

**Balabalagan Islands** (also **Little Paternosters**) an archipelago of c. 30 low-lying Indonesian coral islands in the Makassar (Ujungpandang) Strait between Borneo and the Celebes (Sulawesi).

**Balaclava** /ˌbæləˈklɑːvə/ (also **Balaklava**) a village on the south-west coast of the Crimean peninsula in southern Ukraine, scene of a battle (1854) in the Crimean War during which the famous Charge of the Light Brigade took place. The woollen Balaclava helmet was originally worn by soldiers during the Crimean War.

**Balakovo** /bəˈlɑːkəvəʊ/ a town in the Caspian lowlands of western Russia, north-east of Saratov and east of the Volga River; pop. (1990) 200,000.

**Balashikha** /ˌbæləˈʃiːkə/ a town in western Russia, north-east of Moscow; pop. (1990) 137,000.

**Balaton** /ˈbɒləˌtɒn/, **Lake** a lake in west-central Hungary, situated in a leading resort and wine-producing region to the south of the Bakony Mountains. It is the largest and shallowest lake in central Europe; area 596 sq. km. (230 sq. miles).

**Balboa** /bælˈbəʊæ/ a town at the western Pacific entrance to the Panama Canal; pop. (1990) 2,750. It is named after the Spanish explorer Vasco Nuñez de Balboa.

**Balbriggan** /ˌbælˈbrɪgən/ a resort town on the east coast of Ireland between Dublin and Drogheda. It gives its name to a knitted cotton fabric used for stockings, underwear, etc.

**Baldwin Park** /ˈbɔːldwɪn/ a residential suburb of Los Angeles County in the San Gabriel valley, southern California, USA; pop. (1990) 69,330.

**Baldy Mountain** /ˈbɔː(l)dɪ/ a mountain in south-west Manitoba, Canada. Rising to 832 m. (2,730 ft.), it is the highest peak in the province.

**Balearic Islands** (also **Balearics**, Spanish **Islas Baleares**) a group of Mediterranean islands off the east coast of Spain, forming an autonomous region of that country, with four large islands (Majorca, Minorca, Ibiza, and Formentera) and seven smaller ones; area 5,014 sq. km. (1,937 sq. miles); pop. (1986) 754,800; capital, Palma (on Majorca). The Balearic dialect is derived from Catalan. Occupied by the Romans after the destruction of Carthage, the islands were subsequently conquered by Vandals and Moors, and then by Aragon in the 13th c. Tourism, fishing, and the production of wine, fruit, timber, textiles, grain, and cattle are important.

**Bali** /ˈbɑːlɪ/ a mountainous island of Indonesia, lying between Java to the west and Lombok to the east; area 5,561 sq. km. (2,148 sq. miles); pop. (est. 1993) 2,856,000; chief town, Denpasar. Bali is dominated by the volcanic peaks of Mt. Agung (= Holy Mountain) which rises to a height of 3,142 m. (10,308 ft.) and Mt. Batur (1,740 m., 5,700 ft.). In the north, rice, vegetables, and copra are grown by islanders. Tourist resorts have developed on the south coast at Sanur, Kuta, and Nusa Dua. The predominant religion is a form of Hindu known as Agama-Hindu.
**Balinese** adj. & n.

**Balikesir** /ˌbælɪkəˈsiːr/ **1.** a province in north-west Turkey, on the Sea of Marmara; area 14,292 sq. km. (5,520 sq. miles); pop. (1990) 973,314. **2.** its capital, which trades in textiles, minerals, and cereals; pop. (1990) 170,589.

**Balikpapan** /ˌbɑːlɪkˈpɑːpən/ a port and oil-refining centre on the east coast of the island of Borneo, in the Indonesian province of East Kalimantan; pop. (1980) 281,000.

**Balkan Mountains** /ˈbɒlkən/ (Bulgarian **Stara Planina**) a range of mountains stretching eastwards across Bulgaria from the Serbian frontier to the Black Sea. Its highest point is Botev Peak (2,375 m., 7,793 ft.).

**Balkans** (also **Balkan States**) the countries occupying the Balkan peninsula of south-eastern Europe, lying south of the Danube and Sava rivers, between the Adriatic and Ionian Seas in the west, the Aegean and Black Seas in the east, and the Mediterranean in the south. It is the home of various peoples including Albanians, Vlachs, Greeks, Serbs, Bulgars, and Turks. From the 3rd to 7th c. the Balkan peninsula, nominally ruled by the Byzantine emperors, was invaded by successive migrations of Slavs; later, parts of it were conquered by Venice and other states. In 1356 the Ottoman invasion began. Constantinople fell to the Turks in 1453, and by 1478 most of the peninsula was in their power; the subject nations, though largely retaining their languages and religions, did not recover independence until the 19th c. In 1912–3 Turkey was attacked and defeated by other Balkan peoples in alliance, then the former allies fought over their gains. After World War I the peninsula was divided between Greece, Albania,

Bulgaria, and Yugoslavia, with Turkey retaining only Constantinople and the surrounding land. In 1991–2 instability returned to the Balkans as Yugoslavia's constituent republics struggled to regain their independence against a background of ethnic conflict.

**Balkh** /bɔːk/ a town in northern Afghanistan to the west of Mazar-e-Sharif, close to the site of the ancient city of Bactra, capital of the central Asian kingdom of Bactria. Once a great centre of Buddhism, Bactra was the birthplace of the prophet Zoroaster, founder of the Parsee religion. The city was taken by the Arabs in the 7th c. and later devastated by Genghis Khan in 1221. In the early 16th c. Bactra was rebuilt on its present site by Tamerlane.

**Balkhash** /bæl'kæʃ/, **Lake** a shallow salt lake with no outlet in Kazakhstan, Central Asia; area 18,428 sq. km. (7,115 sq. miles). It is fed by the River Ili which flows north-westwards into the lake from the Tien Shan range. The copper-mining town and fishing port of Balkhash lies on its northern shore. Like the Aral Sea it has been shrinking in size owing to the extraction of water upstream on the River Ili.

**Ballarat** /'bælə‚ræt/ a mining and sheep-farming centre in the state of Victoria, Australia; pop. (1991) 64,980. The largest gold reserves in Australia were discovered here in 1851. There is a memorial to the Eureka Stockade, site of an armed rebellion by gold miners in 1854.

**Ballina** /bæ'liːnə/ a resort town and fishing port on the coast of New South Wales, south-east Australia, situated at the mouth of the Richmond River east of Lismore; pop. (1991) 14,550.

**Ballymahon** /‚bælɪ'mɑːn/ a village on the River Inny, in County Longford, the Republic of Ireland. The playwright, poet, and novelist Oliver Goldsmith (1728–74) was born at nearby Pallas.

**Ballymena** /‚bælɪ'miːnə/ (Gaelic **An Baile Meánach**) a market town in County Antrim, north-east Northern Ireland; pop. (1981) 18,150. It has textile and engineering industries. The Irish nationalist Roger Casement (1864–1916), executed for high treason by the British, was born in Ballymena.

**Ballymote** /‚bælɪ'mɒtə/ (Gaelic **Baile an Mhota**) a village near Templehouse Lough in County Sligo, north-west Ireland. There are ruins of a 14th c. stronghold of the Earls of Ulster and a Franciscan friary within which was written the *Book of Ballymote*, an Irish history that included the key to reading Ogham script.

**Balmoral Castle** /bæl'mɒr(ə)l/ a holiday residence of the British royal family on the River Dee near Braemar in north-east Scotland. The estate was bought in 1847 by Prince Albert who rebuilt the castle. Balmoral lends its name to a highland bonnet and a leather walking-boot with laces up the front.

**Balquhidder** /bæl'wɪdə(r)/ a small village near Loch Earn in central Scotland, that was the burial place of Robert Campbell or Macgregor (1671–1734) better known as Rob Roy.

**Balt** /bɔːlt/ a native of one of the Baltic States of Lithuania, Latvia, and Estonia.

**Baltic Sea** an almost land-locked shallow sea in northern Europe, connected with the North Sea by the Kattegat and Skagerrak straits and by the Kiel Canal across the Jutland peninsula, and bordered by Sweden, Finland, Russia, the Baltic States, Poland, Germany, and Denmark. Its chief ports include Copenhagen, Stockholm, Turku, Helsinki, Tallinn, Riga, Klaipeda, Kaliningrad, Gdansk, and Rostock.

**Baltic states 1.** the independent states of Lithuania, Latvia, and Estonia. **2.** the littoral states of the Baltic, as in the 10-member Council of Baltic States established in 1992 (Denmark, Estonia, Finland, Germany, Latvia, Lithuania, Norway, Poland, Russia, and Sweden).

**Baltimore** /'bɔːltɪ‚mɔː(r)/ a commercial city and industrial seaport in north Maryland, USA, on the Patapsco River; pop. (1990) 736,000. First settled in the 1660s, it was named after Lord Baltimore (1606–75), the English proprietor of territory that later became the state of Maryland. During the 19th c. it was a noted centre of shipbuilding. At anchor in the Inner Harbor lies the US Frigate *Constellation*, the first ship of the US Navy (built in 1797) and the oldest warship in the world still afloat. The sight of an American flag still flying over Fort McHenry after a British naval bombardment in 1814 inspired Francis Scott Keys to write *The Star-Spangled Banner*. Mount Clare Station (1851) was the first passenger railway station to be built in the USA and the Basilica of the Assumption of the Blessed Virgin Mary the first Roman Catholic cathedral (1806–21) in the US. The world's first shopping centre was built at Roland Park in 1896. Baltimore was the birthplace of the journalist H. L. Mencken (1880–1956) and the baseball player Babe Ruth. It was also the home of the author Edgar Allan Poe (1809–49) who lies buried in Westminster Cemetery. Johns Hopkins University (1876), Morgan State University (1867), and the University of Maryland at Baltimore are important centres of education. Coal, grain, and iron, steel, and copper products are exported. Industries include shipbuilding, oil refining, steel, chemicals, aerospace equipment, and food processing.

**Baltistan** /‚bɔːltɪ'stɑːn/ (also **Little Tibet**) a region of Pakistani-held Kashmir in the Karakoram range of the Himalayas, to the south of Mt. K2, western Ladakh. It is the home of the Baltis, a Muslim tribe of Tibetan origin. The chief town is Skardu.

**Baltoro Glacier** /bæl'təʊrəʊ/ a large glacier to the south of Mt. K2 in the Pakistani-held part of

Kashmir in the Karakoram Range of the Himalayas.

**Baluchistan** /bəˌluːkɪˈstɑːn/ **1.** a mountainous and arid region of western Asia that includes part of south-east Iran, south-west Afghanistan, and west Pakistan. **2.** a province of west Pakistan, bounded in the south by the Arabian Sea, the north by Afghanistan, and the west by Iran; area 347,190 sq. km. (134,102 sq. miles); pop. (1981) 4,332,000; capital, Quetta.

**Bamaga** /bæˈmɑːgə/ the most northerly settlement on the Australian mainland, 40 km. (25 miles) south of Cape York. It is the centre of an Aboriginal community.

**Bamako** /ˈbæməˌkəʊ/ the capital and commercial centre of the African state of Mali, on the River Niger; pop. (1987) 646,000. It is the country's main cattle and kola nut market, and has light industries.

**Bamberg** /ˈbæmbə(r)g/ an industrial port on the River Regnitz in Bavaria, southern Germany; pop. (1991) 70,690. The former seat of the Counts of Bamberg, its 13th-c. cathedral is noted for its sculptures and imperial tombs. Once a famous ecclesiastical centre, Bamberg is now an industrial and commercial city producing electronic equipment and textiles.

**Bamburgh** /ˈbæmb(ə)rə/ a small town on the coast of Northumberland, north-east England, noted for its prominent castle. It was the capital of ancient Bernicia and for a time the capital of Northumbria. Bamburgh was the birthplace of the heroine Grace Darling (1815–42) who, with her father, rescued the survivors of the *Forfarshire* in 1838.

**Bamenda** /bəˈmendə/ a resort town in the North-West province of Cameroon, situated at the western end of the Cameroon Ridge to the north of Mount Lefo; pop. (1991) 138,000.

**Bamian** /ˌbæmɪˈɑːn/ **1.** a province of central Afghanistan; area 17,414 sq. km. (6,726 sq. miles); pop. (1984) 291,476. **2.** its capital, on an ancient caravan route linking Central Asia with Afghanistan; pop. (1984) 8,000. Statues of the Buddha carved on a valley wall are the tallest of their kind in the world.

**Banaba** /bəˈnɑːbə/ (also **Ocean Island**) an island in the Pacific Ocean just south of the equator; area 5 sq. km. (2 sq. miles); pop. (1990) 284. Now part of the Kiribati group, Banaba was the capital of the former British colony of Gilbert and Ellice.

**Bananal** /ˌbænəˈnɑːl/, **Ilha do** one of the largest river islands in the world, lying between two branches of the River Araguaia in the state of Tocantins, central Brazil.

**Banat** /ˈbænət/ a former region of southern Hungary to the east of the River Tisza, which became an Austrian Crown land in 1849 before

reverting to Hungary in 1860. After World War I it was divided between Romania and Yugoslavia. In Hungary during the 18th c. the name *Banat* was generally applied to any frontier district under a *ban* or military governor.

**Banbury** /ˈbænbərɪ/ a market town in Oxfordshire, central England, on the River Cherwell; pop. (1981) 38,200. It is famous for its Banbury cakes and its market cross (restored in 1858) which features in a well-known children's rhyme. It has a large cattle market and an aluminium industry.

**Banda Aceh** /ˈbændə ˈɑːtʃeɪ/ the capital of the Indonesian special territory of Aceh at the northern tip of the island of Sumatra; pop. (1980) 53,668. Formerly known as Kutaraja or Koetaradja, it is a predominantly Muslim community.

**Banda Islands** /ˈbændə/ a group of ten volcanic islands in the Indonesian Moluccas, to the south-east of the island of Seram. It comprises Great Banda, Bandanaira, Agung Api, and seven small islands which were discovered by the Portuguese in 1512. In 1619 the islands were taken over by the Dutch who exterminated the indigenous population in order to gain control of the nutmeg trade. The chief port is Bandanaira.

**Banda Oriental** the former Spanish name for the South American republic of Uruguay which lies on the 'eastern bank' of the Uruguay River.

**Bandar Abbas** /ˈbænd(ə)r əˈbɑːz/ (also **Benderabbas**, formerly **Gombroon**) a strategic seaport on the northern shore of the Strait of Hormuz with fishing and textile industries, in the south Iranian province of Hormozgan; pop. (1991) 250,000.

**Bandar Lampung** /ˈbænd(ə)r læmˈpʊŋ/ a city at the southern tip of the Indonesian island of Sumatra, created during the 1980s as a result of the amalgamation of the hillside city of Tanjungkarang and its port at Telukbetung, 5 km. (3.1 miles) to the south; pop. (1980) 284,275.

**Bandar Seri Begawan** /ˈbændə ˌserɪ ˈbəgɑːwən/ (formerly **Brunei Town**) the capital of the sultanate of Brunei on the island of Borneo; pop. (1991) 46,000. A deep-water port was opened in 1972 at nearby Muara. There is a vast new royal palace and the largest mosque in south-east Asia.

**Banda Sea** /ˈbændə/ a sea in eastern Indonesia, between the central and south Molucca Islands.

**Bandung** /ˈbændʊŋ/ the capital of the province of West Java, Indonesia, situated at an altitude of 715 m. (2,346 ft.); pop. (1990) 2,056,915. Founded by the Dutch in 1810, it was the capital of the Dutch East Indies. It is the third-largest city in Indonesia and the chief centre of the Sundanese people of western Java. Textiles, tea, and quinine are produced.

**Banff** /bamf/ **1.** a national park in the Rocky Mountains of south-west Alberta, Canada; area 6,641 sq. km. (2,565 sq. miles). Established in 1885, it is the oldest national park in Canada. **2.** a small resort town at the entrance to Banff National Park, near Lake Louise; pop. (1991) 5,700.

**Banffshire** a former county of north-east Scotland which formed part of a district (with Buchan) in Grampian Region (1975–96). The former county town was the seaport and fishing port of Banff which lies at the mouth of the River Deveron.

**Bangalore** /ˌbæŋɡəˈlɔː(r)/ the capital of the state of Karnataka in central India; pop. (1991) 2,651,000. Under British rule it was formerly the administrative centre of the state of Mysore. Today it is a prosperous industrial city with aircraft, electronics, machine tools, agricultural implements, paper, and textile industries.

**Bangkok** /bænˈkɒk/ the capital and chief port of Thailand, on the Chao Phraya River, 40 km. (25 miles) upstream from its outlet into the Gulf of Thailand; pop. (1990) 5,876,000. Rice, rubber, tin, and timber are the chief exports. Originally a small port serving Ayutthaya the former capital of Siam, Bangkok became capital in 1782 when the founder of the Chakri dynasty, King Rama I, built his palace there. The city is rich in Thai culture and is a popular tourist destination. Its principal modern industries include rice mills, oil refineries, sawmills, shipyards, and textile factories. There is also a famous trade in jewellery.

**Bangla** see BENGALI.

## Bangladesh
/ˌbæŋɡləˈdeʃ/ official name **The People's Republic of Bangladesh** a Muslim country of the Indian subcontinent, in the delta of the Ganges and Brahmaputra rivers,  on the northern coast of the Bay of Bengal, with India to the north, west, and east and Burma to the south-east; area 143,998 sq. km. (55,813 sq. miles); pop. (est. 1991) 116,600,000; official language, Bangla (Bengali); capital, Dhaka. The largest cities are Dhaka, Chittagong, Khulna, and Rajshahi. Although the alluvial soils of Bangladesh are extremely fertile the region is subject to frequent cyclones and tropical monsoons which cause immense damage and loss of life and crops. Rice, jute, tea, and cotton goods are the chief exports of a predominantly agricultural economy. There are virtually no mineral resources, and with a limited industrial base Bangladesh remains one of the poorest countries in the world. From 1857 the area formed part of India under British rule, until 1947 when it became (as East Pakistan) one of the two geographical units of Pakistan separated by more than 1,600 km. (1,000 miles). In response to a rising tide of nationalism an independent republic was proclaimed in East Pakistan in 1971. Taking

the name of Bangladesh (Bangla = land of Bengal), it became a member state of the Commonwealth in 1972. In 1982 the army chief of staff, General Hussain Mohammed Ershad, assumed control of the country following a bloodless coup that took place a year after the assassination of President Zia. In 1990 Ershad resigned making way for an election that swept to power the Bangladesh Nationalist Party led by President Zia's widow, Begum Khaleda Zia. A new constitution in 1991 restricted the powers of the president and restored power to the unicameral legislature (*Jatiya Sangsad*).
**Bangladeshi** *adj. & n.*
Bangladesh is divided into 4 divisions:

| Division | Area (sq. km.). | (1991) |
| --- | --- | --- |
| Chittagong | 45,415 | 28,811,450 |
| Dhaka | 30,772 | 33,593,100 |
| Khulna | 33,575 | 20,804,515 |
| Rajshahi | 34,239 | 26,667,910 |

**Bangor** /ˈbæŋɡɜː(r)/ **1.** a resort town in County Down, Northern Ireland, on the southern shore of Belfast Lough. A monastery was founded here by St. Comgall in the 6th c. **2.** a town in the county of Gwynedd, north-west Wales, opposite the island of Anglesey; pop. (1981) 46,585. Its cathedral (built *c.* 1500 and restored 1869–90) contains tombs of the Welsh princes. There is a University College founded in 1884. Nearby are Penrhyn Castle and the Menai Bridge connecting the mainland with Anglesey.

**Bangor** /ˈbæŋɡɜː(r)/ the third-largest city in the state of Maine, USA, a port on the Penobscot River; pop. (1990) 33,181. First settled in 1769, Bangor developed as a lumber port in the 19th c. and also has shoe, paper, and printing industries. Originally to be called Sunbury, it is said inadvertently to have been named Bangor after a tune the Reverend Seth Noble was whistling when he went to register the new town.

**Bangui** /ˈbæŋɡiː/ the capital of the Central African Republic, on the Ubangi River; pop. (1988) 576,780. Founded by the French in 1889, it was formerly a centre of the ivory trade. It is a market and university (1970) town and exports cotton and timber.

**Baniyas** /ˈbænjɑːs/ a village in the Israeli-occupied Golan Heights, on the site of the ancient city of CAESAREA PHILIPPI.

**Banja Luka** /ˈbænɪə ˈluːkə/ a spa town in northern Bosnia and Herzegovina, on the River Vrbas; pop. (1991) 143,000. (= St. Luke's Bath.)

**Banjarmasin** /ˌbændʒəˈmɑːsɪn/ (also **Bandjarmasin**) a deep-water port and capital of the Indonesian province of South Kalimantan situated on a delta island near the junction of the Martapura and Barito rivers close to the south coast of the island of Borneo; pop. (1990) 480,740.

It is the centre of a fertile agricultural region and a fishing port.

**Banjul** /bæn'dʒu:l/ (until 1973 **Bathurst**) the capital of the Gambia, on St. Mary's Island at the mouth of the Gambia River, where it meets the Atlantic Ocean; pop. (1983) 44,536. It was founded by the British in 1816 as a trading station and base for suppressing the slave trade, and was named after the 3rd Earl of Bathurst (1762–1834) who was Secretary of State for the Colonies (1812–28). It is the Gambia's commercial centre and has groundnuts processing plants. The tourist industry has also recently developed with new hotels being built for European sunseekers.

**Banks Island** /bæŋks/ an island in the Northwest Territories, Canada, the westernmost of the islands of the Canadian Arctic; area 70,028 sq. km. (27,038 sq. miles). Dominated by tundra vegetation, it has the world's largest population of muskoxen. Its first permanent settlement was established at Sachs Harbour in 1929.

**Bann** /ba:n/ the principal river of Northern Ireland. It rises in the Mourne Mountains and flows 103 km. (65 miles) northwards through L. Neagh and L. Beg before meeting the Atlantic Ocean beyond Coleraine.

**Bannock** /'bænək/ a North American Indian tribe related to the Shoshone of the Great Basin in southern Idaho. They now occupy the Wind River Reservation in Wyoming where they number c. 2,250.

**Bannockburn** /'bænək,bɜ:n/ a village in central Scotland, scene of a decisive Scottish victory over the English when the much larger army of Edward II, advancing to break the siege of Stirling Castle in 1314, was outmanoeuvred and defeated by Robert the Bruce on difficult ground a few miles south of Stirling. Bruce's victory ended for several decades the Plantagenet attempt to reduce Scotland to the status of a vassal kingdom.

**Banqiao** /ba:ŋ'kjaʊ/ a town in Yunnan province, southern China, in the Wumeng Mountains north-east of Zhaotong; pop. (1986) 115,000.

**Banská Bystrica** /'ba:nska: 'bɪstrɪtsa:/ the chief town of central Slovakia, in the Low Tatras, at the confluence of the Hron and Bystrica rivers; pop. (1991) 177,578. Noted in medieval times for its copper and silver mines, Banská Bystrica is now a leading cultural and economic centre.

**Banten** /'ba:nten/ (formerly **Bantam**) an abandoned seaport on the north-west coast of the island of Java, Indonesia, 95 km. (60 miles) west of Jakarta. Once the capital of a Muslim sultanate, it was developed as a Portuguese trading station after 1545 before becoming the first Dutch settlement on Java in 1596. It gives its name to several breeds of small domestic fowl known as 'bantams'.

**Bantry Bay** /'bæntrɪ beɪ/ an inlet of the Atlantic Ocean in County Cork on the south coast of the Republic of Ireland.

**Bantu** /bæn'tu:/ a large group of Negroid peoples of south and central Africa speaking some 300 languages (with 100 million speakers) within the Niger-Kordofanian family of languages including Bemba, Ganda, Kikuyu, Kongo, Lingala, Luba, Makua, Mbundu, Ruanda, Rundi, Shona, Sotho, Swahili, Thonga, Xhosa, and Zulu. Of these, Swahili is the most important. Bantu languages are characterized by words that are nearly all tonal, and nouns that belong to one of a set of clauses, usually about 18. Most Bantu languages were not written down until the 19th c. Originally Arab traders introduced their Arabic script, which was used for Swahili along the coast, but elsewhere the Roman alphabet has been used, sometimes with additional characters. Linguistic evidence suggests that the original home of these languages may have been in the Cameroon region. The Bantu people migrated to southern Africa, through the lake region of East Africa, by the 3rd c. AD. It is believed that the Bantu introduced iron metallurgy to southern Africa at the time of their entry.

**Bantustan** /,bæntu:'sta:n/ a name, often applied offensively, to the former partially self-governing homelands reserved for Black South Africans.

**Baoding** /baʊ'dɪŋ/ a city in Hebei province, eastern China, south-west of Beijing; pop. (1986) 548,000.

**Baoji** /baʊ'dʒi:/ a city in Shaanxi province, central China, in the northern foothills of the Qin Ling Mountains west Xian; pop. (1986) 368,000.

**Baoshan** /baʊ'ʃa:n/ an industrial city in Yunnan province, southern China, situated to the west of the Qingshuilang Mountains south-west of Xiaguan, the site of China's most modern iron and steel complex; pop. (1986) 697,000.

**Baotou** /baʊ'təʊ/ an industrial city in Inner Mongolia, northern China, on the Yellow River; pop. (1990) 1,200,000. Iron, steel, chemicals, and textiles are produced.

**Bar** /ba:r/ (Italian **Antivari**) a seaport south-east of Podgorica (Titograd) on the Adriatic coast of Montenegro, Yugoslavia; pop. (1981) 32,535. There are ferry links to the Greek island of Corfu and the Italian port of Brindisi.

**Baracaldo** /,bærə'ka:ldəʊ/ an industrial city in the Basque province of Vizcaya, northern Spain, on the River Nervion; pop. (1991) 105,170. Iron and steel are the main industrial products.

**Barahona** /,bærə'haʊnə/ a port and resort town on the south coast of the Dominican Republic; pop. (est. 1982) 74,630. Sugar and coffee are grown in the surrounding area.

**Baranavichiy** /,bərə:nə'vji:tʃi:/ an industrial city in Belorussia (Belarus), on the railway line between Minsk and Brest; pop. (1990) 162,800. Founded in 1870, the city was part of Poland from 1920 to 1939.

## Barbados

/bɑːˈbeɪdɒs/ the most easterly of the Caribbean islands, c. 483 km. (300 miles) north of Venezuela in the Windward Islands; area 431 sq. km. (166 sq. miles); pop. (est. 1991) 300,000; offi-

cial language, English; capital, Bridgetown. A largely flat island with no rivers, Barbados is circled by a narrow coastal plain and fine beaches that attract large numbers of tourists. The climate is tropical with a hot rainy season from June to December. During the dry season the north-east trade winds blow steadily across the island. In addition to tourism, fishing and the production of sugar-cane, molasses, and rum are important economic activities. The geographical position of Barbados has influenced its history. Difficult of access in the days of sailing-ships, it became a British colony in 1652 and remained British without interruption until 1966 when it gained independence as a member state of the Commonwealth.

**Barbadian** *adj. & n.*
The island of Barbados is divided into 11 districts:

| District | Area (sq. km.) | Pop. (1980) |
| --- | --- | --- |
| St. Michael | 38.9 | 99,953 |
| Christ Church | 57.1 | 40,790 |
| St. George | 44.0 | 17,361 |
| St. Philip | 59.5 | 18,662 |
| St. John | 33.7 | 10,330 |
| St. James | 31.1 | 17,255 |
| St. Thomas | 33.7 | 10,709 |
| St. Joseph | 25.9 | 7,211 |
| St. Andrew | 36.2 | 6,731 |
| St. Peter | 33.7 | 10,717 |
| St. Lucy | 36.2 | 9,264 |

## Barbary Coast

/ˈbɑːbərɪ/ **1.** a name given to the Mediterranean coast of North Africa from Morocco to Egypt, noted in the 16th–18th c. for its pirates. **2.** a name given to the wild and notorious waterfront area of San Francisco after the 1849 gold-rush.

## Barbican

/ˈbɑːbɪkən/ a part of London near the site of the ancient city walls, to the north-east of St. Paul's Cathedral. It is noted for its post-war luxury apartment blocks and the Barbican Centre, a complex of theatres, cinemas, and galleries that was opened in 1982. Its name is derived from a term used to describe the outer defence of a city or castle, especially a double tower above a gate or drawbridge.

## Barbizon

/ˈbɑːbiːzɔ̃/ a village in the forest of Fontainebleau, Seine-et-Marne department, north-central France; pop. (1982) 1,270. It gave its name to the Barbizon school of French landscape painters who came together here in the 1840s. Théodore Rousseau (1812–67) was the leader of the group which included Daubigny, Corot, Diaz, Millet, and Dupré.

## Barbuda

/bɑːˈbjuːdə/ an island in the Caribbean which, with Antigua (40 km., 25 miles to the south) and Redonda, forms an independent state in the Leeward group of the Lesser Antilles; area 161 sq. km. (101 sq. miles); pop. (1991) 1,400; chief town, Codrington.

## Barcelona

/ˌbɑːsəˈləʊnə/ the second-largest city of Spain and chief city of the region of Catalonia, situated on the Mediterranean coast of north-east Spain between the Llobregat and Bésos rivers; pop. (1991) 1,653,175. It is also the largest seaport and industrial city in Spain, producing vehicles, textiles, petrochemicals, and electrical equipment. Allegedly founded by the Phoenicians, Barcelona was held by Carthaginians, Romans, and Visigoths before falling to the Moors in the 8th c. It was taken by Charlemagne in 801 and during the succeeding two centuries became part of the independent Spanish March held by the counts of Barcelona who freed most of Catalonia from Arab rule. Noted as a centre of radical politics, it was the seat of the Spanish Loyalist government during 1938–9. Barcelona, a leading cultural centre of Spain, hosted the 1992 Olympic Games. Antonio Gaudí (1852–1926) studied architecture here and notable buildings include the 14th–15th-c. cathedral of Santa Eulalia, the Pedralbes Palace, and Gaudí's Church of the Holy Family.

## Barcelona

a mining town and capital of Anzoátegui state, northern Venezuela, on the Neveri River, 238 km. (150 miles) east of Caracas; pop. (1989) 442,677. Its seaport is Guanta.

## Barcelos

/bɑːˈsɛləs/ a town in Braga district, northern Portugal, on the River Cávado; pop. (1991) 4,660. The Barcelos cockerel is the national emblem of Portugal.

## barchan

/ˈbɑːkən/ a crescent-shaped dune of sand formed across the prevailing wind with its tips extending downwind. Barchans are the most mobile of sand dunes, migrating as much as 15 m. (50 ft.) per year.

## Barddhaman

/bɜːdəˈmɑːn/ (formerly **Burdwan**) a town in West Bengal, north-east India, on the Damodar River north-west of Calcutta; pop. (1991) 244,790.

## Bardejov

/ˈbɑːrdjəjəf/ (German **Bartfeld**) the chief town of eastern Slovakia, on the River Topla near the Polish frontier; pop. (1991) 79,000.

## Bardo

/ˈbɑːdəʊ/ (also **Le Bardo**) a town in northern Tunisia forming a north-western suburb of the city of Tunis. The National Museum of the Bardo, founded in 1882 and located in a palace of the former beys of Tunis, features one of the world's largest collections of mosaics.

## Bardolino

/ˌbɑːrdəʊˈliːnəʊ/ a resort town in Venetia, north-east Italy, situated on the eastern shore of Lake Garda in the province of Verona; pop. (1990) 5,975. In addition to its medieval

Romanesque churches the town is perhaps best known for its red wine which is largely made from the Corvina, Negrara, Molinara, and Rondinella grapes.

**Bareilly** /bəˈreɪlɪ/ (also **Bareli**) an industrial city in the state of Uttar Pradesh, northern India; pop. (1991) 583,000. It was a capital of the Afghan region of Rohilkand until taken by the British in 1801, and a leading centre of disaffection during the Indian Mutiny of 1857.

**Barents Sea** /ˈbærənts/ a part of the Arctic Ocean to the north of Norway and Russia, named after the Dutch explorer Willem Barents (d. 1597) who led several expeditions in search of a north-east passage to Asia. In 1993 the governments of Denmark, Finland, Iceland, Norway, Russia, and Sweden set up the Barents Euro-Arctic Council to renew regional trade and economic co-operation in the Barents Sea area.

**Bari** /ˈbɑːrɪ/ an industrial seaport on the Adriatic Sea in the Apulia region of south-east Italy; pop. (1990) 353,030. It is capital of the province of Bari. The Romanesque basilica (1087–1197) with relics of St. Nicholas of Bari is a place of pilgrimage. In addition to traditional industries such as shipbuilding and the manufacture of textiles, Bari is the site of Italy's first atomic power station, and an important centre of the petrochemical industry. High-tech industries flourish in that part of the town known as 'Tecnopolis'.

**Bariloche** SEE SAN CARLOS DE BARILOCHE.

**Barinas** /bæˈriːnəs/ the capital city of Barinas state in western Venezuela, in the eastern foothills of the Cordillera de Mérida; pop. (1981) 110,462. The city is situated on the edge of the llanos plains in an area noted for cattle ranching and oil production.

**Barisal** /ˈbʌrɪˌsæl/ a riverport in southern Bangladesh, on the Ganges delta; pop. (1991) 163,480. It gives its name to the natural phenomenon known as the 'Barisal guns', a sound like cannon-fire or thunder, possibly of seismic origin and heard at the rising of the tide.

**Barking and Dagenham** /ˈbɑːkɪŋ, ˈdæg(ə)nəm/ an industrial outer borough of north London, England, on the River Roding; pop. (1991) 139,900. It is the site of a major car factory.

**Barkly Tableland** /ˈbɑːklɪ/ a plateau region lying to the north-east of Tennant Creek in Northern Territory, Australia; area c. 103,560 sq. km. (40,000 sq. miles). Dominated by tussocky grass, the area is grazed by open-range cattle which are bred here. The 640-km. (403-mile) **Barkly Highway** links Mt. Isa with the Stuart Highway.

**Barlavento** /ˌbærləˈventəʊ/ the windward islands of Santo Antão, São Vicente, Santa Luzia, São Nicalau, Sal, and Boa Vista which together form a district of the Cape Verde Islands in the Atlantic Ocean off the west coast of Africa; area 2,230 sq. km. (861 sq. miles); pop. (1980) 108,000.

**Bar-le-Duc** /bɑːr lə dʊk/ a market town in the Meuse department of Lorraine, north-east France, on the River Ornain; pop. (1982) 20,029. Formerly capital of the Duchy of Bar, it has many houses with fine 16th–18th c. façades. Surrounded by a rich dairy-farming region, Bar-le-Duc is now one of the largest cheese depots in Europe.

**Barletta** /bɑːˈletə/ an Adriatic seaport in the Apulia region of south-eastern Italy; pop. (1990) 88,750. The famous *Disfida di Barletta* or duel between French and Italian knights took place near here in 1503. There is a huge 4th-c. bronze statue (thought to be of the Emperor Valentinian I) brought from Constantinople by Venetians in the 13th c.

**Barnanez** /ˈbɑːnənəs/ a prehistoric tomb near Brignogan-Plage on the Channel coast of Brittany, north-west France. Built c. 4,700 BC, it is one of the oldest neolithic stone monuments in western Europe.

**Barnaul** /ˌbɑːnɑːˈuːl/ the capital of Altai in eastern Russia, on the River Ob in southern Siberia; pop. (1990) 603,000. Founded in the 18th c. as a silver-smelting town, Barnaul is now a major railway junction and commercial centre serving an agricultural region that produces cotton, grain, and sugar-beets.

**Barnet** /ˈbɑːnət/ a largely residential outer borough of north London, England; pop. (1991) 283,000.

**Barnsley** /ˈbɑːnzlɪ/ the county town of South Yorkshire, England, on the River Dearne; pop. (1991) 217,300. Previously a leading coal-mining centre.

**Barnstaple** /ˈbɑːnstəp(ə)l/ a market town on the north coast of Devon, south-west England, on the River Tow; pop. (1981) 24,878. It was the birthplace of the English poet John Gay (1685–1732) who wrote the libretto to *The Beggar's Opera* in 1728.

**Baroda** SEE VADODARA.

**Barossa Valley** /bæˈrɒsə/ Australia's most famous wine-making area, situated to the north of Adelaide in South Australia. First settled in 1842 by predominantly German colonists, the area was named (with incorrect spelling) after Barrosa in Spain.

**Barquisimeto** /ˌbɑːkiːsiːˈmeɪtəʊ/ the capital of the state of Lara in northern Venezuela, on the Trans-Andean highway at the centre of a rich coffee, cacao, and cattle-ranching region; pop. (1991) 602,620; 787,360 (metropolitan area). Founded in 1522, the city was devastated by an earthquake in 1812.

**Barra** /ˈbærə/ an island at the southern end of the Outer Hebrides off the west coast of Scotland, separated from South Uist by the Sound of Barra and named after St. Finnbar; area 91 sq. km. (35 sq. miles); pop. (est. 1984) 1,200. The chief town is

Castlebay near which is Kisimul Castle, seat of the Clan Macneil. Sir Compton Mackenzie the novelist, who lived on the island during World War II, was buried here in 1972. There are ferry links with South Uist and Oban.

**Barrancabermeja** /bə,raːŋkəbər'meɪhaː/ a port and oil town on the Magdalena River in Santander department, north-east Colombia; pop. (est. 1984) 64,400. The nearby De Mares oilfields are linked by pipeline to the port of Cartagena on the Caribbean coast.

**Barranquilla** /,bærən'kiːjə/ the leading industrial seaport of Colombia, at the mouth of the Magdalena River, on the Caribbean coast of Atlantico department; pop. (1985) 899,800. Founded in 1629, Barranquilla was the site of the first air terminal to be built in South America. It has shipbuilding, chemical, textile, and food industries.

**Barren Grounds** /'bærən/ (also **Barren Lands**) a name given to the low-lying, sparsely inhabited land of northern Canada between the Mackenzie River and Hudson Bay.

**Barrie** /'bærɪ/ a city in Ontario, Canada, to the north of Toronto; pop. (1991) 57,400. It is the unofficial gateway to Toronto's cottage-vacation country around Lake Simcoe, Lake Muskoka, and Georgian Bay.

**barrio** /'baːrɪəʊ/ the Spanish-speaking quarter of a town or city. (Spanish = district of a town.)

**Barrow** /'bærəʊ/ a river in the Irish Republic, rising in the Slieve Bloom Mountains and flowing 190 km. (120 miles) east and south to St. George's Channel at Waterford Harbour.

**Barrow** a town on Point Barrow, the most northerly peninsula of the state of Alaska and the USA; pop. (1990) 3,469. A naval base and centre of Arctic research, Barrow is the northernmost town in the USA.

**Barrow-in-Furness** /-'fɜːnəs/ an industrial seaport on the Cumbrian coast of north-west England, on the Furness peninsula. Shipbuilding, steel, offshore gas, engineering, paper making, and chemical production are important industries.

**Barrow Strait** an arm of the Arctic Ocean lying between Bathurst, Cornwallis, and Devon islands to the north and Prince of Wales and Somerset islands to the south.

**Barsac** /'baːsæk/ an area to the south of Bordeaux in the department of Gironde, southwest France noted for its sweet white wine. It is one of five locations bearing the Sauternes appellation.

**Barysaw** /'bɒrɪˌsɔː/ an industrial city in central Belorussia (Belarus), on the Berezina River northeast of Minsk; pop. (1990) 147,000. It was known as Borisov until 1993.

**barysphere** /'bærɪˌsfɪər/ the dense interior of the earth, including the mantle and core, enclosed by the lithosphere.

**Basel** the German name for BASLE.

**Bashkir** /'bæʃkɪə(r)/ a member of a people, the majority of whom live in the southern Urals. Some 70 per cent are to be found in the republic of Bashkortostan where they account for about one quarter of the population. They are Sunni Muslims of the Hanafi school. The northern and western Bashkirs are descended from Finnish-speaking tribes while the southern and eastern Bashkirs are the descendants of Turkic nomadic tribes.

**Bashkortostan** /bæʃ'kɔːtəˌstaːn/ (formerly **Bashkiria** /bæʃ'kɪrjə/) a republic of the Russian Federation to the south-east of the Udmurt and Tartar republics in western Russia and to the west of the Urals; area 143,600 sq. km. (55,465 sq. miles); pop. (1990) 3,964,000; capital, Ufa. Annexed to the Russian empire in 1557, it was constituted as an Autonomous Soviet Socialist Republic in 1919. Following the breakup of the Soviet Union it changed its name to Bashkortostan and was given federal republic status. It is an important centre of oil, coal, timber, paper, steel, and chemical production.

**Basildon** /'bæz(ə)ldən/ a town in Essex, southeast England, developed as a new town after 1949 with diverse light industries; pop. (1991) 157,500.

**Basilicata** /bə,sɪlɪ'kaːtə/ (Latin **Lucania**) a mountainous region of southern Italy, lying between the 'heel' of Apulia and the 'toe' of Calabria; area 9,990 sq. km. (3,859 sq. miles); pop. (1990) 624,519; capital, Potenza. It comprises the provinces of Potenza and Matera.

**basin** /'beɪs(ə)n/ **1.** an area of land drained by a river and its tributaries, the boundary between one basin and another being the watershed. **2.** a geological term describing a rock formation where the strata dip towards the centre.

**Basle** /baːl/ (German **Basel** /'baːz(ə)l/) a commercial, cultural, and industrial city on the Rhine in north-east Switzerland; pop. (1990) 171,000. It has many museums and art galleries and Switzerland's oldest university (1459). It is the focal point of the three-nation Regio Basiliensis which was set up in 1963 to co-ordinate the cultural and economic development of French, German, and Swiss districts in the Upper Rhine Valley. It is a world centre of the pharmaceutical industry and also has textile and publishing industries.

**Basque Country** /bæsk/ (French **Pays Basque**, Spanish **Pais Vasco**, Basque **Euskadi**) that part of France and Spain on both sides of the western Pyrenees occupied by the Basque people. It comprises the Basque Provinces of northern Spain and the greater part of Pyrénées-Atlantique department in the Aquitaine region of south-west France. Culturally the Basques are one of the most distinct groups in Europe. While they do not differ physically from other European groups, their language, Basque (Euskara), is not of the Indo-European language family and is unrelated to any other known tongue, though some similarities with Caucasian languages have been noted. This complex language inherited from the ancient Vascones and predating the Roman conquest of the Iberian peninsula, is the only remnant of the languages spoken in south-west Europe before the region was Romanized. It is spoken by some 700,000 people in the Pyrenees, but evidence of place-names suggests that it was originally current in a much wider area.

**Basque Provinces** (Spanish **Provincias Vascongadas**) an autonomous region of northern Spain comprising the three provinces of Alava, Guipúzcoa, and Vizcaya; area 7,261 sq. km. (2,804 sq. miles); pop. (1991) 2,104,040. The chief cities are Bilbao and San Sebastian.

**Basra** /ˈbæzrə/ an oil port of Iraq, on the Shatt al-Arab waterway; pop. (est. 1985) 616,700. Severely damaged during the Iran–Iraq and Gulf wars, it is one of only two shipping outlets to the Persian Gulf from Iraq.

**Bas-Rhin** /bɑːˈræ̃/ a department in the region of Alsace, north-east France, between the River Rhine and the eastern slopes of the Vosges Mountains; area 4,787 sq. km. (1,849 sq. miles); pop. (1990) 953,050; capital, Strasbourg.

**Bassas da India** /ˈbɑːsəs dæ ˈiːndjə/ an uninhabited tropical French atoll surrounded by reefs in the Mozambique Channel, administered as a dependency of Réunion but claimed by Madagascar.

**Bas St.-Laurent** /bɑː sæ ləˈrɑ̃/ the name given to the highly cultivated part of Quebec in eastern Canada lying between the St. Lawrence River and the Appalachians.

**Bassein** /bæˈseɪn/ (Burmese **Puthein**) a seaport on the Bassein River in the delta of the Irrawaddy, south-west Burma, a rice-milling and exporting centre, 143 km. (90 miles) west of Rangoon; pop. (1983) 355,600.

**Basse-Normandie** /ˌbæsnɔːmãˈdiː/ a region in northern France, comprising the departments of Calvados, Manche, and Orne; area 17,583 sq. km. (6,788 sq. miles); pop. (1990) 1,391,320; capital, Caen.

**Basse-Terre** /bæsˈteə(r)/ the chief port and capital of the French overseas department of Guadeloupe in the Caribbean; pop. (est. 1988) 13,800. It is situated on the south-west corner of an island of the same name.

**Basseterre** /bæsˈteə(r)/ the chief port and capital of St. Kitts-Nevis in the Caribbean; pop. (1980) 14,300. It is situated on the south-west coast of the island of St. Kitts.

**Bass Rock** /bæs/ a rocky islet with a lighthouse and large numbers of sea birds at the mouth of the Firth of Forth, east Scotland. Of volcanic origin, it rises to a height of 95 m. (313 ft.) above sea-level. It has been used on various occasions as a prison.

**Bass Strait** a channel separating the island of Tasmania from the Australian mainland. It is named after the English explorer George Bass who discovered the strait in 1798.

**Bastia** /bæˈstiːə/ the chief port of the French island of Corsica in the Mediterranean, situated on the north-east corner of the island; pop. (1990) 38,730. Founded by the Genoese in the 14th c. and capital of Corsica until the late 18th c., it is now capital of the department of Haute-Corse and the island's second-largest town after Ajaccio. The port is dominated by the Genoese fortress (*bastaglia*) that gives the town its name. It has fishing and commercial harbours.

**Bastide towns** /bɑːsˈtiːd/ (also **Bastides**) a series of fortified towns in Aquitaine, south-west France, built by the kings of France and England in the Middle Ages. These strongholds, which outlined the frontier between English and French territory, were all built to the same chequered plan with a fortified church and a market place surrounded by covered arcades. The best preserved are Monpazier, Villeréal, and Puylaroque.

**Bastille** /bæsˈtiːl/ a fortified prison built on the city wall of Paris, France, between 1370 and 1382 in the reign of Charles V. Used by Cardinal Richelieu, Louis XIII's Minister, it became an infamous state prison in the 17th c. During the French Revolution it was completely demolished after being stormed on 14 July 1789. The prison is remembered in the name of a huge square, the Place de la Bastille, and a national holiday (Bastille Day) held annually on 14 July.

**Basutoland** /bəˈsuːtəʊˌlænd/ the former name (until 1966) of LESOTHO in southern Africa.

**Bata** /ˈbɑːtə/ the chief port of the province of Río Muni on the mainland of Equatorial Guinea; pop. (est. 1986) 17,000.

**Batak** /ˈbætək/ an ethnic group of northern Sumatra, Indonesia, speaking a variety of distinct but related Malayo-Polynesian languages.

**Batala** /bəˈtɑːlə/ a town in Punjab state, northwest India, north-east of Amritsar; pop. (1991) 106,060.

**Batalha** /bəˈtɑːljə/ a small town in the district of Leira, central Portugal; pop. (1991) 3,150. It is noted for its famous Dominican abbey which was founded in 1388 as a tribute to the re-establishment of Portuguese independence from Spain. Nearby is the battlefield of Aljubarrota where King John I of Portugal defeated King John I of Castile on 14 August 1385. Prince Henry the Navigator is buried in the abbey.

**batang** /bəˈtɑːŋ/ a Malay word for a river.

**Batan Islands** /bəˈtɑːn/ the most northerly islands of the Philippines, lying between the Babuyan Islands and Taiwan. Batan, Sabtang, and Itbayat are the principal islands and Basco (on Batan Island) is the chief town.

**Batangas City** /bəˈtæŋɡəs/ a market town, port, and capital of a province of the same name on the island of Luzon in the Philippines; pop. (1990) 143,570. It is situated at the south-west corner of the island on Batangas Bay and has a large oil refinery and steel works.

**Batavia** /bəˈteɪvɪə/ the former name (until 1949) of JAKARTA in Indonesia.

**Batavian Republic** the name given to the Netherlands by the French who occupied that country from 1795 until 1806 when Napoleon installed his brother Louis as King of Holland.

**Batdambang** see BATTAMBANG.

**Bath** /bɑːθ/ a spa town in the county of Avon, south-west England; pop. (1991) 79,900. Known to the Romans as Aquae Sulis or Aquae Calidae, Bath has long been famous for its hot springs. The remains of Roman baths, a 15th–16th-c. abbey church, and notable 18th-c. Georgian crescents and squares are features of the town which is the site of the University of Bath (1966). It was the birthplace of the Arctic explorer Sir William Parry (1790–1855). It has light industries and tourism is important.

**Bathurst** /ˈbæθɜːrst/ the former name (until 1973) of BANJUL, capital of the Gambia. It is one of several places named after Earl Bathurst who was British Colonial Secretary from 1812 to 1828.

**Bathurst** a town in New South Wales, Australia, on the Macquarie River, 209 km. (131 miles) west of Sydney; pop. (1991) 24,680. It is a former gold-mining town, now situated at the centre of a pastoral, fruit, and grain-growing region.

**Bathurst Island** **1.** an island in the Canadian Arctic, one of the Parry Islands to the north of Viscount Melville Sound; area 16,042 sq. km. (6,194 sq. miles). **2.** an island off the coast of Northern Territory, Australia, situated in the Timor Sea, to the west of Melville Island and separated from Darwin by the Beagle Gulf. It is reserved as an Aboriginal Land.

**Batman** /bætˈmɑːn/ (also **Iluh**) a city in the province of Siirt, eastern Turkey; pop. (1990) 147,350.

**Batna** /bətˈnɑː/ a city in northern Algeria, south-west of Constantine; pop. (1989) 122,000. It was founded by the French in 1748 as a military post. Nearby are the ruins of the ancient Roman city of Timgad.

**Baton Rouge** /ˌbæt(ə)n ˈruːʒ/ the capital of the state of Louisiana, USA, on the east bank of the Mississippi; pop. (1990) 219,530. It is a major transportation centre with oil-refining, gas, petro-chemical, engineering, and food-processing industries. Founded in 1719 by French settlers, the city was named after a red post that marked the boundary between the lands of two Indian tribes. The painter-naturalist John James Audubon lived for a time in Baton Rouge which is home to Louisiana State University (1860).

**Battambang** /ˈbætəmˌbæŋ/ (also **Batdambang**) the capital of Battambang province in western Cambodia; pop. (1981) 551,860. Situated on the main supply route to Phnom Penh, it is the second-largest city in Cambodia and a centre for the milling of rice and production of textiles.

**Battenberg** /ˈbæt(ə)nˌbɜːg/ a village in the state of Hesse, western Germany, a seat of aristocracy whose title was revived in 1851 for a branch of the German royal family. Members of the British royal household bearing this name renounced it in 1917, assuming the surname Mountbatten. Battenberg gives its name to a type of sponge cake covered with marzipan.

**Battersea** /ˈbætə(r)sɪ/ a district of the Inner London borough of Wandsworth, England, on the south bank of the River Thames. It is noted for its Dogs' Home (established in 1860) and its huge power-station (now disused) which was designed by Sir Giles Gilbert Scott.

**Battery** /ˈbætərɪ/, **the** a park at the southern tip of Manhattan Island, New York City, USA, site of a fort once built for the protection of New York harbour; area 8.5 hectares (21 acres).

**Batticaloa** /ˌbætɪkəˈləʊə/ a city on the east coast of Sri Lanka, on Batticaloa Lake, an inlet of the Bay of Bengal; pop. (1981) 42,900.

**Battle** /ˈbæt(ə)l/ a town in East Sussex, southeast England, to the north of Hastings. It takes its name from the Battle of Hastings which was fought here in 1066. There are the remains of a Benedictine abbey founded by the victor, William of Normandy.

**Battle Creek** a city in south Michigan, USA, at the junction of the Battle Creek and Kalamazoo rivers; pop. (1990) 53,540. It is the centre of the Kellog and Post breakfast-cereal producing plants.

**Batumi** /bəˈtuːmiː/ a Black Sea port and capital of Adzharia in the Republic of Georgia; pop. (1991) 138,000. Shipbuilding and oil refining are important industries and the port is used as a Russian naval base.

**Bat Yam** /bæt yæm/ an industrial town and resort on the Mediterranean coast of Israel; pop. (1982) 134,500. Founded in 1925, it is a southern suburb of Tel Aviv.

**Bauchi** /ˈbaʊtʃɪ/ **1.** a state in north-east Nigeria; area 64,605 sq. km. (24,954 sq. miles); pop. (1991) 4,294,400. Known as the 'land of slaves', the Bauchi plateau was a former Fulani kingdom. Tin and columbite are mined and cattle, groundnuts, cereals, and cotton are the chief agricultural products. **2.** its capital; pop. (1981) 186,000. Founded in 1809, it was formerly named Yakoba. It grew rapidly with the demand for tin during World War I.

**Baurú** a city in the state of São Paulo, southern Brazil, 280 km. (175 miles) north-west of São Paulo; pop. (1990) 265,120.

**Bavaria** /bə'veɪrɪə/ (German **Bayern** /'baɪ3:n/) a state of southern Germany; area 70,553 sq. km. (27,251 sq. miles); pop. (1990) 11,221,000; capital, Munich. It was until 1918 a kingdom of the German empire. Watered by the Main and Danube rivers Bavaria is bounded to the south by the Bavarian Alps. The heartland of Bavaria, which has its own distinctive culture, is confined to the regions of Upper and Lower Bavaria. Industries are concentrated in the major cities of MUNICH and NUREMBERG. Forestry, agriculture, and tourism are also important.
**Bavarian** adj. & n.

**Bayamo** /bæ'jɑːməʊ/ a city on the Caribbean island of Cuba; pop. (est. 1986) 105,000. It is capital of the south-eastern province of Granma and was the focal point of resistance against Spain in the 1860s.

**Bayamón** /ˌbɑːjɑː'məʊn/ a city on the Caribbean island of Puerto Rico, on the River Bayamón; pop. (1990) 220,260. Founded in 1772, it is now a residential suburb of San Juan.

**Bayan Har** /'bɑːjən hɑː(r)/ a range of mountains forming an eastern offshoot of the Kunlun Shan on the edge of the Tibetan plateau in Qinghai province, west-central China. Its highest peak is Mt. Yagradaze (5,442 m., 17,854 ft.). The Yellow River (Huang He) rises in this range at an altitude of c.4,267 m. (14,000 ft.).

**Bayan Hongor** /'bɑːjən 'hʌŋgə(r)/ the capital of Bayan Hongor county in south-west Mongolia, on the Urd Tamir River; pop. (1990) 21,900. Mining, food processing, timber, and livestock are the chief industries.

**Bayan-Ölgiy** /'bɑːjən 'ʌlgɪ/ (also **Bayan Oelgi** or **Ölgiy**) the capital of Bayan-Ölgiy county in the Altai mountains of western Mongolia; pop. (1990) 29,400. It is an important centre of the livestock trade.

**Bay City** a port in east Michigan, USA, on the shore of Lake Michigan, at the mouth of the Saginaw River; pop. (1990) 38,936. Shipbuilding and the manufacture of electronics, petrochemicals, and vehicle parts are the chief industries.

**Bayern** /'baɪ3:n/ the German name for BAVARIA.

**Bayeux** /baɪ'j3:/ a market and tourist town in the department of Calvados, Basse-Normandie region, north-west France; pop. (1982) 15,240. It has a 13th-c. Gothic cathedral and the William the Conqueror Cultural Centre houses the famous Bayeux tapestry (an embroidery in fact) which depicts 58 scenes covering a length of 70 m. (230 ft.) telling the story of William of Normandy's conquest of England in 1066. Bayeux was the first town in Europe to be liberated by Allied Forces during World War II.

**Bay Islands** (Spanish **Islas de la Bahia**) a group of Caribbean islands lying c.48 km. (30 miles) north of the coast of Honduras; area 261 sq.

km. (100 sq. miles); pop. (1988) 22,060. Roatán, Guanaja, and Utila are the principal islands. Christopher Columbus landed on Guanaja in 1502 and throughout the 17th c. the islands were frequented by British pirates and logwood cutters. In 1850 Britain gained control of the islands under the terms of the Clayton–Bulwer Treaty, but in 1859 territorial rights were relinquished. The islands, which now form a department of Honduras, are dependent on tourism, fishing, fruit, and timber.

**Bay of Pigs** (also **Cochinos Bay**) a bay on the southern coast of the island of Cuba in the Caribbean Sea, the scene of an unsuccessful invasion attempt in April 1961 by US-backed Cuban exiles seeking to oust the Communist government of Fidel Castro.

**Bay of Plenty** a region of North Island, New Zealand stretching in a curve eastwards from the Coromandel Peninsula to Cape Runaway on the opposite side of the bay of the same name. Created in 1989, it comprises the districts of Tauranga, Western Bay of Plenty, Kawerau, Whakatane, Opotoki, and parts of Rotorua and Taupo; pop. (1991) 208,160.

**Bayonne** /bɑː'jɒn/ (anc. **Lapurdum**) a port in the department of Pyrénées-Atlantiques, part of the Basque region of south-west France, at the junction of the Adour and Nive rivers; pop. (1990) 41,850. In addition to exporting sulphur, phosphates, grain, and cement, it is a centre of the chemical and aeronautical industries. During the 16th and 17th c. it was noted for its cutlery and armaments, giving its name to the bayonet which was invented there.

**Bayonne** /beɪ'əʊn/ a city and petroleum-refining centre in north-east New Jersey, USA; pop. (1990) 61,444. It is connected to Staten Island, New York City, by the Bayonne Bridge.

**bayou** /'baɪʊ/ a term used on the gulf coast of the USA to describe a sluggish backwater or marshy offshoot of a river.

**Bayreuth** /'baɪrɔɪt, -'rɔɪt/ a town in Bavaria, southern Germany; pop. (1991) 72,780. The composer Richard Wagner (1813–83) made his home in Bayreuth from 1874 and is buried here. Festivals of his operas are held regularly in a theatre (Festspielhaus) specially built (1872–6) to house performances of Der Ring des Nibelungen. The Hungarian composer Franz Liszt (1811–86) and the novelist Jean Paul Richter (1763–1825) are also buried in Bayreuth. Textiles and cigarettes are local industries together with tourism.

**Bayswater** /'beɪzwɔːtə(r)/ a residential district of west London, England, between Paddington Station and the north side of Kensington Gardens. It is named after Baynard's Water the former name of the Westbourne which flows into the Serpentine.

**Baytown** a city in south-east Texas, USA, on Galveston Bay; pop. (1990) 63,850. It was a sawmill

75 BEBINGTON

town and Confederate shipyard before developing into an oil town after 1916.

**BC** *abbr.* British Columbia.

**Beach-la-Mar** /ˌbiːtʃləˈmɑː(r)/ an English-based Creole language spoken in the western Pacific.

**Beachy Head** /ˈbiːtʃɪ/ a high chalk cliff headland on the coast of East Sussex, southern England, between Seaford and Eastbourne; height, 162 m. (535 ft.). The French defeated a combined English and Dutch fleet in a naval encounter off Beachy Head in 1690.

**Beaconsfield** /ˈbekənzfiːld/ a town in Buckinghamshire, England, 44 km. (28 miles) north-west of London; pop. (1981) 10,900. The poet Edmund Waller (1606–87) and the statesman Edmund Burke both lived in Beaconsfield and are buried there. G. K. Chesterton, who also lived in the town from 1909 to 1935, wrote his *Father Brown* crime stories there. Beaconsfield gave Benjamin Disraeli his earl's title.

**Beagle Channel** /ˈbiːɡ(ə)l/ a channel in the islands of Tierra del Fuego at the southern tip of South America. It is named after the ship of Darwin's voyage.

**Beaker people** /ˈbiːkər/ (also **Beaker Folk**) a neolithic people of western Europe identified by wide-mouthed pottery vessels found in graves dating from the 3rd millenium BC.

**Beardmore Glacier** /ˈbɪədmɔː(r)/ one of the world's largest glaciers moving from the Queen Maude Mts. towards the Ross Sea Ice Shelf in Antarctica; length, 418 km. (260 miles). It was discovered by Ernest Shackleton in 1908.

**Béarn** /beɪˈɑː(r)n/ an ancient province of south-west France adjoining Gascony and now extending over the greater part of the modern French department of Pyrénées-Atlantique.

**Bearsden** /beɪrzˈden/ a residential town north-west of Glasgow, Scotland; pop. (1981) 27,200; Situated at the western end of the Roman Antonine Wall, it was the administrative centre of Bearsden and Milngavie District in Strathclyde Region (1975–96).

**Beas** /ˈbiːɑːs/ a river of northern India that rises in the Himalayas and flows through Himachal Pradesh to join the Sutlej River in the state of Punjab. It is the easternmost of the 'five rivers' that give the Punjab its name. In ancient times, called the Hyphasis, it marked the eastern limit of Alexander the Great's conquests.

**Beauce** /bəʊs/ a thinly populated flat limestone plain in the Ile-de-France region of north-central France. The chief town of this fertile wheat-producing area is Chartres.

**Beaufort Scale** /ˈbəʊfət/ a scale of wind speed ranging from 0 (calm) to 12 (hurricane). It is named after the English admiral Sir Francis Beaufort (1774–1857) who devised it.

**Beaufort Sea** a part of the Arctic Ocean lying to the north of Alaska and Canada. It is named after Sir Francis Beaufort who was hydrographer to the British navy (1829–55).

**Beaujolais** /ˈbəʊʒəˌleɪ/ a notable wine-making area in the Rhône-Alpes region of south-east France, on the north-eastern edge of the Massif Central, to the west of the River Saône and to the south of Mâcon. Formerly a part of the ancient province of Lyonnais, its chief town is Villefranche.

**Beaulieu** /ˈbjuːlɪ/ a village in Hampshire, southern England, on the edge of the New Forest, 9 km. (6 miles) south-west of Southampton; pop. (est. 1985) 1,200. The remains of a Cistercian abbey, founded here c. 1204 by King John, sits in the grounds of the former home of Lord Montagu of Beaulieu alongside the National Motor Museum.

**Beauly Firth** /ˈbjuːlɪ/ an inlet of the North Sea forming a continuation of the Moray Firth on the north-east coast of Scotland, to the west of Inverness. It is spanned by the Kessock Bridge which was completed in 1982.

**Beaumaris** /bəʊˈmɑːrəs/ a resort town on the Island of Anglesey, north Wales, at the northern end of the Menai Strait. There is a moated castle built by Edward I in 1295.

**Beaumes de Venise** /bəʊn də vəˈniːz/ a town in the department of Vaucluse, Provence-Alpes-Côte d'Azur region, south-east France. It is famous for its sweet dessert wines made from the Muscat grape.

**Beaumont** an industrial oil centre and inland port on the Neches River, eastern Texas, USA; pop. (1990) 114,323. It is linked to the Gulf of Mexico via coastal waterways that include the Sabine-Neches deep-water channel. A monument commemorates the discovery of the first major oilfield on the Gulf coastal plain in 1901.

**Beaune** /bəʊn/ a town in the department of Côte-d'Or, Burgundy, eastern France, centre of the Burgundy vineyards; pop. (1990) 22,170. There is a medieval infirmary that was used continuously from its founding in 1443 until 1971.

**Beauvais** /ˈbəʊveɪ/ (anc. **Caesaromagnus** or **Bellovacum**) a town in the department of Oise, in the Ile-de-France region of north-central France, to the north of Paris; pop. (1990) 56,280. The Gothic cathedral, begun in 1247 but never completed, is the tallest in France (68 m., 223 ft.) and has the highest choir in the world. Famous tapestry works established there by Louis XIV's Minister of Finance, Jean-Baptiste Colbert (1619–83), were moved to the Gobelins textile works in Paris in 1940.

**Beaverton** /ˈbiːvɜːrtən/ a city lying to the west of Portland, Oregon; pop. (1990) 53,310.

**Bebington** /ˈbebɪŋtən/ a borough town in Merseyside, England, on the Wirral Peninsula to the south of Birkenhead; pop. (1981) 64,170. The nearby model village of Port Sunlight was built in

1888 to house workers at the Lever Bros. (later Unilever) soap and margarine factory.

**Bec Abbey** /bek/ a Benedictine abbey at Le Bec-Hellouin in the Eure department, Haute-Normandie, northern France, 32 km. (20 miles) south-west of Rouen. Founded in 1034, Lanfranc and Anselm, who became archbishops of Canterbury in the 11th c., were both priors at Bec.

**Béchar** /beɪ'ʃɑːr/ an oasis town on the northern edge of the Sahara Desert, in a department of the same name, western Algeria. Established as a French military post in 1905, it is a centre for the coal, iron, copper, and magnesium mines of the surrounding area.

**Becharre** /bəˈxɑːr/ (also **Bcharre**) a town in the province of Ash Shamal, north Lebanon, 20 km. (12 miles) south-east of Tripoli. Situated at an altitude of 1,400 m. (4,600 ft.) in the Lebanon Mountains, the town stands amidst forest that is dominated by the Cedar of Lebanon which is the national emblem of Lebanon.

**Bechuanaland** /ˌbetʃʊˈɑːnəˌlænd/ the former name (until 1966) of BOTSWANA.

**Beckenham** /ˈbekənəm/ a residential town in Kent, south-east England, forming a suburb of Greater London. The famous Hospital of St. Mary of Bethlehem ('Bedlam') was moved here in 1931.

**Bedford** /ˈbedf(ə)d/ the county town of Bedfordshire in southern England, on the River Ouse; pop. (est. 1983) 89,200. John Bunyan wrote *The Pilgrim's Progress, Grace Abounding*, and other works while imprisoned in the county gaol from 1660 to 1672 for preaching without a licence. The town gives its name to Bedford cord, a tough woven fabric similar to corduroy. It is the site of the Cranfield Institute of Technology (1969).

**Bedfordshire** a county of southern England; area 1,235 sq. km. (477 sq. miles); pop. (1991) 514,200; county town, Bedford. The county is divided into four districts:

| District | Area (sq. km.) | Pop. (1991) |
|---|---|---|
| Luton | 43 | 167,300 |
| Mid Bedfordshire | 503 | 108,000 |
| North Bedfordshire | 476 | 132,100 |
| South Bedfordshire | 213 | 106,800 |

**Bedlam** /ˈbedləm/ the popular name of the Hospital of St. Mary of Bethlehem, founded as a priory in 1247 at Bishopsgate, London, and by the 14th c. a mental hospital. In 1675 a new hospital was built at Moorfields, and this in turn was replaced by a building in the Lambeth Road in 1815 (now the Imperial War Museum), and transferred to Beckenham in Kent in 1931.

**Bedlington** /ˈbedlɪŋt(ə)n/ a former coal-mining town in Northumberland, north-east England, that gives its name to a breed of terrier dog; pop. (est. 1985) 14,800.

**Bedouin** /ˈbeduɪn/ a nomadic Arab people of the deserts of Arabia and North Africa. Until the early 20th c. the Bedouin supplied pack camels to the caravan trade and provided military protection to caravan cities and trade routes. The decline in the use of camels to transport cargo and the development of independent nation states has forced the Bedouin to adopt a more settled way of life.

**Beds.** *abbr.* Bedfordshire.

**Bedworth** /ˈbedwərθ/ an industrial town south of Nuneaton in Warwickshire, central England; pop. (1981) 42,500.

**Beenleigh** /ˈbiːnli/ a town in Queensland, eastern Australia, on the Pacific Highway south of Brisbane; pop. (1991) 16,390. Sugar and rum are produced.

**Beersheba** /bɪəˈʃiːbə/ a town in southern Israel on the northern edge of the Negev Desert; pop. (1987) 114,600. In Old Testament times it marked the southern limit of Israelite territory (Judges 20; see also Daniel 3).

**Bei'an** /berˈɑːn/ a city in Heilongjiang province, north-east China, in the western foothills of the Xiao Hinggan Ling Mountains north of Harbin; pop. (1986) 439,000.

**Beihai** /berˈhaɪ/ a city and port in Guangxi autonomous region, southern China, on the Beibu Gulf south-east of Nanning; pop. (1986) 180,000.

**Beijing** /berˈdʒɪŋ/ the pinyin form of PEKING, capital of China.

**Beipiao** /berˈpjaʊ/ a town in Liaoning province, north-east China, situated to the west of Fuxin; pop. (1986) 605,000.

**Beira** /ˈbeərə/ a deep-water seaport on the east coast of Mozambique; pop. (1990) 299,300. It was founded in 1891 by the Portuguese Mozambique Company which administered that part of Africa until 1942. A railway, road, and oil-pipeline along the so-called **Beira Corridor** link landlocked Zimbabwe with the port of Beira.

**Beira** /ˈbeərə/ an historic region of north-central Portugal, stretching from the Serra da Estrela mountains to the Atlantic coast and comprising the three provinces of Beira Alta, Beira Baixo, and Beira Litoral.

**Beirut** /beəˈruːt/ the capital and chief port of Lebanon, on the Mediterranean Sea; pop. (1989) 1,500,000. A major commercial centre since Phoenician times, Beirut became famous under the Romans for its trade in linen and wine and for its school of Roman law. It was captured by the Arabs in AD 635, taken by the Crusaders in 1110, and from the early 16th c. controlled by the Druses under Ottoman Rule. In 1918 Beirut was captured by the French and two years later made capital of Lebanon under French mandate. Once a prominent financial and cultural centre, the city was ravaged by the civil war that began in 1975 and has driven away its thriving tourist industry. Beirut has four universities, is a free port, and small-scale industries continue.

**Beja** /'beɪʒə/ **1.** a district in the Baixo Alentejo of southern Portugal; area 10,240 sq. km. (3,955 sq. miles); pop. (1989) 173,200. **2.** its capital in south-east Portugal, midway between the Sado and Guadiana rivers; pop. (1981) 19,700. Known to the Romans as Pax Julia, it was the birthplace of King John I and King Manuel I.

**Béja** /beɪ'ʒə/ (anc.**Vacca**) a town in northern Tunisia, 90 km. (57 miles) west of Tunis; pop. (1984) 46,700. It is capital of a governorate of the same name.

**Bejaïa** /bə'dʒɑ:jə/ (formerly **Bougie** /bu:'ʒi:/) a port on the Mediterranean coast of north-east Algeria; pop. (1989) 124,000. Capital of the Vandals in the 5th c., the city was rebuilt by the Berbers in the 11th c. and was an important cultural and commercial centre. It later became a stronghold of the Barbary pirates and in the 20th c. developed as a seaport trading in oil, minerals, grain, and fruit.

**Bekaa** /bɪ'kɑ:/ (also **El Beqa'a**) a fertile valley in central Lebanon through which the Litani River flows NE–SW between the Lebanon and Anti-Lebanon mountains. The chief towns are Zahlé, Baalbek, and Hermel.

**Békéscsaba** /'beɪkeɪʃˌtʃɔ:bə/ the county town of Békés in south-east Hungary, on the Great Plain; pop.(1989) 71,000. It is an agricultural centre with textile, food-processing, and engineering industries. The Hungarian painter Mihály Munkácsy (1846–1900) served part of his apprenticeship here.

**Bel Air** /bel 'eə(r)/ a wealthy residential district of Los Angeles, southern California, USA, in the Santa Monica Mountains north of Westwood and west of Beverly Hills.

**Belarus** /belə'ru:s/, **The Republic of** the official long-form name for BELORUSSIA.

**Belau** /bə'laʊ/ (formerly **Palau**) a group of islands in the western Pacific Ocean, formerly held by Spain, Germany, and Japan, but part of the US Trust Territory of the Pacific Islands from 1947 until achieving independence as a self-governing state in 1994; area 488 sq. km. (188 sq. miles); pop. (1986) 13,870; official languages, English and Palauan; provisional capital, Koror (capital designate, Babelthuap). The group comprises 26 islands and over 300 small islets, the largest island being Babelthuap. The islands were the last to be held under UN Trusteeship and now maintain a compact of free association with the USA. The republic has a bicameral legislature comprising a Senate and a House of Delegates.

**Belaya** /'bjelæjə/ a river that rises in the southern Urals of Russia and flows 1,120 km. (700 miles) north-west through Bashkortostan and Tatarstan to meet the River Kama near Naberezhnyye Chelny.

**Belaya Tserkov** /ˌbjelæjə 'tsɜ:rkəf/ an industrial city in the Ukraine, 72 km. (45 miles) south of Kiev; pop. (1990) 200,500. It is a rail junction and centre of light industries.

**Belém** /be'lem/ (also **Pará** /pə'rɑ:/) a city and port at the mouth of the Amazon, 120 km. (75 miles) from the Atlantic, the chief commercial centre of northern Brazil and capital of the mineral-rich state of Pará; pop. (1991) 1,245,000. The Portuguese landed here in 1616 and established a colony that united with Brazil in 1775 and developed a prosperous trade in cacao, vanilla, cinnamon, and cassia. During the 19th c. rubber became an important export and the city grew towards a population of c. 100,000. It processes and exports rubber, nuts, timber, fish, and vegetable oils.

**Bélep Islands** /'beɪləp/ a group of islands forming a dependency to the north of the French overseas territory of New Caledonia in the south-west Pacific Ocean; area 70 sq. km. (27 sq. miles); pop. (1983) 686. The chief islands are Art, Pott, and Nienane.

**Belfast** /bel'fɑ:st/ the capital of Northern Ireland, a port at the mouth of the River Lagan where it flows into Belfast Lough; pop. (1991) 280,970. Chartered by King James in 1613, Belfast grew after the arrival of Huguenot linen weavers in 1685. After the Act of Union in 1800 it expanded into an industrial centre with world-famous shipyards. Queen's University was founded in 1849. Belfast became a city in 1888 and capital of Northern Ireland in 1920. The Port of Belfast has seven miles of quays approached by a deep-water channel. Engineering, particularly aircraft manufacture, is a major industry and there are numerous light industries.

**Belfort** /bel'fɔː(r)/ **1.** a department (Territoire de Belfort) in the Franche Comté region of eastern France; area 610 sq. km. (236 sq. miles); pop. (1990) 134,100. Outside the urban departments of the Paris Basin it is the smallest department in France. **2.** its capital on the River Savoureuse, commanding a strategic position in the Belfort Gap between the Jura and Vosges mountains; pop. (1990) 51,910. The city's symbol (which commemorates three sieges in 1814, 1815, and 1870) is a huge sandstone lion carved by Frédéric Bartholdi (1834–1904) sculptor of the Statue of Liberty in New York. The town has a system of fortifications established by Louis XIV's military engineer Vauban (1633–1707).

**Belgae** /'beldʒaɪ/ an Iron Age Celtic people of north-west Europe occupying part of ancient Gaul to the north of the Seine and Marne rivers. They were defeated by Julius Caesar in 57 BC.

**Belgaum** /'belgɔ:m/ an agricultural market and industrial city in the state of Karnataka, southern India, on the Goa–Bombay railway line; pop. (1991) 326,000.

**Belgian Congo** the former name (1908–60) of ZAIRE.

**Belgic** /'beldʒɪk/ a general term used to describe the Low Countries of north-west Europe.

## Belgium

/'beldʒəm/ (French **Belgique** /bel'ʒi:k/, Flemish **België** /'belgɪə/) official name **The Kingdom of Belgium** a coun-try in western Europe on the south shore of the North Sea,

bounded north by the Netherlands, south by France, and east by Germany and Luxembourg; area 30,540 sq. km. (11,796 sq. miles); pop. (1991) 9,978,700; official languages, Flemish and French; capital, Brussels. The largest cities are Brussels, Antwerp, Ghent, Charleroi, Liège, and Bruges. A low-lying coastal plain extends over the northern one-third of the country and in the south lies the heavily forested Ardennes plateau. The French lan-guage is spoken in the south (Wallonia), with pock-ets of German-speakers in the eastern Ardennes, while Flemish predominates in the north (Flanders). Engineering, oil-refining, and the manufacture of iron, steel, chemicals, textiles, and plastics are important industries. The country takes its name from the Belgae, a Celtic people con-quered by the Romans in the 1st c. BC. Prosperous in medieval times as a result of textile production and commerce, Belgium was on the border of French, Dutch, and Habsburg spheres of influence in the 16th–18th c. and, as a result, frequently the site of military operations. After falling at various times under the rule of Burgundy, Spain, Austria, France, and the Netherlands it gained formal independence in 1839 as a consequence of a nation-alist revolt that began in 1830, and Prince Leopold of Saxe-Coburg was elected as king. Occupied and devastated during both world wars, Belgium made a quick recovery after 1945, taking the first step towards European economic integration with the formation of the Benelux customs union with the Netherlands and Luxembourg in 1948. Belgium is a constitutional monarchy with a bicameral legis-lature comprising a Chamber of Deputies and a Senate. It is a member state of the European Union.

**Belgian** *adj. & n.*
The country is divided into nine provinces:

| Province | Area (sq. km.) | Pop. (1991) | Capital |
| --- | --- | --- | --- |
| Antwerp | 2,867 | 1,605,167 | Antwerp |
| Brabant | 3,358 | 2,245,890 | Brussels |
| Hainaut | 3,788 | 1,278,791 | Mons |
| Liège | 3,863 | 999,646 | Liège |
| Limburg | 2,422 | 750,435 | Hasselt |
| Luxembourg | 4,441 | 232,813 | Arlon |
| Namur | 3,666 | 423,317 | Namur |
| East Flanders | 2,982 | 1,335,793 | Ghent |
| West Flanders | 3,134 | 1,106,829 | Bruges |

**Belgorod** /'bjelgərət/ an industrial city on the North Donets River, 72 km. (45 miles) north of Kharkov, western Russia; pop. (1990) 306,000. The surrounding region has one of the world's largest deposits of iron ore and extensive areas of chalk and limestone which are used to manufacture cement and building materials.

**Belgrade** /bel'greɪd/ (Serbo-Croat **Beograd**) the capital of Serbia, at the junction of the River Sava with the Danube; pop. (1981) 1,455,000. Bel-grade occupies a strategic location on the trade route between central Europe and the Balkans. It was an important river port to the Romans who called it Singidinum and was occupied by Huns, Goths, Franks, and Bulgars before becoming capital of Serbia in the 12th c. In 1521 it fell to the Ottoman Turks who made it their leading fortress town in Europe and from 1929 to 1991 it was cap-ital of the Socialist Federal Republic of Yugoslavia. Its university was founded in 1860 and it has an outstanding national museum. Its industries in-clude oil refining, metal manufactures, textiles, chemicals, electrical goods, and machine tools.

**Belgravia** /bel'greɪvjə/ a district of London, England, to the south of Knightsbridge, laid out between 1825 and 1830 by the builder Thomas Cubitt (1788–1855) who was also responsible for the east front of Buckingham Palace. Matthew Arnold, Noël Coward, Charles Dickens, W. S. Gilbert, George Meredith, Margaret Oliphant, and A. C. Swinburne are some of the well known authors who have lived in Belgravia.

**Belitung** /bə'li:tɔ:ŋ/ (also **Billiton**) an Indonesian island in the Java Sea between Sumatra and Borneo; area 4,833 sq. km. (1,866 sq. miles); chief town, Tanjungpandan. Once an important source of tin, many of its people are descended from Chinese who came to work the mines which opened in 1851.

**Belize** /bə'li:z/ a country on the Caribbean coast of Central America bounded north by Mexico and west and south by Guatemala; area 22,965 sq. km. (8,867 sq. miles); pop. (1991) 190,792;

official language, English; capital, Belmopan. The chief settlements are Belize City, Orange Walk, Dangriga, and Corozal. Offshore cays and the second-longest barrier reef in the world protect shallow inshore waters which give way to a narrow fringe of mangrove forest that helps stabilize a coastline that is occasionally battered by hurric-anes. The coastal plain, swampy in the north, gradually gives way to more fertile flat land. In the south-west, a hilly backbone formed by the Maya Mountains rises to 1,121 m. (3,681 ft) at Victoria

Peak. Much of the interior is covered in hardwood forest that has in the past been cut over for mahogany, logwood, Spanish cedar, and rosewood, but today is being cleared in some areas for both small-scale farming and large-scale commercial plantations producing citrus, bananas, and sugar-cane. The climate is sub-tropical, tempered by trade winds, with rainfall varying from an annual average of 1,295 mm. in the south to 4,445 mm in the north. There is a dry season from December to June. Since the mid-1980s the country's natural environment and ancient Mayan ruins have formed the basis of a rapidly expanding eco-tourism industry. Frequented by pirates and settled by British logwood cutters in the 17th c., the area (as British Honduras) was proclaimed a Crown Colony in 1862. It adopted the name Belize in 1973, and in 1981 became an independent state within the Commonwealth. Guatemala has always claimed the territory on the basis of former Spanish treaties. It is governed by a bicameral National Assembly comprising a Senate and House of Representatives. **Belizean** *adj. & n.*
There are six districts in Belize:

| District | Area (sq. km.) | Pop. (1991) | Chief Town |
|---|---|---|---|
| Belize | 4,202 | 59,220 | Belize City |
| Cayo | 5,336 | 37,255 | Belmopan |
| Corozal | 1,859 | 28,500 | Corozal |
| Orange Walk | 4,735 | 30,260 | Orange Walk |
| Stann Creek | 2,175 | 17,910 | Dangriga |
| Toledo | 4,647 | 17,640 | Punta Gorda |

**Belize City** the largest town and chief port of Belize in Central America, at the mouth of the Belize River; pop. (1991) 46,000. It was the capital of Belize until 1970.

**Bellagio** /bəˈlɑːdʒiːəʊ/ a resort town on a promontory separating the two branches of Lake Como in Lombardy, northern Italy; pop. (1990) 3,050.

**Bellary** /bəˈlɑːriː/ an industrial city in north-east Karnataka, south-west India at the centre of an iron- and manganese-mining region; pop. (1991) 245,760.

**Bellevue** /belˈvjuː/ a city in the state of Washington, north-west USA, on Lake Washington, opposite Seattle to which it is linked by the Evergreen Floating Bridge; pop. (1990) 86,874. It is a largely residential city but produces medical and aerospace equipment in addition to electronic and computing products.

**Bellflower** /ˈbelflaʊər/ a city in the Los Angeles conurbation, to the north of Long Beach, southern California, USA; pop. (1990) 61,815.

**Belle-Ile** /belˈiːl/ (also **Belle-Ile-en-Mer**) a resort island in the Bay of Biscay off the Brittany coast of France; area 90 sq. km. (35 sq. miles); pop. (1980) 5,500. The chief town and port of entry is Le Palais. It is linked by ferry to Quiberon on the mainland.

**Belleville** /ˈbelviːl/ a town in Ontario, Canada, to the north of Lake Ontario between Ottawa and Toronto; pop. (1991) 62,700. It is a departure point for the rolling farmland of Quinte's Isle (Prince Edward County) to the south.

**Bellingham** /ˈbelɪŋəm/ an industrial city in north-west Washington state, USA, on Bellingham Bay, 29 km. (18 miles) south of the Canadian frontier; pop. (1990) 52,180. Named after Sir William Bellingham, the city was created in 1903 with the amalgamation of the adjoining settlements of New Whatcom and Fairhaven. Fishing, boat building, and paper making are important industries.

**Bellingshausen Sea** /ˈbelɪŋzˌhaʊz(ə)n/ a sea in the south-east Pacific, off the coast of Antarctica to the west of the Antarctic Peninsula and north of Ellsworth Land. It is named after the Russian Antarctic explorer Fabian von Bellingshausen (1778–1852) who was the first to circumnavigate the Antarctic continent during 1819–21.

**Bellinzona** /belɪntˈsəʊnə/ the capital of the canton of Ticino in southern Switzerland, in the valley of the Ticino River, east of Locarno; pop. (1990) 16,935.

**Belluno** /bəˈluːnəʊ/ the capital of Belluno province in the Venetia region of north-eastern Italy, at the junction of the Ardo and Piave rivers; pop. (1990) 35,860.

**Belmopan** /ˌbelməʊˈpæn/ the capital of Belize, Central America. Founded in 1970 in the interior of Belize, it is one of the smallest capital cities in the world; pop. (1991) 4,000.

**Belo Horizonte** /ˈbeləʊ ˌhɒrɪˈzɒnteɪ/ a city in eastern Brazil, capital of the state of Minas Gerais, situated at the centre of a rich mining and agricultural region; pop. (1991) 2,107,000. Built in 1895–7, it was Brazil's first planned modern city. Its industries include steel, vehicles, electric trains, textiles, and cement.

**Belorussia**
/ˌbeləʊˈrʌʃə/ (also
**Belarus, Byelarus,
Byelorussia**, or
**White Russia**) official name **The
Republic of
Belarus** an
independent republic
on the flat plains of

eastern Europe, bounded east by the Russian Federation, west by Poland, south by Ukraine, and north-west by Lithuania and Latvia; area 207,600 sq. km. (80,185 sq. miles); pop. (1990) 10,259,300; official language, Belorussian (an East Slavic language); capital, Minsk. The largest cities are Gomel, Vitebsk, Mogilev, Bobruysk, Grodno, and Brest. Belorussia, which has vast areas of marsh and peatland, is watered by the Dnieper River and its tributaries which include the Pripet, Neman, and Sozh rivers. Nearly half the country is farmed,

producing meat, dairy products, and flax. Manufactures include textiles, chemicals, vehicles, and
timber products. Settled by East Slavic tribes after
the 5th c., Belorussia was dominated from the 9th
to the 14th c. by Kiev before being absorbed into
the grand duchy of Lithuania. Merged with Poland
in 1569, it was subsequently annexed by Russia
during the partitions that took place in 1772, 1793,
and 1795. In 1921 western Belorussia was awarded
to Poland, the eastern and larger part becoming a
republic of the USSR. With the breakup of the
Soviet Union in 1991, Belorussia gained independence as a member of the Commonwealth of
Independent States.
**Belorussian** or **Belarussian** *adj. & n.*
Belorussia is divided administratively into the city
of Minsk and six regions (*oblasts*):

| Region | Area (sq. km.) | Pop. (1990) | Capital |
| --- | --- | --- | --- |
| Brest | 32,300 | 1,472,000 | Brest |
| Gomel | 40,400 | 1,674,300 | Gomel |
| Grodno | 25,000 | 1,179,100 | Grodno |
| Minsk | 40,800 | 1,590,300 | Minsk |
| Mogilev | 29,000 | 1,283,700 | Mogilev |
| Vitebsk | 40,100 | 1,423,000 | Vitebsk |

**Belovo** /bə'ləʊvəʊ/ an industrial city in west
Siberia, Russia, in the Kuznetsk Basin 88 km. (55
miles) north-west of Novokuznetsk; pop. (1989)
118,000. Coal mining, zinc smelting, and engineering are the chief industries.

**Belsen** /'bels(ə)n/ a village in Lower Saxony,
north-west Germany, which was the site of a Nazi
concentration camp in World War II.

**Beltsy** /'beltsi:/ (Romanian **Bălţi**) a city in
northern Moldova (Moldavia), on a tributary of
the Dniester; pop. (1990) 164,800.

**Benares** see VARANASI.

**Benbecula** /ben'bekjʊlə/ a flat boggy island
with a deeply indented coastline in the Western
Isles of Scotland between North and South Uist;
area 93 sq. km. (36 sq. miles). There are the
remains of medieval church sites at Balivanich and
Nunton.

**Bendery** /ben'dɜ:ri:/ the former Russian name
for TIGHINA in Moldova.

**Bendigo** /'bendɪɡəʊ/ a former gold-mining
town in the Central Uplands of the state of
Victoria, Australia; pop. (1991) 57,430. Originally
called Sandhurst, the town was renamed after a
local boxer who adopted the nickname of a well-
known English prize-fighter William Thompson
(1811–89). Although gold is no longer mined,
Bendigo now lies at the centre of a prosperous agricultural and wine-producing region.

**Benelux** /'benɪˌlʌks/ a collective name for
Belgium, the Netherlands, and Luxembourg, especially with reference to their economic co-
operation established in 1948.

**Benevento** /beɪneɪ'ventəʊ/ (anc.
**Beneventum**) the capital of the province of
Benevento in Campania, southern Italy, 57 km.
(32 miles) north-east of Naples; pop. (1990) 64,690.
Originally known as Maleventum (= ill wind), its
name was changed to Beneventum (= fair wind) by
the Romans who defeated Pyrrhus, King of Epirus,
near the town in 275 BC. The Strega liqueur is produced in Benevento.

**Bengal** /ben'ɡɔ:l/ a former province of British
India divided in 1947 into the predominantly
Hindu West Bengal, which became a state of India,
and the largely Muslim East Bengal, which became
part of East Pakistan and ultimately the independent nation of Bangladesh in 1971. The Bengali or
Bangla language is a descendant of Sanskrit,
written in a version of the Sanskrit Devanagari
script. It is spoken by some 125 million people and
is the official language of Bangladesh.
**Bengali** adj. & n.

**Bengal, Bay of** an arm of the Indian Ocean
bounded west by India and Sri Lanka, north by
Bangladesh, and east by Burma and Thailand. It
is separated from the Andaman Sea by the
Andaman and Nicobar Islands. Calcutta,
Madras, Chittagong, and Trincomalee are the
chief ports.

**Bengbu** /ben'bu:/ a city in Anhui province, eastern China, on the Huai River north-west of
Nanjing; pop. (1986) 623,000.

**Benghazi** /ben'ɡɑ:zɪ/ a Mediterranean port in
Cyrenaica, north-east Libya; pop. (1984) 485,000.
The Greeks founded the colony of Hesperides here
in the 7th c. BC. Later renamed Berenice after the
wife of Ptolemy III of Egypt, it was conquered by
Romans, Vandals, Arabs, Ottoman Turks, and
Italians before Libya gained full independence
in 1951. It was the co-capital (with Tripoli) of
Libya from 1951 to 1972. Benghazi is an administrative and commercial centre with diverse light
industries.

**Benguela** /ben'ɡwelə/ a port and railway terminal on the Atlantic coast of Angola, to the south
of Lobito; pop. (1983) 155,000. The Benguela railway line provides a link with the interior copper-
mining regions of Zambia and Zaire. The town has
food-processing plants.

**Benguela current** a cold ocean current that
flows northwards from Antarctica along the coast
of south-west Africa before meeting the warmer
equatorial current at a latitude of 15° S. Its waters
are rich in fish and plankton.

**Benha** /'benhə/ a city in northern Egypt, in the
Nile delta north of Cairo; pop. (1991) 133,000.

**Benidorm** /'benɪˌdɔ:m/ a popular
Mediterranean resort town in the province of
Alicante, eastern Spain, on the Costa Blanca; pop.
(1991) 74,900.

**Benin** /be'nɪn/ offi-
cial name **The
Republic of Benin**
a country of western
Africa, on the Gulf
of Guinea, between
Nigeria (east) and
Togo (west) with
Burkina and Niger to
the north; area

112,622 sq. km. (43,483 sq. miles); pop. (est. 1991)
4,800,000; official language, French; capital, Porto
Novo. Cotonou is the chief commercial and political centre of the country. A narrow coastal strip
with lagoons rises towards an inland plateau
covered with swamp and forest. The climate is tropical with two rainy seasons in the south during
April–July and October–November and a single
wet season in the north during June–October. The
economy is largely dependent on the export of
cotton, palm oil, cocoa, and petroleum. About 80
per cent of the population is engaged in subsistence
agriculture based on maize, sorghum, yams, rice,
beans, and cassava crops. Known as Dahomey, and
formerly a centre of the slave-trade, the country
was conquered by the French in 1893 and became
part of French West Africa. In 1960 it achieved full
independence and in 1975 adopted the name
Benin, the name of a former African kingdom (in
what is now southern Nigeria) that was powerful in
the 14th–17th c. and was famous for its bronze and
ivory sculptures. From 1972 to 1990 Benin was
ruled as a one-party state on Marxist-Leninist
lines. In 1990 multi-party politics were reintro-
duced and in 1991 Benin was the first mainland
African country to vote an incumbent president
out of power in a democratic election.
**Beninese** adj. & n.
Benin is divided into six provinces:

| Province | Area (sq. km.) | Pop. (est.1987) | Capital |
| --- | --- | --- | --- |
| Atakora | 31,200 | 622,000 | Natitingou |
| Borgou | 51,000 | 630,000 | Parakou |
| Zou | 18,700 | 731,000 | Abomey |
| Mono | 3,800 | 610,000 | Lokossa |
| Atlantique | 3,200 | 909,000 | Cotonou |
| Ouémé | 4,700 | 806,000 | Porto Novo |

**Benin City** the capital of the state of Edo in
southern Nigeria; pop. (1981) 183,000. Early trade
with Portuguese was in slaves and ivory; now Benin
City is a market for palm oil and rubber. It is also a
centre of handicrafts. Bronze portrait busts, some
dating from the 13th c. are among Africa's finest
works of art.

**Beni Suef** /ˌbeni 'sweɪf/ the capital of a province of the same name in the Nile Valley, Egypt, 130
km. (82 miles) south of Cairo; pop. (1991) 174,000.
It has cotton mills and sugar refineries.

**Ben Macdhui** /ben mək'duːɪ/ a peak in the
Cairngorm Mountains of Scotland. At 1,309 m.

(4,296 ft.), it is the second-highest mountain in the
British Isles.

**Ben Nevis** /ben 'nevɪs/ the highest mountain in
the British Isles rising to 1,343 m. (4,406 ft.) near
Fort William in western Scotland. At its summit,
amidst massive boulders, are the ruins of an
observatory built in 1883 and in use until 1904.

**Benoni** /bə'nəʊnɪ/ a city in the South African
province of Transvaal; pop. (1980) 206,800. Engineering and gold mining are the main industries.

**Benue** /beɪ'nuːɪ/ **1.** a state in central Nigeria;
pop. (1991) 2,780,400. **2.** a tributary of the Niger
River in west Africa that rises in Cameroon and
flows north then south-west into central Nigeria
where it meets the Niger near Okoja. **3.** a 180,000-
hectare (444,450-acre) national park in northern
Cameroon designated in 1968. It comprises rugged
ranges of hills that rise to the 1,100-m. (3,609-ft.)
peak of Mount Garoua.

**Benxi** /ben'ʃi:/ an industrial city in the province
of Liaoning, north-east China, south-east of
Shenyang; pop. (1990) 920,000. It lies in a coal-
mining area and has major iron and steel industries.

**Beograd** SEE BELGRADE.

**Berat** /beɪ'rɑːt/ (anc. **Antipatria** and later
**Pulcheriopolis**) the capital of a district of the
same name in south-central Albania, at the foot of
Mt. Tomori; pop. (1990) 43,800. It is a market town
for the surrounding area which produces wine,
tobacco, and vegetables.

**Berber** /'bɜːbə(r)/ (Berber **Tamazirght**) a
Muslim Hamito-Semitic people of the Maghreb
region of North Africa, now largely to be found in
the Atlas Mountains of Morocco and Algeria.
Speaking a language which they call Amzirght, the
Berbers have a largely oral culture.

**Berbera** /'bɜːbə(r)ə/ a port on the north coast of
Somalia, until 1941 the winter capital of British
Somaliland; pop. 65,000.

**Berbice** /bɜː'biːs/ a river in Guyana, South
America, that rises in the Guiana Highlands and
flows 480 km. (300 miles) north to meet the
Atlantic at New Amsterdam.

**Berchtesgaden** /'berktəsˌgɑːd(ə)n/ a town in
south-east Bavaria, southern Germany, in the
Bavarian Alps, 16 km. (10 miles) south of Salzburg.
Salt has been continuously mined in the area since
1517. Nearby is the site of a villa built as a retreat
for Adolf Hitler.

**Berdyansk** /bɜː'djɑːnsk/ a port in Ukraine, on
the north coast of the Sea of Azov; pop. (1990)
134,000. It was known as Osipenko from 1930 to
1958.

**Berenice** /ˌbɜːrə'niːsɪ/ a small port and military
town on the Red Sea coast of Egypt. Founded in
275 BC by Ptolemy II who named it after his
mother, Berenice flourished as a trading post until
the 5th c. AD. Nearby are the ruins of the Temple of
Seramis.

**Berezniki** /bjɜːrˈjɔːznjɪkɪ/ an industrial city in the west-central Urals of Russia, on the River Kama; pop. (1990) 201,000. Nearby deposits of sodium, potassium, and magnesium salts make this one of Russia's leading centres of the chemical industry.

**Bergama** /bərˈɡɑːmə/ (anc. **Pergamum**) a market town in the province of Izmir, western Turkey; pop. (1990) 101,421. Nearby are the ruins of ancient Pergamum which was capital of the Mysian kingdom of Pergamum and later the Roman province of Asia. The city which developed under Eumenes II (197–159 BC) was famous for its library which rivalled the great collection of manuscripts at Alexandria. The city gave its name to parchment which was used as a writing surface here as early as the 2nd c. BC.

**Bergamo** /ˈbɜːɡəˌməʊ/ the capital of the province of Bergamo in Lombardy, northern Italy, at the foot of the Bergamo Alps; pop. (1990) 117,890. The upper walled town contains historic buildings; the lower town is commercial and industrial. The town gives its name to an oily perfume (bergamot) extracted from the rind of the fruit of the citrus tree *Citrus bergamia*, a dwarf variety of the Seville orange tree. Gaetano Donizetti (1797–1848) the Italian composer spent his whole life in Bergamo.

**Bergen** /ˈbɜːɡən/ a seaport and capital of Hordaland county in south-west Norway; pop. (1991) 213,344. Founded in 1070 by King Olaf Kyrre it has developed into Norway's third-largest city as an important centre of the fishing and North Sea oil industries. It was the birthplace of the composer Edward Grieg (1843–1907).

**Bergen** see MONS.

**Bergerac** /ˈbɜːʒɜːrɑːk/ **1.** a district of the Dordogne valley in south-west France, dominated by vineyards and orchards. **2.** a town in the Dordogne department of Aquitaine, south-west France, on the Dordogne River; pop. (1990) 27,890. Famous for its truffles and wine (including the sweet Monbazillac), it is the chief town of southern Périgord.

**Bergisches Land** /ˈbɜːɡɪʃəs/ a region of North Rhine-Westphalia, western Germany, on the east bank of the Rhine between Düsseldorf and Cologne (Köln). Formerly the duchy of Berg, the chief town is Bergisch Gladbach.

**Bergisch Gladbach** /ˌbɜːɡɪʃˈɡlɑːtbɑːk/ an industrial city in North Rhine-Westphalia, western Germany, north-east of Cologne; pop. (1991) 104,000. It has electrical, metal, and paper industries.

**Bergstrasse** /ˈbɜːɡstrɑːsə/ (Latin **Strata Montana**) a region of Hesse and Baden-Württemberg, Germany, in the upper Rhine valley, stretching from Darmstadt to Heidelberg. It is a region of fruit, wine, and vegetables.

**berg wind** /bɜːɡ/ a dry wind that blows from the interior to the coastal districts of South Africa and Namibia, particularly during the winter season.

**Bering Glacier** /ˈbeərɪŋ/ a glacier in the Chugach-St. Elias Mountains, southern Alaska. It is the largest glacier in North America.

**Bering Sea** /ˈbeərɪŋ/ an arm of the north Pacific lying between Siberia and Alaska and bounded to the south by the Aleutian Islands. It is linked to the Arctic Ocean via the Bering Strait and Chukchi Sea, and takes its name from the Danish explorer Vitus Bering (1681–1741) who led several Russian expeditions to discover whether Asia and North America were connected by land. Bering died after being shipwrecked on an island (later named Bering Island) in the Russian Komandorskie group.

**Berkeley** /ˈbɜːrklɪ/ an educational and industrial city in central California, USA, on San Francisco Bay north of Oakland; pop. (1990) 102,724. First settled in 1841 and named after the Irish philospher George Berkeley, Bishop of Cloyne, it is the principal campus of the University of California (1873). It has chemical, pharmaceutical, metal, and food industries.

**Berkhamsted** /ˈbɜːkəmsted/ a town in Hertfordshire, south-east England, in the Chiltern Hills; pop. (1981) 16,900. There are remains of a castle in which Chaucer lived. It was the birthplace of the poet William Cowper (1731–1800).

**Berks.** /bɑːks/ *abbr.* Berkshire.

**Berkshire** /ˈbɑːkʃɪə(r)/ (also **Royal Berkshire**) an inland county of southern England; area 1,259 sq. km. (486 sq. miles); pop. (1991) 716,500; county town, Reading. The county is divided into six districts:

| District | Area (sq. km.) | Pop.(1991) |
| --- | --- | --- |
| Bracknell Forest | 109 | 93,800 |
| Newbury | 705 | 136,400 |
| Reading | 40 | 122,600 |
| Slough | 28 | 98,600 |
| Windsor and Maidenhead | 198 | 128,700 |
| Wokingham | 179 | 136,300 |

**Berlin** /bɜːˈlɪn/ the capital of Germany; pop. (1991) 3,446,000. Founded in the 13th c. it was a seat of the royal Hohenzollerns, capital of Brandenburg, then capital of Prussia. From World War II until the reunification of Germany in 1990 it was divided into two parts: West Berlin (a state of the Federal Republic of Germany, forming an enclave within the German Democratic Republic) and East Berlin (the zone of the city that was Soviet-occupied at the end of the war, and later became capital of the German Democratic Republic). Despite blockade by the Communists, West Berlin was successfully supplied by a large-scale Allied 'airlift' in 1949. A fortified wall separating the two sectors was erected in 1961 by the Communist authorities to curb the flow of refugees to the West, and many people were killed or wounded while attempting to cross. Long regarded as a symbol of the East–West division of Europe, it was opened in November 1989 after the collapse of the Communist regime in East Germany, and subsequently dismantled. Berlin is a commercial, educational, and industrial centre. It has three airports, two universities (1810, 1946), the Academy of Sciences (1700), and numerous museums, including the Pergamum, art galleries, two opera houses, symphony orchestras and theatres, a famous zoo, and many historic buildings. Its diverse industries include chemicals, electronic and electrical equipment, machinery, textiles, and publishing.

**Bermejo** /bɜ:ˈmeɪhəʊ/ a river of South America that rises in northern Argentina and flows c. 1,045 km. (650 miles) south-eastwards to join the Paraguay River on the frontier with Paraguay opposite Pilar.

**Bermuda**
/bɜ:ˈmju:də/ (also **Bermuda Islands** or **Bermudas**, formerly **Somers Islands**) a dependent territory of the UK comprising a group of about 150 small islands in the

western Atlantic off the coast of North Carolina, USA; area 53 sq. km. (20.5 sq. miles); pop. (est. 1988) 58,100; official language, English; capital, Hamilton. The seven main islands are mostly linked by bridges to form a single cluster 39 km. (24 miles) long and averaging less than 1.6 km. (1 mile) wide. The climate is subtropical with high winds often blowing during December–April. In addition to tourism, fishing, international finance and insurance, there are light industries producing paint, perfume, and furniture. The islands were sighted early in the 16th c. by the Spaniard, Juan Bermúdez, from whom they take their name, but remained uninhabited until 1609 when an English expedition, on its way to Virginia, was shipwrecked there; its leader Sir George Somers, later returned from Virginia to claim the islands for Britain. King James I granted a charter to the Virginia Company and in 1684 the government of Bermuda passed to the British Crown. It is Britain's oldest colony. Granted internal self-government in 1968, the islands are governed by an executive prime minister and a bicameral legislature comprising a Senate and House of Assembly. The UK sovereign is represented by a Governor.
**Bermudian** *adj. & n.*

**Bermuda Triangle** the name given to an area of the western Atlantic between Bermuda and Florida, credited since the mid-19th c. with a number of unexplained disappearances of ships and aircraft.

**Berne** /beən/ (also **Bern**) a city on the River Aar, founded in 1191 and the capital of Switzerland

since 1848; pop. (1990) 134,620. It is the administrative centre of Switzerland and has national museums and libraries. The 'old town', which is largely unspoilt, has medieval and 18th c. buildings. Berne has light industries including watch-making and tourism. It is the headquarters of the Universal Postal Union which was founded in 1874.

**Bernese Alps** /ˈbɜ:ni:z/ (German **Berner Alpen**) a northern range of the central Alps in the Swiss cantons of Bern and Valais. It is divided into the West Bernese Alps, a ridge running parallel to the Rhône valley from Lake Geneva to the Gemmi Pass, and the East Bernese Alps or Bernese Oberland, which forms the main group of the Bernese range. Finsteraarhorn (4,274 m., 14,022 ft.) is the highest peak, although the most prominent mountains are the Jungfrau and the Eiger. The Aletsch glacier north of the Rhône is one of the largest in Europe.

**Bernkastel** /ˈbɜ:nkəstel/ a small town in the Rhineland-Palatinate, Germany, north-east of Trier, in an area renowned for its wines. It is linked to the town of Kues by a bridge over the Mosel River. Bernkastel has many half-timbered houses, while Kues owes its fame to the Gothic St. Nikolaus Hospital endowed in 1447 by the cardinal-philosopher Nicolaus von Kues.

**Berry** /ˈberɪ/ a former province of central France, now part of Centre region, centred around the city of Bourges.

**Berry Islands** a group of islands in the Bahamas, extending in an arc northwards from Andros Island; area 31 sq. km. (12 sq. miles); pop. (1990) 634.

**Bertoua** /bɜ:ˈtʊə/ the administrative centre of Est province in Cameroon; pop. (est. 1984) 22,000. It is also a centre of the timber industry.

**Berwickshire** /ˈberɪkʃɪə(r)/ a former county of Scotland and from 1975 to 1996 a district in the Borders Region; area 907 sq. km. (350 sq. miles); pop. (1991) 18,781. Its chief town is Duns.

**Berwick-upon-Tweed** /ˈberɪk/ a town at the mouth of the River Tweed in the county of Northumberland, north-east England, 5 km. (3 miles) south of the Scottish border; pop. (1981) 13,000. A fortified town held alternately by England and Scotland for centuries until it became a neutral town in 1551. From that date until 1746 it was mentioned separately in Acts of Parliament.

**Besançon** /bezãˈsɔ̃/ (anc. **Besontium**) the capital of the department of Doubs in the Franche-Comté region of north-east France, on the River Doubs; pop. (1990) 119,190. The world's first factory producing artificial fibres was established here in 1890. It was the birthplace of the French author Victor Hugo (1802–85) and the chemists Auguste and Louis Lumière who invented the cine camera in 1893 and a process of colour photography. It has textile and watch-making industries, and a world-famous 'watch school'.

**Beskids** /'beskɪdz/ a group of mountains in the western Carpathians, on the frontier between Poland and Slovakia. The highest peak is Babia Góra (1,725 m., 5,659 ft.).

**Bessarabia** /ˌbesə'reɪbɪə/ a region in eastern Europe between the Dniester and Prut rivers. It chose to become part of Romania in 1918 but was forced to cede to the Soviet Union in 1940. Most of it now forms part of the Republic of Moldova (Moldavia), the remainder is in the Ukraine. **Bessarabian** adj. & n.

**Bethesda** /bə'θezdə/ a residential suburb in central Maryland, USA, to the north of Washington DC; pop. (1990) 62,936. The National Library of Medicine has the world's largest biomedical library.

**Bethlehem** /'beθlɪˌhem/ (Arabic **Bayt Lahm**) a small town 8 km. (5 miles) south of Jerusalem in the Israeli-occupied West Bank of the Jordan, first mentioned in Egyptian records of the 14th c. BC; pop. (est. 1980) 14,000. The native city of King David and reputed birthplace of Jesus Christ, it contains a church built by Constantine in 330 over the supposed site of Christ's birth. St. Jerome lived and worked in Bethlehem from 384, and it became a monastic centre.

**Bethlehem** a city in east Pennsylvania, USA, on the Lehigh river; pop. (1990) 71,428. Founded by members of the Protestant Moravian sect in 1741, the city is famous for its steel products and its music festivals.

**Beverley** the administrative centre of Humberside in north-east England, 12 km. (8 miles) north of Hull; pop. (1981) 19,690.

**Beverly Hills** /'bevəlɪ/ an affluent and largely residential city in southern California, surrounded by the city of Los Angeles; pop. (1990) 31,970. It gained city status in 1913 after which it became famous as the home of Hollywood film stars.

**Bexley** /'beksli/ a borough of Outer London, England, comprising the south-east London suburbs of Bexley, Crayford, Erith, and part of Sidcup; pop. (1991) 211,200. Erith and Crayford are industrial centres with engineering and chemical works, and miscellaneous light industries. At Bexley Heath is a house built for the poet William Morris (1834–96) by Philip Webb.

**Béziers** /'beɪzjeɪ/ (Latin **Julia Septimania Biterae**) a town in the department of Hérault, Languedoc-Roussillon, southern France, on the River Orb; pop. (1990) 72,360. It is the centre of the wine and spirit trade in the Languedoc.

**Bhadgaon** /'bætgaʊn/ (also **Bhatgaon** or **Bhaktapur**) a town and Hindu religious centre in central Nepal, on the Hanumante River, 12 km. (8 miles) east of Kathmandu; pop. (1981) 48,500. Situated at an altitude of 1,220 m. (4,000 ft.) above sea-level, the town is noted for its temples and royal palace.

**Bhadravati** /bəd'rɑːvəti:/ an industrial town in Karnataka, south-west India, south-east of Shimoga on the edge of the Baba Bhudan Hills; pop. (1991) 149,130. It has iron and steel and paper industries.

**Bhagalpur** /'bɑːgəlˌpʊə/ a market and administrative city in the state of Bihar, north-east India, on the Ganges; pop. (1991) 261,855.

**Bhamo** /'bɑːməʊ/ a market town in the state of Kachin, north-east Burma, at the head of navigation on the Irrawaddy River.

**Bharat** /'bərət/ the Hindi name for INDIA.

**Bharatpur** /'bərətˌpʊər/ a town in Rajasthan, north-west India, 56 km. (35 miles) west of Agra; pop. (1991) 156,840. It was capital of a former state of the same name. Its industries manufacture railway equipment, glass, and handicrafts. There is a sanctuary for migratory birds nearby.

**Bharuch** /bə'rəʊtʃ/ (also **Bharoch** or **Broach**) a port in Gujarat, western India, at the mouth of the Narmada River; pop. (1991) 138,250.

**Bhatinda** /bə'tɪndə/ a town in Punjab state, north-west India, situated to the south of Amritsar; pop. (1991) 159,110.

**Bhatpara** /bət'pɑːrə/ an industrial town in West Bengal, eastern India on the Hooghly River, once famous as a seat of Sanskrit learning, now a jute-manufacturing centre; pop. (1991) 304,300.

**Bhavnagar** /baʊ'nʌgər/ an industrial port on the Gulf of Cambay in the state of Gujarat, western India; pop. (1991) 400,640. It manufactures building materials and metal products. It was the capital of the former Rajput princely state of Bhavnagar.

**Bhils** /bɪlz/ an indigenous people of Rajasthan in western India, comprising nearly 40 per cent of the tribal population of that area. Noted for their skills in archery, their name is derived from the word bil (= bow).

**Bhiwandi** /bɪ'wɑːndɪ/ a city in Maharashtra, western India, north-east of Bombay; pop. (1991) 391,670.

**Bhiwani** /bɪ'wɑːni:/ a town in Haryana, northern India, west of Delhi; pop. (1991) 121,450.

**Bhopal** /bəʊ'pɑːl/ an industrial city in central India, the capital of the state of Madhya Pradesh; pop. (1991) 1,064,000. The city is said to have derived its name from its 11th-c. founder Raja Bhoj who created lakes by building dams or pals. It has heavy electrical equipment industries. In December 1984 leakage of poisonous gas from an American-owned pesticide factory caused the death of about 2,500 people and thousands suffered injury in the world's worst industrial disaster.

**Bhubaneswar** /ˌbu:bə'neʃwər/ the capital of the state of Orissa in east India, south of the Mahanadi River; pop. (1991) 412,000. It is noted for its Hindu temples of which it is said there were once 7,000. Of the 500 temples that remain, the great Lingaraj Temple dedicated to Bhubaneswar

('Lord of the Three Worlds') is one of the finest in India. Nearby are the ancient Udayagiri and Khandagiri Bhuddist and Jain caves. It has an agricultural and technological university.

**Bhusawal** /buːˈsɑːv(ə)l/ a town and railway junction with large workshops in Maharashtra, northern India, on the Tapti River east of Jalgaon; pop. (1991) 159,460.

**Bhutan** /buːˈtɑːn/ (Bhutanese **Druk-Yul**) official name **The Kingdom of Bhutan** a small independent kingdom, a protectorate of the Republic of India, lying on the south-eastern slopes

of the Himalayas where it is bordered on the north by Tibet and on the south, east, and west by India; area 46,620 sq. km. (18,000 sq. miles); pop. (est. 1991) 700,000; official language, Dzongkha; capital, Thimphu. Lofty mountain peaks running north to south and rising to heights in excess of 7,315 m. (24,000 ft.) in the north are separated by deep valleys. Over 90 per cent of the population is engaged in subsistence farming, growing rice, vegetables, and fruit. Nepalis who arrived in the late 19th and early 20th c. farm the southern foothill regions, while the Sharchop people of early Indian origin live in the east, and the Ngalops of Tibetan stock are mostly found in the northern two-thirds of the country. Buddhism, which was introduced from Tibet in the 8th c., has strongly influenced the political history of Bhutan which was consolidated as one country by a Tibetan lama in the 17th c. An hereditary monarchy replaced religious rule in 1907 and in 1910 a treaty was signed by which Bhutan agreed to be guided by Britain in its foreign affairs. There are no political parties in this constitutional monarchy which is ruled by the King and a Council of Ministers. **Bhutanese** *adj. & n.*

**Bia** /ˈbɪə/ a national park in western Ghana protecting the headwaters of the Tawya, Panabo, and Sukusuku rivers. It was designated a forest reserve in 1935 and a park in 1974.

**Biafra** /bɪˈæfrə/ a state proclaimed in 1967 when part of eastern Nigeria, inhabited chiefly by the Ibo people, sought independence from the rest of the country. In the ensuing civil war the new state's troops were overwhelmed by numerically superior forces, and by 1970 it had ceased to exist. **Biafran** *adj. & n.*

**Biafra, Bight of,** an eastern bay of the Gulf of Guinea extending from the mouth of the River Niger to Gabon.

**Białystok** /bjɑːˈwɪstɒk/ an industrial city and capital of a province of the same name in north-

east Poland, on the Podlasie plain; pop. (1990) 270,570. Largely destroyed during World War II, it has subsequently developed into the largest city in north-eastern Poland. Engineering and the manufacture of textiles and chemicals are the main industries.

**Biarritz** /bɪəˈrɪts/ a seaside resort and fishing port in Pyrénées-Atlantique department, Aquitaine, south-west France, on the Bay of Biscay; pop. (1990) 28,890. It became a fashionable resort in the 1850s after Napoleon III's wife Eugénie built a villa there.

**Bible Belt** a region of the southern and central US, including Arkansas, Oklahoma, Texas, Tennessee, and parts of Kentucky noted for its religious fundamentalism and its Bible salesmen.

**Bicester** /ˈbɪstər/ a market town in Oxfordshire, England, 21 km. (13 miles) north of Oxford, on the edge of the Vale of Aylesbury; pop. (est. 1984) 17,000. Nearby is the site of the Roman town of Alchester, on the line of Akeman Street.

**Bideford** /ˈbɪdəˌfə(r)d/ a port and resort town on the Bristol Channel in the county of Devon, south-west England, at the mouth of the River Torridge; pop. (1981) 13,000. Charles Kingsley is said to have written part of *Westward Ho!* while staying here in 1854.

**Biel** /biːl/ (French **Bienne** /bjen/) a town in Bern canton, west Switzerland, at the foot of the Jura Mountains, on the River Schüss near Lake Biel; pop. (1990) 52,000. It is a watch-making centre.

**Bielefeld** /ˈbiːləˌfelt/ an industrial city in North Rhine-Westphalia, western Germany, near the Teutoburg Forest, east of Münster; pop. (1991) 322,130. Its industries include textiles, machinery, and glass.

**Bielsko-Biała** /ˌbjelˈʃkəʊ ˈbjaʊə/ (German **Bielitz** /ˈbiːlɪts/) the capital of the province of Bielskie in southern Poland; pop. (1990) 181,280. The chief industries are engineering and the manufacture of textiles and vehicles.

**Bienne** see BIEL.

**Big Bend National Park** a national park with dramatic canyons in the desert lands to the north of the Rio Grande in southern Texas, USA. Established in 1935, the park extends to 299,748 hectares (740,118 acres). In 1975 fossil remains of the pterosaur, the largest flying creature ever known, were discovered here.

**Bihar** /bɪˈhɑː(r)/ a state in north-east India, bounded north by Nepal, east by West Bengal, south by Orissa, and west by Uttar Pradesh and Madhya Pradesh. It has many coal-mines and steel plants. Wheat and rice are grown but food also has to be imported; area 173,877 sq. km. (57,160 sq. miles); pop. (1991) 86,338,850; capital, Patna. **Bihari** *adj. & n.*

**Bihari** /bɪˈhɑːrɪ/ a group of three closely related languages, descended from Sanskrit, spoken principally in Bihar. The three languages are Bhojpuri with 20 million speakers in western Bihar and eastern Uttar Pradesh, Maithili with 15 million speakers in northern Bihar and Nepal, and Magahi with 5 million speakers in central Bihar.

**Bigorre** /bɪˈgɔː(r)/ a mountainous district of the Pyrenees in south-west France, centred on the department of Hautes-Pyrénées whose capital is the town of Tarbes, but whose most famous location is the pilgrimage centre of Lourdes.

**Biisk** see BIYSK.

**Bijagós, Ilhas dos,** the Portuguese name for the BISSAGOS ISLANDS.

**Bijapur** /bɪˈdʒɑːpər/ a Muslim town in Karnataka, south-west India; pop. (1991) 193,040. The Gol Gumbaz tomb of Adil Shah has the world's second-largest dome unsupported by pillars.

**Bikaner** /bɪkəˈneə(r)/ a walled city in the state of Rajasthan, north-west India, on the edge of the Thar Desert; pop. (1991) 415,000. Once capital of the Rajput state of Bikaner and an important trading post on the great caravan trade routes, it was merged with Rajasthan in 1949. The city is noted for its textile products and its camels which are bred locally.

**Bikini** /bɪˈkiːnɪ/ an atoll in the Marshall Islands in the Pacific where the US tested atom bombs from 1946 to 1958; area 5.2 sq. km. (2 sq. miles). The island gives its name to a two-piece swimsuit for women.

**Bilaspur** /bəˈlɑːspʊ(ə)r/ a market and administrative town in Madhya Pradesh, central India, north of Raipur; pop. (1991) 233,570.

**Bilbao** /bɪlˈbɑːəʊ/ a seaport and capital of the Basque Province of Vizcaya in northern Spain, on the Nervión estuary; pop. (1991) 372,200. It stands at the centre of a large industrial and coal-mining area. Greater Bilbao includes all the towns between Basauri and Galdakao. For centuries a wool port for Castile, Bilbao is now Spain's largest port as well as a major centre for oil-refining and ship-building. The city gives its name to the Bilbao sword noted for the temper and elasticity of its blade.

**billabong** /ˈbɪləˌbɒŋ/ an Australian term of Aboriginal origin for the branch of a river that forms a backwater or a stagnant pool.

**Billings** /ˈbɪlɪŋz/ a city in Montana, USA, on the west bank of the Yellowstone River; pop. (1990) 81,150. Built by the Northern Pacific Railway, it was given the name of the railroad president, Frederick K. Billings. It is the largest city in the state and a major distribution point for Wyoming and Montana strip-mines. It has oil-refining and food-processing industries.

**Billingsgate** /ˈbɪlɪŋzˌgeɪt/ a fish market near London Bridge, London, England, on the site of a Roman river-wall. Dating from the 16th c. it has long been known for the invective traditionally ascribed to its fish-porters.

**Billiton** See BELITUNG.

**Billund** /ˈbɪlʌnt/ a small town in central Jutland, Denmark, site of the 'Legoland' factory which produces the world famous plastic bricks for children and Legoland Park (1968); pop. (1990) 5,170.

**Binche** /bɪnʃ/ a small town in the province of Hainaut, Belgium, 16 km. (10 miles) east of Mons; pop. (1991) 32,840. It is famous for its pre-Lent carnival feast that may be the origin of the English word 'binge'.

**Binga** /ˈbɪŋə/, **Mount** the highest mountain in Mozambique, rising to a height of 2,436 m. (7,992 ft.) near the border with Zimbabwe in Manica province.

**Bingerville** /ˈbɪŋɜːvɪl/ a town in southern Ivory Coast, east of Abidjan. It was capital of the French Ivory Coast from 1900 to 1935. It has an agricultural research centre.

**Binghamton** /ˈbɪŋəmtən/ a city in southern New York state, USA, at the junction of the Chenango and Susquehanna rivers; pop. (1990) 53,000. The opening of the Chenango Canal in 1837 made it an important link between the Pennsylvania coalfields and the Erie Canal. Shoes and electronic products are the main industries.

**Binzhou** /bɪnˈdʒəʊ/ a city in Shandong province, eastern China, on the Yellow River north-east of Jinan; pop. (1986) 186,000.

**Bío-Bío** /ˈbiːəʊ ˈbiːəʊ/ a South American river that rises in the Andes on the Chile–Argentina frontier and flows 352 km. (220 miles) north-west to meet the Pacific near Concepción.

**Bioko** /bɪˈəʊkəʊ/ an island of Equatorial Guinea, in the eastern part of the Gulf of Guinea; area 2,017 sq. km. (779 sq. miles). Its chief town is Malabo (capital of Equatorial Guinea) and its main products are coffee, cocoa, and copra. It was known as Fernando Póo until 1973 and Macias Nguema Bijogo 1973–9.

**bir** /bɪə(r)/ an Arabic word for a spring or well.

**Birchington** /ˈbɜːtʃɪŋˌtən/ a resort town near Margate in Kent, south-east England, where the poet and painter Dante Gabriel Rossetti (1828–82) spent his last days and was buried.

**Birkenhead** /ˈbɜːk(ə)nˌhed/ a port and industrial town on the south bank of the River Mersey, England, on the Wirral peninsula, opposite Liverpool to which it is connected by the Queensway road tunnel (1934) and the Mersey rail tunnel (1886); pop. (1981) 123,884. Shipbuilding and engineering have been important to the development of Birkenhead.

**Birmingham** /ˈbɜːmɪŋəm/ a city in the West Midlands of central England; pop. (1991) 934,900. It is the second-largest city in Britain and a major centre of industries which include the manufacture of vehicles, chemicals, plastics, machine tools, aerospace components, and electrical equipment. Locally it is known as Brum which is an abbreviation of Brummagem, a form that passed into English usage to describe anything that is cheap or fake. For many years it was a noted centre for the manufacture of swords and later firearms. Birmingham is the site of the National Exhibition Centre and a cultural city with its own symphony orchestra. It is the home of the University of Birmingham (1900), Aston University (1966) and the University of Central England in Birmingham (formerly Birmingham Polytechnic) which was established in 1992.

**Birmingham** /ˈbɜːmɪŋəm/ an industrial and commercial city in the state of Alabama, USA; pop. (1990) 265,968. It was founded in 1870 at a railroad junction and developed as a steel city using the local Red Mountain iron ore. The University of Alabama (1831) is a major centre of medical research.

**Biscay** /ˈbɪskeɪ/, **Bay of** (French **Golfe de Gascogne**, Spanish **Golfo de Vizcaya**) part of the North Atlantic between the north coast of Spain and the west coast of France, noted for its strong currents and storms.

**Biscayne Bay** /bɪˈskeɪn/ an inlet of the Atlantic Ocean forming a bay in south-east Florida, USA. The city of Miami lies on its north-western shore. The southern part of the bay was designated a national park in 1980 to protect mangrove forest, migrating birds, and the only living coral reefs in the continental US.

**Bishkek** /ˈbɪʃkek/ the capital city of Kyrgyzstan in Central Asia; pop. (1990) 625,000. From 1926 to 1991 the city was named Frunze, after the Red Army general Mikhail Vasilyevich Frunze (1885–1925). Before 1926 it was known as Pishpek. It has metal, electrical, machinery, textile, and food industries.

**Bishopsbourne** /ˈbɪʃəps.bɔː(r)n/ a village in the Stour Valley, Kent, south-east England, south of Canterbury, where the Polish-born novelist Joseph Conrad (1857–1924) spent the last four years of his life.

**Bishop's Stortford** /-ˈstɔːrfə(r)d/ a town in Hertfordshire, south-east England, on the River Stort; pop. (1981) 22,800. It was the birthplace of Cecil Rhodes (1853–1902). Stansted airport is nearby.

**Biskra** /ˈbɪskrə/ an oasis town in the southern foothills of the Aurès Mountains of northern Algeria, at the northern edge of the Sahara Desert; pop. 60,000.

**Bisley** /ˈbɪzlɪ/ a village in Surrey, south-east England, 5 km. (3 miles) west of Woking. The National Rifle Association has held regular competitions at Bisley Camp since 1890.

**Bismarck** /ˈbɪzmɑːk/ the capital of North Dakota, USA, on the Missouri River; pop. (1990) 49,256. It developed first as a steamboat port and then as a terminus of the Northern Pacific Railway,

taking the name of the German Chancellor in order to attract German capital for railroad building. In 1876 General Custer rode out from here to confront Chief Sitting Bull at Little Bighorn. It is a trade and distribution centre for a large agricultural and oil-reserves region.

**Bismarck Sea** an arm of the Pacific Ocean north-east of New Guinea and north of New Britain. The Admiralty Islands and other islands of the Bismarck Archipelago were part of a German dependency that existed 1884–1919.

**Bissagos Islands** /bɪˈsɑːgəs/ (Portuguese **Ilhas dos Bijagós** /ˌviːzəˈɡɒʃ/) a group of islands off the coast of Guinea-Bissau, West Africa.

**Bissau** the capital of Guinea-Bissau, on Bissau Island at the mouth of the River Geba; pop. (est. 1980) 110,000. It was established as a slave trading port in 1687 and developed as a free port after 1869. It is the country's main commercial centre and handles most of its trade. There is a massive Roman Catholic cathedral.

**Bistriţa** the capital of Bistriţa-Nasaud county in northern Romania; pop. (1989) 79,540. Founded by German colonists in the 12th–13th c., it trades in timber, wine, and agricultural produce.

**Bithynia** /bɪˈθɪnɪə/ the ancient name for the region of north-west Asia Minor west of Paphlagonia and bordering the Black Sea and the Sea of Marmara.

**Bitola** /ˈbiːtəˌljɑː/ (also **Bitolj**, Turkish **Monastir**) the second-largest town in the Balkan republic of Macedonia; pop. (1981) 137,835. It processes local agricultural products and has many light industries including carpets and clothing.

**Bitter Lakes** /ˈbɪtə(r)/ two lakes in north-east Egypt, situated in depressions to the north of Suez and traversed by the Suez Canal. The **Great Bitter Lake** lies to the north of the **Little Bitter Lake**.

**Biwa** /ˈbiːwə/, **Lake** (Japanese **Biwako**) a lake in the Kinki region of central Honshu Island, Japan, 8 km. (5 miles) north-east of Kyoto. With an area of 676 sq. km. (261 sq. miles) it is the largest lake in Japan. Its only natural outlet is the River Seta.

**Biysk** /biːsk/ (also **Biisk** or **Bisk**) a town in East Siberia, in the Altai Territory of the Russian Federation, on the Biya River south-east of Barnaul; pop. (1990) 234,000. Established in 1708 as a military fortress it has developed into an industrial town producing chemicals and textiles.

**Bizerta** /bɪˈzɜːtə/ (also **Bizerte**) a Mediterranean seaport on the northern coast of Tunisia, 60 km. west of Tunis; pop. (1984) 94,500. Founded by the Phoenicians, it was taken in 1881 by the French who maintained an important strategic naval base there until 1963. It has a 16th-c. fort and a 17th c. mosque. Its principal industries are oil refining, steel, and cement, and iron ore is the main export.

**Bjorneborg** the Swedish name for the Finnish town of PORI on the Gulf of Bothnia.

**Blackburn** /'blækbɜːn/ an industrial town in Lancashire, north-west England, on the Leeds–Liverpool Canal; pop. (1991) 132,800. Textiles, paper, electronics, and paint are the main products.

**Blackburn, Mount** a mountain peak in southeast Alaska in the Wrangell-St. Elias National Park. Rising to 5,160 m. (16,929 ft.), it is the highest of the Wrangell Mountains.

**Black Country** a name applied to the industrial heart of the West Midlands of England derived from the soot and smoke produced by the original heavy industries.

**Blackfoot** a North American Indian tribe of the Great Plains and prairies of northern Montana and southern Alberta. Divided into Blackfoot Proper, Blood Blackfoot, and Piegan subgroups, the Blackfoot are among the westernmost of the Algonquian-speaking Indians. They were formerly almost entirely dependent on buffalo and other large game. The principal Blackfoot city is Browning, Montana, which is home to the Museum of the Plains Indians.

**Black Forest** (German **Schwarzwald** /'ʃvɑːtsvɑːlt/) a hilly wooded region of south-west Germany lying to the east of the Rhine valley. The spa town of Baden-Baden lies in the Black Forest and the highest point is the Feldberg (1,493 m., 4,898 ft.). It is a popular tourist and holiday area and is famous for its clocks and toys. Lumbering is an important industry.

**Blackfriars** /'blæk͵fraɪəz/ a district of London on the north bank of the Thames named after a Black Friar or Dominican priory founded there in 1238. James Burbage established a famous theatre in 1595, but the buildings of the district were mostly destroyed during the Great Fire of 1666.

**Blackheath** /blæk'hiːθ/ a residential suburb of London, England, in the boroughs of Greenwich and Lewisham, named after a common on which Wat Tyler camped during the Peasants' Revolt of 1381.

**Black Hills** a range of mountains in east Wyoming and west South Dakota, USA, so called because the densely forested slopes look dark from a distance. The highest point is Harney Peak (2,207 m., 7,242 ft.) and on the granite face of Mt. Rushmore (1,890 m, 6,200 ft.) are sculpted the giant heads of Presidents Washington, Lincoln, Jefferson, and Theodore Roosevelt.

**Black Isle** a peninsula in Highland Region, northern Scotland, between the Cromarty Firth to the north and the Beauly and Moray Firths to the south and east. The fishing port of Cromarty was the birthplace of the Scottish geologist and writer Hugh Miller (1802–56).

**Black Mountain** a ridge in the Brecon Beacons, Dyfed, south Wales, stretching *c.* 20 km. (12 miles) north-eastwards from the Amman River.

**Black Mountains** (French **Les Montagnes Noire**) a range of wooded hills in Brittany, France, between Quimper and Rostrenan. The Aulne and Odet rivers meet near Châteauneuf-du-Faou.

**Black Mountains** a group of mountains in Powys, south Wales, between Offa's Dyke and Brecon. The highest peak is Waun Fach (811 m., 2,660 ft.).

**Blackpool** /'blækpuːl/ a seaside resort on the coast of Lancashire, north-west England; pop. (1991) 144,500. It is the largest and most popular holiday resort in northern England with famous autumn illuminations and a 173-m. (568-ft.) observation tower built in 1894 and modelled on the Eiffel Tower in Paris.

**Black Sea** (also **Euxine Sea**, Russian **Chernoye More**, Turkish **Karadeniz**) a tideless virtually landlocked sea bounded by Ukraine, Russia, Georgia, Turkey, Bulgaria, and Romania, and connected to the Mediterranean Sea through the Bosporus and the Sea of Marmara; area 413,365 sq. km. (159,662 sq. miles). It reaches a maximun depth of 2,246 m. (7,369 ft.) and receives a number of rivers including the Danube, Volga, Dniester, and Dnieper which give its upper layers a low salt content.

**Blackwall** /'blækwɔl/ a district in east London, England, at the northern end of the Isle of Dogs. There is a road tunnel under the Thames to Greenwich. Until modern times famous for building sailing ships.

**Blackwater** /'blækwɔːtər/ **1.** a river in the Republic of Ireland that rises in County Kerry and flows 166 km. (104 miles) through County Cork and County Waterford before meeting the Atlantic at Youghal. **2.** a river in the Republic of Ireland and Northern Ireland that rises in Tyrone and flows 80 km. (50 miles) east and north to the southwest corner of Lough Neagh.

**Blaenau-Ffestiniog** /͵blaɪnau fəs'tɪnjəg/ a slate-mining town in the Ffestiniog valley, Gwynedd, north Wales, 27 km. (17 miles) southeast of Caernarvon. The oldest narrow-gauge railway in the world was built in 1836 to carry slate from Blaenau-Ffestiniog to the port of Porthmadoc.

**Blagoevgrad** /bləg'əʊjəvgrɑːt/ a spa town in the Pirin Mountains of south-west Bulgaria; pop. (1990) 86,160. Built on the ruins of the ancient Thracian town of Scaptopara, it was known by its Turkish name Gorna Dzhumaya until 1950.

**Blagoveshchensk** /bləgə'vjeʃtʃɪnsk/ a city in east Siberia, in the Russian Federation, close to the Sino-Russian frontier at the junction of the Amur and Zeya rivers; pop. (1990) 208,000. First settled by Russians in 1644, the city was ceded to China from 1689 until 1856. It is a transport centre on a branch of the Trans-Siberian Railway, and has saw-milling, machinery, and food-processing industries.

**Blair Atholl** /bleɪr 'æθ(ə)l/ a small town in Perthshire, Scotland, close to the junction of the Tilt and Garry rivers. Nearby is Blair Castle, the seat of the Dukes of Atholl who retain the privilege of maintaining the only private army in Britain.

**Blaj** /blɑːʒ/ a town in the county of Alba, west-central Romania; pop. (1983) 22,800.

**Blantyre** /blæn'taɪə(r)/ the chief commercial and industrial city of Malawi; pop. (1987) 331,588 (with Limbe). Founded by Scottish missionaries in 1876 and named after Livingstone's birthplace. It is the centre of a rich agricultural region with food-processing industries.

**Blantyre** a town in west-central Scotland, north-west of Hamilton, the birthplace of the missionary-explorer David Livingstone (1813–73); pop. (1981) 19,900.

**Blarney** /'blɑːnɪ/ a village in County Cork, southern Ireland, 8 km. (5 miles) north-west of Cork; pop. (1981) 1,500. Those who kiss the Blarney stone at Blarney Castle are said to be conferred with a cajoling tongue.

**Blasket Islands** /'blɑːskət/ a group of islands off the south-west tip of the Dingle Peninsula, County Kerry, Ireland, forming the most westerly point of Europe. The largest island, the Great Blasket, was inhabited until 1953.

**Blayais** /bleɪ'jeɪ/ a region of France lying be-tween Charentes and Entre-Deux-Mers on the right bank of the Gironde. The chief towns are Blaye and Bourg.

**Bled** /bled/ (Serbo-Croat **Blejsko Jezero** /'bletskəʊ jə'zɜːrəʊ/) a lake in north-west Slovenia at the centre of a summer resort and winter-sports region.

**Blenheim** /'blenɪm/ (German **Blindheim** /'blɪnthaɪm/) a village in Bavaria, southern Germany, that gave its name to a battle in 1704 at which John Churchill, 1st Duke of Marlborough, commanded a British and Austrian army that de-feated the French forces of Louis XIV. Blenheim Palace, the Duke's seat at Woodstock in Oxfordshire, England, was named after this vic-tory. Begun in 1705, the building was designed by the English architects Sir John Vanbrugh and Nicholas Hawksmoor. The park was laid out by 'Capability' Brown.

**Blésois** /bleɪ'swɑː/, **the** a region of the Loire Valley in France lying between Touraine and Orléanais, largely in the department of Loir-et-Cher.

**Blida** /'bliːdə/ (Arabic **El Boulaida**) a town in the foothills of the Atlas Mountains of northern Algeria, 48 km. (30 miles) south-west of Algiers; pop. (1989) 191,000. Built on the site of a Roman camp, Blida was founded in 1553 by Andalusians

who cultivated the fruits, vines, and flowers for which the city has become famous.

**Bloemfontein** /'bluːmfɒnteɪn/ the capital of Orange Free State and judicial capital of the Republic of South Africa; pop. (1985) 233,000. Founded in 1846, it was the venue (in 1909) for the final negotiations that led to the formation of the Union of South Africa in 1910. It is a commercial centre with light industries.

**Blois** /blwɑː/ (anc. **Blesae**) an historic market and tourist town on the Loire River, central France; pop. (1990) 51,550. It is the capital of the department of Loire-et-Cher, noted for its manu-facture of chocolate and its trade in wine, grain, fruit, and vegetables. Between the 10th c. and the late 14th c. the Counts of Blois were amongst the most powerful of the feudal families of France. The lands of Blois eventually passed to the Duke of Orléans whose grandson Louis XII of France was born in the Renaissance château, a favourite royal residence, in 1462.

**Bloomington** /'bluːmɪŋtən/ **1.** a commercial and industrial city in central Illinois, USA; pop. (1990) 51,970. Founded as a prairie settlement in 1843 and originally known as Blooming Grove, it was here that Abraham Lincoln made his famous electioneering 'lost speech' in 1856. Illinois Wesleyan University was founded in 1850 and Illinois State University in 1857. Bloomington was the home of Adlai Stevenson, US Vice-president under Grover Cleveland, and the burial place of his grandson Governor Adlai Stevenson who was US ambassador to the UN. **2.** an industrial town in south-central Indiana, USA; pop. (1990) 60,633. Settled in 1818, it developed in association with the limestone industry. Today electronics and tourism are important. Indiana University was founded in 1820. **3.** a suburb of Minneapolis, south-east Minnesota, USA, incorporated as a separate city in 1953; pop. (1990) 86,335. It manufactures elec-tronic equipment and lawn mowers.

**Bloomsbury** /'bluːmzbərɪ, -brɪ/ a district in the London borough of Camden, England, noted for its large squares and gardens which include Bedford Square, Russell Square, and Bloomsbury Square. The British Museum (founded in 1753) is located here and Dr Peter Mark Roget, author of the *Thesaurus*, lived here from 1808 to 1843. The Bloomsbury Group of writers, artists, and philo-sophers lived in or were associated with Blooms-bury during the early 20th c.

**Bluefields** /'bluːfiːldz/ a port on the Miskito coast of Nicaragua, situated on an inlet of the Caribbean Sea, at the mouth of the Bluefields or Escondido River; pop. (1985) 18,000. Named after the Dutch pirate Bleuwveldt, its chief outlet is the outer port of El Bluff from which timber, fish, and bananas are shipped.

**Blue Mosque** (also **Sultan Ahmet Mosque**) an Islamic mosque with six minarets in Istanbul,

Turkey, said to be one of the finest in the world. Built by Sultan Ahmet I in 1609–16, its dome is 43 m. (141 ft.) high and 23.5 m. (77 ft.) in diameter.

**Blue Mountains 1.** a section of the Great Dividing Range in New South Wales, Australia. The mountains appear blue because the fine droplets of oil that are dispersed from the Eucalyptus trees cause the blue light rays of the sun to be scattered more effectively. Now a popular resort area, the range was first traversed in 1813 by Blaxland, Lawson, and Wentworth. The **Blue Mountains National Park,** which extends over an area of 2,160 sq. km. (834 sq. miles), is a sanctuary for kangaroos, wallabies, platypuses, and many species of bird. **2.** a range of mountains in eastern Jamaica rising to 2,256 m. (7,402 ft.) at Blue Mountain Peak which is the highest mountain on the island. **3.** a range of mountains running from central Oregon to south-east Washington, USA.

**Blue Nile** one of the two principal headwaters of the River Nile. It rises in Lake Tana in the Ethiopian Highlands and flows c. 1,600 km. (1,000 miles) south through Ethiopia then northwestwards into Sudan where it meets the White Nile at Khartoum. The Roseires Dam close to the Ethiopian frontier supplies the greater part of Sudan's hydroelectric power.

**Blue Ridge Mountains** a range of the Appalachian Mountains in the eastern USA, stretching 1,040 km. (650 miles) from south Pennsylvania to north Georgia. Mt. Mitchell (2,039 m., 6,684 ft.) is the highest peak. The Great Ridge Parkway links the Shenandoah valley with the Great Smoky Mts.

**Blumenau** /ˌbluːməˈnaʊ/ a city in the state of Santa Catarina, southern Brazil, on the Itajaí River 140 km. (88 miles) from Florianópolis; pop. (1990) 206,100. It was founded by German settlers in 1851.

**Boa Vista** /ˈbəʊə ˈviːʃtə/ the chief town of the Roraima district in northern Brazil, on the Río Branco; pop. (1991) 143,000. It has grown rapidly in association with the mining of bauxite and other minerals nearby.

**Bobigny** /bɔːbiːˈnjiː/ an industrial suburb of north-east Paris and capital of the department of Seine-St. Denis, France; pop. (1990) 44,880.

**Bobo-Dioulasso** /ˈbɒbə djuːˈlɑːsəʊ/ a city in south-west Burkina on the railway line linking Ouagadougou with Abidjan on the Guinea coast; pop. (1985) 228,668. It is the second-largest city in Burkina. It is a marketing and industrial centre processing local agricultural products.

**Bobruysk** /bəˈbruːəsk/ (also **Bobruisk**) see BABRUYSK.

**bocage** /bɒˈkɑːʒ/ a French term for a small woodland used to describe cultivated landscapes with copses and hedgerows as in the Bocage Vendéen north-west of Poitou or the Bocage Normand of the departments of Calvados and Orne.

**Boca Raton** /ˈbəʊkə rætɒn/ a resort town on the Atlantic coast of south-east Florida, USA, 25 km. (16 miles) north of Fort Lauderdale; pop. (1990) 61,492. It is a centre for high-tech electronics and data systems, and home of Florida Atlantic University (1964).

**Bochum** /ˈbəʊxʊm/ a commercial and industrial city in the Ruhr Valley, North Rhine-Westphalia, western Germany; pop. (1991) 398,580. Once Germany's leading iron and steel town, Bochum lies close to the Ruhr coalfields. It has steel and vehicle industries.

**Boden** /ˈbəʊd(ə)n/ a major railway junction in Norrbotten county, northern Sweden, on the Lule River.

**Bodensee** /ˈbəʊdənzeɪ/ the German name for Lake Constance. See CONSTANCE, LAKE.

**Bodhgaya** /ˌbɒdgəˈjɑː/ (also **Buddh Gaya** /ˌbʊd/) a village in the state of Bihar, in India, where Buddha attained enlightenment. A bo-tree here is said to be a descendant of the tree under which he meditated.

**Bodleian Library** /ˈbɒdlɪən/ (colloq. **Bodley** /ˈbɒdlɪ/) the library of Oxford University in England. The first library was founded in the 14th c. and benefited from the manuscript collections donated by Humphrey, duke of Gloucester (1391–1447). It was refounded by Sir Thomas Bodley (1545–1613), diplomat and scholar, for the use both of the University of Oxford and the 'republic of the learned', and opened in 1602. In 1610 the Stationers' Company agreed to give the library a copy of every book printed in England, and by various Copyright Acts it is now one of the six libraries entitled to receive on demand a copy of every book published in the UK. It also houses one of the world's most extensive collections of Western and Oriental manuscripts.

**Bodmin** /ˈbɒdmɪn/ a town in Cornwall, south-west England, on the south-west edge of Bodmin Moor; pop. (est. 1984) 15,000. Sir Arthur Quiller-Couch (1863–1944) was born here.

**Bodnath** /bədˈnæθ/ the site of a huge Buddhist stupa to the east of Kathmandu in Nepal, the religious centre for Nepal's Tibetan population. It is the largest stupa in Nepal and one of the largest in the world.

**Bodo** /ˈbəʊdəʊ/ a Tibeto-Burman ethnic group of the Brahmaputra flood plain largely found in the Indian state of Assam where they number c. 4 million. Since the 1960s Bodo militant groups have agitated for a separate state.

**Bodø** /ˈbəʊdəʊ/ a fishing port in northern Norway, at the mouth of the Saltfjord opposite the Lofoten Islands; pop. (1991) 36,950. It is capital of Nordland county.

**Bodrum** /ˈbɒdrəm/ a resort town on the Aegean coast of western Turkey, site of the ancient city of HALICARNASSUS.

**Boeotia** /bɪˈəʊʃə/ (Greek **Voiotía**) a department in central Greece, to the north of the Gulf of Corinth; area 2,952 sq. km. (1,140 sq. miles); pop. (1991) 134,000; capital, Levádhia. Hesiod, Pindar, and Plutarch were natives of ancient Boeotia.
**Boeotian** *adj. & n.*

**Boer** /ˈbəʊə(r), bʊə(r)/ a South African of Dutch descent. (Dutch *boer* = farmer.)

**Bofors** /ˈbəʊfəz/ a town in south-central Sweden, 50 km. (31 miles) west of Örebro. Alfred Nobel (1833–96), founder of the Nobel prizes, owned a steel and armament plant in Bofors which gave its name to a rapid-firing anti-aircraft gun.

**boğazi** /ˌbəʊgaˈziː/ the Turkish word for a strait, as in Çanakkale Boğazi (the Dardanelles).

**Bogazköy** /bɜːˈaːzkɔɪ/ a village in central Turkey, 145 km. (90 miles) east of Ankara. It is built on the site of ancient Hattusas, capital of the Hittite empire *c.* 1400–1200 BC.

**Bognor Regis** /ˌbɒgnər ˈriːdʒɪs/ a resort town in West Sussex on the south coast of England, east of Chichester. Originally known as Bognor, the word *Regis* was added after King George V came to recuperate near here in 1929. The composer Eric Coates lived here from 1952 until his death in 1957.

**Bogong** /ˈbəʊgɒŋ/, **Mount** a mountain in the Australian Alps, south-east Australia. Rising to 1,985 m. (6,508 ft.) it is the highest peak in the state of Victoria.

**Bogor** /ˈbəʊgər/ a town on the Indonesian island of Java, 48 km. (30 miles) south of Jakarta; pop. (1980) 247,000. Now a research centre with a noted botanical garden, the highland resort of Bogor was the residence of the governor-general of the former Dutch East Indies.

**Bogotá** /ˌbɒgəˈtaː/ the capital and largest city of Colombia, situated in the eastern Andes at *c.* 2,610 m. (8,560 ft.); pop. (1985) 3,982,900. Founded by the Spanish in 1538 on the site of a pre-Columbian centre of the Chibcha culture, it was originally known as Santa Fe de Bogotá. The home of the liberator Simon Bolivar and the famous 'El Dorado' treasures in the Gold Museum are major attractions. The city is a mixture of Spanish colonial and modern architecture. It is the political, social, financial, and marketing centre of the republic; it has several universities. Its industries include textiles, vehicles, chemicals, engineering, and food processing.

**Bo Hai** see CHIHLI, GULF OF.

**Bohemia** /bəʊˈhiːmɪə/ (Czech **Cechy** /ˈtseki:/) the western part of the Czech Republic, divided into the administrative regions of Central, East, West, North, and South Bohemia; pop. (1991) 6,288,350. Formerly a Slavonic kingdom, it fell under Austrian rule in 1526, and by the Treaty of Versailles (1919) became a province of Czechoslovakia. Its chief centre is the city of Prague.
**Bohemian** *adj. & n.*

**Bohemian Forest** (Czech **Cechy Les**, Ger. **Böhmerwald** /ˈbɜːməˌvaːlt/) a wooded mountain range on the frontier between Germany and the Czech Republic, separating Bohemia from Bavaria. It is *c.* 190 km. (120 miles) long and rises to a height of 1,458 m. (4,785 ft.) at Arber.

**Bohinj** /bɒˈhɪnjə/ a lake at the centre of a resort area in the Julian Alps, north-west Slovenia, north-west of Ljubljana.

**Bohol** /bəʊˈhɒl/ an island lying to the north of Mindanao in the central Philippines; chief town, Tagbilaran. It is the tenth-largest island in the Philippines. The limestone Chocolate Hills are the island's main attraction.

**bohorok** /bəˈhɒrək/ a hot dry wind that blows onto the north-west coast of Sumatra, Indonesia, during the north-west monsoon season (June–Sept.).

**Bois de Boulogne** /bwæ də bʊˈlɒnjə/ a park in the centre of Paris, France, to the south of the Avenue Charles de Gaulle; area 865 hectares (2,137 acres). Once part of a royal hunting ground, it developed a reputation as the resort of duellists and robbers before being laid out in 1852 with lakes, avenues, and gardens. The Abbey of Longchamp (1256), the Château de Bagatelle (1777), and the racecourses of Longchamp and Auteil all lie within the park.

**Boise** /ˈbɔɪzi/ the capital and largest city of Idaho, USA, on the Boise River; pop. (1990) 125,738. Established as a gold-mining town in 1862, the area was originally named *Les Bois* (= the woods) by French fur trappers. Electronics, steel fabrication, and the construction of mobile homes are the chief industries. It is the home of Boise State University (1932) and North America's only Basque heritage museum.

**Bois-le-Duc** the French name for 'S-HERTOGEN-BOSCH.

**Bokaro Steel City** /bəʊˈkaːrəʊ/ an industrial steel-producing city in the coalfields of Bihar state, eastern India; pop. (1991) 415,690.

**Bokhara** see BUKHARA.

**Bolan Pass** /bəʊˈlaːn/ a deep and narrow gorge *c.* 87 km. (55 miles) long through the Brahui Range, on the route linking Afghanistan with the lower Indus valley of Pakistan. It climbs to a height of *c.* 1,798 m. (5,900 ft.). The city of Quetta lies close to its eastern entrance.

**Bole** /bəʊl/ (also **Bortala**) a Khazak town in Xinjiang autonomous region, north-west China, situated to the north of the Tien Shan Range; pop. (1986) 141,000.

**Bolívar** /bəˈliːvaː(r)/, **Pico** a mountain in the Cordillera de Mérida, western Venezuela. At 5,775 m. (18,949 ft.) it is the highest peak in the country.

**Bolivia** /bə'lɪvɪə/
official name
**Republic of Bolivia**
a landlocked country
in South America
with Brazil to the
east and north, Chile
and Peru to the west,
and Paraguay and
Argentina to the

south; area 1,098,580 sq. km. (424,162 sq. miles);
pop. (est. 1991) 7,500,000; languages, Spanish (official), Aymara, and Quechua; administrative capital, La Paz; judicial and legal capital, Sucre; largest
cities, La Paz, Santa Cruz, Cochabamba, and
Oruro. Bolivia's chief topographical feature is the
*altiplano*, the great central plateau between the
eastern and western chains of the Andes. With an
average altitude of 3,650 m. (12,000 ft.) above sea-
level the *altiplano* has a clear atmosphere and a
cool climate suited to growing cereals and potatoes
and rearing livestock such as sheep, alpacas, llamas,
and vicunas. The *yungas* hills and valleys separate
the high plateau from the tropical lowland plains to
the east (the *llano* region) and south-east (the
Chaco plain). Most of Bolivia's deposits of oil, gas,
and iron ore are located in the lowland plain while
lithium-rich salts and minerals such as tin, zinc,
silver, and tungsten are mined in the high plateau.
The coca plant, from the leaves of which cocaine is
produced, is grown extensively as a cash crop. Part
of the Inca empire, Bolivia became one of the most
important parts of Spain's American empire following the discovery of major silver deposits soon after
Pizarro's destruction of the Incas. It was freed from
the Spanish in 1825 and named after the great liberator Simon Bolivar, but since then it has been crippled by endemic poverty and political instability,
losing land (including its Pacific coast) to surrounding countries during the War of the Pacific (1879–
84) and the Chaco War (1932–5), and suffering
from almost continual *coups* and changes of government. It is governed by a bicameral legislature
comprising a Senate and a Chamber of Deputies.
**Bolivian** *adj. & n.*
Bolivia is divided into nine departments:

| Department | Area (sq. km) | Pop. (est. 1988) | Capital |
|---|---|---|---|
| Beni | 213,564 | 215,400 | Trinidad |
| Chuquisaca | 51,524 | 442,600 | Sucre |
| Cochabamba | 55,631 | 982,000 | Cochabamba |
| La Paz | 133,985 | 1,926,200 | La Paz |
| Oruro | 53,588 | 388,300 | Oruro |
| Pando | 63,827 | 41,000 | Cobija |
| Potosí | 118,218 | 667,800 | Potosí |
| Santa Cruz | 370,621 | 1,110,100 | Santa Cruz |
| Tarija | 37,623 | 246,600 | Tarija |

**Bologna** /bə'ləʊnjə/ an historic city in north
Italy, capital of Emilia-Romagna; pop. (1990)
411,800. Its university, which dates from the 11th

c., is one of the oldest in Europe. Dante and
Petrarch were among its scholars. Guglielmo
Marconi (1874–1937), Italian inventor, was born
here. Engineering, electrical equipment, and food-
processing are the main industries.

**Bolsover** /'bɒlzəʊvə/ a mining town in
Derbyshire, central England, 32 km. (20 miles)
north-east of Derby; pop. (1981) 11,000.

**Bolton** /'bəʊltən/ a town in Greater Manchester,
England, north-west of Manchester; pop. (1991)
253,300. Formerly a major centre of wool and
cotton production, engineering, and the manufacture of chemicals, textiles, and paper are now
the chief industries.

**Bolu** /bɒ'luː/ **1.** a province in northern Turkey,
on the Black Sea; pop. (1990) 536,869; area 11,051
sq. km. (4,268 sq. miles); pop. (1990) 536,870. **2.** its
capital, on the Devrek River; pop. (1990) 60,790.
Its industries include timber and leather goods.

**Bolzano** /bɒl'tsaːnəʊ/ (German **Bozen**
/'bəʊtsen/) **1.** an autonomous, largely German-
speaking province in the Trentino-Alto Adige
region of north Italy; area 7,400 sq. km. (2,858 sq.
miles); pop. (1990) 441,670. The province includes
the Dolomite and Ortler ranges. **2.** its capital, on
the River Isarco south of the Brenner Pass; pop.
(1990) 100,380. It is a cultural centre with numerous museums, libraries, and institutions.

**Boma** /'bəʊmə/ a port in western Zaire, on the
north bank of the Congo (Zaïre) River; pop. (1976)
94,000. Founded as a slave-trading town, it was
capital of the Belgian Congo until 1923. It now exports tropical produce such as bananas, cacao, and
timber.

**Bombay** /bɒm'beɪ/ a city and port on the west
coast of India, the country's second-largest city
and a commercial centre long noted for its textile
industry; pop. (1991) 9,990,000. It is capital of the
state of Maharashtra. Ceded to Portugal by the
Sultan of Gujarat, Bombay was given in 1661 as a
wedding gift to King Charles I who married the
daughter of the Portuguese king. It was the headquarters of the British East India Company from
1685 to 1708 and developed as the 'Gateway to
India' after the opening of the Suez Canal in 1869.
Its principal public buildings are built in Victorian
styles, and Bombay is considered to be the most
'westernized' of Indian cities. It is also a major cultural, financial, and industrial centre with oil-
refining, chemical, textile, and vehicle industries
plus all kinds of consumer goods. Tourism is also
important. It has two universities and is the centre
of the considerable Hindi film industry.

**bombora** /bɒm'bɔːrə/ an Australian Aboriginal
term describing a dangerous sea area where waves
break over a submerged reef.

**Bonaire** /bɒ'neə(r)/ one of the two principal
islands of the Netherlands Antilles, situated in the
Caribbean Sea, 60 km. (37 miles) north of the
Venezuelan coast; area 288 sq. km. (111 sq. miles);

pop. (est. 1990) 11,060; chief town, Kralendijk. Tourism is important.

**Bonampak** /bɒnəm'pæk/ the site of an ancient Mayan city on the Usumacinta River, in the tropical lowlands of eastern Guatemala. Rediscovered in 1948, its wall paintings depict violent scenes of battle and sacrifice.

**Bonavista Peninsula** /ˌbəʊnə'vɪstə/ a peninsula on the rugged east coast of the island of Newfoundland, Canada. At Cape Bonavista stands a statue of John Cabot who is supposed to have sighted this part of the New World for the first time in 1497.

**Bonchurch** /'bɒntʃɜːtʃ/ a coastal resort on the Isle of Wight, southern England, just east of Ventnor. The town has associations with Charles Dickens who wrote part of *David Copperfield* here. The poet Swinburne (1837–1909) is buried in the new church (built in 1847).

**Bondi** /'bɒndɪ/ a coastal resort in a suburb of Sydney, New South Wales, Australia, with a popular beach, and famous for its surfing.

**Bône** /bəʊn/ the former name of the Algerian port of ANNABA.

**Bongor** /bɒŋ'gɔː(r)/ a market town in southwest Chad on the Logone River, capital of Mayo-Kebbi prefecture; pop. (1993) 195,000.

**Bonifacio** /ˌbɒnə'fætʃəʊ/, **Strait of** an arm of the Mediterranean Sea separating the islands of Corsica and Sardinia.

**Bonin Islands** /'bəʊnən/ (Japanese **Ogasawara-gunto**) a group of 27 volcanic islands in the Pacific Ocean between Japan and the Northern Marianas; area *c.* 100 sq. km. (40 sq. miles). The largest island is Chichi-shima. Colonized by Europeans and Hawaiians in the 1830s, the islands were annexed by Japan in 1876. Between 1945 and 1968 they were administered by the US Navy.

**Bonn** /bɒn/ a city in North Rhine-Westphalia, western Germany; pop. (1991) 296,240. Founded by the Romans in the 1st c. AD, it later became the seat of the electors of Cologne (1238–1794) whose baroque-style palace is now one of the main buildings of a university founded in 1786. From 1949 until the reunification of Germany in 1990 Bonn was the capital of the Federal Republic of Germany. It was the birthplace in 1770 of the composer Beethoven.

**Bonneville Flats** /'bɒnəvɪl/ the salt flats surrounding the Great Salt Lake in Utah, USA, scene of several attempts to break the world land-speed record.

**Bonny** /'bɒnɪ/ a port and oil terminal in southeast Nigeria, situated on the Bonny River in the Niger delta south of Port Harcourt.

**Bontebok National Park** /'bɒntəbɒk/ a national park on the Bree River in south-west Cape Province, South Africa, established in 1960 to protect a small herd of the endangered bontebok.

**boondock** /'buːndɒk/ US slang for rough or isolated country derived from a Philippine Tagalog word (*bundok* = mountain).

**Boothia** /'buːθjə/, **Gulf of** a gulf in the Canadian Arctic separating north-west Baffin Island from the Boothia Peninsula of Keewatin district in the Northwest Territories. The gulf and peninsula were named after Sir Felix Booth (1775–1850) who was patron of Sir John Ross's expedition of 1829–33.

**Bootle** /'buːt(ə)l/ a port on the outskirts of Liverpool in Merseyside, England, situated at the mouth of the River Mersey; pop. (1981) 62,400. The National Girobank headquarters are located here.

**Bophuthatswana** /bəʊˌpuːtə'tswɑːnə/ a former independent homeland of the Tswana people of South Africa, created in 1977 and comprising seven separate territories, now part of Northern Transvaal. Its capital was Mmabatho. The territory is one of the world's major producers of platinum as well as an important source of minerals such as chrome, copper, asbestos, coal, diamonds, nickel, and gold. The internationally famous Sun City holiday complex lies to the northwest of Mmabatho.

**bora** /'bɔːrə/ a strong cold dry north-easterly wind blowing in the upper Adriatic, particularly during winter and spring.

**Bora-Bora** /ˌbɔːrə'bɔːrə/ an island in the South Pacific, situated in the leeward group of the Society islands, French Polynesia. The remnants of a volcano rising to 655 m. (2,100 ft.) are surrounded by a circular coral reef to form what James Michener described as 'the most beautiful island in the world'.

**Borås** /bʊ'rɜːs/ a textile manufacturing centre in Älvsborg county, south-west Sweden, on the Viskan River 56 km. (35 miles) east of Gothenburg (Göteborg); pop. (1990) 101,766.

**Bordeaux** /bɔː'dəʊ/ an inland port on the River Garonne in south-west France; pop. (1990) 213,270. It is capital of the department of Gironde and a major commercial centre for the Aquitaine region. Oil-refining, shipbuilding, and the manufacture of chemicals and aeronautical equipment are the chief industries of the city. The surrounding area is noted for its wines, notably those in the regions of Médoc, St. Emilion, Pomerol, Graves, Barsac, Sauternes, and Entre-Deux-Mers. Bordeaux was held by the English for three centuries before falling to the French in 1453. It was the birthplace of the French dramatist Jean Anouilh. It has a Gothic cathedral dating from the 11th c., a university founded in 1441, and several medieval churches.

**Bordelais** /'bɔː(r)dəleɪ/ an area of northern Aquitaine in south-west France centred around Bordeaux.

**Borders 1.** a general name given to the lands lying on either side of the frontier between England

and Scotland. **2.** a local government region in southern Scotland created in 1975; area 4,712 sq. km. (1,829 sq. miles); pop. (1991) 102,649; capital, Newtown St. Boswells. Between 1975 and 1996 it comprised four districts:

| District | Area (sq. km.) | Pop. (1991) | Administrative Centre |
|---|---|---|---|
| Berwickshire | 907 | 18,781 | Duns |
| Ettrick and Lauderdale | 1,365 | 33,939 | Galashiels |
| Roxburgh | 1,540 | 34,615 | Hawick |
| Tweeddale | 899 | 15,314 | Peebles |

**boreal** /'bɔːrɪəl/ **1.** a term loosely used to describe cold northern regions, derived from the name of the Greek god of the wind, *Boreas*. The northern coniferous forest of Eurasia and North America is known as the boreal forest. **2.** the name of a post-glacial climatic period ranging from *c.*7,500 to 5,500 BC.

**Borgå** /'bɒrgəʊ/ the Swedish name for the town of PORVOO in Finland.

**Borisov** /bə'riːsəf/ the former name of BARYSAW in Belorussia.

**Borneo** /'bɔːnɪˌəʊ/ a large densely forested and mountainous island of the Malay archipelago, comprising Kalimantan (a region of Indonesia), Sabah and Sarawak (now parts of Malaysia), and Brunei. It is the second-largest non-continental island in the world; area 751,100 sq. km. (290,000 sq. miles).
**Bornean** *adj.*

**Bornholm** /'bɔːnhəʊm/ a detached Danish island in the Baltic Sea, south-east of Sweden; 588 sq. km. (227 sq. miles); pop. (1990) 46,100; chief town and ferry port, Rønne. Fishing, agriculture, handicrafts, and tourism are the chief occupations.

**Borno** /'bɔːnəʊ/ (also **Bornu**) a state in north-east Nigeria; pop. (1991) 2,596,600; capital, Maiduguri. From the 9th to the 19th c. the much larger kingdom of Borno extended to the west and south of Lake Chad in parts of present day Niger, Nigeria, and Cameroon. Converted to Islam in the 11th c., the Borno empire reached the peak of its power in the 15th–18th c. before being absorbed into British, French, and German colonies.

**Borobudur** /ˌbɒrəʊbʊ'dʊə(r)/ a Buddhist monument in central Java, built *c.*800, abandoned *c.*1000, and restored in 1907–11 and again in the 1980s. Designed for the purpose of worship, veneration, and meditation, it consists of five square successively smaller terraces, one above the other, surmounted by three concentric galleries with open stupas culminating in a supreme closed stupa. Each of the square terraces is enclosed by a high wall; bas-reliefs on its vertical surfaces depict, in a continuous series, the life of the Buddha and successive stages towards the perfection of Nirvana. It is the largest religious monument in south-east Asia.

**Borodino** /ˌbɒrə'diːnəʊ/ a village in western Russia, 111 km. (70 miles) west of Moscow; site of a bloody battle between Russian and French armies prior to Napoleon's occupation of Moscow in September 1812.

**borough** /'bʌrə/ **1.** a British town represented in the House of Commons. **2.** a British town with a municipal corporation and privileges conferred by a royal charter. **3.** a municipal corporation in certain states of the USA. **4.** each of the five divisions of New York City. **5.** a division corresponding to a county in Alaska, USA. See also BURGH.

**Borovets** /'bɒrəvets/ a ski resort in the Rila Mountains of western Bulgaria.

**Borrowdale** /'bɒrəʊˌdeɪl/ a valley to the south of Keswick in the Lake District of Cumbria, north-west England. The Derwent Water flows into the valley from the Borrowdale Fells.

**Borstal** /'bɔːst(ə)l/ a village near Rochester in Kent, south-east England, the site of a reformatory for young offenders founded in 1902.

**Borujerd** /ˌbəʊrə'dʒɑːd/ a city in Lorestan province, western Iran, in the Zagros Mountains north-east of Khorramabad; pop. (1991) 201,000.

**Bose** /bəʊz/ a city in Guizhou autonomous region, southern China, situated between Guiyang and the frontier with Vietnam; pop. (1986) 275,000.

**Bosnia and Herzegovina** /'bɒznɪə, ˌhɜːtsɪgə'viːnə/ (Serbo-Croat **Bosna-I-Hercegovina**) official name **The Republic of Bosnia and Herzegovina** a  former constituent republic of Yugoslavia, bounded north and west by Croatia, east by Serbia and south-east by Montenegro; area 51,128 sq. km. (19,748 sq. miles); pop. (1981) 4,124,256; capital, Sarajevo. Settled by Slavs in the 7th c., Bosnia was conquered by the Turks in 1463. Its annexation by Austro-Hungary in 1908 contributed towards the outbreak of World War I, but in 1918 it became part of the Kingdom of Serbs, Croats, and Slovenes which changed its name to Yugoslavia in 1929. In 1992 it followed Slovenia and Croatia in declaring independence, but ethnic conflict amongst Muslims, Serbs, and Croats quickly reduced the republic to a state of civil war forcing thousands of people to flee into neighbouring countries.

**Bosporus** /'bɒspərəs/ (also **Bosphorus** /-fərəs/, Turkish **Karadeniz Boğazi** /ˌkɑːrədə'niːz ˌbəʊgɑː'ziː/) a strait, *c.* 32 km. (20 miles) in length, connecting the Black Sea and the Sea of Marmara, with Istanbul at its south end. It separates Europe from Asia Minor which are linked by two bridges completed in 1973 and 1988.

**Bosra** /'bɒzrə/ a ruined city in the plain of the Howran, south-western Syria. It was a leading city of the Nabateans in the 1st century, capital of the Roman province of Arabia, and the first Syrian city to become Muslim. Its impressive Roman theatre was incorporated into a 12th-c. fortress of the Saladin (Ayyubid) dynasty and there are also Roman baths, colonnaded streets, Nabatean and Roman gateways, and churches dating from the 3rd, 4th, and 5th c.

**Bossier City** /'bəʊʒɜ:/ a city in north-west Louisiana, USA; pop. (1990) 52,721. Nearby Barksdale Air Force Base is the home of the US 8th Air Force and the 2nd Bomb Wing.

**Boston** /'bɒst(ə)n/ a market town on the Witham River, Lincolnshire, east England; pop. (est. 1985) 27,000. John Cotton led a party of Puritans who sailed from Boston to Massachusetts Bay in 1633. St. Botolph's Church is said to be England's largest parish church.

**Boston** the state capital of Massachusetts, USA, on Boston Bay; pop. (1990) 574,283; metropolitan area (1990) 2,870,670. Founded c. 1630 as the principal settlement of the Massachusetts Bay Company, Boston was an early centre of New England Puritanism. Faneuil Hall Marketplace, bequeathed to the city as a public meeting-hall and market place in 1742, is known as the 'Cradle of Liberty'. The Hall was the scene of mass protest meetings held before the American War of Independence which broke out near here in 1775. The USS *Constitution*, launched in 1797 is the oldest commissioned navy vessel afloat in the world. Boston was the birthplace of the Christian Science movement and is the home of Boston University (1839), Harvard Medical School, numerous colleges, institutions, and museums. Harvard university and the Massachusetts Institute of Technology are located at nearby CAMBRIDGE. Boston had the first public library (1653) and the first newspaper (1704) in the New World. Its Symphony Orchestra is world-renowned. Its industries include electronics, machinery, publishing, and food processing. Paul Revere, Ralph Waldo Emerson, and Oliver Wendell Holmes were all natives of the city.

**Boswash** /'bɒzwɒʃ/ a name sometimes applied in the USA to the urban area stretching from Boston, Massachusetts, to Washington DC.

**Bosworth Field** /'bɒzwəθ/ the scene, near Market Bosworth in Leicestershire, of a battle (1485) in the Wars of the Roses, at which Henry Tudor defeated the Yorkist king Richard III, who died there. The battle is generally considered to mark the end of the Wars of the Roses, but Henry crowned soon afterwards as Henry VII, was not really secure until a last Yorkist challenge was crushed at the battle of Stoke two years later.

**Botany Bay** /'bɒtənɪ/ an inlet of the Tasman Sea on the coast of New South Wales, south-east Australia, just south of Sydney. In 1770 Captain James Cook landed here naming the bay after the large variety of plants collected by Sir Joseph Banks. Chosen as the site for a penal settlement in 1787, it proved to be unsuitable and a location at nearby Sydney Cove was selected.

**Botev Peak** /'bɒtəf/ a mountain in Bulgaria to the east of Sofia. At 2,376 m. (7,793 ft.) it is the highest peak in the Balkan Mountains (Stara Planina). Until 1950 it was known as Yumrukchal.

**Bothnia** /'bɒθnɪə/, **Gulf of** a northern arm of the Baltic Sea between Sweden and Finland.

**Botosani** /bəʊtəʊ'ʃɑːn/ a market town in north-east Romania, situated on the Moldavian Plain near the border with Ukraine; pop. (1989) 119,560. Its name is said to be derived from that of Batu Khan, a grandson of Genghis Khan. It is the capital of a county of the same name with industries producing textiles, clothing, flour, and processed food.

**Botou** /bəʊ'taʊ/ a city in Hebei province, eastern China, on the Grand Canal south of Tianjin; pop. (1986) 1,593,000.

## Botswana

/bɒt'swɑːnə/ official name **The Republic of Botswana** an inland country of southern Africa, bounded west and north by Namibia, north-east by Zambia and Zimbabwe, and south by South Africa; area 600,360 sq. km. (231,800 sq. miles); pop. (est. 1991) 1,300,000; languages, English (official) and Setswana; capital, Gaborone. The chief towns are Gaborone, Mahalapye, Serowe, Tutume, and Bobonong. Botswana is a largely arid, subtropical tableland with the Kalahari Desert occupying the western half of the country. There are hills to the east and salt lakes in the north. Rainfall, chiefly during October–April, is greatest in the north and east. Most of the population, 95 per cent of whom are of the Tswana tribe, lives in the east where the chief agricultural products are cattle, corn, millet, sorghum, beans, and cowpeas. Since the 1960s minerals such as copper, nickel, diamonds, salt, soda ash, and potash have become sources of export income. Threatened by the Transvaal Boers, the area was made the British Protectorate of Bechuanaland in 1885. Self government was granted in 1965 and a year later the country became independent as a republic within the Commonwealth. Botswana is governed by a unicameral National Assembly, although a House of Chiefs voices opinions on matters relating to tribal affairs.

**Botswana** *adj. & n.*

Botswana is divided into 10 districts:

| District | Capital |
| --- | --- |
| Ngamiland | Maun |
| Chobe | Kasane |
| Ghanzi | Ghanzi |
| Central | Serowe |
| North-east | Francistown |
| Kweneng | Molepolole |
| Kgatleng | Mochudi |
| Southern | Kanye |
| South-east | Ramotswa |
| Kgalagadi | Tshabong |

**Bottrop** /'bɒtrəp/ an industrial city in North Rhine-Westphalia, western Germany, 8 km. (5 miles) north of Essen; pop. (1991) 118,760. It developed from a coal-mining centre in the 1860s to an industrial centre producing chemicals, textiles, and electrical equipment.

**Bouaké** /'bwɑːkeɪ/ a city in central Ivory Coast, West Africa, on the main railway line from Burkina to the coastal port of Abidjan; pop. (1986) 390,000. It is the second-largest city in the country and a centre of the textile industry.

**Bouba Ndjida National Park** /bubə (ə)n'jiːdə/ a national park on a large rugged plain in northern Cameroon, established in 1968 to protect the endangered black rhino and giant eland.

**Bouches-du-Rhône** /ˌbuːʃduˈrəʊn/ a department on the Rhône delta in the region of Provence-Alpes-Cote d'Azur, south-east France; area 5,112 sq. km. (1,974 sq. miles); pop. (1990) 1,759,370; chief town, Marseilles.

**Boucle de la Pendjari National Park** /'bʊklə də læ penˈdʒɑːrɪ/ a national park in the Volta depression, north-west Benin, designated in 1961 to protect dry-savanna woodland and the quartzite cliffs of the Atakora Mts.

**Boucle du Baoulé National Park** /'bʊklə də læ 'baʊleɪ/ a national park on the Baoulé River which waters the Madingue plateau of western Mali. It was designated in 1953 to protect grassland and riverine forest.

**Bougainville** /'buːɡənvɪl/ a volcanic island in the South Pacific Ocean at the north-west end of the Solomon Islands. With the island of Buka it forms a province of Papua New Guinea; area 10,050 sq. km. (3,880 sq. miles); pop. (est. 1990) 128,000. Named after the French explorer Louis de Bougainville who visited the island in 1768, Bougainville became part of German New Guinea in 1884 while the rest of the Solomons came under British rule. Under Australian mandate after 1920, it became part of independent Papua New Guinea in 1975. It is one of the world's largest producers of copper and potentially one of the greatest producers of gold outside South Africa. In 1989 Melanesian nationalists declared unilateral independence at the height of a guerrilla war that forced the island's mines to close down.

**Bougie** see BEJAÏA.

**Bou Kraa** /buːˈkrɑː/ (also **Bu Cra'a**) the leading phosphate-mining centre of Western Sahara, north-west Africa, 120 km. (75 miles) south-east of La'youn to which it is linked by a conveyor belt.

**Boulder** /'bəʊldə(r)/ a mining town adjacent to Kalgoorlie in Western Australia, situated at the centre of the Coolgardie goldfield; pop.(1991) 21,020 (with Kalgoorlie).

**Boulder** a city in the US state of Colorado, 40 km. (25 miles) north-west of Denver; pop. (1990) 93,312. Situated in a rich agricultural region at the foot of the Rocky Mountains, Boulder claims to be the only city in the world that obtains part of its water supply from a city-owned glacier (Arapho Glacier). The University of Colorado (1876), the National Institute of Standards and Technology, and the National Center for Atmospheric Research are all based in Boulder which is a centre of high-tech industry.

**Boulder Dam** the former name (1937–47) for the HOOVER DAM.

**Boulogne** /bʊˈlɔɪn/ (also **Boulogne-sur-Mer** /sjʊə ˈmer/) a fishing and English Channel ferry port on the north-west coast of France, at the mouth of the River Liane; pop. (1990) 44,240. Julius Caesar set out from here to invade England in 55 BC. The town, which is a leading European fishing port, is France's principal fish-processing centre.

**Boundary Peak** /'baʊndərɪ/ a mountain on the frontier between the US states of Nevada and California. Rising to 4,006 m. (13,143 ft.) it is the highest peak in Nevada.

**Bounty Islands** /'baʊntɪ/ a group of 13 small uninhabited islands in the South Pacific 640 km. (400 miles) south-east of New Zealand, named after HMS *Bounty* which visited the islands in 1788.

**Bourbonnais** /'bʊəbɒneɪ/ a former province of central France now largely occupied by the department of Allier.

**Bourg-en-Bresse** /ˌbʊəkãˈbres/ a market town in the department of Ain, eastern France, on the River Reyssouze; pop. (1990) 43,955. Known for its gourmet food and enamel jewellery.

**Bourges** /bʊəʒ/ the capital of the department of Cher in central France, at the junction of the Auron and Yèvre rivers; pop. (1990) 78,770. Known to the Romans as Avaricum, it was capital of the province of Aquitania. It is noted for its Renaissance buildings, its Gothic cathedral (1192–1324), and its ducal palace where Louis XI was born. The religious reformer Calvin studied law here. Its industries include aircraft and missiles, metals, textiles, tyres, brewing, and food processing.

**Bourget** /'bʊəʒeɪ/, **Lake** a lake in the Savoy region of eastern France, to the east of the Mont du Chat. The spa town of Aix-les-Bains lies on its south-eastern shore and on its western shore stands the Abbaye de Hautecombe which houses the tombs of the Princes of the House of Savoy.

**Bourgogne** /buə'gɒnjə/ the French form of BURGUNDY.

**Bournemouth** a resort town on Poole Bay, an inlet on the Dorset coast of southern England; pop. (1991) 154,400. It was the birthplace of the composer Sir Charles Parry (1848–1918). Robert Louis Stevenson lived in Bournemouth 1884–7 and Mary Shelley is buried in St. Peter's churchyard. Bournemouth University (formerly Bournemouth Polytechnic) was established in 1992.

**Bournville** /'bɔːnvɪl/ a planned village in Warwickshire, central England, established by George and Richard Cadbury in 1879 for those working in the famous Cadbury cocoa and chocolate factory.

**Bourse** /buəs/ (fully **Palais de la Bourse**) the Paris stock exchange in the Rue Vivienne, Paris, France. Built in the style of a Graeco-Roman temple in 1808–27 by the architect A.-Th. Brongniart, it was later enlarged in 1902–3.

**Bouvet Island** /'buːveɪ/ an uninhabited Norwegian island in the South Atlantic, named after the French navigator François Lozier-Bouvet who visited the island in 1739; area 48 sq. km. (19 sq. miles). Once used as a whaling station, it has been a dependency of Norway since 1930.

**Bow** /bəʊ/ the name of several locations in London, England. **1.** a district (also **Stratford-le-Bow**) in Tower Hamlets, east London, named after the bows of a bridge built during the reign of Queen Matilda. **2.** the Bow Church or City parish church of St. Mary-le-Bow in Cheapside within earshot of which the true cockney is supposed to be born. **3.** Bow Street in the Covent Garden area of Westminster, famous for its police court.

**Bow** a river in Canada that rises in the Rocky Mountains of southern Alberta and flows 507 km. (315 miles) south-east through Calgary before it meets the Belly River to become the South Saskatchewan River.

**Bowery** /'baʊərɪ/, **the** a street in lower Manhattan, New York City, USA. Once the road to the farm or *bouwerie* of Peter Stuyvesant, it became part of the mail road to Boston in the 1670s. It later gained a reputation for its theatres, saloons, drunks, and down-and-outs.

**Bowling Green 1.** a city in southern Kentucky, USA, on the Barren River; pop. (1990) 40,641. Founded in 1780, it is a market centre for livestock, dairy produce, and tobacco from the surrounding area. Western Kentucky University (1906) is built around the site of a Civil War fort. **2.** an educational and industrial city in north-west Ohio; pop. (1990) 28,176.

**Boyne** /bɔɪn/ a river in the Republic of Ireland near which the Protestant army of William of Orange defeated the Catholic supporters of James

II in 1690. It rises in the Bog of Allen and flows 128 km. (80 miles) north-eastwards to meet the Irish Sea near Drogheda.

**Boys Town** a village for homeless boys 16 km. (10 miles) west of Omaha, Nebraska, USA, founded in 1917 by Father E. J. Flanagan.

**Bozcaada** /ˌbəʒjɑ'dɑ/ (anc. **Tenedos**) a Turkish island in the Aegean, off the west coast of Turkey, just south of the entrance to the Dardanelles Strait; area 39 sq. km. (15 sq. miles); chief town, Bozcaada. It was alleged to have been used as a base for the Greek fleet during the siege of Troy.

**Bozen** the German form of BOLZANO in Italy.

**Brabant** /brə'bænt/ (Flemish **Braband**) **1.** a former duchy in western Europe between the Meuse and Scheldt rivers, now divided between Belgium and the Netherlands. **2.** a province of central Belgium; area 3,358 sq. km. (1,297 sq. miles); pop. (1991) 2,245,890; capital, Brussels. **3. North Brabant** is a province of the Netherlands; area 4,963 sq. km. (1,917 sq. miles); pop. (1991) 2,209,000; capital, 's-Hertogenbosch.

**Brac** /brɑːtʃ/ (also **Brach**, Italian **Brazza** /'brætzə/) the largest of the Adriatic islands off the Dalmatian coast of Croatia; area 394 sq. km. (152 sq. miles). Its chief town in Supetar. There is a ferry link with Split on the mainland.

**Bracknell** /'bræknəl/ a town 16 km. (10 miles) south-east of Reading in Berkshire, southern England, established in 1949 as a 'new town'; pop. (1981) 49,000. It is the headquarters of the Meteorological Office.

**Bradford** /'brædfəd/ an industrial city with a university (1966) in West Yorkshire; pop. (1981) 281,000. It developed in medieval times as a wool and cloth-manufacturing town. Since the decline of the textile industry in the 1970s engineering, printing, and the manufacture of electronics have become important. The University of Bradford was founded in 1966.

**Braemar** /breɪ'mɑːr/ a Deeside village in north-east Scotland. Situated near Balmoral Castle, its Braemar Gathering is the most famous of the Highland Games held every summer. The standard for the first Jacobite Rising of 1715 was raised at Braemar by the 6th Earl of Mar whose family seat was at Braemar Castle.

**Braga** /'brɑːgə/ a market city in northern Portugal; pop. (1991) 90,535. It is the seat of the Primate of Portugal and capital of a mountainous district of the same name. Known to the Romans as Bracara Augusta, it was capital of the province of Lusitania.

**Braganza** /brə'gænzə/ (Portuguese **Bragança**) a city in north-east Portugal near the Spanish frontier; pop. (1991) 16,550. It is the capital of a district of the same name and was the original seat of the Braganzas who ruled Portugal from 1640 till the end of the monarchy in 1910, and Brazil (upon its independence from Portugal) from 1822 until the formation of the republic in 1889.

**Brahmaputra** /ˌbrɑːməˈpuːtrə/ (Bengali **Jamuna**, Chinese **Yarlung Zangbo**) a river of southern Asia, which rises in Tibet and flows 2,735 km. (1,700 miles) through the Himalayas and north-east India to join the Ganges at its delta (in Bangladesh) on the Bay of Bengal.

**Brahminism** /ˈbrɑːməˌnɪz(ə)m/ the complex sacrificial religion that emerged in post-Vedic India (c.900 BC) under the influence of the dominant priesthood (Brahmans). It was as a reaction to Brahman orthodoxy that heterodox sects such as Buddhism and Jainism were formed.

**braided river** a shallow river course that is interlaced with water channels that are separated by bars of alluvial material.

**Braila** /brəˈiːlə/ an industrial city in south-east Romania, one of the country's two leading ports on the Danube; pop. (1989) 242,595. It is the capital of a county of the same name. Among its chief industries are fishing, shipbuilding, and the manufacture of pulp, textiles, rolling stock, and iron and steel. It is accessible to ocean-going ships from the Black Sea.

**Braintree** /ˈbreɪntriː/ a town on the River Blackwater in Essex, south-east England; pop. (1981) 31,100. Printing, engineering, and the making of nylon have replaced wool manufacture as the chief industries. Nicholas Udall, author of the earliest-known English comedy (*Ralph Roister Doister*) was vicar here from 1537 to 1544.

**Bramber** /ˈbræmbə(r)/ a village on the River Adur in West Sussex, north-east of Worthing. It was the birthplace of Nicholas Barbon who first introduced fire insurance in 1680 (14 years after the Great Fire of London).

**Brampton** /ˈbræmtən/ an industrial town in Ontario, west of Toronto; pop. (1991) 234,400. Its industries include motor vehicles, optical goods, and market gardening.

**Brandenburg** /ˈbrændən ˌbɜːg/ **1.** a former region of north-west Europe whose Hohenzollern rulers became kings of Prussia and emperors of Germany. Its eastern part was ceded to Poland after World War II. **2.** a state of Germany, part of East Germany 1952–90; area 29,060 sq. km. (11,224 sq. miles); pop. (est. 1990) 2,799,000; capital, Potsdam.

**Brandenburg Gate** one of the city gates of Berlin, the only one that survives. It was built in 1788–91 by Carl Langhans (1732–1808), chief architect to Frederick William II of Prussia, in neo-classical style, and surmounted by the Quadriga of Victory, a chariot drawn by four horses. After the construction of the Berlin Wall (1961) it stood in East Berlin, a conspicuous symbol of a divided city; it was reopened on 21 December 1989.

**Brandon** /ˈbrændən/ the second-largest city in Manitoba province, central Canada, situated on the Assiniboine River, in the Great Plains between Regina and Winnipeg; pop. (1991) 38,570. Founded in 1778, it developed as a grain-trading centre for the surrounding farmland. Nearby is the Agricultural Canada Research Station. Its industries include oil refining, chemicals, and farm machinery.

**Brands Hatch** /brændz hætʃ/ a motor circuit near Farningham in Kent, south-east England, opened for Formula Three racing in 1949 and now used both for motor-racing and test-driving.

**Brantford** /ˈbræntfɜːd/ an industrial city in Ontario, Canada, to the west of Hamilton; pop. (1991) 82,000. It is named after Chief Joseph Brant leader of the Six Nations Indians and has the only Royal Indian Chapel in the world (Her Majesty's Chapel of the Mohawks). Alexander Graham Bell, inventor of the telephone lived here and his home is a museum. It has a large farm implement industry.

**Brasilia** /brəˈzɪliə/ the capital (since 1960) of Brazil; pop. (1990) 1,841,000. Designed by Lucio Costa (1902–63) it was built in an unpopulated region, on a site at the geographical centre of the country, chosen (in 1956) in an unsuccessful attempt to draw commerce away from the crowded coastal areas. It was laid out in the shape of an aeroplane with the most impressive buildings, designed by the Brazilian architect Oscar Niemeyer, at its 'nose'.

**Brasov** /bræˈʃɒv/ (Hungarian **Brassó**, German **Kronstadt**) the second-largest city in Romania, an important transportation centre in the central Carpathians; pop. (1989) 352,640. It was held by Hungary from the 11th c. until 1918, when it was ceded to Romania, many of its inhabitants being descended from 13th c. German settlers. During 1950–60 it was known as Orasul Stalin (Romanian = Stalin City). Its industries produce chemicals, textiles, trucks, tractors, sawn timber, electrical goods, and processed food.

**Bratislava** /ˌbrætɪˈslɑːvə/ (German **Pressburg**) a port on the Danube, the capital city of Slovakia; pop. (1991) 441,453. In the Middle Ages it was a frontier town of the Magyar state and from 1536 to 1784 was the capital of Hungary. Its university was founded in 1467. It was incorporated into Czechoslovakia in 1918, becoming capital of the Slovak Socialist Republic in 1969 and capital of independent Slovakia in 1992. Its industrial suburbs produce chemicals, oil, rubber, electrical and engineering goods.

**Bratsk** /brætsk/ a city in central Siberia, in the Russian Federation, on the River Angara; pop. (1990) 258,000. Its industries are largely based on the processing of timber.

**Braunschweig** the German name for BRUNSWICK.

**brave west winds** the strong westerly winds
that blow over oceans in the mid-latitudes of the
southern hemisphere.

**Bray** /breɪ/ **1.** a village on the River Thames in
Berkshire, southern England. The church, which has
a 15th c. lych-gate, is associated with the 'Vicar of
Bray'. **2.** a resort town in County Wicklow, Ireland,
on the Irish Sea coast, south of Dublin; pop. (1991)
25,100. James Joyce lived here from 1888 to 1891

**Brazil** /brə'zɪl/
(Portuguese **Brasil**)
official name **The
Federative Repub-
lic of Brazil** a coun-
try in north-east
South America, the
largest of that contin-
ent, comprising
almost half its total

area, and the fifth-largest in the world; area
8,511,965 sq. km. (3,287,742 sq. miles); pop. (1990)
155,566,100; official language, Portuguese; capital,
Brasilia. The largest cities are São Paulo, Río de
Janeiro, Belo Horizonte, Salvador, Fortaleza,
Brasilia, Nova Iguaçu, Pôrto Alegre, Recife, Belém,
and Manaus. The northern half of Brazil is drained
by the River Amazon and its tributaries, the southern half is drained by the Paraná, Paraguay, and
Uruguay rivers. One-third of the world's remaining
tropical rainforest is located in the Amazon Basin.
Economically, Brazil is still mainly an agricultural
country, but is rich in mineral resources including
iron, gold, phosphates, and uranium. The land is
split into an industrialized coastal belt, which
makes it the most industrialized country in South
America, and a vast underdeveloped interior.
Colonized by the Portuguese in the 16th c., Brazil
became an independent kingdom in 1826, remaining a liberal monarchy until the institution of a

republic in 1889. It fell under dictatorial rule between the World Wars, and although not as troubled by instability as some of its neighbours, is still prone to socio-political unrest. The country, which is named after Brazil-wood from which a red dye was extracted, is governed by a bicameral National Congress.
**Brazilian** *adj. & n.*
The country is divided into 27 federal units:

| Federal Unit | Area (sq. km.) | Pop. (1991) | Capital |
| --- | --- | --- | --- |
| **Norte** | | | |
| Rondônia | 243,044 | 1,130,870 | Pôrto Velho |
| Acre | 152,589 | 417,165 | Río Branco |
| Amazonas | 1,564,455 | 2,102,900 | Manaus |
| Roraima | 230,104 | 215,950 | Boa Vista |
| Pará | 1,250,722 | 5,181,570 | Belém |
| Amapá | 140,276 | 288,690 | Macapá |
| Tocantins | 269,911 | 920,120 | Palmas |
| **Nordeste** | | | |
| Maranhão | 328,663 | 4,929,030 | São Luis |
| Piauí | 250,934 | 2,581,215 | Teresina |
| Ceará | 150,630 | 6,362,620 | Fortaleza |
| Río Grande do Norte | 53,015 | 2,414,120 | Natal |
| Paraíba | 56,372 | 3,200,680 | João Pessoa |
| Pernambuco | 98,281 | 7,122,550 | Recife |
| Alagoas | 27,731 | 2,512,990 | Maceió |
| Sergipe | 21,994 | 1,491,870 | Aracajú |
| Bahia | 561,026 | 11,855,160 | Salvador |
| **Sudeste** | | | |
| Minas Gerais | 587,172 | 15,731,960 | Belo Horizonte |
| Espírito Santo | 45,597 | 2,598,505 | Vitória |
| Río de Janeiro | 44,268 | 12,783,760 | Río de Janeiro |
| São Paulo | 247,898 | 31,546,470 | São Paulo |
| **Sul** | | | |
| Paraná | 199,544 | 8,443,300 | Curitiba |
| Santa Catarina | 95,985 | 4,538,250 | Florianópolis |
| Río Grande do Sul | 282,184 | 9,135,480 | Pôrto Alegre |
| **Centro-Oeste** | | | |
| Mato Grosso do Sul | 350,548 | 1,778,740 | Campo Grande |
| Mato Grosso | 881,001 | 2,022,520 | Cuiabá |
| Goiás | 372,181 | 4,012,560 | Goiânia |
| Federal District | 5,814 | 1,598,415 | Brasilia |

**Brazos** /ˈbræzəs/ a river of the USA, formed in northern Texas at the junction of the Salt Fork and Double Mountain Fork rivers. It flows south-east for 2,106 km. (1,309 miles) before entering the Gulf of Mexico.

**Brazzaville** /ˈbræzəvɪl/ the capital and a major port of the Republic of the Congo, at the lowest navigable point on the Congo (Zaïre) River; pop. (est. 1984) 585,800. It was founded in 1880 by the French explorer Savorgnan de Brazza and was capital of French Equatorial Africa from 1910 to 1958. The city developed after World War II when it was used as a base for the Free French forces in Africa as a trans-shipment point of goods for other Central African countries. Its university was founded in 1972. Industries include railway repair works, shipyards, and consumer goods.

**Breckland** /ˈbreklənd/ a term used to describe a tract of heathland with thicket in east England on the border between Norfolk and Suffolk.

**Brecon Beacons** /ˈbrek(ə)n/ an area of the Welsh countryside dominated by the two highest peaks in south Wales—Pen y Fan (886 m., 2,906 ft.) and Corn Dû (873 m., 2,863 ft.). The Brecon Beacons National Park (1957) stretches from the Tywi valley in the west to the Black Mountains in the east, covering an area of 1,344 sq. km. (519 sq. miles).

**Breda** /ˈbreɪdə/ a manufacturing town in the province of North Brabant, south-west Netherlands, at the junction of the Mark and Aa rivers; pop. (1991) 124,800. It is remembered for the Compromise of Breda (1866), a protest against Spanish rule; the manifesto of Charles II (who lived there in exile), stating his terms for accepting the throne of Britain (1660); and the Treaty of Breda, which ended the Anglo-Dutch war of 1665–7. Its industries include textiles, chocolate, and metal goods.

**Brega** /ˈbreɪgə/ (also **Mersa Brega**, Arabic **Al Brayqah**) a port on the Mediterranean coast of northern Libya, situated on the Gulf of Sirte to the south of Benghazi. It has oil-refineries and is linked by pipeline to the oilfields of the Libyan Desert.

**Bregenz** /breɪˈgents/ the capital of the state of Vorarlberg in western Austria, at the eastern end of Lake Constance (Bodensee); pop. (1991) 27,240.

**Bregenz Forest** (German **Bregenzerwald**) the meadow-covered lower slopes of the northern part of the Vorarlberg Alps between Lake Constance and the Arlberg in western Austria.

**Bremen** /ˈbreɪmən/ **1.** a state of the Federal Republic of Germany surrounded on all sides by Lower Saxony; area 404 sq. km. (156 sq. miles); pop. (1991) 552,750. **2.** its capital, an industrial city and port on the River Weser; pop. (1989) 537,600. It is a major trade outlet to the North Sea and has oil refineries, shipbuilding, textiles, vehicles, electronics, and food processing.

**Bremerhaven** /ˈbreɪmərˌhɑːvən/ a port in Lower Saxony, on the North Sea coast of Germany, north of Bremen; pop. (1991) 130,940. Fishing, engineering, and shipbuilding are the main industries. Founded in 1827, the first regular shipping service between continental Europe and the USA began here in 1847.

**Brenner Pass** /ˈbrenə(r)/ an Alpine pass on the Austro-Italian frontier, at an altitude of 1,371 m. (4,450 ft.) on the route between Innsbruck and Bolzano. It is the lowest and one of the oldest routeways over the main chain of the Alps.

**Brent** /brent/ an outer borough of north-west London, England; pop. (1991) 226,100. The Wembley football stadium is located here.

**Brentford** /ˈbrentfə(r)d/ a western suburb of Greater London, England, on the north bank of the River Thames and a centre of light industry. A stone marks the place where Julius Caesar is said to have crossed the Thames.

**Brentwood** /'brentwʊd/ a mainly residential town in Essex, south-east England, 17 km. (11 miles) south-west of Chelmsford; pop. (1981) 51,643.

**Brescia** /'breʃə/ an industrial city and railway junction in Lombardy, northern Italy; pop. (1990) 196,770. Known to the Romans as Brixia, there are fine examples of Roman, medieval, and Renaissance buildings. For centuries the city has been a noted centre for the production of iron and weapons.

**Breslau** /'brezlaʊ/ the German name for WROCLAW in Poland.

**Bresse** /bres/ a district of forest and pastureland in the Rhône-Alpes region of eastern France, between the River Saône and the Jura Mountains. Centred on the town of Bourg-en-Bresse, the Bresse countryside is noted for its blue cheese.

**Brest** /brest/ a commercial port, arsenal, and naval base on the Atlantic coast of Brittany in north-west France; pop. (1990) 153,100. Originally a Roman military outpost, Brest was developed as a major French port by Cardinal Richlieu in the 1630s. It has shipyards, engineering, and chemical factories as well as a Naval School, Maritime Museum, Oceanographic Research Centre, and university. Brest has been largely rebuilt after the devastation of World War II when it was a German submarine base.

**Brest** (also **Brest-Litovsk** /ˌbrestlɪ'tɒfsk/, Polish **Brzescnad Bugiem**) a port and industrial city in western Belorussia (Belarus), situated close to the Polish border at the junction of the Bug and Mukhavets rivers; pop. (1990) 268,800. A treaty of peace between Germany and Russia was signed here in 1918. It was the birthplace of the Israeli prime minister Menachem Begin (1913–92). Its industries include engineering, sawmilling, textiles, and food processing.

**Bretagne** the French name for BRITTANY.

**Breton** /'bret(ə)n/ (also **Brezhoneg**) a native of Brittany in north-west France. The language of the Bretons belongs to the Brythonic branch of the Celtic language group. It is the only Celtic language now spoken on the European mainland, representing the modern development of the language brought from Cornwall and south Wales in the 5th and 6th c. by Britons fleeing from the Saxon invaders. Until the 20th c. it was widely spoken in Brittany, but official encouragement of the use of French contributed to its decline, although there has recently been some revival of the language. Spoken by some 800,000 people, it has four dialects: Cornouaillais, Léonard, Trégorrois, and Vannetais.

**breva** /'bri:və/ a damp, valley breeze that blows upwards from the Italian lakes.

**Brezhoneg** see BRETON.

**Briansk** see BRYANSK.

**brickfielder** /'brɪkfi:ldə(r)/ a hot, dusty wind in south-east Australia. It usually blows southwards from the interior in front of depressions during the summer.

**Bridgend** /brɪdʒ'end/ a market town on the River Ogmore in Mid Glamorgan, south Wales; pop. (1981) 31,600.

**Bridgeport** /'brɪdʒpɔ:t/ a seaport, residential and industrial city on Long Island Sound, Connecticut, USA; pop. (1990) 141,686. Bridgeport was the home of the showman P. T. Barnum (1810–91) whose 'Greatest Show on Earth' included the 28-inch Charles S. Stratton (better known as General Tom Thumb), also a native of the city. Its industries include helicopters, firearms, gas-turbine engines, metal products, electrical equipment, and stage scenery.

**Bridgetown** /'brɪdʒtaʊn/ a port and capital of the island of Barbados in the Caribbean; pop. (1990) 6,720.

**Bridgwater** /'brɪdʒwɔ:tə(r)/ a town in the county of Somerset, south-west England, on the Parrett River; pop. (1981) 31,000. The Duke of Monmouth proclaimed himself king here in 1685, but was defeated at Sedgemoor which lies 5 km. (3 miles) to the south-east. It was the birthplace of Admiral Robert Blake (1599–1657). There is a nuclear power-station at Hinkley Point on Bridgwater Bay.

**Bridlington** /'brɪdlɪŋtən/ a port and resort town on the North Sea coast of Humberside, England; pop. (1981) 28,970. It was the birthplace of the painter, gardener, and architect William Kent (1684–1748).

**Brie** /bri:/ a district of northern France in the departments of Marne and Seine-et-Marne east of Paris, noted for its soft cheese.

**Brighouse** /'brɪghaʊs/ a town in West Yorkshire, England, on the River Calder; pop. (1981) 32,550. Engineering and the manufacture of textiles are the chief industries. The grave of Robin Hood is said to be near the 13th-c. Kirklees Priory.

**Brighton** /'braɪt(ə)n/ a residential town and resort on the south coast of England, in East Sussex; pop. (1991) 133,400. It was patronized by the Prince of Wales (later George IV) from c. 1780 to 1827, and has much Regency architecture and a royal pavilion rebuilt for him by John Nash in Oriental style. The University of Sussex was founded in 1961 and the University of Brighton (formerly Brighton Polytechnic) was established in 1992.

**Brindisi** /'bri:ndəsi:/ an Adriatic port and capital of Brindisi province, Apulia, on the 'heel' of south-east Italy; pop. (1991) 93,290. The Romans developed a harbour here at the southern end of the Appian Way. It was later used as a point of departure for Crusaders during the 12th–13th c., and as a naval base during World War I. There is a ferry link with Greece and a petrochemicals industry. The poet Virgil died here in 19 BC.

**Brisbane** /'brɪzbən/ a port on the east coast of Australia, on the Brisbane River, the capital and largest city of Queensland; pop. (1991) 1,145,540. Founded in 1824 as a penal colony, it is named after the Scottish soldier and patron of astronomy Sir Thomas Brisbane, governor of New South Wales 1821–5. Its university was founded in 1909 and the city has oil-refining, shipbuilding, textiles, and agricultural machinery industries.

**Bristol** /'brɪst(ə)l/ the county town of Avon in south-west England, at the junction of the Avon and Frome rivers; pop. (1991) 370,300. A leading port and commercial centre since the 12th c., Bristol was the second most important town in England between the 15th and 18th c. It was given the status of a county by Edward III in 1373. It developed as one of the 'corners' of the triangular colonial trade which included the shipping of slaves from Africa to the Americas. It is particularly rich in old churches: its cathedral dates back to the 12th c. and St. Mary Redcliffe to the 13th c. The *Great Western*, which was one of the world's first transatlantic steamships, was launched in Bristol and at anchor in Bristol shipyard is the *Great Britain*, the first iron-built ship. John Cabot set out from here in 1497 on his expedition to North America. It is the site of the University of Bristol (1909) and the University of the West of England, Bristol (formerly Bristol Polytechnic) which was established in 1992. The city has many light industries; its suburb of Filton has a major aerospace complex. Clifton has Brunel's suspension bridge, completed after his death.

**Bristol** a city in Connecticut, USA, 22 km. (14 miles) south-west of Hartford; pop. (1990) 60,640. It has been a noted centre of clock-making since 1790. Cable television and the manufacture of ball-bearings, springs, and electrical equipment are also important.

**Bristol Channel** an extension of the River Severn estuary separating England and Wales.

**Britain** /'brɪt(ə)n/ (in full **Great Britain**) the island containing England, Wales, and Scotland, and including the small adjacent islands. After the Old English period *Britain* was used only as an historical term until about the time of Henry VIII and Edward VI, when it came into practical politics in connection with the efforts made to unite England and Scotland. In 1604 James I was proclaimed 'King of Great Britain', and this name was adopted for the United Kingdom at the Union of 1707, after which *South Britain* and *North Britain* were frequent in Acts of Parliament for England and Scotland respectively.
**British** *adj. & n.*

**British Antarctic Territory** that part of Antarctica claimed by Britain. Designated in 1962 from territory formerly administered as part of the Falklands Islands Dependencies, it includes some 388,500 sq. km. (150,058 sq. miles) of the continent of Antarctica as well as adjacent South Orkney Islands and South Shetland Islands in the South Atlantic. Also in 1962 the former Falklands Islands Dependencies Survey, which had established its first shore-stations in 1944, became the British Antarctic Survey.

**British Columbia** /kə'lʌmbɪə/ a province of Canada on the west coast of North America, formed in 1866 by the union of Vancouver Island (a British colony from 1849) and the mainland area which was then called New Caledonia; area 947,800 sq. km. (365,947 sq. miles); pop. (1991) 3,282,060; capital, Victoria. British Columbia is Canada's westernmost and third-largest province. Off its 7,022-km. (4,419-mile) Pacific coast lie Vancouver Island and Queen Charlotte Islands. It is a largely mountainous province, with the Rocky Mountains in the south-east, the Coast Mountains along the Pacific coast, and the Stikine Mountains in the north-west. Its highest peak is Fairweather Mountain (4,663 m., 15,298 ft.). There are over two million hectares of lakes and waterways which support fishing, farming, recreation, and the generation of hydroelectric power, the largest river being the Fraser River. Commercial forest covers more than half of the province which contains 50 per cent of Canada's softwood timber. Coal, oil, gas, copper, zinc, and molybdenum are the most important mineral resources.

**British Commonwealth** (fully **British Commonwealth of Nations**) the former name of the COMMONWEALTH or Commonwealth of Nations.

**British East Africa** a general term for the former British East African territories of Kenya, Uganda, Tanganyika, and Zanzibar.

**British Guiana** /gaɪ'ænə/ the former name (until 1966) of GUYANA in South America.

**British Honduras** /hɒn'djʊərəs/ the former name (until 1973) of BELIZE in Central America.

**British Indian Ocean Territory** a British dependency in the Indian Ocean, comprising the islands of the Chagos Archipelago. Ceded to Britain by France in 1814, the islands were administered  from Mauritius until the designation of a separate dependency in 1965. There are no permanent inhabitants, but British and US naval personnel occupy the island of Diego Garcia.

**British Isles** the islands lying off the west coast of Europe from which they are separated by the

English Channel and the North Sea. The islands comprise the United Kingdom of Great Britain and Northern Ireland (including the Channel Islands and the Isle of Man) and the Republic of Ireland.

**British Library** the national library of Britain containing the former library departments of the British Museum, to which George II presented the royal library in 1757. It is one of the six copyright libraries to receive a copy of every book published in the UK. Its very expensive, and much derided, new building is in Euston Road, London.

**British Museum** a national museum of antiquities etc. in Bloomsbury, London, occupying the site of Montagu House, which was acquired in 1753 to house the library and collections of Sir Hans Sloane and the Harleian manuscripts purchased with funds granted by Parliament. The present buildings were erected from 1823 onwards.

**British Somaliland** a former British protectorate established on the Somali coast of East Africa in 1884. In 1960 it united with Italian Somaliland to form the independent state of Somalia.

**British Virgin Islands** the northern and eastern islands of the Virgin Islands group in the Caribbean, comprising the four larger islands of Tortola, Virgin Gorda, Anegada,  and Jost Van Dyke, and about 36 smaller islets and cays, all of which form a British dependent territory at the north-west end of the Lesser Antilles; area 153 sq. km. (59 sq. miles); pop. (1991) 16,750; official language, English; capital, Road Town (on Tortola Island). First settled by the Dutch in 1648, the islands were later occupied by British planters in 1666. It remained part of the colony of the Leeward Islands until 1956 when it became a separate Crown Colony. Tourism, the mining of stone and gravel, and the production of sugar-cane, coconuts, fruit, and vegetables are the main industries.

**British West Africa** a general term for the former British West African territories of Gold Coast, Gambia, Togoland, Nigeria, Sierra Leone, and Cameroons.

**Briton** /'brɪt(ə)n/ **1.** one of the people of southern Britain before the Roman conquest. **2.** a native or inhabitant of Great Britain or (formerly) of the British Empire.

**Brive-la-Gaillarde** /ˌbriːvlæ'gaɪjɑːd/ a town in the department of Corrèze, Limousin region, south-central France, on the River Corrèze; pop. (1990) 52,680. It is a noted centre of market gardening and fruit growing.

**Brittany** /'brɪtənɪ/ (French **Bretagne** /bre'tænjə/) a region of north-west France forming a peninsula between the Bay of Biscay and the English Channel. It comprises the departments of Côtes-d'Armor, Finistère, Ille-et-Vilaine, and Morbihan; area 27,208 sq. km. (10,509 sq. miles) and is noted for market gardening, fishing, tourism, and industries including motor vehicles and electronics; pop. (1990) 2,175,800. The chief towns are Nantes, Rennes, Lorient, Quimper, and Brest.

**Brixham** /'brɪksəm/ a resort town near Torquay in Devon, south-west England; pop. (1981) 15,500. William of Orange landed here in 1688 before ascending the throne of Great Britain. The town is associated with H. F. Lyte, composer of the hymn *Abide with me*.

**Brixton** /'brɪkstən/ a suburb of south-west London, England, the location of a major prison.

**Brno** /'bɜːnəʊ/ (German **Brünn**) an industrial city of South Moravia in the Czech Republic, situated at the junction of the Svratka and Svitava rivers; pop. (1991) 387,990. Founded in the 10th century and later capital of the Austrian Crownland of Moravia, it is now the second-largest city in the country. The Austrian biologist Gregor Mendel (1822–84) devised his theory of inheritance while an abbott in Brno. The Bren gun, which was developed here, is named after the city. As well as armaments, the city has textile, chemical, and machinery industries.

**Broad Peak** /brɔːd/ a mountain peak of the Karkoram Range rising to 8,047 m. (26,400 ft.). Known locally as Palchan Ri, it was given its English name by the Conway expedition of 1892 and was first climbed by an Australian team in 1957.

**Broads** /brɔːdz/, **the** a name given to that part of East Anglia in England typified by shallow freshwater lakes that are created by the broadening out of slow-moving rivers. The largest of the lakes is Hickling Broad and there are over 320 km. (200 miles) of navigable waterways.

**Broadstairs** /'brɔːdsteɪrz/ a coastal resort near Ramsgate in the Isle of Thanet, Kent, south-east England; pop. (1981) 25,326. The town has associations with Charles Dickens who wrote some of his novels here and the composer and pianist Richard Rodney Bennet who was born here in 1936.

**Broadway** /'brɔːdweɪ/ a street traversing the length of Manhattan Island, New York City, USA. One of the longest streets in the world, it extends for about 21 km. (13 miles), and is famous for its theatres which formerly made its name synonymous with showbusiness.

**Brocken** /'brɒkən/ the highest peak (1,143 m., 3,747 ft.) in the Harz Mountains in northern Germany, reputed to be the scene of witches'

Walpurgis-night revels. It gives its name to the *Brocken spectre*, a magnified shadow of the spectator thrown on a bank of cloud in high mountains when the sun is low, and often encircled by rainbow-like bands.

**Brockton** /'brɒktən/ an industrial city in east Massachusetts, USA, south of Boston; pop. (1990) 92,788. Once noted for its manufacture of shoes, it is now a centre for the production of plastics, paper products, and electronic equipment. The boxers Rocky Marciano and Marvin Hagler were born in Brockton.

**Broken Arrow** an oil city in eastern Oklahoma, USA, situated 22 km. (14 miles) south-east of Tulsa; pop. (1990) 58,000.

**Broken Hill** a mining town in New South Wales, Australia; pop. (1991) 23,260. It was founded in 1884 as a lead-, zinc-, and silver-mining settlement and has a School of the Air and Royal Flying Doctor Service.

**Broken Hill** the former name of KABWE in Zambia.

**Bromberg** /'brɒmbeək/ the German name for the city of BYDGOSZCZ in Poland.

**Bromley** /'brɒmlɪ/ an outer residential borough of south-east London, England; pop. (1991) 281,700. The novelist H. G. Wells was born here in 1866.

**Bromo** /'brəʊməʊ/, **Mount** a volcano on the Indonesian island of Java, rising to 2,614 m. (8,576 ft.) in the Tengger Mountains. Live animals are thrown into the crater to placate the gods in the annual Kasada Festival. The last major eruption was in 1930.

**Brompton** /'brɒmtən/ a suburb of Kensington in west London, England.

**Bromsgrove** /'brɒmzgrəʊv/ a market and residential town in Hereford and Worcester, west-central England; pop. (1991) 89,800.

**Bronx** /brɒŋks/, **the** a borough of New York City, USA, north-east of the Harlem River; area 109 sq. km. (42 sq. miles); pop. (1990) 1,203,790. It was named after a Dutch settler Jonas Bronck, who purchased land here in 1641. It is a crowded residential area with factories, warehouses, and a vast wholesale produce market. It has New York's zoo and botanical gardens, Yankee Stadium, and many educational institutions.

**Brooklands** /'brʊkləndz/ a motor-racing track opened in 1907 near Weybridge in Surrey, south-east England. Laid out in the shape of an oval horse-racing track, it was the world's first special motor-racing circuit. The course proved invaluable to British motor manufacturers and inventors who were hampered in testing their products by the prevailing speed limit of 20 m.p.h. on roads. The first British Grand Prix was held here in 1926. During World War II the course was converted (and subsequently sold) for aeroplane manufacture.

**Brookline** /'brʊklaɪn/ a residential city just west of Boston, Massachusetts, USA; pop. (1990) 54,718. Settled in the 1630s, it was known as Muddy River when part of Boston. Brookline, which became a separate city in 1705, was the birthplace of President John F. Kennedy.

**Brooklyn** /'brʊklɪn/ a borough of New York City, USA, at the south-west corner of Long Island; area 182 sq. km. (70 sq. miles); pop. (1990) 2,292,160. The **Brooklyn Bridge** (1883), Manhattan Bridge, and **Brooklyn Battery Tunnel** (the longest vehicular tunnel in the US) link Brooklyn with Lower Manhattan and the Verrazano-Narrows Bridge (1964) links Brooklyn with Staten Island. It is both a residential and industrial borough with machinery, paper, chemical, and textile industries. It has notable museums and libraries, and many educational institutions, as well as botanical gardens, old churches, and the New York Aquarium.

**Brooklyn Park** a suburb of Minneapolis, Minnesota, USA; pop. (1990) 56,381. It became a separate city in 1969.

**Brooks Range** /brʊks/ a mountain range in northern Alaska between the Bering Strait and the Canadian border. It includes the smaller Endicott, Baird, and De Long mountain ranges. Its highest peak is Mt. Chamberlain (2,749 m., 9,020 ft.).

**Browning** /'braʊnɪŋ/ a town at the eastern entrance to Glacier National Park, Montana, USA; pop. (1990) 1,170. Named after a US Commissioner of Indian Affairs, it is home to the Museum of the Plains Indian and nearby is a Blackfoot Indian reservation.

**Browns Ferry** /ˌbraʊnz 'ferɪ/ the site of a nuclear power-station on the Alabama River, central Alabama, USA. It was the scene of a near-disastrous nuclear accident in 1975 when Browns Ferry was the home of the world's largest nuclear power-station. This event marked the beginning of a decline in the construction of new reactors.

**Brownsville** /'braʊnzvɪl/ a city in southern Texas, USA, situated near the mouth of the Rio Grande, close to the Mexican border opposite Matamoros; pop. (1990) 98,962. Founded in 1846 the construction of Fort Taylor precipitated the Mexican War which is commemorated nearby at the battlefield site of Palo Alto where the first engagement took place. Port Brownsville, which is an important shrimp port and deep-sea fishing centre, is linked to the Gulf of Mexico by a canal along which is shipped grain, fruit, and vegetables.

**Bruce** /bruːs/, **Mount** one of the highest peaks in the state of Western Australia, rising to 1,226 m. (4,024 ft.) between the Ashburton and Fortescue rivers.

**Bruce Trail** a 437-km. (271-mile) walking route that follows the Niagara escarpment in eastern Canada from Niagara to Tobermory, passing through Hamilton, Burlington, and Dundas.

**Bruges** /bruːʒ/ (Flemish **Brugge** /ˈbrʊxə/) an historic and commercial city in north-west Belgium, capital of the province of West Flanders; pop. (1991) 117,000. In medieval times Bruges was the chief city of the Hanseatic League and a major centre of the textile industry. Its trade declined in the 15th c. in the face of competition with Antwerp and the silting-up of the River Zwyn which linked it to the North Sea. Every year on Ascension Day the drops of Christ's blood gifted to the city in 1150 are paraded through the streets. The well-preserved medieval buildings make it a popular tourist destination. Other industries include chemicals, textiles, and electronics.

**Brunei** /ˈbruːnaɪ/ official name **The State of Brunei Darussalam** a small oil-rich sultanate on the north coast of Borneo, between the Malaysian states of Sabah and Sarawak, facing the South

China Sea; area 5,765 sq. km. (2,226 sq. miles); pop. (est. 1991) 300,000; capital, Bandar Seri Begawan. Some 65 per cent of the population are of Malay origin and Islam is the official religion. Largely covered in tropical forest, its principal exports are petroleum and natural gas. By the early 16th c. Brunei's power extended over the whole of the island of Borneo and parts of the Philippines, but declined as Portuguese and Dutch influence grew, and in 1888 it was placed under British protection; it became fully independent in 1984. The Sultan, who has supreme executive authority, presides over a Council of Cabinet Ministers, a Religious Council, and a Privy Council.
**Bruneian** *adj. & n.*

**Brunei Town** the former name (until 1970) of BANDAR SERI BEGAWAN, capital of Brunei.

**Brunswick** /ˈbrʌnzwɪk/ (German **Braunschweig** /ˈbraʊnʃvaɪk/) **1.** a former duchy and state of Germany mostly incorporated into Lower Saxony in 1946. **2.** an industrial city in Lower Saxony, north-west Germany, on the Oker River; pop. (1991) 259,130. Henry the Lion (d. 1195), Emperor Otto IV (d. 1218) and the philosopher Gotthold Lessing (1729–81) are buried in Brunswick. Manufactures include pianos, computers, vehicle parts, and cameras.

**Brussels** /ˈbrʌs(ə)lz/ (French **Bruxelles** /bruːˈsel/, Flemish **Brüssel**) a city on the River Senne, the capital of Brabant since the 14th c. and of Belgium since it achieved independence in 1830; pop. (1991) 954,000. It was an important textile city in medieval times and was the seat of the dukes of Burgundy and the governors of the Spanish Netherlands. The North Atlantic Treaty Organization (NATO) and the Commission of the European Communities have their headquarters here. Brussels is a major administrative, commercial, cultural, and industrial centre. It has many medieval and Renaissance-style buildings, churches, art galleries, and museums. Its cathedral dates from the 13th c. and its university from 1834. Industries, largely in the suburbs, include electronic and electrical equipment, textiles, chemicals, machinery, rubber, brewing, and food processing.

**Bryansk** /briːˈɑːnsk/ (also **Briansk**) an industrial city in western Russia, on the Desna River south-west of Moscow; pop. (1990) 456,000. It was formerly named Bryn' and later Debriansk.

**Bryce Canyon** /braɪs/ a canyon with notable rock formations on the edge of the Paunsaugunt Plateau, southern Utah, USA. Named after an early settler, Ebenezer Bryce, 14,841 hectares (37,102 acres) were designated as a national park in 1924.

**Brythonic** /brɪˈθɒnɪk/ the southern group of the Celtic languages, including Welsh, Cornish, and Breton. It grew from the language spoken by the Britons at the time of the Roman invasion, and borrowed a number of Latin words during the Roman occupation. When in the 5th c. Britain was invaded by Germanic-speaking peoples the language of the Britons died out in most parts but survived in the mountainous and more remote parts of Wales, Cumberland, the Scottish lowlands, and Cornwall, and was carried by British emigrants across the Channel, where it survives as the Breton language in Brittany.

**Brzeg** /bəˈʒek/ (German **Brieg** /briːk/) an industrial city in the county of Opole, south-west Poland, on the Oder River; pop. (1990) 38,440. It was the seat of the Piast dukes of Brzeg from 1311 to 1675. In the 18th c. it was an important centre of Polish publishing.

**BST** *abbr.* British Summer Time.

**Bucaramanga** /ˌbuːkərəˈmɑːŋgə/ a commercial city and capital of the department of Santander in north-central Colombia; pop. (1985) 352,526. Known as the 'garden city' of Colombia, it lies at the centre of a major coffee-, cotton-, and tobacco-growing region.

**Bucelas** /buːˈseləs/ a village in central Portugal, situated to the north of Lisbon in a small but noted wine-producing region; pop. (1991) 1,970.

**Buchan** /ˈbʌxən/ an area of north-east Scotland to the north of the Ythan River. The **Buchan Ness** headland south of Peterhead is the eastern-most point of Scotland and the **Bullers of Buchan** is a rocky hollow on the Buchan coast.

**Buchanan** /ˌbjuːˈkænən/ a port on the south-east coast of Liberia in west Africa. It was formerly known as Grand Bassa.

**Bucharest** /ˌbuːkəˈrest/ (Romanian **Bucureşti** /buːkuːˈreʃt/) a city on the Dambovita River, capital of Romania; pop. (1989) 2,318,890. Founded in the 14th c. on the trade route between Europe and Constantinople, Bucharest became capital of the principality of Walachia in 1698 and of Romania in 1861. It is a cultural centre with theatres, museums, galleries, and old churches. Engineering, oil refining, food processing, and the manufacture of textiles and chemicals are the chief industries.

**Buchenwald** /'bu:kən‚vɑːlt/ a village in central Germany near Weimar in Thuringia, site of a Nazi concentration camp in World War II.

**Buckingham** /'bʌkɪŋəm/ a market town in Buckinghamshire, England, on the River Ouse. The University of Buckingham (founded as University College at Buckingham in 1976) was established in 1983.

**Buckingham Palace** the London residence of the British sovereign since 1837, adjoining St. James's Park, Westminster. It was built for the Duke of Buckingham in the early 18th c., bought by George III in 1761, and redesigned by John Nash for George IV in 1825; the façade facing the Mall was redesigned in 1913.

**Buckinghamshire** /'bʌkɪŋəm‚ʃɪə(r)/ a southern county of England, situated to the north of the Chiltern Hills; area 1,883 sq. km. (727 sq. miles); pop. (1991) 619,500; county town, Aylesbury. Buckinghamshire is divided into five districts:

| District | Area (sq. km.) | Pop. (1991) |
| --- | --- | --- |
| Aylesbury Vale | 904 | 143,600 |
| Chiltern | 200 | 88,700 |
| Milton Keynes | 310 | 172,300 |
| South Bucks | 144 | 60,300 |
| Wycombe | 324 | 154,500 |

**Buck Island Reef** a coral reef off the north-east coast of the Caribbean island of St. Croix in the US Virgin Islands. The reef, which is a national monument, features an underwater nature trail.

**Bucks.** /bʌks/ abbr. Buckinghamshire.

**Budapest** /‚bu:də'pest/ the capital of Hungary, formed in 1873 by the union of the hilly Buda on the right bank of the Danube with the low-lying Pest on the left bank (they are connected by several bridges including the Chain Bridge built by British engineers (1839–49), and modelled on that across the Thames at Marlow, Bucks.); pop. (1989) 2,000,000. Its old town is a mixture of Roman-esque, Gothic, and baroque buildings. Its principal landmarks are Buda Castle, 13th-c. Matthias Church, the Fisherman's Bastion, the neo-Gothic Parliament, the remains of the Roman town of Aquincum, the Liberation Monument on Gellért Hill, and the Hungarian National Museum. The city is associated with the composers Béla Bartók, Zoltán Kodály, and Franz Liszt, and was the birth-place in 1885 of the literary historian Georg Lukács. Its international airport is at Ferihegy,

14 km. (9 miles) south-east of the city centre. It is the economic, political, and cultural centre of Hungary and produces nearly half of its industrial products. Its suburban industries include oil refin-ing, chemicals, pharmaceuticals, textiles, engineer-ing, and foodstuffs.

**Buddh Gaya** see BODHGAYA.

**Buddhism** /'bʊdɪz(ə)m/ a widespread Asian religion or philosophy, founded by Siddhartha Gautama, entitled the Buddha, in north-east India in the 5th c. BC as a reaction against the sacrificial religion of orthodox Brahminism. It is a religion without a god, in which human mistakes and human doom are linked in a relentless chain of cause and effect. There are two major traditions, namely: *Theravada* (often called *Hinayana*), and *Mahayana*; and emerging from the latter, *Vajrayana*. The basic teachings of Buddhism are contained in the 'four noble truths': all existence is suffering; the cause of suffering is desire; freedom from suffering is nirvana; and the means of attain-ing nirvana is prescribed in the 'eightfold path' that combines ethical conduct, mental discipline, and wisdom. Central to this religious path are the doc-trine of 'no self' (*anatta*) and the practice of meditation. The three 'jewels' of Buddhism are the Buddha, the doctrine (*dharma*), and the sangha. There are approximately 300 million adherents of Buddhism worldwide.
**Buddhist** adj. & n.

**Bude** /bjuːd/ a resort town on the north coast of Cornwall, south-west England; pop. (est. 1985) 4,624.

**Budweis** the German name for CESKÉ BUDEJOVICE in the Czech Republic.

**Buena Park** /'bweɪnə/ a city in southern California, USA, situated between Los Angeles and Anaheim; pop. (1990) 68,784. It is the site of the Los Alamitos Race Course and the historic gold-rush settlement of Knott's Berry Farm.

**Buenaventura** /‚bweɪnəven'tʊərə/ the chief Pacific port of Colombia, trading in tobacco, sugar, and coffee from the Cauca valley; pop. (1985) 122,500.

**Buenos Aires** /'bweɪnəs 'aɪriːz/ the capital city, chief port, commercial, industrial, and cul-tural centre of Argentina, on the south bank of the River Plate; pop. (1991) 2,960,980; metropolitan area pop. (1991) 11,256,000. The first permanent settlement was established here by the Spanish in 1580 and in 1776 it was made capital of the new viceroyalty of the Río de la Plata. In 1862 it became capital of a united Argentina. The subsequent con-struction of railways attracted large numbers of immigrants to the surrounding pampas and the city developed as a major outlet and processing centre for cattle, grain, and dairy products. Its in-dustries include motor vehicles, engineering, oil, chemicals, textiles, paper, and food processing with large meat-packing and refrigeration plants. It is a major cultural centre with several universities, The National Library, and a world-famous opera house.

**Buffalo** /'bʌfə‚ləʊ/ an industrial city and major port of the St. Lawrence Seaway at the eastern end of Lake Erie, in north-west New York State, USA; pop. (1990) 328,120. It is the second-largest city in the state of New York and one of the largest railroad centres in the US. In 1679 the first ship to sail on the Great Lakes was launched from here by the French and in 1816 the first Great Lakes steamboat was built. The opening of the Erie Canal in 1825 turned Buffalo into a major transportation centre and the development of the steam-powered grain elevator in 1843 led to a boom in the grain-processing industry. When President William McKinley was assassinated at the Pan-American Exposition in 1901, Theodore Roosevelt took the presidential oath in Buffalo. The National Center for Earthquake Research is located at the State University of New York at Buffalo (1846). Its industries include steel, chemicals, grain milling, and feedstuffs.

**Bug** /bu:g/ (also **Western Bug**) a river of eastern Europe that rises in west Ukraine and flows north to Brest then west into Poland to meet the Vistula north-west of Warsaw.

**Bug** (also **Southern Bug**) a river that rises in south-west-central Ukraine and flows south-east for 845 km. (532 miles) to meet the Dnieper estuary near Nikolayev.

**Buganda** /bu:'gændə, bju:-/ a former powerful kingdom of East Africa, on the north shore of Lake Victoria, now part of Uganda.

**Bugis** /'bu:gɪz/ a seafaring tribe of the Indonesian archipelago of South-East Asia. Early European spice traders, who were terrified of the ferocity of the Bugis, coined the word 'Boogie man' or 'bogeyman' to describe any person (real or imaginary) causing fear.

**Bujumbura** /‚bu:dʒəm'bʊərə/ the capital and largest city of Burundi, on the Ruzizi Plain at the north-east corner of Lake Tanganyika; pop. (1989) 241,000. Formerly known as Usumbura (until 1962), the modern city developed after 1899 when it became a military post of German East Africa. After World War I it became the administrative centre of the Belgian mandate of Ruanda-Urundi.

**Bukavu** /bu:'kɑ:vu:/ a mining town and capital of Kivu region in eastern Zaire; pop. (1984) 171,000. Until 1966 it was known as Costermansville.

**Bukhara** /bʊ'kɑ:rə/ (also **Bokhara**, Uzbek **Bukhoro**) a city in Uzbekistan, in the valley of the Zeravshan River; pop. (1990) 246,200. Situated in a large cotton-growing district, it is a leading centre of karakul lambskin processing and one of the oldest trade centres in central Asia. From the 16th c. to 1920 it was capital of the khanate of Bukhara which was incorporated into the Russian empire in 1868.

**Bukittinggi** /‚bu:kə'tɪŋgɪ/ a town on the Indonesian island of Sumatra, in the mountains to the north of Padang on the west coast. It is the centre of a rich agricultural area producing rice, coffee, and tobacco. It is the cultural centre of the Minangkabau people.

**Bükk** /bʌk/ a range of mountains to the north-east of Eger in the Northern Highlands of Hungary.

**Bukovina** /‚bʊkə'vi:nə/ a region of south-east Europe, divided between Romania and Ukraine. Formerly a province of the principality of Moldavia, it was ceded to Austria by the Turks in 1777. Known for a time as the circle of Chernowitz, it became an Austrian duchy in 1849. After World War I it was made part of Romania and so remained until World War II, when the northern part was occupied by the Soviet army, who incorporated this section into the Ukrainian SSR. The region is noted for its painted churches.

**Bulawayo** /‚bu:lə'weɪəʊ/ an industrial city and transportation centre in western Zimbabwe, the administrative and commercial capital of Matabeleland North and South; pop. (1982) 414,000. Formerly the capital of the Matabele chiefs and originally known as GuBulawayo (= place of slaughter), the city developed into the country's second-largest city after 1893 when it was occupied by the British South Africa Company as a mining settlement. It has varied industries including motor vehicles, metals, machinery, textiles, tyres, building materials, and food processing.

**Bulgan** /'bu:lgɑ:n/ the capital of a county of the same name in northern Mongolia; pop. (1990) 13,800. Mining, timber, and livestock are important local industries.

**Bulgar** /'bʌlgɑ:(r)/ an ancient Finnish tribe that conquered the Slavs of the lower Danube area in the 7th c. AD and settled in what is now Bulgaria, becoming Slavonic in language.

**Bulgaria**
/bʌl'geərɪə/
(Bulgarian
**Bulgariya**) official
name **Republic of
Bulgaria** a country
in south-east Europe
on the western shores
of the Black Sea,
with Romania to the

north, Greece and Turkey to the south, and Serbia and Macedonia to the west; area 110,912 sq. km. (42,840 sq. miles); pop. (est. 1991) 9,000,000; official language, Bulgarian; capital, Sofia. Its largest cities are Sofia, Plovdiv, Varna, Burgas, and Ruse. The Balkan Range (Stara Planina) crosses the country from east to west separating the plain of the River Danube (which flows along the greater part of Bulgaria's northern frontier) from the valley of the Maritsa River. To the west and south, the Rhodope, Rila, and Pirin mountains separate Bulgaria from its neighbours. The climate is largely continental with hot summers and cold winters, but in the south and along the Black Sea coast winters are milder. Until World War II Bulgaria was predominantly an agricultural country, but since then the industrial sector has been effectively built up (initially with Soviet assistance) and a substantial engineering industry developed. About 40 per cent of the land is arable producing wheat, corn, barley, and tobacco (the world's fourth-largest exporter). Conquered during the Dark Ages by Bulgar tribes from the east, the country became part of the Ottoman empire in the 14th c., remaining under Turkish rule until the Russo-Turkish wars of the late 19th c. Bulgaria fought on the German side in both World Wars, generally not enjoying good relations with her Balkan neighbours. Occupied by the Soviets after World War II, the state was one of the most consistently pro-Soviet members of the Warsaw Pact until the general collapse of Communism in Eastern Europe in 1989 and the introduction of a multi-party political system.

**Bulgarian** *adj. & n.*

Bulgaria has been divided since 1987 into nine regions (*oblasts*):

| Region | Area (sq. km.) | Pop. (1990) |
|---|---|---|
| Burgas | 14,657 | 875,430 |
| Khaskovo | 13,892 | 1,054,400 |
| Lovech | 15,150 | 1,048,670 |
| Mikhailovgrad | 10,607 | 655,800 |
| Plovdiv | 13,628 | 1,287,610 |
| Razgrad | 10,842 | 843,580 |
| Sofia (city) | 1,331 | 1,220,900 |
| Sofia | 18,979 | 1,010,950 |
| Varna | 11,929 | 989,820 |

**Bull Run** /bʊl/ a small river in east Virginia, scene of two Confederate army victories (1861 and 1862) during the American Civil War.

**Bunbury** /'bʌnbərɪ/ a seaport and resort on Koombana Bay to the south of Perth in Western Australia; pop. (1991) 24,000. Named after a Lieut. Bunbury who first explored the area in the 1830s, the town was originally a timber port.

**Buncombe** /'bʌnkəm/ a county in the Blue Ridge Mountains of North Carolina, USA, mentioned in a filibustering speech by its Congressman, *c.*1820, giving rise to the expression *Bunkum* meaning nonsense or humbug. Its county town is Asheville.

**Bundaberg** /'bʌndə,bɜːg/ a town in Queensland, eastern Australia, 375 km. (236 miles) north of Brisbane in the fertile plain of the Burnett River; pop. (1991) 38,070. It is the southernmost access point to the Great Barrier Reef and a centre

for the production of sugar and rum. There is a port facility at **Port Bundaberg** to the north-east. It was the home of Bert Hinkler who in 1928 was the first man to fly solo from England to Australia.

**Bundoran** /bən'dəʊrən/ a resort town in County Donegal in the north of the Republic of Ireland, situated on the southern shore of Donegal Bay; pop. (1991) 1,458.

**Bungle Bungle Mountains** /'bʌŋg(ə)l bʌŋg(ə)l/ a range of sandstone mountains in the Kimberley region of north Western Australia. Its unusual banded rock walls and domed peaks form part of the Purnululu National Park which was designated in 1987.

**Bungo Strait** /'bʌŋgəʊ/ a channel separating the Japanese islands of Kyushu and Shikoku.

**Bunker Hill** /'bʌŋkə(r)/ a hill (33 m., 107 ft.) near Boston, Massachusetts, that gave its name to the first pitched battle (1775) of the War of American Independence (actually fought on nearby Breed's Hill). Although the British were able to drive the American rebels from their positions, the good performance of the untrained American irregulars gave considerable impetus to the revolution.

**Burakumin** /bɜːˌræku'mɪn/ a social minority group in Japan with a total population of *c.*3 million, most of whom live in Baraku communities throughout the country. Over 40 per cent of all Burakumin, Japan's largest minority group, are found in the Kinki region of central Japan. Originally of outcaste status, the Burakumin have a long history of political militancy designed to combat discrimination.

**buran** /bʊə'rɑːn/ the Russian name for a strong, cold north-easterly wind that blows in Central Asia. A winter blizzard of this kind is known as a *white buran* or *poorga*.

**Burbank** /'bɜːbæŋk/ a city in southern California, USA, to the north of Los Angeles; pop. (1990) 93,640. It is a centre of the film and television industries.

**Burdur** /bʊər'dʊər/ **1.** a province in south-west Turkey; area 7,449 sq. km. (2,876 sq. miles); pop. (1990) 254,900; . **2.** its capital, between Denizli and Isparta near **Lake Burdur**; pop. (1990) 56,430.

**Burdwan** /bɜː'dwɑːn/ the former name of BARDDHAMAN.

**Burgas** /bʊə'gæs/ (also **Bourgas**) an industrial port and resort on the Black Sea coast of Bulgaria; pop. (1990) 226,120. Built on the site of ancient Thracian and Roman settlements, the modern city developed after the construction of a harbour in 1903–6. It is the chief city of a region of the same name and has industries producing rolling stock, cables, and other engineering products.

**Burgenland** /'bʊəgən,lænt/ a largely agricultural state of eastern Austria on the frontier

with Hungary; area 3,966 sq. km. (1,532 sq. miles); pop. (1991) 273,540; capital, Eisenstadt.
**Burgenlander** *adj. & n.*

**burgh** /ˈbʌrə/ any town in Scotland that has been granted a charter giving it special privileges as a royal burgh, ecclesiastical burgh, or burgh of barony.

**Burgos** /ˈbʊə(r)gɒs/ **1.** a province in Castilla-León region, northern Spain, lying between the Cantabrian Mountains in the north and outliers of the central meseta in the south, and bounded north by Santander and the Basque Provinces, west by Palencia, south by Segovia, south-east by Soria, and east by Rioja; area 14,309 sq. km. (5,527 sq. miles); pop. (1991) 352,770. **2.** its capital on the River Arlanzón; pop. (1991) 169,279. Founded in the 9th c., it was the capital of Castile during the 11th c. and the burial place in 1099 of the Spanish hero El Cid. Its 13th-c. cathedral is regarded as one of Europe's finest Gothic buildings. During the Spanish Civil War (1936–9) it was General Franco's capital city. It has numerous light industries.

**Burgundy** /ˈbɜːgəndɪ/ (French **Bourgogne** /buəˈgɒnjə/) a former kingdom, now a region of east-central France, comprising the departments of Côte-d'Or, Nièvre, Saône-et-Loire, and Yonne; area 31,582 sq. km. (12,198 sq. miles); pop. (1990) 1,609,650. Dijon is the chief town. It is a notable wine-producing region.

**Buriat** see BURYATIA.

## Burkina

/bɜːˈkiːnə/ (formerly **Upper Volta**) official name **People's Democratic Republic of Burkina** or **Burkina Faso** an inland country of western Africa, lying in the  Sahel region between the Sahara Desert and the Gulf of Guinea, south of the Niger River. It is bounded to the south by the Ivory Coast, Ghana, Togo, and Benin, to the north and west by Mali, and to the east by Niger; area 274,200 sq. km. (105,870 sq. miles); pop. (est. 1991) 9,400,000; official language, French; capital, Ouagadougou. The land is fertile in the south with an annual average rainfall of 100 cm. (40 in.) but semiarid in the north with an average rainfall of only 25 cm. (10 in.) per year, most of central Burkina lying on a savanna plateau. Tribes of the Voltaic and Mandé groups make up the greater part of the population, most of which lives in the south and centre of the country. It is one of the poorest countries in Africa with *c.*80 per cent of the people dependent on subsistence farming that produces millet, maize, sorghum, and rice. Cash crops include cotton, ground nuts, sesame, and shea nuts, and gold is a leading export. Ouagadougou is connected to the deep-water port

of Abidjan in the Ivory Coast by a 1,150-km. (712-mile) railway line. The country was a French protectorate from 1898, originally attached to Soudan (now Mali) and later partitioned between the Ivory Coast, Soudan, and Niger. In 1958 it became an autonomous republic within the French Community and a fully independent republic in 1960. The civilian government was overthrown by a military *coup* in 1980 and military rule continued until 1991 when a new multiparty constitution was adopted restoring the legislative National Assembly.
**Burkinan** or **Burkinabè** *adj. & n.*
Burkina is divided into 30 provinces:

| Province | Area (sq. km.) | Pop. (1985) | Capital |
|---|---|---|---|
| Bam | 4,017 | 164,263 | Kongoussi |
| Bazéga | 5,313 | 306,976 | Kombissiri |
| Bougouriba | 7,087 | 221,522 | Diébougou |
| Boulgou | 9,033 | 403,358 | Tenkodogo |
| Boulkiemde | 4,138 | 363,594 | Koudougou |
| Comoé | 18,393 | 250,510 | Banfora |
| Ganzourgou | 4,087 | 196,006 | Zorgo |
| Gnagna | 8,600 | 229,249 | Bogandé |
| Gourma | 26,613 | 294,123 | Fada-N'Gourma |
| Houet | 16,472 | 585,031 | Bobo-Dioulasso |
| Kadiogo | 1,169 | 459,138 | Ouagadougou |
| Kénédougou | 8,307 | 139,722 | Orodaro |
| Kossi | 13,177 | 330,413 | Nouna |
| Kouritenga | 1,627 | 197,027 | Koupéla |
| Mouhoun | 10,442 | 289,213 | Dédougou |
| Nahouri | 3,843 | 105,273 | Pô |
| Namentenga | 7,755 | 198,798 | Boulsa |
| Oubritenga | 4,693 | 303,229 | Ziniaré |
| Oudalan | 10,046 | 105,715 | Gorom Gorom |
| Passoré | 4,078 | 225,115 | Yako |
| Poni | 10,361 | 234,501 | Gaoua |
| Sanguie | 5,165 | 218,289 | Réo |
| Sanmatenga | 9,213 | 368,365 | Kaya |
| Sèno | 13,473 | 230,043 | Dori |
| Sissili | 13,736 | 246,844 | Léo |
| Soum | 13,350 | 190,464 | Djibo |
| Sourou | 9,487 | 267,770 | Tougan |
| Tapoa | 14,780 | 159,121 | Diapaga |
| Yatenga | 12,292 | 537,205 | Ouahigouya |
| Zoundwéogo | 3,453 | 155,142 | Manga |

**Burlington** /ˈbɜːlɪntən/ **1.** a city in southern Ontario, a suburb of Hamilton, Canada, 48 km. (30 miles) west of Toronto, on Lake Ontario; pop. (1991) 129,600. **2.** a city in south-east Iowa, USA, on the Mississippi River; pop. (1990) 27,200. It was formerly capital of the Wisconsin Territory (1837) and the Iowa Territory (1838–41). Chief industries include the manufacture of furniture, chemicals, tractors, and electronic instruments. A street named Snake Alley is said to be the 'crookedest street in the world'. **3.** a city on the shore of Lake Champlain, north-west Vermont, USA; pop. (1990) 39,130. It is the largest city in Vermont and has steel, missile, machinery, and textile industries. The philosopher John Dewey (1859–1952) was born here.

**Burma** /'bɜːmə/ (Burmese **Myanmar**) official name **Union of Myanmar** a country in south-east Asia on the Bay of Bengal, centred on the Irrawaddy River, and bounded east by China, Laos, and

Thailand and north-west by India and Bangladesh; area 676,560 sq. km. (261,220 sq. miles); pop. (est. 1991) 42,100,000; official language, Burmese; capital, Yangon (Rangoon). Occupying the north-west corner of the Indo-Chinese peninsula, Burma is separated from India by the Arakan Mountains. A central basin extends the length of the Irrawaddy River and widens out into a flat fertile delta in the south. In the east the Shan plateau, watered by the Salween River, stretches southwards into the Malay peninsula. Burma has a tropical monsoon climate with a rainy season from May to Oct. and extreme heat in the central basin during March–May. Rainfall is highest in the Arakan and Tenasserim mountains in the north. Rice has traditionally been the mainstay of the country's economy, and teak is a valuable export. Burma is rich in minerals including lead and zinc; petroleum products are also important. An independent empire under the Pagan dynasty in the 11th–13th c., Burma fell to the Mongols and was generally split into small rival states until unified once again in 1757. As a result of the Burmese Wars of 1823–86 Burma was gradually annexed by the British, remaining under British administration until World War II. Occupied by the Japanese in 1942, the country became an independent republic in 1948, taking the formal name of the Union of Burma, changed in 1989 to the Union of Myanmar. In 1962 an army *coup* led by Ne Win overthrew the government and established an authoritarian state that continued to maintain a policy of neutrality and limited foreign contact. In the late 1980s the pro-democracy movement gathered momentum and following widespread demonstrations against the government in 1988 the army formally imposed military rule. Although the opposition National League for Democracy succeeded in winning an election in 1990, its leaders were imprisoned and the military government remained in office. In the regions the government faces armed opposition from separatist movements among ethnic minorities such as the Kachin, Shan, and Karen people.
**Burmese** or **Burman** *adj. & n.*
Burma is divided into seven states and seven divisions:

| State | Pop. (1983) | Capital |
| --- | --- | --- |
| Kachin | 904,000 | Myitkyina |
| Kayah | 168,350 | Loikaw |
| Karen | 1,057,500 | Pa-an |
| Chin | 368,985 | Haka |
| Mon | 1,682,000 | Moulmein |
| Rakhine | 2,045,900 | Akyab |
| Shan | 3,718,700 | Taunggyi |
| Division | | |
| Sagaing | 3,856,000 | Sagaing |
| Tenasserim | 917,600 | Tavoy |
| Pegu | 3,800,250 | Pegu |
| Magwe | 3,241,100 | Magwe |
| Mandalay | 4,580,900 | Mandalay |
| Yangon | 3,973,800 | Yangon |
| Irrawaddy | 4,991,000 | Bassein |

**Burma Road** a highway linking the railhead at Lashio near Mandalay in east Burma to Kunming and Chongqing in China, a total distance of 2,195 km. (1,381 miles). It was constructed between 1936 and 1938 as a supply route for the Chinese government. Under Japanese control (1942–5) the route was extended towards India with the building of the Stilwell and Ledo roads using prisoner-of-war labour.

**Burnaby** /'bɜːnəbɪ/ an eastern suburb of Vancouver in the Canadian province of British Columbia; pop. (1988) 145,160. It is the home of the Simon Fraser University (1963).

**Burnie** /'bɜːnɪ/ a deep-water port on the north coast of Tasmania, Australia, situated on the Bass Strait west of Devonport; pop. (1991) 20,505 (with Somerset). Industries include food-processing and the manufacture of pulp, paper, and titanium oxide pigments.

**Burnley** /'bɜːnlɪ/ an industrial town in Lancashire, north-west England; pop. (1991) 89,000. A former cotton-manufacturing town with engineering and chemical industries.

**Burnsville** /'bɜːnzvɪl/ a city in south-east Minnesota, USA, 25 km. (16 miles) south of Minneapolis; pop. (1990) 51,288.

**Bursa** /'bɜːsə/ **1.** a province in north-west Turkey, to the south of the Sea of Marmara; area 11,043 sq. km. (4,265 sq. miles); pop. (1990) 1,603,137. **2.** its capital; pop. (1990) 834,576. Originally named Prusa by the Byzantines, after its capture by the Turks in 1326 it was called Brusa or Bursa, and became the first capital of the Ottoman empire. It was sacked by Tamerlane in 1402, and in 1423 the capital was moved to Adrianople (Edirne). Its oldest industry is the manufacture of silk, but modern industries include the production of automobiles and soft drinks.

**Burton upon Trent** a town in east Staffordshire, central England, on the River Trent; pop. (1981) 59,600. It has long been noted for its breweries.

**Burundi** /buˈrʌndɪ/ official name **Republic of Burundi** a small African country on the east side of Lake Tanganyika, bounded north-west by Zaire, north by Rwanda, and east and south by Tanzania; area 27,834 sq. km. (10,747 sq. miles); pop. (est. 1991) 5,800,000; official languages, Kirundi and

French; capital, Bujumbura. Burundi is situated on a high rolling plateau in the Great Rift Valley where there is a major dry season from May to September and a short dry season in
January. The majority of the population are Hutu farmers whose Bantu-speaking ancestors migrated to Burundi nearly 1,000 years ago. The remainder are pastoral Tutsi and pygmy Twa. The country's chief agricutural products are coffee, tea, sorghum, bananas, and cotton. Once ruled by a king (*mwami*) who was drawn from one of a number of princely dynastic families, Burundi came under European administration in the 1890s as part of German East Africa. After World War I it was mandated to Belgium as part of the territory of Ruanda-Urundi (subsequently a UN Trust Territory) and in 1962 it became independent as a constitutional monarchy. In 1966 the monarchy was overthrown and a republic declared under a Tutsi-led military government. Thereafter, political instability and inter-tribal conflict accompanied by soil erosion and famine have crippled the country which has the second densest population in sub-Saharan Africa and is one of the poorest in the world.

**Bury** /'berɪ/ a town in Greater Manchester, north-west England, on the River Irwell; pop. (1981) 62,181. It was the birthplace of the English statesman Sir Robert Peel (1788–1850), founder of the police force, and John Kay, inventor of the flying-shuttle weaving loom.

**Buryatia** /bʊə'jɑːtɪə/ a republic of the Russian Federation in Siberia, between Lake Baikal and the Yablonovy Mountains on the frontier with Mongolia; area 351,300 sq. km. (135,600 sq. miles); pop. (1990) 1,049,000; capital, Ulan-Udé. Settled by Russians during and after the 1620s, Buryatia was annexed from China by treaties of 1689 and 1727. From 1923 to 1958 it was named the Buryat-Mongol Autonomous Soviet Socialist Republic. Therafter it was styled the Buryat (Buriat) Autonomous Soviet Socialist Republic until the breakup of the Soviet Union in 1991. The Buddhist and shamanist Buryat people rear sheep, cattle, and reindeer.

**Bury St. Edmunds** a market town in Suffolk, east England, on the River Lark; pop. (1981) 31,178. The 7th-c. monastery (later a Benedictine abbey) was the burial place of King Edmund (later St. Edmund).

**Bushehr** /bu:'ʃeər/ a city in southern Iran, a port on the Persian Gulf; pop. (1991) 133,000. It is capital of Bushehr province. It was at one time the principal port and naval base of Persia.

**Bushmen** /'bʊʃmən/ a nomadic people speaking a Khoisan or Click language and, before the coming of the Bantu and the Europeans, found throughout southern Africa, but now largely found in Namibia and Botswana in the neighbourhood of the Kalahari Desert.

**bushveld** /'bʊʃfelt/ a South African term for savanna or open country consisting largely of bush.

**Bute** /bju:t/ an island in the Firth of Clyde, part of Argyll and Bute district in the west of Scotland; area 129 sq. km. (50 sq. miles). Its chief town is the royal burgh of Rothesay after which the Prince of Wales takes his ducal title.

**butte** /bju:t/ a US term for a high isolated steep-sided hill.

**Buxton** /'bʌkstən/ a former spa town in Derbyshire, central England, on the River Wye; pop. (1981) 20,800. Its springs, which have been used since Roman times, supply bottled mineral water. The town has associations with Anna Sewell (1820–78), author of *Black Beauty*.

**Buyi** /bu:'ji:/ (also **Bouyei**) a minority nationality of southern China, mostly found in Guizhou province where the Buyi people number *c.* 2.1 million.

**Buzau** /bə'zaʊ/ (Hungarian **Bodza** /'bəʊdzə/) an industrial town and capital of Buzau county in south-east-central Romania, on the River Buzau; pop. (1989) 145,420. The city is located at the centre of a major oil-producing region.

**Byblos** an ancient Phoenician city 32 km. (20 miles) north of Beirut in Lebanon on the site of present-day Jebeil. Known to the Assyrians and Babylonians as Gubla, it became the principal city of the Phoenicians in the 2nd millenium BC and had a thriving export of cedar to Egypt. It was later named Byblos by the Romans for whom it became the chief centre of the worship of Adonis. It is suggested that the Bible takes its name from this city whose papyruses were used in the production of books.

**Bydgoszcz** /bɪd'gɒʃt/ (German **Bromberg** /'brɒmbeək/) an industrial port on the Brda River in north-central Poland; pop. (1990) 381,534. Medieval and Gothic buildings have survived the devastation of World War II. A monument commemorates the massacre of 20,000 of its citizens by Nazis in September 1939. The Bydgoszcz Canal links the Vistula and Oder river basins with other Central European waterways. Industries include machinery and machine tools, electrical equipment, chemicals, precision instruments, and domestic equipment.

**Byelorussia** see BELORUSSIA.

**Bylot Island** /'baɪlɑːt/ an island in the Canadian Arctic situated off the north-east coast of Baffin Island at the entrance to Lancaster Sound; area 11,067 sq. km. (4,273 sq. miles). It was named after Robert Bylot, a British sea captain who sailed with William Baffin and Henry Hudson in the 17th c. The island is noted for its colonies of breeding greater snow geese.

**Bytom** /ˈbɪtəm/ (German **Beuthen** /ˈbɔɪt(ə)n/) a city in Katowice county, south-west Poland; pop. (1990) 231,200. A former medieval fortress town that developed with the mining of coal, lead, and zinc in the vicinity. Formerly part of Prussia, it was incorporated into Poland in 1945. Its factories produce metal goods and furniture.

**Byzantium** /bɪˈzæntɪəm/ an ancient Greek city on the European side of the south end of the Bosporus, founded in the 7th c. BC and refounded as Constantinople by Constantine in AD 330. It became capital of the Eastern Roman or Byzantine Empire which survived until the city was captured by the Turks in 1453. See ISTANBUL.

**Byzantine** adj. & n.

# C *c*

**CA** *abbr.* US California (in official postal use).

**caatinga** /kɑː'tɪŋgə/ a type of thorn forest or scrub found in arid regions of north-eastern Brazil.

**Cabimas** /kə'biːməs/ a city on Lake Maracaibo, in the state of Zulia, western Venezuela; pop. (1981) 140,435.

**Cabinda** /kə'bɪndə/ **1.** an enclave of Angola at the mouth of the Congo (Zaïre) River, separated from the rest of Angola by a wedge of Zaire; area 7,270 sq. km. (2,808 sq. miles); pop. (1991) 163,000. Rich oilfields lie off the coast of Cabinda which claims independence from Angola on the basis of the legitimacy of the 1885 Simulambuco Treaty which first linked Cabinda and Angola. **2.** its capital city; pop. (1980) 81,300. It is Angola's chief oil-refining centre.

**caboclo** /kə'bɒkləʊ/ literally meaning copper-coloured, it is a Brazilian word used to describe someone of mixed Amerindian and European descent.

**Cabora Bassa** /kə‚bɔːrə 'bæsə/ a lake on the Zambezi River in western Mozambique. Its waters are impounded by a dam and massive hydroelectric complex supplying power mainly to South Africa and to Mozambique.

**cabotage** the reservation to a country of traffic (especially air) operation within its territory.

**Cabot Trail** /'kæbət/ a scenic trail on Cape Breton Island, Canada, which stretches a distance of 300 km. (190 miles) across the north-west of the island from the town of Baddeck. It is named after the seafarer John Cabot who first landed in North America in 1497.

**Cáceres** /'kæθərəs/ **1.** a province in the auto-nomous region of Extremadura, western Spain; area 19,945 sq. km. (7,704 sq. miles); pop. (1991) 411,460. **2.** its capital, a walled city on the River Cáceres; pop. (1991) 80,700. Founded by the Romans in the 1st c. AD, it fell to the Moors in the 8th c. but was recaptured by Alfonso IX in 1229. Industries include the manufacture of chemicals, pharmaceuticals, and textiles.

**cachoeira** /‚kæʃə'weərə/ a Brazilian word for a waterfall, often used in place-names such as the city of Cachoeira in the state of Bahia and Cachoeira do Sul near Pôrto Alegre in the state of Rio Grande do Sul.

**cadastral map** /kə'dæstrəl/ any map that is large enough to represent accurately the bound-aries of property.

**Cader Idris** /'kɑːdə(r) 'aɪdrɪs/ a mountain ridge in north-west Wales that rises to 892 m. (2,926 ft.) at Pen-y-Gader. (Welsh = the chair of Idris)

**Cadiz** /kə'dɪz/ a city and port on the Andalusian coast of south-west Spain; pop. (1991) 156,558. It is the capital of a province of the same name. Originally a Phoenician settlement, it reached its highest importance in the 16th–18th c. as the head-quarters of the Spanish naval fleets. In 1587 Sir Francis Drake burnt the ships of Philip II at anchor here. There are ferry links with Casablanca and the Canary Islands. Shipbuilding and the export of sherry, salt, fish, and olives are the chief economic activities, together with tourism.

**Caen** /kɑ̃/ a port, commercial, and industrial city on the coast of Normandy in north-west France, on the River Orne; pop. (1990) 115,620. It is capital of the department of Calvados in the Basse-Normandie region. William the Conqueror is buried in the abbey church of St. Etienne and Beau Brummel died here in the pauper lunatic asylum in 1840. Manufactures include steel and electronics. Caen was largely rebuilt after massive destruction during the Normandy campaign of 1944.

**Caernarvon** /kə'nɑːvən/ (Welsh **Caernarfon**) the county town and tourist centre of Gwynedd in north-west Wales, on the shore of the Menai Strait; pop. (1981) 9,400. The seat of the native princes of Wales until the 9th c., its 13th-c. castle (built by Edward I) was the birthplace of Edward II, the first English Prince of Wales. Nearby are the remains of the Roman fort of Segontium. It was the adminis-trative centre of the former county of Caernarvon until 1974.

**Caerphilly** /keə'fɪlɪ/ a market town in Mid Glamorgan, south Wales, 10 km. (7 miles) north-west of Cardiff. It gives its name to a kind of mild white cheese made in the area. Caerphilly Castle, built in the 13th c. by Edward I, is said to be the second-largest castle in England and Wales.

**Caesarea** /‚siːzə'riːə/ (formerly **Caesarea Palestinae** /-pæləs'tiːnaɪ/) a seaport on the Medi-terranean coast of Israel midway between Haifa and Tel Aviv. Originally founded by Phoenicians in the 4th c. BC, it was later occupied by the Greeks. In 22 BC Herod the Great founded a new port that became one of the chief cities of Roman Palestine and named it after Caesar Augustus. When Judea became a Roman province its governors resided here. Caesarea was the birthplace of the Byzantine historian Procopius (*c.* 499–565) and home of a school of literature, philospohy, and theology founded by Origen (AD 185–254). After its capture by the Arabs in AD 637 it lost its importance and the harbour silted up. Although partially refortified during the Crusades, it was not resettled until the founding of the Sedot Yam kibbutz in 1940.

**Caesarea Mazaca** /ˌsiːzəriːə ˈmæzəkə/ an ancient name for KAYSERI in Turkey.

**Caesarea Philippi** an ancient city of Palestine on the site of the modern village of BANIYAS in the Israeli-occupied Golan Heights. Formerly known as Paneas, it was an important Hellenistic shrine to the god Pan before being rebuilt by Herod the Great and named in honour of the Roman emperor Augustus.

**Cagayan de Oro** /ˌkɑːɡəˈjɑːn deɪ ˈəʊrəʊ/ an administrative, transport, and market city on the north-west coast of the island of Mindanao in the Philippines; pop. (1990) 339,600.

**Cagayan Islands** a group of seven small islands in the Sulu Sea in the western Philippines.

**Cagliari** /ˈkælˈjɑːrɪ/ a seaport and capital of the Italian island of Sardinia, situated on the southern coast and surrounded by beaches and lagoons; pop. (1990) 211,720. Its position at the centre of the western Mediterranean has made it of strategic importance since ancient times. It has a 13th-c. cathedral and a 5th-c. basilica. The nearby saltworks of Santa Gilla are among the largest in Italy, and a large petrochemical industry is sited to the west of the city.

**Cagnes-sur-Mer** /ˈkæn sjʊə ˈmeə/ a fishing port and seaside resort in the Alpes-Maritimes department of south-east France; pop. (1990) 41,300. The artist Auguste Renoir (1841–1919) died here.

**Caguas** /ˈkæɡwɑːs/ a commercial and light-industrial city on the Caribbean island of Puerto Rico; pop. (1990) 133,450. Named after an Amerindian chief, the city lies in a fertile valley in the foothills of the Cordillera Central to the south of San Juan.

**Cahors** /kæˈɔː(r)/ a centre of light industries and the capital of the department of Lot in the Midi-Pyrénées region of south-central France, on a loop of the River Lot; pop. (1990) 20,790. Noted for its medieval buildings and wine, it was the birthplace of the radical statesman Léon Gambetta (1838–82).

**Cairngorm Mountains** /ˈkeəngɔːm/ (also **Cairngorms**) a mountain range forming part of the larger Grampian Range in northern Scotland. The highest peak is Ben Macdhui (1,309 m., 4,295 ft.). The mountains give their name to a wine-coloured semi-precious form of quartz found there.

**Cairns** /keənz/ a resort town on the north-east coast of Queensland, Australia, on Trinity Bay; pop. (1991) 64,430. An embarkation point for tours of the Barrier Reef, it is also a trading centre for agricultural produce, sugar, timber, fish, and minerals.

**Cairo** /ˈkaɪrəʊ/ (Arabic **El Qâhira**) the capital of Egypt, a port on the Nile near the head of the delta, and the largest city in Africa; pop. (1991) 6,663,000. Founded by the Fatamid dynasty in 969 it was later fortified against the Crusaders by Saladin, whose citadel (built c. 1179) still survives. Cairo's mosques include that of Al Azhar (972), housing an Islamic university said to be the oldest in the world and the leading centre of Koranic studies. Islamic Cairo has been designated a world heritage site by UNESCO. Old Cairo, a crowded maze of ancient houses and 400 mosques lies in the south of the built-up area; new Cairo with its modern hotels and office buildings, and three universities, lies to the north and west. Cairo has many light industries including tourism.

**Caithness** /ˈkeɪθnes/ a former county in the far north of Scotland now part of Highland Region; area 1,776 sq. km. (686 sq. miles); pop. (1991) 26,100. Its chief town is the fishing port of Wick.

**Cajamarca** /ˌkɑːhəˈmɑːkə/ a commercial town in the Andes of northern Peru, at an altitude of 2,745 m. (9,000 ft.); pop.(1990) 92,600. It is the chief town of the northern mountains of Peru, producing textile and leather goods. Gold, silver, and copper are mined nearby. Pizarro captured the Inca chief Atahualpa here in 1533.

**Calabar** /ˈkæləˌbɑː(r)/ a port and capital of Cross River State in south Nigeria, at the mouth of the **Calabar River** (the most easterly mouth of the Niger) where it flows into the Gulf of Guinea; pop. (1983) 126,000.

**Calabria** /kəˈlæbrɪə/ a region of south-west Italy comprising the provinces of Catanzaro, Cozenza, and Reggio di Calabria; area 15,079 sq. km. (5,824 sq. miles); pop. (1990) 2,153,656; capital, Reggio di Calabria. In antiquity the name was applied to the flat and arid but fertile south-eastern promontory or 'heel' of Italy. The Lombards seized Calabria c. AD 700, whereupon the Byzantines transferred its name to the south-west promontory or 'toe' of Italy, the Calabria of today.
**Calabrian** adj. & n.

**Calais** /ˈkæleɪ/ a Channel ferry-port in the department of Pas-de-Calais, north-west France; pop. (1990) 75,840. Captured by Edward III in 1347 after a long siege, it was saved from destruction by the surrender of six burghers (commemorated in Rodin's sculpture), and remained an English possession until retaken by the French in 1558 in the reign of Mary. The French terminal of the Channel Tunnel is at Fréthun, to the south of Calais.

**Calama** /kəˈlɑːmə/ a town in the Antofagasta region, northern Chile, situated on a high plain in the Atacama Desert north-east of Antofagasta; pop. (1991) 118,000. It serves the nearby opencast copper mines of Chuquicamata which are amongst the largest in the world.

**Calamata** (Greek **Kalámai** or **Kalamáta**) the capital and principal trading port of the Messinia prefecture in the Peloponnese of southern Greece; pop. (1981) 41,100.

**Calarasi** /kælə'rɑːʃ/ (also **Kalarash**) the capital of Calarasi county in south-east Romania, on the River Byk; pop. (1989) 76,240.

**Calcutta** /kæl'kʌtə/ the capital of the state of West Bengal in north-east India, on the east bank of the Hugli River; pop. (1991) 10,916,000. It is a major port and the largest city of India. Founded c. 1690 by the East India Company, it was the capital of British India from 1833 until 1912 when it was replaced by Delhi. Its striking buildings include Fort William in the centre of the Maidan or Great Park, palaces of former princes, the Law Courts and Government House, relics of British rule; its educational institutions include the University of Calcutta (1857), the oldest of three universities, the Visva Bharati, the Bose Research Institute, and the Indian Museum. Calcutta is a major commercial and industrial centre with jute mills, and textile, chemical, metal, and paper industries. Other industries lie across the Hugli at HAORA and at Haldia, a new outport developed because of the silting of the river. It handles bulk cargoes and has oil refineries and petrochemical plants. The Black Hole of Calcutta was a dungeon in Fort William where, following the capture of Calcutta by the Nawab of Bengal in 1756, 156 English prisoners were confined in a narrow cell 6 m. (20 ft.) square for the night of 20 June, only 23 of them still being alive next morning.

**caldera** /kɑːl'deərə/ a large volcanic depression left after the removal of a mountain peak by immense volcanic activity.

**Caledonia** /ˌkælɪ'dəʊnɪə/ a Roman name for the northern part of Britain that is now Scotland.

**Caledonian Canal** a system of lochs and man-made canals in Scotland stretching for nearly 100 km. (63 miles) from Inverness south-westwards to Fort William, linking the North Sea with the Atlantic Ocean. The work of Thomas Telford, it was opened in 1822.

**Caledonian folds** (also **Caledonian orogeny**) the north-east to south-west alignment of folds, faults, and mountains created in Europe during the late Silurian and early Devonian periods of geological time.

**Calgary** /'kælgərɪ/ a commercial and industrial city in southern Alberta, south-west Canada, situated to the east of the Rocky Mountains, on the edge of a rich agricultural and stock-raising area; pop. (1991) 754,030 (metropolitan area). Originally known as Fort Brisebois, Calgary was founded in 1875 as a fort of the Northwest Mounted Police. It is the centre of Alberta's oil business with oil-refining, timber-processing, and flour-milling

industries. The Calgary Stampede, inaugurated in 1912, is an annual rodeo.

**Cali** /'kɑːliː/ a city at the centre of the fertile Cauca river valley in western Colombia; pop. (1985) 1,429,000 Founded in 1536, it is now the third-largest city in Colombia. Trading in tobacco, sugar, livestock, and minerals, it has since the early 1980s gained a reputation as the base of a drug cartel supplying cocaine to North America, chiefly New York City.

**Calicut** /'kælɪˌkʌt/ (also **Kozhikode** /'kəʊʒəˌkəʊd/) a seaport in the state of Kerala, south-west India, on the Malabar Coast; pop. (1991) 420,000. This was Vasco da Gama's first port of call when he visited India in 1498. It subsequently developed as a European trading town which gave its name to the cotton cloth known as calico. It manufactures ropes and nets and exports tea, coffee, spices, and timber.

**California** /ˌkælɪ'fɔːnɪə/ a state on the Pacific coast of the USA, bounded north by Oregon, east by Nevada, south-east by Arizona, and south by Mexico; area 411,049 sq. km. (158,706 sq. miles); pop. (1990) 29,760,000; capital, Sacramento. The largest cities are Los Angeles, San Diego, San José, and San Francisco. California is also known as the Golden State. It was ceded by Mexico in 1847, a year before the discovery of gold that brought large numbers of settlers to the territory. In 1850 it became the 31st state of the union. By 1964 it had become not only the most populous US state but the state with the greatest per capita income and expenditure. The chief products are timber, natural gas, petroleum, electronics, transportation equipment, and food. Major tourist attractions include Disneyland, the Golden Gate Bridge, and Yosemite, Sequoia, and Kings Canyon National Parks. The state is divided into 58 counties:

| County | Area (sq. km.) | Pop. (1990) | County Seat |
| --- | --- | --- | --- |
| Alameda | 1,914 | 1,279,180 | Oakland |
| Alpine | 1,919 | 1,110 | Markleeville |
| Amador | 1,531 | 30,040 | Jackson |
| Butte | 4,280 | 182,120 | Oroville |
| Calaveras | 2,655 | 32,000 | San Andreas |
| Colusa | 2,995 | 16,275 | Colusa |
| Contra Costa | 1,898 | 803,730 | Martinez |
| Del Norte | 2,618 | 23,460 | Crescent City |
| El Dorado | 4,459 | 125,995 | Placerville |
| Fresno | 15,543 | 667,490 | Fresno |
| Glenn | 3,429 | 24,800 | Willows |
| Humboldt | 9,305 | 119,120 | Eureka |
| Imperial | 10,850 | 109,300 | El Centro |
| Inyo | 26,580 | 18,280 | Independence |
| Kern | 21,138 | 543,480 | Bakersfield |
| Kings | 3,619 | 101,470 | Hanford |
| Lake | 3,281 | 50,630 | Lakeport |
| Lassen | 11,838 | 27,600 | Susanville |
| Los Angeles | 10,582 | 8,863,160 | Los Angeles |
| Madera | 5,577 | 88,090 | Madera |
| Marin | 1,360 | 230,100 | San Rafael |

*(cont.)*

| County | Area (sq. km.) | Pop. (1990) | County Seat |
|---|---|---|---|
| Mariposa | 3,786 | 14,300 | Mariposa |
| Mendocino | 9,131 | 80,345 | Ukiah |
| Merced | 5,054 | 178,400 | Merced |
| Modoc | 10,566 | 9,680 | Alturas |
| Mono | 7,847 | 9,960 | Bridgeport |
| Monterey | 8,588 | 355,660 | Salinas |
| Napa | 1,934 | 110,765 | Napa |
| Nevada | 2,496 | 78,510 | Nevada City |
| Orange | 2,075 | 2,410,560 | Santa Ana |
| Placer | 3,682 | 172,800 | Auburn |
| Plumas | 6,690 | 19,740 | Quincy |
| Riverside | 18,756 | 1,170,410 | Riverside |
| Sacramento | 2,525 | 1,041,220 | Sacramento |
| San Benito | 3,609 | 36,700 | Hollister |
| San Bernardino | 52,166 | 1,418,380 | San Bernardino |
| San Diego | 10,951 | 2,498,020 | San Diego |
| San Francisco | 120 | 723,960 | San Francisco |
| San Joaquin | 3,679 | 480,630 | Stockton |
| San Luis Obispo | 8,601 | 217,160 | San Luis Obispo |
| San Mateo | 1,162 | 649,620 | Redwood City |
| Santa Barbara | 7,145 | 369,600 | Santa Barbara |
| Santa Clara | 3,362 | 1,497,580 | San José |
| Santa Cruz | 1,160 | 229,730 | Santa Cruz |
| Shasta | 9,844 | 147,040 | Redding |
| Sierra | 2,493 | 3,320 | Downieville |
| Siskiyou | 16,331 | 43,530 | Yreka |
| Solano | 2,168 | 340,420 | Fairfield |
| Sonoma | 4,170 | 388,220 | Santa Rosa |
| Stanislau | 3,916 | 370,520 | Modesto |
| Sutter | 1,565 | 64,415 | Yuba City |
| Tehama | 7,678 | 49,625 | Red Bluff |
| Trinity | 8,294 | 13,060 | Weaverville |
| Tulare | 12,501 | 311,920 | Visalia |
| Tuolumne | 5,808 | 48,460 | Sonora |
| Ventura | 4,841 | 669,020 | Ventura |
| Yolo | 2,636 | 141,090 | Woodland |
| Yuba | 1,664 | 58,230 | Marysville |

**California, Gulf of** an arm of the Pacific Ocean separating the Baja California peninsula from mainland Mexico. It stretches for about 1,125 km. (700 miles) and has a width of 80–210 km. (50–130 miles). Deepening from north to south, the gulf reaches a depth of c. 2,595 m. (8,500 ft.).

**California current** a cold ocean current of the eastern Pacific that flows south along the west coast of North America.

**calina** /kæˈliːnə/ a form of sandy dust that blows from North Africa to Europe. (Spanish = haze.)

**Callanish** /kæˈlɑːnɪʃ/ a village on the west coast of the island of Lewis in the Outer Hebrides of Scotland, adjacent to a prehistoric site dating from c. 2,500 BC. The Callanish standing stones form avenues radiating from a central stone circle.

**Callao** /kəˈljɑːəʊ/ the principal seaport of Peru, on the Pacific coast west of Lima; pop. (1990) 588,600. Callao handles the greater part of Peru's export trade and has a large oil refinery, and dockyard. The Lima-Callao metropolitan area produces three-quarters of all Peru's manufactures. Callao has been subjected to damaging earthquakes, the last in 1940.

**Caloocan** /ˌkæləˈəʊkən/ (also **Kalookan**) a city on the island of Luzon in the Philippines, situated in the National Capital Region north of Manila; pop. (1990) 763,415.

**Caloundra** /kəˈluːndrə/ a beach resort on the Sunshine Coast of Queensland, eastern Australia, situated 96 km. (60 miles) north of Brisbane; pop. (1991) 22,090.

**Calpe** /ˈkælpiː/ an ancient name for the Rock of Gibraltar.

**Caltanisetta** /ˌkæltəniːˈsetə/ a mining town in the hills of central Sicily; pop. (1990) 62,850. Sulphur, potash and magnesium are mined nearby. Originally known as Nissa, the Arabs renamed the town Caltanisetta. (Arabic *Kalat* = castle.)

**Calvados** /ˈkælvədɒs/ a low-lying department on the English Channel in the Basse-Normandie region of north-west France; area 5,548 sq. km. (2,143 sq. miles); pop. (1990) 618,480; capital, Caen. The dangerous **Calvados Reef** off the Normandy coast between the mouths of the Orne and Vire rivers takes its name from a ship of the Spanish Armada which was wrecked there in 1588. Textiles, dairy produce, and the Calvados liqueur are the chief products of the area. Tourism is also important.

**Calvary** /ˈkælvəriː/ (Hebrew **Golgotha**) a place just outside the city of Jerusalem where the crucifixion of Jesus took place. The Church of the Sepulchre is alleged to stand on the site.

**Calvi** /ˈkælviː/ a small seaport and resort town in northern Corsica; pop. (1982) 3,600. Nelson lost an eye during the siege of Calvi in 1794.

**Calymnos** /kəˈlɪmnɔːs/ (Greek **Kálymnos**) an island in the Dodecanese between Leros and Cos; area 109 sq. km. (42 sq. miles); pop. (1981) 14,500; chief town, Pothiá.

**Cam** /kæm/ (anc. **Granta**) a river in east England that rises west of Thaxted and flows 65 km. (40 miles) north-eastwards through Cambridge to meet the River Ouse near Ely.

**Camagüey** /ˌkɑːmæɡˈweɪ/ a commercial centre and capital of Camagüey province eastern Cuba; pop. (est. 1986) 260,800. It is the third largest city in Cuba with an economy based on its trade in livestock and agricultural produce from the surrounding area. Founded in 1515 as Santa Maria del Puerto Príncipe, it was rebuilt in 1528 on its present site and renamed after the Indian village that previously existed there. During the 19th c. it was capital of the Spanish West Indies. Its port lies at nearby Nuevitas.

**Camargue** /kæˈmɑːɡ/**, the** the area of the Rhône delta in south-east France, characterized by numerous shallow salt lagoons. The region is known for its white horses and as a nature reserve for migratory birds.

**Camarillo** /ˌkæməˈrɪləʊ/ a city in southern California, USA, between Santa Barbara and Los Angeles; pop. (1990) 52,300. Situated in a citrus-farming and horticultural area, it also produces electronic equipment.

**Cambay** /kæmˈbeɪ/, **Gulf of** (also **Gulf of Khambat**) an inlet of the Arabian Sea on the Gujarat coast of western India, north of Bombay. The Narmada River flows into the gulf whose ports have largely been silted up.

**Camberley** /ˈkæmbɜːlɪ/ a residential town in Surrey, south-east England, near Aldershot; pop. (1981) 45,700. The Royal Staff College is located here.

**Cambodia** /kæmˈbəʊdɪə/ official name **The Kingdom of Cambodia** a country in south-east Asia between Thailand in the north-west and the south of Vietnam in the east, with Laos in the

north-east and the Gulf of Thailand in the south-west; area 181,040 sq. km. (69,884 sq. miles); pop. (est. 1991) 7,100,000; official language, Khmer; capital Phnom Penh. The economy is chiefly agricultural with rice as the staple crop grown on the flat central alluvial plain which is formed by the basin of the Mekong River and Tonle Sap (Great Lake). Ringed by mountains, which include the Cardamom Mountains and the Dangrek Range, Cambodia has a tropical monsoon climate with a dry season from November to May. There is little industry except for rice milling, fishing, and the production of timber, textiles, and cement. About 90 per cent of the people are ethnic Khmer including hill tribes (Khmer Loeu), the people of the central ricelands (Khmer Kandal), and the people of the Mekong delta (Khmer Krom). Formerly part of the Khmer empire, the country was made a French protectorate in 1863 and remained under French influence until it became fully independent in 1953. Civil war in 1970–5 undermined and finally overthrew the government, but the victorious Communist Khmer Rouge regime was itself toppled by a Vietnamese invasion in 1979. The country continued to be plagued by intermittent guerrilla activity until Vietnam withdrew its forces in 1989 after international pressure to do so and a UN peace plan was accepted in 1990. A new constitution was adopted in 1993 and Norodom Sihanouk, who had abdicated in 1955, returned to the throne. Cambodia was officially known as the Khmer Republic (1970–5), Democratic Kampuchea (1976–9), and the People's Democratic Republic of Kampuchea (1979–92).
**Cambodian** *adj. & n.*

**Camborne** /ˈkæmbɔːn/ a former tin-mining town near Redruth in Cornwall, south-west England; pop. (1981) 34,800. Robert Trevithick, pioneer of steam locomotives, was born here in 1771.

**Cambrai** /kæmˈbreɪ/ (Flemish **Kambryk** /ˈkɑːmbrɪk/) an industrial town in north-west France, situated on the River Escaut in the Nord department of Nord-Pas-de-Calais region; pop. (1990) 34,210. The Flemish style, Kambryk, gives its name to a fine white linen or cotton fabric known as cambric.

**Cambrian** /ˈkæmbrɪən/ **1.** of Cambria, the ancient name for Wales which is mostly occupied by the rugged upland plateau of the **Cambrian Mountains. 2.** a geological term relating to the first period in the Palaeozoic era, following the Precambrian era and preceding the Ordovician period. Lasting from about 590 to 505 million years ago. It was a time of widespread seas, and is the first period in which fossils (notably trilobites) can be used in geological dating. Rocks of this period were first recognized in Wales (whence its name).

**Cambridge** /ˈkeɪmbrɪdʒ/ a town in south-east Ontario, Canada, situated to the west of Lake Ontario between Hamilton and Waterloo; pop. (1991) 92,800.

**Cambridge** (anc. **Cantabrigia**) a city in Cambridgeshire, England, on the River Cam, the seat of a major English university organized as a federation of colleges; pop. (1991) 101,000. The first historical trace of Cambridge as a University (*studium generale*) is in 1209; a number of scholars migrated from Oxford to Cambridge in 1209–14 after a conflict with townsmen during which two or three students were hanged. Its first recognition came in a royal writ to the Chancellor of Cambridge in 1230. The first college, Peterhouse, was founded in 1284 and another nine followed in the 14th and 15th centuries, but the university did not achieve real eminence until the 16th-c. Reformation when it produced Tyndale, Coverdale, Cranmer, and Latimer. After a prolonged period of stagnation, Cambridge was revived by its growth as a centre of scientific research in the late 19th and early 20th c. Women's colleges were founded in the mid-19th c., but women did not receive full academic status until 1948. Cambridge today also processes agricultural produce, and has computer-based high-tech industries.

**Cambridge** an industrial and educational city in eastern Massachusetts, USA, on the Charles River opposite Boston; pop. (1990) 95,800. Founded in 1630, it was known as New Towne until 1638. Harvard University (the oldest college in the USA) was established here in 1636 and four years later in 1640 the first printing press in the USA was set up. Cambridge is also the home of the distinguished Massachusetts Institute of Technology. Henry Longfellow lived here from 1837 until his death in 1882.

**Cambridgeshire** a county of eastern England; area 3,401 sq. km. (1,314 sq. miles); pop. (1991) 640,700; county town, Cambridge. The former county of Cambridge was united with the Isle of Ely in 1965 and part of Huntingdonshire in 1974. The county is divided into six districts:

| District | Area (sq. km.) | Pop. (1991) |
|---|---|---|
| Cambridge | 41 | 101,000 |
| East Cambridgeshire | 655 | 59,300 |
| Fenland | 547 | 72,900 |
| Huntingdonshire | 924 | 140,700 |
| Peterborough | 333 | 148,800 |
| South Cambridgeshire | 902 | 118,100 |

**Camden** /'kæmdən/ an inner borough of London, England; pop. (1991) 170,500. Situated to the north of the City of Westminster, it includes the suburbs of Bloomsbury, Hampstead, St. Pancras, Highgate, and Holborn. It is named after Sir Charles Pratt, 1st Earl Camden (1713–94) who was Lord Chancellor from 1766 to 1770.

**Camden** a port and centre of light industries on the east bank of the Delaware River in the state of New Jersey, USA; pop. (1990) 87,500. It was the home of the poet Walt Whitman from 1873 to 1892.

**Camelot** /'kæmɪ͵lɒt/ (in Arthurian legend) the place where the legendary King Arthur held his court, stated by Malory to be Winchester.

**Camembert** /'kæməmbɜ:(r)/ a village of Normandy in north-west France, situated near Falaise in the department of Orne in the Basse-Normandie region. It gives its name to a kind of soft creamy cheese with a strong flavour.

**Cameron Highlands** /'kæmərən/ a hill-resort region in the state of Pahang, central Peninsular Malaysia, named after the surveyor, William Cameron, who mapped the area in 1885.

**Cameroon** /͵kæmə'ru:n/ official name **The Republic of Cameroon** a country on the west coast of Africa bounded north-west by Nigeria, north-east by Chad, east by the Central African  Republic, south-east by Congo, south by Gabon and Equatorial Guinea, and west by the Gulf of Guinea; area 475,442 sq. km. (183,569 sq. miles); pop. (est. 1991) 11,400,000; official languages, French and English; capital, Yaoundé. The largest cities are the seaport of Douala and Yaoundé. The terrain rises from a low coastal plain in the south through an interior plateau to high mountains in the west. In the north, rolling savanna gradually slopes down to desert and marshland near Lake Chad. The climate is equally varied, ranging from a humid coast with an annual average rainfall of 1,150 cm. (460 inches) to very dry conditions in the far north. Agriculturally self sufficient, Cameroon exports a wide range of products including oil, aluminium, coffee, cocoa, bananas, rubber, cotton, peanuts, palm oil, and timber. Inhabited by Muslim people of Hamitic and Semitic stock in the north and by Bantu people in the south, Cameroon was a German protectorate from 1884 to 1916. It was subsequently administered under the League of Nations, later under UN trusteeship, part by France and part by Britain. In 1960 French Cameroons became an independent republic, to be joined in 1961 by part of the British Cameroons; the remainder became part of Nigeria. The French and British halves of the territory (West and East Cameroon) at first had separate governments but in 1972 merged as a united republic governed by a single-party National Assembly which is dominated by the Cameroon People's Democratic Movement.
**Cameroonian** *adj. & n.*
Cameroon is divided into 10 provinces:

| Province | Area (sq. km.) | Pop. (1987) | Capital |
|---|---|---|---|
| Adamaoua | 63,691 | 495,200 | Ngaoundéré |
| Centre | 68,926 | 1,651,600 | Yaoundé |
| Est | 109,011 | 517,200 | Bertoua |
| Extrême-Nord | 34,246 | 1,855,700 | Maroua |
| Littoral | 20,239 | 1,354,800 | Douala |
| Nord | 65,576 | 832,200 | Garoua |
| Nord-Ouest | 17,810 | 1,237,300 | Bamenda |
| Ouest | 13,872 | 1,339,800 | Bafoussam |
| Sud | 47,110 | 373,800 | Ebolowa |
| Sud-Ouest | 24,471 | 838,000 | Buéa |

**Cameroon, Mount** a volcanic peak rising to a height of 4,070 m. (13,354 ft.) at the centre of a large massif in southern Cameroon. It is the highest peak in sub-Saharan West Africa and the highest active volcano in Africa. First climbed by Richard Burton in 1861, its last major eruption took place in 1982.

**Camino Real** /kə'mi:nəʊ reɪ'æl/ a name used to describe a number of so-called 'royal roads' in the Americas, in particular the Spanish routeway linking Chihuahua in Mexico with Santa Fe in New Mexico (first used in 1581), and the ancient Inca routeway between the Andean cities of Quito (in Ecuador) and Cuzco (in Peru).

**Camlan** /'kæmlən/ an unidentified location in England (but possibly near Camelford in Cornwall) where King Arthur is said to have died in battle in 537.

**Camp, the** the name given to the open country of the Falkland Islands

**Campagna di Roma** /kæm'pænjə di: 'rəʊmə/ a plain surrounding the city of Rome in the Latium region of central Italy, stretching from the Sabine Hills to the Tyrrhenian Sea. Drained by the River Tiber, it had been a prosperous area in Roman times before becoming an impoverished mosquito-ridden wilderness. It was later improved by large-scale land reclamation and drainage in the 19th and 20th centuries.

**Campania** /kæm'peɪnɪə/ a region of west-central Italy comprising the provinces of Caserta, Benevento, Napoli, Avellino, and Salerno; area 13,598 sq. km. (5,252 sq. miles); pop. (1991) 5,853,900; capital, Naples. The ancient cities of Pompeii, Herculaneum, Paestum, and Velia are located in the fertile Campania region which produces, grain, fruit, wine, tobacco, and vegetables.

**Campbell Island** /'kæmbəl/ an uninhabited volcanic island of New Zealand lying in the Southern Ocean to the south-east of Auckland Island and 720 km. (453 miles) south of Invercargill at the tip of South Island; area 114 sq. km. (44 sq. miles). Discovered in 1810, it is visited by seal hunters.

**Camp David** the retreat in the Appalachian Mountains, Maryland, of the President of the USA. It was first used as a summer residence by Franklin D. Roosevelt who named it Shangri-La. Under President Truman it became an official residence. Historic encounters took place between Roosevelt and Churchill in 1943 and Eisenhower and Kruschev in 1959, and in 1978 President Carter hosted a series of talks between the leaders of Israel and Egypt in an attempt to resolve the Arab-Israeli conflict. The resulting Camp David agreements formed the basis of the subsequent Egypt–Israel peace treaty of 1979.

**Campeche** /kæm'peɪtʃeɪ/ **1.** a state in south-east Mexico on the Yucatán peninsula; area 50,812 sq. km. (19,626 sq. miles); pop.(1990) 528,820. The region gives its name to a type of logwood known as Campeachy wood which was first exported from here. **2.** its capital, a seaport on the Bay of Campeche in the Gulf of Mexico; pop.(1990) 172,200. It has fishing, textile, and handicraft industries.

**Camperdown** /'kæmpə(r),daʊn/ (Dutch **Camp**) a village in the province of North Holland, on the North Sea coast of the Netherlands, north-west of Alkmaar. In 1797 the British defeated the Dutch in a naval battle near here.

**Campina Grande** /kæm'piːnə 'grɑːndɪ/ a commercial city in the state of Paraíba, north-east Brazil, north-west of Recife; pop. (1990) 335,669. It is a centre for light industry and trade in goods from the north-eastern *sertão* region.

**Campinas** /kæm'piːnəs/ a commercial city 88 km. (55 miles) north-west of São Paulo in south-east Brazil; pop. (1990) 835,000. It is a major centre of the Brazilian coffee trade and the base for multi-national companies specializing in electronics. It has diverse light industries.

**campo** /'kæmpəʊ/ the word for a plain in Spanish and Portuguese. In Brazil campo is a term used to describe savanna grassland and campo cerrado is a shrubby or arboreal type of savanna.

**Campo Grande** /ˌkæmpəʊ 'grɑːndɪ/ the capital of the state of Mato Grosso do Sul in west-central Brazil; pop. (1991) 525,000. A regional museum features the Xavante and Bororo Indians of the Pantanal and Mato Grosso.

**Campobasso** /ˌkæmpəʊ'bæsəʊ/ the capital of a province of the same name in the Molise region of central Italy; pop. (1990) 51,300. It is noted for its annual *Sagra dei Misteri* procession on the feast of Corpus Christi.

**campos** /'kæmpəs/ the savanna plains of central Brazil.

**Campos** /'kæmpəs/ (fully **Campos dos Goytacazes**) a city to the north-east of Río de Janeiro in south-east Brazil; pop. (1990) 400,600. It lies at the centre of a large sugar-producing area and services the offshore oilfields.

**Camranh Bay** /kæm'ræn/ an inlet of the South China Sea on the south-east coast of Vietnam, used at various times by the French, Japanese, USA, and Soviet Union as a strategic naval base.

**Camster** /'kæmstə(r)/ a prehistoric site on open moorland near Lybster in Caithness, northern Scotland, comprising two great burial cairns known as the Grey Cairns of Camster.

**Cana** /'keɪnə/ a small town in Galilee in northern Israel, north-east of Nazareth, where Christ is said to have performed his first miracle by changing water into wine during a marriage feast (John 2: 1–11).

**Canaan** /'keɪnən/ a name often applied to the whole of ancient Palestine, but more specifically to the land lying between the River Jordan and the Mediterranean. Occupied in the 3rd millenium BC by the Canaanites, a Semitic-speaking people, it was conquered and occupied during the latter part of the 2nd millenium BC by the Israelites who described it as their 'Promised Land' (Exodus 3: 8). The earliest-known mention of the country by this name is in the Mari documents of the 18th c. BC. **Canaanite** *adj. & n.*

**Canada** /'kænədə/ a country covering the entire northern half of North America with the exception of Alaska and the French dependency of St. Pierre and Miquelon; area 9,976,186 sq.  km. (3,851,809 sq. miles); pop. (1991) 27,296,860; official languages, English and French; capital, Ottawa. Its largest cities are Toronto, Montreal, Vancouver, Ottawa, Edmonton, Calgary, Winnipeg, and Quebec. Canada is the world's largest source of nickel and zinc and the second-largest source of asbestos. Major exports also

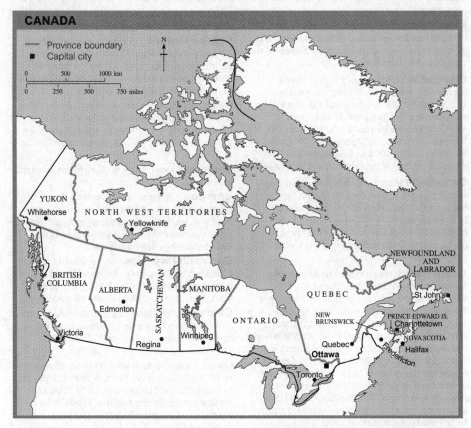

CANADA

— Province boundary
■ Capital city

0    500    1000 km
0  250   500  750 miles

YUKON
Whitehorse
NORTH WEST TERRITORIES
Yellowknife
BRITISH
COLUMBIA
ALBERTA
SASKATCHEWAN
MANITOBA
Edmonton
Victoria
Regina
Winnipeg
ONTARIO
QUEBEC
NEW
BRUNSWICK
NEWFOUNDLAND
AND
LABRADOR
St John's
PRINCE EDWARD IS.
Charlottetown
NOVA SCOTIA
Quebec
Ottawa
Halifax
Fredericton
Toronto

include grain, livestock, and timber. Occupied since prehistoric time by Inuit and Indian nations, a settlement on the north-east tip of Newfoundland was briefly established by Vikings *c.*AD 1000. Five centuries later in 1497 John Cabot reached the east coast. Jaques Cartier explored the St. Lawrence in 1535 and Samuel de Champlain founded Quebec in 1608 and penetrated the interior (1609–16). Eastern Canada was colonized by the French mainly in the 17th c., with the British emerging as the ruling colonial power after the Seven Years War which concluded with the Treaty of Paris in 1763. Formerly known as British North America, Canada became a federation of provinces in 1867, and the last step in the attainment of its legal independence from the UK was taken with the signing of the Constitution Act of 1982. Through the late 19th and early 20th centuries the vast Canadian West was gradually opened up, but the country remains sparsely populated for its size. Although periodically affected by the separatist aspirations of the French-speaking people of Quebec and the territorial claims of Inuit and Indian minorities, Canada has generally remained both stable and prosperous.

**Canadian** *adj. & n.*
Canada is a federation of 10 provinces and two territories:

| Province/ Territory | Area (sq. km.) | Pop. (1991) | Capital |
|---|---|---|---|
| Alberta | 661,190 | 2,545,550 | Edmonton |
| British Columbia | 947,800 | 3,282,060 | Victoria |
| Manitoba | 649,950 | 1,091,940 | Winnipeg |
| New Brunswick | 73,440 | 723,900 | Fredericton |
| Newfoundland | 405,720 | 568,470 | St. John's |
| Nova Scotia | 55,490 | 899,940 | Halifax |
| Ontario | 1,068,580 | 10,840,300 | Toronto |
| Prince Edward Island | 5,660 | 129,765 | Charlottetown |
| Quebec | 1,540,680 | 6,895,960 | Quebec |
| Saskatchewan | 652,330 | 988,930 | Regina |
| Northwest Territories | 3,426,320 | 57,650 | Yellowknife |
| Yukon Territory | 483,450 | 27,800 | Whitehorse |

**Canadian** /kə'neɪdɪən/ a river of south-west USA rising in southern Colorado and flowing 1,458 km. (906 miles) south and east through New Mexico and northern Texas to join the Arkansas River in eastern Oklahoma.

**Canadian Shield** a region of ancient Precambrian rock underlying nearly half of Canada from the Canadian Arctic around Hudson Bay to the Great Lakes. During the Ice Age large continental ice sheets depressed the area, carried away most of the region's fertile soil, and gouged out large numbers of hollows that now form lake basins. Its bare rock, thin soil, and muskeg swamp have not encouraged settlement but have provided Canada with natural resources such as timber, minerals, and water power and with a landscape that attracts an increasing number of tourists.

**Çanakkale** /tʃəˈnækəlɪ/ **1.** a province of northwest Turkey between the Aegean and the Sea of Marmara; area 9,737 sq. km. (3,761 sq. miles); pop. (1990) 432,260. **2.** its capital (also **Dardanelli**); pop. (1990) 54,000.

**Canandaigua** /kænənˈdeɪgwə/ a resort city in west-central New York state, USA, at the north end of Canandaigua Lake in the Finger Lakes region; pop. (1990) 10,725. First settled in 1789, the treaty forming the Iroquois Confederacy was signed here in 1794.

**Canaries current** a cold ocean current in the North Atlantic that flows south-westwards from Spain to meet equatorial waters near the Canary Islands.

**Canary Islands** /kəˈneərɪ/ (also **Canaries**, Spanish **Islas Canarias** /ˈiːzlɑːs kəˈnɑːrɪəs/) a group of islands in Spanish possession since the 15th c., situated in the Atlantic Ocean off the north-west coast of Africa. Forming an autonomous region of Spain, the archipelago comprises the islands of Tenerife, Gomera, La Palma, Hierro, Gran Canaria, Fuerteventura, Lanzarote, and the uninhabited islands of Alegranza, Graciosa, and Isla de Lobos; area 7,273 sq. km. (2,809 sq. miles); pop. (1991) 1,493,780; capital, Las Palmas. Tourism and the export of fruit and vegetables are the main industries. It is said to have derived its name from the many dogs (Latin *canis* = dog) that existed on Gran Canaria.

**Canberra** /ˈkænbərə/ the capital and seat of the federal government of Australia in Australian Capital Territory, south-east Australia. It was planned by Walter Burley Griffin, an American architect, and in 1927 it succeeded Melbourne as the capital of Australia, construction having been delayed by World War I; pop. (1991) 299,890 (with Queanbeyan). The old Parliament House (1927) was replaced by a new one completed in 1988. Other notable buildings include the Australian National Gallery, National Library, High Court of Australia, Academy of Science, National Science and Technology Centre, and Australian War Memorial.

**Cancún** /kænˈkuːn/ a Caribbean resort in southeast Mexico, on the north-east coast of the Yucatán peninsula; pop. (1980) 27,500.

**Candia** /ˈkændɪə/ the Venetian name for the island of CRETE, the city of HERAKLION, and that part of the southern Aegean Sea lying between the Cyclades and Crete.

**Canea** /kəˈniːə/ (Greek **Khaniá** /ˈxɑːnjɑː/, also **Chania**) a port on the north coast of Crete shipping olive oil, fruit, and wine; pop. (1981) 47,340.

Founded by the Venetians in the 13th c., it was capital of Crete from 1841 to 1971.

**Canelones** /kænəˈləʊnez/ the capital of the grain-growing department of Canelones in southern Uruguay, 45 km. (28 miles) from Montevideo; pop. (1985) 17,300.

**Cangzhou** /kænˈdʒəʊ/ a city in Hebei province, eastern China, on the Grand Canal south of Tianjin; pop. (1986) 303,000.

**Çankiri** /ˈtʃænkərə/ **1.** a mountainous province of northern Turkey, north-east of Ankara; area 8,454 sq. km. (3,265 sq. miles); pop. (1990) 279,100. **2.** its capital; pop. (1990) 45,500.

**Canna** /ˈkɑːnə/ an island in the Inner Hebrides off the west coast of Scotland, separated from the island of Rhum by the Sound of Canna and from the island of Skye by the Cuillin Sound. A ferry service to Mallaig links it to the Scottish mainland. The iron in the basalt of Compass Hill is known to navigators for its distortion of compass readings.

**Cannes** /kæn/ a coastal resort on the Riviera in the Alpes-Maritime department of southern France, made fashionable in the 19th c. by visiting royalty and aristocracy, the first of whom was Lord Brougham; pop. (1990) 69,360. An important international film festival is held here annually.

**Cannock Chase** /ˈkænək/ a district in the midland county of Staffordshire, central England; area 789 sq. km. (305 sq. miles); pop. (1991) 87,400. It takes its name from a moorland with rich coal deposits.

**Cano** /ˈkænəʊ/ a volcanic peak on the Atlantic island of Fogo, Cape Verde. Rising to 2,829 m. (9,281 ft.) it is the highest peak in the Cape Verde Islands.

**Canoas** a northern suburb of Pôrto Alegre in the State of Rio Grande do Sul, southern Brazil; pop. (1990) 260,360.

**Cantab.** an abbreviation of *Cantabrigiensis* which is the Latin name for Cambridge.
**Cantabrigian** *adj. & n.*

**Cantabria** /kænˈtæbrɪə/ an autonomous region of northern Spain, between Asturias in the west and the Basque Provinces in the east; area 5,289 sq. km. (2,043 sq. miles); pop. (1991) 527,330; capital, Santander.

**Cantabrian Mountains** (Spanish **Cordillera Cantabrica**) a mountain range in northern Spain extending eastwards from Galicia for a distance of 500 km. (190 miles) through the regions of Asturias, Cantabria, and the Basque Provinces. Rising to 2,648 m. (8,688 ft.) in the Picos de Europa, the Cantabrian Mountains are the source of the Ebro, Sil, Esla, and Carrión rivers.

**Cantal** /kænˈtæl/ a department in the Auvergne region of central France; area 5,726 sq. km. (2,212 sq. miles); pop. (1990) 158,720; capital, Aurillac.

**Canterbury** /ˈkæntəbərɪ/ (anc. **Durovernum** or **Cantuaria**) an historic city in Kent, south-east

England; pop. (1981) 39,700. It was St. Augustine's centre for the conversion of England to Christianity, now the seat of the Anglican archbishop, 'Primate of All England'. St. Augustine had been ordered to organize England into two ecclesiastical provinces, with archbishops at London and York. From the first, however, the place of London was taken by Canterbury. The 11th–15th-c. cathedral was the scene of the murder of Thomas à Becket in 1170 and became thereafter a centre of pilgrimage. Chaucer stayed here in 1360–1 as part of the Royal Household and wrote his *Canterbury Tales*. Canterbury was the birthplace of Christopher Marlowe (1564–93) and R. H. Barham (1788–1845) author of the *Ingoldsby Legends*. The University of Kent at Canterbury was founded here in 1965. The city is a major tourist destination.

**Canterbury Plains** a region on the central east coast of South Island, New Zealand, stretching southwards for 193 km. (121 miles) from the Banks Peninsula. The lower parts of the plain contain the widest area of flat land in New Zealand, while the northern and southern extremities merge into rolling downs. It derives its name from the Canterbury Association formed in 1848 under the presidency of the Archbishop of Canterbury for the purpose of settling the region with members of the Church of England. The **Canterbury** local government region, constituted in 1989, comprises Christchurch and the districts of Mackenzie, Waimate, Timaru, Ashburton, Selwyn, Waimakariri, Banks Peninsula, and parts of Hurunui and Waitaki; pop. (1991) 442,390.

**Canton** /kæn'tɒn/ see GUANGZHOU.

**Canton** a city in north-east Ohio, USA at the meeting place of three branches of the Nimishillen Creek; pop. (1990) 84,161. It is one of the largest producers of speciality steels in the world and was the boyhood home of W. H. Hoover founder of the Hoover Company. After his assassination in 1901, President William McKinley was buried here.

**Canton and Enderbury** two Pacific islands in the Phoenix group, Kiribati, administered from 1939 to 1980 as a joint UK-USA condominium.

**Canvey Island** /'kænvɪ/ an island on the north side of the Thames estuary, south-east England, to the west of Southend.

**canyon** /'kænjən/ (Spanish **cañon**) a deep narrow gorge, often with a stream or river, often found in arid areas.

**Canyon de Chelly** /-ʃeɪ/ an area in north-east Arizona, USA, with ancient Indian cliff-dwellings built between AD 350 and 1300. Still occupied by Navajo Indians, 33,955 hectares (83,840 acres) have been designated a National Monument.

**Canyonlands National Park** a national park at the junction of the Green and Colorado rivers in southern Utah, USA, established in 1964; area 136,716 hectares (337,570 acres).

**Cape Aghulas** /ə'gʌləs/ the most southerly point of the continent of Africa, at the tip of Western Cape, South Africa.

**Cape Almadies** /ˌælmə'diːəs/ the westernmost point of the continent of Africa, at the tip of the Cape Vert peninsula, north-west of Dakar in Senegal.

**Cape Bon** /bɒn/ a peninsula of north-east Tunisia, extending into the Mediterranean Sea, noted for its resorts and its wine.

**Cape Breton Island** an island that forms the north-eastern part of the Canadian province of Nova Scotia from which it is separated by the Strait of Canso. Discovered by John Cabot in 1497, it was a French possession until 1763 and a separate colony from 1784 to 1820. Sydney is the chief town. The Cape Breton Highlands National Park covers 958 sq. km. (370 sq. miles) between the Gulf of St. Lawrence and the Atlantic.

**Cape Byron** /'baɪrən/ the most easterly point of the continent of Australia, in New South Wales.

**Cape Canaveral** /kə'nævər(ə)l/ a cape on the east coast of Florida, USA, known as Cape Kennedy from 1963 until 1973. It is the location of the John F. Kennedy Space Center which has been the principal US launching site for manned space flights since 1961.

**Cape Chelyuskin** /tʃe'ljuːskɪn/ the northernmost point on the mainland of Asia, at the northern tip of the Taimyr Peninsula in Siberian Russia.

**Cape Cod** /kɒd/ a sandy peninsula in south-east Massachusetts, which forms a wide curve enclosing Cape Cod Bay. The Cape Cod Canal, completed in 1914, links the bay with Buzzard's Bay on the south-west. The Pilgrim Fathers landed on the northern tip of Cape Cod in November 1620.

**Cape Coloured** a term used in Cape Province, South Africa, to describe people of mixed African and European descent.

**Cape Comorin** /'kɒmərɪn/ a cape at the southern tip of India, in the state of Tamil Nadu.

**Cape Coral** a city in south-west Florida, USA, on the Caloosahatchee River near its junction with the Gulf of Mexico. pop. (1990) 74,991. Founded in 1958.

**Cape Dezhnev** /'deʒnef/ (also **East Cape**) a cape on the Chukchi Peninsula at the far north-eastern tip of Siberia, in the Russian Federation, on the Bering Strait. Named after a Russian navigator, it is the north-easternmost point of Asia.

**Cape doctor** a strong wind that blows outwards from the plateau of southern Africa to the coast.

**Cape Finisterre** a point on the north-west coast of Spain, in the province of La Coruña.

**Cape Gracias à Dios** /-ˌgrɑːʃɪəs ɑː ˈdiːəs/ the most easterly point of Honduras on the Mosquito Coast of the Caribbean Sea. Columbus is said to have named the point when, after being becalmed for a long period, his ship picked up wind.

**Cape Hafun** /hæˈfuːn/ (Arabic **Ras Hafun**) a peninsula on the north-east coast of Somalia. It is the most easterly point on the continent of Africa.

**Cape Horn** /hɔːn/ the southernmost point of South America, on an island south of Tierra del Fuego, belonging to Chile. It was discovered by the Dutch navigator Schouten in 1616 and named after Hoorn, his birthplace. The ocean region is notorious for storms, and until the opening of the Panama Canal in 1914 lay on a sea route between the Atlantic and Pacific Oceans.

**Cape Johnson Depth** /ˈdʒɒns(ə)n/ the deepest point of the Philippine Trench which drops to 10,497 m. (34,440 ft.) below-sea-level off the coast of the Philippines. It is named after the USS *Cape Johnson* which took soundings there in 1945.

**Cape Leeuwin** /ˈluːən/ the extreme southwestern point of the continent of Australia.

**Cape May** a peninsula on the Atlantic coast of New Jersey, USA, which became popular as a beach resort in the mid-19th c.

**Cape of Good Hope** (Afrikaans **Kaap die Goeie Hoop**) a mountainous promontory near the southern extremity of Africa, south of Cape Town. It was sighted towards the end of the 15th c. by the Portuguese explorer Dias and named Cape of Storms, and was rounded for the first time by Vasco da Gama in 1497.

**Cape Piai** /piːˈaɪ/ the southernmost point of the mainland of Asia, at the southern tip of the Malay peninsula.

**Cape Province** (Afrikaans **Kaapprovinsie**) a former province of the Republic of South Africa; area 641,379 sq. km. (247,332 sq. miles); pop. (1985) 5,041,100. Its capital was Cape Town. Ceded to the British by the Dutch in 1814, it joined the Union of South Africa in 1910 and in 1994 was divided into the provinces of Eastern Cape, Western Cape, and Northern Cape.

**Capernaum** /kəˈpɜːn(ə)m/ (Hebrew **Kefar Nahum**) the site of an ancient village on the northern shores of the Sea of Galilee, Israel. It was the centre of Jesus' ministry in Galilee, where he healed the servant of the centurion who had built a synagogue (Luke 7: 1–10), and where he found his first disciples Simon and Andrew casting their nets into the water (Matthew 4: 19).

**Cape Roca** /ˈrɒkə/ a peninsula on the Atlantic coast of Portugal, west of Lisbon. It is the most westerly point on the mainland of Europe.

**Cape Tarifa** /tæˈriːfə/ a peninsula on the Andalusian coast of southern Spain. It is the southernmost point of mainland Europe.

**Cape Town** (Afrikaans **Kaapstad**) the legislative capital of the Republic of South Africa and administrative capital of the Western Cape Province, situated on Table Bay at the foot of Table Mountain (1,080 m., 3,543 ft.); pop. (1985) 776,600. Founded as a victualling station by the Dutch East India Company in 1652, Cape Town was eventually occupied by the British in 1795. Capital of the Western Cape since 1994, it was capital of the former Cape Province. Its castle (1666) is South Africa's oldest building; the Dutch Reformed church dates from 1699. Groote Schuur, the former estate of Cecil Rhodes, contains the University of Cape Town, the Rhodes Memorial, a hospital, and museum. The National Botanic Gardens (1913) contain a famous collection of South African flora. Cape Town is the chief port, commercial, and industrial centre for the surrounding region. Its industries include food processing, wine making, clothing, printing, and tourism.

**Cape Verde**
/vɜːd/ official name
**The Republic of
Cape Verde** a country consisting of a group of 10 islands and five islets in the Atlantic, 620 km. (385 miles) off the coast of Senegal,
named after the most westerly peninsula of Africa; area 4,033 sq. km. (1,557 sq. miles); pop. (est. 1991) 400,000; official language, Portuguese; capital, Praia (on São Tiago Island). The largest city is Mindelo (on São Vicente Island) which is the chief port. Divided into the windward (Barlavento) and leeward (Sotavento) groups, the islands experience long periods of drought with sand storms blowing from the Sahara in winter. The low-lying islands of Sal, Boa Vista, and Maio are without natural water supplies and all of the islands have suffered from soil erosion. Corn, beans, sweet potatoes, and manioc are staple crops and small quantities of fish are exported. Salt, limestone, and possolana (a volcanic rock used in cement production) are the chief mineral resources. Despite the islands' meagre resources, Cape Verde lies at a strategic location at the cross-roads of mid-Atlantic air and sea routes. Settled by the Portuguese in the 15th c., the islands formed a Portuguese colony until they became independent in 1975. They have links with Guinea-Bissau with which they were formerly administered, but the plans for a federation with Guinea-Bissau were dropped in 1980. Governed by a National Assembly, Cape Verde's African Party, which had ruled since independence, was swept from power in the country's first multi-party elections held in 1991.
**Cape Verdean** *adj. & n.*

**Cape Wrath** /rɒθ/ a promontory at the northwest extremity of Scotland.

**Cape York** the northernmost point of the continent of Australia, on the Torres Strait, at the tip of the sparsely-populated Cape York Peninsula in Queensland.

**Cap Haïtien** /'heɪʃən/ (Locally **Le Cap**) a commercial port and capital of Nord department in northern Haiti; pop. (1988) 133,230. Settled by the French in 1670, the town was devastated by an earthquake in 1842. It exports coffee, bananas, sugar-cane, cocoa, and sisal.

**Capitol** /'kæpɪt(ə)l/ the seat of the US Congress in Washington DC. Its site was chosen by George Washington, who laid the first stone in 1793.

**Capitoline Hill** /'kæpɪtə͵laɪn/ the highest of the seven hills of Rome.

**Capitol Reef National Park** a national park in south-central Utah, USA, noted for its geological formations, principally the monocline known as the Waterpocket Fold. It was designated a national monument in 1937 and a park in 1971; area 97,955 hectares (241,865 acres).

**Capo di Monte** /͵kæpəʊ dɪ 'mɒnteɪ/ a village near Naples in Italy, which lends its name to a type of porcelain first produced there in the mid-18th c.

**Cappadocia** /͵kæpə'dəʊʃə/ the ancient name for the region in the centre of Asia Minor, now in modern Turkey, between Lake Tuz and the Euphrates, north of Cilicia. During the 3rd c. BC it became a kingdom that maintained its independence until annexed by Rome in AD 17. It was an important centre of early Christianity. **Cappadocian** *adj. & n.*

**Caprese Michelangelo** /kə'preɪzɪ ͵maɪkl'ɑ:nʒələʊ/ a village in the eastern Alpe di Catenaia of Tuscany, Italy, north-east of Arezzo; pop. (1990) 1,716. It was the birthplace of the Italian artist Michelangelo (1474–1564).

**Capri** /'kæpri:, kə'pri:/, **Isle of** an island off the west coast of Italy in the Bay of Naples. Its chief towns are Capri and Anacapri. The Swedish writer Axel Munthe (1857–1949) lived at the Villa of San Michele.

**Caprivi Strip** /kə'pri:vɪ/ a narrow strip of Namibia that extends towards Zambia from the north-east corner of Namibia and reaches the Zambezi River. It was part of German South West Africa until after World War I, having been ceded by Britain in 1893 in order to give the German colony access to the Zambezi, and is named after Leo Graf von Caprivi, German imperial chancellor 1890–4.

**Capsian** /'kæpsɪən/ the palaeolithic industry of North Africa and southern Europe (c. 8,000–4,500 BC) noted for its microliths. The Capsian culture takes its name from the town of GAFSA in Tunisia.

**Capua** /'kæpu:ə/ a town in the Campania region of southern Italy, on a loop of the River Volturno; pop. (1990) 19,520. On the site of ancient Casilinum, the Roman Appian Way crossed the river here. The city was rebuilt after old Capua was destroyed by the Arabs in AD 841. In ancient times Capua was noted for its perfume made from wild roses.

**Caracas** /kə'rækəs/ the capital and largest city of Venezuela; pop. (1991) 1,824,890; 3,435,795 (metropolitan area). Founded in 1567 as Santiago de León de Caracas, the city developed rapidly during the oil boom of the 1950s. It was the birthplace in 1783 of the revolutionary leader Simón Bolívar who is buried in the Panteón Nacional and whose home has been reconstructed as a museum. The cathedral dates from 1614, and the city is a contrasting mixture of skyscrapers and shanty towns. Main industries are oil refining, textiles, vehicle assembly, chemicals, and food processing.

**Caracol** /͵kærə'kɒl/ the remains of an ancient Mayan city in the tropical forest of western Belize, Central America, rediscovered in 1936.

**Carajás** /͵kærə'ʒɑ:s/ a mining region in the state of Pará in north Brazil, the site of one of the richest deposits of iron ore in the world.

**Caravaggio** /͵kærə'vædʒɪəʊ/ an agricultural and industrial town in the province of Bergamo, northern Italy, situated on the Lombardy Plain east of Milan; pop. (1990) 13,720. It was the birthplace of the painter Caravaggio (1573–1610). Near the town is a supposedly miraculous spring where the Virgin Mary appeared to a peasant woman during the Middle Ages.

**Carboniferous** a period of geological time (345–280 million years BP) between the Devonian and Permian epochs when the first amphibians began to make their appearance and coal was extensively formed.

**Carcassonne** /͵kɑ:kə'sɒn/ (anc. **Carcaso**) an ancient city, market and tourist centre on the River Aude in south-west France, noted for its (much restored) medieval fortifications; pop. (1990) 44,990. It is the capital of Aude department in the Languedoc-Roussillon region.

**Carchemish** /'kɑ:kɪmɪʃ/ an ancient city north-east of Aleppo near the modern Turkish town of Karkamis, situated in a strategic position on the upper Euphrates. It was a Hittite stronghold, annexed by Sargon II of Assyria in 717 BC.

**Cardamom Mountains** /'kɑ:dəməm/ a range of mountains in western Cambodia, rising to a height of 1,813 m. (5,886 ft.) at Phnomh Aural near the Thai frontier.

**Cardiff** /'kɑ:dɪf/ (Welsh **Caerdydd**) the capital of Wales, an administrative and commercial centre on the Bristol Channel at the mouth of the Taff, Ely, and Rhymney rivers; pop. (1991) 272,600. Among its chief industries are the manufacture of steel, engineering, and food processing, and among its principal landmarks are Llandaff Cathedral, Cardiff Castle, the National Museum of Wales, and the Welsh National Folk Museum. The

administrative headquarters of Mid Glamorgan
and South Glamorgan are in Cardiff at Cathays
Park and Atlantic Wharf. Its University Colleges
were founded in 1884 and 1893. Cardiff Arms Park
rugby stadium is world famous and the Royal Mint
is near Cardiff at Llantrisant. The composer and
dramatist Ivor Novello was born in Cardiff in 1893.

**Cardigan** /'kɑ:dɪg(ə)n/ a market town in Dyfed,
south Wales, on the River Teifi; pop. (1981) 4,000.
It was the former county town of Cardiganshire.

**Cardiganshire** a former county of south
Wales stretching from the River Dovey in the north
to the River Teifi in the south. It became part of
Dyfed in 1974.

**Carefree** a small town in central Arizona,
USA, on the edge of the Tonto National Forest
north-east of Phoenix; pop. (1990) 1,666. Its chief
landmarks are the largest sundial in the Western
Hemisphere and the world's tallest kachina (spirit
doll).

**Caria** /'keərɪə/ the ancient name for the region of
south-west Asia Minor south of the River
Maeander and north-west of Lycia. Halicarnassus
and Miletus were two of its chief cities.
**Carian** *adj. & n.*

**Cariacica** /ˌkɑ:rɪə'si:kə/ a city in the state of
Espiritu Santo, eastern Brazil, to the west of
Vitória; pop. (1990) 251,780.

**Carib** /'kærɪb/ a member of the pre-Columbian
American Indian inhabitants of the Lesser Antilles
and parts of the neighbouring South American
coast, or of their descendants. A fearsome maritime people, the Caribs forced the peaceful
Arawak-speaking peoples of the Antilles to mi-
grate to South America to escape their depredations. Still expanding at the time of the Spanish
conquest the Caribs were supplanted, in turn, by
European colonialism and have all but disappeared
in the West Indies (where only a few hundred still
remain on the island of Dominica). On mainland
South America Carib-speaking groups occupy
territory in the north-east and Amazon regions,
living in small autonomous communities. Peculi-
arly, the Carib language was spoken only by men;
their women, who were captured in raids on other
tribes, spoke only Arawak. Male captives were tor-
tured and eaten—hence the Carib name not only
applied to the Caribbean Sea but also to the root of
the English word 'cannibal'.

**Caribbean Sea** /ˌkærɪ'bi:ən, kə'rɪbɪən/ an arm
of the Atlantic Ocean lying between the Antilles
and the mainland of Central and South America.
It reaches a depth of 7,680 m. (25,197 ft.) in the
Cayman Trench between Cuba and Jamaica.

**Caribbees Islands** /kærə'bi:z/ (also
**Caribbees**) an early name for islands of the
Caribbean, especially the easternmost islands of
the West Indes now lying within the Leeward and
Windward groups of islands.

**Cariboo Highway** /'kærɪbu:/ a roadway
(Highway 97) in British Columbia, western Canada, linking Vancouver with the gold-rush region
of the Cariboo Mountains. It follows the route of
the old Cariboo Trail and the later Cariboo
Waggon Road along the Fraser River, from the
Trans-Canada Highway near Cache Creek to the
Yellowhead Highway near Prince George, a distance of *c.*445 km. (276 miles).

**CARICOM** *abbr.* Caribbean Community and
Common Market. An organization established in
1973 to promote co-operation in economic affairs
and social services etc. and to co-ordinate foreign
policy among its members, all of which are
independent states of the Caribbean region. Its
headquarters are at Georgetown, Guyana.

**Carinthia** /kə'rɪnθɪə/ (German **Kärnten**
/'keənt(ə)n/) an alpine province of southern
Austria; area 9,533 sq. km. (3,682 sq. miles); pop.
(1991) 552,420; capital, Klagenfurt.

**Carioca** /ˌkærɪ'əukə/ a native of Río de Janeiro.

**Carlisle** the county town and market centre of
Cumbria in north-west England, at the junction of
the Eden, Caldew, and Petteril rivers; pop. (1991)
99,800. It was the site of the Roman camp of
Luguvallum at the western end of Hadrian's Wall.
Its cathedral dates from the 12th c. Carlisle
changed hands frequently between Scots and
English in the Middle Ages. Today it manufactures
textiles, metal products, and biscuits.

**Carlow** /'kɑ:ləu/ (Gaelic **Cheatharlach**) **1.** a
county in the province of Leinster in the Republic
of Ireland; area 896 sq. km. (346 sq. miles); pop.
(1991) 40,946. **2.** its capital, on the River Barrow;
pop. (1991) 11,275.

**Carlsbad** the German name for KARLOVY VARY.

**Carlsbad** /'kɑ:lzbæd/ a resort town on the
Pacific coast of southern California, USA; pop.
(1990) 63,130. Founded in the 1880s, it was named
after the spa town of Carlsbad (Karlovy Vary) in
the Czech Republic following the discovery of mineral springs identical to the water found there.

**Carlsbad Caverns National Park** a national park protecting a system of limestone caves
in southern New Mexico, USA. Designated a national monument in 1923 and a park in 1930, it includes one of the world's largest underground cave
systems; area 18,935 hectares (46,753 acres).

**Carmarthen** /kə'mɑ:ðən/ the administrative
centre of Dyfed county, south Wales; pop. (1991)
54,800. It is a dairying centre and cattle market.

**Carmarthenshire** a former county of Wales
which became part of Dyfed in 1974. Its county
town was Carmarthen.

**Carmel** /kɑ:'mel/ a resort town popular with
writers and artists on the Pacific coast of California, USA, to the south of San Francisco; pop.
(1990) 4,240. Named after the Carmelite Friars by
early Spanish settlers, its Mission San Carlos

Borromeo del Rio Carmelo was founded in 1770 and was the headquarters of the California missions.

**Carmel** /ˈkɑːm(ə)l/, **Mount** a group of mountains in north-west Israel near the Mediterranean coast, rising to a height of 552 m. (1,812 ft.) and sheltering the port of Haifa. On its south-west slopes are caves that have provided evidence of human occupation dating from the palaeolithic down to the mesolithic periods. The Carmelite Order of Our Lady of Mount Carmel was founded on Mount Carmel by St. Berthold during the Crusades.

**Carnaby Street** /ˈkɑːnəbɪ/ a street in the West End of London, England, made famous in the 1960s as a centre of the teenage fashion industry.

**Carnac** /ˈkɑːnæk/ a village in north-west France, near the Atlantic coast of Brittany; pop. (1982) 4,000. It is the site of a group of stone monuments dating from prehistoric times, chiefly the neolithic period. Out of an original complex of some 10,000 stones 2,671 survive. They include single standing stones (menhirs), dolmens, and long avenues of grey monoliths which march across the countryside, arranged in order of height so that they decrease steadily from about 3–3.7 m. (10–12 ft.) to 1–1.2 m. (3–4 ft.); some of these avenues end in semicircular or rectangular enclosures of standing stones. It was at Carnac that scientists first proposed that neolithic architects used as their unit of measure a prehistoric yard of 0.829 m.

**Carnatic** /kɑːˈnætɪk/ (also **Karnatic**) a name sometimes applied to the whole of southern India, but more specifically to the plains of south-east India to the east of the eastern Ghats where the struggle between France and Britain for control of India took place during the 18th c.

**Carnic Alps** /ˈkɑːnɪk/ (German **Karnische Alpen**) a range of the eastern Alps in southern Austria and north-eastern Italy, rising to 2,781 m. (9,124 ft.) at Monte Coglians. The Plocken Pass links the Ober Gailtal to the Tagliamento valley.

**Carniola** /kɑːniˈəʊlə/ (Serbo-Croat **Kraniska** /ˈkrænskə/, Slavic **Krajina**) an historic region of Slovenia on the frontier with Italy that formed part of the Roman province of Pannonia and was later settled by Slovenes during the 6th c. It became an Austrian crown-land and was divided between Italy and Yugoslavia in 1919. Since 1947 it has been entirely within Slovenia. Ljubljana is the chief city.

**Carolina** /kærəˈlamə/ a city on the Caribbean island of Puerto Rico, south-east of San Juan; pop. (1990) 177,800.

**Caroline Islands** /ˈkærəˌlaɪn/ (also **Carolines**) a group of islands in the western Pacific Ocean, north of the equator, forming (with the exception of Palau and some smaller islands) the FEDERATED STATES OF MICRONESIA.

**Caroni** /kɑːrəˈniː/ a river of eastern Venezuela that rises at the Pacaraima Range and flows northwards for 880 km. (550 miles) through the Guri Reservoir to join the Orinoco near its mouth at Ciudad Guayana.

**Carpathian Mountains** /kɑːˈpeɪθɪən/ (also **Carpathians**) a mountain system extending in an arc south-eastwards from southern Poland and the Czech Republic into Romania and the Ukraine. They are divided into the White Carpathians (Bílé Karpaty) in the Czech Republic, the Little Carpathians (Malé Karpaty) in Slovakia, the Beskids (Beskydy) in southern Poland, the High Tatra (Vysoké Tatry) and Low Tatra (Nizké Tatry) of southern Poland and Slovakia, the Transylvanian Carpathians (Carpatii Meridionali), and the Eastern or Romanian Carpathians (Carpatii Orientali). The highest peak is Gerlachovsky which rises to 2,655 m. (8,711 ft.) in the Tatra Mountains of Slovakia. In 1993 the governments of Poland, Hungary, and Ukraine signed a regional economic, cultural, and environmental protection agreement establishing an area known as the Carpathian Euroregion.

**Carpathos** /ˈkærpəθəs/ (Greek **Kárpathos**, formerly **Scarpanto**) the largest of the Greek islands of the Dodecanese in the Aegean Sea; area 301 sq. km. (116 sq. miles); pop. (1981) 4,645; capital, Pigádhia.

**Carpentaria** /ˌkɑːpənˈteərɪə/, **Gulf of** a large bay indenting the eastern part of the north coast of Australia, between Arnhem Land and Cape York Peninsula. Discovered by Abel Tasman in 1606, it was named after Pieter Carpentier, Governor-General of the Dutch East Indies.

**Carrara** /kəˈrɑːrə/ a town in Tuscany, north-west Italy, at the foot of the Apuan Alps north of Massa, famous for its white marble which has been worked since Roman times and was a favourite material of Michelangelo; pop. (1990) 68,480. **Carrarese** adj. & n.

**Carriacou** /kærˈjɑːkuː/ the largest of the Grenadine islands in the Caribbean 37 km. (23 miles) north-east of Grenada; area 21 sq. km. (13 sq. miles); pop. (1981) 7,000. Its chief town is Hillsborough. The island is noted for its traditional African Big Drum Dances, Tombstone Feasts, and annual schooner regatta.

**Carrickfergus** /ˌkærɪkˈfɜːgəs/ (Gaelic **Carraig Fhearghais**) a port in County Antrim. Northern Ireland, on the north shore of Belfast Lough; pop. (1981) 17,600. It is built on Fergus's rock where legend has it that the progenitor of the royal house of Scotland was drowned. William II landed here before the battle of the Boyne in 1690.

**Carrick-on-Shannon** (Gaelic **Cora Droma Rúisc**) the county town of Leitrim in the Republic of Ireland, on the River Shannon; pop. (1991) 6,168.

**Carrick-on-Suir** /-sʊər/ (Gaelic **Carraig na Siúire**) a town in County Tipperary, Ireland, on the River Suir; pop. (1991) 5,145. Its ruined castle was the seat of the Dukes of Ormonde.

**Carrollton** /ˈkær(ə)ltən/ an industrial suburb of Dallas in northern Texas, USA; pop. (1990) 82,169. It produces electronic equipment and aircraft parts.

**carse** /kɑːs/ in Scotland the term used to describe a fertile alluvial river valley as in the Carse of Gowrie.

**Carson City** /ˈkɑːs(ə)n/ the capital of the US state of Nevada, near Lake Tahoe; pop. (1990) 40,443. Founded as a trading post in 1851 on the route from Salt Lake City to California, it is now a commercial centre at the heart of a mining and agricultural region. Named after Kit Carson, it became state capital in 1864.

**Cartagena** /ˌkɑːtəˈxenə/ (fully **Cartagena de los Indes**) a port, resort, and oil-refining centre on the Caribbean coast of north-west Colombia; pop. (1985) 529,600. Once a storehouse for Spanish treasure *en route* to Europe the old walled town was frequently attacked by British privateers and was sacked by Sir Francis Drake in 1586.

**Cartagena** /ˌkɑːtəˈxenə/ a port in the province of Murcia, on the Mediterranean coast of south-east Spain; pop. (1991) 172,152. Originally named Mastia, it was refounded as New Carthage (*Carthago Nova*) by Hasdrubal in 228 BC as a base for the Carthaginian conquest of Spain. It has a fine natural harbour and has been a naval port since the 16th c. Its industries include shipbuilding, oil refining, metal working, and chemicals.

**Carthage** /ˈkɑːθɪdʒ/ the ruins of an ancient city on the north coast of Africa in Tunisia, situated to the west of Tunis. Traditionally founded by Phoenicians from Tyre (in modern Lebanon) in 814 BC, it became a major centre of the Mediterranean, with interests in North Africa, Spain, and Sicily which brought it into conflict with Greece until the 3rd c. BC and then with Rome in the Punic Wars, until the Romans finally destroyed it in 146 BC.
**Carthaginian** *adj. & n.*

**cartography** /kɑːˈtɒɡrəfɪ/ the art and science of drawing maps, plans, and charts.

**Casablanca** /ˌkæsəˈblæŋkə/ a seaport and commercial centre on the Atlantic coast of north-west Africa, the largest city of Morocco; pop. (1982) 2,139,200. It was founded in 1515 by the Portuguese who had in 1468 destroyed the older city of Anfa. The King Hassan Mosque, completed in 1993, is the world's largest mosque. Casablanca is a mixture of old Muslim quarter, modern European city, and outlying shanty towns. It handles three-quarters of the country's commerce and has textile, glass, and tourist industries. It was the site of an Allied landing in 1942 and of a conference between Roosevelt and Churchill in 1943.

**Cascade Range** /kæsˈkeɪd/ a range of mountains to the east of the Coast Range on the Pacific coast of North America, running north-south from the Canadian frontier to northern California. The range, which includes Crater Lake and volcanic peaks such as Mt. St Helens, Mt. Hood, Mt. Shasta, and Mt. Adams, rises to 4,392 m. (14,409 ft.) at Mt. Rainier.

**Cascais** /kæʃˈkaɪʃ/ a resort and fishing village on the Atlantic coast of central Portugal, west of Lisbon; pop. (1991) 19,480.

**Casentino** /ˌkæzənˈtiːnəʊ/ the name given to the upper valley of the River Arno in Tuscany, Italy, between Florence and Arezzo.

**Caserta** /kæˈzɜːtə/ a commercial centre in Campania, south-central Italy, capital of Caserta province; pop. (1990) 69,350. The town developed around a royal palace built in the 18th c. Nearby is the original town of Caserta now known as Caserta Vecchia, a medieval town with a Romanesque cathedral.

**Cashel** /ˈkæʃəl/ a town in County Tipperary, in the south of the Republic of Ireland, east of the River Suir; pop. (1991) 2,470. The town is dominated by the **Rock of Cashel**, a limestone outcrop that rises to a height of 60 m. (200 ft.) and on which stands the 12th-c. Cormac's Chapel. The Rock was the seat of the Munster kings from about 370 to 1101.

**Casos** /ˈkæsəs/ (Greek **Kásos**) the most southerly of the Greek Dodecanese islands in the Aegean Sea, between Carpathos and Crete; area 66 sq. km. (25 sq. miles); pop. (1981) 1,184. In 1824 the island was devastated by the Egyptians.

**Casper** /ˈkæspə(r)/ a town on the North Platte River, east-central Wyoming, USA; pop. (1990) 46,742. Founded in 1888 at a railroad terminus in cattle country, Casper quickly expanded after the discovery of oil in 1890. Coal, bentonite, and uranium are mined nearby.

**Caspian Gates** /ˈkæspɪən/ (anc. **Caspiae Pylae**) a narrow pass in south-eastern Europe used for centuries as a trade route across the western Caucasus to the Caspian Sea near Derbent.

**Caspian Sea** /ˈkæspɪən/ a land-locked salt lake enclosed by Russia, Kazakhstan, Turkmenistan, Azerbaijan, and Iran. It is the world's largest body of inland water with an area of *c.* 370,992 sq. km. (143,524 sq. miles). Its surface lies 28 m. (92 ft.) below sea-level.

**Cassian Way** /ˈkæsɪən/ (Latin **Via Cassia**) an ancient Roman road linking Florence with Rome.

**Cassino** /kæˈsiːnəʊ/ a town of Latium in west-central Italy, in the province of Frosinone 130 km. (80 miles) south-east of Rome; pop. (1990) 34,590. An important centre of learning in the Middle Ages, the Benedictine abbey of Monte Cassino on a hill above the town was founded by St. Benedict of Nursia in 529. Cassino was rebuilt after being completely destroyed during World War II. (See also MONTE CASSINO.)

**Castalia** /kæ'steɪlɪə/ a spring on Mount Parnassus in Greece, sacred to Apollo and the Muses.

**Castel Gandolfo** /'kæstel gæn'dɒlfəʊ/ the summer residence of the pope, situated in the Alban Hills, on the western edge of Lake Albano in central Italy, 16 km. (10 miles) south-east of Rome.

**Castelli Romani** /kæs'telɪ rəʊ'mɑːniː/ region of vineyards, olive groves, and chestnut forests in the Alban Hills to the east of Rome, central Italy. It takes its name from the castles of popes and Roman patrician families including Castel Gandolfo, Frascati, Marino, Albano, Ariccia, Rocca di Pappa, and Monte Cómpatri.

**Castellón de la Plana** /kɑːstel'jəʊn deɪ lɑː 'plɑːnə/ **1.** a province in the Valencia region of eastern Spain; area 6,679 sq. km. (2,580 sq. miles); pop. (1991) 446,740. **2.** its capital, a Mediterranean seaport and industrial city; pop. (1991) 137,456.

**Castile** /kæs'tiːl/ the central plateau of the Iberian peninsula, a former Spanish kingdom. Castile became an independent Spanish kingdom in the 10th c. and, with Aragon to the east, dominated the Spanish scene during the Middle Ages. The marriage of Isabella of Castile to Ferdinand of Aragon in 1469 effectively unified Spain into a single country.
**Castilian** *adj. & n.*

**Castilian** /kəs'tɪljən/ (Spanish **Castellano**) the language of Castile which is the standard spoken and literary Spanish.

**Castilla-La Mancha** /kæˌstiːljə lɑː 'mæntʃə/ an autonomous region in central Spain comprising the provinces of Albacete, Ciudad Real, Cuenca, Guadalajara, and Toledo; area 79,230 sq. km. (30,602 sq. miles); pop. (1991) 1,658,450; capital, Toledo.

**Castilla-León** /kæ'stiːljəleɪˌɒn/ an autonomous region of northern Spain comprising the provinces of Avila, Burgos, León, Palencia, Salamanca, Segovia, Soria, Valladolid, and Zamora; area 94,147 sq. km. (36,364 sq. miles); pop. (1991) 2,545,930; capital, Valladolid.

**Castlebar** /kæs(ə)l'bɑː(r)/ the county town of County Mayo in the Republic of Ireland, on the Castlebar River to the east of Castlebar Lough; pop. (1991) 6,070. In 1798 a French force routed the English in an engagement known as the 'Races of Castlebar'. John Moore, who for a week in the same year was president of the Provisional Republic of Connaught, is buried here. (Irish *Caislean ab Bharraigh* = Barry's Castle.)

**Castlemaine** /'kɑːs(ə)l,meɪn/ a former gold mining town in central Victoria, Australia, at the foot of Mt. Alexander; pop. (1986) 7,650. It was the scene of some of the earliest strikes during the gold-rush of the 1850s.

**Castlerigg** /'kɑːs(ə)lrɪg/ a prehistoric site near Keswick in Cumbria, north-west England. Built c. 3,000 BC, it comprises a circle of 38 stones measuring 30 m. (100 ft.) in diameter.

**Castries** /'kæstriːs/ a seaport in the Caribbean, capital of the island of St. Lucia; pop. (1988) 52,900. Built on the shores of an almost-landlocked harbour and named in 1758 after Marechal de Castries, a Minister of the French Navy and the Colonies, its strategic position at the centre of the Eastern Caribbean has attracted shipping. It was originally known as Le Carenage, a place for careening ships.

**Catalan** /'kætəlæn/ **1.** a native of Catalonia in Spain. **2.** a Romance language most closely related to Provençal. Traditionally it is the language of Catalonia, but it is also spoken in Andorra, the Balearic Islands, and some parts of southern France.

**Catalonia** /ˌkætə'ləʊnɪə/ (Catalan **Catalunya**, Spanish **Cataluña**) an autonomous region of north-east Spain, comprising the provinces of Barcelona, Gerona, Lérida, and Tarragona; area 31,932 sq. km. (12,334 sq. miles); pop. (1991) 6,059,450; capital, Barcelona. The region includes the Mediterranean resorts of the Costa Brava.

**Catamarca** /kætə'mɑːkə/ **1.** a province in north-west Argentina; area 99,818 sq. km. (38,555 sq. miles); pop. (1991) 265,571. **2.** its capital, a mining centre and market town in the eastern foothills of the Andes; pop. (1991) 110,500.

**Catania** /kə'tɑːnɪə/ a seaport situated at the foot of Mount Etna, on the east coast of Sicily; pop. (1990) 364,180. Destroyed by earthquakes in 1169 and 1693, the city was rebuilt to a design by the Palermo architect Giovanni Battista Vaccarini (1702–68). It was the birthplace of the Italian composer Vincenzo Bellini (1801–35). Catania is a major commercial and industrial centre with chemical, textile, and light industries.

**Catanzaro** /ˌkætən'zɑːrəʊ/ the chief town of the Calabria region of southern Italy, overlooking the Ionian Sea; pop. (1990) 103,800. It is capital of Catanzaro province, and is a commercial centre with flour mills and distilleries.

**cataract** /'kætə,rækt/ a large waterfall or a series of rapids on a river such as the Nile.

**Catawba** /kə'tɔːbə/ a river that rises in the Blue Ridge Mountains of North Carolina, USA, and flows 402 km. (250 miles) southwards into South Carolina where it becomes the Wateree River. It gives its name to a variety of grape found in the US.

**catchment area** a drainage basin or area from which water flows into a river. The term is also used to describe an area served by a business or public facility such as a school or a hospital.

**Cathay** /kæ'θeɪ/ (also **Khitai**) the name by which China was known to medieval Europe, the

Khitans being a people of Manchu race, to the north-east of China, who established an empire over northern China during the two centuries ending in 1123.

**Catherine** /'kæθɜ:rɪn/, **Mount** (Arabic **Gebel Katherîna**) a mountain at the southern end of the Sinai peninsula in Egypt. Rising to 2,637 m. (8,652 ft.), it is the highest peak in Egypt. On its lower slopes stands the Monastery of St. Catherine founded in the 4th c. AD by the Byzantine empress Helena near the alleged site of the burning bush from which God spoke to Moses.

**Catskill Mountains** /'kætskɪl/ a northern arm of the Appalachian Mountains in south-east New York State, USA, to the west of the Hudson River. Rising to 1,282 m. (4,206 ft.) at Mt. Slide, the wooded rolling mountains of this dissected plateau are a popular resort area. The legendary Rip Van Winkle is said to have slept for 20 years near the village of Catskill at the entrance to the Catskill Mountains.

**Catterick** /'kætɜ:rɪk/ a village in North Yorkshire, England, 56 km. (35 miles) north-west of York, noted for its military camp and race-course.

**Cauca** /'kaʊkə/ a river in Colombia that flows northwards between the central and western Cordilleras of the Andes to meet the Magdalena River south of San Jacinto.

**Caucasus** /'kɔ:kəsəs/ (also **Caucasia**) a region of south-east Europe in Russia, Georgia, Armenia, and Azerbaijan, lying between the Black Sea and the Caspian Sea. It is dominated by the mountain ranges of the **Great Caucasus** (Russian **Bolshoy Kavkaz**) and **Little Caucasus** (Russian **Maly Kavkaz**). Mt. Elbrus in the Great Caucasus (5,642 m., 18,480 ft.) is the highest mountain in Europe. The Caucasian languages are a group of languages spoken in the region of the Caucasus. Of the 40 known only a few are committed to writing. The main language of the group is Georgian, which belongs to the southern sub-group. The term Caucasian is also used to describe one of the major racial divisions of man as defined by the German anthropologist Johan Blumenbach (1752–1840). The original distribution of this white or light-skinned Caucasoid race extended from the Arctic to Africa north of the Sahara, and from the Azores in the North Atlantic to Samarkand in Central Asia.
**Caucasian** *adj. & n.*

**causses** /kɔʊs/ a term used in France to describe limestone country as in **Les Causses**, a limestone plateau at the southern edge of the Massif Central that is deeply incised by rivers.

**Cauto** /'kaʊtəʊ/ a river of south-east Cuba that flows westwards for *c.* 240 km. (150 miles) into the Gulf of Guacanayabo. It is the longest river on the island of Cuba.

**Cauvery** /'kɑ:vərɪ/ (also **Kaveri**) a sacred river in south India that rises in north Kerala and flows

east and south-east to the Bay of Bengal south of Pondicherry.

**Cavan** /'kævən/ (Gaelic **Cabhán**) **1.** an inland county of the Republic of Ireland, forming part of the province of Ulster; area 1,890 sq. km. (730 sq. miles); pop. (1991) 52,756. **2.** its county town near Swellan Lough; pop. (1991) 3,332. To the north-east on Shantemon Hill are the prehistoric standing stones known as 'Finn MacCool's Fingers'.

**Cawdor** /'kɔ:də(r)/ a village near Nairn in northern Scotland. Nearby Cawdor castle, home of the Earls of Cawdor, was alleged by Shakespeare to be the scene of the murder of King Duncan by Macbeth in 1040.

**Cawnpore** see KANPUR.

**Caxias do Sul** /kə'ʃɪəs dəʊ 'sʊl/ a city to the north of Pôrto Alegre in the state of Rio Grande do Sul, southern Brazil; pop. (1990) 262,920. It is a metal-working centre with extensive vineyards.

**cay** /ki:/ (also **caye**) a low-lying island of coral and sand in the Caribbean Sea.

**Cayenne** the capital and chief port of French Guiana, on an island on the Atlantic coast at the mouth of the Cayenne River; pop. (1990) 41,660. It gives its name to a type of pepper.

**Cayman Islands** /'keɪmən/ (also **Caymans**) three islands (Grand Cayman, Cayman Brac, and Little Cayman) in the Caribbean Sea, a British dependency, south of Cuba; area

259 sq. km. (100 sq. miles); pop. (est. 1992) 27,000; official language, English; capital, George Town. Columbus, discovering the islands in 1503, named them Las Tortugas (Spanish = the turtles) because of their abundance of turtles. A British colony was established towards the end of the 17th c., and in the 19th c. the Caymans became noted for the building of schooners. The islands have been administered as a separate colony since Jamaica gained independence in 1962. Tourism, international finance (the islands are a tax-haven for off-shore companies), the trans-shipment of oil, and the export of fish are the main economic activities.

**Cayman Trench** a deep oceanic trench in the north-west Caribbean Sea, containing the deepest point in the Caribbean at 7,680 m. (25,197 ft.) below sea level.

**cayo** /'kaɪjəʊ/ the word for a small island in Spanish.

**Ceanannus Mor** /ˌsiːəˈnænəs mɒr/ (also **Kells**) a town on the River Blackwater in County Meath, the Republic of Ireland; pop. (1991) 2,187. A former residence of Irish kings, there are the remains of a Celtic monastery founded by

St. Columba in the 6th c. The *Book of Kells*, a Latin copy of the Gospels written here *c.* AD 800 (and now in Trinity College Library, Dublin), is said to be 'the most beautiful book in the world'.

**Ceará** /ˌseɪəˈrɑː/ a federal state of north-east Brazil; area 148,016 sq. km. (57,149 sq. miles); pop. (1991) 6,362,620; capital, Fortaleza.

**Cebu** /seɪˈbuː/ **1.** an island of the Visayan group in the southern Philippines, between Negros and Bohol; area 4,419 sq. km. (1,707 sq. miles). Sugarcane, peanuts, rice, corn, fertilizer, copper, and coal are the main products. **2.** the chief city and seaport of Cebu Island; pop. (1990) 610,420. After Magellan landed (and was killed) here in 1521 it became capital of the Spanish Philippines. It exports copra, maize, rice, and fish.

**Cedar Rapids** /ˈsiːd(ə)r/ a city in east-central Iowa, USA, on the Cedar River; pop. (1990) 108,751. It is a centre for the production of meat, cereals, farm machinery, and electronic equipment. The city has a large population of Czech descent.

**Celaya** /seɪˈlɑːjə/ a city in the state of Guanajuato, west-central Mexico; pop. (1990) 315,580. Founded by the Spanish in 1571, the city is noted for its fine baroque churches.

**Celebes** /ˈseləbiːz/ see SULAWESI.

**Celebes Sea** (also **Sulawesi Sea**) an arm of the western Pacific extending westwards as far as Borneo and separating the Philippines from the Celebes (Sulawesi). It is linked to the Java Sea by the Makassar Strait.

**Celje** /ˈtʃeljə/ a spa and light industrial town in central Slovenia, on the River Savinja; pop. (1991) 40,700. Founded by the Roman Emperor Claudius in the 1st c. AD, it was part of Austria until 1918.

**Celt** /kelt, selt/ (also **Kelt**) a member of a group of west European peoples, including the pre-Roman inhabitants of Britain and Gaul and their descendants, especially in Ireland, Scotland, Wales, Cornwall, Brittany, and the Isle of Man. The Celtic language is a sub-group of the Indo-European language group, divided into two groups, Goidelic (consisting of Irish, Scots Gaelic, and Manx) and Brythonic (consisting of Welsh, Cornish, and Breton).

The Celts occupied a large part of Europe in the Iron Age. Their unity is recognizable by common speech and common artistic tradition, but they did not constitute one race or group of tribes ethnologically. The origins of their culture can be traced back to the Bronze Age of the upper Danube in the 13th c. BC, with successive stages represented by the urnfield and Hallstatt cultures. Spreading over western and central Europe from perhaps as early as 900 BC, they reached the height of their power in the La Tène period of the 5th–1st c. BC. The ancients knew them as fierce fighters and superb horsemen, with savage religious rites conducted by the Druid priesthood. They were farmers, who cultivated fields on a regular basis with ox-drawn

ploughs in place of manual implements, revolutionary changes which permanently affected people's way of life. But Celtic political sense was weak, and the numerous tribes, continually warring against each other, were crushed between the migratory Germans and the power of Rome, to be ejected or assimilated by the former or conquered outright by the latter.

**Celtic** *adj. & n.*

**Celtic Sea** the part of the Atlantic Ocean between southern Ireland and England.

**Cenozoic** /ˌsiːnəˈzəʊɪk/ (also **Cainozoic** or **Caenozoic**) the most recent geological era, following the Mesozoic and lasting from about 65 million years ago to the present day. It includes the Tertiary and Quaternary periods, and is characterized by the rapid evolution of mammals (Greek *kainos* new + *zoion* animal).

**Central** a local government region of central Scotland from 1975 to 1996; area 2,634 sq. km. (1,017 sq. miles); pop. (1991) 267,960. Its chief town is Stirling. Central Region is divided into three districts:

| District | Area (sq. km.) | Pop. (1991) | Administrative Centre |
|---|---|---|---|
| Clackmannan | 161 | 47,209 | Alloa |
| Falkirk | 301 | 139,038 | Falkirk |
| Stirling | 2,170 | 81,717 | Stirling |

**Central African Republic** official name **The Central African Republic** a country in the Sahel region of central Africa, bounded by Chad, Sudan, Zaire, Congo, and Cameroon; area 625,000 sq. km. (241,313 sq. miles); pop. (est. 1991) 3,000,000; official language, French; national language, Sangho; capital, Bangui. Situated just north of the equator, the Central African Republic is covered by tropical forest in the extreme south-west and semidesert in the north-east and east. It is drained by two river systems, the first flowing northwards to Lake Chad, the second draining southwards into the Oubangui which is a tributary of the Congo (Zaire) River. There is a rainy season from June to November during which the Oubangui rises about 6 m. (20 ft.). More than two-thirds of the population lives in rural areas where peanuts, corn, manioc, sorghum, and sesame are staple food crops. The principal export crops are coffee, cotton, tobacco, timber, and livestock. Diamonds are also a major source of income. Formerly the French colony of Ubanghi Shari, it became a republic within the French Community in 1958 and a fully independent state in 1960. In 1976, its president Jean Bédel Bokassa, who had come to

power after a military *coup* in 1966, declared himself Emperor and changed his country's name to Central African Empire, but it reverted to the name of Republic after he had been ousted in 1979 following widespread unrest and allegations of atrocities. The country was governed by the mil-itary until 1986 when a new constitution signalled a return to civilian rule with the introduction of civilians to the government and the creation of a single political party, the Central African Democratic Assembly. The country is divided into the autonomous commune of Bangui and 16 prefectures:

| Prefecture | Area (sq. km.) | Pop. (1988) | Capital |
|---|---|---|---|
| Bangui | 67 | 451,700 | Bangui |
| Ombella-M'poko | 31,835 | 180,900 | Boali |
| Lobaye | 19,235 | 30,200 | M'baiki |
| Sangha | 19,412 | 66,000 | Nola |
| Mambere Kaedéi | 30,203 | 230,400 | Berbérati |
| Nana-Mambere | 26,600 | 191,200 | Bouar |
| Ouham-Pende | 32,100 | 287,650 | Bozoum |
| Ouham | 50,250 | 262,950 | Bossangoa |
| Nana Gribizi | 19,996 | 95,500 | Kaga-Bandoro |
| Bamingui-Bangoran | 58,200 | 28,600 | Ndele |
| Vakaga | 46,500 | 32,100 | Birao |
| Kemo | 17,204 | 82,900 | Sibut |
| Ouaka | 49,900 | 208,300 | Bambari |
| Basse-Kotto | 17,604 | 194,750 | Mobaye |
| Haute-Kotto | 86,650 | 58,800 | Bria |
| M'bomou | 61,150 | 119,250 | Bangassou |
| Haut-M'bomou | 55,530 | 27,100 | Obo |

**Central America** the narrow strip of land to the south of Mexico, linking North and South America and including Guatemala, Belize, Honduras, El Salvador, Nicaragua, Costa Rica, and Panama.

**Central Asian States** an economic union involving the Central Asian republics of Kazakhstan, Uzbekistan, and Kyrgyzstan, created in 1994. Rich in mineral and energy resources, the union has a total population of some 48 million people.

**Central Lancashire** a development area in Lancashire, north-west England, incorporating the towns of Preston, Chorley, and Leyland. Established in 1970, it covers an area of 142 sq. km. (55 sq. miles). The University of Central Lancashire (formerly Lancashire Polytechnic) was established in 1992.

**Central Park** a park on Manhattan Island, New York City, USA, between Fifth Avenue and Central Park West on Eighth Avenue. It was laid out in 1856 by the landscape architects Frederick L. Olmsted and Calvert Vaux; area 340.2 hectares (840 acres).

**Central Powers** a Triple Alliance of Germany, Austria, and Hungary agreed in 1882.

**Centre** /'sātrə/ an administrative region of central France comprising the departments of Cher, Eure-et-Loire, Indre, Indre-et-Loire, Loire-et-Cher, and Loiret; area 39,151 sq. km. (15,122 sq. miles); pop. (1990) 2,371,040.

**Centre Pompidou** /ˌsãtrə 'pɒmpɪdu:/ (or **Centre Beaubourg**, in full **Centre National d'Art et de Culture Georges Pompidou**, English **George Pompidou National Centre for Art and Culture**) a modern exhibition centre housing the French National Gallery of Modern Art and the Centre for Industrial Design, situated between the Halles and Marais areas of Paris, France. Opened in 1977 and named after a former president of France, the building was designed in glass and steel by Richard Rogers and Renzo Piano.

**Cephalonia** /ˌsefə'ləʊnɪə/ (Greek **Kefallinia** /ˌkefəlɪ'ni:ə/) a hilly Greek island in the Ionian Sea; area 781 sq. km. (302 sq. miles); pop. (1981) 31,300. Its capital is Argostólion.

**Ceram Sea** /'seɪrəm/ (also **Seram**) a section of the western Pacific Ocean in the central Molucca Islands.

**Cerignola** /ˌtʃerɪ'njəʊlə/ a market town on the fertile Tavoliere plateau in the Apulia region of south-east Italy, south-east of Foggia; pop. (1990) 54,830.

**Cerigo** See CYTHERA.

**Cerne Abbas** /sɜːn 'æbəs/ a village in Dorset, southern England, north-west of Dorchester, near which is the *Cerne Giant*, a prehistoric figure cut in the chalk hillside.

**cerro** /'sɜːrəʊ/ a Spanish word for a mountain.

**Cerro de Pasco** /ˌsɜːrəʊ deɪ 'pæskəʊ/ **1.** a mountain in central Peru, rising to a height of 4,602 m. (15,100 ft.) in the Andes. **2.** (also **Pasco**) a mining town in the Andes of central Peru at an altitude of 4,333 m. (14,216 ft.); pop. (1990) 77,700. It is the highest major town in Peru and capital of the department of Pasco.

**Certaldo** /tʃɜː'tɑːldəʊ/ a village in Tuscany, Italy, 29 km. (18 miles) south-west of Florence; pop. (1990) 16,100. It was the birthplace of the Italian writer Giovanni Boccaccio (1313–75), author of the *Decameron*.

**Cesena** /tʃə'zeɪnə/ a town in the Emilia-Romagna region of northern Italy, on the right bank of the River Savio, between Forlì and Rimini; pop. (1990) 89,500. It produces wine and agricultural machinery. The Malatesta Library (1452) is one of the oldest monastic libraries in existence.

**České Budějovice** /'tʃeʃkɪ ˌbʊdje'jaʊətsə/ (German **Budweis** /'bʊtvaɪs/) the chief town of South Bohemia in the Czech Republic, on the River Vltava; pop. (1991) 173,400. Founded as a fortress town in 1265, the city developed through trading salt and wine with Austria. It is the original home of Budvar or Budweiser beer which is still produced. The first horse-drawn railway in continental Europe ran from České Budějovice to Linz in Austria. To the north-west is the birthplace of John Huss (1369–1415) the Bohemian religious reformer.

**Český Krumlov** /ˌtʃeskɪ ˈkrʌmlɒf/ a picturesque medieval town in the South Bohemia region of the Czech Republic, on the River Vltava; pop. (1991) 14,100.

**Cessnock** /ˈsesnɒk/ a town in New South Wales, south-eastern Australia, situated on Black Creek to the west of Newcastle; pop. (1991) 17,930 (with Bellbird). Formerly a coal-mining town, it now lies at the centre of a noted wine-producing region.

**Cetinje** /ˈset(ə)njə/ a town in the mountains of Montenegro, Yugoslavia; pop. (1981) 20,200. Founded by the Montenegrin King Ivan the Black in 1484, it was capital of Montenegro until 1918.

**Ceuta** /seɪˈuːtə, ˈθeɪ-/ a Spanish enclave in Morocco, held since 1580, on the coast of North Africa; area 18 sq. km. (7 sq. miles); pop. (1991) 67,615. It consists of a free port and a military post, and overlooks the Mediterranean approach to the Strait of Gibraltar.

**Cévennes** /seɪˈven/ a mountain range on the south-eastern edge of the Massif Central in France, largely in the departments of Ardèche and Lozère. Its highest peak is Mt. Mézenc (1,754 m., 5,755 ft.).

**Ceyhan** /dʒeɪˈhɑːn/ **1.** a river that flows from the Anti-Taurus Mountains south-westwards through Cilicia in southern Turkey to the Gulf of Iskenderun. **2.** a city in the province of Adana, southern Turkey, on the Ceyhan River; pop. (1990) 85,300.

**Ceylon** /sɪˈlɒn/ the former name (until 1972) of SRI LANKA.

**Chablais** /ʃæˈbleɪ/ a part of the Savoy region of eastern France near Lake Geneva. It is divided into the Bas (Lower) Chablais, which occupies the vine-clad lower slopes to the south of the lake, and the Haut (Upper) Chablais of upland forest and pastureland around Morzine. Thonon is the chief town.

**Chablis** /ˈʃæblɪ/ a village in the Yonne department of Burgundy in central France, noted for its dry white wine.

**Chachapoyas** /ˌtʃɑːtʃəˈpəʊjəs/ the capital of the department of Amazonas in northern Peru, situated at an altitude of 1,834 m. (6,017 ft.) in the Andes; pop. (1990) 14,000. It is a base for visiting the pre-Inca ruins of Kuelap which lie on a ridge above the River Utcubamba.

**Chaco** see GRAN CHACO.

**Chaco** /ˈtʃækəʊ/ a province of northern Argentina, forming the southern part of the Gran Chaco region of South America; area 99,633 sq. km. (38,483 sq. miles); pop. (1991) 838,300; capital, Resistencia.

**Chad** /tʃæd/ official name **The Republic of Chad** a landlocked country in north-central

Africa, bounded by Libya, Sudan, the Central African Republic, Cameroon, Nigeria, and Niger; area 1,284,000 sq. km. (495,752 sq. miles); pop. (est. 1991) 5,100,000; official languages, French and Arabic; capital, N'Djamena. The country, which takes its name from Lake Chad on its western frontier, lies in a shallow basin that rises gradually from south to north, reaching heights in excess of 3,658 m. (12,000 ft.) in the Tibesti Mountains. The northern half of the country is in the Sahara Desert and is sparsely populated. The southern half of the country lies in the watershed of Lake Chad. Cotton, livestock, fish, and gum arabic are the chief exports, but over 95 per cent of the people survive on subsistence crops which include millet, sorghum, peanuts, cassava, yams, and manioc. There are deposits of uranium, tungsten, natron, kaolin, and perhaps oil. There are more than 200 ethnic groups in Chad ranging from Muslim Arabs in the arid north to animist Bantu tribes in the tropical south. French expeditions entered the area in 1890, and by 1920 the country was organized as the largest colony of French Equatorial Africa. It became autonomous within the French Community in 1958, and fully independent as a republic in 1960. In 1965 the divide between the Muslim north and the government in the south led to an outbreak of civil war and in 1973 Libya lent its support to the northern rebels and occupied the Aozou Strip. Political instability and the damage to infrastructure caused by years of civil war continue to prevent economic development.

**Chadian** *adj. & n.*

Chad is divided into 14 prefectures:

| Prefecture | Area (sq. km.) | Pop. (1993) | Capital |
|---|---|---|---|
| Bourkou-Ennedi-Tibesti | 600,350 | 70,600 | Faya-Largeau |
| Biltine | 46,850 | 167,100 | Biltine |
| Ouaddaï | 76,240 | 549,900 | Abéché |
| Batha | 88,800 | 288,100 | Ati |
| Kanem | 114,520 | 280,800 | Mao |
| Lac | 22,320 | 268,200 | Bol |
| Chari-Baguirmi | 82,910 | 1,252,100 | N'Djamena |
| Guéra | 58,950 | 306,650 | Mongo |
| Salamat | 63,000 | 186,000 | Am Timan |
| Moyen-Chari | 45,180 | 744,700 | Sarh |
| Logone Oriental | 28,035 | 440,300 | Doba |
| Logone Occidental | 8,695 | 455,100 | Moundou |
| Tandjilé | 18,045 | 458,200 | Laï |
| Mayo-Kabbi | 30,105 | 820,200 | Bongor |

**Chad, Lake** a shallow lake on the frontiers of Chad, Niger, and Nigeria in north-central Africa. Its size varies seasonally from *c.* 10,360 sq. km.

(4,000 sq. miles) to *c.* 25,900 sq. km. (10,000 sq. miles).

**Chadic**  a group of languages spoken in the region of Lake Chad in north-central Africa, of which the most important is Hausa.

**Chafarinas Island**  /ˌtʃɑːfəˈriːnəs/ (also **Zafarin Islands**) a group of small islands in the Mediterranean Sea off the north coast of Morocco near Melilla. They are administered by Spain with Ceuta and Melilla.

**Chaghcharan**  /ˌtʃæɡtʃəˈrɑːn/ the capital of the province of Ghowr in central Afghanistan; pop. (est. 1984) 3,260.

**Chagos Archipelago**  /ˈtʃeɪɡəs/ an island group in the Indian Ocean, formerly a dependency of Mauritius and now part of the strategic BRITISH INDIAN OCEAN TERRITORY.

**Chalatenango**  /ˌtʃɑːlətəˈnæŋɡəʊ/ a town in northern El Salvador, near the frontier with Honduras; pop. (1980) 28,675. It is capital of a department of the same name and was a remote haven for anti-government guerrillas during the civil war of the 1980s.

**Chalcedon**  /ˈkælsɪdʒ(ə)n/ (Turksih **Kadiköy**) a city in Asia Minor, on the Bosporus near present-day Istanbul, where the fourth ecumenical council of the Church was held in AD 451, at which was drawn up the important statement of faith affirming the two natures, human and divine, united in the single person of Christ.
**Chalcedonian** *adj. & n.*

**Chalcidice**  /kælˈsɪdəsi/ (Greek **Khalkidhikí** /ˌkɑːlkjəˈðiˈkiː/) a peninsula in Macedonia, northern Greece, that projects with three long headlands into the Aegean Sea south-east of Salonica.

**Chalcis**  /ˈkælsɪs/ (Greek **Khalkis** /xælˈkiːs/) the chief town of the island of Euboea, on the coast opposite mainland Greece; pop. (1981) 44,800. Aristotle died here in 322 BC.

**Chaldea**  /kælˈdiːə/ the country of the Chaldeans, the southern part of Babylonia. The Chaldeans were a Semitic people originating from Arabia, who settled in the neighbourhood of Ur *c.* 800 BC and ruled Babylonia 625–538 BC. They were famous as astronomers. The biblical reference to 'Ur of the Chaldees' in the time of Abraham is an anachronism.

**Chaldee**  /kælˈdiː/ **1.** the language of the Chaldeans. **2.** a native of ancient Chaldea. **3.** the Aramaic language as used in Old Testament books.

**Chaleur Bay**  /ʃæˈlɜː(r)/ an inlet of the Gulf of St. Lawrence between the island of New Brunswick and the Gaspé peninsula of south-east Quebec, Canada.

**Challenger Deep**  /ˈtʃælɪndʒə(r)/ the deepest part of the Mariana Trench in the Pacific Ocean (11,034 m., 36,197 ft.), surveyed by and named after HMS *Challenger II* in 1948.

**Châlons-sur-Marne**  /ʃæˌlɔ̃sʊəˈmɑːn/ the capital of the department of Marne in the Champagne-Ardenne region of north-east France, on the River Marne; pop. (1990) 51,530. Attila was defeated by the Romans here in AD 451. Its industries include champagne-making, brewing, electrical engineering, and textiles.

**Châlon-sur-Saône**  /-sɔʊn/ an industrial town in the department of Saône-et-Loire, Burgundy, east-central France, at the junction of the Saône and Loire rivers; pop. (1990) 56,260. It was the birthplace of the chemist and pioneer photographer Nicéphore Niepce (1765–1833). It is an inland port trading in grain and wine. Its industries include electrical equipment, barges, chemicals, metal products, and glass.

**Chalosse**  /ʃæˈlɒs/ the southern part of the department of Landes in the Aquitaine region of south-west France, noted for its *foie gras*. The chief town is Dax.

**Chambéry**  /ˌʃɑːmbeɪˈriː/ a commercial town in the Savoy region of eastern France; pop. (1990) 55,600. It is capital of the Savoie department and was capital of the former Duchy of Chambéry. Its old town contains a huge 13th-c. château and old houses. It has aluminium and cement industries.

**Chamonix**  /ˈʃæməni/ a resort town in the department of Haute-Savoie, eastern France, on the River Arve near the Swiss frontier; pop. (1982) 9,255. It lies at the foot of Mont Blanc. The highest cable-car in the Alps rises from Chamonix to the summit of the Aiguille du Midi.

**Champagne-Ardenne**  /ʃæmˈpeɪnɑːˈden/ a region of north-east France comprising the departments of Ardennes, Aube, Marne, and Haute-Marne; area 25,606 sq. km. (9,890 sq. miles); pop. (1990) 1,347,850; capital, Rheims. It includes part of the Ardennes forest and the vine-growing Plain of Champagne. Champagne wine was first made in the 17th c. from grapes grown in a small area around Épernay and Rheims.

**Champagne Castle**  /ʃæmˈpeɪn/ a mountain peak in the Drakensberg Range, South Africa. Rising to a height of 3,375 m. (11,073 ft.), it is the highest peak in the country.

**Champlain**  /ʃæmˈpleɪn/ **, Lake** a North American lake lying between the Adirondacks and the Green Mountains where it forms part of the frontier between the states of New York and Vermont. Extending northwards into Quebec, Canada, the lake is 201 km. (125 miles) in length. It is linked to the St. Lawrence by the Richelieu River and to the Hudson River by the Barge Canal, and is named after Samuel de Champlain who discovered it in 1609.

**Champs-de-Mars**  /ˌʃɑ̃dəˈmɑːs/ a former military parade ground between the Eiffel Tower and the École Militaire in the centre of Paris, France. On 14 July 1790 it was the scene of the Festival of the Federation at which Louis XVI swore to uphold the new constitution. Numerous expositions and world fairs have been held here.

**Champs Elysées** /ʃɑ̃zeɪli:ˈzeɪ/ (in full **Avenue des Champs Elysées**) a celebrated avenue 1.88 km. in length between the Place de la Concorde and the Arc de Triomphe in the city of Paris, France, built in open countryside (Elysian Fields) by André Le Nôtre (the landscape gardener of Versailles) after the completion of the Palace of the Tuileries in the 17th c. It forms part of the 'voie triomphale' (= triumphal way) completed under Napoleon III, linking the Arc de Triomphe de l'Etoile with the Arc de Triomphe du Carrousel. The upper part is flanked by luxury shops, hotels, restaurants, theatres, and pavement cafés.

**Chan Chan** /tʃæn tʃæn/ the capital of the pre-Inca kingdom of Chimu, built c. AD 1300. Its extensive adobe ruins are situated on the north coast of Peru, near Trujillo. It was the largest pre-Columbian city in the Americas and the largest mud-built city in the world.

**Chandernagore** /ˌtʃændənəˈgɔː(r)/ (also **Chandannagar**) a town in West Bengal, India, situated on the Hugli River and a northern suburb of Calcutta; pop. (1991) 122,350. Originally a French colony founded in 1673, it was not handed over to India until after a referendum in 1950.

**Chandigarh** /ˌtʃʌndɪˈgɑː(r)/ **1.** a Union Territory of northern India, created in 1966; area 114 sq. km. (44 sq. miles). **2.** a city in this Territory, on the edge of the Siwalik Hills, capital of both Punjab and (at present) Haryana states; pop. (1991) 503,000. The city was laid out during the 1950s to a design by the French architect Le Corbusier. Its site was chosen for its healthy climate and good water supply.

**Chandler** /ˈtʃændl(ə)r/ a winter resort city in the valley of the Salt River, south-central Arizona, USA; pop. (1990) 90,530. Cotton, citrus fruits, pecans, and sugar-beets are grown in the surrounding area and Williams Air Force Base lies to the east.

**Chang** (also **Ko Chang**) an island resort in the Gulf of Thailand. It is the second-largest island in Thailand.

**Chang'an** /tʃæŋˈɑːn/ the original name of the city of XI'AN in Shaanxi province, China. Built by the first emperor of the Han dynasty, it was the first capital of a unified China and the starting point of the Silk Road to Persia.

**Changchun** /ˌtʃæŋˈtʃʊn/ an industrial city in north-east China, capital of Jilin province; pop. (1990) 2,110,000. Under Japanese occupation (1932–45) it was capital of the state of Manchukuo and was known as Hsing-King. The chief industries are engineering, and the production of chemicals, machinery, electrical appliances, vehicles, and textiles.

**Changde** /ˌtʃæŋˈdeɪ/ a city and river port in Hunan province, south-east-central China, on the Yuan River north-west of Changsha; pop. (1986)

230,000. Its industries include ceramics, machine tools, textiles, leather, and foodstuffs.

**Changji** /ˌtʃæŋˈdʒiː/ a city in Xinjiang autonomous region, north-west China, in the northern foothills of the Tien Shan Range north-west of Urumqi; pop. (1986) 237,000.

**Chang Jiang** /tʃæŋ dʒæŋ/ the Chinese name for the YANGTZE RIVER.

**Changsha** /tʃæŋˈʃɑː/ the capital of Hunan province in south-east-central China, on the Xiang River; pop. (1990) 1,330,000. It is a river port and major distribution centre on the railway line linking Beijing and Canton (Guangzhou). A noted centre of education for a thousand years, Mao Zedong studied here 1912–18. It has a wide variety of light industries.

**Changshu** /ˌtʃæŋˈʃuː/ a town in Jiangsu province, eastern China, near the mouth of the Yangtze River north-west of Shanghai; pop. (1986) 1,004,000.

**Changzhi** /ˌtʃæŋˈʒiː/ a city in Shanxi province, east-central China, west of Anyang; pop. (1986) 474,000.

**Changzhou** /ˌtʃæŋˈdʒəʊ/ a city in Jiangsu province, eastern China, on the Grand Canal north-west of Shanghai; pop. (1990) 670,000.

**Chania** see CANEA.

**Channel Country** an area of south-west Queensland and north-east South Australia watered intermittently by channels such as Cooper's Creek and Warburton Creek. The rich grasslands produced by the summer rains provide grazing for cattle. The region is traversed by 'beef roads' such as the Strzelecki Track and the Diamanta Devel Road, down which beasts for slaughter are conveyed in 'trains' of linked cattle trucks.

**Channel Islands** (French Îles Normandes /ˌiːl nɔːˈmɑ̃d/ a group of islands in the English Channel off the north-west coast of France, of which the largest are Jersey, Guernsey, and  Alderney; area 194 sq. km. (75 sq. miles); pop. (1981) 128,900; chief towns, St. Helier (Jersey), St. Peter Port (Guernsey). Other smaller islands include Sark, Herm, Jethou, Brechou, Lihou, and the Minquiers. Divided administratively into the Bailiwicks of Jersey and Guernsey, they are the only portions of the former Duchy of Normandy that still owe allegiance to England, to which they have been attached since the Norman Conquest in 1066.

**Channel Islands National Park** a group of 8 small islands off the coast of southern California, USA, designated a national park in 1980 to protect bird- and seal-breeding colonies. A geological extension of the Santa Monica Mts., the islands were discovered by Juan Rodriguez Cabrillo in 1542, when they were still inhabited by the seafaring Chumash Indians.

**Channel Tunnel** a tunnel under the English Channel providing a direct rail link between London and Paris. Officially opened in 1994, work began in 1986 on the construction of a pair of railway tunnels linking the English coast at Holywell near Folkestone with the French coast at Sangatte near Calais. Such a scheme was first put forward in 1802 by a French engineer, who perceived the possibility of tunnelling through the layer of soft chalk rock that is continuous from one side of the Channel to the other. Napoleon showed interest, but Britain was again at war with France in 1803 and no move was made. The proposal was revived again at intervals (i.e. the 1857 scheme of Thome de Camond) and digging actually started in 1882, but fear of invasion from the Continent brought hostile reaction in Britain until the 1950s, when the development of air power and guided missiles made the Channel no longer the natural defence that it had once been. The tunnel is 49 km. (31 miles) long.

**Chantilly** /ʃænˈtɪlɪ, ʃɑ̃tiːˈjiː/ a town in the department of Oise to the north of Paris, France; pop. (1982) 10,200. Situated on the edge of one of the great forests of France, it is noted for its château, which was the seat of the Princes of Condé (a branch of the royal house of Bourbon), and its race-course. A porcelain factory was founded here in 1725 by Louis Henri, duc de Bourbon. Chantilly gives its name to a type of bobbin-lace and a sweetened or flavoured whipped cream.

**Chaohu** /tʃaʊˈhuː/ a city in Anhui province, eastern China, on the eastern shore of Lake Chao; pop. (1986) 741,000.

**Chao Phraya** /tʃaʊ ˈpraɪə/ a major waterway of central Thailand, formed by the junction of the Ping and Nan rivers near the port of Nakhon Sawan. It flows for a distance of 365 km. (230 miles) before meeting the Gulf of Thailand near Bangkok.

**Chaoyang** /tʃaʊˈjɑːŋ/ a city in Liaoning province, north-eastern China, on the Daling River north-east of Beijing; pop. (1986) 328,000.

**chaparral** /ˌtʃæpəˈræl, ˌʃæp-/ a type of vegetation found in areas of low to moderate rainfall in the US states of California and Oregon. It is dominated by scrub or low-growing trees, the majority of which are drought-resistant evergreens.

**Chappaquiddick Island** /ˌtʃæpəˈkwɪdɪk/ an island in the Nantucket Sound off the coast of Martha's Vineyard, Massachusetts, USA.

**Chapultepec** /ˌtʃæˈpʊltəpek/ a park in Mexico City at the centre of which is a hill that was the ancient seat of the Aztec emperors. A castle built on the hill 1783–1840 was captured by US forces in 1847 and was the royal residence of the Emperor Maximilian. The park is said to be the oldest natural park in North America and one of the largest in the world (840 hectares).

**Chardzhou** see CHÄRJEW.

**Charente** /ʃæˈrɑ̃t/ **1.** a river of western France, that rises in the Massif Central and flows 360 km. (225 miles) westwards to the Bay of Biscay, near Rochefort. **2.** a department in the Poitou-Charentes region of western France; area 5,956 sq. km. (2,300 sq. miles); pop. (1990) 341,990; capital, Angoulême.

**Charente Maritime** a department on the Atlantic coast of the Poitou-Charentes region, western France; area 6,864 sq. km. (2,651 sq. miles); pop. (1990) 527,150; capital, La Rochelle. It was known as Charente-Inférieure until 1941.

**Chari** see SHARI.

**Charikar** /ˈtʃɑːrɪˌkɑː/ a city in eastern Afghanistan, in the Hindu Kush Mountains to the north of Kabul; pop. (est. 1988) 100,000.

**Charing Cross** /ˈtʃærɪŋ/ a district in central London, England, between Trafalgar Square and Whitehall, on the site of the former village of Cheringe. Road distances from London are traditionally measured from Charing Cross.

**Chärjew** /tʃɑːˈdʒuː/ (also **Charjui**) a city in eastern Turkmenistan, on the Amu Darya River near the border with Uzbekistan; pop. (1990) 164,000. Formerly known as Chardzhou, it is a leading centre of the cotton trade.

**Charleroi** /ˈʃɑːləˌrwɑː/ an industrial city in the province of Hainaut in south-west Belgium, on the River Sambre; pop. (1991) 206,200. Founded in 1666, it was named after Charles II of Spain. It has steel, electrical equipment, and glass industries.

**Charlesbourg** /ˈʃɑːlbʊ(ə)r/ a city in southern Quebec, Canada, to the north of Quebec; pop. (1991) 70,800.

**Charleston** /ˈtʃɑːlst(ə)n/ a city and port in south-east South Carolina, USA, where the Ashley and Cooper rivers meet the Atlantic; pop. (1990) 80,410. Founded by the Earl of Shaftesbury in the 1670s, it was the first permanent settlement in the Carolinas. As a provincial capital it developed around the rice and indigo trade. It has many light industries and a large naval base. Fort Sumter, scene of the opening engagement of the Civil War in 1861, is on an island at the entrance to the harbour. The city gave its name to a lively American dance of the 1920s.

**Charleston** a city in west-central West Virginia, USA, at the junction of the Kanawha and Elk rivers; pop. (1990) 57,290. The city developed around the site of Fort Lee which was established in 1788 and was state capital in 1870 and again in 1885. It became an important centre for the production of salt in 1824 and during World War I manufactured plate, bottle glass, and high explosives. Charleston is now a major industrial and commercial centre producing oil, gas, and coal.

**Charlestown** the chief town and port of the Caribbean island of Nevis in the federation of St. Kitts-Nevis; pop. (1980) 1,243. Linked by ferry to Basseterre on St. Kitts, it was the birthplace of Alexander Hamilton, architect of the US Constitution.

**Charleville-Mézières** /ˌʃaːlviːlmeɪˈzjeə(r)/ the capital of the department of Ardennes in the Champagne-Ardenne region of north-east France, on the River Meuse; pop. (1990) 59,440. It was the birthplace of the poet Arthur Rimbaud (1854–91). It has metallurgical industries.

**Charlevoix** /ʃaːləˈvwæ/ the name given to the stretch of mountainous and forested countryside along the left bank of the St. Lawrence River in Quebec, Canada, from Côte de Beaupré as far as the Saguenay River. It is named after the Jesuit François Xavier de-Charlevoix (1682–1761), who published the first history of Canada in 1744.

**Charlotte** /ˈʃaːlət/ a commercial city and transportation centre in southern North Carolina, USA; pop. (1990) 395,934. First settled in the 1740s it developed as a textile-manufacturing town and trading centre. The city is named after the wife of George III. In 1799 with the discovery of gold it became the nation's leading gold producer until the California gold-rush of 1848. President James K. Polk (1795–1849) was born in Charlotte and the last Confederate Cabinet meeting was held here in 1865. The US mint was located in Charlotte during the years 1837–1861, 1867–1913. Local hydro-electric power serves textile, chemical, clothing, and machinery industries.

**Charlotte Amalie** /-ˈæməliː/ the capital of the US Virgin Islands, on the south coast of the Caribbean island of St. Thomas; pop. (1985) 52,660. Originally known to its Danish settlers as Tap Hus (= rum house), it was renamed in 1730 after the wife of King Christian V of Denmark. From 1921 to 1937 it was named St. Thomas. Its port is frequently visited by cruise ships.

**Charlottetown** /ˈʃaːlətˌtaʊn/ the capital, chief port, and tourist centre of the Canadian province of Prince Edward Island; pop. (1991) 15,400. First settled by the French c. 1720, it was laid out by the British in 1768. The town developed with the fishing and timber industries during the 19th c. and was the venue in 1864 for the Charlottetown Conference of the Maritime Provinces which led to the eventual confederation of Canada. It is the smallest of Canada's provincial capitals.

**Chartres** /ʃaːtr/ an historic, market town and the capital of Eure-et-Loire department in the Centre region of northern France, on the River Eure; pop. (1990) 41,850. It is noted for its vast twin-spired 12th–13th-c. Gothic cathedral (a world heritage monument) in which Henry IV was crowned King of France in 1594. It is said to have been built in 30 years by communal labour, and its stained glass and carved portals are consummate works of art.

**Chartreuse** /ʃaːˈtrɜːz/, **Grande** a mountainous region in the department of Isère, south-east France, rising to 2,088 m. (6,847 ft.) at Chamechaude Peak in the Dauphiné Alps. The Carthusian monastery of La Grande Chartreuse near Grenoble was founded by St. Bruno in 1084. Its monks perfected the recipe for distilling the famous green and yellow Chartreuse liqueurs.

**Charybdis** /kəˈrɪbdɪs/ in Greek legend a dangerous whirlpool opposite the cave of Scylla in a narrow channel of the sea. It was later identified with Galofalo on the Strait of Messina near Cape Faro in Sicilly.

**Châteaugay** /ˈʃætəʊˌgeɪ/ (also **Châteauguay**) a town in southern Quebec, Canada, on the Châteaugay and St. Lawrence rivers south-west of Montreal; pop. (1991) 60,500. It was the site in 1813 of a defeat of American forces attempting to invade Canada.

**Châteauroux** /ˈʃaːtəʊˌruː/ the capital of the department of Indre in the Centre region of northern France, on the River Indre; pop. (1990) 52,950. The French *Gitane* cigarettes are made here.

**Château-Thierry** /-tjəˈriː/ a town in the department of Aisne in the Picardy region of northern France, on the River Marne; pop. (1982) 14,900. It was the birthplace of the writer of fables, Jean de la Fontaine (1621–95).

**Châtellerault** /ˌʃaːtəlˈrəʊ/ (also **Châtelherault**) an ancient trading port on the River Vienne in the Poitou-Charentes region of western France; pop. (1990) 3,690. The philosopher Descartes lived here.

**Chatham** /ˈtʃætəm/ a town with a former naval base on the estuary of the River Medway, 45 km. (28 miles) east of London, England; pop. (1981) 66,100.

**Chatham Islands** an island group comprising the islands of Pitt (Rangihaute) and Chatham (Whairikauri), situated in the south-west Pacific Ocean to the east of New Zealand to which they belong; area 965 sq. km. (372 sq. miles); pop. (1991) 769. The islands were discovered in 1791 by the British sailor Lt. William Broughton who named them after his ship, the *Chatham*. The last of the islands' indigenous Moriori people died in 1933.

**Chatsworth** /ˈtʃætswəθ/ the seat of the Dukes of Devonshire, near the River Derwent in Derbyshire, central England.

**Chattanooga** /ˌtʃætəˈnuːgə/ an industrial city in the mountains of eastern Tennessee, USA, on the Tennessee River; pop. (1990) 152,470. Founded as a trading post in 1810, it was a centre for the shipping of salt and cotton before the introduction of the iron industry in the 1870s. After an increase in the generation of hydroelectric power was made possible by the Tennessee Valley Authority project in the 1930s, the city's manufacturing industries expanded. The first Coca-Cola bottling plant was located in Chattanooga. The world's steepest passenger railroad incline climbs nearby Lookout Mountain. Chattanooga was the birthplace of the blues singer Bessie Smith (1895–1937). Today it manufactures textiles, metal products, primary metals, and chemicals.

**Chaudière Falls** /ʃəʊˈdjeə(r)/ a series of cascades on the Ottawa River as it passes through the centre of the city of Ottawa, Canada.

**Chaumont** /ˈʃəʊmɑ̃/ the capital of the department of Haute-Marne in the Champagne-Ardenne region of north-east France, near the junction of the Marne and Suize rivers; pop. (1990) 28,900. The Basilica of St. Jean houses the 16th-c. Tree of Jesse, a genealogy of Christ. It was the headquarters of the US Expeditionary Force during World War I.

**Chavín de Huántar** /ˌtʃæviːn deɪ ˈwɑːntæ(r)/ a village near Huaraz in north-central Peru that gives its name to the pre-Inca Chavín culture of northern Peru whose people were skilled artists and built a city here c. 3,000 years ago.

**Chawton** /ˈtʃɔːt(ə)n/ a village near Alton in Hampshire, England. It was the home of the novelist Jane Austen from 1809 to 1817.

**Cheadle** /tʃiːd(ə)l/ **1.** a residential and light industrial town near Stockport in Greater Manchester, England; pop. (1981) 59,800. **2.** a market town in Staffordshire, England, 13 km. (8 miles) east of Stoke-on-Trent.

**Cheam** /tʃiːm/ a residential district in the London borough of Sutton.

**Cheapside** a business district in the city of London, England, near St. Paul's Cathedral, noted in medieval times for its markets and its tournaments, and was the site of the famous Mermaid Tavern.

**Cheb** /xep/ (German **Eger**) an industrial town and railway centre on the River Ohre, in western Slovakia; pop. (1991) 31,800. The German general-prince Wallenstein was murdered here in 1634.

**Cheboksary** /ˌtʃebəkˈsɑːriː/ (or **Shupashkar**) a river port and the capital of Chuvashia (the Chuvash Republic) in central Russia, situated on the River Volga, west of Kazan; pop. (1990) 429,000. It is the marketing centre of an agricultural region.

**Chechenya** /tʃəˈtʃenɪə/ (also **Chechnya** and **The Chechen Republic**) a republic of the Russian Federation, in the northern Caucasus; area 19,300 sq. km. (7,350 sq. miles); pop. (1990) 1,290,000 (including Ingushetia); capital, Groznyy. Absorbed into the Russian empire during the 1850s, the Chechen and Ingush people maintained separate autonomous regions after the Russian

Revolution, but were united in 1934 into a single autonomous republic. Large numbers of Chechens were moved into Central Asia by Stalin in 1944. Following the breakup of the Soviet Union in 1991 Chechenya and Ingushetia split apart again, declaring themselves unilaterally independent of the Russian Federation. This move eventually led to bloody conflicts with Russian troops which invaded Chechenya in 1994. Chief industries include engineering, oil production, food processing, and the manufacture of chemicals, building materials, and timber products.

**Cheddar** /ˈtʃedə(r)/ a village in the Mendip Hills of Somerset, south-west England, near the dramatic cliffs of the Cheddar Gorge. It gives its name to a kind of firm smooth cheese originally made here.

**Cheektowaga** /ˌtʃiːktəˈwɑːgə/ an urban area to the east of Buffalo in western New York state, USA; pop. (1990) 84,387.

**Chefchaouen** /ˌʃefʃaʊˈen/ (also **Chechaouen** or **Chaouen**) a town in the Rif Mountains of north-east Morocco; pop. (1982) 23,560. Known as 'the town of fountains', it was founded in 1471 by Moulay Ali Ben Rachid as a base for attacking Portuguese settlements.

**Chefoo** See YANTAI.

**Cheju** /tʃeɪˈdʒuː/ **1.** a subtropical volcanic island off the southern tip of the Korean peninsula; area 1,824 sq. km. (704 sq. miles); pop. (1984) 514,600. Mount Halla, at the centre of the island, is the highest peak in Korea (1,950 m., 6,398 ft.). The island is noted for its ancient black lava statues (*harubang stones*), produces citrus fruit, and raises cattle and horses. **2.** its capital city, a fishing port, on the north coast of the island; pop. (1990) 232,690.

**Chekiang** see ZHEJIANG.

**Chelan, Lake** /ʃəˈlɑːn/ a lake occupying a deep narrow gorge in the Cascade Range, north-west Washington state, USA. It is linked to the Columbia River by its outlet, the Chelan River, and is the third-deepest lake in the USA.

**Chelles** /ʃel/ a town in the department of Seine-et-Marne, northern France, east of Paris on the River Marne, that gives its name to the Chellean archaeological period.

**Chełm** /xelm/ the capital of the county of Chełm in eastern Poland; pop. (1990) 66,400. Situated near the border with Ukraine, it has been part of Poland, Austria, and Russia in the past.

**Chełmno** /ˈxelmnəʊ/ **1.** an industrial city in Torun county, north-central Poland, in the valley of the River Vistula; pop. (1990) 21,560. The Teutonic Knights started their conquest of Prussia from here in the 13th c. **2.** the site of a World War II Nazi concentration camp on the road from Konin to Łodz, central Poland.

**Chelmsford** /'tʃelmzfəd/ the county town of Essex, south-east England; pop. (1991) 150,000. Its cathedral dates from 1424. It is the site of the Anglia Polytechnic University (1992).

**Chelsea** /'tʃelsɪ/ a district of London, England, on the north bank of the River Thames, associated with writers and artists. It gives its name to the Chelsea bun and to the 18th-c. porcelain Chelsea-ware once made here. Chelsea pensioners are retired or disabled soldiers who live in the Chelsea Royal Hospital which was designed by Christopher Wren.

**Cheltenham** /'tʃeltenəm/ a residential, commercial, and resort town in Gloucestershire, west-central England; pop. (1991) 85,900. Formerly noted as a spa town, its saline waters became fashionable after a visit by George III in 1788. It has many Georgian and Regency buildings. Cheltenham was the birthplace in 1874 of the composer Gustav Holst, and the poet James Elroy Flecker (1884–1925) lived and was buried here. It is the headquarters of the UK electronic surveillance service (GCHQ), and at nearby Prestbury Park is a steeplechase course, scene of the annual Cheltenham Gold Cup.

**Chelyabinsk** /ˌtʃel'jæbɪnsk/ an industrial city in central Russia, on the eastern slopes of the Ural Mountains; pop. (1990) 1,148,000. Founded as a frontier post it developed as an industrial town on the trans-Siberian railway, with iron and steel, vehicle, engineering, and chemical industries.

**Chelyuskin Point** /tʃel'juːskɪn/ (also **Cape Chelyuskin**) a cape at the tip of the Taimyr Peninsula, northern Russia. Named after a Russian explorer who discovered it in 1742, it is the most northerly point of the Asian continent.

**Chemnitz** /'kemnɪts/ an industrial city in Saxony, south-east Germany, on the Chemnitz River; pop. (1991) 287,510. It was called Karl-Marx-Stadt from 1953 until the reunification of Germany in 1990. It has old-established textiles and engineering as well as modern chemical and electronics industries.

**Chenab** /tʃɪ'næb/ a river of northern India that rises in the Himalayas and flows through Himachal Pradesh and Jammu-Kashmir to join the Sutlej River (in Punjab) to become the Panjnad. It is one of the 'five rivers' that give Punjab its name.

**Chengchow** see ZHENGZHOU.

**Chengde** /'tʃeŋdə/ a city in Hebei province, northern China; pop. (1986) 337,800. Once the site of the summer palace of the Qing emperor, Kang Xi, it is now a city trading in agricultural and forest produce.

**Chengdu** /tʃeŋ'duː/ the capital of Sichuan province in central China; pop. (1990) 4,025,000. Formerly the capital of the Zhou dynasty, it has since 1949 developed as an industrial city trading in agricultural goods and producing iron, steel,

paper, machinery, chemicals, electronic goods, and textiles. A cultural centre since ancient times, the city is associated with the Tang poet Du Fu (712–70).

**Cheops** /'tʃiːɒps/, **Pyramid of** a great pyramid in the Nile valley near Giza in northern Egypt, built c. 2,600 BC and comprising some 2.5 million limestone blocks weighing c. 6 million tonnes. With a height of 146.5 m. (480 ft.) it is the tallest pyramid in Egypt. It has been designated a world-heritage site by UNESCO.

**Chequers** /'tʃekəz/ a Tudor mansion in the Chiltern Hills near Princes Risborough, Buckinghamshire, central England, presented to the British nation in 1917 by Lord and Lady Lee of Fareham to serve as a country seat for the Prime Minister in office.

**Cher** /ʃeə(r)/ **1.** a river of central France that rises in the Massif Central and flows 350 km. (220 miles) northwards to meet the Loire near Tours. **2.** a department in the Centre region of central France; area 7,235 sq. km. (2,794 sq. miles); pop. (1990) 321,560; capital, Bourges.

**Cherbourg** /'ʃɜːbʊəg/ a seaport, naval base, and resort in the Manche department on the Normandy coast of north-west France; pop. (1990) 28,770. Developed by Vauban in the 17th c. and by Napoleon over a century later, Cherbourg is linked by ferries to Portsmouth, Poole, and Weymouth in England.

**Cherepovets** /tʃərɪpə'vjets/ a city on the Volga-Baltic waterway, north-west Russia; pop. (1990) 313,000. The city, which developed around a monastery in the 14th c., is a transportation and industrial centre producing chemicals and metal products.

**Cherkassy** /tʃɜː'kɑːsɪ/ a port on the Dnieper River, central Ukraine; pop. (1990) 297,000. Situated at the north-west end of the Kremchung reservoir, the city produces chemicals, clothing, and fertilizers.

**Cherkess** /tʃɜː'kes/ a mountainous region in the north-west Caucasus Mountains of southern Russia, in the valley of the upper Kuban River. It is largely occupied by Cherkess people of Circassian descent. See also KARACHAY-CHERKESSIA which is a republic of the Russian Federation.

**Cherkessk** /tʃɜː'kesk/ the capital of the Karachay-Cherkess Republic in southern Russia, on the Kuban River; pop. (1990) 113,000. It has electrical equipment and light industries.

**Chernigov** /tʃɜː'njegəf/ a railway junction, market centre, and port on the River Desna, north-east Ukraine; pop. (1990) 301,000. It is an ancient city with buildings dating from the 12th c. and has numerous light industries including the making of musical instruments.

**Cherni Vruh** /tʃɜːni 'vræx/ the highest peak of the Vitosha Mountains in west Bulgaria, rising to a height of 2,290 m. (7,513 ft.) south-west of Sofia. The mountain is popular both as a national park and a skiing centre.

**Chernivtsi** /tʃɜːˈnɪftsi:/ (formerly **Chernovtsy**) the economic and cultural centre of the Bukovina region of south-west Ukraine; situated on the River Prut, in the eastern foothills of the Carpathian Mts.; pop. (1990) 257,000. The city was part of Romania from 1918 to 1940, and has sawmilling, engineering, textile, rubber, and food-processing industries.

**Chernobyl** /tʃɜːˈnɒbɪl/ a city near Kiev in north-central Ukraine, where in April 1986 explosions at a nuclear power-station resulted in a serious escape of radioactivity which spread in the atmosphere to neighbouring republics of the former Soviet Union and a number of countries of Europe. The city, which had a population of 244,000 in 1985, was subsequently evacuated.

**chernozem** /ˈtʃɜːnəʊˌzem/ a fertile black soil rich in humus, found in semiarid regions, especially southern Russia and tapering to the east in Western Siberia and northern Kazakhstan. It is also called a black earth soil.

**Cherokee** /ˈtʃerəkɪ/ a North American Iroquoian-speaking Indian tribe, one of the largest of the tribes of south-east USA, once occupying parts of Georgia, Tennessee, and the Carolinas and constituted as a Cherokee Nation from 1839 to 1914 following their forced removal to Oklahoma. They number 95,000 in Oklahoma and 10,000 in North Carolina.

**Cherrapunjee** /tʃerəˈpundʒi:/ a village in Meghalaya state in north-east India, reputedly the world's wettest inhabited place with an average recorded annual rainfall of 10,719 mm. (422 inches), although 22,990 mm. (905 inches) were recorded for 1861.

**Cherry Hill** an urban area in west-central New Jersey, USA, to the east of Camden; pop. (1990) 69,320.

**Cherski Range** /ˈtʃɜːskɪ/ (Russian **Khrebet Cherskogo**) a mountain range in north-east Siberia, between the Yana and Kolyma rivers.

**Chersonese** /ˈkɜːsəˌniːs/ an ancient name applied to several peninsulas including: **1.** the Thracian or Gallipoli peninsula on the north side of the Hellespont, **2.** the Crimea (Tauric Chersonese). See also the GOLDEN CHERSONESE.

**Chesapeake** /ˈtʃes(ə)piːk/ a residential city with light industries in south-east Virginia, USA, at the north-eastern end of the Great Dismal Swamp; pop. (1990) 151,980.

**Chesapeake Bay** a large inlet of the Atlantic Ocean on the coast of the USA, 320 km. (200 miles) in length, bordering on Virginia and Maryland.

**Chesham** /ˈtʃeʃəm/ a residential and market town in Buckinghamshire, England, on the River

Chess, 40 km. (25 miles) north-west of London; pop. (1981) 21,000.

**Cheshire** /ˈtʃeʃə(r)/ a north-west midlands county of England; area 2,333 sq. km. (901 sq. miles); pop. (1991) 937,300; county town, Chester. It is divided into eight districts:

| District | Area (sq. km.) | Pop. (1991) |
| --- | --- | --- |
| Chester | 448 | 115,000 |
| Congleton | 211 | 82,900 |
| Crewe and Nantwich | 431 | 101,800 |
| Ellesmere Port and Neston | 86 | 78,800 |
| Halton | 74 | 121,400 |
| Macclesfield | 525 | 147,000 |
| Vale Royal | 381 | 111,100 |
| Warrington | 176 | 179,500 |

**Chesil Bank** /ˈtʃez(ə)l/ a shingle beach forming a spit of land that stretches for 25 km. (17 miles) from Portland to Abbotsbury on the Dorset coast of England. Protecting a tidal lagoon noted for its wintering wildfowl, it is one of the longest storm beaches in Europe.

**Chester** /ˈtʃestə(r)/ (anc. **Deva**) the county town and tourist city of Cheshire in the north midlands of England, on the River Dee; pop. (1991) 115,000. It is a well-preserved walled city with many ancient buildings including a Roman amphitheatre, a castle, a 12th-c. cathedral, and fine medieval shops and houses. The conductor Sir Adrian Boult was born here in 1889.

**Chesterfield** /ˈtʃestə(r)ˌfiːld/ a town in Derbyshire, central England; pop. (1991) 99,700. Its All Saints Church has an unusual twisted spire. The locomotive engineer George Stephenson (1781–1848) lies buried here.

**Chesterfield Islands** a group of 11 uninhabited coral islands in the South Pacific Ocean, 550 km. (350 miles) north-west of the French Overseas Territory of New Caledonia.

**Chetumal** /ˌtʃetuˈmaːl/ the capital of the state of Quintana Roo on the Yucatán peninsula of south-east Mexico; pop. (1981) 40,000. It is a freeport on the shallow Chetumal Bay, an inlet of the Caribbean Sea.

**Cheviot Hills** /ˈtʃiːvɪət/ (also **Cheviots**) a range of hills on the border between Scotland and England, rising to 816 m. (2,677 ft.) in The Cheviot.

**Cheyenne** /ʃaɪˈæn/ an Algonquian-speaking tribe of North American Indians that formerly lived on the Great Plains between the Missouri and Arkansas rivers. The majority (4,500) live in Montana, others live in Oklahoma.

**Cheyenne** the capital of the state of Wyoming, USA; pop. (1990) 50,010. Developed as a railroad town in 1867, it became the banking centre of a vast cattle and sheep ranching area. Coal, oil, and timber are also important commodities.

**Chiangmai** /dʒɪæŋˈmaɪ/ a city on the Ping River in north-west Thailand, principal city of the region since 1296 when it was capital of the kingdom of Lan Na, powerful until the 16th c.; pop. (1990) 164,900. It is now a popular tourist destination.

**Chianti** /kɪˈæntɪ/ an area of Tuscany to the north-west of Siena in northern Italy, noted for its dry red wine. Gaiole, Radda, and Castellina are the chief towns.

**Chiapas** /tʃɪˈɑːpəs/ a state on the Pacific coast of southern Mexico; area 74,211 sq. km. (28,664 sq. miles); pop. (1990) 3,203,915; capital, Tuxtla Gutiérrez. In 1994 it was the scene of a Mayan Indian uprising which led to confrontation between Mexican troops and soldiers of the so-called Zapatista National Liberation Army.

**Chiba** /ˈtʃiːbə/ a city in the Kanto region of east Honshu Island, Japan, at the north-east end of Tokyo Bay, 40 km. (25 miles) east of Tokyo; pop. (1990) 829,470.

**Chibcha** /ˈtʃɪbtʃə/ an Indian people of Colombia with an ancient civilization that was flourishing at the time the Spaniards first encountered them in 1537.

**Chicago** /ʃɪˈkɑːgəʊ/ a city in Illinois, on Lake Michigan, the third-largest city of the USA, known as the 'Windy City', and the original home of the skyscraper; pop. (1990) 2,783,726. Originally a trading post, then a military fort, Chicago first developed in the early 1800s after it was chosen as the terminal site of the Illinois and Michigan canal (completed in 1848). It became the largest grain market in the world and a major centre for iron and steel, electronics, food-processing and the transportation of livestock. Despite the Great Fire of 1871 which destroyed over 15,000 houses, the city continued to expand in the 20th c. It is a major Great Lakes port and its airport is the busiest in the world. The Sears Tower, built in 1974, is the tallest inhabited building in the world at 443 m. (1,454 ft.), and the Union States Post Office is the largest in the world under one roof.

**chicano** /tʃɪˈkɑːnəʊ/ a term used in the USA to describe an American of Mexican origin.

**Chichén Itzá** /ˈtʃɪtʃen ɪtˈsɑː/ a site in northern Yucatán, Mexico, which was the centre of the Maya empire until abandoned in 1200, with elaborate ceremonial buildings that centre on a sacred well (*cenote*). Built c. AD 400, it was taken by the Toltecs c. 900.

**Chichester** /ˈtʃɪtʃɪstə(r)/ the county town of West Sussex, near the south coast of England, east of Portsmouth; pop. (1981) 27,200. There are Roman remains at Fishbourne nearby and an 11th–12th-c. cathedral. It was the birthplace of the poets William Collins (1721–59) and Charles Crocker (1797–1861).

**Chichimec** /tʃiːtʃɪˈmek/ a horde of invaders who entered the central valley of Mexico from the north-west c. 950–1300, and came to be known as the Toltec after the founding of their capital, Tula, in 986. In 1300 Chichimec farmers left their drought-stricken land and converged on Tula, contributing to its destruction.

**Chiclayo** /tʃiːˈklɑːjəʊ/ the capital of the department of Lambayeque in north-west Peru, on the arid coastal lowlands north of Trujillo; pop. (1990) 426,300. In 1987 a royal Moche tomb was discovered at Sipán c. 30 km. (19 miles) south-east of the city.

**Chicopee** /ˈtʃɪkəpiː/ an industrial city in south-west Massachusetts, USA, at the junction of the Chicopee and Connecticut rivers north of Springfield; pop. (1990) 56,630. Its industries include rubber and sporting goods, firearms, and machinery.

**Chicoutimi** /ʃəˈkuːtəmi/ a commercial and industrial city on the Chicoutimi and Saguenay rivers to the north of Quebec, Canada; pop. (1991) 62,700; 160,930 (metropolitan area with Jonquière). Notable buildings include the cathedral dedicated to St. François-Xavier (1921) and the wigwam-shaped Notre-Dame-de-Fatima. It has aluminium plants and paper mills.

**Chiem** /kiːm/, **Lake** (German **Chiemsee** /ˈkiːmseɪ/) the largest lake in Bavaria, southern Germany, at the centre of a resort area 60 km. (38 miles) south-east of Munich; area, 81 sq. km. (31 sq. miles). It is fed by the River Ache and drained by the River Alz.

**Chieti** /ˈkjeɪti/ the capital town and commercial centre of Chieti province in the Abruzzi region of central Italy, on the Pescara River; pop. (1990) 57,535. There are the remains of a Roman theatre, temple, and baths.

**Chifeng** /tʃiːˈfeŋ/ (also **Ulanhad**) a city in Inner Mongolia, north-east China, north-east of Beijing; pop. (1986) 896,000.

**Chigasaki** /ˌtʃiːgəˈsɑːkɪ/ a resort and industrial city in Kanagawa prefecture, central Honshu Island, Japan, south-west of Yokohama; pop. (1990) 201,670. It has a large electronics industry.

**Chihli** /tʃiːˈliː/, **Gulf of** (also **Bo Hai** /bəʊ haɪ/) a north-western arm of the Yellow Sea in north-east China. It is enclosed on three sides by the Chinese provinces of Shandong, Hebei, and Liaoning and the municipality of Tianjin. Since 1993 the Bo Hai Economic Rim has been a key area of development with Beijing, Tianjin, and Tangshan at its centre and the Liaodong and Shandong peninsulas as its two wings. The rim extends over 12 million sq. km. with a population of c. 240 million.

**Chihuahua** /tʃɪˈwɑːwə/ **1.** the largest state in Mexico; area 244,938 sq. km. (94,607 sq. miles); pop. (1990) 2,439,950. **2.** its capital, the leading city of north-central Mexico; pop. (1990) 530,490. Founded in 1709, it became the centre of a rich silver-mining, lumbering, and cattle-raising area. Miguel Hidalgo y Costilla, father of Mexican independence, was executed here in 1811 and Benito Juarez made his headquarters in the city when French troops invaded Mexico 1862–7. The city gives its name to a breed of small dog.

**Chile** /'tʃɪlɪ/ official name **The Republic of Chile** a country occupying a long coastal strip down the southern half of the west of south America, between the Andes and the Pacific Ocean,

bounded east by Argentina, north-east by Bolivia, and north by Peru; 756,622 sq. km. (292,132 sq. miles); pop. (est. 1991) 13,400,000; official language, Spanish; capital, Santiago. Its largest cities are Santiago, Viña del Mar, Concepción, Valparaiso, Talcahuano, Temuco, and Antofagasta. In northern Chile the arid Atacama Desert contains great mineral wealth, chiefly copper, iron ore, and nitrate of soda, while southern Chile is rich in forest and grazing land and the chief source of bituminous coal. In the far south, where the Andes meet the Pacific, the coastline is deeply indented with fjords and inlets. The relatively small central region dominates the country in terms of population and agricultural resources which include grain, fruit, and vegetables. Most of Chile was incorporated in the Inca empire and became part of the Spanish Viceroyalty of Peru after Pizarro's conquest, although the tribes of the south (including the Araucanians) generally held out successfully against both imperial powers. Chilean independence was proclaimed in 1810 by Bernardo O'Higgins and finally achieved in 1818 with help from Argentina. Chilean territory was pushed northwards in 1879–83 at the expense of Bolivia, and although difficulties with Argentina were solved without war in 1902, relations with her eastern neighbour have since periodically deteriorated. Chile was ruled by a right-wing military dictatorship after the overthrow of the Marxist democrat Allende in 1973 until a democratically elected president took office in March 1990. The country is now governed by an executive president and a bicameral National Congress comprising a Senate and a Chamber of Deputies.
**Chilean** *adj. & n.*
Chile is divided into 13 regions:

| Region | Area (sq. km.) | Pop. (1991) | Capital |
| --- | --- | --- | --- |
| Tarapaca | 58,786 | 363,425 | Iquique |
| Antofagasta | 125,253 | 391,740 | Antofagasta |
| Atacama | 74,705 | 201,450 | Copiapó |
| Coquimbo | 40,656 | 489,360 | La Serena |
| Valparaiso | 16,396 | 1,415,570 | Valparaiso |
| Santiago | 15,549 | 5,342,910 | Santiago |
| Bernardo O'Higgins | 16,456 | 655,930 | Rancagua |
| Maule | 30,518 | 857,590 | Talca |
| Bío-Bío | 36,939 | 1,692,400 | Concepción |
| Araucanía | 31,846 | 798,400 | Temuco |
| Los Lagos | 67,247 | 934,600 | Puerto Montt |
| Aisén | 108,997 | 80,830 | Coíhaique |
| Magallanes | 132,034 | 161,800 | Punta Arenas |

**Chillán** /tʃɪl'ɑːn/ a marketing city in the Bío-Bío region of south-central Chile, to the north of Concepción; pop. (1991) 145,970. It was the birthplace in 1778 of the liberator Bernardo O'Higgins, and has been subjected to severe earthquakes, the last in 1939.

**Chilpancingo** /ˌtʃiːlpænˈsɪŋɡəʊ/ an agricultural market town in southern Mexico, capital of the state of Guerrero; pop. (1980) 120,000. The first Mexican Revolutionary Congress met here in 1813. Nearby are the Juxtlahuaca Caves with 3,000-year-old Olmec paintings.

**Chiltern Hills** /'tʃɪlt(ə)n/ (also **Chilterns**) a range of chalk hills in east-central England, north of the Thames, between the Berkshire Downs and the East Anglian Ridge. Coombe Hill (260 m., 853 ft.) near Wendover is the highest point. When an MP wishes to resign from Parliament he applies for the Chiltern Hundreds, the stewardship of a district (formerly called a *hundred*) which includes part of the Chiltern Hills and is Crown property. Resignation is not normally permitted once an MP has been elected, but the holding of an office of profit under the Crown disqualifies a person from being an MP, and by a legal fiction this stewardship is held to be such an office.

**Chilung** /'dʒiːluːŋ/ (also **Keelung**) the chief port and naval base of Taiwan, at the northern tip of the island; pop. (1982) 351,700. Shipbuilding, chemicals, machinery, and fertilizers are important industries.

**Chimanimani National Park** /tʃɪmænɪˈmænɪ/ a national park in the Chimanimani Range, eastern Zimbabwe, near the frontier with Mozambique. Designated a park in 1954, its montane forest supports a variety of birdlife as well as populations of sable and eland.

**Chimborazo** /ˌtʃɪmbəˈrɑːzəʊ/ an inactive volcano, the highest peak of the Andes in Ecuador, rising to a height of 6,310 m. (20,487 ft.) near Riobamba.

**Chimbote** /tʃiːmˈbəʊteɪ/ the chief fishing port of Peru, situated in the department of Ancash, 450 km. (283 miles) north of Lima; pop. (1990) 297,000. Fishmeal and steel are its chief products.

**Chimkent** /tʃɪmˈkjent/ see SHYMKENT.

**Chimu** /'tʃiːmuː/ the largest and most important civilization of Peru before the Inca. The large-scale irrigation systems and increased urbanization which marked their great efflorescence in the 14th c. anticipated subsequent developments by their

Inca conquerors, to whom they passed their culture and engineering skills. Chimu social organization, with its distinctive hierarchical structure, was imperfectly copied by the Inca who had not yet established a permanent ruling class at the time of the Spanish conquest. The Chimu language died out in the 19th c.

**China** /'tʃaɪnə/ official name **The People's Republic of China** a country in eastern Asia, the third-largest and most populous in the world, bounded by Mongolia and Russia in the north, North

Korea in the north-east, Vietnam, Laos, Burma, India, Bhutan, Pakistan, and Nepal in the south, and Afghanistan, Tajikistan, Kyrgyzstan, and Kazakhstan in the west; area 9,571,300 sq. km. (3,695,300 sq. miles); pop. (est. 1991) 1,151,300,000; official language, modern standard Chinese (based on the dialect of Beijing); capital, Beijing (Peking). The largest cities are Shanghai, Beijing, Tianjin, Guangzhou (Canton), Wuhan,

and Shenyang. Ninety per cent of the people live on one-sixth of the land area of China, chiefly in the eastern lowlands where the Yangtze, Yellow, and Pearl rivers flow through fertile plains to the sea. The western two-thirds of the country is mountainous or semidesert. Of the 14 mountains in the world that are over 8,000 m. (26,000 ft.) in height, nine are in China or on its borders. The greater part of China lies within the temperate zone, although parts of the southern provinces of Yunnan and Guangdong and the autonomous region of Guangxi have a tropical climate that is affected by seasonal monsoons. Most of the country's rainfall is in the summer months and floods are more common in the south. China is essentially an agricultural country and is the world's largest producer of rice, millet, sorghum, barley, tea, and potatoes which, in addition to cotton and oilseed, are major export crops. Mineral resources have been largely developed since 1949, China being a major producer of coal, oil, natural gas, tin, antimony, tungsten, and fluorspar. Chinese civilization stretches back until at least the 3rd millenium BC, the country being ruled by a series of dynasties, including a Mongol one in the 13th-14th c., until the Ch'ing (or Manchu) dynasty

**CHINA**

was overthrown by Sun Yat-sen in 1912. The country was stricken by civil war (1927–37 and 1946–9), and by Japanese invasion, and soon after the end of World War II the corrupt and ineffect-ive Kuomintang government was overthrown by the Communists, the People's Republic of China being declared in 1949. For many years China remained generally closed to Western economic or political penetration, both under its old imperial rulers and its new Communist ones. Legislative authority is vested in a National People's Congress and executive power is exercised by the State Council.

**Chinese** *adj. & n.*
China is divided into three special municipalities (Beijing, Tianjin, and Shanghai), 21 provinces, and five autonomous regions:

| Province | Area (sq. km.) | Pop. (1990) | Capital |
|---|---|---|---|
| Anhui | 139,900 | 56,181,000 | Hefei |
| Fujian | 123,100 | 30,048,000 | Fuzhou |
| Gansu | 530,000 | 22,371,000 | Lanzhou |
| Guangdong | 231,400 | 62,829,000 | Guangzhou |
| Guizhou | 174,000 | 32,392,000 | Guiyang |
| Hebei | 202,700 | 61,082,000 | Shijiazhuang |
| Heilongjiang | 463,600 | 35,215,000 | Harbin |
| Henan | 167,000 | 85,510,000 | Zhengzhou |
| Hubei | 187,500 | 53,969,000 | Wuhan |
| Hunan | 210,500 | 60,660,000 | Changsha |
| Jiangsu | 102,200 | 67,057,000 | Nanjing |
| Jiangxi | 164,800 | 37,710,000 | Nanchang |
| Jilin | 187,000 | 24,659,000 | Changchun |
| Liaoning | 151,000 | 39,460,000 | Shenyang |
| Qinghai | 721,000 | 4,457,000 | Xining |
| Shaanxi | 195,800 | 32,882,000 | Xian |
| Shandong | 153,300 | 84,393,000 | Jinan |
| Shanxi | 157,100 | 28,759,000 | Taiyuan |
| Sichuan | 569,000 | 107,218,000 | Chengdu |
| Yunnan | 436,200 | 36,973,000 | Kunming |
| Zhejiang | 101,800 | 41,446,000 | Hangzhou |

| Aut. Region | Area (sq. km.) | Pop. (1990) | Capital |
|---|---|---|---|
| Guangxi | 220,400 | 42,246,000 | Nanning |
| Inner Mongolia | 1,183,000 | 21,457,000 | Hohhot |
| Ningxia | 77,800 | 4,655,000 | Yinchuan |
| Xinjiang | 1,646,800 | 15,156,000 | Urumqi |
| Tibet | 1,221,600 | 2,196,000 | Lhasa |

**Chinan** See JINAN.

**China Sea** a part of the Pacific Ocean off the coast of China, divided by the island of Taiwan into the East China Sea in the north and the South China Sea in the south. The Spratly Islands and Paracel Islands in the South China Sea are disputed islets (all or partly claimed by China, Taiwan, Malaysia, Vietnam, Philippines, and Brunei) on the shipping lanes that link Japan, China, and Korea with the Middle East.

**Chinatown** /ˈtʃaɪnəˌtaʊn/ a district of any non-Chinese town, especially a city or seaport, in which the population is predominantly Chinese.

**Chindwin** /ˈtʃɪndwən/ the chief tributary of the Irrawaddy River in Burma. Rising in the hills of northern Burma it flows southwards for 885 km. (550 miles) before meeting the Irrawaddy 550 km. (350 miles) north of Rangoon.

**Chinese** /tʃaɪˈniːz/ a member of the Sino-Tibetan language group, a tonal language with no inflexions, declensions, or conjugations. There are many dialects, including Mandarin (based on the pronunciation of Beijing), and Cantonese (spoken in the south-east and in Hong Kong). Written in Han characters, Chinese script is ideographic; the characters were in origin pictographic, with each sign standing for an object, and they gradually gave way to non-pictorial ideographs representing not only tangible objects but also abstract concepts. Despite its complexity the script makes written communication possible between people speaking mutually incomprehensible dialects. Examples of Chinese writing date back well beyond 1,000 BC. Traditionally Chinese books were arranged in vertical columns and read from right to left, but they are now usually composed horizontally. Until the beginning of the 20th c. the greater part of written Chinese was in a style which imitated that of the Chinese classics, most of which were written before 200 BC, and this written style became far removed from current speech. A reform movement was started to make the literature available to the masses, and many simplified characters were introduced. There are several systems of romanization, chief amongst these formerly being the Wade-Giles system which was used on official UK and US maps of China from 1942. This system was first published by Sir Thomas Wade in 1859 and modified by H. A. Giles in 1912. A system of romanization known as *Pinyin* was officially adopted by China in 1958, but it was not fully accepted throughout the world until 1979. Place-names on mainland China are now usually rendered in Pinyin although names on Taiwan are still commonly rendered in the Wade-Giles form.

**Ch'ing** /tʃɪŋ/ the name of a Chinese dynasty established by the Manchus, 1644–1912. Its overthrow in 1912 ended imperial rule in China and plunged the country into prolonged civil war.

**Chin Hills** /tʃɪn/ (Burmese **Rongklang**) a range of hills in west Burma, close to the frontier with Bangladesh. Forming part of the larger Arakan Yoma range, they rise to a height of 3,053 m. (10,016 ft.) at Mt. Victoria.

**Chinju** /tʃɪnˈdʒuː/ (also **Jinju**) the capital of the province of South Kyongsang, southern South Korea; pop. (1990) 258,400. It is an agricultural and transport centre with light industries.

**Chinnampo** see NAMPO.

**Chino** /ˈtʃiːnəʊ/ an agricultural and business centre in southern California, USA, situated in the San Bernardino valley to the east of Los Angeles; pop. (1990) 59,680.

**Chinon** /ʃiː'nɔ̃/ a medieval town in the department of Indre-et-Loire, Centre Region, west-central France, on the River Vienne; pop. (1982) 8,700. It has associations with Joan of Arc and was the birthplace of the French satirist Rabelais.

**Chinook** /ʃə'nʊk, tʃə-, -'nuːk/ a North American Indian tribe originally inhabiting the region around the Columbus River in Oregon and Washington. Their livelihood was traditionally dependent on the king or chinook salmon which spawned every year in the river.

**chinook** a warm dry wind that blows from west to east across the Rocky Mountains in North America.

**Chios** /'kaɪɒs/ (Greek **Khios** /'kiːɒs/) a Greek island in the Aegean Sea; area 842 sq. km. (325 sq. miles); pop. (1981) 29,700. Tourism, wine production, and boat-building are the chief industries.

**Chippewa** /'tʃɪpəwæ/ (also **Ojibwa**) a North American Algonquian-speaking Indian people, once the most powerful tribe in the Great Lakes region, now numbering c. 80,000 and living in Canada and reservations in North Dakota, Wisconsin, and Minnesota.

**Chipping Campden** /ˌtʃɪpɪŋ 'kæmd(ə)n/ a picturesque old Cotswold village in Gloucestershire, England, a centre of local handicrafts.

**Chirchik** /tʃɜːtʃiːk/ (Uzbek **Chirchiq**) a town in Uzbekistan, 32 km. (20 miles) north-east of Tashkent; pop. (1990) 159,000.

**Chirripó Grande** /tʃiːrɪ'pəʊ 'grɑːndɪ/ a mountain in the Talamanca Range in central Costa Rica. Rising to a height of 3,819 m. (12,530 ft.), it is the highest peak in Central America.

**Chisholm Trail** /'tʃɪzəm/ a famous 19th-c. cattle trail linking San Antonio, Texas, to the railhead at Abilene, Kansas.

**Chisinau** /'tʃɪsnaʊ/ (Russian **Kishinev** /kɪsɪ'njef/) the capital of the Republic of Moldova (Moldavia), on the River Byk; pop. (1990) 676,000. Founded in 1420 around a monastery, it became the chief town of Bessarabia under Russian rule and was part of Romania 1918–40. It has a 19th-c. Orthodox cathedral and numerous light industries.

**Chiswick** /'tʃɪzɪk/ a residential and commercial district of west London, England, on the north bank of the River Thames. The English statesmen Charles James Fox (1749–1806) and George Canning (1770–1827) both died in Chiswick House, an Italianate villa built in 1725–9 by the Earl of Burlington. Chiswick also has associations with William Thackeray, William Morris, Alexander Pope, and William Hogarth all of whom lived for a time in the district.

**Chita** /tʃiː'tɑː/ an industrial city in east Siberia, Russia, at the junction of the Ingoda and Chita rivers; pop. (1990) 372,000. It has machinery and food-processing industries.

**Chitral** /tʃɪ'trɑːl/ (also **Kunar**) a river in northeast Afghanistan and northern Pakistan that flows southwards from the Hindu Kush through Nuristan for c. 480 km. (300 miles) before joining the Kabul River near Jalalabad.

**Chittagong** /'tʃɪtəˌgɒŋ/ a seaport in south-east Bangladesh, on the Bay of Bengal; pop. (1991) 1,566,070.

**Chizarira National Park** a national park extending over a plateau cut by rivers on their way to join the Zambezi in Matabeleland, Zimbabwe. The 191,000-hectare (471,605-acre) park was designated in 1975.

**Chobe** /'tʃəʊbɪ/ a district in northern Botswana adjacent to the lower course of the Cuando River which flows into the Zambezi 80 km. (50 miles) west of the Victoria Falls. The 1,087,800-hectare (2,685,926-acre) Chobe National Park, designated in 1967, encompasses the Nogatosau floodplains and the sandy Mababe Depression.

**Chocolate Hills** a weathered marine limestone formation standing about 30 m. (98 ft.) high at the centre of the island of Bohol in the Philippines.

**Choctaw** /'tʃɒktɔː/ a North American Algonquian-speaking Indian tribe originally inhabiting the lower Mississippi and known as the 'okla homa' (= red people). There are nearly 39,000 Choctaw living in Oklahoma and Mississippi.

**Choibalsan** /ˌtʃɔɪb(ə)l'sɑːn/ (also **Choybalsan**) a city, the capital of Dornod county, in north-east Mongolia, on the River Kerulen.

**Choiseul** /ʃwaː'zɜːl/ a volcanic island of the Solomon Islands group in the Pacific Ocean, situated between Bougainville and Santa Isabel; area 2,589 sq. km. (1,000 sq. miles).

**Cholula** /tʃɒ'luːlə/ a town in the state of Puebla, central Mexico, at an altitude of 1,360 m. (4,462 ft.), and built on the site of a great pre-Columbian ceremonial centre; pop. (1980) 20,000. First occupied c. 400 BC, the city was built by the Cholutecas, a mixture of Olmec, Mixtec, and other Mexican people. The Tepanapa pyramid is one of the largest in the New World. Cholula is the site of the University of the Americas (1895).

**Chongjin** /tʃʊŋ'dʒɪn/ the capital of north Hamgyong province, on the north-east coast of North Korea; pop. (est. 1984) 754,100.

**Chongju** /tʃʊŋ'dʒuː/ the capital of North Chungchong province, west-central South Korea; pop. (1990) 497,430. It is a marketing and processing centre.

**Chongqing** /tʃʊŋ'kɪŋ/ (also **Chungking**) a city in Sichuan province in central China, on the Yangtze River; pop. (1990) 6,511,000. Founded in the 12th c. it was capital of China 1938–46. It is now a leading industrial city producing steel, chemicals, textiles, and motor cycles.

**Chonju** /tʃʊn'dʒuː/ the capital of North Cholla province, south-west South Korea; pop. (1990) 517,100. It is the agricultural centre of a densely populated rice-growing area with light industries.

**Cho Oyu** /ˌtʃəʊ əʊ'juː/ a mountain of the Himalayas rising to 8,150 m. (26,750 ft.) on the frontier between China and Nepal. Known as the 'Goddess of the Turquoise', it was first climbed by an Austrian team in 1954.

**Chorley** /'tʃɔːlɪ/ a town in Lancashire, England, 16 km. north-west of Bolton; pop. (1981) 33,700. Once noted as a cotton-weaving centre, it was the birthplace in 1819 of Henry Tate, founder of the Tate Gallery in London.

**Chorzów** /xəʊ'ʃuːf/ an industrial city in the Upper Silesian county of Katowice, southern Poland; pop. (1990) 131,900. Railway engineering and the manufacture of iron, steel, and chemicals are the chief industries.

**Chotts** /ʃɒts/ (also **Shotts**) a series of shallow salt lakes stretching across southern Tunisia and Algeria. Often below sea-level, they remain dry for the greater part of the year.

**Christadelphian** /ˌkrɪstə'delfɪən/ a member of a Christian sect founded in America in 1848 by John Thomas, rejecting the beliefs and development associated with the term 'Christian', calling themselves 'Christadelphians' (= brothers of Christ) and claiming to return to the beliefs and practices of the earliest disciples. The core of their faith is that Christ will return in power to set up a worldwide theocracy beginning at Jerusalem, and that belief in this is necessary for salvation.

**Christchurch** /'kraɪstˌtʃɜːtʃ/ an old town and resort in Dorset, southern England, 8 km. east of Bournemouth; pop. (1981) 33,500.

**Christchurch** the largest city in South Island, New Zealand, at the junction of the Heathcote and Avon rivers, at the southern end of Pegasus Bay; pop. (1991) 307,130. The city, which is the centre of administration and commerce for the Canterbury region, was founded in 1850 by English Anglican colonists whose leader, John Robert Godley, named it after his old university college of Christ Church, Oxford. Today it has numerous industries including woollen mills, carpets, furniture, fertilizers, and food processing.

**Christianity** /ˌkrɪstɪ'ænɪtɪ/ a religion whose adherents believe in or follow the religion of Jesus Christ. At first Christianity was simply a Jewish sect which believed that Jesus of Nazareth was the Messiah (or 'Christ' = anointed one). Largely owing to the former Pharisee, Paul of Tarsus, it quickly became an independent, mainly gentile, organization. In the early centuries Christians experienced intermittent persecution by the state, though there was no clear legal basis for this until the reign of the Emperor Decius (AD 250). By the 3rd c. Christianity was widespread throughout the Roman Empire; in 313 Constantine ended

persecution and in 380 Theodosius recognized it as the state religion. There were frequent disputes between Christians mainly over the status of Christ and the nature of the Trinity, and later over grace and church organization. Division between East and West, in origin largely cultural and linguistic, intensified, culminating in the Schism of 1054, sealed by the Crusades. In the West the organization of the church, focused on the Roman papacy, was fragmented by the Reformation of the 16th c. In the 20th c. the ecumenical movement has sought to heal these ancient wounds.

**Christian Science** the doctrine of the Church of Christ, Scientist, a Christian sect founded in Boston in 1879 by Mrs Mary Baker Eddy to 'reinstate primitive Christianity and its lost element of healing'. She taught that God and his perfect spiritual creation are the only ultimate reality, and that his law is always available to bring regeneration and healing to humanity. The movement flourished and spread to other English-speaking countries, to Germany, and to many other countries. Since her death (1910) the affairs of the organization have been administered by a board of directors. Worship includes readings from *Science and Health with Key to the Scriptures* by the foundress.

**Christianshaab** /'krɪstʃənzhɔːb/ (Inuit **Qasigiannguit**) a fishing settlement on the west coast of Greenland, opposite Disko Island; pop. (1992) 1,681.

**Christiansted** /'krɪstʃənsted/ a port on the north-east coast of the island of St. Croix, largest of the US Virgin Islands; pop. (1980) 2,856. Capital of the Danish West Indies during the 18th c., it is the island's chief town.

**Christmas Island 1.** an Australian dependency in the Indian Ocean 350 km. (200 miles) south of the western end of Java; area 135 sq. km. (52 sq. miles); pop. (1991) 1,275. Discovered on Christmas Day 1643 and annexed by the UK in 1888, the administration of the island was handed over to Australia in 1958. In 1991 It became subject to the laws of Western Australia. The island's income is mostly derived from the mining of rock phosphate. **2.** (also **Kiritimati**) a Pacific island in the Line Islands group, Kiribati, the largest atoll in the world; area 578 sq. km. (223 sq. miles); pop. (1990) 2,530. Fishing and the production of copra are important industries.

**Christmas Pie** a small village to the east of Ash in Surrey, south-east England.

**Christ's Hospital** a boys' school founded in London in 1552 for poor children, which has since moved to Horsham, Sussex. Pupils wear a distinctive uniform of long dark-blue belted gowns and yellow stockings.

**chronometer** /krə'nɒmɪtə(r)/ a time-measuring instrument, especially one keeping accurate time in spite of movement or of variations in temperature, humidity, and air pressure. The longitude of a ship at sea may be found by comparing local time with Greenwich Mean Time; the former can be computed by astronomical observation, but without an accurate marine timekeeper it was not easy to ascertain Greenwich time. By 1785 French and English clockmakers had evolved a chronometer with an accuracy of better than one second a day, employing special balance wheels and springs. Modern chronometers use a quartz crystal kept in oscillation at a constant frequency by electronic means. Since the advent of radio time-signals the need for expensive marine chronometers scarcely exists.

**Chubu** /'tʃuːbuː/ a mountainous region of central Japan on the island of Honshu; area 66,743 sq. km. (25,779 sq. miles); pop. (1990) 21,022,000; chief city, Nagoya. The highest section of the Japan Alps rises to 3,180 m. (10,433 ft.) at Yariga-take peak in northern Chubu. The region is divided into nine prefectures:

| Prefecture | Area (sq. km.) | Pop. (1990) | Capital |
| --- | --- | --- | --- |
| Aichi | 5,114 | 6,690,000 | Nagoya |
| Fukui | 4,188 | 824,000 | Fukui |
| Gifu | 10,596 | 2,067,000 | Gifu |
| Ishikawa | 4,196 | 1,165,000 | Kanazawa |
| Nagano | 13,585 | 2,157,000 | Nagano |
| Niigata | 12,577 | 2,475,000 | Niigata |
| Shizuoka | 7,772 | 3,671,000 | Shizuoka |
| Toyama | 4,252 | 1,120,000 | Toyama |
| Yamanashi | 4,463 | 853,000 | Kofu |

**Chubut** /tʃə'buːt/ **1.** a river that rises in the Andes of South America and flows eastwards across Argentina to meet the Atlantic Ocean near Rawson. **2.** a Patagonian province of south-central Argentina; area 224,686 sq. km. (86,785 sq. miles); pop. (1991) 356,600; capital, Rawson. Welsh settlers established towns such as Madryn and Trelew in the 1860s.

**Chudo** /'tʃuːtəʊ/, **Lake** (also **Lake Peipus** /'paɪpəs/, Estonian **Peipsi** /'pɑːpsiː/) a lake in eastern Estonia on the border with Russia. Its southern extension in Russia is Lake Pskov and its outlet is the Narva River which flows northwards to the Gulf of Finland.

**Chugoku** /tʃuː'gəʊkuː/ a region of Japan at the western tip of the island of Honshu; area 31,847 sq. km. (12,300 sq. miles); pop. (1990) 7,746,000; chief city, Hiroshima. The region is divided into five prefectures:

| Prefecture | Area (sq. km.) | Pop. (1990) | Capital |
| --- | --- | --- | --- |
| Hiroshima | 8,455 | 2,850,000 | Hiroshima |
| Okayama | 7,079 | 1,926,000 | Okayama |
| Shimane | 6,627 | 781,000 | Matsue |
| Tottori | 3,492 | 616,000 | Tottori |
| Yamaguchi | 6,095 | 1,573,000 | Yamaguchi |

**Chukchi Peninsula** /'tʃuːktʃɪ/ (Russian **Chukotskiy Poluostrov**) a peninsula at the north-eastern extremity of both Russia and the continent of Asia, forming an extension of the Anadyr mountain range which terminates in Cape Dezhnev. The peninsula lies astride the Arctic Circle. It is home to some 10,000 reindeer-herding Chukchi, a Paleo-Asiatic people related to the American Eskimo.

**Chukchi Sea** an arm of the Arctic Ocean lying between North America and Russia and to the north of the Bering Strait.

**Chukot** a district in north-east Siberia, Russia, comprising the Chukot Range and the Chukot Peninsula, and lying astride the Arctic Circle. Its chief port is Anadyr.

**Chula Vista** /ˌtʃuːlə 'vɪstə/ a city to the south of San Diego, in southern California, USA; pop. (1990) 135,163. It is a trading centre for citrus fruit and vegetables grown in the surrounding area.

**Chunchon** /tʃʊn'tʃɒn/ (also **Chuncheon**) the capital of Kangwon province north-east South Korea, on the Pukhan River; pop. (1990) 174,150.

**Chungking** see CHONQING.

**Churchill** **1.** a settlement at the mouth of the Churchill River, on the west shore of Hudson Bay, Manitoba, Canada; pop. (1981) 1,186. Established in 1718 as a Hudson's Bay trading post, it replaced an earlier settlement further up river. The present town grew up after the completion of the Hudson Bay rail terminal and harbour facility in 1931. **2.** a river rising in north-west Saskatchewan, Canada, and flowing 1,609 km. (1,012 miles) south-east, east, then north-east into Hudson Bay at Churchill. It was named after John Churchill, first Duke of Marlborough and was pioneered by Frobisher as a trade link with Montreal. **3.** the longest river in Labrador, Canada; rising in Ashuanipi Lake it flows 856 km. (539 miles) east to Lake Melville. Originally named after Sir Charles Hamilton, it was renamed in 1965 after Sir Winston Churchill.

**Churchill** /'tʃɜːtʃɪl/ **1.** a village in Oxfordshire, England, south-west of Chipping Norton. It was the birthplace of Warren Hastings (1732–1818) and the geologist William Smith (1769–1839). **2.** a village in Somerset, England, south-west of Bristol. It is associated with a branch of the Churchill family, ancestors of Sir Winston Churchill and the Dukes of Marlborough.

**Chuuk** /tʃʊk/ see TRUK.

**Chuvashia** /tʃuː'vɑːʃɪə/ (also **Chuvash Republic**) a republic in European Russia, in the valley of the River Volga; area 18,300 sq. km. (7,064 sq. miles); pop. (1990) 1,340,000; capital, Cheboksary. Annexed by Russia in the 16th c., it became an autonomous region in 1920 and was a Soviet autonomous republic from 1925 until 1991 when it became an autonomous republic of Russia. About 70 per cent of the population are Chuvash people of Bulgar descent. Railway-repair industries, engineering, the manufacture of textiles and chemicals, and the production of grain and fruit are important.

**Chuvash** *adj. & n.*

**Chuxiong** /ˌtʃʊʃiːˈɒŋ/ a city in Yunnan province, southern China, situated on a tributary of the Jinsha River west of Kunming; pop. (1986) 383,000.

**Chuzhou** /tʃʊˈdʒəʊ/ a city in Anhui province, eastern China, 50 km. (30 miles) north-west of Nanjing; pop. (1986) 370,000.

**Cicero** /ˈsɪsəˌrəʊ/ an industrial and residential city in Illinois, USA, 11 km. (7 miles) west of Chicago; pop. (1990) 67,400.

**cicerone** /ˌtʃɪtʃəˈrəʊnɪ/ a guide who gives information about antiquities, places of interest, etc. to sightseers.

**Cienfuegos** /sjen ˈfweɪɡɒs/ a port and naval base on the south coast of Cuba; pop. (est. 1987) 109,000. Tobacco, sugar, coffee, and citrus are the principal export crops. The city was founded in 1819 by French emigrants from Louisiana.

**Cilicia** /sɪˈlɪʃə/ the ancient name for the eastern half of the south coast of Asia Minor. Between 1080 and the occupation of the region by Ottoman Turks in the 15th c., Cilicia was ruled first as an independent Armenian principality then as a kingdom known as Little Armenia.

**Cilician** *adj.*

**Cilician Gates** /sɪˈlɪʃ(ə)n, saɪ-/ a mountain pass north of Adana in the Taurus Mountains of Cilicia in southern Turkey. It has for centuries formed a natural highway linking Anatolia with the Mediterranean coast.

**cima** /ˈsiːmə/ an Italian word for a mountain peak.

**Cimarron** /ˈsɪmərən/ a river of the USA that rises in north-east New Mexico and flows 1,123 km. (698 miles) across Kansas into Oklahoma where it joins the Arkansas River.

**Cimini Mountains** /ˈtʃiːmənɪ/ a range of hills in Latium, west-central Italy, east of Viterbo. Monte Cimino is the highest peak (1,053 m., 3,455 ft.).

**Cimmerian** /sɪˈmɪərɪən/ **1.** a member of an ancient nomadic people, the earliest-known inhabitants of the Crimea, who overran Asia Minor in the 7th c. BC. They overthrew Phrygia c. 676 BC, and terrorized Ionia, but were gradually destroyed by epidemics and in wars with Lydia and Assyria. The Kerch Strait linking the Azov and Black Seas was known in ancient times as the Cimmerian Bosphorus. **2.** in Greek legend, a member of a people who lived in perpetual mist and darkness, near the land of the dead.

**Cîmpulung** /ˌkəmpuˈluːŋ/ a resort town on the southern slopes of the Transylvanian Alps, central Romania; pop. (1983) 40,000. Founded in the 12th c. by German colonists, it became capital of Walachia a century later.

**Cincinnati** /ˌsɪnsɪˈnætɪ/ an industrial and commercial city in southern Ohio, USA, on the Ohio River; pop. (1990) 364,000. Founded near an Indian river-crossing in 1788–9, Cincinnati grew from three small frontier riverboat settlements (Columbia, North Bend, and Losantiville). After the opening of the Miami and Erie Canal in 1832 it became one of the largest cities in the US, being described by the poet Longfellow as the 'Queen City of the West'. It was the birthplace of William Howard Taft (1857–1930), 27th President of the USA. Its industries include machine tools, vehicles and aircraft engines, electronic and electrical equipment, and metal goods. It is also a cultural centre with the University of Cincinnati and several other institutions and museums.

**Cingalese** an archaic form of SINHALESE.

**Cinque Ports** /sɪŋk ˈpɔːts/ a group of medieval ports in south-east England (originally five: Dover, Hastings, Hythe, Romney, and Sandwich; Rye and Winchelsea were added later) formerly allowed various trading privileges in exchange for providing the bulk of England's navy. The origins of the association are unknown, but it existed long before its first real charter was granted by Edward I. Most of the old privileges were abolished in the 19th c. and the Wardenship of the Cinque Ports is now a purely honorary post.

**Cinqueterre** /tʃiːŋkwɪˈtɜːrə/ that part of the Mediterranean coast of north-west Italy lying between La Spezia and Levanto. It comprises the five villages of Corniglia, Manarola, Monterosso al Mare, Riomaggiore, and Vernazza.

**Cintra** See SINTRA.

**Cipango** /sɪˈpæŋɡəʊ/ (also **Zipango**) the medieval name for a legendary island east of Asia described by Marco Polo and generally considered to be Japan.

**Circassia** /sɜːˈkæsɪə/ a region of the north-west Caucasus, on the north-east shore of the Black Sea, inhabited by people who maintained their independence from the 15th c. until subjugated by Russia in the mid-19th c. The Adygey and Cherkess people are their descendants.

**Circassian** *adj. & n.*

**Cirebon** /sɪrəˈbɒn/ an industrial port on the north coast of western Java, Indonesia; pop. (1980) 224,000.

**Cirencester** /ˈsaɪərənˌsestə(r)/ a market town in Gloucestershire, England on the River Churn; pop. (1981) 14,000. As Corinium Dobunorum it was an important road junction and the second-largest town in Roman Britain. It has a major museum with many locally found Roman artefacts.

**cirque** /sɜːk/ (also **corrie** and **cwm**) a deep bowl-shaped hollow at the head of a valley or on a mountainside; formed during the Ice Age by high-level glaciers.

**cirrocumulus** /ˌsɪrəʊˈkjuːmjuːləs/ a form of usually high cloud consisting of small roundish fleecy clouds in contact with one another, known as 'mackerel sky'.

**cirrostratus** /ˌsɪrəʊˈstreɪtəs/ a thin usually high white cloud formation composed mainly of fine ice-crystals and producing halo phenomena.

**cirrus** /ˈsɪrəs/ a form of high altitude white wispy cloud.

**CIS** *abbr.* COMMONWEALTH OF INDEPENDENT STATES.

**cisalpine** /sɪsˈælpaɪn/ on the southern side of the Alps. The Cisalpine Republic was created by Napoleon in 1797 by uniting territory on either side of the River Po. With its capital at Milan, this territory formed part of the Kingdom of Italy created in 1805 but broken up ten years later in 1815.

**cisatlantic** /ˌsɪsətˈlæntɪk/ on one's own side of the Atlantic.

**Ciskei** /sɪsˈkaɪ/ a former tribal homeland of the Xhosa people in north-east Cape Province, South Africa, designated an independent republic in 1981 but now part of the Eastern Cape province.

**cislunar** /sɪsˈluːnə(r)/ between the earth and the moon.

**cispontine** /sɪsˈpɒntaɪn/ on the north side of the Thames in London.

**Cistercian** /sɪˈstɜːʃ(ə)n/ a religious order founded in 1098 at Cîteaux (Cistercium) near Dijon in France. Observing the Rule of St. Benedict, Cistercian houses spread throughout Europe in the 12th–13th c.

**Citlaltépetl** /ˈsiːtlælˈteɪpet(ə)l/ (also **Pico de Orizaba**) the highest peak in Mexico, in the east of the country, north of the city of Orizaba after which it is sometimes named. It rises to a height of 5,610 m. (18,405 ft.) and is an extinct volcano, inactive since 1687. Its Aztec name means 'star mountain'.

**Ciudad Bolivar** /sjuːˌdɑːd bɒˈliːvɑː(r)/ a city in south-east Venezuela, capital of the state of Bolivar, on the Orinoco River; pop. (1991) 225,850. Its name was formerly ANGOSTURA (= narrows) and was changed in 1846 to honour the country's liberator Simón Bolívar. It is an inland port and commercial centre of a wide region.

**Ciudad del Este** /sjuːˌdɑːd del ˈestɪ/ a port on the Paraná River, eastern Paraguay, capital of the department of Alto Paraná; pop. (1984) 110,000. Situated opposite Foz do Iguaçu in Brazil, it developed rapidly with the building of the nearby Itaipú Dam. It was known as Puerto Presidente Stroessner until 1989, the year in which a *coup* deposed the dictator who had ruled Paraguay for 34 years.

**Ciudad Guayana** /sjuːˌdɑːd geɪˈɑːnə/ an industrial city in eastern Venezuela, on the Orinoco River; pop. (1991) 542,710. It is the site of major steel and aluminium plants.

**Ciudad Madero** /sjuːˌdɑːd məˈdeɪrəʊ/ a city in the state of Tamaulipas in eastern Mexico, forming a northern suburb of Tampico; pop. (1990) 159,640.

**Ciudad Obregón** /sjuːˌdɑːd ɒbreɪˈgəʊn/ a city in the state of Sonora, north-west Mexico, situated in the valley of the Yaqui River; pop. (1990) 311,080. Until 1924 it was named Cajeme after a Yaqui Indian chief of the 1880s. The Alvaro Obregón Dam, 56 km. (35 miles) north-east on the Yaqui River, irrigates a large area of reclaimed land growing cotton, wheat, rice, corn, alfalfa, flax, and sesame.

**Ciudad Real** /sjuːˌdɑːd reɪˈɑːl/ **1.** a province in the Castilla-La Mancha region of central Spain; pop. (1991) 475,435; area 19,749 sq. km. (7,628 sq. miles); pop. (1991) 475,435. **2.** its capital on the La Mancha plain between the Guadiana and Jablón rivers; pop. (1991) 59,400. It is a market town with flour mills and brandy distilleries.

**Ciudad Victoria** /sjuːˌdɑːd vɪkˈtɔːrɪə/ the capital of the state of Tamaulipas in east-central Mexico; pop. (1990) 207,830. It is a major transportation centre in a mining and agricultural region and has a university founded in 1950. The city was named in 1825 after Guadalupe Victoria, first president of Mexico.

**Civitavecchia** /ˌtʃiːviˈtɑːˈvekjə/ (anc. **Trajani Portus** or **Centum Cellae**) a port on the coast of Latium, west-central Italy; pop. (1990) 51,240. Built by the Emperor Trajan as the chief port of Rome, it has a citadel completed by Michelangelo and an arsenal designed by Bernini. The writer Marie Stendhal (1783–1842) lived here as French consul for 20 years.

**Clackmannan** /klækˈmænən/ **1.** a local government area in central Scotland, formerly the smallest county (Clackmannanshire) in Scotland, and from 1975 to 1996 a district of Central Region; area 907 sq. km. (350 sq. miles); pop. (1991) 47,200; administrative centre, Alloa. **2.** a town in Clackmannan district on the River Devon, east of Alloa.

**Clactonian** /klækˈtəʊnɪən/ the lower palaeolithic industries represented by the flint implements found at Clacton in Essex, south-east England, dated c. 250,000–200,000 BC.

**Clapham** /ˈklæpəm/ a residential district in the London borough of Wandsworth, with a large common and major rail junction. William Wilberforce (1759–1833) lived in Clapham, his Evangelical party being known as the 'Clapham Sect'.

**Clare** /kleə(r)/ a county in the province of Munster in the Republic of Ireland, between the River Shannon and Galway Bay; area 3,188 sq. km, (1,231 sq. miles); pop. (1991) 90,800; capital, Ennis. The county is named after an Anglo-Norman family which settled here in the 13th c.

**Clarksville** a city in north-west Tennessee, USA, at the junction of the Cumberland and Red

Rivers; pop. (1990) 75,500. Founded in 1796 and named after General George Rogers Clark, Clarksville developed as a commercial centre trading in livestock, grain, and tobacco. Fort Campbell Military Reservation is the home of the US 101st Airborne Division.

**Clearwater** /'kli:rwɔ:t(ə)r/ a resort city in west Florida, USA, on the Gulf of Mexico; pop. (1990) 98,800.

**Cleethorpes** /'kli:θɔ:ps/ a resort town on the Humber estuary, adjacent to Grimsby in Humberside, north-east England; pop. (1991) 67,500.

**Cleopatra's Needle** the name given to two ancient obelisks erected at Heliopolis in the 15th c. BC by Thothmes III and later transported by the Roman Emperor Augustus to Alexandria c. 14 BC. One of the granite obelisks was removed to the Victoria Embankment, London, in 1878; the other was gifted to the USA in 1881 and erected in Central Park, New York.

**Clerkenwell** /'klɑ:kən,wel/ a district in the borough of Islington, London, England, that takes its name from a well near which clerks held performances of miracle plays in medieval times.

**Clermont-Ferrand** /'kleəmɔ̃fe'rɑ̃/ a city in the Puy-de-Dôme department, at the centre of the Massif Central, central France, capital of the Auvergne region; pop. (1990) 140,170. Agricultural trade and the manufacture of rubber goods are important industries. The philosopher Blaise Pascal was born here in 1623.

**Cleveland** /'kli:vlənd/ a county in north-east England, on the North Sea coast, between Durham and North Yorkshire; area 583 sq. km. (225 sq. miles); pop. (1991) 541,100; county town, Middlesborough. Industries include the manufacture of steel and chemicals. The county is divided into four districts:

| District | Area (sq. km.) | Pop. (1991) |
| --- | --- | --- |
| Hartlepool | 94 | 88,200 |
| Langbaurgh | 240 | 141,700 |
| Middlesborough | 54 | 141,100 |
| Stockton-on-Tees | 195 | 170,200 |

**Cleveland** /'kli:vlənd/ a major port and industrial city in north-east Ohio, USA, situated on the southern shore of Lake Erie; pop. (1990) 505,600. Founded by Moses Cleaveland in 1796, Ohio developed rapidly after the opening (in 1827) of the Ohio Canal linking Lake Erie with the Ohio River. The International Exposition Center is the world's largest exhibition centre. It is a leading iron and steel centre and has metal-manufacturing, oil-refining, chemical, vehicle, and electrical industries.

**Cleveland Heights** a city in north-east Ohio, USA, east of Cleveland; pop. (1990) 54,000.

**Cleves** /kli:vz/ (German **Kleve**) a town in North Rhine-Westphalia, western Germany, between the Rhine and the Dutch frontier. It was the birthplace of Anne of Cleves, fourth wife of Henry VIII of England.

**Clifden** /'klɪfd(ə)n/ a village in County Galway, the Republic of Ireland, situated in the Connemara district on Arbear Bay. Sir John Alcock and Sir Arthur Whitten Brown landed near the village after their first crossing of the Atlantic by air in 1919.

**Clifton** /'klɪftən/ a suspension bridge over the Avon Gorge, Bristol, south-west England.

**Clifton** a city in eastern New Jersey, USA, adjacent to the city of Passaic; pop. (1990) 71,700.

**Clipperton Island** /'klɪpɔ:tən/ an uninhabited French island in the eastern Pacific, 1,065 km. (670 miles) south-west of Mexico, discovered in the 18th c. by an English pirate, John Clipperton, but claimed by France in 1858 and Mexico in 1897. Valued for its phosphates, the island was awarded to France in 1930 and is administered from French Polynesia.

**Cloisters** /'klɔɪstə(r)z/, **the** a collection of European medieval buildings transported to the USA and assembled in Fort Tryon Park in Manhattan, New York City. The Cloisters form a branch of the Metropolitan Museum of Art.

**Clonakilty** /klɒnə'kɪltɪ/ a town at the head of Clonakilty Bay, on the south coast of County Cork in the Republic of Ireland; pop. (1991) 2,400. Founded by the Earl of Cork in 1614, it developed as a linen-weaving town and agricultural centre. The Irish politician Michael Collins (1890–1922) spent his boyhood days at Sam's Cross to the west of the town.

**Cloncurry** /klɒn'kʌrɪ/ a mining town and railhead in north Queensland, Australia, 124 km. (78 miles) east of Mount Isa; pop. (1986) 2,300. In 1916 it was the largest source of copper in Australia, but when the price of copper fell after World War I it reverted to a cattle-farming economy and became a base for the Royal Flying Doctor Service. Since 1974 it has been the source of an exceptionally rare type of 22-carat gold.

**Clonfert** /'klɒnfer/ an ancient ecclesiastical settlement north-west of Banagher in County Galway, the Republic of Ireland. St. Brendan the Navigator (484–577) founded a monastery here in 558–64.

**Clonmacnoise** /klɒnmək'nɔɪz/ an ancient ecclesiastical centre on the River Shannon, south of Athlone in County Offaly, the Republic of Ireland. A monastery founded here in AD 547 by St. Ciaran became one of Ireland's leading seats of learning.

**Clonmel** /klɒn'mel/ the county town of Tipperary (South Riding) in the Republic of Ireland, on the River Suir; pop. (1991) 14,500.

**Clouds Hill** a village in Dorset, southern England, associated with the soldier and Arabic scholar T. E. Lawrence (1888–1935) who first rented a cottage here in 1923 and later retired to live in the village shortly before his death in 1935.

**Clovelly** /kləˈvelɪ/ a picturesque cliff village on the coast of Devon, south-west England. Its single street descends 122 m. (400 ft.) to a tiny quay. The novelist Charles Kingsley lived here as a boy.

**Clovis** /ˈkləʊvɪs/ a city north-east of Fresno in the San Joaquin valley, central California, USA; pop. (1990) 50,300.

**Club of Rome** a 100-member international association of environmental scientists and policy-makers founded by Aurelio Peccei in 1968 for the purpose of fostering a better understanding of the problems faced by the developing and indus-trialized world.

**Cluj-Napoca** /kluːʒ ˈnæpəkə/ (Hungarian **Kolozsvár** /ˈkɒlɒʒˌvaː(r)/) an industrial city in west-central Romania, at the foot of the eastern slopes of the Western Carpathians; pop. (1989) 317,910. Founded in the 12th c. by German colonists who called it Klausenberg, Cluj-Napoca became a noted centre of learning and cultural cap-ital of Transylvania. The city was built on the site of the former Dacian town of Napoca which dates from the 2nd c. BC. The modern city has engineer-ing, chemical, and timber industries. It was the birthplace in 1440 of Matthias I Corvinus who be-came king of Hungary and it is the home of a uni-versity founded in 1872.

**Cluny** /ˈkluːnɪ/ a town in the department of Saône-et-Loire in the Burgundy region of eastern France; pop. (1982) 4,700. A powerful monastery was founded here in 910 by the Duke of Aquitaine with the object of returning to the strict Benedict-ine rule. Other houses followed suit, and the order became centralized and influential in the 11th–12th c.
**Clunaic** *adj. & n.*

**Clutha** /ˈkluːθə/ a river at the southern end of South Island, New Zealand. It is the second-longest river (338 km., 213 miles) in New Zealand but the largest in terms of annual water discharge (650 cu. m./sec). Taking its name from an ancient form of the River Clyde in Scotland, the Clutha is a gold-bearing river.

**Clwyd** /ˈkluːɪd/ a county in north-east Wales; area 2,428 sq. km. (937 sq. miles); pop. (1991) 401,500; county town, Mold. Created in 1974, the county is divided into six districts:

| District | Area (sq. km.) | Pop. (1991) |
| --- | --- | --- |
| Alyn and Deeside | 154 | 71,700 |
| Colwyn | 552 | 54,600 |
| Delyn | 281 | 66,200 |
| Glyndwr | 967 | 41,500 |
| Rhuddlan | 108 | 54,000 |
| Wrexham Maelor | 367 | 113,600 |

**Clyde** /klaɪd/ a river in west-central Scotland that rises in the Southern Uplands and flows north

and west for 170 km. (106 miles) through Glasgow to the Firth of Clyde. The district of Clydebank on the north side of the river developed around the shipbuilding industry.

**Clydesdale** /ˈklaɪdzdeɪl/ a district of central Scotland that gives its name to a breed of draught horse and a breed of terrier dog; pop. (1991) 57,000.

**CN Tower** the tallest free-standing man-made structure in the world, built during 1973–6 in Toronto, Canada. Its height to the top of the steel communication mast is 553 m. (1,814 ft.).

**CO** *abbr.* US Colorado (in official postal use.)

**Coahuila** /ˌkəʊʊəˈwiːlə/ a state of northern Mexico, to the south of the Rio Grande and dominated by the Sierra Madre Oriental; area 149,982 sq. km. (57,930 sq. miles); pop. (1990) 1,971,340; capital, Saltillo. Cotton, grain, fruit, cattle, and coal are important products.

**Coalport** /ˈkəʊlpɔːt/ a town in Shropshire, west-central England, 24 km. (15 miles) south-east of Shrewsbury, that gives its name to a type of china and porcelain produced there until 1926.

**Coast Mountains** /kəʊst/ a mountain range on the Pacific coast of north-west America extend-ing northwards from the Cascade Range through British Columbia and into Alaska. It rises to 4,042 m. (13,261 ft.) at Mount Waddington in British Columbia.

**Coast Ranges** a series of mountain ranges running parallel to the Pacific coast of North America from Alaska to Baja California in Mexico.

**Coatbridge** /kəʊtˈbrɪdʒ/ a town in central Scotland east of Glasgow, from 1975 to 1996 the administrative headquarters of Monklands dis-trict, Strathclyde; pop. (1981) 51,000.

**Coatzacoalcos** /ˌkwætzəˈkwɑːlkəs/ (formerly **Puerte Mexico**) an oil port in the state of Veracruz, Mexico, on the Gulf of Campeche; pop. (1990) 232,310.

**Cobán** /kəʊˈbɑːn/ the capital of the department of Alta Verapaz in the highlands of central Guatemala; pop. (1989) 120,000. It is situated at the centre of tea, coffee, and vanilla plantations.

**Cóbh** /kəʊv/ a seaport and yachting centre in County Cork, the Republic of Ireland, on the south shore of Great Island in Cork Harbour; pop. (1991) 6,200. Formerly known as Cove of Cork, it was named Queenstown from 1849 to 1922. Accessible to Atlantic liners, it is the headquarters of the Royal Cork Yacht Club, the oldest yacht club in the world.

**Coblenz** /kəˈblents/ (German **Koblenz**) a city at the junction of the Mosel and Rhine rivers, in the Rhineland-Palatinate, western Germany; pop. (1991) 109,050. It is an important wine-trading centre.

**Coburg** /'kəʊbɜːg/ a city in the state of Bavaria, southern Germany, on the Itz River; pop. (1991) 44,690. It alternated with Gotha as the capital of Saxe-Coburg-Gotha from 1826 to 1918 and its castle (Veste Coburg) is one of the largest in Germany. Coburg has associations with Martin Luther, the poet Friedrich Rückert, and the novelist Jean Paul. It has light industries including ceramics and toys.

**Cocanada** the former name of KAKINADA.

**Cochabamba** /ˌkɒtʃə'bæmbə/ the third-largest city in Bolivia, situated at the centre of a rich agricultural region producing grain and fruit, at an altitude of 2,500 m. (8,200 ft.); pop. (1990) 413,250. Founded in 1542, it is capital of a department of the same name. It has several museums including one specializing in pre-Columbian arts. It is a manufacturing centre with vehicle-assembly and food-processing plants, as well as an oil refinery.

**Cochin** /'kəʊtʃɪn/ (also **Kochi**) a seaport and naval base on the Malabar coast of south-west India, in the state of Kerala; pop. (1991) 564,000. The first European settlement was established at Fort Cochin in 1502 by the Portuguese navigator Vasco da Gama who is buried here. Oil-refining, shipbuilding, and trade in agricultural products are important.

**Cochin-China** /ˌkəʊtʃɪn'tʃaɪnə/ the former name for the southern region of what is now Vietnam. Part of French Indo-China from 1862, it became a French overseas territory in 1946 before merging officially with Vietnam in 1949. It gives its name to a breed of Asian fowl with feathery legs.

**Cochinos Bay** See BAY OF PIGS.

**Cockaigne, Land of** a mythical land of idle pleasure described in medieval English folklore.

**Cockburnspath** /ˌkəʊbɜːnz'pɑː.θ/ a village on the North Sea coast of Borders Region, Scotland, 12 km. (8 miles) south-east of Dunbar. It was the birthplace in 1732 of John Broadwood, founder of the famous firm of piano makers.

**Cockermouth** /'kɒkə(r)maʊθ/ a market town at the junction of the Cocker and Derwent rivers, Cumbria, north-west England; pop. (1981) 7,000. It was the birthplace of William and Dorothy Wordsworth.

**Cockscomb Range** /'kɒkskəʊm/ an eastern outlier of the Maya Mountains of Belize, Central America, rising to 1,120 m. (3,674 ft.) at Victoria Peak. The Cockscomb Basin Wildlife Sanctuary, designated in 1986, was the world's first jaguar reserve.

**Coco** /'kəʊkəʊ/ a river that rises in south-west Honduras and flows 720 km. (450 miles) along the Honduras–Nicaragua frontier to meet the Caribbean at Cape Gracias à Dios.

**Cocos Island** /'kəʊkəs/ an uninhabited island in the Pacific Ocean between Central America and the Galapagos Islands. It is the only Pacific island belonging to Costa Rica.

**Cocos Islands** /'kəʊkəs/ (also **Keeling Islands** /'kiːlɪŋ/) a group of 27 small coral islands in the Indian Ocean, administered as an external territory of Australia since 1955; area 14 sq. km. (9 sq. miles); pop. (1992) 586. The islands were discovered in 1609 by Captain William Keeling of the East India Company. Its largely Malay population voted to have closer integration with Australia in 1984 and in 1992 became subject to the laws of Western Australia. Copra is the chief product.

**Codrington** /'kɒdrɪŋtən/ the only settlement on the island of Barbuda in the eastern Caribbean; pop. (est. 1986) 1,200. It takes its name from the Codrington family who maintained the island as a private estate from 1674 to 1870, paying rent to the British Crown of 'one fat sheep, if demanded'. Nearby is Codrington lagoon which is noted for its large colony of frigate birds.

**Coff's Harbour** /kɒfs/ a resort town in New South Wales, south-east Australia, situated on the Holiday Coast 580 km. (365 miles) north of Sydney; pop. (1991) 20,325.

**Cognac** /'kɒnjæk/ a city in the department of Charente, western France, on the River Charente, noted for the production of high-quality brandy since the 17th c.; pop. (1982) 23,000. François I of France was born here in 1494.

**Coihaique** /kɔː'haɪkeɪ/ a military and administrative centre in southern Chile, capital of the Aisén region; pop. (1982) 31,170. It is the largest town in Chile south of Puerto Montt.

**Coimbatore** /ˌkəʊɪmbə'tɔː(r)/ a city in the state of Tamil Nadu, southern India, at the foot of the Nilgiri Mts.; pop. (1991) 853,000. Tea and cotton are traded.

**Coimbra** /kəʊ'ɪmbrə/ (Latin **Conimbriga**) a university city in central Portugal, on the River Mondego; pop. (1991) 96,140. The university, which was founded in Lisbon in 1290, was transferred to Coimbra in 1537. It has a 12th-c. cathedral and is a market centre.

**col** /kɒl/ a ridge or high pass between two higher summits.

**Colca Canyon** /'kɒlkə/ (Spanish **El Cañón de Colca**) a deep gorge in the Peruvian Andes north of Arequipa. With sides rising to a height of 4,360 m. (14,300 ft.), it is the deepest canyon in the world.

**Colchester** /'kəʊltʃest(ə)r/ a market town for grain and cattle in Essex, south-east England, on the Colne River; pop. (1981) 82,000. Claiming to be the oldest town in England, it retains well-preserved Roman walls and a Norman castle. The University of Essex was established here in 1964. It has engineering and food-processing industries.

**Colchis** /'kɒlkɪs/ (Greek **Kolkhis**) the ancient Greek name for the region south of the Caucasus mountains at the eastern end of the Black Sea, the goal of Jason's expedition for the Golden Fleece.

**cold front** the boundary between warm air and an advancing wedge of cold air.

**Colditz** /'kəʊldɪts/ a town in the state of Saxony, east Germany, south-east of Leipzig, noted for its castle which was used as a top-security camp for Allied prisoners in World War II.

**Coleraine** /kəʊl'reɪn/ a town in County Derry, Northern Ireland, on the River Brann; pop. (1981) 16,000. The New University of Ulster established here in 1965 amalgamated with Ulster Polytechnic in 1984 to form the University of Ulster.

**Colima** /kɒ'liːmə/ **1.** a state of south-west Mexico; area 5,191 sq. km. (2,005 sq. miles); pop. (1990) 424,660. **2.** its capital, 45 km. (28 miles) from the Pacific coast near the foot of the twin volcanic peaks of **Nevado de Colima** (4,330 m., 14,206 ft.) and **Fuego de Colima** (3,960 m., 12,992 ft.); pop. (est. 1984) 58,000. Designated in 1527 by Cortés to be the third city of New Spain, Colima was named in honour of King Coliman, a former Nahua Indian ruler of the area.

**Coll** /kɒl/ an island in the Inner Hebrides off the west coast of Scotland, north-east of Tiree. The chief settlement is Arinagour and the highest point is Ben Hogh (103 m., 338 ft.). It is linked by boat with Oban.

**College Station** an industrial city in east-central Texas, USA, south of Bryan; pop. (1990) 52,450. Situated in a rich farming region, it is a centre for space research and the wholesale-retail trade.

**Coloane** the southernmost of the islands of Macau; area 5 sq. km. (2 sq. miles).

**Cologne** /kə'ləʊn/ (German **Köln** /kɜːln/) an industrial and commercial city and transportation centre in the German state of North Rhine-Westphalia, on the west bank of the Rhine; pop. (1991) 956,690. Founded by the Romans, Cologne rose to prominence through the see established there, the Archbishop of Cologne becoming one of the most powerful German secular princes in the Middle Ages. At that time it was famous for the shrine of the Wise Men of the East, the 'Three Kings of Cologne'. The twin spires of its Gothic cathedral (which took 600 years to build) rise to 157 m. (515 feet). Its university was founded in 1388. Cologne is a river port with heavy industries including iron and steel, machinery, and chemicals.

**Colombes** /kə'lɔ̃mb/ an industrial suburb of north-west Paris, in the department of Hauts-de-Seine; pop. (1990) 79,060. It has oil refineries, foundries, and an international sports stadium.

**Colombia** /kə'lɒmbɪə/ official name **The Republic of Colombia** a country in the extreme north-west of South America, having a coastline on both the Atlantic and Pacific Ocean; area 1,140,105 sq. km. (440,365 sq. miles); pop. (1985)

27,867,300; official language, Spanish; capital, Bogotá. The largest cities are Bogotá, Medellín, Cali, Barranquilla, Bucaramanga, and Cartagena. The Pacific coastal plain is humid and swampy, and most of the population is concentrated in the temperate valleys of the high Andes which run north–south in three ranges that merge on the border with Ecuador. To the east a low jungle-covered plain is drained by tributaries of the Amazon and Orinoco. The principal rivers flowing northwards through the Andes to the Caribbean are the Cauca and Magdalena. Islands in the Caribbean include San Andrés, Providencia, San Bernardo, Islas del Rosario, and Isla Fuerte; and islands in the Pacific include Malpelo, Gorgona, and Gorgonilla. The economy is mainly agricultural, coffee being the chief export. Mineral resources are rich and include gold, silver, platinum (one of the world's richest deposits), emeralds, and salt, as well as oil, coal, and natural gas. Inhabited by the Chibcha and other Indian peoples, Colombia was conquered by the Spanish in the early 16th c., and under Spanish rule the capital Bogotá developed such a reputation for intellectual and social life as to be called the 'Athens of South America'. Like the rest of Spain's South American empire, Colombia achieved independence in the early 19th c., although the resulting Republic of Great Colombia lasted only until 1830, when first Venezuela and then Ecuador broke away to become independent states in their own right. The remaining state was known as New Granada, changing its name to Colombia in 1863. The country was stricken with civil war between 1949 and 1968, and since then there has been open conflict between the government and drug traffickers who monopolize the world trade in narcotics. With a constitution dating from 1886 Colombia is the second-oldest democracy in the western hemisphere. The country is governed by a bicameral Senate comprising an Upper House of Congress and a House of Representatives.
**Colombian** adj. & n.

Colombia is divided into 23 departments, 4 intendencies and 5 territories:

| Department | Area (sq. km.) | Pop. (1985) | Capital |
|---|---|---|---|
| Antioquia | 63,612 | 3,999,100 | Medellín |
| Atlántico | 3,388 | 1,428,600 | Barranquilla |
| Bolívar | 25,978 | 1,197,600 | Cartagena |
| Boyacá | 23,189 | 1,097,600 | Tunja |
| Caldas | 7,888 | 838,100 | Manizales |
| Caquetá | 88,965 | 214,500 | Florencia |
| Cauca | 29,308 | 795,800 | Popayán |
| César, El | 22,905 | 584,600 | Valledupar |

| | | | |
|---|---|---|---|
| Chocó | 46,530 | 242,800 | Quibdó |
| Córdoba | 25,020 | 913,600 | Montería |
| Cundinamarca | 22,478 | 1,382,400 | Bogotá |
| Guajira, La | 20,848 | 255,300 | Riohacha |
| Huila | 19,890 | 647,800 | Neiva |
| Magdalena | 23,188 | 769,100 | Santa Marta |
| Meta | 85,635 | 412,300 | Villavicencio |
| Nariño | 33,268 | 1,019,100 | Pasto |
| Norte de Santander | 21,658 | 883,900 | Cúcuta |
| Quindío | 1,845 | 377,900 | Armenia |
| Risaralda | 4,140 | 625,500 | Pereira |
| Santander | 30,537 | 1,438,200 | Bucaramanga |
| Sucre | 10,917 | 529,100 | Sincelejo |
| Tolima | 23,562 | 1,051,900 | Ibagué |
| Valle del Cauca | 22,140 | 2,847,100 | Calí |

| Intendency | Area (sq. km.) | Pop. (1985) | Capital |
|---|---|---|---|
| Arauca | 23,818 | 70,100 | Arauca |
| Casanare | 44,640 | 110,300 | El Yopal |
| Putumayo | 24,885 | 119,800 | Mocoa |
| San Andrés & Providencia | 44 | 35,900 | San Andrés |

| Territory | Area (sq. km.) | Pop. (1985) | Capital |
|---|---|---|---|
| Amazonas | 109,665 | 30,300 | Leticia |
| Guainía | 72,238 | 9,200 | Obando |
| Guaviare | 53,460 | 35,300 | San José del Guaviare |
| Vaupés | 54,135 | 18,900 | Mitú |
| Vichada | 100,242 | 13,800 | Puerto Carreño |

**Colombo** /kə'lʌmbəʊ/ the capital city and chief port of Sri Lanka; pop. (1990) 615,000. The government of the country has been based in the outer suburb of Sri-Jayawardenapura since 1983. Settled by the Portuguese and then the Dutch, the British took control in 1796. It was the location in 1950 of a Commonwealth conference that devised a plan for economic assistance of countries in Asia known as the Colombo Plan. The city is a mixture of old colonial buildings, modern blocks, and shanty towns. It has three universities, an outstanding zoological gardens, temples, bazaars, and markets. It has many light and handicraft-based industries such as gem-cutting.

**Colón** /kɒ'lɒn/ the chief port and a commercial centre of Panama, at the Caribbean end of the Panama Canal; pop.(1990) 140,900. Founded in 1850, it was originally named Aspinwall after the railway builder William Aspinwall. Its present name (since 1903) is the Spanish form of 'Columbus'; that of the neighbouring port Cristóbal is Spanish for 'Christopher'. It is the second-largest city in Panama and capital of a department of the same name, and has been a free-trade zone since 1953.

**Colón, Archipélago de** the official Chilean name for the GALAPAGOS ISLANDS.

**Colonia** /kə'ləʊnjə/ (fully **Colonia del Sacramento**) a resort city on the River Plate, southern Uruguay, at the mouth of the Uruguay River opposite Buenos Aires; pop. (1985) 19,000. The city, which is capital of the department of Colonia, was founded by Portuguese settlers from Brazil in 1680.

**colony** /'kɒlənɪ/ a group of settlers in a new country (whether or not already inhabited) fully or partly subject to the mother country.

**Colorado** /ˌkɒlə'rɑːdəʊ/ a state in central USA, named from the great Colorado River which rises there and flows into the Gulf of California; area 269,595 sq. km. (104,091 sq. miles); pop. (1990) 3,294,400; capital, Denver. The largest cities are Denver, Colorado Springs, Boulder, and Fort Collins. Colorado is also known as the Centennial State. Part of it was acquired by the Louisiana Purchase in 1803 and the rest ceded by Mexico in 1848. It was organized as a territory in 1861 and became the 38th state in 1876. Traversed north-south by the Rocky Mountains, there are more than 1,000 peaks over 3,048 m. (10,000 ft.) high. Tourism, advanced technology, defence industries, gold mining, livestock, and grain production are important. The principal tourist attractions are the Rocky Mountain National Park, Mesa Verde National Park, and the Great Sand Dunes and Dinosaur National Monuments. The state is divided into 63 counties:

| County | Area (sq. km.) | Pop. (1990) | County Seat |
|---|---|---|---|
| Adams | 3,211 | 265,040 | Brighton |
| Alamosa | 1,869 | 13,620 | Alamosa |
| Arapahoe | 2,080 | 391,510 | Littleton |
| Archuleta | 3,518 | 5,345 | Pagosa Springs |
| Baca | 6,640 | 4,560 | Springfield |
| Bent | 3,944 | 5,050 | Las Animas |
| Boulder | 1,929 | 225,340 | Boulder |
| Chaffee | 2,621 | 12,680 | Salida |
| Cheyenne | 4,636 | 2,400 | Cheyenne Wells |
| Clear Creek | 1,030 | 7,620 | Georgetown |
| Conejos | 3,338 | 7,450 | Conejos |
| Costilla | 3,190 | 3,190 | San Luis |
| Crowley | 2,054 | 3,950 | Ordway |
| Custer | 1,924 | 1,930 | Westcliffe |
| Delta | 2,967 | 20,980 | Delta |
| Denver | 288 | 467,610 | Denver |
| Dolores | 2,766 | 1,500 | Dove Creek |
| Douglas | 2,187 | 60,390 | Castle Rock |
| Eagle | 4,394 | 21,930 | Eagle |
| Elbert | 4,813 | 9,650 | Kiowa |
| El Paso | 5,535 | 397,010 | Colorado Springs |
| Fremont | 3,999 | 32,270 | Canon City |
| Garfield | 7,675 | 29,970 | Glenwood Springs |
| Gilpin | 387 | 3,070 | Central City |
| Grand | 4,820 | 7,970 | Hot Sulphur Springs |
| Gunnison | 8,419 | 10,270 | Gunnison |
| Hinsdale | 2,899 | 467 | Lake City |
| Huerfano | 4,118 | 6,010 | Walsenburg |
| Jackson | 4,196 | 1,605 | Walden |
| Jefferson | 1,997 | 438,430 | Golden |
| Kiowa | 4,571 | 1,690 | Eads |
| Kit Carson | 5,616 | 7,140 | Burlington |

(cont.)

| County | Area (sq. km.) | Pop. (1990) | County Seat |
|---|---|---|---|
| Lake | 985 | 6,010 | Leadville |
| La Plata | 4,399 | 32,280 | Durango |
| Larimer | 6,770 | 186,140 | Fort Collins |
| Las Animas | 12,405 | 13,765 | Trinidad |
| Lincoln | 6,724 | 4,530 | Hugo |
| Logan | 4,727 | 17,570 | Sterling |
| Mesa | 8,603 | 93,145 | Grand Junction |
| Mineral | 2,280 | 558 | Creede |
| Moffat | 12,303 | 11,360 | Craig |
| Montezuma | 5,299 | 18,670 | Cortez |
| Montrose | 5,824 | 24,420 | Montrose |
| Morgan | 3,318 | 21,940 | Fort Morgan |
| Otero | 3,242 | 20,185 | LaJunta |
| Ouray | 1,409 | 2,295 | Ouray |
| Park | 5,699 | 7,170 | Fairplay |
| Philips | 1,789 | 4,190 | Holyoke |
| Pitkin | 2,517 | 12,660 | Aspen |
| Prowers | 4,235 | 13,350 | Lamar |
| Pueblo | 6,180 | 123,050 | Pueblo |
| Rio Blanco | 8,377 | 5,970 | Meeker |
| Rio Grande | 2,374 | 10,770 | Del Norte |
| Routt | 6,154 | 14,090 | Steamboat Springs |
| Saguache | 8,234 | 4,620 | Saguache |
| San Juan | 1,009 | 745 | Silverton |
| San Miguel | 3,346 | 3,650 | Telluride |
| Sedgwick | 1,404 | 2,690 | Julesburg |
| Summit | 1,578 | 12,880 | Breckenridge |
| Teller | 1,453 | 12,470 | Cripple Creek |
| Washington | 6,552 | 4,810 | Akron |
| Weld | 10,374 | 131,820 | Greeley |
| Yuma | 6,149 | 8,950 | Wray |

**Colorado** a river that rises in the Andes of South America and flows 860 km. (540 miles) south-eastwards across Argentina to meet the Atlantic Ocean south of Bahía Blanca.

**Colorado 1.** a river that rises in the Rocky Mountains of north Colorado, USA, and flows 2,333 km. (1,450 miles) south-west through the Grand Canyon and on into Mexico before entering the Gulf of California. **2.** a river that rises in north-west Texas, USA, and flows 1,438 km. (894 miles) south-eastwards to meet the Gulf of Mexico between Galveston and Corpus Christi.

**Colorado depressions** storms that form on the Atlantic Polar Front over the plains to the west of the Mississippi, USA, and travel north-eastwards into Ontario and Quebec in Canada.

**Colorado Springs** a resort city in central Colorado, USA, at the foot of Pikes Peak; pop. (1990) 281,140. Noted for its mineral springs, it was originally founded in 1859 as a gold-mining settlement known as El Dorado.

**Colosseum** /ˌkɒlə'siːəm/ the medieval name given to the *Amphitheatre Flavium*, a vast amphitheatre in Rome begun by Vespasian *c.*AD 75 and continued and completed by Titus and Domitian. It was capable of holding 50,000 people, with seating in three tiers and standing-room above; an

elaborate system of staircases served all parts. The arena, floored with timber and surrounded by a fence, was the scene of gladiatorial combats, fights between men and beasts, and large-scale mock battles.

**Colossae** /kə'lɒsaɪ/ an ancient city of Asia Minor in south-west Phrygia in what is now western Turkey. It was the seat of an early Christian Church to which St. Paul wrote the *Epistle to the Colossians*.

**Colossus of Rhodes** a huge bronze statue of the sun-god Helios, one of the Seven Wonders of the World, said by Pliny to have been over 30.5 m. (100 ft.) high. Built *c.*292–280 BC, it commemorated the raising of the siege of Rhodes in 305–304 BC, and stood beside the harbour entrance at Rhodes for about 50 years but was destroyed in an earthquake in 224 BC.

**Columbia** /kə'lʌmbɪə/ a poetic name for America.

**Columbia** the capital of South Carolina, USA, at the junction of the Broad and Saluda rivers which form the River Congaree; pop. (1990) 98,000. Founded in 1786, the city was reduced to ashes in 1865 by General William T. Sherman. It is the home of the University of South Carolina (1801) and the Fort Jackson US Army training centre.

**Columbia, District of** See DISTRICT OF COLUMBIA.

**Columbia** a river rising in Columbia Lake in the Rocky Mountains of south-east British Columbia. It flows 2,000 km. (1,258 miles) north-west then south into the USA before turning west along the Washington–Oregon frontier, entering the Pacific Ocean south-west of Tacoma. It flows a distance of 801 km. (504 miles) within Canada.

**Columbus** /kə'lʌmbəs/ **1.** an industrial city in west Georgia, USA, at the head of navigation on the Chattahoochee River; pop. (1990) 179,300. Originally a Creek Indian settlement, it was a Confederate supply-town during the American Civil War, later developing in association with the cotton and iron industries. **2.** the state capital of Ohio, USA, at the junction of the Scioto and Olentangy rivers; pop. (1990) 632,900. Founded in 1812, the growth of Columbus was stimulated first by stagecoach travel and then by the arrival of the railroad in 1850. It is the home of Ohio State University (1870). Printing, publishing, food-processing and the manufacture of transportation equipment, chemicals, and machinery are the chief industries.

**Comanche** /kə'mæntʃɪ/ a North American Uto-Aztecan Indian people of the plains and prairies of Texas and Oklahoma. An offshoot of the Shoshone, they migrated to the plains from the Rocky Mountains to hunt buffalo. Their name is derived from the Spanish *camino ancho* (= wide trail).

**Colwyn Bay** /'kɒlwɪn/ a resort town on the coast of Clwyd, north Wales; pop. (1981) 27,700. It is often referred to as the 'garden resort of Wales'.

**Coma Pedrosa** /'kəʊmə peɪ'drəʊzə/ the highest peak in Andorra, rising to 2,946 m. (9,665 ft.) in the east-central Pyrenees.

**Comayagua** /ˌkəʊmə'jɑ:gwə/ a town in west-central Honduras, capital of the department of Comayagua; pop. (1988) 32,900. A former Conservative stronghold in the years following independence from Spain in 1821, it was capital of Honduras on several occasions before Tegucigalpa became the permanent capital. It is situated in a mining and agricultural region.

**Comecon** /'kɒmɪˌkɒn/ *abbr. C*ouncil for *M*utual *Econ*omic Assistance; the English name for a former economic organization of Soviet-bloc countries, that operated between 1949 and 1991 and was analagous to the European Economic Community. Its headquarters were in Moscow.

**Comédie Française** /'kɒmeɪdi: frɑ̃'seɪz/ the French national theatre (used for both comedy and tragedy), in Paris, founded in 1680 by Louis XIV and reconstituted by Napoleon in 1803. It is organized as a co-operative society in which each actor holds a share or part-share.

**Comilla** /ku:'mɪlə/ the capital city of Comilla region, east Bangladesh, 115 km. (72 miles) south-east of Dacca; pop. (1991) 164,510. It is a commercial centre producing pharmaceuticals. The Academy for Rural Development is based here.

**Comino** /kɒ'mi:nəʊ/ the smallest of the three main islands of Malta, lying between Malta and Gozo; area 2.7 sq. km. (1 sq. mile).

**Commonwealth, the** (in full **The Commonwealth of Nations**) a voluntary association of 48 independent sovereign states consisting of the UK together with states and dependencies that were previously part of the British Empire. The recognition of full independent status within the former British Commonwealth was first recognized with the passage by the British Parliament of the Statute of Westminster in 1931. In 1971 its principles were spelt out in the Singapore Declaration which established the role of the Commonwealth in promoting international understanding and world peace.

**Commonwealth of Independent States** *abbr.* **CIS** a confederation of independent states, formerly among the constituent republics of the Soviet Union, established in 1991 following a summit in the Belorussian city of Brest at which the USSR was dissolved. The 12 member-states are Armenia, Azerbaijan, Belorussia (Belarus), Georgia, Kazakhstan, Kyrgyzstan, Moldova (Moldavia), Russia, Tajikistan, Turkmenistan, Ukraine, and Uzbekistan. The administrative headquarters of the CIS is in the Belorussian city of Minsk.

**Communism Peak** (Russian **Pik Kommunizma** /kɑ:mu:'ni:zmə/) a mountain rising to 7,495 m. (24,590 ft.) in the Pamirs of south-east Tajikistan. Known as Mt. Garmo until 1933 and Stalin Peak until 1962, it was the highest mountain in the former Soviet Union.

**Como** /'kəʊməʊ/, **Lake** a lake in the foothills of the Bernese Alps in Lombardy province north Italy, formed by a natural widening of the River Adda. The medieval resort town of Como lies on its south-west shore.

**Comoe National Park** an area of savanna grassland and forest watered by the Comoe River in north-east Ivory Coast, designated a national park in 1968. The park supports populations of elephant, leopard, buck, and baboon.

**Comodoro Rivadavia** /'kəʊmə'dɒ:rəʊ ˌri:və'dɑ:vɪə/ the largest seaport in Patagonia and chief centre of oil production in Argentina, situated on the Atlantic coast of Chubut province; pop. (1991) 124,000.

**Comoros** /kɒ'mɔ:rəʊz/ official name **The Federal Islamic Republic of the Comoros** a country consisting of a group of three volcanic islands (Grande Comoro, Anjouan, and Mohéli) in the Indian Ocean north-west of Madagascar; area 1,787 sq. km. (690 sq. miles); pop. (est. 1991) 500,000; official languages, French and Arabic; capital, Moroni. The islands have a tropical marine climate and a plantation-based economy that produces copra, vanilla (the world's second largest producer), cloves, and the perfume essence ylang-ylang (the world's largest producer) for export. Principal food crops include cassava, bananas, and coconuts. Dominated for centuries by Arabs, the islands were visited by the English at the end of the 16th c. but later came under French protection in 1886. In 1961 internal political autonomy was granted to the islands and in 1974 all but one (Mayotte) of the French islands voted for independence which was scheduled for 1978. The Comorian Parliament declared unilateral independence in 1975 but the island of Mayotte elected to remain under French administration. Comoros is an Islamic republic with a unicameral National Assembly.
**Comoran** *adj. & n.*

| Island | Area (sq. km.) | Pop. (1993) | Chief Town |
|---|---|---|---|
| Grande Comore (Njazídja) | 1,148 | 265,500 | Moroni |
| Mohéli (Mwali) | 290 | 26,100 | Fomboni |
| Anjouan (Nzwani) | 424 | 205,400 | Mutsamudu |

**compass** /'kʌmpəs/ an instrument showing the direction of magnetic north and bearings from it, used as an aid to navigation. In early times navigation was by observation of landmarks or of the stars. The mariner's compass is reported in China *c.* 1100, western Europe 1187, Arabia *c.* 1220, and Scandinavia *c.* 1300; its actual use may well be considerably earlier in each of these areas. In very small and simple compasses the compass card is fixed and the magnetic needle swings round above it; in all aircraft and ships' magnetic compasses, however, the card is laid on top of the needle and attached to it, so that the needle swings it round. In a ship the compass card not only rotates on a pivot but is arranged so that it nearly floats on a quantity of alcohol; this liquid lessens the weight on the pivot, making the compass more sensitive, and the casing of the whole is swung on gimbals so that it remains face upwards in spite of the rocking of the ship. This kind of compass, which points to the magnetic north (whose position varies over the years) is subject to a number of errors (deviations can be caused by adjacent metal fitments etc.) but is carried as an emergency instrument even when a gyro-compass is fitted.

**Conakry** /'kɒnəˌkrɪ/ the capital and chief port of Guinea, established by the French in 1887 on Tombo Island; pop. (1983) 705,300. It exports iron ore, fruit, kola nuts, groundnuts, and coffee.

**Concepción** /kɒnˌsepsɪ'əʊn/ an industrial city in south-central Chile on the Bío-Bío River; pop. (1991) 306,460. It is the third-largest city in Chile and capital of an industrialized province of the same name in the region of Bío-Bío. Its port, on the Pacific coast, is Talcahuano. It has textile, glass, and cement industries, and is a tourist resort.

**Concepción** a river port on the east bank of the Paraguay River, in the Oriental region of north-central Paraguay; pop. (1984) 25,600. It ships grain and beef.

**Concord** /'kɒnkɔːd/ **1.** a city in Contra Costa county, west-central California, USA, to the east of San Francisco; pop. (1990) 111,350. It lies adjacent to a naval weapons station. **2.** a town in north-east Massachusetts, USA, on the Concord River; pop. (1990) 17,080. Settled in 1635, the town was named after a 'concord' with local Indians. Battles here and at Lexington in April 1775 marked the start of the American War of Independence. **3.** the capital of the state of New Hampshire, USA, on the Merrimack River; pop. (1990) 36,000. The legislature which meets here every two years is the largest of any US state with 400 seats. There is a living museum of Shaker crafts, architecture, and inventions.

**Concordia** /kɒn'kɔːdɪə/ a port on the Uruguay River in the province of Entre Rios, north-east Argentina; pop. (1981) 93,600.

**condominium** a territory administered jointly by two or more countries. For example, between 1906 and 1980 the New Hebrides (now Vanuatu) was governed as an Anglo-French condominium.

**Coney Island** /'kəʊnɪ/ a resort on the US Atlantic coast in Brooklyn, New York City, forming part of Long Island since the silting up of a creek. It has been developed as a pleasure ground since the 1840s but is now in decline.

**Confederate States** /kən'fedərət/ the 11 Southern States (Alabama, Arkansas, Florida, Georgia, Louisiana, Mississippi, North Carolina, South Carolina, Tennessee, Texas, Virginia) which seceded from the United States in 1860–1 and formed a confederacy of their own (thus precipitating the American Civil War) which was finally overthrown in 1865, after which they were reunited to the USA.

**Confucianism** /kən'fjuːʃənɪz(ə)m/ a system of philosophical and ethical teachings founded by Confucius in the 6th c. BC and developed by Mencius (Meng-tzu) in the 4th c. BC, one of the two major Chinese ideologies (see TAOISM). The basic concepts are ethical ones: love for one's fellows, filial piety, decorum, virtue, and the ideal of the superior man. The publication in AD 1190 of the four great Confucian texts revitalized Confucianism throughout China. A second series of texts, the 'five classics', includes the I Ching. There are an estimated 5,800,000 followers of Confucianism in the world.
**Confucianist** *n.*

**Congaree Swamp** /'kɒndʒəriː/ a floodplain containing a rare remnant of river-forest, 32 km. (20 miles) south of Columbia, South Carolina, USA. The area was established as a national monument in 1976.

**Congo** /'kɒŋɡəʊ/ (also **Zaïre** /zɑː'ɪə(r)/) a major river of central Africa formed by the waters of the Lualaba River and its tributary, the Luvua River. It lies largely within the republic of Zaire and flows north, west, and south-west in a great curve for 4,374 km. (2,718 miles) before emptying into the Atlantic Ocean. Known internationally as the Congo, it was named the Zaïre River by the Zaire government in 1971. Its headwaters were explored by David Livingstone (1871) and later by Henry Stanley (1874–7) who proved that the Lualaba was the source of the Congo and not the Nile.

**Congo** /'kɒŋɡəʊ/ official name **The Republic of the Congo** a country in central Africa, with a short Atlantic coastline, lying on the Equator with Zaire to the east, and the Congo (Zaïre) River  and its tributary the Ubangi forming most of its eastern boundary; area 342,000 sq. km. (132,046 sq. miles); pop. (est. 1991) 2,300,000; official language, French; capital, Brazzaville. Pointe-Noire is the country's principal Atlantic seaport. The

densely forested Congo has a hot, humid equatorial climate and its chief exports are oil, timber, coffee, and tobacco. Largely occupied by Bantu peoples, the Congo was colonized in the 19th c. by France. After gaining independence in 1960 it was the scene of internal conflict for nearly two decades. In 1990 the leaders of the single ruling party (Congolese Labour Party) voted to end the one-party system.
**Congolese** *adj. & n.*
In addition to the federal district of Brazzaville, the Congo is divided into 9 regions:

| Region | Area (sq. km.) | Pop. (1984) | Capital |
| --- | --- | --- | --- |
| Kouilou | 13,694 | 369,000 | Pointe-Noir |
| Niari | 25,942 | 173,600 | Loubomo |
| Lékoumou | 20,950 | 68,300 | Sibiti |
| Bouenza | 12,265 | 187,100 | N'kayi |
| Pool | 33,990 | 184,300 | Kinkala |
| Plateaux | 38,400 | 109,700 | Djambala |
| Cuvette | 74,850 | 135,700 | Owando |
| Sangha | 55,800 | 46,100 | Ouesso |
| Likouala | 66,044 | 49,500 | Impfondo |

**Conjeeveram**  the former name of KANCHI-PURAM.

**Connaught**  (also **Connacht**) a province of the Republic of Ireland, comprising Galway, Leitrim, Mayo, Roscommon, and Sligo counties; area 17,121 sq. km. (6,613 sq. miles); pop. (1991) 422,900.

**Connecticut**  /kə'netɪkət/ a state of north-east USA with the Atlantic to the south, Massachusetts to the north, Rhode Island to the east, and New York to the west; area 12,997 sq. km. (5,018 sq. miles); pop. (1991) 3,287,100; capital, Hartford. The largest cities are Bridgeport, Hartford, New Haven, Waterbury, and Stamford. It is also known as the Constitution State or the Nutmeg State. Major products include hardware, vehicles, weapons, poultry, fruit, and dairy produce. A Puritan settlement in the 17th c., it was one of the original 13 states of the US (1788). The state is divided into 8 counties:

| County | Area (sq. km.) | Pop. (1990) | County Seat |
| --- | --- | --- | --- |
| Fairfield | 1,643 | 827,645 | Bridgeport |
| Hartford | 1,921 | 851,780 | Hartford |
| Litchfield | 2,395 | 174,090 | Litchfield |
| Middlesex | 970 | 143,200 | Middletown |
| New Haven | 1,586 | 804,220 | New Haven |
| New London | 1,739 | 254,960 | Norwich |
| Tolland | 1,071 | 128,700 | Rockville |
| Windham | 1,339 | 102,525 | Putnam |

**Connecticut**  a river rising in the Connecticut Lakes of New Hampshire, USA, and flowing south for 655 km. (407 miles) across Massachusetts and Connecticut to enter Long Island Sound at Old Saybrook. It is the longest river in New England.

**Connemara**  /ˌkɒnə'mɑːrə/ a mountainous district of County Galway in the Republic of Ireland.

**Constance**  /'kɒnstəns/, **Lake** (German **Bodensee** /'bəʊdən,zeɪ/) a lake on the north side of the Swiss Alps, at the meeting point of Germany, Switzerland, and Austria, forming part of the course of the River Rhine; area 541 sq. km. (209 sq. miles).

**Constantine**  /'kɒnstən,taɪn/ a city in north-east Algeria; pop. (1989) 449,000. As Cirta (or Kirtha) it was the capital of the Roman province of Numidia. It was destroyed in 311 but rebuilt soon afterwards by Constantine the Great, and given his name. Its port is Skikda. It is the third city of Algeria and a communications centre and a market for woollen textiles and grain. Its leatherwork is highly esteemed.

**Constantinople**  /ˌkɒnstæntɪ'nəʊp(ə)l/ a city (modern ISTANBUL) on the European side of the south end of the Bosporus, founded in 324 and inaugurated (330) as the second capital of the Roman Empire by Constantine the Great on the site of BYZANTIUM. Subsequently the seat of the Byzantine emperors, it was captured by the Ottoman Turks in 1453 and renamed Istanbul in 1930.

**Constanza**  /kɒn'stæntsə/ (Romanian **Constanţa**) the chief port of Romania, on the Black Sea; pop. (1989) 315,920. It was established as a Greek colony in the 7th c. BC but was later held by the Romans. The Roman poet Ovid (43 BC–AD 17) lived in exile here and there are magnificent Roman remains including a very large mosaic. Constanza is a resort and industrial city, and naval base with oil refineries and shipyards.

**Contadora**  /ˌkɒntə'dɔːrə/ one of the Pearl Islands of Panama, in the Gulf of Panama. It gave its name to the Contadora Group, a group of countries (Colombia, Panama, Venezuela, and Mexico) whose representatives met on the island in January 1983 with the aim of finding a means of bringing peace and stability to Central America.

**Contagem**  /kɒntə'ʒem/ a western suburb of Belo Horizonte in the state of Minas Gerais, Brazil; pop. (1990) 433,800.

**continent**  /'kɒntɪnənt/ any of the main continuous expanses of land (Europe, Asia, Africa, North and South America, Australia, Antarctica). Asia has the largest area, largest population, and highest and lowest elevations; Australia is the smallest continent. In Britain **the Continent** refers to the mainland of Europe as distinct from the British Isles.

**continental climate**  climatic conditions associated with continental rather than maritime areas, and characterized by marked contrasts between summer and winter.

**Continental Divide**  (also **Great Divide**) the main series of mountain ridges in North America, chiefly the crest of the Rocky Mountains, which forms a watershed separating the rivers flowing eastwards into the Atlantic Ocean or the Gulf of

Mexico from those flowing westwards into the Pacific.

**continental drift** the postulated movement of the existing continents to their present positions after having at one time formed a single land mass. The idea of such lateral displacement is generally ascribed to the German meteorologist Alfred Wegener, although similar but less detailed suggestions had been put forward by earlier writers. Wegener's theory was based on similarities in the types of rock forming the continents, and in the correspondence of the outline of the coasts of South America and Africa, but the concept that the masses of rock forming the continents could drift across the rocks that form the weaker sub-oceanic portion of the earth's crust gained little credence before the 1960s. Since then information from the floors of the oceans, from seismic studies, from palaeomagnetic surveys, and from radiometric dating of rocks have shown that the theory is valid. It is now evident that the continental land masses of South America, Africa, Australia, Antarctica, and the Indian subcontinent once formed a single supercontinent, termed Gondwanaland, which began splitting up about 200–150 million years ago. The precise geophysical mechanisms involved in the drift of the continents and, indeed, plate tectonics—a theory which expands upon that of continental drift—are still hotly debated.

**continental shelf** a gently sloping submarine plain stretching from the coastline of continents to the crest of the continental slope which drops down steeply to the ocean depths of the abyssal plain. The continental shelf is covered by sedimentary deposits which can be as deep as 3,650 m. (12,000 ft.) and can occasionally include deposits of oil. Continental shelves tend to be narrower on the sides of continents nearest subduction zones or deep trenches where the edges of continental plates converge.

**Conwy** /ˈkɒnwɪ/ (also **Conway**) a market town in north Wales, on the River Conwy; pop. (1981) 12,950. A suspension bridge built by Telford in 1826 and a railway bridge built by Stephenson in 1848 span the river here.

**Coober Pedy** /ˌkuːbə(r) ˈpedɪ/ a town in South Australia, in an area of the Stuart Range which produces 90 per cent of Australia's opals.

**Cooch Behar** /ˌkuːtʃ bəˈhɑː(r)/ a former state of north-east India, now part of West Bengal.

**Cooee** /ˈkuːiː/ a bay on the coast of Queensland, Australia, north of Rockhampton. It is named after the call of the bushmen.

**Cook** /kʊk/, **Mount** the highest peak in New Zealand, a mountain in the Southern Alps on South Island, rising to a height of 3,754 m. (12,316 ft.). It is named after Capt. James Cook, the explorer. A major avalanche on 14 December 1991 resulted in the height of Mt. Cook being reduced by 10 m.

**Cook Islands** a group of 15 islands in the south-west Pacific Ocean between Tonga and French Polynesia with the status of a self-governing territory in free association with New Zealand; area 238 sq. km. (92 sq. miles); pop. (est. 1992) 18,000; capital, Avarua. The islands have a tropical maritime climate with a hurricane season from November to April. Fruit and copra are the main exports. The islands were visited by Captain Cook in 1773 and were placed under British protection 1888–1901. In 1965 the Cook Islands became internally self-governing.

**Cookstown** a town in County Tyrone, Northern Ireland, on the Ballinderry River; pop. (1981) 7,600.

**Cook Strait** a passage separating the North and South Islands of New Zealand. It was visited in 1642 by the Dutch explorer Abel Tasman, who believed it to be a bay; Captain Cook discovered in 1770 that it was in fact a strait.

**Cooktown** a town on the north-east coast of Queensland, Australia, where Captain James Cook beached his ship the *Endeavour* in 1770 to repair damage. Gold was discovered near here in the 1870s and a gold-rush port developed; pop. (1986) 964.

**coomb** /kuːm/ (also **cwm**) a valley or hollow on the side of a hill or a short valley running up from the coast.

**Coonawarra** /ˌkuːnəˈwɒrə/ a noted wine-producing region of South Australia whose name is derived from an Aboriginal word meaning 'wild honeysuckle'.

**Coon Rapids** a city in south-east Minnesota, USA, on the Mississippi River; pop. (1990) 52,980. It is a northern outer suburb of Minneapolis-St. Paul.

**Coorong** /kuːˈrɒŋ/, **the** a coastal region of south-east South Australia stretching from Lake Alexandrina in the north to Kingston S.E. in the south. It largely comprises a long shallow lagoon separated from the Great Australian Bight by the narrow Younghusband Peninsula. The **Coorong National Park** is a sanctuary for birds such as giant pelicans, terns, swans, and ibis.

**Cootamundra** /ˌkuːtəˈmuːndrə/ a town in New South Wales, south-east Australia, situated at the centre of a farming and livestock-rearing region on the Olympic Highway north-east of Wagga Wagga; pop. (1986) 6,300. It gives its name to the Cootamundra Wattle (*Acacia baileyana*) and was the birthplace in 1908 of the Australian cricketer Sir Donald Bradman.

**Copacabana Beach** /ˌkɒpəkəˈbænə/ a beach resort on the Atlantic coast of Brazil, near the entrance to Guanabara Bay, Rio de Janeiro.

**Copán** /kəʊˈpæn/ an ancient Mayan city, flourishing c. 300–900, that was the southernmost point of the Mayan empire, in western Honduras near the Guatemalan frontier. The site was bought by the American writer John Stephens in the 1820s for $50.

**Copenhagen** /ˌkəʊpən'heɪgən/ (Danish **København** /ˌkɑ:bən'haʊn/) the capital and chief port of Denmark, on the east coast of the island of Zealand and the northern part of Amager Island; pop. (1990) 466,700. Capital of Denmark since 1443, its airport (Kastrup) is a focal point of air travel in Scandinavia. Its principal attractions are the Tivoli amusement park, the Little Mermaid statue, Amalienborg Palace (home of the Danish royal family), Christiansborg Palace, and Rosenborg Castle. Its university was founded in 1497 and there are several major museums including the Toy Museum and Zoological Museum. Its industries include shipbuilding, furniture, clothing, silverware, and porcelain. It is a free port and popular tourist destination.

**Copiapó** /kɒpɪə'pəʊ/ a town at the southern end of the Atacama Desert in northern Chile, capital of the Copiapó region; pop. (1982) 70,240. It grew as the centre of local silver- and copper-mining.

**Copperbelt** /'kɒpə,belt/ a province of central Zambia in one of the richest copper mining areas of the world; pop. (1989) 1,866,490; capital, Ndola. Copper, cobalt, and uranium are mined here.

**Copt** /kɒpt/ **1.** a native Egyptian in the Hellenistic and Roman periods. **2.** a native Christian of the independent Egyptian (Coptic) Church. Traditionally founded by St. Mark, the Coptic Church became isolated from the rest of Christendom in 451 when it adhered to the Monophysite doctrine condemned by the Council of Chalcedon. The language of the Copts, surviving only as the liturgical language of the Coptic Church, represents the final stage of ancient Egyptian, with an alphabet largely based on Greek but with some letters borrowed from Egyptian demotic.

**Coquilhatville** /ˌkəʊkiː'ætviːl/ the former name (until 1966) of MBANDAKA in Zaire.

**Coquimbo** /kəʊ'kiːmbəʊ/ a Pacific port in the Coquimbo region of central Chile, situated immediately south of La Serena; pop. (1991) 117,100. It is the outlet of a copper- and manganese-mining region.

**Coral Sea** /'kɒr(ə)l/ a part of the western Pacific Ocean lying between Australia, New Guinea, and Vanuatu. The Territory of the Coral Sea Islands is an uninhabited territory comprising the islands and reefs (including the Great Barrier Reef) of the Coral Sea and administered by Australia.

**Coral Springs** a city in south-east Florida, USA, south-west of Boca Raton; pop. (1990) 79,400.

**Corbett National Park** /'kɔ:bət/ a national park in Uttar Pradesh, northern India. Designated in 1936 and originally named Hailey National Park after the governor of the United Provinces, it was India's first national park. Known as Ramganga

National Park after independence, it was later renamed in honour of Jim Corbett whose efforts to conserve the habitat of tigers and leopards resulted in 500 sq. km. (193 sq. miles) gaining protected-area status. The park centre is located at Dhikala.

**Corbières** /kɔ:'bjer/ a noted wine-producing district in the south of the Languedoc region of France, between Narbonne and the Spanish frontier.

**Corby** /'kɔ:bɪ/ a town in Northamptonshire, England, designated a New Town in 1950; pop. (1981) 48,800. It was formerly a centre of the steel industry and now has diverse light industries.

**Corcovado** /ˌkɔ:kə'vɑ:dəʊ/ a peak rising to 711 m. (2,310 ft.) on the south side of Rio de Janeiro, Brazil. It is topped by the 40-m. (131-ft.) statue of 'Christ the Redeemer'.

**Corcyra** /kɔ:'saɪərə/ the former name of CORFU.

**Cordilleras** /ˌkɔrdɪl'jeɪrəz/ a general term applied to the mountain systems extending the entire length of the west coasts of North, Central, and South America. It is derived from the Spanish word *cordillera* (= mountain range).

**Córdoba** /'kɔ:dəbə/ a city in central Argentina, capital of Córdoba province; pop. (1990) 1,198,000. Its university has been one of the principal centres of learning in South America since it was founded in 1613.

**Córdoba** (also **Cordova**) a city in Andalusia, southern Spain, on the Guadalquivir River; pop. (1991) 309,200. It was founded by the Carthaginians and held by the Moors from 711 to 1236. As capital of the most powerful of the Arab Spanish states it flourished as a centre of learning, earning the title of the 'Athens of the West'. It began to decline after the overthrow of the caliphate in 1031. Textiles, olive oil and pharmaceuticals are produced.

**Corfu** /kɔ:'fu:/ (anc. **Corcyra**, Greek **Kérkira** /'keəkɪrə/) one of the largest of the Ionian Islands, off the west coast of Greece; area 592 sq. km. (229 sq. miles); pop. (1981) 96,500; chief town, Kérkira. It is a popular tourist resort.

**Corinth** /'kɔ:rɪnθ/ (Greek **Kórinthos**) a city in the north-east Peloponnesus, capital of the prefecture of Corinth, Greece, on the Gulf of Corinth; pop. (1981) 22,700. Rebuilt after earthquake damage in 1858 and again in 1928 and 1933, it is situated north-east of the ancient city of Corinth which dates from Homeric times. St. Paul preached here and later wrote two epistles to the Corinthian church.
**Corinthian** *adj. & n.*

**Corinth, Gulf of** (also **Gulf of Lepanto**, Greek **Korinthiakos Kólpos**) an inlet of the Ionian Sea *c.* 130 km. (80 miles) long, separating the Peloponnese from mainland Greece.

**Corinth, Isthmus of** (Greek **Isthmos Korinthou**) a narrow neck of land linking the

Peloponnese with central Greece and separating the Gulf of Corinth from the Saronic Gulf.

**Corinth Canal** a man-made channel across the Isthmus of Corinth, linking the Gulf of Corinth and the Saronic Gulf. Built between 1881 and 1893, it is 6.4 km. (4 miles) long.

**Corinto** /kɒˈriːntəʊ/ the principal port of Nicaragua on the Pacific Coast; pop. (1985) 24,000. Founded in 1840, it was formerly known as Punta Icacos.

**Coriolis wind** an effect created by the rotation of the earth from west to east that deflects winds and ocean currents to the right of their direction of travel in the Northern Hemisphere and to the left in the Southern Hemisphere. It was named after the French mathematician Gaspard Coriolis (1792–1843).

**Cork** /kɔːk/ a city in the Republic of Ireland, capital of Cork county in the province of Munster, on the Lee River; pop. (1991) 127,000. St. Finbarr is said to have founded an abbey here in the 7th c. It has both Catholic and Protestant cathedrals, and diverse light industries. Cork Harbour to the south of the city is a centre for offshore oil exploration.

**Corn Belt** a name given to the principal agricultural region of the USA which stretches across the northern plains of the Midwest from Ohio to Nebraska.

**corniche** /kɔːˈniːʃ/ a term used to describe steep or high roads overlooking the Mediterranean Sea, especially the road between Nice and Genoa.

**Corn Islands** (Spanish **Islas del Maiz** /-maɪz/) two small islands (Great Corn Island and Little Corn Island) in the Caribbean Sea off the east coast of Nicaragua. They were used by the US as a marine base from 1916 to 1971.

**Cornwall** /ˈkɔːnw(ə)l/ a town in eastern Ontario, Canada, to the south-east of Ottawa and north of the St. Lawrence River; pop. (1991) 47,100.

**Cornwall** /ˈkɔːnw(ə)l/ a county occupying the extreme south-west peninsula of England; area 3,564 sq. km. (1,377 sq. miles); pop. (1991) 469,300 (with the Isles of Scilly); county town, Truro. The ancient Celtic language of Cornwall, belonging to the Brythonic branch of the Celtic language group, was formerly spoken in Cornwall but gradually died out in the 17th-18th c.
**Cornish** *adj. & n.*
The county is divided into 7 districts:

| District | Area (sq. km.) | Pop. (1991) |
|---|---|---|
| Caradon | 664 | 75,800 |
| Carrick | 461 | 82,700 |
| Kerrier | 473 | 86,400 |
| North Cornwall | 1,195 | 73,700 |
| Penwith | 303 | 59,400 |
| Restormel | 452 | 88,300 |
| Isles of Scilly | 16 | 2,900 |

**Coromandel Coast** /ˌkɒrəˈmænd(ə)l/ the name given to the east coast of Tamil Nadu in south-east India, from Point Calimere to the mouth of the Krishna River.

**Coromandel Peninsula** a peninsula of North Island, New Zealand, to the east of Auckland, comprising an area of densely forested hills. Taking its name from HMS *Coromandel* which anchored there in 1820 to collect Kauri timber, its chief settlements are the former gold-mining towns of Thames and Coromandel.

**Corona** /kəˈrəʊnə/ a city in southern California, USA; pop. (1990) 76,100. It is a processing centre for citrus fruits.

**Corozal** /kɒrəʊˈzɑːl/ the chief town of the department of Corozal in northern Belize, on Corozal Bay; pop. (1991) 7,200. The town lies at the centre of a sugar-producing area.

**Corpus Christi** /ˈkɔːpəs ˈkrɪstɪ/ an industrial centre and fishing port on the coast of southern Texas, USA; pop. (1990) 257,400. Situated on Corpus Christi Bay, it is linked to the Gulf of Mexico through the Aransas Pass. It was established as a trading post in 1839 and it developed with ranching and with the discovery of oil and gas nearby in the early 1900s. It has oil refineries and petrochemical industries.

**Corregidor** /kəˈregəˌdɔː/ an island of the Philippines to the south of the Bataan Peninsula, Luzon Island. It divides the entrance to Manila Bay into two channels (Boca Chica and Boca Grande) and has been used as a fortification to protect the bay. It was the scene of heavy fighting during 1942 between Japanese and US Forces.

**Corrèze** /kɒˈrez/ a department in the Limousin region of central France; area 5,857 sq. km. (2,262 sq. miles); pop. (1990) 237,900; capital, Tulle.

**Corrib** /ˈkɒrɪb/ the largest freshwater lough in the Republic of Ireland, a lake in Mayo and Galway counties; area 168 sq. km. (65 sq. miles).

**Corrientes** /kɒrˈjenteɪz/ a port on the Paraná River, north-east Argentina; pop. (1991) 268,600. Founded by the Spanish in 1588, it is capital of a province of the same name and the commercial and cultural centre of a rich agricultural region.

**Corsica** /ˈkɔːsɪkə/ (French **Corse**) a mountainous island off the west coast of Italy, under French rule; area 8,680 sq. km. (3,353 sq. miles); pop. (1990) 249,740; capital, Ajaccio. The highest peak on the island is Mont Cinto (2,710 m., 8,891 ft.). Ajaccio was the birthplace of Napoleon I (who was known as 'the Corsican'). Since 1974 the island has been divided into the departments of **Corse-du-Sud** and **Haute-Corse**. It produces olive oil, wine, timber, wheat, cheese, and fish, and has many tourist resorts along its coasts.
**Corsican** *adj. & n.*

**Çorum** /tʃəˈruːm/ **1.** a province of north-central Turkey, between Ankara and the Black Sea port of Samsun; area 12,820 sq. km. (4,952 sq. miles); pop. (1990) 609,900. **2.** its capital; pop. (1990) 116,800.

**Corunna** /kə'rʌnə/ (Spanish **La Coruña** /ˌlæ kə'rʊnjə/) a seaport in Galicia, north-west Spain, capital of La Coruña province; pop. (1991) 251,300. The Armada sailed from here to attack England in 1588, and the town was sacked by Francis Drake in 1589. It was the site of a battle (1809) in the Peninsular War. Sir John Moore, who died at the battle, is buried in San Carlos Gardens. There are car ferries to the Canary Islands. Its fisheries specialize in sardines and there are canning, cigar-making, textiles, and glass-making industries.

**Corvo** /'kɔːvəʊ/ the most northerly and smallest of the Portuguese islands of the Azores; area 17.5 sq. km. (6.8 sq. miles). The island is the remnant of a single extinct volcano, Monte Gordo which rises to 777 m. (2,549 ft.). Vila Nova de Corvo is the only settlement.

**Cos** /kɒs/ (Greek **Kos**) a Greek island in the south-east Aegean Sea, in the Dodecanese group off the coast of Turkey; area 290 sq. km. (112 sq. miles). The chief town is the port of Kos. In ancient times it was associated with Hippocrates and the Asklepius school of medicine.

**Cosenza** /kɒ'sentzə/ a market town in Calabria, southern Italy, at the confluence of the Crati and Busento rivers, capital of Cosenza province; pop. (1990) 104,480. Cereals, fruit, olive oil, and cloth are traded.

**cosmography** /kɒz'mɒgrəfɪ/ a description or mapping of general features of the universe.

**cosmology** /kɒz'mɒlədʒɪ/ the science or theory of the creation and development of the universe. While ancient cosmologies supposed the world to be supported on the backs of elephants standing upon tortoises, or placed earth at the centre of a universe of concentric crystal spheres, modern science debates whether an infinite and unchanging universe is maintained by the continuous creation of matter from the void, or whether a big bang both created and dispersed matter in an expansion which continues today, and which may be reversed if the universe is dense enough. The last of these interpretations is favoured by the detection of a radiation field permeating the universe, believed to be the cool remnant of the initial fireball.

**Cossack** /'kɒsæk/ originally, a member of those Russians who sought a free life in the steppes or on the frontiers of Imperial Russia in the 15th–16th c. and were allowed privileges by the Tsars, including autonomy for their settlements in southern Russia (especially the Ukraine) and Siberia in return for service in protecting the frontiers. Suppressed along with Ukrainian autonomy from the mid-18th c., Ukrainian Cossackdom experienced a revival following the breakup of the Soviet Union in

1991. There are 15,000 registered Cossacks in the Ukraine. Russian Cossacks, of whom the largest group are the Don Cossacks, intermarried with the various minority peoples among whom they lived and were also suppressed from the early 1920s. Kuban Cossacks are descended from Ukrainian Cossacks who were forcefully deported to the Kuban region of southern Russia.

**Costa Blanca** /'kɒstə 'blæŋkə/ a major resort region on the Mediterranean coast of south-east Spain. (Spanish = white coast)

**Costa Brava** /'kɒstə 'brɑːvə/ a major resort region to the north of Barcelona, on the Mediterranean coast of north-east Spain. (Spanish = wild coast)

**Costa del Sol** /'kɒstə del 'sɒl/ a major resort region on the Mediterranean coast of south Spain. Marbella and Torremolinos are the principal resort towns. (Spanish = coast of the sun)

**Costa Dorada** /'kɒstə dɒ'rɑːdə/ a resort region on the Mediterranean coast of Spain to the south of Barcelona. (Spanish = golden coast)

**Costa Mesa** /'kɒstə 'meɪzə/ a city on the south-west coast of California, USA, south of Santa Ana; pop. (1990) 96,360. It has boat-building and electronics industies.

## Costa Rica

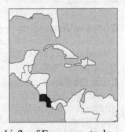

/ˌkɒstə 'riːkə/ official name **The Republic of Costa Rica** a country in Central America on the Isthmus of Panama, with Nicaragua to the north and Panama to the south-east. The population is chiefly of European stock; area 51,022 sq. km. (19,707 sq miles); pop. (est. 1991) 3,100,000; official language, Spanish; capital, San José. The largest towns are San José, Limón, and Alajuela. Rugged mountains and hills separate a wide coastal plain facing the Caribbean from a narrower coastal plain facing the Pacific. The coastal regions have a tropical climate with a wet season from May to November while the highland region is more temperate. The economy is chiefly agricultural, and the forests which cover most of the land produce valuable timber. Principal exports include coffee, cocoa, sugar, bananas, and beef. Colonized by Spain in the early 16th c., Costa Rica achieved independence in 1823 and finally emerged as a separate country in 1838 after 14 years within the Federation of Central America. Since then it has been one of the most stable and prosperous states in the region. Although there are civil and rural guards, the army was abolished in 1948. The country is governed by a unicameral legislative assembly.

**Costa Rican** *adj. & n.*

Costa Rica is divided into 7 provinces:

| Province | Area (sq. km.) | Pop. (est. 1991) | Capital |
|---|---|---|---|
| San José | 4,960 | 1,105,840 | San José |
| Alajuela | 9,753 | 539,375 | Alajuela |
| Cartago | 3,125 | 340,300 | Cartago |
| Heredia | 2,656 | 243,680 | Heredia |
| Guanacaste | 10,141 | 242,680 | Liberia |
| Puntarenas | 11,277 | 338,380 | Puntarenas |
| Limón | 9,188 | 219,485 | Limón |

**Costermanville** the former name (until 1966) of BUKAVU in Zaire.

**Côte d'Azur** /ˌkəʊt dæˈzjʊə(r)/ a name applied to the coastline of the French Riviera in the departments of Alpes-Maritimes and Var. The chief resorts are Antibes, Cannes, Nice, Juan-Les-Pins, and Monte Carlo in Monaco.

**Côte d'Ivoire** See IVORY COAST.

**Côte d'Or** /kəʊt dɔ:/ a department in the Burgundy (Bourgogne) region of central France famous for its vineyards and red wines; area 8,763 sq. km. (3,385 sq. miles); pop. (1990) 493,870; capital, Dijon.

**Cotentin** /ˌkəʊtɑ̃ˈtæ/ a region of Normandy in north-west France, forming a peninsula that juts into the English Channel with the port of Cherbourg at its northern tip.

**Côtes-d'Armor** /ˌkəʊt dɑːˈmɔː/ a department in Brittany, north-west France, formerly known as Côtes-du-Nord; area 6,877 sq. km. (2,656 sq. miles); pop. (1990) 538,400; capital, Saint-Brieuc.

**Coto Doñana** /ˌkəʊtəʊ dənˈjɑːnə/ an area of marshland, woods, lakes, and scrubland in southern Spain, to the north of the mouth of the Guadalquivir River. Extending over 500 sq. km. (190 sq. miles), the Coto Doñana National Park is a stopover point for over 200 species of migrating birds. It was once the hunting ground of the dukes of Medina Sidonia and is named after Doña Ana, the wife of the 7th duke who was the commander of the Spanish Armada.

**Cotonou** /ˌkɒtəˈnuː/ the largest city, chief port, and *de facto* capital of Benin, on the Guinea coast of West Africa; pop. (1982) 487,000. The National Assembly, Presidency, and foreign embassies are all located here due to the decline of PORTO NOVO. Light industries are developing to the east of the port.

**Cotopaxi** /ˌkɒtəˈpæksɪ/ one of the highest active volcanoes in the world, rising to 5,897 m. (19,347 ft.) in the Andes of central Ecuador. Its Quechua name means 'shining peak'.

**Cotswold Hills** /ˈkɒtswəʊld/ (also **Cotswolds**) a range of limestone hills, largely in Gloucestershire, England, noted for its sheep pastures and its picturesque villages which were formerly centres of the woollen industry. The Cotswolds rise to 333 m. (1,092 ft.) at Cleeve Cloud near Cheltenham.

**Cottbus** /ˈkɒtbʊs/ an industrial city in the state of Brandenburg, south-east Germany, on the River Spree; pop. (1991) 123,320. Textiles, metal products, and electrical goods are produced.

**Cottian Alps** /ˈkɒtɪən/ a region of the western Alps on the frontier between south-east France and north-west Italy. Mt. Viso, rising to 3,851 m. (12,634 ft.), is the highest point. The Col de la Traversette was probably the route taken by Hannibal when he crossed the Alps in 218 BC.

**Council Bluffs** a city in south-west Iowa, USA, on the Missouri River opposite Omaha, Nebraska; pop. (1990) 54,300. Originally named Hart's Bluff, this trading community was renamed Kanesville when Mormons settled here in 1846. After the Mormons left in 1852 to join Brigham Young in Salt Lake City, it was given its present name. Thereafter, Council Bluffs developed as a railway junction.

**Council of Europe** an association of European states, independent of the European Community. It meets in Strasbourg. Founded in 1949, it is committed to the principles of freedom and the rule of law, and to safeguarding the political and cultural heritage of Europe. Its executive organ is the Committee of Ministers, and most of its conclusions take the form of international agreements (known as *European Conventions*) or recommendations to governments. One of the Council's principal achievements is the European Convention of Human Rights (1950) under which was established the European Commission and the European Court of Human Rights.

**Courtrai** See KORTRIJK.

**Covent Garden** /ˈkʌvənt/ a district in central London, originally the convent garden of the Abbey of Westminster. It was the site for 300 years of London's chief fruit and vegetable market, which in 1974 was moved to Nine Elms, Battersea. The first Covent Garden Theatre was opened in 1732 and such famous plays as Goldsmith's *She Stoops to Conquer* (1773) and Sheridan's *The Rivals* (1775) were first performed there. It was several times destroyed and reconstructed, and since 1946 has been the home of London's chief opera and ballet companies. The market site has now been developed as shops and restaurants.

**Coventry** /ˈkɒvəntrɪ/ an industrial city in the West Midlands, central England; pop. (1991) 292,600. Formerly a centre of the clothing industry, Coventry now produces vehicles, machinery and telecommunications equipment in addition to man-made fibres. Its cathedral (1443), badly damaged during World War II, was replaced by a new cathedral consecrated in 1962. It is the site of the University of Warwick (1965) and Coventry University (formerly Coventry Polytechnic) which was established in 1992.

**Covilhã** /kuːviːlˈjɑː/ a winter-sports centre in the Sierra Estrela Mountains, central Portugal; pop. (1991) 22,030.

**Cowes** /kaʊz/ a town on the Isle of Wight, England, on the River Medina; pop. (1981) 16,300. It is internationally famous as a yachting centre and hosts the annual Cowes Week in August. Built by Henry VIII, Cowes Castle is the home of the Royal Yacht Squadron.

**Cox's Bazar** /ˈkɒksɪz/ a seaport and resort town in the Chittagong region of south-east Bangladesh; pop. (1981) 29,600. It derives its name from Captain Hiram Cox who settled the area with Arakanese immigrants from Burma in 1798. It is famous for cigar-making.

**Cozumel** /ˌkɒzʊˈmel/ a resort island in the Caribbean off the north-east coast of the Yucatán peninsula, Mexico; pop. (1980) 32,000; port of entry and chief town, San Miguel. Formerly a port of call on the chicle export route to North America and a military base during World War II, it developed as a resort area in the 1960s.

**Crac des Chevaliers** /ˌkræk deɪ ʃəˈvæljeɪ/ (also **Krak des Chevaliers**, Arabic **Qalaat al-Hosn**) a ruined fortress between Homs and the Mediterranean coast of western Syria. Built in the Middle Ages on the site of a former Kurdish castle by the Crusader Knights Hospitalers, it commanded a strategic position in the Homs Gap between inland Syria and the sea.

**crachin** /ˈkræʃæ̃/ a French term describing the light rain that occurs on the coast and northern mountain slopes of Vietnam during the cool season.

**Cracow** /ˈkrækaʊ/ (Polish **Kraków** /ˈkraːkuːf/) an industrial and tourist city in southern Poland, at the head of navigation on the upper Vistula River; pop. (1990) 750,540. Originally an important commercial centre, Cracow was capital of Poland from 1302 to 1609. With the growth of Warsaw and the destruction of the city by the Swedes in 1655, the city went into decline but recovered in the 19th c. when it developed into an industrial and railway centre. During the Communist period its industry was promoted by the building of a new town, Nova Huta, housing the Lenin steel works. It also has chemical, printing, and ceramic industries. The large medieval market place, which is one of the biggest in Europe, is surrounded by historic buildings including the 14th-c. Cloth Hall (incorporating the Gallery of Polish Art), the 13th-c. Church of St. Mary and the Romanesque Church of St. Adalbert. There is also a National Museum, royal castle, and cathedral with tombs of Polish kings and national figures such as John Sobieski and Tadeusz Kosciuszko. In 1364 King Casimir established the Jagiellonian University, one of the oldest in Europe.

**Craigavon** /kreɪgˈæv(ə)n/ a new town in County Armagh, Northern Ireland, created in 1965 with a view to merging the industrial settlements of Lurgan and Portadown and relieving congestion in Belfast; pop. (1981) 10,200.

**Craiova** /krəˈjəʊvə/ (also **Krajova**) an industrial city in the mineral-rich Oltenia region of south-west Romania, on the River Jiu; pop. (1989) 300,030. It is the capital of Dolj county and has a university founded in 1966. Its industries include vehicles, railway equipment, electrical goods, and textiles.

**Cranbourne** /ˈkrænbɔːn/ a town in Victoria, south-east Australia, situated at the head of the Mornington Peninsula to the south of Melbourne; pop. (1991) 18,890. It is the site of the Royal Botanical Gardens Cranbourne Garden.

**Cranwell** /ˈkrænwəl/ a village in Lincolnshire, England, home of the Royal Air Force College.

**Crater Lake** a lake with no inlet or outlet in a volcanic crater in the Cascade Range, south-west Oregon, USA. It is 9.5 km. (6 miles) in diameter and at over 600 m. (1,968 ft.) deep is the deepest lake in the USA. Crater Lake lies within a 74,188-hectare (183,180-acre) national park created in 1902.

**Crathie** /ˈkræθɪ/ a village in the Dee valley, north-east Scotland, 1 km. east of Balmoral Castle. Its church is attended by the royal family when in residence at Balmoral.

**Crawley** /ˈkrɔːlɪ/ a town in West Sussex, southern England, nearly 45 km. (28 miles) south of London; pop. (1981) 73,400. Created as a New Town in 1947, it lies adjacent to Gatwick Airport and has numerous light industries.

**Crays Malville** /ˈkreɪz mælˈviːl/ the site of the world's first commercial-scale fast nuclear reactor known as 'Super-Phénix', situated 40 km. (25 miles) from Lyons in the Rhône-Alpes region of eastern France.

**Crécy** /ˈkresɪ/ (in full **Crécy-en-Ponthieu**) a village in Picardy in northern France, scene of the first great English victory (1346) of the Hundred Years War when Edward III defeated Philip VI.

**Cree** /kriː/ an Algonquian-speaking Indian tribe of North America. Traditionally dependent on caribou and moose, they are the southernmost of the major subarctic tribes of Manitoba and Saskatchewan in Canada.

**Creek** /kriːk/ a Muskogean North American Indian confederacy, originally one of the dominant groups of the mid-south. In the 18th c. they were pushed westwards from the coasts of Carolina and Georgia, eventually settling in Indian Territory in Oklahoma where they number 50,000.

**creek** a small bay or harbour on a sea-coast, or a narrow inlet on a sea-coast or river-bank. In the US it usually refers to a stream or tributary of a river.

**Cremona** /krəˈməʊnə/ a market town in Lombardy, northern Italy, on the River Po; pop. (1990) 75,160. Situated at the centre of a rich dairy-farming area, it is linked to Milan by the Milan–Po Canal. From the 16th to the 18th c. it was, and still is, noted for the production of stringed instruments. There is a museum dedicated to the Stradivari family of violin-makers.

**Creole** /'kriːəʊl/ **1. a** a descendant of European (especially Spanish) settlers in the West Indies or Central or South America. **b** a White descendant of French settlers in the southern USA. **c** a person of mixed European and Black descent. **2.** a language formed from the contact of a European language (especially English, French, or Portuguese) with another (especially African) language.

**Cresta run** /'krestə/ a hazardously winding steeply banked channel of ice built each year as a tobogganing course at St. Moritz, Switzerland, by the St. Moritz Tobogganing Club, who draw up rules for racing on it. A run down the Cresta valley was first built in 1884.

**Cretaceous** /krɪ'teɪʃəs/ of or relating to the last period of the Mesozoic era, following the Jurassic and preceding the Tertiary, lasting from about 144 to 65 million years ago, during which time the climate was warm and the sea-level rose. It is characterized especially in north-west Europe by the deposition of chalk (whence its name). This period saw the emergence of the first flowering plants and the continued dominance of dinosaurs, although they died out before the end of it.

**Crete** /kriːt/ (Greek **Kríti** /'kriːtɪ/, formerly **Candia**) a Greek island in the eastern Mediterranean, noted for remains of the Minoan civilization; area 8,336 sq. km. (3,220 sq. miles); pop. (1981) 502,100; capital, Heraklion. The highest point on the island is Psilorítis (Mt. Ida) which rises to 2,456 m. (8,058 ft.). It fell to Rome in 67 BC and was subsequently ruled by Byzantines, Venetians, and Turks; it has been part of Greece since 1913. Fruit, olives, olive oil, raisins, and tourism are economically important.
**Cretan** *adj. & n.*

**Créteil** /krə'teɪ/ a southern suburb of Paris, France, on the River Marne, the capital of Val-de-Marne department; pop. (1990) 82,390. It has light industries including gold and silverware.

**Creuse** /krɜːz/ **1.** a department in Limousin region, central France; area 5,565 sq. km. (2,149 sq. miles); pop. (1990) 131,350; capital, Guéret. **2.** a river rising in the Millevaches plateau of the Massif Central in the Limousin region of central France. It flows 255 km. (160 miles) north-westwards to meet the Vienne near La Haye-Descartes.

**Crewe** /kruː/ an industrial town and railway junction in Cheshire, England; pop. (1981) 47,800. It has important engineering industries.

**Crimea** /kraɪ'mɪə/ (Russian **Krym** /krɪm/) **1.** a peninsula of the Ukraine lying between the Sea of Azov and the Black Sea. Settled successively by Goths, Huns, Khazars, Greeks, Tartars, Russians, and Ukrainians it became a khanate of the Turkic-speaking Tatar people in the 13th c. It was the scene of inconclusive but bloody fighting between Russia

and Turkey, France and Britain during the Crimean War of 1854–6 and in 1921 became an autonomous republic of the Russian republic. Under Stalin it was transferred to the Ukrainian Soviet Socialist Republic. Its resorts were much favoured by the Communist party élite. **2.** an autonomous republic of Ukraine; area 26,990 sq. km. (10,425 sq. miles); pop. (1989) 2,456,000; capital, Simferopol. Following the breakup of the Soviet Union in 1991 the Crimea became an autonomous republic of Ukraine, but its predominantly Russian-speaking population favour secession from the Ukraine and union with Russia.

**Cristóbal** /krɪstəʊ'bæl/ a town in Panama, at the Caribbean end of the Panama Canal opposite Colón.

**Croagh Patrick** /krəʊ'pætrɪk/ a mountain near Clew Bay in County Mayo, Ireland, 9.5 km. (6 miles) from Westport. Associated with St. Patrick, it is the scene of an annual pilgrimage.

**Croatia**  /krəʊ'eɪʃə/ (Serbo-Croat **Hrvatska** /'hɜːvɑːtskə/) official name **The Republic of Croatia** an independent state in south-east Europe bounded by Hungary and Slovenia to the north, Serbia and Bosnia to the east, and the Adriatic Sea to the west; area 56,538 sq. km. (21,838 sq. miles); pop. (1985) 4,660,000; official language, Serbo-Croat; capital, Zagreb. The interior of Croatia, which extends as far east as the Danube is separated from a long Adriatic coastline by the Dinaric Alps. The country produces, coal, oil, grain, livestock and timber. The Croats who migrated to this area of Europe in the 6th c. were conquered by Hungary in the 11th c. They remained under Hungarian rule until 1918 when the Republic of Yugoslavia was formed, but during World War II established an independent Croatian state that allied itself with the Axis. In 1946 Croatia became part of Yugoslavia once more and remained a constituent republic until it declared itself independent in 1991. The secession of Croatia led to ethnic conflict between Croats and the Serb minority which tried to divorce itself from Croatia by establishing the Serbian Republic of Krajina.
**Croatian** *adj.* **Croat** *n.*

**Cro-Magnon** /krəʊ'mænjɒn, -'mægnən/ the name of a hill of Cretaceous limestone in the Dordogne department of France, in a cave at the base of which skeletons of five individuals were found in 1868 among deposits of upper palaeolithic age. It had previously been supposed that modern man did not exist in palaeolithic times. The name is now applied in a more general sense to describe a particular race of modern man (*Homo sapiens sapiens*) that is associated with the upper palaeolithic Aurignacian industry found throughout western Europe and particularly south-west France from between c. 34,000 and 29,000 years BC. The geographical origin of the fully modern Cro-Magnon 'race' is uncertain but its appearance in western Europe heralded the apparent decline and disappearance of the existing Neanderthal populations and their middle palaeolithic industries. The group persisted in mesolithic and neolithic times, and some authorities consider that it survived in the Guanches, the earliest inhabitants (now extinct) of the Canary Islands.

**Cromarty Firth** an inlet of the Moray Firth between the Black Isle and the mainland of Ross and Cromarty in Highland Region, northern Scotland. The principal settlements on its coastline are Invergordon, Dingwall, and Cromarty which was the birthplace of the geologist and writer Hugh Miller (1802–56).

**Crosby** /'krɒzbɪ/ (also **Great Crosby**) a residential suburb of Sefton at the mouth of the River Mersey, north-west England; pop. (1981) 53,500.

**Cross Fell** the highest peak in the Pennine Chain, northern England, rising to 893 m. (2,892 ft.) in Cumbria.

**Cross River** a state in south-east Nigeria between the Cross River and the frontier with Cameroon; area 20,156 sq. km. (7,785 sq. miles); pop. (1991) 1,865,600; capital, Calabar.

**Crosthwaite** /'krɒsθweɪt/ a village in Cumbria, north-west England, to the north-west of Keswick in the Lake District. The poet and writer Robert Southey (1774–1843) lies buried here.

**Crow** /krəʊ/ a Siouan North American Indian tribe of the plains and prairies of Montana and North Dakota, USA.

**Croy Brae** /krɔɪ breɪ/ (also **Electric Brae**) a hillside on the coast between Ayr and Girvan in south-west Scotland, where by an optical illusion a downward sloping road appears to slope upwards.

**Croydon** /'krɔɪd(ə)n/ a residential and commercial outer borough of Greater London, England, to the south of Lambeth; pop. (1991) 299,600. The Saxon market town of Crogedene (= valley of saffron) became a powerful medieval trading post, a home of the Archbishops of Canterbury, a London borough (1883), and in the 1960s the centre of south-east England's financial and insurance services. It was the site of London's first airport in 1915.

**Crozet Islands** /krəʊ'zeɪ/ a group of 5 small islands in the Southern Ocean forming part of the French Southern and Antarctic Lands; area 505 sq. km. (195 sq. miles). Discovered by Marion-Dufresne in 1772, they were annexed to France by Crozet. There is a scientific and meteorological base on Ile de la Possession.

**Crystal Palace** a large building of iron and glass, like a giant greenhouse, designed by (Sir) Joseph Paxton for the Great Exhibition of 1851 in Hyde Park, London, and re-erected at Sydenham near Croydon; it was accidentally burnt down in 1936.

**CT** *abbr.* US Connecticut (in official postal use.)

**Ctesiphon** /'tesɪf(ə)n/ an ancient city on the Tigris near Baghdad, Iraq, capital of the Parthian kingdom from c. 224 and then of Persia under the Sassanian dynasty. It was taken by the Arabs in 636.

**Cuba** /'kju:bə/ official name **The Republic of Cuba** a Caribbean country, the largest and furthest west of the islands of the West Indies, situated at the mouth of the Gulf of Mexico; area 110,860  sq. km. (42,820 sq. miles); pop.(est. 1990) 10,600,000; official language, Spanish; capital, Havana. The largest cities are Havana, Santiago de Cuba, Camagüey, and Holguín. Flat or gently rolling plains rise to mountains reaching 2,000 m. (6,000 ft.) in the south-east. The climate is tropical with a rainy season from May to October, but is moderated by trade winds. Sugar is the mainstay of the economy and is the principal export; other exports include nickel, citrus, seafood, and tobacco. One of the first parts of the New World to be discovered and colonized by Spain, Cuba remained under Spanish rule until the Spanish–American War of 1898. Thereafter it was nominally independent but heavily under American influence, until granted full autonomy in 1934. The country was stricken by instability, however, and after several periods of dictatorship was taken over by a Communist rebellion in 1959, after which time it lent heavily on Soviet aid under the presidency of Fidel Castro. In 1962 Cuba became the focus of cold war manœuvres when on 22 October President Kennedy announced a US blockade of the island in order to compel the USSR to dismantle the missile bases which it had installed there. On 28 October Khrushchev agreed to do so, and nuclear war was averted. With the breakup of the Soviet Union in 1991, Russian troops and economic support were withdrawn. The Communist Party of Cuba is the only authorized political party.
**Cuban** *adj. & n.*
In addition to the city of Havana, Cuba has 14 provinces:

| Province | Area (sq. km.) | Pop. (1989) |
| --- | --- | --- |
| Pinar del Rio | 10,860 | 681,500 |
| La Habana | 5,671 | 633,400 |
| Isla de la Juventud | 2,199 | 70,900 |
| Matanzas | 11,669 | 599,500 |

(cont.)

| Province | Area (sq. km.) | Pop. (1989) |
|---|---|---|
| Cienfuegos | 4,149 | 356,700 |
| Villa Clara | 8,069 | 788,800 |
| Sancti Spiritus | 6,737 | 422,300 |
| Ciego de Avila | 6,485 | 355,500 |
| Camagüey | 14,134 | 727,700 |
| Las Tunas | 6,373 | 481,500 |
| Holguín | 9,105 | 927,700 |
| Granma | 8,452 | 777,300 |
| Santiago de Cuba | 6,343 | 974,100 |
| Guantánamo | 6,366 | 487,900 |

**Cubango** the Angolan name for the OKAVANGO River.

**Cuddalore** /'kʌdə,lɔ:(r)/ a port on the Coromandel Coast of Tamil Nadu, southern India, south of Pondicherry; pop. (1991) 143,770. It was founded as a trading settlement by the East India Company in 1684.

**Cuddapah** /'kʌdəpə/ a town in Andhra Pradesh, southern India, north-west of Madras; pop. (1991) 215,545. It is an administrative and market centre with paint and varnish industries.

**cuenca** /'kweŋkə/ a Spanish word for a valley.

**Cuenca** /'kweŋkə/ the third-largest city in Ecuador, founded in 1557 and known as the marble city because of its many fine buildings; pop. (1990) 332,920. Situated in a valley in the Andes, it is capital of Azuay province and a major centre of handicrafts, particularly panama hats, textiles, and leatherwork.

**Cuenca 1.** a province in the Castilla-La Mancha region of central Spain; area 17,061 sq. km. (6,590 sq. miles); pop. (1991) 205,200. **2.** its capital on the River Júcar; pop. (1991) 45,800. It is a picturesque town with a 12th-c. cathedral.

**Cuernavaca** /kwɜ:nəˈvɑːkə/ a resort town in the Mexican state of Morelos at an altitude of 1,542 m. (5,060 ft.) in the hills to the south of Mexico City pop. (1990) 282,000. It is capital of the state of Morelos and a favourite residence of Mexican officials and foreign diplomats.

**cuesta** a gentle slope, especially one ending in a steep drop.

**Cuiabá** /,ku:jəˈbɑː/ a city in west-central Brazil, on the Cuiabá River, capital of the state of Mato Grosso; pop. (1990) 389,070. Founded by slave-traders and gold-miners in the early 1700s, it is now a base from which to explore the Pantanal region.

**Culiacán** /kʊljəˈkɑːn/ (in full **Culiacán Rosales**) the capital of the state of Sinaloa in north-west Mexico, on the River Culiacán; pop. (1990) 602,110. A trading centre for fruit, cattle, cotton, and winter vegetables.

**Culloden** /kəˈlɒd(ə)n/ a village and moor near Inverness in north-east Scotland, site of the final engagement of the Jacobite uprising of 1745–6, the last pitched battle fought on British soil.

**Cumberland** /'kʌmb(ə)rlənd/ a former county of north-west England united with Westmorland and part of Lancashire in 1974 to form the county of Cumbria.

**Cumberland** a river in eastern USA, formed at the junction of the headwaters in south-eastern Kentucky. It flows 1,105 km. (687 miles) west and south in a great loop that enters Tennessee and returns to western Kentucky where it joins the Ohio River.

**Cumberland Gap** a high pass through the Appalachian Mts. in the eastern US, used by early pioneers to the west. It crosses the Cumberland Plateau near the junction of the boundaries of the US states of Virginia, Kentucky, and Tennessee.

**Cumbernauld** /kʌmb(ə)rˈnɔːld/ a New Town in central Scotland established in 1955, the administrative centre of Cumbernauld and Kilsyth District, Strathclyde Region from 1975 to 1996; pop. (1981) 47,900.

**Cumbria** /'kʌmbrɪə/ a county of north-west England formed in 1974 from the former counties of Cumberland, Westmorland, and part of Lancashire; area 6,824 sq. km. (2,636 sq. miles); pop. (1991) 486,900; county town, Carlisle. Separated from Northumberland by the Pennine Range, the county is dominated by the Cumbrian Mountains and the Lake District. Cumbria is divided into six districts:

| District | Area (sq. km.) | Pop. (1991) |
|---|---|---|
| Allerdale | 1,259 | 96,300 |
| Barrow-in-Furness | 770 | 71,900 |
| Carlisle | 1,040 | 99,800 |
| Copeland | 737 | 70,700 |
| Eden | 2,158 | 46,300 |
| South Lakeland | 1,553 | 101,900 |

**cumulonimbus** /,kju:mjʊləʊˈnɪmbəs/ a form of cloud consisting of a tall dense mass, present during thunderstorms.

**cumulus** /'kju:mjʊləs/ a cloud formation consisting of round masses heaped on each other above a horizontal base.

**Cunene** /kju:ˈeɪnə/ a river of Angola which rises near the city of Huambo and flows 250 km. (156 miles) south as far as the frontier with Namibia, which it then follows westwards to the Atlantic.

**Cuneo** /ku:ˈneɪəʊ/ an industrial and market town in the Piedmont region of northern Italy, capital of Cuneo province, on a high terrace between the Gesso and Stura di Demonte rivers; pop. (1990) 55,840. It has agriculturally based light industries.

**Curaçao** /,kjʊərəˈsaʊ/ the largest island of the Netherlands Antilles, situated in the Caribbean Sea 60 km. (37 miles) north of the Venezuelan coast; area 444 sq. km. (171 sq. miles); pop. (1990) 144,960; chief town, Willemstad. Curaçao's economy is based on refining of crude oil imported from Venezuela, and on tourism.

**Curepipe** /kjʊərˈpiːp/ a town in the uplands of west-central Mauritius, developed in the 19th c. when outbreaks of disease forced settlers to move away from the hot coastal port of Port Louis; pop. (1989) 66,700.

**Curia** /ˈkjʊərɪə/ the papal court and government departments of the Vatican City in Rome. It was also the name of an ancient Roman tribe, the senate house in Rome, and a feudal court of justice.

**Curicó** /kuːriəˈkəʊ/ a town in the wine-producing province of Curicó in the Maule region of central Chile; pop. (1991) 109,000.

**Curitiba** /ˌkjʊərɪˈtiːbə/ a city in south-east Brazil, capital of Paraná state; pop. (1990) 1,248,400. Paper, textiles, and chemicals are produced.

**Curragh** /ˈkʌrə/, **the** a plain in County Kildare in the Republic of Ireland, noted for the breeding of racehorses. The Irish Derby is run annually on its racecourse.

**Cushitic** /kʊˈʃɪtɪk/ a group of east African languages of the Hamitic type, spoken mainly in Ethiopia and Somalia.

**customs union** a group of countries forming an economic union that allows member-states to trade freely with each other while applying a common tariff to goods from outside the union.

**Cuttack** /ˈkʌtək/ a port at the head of the Mahanadi river delta in the state of Orissa, eastern India; pop. (1991) 402,000. Founded in the 10th c. it is noted for its gold and silver filigree work.

**Cuyo** /ˈkuːjəʊ/ the name given to a fruit-growing region of western Argentina comprising the provinces of San Juan, San Luis, and Mendoza. The name is derived from an Araucanian Indian word meaning 'sandy land'.

**Cuzco** /ˈkʊskəʊ/ an historic city in the Andes of southern Peru that was the capital of the Inca empire and the beginning of the 'Inca Trail' to MACHU PICCHU until the Spanish conquest (1533); pop. (1990) 275,300. It is capital of a department of the same name. It has a magnificent baroque cathedral and church built in 1668, and holds both Catholic and Inca festivals. It was heavily damaged by a severe earthquake in 1950 but the major buildings have been restored.

**cwm** /kʊm/ a Welsh word for a valley.

**Cwmbran** /kəmˈbrɑːn/ the administrative centre of Gwent in south Wales, on the Afon Lywel north-west of Newport; pop. (1981) 44,800. It was established in 1949 as a New Town to accommodate steel workers.

**Cyclades** /ˈsɪklədiːz/ (Greek **Kikládhes** /kɪkˈlɑːðiːs/) a group of Greek islands in the Aegean Sea, regarded in antiquity as circling around the sacred island of Delos. They are the site of a Bronze Age civilization noted for developments in metallurgy and for angular figurines in white marble. The Cyclades form a department of modern Greece; pop. (1991) 100,100.

**cyclone** /ˈsaɪkləʊn/ **1.** a depression or a system of winds rotating inwards to an area of low barometric pressure. In the Northern Hemisphere cyclones spin in an anticlockwise direction; in the Southern Hemisphere cyclones turn clockwise. **2.** a violent hurricane of limited diameter created when cold polar air meets warm air of the temperate zone.
**cyclonic** adj.

**Cymru** /ˈkʌmrɪ/ the Welsh name for WALES.
**Cymric** adj.

**Cyprus** /ˈsaɪprəs/ (Greek **Kapros**, Turkish **Kibris**) a large island in the eastern Mediterranean about 80 km. (50 miles) south of the Turkish coast; area 9,251 sq. km. (3,573 sq. miles); 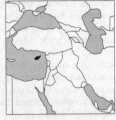 pop. (est. 1991) 700,000; languages, Greek (80%) and Turkish (18%); capital, Nicosia. The third-largest island in the Mediterranean, Cyprus is traversed from east to west by two mountain ranges that are separated by the fertile Mesaoria plain. The Kyrenia range in the north rises to 1,024 m. (3,360 ft.) at Mt. Kyparissovouno and the Troödos Mts. in the south-west rise to 1,951 m. (6,400 ft.) at Mt. Olympus. The island's principal exports are citrus fruit, grapes, potatoes, wine, and clothing. Paphos and Ayia Napa are the island's principal tourist resorts. Cyprus was colonized from Greece in the first half of the 14th c. BC. In classical times it was noted for its copper (which is named after it) and its cult of Aphrodite. Placed at the crossroads of a number of civilizations, its Greek population was successively subject to Assyrian, Egyptian, Persian, Ptolomaic, and Roman overlordship. In medieval times it was ruled by Byzantines, Arabs, Franks, and Venetians, until conquered in 1571 by the Turks, who held it until 1878 when it was placed under British administration. It was annexed by Britain in 1914 and made a Crown Colony in 1925. The island's recent history has been dominated by tension between the two major communities, the Greek Cypriots, 78 per cent of the population, (some of whom favour *enosis* or union with Greece) and the Turkish Cypriots. After a period of virtual civil war from 1955 Cyprus became an independent republic within the Commonwealth in 1960, but its constitution proved unworkable. Britain continued to maintain military bases at Akrotiri and Dhekelia, but violence escalated and in 1964 a UN peace-keeping force was sent to the island. In 1974 Turkey invaded the island and established a 'Turkish Federated State' over the northern 37 per cent of Cyprus. Intercommunal talks failed to resolve the situation and in 1983 the Turkish Cypriot community established the 'Independent Turkish Republic of Northern Cyprus (pop. 175,000); this has not been recognized by the UN.

**Cyrenaica** /ˌsaɪrəˈneɪkə/ (anc. **Cyrene**) a region of north-east Libya, bordering on the Mediterranean Sea. Settled by Greeks c. 640 BC, the colony of Cyrene gave its name to the Cyrenaic school of philosphy which flourished in the 4th c. BC. Under Egyptian rule it was known as Pentopolis after the five cities of Cyrene, Arsinoë, Berenice, Ptolemaïs, and Apollonia.

**Cyrillic** /sɪˈrɪlɪk/ one of the two principal Slavonic scripts or alphabets (the other is the Roman) in use today. It was based on Greek uncials, and was reputedly introduced by St. Cyril and his brother St. Methodius in their missionary work among the southern Slavs. It has remained, with some changes, the method of writing the languages (which include Russian) of those Slavonic peoples whose Christianity and culture came, directly or indirectly, from the Greek civilization of medieval Constantinople.

**Cythera** /səˈθiːrə/ (Greek **Kíthira**, also **Cerigo**) an island in the Aegean Sea off the south-east coast of the Peloponnese of southern Greece; area 278 sq. km. (107 sq. miles). It is linked to Piraeus by ferry.

**Czechoslovakia** /ˌtʃekəsləˈvækɪə/ (Czech **Ceskoslovensko**) a former state of central Europe comprising the Czech Republic and Slovakia which separated and became independent republics in 1993; area 127,896 sq. km. (49,399 sq. miles); pop. (1991) 15,567,600; capital, Prague. Czechoslovakia was created out of the northern part of the old Austro-Hungarian empire after the latter's collapse at the end of World War I. It incorporated the Czechs (who had enjoyed freedom within their own state of Bohemia until the rise of Habsburg power in the 16th and 17th c.) of Bohemia and Moravia with the Slovaks of Slovakia. Czech history between the two World Wars represents a brave and enlightened attempt at integration, undermined by economic trouble and eventually crushed by the Nazi takeover of first the Sudetenland (1938) and then the rest of Bohemia and Moravia (1939). After World War II power was seized by the Communists and Czechoslovakia remained under Soviet domination, an attempt at liberalization being crushed by Soviet military intervention in 1968, until Communist supremacy was overthrown in a peaceful revolution in December 1989, followed by the introduction of democratic reforms and the eventual separation of Slovakia and the Czech Republic into independent states in 1993.
**Czechoslovakian** or **Czechoslovak** *adj. & n.*

**Czech Republic** /tʃek/, **The** (Czech **Ceská Republika**)

an independent state in central Europe, formerly one of the two constituent republics of Czechoslovakia, surrounded by Slovakia to the east, Poland to the north, Austria to the south, and Germany to the west; area 78,864 sq. km. (30,461 sq. miles); pop.(1991) 10,298,700; official language, Czech; capital, Prague. Its largest cities are Prague, Brno, Ostrava, Pilsen (Plzen), and Olomouc. The Czech Republic is separated from Germany by the Bohemian Forest and from Poland by the Sudetic Mts.; Bohemia and Moravia, the two divisions of the Czech Republic, are separated by the Bohemian-Moravian Highlands. Formerly part of the Austrian Empire, the provinces of Bohemia and Moravia united with Slovakia in the east to form the republic of Czechoslovakia in 1918. During World War II western Czechoslovakia, as Bohemia and Moravia, was a German protectorate. As part of post-war Czechoslovakia, it formed close ties with the Soviet Union until the collapse of Communism in 1989. Designated as the Czech Socialist Republic under the 1968 federal constitition, it separated from Slovakia in 1993 to become an independent state.
**Czech** *adj. & n.*

The Czech Republic is divided into seven regions:

| Region | Area (sq. km.) | Pop. (1991) | Capital |
|---|---|---|---|
| Central Bohemia | 11,003 | 1,112,400 | Prague |
| South Bohemia | 11,345 | 697,300 | Ceske Budejovice |
| West Bohemia | 10,876 | 860,300 | Pilsen |
| North Bohemia | 7,810 | 1,173,700 | Usti nad Labem |
| East Bohemia | 11,240 | 1,232,600 | Hradec Králové |
| South Moravia | 15,028 | 2,048,900 | Brno |
| North Moravia | 11,067 | 1,961,500 | Ostrava |

**Częstochowa** /ˌtʃenstəˈkəʊvə/ an industrial city, capital of Częstochowa county in central Poland, on the River Warta; pop. (1990) 258,000. The Paulite monastery on Jasna Góra Hill contains a noted shrine of the Virgin Mary. Steel, chemicals, and textiles are produced.

# D*d*

**Dąbrowa Górnicza** /dəmˈbrɒvə gʊəˈniːtʃə/ a mining and steel-manufacturing city in the province of Katowice, southern Poland; pop. (1990) 136,900.

**Dacca** See DHAKA.

**Dachau** /ˈdæxaʊ, -kaʊ/ a city in southern Bavaria, Germany, on the River Amper near Munich, site of a Nazi concentration camp from 1933 and during World War II.

**Dachstein** /ˈdæxstaɪn/ **1.** a mountainous alpine region of central Austria on the frontiers of Styria, Upper Austria, and Salzburg states, noted for its mountain lakes, glaciers, and ice caves. **2.** its highest peak rising to a height of 2,996 m. (9,829 ft.).

**Dacia** /ˈdeɪʃə/ an ancient country of south-east Europe in what is now the northern and western part of Romania. It was inhabited by an Indo-European people known to the Romans as Daci and the Greeks as Getae.

**Dadès Gorge** /deɪˈdez/ a narrow gorge 500 m. (1,600 ft.) deep in the High Atlas Mountains of Morocco, north of Boumalne. From November to January its river-bed is flooded with seasonal rain.

**Dadra and Nagar Haveli** / ˈdɑːdrə, ˌnɑːgə həˈveɪlɪ/ a Union Territory in western India, on the Arabian Sea; area 491 sq. km. (188 sq. miles); pop. (1991) 138,500; administrative headquarters, Silvassa. Formerly Portuguese territory, the two enclaves were occupied by Indian nationalists in 1954 and officially incorporated into India as a centrally administered Union Territory in 1961. Tourism and agriculture are the chief economic activities.

**Dagestan** /ˌdægɪˈstɑːn/ a republic in the Russian Federation, on the western shore of the Caspian Sea; area 50,300 sq. km. (19,416 sq. miles); pop. (1990) 1,823,000; capital, Makhachkala. Engineering, agriculture, and the production of oil, textiles, chemicals, and food are the chief industries.

**dağlari** /ˌdɑː(g)lɑːˈriː/ a Turkish word for a mountain range, as in Toros Dağlari (Taurus Mountains).

**Dahlak Islands** /ˈdɑːlək/ (also **Dehalak' Deset**) a group of islands in the Red Sea opposite the Eritrean port of Massawa.

**Dahna** /ˈdɑːnə/ a corridor of gravel plains and sand dunes between the Nejd and the Persian Gulf, linking the great desert (Rub' al Khali) of southern Arabia to the Nafud desert at the northern end of the Arabian peninsula.

**Dahomey** /dəˈhəʊmɪ/ the former name (until 1975) of BENIN.

**Dáil** /dɔɪl/ (in full **Dáil Eireann** /ˈeɪrən/) the lower house of parliament in the Republic of Ireland, composed of 166 members elected on a basis of proportional representation. It was first established in 1919 when the Irish republicans elected to Westminster in the 1918 election proclaimed an Irish State.

**Dairen** /daɪˈren/ the former Western name for DALIAN in north-east China.

**Dakar** /ˈdæka:(r)/ the capital of Senegal, a port on the Atlantic coast of West Africa; pop. (est. 1985) 1,382,000. It was founded by the French in 1857 on the site of a fishing village. It has one of the best Atlantic harbours in Africa and became the capital of French West Africa in 1902. It has a naval base and a railway link to the Senegal River. It is one of the largest industrial centres of West Africa with oil refining, sugar refining, groundnut crushing, textiles, fertilizer manufacturing, fishing, and tourism.

**Dakhla** (also **Ad Dakhla**) a town on the Atlantic coast of Western Sahara, known as Villa Cisneros until 1976; pop. (1982) 17,800. It is capital of the Moroccan province of Oued Addahab and was chief town of the former Spanish territory of Rio de Oro.

**Dakota** /dəˈkəʊtə/ a former territory of the US, organized in 1889 into the states of North Dakota and South Dakota.

**Dakota** a river of North and South Dakota, USA. See JAMES.

**Dakota, the** a luxury apartment building on Central Park West from 72nd to 73rd streets, New York City, USA. It was built by William Randolph Hearst as an investment for his mistress, Marion Davies. After World War II it became a co-operative occupied by the rich and the famous. In 1975 the singer-songwriter John Lennon was murdered here.

**Dalandzadgad** /ˌdælənˈzaːdəgət/ a market town, capital of the Gobi Desert region of southern Mongolia.

**Dales, the** the name given to a series of river valleys in northern England whose rivers drain the Pennine Hills through Yorkshire to the North Sea. Valleys include Teesdale, Swaledale, Wensleydale, Wharfedale, Nidderdale, and Airedale.

**Dali** /ˌdɑːˈliː/ a city in Yunnan, southern China, north-west of Kunming; pop. (1986) 399,000.

**Dalian** /dɑːlˈjen/ (formerly **Dairen**) a deep-water port on the Liaodong peninsula in Liaoning province, north-east China, one of the chief ship-building centres of China. With the port of Lüshun (formerly Port Arthur) it is sometimes known as Lüda; pop. (1986) 4,619,000.

**Dalkeith** /dælˈkiːθ/ a market town in Lothian Region, central Scotland, on the North and South Esk rivers, 10 km. (6 miles) south of Edinburgh. Dalkeith House was formerly the seat of the Dukes of Buccleuch.

**Dallas** /ˈdæləs/ an industrial, commercial, and cultural city in north-east Texas, on the Trinity River, noted as a major centre of banking and the oil, aerospace, and fashion industries; pop. (1990) 1,006,900. The Dallas–Fort Worth Airport is the largest commercial airport in the world. Dallas has several educational institutions, museums, and theatres. Founded as a trading post in 1841, Dallas was settled in 1855 by French, Swiss, and Belgians seeking to found a Utopian colony. President John F. Kennedy was assassinated here on 22 November 1963.

**Dalmatia** /dælˈmeɪʃə/ a region of Croatia comprising mountains and a narrow lowland plain that stretches down the east coast of the Adriatic Sea from Rijeka (Fiume) to the Montenegrin frontier. Split and Dubrovnik are two of its chief centres. Dalmatia is noted for its scenic beauty, its resort towns, and its offshore islands.
**Dalmatian** adj. & n.

**Dalriada** /dælˈriːədə/ an ancient Gaelic kingdom in northern Ireland whose people (known as *Scoti*) established a colony in south-west Scotland from about the late 5th c. By the 9th c. Irish Dalriada had declined but the people of Scottish Dalriada gradually acquired dominion over the whole of Scotland, giving that country its present name. The kings of the Scots were crowned at Dunadd, capital of Dalriada until the 9th c.

**Dalton Highway** /ˈdɔːlt(ə)n/ a road in the US state of Alaska, linking Fairbanks with the oilfields of Prudhoe Bay on the Arctic Ocean coast. Built in 1974 to service the Trans-Alaskan pipeline, the Dalton Highway stretches for a distance of 666 km. (420 miles).

**Daly City** /ˈdeɪlɪ/ a southern suburb of San Francisco, California, USA; pop. (1990) 92,300.

**Daman and Diu** /deˌmɑːn, ˈdiːuː/ a Union Territory on the Gujarat coast of west India, north of Bombay; area 112 sq. km. (43 sq. miles); pop. (1991) 101,400; administrative headquarters, Daman. Until 1987 the district of Daman and the island of Diu were administered with the former Portuguese colony of Goa, which now forms a separate state.

**Damanhur** /ˌdæmənˈhʊə(r)/ a cotton-processing and market city in northern Egypt, in the Nile delta west of the Rosetta Branch; pop. (1991) 216,000. It lies on the site of ancient Hermopolis Parva.

**Damaraland** /dəˈmɑːrəˌlænd/ a plateau region of central Namibia inhabited chiefly by Damara Hottentots and Bantu Herero people.

**Damascus** /dəˈmɑːskəs/ (Arabic **Dimashq**) the capital city of Syria since the country's independence in 1946; pop. (est. 1987) 1,292,000. Situated immediately east of the Anti-Lebanon Mts. on the Barada River, it has existed as a city for over 4,000 years. Under Roman rule it flourished as a commercial centre noted for its grain and its woven fabric which came to be known throughout the world as damask. Today it is Syria's administrative, financial, and communications centre. The old walled city which contains Christian churches as well as the Great Mosque built in 708 lies south of the river and the modern city with its office blocks, apartments, and university buildings (1924) lies to the north. Most of its main industries have a long tradition and include textiles, metal working, glass, leather goods, and foodstuffs.

**Damavand** /ˈdeməˌvend/ the highest peak in the Elburz Mts. of northern Iran, rising to 5,601 m. (18,376 ft.) north-east of Tehran.

**Dambulla** /dəmˈbuːlə/ a cave temple 72 km. (45 miles) north of Kandy in Sri Lanka. Five caves contain 150 Buddha images thought to date from the first century BC when King Valagam Bahu sought refuge here after being driven out of the Sinhalese capital of Anuradhapura.

**Damietta** /ˌdæmɪˈetə/ (Arabic **Dumyât** /dʊmˈjɑːt/) **1.** the partially silted up eastern branch of the Nile delta. **2.** a port at the mouth of the Nile on the north coast of Egypt; pop.(1991) 113,000. Once a prosperous Arab trading port, Damietta's importance declined after the building of the Suez Canal and the subsequent development of Port Said.

**Damodar** /ˈdæmədɑː/ a river of north-east India, which rises in the Chota Nagpur plateau of Bihar and flows 560 km. (350 miles) eastwards through West Bengal to meet the Hooghly River south-west of Calcutta.

**Dampier** /ˈdæmpɪə(r)/, **Mount** a mountain peak on South Island, New Zealand rising to 3,447 m. (11,309 ft.) on the main divide of the Southern Alps. It is the third largest mountain in New Zealand.

**Dan** /dæn/ a city of ancient Palestine, once the northernmost city of the Holy Land, thought to lie just west of present day Baniyas in Syria (Judges 20: 1).

**Danakil Depression** /ˈdænəkɪl/ a long low-lying desert region of north-east Ethiopia and northern Djibouti between the Red Sea and Africa's Great Rift Valley. The region is occupied by Danakil and Afar people who exploit natural reserves of salt. Lake Karum lies at its lowest point 120 m. (400 ft.) below sea-level and to the south rise the volcanic peaks of Erta Alé

**Da Nang** /dɑː næŋ/ a port and city (formerly called Tourane, Cua Han, and Thai Pien) in central Vietnam, on the South China Sea; pop. (est. 1991) 400,000. During the Vietnam War it was used as a US military base, the first US marines landing here on 8th March 1965.

**Danbury** /ˈdænbərɪ/ a city in south-west Connecticut, USA; pop. (1990) 65,590. Settled in 1685, it was a famous centre of hat production until the 1950s. During the American War of Independence it was an important supply depot and the site of a military hospital used by the Continental Army.

**Dandong** /dænˈdʊŋ/ (formerly **Antung**) a port in Liaoning province, north-east China, near the mouth of the Yalu River opposite Sinuiju in North Korea; pop. (1986) 2,574,000. It is China's northernmost ice-free deep-water harbour. Silk, synthetic fibres, electronic goods, and vehicles are produced.

**Dane** /deɪn/ a native or national of Denmark.

**Danelaw** /ˈdeɪnlɔː/ the part of north and east England occupied or administered by Danes from the late 9th c. and administered according to their laws until the Norman Conquest.

**Danger Island** (also **Pukapuka**) an island in the northern group of the Cook Islands in the central Pacific.

**Dangerous Islands** the English name for the TUAMOTU ISLANDS in French Polynesia.

**Dangrek Mountains** /tɒŋˈrek/ (also **Phanom Dong Rak** /ˈpɑːnəm tɒŋˈrɑːk/) a range of mountains stretching a distance of c. 320 km. (200 miles) along the frontier between Thailand and north-west Cambodia.

**Dangriga** a town on the Caribbean coast of Stann Creek District, Belize; pop. (1990) 6,400. It was known as Stann Creek until 1984.

**Danish** /ˈdeɪnɪʃ/ the official language of Denmark (where it is spoken by over 5 million people) and also of Greenland and the Faeroes.

**Danish West Indies** the former name of the US Virgin Islands which were established as a Danish colony in 1754 and later sold to the US in 1917 for $25 m.

**Danjiangkou** /dændʒæŋˈkəʊ/ (also **Jun Xian**) a city in Hubei province, east-central China, at the southern end of the Danjiangkou Reservoir; pop. (1986) 431,000.

**Danube** /ˈdænjuːb/ a river 2,857 km. (1,775 miles) long that rises in the Black Forest in southwest Germany and flows generally south-eastwards to the Black Sea. The Danube, which is Europe's second-longest river, is known as the **Donau** in Germany and Austria, **Dunaj** in Slovakia, **Duna** in Hungary, and **Dunarea** in Romania. The capital cities of Vienna, Budapest, and Belgrade are situated on it. For centuries it has been a vital traffic artery and is now linked to the Rhine by canal. In 1990, regions through which the Danube flows formed a 'working community' to promote co-operation.
**Danubian** *adj.*

**Danubian principalities** the name given to the former principalities of Wallachia and Moldavia in eastern Europe, united in 1859 to form the state of Romania.

**Danville** a city in south Virginia, USA, on the Dan River; pop. (1990) 53,000. Founded in 1792, it is a textile and tobacco centre with one of the nation's largest tobacco auction markets, and the largest single-unit textile mill in the world.

**Danzig** the German name for the port of GDANSK on the Baltic coast of Poland.

**Dão** /daʊ/ a river and noted wine-producing region of north-central Portugal. The Dão rises in the Serra de Lapa and flows 80 km. (50 miles) south-west to join the River Mondego near the town of Coimbra.

**Daqing** /dɑːˈkɪŋ/ (formerly **Taching**) a major industrial city in Heilongjiang province, north-east China, north-west of Harbin, producing oil, gas, and petrochemicals; pop. (1990) 940,000. It was developed by the state as a model agro-industrial complex after the discovery of oil in 1959.

**Darbhanga** /dɜːˈbæŋgə/ a city in the state of Bihar, north-east India, north-east of Patna; pop. (1991) 218,270.

**Dardanelles** /ˌdɑːdəˈnelz/ (Turkish **Çanakkale Boğazi** /ˌtʃɑːnəkəˈleɪ ˌbəʊ(g)ɑːˈziː/) a narrow strait between Europe and Asiatic Turkey, anciently called the Hellespont. Linking the Sea of Marmara with the Aegean Sea, it is 60 km. (38 miles) long. It was the scene of an unsuccessful attack on Turkey by British and French troops in 1915, with Australian and New Zealand contingents playing a major part.

**Dar es Salaam** /dɑːr es səˈlɑːm/ the former capital (until 1974) and chief port of Tanzania, founded in 1866 by the Sultan of Zanzibar, who built his summer palace there; pop. (1988) 1,360,850. In Arabic its name means 'haven of peace'. It handles most of Zambia's trade since the building of the Tanzam railway, as well as Tanzania's, and has oil-refining, textile, pharmaceutical, and food industries.

**Darfur** /dɑːˈfʊə(r)/ a former independent kingdom that became a province of Egypt in 1874 and later a region of west Sudan; area 196,555 sq. km. (75,919 sq. miles); pop. (1983) 3,093,700; capital, El Fasher.

**Darien** /ˈdeərɪən/ a sparsely populated province of eastern Panama; area 16,671 sq. km. (6,439 sq. miles); pop. (1990) 43,800; capital, La Palma. Originally known to the Spanish as Santa María la Antigua del Darién, the name was formerly applied to the whole of the the Isthmus of Panama. At the end of the 17th c. an unsuccessful attempt was made by Scottish settlers to establish a colony in the tropical wilderness of the eastern region with the aim of controlling trade between the Atlantic and Pacific Oceans.

**Darien, Gulf of** a part of the Caribbean Sea, between Panama and Colombia.

**Darjeeling** /dɑː'dʒiːlɪŋ/ (also **Darjiling**) a hill station at an altitude of 2,150 m. (7,054 ft.) in West Bengal, north-east India, near the Sikkim frontier; pop. (1991) 73,090. The surrounding area produces a high-quality tea for export.

**Darkhan** /dɑː'kɑːn/ (also **Darhan**) an industrial and mining city in northern Mongolia, established in 1961; pop. (1990) 80,100.

**Darling Downs** /ˌdɑːlɪŋ 'daʊnz/ a fertile low-lying plain in south-eastern Queensland, Australia, noted for its black volcanic soil and its landscape of lush pasture and cultivated fields which produce wheat, oats, tobacco, fruit, cotton, soybeans, sheep, and dairy produce.

**Darling River** /'dɑːlɪŋ/ a river of south-east Australia, whose headstreams rise in the Great Dividing Range and which flows 1,867 km. (1,160 miles) in a generally south-westward course to join the Murray River north-west of Mildura. It was named after Sir Ralph Darling (1775–1858), Governor-General of New South Wales from 1825 to 1831.

**Darlington** /'dɑːlɪŋtən/ an industrial town in the county of Durham, north-east England, at the junction of the Skerne and Cocker Beck rivers; pop. (1991) 96,700. The world's first passenger railway built by George Stephenson linked Darlington and Stockton in 1825.

**Darmstad** /'dɑːmstæt/ an industrial town and transport centre in the state of Hesse, Germany, with wine-making, machinery, and chemical industries. It is also the centre of the European space industry; pop. (1991) 140,040.

**Dartford** a residential and industrial town in Kent south-east England, to the south of the River Thames and east of London; pop. (1981) 42,000. Built in 1963, the **Dartford Tunnel** runs under the Thames to Purfleet in Essex. There is also a bridge across the river.

**Dartmoor** /'dɑːtmʊə(r)/ **1.** a moorland district in Devon, south-west England, which is famous for its wild ponies and was a royal forest in Saxon times, now (since 1951) a national park. **2.** a major long-term prison near Princetown in this district, originally built to hold French prisoners of war during the Napoleonic Wars.

**Dartmouth** /'dɑːtməθ/ a fishing port and resort town in Devon, south-west England, on the estuary of the River Dart opposite Kingswear. The *Mayflower* and *Speedwell* sailed from here with the Pilgrim Fathers in August 1620. There is a Tudor castle and the Royal Naval College (opened in 1905).

**Darwin** /'dɑːwɪn/ the capital of the Northern Territory, Australia, on the Beagle Gulf; pop. (1991) 67,950. Originally known as Palmerston or Port Darwin, its name was changed to Darwin in 1911. Development has largely been linked to the exploitation of the territory's mineral wealth. Devastated by a hurricane in 1879, it was again almost completely destroyed by Cyclone Tracy in 1974.

**darya** /'dɑːrjə/ a Persian word for a river, as in Amu Darya.

**Dashhowuz** /dɑː'ʃaʊz/ a city in northern Turkmenistan, in the valley of the Amu Darya near the frontier with Uzbekistan; pop. (1990) 114,000. It was known as Tashauz until 1991.

**dasht** a Persian word for a desert, as in the Dasht-e Lut of central Iran.

**Date Line** see INTERNATIONAL DATE LINE.

**Datong** /dɑː'tuːŋ/ (formerly **Ta-T'ung**) a coal-mining and industrial city in northern Shanxi province, China; pop. (1990) 1,110,000. Formerly capital of the Northern Wei Dynasty (until AD 494), Datong developed into an important industrial centre in the 1920s, being particularly developed as a railway and locomotive-building centre. The Upper Huayan monastery is one of the largest temples in China. At the foot of the Wuzhou Hills 16 km. (10 miles) west of the city lie the Yungang cave temples with the earliest Buddhist stone carvings in China.

**Daugava** /'daʊgəvə/ the Lettish name for the Western Dvina River (see DVINA).

**Daugavpils** /'daʊgəfˌpɪls/ a marketing city in east Latvia, on the Western Dvina River; pop. (1989) 127,000. A trading centre for timber, grain, and flax with engineering and textile industries, it was known as Dvinsk until 1920, Latgale (1920–40), and Dünaburg (1941–4).

**Dauphiné** /ˌdəʊfiˈneɪ/ a former province of south-east France deriving its name from the title (dauphin) borne by the eldest son of the king of France from 1349, when the French Crown acquired the lands, to 1830. Charles V ceded the Dauphiné to his eldest son in 1368, establishing the practice of passing both title and lands to the Crown prince. Its capital was the town of Grenoble. The name is still applied to an area of the western Alps which rises to a height of 4,101 m. (13,455 ft.) at the Barre des Ecrins.

**Davangere** /dəˈvæŋgəˌreɪ/ a city in the state of Karnataka, southern India, north-west of Bangalore; pop. (1991) 287,110. It is a market town for cotton, millet, sugar-cane, and peanuts.

**Davao** /'dɑːvaʊ/ a seaport in the southern Philippines, on the island of Mindanao; pop. (1990) 849,950. Founded in 1849, it is the largest city on the island and the third-largest city in the Philippines. Its land area of 1937 sq. km. (748 sq. miles) makes it one of the most extensive cities in the world. It exports hemp, coffee, cocoa, and timber.

**Davenport** /'dævənpɔːt/ a city in eastern Iowa, USA, on the Mississippi River; pop. (1990) 95,300. It is part of the Quad cities metropolitan area which also includes Bettendorf in Iowa and Moline and Rock Island in Illinois. Founded in 1808, the city is named after a US Army officer who explored this area. It developed rapidly after the railroad crossed the Mississippi in 1854 and manufactures heavy industrial and agricultural equipment.

**David** /dɑːˈviːd/ the principal city of western Panama, on the River David; pop. (1980) 50,600. Founded as a gold-mining town in 1738, it is capital of the province of Chiriqui.

**Davis Strait** /'deɪvɪs/ a sea passage 645 km. (400 miles) long separating Greenland from Baffin Island and connecting Baffin Bay with the Atlantic Ocean. The strait is named after the English explorer John Davis (1559–1605) who sailed through it in 1587.

**Davos** /'dɑːvəʊs/ a resort and winter sports centre in Graubünden canton, eastern Switzerland; pop. (1990) 10,500. It is linked to the resort of Klosters by the Parsenn ski area.

**Dawson** /'dɔːsən/ (formerly **Dawson City**) a former gold-mining town in west Yukon Territory, northern Canada, at the junction of the Klondike and Yukon rivers; pop. (1991) 1,900. Capital of the Yukon until 1953, gold was discovered here in 1896. The town is associated with the writer Jack London and the poet Robert Service both of whom lived here for some time.

**Dawson Creek** a town in north-east British Columbia, Canada, in the eastern foothills of the Rocky Mountains on the Alaska Highway; pop. (1991) 10,980.

**Daxian** /ˌdɑːʃiːˈɑːn/ a city in Sichuan province, central China, on the Zhou River north of Chongqing; pop. (1986) 218,000.

**Daya Bay** /'dæɪə/ (Chinese **Daya Wan**) a bay on the coast of Guandong province, southern China, an inlet of the South China Sea south-east of Guangzhou (Canton). A nuclear power-station (completed in 1993) at the head of the bay is one of the largest in China.

**Dayton** /'deɪt(ə)n/ a city in western Ohio, USA, at the junction of the Great Miami and Stillwater rivers; pop. (1990) 182,000. Founded in 1796, Dayton was the home of James Ritty, inventor of the cash register, and the Wright brothers who pioneered aviation. Wright-Paterson Air Force Base is a centre of research and aerospace logistics. It is the industrial and trading hub of a fertile agricultural area.

**Daytona Beach** /deɪˈtəʊnə/ a resort city on the Atlantic coast of Florida, USA; pop. (1990) 61,900. In the early days of the motor car its 36-km. (23-mile) beach was used as a natural speedway on which Alexander Winton set the world record of 68 m.p.h. in 1903. The Daytona International Speedway is a modern 4-km. (2.5-mile) speedway track.

**Dazu** /dɑːˈzuː/ an important Buddhist archaeological site in the hills 160 km. (100 miles) northwest of Chongqing in Sichuan province, central China. There are more than 50,000 stone carvings dating from the 9th to the 13th c.

**DC** *abbr.* US District of Columbia.

**DE** *abbr.* US Delaware (in official postal use).

**Dead Sea** a bitter salt-lake or inland sea in the Jordan valley on the Israel–Jordan border. At 400 m. (1,300 ft.) below sea-level, it is the lowest point in the world.

**Deal** /diːl/ a resort town, one of the Cinque Ports, in Kent on the south coast of England; pop. (1981) 26,500. In 1852 the Duke of Wellington died at Walmer Castle, official home of the Lord Warden of the Cinque Ports.

**Dearborn** /'dɪəbɔːn/ a suburban area of Detroit, Michigan, USA; pop. (1990) 89,300. It was the birthplace in 1863 of Henry Ford and home of the Ford Motor Company. Over 80 17th–19th c. historic homes from all corners of the USA have been reconstructed at Greenfield Village. Its industries include automobiles, steel, machine tools, and metal products.

**Dearborn Heights** a suburban area of Detroit, in Michigan, USA, pop. (1990) 60,840.

**Death Valley** a deep arid desert basin in southeast California and south-west Nevada, USA, the hottest and driest part of North America and one of the hottest places on earth. At 86 m. (282 ft.) below sea-level, it is the lowest elevation in North America. It formed an obstacle to the movements of pioneer settlers, whence its name.

**Deauville** /'dəʊviːl/ a resort town on the Normandy coast of north-west France, on the estuary of the River Seine; pop. (1982) 4,770. It is noted for its race-course, its boardwalk (Promenade des Planches) which runs the whole length of the 3 km. beach, and casinos.

**Debrecen** /'debrət‚sen/ an industrial, commercial, and cultural city in eastern Hungary, at the heart of the Great Plain region; pop. (1993) 217,290. It is capital of Hajdú-Bihar county and the third-largest city in Hungary. It was the centre of 16th-c. Hungarian Protestantism and its Calvinist college became the present university. The old town contains many ancient buildings. The industrial zone produces machinery, medical instruments, pharmaceuticals, and foodstuffs.

**Decatur** /dɪˈkɑːtə(r)/ a city in central Illinois, USA, on the Sangamon River; pop. (1990) 83,900. Founded in 1829, it is an agricultural trade and food-processing centre. Abraham Lincoln lived and worked in the area and made his first political speech in Decatur.

**Deccan** /'dekən/ a triangular plateau region of southern India, bounded by the Malabar and Coromandel coasts, and by the Vindhaya mountains in the north.

**Dee** /di:/ **1.** a river in north-east Scotland that rises in the Grampian Mts. and flows eastwards to meet the North Sea at Aberdeen. **2.** a river that rises in Loch Dee in the Southern Uplands of south-west Scotland and flows southwards to the Solway Firth at Kirkcudbright. **3.** a river that rises in Lake Bala, North Wales and flows east then north along the Welsh border before passing through Chester and on into the Irish Sea.

**Deep South, the** a name given to the south-eastern states of the USA that were generally associated with slavery before the Civil War, including South Carolina, Tennessee, Louisiana, Mississippi, Alabama, and Georgia.

**Defense** /deɪ'fɒns/, **La** a commercial district of western Paris, France.

**deflation** /dɪ'fleɪʃən/ the removal by wind of fine dust and sand deposits on the land surface.

**Dehiwala** /ˌdeɪhi:'wɑːlə/ a resort town on the west coast of Sri Lanka, just south of Colombo; pop. (1981) 174,400.

**Dehra Dun** /ˌdeɪrə 'duːn/ a city in the state of Uttar Pradesh, northern India; pop. (1991) 270,030. Founded in the 17th c. by the Sikh Guru Ram Rai, it is noted for its military academy and its forest research institute.

**Delaware** /'deləˌweə(r)/ a state of the US on the Atlantic coast between Maryland and Delaware Bay, one of the original 13 states of the US (1787); area 5,295 sq. km. (2,044 sq. miles); pop. (1990) 666,168; capital, Dover. Its largest cities are Wilmington, Dover, and Newark. Delaware is also known as the First State or the Diamond State. Industrial products include textiles, chemicals, machinery, and vehicles; agricultural products include, fish, fruit, vegetables, corn, chickens, and dairy produce. Colonized by Dutch and Swedish settlers, Delaware was named after an early 17th c. governor of Virginia, Thomas West, Baron De La Warr. It was taken by the British in 1664 and was the first state to ratify the constitution in 1787. The state is divided into three counties:

| County | Area (sq. km.) | Pop. (1990) | County Seat |
| --- | --- | --- | --- |
| Kent | 1,547 | 110,990 | Dover |
| New Castle | 1,030 | 441,950 | Wilmington |
| Sussex | 2,449 | 113,230 | Georgetown |

**Delaware** /'deləˌweə(r)/ a river of eastern USA that flows along the frontiers of Pennsylvania, New York, and New Jersey before entering Delaware Bay, an inlet of the North Atlantic.

**Delaware** an Algonquian-speaking tribe of North American Indians whose original homelands lay along the Atlantic coast where they cultivated maize. During the 19th c. they moved to Kansas and Oklahoma and today others live in Wisconsin and Ontario. Known to the British as Deleware and the French as Loupe (= wolves), they called themselves Lenni-Lenape (= men of our nation).

**Delaware Water Gap** a gorge on the course of the Delaware River as it passes through the Kitatinny Mountains of eastern Pennsylvania, USA, close to the New Jersey frontier.

**Delft** /delft/ a town in the province of South Holland in the Netherlands, 5 km. (3 miles) south-east of the Hague; pop. (1991) 89,400. Since the 17th c. the town has been noted for its pottery. The painters Pieter de Hooch (1629–83) and Jan Vermeer lived here and much of the old town they knew has survived; William the Silent, who freed the Netherlands from Spanish rule was assassinated in Delft in 1584. Delft manufactures spirits, pharmaceuticals, cables, and ceramics.

**Delhi** /'deli/ **1.** a Union Territory of India; area 1,483 sq. km. (573 sq. miles); pop. (1991) 9,370,475. **2.** the capital of India comprising **Old Delhi**, a walled city on the River Jumna, and **New Delhi** (pop. 294,150), the present seat of the government of India, built 1912–29 to the design of Sir Edwin Lutyens (1869–1944), to replace Calcutta as the capital of British India; pop. (1991) 8,375,200. Delhi was made the capital of the Mughal empire in 1638 by Shah Jahan, who built the Red Fort containing the imperial Mughal palace. Other places of interest include the Jami Majid mosque, the Rashtrapati Bhawan (the former Viceroy's Palace), Rajpath Avenue, the Qutb Minar—the highest stone tower in the world, and the observatory of Jai Singh. The University of Delhi, which has 74 constituent colleges was founded in 1922 and is located in the southern part of New Delhi as are the airport, and the arenas built for the 1982 Asian Games. The place of Gandhi's cremation after his assassination in 1948 is a national shrine. Delhi's industries, mainly of consumer goods of all kinds are sited in satellite towns. Old Delhi is a centre for skilled crafts.

**Delmenhorst** /'delmənˌhɔːst/ an industrial city in Lower Saxony, north-west Germany, west of Bremen; pop. (1991) 75,970.

**Delos** /'diːlɒs/ a small Greek island in the Aegean, at the centre of the Cyclades group. According to legend the birthplace of Apollo and Artemis, it was from earliest historical times sacred to Apollo.
**Delian** *adj. & n.*

**Delphi** /'delfɪ, -faɪ/ (Greek **Dhelfoí** /ðel'fiː/) one of the most important sanctuaries of the ancient Greek world, dedicated to Apollo and situated on the lower southern slopes of Mount Parnassus above the Gulf of Corinth. Reputedly the navel of the earth, it was the seat of the Delphic Oracle, whose often riddling responses to a wide range of religious, political, and moral questions were delivered in a state of ecstasy by the Pythia, the priestess of Apollo; a male prophet put the question to her and interpreted her answer. Influential in the earlier periods of Greek history, its influence declined in Hellenistic times although it was still a centre of information for the Greek World. Under the Roman empire there were other oracles and other methods of divination (e.g. astrology) which provided alternative sources of prophecy, and its decline was almost complete when Christianity became the official religion under Constantine. **Delphic** or **Delphian** *adj.*

**delta** /'deltə/ a triangular tract of deposited earth, alluvium, etc., at the mouth of a river, formed by its diverging outlets.

**Demerara** /ˌdeməˈrɑːrə/ a river of Guyana in South America that flows *c.* 320 km. (200 miles) northwards to the Atlantic Ocean from the Guiana Highlands.

**demography** /dɪˈmɒgrəfɪ/ the study of the statistics of births, deaths, disease, etc., as illustrating the conditions of life in communities. **demographic** *adj.*

**Dempster Highway** /'demstə(r)/ a highway in northern Canada that stretches *c.* 740 km. (460 miles) from near Dawson in the Yukon Territory to Inuvik at the mouth of the Mackenzie River on the Arctic coast of the Northwest Territories. It is the only public road in North America to extend north of the Arctic Circle. Following an old Indian trade route, it is named after Corporal W. D. Dempster who led a patrol in the winter of 1911 in search of a missing Northwest Mounted Police patrol.

**Denali National Park** a national park in the Kichatna Mountains of Alaska that includes Mount McKinley which is known to the Aleuts as Denali. Established in 1917 as the Mount McKinley National Park, its name was officially changed in 1980.

**Denbigh** /'denbɪ/ a town in Clwyd, north Wales, 16 km. (10 miles) south of Rhyl. It was the birthplace of the African explorer H. M. Stanley (1841–1904) who was brought up in the workhouse here.

**Denbigh** (also **Denbighshire**) a former county of north Wales, divided between Clwyd and Gwynedd in 1974.

**Den Haag** See the HAGUE.

**Den Helder** /dən ˈheldə(r)/ the chief North Sea naval base of the Netherlands, in the province of North Holland opposite the island of Texel; pop. (1991) 61,500. It is linked to Amsterdam by the North Holland Canal.

**Denison** /'denɪsən/ a city in north-east Texas, USA, near the Red River; pop. (1990) 21,505. It was the birthplace of President Dwight D. Eisenhower (1890–1969). It has numerous light industries.

**deniz** a Turkish word for a sea or lake.

**Denizli** /dəˈniːzlɪ/ **1.** a province of south-west Turkey; area 11,868 sq. km. (4,584 sq. miles); pop. (1990) 750,900. **2.** its capital, a market town 176 km. (110 miles) south-east of Izmir; pop. (1990) 204,100. Nearby are the ruins of ancient Laodicea.

**Denmark**
/'denmɑːk/ (Danish **Danmark**) official name **The Kingdom of Denmark** a Scandinavian country consisting of the greater part of the Jutland peninsula and the neighbour-ing islands, between the North Sea and the Baltic; area 43,075 sq. km. (16,631 sq. miles); pop. (est. 1991) 5,100,000; official language, Danish; capital, Copenhagen. Its largest cities are Copenhagen, Aarhus, Odense, and Ålborg. Denmark emerged as a separate country during the Viking period of the 10th and 11th c. In the 14th c. Denmark and Norway were united under a Danish king, the union being joined between 1389–97 and 1523 by Sweden. Territory was lost to Sweden as a result of wars in the mid-17th c. and Norway was ceded to Sweden after the Napoleonic Wars. More territory was lost to the south when Schleswig-Holstein was taken by Prussia in 1864 (although the northern part of Schleswig was returned to Denmark in 1920). Denmark remained neutral in World War I, but was occupied by the Germans for much of World War II. Since the war, however, Denmark has been stable and prosperous, her economy built around oil, textiles, and agriculture, particularly dairy products. Greenland was created an autonomous region in 1979. The country is a constitutional monarchy with a unicameral parliament.
**Danish** *adj.*
In addition to the city of Copenhagen and the borough of Frederiksberg Denmark is administratively divided into 14 counties:

| County | Area (sq. km.) | Pop. (1990) | Capital |
|---|---|---|---|
| Copenhagen | 522 | 601,670 | Copenhagen |
| Frederiksborg | 1,347 | 221,400 | Hillerød |
| Roskilde | 891 | 152,700 | Roskilde |
| West Jutland | 2,984 | 283,650 | Soro |
| Storstrøm | 3,398 | 257,000 | Nykøbing |
| Bornholm | 588 | 45,900 | Rønne |
| Fyn | 3,486 | 459,350 | Odense |
| South Jutland | 3,930 | 250,400 | Aabenraa |
| Ribe | 3,131 | 218,600 | Ribe |
| Vejle | 2,997 | 330,400 | Vejle |
| Ringkøbing | 4,853 | 267,300 | Ringkøbing |
| Aarhus | 4,561 | 597,000 | Aarhus |
| Viborg | 4,122 | 229,800 | Viborg |
| North Jutland | 6,173 | 484,500 | Aalborg |

**Denmark Strait** an arm of the North Atlantic separating Greenland and Iceland. During World War II HMS *Hood* was sunk here by the German battleship *Bismarck*.

**Denpasar** /den'pɑːsɑː(r)/ the capital, market, and cultural centre of the Indonesian island of Bali; pop. (1980) 261,300. It has two art galleries and a large open-air theatre.

**Dent Blanche** /dɔːn blɑːnʃ/ a mountain rising to 4,367 m. (14,318 ft.) in the Pennine Alps of southern Switzerland.

**Denton** /'dentən/ a city in north Texas, USA, 56 km. (35 miles) north-west of Dallas; pop. (1990) 66,300. It is an agricultural trading centre and university town.

**Dents du Midi** /ˌdɑ̃ du: 'miːdiː/ a mountain group in the western Alps between the River Rhône at Martigny and Mont Blanc. Its highest peak rises to a height of 3,257 m (10,686 ft.).

**D'Entrecasteaux Islands**
/ˌdɔːntrə'kæstəʊ/ a group of volcanic islands in the western Pacific off the south-east coast of New Guinea, the largest of which are Goodenough, Fergusson, and Normanby islands. They form part of the Papua New Guinea province of Milne Bay.

**Denver** /'denvə(r)/ the capital and largest city of Colorado, USA, at the junction of the South Platte River and Cherry Creek; pop. (1990) 467,600. Known as the 'Mile High City', Denver is situated at an altitude of 1,608 m. (5,280 ft.) on the eastern edge of the Rocky Mountains. It first developed as a silver-mining town in the 1870s and later became an important centre for transportation, tourism, commerce, and research. Its manufactures include aircraft, chemicals, and electronics. The national Mint is located here and Denver International Airport is the world's largest airport.

**Deolali** /du:'læli/ a town in Maharashtra, western India, north-east of Bombay; pop. (1991) 51,115. It was a transfer camp for British soldiers going home during World Wars I and II. Those who spent time there, especially in its mental hospital, were said to go crazy with boredom, an infliction that came to be known as 'Doolally Tap'.

**Dera Ghazi Khan** /ˌdeɪrə 'gɑːzi: xɑːn/ an agricultural market town in the Indus valley of Punjab province, Pakistan; pop. (1981) 103,000. It was rebuilt to the west of the river after being destroyed by floods in 1908–9.

**Derbent** /də'bent/ (also **Derbend**) a city of Dagestan in southern Russia, on the western shore of the Caspian Sea; pop. (1985) 80,000. The city, formerly on an important land route for trade between Europe and Asia, is approached from the west through a pass known as the **Derbent Gateway**. A great wall, said to have been built in the 6th c. and named the Caspian Gates, once defended the city against the attacks of nomadic tribes.

**Derby** /'dɑːbɪ/ a city in the Derbyshire Peak District, central England, on the River Derwent; pop. (1991) 214,000. Known to the early Saxons as Northworthy, its name was changed to Deoraby by the Danes in the 9th c. Derby was the birthplace of the philosopher Herbert Spencer (1820–1903) and the painter Joseph Wright (1734–97). It is the headquarters of Rolls-Royce cars and aero engines.

**Derbyshire** /'dɑːbɪʃɪə(r)/ a county of central England; area 2,631 sq. km. (1,016 sq. miles); pop. (1991) 915,000; county town, Matlock. The county is divided into 9 districts:

| District | Area (sq. km.) | Pop. (1991) |
| --- | --- | --- |
| Amber Valley | 265 | 109,700 |
| Bolsover | 160 | 69,000 |
| Chesterfield | 66 | 99,700 |
| Derby | 78 | 214,000 |
| Derbyshire Dales | 795 | 67,700 |
| Erewash | 109 | 104,400 |
| High Peak | 541 | 83,800 |
| North East Derbyshire | 277 | 95,600 |
| South Derbyshire | 339 | 71,100 |

**Derry** see LONDONDERRY.

**Derwent** /'dɜːwənt/ the name of four English rivers **1.** a river that rises in the Borrowdale Fells in Cumbria, and flows northwards through Derwent Water and Bassenthwaite to the Irish Sea at Workington. **2.** a river that rises in the Derbyshire Peak District and flows southwards past Derby to join the River Trent on the Leicestershire border. **3.** a river that rises in the Pennines and flows north-eastwards to join the River Tyne near Newcastle. **4.** a river that rises in the North Yorkshire Moors and flows south-westwards to join the River Ouse near Selby.

**Derwent Water** a lake south-west of Keswick in the Lake District of Cumbria, north-west England, formed by the River Derwent. It is 5 km. (3 miles) long and up to 2 km. wide.

**desert** /'dezət/ a dry, barren, often sand-covered area of land in hot or mid-latitude areas of the world, characteristically desolate, lacking in water, and with little or no vegetation. About 30 per cent of the world's land surface is arid or semiarid desert.

**desertification** the process of making or becoming a desert as a result of a lack of rainfall or human actions such as overgrazing by livestock and cutting vegetation for fuelwood. The world's arid, semiarid, and sub-humid zones are most susceptible to desertification which is a term that was first used in 1949 by the French forester, Aubreville, who was working in West Africa.

**Des Moines** /dɪ 'mɔɪn/ the capital and largest city of Iowa, USA, at the junction of the Raccoon and Des Moines rivers; pop. (1990) 193,200. Established as a military garrison in 1843, Des Moines later developed as the industrial and retail centre of the Corn Belt, an extensive agricultural region. It replaced Iowa City as state capital in 1857.

**Desna** /də'snɑ:/ a river that rises in Russia to the east of Smolensk and flows 875 km. (550 miles) southwards through Ukraine to join the Dnieper near Kiev.

**Desolation Islands** see KERGUELEN ISLANDS.

**Dessau** /'desaʊ/ an industrial city in the state of Anhalt, Germany, at the junction of the Elbe and Mulde rivers, about 112 km. (70 miles) south-west of Berlin; pop. (1991) 95,100. Dessau was the seat of the Bauhaus art school from 1925 to 1932. It produces vehicles, machinery, and instruments.

**Dessye** /'deseɪ/ (also **Dessie** or **Dese**) a market town in the Welo region of north-central Ethiopia, at the junction of roads leading from the Red Sea ports of Massawa and Assab to Addis Ababa; pop. (est. 1980) 75,000.

**Detmold** /'detmɔʊld/ the capital of the German state of North Rhine-Westphalia and resort, at the northern edge of the Teutoburg Forest; pop. (1983) 67,000. Nearby is the huge statue of the German chieftain Arminius who defeated the Romans in AD 9. Detmold was the birthplace of the dramatist Christian Dietrich Grabbe (1801–36) and the poet Ferdinand Freiligrath (1810–76). It is a furniture-manufacturing centre.

**Detroit** /dɪ'trɔɪt/ a major industrial city and Great Lakes shipping centre in north-east Michigan, USA, on the Detroit River; pop. (1990) 1,028,000. Founded in 1701 by Antoine de la Motha Cadillac, it was named Le Place du Détroit (French = the place of the strait). It is the centre of the US automobile industry, containing the head-quarters of Ford, Chrysler, and General Motors—whence its nickname 'Motown' (short for motor town). It was a famous centre for jazz and later for rock and soul music.

**Dettingen** /'detɪŋən/ a village in north-west Bavaria, Germany, near which English, Austrian, and Hanoverian troops under George II defeated the French in 1743.

**Deux Balés National Park** /də 'bæleɪ/ a national park in central-western Burkina established in 1967 to protect savanna plain and gallery forest.

**Deutschland** /'dɔɪtʃlɑ:nt/ the German name for GERMANY.

**Deux-Sèvres** /də 'sev(r)/ a department in the Poitou-Charentes region of western France; area 6,004 sq. km. (2,319 sq. miles); pop. (1990) 345,965; capital, Niort.

**Deva** /'deɪvə/ a market town on the River Mures in west-central Romania, capital of Hunedoara county; pop. (1989) 77,340.

**Devanagari** /ˌdeɪvə'nɑ:gərɪ/ the alphabet used for Sanskrit, Hindi, and other Indian languages.

**Deventer** /'deɪfəntə(r)/ an industrial city in the Dutch province of Overijssel, on the IJssel River;

pop. (1991) 67,500. It was the birthplace of Geert Groote (1340–84), founder of the Brotherhood of Common Life.

**Devil's Island** (French **Ile du Diable**) a rocky island off the coast of French Guiana in the Iles du Salut group. From 1852 it was part of a penal settlement, originally for prisoners suffering from contagious diseases, especially leprosy; later it was used largely for political prisoners, of whom the most famous was Alfred Dreyfus, and became notorious for its harsh conditions. No prisoners were sent there after 1938, and the last one was released in 1953. The island is now chiefly a tourist attraction.

**Devil's Postpile National Monument** a national monument in California, USA, in the eastern Sierra Nevada to the south-east of Yosemite. It protects some of the world's finest examples of columnar basalt.

**Devil's Tower National Monument** a national monument in north-east Wyoming, USA, protecting a 264-m. (865-ft.) tower of volcanic rock. Designated in 1906, it was the first national monument to be established in the USA.

**Devon** /'devən/ (also **Devonshire**) a county of south-west England; area 6,711 sq. km. (2,592 sq. miles); pop. (1991) 1,008,300; county town, Exeter. It is divided into 10 districts:

| District | Area (sq. km.) | Pop. (1991) |
|---|---|---|
| East Devon | 815 | 116,300 |
| Exeter | 47 | 101,100 |
| Mid Devon | 915 | 63,600 |
| North Devon | 1,086 | 85,100 |
| Plymouth | 79 | 238,800 |
| South Hams | 887 | 77,300 |
| Teignbridge | 674 | 107,100 |
| Torbay | 63 | 122,500 |
| Torridge | 985 | 52,100 |
| West Devon | 1,160 | 44,400 |

**Devonian** *adj. & n.*

**Devonian** /dɪ'vəʊnɪən/ the fourth period of the Palaeozoic era of geological time, following the Silurian and preceding the Carboniferous, lasting from about 408 to 360 million years ago. During this period fish became abundant, the first amphibians evolved, and the first forests appeared.

**Devon Island** an island in the Canadian Arctic, the second-largest of the Queen Elizabeth Islands; area 55,247 sq. km. (21,330 sq. miles). The island was visited in 1616 by William Baffin and later named after the English county by W. E. Parry.

**Devonport** /'devənˌpɔːt/ **1.** a port on the north coast of Tasmania, Australia, situated at the mouth of the River Mersey; pop. (1991) 22,660. It is linked by ferry to Melbourne. **2.** a suburb of Plymouth in Devon, England, with an important naval dock-yard and ferry port. It was the birthplace of the Antarctic explorer Captain R. F. Scott (1868–1912). **3.** a suburb of Auckland, North

Island, New Zealand, home of the Royal New Zealand Navy.

**Deyang** /de'ja:ŋ/ a city in Sichuan province, central China, to the north of Chengdu; pop. (1986) 768,000. It is the site of a wall 1,000 m. (3,280 ft.) in length, the largest artistic wall in China, built in 1993 by descendants of those who took part in the construction of the Forbidden City in Beijing and the Summer Palace.

**Dewsbury** /'dju:zbərɪ/ a textile-manufacturing town in West Yorkshire, England, on the River Calder near Leeds; pop. (1981) 50,000.

**Dezful** /dɪz'fʊl/ (also **Desful**) a market town in Khuzestan, western Iran, on the River Dez near the site of ancient Susa; pop. (1991) 181,000.

**Dezhou** /de'ʒəʊ/ a city in Shandong province, eastern China, on the Grand Canal north-west of Jinan; pop. (1986) 283,000.

**Dhahran** a town on the Gulf coast of Saudi Arabia developed as a pipeline station serving Saudi Arabia's oilfields. It was used as a military base and port of entry by Allied forces during the Gulf War of 1991.

**Dhaka** /'dækə/ (also **Dacca**) the capital of Bangladesh, on the Ganges delta; pop. (1991) 3,397,200. Formerly a French, Dutch, and British trading post, capital of the Mogul province of East Bengal (1608–1704), capital of the British province of East Bengal and Assam (1905–12), it became capital of East Pakistan in 1947 and Bangladesh in 1971. The city has a striking mixture of architectural styles. Impressive buildings include the 17th-c. Lal Bagh Fort and several mosques, the early 20th-c. supreme court and university, and the recently constructed Parliament buildings and railway station. Much of the city is low-lying and subject to flooding but this has not deterred the development of shanty towns. Jute-processing, tanning, and the manufacture of chemicals, textiles, and glass are the chief industries in addition to trade in agricultural crops such as rice, oilseed, sugar, and tea.

**Dhanbad** /'dɑːnbæd/ a coal-mining city in the state of Bihar, north-east India; pop. (1991) 817,550.

**Dharamsala** /ˌdɑːrəm'sɑːlə/ a town in north-west Himacahal Pradesh, northern India, headquarters of the Dalai Lama's Tibetan government in exile; pop. (1991) 17,320.

**Dharwar** /dɑː'wɑː(r)/ a city in Karnataka, southern India, twinned with Hubli; pop. (1991) 647,640. A centre of textile manufacture, Hubli-Dharwar is the site of the State University founded in 1949.

**Dhaulagiri** /ˌdaʊlə'gɪrɪ/ a Himalayan mountain massif with six peaks rising to 8,172 m. (26,810 ft.) at its highest point 224 km. (140 miles) north-west of Kathmandu. In the early 19th c. it was thought to be the highest mountain in the world. Each

of the peaks was first climbed between 1960 and 1975.

**Dhelfoí** the Greek name for DELPHI.

**Dhivehi** /də'veɪhɪ/ (also **Divehi**) the Sinhalese language of the Maldives in the Indian Ocean.

**Dhofar** /dəʊ'fɑː(r)/ the fertile south-western province of Oman on the Arabian Peninsula. Its chief town is the port of Salalah.

**Dhule** /'du:li:/ a town in Maharashtra, western India, north-east of Bombay; pop. (1991) 277,960.

**Diamantina** /ˌdi:əmæn'ti:nə/ a river that rises in central Queensland, Australia, and flows south-westwards for 890 km. (560 miles) through the Channel Country to become Warburton Creek on meeting Eyre Creek in South Australia.

**Diamond Head** a volcanic crater 232 m. (761 ft.) high, overlooking the port of Honolulu on the Hawaiian island of Oahu.

**diaspora** /daɪ'æspərə/ any group of people dispersed throughout the world. The Diaspora usually refers to the dispersion of the Jews among the Gentiles mainly in the 8th–6th c. BC.

**Didyma** /'dɪdɪmə/ an ancient sanctuary of Apollo to the south of Miletus, site of one of the most famous oracles of the Aegean region, close to the west coast of Asia Minor. After the area was conquered by Alexander the Great, work began (c. 300 BC) on a massive new temple, which was never completed.

**Diego Garcia** /dɪˌeɪgəʊ gɑː'si:ə/ the largest island of the Chagos Archipelago in the Indian Ocean, site of a strategic Anglo-American naval base established in 1973.

**Diekirch** /'di:kɜːx, -kɜːk/ a resort town in Luxembourg, on the River Sûre 35 km. (22 miles) north of Luxembourg; pop. (1991) 5,650. It is capital of a canton and district of the same name.

**Dien Bien Phu** /ˌdjen bjen 'fu:/ a village in Lai Chau province, north-west Vietnam, near the Laos frontier, with a military post held by the French until captured by Vietminh forces after a famous 55-day siege in 1954.

**Dieppe** /dɪ'ep/ a resort and channel commercial and fishing port of Normandy in the department of Seine-Maritime, northern France, situated at the mouth of the River Arques; pop. (1990) 36,600. There are ferry links with England. The town has been rebuilt after devastation during World War II, particularly during an unsuccessful commando attack in 1942.

**Digne** /'di:njə/ (also **Digne-les-Bains**) a resort town and thermal spa, capital of the department of Alpes-de-Haute-Provence in south-east France; pop. (1982) 16,400.

**Digya** /'dɪgjə/ a national park in West Africa protecting a savanna woodland peninsula on the western shore of Lake Volta in Ghana.

**Dijon** /'di:ʒɔ̃/ an old industrial city in the Côte d'Or department of east-central France; pop. (1990) 151,640. The chief city of the Burgundy region, it is noted for its wine trade and its cuisine.

**Díli** /'dɪli/ a seaport on the Indonesian island of Timor that was (until 1975) the capital of the former Portuguese colony of East Timor; pop. (1980) 60,150.

**Dimitrovgrad** /də'mi:trəfgrɑ:t/ a chemical industry town in western Russia, situated east of the Volga and north-west of Samara; pop. (1990) 133,000.

**Dinajpur** /dɪ'næḓʒpʊə/ a city, capital of Dinajpur in north-west Bangladesh, on the River Punarbhaba; pop. (1981) 96,700. Rice, jute, sugar-cane, and oilseed are traded.

**Dinan** /'di:nɑ̃/ an old fortified market and tourist town in the department of Côtes-du-Nord, Brittany, north-west France, on the River Rance; pop. (1982) 14,150. The town has textile industries and many associations with Bertrand du Guesclin who was born nearby in 1320.

**Dinant** /'di:nɑ̃/ a resort town in the province of Namur, southern Belgium, on the River Meuse; pop. (1991) 12,200.

**Dinard** /'di:nɑ:(r)d/ a resort town and fishing port in the department of Ille-et-Vilaine on the coast of Brittany, north-west France, made fashionable in the Victorian era by English aristocracy; pop. (1982) 10,000.

**Dinaric Alps** /dɪ'nærɪk/ (Serbo-Croat **Dinara Planina**) an Alpine range running parallel to the Adriatic coast of Croatia, Montenegro, and north-west Albania. The range, which includes the limestone Karst region, rises to a height of 2,522 m. (8,274 ft.) at Durmitor.

**Dindigul** /'dɪndɪˌgəl/ a market town in Tamil Nadu, southern India, in the Sirumalai Hills north-west of Madurai; pop. (1991) 182,290. Noted for its cheroots, tobacco, tanning, and cotton are its chief industries.

**Ding Gong** /dɪŋ 'gɒŋ/ an archaeological site in Shandong province, China, near the Yellow River east of Jinan. Simple pictograms on pottery, dating from c. 5,500 BC and thought to be the world's earliest form of writing, were discovered here in 1993.

**Dingle** /'dɪŋg(ə)l/ a port on the west coast of County Kerry, south-west Ireland, the most westerly town in Europe; pop. (est. 1980) 1,500. It lies on the north shore of **Dingle Bay**.

**Dingwall** /'dɪŋwəl/ a town in northern Scotland at the head of the Cromarty Firth, the administrative centre of Ross and Cromarty district in Highland Region from 1975 to 1996; pop. (1981) 4,842. Nearby is Foulis Castle, seat of the Chiefs of the Clan Munro.

**Dinka** /'dɪŋkə/ a people of the southern Sudan whose language is a Nilotic subgroup of the Eastern Sudanic branch of the Nilo-Saharan language group. Subjected to slavery by Arabs from the north, these people have continued to suffer as a result of Sudan's civil war.

**Diredawa** /ˌdɪrɪdə'wɑ:/ a trading town in Harar province, central Ethiopia, on the railway from Addis Ababa to Djibouti; pop. (est. 1990) 127,000.

**Disko** /'dɪskəʊ/ an island with extensive coal resources on the west coast of Greenland. Its chief settlement is Godhavn; area 8,285 sq. km. (3,200 sq. miles).

**Dismal Swamp** a vast area of swamp land, one of the largest in the USA, in south-east Virginia and north-east Carolina. Covering an area of 1,942 sq. km. (750 sq. miles), it is traversed by the 35-km. (22-mile) long Dismal Swamp Canal which links Chesapeake Bay with the Albemarle Sound.

**Disneyland** an amusement park in California, USA, incorporating all the elements of fantasy associated with the films of Walt Disney (1901–66). Opened in 1955, it covers an area of 74 hectares (184 acres).

**Disney World** (in full **Walt Disney World**) an amusement park in Florida, USA, 35 km. (22 miles) south-west of Orlando, comprising The Magic Kingdom (1971), Epcot Center (1982), and Disney-MGM Studios (1989) in addition to resort hotels, golf courses, outdoor sports, and a 3,030-hectare (7,500-acre) wilderness area.

**Dispura** /dɪs'pʊərə/ the temporary capital of Assam, situated 10 km. (6 miles) south of the city of Guwahati.

**District of Columbia** /kə'lɒmbɪə/ (abbr. DC) a federal district of the USA, co-extensive with the city of WASHINGTON, the federal capital. Established 1790–1 from land ceded by the states of Maryland and Virginia.

**Divehi** see DHIVEHI.

**Divinópolis** /dɪvɪ'nɔ:pəlɪs/ an industrial town in the state of Minas Gerais, south-east Brazil; pop. (1990) 160,900.

**Diyarbakir** /dɪ'jɑ:bəkə(r)/ **1.** a province in a predominantly Kurdish region of south-eastern Turkey; area 15,355 sq. km. (5,931 sq. miles); pop. (1990) 750,900. **2.** its capital, a market town on the River Tigris; pop. (1990) 381,100.

**Dixie** /'dɪksɪ/ (also **Dixieland**) a name given to the southern states of the USA, said to be derived from the local Creole pronunciation of the name of Jeremiah Dixon who surveyed the border between the states of Maryland and Pennsylvania (Mason-Dixon Line). The name is used in the song *Dixie* (1859) by Daniel D. Emmett, a popular marching song sung by Confederate soldiers in the American Civil War. The name Dixieland is also given to a kind of jazz with a strong two-beat rhythm and collective improvisation.

**Djajapura** /ˌdʒæjə'pʊərə/ (also **Jayapura**) the seaport capital of the Indonesian province of West

New Guinea (Irian Jaya), situated on the north coast of the island of New Guinea near the frontier with Papua New Guinea; pop. (1980) 45,800. Known to the Dutch as Hollandia, it was named Sukarnapura from 1963 to 1969.

**Djakarta** see JAKARTA.

**Djambi** /'dʒæmbɪ/ the capital of a province of the same name on the Indonesian island of Sumatra, situated at the head of navigation on the River Hari; pop. (1980) 158,550. It is a transportation centre for oil, timber, and rubber.

**djebel** see JABAL.

**Djerba** /'dʒɜːbə/ (also **Jerba**) a resort island in the Gulf of Gabès off the coast of Tunisia.

**Djibouti**
/dʒɪ'buːtɪ/ (also
**Jibouti**) official
name **The Republic
of Djibouti** a coun-
try on the north-east
coast of Africa
bounded by
Ethiopia, Somalia,
and the Gulf of

Aden; area 23,310 sq. km. (9,003 sq. miles); pop. (est. 1991) 400,000; official language, French; capital, Djibouti. The chief cities are Djibouti, Dikhil, Ali-Sabieh, Obock, and Tadjoura. A coastal plain gives way to mountains with peaks that rise to 1,500 m. (5,000 ft.). Beyond the mountains lies an extensive plateau area. Nearly 90 per cent of Djibouti is desert wasteland and at Lake Assal the land falls to 153 m (503 ft.) below sea-level, the lowest elevation in Africa. The climate is hot and humidity is high throughout the year but rainfall is sparse and erratic. The country is largely populated by Cushtic-speaking Somalis (mostly of the Issa tribe), Danakils, and Afars who are dependent on a pastoral economy or employment in commercial activities associated with the railway, port, and airport of Djibouti. After the opening of the Suez Canal in 1869 France expanded its interest in north-east Africa offering friendship and assistance to the sultans around the Gulf of Tadjoura. By 1897 the boundaries of a protectorate had been agreed and the area was designated as French Somaliland. Between 1897 and 1917 a Franco-Ethiopian railway was built linking Addis Ababa with the port of Djibouti. In 1958 the colony gained a degree of self-rule when it became an overseas territory of France and in 1967 its name was changed to the French Territory of Afars and Issas. After a referendum in 1977 it gained full independence from France as the Republic of Djibouti. Since then the country has been ruled as a one-party state by a 65-member National Assembly. Djibouti is administratively divided into the five districts of Djibouti, Dikhil, Ali-Sabieh, Obock, and Tadjoura.
**Djiboutian** *adj. & n.*

**Djibouti** the capital of Djibouti on a peninsula at the mouth of the Gulf of Tadjoura; pop. (1988) 290,000. Built between 1886 and 1900, Djibouti succeeded Obock as capital in 1896 because it had a better natural harbour and ready access to the Ethiopian Highlands. Its economy is based on its role as the transit port for Ethiopia.

**Dnieper** /də'niːpə(r)/ (also **Dnepr**) a river in eastern Europe that rises in the Valdai Hills west of Moscow and flows some 2,202 km. (1,368 miles) southwards through Belorussia and Ukraine to the Black Sea. The cities of Kiev, Dneprodzerzhinsk, and Dnepropetrovsk are situated on it. Dams have been built at a number of points to provide hydro-electric power and water for Ukraine's industries.

**Dniester** /də'niːstə(r)/ (also **Dnestr**) a river that rises in the Carpathian Mts. of western Ukraine and flows 1,410 km. (876 miles) south-eastwards through Moldova (Moldavia) to meet the Black Sea just south of Odessa.

**Dniprodzerzhinsk** /də,njiːprədzɜː'ʒɪnsk/ (formerly **Dneprodzherzhinsk**) an industrial port in Ukraine, on the Dnieper River; pop. (1990) 283,600. It was known as Kamensoye until 1936.

**Dnipropetrovsk** /də,njiːprəpe'trɒfsk/ (formerly **Dnepropetrovsk**) an industrial port in Ukraine, on the Dnieper River; pop. (1990) 1,200,000. Until 1926 it was known as Ekaterinoslav. Founded in 1787 by Potemkin, it was also called Novorosiysk between 1791 and 1802.

**Dobrich** /dɒ'brɪtʃ/ a commercial town in Varna region, north-east Bulgaria; pop. (1990) 30,760. From 1949 to 1991 it was named Tolbukhin in honour of the Russian general who captured it during World War II.

**Dobruja** /'dɒbruːjə/ a district in south-east Romania and north-east Bulgaria bounded on the east by the Black Sea and on the north and west by the Danube. In 1878 the Congress of Berlin awarded northern Dobruja to Romania and southern Dobruja to Bulgaria.

**Dodecanese** /,dəʊdɪkə'niːz/ a group of islands in the south-east Aegean, of which the largest is Rhodes, which were occupied by Italy in 1912 during the war with Turkey and ceded to Greece in 1947. Despite its name (Greek = twelve islands) there are, in addition to the 12 main islands, numerous small islands in the group which comprises the greater part of the Southern Sporadhes; area 2,682 sq. km. (1,036 sq. miles); capital, Rhodes.

**Dodge City** /dɒdʒ/ a city in south-west Kansas, USA, pop. (1990) 21,130. Established in 1872 as a railhead on the Santa Fe Trail, it gained a reputation as a rowdy frontier town and was known as the 'cowboy capital'. The city hall is built on the site of Boot Hill, the famous cowboy burial ground. Once noted for its buffalo hunts and its cattle ranches, the surrounding area now produces large quantities of wheat.

**Dodoma** /də'dəʊmə/ the capital of Tanzania, situated at an altitude of 1,120 m. (3,675 ft.) in the centre of the country; pop. (1984) 54,000. It was designated to replace the port of Dar es Salaam as capital in 1974.

**Dogger Bank** /'dɒgə(r)/ a submerged sandbank in the North Sea, about 115 km. (70 miles) off the north-east coast of England.

**Doha** /'dəʊhə/ (Arabic **Ad Dawhah**) the capital of the State of Qatar in the Persian Gulf, on the east coast of the Qatar peninsula; pop. (est. 1990) 300,000. It developed from a small fishing village into a modern city after the discovery of oil in 1949 and is now a major shipping, engineering, oil-refining, and food-processing centre.

**Doi Inthanon** /dɔɪ 'ɪntənən/ a mountain in north-west Thailand. Rising to 2,594 m. (8,510 ft.), it is the highest peak in the country.

**doldrums** /'dɒldrəmz/ an equatorial ocean region of calms, sudden storms, and light unpredictable winds situated between the north-east and south-east trade winds.

**dolina** /də'li:nə/ (also **doline** /də'li:n/) an extensive shallow depression or basin in limestone (Russian = valley).

**Dolomite Mountains** /'dɒlə‚maɪt/ (also **Dolomites**, Italian **Alpi Dolomitiche**) a range of the Alps in northern Italy extending over Trentino, Bolzano, Cadorino, and parts of Venetia. The mountains are so named because the characteristic rock is dolomitic limestone, the term dolomite being derived from the name of the French geologist Déodat de Dolomieu who identified the rock composition as largely calcium and magnesium carbonate. At 3,342 m. (10,965 ft.) Marmolada is the highest point of the Dolomites and the only glaciated peak in the area. The Brenta Dolomites lie to the south-west of Bolzano.

**Dolores** /də'lɔ:rez/ a tributary of the Colorado River that rises in the San Juan Mts. and flows for a distance of 365 km. (230 miles) across the US states of Colorado and Utah.

**Dolores Hidalgo** /də'lɔ:rez hi:'dɑ:lgəʊ/ a town in the state of Guanajuato, central Mexico, north-west of Mexico City; pop. (1980) 20,000. Known as the 'cradle of national independence,' it was here in 1810 that Father Miguel Hidalgo y Costilla gave the famous *Grito de Dolores* at the beginning of the 11-year war that led to Mexican independence.

**Dom** /dəʊm/ a mountain in the Mischabelhörner group of the Pennine Alps, southern Switzerland. Rising to 4,545 m. (14,911 ft.) north-east of Zermatt, it is the highest mountain entirely in Switzerland.

**Dome of the Rock** an Islamic shrine in Jerusalem, surrounding the sacred rock on which, according to tradition, Abraham prepared to sacrifice his son (Genesis 22: 9) and from which the prophet Muhammad made his miraculous midnight ascent into heaven. Built in the area of Solomon's Temple and dating from the end of the 7th c., to Muslims it is the third most holy place, after Mecca and Medina, and stands on a sacred site called 'the furthest mosque'. The expanse of rough irregular rock that forms its centre contrasts starkly with the strict Byzantine geometry and ornate decoration of the surrounding structure, while the exterior is of rich mosaic work capped by a golden dome which was restored in 1994 and is the largest of its kind in the world.

**Dominica** /‚dɒmɪ'ni:kə/ (French **Dominique**) official name **The Commonwealth of Dominica** a mountainous island in the West Indies between the French islands of Martinique and  Guadeloupe, the loftiest of the Lesser Antilles and the northernmost and largest of the Windward Islands; area 751 sq. km. (290 sq. miles); pop. (est. 1988) 97,800; English is the official language although French is widely spoken; capital, Roseau. Dominated by high volcanic peaks that are covered with lush forest, Dominica has few beaches. The climate, which is tropical, is moderated by northeast trade winds, with the greatest rainfall occurring between May and August. Bananas, citrus fruit, cocoa, and soap are the chief exports. It was named by Columbus who discovered it on Sunday, 3 November 1493 (Latin *dies domenica* = the Lord's day), and after much Anglo-French rivalry came into British possession at the end of the 18th c., becoming an independent republic within the Commonwealth in 1978. Dominica is a parliamentary democracy governed by a unicameral House of Assembly.
**Dominican** *adj. & n.*

**Dominican** /də'mɪnɪkən/ an order of preaching friars founded by the Spanish priest St. Dominic in 1215–16.

**Dominican Republic** (Spanish **República Dominicana**) a country in the Caribbean, the Spanish-speaking eastern two-thirds of the island named Hispaniola by  Columbus, who discovered it in 1492; area 48,442 sq. km. (18,704 sq. miles); pop. (est. 1991) 7,300,000; official language, Spanish; capital, Santo Domingo. The largest cities are Santo Domingo and Santiago de los Caballeros. The Dominican Republic is crossed from north-west to south-east by mountains which rise to 3,175 m. (10,417 ft.) at Pico Duarte, the highest peak in the Caribbean. Between the Central and Septentrional Mountains lies the Cibao, a large fertile valley. The maritime tropical climate is moderated year-round by trade winds, with most rainfall occurring between May and November. The country's chief exports are sugar, coffee, cacao, tobacco, meat, gold, silver, and ferronickel. The republic is the former Spanish colony of Santo Domingo, the part of Hispaniola which Spain retained when she ceded the western portion (now Haiti) to France in 1697. After the colony of Santo Domingo had itself been made over to France in 1795, and twice been overrun by Haiti, a Republic was proclaimed in 1844. The history of the republic has been turbulent, culminating in the ruthless dictatorship (1930–61) of Rafael Trujillo Molina. An unsettled period followed, with civil war and US military intervention; governed by a bicameral congress, a new constitution was introduced in 1966. The country occupies a strategic position on major sea-routes leading from both Europe and the US to the Panama Canal.

**Don** /dɒn/ **1.** a river that rises near Penistone in the Pennines of northern England and flows 112 km. (70 miles) eastwards to join the River Ouse at Goole. **2.** a river in north-east Scotland that rises in the Grampians and flows 131 km. (82 miles) eastwards to enter the North Sea at Aberdeen. **3.** a river of eastern Europe that rises near Tula in western Russia and flows 1,967 km. (1,222 miles) southwards to enter the Sea of Azov beyond Rostov. It is linked by canal to the River Volga.

**Donatist** /'dəʊnətɪst/ a member of a Christian sect which arose in North Africa in AD 311 out of a dispute about the election of the bishop of Carthage, and which maintained that it was the only true and pure Church and that the ordinations of others were invalid.

**Donau** see DANUBE.

**Donbas** see DONETS BASIN.

**Doncaster** /'dɒnkəst(ə)r/ an industrial (railway) town on the River Don, South Yorkshire, England; pop. (1991) 284,300. The race for the St. Leger is run annually on the racecourse.

**Dondra Head** /'dɑːndrə/ the southernmost tip of the island of Sri Lanka projecting into the Indian Ocean.

**Donegal** /ˌdɒnɪ'gɔːl/ a county in the province of Ulster in the extreme north-west of the Republic of Ireland; area 4,830 sq. km. (1,866 sq. miles); pop. (1991) 128,000; capital, Lifford.

**Donets** /dɒ'njets/ a river in Europe that rises near Belgorod in Russia and flows south-eastwards for 1,000 km. (630 miles) to meet the River Don near Rostov.

**Donets Basin** (also **Donbas** or **Donbass** /dɒn'bæs/) a coal-mining region of eastern Ukraine and southern Russia, in the valley of the Donets and lower Dnieper Rivers.

**Donetsk** /dɒ'njetsk/ the leading industrial city of the Donbas mining region of Ukraine; pop. (1990) 1,116,900. It has heavy industries including coal, iron and steel, machinery, chemicals, and cement.

**Dong** /dʊŋ/ a minority nationality of southern China, mostly found in Guizhou, Hunan, and Guangxi where the Dong people number c. 1.4 million.

**Dongchuan** /dʊŋ'ʃwɑːn/ a city in Yunnan province, southern China, in the western foothills of the Wumeng Mountains north of Kunming; pop. (1986) 277,000.

**Dongguang** /dʊŋ'gwæn/ a city in Hebei province, eastern China, on the Grand Canal north-east of Dezhou; pop. (1986) 1,230,000.

**Dongsheng** /dʊŋ'ʃen/ a town in Inner Mongolia, northern China, at a crossroads on the northern steppes in the loop of the Yellow River; pop. (1986) 130,000.

**Dongting** /dʊŋ'tɪŋ/ a lake in the province of Hunan, east-central China, the second-largest freshwater lake in China; area 2,820 sq. km. (1,089 sq. miles).

**Dongying** /dʊŋ'jɪŋ/ a city in Hebei province, eastern China, near the mouth of the Yellow River; pop. (1986) 540,000.

**Doornik** the Flemish name for TOURNAI.

**Dorchester** /'dɔːtʃəst(ə)r/ the county and market town of Dorset in southern England, on the River Frome; pop. (est. 1985) 14,000. The town has associations with Judge Jeffreys whose 'Bloody Assizes' were held here in 1685, and in 1834 the Tolpuddle Martyrs were sentenced in the local court house. The Stone Age earthworks of Maiden Castle lie 3 km. to the south-west. Dorchester became 'Casterbridge' in Thomas Hardy's novels.

**Dordogne** /dɔː'dɔɪn/ **1.** an inland department of Aquitaine in south-west France containing numerous caves and rock-shelters that have yielded abundant remains of early humans and their artefacts and art; area 9,060 sq. km. (3,499 sq. miles); pop. (1990) 386,365; capital, Périgeux. **2.** a river that rises in the Auvergne Hills of south-west France and flows 472 km. (297 miles) generally westwards through the vineyards of St. Emilion, Bergerac, and Pomerol to meet the River Garonne where it forms the Gironde estuary.

**Dordrecht** /'dɔː drext/ (*abbr.* **Dort** /dɔːt/) an industrial city and river-port near the mouth of the River Rhine, 20 km. (12 miles) south-east of Rotterdam in the Dutch province of South Holland; pop. (1991) 110,500. Situated on one of the busiest river junctions in the world, it was the wealthiest town in the Netherlands until surpassed by Rotterdam in the 18th c. It has shipyards, and machinery and chemical industries.

**Dorian** /'dɔːrɪən/ the tribes speaking the Doric dialect of Greek who probably entered Greece from the north *c.* 1,100–1,000 BC and by the 8th c. BC had settled most of the Peloponnese, the southernmost Aegean islands, and the south-west corner of Asia Minor. While culturally distinct in architecture and dialect, the Dorians retained their political system only in Sparta and Crete where the ruling military class subjected the local peoples as serfs and dependants.

**Doric** /'dɒrɪk/ **1.** the dialect of the Dorians in ancient Greece. **2.** a term used to describe a broad or rustic dialect, especially in England and Scotland. **3.** the oldest, sturdiest, and simplest of the Greek orders of architecture.

**Dornbirn** /'dɔːnbɪrn/ a town in the state of Vorarlberg, western Austria, in the Rhine valley near Bregenz; pop. (1991) 40,880.

**Dorset** /'dɔːsɪt/ a county of south-west England; area 2,654 sq. km. (1,025 sq. miles); pop. (1991) 645,200; county town, Dorchester. Dorset is divided into eight districts:

| District | Area (sq. km.) | Pop. (1991) |
| --- | --- | --- |
| Bournemouth | 46 | 154,400 |
| Christchurch | 50 | 40,500 |
| East Dorset | 355 | 77,200 |
| North Dorset | 610 | 52,200 |
| Poole | 64 | 130,900 |
| Purbeck | 405 | 42,600 |
| West Dorset | 1,083 | 86,300 |
| Weymouth and Portland | 41 | 61,000 |

**Dort** see DORDRECHT.

**Dortmund** /'dɔːtmʊnd/ an industrial city and inland port in North Rhine-Westphalia, north-west Germany, the southern terminus of the Dortmund-Ems Canal which links the Ruhr industrial area with the North Sea; pop. (1991) 601,000. It has a major steel industry and Europe's largest brewery.

**Douai** /'duːeɪ/ an ancient town in the Nord department of north-west France, on the Scarpe River near Lille; pop. (1990) 44,195. It was the centre of the cloth trade in the Middle Ages. Douai's 14th c. bell-tower (with 62 bells) is reputed to have the largest carillon in Europe. It has many light industries including metal goods of all kinds.

**Douala** /duː'ælə/ the chief port and largest city of Cameroon, at the mouth of the Wouri River; pop. (1991) 884,000. As capital of German West Africa it was known as Kamerunstadt from 1885 to 1901. Its name was changed to Douala in 1907 and it later became capital of French Cameroon (1940–6). It is a mixture of expensive shops, modern buildings, African markets, and slums.

**Doubs** /duː/ **1.** a department in the Franche-Comté region of eastern France; area 5,234 sq. km. (2,022 sq. miles); pop. (1990) 484,770; capital, Besançon. **2.** a river in eastern France that rises in the Jura Mts. and flows north-eastwards through limestone gorges into Switzerland before turning

westwards back into France where it joins the Saône near Chalons-sur-Saône.

**Douglas** /'dʌɡləs/ a resort town on the Irish Sea, capital of the Isle of Man; pop. (1991) 22,210.

**Dounreay** /duːn'reɪ/ a location on the north coast of Caithness, Scotland, 13 km. (8 miles) west of Thurso. It was the site of the UK's only two experimental fast-breeder nuclear reactors. The first, the Dounreay Fast Reactor, operated from 1959 to 1977. The second, the Prototype Fast Reactor, operated from 1974 to 1994. In 1995 the world's first wave-power station in open sea began operating in the Pentland Firth off Dounreay.

**Douro** /'dʊərəʊ/ (Spanish **Duero** /'dʊerəʊ/) a river of the Iberian peninsula, which rises in central Spain and flows west for 900 km. (556 miles) through Portugal to the Atlantic Ocean near Oporto. In its valley in Portugal grow the grapes from which port wine is made.

**Dover** /'dəʊvə(r)/ a ferry port and resort in Kent, the largest of the Cinque Ports, on the coast of the English Channel its chalk cliffs are world famous; pop. (1981) 34,300. Dover has been fortified since Roman times and many ancient buildings survive. It is mainland Britain's nearest point to the Continent, being only 35 km. (21 miles) from Calais.

**Dover** the capital of the US state of Delaware; pop. (1990) 27,630. Settled in 1683 and laid out in 1717 by William Penn, it became state capital in 1777. Dover Air Force Base has one of the largest cargo-terminals in the world.

**Dover, Strait of** a stretch of water between England and France connecting the English Channel with the North Sea. At its narrowest it is 35 km. (21 miles) wide.

**Down** /daʊn/ a county of Northern Ireland; area 2,448 sq. km. (945 sq. miles); pop. (1981) 339,200; county town, Downpatrick.

**Down Ampney** /daʊn 'æmpnɪ/ a village near Cirencester in Gloucestershire, England, the birthplace of the composer Ralph Vaughan Williams (1872–1958).

**Downe** /daʊn/ a village near Sevenoaks in Kent, south-east England, the home of the naturalist Charles Darwin (1809–82).

**Downend** /daʊn'end/ a town near Bristol in Avon, England, the birthplace of the famous cricketer W. G. Grace (1848–1915).

**Downey** /'daʊnɪ/ a residential and industrial city in the Los Angeles conurbation, southern California, USA, situated to the east of the Rio Hondo and south of the Santa Ana Freeway; pop. (1991) 91,400. It has aerospace and metal industries.

**Downing Street** /'daʊnɪŋ/ a street in Westminster, London, between Whitehall and St. James's Park. It was built by the diplomat Sir George Downing (d. 1684), described by Pepys as 'a most ungrateful villain'. His friend and bene-factor Colonel Okey was one of the people who had signed the death warrant of Charles I; Downing betrayed him to the Royalists (who then executed Okey), and the street now named after him was his reward. In 1732 No. 10 was acquired on a Crown lease by Sir Robert Walpole, Britain's first Prime Minister, who accepted it on behalf of all future Lords of the Treasury (still the formal title of the Prime Minister). This house is the offi-cial town residence of the Prime Minister, No. 11 that of the Chancellor of the Exchequer, and the Foreign and Commonwealth Office is also situ-ated in this street, whence the allusive use of its name to refer to the British government, Prime Minister, etc.

**Downpatrick** /daʊn'pætrɪk/ the county town of Down in Northern Ireland, in the valley of the Quoile River; pop. (1981) 7,400. Once the royal seat of the Macdonlevys, it was named Downpatrick in 1177 by the Anglo-Norman John de Courcy. St. Patrick, who began his mission to Ireland near here in 432, is reputed to have been buried in Down-patrick.

**Downs** /daʊnz/ a region of chalk hills in south-ern England forming parallel ranges in Surrey and Kent (**North Downs**) and Sussex (**South Downs**).

**Drachenfels** /'drɑːkənˌfelz/ a hill near Bonn in North Rhine-Westphalia, western Germany, rising to 321 m. (1,053 ft.) to the east of the Rhine. The legendary Siegfried is said to have slain the dragon here.

**dragoman** /'drægəmən/ an interpreter or guide, especially in countries speaking Arabic, Turkish, or Persian.

**Drakensberg Mountains** /'drɑːkənzˌbɜːg/ a range of mountains at the southern edge of the African plateau, stretching in a NE–SW direction for a distance of c. 1,126 km. (700 miles) through Lesotho and the South African provinces of Natal, Orange Free State, and Transvaal. The highest peak is Thabana Ntlenyana (3,482 m., 11,425 ft.).

**Drake Passage** /dreɪk/ a channel separating the southern tip of South America from the Antarctic Peninsula and connecting the South Atlantic and South Pacific Oceans. It is named after Sir Francis Drake who sailed to the south of Tierra del Fuego in 1578.

**Drama** /'drɑːmə/ the capital of a department of the same name in Macedonia, northern Greece, be-tween the Strymon and Nestos rivers; pop. (1981) 36,100.

**Drammen** /'drɑːmən/ a seaport in south-east Norway, capital of Buskerud county; pop. (1991) 51,900. It is a major port of the timber and paper trades.

**Drammen** /'drɑːmən/ a river in southern Norway that rises on the southern slopes of the Hallingskarvet range and flows 309 km. (194 miles)

eastwards to the Drammensfjord, an inlet of the Oslo Fjord.

**Drava** /'drɑːvə/ (also **Drave**, Austrian **Dau**) a river that rises in the Carnic Alps of northern Italy and flows c. 725 km. (456 miles) eastwards through southern Austria, Slovenia, and Croatia before meeting the Danube near Osijek. For part of its course it follows the frontier between Hungary and Croatia.

**Dravidian** /drə'vɪdɪən/ **1.** a member of an ethnic group of southern India and Sri Lanka (including the Tamils and Kanarese). **2.** any of the group of languages spoken by this people, including Tamil, Telugu, and Kanarese. It is thought that before the arrival of speakers of Indo-Aryan languages c. 1,000 BC the Dravidian languages were spoken over much of India.

**Drenthe** /'drentə/ an agricultural north-eastern province of the Netherlands; area 2,680 sq. km. (1,035 sq. miles); pop. (1991) 443,500; capital, Assen.

**Dresden** /'drezd(ə)n/ a city in east Germany, the capital of the state of Saxony, on the River Elbe; pop. (1991) 485,130. Dresden china, with elaborate decoration and delicate coverings, was originally made at Dresden but from 1710 at nearby Meissen. The city has been rebuilt after being almost totally destroyed by bombing in 1945.

**drift** /drɪft/ **1.** a slow-moving surface-water cur-rent under the influence of wind. **2.** superficial de-posits of material spread over the land by wind, water, or ice. It is a term used by geomorphologists to describe unstratified Pleistocene deposits (boul-der clay) derived from ice that has melted *in situ*.

**Drin** /driːn/ a river in the Balkans that flows northwards out of Lake Ohrid, then westwards to the Adriatic Sea near Lezhe. It is the longest river in Albania.

**Drina** /'driːnə/ a river of the Balkans, which rises as the Tara and Piva rivers in the mountains of Montenegro and flows northwards along the Serbia–Bosnia frontier to meet the Sava west of Belgrade.

**Drogheda** /'drɔɪdə/ a port near the mouth of the Boyne River in Louth County, the Republic of Ireland; pop. (1991) 23,800. The Battle of the Boyne was fought near Drogheda in 1690.

**Droitwich** /'drɔɪtwɪtʃ/ a spa town in Hereford amd Worcester, England, situated on the Salwarpe River north-east of Worcester; pop. (1981) 18,100. There are brine baths and radioactive springs. In medieval times, tracks known as 'Saltways' radi-ated from the town.

**Drôme** /drəʊm/ a department in the Rhône-Alpes region of eastern France; area 6,525 sq. km. (2,520 sq. miles); pop. (1990) 414,070; capital, Valence. It is crossed by the Drôme River which rises in the Cottian Alps and flows north-westwards to meet the River Rhône near Montélimar.

**Drottningholm Palace** /'drɒtnɪŋˌhɒm/ the winter palace of the Swedish kings, on the island of Lovö west of Stockholm. It was built for Queen Eleonora in 1662 by Nicodemus Tessin the Elder.

**Drouzhba** /'dru:ʒbə/ (also **Druzba**) a resort town on the Black Sea coast of Bulgaria, 10 km. (6 miles) north of the port of Varna. It was the first international tourist resort built on the Black Sea coast of Bulgaria.

**Drury Lane** /'drʊərɪ/, **Theatre Royal** London's most famous theatre. The first theatre on the site opened in 1663, the second—notable for David Garrick's association with it—in 1674, and the third in 1794. The present theatre, dating from 1812, was not particularly successful until the 1880s, when it became famous for its melodramas and spectacles. Since the 1920s it has staged numerous musicals.

**Druse** /dru:z/ (also **Druze**) a member of a political and religious sect of Muslim origin, concentrated in Lebanon, with smaller groups in Syria and Israel. The sect broke away from Ismaili Shiite Islam in the 11th c. over a disagreement about the succession to the imamate (leadership), a position in which spiritual and political leadership were and are indissolubly linked. The Druses followed the seventh caliph of the Fatimid dynasty, al-Hakim b'illah (996–1021), who is claimed to have disappeared and whose return is expected. They regard al-Hakim as a deity, and thus are considered heretics by the Muslim community at large.

**Druzba** see DROUZHBA.

**Dryburgh Abbey** /'draɪbərə/ a ruined Premonstratensian abbey near Melrose in the Borders Region of Scotland, on the River Tweed. Sir Walter Scott and the 1st Earl Haig are buried here.

**Duarte** /'dwɑ:tɪ/, **Pico** a mountain in the Cordillera Central of the Dominican Republic. Rising to a height of 3,175 m. (10,417 ft.) it is the highest peak in the Caribbean.

**Dubai** /du:'baɪ/ **1.** one of the seven member-states of the United Arab Emirates; area 3,900 sq. km. (1,506 sq. miles); pop. (1985) 419,100. Since the discovery of oil in 1966 major port facilities have developed at Port Rashid and Mina Jebel Ali. **2.** its capital, a port on the Persian Gulf; pop. (1980) 265,700.

**Dubbo** /'dʌbəʊ/ a city in New South Wales, south-east Australia, on the Macquarie River 420 km. (264 miles) north-west of Sydney; pop. (1991) 28,060.

**Dublin** /'dʌblɪn/ the capital of the Republic of Ireland, situated on the Irish Sea at the mouth of the River Liffey; pop. (1991) 477,700. It is linked by ferry to Holyhead and Liverpool. Built on the site of a Viking settlement, Dublin prospered during the late 18th c. when its parliament was temporarily independent of England. It was the birthplace

of many poets, playwrights, and authors including Jonathan Swift (1667–1731), Thomas Parnell (1679–1718), Edmund Burke (1729–97), Richard Sheridan (1751–1816), Oscar Wilde (1854–1900), J. M. Synge (1871–1909), Sean O'Casey (1880–1964), James Joyce (1882–1941), and Brendan Behan (1923–64). Swift was dean of 14th-c. St Patrick's (Protestant) cathedral for many years and is buried there; the University of Dublin (Trinity College) was founded in 1591 and its library contains the famous *Book of Kells*. The National University (Catholic) was founded in 1909. Dublin has seen much bloodshed in its attempts to secure Irish independence. Today it is the centre of Irish commerce and industry, as well as political and cultural life. It has a major airport and ferry terminal and its industries include textiles, brewing and distilling, electrical products, printing, glass, cigarettes, food processing, and tourism.

**Dubrovnik** (Italian **Ragusa**) an historic Adriatic resort and seaport on the Dalmatian coast of Croatia; pop. (1991) 49,730. Founded in the 7th c., Dubrovnik became an important trading republic in the Middle Ages, linking the Latin and Slavic worlds. As such, it was a major centre of Serbo-Croatian culture. During the 20th c. it developed as a tourist resort but much of its medieval architecture was severely damaged when the city was besieged by Serbs in 1991.

**Dubuque** /də'bjʊk/ a city in eastern Iowa, USA, on the Mississippi River; pop. (1991) 57,500. It takes its name from the French Canadian Julien Dubuque who came from Quebec to mine lead in 1788. Formerly a mining town, it is now a centre for farm products and food-processing.

**Dudley** /'dʌdlɪ/ an industrial borough in the West Midlands of England, near Birmingham; pop. (1981) 187,000. Its industries include steel and engineering.

**Duero** the Spanish name for the DOURO.

**Duffel** /'dʌf(ə)l/ a town to the south of Antwerp in north Belgium; pop. (1991) 7,200. A coarse woollen cloth known as *duffel* was originally made here.

**Dufourspitze** /dʊ'fʊərʃpɪtzə/ a mountain peak in the Monta Rosa group of the Pennine Alps in Valais canton, Switzerland. Rising to 4,634 m. (15,203 ft.) it is the second highest peak in the Alps.

**Duisburg** /'du:sbʊəg/ the largest inland port in Europe, situated at the junction of the Rhine and Ruhr rivers in North Rhine-Westphalia, north-west Germany; pop. (1991) 537,440. Engineering, brewing, oil-refining, and the manufacture of steel, copper, and plastics are all important industries. The cartographer Gerhard Kremer (Mercator) (1512–94) lived in Duisburg.

**Dukeries** /'dju:kərɪz/, **the** a district including part of Sherwood Forest in north-west Nottinghamshire, England, comprising the parks of the former ducal seats of Welbeck, Clumber, Rufford, and Thoresby.

**Dukou** /ˌduˈkəʊ/ a city in south Sichuan province, southern China, on the Anning River north-west of Kunming; pop. (1986) 546,000.

**Duluth** /dəˈluːθ/ a city in north-east Minnesota, USA, on the west shore of Lake Superior; pop. (1991) 85,500. The twin ports of Duluth and Superior, which are the leading grain-exporting ports of the US, form the westernmost water terminus for goods destined for north-west USA. Originally a fur-trading post, the city takes its name from Daniel Greyson, Sieur Du Lhut, who landed here in 1679. It was the birthplace of the rock singer Bob Dylan in 1941.

**Dulwich** /ˈdʌlɪtʃ/ a district of Southwark in south London, England, with a college founded in 1619 by the actor Edward Alleyn. Its famous art gallery was the first to be opened to the public in Britain.

**Dum Dum** a city in West Bengal, north-east India, with an airport serving Calcutta; pop. (1991) 40,940. Once the north-eastern headquarters of the British artillery, the soft-nosed 'dum-dum' bullet was first made at the arsenal here.

**Dumfries** /dʌmˈfriːs/ a market town in south-west Scotland, on the River Nith, capital of Dumfries and Galloway Region; pop. (1981) 32,100. The poet Robert Burns died here in 1795.

**Dumfries and Galloway** /dʌmˈfriːs, ˈɡælə‚weɪ/ a local government region in south-west Scotland; area 6,396 sq. km. (2,470 sq. miles); pop. (1991) 147,000; capital, Dumfries. From 1975 to 1996 the region was divided into four districts:

| District | Area (sq. km.) | Pop. (1991) |
|---|---|---|
| Annandale and Eskdale | 1,553 | 36,800 |
| Nithsdale | 1,433 | 56,600 |
| Stewartry | 1,671 | 23,600 |
| Wigtown | 1,738 | 30,000 |

**Dumfriesshire** /dʌmˈfriːsʃɪə(r)/ a former county (until 1975) in the Scottish Borders, now part of Dumfries and Galloway.

**Dumyat** see DAMIETTA.

**Dunaújváros** /ˌdunəwɪˈvaːrɒʃ/ an industrial town in Fejér county, central Hungary, on the Danube; pop. (1984) 62,000. A major iron and steel and cement town which was created by the communist government in the 1950s.

**Dunbartonshire** /dʌnˈbaːt(ə)n‚ʃɪə(r)/ a former county on the Clyde estuary of west-central Scotland, In 1975 it became part of Strathclyde region and in 1996 the local government area of Dumbarton and Clydebank.

**Dundalk** /dʌnˈdɔːk/ a port, the county town of Louth in the Republic of Ireland, on Dundalk Bay at the mouth of the Castletown River; pop. (1991) 25,800. Edward Bruce was crowned King of Ireland here in 1315. Dundalk was the birthplace of the Arctic explorer Sir Francis McClintock (1819–1907).

**Dundee** /dʌnˈdiː/ a city in east-central Scotland on the Tay estuary, the administrative centre of Tayside region from 1975 to 1996; pop. (1991) 165,500. A royal burgh since the 12th c., Dundee developed from a whaling port during the 19th c. with the expansion of the textile and jute industries. Its university, which was founded in 1881 as University College, was incorporated with St. Andrews until 1967. Dundee was the birthplace of Admiral Adam Duncan of Camperdown (1731–1804), the historian Hector Boece (c. 1465–1536), the doggerel poet William McGonagall (1830–1902), and John Graham of Claverhouse, 1st Viscount Dundee (c. 1649–89). Anchored at the Victoria Dock is the Frigate *Unicorn*, the oldest British warship afloat, and nearby is Scott's *Discovery* built, like his later ship, *Terra Nova*, in Dundee's shipyards. Dundee's industries include engineering, textiles, electrical products, printing and publishing, and food processing. Its famous jam industry began in 1797 with Mrs Keiller's marmalade. The Tay road bridge, one of the longest in Europe, was completed in 1966.

**Dunedin** /dʌˈniːdɪn/ a city and port of South Island, New Zealand, at the head of Otago Harbour; pop. (1991) 109,500. It was founded in 1848 by Scottish settlers; its name, which reflects the Gaelic word (Duneideann) for Edinburgh, was suggested by the Edinburgh publisher William Chambers. Stimulated by discoveries of gold nearby in the 1860s, Dunedin became the first industrialized city in New Zealand.

**Dunfermline** /dʌnˈfɜːmlɪn/ an industrial city in Fife, central Scotland, near the Firth of Forth; pop. (1981) 52,000. A number of Scottish monarchs including Queen Margaret and Robert the Bruce are buried in its Benedictine abbey. The philanthropist Andrew Carnegie was born in the city in 1835, and it is the headquarters of all the Carnegie trusts. In the 19th c. Dunfermline developed as a textile town.

**Dungarvan** the administrative centre of County Waterford in the Republic of Ireland; pop. (1991) 6,920. Situated on Dungarvan Harbour, it lies to the south of the Comeragh and Monavullagh mountains on the River Colligan. The chief landmarks are a 13th-c. Augustinian priory and Dungarvan Castle which was originally built in 1185 by King John.

**Dunhua** /dʊnˈhwaː/ a city in Jilin province, north-east China, on the Mudan River north-west of Yanji; pop. (1986) 450,000.

**Dunhuang** /dʊnˈhwaːŋ/ a town in western Gansu province, China, formerly an important caravan stop on the Silk Road. The nearby cave temples of Mogao (which number 492 and date from the 4th c.) are the oldest Buddhist shrines in China. Discovered in the early 20th c., the caves were excavated by Sir Aurel Stein.

**Dunkirk** /dʌnˈkɜːk/ (French **Dunkerque**) a French channel port, the third-largest in France, situated in the Nord department of Nord-Pas-de-Calais region; pop.(1990) 71,070. It was the scene of the evacuation of the British Expeditionary Force in 1940. Forced to retreat to the Channel by the German breakthrough at Sedan, 225,000 British troops, as well as 110,000 of their French allies, were evacuated from Dunkirk between 27 May and 2 June by warships, requisitioned civilian ships, and a host of small boats, under constant attack from the air. There are ferry links with Dover and Harwich in England.

**Dun Laoghaire** /dʌnˈliːrɪ/ a resort town on the south shore of Dublin Bay in the Republic of Ireland; pop. (1991) 185,400 (Dun Laoghaire–Rathdown). In 1821 its name was changed to Kingstown to commemorate a visit by King George IV, but in 1920 it reverted to Dun Laoghaire. It has a notable yachting harbour and is linked by ferry to Holyhead.

**Dunmow** /ˈdʌnməʊ/ the name of a market town and village in Essex, south-east England. **Great Dunmow** on the River Chelmer near Chelmsford is the scene of the Dunmow Flitch, which has been awarded to happily married couples since the 13th c. **Little Dunmow** lies to the east of Great Dunmow.

**Dunnet Head** /ˈdʌnɪt/ the most northerly point on the British mainland, north-east of Thurso in the Caithness district of Highland Region, Scotland. Its 122-m. (400-ft.) Old Red Sandstone cliffs have a large breeding population of seabirds.

**Dunsinane** /ˈdʌnsɪneɪn/ a hill rising to 309 m. (1,012 ft.) at the western end of the Sidlaws in Angus, Scotland, described by William Shakespeare as the scene of Macbeth's final defeat.

**Dunstable** /ˈdʌnstəb(ə)l/ a residential and industrial town in Bedfordshire, southern England, to the north of the Chiltern Hills, at the junction of the ancient routeways of Watling Street and Icknield Way; pop. (1981) 48,600. The divorce proceedings of King Henry VIII against Catherine of Aragon took place here, and in 1533 Cranmer pronounced his judgment in the church. Dunstable has automobile and printing industries. Nearby to the south is Whipsnade Park Zoo.

**Dunwich** /ˈdʌnɪtʃ/ a village on the coast of Suffolk, eastern England, near Minsmere, the remains of a prosperous town engulfed by the sea in 1328. Sir John Downing who gave his name to Downing Street in London was born here.

**Duque de Caxias** /ˌduːkiə də kəˈʃɪəs/ a city in the state of Rio de Janeiro, eastern Brazil, a north-ern residential and commercial suburb of Rio de Janeiro; pop. (1990) 594,380.

**Durance** /djʊˈrãs/ a river that rises in south-east France on the Italian frontier and flows 305 km. (192 miles) westwards to join the Rhône near Avignon.

**Durand Line** /djuːˈrænd/ a name given to the frontier between Afghanistan and the North-West Frontier province of Pakistan agreed by a bound-ary commission in 1893 and named after the diplo-mat Sir Henry Durand (1850–1924).

**Durango** /dʊəˈræŋgəʊ/ **1.** a state of north-central Mexico; area 123,181 sq. km. (47,579 sq. miles); pop. (1990) 1,352,160. **2.** (in full **Victoria de Durango**) its capital, a mining town founded in 1563 by Don Francisco de Ibarra; pop. (1990) 414,000. A popular location for film makers, its cathedral was completed in 1750.

**Duras** /djʊˈrɑːs/ a small town in the department of Lot-et-Garonne, in the Aquitaine region of south-west France; pop. (1982) 1,245. It is situated at the centre of a notable wine-growing district.

**Durazno** /duːˈræznəʊ/ an agricultural trading centre, capital of Durazno department in central Uruguay, on the Yí River; pop. (1985) 27,600.

**Durazzo** the Italian name for DURRËS.

**Durban** /ˈdɜːbən/ a seaport and resort in the Republic of South Africa, on the coast of KwaZulu-Natal province; pop. (1985) 634,300. Formerly known as Port Natal, it was renamed in 1835 after Sir Benjamin d'Urban, then governor of Cape Colony. It is South Africa's third-largest city and capital (since 1994) of the province of KwaZulu-Natal. Its heavy industries include ship repairing, oil refining, vehicle assembly, fishing, and chemicals; it also has a wide variety of light industries.

**Düren** /ˈdjʊərən/ a transportation centre and industrial city on the River Ruhr, North Rhine-Westphalia, west Germany; pop. (1983) 85,600.

**Durg** /dʊərg/ a town in Madhya Pradesh, central India, west of Raipur, joined to the steel town of Bhilainagar; pop. (1991) 688,670 (with Bhilainagar).

**Durgapur** /ˌdʊərgəˈpʊər/ a city in West Bengal, north-east India, on the Damodar River; pop. (1991) 415,990. Mining, steel production, and the generation of hydroelectric power are the chief industries.

**Durham** /ˈdʌrəm/ a county of north-east England between the Pennines and the North Sea; area 2,434 sq. km. (940 sq. miles); pop. (1991) 589,800; capital, Durham. Durham is divided into eight districts:

| District | Area (sq. km.) | Pop. (1991) |
| --- | --- | --- |
| Chester-le-Street | 68 | 51,600 |
| Darlington | 198 | 96,700 |
| Derwentside | 271 | 84,800 |
| Durham | 187 | 85,000 |
| Easington | 144 | 96,300 |
| Sedgefield | 218 | 89,200 |
| Teesdale | 843 | 24,200 |
| Wear Valley | 505 | 62,100 |

**Durham** city and county town of Durham, north-east England, on the River Wear; pop. (1991) 85,800. Founded by monks in the 10th c. its Norman cathedral was built at the end of the 11th c. and contains the tomb of the Venerable Bede (d. 735). It has a university founded in 1832 and the Gulbenkian Museum of Oriental Art.

**Durham** a city in the piedmont region of North Carolina, USA; pop. (1991) 136,600. Known as 'the City of Medicine', Durham is the home of the Duke University Medical Center, the Burroughs Wellcome Company, the National Institute of Environmental Health Sciences, and the Environmental Protection Agency.

**Durrës** /'dʊrɛs/ (Italian **Durazzo**, Turkish **Draj**) a port and resort on the Adriatic coast of Albania, capital of the province of Durrës; pop. (1990) 85,400. In ancient times, as Epidamnos and later as Dyrrhachium, it was an important seaport. Under Italian and Austrian occupation it was capital of Albania from 1912 to 1921.

**Dushanbe** /du:'ʃænbeɪ/ the capital of Tajikistan in Central Asia; pop. (1990) 602,000. The city was known as Stalinabad from 1929 to 1961. It is an industrial city with textiles, engineering, and food processing.

**Düsseldorf** /'dʊsəl,dɔ:f/ an industrial, commercial, and cultural city, capital of the state of North Rhine-Westphalia in north-west Germany, at the junction of the Rhine and Düssel rivers; pop. (1991) 577,560. It has theatres, museums, art galleries, a university, and an avant-garde film industry. The poet Heinrich Heine was born here in 1797. Its industries include engineering, chemicals, and textiles.

**dust bowl** an arid or unproductive dry region. The term is applied specifically to an area in the prairie states of the USA that was subject to dust storms and drought in the 1930s when the land was returned to grazing after being cultivated since World War I, and the hooves of animals pulverized the unprotected soil. A graphic and moving description is given in John Steinbeck's novel *The Grapes of Wrath* (1939). Increased rainfall, regrassing, and erosion-preventing measures such as contour ploughing have since reduced the area.

**Dutch** relating to, or associated with the Netherlands or its people or language, which belongs to the Germanic language group and is mostly related to German and English. Dutch is spoken by the 13 million inhabitants of the Netherlands and is also the official language of Surinam in South America and the Netherlands Antilles in the Caribbean. The same language is also spoken in parts of Belgium where it is called Flemish. An offshoot of Dutch is Afrikaans which was taken to Africa by Dutch settlers in the 17th c.

**Dutch East Indies** the former name (until 1949) of INDONESIA under Dutch colonial rule.

**Dutch Guiana** the former name of SURINAM.

**Duyun** /dʊ'jʊŋ/ a city in Guizhou province, southern China, on the Longtou River south-east of Guiyang; pop. (1986) 392,000.

**Dvina** /də'vi:nə/ the name of two rivers in Russia. **1.** The **Northern Dvina**, which flows into the White Sea near Archangel in northern Russia, is formed by the junction of the Sukhona and Yug rivers near Kotlas; length, 744 km. (468 miles). **2.** The **Western Dvina**, which is known as the Daugava in Latvia, rises in the Valdai Hills of north-west European Russia and flows south-westwards through Belorussia (Belarus) and Latvia to enter the Gulf of Riga; length, 1,008 km. (634 miles).

**Dyak** /'daɪæk/ (also **Dayak**) the indigenous non-Muslim peoples of Borneo, subdivided into several named groups including the Land Dyak of south-west Borneo and the Sea Dyak of Sarawak. Reckoned to be early inhabitants of the island, forced inland by subsequent migrations of Malays to the coasts, the people live in long-house communities. Intertribal warfare and head-hunting were formerly characteristic of Dyak society. The term 'Sea Dyak' is a misnomer, since the population to which it is applied is primarily a riverine hill-dwelling people whose economy is based on rice cultivation; it was introduced originally to distinguish the more aggressive peoples of the interior, who carried out raids on their coastal neighbours by going down to the sea and then mounting expeditions, from the more passive Land Dyaks of the coast.

**Dyfed** /'dʌfɪd/ a county of south-west Wales, comprising the former counties of Cardiganshire, Carmarthenshire, and Pembrokeshire; area 5,766 sq. km. (2,227 sq. miles); pop. (1991) 341,600; capital, Carmarthen. Dyfed is divided into six districts:

| District | Area (sq. km.) | Pop. (1991) |
| --- | --- | --- |
| Carmarthen | 1,180 | 54,800 |
| Ceredigion | 1,794 | 63,600 |
| Dinefwr | 972 | 38,000 |
| Llanelli | 233 | 73,500 |
| Preseli Pembrokeshire | 1,151 | 69,600 |
| South Pembrokeshire | 436 | 42,100 |

**Dzaoudzi** /'dʒaʊdʒɪ/ the former capital of the French territory of Mahore (Mayotte) and of the Comoros Islands in the Indian Ocean, situated on the small islet of La Petite Terre (Pamanzi); pop. (1985) 5,675. In 1977 it was officially replaced as capital by the larger town of Mamoutzu on the island of La Grande Terre.

**Dzerzhinsk** /dʒɜ:'ʒɪnsk/ an industrial city in west-central Russia, on the Oka River to the west of Nizhniy Novgorod; pop. (1990) 286,000. Named after the head of the first Soviet secret police, it was known as Chernorechye (until c. 1919) and

Rastyapino (until 1929). It is the centre of a major chemical industry.

**Dzhambul** /dʒəm'buːl/ the former name of ZHAMBYL.

**Dzhezkazgan** /ˌdʒeskəs'gɑːn/ the former name of ZHEZQAZGHAN.

**Dzongkha** /'zɒŋkə/ a Tibetan dialect that is the official language of Bhutan.

**Dzungaria** /zʊŋ'gærɪə/ (also **Zungaria, Sungaria** or **Junggar Basin**, Chinese **Junggar Pendi**) a sparsely inhabited semidesert region of Xinjiang autonomous region, north-west China, lying between the Tien Shan and Altai Shan ranges.

**Dzunnmod** /'zʊnməd/ (also **Töv**) the capital of Töv county in central Mongolia; pop. (1990) 18,200.

# E*e*

**Ealing** /'iːlɪŋ/ a residential and commercial outer borough of Greater London; pop. (1991) 263,600. Noted as a centre of British film-making, the first British sound-film studio was built here in 1931. Ealing was the birthplace of the biologist Thomas Huxley (1825–95).

**Earl's Court** /ɜːlz 'kɔːt/ a largely residential district of Greater London between Kensington and Fulham, with a noted exhibition hall. It probably takes its name from the Earls of Warwick who had a mansion house here.

**Earlston** /'ɜːlstən/ a small town near Melrose in the Borders Region of Scotland; pop. (1981) 1,610. Its ruined tower house was the home of the 13th-c. poet and seer Thomas Learmont who was known as Thomas of Ercildoune (Earlston), True Thomas, or Thomas the Rhymer.

**Earn** /ɜːn/ a river in Perthshire, Scotland. It flows 73 km. (46 miles) eastwards through Strathearn from Loch Earn to the Tay estuary near Perth.

**earthquake** /'ɜːθkweɪk/ a violent movement of the surface of the earth due to the release of accumulated stress as a result of faults in strata or volcanic action. While gentle earth tremors can occur in any region of the globe, the more severe ones usually occur near the edges of the major 'plates' that make up the earth's crust. The point at which an earthquake shock originates is called the focus and the point immediately above this on the earth's surface is the epicentre. The intensity of the earthquake is reported as measured by the Richter scale. Major earthquakes generally measure between about 7 and 9, though in theory there is no upper limit on the scale.

**Eas Coul Aulin** /ɪəs kuːl 'æl(ə)n/ (also **Eas a' Chual Aluinn**) a waterfall in northern Scotland, situated on the Abhainn an Loch Bhig to the south-east of Glencoul near Unapool in Highland Region. With a height of 201 m. (658 ft.) it is the highest waterfall in Britain.

**East Anglia** /'æŋglɪə/ an ancient division of England, now a region of eastern England consisting of the counties of Norfolk, Suffolk, Cambridgeshire, and parts of Essex. Founded in 1963, the University of East Anglia is based in Norwich.

**East Bengal** a part of the former Indian province of Bengal that was ceded to Pakistan in 1947. It formed the greater part of the province of East Pakistan which gained independence as Bangladesh in 1971.

**East Bergholt** /'bɜːghəʊlt/ a village in Suffolk, east England, in the Stour valley. It was the birthplace of the artist John Constable in 1776.

**Eastbourne** /'iːstbɔːn/ a resort town in East Sussex, on the south coast of England; pop. (1981) 78,000. Beachy Head is nearby.

**East Budleigh** /'bʌdlɪ/ a village in Devon, south-west England, near Budleigh Salterton. The nearby manor house of Hayes Barton was the birthplace of Sir Walter Raleigh (1552–1618).

**East Cape** a peninsula on the coast of Gisborne Region, New Zealand, forming the easternmost point of North Island. Named by Captain James Cook in 1769, East Cape was an administrative region until the local authority reforms of 1989.

**East China Sea** SEE CHINA SEA.

**East Coker** /'kəʊkə(r)/ a village in Somerset, England, 5 km. (3 miles) south of Yeovil. It was the birthplace of the explorer William Dampier (1652–1715) and buried here are the ashes of T. S. Eliot, whose ancestors left the village for North America.

**East Dereham** /'dɪrəm/ a town in Norfolk, England, the burial place of the poet William Cowper (1731–1800).

**East End** the name given to the eastern part of London north of the Thames, associated in the 19th c. with Victorian slums, poverty, and a particular breed of cheerful cockney humour.

**Easter Island** (Spanish **Isla de Pascua** /ˌiːzlɑː ðeɪ 'pɑːskwə/, Polynesian **Rapa Nui** /ˌrɑːpə 'nuːiː/) an island in the south-east Pacific west of Chile, named by the Dutch navigator Roggeveen who visited it on Easter Day, 1722; area 117 sq. km. (45 sq. miles); pop. (est. 1988) 2,000. Administered by Chile since 1888, it is famous for its many monolithic statues (*moai*) of human heads (up to 10 metres high). Between 1888 and 1952 the greater part of the island was leased to a Chilean-Scottish sheep-ranching company. Nearly 70 per cent of the population lives in the chief town, Hanga Roa.

**easterly** a wind blowing from the east.

**Eastern Cape** a province of South Africa created in 1994 from part of the former Cape Province. Its capital is East London.

**Eastern Island** SEE MIDWAY ISLANDS.

**Eastern Time** standard time used in eastern Canada and the US or in eastern Australia.

**Eastern Desert** (also **Arabian Desert**) a desert in eastern Egypt, lying between the Nile and the Red Sea.

**Eastern Transvaal** a province of South Africa created in 1994 from part of the former province of Transvaal. Its capital is Nelspruit.

**East Germany** the former name of that part of Germany constituted as an independent state (German Democratic Republic) in the Soviet-dominated Eastern Bloc after World War II. Created in 1949, it remained largely unrecognized by non-Communist countries until 1972–3 and in 1990, with the collapse of Communism in Eastern Europe, it reunited with West Germany once again. Its capital was East Berlin and its area was 108,568 sq. km. (41,757 sq. miles).

**East Indies** the many islands off the south-east coast of Asia, now sometimes called the Malay Archipelago. The Netherlands East Indies or Dutch East Indies was the former name (until 1949) for Indonesia.

**easting** /ˈiːstɪŋ/ a nautical term used to describe the distance travelled or the angle of longitude measured eastward from either a defined north–south grid line or a meridian.

**East Kilbride** /kɪlˈbraɪd/ a town in central Scotland, south of Glasgow; pop. (1991) 81,400. It was designated a New Town in 1947.

**East Lansing** /ˈlænsɪŋ/ a town in south-central Michigan, USA, adjacent to Lansing; pop. (1990) 13,500.

**East London** a port and resort on the south-east coast of South Africa developed in the 19th c. from a military post, capital (since 1994) of the Eastern Cape province; pop. (1985) 193,800. Its industries include vehicle assembly, furniture, textiles, clothing, and fishing.

**East Lothian** /ˈləʊðɪən/ a local government area of east-central Scotland; area 1,716 sq. km. (663 sq. miles); pop. (1991) 83,000. Its chief towns are Haddington and Tranent.

**East Orange** a residential city near Newark in the state of New Jersey, USA; pop. (1990) 73,500.

**East Providence** a suburb of Providence, Rhode Island, USA; pop. (1990) 50,400.

**East River** an arm of the Hudson River in New York State, USA, separating Manhattan and the Bronx from Brooklyn and Queens on Long Island.

**East Siberian Sea** that part of the Arctic Ocean lying between the New Siberian Islands and Wrangel Island, to the north of the Yakutsk and Chukot regions of Russian Siberia.

**East Side** that part of Manhattan Island in New York, USA, lying between Fifth Avenue and the East River. The Lower East Side between 14th Street and Canal Street and east of Lafayette Street was settled by Jewish immigrants from the 1870s to the 1930s and later by Blacks, Puerto Ricans, and other Hispanics. Generally associated with

poverty, the Lower East Side was the childhood home of many famous Americans, especially musicians and entertainers such as Irving Berlin, Al Jolson, Fanny Brice, and George and Ira Gershwin.

**East Sussex** /ˈsʌsɪks/ a county of south-east England; area 1,795 sq. km. (693 sq. miles); pop. (1991) 670,600; county town, Lewes. East Sussex is divided into seven districts:

| District | Area (sq. km.) | Pop. (1991) |
| --- | --- | --- |
| Brighton | 58 | 133,400 |
| Eastbourne | 44 | 83,200 |
| Hastings | 30 | 78,100 |
| Hove | 24 | 82,500 |
| Lewes | 292 | 85,400 |
| Rother | 510 | 80,200 |
| Wealden | 837 | 127,700 |

**East Timor** see TIMOR.

**Eastwood** a mining village in Nottinghamshire, central England, the birthplace in 1885 of the writer D. H. Lawrence; pop. (1981) 18,100.

**Eau Claire** /əʊ ˈkleɪr/ a city in west-central Wisconsin, USA, at the junction of the Eau Claire and Chippewa rivers; pop. (1990) 56,900. It was founded in 1844 as a lumber and sawmilling town.

**Ebbw Vale** /ˌebʊ ˈveɪl/ an industrial town in Gwent, south-east Wales, 33 km. (20 miles) north of Cardiff; pop. (1981) 21,145. Formerly (until the 1970s) a centre of coal, and iron and steel production, the industry of the town is now based around engineering and printing.

**Ebla** /ˈeblə/ the ancient name of IDLIB in Syria.

**Ebro** /ˈiːbrəʊ/ the principal river of north-east Spain, which rises in the Cantabrian Mountains and flows south-east for 910 km. (570 miles) into the Mediterranean Sea. It is the longest river flowing entirely within Spain.

**EC** abbr. **1.** East-Central (London postal district). **2.** the European Community.

**Ecclefechan** /ˌek(ə)lˈfexən/ a village in Dumfries and Galloway, southern Scotland, 8 km. (5 miles) north of Annan, the birthplace of Thomas Carlyle (1795–1881).

**Ech Chlef** (also **Ech Chéliff**) a market city in northern Algeria, on the Chéliff River to the west of Algiers; pop. (1983) 119,000. It was known by its French name Orléansville, until 1962 and also by the Arabic name, El Asnam. It is the centre of an important citrus-fruit and grain-producing region.

**Eccles** /ˈeklz/ an industrial town in Lancashire, England, at the junction of the Bridgewater Canal and Manchester Ship Canal; pop. (1981) 37,800. It is known for its Eccles cakes which are round pastries filled with dried fruit.

**ecology** /iːˈkɒlədʒɪ/ the branch of biology dealing with the relations of organisms to one another and to their physical surroundings. Human ecology is the study of the interaction of people with their environment.

**ecosphere** /'iːkəʊˌsfɪər/ the region of space including planets where conditions are such that living things can exist.

**ecosystem** /'iːkəʊˌsɪstəm/ a biological community of interacting organisms and their physical environment. The term was coined by the Oxford ecologist A. G. Tansley in 1934.

## Ecuador

/'ekwəˌdɔː(r)/ official name **The Republic of Ecuador** an equatorial country in South America, on the Pacific coast, between Peru and Colombia; area 270,670 sq. km.

(109,484 sq. miles); pop. (est. 1991) 10,800,000; official language, Spanish; capital, Quito. The largest cities are Guayaquil, Quito, and Cuenca. Ranges and plateaux of the Andes separate the coastal plain from the tropical jungles of the Amazon Basin. Despite the sale of petroleum after major oilfields were discovered in 1972, the economy is largely agricultural and dependent on exports of coffee, bananas, and fish. Incorporated in the late 16th c. into the Inca empire, Ecuador was conquered by the Spanish in 1534 and remained part of Spain's American empire until independence was won in 1822. The country has remained independent since leaving the Federation of Grand Colombia in 1830, but has since lost territory in border disputes with its more powerful neighbours. The Galápagos Islands (or Colón Archipelago) in the Pacific became part of Ecuador in 1832. The country is governed by an executive president and a unicameral National Congress.
**Ecuadorean** adj. & n.

Ecuador is divided into 21 provinces:

| Province | Area (sq. km.) | Pop. (1990) | Capital |
| --- | --- | --- | --- |
| Azuay | 8,125 | 506,550 | Cuenca |
| Bolívar | 3,940 | 170,590 | Guaranda |
| Cañar | 3,122 | 189,110 | Azogues |
| Carchi | 3,605 | 141,990 | Tulcán |
| Chimborazo | 6,569 | 360,600 | Riobamba |
| Cotopaxi | 6,072 | 283,290 | Latacunga |
| El Oro | 5,850 | 415,070 | Machala |
| Esmeraldas | 15,239 | 307,190 | Esmeraldas |
| Guayas | 20,502 | 2,463,420 | Guayaquil |
| Imbabura | 4,559 | 273,260 | Ibarra |
| Loja | 11,026 | 389,680 | Loja |
| Los Ríos | 7,175 | 530,840 | Babahoyo |
| Manabí | 18,879 | 1,026,070 | Portoviejo |
| Morona Santiago | 25,690 | 95,685 | Macas |
| Napo | 33,931 | 102,620 | Tena |
| Pastaza | 29,774 | 40,710 | Puyo |
| Pichincha | 12,915 | 1,734,940 | Quito |
| Sucumbíos | 18,327 | 77,450 | Nueva Loja |
| Tungurahua | 3,335 | 366,520 | Ambato |
| Zamora Chinchipe | 23,111 | 66,730 | Zamora |
| Galápagos Islands | 8,010 | 9,750 | San Cristóbal |

**Edam** /'iːdæm/ a market town in the Netherlands, situated in the province of North Holland, north-east of Amsterdam; pop. (1987) 24,400 (with Volendam). It is noted for its round, pale yellow cheese with a red rind.

**Eddystone Rocks** /'edɪstən/ a rocky reef off the Cornish coast of south-west England, 22 km. (14 miles) south-west of Plymouth. A lighthouse built here by Winstanley was swept away in a storm in 1703 and a successor was burned in 1755. The lighthouse erected by John Smeaton in 1757–9 was removed to Plymouth Hoe and replaced by another in 1882.

**Ede** /'eɪdə/ an industrial city in the Dutch province of Gelderland; pop. (1991) 94,750. Food processing and the manufacture of rayon and metal goods are the chief industries.

**Eden** /'iːdən/ **1.** a river in northern England flowing 104 km. (65 miles) north-westwards from the Pennines to the Solway Firth. **2.** a river in south-east England that rises in Surrey and flows 19 km. (12 miles) east to the River Medway. **3.** a river in central Scotland that flows 48 km. (30 miles) eastwards through north Fife to meet the North Sea at St. Andrews.

**Eden** (also **Garden of Eden**) a name applied to a paradise or place of great happiness. Eden is associated with the abode of Adam and Eve in the biblical account of the Creation.

**Edgehill** /edʒ'hɪl/ a locality in Warwickshire, central England, 11 km. (7 miles) north-west of Banbury, at which the first pitched battle of the English Civil War was fought in 1642.

**Edinburgh** /'edɪnbərə/ the capital of Scotland from 1437, lying close to the southern shore of the Firth of Forth; pop. (1991) 421,200. The city grew up round the 11th-c. castle built by Malcolm III on a rocky ridge which dominates the landscape. The 'Royal Mile', which links the castle with the Palace of Holyroodhouse at the bottom of the ridge, passes through the old medieval burghs of Edinburgh and the Canongate. Princes Street, to the north, is the main thoroughfare in the 'New Town' which was built in the 18th and 19th c. It was the birthplace of the founder of the Bank of France, John Law (1671–1729), the painter Sir Henry Raeburn (1756–1823), Robert Louis Stevenson (1850–94), and Sir Walter Scott (1771–1832). Edinburgh has hosted a famous international festival annually since 1947. It is the headquarters of the Scottish Office, the Forestry Authority, and the British Geological Survey and home of the University of Edinburgh (1583), Heriot-Watt University (1966), and Napier University (1992). Finance, brewing, tourism, and light industry are important.

**Edirne** /e'dɪrnɪ/ **1.** a province of north-west Turkey bounded to the north and west by Bulgaria and Greece; area 6,276 sq. km. (2,424 sq. miles); pop. (1990) 404,600. **2.** its capital at the junction of the Tundzha and Maritsa rivers; pop. (1990) 102,300. Originally a Thracian city, it was rebuilt by the Romans in the 2nd c. AD and named Adrianopolis after the emperor Hadrian. It has numerous industries including textiles and carpets.

**Edmond** /'edmənd/ a market city in central Oklahoma, USA, to the north of Oklahoma City and close to a major oilfield; pop. (1990) 52,315.

**Edmonton** /'edmənt(ə)n/ the capital (since 1905) and largest city of Alberta, Canada, 300 km. (116 miles) east of the Rockies, on the North Saskatchewan River; pop. (1991) 616,700; 839,920 (metropolitan area). Founded by the Hudson's Bay Company as a fur-trading settlement in 1795, it developed after the area was opened up for pioneers in the 1870s and when the railway arrived from Calgary in 1891. A major centre of oil development and petrochemical industries in the 1960s and 1970s, Edmonton's main annual event is the 'Klondike Days' which commemorates the gold-rush of 1898 when the Klondike Trail to Dawson City in the Yukon put Edmonton on the map. The University of Alberta was founded here in 1907.

**Edo** /'i:dəʊ/ the former name (until 1868) of Tokyo, capital of Japan. It gave its name to the Edo Period of Japanese history which existed prior to the birth of modern Japan. Under the feudal Tokugawa Shogunate, which lasted from 1603 to 1867, local warlords were kept in check and Japan remained largely isolated from the outside world. The Edo period is characterized by the development of Kabuki drama and craftwork such as wood-block prints, silk brocade, and lacquerware.

**Edom** /'i:dəm/ (also **Seir**) an ancient region of the Middle East to the south of the Dead Sea whose people were traditionally descended from Esau and whose capital was Petra.

**Edomite** *adj. & n.*

**Edward** /'edwəd/, **Lake** (also **Lake Rutanzige**) a lake in the Rift Valley of East Africa, situated at an altitude of 912 m. (2,992 ft.) on the frontier between Uganda and Zaire. It is 80 km. (50 miles) long and 50 km. (31 miles) wide, with an area of 2,149 sq. km. (830 sq. miles). After its European discovery by H. M. Stanley in 1889 it was known as the Albert Edward Nyanza and from 1973 to 1979 it was known to Ugandans as Lake Idi Amin. It is linked to Lake Albert by the Semliki River.

**EEC** *abbr.* EUROPEAN ECONOMIC COMMUNITY. (The former term for the European Union.)

**Eelam** the homeland of the Tamil people of Sri Lanka, named after Elara, the last Tamil king of Anuradhapura. Although the Tamil history of Sri Lanka refers to the whole of the island as Eelam, present-day demands for a separate Tamil State of Eelam extend only to the northern and eastern provinces of Sri Lanka.

**Efate** /eɪ'fɑːtiː/ an island in the south-west Pacific whose chief town is the port of Vila, capital of Vanuatu; area 914 sq. km. (353 sq. miles).

**Egadi Islands** (Italian **Isole Egadi**) a group of small Italian islands off the west coast of Sicily. The chief islands are Marettimo, Favignana, Levanzo, and Stagnone.

**Eger** /'egə(r)/ a spa town on the River Eger northern Hungary, noted for its red 'Bull's Blood' wine; pop. (1993) 63,365.

**Egmont** /'egmənt/, **Mount** see TARANAKI.

**Egnatian Way** /eg'neɪʃən/ (Latin **Via Egnatia**) a Roman road through the Balkans, linking Durrës in Albania with Salonica and Constantinople in the east.

**Egypt** /'i:dʒɪpt/ official name **The Arab Republic of Egypt** a country in north-east Africa bordering on the Mediterranean Sea, consisting largely of desert, with its population concentrated 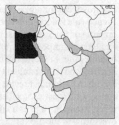 chiefly along the fertile valley of the River Nile; area 1,002,000 sq. km. (386,900 sq. miles); pop. (est. 1991) 56,500,000; official language, Arabic; capital, Cairo. The largest cities are Cairo, Alexandria, and Giza all of which lie in the Nile delta. The chief cash crop is cotton, and Egypt is self-sufficient in energy, having considerable reserves of petroleum and natural gas as well as hydroelectric power produced by the Aswan High Dam. Its antiquities make tourism a major industry in addition to textiles and food processing.

Egypt's history spans 5,000 years, dating back to the neolithic period when nomadic hunters settled in the Nile valley. The ancient kingdoms of Upper and Lower Egypt became united, according to tradition, under Menes (c. 3,000 BC), founder of the first of the 31 dynasties which successively ruled ancient Egypt. The period of the Old Kingdom (c. 2575–2134 BC, 4th–8th Dynasty), the 'Pyramid Age', was characterized by strong central government, with the political and religious centre at Memphis. The Middle Kingdom (c. 2040–1640 BC, 11th–14th Dynasty) is considered to be the classical age of ancient Egyptian culture; its collapse was brought about by infiltration of Asiatics, culminating in the Hyksos usurpation. The New Kingdom (c. 1550–1070 BC, 18th–20th Dynasty), the 'empire' period, with its capital at Thebes, begins with the expulsion of the Hyksos. Egypt's claim over territory in Syria and Palestine brought it into direct confrontation with its principal rivals, Mitanni and the Hittites; Nubia was administered directly from Egypt. These foreign interests brought Egypt considerable wealth as well as technological and cultural innovations, but by the end of the period a decline in the power of the Pharaohs and an increase in that of the priests resulted in a weakening of the central government. Egypt fell successively to Libyans, Ethiopians, Assyrians, and Persians, and indigenous rule was finally ended by Alexander the Great, who took Egypt in 332 BC. From then until AD 1922 some people other than the Egyptians ruled Egypt.

On Alexander's death the Macedonian Ptolemy I acquired Egypt, and for three centuries the country was the centre of Hellenistic culture because of the considerable role played by Alexandria, home of a cosmopolitan Greek-speaking population who cultivated the arts and sciences, until on the death of Cleopatra it became a Roman province. After the Arab conquest in 642 Egypt was an Islamic country. From 1517 it formed part of the Ottoman empire except for a brief period (1798–1801) under French rule following Napoleon's invasion. The opening of the Suez Canal in 1869 made Egypt strategically important, and when the Turks became allies of Germany in World War I the British (who had installed themselves following an Egyptian nationalist revolt in 1882) declared the country a British protectorate. Egypt became fully independent in 1936 as a kingdom, but with the overthrow of the monarchy in 1952 a republic was created. Gamal Abdel Nasser, who ruled Egypt until his death in 1970, developed a policy of pan-Arab socialism and succeeded in uniting Egypt and Syria into the United Arab Republic from 1958 until its formal dissolution in 1984. Conflict with Israel in 1948, 1956, 1967, and 1973 was eventually resolved with the signing of an Egypt-Israel Peace treaty in 1979. The country is governed by a legislative People's Assembly and a consultative Shura Council both of which have elected and presidentially appointed members.

**Egyptian** *adj. & n.*

Egypt is divided into 26 governorates:

| Governorate | Area (sq. km.) | Pop. (est.1991) | Capital |
| --- | --- | --- | --- |
| North Sinai | 33,140 | 223,000 | Af-Tur |
| South Sinai | 25,574 | 41,000 | Al-Arish |
| Suez | 17,840 | 376,000 | Suez |
| Ismâilîya | 1,442 | 632,000 | Ismâilîya |
| Port Said | 72 | 449,000 | Port Said |
| Sharqîya | 4,180 | 3,899,000 | Zagâziq |
| Daqahlîya | 3,471 | 3,939,000 | Mansûra |
| Damietta | 589 | 836,000 | Damietta |
| Kafr el-Sheikh | 3,437 | 2,054,000 | Kafr el-Sheikh |
| Alexandria | 2,679 | 3,295,000 | Alexandria |
| Behera | 10,130 | 3,730,000 | Damanhur |
| Gharbîya | 1,942 | 3,240,000 | Tanta |
| Menûfîya | 1,532 | 2,532,000 | Shibin el-Kom |
| Qalyûbîya | 1,001 | 2,880,000 | Benha |
| Cairo | 214 | 6,663,000 | Cairo |
| Gîza | 85,105 | 4,182,000 | El Gîza |
| Faiyûm | 1,827 | 1,805,000 | El Faiyûm |
| Beni Suef | 1,322 | 1,656,000 | Beni Suef |
| Minyâ | 2,262 | 3,003,000 | Minyâ |
| Asyût | 1,530 | 2,532,000 | Asyût |
| Sohag | 1,547 | 2,763,000 | Sohag |
| Qinâ | 1,851 | 2,598,000 | Qinâ |
| Aswan | 679 | 925,000 | Aswan |
| Red Sea | 203,685 | 112,000 | Al-Ghurdaqah |
| New Valley | 376,505 | 130,000 | Al-Kharijah |
| Mersa Matrûh | 212,112 | 193,000 | Matrûh |

**Eider** /'aɪdə(r)/ a river in north-west Germany which rises to the south of Kiel, flows north to the Kiel Canal and then west to meet the North Sea near Tönning. Its length is 187 km. (117 miles).

**Eidsvoll** /'eɪtsvɒl/ a town in Akershus county, south-east Norway, on the River Vorma near Lake Mjøsa. The constitution of Norway was proclaimed here in 1814.

**Eiffel Tower** /'aɪf(ə)l/ a wrought-iron structure designed by Alexandre Gustave Eiffel (1832–1923) and erected in Paris for the centenary exhibition of 1889. Still a famous landmark though at first greatly disliked, it was, with a height of 300 m. (984 ft.), the tallest man-made structure for many years.

**Eiger** /'aɪgə(r)/ a mountain peak in the Bernese Alps of Central Switzerland, first climbed by C. Barrington in 1858. It is a mountain with three ridges the highest of which rises to 3,970 m. (13,101 ft.).

**Eigg** /eg/ an island in the Small Isles Parish of the Inner Hebrides, lying off the west coast of Scotland to the south of Skye. Kildonan is the chief settlement and the Sgurr of Eigg is the highest point (393 m., 1,289 ft.). It is linked by ferry with Mallaig on the mainland.

**Eilat** /eɪ'læt/ (also **Elat**) the southernmost town in Israel, a port and resort at the head of the Gulf of Aqaba; pop. (est. 1982) 19,500. Founded in 1949 near the ruins of biblical Elath, it is Israel's only outlet to the Red Sea.

**Eilean Donan** /ˌiːlən 'dəʊnən/ a small islet at the mouth of Loch Duich on the Kintail coast of Wester Ross, Scotland, on which stands a picturesque castle of the Clan Macrae reduced to rubble during a naval bombardment in 1719 and restored in the 1930s.

**Eildon Hills** /'iːldən/ a group of three peaks rising to 422 m. (1,385 ft.) near Melrose in the Borders Region of Scotland.

**Eindhoven** /'aɪnthəʊv(ə)n/ the chief industrial city of the province of North Brabant, in the Netherlands, situated on the River Dommel 88 km. (55 miles) south-east of Rotterdam; pop. (1991) 192,900. The city is a major producer of electrical and electronic goods.

**Eire** /'eərə/ (Gaelic **Eire**) the former name of the Republic of Ireland still often used in newspapers etc. to distinguish the country from Northern Ireland and from the island as a whole.

**Eisenach** /'aɪzenæx/ a resort and industrial town in the state of Thuringia, central Germany, situated west of Erfurt; pop. (1981) 50,700. It was the birthplace in 1735 of the composer Johann Sebastian Bach. Its industries include vehicles, machinery, chemicals, and electronics.

**Eisenhüttenstadt** /'aɪz(ə)n‚hjuːt(ə)n‚ʃtɑːt/ a residential and industrial city in the state of Brandenburg, eastern Germany, situated near the Polish frontier south of Frankfurt an der Oder; pop. (1991) 49,060. It has iron and steel industries.

**Eisenstadt** /'aɪz(ə)n‚ʃtɑːt/ the capital (since 1925) of the province of Burgenland in eastern Austria; pop. (1991) 10,500. It was a Hungarian city until ceded to Austria in 1920, and in the 17th–18th c. was the principal seat of the Esterházy princes, patrons of the composer Joseph Haydn who himself lived here for many years. It is the centre of a fertile fruit and wine region.

**Eisriesenwelt** /'aɪs'riːz(ə)n‚velt/ a system of caves extending 40 km. (25 miles) into the Tennen massif, south of the Austrian city of Salzburg. Filled with ice formations, it is thought to be the largest ice-cave system in Europe. Its name in German means 'the world of the ice giants'. The caves were first explored in 1879 by Anton von Posselt-Czorich.

**Ekibastuz** /‚ekə'bɑːstəs/ a coal-mining town in north-east Kazakhstan; pop. (1990) 137,000.

**El Aaiún** see LA'YOUN.

**El Alamein** /el 'ælə‚meɪn/ the site of the decisive British victory in the North African campaign of 1940–3, 90 km. (60 miles) west of Alexandria, where the German Afrika Korps under Rommel was checked in its advance towards the Nile by the British Eighth Army under Montgomery.

**Elam** /'iːlæm/ an ancient kingdom east of the Tigris, established in the 4th millenium BC, with its capital at Susa.

**El Asnam** /el æs'nɑːm/ see ECH CHLEF.

**Elat** see EILAT.

**Elâziğ** /‚elə'zə/ **1.** a mountainous province of east central Turkey to the east of the Euphrates; area 9,153 sq. km. (3,535 sq. miles); pop. (1990) 498,200. **2.** its capital, a textile manufacturing and agricultural market town 250 km. (160 miles) west of Lake Van; pop. (1990) 204,600.

**Elba** /'elbə/ a small island off the west coast of Italy, famous as the place of Napoleon's first exile (1814–15). Its chief town and port is Portoferraio and its highest peak is Mt. Capanne (1,108 m., 3,340 ft.).

**Elbasan** /‚elbə'sɑːn/ a market town in central Albania, 32 km. (20 miles) south-east of Tirana in the valley of the River Shkumbin; pop. (1990) 83,300. It is capital of a province of the same name.

**Elbe** /elb/ (Czech **Labe**) a river of Central Europe which rises in the Czech Republic and flows 1,159 km. (720 miles) through Germany to the North Sea. Major cities upon it are Dresden, Magdeburg, and Hamburg. From 1945 until the re-unification of Germany in 1990 it formed part of the frontier between East and West Germany.

**Elblag** /el'blɑ̃/ (German **Elbing**) a port on the Elblag River, northern Poland, situated near the Baltic Sea south-east of Gdansk; pop. (1990) 126,000. It is capital of Elblag county and a centre of marine engineering.

**Elbrus, Mount** /el'bruːs/ a peak in the Caucasus Mountains on the frontier between Russia and the Republic of Georgia. Rising to 5,642 m. (18,510 ft.), it is the highest mountain in Europe.

**Elburz Mountains** /el'buəz/ (Persian **Reshteh ye Alborz**) a mountain range in north-west Iran, close to the southern shore of the Caspian Sea. Its highest peak, Damavand, rises to a height of 5,601 m. (18,376 ft.).

**El Capitan** /el kæpɪ'tɑːn/ a peak of the Sierra Nevada in Yosemite Valley, California, USA. Rising 1,098 m. (3,604 ft.) above the valley floor, it is the tallest monolithic rock face in the world.

**El Cajon** /‚elkə'həʊn/ an industrial city in southern California, USA, east of San Diego; pop. (1990) 88,700. It is a rapidly growing centre of aerospace and electronic industries.

**El Centro** a market town in the Imperial Valley, southern California, USA; pop. (1990) 31,380. It is the largest town entirely below sea-level in the USA and lies amidst farmland irrigated by water from the All-American Canal and Hoover Dam.

**Elche** /'eltʃeɪ/ a town in the province of Alicante, eastern Spain, on the River Vinalapó; pop. (1991) 181,200. It is noted for its elegant palm trees and its 13th-c. mystery play which is performed every August in the church of Santa María. It has diverse agriculturally based light industries.

**Elda** /'eldə/ a town with a Moorish castle in the province of Alicante, eastern Spain; pop. (1991) 54,000. The manufacture of shoes is a leading industry.

**El Djem** /el 'dʒem/ (also **El Jem**) a town in eastern Tunisia noted for its vast, well-preserved Roman amphitheatre.

**El Dorado** /el də'rɑːdəʊ/ the name of a fictitious country (according to some, a city) abounding in gold, believed by the Spanish and by Sir Walter Raleigh to exist upon the Amazon. The origin of the belief, which led Spanish conquistadors to converge on the area in search of treasure, appears to have been rumours of an Indian ruler, in what is now Colombia, who ritually coated his body with gold dust and then plunged into a sacred lake while his subjects threw in gold and jewels.

**Elea** /'iːlɪə/ the site of an ancient Greek city to the south of Salerno in the Campania region of south-west Italy. Founded in 536 BC, it was the home of the Eleatic school of philosophers led by Xenophanes, Parmenides, and Zeno. Roman aristocracy later built the resort town of Velia on this site.

**Eleatic** *adj. & n.*

**Eleanor Cross** /ˈelɪnə(r)/ any of the stone crosses erected by Edward I to mark the stopping-places of the cortège that brought the body of his queen, Eleanor of Castile, from Nottinghamshire to London in 1290. Three of the twelve crosses survive.

**Electric Brae** see CROY BRAE.

**Elektrostal** /elˌjektrəˈstɑːl/ an industrial town in western Russia, 48 km. (30 miles) east of Moscow; pop. (1990) 153,000. It was known as Zatishye until 1938.

**Elephanta Island** /ˌeləˈfæntə/ (Hindu **Gharapuri**) a small island with four rock-cut temples in Bombay Harbour on the west coast of India. Sculptured panels are thought to date from between AD 450 and 750. It has been designated a world heritage site by UNESCO.

**Elephantine Island** an island in the Nile, Egypt, situated below the First Cataract, opposite Aswan. It was the site of an ancient town which was the centre of the cult of the ram-headed Khnum, god of the cataracts and creator of mankind.

**Elephant Pass** a narrow strip of land linking the Jaffna peninsula with the mainland at the north end of Sri Lanka.

**El Escorial** /el esˈkɔʊrɪˌæl/ a town in the Sierra Guadarrama of central Spain, situated 40 km. (25 miles) north-west of Madrid, adjacent to a royal palace and monastery built by King Philip II between 1563 and 1584.

**Eleusis** /elˈjuːsɪs/ (also **Elefsína** or **Elévsis**) an industrial town 22 km. (14 miles) north of Athens, Greece; pop. (1981) 20,300. The ancient city of Eleusis was the birthplace of the Greek dramatist Aeschylus (525–456 BC) and home of the sanctuary of the corn goddess Demeter who was celebrated in the annual Eleusinian Mysteries. Industries in the modern town include shipbuilding and the production of petrochemicals, iron, and steel.

**Eleusinian** *adj.*

**Eleuthera** /iːˈluːθrə/ an island in the Bahamas, the first to be settled when the company of Eleutherian Adventurers arrived in 1648, escaping religious persecution in England and Bermuda. They named the island after the Greek word for freedom. The island is 160 km. (100 miles) long and on average 3.2 km. (2 miles) wide; area 518 sq. km. (200 sq. miles); pop.(1990) 9,300 (with Harbour Island and Spanish Wells).

**El Faiyûm** /el faɪˈjuːm/ (also **Fayum**) a city in northern Egypt, 100 km. (63 miles) south-west of Cairo in a depression entirely below sea-level; pop. (1991) 244,000. It is Egypt's largest oasis settlement. The Pharaohs of the 12th dynasty reclaimed the surrounding land by regulating the flow of the Nile and the Pharaohs of the 13th dynasty built several fine palaces here. Once a centre of worship for the ancient crocodile-headed god Sobek, the Greeks named the place Crocodilopolis. Many ancient papyri have been found here. The city has many light industries.

**El Ferrol** /el fəˈrɒl/ (in full **El Ferrol de Caudillo**) a city in the province of La Coruña, Galicia, north-west Spain; pop. (1991) 84,500. It is Spain's leading naval base on the Atlantic coast, with shipyards and a naval academy. General Franco was born here in 1892.

**Elgin** /ˈelgɪn/ a burgh town and cathedral city on the River Lossie in the Moray District of northern Scotland; pop. (1981) 18,900.

**Elgin** a city in north-east Illinois, USA, in the Fox River valley; pop. (1990) 77,000. Founded in 1835, Elgin is associated with watch-making and the invention of condensed milk.

**El Giza** see GIZA.

**Elgon** /ˈelgɒn/, **Mount** an extinct volcano with a massive caldera on the Kenya–Uganda frontier, rising to a height of 4,321 m. (14,178 ft.). The Mount Elgon National Park, extending to 16,923 hectares (41,785 acres), was designated in 1968 to protect wet montane forest, bamboo and giant podocarpus, moorland, and heathland.

**Elis** /ˈelɪs/ the ruins of an ancient Greek city situated near the modern village of Boukhióti on the Kyllini peninsula of the Peloponnesos, south-western Greece. It was the centre of the holy land of Elis famous for its temple of Zeus at Olympia.

**Elisabethville** /ɪˈlɪzəbəθˌvɪl/ the former name (until 1966) of LUBUMBASHI in Zaire.

**Elista** /iːˈlɪstə/ the capital of the Republic of Kalmykia-Khalmg Tangch (Kalmykia) in southern Russia, situated to the west of Astrakhan; pop. (1990) 85,000. It was known as Stepnoy from 1944 to 1957.

**Elizabeth** an industrial city in north-east New Jersey, USA, on Newark Bay; pop. (1990) 110,000. It was the first English settlement in New Jersey, and was state capital from 1664 to 1686. The first Colonial Assembly met here from 1669 to 1692 and Princeton University was founded here in 1746 as the College of New Jersey. Elizabeth Port Authority Marine Terminal is the largest container port in the US, and the city has a very wide range of light industries.

**Elizavetgrad** /eˈliːzəvetˌɡrɑːd/ see KIROVOHAD.

**El Jadida** /el dʒəˈdiːdə/ a resort town on the Atlantic coast of Morocco, south-west of Casablanca; pop. (1982) 81,450. The Portuguese built a fort here in 1502 and founded a town which they named Mazagan. In 1815 it was rebuilt and renamed by Moulay Abd Er Rahman who repopulated it with members of the Doukala tribe and with a colony of Jews.

**Elk** /elk/ **1.** a river that rises on the western slopes of the Cumberland Mountains in Tennessee, USA, and flows c. 320 km. (200 miles) south-westwards to Wheeler Lake in Alabama. **2.** a river that rises in the Alleghany Range, West Virginia, USA, and flows 277 km. (172 miles) generally north-west before meeting the Kanawha River at Charleston.

**El Kef** /el kef/ a city in north-west Tunisia, capital of the Kaf governorate; pop. (1984) 43,500. Features include the Turkish citadel and the mosque of Sidi Bou Makhlouf.

**Ellef Ringnes Island** /ˌeləf ˈrɪŋneɪs/ an island in the Canadian Arctic, in the Queen Elizabeth Islands west of Ellesmere Island; area 11,295 sq. km. (4,361 sq miles).

**Ellen's Isle** a small island in Loch Katrine in the Trossachs area of central Scotland. It is associated with Sir Walter Scott's poem *The Lady of the Lake*.

**Ellesmere Island** /ˈelzmɪə(r)/ the northernmost island of the Canadian Arctic and third-largest island in Canada; area 196,236 sq. km. (75,796 sq. miles). Cape Columbia is Canada's most northerly point and Barbeau Peak (2,616 m., 8,445 ft.) is the highest mountain in eastern North America. Established in 1953, Grise Fiord is the most northerly settlement in Canada and Lake Hazen is the largest lake within the Arctic Circle. Discovered in 1616 by William Baffin, the island was in 1852 named after the statesman and poet Francis Egerton, Earl of Ellesmere (1800–1857). Fort Conger was the base from which Robert Peary led the first expedition to reach the North Pole in 1909.

**Ellesmere Port** a port on the estuary of the River Mersey in Cheshire, England; pop. (1981) 65,800. It lies to the south-east of Liverpool at the junction of the Manchester Ship Canal and the Shropshire Union Canal. It is an oil-refining and distribution centre.

**Ellice Islands** /ˈelɪs/ the former name (until 1976) of the TUVALU island group in the Pacific.

**Ellis Island** /ˈelɪs/ an island in New York Bay. Long used as an arsenal and a fort, from 1892 until 1943 it served as an point of entry for immigrants to the US, then (until 1954) as a detention centre for aliens and those awaiting deportation. In 1965 it became part of the Statue of Liberty National Monument, open to sightseers. The island is named after Samuel Ellis, a Manhattan merchant who owned it in the 1770s.

**Ellora** /eˈlɔːrə/ a series of 34 Buddhist, Hindu, and Jain caves with sculptured figures dating from 600–800 AD, situated about 30 km. (19 miles) north-west of Aurangabad in the Indian state of Maharashtra.

**Ellsworth Land** a plateau region of Antarctica between the Walgreen Coast and Palmer Land. It rises to 5,140 m. (16,863 ft.) in the Vinson Massif which is the highest mountain in Antarctica. The area was discovered in 1935 by the American explorer Lincoln Ellsworth (1880–1951), who named it after his father. Chile and the UK maintain claims over parts of Ellsworth Land.

**El Mahalla el Kubra** /el məˈhɑːlə el ˈkuːbrə/ a city in northern Egypt, in the Nile delta west of the Damietta Branch; pop. (1991) 400,000.

**El Mansura** /el mænˈsʊərə/ a city in north-east Egypt in the Nile delta, a major centre of the cotton trade; pop. (1991) 362,000. The Crusaders under Louis IX of France were defeated here in 1249.

**El Minya** /el ˈmɪnjə/ an industrial city in Egypt, on the River Nile 247 km. (155 miles) south of Cairo; pop. (1991) 203,000. Sugar-processing and the manufacture of soap and perfume are the chief industries. Nearby are the temples and tombs of Hermopolis, Hasan, and Tuna el Gebel.

**El Misti** /el ˈmiːstiː/ (also **El Volcán de Arequipa**) a dormant volcano rising to 5,822 m. (19,031 ft.) north-east of Arequipa in southern Peru.

**El Monte** /el ˈmɒntɪ/ an industrial and commercial city in the Los Angeles conurbation, southern California, USA, situated in the San Gabriel Valley to the east of downtown Los Angeles; pop. (1990) 106,200. Known for its walnut groves, it was first settled in 1852.

**El Niño** /el ˈniːnjəʊ/ (pl. **El Niños**) an irregularly occurring and complex series of climatic changes affecting the equatorial Pacific region. The name was originally applied to a warm ocean current which affected the waters of northern Peru and Ecuador annually, beginning usually in late December. Every few years, this warming is very marked, and the nutrient-poor warmer water has a disastrous effect on fisheries and the breeding success of seabirds. This warm current is now recognized to be one manifestation of a much larger cycle of abnormal phenomena, sometimes lasting for more than a year, in which cause and effect have not been fully distinguished. The effects of El Niño, which may reach beyond the Pacific region, include reversal of wind patterns across the Pacific, drought in Australasia, and unseasonal heavy rain in North and South America. Commonly occurring around Christmas, it takes its name from the Spanish for the (Christ) child.

**El Obeid** /el əʊˈbeɪd/ (also **Al Ubayyid**) a city in the Kordofan region of central Sudan; pop. (1983) 140,000. Surrounded by desert, the city is a centre for the collection of gum arabic.

**El Paso** /el ˈpæsəʊ/ an industrial city in western Texas, USA, on the Rio Grande opposite the Mexican city of Ciudad Juárez; pop. (1990) 515,300. Named El Paso del Norte in 1598, it developed as a mission and then a ranching centre before a proper town was founded in 1827. In 1846 Mexico surrendered the town to the US. A military post was immediately established and a trading post set up six years later in 1852. Dating from

1682, Ysleta is the oldest mission in Texas. Fort Bliss is one of the largest air-defence centres in the world. Modern industry includes oil refining and food processing.

**El Salvador** /el
ˈsælvəˌdɔː(r)/ official
name **The Republic
of El Salvador** a
country on the
Pacific coast of
Central America,
bounded to the
north-west by
Guatemala and the
east and north-east by Honduras; area 21,393 sq. km. (8,260 sq. miles); pop. (est. 1991) 5,400,000; official language, Spanish; capital San Salvador. The only Central American country without an Atlantic seaboard, El Salvador is dominated by volcanic mountain ranges running east to west. Most of the people live in the subtropical valleys of the central region and a narrow tropical coastal belt fronts onto the Pacific. Its economy is mainly agricultural, coffee, cotton, and sugar-cane being the chief crops. Conquered by the Spanish in 1524, El Salvador gained its independence in 1821 and joined the Central American Federation in 1824, before finally emerging as an independent republic in 1839. For many years the country was ruled by a small number of wealthy landowners known as 'the fourteen families' and a peasant rebellion led by the popular hero Farabundo Martí was brutally suppressed in 1932. When a military *coup* ousted the newly elected centre-left coalition in 1972 El Salvador gradually dissolved into a civil war marked by right-wing death squad killings, the resistance activities of left-wing FMLN guerrillas, and the existence of a large number of refugees. A UN-brokered peace accord was eventually agreed in 1992. El Salvador is governed by an executive president and a unicameral Legislative Assembly.

**Salvadorean** *adj. & n.*
El Salvador is divided into 14 departments:

| Department | Area (sq. km.) | Pop. (1992) | Capital |
|---|---|---|---|
| Ahuachapán | 1,240 | 260,560 | Ahuachapán |
| Sonsonate | 1,226 | 354,640 | Sonsonate |
| Santa Ana | 2,023 | 451,620 | Santa Ana |
| La Libertad | 1,653 | 522,020 | Nueva San Salvador |
| San Salvador | 886 | 1,477,770 | San Salvador |
| Chalatenango | 2,017 | 180,630 | Chalatenango |
| Cuscatlán | 756 | 167,290 | Cojutepeque |
| La Paz | 1,224 | 244,150 | Zacatecoluca |
| San Vicente | 1,184 | 135,470 | San Vicente |
| Cabañas | 1,140 | 130,290 | Sensuntepeque |
| Usulután | 2,130 | 317,080 | Usulután |
| San Miguel | 2,077 | 380,440 | San Miguel |
| Morazán | 1,447 | 166,770 | San Francisco |
| La Unión | 2,074 | 251,140 | La Unión |

**Elsene** see IXELLES.

**Elsinore** /ˈelsɪˌnɔː(r)/ (Danish **Helsingør** /ˈhelsɪŋˌɜː(r)/) a port on the north-east coast of the island of Zealand, Frederiksborg county, Denmark; pop. (1990) 56,750. The 16th-c. Kronborg Castle was the setting for Shakespeare's *Hamlet*.

**Elstow** /ˈelstəʊ/ a village in Bedfordshire, England, to the south of Bedford, the birthplace in 1628 of John Bunyan.

**Elstree** /ˈelztriː/ a residential suburb of north-west London to the west of Barnet, noted for its film studios which were established in 1927.

**Eluru** /eˈlʊ(ə)ruː/ (formerly **Ellore**) a trading town in Andhra Pradesh, eastern India, north of Madras; pop. (1991) 212,920. It is noted for carpet-making and leatherwork.

**Elvas** a market town in the district of Portalegre, eastern Portugal; pop. (1981) 12,700. It was built as a fortress town on the Spanish frontier opposite Badajoz, its medieval walls and 13th-c. Moorish castle still remaining.

**Ely** a cathedral city in the fenland of Cambridgeshire, eastern England, on the River Ouse; pop. (1981) 9,100. The King's School, which originated as a monastic school in the 11th c., was refounded here in 1541 by Henry VIII. Oliver Cromwell lived in the old vicarage for 10 years and tradition has it that Hereward the Wake was killed here in what was one of the last Saxon strongholds in Norman England. The beautiful cathedral dates from the 11th c. and has a unique octagonal lantern tower.

**Ely, Isle of** a former county of England extending over the northern part of present day Cambridgeshire which, before widespread drainage, stood out as a fertile 'island' amidst the surrounding fenland.

**Elyria** /ɪˈlɪrɪə/ an industrial city in northern Ohio, USA, at the junction of the east and west branches of the Black River; pop. (1990) 56,700. In addition to trade in poultry, fruit, vegetables, and dairy-produce the city manufactures aircraft parts, metal castings, and golf balls.

**Elysium** /ɪˈlɪzɪəm/ (also **Elysian Fields**) in Greek mythology the fields at the ends of the earth to where (according to Homer and Hesiod) certain favoured heroes, exempted from death, were translated by the gods. This concept appears to be a survival from Minoan religion. When a later age concerned itself with the fate of the blessed dead, Elysium was transferred to the nether regions, in conformity with Greek ideas and the Homeric picture of the House of Hades. The name is still synonymous with a place or state of ideal happiness.

**Emba** /emˈbɑː/ a river that rises in the Mugodzhar Hills of western Kazakhstan and flows 614 km. (384 miles) south-westwards through the

Emba oil-fields to the north-east corner of the Caspian Sea.

**Emden** /'emdən/ a North Sea port in the German state of Lower Saxony, on the estuary of the River Ems; pop. (1991) 51,100. The port developed rapidly after the industrialization of the Ruhr valley and the building of the Dortmund-Ems Canal.

**Emerald Coast** (French **Côte d'Emeraud**) the name given to that part of the coast of Brittany in north-west France to the west of Saint-Malo. It includes the resort towns of Dinard, Paramé, Saint-Briac, and Saint-Lunaire.

**Emi Koussi** /ˌeimiː 'kuːsə/ the highest peak in the Tibesti massif, northern Chad. Rising to 3,415 m. (11,204 ft.), it is of volcanic origin.

**Emilia-Romagna** /ˌemiːljərəʊˈmænjə/ a region of north Italy, to the north of Tuscany and south of Lombardy and Venetia; area 22,119 sq. km. (8,540 sq. miles); pop. (1991) 3,928,700; capital, Bologna. The region was created in 1947 when Emilia and Romagna were united. Most of the region's major cities lie along the ancient **Via Emilia** which stretches from Piacenza to Rimini and takes its name from Marcus Emilius Lepidus who first traced its route.

**Emmental** /'emənˌtɑːl/ the valley of the Emme River in west-central Switzerland which gives its name to a hard Swiss cheese with many holes in it.

**Empire State Building** a skyscraper on Fifth Avenue, New York City, USA, which was for long the tallest building in the world. When first erected in 1930–1, it measured 381 m. (1,250 ft.); the addition of a television mast in 1951 brought its height to 449 m. (1,472 ft.). It is named after New York, the 'Empire State'.

**Empty Quarter** an alternative name for the GREAT SANDY DESERT of the southern Arabian Peninsula.

**Ems** see BAD EMS.

**Enare** see INARE.

**Encarnación** /ˌenkə(r)næsˈjəʊn/ a port on the Paraná River in south-east Paraguay; pop. (1984) 31,445. It is capital of the department of Itapúa.

**Encinitas** /ˌensəˈniːtəs/ a city in southern California, USA, on the Pacific coast north of San Diego; pop. (1990) 55,400. It lies at the centre of a farming area known for its flowers.

**enclave** /'enkleɪv/ **1.** a portion of territory of one state surrounded by territory of another or others, as viewed by the surrounding territory. **2.** a group of people who are culturally, intellectually, or socially distinct from those surrounding them.

**endemic** /en'demɪk/ regularly or only found among a particular people or in a certain region.

**Enderby Land** /'endəbɪ/ a part of Antarctica, claimed by Australia. Its coast was discovered in 1831–2 by the English navigator John Biscoe, sailing for the London whaling firm of Enderby Brothers; he named it after his employers.

**Enfield** /'enfiːld/ a residential northern outer borough of Greater London; pop. (1991) 249,100. To the north is Enfield Chase, a former forest of the Duchy of Lancaster incorporated into the London Green Belt scheme.

**Engels** the former name (1931–1992) of POKROVSK GLAZOV.

**England** /'ɪŋglənd/ a part of Great Britain and the United Kingdom, largely made up of the area south of the River Tweed and containing the capital, London; area 130,478 sq. km. (50,397 sq. miles); pop. (1991) 46,170,300. The north of England is dominated by upland regions such as the Cheviot Hills which rise to 816 m. (2,674 ft.) at The Cheviot, the Cumbrian Mountains which rise to 977 m. (3,210 ft.) at Scafell Pike (England's highest peak), and the Pennine Range which stretches south to the Peak District, rising to 636 m. (2,088 ft.) at Kinder Scout. Extensive areas of upland and moorland also dominate the Welsh border and south-west England, with ranges of low rolling hills such as the Cotswolds, the Chilterns, and the Downs stretching across the south of England. Large areas of flat low-lying land occupy eastern England from the Vale of York to the fenlands of the Wash and East Anglia. The longest river wholly in England is the Thames. England has a mild temperate climate with the highest rainfall in the west. In winter average temperatures are higher in the south and west while in summer the warmest weather is to be found in southern and inland areas. There were settlements in England from at least palaeolithic times, and considerable remains exist of neolithic and Bronze Age cultures. These were followed by the arrival of the Celtic peoples whose civilization spread over the whole country. The Romans under Julius Caesar raided the south of Britain in 55 and 54 BC, but full-scale invasion did not take place until a century later; the country was then administered as a Roman province until the Teutonic conquest of Gaul in the early 5th c. and the subsequent withdrawal of the last Roman garrison. In the 3rd to 7th c. Germanic-speaking tribes, traditionally known as Angles, Saxons, and Jutes, raided and then settled, establishing independent kingdoms, and when that of Wessex became dominant in the 9th c. England emerged as a distinct political entity before being conquered by William, Duke of Normandy, in 1066. The neighbouring principality of Wales was gradually conquered during the Middle Ages and politically incorporated in the 16th c. During the period of Tudor rule (1485–1603) England emerged as a Protestant state with a strong stable monarchy and as a naval power. Scotland and England have been ruled by one monarch from 1603, and the two parliaments were formally united in 1707.

**English** *adj. & n.*

England is divided into seven metropolitan areas and 39 counties:

# ENGLAND

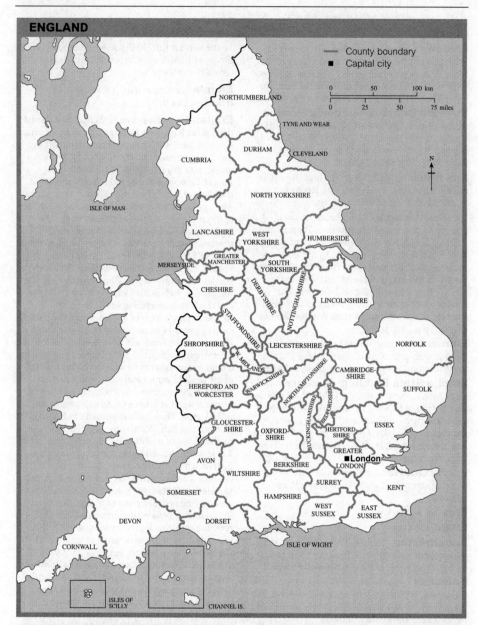

County boundary
■ Capital city

| County | Area (sq. km.) | Pop. (1991) | County Town |
|---|---|---|---|
| Avon | 1,346 | 919,800 | Bristol |
| Bedfordshire | 1,235 | 514,200 | Bedford |
| Berkshire | 1,259 | 716,500 | Reading |
| Buckinghamshire | 1,883 | 619,500 | Aylesbury |
| Cambridgeshire | 3,402 | 640,700 | Cambridge |
| Cheshire | 2,333 | 937,300 | Chester |
| Cleveland | 591 | 541,100 | Middlesborough |
| Cornwall & Isles of Scilly | 3,564 | 469,300 | Truro |
| Cumbria | 6,824 | 486,900 | Carlisle |
| Derbyshire | 2,631 | 915,000 | Matlock |
| Devon | 6,711 | 1,008,300 | Exeter |
| Dorset | 2,654 | 645,200 | Dorchester |
| Durham | 2,434 | 589,800 | Durham |
| East Sussex | 1,795 | 670,600 | Lewes |
| Essex | 3,672 | 1,495,600 | Chelmsford |
| Gloucestershire | 2,643 | 520,600 | Gloucester |
| Hampshire | 3,780 | 1,511,900 | Winchester |
| Hereford and Worcester | 3,926 | 667,800 | Worcester |
| Hertfordshire | 1,636 | 951,500 | Hertford |
| Humberside | 3,513 | 845,200 | Beverley |
| Isle of Wight | 381 | 126,600 | Newport |

| Kent | 3,731 | 1,485,600 | Maidstone |
| Lancashire | 3,061 | 1,365,100 | Preston |
| Leicestershire | 2,553 | 860,500 | Leicester |
| Lincolnshire | 5,918 | 573,900 | Lincoln |
| Norfolk | 5,375 | 737,700 | Norwich |
| Northamptonshire | 2,367 | 568,900 | Northampton |
| Northumberland | 5,032 | 300,600 | Morpeth |
| North Yorkshire | 8,312 | 698,800 | Northallerton |
| Nottinghamshire | 2,161 | 980,600 | Nottingham |
| Oxfordshire | 2,608 | 553,800 | Oxford |
| Shropshire | 3,490 | 401,600 | Shrewsbury |
| Somerset | 3,452 | 459,100 | Taunton |
| Staffordshire | 2,716 | 1,020,300 | Stafford |
| Suffolk | 3,797 | 629,900 | Ipswich |
| Surrey | 1,679 | 997,000 | Kingston upon Thames |
| Warwickshire | 1,980 | 477,000 | Warwick |
| West Sussex | 1,989 | 692,800 | Chichester |
| Wiltshire | 3,479 | 553,300 | Trowbridge |

**Metropolitan counties**

| County | Area (sq. km.) | Pop. (1991) |
| --- | --- | --- |
| Greater London | 1,579 | 6,378,600 |
| Greater Manchester | 1,287 | 2,445,200 |
| Merseyside | 654 | 1,376,800 |
| South Yorkshire | 1,560 | 1,249,300 |
| Tyne and Wear | 540 | 1,087,000 |
| West Midlands | 899 | 2,500,400 |
| West Yorkshire | 2,035 | 1,984,700 |

**English** /'ɪŋglɪʃ/ the principal language of Great Britain, the USA, Canada, Ireland, Australia, New Zealand, and many other countries. There are some 300 million native speakers, and it is the medium of communication for many millions more in all parts of the world. Its history can be divided into three stages: Old English (up to 1150), Middle English (1150–1500), and Modern English (1500 onwards). Old English is usually said to have begun with the settlement of Germanic-speaking tribes (Angles, Saxons, and Jutes) in Britain in the mid-5th c. It was an inflected language, and the gradual decay of these endings is one of the chief changes that took place over the centuries, until by the 15th c. most of them had been lost. Old English was essentially a spoken language, but by the time of Alfred the Great something like a standard literary language was emerging, and by the late 10th c. the dialect of Wessex was becoming dominant. In addition to native Celtic elements and words surviving from the period of Roman rule, extension of vocabulary was brought by the spread of Christian culture, with some words adopted or translated from Latin, and by Scandinavian invaders in the 9th–10th c. After the Norman Conquest, Anglo-Norman was the language of the ruling classes, but from the 14th c. English again became the standard. Despite the influence of French, the Germanic nature of English has been maintained in its syntax and morphology. All changes were gradual, including those in pronunciation; by the 16th c. many vowels were sounded much as they are today.

The spread of the language has its origins in colonization from the Middle Ages onwards and the consolidation of the British Empire particularly in the 19th c. It developed locally (as it has in the British Isles) into many different varieties. Even since the breakup of the Empire, English has gained in influence largely through its use as a medium of international communication and now probably ranks as the world's unofficial lingua franca.

**English Channel** (French **La Manche** /læ mãʃ/) the sea channel separating southern England from northern France. It is 35 km. (21 miles) wide at its narrowest point. In 1875 Matthew Webb was the first to swim across the Channel and in 1907 Louis Blériot made the first air crossing in a plane. There are memorials to both at Dover. A tunnel under the English channel linking France and England was opened in 1994.

**Eniwetok** /e'ni:wətɒk/ an uninhabited island in the North Pacific Ocean forming part of the Ralik Chain in the Marshall Islands. Cleared of its native population, it was used as a testing ground for atomic bombs from 1948 to 1954.

**Ennis** /'enɪs/ the county town of County Clare in the Republic of Ireland, on the River Fergus; pop. (1991) 13,750. Its Franciscan abbey was founded in 1241 by Donough Cairbreach O'Brien.

**Enniskillen** /ˌenɪs'kɪlɪn/ (Gaelic **Inis Ceithleann**) the county town of Fermanagh in Northern Ireland, situated between two channels of the river joining Upper and Lower Lough Erne; pop. (1981) 10,400. A former stronghold of the Maguires, the town was confiscated early in the 17th c. and given to Sir William Cole. In 1613 it was chartered by King James and settled with English families. Following the defence of Enniskillen by its townsmen in 1689 there emerged the military regiment known as the Royal Inniskilling Fusiliers. Oscar Wilde and Samuel Beckett were both pupils at the Portora Royal School (founded in 1618) on the shore of Lower Lough Erne.

**Enschede** /'enskəˌdeɪ/ a university city in the province of Overijssel, in the eastern Netherlands, situated on the Twente Canal; pop. (1991) 146,500. Chartered in 1325, the city developed rapidly with the expansion of textile industries in the 19th c. The Twente University of Technology was established in 1961.

**Ensenada** /ˌensə'nɑːdə/ a resort town on the Pacific coast of Baja California, north-west Mexico, situated on Todos Santos Bay 100 km. (64 miles) south of the US border; pop. (1990) 175,000. Tourism, fishing, and wine production are its chief industries.

**Enshi** /'enʃɪ/ a city in west Hubei province, central China, on the Qing River south-west of Yichang; pop. (1986) 686,000.

**Entebbe** /en'tebɪ/ a town in southern Uganda, on the north shore of Lake Victoria; pop. (1980) 20,500. Founded in 1893, it was capital of Uganda under British rule from 1894 to 1962 when self-government was granted.

**Entre-Deux-Mers** an area of south-west France between the Garonne and Dordogne rivers noted for its Bordeaux wines.

**entrepôt** /'ɒntrə‚pəʊ/ a commercial centre, usually a port, for import and export and for collection and distribution.

**Enugu** /ə'nuːguː/ an industrial city in south-east Nigeria; pop. (est. 1981) 256,000. Developed after the discovery of coal in 1909, it is capital of a state of the same name producing textiles, shoes, steel, and cement. During 1967–70 it was capital of the secessionist state of Biafra. Its university was established in 1960.

**environment** a term used by ecologists to describe the external conditions affecting the growth of plants and animals.

**Epcot Center** one of the three main theme parks of Disney World, near Orlando in the US state of Florida. It features the future technologies of the world using state-of-the-art computerized simulations.

**Épernay** /‚eɪpə(r)'neɪ/ a town in the department of Marne, north-east France, on the River Marne; pop. (1990) 27,740. It is the headquarters of many of the best known champagne producers in France and its underground wine cellars are a major tourist attraction.

**Ephesus** /'efɪsəs/ (Turkish **Efes**) an ancient Greek city and seaport of Asia Minor on the west coast of modern Turkey, site of the temple of Artemis that was one of the Seven Wonders of the World, and an important centre of early Christianity. St. Paul visited it several times and St. John is said to be buried here. Because of silting the remains of the city are now more than 5 km. (3 miles) inland. The resort village of Kuşadasi (New Ephesus) lies 12 km. (7 miles) south-west.

**epicentre** /'epɪ‚sentə(r)/ the point at which an earthquake reaches the earth's surface.

**epicontinental** /‚epɪkɒntɪ'nentəl/ that part of the sea lying over the continental shelf.

**Epidaurus** /‚epɪ'dɔːrəs/ an ancient Greek city and port on the north-east coast of the Peloponnese, famous for its temple of Asclepius and site of a well-preserved Greek theatre dating from the 4th c. BC.

**Épinal** the capital of the department of Vosges in Lorraine, eastern France, on the Moselle River; pop. (1990) 39,480. Known in the 18th and 19th c. for its *Images d'Épinal*, coloured pictures with patriotic or religious themes, the city now produces metal goods, leather, and textiles.

**Epirus** /ɪ'paɪrəs/ (Greek **Ipiros**) **1.** an ancient country located in the coastal region of north-west Greece and southern Albania. Its most famous ruler was Pyrrhus. **2.** an administrative region of modern Greece, comprising the departments of Arta, Thesprotia, Ioannina, and Preveza; area 9,203 sq. km. (3,555 sq. miles); pop. (1991) 339,200; capital, Ioannina.

**Epping** /'epɪŋ/ a residential town at the northern end of Epping Forest in Essex, England, 27 km. (17 miles) north of central London. Epping forest, which extends over 2,000 hectares (5,000 acres) was acquired in 1863 by the City of London.

**Epsom** /'epsəm/ a residential town in Surrey, south-east England; pop. (1981) 68,500. A noted spa town in the 17th c., it gave its name to Epsom salts, a preparation of magnesium sulphate used as a purgative and first found occurring naturally here. Its racecourse on Epsom Downs is the venue for the annual Derby and Oaks horse-races.

**Epworth** /'epwɜːθ/ a small town in the Isle of Axholme, Humberside, England, which was the boyhood home of the Methodists John and Charles Wesley.

**equator** /ɪ'kweɪtə(r)/ an imaginary line round the earth equidistant from the poles and dividing the earth into Northern and Southern Hemispheres. Latitude is measured in degrees north or south of the equator which has a latitude of 0°. It has a length of 40,075 km. (24,902 miles). The celestial equator or equinoctial line is the great circle in the sky in the same plane as the equator.

**equatorial climate** the climate prevailing over the equatorial belt which stretches from about 15°N to 5°S of the equator. It is characterized by high temperature and humidity with small seasonal variations and an even distribution of rainfall. Further from the equator a tropical climate with a more pronounced rainy season occurs.

**Equatorial Guinea** official name **The Republic of Equatorial Guinea** a small equatorial country of West Africa on the Gulf of Guinea, comprising several offshore islands in-  cluding Bioko (formerly Fernando Póo), Annabón, Corisco, Elobey Chico, and Elobey Grande, and the coastal settlement of Río Muni which lies between Cameroon and Gabon; area 28,051 sq. km. (10,830 sq. miles); pop. (1991) 400,000; languages, Spanish (official), pidgin English, Fang, Ibo, and Bubi; capital, Malabo (on the island of Bioko). Split in two by the Rio Benito (Mbini), the continental region rises inland from a coastal plain through a series of valleys separated by low hills of the Crystal Mountains. The climate is tropical, but temperature and humidity is usually higher on the island of Bioko. With limited industrial production, exports are dominated by plantation-grown cocoa, coffee grown on small farms, and timber.

Formerly a Spanish colony the country became fully independent in 1968. Governed by a Supreme Military Council, it is the only independent Spanish-speaking state in the continent of Africa.

**equinox** /'ekwɪˌnɒks/ the time or date (twice each year) at which the sun crosses the celestial equator, when day and night are of equal length.

**Erebus** /'erəbəs/, **Mount** a volcanic peak on Ross Island, Antarctica. Rising to 3,794 m. (12,450 ft.), it is the southernmost active volcano in the world.

**Erechtheum** /ɪ'rekθɪəm/ a marble temple built on the Acropolis in Athens in c. 421–c. 406 BC, with shrines to Athene, Poseidon, and Erechtheus, a legendary king of Athens. A masterpiece of the Ionic order, it is most famous for its southern portico in which the entablature is supported by six caryatids.

**Erfurt** /'eəfʊət/ an industrial city and capital of the state of Thuringia in central Germany, on the River Gera; pop. (1991) 204,910. Market gardening and the manufacture of textiles, electronic goods, and precision tools are the chief industries.

**erg** /ɜːg/ an Arabic word for the sandy deserts of the Sahara, occasionally forming an element of place-names such as the Erg du Djourab in northern Chad, the Grand Erg de Bilma in eastern Niger, and the Grand Erg Occidental and Grand Erg Oriental in Algeria.

**Erie** /'ɪərɪ/, **Lake** the fourth-largest and shallowest of the five Great Lakes of North America, situated on the frontier between Canada and the USA; area 25,812 sq. km. (9,966 sq. miles); area on the Canadian side of the border, 12,880 sq. km. (4,973 sq. miles); maximum depth 64 m. (210 ft.). It is linked to Lake Huron by the Detroit River via Lake St. Clair and to Lake Ontario by the Welland Canal and the Niagara River which is its only natural outlet. The chief industrial cities on or close to its shores include Detroit, Toledo, Cleveland, Erie, and Buffalo in the USA and Windsor and Port Colborne in Canada and the lake has been heavily polluted. The lake takes its name from the Eriez Indians who were ousted by the Seneca in 1654.

**Erie** an industrial city in north-west Pennsylvania, USA, on Lake Erie; pop. (1990) 108,700. It is the third-largest city and largest port in the state. First settled by the French who built Fort Presque Isle on the south shore of Presque Isle Bay, the site was taken by the British in 1753, destroyed by Indians in 1763, and later laid out as a town in 1795. Commodore Oliver Hazard Perry built a fleet here and defeated the British at the Battle of Lake Erie in 1813. It has engineering and foundry industries and handles coal, iron ore, grain, oil, timber, and heavy machinery.

**Erin** /'erɪn/ an archaic literary or poetic name for Ireland.

**Eritrea** /ˌerɪ'treɪə/ (Amharic **Ertra**) official name **The State of Eritrea** an independent state, formerly a province of northern Ethiopia, on the Red

Sea; area 93,679 sq. km. (36,183 sq. miles); pop. (est. 1991) 3,500,000; official languages, Arabic and English; capital, Asmara. The people of Eritrea are a mixture of Afar, Tigre, Beja, and Kunama; 50 per cent are Muslim and 50 per cent are Christian. An Italian colony from 1890, it federated with Ethiopia in 1952 and became a province in 1962. For 30 years secessionist rebels waged a guerrilla war against the government until democracy was restored in 1991 and separatists took control of the province. Its people voted for independence from Ethiopia which took place in 1993. Eritrea is governed by a unicameral National Assembly and an executive State Council. A largely agricultural country, Eritrea has reserves of iron, potassium, copper, and gold.
**Eritrean** *adj. & n.*

**Erlangen** /'ɜːlæŋən/ a city in Bavaria, southern Germany, on the River Regnitz 16 km. (10 miles) north of Nuremberg; pop. (1991) 102,430. It produces electronics, textiles, and beer.

**Ermine Street** /'ɜːmɪn/ the name given to **1.** the Roman road between London and Lincoln via Huntingdon and **2.** the Roman road connecting Silchester with Gloucester.

**Erne** /ɜːn/, **Lough** a lake in County Fermanagh, Northern Ireland, comprising two small basins (Upper and Lower Lough Erne) linked by part of the course of the River Erne. On Devinish Island in Lower Lough Erne are the remains of a monastery founded in the 6th c. by St. Molaise.

**Erne** a river that rises in Lough Gowna in the Republic of Ireland and flows 115 km. (72 miles) north-west through Northern Ireland to meet the Atlantic Ocean at Donegal Bay.

**Erode** /ɪ'rəʊd/ a cotton-processing city in Tamil Nadu, southern India, on the Cauvery River north-east of Coimbatore; pop. (1991) 357,430.

**erosion** /ɪ'rəʊʒ(ə)n/ the wearing away of the earth's surface by the action of water, wind, etc. Under natural conditions erosion is a slow process but as a result of overgrazing, deforestation, and inappropriate agricultural practices the earth's topsoil is eroded at a much faster rate. It is estimated, for example, that in India 6,000 million tonnes of soil are lost each year and in the USA 4,000 million tonnes are being eroded annually.

**Erse** /ɜːs/ the Gaelic language of Ireland or the Scottish highlands and islands.

**Ertis** the Kazakh name for the Irtysh River. See IRTYSH.

**Erzgebirge** see ORE MOUNTAINS.

**Erzincan** /'eəzɪnˌdʒæn/ **1.** a mountainous province in east-central Turkey; area 11,903 sq. km. (4,597 sq. miles); pop. (1990) 299,250. **2.** its capital, at an altitude of 1,200 m. (3,940 ft.) to the north of the Euphrates River; pop. (1990) 91,800.

**Erzurum** /'eəzʊˌrʊm/ **1.** a mountainous province in north-east Turkey; area 25,066 sq. km. (9,682 sq. miles); pop. (1990) 848,200. **2.** its capital, the largest city in eastern Anatolia; pop. (1990) 242,400. An ancient city with a chequered history, it is a market centre with diverse light industries.

**Esbjerg** /'esbjɜːg/ a commercial and ferry port, oil exploration centre, and fishing port in Denmark, on the west coast of Jutland; pop. (1990) 81,500. There are ferry links with Britain and the Faeroe Islands and it has a university and maritime museum.

**escarpment** /ɪ'skɑːpmənt/ a long steep slope at the edge of a plateau.

**Escaut** the French name for the SCHELDT.

**Esch-sur-Alzette** /ˌeʃsʊəræl'zet/ the second-largest town in Luxembourg, situated at the centre of a mining region; pop. (1991) 23,900.

**Escondido** /ˌeskən'diːdəʊ/ a city in southern California, USA, situated to the north of San Diego; pop. (1990) 108,600. It lies at the centre of a major fruit-producing region. To the north-east is the Palomar Observatory.

**Escuintla** /eɪs'kwiːntlə/ a market town in southern Guatemala near the Agua volcano, 45 km. (28 miles) south-west of Guatemala City. It is capital of a Pacific coast department of the same name. Industry is based on the processing of sugar and cotton grown in the surrounding area.

**Esfahan** see ISFAHAN.

**Esher** /'iːʃə(r)/ a residential outer suburb of London in the county of Surrey; pop. (1981) 46,800.

**Esk** /esk/ the name given to several rivers in England and Scotland: **1.** a river flowing south-westwards to the Irish Sea from Scafell in the Lake District. **2.** a river on the Scottish–English border formed by the union of the White and Black Esk. It flows for 58 km. (36 miles) before entering the Solway Firth. **3.** a river that rises in the Cleveland Hills of England and flows eastwards to the North Sea at Whitby. **4.** a river that rises in the Pentland Hills just south of Edinburgh, Scotland, and flows north-east for 34 km. (21 miles) to join the Firth of Forth at Musselburgh. **5.** the North Esk river rises in the Grampians of northern Scotland and flows south-east for 46 km. (29 miles) to the North Sea just north of Montrose. **6.** the South Esk rises in the Grampians and flows 78 km. (49 miles) south-east and east to the North Sea at Montrose.

**esker** /'eskə(r)/ a long ridge of sand and gravel deposited by subglacial streams during the Ice Age.

**Eskimo** /'eskɪˌməʊ/ a member of a people inhabiting northern Canada, Alaska, Greenland, and eastern Siberia, whose name is derived from an Algonquian word literally meaning 'eaters of raw flesh'. See INUIT.

**Eskişehir** /es'kɪʃəhɪr/ **1.** a province in north-west Turkey to the west of Ankara; 13,477 sq. km. (5,390 sq. miles); pop. (1990) 641,000. **2.** its capital, a spa town and industrial city on the River Porsuk; pop. (1990) 413,100. The main industries are sugar refining and the manufacture of agricultural machinery.

**Esmeraldas** /ˌezmə'rɑːldəs/ a port and provincial capital on the Pacific coast of north-west Ecuador, at the mouth of the Esmeraldas River; pop. (1990) 172,650. Its main exports are timber, bananas, and oil which is piped from the oilfields of the Oriente on the far side of the Andes.

**Esperanto** /ˌespə'ræntəʊ/ an artificial language devised in 1887 by L. L. Zamenhof, a Polish physician, as a medium of communication for persons of all languages. Its words are based mainly on roots commonly found in Romance and other European languages, and while it has the advantage of grammatical regularity and ease of pronunciation it retains the structure of these languages, which makes Esperanto no easier than any other European language for a speaker whose native tongue falls outside this group.

**Espírito Santo** /es'piːrɪtəʊ 'sæntəʊ/ a state on the south-east coast of Brazil; area 45,597 sq. km. (17,612 sq. miles); pop. (1991) 2,598,505; capital, Vitória.

**Espiritu Santo** a volcanic island of the south-west Pacific Ocean, in the Vanuatu group; area 3,947 sq. km. (1,524 sq. miles). Its chief town is Santo. Coffee, cocoa, and copra are the chief products.

**Espoo** /es'pəʊ/ (Swedish **Esbo**) a city that forms an outer western suburb of Helsinki in the Finnish province of Uudenmaa; pop. (1990) 172,600. It is the second-largest city in Finland and the location of Helsinki's technical university.

**Esquipulas** /ˌeski:'pjuːlæs/ a town in south-east Guatemala, near the frontier with Honduras; pop. (1981) 18,840. Thought to have been a Mayan religious centre, its church contains a black image of Christ which is a symbol of peace. A series of miracles attributed to the 'Black Christ of Esquipulas' led to the building of a sanctuary (completed in 1758) which is visited by pilgrims from all over Central America. In 1983 the town was the venue for a summit of Central American presidents who assembled to endorse the Contadora peace process.

**Essaouira** /ˌesə'wiːrə/ a fishing port and resort town on the Atlantic coast of Morocco, 172 km. (108 miles) north of Agadir; pop. (1982) 42,000. Frequented from early times by Phoenician traders, it developed a trade in purple dye derived from the purpura shellfish. Essaouira rivalled the port of Agadir and was an important trade outlet until the French opened up ports in West Africa. Known to the Portuguese and Spanish as Mogador, US forces landed here in 1942 to engage in the liberation of North Africa from the Germans.

**Essen** /'es(ə)n/ a city in the state of North Rhine-Westphalia, north-west Germany, the hub of the industrial Ruhr valley; pop. (1991) 626,990. The city developed around a Benedictine convent founded in the 9th c., but its modern industrial growth dates from the mid-19th c. Located at the heart of a major European coalfield, it is an important centre of trade and industry and the headquarters of companies such as the Krupp steelworks. Essen's cathedral was dedicated in 873. The city was heavily bombed in World War II and has been imaginatively rebuilt.

**Essene** /'esi:n, e'si:n/ a member of an ancient Jewish ascetic sect of the 2nd c. BC–2nd c. AD in Palestine, who lived in highly organized groups and held property in common.

**Essequibo** /ˌesɪˈkiːbəʊ/ the longest river of Guyana, rising in the Guiana Highlands and flowing c.965 km. (600 miles) northwards to the Atlantic Ocean.

**Essex** /'esɪks/ a county of eastern England to the north of the Thames estuary; area 3,672 sq. km. (1,418 sq. miles); pop. (1991) 1,495,600; county town, Chelmsford. It is divided into 14 districts:

| District | Area (sq. km.) | Pop. (1991) |
|---|---|---|
| Basildon | 110 | 157,500 |
| Braintree | 612 | 115,700 |
| Brentwood | 149 | 68,600 |
| Castle Point | 45 | 84,200 |
| Chelmsford | 342 | 150,000 |
| Colchester | 333 | 141,100 |
| Epping Forest | 340 | 113,100 |
| Harlow | 30 | 73,500 |
| Maldon | 359 | 50,800 |
| Rochford | 169 | 74,000 |
| Southend-on-Sea | 42 | 153,700 |
| Tendring | 336 | 125,100 |
| Thurrock | 163 | 124,300 |
| Uttlesford | 641 | 63,900 |

**Esslingen** /'eslɪŋən/ an industrial city in the state of Baden Württemberg, Germany, on the Neckar River 10 km. (6 miles) from Stuttgart; pop. (1983) 88,400. Established in the 8th c., it became a free imperial city in the 13th c. and was the scene of the founding of the Great Swabian League in 1488. Textiles, vehicle parts, machinery, and electrical goods are the chief products.

**Essonne** /e'sɒn/ a department to the south of Paris in the Ile-de-France region of France; area 1,804 sq. km. (697 sq. miles); pop. (1990) 1,084,820; capital, Évry.

**Estonia** (Estonian **Esti**) official name **The Republic of Estonia** an independent Baltic state on the south coast of the Gulf of Finland, with Russia to the east and Latvia to the south; area 45,100 sq. km. (17,420 sq. miles); pop. (1989) 1,573,000; languages, Estonian (official), Russian; capital, Tallinn. A flat lowland country, with marshland, forest, and lakes, the largest

of which is Lake Peipus (Chudskoye Ozero). In addition to shipbuilding, fishing, and the production of fertilizers and timber products, Estonia is a major world producer of oil shale. Ruled by the German Teutonic Knights from the 13th c., by the Swedes from 1521, and by Russia from 1721, Estonia finally gained independence at the end of World War I. Invaded by Russian troops at the outset of World War II, Estonia was absorbed into the Soviet Union as a Soviet Socialist Republic. With the breakup of the Soviet Union in 1991 Estonia regained its independence. The country is governed by a 105-member Supreme Council (*Ulemnoukogu*).
**Estonian** *adj. & n.*

**Estoril** /ˌeʃtəˈrɪl/ a fashionable resort town with a mild climate and radioactive hot springs on the Atlantic coast of Portugal, west of Lisbon; pop. (1991) 24,850. Since the early 1900s its luxurious villas and hotels have played host to an elegant international circle that has included some of the exiled crowned heads of Europe. Since 1984 it has been the venue for Portugal's annual Formula One Grand Prix motor-racing event.

**estrecho** /es'tretʃəʊ/ the Spanish word for a strait.

**Estremadura** /ˌeʃtreməˈdʊərə/ a coastal region and former province of west-central Portugal stretching northwards from the mouth of the River Tagus across the districts of Setúbal, Lisbon, and Leiria. It contains much of Portugal's heavy industry, produces wheat, maize, olives, and grapes, and has on its coasts numerous small fishing villages and resorts.

**Estrie** /'estrɪ/ (also **Cantons de l'Est** or **Eastern Townships**) a sparsely populated geographical region of Quebec, Canada, extending over an area of 13,000 sq. km. (5,000 sq. miles) to the east of Montreal. Popular with skiers in winter, its small towns (which include Granby and Magog) are predominantly French-speaking.

**estuary** /'estʊərɪ/ a wide tidal mouth of a river.

**Esztergom** /ˌestəˈgɒm/ (also **Gran**) a town and river port in Hungary, on a bend of the Danube 40 km. (25 miles) north-west of Budapest; pop. (1993) 29,730. From the 10th c. until c.1300 it was the capital of Hungary. It was the birthplace in 1001 of Hungary's patron saint who, as King Stephen I, was crowned here. Historic sites include the former Royal Palace, Archbishop's Palace, and Cathedral (completed in 1856). Engineering and tourism are the chief industries.

**étang** /eɪˈtɑ̃/ the French word for a shallow lake such as those commonly found in the south of France in the Rhône delta.

**Etawah** /ɪˈtɑːwə/ a market town in Uttar Pradesh, northern India, south-east of Agra; pop. (1991) 124,030.

**etesian** /ɪˈtiːzɪən/ (also **etesian winds**) strong north to north-westerly winds blowing each summer in the eastern Mediterranean.

## Ethiopia

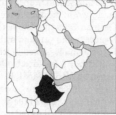

/ˌiːθɪˈəʊpɪə/ a country in north-east Africa bordered by Sudan, Kenya, Somalia, Eritrea, and Djibouti; area 1,223,600 sq. km. (472,432 sq. miles); pop. (est. 1993) 45,892,000; languages, Amharic (official), Orominga, Tigrinya, Somali; capital, Addis Ababa. Its largest cities are Addis Ababa, Asmara, Jimma, and Diredawa. The western half of Ethiopia is a high plateau with mountain ranges and lakes, the largest of which is Lake Tana, source of the Blue Nile. To the east the land falls towards the Ogaden desert on the frontier with Somalia and the Danakil Depression between the plateau and the Red Sea. Most of the country has a tropical climate that is moderated by altitude but the north-eastern lowlands and eastern desert have a hot semiarid climate. In the highlands there is a wet season from April to September. The economy is based on agriculture, with over 90 per cent of production in the hands of peasant farmers and the country's chief export being coffee. During the 1980s drought and famine compelled thousands of Ethiopians to seek refuge in other countries despite a massive relief operation mounted by the UN and Western aid agencies. Formerly known as Abyssinia, Ethiopia is the oldest independent country in Africa. Its earliest recorded civilization, known to the ancient Egyptians as Punt, dates from the 2nd millennium BC. In ancient times Ethiopians (= burnt-faced men) were often confused with Indians. Christianized in the 4th c., Ethiopia was isolated by Muslim conquests to the north three centuries later, remaining remote and little known until the late 19th c. It successfully resisted Italian attempts at colonization in the 1890s but was conquered by Italy in 1935. The Emperor Haile Selassie was restored by the British in 1941 and ruled until overthrown in a Marxist *coup* in 1975. The new military rulers of Ethiopia abandoned the constitution and initiated a widespread programme of land reform and nationalization, but drought combined with separatist insurgencies in the provinces of Eritrea and Tigré, and a brief conflict with Somalia in

1977–8 reduced the country to a state of disarray. The withdrawal of Soviet aid weakened the government's capacity to resist rebel opponents who had united under the banner of the Ethiopian People's Revolutionary Democratic Front and in 1991 the military dictator Mengistu Haile Miriam was finally overthrown. In the aftermath of the civil war the separatist guerrilla organization, the Eritrean People's Liberation Front, immediately took control of Eritrea in advance of independence for that region of the country in 1993.
**Ethiopian** *adj. & n.*

**Ethiopic** /ˌiːθɪˈɒpɪk/ the liturgical language of the Coptic Church of Ethiopia.

**ethnic** /ˈeθnɪk/ **1.** a social group with a common national or cultural tradition. **2.** a term denoting origin by birth or descent rather than nationality. **3.** relating to race or cultural.

**ethnic minority** a group differentiated from the main population of a community by racial origin or cultural background.

**ethnoarchaeology** /ˌeθnəʊˌɑːkɪˈɒlədʒɪ/ the study of a society's institutions based on examination of its material attributes.

**ethnocentric** /ˌeθnəʊˈsentrɪk/ evaluating other races and cultures by criteria specific to one's own.

**ethnography** /eθˈnɒɡrəfɪ/ the scientific description of the races and cultures of mankind.

**ethnology** /eθˈnɒlədʒɪ/ the comparative scientific study of human peoples.

**Etna** /ˈetnə/, **Mount** a snow-capped volcano on the east coast of the island of Sicily in the Italian province of Catania, the highest and most active European volcano (3,323 m., 10,902 ft.). Over 135 serious eruptions have been recorded since the 5th c. BC.

**Eton College** /ˈiːt(ə)n/ a school near Windsor in Berkshire, England, founded in 1440 by Henry VI to prepare scholars for King's College, Cambridge. Its library preserves the original *Gray's Elegy* among its manuscripts. The Eton wall game, one of the oldest forms of football in existence, is played only on a site at Eton College where scholars (or Collegers) have played non-scholars (Oppidians) on St. Andrew's Day (30 November) since *c.* 1820. Many famous British politicians were educated at the College.
**Etonian** *adj. & n.*

**Etosha Pan** /ɪˈtəʊʃə/ a depression of the great African plateau, filled with salt water and having no outlets, extending over an area of 4,800 sq. km. (1,854 sq. miles) in northern Namibia. Supporting a large variety of animals and waterfowl, Etosha was established as a game reserve in 1907 and declared a national park in 1958. The wetlands of Etosha are home to the world's largest breeding population of greater flamingo.

**Etruria** /ɪˈtruːrɪə/ an ancient state in west-central Italy which spread its civilization throughout most

of Italy in the 6th c. BC. It is now part of modern Tuscany and Umbria.
**Etruscan** *adj. & n.*

**Etruria** a town in the Potteries, Staffordshire, England, forming a district of Stoke-on-Trent. In 1769 a famous pottery was founded here by Josiah Wedgwood who built houses for his workers and named the location after ancient Etruria in Italy where Estruscans produced a well known pottery.

**EU** *abbr.* the European Union.

**Euboea** /juːˈbiːə/ (Greek **Évvoia** /ˈeɪvɪə/) an island of Greece, in the western Aegean Sea, almost parallel to the mainland, from which it is separated by only a narrow channel for most of its length. With an area of 3,379 sq. km. (1,305 sq. miles), it is the second-largest Greek island. Euboea and its surrounding islands form a department of Greece with pop. (1991) 209,130. Its capital is Khalkis.

**Euclid** /ˈjuːklɪd/ an industrial city in north-east Ohio, USA, on Lake Erie adjacent to Cleveland; pop. (1990) 54,875. Machinery and motor vehicle parts are produced and the National Shrine of Our Lady of Lourdes is located here.

**Eugene** /ˈjuːdʒiːn/ a city in west Oregon, USA, on the west bank of the Williamette River opposite Springfield; pop. (1990) 112,700. It is the seat of the University of Oregon (founded in 1876) and a transportation centre for timber and food products from the surrounding area.

**Euphrates** /juːˈfreɪtiːz/ a river of south-west Asia that rises in the mountains of eastern Turkey and flows through Syria and Iraq to join the Tigris near Basra, forming the Shatt al-Arab waterway which flows into the Persian Gulf. In Turkey the Euphrates forms a major element of the Grand Anatolian Project to supply irrigation water and hydroelectric power. The Ataturk dam, the largest of Turkey's dams, was completed in 1989. In Syria the Euphrates is the main single source of water for domestic use, irrigation, and industry. The river is about 2,736 km. (1,700 miles) long.

**Eurasia** /jʊəˈreɪʒə/ a term used to describe the total continental land mass of Europe and Asia combined.
**Eurasian** *adj. & n.*

**Eure** /ɜː(r)/ **1.** a department in the Haute Normandie region of north-west France; area 6,040 sq. km. (2,333 sq. miles); pop. (1990) 513,820; capital, Évreux. **2.** a river of north-west France rising in the Perche Hills in the department of Orne. It flows 225 km. (142 miles) through Chartres to join the Seine near Rouen.

**Eure-et-Loir** /ˌɜːreɪˈlwɑː(r)/ a department in the Centre Region of northern France; area 5,880 sq. km. (2,271 sq. miles); pop. (1990) 396,070; capital, Chartres.

**Eureka Stockade** /juːˈriːkə/ the site of Australia's only major civil riot which took place to the east of the gold-mining town of Ballarat, Victoria, in 1854 when aggrieved miners took up arms against police and troops.

**Euro Disney Resort** /ˈjʊərəʊ ˌdɪznɪ/ (also **Disneyland Paris**) an American-style pleasure park in France, situated at Marne-la-Vallée, 30 km. (19 miles) east of Paris. Opened in 1992 and occupying an area of 1,943 hectares (4,776 acres), its entertainments are based on the films of Walt Disney.

**Europa Island** an uninhabited tropical French island in the Mozambique Channel, 340 km. (214 miles) west of Madagascar; area 28 sq. km. (10.8 sq. miles). It is administered as a dependency of Réunion.

**Europe** /ˈjʊərəp/ a continent of the northern hemisphere consisting of the western part of the land mass of which Asia forms the eastern (and greater) part, and including Scandinavia, that part of Russia west of the Urals, and the British Isles; area 9.9 million sq. km. (3.8 million sq. miles); pop. (est. 1988) 496 million. It contains approximately 20 per cent of the world's population and is the second smallest continent after Australia. Falling largely within the northern temperate climatic zone, over two-thirds of Europe is a great plain that stretches E–W between the Scandinavian Highlands in the north and the mountain ranges of the Pyrenees, Alps, and Carpathians in the south. Europe's highest peak is Mt. Elbrus in the Caucasus (5,642 m., 18,510 ft.); the most westerly point of the mainland is Cape Roca in Portugal; the northernmost point is the tip of Nordkynn in Norway, and the southernmost point is Tarifa Point in Spain. The largest cities in Europe are Moscow, Paris, London, St. Petersburg, Berlin, Madrid, Athens, Rome, Kiev, and Budapest. The western part of Europe was consolidated within the Roman Empire, but the subsequent barbarian invasions brought political chaos which was only gradually resolved in the medieval and post-medieval periods, the last modern European nation states emerging in the 19th c. Politically and economically preeminent in the 18th and 19th centuries, Europe was overshadowed for much of the 20th c. as a result of the rise of the superpowers, but it still maintains a general standard of living and political stability well in advance of most of the Third World.
**European** *adj. & n.*

**European Community** (**EC**) an organization of Western European countries, which came into being in 1967 through the merger of the European Economic Community (Common Market or EEC), European Atomic Energy Community (Euratom), and European Coal and Steel Community (ECSC), and was committed to economic and political integration as envisaged by the Treaties of Rome. It was superseded in 1993 by the EUROPEAN UNION.

**European Economic Area** (**EEA**) an economic union agreed between the 12 member states of the European Community and the seven EFTA states (Austria, Finland, Iceland, Liechtenstein, Norway, Sweden, and Switzerland) at a meeting in Oporto, Portugal in May 1992 for the purpose of strengthening trade and economic relations by promoting the free movement of goods, services, capital, and people. The EEA extends the EC's Single European Market principles, known collectively as the *acquis*, to over 380 million people.

## European Free Trade Association

**(EFTA)** a customs union of Western European countries, established in 1960, created by a British initiative as a trade grouping unencumbered by the political implications of the EC. In 1973 Britain and Denmark entered the EC and left EFTA. Free trade between its original members was achieved by the end of 1966, and all tariffs between EFTA and EC countries were finally abolished in 1984.

**European Union** an economic and political union of countries in Western Europe established by the Maastricht Treaty which came into force on 1 November 1993. It is a closer integration of the three European Communities (EC, ECSC, and EURATOM) providing frameworks for inter-governmental co-operation on foreign and security affairs as well as justice and home affairs. The European Parliament (first elected in 1979) meets in Strasbourg and Luxembourg while the Commission and Council of Ministers meets in Brussels.

**Europoort** /'jʊərəʊˌpɔːt/ a major European port facility created since 1958 at the mouth of the New Waterway opposite the Hook of Holland, near Rotterdam in the Netherlands. It can handle the world's largest bulk carriers and container ships and has oil and metal refineries, as well as engineering, ship repair, chemicals, and food-processing plants.

**Euskadi** the Basque name for the BASQUE COUNTRY.

**eustasy** /juːˈsteɪzɪ/ a change of sea-level that occurs as a result of melting ice, the movement of ocean floors, or widespread sedimentation.

**Evanston** /'evənzt(ə)n/ a residential and cultural city in north-east Illinois, USA, on Lake Michigan, north of Chicago; pop. (1990) 73,200. Originally known as Gross Point, it was renamed in 1853 in honour of John Evans, one of the founders of Northwestern University. It is the headquarters of Rotary International and the Methodist Church.

**Evansville** /'evənzˌvɪl/ a city in south-west Indiana, USA, on the Ohio River; pop. (1990) 126,300. Founded in 1819, it is the largest city in southern Indiana and a major transportation and industrial centre producing agricultural equipment, textiles, plastics, furniture, and pharmaceutical products.

**Everest** /'evərɪst/, **Mount** (Nepali **Sagarmatha**, Chinese **Qomolangma**) the highest mountain in the world (8,848 m., 29,028 ft.), in the

Himalayas on the border of Nepal and Tibet. It is named after Sir George Everest (1790–1866), surveyor-general of India, and was first climbed in 1953 by the New Zealand mountaineer and explorer (Sir) Edmund Hillary and the Sherpa mountaineer Tenzing Norgay.

**Everglades** /'evəˌgleɪdz/, **the** a vast area of marshland and coastal mangrove forest in south Florida, USA, extending from Lake Okeechobee southwards to Florida Bay. A national park established in 1947 protects endangered species such as the alligator, bald eagle, and egret.

**Eversley** /'evɜːzlɪ/ a village in Hampshire, southern England, south-east of Reading. The novelist Charles Kingsley (1819–75), who was rector of the church from 1844 to 1875, was buried in the churchyard.

**Evesham** /'iːvʃəm/ a market town on the River Avon in the Vale of Evesham, Hereford and Worcester, England; pop. (1981) 15,280. Simon de Montfort, founder of the English parliament, was killed in battle here in 1265.

**Évian** /'ervjæ/ (in full **Évian-les-Bains**) a spa town on Lake Geneva in the Haute-Savoie department of eastern France; pop. (1982) 6,100. It is famous for its mineral water and as a centre for bathing, sailing, and sports. A ceasefire between the French and Algerians was signed here in 1962.

**Évora** /'ervʊərə/ a market town in the Alto Alentejo region of central Portugal; pop. (1981) 34,100. It is capital of a district of the same name. Known as Ebora or Liberalitas Julia to the Romans who built a temple dedicated to Diana, Évora was taken by the Moors who developed the town as a centre of trade. Recaptured 1166, it later became a favourite seat of the Portuguese royal family. Wool, carpets, and cork are produced.

**Évreux** /er'vrɜː/ the ancient capital town of the department of Eure in Haute-Normandie, northern France, on the River Iton; pop. (1990) 51,450. It was founded by the Romans who called it Civitas Eburovicum. During the 14th–15th c. the counts of Évreux were also Kings of Navarre. It has engineering and electrical industries which have moved out from Paris since 1955.

**Évros** /'evrɒs/ a department of Thrace in north-eastern Greece; area 4,242 sq. km. (1,638 sq. miles); pop. (1991) 143,800; capital, Alexandroúpolis. The department includes the island of Samothrace.

**Évry** /er'vriː/ the capital of the department of Essonne in the Ile-de-France region of north-central France and a new town, south of Paris; pop. (1990) 45,850. It manufactures aerospace equipment.

**Évvoia** the Greek name for EUBOEA.

**Exeter** /'eksɪtər/ (Latin **Isca Dumnoniorm**, Saxon **Escancestre**) the county town of Devon, south-west England, on the River Exe; pop. (1991) 101,100. Founded by the Romans, it was the western headquarters of Royalist forces during the Civil War. There are the ruins of Roman walls and Rougemont Castle built by William the Conqueror in 1068. It has a university founded in 1955. The library of the Norman cathedral contains the *Exeter Book*, the largest surviving collection of Anglo-Saxon poems. Exeter is an administrative, marketing, and transport centre with various light industries including tourism.

**Exmoor** /'eksmʊə(r)/ an area of moorland in north Devon and west Somerset, south-west England, rising to a height of 520 m. (1,706 ft.) at Dunkery Beacon. Together with the adjacent coastline of the English Channel it was designated a national park in 1954.

**Exmouth** /'eksməθ/ a port and summer resort town at the mouth of the River Exe in Devon, south-west England.

**Extremadura** /ˌekstreɪmə'dʊərə, ˌes-/ an autonomous region of western Spain, comprising the frontier provinces of Badajoz and Cáceres; area 41,602 sq. km. (16,069 sq. miles); pop. (1991) 1,061,850; chief city, Mérida.

**Exuma Cays** /eks'juːmə/ (also **Exumas**) a group of some 350 small Caribbean islets or cays in the Bahamas, stretching for a distance of 160 km. (100 miles) in a line running south-east, starting 80 km. (50 miles) east of Nassau; area 290 sq. km. (112 sq. miles); pop. (1990) 3,539. The chief town is George Town on Great Exuma, the largest of the islands. Deep-sea fishing and sailing are the main activities.

**Eyre** /eə(r)/, **Lake** a lake in South Australia, named after E. J. Eyre (1815–1901) who explored the interior of Australia in the 1840s. The largest of Australia's salt lakes, it lies in two basins (Lake Eyre North and Lake Eyre South) covering an area of 9,320 sq. km. (3,600 sq. miles) and at 16 m. (52 ft.) below sea level is the lowest elevation in Australia. In 1964 Donald Campbell in the *Bluebird* set a land speed record of 429.3 m.p.h. on the dry salt flats of Lake Eyre North.

**Eyre Highway** a 1,900-km. (1,200-mile) road that stretches across the Nullarbor Plain from Port Augusta in Southern Australia to Norseman in Western Australia.

**Eyre Peninsula** a triangular lowland peninsula south of the Gawler Range, South Australia, bounded in the south by the Southern Ocean and in the east by the Spencer Gulf which separates it from the Yorke Peninsula. Its southernmost point is Cape Catastrophe. Grain grown on the peninsula is shipped out through Port Lincoln.

**Eysturoy** /'ɒstəruː/ (also **Ostero**) the second-largest of the Faeroe Islands, lying to the east of Streymoy; area 266 sq. km. (103 sq. miles); pop. (est. 1990) 10,000.

**Ezhou** /e'dʒəʊ/ a city in Hubei province, east-central China, on the Yangtze River south-east of Wuhan; pop. (1986) 922,000.

# F*f*

**Faenza** /fɑ:ˈentsə/ a town in Emilia-Romagna, northern Italy, on the Lamone River in the province of Ravenna; pop. (1990) 54,050. It lends its name to a type of richly coloured pottery known as faïence.

**Faero Islands** /ˈfeərəʊ/ (also **Faeroes** or **Faroes**) a group of 18 islands in the North Atlantic between Iceland and the Shetlands, forming a self-governing community within the Kingdom of Denmark; area 1,399 sq. km. (540 sq. miles); pop. (est. 1992) 46,800; official language, Faeroese (*Føroyskt*); capital, Thorshavn (Tórshavn). The largest islands are Streymoy and Eysturoy. Situated in the stormiest part of the North Atlantic the climate is mild for its latitude because of the influence of the warm ocean current of the Gulf Stream. The islands are cloudy, wet and windy throughout the year, with a daily average of four hours of sunshine during the summer. Fishing, textiles, and tourism are the chief economic activities. First settled by Irish monks in the 7th c., the islands were later colonized by the Norse who attached them to the kingdom of Norway in the 11th c. With the Union of Kjalmar in 1380 the Faeroes became part of Denmark. In 1948 they obtained a large degree of autonomy from Denmark and now have their own flag, currency, and stamps. Denmark retains control of finance, justice, defence, and foreign relations.
**Faeroese** *adj. & n.*

**Fagatogo** /ˈfæŋəˌtɒŋə/ the administrative capital of American Samoa, on the south side of Pago Pago Harbor on the east coast of the Pacific Island of Tutuila. Local chiefs ceded the island to the US here in 1900.

**Faial** /faɪˈæl/ an island of the Portuguese Azores in the Atlantic; area 172 sq. km. (66 sq. miles); pop (1981) 18,000. Dominated by the Pico Gordo volcano (1,043 m., 3,422 ft.), its chief town is Horta.

**Fairbanks** /ˈfeɪrbæŋks/ a city in central Alaska, USA, at the end of the Alaska Highway; pop. (1990) 30,800. Founded in 1902 as a gold-mining town, it now serves the oil industry.

**Fairfield** /ˈfeɪrfiːld/ a city in California, USA, between San Francisco and Sacramento; pop. (1990) 77,200. It is the site of Travis Air Force Base.

**Fair Isle** /ˈfeɪr aɪl/ a small island about half way between the Orkneys and Shetlands, noted for the characteristic coloured designs in knitting which are named after it. There is a legend that a Spanish galleon was wrecked there after the defeat of the Armada in 1588, and that the designs were learnt from its survivors. The island, which has a permanent bird observatory, belongs to the National Trust for Scotland.

**Fairweather Mountain** a mountain in North America, on the frontier between Alaska and British Columbia. At 4,663 m. (15,298 ft.) it is the highest peak in British Columbia.

**Faisalabad** /ˌfaɪsæləˈbæd/ an industrial city in the Punjab province of Pakistan; pop. (1981) 1,092,000. Formerly known as Lyallpur, the city was founded in 1892 and laid out by the British in the shape of a Union Jack. It is a major trading centre for textiles, grain, and other agricultural produce.

**Faizabad** /ˈfaɪzəˌbæd/ a market town in Uttar Pradesh, northern India, on the Ghaghara River east of Lucknow; pop. (1991) 177,500. It was formerly the capital of the state of Oudh.

**Falaise** /fəˈleɪz/ a market town in the department of Calvados, Normandy, northern France; pop. (1982) 8,820. William the Conqueror was born near here in 1027. The 'Falaise pocket' was the scene of heavy fighting during the German retreat from Normandy in August 1944.

**Falasha** /fæˈlɑːʃə/ a member of a group of people in Ethiopia holding the Jewish faith. After much persecution, most were airlifted to Israel in 1984–5. Their name is derived from the Amharic word for an exile or immigrant.

**Falkirk** /ˈfɒlkɜːk/ an industrial town in central Scotland, between Edinburgh and Glasgow; pop. (1981) 36,880. Edward I defeated the Scots here in 1298. It has modern business parks with financial and computing businesses.

**Falkland Islands** /ˈfɔːlklænd, ˈfɒl-/ (also **Falklands**, Spanish **Islas Malvinas** /ˈiːləs mælˈviːnəs/) a group of two main islands and over 100 smaller ones forming a  British Crown Colony in the South Atlantic, about 650 km. (400 miles) east of the Magellan Strait; area 12,170 sq. km. (4,700 sq. miles); pop.(1991) 2,121; language, English; capital, Stanley (on East

Falkland). The climate is bleak, with long winters and much snow. Formerly dependent on sheep farming, the islands have, since 1986, derived considerable income from fishing licences granted by the Falkland Islands Government over its exclusive maritime zone. There are direct air cargo links from the UK to Mount Pleasant Airport which was completed in 1988. First visited by European explorers in the late 16th c., the islands were successfully colonized by the French and Spanish before final occupation by Britain in 1833, following the expulsion of an Argentinian garrison. Argentina has since refused to recognize British sovereignty. In 1982 an Argentinian invasion led to a two-month war ending in a successful British reoccupation. The island is administered by a Governor, Executive Council, and Legislative Council.

**Fall River** /ˈfɔːl/ a town and port in south-east Massachusetts, USA, at the mouth of the Taunton River on Mt. Hope Bay; pop. (1990) 92,700. Founded in 1656, the city became a major centre of the cotton industry in the 19th c. It still has textile and other light industries. It was the scene of the famous murder trial of Lizzie Borden in 1892.

**Falmouth** /ˈfælməθ/ a historic port and sailing centre on the coast of Cornwall, south-west England; pop. (1981) 18,548. It was formerly important as the first and last port of call for ships sailing through the English Channel. It is the headquarters of the Royal Cornwall Yacht Club. The harbour entrance is guarded by Pendennis and St. Mawes castles. Falmouth has ship-repairing and engineering industries.

**Falster** /ˈfɑːlstə(r)/ a Danish island with sandy beaches in the Baltic Sea, south of Zealand from which it is separated by the Storstrøm Strait; area 512 sq. km. (198 sq. miles). Gedser Odde, its southern tip, is the most southerly point of Denmark.

**Famagusta** a port and resort town on the east coast of Cyprus; pop. (est. 1985) 8,000. Following the Turkish invasion of 1974 the greater part of the town was evacuated.

**Faneuil Hall** /ˈfænɪ/ a historic marketplace on the Freedom Trail in the centre of Boston, Massachusetts, USA. Built in 1740–2, it served as a political forum for revolutionary leaders during the American War of Independence.

**Fanti** /ˈfæntɪ/ (also **Fante** /ˈfæntiː/) a coastal tribe of Ghana belonging to the Akans people, a Kwa-speaking African branch of the Niger-Congo linguistic group.

**Fao** /fɔː/ (also **Faw**) a port on a peninsula at the mouth of the Shatt al-Arab waterway in south-east Iraq.

**Far East** a region of eastern Asia bordering the North Pacific and comprising China, Japan, Mongolia, North Korea, South Korea, and Siberian Russia, but occasionally extended to include other countries in Indo-China and South-East Asia.

**Farewell** /feəˈwel/, **Cape 1.** (Danish **Kap Farvel** /ˌkæp ˈfɑːˈvel/, Eskimo **Uummannarsuaq**) the southernmost point of Greenland. **2.** the northernmost point of South Island, New Zealand. Charted by Abel Tasman in 1642, the cape was named by Captain Cook as the last land sighted before he left for Australia at the end of his first voyage on 31 March 1770. A 24-km. sandspit stretching eastwards is designated a wildlife refuge to protect nesting godwits.

**Farghona** the Uzbek name for FERGANA.

**Fargo** /ˈfɑːɡəʊ/ a city and port on the Red River in south-east North Dakota, USA; pop. (1990) 74,100. Founded in 1872, it is named after William G. Fargo of the Wells-Fargo Express Company. Fargo is the largest city in North Dakota and a leading retail centre in the Red River valley trading in farm products. It is also noted for its many casinos.

**Faridabad** /fəˈriːdəˌbɑːd/ an industrial city in northern India, south of Delhi in the state of Haryana; pop. (1991) 614,000.

**Farnborough** /ˈfɑːnbərə/ a town in Hampshire, southern England, in a military area north of Aldershot; pop. (1990) 48,300. Its air-force base is noted for its annual air displays.

**Farndon** /ˈfɑːndən/ a village in Cheshire, England, on the River Dee 9 km. (6 miles) north-east of Wrexham. It was the birthplace in 1552 of the cartographer John Speed.

**Farne Islands** /fɑːn/ (also **The Staples**) a group of small islands off the coast of Northumberland, north-east England. Noted for their grey seals and sea birds, the islands' wildlife has been protected since St. Cuthbert passed an edict protecting the eider duck.

**Farnham** /ˈfɑːnəm/ a residential town in Surrey, south-east England, on the River Wey; pop. (1981) 34,850. William Cobbett was born here in 1762 and James Barrie wrote *Peter Pan* in a house near here in 1904.

**Faro** /ˈfæruː/ a seaport on the south coast of Portugal, capital of the Algarve region; pop. (1990) 31,970. It trades in cork, fish, wine, and fruit and is a tourist centre with an international airport.

**Farraka Barrage** /fəˈrækə/ a dam on the frontier between India and Bangladesh, built on the Ganges to prevent silty water from reaching the port of Calcutta. Opened in 1975, it became a source of controversy because it reduced the flow of water in Bangladesh, permitting salt water to flow further up the Ganges delta.

**Farrukhabad** /fəˈruːkəˌbɑːd/ a market town in Uttar Pradesh, northern India, on the Ganges north-west of Lucknow; pop. (1991) 207,780 (with Fategarh).

**Fars** /fɑː(r)z/ (also **Farsistan**) a province of south-west Iran; area 133,300 sq. km. (51,497 sq.

miles); pop. (1986) 3,193,770; capital, Shiraz. As Persis it was the focal point of ancient Persia with its chief cities at Persepolis and Pasargadae.

**Farsi** /'fɑːsiː/ the modern Persian language, spoken by over 25 million people in Iran and Afghanistan. It belongs to the Indo-Iranian language group and dates from the 6th c. BC when Old Persian was the language of the Persian Empire, which at one time stretched from the Mediterranean to India. Old Persian was written in cuneiform, but in the 2nd c. BC the Persians created their own alphabet (Pahlavi), which remained in use until the Islamic conquest of the 7th c.; since then Persian or Farsi has been written in the Arabic script.

**Farvel, Kap** see FAREWELL, CAPE 1.

**Fashoda** see KODOK.

**Fassi** /'fɑːsiː/ the name given to an inhabitant of Fez in Morocco.

**Fastnet** /'fɑːs(t)net/ (Gaelic **Carraig Aonair** = Lone Rock) a rocky islet off the south-west coast of the Republic of Ireland that is a familiar sight to yachtsmen and transatlantic travellers. Its name is applied to a shipping forecast area in the Atlantic.

**Fátima** /'fætɪmə/ a town in the district of Santarém, central Portugal; pop. (1991) 5,445. A sighting of the Virgin Mary near here in 1917 turned the place into a centre of pilgrimage and the building of a huge basilica began in 1928.

**Fatimid** /'fætɪmɪd/ (also **Fatimite**) a descendant or Arabian dynasty claiming descent from Fatima, the daughter of the Prophet Muhammad. The Fatimids ruled in parts of North Africa from 908 to 1171, and during some of that period in Egypt and Syria.

**fault** /fɔːlt/ a geological term describing an extended break in the earth's crust, on either side of which movement has displaced rock strata.

**favela** /fə'velə/ a Brazilian shack, slum, or shanty town.

**Fayetteville** /'feɪət̩vɪl/ an industrial city, inland port, and marketing centre on the Cape Fear River, North Carolina, USA; pop. (1990) 75,700. Founded by Scottish settlers in 1739, it was originally known as Cross Creek City. In 1783 it was re-named in honour of the Marquis de Lafayette and in 1789–93 it was state capital. Nearby is the Fort Bragg Airforce Base. It is connected to the Intra-coastal Waterway and has large textile and lumber industries as well as varied light industries.

**fazenda** /fə'zendə/ a large ranch or farm in Brazil.

**Fécamp** /feɪˈkã/ a fishing port and resort town in the department of Seine-Maritime, northern France; pop. (1990) 21,140. The novelist Guy de Maupassant (1850–93) lived here and monks of the Benedictine Abbey of the Trinity first distilled Benedictine liqueur here in the 16th c.

**Federally Administered Tribal Areas** an adminstrative region of north-west Pakistan on the frontier with Afghanistan, comprising the tribal areas of Khyber, Kurram, Malakand, Mohmand, North Waziristan, and South Waziristan; area 27,220 sq. km. (10,514 sq. miles); pop. (1981) 2,199,000. Miram Shah is the chief town.

**Feira de Santana** /feɪˈiːrə də sænˈtænə/ a city in the interior of the state of Bahia, north-east Brazil; pop. (1990) 393,100. Its cattle market is the largest in Brazil and dried beef is produced.

**fejbej** see FESH-FESH.

**Feldberg** /'feltbɜːg/ a mountain in Baden-Württemberg, Germany, south-east of Freiburg. At 1,493 m. (4,898 ft.) it is the highest peak in the Black Forest.

**Feldkirch** /'feltkɪəx/ a town in the state of Vorarlberg, western Austria, on the River Ill close to the border with Liechtenstein; pop. (1991) 26,740. Situated on the route from Lake Constance to the Arlberg, it is the site of the Jesuit Stella Matutina College (1855).

**Felixstowe** /'fiːlɪkˌstəʊ/ a North Sea port on the coast of Suffolk, east England; pop. (1981) 24,460. There are ferry links with Sweden and the Netherlands.

**fell** /fel/ the name given to a hill, stretch of hills or moorland in northern England.

**Fennoscandia** /ˌfenəʊˈskændɪə/ a term used to describe Finland and Scandinavia considered as a single geological unit.

**Fens** /fenz/, **the** the name given to the flat low-lying areas of Lincolnshire, Cambridgeshire, and neighbouring counties in eastern England. Formerly marshland, they have been drained for agriculture since the 17th c., originally by Dutch engineers.

**Fergana** /fɜːˈgɑːnə/ (also **Ferghana**, Uzbek **Farghona**) **1.** a region in the mountains of Uzbekistan, comprising fertile irrigated land to the south-east of Tashkent. Standing astride the old Silk Route, it is one of the world's oldest cultivated areas as well as a routeway used in the past by invading armies. Oil, coal, and uranium occur in the region. **2.** the chief town of the Fergana Valley region of eastern Uzbekistan; pop. (1990) 183,000. It was known as Novy Margelan until 1910 and Skobelev from 1910 to 1924, and has textile industries.

**Fermanagh** /fəˈmænə/ a hilly county of south-west Northern Ireland drained by the River Erne; area 1,676 sq. km. (647 sq. miles); pop. (1981) 51,000; county town, Enniskillen.

**Fernando de Noronha** /fɜːˈnændəʊ deɪ nəˈrɒnɪə/ a federal territory of north-eastern Brazil, comprising a group of volcanic islands in the Atlantic Ocean; area 26 sq. km. (10 sq. miles). Its principal island was once a penal colony.

**Fernando Póo** /fəˈnændəʊ ˈpəʊ/ the former name (until 1973) of the island of Bioko in Equatorial Guinea.

**Ferrara** /fəˈrɑːrə/ a walled medieval town, the capital of Ferrara province, Emilia-Romagna, northern Italy, on the Adriatic near the Po delta; pop. (1990) 140,600. A free state in the 12th c., it became a powerful commercial and cultural city under the Este family a century later. It has several fine medieval buildings including a Romanesque-Gothic cathedral dating from 1135. It has petro-chemical and food, as well as tourist industries. Savonarola was born here in 1452.

**Fertile Crescent** a name given to the fertile land stretching from the Mediterranean coast of Syria, Lebanon, and Israel down the valley of the Tigris and Euphrates rivers to the Persian Gulf. The term was coined by the archaeologist James H. Breasted to describe that part of the Middle East that formed the cradle of early civilizations such as the Assyrian, Sumerian, Phoenician, Babylonian, Hittite, and Hebrew.

**Fertö** the Hungarian name for the NEUSIEDLER SEE on the Austro-Hungarian frontier.

**Fès** see FEZ.

**fesh-fesh** (also **fejbej**) the name given to a fine sand that often creates treacherous conditions for drivers in the Sahara Desert unless a track is laid.

**Fez** /fez/ (also **Fès**) the oldest of the four imperial cities of Morocco, 160 km. (100 miles) east of Rabat; pop. (1982) 448,800. Founded in 808 by Moulay Idriss II, it was a former capital of Morocco and its mosque became the focal point of a famous Muslim university. Fez gives its name to a flat-topped conical red hat with a tassel worn by men in some Muslim countries. Carpets, textiles, and leather goods are produced.

**Fezzan** /fəˈzɑːn/ a historic region of south-west Libya on the trans-Saharan caravan route to the north coast of Africa.

**Fianarantsoa** /ˌfɪənɑːrənˈtsəʊə/ (locally **Fianar**) a town in the highlands of east-central Madagascar; pop. (1990) 124,000. It was founded in 1830 on the site of an earlier village named Ivoneha and became the second capital of Mada-gascar. A noted centre of learning, its name liter-ally means 'the town where good is learnt'. The surrounding area produces wine.

**Fier** /fɪˈɜː/ a market town and capital of Fier province in south-central Albania, on the edge of the Muzaki (Myzeque) plain; pop. (1990) 45,200. Nearby are the ruins of ancient Apollonia. Cotton, bricks, and chemicals are produced.

**Fife** /faɪf/ a local government region in east-central Scotland, between the estuaries of the Forth and Tay; area 1,312 sq. km. (507 sq. miles); pop. (1991) 339,280; capital, Glenrothes. Often re-ferred to as the 'Kingdom of Fife', it has maintained a distinct identity since Pictish times. From 1975 to 1996 it was divided into three districts:

| District | Area (sq. km.) | Pop. (1991) |
|---|---|---|
| Dunfermline | 301 | 125,530 |
| Kirkcaldy | 245 | 144,570. |
| North East Fife | 765 | 69,180 |

**Fifth Avenue** one of the main thoroughfares of Manhattan Island, New York, stretching from Washington Square to the Harlem River. From 59th to 110th Streets it borders Central Park. The Flatiron Building, Empire State Building, New York Public Library, St. Patrick's Cathedral, Frick Collection, Guggenheim Museum, and Museum of the City of New York all overlook Fifth Avenue.

**Fiji** /ˈfiːdʒɪ/ official name **Republic of Fiji** a group of some 330 Melanesian is-lands, of which about 100 are inhabited, in the South Pacific, 3,152 km. (1,960 miles) north-east of Sydney, Australia;  area 18,333 sq. km. (7,078 sq. miles); pop. (est. 1990) 800,000; languages, Fijian, Hindustani, English; capital, Suva (on Viti Levu). The prevail-ing wind blows from the east or south-east and there is a wet season between November and April during which tropical hurricanes can develop. To the windward the islands are covered with dense tropical forest and to the leeward, where there is a more clearly defined wet and dry season, the islands are mostly dry and treeless. The two largest volcanic islands are Viti Levu and Vanua Levu, most of the population living on the island coasts, either in the capital or in smaller urban centres. The island interiors are sparsely populated because of the mountainous, rough terrain. About 46 per cent of the people of Fiji are indigenous Pacific Islanders (Fijians), the remainder being descend-ants of Indians brought in to work the sugar planta-tions in the 1870s. The majority of the population are subsistence farmers, but sugar, rice, copra, and ginger are exported. Discovered by Tasman in 1643 and visited by Captain Cook in 1774, the Fiji Islands became a British Crown Colony in 1874 and an independent state and member of the Commonwealth in 1970. In 1987, following a *coup*, Fiji was declared a republic and its membership of the Commonwealth was withdrawn. Situated in the heart of the South Pacific, Fiji has become a cross-roads for air and sea travel between Australasia and North America. The country is governed by a bicameral legislature although considerable power is also vested in the traditional *Bose Levu Vakaturaga* (Great Council of Chiefs).

**Filipino** /ˌfɪlɪˈpiːnəʊ/ (*feminine* **Filipina** /-nə/) a native or national of the Philippines.

**Fingal's Cave** /'fɪŋg(ə)lz keɪv/ a cave on Staffa Island in the Inner Hebrides of Scotland, famous for the clustered basaltic pillars that are its cliffs. It is said to have been the inspiration for Mendelssohn's overture *The Hebrides*, but in fact he noted down the principal theme before his visit to Staffa in 1829.

**Finger Lakes** a group of long, narrow finger-like lakes in upper New York state, USA, to the south of Lake Ontario. Cayuga and Seneca are the largest lakes in this wine-producing area which is also noted for its truck-farming.

**Finisterre** /ˌfɪnɪ'steə(r)/ the westernmost point of mainland Spain, a promontory on the Atlantic north-western coast of the province of Galicia. British fleets defeated the French near here in 1747 and 1805.

**Finistère** /ˌfɪnɪ'steə(r)/ a department of Brittany in north-west France; area 6,733 sq. km. (2,600 sq. miles); pop. (1990) 838,690; capital, Quimper. It is the most westerly department of France.

**Finland** /'fɪnlənd/ (Finnish **Suomi** /su:'əʊmɪ/) official name **The Republic of Finland** a Scandinavian country with a coastline on the Baltic Sea and an extensive network of inland waterways,  bounded to the west by the Baltic Sea and Sweden, to the north by Norway, to the east by Russia, and to the south by the Gulf of Finland; area 338,145 sq. km. (130,608 sq. miles); pop. (1990) 4,998,500; official languages, Finnish and Swedish; capital, Helsinki (Helsingfors). The largest cities are Helsinki, Espoo, Tampere, Turku, Vantaa, and Oulu. The most sparsely populated country in mainland Europe, the greater part of Finland is flat lowland covered with lakes and forest. The northern one-third of the country lies north of the Arctic Circle and off the south-west coast are *c.* 17,000 small islands and skerries including the Swedish-populated Åland Islands. Winters are long and cold but summers are warm, particularly in the south of the country. Since 1945 Finland has become highly industrialized, principal export earnings being derived from timber, paper and pulp, ships, machinery, and textiles. Converted to Christianity by Eric IX of Sweden in the 12th c., Finland became an area of Swedish-Russian rivalry. A Grand Duchy from the 16th c., it was ceded to Russia in 1809, regaining full independence after the Russian Revolution. Wars with the USSR in 1939–40 and 1941–4 cost Finland Karelia and Petsamo, and thereafter it remained neutral during the Cold War. Since the collapse of the Soviet Union in 1991 Finland has moved closer to economic integration with the rest of Europe,

joining the European Union in 1995. The country is governed by a single-chamber *Eduskunta* (Diet) with 200 elected members.
**Finnish** *adj.*
Finland is divided into 12 *lahni* (provinces):

| Province | Area (sq. km.) | Pop. (1990) | Capital |
|---|---|---|---|
| Uusimaa | 10,404 | 1,248,041 | Helsinki |
| Turku-Pori | 23,166 | 728,157 | Turku |
| Häme | 19,802 | 681,588 | Hämeenlinna |
| Kymi | 12,828 | 335,159 | Kouvola |
| Mikkeli | 21,660 | 208,223 | Mikkeli |
| Pohjois-Karjala | 21,585 | 176,836 | Joensuu |
| Kuopio | 19,956 | 256,781 | Kuopio |
| Keski-Suomi | 19,356 | 252,825 | Jyväskylä |
| Vaasa | 27,319 | 445,685 | Vaasa |
| Oulu | 61,579 | 439,905 | Oulu |
| Lappi | 98,938 | 200,674 | Rovaniemi |
| Ahvenanmaa (Åland) | 1,552 | 24,604 | Mariehamn |

**Finland, Gulf of** an arm of the Baltic Sea stretching eastwards to Russia between Estonia and Finland. It is shallow and ice-bound during much of the winter.

**Finnish** /'fɪnɪʃ/ of the Finns or their language which is spoken by some five and a half million people in Finland (where it is one of the two official languages), north-west Russia, and Sweden. It belongs to the Finno-Ugric group, is related to Estonian, and is noted for its complexity; a Finnish noun has 15 different case forms.

**Finno-Ugric** /ˌfɪnəʊ'u:grɪk, -ju:grɪk/ (also **Finno-Ugrian** /-'u:grɪən/) a group of Ural-Altaic languages, divided into Finnish languages (of which the most important are Finnish and Estonian), and Ugrian (or Ugric) languages of which the most important is Hungarian. The languages are also spoken in scattered areas of central Russia, which is thought to be the original homeland of their speakers.

**Finsteraarhorn** /ˌfɪnstər'ɑ:hɔ:n/ a mountain in Switzerland rising to 4,280 m. (14,032 ft.), the highest peak of the Bernese Alps.

**fiord** /'fi:ɔ:d/ (also **fjord**) a long, narrow inlet of sea between high cliffs, the result of glacial erosion, as in Norway.

**Firenze** the Italian name for FLORENCE.

**firn** /fɜ:n/ a German term for an accumulation of snow above glacier ice that is partially compacted by freeze and thaw action.

**Firozabad** /fə'rəʊzəˌbæd/ a market and industrial town in Uttar Pradesh, northern India, east of Agra; pop. (1991) 270,530. It produces electrical, leather, and cotton goods.

**firth** /fɜ:θ/ (also **frith** /frɪθ/) a Scottish term derived from Old Norse for an estuary or narrow inlet of the sea as in the Firth of Forth and the Firth of Clyde.

**Fish River** /fɪʃ/ (Afrikaans **Vis**) a river in south-west Africa, which rises in central Namibia and flows southwards for 480 km. (300 miles) to meet the Orange River on the frontier with South Africa.

**Fitzroy Mountains** /'fɪtsrɔɪ/ (Spanish **Cerro Fitzroy**) a range of mountains in southern Patagonia, to the north of Lake Viedma on the border between Argentina and Chile. Its jagged peaks which rise to 3,375 m. (11,073 ft.) are a challenge to climbers who approach the range from the small town of Chalten.

**Fiume** the Italian name for the port of RIJEKA in Croatia.

**FL** *abbr.* US Florida (in official postal use).

**Flagstaff** /'flægstɑːf/ a town in northern Arizona, USA, on Route 66 north of Phoenix; pop. (1990) 45,860. First settled in 1876 when a group of army scouts raised the US flag on a tall pine tree, Flagstaff developed as a railway town on the Atlantic and Pacific Railroad (now the Santa Fe) line. It is the site of the Northern Arizona University (1899) and a centre of tourism. To the west is the Lowell Observatory established in 1894 by Percival Lowell.

**Flaminian Way** /flə'mɪnɪən/ a road from Rome to Cisalpine Gaul, built by Caius Flaminius *c.* 220 BC. It is 346 km. (215 miles) in length.

**Flanders** /'flɑːndəz/ a medieval principality of Western Europe in the south-western part of the Low Countries, extending along the North Sea coast and lying west of the River Scheldt. Now divided between Belgium, France, and the Netherlands, Flanders developed in medieval times with the expansion of the textile trade. In 862 Baldwin Bras-de-Fer became the first Count of Flanders which was ruled in turn by France, Spain, and Austria. In 1815 that part of Flanders formerly held by the Austrian Habsburgs was granted to the Netherlands, the French having annexed western Flanders between 1668 and 1678. The area was the scene of considerable military activity during World War I when British troops held the sector of the Western Front round the town of Ypres.

**Flatford Mill** /'flætfə(r)d/ a water-mill on the River Stour in Suffolk, eastern England, famous as the subject of one of John Constable's best known paintings, *The Hay Wain*.

**Flathead** a tribe of North American Indians of the Salishan linguistic group from the Flathead Lake area of western Montana. They number 7,000 on the Flathead reservation. As hunters of buffalo they were known for their horsemanship. Originally known as Salish, their name derives from the fact that they did not practise head deformation unlike neighbouring peoples.

**F-layer** /'ef‚leɪə(r)/ the highest and most strongly ionized region of the ionosphere.

**Fleet Street** /fliːt/ a London street between the Strand and the City, in or near which most of the leading national newspapers formerly (until the mid-1980s) had offices, whence the allusive use of its name to refer to the British press. It is named after the River Fleet which is now covered in.

**Flemish** /'flemɪʃ/ relating to Flanders, or its people or their language. Spoken by 57 per cent of the people of Belgium (mostly in the north), it is one of the two official languages of that country, the other being French. It is essentially the same language as Dutch; the apparent differences being a matter of spelling convention.

**Flensburg** an industrial seaport in Schleswig-Holstein, north-west Germany, on an inlet of the Baltic Sea; pop. (1991) 87,240. It was part of Denmark until 1867. Shipbuilding and trade in coal, timber, and food products are the chief economic activities.

**Flevoland** /'fleɪvə‚lɑːnt/ a province of the Netherlands, created in 1986 and comprising an area reclaimed from the Zuider Zee in 1950–7 and 1959–68; area 1,411 sq. km. (544 sq. miles); pop. (1991) 221,500. Its chief settlement is Lelystad.

**Flinders Chase** /‚flɪndəz 'tʃeɪs/ a national park at the western end of Kangaroo Island in South Australia.

**Flinders Island** /'flɪndəz/ the largest island in the Furneaux Group, situated in the Bass Strait between Tasmania and mainland Australia; area *c.* 2,071 sq. km. (800 sq. miles). It is named after the explorer Matthew Flinders (1774–1814). Aboriginal Tasmanians were forced to take refuge here in 1831.

**Flinders Ranges** a range of mountains in South Australia running in a north–south direction to the north of Adelaide and the Mount Lofty Ranges. Copper was discovered here in 1841 and brown coal first mined in 1945. The **Flinders Ranges National Park**, with a total area of 80,265 hectares (32,507 acres), includes the Wilepena Pond, a natural rock bowl surrounded by sheer cliffs, created in the Cambrian geological period.

**Flinders Reef** an outer reef of the Australian Great Barrier Reef.

**Flinders River** the longest river in Queensland Australia, rising on the south-west slopes of the Gregory Range. It flows seasonally for 826 km. (520 miles) to the Gulf of Carpentaria. It was named in 1841 by the surveyor John Stokes.

**Flin Flon** a mining town straddling the frontier between Manitoba and Saskatchewan, Canada; pop. (1991) 14,550. Named after Josiah Flintabbatey Flonatin, a fictional character in a penny novel, Flin Flon has been a centre for the mining of gold, silver, copper, and zinc since the early 1900s.

**Flint** /flɪnt/ a city in east Michigan, USA, on the River Flint; pop. (1990) 140,760. Founded in 1819 as a fur-trading and lumber town, Flint became a centre for the production of wagons and carriages, and later automobiles, when the Buick car plant of General Motors was founded here.

**Flint** a town in Clwyd, north-east Wales, on the River Dee estuary; pop. (1981) 11,400. There is a 13th-c. castle. Chemicals, paper, and rayon are produced.

**Flodden** /'flɒd(ə)n/ the scene of the decisive battle of the Anglo-Scottish war of 1513. A Scottish army under James IV was defeated by a smaller but better-led English force under the Earl of Surrey (sent northwards by Henry VIII, who was on a campaign in France) near the Northumbrian village of Branxton. The Scottish king and most of his nobles were among the heavy Scots losses.

**Florence** /'flɒrəns/ (Italian **Firenze** /fiə'rentseɪ/) the capital city of Tuscany in northern Italy, situated on the River Arno at the foot of the Fiesole Hills; pop. (1990) 408,400. Built near the Etruscan town of Faesulae, Florence (= City of Flowers) stood at the heart of the Roman colony of Florentia from the 1st c. BC to the 5th c. AD. During early medieval times it became a centre of the Carolingian princedom of Tuscany prior to its emergence as a republic in the 12th c. From 1414 to 1527 Florence was ruled by the rich Medici family and under them it became the leading artistic and architectural city of Italy. From the 13th to the 16th c. many of the city's fine buildings were created. These include the Ponte Vecchio (1345), the Campanile (1334), the Duomo (1296), Medici Palace (1444), the church of Santa Maria Novella (1268), and the Franciscan church of Santa Croce (1295) with the tombs of Michelangelo, Macchiavelli, and Rossini. Many historic buildings were severely damaged by floods in 1966. Florence ceased to be independent and became the capital of the Grand Duchy of Tuscany in 1532. It was the birthplace of opera at the end of the 16th c. and home of the literary Accademia della Crusca (1582). Florence is generally regarded as the world's greatest repository of art; it abounds in famous churches, palaces, museums, and monuments. Its city-centre is a world heritage site.
**Florentine** adj. & n.

**Florencia** /flɒ'rensɪə/ the capital of the department of Caquetá in southern Colombia, on the Orteguaza River; pop. (1985) 77,600. Situated on the edge of the Colombian Amazon, the town was founded by Italian missionaries in 1902.

**Flores** /'flɔːrez/ a town on an island in Lake Flores (Petén Itzá), north Guatemala, capital of the department of El Petén; pop. (1980) 5,000. Nearby are the Mayan ruins of Tikal.

**Flores** /'flɔːrez/ a mountainous volcanic island, the largest island of the Lesser Sunda group in the province of East Nusa Tenggara, Indonesia; area 17,144 sq. km. (6,622 sq. miles); pop. (est. 1990)

1,500,000. Known locally as Nusa Nipa (= Serpent Island) it is 350 km. (220 miles) in length but only 70 km. (44 miles) wide. Its chief town is Ende and coffee, copra, cattle, and rice are its chief products. The east and centre of the island is mostly populated by Papuan-Melanesians while the west is dominated by Malays.

**Flores** /'flɔːriːʃ/ the most westerly of the Portuguese islands of the Azores in the Atlantic Ocean; area 142 sq. km. (55 sq. miles). Santa Cruz dos Flores on the east coast is the chief town and Morro Grande (942 m., 3,090 ft.) is the highest point.

**Flores Sea** a sea in south-east Asia between the islands of Sulawesi (Celebes) and the Lesser Sunda group in Indonesia. The Java Sea lies to the west and the Banda Sea to the east.

**Florianópolis** /ˌflɒrɪən'ɒpəlɪs/ a city and resort on the Atlantic coast of southern Brazil, capital of the state of Santa Caterina; pop. (1990) 293,300. It was founded in 1673 by colonists from São Paulo.

**Florida** /'flɒrɪdə/ a state forming a peninsula of the south-eastern USA; area 151,939 sq. km. (58,664 sq. miles); pop. (1990) 12,937,900; capital, Tallahassee. The largest cities are Miami, Tampa, St. Petersburg, and Cape Coral. Florida is also known as the 'Sunshine State'. Held by Spain after it was explored in 1513 by Ponce de León, Florida was sold to the United States in 1819. It entered the Union as the 27th state in 1845. Fruit, vegetables, cattle, and forest products are the state's chief produce, but tourism is the most important sector of the economy. Chief attractions are Disney World, the Epcot Centre, Miami Beach, Daytona Beach, the Everglades, and the NASA Kennedy Space Center's Spaceport USA. The state is divided into 67 counties:

| County | Area (sq. km.) | Pop. (1990) | County Seat |
|---|---|---|---|
| Alachua | 2,343 | 181,600 | Gainesville |
| Baker | 1,521 | 18,490 | Maccleny |
| Bay | 1,971 | 126,990 | Panama City |
| Bradford | 762 | 22,515 | Starke |
| Brevard | 2,587 | 398,980 | Titusville |
| Broward | 3,149 | 1,255,490 | Fort Lauderdale |
| Calhoun | 1,477 | 11,010 | Blountstown |
| Charlotte | 1,794 | 110,975 | Punta Gorda |
| Citrus | 1,635 | 93,515 | Inverness |
| Clay | 1,539 | 105,990 | Green Cove Springs |
| Collier | 5,184 | 152,100 | Naples |
| Columbia | 2,070 | 42,610 | Lake City |
| Dade | 5,083 | 1,937,090 | Miami |
| De Soto | 1,654 | 23,865 | Arcadia |
| Dixie | 1,823 | 10,585 | Cross City |
| Duval | 2,018 | 672,970 | Jacksonville |
| Escambia | 1,716 | 262,800 | Pensacola |
| Flagler | 1,278 | 28,700 | Bunnell |
| Franklin | 1,417 | 8,970 | Apalachicola |
| Gadsden | 1,347 | 41,105 | Quincy |
| Gilchrist | 920 | 9,670 | Trenton |

| Glades | 1,984 | 7,590 | Moore Haven |
|---|---|---|---|
| Gulf | 1,453 | 11,500 | Port St. Joe |
| Hamilton | 1,344 | 10,930 | Jasper |
| Hardee | 1,656 | 19,500 | Wauchula |
| Hendry | 3,024 | 25,770 | La Belle |
| Hernando | 1,240 | 101,115 | Brooksville |
| Highlands | 2,675 | 68,430 | Sebring |
| Hillsborough | 2,738 | 834,050 | Tampa |
| Holmes | 1,269 | 15,780 | Bonifay |
| Indian River | 1,292 | 90,210 | Vero Beach |
| Jackson | 2,449 | 41,375 | Marianna |
| Jefferson | 1,583 | 11,300 | Monticello |
| Lafayette | 1,417 | 5,580 | Mayo |
| Lake | 2,480 | 152,100 | Tavares |
| Lee | 2,088 | 335,110 | Fort Myers |
| Leon | 1,758 | 192,490 | Tallahassee |
| Levy | 2,860 | 25,920 | Bronson |
| Liberty | 2,176 | 5,570 | Bristol |
| Madison | 1,846 | 16,660 | Madison |
| Manatee | 1,942 | 211,710 | Bradenton |
| Marion | 4,186 | 194,830 | Ocala |
| Martin | 1,443 | 100,900 | Stuart |
| Monroe | 2,688 | 78,200 | Key West |
| Nassau | 1,687 | 43,940 | Fernandina Beach |
| Okaloosa | 2,434 | 143,780 | Crestview |
| Okeechobee | 2,002 | 29,630 | Okeechobee |
| Orange | 2,366 | 677,490 | Orlando |
| Osceola | 3,510 | 107,730 | Kissimmee |
| Palm Beach | 5,182 | 863,520 | West Palm Beach |
| Pasco | 1,919 | 281,130 | Dade City |
| Pinellas | 728 | 851,660 | Clearwater |
| Polk | 4,740 | 405,830 | Bartow |
| Putnam | 1,906 | 65,070 | Palatka |
| St. Johns | 1,604 | 83,830 | Saint Augustine |
| St. Lucie | 1,511 | 150,170 | Fort Pierce |
| Santa Rosa | 2,662 | 81,600 | Milton |
| Sarasota | 1,490 | 277,780 | Sarasota |
| Seminole | 775 | 287,530 | Sanford |
| Sumter | 1,459 | 31,580 | Bushnell |
| Suwannee | 1,794 | 26,780 | Live Oak |
| Taylor | 2,751 | 17,110 | Perry |
| Union | 640 | 10,250 | Lake Butler |
| Volusia | 2,894 | 370,710 | De Land |
| Wakulla | 1,563 | 14,200 | Crawfordville |
| Walton | 2,772 | 27,760 | De Funiak Springs |
| Washington | 1,534 | 16,920 | Chipley |

**Florida Keys** /kiːz/ a chain of small coral lime-stone islands stretching a distance of some 240 km. (150 miles) from Virginia Key to Key West around the Florida peninsula, south-eastern USA. Linked to the mainland by a highway, Key Largo is the largest island.

**Florida, Straits of** a sea-passage between the Florida Keys and the Bahamas, linking the Caribbean Sea with the Atlantic Ocean. The Gulf Stream flows north-eastwards through the straits.

**Florissant** /ˈflɒrəs(ə)nt/ a residential suburb of St. Louis, Missouri, USA, on the Missouri River; pop. (1990) 51,200. It was first settled in the 1760s by French farmers and fur trappers.

**Florissant Fossil Beds** a national monu-ment in Colorado, USA, 35 km. (22 miles) west of Manitou Springs, with over 2,430 hectares (6,000 acres) of prehistoric lake beds comprising organ-isms from the Oligocene epoch fossilized in vol-canic ash and lava.

**Fluminense** /fluːmɪnˈensɪ/ a native of the state of Rio de Janeiro in Brazil.

**Flushing** /ˈflʌʃɪŋ/ (Dutch **Vlissingen**) a naval base and industrial seaport in Zeeland province, the Netherlands, on the Scheldt estuary; pop. (1991) 43,800. It was the birthplace of Admiral Michiel de Ruyter (1607–76) and the poet Jacobus Bellamy (1557–86). It has shipbuilding, fishing, and tourist industries.

**fluvio-glacial** /ˌfluːvɪəʊˈɡleɪsɪəl/ of or caused by streams from glacial ice, or the combined action of rivers and glaciers.

**Fly** /flaɪ/ the longest river on the island of New Guinea. Rising in the highlands of western Papua New Guinea, it flows south and south-east for 1,200 km. (750 miles) into the Gulf of Papua. For a short distance the river enters the Indonesian province of Irian Jaya. At its mouth it forms an estuary 80 km. (50 miles) wide surrounding a number of islands the largest of which is Kiwai.

**Foggia** /ˈfɒdʒə/ a town in Puglia south-east Italy, capital of Foggia province; pop. (1990) 159,540. Food processing, engineering, and paper-making are the chief industries.

**Fogo** /ˈfɒɡuː/ an island in the leeward group of the Cape Verde Islands; area 476 sq. km. (184 sq. miles); pop. (1980) 31,100. Its chief town is São Filipe and its highest point is Cano Peak (2,829 m., 9,280 ft.).

**föhn** /fɜːn/ (also **foehn**) **1.** a hot southerly wind on the northern slopes of the Alps. **2.** a warm dry wind on the lee side of mountains.

**Foix** /fwæ/ the capital of the department of Ariège, Midi-Pyrénées, southern France, on the River Ariège; pop. (1982) 10,000. It has an im-posing 12th-c. château and is a tourist centre.

**fold** a geological term describing a bend in the strata of rock caused by compression of the earth's surface.

**Folies-Bergère** /ˌfɒlibeəˈʒeə(r)/ a variety theatre in Paris, opened in 1869. In an age of de-corum its reputation was for lavish productions and pleasurable impropriety.

**Folkestone** /ˈfəʊkst(ə)n/ a seaport and resort in Kent, on the south-east coast of England; pop. (1981) 44,000. The English terminal of the Channel Tunnel is at Cheriton, near Folkestone. To the east are picturesque cliffs known as the Warren. There is a racecourse and a cross-Channel ferry link with France. It was the birthplace of the physician William Harvey (1578–1657) who discovered the circulation of blood.

**Folsom** /ˈfəʊlsəm/ the name of a village in north-east New Mexico, USA, applied to the remains of a prehistoric industry first found there, and especially to a distinctive type of fluted lanceo-late projectile point or spearhead, flaked from stone, found at the site in association with the bones of an extinct bison. These points have now been found throughout much of central North America but are commonest in eastern Colorado and New Mexico. The industry dates from *c.*11,000–10,000 to 8,000 BC. It is generally thought that the development of the Folsom industry reflects a change in prehistoric economy from the hunting of mammoth, prevalent during the preced-ing period, to the hunting of bison. The direct association of the Folsom point with an extinct late-Pleistocene bison clearly demonstrates man's presence in the New World at an early date.

**Fonseca** /fɒn'sekə/, **Gulf of** a large inlet of the Pacific Ocean on the coast of Central America whose waters are subject to the joint sovereignty of Nicaragua, El Salvador, and Honduras. In 1914 the USA negotiated a treaty giving it an option on a canal route from here through Nicaragua to the Caribbean as well as the right to maintain a naval base in the Gulf. Between 1916 and 1933 US troops were based there, but in 1970 the treaty was termin-ated. A long-standing boundary dispute between Honduras and El Salvador was resolved in 1992 when El Salvador was awarded the islands of Meanguera and Meanguerita and Honduras awarded the Isla el Tigre.

**Fontainebleau** /'fɒntənbləʊ/ a town in the Seine-et-Marne department of northern France; pop. (1982) 18,750. It was a resort of the French kings who enjoyed hunting in the Forest of Fontainbleau, Francis I eventually building a magnificent French Renaissance palace here. The revocation of the Edict of Nantes was signed in the palace by Louis XIV in 1685 and Napoleon signed his first abdication here in 1814.

**Fontana** /fɒn'tænə/ an industrial city in the Los Angeles conurbation, southern California, USA, to the west of San Bernardino; pop. (1990) 87,500. It produces steel and industrial gases.

**Foochow** see FUZHOU.

**Foraker** /'fɒrɪkə(r)/, **Mount** a mountain peak at the northern end of the Aleutian Range in Alaska, USA. It rises to 5,304 m. (17,042 ft.) south-west of Mount McKinley.

**Forest Lawn** a cemetery in the city of Glendale near Los Angeles, California, USA, occupying an area of 486 hectares (1,200 acres). It is the last rest-ing place of many Hollywood celebrities.

**Forest of Dean** /di:n/ a heavily wooded area in Gloucestershire between the Severn and Wye rivers, formerly a royal hunting-ground and coal-mining area which had small, private mines.

**Forlì** /fɔː'li:/ an industrial town in Emilia-Romagna, north-east Italy, in the eastern foothills of the Apennines on the River Montone; pop. (1990) 109,755. It is capital of a province of the same name. Textiles, furniture, and footwear are its chief products.

**Formentera** /ˌfɔːmən'teərə/ a Spanish island in the Mediterranean, situated to the south of Ibiza in the Balearic Islands; area 100 sq. km. (39 sq. miles); pop. (1981) 3,500. Its chief town is San Francisco Javier.

**Formigas** /fɜːˈmiːgəs/ a group of uninhabited Portuguese islets in the Atlantic, forming a rocky reef to the north of Santa Maria Island in the Azores.

**Formosa** /fɔːˈməʊsə/ a city in north-eastern Argentina, on the River Paraguay, capital of a province of the same name; pop. (1991) 166,000.

**Formosa** /fɔːˈməʊsə/ the former name (from Portuguese *formosa* = the beautiful) of TAIWAN.

**Formosa Channel** SEE TAIWAN STRAIT.

**Forster-Tuncurry** /'fɔːst(ə)r-tən'kʌrɪ/ twin towns in the Great Lakes resort district on the east coast of New South Wales, south-east Australia, situated on either side of Wallis Lake north-east of Newcastle; pop. (1991) 14,580.

**Fortaleza** /fɔːtə'leɪzə/ a port and resort on the Atlantic coast of north-east Brazil, capital of the state of Ceará; pop. (1991) 1,766,000. First colon-ized in 1612 by Portuguese sailing from the Azores, Fortaleza was taken by the Dutch in 1635 but reclaimed by the Portuguese in 1654. A sugar-plantation town subsequently developed around the Fortress of Our Lady of the Assumption and in the early 1800s its port was opened to international trade. It has a thriving tourist industry but many of its inhabitants are poor migrants living in shanty towns.

**Fort Archambault** /'ɑːʃəmˌbəʊ/ the name (until 1973) of Sarh in southern Chad.

**Fort Bragg** /bræg/ a US military base north of Fayetteville, North Carolina, established in 1918. It is a major centre for airborne training.

**Fort Collins** /'kɒlɪnz/ a town in northern Colorado, USA, in the foothills of the Rocky Mountains; pop. (1990) 87,750. Settled in 1864, Fort Collins was a favourite camping ground for pioneers moving west. It is now a major centre for the production of lamb and sugar-beet.

**Fort-de-France** /ˌfɔːdə'frɑːs/ the capital of the French overseas department of Martinique, situ-ated at the head of a bay on the leeward side of the island; pop. (1990) 101,540. The original settlement developed around Fort St. Louis which was estab-lished in 1639. Although an administrative centre since 1681, its population and importance only be-came significant after the eruption of Mont Pelée which destroyed the commercial and cultural town of St. Pierre at the north end of the island in 1902. **Foyalais** *adj. & n.*

**Forth** /fɔːθ/ a river of central Scotland that rises on Ben Lomond and flows eastwards through Stirling into the North Sea. Its estuary, the **Firth of**

**Forth**, separates the Lothians from Fife and is spanned by a railway bridge (1890) and a road bridge (1964). Its chief tributaries are the Almond, Leven, Esk, Carron, Allan Water, and Teith rivers.

**Fort Knox** /nɒks/ a US military reservation in Kentucky, famous as the site of the US Depository (built in 1936) which holds the bulk of the nation's gold bullion in its vaults.

**Fort Lamy** /læ'mɪ/ the former name (until 1973) of N'DJAMENA, capital of Chad.

**Fort Lauderdale** /'lɔːdə(r)ˌdeɪl/ a city on the Atlantic coast of Florida, USA, 40 km. (25 miles) north of Miami; pop. (1990) 149,400. Situated on the edge of a vast network of rivers, inlets, and canals, the city was named after Major William Lauderdale who built a fort here in 1838 during the Seminole War. Fort Lauderdale became popular with students on vacation in the 1950s and 1960s, and subsequently developed as a recreation area with commerce, and high-tech industries. Its harbour at Port Everglades is the world's second-largest passenger cruise port.

**Fort Raleigh** /'rɔːlɪ/ the site of the first attempted English colony in the US, established on Roanoke Island, North Carolina in 1587 by 150 men and women sent out by Sir Walter Raleigh. The legendary 'Lost Colony' is now a national historic site.

**Fort Smith** /smɪθ/ a city in western Arkansas, USA, at the junction of the Poteau and Arkansas rivers; pop. (1990) 72,800. A fort was established here in 1817 to protect traders from the Osage and Cherokee Indians and in 1848, with the discovery of gold in California, the town became a supply centre and starting point on the gold-rush trail. It is a trading and industrial centre.

**Fort Victoria** the former name of MASVINGO in Zimbabwe.

**Fort Wayne** /weɪn/ a city in north-east Indiana, USA, where the St. Mary and St. Joseph rivers meet to form the Maumee; pop. (1990) 173,100. Settled by French fur traders c. 1690, it was named Miami Town (after the local Indian tribe) and then Frenchtown. In the 1790s the site was taken by General Anthony Wayne who established a US fort. The city developed after it was linked to Chicago and Pittsburgh in the 1850s. Vehicles, wire die tools, and tyres are produced. Fort Wayne is home to Indiana University-Purdue University which was founded in 1964.

**Fort William** a town on the shore of Loch Linnhe, western Scotland, chief town of Lochaber in Highland Region; pop. (est. 1985) 4,400. Ben Nevis, Britain's highest mountain rises near the town.

**Fort Worth** /wɜːθ/ a city in north-east Texas, USA, on the Trinity River; pop. (1990) 447,600. Settled in 1849 and named after General William J. Worth, a Mexican War hero, the city developed after the Civil War when herds of cattle were driven through the area *en route* to the Kansas railheads. In 1876, with the arrival of the railway, Fort Worth became a major shipping point. In addition to cattle, the city's economy is dependent on oil, aircraft industries, and the grain trade.

**forty-ninth parallel** the parallel of latitude 49° north of the equator, especially as forming the boundary between Canada and the US west of the Lake of the Woods.

**Foshan** /fʊ'ʃɑːn/ (formerly **Fatshan** or **Namhoi**) a city in Guangdong province, southern China, south-west of Guangzhou (Canton); pop. (1986) 323,000.

**Fosse Way** /fɒs/ an ancient road in Britain, so called from the fosse or ditch on each side. It probably ran from Axminster to Lincoln, via Bath and Leicester (about 300 km., 200 miles), and marked the limit of the first stage of the Roman occupation (mid-1st c. AD).

**Fotheringhay** /'fɒðərɪŋˌɡeɪ/ a village in Northamptonshire, England, on the River Nene 6 km. (4 miles) north-east of Oundle. Fotheringhay Castle was the birthplace in 1452 of Richard III, and Mary Queen of Scots was imprisoned in the castle before her execution here in 1587.

**Fou-Hsin** see FUXIN.

**Fountain Valley** a residential city in the Los Angeles conurbation, southern California, USA, situated between Huntington Beach and Santa Ana; pop. (1990) 53,700. It has light industries.

**Fountains Abbey** /'faʊntənz/ a ruined medieval abbey in North Yorkshire, England, situated by the River Skell 5 km. (3 miles) south-west of Ripon.

**Foxe Basin** a shallow basin of water forming a north-eastern extension of Hudson Bay and separating Baffin Island from the mainland of the Northwest Territories of Canada. It is named after Luke Foxe who explored the area in 1631.

**France** /frɑːns/ official name **The Republic of France** a country in western Europe, with coastlines on the Atlantic Ocean, the English Channel, and the Mediterranean Sea; area 547,026 sq. km.  (211,208 sq. miles); pop. (est. 1991) 56,700,000; official language, French; capital, Paris. Its largest cities are Paris, Marseilles, Lyons, Toulouse, and Nice. Extending 1,000 km. (600 miles) from north to south, France is generally low-lying except in the south and east where the Pyrenees and the western Alps rise on opposite sides of the Massif Central. Southern France has a Mediterranean-type climate that is warmer than the north, where the influence of the Atlantic gives rise to more changeable weather. Central France has a typical continental

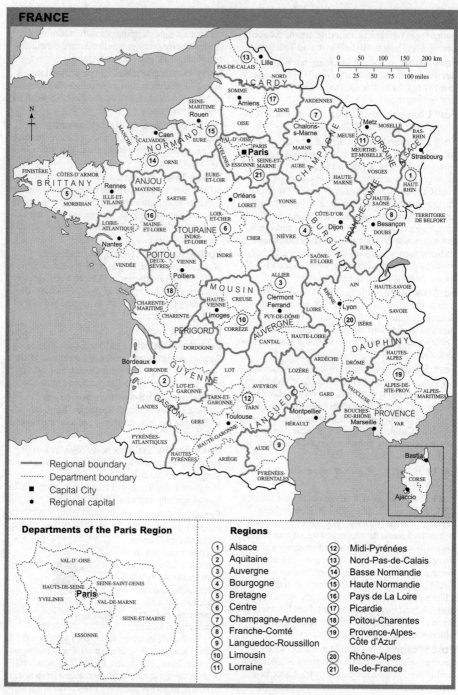

**FRANCE**

| 0 | 50 | 100 | 150 | 200 km |
| 0 | 25 | 50 | 75 | 100 miles |

Regional boundary
Department boundary
■ Capital City
● Regional capital

**Departments of the Paris Region**

VAL-D'-OISE
HAUTS-DE-SEINE
SEINE-SAINT-DENIS
YVELINES
Paris
VAL-DE-MARNE
SEINE-ET-MARNE
ESSONNE

**Regions**

① Alsace
② Aquitaine
③ Auvergne
④ Bourgogne
⑤ Bretagne
⑥ Centre
⑦ Champagne-Ardenne
⑧ Franche-Comté
⑨ Languedoc-Roussillon
⑩ Limousin
⑪ Lorraine

⑫ Midi-Pyrénées
⑬ Nord-Pas-de-Calais
⑭ Basse Normandie
⑮ Haute Normandie
⑯ Pays de La Loire
⑰ Picardie
⑱ Poitou-Charentes
⑲ Provence-Alpes-Côte d'Azur
⑳ Rhône-Alpes
㉑ Ile-de-France

climate with warm summers and winters that
become colder towards the east. Although it is an
industrial country, agriculture remains important,
and many regions are famous for their wines.
Additional exports include grain, vegetables, fruit,
dairy produce, textiles, chemicals, and machinery.

Prehistoric remains, cave paintings, and megalithic
monuments attest the long history of human
habitation. Julius Caesar subdued the area in the
1st c. BC and it became the Roman province of
Gaul. It was politically splintered by barbarian
invasions from the 3rd c. onwards and, although

briefly united under the Merovingian and
Carolingian kings, it did not emerge as a permanently unified state until the ejection of the English
and Burgundians at the end of the Middle Ages.
Under the Valois and Bourbon dynasties France
rose to contest European hegemony in the
16th–18th c., and after the overthrow of the monarchy in the French Revolution briefly dominated
Europe under Napoleon. Defeated in the Franco-
Prussian war (1870–1), and weakened by two world
wars, France has emerged in the post-war era as a
major power and leading member of the European
Union. The country is governed by a bi-cameral
Parliament comprising the National Assembly and
the Senate. Executive power of the Fifth Republic
is vested in the President.

**French** *adj.*

Metropolitan France is divided into 22 regions and
96 departments:

| Region | Area (sq. km.) | Pop. (1990) | Capital |
|---|---|---|---|
| Alsace | 8,280 | 1,624,000 | Strasbourg |
| Aquitaine | 41,308 | 2,796,000 | Bordeaux |
| Auvergne | 26,013 | 1,321,000 | Clermont Ferrand |
| Basse-Normandie | 17,589 | 1,391,000 | Caen |
| Haute Normandie | 12,317 | 1,737,000 | Rouen |
| Bourgogne | 31,582 | 1,609,000 | Dijon |
| Bretagne | 27,208 | 2,796,000 | Rennes |
| Centre | 39,151 | 2,371,000 | Orléans |
| Champagne-Ardenne | 25,606 | 1,348,000 | Châlons-sur-Marne |
| Corse | 8,680 | 250,000 | Ajaccio |
| Franche-Comté | 16,202 | 1,097,000 | Besançon |
| Ile-de-France | 12,012 | 10,660,000 | Paris |
| Languedoc-Roussillon | 27,376 | 2,115,000 | Montpellier |
| Limousin | 16,942 | 723,000 | Limoges |
| Lorraine | 23,547 | 2,306,000 | Metz |
| Midi-Pyrénées | 45,348 | 2,431,000 | Toulouse |
| Nord-Pas-de-Calais | 12,414 | 3,965,000 | Lille |
| Pays de la Loire | 32,082 | 3,059,000 | Nantes |
| Picardie | 19,399 | 1,811,000 | Amiens |
| Poitou-Charentes | 25,809 | 1,595,000 | Poitiers |
| Provence-Alpes-Côte d'Azur | 31,400 | 4,258,000 | Marseille |
| Rhône-Alpes | 43,698 | 5,351,000 | Lyon |

| Code | Department | Pop. (1990) | Capital |
|---|---|---|---|
| 01 | Ain | 471,020 | Bourg-en-Bresse |
| 02 | Aisne | 537,260 | Laon |
| 03 | Allier | 357,710 | Moulins |
| 04 | Alpes-de-Haute-Provence | 130,880 | Digne |
| 05 | Hautes-Alpes | 113,300 | Gap |
| 06 | Alpes-Maritimes | 971,830 | Nice |
| 07 | Ardèche | 277,580 | Privas |
| 08 | Ardennes | 296,360 | Charleville-Mézières |
| 09 | Ariège | 136,455 | Foix |
| 10 | Aube | 289,210 | Troyes |
| 11 | Aude | 298,710 | Carcassonne |
| 12 | Aveyron | 270,140 | Rodez |
| 13 | Bouches-du-Rhône | 1,759,370 | Marseille |
| 14 | Calvados | 618,480 | Caen |
| 15 | Cantal | 158,720 | Aurillac |
| 16 | Charente | 341,990 | Angoulème |
| 17 | Charente-Maritime | 527,150 | La Rochelle |
| 18 | Cher | 321,560 | Bourges |
| 19 | Corrèze | 237,910 | Tulle |
| 20a | Corse du Sud | 118,170 | Ajaccio |
| 20b | Haute Corse | 131,560 | Bastia |
| 21 | Côte-d'Or | 493,870 | Dijon |
| 22 | Côtes-d'Armor | 538,395 | Saint-Brieuc |
| 23 | Creuse | 131,350 | Guéret |
| 24 | Dordogne | 386,365 | Périgueux |
| 25 | Doubs | 484,770 | Besançon |
| 26 | Drôme | 414,070 | Valence |
| 27 | Eure | 513,820 | Évreux |
| 28 | Eure-et-Loir | 396,070 | Chartres |
| 29 | Finistère | 838,690 | Quimper |
| 30 | Gard | 585,050 | Nimes |
| 31 | Haute Garonne | 925,960 | Toulouse |
| 32 | Gers | 174,590 | Auch |
| 33 | Gironde | 1,213,500 | Bordeaux |
| 34 | Hérault | 794,600 | Montpellier |
| 35 | Ille-et-Vilaine | 798,720 | Rennes |
| 36 | Indre | 237,510 | Chateauroux |
| 37 | Indre-et-Loire | 529,345 | Tours |
| 38 | Isère | 1,016,230 | Grenoble |
| 39 | Jura | 248,760 | Lons-Le Saunier |
| 40 | Landes | 311,460 | Mont-de-Marsan |
| 41 | Loir-et-Cher | 305,940 | Blois |
| 42 | Loire | 746,290 | St.-Étienne |
| 43 | Haute-Loire | 206,570 | Le Puy |
| 44 | Loire-Atlantique | 1,052,180 | Nantes |
| 45 | Loiret | 580,610 | Orléans |
| 46 | Lot | 155,810 | Cahors |
| 47 | Lot-et-Garonne | 305,990 | Agen |
| 48 | Lozère | 72,825 | Mende |
| 49 | Maine-et-Loire | 705,880 | Angers |
| 50 | Manche | 479,640 | Saint-Lo |
| 51 | Marne | 558,220 | Châlons-sur-Marne |
| 52 | Haute-Marne | 204,070 | Chaumont |
| 53 | Mayenne | 278,040 | Laval |
| 54 | Meurthe-et-Moselle | 711,820 | Nancy |
| 55 | Meuse | 196,340 | Bar-le-Duc |
| 56 | Morbihan | 619,840 | Vannes |
| 57 | Moselle | 1,011,300 | Metz |
| 58 | Nièvre | 233,280 | Nevers |
| 59 | Nord | 2,531,855 | Lille |
| 60 | Oise | 725,600 | Beauvais |
| 61 | Orne | 293,200 | Alençon |
| 62 | Pas-de-Calais | 1,433,200 | Arras |
| 63 | Puy-de-Dôme | 598,210 | Clermont-Ferrand |
| 64 | Pyrénées-Atlantique | 578,520 | Pau |
| 65 | Haute-Pyrénées | 224,760 | Tarbes |
| 66 | Pyrénées-Orientales | 363,800 | Perpignan |
| 67 | Bas-Rhin | 953,050 | Strasbourg |
| 68 | Haut-Rhin | 671,320 | Colmar |

(cont.)

| 69 | Rhône | 1,508,970 | Lyon |
|----|-------|-----------|------|
| 70 | Haute-Saône | 229,650 | Vesoul |
| 71 | Saône-et-Loire | 559,410 | Mâcon |
| 72 | Sarthe | 513,650 | Le Mans |
| 73 | Savoie | 348,260 | Chambéry |
| 74 | Haute-Savoie | 568,290 | Annecy |
| 75 | Paris | 2,175,200 | Paris |
| 76 | Seine-Maritime | 1,223,430 | Rouen |
| 77 | Seine-et-Marne | 1,078,170 | Melun |
| 78 | Yvelines | 1,307,150 | Versailles |
| 79 | Deux-Sèvres | 345,965 | Niort |
| 80 | Somme | 547,825 | Amiens |
| 81 | Tarn | 342,720 | Albi |
| 82 | Tarn-et-Garonne | 200,220 | Montauban |
| 83 | Var | 815,450 | Toulon |
| 84 | Vaucluse | 467,075 | Avignon |
| 85 | Vendée | 509,360 | La Roche-sur-Yon |
| 86 | Vienne | 379,980 | Poitiers |
| 87 | Haute-Vienne | 353,590 | Limoges |
| 88 | Vosges | 386,260 | Épinal |
| 89 | Yonne | 323,100 | Auxerre |
| 90 | Territoire de Belfort | 134,100 | Belfort |
| 91 | Essonne | 1,084,820 | Évry |
| 92 | Hauts-de-Seine | 1,391,660 | Nanterre |
| 93 | Seine-Saint-Denis | 1,381,200 | Bobigny |
| 94 | Val-de-Marne | 1,215,540 | Créteil |
| 95 | Val-d'Oise | 1,049,600 | Pontoise |

In addition to these regions and departments there are also four overseas departments (French Guiana, Guadeloupe, Martinique, and Réunion); four overseas territories (French Polynesia, French Southern and Antarctic Lands, New Caledonia, and Wallis and Fatuna); and two overseas territorial collectivities (Mahore and St. Pierre and Miquelon).

**Franche-Comté** /ˌfrɑ̃ʃkɒnˈteɪ/ a region of eastern France in the northern foothills of the Jura Mountains; area 16,202 sq. km. (6,257 sq. miles); pop. (1990) 1,097,280; capital, Besançon. It comprises the departments of Doubs, Jura, Haute-Saône, and the Territoire de Belfort.

**Franciscan** (also **Grey Friar**) a monk, nun, or sister of a religious order founded in 1209 by St. Francis of Assisi. The nuns are known as Poor Clares, after their founder, St. Clare (1215).

**Francistown** /ˈfrænsɪstaʊn/ a town in eastern Botswana, founded as a gold, copper, and nickel mining settlement but now a centre of industry and commerce; pop. (1991) 65,240. It is the second-largest town in Botswana, with diamond-mining and the extraction of soda ash nearby.

**Franconia** /frænˈkəʊnɪə/ a medieval duchy of south-west Germany between the Rhine and Main rivers. It was partitioned in 939 into Western or Rhenish Franconia and Eastern Franconia and later became part of the Franconian circle of the Holy Roman Empire. The name is still used today to describe a German wine region centred on Würzburg.

**Francophile** /ˈfræŋkəˌfaɪl/ a person who is fond of France or the French.

**Francophone** /ˈfræŋkəˌfəʊn/ a French-speaking person.

**Frankenthal** /ˈfræŋkənˌtɑːl/ an industrial city in Rhineland-Palatinate, western Germany, northwest of Mannheim; pop. (1991) 47,090.

**Frankfort** /ˈfræŋkfɜːt/ the capital of the US state of Kentucky, on the Kentucky River; pop. (1990) 26,000. Founded in 1786, it was chosen as state capital in 1792 as a compromise to settle the rival claims of Louisville and Lexington. Bourbon is distilled here and there are varied light industries.

**Frankfurt** /ˈfræŋkfɜːt/ (in full **Frankfurt am Main** /æm ˈmaɪn/) a port and commercial city on the River Main in the state of Hesse, western Germany; pop. (1991) 654,080. It has been a major trading centre since the Roman occupation and for 400 years the Holy Roman Emperors were elected here. It was the birthplace of the poet and dramatist Johann Goethe (1749–1832). It is Germany's financial centre with the headquarters of the Bundesbank and the European Monetary Institute. Since medieval times it has hosted national and international fairs and is a major transportation centre with a large airport. Frankfurt is also a cultural and tourist centre.

**Frankfurt** (in full **Frankfurt an der Oder**) an industrial city in Brandenburg, Germany, situated close to the Polish frontier on the River Oder; pop. (1991) 85,360. Engineering and food processing are its chief industries.

**Franz Joseph Land** /frænts ˈdʒəʊsef/ (Russian **Zemlya Frants-Iosifa**) a group of uninhabited Russian islands in the Arctic Ocean, discovered in 1873 by an Austrian expedition and named after the Austrian emperor. The islands were annexed by the USSR in 1928; area 20,720 sq. km. (8,000 sq. miles). The largest island is Graham Bell Island.

**Frascati** /frəsˈkɑːtɪ/ a resort town in Latium, Italy, 20 km. (12 miles) south-east of Rome; pop. (1990) 20,065. It was one of the best-known of the Castelli Romani that belonged to the popes and patrician families of Rome. The missionary and explorer of Ethiopia, Cardinal Massaia, is buried here and the surrounding Frascati region produces one of Italy's most famous wines.

**Fraser River** /ˈfreɪzə(r)/ the chief river of British Columbia, north-west Canada. Rising at Yellowhead Pass in the Rocky Mts., it flows 1,370 km. (862 miles) north-west, south, and then west to the Strait of Georgia just south of Vancouver. The Fraser River was explored by Sir Alexander Mackenzie in 1793, but is named in honour of Simon Fraser who followed its course to the river mouth in 1808, establishing trading posts *en route*.

**Frauenfeld** /'frauənfelt/ an industrial town and capital of Thurgau canton, north-east Switzerland, on the Murg River 34 km. (21 miles) north-west of Zurich; pop. (1990) 19,600.

**Fray Bentos** /fraɪ 'bentɒs/ a port and meat-packing centre on the Uruguay River in western Uruguay; pop. (1985) 20,000. It is capital of the Rio Negro department. A bridge built in 1976 links it with the town of Puerto Unzué in Argentina.

**Fredericia** /fred'ri:tsjə/ an industrial port in Jutland, central Denmark, on the Little Belt (Lille Baelt); pop. (1990) 28,000. Built in 1650 by Frederick III as the principal fortress town of Jutland, the city developed as a rail junction, oil-refining, and manufacturing centre in the 20th c.

**Fredericksburg** /'fredriks,bɜ:g/ an historic city on the Rappahannock River, northern Virginia, USA, between Richmond and Washington DC; pop. (1990) 19,030. It was laid out in 1727 and named after the Prince of Wales. Guns for the War of American Independence were made here and a resolution declaring independence from Britain was passed here in April 1775. George Washington went to school in Fredericksburg and James Monroe practised law in the town 1786–9. A military park nearby commemorates four of the hardest-fought battles of the Civil War: the Battle of Fredericksburg (1862), Battle of Chancellorsville (1863), Battle of the Wilderness (1864), and Battle of Spotsylvania (1864).

**Fredericton** /'fredərɪkt(ə)n/ the capital of the province of New Brunswick in eastern Canada, on the St. John River; pop. (1991) 45,360. Originally settled by Acadians in 1731 and called Pointe Ste.-Anne, it was later refounded by United Empire Loyalists who named it after Frederick Augustus, second son of George III. Canada's oldest observatory stands on the campus of the University of New Brunswick which is the third-oldest university in Canada (1785). Lord Beaverbrook, the newspaper proprietor was a benefactor of the town and the university.

**Frederiksberg** /'fredrɪksbɜ:k/ a western suburb of Copenhagen in east Zealand, Denmark; pop. (1990) 85,600.

**Frederikshavn** /'fredrɪkshaʊn/ an industrial port on the Kattegat in north-east Jutland, Denmark; pop. (1990) 25,100.

**Frederiksted** /'fredrɪk,stəd/ a commercial centre on the west coast of the island of St. Croix in the US Virgin Islands. Founded in 1751, it is the island's chief port and exports sugar.

**Fredrikstad** /,fredrɪk'stɑ:/ a port in Østfold county, southern Norway, on the Oslo Fiord, at the mouth of the Glåma River; pop. (1991) 26,500. It was founded by Frederick II in 1567. Shipbuilding, fishing, and the timber trade are important industries.

**Freedom Trail** a historic route through Boston, Massachusetts, USA, which begins and ends at the Faneuil Hall where Bostonians met to protest against British 'taxation without representation' in the months preceding the War of American Independence.

**Freeport** /'fri:pɔ:t/ **1.** the chief settlement on Grand Bahama Island in the Bahamas; pop. (1980) 24,420. **2.** a port on Ireland Island, Bermuda.

**Freetown** /'fri:taʊn/ the capital and chief port of Sierra Leone; pop. (est. 1988) 469,800. It was founded by the British on the Sierra Leone peninsula in 1787 as a settlement for freed slaves. Subsequently it became a naval base. West Africa's oldest university is located on a campus at Fourah Bay in the hills behind the city. It was founded in 1827 and became part of the University of Sierra Leone in 1967. Freetown has an oil refinery and light industries.

**Freiberg** /'fraɪbɜ:k/ a town in the northern foothills of the Ore Mts. in the state of Saxony, east Germany; pop. (1981) 51,400. Situated at the centre of a lead- and silver-mining region, it has a mining academy founded in 1765.

**Freiburg** /'fraɪbʊək/ (in full **Freiburg im Breisgau**) an industrial city on the western edge of the Black Forest, in the state of Baden-Württemberg, south-west Germany; pop. (1991) 193,775. Founded in 1120, it has a notable university established in 1457. Pharmaceuticals, textiles, and precision instruments are manufactured.

**Fremantle** /'fri:mænt(ə)l/ the principal port of Western Australia, on the Swan River; pop. (1986) 24,000. The city is named after Capt. Charles Fremantle who arrived in 1829 immediately prior to the establishment of Australia's first colony of European free settlers. Superseding Albany as Western Australia's leading port in 1897, its harbour has become an important passenger port and the 'Western Gateway to Australia'.

**Fremont** /'fri:mɒnt/ a city in Alameda County, California, USA, 55 km. (21 miles) south of San Francisco; pop. (1990) 173,300. Created in 1956 from five communities, it is a high-tech centre for the production of micro-electronics and computer software in California's 'Silicon Valley'. It is the site of the reconstructed Mission San Jose (1797).

**French** /frentʃ/ of or relating to France or its people or language. French is spoken as a native language by some 75 million people in France and its overseas territories as well as in neighbouring countries and in Canada. It is also the official language of a number of African states, having spread as a result of French colonization. It is a Romance language which has developed from the version of the Latin spoken in Gaul after its conquest in 58–51 BC. A number of dialects of French arose, but in recent centuries, since Paris became the French capital, the northern dialects have gained the ascendancy. A feature of French which began in the Middle Ages is the nasal pronunciation of certain vowels, found in no other living west European speeches except Portuguese. From the 11th to the 14th c. France was the leading country in Europe. Its influence and language spread, and in most European countries it became customary for the upper classes to learn French. From the 13th c. until well into the 20th c. it was the language of diplomacy, used for international negotiations. In 1635 the French Academy was founded determining what should be considered correct French, and although modern writers continue to experiment with the language modern literary French remains much the same as the language of the 17th c. French is the international postal language (whence the use of *aérogramme* on air-letter forms)—a status that it has held since a decision of the Universal Postal Union on its foundation in 1875.

**French Community** a political union superseding the French Union, established by France in 1958 and comprising metropolitan France, its overseas departments and territories, and seven former French colonies in Africa, namely, Central African Republic, Chad, Comoros, Congo, Gabon, Madagascar, and Senegal.

**French Equatorial Africa** a federation of French colonies created in 1910 to consolidate French territories in west-central Africa. Originally called French Congo, its constituent territories were Gabon, Middle Congo, Chad, and Ubangi-Shari (now the Central African Republic). The federation was dissolved in 1958.

**French Guiana**
/gɪˈɑːnə/ (French **Guyane Française**) an overseas department of France in South America, lying to the north of Brazil and east of Surinam; area 90,976 sq. km. (35,126 sq. miles);

pop. (est. 1990) 94,700; official language, French; capital, Cayenne. A low-lying territory, French Guiana has a humid tropical climate with a wet season from December to June. Its chief exports are timber, rum, and shrimps. First settled in 1604, it became a territory of France in 1817. It was an official penal colony from 1852 to 1946 when it became an overseas department of France.

**French Polynesia** (French **Territoire de la Polynésie Française**, formerly **French Oceania**) an overseas territory of France in the South Pacific, comprising five island groups: the Windward Islands (including Tahiti), the Leeward Islands, the Tuamotu Archipelago, the Austral or Tubuai Islands, and the Marquesas Islands; area 3,941 sq. km. (1,522 sq. miles); pop. (est. 1991) 200,000; official language, French; capital, Papeete (on the island of Tahiti). In addition to tourism, the production of copra, vanilla, and mother-ofpearl is important. Under French protection from 1843, the islands were annexed by France in 1880–2 to form the French Settlements in Oceania. Placed under a single administration in 1903, they were accorded the status of overseas territory in 1958. Since 1966 the French have carried out nuclear test explosions on the Mururoa atoll. French Polynesia is administered by a Territorial Assembly which elects a Council of Government.

**French Somaliland** the former name (until 1967) of DJIBOUTI.

**French Southern and Antarctic Lands** (French **Terres Australes et Antarctiques Françaises**) an overseas territory of France in Antarctica. Created in 1955, it comprises the Kerguelen and Crozet archipelagos and the islands of Saint Paul and Amsterdam in the Southern Ocean, and the sector of the Antarctic continent known as Terre Adélie which was explored by Dumont D'Urville in 1840. The territories are administered from Paris and are only occupied by scientific research staff.

**French Territory of the Afars and Issas** /ˈɑːfɑːz, iːˈsɑːz/ the name of DJIBOUTI from 1967 to 1977.

**French Union** a federation created by France in 1946, comprising France and its overseas departments and territories. The federation was superseded in 1958 by the FRENCH COMMUNITY.

**French West Africa** a former federation of eight French colonies created in 1895 to consolidate French territory in north and west Africa. Its constituent territories were Dahomey (now Benin), French Guinea, French Sudan, Ivory Coast, Mauritania, Niger, Senegal, and Upper Volta (now Burkina). The federation was dissolved in 1959.

**Fresno** /ˈfreznəʊ/ a city in the San Joaquin valley at the geographical centre of California, USA; pop. (1990) 354,200. It was founded in 1874 when the people of Millerton decided to move closer to the railway line. Major industries include food processing (especially dried fruit), wine production, and trade in agricultural produce. It is the centre of oil and natural-gas fields.

**Fribourg** /ˈfriːbʊə/ the capital of Fribourg canton in west Switzerland, on the Sarine River; pop. (1990) 34,000.

**Friendly Islands** see TONGA.

**Friesland** /ˈfriːzlənd/ a northern province of the Netherlands, bounded to the north by the Wadden Sea and south by Lake IJssel; area 3,357 sq. km. (1,297 sq. miles); pop. (1991) 600,000; capital, Leeuwarden.
**Frisian** *adj. & n.*

**Frisian** /ˈfrɪzɪən/ the Germanic language of Friesland, most closely related to English and Dutch, with some 300,000 speakers.

**Frisian Islands** /'frɪzɪən/ a line of islands in the North Sea off the coast of Denmark, Germany, and the Netherlands, stretching from the Wadden Sea to Jutland. Fishing, cattle-raising, and tourism are important.

**Friuli** /fri:'u:lɪ/ a historic region of south-east Europe now divided between Slovenia and the Italian region of Friuli-Venezia Giulia.

**Friuli-Venezia Giulia** /fri:ˌu:lɪve'netsɪə 'dʒu:lɪə/ an autonomous region of north-east Italy, comprising the provinces of Gorizia, Pordenone, Trieste, and Udine; area 7,843 sq. km. (3,029 sq. miles); pop. (1990) 1,201,000; capital, Trieste. Granted the status of an autonomous region in 1966, it has a Slavic minority of c. 100,000 people.

**Frobisher Bay** /'frəʊbɪʃə(r)/ an inlet of the Atlantic at the south-east end of Baffin Island in the Canadian Arctic. It is named after Sir Martin Frobisher who explored it in 1576. The settlement of Iqaluit (formerly Frobisher Bay) lies at the head of the bay.

**Fronsac** /'frɒnsæk/ an district to the west of Pomerol in the Bordeaux region of south-west France, noted for its red wines.

**Frunze** /'fru:nzjə/ the former name (until 1991) of BISHKEK, capital of Kyrgyzstan in Central Asia.

**Fuerteventura** /ˌfwɜ:tɪven'tʊəræ/ the second-largest of the Spanish Canary Islands in the Atlantic, situated between Lanzarote and Grand Canary Island; area 1,722 sq. km. (665 sq. miles). Its chief town and port is Puerto del Rosario.

**Fujairah** /fu:'dʒaɪrə/ **1.** one of the seven member-states of the United Arab Emirates whose people are largely of the Sharqiyin tribe; area 1,300 sq. km. (502 sq. miles); pop. (1985) 54,400. Recognized as a separate emirate in 1952, it is the only emirate with no coastline on the Persian Gulf. **2.** its capital in the eastern foothills of the Hajar Mountains on the Gulf of Oman. Since its completion in 1983, the port has become a major trans-shipment centre.

**Fuji** /'fu:dʒɪ/, **Mount** (Japanese **Fujisan**, also **Fujiyama** /ˌfu:dʒɪ'ja:mə/) an active volcano in Chubu Region on the island of Honshu, Japan, 88 km. (52 miles) west of Tokyo. It is the highest peak in Japan (3,776 m., 12,385 ft.), forming a snow-capped cone of exceptional beauty. A sacred mountain which has inspired Japanese poets and artists for centuries. Its last eruption was in 1707.

**Fujian** /ˌfu:dʒɪ'æn/ (formerly **Fukien** /fu:'kjen/) a mountainous province of south-east China facing the China Sea; area 123,100 sq. km. (47,547 sq. miles); pop. (est. 1986) 27,490,000; capital, Fuzhou. Timber, rubber, oils and resins, rice, sugar-cane, tobacco, fruit, and fish are its chief products.

**Fujisawa** /fu:dʒi:'sa:wə/ a city and resort in Kanto region, a suburb of Tokyo, central Japan, situated on Sagami Bay on the east coast of Honshu Island, south-west of Tokyo; pop. (1990) 350,335.

**Fukui** /fu:'ku:i:/ the capital of Fukui prefecture in the Chubu region of Honshu Island, central Japan; pop. (1990) 252,750. Food processing and the manufacture of paper and textiles are its chief industries.

**Fukuoka** /ˌfu:ku:'əʊkə/ (formerly **Hakata**) a commercial and industrial city on the north coast of Kyushu Island, southern Japan; pop.(1990) 1,237,100. It is a port and capital of a prefecture of the same name with ferry links to other Japanese islands and to Pusan in Korea.

**Fukushima** /fu:kə'ʃi:mə/ a major commercial and textile city in the Tohoku region of north Honshu Island, Japan, north-east of the Azuma Mts.; pop. (1990) 277,530.

**Fukuyama** /fu:kə'ja:mə/ an industrial port in the Chugoku region, south-west Honshu Island, Japan, at the mouth of the River Ashida; pop. (1990) 365,615. There is a ferry link with Shikoku Island and Fukuyama has a large electronics industry.

**Fulani** a nomadic cattle-herding people of the Sahel region of West Africa, especially in Senegal, Guinea, Niger, Mali, Chad, and Nigeria, whose language belongs to the Niger-Kordofanian language group.

**Fulda** /'fu:ldə/ a headwater of the Weser River in the state of Hesse, west Germany. It flows for 218 km. (137 miles) through the town of Fulda before joining the River Werra to form the Weser.

**Fuling** /fʊ'lɪŋ/ a city in Sichuan province, central China, on the Yangtze River at its junction with the Wu River; pop. (1986) 986,000.

**Fullerton** /'fʊlə(r)tən/ a city in the Los Angeles conurbation of southern California, USA, situated to the north of Anaheim; pop. (1990) 114,150. Founded in 1887, it is a centre for the production of electrical equipment, food products, musical instruments, and paper. It is the site of the California State University.

**fumarole** /'fju:mərˌrəʊl/ an opening in or near a volcano, through which hot vapours emerge.

**Funabashi** /fu:nə'ba:ʃɪ/ a residential and industrial suburb of Tokyo, on the east coast of Honshu Island, central Japan; pop. (1990) 533,270.

**Funafuti** /ˌfu:nə'fu:tɪ/ the capital of the islands of Tuvalu in the South Pacific, on Funafuti Island. The population of the island (est. 1985) is 2,810.

**Funan** /fu:'na:n/ a former kingdom of South-East Asia extending over much of present-day Cambodia and southern Vietnam from the 1st to the 6th centuries. It owed its prosperity to its position on the great trade route between India and China and subsequent Khmer dynasties viewed Funan as the state from which they were descended. The name is a transliteration of the ancient Khmer form of the word *phnom* (= hill).

**Funchal** /fʊn'ʃa:l/ the capital and chief port of the Portuguese island of Madeira in the Atlantic;

pop. (1991) 109,960. Situated on the south coast of the island, the city was founded in 1421. It is a year-round tourist resort and port of call for cruise ships.

**Fundy** /'fʌndɪ/, **Bay of** an inlet of the Atlantic Ocean between the Canadian provinces of New Brunswick and Nova Scotia. It is subject to fast-running tides, the highest in the world, reaching 21 m. (70 ft.) and now used to generate electricity.

**Furneaux Islands** /'fʊənəʊ/ a group of islands in the Bass Strait between Tasmania and the mainland of Australia, discovered in 1773 by Tobias Furneaux. Flinders Island is the largest island in the group.

**Furness** /fɜ:'nes/ a peninsula between the estuaries of the Leven and Duddon rivers, to the north-west of Morecambe Bay in Cumbria, north-west England. Its chief towns are Barrow-in-Furness, Dalton-in-Furness, and Ulverston.

**Fürth** /'fʊə(r)t/ an industrial city in Bavaria, southern Germany, a suburb of Nuremberg; pop. (1991) 105,300. It specializes in the manufacture of toys and glass.

**Fushun** /fu:'ʃʊn/ a coal-mining and industrial city in Liaoning province, north-east China, east of Shenyang; pop. (1986) 2,045,000. It has engineering, oil-refining, vehicle, aluminium, chemical, and textile industries. Its opencast coal-mines are the largest in the world.

**Futurescope** /'fju:tjə,skəʊp/ a leisure and discovery park in central France, situated at Jaunay-Clan to the north of Poitiers.

**Fuxin** /fu:'ʃɪn/ (formerly **Fou-Hsin**) an industrial city in Liaoning province, north-east China; pop. (1986) 1,693,000.

**Fuzhou** /fu:'dʒəʊ/ **1.** (formerly **Foochow**) the capital of Fujian province in eastern China, a port on the Min River; pop. (1986) 1,652,000. Founded in 202 BC as the capital of the state of Minyue, Fuzhou was a focal point of the First Opium War in 1839. Sugar, rice, tea, and fruit grown in the surrounding area form the basis of the city's food-processing industries. Machinery, electronics, chemicals, textiles, and lacquerware are also produced. **2.** a city in Jiangxi province, south-east China, on the Fu River south of Nanchang; pop. (1986) 174,000.

**Fyn** /fu:n/ (German **Fünen** /'fju:nən/) a Danish island between Jutland and Zealand with the Little Belt to the west and the Great Belt to the east; area 3,846 sq. km. (1,485 sq. miles); pop. (1990) 459,350. Its chief town is Odense.

# G g

**Ga** a people of south-east Ghana speaking the Kwa branch of the Niger-Congo language group. Originally a farming people, they inhabit six so-called Ga towns including the capital Accra.

**GA** *abbr.* US Georgia (in official postal use).

**Gabcikovo** /gæbtʃɪ'kəʊvəʊ/ a hydroelectric dam on the River Danube, on the frontier between Hungary and Slovakia. Its construction was agreed between Hungary and Czechoslovakia in 1977 but work was terminated following protests by environmentalists who claimed the project would destroy valuable wetlands in the Danube valley. Slovakia eventually decided to resume work on this controversial scheme in 1991.

**Gabès** /'gɑːbez/ (also **Qabis**) an oasis town and industrial seaport in eastern Tunisia, on the Gulf of Gabès 140 km. (88 miles) south-west of Sfax; pop. (1984) 92,250. Originally a Phoenician trading-post, the town stands on the site of the Roman town of Tacapae; it was for centuries a coastal outlet for Saharan nomads. The principal attraction is the mosque of Sidi Bou El Baba with the tomb of the Prophet's barber. Its chief industries include oil refining, potassium processing, and the manufacture of bricks and cement.

**Gabon** /gə'bɒn/ official name **The Gabonese Republic** a country in West Africa bounded north by Equatorial Guinea and Cameroon, south and east by Congo, and west by  the South Atlantic; area 267,667 sq. km. (103,386 sq. miles); pop. (est. 1991) 1,200,000; languages, French (official), Fang, and other indigenous languages; capital, Libreville. Straddling the equator, Gabon rises in a series of steps from a coastline with lagoons and mangrove swamps to the African central plateau in the east. Covered by dense tropical rainforest, its chief river is the Ogooué which flows into the Atlantic south of Libreville. The climate is typically equatorial with high temperature and humidity. Gabon's chief exports are petroleum, timber, and minerals such as manganese, gold, and uranium. French traders gained a foothold in the 1830s and 1840s, and in 1888 Gabon became a French Territory. It gained its independence as a republic in 1960 and in 1968 a single-party system of government was established. Following a National Conference in 1990 a multi-party constitution was adopted. Legislative power is vested in a 120-member National Assembly.

**Gaborone** /gæbə'rəʊnɪ/ a city in southern Africa, capital of Botswana, situated near the Ngotwane River on the main railway line linking South Africa with the Frontline States; pop. (1991) 133,470. Established in the 1890s and named after the chief of the Batlokwa tribe, Gaborone was chosen in 1962 as the site of the new capital of Botswana in preparation for independence in 1966. For a year prior to independence it was capital of the Bechuanaland Protectorate. It is one of the fastest growing cities in Africa and contains the University College of Botswana (1976), the National Museum, and Art Gallery.

**Gabrovo** /'gæbrəvəʊ/ an industrial city in the Lovech region of central Bulgaria, on the Yantra River in the northern foothills of the Balkan Mts.; pop. (1990) 88,150. Founded in the 14th c., Gabrovo became an important craft centre under Ottoman rule, producing textiles, rugs, wooden products, and iron goods. It has a noted Theatre of Humour and Satire founded in 1972.

**Gadag** /'gədəg/ a cotton-market town in Karnataka, south-west India, east of Hubli; pop. (1991) 133,920 (with Betgeri).

**Gadsden Purchase** /'gædzdən/ an area in New Mexico and Arizona, near the Rio Grande. Extending over 77,700 sq. km. (30,000 sq. miles), it was purchased from Mexico for the sum of $10 million by the United States in 1853. The deal was negotiated by James Gadsden in order to ensure a southern railroad route to the Pacific Ocean.

**Gael** /geɪl/ a Scottish or Gaelic-speaking Celt.

**Gaelic** /'geɪlɪk, 'gæ-/ a language spoken in Ireland and Scotland in two distinct varieties, referred to also as Irish (or Erse) and Scots Gaelic respectively, forming, together with Manx, the Goidelic group of the Celtic language group. From about the 5th c. AD the language was carried to Scotland by settlers from Ireland (see DALRIADA), and became the language of most of the highlands and islands; in time the Scottish variety diverged to the point where it was clearly a different dialect. Scots Gaelic is spoken by only about 75,000 people in the far west of Scotland; there is a small flourishing literary movement. A number of English words are taken from it, e.g. *bog, cairn, slogan, whisky*.

**Gaeltacht** /'geɪltəxt/ (Irish **Gaedhealtacht**) any of the regions in Ireland where the vernacular language is Irish.

**Gaetulia** /dʒɪ'tjuːliːə/ a region of ancient Numidia in North Africa occupying the northern part of present-day Libya.

**Gafsa** /'gæfsə/ an oasis and industrial town in central Tunisia, on the edge of the pre-Sahara, 180 km. (115 miles) south-west of Sfax; pop. (1984) 61,000. It was known to the Romans as Capsa and to the Byzantines as Justiniana, the former name being applied to a period of prehistory (Capsian) identified with a palaeolithic culture of North Africa. It is the centre of a phosphate-mining region.

**Gagauz** a people of Turkish origin, 90 per cent of whom form an ethnic minority in southern Moldova (Moldavia) where they numbered about 153,000 in 1989. Fearing a resurgence of Romanian nationalism in the months leading up to the collapse of the Soviet Union, Gagauz separatists unilaterally declared an independent republic in 1990. The 1994 constitution of Moldova gave autonomy to the Gagauz region whose chief city is Comrat.

**Gaia** /'geɪə, 'gaɪə/ (also **Gaea**, **Ge**) a name in Greek mythology for the Earth, personified as a goddess, daughter of Chaos. She was the mother and wife of Uranus (Heaven); their offspring included the Titans and the Cyclopes.

**Gaia hypothesis** the theory, put forward by the British scientist James Lovelock in 1969, that the entire range of living matter on earth defines the material conditions needed for its survival, functioning as a vast organism (which he named after the goddess Gaia) capable of modifying the biosphere, atmosphere, oceans, and soil to produce the physical and chemical environment that suits its needs.

**Gaillac** /'gaɪæk/ a town in the department of Tarn in the Midi-Pyrénées region of southern France, on a loop of the River Tarn; pop. (1982) 10,650.

**Gaillard Cut** /gæl'jɑːd/ a south-eastern section of the Panama Canal 13 km. (8 miles) in length, passing through Culebra Mt., from Gamboa to the locks at Pedro Miguel. It is named after David du Bose Gaillard who supervised the excavation of this part of the canal. It was widened in 1969.

**Gainesville** /'geɪnzvɪl/ a university city and farming centre in northern Florida, USA; pop. (1991) 84,770. Originally known as Hogtown, the city was renamed in honour of General Edmund P. Gaines, a hero of the Seminole War. The University of Florida was founded here in 1853.

**Gairdner** /'gærdnə(r)/, **Lake** a saline mudflat which becomes a salt lake after heavy rains, in South Australia to the north of the Eyre Peninsula and to the south-west of Woomera; area 4,764 sq. km. (1,840 sq. miles).

**Galapagos Islands** /gə'læpəgəs/ (official Spanish name **Archipiélago de Colón**) a Pacific archipelago on the equator, about 1,045 km. (650 miles) west of Ecuador, to which it belongs; area 7,812 sq. km. (3,017 sq. miles); pop. (1990) 9,750. The group comprises the islands of San Cristóbal, Santa Cruz, Isabela, San Salvador, Fernandina, Santa Maria, and some 50 small islands and islets most of which are uninhabited. Its chief town is Baquerizo Moreno on San Cristóbal, its chief port is Puerto Ayora, and its highest peak is Volcán Wolf on Isabela (1,707 m., 5,633 ft.). The abundant wildlife of the islands includes giant tortoises, flightless cormorants, marine iguanas, and many other endemic species. The observations made here by Charles Darwin in 1835, when official naturalist on HMS *Beagle*, helped him to form his theory of natural selection. In 1985 the island of Isabela was severely damaged by fire. Fragments of pottery found there, made by the Chimu Indians, indicate that the islands were visited by people who travelled from the mainland of South America before the Spanish conquest. The islands' name is derived from the Spanish word for tortoises.

**Galashiels** /gælə'ʃiːlz/ a town in the Borders Region of Scotland, on the Gala Water 9 km. (6 miles) north of Selkirk; pop. (1981) 12,200. Abbotsford, the home of the novelist Sir Walter Scott, is nearby. Electronics and textiles are the chief industries.

**Galata Bridge** /gə'lætə/ a pontoon bridge across the mouth of the Golden Horn, north-west Turkey, linking the northern part of Istanbul with the old town. Built in 1909–12 by a German firm, it is 468 m. (512 yards) long. Its middle section swings open to allow large ships to pass. To the north of the bridge is the **Galata Tower** which was built in Byzantine times and was later restored by the Genoese in 1423 and by the Ottoman Turks in 1875.

**Galatia** /gə'leɪʃə/ an ancient region in central Asia Minor, settled by invading Gauls (the Galatians) in the 3rd c. BC. In 64 BC it became a protectorate of Rome and, in 25 BC, with the addition of some further territories, was made a province of the Roman empire.
**Galatian** *adj. & n.*

**Galatz** /gæ'læts/ (Romanian **Galaţi**) an industrial city on the lower Danube in eastern Romania; pop. (1989) 307,380. Founded in the 3rd c. BC, it was occupied by the Romans who developed it as an important centre of trade. It became a free port in 1837 and in 1856 the city became the headquarters of the European Danube Commission which regulated the usage of the River Danube. Its chief industries include food processing, oil refining, shipbuilding, and the manufacture of iron and steel, chemicals, and textiles. It is also a major river port for the trans-shipment of coal, timber, grain, and petroleum products.

**Galdhøpiggen** /'gɑːlhɜːˌpɪgən/ a mountain in the Jottunheim range of south-central Norway rising to 2,469 m. (8,097 ft.). It is the second-highest peak in Norway, but would be the highest if glacier ice on the summit of nearby Glittertind melted.

**Galena** /gæ'liːnə/ a historic city in north-west Illinois, on the Galena River; pop. (1990) 3,647. Prior to the Civil War it was a major centre for the exploration of the north-western states and a leading producer of lead. General Ulysses S. Grant lived here after the Civil War.

**Galicia** /gə'lɪsɪə/ an historic region of east-central Europe on the northern slopes of the Carpathians, in south-east Poland and western Ukraine. Following the First Partition of Poland in 1772 it became an Austrian crown land and in 1861 it gained a degree of autonomy. In 1918 western Galicia was taken by Poland which in 1920 acquired title to eastern Galicia. In 1939 eastern Galicia was incorporated into the Ukraine.

**Galicia** /gə'lɪsɪə/ an autonomous region and former kingdom on the Atlantic coast of north-west Spain, to the north of Portugal and comprising the provinces of La Coruña, Lugo, Orense, and Pontevedra; area 29,434 sq. km. (11,369 sq. miles); pop. (1991) 2,731,670; capital, Santiago de Compostela.
**Galician** *adj. & n.*

**Galilee** /'gælɪlɪ/ (Hebrew **Galil**) a northern region of ancient Palestine, west of the Jordan River, associated with the ministry of Jesus.

**Galilee, Sea of** (also **Lake Tiberias**) a salt lake in northern Israel, north of the plain of Esdraelon. The River Jordan flows through it from north to south; area 166 sq. km. (64 sq. miles). Its surface is 215 m. (705 ft.) below sea-level.

**Galle** /'gɑːlə/ a seaport on the south-west coast of Sri Lanka, 115 km. (72 miles) south of Colombo; pop. (1981) 76,800. Formerly the leading port of Sri Lanka, it has a large fort built by the Dutch in 1663 which survives together with many colonial mansions. It is a centre of lacemaking, wood-carving, and gem-cutting.

**Gallia Narbonensis** /'gælɪə 'nɑːbənensɪs/ see GAUL.

**Gallic** /'gælɪk/ a term used to describe anything French or typically French. A Gallicism is a French idiom.

**Gallipoli** /gə'lɪpəlɪ/ (Turkish **Gelibolu**) a peninsula on the European side of the Dardanelles, the scene of heavy fighting during World War I. In an attempt to remove Turkey from the war in 1915–16 both the Turks and the Allies, notably Australian and New Zealand troops, suffered a quarter of a million casualties.

**Gällivare** /'jeləˌvɑːrə/ a mining town in Norbotten province, Swedish Lapland, on Lake

Vásara; pop. (1990) 22,400. Iron ore has been mined here since the 18th c.

**Galloway** /'gæləˌweɪ/ an area of south-west Scotland consisting of the two former counties of Kirkcudbrightshire and Wigtownshire, and now part of Dumfries and Galloway region. The area is noted for its western peninsula, called the Rhinns, of which the southern tip, the Mull of Galloway, is the most southerly point of Scotland. Galloway gives its name to a breed of hornless black cattle.

**Galt** /gɒlt/ a town in south-east Ontario, Canada, on the Grand River south-east of Kitchener. Originally called Shade's Mill when it was founded in 1816, its name was changed in 1827 by its Scottish settlers in honour of the novelist John Galt who founded the city of Guelph in Upper Canada (Ontario).

**Galveston** /'gælvɪstən/ a city and port in Texas, USA, south-east of Houston at the entrance to Galveston Bay, an inlet of the Gulf of Mexico; pop. (1990) 59,100. Occupied by Jean Lafitte in 1817, it was a base for pirates and slave-traders until captured by the US Navy in 1821. After the Civil War it was developed as a deep-water port, but in 1900 it was devastated by a hurricane that killed 6,000 people. Rebuilt on higher ground and protected by a sea-wall, Galveston became a leading medical centre and sea-port trading in cotton, sulphur, and grain.

**Galway** /'gɔːlweɪ/ **1.** a county of the Republic of Ireland, on the west coast of the province of Connaught; area 5,939 sq. km. (2,294 sq. miles); pop. (1991) 180,300. **2.** its county town, a sea-port and resort town on the River Corrib at the head of Galway Bay; pop. (1991) 50,800. Developed as an Anglo-Norman colony by Richard de Burgh in the 13th c. and settled by the '14 Tribes of Galway', it became a noted centre of education in the 16th c. Renowned in medieval times as a centre of learning, its University College was founded in 1845.

**Galway Bay** a bay on the west coast of Ireland, an inlet of the Atlantic Ocean from which it is separated by the Aran Islands. Bounded by the counties of Galway and Clare, its chief port is Galway.

**Gambia**
/'gæmbɪə/ (also **The Gambia**) a country on the Atlantic coast of West Africa, forming an enclave in Senegal; area 11,295 sq. km. (4,363 sq. miles); pop. (est. 1991) 900,000; lan-

guages, English (official), Malinke, and other indigenous languages; capital, BANJUL. The smallest country in Africa, Gambia consists of a narrow strip on either side of the Gambia River extending 320 km. (200 miles) upstream from its mouth. The river is fringed with mangrove swamp backed by river flats that are submerged during the wet season from June to Oct. The climate is subtropical. Tourism and the export of fish and peanuts form the basis of the economy. A British trading post from the 17th c., Gambia was created a British colony in 1843. It became an independent member of the Commonwealth in 1965, and a republic in 1970. The chief legislative body is a 50-member unicameral House of Representatives. **Gambian** *adj. & n.*

**Gambia River** a river of West Africa that rises in the Fouta Djallon Massif near Labé in Guinea and flows 800 km. (500 miles) north-west and west through Senegal and Gambia to meet the Atlantic at Banjul.

**Gambier Islands** /'gæmbɪə(r)/ a group of coral islands in the South Pacific, part of the Tuamoutu Archipelago in French Polynesia; pop. (1988) 582. The chief settlement is Rikitea on the island of Mangareva. Discovered by Captain James Wilson in 1797, the islands were named after the British naval commander, James Gambier, 1st Baron Gambier (1756–1833) who led the bombardment of Copenhagen in 1807.

**Gamlakarleby** the Swedish name for the town of KOKKOLA in Finland.

**Gäncä** /'gændzə/ (also **Gänjä, Gandzhe,** or **Gyandzhe**) an industrial city in Azerbaijan, on a tributary of the Kura River; pop. (1990) 281,000. The city was formerly called Elizavetpol (1804–1918) and Kirovabad (1935–89). It produces textiles, chemicals, and processed food.

**Gand** the French name for GHENT.

**Gander** /'gændə(r)/ a town in eastern Newfoundland, Canada, on the shore of Lake Gander, northwest of St. John's; pop. (1991) 10,100. Its airport served the first regular transatlantic flights and planes heading for Europe during World War II.

**Gandhinagar** /'gɑːndɪˌnægər/ a new town developed since 1961 as the capital of the state of Gujarat in western India, 25 km. (16 miles) north of Ahmadabad; pop. (1991) 121,750.

**Gandzhe** /'gɑːndzə/ see GÄNCÄ.

**Ganga** /'gʌŋgə/ the Hindi name for the GANGES.

**Ganganagar** /'gəŋgəˌnəgə(r)/ a town in Rajasthan, north-west India, north-west of Delhi near the border with Pakistan; pop. (1991) 161,380.

**Ganges** /'gændʒiːz/ (Hindi **Ganga**) a river in the north of India, held sacred by the Hindus who seek to wash away their sins in its waters. It flows 2,494 km. (1,550 miles) from the Gangotri Glacier in the Himalayas south-east to Bangladesh, where it reaches the Bay of Bengal in the world's largest delta. Many of India's largest cities lie in the valley of the Ganges. Thousands of pilgrims visit the 18th-c. temple near the source of the Ganges at **Gangotri** where Hindu legend claims the daughter of heaven came down to earth.

**Gangetic Plain** /gæn'dʒetɪk/ a flat, featureless plain in northern India, extending over the greater part of the state of Uttar Pradesh. Drained by the Ganges and its tributaries, its elevation falls from 365 m. (1,200 ft.) in the west to 80 m. (260 ft.) in the east at Varanasi. The region is hot, dry, and dusty in summer, but due to irrigation and natural fertility it is one of the world's most densely populated regions. Its main crops are rice, grains, oilseed, sugar-cane, and cotton.

**Gangtok** /gæŋ'tɒk/ the capital of the Himalayan state of Sikkim in northern India, in the foothills of the Kanchenjunga Range on the Ranipool River; pop. (1991) 24,970. The Namgyalk Institute of Tibetology established in 1958 has one of the world's largest collections of books and rare manuscripts on the subject of Mahayana Buddhism.

**Gänjä** see GÄNCÄ.

**Gansu** /gæn'suː/ (also **Kansu**) a province of north-west-central China, between Mongolia and Tibet; area 454,000 sq. km. (175,290 sq. miles); pop. (1990) 22,371,000; capital, Lanzhou (Lanchow). This narrow, mountainous province, traversed by the valleys of the upper Yellow River, forms a corridor through which passed, in ancient times, the route to the west known as the Silk Road. Wheat, millet, and sorghum are grown on fertile loess soils and there are rich deposits of minerals.

**Ganvie** /'gænvɪ/ a picturesque traditional fishing village of the Tofinu people of southern Benin, built on stilts in Lake Nokoué north-west of Cotonou; pop. (est. 1984) 12,000.

**Gao** /gaʊ/ the capital of Gao region in north Mali, a port and market town on the River Niger; pop. (1976) 30,700. It was once the capital of the Songhai empire.

**Gap** /gæp/ the capital of the Hautes-Alpes department in the Provence-Alpes-Côte d'Azur region of south-east France, on the Luye River in the foothills of the Dauphiné Alps; pop. (1990) 35,650. Industries include textiles, flour milling, and leather goods.

**Gard** /gɑː(r)/ a department in the Languedoc-Roussillon region of southern France, in the lower Rhône valley; area 5,853 sq. km. (2,260 sq. miles); pop. (1990) 585,049; capital, Nîmes.

**Garda** /'gɑːdə/, **Lake** (Italian **Lago di Garda**) the largest lake in Italy, situated on the frontier between the northern regions of Lombardy and Venetia; area 370 sq. km. (143 sq. miles). It is fed by the River Sarca and its outlet is the River Mincio, a tributary of the Po.

**Garden Grove** a residential city in southern California, USA, to the north-west of Santa Ana; pop. (1990) 143,000.

**Gardner Island** the former name of the Pacific island of NIKUMARORO in the Kiribati group.

**garh** /gɑːr/ a Hindi word for a hill.

**Garland** /'gɑ:(r)lənd/ a north-eastern suburb of Dallas, Texas, USA; pop. (1990) 180,650. A centre for electronics research and avionics production.

**Garonne** /gæ'rɒn/ a river of south-west France, which rises in the Pyrenees and flows 645 km. (400 miles) north-westwards through Toulouse and Bordeaux to join the Dordogne at the Gironde estuary.

**Garoua** /gə'ruə/ a market town and river port of northern Cameroon, on the Benue River north-west of Lagdo Reservoir; pop. (1981) 77,850. Linked to the Niger, it trades in cotton, salt, and groundnuts produced in the surrounding area.

**garrigue** /gə'ri:g/ a type of evergreen scrub vegetation characterized by aromatic herbaceous plants that grow on limestone soils around the Mediterranean, especially in southern France, Corsica, Sardinia, and Malta.

**Gary** /'gærɪ/ an industrial city in north-west Indiana, USA, on Lake Michigan south-east of Chicago; pop. (1990) 116,600. Founded as a major centre of steel production in 1906 and located mid-way between the coal beds of the east and the iron-ore mines of the north-west, it is named in honour of E. H. Gary (1846–1927), chairman of the US Steel Corporation.

**Gascogne** the French name for GASCONY.

**Gascony** /'gæskənɪ/ (French **Gascogne** /gæs'kɒnjə/) a former province of south-west France, in the northern foothills of the Pyrenees. Having united with Aquitaine in the 11th c., it was held by England between 1154 and 1453. **Gascon** *adj. & n.*

**Gasherbrum** /'gəsəbru:m/ a mountain peak of the Karakoram rising to 8,068 m. (26,470 ft.) south-east of Mt. K2. It was first climbed by an American expedition in 1958.

**Gaspé Peninsula** /gæs'peɪ/ a peninsula forming a mountainous wilderness in eastern Quebec, Canada, lying between the St. Lawrence River and Chaleur Bay. Extending for a length of *c.* 240 km. (150 miles), it is an extension of the Appalachian Mountains.

**Gastein Valley** /'gæstaɪn/ (German **Gasteiner Tal**) an alpine river valley with mineral springs and beautiful scenery in the uplands of the north Hohe Tauern range, Salzburg state, Austria. Its chief spas are at Bad Hofgastein and Badgastein.

**Gastonia** /gæs'təʊnjə/ an industrial city in the Piedmont of south-western North Carolina, USA; pop. (1990) 54,730. Textiles, textile machinery, plastics, and vehicle parts are produced.

**Gateshead** /'geɪtshed/ an old industrial town in the Tyne and Wear metropolitan region, north-east England, on the south side of the River Tyne opposite Newcastle upon Tyne; pop. (1991) 196,500. Its heavy industries have given way to light industries.

**Gath** /gæθ/ one of the five city-states of ancient Palestine, to the east of Ashdod in modern Israel. It was the home of Goliath.

**Gatineau** /'gætɪnəʊ/ **1.** a river in south-west Quebec, Canada, that flows *c.* 385 km. (240 miles) southwards to meet the Ottawa River at Hull. **2.** a town in south-west Quebec, Canada, near the mouth of the Gatineau River; pop. (1991) 92,300.

**GATT** *abbr.* **General Agreement on Tariffs and Trade** a multilateral treaty that lays down a code of conduct for international trade and forms the basis of a forum for resolving world trade problems and lowering trade barriers. GATT was formed in 1948 by members of the UN Economic and Social Council who originally came together to establish an International Trade Organization. About 100 countries are party to the treaty (others apply it *de facto*).

**Gattinara** /ˌgætɪ'nɑːrə/ a town in the Piedmont region of northern Italy; pop. (1990) 8,800. It gives its name to a red wine made near the town from grapes grown in the Nebbiolo vineyards.

**Gatún Lake** /gɑ:'tu:n/ a man-made lake on the Chagres River, Panama, created in 1912 with the building of the Gatún Dam during the construction of the Panama Canal.

**Gatwick** /'gætwɪk/ an international airport in West Sussex, south-east England, to the south of London. It was constructed in 1956–8 as a second London airport.

**gaucho** /'gaʊtʃəʊ/ the name given to a South American cattle herder of the Argentine and Uruguayan pampas.

**Gauhati** see GUWAHATI.

**Gaul** /gɔ:l/ an ancient region of Europe, corresponding to modern France, Belgium, the south Netherlands, south-west Germany, and northern Italy. The area was settled by groups of Celts, who had begun migration across the Rhine in 900 BC, spreading further south beyond the Alps from 400 BC onwards and ousting the Etruscans. The area south of the Alps was conquered in 222 BC by the Romans, who called it *Cisalpine Gaul*. The area north of the Alps, known to the Romans as *Transalpine Gaul*, was taken by Julius Caesar between 58 and 51 BC, remaining under Roman rule until the 5th c. AD. Within Transalpine Gaul the southern province, parts of which had fallen to the Romans in the previous century, became known as *Gallia Narbonensis*.

**Gaunt** /gɔ:nt/ the former English name of GHENT.

**Gävle** /'jevlə/ a seaport in east-central Sweden, on the Gulf of Bothnia, 160 km. (100 miles) north of Stockholm; pop. (1990) 88,600. It is the capital of Gävleborg county and a major centre for the export of timber and metal ore.

**gawa** /'gɑ:wə/ (also **kawa**) a Japanese word for a river.

**Gawler Ranges** /'gɔ:lə(r)/ a range of mountains to the north of the Eyre Peninsula in South Australia, named after George Gawler, governor of South Australia from 1838 to 1841.

**Gaya** /gə'jɑː/ a city in the state of Bihar, north-east India, on the Falgu River between the Ganges and the Rajmahal Hills, 100 km. (63 miles) south of Patna; pop. (1991) 291,000. Hindu pilgrims visit Gaya in order to make offerings that will free their ancestors from bondage to the earth. BODHGAYA, one of the holiest sites of Buddhism, is nearby.

**Gazankulu** /ˌgæzən'kuːluː/ a former self-governing homeland of the Tsonga people, created in the province of Transvaal, South Africa in 1973; pop. (1985) 495,000.

**Gaza Strip** /'gɑːzə/ a strip of coastal territory in the south-east Mediterranean, including the town of Gaza; area 363 sq. km. (140 sq. miles); pop. (est. 1988) 564,000. Administered by Egypt from 1949, it was occupied by Israel in 1967. Over 50 per cent of the Palestinian Arabs of Gaza live in refugee camps which were created after the 1948–9 Arab-Israeli war. Used as a base for Arab fedayeen guerrilla attacks on Israel during the 1950s, Gaza was the focal point of the anti-Israeli *intifada* or Palestinian uprising which began in 1987. In 1991 Israeli troops were withdrawn from Gaza as part of an agreement transferring power from Israel to the Palestinians.

**gazetteer** /ˌgæzɪ'tɪə(r)/ a geographical index or dictionary of place-names.

**Gazientep** /ˌgæziːən'tep/ **1.** a province in southern Turkey, on the frontier with Syria; area 7,642 sq. km. (2,952 sq. miles); pop. (1990) 1,140,600. **2.** its capital near the border with Syria, a manufacturing and trading centre on the Bağirsak River, a tributary of the Euphrates; pop. (1990) 603,400. Until 1921 it was called Aintab.

**GB** *abbr.* Great Britain.

**Gdańsk** /gdænsk/ (German **Danzig** /'dæntsɪg/) an industrial port and shipbuilding centre in northern Poland, on an inlet of the Baltic Sea; pop. (1990) 465,100. Originally a member of the Hanseatic League, it was disputed between Prussia and Poland during the 19th c. It was a free city under a League of Nations mandate from 1919 until 1939, when it was annexed by Nazi Germany, precipitating hostilities with Poland and the outbreak of World War II. It passed to Poland in 1945. In the 1980s the Gdańsk shipyards were the site of the activities of the Solidarity movement, which eventually led to the collapse of the Communist regime in Poland in 1989.

**GDR** *abbr.* the **German Democratic Republic**, official name of the former state of East Germany.

**Gdynia** /'gdɪnjə/ a seaport and naval base in northern Poland, on the Baltic Sea, 20 km. northwest of Gdańsk; pop. (1990) 251,500.

**gebirge** /gə'bɪrgə/ a German word for a mountain range, as in the Erzgebirge (Ore Mountains).

**Gedrosia** /jə'drəʊʒ(iː)ə/ an ancient country of south-west Asia and former province of Persia, on the Arabian Sea in modern Pakistan and south-east Iran.

**Geelong** /dʒiː'lɒŋ/ a port and oil-refining centre on Corio Bay on the south coast of Australia, the largest city in the state of Victoria; pop. (1991) 126,300. First settled in the 1830s, it is also a major wool-selling centre.

**geest** /giːst/ the German name for an area of sand, gravel, or heathland applied from the Netherlands to the north coast of Poland.

**Ge'ez** /'giːez/ the classical literary language of Ethiopia, a Semitic language thought to have been introduced from Arabia in the 1st c. BC. It is the ancestor of all the modern Ethiopian languages such as Amharic, and survives in the liturgical language of the Coptic Church in Ethiopia.

**Gehenna** /gɪ'henə/ the name of the valley of Hinnom near Jerusalem, Israel, where children were burnt in ancient times in sacrifice to pagan gods. The name is sometimes used to refer to a place of burning, torment, or misery.

**Gejiu** /ge'dʒuː/ (also **Geju**) a mining city in Yunnan province, south-west China, near the border with Vietnam; pop. (1986) 349,700. It is a major centre of tin production and was in the 18th c. the location of a royal mint producing bronze coins.

**Gelderland** /'geldəˌlænd/ a province of the Netherlands on the German border; area 5,015 sq. km. (1,937 sq. miles); pop. (1991) 1,816,900; capital, Arnhem.

**Gelsenkirchen** /'gelz(ə)nˌkɪəx(ə)n/ an industrial city in North Rhine-Westphalia, Germany, in the Ruhr valley north-east of Essen; pop. (1991) 293,840. Coal, chemicals, and steel are the chief products.

**Gemsbok** /'gemzbɒk/ a national park established in 1971 on the frontier between South Africa (Kalahari Gemsbok) and Botswana (Botswanan Gemsbok) and characterized by fossil river beds and high sand dunes; area 24,800 sq. km. (9,580 sq. miles).

**Geneva** /dʒə'niːvə/ (French **Genève** /ʒə'nev/, German **Genf**, Italian **Ginevra**) a city of south-west Switzerland, on Lake Geneva; pop. (1990) 167,200. For long a cultural centre of French-speaking Switzerland (la Suisse romande), it was in the 16th c. a stronghold of the reformer John Calvin, who rewrote its laws and constitution and founded an Academy (1559) which later became a university. More recently it has become the headquarters of international bodies such as the Red Cross, the League of Nations (1922–46), and the World Health Organization. A series of international agreements, known as the Geneva

Conventions, were concluded at Geneva between 1846 and 1949 with the object of mitigating the harm done by war to both service personnel and civilians by governing the status of hospitals, ambulances, the wounded, etc. Its light industries include the manufacture of watches, jewellery, precision instruments, machinery, clothing, and confectionery.

**Geneva, Lake** (French **Lac Léman** /leɪˈmã/) a lake in south-west Switzerland and eastern France, surrounded by the Alpine ranges of the Savoy Alps, Vaud Alps, and Jura Mts.; area 581 sq. km. (224 sq. miles). The River Rhône flows into the lake and leaves it at Geneva. Its southern shore forms part of the border between France and Switzerland.

**Genk** /geŋk/ a town in the province of Limburg, north-east Belgium, north of Liège; pop. (1991) 61,300.

**Genoa** /ˈdʒenəʊə/ (Italian **Genova** /ˈdʒenəvə/) a commercial and industrial city and seaport on the Ligurian coast of north-west Italy, capital of Liguria region; pop. (1990) 701,030. During the 13th c. it competed with Venice as the leading Mediterranean port and in the 20th c. its position as one of the largest of the modern ports in the Mediterranean was restored when container facilities were built in 1969. It has oil-refining, chemical, vehicle, and textile industries. The heavy industries of shipbuilding and steel are in decline. Genoa gave its name to the twilled cotton cloth now used to make jeans and was the birthplace of Christopher Columbus in c.1451.

**Genova** the Italian name for GENOA.

**Gent** the Flemish name for GHENT.

**Genting Highlands** /ˈdʒentɪŋ/ a recreational hill resort in Malaysia, on the border between the states of Pahang and Selangor, built at an altitude of 1,700 m. (5,520 ft.) in 1971.

**geo** /ˈdʒiːəʊ/ (Norse **Gya**) a narrow inlet or steep-sided coastal cliff formed by marine erosion. The term is used in Scotland and the Faeroes.

**geodesy** /dʒɪˈɒdɪsɪ/ that branch of science that deals with the shape and size of the earth.

**geography** /dʒɪˈɒɡrəfɪ/ the study of phenomena at or near the surface of the earth with special reference to the spatial dimension and the significance of space as a variable; generally divided into physical and human geography.

**geoid** /ˈdʒiːɔɪd/ the shape of the earth or an earth-shaped body.

**Geological Survey, US** a bureau organized under the US Department of the Interior in 1879 for the purpose of co-ordinating surveys of geology, topography, and natural resources in the USA.

**geology** /dʒɪˈɒlədʒɪ/ the science of the earth, including the composition, structure, and origin of its rocks.

**geomagnetism** /ˌdʒiːəʊˈmæɡnɪˌtɪz(ə)m/ the study of the magnetic properties of the earth.

**geomorphology** /ˌdʒiːəʊmɔːˈfɒlədʒɪ/ the study of the physical features of the surface of the earth and their relation to its geological structures.

**geopolitics** /ˌdʒiːəʊˈpɒlɪtɪks/ the study of the politics of a country with reference to its geographical features. Any programme or policy based on this, e.g. Nazi doctrines meant to lead to world domination.

**Georgetown** /ˈdʒɔːdʒtaʊn/ the capital of Guyana, a port at the mouth of the Demerara River; pop. (est. 1983) 188,000. Fishing and food processing are the chief industries.

**George Town** the capital of the Cayman Islands, on the Caribbean island of Grand Cayman; pop. (est. 1988) 12,000.

**George Town** (also **Penang** or **Pinang**) the former chief port of Malaysia and capital of the state of Penang, on Penang Island (Pulau Pinang); pop. (1980) 250,500. It was founded in 1786 by the British East India Company. Most of its port trade has moved to Butterworth and George Town today is primarily a tourist centre.

**Georgia**

/ˈdʒɔːdʒɪə/ (Russian **Gruziya**) official name **The Republic of Georgia** a country of south-east Europe, on the eastern shore of the Black Sea and bounded by Russia to the north and Turkey, Armenia, and Azerbaijan to the south; area 69,700 sq. km. (26,905 sq. miles); pop. (1989) 5,449,000; languages, Georgian (official), Russian, and Armenian; capital, Tbilisi. Georgia is a mountainous country with a climate that ranges from perpetual snow on the high peaks to subtropical on the Black Sea coast. Two-thirds of the country is covered by forest and, except for the fertile Kolkhida plain, agricultural land is limited. The chief products are tobacco, tea, grapes, citrus fruit, and machinery. An independent kingdom in medieval times, it was divided between Persia and Turkey in 1555 and absorbed into the Russian Empire in the 19th c. It was a constituent republic of the USSR until the breakup of the Soviet Union in 1991 when it regained its independence. Since then separatist movements amongst the Abkhaz and South Ossetian minorites have led to outbursts of ethnic conflict.

**Georgian** adj. & n.

**Georgia** a state of the south-eastern US, on the Atlantic coast; area 152,576 sq. km. (58,910 sq. miles); pop. (1990) 6,478,220; capital, Atlanta. Its largest cities are Atlanta, Columbus, Savannah, and Macon. Georgia is also known as the Peach State or Empire State of the South. Founded in 1733 as an English colony and named after George II, it was one of the original 13 states of the US.

The chief products of the state are paper and board, textiles, food products, resin, turpentine, bauxite, marble, and kaolin. The principal tourist attractions include the Confederate memorial at Stone Mountain, Okefenokee National Wildlife Refuge, and the Little White House at Warm Springs where President F. D. Roosevelt died in 1945. Georgia is divided into 159 counties:

| County | Area (sq. km.) | Pop. (1990) | County Seat |
|---|---|---|---|
| Appling | 1,326 | 15,740 | Baxley |
| Atkinson | 894 | 6,210 | Pearson |
| Bacon | 744 | 9,570 | Alma |
| Baker | 902 | 3,615 | Newton |
| Baldwin | 668 | 39,530 | Milledgeville |
| Banks | 608 | 10,310 | Horner |
| Barrow | 424 | 29,720 | Winder |
| Bartow | 1,186 | 55,910 | Cartersville |
| Ben Hill | 660 | 16,245 | Fitzgerald |
| Berrien | 1,186 | 14,150 | Nashville |
| Bibb | 658 | 149,970 | Macon |
| Bleckley | 569 | 10,430 | Cochran |
| Brantley | 1,157 | 11,080 | Nahunta |
| Brooks | 1,278 | 15,400 | Quitman |
| Bryan | 1,147 | 15,440 | Pembroke |
| Bulloch | 1,763 | 43,125 | Statesboro |
| Burke | 2,166 | 20,580 | Waynesboro |
| Butts | 486 | 15,330 | Jackson |
| Calhoun | 738 | 5,010 | Morgan |
| Camden | 1,687 | 30,170 | Woodbine |
| Candler | 645 | 7,740 | Metter |
| Carroll | 1,303 | 71,420 | Carrollton |
| Catoosa | 421 | 42,460 | Ringgold |
| Charlton | 2,028 | 8,500 | Folkston |
| Chatham | 1,152 | 216,935 | Savannah |
| Chattahoochee | 650 | 16,930 | Cusseta |
| Chattooga | 814 | 22,240 | Summerville |
| Cherokee | 1,102 | 90,200 | Canton |
| Clarke | 317 | 87,590 | Athens |
| Clay | 519 | 3,360 | Fort Gaines |
| Clayton | 385 | 182,050 | Jonesboro |
| Clinch | 2,135 | 6,160 | Homerville |
| Cobb | 892 | 447,745 | Marietta |
| Coffee | 1,565 | 29,590 | Douglas |
| Colquitt | 1,448 | 33,645 | Moultrie |
| Columbia | 754 | 66,030 | Apping |
| Cook | 606 | 13,460 | Adel |
| Coweta | 1,154 | 53,850 | Newman |
| Crawford | 853 | 8,990 | Knoxville |
| Crisp | 715 | 20,010 | Cordele |
| Dade | 458 | 13,150 | Trenton |
| Dawson | 546 | 9,430 | Dawsonville |
| De Kalb | 702 | 545,840 | Decatur |
| Decatur | 1,524 | 25,510 | Bainbridge |
| Dodge | 1,310 | 17,610 | Eastman |
| Dooly | 1,032 | 9,900 | Vienna |
| Dougherty | 858 | 96,310 | Albany |
| Douglas | 528 | 71,120 | Douglasville |
| Early | 1,342 | 11,850 | Blakely |
| Echols | 1,095 | 2,330 | Statenville |
| Effingham | 1,253 | 25,690 | Springfield |
| Elbert | 954 | 18,950 | Elberton |
| Emanuel | 1,789 | 20,550 | Swainsboro |
| Evans | 484 | 8,720 | Claxton |
| Fannin | 998 | 15,990 | Blue Ridge |
| Fayette | 517 | 62,415 | Fayetteville |
| Floyd | 1,349 | 81,250 | Rome |
| Forsyth | 588 | 44,080 | Cumming |
| Franklin | 686 | 16,650 | Carnesville |
| Fulton | 1,388 | 648,950 | Atlanta |
| Gilmer | 1,110 | 13,370 | Ellijay |
| Glascock | 374 | 2,360 | Gibson |
| Glynn | 1,071 | 62,500 | Brunswick |
| Gordon | 923 | 35,070 | Calhoun |
| Grady | 1,193 | 20,280 | Cairo |
| Greene | 1,011 | 11,790 | Greensboro |
| Gwinnett | 1,131 | 352,910 | Lawrenceville |
| Habersham | 723 | 27,620 | Clarkesville |
| Hall | 985 | 95,430 | Gainesville |
| Hancock | 1,222 | 8,910 | Sparta |
| Haralson | 736 | 21,970 | Buchanan |
| Harris | 1,206 | 17,790 | Hamilton |
| Hart | 598 | 19,710 | Hartwell |
| Heard | 759 | 8,630 | Franklin |
| Henry | 835 | 58,740 | McDonough |
| Houston | 988 | 89,210 | Perry |
| Irwin | 941 | 8,650 | Ocilla |
| Jackson | 889 | 30,005 | Jefferson |
| Jasper | 965 | 8,450 | Monticello |
| Jeff Davis | 871 | 12,030 | Hazelhurst |
| Jefferson | 1,375 | 17,410 | Louisville |
| Jenkins | 918 | 8,250 | Millen |
| Johnson | 796 | 8,330 | Wrightsville |
| Jones | 1,024 | 20,740 | Grey |
| Lamar | 484 | 13,040 | Barnesville |
| Lanier | 504 | 5,530 | Lakeland |
| Laurens | 2,122 | 39,990 | Dublin |
| Lee | 931 | 16,250 | Leesburg |
| Liberty | 1,344 | 52,745 | Hinesville |
| Lincoln | 510 | 7,440 | Lincolnton |
| Long | 1,045 | 6,200 | Ludiwici |
| Lowndes | 1,318 | 75,980 | Valdosta |
| Lumpkin | 746 | 14,570 | Dahlonega |
| McDuffie | 666 | 20,120 | Thomson |
| McIntosh | 1,105 | 8,630 | Darien |
| Macon | 1,050 | 13,110 | Oglethorpe |
| Madison | 741 | 21,050 | Danielsville |
| Marion | 952 | 5,590 | Buena Vista |
| Meriwether | 1,316 | 22,410 | Greenville |
| Miller | 738 | 6,280 | Colquitt |
| Mitchell | 1,331 | 20,275 | Camilla |
| Monroe | 1,032 | 17,110 | Forsyth |
| Montgomery | 634 | 7,160 | Mount Vernon |
| Morgan | 907 | 12,880 | Madison |
| Murray | 897 | 26,150 | Chatsworth |
| Muscogee | 567 | 179,300 | Columbus |
| Newton | 720 | 41,810 | Covington |
| Oconee | 484 | 17,620 | Watkinsville |
| Oglethorpe | 1,149 | 9,760 | Lexington |
| Paulding | 811 | 41,610 | Dallas |
| Peach | 395 | 21,190 | Fort Valley |
| Pickens | 603 | 14,430 | Jasper |
| Pierce | 894 | 13,330 | Blackshear |
| Pike | 569 | 10,220 | Zebulon |
| Polk | 809 | 33,815 | Cedartown |
| Pulaski | 647 | 8,110 | Hawkinsville |
| Putnam | 894 | 14,140 | Eatonton |
| Quitman | 380 | 2,210 | Georgetown |
| Rabun | 962 | 11,650 | Clayton |
| Randolph | 1,121 | 8,020 | Cuthbert |

| Richmond | 848 | 189,720 | Augusta |
|---|---|---|---|
| Rockdale | 343 | 54,090 | Conyers |
| Schley | 439 | 3,590 | Ellaville |
| Screven | 1,703 | 13,840 | Sylvania |
| Seminole | 585 | 9,010 | Donalsonville |
| Spalding | 517 | 54,460 | Griffin |
| Stephens | 460 | 23,260 | Toccoa |
| Stewart | 1,175 | 5,650 | Lumpkin |
| Sumter | 1,271 | 30,230 | Americus |
| Talbot | 1,027 | 6,520 | Talbotton |
| Taliaferro | 510 | 1,915 | Crawfordville |
| Tattnall | 1,258 | 17,720 | Reidsville |
| Taylor | 993 | 7,640 | Butter |
| Telfair | 1,154 | 11,000 | MacRae |
| Terrell | 876 | 10,650 | Dawson |
| Thomas | 1,433 | 38,990 | Thomasville |
| Tift | 697 | 35,000 | Tifton |
| Toombs | 965 | 24,070 | Lyons |
| Towns | 429 | 6,750 | Hiawassee |
| Treutlen | 525 | 5,990 | Soperton |
| Troup | 1,076 | 55,540 | La Grange |
| Turner | 751 | 8,700 | Ashburn |
| Twiggs | 941 | 9,800 | Jeffersonville |
| Union | 832 | 11,990 | Blairsville |
| Upson | 848 | 26,300 | Thomaston |
| Walker | 1,160 | 58,340 | La Fayette |
| Walton | 858 | 38,590 | Monroe |
| Ware | 2,358 | 35,470 | Waycross |
| Warren | 744 | 6,080 | Warrenton |
| Washington | 1,778 | 19,110 | Sandersville |
| Wayne | 1,682 | 22,360 | Jesup |
| Webster | 546 | 2,260 | Preston |
| Wheeler | 777 | 4,900 | Alamo |
| White | 629 | 13,010 | Cleveland |
| Whitfield | 757 | 72,460 | Dalton |
| Wilcox | 993 | 7,010 | Abbeville |
| Wilkes | 1,222 | 10,600 | Washington |
| Wilkinson | 1,173 | 10,230 | Irwinton |
| Worth | 1,495 | 19,745 | Sylvester |

**Georgian Bay** a bay in Ontario, Canada, separated from Lake Huron by the Bruce Peninsula and Manitoulin Island and named after King George IV. Its shores, originally the home of Huron Indians, are now studded with popular holiday resorts such as Owen Sound, Wasaga Beach, Parry Sound, and Collingwood.

**geosphere** /'dʒiːəˌsfɪə(r)/ **1.** the solid surface of the earth. **2.** any of the almost spherical concentric regions of the earth and its atmosphere.

**geostrophic** /ˌdʒiːəʊˈstrɒfɪk/ a meteorological term describing a phenomenon depending upon the rotation of the earth.

**geothermal energy** /ˌdʒiːəʊˈθɜːm(ə)l/ energy originating from, or produced by the internal heat of the earth. Installations for obtaining heat from dry rock or from hot water deep below the earth's surface exist in many parts of the world as alternative energy sources.

**Gera** /'geɪrə/ an industrial city on the Weisse Elster River, Thuringia, east-central Germany; pop. (1991) 126,520. Industries include engineering, food processing, and the manufacture of textiles.

**Geraldton** /'dʒerəldt(ə)n/ a seaport and winter resort 424 km. (267 miles) north of Perth on the west coast of Australia; pop. (1991) 24,360.

**Gerasa** see JERASH.

**German** /'dʒɜːmən/ a Germanic language spoken by some 100 million people mainly in Germany, Austria, and Switzerland, although there are large German-speaking communities in the US. It is the official language of Germany and of Austria, and one of the official languages of Switzerland. **High German** is the variety of Teutonic speech, originally confined to 'High' or southern Germany, now accepted as the literary language of the whole country. Its chief distinctive characteristic is that certain consonants have been altered from their original Teutonic sounds which the other dialects in the main preserve. The spread of this form of the language owes much to the Biblical translations of Martin Luther in the 16th c. **Low German** is the collective name for the dialects of Germany which are not High German. It is spoken in the lowland areas of northern Germany, and is most closely related to Dutch and Friesian.

**German Bight** a shipping forecast area covering the eastern North Sea off the northern Netherlands, Germany, and southern Denmark.

**German Democratic Republic** (*abbr.* **GDR**) see EAST GERMANY

**German East Africa** a former German protectorate in East Africa (1891–1918), corresponding to present-day Tanzania, Rwanda, and Burundi. Conquered by Britain during World War I, it was administered thereafter under League of Nations mandates by Britain and Belgium.

**Germanic** /dʒɜːˈmænɪk/ the branch of Indo-European languages including English, German, Dutch, and the Scandinavian languages. These different languages reflect a dialectal split into West Germanic (English and German), North Germanic (the Scandinavian languages for which the oldest evidence is that of Old Norse), and East Germanic, which has died out but for which Gothic provided the oldest evidence.

**German South West Africa** a former German protectorate in south-west Africa (1884–1918), corresponding to present-day Namibia. Administered by South Africa under a League of Nations mandate until 1968.

**Germany** (German **Deutschland** /'dɔɪtʃlɑːnt/) official name **The Republic of Germany** a country in central Europe stretching northwards from the Alps to the North Sea and the Baltic, and bounded by Denmark, the Netherlands, Belgium, France, Luxembourg,

GERMANY

— State boundary (Länder)
■ Capital city

Kiel

SCHLESWIG-
HOLSTEIN

BREMEN

Hamburg          Schwerin

MECKLENBURG-WEST
POMERANIA

Bremen    HAMBURG

BRANDENBURG

LOWER SAXONY

Hanover          Magdeburg

Berlin

Potsdam    BERLIN

SAXONY-ANHALT

NORTH RHINE-WESTPHALIA

Düsseldorf

SAXONY

Dresden

Erfurt

THURINGIA

HESSE

RHINELAND-
PALATINATE

Wiesbaden

Mainz

Saarbrücken

SAARLAND

Stuttgart

BAVARIA

BADEN-
WÜRTTEMBERG

Munich

Switzerland, Austria, the Czech Republic, and Poland; area 357,000 sq. km. (137,838 sq. miles); pop. (1991) 78,700,000; official language, German; capital, Berlin; seat of government, Bonn. Germany's largest cities are Berlin, Hamburg, Munich, Cologne, Frankfurt, Essen, Dortmund, Düsseldorf, Stuttgart, Leipzig, Bremen, Duisberg, Dresden, and Hanover. A wide northern plain, traversed by navigable rivers such as the Rhine, Elbe, Weser, and Oder, gradually gives way to hills further south and to high alpine mountains along the frontier with Switzerland and Austria. Germany

has a variable temperate climate, with summers marginally the wettest season over much of the country. As one of the world's leading economic powers, Germany has an expanding economy based on its position as a major exporter of chemicals, motor vehicles, iron and steel products, electrical goods, and other manufactured products. German tribes came repeatedly into conflict with the Romans, and after the collapse of the Roman Empire they overran the Rhine which had been its northern frontier. Loosely unified under the Holy Roman Empire during the Middle Ages, the multi-

plicity of small German states achieved real unity only in the mid-19th c. Defeated in World War I, in the 1930s Germany was taken over by the Nazi dictatorship which led her into a policy of expansionism and eventually complete defeat in World War II. After the war Germany was divided into the Federal Republic of Germany (West Germany) and the German Democratic Republic (East Germany). West Germany emerged as a European industrial power within the western defence community, and was a founder member of the EEC, while the East remained to a considerable extent under Soviet domination. After the general collapse of Communism in Eastern Europe towards the end of 1989, East and West Germany reunited on 3 October 1990. Germany is governed by a bicameral parliament headed by a chancellor who is the executive head of government.
**German** *adj. & n.*
The country is divided into 16 federal states (*Länder*):

| State | Area (sq. km.) | Pop. (1991) | Capital |
|---|---|---|---|
| Baden-Württemberg | 35,751 | 10,001,840 | Stuttgart |
| Bavaria | 70,553 | 11,595,970 | Munich |
| Berlin | 883 | 3,446,030 | Berlin |
| Brandenburg | 25,900 | 2,542,720 | Potsdam |
| Bremen | 404 | 683,680 | Bremen |
| Hamburg | 755 | 1,668,760 | Hamburg |
| Hesse | 21,115 | 5,837,330 | Wiesbaden |
| Lower Saxony | 47,438 | 7,457,790 | Hanover |
| Mecklenburg-West Pomerania | 22,887 | 1,891,660 | Schwerin |
| North Rhine-Westphalia | 34,068 | 17,509,870 | Düsseldorf |
| Rhineland-Palatinate | 19,848 | 3,821,235 | Mainz |
| Saarland | 2,569 | 1,076,880 | Saarbrücken |
| Saxony | 17,036 | 5,678,880 | Dresden |
| Saxony-Anhalt | 25,900 | 2,823,320 | Magdeburg |
| Schleswig-Holstein | 15,727 | 2,648,530 | Kiel |
| Thuringia | 15,482 | 2,572,070 | Erfurt |

**Germiston** /ˈdʒɜːmɪstən/ a city in the Transvaal province of South Africa, at the centre of the Witwatersrand gold-mining region to the southeast of Johannesburg; pop. (1980) 155,400. Its refineries produce three-quarters of the Western world's gold bullion.

**Gerona** /xerˈrəʊnə/ an industrial city in the Catalonia region of north-east Spain, on the Oñar River, 88 km. (55 miles) north-east of Barcelona; pop. (1991) 66,800. Founded in pre-Roman times, the town held out against the French during a siege in 1809 that earned it the heroic title of 'immortal Gerona'. It is the capital of a province of the same name and has textile, chemical, and electronics industries.

**Gers** /ʒer/ a department in the Midi-Pyrénées region of south-west France; area 6,254 sq. km. (2,416 sq. miles); pop. (1990) 174,587; capital, Auch.

**Gersoppa Falls** /dʒɜːˈsɒpə/ a cataract on the Sharavati River in the state of Karnataka, southwest India.

**Getafe** /heɪˈtɑːfɪ/ an industrial town at the geographical centre of Spain, 12 km. (7 miles) south of Madrid; pop. (1991) 140,100. Chemicals, agricultural equipment, and motor vehicles are its chief products.

**Gethsemane** /geθˈsemənɪ/, **Garden of** the garden to which Christ went with his disciples after the Last Supper, and which was the scene of his agony and betrayal. It lies in the valley between Jerusalem and the Mount of Olives.

**Gettysburg** /ˈgetɪzˌbɜːg/ a small town in Pennsylvania, USA, scene of a decisive battle of the American Civil War, fought in the first three days of July 1863. The Confederate Army of Northern Virginia, commanded by General Lee, was repulsed in a bloody engagement by the Union Army of the Potomac, commanded by General Meade, forcing Lee to abandon his invasion of the north. The famous Gettysburg address was a speech delivered on 18 November 1863 by President Abraham Lincoln at the dedication of the National Cemetery on the battlefield.

**Gevrey-Chambertin** /ˌʒevreɪ, ʃɑ̃beəˈtæ̃/ a notable wine-producing district in the Côte de Nuits region of Burgundy, central France.

**Geysir** /ˈgeɪzɪr/ (also **Great Geysir**) a hot spring in south-west Iceland which gives its name to the *geyser*, an intermittently gushing hot spring that throws up a tall column of water which occurs in volcanic regions.

**Gezhouba** /gəˈʒuːbə/ a large dam and hydroelectric plant on the Yangtze River, near Yichang in Hubei province, China. With a maximum capacity of 2,715 MW, it came into operation in 1981.

**Ghadamis** /gəˈdɑːmɪs/ (also **Ghadames**) a Saharan oasis in western Libya, near the frontier with Algeria and Tunisia; pop. (1984) 52,200.

**Ghaghara** /ˈgægərə/ (also **Gogra**, Nepalese **Karnali** /kɑːˈnɑːlɪ/) a river that rises in south-west Tibet and flows c.900 km. (570 miles) southwards through Nepal into the state of Uttar Pradesh, India, where it meets the Ganges near Chapra.

**Ghana** /ˈgɑːnə/ official name **The Republic of Ghana** a country of West Africa with its southern coastline bordering on the Atlantic Ocean and lying between the Ivory Coast and Togo, with  Burkina to the north; area 238,537 sq. km. (92,100 sq. miles); pop. (est. 1991) 15,500,000; languages, English (official) and over 50 local dialects; capital, Accra. Ghana's population is concentrated along

the coast, in the northern areas near the Ivory Coast, and in the principal cities which include Accra, Kumasi, and Tamale. The country is generally flat, covered by tropical rainforest, and intersected by rivers which in the east have been dammed to create the great Volta Lake. The climate is tropical with a rainy season in the north from May to Sept. and two distinct rainy seasons in the south during May–June and Aug.–Sept. A dry north-easterly Harmattan wind blows in Jan.–Feb. Ghana is mainly agricultural with 55 per cent of its people engaged in farming. Exports include cocoa, coffee, coconuts, and timber. In the 15th c. it was visited by Portuguese and other European traders, who called it the Gold Coast, and it was a centre of the slave-trade until the 19th c. Britain established control over the area and it became the British colony of Gold Coast in 1874. In 1957 it gained independence as a member-state of the Commonwealth, the first British colony to do so, under the leadership of Dr Kwame Nkrumah, taking the name of Ghana from an important kingdom (said to date from the 4th c.) that had flourished in that region in medieval times. Ghana became a republic in 1960 and experienced a series of military *coups* between 1966 and 1981. Governed as a one-party military state for over a decade, Ghana's military regime relinquished power in 1993 after multiparty elections.
**Ghanaian** *adj. & n.*
Ghana is divided into 10 regions:

| Region | Area (sq. km.) | Pop. (1984) | Capital |
|---|---|---|---|
| Eastern | 19,977 | 1,680,900 | Koforidua |
| Western | 23,921 | 1,157,800 | Sekondi-Takoradi |
| Central | 9,826 | 1,142,300 | Cape Coast |
| Ashanti | 24,390 | 2,090,100 | Kumasi |
| Brong-Ahafo | 39,557 | 1,206,600 | Sunyani |
| Northern | 70,383 | 1,164,600 | Tamale |
| Volta | 20,572 | 1,211,900 | Ho |
| Upper East | 8,842 | 772,700 | Bolgatanga |
| Upper West | 18,477 | 438,000 | Wa |
| Greater Accra | 2,593 | 1,431,100 | Accra |

**Ghardaïa** /gɑːˈdɑːjə/ a market and tourist town in the M'Zab region of northern Algeria, to the south of the Saharan Atlas Mountains on the trans-Saharan caravan route. Once a stronghold of the dissident Islamic *Khawarij* sect, it produces dates and textiles.

**Gharyan** /gɑːˈjæn/ a city in north-west Libya, to the south of Tripoli; pop. (1984) 118,000.

**Ghassanid** /gəˈsɑːnɪd/ a dynasty ruling the Arab kingdom of Ghassan which flourished during the 6th–7th c. in what is now Syria, Jordan, and part of Israel. The Ghassanids, who supported the Byzantines against the Persians, were eventually overthrown by the Muslims in the 7th c.

**ghat** a term used to describe a range of mountains, a river landing, or a mountain pass in India.

**Ghats** /gɔːts, gɑːts/ two mountain ranges in central and southern India that run parallel to the coast on either side of the Deccan Plateau. The **Eastern Ghats** stretch southwards from Orissa to the Nilgiri Hills in the states of Kerala and Tamil Nadu. The **Western Ghats** extend southwards from Maharashtra state to the southern tip of India. At Anai Mudi Peak in the Cardamon Hills the Ghats reach a height of 2,695 m. (8,842 ft.).

**Ghazi** /ˈgɑːzɪ/ the Arab name for a Muslim fighter against non-Muslims.

**Ghaziabad** /ˈgɑːziːəˌbæd/ a market city in the state of Uttar Pradesh, north-central India, to the east of Delhi; pop. (1991) 461,000.

**Ghazni** /ˈgɑːzniː/ a market town in east-central Afghanistan, on the River Ghazni between Kabul and Kandahar; pop. (est. 1984) 33,350. It is capital of a province of the same name, and is known for its sheepskin coats and handicrafts.

**Ghent** /gent/ (Flemish **Gent**, French **Gand** /gɑ̃/) a city and port in west Belgium at the junction of the Leie and Scheldt Rivers; pop. (1991) 230,200. Connected to the North Sea by canals, Ghent is the historic capital of Flanders and capital of the modern Belgian province of East Flanders. It was founded in the 10th c. around a fortress built by the first count of Flanders and became a major centre of wool production in the Middle Ages. In English it was sometimes called Gaunt. With the development of river port facilities and canals in the 19th c. Ghent's trade and industry expanded to include the manufacture of steel, chemicals, vehicles, paper, and food products.

**ghetto** /ˈgetəʊ/ a part of a city, especially a slum area, occupied by a minority group or groups. The term (Italian = foundry) was first applied to a site in Venice in 1516.

**ghibli** an Arabic name for the hot, dry sirocco winds blowing northwards from the Sahara into Libya and Tunisia.

**Ghirardelli Square** /giːrəˈdelɪ/ a square in San Francisco, USA, that became a model for urban renewal in the 1960s. Originally the site of a woollen-mill that later became a chocolate factory, the square was restored between 1962 and 1967 as a modern shopping and restaurant complex.

**Ghor** /gɔː(r)/, **the** a region of the Jordan River valley between the Dead Sea and the Sea of Galilee. Situated between the steep escarpments of the Great Rift Valley, it lies below sea-level.

**Ghulghuleh** SEE BAMIAN.

**Giant's Causeway** a formation of basalt columns dating from the tertiary period on the coast of Antrim, Northern Ireland. It was once believed to be the end of a road made by a legendary giant to Staffa in the Inner Hebrides, where there is a similar formation.

## Gibraltar

/dʒɪˈbrɔːltə(r)/ a British dependency near the southern tip of the Iberian peninsula, at the eastern end of the Strait of Gibraltar; area 5.86 sq. km. (2.26 sq. miles); pop. (1991) 28,075; official languages English and Spanish. Occupying a site of great strategic importance, Gibraltar consists of a fortified town and military base at the foot of a rocky headland (the *Rock of Gibraltar*) 426 m. (1,398 ft.) high. In Arabic the territory is known as Gebel-al-Tarik (= hill of Tarik), taking its name from a Saracen commander of the 8th c. The site has been in British hands since it was captured during the War of the Spanish Succession in 1704 and formally ceded to Britain by the Treaty of Utrecht (1713); Britain is responsible for defence, external affairs, and internal security. Since World War II Spain has pressed her claim to the territory. Remains of what was later called Neanderthal man were first discovered in Gibraltar in 1848 but were not recognized to be this species until the discovery of other remains in the Neander Valley in 1857. Gibraltar is a popular tourist and cruise ship destination.

## Gibraltar, Strait of (Arabic **Bab al Zakak**) a

channel between the southern tip of the Iberian peninsula and North Africa, forming the only outlet of the Mediterranean Sea to the Atlantic. Varying in width from 24km. (15 miles) to 40 km. (25 miles) at its western extremity, it stretches east–west for some 60 km. (38 miles).

## Gibson Desert /ˈgɪbs(ə)n/ a desert region in

Western Australia, situated between the Nullarbor Plain and the Great Sandy Desert. It was named by William Giles after a companion who was lost during an expedition into the desert in 1873.

## Gifu /ˈgiːfuː/ a city in Chubu region, Honshu

Island, central Japan, on the Nagara River northwest of Nagoya; pop. (1990) 410,300. It is the capital of Gifu prefecture and located at the geographic centre of Japan. Devastated by an earthquake in 1891 and during World War II, Gifu is noted for its paper crafts and its 1,000 kg. statue of Buddha made of paper *sutras* (prayers). It is promoted as a convention centre and produces clothes, pharmaceuticals, and cutlery.

## Gigha /ˈgiːæ/ an island in the Inner Hebrides of

Scotland off the west coast of Kintyre. Its chief settlement is Ardminish. The garden at Achamore House, established by Sir James Horlicks after he bought the island in 1944, is noted for its collection of rhododendrons and azaleas.

## Gijón /hiːˈhəʊn/ a port and industrial city of

Asturias in northern Spain, on the Bay of Biscay; pop. (1991) 260,250. In addition to shipbuilding,

fishing, and the manufacture of steel, vehicles, and electrical goods, Gijón is a major outlet for the coal-mines of Asturias.

## Gila /ˈhiːlə/ a river of the US that rises in western

New Mexico and flows 1,014 km. (630 miles) westwards across Arizona to meet the Colorado River at Yuma.

## Gila Cliff Dwellings a national monument in

south-west New Mexico, USA, preserving natural caves in an overhanging volcanic cliff, occupied in the 13th–14th c. by people of the Mogollon Culture.

## Gilbert and Ellice Islands a former British

colony (1915–75) in the central Pacific, consisting of two groups of islands straddling the equator: the Gilbert Islands, now a part of Kiribati, and the Ellice Islands, now Tuvalu.

## Gilbert Islands a group of 17 atolls in the

Pacific Ocean straddling the equator and lying immediately west of the International Date Line; area 264 sq. km. (102 sq. miles); pop. (1985) 29,900. Spread over a distance of 680 km. (428 miles), they form a western group of Kiribati. Thought to have been occupied by Samoans in the 13th c., the Gilbert Islands became a British protectorate in 1892 and a colony (with the Ellice Islands) in 1915. Separated from the Ellice Islands in 1975, they (along with the Phoenix and Line Islands) became part of the independent republic of Kiribati in 1979.

## Gilboa /gɪlˈbəʊə/, Mount (Hebrew **Har Gilboa**)

an arm of the Samarian highlands of Israel rising to 508 m. (1,667 ft.) above sea-level to the northwest of the Jezreel Plain. The Israelites under King Saul were defeated here by the Philistines.

## Gilgit /ˈgɪlgɪt/ 1. a mountainous district in

northern Kashmir between the Indus River and the Wakhan Salient. Administered by Pakistan, it has a largely Muslim population. 2. its capital, a trading and administrative centre that was formerly capital of the Patola dynasty during the 4th–8th centuries and of Dardistan during the 9th–10th centuries.

## Gillingham /ˈdʒɪlɪŋəm/ a residential town in

Kent, England, on the Medway estuary south-east of London; pop. (1981) 93,700.

## Gippsland /ˈgɪpslænd/ a region of south-east

Victoria, Australia, lying to the east of Melbourne between the foothills of the Australian Alps and the sea. Shallow coastal lagoons, known as the **Gippsland Lakes**, are separated from the Bass Strait by the Ninety Mile Beach and associated sand ridges. The region is named after Sir George Gipps, Governor of New South Wales from 1838 to 1846.

## Giresun /ˌgɪrəˈsuːn/ 1. a mountainous province

of Anatolia in northern Turkey, on the southern edge of the Black Sea; area 6,934 sq. km. (2,678 sq. miles); pop. (1990) 499,100. 2. its capital on the Black Sea coast; pop. (1990) 67,600.

**Gironde** /ʒɪˈrɒnd/ a river estuary in Aquitaine, south-west France, formed at the junction of the Garonne and Dordogne rivers north of Bordeaux. It flows north-westwards for 72 km. (45 miles) into the Bay of Biscay between the Médoc and Côtes vineyards.

**Gironde** a department in Aquitaine, south-west France; area 10,000 sq. km. (3,862 sq. miles); pop. (1990) 1,213,500; capital, Bordeaux.

**Gisborne** /ˈgɪzbɜːn/ **1.** a region of North Island, New Zealand, created in 1989; pop. (1991) 44,390. **2.** a seaport and resort on the east coast of North Island, New Zealand, on the north shore of Poverty Bay; pop. (1991) 31,480. Founded as a trading post in the 1800s, the town was named after the Colonial Secretary, William Gisborne (1825–98). Capt. James Cook landed here in 1769. Engineering, fishing, brewing, food processing, and canning are the chief industries.

**Gitega** /giːˈteɪgə/ a town in central Burundi; pop. (1986) 95,300. It was formerly a royal residence.

**Giurgiu** /ˈdʒʊədʒuː/ a port on the Danube and capital of a county of the same name in southern Romania; pop. (1995) 72,275. Founded by Genoese merchants in the 10th c., it produces and trades in chemicals, textiles, processed-food, and timber products.

**Giza** /ˈgiːzə/ (also **El Giza**; Arabic **Al Jizah**) a suburban city south-west of Cairo in northern Egypt, on the west bank of the Nile, site of the Pyramids of Khufu, Khephren, and Menkaure and of the Great Sphinx; pop. (est. 1989) 1,670,800. The pyramid area has been designated a world heritage site by UNESCO.

**Gjirokastër** /gjiːrəʊˈkɑːstə(r)/ (also **Argyrocastro**) a town in southern Albania, on the River Vijosë; pop. (1990) 24,900. It was the birthplace of the former Communist leader of Albania, Enver Hoxha. Tobacco, chemicals, and shoes are produced.

**Glace Bay** /glæs/ a former coal-mining town on Cape Breton Island, Nova Scotia, Canada; pop. (1991) 19,500. Vast deposits of coal (mined until the 1950s) were discovered by the French who named the site after the ice found in the bay during winter. The first west–east transatlantic wireless message was sent from a transmitter at nearby Table Head in 1902.

**glacial period** a period in the earth's history characterized by an unusual extension of polar and mountain ice sheets over the earth's surface. The Pleistocene and the preceding Pliocene epoch included a number of such periods, interrupted by warmer phases called interglacials, and it may be that the climate of the present day represents such a warm phase and that another ice age is to follow. During the coldest time, about 18,000 years ago, extensive ice sheets covered much of Europe, North America, and Asia, and sea-levels were as much as 200 m. lower than they are today. In the southern hemisphere glaciation was less extensive owing to the isolation of the Antarctic ice sheet from the other southern continents. Although the glacial periods of the Pleistocene epoch are the most important in terms of their effect upon present-day topography, there is evidence of earlier glaciations in Palaeozoic and Precambrian times. Their causes are not fully understood but it is thought that their onset may be affected by the position of the continents relative to the pole and by variations in the brightness of the sun.

**glacier** /ˈglæsɪə(r)/ a mass of moving land ice formed by the accumulation of snow on high ground and in polar regions. Glacier ice can be a powerful agent of erosion, cutting deep valleys, plucking blocks of rock from the ground, and smoothing rock surfaces by abrading or breaking off small fragments. Glacial deposits formed when ice melts create distinct landforms that range from sediments of glacial till covering extensive areas of land to ridge and hill features such as moraines, drumlins, and eskers.

**Glacier Bay National Park** a national park on the Pacific coast of south-east Alaska, USA, at the terminus of the Grand Pacific Glacier. Designated a national monument in 1925 and a national park in 1980, it extends over an area of 12,880 sq. km. (4,975 sq. miles). Glacier ice recedes here more rapidly than anywhere else on earth.

**Glacier National Park** **1.** a national park established in 1886 in the northern Selkirk Range of the Columbia Mountains, British Columbia, Canada. Over 400 glaciers and glacier-fed lakes are fed by constant rain in the summer and daily snowfalls in the winter. The Rogers Pass (1,327 m., 4,355 ft.), which forms part of the Trans-Canada Highway running through the park, was discovered in 1881 by Major A. J. Rogers in search of a route over the mountains. Mountain goat, caribou, black bear, and grizzly bear are found in the park which covers an area of 1,350 sq. km. (520 sq. miles). **2.** a national park on the US–Canada frontier in Montana and Alberta. Established in 1910 as the Waterton-Glacier International Peace Park, it covers an area of 4,100 sq. km. (1,584 sq. miles) and is home to bighorn sheep, grizzly bears, deer, mountain goats, moose, and elk.

**glaciology** /ˌgleɪsɪˈɒlədʒɪ/ the science of the internal dynamics and effects of glaciers.

**Gladstone** /ˈglædstən/ an industrial deep-water port on the coast of Queensland, eastern Australia, south-east of Rockhampton; pop. (1991) 23,460. It was founded as a colony in 1847 by W. E. Gladstone who was then Secretary of State for the Colonies and is now a major centre for the processing of bauxite and an outlet for coal, minerals, and agricultural produce. There is an annual Brisbane to Gladstone yacht race.

**Glamis** a village in the Strathmore valley, Angus, north-east Scotland adjacent to which is Glamis Castle, home of the family of the earls of Strathmore since 1372. Glamis Castle was the childhood home of Queen Elizabeth the Queen Mother and the birthplace of Princess Margaret.

**Glarner Alps** /'glɑːnə(r)/ (German **Glarner Alpen**) a range of the central European Alps in north-east Switzerland between Lake Lucerne and the Rhine. The face of Glärnisch (2,914 m., 9,560 ft.) is one of the highest and steepest in the Alps, rising 1,980 m. (6,496 ft.) at an angle of 45°.

**Glarus** /'glɑːrəs/ (French **Glaris**) an ancient town in north-east Switzerland at the foot of Glärnisch in the northern Glarner Alps; pop. (1980) 5,800. It is capital of Glarus canton. Ulrich Zwingli, the Protestant reformer, was priest here from 1506 to 1515.

**Glasgow** /'glæsgəʊ/ the largest city in Scotland; pop. (1991) 654,500. Situated on the River Clyde, the city owes its growth successively to the tobacco, cotton, iron and steel, and shipbuilding industries. Although these industries are no longer of major significance, Glasgow has remained an important commercial and cultural centre with attractions that include the Glasgow School of Art, product of Charles Rennie Mackintosh the art nouveau designer and architect, the Burrell Collection, Kelvingrove Art Gallery and Museum, the Hunterian Museum, Provands Lordship (the oldest house in Glasgow), and Glasgow Cathedral (12th c.). It is the site of the University of Glasgow (1451), the University of Strathclyde (1964), and the Queen's University, and the headquarters of the Royal Scottish Geographical Society. The city has undergone a massive programme of slum clearance and road building. It has numerous light industries including electronics, carpets, textiles, printing, chemicals, and tourism
**Glaswegian** *adj. & n.*

**Glastonbury** /'glæstənbərɪ/ a town in Somerset, England; pop. (1981) 6,770. It is the legendary burial place of King Arthur and Queen Guinevere and the site of a ruined abbey held by legend to have been founded by Joseph of Arimathea. It was also identified in medieval times with the mythical Avalon. It has a leather industry making sheepskin products.

**Glaswegian** /glæz'wiːdʒən, glɑːz-/ a native or citizen of the city of Glasgow in Scotland.

**glen** the Scottish word for a narrow valley.

**Glencoe** /glen'kəʊ/ a glen in the Scottish Highlands to the south-east of Fort William, scene of the massacre in 1692 of Jacobite Macdonald clansmen by Campbell soldiers acting for the government of William III. While this massacre has often been considered a particularly foul violation of the rules of Highland hospitality in continuation of the long-standing feud between the Campbells and the Macdonalds, it was in fact a deliberate government

attempt to make an example of one of the most notorious Jacobite clans, badly botched by the men on the spot (who killed less than a third of about 140 intended victims).

**Glendale** **1.** a city in south-central Arizona, USA, to the north-west of Phoenix; pop. (1990) 148,100. Luke Air Force Base is nearby. **2.** a city in the San Fernando Valley, south-west California, USA, forming a residential suburb to the north of Los Angeles; pop. (1990) 180,000.

**Glendalough** /glen'dɑːləx/ a valley in County Wicklow, the Republic of Ireland, with several religious buildings (Kevin's Cell, Reefert Church, The Church of the Rock, St. Mary's Church, and St. Kevin's Church) associated with St. Kevin who lived as a hermit here in the 6th–7th c. Named after its two lakes, it became a famous centre of learning in the 7th c.

**Gleneagles** /glen'iːg(ə)lz/ a glen in Perthshire, Scotland, near the village of Auchterarder, site of a noted hotel and golfing centre.

**Glen Fiddich** /glen'fɪdɪx/ a glen in the Grampians of northern Scotland to the south of Dufftown near which is the Glenfiddich whisky distillery.

**Glen Finnan** /glen'fɪnən/ a glen in the Lochaber district of Highland Region, Scotland. At the head of Loch Shiel is a monument commemorating the raising of Prince Charles Edward Stuart's standard at the beginning of the second Jacobite rebellion in 1745.

**Glen Garry** /glen'gærɪ/ a glen in the Scottish Highlands to the north of Fort William, extending westwards from the Great Glen to Loch Quoich. To the south of Loch Garry, Ben Tee rises to a height of 901 m. (2,956 ft.) in the Glengarry deer forest. The glengarry, brimless Scottish hat with a cleft down the centre and two ribbons hanging down the back, takes its name from this locality.

**Glenlivet** /glen'lɪvɪt/ a glen in the Grampians of northern Scotland, to the north-east of Tomintoul.

**Glenmore** a glen in the Scottish Highlands between the River Spey and the Cairngorm Mountains. It links the resort town of Aviemore with the Cairngorm ski slopes and includes Loch Morlich and the Glen More Forest Park.

**Glen More** see GREAT GLEN.

**Glenrothes** /glen'rɒθəs/ a town in central Fife, east Scotland, capital of Fife region; pop. (1981) 33,000. Designated a New Town in 1948, its industries include light engineering and the manufacture of clothing, paper, and electronics.

**Glen Roy** /glen'rɔɪ/ a glen in the Scottish Highlands to the north-east of Fort William noted for its 'Parallel Roads' which are terraces marking successive shore lines of an ice-dammed lake formed during the Ice Age.

**Glen Shee** /glen ʃiː/ a glen with winter skiing facilities in the eastern Grampian Mountains of

Scotland, between Blairgowrie and Braemar, in the upper valley of the Shee Water.

**Glen Trool** /glen truːl/ a national forest park to the north of Newton Stewart in south-west Scotland.

**Glenveagh** /glenˈveɪ/ a picturesque valley with a lake in County Donegal, the Republic of Ireland, to the south of the Derryveagh range.

**Glittertind** /ˈɡlɪtə(r)tɪn/ a mountain in the Jotunheim range of south-central Norway. Rising to a height of 2,472 m. (8,110 ft.), it is the highest peak in both Norway and Scandinavia.

**Gliwice** /ɡliːˈviːtsɪ/ a coal-mining and industrial city in the Katowice region of southern Poland, near the border with the Czech Republic; pop. (1990) 214,200. Its industries include steel, machinery, and chemicals.

**globe** /ɡləʊb/, **the** a name given to the planet earth or to a spherical representation of the earth (terrestrial globe) or of the constellations (celestial globe) with a map on the surface. The earliest globe was probably constructed by the Greek geographer Crates of Mallus in the 2nd c. BC, and the first globes of modern times were made in the 15th–16th c. by Leonardo da Vinci, Martin Behaim of Nuremberg, and Willem Blaeu.

**global warming** an increase in temperature of the earth's atmosphere attributed to the GREEN-HOUSE EFFECT.

**Globe Theatre** the Burbages's theatre at Bankside in Southwark, London, erected in 1599 with materials from the old theatre on the north side of the river. It was a large thatched circular building, with the centre open to the sky, and was used only during the summer months. The thatch caught fire in 1613 from a discharge of stage gunfire during a play, and the whole building was destroyed. It was rebuilt in 1614 and was in constant use until all the London theatres were closed on the outbreak of the Civil War in 1642. Shakespeare had a share in the theatre and acted there.

**Glomach** /ˈɡləʊmæx/, **Falls of** a waterfall in north-west Scotland, on a tributary of the River Elchaig; height 113 m. (370 ft.).

**Glomma** /ˈɡləʊmæ/ (also **Glåma**) the longest river in Norway, rising in south-east Norway and flowing southwards for c. 590 km. (365 miles) to the Skagerrak at Frederikstad.

**Gloucester** /ˈɡlɒstə(r)/ an ancient city in south-west England, the county town of Gloucestershire, situated on the River Severn north-east of Bristol; pop. (1991) 91,800. It has a major aircraft industry. Gloucester was founded by the Romans, who called it Glevum, in AD 96. Its Norman cathedral contains the tomb of King Edward II and a cross commemorates Bishop Hooper, martyred in 1555. The Three Choirs Music Festival takes place every three years at Gloucester.

**Gloucestershire** /ˈɡlɒstəˌʃɪə(r)/ a county of south-west England; area 2,643 sq. km. (1,021 sq. miles); pop. (1991) 520,600; county town, Gloucester. It gives its name to a kind of hard cheese originally made in Gloucestershire. The county is divided into six districts:

| District | Area (sq. km.) | Pop. (1991) |
|---|---|---|
| Cheltenham | 34 | 85,900 |
| Cotswold | 1,143 | 73,000 |
| Forest of Dean | 528 | 74,200 |
| Gloucester | 33 | 91,800 |
| Stroud | 454 | 108,300 |
| Tewkesbury | 450 | 87,400 |

**Glyndebourne** /ˈɡlaɪndbɔːn/ an estate near Lewes in Sussex, England, where an annual festival of opera is held. Rebuilt in 1994, the original opera house was built by the owner of the estate, John Christie (d. 1962), who founded the festival in 1934 to stage ideal performances in a beautiful setting. The inspiration for the enterprise was his wife, the soprano Audrey Mildmay. Nearby is the village of Glynde.

**GMT** *abbr.* GREENWICH MEAN TIME.

**Gneizeno** /ˈnjeznəʊ/ an ancient town in Poznan county, west-central Poland; pop. (1990) 70,400. It was the first capital of Poland, allegedly founded by a chief of the Polanie tribe after sighting a nesting white eagle there. The kings of Poland were crowned at Gneizeno until 1320 and the archbishops of Gneizeno acted as Protectors of Poland until the early 19th c. The city was part of Prussia from 1793 until 1919. It has light industries.

**gnamma** /ˈnæmə/ (also **namma**) an Australian Aborigine word for a waterhole or a natural hole in a rock, containing water.

**Goa** /ˈɡəʊə/ a state on the west coast of India; area 3,702 sq. km. (1,430 sq. miles); pop. (1991) 1,168,600; capital, Panaji. Formerly a Portuguese territory, it was seized by India in 1961, and together with two other Portuguese territories, Daman and Diu, formed a Union Territory of India until it achieved separate statehood in 1987. Goa's population is racially mixed and predominantly Catholic. St. Francis Xavier is buried in its baroque cathedral which, together with colonial churches and convents, are world heritage monuments. The state's main industrial products are pharmaceuticals, clothing, footwear, pesticides, and fishing nets. Tourism is of major importance. **Goan** or **Goanese** *adj. & n.*

**Goajiro** /ɡwæˈhiːrəʊ/ an Arawakan Indian people of northern Colombia and Venezuela.

**Goat Fell** /ɡəʊtˈfel/ a mountain rising to 874 m. (2,866 ft.), north-west of Brodick on the Scottish island of Arran.

**Gobi Desert** /ˈɡəʊbɪ/ a barren plateau of southern Mongolia and northern China, extending over an area of *c.* 1,295,000 sq. km. (500,200 sq. miles). Its name means 'Stony desert'.

**Godalming** /ˈgɒdɔːmɪŋ/ a residential town in Surrey, south-east England, on the River Wey 7 km. (4 miles) south-west of Guildford; pop. (1981) 18,900. The town is noted for its old almshouses, its town hall (1814), and its Norman church.

**Godavari** /gəʊˈdɑːvərɪ/ a river in central India which rises in the state of Maharashtra at the northern end of the Western Ghats and flows *c.* 1,440 km. (900 miles) south-east across the Deccan plateau to the Bay of Bengal. To the Hindus it is a holy river.

**Godhavn** /ˈgəʊdhaʊn, ˈgɒ-/ a town in western Greenland, on the south coast of the island of Disco; pop. (1992) 1,185. It is a fishing base and has an Arctic research station.

**Godthåb** /ˈgɒthɔːb/ (also **Godthaab**) the former Danish name, until 1979, of NUUK, capital of Greenland.

**Godoy Cruz** /gəˌdɔɪ ˈkruːz/ a city to the south of Mendoza in the province of Mendoza, western Argentina; pop. (1991) 179,500. It is a centre of wine production.

**Godwin-Austen** /ˌgɒdwɪn ˈɔːstɪn/, **Mount** see K2.

**Gog and Magog** /gɒg, ˈmeɪgɒg/ **1.** the names of various people and lands in the Old Testament. **2.** nations under the dominion of Satan (Rev. 20: 8), opposed to the people of God. **3.** (in medieval legend) opponents of Alexander the Great, living north of the Caucasus. **4.** the names given to two giant statues standing in Guildhall, London, from the time of Henry V (destroyed in 1666 and 1940; replaced in 1953), either (according to Caxton) the last two survivors of a race of giants inhabiting Britain before Roman times, or (in another account) Gogmagog, chief of the giants, and Corineus, a Roman invader.

**Gogo** /ˈgəʊgəʊ/ (also **Wagogo**) a Bantu-speaking people of central Tanzania.

**Gogra** see GHAGHARA.

**Goiânia** /gəʊˈjɑːnjə/ the capital of the state of Goiás in west-central Brazil, at the centre of a rice-growing, cattle-raising, and mining area; pop. (1990) 998,500. Founded as a new city in 1933, it succeeded Goiás Velho as state capital in 1942.

**Goiás** a state in west-central Brazil to the south of the River Tocantins; area 372,181 sq. km. (143,755 sq. miles); pop. (1990) 4,516,000; capital, Goiânia. In addition to cattle, rice, and coffee, the state produces minerals such as gold, nickel, manganese, and tin.

**Goidel** /ˈgɔɪd(e)l/ a member of the Gaelic people that comprise the Scots, Irish, and Manx Celts. **Goidelic** *adj. & n.*

**göl** /gəl/ (also **gölu** /gəlˈjuː/) a Turkish word for a lake.

**Golan Heights** /gəʊˈlɑːn/ a range of hills on the border between Syria and Israel, north-east of the Sea of Galilee. Formerly under Syrian control, the area was occupied by Israel in 1967 and annexed in 1981; pop. (1983) 19,700.

**Golconda** /gɒlˈkɒndə/ an ancient ruined fort 8 km. (5 miles) west of Hyderabad in Andhra Pradesh, south-central India. It was the capital (1512–90) of one of the five Muslim kingdoms of the Deccan. The tombs of the Qutab Shahi kings lie to the north of the citadel fort which stands on a granite hill 120 m. (394 ft.) high. Golconda, once famous for its diamonds, lends its name to a word describing any mine or source of wealth, advantages, etc.

**Gold** /gəʊld/ the name given to part of the Normandy beaches of France where Allied troops (the British 50th Division) landed on 6 June 1944. There are remains of the Mulberry artificial harbour at Arromanches-les-Bains.

**Gold Coast 1.** the former name (until 1957) of GHANA. **2.** a resort region on the east coast of Australia between Brisbane and Sydney; pop. (1991) 256,275.

**Golden Chersonese** /ˈkɜːsəˌniːs/, **the** a name formerly given to the Malay peninsula and arising from a line in Milton's *Paradise Lost*: 'Thence to Agra and Lahor of Great Mogul, down to the golden Chersonese'.

**Golden Gate** a deep channel connecting San Francisco Bay with the Pacific, spanned by a suspension bridge completed in 1937. It was named during the gold-rush of 1849.

**Golden Horde, the** see KIPCHAK EMPIRE.

**Golden Horn, the** (Turkish **Haliç** /hɑːˈliːtʃ/) a curved inlet of the Bosporus, separating the northern and southern districts of of Istanbul, Turkey. It is crossed by the Galata, Ataturk, and Haliç bridges and forms a natural harbour 8 km. (5 miles) in length.

**Golden Isles** a chain of subtropical resort islands off the Atlantic coast of Georgia, USA. Stretching from Savannah southwards to Brunswick, they include Sea Island, St. Simon's Island, and Jekyll Island.

**Golden Mile, the 1.** a name given to the gold-bearing reef that stretches 5 km. (2 miles) from Kalgoorlie to Boulder in Western Australia. **2.** a name given to the sea front at the resort town of Blackpool in north-west England.

**Golden Sands** (Bulgarian **Zlatni Pyasutsi** /ˌzlætnɪ pjəˈsʊtsɪ/) a modern resort town and conference centre in eastern Bulgaria, situated on the Black Sea north-east of Varna.

**Golgotha** /ˈgɒlgəθə/ the Hebrew name of Calvary near Jerusalem where the crucifixion of Jesus took place (Hebrew *Gulgoleth* = skull).

**Gomati** /ˈgɑːmətiː/ (also **Gumti**) a river of northern India rising in Uttar Pradesh in the foothills of the Himalayas and flowing *c.* 800 km. (500 miles) south-east past Lucknow to meet the Ganges below Varanasi.

**Gomel** /ˈɡəʊm(ə)l/ see HOMYEL.

**Gomera** /ɡəʊˈmɜːrə/ an island in the Atlantic to the west of Tenerife, one of the Canary Islands; area 378 sq. km. (146 sq. miles); chief port and settlement, San Sebastián. It lies in the Spanish province of Santa Cruz de Tenerife and its highest point is the Alto de Garajonay (1,375 m., 4,501 ft.) at the centre of the island.

**Gómez Palacio** /ˈɡəʊmez pəˈlɑːsɪəʊ/ a city in the state of Durango, northern Mexico, situated on the railway from Mexico City to El Paso, midway between the Sierra Madre Occidental and the Sierra Madre Oriental; pop. (1990) 232,550. It trades in wheat and cotton.

**Gomorrah** /ɡəˈmɒrə/ a town of ancient Palestine, probably south of the Dead Sea, destroyed by fire from heaven (according to Genesis 19: 24), along with Sodom, for the wickedness of its inhabitants.

**Gonaïves** /ˌɡəʊnəˈiːv/ a port on the Gulf of Gonâve and capital of the department of L'Artibonite, western Haiti; pop. (1982) 34,200. The independence of Haiti from France was declared here on 1 January 1804.

**Gond** /ɡɒnd/ a culturally diverse people of central India numbering *c.* 3,000,000 in the states of Madhra Pradesh, Andhra Pradesh, Orissa, and Maharashtra.
**Gondi** *adj. & n.*

**Gondar** /ˈɡɒndɜː/ (also **Gonder**) a town in northern Ethiopia to the north of Lake Tana; pop. (est. 1984) 68,950. It was a centre of Christian culture and capital of Ethiopia from 1732 till 1855.

**Gondia** /ˈɡɑːndɪə/ (also **Gondiya**) a town in Maharashtra, central India, north-east of Nagpur; pop. (1991) 109,270.

**Gondwana** /ɡɒnˈdwaːnə/ (also **Gondwana-land**) a vast continental area thought to have once existed in the southern hemisphere and to have broken up in Mesozoic or late Palaeozoic times to form Arabia, Africa, South America, Antarctica, Australia, and peninsular India. (*Gondwana* = land of the Gonds, a Dravidian people of central India.) See also CONTINENTAL DRIFT.

**Good Hope, Cape of** see CAPE OF GOOD HOPE.

**Goodwin Sands** /ˈɡuːdwɪn/ an area of sandbanks in the Strait of Dover, off the coast of south-east England. Often exposed at low tide, the sandbanks are a hazard to shipping.

**Goodwood** /ˈɡuːdwʊd/ a racecourse near Chichester in West Sussex, south-east England, at the north end of Goodwood Park. It is the scene of an annual summer race-meeting. Nearby Goodwood House was built in 1739 by the Earl of Richmond.

**Goonhilly Downs** an area of barren uplands on the Lizard Peninsula in Cornwall, south-west England. The area is noted for its many ancient earthworks and modern satellite tracking station with its prominent communications transmitter-receiver .

**Goose Bay** a settlement in south-east Labrador, Canada, at the mouth of the Hamilton River on Goose Bay, an inlet of Lake Melville. A military airbase established here during World War II was later developed as a facility for transatlantic commercial aircraft.

**Gorakhpur** /ˈɡɔːrək͵pʊə(r)/ an industrial city in Uttar Pradesh, north-east India, on the River Rapti near the border with Nepal; pop. (1991) 490,000. Founded in 1400, it was named after a Hindu deity. Railway engineering and the production of paper, textiles, and Hindu literature are its chief industries.

**Gorazde** /ɡɒˈræʒdə/ a predominantly Muslim town in eastern Bosnia-Herzegovina, on the River Drina south-east of Sarajevo. Despite being declared a safe haven by the UN, it was the subject of a prolonged siege by Bosnian Serbs during 1993–4.

**Gorbals** /ˈɡɔːb(ə)lz/, **the** a district on the south bank of the River Clyde in the city of Glasgow, Scotland, originally laid out as an elegant residential area by wealthy 18th-c. merchants, but noted by the 1920s for its slums which housed the workforce for the former Clydeside shipbuilding and engineering industries. Its notorious poverty and street life featured in the novels of several writers including Alexander McArthur (*No Mean City*) and Jeff Torrington (*Swing Hammer Swing*). In more recent times it has been the focus of urban regeneration schemes such as the building of 24-storey tower blocks (designed by Sir Basil Spence) in the 1960s and their replacement with low-rise housing in the 1980s and 1990s.

**Gordium** /ˈɡɔːdɪəm/ an ancient city of Asia Minor, the capital of Phrygia in the 8th and 9th c. BC. According to Greek legend the city was founded by King Gordius, who tied the knot cut by Alexander the Great during his expedition of 334 BC. The city, now in ruins, lies beside the River Sakarya in north-west Turkey 80 km. (50 miles) west of Ankara.

**Gordon** /ˈɡɔːdən/ a district of Grampian Region, north-east Scotland from 1975 to 1996; area 2,214 sq. km. (855 sq. miles); pop. (1991) 74,000. Its chief town is Inverurie.

**Gordonstoun** /ˈɡɔːdənstən/ a school 6 km. (4 miles) west of Lossiemouth in north-east Scotland. The Duke of Edinburgh and Prince Charles were educated here.

**Göreme** /ˈɡɜːriːmɪ/ a valley in Cappadocia in central Turkey, noted for its cave-dwellings. Originally the name was applied to a larger area which was a major centre of early Christianity; in the Byzantine era it contained hermits' cells, monasteries, and over 400 churches, all hollowed out of the soft tufa rock.

**Gorgan** /gəʊrˈgɑːn/ (also **Gurgan**) a town in the province of Mazandaran in northern Iran, in the north-eastern foothills of the Elburz Mountains; pop. (1991) 162,000. Formerly known as Asterabad, it is the terminus of the railway linking Tehran with the Caspian provinces.

**gorge** /ˈgɔːdʒ/ a narrow opening between hills or a rocky ravine, often with a stream running through it.

**Gorgio** /ˈgɔːdʒɪˌəʊ/ the Romany name for a non-gypsy.

**Gorgonzola** /ˌgɔːgənˈzəʊlə/ a village in Lombardy, northern Italy, 18 km. (11 miles) north-east of Milan, famous for its rich Strachino or Gorgonzola cheese with bluish-green veins; pop. (1990) 16,190.

**Gorizia** /gɔːˈriːtsɪə/ (German **Görz** /gɜːts/) a town in north-east Italy, 35 km. (22 miles) north-west of Trieste. It is capital of the province of Gorizia in Friuli-Venezia Giulia region and is situated at the easternmost point of Italy; pop. (1990) 39,000. It is a commercial and tourist centre with light industries.

**Gorky** /ˈgɔːkɪ/ the former name (1932–91) of the Russian city of NIZHNIY NOVGOROD.

**Görlitz** /ˈgɜːlɪts/ an industrial town in Saxony, eastern Germany, on the River Neisse east of Dresden; pop. (1991) 70,450. It is situated on the Polish border. Its industries include railway equipment, machinery, textiles, and precision instruments.

**Gorlovka** /gɜːrˈlɒfkə/ an industrial city in the Donets Basin, south-east Ukraine, 45 km. northeast of Donetsk; pop. (1990) 337,900. Mining, engineering, and the manufacture of chemicals and fertilizers are the chief industries.

**Gorno-Altaisk** /ˌgɔːnəʊælˈtaɪsk/ the capital of the Republic of Gorno-Altai in Siberian Russia, on the Katun River; pop. (1990) 39,000. It was known as Ulala until 1932 and Oirot-Tura 1932–48.

**Gorno-Altai** /ˌgɔːnəʊælˈtaɪ/ (also **Gornyy-Altay**) a republic of the Russian Federation in Siberia on the frontier with Mongolia; area 92,600 sq. km. (35,740 sq. miles); pop. (1989) 192,000; capital, Gorno-Altaisk. Established as the Oirot Autonomous Region in 1922, its name was changed in 1948. After the breakup of the Soviet Union it was declared a republic of the Russian Federation in 1992. Cattle-farming, timber production, and the mining of gold, mercury, and coal are the chief industries.

**gorod** /gəˈrɒd/ a Russian word for a city.

**Goroka** /gɜːˈrɒkə/ the commercial centre of the Eastern Highlands of central Papua New Guinea; pop. (est. 1985) 11,000.

**Gort** /gɔːt/ a village in County Galway, the Republic of Ireland, 24 km. (15 miles) south-east of Loughrea. Its ruined palace was the residence of the 7th c. king of Connaught, Guaire. Ballylea

Castle to the north-east was once the home of W. B. Yeats.

**Gorzów Wielkopolski** /ˈgɔːzuːf ˌvjelkəˈpɒlskɪ/ (German **Landsberg**) a market town and port on the River Warta, capital of the Polish county of Gorzów; pop. (1990) 124,300. It has chemical and light industries.

**Gosainthan** /ˌgəʊsaɪnˈtɑːn/ (also Shishma Pangma) a mountain peak of the Himalayas in southern Tibet near the Nepal frontier. Rising to 8,012 m. (26,287 ft.), it is the only 8,000 m. peak in China. Its summit was first reached in 1964.

**Gosport** /ˈgɒspɔːt/ a residential town and former naval base in Hampshire, southern England, at the entrance to Portsmouth Harbour; pop. (1981) 70,700.

**Gosse Bluff** /gɒs/ a rock-rimmed crater in Northern Territory, central Australia, to the west of Alice Springs, said to have been gouged out by the impact of a meteorite 130 million years ago.

**Göteborg** see GOTHENBURG.

**Goth** /gɒθ/ a member of a Germanic tribe that invaded the Roman Empire from the east between the 3rd and 5th centuries. The eastern half of the tribe, the Ostrogoths, eventually founded a kingdom in Italy, while the Visigoths, their western cousins, went on to found one in Spain.
**Gothic** adj. & n.

**Gotha** /ˈgəʊtə/ a city in the German state of Thuringia, 24 km. (15 miles) west of Erfurt; pop. (1981) 57,600. Founded in the 12th c., it was the former residence of the dukes of Saxony-Gotha and Saxe-Coburg-Gotha. Textiles, chemicals, and precision instruments are manufactured.

**Gotham** /ˈgɒθəm/ a village in Nottinghamshire, England, 10 km. (6 miles) north of Loughborough, associated with the English folk-tale of the *Wise Men of Gotham* in which the inhabitants of the village demonstrated cunning by feigning stupidity.

**Gothenburg** /ˈgɒθənˌbɜːg/ (Swedish **Göteburg** /ˈjɜːtəˌbɔːr/) a seaport in south-west Sweden, on the Kattegat at the mouth of the River Göta; pop. (1990) 433,000. It is the second-largest city in Sweden and capital of Göteborg och Bohus county. Shipbuilding, engineering, and the manufacture of chemicals and vehicles are its chief industries.

**Gothic** /ˈgɒθɪk/ a language which constitutes the oldest manuscript evidence for the Germanic language group. It belongs to the East Germanic group and was spoken in the area to the north and west of the Black Sea. The evidence is fragmentary, the main text being part of a Gothic translation of the Greek Bible written in the 4th century by Bishop Wulfila.

**Gotland** /ˈgɒtlənd/ an island of Sweden, in the Baltic Sea. The county of Gotland also includes the islands of Fårö and Karlsö; area 3,140 sq. km. (1,213 sq. miles); pop. (1990) 57,100; capital, Visby.

Held successively by Sweden and Denmark, and once the haunt of pirates, Gotland has been part of Sweden since 1645. The cement industry and tourism are important.

**Göttingen** /'gɜ:tɪŋən/ a historic university town in Lower Saxony, north-central Germany, on the River Leine; pop. (1991) 124,000. It has many unspoilt old buildings and a university founded in 1734 by the Elector George Augustus (later King George II of Britain). Max Planck (1858–1947), formulator of the quantum theory, is buried in the city which is the headquarters of the Max Planck Society. Its light industries include optical and precision instruments.

**Gottwaldov** /'gɑ:tvəldəf/ the former name of ZLIN (1948–90) in the Czech Republic.

**Gouda** /'gaʊdə/ a market town in the Dutch province of South Holland, 15 km. (9 miles) northeast of Rotterdam, noted for its cheese and its stained-glass windows; pop. (1991) 65,900.

**Gough Island** /'gɑ:f/ a small uninhabited island to the south of Tristan da Cunha in the South Atlantic. In 1938 it became a dependency of the British Crown Colony of St. Helena. Because of its scientific interest it was declared a world heritage site by UNESCO.

**Goulburn** /'gəʊlbɜ:n/ **1.** a river in Victoria, Australia that rises in the Australian Alps c. 130 km. (80 miles) north-east of Melbourne and flows north-westwards for 445 km. (280 miles) to the Murray River. Named after Henry Goulburn (1784–1856), Under-Secretary for the Colonies (1812–21), much of its water is used to irrigate farmland in Victoria. **2.** a wool-market town in New South Wales, south-eastern Australia, on the Hume Highway 210 km. (132 miles) south-west of Sydney; pop. (1991) 21,450.

**Gourniá** /'gu:rnɪə/ the ruins of an ancient Minoan town on a hill overlooking the Bay of Mirabéllo on the north-east coast of the Mediterranean island of Crete. Lying 18.5 km. (11.5 miles) south-east of Ayios Nikólaos, it has a well-preserved street plan that was extensively excavated during 1901–4 to reveal evidence of occupation from the 3rd millenium BC.

**Gourock** /'gu:rək/ a town and ferry port on the south shore of the Firth of Clyde, central Scotland; pop. (1981) 11,200.

**Gove Peninsula** /'gəʊv/ a peninsula at the north-eastern extremity of Arnhem Land in the Aboriginal Land of Northern Territory, Australia. Its chief settlements are Nhulunbuy and Yirrkala. It is named after W. H. J. Gove, an Australian airman killed here in World War II.

**Gower** /'gaʊər/ a limestone peninsula on the coast of south Wales, projecting into the Bristol Channel between Swansea Bay and Carmarthen Bay, and a popular holiday resort.

**Gozo** /'gəʊzəʊ/ (Maltese **Ghaudex** /'gaʊdeʃ/) one of the three main islands of Malta, situated north-west of the island of Malta; area 67 sq. km. (26 sq. miles); pop. (1987) 25,160 (with Comino).

**graben** /'grɑ:bən/ a rift valley or depression of the earth's surface between faults.

**Graceland** /'greɪslænd/ a mansion house in Memphis in the US state of Tennessee, maintained as a museum to the memory of the rock singer Elvis Presley (1935–77) who lived there and was buried in the adjacent Meditation Gardens.

**Gracias a Dios** /'grɑ:sɪˌɑ:s ɑ: 'di:ɒs/, **Cape** the easternmost extremity of the Mosquito Coast in Central America, on the border between Nicaragua and Honduras. The cape was named by Columbus who, in 1502, had been becalmed off the coast but was able to continue his voyage with the arrival of a following wind. (Spanish = thanks (be) to God.)

**Graeco-** /'gri:kəʊ/ (also **Greco**) of or relating to Greece or the Greeks; used in combination with other words such as Graeco-Roman.

**Grafton** /'græftən/ a town in north-east New South Wales, Australia, on the River Clarence, famous for its jacaranda trees; pop. (1991) 16,640.

**Graham Land** /'greɪəm/ the northern part of the Antarctic Peninsula, the only part of the Antarctic continent lying outside the Antarctic Circle. Discovered in 1831 by the English navigator John Biscoe, it now forms part of British Antarctic Territory, but is claimed also by Chile and Argentina. At one time the whole peninsula was named by the British in honour of a First Lord of the admiralty, Sir James Graham (1792–1861). The Americans preferred to call the peninsula the Palmer Peninsula after the US explorer, Nathaniel Palmer, but in 1964 place-name committees in the USA and the UK agreed to name the northern half Graham Land and the southern half Palmer Land.

**Graian Alps** /'graɪən/ a western range of the Alps, to the south of the Mont Blanc group on the frontier between France and Italy. Its highest peak is Gran Paradiso (4,061 m., 13,323 ft.).

**Grain Coast** the name formerly given to the coast of Liberia in West Africa which traded in melegueta pepper grain.

**Grampian** /'græmpɪən/ a local government region in north-east Scotland from 1975 to 1996; area 8,698 sq. km. (3,360 sq. miles); pop. (1991) 493,150; capital, Aberdeen. The region is divided into five districts:

| District | Area (sq. km.) | Pop. (1991) |
| --- | --- | --- |
| Aberdeen City | 184 | 202,000 |
| Banff and Buchan | 1,526 | 82,950 |
| Gordon | 2,214 | 74,000 |
| Kincardine and Deeside | 2,548 | 52,600 |
| Moray | 2,224 | 82,500 |

**Grampian Mountains** /ˈgræmpiən/ (also **Grampians**) **1.** a mountain range in north-central Scotland. Its southern edge forms a natural boundary between the Highlands and the Lowlands. **2.** a mountain range in Victoria, south-east Australia, forming a spur of the Great Dividing Range at the western extremity of the Eastern Highlands.

**Gramsh** /græmʃ/ a town in central Albania, on the River Devoll. It is capital of a province of the same name.

**Granada** /grəˈnɑːdə/ a city in Nicaragua on the north-west shore of Lake Nicaragua, founded in the Spanish colonial period; pop. (1985) 88,600. It has light industries and is linked by rail to the Pacific port of Corinto. Many of its colonial buildings survive.

**Granada** an ancient city at the foot of the Sierra Nevada in Andalusia, southern Spain; pop. (1991) 286,700. Founded in the 8th c., it became the capital of the Moorish kingdom of Granada in 1238. The Palace of the Alhambra, residence of the Moorish rulers of Granada, is one of Spain's major tourist attractions. The city's 16th-c. cathedral contains the tombs of Ferdinand and Isabella. The poet Federico Garcia de Lorca was born in Granada in 1898.

**Gran Chaco** /græn ˈtʃɑːkəʊ/ a vast, sparsely populated lowland plain in central South America, extending from southern Bolivia through Paraguay to northern Argentina. The discovery of oil in the Chaco Boreal to the north of the Pilcomayo River precipitated the Chaco War (1932–5) between Paraguay and Bolivia in a dispute about the interstate boundary. (Spanish = great hunting-ground or riches.)

**Gran Colombia** a country formed in north-west South America following the wars of independence against Spain. Created in 1819 and initially known as the Republic of Colombia, it comprised what is now Colombia, Ecuador, Panama, and Venezuela. Gran Colombia was dissolved following the secession of Venezuela in 1829 and Ecuador in 1830. Its capital was the city of Bogota.

**Grand Bahama** the fourth-largest island in the Bahamas; area 1,372 sq. km. (530 sq. miles); pop. (1980) 33,100. Its chief town is the tourist resort of Freeport-Lucaya which developed in the 1950s.

**Grand Banks** a submarine plateau of the continental shelf off the south-east coast of Newfoundland, Canada. It is a meeting place of the warm Gulf Stream and the cold Labrador Current; this promotes the growth of plankton, making the waters an important feeding area for fish. It has been visited by European cod-fishers since the end of the 15th c. and was the scene of a dispute between Canadian and Spanish fishermen in 1995.

**Grand Caicos** /ˈkeɪkɒs/ (also **Middle Caicos**) the largest of the Turks and Caicos Islands in the eastern Caribbean. Conch Bar and Lorimer are the chief settlements.

**Grand Canal** **1.** a series of waterways in eastern China, extending from Beijing southwards to Hangzhou, a distance of 1,747 km. (1,092 miles). First constructed in 486 BC as a link between the Yangtze and Yellow rivers, it was extended over the centuries until its present length was reached in AD 1327. Its original purpose was to transport rice from the river valleys to the cities. It is the longest artificial waterway in the world. **2.** the main waterway of Venice in Italy. It is lined on each side by fine palaces and is spanned by the Rialto Bridge. A gondola race is held on the Grand Canal every September.

**Grand Canary** (Spanish **Gran Canaria** /græn kəˈnɑːrjə/) a volcanic island of the Canary Islands in the Atlantic Ocean off the west coast of Africa; area 1,532 sq. km. (592 sq. miles). Its chief town is the port and resort of Las Palmas de Gran Canaria and its highest peak is the Pozo de las Nieves (1,980 m., 6,496 ft.).

**Grand Canyon** a deep gorge about 440 km. (277 miles) long formed by the Colorado River in Arizona, USA. It is 8–24 km. (5–15 miles) wide and, in places, 1,800 m. (6,000 ft.) deep. The oldest sedimentary rocks in the canyon date back almost 2,000 million years. It was designated a national monument in 1908 and a national park in 1919. It is visited by 3 million people each year.

**Grand Cayman** the largest of the Cayman Islands in the western Caribbean; area 197 sq. km. (76 sq. mile). Its chief settlement is George Town.

**Grand Comore** (Comoran **Njazidja**) the largest of the Comoros Islands in the Indian Ocean to the north-west of Madagascar; area 1,148 sq. km. (443 sq. miles); pop. (1980) 189,000. Its chief town is Moroni.

**Grand Coulee** /ˈkuːliː/ a deep gorge 48 km. (30 miles) in length cut in the Columbia Plateau by the Columbia River as it flows through north-central Washington state, USA. The Grand Coulee Dam, completed in 1942, is 168 m. (550 ft.) high.

**Grande Chartreuse** see CHARTREUSE.

**Grande-Terre** /grɑ̃dˈteə(r)/ the easternmost of the two main islands of the French overseas department of Guadeloupe in the eastern Caribbean; area 585 sq. km. (226 sq. miles); pop. (1982) 157,700. Its chief town is Point-à-Pitre.

**Grand Prairie** /ˈpreɪrɪ/ a city in northern Texas, USA, between Dallas and Fort Worth; pop. (1990) 99,620. It produces plastics, metal goods, medical supplies, and has a large aerospace industry.

**Grand Rapids** an industrial city and distribution centre in west-central Michigan, USA, on the Grand River; pop. (1990) 189,130. Settled in 1826 on the site of an Indian trading post, the city produces furniture, vehicle parts, and electronic equipment. It is also a noted convention centre. Gerald Ford, 38th president of the US, practised law here.

**Grand Teton** a national park established in Wyoming in 1929 to protect the most scenic part of the snow-covered Teton Range which rises to 4,199 m. (13,766 ft.) at Grand Teton. The Snake River passes through the park.

**Grand Turk** the principal island of the Turks in the Turks and Caicos Islands at the south-eastern tip of the Bahamas archipelago; pop. (1980) 5,800. Its chief settlement is Cockburn Town. Astronaut John Glenn came ashore here after the first US manned-flight into space in 1962.

**Grangemouth** /'greɪndʒmaʊθ/ an oil-refining town with container port facilities on the south bank of the Firth of Forth, central Scotland; pop. (1981) 21,600.

**Gran Sasso d'Italia** /græn ˌsɑːsəʊ dɪˈtæljə/ a snow-capped limestone massif in the Apennine Range of east-central Italy, to the north of L'Aquila in the Abruzzi region. Its highest peak is the Corno Grande (2,914 m., 9,554 ft.) and its glacier is the only one in the Apennines.

**Granta** /'græntə/ an alternative name for the River Cam in east England. (See CAM.)

**Grantha** /'grʌntə/ a south Indian alphabet dating from the 5th c. AD, used by the Tamil brahmins for the Sanskrit transcriptions of their sacred books.

**Grantham** /'grænθ(ə)m/ a market and engineering town in Lincolnshire, east-central England; pop. (1981) 30,080. It was the birthplace in 1925 of Margaret Thatcher, Britain's first woman prime minister (1979–90).

**Grasmere** /'grɑːsmiːr/ a village in the Lake District of Cumbria, north-west England, beside Lake Grasmere; pop. (1981) 1,100. It is associated with William and Dorothy Wordsworth who settled there in 1799.

**Grasse** /grɑːs/ a town near Cannes in the department of Alpes-Maritimes, south-east France, centre of the French perfume industry; pop. (1990) 42,080.

**Graubünden** see GRISONS.

**Grauspitze** /'graʊʃpɪtsə/ a mountain rising to 2,599 m. (8,527 ft.) in the Rhätikon Alps, the highest peak in the Principality of Liechtenstein.

**Graves** /grɑːv/ a district in the department of Gironde, south-west France, on the banks of the Garonne to the south of Bordeaux. It is a predominantly gravelly district noted for its wines.

**Gravesend** /greɪv'zend/ an industrial town in Kent, south-east England, on the River Thames to the east of London; pop. (1981) 53,640. Pocohontas, the North American Indian princess, died here in 1617 and was buried in St. George's Church. It has engineering, paper-making, and cement industries.

**Gravettian** /grə'vetɪən/ an upper palaeolithic industry in Europe, following the Aurignacian, named after the type-site at La Gravette in the Dordogne, France.

**Graz** /grɑːts/ a city in southern Austria, capital of the state of Styria; pop. (1991) 232,155. Situated on the River Mur, it is the second-largest city in Austria. Its old buildings include a 15th-c. Gothic cathedral and several medieval churches. The famous Lippizaner horses are bred near here for the Spanish Riding School in Vienna, and the German astronomer Johannes Kepler lived here from 1594 to 1600. Its industries include iron and steel, machinery, and chemicals.

**Great Alföld** /'ɔ:lfəld/ (also **Great Plain**) the wide central plain that occupies more than half of Hungary, extending eastwards from the Danube to the eastern frontier of Hungary with Ukraine and northern Romania. It is divided in two by the River Tisza. An important agricultural region rich in oil and gas, its largest town is Nyirégyháza.

**Great Ararat** see ARARAT, MOUNT.

**Great Arber** /'ɑ:bɜ:/ (German **Grosser Arber**) a mountain in eastern Bavaria, Germany, the highest peak in the Bohemian Forest (1,456 m., 4,777 ft.).

**Great Australian Bight** a wide bay on the south coast of Australia, part of the Southern Ocean. Underlain by the continental shelf, its coast is lined with the cliffs of the Nullarbor Plain.

**Great Barrier Reef** a coral reef in the western Pacific, off the coast of Queensland, Australia. It extends for about 2,000 km. (1,250 miles), roughly parallel to the coast and is the largest coral reef in the world. It is studded with some 700 small islands or 'cays' formed by the deposition of detritus on the reef exposed at low tide and anchored by vegetation. Island groups from north to south include the Tropical North Islands, Whitsunday Islands, Southern Reef Islands, and Fraser and Moreton Bay Islands. There are only 10 navigable passages penetrating the reef, often found opposite river mouths where fresh water and silt inhibit coral growth. The Great Barrier Reef was declared a marine park in 1979 and a world heritage site by UNESCO.

**Great Basin** an arid, sparsely populated region of the western USA between the Sierra Nevada and the Wasatch Range, lying mainly in Nevada and western Utah. Explored and named in 1843–5 by J. C. Frémont, it includes Death Valley and the Mojave Desert. The Great Basin National Park extending over an area of 307 sq. km. (118 sq. miles) in Nevada was established in 1986 to protect limestone caverns, sagebrush, alpine meadows, aspen forests, and glacial lakes.

**Great Bear Lake** a large lake in the Northwest Territories, Canada, the largest lake wholly in Canada and fourth-largest in North America; area 31,328 sq. km. (12,095 sq. miles). It drains into the Mackenzie River via the Great Bear River.

**Great Belt** (Danish **Store Bëlt**) a strait separating the Danish islands of Zealand and Fyn.

**Great Britain** England, Wales, and Scotland considered as a unit (see also BRITAIN); the name is also often used loosely to refer to the United Kingdom. Wales was politically incorporated with England in the 16th c., and the Act of Union formally united Scotland with England in 1707. (See ENGLAND, SCOTLAND, WALES.) Constitutional monarchy was established by the 'Glorious Revolution' of 1688, with parliamentary supremacy guaranteed by the passing of the Bill of Rights (1689). Although the American colonies broke away in 1783, in the 18th c. Great Britain was the leading naval and colonial power in the world, while the Industrial Revolution which was then beginning made it the first industrialized country, with improvements also in agriculture and communications.

**Great Dismal Swamp** see DISMAL SWAMP.

**Great Divide** 1. see CONTINENTAL DIVIDE. 2. see GREAT DIVIDING RANGE.

**Great Dividing Range** (also **Great Divide**) the crest of the Eastern Highlands of Australia, curving roughly parallel to the coast for almost its entire north–south length from Cape York in Queensland to the Grampians of Victoria.

**Greater Antilles** see ANTILLES.

**Greater London** a metropolitan area comprising central London and the surrounding regions; area 1,579 sq. km. (610 sq. miles); pop. (1991) 6,378,600. From 1965 to 1986 the whole metropolitan area was administered by the Greater London Council. Greater London is administratively divided into the City of London, 13 Inner London Boroughs, and 19 Outer London Boroughs:

| Borough | Area (hectares) | Pop.(1991) |
|---|---|---|
| City of London | 274 | 4,000 |
| **Inner London** | | |
| Camden | 2,171 | 170,500 |
| Hackney | 1,948 | 164,200 |
| Hammersmith and Fulham | 1,617 | 136,500 |
| Haringey | 3,031 | 187,300 |
| Islington | 1,489 | 155,200 |
| Kensington and Chelsea | 1,195 | 127,600 |
| Lambeth | 2,727 | 220,100 |
| Lewisham | 3,473 | 215,300 |
| Newham | 3,637 | 200,200 |
| Southwark | 2,880 | 196,500 |
| Tower Hamlets | 1,973 | 153,500 |
| Wandsworth | 3,491 | 237,500 |
| City of Westminster | 2,158 | 181,500 |
| **Outer London** | | |
| Barking and Dagenham | 3,419 | 139,900 |
| Barnet | 8,953 | 283,000 |
| Bexley | 6,065 | 211,200 |
| Brent | 4,421 | 226,100 |
| Bromley | 15,179 | 281,700 |
| Croydon | 8,658 | 299,600 |

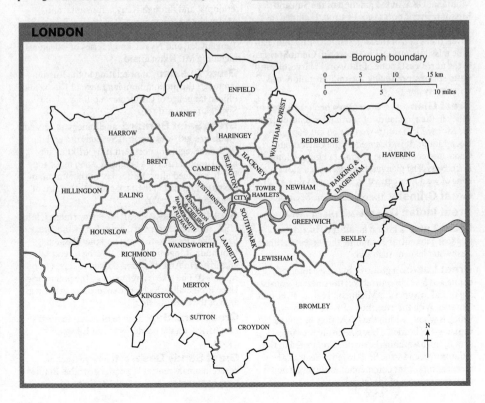

LONDON

Borough boundary
0    5    10    15 km
0              5              10 miles

ENFIELD

BARNET

HARROW

HARINGEY

WALTHAM FOREST

REDBRIDGE

HAVERING

BRENT

HACKNEY

ISLINGTON

CAMDEN

HILLINGDON

EALING

WESTMINSTER

TOWER HAMLETS

NEWHAM

BARKING & DAGENHAM

KENSINGTON & CHELSEA

HAMMERSMITH & FULHAM

CITY

SOUTHWARK

GREENWICH

HOUNSLOW

WANDSWORTH

LAMBETH

BEXLEY

RICHMOND

LEWISHAM

MERTON

KINGSTON

SUTTON

BROMLEY

CROYDON

N

(cont.)

| | | |
|---|---|---|
| Greenwich | 4,744 | 200,800 |
| Harrow | 5,082 | 194,300 |
| Havering | 11,776 | 224,400 |
| Hillingdon | 11,037 | 225,800 |
| Hounslow | 5,852 | 194,100 |
| Kingston upon Thames | 3,756 | 130,300 |
| Mertin | 3,796 | 161,800 |
| Redbridge | 5,647 | 220,600 |
| Richmond upon Thames | 5,526 | 154,600 |
| Sutton | 4,342 | 164,300 |
| Waltham Forest | 3,966 | 203,400 |

**Greater Manchester** a metropolitan county of north-west England; area 1,287 sq. km. (497 sq. miles); pop. (1991) 2,445,200. It is divided into 10 administrative metropolitan districts:

| District | Area (hectares) | Pop. (1991) |
|---|---|---|
| Bolton | 13,973 | 253,300 |
| Bury | 9,918 | 172,200 |
| Manchester | 11,621 | 397,400 |
| Oldham | 14,112 | 211,400 |
| Rochdale | 15,975 | 196,900 |
| Salford | 9,687 | 217,900 |
| Stockport | 12,605 | 276,800 |
| Tameside | 10,323 | 211,700 |
| Trafford | 10,565 | 205,700 |
| Wigan | 19,895 | 301,900 |

**Great Falls** an industrial city in north-central Montana, USA, at the junction of the Sun and Missouri rivers; pop. (1990) 55,100. Founded in 1884, the city was named after falls on the Missouri River. It has one of the largest intercontinental ballistic missile complexes in the world. Giant Springs to the north-east is one of the world's largest freshwater springs, producing 290 million gallons of water every day.

**Great Glen** (also **Glen More** /mɔː(r)/) a glen or valley in the Highlands of Scotland extending from the Moray Firth south-west for 96 km. (60 miles) to Loch Linnhe. It is traversed by the Caledonian Canal and contains the 37 km.- (23 miles-) long Loch Ness. The glen has been excavated along a zone of weakness caused by the Great Glen Fault.

**Great Grimsby** the official name of GRIMSBY.

**Great Indian Desert** see THAR DESERT.

**Great Lake** a lake at an altitude of 1,030 m. (3,380 ft.) in central Tasmania, the largest natural freshwater lake in Australia.

**Great Lakes** a group of five large interconnected lakes in central North America, consisting of Lakes Superior, Michigan, Huron, Erie, and Ontario. With the exception of Lake Michigan, which is wholly within the USA, they lie on the Canada–US border. They constitute the largest area of fresh water in the world. Connected to the Atlantic Ocean by the St. Lawrence Seaway, they form an important commercial waterway. The total surface area of the lakes is c. 245,300 sq. km.

(94,747 sq. miles). Lake Superior, the largest and deepest of the lakes, is the largest lake in North America and second-largest lake in the world. The Great Lakes were formed at the end of the last Ice Age when glacially eroded basins were filled with meltwater. The first Europeans to explore the Great Lakes in the 17th c. were French fur traders, notably Etienne Brulé, Samuel de Champlain, and Robert LaSalle.

| Lake | Length (km.) | Breadth (km.) | Area (sq. km.) | Max.Depth (m.) |
|---|---|---|---|---|
| Superior | 563 | 257 | 84,243 | 405 |
| Michigan | 494 | 190 | 57,757 | 281 |
| Huron | 332 | 295 | 63,096 | 229 |
| Erie | 388 | 92 | 25,812 | 64 |

**Great Malvern** /ˈmɔː(l)vɜːn/ a spa town in the Malvern Hills of Hereford and Worcester, west-central England, noted for its mineral water; pop. (1981) 30,470.

**Great Ouse** see OUSE 3.

**Great Plains** a vast area of plains to the east of the Rocky Mountains in North America, extending from the valley of the Mackenzie River in Canada to southern Texas.

**Great Rift Valley** the most extensive system of rift valleys in the world, a geological fault system running some 6,400 km. (4,000 miles) from the Jordan valley in Israel, along the Red Sea into Ethiopia, and through Kenya, Tanzania, and Malawi into Mozambique. It is marked by a series of steep-sided lakes such as Lakes Turkana, Tanganyika, and Nyasa, and a series of volcanoes including Mt. Kilimanjaro.

**Great Russian** of or relating to the Russian language, the predominant language of Russia and official language of the former republics of the Soviet Union until 1991.

**Great Saint Bernard** an alpine pass between Valais in south-west-central Switzerland and the Piedmont region of northern Italy. 61 km. (38 miles) long, it rises to a height of 2,469 m. (8,100 ft.). It is named after the hospice at the summit of the pass, founded in the 11th c. by St. Bernard of Menthon (923–1008).

**Great Salt Lake** a salt lake in northern Utah, USA, near Salt Lake City, bounded by the Great Salt Lake Desert to the west and the Wasatch Mountain Range to the east. It is the largest salt lake in north America; area c. 2,590 sq. km. (1,000 sq. miles). The lake is a remnant of the prehistoric Lake Bonneville which once covered an extensive area of the Great Basin.

**Great Sand Sea** an area of desert in north-east Africa, on the border between Libya and Egypt.

**Great Sandy Desert 1.** a large tract of desert in north-central Western Australia. **2.** (also **Empty Quarter**, Arabic **Rub' al Khali**) a vast sandy desert on the Arabian peninsula stretching from the Nejd of central Saudi Arabia to the Hadhramaut of Yemen and frequented by Bedouin of the Murra and Rashidi tribes. The first European crossing was made by Bertram Thomas in 1930–1, with later explorations by Harry St. John Philby and William Thesiger.

**Great Slave Lake** a lake in the Northwest Territories of Canada, the deepest lake in North America, with a depth of 615 m. (2,015 ft.). Named after the Slave Indians who used to live on its shores, it is the fifth-largest lake in North America; area 28,568 sq. km. (11,030 sq. miles).

**Great Smoky Mountains** (also **Great Smokies**) a range of the Appalachian Mountains on the frontier between the US states of North Carolina and Tennessee. Its highest peak is Clingmans Dome (2,025 m., 6,643 ft.). A national park with an area of 2,068 sq. km. (800 sq. miles) was created in 1926.

**Great Victoria Desert** a desert region of Australia, which straddles the boundary between Western Australia and South Australia.

**Great Wall of China** a defensive wall in northern China, extending over a total distance of 6,700 km. (4,187 miles) from the Jiayuguan Pass in Gansu province to Shanhaiguan on the Yellow Sea north of Beijing. Its origin dates from c. 210 BC when the country was unified under one ruler (Qin Shi Huang), and the northern walls of existing rival states were linked to form a continuous protection against nomad invaders. It was rebuilt in medieval times largely against the Mongols, and the present wall dates from the Ming Dynasty (1368–1544). Although principally a defensive wall it served also as a means of communication, and is said to be the only man-made feature that would be visible from a space orbit.

**Great Yarmouth** /'jɑːməθ/ a port and resort town on the coast of Norfolk, eastern England; pop. (1981) 55,400. Once an important fishing port, it now services the North Sea oil industry.

**Great Zimbabwe** /zɪmˈbɑːbwɪ/ the massive ruins of a city in Zimbabwe, 28 km. (17 miles) south-east of Masvingo, dating from the 13th–15th c. when it prospered in connection with the Arab gold trade.

**Greece** /griːs/  (Greek **Ellás** /eˈlɑːs/) official name **The Hellenic Republic** a country in south-east Europe comprising a peninsula bounded by the Ionian, Mediterranean, and Aegean Seas, and numerous outlying islands; area 130,714 sq. km. (50,488 sq. miles); pop. (1991) 10,269,000; official language, Greek; capital,

Athens. Its largest cities are Athens, Salonika, Patras, Volos, Heraklion, and Larisa. The coastal climate is generally Mediterranean with mild rainy winters and hot dry summers; mountain areas are cooler. Agriculture remains important to the economy, though there has been a substantial increase in industrial activity since Greece joined the EC in 1981. In addition to grain, fruit, olive oil, cotton, dairy products, and wine, Greece produces textiles, chemicals, pharmaceuticals, and metal and electrical goods for export.

The country was invaded by Greek-speaking peoples c. 2000–1700 BC, and thereafter enjoyed settled conditions which allowed the Mycenean civilization to develop and flourish until the arrival in the 12th c. of the Dorians. Village settlements developed into city-states, of which the most prominent were Athens and Sparta, and rising populations and expanding trade led to overseas colonization, especially in Ionia. Although the city-states showed themselves able to combine in a crisis, as against the Persian expeditionary force which they unexpectedly defeated in 480 BC, they were weakened by rivalries and conflicts with each other and by internal political turmoil. In 338 BC they fell to the superior military power of Philip II of Macedon, and formed part of the empire of his successor Alexander the Great. Towards the end of the 3rd c. BC Macedonia came into conflict with the expanding power of Rome, and in 146 BC Greece was made a Roman province; the liberties of the Greek city-states were at an end.

In AD 395 the Roman Empire was divided and Greece became part of the Eastern Empire, centred on Constantinople. It was conquered by the Ottoman Turks (1466) and remained under Turkish rule until the successful war of independence between 1821 and 1830, after which it became a monarchy and then in 1973 a republic. It is a member state of the European Union. Greece is a presidential parliamentary republic with an executive president and a unicameral parliament (*Vouli*).

**Greek** *adj. & n.*

The country is divided into 51 prefectures (*nomi*):

| Prefecture | Area (sq. km.) | Pop. (1991) | Capital |
|---|---|---|---|
| **Central Greece and Euboea** | | | |
| Aetolia and Acarnina | 5,461 | 230,690 | Agrinion |
| Attica | 3,381 | 425,990 | Athens |
| Boeotia | 2,952 | 134,030 | Levádhia |
| Euboea | 4,167 | 209,130 | Khalkís |
| Evritania | 1,869 | 23,530 | Karpenísi |
| Phthiotis | 4,441 | 168,290 | Lamía |
| Phocis | 2,120 | 43,880 | Amfissa |
| **Peloponnese** | | | |
| Argolid | 2,154 | 95,250 | Nauplia |
| Arcadia | 4,419 | 103,840 | Trípolis |
| Achaea | 3,271 | 297,320 | Patras |
| Elis | 2,618 | 174,020 | Pírgos |

(cont.)

| | | | |
|---|---|---|---|
| Corinth | 2,290 | 142,360 | Corinth |
| Laconia | 3,636 | 94,920 | Sparta |
| Messenia | 2,991 | 167,290 | Kalamáta |
| **Ionian Islands** | | | |
| Zákynthos | 406 | 32,750 | Zákynthos |
| Corfu | 641 | 105,040 | Corfu |
| Cephalonia | 904 | 32,310 | Argostóli |
| Lévkas | 356 | 20,900 | Lévkas |
| **Aegean Islands** | | | |
| Chios | 904 | 52,690 | Chios |
| Cyclades | 2,572 | 100,080 | Ermoupolis |
| Lesbos | 2,154 | 103,700 | Mytilíni |
| Samos | 778 | 41,850 | Vathy |
| Dodecanese | 2,714 | 162,440 | Rhodes |
| **Epirus** | | | |
| Arta | 1,662 | 78,880 | Arta |
| Thesprotia | 1,515 | 44,200 | Igoumenítsa |
| Ioánnina | 4,990 | 157,210 | Ioánnina |
| Préveza | 1,036 | 58,910 | Préveza |
| **Thessaly** | | | |
| Kardhítsa | 2,636 | 126,500 | Kardhítsa |
| Lárisa | 5,381 | 369,300 | Lárisa |
| Magnesia | 2,636 | 197,610 | Vólos |
| Tríkkala | 3,384 | 137,820 | Tríkkala |
| **Macedonia** | | | |
| Grevená | 2,291 | 37,020 | Grevená |
| Dráma | 3,468 | 96,980 | Dráma |
| Emathia | 1,701 | 138,070 | Véroia |
| Salónika | 3,683 | 977,530 | Salónika |
| Kaválla | 2,111 | 135,750 | Kaválla |
| Kastoriá | 1,720 | 52,720 | Kastoriá |
| Kilkís | 2,519 | 81,850 | Kilkís |
| Kozáni | 3,516 | 150,160 | Kozáni |
| Pélla | 2,506 | 138,260 | Edhessa |
| Pieria | 1,516 | 116,820 | Kateríni |
| Sérres | 3,968 | 191,890 | Sérres |
| Flórina | 1,924 | 52,770 | Flórina |
| Chalcidice | 2,918 | 91,650 | Políyiros |
| Mount Athos | 336 | 1,560 | Kariai |
| **Thrace** | | | |
| Evros | 4,242 | 143,790 | Alexandroúpolis |
| Xánthi | 1,793 | 90,450 | Xánthi |
| Rhodope | 2,543 | 103,290 | Komotiní |
| **Crete** | | | |
| Heraklion | 2,641 | 263,870 | Heraklion |
| Lasithi | 1,823 | 70,760 | Ayios Nikólaos |
| Khania | 2,376 | 133,060 | Khania |
| Rethymnon | 1,496 | 69,290 | Rethymnon |
| Greater Athens | 427 | 3,096,770 | Athens |

**Greek** /griːk/ the Indo-European language of Greece, in its ancient form spoken in the Balkan peninsula from the 2nd millenium BC; the earliest evidence is to be found in the Linear B tablets dating from 1500 BC. Like Latin, it was a highly inflected language with strict rules and rather complicated grammar. The alphabet normally used as adapted from the Phoenician c. 1000 BC; the capitals have remained unaltered, and the lower case letters have developed from them. There were four main dialects, but with the rise of Athens the dialect of the city (Attic) predominated and formed the basis of the Koine which became the standard dialect from the 3rd c. BC onwards. It was the official language of the Byzantine empire, but in the four centuries when Greece was under Turkish rule oral speech and dialects developed unchallenged. Today Greek is spoken by some 10 million people in mainland Greece and the Aegean archipelago, and is the official language of Greece. Modern Greek has changed from ancient Greek in various ways; some vowels, dipthongs, and consonants have changed or modified their sounds, there are fewer grammatical forms, and the structure is simpler. Two forms of the language are in use: demotic, the common language, and *katharevousa*, an imitation of classical Greek which has been revived for literary purposes. Demotic is gaining ground not only for conversation but also in literature.

**Greeley** /ˈgriːlɪ/ a city in northern Colorado, USA, founded in 1870 by Horace Greeley as a co-operative farming and temperance colony; pop. (1990) 60,540. It is marketing and processing centre for a fertile irrigated region.

**Green** /griːn/ a river of north-west USA that rises in Wyoming in the Wind River Range of the Rocky Mountains and flows 1,175 km. (730 miles) generally southwards across the north-west corner of Colorado and into Utah before joining the Colorado River.

**Greenham Common** /ˈgriːnəm/ the site of a former US airbase near Newbury in Berkshire, southern England, the scene of a protest against the deployment of US cruise missiles that lasted from 1981 until the withdrawal of missiles in 1990 following the end of the Cold War.

**greenhouse effect** the trapping of the sun's warmth in the lower atmosphere of the earth caused by an increase in carbon dioxide, which is more transparent to solar radiation than to the reflected radiation from the earth.

**Greenland**
/ˈgriːnlənd/ (Danish
**Grønland** /ˈgrɜːnlɑːn/,
Inuit **Kalaallit
Nunaat** /kəˌlɑːlɪt
nəˈnɑːt/) an island,
the largest in the
world, lying to the
north-east of North
America and mostly

within the Arctic Circle; area c. 2,175,600 sq. km. (840,325 sq. miles), of which 16 per cent is ice-free; pop. (1992) 55,385, mostly Inuit; capital, Nuuk (Godthåb). It was discovered and named by the Norse explorer Eric the Red in 986 and settled in coastal pockets by Norse colonists. Although only five per cent of Greenland is habitable, it was from 1721 resettled by the Danes, and became part of Denmark in 1953, with internal autonomy from 1979; it withdrew from the EC in 1985. The economy of Greenland is largely based on inshore and deep-water fishing.
**Greenlander** *n.*

**Greenland Sea** a sea between Greenland and the Svalbard islands, linking the Arctic and Atlantic Oceans.

**Greenock** /'griːnək, 'gren-/ a port on the south bank of the River Clyde in west-central Scotland; pop. (1981) 57,300. The engineer James Watt, inventor of the steam-engine, was born here in 1736.

**Greensboro** an industrial city in the Piedmont of north-central North Carolina, USA, producing textiles, cigarettes, machinery, and electrical components; pop. (1990) 183,520. Founded in 1808, it was settled by Quakers, Germans, Scots, and Irishmen. The author William Sydney Porter (O. Henry) was born near here.

**Greenville** /'griːnvɪl/ a port on the coast of Liberia, at the mouth of the River Sinoe.

**Greenville** /'griːnvɪl/ an industrial city in north-west South Carolina, USA, on the Reedy River; pop. (1990) 58,280. Founded in 1797, its industries produce clothing, nylon, chemicals, plastic film, and machinery. The Bob Jones University (1927) has a collection of religious art and rare bibles.

**Greenwich** /'grenɪtʃ, grɪnɪdʒ/ a borough of east-central London, England, to the south of the River Thames; pop. (1991) 200,800. It was the site of the Royal Observatory, founded in 1675 by Charles II, in a building designed by Christopher Wren. Soon after World War II the observatory was moved to Herstmonceux in East Sussex. The buildings at Greenwich itself, together with many of the old instruments, now form part of the National Maritime Museum. The Royal Naval College (Christopher Wren) and Queen's House (Inigo Jones) stand on the site of a Tudor royal palace. The *Cutty Sark* tea clipper and *Gipsy Moth IV* are popular tourist attractions.

**Greenwich Mean Time** (GMT) the mean solar time on the Greenwich Meridian of longitude which was defined to pass through the Airy Transit Circle at Greenwich in England and was adopted internationally as the zero of longitude at a conference in Washington in 1884. Its acceptance was facilitated by the overwhelming use of the Greenwich Meridian in navigation and the adoption, in the US and Canada, of time zones based on Greenwich. Originally different towns in Great Britain kept their own local time, varying according to longitude. In the mid-19th c. Greenwich time was adopted by railways throughout Britain for the sake of uniformity. However, it was only in 1880 that Greenwich Mean Time became the legal time throughout Great Britain. The international reference time-scale for civil use is now based on atomic clocks but is subject to step adjustments (leap seconds) to keep it close to mean solar time on the Greenwich Meridian. The formal name of the time-scale is UTC (a language-independent abbreviation of co-ordinated universal time) but it is still widely known as Greenwich Mean Time.

**Greenwich Village** a district of New York City, USA, on the lower west side of Manhattan, to the south of 14th Street and west of Washington Square. Once a separate village, it became an exclusive residential area associated with writers and musicians. Some of the few surviving wooden houses built in Manhattan (built in the 1840s) are located in Greenwich Village.

**Greifswald** /'griːfsvɑːlt/ a town in Mecklenburg-West Pomerania, north-east Germany, south-east of Stralsund; pop. (1991) 65,530.

**Grenada**
/grə'neɪdə/ a country in the West Indies, consisting of the island of Grenada (the southernmost of the Windward Islands) and the southern Grenadines; area 345 sq. km. (133 sq. miles);

pop. (est. 1990) 94,000; official language, English; capital, St. George's. The climate is subtropical with a dry season from January to May. Although declining in importance, Grenada's principal exports are agricultural products such as cocoa, spices, bananas, fruit, and vegetables. The island was sighted in 1498 by Columbus on 15 August which is now Grenada's national day. Colonized by the French, it was ceded to Britain in 1763, recaptured by the French, and restored to Britain in 1783. It became an independent state within the Commonwealth in 1974. Seizure of power by a left-wing military group in 1983 prompted an invasion by US and some Caribbean countries, fearful of instability and Communist influence in the region; they withdrew in 1985. The UK sovereign, represented by a Governor-General, is head of state and legislative power is vested in a bicameral parliament comprising a House of Representatives and a Senate.
**Grenadian** adj. & n.

**Grenadine Islands** /'grenə,diːn/ (also **Grenadines**) a chain of small islands, reefs, and sand bars in the West Indies, part of the Windward Islands. They are divided between St. Vincent and Grenada. The principal islands are Bequia, Mustique, Canouan, Mayreau, Union Island, Carriacou, Little Martinique, and Ronde Island.

**Grenoble** /grə'nəʊb(ə)l/ a resort and industrial city and capital of the department of Isère in the Dauphiné Alps of south-east France, at the junction of the Drac and Isère rivers; pop. (1991) 153,970. Grenoble developed in the 19th c. in association with its soap factories and oil mills, and pioneered the use of hydroelectric power. It is now an important winter-sports and tourist centre with industries based around nuclear research, engineering, chemistry, and computer technology. The novelist Stendhal was born here in 1783.

**Gresham** /'greʃəm/ a city in north-west Oregon, USA, to the east of Portland; pop. (1990) 68,235. Food processing and the manufacture of aluminium and rubber products are its chief industries.

**Gretna Green** /'gretnə/ a village just north of the Scottish–English border near Carlisle, formerly a popular place for runaway couples from England to be married according to Scots Law without the parental consent required in England for those who had not attained their majority. A valid marriage could be contracted in Scotland merely by a declaration of consent by the two parties before a witness (traditionally the village blacksmith, who also read the marriage service to couples for sentiment's sake). The practice began after 1753, when English law made it impossible to conduct a marriage clandestinely, and lapsed after 1857 when Scots Law prescribed certain conditions for 'irregular' marriages, though it recognized such marriages until 1939.

**Grevená** /ˌgrevəˈnɑː/ the capital town of the department of Grevená in Macedonia, northern Greece, at the junction of two branches of the Greveniotikos River; pop. (1981) 7,430. It was a centre of Greek learning in the Middle Ages and was the headquarters of a Byzantine irregular militia known as the *Armatoles*. The town has a school of forestry.

**Grevenmacher** /'greɪvənˌmæxɜː/ a port on the Mosel River at the centre of a wine-producing region in eastern Luxembourg; pop. (1991) 3,045. It is capital of a district of the same name.

**Grimsby** /'grɪmzbɪ/ (official name **Great Grimsby**) a port on the south shore of the Humber estuary, Humberside, east England; pop. (1991) 88,900. It trades in fish, grain, coal, and timber.

**Grindelwald** /'grɪndəlvɑːlt/ a skiing resort and climbing centre in the Jungfrau region of west-central Switzerland, situated at an altitude of 1,042 m. (3,420 ft.) in the Bernese Alps.

**gringo** /'grɪŋgəʊ/ a foreigner, especially a British or North American person, in a Spanish-speaking country. (Spanish = gibberish.)

**Grisons** /griː'zɔ̃/ (German **Graubünden** /grɑʊˈbʊnd(ə)n/) a mountainous canton of south-west Switzerland; area 7,109 sq. km. (2,746 sq. miles); pop. (1990) 170,410; capital, Chur. It is the largest of the Swiss cantons and amongst its notable resorts are St. Moritz and Davos.

**Griqualand** /'griːkwəˌlænd/ a region of Cape Province, South Africa, settled by the Griqua Bushmen in 1862 under their leader Adam Kok. East Griqualand, in east Cape Province, joined Cape Colony in 1879 and West Griqualand, in north Cape Province, followed a year later. Its chief towns are Kokstad and the diamond-mining town of Kimberley.

**Grodno** /'grɒdnə/ see HRODNA.

**Groningen** /'grəʊnɪŋən/ **1.** an agricultural province of north-east Netherlands; pop. (1991) 554,604; area 2,346 sq. km. (906 sq. miles); pop. (1991) 554,604. **2.** its capital city, at the junction of the Hoornse Diep and Winschoter Diep; pop. (1991) 168,700. The leading city in the northern Netherlands, it is the headquarters of the Dutch Grain Exchange and has one of the largest markets in the country. Its university was founded in 1614, and it is a picturesque city with fine churches. It is linked to its port at Delfzijl by the Eems canal and lies on the western edge of a large natural-gas field. Its industries include machinery and printing.

**Grønland** the Danish name for GREENLAND.

**Groote Eylandt** /gruːt 'aɪlənd/ an island in the Gulf of Carpentaria off the coast of Arnhem Land, north Australia; area 2,459 sq. km. (950 sq. miles). Named by Tasman in 1644, the island has large reserves of manganese.

**Grootfontein** /'gruːtfɒntiːn/ a mining town in north-east Namibia, developed by the South West Africa Company on the site of a German fort. Copper and lead are mined nearby.

**Gros Morne National Park** /grəʊ mɔːn/ a national park in Newfoundland, eastern Canada, protecting a magnificent landscape of mountains, fiords, and forests; area 1,943 sq. km. (750 sq. miles). (French = big bleak hill.)

**Grosser Arber** See GREAT ARBER.

**Grossetto** /grəʊ'seɪtəʊ/ a marketing centre and the capital of Grossetto province in Tuscany, west-central Italy, at the heart of the reclaimed Maremma coastal region; pop. (1990) 71,370.

**Grossglockner** /'grəʊsˌglɒknə(r)/ the highest mountain in Austria, rising to a height of 3,797 m. (12,457 ft.) in the east Tyrolean Alps.

**Group of Seven, G-7** the name given to the seven leading industrial nations of the world, namely, the US, Japan, Germany, France, the UK, Italy, and Canada.

**Groznyy** /'grɒzniː/ a city in south-west Russia, on the Terek River near the border with Georgia, capital of the Chechen Republic; pop. (1990) 401,000. Founded as a frontier fortress town, it has (since 1893) grown into a major oil centre with petrochemical industries. The city was badly damaged during the confrontation between Chechen nationalists and Russian forces in 1994–5.

**Gruyère** /gruː'jeə(r)/ (also **Gruyères**) a village in western Switzerland, 23 km. (15 miles) southwest of Fribourg, that gives its name to a firm pale cheese originally made in the surrounding area.

**Grytviken** /'grɪtˌviːkən/ a base on the island of South Georgia, in the South Atlantic. It was the site of a whaling station between 1904 and 1966. During the Falklands War of 1982 it was occupied by British military personnel.

**Gstaad** /gəˈʃtɑːt/ a famous winter-sports resort in western Switzerland, in the Bernese Alps at an altitude of 1,005 m. (3,300 ft.) and lying in the valley of the Saane River. Many of its chalets are owned by royalty, celebrities, and other fashionable people.

**Guadalajara** /ˌgwædələˈhɑːrə/ **1.** the capital of the state of Jalisco in west-central Mexico; pop. (1990) 2,846,720. Situated at an altitude of 1,567 m. (5,141 ft.), it is the second-largest city in Mexico. It is the commercial and industrial centre of the western highland area and is a spacious city with many Spanish colonial buildings, parks, and squares. It has a 16th-c. cathedral and an 18th-c. university. Guadalajara's industries include vehicle assembly, photographic equipment, textiles, and clothing. It is also famous for its glassware, pottery, and other handicrafts. The warm, dry climate makes it a popular health resort. **2.** a province in the Castilla-La Mancha region of central Spain, watered by the River Tagus (Tejo); area 12,190 sq. km. (4,708 sq. miles); pop. (1991) 145,590. **3.** a market town, the capital of the province of Guadalajara in central Spain, to the north-east of Madrid; pop. (1991) 67,200.

**Guadalaviar** /ˌgwædələˈvjɑː(r)/ (also **Turia**) a river of eastern Spain that rises in the Sierra de Gudar and flows southwards through Teruel before turning south-eastwards to the coastal lowlands of Valencia where it meets the Mediterranean at the city of Valencia.

**Guadalcanal** /ˌgwædəlkəˈnæl/ an island in the western Pacific, the largest of the Solomon Islands; area 5,302 sq. km. (2,048 sq. miles); pop. (est. 1987) 71,300. Its chief town is Honiara. During World War II it was the scene of the first major US offensive against the Japanese (August 1942).

**Guadalquivir** /ˌgwædəlkwɪˈvɪə(r)/ a river of Andalusia in southern Spain, which rises in the Sierra de Cazorla and flows west and south-west for 657 km. (410 miles) to meet the Atlantic at Sanlúcar de Barrameda.

**Guadalupe Hidalgo** /ˌgwædə.luːp hɪˈdɑːlgəʊ/ a northern suburb of Mexico City surrounding the Churches of Our Lady of Guadalupe, a leading centre of pilgrimage in Mexico. The old basilica dates from 1533 and the modern building from 1976.

**Guadalupe Mountains** a range of mountains on the border between western Texas and New Mexico, USA, 176 km. (110 miles) east of El Paso. A national park was established here in 1966 to protect one of the world's most extensive fossil reefs dating from the Permian era. Guadalupe Peak is the highest point in Texas at 2,667 m. (8,749 ft.).

**Guadeloupe** /ˌgwɑːdəˈluːp/ a group of islands in the Lesser Antilles, forming an overseas department of France in the eastern Caribbean; area 1,779 sq. km. (687 sq. miles); pop. (1991) 386,990; official language, French. Its capital is Basse-Terre

on the south-west coast of Basse-Terre but its largest town and commercial centre is Pointe-à-Pitre on Grande-Terre. In addition to the two largest islands of Basse-Terre and Grande-Terre, which lie adjacent to each other and are only separated by the Rivière Salée, Guadeloupe includes the islands of Marie Galante, La Désirade, the Iles de la Petite Terre, the Les Saintes group, and a number of small islets. The island of St. Barthélemy and the northern part of St. Martin, 250 km. (155 miles) to the north-east, are administered as part of the French department of Guadeloupe. In addition to tourism, the islands depend on agricultural exports such as tropical fruit, sugar, rum, and cocoa. Known to the Caribs as Karukera (isle of beautiful waters), the islands were christened Santa Maria de Guadaloupe de Extremadura by Columbus in 1493. They were settled in 1635 by the French and administered from Martinique, later held by Britain and Sweden for a short while, and in 1816 returned to France. In 1946 Guadeloupe gained the status of a department of France.
**Guadeloupian** *adj. & n.*

**Guadiana** /gwɑːˈdjɑːnɑː/ a river in the Iberian Peninsula that rises in the La Mancha plateau then flows westwards to Badajoz on the Portuguese frontier where it turns southward to enter the Gulf of Cadiz at Ayamonte on the Costa de la Luz.

**Guallatiri** /ˌgwɑːləˈtiːrɪ/ a volcano in the Cordillera Occidental of the Andean Mountains in northern Chile. Rising to 6,063 m. (19,892 ft.), it is the highest active volcano in South America. Its last significant eruption took place in 1987.

**Guam** /gwɑːm/ the largest and southernmost of the Mariana Islands in the western Pacific Ocean, administered as an unincorporated territory of the US and serving as a general trans-shipment centre for goods crossing the Pacific; area 541 sq. km. (209 sq. miles); pop. (1990) 132,000; official language, English; native language, Chamorro; capital, Agaña. Discovered by Magellan in 1521, Guam was ceded to the US by Spain in 1898. Its economy is based on financial services, petroleum refining, and the servicing of a military installation. Agricultural exports include copra, palm oil, and fish.

**Guanabara Bay** /ˌgwænəˈbɑːrə/ an inlet of the Atlantic Ocean at Rio de Janeiro, south-east Brazil.

**Guanacaste** /gwænə'kɑ:stɪ/ a region of north-west Costa Rica; area 10,141 sq. km. (3,917 sq. miles); pop. (1984) 195,200; capital, Liberia. It is the principal tourist region of Costa Rica, featuring coastal resorts and wildlife reserves.

**Guanajuato** /ˌgwænə'hwɑ:təʊ/ **1.** a state of central Mexico; area 30,491 sq. km. (11,777 sq. miles); pop. (1990) 3,980,200. **2.** its capital in the Sierra Madre Occidental, noted for its Spanish colonial architecture and its subterranean streets and passageways; pop. (est. 1983) 45,000. The city developed after one of the Hemisphere's richest veins of silver was discovered near here in 1558. It was the birthplace in 1886 of the Mexican artist Diego Rivera.

**Guanche** /gwɑ:ntʃ/ an extinct group of neolithic-type people that occupied the western Canary islands at the time of the arrival of the Spanish in the 15th c.

**Guang** /gwæŋ/ (also **Guan** or **Gonja**) a people of northern Ghana, descendants of the Gonja state established in the 16th c. They speak Voltaic and Guang languages of the Niger-Congo family of languages.

**Guangdong** /gwæŋ'dʊŋ/ (formerly **Kwang-tung** /kwæŋ'tʊŋ/) a province of southern China, bordering the South China Sea opposite the island of Hainan; area 231,400 sq. km. (89,378 sq. miles); pop. (est. 1986) 63,640,000; capital, Guangzhou (Canton). The Pearl River delta is a rich agricultural area producing rice, tubers, sugar-cane, rubber, and fruits.

**Guangxi** /gwæŋ'ʃi:/ (formerly **Kwangsi** /kwæŋ'si:/) a mountainous region in southern China, on the border with Vietnam; area 220,400 sq. km. (85,129 sq. miles); pop. (est. 1986) 39,460,000; capital, Nanning. In 1958 it was made an autonomous region for the Zhuang people, China's largest minority nationality. Its chief products are timber, pine resin, wood oils, tin, coal, rice, sugar-cane, and fruit.

**Guangzhou** /gwæŋ'dʒəʊ/ (also **Canton** /kæn'tɒn/, formerly **Kwangchow**) a city in southern China, the capital of Guangdong province, situated on the Pearl River (Zhu Jiang) delta; pop. (1986) 3,290,000. It is the leading industrial and commercial centre of southern China. The Chinese revolutionary Sun Yat-Sen (1866–1925) was born at Tsuiheng near the city. The Huaisheng mosque, built in AD 670, is said to be the oldest in China. It has shipyards, a steel complex, paper and textile mills, chemicals, and diverse light industries.

**Guantánamo Bay** a bay on the south-east coast of Cuba, one of the largest natural harbours in the world, and occupying a location of strategic importance on the waterway linking the Atlantic with the Caribbean. It is the site of a US naval base established in 1903 and the source of friction between Cuba and the USA since Fidel Castro came to power in 1959.

**Guaporé** /ˌgwæpə'reɪ/ a river of South America that rises in the Mato Grosso of south-west Brazil and flows north-westwards for 1,745 km. (1,090 miles) to join the River Mamoré. For part of its course it follows the frontier between Brazil and Bolivia.

**Guarani** a South American Indian people, originally of the tropical forest but now largely occupying eastern Paraguay and parts of adjacent Brazil and Argentina on the banks of the Paraguay River where they number c. 100,000.

**Guarda** /'gwɑ:rdə/ a town in north-east Portugal, capital of a district of the same name; pop. (1991) 18,215. At an altitude of 1,057 m. (3,468 ft.) on the slopes of the Serra da Estrela, it is the highest town in Portugal.

**Guatemala** /ˌgwætɪ'mɑ:lə/ official name **The Republic of Guatemala** a country to the south of Mexico in the north of Central America, bordering on the Pacific Ocean and  with a short coastline on the Caribbean; area 108,889 sq. km. (42,056 sq. miles); pop. (est. 1990) 9,200,000; official language, Spanish; capital, Guatemala City. Its largest cities and towns are Guatemala City, Escuintla, Quezaltenango, and Cobán. A narrow coastal plain separates the Pacific from a heavily populated highland region that constitutes about one-fifth of the country's land surface. The more sparsely populated lowlands to the east have fertile river valleys and to the north lies the densely forested Petén region. While January and February are the driest months in the west, rainfall is plentiful all year round in the tropical eastern lowlands. In addition to oil, which was discovered in the 1970s, Guatemala exports agricultural products including coffee, cotton, sugar, meat, and bananas. A former centre of Mayan civilization, Guatemala was conquered by the Spanish in 1523–4. After independence it formed the core of the short-lived Central American Federation (1828–38) before becoming an independent republic in its own right. Its history since then has frequently been characterized by dictatorship and revolution, and since the 1960s the military has had to contend with rural guerrilla movements that have united under the umbrella grouping known as the Guatemalan National Revolutionary Unity (URNG). After a succession of military administrations the first transfer of power from one elected civilian president (elected in 1985) to another took place in 1991. Guatemala is governed by an executive president and a unicameral National Congress.

**Guatemalan** adj. & n.

Guatemala is divided into 22 departments:

| Department | Area (sq. km.) | Pop. (1991) | Capital |
|---|---|---|---|
| Alta Verapaz | 8,686 | 591,910 | Cobán |
| Baja Verapaz | 3,124 | 184,460 | Salamá |
| Chimaltenango | 1,979 | 343,820 | Chimaltenango |
| Chiquimula | 2,376 | 252,050 | Chiquimula |
| El Progresso | 1,922 | 108,400 | El Progresso |
| Escuintla | 4,384 | 542,090 | Escuintla |
| Guatemala | 2,126 | 2,018,180 | Guatemala City |
| Huehuetenango | 7,403 | 716,670 | Huehuetenango |
| Izabal | 9,038 | 326,400 | Puerto Barrios |
| Jalapa | 2,063 | 190,850 | Jalapa |
| Jutiapa | 3,219 | 354,340 | Jutiapa |
| Petén | 35,854 | 253,330 | Flores |
| Quezaltenango | 1,951 | 557,830 | Quezaltenango |
| Quiché | 8,378 | 574,750 | Santa Cruz del Quiché |
| Retalhuleu | 1,858 | 238,860 | Retalhuleu |
| Sacatepéquez | 465 | 180,150 | Antigua Guatemala |
| San Marcos | 3,791 | 702,290 | San Marcos |
| Santa Rosa | 2,955 | 267,790 | Cuilapa |
| Sololá | 1,061 | 242,020 | Sololá |
| Suchitepéquez | 2,510 | 361,680 | Mazatenango |
| Totonicapán | 1,061 | 297,480 | Totonicapán |
| Zacapa | 2,690 | 161,640 | Zacapa |

**Guatemala City** the capital city of Guatemala, in the Guatemalan Highlands at an altitude of 1,500 m. (4,920 ft.); pop. (est. 1990) 1,900,000. It is the largest city in Central America and has an equable climate. It was founded in 1776 to replace the former capital, Antigua Guatemala, destroyed by an earthquake in 1773. The city was severely damaged by earthquakes in 1917–18 and again in 1976. To the west of the city lie the Mayan ruins of Kaminal Juyú. Guatemala city is a commercial and industrial centre. Its industries account for half the country's output and include textiles, silverware, and food processing.

**Guaviare** /gwæv'jɑːrɪ/ a river of South America that rises in the Colombian Andes and flows 1,040 km. (650 miles) eastwards to meet the Orinoco on the Venezuela–Colombia frontier.

**Guayaquil** /ˌgwaɪə'kiːl/ a city in Ecuador, the country's principal Pacific seaport and second-largest city, situated at the mouth of the Guayas River; pop. (1982) 1,300,900. Named after the legendary Indian prince and princess Guayas and Quil, the city was founded in 1537 by Francisco de Orellana, a Spaniard who made one of the earliest European descents of the Amazon. A monument marks the meeting in 1822 of the liberators Simón Bolívar and José de San Martin. In addition to trading in fruit and oil refining, Guayaquil has many industries producing plastics, textiles, pharmaceuticals, food products, vehicles, and electrical equipment.

**Guayas** /'gwaɪæs/ a river of South America that rises in the Andes of Ecuador and flows westwards for 160 km. (100 miles) to meet the Pacific at

Guayaquil. It is the longest river to the west of the Andes.

**Guaymas** /gwaɪ'mɑːs/ a port and resort town on the coast of Sonora state, north-west Mexico; pop. (1980) 54,820.

**Guaymi** /'gwaɪmɪ/ a native Central American people living in Panama where they engage in hunting and subsistence farming. They speak a branch of the Chibchan group of languages and are divided into northern and southern groups.

**Gubbio** /'guːbiːəʊ/ a well-preserved old town in the Umbrian province of Perugia, central Italy, situated on the slopes of Mt. Ingino in the Apennines; pop. (1990) 31,770. It has an ancient Roman theatre and St. Francis is said to have 'tamed the savage wolf' here. It has a 13th-c. cathedral and a 15th-c. palace. Its *Corsa dei Ceri* held on 15 May is one of the leading annual festivals of Italy.

**Gudbrand Valley** /'gʊdbrænd/ (Norwegian **Gudbrandsdalen** /'gʊdbræns, daːlən/) a valley in Oppland county, south-central Norway, to the east of the Jotunheim Range and north of Lillehammer. The valley has formed a routeway since Viking times linking Trondheim with the south.

**Gudenå** /'guːðə,nɔː/ the principal river of Denmark, rising in east Jutland and flowing 158 km. (98 miles) northwards through Randers to the Randers Fjørd, an inlet of the Kattegat.

**Guelders** see GELDERLAND.

**Guelph** /gwelf/ an industrial town in southern Ontario, Canada, between Toronto and Kitchener; pop. (1991) 87,980. Founded in 1827 by the Scottish novelist John Galt, it has a university (1964) and hosts an annual spring festival of music. It was the birthplace of the poet John McCrae who wrote the World War I poem *In Flanders Fields*.

**Guéret** /ge'reɪ/ the capital town of the department of Creuse in the Limousin region, central France; pop. (1982) 16,620. It was formerly the capital of the old province of Marche.

**Guernica** /gɜː'niːkə, 'gɜːnɪkə/ (also **Guernica y Luno** /iː 'luːnəʊ/) a town in the Basque Provinces of northern Spain, 25 km. (16 miles) east of Bilbao; pop. (1981) 17,840. Formerly the seat of a Basque parliament, it was bombed in 1937, during the Spanish Civil War, by German planes in support of Franco, an event depicted in a famous painting by Picasso.

**Guernsey** /'gɜːnzɪ/ an island in the English Channel, to the north-west of Jersey; area 63 sq. km. (24 sq miles); pop.(1991) 58,870. Its chief town is St. Peter Port. The island, which is the second-largest of the Channel Islands and a popular holiday resort, gives its name to a breed of dairy cattle.

**Guerrero** /ge'reə,rəʊ/ a state of south-west-central Mexico, on the Pacific coast; area 64,281 sq. km. (24,828 sq. miles); pop. (1990) 2,622,070; capital, Chilpancingo de los Bravos.

**Guiana** /gi:'ɑ:nə/ a region in northern South America, bounded by the Orinoco, Negro, and Amazon rivers, and the Atlantic Ocean. It now comprises Surinam, Guyana, French Guiana, and the Guiana Highlands of south-east Venezuela and northern Brazil. (Amerindian = land of waters.)

**Guiana Highlands** a mountainous plateau region of northern South America, lying between the Orinoco and Amazon rivers in south-east Venezuela and northern Brazil. Its highest peak is Roraima (2,774 m., 9,094 ft.).

**Guienne** see GUYENNE.

**Guildford** /'gɪlfəd/ an old residential town in Surrey, south-east England, on the River Wey, 45 km. (28 miles) south-west of London; pop. (1981) 63,090. The Revd Charles Dodgson (Lewis Carroll) lies buried here. It has a modern brick-built cathedral (1964) and the Royal King Edward Grammar School (1557). The University of Surrey was founded in 1966 and the Yvonne Arnaud Theatre opened in 1965.

**Guilin** /gweɪ'lɪn/ (formerly **Kweilin** /kweɪ'lɪn/) a city in southern China, on the Li River in the autonomous region of Guangxi Zhuang; pop. (1986) 686,000. Guilin, which has a large Muslim population, produces grain, pharmaceuticals, textiles, and machinery. It is noted for the unusual limestone caves and hills which surround it. Guilin is the fourth tourist city of China.

**Guimarães** /gi:mə'rænʃ/ a city in the district of Braga, north-west Portugal, 21 km. south-east of Braga; pop. (1991) 48,160. It was the first capital of Portugal and birthplace in 1110 of Portugal's first king, Alfonso Henriques. It has textile and cutlery industries.

**Guinea** /'gɪnɪ/ (French **Guinée** /gi:'neɪ/) official name **The Republic of Guinea** a country on the west coast of Africa, bounded by Guinea-Bissau, Senegal, Mali, Ivory Coast, Liberia,  Sierra Leone, and the Atlantic Ocean; area 245,857 sq. km. (94,962 sq. miles); pop. (est. 1990) 5,800,000; official language, French; capital, Conakry. Comprising a coastal lowland plain that is separated from a savanna interior in the north and south-east by the pastoral Fouta Djallon highlands, Guinea has a humid tropical climate with a rainy season from April to November. The principal ethnic groups of Guinea include the Foulani of the Fouta Djallon highlands, the Mandingos of the savanna, and the coastal Soussos. Although fruit, palm products, and coffee are important exports, bauxite and alumina account for 90 per cent of the country's foreign exchange. Guinea is estimated to have one-third of the world's proven reserves of bauxite as well as significant reserves of high-grade iron ore, diamonds, gold, and uranium. Formerly part of French West Africa, Guinea became an independent republic in 1958, the only former French colony to vote against membership of the French Community. The development of mineral resources began in the 1960s under President Sékou Touré who ruled the country from independence until his death in 1984. Guinea was subsequently governed by a Military Committee for National Redressment (CMRN) and in 1993 the country's first multiparty elections were held. **Guinean** adj. & n.

**Guinea-Bissau** /ˌgɪnɪbɪ'saʊ/ (Portuguese **Guiné-Bissau**, formerly **Portuguese Guinea**) official name **The Republic of Guinea-Bissau** a country on the west coast of Africa, be-  tween Senegal and Guinea; area 36,125 sq. km. (13,953 sq. miles); pop.(est. 1990) 1,000,000; official language, Portuguese; capital, Bissau. Largely comprising a lowland coastal plain watered by many rivers, the land rises towards savanna in the east. Offshore lie the Bijagós Islands. The climate is tropical with a dry season from November to May during which the dust-laden Harmattan wind blows southwards from the Sahara. Among the world's least developed countries, Guinea-Bissau is dependent on fishing and agriculture. Rice is the most important staple food and its chief exports are peanuts, cashews, palm kernels, and timber. The area was explored by the Portuguese in the 15th c. and became a colony in 1879. It gained independence, as a republic, in 1974 and after a *coup* in 1980 was separated from Cape Verde. The country was ruled by a transitional Revolutionary Council until 1984 when a National Popular Assembly was constituted. The introduction of multiparty democracy was formally approved in 1991.

**Guinea, Gulf of** a large inlet of the Atlantic Ocean bordering on the southern coast of West Africa.

**Guipúzcoa** /gi:'pʊθkəʊə/ the smallest of the three Basque Provinces in northern Spain; area 1,997 sq. km. (771 sq. miles); pop. (1991) 676,490; capital, San Sebastian.

**Guise** /gi:z/ a town with a medieval castle in the department of Aisne in northern France that gave its name to the dukes of Guise in 1528.

**Guiyang** /gweɪ'jæŋ/ (formerly **Kweiyang** /kweɪ'jæŋ/) an industrial city in southern China, capital of Guizhou province; pop. (1990) 1,530,000. It is an important railway centre with iron and steel works.

**Guizhou** /gweɪ'dʒəʊ/ (formerly **Kweichow** /kweɪ'dʒəʊ/) a mountainous province of southern China; area 176,000 sq. km. (67,980 sq. miles); pop. (1990) 32,392,000; capital, Guiyang. Although one of the poorest provinces in China, it has rich deposits of coal, iron ore, phosphorus, manganese, aluminium, and mercury. Rice, maize, potatoes, oilseed rape, and tobacco are the chief agricultural crops.

**Gujarat** /ˌguːdʒə'rɑːt/ a highly industrialized state in western India, with an extensive coastline on the Arabian Sea; area 196,024 sq. km. (75,714 sq. miles); pop. (1991) 41,174,060; capital, Gandhinagar. Its principal port is Kandla. It was formed in 1960 from the northern and western parts of the former state of Bombay. One of the leading industrial states of India, Gujarat, which has large reserves of coal, oil, gas, fluorite, bauxite, and china clay, is a major producer of salt and soda-ash. **Gujarati** *adj. & n.*

**Gujarati** /ˌguːdʒə'rɑːtɪ/ a language descended from Sanskrit and so belonging to the Indo-Iranian language group, spoken by over 25 million people mainly in the Indian state of Gujarat. It is written in a form of the Devanagari script.

**Gujranwala** /ˌgʊdʒrən'wɑːlə/ a commercial market city of Pakistan in Punjab province northwest of Lahore; pop. (1981) 597,000. It was the birthplace of the Sikh ruler Ranjit Singh (1780–1839), and was an important centre of Sikh influence in the early 19th c.

**Gujrat** /'guːdʒrɑːt/ a city of Pakistan in Punjab province north of Lahore; pop. (1981) 154,000. It is a market town for grain grown in the surrounding region.

**Gulbarga** /'guːlbɑːgɑː/ a city in the state of Karnataka, south-central India; pop. (1991) 303,000. It was part of the Muslim sultanate of Delhi in the early 14th c., becoming the seat of the Bahmani kings of the Deccan in 1347 (until *c.* 1424). It is a centre of the cotton trade.

**gulf** /gʌlf/ a stretch of sea consisting of a deep inlet with a narrow mouth.

**Gulf, The** see PERSIAN GULF.

**Gulf Co-operation Council** an international organization founded in May 1981 with the aim of promoting closer cultural and economic links among the Gulf States excluding Iraq and Iran. Its Supreme Council, comprising heads of state of member countries, meets annually.

**Gulf Country** a region of Queensland and Northern Territories, Australia comprising the lowland coastal region around the Gulf of Carpentaria.

**Gulf States** **1.** the states with a coastline on the Persian Gulf (Bahrain, Kuwait, Oman, Qatar, Saudi Arabia, and the United Arab Emirates; sometimes also including Iran and Iraq). **2.** the states of the USA bordering on the Gulf of Mexico (Florida, Alabama, Mississippi, Louisiana, and Texas).

**Gulf Stream** a warm ocean current which flows from the Gulf of Mexico parallel with the North American coast towards Newfoundland, continuing (as the North Atlantic Drift) across the Atlantic Ocean and along the coast of north-west Europe, where it has a significant effect upon the climate.

**Gullah** /'gʌlə/ a creole language spoken by Black people who live on the coast of southern Carolina, USA, or the nearby Sea Islands.

**gully** /'gʌlɪ/ a water-worn ravine or artificial channel. In Australia and New Zealand it often refers to a river valley.

**gumland** a term used in New Zealand to describe scrub land from which fossil kauri gum has been obtained.

**Gumti** see GOMATI.

**Gümüşhane** /ˌgjuːməʃə'neɪ/ **1.** a province of north-east Turkey to the north of the Erzincan Mts.; area 10,227 sq. km. (3,950 sq. miles); pop. (1990) 169,375. **2.** its capital, 130 km. (81 miles) south of Trabzon (Trebizond); pop. (1990) 26,000.

**Guntur** /guːn'tʊə(r)/ a commercial city and railway centre in the state of Andhra Pradesh, southeast India; pop. (1991) 471,000. Founded by the French in the 18th c. it was the capital of the region known as the Northern Circars ruled from 1766 by the Muslim Nizam of Hyderabad. It trades in tobacco and cotton.

**Gunung** /'guːnʌŋ/ a Malay and Indonesian word for a mountain.

**Gupta** /'gʊptə/ the name of a Hindu dynasty established in 320 by Chandra Gupta I in Bihar. The Gupta empire eventually stretched across most of northern India, but began to disintegrate towards the end of the 5th c., only north Bengal being left by the end of the 6th c.

**Gur** see VOLTAIC LANGUAGES.

**Gurkha** /'gɜːkə/ a military people of Hindi descent and Sanskritic speech, who settled in the province of Gurkha, Nepal, in the 18th c. and made themselves supreme. The name is applied to a regiment of Nepalese soldiers in the British Army.

**Gustavia** /guː'stæviə/ the capital of the French island of St. Barthélémy in the West Indies. Formerly known as Carénage, it was renamed in honour of an 18th-c. King of Sweden.

**Gutland** /'guːtlænt/ (French **Pays Gaumais**) the name given to a fertile region occupying the southern two-thirds of Luxembourg.

**Guwahati** /gaʊ'hɑːtɪ/ (also **Gauhati**) the largest city of the state of Assam, north-east India, on the Brahmaputra River; pop. (1991) 578,000. It is a centre for oil refining, the grain trade, and the production of textiles. Its Kamakshya Temple is a centre for Tantric Hinduism attracting many pilgrims and the Navagrah Temple was an ancient seat of astronomy and astrology. The state capital lies 10 km. (6 miles) south at Dispur.

**Guyana** /gaɪ'ænə/  official name **The Co-operative Republic of Guyana** a country on the north-east coast of South America to the east of Venezuela and west of Surinam, with Brazil to the south and the Atlantic Ocean to the north; area 214,969 sq. km. (83,032 sq. miles); pop. (est. 1991) 800,000; official language, English; capital, Georgetown. A lowland coastal plain, watered by the Essequibo, Demerara, Berbice, and Corentyne rivers, rises through forest and savanna to the Guiana Highlands in the south. Much of the country is covered with dense forest. The climate is tropical with wet seasons on the coast during April–July and November–January. Agriculture and mining are the most important sectors of the economy, with sugar, rice, bauxite, shrimp, and timber accounting for the greater part of export earnings. The Spanish explored the area in 1499, and the Dutch settled there in the 17th c. It was occupied by the British from 1796 and established, with adjacent areas, as the colony of British Guiana in 1831. From the abolition of slavery in 1834 until 1917 indentured workers were brought to the colony, chiefly from India, China, and Portugal. In 1966 it gained independence as Guyana, and became a Co-operative Republic within the Commonwealth in 1970. Guyana is governed by an executive president and an elected unicameral National Assembly.
**Guyanese** *adj. & n.*

**Guyenne** /gi:'en/ (also **Guienne**) a former province of southern France centred on Bordeaux and stretching from the Bay of Biscay across Aquitaine to the south-west edge of the Massif Central.

**guyot** /'gi:əʊ/ a flat-topped mountain of volcanic origin rising from the ocean floor, particularly in the Pacific. The term is named after the Swiss-American scientist, Arnold Guyot (1807–89).

**Gwalior** /'gwɑ:lɪ,ɔ:(r)/ a city in a district of the same name in Madhya Pradesh, central India, between the Sind and Chambal rivers; pop. (1991) 693,000. It is noted for its fortress, dating from AD 525, which includes several palaces, temples, and shrines. The district of Gwalior corresponds to a former princely state of the same name. The city has textile, footwear, foodstuffs, and leather industries.

**Gwent** /gwent/ a county of south-east Wales formed in 1974 from most of Monmouthshire, part

of Breconshire, and Newport; area 1,376 sq. km. (531 sq. miles); pop.(1991) 432,300; administrative centre, Cwmbran. Gwent is divided into five districts:

| District | Area (sq. km.) | Pop. (1991) |
|---|---|---|
| Blaenau Gwent | 127 | 74,400 |
| Islwyn | 102 | 64,900 |
| Monmouth | 831 | 75,000 |
| Newport | 190 | 129,900 |
| Torfaen | 126 | 88,200 |

**Gweru** /'gweru:/ (formerly **Gwelo**) the third-largest city in Zimbabwe and administrative capital of the Midlands province; pop. (1982) 78,920. Established in the 1890s as a coaching station on the Harare–Bulawayo route, Gweru developed in association with the nearby gold mines. The Dabuka rail marshalling yard is the biggest container-handling facility in the country. It changed its name from Gwelo to Gweru in 1982.

**Gwynedd** /'gwɪnəð/ a county of north-west Wales formed in 1974 from Anglesey, Caernarvonshire, part of Denbighshire, and most of Merionethshire; area 3,863 sq. km. (1,492 sq. miles); pop. (1991) 238,600; administrative centre, Caernarvon. Gwynedd is divided into five districts:

| District | Area (sq. km.) | Pop. (1991) |
|---|---|---|
| Aberconwy | 601 | 54,100 |
| Arfon | 410 | 54,600 |
| Dwyfor | 620 | 28,600 |
| Meironnydd | 1,517 | 33,400 |
| Isle of Anglesey | 715 | 67,800 |

**Gyandzha** /'gɑ:ndʒə/ see GÄNCÄ.

**Győr** /dʒɜ:/ an industrial city in north-west Hungary, at the junction of the Raba and Repce rivers with the Danube near the frontier with Slovakia; pop. (1993) 130,560. It is capital of Győr-Sopron county. Vehicles, steel, textiles, and food are produced.

**gypsy** /'dʒɪpsɪ/ (also **gipsy**) a travelling people with dark skin and hair, and speaking Romany, a language related to Hindi. Their original home was the Indian subcontinent which they left in three separate migrations. With their distinctive language and customs the gypsies continue to resist assimilation and their dispersion has been accelerated in modern times by prejudice and by persecution. The English began a policy of transportation in 1544 and sent them to the West Indies, the American colonies, and later to Australia. Similar forced migration was practised by the Portuguese (to Brazil and Angola), the Dutch, Germans, etc.; Nazi extermination campaigns directed against the gypsies reduced their numbers in Europe by 400,000 between 1939 and 1945. Estimated to number *c.* 3,000,000, gypsies are largely to be found in Europe, especially in Romania.

**Gyumri** /kuːmˈriː/ (also **Kumayri**) an industrial city in north-west Armenia, near the Turkish frontier north-west of Yerevan; pop. (1990) 123,000. Founded as a fortress town in 1837 and formerly called Alexandropol, it was known as Leninakan from 1924 to 1991. The city was devastated by an earthquake in 1988. It manufactures textiles, carpets, and copper utensils.

# H *h*

**Haaf** /hɑːf/ **1.** a term used by geographers to describe a coastal lagoon separated from the sea by a spit of sand. **2.** a word used by fishermen of Orkney and Shetland to describe their deep-sea fishing grounds.

**Haardt Mountains** /hɑːrt/ a range of hills to the east of the Rhine in the Rhineland-Palatinate of south-west Germany. A continuation of the Vosges, the densely forested slopes of the Haardt Mts. rise to 673 m. (2,208 ft.) at Mt. Kalmit.

**Haarlem** /'hɑːləm/ a commercial and industrial city in the Netherlands, capital of the province of North Holland and commercial centre of the Dutch bulb industry, 20 km. (12 miles) west of Amsterdam; pop. (1991) 149,470. It was a centre of Dutch painting in the 16th and 17th c. and of a school of architecture founded by Lieven de Key (1560–1627). The painter Frans Hals (c. 1580–1666) lived all his life in the city. Its 15th-c. church is said to be one of the largest in the Netherlands. Haarlem has shipyards and machinery industries.

**Haarlemmermeer** /'hɑːləmə:ˌmiːr/ a city in the Dutch province of North Holland, 10 km. (6 miles) south-east of Haarlem; pop. (1991) 98,070. The city developed around the village of Hoofddorp on fenland drained in the early 19th c.

**Habana, La** see HAVANA.

**Habikino** /ˌhæbɪˈkiːnəʊ/ a city in Kinki region, Japan, situated south-east of Osaka, on the island of Honshu; pop. (1990) 115,000.

**Habsburg** /'hæpsbɜːg/ a castle in Switzerland that gave its name to a German family to which belonged rulers of various countries of Europe from 1273, when they first became kings of Germany, until 1918, and various Holy Roman Emperors from 1483. A branch of the family ruled in Spain (1504–1700).

**Hachinohe** /ˌhætʃiːˈnəʊheɪ/ a city and deep-sea fishing port in Tohoku region, north-eastern Honshu Island, Japan; pop. (1990) 241,000. Its chief products are chemicals, iron, and steel. There is a ferry link with Tomakomai on Hokkaido Island.

**Hachioji** /ˌhætʃiːˈəʊdʒɪ/ a city in the Kanto region of Honshu Island, Japan, to the west of Tokyo; pop. (1990) 466,000. It is noted for its tradition of silk weaving.

**Hackensack** /'hækənˌsæk/ **1.** a river of the USA that rises in south-east New York and flows southwards for c. 25 km. (40 miles) through New Jersey to Newark Bay. **2.** an industrial city on the Hackensack River in north-east New Jersey; pop. (1990) 37,050. Known as New Barbados until 1921, its name is derived from that of a former Indian village and tribe. It is the site of the New Jersey Naval Museum.

**Hackney** /'hækni/ a borough of north-east London, England, said to have given its name to the hackney coach which began to ply in London in 1625. By the reign of George III the number of hackney coaches had risen to 1,000, operating by licence and paying duty of five shillings a week to the king. Horses were pastured at Hackney.

**Hadano** /hæˈdɑːnəʊ/ a marketing city in Kanto region, Japan, situated south-west of Tokyo on the island of Honshu; pop. (1990) 156,000. It makes sake and soy-sauce.

**Haddington** /'hædɪŋtən/ a town and royal burgh in East Lothian, Scotland, on the River Tyne; pop. (1981) 8,140. It was the birthplace in 1505 of the Scottish reformer John Knox.

**Hades** /'heɪdiːz/ (Greek **Aïdes**) in Greek mythology the kingdom of one of the sons of Cronus, lord of the lower world (which is known as the House of Hades).

**Hadhramaut** /ˌhɑːdrəˈmaʊt/ (also **Hadramaut**) a narrow coastal plain on the arid south-eastern coast of the Arabian Peninsula, stretching from Aden in Yemen to Cape Ra's al Hadd in Oman.

**Hadrianopolis** /ˌheɪdrɪənˈɒpəlɪs/ the former Roman name for the present-day city of EDIRNE in north-west Turkey.

**Hadrian's Wall** /'heɪdrɪənz/ a Roman defensive wall across northern England from the Solway Firth in the west to the mouth of the River Tyne in the east (about 120 km., 74 miles). It was begun in AD 122, after the emperor Hadrian's visit, to defend the province of Britain against invasions of tribes from the north. There were forts and fortified posts at intervals, a ditch on the north and a wider ditch on the south, and the wall itself (2.5–3 m. thick) was eventually built of stone throughout its length. After Hadrian's death the frontier was advanced to the Antonine Wall, which the Romans proved unable to hold; after being overrun and restored several times Hadrian's Wall was abandoned c. AD 410.

**Hadrumetum** /ˌhædrəˈmiːtəm/ the ancient Carthaginian name for the city of Sousse in Tunisia. Its name was changed to Justinianopolis in 533 after the Roman reoccupation of North Africa.

**Haeju** /'haɪdʒuː/ a city in south-west North Korea, capital of South Hwanghai province; pop. (est. 1984) 131,000. During the winter it is the only ice-free port on the west coast of North Korea.

**Haerphin** see HARBIN.

**Hafsid** /'hæfsiːd/ a Berber dynasty ruling part of Tunisia and eastern Algeria in the 13th–16th c.

**Hagen** /'hɑːg(ə)n/ an industrial city in North Rhine-Westphalia, Germany, on the Ennepe River 48 km. (30 miles) north-east of Düsseldorf; pop. (1991) 214,085. Its chief products are textiles, iron and steel, chemicals, and paper.

**Hagia Sophia** /ˌhægɪə səˈfiːə/ see ST. SOPHIA.

**Hague** /heɪg/, **The** (Dutch **Den Haag** /den 'hɑːg/; also called **'s-Gravenhage** /'sxrɑːvənˌhɒxə/) the seat of government and administrative centre of the Netherlands, on the North Sea coast in the province of South Holland; pop. (1991) 444,240. It is the third-largest city in the Netherlands and seat of the International Court of Justice which is housed in the Palace of Peace (1913). The Hague Convention of 1907 formulated much of the law governing the conduct of international warfare. The city's two names *'s-Gravenhage* 'the counts' park', and *Den Haag* 'the hedge', refer to a wooded former hunting preserve, site of a royal palace since 1250.

**Hai** /haɪ/ (Chinese **Hai He**) a river of eastern China that rises in the Taihang Shan Mts. and flows north-eastwards for 1,090 km. (677 miles) before emptying into the Bohai Sea east of Tianjin.

**Haicheng** /haɪˈtʃeŋ/ a city in Liaoning province, north-east China, in the western foothills of the Qian Shan Range east of Yingkou; pop. (1986) 992,000.

**Haifa** /'haɪfə/ the chief port of Israel, in the north-west of the country on a peninsula jutting into the Mediterranean Sea; pop. (1988) 222,600. It is the third-largest city in Israel and site of the Baha'i Shrine. Its industries include chemicals, textiles, and electrical equipment.

**Haikou** /haɪˈkəʊ/ an industrial seaport on the island of Hainan in Guandong province, southern China; pop. (1986) 300,000. It has a large integrated steel complex, machine shops, and cement plants.

**Ha'il** /hæˈiːl/ an oasis and market town in north-west Saudi Arabia, on the pilgrimage route from Iraq to Mecca. In the 1890s it became capital of desert Arabia, but in the 1920s its importance began to decline when the Saudi kings made Riyadh their capital.

**Hailar** /haɪˈlɑː/ a market town in Inner Mongolia, north-east China, on the Hailar River west of the Da Hinggang Mountains; pop. (1986) 185,000.

**Hainan** /haɪˈnæn/ an island in the South China Sea forming an autonomous region of China; area 34,000 sq. km. (13,132 sq. miles); pop. (1986) 6,000,000; capital, Haikou. Produce includes rubber, sugar, fruit, coffee, cocoa, and minerals such as iron ore, limestone, marble, and china clay.

**Hainaut** /eɪˈnəʊ/ (Flemish **Henegouw** /'heɪnəgaʊ/) a province in southern Belgium to the north of the Ardennes; area 3,788 sq. km. (1,463 sq. miles); pop. (1991) 76,785; capital, Mons.

**Haining** /haɪˈnɪŋ/ a city in Zhejiang province, eastern China, between Shanghai and Hangzhou; pop. (1986) 600,000.

**Haiphong** /haɪˈfɒŋ/ a port in northern Vietnam on the Cam River which forms part of the delta of the Red River (Bac Bo); pop. (1989) 456,050. Developed by the French, who took possession of a small market town here in 1874, it is the third-largest city in the country and the leading industrial centre of north Vietnam. Its industrial development has been partly dependent on nearby supplies of coal. The city was badly damaged during air raids in 1946 and from 1965 to 1972, during the Vietnam War.

**Haiti** /'heɪtɪ/ (French **Haïti** /aˈiːtiː/) official name **The Republic of Haiti** a country in the Caribbean, the French-speaking western part of the island of Hispaniola; area 27,750 sq. km.  (10,718 sq. miles); pop. (est. 1990) 6,500,000; official language, Haitian Creole and French; capital, Port-au-Prince. Two mountainous peninsulas are separated by the Golfe de la Gonâve and the low-lying Plaine du Cul-de-Sac. The climate is tropical with a wet season from May to September, but the country is generally semiarid. A predominantly agricultural economy, Haiti's chief exports are bananas, coffee, fish, timber, and bauxite. In 1492 Columbus discovered the island that now comprises Haiti and the Dominican Republic, and named it La Isla Española (the Spanish Island). The indigenous inhabitants were enslaved or killed by the Spaniards, who established some not very successful settlements at the east end of the island, while French pirates were more successful in establishing plantations in the west. In 1697 the western area was ceded to the French (as Saint Domingue), who introduced large numbers of slaves from West Africa to work in the sugar plantations. In 1791 the slaves rose in rebellion; they swept to victory under Black leaders such as Toussaint L'Ouverture and in 1804 the colony was proclaimed an independent state, under the aboriginal name of Haiti, the first country in the Americas (after the US) to achieve freedom from colonial rule. Haiti's West African heritage is shown by the great preponderance of pure Blacks in the population (in contrast to the largely mulatto Dominican Republic) and the practice of voodoo rites. Following a succession of corrupt dictatorships Haiti became bankrupt and was governed by the USA from 1915 to 1934. In 1957 François Duvalier succeeded General Paul Magloire as dictator of Haiti and under his repressive rule the country was reduced to the status of poorest nation in the western hemisphere. The Duvalier family dictatorship came to an end in 1986 when his son Jean-Claude ('Baby-Doc') was ousted. Since then military interference has prevented stable government, most notably in 1991 when Father Jean-Bertrand Aristide was ousted after becoming Haiti's first democratically elected president. Aristide was restored to power with US help in 1994. Haiti is governed by an executive Council of National Government and a bicameral legislature.

**Haitian** *adj. & n.*

The country is divided into nine departments:

| Department | Area (sq. km.) | Pop. (1982) | Capital |
| --- | --- | --- | --- |
| Nord-Ouest | 2,094 | 293,530 | Port-de-Paix |
| Nord | 2,175 | 564,000 | Cap-Haïtien |
| Nord-Est | 1,698 | 189,570 | Fort-Liberté |
| L'Artibonite | 4,895 | 732,930 | Gonaïves |
| Centre | 3,597 | 361,470 | Hinche |
| Ouest | 4,595 | 1,551,790 | Port-au-Prince |
| Sud-Est | 2,077 | 367,910 | Jacmel |
| Sud | 2,602 | 502,620 | Les Cayes |
| Grande Anse | 3,100 | 489,960 | Jérémie |

**Haitian Creole** a French-based creole language spoken by 90 per cent of the people on the island of Hispaniola in the Caribbean. It has been the official language of Haiti since 1987.

**Hajar** /'hædʒ(ə)r/ a mountain range in northern Oman rising to 3,018 m. (9,902 ft.) at Jabal Akhadar.

**hajj** /hædʒ/ (also **hadj**) an Islamic pilgrimage to Mecca required of Muslims once in a lifetime. A **hajji** is someone who has been to Mecca as a pilgrim.

**Hakkâri** /ˌhækjə'ri:/ **1.** a mountainous province of south-eastern Turkey, on the frontier with Iran and Iraq; area 9,521 sq. km. (3,677 sq. miles); pop. (1990) 172,480. **2.** its capital; pop. (1990) 30,400.

**Hakodate** /hækəʊ'dɑ:tɪ/ a port on the south-west coast of the island of Hokkaido, northern Japan; pop. (1990) 307,000. Its chief industries are fishing, shipbuilding, and food processing.

**Hakone** /hæ'kəʊnɪ/ a resort town on Honshu Island, Japan, 90 km. (56 miles) south-west of Tokyo. It is situated at the centre of the Fuji-Hakone-Izu National Park, which was designated in 1936 and includes Mt. Fuji, Lake Ashino, and several hot spring resorts.

**Halab** see ALEPPO.

**Halabja** /hə'læbdʒə/ a Kurdish town in the province of Sulaymaniyah, north-eastern Iraq, situated close to the Iranian border. In August 1988 an estimated 5,000 Kurds died when Iraqi planes dropped poison gas on the town.

**Halafian** /hæ'læfɪən/ a chalcolithic culture (c. 5,000–4,500 BC) identified primarily by the use of polychrome pottery (Halaf ware) which was first noted during excavations at Tell Halaf in north-east Syria. Its distribution extends to the Mediterranean coast and the region of Lake Van in eastern Turkey.

**Halden** /'hɑ:ld(ə)n/ a timber-processing town and port in Østfold county, south-east Norway, near the Swedish border on the Iddefjord, an inlet of the Skaggerak; pop. (1991) 25,850. Formerly known as Frederikshald (1665–1927), it was rebuilt on a regular plan in 1826 after a great fire. King Charles XII of Sweden was killed here during a siege of the town in 1718.

**Haleakala** /ˌhæleɪˌækə'lɑ:/ a volcanic peak on the island of Maui, Hawaii, designated a national park in 1960. Rising to 3,058 m. (10,025 ft.), its crater is one of the largest in the world with an area of 49 sq. km. (19 sq. miles). The rare silversword plant grows here.

**Halesowen** /heɪlz'əʊɪn/ an engineering town to the west of Birmingham in the West Midlands of England; pop. (1981) 57,530.

**Half Dome** a granite mountain peak with a precipitous rock face in Yosemite National Park, California, USA, rising to 2,698 m. (8,852 ft.) in the Sierra Nevada. The northern half of the mountain was eroded during the Ice Age when the 610-m. (2,000-ft.) thick Merced and Tenaya glaciers merged near Half Dome and quarried out Yosemite Valley.

**Half Moon Caye** a coral island on Lighthouse Reef in the western Caribbean, off the coast of Belize. Designated a natural monument in 1982, it is the breeding ground of the red-footed booby which occurs here in a rare white-colour phase.

**Haliç** /'hælɪtʃ/ the Turkish name for the GOLDEN HORN.

**Halicarnassus** /ˌhælɪkɑ:'nɑ:səs/ an ancient Greek city on the south-west coast of Asia Minor at what is now the Turkish city of Bodrum. It was the birthplace of the historian Herodotus and is the site of the Mausoleum of Halicarnassus, tomb of the local dynast Mausolus (d. 353 BC), and one of the Seven Wonders of the World.

**Halidon Hill** /'hælɪd(ə)n/ a hill in Northumberland, north-east England, 3 km. (2 miles) north-west of Berwick-upon-Tweed. It was the scene of a battle on 19 July 1333 at which a Scottish army attempting to relieve a garrison at Berwick-upon-Tweed were defeated by the English under Edward III.

**Halifax** /'hælɪˌfæks/ the capital of Nova Scotia, and Canada's principal ice-free port on the eastern seaboard; pop. (1991) 67,800; 320,500 (metropolitan area). It is an educational centre with four universities (founded 1789, 1802, 1818, and 1925). Originally a French fishing station, it was settled in 1749 by the English, who named it after the second earl of Halifax, President of the Board of Trade and Plantations. One of the largest man-made explosions ever to take place before the atom bomb occurred in 1917 when an ammunition ship exploded killing 2,000 people, injuring 20,000 others and destroying the northern half of the city. In 1945 a naval arsenal exploded rocking the city again. In 1912 many victims of the *Titanic* disaster were buried here. The port handles bulk cargoes and container traffic and has oil refineries, iron foundries, and numerous light industries. Fishing is also important.

**Halifax** a town in West Yorkshire, England, on the River Calder near Bradford; pop. (1981) 77,350. It developed in the Middle Ages as a cloth-making town.

**Halle** /'hɑːlə/ **1.** (French **Hal**) a manufacturing town in the province of Brabant, central Belgium, on the River Senne and the Charleroi-Brussels Canal; pop. (1991) 32,770. Its medieval Gothic church is a place of pilgrimage and its chief industries include food processing and the production of textiles and leather. **2.** a city in the state of Saxony-Anhalt, central Germany, on the River Saale north-west of Leipzig; pop. (1991) 303,000. The composer Handel was born here in 1685.

**Hallstatt** a village in the Salzkammergut of Upper Austria, on the Hallstätter See; pop. (1991) 1,153. It gives its name to a phase of the late Bronze–early Iron Age (*c.* 700–500 BC), preceding the La Tène. Remains of that period were found in a necropolis on the nearby Salt Mountain (Salzberg).

**Halmahera** /ˌhælməˈhɜːrə/ the largest of the Molucca (Maluku) Islands of Indonesia, situated on the equator; area 17,936 sq. km. (6,928 sq. miles). The chief settlements are Tobelo and Kao. Halmahera is still largely covered in undeveloped primary forest.

**Halmstad** /'hɑːlmstɑːd/ a port in southern Sweden on the Kattegat at the mouth of the Nissan River; pop. (1990) 80,000. Rebuilt in 1619 after a fire, it produces textiles, paper, and pulp. It is capital of Halland county.

**Hälsingborg** the Swedish name for HELSINGBORG.

**Hama** /'hɑːmə/ (also **Hamah**) a steel-manufacturing city in west-central Syria, on the River Orontes; pop. (1981) 176,640. Originally a Hittite city, it became the Kingdom of Hamath under the Aramaeans in the 11th c. BC and was renamed Epiphania in the 2nd c. BC by the Seleucids. It is noted for its water-wheels which have been used for irrigation since the Middle Ages.

**hamada** /hɑːˈmɑːdə/ the name commonly given to a flat rocky (as opposed to a sandy) desert.

**Hamadan** /ˌhæməˈdɑːn/ a city in western Iran, in the Zagros Mountains between Tehran and Kermanshah; pop. (1991) 350,000. It is capital of the province of Hamadan. Allegedly inhabited since the 2nd millennium BC, it became the capital of Media in the 6th c. BC when it was known as Ecbatana. The shrine of Esther is the most important Jewish pilgrimage site in Iran. It produces carpets, rugs, and leather goods.

**Hamamatsu** /ˌhæməˈmɑːtsuː/ an industrial city in Chubu region, Honshu Island, Japan, situated 90 km. (56 miles) south-east of Nagoya; pop. (1990) 535,000. Promoted as a convention centre, its chief products are tea, textiles, motor cycles, and musical instruments. An annual kite festival is held in May.

**Hamburg** /'hæmˌbɜːg/ a city-state and industrial port of northern Germany, on the River Elbe; area 755 sq. km. (292 sq. miles); pop. (1991) 1,668,760. Founded by Charlemagne in the 9th c., it was a founder member of the Hanseatic League, and became a state of the German Empire in 1871. It was the birthplace of Brahms and Mendelssohn; its university was founded in 1919. At least half of the city was devastated by gigantic fires set off by air raids during World War II. It has been completely reconstructed as the largest port in Germany, with extensive shipyards, petrochemical, electronics, and food-processing industries.

**Hämeenlinna** /'hɑːmˌ(ə)nliˌnə/ (Swedish **Tavastehus** /tæˈvæstəˌhuːs/) a city in south-west Finland, on Lake Vanajavesi; pop. (1990) 43,420. It is capital of Häme province and was the birthplace of the composer Jean Sibelius in 1865. It has textile and plywood industries.

**Hamelin** /'hæmlɪn/ (German **Hameln** /'hɑːməln/) a carpet-making and tourist town in Lower Saxony, north-west Germany, on the River Weser; pop. (1983) 57,000. It was a medieval market town, the setting of the legend of the *Pied Piper of Hamelin*, which may be based on actual events which occurred in 1284.

**Hamersley Range** a mountain range in north-west Western Australia to the south of the Fortescue River. Rising to 1,226 m. (4,022 ft.) at Mt. Bruce, its deep gorges and weathered rock were included in 1969 within a national park extending to 6,176 sq. km. (2,385 sq. miles).

**Hamhung** /hæmˈhuːŋ/ the capital city of South Hamgyong province, eastern North Korea; pop. (est. 1984) 775,000. It was the centre of government of north-east Korea during the Yi dynasty of 1392–1910. It has machinery, textile, and chemical industries.

**Hami** /'hɑːmɪ/ (also **Kumul**) a city in Xinjiang autonomous region, northern China, on the trade route south-east from Urumqi; pop. (1986) 275,000.

**Hamilton** /'hæmɪlt(ə)n/ the capital of the Bermuda Islands in the North Atlantic and chief port of Great Bermuda; pop. (1980) 1,620. Established in 1612, it became capital in 1815.

**Hamilton** a city in south-east Ontario, Canada, at the head of Lake Ontario to the south-west of Toronto; pop. (1991) 318,500; 599,760 (metropolitan area). Founded in 1813 by George Hamilton, a local landowner, it is the home of McMaster University (1887) and a centre for the production of steel, vehicles, chemicals, machinery, textiles, and electrical equipment.

**Hamilton** a city on North Island, New Zealand, on the Waikato River; pop. (1990) 98,500. It is New Zealand's largest inland city and a major centre of communication and marketing. First settled in 1864 by soldiers sent to quell a Maori uprising, the city was named in honour of Captain John Hamilton RN who was killed leading the naval brigade at the Battle of Gate Pa near Tauranga. Hamilton has a number of agricultural research establishments.

**Hamilton** a town in central Scotland, southeast of Glasgow; pop. (1981) 51,720.

**Hamilton** an industrial city in south-west Ohio, USA, on the Miami River; pop. (1990) 61,370. Originally named Fort Hamilton and first settled in 1796, it developed in the 1850s after the completion of the Miami–Erie Canal.

**Hamina** /'hɑːmiːnə/ (Swedish **Frederikshamn** /'freɪdrɪks,hɑːm(ə)n/) a port in the province of Kymi, south-east Finland, on the Gulf of Finland; pop. (1991) 10,100. Founded in 1653, the town was named in honour of the Swedish king Fredrik I in 1753. The 1809 Treaty of Hamina ceded the whole of Finland to Russia.

**Hamite** /'hæmaɪt/ a group of North African peoples, including the ancient Egyptians, Berbers, and Tuareg, supposedly descended from Ham, son of Noah.

**Hamitic** /həˈmɪtɪk/ a group of African languages including ancient Egyptian, Berber, and Cushitic, probably related in the past to the Semitic languages.

**Hamito-Semitic** /ˌhæmɪtəʊsɪˈmɪtɪk/ (also **Afro-Asiatic**) a family of languages spoken in the Middle East and in northern Africa, divided into Semitic, Hamitic, and Chadic subgroups.

**Hamm** /hɑːm/ an industrial city in North Rhine-Westphalia, west Germany, on the Lippe River; pop. (1991) 180,320. It was founded in 1226 and was a member of the Hanseatic League. It has iron and steel, textile, and machinery industries.

**Hammamet** /'hæmə,met/ a Mediterranean resort town of north-east Tunisia, on the Cape Bon peninsula.

**Hammerfest** /'hæmə,fest/ a port in Finnmark county, northern Norway, on Kvaløy Island; pop. (1991) 6,900. It is the northernmost town in Europe.

**Hammersmith** /'hæmə,smɪθ/ a district of London, England, that (since 1965) has formed with Fulham an inner borough to the north of the Thames; pop. (1991) 136,500. The Olympia exhibition centre and the BBC Television centre are located here.

**Hammond** /'hæmənd/ an industrial city near Chicago on the south-west shore of Lake Michigan, Indiana, USA, adjacent to Calumet City in Illinois; pop. (1990) 84,240. Its chief products are steel, car wheels, forgings, surgical goods, and railway supplies.

**Hampshire** /'hæmpʃɪə(r)/ a county on the coast of southern England; area 3,780 sq. km. (1,460 sq. miles); pop. (1991) 1,511,900; county town, Winchester. Its largest cities are Southampton, from which it takes its name, and Portsmouth. It is divided into 13 districts:

| District | Area (sq. km.) | Pop. (1991) |
| --- | --- | --- |
| Basingstoke and Deane | 634 | 140,400 |
| East Hampshire | 515 | 101,100 |
| Eastleigh | 80 | 103,200 |
| Fareham | 74 | 97,300 |
| Gosport | 25 | 72,800 |
| Hart | 215 | 78,700 |
| Havant | 55 | 117,400 |
| New Forest | 753 | 157,000 |
| Portsmouth | 40 | 174,700 |
| Rushmoor | 39 | 80,400 |
| Southampton | 50 | 194,400 |
| Test Valley | 637 | 99,000 |
| Winchester | 661 | 95,700 |

**Hampstead** /'hæmsted/ a residential suburb of north-west London. It contains Hampstead Heath, a large tract of open common land within the city, popular for recreation. It was the birthplace of Evelyn Waugh in 1903 and the home of writers such as John Galsworthy, George Orwell, Aldous Huxley, H. G. Wells, Katherine Mansfield, and John Keats.

**Hampton** /'hæmpt(ə)n/ a city in south-east Virginia, USA, on the Hampton Roads channel, Chesapeake Bay; pop. (1990) 133,790. Settled in 1610 at a place then called Kecoughan, it is alleged to be the oldest English-speaking community in the US. It was a one-time haunt of pirates such as the infamous Blackbeard and was destroyed, first by the British during the war of 1812, and later in 1861 to prevent occupation by Union forces. Later rebuilt, it is now an important centre of commercial fishing. Nearby are Langley Air Force Base, headquarters of the Tactical Air Command, Langley Research Center for the National Aeronautics and Space Administration, and Fort Monroe, headquarters of the US Army's Training and Doctrine Command.

**Hampton Court** /'hæmpt(ə)n/ a palace on the north bank of the River Thames in the London borough of Richmond, England. It was built by Cardinal Wolsey as his private residence but later presented by him to Henry VIII, and was a favourite royal residence until the reign of George II. William III had part rebuilt by Sir Christopher Wren and the gardens laid out in formal Dutch style. Its collections, gardens, and maze are a major tourist attraction.

**Hampton Roads** a deep-water estuary 6.4 km. (4 miles) long, formed by the James River where it joins Chesapeake Bay, on the Atlantic coast of south-east Virginia, USA. It has been used as a natural anchorage since colonial times. The **Port of Hampton Roads** comprises the harbours at Newport News, Norfolk, and Portsmouth.

**Han** /hæn/ the name of the Chinese dynasty that ruled from 206 BC until AD 220 with only a brief interruption. During this period the territory was expanded, administration was in the hands of an organized civil service, Confucianism was recognized as the state philosophy, and detailed historical records were kept. The arts flourished, and technological advances included the invention of paper. It was to this era that later dynasties looked for their model.

**Han** 1. (also **Han Shui**) a river in China that rises in south-west Shaanxi province and flows 1,532 km. (952 miles) south-eastwards into Hubei province where it meets the Yangtze River. **2. Han Chiang** a river in China that rises in south-west Fujian province and flows southwards into Guangdong province where it meets the South China Sea at Shantou. **3.** a river in northern South Korea that flows westwards across the peninsula and through Seoul before entering the Yellow Sea.

**Hanau** /ˈhænaʊ/ (fully **Hanau am Main**) a river port in the German state of Hesse, on the River Main east of Frankfurt; pop. (1989) 84,300. It was founded in 1597 for Protestant Dutch and Walloon refugees. It has machinery, rubber, and jewellery industries.

**Hancheng** /hænˈtʃen/ a city in Shaanxi province, central China, to the west of the Yellow River; pop. (1986) 307,000.

**Handa** /ˈhɑːndə/ a fishing port and industrial city in the Chubu region of Japan, situated on the Chita peninsula, Honshu Island, 32 km. (20 miles) south of Nagoya; pop. (1990) 100,000.

**Handan** /hɑːnˈdɑːn/ a city in southern Hebei province, east China, on the Fuyang River north of Anyang; pop. (1990) 1,110,000.

**Hangzhou** /hænˈdʒaʊ/ (formerly **Hangchow** /hænˈtʃaʊ/) the capital city of Zhejiang province in eastern China, situated on Hangzhou Bay, an inlet of the Yellow Sea, at the southern end of the Grand Canal; pop. (1990) 5,234,000. Its chief industries include oil refining and the manufacture of silk, satins, brocades, iron, steel, electronics, and machinery.

**Hani** /ˈhɑːnɪ/ a minority nationality of southern China, mostly found in Yunnan province where the Hani people number c. 1 million.

**Hanish Islands** /ˈhænɪʃ/ a group of volcanic islands and rocky islets at the southern end of the Red Sea off the south-west coast of Yemen. The four largest islands are Zukur, Great Hanish, Little Hanish, and Suyul.

**Hanko** /ˈhɑːŋkəʊ/ (Swedish **Hangö**) a resort town and industrial port on the south coast of Finland, on the Gulf of Finland; pop. (1990) 11,460. It is Finland's southernmost town.

**Hannover** see HANOVER.

**Hanoi** /hæˈnɔɪ/ the capital and second-largest city of Vietnam, on the Red River; pop. (est. 1984) 925,000, Greater Hanoi pop. (est. 1984) 2,800,000. It was the capital of French Indo-China from 1887 to 1946 and of North Vietnam before reunification of North and South Vietnam in 1975. It manufactures vehicles, machine tools, chemicals, and textiles.

**Hanover** /ˈhænəvə(r)/ (German **Hannover** /hæˈnɒfər/) **1.** an industrial and cultural city and capital of Lower Saxony, northern Germany, on the River Leine; pop. (1991) 517,480. George I of Britain is buried here. It has a trade fair in the spring and its industries manufacture steel, chemicals, rubber, and textiles. **2.** a former state and province in northern Germany. It was an electorate of the Empire from 1692 until 1806, ruled by the Guelph dynasty, and from 1866 until 1945 was a province of Prussia. In 1714 the Elector of Hanover succeeded to the British throne as George I, and from then until 1837 the same monarch ruled both Britain and Hanover. With the succession of Victoria to the British throne, however, Hanover passed to her uncle, Ernest, Duke of Cumberland, the Hanoverian succession being denied to a woman as long as a male member of the Guelph family survived.

**Hanseatic League** /ˌhænsɪˈætɪk/ a medieval association of north German cities (Hanse Towns), formed in 1241 as a commercial alliance for trade between the eastern and western sides of northern Europe. In the later Middle Ages the League, with about 100 member towns, was an independent political power, with its own army and navy, but it began to collapse in the early 17th c. and only three major cities (Hamburg, Bremen, and Lübeck) remained until it was finally broken up in the 19th c.

**Hants** /hænts/ abbr. the county of Hampshire in the south of England.

**Hanzhong** /hænˈdʒʊŋ/ a city in Shaanxi province, central China, south-west of Xi'an in the southern foothills of the Qin Ling Mountains; pop. (1986) 420,000.

**Haora** /ˈhaʊrə/ (also **Howrah**) an industrial city in the state of West Bengal, eastern India, on the Hooghly (Hugli) River opposite Calcutta; pop. (1991) 947,000. It has iron and steel works, textile and paper mills, and railway workshops. Because of its position it, rather than its larger neighbour, is the focus of the rail network. It is the headquarters of the Ramakrishna Mission which was founded in 1899.

**Hapur** /'hɑːpər/ a town in Uttar Pradesh, northern India, east of Delhi; pop. (1991) 146,590.

**Harappa** /həˈræpə/ an ancient city of the Indus Valley civilization (c. 3,000–1,700 BC), to the north of Multan in Punjab province, north-west Pakistan. The site of the ruins was discovered in 1920.

**Harare** /hɑːˈrɑːrɪ/ (formerly **Salisbury**) the capital, largest city, and marketing centre of Zimbabwe, at an altitude of 1,470 m. (4,825 ft.) in the province of Mashonaland East; pop. (1982) 656,000. Originally named Fort Salisbury in honour of the British prime minister Lord Salisbury, the city was first settled by Europeans in 1890. It was designated capital of Southern Rhodesia in 1902. It is a modern city with the world's largest tobacco market and produces a wide range of foodstuffs, building materials, and consumer goods.

**Harbin** /'hɑːbɪn/ (formerly **Haerphin** or **Pinkiang**) the capital of Heilongjiang province in north-east China, on the Sungari (Songhua) River; pop. (1990) 2,830,000. Harbin developed from a small fishing village into a major railway junction and experienced a large influx of Russians after the 1917 Russian Revolution. Food processing, sugar refining, and the manufacture of machinery and paper are the chief industries.

**Hardanger Fiord** /'hɑːdəŋɜː/ a fiord on the south-west coast of Norway, extending 120 km. (75 miles) inland from the North Sea. It is Norway's second-largest fiord.

**Hardwar** /hɑːˈdwɑː(r)/ a city in Uttar Pradesh, northern India, on the Ganges at the foot of the Siwalik Hills; pop. (1991) 188,960. Every 12 years there is a major Hindu pilgrimage (Kumbh Mela) to the city which is situated at the point where the holy Ganges emerges from a gorge and starts its course across the plains after descending from its source in the Himalayas.

**Hargeisa** /hɑːˈgeɪʃə/ (also **Hargeysa**) a market city in north-west Somalia; pop. (est. 1987) 400,000. It was the capital of British Somaliland, 1941–60.

**Haringey** /'hærɪŋgeɪ/ a northern inner borough of Greater London, containing the districts of Hornsey, Wood Green, and Tottenham; pop. (1991) 187,300.

**Harlech** /'hɑː(r)ləx/ a village in Gwynedd, west Wales, on Tremadoc Bay; pop. (1989) 1,310. It was the ancient capital of Merionethshire and has the remains of a famous castle built in the 13th c. by Edward I.

**Harlem** /'hɑːləm/ **1.** a residential and business district of New York City, situated to the north of 96th Street, having a large Black population. Its main thoroughfare is 125th Street which stretches

from the Hudson River eastwards to the Harlem River. In the 1920s and 1930s the district was noted for its night clubs and jazz bands, and in the 1930s Puerto Ricans were encouraged to settle in the area that came to be known as Spanish Harlem. **2. Harlem River** a narrow tidal river channel separating Manhattan Island from the Bronx. It is also known as the East River.

**Harley Street** /'hɑːlɪ/ a street in London, England, long associated with the premises of eminent physicians and surgeons, whence the allusive use of its name to refer to medical specialists.

**Harlow** /'hɑːləʊ/ a town in west Essex, southeast England, 33 km. (21 miles) north of London; pop. (1981) 79,520. It was designated a New Town in 1947 and has numerous light industries.

**harmattan** /hɑːˈmæt(ə)n/ a parching, dusty land-wind blowing off the Sahara to the coast of west Africa from December to March.

**Härnösand** /'hɑːnəsɑːnd/ a port in eastern Sweden, on the Gulf of Bothnia at the mouth of the Ångerman River; pop. (1990) 27,450. It is the capital of Västernorrland county.

**Harpers Ferry** /'hɑːpəz/ a small town in Jefferson County, West Virginia, USA, at the junction of the Potomac and Shenandoah rivers. It is famous for a raid in October 1859 in which John Brown and a group of Abolitionists captured a federal arsenal.

**Harris** /'hærɪs/ the southern part of the largest and northernmost island (Lewis and Harris) of the Outer Hebrides, off the north-west coast of Scotland. The chief settlements are Tarbert and Leverburgh. It is famous for its hand-woven tweed (Harris tweed).

**Harrisburg** /'hærɪsˌbɜːg/ the state capital of Pennsylvania, USA, on the Susquehanna River; pop. (1990) 52,370. A trading post was set up here by John Harris in 1718 and a town established by his son in 1785. A nuclear reactor at nearby Three Mile Island was, in 1979, the scene of a near catastrophic accident that led to a reassessment of US nuclear-safety standards.

**Harrow** /'hærəʊ/ (short for **Harrow School**) a public school at Harrow-on-the-Hill in the north-west London borough of Harrow, England. A traditional rival of Eton College, it was founded and endowed by John Lyon under a charter (1572) granted by Queen Elizabeth I. Lord Byron, Sir Robert Peel, and Sir Winston Churchill were some of the many famous pupils.

**Hartford** /'hɑːtfəd/ the state capital of Connecticut, north-east USA, on the Connecticut River; pop. (1990) 139,740. Founded by Dutch settlers in 1623, the city has developed into a major centre for insurance companies. Samuel Clemens (Mark Twain) and Harriet Beecher Stowe (author of *Uncle Tom's Cabin*) both lived in Hartford. It manufactures aircraft engines, office and domestic equipment, and firearms.

**Hartlepool** /'hɑːtlɪ,puːl/ an industrial town and port on the North Sea coast of Cleveland, north-east England; pop. (1981) 92,130. It was the birthplace in 1883 of the novelist Sir Compton Mackenzie. It has engineering and brewing industries.

**Harvard** /'hɑːvəd/ the oldest American university, founded in 1636 at Cambridge, Massachusetts. It is named after John Harvard (d. 1638), an English settler who bequeathed to it his library and half his estate.

**Harwich** /'hærɪtʃ/ a port in Essex, on the North Sea coast of south-east England; pop. (1981) 17,330. It has an extensive freight terminal and ferry links with northern Europe.

**Haryana** /hʌrɪ'ɑːnə/ a state of northern India, formed in 1966, mostly from the Hindi-speaking part of the state of Punjab; area 44,212 sq. km. (17,077 sq. miles); pop. (1991) 16,317,710; capital, Chandigarh.

**Harz Mountains** /hɑːts/ a range of mountains in central Germany, between the Leine and Saale rivers, the highest of which is the Brocken (1,142 m., 3,747 ft.). The region is the source of many legends about witchcraft and sorcery.

**Hashemite** /'hæʃɪ,maɪt/ an Arab princely family related to the Prophet Muhammad. Hashim was the great-grandfather of Muhammad. Jordan, which is ruled by a branch of this family, is known officially as the Hashemite Kingdom of Jordan.

**Hasidism** /'hæsɪ,dɪz(ə)m/ (also **Chasidism**) **1.** a strictly orthodox Jewish sect in Palestine in the 3rd–2nd c. BC who opposed Hellenizing influences on their faith and supported the Maccabean revolt. **2.** a mystical Jewish movement founded in Poland in the 18th c. in reaction to the rigid academic formation of rabbinical Judaeism. Its founder was Israel ben Eliezer (d. 1760), called Bad-Shem-Tov (Hebrew = master of the good name) because of his reputation as a miraculous healer. The movement was denounced as heretical in 1781 and declined sharply in the 19th c. with the spread of modernism, but fundamentalist communities developed from it are currently a force in Jewish life, particularly in Israel and New York, where they oppose fellow Jews whom they regard as violating the moral and religious principles of their faith.

**Haskovo** see KHASKOVO.

**Hasselt** /'hæselt/ an industrial city in north-east Belgium, capital of the province of Limburg, on the River Demer; pop. (1991) 66,610. Its suburbs have brewing, distilling, and engineering industries.

**Hastings** /'heɪstɪŋz/ a city on North Island, New Zealand, on the Heretaunga plains near the Ngaruroro River; pop. (1991) 57,750. Named after the Indian administrator Warren Hastings, it lies at the centre of a large fruit-growing region. Its chief industries are canning and food processing.

**Hastings** /'heɪstɪŋz/ a resort town on the coast of East Sussex, England, north of which William the Conqueror defeated the Anglo-Saxon king Harold II at a famous battle in 1066; pop. (1981) 75,280. It is a Cinque Port on the Channel coast and former base of the Royal Fleet.

**Hatay** /'hæteɪ/ a Mediterranean province of southern Turkey, on the Syrian frontier; pop. area 5,403 sq. km. (2,087 sq. miles); pop. (1990) 1,109,750; capital Antakya (Hatay). Formerly known as the Sanjak of Alexandretta, it was awarded to Syria in 1920. Following complaints by its Turkish minority it was given autonomous status as a republic in 1937, but rioting in 1938 resulted in its joint military control by Turkey and France and a year later its becoming an integral part of Turkey.

**Hatfield** /'hætfiːld/ a town in Hertfordshire, south-east England, to the north of London; pop. (1981) 33,300. It was designated a New Town in 1948 and is a centre of engineering industries. The University of Hertfordshire (formerly Hatfield Polytechnic) was established here in 1992.

**Hattusas** /'hætuː,sæs/ the capital of the ancient Hittite empire, situated in central Turkey c. 35 km. (22 miles) east of Ankara. It is the site of the modern Turkish village of Boğazköy.

**Hausaland** /'haʊzə,lænd/ a high plateau region of northern Nigeria that was once the centre of an empire of the Hausa people whose Hamito-Semitic Chad language is widely spoken in West Africa.

**Haute-Corse** /əʊt kɔːs/ a department in northern Corsica; area 4,666 sq. km. (1,802 sq. miles); pop. (1990) 131,560; capital, Bastia.

**Haute-Garonne** /əʊt gə'rɒn/ a department in the Midi-Pyrénées region of southern France; area 6,309 sq. km. (2,437 sq. miles); pop. (1990) 925,960; capital, Toulouse.

**Haute-Loire** /əʊt lwɑː(r)/ a department in the Auvergne region of central France; area 4,977 sq. km. (1,922 sq. miles); pop. (1990) 206,570; capital, Le Puy-en-Velay.

**Haute-Marne** /əʊt mɑːn/ a department in the Champagne-Ardenne region of north-eastern France; area 6,211 sq. km. (2,399 sq. miles); pop. (1990) 204,070; capital, Chaumont.

**Haute-Normandie** /əʊt ,nɔːm(ə)nd'iː/ the Upper Normandy region of northern France on the English Channel, comprising the departments of Eure and Seine-Maritime and including the city of Rouen. It was formed from part of the former province of Normandy.

**Hautes-Alpes** /əʊt ɑːlp/ a department in the Provence-Alpes-Côte d'Azur region of south-east France; area 5,549 sq. km. (2,143 sq. miles); pop. (1990) 113,300; capital, Gap.

**Haute-Saône** /əʊt sɔʊn/ a department in the Franche-Comté region of eastern France; area

5,343 sq. km. (2,064 sq. miles); pop. (1990) 229,650; capital, Vesoul.

**Haute-Savoie** /əʊt sə'vwæ/ a department in the Rhône-Alpes region of eastern France, on the frontier with Switzerland; area 4,391 sq. km. (1,696 sq. miles); pop. (1990) 568,290; capital, Annecy.

**Hautes-Pyrénées** /əʊt pɪrə'niːz/ a department in the Midi-Pyrénées region of southern France, on the frontier with Spain; area 4,507 sq. km. (1,741 sq. miles); pop. (1990) 224,760; capital, Tarbes.

**Haute-Vienne** /əʊt vjen/ a department in the Limousin region of central France; area 5,512 sq. km. (2,129 sq. miles); pop. (1990) 353,590; capital, Limoges.

**Haut-Rhin** /əʊt rɑ̃/ a department in the Alsace region of eastern France; area 3,523 sq. km. (1,361 sq. miles); pop. (1990) 671,320; capital, Colmar.

**Hauts-de-Seine** /əʊ də seɪn/ a department in the Ile-de-France region of central France; area 175 sq. km. (68 sq. miles); pop. (1990) 1,391,660; capital, Nanterre.

**Havana** /hə'vænə/ (Spanish **La Habana**) the capital of Cuba and chief port of the West Indies, on the north coast of the island of Cuba; pop. (1989) 2,068,600. Originally located on the south coast, the city was founded in its present location by Diego Velásquez in 1519. It was the principal Spanish port in the West Indies and the blowing up of the US battleship *Maine* in 1898 led to the Spanish–American War. Since 1898 it has been capital of independent Cuba. The novelist Ernest Hemingway lived on the outskirts of the city whose chief exports are cigars, coffee, and sugar. Its industries include oil refining, textiles, rum distilling, and the making of the famous Havana cigars.

**Havant** /'hæv(ə)nt/ an engineering town in Hampshire, southern England, north-east of Portsmouth; pop. (1981) 50,220.

**Haverhill** /'heɪvərəl/ a city in north-east Massachusetts, on the Merrimack River; pop. (1990) 51,420. The Quaker poet John Greenleaf Whittier was born here. It manufactures shoes and high-tech products.

**Havering** /'heɪvɜːrɪŋ/ a residential outer borough at the eastern extremity of Greater London, containing the districts of Hornchurch, Romford, Rainham, and Upminster; pop. (1991) 224,400.

**Hawaii** /hə'waɪɪ/ a state of the US comprising a chain of islands in the North Pacific stretching from the island of Hawaii to Kure Island (but excluding the Midway Islands); area 16,641 sq. km. (6,425 sq. miles); pop. (1990) 1,108,230; capital, Honolulu (on Oahu). Its largest cities are Honolulu and Hilo. The eight principal islands of the group are Oahu, Hawaii, Maui, Kauai, Molokai, Lanai, Kahoolawe, and Niihau. Hawaii is also known as the Aloha State. First settled by Polynesians,

Hawaii was visited in 1778 by Captain Cook who named them the Sandwich Islands. Its indigenous kingdom was abolished in 1894 and the islands were annexed by the US in 1898, becoming the 50th state in 1959. In addition to tourism, the islands depend on the export of agricultural produce such as pineapples, sugar, coffee, bananas, and nuts. **Hawaiian** *adj. & n.*

Hawaii is divided into five counties:

| County | Area (sq. km.) | Pop. (1990) | County Seat |
| --- | --- | --- | --- |
| Hawaii | 10,488 | 120,320 | Hilo |
| Honolulu | 1,550 | 836,230 | Honolulu |
| Kauai | 34 | 51,180 | Lihue |
| Maui | 3,021 | 100,370 | Wailuku |
| (includes Kalawao county, pop. 130) | | | |

**Hawaii** the largest and southernmost of the Pacific islands in the US state of Hawaii; area 10,488 sq. km. (4,050 sq. miles). Its chief town is Hilo. Hawaii Volcanoes National Park contains the active volcanoes Mauna Loa and Kilauea.

**Hawick** /'hɔːɪk/ a town in the Borders Region of Scotland, on the River Teviot; pop. (1981) 16,360. It was the administrative centre of Roxburgh district from 1975 to 1996 and was the birthplace of the composers John McEwen (1868–1948) and Francis George Scott (1880–1958), and the soprano Isobel Baillie.

**Hawke Bay** /hɔːk/ a bay on the east coast of North Island, New Zealand. The port of Napier lies on its southern shore. It was visited in 1769 by Captain James Cook, who named it after Edward Hawke, First Lord of the Admiralty (1766–71).

**Hawkes Bay** an administrative region on the east coast of North Island, New Zealand, created in 1989 and comprising the city of Napier and the districts of Central Hawkes Bay, Hastings, Wairoa, and parts of Taupo and Rangitikei; pop. (1991) 139,480.

**Hawthorne** /'hɔːθɔːn/ a city in the Los Angeles conurbation, south-west California, USA, to the south of Inglewood; pop. (1990) 71,350. Hawthorne was the original home of the famous 1960s rock band, the *Beach Boys*. It has a variety of light industries.

**Hayward** /'heɪwɜːd/ a food-processing city in western California, USA, south-east of Oakland, to the east of San Francisco Bay; pop. (1990) 111,500.

**Hazara** /hə'zɑːrə/ a people of Mongol descent of whom the largest proportion live in the mountains of central Afghanistan where they number *c.* 1,500,000. A further 150,000 are to be found in Iran and Pakistan.

**Heard and McDonald Islands** /hɜːd, mək'dɒnəld/ a group of uninhabited islands in the south Indian Ocean, administered by Australia since 1947 as an external territory; area 412 sq. km. (159 sq. miles). A scientific station set up by the

Australian National Antarctic Research Expedition on Heard Island in 1947 was closed in 1955 following the establishment of a station at Mawson on the continent of Antarctica. Having no introduced organisms, Heard Island is of special interest to ecologists.

**Heathrow** /hiːˈθrəʊ/ an international airport with four terminals situated 25 km. (15 miles) west of the centre of London. It is also known as London Airport.

**Heavenly Mountains** see TIEN SHAN.

**Hebei** /həˈbeɪ/ (formerly **Hopeh** /həˈpeɪ/) a province of north-east China on the Gulf of Chihli (Bo Hai) to the south of Inner Mongolia; area 188,000 sq. km. (72,615 sq. miles); pop. (1990) 61,082,000; capital, Shijiazhuang. Occupying part of the North China Plain, its chief products are cotton, grain, fruit, timber, and oil.

**Hebi** /həˈbiː/ a city in Henan province, China, south-west of Anyang; pop. (1986) 326,000.

**Hebrew** /ˈhiːbruː/ a member of the Hamito-Semitic language family spoken by people who were originally centred in ancient Palestine, traditionally from the middle Bronze Age (mid-18th c. BC). Spoken and written for more than 1,000 years, it is written from right to left in an alphabet consisting of 22 letters, all consonants; not until the 6th c. AD were vowel signs added to the Hebrew text of the Old Testament to facilitate reading. By c. 500 BC it had come greatly under the influence of Aramaic, which largely replaced it as a spoken language by c. 200 AD, but it continued as the religious language of the Jewish people. It was revived as a spoken language in the 19th c., with the modern form having its roots in the ancient language but drawing words from the vocabularies of European languages, and is now the official language of the State of Israel.

**Hebrides** /ˈhebrɪˌdiːz/ a group of about 500 islands off the north-west coast of Scotland. The **Inner Hebrides** are divided between Highland and Strathclyde regions; the largest of the islands is Skye, others include Raasay, Mull, Jura, Islay, Tiree, Coll, Colonsay, Rum, Eigg, Muck, and Iona. The **Outer Hebrides** form part of the Western Isles region, separated from the Inner group by the Little Minch; the largest is Lewis and Harris, others include North and South Uist, Eriskay, Barra, the Flannan Islands, and the remote island group of St Kilda. Until near the end of the 13th c. 'The Hebrides' included also Scottish islands in the Firth of Clyde, the peninsula of Kintyre in south-west Scotland, the Isle of Man, and the (Irish) Isle of Rathlin; they formed part of the kingdom of Scotland from 1266, when they were ceded to the Scottish king Alexander III by Magnus of Norway. Norse occupation has influenced the language, customs, and place-names, although most of the present-day population have Celtic affinities and Gaelic is still spoken on several of the islands. The main occupations are farming, fishing, and the manufacture of textiles and woollens. The shipping-forecast area *Hebrides* covers an area of the Atlantic off the north-west coast of Scotland. **Hebridean** /-ˈdiːən/ adj. & n.

**Hebron** /ˈhebrɒn/ (Hebrew **Hevron**, Arabic **El Khalhil** or **El Khalil**) a city lying in the Judaean Hills between Jerusalem and Beersheba, in the Israeli-occupied West Bank area of Jordan. It is one of the most ancient cities in the Middle East, probably founded in the 18th c. BC and is sacred to both Jews and Arabs who regard themselves as being descended from Abraham who made his home here. Its chief landmark is the Tomb of the Patriarchs which (as the cave of Machpelah) was the family vault created by Abraham and the site of a synagogue built by Herod in 20 BC. It came under Jordanian control in 1948, but was reoccupied by Israel in 1967. During the 20th c. it was the scene of massacres of the Jews by militant Palestinian Arabs in 1929 and 1994. Its chief industries are glass-making and food processing.

**Hechi** /həˈtʃiː/ a city in Guangxi autonomous region, southern China, on the Long River north-west of Liuzhou; pop. (1986) 274,000.

**Heerlen** /ˈheɪrlən/ an industrial city in the province of Limburg in the Netherlands, north-east of Maastricht; pop. (1991) 94,340. It developed in the 19th c. as a coal-mining centre, but now produces chemicals, plastics, and fertilizers.

**Hefei** /heˈfeɪ/ (formerly **Hofei** /həʊˈfeɪ/ or **Luchow**) an industrial city in eastern China, capital of the province of Anhui; pop. (1990) 1,541,000. Its industries produce iron, steel, machinery, electronics, and chemicals.

**Hegang** /həˈgæŋ/ a city in Heilongjiang province, north-east China, north-east of Harbin; pop. (1990) 650,000.

**hegemony** /hɪˈdʒemənɪ/ leadership, especially by one state of a confederacy.

**Heidelberg** /ˈhaɪd(ə)lˌbɜːg/ an industrial city in Baden-Württemberg, south-west Germany, on the River Neckar; pop. (1991) 139,390. It is noted for its university, which received its charter in 1386 and is the oldest in Germany, and for its medieval castle. It is also noted for the manufacture of printing machinery and precision instruments.

**Heihei** /ˌheɪˈheɪ/ a town in Heilongjiang province, north-east China, on the Heilong River opposite the Russian town of Blagovescensk; pop. (1986) 138,000.

**Heilbronn** /ˈhaɪlbrɒn/ an industrial city and river port in Baden-Württemberg, Germany, on the River Neckar north of Stuttgart; pop. (1991) 117,430. Its industries produce wine, paper, chemicals, and metal goods.

**Heilongjiang** /ˌheɪlʊŋdʒɪˈæŋ/ **1.** a province (formerly **Heilungkiang** /ˌheɪlʊŋkɪˈæŋ/) of north-east China on the frontier with Russia; area

469,000 sq. km. (181,151 sq. miles); pop. (1990) 35,215,000; capital, Harbin. It is the most northerly province of China. Its chief products are grain, timber, oil, petrochemicals, coal, and minerals such as copper, aluminium, lead, and zinc. **2.** the Chinese name for the AMUR RIVER on the Sino-Russian frontier.

**Heimay** /ˈhaɪmeɪ/ a volcanic island off the south coast of Iceland in the Westman Islands. Its eruption in January 1973 caused the evacuation of the island's population of 5,300 people.

**Heinola** an industrial town in the province of Mikkeli, south-east-central Finland, on the River Kymi near Lahti; pop. (1990) 16,335. It was founded in 1839.

**Hejaz** /hɪˈdʒæz/ (also **Hijaz**) a coastal region of western Saudi Arabia, extending along the Red Sea and containing the holy cities of Mecca and Medina.

**Hekla** /ˈheklə/ an active volcano in south-west Iceland, rising to a height of 1,491 m. (4,892 ft.). Recent major eruptions occurred in 1947, 1970, and 1991.

**Helena** /ˈhelmə/ the state capital and fourth-largest city of Montana, USA; pop. (1990) 24,570. Established during a gold-rush in 1864, its original name was Last Chance. Its chief industry is the smelting and refining of iron ore.

**Helensburgh** a town and resort in west-central Scotland, at the entrance to the Gare Loch on the Firth of Clyde; pop. (1981) 16,620. Laid out in the 18th c. by Sir Alexander Colquhoun, it became a dormitory resort for the wealthy merchant class of Glasgow. The Hill House was designed for the Glasgow publisher W. Blackie by Charles Rennie Macintosh in 1902–3 and the Scottish novelists Neil Munro and O. H. Mavor (James Bridie) both lived in Helensburgh for many years. John Logie Baird, pioneer of television, was born here in 1888 and Henry Bell, pioneer of steam navigation and designer of the *Comet* (1812), was town provost in 1807.

**Helgoland** the German name for HELIGOLAND.

**Helicon** /ˈhelɪkɒn/, **Mount** (Greek **Helikon**) a mountain range in Boetia, central Greece, to the north of the Gulf of Corinth, rising to 1,750 m. (5,741 ft.) at Palaiovouni. It was believed by the ancient Greeks to be the home of the Muses and on Mount Zagora is the Hippocrene spring which is said to inspire poets.

**Heligoland** /ˈhelɪɡəˌlænd/ (German **Helgoland** /ˈhelɡəˌlɑːnt/) a small island in the North Sea, one of the North Frisian Islands, off the coast of Germany. Originally the home of Frisian seamen, it was Danish from 1714 until seized by the British Navy in 1807 and later ceded officially to Britain. In 1890 it was given to Germany in exchange for Zanzibar and Pemba, and was an important German naval base in both World Wars. Its naval installations were blown up in 1947 in the

largest non-atomic explosion in history, and it was returned to the Federal Republic of Germany in 1952.

**Heliopolis** /ˌhiːlɪˈɒpəlɪs/ **1.** the Greek name for an ancient Egyptian city, situated near the apex of the Nile delta, at what is now Cairo. It was an important religious centre and the centre of sun worship; its name means 'city of the sun'. It was the original site of the obelisks known as Cleopatra's Needles. **2.** the ancient Greek name for BAALBEK in Lebanon.

**Hell** /hel/ **1.** a location at the north end of Seven Mile Beach on the Caribbean island of Grand Cayman. **2.** a village in Nord-Trøndelag county, central Norway, 32 km. (20 miles) east of Trondheim.

**Helladic** /heˈlædɪk/ belonging to the Bronze Age culture of mainland Greece (c. 3,000–1,050 BC), of which the latest period is the equivalent of Mycenaean.

**Hellas** /ˈhelæs/ the Greek name for GREECE.

**Hellene** /ˈheliːn/ a native of modern Greece or an ancient Greek of genuine Greek descent. **Hellenic** *adj.*

**Hellespont** /ˈhelɪsˌpɒnt/ the ancient name for the Dardanelles, the narrow strait in modern Turkey linking the Sea of Marmara with the Aegean, named after the legendary Helle who fell into the strait and was drowned while escaping with her brother Phrixus from their stepmother, Ino, on a golden-fleeced ram. The scene of the legend of Hero and Leander.

**Hell's Canyon** a chasm cut by the Snake River, which runs along the border of Idaho and Oregon, to form the deepest gorge in the USA. Flanked by the Seven Devils Mountains, the canyon drops to a depth of 2,422 m. (7,900 ft.).

**Helmand** /ˈhelmənd/ the longest river in Afghanistan. Rising in the Hindu Kush, it flows 1,125 km. (700 miles) generally south-west before emptying into the marshland surrounding Lake Saberi on the Iran–Afghanistan frontier.

**Helpston** /ˈhelpst(ə)n/ a village in Cambridgeshire, England, 10 km. (6 miles) north-west of Peterborough. It was the birthplace of the peasant poet John Clare (1793–1864).

**Helsingborg** /ˈhelsɪŋˌbɔːɡ/ (Swedish **Hälsingborg**) a sea and ferry port in Malmö county, southern Sweden, situated on the Øresund (Sound) opposite Helsingør in Denmark; pop. (1990) 109,270. It has numerous light industries.

**Helsingfors** the Swedish name for HELSINKI.

**Helsingør** see ELSINORE.

**Helsinki** /ˈhelsɪŋkɪ/ (Swedish **Helsingfors** /ˈhelsɪŋˌfɔːʃ/) the capital of Finland, a seaport on the Gulf of Finland; pop. (1990) 492,400. Founded by Gustavus Vasa of Sweden in 1550, Helsinki was rebuilt by Alexander I of Russia after being destroyed by fire in 1808. It replaced Turku as capital of Finland in 1812. It is Finland's largest port and manufacturing centre with shipbuilding, chemical, textile, sugar-refining, printing, and ceramic industries. It has a neoclassical cathedral (1852) and an impressive railway station designed by Eero Saarinen. It has Finland's largest and oldest university (1849) and a technical university (1908) and many museums, galleries, halls, and stadiums.

**Helvellyn** /hel'velɪn/ a mountain in the Lake District of north-west England, rising to 950 m. (3,117 ft.) between Ullswater and Thirlmere.

**Helvetia** /hel'viːʃ(ə)/ an archaic name used in poetic reference to Switzerland, derived from the Latin name (Helvetii) given by the Romans to the Celtic tribe occupying the plateau between the Alps and the Jura Mts., now part of western Switzerland. The name Helvetia is still used on postage stamps.

**Helwan** /hel'waːn/ an industrial city in northern Egypt, situated to the south of Cairo and east of the River Nile; pop. (1991) 328,000.

**Hemel Hempstead** /ˌhem(ə)l 'hempsted/ a residential and light industrial town in Hertfordshire, south-east England, on the River Gade; pop. (1981) 80,340. It was designated a New Town in 1947.

**hemisphere** /'hemɪˌsfɪə(r)/ a half of the earth, especially as divided by the equator (into *Northern* and *Southern* Hemispheres) or by a line passing through the poles (into *Eastern* and *Western* Hemispheres).

**Hemkund Lake** /'hemkənd/ a lake in northern India, in the Himalayan foothills of Uttar Pradesh. It is regarded as holy by the Sikhs.

**Henan** /hə'næn/ (formerly **Honan** /həʊ'næn/) a province of north-east-central China; area 167,000 sq. km. (64,504 sq. miles); pop. (1990) 85,510,000; capital, Zhengzhou. The Yellow River passes through northern Henan which is China's leading producer of wheat and tobacco.

**Henderson** /'hendɜː,s(ə)n/ a city in south-east Nevada, USA, south-east of Las Vegas; pop. (1990) 64,940. The city was established in 1942 in association with nearby magnesium works.

**Henegouw** see HAINAUT.

**Hengelo** /'heŋgələʊ/ an industrial town in Overijssel province, the Netherlands, north-west of Enschede near the frontier with Germany; pop. (1991) 76,370. It has machinery and metal industries.

**Hengshui** /'heŋ'ʃuːɪ/ a city in Hebei province, eastern China, on the Fuyang River; pop. (1986) 292,000.

**Hengyang** /'heŋ'jɑːŋ/ a city in Hunan province, south-eastern China, on the Xiang River south of Changsha; pop. (1986) 616,000. It is a transportation centre with chemical, machine tool, and textile industries.

**Henley** /'henlɪ/ (fully **Henley-on-Thames**) a town in south Oxfordshire, England, on the River

Thames; pop. (1981) 11,180. It is associated with rowing and especially the Royal Henley Regatta which has been a fashionable annual event since 1839.

**Heraklion** /hɪ'ræklɪən/ (Greek **Iráklion** /i'ræklɪən/) a seaport and administrative centre of the Greek island of Crete, on the north coast of the island; pop. (1991) 117,000. Known as Candia in medieval times, it has been the island's capital since 1971. Its harbour has an impressive Venetian fortress and arsenals, and to the south of the town is the tomb of Níkos Kazantzákis (d. 1957), author of *Zorba the Greek*. It exports wine, olive oil, raisins, and almonds.

**Herald Square** /'herəld/ a square in Manhattan, New York City at the junction of Broadway and Sixth Avenue at 34th Street, immortalized in a song written by George M. Cohan in 1904. Founded in 1858, the department store of R. C. Macy & Co. Ltd. is the largest in the world.

**Herat** /hə'ræt/ the largest city of western Afghanistan and capital of a province of the same name; pop. (est. 1988) 177,000. It lies at the crossroads of ancient trade routes from Persia to India and Central Asia to China. In addition to weaving textiles and carpets, the city trades in fruit grown in the surrounding area.

**Hérault** /eə'rəʊ/ **1.** a department in the Languedoc-Roussillon region of southern France; area 6,101 sq. km. (2,356 sq. miles); pop. (1990) 794,600; capital, Montpellier. **2.** a river of southern France that rises in the Cévennes and flows 160 km. (100 miles) southwards to enter the Mediterranean at Agde.

**Hercegovina** see BOSNIA AND HERZEGOVINA.

**Herculaneum** /ˌhɜːkjʊ'leɪnɪəm/ an ancient Roman town, near Naples, on the lower slopes of Mt. Vesuvius. The eruption in AD 79 buried it deeply under volcanic ash and thus largely preserved it. Excavations have continued since 1709.

**Hercynian** /hɜː'sɪnɪən/ a mountain-forming geological period in the Eastern Hemisphere in the late Palaeozoic era.

**Hereford** /'herɪfəd/ a market city in the county of Hereford and Worcester, west-central England, on the River Wye; pop. (1991) 49,800. Its Norman cathedral has a library of chained books and a famous 14th-c. *Mappa Mundi*. It shares the Three Choirs Festival with Worcester and Gloucester. The actor David Garrick was born here in 1717.

**Hereford and Worcester** /'herɪfəd, 'wʊstə(r)/ a county of west-central England, on the border with Wales; area 3,926 sq. km. (1,516 sq. miles); pop. (1991) 667,800; county town, Worcester. It was formed in 1974 from the former counties of Herefordshire and Worcestershire. The county is divided into nine districts:

| District | Area (sq. km.) | Pop. (1991) |
|---|---|---|
| Bromsgrove | 220 | 89,800 |
| Hereford | 20 | 49,800 |
| Leominster | 933 | 39,000 |
| Malvern Hills | 900 | 87,000 |
| Redditch | 54 | 76,900 |
| South Herefordshire | 905 | 51,200 |
| Worcester | 33 | 81,000 |
| Wychavon | 664 | 99,800 |
| Wyre Forest | 196 | 93,400 |

**Herefordshire** /'herɪfəd,ʃɪə(r), -ʃə(r)/ a former county of west-central England. Since 1974 it has been part of the county of Hereford and Worcester.

**Herero** /he'reɪrəʊ/ a Bantu-speaking people of south-west Africa, especially central Namibia and Botswana, where they lead a pastoral life that is largely dependent on cattle, sheep, and goats.

**Hermitage** /'hɜːmɪtɪdʒ/, **the** a leading art museum in St. Petersburg, Russia, containing the collections begun by Catherine the Great, one of the most voracious collectors of all time. It derives its name from the 'retreat' in which she displayed them to her friends.

**Hermosillo** /ɜːmə'siːljəʊ/ an agricultural centre in north-west Mexico, capital of the state of Sonora; pop. (1990) 449,470. It was founded in 1700 for the resettlement of Pima Indians.

**Herne** /'hɜːnə/ an industrial city in North Rhine-Westphalia, north-west Germany, in the Ruhr valley north-east of Essen; pop. (1991) 179,140.

**Herning** /'hɜːnɪŋ/ a textile manufacturing city in Ringkøping county, central Jutland, Denmark; pop. (1990) 56,690.

**Hertfordshire** /'hɑːfədʃɪə(r)/ one of the Home Counties of south-east England; area 1,636 sq. km. (632 sq. miles); pop. (1991) 951,500; county town, Hertford. The county is divided into 10 districts:

| District | Area (sq. km.) | Pop. (1991) |
|---|---|---|
| Broxbourne | 52 | 79,500 |
| Dacorum | 210 | 129,200 |
| East Hertfordshire | 477 | 114,200 |
| Hertsmere | 98 | 86,100 |
| North Hertfordshire | 375 | 108,600 |
| St. Albans | 161 | 122,400 |
| Stevenage | 26 | 73,700 |
| Three Rivers | 87 | 74,100 |
| Watford | 21 | 72,100 |
| Welwyn Hatfield | 127 | 91,600 |

**Herts** *abbr.* Hertfordshire in England.

**Hervey Bay** /'hɑːvɪ/ a city on the east coast of Queensland, Australia, situated on Hervey Bay between Rockhampton and Brisbane; pop. (1991) 22,205. It comprises the resorts of Gatakers Bay, Pialba, Scarness, Torquay, Urangan, Burrum Heads, Toogoom, Howard, and Torbanlea.

**Herzegovina** see BOSNIA AND HERZEGOVINA.

**Heshan** /hə'ʃɑːn/ a city in Guangxi autonomous region, southern China, on the Xun River north of Nanning; pop. (1986) 112,000.

**Hesperia** /ˌhespə'rɪə/ a city in southern California to the north of San Bernardino, in the north-eastern foothills of the San Gabriel Mts.; pop. (1990) 50,420.

**Hesse** /'hesə/ (German **Hessen** /'hes(ə)n/) a state of western Germany; area 21,115 sq. km. (8,156 sq. miles); pop. (1990) 5,600,000; capital, Wiesbaden. Hesse is a largely agricultural region producing wine, fruit, vegetables, and grain.

**Heze** /hə'ze/ (also **Caozhou**) a city and transportation centre in west Shandong province, eastern China; pop. (1986) 1,017,000.

**HI** *abbr.* US Hawaii (in official postal use).

**Hialeah** /ˌhaɪə'liːə/ a city in south-east Florida, USA, forming a western suburb of Miami; pop. (1990) 188,000. The city was founded in 1921 by the aviation pioneers Glenn Curtiss and James H. Bright. It has miscellaneous light industries.

**Hibernia** /haɪ'bɜːnɪə/ an archaic poetic and literary name for Ireland.
**Hibernian** *adj. & n.*

**Hidalgo** /hɪ'dælgəʊ/ a mountainous state of southern Mexico, formerly noted for its silver mines; area 20,813 sq. km. (8,039 sq. miles); pop. (1990) 1,880,630; capital, Pachuca de Soto.

**Higashimurayama** /hɪˌgɑː'ʃɪˌmʊərə'jaːmə/ a city in Kanto region, Japan, on Honshu Island 29 km. (18 miles) north-west of Tokyo; pop. (1990) 134,000.

**Higashiosaka** /hɪˌgɑːʃɪəʊ'sɑːkə/ an eastern residential and industrial suburb of Osaka on the island of Honshu, Japan; pop. (1990) 518,000.

**high** /haɪ/ a region of high atmospheric pressure usually associated with pressures greater than 1,000 millibars.

**Higher Walton** a village in Cheshire, England, 3 km. (2 miles) south of Warrington. It was the birthplace of the famous contralto singer Kathleen Ferrier in 1912.

**Highgate** /'haɪgeɪt/ a district of north London, north-east of Hampstead Heath, that takes its name from a toll-gate that once operated. The poet Samuel Coleridge, who lived here for 19 years, was buried in St. Martin's Church and Highgate cemetery was the burial place of George Eliot, Christina Rossetti, Herbert Spencer, and Karl Marx.

**Highland** /'haɪlənd/ a local government region of northern Scotland; area 25,398 sq. km. (9,810 sq. miles); pop. (1991) 209,419; administrative centre, Inverness. From 1975 to 1996 Highland Region was divided into eight districts:

| District | Area (sq. km.) | Pop. (1991) |
|---|---|---|
| Badenoch and Strathspey | 2,325 | 12,940 |
| Caithness | 1,776 | 26,110 |
| Inverness | 2,848 | 62,650 |
| Lochaber | 4,407 | 20,800 |
| Nairn | 422 | 10,680 |
| Ross and Cromarty | 4,952 | 49,950 |
| Skye and Lochalsh | 2,701 | 12,540 |
| Sutherland | 5,865 | 13,740 |

**Highlands** /ˈhaɪləndz/, **the** a name applied to the mountainous parts of northern Scotland.

**high latitudes** a term often applied to latitudes near the poles of 60° or more.

**High Point** an industrial city in North Carolina, USA; pop. (1990) 69,500. Founded in 1859, it was the highest point on the North Carolina and Midland Railroad built in 1853. Its chief products are furniture and hosiery. High Point has a Doll Museum and a building known as the Giant Bureau, built in 1926 to look like a huge chest of drawers.

**highveld** /haɪˈvelt/ a name given to the high, treeless plateau land of southern Africa.

**High Wycombe** /haɪ ˈwɪkəm/ a town in Buckinghamshire, England, on the River Wye north-west of London; pop. (1981) 70,200. It has a long tradition of furniture-making and has a Chair and Local History Museum.

**Hijaz** see HEJAZ.

**Hikone** /hɪˈkəʊnɪ/ a city in Kinki region, Honshu Island, Japan, on the east shore of Lake Biwa; pop. (1990) 100,000. It has a notable 17th-c. castle and gardens.

**Hildesheim** /ˈhɪldəʃˌhaɪm/ an industrial city in Lower Saxony, Germany, situated south-east of Hanover on the River Innerste; pop. (1991) 106,000. It has a 9th-c. cathedral rebuilt after war damage. It has diverse light industries.

**Hillerød** /ˈhɪləˌrɜːð/ a tourist town in north Zealand, Denmark, the capital of Frederiksborg county; pop. (1990) 33,390. Its most notable landmark is the 17th-c. Frederiksborg Castle.

**Hillingdon** /ˈhɪlɪŋd(ə)n/ a residential and light industrial outer borough of west Greater London, containing Heathrow Airport, Uxbridge, and the districts of Hayes, Harlington, Harmondsworth, Ruislip, West Drayton, and Yiewsley; pop. (1990) 225,800.

**Hillsborough** a village in County Down, Northern Ireland, between Belfast and Newry, named after Sir Arthur Hill who built a fort here in the 17th c. Hillsborough Castle, the Hill family seat, was the official residence of the Governors of Northern Ireland and scene of talks that led to the Anglo-Irish Agreement between the British and Irish governments in 1985. It was the birthplace of the composer Sir Hamilton Harty in 1879.

**Hilo** /ˈhiːləʊ/ a port on the island of Hawaii; pop. (1990) 37,810. Settled by missionaries in the 1820s, it trades in island produce such as fruit, nuts, and sugar.

**Hilton Head Island** an island in the Atlantic Ocean off the coast of South Carolina, USA. It is the largest resort island on the east coast of the US between New Jersey and Florida; area 109 sq. km. (42 sq. miles).

**Hilversum** /ˈhɪlvəˌsʊm/ a residential town in the Netherlands, in the province of North Holland, 20 km. (12 miles) south-east of Amsterdam; pop. (1991) 84,600. It is the centre of the Dutch radio and television network.

**Himachal Pradesh** /hɪˌmɑːtʃ(ə)l prəˈdeʃ/ a mountainous state in northern India, to the south of Kashmir and west of Tibet; area 55,673 sq. km. (21,504 sq. miles); pop. (1991) 44,817,400; capital, Simla. The chief products are coniferous timber, grain, fruit, and vegetables.

**Himalayas** /ˌhɪməˈleɪəz/ a vast mountain system in southern Asia, extending over 2,400 km. (1,500 miles) from Kashmir eastwards to Assam. It covers most of Nepal, Sikkim, and Bhutan and forms part of the northern boundary of the Indian subcontinent. It is a series of parallel ridges rising up from the Ganges basin to the Tibetan plateau, at over 3,000 m. above sea-level, and includes the Karakoram, Zaskar, and Ladakh ranges. The backbone is the Great Himalayan Range, the highest range in the world, with several peaks rising to over 7,700 m. (25,000 ft.), the highest being Mount Everest (8,848 m., 29,028 ft.) which rises on the frontier between Nepal and Tibet and K2 (8,611 m., 28,250 ft.) in the Karakoram Range of the north-west Himalayas.
**Himalayan** adj.

**Himeji** /hɪˈmedʒɪ/ an industrial city in Kinki region, Japan, on Honshu Island, 54 km. (34 miles) north-west of Kobe; pop. (1990) 454,000. Its castle is one of the finest in Japan. It has steel, oil-refining, and textile industries.

**Hims** see HOMS.

**Hindenburg Line** a defensive barrier of barbed wire, trenches, and pillboxes built on the Western Front by the German army during World War I. It was named after the German field marshal who eventually became president of Germany.

**Hindi** /ˈhɪndɪ/ **1.** a literary form of Hindustani with vocabulary based on Sanskrit, written in the Devanagari script, an official language of India. Hindi is the most widely spoken language in India, with some 180 million speakers. **2.** a group of spoken dialects of northern India, belonging to the Indo-European family of languages and related to Urdu.

**Hindoo** an archaic variation of HINDU.

**Hindu** /ˈhɪnduː, -ˈduː/ a follower of Hinduism.

**Hinduism** /ˈhɪnduːˌɪz(ə)m/ a system of religious beliefs and social customs, with adherents, especially in India, both a way of life and a rigorous system of religious law, developed over a period of about 50 centuries. Unlike most religions, Hinduism requires no one belief regarding the nature of god: it embraces polytheism, monotheism, and monism. More important are the beliefs concerning the nature of the universe and the structure of society. The former is described by the key concepts of *dharma*, the eternal law underlying the whole of existence; *karma*, the law of action by which each cause has its effect in an endless chain reaching from one life to the next; and *moshka*, liberation from this chain of birth, death, and rebirth. The latter is prescribed by the ideals of *varna*, the division of mankind into four classes or types, the forerunner of caste; *ashrama*, the four stages of life; and personal dharma, according to which ones religious duty is defined by birth and circumstance. There are an estimated 705 million Hindus in the world.

**Hindu Kush** /ˌhɪndu: 'ku:ʃ, 'kʊʃ/ a range of high mountains in northern Pakistan and Afghanistan, forming a westward continuation of the Himalayas. Rising to 7,690 m. (25,230 ft.) at Tirich Mir, the Hindu Kush has several peaks exceeding 6,150 m. (20,000 ft.).

**Hindustan** /ˌhɪndʊ'stɑ:n/ literally meaning 'the land of the Hindus', a historic term loosely used to describe the whole of the Indian subcontinent but more specifically referring to India north of the Deccan plateau, especially the plains of the Ganges and Jumna rivers.

**Hindustani** /ˌhɪndʊ'stɑ:nɪ/ a language based on the Western Hindi dialect of the Delhi region with an admixture of Arabic, Persian, etc., current as the standard language and lingua franca in much of northern India and (as colloquial Urdu) Pakistan.

**Hinnøya** /'hɪnɜ:jə/ an island off the north-west coast of Norway, the largest of the Lofoten Islands; area 2,198 sq. km. (849 sq. miles).

**Hino** /'hi:nəʊ/ a city in Kanto region, Japan, on Honshu Island, 32 km. (20 miles) west of Tokyo; pop. (1990) 166,000.

**Hippocrene** /'hɪpəˌkri:n/ a spring on Mount Helicon, west of Thebes in southern Greece, the inspiration of poets. It was fabled to have been produced by a stroke from the hoof of Pegasus.

**Hippo Regius** /ˌhɪpəʊ 'ri:dʒəs/ see ANNABA.

**Hirakata** /ˌhɪrə'kɑ:tə/ a residential city in Kinki region, Honshu Island, Japan, near Osaka; pop. (1990) 391,000.

**Hiratsuka** /hɪ'rɑ:ts(ə)ˌkɑ:/ a commercial city in Kanto region, Honshu Island, Japan, on the Sagami River south-west of Yokohama; pop. (1990) 246,000. It has light industries including electronic equipment.

**Hirosaki** /ˌhɪrəʊ'sɑ:kɪ/ a city in Tohoku region, at the northern end of Honshu Island, south-west of Aomori; pop. (1990) 175,000. Its castle, seat of

the Tsugaru clan, dates from 1611 and its five-storey pagoda from 1672. Hirosaki's chief products are lacquer and fruit. South-east of the city lies the scenic Towada-Hachimantai National Park.

**Hiroshima** /hɪ'rɒʃmə/ the capital of Chugoku region on the south coast of Honshu Island, Japan, at the mouth of the River Ota; pop. (1990) 1,086,000. Founded in 1594, the city served as a military headquarters. It was the target of the first atomic bomb on 6 August 1945, which resulted in the immediate deaths of more than one-third of the city's population of 300,000, and, together with a second attack on Nagasaki three days later, led directly to Japan's surrender and the end of World War II. The event is commemorated in the Peace Memorial Park. It is now a car-making and ship-building centre, with numerous light industries.

**Hispanic** /hɪ'spænɪk/ **1.** of or relating to Spain or to Spain and Portugal. **2.** a Spanish-speaking person, especially one of Latin American descent, living in the USA.

**Hisar** /hɪ'sɑ:(r)/ (formerly **Hissar**) a town in Harayana, north-west India, north-west of Delhi. Founded by Firuz Shah III in 1354, it is widely known for its cattle fairs.

**Hispaniola** /ˌhɪspæn'jəʊlə/ an island of the Greater Antilles in the West Indies, divided into the states of Haiti and the Dominican Republic. It was originally named La Isla Española (= the Spanish Island) by Columbus who discovered it in 1492. The western part of the island was frequented by French pirates who successfully established plantations and in 1697 that part of the island was ceded to France. In 1804, after a slave rebellion, the western third of the island declared itself independent of France as the Republic of Haiti and in 1844 the eastern two-thirds gained its independence from Spain. Pico Duarte in the Cordillera Central is the highest peak in the West Indies (3,175 m., 10,417 ft.); area 76,192 sq. km. (29,430 sq. miles); pop. (est. 1990) 13,700,000. The principal cities are Santo Domingo and Port-au-Prince.

**historical geography** the study of past geographies and of past landscapes involving the analysis of changing patterns and processes over a period of time.

**Hitachi** /hɪ'tɑ:tʃɪ/ an industrial city in Kanto region, Honshu Island, Japan, on the east coast north-east of Mito; pop. (1990) 202,000. It was the site of a major copper mine and has electrical and chemical industries.

**Hitchin** /'hɪtʃɪn/ a town in Hertfordshire, south-east England, north-east of Luton; pop. (1981) 33,740. The growing of lavender was introduced from Naples in the 16th c. Hitchin was the birthplace in 1559 of the poet George Chapman and in 1813 of the steel manufacturer Sir Henry Bessemer.

**Hittite** /'hɪtaɪt/ an ancient empire of Asia Minor that gained control of central Anatolia c. 1800–1200 BC and reached its zenith under the totalitarian rule of Suppiluliuma I (*c.* 1380 BC), whose political influence extended from the capital, Hattusas, situated at Boğazköy (about 35 km. (22 miles) east of Ankara in modern Turkey) west to the Mediterranean coast and south-east into northern Syria. In their struggle for power over Syria and Palestine they clashed with the troops of Rameses II of Egypt in a battle (1285 BC) at Kadesh on the River Orontes which seems to have ended indecisively. The subsequent decline and demise of Hittite power by 700 BC resulted from internal and external dissension, probably following an outbreak of famine.

**Hkakabo Razi** /kæ'kɑːbəʊ 'rɑːziː/ a mountain in the state of Kachin in northern Burma, on the frontier with China. Rising to 5,881 m. (19,295 ft.), it is the highest peak in Burma.

**Hobart** /'həʊbɑːt/ the capital and chief port of Tasmania, Australia, at the mouth of the Derwent River; pop. (1991) 127,130. A penal colony named after Lord Hobart (1760–1816), Secretary of State for the Colonies, was moved to the city's present site on Sullivan Cove in 1804; it became the island's capital in 1812. From a whaling centre it developed into a major yachting, fishing, and trading port exporting fruit, textiles, and processed food. There is an annual Sydney to Hobart Yacht Race.

**Hoboken** /həʊ'bəʊkən/ **1.** an industrial suburb of Antwerp in north Belgium, on the River Scheldt. **2.** an industrial city in New Jersey, USA, on the Hudson River opposite Manhattan Island to which it is linked by tunnel and ferry; pop. (1990) 33,400. Laid out in 1804, Hoboken was a resort town for New Yorkers during the 19th c.

**Ho Chi Minh City** /həʊ tʃɪ 'mɪn/ a city in southern Vietnam, on the Saigon River; pop. (est. 1991) 3,450,000. Made capital of the French colony of Cochin China in 1859, it was known as Saigon until 1975 when it was named after the Vietnamese Communist statesman who led his country in its struggle for independence from French rule. It is now the largest city and one of the chief industrial centres of Vietnam centred on the adjacent town of Cholon. Industries include shipbuilding, textiles, machinery, pharmaceuticals, and the manufacture of diverse consumer goods. The deep-water port on Kanh Ho Island handles almost all the trade of southern Vietnam.

**Ho Chi Minh Trail** a covert road system crossing the Truong Son Mts. on the western frontier of Vietnam, built by the North Vietnamese during the 1960s to act as a supply line for ammunition, food, and medicine *en route* from North Vietnam to revolutionary forces in South Vietnam, Cambodia, and Laos. It comprised five main roads, 21 branches, and many detours with a total length of *c.* 16,000 km. (10,000 miles).

**Hodeida** /həʊ'deɪdə/ (Arabic **Al-Hudayda** /ælhuː'deɪdə/) the chief port of Yemen, on the Red Sea 145 km. (90 miles) south-west of San'a; pop. (1986) 155,100. It is the principal city of the coastal Tihama region, third-largest city in Yemen, and a provincial capital. Hodeida was developed as a port by the Ottoman Turks in the 1830s and rapidly expanded as a port of entry for goods after the end of the civil war in 1970. It has an oil refinery, textile plants, and numerous light industries.

**Hoek van Holland** the Dutch name for the HOOK OF HOLLAND.

**Hof** /hɒf/ a town in Bavaria, southern Germany, on the Saale River north-east of Bayreuth; pop. (1991) 52,860.

**Hofei** SEE HEFEI.

**Hofburg** /'hɒfbɜːg/ a complex of buildings in Vienna, Austria, that was the seat of the rulers of Austria until 1918 and of the emperors of Germany until 1806.

**Hoggar Mountains** /'hɒgə(r)/ (also **Ahaggar Mountains** /ə'hægə(r)/) a mountain range in the Saharan desert of southern Algeria of volcanic origin, rising to a height of 2,918 m. (9,573 ft.) at Tahat north-west of Tamanrhasset. The region is the home of the Tuareg people.

**Hohenzollern** /ˌhəʊən'zɒlɜːn/ a former province of Germany to the south-east of the Black Forest, now part of the state of Baden-Württemberg; its capital was Sigmaringen. The family of Hohenzollern ruled as Emperors of Germany from 1871 to 1918.

**Hohe Tauern** /'həʊə 'taʊɜːn/ a mountain range of the eastern Alps in the provinces of Tyrol and Carinthia, Austria. The highest peak is Grossglockner (3,797 m., 12,457 ft.).

**Hohhot** /hu:'hɒt/ (formerly **Huhehot** /ˌhju:heɪ'hɒt/ or **Kwesui** /gweɪ'sweɪ/) the capital of Inner Mongolia autonomous region in north-eastern China, at the junction of former caravan routes to Mongolia and Xinjiang; pop. (1990) 1,206,000. It is a trading centre with industries that include sugar refining and the manufacture of textiles, and chemicals. The original Mongol city, named Kukukhoto, was founded in the 16th c. and was an important religious centre for Tibetan Buddhism. It was renamed Kwesui by the Chinese in the 18th c. and Hohhot in 1954, when it became a provincial capital. A Stone Age village was discovered near here in 1973.

**Hokkaido** /hɒ'kaɪdəʊ/ the most northerly and second-largest of the four main islands of Japan, constituting an administrative region; area 83,519 sq. km. (32,259 sq. miles); pop. (1990) 5,644,000. Separated from Honshu Island by the Tsugaru Strait but linked by the Seikan Tunnel, its chief cities are Sapporo (regional capital) and Hakodate.

**holarctic** /hə'lɑːktɪk/ of or relating to the geographical distribution of animals in the whole northern or Arctic region.

**Holguin** /əʊl'giːn/ a colonial town in eastern Cuba, capital of a province of the same name; pop. (est. 1986) 194,700.

**Holland** /ˈhɒl(ə)nd/ a former province of the Netherlands now divided into **North Holland** and **South Holland**. Its name is often used interchangeably with the Netherlands as the name of the country.

**Holland, Parts of** one of the three former administrative divisions or 'ridings' of the county of Lincoln, East England, prior to the local government reorganization of 1974 that created the districts of Boston and South Holland. Its chief town was Boston.

**Hollywood** /ˈhɒlɪwʊd/ **1.** a district of Los Angeles, California, USA. American film-making was originally based on New York, but southern California, with its sunshine and scenic variety, appealed to film-makers from as early as 1907. In 1911 the first studio was established in Hollywood and 15 others followed in the same year. The Hollywood studio system reached its peak in the 1930s, but by 1950 television had become a serious competitor, and many films are now made for that medium. Landmarks of Hollywood include the Hollywood Bowl outdoor amphitheatre, the Hollywood Sign (1923), and the Sunset Strip district. **2.** a city in south-east Florida, USA, on the Atlantic coast north of Miami; pop. (1990) 121,700. It was established during a real-estate boom in the 1920s and is noted for its golfing facilities.

**Hollywood Bowl** an outdoor amphitheatre with a seating capacity of 17,000 on Highland Avenue, Hollywood, California. Located in a 47-hectare (116-acre) park, it has hosted concerts since 1923.

**Holne** /həʊn/ a village in Devon, south-west England, to the east of Dartmoor. It was the birthplace of the novelist Charles Kingsley in 1819.

**Holocene** /ˈhɒləˌsiːn/ the second of the two epochs of the Quaternary period, following the Pleistocene and lasting from about 10,000 years ago to the present. Also called Recent, the epoch has seen a rise in world temperatures after the last of the Pleistocene ice-ages, and coincides with the development of human agricultural settlement and civilization.

**Holsteinsborg** /ˈhɒlʃtaɪnzˌbɔːg/ (Inuit **Sisimiut**) a settlement on the west coast of Greenland, the second-largest in Greenland; pop. (1992) 5,220.

**Holyhead** /ˈhɒlɪˌhed/ (Welsh **Caer Gybi**) a port on Holyhead Island, off the coast of Anglesey in the Welsh county of Gwynedd; pop. (1981) 12,652. There is a ferry link with Ireland and a container terminal.

**Holy Island 1.** see LINDISFARNE. **2.** a small island off the western coast of Anglesey, in the county of Gwynedd; chief town, Holyhead.

**Holy Land** a region on the eastern shores of the Mediterranean in what is now Israel and Palestine. It has religious significance for Judaism, Christianity, and Islam. In the Christian religion, the name has been applied by Christians since the Middle Ages with reference both to its having been the scene of the Incarnation and to the existing sacred sites there, especially the Holy Sepulchre at Jerusalem.

**Holy Roman Empire** the empire set up in western Europe following the coronation of Charlemagne as emperor, in the year 800. Of the emperors, after 1250 only five were crowned as such; the dignity was abolished by Napoleon in 1806. In true apocalyptic style the empire lasted about 1,000 years. The creation of the medieval popes, it has been called their greatest mistake; for whereas their intention was to appoint a powerful secular deputy to rule Christendom, in fact they generated a rival. The emperor never ruled the whole of Christendom, nor was there any substantial machinery of imperial government. From Otto I's coronation (962) the Empire was always associated with the German Crown, even after it became a Habsburg/Austrian preserve in the 15th c. Its somewhat mystical ideal was formal unity of government, based on coronation in Rome, memories of the old Roman Empire as well as Charlemagne, and devotion to the Roman Catholic Church.

**Holy See** the papacy or papal court in Rome which constitutes the government of the Roman Catholic Church. (see VATICAN)

**Homburg** /ˈhɒmbɜːg/ (also **Bad Homburg**, in full **Bad Homburg vor der Höhe**) a resort town at the foot of the Taunus Mts. in the state of Hesse, west Germany, noted for its mineral baths and the felt Homburg hats that were first manufactured here; pop. (1983) 50,600.

**Home Counties** the counties surrounding London, England, into which London has extended, comprising chiefly Kent, Surrey, Essex, and Hertfordshire.

**Homs** /hɒms, -z/ (also **Hims**) an industrial city of west-central Syria, on the River Orontes; pop. (1981) 354,500. Known in ancient times as Emesa, it lay at the junction of north–south and east–west trade routes. It was the birthplace of the emperor Elagabalus and was the site of Zenobia's defeat by Aurelian (272). Oil refining, sugar refining, and the manufacture of textiles, fertilizers, and metal goods are its chief industries.

**Homs Gap** a valley in south-western Syria between the Ansariya and Lebanon ranges, the only place at which the mountain barrier between inland Syria and the Mediterranean Sea can be easily crossed. It is cut by the al-Kabir River in whose fertile valley lies the frontier between Syria and Lebanon.

**Homyel** /ˈhɒm(ə)l/ (formerly **Gomel**) an industrial city in south-west Belorussia (Belarus), on the Sozh River; pop. (1990) 506,100. Railway engineering and the manufacture of footwear, electrical goods, and agricultural machinery are its chief industries.

**Honan** see **1.** HENAN. **2.** LUOYANG.

### Honduras

/hɒnˈdjuːrəs/ official name **The Republic of Honduras** a country of Central America, bordering on the Caribbean Sea and lying between Guatemala and Nicaragua; area 112,088 sq. km. (43,294 sq. miles); pop. (est. 1990) 5,100,000; official language, Spanish; capital, Tegucigalpa. Honduras has a 644-km. (400-mile) coast on the Caribbean and a narrower outlet to the Pacific through the Gulf of Fonseca. The tropical lowlands rise up to more temperate regions in the mountain ranges that cross the interior of the country from north to south. There is a dry season from November to May. The economy is largely dependent on the country's extensive range of forest, marine, and agricultural resources, the chief exports being bananas, coffee, sugar, fruit, grain, shrimp, and beef. Discovered by Columbus in 1502, Honduras was a dependency of Spain for nearly three centuries until independence was proclaimed in 1821. Plagued by years of instability Honduras remained one of the most poorly developed countries in Latin America. It is governed by an executive president and a unicameral National Congress.
**Honduran** adj. & n.
The country is divided into a Federal District and 18 departments:

| Department | Area (sq. km.) | Pop. (1988) | Capital |
|---|---|---|---|
| Atlántida | 4,251 | 238,740 | La Ceiba |
| Choluteca | 4,211 | 295,480 | Choluteca |
| Colón | 8,875 | 149,680 | Trujillo |
| Comayagua | 5,196 | 239,860 | Comayagua |
| Copán | 3,203 | 219,455 | Santa Rosa |
| Cortés | 3,954 | 662,770 | San Pedro Sula |
| El Paraíso | 7,218 | 254,295 | Yuscarán |
| Federal District | 1,648 | 576,660 | Tegucigalpa |
| Francisco Morazán | 6,298 | 828,270 | Tegucigalpa |
| Gracias a Dios | 16,630 | 34,970 | Puerto Lempira |
| Intibucá | 3,072 | 124,680 | La Esperanza |
| Bay Islands | 261 | 22,060 | Roatán |
| La Paz | 2,331 | 105,930 | La Paz |
| Lempira | 4,290 | 177,055 | Gracias |
| Ocotepeque | 1,680 | 74,280 | Nueva Ocotepeque |
| Olancho | 24,350 | 283,850 | Juticalpa |
| Santa Bárbara | 5,115 | 278,870 | Santa Bárbara |
| Valle | 1,565 | 119,645 | Nacaome |
| Yoro | 7,939 | 333,510 | Yoro |

**Hong Kong** /hɒŋ ˈkɒŋ/ (Chinese **Xiangjiang** /siːæŋˈdʒæŋ/) a British dependency on the south-

east coast of China, adjoining the Chinese province of Guangdong; area 1,071 sq. km. (414 sq. miles); pop. (est. 1990) 5,900,000; languages, English and Chinese (official). Including over 200 islands and a portion of the mainland east of the Pearl River, it comprises Hong Kong Island, ceded by China under the Treaty of Nanking in 1842, the Kowloon peninsula, acquired by the Convention of Peking in 1860, and the New Territories, leased from China in 1898 for 99 years. The climate is tropical, with a dry sunny season from September to March. Hong Kong is a free port, and a major financial and manufacturing centre, exporting textiles, electronics, toys and re-exported goods. By an agreement between the Chinese and British governments (signed in 1984), China will in 1997 resume sovereignty over Hong Kong which will then become a Special Administrative Region whose basic law will guarantee present systems and life-styles for a period of 50 years.

**Hongze** /ˈhʌntsɪ/ (Chinese **Hongze Hu**) a lake in the province of Jiangsu, eastern China, the third-largest freshwater lake in China; area 3,780 sq. km. (1,460 sq. miles). It is fed by the Huai River and drains southwards into the Yangtze.

**Honiara** /ˌhəʊnɪˈɑːrə/ a seaport and capital of the Solomon Islands, situated at the mouth of the Mataniko River on the north-west coast of the island of Guadalcanal; pop. (est. 1990) 35,290. It replaced the former capital, Tulagi, after World War II.

**Honolulu** /ˌhɒnəˈluːluː/ the capital and principal port of Hawaii, situated on the south-east coast of the island of Oahu; pop. (1990) 836,230. It became capital of the Kingdom of Hawaii in 1845 and capital of the 50th US state in 1959. The Japanese attack on the US naval base at Pearl Harbor on 7 December 1941 brought the USA into World War II. It is the headquarters of the US Pacific Fleet and its landmarks include Diamond Head volcanic crater, Waikiki Beach, the royal palace of Iolani, and the USS *Arizona* Memorial at Pearl Harbor. Tourism is a major industry together with sugar processing and pineapple canning.

**Honshu** / hɒnˈʃuː/ the largest of the four main islands of Japan, comprising the regions of Kanto, Chubu, Kinki, Chugoku, and Tohoku; area 230,897 sq. km. (89,184 sq. miles); pop. (1990) 99,254,000. Its chief cities are Tokyo, Yokohama, Osaka, and Nagoya, and landmarks include Mt. Fuji (3,776 m., 12,385 ft.), the largest mountain in Japan and Lake Biwa, the largest lake in Japan.

**Hood** /hʊd/**, Mount** an extinct volcano in the Cascade Range, north-west Oregon, USA. Rising to 3,424 m. (11,234 ft.) in a symmetrical cone, it is the highest peak in the state.

**Hooghly** /'hu:glɪ/ (also **Hugli**) the most westerly of the rivers of the Ganges delta, in West Bengal, India. It flows 192 km. (120 miles) into the Bay of Bengal and was navigable to Calcutta before silting made it necessary to develop the outport of Hadeida.

**Hook of Holland** (Dutch **Hoek van Holland**) a cape and port of the Netherlands, 15 km. (9 miles) south-east of The Hague, linked by ferry to Harwich, Hull, and Dublin. Its Dutch name means 'corner of Holland'.

**Hoorn** /hʊərn/ a city in the province of North Holland, the Netherlands, on an inlet of the Ijsselmeer; pop. (1991) 58,225. Founded as a fishing and trading settlement in the 14th c., the city expanded during the 16th and 17th c. as a result of trade with the Dutch East Indies. It is now a popular yachting centre. The navigator Willem Schouten, who was born here in 1580, rounded the southern tip of South America in 1616, naming it Cap Hoorn (Cape Horn).

**Hoover Dam** a hydroelectric dam on the Colorado River at Boulder Canyon on the border between the US states of Arizona and Nevada. Completed in 1936, its reservoir (Lake Mead) was then the largest man-made lake in the world. It was known as the Boulder Dam (1937–47). The dam is 221 m. (726 ft.) high.

**Hopeh** see HEBEI.

**Hopi** /'həʊpɪ/ a Uto-Aztecan Indian tribe of North America associated with the pueblos of Arizona, Colorado, and New Mexico. Known as 'the peaceful ones', the Hopi are descended from people who migrated into the south-west before 1,000 BC. They number c.9,000 in Arizona.

**Hormuz** /'hɔ:mʊz/ (also **Hormoz** and **Ormoz** /'ɔ:mʊz/) **1.** an island and small town in the Iranian province of Hormozgan, near the mouth of the Persian Gulf. Once a city of importance, Hormuz now thrives on fishing, smuggling, and the mining of salt and red ochre. **2. Strait of Hormuz** a strait separating Iran from the Arabian peninsula and linking the Persian Gulf with the Gulf of Oman which leads to the Arabian Sea. It is of strategic importance as a waterway through which sea traffic to and from the oil-rich states of the Persian Gulf must pass.

**Horn of Africa, the** a peninsula of north-east Africa separating the Gulf of Aden from the main part of the Indian Ocean. It is also called the **Somali Peninsula** and comprises Somalia and parts of Ethiopia.

**horse latitudes** a belt of calms in each hemisphere at 30–35° north and south of the equator, between the trade winds and the westerlies. The origin of the name is uncertain; some hold that it arose from the alleged practice of throwing overboard horses, which were being transported to the Americas or West Indies, when the ship's voyage was unduly prolonged by lack of a favourable wind.

**Horsens** /'hɔ:sənz/ a port on the east coast of Jutland, Denmark, situated on the Horsens Fjord; pop. (1990) 55,210.

**Horta** /'hɒrtə/ a port on the south-east coast of the island of Faial in the Azores; pop. (1981) 6,910. It trades in wine, fruit, and grain and is capital of a district of the same name that comprises the islands of Faial, Pico, Flores, and Corvo.

**Hortobágy** /'hɔ:tə,bædʒə/ a national park on the Great Plain of north-east Hungary, extending over an area of grassland (*puszta*) noted for its stock breeding and its wildlife.

**Hospet** /'həʊʃ,pet/ a town in Karnataka, southern India, on the Tungabhadra River east of Hubli; pop. (1991) 134,935. Nearby at Hampi are the remains of the seat of the 14th–16th-c. Hindu Vijayanagara empire.

**Hospitalet de Llobregat** /,ɒspi:tə'let ðeɪ ,ljɒvreɪ'gæt/ a southern suburb of Barcelona, Spain, on the River Llobrigat; pop. (1991) 269,345. Its industries produce steel, chemicals, textiles, and leather.

**Hotan** /hɒ'tɑ:n/ a town in Xinjiang autonomous region, north-west China, at the southern edge of the Taklimakan Desert in the northern foothills of the Kunlun Shan range; pop. (1986) 121,000.

**Hot Springs** a national park in west-central Arkansas, USA, established in 1921. Over one million gallons of water with an average temperature of 143°F (62°C) is produced daily by 47 hot springs that were used by Indians for medicinal purposes. The resort town of Hot Springs is located nearby.

**Hottentot** /'hɒtən,tɒt/ a people related to the Bushmen now found chiefly in south-west Africa. They formerly occupied the region near the Cape but were largely dispossessed by Dutch settlers. Their language (also known as *Nama*) which is spoken in Namibia by about 50,000 people has a number of 'click' consonants made by drawing air into the mouth and clicking the tongue.

**Houma** /'həʊmə/ a town in southern Shanxi province, central China, on a tributary of the Fen River which flows westwards into the Yellow River; pop. (1986) 160,000.

**Houston** /'hju:st(ə)n/ an inland deep-water port of Texas, USA, linked to the Gulf of Mexico by the Houston Ship Canal and a great financial, commercial, and industrial centre; pop. (1990) 1,630,550. It is the fourth-largest city in the USA, and has since 1961 been an important centre for space research and manned space flight. The city is named after Samuel Houston (1793–1863), American politician and military leader who led the struggle to win control of Texas (1834–6) and make it part of the USA. It is the home of Rice University (1912), the University of Houston

(1927), and the Johnson (NASA) Space Center. It is one of the world's major oil centres with refineries and petrochemical works; it has steel mills, shipyards, breweries, and meat-packing plants, as well as many electronics and avionics research firms and consumer goods industries. Houston is also a major cultural and tourist centre with a ballet company, symphony orchestra, numerous galleries and museums, arboretum, botanic gardens, and sports and amusement centres.

**Hove** /həʊv/ a resort town and residential suburb on the south coast of England, adjacent to Brighton in East Sussex; pop. (1981) 67,140. The composer Roger Quilter was born here in 1877.

**Howland Island** an uninhabited US island in the North Pacific Ocean, near the equator; area 1.6 sq. km. (1 sq. mile). Claimed by the USA in 1856, it was used as a source of guano in the 19th c. Amelia Earhart and Fred Noonan stopped here to refuel before disappearing during their round-the-world flight in 1937.

**Howrah** see HAORA.

**Hradec Králové** /ˌhrædets ˈkrɑːlɒˌveɪ/ a historic town in the Czech Republic, to the east of Prague at the junction of the Elbe and Orlice rivers; pop. (1991) 161,960. Founded in the 13th c. and formerly the seat of the widowed queens of Bohemia, it is now capital of the administrative region of East Bohemia. Its manufactures include machinery, chemicals, woodwork, and musical instruments.

**Hrodna** /ˈhrɒdnə/ (formerly **Grodno** or **Gardinas**) an industrial port on the River Neman in west Belorussia (Belarus); pop. 220,000. Industries include sugar refining and the manufacture of chemical fibres and fertilizers. Founded in the 10th century, it was for a time the second city of the Grand Duchy of Lithuania and in the 17th and 18th centuries the seat of Polish Diets.

**Hrvatska** the Serbo-Croat name for CROATIA.

**Hsining** see XINING.

**Hsinchu** /sɪnˈtʃuː/ a port on the north-west coast of Taiwan; pop. (est. 1982) 292,740. It has an industrial park manufacturing high-tech products.

**Huai** /hwaɪ/ a river in eastern China that rises in the Tongbai Mts. of south Henan province and flows eastwards for 560 km. (350 miles) across Anhui to Lake Hongze.

**Huaibei** /hwaɪˈbeɪ/ a city in north Anhui province, eastern China, south-west of Xuzhou; pop. (1986) 1,308,000.

**Huaihua** /hwaɪˈhwɑː/ a city in Hunan province, south-central China, situated on a bend of the Wu Shui River; pop. (1986) 436,000.

**Huainan** /hwaɪˈnɑːn/ a city in the province of Anhui, east-central China, on the Huai River; pop. (1986) 1,519,000. It was established in 1949 at the centre of a major coal-mining region.

**Huaiyin** /hwaɪˈjɪn/ a city in Jiangsu province, eastern China, on the Grand Canal north of Nanjing; pop. (1986) 391,000.

**Huallaga** /wɑːˈjɑːɡə/ a river in central Peru, one of the headwaters of the Amazon. Rising near the Andean mining town of Cerro de Pasco, it flows *c.* 1,120 km. (700 miles) generally north-eastwards to meet the Marañon River in northern Peru. The remote upper river valley is one of the world's chief coca-growing regions.

**Huambo** /ˈwæmbəʊ/ a city in the mountains of western Angola, at an altitude of 1,695 m. (5,561 ft.); pop. (1983) 203,000. Founded in 1912, it was known by its Portuguese name, Nova Lisboa, until 1978.

**Huancavelica** /ˌhwænkəˈveliːkə/ a historic town in the Andean Mountains of central Peru, on the Huancavelica River; pop. (est. 1990) 27,400. It is capital of a department of the same name and was an ancient Inca centre before the arrival of the Spanish who discovered silver and mercury nearby. The town was founded in 1571 and named Villa Rica de Oropesa.

**Huancayo** /hwænˈkaɪəʊ/ an old colonial city in the Andean Mountains of central Peru, in the valley of the Mantaro River; pop. (est. 1990) 207,600. It is capital of the department of Junín and an important market centre.

**Huangguoshu Falls** /hwæŋˈgwɒʃuː/ a waterfall on the Bai Shui River in central Guizhou province, southern China. With a drop of 67 m. (220 ft.) and a width of 84 m. (275 ft.) it is one of the largest waterfalls in China.

**Huang He** /hwæŋ ˈhiː/ the Chinese name for the YELLOW RIVER.

**Huangshan** /hwæŋˈʃɑːn/ a town in southern Anhui province, eastern China, situated to the north of Huang Shan Mountain; pop. (1986) 151,000.

**Huang Shan** /hwæŋˈʃɑːn/ (English **Yellow Mountain**) a mountain range in eastern China to the south of the Yangtze River. It has 72 peaks, the highest of which rises to 1,841 m. (6,040 ft.). Its cloud-swept landscape has been popular with Chinese poets and painters.

**Huangshi** /hwæŋˈʃiː/ a city in Hubei province, east-central China, on the Yangtze River southeast of Wuhan; pop. (1986) 1,069,000. A new major industrial centre with iron and steel and other heavy industries.

**Huánuco** /ˈhwænuːkəʊ/ a town in the Andean Mountains of central Peru, in the upper reaches of the Huallaga River; pop. (est. 1990) 86,300. It is capital of the agricultural department of Huánuco and is situated close to one of Peru's oldest Andean archaeological sites, the Temple of Kotosh, which was discovered in 1960.

**Huaraz** /hwəˈrɑːs/ the capital of the department of Ancash in western Peru, on the Santa River;

pop. (est. 1990) 65,600. Situated on a major route-way through the Andes, it has been destroyed on several occasions by earthquakes, the most recent being in May 1970 when half the population of the city was killed. It has now been rebuilt and has a fine archaeological museum.

**Huascarán** /ˌhwæskəˈrɑːn/ (also **Nevado de Huascarán**) an extinct volcano in the Peruvian Andes, rising to 6,768 m. (22,205 ft.). It is the highest peak in Peru.

**Hubei** /huːˈbeɪ/ (formerly **Hupeh**) a province of east-central China, mountainous in the north and west and watered by numerous rivers including the Yangtze; area 186,000 sq. km. (71,815 sq. miles); pop. (1990) 53,969,000; capital, Wuhan. Rice, cotton, grain, tea, and mineral resources such as copper, limestone, and anthracite are its chief products.

**Hubli** /ˈhuːblɪ/ a city and railway junction in the state of Karnataka, southern India; pop. (1991) 648,000. It was united with the city of Dharwar in 1961 and is a centre of the cotton industry.

**Hucknall** /ˈhʌkn(ə)l/ (formerly **Hucknall Torkard**) a small industrial town in Nottinghamshire, England, 10 km. (6 miles) north of Nottingham; pop. (1981) 27,500. The church was the burial place (except for his heart which is in Missolonghi, Greece) of Lord Byron in 1824 and the birthplace of the composer Eric Coates in 1886.

**Huddersfield** /ˈhʌdɜːzˌfiːld/ a town which developed as a textile-manufacturing centre in West Yorkshire, England, on the River Colne; pop. (1981) 148,540. It was the birthplace of the organist and composer Edward Bairstow in 1874. The University of Huddersfield (formerly Polytechnic of Huddersfield) was established here in 1992. It has developed light industries.

**Hudson Bay** /ˈhʌds(ə)n/ a large inland sea in north-eastern Canada, named after the English explorer Henry Hudson (d. 1611) who visited it in 1610; area c. 1,230,250 sq. km. (475,180 sq. miles). It is the largest inland sea in the world and is connected to the Arctic Ocean via Foxe Basin and the North Atlantic Ocean via the Hudson Strait. The Hudson's Bay Company, a British colonial trading company created in 1670, was granted exclusive rights to the land draining into the bay for purposes of commercial exploitation. The company continued to control these lands, amalgamating with the rival North-West Company in 1821, for two centuries, finally handing them over to the new Canadian government in 1869.

**Hudson River** a river of eastern North America, which rises in the Adirondack Mountains of New York state, USA, and flows southwards for 560 km. (350 miles) to meet the Atlantic at New York City. Navigable as far as Albany, it was named after the English explorer Henry Hudson who sailed 240 km. (150 miles) up the river in 1609.

**Hué** /hweɪ/ a port and industrial city in central Vietnam, near the mouth of the Hué River in the province of Binh Tri Thien; pop. (est. 1990) 200,000. A former capital of Vietnam (1802–1945), it was the ancient capital of the Nguyen dynasty. In addition to the imperial city there are many pagodas and royal tombs. It is a market centre of a rich farming area.

**Huehuetenango** /hweɪhweɪtəˈnæŋgəʊ/ a copper- and silver-mining town in western Guatemala, on the Inter-American Highway north-west of Guatemala City. It is capital of a department of the same name.

**Huelva** /ˈhwelvə/ **1.** a province in Andalusia, southern Spain, on the frontier with Portugal; area 10,085 sq. km. (3,895 sq. miles); pop. (1991) 443,480. **2.** its capital, a port on the delta of the Odiel and Tinto rivers; pop. (1991) 143,570. Fishing, fish-canning, oil refining, and the export of mineral ores are important. Columbus sailed from here on his voyages of discovery to the New World.

**Huesca** /ˈhweskə/ **1.** a province in the Aragón region of north-east Spain, on the south-facing slopes of the Pyrenees, to the north of the River Ebro; area 15,613 sq. km. (6,030 sq. miles); pop. (1991) 207,810. **2.** its capital, the former seat of the kings of Aragón and a marketing and light-industry centre; pop. (1991) 50,020.

**Hugli** see HOOGHLY.

**Huhehot** see HOHHOT.

**Hui** /hwiː/ a minority nationality of northern China, mostly found in Ningxia, Gansu, Shanxi, and Xinjiang where the Hui people number c. 7.2 million.

**Huila** /ˈwiːlə/ (also **Nevado de Huila**) a South American volcano in the Andes of central Colombia, rising to 5,750 m. (18,865 ft.) south-east of Cali. It is the second-highest peak in Colombia.

**Huizhou** /hwiːˈdʒəʊ/ a city in Guandong province, southern China, to the east of Guangzhou (Canton); pop. (1986) 188,000.

**Hull** /hʌl/ a city in southern Quebec, eastern Canada, on the Gatineau and Ottawa river opposite Ottawa; pop. (1991) 60,700. It is a French-speaking city and an important centre for administration and the timber and paper industries. It is the site of the Musée Canadien des Civilisations.

**Hull** /hʌl/ (officially **Kingston upon Hull**) a city and port in Humberside, England, situated at the junction of the Hull and Humber rivers; pop. (1991) 252,200. It is linked to the south bank of the estuary by a bridge completed in 1981. Hull was the birthplace of the English philanthropist William Wilberforce (1759–1833). The University of Hull was founded in 1954 and the University of Humberside (formerly Humberside Polytechnic) was established in 1992. Formerly a fishing port its trade is now with northern Europe. It has engineering and chemical industries.

**Humber** /ˈhʌmbə/ **1.** a river estuary in Humberside, north-east England, formed at the junction of the Ouse and Trent rivers near Goole. The Humber flows 60 km. (38 miles) eastwards to enter the North Sea at Spurn Head. **2.** a shipping forecast area covering an area of the North Sea off eastern England, extending roughly from the latitude of north Norfolk to that of Flamborough Head.

**Humberside** /ˈhʌmbəˌsaɪd/ a county of north-east England; area 3,513 sq. km. (1,357 sq. miles); pop. (1991) 845,200; county town, Beverley. It was formed in 1974 from parts of the East and West Ridings of Yorkshire and the northern part of Lincolnshire. It is divided into nine districts:

| District | Area (sq. km.) | Pop. (1991) |
|---|---|---|
| Boothferry | 646 | 63,100 |
| Cleethorpes | 164 | 67,500 |
| East Yorkshire | 1,044 | 83,700 |
| East Yorks Borough of Beverley | 404 | 109,500 |
| Glanford | 580 | 70,000 |
| Great Grimsby | 28 | 88,900 |
| Holderness | 540 | 49,900 |
| Kingston upon Hull | 72 | 252,200 |
| Scunthorpe | 34 | 60,500 |

**Humboldt Current** /ˈhʌmbəʊlt/ (also **Peruvian Current**) a cold ocean current that moves northwards from the Southern Ocean along the Pacific coast of Chile and Peru before being turned westwards into the Southern Equatorial Current by the trade winds. It is named after the German explorer and scientist Baron von Humboldt (1799–1804). The current causes near-desert conditions along the coasts of Peru and northern Chile and also gives rise to the vast shoals of anchovies now depleted by over-fishing.

**Hun** /hʌn/ a warlike Asiatic nomadic people who invaded and ravaged Europe in the 4th–5th c.

**Hunan** /huːˈnæn/ a province of east-central China, to the south of the Yangtze River; area 210,000 sq. km. (81,112 sq. miles); pop. (1990) 60,660,000; capital, Changsha. Its chief products are coal, lead, zinc, antimony, rice, tobacco, sugar-cane, and oil-bearing crops such as rape and sesame.

**Hungarian** /hʌŋˈgeərɪən/ the official language of Hungary, one of the Finno-Ugric languages, spoken by some 11 million people in Hungary and Romania, the only major language of the Ugric branch.

**Hungary** /ˈhʌŋgərɪ/ (Hungarian **Magyarország**) official name **The Republic of Hungary** a country in central Europe, bordering on Slovakia, Ukraine, Romania, Serbia, Croatia, Slovenia, and Austria; area 93,033 sq. km. (35,934 sq. miles); pop. (est. 1990) 10,600,000; offi-

cial language, Hungarian (Magyar); capital, Budapest. Its largest cities are Budapest, Debrecen, and Miskolc. Hungary largely comprises a broad rolling plain (Great Plain) drained by the Danube and Tisza rivers. To the north lie the Northern Highlands and to the north-west, beyond Lake Balaton and the Transdanubian Highlands, lies the Little Plain which is watered by the Rába and the Danube. Formerly a predominantly agricultural economy, Hungary became industrialized during the post-war years and made use of rich bauxite deposits, coal, and natural gas. Its main exports are machinery, consumer goods, and chemical products. Settled by the Magyars in the 9th c., Hungary emerged at the centre of a strong Magyar kingdom in the late Middle Ages, but was conquered first by the Turks in the 16th c. and then by Habsburgs in the 17th c., being incorporated in the Austrian empire thereafter. Nationalist pressure resulted in increased Hungarian power and autonomy within the empire in the 19th c., and following the collapse of Habsburg power in 1918 Hungary finally achieved independence. After participation in World War II on the Axis side, Hungary was occupied by the Soviets and became a Communist state under their strong influence, a liberal reform movement being crushed by Soviet troops in 1956. A reform movement in the late 1980s ultimately led to the abandonment of Communism in 1989, the withdrawal of Soviet troops, and the holding of free multiparty elections in 1990.

**Hungarian** *adj. & n.*

Hungary, which is governed by a unicameral National Assembly and an executive Presidential Council, is divided into 20 counties:

| County | Area (sq. km.) | Pop. (1990) | Capital |
|---|---|---|---|
| Bács-Kiskun | 8,363 | 545,000 | Kecskemét |
| Baranya | 4,487 | 430,000 | Pécs |
| Békés | 5,632 | 410,000 | Békéscaba |
| Borsod-Abaúj-Zemplén | 7,248 | 770,000 | Miskolc |
| Budapest | 525 | 2,115,000 | Budapest |
| Csongrád | 4,263 | 450,000 | Szeged |
| Fejér | 4,374 | 425,000 | Székesfehérvár |
| Győr-Moson-Sopron | 4,012 | 430,000 | Győr |
| Hajdú-Bihar | 6,212 | 550,000 | Debrecen |
| Heves | 3,637 | 335,000 | Eger |
| Komárom-Esztergom | 2,250 | 320,000 | Tatabánya |
| Nógrád | 2,544 | 230,000 | Salgótarján |
| Pest | 6,394 | 970,000 | Budapest |
| Somogy | 6,035 | 350,000 | Kaposvár |
| Szabolcs-Szatmár-Bereg | 5,938 | 570,000 | Nyiregyháza |
| Jasz-Nagykun-Szolnok | 5,608 | 430,000 | Szolnok |
| Tolna | 3,702 | 260,000 | Szekszárd |
| Vas | 3,337 | 280,000 | Szombathely |
| Veszprém | 4,689 | 385,000 | Veszprém |
| Zala | 7,784 | 310,000 | Zalaegerszeg |

**Hunjiang** /hʊn'dʒɑːŋ/ a city in Jilin province, north-east China, near the border with North Korea; pop. (1986) 694,000.

**Huntingdon** /'hʌntɪŋd(ə)n/ a town in Cambridgeshire, England, on the River Ouse 24 km. (15 miles) north-west of Cambridge; pop. (1981) 17,600. It was the birthplace of Oliver Cromwell in 1599.

**Huntingdonshire** a former county of eastern England, that became part of Cambridgeshire in 1974.

**Huntington** /'hʌntɪŋtən/ a city in West Virginia, USA, on the Ohio River; pop. (1990) 54,840. Now the second-largest city in the state, it was established in 1871 as a rail and river terminus by Collis P. Huntington, president of the Chesapeake and Ohio Railroad. It produces glass, metal goods, and railway products.

**Huntington Beach** a city in southern California, USA, on the Pacific coast south-east of Long Beach; pop. (1990) 181,520. It is a noted surfing resort.

**Huntington Park** a city in the Los Angeles conurbation, southern California, USA, an industrial and residential suburb to the west of the Los Angeles River; pop. (1990) 56,065.

**Huntsville** /'hʌntsvɪl/ a city in northern Alabama, USA, north-east of Decatur; pop. (1990) 159,790. Originally a textile town dating from 1805, it is now a centre for space exploration and solar-energy research. The George C. Marshall Space Flight Center of NASA began operations here in 1960. It was the birthplace of the actress Tallulah Bankhead (1903–68).

**Hunza** /'hʌnzə/ a former princely state in Kashmir that came under the sovereignty of the Maharajah of Jammu and Kashmir in 1869, was united with the state of Nagar in 1888, and became part of the Gilgit Agency a year later in 1889. Now part of Pakistani-held Kashmir, its capital was the town of Hunza (Baltit); area 10,100 sq. km. (3,900 sq. miles).

**Hupeh** see HUBEI.

**Huron** /'hjʊərən/ (also **Wyandot**) a confederation of five Iroquoian Indian groups living northeast of Lake Huron. Known to themselves as Wyandot or Wendat (= people of the peninsula) and surviving today in Quebec and Oklahoma, they were named Huron (= bristly-headed ruffian) by the French explorer Samuel de Champlain when he first encountered them in 1615.

**Huron, Lake** the second-largest of the five Great Lakes of North America, divided between Canada and the USA; area 63,096 sq. km. (24,361 sq. miles); area on the Canadian side of the border, 39,473 sq. km. (15,240 sq. miles); maximum depth 229 m. It is linked to Lake Michigan in the west by the Straits of Mackinac, to Lake Superior in the

north by St. Mary's River, and to Lake Erie in the south via Lake St. Clair and the St. Clair River.

**Hurrian** /'hʌrɪən/ a widespread non-Semitic people in the Middle East during the 3rd–2nd millennium BC identified with the Horites of the Bible. Their language, written in cuneiform and of unknown origin, was neither Semitic nor Indo-European.

**hurricane** a storm or violent cyclonic disturbance which originates over tropical waters mostly during late summer and early autumn in the region between the north-east and south-east trade winds. It is defined by meteorologists as a wind of 65 knots (75 m.p.h.) or more, force 12 on the Beaufort scale. Hurricanes are known as **willy-willies** in Australia, **tropical cyclones** in the Arabian Sea and Bay of Bengal, and **typhoons** in the north-west Pacific. The naming of hurricanes dates back many years. For example, in the Caribbean hurricanes took the name of the saint's day on which they occurred. In the US storms were identified and named using letters of the phonetic alphabet for the purpose of radio transmission until 1953 when the practice of giving female names to hurricanes was adopted. Since 1979 both male and female names have been used except those beginning with the letters Q, U, X, Y, and Z.

**Hutu** /'huːtuː/ a Bantu farming people of east Africa who comprise the majority of the people of Rwanda and Burundi.

**Huzhou** /hʊ'dʒəʊ/ (also **Wuxing** /wʊ'ʃɪŋ/) a city in northern Zhejiang province, eastern China, to the south of Lake Tai; pop. (1986) 974,000.

**Hvannadalshnjúkur** /'hwænədæls͵hnjuːkʊə(r)/ a mountain in south-east Iceland, rising to 2,119 m. (6,952 ft.), the highest peak in Iceland.

**Hvar** /hvɑː/ an island in the Adriatic, off the Dalmatian coast of Bosnia-Herzegovina; area 300 sq. km. (116 sq. miles). The towns of Nvar, Stari Grad, Vrboska, and Jelsa were popular tourist resorts prior to the outbreak of civil war following the breakup of Yugoslavia in 1991.

**Hwange** /'wæŋgɪ, 'hw-/ **1.** a town in the province of Matabeleland North, western Zimbabwe, on the railway line between Bulawayo and Victoria Falls; pop. (1982) 39,200. Known as **Wankie** until 1982, and taking its name from a local Ndebele chief, the town has developed alongside coalfields and as a service centre for a cattle-ranching area to the north. **2.** the largest national park in Zimbabwe, situated to the south of the town of Hwange at the north-eastern tip of the Kalahari Desert. The former hunting preserve of the Ndebele chiefs, Hwange became a national park in 1929 to protect 'fossil' sand dunes and river beds, savanna grassland and scrub, mopane woodland, and forests of teak. It has some 35 species of large mammal including one of Africa's largest populations of elephant; area 14,650 sq. km. (5,658 sq. miles).

**Hyde Park** the largest of the royal parks in west-central London, between Bayswater Road to the north and Kensington Road to the south. Once owned by the Church as part of the Manor of Hyde, it was taken by the Crown in 1536. At the instance of Queen Caroline the park was improved in the 1830s with the creation of the Serpentine and the building of walkways, lodges, ponds, and arches to a plan by Decimus Burton. The southeast corner of the park is known as **Hyde Park Corner** and the north-east corner near Marble Arch, with its soap-box orators, is known as Speakers' Corner.

**Hyderabad** /'haɪdərə,bæd/ **1.** a city, capital of the state of Andhra Pradesh in central India, on the River Musi; pop. (1991) 3,005,000. Founded in 1589 as a Muslim stronghold, it was capital of the kingdom of Golconda and of the former state of Hyderabad, and has many ancient buildings including tombs and mosques. It has four universities (founded 1918, 1964, 1972, and 1974) and research institutions. Hyderabad is a commercial centre and a centre of craft industries. **2.** a former large princely state of south-central India occupying the greater part of the Deccan plateau; area 213,108 sq. km. (82,313 sq. miles). It was ruled by Muslim Nizams until its union with India in 1948.

**Hyderabad** (also **Haidarabad**) a city in south-east Pakistan, on the Indus; pop. (1991) 1,000,000. Founded by Ghulam Shah Kalhora in 1768, it was until the arrival of the British in 1843 the capital of the province of Sind. Its university was founded in 1947 and its industries produce clothing, leather shoes, lacquered-wood furniture, and handicrafts.

**Hydra** /'haɪdrə/ (Greek **Idhra**) a Greek island in the Aegean Sea, off the east coast of the Peloponnese; area 50 sq. km. (19 sq. miles). Its chief town is the port of Hydra.

**hydrology** /haɪ'drɒlədʒɪ/ the study of the earth's water, especially water under or on the surface of the ground before it evaporates or reaches the sea.

**Hyères Islands** /jɜː/ (French **Iles d'Hyères**) a group of French islands in the Mediterranean Sea off the south coast of the department of Var.

**Hyksos** /'hɪksɒs/ a people of mixed Semitic-Asiatic stock who settled in the Nile delta c. 1640 BC. They formed the 15th and 16th dynasties of Egypt, and ruled a large part of the country until driven out by the powerful 18th dynasty c. 1532 BC. Described as oppressors by later Egyptians, they nevertheless upheld many Egyptian traditions. During their reign the composite bow, the horse and chariot, and new military techniques were introduced into Egypt.

**Hyphasis** /'hɪfəsəs/ the ancient name for the BEAS.

**hypogean** /,haɪpə'dʒiːən/ existing or growing underground.

**Hyvinkää** /'huːvɪŋkə/ a winter-sports resort to the north of Helsinki in the province of Uudenmaa, southern Finland; pop. (1990) 40,190.

# I *i*

**IA** *abbr.* US Iowa (in official postal use).

**Iaşi** /ˈjæʃɪ/ (German **Jassy** /ˈjɑːsɪ/) the capital city of Iaşi county in eastern Romania, situated close to the frontier with Moldavia on the Bahlui River; pop. (1989) 330,195. Between 1565 and 1859 it was the capital of the principality of Moldavia and after World War I it was a centre of the working-class movement. Its university, the oldest in Romania, was founded in 1860 and its industries produce machinery, chemicals, and processed food.

**Ibadan** /ˌɪbəˈdɑːn/ the second-largest city of Nigeria, situated north-east of Lagos; pop. (est. 1986) 847,000. It is an industrial and commercial city, capital of the state of Oyo, and intellectual and cultural centre of Yorubaland. Its world-famous university was established in 1948.

**Ibagué** /iːbəˈgeɪ/ the capital of the department of Tolima in west-central Colombia, in the Andes at the foot the Quindío Mts.; pop. (1985) 285,410. It has a Conservatory of Music (1906) and hosts an annual Colombian folk festival. It is a market town with agriculturally based light industries.

**Iban** /ˈiːbæn/ a group of non-Muslim indigenous peoples from the island of Borneo; a member of the Sea Dyaks. Their language, which belongs to the Malayo-Polynesian group of languages, is spoken by about 303,000 people.

**Ibaraki** /ˌiːbəˈrɑːkɪ/ a city near Osaka, on the island of Honshu, Japan; pop. (1990) 254,000.

**Ibarra** /iːˈbɑːrə/ (fully **San Miguel de Ibarra**) the capital of the Andean province of Imbabura in northern Ecuador, 135 km. (84 miles) north of Quito; pop. (1990) 117,220. It is an old colonial town, founded in 1597 by Alvarro de Ibarra and a marketing and tourist centre.

**Iberia** /aɪˈbɪərɪə/ the ancient Roman name for what is now Spain and Portugal. It takes its name from *Iberus*, the Roman name for the River Ebro. **Iberian** *adj. & n.*

**Iberian Peninsula** /aɪˈbɪərɪən/ the extreme south-west peninsula of Europe, containing present-day Spain and Portugal. In ancient times it was a centre of Carthaginian colonization until the Third Punic War (149–146 BC), after which it came increasingly under Roman influence. It was invaded by the Visigoths in the 4th–5th c. AD and by the Moors in the 8th c.

**Ibiza** /ɪˈbiːθə/ (also **Iviza**) **1.** the third-largest and westernmost of the Spanish Balearic Islands in the Mediterranean Sea; area 572 sq. km. (220 sq.

miles). **2.** its capital, a port and major tourist resort on the south-east coast of the island; pop. (1981) 25,490.

**Ibo** /ˈiːbəʊ/ (also **Igbo**) a people of south-east Nigeria whose language, spoken by eight million people, belongs to the Niger–Congo language group. (See also BIAFRA.)

**Icaria** /ɪˌkəˈrɪə/ (Greek **Ikaría**) a Greek island in the Aegean Sea, named after the legendary Icarus who plunged into the Icarian Sea while flying from Crete with Daedalus; area 255 sq. km. (98 sq. miles); capital, Ayios Kírikos. It has radioactive hot springs.

**Icefields Parkway** the name given to Highway 93 in the Rocky Mountains of Alberta and British Columbia, Canada. Built as a scenic routeway and completed in 1960, it connects Lake Louise on the Trans-Canada Highway with Jasper on the Yellowhead Highway and passes through Banff and Jasper national parks. Passing through mountain scenery and reaching 2,068 m. (6,787 ft.) at Bow Pass, it stretches for a distance of 230 km. (143 miles).

**İçel** /ɪˈtʃiːl/ a province on the Mediterranean coast of southern Turkey; area 15,853 sq. km. (6,123 sq. miles); pop. (1990) 1,267,000; capital, Mersin.

**Iceland** (Icelandic **Island**) official name **The Republic of Iceland** a volcanic island country in the North Atlantic, just south of the Arctic Circle; area 102,820 sq. km. (39,714 sq. miles); pop. (est.

1990) 300,000; official language, Icelandic; capital, Reykjavik. Situated at the north end of the Mid-Atlantic Ridge, Iceland has several volcanoes, lava flows, and hot springs (*geysers*). It has a heavily in-dented coastline, extensive snowfields, and glacial ice-caps, with only 21 per cent of the country con-sidered habitable or fit for arable farming. The greater part of the island is a desert plateau lying some 400 m. (1,300 ft.) above sea-level. The Gulf Stream warms the south and west coasts but com-bines with relatively cold polar sea air to create generally wet conditions for much of the year. Further north the weather can be clear and sunny, but snow blizzards can develop at almost any time of year. Iceland makes good use of hydroelectric and geothermal power, and exports fish, diatomite, and aluminium. First settled by Norse colonists in the 9th c., Iceland was under Norwegian rule from 1262 to 1380 when it passed to Denmark. Granted internal self-government in 1874, it became a fully fledged independent republic in 1944. In 1972 Iceland unilaterally extended its territorial waters from 12 to 50 nautical miles causing disputes with the UK known as the 'Cod Wars' (1952–6, 1972–3, and 1975–6). Restrictions on fishing within its waters was also a key issue during negotiations to form the European Economic Area in 1991. Iceland is governed by a bicameral parliament (*Althing*), with executive power exercised by a prime minister and a cabinet.

**Icelandic** *adj. & n.*; **Icelander** *n.*

Iceland is divided into eight administrative regions:

| Region | Pop. (1990) |
|---|---|
| Suðurnes | 15,200 |
| Höfuðborgarsvaeði | 145,980 |
| Vesturland | 14,540 |
| Vestfirðir | 9,800 |
| Norðurland vestra | 10,450 |
| Norðurland eystra | 26,130 |
| Austurland | 13,220 |
| Suðurland | 20,400 |

**Ichihara** /iːtʃiːˈhɑːrə/ an industrial city in Kanto region, east Honshu Island, Japan, south-east of Tokyo; pop. (1990) 258,000. It has steel, shipbuilding, and petrochemical industries.

**Ichikawa** /iːtʃiːˈkɑːwə/ an industrial city in Kanto region, east Honshu Island, Japan, on the Edo River north-east of Tokyo; pop. (1990) 437,000. It has metallurgical, chemical, and textile industries.

**Ichinomiya** /iːtʃiːˈnəʊmɪə/ an industrial city and resort in Chubu region, central Honshu Island, Japan, north-west of Nagoya; pop. (1990) 262,000. It has textile and metallurgical industries.

**Icknield Way** /ˈɪkniːld/ an ancient pre-Roman track which crosses England in a wide curve from Wiltshire to Norfolk through the Berkshire Downs and the Chilterns.

**ID** *abbr.* US Idaho (in official postal use).

**Ida** /ˈaɪdə/, **Mount** (Greek **Idha** or **Psilorítis** /ˌsɪlɔːˈriːtɪs/) a mountain in central Crete, associated with the god Zeus. Rising to 2,456 m. (8,058 ft.), it is the highest peak on the island. Excavations at the Idaian Cave have uncovered items dating back to the Minoan period.

**Idaho** /ˈaɪdəˌhəʊ/ a state of the north-western US, bordering on British Columbia to the north and containing part of the Rocky Mountains; area 216,432 sq. km. (83,564 sq. miles); pop. (1990) 1,007,750; capital, Boise. The largest cities are Boise, Pocatello, and Idaho Falls. It is also known as the Gem State, Spud State, or Panhandle State.

Idaho was acquired by the US as part of the Louisiana Purchase in 1803 and became the 43rd state of the Union in 1890. Explored by Lewis and Clark in 1805–6, the first permanent US settlement was eventually established by Mormons at Franklin in 1860. In addition to extensive timber resources the state is rich in minerals such as silver, antimony, cobalt, lead, mercury, vanadium, and zinc. Since World War II irrigated farming (producing one-fourth of the US potato crop) and tourism have become important, the state's chief attractions being the Craters of the Moon National Monument, Nez Percé National Historic Park, Hagerman Fossil Beds National Monument, City of Rocks National Reserve, and the Sun Valley winter-sports resort. Idaho is divided into 44 counties:

| County | Area (sq. km.) | Pop. (1990) | County Seat |
|---|---|---|---|
| Ada | 2,735 | 205,775 | Boise |
| Adams | 3,541 | 3,520 | Council |
| Bannock | 2,891 | 66,030 | Pocatello |
| Bear Lake | 2,574 | 6,080 | Paris |
| Benewah | 2,038 | 7,940 | Saint Maries |
| Bingham | 5,450 | 37,580 | Blackfoot |
| Blaine | 6,848 | 13,550 | Hailey |
| Boise | 4,943 | 3,510 | Idaho City |
| Bonner | 4,488 | 26,620 | Sandpoint |
| Bonneville | 4,784 | 72,210 | Idaho Falls |
| Boundary | 3,297 | 8,330 | Bonners Ferry |
| Butte | 5,814 | 2,920 | Arco |
| Camas | 2,785 | 727 | Fairfield |
| Canyon | 1,518 | 90,080 | Caldwell |
| Caribou | 4,584 | 6,960 | Soda Springs |
| Cassia | 6,656 | 19,530 | Burley |
| Clark | 4,584 | 762 | Dubois |
| Clearwater | 5,814 | 8,505 | Orofino |
| Custer | 12,810 | 4,130 | Challis |
| Elmore | 7,985 | 21,205 | Mountain Home |
| Franklin | 1,726 | 9,230 | Preston |
| Fremont | 4,815 | 10,940 | Saint Anthony |
| Gem | 1,451 | 11,840 | Emmett |
| Gooding | 1,893 | 11,630 | Gooding |
| Idaho | 22,092 | 13,780 | Grangeville |
| Jefferson | 2,842 | 16,540 | Rigby |
| Jerome | 1,563 | 15,140 | Jerome |
| Kootenai | 3,224 | 69,795 | Coeur d'Alene |
| Latah | 2,800 | 30,620 | Moscow |
| Lemhi | 11,866 | 6,900 | Salmon |
| Lewis | 1,243 | 3,520 | Nezpercé |
| Lincoln | 3,133 | 3,310 | Shoshone |
| Madison | 1,217 | 23,670 | Rexberg |
| Minidoka | 1,968 | 19,360 | Rupert |
| Nez Percé | 2,197 | 33,750 | Lewiston |
| Oneida | 3,120 | 3,490 | Malad City |
| Owyhee | 19,872 | 8,390 | Murphy |
| Payette | 1,053 | 16,430 | Payette |
| Power | 3,648 | 7,090 | American Falls |
| Shoshone | 6,867 | 13,930 | Wallace |
| Teton | 1,165 | 3,440 | Driggs |
| Twin Falls | 5,054 | 53,580 | Twin Falls |
| Valley | 9,542 | 6,110 | Cascade |
| Washington | 3,780 | 8,550 | Weiser |

**Idhra** the Greek name for the island of HYDRA in the Aegean Sea.

**Idlib** /ˈɪdləb/ a town in north-west Syria, 55 km. (35 miles) south-west of Aleppo, to the north of the site of ancient Ebla which was destroyed c. 1600 BC. The discovery in 1974–6 of 16,000 clay tablets dating from the 3rd millennium BC provides evidence of the language used by the first great urban culture of Syria.

**Ido** /ˈiːdəʊ/ an artificial universal language based on Esperanto.

**Ieper** the Flemish name for YPRES.

**Ife** /ˈiːfeɪ/ an industrial city and cultural, religious, and marketing centre in south-west Nigeria, east of Ibadan; pop. (1981) 240,600. It was a major centre of the Yoruba kingdom from the 14th to the 17th c. and is noted for its bronze art work which dates back to the 12th c. Its university was established in 1961.

**Ifni** /ˈɪfniː/ a former overseas province of Spain, on the south-west coast of Morocco. Settled by Spain in the late 15th c. and abandoned until reclaimed in 1860, it was formally ceded to Morocco in 1969. Its chief town and port is Sidi Ifni.

**Iguaçu** /ˌiːgwəˈsuː/ (Spanish **Iguazú**) a river of southern Brazil, famous especially for the Iguaçu Falls, a spectacular series of waterfalls close to the frontier between Brazil and Argentina. The river rises near the city of Curitaba in the Serra do Mar mountains and is fed by 30 tributaries as it flows the 1,300 km. (800 miles) to the falls which comprise some 275 individual falls cascading 82 m. (269 ft.) into the gorge below. It eventually joins the River Paraná about 22 km. (14 miles) to the south.

**Igualada** /ˌiːgwəˈlaːdə/ an industrial town in Catalonia, north-east Spain, north-east of Barcelona; pop. (1991) 32,270. It produces textiles, leather, and metal goods.

**Iisalmi** /ˈiːsɑːlmɪ/ (Swedish **Idensalmi**) an industrial town in Kuopio province, central Finland; pop. (1990) 23,980. It was the birthplace in 1861 of Juhani Aho, founder of the realist school of Finnish literature.

**IJssel** /ˈaɪs(ə)l/ a river of the Netherlands. In part it is a distributary of the Rhine, which it leaves at Arnhem, joining the Oude IJssel ('Old IJssel') a few kilometres downstream, and flows 115 km. (72 miles) northwards through the eastern Netherlands to meet Lake IJssel near Kampen.

**IJssel, Lake** (Dutch **IJsselmeer** /ˈaɪs(ə)lmɪə(r)/) a shallow lake in the north-west Netherlands forming part of the Zuyder Zee land-reclamation works. A broad barrier dam stretching 30 km. (19 miles) from the coast of North Holland to the coast of Friesland was completed in 1932, turning the former inland sea (Zuyder Zee) into a lake (Lake IJssel) on the edge of which five great polders were created, increasing the land area of The Netherlands by six per cent; area 1,200 sq. km. (463 sq. miles).

**Ikaría** see ICARIA.

**Ikeda** /ɪˈkeɪdə/ an industrial city on Honshu Island, Japan, on the Ina River north-west of Osaka; pop. (1990) 104,000. It has a large motor-vehicle industry.

**Ikeja** /iˈkeɪdʒə/ an industrial city in southern Nigeria, capital of the state of Lagos and site of its international airport.

**IL** *abbr.* US Illinois (in official postal use).

**Ilam** /iˈlɑːm/ a city in western Iran, in the western foothills of the Zagros Mountains near the border with Iraq; pop. (1991) 116,000. It is the capital of Ilam province.

**Ile-de-France** /ˌiːldəˈfrɑ̃s/ a region of north-central France, incorporating the city of Paris and comprising the departments of Ville de Paris, Seine-et-Marne, Essonne, Yvelines, Hauts-de-Seine, Seine-Saint-Denis, Val-de-Marne, and Val d'Oise; pop. (1990) 10,660,550.

**Ilesha** /ɪˈliːʃə/ a city in south-west Nigeria, east of Ibadan; pop. (1981) 306,200. Formerly a centre of the slave trade, it is now a commercial and agricultural centre trading in cacao and vegetables grown in the surrounding area.

**Ilhas dos Bijagós** the Portuguese name for the BISSAGOS ISLANDS.

**Iliniza** /ɪlɪˈniːtsə/ a volcanic peak in the Andes of central Ecuador rising to 5,263 m. (17,267 ft.) west of Cotopaxi.

**Ilium** /ˈɪlɪəm/ another name for TROY, denoting especially the Greek city built there in the 7th c. BC.

**Ilkley** /ˈɪlklɪ/ a town in Wharfedale, West Yorkshire, England, 16 km. (10 miles) north of Bradford; pop. (1981) 13,527. It lies on the site of the Roman town of Olicana and has three notable Saxon crosses in the churchyard of All Saints' Church. Ilkley Moor lies to the south.

**Ill** /iːl/ a river in eastern France that rises in the Jura Mts. and flows 208 km. (130 miles) through Alsace to join the River Rhine.

**Ille-et-Vilaine** /ˌiːleɪvɪˈlen/ a department of Brittany in western France; area 6,775 sq. km. (2,617 sq. miles); pop. (1990) 798,720; capital, Rennes.

**Illimani** /iːljiˈmɑːnɪ/ a volcanic peak in the Andes of western Bolivia, rising to 6,451 m. (21,151 ft.) south-east of La Paz.

**Illinois** /ɪlɪˈnɔɪ/ a state in the Middle West of the US, to the south and west of Lake Michigan; area 145,934 sq. km. (56,345 sq. miles); pop. (1990) 11,430,600; capital, Springfield. The largest cities are Chicago, Rockford, Peoria, and Springfield. It is also known as the Prairie State. Ceded by France to Britain in 1763 and acquired by the US in 1783, Illinois became the 21st state of the Union in 1818. The state has associations with Abraham Lincoln whose home (1844–61) in Springfield is a national

historic site. Illinois is a leading centre of manufacturing, coal-mining, and agricultural exports.
The state is divided into 102 counties:

| County | Area (sq. km.) | Pop. (1990) | County Seat |
|---|---|---|---|
| Adams | 2,215 | 66,090 | Quincy |
| Alexander | 614 | 10,630 | Cairo |
| Bond | 980 | 14,990 | Greenville |
| Boone | 733 | 30,810 | Belvidere |
| Brown | 796 | 5,840 | Mount Sterling |
| Bureau | 2,259 | 35,690 | Princeton |
| Calhoun | 650 | 5,330 | Hardin |
| Carroll | 1,154 | 16,805 | Mount Carroll |
| Cass | 972 | 13,430 | Virginia |
| Champaign | 2,595 | 173,025 | Urbana |
| Christian | 1,846 | 33,420 | Taylorville |
| Clark | 1,316 | 15,290 | Marshall |
| Clay | 1,219 | 14,460 | Louisville |
| Clinton | 1,227 | 33,940 | Carlyle |
| Coles | 1,323 | 51,640 | Charleston |
| Cook | 2,491 | 5,105,070 | Chicago |
| Crawford | 1,160 | 19,460 | Robinson |
| Cumberland | 900 | 10,670 | Toledo |
| De Kalb | 1,648 | 77,930 | Sycamore |
| De Witt | 1,032 | 16,520 | Clinton |
| Douglas | 1,084 | 19,460 | Tuscola |
| Du Page | 876 | 781,670 | Wheaton |
| Edgar | 1,620 | 19,595 | Paris |
| Edwards | 580 | 7,440 | Albion |
| Effingham | 1,243 | 31,700 | Effingham |
| Fayette | 1,843 | 20,890 | Vandalia |
| Ford | 1,264 | 14,275 | Paxton |
| Franklin | 1,076 | 40,320 | Benton |
| Fulton | 2,265 | 38,080 | Lewiston |
| Gallatin | 845 | 6,910 | Shawneetown |
| Greene | 1,412 | 15,320 | Carrollton |
| Grundy | 1,100 | 32,340 | Morris |
| Hamilton | 1,134 | 8,500 | McLeansboro |
| Hancock | 2,070 | 21,370 | Carthage |
| Hardin | 471 | 5,190 | Elizabethtown |
| Henderson | 970 | 8,100 | Oquawka |
| Henry | 2,142 | 51,160 | Cambridge |
| Iroquois | 2,907 | 30,790 | Watseka |
| Jackson | 1,534 | 61,070 | Murphysboro |
| Jasper | 1,290 | 10,610 | Newton |
| Jefferson | 1,482 | 37,020 | Mount Vernon |
| Jersey | 970 | 20,540 | Jerseyville |
| Jo Davies | 1,568 | 21,820 | Galena |
| Johnson | 900 | 11,350 | Vienna |
| Kane | 1,362 | 317,470 | Geneva |
| Kankakee | 1,765 | 96,255 | Kankakee |
| Kendall | 837 | 39,410 | Yorkville |
| Knox | 1,872 | 56,390 | Galesburg |
| La Salle | 2,961 | 106,910 | Ottawa |
| Lake | 1,180 | 516,420 | Waukegan |
| Lawrence | 972 | 15,970 | Lawrenceville |
| Lee | 1,885 | 34,390 | Dixon |
| Livingston | 2,720 | 39,300 | Pontiac |
| Logan | 1,609 | 30,800 | Lincoln |
| McDonough | 1,534 | 35,240 | Macomb |
| McHenry | 1,576 | 183,240 | Woodstock |
| McLean | 3,081 | 129,180 | Bloomington |
| Macon | 1,511 | 117,210 | Decatur |
| Macoupin | 2,249 | 47,680 | Carlinville |
| Madison | 1,893 | 249,240 | Edwardsville |
| Marion | 1,490 | 41,560 | Salem |
| Marshall | 1,009 | 12,850 | Lacon |
| Mason | 1,394 | 16,270 | Havana |
| Massac | 627 | 14,750 | Metropolis |
| Menard | 819 | 11,160 | Petersburg |
| Mercer | 1,453 | 17,290 | Aledo |
| Monroe | 1,009 | 22,420 | Waterloo |
| Montgomery | 1,833 | 30,730 | Hillsboro |
| Morgan | 1,477 | 36,400 | Jacksonville |
| Moultrie | 845 | 13,930 | Sullivan |
| Ogle | 1,973 | 45,960 | Oregon |
| Peoria | 1,615 | 182,830 | Peoria |
| Perry | 1,152 | 21,410 | Pinckneyville |
| Piatt | 1,142 | 15,550 | Monticello |
| Pike | 2,158 | 17,580 | Pittsfield |
| Pope | 972 | 4,370 | Golconda |
| Pulaski | 528 | 7,520 | Mound City |
| Putnam | 416 | 5,730 | Hennepin |
| Randolph | 1,516 | 34,580 | Chester |
| Richland | 936 | 16,545 | Olney |
| Rock Island | 1,100 | 148,720 | Rock Island |
| St. Clair | 1,747 | 262,850 | Belleville |
| Saline | 1,001 | 26,550 | Harrisburg |
| Sangamon | 2,252 | 178,390 | Springfield |
| Schuyler | 1,134 | 7,500 | Rushville |
| Scott | 653 | 5,640 | Winchester |
| Shelby | 1,942 | 22,260 | Shelbyville |
| Stark | 749 | 6,530 | Toulon |
| Stephenson | 1,466 | 48,050 | Freeport |
| Tazewell | 1,690 | 123,690 | Pekin |
| Union | 1,076 | 17,620 | Jonesboro |
| Vermilion | 2,340 | 88,260 | Danville |
| Wabash | 582 | 13,110 | Mt. Carmel |
| Warren | 1,412 | 19,180 | Monmouth |
| Washington | 1,464 | 14,965 | Nashville |
| Wayne | 1,859 | 17,240 | Fairfield |
| White | 1,292 | 16,520 | Carmi |
| Whiteside | 1,773 | 60,190 | Morrison |
| Will | 2,194 | 357,310 | Joliet |
| Williamson | 1,110 | 57,730 | Marion |
| Winnebago | 1,342 | 252,910 | Rockford |
| Woodford | 1,370 | 32,650 | Eureka |

**Illyria** /ɪˈlɪrɪə/ an ancient region along the east
coast of the Adriatic Sea, including Dalmatia and
what is now Montenegro and northern Albania. It
was subsequently the Roman province of Illyricum.
**Illyrian** *adj. & n.*

**Iloilo** /ˌiːləˈwiːləʊ/ a port, marketing centre, and
old colonial city on the south coast of the island of
Panay in the central Philippines; pop. (1990)
309,500. The city, which is known for its hand-
woven fabrics, takes its name from the lie of the
land between the Iloilo and Batiano rivers which is
shaped 'like a nose' (Ilong-Ilong). Every February
there is a sail-boat race from Iloilo to Guimaras
Island which shelters the harbour.

**Ilopango** /ˌiːləʊˈpæŋɡəʊ/ a volcanic lake in
southern El Salvador, to the east of San Salvador.
It is the largest lake in the country.

**Ilorin** /iːˈlɔːriːn/ an industrial city, capital of
Kwara State, western Nigeria; pop. (est. 1986)

390,000. In the 18th c. it was the capital of a Yoruba kingdom that was eventually absorbed into the Fulani state of Sokoto in the early 19th c. Its university was established in 1975. It has light industries and traditional handicrafts.

**Imabari** /ˌiːməˈbɑːrɪ/ an industrial port on the Kurashima-hanto peninsula, on the north-west coast of the island of Shikoku, Japan; pop. (1990) 123,000. It is linked by ferry with Onomichi and Mihara on Honshu Island.

**Imatra** /ɪˈmɑːtrə/ an industrial town with cellulose and chemical industries in south-east Finland, situated on the Vuoksi River where it enters Lake Saimaa; pop. (1990) 33,570.

**Imbros** /ˈɪmbrɒs/ (Turkish **Imroz** /ˈɪmrɒz/) a Turkish island in the north-east Aegean Sea, near the entrance to the Dardanelles; area 280 sq. km. (108 sq. miles).

**Immingham** /ˈɪmɪŋ(ə)m/ a major container port on the east coast of England, on the Humber estuary north-west of Grimsby; pop. (1981) 11,500.

**Imperatriz** /ˌiːmpeɪrəˈtriːs/ a city to the south of Belém in the state of Maranhão, north-east Brazil; pop. (1990) 262,760. It is a commercial centre serving a region that produces cattle, rice, and timber.

**Imperia** /iːmˈpɪrɪə/ a city, capital of Imperia province in Liguria, north-west Italy, situated on the Ligurian coast; pop. (1990) 41,280. It comprises the Piedmont town of Porto Maurizio and the Savoy town of Oneglia (united in 1923) which are physically separated by the River Imperia. In addition to oil refining, Imperia produces pasta and pharmaceuticals.

**Imphal** /ˈɪmpəl/ the capital of the state of Manipur in the far north-east India, on the River Manipur close to the border with Burma; pop. (1991) 156,620. It was the scene of an important victory in 1944 by Anglo-Indian forces over the Japanese.

**Imroz** the Turkish name for IMBROS.

**IN** *abbr.* US Indiana (in official postal use).

**Inari** /ɪˈnɑːrɪ/, **Lake** (Finnish **Inarijärvi**, Swedish **Enare**) a lake in the province of Lappi, north-east Finland, close to the Russian frontier; area 1,000 sq. km. (386 sq. miles). The lake, which has over 3,000 islands, is fed by the Ivalo River and drained towards the Arctic Ocean by the River Pats.

**Inchcape Rock** /ɪntʃˈkeɪp/ (also **Bell Rock**) a sandstone reef in the North Sea beyond the mouth of the River Tay in Scotland. Robert Stevenson and John Rennie designed a lighthouse that was built in 1807–10. It has associations with R. M. Ballantyne who stayed here before writing his adventure story, *The Lighthouse*, and with Robert Southey, whose poem *The Inchcape Rock* recounts the story of Sir Ralph the Rover.

**Inchon** /ɪnˈtʃɒn/ a port on the west coast of South Korea, on the Yellow Sea west of Seoul; pop. (1990) 1,818,300. Fishing and the manufacture of

steel and textiles are important industries. US forces landed here at the outset of the Korean War in 1950.

**Independence** a residential city to the east of Kansas City, Missouri, USA; pop. (1990) 112,300. It was an outfitting post for wagon trains heading west between 1830 and 1850 and was the home of Harry S. Truman, 33rd US president. Independence is the world headquarters of the Reorganized Church of Jesus Christ of Latter Day Saints.

**Independence Hall** the historic statehouse on Independence Square at the centre of Philadelphia, USA, where the US Declaration of Independence was proclaimed in 1776. The Liberty Bell is located nearby.

**India** /ˈɪndɪə/ (Sanskrit **Bharat** /ˈbɑːrət/) official name **The Republic of India** a country in southern Asia occupying the greater part of the Indian subcontinent, a peninsula to the south of the  Himalayas bounded by the Arabian Sea, the Indian Ocean, and the Bay of Bengal; area 3,185,019 sq. km. (1,229,737 sq. miles); pop. (est. 1991) 859,200,000; official languages, Hindi and English (of the many other languages spoken in India, 14 are recognized as official in certain regions; of these, Bengali, Gujarati, Marathi, Tamil, Telugu, and Urdu have most first-language speakers); capital, New Delhi. Its largest cities are Calcutta, Bombay, Delhi, Madras, Bangalore, Ahmadabad, and Hyderabad. India includes the Nicobar and Andaman islands in the Bay of Bengal and the Laccadive, Minicoy, and Amindvi islands (Lakshadweep) in the Arabian Sea. The Himalayan range, which includes some of the highest peaks in the world extends *c.* 2,400 km. (1,500 miles) with a breadth varying from 240 to 320 km. Immediately to the south, the Indo-Gangetic plain is watered by the Ganges, Indus, and Brahmaputra and their tributaries, and is one of the most densely populated areas of the world. South of this rich alluvial plain lies the peninsula of southern India, a plateau flanked by the Eastern and Western Ghats which meet in the south to form the Nilgiri Hills. The climate of India, which varies from the cold snows of the Himalayas to the hot desert plains of Rajasthan, is generally tropical monsoon with a wet south-western monsoon period during June–September and a north-eastern monsoon period in the southern peninsula during October–December. India has the world's third-largest Muslim population (11%), but the majority of its people are Hindus (83%). Although 70 per cent of the population depend on subsistence farming, India has since 1947 built up a substantial

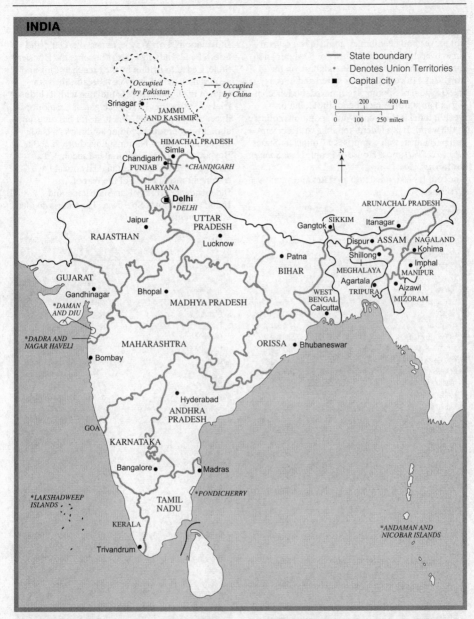

## INDIA

State boundary
* Denotes Union Territories
■ Capital city

0    200    400 km
0    100    250 miles

*Occupied by Pakistan* — *Occupied by China*

Srinagar
JAMMU AND KASHMIR

HIMACHAL PRADESH
Simla
Chandigarh
PUNJAB    *CHANDIGARH

HARYANA
■ Delhi
*DELHI

Jaipur    UTTAR PRADESH    SIKKIM    ARUNACHAL PRADESH
Gangtok    Itanagar
RAJASTHAN    Lucknow    Dispur ● ASSAM    NAGALAND
Patna    Shillong ●    Kohima
GUJARAT    BIHAR    MEGHALAYA    Imphal
Gandhinagar    Bhopal    Agartala    MANIPUR
*DAMAN AND DIU    MADHYA PRADESH    WEST BENGAL    TRIPURA    Aizawl
Calcutta    MIZORAM

*DADRA AND NAGAR HAVELI
MAHARASHTRA    ORISSA ● Bhubaneswar
Bombay

Hyderabad
ANDHRA PRADESH
GOA
KARNATAKA
Bangalore ●    ● Madras
*LAKSHADWEEP ISLANDS    *PONDICHERRY
TAMIL NADU
KERALA    *ANDAMAN AND NICOBAR ISLANDS
Trivandrum ●

industrial base. The textile and jute industries are important; other major industries are based on the exploitation of the country's mineral resources, chiefly coal, oil, iron, and precious stones.

The history of the subcontinent began in the 3rd millennium BC, when the Indus valley was the site of a fully developed civilization. This collapsed *c.*1760 BC when the invading Aryans spread from the west through the northern part of the country. Consolidated first within the Buddhist empire of Asoka and then the Hindu empire of the Gupta dynasty, much of India was united under a Muslim sultanate based on Delhi from the 12th c. until

incorporated in the Mughal empire by Babur and Akbar the Great in the 16th c. The decline of Mughal power in the late 17th and early 18th c. coincided with increasing European penetration, with Britain eventually triumphing over her colonial rivals. British interest had begun in the 17th c. with the formation of the East India Company, which in 1765 acquired the right to administer Bengal and afterwards other parts; in 1858, after the Indian Mutiny, the Crown took over the Company's authority, and in 1877 Queen Victoria was proclaimed Empress of India. Rising nationalism, with Mahatma Gandhi a notable

leader, resulted in independence and partition in
1947, but the new states of India and Pakistan did
not prove good neighbours, going to war several
times over the disputed territory of Kashmir and
the Pakistani enclave (now Bangladesh) in the
north-east. In 1961 Goa was seized and in 1975
the kingdom of Sikkim was annexed, both becoming Indian states. A member of the Commonwealth, India is the second-most populous country
in the world. It is a federal republic with a bicameral parliament that comprises a Council of States
(*Rajya Sabha*) and a House of People (*Lok Sabha*).
**Indian** adj. & n.
The country is divided into 25 states and 7 union
territories:

| State | Area (sq. km.) | Pop. (1991) | Capital |
|---|---|---|---|
| Andhra Pradesh | 275,068 | 66,304,850 | Hyderabad |
| Arunachal Pradesh | 83,743 | 858,350 | Itanagar |
| Assam | 78,438 | 22,294,560 | Dispur |
| Bihar | 173,877 | 86,338,850 | Patna |
| Goa | 3,702 | 1,168,620 | Panaji |
| Gujarat | 196,024 | 41,174,060 | Gandhinagar |
| Haryana | 44,212 | 16,317,710 | Chandigarh |
| Himachal Pradesh | 55,673 | 5,111,080 | Simla |
| Jammu-Kashmir | 222,236 | 7,718,700 | Srinagar |
| Karnataka | 191,791 | 44,817,400 | Bangalore |
| Kerala | 38,863 | 29,011,240 | Trivandrum |
| Madhya Pradesh | 443,446 | 66,135,860 | Bhopal |
| Maharashtra | 307,690 | 78,706,720 | Bombay |
| Manipur | 22,327 | 1,826,710 | Imphal |
| Meghalaya | 22,429 | 1,760,630 | Shillong |
| Mizoram | 21,081 | 686,220 | Aizawi |
| Nagaland | 16,579 | 1,215,570 | Kohima |
| Orissa | 155,707 | 31,512,070 | Bhubaneswar |
| Punjab | 50,362 | 20,190,800 | Chandigarh |
| Rajasthan | 342,239 | 43,880,640 | Jaipur |
| Sikkim | 7,096 | 403,610 | Gangtok |
| Tamil Nadu | 130,058 | 55,638,320 | Madras |
| Tripura | 10,486 | 2,744,830 | Agartala |
| Uttar Pradesh | 294,411 | 138,760,420 | Lucknow |
| West Bengal | 88,752 | 67,982,730 | Calcutta |

| Union Territory | Area (sq. km.) | Pop. (1991) | Capital |
|---|---|---|---|
| Andaman and Nicobar | 8,249 | 277,990 | Port Blair |
| Chandigarh | 114 | 640,720 | Chandigarh |
| Dadra and Nagar Haveli | 491 | 138,540 | Silvassa |
| Daman and Diu | 112 | 101,440 | Daman |
| Delhi | 1,483 | 9,370,470 | Delhi |
| Lakshadweep | 32 | 51,680 | Kavaratti |
| Pondicherry | 492 | 789,420 | Pondicherry |

**Indian** /'ɪndɪən/ **1.** a native or national of India,
or a person of Indian descent. **2.** an American
Indian.

**Indiana** /ˌɪndɪ'ænə/ a state in the Middle West of
the US, to the south of Lake Michigan; area 93,720
sq. km. (36,185 sq. miles); pop. (1990) 5,544,160;
capital, Indianapolis. The largest cities are
Indianapolis, Fort Wayne, Evansville, Gary, and
South Bend. Indiana is also known as the Hoosier
State. Ceded to Britain by the French in 1763 and
acquired by the US in 1783, it became the 19th
state of the Union in 1816. Indiana, with its industrial waterfront on Lake Michigan, is a major producer of iron and steel, limestone for building, and
agricultural products. Major landmarks include
the Indiana Dunes National Lakeshore, Lincoln
Boyhood National Memorial in Lincoln City,
George Rogers Clark National Historical Park
commemorating a hero of the War of
Independence, Turkey Run State Park, and
Indianapolis Motor Speedway. The state is divided
into 92 counties:

| County | Area (sq. km.) | Pop. (1990) | County Seat |
|---|---|---|---|
| Adams | 884 | 31,095 | Decatur |
| Allen | 1,713 | 300,840 | Fort Wayne |
| Bartholomew | 1,063 | 63,660 | Columbus |
| Benton | 1,058 | 9,440 | Fowler |
| Blackford | 432 | 14,070 | Hartford City |
| Boone | 1,100 | 38,150 | Lebanon |
| Brown | 811 | 14,080 | Nashville |
| Carroll | 967 | 18,810 | Delphi |
| Cass | 1,076 | 38,410 | Logansport |
| Clark | 978 | 87,780 | Jeffersonville |
| Clay | 936 | 24,705 | Brazil |
| Clinton | 1,053 | 30,970 | Frankfort |
| Crawford | 798 | 9,910 | English |
| Davies | 1,123 | 27,530 | Washington |
| Dearborn | 798 | 38,835 | Lawrenceburg |
| Decatur | 970 | 23,645 | Greensburg |
| De Kalb | 946 | 35,320 | Auburn |
| Delaware | 1,019 | 119,660 | Muncie |
| Dubois | 1,115 | 36,620 | Jasper |
| Elkhart | 1,212 | 156,200 | Goshen |
| Fayette | 559 | 26,015 | Connersville |
| Floyd | 390 | 64,400 | New Albany |
| Fountain | 1,035 | 17,810 | Covington |
| Franklin | 1,001 | 19,580 | Brookville |
| Fulton | 959 | 18,840 | Rochester |
| Gibson | 1,274 | 31,910 | Princeton |
| Grant | 1,079 | 74,170 | Marion |
| Greene | 1,420 | 30,410 | Bloomfield |
| Hamilton | 1,035 | 108,940 | Noblesville |
| Hancock | 798 | 45,530 | Greenfield |
| Harrison | 1,264 | 29,890 | Corydon |
| Hendricks | 1,063 | 75,720 | Danville |
| Henry | 1,024 | 48,140 | New Castle |
| Howard | 762 | 80,830 | Kokomo |
| Huntington | 952 | 35,430 | Huntington |
| Jackson | 1,334 | 37,730 | Brownstown |
| Jasper | 1,459 | 24,960 | Rensselaer |
| Jay | 998 | 21,510 | Portland |
| Jefferson | 944 | 29,800 | Madison |
| Jennings | 983 | 23,660 | Vernon |
| Johnson | 835 | 88,110 | Franklin |
| Knox | 1,352 | 39,880 | Vincennes |
| Kosciusko | 1,404 | 65,290 | Warsaw |
| Lagrange | 988 | 29,480 | Lagrange |

| | | | |
|---|---|---|---|
| Lake | 1,303 | 475,590 | Crown Point |
| La Porte | 1,560 | 107,070 | La Porte |
| Lawrence | 1,175 | 42,840 | Bedford |
| Madison | 1,178 | 130,670 | Anderson |
| Marion | 1,030 | 797,160 | Indianapolis |
| Marshall | 1,154 | 42,180 | Plymouth |
| Martin | 881 | 10,370 | Shoals |
| Miami | 959 | 36,900 | Peru |
| Monroe | 1,001 | 108,980 | Bloomington |
| Montgomery | 1,313 | 34,440 | Crawfordsville |
| Morgan | 1,063 | 55,920 | Martinsville |
| Newton | 1,043 | 13,550 | Kentland |
| Noble | 1,074 | 37,880 | Albion |
| Ohio | 226 | 5,315 | Rising Sun |
| Orange | 1,061 | 18,410 | Paoli |
| Owen | 1,004 | 17,280 | Spencer |
| Parke | 1,154 | 15,410 | Rockville |
| Perry | 993 | 19,110 | Cannelton |
| Pike | 887 | 12,510 | Petersburg |
| Porter | 1,087 | 128,930 | Valparaiso |
| Posey | 1,063 | 25,970 | Mount Vernon |
| Pulaski | 1,131 | 12,640 | Winamac |
| Putnam | 1,253 | 30,315 | Greencastle |
| Randolph | 1,180 | 27,150 | Winchester |
| Ripley | 1,162 | 24,620 | Versailles |
| Rush | 1,061 | 18,130 | Rushville |
| St. Joseph | 1,193 | 247,050 | South Bend |
| Scott | 497 | 20,990 | Scottsburg |
| Shelby | 1,074 | 40,310 | Shelbyville |
| Spencer | 1,040 | 19,490 | Rockport |
| Starke | 803 | 22,750 | Knox |
| Steuben | 801 | 27,450 | Angola |
| Sullivan | 1,175 | 18,990 | Sullivan |
| Switzerland | 580 | 7,740 | Vevay |
| Tippecanoe | 1,305 | 130,600 | Lafayette |
| Tipton | 676 | 16,120 | Tipton |
| Union | 421 | 6,980 | Liberty |
| Vanderburgh | 614 | 165,060 | Evansville |
| Vermillion | 676 | 16,770 | Newport |
| Vigo | 1,053 | 106,110 | Terre Haute |
| Wabash | 1,035 | 35,070 | Wabash |
| Warren | 952 | 8,180 | Williamsport |
| Warrick | 1,017 | 44,920 | Boonville |
| Washington | 1,342 | 23,720 | Salem |
| Wayne | 1,050 | 71,950 | Richmond |
| Wells | 962 | 25,950 | Bluffton |
| White | 1,316 | 23,265 | Monticello |
| Whitley | 874 | 27,650 | Columbia City |

**Indianapolis** /ˌɪndɪə'næpəlɪs/ the capital of the US state of Indiana, on the White River at the geographical centre of the state; pop. (1990) 741,950. Selected as the site for a new state capital in 1820, Indianapolis was laid out in a wheel pattern similar to Washington DC and in 1825 the capital was moved from Corydon. The city developed as a seat of government and a manufacturing and commercial centre at the heart of a rich agricultural region. It is one of the leading US grain markets, with an important livestock trade and meat-processing industry. Pharmaceuticals, vehicle parts, electronic goods, and medical equipment are also produced. Benjamin Harrison (23rd US president), the poet James Whitcomb Riley, and the novelist Booth Tarkington are buried in Crown Hill Cemetery. The city hosts an annual 500-mile (804.5-km.) motor-race (the Indianapolis 500).

**Indian Ocean** the ocean to the south of India, extending from the east coast of Africa to the East Indies and Australia. It is the third-largest of the world's oceans and was known in ancient times as the Erythræan Sea. Straddling the equator, the Indian Ocean reaches its maximum depth of 7,725 m. (25,345 ft.) in the Java Trench, Indonesia. Its principal islands and island groups are Sri Lanka, Madagascar, La Réunion, Mauritius, the Seychelles, the Maldives, the Andaman and Nicobar Islands, the Laccadive Islands (Lakshadweep), the Cocos Islands, and the Chagos Archipelago.

**Indian summer** a period of unusually dry warm weather sometimes occurring in late autumn in temperate regions.

**Indian subcontinent** the part of Asia south of the Himalayas which forms a peninsula extending into the Indian Ocean, between the Arabian Sea and the Bay of Bengal. Historically forming the whole territory of greater India, the region is now divided between India, Pakistan, and Bangladesh. Geologically, the Indian subcontinent is a distinct unit, formerly part of the ancient supercontinent of Gondwana. As a result of continental drift it became joined to the rest of Asia, perhaps as recently as 40 million years ago, in a collision which created the Himalayas.

**Indic** /'ɪndɪk/ the group of Indo-European languages comprising Sanskrit and the modern Indian languages which are its descendants.

**Indies** /'ɪndɪz/, **the** a name once applied to India and its adjacent regions. See EAST INDIES and WEST INDIES.

**Indigirka** /ˌɪndɪ'gɪəkə/ a river in the Yakut region of far-eastern Siberia. It flows northwards for 1,779 km. (1,112 miles) from the Khrebet Santar Khayata to the East Siberian Sea where it forms a wide delta.

**Indira Gandhi Canal** /ɪn'dɪərə 'gɑːndɪ, 'ɪndərə/ (formerly **Rajasthan Canal**) a massive canal in north-west India, bringing water to the arid Thar Desert from the snow-fed Beas and Sutlej rivers which meet at the Harike Barrage. The canal, which is 650 km. (406 miles) long, was completed in 1986 and is named in honour of the former prime minister of India, Indira Gandhi (1917–84).

**Indo-Arayan** /ˌɪndəʊ'eərɪən/ any of the Arayan peoples of India or the Indic languages.

**Indo-China** /ˌɪndəʊ'tʃaɪnə/ **1.** the peninsula of south-east Asia containing Burma, Thailand, Malaya, Laos, Cambodia, and Vietnam. **2.** (**French Indo-China**) a region of south-east Asia that now consists of Laos, Cambodia, and Vietnam and was a French dependency from 1862 to 1954.

**Indo-European** /ˌɪndəʊ jʊərə'pɪən/ (also **Indo-Germanic** or **Aryan**) a family of languages spoken for at least the last 3,000 years over the greater part of Europe and extending into Asia as far as northern India. The name has become established as a technical term, but it must not be supposed to include all the languages of India and Europe, some of which (e.g. the Dravidian languages, Finnish, and Hungarian) belong to quite different families. Considerably before 2,000 BC there must have existed a relatively small tribe speaking a language which we may call 'Proto-Indo-European'. No records of it survive, nor is there any evidence that it could ever have been written, but its existence can be inferred from a comparison of its daughter languages, and most of its phonology and morphology and some of its vocabulary can be reconstructed with some degree of certainty. The main divisions into which it split up, in the course of time, are the Indo-Iranian or Aryan group, the Hellenic group or Greek, the Italic group (of which the most important element is Latin, together with its daughter languages French and the other Romance languages), the Germanic languages (to which English belongs), the Celtic group, the Baltic languages, and the closely related Slavonic languages. In addition to these, Albanian forms a distinct member of the family and so does Armenian. Two important discoveries of the 20th c. have added to the family the ancient Anatolian languages (from the 2nd millennium BC: Hittite is the oldest attested Indo-European language), and Tocharian, which flourished in Chinese Turkestan more than 1,000 years ago.

Recognition of the breadth of this language family is relatively recent and was first reached when a number of European scholars started studying Sanskrit in the late 18th and early 19th c. In 1786 the English orientalist Sir William Jones pointed out the strong affinity that Sanskrit bore to Greek and Latin, and spoke of a common origin for these languages, but most of the research on which the language groupings and the reconstruction of the parent language are based was the work of German scholars in the 19th c.

**Indo-Germanic** /ˌɪndəʊdʒɜːˈmænɪk/ see INDO-EUROPEAN.

**Indo-Iranian** /ˌɪndəʊɪˈreɪnɪən/ a large group of Indo-European languages spoken chiefly in northern India and Iran. It can be divided into the Indo-Aryan (or Indic) group and the Iranian.

**Indonesia**
/ˌɪndəˈniːzjə, -ʒə, -ʃə/ official name **The Republic of Indonesia** a country in south-east Asia, formerly the Dutch East Indies, comprising a large island group of more than 13,500 islands in the Malay archipelago, chief of which are Java, Sumatra, Kalimantan, Irian Jaya,

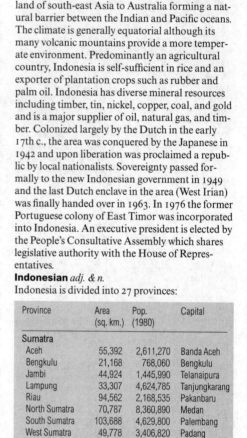

the Moluccas, Sulawesi (Celebes), and Lesser Sunda Islands; area 1,904,569 sq. km. (735,638 sq. miles); pop. (est. 1990) 184,300,000; official language, Bahasa Indonesia (Dutch, English, and over 60 regional languages are spoken); capital, Jakarta (on Java). The largest cities are Jakarta, Surabaya, Bandung, and Medan. The islands of Indonesia stretch along the equator from the mainland of south-east Asia to Australia forming a natural barrier between the Indian and Pacific oceans. The climate is generally equatorial although its many volcanic mountains provide a more temperate environment. Predominantly an agricultural country, Indonesia is self-sufficient in rice and an exporter of plantation crops such as rubber and palm oil. Indonesia has diverse mineral resources including timber, tin, nickel, copper, coal, and gold and is a major supplier of oil, natural gas, and timber. Colonized largely by the Dutch in the early 17th c., the area was conquered by the Japanese in 1942 and upon liberation was proclaimed a republic by local nationalists. Sovereignty passed formally to the new Indonesian government in 1949 and the last Dutch enclave in the area (West Irian) was finally handed over in 1963. In 1976 the former Portuguese colony of East Timor was incorporated into Indonesia. An executive president is elected by the People's Consultative Assembly which shares legislative authority with the House of Representatives.

**Indonesian** adj. & n.
Indonesia is divided into 27 provinces:

| Province | Area (sq. km.) | Pop. (1980) | Capital |
|---|---|---|---|
| **Sumatra** | | | |
| Aceh | 55,392 | 2,611,270 | Banda Aceh |
| Bengkulu | 21,168 | 768,060 | Bengkulu |
| Jambi | 44,924 | 1,445,990 | Telanaipura |
| Lampung | 33,307 | 4,624,785 | Tanjungkarang |
| Riau | 94,562 | 2,168,535 | Pakanbaru |
| North Sumatra | 70,787 | 8,360,890 | Medan |
| South Sumatra | 103,688 | 4,629,800 | Palembang |
| West Sumatra | 49,778 | 3,406,820 | Padang |
| **Java and Madura** | | | |
| Jakarta | 590 | 6,503,450 | Jakarta |
| Central Java | 34,206 | 25,372,890 | Semarang |
| East Java | 47,922 | 29,188,850 | Surabaya |
| West Java | 46,300 | 27,453,525 | Bandung |
| Yogyakarta | 3,169 | 2,750,810 | Yogyakarta |
| **Borneo** | | | |
| Central Kalimantan | 152,600 | 954,350 | Palangkaraya |
| East Kalimantan | 202,440 | 1,218,010 | Samarinda |
| South Kalimantan | 37,660 | 2,064,650 | Banjarmasin |
| West Kalimantan | 146,760 | 2,486,070 | Pontianak |
| **Sulawesi** | | | |
| Central Sulawesi | 69,726 | 1,289,635 | Palu |
| North Sulawesi | 19,023 | 2,115,380 | Menado |
| South-east Sulawesi | 27,686 | 942,300 | Kendari |
| South Sulawesi | 72,781 | 6,062,210 | Ujung Padang |
| **Lesser Sunda Islands** | | | |
| Bali | 5,561 | 2,469,930 | Denpasar |
| East Nusa Tenggara | 47,876 | 2,737,170 | Kupang |

*(cont.)*

| | | | |
|---|---|---|---|
| West Nusa Tenggara | 20,177 | 2,724,660 | Mataram |
| East Timor | 14,874 | 555,350 | Dili |
| Moluccas | | | |
| Malaku | 74,505 | 1,411,000 | Amboina |
| New Guinea | | | |
| West Irian | 421,981 | 1,173,875 | Jayapura |

**Indore** /ɪn'dɔː(r)/ a manufacturing city of Madhya Pradesh in central India, on the Khan and Sarasvati rivers; pop. (1991) 1,087,000. It was the seat of the maharajahs of the house of Holkar and the first city to open its temples, schools, and public wells to the *Harijans* (untouchables) during Mahatma Gandhi's campaign against untouchability. Indore, which is a notable centre of Hindustani classical music, produces chemicals and furniture and is one of India's chief cotton centres.

**Indre** /'ændr(ə)/ **1.** a river in central France that rises in the Massif Central and flows 265 km. (166 miles) north-westwards to meet the Loire near Tours. **2.** a department in the Centre region of central France; area 6,791 sq. km. (2,623 sq. miles); pop. (1990) 237,510; capital, Châteauroux.

**Indre-et-Loire** /'ændr(ə)eɪ'lwɑː/ a department in the Centre region of central France; area 6,127 sq. km. (2,366 sq. miles); pop. (1990) 529,345; capital, Tours.

**Indus** /'ɪndəs/ a river of southern Asia, about 2,900 km. (1,800 miles) in length, flowing from Tibet through Kashmir and Pakistan to the Arabian Sea. Along its valley an early culture flourished from c.2600 to 1760 BC, with important centres at Mohenjo-Daro and Harappa, characterized by towns built to a grid-like plan with granaries, drainage systems, and public buildings, copper-bronze technology, a standard system of weights and measures, and steatite seals with (undeciphered) hieroglyphic inscriptions. Its economic wealth was derived from well-attested sea and land trade with the Indian subcontinent, Afghanistan, the Gulf, Iran, and Mesopotamia. In the early 2nd millennium its power declined, probably because of incursions by Aryans.

**Ingermanland** /'ɪŋɜːmənˌlænd/ (also **Ingria**) a historic region in north-west Russia, to the east of the Gulf of Finland in the valley of the Neva. Named after its Finnic inhabitants, the Ingers, Ingermanland was alternately held by Sweden and Russia until 1721 when it was finally ceded to Russia by the Treaty of Nystad.

**Inglewood** /'ɪŋg(ə)lˌwuːd/ a residential and industrial city in the Los Angeles conurbation, southern California, USA, to the east of Los Angeles International Airport; pop. (1990) 109,600. It is the location of The Forum, a prestigious sports-entertainment complex, and has avionics industries.

**Ingolstadt** /'ɪŋg(ə)lˌʃtæt/ an industrial city in Bavaria, south-west Germany, on the River Danube; pop. (1991) 107,375. It has oil refineries, and vehicle and electronics industries.

**Ingushetia** (also **The Ingush Republic**) an autonomous republic of Russia, to the north of Georgia, largely populated by Ingush people of the northern Caucasus. It was constituted as an autonomous area of the Terek Autonomous Republic of the USSR in 1924 but was united with Chechenya from 1934 until the breakup of the Soviet Union in 1991. Its capital is Nazran. (See also CHECHENYA.)

**Inhambane** /ˌiːjəm'bɑːnɪ/ a port and rail terminus on the coast of Mozambique, capital of a province of the same name; pop. (1980) 56,440.

**Inland Sea** (Japanese **Seto Naikai**) an almost landlocked arm of the Pacific Ocean surrounded by the Japanese islands of Honshu, Shikoku, and Kyushu. Its chief port is Hiroshima.

**Inle Lake** /'ɪnleɪ/ a lake in Shan state, central Burma, noted for its floating villages and colourful markets. It is situated south-west of Taunngyi at an altitude of about 853 m. (2,800 ft.).

**Inn** /ɪn/ a river of western Europe that rises in the Rhaetian Alps in Switzerland and flows 508 km. (320 miles) north-eastwards through the Austrian Tyrol into Bavaria in southern Germany where it joins the Danube at Passau.

**Inner Mongolia** (Chinese **Nei Monggol**) an autonomous region of northern China, comprising grassland and desert on the frontier with Mongolia; area 1,183,000 sq. km. (456,933 sq. miles); pop. (1990) 21,457,000; capital, Hohhot.

**Innsbruck** /'ɪnzbrʊk/ a resort and industrial city of western Austria, on the River Inn; pop. (1991) 115,000. A winter-sports centre and capital of the state of Tyrol, situated on a historic routeway between Germany and Italy and between Vienna and Switzerland. It was founded as a market town in 1180 and was a ducal residence from 1420 to 1665; it has several ancient churches and a 15th-c. castle. There are several museums and a botanical garden specializing in Alpine plants. Innsbruck's industries include metal products, textiles, and printing.

**In Salah** /ɪn'ʃɑːlə/ (also **Ain Salah**) an oasis town in the Tamanrasset department of central Algeria, on the trans-Saharan route from Niger to the coast of North Africa; pop. (1982) 25,500.

**Insein** /ɪn'seɪn/ a city in the Pegu Division of southern Burma, situated on the Irrawaddy River north-west of Rangoon; pop. (1983) 144,000.

**inselberg** /'ɪns(ə)lˌbɜːg/ a mountain that rises abruptly from the earth's surface in arid and semi-arid regions.

**Inter-American Highway** the name given to that part of the Pan-American Highway between Nuevo Laredo on the US–Mexican frontier and Panama City.

**interfluve** /'ɪntɜːˌfluːv/ an area of land that lies between two rivers.

**Interlaken** /'ɪntəˌlaːkən/ the chief resort town of the Bernese Alps in central Switzerland, situated on the River Aare between Lake Brienz and Lake Thun; pop. (1980) 4,850. It has a clock and watch industry.

**International Date Line** an imaginary line on the earth's surface which follows the 180° meridian of longitude and marks a one-day date change. Points immediately to the west lie 12 hours ahead of Greenwich Mean Time and points just east of it are 12 hours behind. Westbound travellers lose a day and eastbound travellers gain one. In order to avoid date changes in populated areas, the Dateline bends to the west of the Aleutian Islands and to the east of various islands in the South Pacific.

**International Nautical Mile** a distance equal to one minute of longitude or latitude at the equator (1,852 m., 6,076 ft.).

**International Phonetic Alphabet** a set of phonetic symbols for international use, introduced in the late 19th c. by the International Phonetic Association, based on the Roman and Greek alphabets with the addition of some special symbols and diacritical marks.

**Inuit** /'ɪnjuːɪt, 'ɪnʊɪt/ (also **Innuit**) a member of a North American people inhabiting Alaska, northern Canada, Greenland, and eastern Siberia. A semi-nomadic hunting and gathering people, they were noted for their adaptation to a harsh environment and were sometimes called Eskimos. Their languages belong to the Inuit-Aleut family and are divided into two main branches: the Inupik or Inuk (spoken in Greenland, Labrador, the Arctic coast of Canada, and northern Alaska) and the Yupik or Yuk (spoken in southern Alaska and Siberia). There are approximately 40,000 Inuit-speakers in Greenland, 25,000 in Alaska, 15,000 in Canada, and several hundred in Siberia. (See also NUNAVUT and ESKIMO.)

**Inuvik** /ɪn'uːvɪk/ a fur-trading and communication centre on the Mackenzie River delta in the Northwest Territories, Canada; pop. (1991) 3,178. The largest Canadian community north of the Arctic Circle, it was built during the late 1950s and early 1960s to replace Aklavik which was threatened by flooding and erosion.

**Invercargill** /ˌɪnvə'kaːgɪl/ a city of New Zealand, on the Waihopai River at the southern tip of South Island; pop. (1991) 51,980. Founded in 1857 and named after William Cargill (1784–1860), Superintendent of Otago, it is the southernmost city of New Zealand and a market centre for the surrounding Southland Plain.

**Inverness** /ˌɪnvə'nes/ a city in northern Scotland, on the River Ness at the mouth of the Beauly Firth; pop. (1981) 40,000. It has diverse light industries and is the administrative centre of Highland Region and lies at the north-eastern end of the Caledonian Canal.

**Inyangani** /ˌɪnjən'gaːni/, **Mount** a mountain in Zimbabwe, rising to 2,592 m. (8,504 ft.) in the Eastern Highlands near the Mozambique frontier. It is the highest peak in Zimbabwe.

**Ioánnina** /jəʊ'aːnjnə/ a town, capital of a department of the same name in Epirus, western Greece, on Lake Ioánnina; pop. (1981) 44,830. It is noted for its filigree silver. It is a military headquarters and a market town for produce grown on the surrounding plain.

**Iona** /aɪ'əʊnə/ an island in the Inner Hebrides, site of a monastery founded by St. Columba c. 563 which became a centre for Celtic Christian missions to Scotland and a place of pilgrimage. There are many Celtic crosses and 60 Scottish, Norse, and Irish kings are said to be buried near the restored cathedral. Iona is now a major tourist destination.

**Ionia** /aɪ'əʊnɪə/ in classical times, the central part of the west coast of Asia Minor. In the 11th c. BC tribes speaking the Ionic dialect of Greek settled in the Aegean Islands and in the coastal area of Asia Minor, later known as Ionia, which was also colonized by the Greeks from the mainland from about the 8th c. BC. They retained their distinctive dialect (Ionic), which was also spoken in Athens, and are noted for their contributions in science, poetry, and architecture. Throughout the eastern Mediterranean 'Yawani' (= Ionians) became the generic word for Greek.
**Ionian** adj. & n.

**Ionian Islands** /aɪ'əʊnɪən/ a chain of about 40 islands off the western coast of Greece, of which the largest are Corfu and Cephalonia. The islands constitute a region of modern Greece and are a major tourist attraction; area 2,307 sq. km. (891 sq. miles); pop. (1991) 191,000.

**Ionian Sea** the part of the Mediterranean Sea between western Greece and southern Italy, at the mouth of the Adriatic. According to one ancient Greek tradition it is named after Io, priestess of Hera, who crossed it in her wanderings, rather than after the Ionians.

**ionosphere** /aɪ'ɒnəˌsfɪə(r)/ an ionized region of the atmosphere above the stratosphere, extending to about 1,000 km. above the earth's surface and able to reflect radio waves for long-distance transmission round the earth.
**ionospheric** adj.

**Ios** /'iːɒs/ (also **Nio**) a Greek island in the Aegean Sea, one of the Cyclades group; area 108 sq. km. (42 sq. miles); capital, Ios. Its chief port is Ormos Iou. Homer is reputed to have died on the island.

**Iowa** /'aɪəwə/ a state in the Middle West of the US, to the north of Missouri; area 145,753 sq. km. (56,275 sq. miles); pop. (1990) 2,776,770; capital, Des Moines. The largest cities are Des Moines, Cedar Rapids, Davenport, and Sioux City. It is also known as the Hawkeye State. The US gained control of Iowa in 1803 as part of the Louisiana Purchase, and it became the 29th state in the Union in 1846. Food processing and manufacturing are the chief industries of Iowa which is a leading grain, soybean, livestock, and hog-marketing state. Timber and minerals such as cement, coal, gypsum, limestone, sand, and gravel are also produced. The state's principal landmarks are the Fort Dodge Historical Museum, the seven Amana Colonies, the birthplace of President Herbert Hoover, and the Effigy Mounds National Monument. Iowa is divided into 99 counties:

| County | Area (sq. km.) | Pop. (1985) | County Seat |
|---|---|---|---|
| Adair | 1,482 | 9,510 | Greenfield |
| Adams | 1,105 | 5,730 | Corning |
| Allamakee | 1,646 | 15,110 | Waukon |
| Appanoose | 1,295 | 15,510 | Centerville |
| Audubon | 1,154 | 8,560 | Audubon |
| Benton | 1,867 | 23,650 | Vinton |
| Black Hawk | 1,490 | 137,960 | Waterloo |
| Boone | 1,490 | 26,180 | Boone |
| Bremer | 1,141 | 24,820 | Waverly |
| Buchanan | 1,487 | 22,900 | Independence |
| Buena Vista | 1,495 | 20,770 | Storm Lake |
| Butler | 1,513 | 17,670 | Allison |
| Calhoun | 1,485 | 13,540 | Rockwell City |
| Carroll | 1,482 | 22,950 | Carroll |
| Cass | 1,469 | 16,930 | Atlantic |
| Cedar | 1,513 | 18,635 | Tipton |
| Cerro Gordo | 1,479 | 48,460 | Mason City |
| Cherokee | 1,500 | 16,240 | Cherokee |
| Chickasaw | 1,313 | 15,440 | New Hampton |
| Clarke | 1,121 | 8,610 | Oscea |
| Clay | 1,479 | 19,580 | Spencer |
| Clayton | 2,025 | 21,100 | Elkader |
| Clinton | 1,807 | 57,120 | Clinton |
| Crawford | 1,856 | 18,935 | Denison |
| Dallas | 1,537 | 29,510 | Adel |
| Davis | 1,310 | 9,100 | Bloomfield |
| Decatur | 3,391 | 9,790 | Leon |
| Delaware | 1,503 | 18,930 | Manchester |
| Des Moines | 1,076 | 46,200 | Burlington |
| Dickinson | 991 | 15,630 | Spirit Lake |
| Dubuque | 1,578 | 93,745 | Dubuque |
| Emmet | 1,024 | 13,340 | Estherville |
| Fayette | 1,901 | 25,490 | West Union |
| Floyd | 1,303 | 19,600 | Charles City |
| Franklin | 1,516 | 13,040 | Hampton |
| Fremont | 1,339 | 9,400 | Sidney |
| Greene | 1,485 | 12,120 | Jefferson |
| Grundy | 1,303 | 14,370 | Grundy Center |
| Guthrie | 1,534 | 11,980 | Guthrie Center |
| Hamilton | 1,498 | 17,860 | Webster City |
| Hancock | 1,485 | 13,830 | Garner |
| Hardin | 1,479 | 21,780 | Eldora |
| Harrison | 1,812 | 16,350 | Logan |
| Henry | 1,134 | 18,890 | Mount Pleasant |
| Howard | 1,230 | 11,110 | Cresco |
| Humboldt | 1,134 | 12,250 | Dakota City |
| Ida | 1,123 | 8,910 | Ida Grove |
| Iowa | 1,526 | 15,430 | Marengo |
| Jackson | 1,659 | 22,500 | Maquoketa |
| Jasper | 1,901 | 36,425 | Newton |
| Jefferson | 1,144 | 16,320 | Fairfield |
| Johnson | 1,596 | 81,720 | Iowa City |
| Jones | 1,498 | 20,400 | Anamosa |
| Keokuk | 1,508 | 12,920 | Sigourney |
| Kossuth | 2,532 | 21,890 | Algona |
| Lee | 1,357 | 43,110 | Fort Madison and Keokuk |
| Linn | 1,882 | 169,775 | Cedar Rapids |
| Louisa | 1,045 | 12,055 | Wapello |
| Lucas | 1,123 | 10,310 | Charlton |
| Lyon | 1,529 | 12,900 | Rock Rapids |
| Madison | 1,464 | 12,600 | Winterset |
| Mahaska | 1,485 | 22,870 | Oskaloosa |
| Marion | 1,456 | 29,670 | Knoxville |
| Marshall | 1,490 | 41,650 | Marshalltown |
| Mills | 1,141 | 13,400 | Glenwood |
| Mitchell | 1,222 | 12,330 | Osage |
| Monona | 1,812 | 11,690 | Onawa |
| Monroe | 1,128 | 9,210 | Albia |
| Montgomery | 1,102 | 13,410 | Red Oak |
| Muscatine | 1,149 | 40,440 | Muscatine |
| O'Brien | 1,492 | 16,970 | Primghar |
| Osceola | 1,037 | 8,370 | Sibley |
| Page | 1,391 | 19,060 | Clarinda |
| Palo Alto | 1,461 | 12,720 | Emmetsburg |
| Plymouth | 2,246 | 24,740 | Le Mars |
| Pocahontas | 1,500 | 11,370 | Pocahontas |
| Polk | 1,513 | 303,170 | Des Moines |
| Pottawattamie | 2,478 | 86,560 | Council Bluffs |
| Poweshiek | 1,521 | 19,310 | Montezuma |
| Ringgold | 1,391 | 6,110 | Mount Ayr |
| Sac | 1,498 | 14,120 | Sac City |
| Scott | 1,193 | 160,020 | Davenport |
| Shelby | 1,537 | 15,040 | Harlan |
| Sioux | 1,999 | 30,810 | Orange City |
| Story | 1,492 | 72,330 | Nevada |
| Tama | 1,875 | 19,530 | Toledo |
| Taylor | 1,396 | 8,350 | Bedford |
| Union | 1,108 | 13,860 | Creston |
| Van Buren | 1,258 | 8,630 | Keosauqua |
| Wapello | 1,128 | 40,240 | Ottumwa |
| Warren | 1,490 | 34,880 | Indianola |
| Washington | 1,482 | 20,140 | Washington |
| Wayne | 1,368 | 8,200 | Corydon |
| Webster | 1,867 | 45,950 | Fort Dodge |
| Winnebago | 1,043 | 13,010 | Forest City |
| Winneshiek | 1,794 | 21,880 | Decorah |
| Woodbury | 2,270 | 100,880 | Sioux City |
| Worth | 1,043 | 9,075 | Northwood |
| Wright | 1,505 | 16,320 | Clarion |

**Iowa City** a city in eastern Iowa, USA, on the Iowa River; pop. (1990) 59,740. Founded in 1838, it was capital of the territory then the state until replaced by Des Moines in 1858. It is the home of the University of Iowa (1847).

**Ipiros** see EPIRUS.

**Ipoh** /ˈiːpəʊ/ a commercial city of northern Malaysia, on the River Kinta between the Main Range and the Keledang Mts.; pop. (1980) 300,700. Developed as a tin-mining town, Ipoh takes its name from the Ipoh or Upa tree from which the

Orang Asli tribe used to extract deadly poison for their blowpipe darts. It replaced Taiping as capital of the state of Perak in 1937.

**Ipswich** /ˈɪpswɪtʃ/ the county town of Suffolk in east England, a port and industrial town on the estuary of the River Orwell; pop. (1991) 115,500. It was a major wool port in the 16th c. and the birth-place of Cardinal Wolsey c. 1475. The 18th c. English painter Thomas Gainsborough lived here. Its trade links are with nearby European ports and its light industries include malting, brewing, flour-milling, and printing.

**Iquique** /iˈkiːkeɪ/ a port on the Pacific coast of northern Chile, capital of a province of the same name in the Tarapacá region; pop. (1991) 148,510. Developed in the 19th c. as a port for the export of minerals, its name is derived from an Aymara Indian word meaning 'place of rest'. The city was badly damaged by an earthquake in 1877. It pro-duces salt and fish products.

**Iquitos** /ɪˈkiːtɒs/ the principal river port and oil exploration centre in the tropical rainforest of east-ern Peru, situated on the west bank of the River Amazon; pop. (est. 1988) 247,000. It is a cultural and tourist centre.

**Iráklion** SEE HERAKLION.

**Iran** /ɪˈrɑːn/ official name **The Islamic Republic of Iran** a country in the Middle East between the Caspian Sea and the Persian Gulf; area 1,648,000 sq. km. (636,539 sq. miles); pop. (est.

1990) 54,600,000; official language, Farsi (Persian), (Turkish, Kurdish, Azerbaijani, and Arabic are also spoken); capital, Tehran. The largest cities are Tehran, Isfahan, Mashhad, and Tabriz. The greater part of the country forms a plateau at c. 1,220 m. (4,000 ft.) above sea-level with large areas of desert and steppe. Lowlands stretch along the Persian Gulf and the shore of the Caspian Sea; in the north the Elburz Mts. rise to 5,601 m. (18,376 ft.) at Mt. Damavand and in the west rise the Zagros Mts. in the western foothills of which lie Iran's major oil-fields. Most of Iran experiences extremes of heat and cold between summer and winter, with rainfall largely confined to the winter and spring. Oil is the chief source of revenue, otherwise the country is largely agricultural. Major industries are petro-chemicals, textiles, and food processing, but the de-veloping industrial output was largely curtailed by the 1979 revolution and the subsequent Gulf War with Iraq. The country was successively the centre of the Persian, Seleucid, Parthian, and Sassanian empires. Following the Muslim conquest in the 7th c. it was part of various Turkish, Persian, Tartar, and Mongol empires. A *coup* in 1925 brought the

Pahlavi family to the throne, but following the overthrow of the Shah in 1979 Iran became an Islamic state under the leadership of Ayatollah Khomeini. From 1980 to 1988 Iran was involved in war with her neighbour Iraq. Following the death of Khomeini in 1989 attempts were made to seek better relations with the West and to revive the economy. Separatist movements exist amongst the 5,000,000 Kurds in north-western Iran and the Baluchis of south-east Iran on the frontier with Pakistan. Iran is governed by an elected president and a unicameral National Consultative Assembly. **Iranian** *adj. & n.*

Iran is divided into 24 provinces (*ostán*):

| Province | Area (sq. km.) | Pop. (1986) | Capital |
| --- | --- | --- | --- |
| East Azerbaijan | 67,102 | 4,114,080 | Tabriz |
| West Azerbaijan | 38,850 | 1,971,680 | Urumiyeh |
| Bakhtaran | 23,667 | 1,462,965 | Bakhtaran |
| Bushehr | 27,699 | 612,180 | Bushehr |
| Chahar Mahall and Bakhtiari | 14,820 | 631,180 | Shahr Kord |
| Ispahan | 104,550 | 3,294,920 | Ispahan |
| Fars | 133,298 | 3,193,770 | Shiraz |
| Gilan | 14,709 | 2,081,040 | Rasht |
| Hamadan | 20,172 | 1,505,830 | Hamadan |
| Hormozgan | 66,870 | 762,200 | Bandar 'Abbas |
| Ilam and Poshtkuh | 19,042 | 382,090 | Ilam |
| Kerman | 186,472 | 1,622,960 | Kerman |
| Khorasan | 313,337 | 5,280,600 | Mashhad |
| Khuzestan | 67,236 | 2,681,980 | Ahvaz |
| Kohkiluyeh and Buyer Ahmadi | 14,261 | 411,828 | Yasuj |
| Kordestan | 24,998 | 1,078,415 | Sanandaj |
| Lorestan | 28,803 | 1,367,030 | Khorramabad |
| Markazi | 39,895 | 1,082,110 | Arak |
| Mazandaran | 46,200 | 3,419,350 | Sari |
| Semnan | 91,214 | 417,035 | Semnan |
| Sistan and Baluchistan | 181,578 | 1,197,060 | Zahedan |
| Tehran | 19,125 | 8,712,090 | Tehran |
| Yazd | 63,455 | 574,030 | Yazd |
| Zanjan | 36,398 | 158,800 | Zanjan |

**Iranian** /ɪˈreɪnɪən/ an Indo-European group of languages including Persian (Farsi), Pashto, Avestan, and Kurdish.

**Irapuato** /ˌiːrəˈpwɑːtəʊ/ an industrial city in the state of Guanajuato, central Mexico, on the Irapuato River south-west of Guanajuato City; pop. (1990) 362,470. Settled by the Spanish in 1547, it lies in a fertile farming area noted for its strawberries, cattle, and pig farms.

**Iraq** /ɪˈræk/ official name **The Republic of Iraq** a country in the Middle East with a short coastline on the Persian Gulf and surrounded by Turkey, Iran, Kuwait, Syria, and Jordan; area 438,317 sq. km. (169,300 sq. miles); pop. (est. 1990) 18,900,000; official language, Arabic (Kurdish and Turkoman are also spoken); capital, Baghdad. The largest cities are Baghdad, Basra, Mosul, and Irbil. A

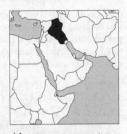

largely flat country, Iraq is drained by the Tigris and Euphrates Rivers which meet north-west of Basra to form the Shatt al-Arab Waterway before entering the Gulf. The north-east is mountainous while the west is largely desert with extreme temperature variations between summer and winter. Most of the country has a desert or steppe climate, with winters becoming milder further south and most rainfall occurring between December and March. Oil is the principal source of revenue, but agriculture is important. The Tigris–Euphrates valley was the site of an early Mesopotamian civilization. It was conquered by Arabia in the 7th c. and from 1534 formed part of the Ottoman empire, becoming an independent state after World War I when the Turks were expelled. Iraq was a kingdom (at first under British administration) until a *coup* in 1958 overthrew the monarchy and a republic was declared. Saddam Hussein came to power as President in 1979. The country was at war with its eastern neighbour Iran in 1980–8, and in August 1990 Iraq invaded Kuwait in an attempt to gain that country's wealth and oilfields and to secure its own access to the sea-outlet of the Gulf; it was expelled from Kuwait by an international coalition of forces in Jan.–Feb. 1991. A large Kurdish minority in the north and Marsh Arabs in the south have been the subject of military attacks. Iraq is governed by the Arab Ba'ath Socialist Party through a Command Council of the Revolution headed by the president who also heads a Council of Ministers.

**Iraqi** *adj. & n.*

Iraq is divided into 18 governorates:

| Governorate | Area (sq. km.) | Pop. (est.1985) | Capital |
|---|---|---|---|
| Al Anbar | 137,723 | 582,060 | Al Ramadi |
| Babil | 5,258 | 739,030 | Al Hillah |
| Baghdad | 5,159 | 4,648,600 | Baghdad |
| Basra | 19,070 | 1,304,150 | Basra |
| Dohuk | 6,120 | 330,360 | Dohuk |
| Dhi Qar | 13,626 | 725,910 | Al Nasiriyah |
| Arbil | 14,471 | 742,680 | Arbil |
| Karbala | 5,034 | 329,234 | Karbala |
| Maysan | 14,103 | 411,840 | Al Amarah |
| Al Muthanna | 51,029 | 253,820 | Al Samawah |
| Al Najaf | 27,844 | 472,100 | Al Najaf |
| Ninawa | 37,698 | 1,358,080 | Mosul |
| Al-Qadisiyah | 8,507 | 511,800 | Al Diwaniyah |
| Salah ad Din | 29,004 | 442,780 | Samarra |
| Al Sulaymaniyah | 15,756 | 906,500 | Sulaymaniyah |
| Ta'mim | 10,391 | 650,965 | Kirkuk |
| Wasit | 17,308 | 483,716 | Al Kut |

**Irazu** /ɪrə'zu:/ a volcanic peak to the east of San José in the Cordillera Central, central Costa Rica.

It rises to a height of 3,432 m. (11,260 ft.) and its summit is within sight of both the Atlantic and Pacific oceans.

**Irbid** /'ɪəbɪd/ a grain-marketing city in northern Jordan, on the east bank of the River Jordan north of Amman; pop. (est. 1986) 680,000. It is the capital of Irbid governorate and seat of Yarmouk University (1977). There are Bronze Age and Roman antiquities.

**Irbil** /'iːəbɪl/ see ARBIL.

**Ireland** /'aɪələnd/ an island of the British Isles, lying west of Great Britain; area 83,694 sq. km. (32,327 sq. miles); pop. (1991) 5,093,370. Four-fifths of it is occupied by the Irish Republic, and the remainder by Northern Ireland which is part of the United Kingdom. The soil is fertile and the pasturage lush, swept by warm damp winds from the Atlantic; the economy relies heavily on agriculture, especially beef production and dairy farming. Settled by the Celts, the country became divided into independent tribal territories over which the lords of Tara exercised nominal suzerainty. Christianity reached Ireland, probably in the 4th c., to be consolidated by the work of St. Patrick, and after the breakup of the Roman Empire the country became for a time a leading cultural centre, with the monasteries fostering learning and missionary work. English invasions began in the 12th c. under Henry II, but the authority that he established was never secure and by the 16th c. was confined to an area around Dublin (the English Pale) until the Tudors succeeded in extending it over the whole of the island. Revolts against English rule, and against the imposition of Protestantism (which met with unexpectedly stubborn resistance), resulted in the 'plantation' of Ireland by English (and later Scottish) families on confiscated land in an attempt to anglicize the country and secure its allegiance. In Ulster in particular the descendants of such settlers retained a distinctive identity. After an unsuccessful rebellion in 1798, political union of Britain and Ireland followed in 1801. In spite of genuine efforts towards its success Ireland sank deeper into destitution. A share of Britain's industrial prosperity reached Protestant Ulster, but the rest of the island found its agricultural assets dropping in value, and at the failure of the potato crop (Ireland's staple) in the 1840s thousands died in the famine, thousands more fled abroad. The Home Rule movement, led by Parnell, failed to achieve its aims in the 19th c. and implementation of a bill passed in 1910 was delayed by the outbreak of World War I. An armed uprising at Easter, 1916, was suppressed. Ireland was partitioned by the Anglo-Irish Treaty of 1921, which gave dominion status to Ireland with the exception of six of the counties of Ulster (Northern Ireland), whose Protestant majority wished to preserve the Union and which remained part of the United Kingdom.

**Irian Jaya** /ˌɪrɪən 'dʒaɪə/ (also **West Irian**) a province of eastern Indonesia comprising the western half of the island of New Guinea together with the adjacent small islands; area 421,981 sq. km. (162,990 sq. miles); pop. (est. 1993) 1,828,700; capital, Jayapura. Prior to its incorporation into Indonesia it was known as Dutch New Guinea. A 1962 agreement between Holland and Indonesia made provision for the Irianese to vote on their joining the Indonesian republic, but the referendum was waived and in 1969 Irian Jaya was fully incorporated into Indonesia. Since then an Irianese separatist movement has been engaged in guerrilla activities and thousands of refugees have fled across the border into Papua New Guinea.

**Iringa** /ɪˈrɪŋɡə/ a market town in central Tanzania, on a highland plateau south-west of Dar es Salaam; pop. (1984) 67,000. Ruaha National Park lies to the west.

**Irish** /ˈaɪərɪʃ/ (also **Erse**) the Celtic language of Ireland, forming a distinct variety of Gaelic. It was brought to Ireland by Celtic invaders c. 1000 BC, and down to the end of the 18th c. was spoken by the great majority of the people especially in areas other than the cities. Its earliest attestation is in inscriptions from the 4th c. AD, written in the Ogham script, and there has been a tradition of literature since the 6th c., with a mass of material from the 9th to 19th c. English gained ground rapidly and Irish is now spoken regularly only in certain areas in the west of Ireland. Since 1922 the Irish government has organized its revival, and it is now taught in all the schools, but despite this active support and the establishment of Irish as an official language there are probably fewer than 60,000 speakers. It is the first official language of the Irish Republic (the second is English). A few words used in the English language are derived from Irish, e.g. *banshee, blarney, galore, leprechaun, and Tory.*

**Irish Free State** the name for southern Ireland from 1921, when it gained dominion status on the partition of Ireland, until 1937, when it became the sovereign state of Eire.

**Irish Republic**
official name **The Republic of Ireland** an independent state occupying the southern four-fifths of the island of Ireland; area 70,282 sq. km. (27,146 sq. miles); pop. (1991)

3,523,400; official languages, Irish and English; capital, Dublin. Its chief exports are dairy products, meat, chemicals, computer equipment, and machinery. From 1801 to 1921 Ireland was an integral part of the United Kingdom, the Anglo-Irish War of 1919–21 leading to the establishment of the Irish Free State that recognized the temporary partition of the 26 counties of Ireland. In 1937 forces opposed to the Anglo-Irish Treaty of 1921 gained

control of the government and in 1948 a republic was declared. Ireland is governed by a bicameral parliament comprising a House of Representatives (*Dáil*) and a Senate (*Seanad*). The Irish Republic is divided into four provinces and 26 counties:

| County | Area (sq. km.) | Pop. (1991) | County Town |
|---|---|---|---|
| **Leinster** | | | |
| Carlow | 896 | 40,950 | Carlow |
| Dublin | 922 | 1,024,430 | Dublin |
| Kildare | 1,694 | 122,520 | Naas |
| Kilkenny | 2,062 | 73,610 | Kilkenny |
| Laois | 1,720 | 52,325 | Port Laoise |
| Longford | 1,044 | 30,290 | Longford |
| Louth | 821 | 90,710 | Dundalk |
| Meath | 2,339 | 105,540 | Navan |
| Offaly | 1,997 | 58,450 | Tullamore |
| Westmeath | 1,764 | 61,880 | Mullingar |
| Wexford | 2,352 | 102,045 | Wexford |
| Wicklow | 2,025 | 97,290 | Wicklow |
| **Munster** | | | |
| Clare | 3,188 | 90,830 | Ennis |
| Cork | 7,459 | 409,810 | Cork |
| Kerry | 4,701 | 121,720 | Tralee |
| Limerick | 2,686 | 161,860 | Limerick |
| Tipperary N.R. | 1,996 | 57,830 | |
| Tipperary S.R. | 2,258 | 74,790 | Clonmel |
| Waterford | 1,839 | 91,610 | Dungarvan |
| **Connaught** | | | |
| Galway | 5,939 | 180,300 | Galway |
| Leitrim | 1,526 | 25,300 | Carrick-on-Shannon |
| Mayo | 5,398 | 110,700 | Castlebar |
| Roscommon | 2,463 | 51,880 | Roscommon |
| Sligo | 1,795 | 54,740 | Sligo |
| **Ulster** | | | |
| Cavan | 1,891 | 52,760 | Cavan |
| Donegal | 4,830 | 127,990 | Lifford |
| Monaghan | 1,290 | 51,260 | Monaghan |

**Irish Sea** the sea separating Ireland from England and Wales.

**Irkutsk** /ɪəˈkʊtsk/ a major industrial and cultural city in east Siberia, inland from Lake Baikal; pop. (1990) 635,000. Founded in the 17th c. as a fortress town and fur-trading centre, it developed industrially with the building of the Trans-Siberian Railway. Its university was founded in 1918 and its heavy industries include aircraft, vehicles, oil refining, chemicals, machine tools, and metals.

**Iron Curtain** a former barrier to the passage of persons and information at the limit of the Soviet sphere of influence. The first 'iron curtain' (in the literal sense) dates from the rebuilding of Drury Lane Theatre in 1794, after its destruction by a fire which started on the stage, and was designed for lowering as a protection. The figurative sense (= an impenetrable barrier) is found from about 25 years later. The first reference to such a barrier in connection with Russia dates from 1920, but its use by Winston Churchill in 1946 fixed it in the language of the Cold War era.

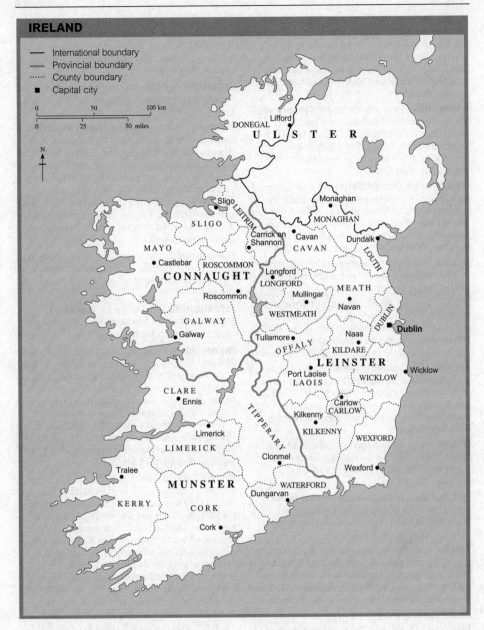

**IRELAND**

— International boundary
— Provincial boundary
······ County boundary
■ Capital city

0        50       100 km
0    25       50 miles

N

DONEGAL Lifford
U L S T E R

Sligo
SLIGO LEITRIM
Monaghan
MONAGHAN

Carrick on Cavan
Shannon CAVAN
Dundalk

MAYO
ROSCOMMON
LOUTH

Castlebar
CONNAUGHT Longford
LONGFORD
M E A T H

Roscommon
Mullingar
Navan

GALWAY
WESTMEATH
DUBLIN

Galway
Tullamore
Naas
■ Dublin

OFFALY
KILDARE

L E I N S T E R

Port Laoise
WICKLOW
Wicklow

CLARE
LAOIS

Ennis
Carlow
CARLOW

TIPPERARY
Kilkenny

Limerick
KILKENNY
WEXFORD

LIMERICK
Clonmel

Tralee
Wexford

MUNSTER
WATERFORD

KERRY
Dungarvan

CORK

Cork

**Iron Gate** (Romanian **Porţile de Fier**, Serbo-
Croatian **Gvozdena Vrata**) a gorge through which
a section of the River Danube flows, forming part
of the boundary between Romania and Serbia.
Navigation was improved by means of a ship canal
constructed through it in 1896, and a joint
Yugoslav–Romanian project completed a dam and
hydroelectric power plant in 1972.

**Iroquoian** /ˌɪrəˈkwɔɪən/ a language family of
eastern North America, including Cherokee and
Mohawk.

**Iroquois** /ˈɪrəˌkwɔɪ/ the collective designation of
the League of Five (later Six) Nations of North
American Indian tribes (i.e. Huron, Mohawk,
Oneida, Seneca, Onondaga, and Cayuga), speaking the Iroquoian languages, which joined in confederacy c. 1570 by the efforts of the Huron prophet
Deganawida and his disciple Hiawatha. A powerful force in early colonial history, the divisions in
the confederacy occasioned by conflicting support
of the various contestants in the War of American
Independence saw the rapid decline of the Six

Nations in the late 18th c., with half the League (i.e. the Cayugas, Mohawks, and Seneca) migrating north to Canada, where they accepted grants of land as allies of the defeated Loyalists and where they continue to live today. Traditional Iroquois society revolved around matrilineal residential and social organization.

**Irrawaddy** /ˌɪrə'wɒdɪ/ (Burmese **Ayeyarwady**) the principal river of Burma, 2,090 km. (1,300 miles) long. Formed at the junction of two headwaters in Kachin State, it flows southwards and eventually forms a large delta that empties into the eastern Bay of Bengal.

**Irtysh** /ɪə'tɪʃ/ (Kazakh **Ertis**) a river of Central Asia that rises on the slopes of the Altai Mts. in northern China and flows westwards into north-east Kazakhstan where it turns north-west into Russia, joining the River Ob near its mouth at the head of the Gulf of Ob; length 4,248 km. (2,655 miles).

**Iruma** /ɪ'ruːmə/ a residential and industrial city on Honshu Island, Japan, 40 km. (25 miles) north-west of Tokyo; pop. (1990) 138,000.

**Irún** /iː'ruːn/ an industrial river port in the Basque Provinces of northern Spain, on the River Bidassoa east of San Sebastian; pop. (1991) 53,570. Its economy is largely based on agro-industry, engineering, and the mining of lead and iron ore.

**Irvine** /'ɜːvɪn/ a town in North Ayrshire, west-central Scotland, at the mouth of the River Irvine west of Kilmarnock; pop. (1981) 32,970. It was designated a New Town in 1966 and was the administrative centre of Cunninghame District from 1975 to 1996.

**Irvine** a city in southern California, USA, south of Santa Ana between the Pacific coast and the Santa Ana Mts.; pop. (1990) 110,330.

**Irving** /'ɜːvɪŋ/ a city in north-east Texas, USA, a western suburb of Dallas to the north of the West Fork Trinity River; pop. (1990) 155,040. The University of Dallas (1956) and the Dallas–Fort Worth Airport are sited in Irving.

**Ischia** /'ɪskɪə/ a volcanic island in the Tyrrhenian Sea off the west coast of Italy, about 26 km. (16 miles) south-west of Naples. Known as the Emerald Isle, it has been noted for centuries for its warm mineral springs which are a major tourist attraction.

**Ischl** see BAD ISCHL.

**Ise** /'iːseɪ/ (also **Iseshi**, formerly **Ujiyamada**) a city in central Honshu Island, Japan, on Ise Bay; pop. (1990) 104,000. It has several noted Shinto shrines including one dedicated to Amaterasu, the sun goddess, from whom the Japanese royal family were once claimed to be descended. A leading producer of cultured pearls is located nearby.

**Ise Bay** an inlet of the Pacific Ocean on the south coast of Honshu Island, Japan. The city of Nagoya lies at its head.

**Isère** /iː'zer/ **1.** a river of eastern France that rises in the Graian Alps near Val d'Isère and flows 290 km. (180 miles) through the Savoy Alps to join the River Rhône near Valence. **2.** a department in the Rhône-Alpes region of eastern France; area 7,431 sq. km. (2,870 sq. miles); pop. (1990) 1,016,230; capital, Grenoble.

**Isesaki** /ˌiːseɪ'sɑːkɪ/ a city on Honshu Island, Japan, 88 km (55 miles) north-west of Tokyo; pop. (1990) 116,000.

**Isfahan** /ˌɪsfə'hɑːn/ (also **Esfahan**, **Ispahan**) an industrial city in west-central Iran, the country's third-largest city; pop. (1991) 1,127,000. Abbas I made it his capital city from 1598, and it became one of the largest and most beautiful cities of this period until captured and destroyed by the Afghans in 1722. It has a Great Bazaar and a large number of mosques, tombs, palaces, and schools. It has traditional industries of carpets and rugs, textiles, and metalwork.

**Ishinomaki** /ˌɪʃɪnəʊ'mɑːkɪ/ a major fishing port on the north-east coast of the island of Honshu, Japan, to the north-east of Sendai; pop. (1990) 122,000.

**Ishizuchino** /ˌiːʃɪ'zuːtʃɪnəʊ/, **Mount** the highest peak on the Japanese island of Shikoku; height 1,981 m. (6,500 ft.).

**Iskenderun** /ɪs'kendəˌruːn/ a port, naval base, and steel-making town of southern Turkey, on the north-east coast of the Mediterranean Sea; pop. (1990) 158,930. Formerly named Alexandretta, it lies on or near the site of Alexandria ad Issum, founded by Alexander the Great in 333 BC. The port was an important outlet for goods from Persia, India, and eastern Asia before the development of sea-routes round the Cape of Good Hope and later through the Suez Canal.

**Islam** /'ɪzlɑːm, -læm, -'lɑːm/ the religion of the Muslims, a monotheistic faith founded by the Prophet Muhammad in the Arabian Peninsula in the 7th c. AD and is now the professed religion of nearly one thousand million people worldwide. To become a Muslim means both to accept and affirm an individual surrender to God, and to live as a member of a social community. The Muslim performs prescribed acts of worship and strives to fulfil good works within the group; the 'Pillars of Islam' include profession of the faith in a prescribed form, observance of ritual prayer (five obligatory prayer sequences each day as well as non-obligatory prayers), giving alms to the poor, fasting during the month of Ramadan, and performing the pilgrimage to Mecca. These ritual observances, as well as a code governing social behaviour, were given to Muhammad as a series of revelations, codified in the Koran and supplemented by the deeds and discourse of the Prophet. Islam is regarded by its adherents as the last of the revealed religions (following Judaism and Christianity), and Muhammad is seen as the last of the Prophets, building upon and perfecting the examples and teachings of Abraham, Moses, and

Jesus. The term Islam carries three interrelated significations: the personal individual submission to Allah; the 'world of Islam' as a concrete historical reality comprising a variety of communities which, however, share not only a common religious outlook but also a common fund of cultural legacies; and finally, the concept of an 'ideal Muslim community' as set forth in the Koran and supporting sources.

**Islamic** *adj.*

**Islamabad** /ɪz'lɑːmə,bɑːd/ the capital of Pakistan, a modern planned city in the north of the country, which replaced Karachi as capital in 1967; pop. (1981) 201,000.

**Isla Mujeres** /'iːslə muː'hɜːrez/ a limestone island in the Gulf of Mexico, situated 7 km. (5 miles) off the east coast of the Mexican state of Quintana Roo. A popular resort island, it was named the 'Island of Women' by Spanish explorers who found the island adorned with terracotta images of women in 1517.

**island** /'aɪlənd/ a piece of land, smaller than a continent, surrounded by water. They can be formed by rising sea-levels, erosional processes, and volcanic activity. The world's largest islands are Greenland, New Guinea, and Borneo.

**Islay** /'aɪlə/ an island in the Inner Hebrides of Scotland, to the south of Jura in Strathclyde Region; area 608 sq. km. (235 sq. miles). Its chief ports of entry are Port Ellen and Port Askaig, and its principal industry is the distillation of whisky. Finlaggan was the former administrative centre of the Lords of the Isles.

**Isle of Man** an island in the Irish Sea which is a British Crown possession enjoying home rule, with its own legislature (the *Tynwald*) and judicial system; area 572 sq. km. (221 sq. miles); pop. (1991) 69,790; capital, Douglas. Its highest point is Snaefell (621 m., 2,036 ft.) and its longest river is the Sulby (117 km., 10.5 miles). The island was part of the Norse kingdom of the Hebrides in the Middle Ages, passing into Scottish hands in 1266 for a time, until the English gained control in the early 15th c. Its ancient language, Manx, is still used for ceremonial purposes. The island hosts an annual series of Tourist Trophy motor cycle races, and is popular with both holiday-makers and tax-exiles.

**Isle of Wight** /waɪt/ an island off the south coast of England, a county since 1974; area 381 sq. km. (147 sq. miles); pop. (1991) 126,600; county town, Newport. It lies at the entrance to Southampton Water and is separated from the mainland by the Solent. It is administratively divided into two districts:

| District | Area (sq. km.) | Pop. (1991) |
|---|---|---|
| Medina | 264 | 70,100 |
| South Wight | 117 | 56,400 |

**Isle Royale** /iːl rɔɪ'ɑːl/ the largest island in Lake Superior, designated a US national Park in 1931. It lies in the state of Michigan; area 2,182 sq. km. (843 sq. miles).

**Isles of Scilly** /'sɪlɪ/ (also **Scillies**) a group of about 40 small islands, situated 28 miles west of the mainland of south-west England off Land's End; area 16 sq. km. (6 sq. miles); pop. (1991) 2,900. Its chief settlement is Hugh Town (on St. Mary's). Five of the islands are inhabited and because they lie in the path of the Gulf Stream they enjoy a mild climate. Numerous prehistoric remains are evidence of their settlement since the Bronze Age and since 1337 the islands have largely belonged to the Duchy of Cornwall.

**Scillonian** *n.*

**Islington** /'ɪzlɪŋt(ə)n/ an inner borough of Greater London, both residential and industrialized, lying to the north of the City of London; pop. (1990) 155,200. John Wesley's chapel and house and the Sadler's Wells Theatre are to be found in Finsbury in the south of the borough.

**Ismaili** /ɪz'maɪlɪ/ a member of a Shiite Muslim sect that seceded from the main group in the 8th c. over the question of succession to the position of imam. They regarded Ismail, eldest son of the sixth imam, as the seventh and final imam, while the rest of the Shiites supported the second son, Musa al-Kazim. The Ismaili movement (which consisted of several groups rather than one unified body) represented a revolutionary political force in its early stages, and its adherents developed an elaborate esoteric doctrine (diverging considerably from the rest of Islam) concerning the believer's place in the cosmos and the highly structured path to spiritual fulfilment. Initiation into the group's doctrines was a long process to which only a few were admitted, and the organization tended to be that of a very hierarchical secret society. It eventually split into many sub-sects, of which the best-known is that headed by the Aga Khan. Today Ismailis are found especially in India, Pakistan, and East Africa, with smaller groups in Syria, Iran, and some other countries.

**Ismailia** /,ɪzmaɪ'iːlə/ (also **Ismailiya**) a city in north-eastern Egypt, to the west of the Suez Canal, midway between Port Said and Suez; pop. (1991) 247,000. It was founded and named after Pasha Ismail, ruler of Egypt during the construction of the Suez Canal in the 1860s.

**isobar** /'aɪsəʊ,bɑː(r)/ a line on a map connecting positions having the same atmospheric pressure at a given time or on average over a given period.

**isochrone** /'aɪsəʊ,krəʊn/ a line on a map connecting places of equal travel time from a given point.

**isohyet** /'aɪsəʊ,haɪt/ a line on a map connecting places having the same amount of rainfall over a given period.

**isopleth** /'aɪsəʊ,pleθ/ a line on a map connecting places having an equal incidence of a particular phenomenon.

**isostasy** /aɪˈsɒstəsɪ/ the general state of equilibrium of the highlands and lowlands of the earth's crust, with the rise and fall of land relative to sea.

**isothere** /ˈaɪsəʊˌθɪə(r)/ a line on a map connecting places having the same average summer temperature.

**isotherm** /ˈaɪsəʊˌθɜːm/ a line on a map connecting places having the same temperature at a given time or on average over a given period.

**Ispahan** see ISFAHAN.

**Isparta** /ɪsˈpɑː(r)tə/ **1.** a mountainous province in south-west Turkey; area 8,933 sq. km. (3,450 sq. miles); pop. (1990) 434,770; . **2.** its capital, Isparta; pop. (1990) 112,120. It has textile and carpet industries.

**Israel** /ˈɪzreɪ(ə)l/ **1.** (also **Children of Israel**) the Hebrew nation of people traditionally descended from the patriarch Jacob (his alternative name was 'Israel'), whose 12 sons became founders of the 12 tribes. **2.** the northern kingdom of the Hebrews (c.930–721 BC, in contrast to Judah), whose inhabitants were carried away to captivity in Assyria. The name Israel is first found on the Moabite Stone (c.850 BC) commemorating the successes of the king Moab against Israel.
**Israelite** adj. & n.

**Israel** official name **The State of Israel** a country in the Middle East, with the River Jordan forming part of its eastern border and with a coastline on the Mediterranean Sea; area 20,770 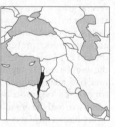 sq. km. (8,022 sq. miles); pop. (est. 1990) 4,600,000; official language, Hebrew (Arabic is spoken by about 15 per cent of the population); capital (not recognized as such by the UN), Jerusalem. In the north a coastal plain is separated from the Jordan Rift Valley by central mountains, while in the south the Negev Desert comprises half of the country's total area. The climate is temperate except in the dry and arid Negev, most rain falling from October to April. Much of the northern half of the country is fertile, and since 1948 massive irrigation programmes have brought large areas of former desert under cultivation. Israel has few natural resources but uses skilled labour to produce a wide range of goods including metal products, electronic equipment, processed food, chemicals, plastic and rubber goods, transport equipment, and oil-based products. The Jewish population of Israel has increased six-fold since independence, with more than half of the increase due to immigration. The 'Holy Land' of Jews and Christians, and with Jerusalem sacred also to Muslims, it contains numerous sites that attract both pilgrims and tourists. Remains of early man were found in caves on Mount Carmel, and the country is rich in archaeological remains of all periods. Although it is the ancient and traditional home of the Jewish people, for most of its history it was controlled by one or other of the powerful nations of each succeeding era, until following the surrender of the British mandate at the end of World War II the independent Jewish State of Israel was proclaimed in 1948. Conflict with the surrounding Arab states led to wars in 1948, 1956, 1967, and 1973, and resulted in Israel's occupation of the West Bank of Jordan, the Gaza Strip, and the Golan heights. Following conflict with Palestinians in Lebanon in 1978 and 1982, Israel established a 'security zone' on its northern frontier and in 1987 Arab opposition to Israeli occupation erupted in a violent uprising (*intifada*) against Israeli security forces. As a result of tensions with its neighbours and containment of the occupied territories Israel has emerged as one of the strongest military powers in the Middle East, and despite a high inflation rate, the development of the economy has made it the most industrialized country in the region. Israel is a parliamentary democracy governed by a unicameral legislature (*Knesset*).
**Israeli** /ɪzˈreɪlɪ/ adj. & n.

Israel is divided into six administrative districts:

| District | Area (sq. km.) | Pop. (1985) | Chief Town |
| --- | --- | --- | --- |
| Central | 1,242 | 907,700 | Ramla |
| Haifa | 854 | 596,100 | Haifa |
| Jerusalem | 627 | 518,200 | Jerusalem |
| Northern | 4,501 | 718,900 | Nazareth |
| Southern | 14,107 | 518,100 | Beersheba |
| Tel Aviv | 170 | 1,018,800 | Tel Aviv |

**Istanbul** /ˌɪstænˈbʊl/ a great historic city, port, and the former capital (until 1923) of Turkey, situated on the Bosporus and partly in Europe, partly in Asia, to which it is linked by two suspension bridges; pop. (1990) 6,620,240. The largest city in Turkey, Istanbul was founded c.660 BC by Dorian Greeks. It was known as Byzantium until it became the second capital of the Roman Empire and was renamed Constantinople in AD 330 by Constantine I. Declared capital of the Eastern Roman Empire in 395, the city was largely rebuilt by Justinian (527–65). Captured by the Turks in 1453, most of its characteristic buildings, such as the Topkapi Palace, the Blue Mosque, and the Mosque of Suleiman the Magnificent, date from the Ottoman period (1453–1923). Istanbul has the world's largest covered bazaar. It is Turkey's commercial, religious, and cultural centre, and as a cosmopolitan city it has many foreign communities. Its port handles two-thirds of Turkey's trade and it has both heavy and light industries, including shipbuilding, cement, textiles, consumer goods of all kinds, and tourism. Istanbul's name is derived from Greek *eis ten polin* meaning 'into the city'.

**isthmus** /ˈɪsməs, ɪsθ-/ a narrow piece of land connecting two larger bodies of land.
**isthmian** adj.

**Itaipu** /iːˈtaɪpuː/ a dam on the Paraná River in south-west Brazil. Operational since 1984, it is the world's largest hydroelectric plant.

**Italian** /ɪˈtæljən/ the official language of Italy, a Romance language which in many ways has remained closer to Latin than have the others of this group. It is spoken by some 60 million people in Italy and Switzerland, and by large numbers of speakers in the US and South America.

**Italiot** /ɪˈtælɪət/ an inhabitant of the Greek colonies in ancient Italy.

**Italy** /ˈɪtəlɪ/ (Italian **Italia**) official name **The Italian Republic** a country in southern Europe comprising a peninsula that juts into the

**ITALY**

Region boundary
■ Capital city

0    50   100   150   200 km
0    25   50   75   100 miles

N

TRENTINO-ALTO ADIGE
Trento

FRIULI-VENEZIA GIULIA

Aosta
VALLE D'AOSTA

LOMBARDY

VENETIA
Venice

Trieste

Turin
Milan

PIEDMONT

LIGURIA
Genoa

EMILIA-ROMAGNA

Bologna

Florence

TUSCANY

Ancona

THE MARCHES

Perugia
UMBRIA

L'Aquila

**Rome**
■

ABRUZZI

LATIUM

MOLISE
Campobasso

Naples
CAMPANIA

Potenza
BASILICATA

Bari
APULIA

SARDINIA

Cagliari

CALABRIA

Palermo

Reggio

SICILY

Mediterranean Sea, and a number of off-shore islands of which the largest are Sicily and Sardinia; area 301,225 sq. km. (116,348 sq. miles); pop. (1990) 57,746,160; official language, Italian

(German is spoken in the South Tyrol and French in the Valle d'Aosta); capital, Rome. The largest cities are Rome, Milan, Naples, and Turin. From the Alpine ranges that form Italy's northern frontier, the Apennines stretch southwards the whole length of the country, separating east and west coasts. In the north-east the Lombardo-Venetian plain, which is watered by many rivers including the Po and the Adige, is the most densely populated and agriculturally productive region. The climate of peninsular Italy is typically Mediterranean in coastal areas, with mild winters and generally dry summers. In winter, mountain regions are cold, wet and often snowy and further south the length and intensity of the summer season increases. The east coast is sometimes affected by the cold Bora winds in winter and spring, and occasionally during summer and autumn all parts experience very high temperatures and humidity when the sirocco winds blow. Italy's principal exports include textiles, clothes, chemicals, metal goods, transport equipment, wine, fruit, and vegetables. The centre of the Roman Empire, Italy was dominated by the city-states and the papacy in the Middle Ages, but fell under Spanish and Austrian rule in the 16th–17th c. Modern Italy was created by the nationalist movement of the mid-19th c., led by Garibaldi and the kingdom of Sardinia, the monarch of the latter country becoming king of Italy in 1861. Italy entered World War I on the Allied side in 1915, but after the war the country was taken over by the Fascist dictator Mussolini; participation in support of Germany during World War II resulted in defeat and much devastation. A republic was established by popular vote in 1946. The country is divided between the industrialized north and the agricultural south, and by European standards has experienced a considerable degree of political instability in recent decades. Italy has an executive Council of Ministers headed by the president, and a bicameral legislature comprising a Senate and a House of Deputies.

**Italian** *adj. & n.*

Italy is divided into 20 regions:

| Region | Area (sq. km.) | Pop. (1990) | Capital |
|---|---|---|---|
| Abruzzi | 10,794 | 1,272,390 | L'Aquila |
| Apulia | 19,347 | 4,081,540 | Bari |
| Basilicata | 9,992 | 624,520 | Potenza |
| Calabria | 15,080 | 2,153,660 | Reggio di Calabria |
| Campania | 13,595 | 5,853,900 | Naples |
| Emilia-Romagna | 22,123 | 3,928,740 | Bologna |
| Friuli-Venezia Giulia | 7,846 | 1,201,030 | Trieste |
| Latium | 17,203 | 5,191,480 | Rome |
| Liguria | 5,416 | 1,719,200 | Genoa |
| Lombardy | 23,856 | 8,939,430 | Milan |
| The Marches | 9,694 | 1,435,570 | Ancona |
| Molise | 4,438 | 336,460 | Campobasso |
| Piedmont | 25,399 | 4,356,230 | Turin |
| Sardinia | 24,090 | 1,664,370 | Cagliari |
| Sicily | 25,708 | 5,196,820 | Palermo |
| Trentino-Alto Adige | 13,613 | 891,420 | |
| Bolzano | 7,400 | 441,670 | Bolzano |
| Trento | 6,213 | 449,750 | Trento |
| Tuscany | 2,992 | 3,562,425 | Florence |
| Umbria | 8,456 | 822,765 | Perugia |
| Valle d'Aosta | 3,262 | 116,000 | Aosta |
| Venetia | 18,364 | 4,398,110 | Venice |

**Itami** /iːˈtɑːmiː/ a city on Honshu Island, Japan, a residential suburb of Osaka on the Muko River; pop. (1990) 186,000.

**Itanagar** /ˌɪtənəˈɡɑː/ a city in the far north-east of India, north of the Brahmaputra River, capital of the state of Arunachal Pradesh; pop. (1991) 17,300.

**Ithaca** /ˈɪθəkə/ (also **Ithaka**, Greek **Itháki**) an Ionian island off the west coast of Greece, separated from Cephalonia by the Ithaca Channel; area 114 sq. km. (44 sq. miles). Its chief port is Vathy. The island was the legendary home of Odysseus who was associated with the Grotto of the Nymphs and the Fountain of Arethusa.

**Ivano-Frankovsk** /ɪˌvɑːnəʊfrɑːŋˈkɒfsk/ (also **Ivano-Frankivsk**) an industrial city in western Ukraine, on a tributary of the Dniester River; pop. (1990) 220,000. It was known as Stanislav until 1962. It has oil refineries, and railway repair shops.

**Ivanovo** /ɪˈvɑːnəvə/ a major textile city in western Russia, north-east of Moscow and south of the Volga; pop. (1990) 482,000.

**Iviza** see IBIZA.

**Ivory Coast** (French **Côte d'Ivoire** /kəʊt diːˈvwɑː/) official name **The Republic of Côte d'Ivoire** a country in West Africa on the Gulf of Guinea, between Liberia and Ghana;

area 322,462 sq. km. (124,550 sq. miles); pop. (est. 1990) 12,000,000; official language, French; capital, Yamoussoukro (formerly Abidjan). Dense forest gives way to savanna in the north and the south-east coast is fringed with numerous lagoons; in the north-west the Guinea Highlands rise to

1,460 m. (4,800 ft.). The Ivory Coast has a tropical climate with high year-round temperatures and humidity and a short rainy season from May to July. One of the more developed of African economies, it is noted for its forest resources which make it a leading exporter of tropical timber. Cash crops such as coffee, cacao, bananas, rubber, and palm oil are also important. The area was explored by the Portuguese in the late 15th c., and subsequently disputed by traders from various European countries who sought the ivory from which the country takes its name, and slaves. It was made a French protectorate in 1842, and became an autonomous republic within the French Community in 1958 and a fully independent republic outside it in 1960. The country is governed by an executive president and a unicameral National Assembly.

**Ivy League** a name applied to a group of long-established eastern US universities of high academic and social prestige, including Harvard, Yale, Princeton, and Columbia.

**Iwaki** /ɪ'wɑːkiː/ an industrial city and former coal-mining centre on Honshu Island, Japan, on the east coast between Mito and Sendai; pop. (1990) 356,000. In 1966 it merged with four other cities including Taira and is a centre of the chemical industry.

**Iwakuni** /ˌiːwɑː'kuːnɪ/ an industrial city on the south-west coast of Honshu Island, on an inlet of the Inland Sea south-west of Hiroshima; pop. (1990) 110,000. Oil-refining and the production of chemical fibres, paper-pulp, and machine tools are its chief industries.

**Iwatsuki** /ˌiːwɑː't'suːkɪ/ a city on Honshu Island, Japan, on the Edo River; pop. (1990) 106,000. It produces textiles.

**Iwo** /'iːwəʊ/ a city in western Nigeria, north-east of Ibadan; pop. (1991) 261,600. It is a centre for the cacao trade.

**Iwo Jima** /ˌiːwəʊ 'dʒiːmə/ a small volcanic island, the largest of the Volcano Islands in the western Pacific, 1,222 km. (760 miles) south of Tokyo. During World War II it was the heavily fortified site of a Japanese airbase, and its attack

and capture in 1944–5 was one of the severest US campaigns. It was returned to Japan in 1968.

**Ixelles** /iːk'sel/ (also **Elsene** /el'sen/) a south-eastern industrial suburb of Brussels in the province of Brabant, central Belgium; pop. (1991) 72,610.

**Ixtaccihuatl** /ˌiːʃtə'siːwæt(ə)l/ (also **Iztaccihuatl**) a volcanic peak in central Mexico, rising to 5,286 m. (17,342 ft.) south-east of Mexico City.

**Izalco** /ɪ'zɑːlkəʊ/ (Spanish **Volcan de Izalco**) a volcano in western El Salvador, one of the most active in Central America. It rises to a height of 1,830 m. (6,004 ft.).

**Izhevsk** /ɪ'ʒevsk/ the capital of the Udmurt Republic (Udmurtia) in European Russia, on the River Izh; pop. (1990) 642,000. Founded in 1760, it was for a few years in the 1980s known as Ustinov. It is a major centre of metal production and the defence industries.

**Izmir** /ɪz'mɪə(r)/ (formerly **Smyrna** /'smɜːnə/) a seaport and naval base in western Turkey, on an inlet of the Aegean Sea; pop. (1990) 1,757,410. It is the third-largest city in Turkey. Founded by the Greeks in c.1000 BC, it was captured by the Ottoman Turks in 1424, occupied by the Greeks in 1919 but retaken by the Turks in 1922 when it was devastated by fire. It produces a wide range of goods including carpets and foodstuffs for export. The province of the same name is rich in minerals; area 12,825 sq. km. (4,952 sq. miles).

**Izmit** /ɪz'mɪt/ (also **Kocaeli**) a city and port in north-west Turkey, situated on the Gulf of Izmit, an inlet of the Sea of Marmara; pop. (1990) 256,880. It is capital of the province of Kocaeli and trades in tobacco and olives.

**Iznik** /ɪz'nɪk/ a town in the province of Bursa, north-west Turkey, situated to the south-east of the Sea of Marmara; pop. (1990) 17,230. Built on the site of ancient Nicaea, it has been a noted centre for the production of coloured tiles since the 16th c.

**Izumi** /iː'zuːmɪ/ a residential and industrial suburb of Osaka on the island of Honshu, Japan; pop. (1990) 138,000. It has textile industries.

# J j

**jabal** /'dʒæbəl/ (also **jebel** or **djebel**) an Arabic word for a hill.

**Jabalpur** /ˌdʒʌbəl'pʊə(r)/ an industrial city and military post in the state of Madhya Pradesh, central India, in the Narmada River valley; pop. (1991) 740,000. It was the capital of the Gond kings during the 12th c. and later the seat of the Kalchuri dynasty. It has firearms and ammunition manufactures.

**Jablonec nad Nisou** /'jæblənets næd ˌnjɪsaʊ/ a city of North Bohemia, in the Czech Republic; pop. (1991) 88,060. It is the centre of the Bohemian glass industry. Engineering and the manufacture of costume jewellery are also important.

**Jaboatão** /ˌʒæbwə'taʊ/ a city in the state of Pernambuco, eastern Brazil, situated to the south-west of Recife; pop. (1990) 467,080.

**Jackson** /'dʒæksən/ **1.** a town in southern Michigan, USA; pop. (1990) 37,450. Founded in 1829, it developed as a rail and road transportation centre and was the site of the official founding of the Republican Party on 6 July 1854. **2.** the state capital of Mississippi, USA, on the Pearl River; pop. (1990) 196,640. Founded as a trading post by the French Canadian trader Louis LeFleur and later named after President Andrew Jackson, the city became state capital in 1822. It developed as a railway junction and administrative centre during the 19th c. and further expanded after the discovery of natural gas nearby in the 1930s. **3.** a railway city in western Tennessee, USA, on the Forked Deer River; pop. (1990) 48,950. It was the home and burial place of the railroad hero John Luther 'Casey' Jones.

**Jacksonville** /'dʒæksən,vɪl/ a major transport centre, and industrial, commercial, and financial city and port in north-east Florida, USA, on the St. Johns River 19 km. (12 miles) inland from its mouth; pop. (1990) 672,970. Formerly known as Cowford, it was renamed in honour of President Andrew Jackson. A very extensive city with shipyards and naval installations, and many light industries including tourism and sports facilities.

**Jacobabad** /'jeɪkəbə,bɑːd/ a city in the province of Sind, south-east Pakistan; pop. (1981) 80,000. Founded as a frontier post by General John Jacob, superintendent of the Upper Sind Frontier Region 1847–58, it is now a market town trading in grain. Because Jacob was highly respected for bringing peace to the region, it is one of the few

remaining towns of Asia that retains the name of an Englishman.

**Jadotville** /ˌʒɑːdəʊ'viː/ the former name (until 1966) of LIKASI.

**Jaén** /hæ'eɪn/ **1.** a province in Andalusia, southern Spain; pop. (1989) 659,940; area 13,498 sq. km. (5,213 sq. miles); pop. (1991) 637,630. **2.** its capital on the River Guadalbullon; pop. (1991) 105,545. Known to the Romans as Auringis, Jaén became capital of the Moorish kingdom of Jayyan. Once famous for its silver mines, it now produces pharmaceuticals, textiles, and olive oil.

**Jaffa** /'dʒæfə/ (Hebrew **Yafo**, ancient **Joppa**) a city and port on the Mediterranean coast of Israel, forming a southern suburb of Tel Aviv. Occupied since prehistoric times, Jaffa was the seat of a bishop of the Byzantine empire until captured by the Arabs in 636 and was a stronghold of the Crusaders. It has associations with Noah's son Japheth who is said to have founded the town after the Flood and with the legendary Perseus who rescued Andromeda here. Jaffa united with Tel Aviv in 1949.

**Jaffna** /'dʒæfnə/ **1.** a district at the northern tip of Sri Lanka, dominated by a Hindu Tamil population; area 983 sq. km. (380 sq. miles); pop. (1990) 863,000; . **2.** its capital city, a port at the western end of the Jaffna Lagoon; pop. (est. 1990) 129,000. The city, which is dominated by a Dutch colonial fort, was the capital of a Tamil monarchy until the 17th c. It exports fruit, cotton, tobacco, and timber.

**Jagannath Temple** /'dʒægənæθ/ a temple to the Hindu God Jagannath, 'Lord of the Universe', in the city of Puri, Orissa, India. Every June/July a chariot carrying a massive wooden image of Jagannath is pulled through the streets by 4,000 men, a vehicle that has given the English language the word *juggernaut*.

**Jain Caves** /'dʒaɪn/ a series of caves to the west of Bhubaneswar, Orissa, India, excavated and occupied by Jainist ascetics in the 2nd c. BC.

**Jainism** /'dʒaɪnɪzm/ a non-theistic religion founded in India in the 6th c. BC by Vardhamana Mahavira as a reaction against the teachings of orthodox Brahminism. Its central doctrine is non-injury to living creatures. Salvation is attained by perfection of the soul through successive lives. Numbering some 3.6 million adherents, its followers in India are mostly found in Gujarat and Maharashtra states. There are two major sects: the white-robed *Svetambaras* and the naked *Digambaras*.

**Jainist** n.

**Jaipur** /dʒaɪˈpʊə(r)/ (formerly **Jeypore**) a city of western India, the capital of Rajasthan; pop. (1991) 1,455,000. Founded in 1725 by Sawai Jai Singh II, maharaja of the Kacchwaha Rajputs, who laid it out according to Hindu rules of town planning with a grid pattern and wide avenues. Pink, a traditional colour of welcome, was added to buildings in 1853 in honour of a visit by Prince Albert. Notable buildings include the Palace of the Winds (Hawa Mahal), the 18th-c. observatory (Jantar Mantar), and the city palace. It is noted for its carpets and handicrafts including jewellery and miniature paintings.

**Jakarta** /dʒəˈkɑːtə/ (also **Djakarta**) the capital of Indonesia, situated in north-west Java on an inlet of the Java Sea; pop. (1990) 8,222,500. Founded by the Dutch in the early 17th c., it was the headquarters of the Dutch East India Company. It was known as Batavia until 1949 when it became capital of the newly independent state of Indonesia. The old city centre with its Dutch colonial architecture is surrounded by residential suburbs and shanty towns. It is the administrative, commercial, and cultural centre of Indonesia with eleven universities founded between 1950 and 1960. Its industries include textiles, metals, and timber. It exports tea and rubber.

**Jakobstad** /ˈjɑːkəbˌstɑːd/ the Swedish name for the Finnish port of PIETARSAARI.

**Jalalabad** /dʒəˈlæləˌbæd/ a city in eastern Afghanistan, situated east of Kabul, near the frontier with Pakistan; pop. (est. 1984) 61,000. The population swelled to nearly one million during the civil war in the 1980s.

**Jalandhar** /ˈdʒələndə(r)/ (formerly **Jullundur**) a road and rail junction in the state of Punjab, northern India; pop. (1991) 519,530. It was an important administrative centre between the Beas and Sutlej rivers, being capital of the ancient kingdom of Trigarta and of the Punjab (1947–54).

**Jalapa** /həˈlɑːpə/ (in full **Jalapa Enriquez** /-enˈriːkez/, also **Xalapa**) a city in east-central Mexico, capital of the state of Veracruz; pop. (1990) 288,330. It is a commercial centre in a coffee- and tobacco-growing area and is known for the plant (*Exogonium purga*) from which the medicinal purgative jalap is made.

**Jalgaon** /ˈdʒɑːlˌgaʊn/ a town and rail junction in Maharashtra, west-central India, on the Tapi River north-east of Bombay; pop. (1991) 241,600.

**Jalisco** /hæˈliːskəʊ/ a state of west-central Mexico, on the Pacific coast; area 80,836 sq. km. (31,223 sq. miles); pop. (1990) 5,278,990; capital, Guadalajara.

**Jalna** /ˈdʒɑːlnə/ a town in Maharashtra, west-central India, south-east of Aurangabad; pop. (1991) 174,960.

**Jamaica**
/dʒəˈmeɪkə/ an island country in the Caribbean Sea, south-east of Cuba; area 10,956 sq. km. (4,230 sq. miles); pop. (est. 1990) 2,500,000; official language, English; capital, Kingston.

The third-largest Caribbean Island, Jamaica is dominated by mountain ranges that rise to 2,221 m. (7,402 ft.) at Blue Mountain. The climate is humid and tropical, but during November to March it can be cooler, particularly along the north coast. Subject to occasional hurricanes, Jamaica was badly affected by Hurricane Gilbert in 1988. The population is largely of African, Afro-European, and East Indian descent and the economy is based on both agriculture (sugar, bananas, citrus, and cocoa) and industry, in the latter respect particularly upon bauxite and aluminium. Discovered by Columbus in 1494, Jamaica remained a Spanish colony until conquered by the British in 1655. British colonial rule was threatened by popular violence in the mid-19th c., which led to the suspension of representative government for two decades, but self- government was granted in 1944, and in 1962 Jamaica became an independent Commonwealth state. The country is governed by an executive prime minister and a bicameral parliament.

**Jamaican** adj. & n.

Jamaica is divided into three counties and 14 parishes:

| Parish | Area (sq. km.) | Pop. (1989) | Capital |
|---|---|---|---|
| **Cornwall** | | | |
| Hanover | 448 | 65,600 | Lucea |
| Westmorland | 787 | 127,700 | Savanna-la-mar |
| St. Elizabeth | 1,207 | 144,900 | Black River |
| St. James | 596 | 155,700 | Montego Bay |
| Trelawny | 874 | 73,700 | Falmouth |
| **Middlesex** | | | |
| Manchester | 827 | 163,100 | Mandeville |
| St. Ann | 1,213 | 149,100 | St. Ann's Bay |
| Clarendon | 1,197 | 216,600 | May Pen |
| St. Catherine | 1,195 | 356,600 | Spanish Town |
| St. Mary | 608 | 112,000 | Port Maria |
| **Surrey** | | | |
| Portland | 812 | 77,200 | Port Antonio |
| St. Thomas | 742 | 86,200 | Morant Bay |
| Kingston | 22 } | 661,600 | Kingston |
| St. Andrew | 430 } | | Half Way Tree |

**Jamalpur** /dʒʌməlˈpʊə(r)/ a city in northern Bangladesh, on the Brahmaputra north-west of Mymensingh; pop. (1991) 101,000.

**Jambi** /ˈdʒæmbɪ/ (also **Djambi**) a city in southern Sumatra, Indonesia, situated on the

Batanghari River north-west of Palembang; pop. (1980) 230,000.

**Jambol** see YAMBOL.

**James** /dʒeɪmz/ (also **Dakota**) a river of northern USA that rises in North Dakota and flows 1,142 km. (710 miles) southwards into South Dakota where it meets the Missouri.

**James Bay** a shallow southern arm of Hudson Bay, Canada, explored in 1610 by Henry Hudson but later named in honour of Captain Thomas James who visited the region in 1631. Trading posts at the mouths of rivers feeding into the bay formerly acted as centres for gathering furs brought down stream by Cree Indians. The controversial James Bay Project, announced in 1971, entailed the flooding of large tracts of land and the diversion of water to reservoirs on the Grande Prairie River which feeds into James Bay. The Indian village of Fort George (Chisasibi) was relocated and a massive underground hydroelectric power plant was constructed.

**Jamestown** /'dʒeɪmztaʊn/ the site of an English colony established on the Virginia Peninsula in 1607 during the reign of James I, the first permament English settlement in the New World. Built on a marshy and unhealthy site, the town suffered badly at the hands of fire, disease, and Indians, and was finally abandoned when the colony's capital was moved to Williamsburg at the end of the 17th c. With Williamsburg and Yorkton, Jamestown is now part of Virginia's Colonial National Historic Park.

**Jamestown** the capital and chief port of the island of St. Helena; pop. (1981) 1,500.

**Jammu** /'dʒʌmu:/ the railhead and winter capital of the state of Jammu and Kashmir in north-west India, on the Tawi River, a tributary of the Chenab; pop. (1991) 206,000. The Old Fort and the maharaja's palace dominate the city.

**Jammu and Kashmir** /'dʒʌmu:, kæʃ'mɪə(r)/ a state in north-west India; area 100,569 sq. km. (38,845 sq. miles); pop. (est. 1991) 7,718,700; capital, Srinagar (summer), Jammu (winter). Over 60 per cent of the predominantly Urdu-speaking population are Muslims. (See KASHMIR.)

**Jamnagar** /dʒʌm'nɑ:gə(r)/ a city in the state of Gujarat, western India, a port on the Gulf of Kutch; pop. (1991) 365,460. It was a pearl-fishing town and capital of the former princely state of Nawanagar whose ruler from 1907 to 1933 was the famous cricketer Ranjitsinghji. The walled city is famous for its tie-dyed fabrics, embroidery, and silverware, and as a centre for the study of herbal medicine.

**Jamshedpur** /'dʒʌmʃed,pʊə(r)/ (also **Tatanagar**) an industrial city in the state of Bihar, north-east India, at the junction of the Karkhai and Subarnarekha rivers; pop. (1991) 834,535. Located close to iron and coal deposits, it was established in 1908 as a steel town by the industrialist Jamshedji Tata. It is the home of India's National Metallurgical Laboratory.

**Janesville** /'dʒeɪnz,vɪl/ a city in southern Wisconsin, USA, on the Rock River; pop. (1990) 52,130. Founded in 1836 by Henry F. Janes, it produces motor vehicles.

**Jan Mayen** /jæn 'maɪən/ a barren and virtually uninhabited island in the Arctic Ocean between Greenland and Norway, annexed by Norway in 1929. It lies 1,000 km. (621 miles) from Norway and was probably first sighted by Henry Hudson in 1607, but is named after a Dutch sea captain, Jan May, who claimed the island for his company and his country in 1614. Situated on the mid-Atlantic ridge, Jan Mayen is subject to earth tremors and volcanic activity, Mount Beerenberg (2,300 m., 7,546 ft.) being Norway's only active volcano. Once used as a whaling and sealing base, it now functions as a station for weather observations and radio services.

**Jansenism** /'dʒænsənɪzm/ a religious movement of the 17th and 18th c., based on the writings of the Dutch Roman Catholic theologian, Cornelius Jansen, and characterized by general harshness and moral rigour. Its most famous exponent was Pascal. The movement received papal condemnation and its adherents were persecuted in France (though tolerated in The Netherlands) during most of the 18th c.

**Japan** /dʒə'pæn/ (Japanese **Nippon**) official name **Japan** a country in eastern Asia, occupying a festoon of islands in the Pacific, stretching some 3,200 km. (2,000 miles) in a line roughly parallel with  the east coast of the Asiatic mainland from which it is separated by the Sea of Japan; area 377,815 sq. km. (145,931 sq. miles); pop. (1990) 123,612,000; official language, Japanese; capital, Tokyo. Its largest cities are Tokyo, Yokohama, Osaka, and Nagoya. Japan comprises the four main islands of Honshu, Hokkaido, Shikoku, and Kyushu, and more than 3,900 smaller islands. About four-fifths of the main islands are mountainous, rising to a height of 3,776 m. (12,385 ft.) at Mt. Fuji. Subject to occasional earthquakes, Japan has a climate that ranges from subtropical on Okinawa to cool temperate on Hokkaido. There is a rainy season in summer associated with the Asiatic monsoon. Japan has few natural resources and less than 20 per cent of its land is suitable for cultivation, but it is now the leading economic power in East Asia and the most highly industrialized country in that region, with a range of manufacturing industries that includes electrical goods, motor vehicles,

chemicals, and shipping. According to Japanese tradition, the empire was founded in 660 BC by the emperor Jimmu, a descendant of the sun goddess. After a long period of courtly rule centred on Kyoto, from the 12th c. onwards the country was dominated by succeeding clans of military warriors. With the restoration of direct Imperial rule in 1868 it entered the modernizing process, which was accelerated by wars with China (1894–5) and Russia (1904–5), but Japan did not become a major world power until the 20th c. Its occupation of the Chinese province of Manchuria in 1931 was followed by full-scale invasion of China in 1937. In 1936 an alliance was formed with Germany and later with Italy. After attacking Pearl Harbor (1941) the Japanese invaded Malaya and captured Hong Kong, Manila, and Singapore. Their advance was halted by a series of US air and naval victories in 1942–4, and Japan surrendered in 1945 after the dropping of atomic bombs on Hiroshima and Nagasaki; a constitutional monarchy was established in 1947 and the country was placed under the international control of the Allied Powers until 1952. In 1972 the USA returned control of the Ryuku, Bonin, and Volcano Islands to Japan, but a dispute still exists with Russia over the Kuriles which were occupied by the former USSR after the war. The country is governed by an executive prime minister and a bicameral Diet that comprises a House of Representatives and a House of Councillors.
**Japanese** *adj. & n.*
Japan is divided into nine regions and 47 prefectures:

| Region | Area (sq. km.) | Pop. (1990) |
| --- | --- | --- |
| Chubu | 66,743 | 21,022,000 |
| Chugoku | 31,847 | 7,746,000 |
| Hokkaido | 83,513 | 5,644,000 |
| Kanto | 32,309 | 38,541,000 |
| Kinki | 33,038 | 22,207,000 |
| Kyushu | 42,084 | 13,296,000 |
| Okinawa | 2,246 | 1,222,000 |
| Shikoku | 18,795 | 4,195,000 |
| Tohoku | 66,959 | 9,738,000 |

**Japan, Sea of** an arm of the Pacific Ocean separating Japan from the mainland of the continent of Asia.

**Japanese** /ˌdʒæpəˈniːz/ the official language of Japan, spoken by virtually the whole population of that country. Japanese is an agglutinative language. It contains many Chinese loan-words and has no genders, no article, and no number in nouns or verbs. It is written vertically or horizontally, in a system that is partly ideographic and partly syllabic. The ideographs (known as *kanji*) were adopted from the Chinese in the early centuries of the Christian era and designate the chief meaningful elements of the language. They are supplemented by two groups of syllabic characters (*kana*), known as *hiragana* and *katakana*, for the agglutinative and inflexional endings. Attempts have been made to abolish characters altogether, but this is thought by many to be unsatisfactory since many words look exactly alike when written in Roman letters. There is no definite link between Japanese and any other language, although it may be related to Korean.

**Japurá** /ˌʒɑːpʊˈrɑː/ a river of South America that rises in south-west Colombia (where it is known as the Caquetá) and flows south-eastwards for 2,414 km. (1,500 miles) into Brazil where it joins the Amazon.

**Jari** /ʒəˈriː/ a river in north-eastern Brazil that rises in the Tumucumaqua Mountains and flows south-eastwards for 576 km. (360 miles) to join the Amazon near its mouth. Its southern reaches around the company town of Monte Dourada have been the focal point of rice and forestry projects since the late 1960s.

**Jarlshof** /ˈjɑːlzhɒf/ the site of a late Bronze Age settlement at the south-western tip of the mainland of Shetland. Occupied for over 3,000 years, its ruins were discovered in 1905 when a storm revealed sections of huge stone walls.

**Jarrow** /ˈdʒærəʊ/ a town and port in Tyne and Wear, north-east England on the Tyne estuary east of Newcastle; pop. (1981) 31,310. From the 7th c. until the Viking invasions its monastery was a centre of Northumbrian Christian culture; the Venerable Bede lived and worked there. Its name is associated with the hunger marches to London by the unemployed during the economic depression of the 1930s.

**Järvenpää** /ˌjɑːvənˈpɑː/ a town in southern Finland, to the north of Helsinki; pop. (1990) 31,525. It was the home of the composer Jean Sibelius.

**Jarvis Island** an uninhabited tropical island in the South Pacific, situated just south of the equator 2,090 km. (1,315 miles) south of Hawaii; area 4.6 sq. km. (1.8 sq. miles). It is an unincorporated territory of the USA.

**Jasper National Park** /ˈdʒæspə(r)/ a national park in the Rocky Mountains of Alberta, Canada; area 10,878 sq. km. (4,199 sq. miles). It is the largest park in the Rockies. The town of Jasper, on the Athabasca River, was originally known to fur traders as Fitzhugh. It developed in 1911 with the arrival of the railway and two years later its name was changed in honour of a resident named Jasper Hawes.

**Jassy** see IAŞI.

**Java** /ˈdʒɑːvə/ (Indonesian **Jawa**) a large island in the Malay Archipelago, forming part of Indonesia; area 132,187 sq. km. (51,057 sq. miles); pop. (est. 1993) 112,158,200 (with Madura). Java contains almost 60 per cent of the population of Indonesia. Over 100 volcanoes, many of them active, traverse the island from east to west; most are densely forested and there are millions of acres of teak plantations. Rubber, tea, coffee, cacao are also grown in the highlands; rice and sugar-cane on fertile lowland soils. Java has been the cultural and economic centre of the region for centuries. The island was chiefly under Dutch rule from the 17th c. and was occupied by Japanese troops during World War II. Its chief city is Jakarta. **Javan** or **Javanese** *adj. & n.*

**Javanese** /ˌdʒɑːvənˈiːz/ the language of Java, which belongs to the Malayo-Polynesian group of languages.

**Java Sea** a sea in the Malay Archipelago of south-east Asia surrounded by the islands of Borneo, Java, and Sumatra.

**Jayapura** /ˌdʒɑːjəˈpʊə(r)ə/ a seaport on the north coast of the island of New Guinea, capital of the Indonesian province of West Irian (Irian Jaya); pop. (1980) 45,790. Under Dutch rule it was known as Hollandia.

**Jaya Peak** /ˈdʒɑːjə/ (Indonesian **Puncak Jaya** or **Victory Peak**) a mountain in western New Guinea in the Indonesian province of West Irian (Irian Jaya). Rising to 5,030 m. (16,503 ft.) in the north-west corner of the Lorentz Reserve, it is the highest peak in Indonesia. It was formerly known as Gunung Carstenz.

**jebel** see JABAL.

**Jedburgh** /ˈdʒedbərə/ an abbey town in the Borders Region of southern Scotland, on the Jed Water. Situated near the English border, where disputes frequently arose between border peoples, it gave its name to *Jedburgh Justice*, a summary procedure whereby a person is sentenced first and tried later.

**Jeddah** /ˈdʒedə/ (also **Jiddah** /ˈdʒɪdə/) a large deep-water seaport on the Red Sea coast of Saudi Arabia, west of Mecca; pop. (est. 1986) 1,400,000. It is the administrative capital of Saudi Arabia, commercial capital of Makkah province, and Saudi Arabia's largest port. It is also a port of entry on the pilgrimage route to Mecca, often through the ultra-modern airport.

**Jefferson City** /ˈdʒefəs(ə)n/ the state capital of Missouri, USA, on the Missouri River; pop. (1990) 35,480. Selected to be state capital in 1821, it was named after President Thomas Jefferson. It is the home of Lincoln University of Missouri (1866).

**Jehol** /dʒeˈhɒl/ a former province of north-eastern China that formed the traditional gateway to Mongolia and now forms part of Inner Mongolia, Hebei, and Liaoning.

**Jehovah's Witness** a member of a sect of American origin, the Watch Tower Tract and Bible Society, founded c. 1879 by Charles Taze Russell (1852–1916) of Pittsburgh, Pennsylvania, denying many of the traditional Christian doctrines and refusing to acknowledge the claims of the state when these conflict with the sect's principles.

**Jena** /ˈjeɪnə/ a university town in Thuringia, central Germany, on the River Saale; pop. (1991) 100,970. It was the scene of a battle (1806) in which Napoleon defeated the Prussians. It produces chemicals and optical instruments.

**Jerash** /dʒɜːˈrɑːʃ/ (also **Jarash** or **Gerash**) a village in the East Bank, north-west Jordan, north of Amman. It is built on the site of the ancient city of Gerasa which flourished in the 2nd and 3rd c. AD and is one of the best-preserved Palestinian cities of Roman times.

**Jerba** see DJERBA.

**Jerez** /ˈhereθ/ (in full **Jerez de la Frontera**) a town in the Andalusian province of Cadiz, southern Spain; pop. (1991) 184,020. It is the centre of the sherry-making industry and gives its name to the wine.

**Jericho** /ˈdʒerɪˌkəʊ/ (Arabic **El Riha**) an ancient oasis town of Palestine, in the West Bank north of the Dead Sea. It has been occupied from at least c. 9000 BC and is reckoned to be one of the oldest continuously inhabited cities in the world. According to the Old Testament, Jericho was destroyed by the Israelites after they crossed the Jordan into the Promised Land, its walls having been flattened by the shout of the army at the blast of the trumpets (Joshua 2–6). Historic sites include the Tell of Old Jericho, the Hisham Palace, and the Mount of the Temptation where Jesus is said to have fasted for 40 days after being baptized by John. In the surrounding area irrigated agriculture produces dates, bananas, and oranges. It was designated the administrative centre for Palestinian self-rule in Gaza and the West Bank in 1993.

**Jersey** /ˈdʒɜːzɪ/ the largest of the Channel Islands; area 116 sq. km. (45 sq. miles); pop. (1990) 82,810; capital, St. Helier. It gives its name to a type of woollen pullover and to a breed of light-brown dairy cattle that originated in Jersey, producing milk with a high fat content. Market gardening is important and the island is a popular holiday resort and tax-haven.

**Jersey City** an industrial city in north-east New Jersey, USA, on a peninsula between the Hudson and Hackensack rivers opposite New York; pop. (1990) 228,540. It is a major US manufacturing and transportation centre, linked to Manhattan Island opposite by the Holland Tunnel and the Port Authority Trans-Hudson (PATH) rapid transit system. It has railway workshops, oil refineries, warehouses, and many factories. A major landmark is the 15.2-m. (50-ft.) diameter Colgate Clock at 105 Hudson Street.

**Jerusalem** /dʒəˈruːsələm/ (Hebrew **Yerushalayim**) the holy city of the Jews, sacred also to Christians and Muslims, lying in the Judaean hills about 30 km. (20 miles) from the Jordan River, proclaimed by the State of Israel its capital; pop. (1987) 482,700. It was a Canaanite stronghold, captured by David (c. 1000 BC) who made it the capital of the national state; after the building of the Temple by Solomon it became a religious as well as a political capital. Since then it has shared the troubled history of its area—destroyed by the Babylonians in 586 BC and by the Romans in AD 70, refounded by Hadrian as a gentile city (AD 135) under the name of Aelia Capitolina, destroyed again by the Persians in 614, and fought over by Saracens and Crusaders in the Middle Ages; Suleiman the Magnificent rebuilt its walls (1542). From 1947 the city was divided between the states of Israel and Jordan until the Israelis occupied the whole city in June 1967. In 1980 it was declared capital of Israel, a status not recognized by the UN and many countries which retain embassies in Tel Aviv. Its Christian history begins with the short ministry of Christ, culminating in his crucifixion. For Muslims Jerusalem is the holiest city after Mecca and Medina, containing the Dome of the Rock (where Muhammad was carried up to heaven), one of Islam's most sacred sites. After World War II it was envisaged by the United Nations as an international city, but was seized by Israel during the Six Day War of 1967 and proclaimed the eternal and indivisible capital of the state of Israel. Jerusalem is an administrative, religious, and cultural centre. Construction and tourism are important industries.

**Jervis Bay Territory** /'dʒɜːvɪs/ a territory on Jervis Bay on the south-east coast of Australia, c. 195 km. (122 miles) south of Sydney; area 70 sq. km. (27 sq. miles); pop. (1991) c. 800. Incorporated in 1915 as a sea outlet for the Australian Capital Territory, it developed as a port and naval base. In 1988 it separated from the Capital Territory and in 1992 some 80 per cent of the territory was designated a National Park.

**Jessore** /dʒəˈsɔː(r)/ the capital city of Jessore region in south-west Bangladesh, on the River Ganges; pop. (1991) 176,400. It is an important road junction and market for local produce such as tobacco, linseed, rice, sugar, and tamarind.

**Jesuit** /'dʒezjʊɪt/ a member of the Society of Jesus, an order of priests founded in 1534 in Paris by Ignatius Loyola, Francis Xavier, and others. The Society became the spearhead of the Counter-Reformation, though originally intended as a missionary order. Its genius is found in Ignatius' *Spiritual Exercises*. The success of Jesuits as missionaries, teachers, scholars, and spiritual directors—as well as the fear they have inspired— manifests how close they have been to their ideal of a disciplined force, effective in the cause of the Roman Church.
**Jesuitical** *adj.*

**Jew** /dʒuː/ a person of Hebrew descent or whose religion is Judaism. Ashkenazim are Jews of European origin and Sephardic Jews are of Afro-Asian origin. European Jews were traditionally the subject of persecution by the Christian majority, partly as a result of religious prejudice but also because of jealousy of Jewish commercial success and because the Jewish community tended to maintain a separate and highly distinct identity. Anti-Semitism was a feature of European life from the Middle Ages, the killing of Jews being a common response to economic or social crisis, and in the modern age anti-Semitism became a central part of many right-wing political philosophies, most notably Nazism. In medieval England, Jews were particularly familiar as money-lenders, their activities being publicly regulated for them by the Crown, whose protégés they were. (In private Christians also practised money-lending, though forbidden to do so by Canon Law.) Thus they came to be associated in the popular mind with usury. There are an estimated 17.4 million Jews throughout the world of which 6.9 million live in North America, 5.4 million in Asia, and 3.7 million in Europe.
**Jewish** *adj.*

**Jewel Cave** a cave in the Black Hills of South Dakota, USA, noted for its lining of sparkling calcite crystal and for its passageways which extend over 96 km. (60 miles). Explored by Herbert and Jan Conn in the 1960s and 1970s the cave system, which is a national monument, is one of the largest in the world.

**Jewish Republic** an autonomous oblast in the Far East of Russia, forming part of Khabarovsk Territory in the basins of the Biro and Bidzhan rivers; area 36,000 sq. km. (13,895 sq. miles); capital, Birobidzhan. It was made a Jewish National District of the USSR in 1928, forming a home territory for Jews and a frontier settlement in the vulnerable Soviet far east, and in 1934 it became an autonomous region, but it never attracted many Jewish settlers who continue to make up a small share of its total population. After the breakup of the Soviet Union in 1991 it was declared an autonomous oblast of the Russian Federation.

**Jewish calendar** a complex ancient calendar in use among Jews. It is a lunar calendar adapted to the solar year, having normally 12 months, but 13 months in leap years which occur 7 times in every cycle of 19 years. The years are reckoned from the Creation (371 BC); the months are Nisan (normally March–April), Iyar (April–May), Sivan (May–June), Tammuz (June–July), Ab (July–Aug.), Elul (Aug.–Sept.), Tishri (Sept.–Oct.), Cheshvan (Oct.–Nov.), Kislev (Nov.–Dec.), Teveth (Dec.–Jan.), Shebat (Jan.–Feb.), Adar (Feb.–March.), 2nd Adar (intercalary month). The ecclesiastical year begins with Nisan and ends with Tishri.

**Jeypore** see JAIPUR.

**Jhansi** a market city and railway centre with metal industries in the state of Uttar Pradesh, northern India; pop. (1991) 368,580. It was the capital of the Maratha principality from 1770 to

1853 and its fort was seized and occupants slaughtered in 1857 during the Sepoy Mutiny.

**Jhelum** /'dʒeɪləm/ a river that rises in the Himalayas and flows for about 720 km. (450 miles) through the Vale of Kashmir into the province of Punjab in Pakistan, where it meets the Chenab River. It is one of the 'five rivers' that gave Punjab its name. In ancient times it was called the Hydaspes.

**Jiamusi** /dʒiæ'mʊsɪ/ a city in Heilongjiang province, north-east China, on the Songhua River north-east of Harbin; pop. (1986) 571,000.

**Ji'an** /dʒi:'ɑ:n/ a city in Jiangxi province, south-east-central China, on the Gan River south-west of Nanchang; pop. (1986) 186,000.

**Jiangmen** /dʒɪæŋ'men/ a city in Guangdong province, southern China, on a branch of the Pearl River south-west of Guangzhou (Canton); pop. (1986) 240,000.

**Jiangsu** /dʒɪæŋ'su:/ (formerly **Kiangsu**) a province of eastern China; area 103,000 sq. km. (39,784 sq. miles); pop. (1990) 67,057,000; capital, Nanjing. It includes the lower reaches of the Yangtze River and is the most densely populated of the provinces of China. It is a major producer of agricultural and industrial goods including rice, wheat, maize, oil seed, silkworm cocoons, textiles, paper, and cigarettes.

**Jiangxi** /dʒɪæŋ'ʃi:/ (formerly **Kiangsi**) a province of south-east China to the south of the Yangtze River; area 169,000 sq. km. (65,276 sq. miles); pop. (1990) 37,710,000; capital, Nanchang. It includes Poyang, China's largest freshwater lake. Coal, porcelain, rice, timber, livestock, and fruit are its chief products.

**Jiaojiang** /dʒaʊ'dʒæŋ/ a city in Zhejiang province, eastern China, a port on the East China Sea; pop. (1986) 158,000.

**Jiaozou** /dʒaʊ'zəʊ/ a city in Henan province, east-central China, north-west of Zhengzhou; pop. (1986) 519,000.

**Jiaxing** /dʒɪæ'ʃɪŋ/ a city in Zhejiang province, eastern China, on the Grand Canal south-west of Shanghai; pop. (1986) 697,000.

**Jiayuguan** /dʒɪæju:'gwɑ:n/ a city in Gansu province, northern China, in the northern foothills of the Qilian Shan Mountains; pop. (1986) 103,000.

**Jibuti** see DJIBOUTI.

**Jiddah** see JEDDAH.

**Jihlava** /'jɪləwə/ a town in the uplands of South Moravia in the Czech Republic, on the River Jihlava; pop. (1991) 108,460. A royal town that developed with the discovery of silver in the Middle Ages, Jihlava has one of the largest squares in Europe. The composer Gustav Mahler spent part of his childhood here.

**Jijiga** /'dʒi:dʒɪgə/ a town in eastern Ethiopia, 80 km. (50 miles) east of Harar.

**Jilin** /dʒi:'lɪn/ **1.** (formerly **Kirin**) a province of north-east China; area 187,000 sq. km. (72,229 sq. miles); pop. (1990) 24,659,000; capital, Changchun. Occupying part of the north-east plain, its chief resources include coal, iron ore, gold, copper, and timber. Agricultural crops include maize, soy beans, sugar beet, rice, millet, and ginseng. **2.** an industrial city in Jilin province, China, east of Changchun; pop. (1986) 3,974,000. A shipping port with oil refineries and large chemical plants.

**jima** /'dʒi:mə/ see SHIMA.

**Jinan** /dʒi:'næn/ (formerly **Tsinan**) a city of eastern China, the capital of Shandong province; pop. (1990) 3,376,000. Dating from neolithic times, Jinan emerged as a commercial centre during the Yang dynasty (618–907). It is noted for its natural springs and silk industries.

**Jinchang** /dʒɪn'tʃæŋ/ a city in Gansu province, northern China, situated near the western end of the Great Wall of China; pop. (1986) 142,000.

**Jincheng** /dʒɪn'tʃeŋ/ a city in southern Shanxi province, east-central China, to the north-west of Zhengzhou; pop. (1986) 621,000.

**Jingmen** /dʒɪŋ'men/ a city in Hubei province, east-central China, situated between the Yangtze and Huan rivers north-west of Wuhan; pop. (1986) 957,000.

**Jinhua** /dʒɪn'hwɑ:/ a city in Zhejiang province, eastern China, situated to the south of Hangzhou; pop. (1986) 869,000.

**Jining** /dʒɪn'ɪŋ/ **1.** a city in Inner Mongolia, northern China, east of Hohhot; pop. (1986) 220,000. **2.** a city in Shandong province, eastern China, on the Grand Canal, to the south of Jinan and the Yellow River; pop. (1986) 166,000.

**Jinja** /'dʒɪndʒə/ a town in the province of Busoga, south-east Uganda, on the north shore of Lake Victoria; pop. (est. 1983) 45,000. Founded as a trading post in 1901, it is now a trading and food processing centre.

**Jinshi** /dʒɪn'ʃi:/ a city in Hubei province, east-central China, north-west of Dongting Lake; pop. (1986) 218,000.

**Jinzhou** /dʒɪn'dʒəʊ/ a city in Liaoning province, north-eastern China; pop. (1986) 4,448,000.

**Jipijapa** /ˌhi:pi:'hɑ:pə/ a small market town in the province of Manabi in the equatorial lowlands of western Ecuador; pop. (1982) 27,150. It is an important centre for the production of Panama hats.

**Jishou** /dʒɪ'ʃəʊ/ a city in Hunan province, south-central China, in the Wuling Shan Mountains west of Changsha; pop. (1986) 199,000.

**Jiujiang** /dʒʊ'dʒæŋ/ a city in north Jiangxi province, east-central China, on the Yangtze River south-east of Wuhan; pop. (1986) 390,000.

**Jiuquan** /dʒʊˈkwɑːn/ a town in Gansu province, northern China, in the northern foothills of the Qilian Shan Mountains east of Jiayaguan; pop. (1986) 280,000.

**Jivaro** /hɪˈvɑːrəʊ/ an Amerindian people of South America living a subsistence life of hunting, fishing, and farming in the tropical forests of eastern Ecuador and Peru. Their language belongs to the Andean-Equatorial group of languages.

**Jixi** /dʒiːˈʃiː/ a city in Heilongjiang province, north-eastern China, on the Muling River east of Harbin; pop. (1990) 860,000.

**João Pessoa** the capital city of Paraíba state, north-east Brazil, on the Atlantic coast 120 km. (75 miles) north of Recife; pop. (1991) 497,000. Founded in 1585, the city's principal attraction is a Franciscan convent, one of Brazil's finest churches. It is a resort city with light industries.

**Jodhpur** /ˈdʒɒdpʊə(r)/ **1.** a former princely state of India, now part of Rajasthan. **2.** a city in the state of Rajasthan, western India, on the southern edge of the Thar Desert; pop. (1991) 648,620. Founded in 1459 by Rao Jodha, chief of the Rathore Tajput clan, it is the second-largest city in Rajasthan and has light industries. Its Indo-Deco style palace was designed by H. V. Lanchester and completed in 1944. The city gives its name to long breeches for riding etc., close-fitting from the knee to the ankle.

**Jodrell Bank** /ˈdʒɒdr(ə)l/ the site in Cheshire, England, of the Nuffield Radio Astronomy Laboratory of Manchester University. It has one of the world's largest radio telescopes, with a giant reflector, 76 m. (250 ft.) in diameter, that can be tilted in any direction.

**Joensuu** /ˈjɒɒnsuː/ a city in the lake district of south-east Finland, capital of the province of Pohjois-Karjala; pop. (1990) 47,550. Established as a copper-mining town in 1848, it is now a commercial centre trading in timber.

**Jogjakarta** see YOGYAKARTA.

**Johannesburg** /dʒəʊˈhænɪsˌbɜːg/ the largest city in South Africa, the centre of its gold-mining industry, and the financial and commercial capital of the prosperous Witwatersrand; pop. (1985) 1,609,000. Founded in 1886 and probably named after Johannes Meyer, the first mining commissioner, it lies at the centre of a large conurbation of municipalities and townships including the township of Soweto, at an altitude of 1,754 m. (5,750 ft.). It was made capital of the province of Pretoria-Witwatersrand-Vereeniging in 1994. It has chemical, pharmaceutical, metal, machinery, and textile industries. It is also a diamond-cutting centre.

**John Hart–Peace River Highway** the name given to the northern extension of the Cariboo Highway in British Columbia, Canada. It starts at Prince George on the Yellowhead Highway and stretches north for 412 km. (256 miles) to join the Alaska Highway at Dawson Creek. A western route follows the Peace River to Fort St. John.

**John o' Groats** /dʒɒn ə ˈɡrəʊts/ a village at the extreme north-east point of the Scottish mainland in the district of Caithness. It is said to be named from a house built there in the 16th c. by a Dutchman, John Groot. (Compare LAND'S END.)

**Johnston Islands** a coral atoll enclosing four small islands—Johnston, Sand, North (Akau), and East (Hikina)—in the central Pacific Ocean, southwest of Hawaii, discovered by Capt. Johnston of the *Cornwallis* in 1807. Claimed by Hawaii, its guano was shipped to the US which eventually established a naval base here in 1941. The islands have been used as a nuclear-testing and waste-disposal site for toxic gas; area 2.8 sq. km. (1 sq. mile).

**Johor** /dʒəˈhɔː(r)/ (also **Johore**) a state of Malaysia, at the southernmost point of mainland Asia, joined to Singapore by a causeway; area 18,985 sq. km. (7,333 sq. miles); pop. (1990) 2,106,000; capital Johor Baharu.

**Johor Baharu** /dʒəˌhɔː ˈbɑːruː/ the capital of the state of Johor in Malaysia, situated at the southern tip of the Malay Peninsula opposite Singapore Island; pop. (1980) 246,400. It is an industrial outlier of Singapore, gateway to Malaysia, and trade centre for local produce.

**Johor, Straits of** (Malay **Selat Tebrau**) the channel separating Singapore from the southern tip of the Malay Peninsula. It was crossed by a causeway in 1924 and bridge in the 1990s.

**Joinville** /ˈʒɔmviːliː/ an industrial city in the state of Santa Catarina, southern Brazil, on the Cachoeira River north of Blumenau; pop. (1990) 321,600.

**jökull** /ˈjəʊkəl/ an Icelandic word for a glacier, as in Vatnajökull.

**Joliet** /ˌdʒɒlɪˈet/ an industrial city in north-east Illinois, USA, on the Des Plaines River; pop. (1990) 76,840. Settled in 1831, its growth was boosted by the building of the Chicago Sanitary and Ship Canal and by the arrival of railroad freight lines. The canal's Brandon Road Locks, to the south of Joliet, are among the largest in the world. It was formerly a major supplier of steel and limestone, but now produces chemicals, petroleum products, and electronic parts. Named after the 17th-c. French-Canadian explorer Louis Joliette, it was incorporated in 1837 as Juliet, companion to the nearby town of Romeo (now Romeoville).

**Joliette** /ˌdʒɒlɪˈet/ a town in the Lanaudière region of Quebec, eastern Canada; pop. (1991) 31,400. A noted centre of art, it was founded in 1841 by Barthélemi Joliette, a descendant of the Louis Joliette who explored Mississippi.

**Jönköping** /jɜːˈnˈtʃɜːpɪŋ/ an industrial city in southern Sweden, at the south end of Lake

Vättern; pop. (1990) 111,490. It is capital of Jönköping county. It produces safety-matches, textiles, paper, and machinery.

**Jonquière** /'ʒɒnkiːer/ a town in Quebec, Canada, on the Saguenay River west of Chicoutimi; pop. (1991) 57,900; 160,930 (with Chicoutimi).

**Joppa** see JAFFA.

**Jordan** /'dʒɔːd(ə)n/ official name **The Hashemite Kingdom of Jordan** a country in the Middle East east of the River Jordan, bordering Syria, Israel, Saudi Arabia, 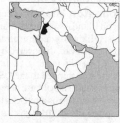 and Iraq; area 89,206 sq. km. (35,475 sq. miles); pop. (est. 1990) 3,060,000; official language, Arabic; capital, Amman. Largely an extension of the Syrian Desert, nearly 90 per cent of Jordan is unfit for cultivation. The climate is Mediterranean with a rainy season from November to March. Its natural resources are meagre, and its only outlet to the sea is the port of Aqaba at the north-east end of the Red Sea. The most important industries are phosphate-mining and tourism. Hittites, Israelites, Egyptians, Assyrians, Babylonians, Persians, Greeks, Romans, Arabs, and Crusaders dominated the area successively until it fell under Turkish rule in the 16th c. In 1916 the land east of the River Jordan was made a British protectorate, the Amirate of Transjordan; this became independent in 1946 as the Hashemite Kingdom of Jordan. During the Arab–Israeli war of 1948–9 the Jordanians overran a large area on the west bank of the river, but were driven from this by Israel in the Six-Day War of 1967. Jordan is a constitutional monarchy with an executive prime minister and a bicameral National Assembly comprising a Senate and a Chamber of Deputies.
**Jordanian** *adj. & n.*

**Jordan** a river flowing from the Anti-Lebanon mountains on the Lebanon–Syria frontier southward for 320 km. (200 miles) through the sea of Galilee and into the Dead Sea. It has many biblical associations, especially with the life of Jesus.

**Jos** /dʒɒs/ a tin- and columbite-mining and trading town on the Jos plateau, central Nigeria; pop. (1991) 149,000. It is capital of Plateau state and, because of its altitude and surrounding scenery, a popular hill resort.

**Joshua Tree** /'dʒɒʃjuə/ a national park in southern California, USA, preserving the Joshua tree, *Yucca brevifolia*, which is only found in the arid lands of California, western Arizona, and southern Utah.

**Jostedal Glacier** /'juːstə͵dɑːl/ a glacier in Sogn og Fjordane County, western Norway, the largest ice field in Europe.

**Jotunheim** /'jəʊtʊn͵haɪm/ (Norwegian **Jotunheimen**) a mountain range in south-central Norway (Norwegian = home of the giants). Its highest peak is Glittertind (2,472 m., 8,110 ft.).

**Juan de Fuca Strait** /hwɑːn deɪ 'fuːkə/ an inlet of the Pacific Ocean between Vancouver Island and the US state of Washington. It is named after a Spanish navigator who allegedly discovered it in 1592.

**Juan de Nova Island** an uninhabited island in the Mozambique Channel, administered as a dependency of France but claimed by Madagascar; area 4.4 sq. km. (1.7 sq. miles). It is a source of guano.

**Juan Fernandez Islands** /hwɑːn fə'nændez/ (Spanish **Archipelago de Juan Fernández**) a group of three islands in the Pacific Ocean, 640 km. (400 miles) west of Chile. The islands, which were frequented by seal-hunters and Dutch and English pirates, take their name from a Spanish navigator who discovered them in 1574 and in 1704 Alexander Selkirk (Daniel Defoe's prototype for *Robinson Crusoe*) was marooned here; area 181 sq. km. (70 sq. miles).

**Juan-les-Pins** /ʒwæn leɪ pæn/ a popular resort on the French Riviera, in the Alpes-Maritimes department of southern France. It lies on a bay of the Cap d'Antibes between Nice and Cannes and has a fine beach. It hosts a famous jazz festival each summer.

**Juba** /'dʒuːbə/ (also **Jubba**) a river of East Africa, rising in the highlands of central Ethiopia and flowing southwards for *c.* 1,600 km. (1,000 miles) through Somalia to the Indian Ocean. In 1925 the surrounding territory of Jubaland was transferred from Kenya to Italian Somaliland.

**Juba** the capital of the southern region of Sudan, on the White Nile; pop. (est. 1990) 100,000. Since 1983 the city has been virtually isolated by the civil war in Sudan.

**Júcar** /'huːkær/ a river of eastern Spain that rises in the Sierra de Albarracin and flows 502 km. (314 miles) through Valencia to the Mediterranean. It is a source of irrigation water and hydroelectric power.

**Judaea** /dʒuː'diːə/ the southernmost region of ancient Palestine whose chief city was Jerusalem. At the end of the second millennium BC it was established by the Israelite tribe of Judah as an independent kingdom, which lasted until it was overrun by the Babylonians in 587 BC. The Jews returned to Judaea in 537 BC after the Babylonian captivity, and in 165 BC the Maccabees again established it as an independent kingdom. It became a province of the Roman Empire in 63 BC, and was subsequently amalgamated with Palestine.
**Judaean** *adj. & n.*

**Judah** /'dʒuːdə/ the most powerful of the 12 tribes of Israel. After the reign of Solomon it formed a separate kingdom, with Benjamin, which outlasted that of the northern tribes.

**Judaism** /'dʒuːdeɪˌɪz(ə)m/ the religion of the Jews, with a belief in one God and a basis in Mosaic and rabbinical teachings. The Jews were a race called to reject polytheism and worship the one God, the Creator, whose will is revealed in the *Torah* which comprises the first five books of the Bible (also known as the Pentateuch). This monotheism, inherited by both Christianity and Islam, is the heart of the Jewish experience. But it is more than a speculative belief: the decisive events of their history, such as the call of Abraham, the Exodus, the witness of the prophets and the Exile, all draw out its radical moral character of abandonment to God and his often mysterious purposes, with rejection of any human self-reliance.

**Juiz de Fora** /ˌʒwiːʒ de 'fɔːrə/ a textile-manufacturing city in the state of Minas Gerais, eastern Brazil, to the north of Rio De Janaeiro; pop. (1990) 383,210. It has a university founded in 1960.

**Jujuy** /huːˈhwiː/ a city in the eastern Andes of north-west Argentina, on the Bermejo River; pop. (1990) 43,620. It lies at the centre of a mining and cattle-ranching region.

**Júktas** /'jʊktɑːs/, **Mount** (also **Ioúktas**) a mountain rising to a height of 811 m. (2,660 ft.) to the south of Knossos at the centre of the Mediterranean island of Crete. Seen as a reclining bearded god, it was said to have been the burial place of the Cretan Zeus. On its peak there is a modern Greek chapel dedicated to the Metamorphosis and the Transfiguration of Christ.

**Julian Alps** /'dʒuːliən/ an Alpine range in north-east Italy and western Slovenia, rising to a height of 2,864 m. (9,395 ft.) at Triglav.

**Julian calendar** a calendar introduced by Julius Caesar in 46 BC and slightly modified under Augustus, in which the ordinary year has 365 days, and every fourth year (with the exception of the century year) is a leap year of 366 days.

**Julian March** the name formerly given to the territory at the head of the Adriatic lying between the Isonzo and Sava rivers, on the frontier between Italy and Slovenia.

**Jullundur** see JALANDHAR.

**Jumna** /'dʒʌmnə/ (also **Yamuna**) a river in northern India, rising in the Himalayas and flowing *c.* 1,370 km. (850 miles) south-eastwards past Delhi and into the Ganges below Allahabad. Its source (Yamunotri) and its confluence with the Ganges are both Hindu holy places.

**Junagadh** /dʒʌ'nɑːɡəd/ (also **Junagarh**) a town in the state of Gujarat, western India, on the Kathiawar Peninsula south-west of Rajkot; pop. (1991) 166,755. A capital of Gujarat from the 2nd to the 4th century AD, its chief landmark is the Uparkot Citadel. It is a market for handicrafts.

**Jundiaí** /ˌʒʊndjə'iː/ a city and transportation centre in the state of São Paulo, southern Brazil, between São Paulo and Campinas; pop. (1990) 285,680.

**Juneau** /'dʒuːnəʊ/ the state capital of Alaska, a seaport on the Gastineau Channel with an ice-free harbour, an inlet of the Pacific Ocean; pop. (1990) 26,750. It developed after the discovery of gold by Joseph Juneau in 1880. It was designated capital of the Territory of Alaska in 1900 and became state capital in 1959. Fishing, lumbering, and tourism are important industries.

**Junggar Basin** see DZUNGARIA.

**Jungfrau** /'jʊŋfraʊ/ a mountain in the Bernese Alps of south-central Switzerland, 5,158 m. (13,642 ft.) high. Ascended by J. R. and H. Meyer in 1811, it was one of the first major mountains of the Alps to be climbed.

**Juno** /'dʒuːnəʊ/ the name given to part of the Normandy beaches of France near the town of Courseulles-sur-Mer (and lying between Gold Beach and Sword Beach) where Allied troops (the Canadian 3rd Division) landed on 6 June 1944.

**Jura** /'dʒʊərə/ a system of mountain ranges, on the border of France and Switzerland, which has given its name to the Jurassic period when most of its rocks were laid down. The highest peak in the Jura Mts. is Crête de la Neige (1,718 m., 5,636 ft.).

**Jura** a department in the Franch Comté region of eastern France; area 4,999 sq. km. (1,931 sq. miles); pop. (1990) 248,760; capital, Lons-le-Saunier.

**Jura** an island of the Inner Hebrides, separated from the west coast of Scotland by the Sound of Jura. Its principal settlement is Craighouse. The author George Orwell (Eric Blair) lived at Barnhill on the north-east coast from 1946 until his death.

**Jura** a French-speaking canton of western Switzerland, created in 1979; area 838 sq. km. (324 sq. miles); pop. (1990) 65,700; capital, Delémont.

**Jurassic** /dʒʊə'ræsɪk/ the second period of the Mesozoic era, following the Triassic and preceding the Cretaceous, lasting from about 213 to 144 million years ago. During this period dinosaurs and other reptiles attained their maximum size and were found on land, in the sea, and in the air. The first birds appeared towards the end of the period which takes its name from the Jura Mts. on the French–Swiss frontier.

**Jurong** /dʒuː'rɒŋ/ a new industrial location on the south-west coast of Singapore Island employing about half of the country's work-force which is housed in a new town development. Industries include shipbuilding, steel, pharmaceuticals, chemicals, plastics, tyres, and textiles.

**Jute** /dʒuːt/ a Low-German tribe that invaded southern England (according to legend under

Horsa and Hengist) in the 5th c. and set up a kingdom in Kent.

**Jutish** *adj.*

**Jutland** /'dʒʌtlənd/ (Danish **Jylland** /'juːlæn/) a peninsula of north-west Europe stretching northwards into the North Sea from Germany to form the mainland of Denmark together with the north German state of Schleswig-Holstein.

**Juventud** /juːven'tʊd/, **Isla de la** an island province off the south-west coast of Cuba, formerly known as the Isle of Pines until renamed in 1958 in honour of the contribution made by youth to the development of the country; area 2,199 sq. km. (849 sq. miles); pop. (1981) 57,880.

**Jylland** see JUTLAND.

**Jyväskylä** /'jʊvæˌskʊlæ/ a port and industrial city at the north end of Lake Päijänne in central Finland, capital of Keski-Suomi province; pop. (1990) 66,530. Paper and wood products are important industries.

# K k

**K2** /ˈkeɪˈtuː/ (also **Dapsang** /ˈdæpsæŋ/) the highest mountain in the Karakoram range, on the border between Pakistan and China. It is the second-highest peak in the world, rising to 8,611 m. (28,250 ft.). Discovered in 1856, it was named K2 because it was the second peak measured in the Karakoram range. It has also been known as Mt. Godwin-Austen, after Col. H. H. Godwin-Austen, who first surveyed it.

**Kaaba** /ˈkɑːəbə/ (also **Caaba**) a building at Mecca, the Muslim Holy of Holies, containing a sacred black stone. It is a pre-Islamic granite and marble shrine shaped like an irregular cube of about 12 x 10 x 15 metres (40 x 33 x 50 ft.), said to have been constructed by Abraham upon divine command (some say it was built by Adam). It is considered by Muslims to be the 'navel' of the earth and indeed as the centre of the cosmos. Now surrounded by the Great Mosque, the Kaaba—or rather its north-west wall—replaced Jerusalem during Muhammad's lifetime as the point which all Muslims face in ritual prayer. The entire cube is covered by a black-cloth covering (*kiswa*) around which the *shahada*, or witness of the faith, is woven in gold. The Egyptian government traditionally provides a new kiswa each year. The Kaaba is the focal point of the first ritual devotions of the pilgrims who walk round it seven times, touching or kissing the sacred black stone. This is a stone of basalt, or possibly a meteorite, originally about 30 cm. (12 inches) in diameter, lodged in the eastern corner of the shrine, said to have been conveyed to Abraham by the angel Gabriel.

**Kabalega Falls** /ˌkæbəˈleɪgə/ a waterfall on the lower Victoria Nile near Lake Albert, in northwest Uganda. It is a central feature of the Kabalega National Park (established 1952) and is formed at a point where the river narrows to 6 m. (20 ft.) and drops 120 m. (400 ft.) in three cascades. It was formerly known as Murchison Falls, being named in honour of Sir Roderick Murchison who was a president of the Royal Geographical Society.

**Kabardino-Balkaria** /kɑːbɜːˌdiːnəʊ bɒlˈkɑːrɪə/ official name **The Kabarda-Balkar Republic** a republic of the Russian Federation in the northern Caucasus on the border with Georgia; area 12,500 sq. km. (4,825 sq. miles); pop. (1990) 768,000; capital, Nalchik. Absorbed into the Russian empire in the 16th c., it was designated an Autonomous Soviet Republic in 1936 and became a federal republic of Russia in 1991.

**Kabul** /ˈkɑːbʊl/ the capital of Afghanistan, a historic city situated on the River Kabul in a narrow mountain valley, commanding the mountain passes through the Hindu Kush, especially the Khyber Pass; pop. (est.1988) 1,424,000. It has existed for more than 3,000 years and has been destroyed and rebuilt several times in its history. It was capital of the Mogul empire, 1504–1738, and in 1773 replaced Kandahar as capital of an independent Afghanistan. It was the scene of bitter fighting during the 19th c. Afghan Wars and again during the civil war that began in 1979. It is Afghanistan's cultural and commercial centre with textile, footwear, and vehicle component industries.

**Kabwe** /ˈkɑːbwɪ/ the capital of Central province and the oldest lead- and zinc-mining town in Zambia; pop. (1987) 190,750. It was known as Broken Hill from 1904 to 1965.

**Kabylia** /kəˈbaɪljə/ the region of the Algerian Atlas Mountains occupied by the Berber Kabyle people.

**Kachin** /kæˈtʃɪn/ a state in northern Burma, on the frontier with India and China; pop. (1983) 803,980; capital, Myitkyina.

**Kachin** /kæˈtʃɪn/ a mountain people of northern Burma and adjacent areas of China and India speaking a variety of Tibeto-Burman languages. They number *c.* 245,000.

**Kadiköy** /ˌkædɪˈkɔɪ/ see CHALCEDON.

**Kadoma** /kæˈdəʊmə/ an industrial and residential suburb of Osaka, Honshu Island, Japan, on the Furu River; pop. (1990) 142,300. It has textile and machinery industries.

**Kaduna** /kəˈduːnə/ an industrial city and capital of Kaduna state in northern Nigeria, on the Kaduna River; pop. (est.1986) 280,000. Founded under British rule in 1913, it was formerly capital of Nigeria's Northern Region. In addition to brewing and oil refining, its industries produce textiles, cement, vehicles, and metal goods.

**Kaesong** /kaɪˈsɒŋ/ a commercial city in southern North Korea, on the 38th parallel; pop. (est.1984) 345,640. It manufactures porcelain and exports ginseng and rice.

**Kaffir** /ˈkæfə(r)/ a member of the Xhosa-speaking peoples of South Africa, many of whom were settled on a Cape Colony reserve known as Kaffraria established by the British in 1847 on land lying between the Keiskamma and Kei rivers. The term came to be used derogatively for a Black African.

**Kafir** /'kæfə(r)/ a native of the Hindu Kush mountains of north-east Afghanistan.

**Kafr el Dauwar** /ˌkæfər el 'daʊɑː(r)/ a city in northern Egypt, in the Nile delta south-east of Alexandria; pop. (1991) 221,000.

**Kafr el Sheikh** /ˌkæfər el 'ʃeɪk/ a city in northern Egypt, in the Nile delta between the Rosetta and Damietta branches; pop. (1991) 103,000.

**Kafue** /kæ'fuːɪ/ a river that rises near Lubumbashi on the Zambia–Zaire frontier and flows c. 965 km. (600 miles) through Zambia to meet the Zambezi. The grassy floodplains of the river were designated part of the Kafue National Park in 1972.

**Kagera** /kə'gɑːrə/ a river in the Rift Valley of east-central Africa, the remotest headwater of the Nile. It flows 400 km. (250 miles) northwards and eastwards following Tanzania's frontiers with Rwanda and Uganda before emptying into Lake Victoria.

**Kagoshima** /ˌkægɒ'ʃiːmə/ a city and port in Japan; pop. (1990) 537,000. It is situated on the southern coast of Kyushu Island, on the Satsuma Peninsula, beside an active volcano, Sakurajima. It has a navy yard and rocket base, and industries producing porcelain, clothing, and tinware.

**Kahramanmaraş** /ˌkærəmən'mɑːræʃ/ **1.** a province in central Turkey; area 14,327 sq. km. (5,534 sq. miles); pop. (1990) 892,950. **2.** its capital; pop. (1990) 228,130.

**Kaieteur Falls** /'kaɪətʊə(r)/ a South American waterfall with a sheer drop of 251 m. (822 ft.) on the River Potaro in the Guiana Highlands, central Guyana. It was discovered in 1870 by Barrington Brown and forms part of the Kaieteur National Park designated in 1929.

**Kaifeng** /kaɪ'feŋ/ an ancient city in Henan province, eastern China, to the east of Zhengzhou and south of the Yellow River; pop. (1990) 690,000. Established in the 4th c. BC, it is one of the oldest cities in China and, from 907 to 960, as Pien Ling, its capital under the Sung dynasty. It has developed into an industrial city producing agricultural machinery, chemicals, electrical goods, and silk.

**Kai Islands** /kaɪ/ a group of Indonesian islands in the Banda Sea south-east of the Moluccas, comprising the main islands of Little Kai (Kai Kecil) and Great Kai (Kai Besar) as well as many small islands. Its administrative centre is Tual on Little Kai.

**Kailas** /kaɪ'lɑːs/ (Chinese **Gangdisê** /gæŋ'tiːsə/) a range of mountains in south-west Tibet near the Nepalese frontier; the source of the Indus and Sutlej rivers and the headwaters of the Brahmaputra. Its highest peak is Kailas (6,714 m., 22,027 ft.) which is a mountain sacred to the Hindus.

**Kaili** /kaɪ'liː/ a city in Guizhou province, southern China, to the east of Guiyang; pop. (1986) 349,000.

**Kainji Lake** /kə'ɪndʒɪ/ a reservoir on the Niger River in western Nigeria. Its area of 1,295 sq. km. (500 sq. miles) makes it one of Africa's largest man-made lakes. The Kainji hydroelectric power-station supplies electricity to a wide area; irrigation and flood control are also part of the project.

**Kairouan** /ˌkaɪruː'ɑːn/ a Muslim holy city in northern Tunisia; pop. (1984) 72,250. Capital of the Aghlabid dynasty in the 9th c., it was a focal point for the caravans of pilgrims and traders and a centre of rug-weaving. Its Great Mosque, one of the oldest in North Africa, is situated at the centre of a walled city that is one of the holiest places in the Muslim world.

**Kaiserslautern** /'kaɪzɜːzˌlaʊtɜːn/ an industrial city in the Palatinate Forest, Rhineland-Palatinate, western Germany, on the Lauter River; pop. (1991) 100,540. Its university was established in 1975 and its industries include ironworks, car factories, and the making of sewing-machines.

**Kaiyuan** /kaɪjʊ'ɑːn/ a city in Yunnan province, southern China, to the south of Kunming; pop. (1986) 219,000.

**Kajaani** /kæ'jɑːnɪ/ a town in the Kainuu region of east-central Finland, on the Kajaani River; pop. (1990) 36,430. Founded close to a castle and river rapids in 1651, the town has sawmills, wood-pulp and paper mills, and cellulose and tar making industries.

**Kakadu National Park** /kə'kɑːduː/ a national park in Northern Territory, Australia, situated to the east of Darwin in the catchment area of the South Alligator River. It is noted for its natural scenery, wildlife, and Aboriginal rock art.

**Kakamigahara** /kæˌkɑːmɪgə'hɑːrə/ a marketing city in Gifu prefecture, central Honshu Island, Japan; pop. (1990) 129,680.

**Kakinada** /ˌkɑːkə'nɑːdə/ (formerly **Cocanada**) a market city in Andhra Pradesh, south-east India, on the delta of the Godavari River; pop. (1991) 327,400.

**Kakogawa** /kæ'kəʊgæwə/ an industrial city in Hyogo prefecture, southern Honshu Island, Japan, on the Kako River; pop. (1990) 239,800. It produces textiles, rubber goods, and fertilizers.

**Kalaallit Nunaat** /kəˌlɑːtlɪt nə'nɑːt/ the Inuit name for GREENLAND.

**Kalahari Desert** /ˌkælə'hɑːrɪ/ a high, vast, arid plateau in southern Africa north of the Orange River covering 582,800 sq. km. (225,000 sq. miles). It comprises most of Botswana with parts in Namibia and South Africa. Fed by seasonal rains, the Kalahari supports grass and occasional trees and is only a desert in the sense that it has little permanent water. It is the site of the Central Kalahari Game Reserve (established 1931) and the

Gemsbok National Park (established 1971) in Botswana, and the Kalahari Gemsbok National Park (established 1931) in South Africa. In the north the only permanent river, the Okavango, flows into the Okavango marshes, rich in wildlife. The Kalahari is peopled by nomadic Bushmen.

**Kalamata** /ˌkælə'maːtə/ (also **Calamata** or **Kalámai**) the capital, principal port, and agricultural trade centre of the department of Messenia in the south-west Peloponnese of southern Greece; pop. (1981) 43,235. Badly damaged by an earthquake in 1986, it was allegedly the first Greek city to revolt against the Turks in 1821.

**Kalamazoo** /ˌkæləmə'zuː/ a city in south-west Michigan, USA, at the junction of the Kalamazoo River and Portage Creek; pop. (1990) 80,280. It produces pharmaceuticals and paper products.

**Kalgoorlie** /kæl'ɡʊəlɪ/ a gold-mining town at the western end of the Nullarbor Plain in Western Australia; pop. (1991) 25,010 (with Boulder). Gold was first discovered here in 1887 and it was a centre of the Coolgardie gold-rush in the 1890s.

**Kali Gandaki** /ˌkaːliː 'ɡəndəkɪ/ a river that rises in Tibet and flows southwards through the Himalayas into India where it joins the River Gandak, a tributary of the Ganges. Where it passes between Annapurna Himal and Dhaulagiri Himal, the river lies in the world's deepest valley some 4,400 m. (14,400 ft.) below the mountain summits.

**Kalimantan** /ˌkælɪ'mæntæn/ a region of Indonesia, comprising the southern part of the island of Borneo; area 539,460 sq. km. (208,366 sq. miles); pop. (est. 1993) 9,959,800.

**Kalinin** /kə'liːnɪn/ the former name (1931–91) of the Russian city of TVER.

**Kaliningrad** /kæ'liːnɪnˌɡraːd/ **1.** a region of Russia, situated on the Baltic coast of eastern Europe; area 15,100 sq. km. (5,832 sq. miles); pop. (1989) 871,000. It shares its borders with Lithuania and Poland and is separated from Russia by the intervening countries of Lithuania, Latvia, and Belorussia (Belarus). **2.** its capital, an industrial seaport on the Baltic coast; pop. (1990) 406,000. It was founded in the 13th c. and in the 15th c. became the capital of East Prussia. It was known by its German name of Königsberg until 1945, when it was ceded to the Soviet Union under the Potsdam Agreement and renamed in honour of President Kalinin. It was the birthplace in 1724 of the German philosopher Immanuel Kant who taught at its university (founded in 1544). Its port is ice-free all the year and is a significant base for the Russian fleet. It is also a major fishing port with shipbuilding and machinery industries. **3.** a town in western Russia, north-east of Moscow; pop. (1990) 161,000.

**Kalisz** /kə'liːʃ/ a city in central Poland, on the River Prosna; pop. (1990) 106,150. Founded on an ancient trade route linking southern Europe with the Baltic, it is one of Poland's oldest towns. It is now an industrial centre with textile, metal, engineering, and piano-making industries and capital of Kalisz county.

**Kalix** /'kaːlɪks/ a river in northern Sweden that rises near the Norwegian frontier and flows 430 km. (270 miles) south-eastwards to meet the Gulf of Bothnia at the town of Kalix.

**Kalmar** /'kælmaː(r)/ (also **Calmar**) a city in south-east Sweden, opposite the island of Oland, capital of Kalmar county; pop. (1990) 56,200. It is a commercial, tourist, and light-industrial centre.

**Kalmyk** /'kælmɪk/ (also **Kalmuck**) a Buddhist Mongolian people of central Asia who invaded Russia in the 17th–18th c. and settled along the lower Volga. Speaking a Ural-Altaic language, many migrated to Chinese Turkestan in the 18th c.

**Kalmykia** /ˌkæl'mɪkɪə/ official name **The Republic of Kalmykia-Khalmg Tangch** a republic in the Russian Federation, on the Caspian Sea south of the Volga; area 75,900 sq. km. (29,300 sq. miles); pop. (1990) 325,000; capital, Elista. Declared an independent republic on the breakup of the Soviet Union in 1991, over 45 per cent of its people are Kalmyks who migrated from western China to the Russian steppe in the 17th c.

**Kaluga** /kə'luːɡə/ an industrial city and river port in western Russia, on the River Oka southwest of Moscow; pop. (1990) 314,000. It produces iron and steel and railway equipment.

**Kalulushi** /kælʊ'luːʃɪ/ a mining town near Kitwe in the Copperbelt province of northern Zambia; pop. (1988) 94,380.

**Kalyan** /kæl'jaːn/ a city on the west coast of India, in the state of Maharashtra, north-east of Bombay; pop. (1991) 1,014,000.

**Kalymnos** /'kaːlɪmnɒs/ (also **Kálimnos**) an island of the Dodecanese in the south Aegean Sea, lying to the north of Kos; area 111 sq. km. (43 sq. miles); pop. (1981) 14,300; chief town, Kalymnos.

**Kama** /'kaːmə/ a river of Russia that rises in the central Urals and flows in a loop north, east, and then south-west for 1,805 km. (1,128 miles) before joining the Volga near Kazan. It is the chief tributary of the Volga.

**Kamakura** /ˌkæmə'kʊərə/ a resort and residential town on the coast of Honshu Island, Japan, at the head of the Miura-hanto peninsula to the south of Tokyo; pop. (1990) 174,300. Capital of Japan from 1192 to 1333, its most famous landmark is the great bronze figure of Buddha, the Kamakura Daibutsu, which was cast in 1252. The city gives its name to a period of Japanese history characterized by the establishment of the first feudal military shogunate based at Kamakura. During the Kamakura Period various sects of Buddhism flourished, the Zen principle in particular greatly influencing art and literature.

**Kamarhati** /ˌkæmɜːˈhɑːtɪ/ a suburb of Calcutta in West Bengal, north-east India; pop. (1991) 266,000.

**Kamchatka** /kæmˈtʃætkə/ a vast mountainous peninsula of the north-east coast of East Siberia in the Russian Federation, separating the Sea of Okhotsk from the Bering Sea; chief port Petropavlovsk-Kamchatskiy. It is a volcanically active zone containing 22 active volcanoes and many hot springs.

**kame** /keɪm/ a short ridge or mound of stratified sands and gravels which have been deposited by glacial meltwater. **Kame terraces** are formed by meltwater deposits laid down between the side of a decaying glacier and a valley wall.

**Kamenskoye** /kæˈmjenskɔɪjə/ a former name (until 1936) of DNIPRODZHERZHYNSK.

**Kamensk-Uralski** /ˈkɑːmensk juːˈrɑːlskɪ/ an industrial city in central Russia, in the eastern foothills of the Urals south-east of Yekaterinburg; pop. (1990) 208,000.

**Kamloops** /kæmˈluːps/ a rail and road junction in southern British Columbia, Canada, on the eastern shore of Lake Kamloops; pop. (1991) 67,100. Founded as a fur-trading post in 1812, it was originally known as Fort Thompson. It is now a centre of tourism, sawmilling, paper manufacturing, and the livestock trade.

**Kampala** /kæmˈpɑːlə/ the capital of Uganda; pop. (1980) 458,400. It is situated on the northern shores of Lake Victoria (Victoria Nyanza), and replaced Entebbe as capital when the country became independent in 1963. It was originally the site of a royal palace and is built on a number of hills.

**Kampen** /ˈkæmpən/ a market and industrial town in the Dutch province of Overijssel, at the mouth of the Ijssel River; pop. (1990) 32,680. There are picturesque remains of the old Hanseatic town and a yacht harbour.

**kampong** /ˈkæmpɒŋ/ a Malay word for an enclosure or village.

**Kampot** /kæmˈpɒt/ a port in southern Cambodia, on the Tuk Chhou River 5 km. (3 miles) from the Gulf of Thailand; pop. (est. 1990) 14,000. It is capital of the province of Kampot and a centre of the pepper trade.

**Kampuchea** /ˌkæmpʊˈtʃɪə/ see CAMBODIA.

**Kamyshin** /kəˈmɪʃən/ a river port in central European Russia, on the River Volga north of Volgograd; pop. (1990) 123,000.

**Kanarese** /ˌkænəˈriːz/ (also **Kannada**) the language of the people of Kanara, a district in south-west India. It is a member of the Dravidian language group, closely allied to Telugu, with about 22 million speakers. Its alphabet is similar to that of Telugu, developed from the Grantha script.

**Kanazawa** /kæˈnɑːzæwə/ a resort city and capital of Ishikawa prefecture, central Honshu Island, Japan, on the Sea of Japan; pop. (1990) 442,870. Once a centre of the Maeda clan, it is noted for its porcelain.

**Kanchenjunga** /ˌkæntʃenˈdʒʊŋgə/ (also **Kangchenjunga** and **Kinchinjunga** /ˌkɪn-/) a mountain in the Himalayas on the border between Nepal and Sikkim. Rising to 8,598 m. (28,209 ft.), it is the world's third-highest mountain. Its summit is split into five separate peaks, whence its name, which in Tibetan means 'the five treasures of the snows'. It was first climbed in 1955 by a British expedition led by Charles Evans.

**Kanchipuram** /kɑːnˈtʃiːpərəm/ (formerly **Conjeeveram**) a town in Tamil Nadu, southern India, south-west of Madras; pop. (1991) 169,810. It is noted for its many temples and its silk.

**Kandahar** /ˌkændəˈhɑː(r)/ (also **Qandahar**) a city in southern Afghanistan, capital of the province of Kandahar; pop. (est. 1988) 226,000. It was the first capital of Afghanistan after it became independent, from 1748 until replaced by Kabul in 1773. It is a wool, grain, and tobacco trading centre of the Pashtun people.

**Kandy** /ˈkændɪ/ **1.** a resort and sacred city in the highlands of central Sri Lanka; pop. (1990) 104,000. Originally known as Senkadagala, it became an important centre of Buddhist political power in the 15th c. Since 1542 it has been the home of the Buddha's Tooth which is paraded through the streets each July–August during the 15-day festival of Esala Perahera, Sri Lanka's greatest festival. **2.** a former independent kingdom in Ceylon. The city of Kandy was its capital from 1480 to 1815.

**Kangar** /ˈkɑːŋɑː/ the capital of the state of Perlis in north-west Malaysia; pop. (1980) 12,950. The royal capital of Perlis is at nearby Arau.

**Kangaroo Island** /ˌkæŋgəˈruː/ an island in the Southern Ocean at the mouth of the Gulf of St. Vincent, Southern Australia, 110 km. (69 miles) south of Adelaide; area 4,350 sq. km. (1,680 sq. miles). It was visited by the French explorer Nicolas Baudin in 1803 and settled by whalers and fishermen of the South Australia Company in 1836. To the west lies the Flinders Chase National Park which was established in 1919 to protect eucalyptus forest. Its chief settlements are Kingscote, American River, and Penneshaw.

**KaNgwane** /ˌkɑːˈŋgwɑːneɪ/ a former self-governing state of the Swazi people established in eastern Transvaal in 1971. Its capital was Nyamasane.

**kanji** /ˈkændʒɪ/ Japanese writing using Chinese characters.

**Kankan** /kænˈkæn/ a town in Guinea, a port on the Milo river and capital of the province of Haute-Guinée; pop. (1983) 88,760. It is the second-largest town in the country, and trading centre for local produce.

**Kannada** see KANARESE.

**Kano** /'kɑːnəʊ/ the chief city of northern Nigeria, capital of Kano state, and Nigeria's third city; pop. (est. 1986) 553,100. Originally a Hausa settlement, it was captured by the Fulani in the 19th c. and developed as the terminus of a trans-Saharan trade route. It is a major commercial and industrial city, particularly famous for its leather work and its great market, and is in addition a Muslim educational and religious centre. Tourism is also important.

**Kanpur** /kɑːnˈpʊə(r)/ (formerly **Cawnpore** /kɔːnˈpɔː(r)/) a city in Uttar Pradesh, northern India, on the River Ganges; pop. (1991) 2,111,280. An important garrison town under British rule, it was the site of a massacre of British soldiers and European families in July 1857, during the Indian Mutiny. Kanpur is now a major industrial city with sugar, vegetable oil, textile, leather, aviation, and chemical industries.

**Kansas** /'kænsəs/ a state in the Middle West of the USA, between the Missouri River and the Rocky Mountains; area 213,098 sq. km. (82,277 sq. miles); pop. (1990) 2,477,570; capital, Topeka. The largest cities are Wichita, Kansas City, Topeka, and Overland Park. Kansas is also known as the Sunflower State or the Jayhawk State. Ceded to Spain by France in 1763, the territory reverted back to France in 1800 before being sold to the US as part of the Louisiana Purchase in 1803. It was organized as a territory in 1854 and became the 34th state of the Union in 1861. Early settlements such as Fort Larned, Fort Scott, and Dodge City were designed to protect westbound travellers on the Oregon and Santa Fe trails. Grain, cattle, and vegetables are important products of the state which also produces oil, coal, zinc, lead, salt, and the country's largest quantities of helium. Its chief landmarks are the Eisenhower boyhood home in Abilene, the 'cowboy capital' Dodge City, and the historic frontier posts at Fort Scott and Fort Larned. Kansas is divided into 105 counties:

| County | Area (sq. km.) | Pop. (1990) | County Seat |
|---|---|---|---|
| Allen | 1,313 | 14,640 | Iola |
| Anderson | 1,518 | 7,800 | Garnett |
| Atchison | 1,121 | 16,930 | Atchison |
| Barber | 2,954 | 5,870 | Medicine Lodge |
| Barton | 2,327 | 29,380 | Great Bend |
| Bourbon | 1,659 | 14,970 | Fort Scott |
| Brown | 1,487 | 11,130 | Hiawatha |
| Butler | 3,752 | 50,580 | El Dorado |
| Chase | 2,020 | 3,020 | Cottonwood Falls |
| Chautauqua | 1,674 | 4,410 | Sedan |
| Cherokee | 1,534 | 21,370 | Columbus |
| Cheyenne | 2,655 | 3,240 | Saint Francis |
| Clark | 2,535 | 2,420 | Ashland |
| Clay | 1,643 | 9,160 | Clay Center |
| Cloud | 1,867 | 11,020 | Concordia |
| Coffey | 1,599 | 8,400 | Burlington |
| Comanche | 2,051 | 2,310 | Coldwater |
| Cowley | 2,933 | 36,915 | Winfield |
| Crawford | 1,547 | 35,570 | Girard |
| Decatur | 2,324 | 4,020 | Oberlin |
| Dickinson | 2,215 | 18,960 | Abilene |
| Doniphan | 1,009 | 8,130 | Troy |
| Douglas | 1,199 | 81,800 | Lawrence |
| Edwards | 1,612 | 3,790 | Kinsley |
| Elk | 1,690 | 3,330 | Howard |
| Ellis | 2,340 | 26,000 | Hays |
| Ellsworth | 1,864 | 6,590 | Ellsworth |
| Finney | 3,385 | 33,070 | Garden City |
| Ford | 2,857 | 27,460 | Dodge City |
| Franklin | 1,500 | 21,990 | Ottawa |
| Geary | 980 | 30,450 | Junction City |
| Gove | 2,787 | 3,230 | Gove |
| Graham | 2,335 | 3,540 | Hill City |
| Grant | 1,495 | 7,160 | Ulysses |
| Gray | 2,257 | 5,400 | Cimarron |
| Greeley | 2,023 | 1,770 | Tribune |
| Greenwood | 2,951 | 7,850 | Eureka |
| Hamilton | 2,595 | 2,390 | Syracuse |
| Harper | 2,085 | 7,124 | Anthony |
| Harvey | 1,404 | 31,030 | Newton |
| Haskell | 1,503 | 3,890 | Sublette |
| Hodgeman | 2,236 | 2,180 | Jetmore |
| Jackson | 1,711 | 11,525 | Holton |
| Jefferson | 1,391 | 15,905 | Oskaloosa |
| Jewel | 2,366 | 4,250 | Mankato |
| Johnson | 1,243 | 355,050 | Olathe |
| Kearny | 2,257 | 4,030 | Lakin |
| Kingman | 2,249 | 8,290 | Kingman |
| Kiowa | 1,880 | 3,660 | Greensburg |
| Labette | 1,698 | 23,690 | Oswego |
| Lane | 1,864 | 2,375 | Dighton |
| Leavenworth | 1,204 | 64,370 | Leavenworth |
| Lincoln | 1,872 | 3,650 | Lincoln |
| Linn | 1,563 | 8,250 | Mound City |
| Logan | 2,790 | 3,080 | Oakley |
| Lyon | 2,194 | 34,730 | Emporia |
| McPherson | 2,340 | 27,270 | McPherson |
| Marion | 2,454 | 12,890 | Marion |
| Marshall | 2,283 | 11,705 | Marysville |
| Meade | 2,545 | 4,250 | Meade |
| Miami | 1,534 | 23,470 | Paola |
| Mitchell | 1,864 | 7,200 | Beloit |
| Montgomery | 1,680 | 38,820 | Independence |
| Morris | 1,802 | 6,200 | Council Grove |
| Morton | 1,901 | 3,480 | Elkhart |
| Nemaha | 1,869 | 10,450 | Seneca |
| Neosho | 1,498 | 17,035 | Erie |
| Ness | 2,792 | 4,030 | Ness City |
| Norton | 2,270 | 5,950 | Norton |
| Osage | 1,807 | 15,250 | Lyndon |
| Osborne | 2,293 | 4,870 | Osborne |
| Ottawa | 1,875 | 5,630 | Minneapolis |
| Pawnee | 1,963 | 7,555 | Larned |
| Phillips | 2,306 | 6,590 | Phillipsburg |
| Pottawatomie | 2,153 | 16,130 | Westmoreland |
| Pratt | 1,911 | 9,700 | Pratt |
| Rawlins | 2,779 | 3,400 | Atwood |
| Reno | 3,273 | 62,390 | Hutchinson |
| Republic | 1,869 | 6,480 | Belleville |
| Rice | 1,893 | 10,610 | Lyons |
| Riley | 1,542 | 67,140 | Manhattan |

(cont.)

| | | | |
|---|---|---|---|
| Rooks | 2,309 | 6,040 | Stockton |
| Rush | 1,867 | 3,840 | LaCrosse |
| Russell | 2,259 | 7,835 | Russell |
| Saline | 1,875 | 49,300 | Salina |
| Scott | 1,867 | 5,290 | Scott City |
| Sedgwick | 2,618 | 403,660 | Wichita |
| Seward | 1,664 | 18,740 | Liberal |
| Shawnee | 1,427 | 160,980 | Topeka |
| Sheridan | 2,330 | 3,040 | Hoxie |
| Sherman | 2,748 | 6,300 | Goodland |
| Smith | 2,332 | 5,080 | Smith Center |
| Stafford | 2,049 | 5,365 | Saint John |
| Stanton | 1,771 | 2,330 | Johnston |
| Stevens | 1,890 | 5,050 | Hugoton |
| Sumner | 3,076 | 25,840 | Wellington |
| Thomas | 2,795 | 8,260 | Colby |
| Trego | 2,314 | 3,690 | Wakeeney |
| Wabaunsee | 2,072 | 6,600 | Alma |
| Wallace | 2,376 | 1,820 | Sharon Springs |
| Washington | 2,335 | 7,070 | Washington |
| Wichita | 1,869 | 2,760 | Leoti |
| Wilson | 1,495 | 10,290 | Fredonia |
| Woodson | 1,295 | 4,120 | Yates Center |
| Wyandotte | 387 | 161,990 | Kansas City |

**Kansas City** two adjacent cities with the same name situated at the junction of the Missouri and Kansas rivers, one in north-east Kansas (1990 pop. 149,770) and the other in north-west Missouri (1990 pop. 435,150). Kansas City (Kansas) is an amalgamation of eight separate towns, the oldest of which, Wyandot City, was settled in 1843 by the Wyandot Indians. Now an industrial railway centre, it produces steel, vehicles, grain, and soap. Kansas City (Missouri) is a major industrial and distribution centre, trading in grain and livestock and producing refined petroleum, steel, vehicles, and processed food. It was laid out in 1838 as the easternmost outfitting post on the Santa Fe Trail. Alexander Majors, founder of the pony express, lies buried in Union Cemetery.

**Kansk** /kɑːnsk/ a coal-mining and industrial town in west Siberian Russia, east of Krasnoyarsk; pop. (1990) 110,000. Its industries include machinery, chemicals, and textiles.

**Kansu** see GANSU.

**Kanto** /kæn'təʊ/ a region of Japan on the island of Honshu; area 32,309 sq. km. (12,479 sq. miles); pop. (1990) 38,541,000; chief city, Tokyo. It is divided into seven prefectures:

| Prefecture | Area (sq. km.) | Pop. (1990) | Capital |
|---|---|---|---|
| Chiba | 5,115 | 5,555,000 | Chiba |
| Gumma | 6,356 | 1,966,000 | Maebashi |
| Ibaraki | 6,090 | 2,845,000 | Mito |
| Kanagawa | 2,391 | 7,980,000 | Yokohama |
| Saitama | 3,799 | 6,405,000 | Urawa |
| Tochigi | 6,414 | 1,935,000 | Utsunomiya |
| Tokyo | 2,145 | 11,855,000 | Tokyo |

**Kanye** /'kɑːnjeɪ/ a town in southern Botswana, south-west of Gaborone; pop. (1988) 26,300. It is capital of Ngwaketse district. Asbestos is mined nearby.

**Kaohsiung** /ˌkaʊʃɪ'ʊŋ/ the chief port of Taiwan, situated on the south-west coast of the island; pop. (1990) 1,390,000. It has dry-dock, container-handling, and shipbreaking facilities.

**Kapachira Falls** /kæpə'tʃɪərə/ a series of rapids on the Shire River in the Majete Game Reserve to the west of Blantyre in southern Malawi, formerly known as the Murchison Falls or Murchison Rapids.

**Kap Farvel** see FAREWELL, CAPE I.

**Kapfenberg** /'kæpfənbɜːk/ a town in Carinthia, south-eastern Austria, situated on the River Mur north-west of Graz; pop. (1991) 23,490.

**Kaposvar** /ˌkɒpɒʃ'vɑː(r)/ a city in south-west Hungary on the River Kapos; pop. (1989) 74,000. Trading in tobacco, fruit, and wine, it is the capital of Somogy county.

**Kapuas** /'kɑːpəwæs/ a river that rises in north-west-central Borneo and flows westwards for 1,243 km. (777 miles) to meet the South China Sea at Pontianak. Logging and gold-panning are important activities along its banks.

**karaburan** /ˌkærəbu:'rɑːn/ a strong, warm, north-easterly wind that blows over central Asia often carrying large amounts of fine-grained soil which is deposited as loess.

**Karachay-Cherkessia** /kɑːrə'tʃaɪ tʃɜː'kesɪə/ official name **The Karachay-Cherkess Republic** a republic of the Russian Federation in the northern Caucasus; area 14,100 sq. km. (5,442 sq. miles); pop. (1989) 418,000; capital, Cherkessk. An autonomous Karachai republic existed until 1943 after which Stalin deported many of its ethnic Muslim Karachai population. After the breakup of the Soviet Union it was declared a republic of the Russian Federation in 1992.

**Karachi** /kə'rɑːtʃɪ/ a major industrial, commercial, and financial city and port in Pakistan, capital of Sind province; pop. (est.1991) 6,700,000. Situated on the Arabian Sea near the mouth of the Indus River, it was capital of Pakistan 1947–59, before being replaced by Islamabad. Muhammad Ali Jinnah, founder of Pakistan was born in Karachi in 1876. Karachi has heavy industries including automobile assembly, oil refining, steel, shipbuilding, as well as textile, printing, food-processing, chemical, and engineering industries.

**Karaganda** /ˌkærəgən'dɑː/ see QARAGHANDY.

**Karaikkudi** /kə'riːkədiː/ a town in the state of Tamil Nadu, southern India, south-east of Madurai; pop. (1991) 110,470.

**Karaite** /'keərəˌaɪt/ a Jewish sect chiefly in the Crimea, founded in the 8th c., rejecting rabbinical tradition and basing its tenets on a literal interpretation of the Scriptures.

**Karaj** /kæ'rɑːdʒ/ a city in northern Iran, on the Karaj River in the southern foothills of the Elburz Mts. north-west of Tehran; pop. (1991) 442,000. It is an agricultural market and chemical industry centre.

**Karakalpakstan** /ˌkærəkɪl'pɑːkstɑːn/ an autonomous region of western Uzbekistan, Central Asia, on the lower Amu Darya (Oxus River); area 164,900 sq. km. (63,920 sq. miles); pop. (1990) 1,244,700; capital, Nukus. Absorbed into the Russian empire in the late 19th c., it became an autonomous region of Kazakhstan in 1925, and an Autonomous Soviet Republic within Uzbekistan in 1936. It is a largely agricultural region producing cattle, sheep, goats, and wine.

**Karaklis** /kə'rɑːklɪs/ an industrial city in Armenia, situated to the north of Yerevan; pop. (1990) 169,000. It was known as Kirovakan from 1935 to 1991.

**Karakoram** /ˌkærə'kɔːrəm/ a great mountain system of central Asia, extending over 480 km. (300 miles) south-eastwards from north-east Afghanistan to Kashmir and forming part of the borders of India and Pakistan with China. One of the highest mountain systems in the world, it consists of a group of parallel ranges, forming a westwards continuation of the Himalayas, with many peaks over 7,900 m. (26,000 ft.), the highest being K2 (8,611 m., 28,250 ft.). Virtually inaccessible, it also contains the highest passes in the world, at elevations over 4,900 m. (16,000 ft.), including the Karakoram Pass and the Khardungla Pass.

**Karakorum** /ˌkærə'kɔːrəm/ the ruins of a city in central Mongolia, which was the ancient capital of the Mongol empire, established by Genghis Khan in 1220. The capital was later moved by Kublai Khan to Khanbaliq (modern Beijing) in 1267, and Karakorum was destroyed by Chinese forces in 1388.

**Kara Kul** /ˌkærə 'kuːl/ a lake in north-eastern Tajikistan, lying at an altitude of 3,960 m. (13,000 ft.) on a plateau between the Pamirs and the Altai Mts.; area 310 sq. km. (120 sq. miles). It gives its name to the Karakul sheep which is bred in the low-lying regions of central Asia for its astrakhan wool.

**Kara-Kum Desert** /ˌkærə 'kuːm/ (also **Garagum**, Russian **Karakumy**) a desert in central Asia, to the east of the Caspian Sea, between the Aral Sea in the north and the frontier between Turkmenistan and Iran in the south. It is separated from the Kyzyl-Kum Desert by the Amu Darya River.

**Karaman** /ˌkærə'mɑːn/ **1.** a province in south-west-central Turkey, created from the southern part of Konya province in the late 1980s; area 9,163 sq. km. (3,539 sq. miles); pop. (1990) 217,540. **2.** its capital; pop. (1990) 76,525. In the 13th c. it was the capital of the independent Armenian state of **Karamania**.

**Karamay** /kɑːrɑː'maɪ/ a city in Xinjiang autonomous region, north-west China; pop. (1986) 189,000. It lies at the centre of a major oil-producing region of the Dzungarian Basin.

**Kara Sea** /'kɑːrə/ an arm of the Arctic Ocean off the northern coast of Russia, bounded to the east by the island of Severnaya Zemlya and to the west by Novaya Zemlya.

**Karawanken Alps** /ˌkɑːrə'væŋken/ (Italian **Caravanche** /ˌkɑːrə'vɑːŋkə/) a range of the eastern Alps on the frontier between Austria and Slovenia, extending eastwards for 80 km. (50 miles) from Treviso, Italy. The highest peak is Hochstuhl (2,238 m., 7,341 ft.).

**Karbala** /'kɑːbələ/ a city in southern Iraq, to the west of the Euphrates; pop. (est.1985) 184,000. A holy city for Shiite Muslims, it is the site of the tomb of Husein, grandson of Muhammad, who was killed here in AD 680.

**Kardhítsa** /kɑː'ðiːtsə/ a market town and capital of a department of the same name in Thessaly, central Greece; pop. (1981) 27,290. It trades in tobacco, grain, cotton, livestock, and silk from the Thessalian plain and the mountainous Agrafa region.

**Karelia** /kə'riːlɪə/ a region on the frontier of Finland and Russia, which formed an independent Finnish state in medieval times and whose folktales were the source of the Finnish epic, the *Kalevala*. In the 16th c. Karelia came under Swedish rule and in 1721 it was annexed by Russia. Following Finland's declaration of independence in 1917, part of Karelia became a region of Finland and part was subsequently designated an autonomous republic of the Soviet Union. After the Russian–Finnish War of 1939–40 the greater part of Finnish Karelia was ceded to the Soviet Union. **Karelian** *adj. & n.*

**Karelia, Republic of** a republic of the Russian Federation; area 172,400 sq. km. (66,589 sq. miles); pop. (1989) 792,000; capital, Petrozavodsk. Formerly known as Olonets Province, it was designated an autonomous republic of the Russian Soviet Federal Socialist Republic in 1923. With the addition of Finnish territory after World War II, it became the Karelo-Finnish Soviet Socialist Republic, but in 1956 it reverted to autonomous republic status. With the breakup of the Soviet Union in 1991, it declared itself the Republic of Karelia.

**Karen** /kæ'ren/ a group of non-Burmese Mongoloid tribes, most of whom live in the Karen or Kawthoolay State in east Burma on the frontier with Thailand, where they have declared themselves independent of the government of Burma. Their language is of the Sino-Tibetan family and their name is derived from the Burmese word *kareng* (= wild, dirty, low-caste man).

**Karen State** (also **Kawthoolay** or **Kawthulei** /ˌkɔː'θuː'leɪ/) a state in south-east Burma, on the border with Thailand; pop. (1983) 1,057,500; capital, Pa-an. Inaugurated as Karen State in 1954, the Karen people of this area wanted independence and rebelled against the Burmese government. In 1964, the state was given the traditional name of Kawthulei but it reverted to Karen after the 1974 Constitution limited its autonomy. The Karen people are still engaged in armed conflict with the Burmese government in an attempt to gain independence.

**Kariba** /kə'ri:bə/ **1.** a town in the district of Mashonaland West, northern Zimbabwe, on the north-eastern shore of Lake Kariba; pop. (1982) 12,400. It was originally built in the mid-1950s to house the 10,000 workers involved in building the Kariba Dam. Now a major tourist resort, many of its people work in the Kariba hydroelectric power plant which supplies Zimbabwe with most of its electricity. **2. Lake Kariba** is a man-made lake, created by the damming of the Zambezi River between 1955 and 1959. Before flooding took place the settlements of the Tonga people were relocated and wild animals were moved to higher ground, rescued from drowning by Operation Noah. Drawing water from a catchment area of 663,000 sq. km. (256,083 sq. miles), it forms a reservoir with a capacity of 180,600 million cubic metres at maximum operating level. It also forms the Lake Kariba Recreational Park with an area of 5,200 sq. km. (2,008 sq. miles). **3.** the **Kariba Dam**, which lies 385 km. downstream from the Victoria Falls at the upper end of the Kariba Gorge, came into operation in 1959, providing hydroelectric power for both Zimbabwe and Zambia. Its construction entailed the excavation of nearly one million cubic metres of rock and the laying down of 975,000 cubic metres of concrete.

**Karimunjawa Islands** /ˌkærɪmən'jɑ:wə/ a group of 27 sparsely-inhabited Indonesian islands forming a national marine park in the Java Sea 150 km. (94 miles) north of Java. The islands are noted for their rare red coral, forest plants, and nesting eagles.

**Karisimbe** /ˌkærə'sɪmbɪ/ **Mount** (also **Karisimbi**) a mountain on the border between Zaire and Rwanda, rising to 4,507 m. (14,787 ft.) in the Virunga Mountains between Lake Kivu and Lake Edward.

**Kariya** /kæ'ri:jə/ an industrial city in Aichi prefecture, central Honshu Island, Japan; pop. (1990) 120,120. It has textile and machinery industries.

**Karl-Marx-Stadt** the former name (1953–90) of CHEMNITZ in Germany.

**Karlovac** /'kɑ:lə,væts/ an industrial town in north-west Croatia, on the River Kupa between Rijeka and Zagreb; pop. (1991) 59,900. Once a garrison town, its fortress was built in the 16th c. to halt the advance of the Turks. Its industries produce leather, textiles, and machinery.

**Karlovy Vary** /ˌkɑ:ləvɪ 'vɑ:rɪ/ (German **Carlsbad** or **Karlsbad** /'kɑ:lzbæd/) a spa town in the West Bohemia region of the Czech Republic, at the junction of the Tepla and Ohre rivers; pop. (1991) 56,290. Famous for its alkaline thermal springs, it was founded in the 14th c. by the Bohemian king and Holy Roman emperor Charles IV. It is also known for its ceramic and glass industries.

**Karlskrona** /kɑ:lz'kru:nə/ a Baltic seaport and capital of the province of Belkinge, southern Sweden, at the entrance to the Kalmar Sound; pop. (1990) 59,050. Founded in 1680 by Charles XI as a headquarters for the Swedish fleet, it became Sweden's second-largest town in the 18th c. After years of decline it developed industries that include fish processing, shipbuilding, and the manufacture of electrical goods.

**Karlsruhe** /'kɑ:lzru:ə/ an industrial town and port on the Rhine in the state of Baden-Württemberg, western Germany; pop. (1991) 278,580. Capital of the former German state of Baden, it is now a centre for oil refining, engineering, and the production of chemicals, textiles, and rubber goods.

**Karlstad** /'kɑ:lstæd/ an industrial town in central Sweden, on the north shore of Lake Vänern; pop. (1990) 76,470. Named after Charles IX who granted its municipal charter in 1584, it is capital of Örebro province. A Peace Monument commemorates the dissolution of the Swedish-Norwegian Union in 1905. Its industries manufacture wooden products, chemicals, and textiles.

**Karnak** /'kɑ:næk/ a village in Egypt, on the east bank of the Nile near Luxor. It is the site of the northern complex of monuments of ancient Thebes, including the great temple of Amun, which comprise the most extensive group of surviving ancient buildings in the world.

**Karnal** /kɜ:'nɑ:l/ a town in the state of Haryana, north-west India, near the Yamuna River north of Delhi; pop. (1991) 176,120. It is a market and cattle-breeding centre.

**Karnataka** /kə'nɑ:təkə/ a state in south-west India that was known as Mysore until 1973; area 191,791 sq. km. (74,079 sq. miles); pop. (1991) 44,817,400; capital, Bangalore. It is a largely agricultural state producing coffee, ragi, groundnuts, cotton, and rice.

**Karnische Alpen** the German name for the CARNIC ALPS.

**Kärnten** the German name for CARINTHIA.

**Karoo** /kə'ru:/ (also **Karroo**) an elevated semi-desert plateau in Cape Province, South Africa, between the Orange River and the Cape of Good Hope which provides grazing land for sheep and, when irrigated, fertile farm land. It is divided into the **Upper Karoo**, the **Great Karoo**, and the **Little Karoo**. The Karoo National Park, in the

Great Karoo near Beaufort West, was established in 1979.

**Karpathos** /'kɑː(r)pəθɒs/ a Greek island in the Aegean Sea between Crete and Rhodes, one of the Dodecanese islands; area 301 sq. km. (116 sq. miles); pop. (1981) 4,645. Its chief settlement is Karpathos (Pigádia) on the east coast.

**Kars** /kɑːs/ **1.** a mountainous province in north-east Turkey, on the frontier with Armenia; area 18,557 sq. km. (7,168 sq. miles); pop. (1990) 662,155; . **2.** its capital on the Kars River; pop. (1990) 78,455. Noted for its cheese, woollen textiles, felt, and carpet-weaving, it was in the 9th–10th c. capital of an independent Armenian principality.

**Karshi** /'kɑːʃiː/ (Uzbek **Qarshi**) a market town in south-eastern Uzbekistan, centre of a fertile oasis; pop. (1990) 163,000. It was known as Bek-Budi from 1926 to 1937.

**Karst** /kɑːst/ (Slovenian **Kras**) an arid limestone region near Trieste in Slovenia noted for its caves, geological formations, and erosional features. It lends its name to a term used by geologists to describe similar limestone regions in other parts of the world.

**Karviná** /'kɑːvɪnɑ/ a city in the North Moravia region of the Czech Republic, near the Polish border 13 km. (8 miles) east of Ostrava; pop. (1991) 68,370. It is an industrial city at the centre of a coal-mining region.

**kasbah** /'kæzbɑː/ a fortified citadel or fort in North Africa.

**Kashan** /kəˈʃɑːn/ an oasis town to the north of Isfahan in central Iran; pop. (1991) 155,000. It is noted for its carpets, silk, ceramic tiles, copper-ware, and rose-water.

**Kashgar** /'kæʃgɑː(r)/ (also **Kaxgar** or **Kashi**) the chief commercial centre of western Xinjiang autonomous region, China, and chief city of Chinese Turkestan, on the Kashgar River; pop. (1986) 202,000. Situated at the junction of several routeways across Asia including the ancient Silk Road, it was for centuries a fertile oasis of the arid western Tarim Basin. Textiles, rugs, and jewellery are manufactured.

**Kashgaria** /ˌkæʃgɜːˈrɪə/ an alternative name for Chinese Turkestan, a region of western Xinjiang autonomous region in north-west China.

**Kashi** see KASHGAR.

**Kashihara** /ˌkæʃɪˈhɑːrə/ a city in Nara prefecture, Honshu Island, Japan, situated south-east of Osaka; pop. (1990) 115,560.

**Kashiwa** /kæˈʃiːwə/ a city in Chiba prefecture, central Honshu Island, Japan, situated north-east of Tokyo; pop. (1990) 305,060.

**Kashmir** /kæʃˈmɪə(r)/ a region on the northern border of India and north-east Pakistan. Formerly a princely state of India, it has been disputed between India and Pakistan since partition in 1947, with sporadic outbreaks of fighting; area 222,236

sq. km. (85,838 sq. miles). The majority of its population are Muslims. The north-western area occupied by Pakistan is administratively divided into the Northern Areas, which is governed by direct rule from Islamabad, and Azad Kashmir (= Free Kashmir) which has its own legislative assembly. That part of Kashmir to the south of the Line of Control was incorporated into the Indian state of Jammu and Kashmir. Aksai Chin, a strategic area of Kashmir in the Himalayas bordering Tibet, was occupied by China in 1950.

**Kassel** an industrial city in the state of Hesse, central Germany, on the River Fulda; pop. (1991) 196,830. Founded c.913, it was the capital of the kingdom of Westphalia (1807–13) and of the Prussian province of Hesse-Nassau (1866–1944). It produces textiles, vehicles, machinery, and optical equipment.

**Kastamonu** /kəˈstɑːmənu/ **1.** a province of northern Turkey, on the Black Sea coast; pop. (1990) 423,610; area 13,108 sq. km. (5,063 sq. miles). **2.** its capital, situated c.70 km. (44 miles) south of the Black Sea coast; pop. (1990) 51,560. It is a centre for the manufacture of textiles and copper utensils.

**Kassite** /'kæsaɪt/ an Elamite people from the Zagros mountains in western Iran who ruled Babylonia from the 18th to the 12th c. BC until overthrown by Assyria.

**Kastoriá** /ˌkæstʊrɪˈɑː/ a town in Macedonia, north-eastern Greece, on a peninsula in Lake Kastoriá, capital of a department of the same name; pop. (1981) 17,130. Under Turkish occupation it was known as Kesriye, and was a centre of the fur trade. It is a market town and fishing port, and woollen carpets are made nearby.

**Kasugai** /kæˈsuːgaɪ/ a city in Aichi prefecture, central Honshu Island, Japan, forming a north-eastern suburb of Nagoya; pop. (1990) 266,600. It produces silk and textiles.

**Kasukabe** /kæˈsuːkəbɪ/ a city in Saitama prefecture, central Honshu Island, Japan, north of Tokyo; pop. (1990) 188,810.

**Kasur** a Pathan city in the province of Punjab, north-east Pakistan, near the Sutlej River south-east of Lahore; pop. (1981) 155,000.

**katabatic wind** /ˌkætəˈbætɪk/ a downward flowing wind of cold dry air.

**Katanga** /kəˈtaːŋgə/ the former name (until 1972) of the south-eastern mining region of the former Belgian Congo that now constitutes the province of Shaba in southern Zaire.

**Kateríni** /kætəˈriːnɪ/ a market town in northern Greece, capital of the department of Pieria in Macedonia; pop. (1981) 39,900.

**Kathiawar** /ˌkætɪəˈwɑː(r)/ a cotton-producing peninsula on the west coast of India, in the state of Gujarat, separating the Gulf of Kutch from the Gulf of Cambay.

**Kathmandu** /ˌkætmænˈduː/ the capital of Nepal, situated at the confluence of the Bagmati and Bishnumati rivers in the Himalayas at *c.*1,370 m. (4,500 ft.); pop. (1981) 235,000. Founded in AD 723 by the Licchavi king Gunakamadeva, it once stood at the junction of important trade routes. The Singha Durbar palace (built in 1901) was once the largest building in Asia. The first surfaced road reached Kathmandu in 1956 and subsequently the city developed as the centre of the country's tourist industry.

**Katihar** /ˈkətəˌhɑː(r)/ a town in Bihar, north-east India, to the north of the Ganges; pop. (1991) 154,100.

**Katmai** /ˈkætmaɪ/ an active volcano in the Aleutian Range on the Alaska Peninsula rising to a height of 2,047 m. (6,715 ft.). It was the scene of a major eruption in June 1912.

**Katoomba** /kəˈtuːmbə/ a tourist resort in the Blue Mountains of New South Wales, south-east Australia; pop. (1991) 16,930 (with Wentworth Falls). Founded as a coal-mining town, it later attracted holiday-makers from Sydney.

**Katowice** /ˌkætəˈviːtseɪ/ a city in south-west Poland, the industrial centre of the Upper Silesian coal-mining region; pop. (1990) 349,360. It is capital of a province of the same name.

**Katsuta** /kætˈsuːtə/ an industrial city in Ibaraki prefecture, central Honshu Island, Japan, on the Naka River east of Mito; pop. (1990) 109,830. It has vehicle, machinery, and electronics industries.

**Kattegat** /ˈkætɪˌɡæt/ a strait, 225 km. (140 miles) in length, between Sweden and Denmark. It is linked to the North Sea by the Skagerrak and to the Baltic Sea by the Øresund, and was once of considerable strategic importance. Its name means 'cat's throat'.

**Katwijk** /ˈkɑːtvaɪk/ (fully **Katwijk aan Zee**) a resort town in the Dutch province of South Holland, on the North Sea coast at the mouth of the Old Rhine, north-west of Leiden; pop. (1991) 49,100.

**Katy** /ˈkeɪtɪ/, **the** the name given to both a railroad track and a motor freeway (Katy Freeway) which head westwards from the centre of Houston, Texas, USA.

**Kauai** /ˈkaʊɪ/ an island in the US state of Hawaii, to the north-west of Oahu from which it is separated by the Kauai Channel. Its chief town is Lihue and its highest peaks are Kawaikini (1,576 m., 5,170 ft.) and Waialeale (1,548 m., 5,080 ft.).

**Kaufbeuren** /ˈkaʊfbɔɪr(ə)n/ a town in Bavaria, southern Germany, on the Wertach River south-west of Munich; pop. (1991) 41,170.

**Kaunas** /ˈkaʊnɑːs/ an old industrial city and river port in southern Lithuania, at the junction of the Vilnya and Neman rivers; pop. (1991) 430,000. A trading centre in medieval times, Kaunas was the provisional capital of Lithuania from 1918 to 1940.

It has a 13th-c. castle and its university was founded in 1922. It produces electrical machinery, metal goods, textiles, and paper.

**Kaválla** /kəˈvælə/ a port on the Aegean coast of north-east Greece, the second-largest city of Macedonia; pop. (1981) 56,375. Originally a Byzantine city and fortress controlling Macedonia, it was Turkish until 1912, when it was ceded to Greece. Now a centre of the tobacco and cotton trade, it occupies the site of Neapolis, the port of ancient Philippi. It was a port of arrival and departure on the journey between Europe and the Levant, and was the birthplace in 1769 of Mehmet Ali who later became pasha of Egypt.

**Kavaratti** /ˌkəvəˈrəti:/ an Indian island in the Arabian Sea, administrative centre of the Union Territory of Lakshadweep. The island is noted for its masons and craftsmen.

**Kaveri** see CAUVERY.

**Kavieng** /ˌkæviːˈeŋ/ the chief town of the island and province of New Ireland in the Bismarck Archipelago, Papua New Guinea.

**Kavkaz** /kəfˈkɑːz/ see CAUCASUS.

**Kawachinagano** /kəˈwætʃɪnəˌɡɑːnəʊ/ a city on Honshu Island, Japan, to the south of Osaka; pop. (1990) 108,770.

**Kawagoe** /kəˈwɑːɡəʊə/ a city in Saitama prefecture, central Honshu Island, Japan, north-west of Tokyo; pop. (1990) 304,860.

**Kawaguchi** /ˌkæwəˈɡuːtʃɪ/ a northern industrial suburb of Tokyo, in Saitama prefecture, central Japan; pop. (1990) 438,670.

**Kawanishi** /ˌkæwəˈniːʃɪ/ a city in Hyogo prefecture, Honshu Island, Japan, situated on the Ina River to the north of Osaka; pop. (1990) 141,250.

**Kawasaki** /ˌkæwəˈsɑːkɪ/ a major industrial city on the south-east coast of Honshu Island, Japan, situated north-west of Tokyo; pop. (1990) 1,174,000. It is the capital of Kanagawa prefecture in Kanto Region and has steel mills, oil refineries, electrical, and engineering works.

**Kawthoolay** see KAREN STATE.

**Kayseri** /ˈkaɪsəri:/ **1.** a mountainous province in central Anatolia, Turkey, noted for its fine carpets; area 16,917 sq. km. (6,534 sq. miles); pop. (1990) 943,480. **2.** its capital, at the foot of Mount Aergius; pop. (1990) 421,360. The ancient Hittite city of Mazaca built on this site and later known as Eusebeia or Caesaraea Mazaca, eventually became capital of Cappadocia. It was the birthplace of St. Basil the Great.

**Kazakh** /ˈkæzɑːk/ a people of central Asia known as Kirgiz until 1925 and comprising an ethnic mixture of Turkish and Mongol tribes who speak a Turkic language. Traditionally clan-based nomadic herders, they practise a religion that combines Islam and shamanistic beliefs.

## Kazakhstan

/ˌkæzɑːkˈstɑːn/ (Russian **Kazakhskaya Republika**) official name **The Republic of Kazakhstan** an independent republic in central Asia, to the south of Russia and

extending east from the Caspian Sea to the Altai Mountains; area 2,717,300 sq. km. (1,049,555 sq. miles); pop. (1990) 16,691,000; official language, Kazakh; capital, Almaty (Alma Ata). The largest cities are Almaty, Qaraghandy (Karaganda), Semipalatinsk, and Shymkent (Chimkent). A largely low-lying country in the north and west, with rolling hills and plateaux that give way to mountainous areas in the south and east, Kazakhstan has a continental climate with hot summers. Its agriculture has changed from nomadic sheep and cattle rearing to the production of cash crops such as grain, cotton, and tobacco and its rich reserves of natural resources have encouraged the development of industries that produce chemicals, fertilizers, iron and steel, and a wide range of consumer goods. The Turkic tribes of Kazakhstan were overrun by Mongols in the 13th c. and ruled by a series of khanates until absorbed into the Russian empire during the 18th and 19th c. It became an autonomous Soviet republic in 1925, a constituent republic of the USSR in 1936, and an independent republic within the Commonwealth of Independent States in 1991 following the breakup of the Soviet Union. Just under 40 per cent of the population are Kazakh and nearly 38 per cent are Russians, many of whom were settled in Kazakhstan during the Virgin Lands campaign of Nikita Krushchev 1954–63. It is governed by a legislative Supreme Parliament (*Kenges*). **Kazakh** *adj. & n.*

**Kazan** /kəˈzæn, -ˈzænjə/ a city and port on the River Volga, capital of the autonomous republic of Tatarstan in western Russia; pop. (1990) 1,103,000. Founded in 1401, it became capital of the powerful Tatar khanate in 1445 and later a frontier capital of the Russian Volga region. Its university was founded in 1804 and its students have included Leo Tolstoy (1828–1910) and Vladimir Ulyanov (Lenin) (1870–1924). Kazan has chemical, electrical, shipbuilding, oil refining, and machine tools industries as well as traditional handicrafts.

**Kebnekaise** /ˌkebnəˈkaɪsə/ the highest peak in Sweden, in Norrbotten county, rising to a height of 2,117 m. (6,962 ft.).

**Kecskemét** /ˈkexkəmeɪt/ a city, capital of Bács-Kiskun county, southern Hungary; pop. (1993) 105,240. It is a centre of art, music, and education with a livestock trade and industries producing liqueurs, processed food, and textiles.

**Kedah** /ˈkedə/ a state of Malaysia, in the northwest of the Malay peninsula between Thailand and

the Strait of Malacca; area 9,425 sq. km. (3,640 sq. miles); pop. (1990) 1,412,800; capital, Alor Setar.

**Kediri** /keɪˈdɪəri/ a city in eastern Java, Indonesia, on the Brantas River south-west of Surabaya; pop. (1980) 222,000. During the 11th–13th centuries it was the centre of a powerful maritime kingdom trading in spices with the Moluccas and India. It is famous for handicrafts such as batik, silverware, and rattan.

**Keeling Islands** an alternative name for the COCOS ISLANDS.

**Keelung** /kiːˈluːŋ/ a major seaport and industrial centre at the northern tip of Taiwan; pop. (1982) 351,700. It is the second-largest port on the island and when held by the Spanish (1626–41) was known as Santissima Trinidad. Shipbuilding, chemicals, and machinery are important industries.

**Keetmanshoop** /ˈkeɪtmɑːnsˌhəʊp/ a market town in a sheep-rearing area of southern Namibia, founded in 1866 by German missionaries; pop. (est. 1988) 14,000. Named after the German industrialist Johann Keetman who helped fund the original settlement, it is the largest town in Namibia south of Windhoek.

**Keewatin** /kiːˈwɑːtɪn/ an administrative district of the Northwest Territories of Canada, to the west of Hudson Bay; area 590,934 sq. km. (228,160 sq. miles).

**Kefallinía** the Greek name for CEPHALONIA.

**Keflavik** /ˈkefləˌviːk/ a fishing port in south-west Iceland, 40 km. (25 miles) west of Reykjavik; pop. (1990) 7,525. Iceland's international airport is located nearby.

**Kelang** see PORT KELANG.

**Kelantan** /keˈlænt(ə)n/ a state of northern Malaysia on the east coast of the Malay peninsula; area 14,796 sq. km. (5,715 sq. miles); pop. (1990) 1,220,100; capital, Kota Baharu.

**Kells** /kelz/ (Gaelic **Ceannanus Mor** /ˌkiːəˈnɑːnəs mɔː/) a town in County Meath, north-east Ireland, in the valley of the Blackwater River; pop. (1991) 2,187. A monastic settlement was founded here in the 6th c. by St. Columcille. About the beginning of the 9th c. an illuminated Latin manuscript of the four gospels, the famous *Book of Kells*, was produced here. There are remains of St. Columcille's House, a round tower, and several Celtic Crosses.

**Kelowna** /kəˈləʊnə/ a resort in the Columbia Mountains of southern British Columbia, Canada, on the eastern shore of Lake Okanagan; pop. (1991) 76,000. Winter sports and yachting are important vacation activities.

**Kemerovo** /ˈkemərəvə/ an industrial city in west Siberia, in the Russian Federation, to the east of Novosibirsk; pop. (1990) 521,000. Based on the nearby Novokuznetsk coalfield, its industries include chemicals and farm machinery.

**Kemi** /'keɪmɪ/ a seaport at the head of the Gulf of Bothnia in the province of Lappi, northern Finland; pop. (1990) 25,370. It is a steel-producing centre, trading in iron ore and timber products.

**Kemi** /'keɪmɪ/ (Finnish **Kemijoki**) a river of Lapland in northern Finland that rises near the Russian frontier and flows 480 km. (300 miles) westwards past Rovaniemi to the Gulf of Bothnia.

**Kempten** /'kemt(ə)n/ (in full **Kempten im Allgäu**) an ancient town in Bavaria, southern Germany, on the River Iller south-west of Munich; pop. (1991) 62,230. It is the chief town of the Allgäu dairy-farming region in Upper Swabia and has textile and machinery industries. It has a 17th-c. Baroque palace.

**Kendal** /'kend(ə)l/ a town in the Lake District of Cumbria, north-west England, on the River Kent; pop. (1981) 24,200. There are remains of a Norman castle which was the birthplace in 1512 of Catherine Parr, sixth wife of Henry VIII.

**Kenilworth** /'ken(ə)lwɜ:θ/ a market town in Warwickshire, central England, 8km. (5 miles) south-west of Coventry; pop. (1981) 18,920. Its ruined 12th-c. castle, in which Edward II was forced to abdicate, featured in Sir Walter Scott's novel *Kenilworth*.

**Kenitra** /kə'ni:trə/ a river port near the north-west coast of Morocco, 16 km. (10 miles) from the mouth of the Sebou River north-east of Rabat; pop. (1982) 188,190. It was founded by the French in 1913 and until c. 1958 was named Port Lyautey after the French Marshal and former Governor who built the modern city. It has textile, fish-processing, and fertilizer industries.

**Kennedy, Cape** see CAPE CANAVERAL.

**Kenner** /'ken(ə)r/ a city in south-east Louisiana, USA, on the Mississippi west of New Orleans; pop. (1990) 72,030. It is a centre for thoroughbred racing.

**Kenosha** /kə'nəʊʃə/ an industrial city in south-east Wisconsin, USA, a port and transportation centre on Lake Michigan south of Milwaukee; pop. (1990) 80,350. It was first settled by New Englanders in 1835.

**Kensal Green** /'kens(ə)l/ a district to the north of Notting Hill in north-west London whose cemetery contains the graves of Isambard Kingdom Brunel, W. H. Smith, Charles Babbage, and notable writers such as Thomas Hood, Sydney Smith, Leigh Hunt, William Thackeray, Anthony Trollope, and Wilkie Collins.

**Kensington** /'kenzɪŋtən/ a fashionable residential district in central London. Part of the borough of Kensington and Chelsea, it lies to the west and south of Hyde Park. At the west end of Kensington Gardens is Kensington Palace, originally known as Nottingham House, the seat of a 17th-c. Lord Chancellor, and birthplace of Queen Victoria. The Natural History Museum, the Victoria and Albert Museum, the Science Museum, the Royal Albert Hall, and the headquarters of the Royal Geographical Society are all in Kensington which was the birthplace of Sir Max Beerbohm in 1872, G. K. Chesterton in 1874, and Virginia Woolf in 1882.

**Kent** /kent/ a county on the south-east coast of England; area 3,731 sq. km. (1,441 sq. miles); pop. (1991) 1,485,600; county town, Maidstone. **Kentish** *adj*.

Kent is divided into 14 districts:

| District | Area (sq. km.) | Pop. (1991) |
| --- | --- | --- |
| Ashford | 580 | 90,900 |
| Canterbury | 309 | 127,100 |
| Dartford | 73 | 78,400 |
| Dover | 314 | 102,600 |
| Gillingham | 32 | 93,300 |
| Gravesham | 99 | 90,000 |
| Maidstone | 393 | 133,200 |
| Rochester upon Medway | 160 | 142,000 |
| Sevenoaks | 368 | 106,100 |
| Shepway | 357 | 89,200 |
| Swale | 369 | 113,700 |
| Thanet | 103 | 121,700 |
| Tonbridge and Malling | 240 | 99,100 |
| Tunbridge Wells | 332 | 98,300 |

**Kenting National Park** /ken'tɪŋ/ a national park at the southern tip of Taiwan. It extends over an area of 326.4 sq. km. (126 sq. miles) and includes a marine area of 149 sq. km. (57.5 sq. miles). Designated in 1984, it was the first national park to be created in Taiwan.

**Kentish Town** a district of Camden in north London, England, to the north of St. Pancras and Regent's Park.

**Kentucky** /ken'tʌkɪ/ a state in the south-eastern USA; area 104,660 sq. km. (49,409 sq. miles); pop. (1990) 3,685,300; capital, Frankfort. The largest cities are Louisville and Lexington. Kentucky is also known as the Bluegrass State. Ceded by the French in 1763 and first settled in the 1770s, Kentucky entered the Union as the 15th state in 1792. Coal-mining and agriculture are important and the Bluegrass country around Lexington is a noted centre of race-horse breeding. The state's principal landmarks are the Mammoth Cave National Park, the Big South Fork National River and Recreation Area, Cumberland Gap National Historic Park, and the Abraham Lincoln Birthplace National Historic Site. Kentucky is divided into 120 counties:

| County | Area (sq. km.) | Pop. (1990) | County Seat |
| --- | --- | --- | --- |
| Adair | 1,058 | 15,360 | Columbia |
| Allen | 879 | 14,630 | Scottsville |
| Anderson | 530 | 14,570 | Lawrenceburg |
| Ballard | 660 | 7,900 | Wickliffe |
| Barren | 1,253 | 34,000 | Glasgow |
| Bath | 720 | 9,690 | Owingsville |
| Bell | 939 | 31,060 | Pineville |

| | | | |
|---|---|---|---|
| Boone | 640 | 57,590 | Burlington |
| Bourbon | 759 | 19,240 | Paris |
| Boyd | 416 | 51,150 | Catlettsburg |
| Boyle | 473 | 25,640 | Danville |
| Bracken | 528 | 7,770 | Brooksville |
| Breathitt | 1,287 | 15,700 | Jackson |
| Breckinridge | 1,469 | 16,310 | Hardinsburg |
| Bullitt | 780 | 47,570 | Shepherdsville |
| Butler | 1,121 | 11,245 | Morgantown |
| Caldwell | 902 | 13,230 | Princeton |
| Calloway | 1,004 | 30,735 | Murray |
| Campbell | 395 | 83,870 | Alexandria |
| Carlisle | 497 | 5,240 | Bardwell |
| Carroll | 338 | 9,290 | Carrollton |
| Carter | 1,058 | 24,320 | Grayson |
| Casey | 1,157 | 14,210 | Liberty |
| Christian | 1,877 | 68,940 | Hopkinsville |
| Clark | 663 | 29,500 | Winchester |
| Clay | 1,225 | 21,750 | Manchester |
| Clinton | 510 | 9,135 | Albany |
| Crittenden | 936 | 9,200 | Marion |
| Cumberland | 790 | 6,780 | Burkesville |
| Davies | 1,204 | 87,190 | Owensboro |
| Edmonson | 785 | 10,360 | Brownsville |
| Elliott | 608 | 6,455 | Sandy Hook |
| Estill | 666 | 14,610 | Irvine |
| Fayette | 741 | 225,370 | Lexington |
| Fleming | 913 | 12,300 | Flemingsburg |
| Floyd | 1,022 | 43,590 | Prestonsburg |
| Franklin | 551 | 43,780 | Frankfort |
| Fulton | 549 | 8,270 | Hickman |
| Gallatin | 257 | 5,390 | Warsaw |
| Garrard | 603 | 11,580 | Lancaster |
| Grant | 673 | 15,740 | Williamstown |
| Graves | 1,448 | 33,550 | Mayfield |
| Grayson | 1,282 | 21,050 | Leitchfield |
| Green | 751 | 10,370 | Greensburg |
| Greenup | 902 | 36,740 | Greenup |
| Hancock | 491 | 7,800 | Hawesville |
| Hardin | 1,635 | 89,240 | Elizabethtown |
| Harlan | 1,217 | 36,570 | Harlan |
| Harrison | 806 | 16,250 | Cynthiana |
| Hart | 1,071 | 14,890 | Munfordville |
| Henderson | 1,139 | 43,040 | Henderson |
| Henry | 757 | 12,820 | New Castle |
| Hickman | 637 | 5,570 | Clinton |
| Hopkins | 1,435 | 46,130 | Madisonville |
| Jackson | 900 | 11,955 | McKee |
| Jefferson | 1,004 | 664,940 | Louisville |
| Jessamine | 452 | 30,510 | Nicholasville |
| Johnson | 686 | 23,250 | Paintsville |
| Kenton | 424 | 142,030 | Independence |
| Knott | 915 | 17,910 | Hindman |
| Knox | 1,009 | 29,680 | Barbourville |
| Larue | 684 | 11,680 | Hodgenville |
| Laurel | 1,128 | 43,440 | London |
| Lawrence | 1,092 | 13,990 | Louisa |
| Lee | 549 | 7,420 | Beattyville |
| Leslie | 1,045 | 13,640 | Hyden |
| Letcher | 881 | 27,000 | Whitesburg |
| Lewis | 1,258 | 13,030 | Vanceburg |
| Lincoln | 876 | 20,045 | Stanford |
| Livingston | 811 | 9,060 | Smithland |
| Logan | 1,446 | 24,420 | Russellville |
| Lyon | 543 | 6,620 | Eddyville |
| Marion | 902 | 16,500 | Lebanon |
| Marshall | 790 | 27,205 | Benton |
| Martin | 598 | 12,530 | Inez |
| McCracken | 653 | 62,880 | Paducah |
| McCreary | 1,110 | 15,600 | Whitely City |
| McLean | 666 | 9,630 | Calhoun |
| Madison | 1,152 | 57,510 | Richmond |
| Magoffin | 806 | 13,080 | Salyersville |
| Mason | 627 | 16,670 | Maysville |
| Meade | 796 | 24,170 | Brandenburg |
| Menifee | 528 | 5,090 | Frenchburg |
| Mercer | 650 | 19,150 | Harrodsburg |
| Metcalfe | 757 | 8,960 | Edmonton |
| Monroe | 861 | 11,400 | Tompkinsville |
| Montgomery | 517 | 19,560 | Mount Sterling |
| Morgan | 993 | 11,650 | West Liberty |
| Muhlenberg | 1,243 | 31,320 | Greenville |
| Nelson | 1,102 | 29,710 | Bardstown |
| Nicholas | 512 | 6,725 | Carlisle |
| Ohio | 1,550 | 21,105 | Hartford |
| Oldham | 494 | 33,260 | La Grange |
| Owen | 920 | 9,035 | Owenton |
| Owsley | 515 | 5,040 | Booneville |
| Pendleton | 731 | 12,040 | Falmouth |
| Perry | 887 | 30,280 | Hazard |
| Pike | 2,041 | 72,580 | Pikeville |
| Powell | 468 | 11,690 | Stanton |
| Pulaski | 1,716 | 49,490 | Somerset |
| Robertson | 260 | 2,120 | Mount Olivet |
| Rockcastle | 827 | 14,800 | Mount Vernon |
| Rowan | 733 | 20,350 | Morehead |
| Russell | 650 | 14,720 | Jamestown |
| Scott | 744 | 23,870 | Georgetown |
| Shelby | 1,001 | 24,820 | Shelbyville |
| Simpson | 614 | 15,145 | Franklin |
| Spencer | 499 | 6,800 | Taylorsville |
| Taylor | 702 | 21,150 | Campbellsville |
| Todd | 980 | 10,940 | Elkton |
| Trigg | 1,095 | 10,360 | Cadiz |
| Trimble | 385 | 6,090 | Bedford |
| Union | 887 | 16,560 | Morganfield |
| Warren | 1,425 | 76,670 | Bowling Green |
| Washington | 783 | 10,440 | Springfield |
| Wayne | 1,160 | 17,470 | Monticello |
| Webster | 874 | 13,955 | Dixon |
| Whitley | 1,152 | 33,330 | Williamsburg |
| Wolfe | 580 | 6,500 | Campton |
| Woodford | 499 | 19,955 | Versailles |

**Kenya** /ˈkenjə/ official name **The Republic of Kenya** a country in East Africa, bisected by the equator and with a coastline on the Indian Ocean; area 582,646 sq. km. (225,047 sq. miles); pop. (est. 1991) 25,200,000; official language, English (Swahili is the national language); capital, Nairobi. The largest cities are Nairobi, Mombasa, and Kisumu. The northern three-fifths of Kenya is arid semi-desert which supports nomadic

pastoralists, but the majority of the population lives in the south. The Great Rift Valley extends southwards from Lake Turkana and the high plateaux that stretch between the mountain ranges have fertile soils. West of the Aberdare Mts., whose highest peaks are Mt. Kenya and Mt. Elgon, the land gradually falls to the shores of Lake Victoria. Kenya has two rainy seasons from April to June and from October to December, with temperatures varying from the tropical coastline to the more temperate upland region around Nairobi at 1,646 m. (5,400 ft.). The economy is largely based upon agriculture, the tea and coffee crops being particularly important, but in recent years population growth (the world's highest) and crop failures as a result of drought have led to large-scale food imports. Tourism is also very important, the main attractions being wildlife parks and reserves such as the Tsavo, Aberdare, Lake Nakuru, and Mount Kenya national parks and the Maasai Mara, Rahole, Losai, and Bisanadi national reserves. Largely populated by Bantu peoples, Kenya was not exposed to European influence until the arrival of the British in the late 19th c. After the opening up of the interior it became a Crown Colony in 1920. The demands made on the land by European settlers caused discontent, resulting in the Mau Mau rebellion of the 1950s. Kenya became an independent state within the Commonwealth in 1963, and a republic was established the following year. Kenya is governed by an executive president and a unicameral National Assembly.
**Kenyan** *adj. & n.*
Kenya is divided into eight provinces:

| Province | Area (sq. km.) | Pop. (est. 1987) | Capital |
|---|---|---|---|
| Central | 13,173 | 3,284,800 | Nyeri |
| Coast | 83,040 | 1,904,100 | Mombasa |
| Eastern | 155,760 | 3,864,700 | Embu |
| Nairobi | 684 | 1,288,700 | Nairobi |
| North-Eastern | 126,902 | 554,000 | Garissa |
| Nyanza | 12,526 | 3,892,600 | Kisumu |
| Rift Valley | 171,108 | 4,702,400 | Nakuru |
| Western | 8,223 | 2,535,900 | Kakamega |

**Kenya, Mount** (also **Kirinyaga**) a mountain in central Kenya of volcanic origin, just south of the equator, rising to a height of 5,200 m. (17,058 ft.). The second-highest mountain in Africa, it gave its name to the country, Kenya. Its first sighting by European explorers was in 1849 and in 1899 it was climbed by an expedition led by Sir Halford McKinder.

**Kerala** /ˈkerələ/ a state on the coast of south-west India; area 38,863 sq. km. (15,010 sq. miles); pop. (1991) 29,011,230; capital, Thiruvananthapuram (Trivandrum). It was created in 1956 from the former state of Travancore-Cochin and part of Madras.
**Keralite** *adj. & n.*

**Kerava** /ˈkerəvɑː/ (Swedish **Kervo**) a town in southern Finland, a northern suburb of Helsinki; pop. (1990) 27,600. It has a garlic festival in August.

**Kerch** /kɜːtʃ/ **1.** a peninsula of the eastern Crimea in Ukraine, between the Black Sea and the Sea of Azov. **2.** the chief port and industrial centre of the Crimea, at the eastern end of the Kerch Peninsula; pop. (1990) 176,000. Founded in the 6th c. BC by Greek colonists, it was capital of the European part of the Kingdom of Bosporus in the 5th–4th c. BC. It was developed as a Genoese trading centre (renamed Korchev) in the Middle Ages before being captured by the Crimean Tatars in 1475 and then absorbed into the Russian empire in 1772. Its industries include iron, shipbuilding, chemicals, and fishing.

**Kerguelen Islands** /kɜːˈɡeɪlən/ a group of almost uninhabited islands in the southern Indian Ocean, comprising the island of Kerguelen (Grande Terre) and some 300 small islets, forming part of the French Southern and Antarctic Territories; area 7,215 sq. km. (2,787 sq. miles). Occupied by French research scientists in 1949, they are named after the Breton navigator Yves-Joseph de Kerguélen-Trémarec, who discovered them in 1772.

**Kerinci** /kəˈrɪntʃiː/ a volcanic peak in the Barisan Mountains of west-central Sumatra, Indonesia. Rising to a height of 3,806 m. (12,487 ft.) it is the highest mountain on Sumatra and the highest active volcano in Indonesia.

**Kérkira** the Greek name for CORFU.

**Kerkrade** /ˈkɜːkrɑːdə/ a coal-mining town in the Dutch province of Limburg, situated on the German border 30 km. (19 miles) east of Maastricht; pop. (1991) 53,280. An international music competition is held here every four years.

**Kermadec Islands** /kɜːˈmædək/ a group of uninhabited islands in the western South Pacific, north of New Zealand, administered by New Zealand since 1887; area 34 sq. km. (13 sq. miles). The largest of the group is Raoul or Sunday Island on which there is a meteorological station.

**Kerman** /kɜːˈmɑːn/ a desert city in Kerman province, south-east Iran; pop. (1991) 312,000. Its products include carpets and brassware.

**Kermanshah** /ˌkɜːmənˈʃɑː/ (also **Bakhtaran** /ˌbæxtəˈrɑːn/) a city in western Iran, in the Zagros Mountains; pop. (1991) 624,000. Now one of the largest cities of western Iran, it lay on an ancient trading route to Baghdad. Known throughout its long history as Kermanshah (= city of the king), its alternative provincial name was used for nearly a decade after the 1979 Islamic revolution. It is the centre of a rich agricultural region and also manufactures carpets, shoes, and textiles.

**Kerry** /ˈkerɪ/ a county of south-west Ireland, in the province of Munster; area 4,701 sq. km. (1,816 sq. miles); pop. (1991) 121,720; county town, Tralee. It gives its name to a breed of small black dairy cattle and to the Kerry blue, a terrier of a breed with a silky blue-grey coat.

**Kesteven** /kəˈstiːvən/, **Parts of** one of the three former administrative divisions or 'ridings' of the county of Lincoln, east England, prior to the local government reorganization of 1974 that created the districts of North and South Kesteven. Its chief town was Sleaford.

**Keswick** /ˈkezɪk/ a market town and tourist centre near the north end of Derwent Water in Cumbria, north-west England, on the River Greta; pop. (1981) 5,645. The poet Robert Southey lived here from 1809 until his death in 1843 and the novelist Sir Hugh Walpole is buried in St. John's churchyard.

**Kettering** /ˈketərɪŋ/ an industrial and manufacturing town in Northamptonshire, central England, on the River Ise north-east of Northampton; pop. (1981) 45,390.

**Kettering** /ˈketərɪŋ/ a manufacturing city in western Ohio, USA, just south of Dayton; pop. (1990) 60,570. It has numerous engineering industries.

**Kew Gardens** /kjuː/ the Royal Botanic Gardens at Kew, in Richmond upon Thames, London, England. Originally the garden of Kew House, it was established in 1759 as a botanic garden by the mother of George III, with the aid of Sir Joseph Banks. It was presented to the nation in 1841 and continued to develop into a major institution with important reference collections, archives, library, and research laboratories. The palace in Kew Gardens was built by George III.

**Key Biscayne** /kiː ˈbɪskeɪn/ a mangrove-fringed resort island in south-east Florida, USA, on Biscayne Bay opposite Miami; pop. (1990) 8,850. It is a noted centre of international championship tennis. Crandon Park at the north end of the island has golfing and marina facilities. To the south is the Cape Florida lighthouse and the Bill Baggs Cape Florida Recreation Area.

**Key Largo** /kiː ˈlɑːgəʊ/ a resort island off the south coast of Florida, USA, the northernmost and the longest of the Florida Keys; pop. (1990) 11,330. John Pennekamp Coral Reef State Park, the first underwater marine park designated in the US, lies just off the east coast.

**Key West** a fishing port and tourist city in southern Florida, USA, at the southern tip of the Florida Keys; pop. (1990) 24,800. Originally known as Cayo Hueso (Spanish = bone island), it is the southernmost city in continental USA, linked to the southern tip of Florida by the Over-seas Highway which was completed in 1938. It has associations with the ornithologist John Audubon and the novelist Ernest Hemingway who wrote *For Whom the Bell Tolls* here.

**Khabarovsk** /kəˈbɑːrɒfsk/ **1.** a territory in east Siberian Russia, to the north of Manchuria and with the Sea of Okhotsk to the east; area 789,950

sq. km. (305,000 sq. miles); pop. (1990) 1,840,000; . **2.** its capital, on the Amur River; pop. (1990) 608,000. Oil refining, shipbuilding, and engineering are important industries.

**Khakassia** /kəˈkæsɪə/, **Republic of** a republic of the Russian Federation, to the west of the upper Yenesei River in East Siberia; area 61,900 sq. km. (23,855 sq. miles); pop. (1990) 569,000; capital, Abakan. It became an autonomous region of the Soviet Union in 1930 and following the breakup of the USSR in 1991 it became a republic of the Russian Federation.

**Khalkidhiki** the Greek name for CHALCIDICE.

**Khalkis** the Greek name for CHALCIS.

**Khambat, Gulf of** see CAMBAY, GULF OF.

**khamsin** /ˈkæmsɪn/ (also **hamsin** /ˈhæ-/) an oppressive hot south or south-east wind occurring in Egypt for about 50 days in March, April, and May.

**Khandwa** /ˈkəndwɑː/ a market town in Madhya Pradesh, central India, south-east of Indore; pop. (1991) 145,110.

**Khaniá** the Greek name for CANEA.

**Khankendi** /kɑːnˈkendɪ/ see XANKÄNDI.

**Kharagpur** /ˈkərəɡˌpʊ(ə)r/ an industrial town in West Bengal, north-east India, on the Kasai River west of Calcutta; pop. (1991) 279,740. It has a scientific research centre.

**Khardangla Pass** a high-altitude pass in the western Himalayas of Kashmir to the north of the Indus. Reaching a height of 5,662 m. (18,576 ft.), it is reckoned to be one of the highest passes in the world. It is used by the Indian Army as a supply route linking the town of Leh with outposts on the Siachen Glacier near Mt. K2.

**Kharg Island** /kɑːɡ/ a small island at the head of the Persian Gulf, site of Iran's principal deep-water oil terminal.

**Kharkiv** /ˈkɑːkɪv/ (formerly **Kharkov**) an industrial and market city, and railway junction in north-east Ukraine, situated to the east of Kiev in the Donets coal basin at the confluence of the Kharkov, Lopan, and Udy rivers; pop. (1990) 1,618,000. Founded in 1665 as a Cossack frontier headquarters, its coal and metal industries developed in the mid-19th c. It was the first capital of the Ukrainian Soviet Socialist Republic from its establishment in 1919 until replaced by Kiev in 1934. It produces agricultural and mining machinery, machine tools, railway wagons, electrical equipment, and foodstuffs.

**Khartoum** /kɑːˈtuːm/ the capital of Sudan, situated at the junction of the Blue Nile and the White Nile; pop. (1983) 476,220. Originally established in 1821 as an Egyptian army camp, it developed into a garrison town. In 1885 a British and Egyptian force under the command of General Charles Gordon (1833–85) was besieged here for ten months by the Mahdists, who eventually stormed the garrison, killing most of the defenders, including Gordon. It remained under the control of the Mahdists until they were defeated by the British in 1898 and the city was recaptured by General Kitchener. It was the capital of the Anglo-Egyptian government of Sudan until 1956, when it became capital of the independent Republic of Sudan. The city centre lies on a curved strip of land like an elephant's trunk which gives its name to the city (Arabic *Ras-al-hartum* = end of the elephant's trunk). **Khartoum North** across the Blue Nile is a modern industrial zone with pharmaceutical, textile, leather, and food-processing industries; pop. (1983) 341,150.

**Khasi Hills** /'kɑːziː/ a range of hills in the states of Assam and Meghalaya, north-east India. They give their name to an Austro-Asiatic tribe, the Khasis, who live in the area.

**Khaskovo** /'xɑːskəvəʊ/ (also **Haskovo**) the capital city of Khaskovo province, central Bulgaria, in the northern foothills of the Rhodpe Mts.; pop. (1989) 95,030. It is a major tobacco-producing centre.

**Khaylitsa** /kaɪˈlɪtsə/ a township 40 km. (25 miles) south-east of Cape Town, South Africa. Designed to accommodate 250,000 people, it was built in 1983 for black Africans from the squatter camps of Crossroads, Langa, and KTC.

**Kherson** /kɪəˈsɒn/ a port in southern Ukraine, on the Dnieper estuary 24 km. (15 miles) from the Black Sea; pop. (1990) 361,000. It is a centre of oil refining, shipbuilding, engineering, and textile production.

**Khios** the Greek name for CHIOS.

**Khitai** see CATHAY.

**Khiva** /'kiːvə/ an oasis town in north-west Uzbekistan, west of the lower Amu Darya and north of the Kara Kum Desert. It was capital of the former khanate of Khiva or Kharesm which became a Republic in 1920 before being absorbed into the Soviet Republic of Uzbekistan in 1924.

**Khmelnytskyy** /kəmelˈnɪtskiː/ (also **Khmelnitskiy**) a city in western Ukraine, south-west of Kiev; pop. (1990) 241,000. It was known as Proskurov until 1954. It has metal, machine tool, and heavy engineering industries.

**Khmer** /kmeə(r)/ **1.** an ancient kingdom in South-East Asia, which reached the peak of its power in the 11th c., ruling over the entire Mekong valley from the capital at Angkor, and was destroyed by Siamese conquests in the 12th and 14th c. **2.** the indigenous people of Cambodia and parts of Vietnam whose monosyllabic language belongs to the Mon-Khmer group of the Austro-Asiatic family. The **Khmer Kandal** (centre Khmer) are people of the ricelands of west and central Cambodia; the **Khmer Krom** (lower Khmer) are people of Vietnam's Mekong delta; and the **Khmer Loeu** (upper Khmer) are the hill people of north-east Cambodia.

**Khmer Republic** the former official name (1970–75) for CAMBODIA.

**Khodzhent** see KHUDZHAND.

**Khoisan** /hɔɪˈsɑːn/ a group of 'click' languages spoken in southern and eastern Africa, chiefly by Bushmen and Hottentots.

**Khorramabad** /kəʊˈrɑːməˌbɑːd/ a market city in western Iran, in the Zagros Mountains northwest of Isfahan; pop. (1991) 249,000. It is capital of Lorestan province.

**Khorramshahr** /ˌxɔːrəmˈʃɑː(r)/ an oil-port and trading centre in the Khuzestan province of western Iran, at the junction of the River Karun with the Shatt al-Arab waterway; pop. (1986) 151,000. Known as Mohammerah until 1924, it was almost totally destroyed during the Iran–Iraq War of 1980–8.

**Khouribga** /kʊ(ə)riːbˈgɑː/ an industrial town on the coastal plain of north-west Morocco, southeast of Casablanca; pop. (1982) 230,000. It lies at the centre of Morocco's chief phosphate-mining region.

**khrebet** /krəˈbjet/ a Russian word for a mountain range, as in Anadyrski Khrebet (the Anadyr Range).

**Khudzhand** /kuːdˈʒɑːnd/ (also **Kojend**, Russian **Khodzhent**) a city in north-west Tajikistan, on the Syr Darya River south of Tashkent; pop. (1991) 165,000. Situated on an ancient caravan route, it is a major centre for textile and silk production. It was known as Leninabad from 1936 to 1991.

**Khulna** /'kuːlnə/ an industrial city in southern Bangladesh, on the Ganges delta; pop. (1991) 601,050. It is capital of an administrative division of the same name, trading in jute, rice, oil seed, salt, and sugar.

**Khunjerab Pass** /'kʌnəˌjaːb/ a pass through the Himalayas at an altitude of 4,900 m. (16,080 ft.) to the north-west of Mt. K2, on the Karakoram highway linking China and Pakistan.

**Khuzestan** /ˌkuːzɪsˈtɑːn/ an oil-producing province of south-west Iran, on the frontier with Iraq from which it is separated by the Shatt al-Arab Waterway; area 67,236 sq. km. (25,970 sq. miles); pop. (1982) 2,197,000; capital, Ahvaz. Between 1890 and 1925 the predominantly Arab Khuzestanis maintained their autonomy under a tribal sheik. Subsequently absorbed into Iran, their claim to autonomy has been supported by Iraqis who have named the region Arabistan.

**Khyber Pass** /'kaɪbə(r)/ a mountain pass in the Hindu Kush, on the border between Pakistan and Afghanistan at a height of 1,067 m. (3,520 ft.). The pass was for long of great commercial and strategic importance, the route by which successive invaders entered India, and was garrisoned by the British intermittently between 1839 and 1947.

**Kiangsu** see JIANGSU.

**Kibo** /'ki:bəʊ/ the highest peak of Mt. Kilimanjaro in Tanzania, East Africa (5,895 m., 19,340 ft.). Once an active volcano, its summit is permanently snow-covered although only just south of the equator.

**kibbutz** a communal type of self-supporting farming settlement in Israel, conceived and developed in the early years of the 20th c. by Professor Franz Oppenheimer. After an initial experiment in 1908, the first kibbutz farmers settled on land at Kinneret on the south-west shore of the Sea of Galilee.

**kibbutznik** *adj. & n.*

**Kidderminster** /'kɪdə,mɪnstə(r)/ a town of west-central England, in Hereford and Worcester, on the River Stour; pop. (1981) 50,750. It gives its name to a type of reversible carpet made of two cloths of different colours woven together. It was the birthplace in 1795 of Sir Rowland Hill who initiated the 'penny-post'.

**Kiel** /ki:l/ a naval port with large shipyards in northern Germany, capital of the state of Schleswig-Holstein; pop. (1991) 247,100. Situated on the Baltic Sea coast at the eastern end of the Kiel Canal, it was Germany's chief naval base from 1871 to 1945. Now an international yachting centre.

**Kiel Canal** a man-made waterway 98 km. (61 miles) in length in Schleswig-Holstein, north-west Germany, running westwards from Kiel to Brunsbüttel at the mouth of the Elbe. It connects the North Sea with the Baltic and was constructed in 1887–95 to provide the German navy with a shorter route between these two seas.

**Kielce** /ki:'eltseɪ/ an industrial city and transportation centre in southern Poland, to the south of Warsaw; pop. (1990) 214,200. Mining, smelting, engineering, and the manufacture of chemicals, machinery, and vehicles are its chief industries.

**Kielder Water** /'ki:ldə/ a reservoir in Northumberland, north-east England, created by the damming of the River Tyne and constructed between 1974 and 1982 to supply water to the industrial towns of the north-east. It is one of the largest man-made lakes in Europe and the nearby Kielder Forest, which stretches to the Scottish border, is with neighbouring planted areas one of the largest forest plantations in Europe.

**Kiev** /'ki:ef/ (also **Kiyev**) the capital of Ukraine, an ancient industrial and university (1834) city, and port on the River Dnieper; pop. (1990) 2,616,000. Founded in the 8th c., it developed as an early commercial centre on the trade route between Scandinavia and Constantinople, and in the Middle Ages became capital of the state of Kievan Rus. Destroyed by the Mongols in 1240, it was successively held by Lithuania and Poland until the Cossack revolt of 1648 when it briefly became the capital of a Ukrainian state. Under Russian control in 1654,

it eventually became the capital of the Ukrainian Soviet Socialist Republic in 1934. In 1991 it became capital of an independent Ukraine. Its important industries include engineering, food processing, chemicals, and electrical engineering.

**Kigali** /kɪ'gɑ:lɪ/ the capital and chief commercial centre of Rwanda in central Africa; pop. (1981) 156,650. It is situated to the east of Lake Kivu.

**Kigoma** /ki:'gəʊmə/ a port on the shores of Lake Tanganyika, western Tanzania. Formerly an important Arab trading town it developed as a trans-shipment centre for tin and gold from the Belgian Congo. Today it handles timber, cotton, and tobacco from Zaire, Rwanda, and Burundi.

**Kikládhes** the Greek name for the CYCLADES.

**Kikuyu** /kɪ'ku:ju:/ an agricultural people of East Africa, the largest Bantu-speaking group in Kenya.

**Kilbrennan Sound** /kɪl'brenən/ (also **Kilbrannan Sound**) an arm of the Firth of Clyde forming a channel between the island of Arran and the Kintyre peninsula, west-central Scotland.

**Kildare** /kɪl'deə(r)/ a county of the Republic of Ireland, in the east, in the province of Leinster; area 1,694 sq. km. (654 sq. miles); pop. (1991) 122,520; county town, Naas.

**Kilifi** /ke'li:fɪ/ a small town on the east coast of Kenya, at the mouth of Kilifi Creek north of Mombasa. It is a popular yachting anchorage and nearby are the ruins of the Swahili city of Mnarani occupied during the 14th–17th c.

**Kilimanjaro** /,kɪlɪmən'dʒɑ:rəʊ/, **Mount** an extinct volcano in northern Tanzania. It has twin peaks, the higher of which, Kibo (5,895 m., 19,340 ft.), is the highest mountain in Africa. Its lower southern slopes are intensively cultivated, coffee and plantains being the chief crops.

**Kilkenny** /kɪl'kenɪ/ **1.** a county of the Republic of Ireland, in the south-east, in the province of Leinster; area 2,062 sq. km. (796 sq. miles); pop. (1991) 73,610. **2.** its county town, on the River Nore; pop. (1991) 8,510. Capital of the pre-Norman kingdom of Ossary, Kilkenny is named after the 6th-c. church founded by St. Canice. In 1366 the Statute of Kilkenny made it high treason for an Anglo-Norman to marry an Irishwoman and for an Irishman to live in a walled town. The Irish National Design Centre is located in the stables of 13th-c. Kilkenny Castle.

**Kilkís** /ki:l'ki:s/ a town in Macedonia, northern Greece, capital of the department of Kilkís; pop. (1981) 11,150. Situated north of Salonica, the town was formerly known as Avrathisari.

**Killarney** /kɪl'ɑ:nɪ/ a resort town and market centre on Lough Leane in County Kerry, in the south-west of the Republic of Ireland; pop. (1991) 7,250. Set amidst scenic lakes and hills, the Killarney area has long been popular with poets, writers, and artists.

**Killiecrankie** /ˌkɪlɪ'kræŋkɪ/, **Pass of** a wooded gorge south-east of Blair Atholl in Perthshire, Scotland; the site of a battle in 1689 in which the forces of William III were defeated by the Jacobites under Graham of Claverhouse who was killed during the battle. The River Garry flows through the pass.

**Kilmarnock** /kɪl'mɑːnək/ a town in west-central Scotland, the administrative centre of Kilmarnock and Loudon District from 1975 to 1996; pop. (1981) 52,080. The first book of poems by Robert Burns was published here in 1786.

**Kimberley** /'kɪmbəlɪ/ (also **The Kimberleys**) a mining and cattle-rearing region in the far north of Western Australia, situated to the north of the Great Sandy Desert between the Fitzroy and Ord rivers. Its chief settlements are the port of Wyndham (which is the terminus of the Great Northern Highway), the old pearling town of Broome, the cattle town of Derby, and Halls Creek, scene of the first gold-rush in Western Australia in 1885. The meteorite crater at Wolf Creek is the second-largest in the world.

**Kimberley** /'kɪmbəlɪ/ a city in South Africa, capital (since 1994) of the Northern Cape province; pop. (1985) 149,700. Named after the 1st Earl of Kimberley (British Colonial Secretary), it has been a diamond-mining centre since the early 1870s and gave its name to kimberlite, a rare blue-tinged igneous rock that sometimes contains diamonds.

**Kimchaek** /ki:m'tʃæk/ a port on the east coast of North Korea, at the mouth of the Susong River where it meets the Sea of Japan; pop. (est. 1984) 281,000. It has iron-smelting and fish-processing industries.

**Kinabalu** /ˌkɪnəbə'luː/, **Mount** a mountain in the state of Sabah in eastern Malaysia, the highest peak of Borneo and of South-East Asia, rising to a height of 4,094 m. (13,431 ft.). First climbed in 1888 by a zoologist, John Whitehead, it was designated part of the 754-sq. km. (290-sq. mile) Mt. Kinabalu National Park in 1964.

**Kinchinjunga** see KANCHENJUNGA.

**Kineshma** /'ki:nɪʃmə/ an industrial town and river port in western Russia, on the Volga northwest of Nizhniy Novgorod; pop. (1990) 105,000. It has sawmills and textile industries.

**Kingman Reef** an uninhabited series of reefs in the North Pacific, halfway between Hawaii and American Samoa; area 1 sq. km. Administered as an unincorporated territory of the USA, it has an airbase formerly used by flying boats crossing the Pacific.

**King's Canyon** a national park in the Sierra Nevada, California, USA, to the north of, and adjoining the Sequoia National Park. Established in 1940, it preserves groves of ancient sequoia trees amongst which stands the General Sherman Tree, the world's largest tree. Within the park is Mt.

Whitney (4,418 m., 14,494 ft.), the highest peak in the 48 contiguous states of the USA.

**King's Cliffe** a village in Northamptonshire, central England. It was the home of John Fane, 11th Earl of Westmorland (1784–1859), founder of the Royal Academy of Music.

**King's Cross** a district of north London, England, to the east of Regent's Park, site of a large railway terminus built in 1852. Known as Battlebridge until the 1830s, it is named after a statue to King George IV that once stood at a crossroads here.

**King's Lynn** a market town and port in Norfolk, eastern England, on the River Ouse just south of the Wash; pop. (1981) 37,970. Nearby is the royal palace of Sandringham. It was the birthplace of the mystic writer Margery Kempe in 1364, the theologian John Capgrave in 1393, and the novelist Fanny Burney in 1752.

**Kingston** /'kɪŋst(ə)n/ an industrial city in south-east Ontario, Canada, a port on the northeast shore of Lake Ontario at the south-western end of the St. Lawrence River; pop. (1991) 56,600. Founded by United Empire Loyalists in 1783 on the site of a fort (Fort Catasaqui or Fort Frontenac), Kingston was capital of Upper Canada 1841–4. It is the home of a Royal Military College established in 1876. It is an important grain processing and shipping port with heavy industries including locomotive building, shipbuilding, and diesel engines.

**Kingston** /'kɪŋst(ə)n/ the capital and chief port of Jamaica; pop. (1991) 588,000. Situated on the south-east coast of the island and capital since 1870, it was founded in 1693 after the destruction of Port Royal during an earthquake. It is the home of the University of the West Indies (1948) and is the largest English-speaking city in the Americas south of Miami. Its industries include oil refining, food and tobacco processing, shoes and clothing. It is the commercial centre for the coffee trade.

**Kingston upon Hull** /ˌkɪŋst(ə)n, 'hʌl/ the official name of HULL.

**Kingston upon Thames** an outer borough of London, England, on the south bank of the Thames opposite Hampton Court; pop. (1991) 130,300. It was the coronation place of at least six Anglo-Saxon kings. Kingston University (formerly Kingston Polytechnic) was established in 1992.

**Kingstown** /'kɪŋstaʊn/ the capital and chief port of St. Vincent in the Windward Islands of the Caribbean; pop. (1989) 29,370. Situated on Kingstown Bay at the south-west corner of the island, the town is surrounded by a ring of steep hills. Its Botanical Gardens, founded in 1763, are the oldest in the Americas.

**King William Island** a lake-studded island in the Canadian Arctic, situated south-west of the Boothia Peninsula; area 13,111 sq. km. (5,062 sq. miles). Named after King William IV, some of the remains of the ill-fated Franklin expedition were discovered here.

**Kinki** /'ki:nki:/ a region of Japan, in the south of Honshu Island; area 33,080 sq. km. (12,782 sq. miles); pop. (1990) 22,207,000; chief city, Osaka. It is divided into seven prefectures:

| Prefecture | Area (sq. km.) | Pop. (1990) | Capital |
| --- | --- | --- | --- |
| Hyogo | 8,363 | 5,405,000 | Kobe |
| Kyoto | 4,613 | 2,603,000 | Kyoto |
| Mie | 5,774 | 1,793,000 | Tsu |
| Nara | 3,692 | 1,375,000 | Nara |
| Osaka | 1,858 | 8,735,000 | Osaka |
| Shiga | 4,016 | 1,222,000 | Otsu |
| Wakayama | 4,722 | 1,074,000 | Wakayama |

**Kinnesswood** /kɪ'neswu:d/ a village in Kinross-shire, east-central Scotland, to the east of Loch Leven. It was until the early 1900s the centre of Scotland's parchment and vellum industry and was the birthplace in 1746 of the poet Michael Bruce, and in 1829 of the meteorologist Alexander Buchan.

**Kinross** /kɪn'rɒs/ a town in Kinross-shire, east-central Scotland, on the north-west shore of Loch Leven; pop. (1981) 3,500. Kinross House was built by Sir William Bruce, architect royal to King Charles II. It is an agricultural centre with a cashmere spinning mill.

**Kinross-shire** /kɪn'rɒsʃɪə/ a former county of east-central Scotland, since 1975 part of Perth and Kinross District. Its county town was Kinross.

**Kinshasa** /kɪn'ʃɑ:sə/ the capital of Zaire, a port on the Zaïre River; pop. (est.1984) 2,653,560. Founded in 1881 by the explorer H. M. Stanley, it was known until 1966 as Leopoldville and became capital of the Republic of Zaire in 1960. It is a communications focus and a major industrial and cultural centre.

**Kintyre** /kɪn'taɪə/ a peninsula on the west coast of Scotland, to the west of Arran, extending southwards for 64 km. (40 miles) from West Loch Tarbert to the Mull of Kintyre and separating the Firth of Clyde from the Atlantic Ocean. Its chief town is Campbeltown. There are ferry links to the islands of Arran, Gigha, Islay, and Jura.

**Kinyeti** /kɪn'jetɪ/, **Mount** a mountain in southern Sudan, south-east of Juba. At 3,187 m. (10,456 ft.) it is the highest peak in the country.

**Kiowa** /kaɪ'əʊwə/ a Tanoan-language Indian tribe of the North American plains and prairies who once hunted buffalo but now mostly live on the Andarko Agency in Oklahoma where they numbered nearly 4,000 in 1985.

**Kipchak Empire** /'kɪptʃæk/, **the** (also **The Golden Horde**) a Turkish khanate established over central and southern European Russia in the 13th c. by Batu, one of the sons of Genghis Khan. Uniting with the Kingdom of the White Horde (East Kipchak) a century later, it eventually fell to the Tatar conqueror Tamerlane. Its capital was Sarai on the lower Volga.

**Kirghiz** /kɪə'gɪz, 'kɜ:gɪz/ a Mongol people living in central Asia between the Volga and the Irtysh rivers. Closely related to the Kazakhs and making up 52 per cent of the population of Kyrgyzstan, they speak a Turkic language. Until the 20th c. they were a nomadic herding people.

**Kirghizia** /kɪə'gɪzɪə/ a former name for KYRGYZSTAN in Central Asia while it was part of the Soviet Union.

**Kiribati** /'kɪrɪˌbæs/ official name **The Republic of Kiribati** a country in the south-west Pacific, consisting of groups of islands including the Gilbert Islands, the Line Islands, the Phoenix Islands, and Banaba (Ocean Island); area 717 sq. km. (277 sq. miles); pop. (1990) 72,300; official languages, English and I-Kiribati; capital, Bairiki (on South Tarawa). All except one of the islands are low-lying coral atolls. The Gilbert Islands have a tropical climate while the Line Islands, Phoenix Islands, and Banaba, which lie closer to the equator, have a maritime equatorial climate with a higher mean annual rainfall. The islands were a major source of phosphates, but now tuna fishing and the production of copra are the chief economic activities of the islanders who are mostly Micronesian. First sighted by the Spaniards in the mid-16th c., the islands were visited by the British in the 18th c. and named after Thomas Gilbert, an English adventurer who arrived there in 1788; they became a favourite centre for the hunting of sperm whales. Britain declared a protectorate over the Gilbert and Ellice Islands in 1892 and they became a colony in 1915. Links with the Ellice Islands (now Tuvalu) ended in 1975, and in 1979 Kiribati became an independent republic within the Commonwealth. Kiribati is governed by an executive president and a unicameral House of Assembly (*Maneaba*).

**Kiribatian** *adj. & n.*

**Kirikkale** /kə'rɪkəlɪ/ **1.** a province in central Turkey; area 4,365 sq. km. (1,686 sq. miles); pop. (1990) 349,400. **2.** its capital, east of Ankara; pop. (1990) 185,430.

**Kirin** see JILIN.

**Kiritimati** see CHRISTMAS ISLAND.

**Kirkcaldy** /kɜ:'kɔ:dɪ/ an industrial town in Fife, eastern Scotland, a port on the north shore of the Firth of Forth; pop. (1981) 46,500. Often called 'the Lang Toun' from its 4-mile-long main street, it was the birthplace of the economist Adam Smith (1723–90) and the architect Robert Adam (1728–92). Developed as a textile-manufacturing town in the 19th c., its industries today produce linoleum, clothing, and plastics.

**Kirkcudbright** /kɜ:ˈku:brɪ/ a town in Dumfries and Galloway, southern Scotland, administrative centre of the Stewartry District from 1975 to 1996; pop. (1981) 3,430. It is situated on the estuary of the River Dee. The American sailor John Paul Jones was born in the nearby village of Kirkbean in 1747.

**Kirkcudbrightshire** /kɜ:ˈku:brɪʃɪə/ a former county of south-west Scotland, since 1975 part of Dumfries and Galloway.

**Kirkenes** /ˈki:rkəneɪs/ a town in Finnmark county in the far north-east of Norway; pop. (1991) 9,700. Situated on an inlet of the Varanger Fiord, it is a major iron-mining centre.

**Kirklareli** /kɪrkˈlɑ:rəlɪ/ **1.** a province in north-west Turkey, on the frontier with Bulgaria; area 6,378 sq. km. (2,463 sq. miles); pop. (1990) 309,510. **2.** its capital; pop. (1990) 43,020.

**Kirkuk** /kɜ:ˈku:k/ a Kurdish industrial city in northern Iraq, a centre of the country's oil industry; pop. (1985) 208,000.

**Kirkwall** the chief town and port of the Orkneys, situated on the mainland of Orkney, on a narrow neck of land between the Bay of Kirkwall and Scapa Flow; pop. (1981) 6,000. Its principal landmarks are the 12th-c. St. Magnus Cathedral and the 17th-c. Earl Patrick's palace.

**Kirov** /ˈkɪərɒf/ see VYATKA.

**Kirovabad** /ˌkɪrəuvəˈbæd/ see GÄNCÄ.

**Kirovograd** /ˌkɪrəuvəˈgræd/ see KIROVOHAD.

**Kirovohad** /ˌkɪrəuvəˈhæd/ a city in central Ukraine, on the River Ingul; pop. (1990) 274,000. Founded in 1761 as Elizavetgrad, it was known as Zinoviesk (1924–36), Kirovo (1936–9), and Kirovograd (1939–92). It is a major producer of farm machinery.

**Kirriemuir** /ˌkɪrɪˈmjʊə/ a small town in Angus, east-central Scotland; pop. (1981) 5,120. It was the birthplace in 1860 of the novelist and dramatist J. M. Barrie.

**Kirşehir** /kɜ:ʃəˈhi:r/ **1.** a mountainous province in central Turkey; area 6,501 sq. km. (2,511 sq. miles); pop. (1990) 256,860; . **2.** its capital, south-east of Ankara; pop. (1990) 73,540.

**Kiruna** /kɪˈru:nə/ the northernmost town of Sweden, in Norrbotten county at the centre of the Lapland iron-mining region; pop. (1990) 26,150. It is sometimes referred to as the 'world's largest town' because of its extensive administrative district.

**Kirundi** /kɪˈrʊndɪ/ a Bantu language, the official language of Burundi.

**Kiryu** /kɪrˈju:/ a city in Gumma prefecture, central Honshu Island, Japan, east of Maebashi; pop. (1990) 126,440. It is a noted centre of silk production.

**Kisangani** /ki:sənˈgɑ:nɪ/ a city in north-central Zaire, on the Zaïre River; pop. (1984) 282,650.

Founded in 1882 by the explorer H. M. Stanley, it was known as Stanleyville until 1966. Now a manufacturing, commercial, and communications centre.

**Kisarazu** /ki:sɑ:ˈrɑ:zu:/ a residential city in Chiba prefecture, east-central Honshu Island, Japan, on the Boso Peninsula to the south of Tokyo; pop. (1990) 123,430.

**Kishinev** /kɪʃɪˈnjef/ see CHISINAU.

**Kishiwada** /ki:ʃi:ˈwɑ:də/ a residential suburb of Osaka, south-west Honshu Island, Japan, on Osaka Bay; pop. (1990) 188,550.

**Kislovodsk** /kɪsləˈvɒtsk/ a health resort city in Stavropol Kray, south-western Russia, in the northern foothills of the Caucasus; pop. (1990) 116,000.

**Kismayu** /kɪsˈmi:ju:/ (also **Kismaayo**) a port on the Indian Ocean coast of southern Somalia, near the mouth of the Juba River; pop. (1982) 70,000. It was founded by the Sultan of Zanzibar in 1872.

**Kisumu** /ki:ˈsu:mu:/ the capital of Nyanza province, south-west Kenya, on an inlet of Lake Victoria; pop. (est.1986) 198,000. Formerly known as Port Florence, it is a trading centre for cotton, grain, and fish.

**Kiswahili** /ˌkɪswɑ:ˈhi:lɪ/ a Bantu language of the Niger-Congo group of languages spoken in East Africa. It is one of the six languages preferred for use in Africa by the Organization of African Unity.

**Kitakyushu** /ˌki:təkjuːˈʃuː/ an industrial city and seaport in Fukuoka prefecture, north Kyushu Island, Japan, on the Shimonoseki Strait; pop. (1990) 1,026,470. It is the leading Japanese iron and steel producer and the chief industrial centre of Kyushu; it comprises the five formerly separate towns of Kokura, Moji, Tobata, Wakamatsu, and Yawata. There are ferry links with other Japanese islands and with Pusan in Korea.

**Kitami** /ki:ˈtɑ:mi:/ a city on the north-east coast of Hokkaido Island, Japan, on the Tokoro River; pop. (1990) 107,250. It is a noted centre for the production of peppermint.

**Kitchener** /ˈkɪtʃɪnə(r)/ a city in south-east Ontario, Canada, 88 km. (55 miles) west of Toronto; pop. (1991) 168,300; 356,420 (metropolitan area). Settled by German Mennonites in 1805, it bore several names before being changed from Berlin to Kitchener, in honour of Field Marshal Kitchener, in 1916.

**Kithira** see CYTHERA.

**Kitty Hawk** /ˈkɪtɪ ˌhɔ:k/ a small town on a narrow sand peninsula on the Atlantic coast of North Carolina, USA. It was here that, in 1903, the Wright Brothers made their first powered aeroplane flight in the US, which is commemorated by the Wright Brothers National Memorial.

**Kitwe** /ˈki:tweɪ/ a city in the Copperbelt province of northern Zambia, 50 km. (31 miles) north of

Ndola; pop. (1987) 449,440. The second-largest city in Zambia, it is a centre of copper-mining and industry.

**Kitzbühel** /ˈkɪtsbjʊəl/ a winter sports resort in the state of Tyrol, western Austria; pop. (1981) 7,840. Founded in the 12th c., it was a prosperous town, with copper and silver mining.

**Kivu** /ˈkiːvuː/, **Lake** a lake in central Africa, on the Zaire–Rwanda frontier; area 2,699 sq. km. (1,042 sq. miles). Drained by the Ruzzi River, it is the highest lake in Africa at 1,460 m. (4,788 ft.).

**KL** *abbr. colloq.* Kuala Lumpur.

**Kladno** /ˈklædnəʊ/ a city north-west of Prague in the central Bohemia region of the Czech Republic; pop. (1991) 71,735. It is an industrial city in a coal-mining area. Lidice, the village destroyed in 1942 by the Nazis, lay 8 km. (5 miles) to the west.

**Klagenfurt** /ˈklɑːɡənˌfʊət/ the capital city of the state of Carinthia (Kärnten) in southern Austria, on the Glan River; pop. (1991) 89,500.

**Klaipeda** /ˈklaɪpɪdɑː/ the chief port and industrial city of Lithuania, on the Baltic Sea at the entrance to the Kurskiy Lagoon; pop. (1991) 206,000. Under German control it was known as Memel (1918–23 and 1941–4). It is the exporting terminal of the Volga–Urals oil pipeline.

**Klang** /kəˈlɑːŋ/ see PORT KELANG.

**Klausenberg** /ˈklaʊz(ə)nberk/ the German name for CLUJ-NAPOCA.

**Klerksdorp** /ˈkɜːksdɔːp/ a city in the North-West Province of South Africa, situated on the Schoon Spruit River south-west of Johannesburg; pop. (1980) 238,865. It is the marketing and processing centre for the surrounding agricultural area and for the gold and uranium mines.

**Klondike** /ˈklɒndaɪk/ an eastern tributary of the Yukon River, flowing 150 km. (93 miles) from its source in the Tintina to the Yukon at Dawson City. It gives its name to a region of Yukon Territory, north-west Canada, noted as the focal point of a celebrated gold-rush in 1897–8 that was known as the Klondike stampede.

**Klondike Highway** a 717-km. (445-mile) highway in northern Canada, linking Skagway (Alaska) with Dawson City in the Yukon Territory of Canada. Completed in 1979, it follows a route taken by gold prospectors in 1898.

**kloof** /kluːf/ an Afrikaans term used in southern Africa to describe a deep narrow ravine.

**Klosterneuburg** /ˌkləʊstəˈnɔɪbʊəɡ/ a town of Lower Austria in north-eastern Austria, on the River Kierlingbach north-west of Vienna; pop. (1991) 24,590. It has a wine-making college and a 12th-c. Augustinian abbey.

**Klosters** /ˈkləʊstəz/ an Alpine winter sports resort near Davos in Graubünden canton, eastern Switzerland, on the River Lanquart.

**Kluane National Park** /kluːˈɑːnɪ/ a national park in south-west Yukon Territory, Canada, that contains the world's largest icefields outside polar regions. It extends over an area of 2,205 sq. km. (8,498 sq. miles) and comprises some 4,000 glaciers, the deepest of which are up to 1.6 km. (1 mile) thick. The park, which was designated in 1976, is dominated by the St. Elias Mountains which rise to 6,050 m. (19,856 ft.) at Mount Logan, Canada's highest peak.

**Klyuchevskaya Sopka** /klɪəˈtʃefskəjə ˈsɒpkə/ a volcanic peak on the Kamchatka Peninsula, far-eastern Russia. Rising to a height of 4,750 m. (15,584 ft.), it is the highest active volcano in Russia and the continent of Asia.

**Knesset** /ˈknesɪt/ the parliament of the state of Israel. Its name is derived from a Hebrew word meaning a 'gathering'.

**Knightsbridge** /ˈnaɪtsbrɪdʒ/ a district in the West End of London, England, to the south of Hyde Park and west of Piccadilly. It is noted for its fashionable and expensive shops and stores including Harrods which was founded by Charles Harrod in 1849 and is the largest department store in Britain.

**Knock** /nɒk/ a locality in County Mayo, Ireland, a holy shrine since 1879 when an apparition of the Virgin Mary was sighted at the parish church. In 1979 it was visited by Pope John Paul II who was the first pope to set foot on Irish soil. Since then the shrine has been known as the Basilica of Our Lady, Queen of Ireland. It is one of Ireland's leading centres of pilgrimage and has an international airport.

**Knossos** /ˈknɒsəs/ the principal city of Minoan Crete, near the port of Heraklion. It was occupied from neolithic times until *c.* 1200 BC. Excavations by Sir Arthur Evans from 1900 onwards revealed remains of a luxurious and spectacular decorated complex of buildings which he named the Palace of Minos, with frescoes of landscapes, animal life, and the sport of bull-leaping. In *c.* 1450 BC Crete was overrun by the Mycenaeans, but the palace was not finally destroyed until the 14th c. or early 13th c. BC, possibly by an earthquake.

**Knoxville** /ˈnɒksvɪl/ a city in eastern Tennessee, USA, a port on the Tennessee River; pop. (1990) 165,120. Founded as an outpost on the frontier of the Cherokee Indian nation, it developed first as a provisioning place for westward-bound wagons and then as a centre of the livestock and tobacco trade. It was named after Secretary of War Henry Knox. It was twice the state capital, in 1796–1812 and 1817–19, and is now the headquarters of the Tennessee Valley Authority. It is the trade and shipping centre for a productive coal-mining and farming area.

**Kobe** /ˈkəʊbeɪ/ a seaport in Hyogo prefecture, central Honshu Island, Japan, on Osaka Bay; pop. (1990) 1,477,420. Since it was built in 1868 its harbour has become one of the leading ports of

Japan. It has steel and shipbuilding industries. It was devastated by a major earthquake in 1995.

**København** see COPENHAGEN.

**Koblenz** see COBLENZ.

**Kocaeli** /kɒdʒə'eɪlɪ/ a province of north-western Turkey, at the east end of the Sea of Marmara; area 3,626 sq. km. (1,400 sq. miles); pop. (1990) 936,160; capital, Izmit.

**Kochi** see COCHIN.

**Kochi** /'kəʊtʃiː/ a port and market city at the head of an inlet on the south coast of the island of Shikoku, Japan; pop. (1990) 317,090. It is capital of a prefecture of the same name. It exports dried fish, coral, cement, and paper.

**Kodaira** /kəʊ'daɪrə/ a city forming an eastern suburb of Tokyo on the island of Honshu, Japan; pop. (1990) 164,020.

**Kodiak Island** /'kəʊdɪæk/ an island of Alaska, USA, home of the Kodiak bear which is the largest living carnivorous animal; area 13,921 sq. km. (5,375 sq. km). Its chief settlement is Kodiak.

**Kodok** /'kəʊdɒk/ a town in the Upper Nile province of south-east Sudan, on the White Nile northeast of Malakal. It was formerly known as Fashoda and was the scene of the Fashoda incident of 1899 which brought Britain and France to the brink of war.

**Koforidua** /kəʊfəʊriː'dʊə/ the capital of the Eastern Region of Ghana; pop. (1984) 58,730. It is the centre of cocoa, palm oil, and kola nut production.

**Kofu** /kəʊ'fuː/ a city to the west of Tokyo in Yamanashi prefecture, south-central Honshu Island, Japan; pop. (1990) 200,630.

**Koganei** /ˌkəʊgɑː'neɪ/ a city to the west of Tokyo, central Honshu Island, Japan; pop. (1990) 105,890.

**Kohima** /'kəʊhiːmə/ a city in the far north-east of India, capital of the state of Nagaland; pop. (1991) 53,000. The Japanese advance into India during World War II was halted here by British and Indian forces.

**Koil** /kɔɪl/ see ALIGARH.

**Kokand** /kəʊ'kaːnd/ (also **Khokand**, Uzbek **Qŭqon**) a city in eastern Uzbekistan, in the Fergana valley south-east of Tashkent; pop. (1990) 175,700. It was founded in 1732 as the centre of a powerful Uzbek khanate, the last Central Asian khanate to be absorbed into the Russian empire in 1876. It is a centre of cotton, chemical, and fertilizer production.

**Kokchetav** /kɑː:ktʃə'tɑːv/ see KÖKSHETAU.

**Kokkola** /'kɒkvlə/ (Swedish **Gamla Karleby**) a town in western Finland, at the head of an inlet of the Gulf of Bothnia; pop. (1990) 34,635. It exports timber and has chemical and metal goods industries.

**Koko Nor** see QINGHAI.

**Kökshetau** /ˌkɑː:ktʃə'taʊ/ (Russian **Kokchetav**) a city in northern Kazakhstan, at the centre of a mining and dairy-farming region; pop. (1990) 139,400.

**Kokubunji** /ˌkəʊkə'buːndʒiː/ a city to the west of Tokyo, Honshu Island, Japan; pop. (1990) 100,960. It has a famous Buddhist temple.

**Kola Peninsula** /'kəʊlə/ a peninsula on the north coast of Russia, separating the White Sea from the Barents Sea. The port of Murmansk lies on its northern coast.

**Kolhapur** /ˌkɒlhɑː'pʊə/ an industrial city in the state of Maharashtra, western India; pop. (1991) 417,290. It was capital of the former Deccan state of Kolhapur which was founded in the 10th c. and which merged with Maharashtra in 1960. It lies at the centre of a bauxite-mining region.

**Kolkhis** The Greek name for COLCHIS.

**Kollam** /'kɑːləm/ see QUILON.

**Köln** the German name for COLOGNE.

**Kolomna** /kə'lɒmnə/ an industrial city in central Russia, on the Moskva River near its junction with the Oka south-east of Moscow; pop. (1989) 162,000.

**kólpos** /'kɒlpɒs/ a Greek word for a gulf as in Korinthiakós Kólpos (the Gulf of Corinth).

**Kolyma** /kɒlɪ'mɑː/ a river that rises in the Kolyma and Cherskogo ranges in far eastern Russia, and flows 2,513 km. (1,562 miles) northwards through Russia's principal gold-mining region to the Arctic Ocean.

**Komaki** /kəʊ'mɑːkiː/ a market city to the northeast of Nagoya in Aichi prefecture, central Honshu Island, Japan; pop. (1990) 124,440.

**Komarno** /'kɒmɑːnəʊ/ (Hungarian **Komarom**) a city on both sides of the Danube at its junction with the Nitra and Vah rivers. Komarno lies in Slovakia (1991 pop. 37,370) and Komarom in Hungary. It has chemical and aluminium industries.

**Komatsu** /kəʊ'mɑːtsuː/ a city in Ishikawa prefecture, north-central Honshu Island, Japan, between Fukui and Kanazawa; pop. (1990) 106,070.

**Komi** /'kəʊmiː/ a republic of the Russian Federation in the northern Urals; area 415,900 sq. km. (160,641 sq. miles); pop. (1990) 1,265,000; capital, Syktyvkar. Annexed to Moscow in the 14th c., it became an autonomous region of the USSR in 1921 and an autonomous republic in 1936. Following the breakup of the Soviet Union in 1991 it declared itself a republic of Russia. It has a wide range of natural resources including coal, gas, oil, asphalt, and timber, and dairy farming is important. About 23 per cent of the population are Finno-Ugrian Komi people.

**Kommunizma, Pik** see COMMUNISM PEAK.

**Komodo** /kə'məʊdəʊ/ a small island in Indonesia, in the Lesser Sundas, situated between the islands of Sumbawa and Flores; area 375 sq. km. (145 sq. miles). It is the home of the komodo dragon (*Varanus komodoensis*), the largest extant species of lizard (3m. (10ft.) long).

**Komotiní** /kɒmɒtɪ'niː/ a market centre and garrison town near the Bulgarian frontier of northeastern Greece, capital of the Rhodope department in Thrace; pop. (1981) 34,050.

**Kompong Cham** /ˌkɒmpɒŋ 'tʃæm/ (also **Kampong Cham**) a port on the Mekong River in central Cambodia; pop. (est. 1990) 30,000.

**Kompong Som** /ˌkɒmpɒŋ 'sɒm/ (also **Kampong Som**) the chief commercial centre and only deep-water port of Cambodia, situated on the Gulf of Thailand; pop. (est. 1990) 16,000. Until 1970 it was known as Sihanoukville.

**Komsomolsk** /ˌkɑːmsə'mɒlsk/ (in full **Komsomolsk-na-Amur**) an industrial city in the Khabarovsk region of the Far East, in Russia, on the Amur River; pop. (1990) 318,000. It was built in 1932 by members of the Komsomol (Communist Youth League) on the site of the village of Permskoya. It produces chemicals, wood pulp, and steel.

**Konduz** See KUNDUZ.

**Königsberg** /'kɜːnɪgzˌbeəg/ the former German name (until 1946) of KALININGRAD in Russia.

**Konin** /kɒ'njiːn/ an industrial mining city in central Poland, on the River Warta; pop. (1990) 80,290. It is capital of a county of the same name.

**Konstantinovka** /ˌkɑːnstən'tiːnəfkə/ an industrial city in the Donets Basin of Ukraine; pop. (1990) 108,000. It is a zinc-refining and phosphate-producing centre.

**Konya** /'kɒnjə/ **1.** a province of west-central Turkey; area 40,451 sq. km. (15,624 sq. miles); pop. (1990) 1,750,300. **2.** its capital on the south-west edge of the central plateau of Turkey; pop. (1990) 513,350. Originally settled by Phrygians in the 8th c. BC and known in Roman times as Iconium, it became the capital of the Seljuk sultans of Rum towards the end of the 11th c. and was renamed Konya. In the 13th c. it was the home of the Islamic poet and mystic Jalal al-Din Rumi, founder of the sect of whirling dervishes. Besides being a market for agricultural produce, Konya is an important carpet-making centre.

**Kootenay National Park** /'kʊtneɪ/ a national park in the western Rocky Mountains of south-east British Columbia, Canada, adjoining Banff National Park and extending over an area of 1,406 sq. km. (543 sq. miles). Designated in 1920, the park protects scenery and wildlife on either side of the Vermilion and Kootenay river valleys. The River Kootenay flows southwards through the park into north-west Montana, USA, then turns west and north through Idaho and back into Canada where it empties into the southern end of Lake Kootenay.

**kop** /kɒp/ an Afrikaans word for a hill.

**kopje** /'kɒpɪ/ an Afrikaans term used in southern Africa to describe a small isolated hill.

**Korbu** /kɒr'buː/, **Mount** a mountain in Perak state, Malayasia, the second-highest peak in the Malay Peninsula (2,148 m., 7,047 ft.).

**Korçë** /'kɔːsə/ (also **Koritsa**) an industrial town in south-east Albania; pop. (1990) 65,400. Formerly known as Koritsa, it was an important centre of the Orthodox Church and a commercial centre *en route* to the Adriatic. It has light industries including leather, tobacco, glass, and knitwear.

**Kordofan** /ˌkɔːdə'fɑːn/ (also **Kurdufan**) a region of central Sudan, sparsely occupied by Arabic-speaking semi-nomadic Baggara and camel-raising Kababish (in the north) and by Negroid Nuba (in the south); area 146,932 sq. km. (56,752 sq. miles); pop. (1983) 3,093,300; capital El Obeid.

**Kordofanian** /ˌkɔːdə'fænɪən/ a group of languages of the Niger-Kordofanian family spoken in Sudan.

**Korea** /kə'riːə/ a region of eastern Asia forming a peninsula between the Sea of Japan and the Yellow Sea, now divided along the 38th parallel into KOREA (South Korea) and NORTH KOREA. Possessed of a distinct national and cultural identity and ruled from the 14th c. by the Korean Yi dynasty, Korea has suffered from its position between Chinese and Japanese spheres of influence. Chinese domination was ended by the Sino-Japanese War (1894–5) and after the Russo-Japanese War a decade later the country was finally annexed by Japan in 1910. After the Japanese surrender at the end of World War II, the northern half of the country was occupied by the Soviets and the southern half by the Americans. Separate countries were created in 1948 and two years later the Northern invasion of the South resulted in the Korean War (1950–3). A 250 km.-long demilitarized zone was established between the two countries at the end of hostilities but both North Korea and South Korea were some time in recovering from the devastation caused by military operations. While North Korea remains under Communist rule, South Korea is now one of the most rapidly growing industrial nations in the world.

**Korea** /kə'riːə/ (also **South Korea**) official name **The Republic of Korea** an independent state on the Korean peninsula to the south of the 38th parallel; area 99,263 sq. km. (38,340 sq. miles);  pop. (est. 1990) 42,793,000; official language, Korean; capital, Seoul. The largest cities are Seoul,

Pusan, Taegu, and Inchon. Korea's centres of population are mostly in the fertile plains of the north-west. In the east a mountain range extends the full length of the peninsula and off the south and west coasts there are many islands. Winters are cold, dry, and windy with light falls of snow, while summer is hot and rainy. An expanding industrial sector produces ships, steel, textiles, footwear, and electronics for export. The Republic of Korea was established in 1948 following the post-war partitioning of the Korean peninsula. It is governed by an executive president and a unicameral National Assembly.

**South Korean** *adj. & n.*

Korea is divided into nine provinces and six cities with provincial status (Seoul, Pusan, Taegu, Inchon, Kwangju, and Taejon):

| Province | Area (sq. km.) | Pop. (1990) | Capital |
|---|---|---|---|
| Kyonggi | 10,769 | 6,154,320 | Seoul |
| Kangwon | 16,898 | 1,592,510 | Chunchon |
| North Chungchong | 7,437 | 1,414,300 | Chongju |
| South Chungchong | 8,317 | 2,027,770 | Taejon |
| North Cholla | 8,052 | 2,069,850 | Chonju |
| South Cholla | 11,812 | 2,522,515 | Kwangju |
| North Kyongsang | 19,443 | 2,865,680 | Taegu |
| South Kyongsang | 11,771 | 3,679,400 | Pusan |
| Cheju | 1,825 | 514,610 | Cheju |

**Korean** /kəˈrɪən/ the language of North and South Korea spoken by some 65 million people. Its linguistic affiliations are uncertain although it seems most similar to Japanese. Its vocabulary and orthography have been heavily influenced by Chinese. The Korean Alphabet is the only true alphabetical script native to the Far East and the two systems of romanization employed are the Ministry of Education system and the internationally accepted McCune-Reischauer system.

**Korhogo** /kɔːˈrəʊgəʊ/ a town in northern Ivory Coast, West Africa, situated at the foot of Mount Korhogo; pop. (1986) 280,000. It is the chief town of the Senoufou people who are noted for their craftsmanship.

**Kórinthos** the Greek name for CORINTH.

**Koritsa** see KORÇË.

**Koriyama** /kəʊrɪˈjaːmə/ a city in Fukushima prefecture, north-central Honshu Island, Japan, south-west of Fukushima; pop. (1990) 314,650.

**Korla** /ˈkɔːlə/ a city in Xinjiang autonomous region, north-west China, to the north of the Taklimakan Desert; pop. (1986) 230,000.

**Koror** /ˈkəʊrɜː/ the capital of the Republic of Belau, on Koror Island in the Caroline Islands of the western Pacific.

**Kortrijk** /ˈkɔːtraɪk/ (French **Courtrai** /ˈkʊrtraɪ/) a textile-manufacturing city in West Flanders, Belgium, on the River Leie; pop. (1991) 76,140.

**Korup** /ˈkɒrəp/ a national park in western Cameroon, on the border with Nigeria, established in 1961 to protect a large area of tropical rainforest.

**Kos** the Greek name for COS.

**Kosciusko** /kɒsˈtʃʊskəʊ/, **Mount** a mountain in south-east Australia, in the Great Dividing Range in south-east New South Wales. Rising to a height of 2,228 m. (7,310 ft.), it is the highest mountain in Australia. Located in Kosciusko National Park, it was named by the explorer Sir Paul Edmund de Strzelecki (1797–1873) who thought the peak resembled the grave of the Polish patriot Thaddeus Kosciusko (1746–1817).

**Koshigaya** /kəʊʃiˈɡaːjə/ a suburban city north of Tokyo in Saitama prefecture, central Honshu Island, Japan; pop. (1990) 285,280. It is noted for peach production.

**Kosice** /ˈkɒʃətˌseɪ/ an industrial city on the River Hornad in southern Slovakia, capital of the East Slovakia region; pop. (1991) 234,840. An important trading centre in the Middle Ages, it is now the second-largest city in Slovakia. It has steel, heavy engineering, and chemical industries and is also a cultural centre.

**Kosovo** /ˈkɒsəˌvəʊ/ a province of southern Serbia; area 10,887 sq. km. (4,205 sq. miles); pop. (1987) 1,850,000; capital, Pristina. Kosovo was granted a degree of autonomy by the former Yugoslav government in 1974, but following ethnic conflict between Albanians (who make up over 75 per cent of the population) and Serbs the Serbian government dissolved the Kosovo Assembly in 1990 and imposed direct rule.

**Kostroma** /ˌkɑːstrəˈmaː/ an industrial city in the north-west of European Russia, at the junction of the Kostroma and Volga rivers north-east of Moscow; pop. (1990) 280,000. One of the oldest cities in Russia (founded in 1152), it became one of Russia's leading linen manufacturing centres in the 16th c.

**Koszalin** /kɒˈʃaːliːn/ a city on the Baltic coast of north-west Poland; pop. (1990) 108,700. Founded in the 12th c., its landmarks include a Gothic cathedral and the castle of the Pomeranian dukes. It has chemical, metal products, and food-processing industries.

**Kota** /ˈkəʊtə/ a market and industrial city in Rajasthan, north-west India, on the Chambal River; pop. (1991) 536,440. It has a fort built after 1625 and a palace constructed in 1904.

**Kota Baharu** /ˌkəʊtə ˈbaːruː/ the capital of the state of Kelantan, on the north-east coast of the Malay Peninsula near the mouth of the Kelantan River; pop. (1980) 170,560. It is the centre of Malay arts and crafts.

**Kota Kinabalu** /ˈkəʊtə ˌkɪnəbəˈluː/ a seaport of Malaysia on the north coast of Borneo, capital of the state of Sabah; pop. (1980) 56,000. Its name means 'fort of (Mount) Kinabalu'. Originally established as a trading post on Pulau Gaya island in 1881, it was rebuilt on the mainland by the North Borneo Chartered Company and named Jesselton after one of the company directors, Sir Charles Jessel. It was renamed Kota Kinabalu in 1967.

**Kotka** /'kɒtkə/ a port in the province of Kymi, south-east Finland, situated on an island in the Gulf of Finland to the east of Helsinki; pop. (1990) 56,630. Shipbuilding and trade in timber, paper, and pulp are important.

**Koudougou** /ku:'du:gu:/ a town in west-central Burkina, situated east of the Black Volta between Ouagadougou and Bobo Dioulasso; pop. (1985) 51,670.

**Kourou** /kʊ'ru:/ a town on the north coast of French Guiana, at the mouth of the River Kourou; pop. (1990) 11,200. Nearby is a satellite-launching station of the European Space Agency established in 1967. The site was chosen because of its nearness to the equator where the Earth is moving fastest.

**Kouvola** /'kəʊvə‚la:/ a town and railway junction in western Finland, capital of the province of Kymi; pop. (1990) 31,740.

**Kovrov** /kəv'rɒf/ an industrial city and transportation centre in central Russia, on the Klyazma River, between Moscow and Nizhniy Novgorod; pop. (1990) 161,000. It manufactures excavating machines, textiles, and machine tools.

**Kowloon** /kaʊ'lu:n/ a densely populated peninsula on the south-east coast of China, forming part of Hong Kong. It is separated from Hong Kong island by Victoria Harbour which is crossed by ferries and a road tunnel. Kowloon has a population density of 28,500 people per sq. km. Asia's largest container port is located at Kwai Chung; Kai Tak, Hong Kong's international airport, is to the east of Kowloon, partly built over the sea. There is a rail link to Guangzhou on the Chinese mainland.

**Kozáni** /kɒz'ɑ:ni:/ the capital of the department of Kozáni in Macedonia, north-western Greece; pop. (1981) 30,990. Textiles and farming tools are its chief products.

**Kozhikode** see CALICUT.

**Kra** /krɑ:/, **Isthmus of** the narrowest part of the Malay Peninsula, in south-west Thailand and southern Burma.

**kraal** /krɑ:l/ an Afrikaans term used in southern Africa to describe a village or enclosure.

**Krafla** /'kræflə/ an active volcano in north-east Iceland rising to a height of 654 m. (2,145 ft.). After being dormant for over two centuries it erupted in 1975 and again in 1984. During the 1970s a geothermal power-station was established nearby.

**Kragujevac** /krɑ'gu:jə‚væts/ a city in central Serbia, south of Belgrade; pop. (1981) 164,820. It was formerly the capital of Serbia, 1818–39.

**Krajina** /krɑ:'ji:nə/ **1.** see CARNIOLA. **2.** a region of Croatia with predominantly Serbian population which designated itself the **Republic of Serbian Krajina** following Croatia's declaration of independence from Yugoslavia in 1991.

**Krakatoa** /‚krækə'təʊə/ a small volcanic island in Indonesia, lying between Java and Sumatra, scene of a great eruption in 1883 (the world's greatest recorded explosion) which destroyed most of it. The tsunamis generated by the explosion are calculated to have killed 36,000 people.

**Krákow** see CRACOW.

**Kralendijk** /'krɑ:l(ə)n‚daɪk/ the chief town of the Caribbean island of Bonaire in the Netherlands Antilles; pop. (1981) 1,200. It derives its name from a Dutch word meaning a 'coral dike'.

**Kraljevo** /krɑ:l'jeɪvəʊ/ a market town in central Serbia, on the River Ibar near its confluence with the Morava; pop. (1981) 121,620. It lies at the centre of a dairy-farming region and its factories produce wood and metal goods. In the Middle Ages the kings of Serbia were crowned at the nearby 12th-c. Zica monastery.

**Kramatorsk** /‚kræmə'tɔ:sk/ an industrial city and transportation hub at the centre of the Donets Basin in Ukraine; pop. (1990) 199,000. It is an iron and steel centre and manufactures coal-mining and chemical industry equipment.

**Kranj** /'kraɪnjə/ a market town in northern Slovenia, on the River Sava 25 km. (16 miles) north-west of Ljubljana, at the junction of Alpine routes from the Loibl tunnel and the Wurzen pass; pop. (1991) 36,400. Under Austro-Hungarian rule it was known as Krainburg. It was the home of the Slovenian poet France Preşeren (1800–49). Industries produce textiles and electrical goods.

**Kranjska Gora** /'kraɪnskə 'gɒrə/ a winter sports resort near Mt. Vitranc in the Karawanken Alps of north-west Slovenia; pop. (1981) 1,200.

**Krasnodar** /'kræsnə‚dɑ:(r)/ **1.** a kray (territory) of southern Russia in the north Caucasus; area 88,578 sq. km. (34,200 sq. miles); pop. (1990) 5,135,000. **2.** its capital city, a port on the lower Kuban River; pop. (1990) 627,000. Founded in 1794 as a military outpost on Russia's southern frontier, it was known as Yekaterinodar until 1920. Its industries include oil refining, chemical production, railway engineering, and food processing, and it is an important centre of a wheat-growing region.

**Krasnoyarsk** /'kræsnə‚jɑ:sk/ **1.** a kray (territory) of the Russian Federation in west Siberia; area 2,404,000 sq. km. (928,000 sq. miles); pop. (1990) 3,612,000. There are extensive mineral and timber resources. **2.** its capital city, a port and rail centre on the Yenisei River; pop. (1990) 922,000. Founded in 1628, it expanded with the discovery of gold and the development of the Trans-Siberian Railway. It builds heavy railway equipment.

**Krasnyy Luch** /ˌkræsni:ˈlʊx/ a mining town in the Donets Basin of Ukraine; pop. (1990) 114,000.

**kray** /kraɪ/ a first-order administrative division of Russia equivalent to a territory. In addition to autonomous republics and oblasts Russia's first order administrative divisions include the six krays of Altay, Khabarovsk, Krasnodar, Krasnoyarsk, Primorye, and Stavropol.

**Krefeld** /ˈkreɪfelt/ an industrial town and port on the Rhine in North Rhine-Westphalia, western Germany; pop. (1991) 245,770. Its industries produce textiles, steel, vehicles, and chemicals.

**Kremenchuk** /ˌkremənˈtʃuːk/ (formerly **Kremenchug**) an industrial city in east-central Ukraine, on the River Dnieper; pop. (1990) 238,000. It is the centre of an industrial complex based on a hydroelectric plant.

**Kremlin** /ˈkremlɪn/, **the** the citadel in Moscow, centre of administration of the Russian government and formerly of the Soviet Communist government. Covering an area of 28 hectares, its palaces, churches, and monuments are surrounded by a wall 2,235 m. (7,333 ft.) in length. The building of the Kremlin began in 1156 when Prince Yuri Dolgoruky ordered a wooden fort to be built on Borovitsky Hill. This later became the residence of the Grand Dukes of Moscow and the site where Russian emperors and empresses came to be crowned.

**Krems an der Donau** /kremz æn dɜː(r) ˈdɒnaʊ/ an industrial town in Lower Austria, situated at the junction of the Kremstal with the Danube (Donau) west of Vienna; pop. (1991) 22,830. It lies at the centre of a fruit-growing and wine-producing region.

**Krimml Falls** /ˈkrɪm(ə)l/ (German **Krimmler Wasserfälle**) a waterfall on the Krimmler Ache near the resort town of Krimml in western Austria. It falls 380 m. (1,250 ft.) in three cascades and is one of the highest waterfalls in the eastern Alps.

**Krishna** /ˈkrɪʃnə/ (also **Kistna**) a river which rises in the Western Ghats of southern India and flows 1,288 km. (805 miles) generally eastwards to the Bay of Bengal through the state of Andhra Pradesh.

**Kristiansand** /ˌkriːstjənˈsɑːn/ a ferry port on the south coast of Norway, on the Skaggerak; pop. (1991) 65,690. Founded in 1641 by Christian IV, it is capital of Vest-Agder county.

**Kristianstad** /ˌkriːstjənˈstɑːd/ an industrial and commercial town, capital of Kristianstad county in south-east Sweden, on the River Helge; pop. (1990) 71,750. It was founded in 1614 by Christian IV, and produces machinery and textiles.

**Kristiansund** /ˌkriːstjənˈsuːnd/ an Atlantic fishing port in Møre og Romsdal county, west Norway, south-west of Trondheim; pop. (1991) 17,180.

**Kriti** the Greek name for CRETE.

**Krivoy Rog** /krɪˈvɔɪ rɒg/ see KRYVYY RIH.

**Kronstadt** see BRAŞOV.

**Krosno** /ˈkrɔʊʃˈnjɒ/ a town in south-east Poland, on the River Wisłok; pop. (1990) 49,680. It is capital of a county of the same name and the centre of the Carpathian oilfield.

**Kru** /kruː/ (also **Kroo**) an African seafaring people on the coast of Liberia.

**Kru Coast** /kruː/ a section of the south-east coast of Liberia, north-west of Cape Palmas, part of the region formerly known as the Grain Coast.

**Kruger National Park** /ˈkruːɡə(r)/ a national park in South Africa, in north-east Transvaal. Designated a national park in 1926, it was originally a game reserve, established in 1898 by President Kruger. It extends over an area of 19,485 sq. km. (7,526 sq. miles) along the Mozambique border.

**Krugersdorp** /ˈkruːɡə(r)zˌdɔːp/ a mining town in the Witwatersrand region of Transvaal, South Africa, west of Johannesburg producing gold, asbestos, and uranium; pop. (1980) 102,940. It is named in honour of the last president of the former Transvaal Republic.

**Krusevac** /ˈkruːʃəvɑːts/ an industrial town in south-central Serbia, on the River Rasina near its confluence with the Morava; pop. (1981) 132,970. It was capital of Serbia during the 14th c. and has a motor-vehicle industry.

**Kryvyy Rih** /krɪˌviː ˈrɪx/ (formerly **Krivoy Rog**) an industrial city in southern Ukraine, on the Ingulets River at the centre of an iron-ore mining region; pop. (1990) 717,000. Its industries include steel, mining machinery, foodstuffs, and cement.

**KS** *abbr.* US Kansas (in official postal use).

**ksar** /kəˈsɑː/ a fortified village in north-west Africa.

**Kuala Lumpur** /ˈkwɑːlə ˈlʊmpʊə(r)/ the capital city of Malaysia, at the junction of the Klang and Gombak rivers in the south-west of the Malay Peninsula; pop. (1990) 1,237,900. Founded in 1857 by Chinese tin miners, it became capital of the Federated Malay States in 1896. It is a major transportation and commercial city at the centre of a rubber-growing and tin-mining region.

**Kuala Trengganu** /ˈkwɑːlə treŋˈɡɑːnuː/ (also **Kuala Terengganu**) the capital of the state of Terengganu in Malaysia, on the east coast of the Malay Peninsula at the mouth of the Trengganu River; pop. (1980) 180,300. A centre for arts and crafts, the settlement expanded rapidly in the 1980s with the discovery of oil.

**Kuantan** /kwɑːnˈtɑːn/ the capital of the state of Pahang in Malaysia, at the mouth of the Kuantan River on the east coast of the Malay Peninsula; pop. (1981) 131,550. It has a largely Chinese population and is the principal transportation and business centre of eastern peninsular Malaysia.

**Kuban** /ku:'bɑːn/ a river of southern Russia that rises on Mt. Elbrus in the Greater Caucasus and flows 934 km. (584 miles) north then west to meet the Sea of Azov where it forms a wide swampy delta.

**Kuching** /'ku:tʃɪŋ/ a port on the Sarawak River in Malaysia, near the north-west coast of the island of Borneo, capital of the state of Sarawak; pop. (1989) 157,000. It developed from the 1830s as an outlet for antimony *en route* to the tin-plate industry of Singapore. Pepper, rubber, sago, and copra are exported.

**Kufic** /'kju:fɪk/ (also **Cufic**) an early angular form of the Arabic alphabet found chiefly in decorative inscriptions. It takes its name from Kufa, an ancient city to the south of Baghdad in Iraq.

**Kuibishev** /'ku:ɪbɪˌʃef/ (also **Kuybyshev**) a former name (1935–93) of SAMARA. It was the wartime Soviet capital during German invasions (1941–3).

**kum** /ku:m/ (also **qum**) a Turkic name given to sandy desert regions of central Asia.

**Kumagaya** /kə'mɑːgəjə/ a city to the north-west of Tokyo in Saitama prefecture, Honshu Island, Japan; pop. (1990) 152,120.

**Kumamoto** /ku:mə'məʊtəʊ/ a market and industrial city in southern Japan, on the west coast of Kyushu Island on the Shira River; pop. (1990) 579,300. A provincial centre since the 7th c., it was one of Japan's foremost castle towns. It manufactures electrical and electronic components.

**Kumasi** /kʊ'mɑːzɪ/ a city in southern Ghana, capital of Ashanti Region and commercial centre for the cocoa-producing region; pop. (1984) 376,250. The Ashanti tribal King's court is held at Mantriya Palace. Kumasi also has Ghana's largest market, a museum, zoo, and open-air theatre.

**Kumayri** /ku:m'ri:/ see GYOMRI.

**Kumbakonam** /ˌkʊmbə'kəʊnəm/ (also **Combaconum**) a city in south-east Tamil Nadu, southern India, noted for its temples, the oldest of which dates from the 9th c.; pop. (1991) 150,500. The god Siva is said to have broken a water pot (*kumbh*) here after it had been brought down by a great flood and water from the pot is reputed to have filled the holy Mahamakan Tank which is a site of pilgrimage. Textiles and gold and silver jewellery are produced.

**Kunduz** /kən'dʊz/ (also **Konduz** or **Qonduz**) the capital of the province of Kunduz in north-eastern Afghanistan; pop. (est. 1988) 108,000. It lies near the Kunduz River which is a tributary of the Amu Darya rising in the Hindu Kush.

**Kunlun Shan** /'kʊnlʊn ʃɑːn/ a range of mountains in western China, on the northern edge of the Tibetan plateau and south of the Tarim Basin. Its highest peak is Muztag (7,723 m., 25,338 ft.).

**Kunming** /kʊn'mɪŋ/ a city on Lake Dianchi in south-west China, capital of Yunnan province; pop. (1990) 1,976,000. First settled in the 3rd c. BC and situated at an altitude of 1,890 m. (6,200 ft.), it is known as the 'city of eternal spring' because of its pleasant climate. Its industries produce textiles, chemicals, machinery, and optical instruments and air links with other cities have encouraged its development since the 1970s.

**Kuopio** /'kwəʊpɪˌəʊ/ **1.** a province of central Finland; area 19,956 sq. km. (7,708 sq. miles); pop. (1990) 256,780. **2.** its capital city and tourist resort, on the western shore of Lake Kalla (Kallavesi); pop. (1990) 80,610. It is the seat of the Orthodox archbishopric, and has a Lutheran Cathedral, and a university (1966). Its industries are based on timber.

**Kurashiki** /kʊrə'ʃiːkiː/ a city in Okayama prefecture, west Honshu Island, Japan; pop. (1990) 414,690. The old city was an important port in feudal times and has been carefully preserved. The new city is an important industrial centre.

**Kurdistan** /ˌkɜːdɪ'stɑːn/ an extensive plateau and mountainous region of the Middle East, south of the Caucasus, including large parts of Turkey, northern Iraq, western Iran, eastern Syria, Armenia, and Azerbaijan. For centuries it has been the traditional home of the Kurdish people. The creation of a separate state of Kurdistan was proposed by the Allies after World War I, but this was abandoned in 1923 when Turkey reasserted its territorial authority in the region. Although not officially recognized as a state, this region is called Kurdistan by its inhabitants.

**Kurds** /kɜːdz/ a mainly pastoral Aryan Islamic people speaking a dialect of Persian and inhabiting the region known as Kurdistan. Claiming descent from Noah and numbering nearly 20 million, they have maintained their own cultural tradition and language for some 3,000 years but have never been united under one ruler. During the 19th c. Kurdish nationalist movements generally operated independently of each other in each of the countries encompassed by Kurdistan. The first major Kurdish revolt took place in Turkey in 1925, but it was not until the illegal establishment of a Kurdish Democratic Party in Turkey in 1967 that militant nationalism gripped the five south-eastern provinces of Turkey. During the 1960s and early 1970s there were risings against the Iraqi government, and after the Iranian revolution of 1979 there was an increase in Kurdish dissidence in Iran. International attention focused on the Kurds in 1988–9, when Iraq initiated a policy of depopulating Kurdish areas on the frontier with Turkey, and in 1991 when, after the Gulf War, the Iraqi government relaunched its campaign against the Kurds in northern Iraq. Subsequently, 'safe havens' were established for the Kurds of northern Iraq. **Kurdish** *adj. & n.*

**Kŭrdzhali** /kɜ'dʒɑːlɪ/ (also **Kardjali**) an industrial city in the Khaskovo region of south-east Bulgaria, situated on the Arda River in the Rhodope Mountains south-east of Plovdiv; pop. (1990) 112,530. It is a major lead- and zinc-mining and processing centre.

**Kure** /'kuːreɪ/ a city in southern Japan, on the south coast of Honshu Island, near Hiroshima; pop. (1990) 216,720. A former naval base, it now builds some of the world's largest ships.

**Kurgan** /kʊə'gɑːn/ a city in west Siberia, Russia, east of the Urals on the Tobol River; pop. (1990) 360,000. It is a commercial centre for an agricultural region.

**Kuria Muria Islands** /ˌkʊərɪə 'mʊərɪə/ a group of five islands in the Arabian Sea, with few inhabitants, belonging to Oman. They were ceded to Britain in 1854 by the Sultan of Oman, and returned to Oman in 1967.

**Kurile Islands** /'kjʊəriːl/ (also **Kuril Islands** or **Kurils**) a chain of 56 islands, many uninhabited, between the Sea of Okhotsk and the North Pacific Ocean, stretching from the southern tip of the Kamchatka peninsula in east Siberia, Russia, to the north-east corner of the Japanese island of Hokkaido. The islands were given to Japan in exchange for the northern part of Sakhalin Island in 1875, but were retaken by the Soviet Union at the end of World War II. Japan ceded the Kurils to the USSR in 1951 at the San Francisco Peace Conference but reversed its position in the mid-fifties on the southern Kurile Islands of Etorofu (Iturup), Kunashiri, Shikotan, and Habomai, claiming that historically they had always been Japanese. Since then the islands have been a source of dispute between Russia and Japan which calls the islands its Northern Territories.

**Kurnool** /kɜ'nuːl/ (also **Karnul**) a market town in Andhra Pradesh, southern India, at the junction of the Hindri and Tungabhadra rivers south of Hyderabad; pop. (1991) 274,800. It was capital of the former state of Andhra Desa prior to the creation of Andhra Pradesh in 1953.

**Kursk** /kʊəsk/ an industrial city and commercial centre in western Russia, situated on the Siem River between Moscow and Kharkhov; pop. (1990) 430,000. Kursk is the centre of a major iron-ore field (Kursk Magnetic Anomaly) and steel industries.

**Kurume** /kə'ruːmeɪ/ a city on Kyushu Island, Japan, to the south of Fukuoka; pop. (1990) 228,350. Its industries include the manufacture of rubber goods.

**Kusadasi** /kuː'ʃædəsɪ/ a port and resort town on an inlet of the Aegean Sea in western Turkey, south of Izmir; pop. (1990) 31,910. It is one of Turkey's leading holiday centres and has a large anchorage and yachting marina. Nearby are the ruins of ancient Ephesus.

**Kushiro** /kə'ʃiːrəʊ/ a fishing port on the southeast coast of Hokkaido Island, Japan; pop. (1990) 205,640. There are pulp and paper industries.

**Kuskokwim** /'kəskəˌkwɪm/ a river of Alaska that rises in headwaters in the Alaska Range near Mount McKinley and flows 1,287 km. (800 miles) south-westwards to Kuskokwim Bay, an inlet of the Bering Sea.

**Kustanay** /ˌkʊstə'naɪ/ see QOSTANAY.

**Kütahya** /kə'taɪə/ **1.** a province of western Turkey; area 11,875 sq. km. (4,587 sq. miles); pop. (1990) 578,020. **2.** its capital, on the Porsuk River south-east of Bursa; pop. (1990) 130,940. Its industries produce carpets, cotton, ceramics, and Meerschaum clay.

**Kutaisi** /kuː'taɪsɪ/ a city of central Georgia, on the River Rioni; pop. (1990) 236,100. One of the oldest cities in Transcaucasia, it has been the capital of various kingdoms, including Colchis and Abkhazia. Its industries produce chemicals, machinery, vehicles, and food.

**Kutch** /kʊtʃ/, **Rann of** a vast salt-marsh on the frontier between India and Pakistan flooded in the monsoon season. Most of it lies in the Indian state of Gujarat, the remainder in the province of Sind in south-east Pakistan.

**Kuwait** /kuː'weɪt/ official name **The State of Kuwait** a country on the north-west coast of the Persian Gulf, bounded by Iraq to the north and west and Saudi Arabia to the south; area  17,818 sq. km. (6,880 sq. miles); pop. (est.1991) 1,200,000; official language, Arabic; capital, Kuwait City. A largely flat, dry, and arid country, Kuwait is dissected by wadi systems that generally drain towards the interior. Rainfall is limited to light showers in the winter and during the summer temperature and humidity can be extremely high. Since the discovery of oil in the 1930s Kuwait has become one of the world's leading oil and gas producing countries. In addition to this the traditional entrepôt trade and pearl fishing have given way to the production of petrochemicals, boat building, shrimp fishing, and agriculture. Kuwait has been an autonomous sheikdom since the 18th c., its present ruling dynasty being founded by Sheikh Sabah al-Owel who ruled from 1752 to 1772. Its ruler concluded a treaty of protection with Britain in 1899 and although it was recognized as a sovereign state in 1914 it did not break off its affiliation with Britain until 1961 when it gained full control over external and internal affairs. In August 1990 it was invaded by Iraqi forces which were ejected in January–February 1991 by a UN-backed international coalition. The reinstated rulers of Kuwait began a programme of reconstruction and adopted a population policy designed to restrict the size of the population and the proportion of non-Kuwaitis living in Kuwait. Advised by a cabinet, the Amir of Kuwait ruled the country by decree after the dissolution of the National Assembly in 1986. Following elections in 1992 a new National Assembly was convened. **Kuwaiti** *adj. & n.*

Kuwait is divided into four governorates:

| Governorate | Area (sq. km.) | Pop. (1985) |
|---|---|---|
| Hawalli | 620 | 943,250 |
| Ahmadi | 4,665 | 304,660 |
| Jahra | 11,550 | 279,470 |
| Kuwait City and offshore islands | 983 | 167,750 |

**Kuwait City** the capital of the Gulf state of Kuwait, on the south side of Kuwait Bay, an inlet of the Arabian Gulf; pop. (1985) 44,335. Its deep-water port lies in the industrial suburb of Shuwaikh and its international airport is 16 km. (10 miles) from the city centre.

**Kuybyshev** the former name (1935–91) of SAMARA in Russia.

**Kuytun** /kuɪˈtʊn/ a city in the far north-west of Xinjiang autonomous region, north-west China, situated in the northern foothills of the Tien Shan Mountains; pop. (1986) 221,000.

**Kuznetz Basin** /kʊzˈnjets/ (also **Kuznetsk** or **Kusbas** /kʊzˈbæs/) an industrial region of West Siberia, Russia, situated in the valley of the Tom River, between Tomsk and Novokuznetsk. The region is rich in high quality coking-coal deposits.

**Kwa** /kwɑː/ a language group of the Niger-Congo family of languages spoken in west Africa. It includes Akan, Ashanti, Bini, Ewe, Ibo, Ijo, Nupe, and Yoruba.

**KwaNdebele** /ˌkwɑːəndəˈbiːlɪ/ a former self-governing state of the Southern Ndebele people created in north-east Transvaal in 1981. Its capital was Moutjana.

**Kwangchow** see GUANGZHOU.

**Kwangju** /kwæŋˈdʒəʊ/ (also **Kwangchu**) a city in south-west Korea, capital of South Cholla province; pop. (1990) 1,144,700. Its industries include motor vehicles and textiles.

**Kwangsi Chuang** see GUANGXI ZHUANG.

**Kwangtung** see GUANGDONG.

**KwaZulu-Natal** /kwɑːˈzuːluːnəˈtɑːl/ an eastern province of South Africa between the Indian Ocean and the Drakensberg Mountains created in 1994 from the former province of Natal and the former Zulu homeland of KwaZulu. Its capital is Durban. Annexed to the Cape Colony in 1844, Natal became a separate colony in 1856 and a province of the Union of South Africa in 1910, its capital (until 1994) being Pietermaritzburg. The

self-governing national state of KwaZulu, formerly known as Zululand, was created in 1971 but was re-united with Natal in 1994.

**Kweichow** see GUIZHOU.

**Kweilin** see GUILIN.

**Kweiyang** see GUIYANG.

**Kwesui** see HOHHOT.

**KY** *abbr.* US Kentucky (in official postal use).

**kyle** a Gaelic term used in Scotland to describe a channel or body of water separating two islands or an island from the mainland as in Kyles of Bute (separating Bute from the mainland) or Kyle Akin (separating Skye from the mainland).

**Kyongju** /kjɒŋˈdʒuː/ a historic city in south-east Korea, situated east of Taegu; pop. (1990) 141,900. It was the capital of the Silla dynasty from 57 BC to AD 935 and of the whole of Korea from 668 to 935. There are the remains of Silla tombs, Buddhist pagodas and temples, and one of the oldest observatories in the world dating from the early 7th c.

**Kyoto** /kɪˈəʊtəʊ/ an industrial city in the Kinki region of central Honshu Island, Japan; pop. (1990) 1,461,140. Founded in the 6th c., it was capital of Japan from 794 until 1868. There are many historic landmarks including the 14th-c. Golden Pavilion, 15th-c. Ryoanji temple of the Zen sect, and the 17th-c. Nijo Castle. Kyoto Imperial University was founded in 1897. Uniquely undamaged during World War II, its many industries include manufacture of electrical equipment, precision tools, and cameras, as well as food processing, chemicals, and textile machinery.

**Kyrenia** /kaɪˈriːnɪə/ a port on the central part of the north coast of the island of Cyprus, in the Turkish Republic of Northern Cyprus; pop. (1985) 6,900. In July 1974 Turkish forces invading the island landed here. Its many old buildings and picturesque ruins made it a popular tourist destination.

**Kyrgyzstan**
/ˌkɪrɡəˈstɑːn/ (also **Kirghizistan**, formerly **Kirghizia** or **Kirgizia**) official name **The Kyrgyz Republic** a mountainous country of central Asia lying at the western end of

the Tien Shan mountain range on the north-west border of China; area 198,500 sq. km. (76,640 sq. miles); pop. (1990) 4,367,000; official language, Kirgizian; capital Bishkek. The largest cities are Bishkek and Osh. Kyrgyzstan is a mountainous country with an economy based on the cultivation of cotton, sugar beet, tobacco, and opium, the mining of coal, antimony, and mercury, and the production of machinery and hydroelectric power. Over half the population are Kirgiz of Turkic origin whose lands were annexed by Russia in 1864. Included as part of Soviet Turkestan in 1918, it became a separate Autonomous Soviet Socialist Republic within the Russian Republic in 1924 and a constituent republic of the USSR in 1936. Following the breakup of the Soviet Union, Kyrgyzstan declared its independence in 1991. The country is governed by an elected Supreme Soviet. **Kyrgyz** or **Kirgiz** *adj. & n.*

**Kyushu** /kɪˈuːʃuː/ the most southerly of the four main islands of Japan, constituting an administrative region; area 42,084 sq. km. (16,255 sq. miles); pop. (1990) 13,296,000; chief city, Fukuoka. Kyushu is divided into seven prefectures:

| Prefecture | Area (sq. km.) | Pop. (1990) | Capital |
| --- | --- | --- | --- |
| Fukuoka | 4,946 | 4,811,000 | Fukuoka |
| Kagoshima | 9,153 | 1,798,000 | Kagoshima |
| Kumamoto | 7,399 | 1,790,000 | Kumamoto |
| Miyazaki | 7,734 | 1,169,000 | Miyazaki |
| Nagasaki | 4,102 | 1,563,000 | Nagasaki |
| Oita | 6,331 | 1,237,000 | Oita |
| Saga | 2,418 | 878,000 | Saga |

**Kyustendil** /ˌkjuːstenˈdiːl/ a spa town in the Rila Mountains of western Bulgaria. It has been a health resort since Roman times and is capital of a province of the same name. Fruit, grapes, and tobacco are grown in the surrounding area.

**Kyzyl** /kəˈzɪl/ (also **Krasny**) the capital of the Republic of Tuva in south-central Russia, at the junction of the Bei and Khua rivers; pop. (1989) 80,000. Its industries include brick making, timber, and food processing.

**Kyzyl-Kum** /kəˈzɪlkuːm/ (also **Qizilkum**) an arid desert region of central Asia in Uzbekistan and southern Kazakhstan, extending north of the Amu Darya to the valley of the Syr Darya and lying between the Aral Sea and the western foothills of the Pamirs.

**Kyzyl-Orda** /kəˈzɪl ɔːˈdɑː/ see QYZYLORDA.

# L *l*

**LA** *abbr.* US Louisiana (in official postal use).

**Laayoune** see LA'YOUN.

**Labrador** /'læbrə,dɔ:(r)/ the north-eastern peninsula of Canada, from Hudson Bay to the mouth of the St. Lawrence, forming the mainland section of the province of Newfoundland. It has a deeply indented Atlantic coastline some 1,125 km. (703 miles) in length and comprises a granite plateau rising 300 m. above sea-level. Forming part of the Canadian shield, it is mostly barren rock and tundra although its river valleys are forested. The Torngat Mountains include the highest peaks east of the Rockies. Labrador was the subject of a territorial dispute between Newfoundland and Quebec which arose in 1902 and was settled in Newfoundland's favour in 1927. Cod, salmon, and trout fishing are important.

**Labrador Current** a cold ocean current which flows southwards from the Arctic Ocean along the north-east coast of North America during December to May. It meets the warm Gulf Stream in an area off the coast of Newfoundland which is noted for its dense fog.

**Labrador Peninsula** (also **Labrador-Ungava** /ʊŋ'gɑ:və/) a broad peninsula of eastern Canada, between Hudson Bay, the Atlantic, and the Gulf of St. Lawrence. Consisting of the Ungava Peninsula and Labrador, it contains most of Quebec and mainland Newfoundland. It is very sparsely inhabited.

**Labrador Sea** a body of water between Greenland and the coast of Labrador, Canada. It is 1,000 km. (625 miles) wide and 3,400 m. (11,155 ft.) deep where it meets the North Atlantic. Covered with pack ice during December to June, it is a breeding ground for seals. The Labrador and Greenland banks are commercially fished for cod and shrimp.

**La Brea** /læ 'breɪə/ an asphalt pit containing Pleistocene plant and animal remains in Hancock Park, Los Angeles, southern California, USA.

**Labuan** /lə'bu:ən/ a small island off the north coast of Borneo, forming a Federal Territory of Malaysia; area 98 sq. km. (38 sq. miles); pop. (1990) 16,500; capital, Victoria.

**Laccadive Islands** /'lækədɪv/ see LAKSHAD-WEEP ISLANDS.

**La Ceiba** /læ 'seɪbə/ a seaport on the Caribbean coast of Honduras; pop. (1988) 68,200. It is capital of the department of Atlántida and has boat connections with the Bay Islands.

**Lachlan** /'læxlən/ a river of New South Wales, Australia, that rises in the Great Dividing Range and flows some 1,472 km. (920 miles) north-west then south-west to join the Murrumbidgee River near the border with Victoria. It is named after Lachlan Macquarie, the governor of New South Wales from 1810 to 1821.

**La Ciotat** /læ sjə'tɑ:/ a town with a naval shipyard on the Mediterranean coast of southern France, in the department of Bouches-du-Rhône south-east of Marseilles; pop. (1990) 30,750.

**Laconia** /lə'kəʊnɪə/ (also **Lakonia**) a modern department and ancient region of Greece, in the south-east Peloponnese; area 3,636 sq. km. (1,414 sq. miles); pop. (1991) 94,910. Throughout the classical period the region was dominated by its capital, Sparta, which remains the administrative centre of the modern department.
**Laconian** *adj. & n.*

**La Coruña** /,læ kə'rʊnjə/ the Spanish name for CORUNNA.

**La Crosse** /læ 'krɒs/ an agricultural, commercial, and industrial city in western Wisconsin, USA, at the junction of the Black and La Crosse rivers with the Mississippi; pop. (1990) 51,000. Originally a trading post, it was named after the Indian game the French called lacrosse. Its industries include brewing and wine-making.

**Lac Saint-Jean** /læk sæ ʒæ̃/ a lake in southern Quebec, Canada, north of Quebec; area 1,003 sq. km. (387 sq. miles). It is the source of the Saguenay River which flows eastwards to the St. Lawrence through the scenic Saguenay Fiord. It is the scene of an annual marathon swim.

**Ladakh** /lə'dɑ:k/ a high-altitude region of north-west India, Pakistan, and China, containing the Ladakh and Karakoram mountain ranges and the upper Indus River valley; chief town Leh (in India). It lies at the western extremity of Tibet to which it was attached until the mid-19th c. The people of Ladakh are predominantly Buddhist except in the western region of Baltistan where Islam is the dominant religion.

**Ladin** /lə'di:n/ the Rhaeto-Romanic dialect of the Engadine in Switzerland.

**Ladino** /lə'di:nəʊ/ **1.** the Spanish dialect of the Sephardic Jews. **2.** a mestizo or Spanish-speaking White person in Central America.

**Ladoga** /'lɑ:dəgə/ (Russian **Ozero Ladozhskoye**) a large lake in north-west Russia, north-east of St. Petersburg, near the border with Finland. It is the largest lake in Europe, with an area of 17,703 sq. km. (6,835 sq. miles).

**Ladysmith** /'leɪdɪˌsmɪθ/ a town in eastern South Africa, in KwaZulu-Natal. It was founded in the early 19th century and named after the wife of the governor of Natal, Sir Harry Smith. It was subjected to a four-month siege by Boer forces during the Second Boer War and was finally relieved on 28 February 1900 by Lord Roberts, who replaced General Sir Redvers Buller as commander of the British forces.

**Lae** /'lɑːeɪ/ an industrial seaport on the east coast of Papua New Guinea, on the Huon Gulf; pop. (1980) 61,620. Founded in 1927 to serve the Morobe gold-fields, it is the second-largest town in the country. It exports gold, timber, plywood, cattle, cocoa, and coffee.

**Lafayette** /læfə'jet/ a commercial city in south-central Louisiana, USA, on the Vermilion River; pop. (1990) 94,440. Many of its citizens are Louisiana Cajuns, descended from Acadians who came from Nova Scotia in the 18th c. It is a centre of light industry, agriculture, and the oil industry.

**lagoon** /lə'guːn/ **1.** a stretch of salt water separated from the sea by a low sandbank, coral reef, etc. **2.** the enclosed water of an atoll. **3.** *US, Australia, and NZ* a small freshwater lake near a larger lake or river. **4.** an artificial pool for the treatment of effluent or to accommodate an over-spill from surface drains during heavy rain.

**Lagos** /'leɪɡɒs/ the chief city of Nigeria, a seaport on the Gulf of Guinea, situated on islands interconnected by causeways; pop. (est. 1986) 1,739,000. A former Yoruba town and centre of the slave-trade between the 16th and 19th c., it was held by Britain from 1851 until 1960. It was capital of Nigeria from 1960 till the designation of a new federal capital at Abuja in 1982. Its overcrowded slums contrast with modern developments and its traffic congestion is notorious. It has many light industries and craft products.

**Lagos** /læ'ɡuʃ/ a fishing port and resort town on the Algarve coast of southern Portugal, at the mouth of the River Alvor; pop. (1991) 12,950. Henry the navigator was originally buried here in the church of Santa Maria before being transferred to the Batalha Abbey.

**Laguna Beach** /lə'guːnə/ a residential and resort town in the USA, on the coast of Orange County, Southern California; pop. (1990) 23,170. It is noted for its beautiful surfing beaches, art galleries, and annual arts festivals.

**La Habana** see HAVANA.

**La Habra** /læ 'hæbrə/ a city in the Los Angeles conurbation, California, USA, in the southern foothills of the Puente Hills north of Anaheim; pop. (1990) 51,270.

**lahar** /'lɑːhɑː(r)/ a mud-flow composed mainly of volcanic debris.

**Lahore** /lə'hɔː(r)/ the capital of Punjab province and second-largest city of Pakistan, situated on the Ravi River near the border with India; pop. (est. 1991) 3,200,000. In Hindu legend it was founded by Loh, son of Rama, and in the 16th c. it became a capital of the Moghul empire. In 1767 it was taken by the Sikhs and in 1849 it came under British control. Following independence in 1947 Lahore was capital of West Punjab and from 1955 to 1970 it was capital of West Pakistan. It has many fine public buildings dating from the imperial era. Lahore is a commercial, banking, and marketing centre with diverse industries.

**Lahti** /'lɑːtɪ/ a city in the province of Häme, southern Finland, at the southern end of Lake Päijänne; pop. (1991) 93,150. Its industries produce textiles, glass, furniture, and electrical goods.

**Laibach** /'laɪbæx/ the German name for LJUBLJANA.

**Laiwu** /laɪ'wuː/ a city in Shandong province, eastern China, to the south-east of Jinan; pop. (1986) 1,054,000.

**La Jolla** /læ 'hɔɪə/ a resort town on the Pacific coast of southern California, USA, adjacent to San Diego. It is a centre for scientific research and home of the University of California, San Diego (1960).

**Lake Charles** a city in south-west Louisiana, USA, at the north end of Lake Calcasieu; pop. (1990) 70,580. Named after Charles Sallier who settled there in 1781, the town's development was stimulated by the completion of the Southern Pacific Railroad's link between Houston and New Orleans in the 1880s. It is a centre of oil, rubber, timber, rice, and cattle production.

**Lake Clark** /klɑːk/ a US national park in southern Alaska, at the heart of the Chigmit Mountains where the Alaska Range meets the Aleutian Range. It was established in 1980 and includes the active volcanoes Mt. Iliamna and Mt. Redoubt, both of which rise over 3,048 m. (10,000 ft.).

**Lake District** (also **Lakeland**) a region of lakes and mountains in Cumbria, north-west England, made popular in the 19th c. by poets such as Wordsworth, Coleridge, and Southey. Now one of the most popular tourist destinations in England, 866 sq. km. (335 sq. miles) are protected within the bounds of a National Park (designated in 1951). The most prominent lakes are Windermere, Ullswater, Bassenthwaite, Derwent Water, Coniston Water, and Thirlmere and its peaks include Helvellyn, Honister, the Langdales, High Street, and England's highest mountain, Scafell Pikes (977 m., 3,206 ft.).

**Lakeland** /'leɪklænd/ a city in central Florida, USA, east of Tampa; pop. (1990) 70,580. Situated at the centre of a citrus-growing and phosphate-mining area, it takes its name from the 13 lakes within its city limits.

**Lake of the Woods** a lake on the border between Canada and the USA, to the west of the Great Lakes and south-east of Winnipeg. It is bounded to the west by Manitoba, to the north and east by Ontario, and to the south by Minnesota; area 4,472 sq. km. (1,727 sq. miles); area within Canada, 3,150 sq. km. (1,216 sq. miles). It is a remnant of the former glacial Lake Agassiz.

**Lake Placid** /ˈplæsɪd/ a winter-sports resort on Mirror Lake in the Adirondack Mountains, New York state, USA.

**Lakewood 1.** a city in the Los Angeles conurbation, California, USA, situated to the north of Long Beach and west of the San Gabriel River; pop. (1990) 73,560. **2.** a residential western suburb of Denver, Colorado, USA; pop. (1990) 126,480. **3.** a residential western suburb of Cleveland, north-east Ohio, USA, on Lake Erie at the mouth of the Rocky River; pop. (1990) 59,720.

**Lakshadweep Islands** /ˌlækʃæˈdwiːp/ a group of islands off the Malabar coast of south-west India, constituting a Union Territory of India; area 32 sq. km. (12 sq. miles); pop. (1991) 51,680; capital, Kavaratti. The islands were formerly known (until 1973) as the Laccadive, Minicoy, and Amindivi Islands. The predominantly Muslim islanders are chiefly engaged in tourism, fishing, and the production of coconut palm products.

**La Laguna** /læ ləˈguːnə/ a university town on the island of Tenerife in the Canary Islands; pop. (1991) 116,540.

**Lallan** /ˈlælən/ (also **Lallans**) a form of Lowland Scots dialect, developed especially as a literary language by modern Scottish writers.

**La Louvière** /læ luvˈjɜːr(r)/ an industrial city in south-west Belgium, in the province of Hainaut west of Charleroi; pop. (1991) 76,430.

**Lamaism** /ˈlɑːmeɪz(ə)m/ a common but (strictly) incorrect term for Tibetan Buddhism.

**La Mancha** /læ ˈmæntʃə/ a flat treeless plain in south-central Spain that once formed a region of New Castile and now lies largely in the autonomous region of Castilla-La Mancha. Cervantes wrote *Don Quixote* in prison at Argamasilla in La Mancha.

**La Manche** /læ ˈmɑ̃ʃ/ the French name for the ENGLISH CHANNEL.

**Lambersart** /ˈlɑːmbɜːsɑː(r)/ a town in the Nord department of north-west France, 3 km. north-west of Lille; pop. (1990) 28,460.

**Lambeth** /ˈlæmbəθ/ a borough of inner London, England, on the south bank of the Thames between Wandsworth and Southwark; pop. (1991) 220,100. Landmarks include Lambeth Palace, St. Thomas's Hospital, The Oval, the Old Vic Theatre, the Royal Festival Hall, and the Imperial War Museum.

**Lambeth Palace** a palace in the London borough of Lambeth, that since 1197 has been the London residence of the Archbishop of Canterbury.

**La Mesa** /læ ˈmeɪsə/ a city in southern California, USA, an affluent suburb to the east of San Diego; pop. (1990) 52,930.

**Lamía** /lɑːˈmɪə/ the capital of the department of Pthiotis in central Greece, at the foot of Mt. Othris; pop. (1981) 41,670. It is a market town trading in grain, cotton, and garden produce. Lamía is associated with the legendary Achilles and the Lamian War between the Athenians and the Macedonians in 323–322 BC.

**Lammermuir Hills** /ˈlæmɜːˌmjʊə(r)/ a range of hills in East Lothian and the Borders, south-east Scotland rising to 533 m. (1,749 ft.) at Meikle Says Law.

**Lampedusa** /læmpəˈduːzə/ an island of the Pelagian group in the Mediterranean Sea between Malta and North Africa, administered by Italy. Settled in 1843, its only town is Il Porto; area 20 sq. km. (8 sq. miles); pop. (1981) 4,170.

**Lanai** /ləˈnaɪ/ an island of Hawaii to the west of Maui in the Pacific Ocean; area 365 sq. km. (140 sq. miles); pop. (1980) 2,120. Its chief export is pineapple.

**Lanarkshire** a former county of south-central Scotland, incorporated into Strathclyde Region in 1975 and the local government areas of North and South Lanarkshire in 1996.

**Lancang Jiang** /ˌlæŋkæŋ ˈdʒjæŋ/ the Chinese name for the MEKONG RIVER.

**Lancashire** /ˈlæŋkəʃɪə(r)/ a county of north-west England, on the Irish Sea; area 3,070 sq. km. (1,186 sq. miles); pop. (1991) 1,365,100; county town, Preston. The county was noted for the production of textiles, especially cotton goods, between the 16th and 19th centuries. Both cotton manufactures and coal-mining have virtually ceased. Tourism is important on the coast and Pennine hills. Lancashire is divided into 14 districts:

| District | Area (sq. km.) | Pop. (1991) |
|---|---|---|
| Blackburn | 137 | 132,800 |
| Blackpool | 35 | 144,500 |
| Burnley | 111 | 89,000 |
| Chorley | 203 | 96,500 |
| Fylde | 165 | 70,100 |
| Hyndburn | 73 | 76,500 |
| Lancaster | 577 | 125,600 |
| Pendle | 169 | 82,700 |
| Preston | 142 | 126,200 |
| Ribble Valley | 585 | 51,000 |
| Rossendale | 138 | 64,000 |
| South Ribble | 113 | 99,800 |
| West Lancashire | 338 | 106,600 |
| Wyre | 283 | 99,700 |

**Lancaster** /ˈlæŋˌkæstə(r)/ a city in Lancashire, north-west England, on the estuary of the River

Lune; pop. (1981) 44,450. The town developed around a castle and a Benedictine priory built in the 11th c. on the site of a former Roman fortification. It was the county town and administrative centre of Lancashire until 1974. It has a university founded in 1964, and numerous light industries.

**Lancaster** /ˈlæŋˌkæstə(r)/ **1.** a city in southern California, USA, in the western Mojave Desert north of Los Angeles; pop. (1990) 97,290. To the north is Edwards Air Force Base, landing site for the NASA space-shuttle programme. **2.** a city in south-east Pennsylvania, USA, at the heart of the Pennsylvania Dutch area; pop. (1990) 55,550. It developed in the 18th c. as a provisioning and arms manufacturing centre, was state capital (1799–1812), and US capital for one day (27 September 1777).

**Lanchow** see LANZHOU.

**Lancs.** *abbr.* LANCASHIRE.

**Land** /lʌnt/ (*pl.* **Länder** /ˈlendə(r)/) a province of Germany or Austria.

**landes** /lɑ̃d/ a term used in south-west France to describe wastelands or lowlands comprising sand dunes and lagoons.

**Landes** /lɑ̃d/ a coastal department of Aquitaine in south-west France; area 9,243 sq. km. (3,570 sq. miles); pop. (1990) 331,460; capital, Mont-de-Marsan. Main activities are forestry, farming, and tourism.

**Land's End** a rocky promontory in south-west Cornwall, which forms the westernmost point of England. The approximate distance by road from Land's End to John o' Groats, at the north-east tip of Scotland, is 1,400 km. (876 miles).

**Landshut** /ˈlɑːntsˈhuːt/ a city in Bavaria, southern Germany, on the Isar River north-east of Munich; pop. (1991) 59,670. The former residence of the dukes of Bavaria-Landshut, its industries include engineering and the manufacture of textiles, vehicles, and dyestuffs.

**Landskrona** /lɑːnzˈkruːnə/ an industrial seaport in south-west Sweden, in Malmöhus county; pop. (1990) 36,340. Industries include shipbuilding, sugar refining, and the manufacture of chemicals and machinery.

**Langdale** /ˈlæŋdeɪl/ a valley in the Lake District of north-west England with a background of high fells including the **Langdale Pikes**.

**Langfang** /ˌlæŋˈfæŋ/ a city in Hebei province, eastern China, to the north of Tianjin; pop. (1986) 533,000.

**Langkawi** /ˈlæŋˈkɑːwɪ/ a group of 99 tropical islands in Malaysia, situated at the northern end of the Straits of Malacca off the coast of Kedah. The islands, which have many fine beaches, have become one of Malaysia's leading resort areas.

**Languedoc** /lɑ̃ɡˈdɒk/ a former province of southern France, which extended from the Rhône valley to the northern foothills of the eastern Pyrenees and formed a broad coastal plain lying between the Cévennes Mountains and the Mediterranean. It derives its name from the *langue d'oc*, a form of medieval French spoken south of the Loire, the basis of modern Provençal. Lower Languedoc has united with the former province of Roussillon to form the modern French region of Languedoc-Roussillon which comprises the departments of Aude, Gard, Herault, Lozère, and Pyrénées-Orientales; area 27,376 sq. km. (10,574 sq. miles); pop. (1990) 2,114,985. Its chief town is Montpellier.

**Lansing** /ˈlænsɪŋ/ the state capital of Michigan, USA, on the Grand River; pop. (1990) 127,320. First settled in 1847, the city developed after 1887 when R. E. Olds began to build and sell one of America's earliest automobiles, the Oldsmobile. Its heavy industries produce vehicles, metal goods, and machinery. East Lansing is the home of Michigan State University (1855).

**Lantau** /lænˈdaʊ/ (Chinese **Tai Yue Shan**) an island of Hong Kong situated to the west of Hong Kong Island from which it is separated by the Lamma Channel. It is linked to the mainland at Tsuen Wan by a causeway that crosses Tsing Yi Island. It forms part of the New Territories which were ceded to Britain by China in 1898.

**Lanzarote** /ˈlɑːnzəˌrɒtɪ/ one of the Canary Islands, the most easterly island of the group, part of the Spanish province of Las Palmas; area 795 sq. km. (307 sq. miles); chief town, Arrecife. It is a popular tourist resort. The island's landscape was dramatically altered after a series of volcanic eruptions in about 1730. It is noted for the black sand of its beaches and for the 'Mountains of Fire' in the south-west, an area of several hundred volcanoes which still emit heat.

**Lanzhou** /lænˈdʒəʊ/ (formerly **Lanchow** /lænˈtʃaʊ/) a city of northern China, on the upper Yellow River, capital of Gansu province; pop. (1990) 1,480,000. Its chief industries are engineering, oil refining, and atomic energy.

**Laohekou** /laʊˈhekəʊ/ a city in Henan province, east-central China, on the Han River east of the Wudang Shan Mountains; pop. (1986) 423,000.

**Laon** /lɑ̃/ a historic town, capital of Aisne department in northern France, situated on a hill overlooking the Champagne plain; pop. (1990) 28,670. It was capital of France in the 8th–10th c.

**Laois** /liːʃ/ (also **Laoighis**, **Leix**) a county of the Republic of Ireland, in the province of Leinster; area 1,720 sq. km. (664 sq. miles); pop. (1991) 52,325; county town, Portlaoise. It was formerly (until 1920) called Queen's County.

**La Oroya** /lɑː əʊˈrɔɪə/ an industrial mining town in the central highlands of Peru, at an altitude of 3,700 m. (12,140 ft.); pop. (1990) 35,000. The railway line that links La Oroya with Lima passes through La Galera station, the world's highest station on a standard-gauge track (4,781 m., 15,686 ft.).

**Laos** /laʊs, 'lɑːɒs/ official name **The Lao People's Democratic Republic** a land-locked country in south-east Asia, bounded by China, Burma, Vietnam, Cambodia, and

Thailand; area 236,800 sq. km. (91,464 sq. miles); pop. (est. 1991) 4,279,000; official language, Laotian; capital, Vientiane. Forming part of the watershed of the Mekong River, Laos is dominated by dense forest and a mountain chain rising to heights over 2,700 m. (9,000 ft.). The climate is monsoonal with heavy rain from May to September and a marked hot and dry season from February to April. Although less than ten per cent of the land is available for cultivation nearly 85 per cent of the population engage in subsistence agriculture. Rich in undeveloped resources, its chief exports are timber, hydroelectric power, tin, and coffee. Nearly half of the population are Lao people who are descended from the Thais who migrated southwards from China in the 13th c. The Lao kingdom (Lan Xang) was first united in 1353 by King Fa Ngum who made his capital at Luang Prabang and introduced Buddhism as the state religion. In decline from the 16th c., Laos eventually came under direct French rule in 1899. In 1949 France recognized the independence of Laos which stayed within the French Union until 1953, but for most of the next two decades it was torn by strife and civil war between the communist Pathet Lao movement (latterly aided by the North Vietnamese) and government supporters (aided by the US and Thai mercenaries). At the conclusion of the Vietnam war in 1975 the monarchy was abolished and the communist Lao People's Democratic Republic was established. A harsh Soviet-style economic system was imposed until 1985 when free market reforms were introduced as part of a 'new economic mechanism' designed to boost exports. The country is governed by a single party Supreme People's Assembly and an executive Council of Ministers. Laos exports tin, coffee, and timber; also, illegally, opium.
**Lao** or **Laotian** *adj. & n.*

**La Paz** /læ 'pæz/ **1.** the capital of Bolivia, in the north-west of the country near the border with Peru; pop. (1990) 1,126,000. Situated in the Andes at an altitude of 3,660 m. (12,000 ft.), La Paz is the highest capital city in the world. It was founded by the Spanish in 1548 on the site of an Inca settlement. Its industries include textiles, electrical appliances, and chemicals. **2.** a city in north-west Mexico, a port near the southern tip of the Baja California peninsula; pop. (est. 1984) 100,000. It is

capital of the state of Baja California Sur. It is a fishing and pearling centre, and winter resort.

**La Pérouse Strait** /læ peɪˈruːz/ a stretch of water separating the Japanese island of Hokkaido from the Russian island of Sakhalin. It is named after the French explorer François de La Pérouse who sailed through the strait in 1787.

**Lapland** /'læplænd/ the region of northern Europe which extends from the Norwegian Sea to the White Sea and lies mainly within the Arctic Circle. It consists of the northern parts of Norway, Sweden, and Finland, and the Kola Peninsula of Russia.
**Laplander** *n.*

**La Plata** /læ 'plɑːtə/ a port in Argentina, on the River Plate, south-east of Buenos Aires; pop. (1991) 640,000. Founded in 1882, it was known as Eva Perón from 1946 to 1955. It is one of the chief outlets for produce from the pampas of Argentina such as grain and refrigerated meat; it is a major oil-refining centre. It is also a cultural centre, with a national university (1897), colleges, and museums.

**Lapp** /læp/ a member of the indigenous population of the extreme northerly part of Scandinavia who originated in the region of Lake Onega in Russia and moved westwards 10,000 years ago. Although nominally under Swedish and Norwegian control since the Middle Ages, their Christianization was not completed until the 18th c. The Lappish language, of which there are several mutually unintelligible dialects, is related to Finnish. Today the majority of Lapps live in Norway and Sweden with small communities in Finland and Russia. Traditionally associated with the herding and domestication of reindeer, few Lapps continue the nomadic herding of the animals. Approximately 50 per cent of the Lapps now live in permanent settlements with year-round pasture, and another 40 per cent live on the coasts and derive their livelihood from a combination of fishing, hunting, trapping, and farming. Scandinavian industrialization—particularly hydroelectric schemes, mining, and new roads—has severely disrupted the Lapps' traditional lifestyle.

**Lappeenranta** /'lɑːpeɪnˌræntə/ (Swedish **Villmanstrand**) a town in Kymi province, south-east Finland, on Lake Saimaa; pop. (1990) 54,940.

**Lappi** /'lɑːpɪ/ a province of northern Finland; area 98,938 sq. km. (38,215 sq. miles); pop. (1991) 200,670; capital, Rovaniemi.

**Laptev Sea** /'læptef/ a part of the Arctic Ocean, which lies to the north of Russia between the Taimyr Peninsula and the New Siberian Islands.

**L'Aquila** see AQUILA.

**Laramie** /'lærəmɪ/ a city in south-east Wyoming, USA; pop. (1990) 26,690. First settled in 1868, during the construction of the Union Pacific Railroad, its early years were associated with the lawlessness of the Wild West. It is now a centre for agriculture, mining, tourism, and timber production and is home of the University of Wyoming (1886).

**Larache** /ləˈrɑːʃ/ a port on the Atlantic coast of northern Morocco, on the Oued Loukkos; pop. (1982) 63,900. Originally the site of a Phoenician trading settlement, it was successively occupied by Portugal, Spain, and Morocco, flourishing in the 16th–18th c. as a port of call for Algerian and Tunisian pirates.

**Laredo** /ləˈreɪdəʊ/ a town on the US–Mexico frontier of southern Texas, on the Río Grande; pop. (1990) 122,900. Founded in 1755 by Thomas Sanchez who established a ferry across the river, it is now a major US gateway to and from Mexico, and is an import–export trade centre.

**Largo** /ˈlɑː(r)gəʊ/ a city in western Florida, USA, on the Pinellas Peninsula; pop. (1990) 65,670. It is a citrus-processing and shipping centre.

**La Rioja** /læ rɪˈɒxə/ **1.** an autonomous region of northern Spain, in the wine-producing valley of the River Ebro; area 5,034 sq. km. (1,944 sq. miles); pop. (1991) 263,430; capital, Logroño. **2.** a city in north-western Argentina, capital of a province of the same name in the eastern Andes; pop. (1991) 104,000.

**Larissa** /ləˈrɪsə/ (Greek **Lárisa**) a city of north-eastern Greece, capital of a department of the same name and chief town of Thessaly; pop. (1991) 113,000. It is situated on the Piniós River near Mount Olympus and is an agricultural trade centre.

**Larkana** /lɑːˈkɑːnə/ a city in the province of Sind, south-central Pakistan; pop. (est. 1991) 275,000. It was the home town of Zulfikar Ali Bhutto, a former prime minister (1973–7) and first civilian president (1971–3) of Pakistan. Nearby is the ancient prehistoric city of Mohenjo Daro. Larkana is an important rice market and textile trade centre.

**Larnaca** /ˈlɑːnəkə/ a port, industrial town, and resort on the south coast of Cyprus, on Larnaca Bay; pop. (1990) 62,600. It was the birthplace of Zeno the Stoic in 335 BC, and of Apollonius the Alexandrian physician c. 50 BC. Since the partition of Cyprus Greek Cypriots have developed Larnaca as the principal international tourist airport.

**Larne** /lɑːn/ a seaport and resort town in County Antrim, Northern Ireland, near the mouth of Lough Larne; pop. (1981) 18,220. There is a ferry link with Stranraer in south-west Scotland.

**La Rochelle** /læ rɒˈʃel/ a seaport on the Bay of Biscay, capital of the department of Charente-Maritime, western France; pop. (1990) 73,740. A former Huguenot stronghold, it was besieged and devastated by Richlieu in 1627–8. Nearby La Palice is the departure point for the Ile de Ré. La Rochelle has shipbuilding, fish-canning, and saw-milling industries.

**La Roche-sur-Yon** /læ rɒʃ sʊ(ə)rˈjɒn/ the capital town of the department of Vendée in the Pays de la Loire of western France; pop. (1990) 48,568.

**Larvik** /ˈlɑːvɪk/ a seaport in Vestfold county, on the south coast of Norway; pop. (1990) 38,230. It was the birthplace in 1914 of the anthropologist Thor Heyerdahl.

**Lascaux** /ˈlæskəʊ/ a cave with palaeolithic drawings and paintings generally held to be the finest examples of prehistoric art; discovered in 1940 in the Dordogne region of south-west-central France. Now closed for reasons of preservation, its artwork is reproduced in caves nearby (Lascaux II).

**Las Cruces** /læs ˈkruːsɪs/ a city in south-west New Mexico, USA, on the Río Grande; pop. (1990) 62,130. It takes its name from 'the crosses' which commemorate an Apache Indian massacre that took place in 1830. The first atomic bomb was tested at a nearby military range.

**La Serena** /læ səˈreɪnə/ a resort town on the Pacific coast of central Chile, capital of the Coquimbo Region; pop. (1991) 105,590. Chilean independence was declared here in 1818. It has been rebuilt in the colonial style.

**La Seyne-sur-Mer** /læ ˌseɪn sʊ(ə)r ˈmer/ a port in the department of Var, south-east France, on the Mediterranean coast south-west of Toulon; pop. (1990) 60,570.

**Lasíthi** /ləˈsiːθɪ/ a fertile upland plateau in east-central Crete, irrigated by wind-pumps and a grid of drainage ditches that date from the 1630s when the island was part of the Venetian empire. Apples and potatoes are grown. Its chief town is Tzermiádo and above the village of Psykhró is a cave where Zeus is said to have been born. Over-looking the Pediáda plain on the western wall of the plateau are the remains of the Graeco-Roman city of Lyttos.

**Las Marismas** /læs məˈriːzməs/ a region of marshy wetland extending over an area of 388 sq. km. (150 sq. miles) in south-west Spain where the Guadalquivir River meet the Gulf of Cadiz. Noted for its migratory birds, it forms part of the Doñana National Park.

**Las Palmas** /læs ˈpælmɑːs/ (in full **Las Palmas de Gran Canaria** /də græn kəˈnɑːrɪə/) a port and resort on the north-east coast of the island of Gran Canaria, capital and largest city of the Canary Islands; pop. (1991) 347,670. Exports sugar, bananas, and tomatoes.

**La Spezia** /læ ˈspetsɪə/ an industrial port at the head of the Gulf of La Spezia in Liguria, north-western Italy; pop. (1990) 103,000. Since 1861 it has been Italy's chief naval station. There is a ferry link with Corsica.

**Lassa** /ˈlæsə/ a village in Nigeria that gives its name to an acute virus disease of tropical Africa, first reported here in 1969.

**Lassen Peak** /ˈlɑːsən/ the southernmost of a chain of volcanic mountains in the Cascade Range on the Pacific coast of North America. It rises to 3,187 m. (10,457 ft.) in northern California and lies within the **Lassen Volcanic National Park** which was designated in 1916 after a series of eruptions. It is named after the Danish pioneer Peter Lassen.

**Las Vegas** /læs 'veɪgəs/ a desert city in southern Nevada, USA, noted for its casinos and nightclubs; pop. (1990) 258,295. An early camping site on the westward-bound trail across the continent, Las Vegas was settled in 1855–7 by Mormons. It later became a centre of mining and ranching and was purchased by a railway company in 1903.

**Latacunga** /ˌlætəˈkʊŋgə/ a commercial town in central Ecuador, capital of the Andean province of Cotopaxi; pop. (1990) 128,950.

**Latakia** /ˌlætəˈkiːə/ (Arabic **Al Ladhiqiyah**) a seaport on the coast of western Syria, opposite the north-eastern tip of Cyprus; pop. (1981) 196,800. It is famous for its tobacco.

**La Tène** /lɑː ˈten/ the second phase of the European Iron Age, named after the type-site at the east end of Lake Neuchâtel, Switzerland, and dating from the mid-5th c. BC until the Roman conquest. The culture of this period (which follows the Hallstatt) represents the height of early Celtic achievement. It is characterized by hill-forts, developments in agriculture, rich and elaborate burials, and artefacts of excellent craftsmanship and artistic design.

**Lateran** /ˈlætərən/ the site in Rome containing the basilica of St. John the Baptist (St. John Lateran) which is the cathedral church of Rome, and the Lateran Palace where the popes resided until the 14th c. Five general ecclesiastical councils of the Western Church were held in the basilica (1123, 1139, 1179, 1215, 1512–17). The Lateran Treaty, signed in the Lateran Palace in 1929, was a concordat between the kingdom of Italy and the Holy See, recognizing as fully sovereign and independent a new (papal) state called Vatican City.

**Latin** /ˈlætɪn/ an Indo-European language, inflected and with complex syntax, the ancestor of all the Romance languages. It was originally the dialect of the people of Latium (*Latini*), a district of Italy lying south of the Apennines and east of the Tiber, and the rise of Rome led to its spread as the official and literary language of the Roman Empire. In the Middle Ages it remained the international medium of communication in western Europe, the language of law, the sciences, and in particular of liturgy; it was the official language of the Roman Catholic Church until the mid-20th c. Latin of the post-classical period is distinguished chronologically as late Latin (*c.* AD 200–600) and medieval Latin (*c.* 600–1500); silver Latin is the literary language and style of the century following the death of Augustus in AD 14; the term Low or Vulgar Latin is applied to popular and provincial forms of Latin used in the Middle Ages, especially those from which the Romance languages developed.

**Latina** /læˈtiːnə/ a town in Latium, west-central Italy, capital of the province of Latina; pop. (1990) 103,630.

**Latin America** the parts of Central and South America where Spanish or Portuguese is the main language.
**Latin American** *adj. & n.*

**Latin American Economic System** a Latin American organization established in Panama City in 1975 to promote economic and social progress. Its headquarters are in Caracas, Venezuela.

**Latin American Integration Association** an economic grouping of Latin American countries set up in 1980 by the Treaty of Montevideo for the purpose of identifying and supporting areas in need of preferential economic treatment. It replaced the earlier Latin American Free Trade Association, but still has the long-term aim of establishing a Latin American Common Market. Its headquarters are in Montevideo, Uruguay.

**latitude** /ˈlætɪˌtjuːd/ the angular distance on a meridian north or south of the equator, expressed in degrees and minutes. **High latitudes** are regions near the poles and **low latitudes** are regions near the equator.

**Latium** /ˈleɪʃəm/ (Italian **Lazio** /ˈlætsɪˌəʊ/) a region of west-central Italy, west of the Apennines and south of the River Tiber, comprising the provinces of Frosinone, Latina, Rieti, Roma, and Vitebor; area 17,203 sq. km. (6,645 sq. miles); pop. (1990) 5,191,480; capital, Rome. The ancient region of Latium was settled during the early part of the first millennium BC by a branch of the Indo-European people known as the Latini. By the end of the 4th c. BC the region had become dominated by Rome.

**Látrabjarg** /laʊtrəˈbjɑːk/ the westernmost point of Iceland, a headland with one of the world's highest cliff faces. The rescue of the crew of the British trawler *Dhoon* via this cliff in 1947 was one of the most daring of its kind.

**Latur** a town in Maharashtra, south-central India, north-west of Hyderabad; pop. (1991) 197,160.

**Latvia** /ˈlætvɪə/ (Latvian **Latviya**) official name **The Republic of Latvia** a country on the eastern shore of the Baltic Sea, between Estonia and Lithuania; area 64,589 sq. km.

(24,947 sq. miles); pop. (est. 1991) 2,693,000; official language, Latvian (Lettish); capital, Riga. The largest cities are Riga, Daugavpils, and Liepaja. Situated on the edge of the east European Plain,

Latvia rises from coastal lowlands to undulating tree-covered hills that are watered by over 12,000 rivers, the largest of which is the Daugava. In the west the climate is moderated by its closeness to the sea. Latvia is not rich in natural resources although there are exploitable deposits of limestone, gypsum, sand, and gravel. Its location on ancient trade routes leading to the Baltic Sea has resulted in the development of a communications network that facilitates the movement of the country's chief agricultural products which are largely derived from pig-breeding and dairy-farming. After being under Polish and Swedish rule Latvia became a Baltic province of Russia at the end of the Great Northern War of 1700–21. It was proclaimed an independent republic in 1918 but in 1940 was annexed by the USSR as a constituent republic. Following the breakup of the Soviet Union in 1991 Latvia established itself as an independent republic once again. Some 52 per cent of the population is Latvian and 34 per cent Russian, the remainder largely comprising Belorussians, Ukrainians, and Poles. Latvia is governed by a legislative Supreme Council (*Augstake Padome*) and an executive Council of Ministers.
**Latvian** *adj. & n.*

**Latvian** /ˈlætvɪən/ the language of Latvia, also called Lettish, spoken by some 1,500,000 people, most closely related to Lithuanian with which it constitutes the Baltic language group.

**Launceston** /ˈlɔːnsəst(ə)n/ a city in northern Tasmania, at the confluence of the North and South Esk rivers which join to form the 64-km. (40-mile) tidal estuary of the Tamar; pop. (1991) 66,750. Dating from 1824, Launceston has developed into the second-largest city on the island. It is a centre of communication and textile production.

**Laurasia** /lɔːˈreɪʃə/ a vast continental area thought to have once existed in the northern hemisphere and to have broken up in Mesozoic or late Palaeozoic times, forming North America, Greenland, Europe, and most of Asia north of the Himalayas.

**Laurentian Highlands** /lɒˈrenʃ(ə)n/ (also **Laurentians**, French **Les Laurentides**) part of the plateau and southern rim of the Canadian Shield, in southern Quebec, eastern Canada. Lying north of the St. Lawrence, they stretch from Ottawa in the west to the Saguenay River in the east. That part of the region north of Montreal has developed as a leading resort area, and to the north of Quebec City the Laurentides wildlife conservation area (1895) extends over 10,514 sq. km. (4,058 sq. miles) of lakes and forest. See also CANADIAN SHIELD.

**Lausanne** /ləʊˈzɑːn/ a resort town on the north shore of Lake Geneva, south-west Switzerland, capital of the Vaud canton; pop. (1990) 122,600. It is the seat of the International Olympic Committee.

**Laval** a city in Quebec, Canada, on an island in the St. Lawrence River west of Montreal; pop. (1991) 314,400. It is a residential suburb of Montreal and has many tourist facilities.

**Laval** /ləˈvɑːl/ the capital of the department of Mayenne in north-west France, on the River Mayenne; pop. (1990) 53,480. It was the birthplace in 1509 of Ambroise Paré, 'the father of modern surgery', and the painter Henri Rousseau (1844–1910).

**Lawrence** /ˈlɒrəns/ **1.** a city in eastern Kansas, USA, on the Kansas River east of Topeka; pop. (1990) 65,600. Founded in 1854 by the New England Emigrant Aid Company, it is the home of the University of Kansas (1866). **2.** a city in north-east Massachusetts, USA, on the Merrimack River; pop. (1990) 70,200. Founded by a group of Boston financiers in 1847, the water of the Merrimack was initially used to power large textile mills. It now has diverse light industries.

**Lawton** /ˈlɔːt(ə)n/ a city in south-west Oklahoma, USA, founded during the land-rush of 1901; pop. (1990) 80,560. Nearby is the Fort Sill Military Reservation (established in 1869), base of the US Army Field Artillery, with an Apache cemetery in which the Indian chief Geronimo lies buried.

**LAX** a code used by airlines to identify the Los Angeles International Airport in California, USA.

**Laxton** /ˈlækst(ə)n/ a village in Nottinghamshire, central England, 7 km. (4 miles) east of Ollerton, where an ancient openfield system of cultivation is maintained. Known as the 'three-field system', it is England's only surviving traditionally run semi-communal medieval farming complex. The system is administered by a 'jury' of villagers sworn in each November, and a special village court of law known as a 'court leet'.

**La'youn** /lɑːˈjuːn/ (also **Laayoune**, Arabic **El Aaiún** /ˌel aɪˈuːn/) the capital of Western Sahara, on the Atlantic coast of north-west Africa; pop. (1982) 96,800.

**Lazio** the Italian name for LATIUM.

**League of Nations** an association of self-governing states, dominions, and colonies established in 1919 by the Treaty of Versailles, at the instigation of the US President Woodrow Wilson, 'to promote international co-operation and to achieve international peace and security'. Although the League accomplished much of value in post-war economic reconstruction, it failed in its prime purpose through the refusal of member-nations to put international interests before national ones, and was powerless in the face of Italian, German, and Japanese expansionism. By the outbreak of World War II the League of Nations was little more than a helpless spectator, and the war itself destroyed it entirely.

**Leamington Spa** /ˈlemɪŋt(ə)n/ (also **Royal Leamington Spa**) a residential town in Warwickshire, central England, on the River Leam south-east of Birmingham; pop. (1981) 57,350. Noted for its saline springs, it was granted the status of royal spa after a visit by Queen Victoria in 1838.

## Lebanon

/'lebənən/ official name **The Lebanese Republic** a country in the Middle East with a coastline on the Mediterranean Sea; area 10,452 sq. km. (4,037 sq. miles); pop. (est. 1990) 2,700,000; official language, Arabic (French, Kurdish, and Armenian are also spoken); capital and major port, Beirut. To the east of a narrow coastal plain rise the Lebanon Mountains which are separated from the Anti-Lebanon Mountains on the Syrian frontier by the Bekaa Valley. The Litani River, which flows southwards into the sea near Tyre, is Lebanon's principal river and the only river in the Near East that does not cross an international boundary. Summers are hot with a high humidity on the coast while mountain areas are cooler. Winters are mild along the coast with snow more frequent at higher altitudes inland. Lebanon was the historic home of the Phoenicians whose maritime culture was based there for more than 2,000 years (c. 2700–450 BC). Christians established a refuge in the Lebanon Mountains and crusaders built several strongholds there in the Middle Ages. Following the collapse of the Ottoman empire after World War I, the Lebanon was mandated to France by the League of Nations before gaining full independence in 1943. Characterized by political turmoil Lebanon eventually collapsed into civil war in 1975 as a result of difficulties arising from the presence of large numbers of Palestinian refugees. Coupled with the Palestinian problem, differences between Christian and Muslim communities grew more intense with the development of sectarian militias. Complicated by the intervention of Syrian and Israeli forces, a ceasefire was eventually agreed following a meeting of Lebanese parliamentarians in Ta'if, Saudi Arabia, in 1989. In 1991 the Lebanese government with the support of Syrian forces regained control over the greater part of the country although Israeli troops refused to withdraw from a security zone which they had established in the south. The first general elections for twenty years were held in 1992. Until the civil war Lebanon was the financial and commercial centre of the Middle East. Its major industries include banking, food processing, and the manufacture of textiles. Tourism was a major industry before the civil war. The country is governed by an executive president and Cabinet of Ministers who are responsible to a unicameral parliament.
**Lebanese** *adj. & n.*

## Lebanon Mountains

a range of mountains in Lebanon. Running parallel to the Mediterranean coast, it rises to a height of 3,087 m. (10,022 ft.) at Qornet es Saouda. It is separated from the Anti-Lebanon range, on the border with Syria, by the Bekaa valley.

**Le Bourget** /lə 'buə(r)ʒeɪ/ an airport situated 40 km. (25 miles) north of Paris, France. Charles Lindbergh landed here on 21 May 1927 after making the first non-stop solo transatlantic flight.

**Lebowa** /le'bəuə/ a homeland of the North Sotho people in north-east Transvaal, South Africa, designated a self-governing national state in 1972; pop. (1985) 1,842,000.

**Le Cannet** /lə 'kæneɪ/ a town in the Alpes-Maritimes department of south-eastern France, 3 km. north of Cannes; pop. (1990) 42,000.

**Lecce** /'letʃɪ/ an ancient market town in Apulia, south-eastern Italy, capital of the province of Lecce; pop. (1990) 102,340. Many of its fine buildings are decorated in Baroque style. Nearby is the site of Rudiae, an ancient Roman town with tombs and an amphitheatre.

**Lech** /lex/ a river that rises in western Austria and flows 280 km. (175 miles) north-eastwards into Germany where it meets the Danube.

**Lechtal Alps** /'lext(ə)l/ (German **Lechtaler Alpen**) a range of mountains in the eastern Alps, in the Austrian state of Tyrol. Its highest peak is Parseierspitze (3,036 m., 9,961 ft.).

**Le Creusot** /ˌlə krɜː'zəu/ an industrial town in the Saône-et-Loire department, in the Burgundy region of east-central France; pop. (1990) 29,230. From the 17th c. to the early 20th c. it was a noted centre for the manufacture of steel, glass, and ceramics.

**Leeds** /liːdz/ an industrial city in West Yorkshire, England, on the River Aire; pop. (1981) 449,000. Founded in Roman times, Leeds developed as a wool town in the Middle Ages, becoming a centre of the clothing trade in the Industrial Revolution. It was the birthplace in 1545 of Lord Darnley, husband of Mary Queen of Scots, and in 1758 the first railway line in the world was opened here, transporting coal from Middleton. Every three years Leeds hosts an international piano competition. The University of Leeds was founded in 1904 and the Leeds Metropolitan University (formerly Leeds Polytechnic) was established in 1992. Until recently Leeds was Britain's major producer of ready-made clothing and textile machinery. It now has diverse light industries and is a cultural centre and commercial city.

**Leeuwarden** /'leɪwɑːd(ə)n/ the capital of the Dutch province of Friesland, on the River Ee; pop. (1991) 85,690. Once a port and noted centre of gold and silver work, it is an important agricultural market town in a dairy-farming region. The spy known as Mata Hari was born here in 1876.

**Leeward Islands** /'liːwəd/ a group of islands in the West Indies, constituting the northern part

of the Lesser Antilles. The group includes
Guadeloupe, Antigua, St. Kitts, and Montserrat.
The name refers to the fact that the islands are further from the direction of prevailing winds, which
are easterly, than the Windward Islands.

**Lefkosia** /ˌlefkə'sɪə/ the Greek name for the city
of **Nicosia**.

**Left Bank** the name given to an area of Paris to
the south of the River Seine, comprising the districts of St-Germain-des-Prés, Montparnasse, and
St-Michel. It is a noted centre of cultural and artistic life. The area known as the Latin Quarter is
dominated by the Sorbonne, the University of
Paris.

**Leghorn** /'leghɔːn/ (Italian **Livorno** /lɪ'vɔːnəʊ/)
a port and industrial town in north-west Italy, on
the Ligurian coast of Tuscany; pop. (1990) 171,265.
It was laid out as an 'ideal' city for the Medici
family by Buontalenti in the 16th c. and subsequently developed as a trading centre between
Europe and the East. It is the site of the Italian
Naval Academy and has heavy industries associated with its port functions.

**Legnica** /leg'niːtsə/ a town in western Poland,
on the River Kaczawa, capital of Legnica county;
pop. (1990) 105,210. Industries include the manufacture of textiles, copper, electronics, and pianos.

**Leh** /leɪ/ a town in Jammu and Kashmir, northern
India, to the east of Srinagar near the Indus River;
pop. (est. 1991) 9,000. It is the chief town of the
Himalayan region of Ladakh and a market town
and supply base for Indian military outposts on the
Siachen Glacier.

**Le Havre** /lə 'hɑːvr/ France's second-largest
port in the Seine-Maritime department of north-
west France, on the English Channel at the mouth
of the Seine; pop. (1990) 197,220. Founded in the
16th c. by François I, the city was largely rebuilt
after destruction in World War II. It has banking,
oil refining and chemical industries, and ferry links
with the UK.

**Leicester** /'lestə(r)/ a city in central England on
the River Soar, the county town of Leicestershire;
pop. (1991) 270,600. It was founded as a Roman
settlement where Fosse Way crosses the Soar (AD
50–100), and has a 14th-c. cathedral. The
University of Leicester was founded in 1957 and
the De Montfort University (formerly Leicester
Polytechnic) was established in 1992. It is noted as
a hosiery, textile, and engineering city.

**Leicestershire** /'lestəˌʃɪə(r)/ a county of central England; area 2,553 sq. km. (986 sq. miles);
pop. (1991) 860,500; county town, Leicester. It is
divided into nine districts:

| District | Area (sq. km.) | Pop. (1991) |
| --- | --- | --- |
| Blaby | 131 | 81,900 |
| Charnwood | 279 | 140,500 |
| Harborough | 593 | 66,200 |
| Hinckley and Bosworth | 297 | 93,600 |
| Leicester | 73 | 270,600 |
| Melton | 482 | 44,500 |
| North West Leicestershire | 280 | 79,400 |
| Oadby and Wigston | 23 | 51,500 |
| Rutland | 394 | 32,400 |

**Leics.** *abbr.* Leicestershire.

**Leiden** /'laɪd(ə)n/ (also **Leyden**) a city in the
west Netherlands, in the province of South
Holland 15 km. (9 miles) north-east of the Hague;
pop. (1991) 111,950. It is the site of the country's
oldest university, founded in 1575. The painter
Rembrandt was born in the city in 1606, and the
Pilgrim Fathers spent eleven years in the city before
sailing to America. The electrical condenser known
as the 'Leyden jar' was invented here in 1745.

**Leinster** /'lenstə(r)/ a province of the Republic
of Ireland, comprising the counties of Carlow,
Dublin, Kildare, Kilkenny, Laois, Longford,
Louth, Meath, Offaly, Westmeath, Wexford, and
Wicklow; area 19,633 sq. km. (7,583 sq. miles);
pop. (1991) 1,860,040; its capital is Dublin.

**Leipzig** /'laɪpzɪg/ an industrial city in the state of
Saxony, east-central Germany, a centre of the publishing and the music trade; pop. (1991) 503,190.
An annual trade fair has been held here since the
12th c. J. S. Bach is buried in St. Thomas' Church.

**Leiria** /ˌleɪə'rɪə/ a town in central Portugal, on
the River Liz, capital of Leiria district; pop. (1991)
27,530. It is dominated by a 12th-c. castle.

**Leitrim** /'liːtrɪm/ a county in the Republic of
Ireland, in the province of Connaught; area 1,526
sq. km. (589 sq. miles); pop. (1991) 25,300; county
town, Carrick-on-Shannon.

**Leix** see LAOIS.

**Le Lamentin** /lə 'læmentæn/ a town on the
French island of Martinique in the West Indies,
situated south-east of Fort-de-France; pop. (1990)
30,600. The island's international airport is at Le
Lamentin.

**Léman, Lac** see GENEVA, LAKE.

**Le Mans** /lə'mɑ̃/ an industrial town in north-
west France, capital of the department of Sarthe;
pop. (1990) 148,465. There are remains of a 3rd–
4th c. Gallo-Roman fortress and a Romanesque
cathedral. It is the site of a motor-racing circuit, on
which a 24-hour endurance race (established in
1923) for GT and sports cars is held each summer.

**Le Marais** /ˌlə mæ'reɪ/ a district of Paris,
France, more or less coextensive with the 4th
arrondissement. It lies to the north of the Seine
between the Louvre and the Place de la Bastille and
is named after the marsh that was turned into an
elegant residential area during the 16th and 17th
centuries. It is noted for its hôtels which were the
Parisian town houses of the landed gentry.

**Lemberg** /'lembɜːg/ the German name for LVOV.

**Lemnos** /'lemnɒs/ (Greek **Límnos** /'liːmnɒs/) a
Greek island in the northern Aegean Sea off the

north-west coast of Turkey; area 476 sq. km. (184 sq. miles). Its chief settlement is Kástron or Mírina (ancient Myrina).

**Lempa** /ˈlempə/ a river in Central America that rises near Esquipulas in Guatemala and flows 320 km. (200 miles) south and east through Honduras and El Salvador to the Pacific Ocean.

**Lena** /ˈliːnə/ a river in Siberia which rises in the mountains on the western shore of Lake Baikal, and flows generally north-east and north for 4,400 km. (2,734 miles) via a vast delta into the Laptev Sea, a part of the Arctic Ocean. It is one of the three great Siberian Rivers flowing to the Arctic Ocean, famous for the gold-fields in its basin. The river is frozen over for 8 months of the year.

**Lengshuijiang** /ˌlenʃwiːˈdʒæŋ/ a city in Hunan province, south-east-central China, south-west of Changsha; pop. (1986) 287,000.

**Lengshuitan** /ˌlenʃwiːˈtɑːn/ a city in Hunan province, south-east-central China, south-west of Hengyang; pop. (1986) 371,000.

**Leninabad** the former name (1936–91) of KHUDZHAND.

**Leninakan** a former name (1924–91) of GYUMRI.

**Leningrad** a former name (1924–91) of ST. PETERSBURG.

**Lens** /lãs/ an industrial town in the department of Pas-de-Calais, northern France, 18 km. (11 miles) north-east of Arras; pop. (1990) 34,010. The centre of a former coal-mining area it now has metallurgical, chemical, and textile industries. Nearby at Vimy is a memorial to Canadian troops who fought at Vimy Ridge.

**Leoben** /leɪˈəʊbən/ an industrial town in Styria, south-eastern Austria, situated on the River Mur north-west of Graz; pop. (1991) 28,500. It is a centre of lignite-mining and the iron industry.

**León** /leɪˈɒn/ (in full **León de los Aldama**) an industrial city in the state of Guanajuato, south-central Mexico, situated at an altitude of 1,800 m. (5,900 ft.); pop. (1990) 872,450. Founded by the Spanish in 1576, it is famous for its shoes.

**León** /leɪˈɒn/ a city in north-west Nicaragua, near the Pacific coast; pop. (1985) 100,980. Founded in 1524, the original settlement was destroyed by an earthquake in 1609. Rebuilt on another site, it was capital until 1858 and has become the second-largest city of Nicaragua. Its university was founded in 1804 and its cathedral is the largest in Central America. Its industries include timber, chemicals, and food processing.

**León** /leɪˈɒn/ a city in northern Spain, capital of northern Spain, at the confluence of the Bernesga and Torio rivers; pop. (1991) 146,270. It is the capital of the province and former kingdom of León, now part of Castilla-León, and manufactures pottery, textiles, and leather goods.

**Leonding** /leɪˈɒntɪŋ/ a town of Upper Austria, northern Austria, to the south-west of Linz; pop. (1991) 21,355.

**Léopoldville** /ˈliːəˌpəʊldvɪl/ the former name (until 1966) of Kinshasa, capital of Zaire.

**Lepanto** /ləˈpæntəʊ/ a strait at the western entrance to the Gulf of Corinth, scene of a naval battle (1751) in which the fleet of the Holy League (the papacy, Venice, and Spain) under the command of Don John of Austria defeated a large Turkish fleet, ending for the time being the Turkish naval threat in the Mediterranean.

**Le Perreux-sur-Marne** /lə peˌrɜːsʊəˈmɑːn/ a south-eastern suburb of Paris, France, situated on the River Marne in the department of Val-de-Marne; pop. (1990) 28,540.

**Lepontine Alps** /ləˈpɒntiːn/ a section of the central Alps, lying on the Swiss–Italian border between the Pennine and Rhaetian Alps. Its highest peak is Monte Leone (3,563 m., 11,683 ft.).

**Leptis Magna** /ˌleptɪs ˈmægnə/ an ancient seaport and trading centre on the Mediterranean coast of North Africa, near present-day Al Khums (Homs) in Libya. Founded by the Phoenicians (perhaps before 600 BC) it was settled from Carthage, becoming one of the three chief cities of Tripolitania. It became a Roman colony under Trajan, most of its impressive remains dating from the reign of Septimus Severus (c. AD 200) who was a native of the city.

**Lérida** /ˈleɪrɪdə/ (also **Lleida**) an industrial city in north-east Spain, on the Segre River, capital of the Catalonian province of Lérida; pop. (1991) 119,170. It is surrounded by irrigated market gardens, and its industries include leather, textiles, paper, and arms.

**Lerwick** /ˈlɜːwɪk/ the capital of the Shetland Islands Area of northern Scotland, situated on the Mainland; pop. (1981) 7,560. The most northerly town in the British Isles, it is a fishing centre and a service port for the oil industry. The annual mid-winter Up-Helly-Aa festival takes place here every January.

**Les Abymes** /leɪz æˈbiːm/ a town on the island of Grande-Terre in the French Overseas Department of Guadeloupe, north-east of Point-à-Pitre; pop. (1990) 62,810. It is the site of the island's international airport.

**Lesbos** /ˈlezbɒs/ (Greek **Lésvos** /ˈlezvɒs/) a Greek island in the eastern Aegean, off the coast of north-west Turkey, the third-largest of the Greek islands; area 1,630 sq. km. (630 sq. miles); chief town, Mytilene. Its artistic golden age of the late 7th and early 6th c. BC produced the poets Alcaeus and Sappho.

**Lesh** /leʃ/ (Albanian **Lezhë**, Italian **Alessio**) a small town in north-west Albania, known in Classical and Illyrian times as Lissus. It is the capital of a district of the same name and was the burial place of the Albanian national hero, Gjergi Kastrioti Skënderbeg who convened the Albanian League here in 1444.

**Leshan** /le'ʃɑːn/ a city in Sichuan province, central China, on the Min River south of Chengdu; pop. (1986) 1,039,000.

**Les Mureaux** /leɪ mʊ'rəʊ/ a town in the department of Yvelines, northern France; pop. (1990) 33,365.

**lesotep** /'lesəʊtep/ the name given to the wooded northern steppe lands between the Carpathian and Altay mountains.

**Lesotho**
/lə'suːtuː/ official name **The Kingdom of Lesotho** a landlocked mountainous country in southern Africa, surrounded by the South African provinces of Orange Free State, Natal,

and Cape Province; area 30,335 sq. km. (11,717 sq. miles); pop. (est. 1991) 1,816,000; official languages, Sesotho and English; capital, Maseru. The Drakensburg Range, which rises in the east and is the source of the Orange River, is separated from the western lowlands by the Mulati Mountains which stretch from north-east to south-west forming a steep escarpment. Most rain falls between October and April. The majority of the Basotho population live in the western lowlands which cover one-fourth of the country, many being employed for several months of the year in mining, farming, or industry in neighbouring South Africa. The remainder of the population are largely engaged in subsistence agriculture, livestock rearing, and the making of handicrafts. Lesotho has few natural resources (though diamonds are found), but its Highland region is a major source of water supplying the Wiwatersrand region of South Africa. The region was settled in the 16th c. by Bantu-speaking people who eventually formed the Basotho nation in the early 19th c. In 1854 the Basotho lands were incorporated into the Orange Free State by the Boers, but in 1868 the country came under British protection with the name Basutoland. Ruled directly by Britain from 1884, Basutoland became an independent kingdom with the name Lesotho in 1966. In 1970 the constitution was suspended and following a South African-backed coup in 1986 the prime minister was ousted and a military government was established.

**Lesser Antilles** see ANTILLES.

**Lesser Slave Lake** a lake in central Alberta, Canada, north-west of Edmonton, drained by the Lesser Slave River into the Athabasca River; area 1,150 sq. km. (444 sq. miles). The Lesser Slave Lake Provincial Park lies on its eastern shore about 5 km. (3 miles) north of the town of Slave Lake.

**Lésvos** the Greek name for LESBOS.

**Letchworth** /'letʃwɜːθ/ a town in Hertfordshire, south-east England; pop. (1981) 38,140. Built in 1903, it was the first English 'garden city'. It has printing industries.

**Lethbridge** /'leθbrɪdʒ/ a town in the foothills of the Rocky Mountains, southern Alberta, Canada, on the Oldman River; pop. (1991) 60,970. Founded in the 1870s as a mining settlement, it was originally named Coalbanks. It later developed into a centre for agriculture and the oil and gas industries. The last great Indian battle in Canada (between the Blackfoot and the Crees) was fought near here in 1870. Amongst its leading attractions is the Nikka Yuko Japanese Garden, one of the largest of its kind in North America.

**Lethe** /'liːθiː/ in Greek mythology one of the rivers of the underworld, whose water when drunk made the souls of the dead forget their life on earth.

**Leticia** /lə'tiːsɪə/ a town and river port at the southern tip of Colombia, on the upper reaches of the Amazon on the border with Brazil and Peru; pop. (1985) 24,090. It is capital of Amazonas department.

**Lettish** see LATVIAN.

**Leuven** /'lɜːv(ə)n/ (French **Louvain** /'lʊvæ̃/) a town in Belgium, in the province of Brabant on the River Dijle east of Brussels, pop. (1991) 85,020. From the 11th to the 15th centuries it was the capital of the former duchy (now province) of Brabant. Its university (founded in 1425) is the oldest in Belgium.

**Levalloisean** /ˌləvæl'wɑːzɪən/ a flint-working technique first employed in the late Acheulian period in western Europe and associated with numerous Mousterian industries throughout the world, named after the type-site of Levallois north-west of Paris in the department of Hautes-de-Seine, northern France.

**Levant** /lɪ'vænt/ **1.** the eastern part of the Mediterranean with its islands and neighbouring countries. **2.** a region of eastern Spain forming an alluvial plain between the Iberian cordillera and the coast of the Gulfs of Valencia, Alicante, and Murcia.
**Levantine** adj. & n.

**levanter** /le'væntə(r)/ (also **the solano**) the name given to the mild and humid east wind that affects the western Mediterranean, especially the south-east coast of Spain and the Balearic Islands.

**leveche** /lə'vetʃɪ/ a hot, dry, southerly wind that blows northwards into Spain from Morocco.

**levée** /'leveɪ/ a term used to describe an artificial river embankment or a broad low ridge of alluvium laid down naturally by a river in flood.

**Leven** /'liːv(ə)n/, **Loch 1.** a loch in Kinross-shire, central Scotland, the largest freshwater loch in lowland Scotland. Mary Queen of Scots was imprisoned in Loch Leven Castle (1567–8) and Prior

Andrew Wyntoun wrote his *Orygynal Chronikyl*, the first history of Scotland, at the priory on St. Serf's Island. The Loch, which is a noted European centre for wildfowl and wintering geese, has been a national nature reserve since 1964. Its only outlet is the **River Leven** which flows 26 km. (16 miles) eastwards to the Firth of Forth at **Leven**, a summer resort famous for its golf links. **2.** a loch on the west coast of Scotland in Lochaber, Highland Region. It opens out into Loch Linnhe and is crossed near its mouth by a bridge between Ballachulish and North Ballachulish.

**Leverkusen** /ˌleɪvɜːˈkuːz(ə)n/ an industrial city and road and rail junction in North Rhine-Westphalia, west Germany, on the River Rhine south-east of Düsseldorf; pop. (1991) 161,150.

**Levittown** /ˈlevət̬ˌtaʊn/ a residential city on Long Island, New York, USA, founded in 1947 for veterans; pop. (1990) 53,290.

**Levkás** /lefˈkɑːs/ (also **Leicas**) one of the Ionian islands of western Greece, situated in the Ionian Sea to the north of Cephalonia; area 303 sq. km. (117 sq. miles); pop. (1981) 19,950. Its chief town is Levkás.

**Lewes** /ˈluːəs/ the county town of East Sussex, on the south coast of England at the mouth of the River Ouse; pop. (1981) 14,970. Simon de Montfort, founder of the English Parliament, defeated Henry III at the Battle of Lewes in 1264.

**Lewis** /ˈluːɪs/ the northern part of the island of Lewis with Harris, in the Outer Hebrides in Scotland. Its chief town is Stornoway.

**Lewis with Harris** (also **Lewis and Harris**) the largest and northernmost island of the Outer Hebrides in Scotland; area 2,134 sq. km. (824 sq. miles); chief town, Stornoway (on Lewis). The island, which is separated from the mainland by the Minch, consists of a northern part, Lewis, and a southern part, Harris.

**Lewisham** /ˈluːɪʃ(ə)m/ a borough of Greater London, England, between Southwark and Greenwich; pop. (1991) 215,300. It has light engineering industries but is mainly residential. It includes the districts of Lewisham and Deptford (where Queen Elizabeth I knighted Francis Drake aboard the *Golden Hind*).

**Lexington** /ˈleksɪŋt(ə)n/ **1.** a city in north-central Kentucky, USA, south-east of Frankfort; pop. (1990) 255,370 (with Fayette). Founded in 1779 and named after the Battle of Lexington (1775), it became a major producer of the hemp used by New England clipper ships. It is now a centre of thoroughbred horsebreeding and has the world's largest tobacco market. Lexington is the home of the University of Kentucky (1865) and of the first jockey club which was founded here in 1797. **2.** a residential town north-west of Boston, Massachusetts, USA, the scene in 1775 of the first battle in the American War of Independence; pop. (1990) 28,970.

**Leyden** see LEIDEN.

**Leyland** /ˈleɪlənd/ an industrial town in Lancashire, north-west England, to the south of Preston; pop. (1981) 37,150.

**Leyte** /ˈleɪtɪ/ an island in the Visayan group in the central Philippines, between Luzon and Mindanao; area 8,003 sq. km. (3,091 sq. miles); pop. (1990) 1,362,050; chief town, Tacloban. Copra is the island's chief export.

**Lezhë** see LESH.

**Lhasa** /ˈlɑːsə/ the capital of Tibet, which since 1959 has constituted an autonomous region of south-west China; pop. (1986) 108,000. It is situated in the Himalayas at *c.* 3,600 m. (11,800 ft.), on a tributary of the Brahmaputra. Enforced immigration of Chinese has greatly increased the population since 1982. Inaccessibility and the hostility of the Tibetan Buddhist priests to foreign visitors—to whom it was closed until the 20th c.—earned Lhasa the title of the Forbidden City. The spiritual centre of Tibetan Buddhism, it was the seat of the Dalai Lama until 1959, when direct Chinese administration was imposed on the city. Its chief landmark is the 17th-c. Potala Palace.

**Lhotse** /ˈləʊtˈseɪ/ two mountain peaks in the Himalayas on the frontier between China and Nepal. The highest, Lhotse I, rises to 8,511 m. (27,923 ft.) opposite Mt. Everest and is the fourth highest mountain in the world. It was first climbed by a Swiss expedition in 1956. Lhotse II reaches 7,589 m. (24,898 ft.).

**Lianyungang** /ˌljɑːnjuːŋˈgæŋ/ a deep-water port in Jiangsu province, eastern China, on the Yellow Sea; pop. (1986) 472,000. It is a special economic zone at the centre of a rich mining and agricultural region.

**Liao** /liːˈaʊ/ a river of north-east China that rises in Inner Mongolia and flows *c.* 1,390 km. (864 miles) east and south to the Gulf of Liaodong at the head of the Gulf of Chihli (Bo Hai).

**Liaocheng** /liːaʊˈtʃeŋ/ a city in Shandong province, eastern China, south-east of Jinan; pop. (1986) 737,000.

**Liaodong Peninsula** /ˌliːaʊˈdʊŋ/ a peninsula in north-east China which extends southwards into the Yellow Sea between the Gulf of Chihli (Bo Hai) and Korea Bay; area 53,000 sq. km. (21,600 sq. miles). Forming part of Liaoning province, its cities include Dalian, the largest trading port and shipbuilding centre in China; Anshan, China's steel capital; Fushun, China's leading coal-mining city; and the Liaohe oilfield. Noted for fruit-growing, sea-salt production, and textile manufactures, the peninsula was declared an open economic zone in 1988.

**Liaoning** /ˌliːaʊˈnɪŋ/ a province of north-east China, separated from North Korea to the east by the Yalu River; area 146,000 sq. km. (56,392 sq. miles); pop. (1990) 39,460,000; capital, Shenyang.

It has become one of China's most important industrial regions and is a leading producer of iron, steel, coke, and chemicals.

**Liaoyang** /liːaʊˈjæŋ/ a city in Liaoning province, north-east China, south-east of Shenyang; pop. (1986) 1,612,000. It has textiles and other light industries; iron and coal are mined.

**Liaoyuan** /liːaʊjʊˈɑːn/ a city in Jilin province, north-east China, in the Jilin Hada Ling Mts. to the south of Changchun; pop. (1986) 378,000.

**Liberec** /ˈlɪbəˌrets/ the largest city of North Bohemia in the Czech Republic, situated on the Lausitzer Neisse north-east of Prague; pop. (1991) 101,930. Its industries include engineering, woodworking, and the manufacture of textiles and glass.

**Liberia** /laɪˈbɪərɪə/ official name **The Republic of Liberia** a country in West Africa bordering on the Atlantic, between the Ivory Coast and Sierra Leone; area 97,754 sq. km. (37,757 sq. miles);

pop. (est. 1991) 2,639,000; official language, English; capital, Monrovia. The country rises from a 595-km. (370-mile) long coastal strip in a series of forested plateaus that reach heights in excess of 1,370 m (4,500 ft.) on the country's eastern frontier. Liberia has a tropical climate with a wet season between April and November. Iron ore, gold, diamonds, rubber, and timber are the country's most important natural resources. Liberia is the oldest republic in the continent of Africa, and the only one never to have known colonial status. Founded in 1822 as a settlement for freed Black slaves from the US, with which it retains a traditional friendship, it was proclaimed independent in 1847. Following a bloody coup that overthrew the predominant American–Liberian élite in 1980, Samuel Doe assumed power for just over a decade before being overthrown and murdered during a civil war that began in 1990. Despite attempts by neighbouring West African states to help restore order Liberia remained in a state of chaos with rival factions vying for power.
**Liberian** *adj. & n.*

**Liberty** /ˈlɪbətɪ/, **Statue of** a statue on an island at the entrance to New York Harbour, a symbol of welcome to immigrants, representing a draped female figure carrying a book of laws in her left hand and holding aloft a torch in her right. Dedicated in 1886, it was the work of the French sculptor F. A. Bartholdi (who used his mother as a model) and was the gift of the French to the American people, commemorating the alliance of France and the US during the War of American Independence and marking its centenary.

**Liberty Bell** a large bell that is the traditional symbol of US freedom, bearing the legend 'Proclaim liberty throughout all the land unto all the inhabitants thereof' (Leviticus 25: 10). Hung in the State House Steeple, Philadelphia, in 1753, it was first rung on 8 July 1776 to celebrate the first public reading of the Declaration of Independence, and cracked irreparably when rung for George Washington's birthday in 1846. It is now housed near Independence Hall, Philadelphia.

**Libreville** /ˈliːbrəˌviːl/ the capital of Gabon in west-central Africa, a major port on the Atlantic coast at the mouth of the Gabon River; pop. (1983) 350,000. Founded in 1849 on the site of a Roman Catholic mission and trading post, it was originally a refuge for slaves. It has expanded rapidly in recent years with the exploitation of Gabon's mineral resources.

**Libya** /ˈlɪbɪə/ official name **The Great Socialist People's Libyan Arab Jamahiriya** a country of North Africa between the Mediterranean Sea and the Sahara Desert, bounded by

Egypt, Sudan, Chad, Niger, Algeria, and Tunisia; area 1,775,500 sq. km. (685,786 sq. miles); pop. (est. 1991) 4,714,000; official language, Arabic; capital, Tripoli. To the south of a narrow coastal strip 1,770 km (1,110 miles) long the country is largely desert or semi-desert with hills in the far south and also in the north to the east of Benghazi and south of Tripoli. Much of Libya is hot and dry, although the coast is influenced by the Mediterranean. With only 1.2 per cent of the country under cultivation, Libya is dependent on food imports and on revenue from the sale of crude oil which was first discovered in 1959. Having formed part of the Roman Empire, Libya was conquered by the Arabs, brought under Turkish domination in the 16th c., annexed by Italy in 1912, and partially colonized by Europeans. During World War II it was the scene of heavy fighting, and, after a brief period of French and British administration, achieved full independence in 1951. After prolonged political disturbances the country emerged following a *coup* in 1969 with a radical revolutionary leadership that has occasionally brought it into conflict with other countries, particularly with respect to its alleged support for international terrorism. Under the 1977 constitution 'people's power' is in the hands of local people's congresses which form an electoral base for the General People's Congress or parliament.
**Libyan** *adj. & n.*

**Lichfield** /ˈlɪtʃfiːld/ a market town with light industries in Staffordshire, central England, southwest of Burton-on-Trent; pop. (1981) 25,740. It was the birthplace in 1709 of the English lexicographer and critic Samuel Johnson, and has a famous three-spired cathedral.

**Lidingö** /ˈliːdɪŋˌɜː/ an island in the Baltic Sea, forming a residential suburb of the Swedish capital, Stockholm; pop. (1990) 38,400. It was the home of the Swedish Sculptor Carl Milles (1875–1955).

**Lidköping** /ˈliːdtʃɜːpɪŋ/ an industrial port in Skaraborg county, south-west Sweden, on the southern shore of Lake Väner; pop. (1990) 35,800. Dating from the 15th c., it is noted for its porcelain.

**Lido** /ˈliːdəʊ/, **the** (in full **Lido di Malamocco** /dɪ ˌmæləˈmɒkəʊ/) an Adriatic town on the outer reef of the Lagoon of Venice, north-east Italy; pop. (1980) 20,950. Formerly Italy's most fashionable beach resort, it gave its name to a word often used in the English language to describe a public open-air swimming pool or bathing beach. In Italy it is commonly used as a place-name element for beach resorts such as the Lido di Jesolo (in Venetia) and the Lido di Ostia (in Latium).

## Liechtenstein

/ˈlɪktənˌstaɪn/ official name **The Principality of Liechtenstein** a small independent principality in the Alps between Switzerland and Austria; area 160 sq. km. (62 sq miles); pop. (1990) 28,880; official language, German; capital, Vaduz. Largely mountainous, it lies in a strategic location in the Rhine valley at the north–south and east–west crossroads of central Europe. Although economically integrated with Switzerland since the signing of the 1923 Swiss–Liechtenstein Customs Treaty, Liechtenstein has a strong economy based on banking, tourism, and the manufacture of highly specialized machinery. Created in 1719 within the Holy Roman Empire, it became independent of the German confederation in 1866. Liechtenstein has a constitutional and hereditary monarchy governed by a unicameral parliament (*Landtag*).

**Liège** /liˈeʒ/ (Flemish **Luik** /ˈlɜːɪk/) **1.** a province of eastern Belgium, comprising the districts of Huy, Liège, Verviers, and Waremme; area 3,863 sq. km. (1,492 sq. miles); pop. (1991) 999,650. Formerly ruled by independent prince-bishops, it became a part of the Netherlands in 1815 and of Belgium in 1830. **2.** its capital city, a major river port and industrial centre at the junction of the Ourthe and Meuse rivers; pop. (1991) 194,600. An early centre of coal-mining, its industries produce chemicals, electronics, textiles, tobacco, and glassware.

**Liepaja** /ˈljepaːjaː/ a Baltic seaport in Latvia, founded by the Teutonic Knights in the 13th c.; pop. (1989) 114,000. In the late 19th and early

20th c. it was the main point of departure of Russian emigrants sailing to America. Its industries produce paper, linoleum, and hardware.

**Liffey** /ˈlɪfɪ/ a river of eastern Ireland, which flows for 80 km. (50 miles) from the Wicklow mountains to Dublin Bay. The city of Dublin is situated at its mouth.

**Lifford** /ˈlɪfə(r)d/ the county town of Donegal in the Republic of Ireland, separated from Strabane in Tyrone, Northern Ireland, by the River Finn; pop. (1986) 1,460. It was a seat of the O'Donnells.

**Liguria** /lɪˈgjʊərɪə/ **1.** an ancient region of north-west Italy and south-east France stretching along the Ligurian Sea and lying between the Rhône and Arno rivers. Prior to occupation by the Celts it was inhabited by Ligurians, a people of pre-Indo-European stock. A strip of the Ligurian coast around Genoa, designated the Ligurian Republic in 1797, was annexed to France between 1805 and 1815. **2.** a region of northern Italy, comprising the provinces of Genova, Imperia, La Spezia, and Savona; area 5,411 sq. km. (2,090 sq. miles); pop. (1991) 1,719,200; capital, Genoa.

**Ligurian Alps** a 60-km (37-mile) long south-western ridge of the European Alps on the frontier between France and Italy, linking the Alps with the Italian Apennines.

**Ligurian Sea** a part of the northern Mediterranean, between Corsica and the north-west coast of Italy.

**Likasi** /lɪˈkaːzɪ/ a copper- and cobalt-mining town in the Shaba region of south-eastern Zaire; pop. (1984) 194,465. It was known as Jadotville until 1966.

**Lille** /liːl/ an industrial city of north-west France, near the border with Belgium, capital of the department of Nord in the Nord-Pas-de-Calais region; pop. (1990) 178,300. It is the home of the Pasteur Institute and was the first place in the world to introduce an automatic metro system (1982). It is a commercial, cultural, and manufacturing centre renowned for its textiles.

**Lille Bælt** SEE LITTLE BELT.

**Lillehammer** /ˈlɪləˌhɑːmər/ capital of Oppland county, southern Norway, on the north shore of Lake Mjøsa; pop. (1991) 22,890. It is a resort town and winter Olympic sports centre with an open-air museum (Maihaugen) and many fine wooden buildings.

**Lilongwe** /lɪˈlɒŋweɪ/ the capital of Malawi, a modern town built after its designation in 1975; pop. (1987) 233,970. It is an agricultural trading centre.

**Lima** /ˈliːmə/ the capital and largest city of Peru, situated on the River Rímac at the foot of the Cerro San Cristóbal; pop. (est. 1990) 426,300. It was founded in 1535 by Francisco Pizarro who named it the 'city of the kings' and was capital of the Spanish colonies in South America until the

19th c. Its port on the Pacific coast is Callao. One of the largest cities of South America, its university (founded 1551) is the oldest in the western hemisphere. Lima is the site of most of Peru's manufacturing industries.

**Limassol** /ˈlɪməˌsɒl/ a port and resort town on the south coast of Cyprus, on Akrotiri Bay; pop. (est. 1990) 135,400. Its economy has expanded considerably since the partition of Cyprus. There is a British military base nearby.

**Limbe** /ˈlɪmbɪ/ a resort town in the south-west province of Cameroon, situated on the Atlantic coast west of Douala; pop. (1981) 32,920. Formerly known as Victoria, it was for a time the capital of British Cameroon.

**Limburg** /ˈlɪmbɜːg/ **1.** a former duchy of Lorraine, divided in 1839 between Belgium and the Netherlands, and now forming: **2.** (French **Limbourg** /læŋˈbʊər/) a province in north-east Belgium, comprising the districts of Hasselt, Maaseik, and Tongeren; area 2,422 sq. km. (935 sq. miles); pop. (1991) 750,435; capital, Hasselt. The province gives its name to the soft white and strong-smelling Limburger cheese which was originally made here. **3.** a southern province of the Netherlands; area 2,207 sq. km. (852 sq. miles); pop. (1991) 1,109,840; capital, Maastricht.

**Limeño** /liːˈmenjəʊ/ an inhabitant of Lima, capital of Peru.

**Limerick** /ˈlɪmərɪk/ **1.** a county of south-west Ireland, in the province of Munster; pop. (1991) 161,856; area 2,686 sq. km. (1,026 sq. miles). **2.** its county town, on the River Shannon; pop. (1991) 52,040. A commercial and food-processing centre, noted for its ham and bacon.

**limestone pavement** a horizontal bare limestone surface, cut into slabs (*clints*) by deep fissures (*grikes*) running at right angles to each other.

**Limfjord** /ˈlɪmfjɔːd/ a waterway across Denmark's Jutland peninsula, linking the Kattegat with the North Sea; length 176 km. (110 miles).

**Límnos** the Greek name for LEMNOS.

**Limoges** /lɪˈməʊʒ/ a city of west-central France, capital of the department of Haute-Vienne and principal city of the Limousin Region; pop. (1990) 136,400. It was famous in the 16th–17th c. for enamel work and later for porcelain. Hydroelectric power, the mining of uranium, and the manufacture of shoes are important industries.

**Limón** /lɪˈməʊn/ (also **Puerto Limón** /pwɜːˈtəʊ/) the chief Caribbean port of Costa Rica; pop. (1984) 64,400. Columbus landed here on his last expedition to the Americas.

**Limousin** /ˌlɪmuːˈsæ̃/ a region of central France, comprising the departments of Corrèze, Creuse, and Haute-Vienne; area 16,942 sq. km. (6,543 sq. miles); pop. (1990) 537,620. Its chief towns are Limoges and Brive-la-Gaillarde. It gives its name

to a caped cloak originally worn here, and to the limousine or large luxurious motor car.

**Limoux** /ˈlɪmuː/ a small town in the Razès district of Languedoc-Roussillon, southern France, noted for its sparkling white Blanquette de Limoux wine.

**Limpopo** /lɪmˈpəʊpəʊ/ a river of south-east Africa that rises in the province of Transvaal, South Africa, and flows 1,770 km. (1,100 miles) in a great curve north and east to meet the Indian Ocean north-east of Maputo in Mozambique. For much of its course it forms the boundary between north-east South Africa and the neighbouring countries of Botswana and Zimbabwe.

**Linares** /liːˈnɑːrez/ an industrial town in the province of Jaén in Andalusia, southern Spain, situated in a mining area in the upper Guadalquivir valley; pop. (1991) 57,210. It was the birthplace in 1893 of the guitarist Andrés Segovia.

**Lincoln** /ˈlɪŋkən/ a city in eastern England, on the River Witham, county town of Lincolnshire; pop. (1991) 81,900. Known to the Romans as Lindum Colonia, it lay at the junction of Fosse Way and Ermine Street. Its 11th-c. cathedral has one of the four original copies of the Magna Carta. The city today specializes in the manufacture of farm machinery.

**Lincoln** /ˈlɪŋkən/ the capital and second-largest city of the US state of Nebraska; pop. (1990) 191,970. Founded in 1856 and originally known as Lancaster, it was renamed in honour of Abraham Lincoln and made state capital in 1867. It is the home of the University of Nebraska (1869). A marketing and financial centre.

**Lincolnshire** /ˈlɪŋkənˌʃɪə(r)/ an eastern county of England; pop. (1990) 573,900; area 5,918 sq. km. (2,286 sq. miles); county town, Lincoln. The county is divided into seven districts:

| District | Area (sq. km.) | Pop. (1990) |
| --- | --- | --- |
| Boston | 360 | 52,600 |
| East Lindsey | 1,762 | 115,600 |
| Lincoln | 36 | 81,900 |
| North Kesteven | 923 | 78,400 |
| South Holland | 737 | 66,000 |
| South Kesteven | 943 | 107,200 |
| West Lindsey | 1,156 | 72,200 |

**Lincoln's Inn** /ˈlɪŋkənz/ one of the Inns of Court in London where legal societies traditionally admit people to the English bar. Thomas de Lincoln, king's sergeant in the 14th c., may have been an early landlord.

**Lincs.** *abbr.* Lincolnshire.

**Lindesnes** see NAZE, THE.

**Lindisfarne** /ˈlɪndɪsˌfɑːn/ (also **Holy Island**) a small island off the coast of Northumberland, north-east England, north of the Farne Islands. It is linked to the mainland by a causeway exposed only at low tide. Lindisfarne is the site of a church and monastery founded by St. Aidan (635), a missionary centre of the Celtic Church. Driven from the island by vikings in 875, the monks returned to rebuild the priory in 1082 renaming the island Holy Island. In 1903 Lindisfarne Castle was restored to a design by Edwin Lutyens for Edward Hudson, the owner and founder of the magazine *Country Life*.

**Lindsey** /'lɪnzi:/ a region of eastern England, in Lincolnshire. An area of early settlement by the Angles, it became an Anglo-Saxon kingdom ruled by its own kings until the 8th c. Known also as the Parts of Lindsey, the region was one of three administrative divisions or 'ridings' of Lincolnshire (the others were Holland and Kesteven) until 1974, when it was divided between Humberside and Lincolnshire. The portion within Lincolnshire is now administered as the districts of Lincoln and East and West Lindsey.

**Linea de la Concepción** (also **La Linea**) a port on Algeciras Bay in the province of Cadiz, Andalusia, southern Spain; pop. (1991) 58,210. Situated near the frontier with Gibraltar, it is a Spanish customs post.

**Line Islands** /laɪn/ a group of eleven islands in the central Pacific, straddling the equator south of Hawaii. Eight of the islands, including Kiritimati (Christmas Island), form part of Kiribati; the remaining three are uninhabited dependencies of the US.

**Linfen** /lɪn'fen/ a city in Shanxi province, east-central China, on the Fen River north-west of Zhengzhou; pop. (1986) 544,000.

**Linhai** /lɪn'haɪ/ a city in Zhejiang province, eastern China, north-west of Jiaojiang; pop. (1986) 1,012,000.

**Linhe** /lɪn'heɪ/ a city in Inner Mongolia, northern China, on the bend of the Yellow River; pop. (1986) 347,000.

**Linlithgow** /lɪn'lɪθɡəʊ/ a town in West Lothian, central Scotland; pop. (1981) 9,580. Its 15th-c. palace was the birthplace in 1542 of Mary Queen of Scots.

**Linköping** /'lɪntʃɜːpɪŋ/ an industrial town (motor vehicles and aircraft) in south-east Sweden, capital of Östergötland county; pop. (1990) 122,270. It was a noted cultural and ecclesiastical centre in the Middle Ages.

**Linqing** /lɪn'kɪŋ/ a city in Shandong province, eastern China, on the Grand Canal west of Jinan; pop. (1986) 611,000.

**Linxia** /lɪnʃi:'ɑː/ a city in Gansu province, central China, south-west of Lanzhou; pop. (1986) 153,000.

**Linyi** /lɪn'ji:/ a city in Shandong province, eastern China, on the Yi River, south-east of Jinan; pop. (1986) 1,385,000.

**Linz** /lɪnts/ the chief industrial city of northern Austria, on the River Danube; pop. (1991) 202,855.

It is capital of the state of Upper Austria. For several years the composer Anton Bruckner was the organist at Linz cathedral. It has iron and steel, chemical, and textile industries.

**Lipari Islands** /'lɪpərɪ/ a group of seven volcanic islands off the north-east coast of Sicily, in Italian possession. Formerly known as the Aeolian Islands, they were believed by the ancient Greeks to be the home of Aeolus, the god of the winds. The only active volcano is on Stromboli. A sweet white Malvasia wine is produced here. The islands have become a fashionable tourist resort.

**Lipetsk** /'li:petsk/ a health resort and industrial city in western Russia, on the Voronezh River; pop. (1990) 455,000. It is a major centre of the iron and steel industries.

**Lipizza** /'lɪpɪtsə/ (Slovenian **Lipica**) a village in Slovenia, formerly the home of the Austrian Imperial Stud where the white Lipizzaner horse was originally bred. Noted since Roman times as a centre of horse breeding, the stud was established in 1580 by Archduke Charles of Austria.

**Lisbon** /'lɪzb(ə)n/ (Portuguese **Lisboa** /liːʃ'bəʊə/) the capital of Portugal, built on seven hills at the mouth of the River Tagus; pop. (1991) 677,790. Occupied by the Romans in 205 and by the Moors in 714, Lisbon became capital of Portugal in the 13th c. when Alfonso III transferred his court from Coimbra. It prospered during the Age of Discovery but was devastated by an earthquake in 1755. Much of the city was subsequently rebuilt by the Marqués de Pombal. Landmarks include St. George's Castle, a 14th-c. cathedral, the elevator built by Eiffel, the Monument of the Discoveries (1960), the 16th-c. Tower of Belém, and the Convento dos Jerónimos de Belém which was built to commemorate Vasco da Gama's voyage to India in 1497. The city's industries include steel, oil refining, and shipbuilding and repair.

**Lisburn** /'lɪsbɜːn/ a town in County Antrim, Northern Ireland, on the Lagan River south-west of Belfast; pop. (1981) 40,390. It developed as a textile town after the arrival of French Huguenots in 1694.

**Lisdoonvarna** /ˌlɪsdʊn'vɑːnə/ a spa town in the Republic of Ireland, in County Clare, noted for its sulphurous water, its summer folk festival, and its October fair; pop. (1981) 607.

**Lishui** /lɪ'ʃwi:/ a city in Zhejiang province, southeast China, west of Jiaojiang; pop. (1986) 303,000.

**Lismore** /'lɪzmɔː(r)/ a town in north-eastern New South Wales, south-east Australia, on Wilson's River south of Brisbane; pop. (1991) 27,250. It lies at the centre of a fertile agricultural area producing dairy products, tropical fruits, beef, and timber.

**Lismore** /lɪz'mɔː(r)/ an island in Loch Linnhe, western Scotland, with a 13th-c. cathedral built by the Bishop of the Isles whose seat was here. In the 6th c. the island was chosen by St. Moluag as the centre of his mission to Scotland.

**lithosphere** /'lɪθəˌsfɪə(r)/ the name given to the crust and upper mantle of the earth. It varies in thickness from 32 km. (20 miles) to 64 km. (40 miles).

**Lithuania**
/ˌlɪθjuː'eɪnɪə/
(Lithuanian
**Lietuvos**) official
name **The Republic
of Lithuania** a
Baltic country in
north-central Europe
between Latvia and
Poland; area 65,200

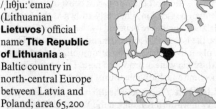

sq. km. (25,183 sq. miles); pop. (est. 1991) 3,765,000; official language, Lithuanian; capital, Vilnius. The largest cities are Vilnius, Kaunas, Klaipeda, and Siauliai. Lying to the east of the Baltic Sea, Lithuania is a country of alternating lowland plains and hilly uplands, studded with some 2,833 lakes and watered by a dense network of rivers, the largest of which is the Neman. Nearly 80 per cent of the population are Lithuanians, the remainder being Russians, Poles, Belorussians, and Ukrainians. Once a predominantly agricultural country producing meat, dairy produce, and timber, Lithuania has since 1940 developed industrially as a producer of steel, ships, paper, and textiles. It is, however, short of energy resources and has to rely on imports, although nuclear power has been developed at the complex at Ignalina. Forming a large state in the Middle Ages, Lithuania united with Poland in 1569 but was absorbed into the Russian empire in 1795. It was occupied by Germany during World War I but emerged as an independent republic in 1918. Poland annexed Vilnius in 1919, and in 1940, following a secret agreement between Russia and Germany, Lithuania came under Soviet rule as a constituent republic of the USSR. In 1991 it declared its independence and was once more recognized as an independent republic. Lithuania is governed by a unicameral parliament (*Seimas*).
**Lithuanian** *adj. & n.*

**Lithuanian** /ˌlɪθjuː'eɪnɪən/ the official language of Lithuania, closely related to Latvian, with which it constitutes the Baltic language group.

**Little Alföld** /'ɔːlfəld/ (also **Kis-Alföld** or **Little Plain**) a plain in north-west Hungary extending northwards from the Transdanubian Highlands to the River Danube.

**Little Ararat** see ARARAT, MOUNT.

**Little Baltistan** /ˌbɒltɪs'taːn/ one of the three principal regions of Ladakh in Kashmir, northern India, comprising the Suru, Wakka, and Bodkarbu valleys.

**Little Belt** (Danish **Lille Bælt** /'lɪlə ˌbelt/) a channel between the Kattegat and the Baltic Sea, separating Fyn Island from the mainland of Denmark.

**Little Big Horn** /'bɪghɔːn/ the site in Montana, USA, of the defeat of General George Custer by Sioux Indians on 25 June 1876, popularly known as 'Custer's Last Stand'.

**Little Minch** see MINCH, THE.

**Little Ouse** see OUSE 4.

**Little Rock** /rɒk/ an industrial centre and the capital of the state of Arkansas, USA, on the Arkansas River opposite North Little Rock; pop. (1990) 175,800. Named by French explorers to differentiate it from larger rock outcroppings further up river, Little Rock became state capital in 1821 when the seat of government was moved from Arkansas Post.

**Little Tibet** see BALTISTAN.

**Liuzhou** /ljuː'dʒəʊ/ (formerly **Liuchow**) a city in Guangxi Autonomous Region, southern China, on the Liu River north-east of Nanning; pop. (1990) 740,000. Founded in 111 BC, Liuzhou is a rapidly expanding industrial city and communication centre with industries producing iron and steel, heavy machinery, household appliances, vehicles, textiles, and pharmaceuticals.

**Livermore** /'lɪvəˌmɔː(r)/ a city and research centre in west-central California; USA, situated east of San Francisco in a wine-producing region; pop. (1990) 56,740.

**Liverpool** /'lɪvəˌpuːl/ a city and seaport in Merseyside, north-west England; pop. (1991) 448,300. Its port trade developed in the 17th c.; it became an important centre of the slave traffic from Africa to the West Indies and later of the textile industry, importing cotton from America and exporting the textiles produced in Lancashire and Yorkshire. Liverpool's traditional industries of shipbuilding and engineering have declined, but it remains one of the chief Atlantic ports of Europe. It was the birthplace of George Stubbs (1794), A. H. Clough (1819), W. E. Gladstone (1809), and was the centre of a lively era of 1960s rock music dominated by the Beatles. The University of Liverpool was founded in 1903 and Liverpool John Moores University (formerly Liverpool Polytechnic) was established in 1992. It has two cathedrals including a Roman Catholic cathedral of modern design.
**Liverpudlian** *adj. & n.*

**Livingston** /'lɪvɪŋstən/ an industrial New Town established in West Lothian, east-central Scotland in 1962; pop. (1981) 38,950. Among its chief industries are engineering and the manufacture of paper, electronics, and scientific instruments.

**Livingstone** the former name of MARAMBA in Zambia.

**Livonia** /lɪ'vəʊnɪə/ (German **Livland** /'lɪvlænd/) a former region on the east coast of the Baltic Sea, north of Lithuania, comprising most of modern Latvia and Estonia. It was named after the Livs, a Finno-Ugrian people living in part of the coastal region, ancestors of the modern Estonians. It was converted to Christianity in the early 13th c. by the Livonian Brothers of the Sword, a crusading order of knights who united with the Teutonic Knights and ruled Livonia until the late 16th c. Between 1558 and 1582 the region was disputed by Poland, Sweden, and Russia in the Livonian War. It was taken by Poland, passing to Sweden in 1692, and was finally ceded to Peter the Great of Russia in 1721. It was divided between Estonia and Latvia in 1918.

**Livonia** /lɪˈvəʊnɪə/ a city in south-east Michigan, USA, an industrial suburb of Detroit with automobile industries; pop. (1990) 100,850.

**Livorno** the Italian name for LEGHORN.

**Lizard** /ˈlɪzəd/, **the** a promontory near the western tip of Cornwall, south-west England, the southernmost point of the British mainland. There is a space-satellite communications station at Goonhilly Downs nearby.

**Ljubljana** /luːbˈljɑːnə/ (German **Laibach**) the capital of the Republic of Slovenia in south-east-central Europe, situated on the Sava and Ljubljanica rivers; pop. (1991) 267,000. It was founded (as Emona) by the Roman emperor Augustus in 34 BC. Under the rule of the Habsburgs from the 13th c., it became capital in 1809 of the Illyrian Provinces and between 1816 and 1849 of the Austrian kingdom of Illyria. It became a part of Yugoslavia in 1918. Its industries produce textiles, electronics, paper, and chemicals.

**Llandudno** /læn'dɪdnəʊ/ a resort town in Gwynedd county, northern Wales, situated on the Irish Sea at the mouth of the River Conwy; pop. (1981) 14,370.

**Llanelli** /læ'nexlɪ/ a town in the county of Dyfed, south-west Wales, on Carmarthen Bay at the mouth of the Burry River; pop. (1981) 45,660. The town grew with steel and tin-plate industries, now in decline.

**Llanfairpwllgwyngyll** /ˌlænfɜːpuːlˈɡwɪŋɪl/ (also **Llanfair P. G.**) a village on the island of Anglesey, in the county of Gwynedd, north-west Wales, famous for its unabbreviated name, Llanfairpwllgwyngyllgogerychwyrndrobwllllantysiliogogogoch, which is the longest name in the UK. The first Women's Institute in Britain was founded here in 1915.

**Llangollen** /læn'ɡɒxlən/ a resort town in Clwyd, north-east Wales, on the River Dee; pop. (1981) 3,070. International *eisteddfods* have been held here since 1947.

**llano** /ˈlɑːnəʊ, ˈljɑː-/ the Spanish-American term for a virtually treeless grassy plain or savanna in tropical South America, notably in the Orinoco basin. It is frequently burnt by graziers to stimulate the growth of new grass during the following wet season. An inhabitant of the llanos is known as a llanero.

**Llano Estacado** /ˈlɑːnəʊ ˌestəˈkɑːdəʊ/ the name given to the semi-arid grassland region of the Great Plains of the USA, on the frontier of New Mexico and Texas between the Pecos River and the Cap Rock escarpment

**Lleida** see LÉRIDA.

**Lobatse** /ləʊ'bætsɪ/ a town in south-east Botswana; pop. (1991) 26,050. Its chief industries are meat processing and the transportation of livestock.

**Lobito** /lʊ'biːtəʊ/ a seaport on the Atlantic coast of Angola, one of the best natural harbours on the west coast of Africa; pop. (1983) 150,000. Dating from 1824, the town expanded after the completion in 1929 of a railway linking it with Zaire, Zambia, and the Mozambique port of Beira. It now exports agricultural products and minerals, and has light industries.

**Locarno** /lə'kɑːnəʊ/ a winter and health resort in Ticino canton, southern Switzerland, at the north end of Lake Maggiore; pop. (1990) 14,150.

**loch** the name given to a freshwater lake or sea inlet in Scotland.

**Loch Leven** see LEVEN, LOCH.

**Loch Lomond** /ˈləʊmənd/ see LOMOND, LOCH.

**Loch Ness** /nes/ a deep loch in the Highlands of Scotland to the south-west of Inverness, forming part of the Caledonian Canal. With a length of 39 km. (24.2 miles) and a maximum depth of 230 m. (755 ft.), it is the longest and largest (by volume of water) lake in Great Britain. There have been reported appearances of an aquatic 'monster' since the time of St. Columba (6th c.).

**Lockerbie** /ˈlɒkəbiː/ a town in south-west Scotland, in Dumfries and Galloway . It was the scene in 1988 of an air crash, caused by a terrorist bomb, in which 276 people died.

**Lodi** /ˈləʊdaɪ/ a city in central California, USA, at the north end of the San Joaquin Valley, east of San Francisco; pop. (1990) 51,870. It lies in a noted wine-producing region.

**Łodz** /wʊtʃ/ an industrial city in central Poland, south-west of Warsaw; pop. (1990) 848,260. It developed as a textile town in the 19th c. and is now the second-largest city in the country. Rebuilt after being destroyed in World War II, its modern factories produce textiles, chemicals, engineering and electrical goods.

**loess** /ˈləʊɪs, lɜːs/ a deposit of fine light-coloured wind-blown dust found especially in the basins of large rivers and very fertile when irrigated.

**Lofoten Islands** /lə'fəʊt(ə)n/ a mountainous island group in the Norwegian Sea, off the north-west coast of Norway, situated within the Arctic Circle south-west of the Vesterålen group. Forming part of Nordland county, they are separated from the mainland by the Vest Fjord. The largest islands of the group are Hinnøy, Austvågøy, Vestvagøy, and Moskenesøya. Rich cod fisheries give rise to a local fish-processing industry. Just south of Moskenesøya is the dangerous whirlpool known as the Maelstrom, made famous by Edgar Allan Poe.

**Logan** /'ləʊgən/, **Mount** a mountain in Kluane National Park, south-west Yukon Territory, Canada. It is the highest peak in Canada and second-highest in North America (5,951 m., 19,524 ft.). Its first ascent in 1925 was achieved after a 44-day trek up the Chitina valley and over glacier ice.

**Logroño** /ləʊ'grəʊnjəʊ/ a market town in northern Spain, on the River Ebro, capital of the wine-producing La Rioja region; pop. (1991) 126,760.

**Loire** /lwɑː(r)/ **1.** a river of west-central France, which rises in the Massif Central and flows 1,015 km. (630 miles) north and west to the Atlantic at St. Nazaire. Principal cities on its route are Orléans, Tours, and Nantes. The longest river in France, it is noted for the châteaux and vineyards that lie along its course. **2.** a department in the Rhône-Alpes region of Eastern France, in the upper Loire valley; area 4,781 sq. km. (1,847 sq. miles); pop. (1990) 746,290; capital, St-Étienne.

**Loire-Atlantique** /ˌlwɑːrætlɑ̃'tiːk/ a department in the Pays de la Loire region of western France; area 6,815 sq. km. (2,632 sq. miles); pop. (1990) 1,052,180; capital, Nantes.

**Loiret** /lwaː'reɪ/ a department in the Centre region of central France; area 6,775 sq. km. (2,617 sq. miles); pop. (1990) 580,610; capital, Orléans.

**Loir-et-Cher** /ˌlwaːreɪ'ʃeə(r)/ a department in the Centre region of central France; area 6,343 sq. km. (2,450 sq. miles); pop. (1990) 305,940; capital, Blois.

**Loja** /'ləʊxə/ a market town in south-west Ecuador, capital of the Andean province of Loja; pop. (1990) 145,280. Founded in 1548 by the Spanish captain, Alonso Mercadillo, it is one of the oldest colonial towns in Ecuador. A Franciscan monk is said to have extracted quinine from a tree near here in order to cure the Countess of Cinchón, wife of a 17th-c. Spanish viceroy, who was dying of malaria. The tree was named the chinchona tree after the countess. The declaration of Ecuadorean independence was signed here in 1820.

**Lolland** /'lɒlɑːn/ (Danish **Laaland**) a Danish island in the Baltic Sea, to the south of Zealand and west of Falster, forming part of the county of Storstrøm; area 1,235 sq. km. (477 sq. miles). Its name means 'low land'.

**Lombard** /'lɒmbɑːd/ a Germanic people from the lower Elbe who invaded Italy in 568 and founded a kingdom (overthrown by Charlemagne in 774) in the valley of the Po.

**Lombard Street** a street in the City of London, England, formerly occupied by bankers from Lombardy and still containing many of the principal London banks.

**Lombardy** /'lɒmbədɪ/ (Italian **Lombardia**) a region of central northern Italy, between the Alps and the River Po, which became part of the kingdom of Italy in 1859; area 23,833 sq. km. (9,205 sq. miles); pop. (1990) 8,939,430; capital, Milan. Founded in the 6th c. by the Germanic Lombards (also known as *Langobards* 'long beards'), it was taken by Spain in the 16th c., was ceded to Austria in 1713, and finally became a part of the kingdom of Italy in 1859.
**Lombard** *adj. & n.*

**Lombok** /'lɒmbɒk/ a volcanic island of the Lesser Sunda group in Indonesia, situated between Bali and Sumbawa; area 4,727 sq. km. (1,826 sq. miles); pop. (1991) 2,500,000. The majority of the population are Muslim Sasaks who converted to Islam in the 16th c. Its principal town is Mataram and its highest point is Mt. Rinjani (3,726 m., 12,224 ft.), the second-highest peak in Indonesia. Chief among its exports are rice, pumice stone, tobacco, cotton, seaweed, and a variety of spices including the chilli peppers that give the island its Javanese name.

**Lomé** /'ləʊmeɪ/ the capital and chief port of Togo in West Africa, on the Gulf of Guinea; pop. (1983) 366,475. In 1975 a trade agreement, subsequently known as the Lomé Convention, was reached here between the EEC and 46 African, Caribbean, and Pacific Ocean States (ACP States), for technical co-operation and development aid. A second agreement was signed in 1979 by a larger group. The modern deep-water port handles primary products from the land-locked states of Mali, Niger, and Burkina.

**Lomond** /'ləʊmənd/, **Loch** a loch in west-central Scotland. It is the largest freshwater lake in Great Britain, with an area of 70 sq. km. (27.5 sq. miles) and a length from north to south of 36.4 km. (22.6 miles).

**London** /'lʌnd(ə)n/ an industrial city in southeast Ontario, Canada, situated on the River Thames to the north of Lake Erie; pop. (1991) 381,520 (metropolitan area). It was founded in 1792 by John Graves Simcoe who named it after London, England. Its industries produce beer, processed food, textiles, and electrical goods.

**London** /'lʌnd(ə)n/ the capital and largest city of the United Kingdom, a port on the River Thames, and a leading world commercial, business, cultural, and tourist centre; pop. (1991) 6,378,600. Greater London, which is divided into the City of London and 32 Boroughs (see GREATER LONDON), was administered by a single Greater London Council from 1965 to 1986. Settled by the Romans at the lowest crossing of the Thames as a port and trading centre (*Londinium*), London has flourished since the Middle Ages. After the plague of 1665 and the fire of 1666 much of it was rebuilt under the direction of Sir Christopher Wren. Air raids in World War II obliterated whole areas of streets and damaged most public buildings; post-war reconstruction has added tower blocks of geometric aspect to the landscape. It is the home of the University of London (1836), the Royal College of Art (1837), the City University (1966), the University of East London (1992), the University of Greenwich (1992), Middlesex University (1992), Southbank University (1992), Thames Valley University (1992), and the University of Westminster (1992). It is the centre of British Government and political power; its many major buildings include Buckingham Palace, Houses of Parliament, British Museum, Westminster Abbey, St. Paul's Cathedral, and the Tower.

**Londonderry** /'lʌnd(ə)n,derɪ/ **1.** a county of Northern Ireland, between Lough Neagh and the Atlantic northern coast of Ireland, formerly an administrative area; area 2,067 sq. km. (798 sq. miles); pop. (1981) 186,750; **2.** its chief town, a city and port on the River Foyle near its outlet on the north coast; pop. (1981) 62,700. Built on the site of an abbey founded by St. Columba in AD 546, it was formerly called Derry, a name still used by many. In 1613 it was granted to the City of London for colonization and became known as Londonderry. In 1689 it resisted a siege by James II for 105 days before being relieved.

**Londrina** /lɒn'dri:nə/ an industrial city in the state of Paraná, southern Brazil, situated to the west of São Paulo; pop. (1990) 355,470.

**Longchamps** /lɒŋ'ʃã/ a world-famous race-course in the Bois de Boulogne, Paris, France, created in 1857. Flat-racing takes place during May, September, and October.

**Long Eaton** /'i:tən/ an industrial town in Derbyshire, central England, east of Derby; pop. (1981) 42,500.

**Long Beach** a port, industrial, and resort city in southern California, situated on the Pacific coast to the south of Los Angeles; pop. (1990) 429,430. In 1967 the ocean liner *Queen Mary* was brought to Long Beach and converted into a hotel and tourist attraction. Its industries include oil refining, air-craft, automobile, and missile manufacturing.

**Longford** /'lɒŋfəd/ **1.** a county of the Republic of Ireland, in the province of Leinster; area 1,044 sq. km. (403 sq. miles); pop. (1991) 30,290. **2.** its county town, on the River Camlin; pop. (1991) 6,390.

**Long Island** an island on the coast of New York State, USA. Its western tip, comprising the New York districts of Brooklyn and Queens, is separated from Manhattan and the Bronx by the East River and is linked to Manhattan by the Brooklyn Bridge and by road tunnels. The island has an area of 3,627 sq. km. (1,400 sq. miles) and extends 190 km. (119 miles) eastwards, roughly parallel to the coast of Connecticut, from which it is separated by Long Island Sound. Largely comprising deposits laid down during the last Ice Age, its southern shore has long beaches backed by dunes and shallow lagoons. The John F. Kennedy

International Airport is situated on the north shore of Jamaica Bay and the semi-derelict entertainment resort of Coney Island lies at the south-western tip of the island. The island is given over to dormitory towns, market gardens, light industries, fishing, and holiday resorts.

**longitude** /'lɒŋɪ,tju:d/ the angular distance, ex-pressed in degrees and minutes east or west, from a standard meridian such as Greenwich to the meri-dian of any place.

**Longleat** /'lɒŋli:t/ a country house in Wiltshire, England, the family home of the Marquis of Bath.

**Longmen** /lɒŋ'men/ a village on the Yi River to the south of Luoyang in Henan province, north-central China. Nearby are the Longmen caves which number over 1,300 and were first excavated and decorated by the Emperor Xiao Wei in AD 494.

**Longmont** /'lɒŋmɒnt/ a city at the centre of an irrigated farming region in northern Colorado, USA; pop. (1990) 51,555.

**Longview** /lɒŋ'vju:/ a city in eastern Texas, USA, in the valley of the Sabine River; pop. (1990) 70,310. Founded in 1870, it is a centre for meat pro-cessing, brewing, oil production, and the manu-facture of earthmoving equipment.

**Longyan** /lɒŋ'jɑ:n/ a city in Fujian province, south-east China, north-west of Xiamen; pop. (1986) 386,000.

**Lons-le-Saunier** /,lɔ̃lə'sɒnjeɪ/ the capital town of the department of Jura in the Franche-Comté region of eastern France; pop. (1990) 210,140. There are salt-mines and vineyards nearby.

**Loop** /lu:p/, **the** the name given to the central business district of Chicago and to an elevated rail-way line adjacent to it built in 1897.

**Lop Nor** /lɒp 'nɔ:(r)/ (also **Lop Nur**) a marshy depression in the arid Tarim Basin of north-west China. Once a large salt lake, which dried up when the Tarim River changed its course, the remote area has been used since 1964 for nuclear-weapons testing.

**Lorain** /lə'reɪn/ an industrial city and port in northern Ohio, USA, on Lake Erie at the mouth of the Black River; pop. (1990) 71,245. Once a centre of shipbuilding, it now manufactures steel and vehicles. The city was devastated by a tornado in 1924.

**Lorca** /'lɔ:kə/ a market town in the province of Murcia, south-east Spain, on the River Guadalentin; pop. (1991) 66,940. It was known to the Romans as Illurco and to the Moors as Lurka.

**Lord Howe Island** /haʊ/ a volcanic island in the Pacific Ocean off the east coast of Australia, administered as part of New South Wales; pop. (1989) 320; area 16.5 sq. km. (6.5 sq. miles). It is named after Admiral Lord Howe (1726–99) who was First Lord of the Admiralty when it was first visited.

**Lord's** /lɔːdz/ a cricket ground in St. John's Wood, north London, England, headquarters since 1814 of the MCC. It is named after the cricketer Thomas Lord (1755–1832).

**Lorelei** /ˈlɔːrəˌlaɪ/ a rock or cliff on the right bank of the Rhine near Sankt Goarshausen. It has a remarkable echo and is held in German legend to be the home of a siren of the same name whose song lures boatmen to destruction.

**Lorestan** /luːrɪsˈtɑːn/ (also **Luristan**) a province in the Zagros Mountains of west-central Iran; area 28,803 sq. km. (11,125 sq. miles); pop. (1986) 1,367,030; capital, Khorramabad.

**Loreto** /ləˈreɪtəʊ/ a town near Ancona in The Marches region of east-central Italy, to which pilgrims travel to see the 'Holy House', said to have been the home of the Virgin Mary in Nazareth and (according to legend) brought to Loreto by angels in 1295. The name of Loreto is derived from the laurel grove (*lauretum*) where the Holy House came to rest. In 1920 Our Lady of Loreto was officially declared to be the patron of aviators; pop. (1990) 10,640.

**Lorient** /lɔːˈrjɑ̃/ a seaport in north-west France, on the south coast of Brittany in the department of Morbihan; pop. (1990) 61,630. Built by Colbert as a naval base in 1666, it became a great centre of shipbuilding and the base of France's India Company which traded in the East.

**Lorraine** /ləˈreɪn/ **1.** a medieval kingdom on the west bank of the Rhine, extending from the North Sea to Italy, and divided in the 10th c. into two duchies, Upper and Lower Lorraine. Upper Lorraine (south of the Ardennes), as a province of France passed to the French Crown in 1766; part of Lorraine was acquired (with Alsace) by Germany in 1871 but was restored to France after World War I. **2.** a region of north-east France between the Plain of Champagne and the Vosges Mountains, comprising the departments of Meurthe-et-Moselle, Meuse, Moselle, and Vosges; area 23,547 sq. km. (9,095 sq. miles); pop. (1990) 2,305,725. Its iron deposits are some of the richest in Europe. Its chief towns are Metz and Nancy.

**Los Alamos** /lɒs ˈæləˌmɒs/ a town in northern New Mexico, USA; pop. (1990) 11,450. It has been a centre for nuclear research since the 1940s, when it was the site of the development of the first atomic and hydrogen bombs.

**Los Angeles** /lɒs ˈændʒɪˌliːz/ a city in the Bío-Bío region of central Chile, to the south of Concepción; pop. (1991) 137,000.

**Los Angeles** /lɒs ˈændʒɪˌliːz/ a city on the Pacific coast of southern California, the second-largest in the USA, and one of the largest built-up areas in the world; pop. (1990) 3,485,400. Founded in 1781, it developed after the arrival of the Southern Pacific Railroad and the discovery of oil in 1894. It has become a major commercial, industrial and urban complex in the 20th c., its metropolitan

area having expanded to include towns such as Beverly Hills, Hollywood, Santa Monica, and Redondo Beach. Its high motor-vehicle density has created a serious problem of 'smog' pollution. Major industries include aircraft, oil refining, and entertainment (film and TV). It is also a cultural and tourist centre.

**Los Glaciares National Park** /lɒs glæsˈjɑːrez/ a national park in southern Argentina. Here the Patagonian ice-cap spawns nine glaciers, the largest of which are the Upsala and Moreno glacier which flow into Lake Argentino. On its northern edge the jagged peaks of the Fitzroy Mountains rise to 3,375 m. (11,073 ft.).

**Los Mochis** /lɒs ˈməʊtʃiːs/ a city on the Pacific coast of the state of Sinaloa, north-west Mexico, founded in 1872 as a socialist utopia by Alfred K. Owens; pop. (1990) 305,500. It is the major coastal terminal of the Chihuahua–Pacific Railway.

**Lot** /lɒt, ləʊ/ **1.** a river of southern France which rises in the Auvergne and flows 480 km. (300 miles) west to meet the Garonne south-east of Bordeaux. **2.** a department in the Midi-Pyrénées region of southern France; area 5,228 sq. km. (2,019 sq. miles); pop. (1990) 155,820; capital, Cahors.

**Lot-et-Garonne** a department in the Aquitaine region of south-west France; area 5,361 sq. km. (2,070 sq. miles); pop. (1990) 305,990; capital, Agen.

**Lothian** /ˈləʊðɪən/ a local government region in east-central Scotland on the Firth of Forth, from 1975 to 1996; area 1,716 sq. km. (663 sq. miles); pop. (1991) 723,680; administrative centre, Edinburgh. It is divided into four districts:

| District | Area (sq. km.) | Pop. (1991) |
|---|---|---|
| East Lothian | 680 | 82,995 |
| Edinburgh City | 261 | 421,210 |
| Midlothian | 350 | 77,970 |
| West Lothian | 425 | 141,500 |

**low** a region of low atmospheric pressure (below 1,000 millibars) usually associated with rain and high winds. Also known as a 'depression'.

**Lozère** /ləʊˈze(r)/ a department in the Languedoc–Roussillon region of southern France, at the southern edge of the Massif Central; area 5,167 sq. km. (1,996 sq. miles); pop. (1990) 72,825; capital, Mende.

**Louangphrabang** SEE LUANG PRABANG.

**Loudi** /ləʊˈdiː/ a city in Hunan province, south-east-central China, south-west of Changsha; pop. (1986) 266,000.

**lough** /lɒx/ the Irish word for a lake, as in Lough Neagh.

**Loughborough** /ˈlʌfbərə/ a town in Leicestershire, central England, on the River Soar; pop. (1981) 46,120. Once noted for lace-making and bell-founding, the bell of St. Paul's Cathedral in London was cast here in 1881. Loughborough University of Technology was founded in 1966. It is now a market town with light industries.

**Louisade Archipelago** a group of islands to the south-east of the island of New Guinea in the south-west Pacific, part of the Papua New Guinea province of Milne Bay; area 1,553 sq. km. (600 sq. miles). Discovered by Torres in 1606, its chief islands are Rossel, Tacuta, and Misima where gold is mined.

**Louisiana** /luːˌiːzɪˈænə/ a state in the southern USA, bordering on the Gulf of Mexico; area 123,677 sq. km. (47,752 sq. miles); pop. (1990) 4,219,970; capital, Baton Rouge. The largest cities are New Orleans, Baton Rouge, and Shreveport. It is also known as the Pelican State, Creole State, or Sugar State. The territory was claimed by France in 1682 and named in honour of Louis XIV. It was sold by the French republic to the US in 1803 (Louisiana Purchase), becoming the 18th state in 1812. Louisiana is a major producer of natural gas, petroleum, salt, and sulphur, and a leading supplier of furs from muskrat, opossum, raccoon, and otter. Its principal tourist attractions are the French Quarter of New Orleans, the coastal bayous, the Jean Lafitte National Historic Park, and the Poverty Point National Monument. Louisiana is divided into 64 parishes:

| Parish | Area (sq. km.) | Pop. (1990) | Capital |
|---|---|---|---|
| Acadia | 1,708 | 55,880 | Crowley |
| Allen | 1,989 | 21,230 | Oberlin |
| Ascension | 780 | 58,210 | Donaldsville |
| Assumption | 889 | 22,750 | Napoleonville |
| Avoyelles | 2,200 | 39,160 | Marksville |
| Beauregard | 3,024 | 30,080 | De Ridder |
| Bienville | 2,122 | 15,980 | Arcadia |
| Bossier | 2,197 | 86,090 | Benton |
| Caddo | 2,324 | 248,250 | Shreveport |
| Calcasieu | 2,813 | 168,130 | Lake Charles |
| Caldwell | 1,407 | 9,810 | Columbia |
| Cameron | 3,684 | 9,260 | Cameron |
| Catahoula | 1,903 | 11,065 | Harrisonburg |
| Claiborne | 1,989 | 17,405 | Horner |
| Concordia | 1,864 | 20,830 | Vidalia |
| De Soto | 2,288 | 25,350 | Mansfield |
| East Baton Rouge | 1,191 | 380,105 | Baton Rouge |
| East Carroll | 1,108 | 9,710 | Lake Providence |
| East Feliciana | 1,183 | 19,210 | Clinton |
| Evangeline | 1,734 | 33,270 | Ville Platte |
| Franklin | 1,651 | 22,390 | Winnsboro |
| Grant | 1,698 | 17,530 | Colfax |
| Iberia | 1,531 | 68,300 | New Iberia |
| Iberville | 1,659 | 31,050 | Plaquemine |
| Jackson | 1,505 | 15,705 | Jonesboro |
| Jefferson | 905 | 448,310 | Gretna |
| Jefferson Davis | 1,703 | 30,720 | Jennings |
| La Salle | 1,659 | 13,660 | Jena |
| Lafayette | 702 | 164,760 | Lafayette |
| Lafourche | 2,967 | 85,860 | Thibodaux |
| Lincoln | 1,227 | 41,745 | Ruston |
| Livingston | 1,719 | 70,530 | Livingston |
| Madison | 1,641 | 12,460 | Tallulah |
| Morehouse | 2,098 | 31,940 | Bastrop |
| Natchitoches | 3,286 | 36,690 | Natchitoches |
| Orleans | 517 | 496,940 | New Orleans |
| Ouachita | 1,630 | 142,190 | Monroe |
| Plaquemines | 2,691 | 25,575 | Pointe a la Hache |
| Pointe Coupée | 1,472 | 22,540 | New Roads |
| Rapides | 3,487 | 131,560 | Alexandria |
| Red River | 1,024 | 9,390 | Coushatta |
| Richland | 1,464 | 20,630 | Rayville |
| Sabine | 2,223 | 22,650 | Many |
| St. Bernard | 1,264 | 66,630 | Chalmette |
| St. Charles | 744 | 42,440 | Hahnville |
| St. Helena | 1,063 | 9,870 | Greensburg |
| St. James | 645 | 20,880 | Convent |
| St. John the Baptist | 554 | 40,000 | Edgard |
| St. Landry | 2,434 | 80,330 | Opelousas |
| St. Martin | 1,947 | 43,980 | St. Martinville |
| St. Mary | 1,594 | 58,090 | Franklin |
| St. Tammany | 2,270 | 144,510 | Covington |
| Tangipahoa | 2,036 | 85,710 | Amite |
| Tensas | 1,620 | 7,100 | Saint Joseph |
| Terrebonne | 3,554 | 96,980 | Houma |
| Union | 2,298 | 20,690 | Farmerville |
| Vermilion | 3,133 | 50,055 | Abbeville |
| Vernon | 3,463 | 61,960 | Leesville |
| Washington | 1,758 | 43,185 | Franklinton |
| Webster | 1,565 | 41,990 | Minden |
| West Baton Rouge | 504 | 19,420 | Port Allen |
| West Carrol | 936 | 12,090 | Oak Grove |
| West Feliciana | 1,056 | 12,915 | St. Francisville |
| Winn | 2,478 | 16,270 | Winnfield |

**Louisiana Purchase** the name given to the US territory between the Mississippi River and the Rocky Mountains and from Canada southwards to the Gulf of Mexico that was purchased from France in April 1803 for the sum of $15,000,000.

**Louisville** /ˈluːɪˌvɪl/ an industrial city in north-west Kentucky, USA, on the Ohio River; pop. (1990) 269,060. Named after Louis XVI of France, it developed as an important portage point around the falls on the Ohio River. The annual Kentucky Derby, the oldest race in the US, takes place on the Churchill Downs race-track. Its university was founded in 1798 and its industries produce bourbon, paint and varnish, home appliances, and synthetic rubber. The largest and oldest publishing house for the blind in the US is located here. Louisville was the birthplace in 1942 of the world-champion heavyweight boxer Muhammad Ali.

**Lourdes** /lʊəd/ a town in the department of Hautes-Pyrénées, south-west France, at the foot of the Pyrenees; pop. (1982) 17,620. In 1858 a peasant girl, Bernadette Soubirous, claimed to have had visions of the Virgin Mary here. At the same time a spring appeared, and miraculous healings were reported. It is now a major centre of pilgimage.

**Lourenço Marques** /ləˈrensəʊ mɑːk/ the former name (until 1976) of Maputo, capital of Mozambique.

**Louth** /laʊθ/ a county of the Republic of Ireland, in the province of Leinster on the frontier with Northern Ireland; area 821 sq. km. (317 sq. miles); pop. (1991) 90,700; county town, Dundalk.

**Louvain** the French name for LEUVEN.

**Louvre** /luːvr/ the national museum and art gallery of France, in Paris, housed in the former royal palace, on the site of an earlier fortress and arsenal, built by Francis I (d.1547) and later extended. When the court moved to Versailles in 1678 its conversion into a museum was begun. It was Francis I who set the pattern for royal collecting and patronage which persisted until the French Revolution, and the royal collections, greatly increased by Louis XIV, formed the nucleus of the national collection which is an epitome of French history and culture.

**Low Countries** a region of north-west Europe comprising the Netherlands, Belgium, and Luxembourg.

**Lowell** /ˈləʊ(ə)l/ a city in north-east Massachusetts, USA, at the junction of the Merrimack and Concord rivers; pop. (1990) 103,440. Settled in 1655, it became a textile town in the 19th c. It was the nation's first large-scale centre for the mechanized production of cotton cloth. It now has diverse light industries. The painter James Whistler was born here in 1834.

**Lower Austria** (German **Niederösterreich** /ˌniːdər ˈ3ːstəˌraɪx/) a federal state of north-east Austria; area 19,172 sq. km. (7,405 sq. miles); pop. (1991) 1,480,930; capital, St. Pölten. It is the largest of the states of Austria, comprising the country's principal agricultural, industrial, and oil producing regions.

**Lower California** see BAJA CALIFORNIA.

**Lower Canada** the mainly French-speaking region of Canada around the St. Lawrence River, in what is now southern Quebec. It was a British colony from 1791 to 1841, when it was united with Upper Canada.

**Lower East Side, the** the name given to an area of New York City between Lafayette Street and the East River and lying south of 14th Street. Generally associated with immigrants and artists, it was the childhood home of many who went on to be famous celebrities.

**Lower Egypt** that part of Egypt north of Cairo, including the Nile delta and the coastland.

**Lower Hutt** /hʌt/ a city on North Island, New Zealand, 10 km. north-east of Wellington; pop. (1986) 63,860. It is both a dormitory town and industrial centre. The prime minister's official residence, Vogel House, is located here.

**Lower Saxony** /ˈsæksənɪ/ (German **Niedersachsen** /ˌniːdər ˈzɑːksən/) a state of north-west Germany; area 47,344 sq. km. (18,286 sq. miles); pop. (est. 1990) 7,238,000; capital, Hanover.

**Lowestoft** /ˈləʊəstɒft/ a fishing port and resort town on the North Sea coast of Suffolk, east England; pop. (1981) 59,875. It is the most easterly English town.

**Lowlands, the** the name given to the lowland region of Scotland.

**Loyalty Islands** /ˈlɔːɪəltɪ/ (French **Iles Loyauté**) a group of islands in the south-west Pacific forming part of the French overseas territory of New Caledonia; pop. (1989) 17,910. The group includes the three main islands of Maré, Lifou, and Uvéa in addition to a large number of small islets. Its chief export is copra.

**Lozère** /ləʊˈzer/ a department in the Languedoc-Roussillon region of southern France; area 5,167 sq. km. (1,996 sq. miles); pop. (1990) 72,825; capital, Mende.

**Lualaba** /ˌluəˈlɑːbə/ a headstream of the Zaïre (Congo) River in central Africa. It rises in south-east Zaire and flows 640 km. (400 miles) northwards before meeting the Lomami to form the Zaïre (Congo) River.

**Luanda** /luːˈændə/ the capital city of Angola, a seaport on the Atlantic coast of West Africa at the mouth of the Cuanza River; pop. (est. 1988) 1,800,000. Founded by the Portuguese in 1575, it became a major centre for the trans-shipment of slaves to Brazil during the 17th and 18th c.

**Luang Prabang** /luːˌæŋ prəˈbæŋ/ (also **Louangphrabang**) a city in north-west Laos, on the Mekong River; pop. (est. 1984) 44,240. It was the capital of a kingdom of the same name from 1707 until the reorganization of 1946–7, when Vientiane became the administrative capital. Luang Prabang remained the royal residence and Buddhist religious centre of Laos until the end of the monarchy in 1975. The former royal palace (1904) now incorporates the National Museum and the royal funeral chapel is located in the grounds of the Buddhist Golden City Temple.

**Luapula** /ˌluəˈpʊlə/ a province of north-west Zambia; area 50,567 sq. km. (19,531 sq. miles); pop. (1989) 526,330; chief town, Mansa.

**Lubango** /lʊˈbæŋɡəʊ/ a town in south-west Angola, capital of Huíla province; pop. (1984) 105,000. Under Portuguese rule it was also known as Serra da Bandeira.

**Lubbock** /ˈlʌbək/ a city in north-west Texas, USA; pop. (1990) 186,200. Originally a centre for buffalo hunters and trail drivers, it is now a major market town for cotton, grain, and vegetables. It was named after Colonel Thomas S. Lubbock, a Confederate officer, and was the birthplace of the rock star Buddy Holly.

**Lübeck** /ˈluːbek/ a port on the Baltic coast of northern Germany, in the state of Schleswig-Holstein north-east of Hamburg; pop. (1991) 211,000. Formerly a Slavonic principality, it became a part of Holstein in 1143. Between the

14th and 19th centuries it was an important city within the Hanseatic League. Its trade is mostly with Scandinavia. Willy Brandt and Thomas Mann were both born in Lübeck.

**Lublin** /'lʊblɪn/ a manufacturing city in eastern Poland, capital of Lublin county; pop. (1990) 351,350.

**Lubumbashi** /ˌluːbʊmˈbæʃɪ/ a city in south-east Zaire, near the border with Zambia; capital of the Shaba cobalt- and copper-mining region; pop. (1984) 543,270. Founded by Belgian colonists in 1910, it was called Elizabethville until 1966.

**Lucania** /luːˈkeɪnɪə/, **Mount** a peak of the St. Elias Mountains in the Yukon Territory, north-west Canada. It rises to 5,226 m. (17,141 ft.) north of Mt. Logan.

**Lucca** /'luːkə/ a town in Tuscany, northern Italy, capital of Lucca province; pop. (1990) 86,440. It was the capital of an independent republic during the 11th–13th c. and was famous for its silk. Lucca was the birthplace in 1858 of the composer Giacomo Puccini. It is the centre of a noted olive oil producing region.

**Lucerne** /luːˈsɜːn/ (German **Luzern**) a resort on the western shore of Lake Lucerne, in central Switzerland, capital of a canton of the same name; pop. (1990) 59,370. It hosts a summer music festival and a winter carnival.

**Lucerne, Lake** (also **Lake of Lucerne**, German **Vierwaldstätter See** /fɪərˈvɑːltˌʃtetər zeɪ/) a lake in central Switzerland, surrounded by the four cantons of Lucerne, Nidwalden, Uri, and Schwyz and sometimes also known as the Lake of the Four Forest Cantons; area 114 sq. km. (44 sq. miles).

**Luchow** see HEFEI.

**Lucknow** /'lʌknaʊ/ a city in northern India, on the Gomti River, capital of the state of Uttar Pradesh; pop. (1991) 1,642,130. In 1775 it became the capital of the province of Oudh and in 1857, during the Indian mutiny, its British residency was twice besieged by Indian insurgents. It is a centre for handicrafts such as silversmithing.

**Lüda** /luːˈdɑː/ an industrial conurbation and port in Liaoning province, north-east China, comprising the cities and ports of Lüshun and Dalian (whence its name); pop. (est. 1986) 1,630,000. It is a heavy engineering centre.

**Lüderitz** /'luːdɜːˌrɪts/ a town on the Atlantic coast of south-west Namibia, named after F. A. E. Lüderitz who established the first German settlement here in 1884. It is a centre for crayfishing, yachting, and carpet weaving.

**Ludhiana** /ˌlʊdiːˈɑːnə/ a city in the Punjab state, north-west India, on the Sutlej River south-west of Amritsar; pop. (1991) 1,012,000. Founded by Lodi princes from Delhi in 1480, it is now a major railway junction and textile and engineering centre with a large grain market.

**Ludwigshafen** /'luːdwɪɡzˌhæf(ə)n/ (fully **Ludwigshafen am Rhein**) an industrial river port in west-central Germany, south-west of Mannheim, on the River Rhine in the state of Rhineland-Palatinate; pop. (1991) 165,370.

**Lugano** /luːˈgɑːnəʊ/ a resort town and financial centre in Ticino canton, southern Switzerland, on the north shore of Lake Lugano (which extends into Italy); pop. (1990) 26,010.

**Lugansk** see LUHANSK.

**Lugo** /'luːgəʊ/ a walled town on the Minho River, capital of the province of Lugo in Galicia, north-west Spain; pop. (1991) 86,960. It lies at the heart of an agricultural region noted for its cheese.

**Luhansk** /luːˈgɑːnsk/ (Ukrainian **Lugansk**) an industrial city of the Donets Basin in east Ukraine, at the junction of the Lugan and Olkhov rivers; pop. (1990) 501,000. Established as a cannon foundry and coal-mining centre in 1795, it was named Voroshilovgrad in honour of the Soviet military and political leader Marshal Voroshilov (1881–1969) from 1935 to 1958 and from 1970 to 1991.

**Luik** the Flemish name for LIÈGE.

**Luleå** /luːˈleɪə/ a seaport on the Gulf of Bothnia, capital of Norrbotten county in northern Sweden; pop. (1990) 68,410. Founded by Gustavus Adolphus in 1621, it is an outlet for the iron ore mined at Gällivare and Kiruna.

**Lumbier Defile** /'lʌmbje(r)/ (Spanish **Hoz de Lumbier**) a gorge cut by the Irati River in the southern foothills of the Pyrenees, in the Navarre region of northern Spain.

**Lumbini** /luːmˈbiːnɪ/ a centre of pilgrimage to the south of the Churia Range in Nepal, birthplace of the Buddha.

**Lund** /lʊnd/ a city in south-west Sweden, just north-east of Malmö in Malmöhus county; pop. (1991) 87,680. It is the site of a university founded in 1666 and a fine Romanesque cathedral.

**Lundy** /'lʌndɪ/ **1.** an uninhabited granite island in the Bristol Channel, south-west England, off the coast of north Devon. Its name is derived from Norse (= Puffin Island). Lundy has one of the most important seabird colonies in southern England and the surrounding waters are a marine nature reserve. **2.** a shipping forecast area covering the Bristol Channel and the eastern Celtic Sea.

**Lüneburg Heath** /'luːnəbɜːg/ a low sandy heathland lying between the Aller and Elbe rivers in northern Germany, partly a nature reserve and partly a military training area.

**Luohe** /ləʊˈheɪ/ a city in Henan province, east-central China, south of Zhengzhou; pop. (1986) 164,000.

**Luoyang** /ləʊˈjæŋ/ (formerly **Honan**) an industrial city in Henan province, north-central China, in the valley of the Luo River; pop. (1990) 1,190,000. It was founded in the 12th c. BC as the imperial capital of the Chou dynasty and was the

capital of several subsequent dynasties. Between
the 4th and 6th c. AD the construction of cave
temples to the south of the city made it an important Buddhist centre.

**Luristan** see LORESTAN.

**Lusaka** the capital city of Zambia; pop. (1989)
1,151,250. Founded in 1905, it was developed as a
railway town, becoming capital of Northern
Rhodesia in 1935. It is the centre of a fertile agricultural region and also has car-assembly and textile plants.

**Lusatian** see WEND.

**Lushnjë** /'lʌʃnɪə/ a town in western Albania,
55 km. (34 miles) from Durrës; pop. (1990) 31,500.
Known in ancient times as Marusium, it is capital
of the district of Lushnjë. It was the seat of a
Congress which met in January 1920 in response to
anti-Italian demonstrations. As a result of this
Congress the capital was moved from Durrës (the
seat of a pro-Italian government) to Tiranë.

**Lüshun** /lu:'ʃu:n/ a port on the Liaodong
Peninsula in north-east China, now part of the
urban complex of Lüda. It was leased by Russia for
use as a Pacific naval port from 1898 until 1905,
when it was known as Port Arthur. Between 1945
and 1955 it was jointly held by China and the
Soviet Union.

**Lusitania** /ˌlu:sɪ'teɪnɪə/ an ancient Roman
province in the Iberian peninsula, corresponding to
modern Portugal.
**Lusitanian** adj. & n.

**Lusuphone States** /'lu:su:fəʊn/ a group of
seven Portuguese-speaking countries—Angola,
Brazil, Cape Verde, Guinea-Bissau, Mozambique,
Portugal, and São Tomé and Príncipe—which
signed an agreement in 1994 as the basis for social,
cultural, and economic co-operation.

**Lutine Bell** /'lu:ti:n/ the bell of HMS *Lutine*,
which sank in 1799. The ship was carrying a large
amount of coin and bullion, and the loss fell on the
underwriters, who were members of Lloyd's of
London. When the bell was recovered during salvage operations it was taken to Lloyd's, where it
now hangs. It is rung (and business is halted) when-
ever there is an important announcement to be
made to the underwriters. It was formerly rung
once if a ship had sunk and twice for good news.

**Lutomer** /'lu:təʊmər/ (also **Ljutomer**) a town in
north-eastern Slovenia, at the centre of a notable
wine-producing area; pop. (1991) 3,600.

**Luton** /'lu:t(ə)n/ an industrial town in
Bedfordshire, southern England, north-west of
London; pop. (1991) 167,300. At one time noted
for millinery, its principal industry now is the
building of cars and trucks. It is the site of a major
airport.

**Luxembourg** /'lʌksəm,bɜ:g/ a province of
south-eastern Belgium; area 4,441 sq. km. (1,715
sq. miles); pop. (1991) 232,810; capital, Arlon.

**Luxembourg**
/'lʌksəm,bɜ:g/ official
name **The Grand
Duchy of
Luxembourg** a
country in western
Europe, situated be-
tween Belgium,
Germany, and
France; area 2,586

sq. km. (999 sq. miles); pop. (1990) 378,400; official
languages, Luxembourgish, French, and German;
capital, Luxembourg. The smallest of the member-
states of the European Community, Luxembourg
extends 57 km. from east to west and 82 km. from
north to south. Approximately one-third of the
territory in the north is an extension of the hilly
Ardennes and forest covers about one-third of the
country. Luxembourg is rich in iron ore and its economic prosperity is based chiefly on its large iron
and steel industries. Becoming a Habsburg possession in the 15th c., Luxembourg was Spanish until
1713 and then Austrian until annexed by France in
1795. As a result of the Treaty of Vienna in 1815 it
became a grand duchy, though in 1839 it lost its
western province to Belgium. Occupied by
Germany during both World Wars, Luxembourg
formed a customs union with Belgium in 1922
which was extended in 1948 into the Benelux
Customs Union which included the Netherlands. It
is a constitutional monarchy with a bicameral
Parliament comprising a Chamber of Deputies and
a Council of State.
**Luxembourger** n.

Apart from its capital, Luxembourg is divided into
12 cantons:

| Canton | Area (sq. km.) | Pop. (1991) |
| --- | --- | --- |
| Luxembourg | 238 | 41,365 |
| Capellen | 199 | 32,000 |
| Esch-sur-Alzette | 243 | 116,820 |
| Mersch | 224 | 19,240 |
| Clervaux | 302 | 10,360 |
| Diekirch | 239 | 23,180 |
| Redange | 268 | 11,170 |
| Vianden | 54 | 2,780 |
| Wiltz | 294 | 9,670 |
| Echternach | 186 | 11,800 |
| Grevenmacher | 211 | 18,270 |
| Remich | 128 | 13,030 |

**Luxembourg** /'lʌksəm,bɜ:g/ the capital of the
Grand Duchy of Luxembourg, on the Alzette and
Petrusse rivers; pop. (1991) 75,620. It is the seat of
the European Court of Justice and the Secretariat
of the Parliament of the EU. It is a commercial,
cultural, and industrial centre with iron and steel
and many light industries.

**Luxor** /'lʌksə(r)/ (Arabic **El Uqsur**) a city in
eastern Egypt on the east bank of the Nile; pop.
(1991) 142,000. It is the site of the southern part of
ancient Thebes and contains the ruins of the

temple built by Amenhotep III between 1411 and 1375 BC and of monuments erected by Rameses II in the 13th c. BC.

**Luzern**  the German name for LUCERNE.

**Luzhou** /luˈdʒəʊ/ a city in Sichuan province, central China, on the Yangtze River south-west of Chongqing; pop. (1986) 369,000.

**Luzon** /luːˈzɒn/ an island in the Philippines; area 104,688 sq. km. (40,420 sq. miles). It is the most northerly and largest of the Philippine islands. Its chief towns are Quezon City and Manila, the country's capital.

**Lviv** /ləˈvɒf/ (formerly **Lvov**, Polish **Lwów** /ləˈvʊf/, German **Lemberg**) an industrial city in western Ukraine, near the Polish frontier; pop. (1990) 798,000. Founded in the 13th c., it was an important trading town on a route linking the Black Sea with the Baltic. It belonged to Poland until 1772 and to Austria-Hungary until 1918. A major communications centre with both heavy and light industries.

**Lyallpur** /ˌlaɪəlˈpʊə(r)/ see FAISALABAD.

**Lycaonia** /ˌlaɪkɪˈəʊnjə/ an ancient region of Asia Minor to the west of Cappadocia that became a Roman province in the 4th c. AD. Its chief cities were Iconium (Konya), Lystra, and Derbe.

**Lyceum** /laɪˈsiːəm/ the garden at Athens in Greece in which Aristotle taught philosophy. It gives its name to a literary institution, lecture-hall, or teaching-place.

**Lycia** /ˈlɪsɪə/ an ancient region on the coast of south-west Asia Minor, between Caria and Pamphylia. Formerly under Persian and Syrian rule, it was annexed by Rome as part of Pamphylia in AD 43, becoming a separate province in the 4th c. **Lycian** adj. & n.

**Lydia** /ˈlɪdɪə/ an ancient region of western Asia Minor, south of Mysia and north of Caria. It became a powerful kingdom in the 7th c. BC but in 546 BC its final king, Croesus, was defeated by Cyrus and it was absorbed into the Persian empire. Lydia was probably the first realm to use coined money. The region gives its name to the Lydian mode, a musical term for the mode represented by the natural diatonic scale. **Lydian** adj. & n.

**Lynchburg** /ˈlɪntʃbɜːg/ a city in central Virginia, USA, on hills overlooking the James River; pop. (1990) 66,050. Settled in 1757, it was named after John Lynch who built a ferryhouse and tobacco warehouse here.

**lynchet**  a term used in England to describe small terraces of land perhaps dating from prehistoric times.

**Lynn** /lɪn/ a city in eastern Massachusetts, USA; pop. (1990) 81,245. First settled in 1629, it became a centre of shoe-making in the 1630s. In 1883 the General Electric Company was established here. Today jet engines, turbines, and electrical goods are manufactured.

**Lynwood** /ˈlɪnwuːd/ a city in southern California, USA, a south-east suburb of Los Angeles; pop. (1990) 61,945.

**Lyon Court** /ˈlaɪən/ the court of the Lord Lyon King of Arms, chief herald of Scotland. It is located in Edinburgh at the east end of Princes Street.

**Lyonnais** /ˌliːɒˈneɪ/ a former province of south-east-central France, centred around the city of Lyons which was its capital.

**Lyons** /ˈliːɒn/ (French **Lyon** /ljɔ̃/) an industrial city and river port in south-east France, situated at the confluence of the Rhône and Saône rivers; pop. (1990) 422,440. It is capital of the department of Rhône, chief city of the Rhône-Alpes region, and third-largest city in France. It was founded by the Romans in AD 43 as Lugdunum, an important city of ancient Gaul situated at a strategic river junction. It is a major trade and gastronomic centre; it also has metallurgical, chemicals, and textiles industries.

**Lys** /liːs/ a river in northern France and Belgium that rises in the Artois Hills in the department of Pas-de-Calais and flows 214 km. (134 miles) north-eastwards along the Franco-Belgian frontier before meeting the River Schelde at Ghent.

**Lytham Saint Anne's** /ˈlɪð(ə)m/ a resort town on the Ribble estuary in Lancashire, north-west England, with a championship golf course; pop. (1981) 40,140.

# M m

**MA** *abbr.* US Massachusetts (in official postal use).

**Ma'anshan** /mɑːnˈʃɑːn/ a city in Anhui province, east-central China, on the Yangtze River south-west of Nanjing; pop. (1986) 375,000.

**Maas** the Flemish and Dutch name for the MEUSE.

**Maasai** see MASAI.

**Maarianhamina** /ˈmɑːrjənhəˌmiːnə/ the Finnish name for MARIEHAMN, capital of the Åland Islands.

**Maastricht** /ˈmɑːstrɪxt/ a multilingual industrial city in the Netherlands, capital of the province of Limburg, situated on the River Maas (Meuse) near the Belgian and German frontiers; pop. (1991) 117,420. Its cathedral, one of the oldest in the Netherlands, dates from the 6th c. An agreement on political, economic, and monetary union in the EC, known as the Treaty on European Union, was signed here in February 1992.

**McAllen** /məˈkɑːl(ə)n/ a winter resort in southern Texas, USA, on the Rio Grande; pop. (1990) 84,020. It lies at the centre of an irrigated agricultural region growing vegetables, cotton, oranges, and grapefruit. Nearby is the Santa Ana National Wildlife Refuge which extends over 810 hectares (2,000 acres) of forest and lakes.

**Macao** /məˈkaʊ/ (also **Macáu**) a peninsula in southeast China, on the west side of the Pearl River estuary, opposite Hong Kong, forming (with the nearby islands of Taipa and Colôane)

an Overseas Special Territory of Portugal; area 17 sq. km. (6.5 sq. miles); pop. (est. 1991) 467,000; official languages, Portuguese and Cantonese; capital, Macao City. First visited by Vasco da Gama in 1497, a trading settlement, the oldest permanent European settlement in the Far East, was established by the Portuguese in 1557. After paying an annual tribute to China for 300 years it was declared a free port by Portugal in 1849, but the silting up of its harbour and the development of Hong Kong on the opposite side of the estuary led to a decline in its importance as a trading centre. Portugal's right of 'perpetual occupation' was recognized by the Manchu government in 1887, but in 1987 Portugal agreed to restore control of Macao to China in 1999. In addition to tourism, gambling, and fishing, its industries produce textiles, electronics, plastics, and fireworks. The territory is administered by a governor appointed by the President of Portugal and by a legislative assembly.
**Macanese** /mækəˈniːz/ *adj. & n.*

**Macapá** /mækəˈpɑː/ a town in northern Brazil, on the Amazon delta north-west of Belém, capital of Amapá Territory; pop. (1991) 179,000. In 1782 the Portuguese built the fort of São José de Macapá as a defence against French incursions from the Guyanas. It is concerned with iron and manganese mining and forest products.

**Macassar** the former name (until *c.* 1970) of UJUNG PADANG.

**Macáu** the Portuguese name for MACAO.

**Macclesfield** /ˈmæklzˌfiːld/ an industrial town in Cheshire, England, on the River Bollin to the south of Stockport, once famous for silk manufacturing; pop. (1981) 48,070. Its industries produce textiles, paper, plastics, and pharmaceuticals.

**Macdonnell Ranges** /məkˈdɒn(ə)l/ a series of mountain ranges extending westwards from Alice Springs in Northern Territory, Australia. The highest peak is Mt. Ziel which rises to a height of 1,510 m. (4,955 ft.). Explored in 1860 by John McDouall Stuart, they were named after Sir Richard Macdonnell who was governor of South Australia at that time.

## Macedonia
/ˌmæsɪˈdəʊnɪə/ **1.** (also **Macedon** /ˈmæsɪd(ə)n/) an ancient country in south-east Europe, at the northern end of the Greek peninsula, including the coastal plain around

Salonica and the mountain ranges behind. In classical times it was a kingdom which under Philip II and Alexander the Great became a world power. The region is now divided between Greece, Bulgaria, and the former Yugoslav Republic of Macedonia (see below). **2.** (Greek **Makedhonia**) a region in the north-east of modern Greece, between the Aegean Sea and the country's north-west frontier; area 34,177 sq. km. (13,200 sq. miles); pop. (1991) 2,263,000; capital, Salonica (Thessaloníki). **3.** official name **The Former Yugoslav Republic**

**of Macedonia** a landlocked republic in the Balkans, bounded by Greece, Albania, Kosovo, Serbia, and Bulgaria; area 25,713 sq. km. (9,932 sq. miles); pop. (est. 1991) 2,038,000; official language, Macedonian; capital, Skopje. Formerly a constituent republic of Yugoslavia, Macedonia became independent after a referendum in 1991.

**Maceió** /mæ'seɪəʊ/ a port on the east coast of Brazil, south of Recife; pop. (1990) 699,760. It is capital of the state of Alagoas and has fine beaches that are protected by an offshore coral reef. The port's main products are sugar, salt, and machinery.

**Macerata** /mætʃeɪ'rɑ:tə/ an agricultural and industrial town in the Marches region of east-central Italy, capital of the province of Macerata; pop. (1991) 43,540. It was built near the site of the Roman City of Helvia Ricina and has a university founded in 1290. Manufactures include musical instruments.

**Macgillicuddy's Reeks** /mə'gɪlɪˌkʌdɪz ri:ks/ a range of hills in County Kerry in south-west Ireland, rising to 1,041 m. (3,415 ft.) at Carrantuohill which is the highest peak in the Republic of Ireland.

**Machakos** /mə'tʃɑ:kɒs/ a town in Kenya to the south-east of Nairobi, the former administrative headquarters of British East Africa; pop. (1979) 84,320.

**Machala** /mə'tʃɑ:lə/ a commercial town in south-west Ecuador, capital of the province of El Oro; pop. (1990) 159,060. Bananas are grown in the surrounding area and the city is served by the port of Puerto Bolívar which lies 6 km. (4 miles) to the west on the Gulf of Guayaquil.

**Macheng** /mɑ:'tʃeŋ/ a city in Hubei province, east-central China, in the southern foothills of the Dabie Shan Mts. north-east of Wuhan; pop. (1986) 1,010,000.

**Machida** /mæ'tʃiːdə/ a suburban city in the Kanto region of Honshu Island, Japan, situated to the south-west of Tokyo; pop. (1990) 349,030.

**Machilipatnam** /ˌməʃəli:'pətnəm/ (formerly **Masulipatnam**) a port on the Coromandel coast of Andhra Pradesh, eastern India, situated on the Bay of Bengal at the mouth of the Krishna River; pop. (1991) 159,000.

**Machu Picchu** /ˌmɑːtʃu: 'pɪktʃu:/ the ruins of a fortified, abandoned Inca town dramatically perched on a steep-sided ridge in the Andes of central Peru. It contains a palace, a temple to the sun, and extensive cultivation terraces. Never found by the Spanish conquistadores, it was discovered by Hiram Bingham in 1911 and named after the mountain that rises above it.

**Mackay** /mə'kaɪ/ a port on the Pacific coast of Queensland in north-east Australia; pop. (1991) 50,300. Situated near the mouth of the Pioneer River, the city was founded in 1862 and named after Captain John Mackay who explored the region in 1860. It developed as a major port after the construction of a breakwater in 1939 and is a major outlet for sugar and coal.

**Mackenzie River** /mə'kenzi/ the longest river in Canada, flowing 1,700 km. (1,060 miles) northwest from the Great Slave Lake to the Beaufort Sea, a section of the Arctic Ocean. It is named after Sir Alexander Mackenzie who visited it in 1789 while exploring Canada for the North West Fur Company. The Mackenzie–Peace–Finlay river system, which rises in the Rockies and flows a total distance of 4,241 km. (2,635 miles), is the second-longest in North America.

**McKinley** /mə'kɪnlɪ/, **Mount** (Aleut **Denali**) a peak in Alaska to the north of Anchorage, the highest in North America, rising to a height of 6,194 m. (20,320 ft.). Situated at the centre of a national park established in 1917, it is named after President William McKinley (1843–1901) and was first climbed in 1913.

**Mâcon** /'mækɔ̃/ the capital of Saône-et-Loire department in southern Burgundy, east-central France, on the River Saône; pop. (1990) 38,500. It is the centre of the Mâconnais wine-producing region.

**Macon** /'mækɒn/ a city in central Georgia, USA, on the River Ocmulgee; pop. (1990) 106,610. Laid out in 1823 on the site of a trading post, Macon developed as a river port, regional cotton market, and railway junction. It was the home town of the poet Sidney Lanier and the rock star Little Richard. Nearby is the Ocmulgee National Monument, the site of an Indian settlement that was occupied from at least 10,000 BC. It is the business and industrial centre of an extensive farm area.

**Macquarie Island** /mə'kwɒrɪ/ an uninhabited Island in the Southern Ocean, c. 1,360 km. (850 miles) south-east of Hobart, a dependency of the state of Tasmania, Australia. In 1948 a scientific research station was established here.

**Macquarie River** a river in New South Wales, Australia, rising on the western slopes of the Great Dividing Range and flowing 960 km. (600 miles) north-west to join the River Darling, of which it is a headwater.

**Mactan** /mæk'tɑ:n/ a coral island in the Philippines, off the coast of Cebu Island, where the Portuguese navigator Ferdinand Magellan was killed in 1521 during the first circumnavigation of the world.

**Madagascar** /ˌmædə'gæskə(r)/ official name **The Democratic Republic of Madagascar** an island country in the Indian Ocean, off the east coast of Africa from which it

is separated by the Mozambique Channel; area 587,041 sq. km. (226,744 sq. miles); pop. (est. 1991) 12,016,000; official languages, Malagasy and French; capital, Antananarivo. Madagascar comprises the world's fourth-largest island and also the small islands of Nosy Be, Nosy Mitsio, Nosy Boraha, Ile Ste. Marie, and Iles Barren. Surrounded by a tropical coastal region, a temperate highland region with a warm rainy season from November to April rises up to 2,880 m. (9,450 ft.) at Mt. Tsaratanana, the east coast falling away abruptly from the highlands and receiving more rainfall. Geologically Madagascar's history is complex and many of its plants and animals are not found elsewhere. Divided into 18 tribal groups, the people are of mixed Polynesian, Arab, and African origin, and the economy is mainly agricultural. Rich in minerals such as mica, graphite, and chromite, its chief exports include vanilla, coffee, cloves, and sugar. Madagascar was heavily influenced by Arab settlers before its discovery by the Portuguese explorer Diego Diaz in the 1500s. Despite rival British and French attempts at domination, the island remained independent until finally colonized by the French in 1896. It regained its independence as the Malagasy Republic in 1960, changing its name back to Madagascar in 1975. The country was ruled for 17 years by a president who came to power during a revolution in 1972, but following opposition that reached a violent climax in 1992 a new multiparty constitution was introduced and a new president elected a year later.

**Malagasy** *adj. & n.*

**Madeira** /mə'dɪərə/ a river in north-west Brazil, which rises on the Bolivian border and flows about 3,241 km. (2,013 miles) to meet the Amazon east of Manaus. It is the longest tributary of the Amazon and is navigable to large ocean-going vessels as far as Pôrto Velho.

**Madeira** (Portuguese **Ilha da Madeira**) the largest of a group of islands (**the Madeiras**) in the Atlantic Ocean off north-west Africa; area 739 sq. km. (285 sq. miles); pop. (1991) 257,690. Its chief port and city is Funchal and its highest mountain is the Pico Ruivo (1,861 m., 6,106 ft.).

**Madeiras** /mə'dɪərəz/ a group of islands in the Atlantic Ocean off the north-west coast of Africa, forming an autonomous region of Portugal and comprising the islands of Madeira and Porto Santo as well as the uninhabited Ilhas Desertas and Ilhas Selvagens; area 794 sq. km. (307 sq. miles); pop. (1991) 262,690. Known to the Phoenicians, the islands were, in the 1st c. BC, called the Insulae Purpuriae after the purple dye produced there. In 1419 they were rediscovered by the Portuguese navigator João Gonçalves Zarco. Occupied by the Spanish (1580–1640) and the British (1807–14), the Madeiras gained a degree of autonomy in 1980. Tourism, fishing, and the production of sugarcane, wine, fruit, and embroidery are important industries. Funchal (the regional capital) and Machico are the chief ports.

**Madhya Pradesh** /ˌmɑːdɪə prə'deʃ/ a state in central India; area 443,446 sq. km. (171,261 sq. miles); pop. (1991) 66,135,860; capital, Bhopal. Formed in 1956, it is the largest of the states of India. Although its economy is dominated by the production of agricultural crops including rice, wheat, pulses, and cotton, Madhya Pradesh is rich in minerals including bauxite, iron ore, manganese, coal, and limestone.

**Madison** /'mædɪs(ə)n/ the state capital of Wisconsin, USA, on an isthmus between Lake Mendota and Lake Monona; pop. (1990) 191,260. Founded as state capital in 1837 and named after President James Madison, it is a cultural and manufacturing centre associated with the architect Frank Lloyd Wright and the Prairie School movement. Madison is the home of the University of Wisconsin-Madison (1845).

**Madison Square Gardens** an arena for sporting events built in 1968 on the site of the former Pennsylvania Station in New York City, USA. It replaced an earlier structure on Eighth Avenue at 50th Street, a popular venue for circuses and boxing matches. The original Madison Square Garden, noted for its roof garden restaurant, occupied a converted station in Madison Square until it was demolished in 1925.

**Madras** /mə'drɑːs, -æs/ **1.** a seaport on the east coast of India, capital of the state of Tamil Nadu; pop. (1991) 5,361,470. Established in 1639 by a British merchant named Francis Day and expanded in the 17th c. as a fortified settlement called Fort St. George, Madras developed as a leading centre of the East India Company to become India's third-largest city. It has textile mills, tanneries, chemical plants, and engineering and car works. **2.** the former name (until 1968) of Tamil Nadu.

**Madrid** /mə'drɪd/ the capital and largest city of Spain, situated on a high plateau almost exactly in the centre of the country; pop. (1991) 2,984,580. It replaced Valladolid as capital of Spain in 1561. Its most noted buildings include the 18th-c. Royal Palace and the Prado art gallery. It is Spain's second-largest industrial centre (after Barcelona) and has aircraft, electrical, and agricultural machinery industries.

**Madura** /mə'dʊərə/ an island of Indonesia off the north-east coast of Java, 160 km. (100 miles) long and 30 km. (19 miles) wide. Its chief town is Pamekasan. Once an important source of salt, the economy of the island is now largely dependent on tobacco farming and cattle breeding. Between August and October tourists visit Madura to see the bull races (*Kerapan Sapi*).

**Madurai** /ˌmɑːdʊ'raɪ/ a city in Tamil Nadu, southern India, on the River Vaigai; pop. (1991) 1,093,700. Once a centre of Tamil culture, Madurai was capital of the Pandiya kingdom until captured in the 14th c. by the Hindu Vijayanagar kings who enriched the architectural heritage of the city with many fine temples. From 1565 until the advent of British rule Madurai was ruled by the warrior Nayaka dynasty.

**Maeander** /miːˈændə(r)/ (Turkish **Menderes**) the ancient name of a river in western Turkey that rises near Afyon and flows west for c. 384 km. (240 miles) to the Aegean. Its legendary wanderings gave rise to the English word 'meander'.

**Maebashi** /maːjəˈbaːʃɪ/ the capital of Gumma prefecture in the Kanto region of central Honshu Island, Japan, situated north-west of Tokyo; pop. (1990) 286,260.

**maelstrom** /ˈmeɪlstrəm/ a term used to describe a great whirlpool or a state of confusion. It takes its name from a powerful current in the Arctic Ocean with a dangerous and legendary tidal race that is funnelled through a channel in the Lofoten Islands off the north-west coast of Norway. Mariners used to tell tall tales of ships from miles around being drawn into its violent whirlpool.

**Mafeking** /ˈmæfɪkɪŋ/ (also **Mafikeng**) a town in the former South African homeland of Bophuthatswana, made famous when a small British force under the command of Baden-Powell was besieged by the Boers for 215 days in 1899–1900. Although the town was of little strategic importance, its successful defence, at a time when the Boer War was going very badly for the British, excited great interest, while its relief was hailed almost with a national sense of jubilation. In 1980 its name reverted to its original form, Mafikeng (Tswana = place of stones), when it was ceded to the newly independent homeland of Bophuthatswana and in 1994 it became capital of the newly created North West province.

**Mafra** /ˈmæfrə/ a town in west-central Portugal, 50 km. (30 miles) north-west of Lisbon, with a massive Baroque convent-palace built in 1717–30 by João V and Queen Maria Ana of Austria in thanksgiving for the birth of a son.

**Magadan** /maːɡəˈdaːn/ a port, naval base, and administrative centre in east Siberia, Russia, on the north shore of the Sea of Okhotsk; pop. (1990) 154,000.

**Magadha** /ˈmaːɡədə/ an ancient kingdom of north-east India that flourished from the 7th c. BC to c. AD 325 when it was conquered by Chandragupta, founder of the Mauryan empire.

**Magadi** /məˈɡaːdɪ/, **Lake** a salt lake in the Great Rift Valley, in southern Kenya, with extensive deposits of sodium and other minerals. It supports many flamingos and other water birds.

**Magdalena** /ˌmæɡdəˈleɪnə/ the principal river of Colombia, rising in the Andes and flowing northwards for about 1,600 km. (1,000 miles) to enter the Caribbean Sea at Barranquilla.

**Magdalenian** /ˌmæɡdəˈliːnɪən/ an archaeological term describing the latest palaeolithic industry of Europe, named after the type-site at La Madeleine in the Dordogne region of France and dated to c. 15,000–11,000 BC. It is characterized by a range of bone and horn tools, including elaborate bone harpoons; cave art reached a zenith during this period.

**Magdeburg** /ˈmæɡdɪˌbɜːɡ/ an industrial city and river port of Germany, the capital of Saxony-Anhalt, situated on the River Elbe and linked to the Rhine and Ruhr by the Mittelland Canal; pop. (1991) 275,240. It produces machinery, chemicals, and scientific instruments. It was the site in 1657 of the famous experiment which demonstrated the pressure of air.

**Magellan** /məˈɡelən/, **Strait of** a passage through the islands of Tierra del Fuego at the southern tip of South America, connecting the Atlantic and Pacific Oceans. It is named after Ferdinand Magellan who discovered it in October 1520. It was a dangerous passage for sailing ships and safer for steamships. Its importance declined with the opening of the Panama Canal.

**Magenta** /məˈdʒentə/ a town in Lombardy, northern Italy, to the west of Milan; pop. (1990) 23,780. It was the site of a battle in 1859 at which the Austrians were defeated by a combined French and Sardinian army. In honour of the victory, the textile town's name was given to a brilliant mauvish-crimson aniline dye.

**Maggiore** /ˌmædʒɪˈɔːreɪ/, **Lake** (Italian **Lago Maggiore**) the second-largest of the lakes of northern Italy, extending into the canton of Ticino in southern Switzerland; area 212 sq. km. (82 sq. miles). Resorts on its shores include Arona, Ispra, Stresa, and Locarno.

**Maghreb** /ˈmæɡrɪb, ˈmʌɡrəb/ (also **Maghrib**) a region of north and north-west Africa between the Atlantic Ocean and Egypt which has both a cultural and geographical unity. It comprises the coastal plain and Atlas Mountains of Morocco, together with Algeria, Tunisia, and sometimes parts of Mauretania, Chad, Mali, and Libya, forming a well-defined zone bounded by sea or desert. It formerly included Moorish Spain. In 1989 Algeria, Morocco, Tunisia, Libya, and Mauretania formed an economic union called the Grand Maghreb, designed to promote a regional common market in an area with a population of c. 62 million people. (Arabic = west)

**Maginot Line** /ˈmæʒɪˌnəʊ/ the line of defensive fortifications built along France's north-eastern frontier from Switzerland to Luxembourg, completed in 1936, in which the French placed excessive confidence. Partly because of objections from the Belgians, who were afraid they would be left in an exposed position, the line was not extended along the Franco-Belgian frontier to the coast. Consequently, although the defences proved impregnable to frontal assault, the line could be outflanked, and this happened when the Germans invaded France in the spring of 1940. It is named after the French Minister of War André Maginot (1877–1932).

**Maglemosian** /ˌmæɡləˈməʊzɪən/ the name given by archaeologists to the first mesolithic industries in northern Europe, named after the type-site Maglemose, a bog (Danish *magle mose* = great moss or bog) at Mullerup in Denmark, and dated to c. 8300–6500 BC. The people were fishers and fowlers, hunting game and gathering natural crops (hazel nuts were relished), but not cultivating crops deliberately nor domesticating animals (except for dogs of a wolfish type).

**Magnesia** /mæɡˈniːzɪə/ the name of two ancient cities of Lydia in Asia Minor (now part of western Turkey): **1. Magnesia on the Maeander**, situated to the south-east of Izmir (Smyrna), was settled by Ionians who built the celebrated temple to Artemis Leukophryne. The Athenian statesman, Themistocles, fled here in 460 BC. **2. Magnesia at Sipylus**, to the north-east of Izmir on the Hermus River at the foot of Mt. Sipylus.

**magnetic pole** each of the points near the extremities of the axis of rotation of the earth where a magnetic needle dips vertically. The position of these poles varies over time, and sometimes the positions of the north and south magnetic poles are reversed.

**Magnitogorsk** /mæɡˌniːtəʊˈɡɔː(r)sk/ an industrial city in south-central Russia, in the southern Ural Mountains on the Ural River close to the border with Kazakhstan; pop. (1990) 443,000. Founded in 1921 near deposits of iron and magnetite, it has developed into a leading centre of metallurgy. Its iron was originally mined from an 'iron mountain' from which the town got is name.

**Magwe** /mæɡˈweɪ/ a port on the Irrawaddy River in the Magwe Division of west-central Burma near important gas and oilfields.

**Magyar** /ˈmæɡjɑː(r)/ a Ural-Altaic people predominant in Hungary.

**Mahabad** /ˌmɑːhəˈbɑːd/ a city in north-west Iran, near the Iraqi border, with a chiefly Kurdish population; pop. (1986) 63,000. Occupied by Soviet troops in 1941, Mahabad became the centre of a short-lived Soviet-supported Kurdish republic in 1945, which was overthrown by the Iranians in 1946.

**Mahajanga** /mæhəˈdʒɑːŋɡə/ (also **Majunga**) a port on the north-west coast of Madagascar, on the Mozambique Channel at the mouth of the Betsiboka which is Madagascar's longest river; pop. (1990) 121,970. Capital and commercial centre of the former Boina kingdom in the mid-18th c., it is now capital of Mahajanga province and one of the chief ports of Madagascar.

**Mahalapye** /mæhəˈlæpjeɪ/ a town on the eastern edge of the Kalahari Desert in eastern Botswana, between Gaborone and Francistown; pop. (1991) 28,000.

**Mahanadi** /məˈhɑːnədiː/ a river in central India that rises in the Eastern Ghats and flows 885 km. (550 miles) north through Orissa to join the Bay of Bengal near Cuttack.

**Maharashtra** /ˌmɑːhəˈræʃtrə/ a large state in western India, bordering on the Arabian Sea, formed in 1960 from the south-eastern part of the former Bombay state; area 307,690 sq. km. (118,845 sq. miles); pop. (1991) 78,748,215; capital, Bombay.
**Maharashtrian** *adj. & n.*

**Mahaweli** /ˌmæhɑːˈweɪlɪ, məˈhɑːvəlɪ/ the largest river in Sri Lanka. Rising in the central highlands, it flows 330 km. (206 miles) to meet the Bay of Bengal near Trincomalee.

**Mahayana** /ˌmɑːhəˈjɑːnə/ the more general form of Buddhism. It survived in India until the Muslim era and also spread to Central Asia, China, Japan, Java, and Sumatra. The stress of the ancient schools (e.g. Theravada) on personal enlightenment is superseded by the ideal of the bodhisattva who postpones his own salvation for the love of others.

**Mahilyou** /ˈmɑːhɪˌljaʊ/ an industrial city and railway centre in eastern Belorussia (Belarus), on the River Dnieper east of Minsk; pop. (1990) 363,000. Until the dissolution of the Soviet Union in 1991 it was known as Mogilev. Industries include metal goods, building materials, and chemicals.

**Mahón** /məˈhɒn/ (also **Port Mahon**) the seaport capital of the island of Minorca in the Balearic Islands; pop. (1991) 21,800. Thought to have been founded by the Carthaginians, the town was held by the Moors between the 8th and 13th centuries and by the British from 1708 to 1783. It gives its name to mayonnaise (*mahonnaise*) a creamy salad dressing made of egg-yolk, oil, and vinegar.

**Mahore**
/məˈhɔː(r)/ (French
**Mayotte** /mæˈjɒt/) a
small island group in
the Indian Ocean
east of the Comoro
Islands, administered
by France. It comprises the main island of La Grande

Terre with an area of 362 sq. km. (140 sq. miles) and pop. (1991) 94,410, and the smaller island of La Petite Terre (or Pamanzi) with an area of 11 sq. km. (4 sq. miles) and pop. (1985) 9,775. Its capital is Mamoutzou (on La Grande Terre); its official language is French and its chief spoken language is Mahorian, an Arabized dialect of Swahili. Mahore became a French colony in 1843 and was attached to the Comoros until that island group became independent in 1974, at which time the people of Mahore voted to remain a French dependency. In

1976 the island became an overseas collectivity of France. Its chief products are coffee, cinnamon, copra, vanilla, cloves, and essence of ylang-ylang.

**Mahratta** see MARATHA.

**Mahratti** see MARATHI.

**Maiden Castle** /'meɪd(ə)n/ a prehistoric fort on a chalk hill in Dorset, southern England, occupied from Neolithic to Iron Age times.

**Maidenhead** /'meɪd(ə)n,hed/ a town in Berkshire, southern England, on the River Thames to the west of London; pop. (1981) 60,460. Printing, boat building, engineering, and the production of chemicals are important industries.

**Maidstone** /'meɪdstəʊn/ the county town of Kent in south-east England, on the River Medway; pop. (1991) 133,200. It was the birthplace of the essayist William Hazlitt (1778–1830). A market town with brewing, paper-making, and agricultural industries.

**Maiduguri** /maɪ'duːgərɪ/ an industrial and market town in north-east Nigeria, capital of Borno state; pop. (est. 1986) 262,000. Has palm oil mills, and shoe and cotton manufactures.

**Maikop** /maɪ'kɒp/ (also **Maykop**) a town in Adygi autonomous region, southern Russia, in the northern foothills of the Caucasus south-east of Krasnodar; pop. (1990) 120,000.

**Main** /maɪn/ a river in western Germany that rises in the Fichtelgebirge in northern Bavaria and flows 500 km. (310 miles) westwards through Frankfurt to meet the Rhine at Mainz.

**Mai-Ndombe** /,maɪən'dɒmbɪ/ a lake in western Zaire formery known as Lake Leopold II. It is subject to seasonal variation in area.

**Maine** /meɪn/ a north-eastern state of the USA, on the Atlantic coast; area 86,156 sq. km. (33,265 sq. miles); pop. (1990) 1,227,930; capital, Augusta. Its largest city is Portland. Maine is also known as the Pine Tree State. Visited by John Cabot in 1498 and colonized from England in the 17th–18th c., it became the 23rd state of the US in 1820. Maine is a major producer of pulp and paper products, sardines, lobsters, and shoes; potatoes, blueberries, apples, dairy products, poultry, and eggs are the chief agricultural products. A popular summer vacation area for hunters, anglers, canoeists, and campers, its major tourist attractions include Acadia National Park, St. Croix Island International Historic Site, and the northernmost section of the Appalachian National Scenic Trail. Maine is divided into 16 counties:

| County | Area | Pop. (sq. km.) | County Seat (1990) |
|---|---|---|---|
| Androscoggin | 1,240 | 105,260 | Auburn |
| Aroostook | 17,475 | 86,940 | Houlton |
| Cumberland | 2,278 | 243,135 | Portland |
| Franklin | 4,417 | 29,010 | Farmington |
| Hancock | 3,996 | 46,950 | Ellsworth |
| Kennebec | 2,278 | 115,900 | Augusta |
| Knox | 962 | 36,310 | Rockland |
| Lincoln | 1,191 | 30,360 | Wiscasset |
| Oxford | 5,338 | 52,600 | South Paris |
| Penobscot | 8,918 | 146,600 | Bangor |
| Piscataquis | 10,364 | 18,650 | Dover-Foxcroft |
| Sagadahoc | 668 | 33,535 | Bath |
| Somerset | 10,218 | 49,770 | Skowhegan |
| Waldo | 1,898 | 33,020 | Belfast |
| Washington | 6,724 | 35,310 | Machias |
| York | 2,621 | 164,590 | Alfred |

**Maine-et-Loire** /meɪn eɪ lwɑː/ a department in the Pays de la Loire region of western France; area 7,166 sq. km. (2,768 sq. miles) pop. (1990) 705,880; capital, Angers.

**Mainz** a city in west Germany at the confluence of the Rhine and the Main, capital of the Rhineland-Palatinate state; pop. (1991) 182,870. An ancient market town, it holds Germany's biggest wine market each year. It has a university founded in 1477. Printing was developed here c. 1448 by Johannes Gutenberg. There is a museum of printing which holds a Gutenberg Bible printed in 1452–5.

**Maipo** /'maɪpəʊ/ (also **Maipú**) **1.** a river in central Chile that flows westwards from the Andes to the Pacific through a valley noted for its wine production. **2.** a volcano in central Chile, rising to a height of 5,290 m. (17,356 ft.) to the south-east of Santiago on the border with Argentina.

**Maitland** /'meɪtlənd/ a town in New South Wales, south-east Australia, on the Hunter River 28 km. (18 miles) north-west of Newcastle; pop. (1991) 41,570. First settled by convicts in 1818, many of its buildings date from the 1800s. It is the centre of an agricultural region.

**Majorca** /mə'jɔːkə/ (Spanish **Mallorca** /mæl'jɔːkə/) the largest of the Balearic Islands in the western Mediterranean; area 3,640 sq. km. (1,406 sq. miles); pop. (1981) 561,215; capital, Palma. Taken by James I of Aragon in 1229, it is administered by Spain as part of the Baleares autonomous region. An early form of the name Majorca, ships of which brought Spanish wares to Italy, was applied to an Italian earthenware (*majolica*) of the Renaissance period with coloured ornamentation on white enamel.

**Majunga** see MAHAJANGA.

**Majuro** /mə'dʒʊ(ə)rəʊ/ the capital of the Marshall Islands in the western Pacific, a tropical atoll in the eastern Ratak chain; pop. (1990) 20,000.

**Makalu** /'məkə,luː/ a mountain of the Himalayas on the frontier between Nepal and China. Rising to 8,481 m. (27,824 ft.), it is the fifth highest mountain in the world. Its peak was first reached in 1955 by a French expedition.

**Makassar** /mə'kæsə(r)/ (also **Makasar** or **Macassar**) the former name (until c. 1970) of UJUNG PANDANG.

**Makassar Strait** a stretch of water separating the islands of Borneo and Sulawesi (Celebes) and linking the Sulawesi Sea in the north with the Java Sea in the south.

**Makgadikgadi Pans** /ˌmægə'di:ˌgədɪ/ an extensive area of shallow salt-pans in north-central Botswana, the remnants of a much larger prehistoric lake. The north-western corner of the Pans has been designated a game reserve and during the dry season from April to October the area attracts large numbers of game animals and birds.

**Makhachkala** /mə'xætʃkəlɑ:/ a port in south-west Russia, on the Caspian Sea, capital of the republic of Dagestan; pop. (1990) 327,000. Situated in the northern Caucasus, it has oil refineries and industries producing chemicals, textiles, machinery, and foodstuffs. It was known as Port Petrovsk until 1922, when it was renamed after the Dagestan revolutionary Makhach.

**Makkah** SEE MECCA.

**Makonde** a Bantu people of the southern Highlands of Tanzania noted for their wood carvings.

**Malabar Coast** /'mælə,bɑ:(r)/ the southern part of the west coast of India, including the coastal region of Karnataka and most of the state of Kerala. It is named from the Malabars, an ancient Dravidian people.

**Malabar Christians** a group of Christians of south-west India, tracing their origin to St. Thomas, who according to their tradition landed in these parts and is supposedly buried in Madras.

**Malabo** /mə'lɑ:bəʊ/ the seaport capital of Equatorial Guinea, situated on the island of Bioko (formerly Fernando Póo) in the Gulf of Guinea; pop. (1988) 37,000. It was formerly (until 1973) known as Santa Isabel and while under British rule in the 1820s was named Port Clarence or Clarence-town. It exports cocoa and timber.

**Malacca** /mə'lækə/ a former Muslim sultanate on the west coast of Malaya, which flourished from about 1403 to 1511, when it was conquered by the Portuguese. It played an important role in the development of trade between Europe and the East, especially China. (See also MELAKA.)

**Malacca, Strait of** the channel between the Malaysia peninsula and the Indonesian island of Sumatra, an important sea passage linking the Indian Ocean to the South China Sea. The ports of Melaka and Singapore lie on this strait.

**Málaga** /'mæləgə/ a seaport at the mouth of the Guadalmedina River on the Andalusian coast of southern Spain, capital of the province of Málaga; pop. (1991) 524,750. It gives its name to a sweet wine produced locally. It has light industries and is a popular resort. There are ferry links with North Africa and Genoa.

**Malagasy** the people of Madagascar or their Malayo-Polynesian language which is related to Malay.

**Malang** /mə'lɑ:ŋ/ a hill resort in eastern Java, Indonesia, situated on the Brantas River 80 km. (50 miles) south of Surabaya at an altitude of 450 m. (1,475 ft.); pop. (1990) 695,100.

**Mälar** /'melɑ:r/, **Lake** (Swedish **Mälaren**) a lake in south-east Sweden, extending inland from the Baltic Sea. The city of Stockholm is situated at its outlet; area 1,140 sq. km. (440 sq. miles).

**Malatya** /mə'lɑ:tjə/ **1.** a mountainous province in east-central Turkey; area 11,752 sq. km. (4,539 sq. miles); pop. (1990) 702,055. **2.** its capital, near the Euphrates in the Taurus Mts.; pop. (1990) 281,780. Known in ancient times as Melitene, it was the capital of a Hittite kingdom and later an important Roman military outpost. It is the commercial centre for a rich agricultural region.

**Malawi** /mə'lɑ:wɪ/ a country of south-central Africa, bounded by Mozambique, Tanzania, and Zambia; area 118,484 sq. km. (45,764 sq. miles); pop. (est. 1991)
8,796,000; official language, English; capital, Lilongwe. Its largest cities are Blantyre and Lilongwe. The Great Rift Valley runs through the country from north to south and much of the eastern border is formed by Lake Malawi (Lake Nyasa), the third-largest lake in Africa. East and west of the Rift Valley are high plateaux and in the south the Shire Highlands rise to 3,048 m. (10,000 ft.) at Mt. Mulanje. The climate is subtropical and the economy is predominantly agricultural, the chief export crops being tobacco, tea, coffee, sugar, cotton, and groundnuts. Malawi, which derives its name from the Maravi, a Bantu people who came from the southern Congo c. 600 years ago, is a land-

MALAYSIA

locked country, heavily dependent on Mozambique for access to the sea. It is the former Nyasaland, a British protectorate from 1891 (following Livingstone's exploration), and from 1953 to 1963 a part of the Federation of Rhodesia and Nyasaland; it became an independent Commonwealth state under President Hastings Banda in 1964, and a republic in 1966. It was ruled as a single-party state until 1994 when the first multiparty elections were held. Malawi is governed by an executive president and a unicameral National Assembly.

**Malawian** *adj. & n.*

Malawi is divided into three regions:

| Region | Area (sq. km.) | Pop. (1987) | Capital |
|--------|------|------|---------|
| Northern | 26,931 | 907,120 | Mzuzu |
| Central | 35,592 | 3,116,040 | Lilongwe |
| Southern | 31,756 | 3,959,450 | Blantyre |

**Malawi, Lake** another name for Lake Nyasa. See NYASA, LAKE.

**Malay** /məˈleɪ/ the language of the Malay people of Malaysia and Indonesia. It belongs to the Malayo-Polynesian language group and is spoken mainly in Malaysia where it is the mother tongue of about half the population (9 million) and the official language. Meaning is shown by the order and grouping of words, not by inflexions. It is virtually the same language as Indonesian. From the 14th c. Malay was written in Arabic script but in the 19th c. the British constructed a roman-based alphabet which is in general use today.

**Malayan** *adj. & n.*

**Malaya** /məˈleɪə/ a former country in south-east Asia, consisting of the southern part of the Malay peninsula and some adjacent islands (originally including Singapore), now forming the western part of the federation of Malaysia, and known as West Malaysia. Malaya was dominated by the Buddhist kingdom of Srivijaya from the 9th to the 14th century and by the Hindu kingdom of Majaphit in the 14th c. Islam was introduced with the rise of the princely states, especially Malacca, in the 15th c. The area was opened up by the Dutch and Portuguese, and eventually Britain became dominant, investing heavily in rubber plantations using much immigrant labour from China and India. The several Malay states federated under British control in 1896. Malaya was occupied by the Japanese from 1941 to 1945. After the war, Britain fought a successful 12-year campaign against Communist guerrillas, mainly Chinese. The country became independent in 1957, the federation expanding into Malaysia in 1963. (See also MALAYSIA.)

**Malayalam** /ˌmæləˈjɑːləm/ the Dravidian language of the state of Kerala in south-west India.

**Malay Archipelago** a very large group of islands, including Sumatra, Java, Borneo, the Philippines, and New Guinea, lying south-east of Asia and north and north-east of Australia. It is the largest island group in the world and constitutes the bulk of the area formerly known as the East Indies.

**Malayo-Polynesian** (also **Austronesian**) a family of languages extending from Madagascar in the west to the Pacific in the east. They are spoken by some 150 million people of whom all but one million speak a language of the Indonesian group, such as Indonesian, Tagalog, or Malagasy. The other groups are Micronesian, Melanesian, and Polynesian.

**Malay peninsula** a peninsula in south-east Asia separating the Indian Ocean from the South China Sea. It extends approximately 1,100 km. (700 miles) southwards from the Isthmus of Kra and comprises the southern part of Thailand and the whole of Malaya (West Malaysia).

**Malaysia** /məˈleɪʒə, -ˈleɪzɪə/ a country in south-east Asia, a federation composed of East Malaysia

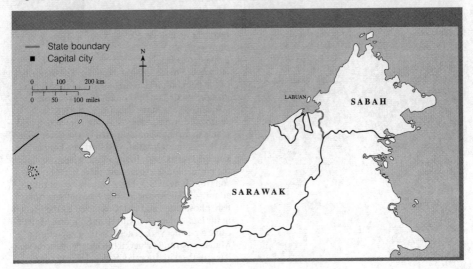

State boundary
Capital city

0  100  200 km
0  50  100 miles

N

LABUAN

SABAH

SARAWAK

(the northern part of Borneo, including Sarawak and Sabah) and West Malaysia (the Malayan Peninsula south of Thailand), separated from each other by 650 km. (400 miles) of the South China

Sea; area 329,758 sq. km. (127,369 sq. miles); pop. (est. 1991) 18,294,000; official language, Bahasa Malaysia; capital, Kuala Lumpur. Its largest cities are Kuala Lumpur, Ipoh, and George Town. West Malaysia, with a central ridge of mountains, and East Malaysia are covered by extensive jungle and swamp producing ebony, teak, sandalwood, and other tropical forest products. West Malaysia is the world's leading producer of palm oil and rubber and leading exporter of tin, while East Malaysia, although considerably less developed, is an important exporter of oil. Dominated by the Buddhist Malay kingdom of Srivijaya from the 9th to 14th c. and by the Hindu kingdom of Majaphit in the 14th c., the Malays were converted to Islam with the rise of the princely state of Malacca in the 15th c. The area was opened up by the Dutch and Portuguese in the 16th and 17th c., but was under British influence from the early 19th c. It federated as an independent state of the Commonwealth in 1963 despite opposition from its neighbours Indonesia and the Philippines. The Federation of Malaysia is a parliamentary monarchy ruled on a five-year rotation by each of the nine hereditary Malay rulers and by a bicameral legislature comprising a Senate (*Dewan Negara*) and a House of Representatives (*Dewan Rakyat*).
**Malaysian** *adj. & n.*

Malaysia is divided into 13 states and two federal territories:

| State | Area (sq. km.) | Pop. (1990) | Capital |
|---|---|---|---|
| Johore | 18,985 | 2,106,500 | Johor Baharu |
| Kedah | 9,425 | 1,412,800 | Alor Setar |
| Kelantan | 14,931 | 1,220,100 | Kota Baharu |
| Melaka | 1,658 | 627,400 | Melaka |
| Negri Sembilan | 6,646 | 723,800 | Seremban |
| Pahang | 35,960 | 1,054,800 | Kuantan |
| Penang | 1,033 | 1,142,200 | George Town |
| Perak | 21,005 | 2,222,200 | Ipoh |
| Perlis | 795 | 187,700 | Kangar |
| Sabah | 73,613 | 1,348,400 | Kota Kinabalu |
| Sarawak | 124,449 | 1,669,000 | Kuching |
| Selangor | 7,956 | 1,978,000 | Shah Alam |
| Terengganu | 12,955 | 752,000 | Kuala Terrengganu |

| Federal Territory | Area (sq. km.) | Pop. (1990) | Capital |
|---|---|---|---|
| Kuala Lumpur | 243 | 1,237,900 | Kuala Lumpur |
| Labuan | 98 | 16,500 | Victoria |

**Maldives**
/'mɔːldaɪvz/ official name **The Republic of Maldives** a country consisting of a chain of coral islands in the Indian Ocean south-west of Sri Lanka; area 298 sq. km. (115 sq. miles);

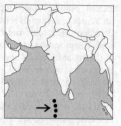

pop. (est. 1991) 221,000; official language, Dhivehi, a form of Sinhalese; capital, Malé. Of the 1,190 islands which are grouped into 19 atolls protected by coral reefs, 202 are inhabited. They are warm and humid and experience south-westerly monsoons from April to October. Fishing, tourism, and the production of copra and coconuts are the islanders' chief sources of income. Inhabited by a seafaring Islamic people, the Maldives were a British protectorate from 1887 until they became independent under the rule of a sultan in 1965 and then a republic in 1968, with a limited form of membership of the Commonwealth since 1982. The country, which has no political parties, is governed by a unicameral Citizens' Assembly (*Majlis*).
**Maldivian** *adj. & n.*

**Maldonado** /ˌmældəˈnɑːdəʊ/ a port at the mouth of the River Plate in Uruguay, capital of the province of Maldonado; pop. (1985) 33,500.

**Malé** /'mɑːli/ the capital and largest atoll of the Maldives, in the Indian Ocean; pop. (est. 1991) 55,130.

**Malegaon** /'mɑːləgaʊn/ a city in the state of Maharashtra, west-central India, at the junction of the Girna and Masam rivers; pop. (1991) 342,430.

**Mali** /'mɑːlɪ/ official name **The Republic of Mali** a landlocked country in West Africa, south of Algeria; area 1,240,192 sq. km. (479,024 sq. miles); pop. (est. 1991) 8,706,000; official

language, French; capital, Bamako. The majority of the population belongs to tribes of the Mande group. Situated on the boundary between the African Sahel and the Sahara, Mali stretches southwards from a desert environment across arid plains to savanna lands watered by the River Niger on the southern frontier with Burkina, Guinea, and the Ivory Coast. In the south, where most of the population is to be found, there is a rainy season from June to October. A largely agricultural country, Mali exports livestock, peanuts, cotton, fish, phosphates, and salt. Colonized by the French in the late 19th c. (and known as Soudan), Mali became a partner with Senegal in the Federation of Mali in 1959 and achieved full independence a year later on the withdrawal of Senegal. From 1968 it

was ruled by a Military Committee for National Liberation which was eventually overthrown during a military coup in 1991. A single-party state since 1979, Mali voted for multiparty rule in 1992. The country is governed by an executive president and a National Assembly.
**Malian** *adj. & n.*

**Malibu** /'mælɪbuː/ a fashionable resort to the west of Los Angeles on the Pacific coast of California, USA; pop. (est. 1990) 7,000. It is noted for its surf and secluded beaches and its private Malibu Beach Colony is home to some of the film industry's biggest stars. The J. Paul Getty Museum, one of the world's greatest private art collections, is in Malibu.

**Malindi** a seaport of Kenya, on the Indian Ocean near the mouth of the Athi River; pop. (1979) 23,000. Vasco da Gama visited Malindi in 1497 and erected a large cross of Lisbon stone as a navigational aid. Nearby is Malindi Marine National Park.

**Malines** the French name for MECHELEN.

**Malin Head** /'mælɪn/ a point on the coast of County Donegal, the northernmost point of Ireland. The shipping forecast area *Malin* covers the Atlantic north of Ireland and west of the southern half of Scotland.

**Mallee Region** /mæ'liː/ a region of north-west Victoria, Australia, between the Wimmera and Murray rivers that takes its name from an Aboriginal word for the bush vegetation dominated by the Mallee Eucalypts. Much of the region, which overlies limestone, has been irrigated and cultivated to grow wheat.

**Mallorca** see MAJORCA.

**Malmaison** /ˌmælmeɪ'zɔ̃/ officially **Musée National du Château de Malmaison**) a French chateau, situated in the west Paris suburb of Rueil-Malmaison. Built in the early Baroque style in 1620, it was the home of Napoleon's wife, Josephine, from 1779 until her death in 1814.

**Malmédy** /ˌmælmeɪ'diː/ a tourist and manufacturing town in the Ardennes hills of eastern Belgium; pop. (1991) 10,290. Formerly in Germany it was ceded to Belgium by the Treaty of Versailles and was the scene of heavy fighting in December 1944.

**Malmesbury** /'mɑːmzbərɪ/ a hill-top town in Wiltshire, southern England, with a 12th-c. Benedictine abbey (partly ruined) in which King Athelstan (d. 940) is reputedly buried; pop. (1981) 2,550.

**Malmö** /'mælmɜː/ a port and fortified city in south-west Sweden, situated on the Øresund (The Sound) opposite Copenhagen, with which it is connected by ferry; pop. (1990) 233,900. It is the third-largest city in Sweden, capital of Malmöhus county, and an industrial centre with shipyards, chemicals, food processing, and textiles.

**Malplaquet** /ˌmælplæ'keɪ/ a village in the department of Nord in northern France, on the border with Belgium about 16 km. (10 miles) south of Mons, scene of the victory in 1709 of allied British and Austrian troops over the French.

**Malta** /'mɔːltə, 'mɒ-/ an island country in the central Mediterranean, lying about 100 km. (60 miles) south of Sicily; area 316 sq. km. (122 sq. miles); pop. (est. 1991) 356,000; official languages,  Maltese and English; capital, Valletta. Malta comprises the three low-lying islands of Malta, Gozo, and Comino and several unihabited islets including Cominotto, Filfla, and St. Paul's Island. It has a climate that is dry in the summer and mild in the winter. Malta was held in turn by Phoenicians, Greeks, Carthaginians, and Arabs, and in 1090 was conquered by Roger of Normandy. Given to the Knights of St. John by the Emperor Charles V in 1530, Malta successfully withstood a long siege by Turkish invaders and remained headquarters for the Order until captured by the French in 1798. It was annexed by Britain in 1814 and subsequently became an important naval base. During World War II the island was awarded the George Cross for its endurance under heavy air attack between 1940 and 1942. Independence was granted in 1964, but since that time, despite income from tourism, the economy has experienced considerable difficulties because of the decline of the naval base. Malta is governed by a House of Representatives.

**Maltese** the language of Malta or a native or national of that country.

**Maluku** see MOLUCCA ISLANDS.

**Malvern Hills** /'mɔːlvɜːn/ a range of hills of ancient volcanic rocks in Hereford and Worcester, west-central England. The highest point is Worcestershire Beacon (425 m., 1,394 ft.). The resort town of Great Malvern lies on its eastern edge. The area has associations with the composer Edward Elgar (1857–1934) who lived at Malvern from 1891 and is buried at Little Malvern. Jenny Lind, the Swedish soprano (1820–87) is buried at Great Malvern.

**Malvinas** /mæl'viːnəs, 'iːzlæs/, **Islas** the name by which the Falkland Islands are known in Argentina. Derived from the French *Malouines* which reflects early connections with fishermen from Saint-Malo, France.

**Mammoth Cave National Park** /'mæməθ/ a national park in west-central Kentucky, USA, designated in 1926 to protect one of the longest known cave systems in the world. Situated on the edge of Kentucky's sinkhole plain, it consists of over 530 km. (330 miles) of charted passageways and contains some spectacular rock formations.

**Mamoré** /'mɑːməʊˌreɪ/ a river of South America with headwaters rising in the Bolivian Andes. It flows c. 965 km. (600 miles) northwards to the Bolivia–Brazil frontier which it follows before joining the Beni River to become the Madeira River.

**Mamoutzu** /məˈmuːtsuː/ (also **Mamoudzou**) the capital of the French territory of Mahore (Mayotte) in the Indian Ocean, situated on the east coast of the island of La Grande Terre; pop. (1985) 12,120. It was designated capital in 1977 pending the transfer of government offices from Dzaoudzi on La Petite Terre.

**Manado** /məˈnɑːdəʊ/ a seaport at the north-east end of Sulawesi, Indonesia, capital of the province of North Sulawesi; pop. (1980) 217,000. A fishing port and processing centre for coconuts, cloves, and nutmeg.

**Managua** /məˈnɑːgwə/ the capital of Nicaragua, on the southern shore of Lake Managua; pop. (1985) 682,110. The city was severely damaged by earthquakes in 1931 and 1972 and also during the civil war in the late 1970s. Besides its administrative functions it is Nicaragua's chief commercial and industrial city.

**Managua, Lake** a lake in western Nicaragua that drains into Lake Nicaragua via the Tipitapa River. Managua, capital of Nicaragua, lies close to its southern shore.

**Manama** /'mænɑːmə/ (Arabic **Al Manamah**) the seaport capital of the state of Bahrain, on Bahrain Island in the Persian Gulf; pop. (est. 1988) 151,500. It is a centre of banking, commerce, and oil refining.

**Mana Pools** /'mɑːnə/ a national park in Zimbabwe, in the Zambezi valley, north-east of Lake Kariba. It was established in 1963.

**Manaslu** /məˈnɑːsluː/ a mountain massif of the Himalayas in central Nepal whose highest peak rises to 8,156 m. (26,760 ft.). It was first climbed by a Japanese expedition in 1956. A later expedition in 1974 was the first ascent of an 8,000 m. peak by women.

**Manas Wildlife Sanctuary** /məˈnɑːs/ a wildlife sanctuary in Assam, north-east India, in the foothills of the Himalayas south and east of the River Manas. Extending over 2,800 sq. km. (1,081 sq. miles) of tall grass and forest, it has at its core the 360-sq. km. (140-sq. mile) Manas Tiger Reserve which was demarcated in 1927 when the conservation programme 'Project Tiger' was launched.

**Manassas** /məˈnæsəs/ a western suburb of Washington, DC, a key railroad junction during the American Civil War and the site of the battles of Bull Run in 1861 and 1862.

**Manaus** /məˈnaʊs/ a city in north-west Brazil, near the junction of the Rio Negro with the

Amazon; pop. (1991) 1,011,000. It is capital of the state of Amazonas and the principal commercial centre of the upper Amazon region. A major (free) port although 1,600 km. (1,000 miles) from the sea. It has a famous opera house, built in 1896 towards the end of the wild-rubber 'boom'.

**Manawatu** /ˌmænəˈwɑːtuː/ a river of North Island, New Zealand, that rises on the eastern slopes of the Ruahine Range and flows eastwards and southwards into the Cook Strait.

**Manawatu Gorge** a ravine separating the Ruahine and Tararua ranges of North Island, New Zealand.

**Manawatu-Wanganui** /-wɑːˈŋgəˈnuːɪ/ a region of North Island, New Zealand, created in 1989 and comprising the city of Palmerston North and districts of Wanganui, Manawatu, Horowhenua, Ruapehu, Tararua, and parts of Rangitikei and Waitomo; pop. (1991) 226,620.

**Manche** /mɑ̃ʃ/ a department in the Basse Normandie region of western France; area 5,938 sq. km. (2,293 sq. miles); pop. (1990) 479,640; capital, St.-Lô.

**Manchester** /'mæntʃestə(r)/ (Latin **Mancunium**) an industrial city in the metropolitan county of Greater Manchester, north-west England, on the River Irwell; pop. (1991) 397,400. Founded in Roman times, it developed in the 17th c. as a textile town that eventually became the centre of the English cotton industry. Manchester's built-up area merges with surrounding towns, such as Salford and Stockport. It is a banking centre second in Britain only to London and also has printing and publishing industries. During the 19th c. it gave its name to the Manchester School of Economics and was the headquarters of the Anti-Corn Law League led by Richard Cobden and John Bright. It was the birthplace in 1785 of the writer Thomas de Quincey. Manchester is the site of the University of Manchester (1880), the University of Manchester Institute of Science and Technology (1824), and Manchester Metropolitan University (formerly Manchester Polytechnic). Its magnificent Victorian public buildings include the Town Hall and Free Trade Hall. It is the home of the famous Hallé Orchestra and the equally f amous Manchester United soccer club. **Mancunian** adj. & n.

**Manchester Ship Canal** a waterway in north-west England, linking the city of Manchester to the Irish Sea. Opened in 1894, it is 57 km. (36 miles) long.

**Manchu** /mænˈtʃuː/ **1.** a member of a Tartar people who conquered China and founded the Ch'ing dynasty (1644–1912). **2.** their language, which belongs to the Tungusic group in the Altaic family of languages. At one time it was an official language of China, but it is now only spoken in parts of northern Manchuria.

**Manchuria** /mænˈtʃʊərɪə/ a mountainous region of north-east China, now comprising the provinces of Jilin, Liaoning, and Heilongjiang. In 1932 it was declared an independent state by Japan and renamed *Manchukuo*; it was restored to China in 1945.

**Mancunian** /mænˈkjuːnɪən/ a native of Manchester in England.

**Mandaean** /mænˈdiːən/ **1.** a member of a Gnostic sect, surviving in Iraq, who revere John the Baptist. **2.** the Aramaic dialect in which their books are written.

**Mandalay** /ˌmændəˈleɪ/ (Burmese **Mandale**) a port on the Irrawaddy River in central Burma (Myanmar); pop. (1983) 533,000. Founded in 1857, it was the capital of the Burmese kingdom 1857–85. It is an important Buddhist religious centre with a pagoda (Kuthodaw Pagoda) within which the entire Buddhist canons are inscribed on marble slabs.

**Mandarin** /ˈmændərɪn/ the most widely spoken form of Chinese and the official language of China.

**Mande** /ˈmændɪ/ a group of Niger-Congo languages spoken in West Africa and including Malinke (Mandingo).

**Mandurah** /mænˈdʊərə/ a resort town on the coast of Western Australia, at the junction of the Murray, Serpentine, and Harvey rivers 80 km. (50 miles) south of Perth; pop. (1991) 23,340.

**Mandya** /ˈmændɪə/ a market town in Karnatka, southern India, north-east of Mysore; pop. (1991) 119,970.

**Mangalore** /ˌmæŋɡəˈlɔː(r)/ a seaport in the state of Karnataka, south-west India, on the Arabian Sea; pop. (1991) 425,785. Formerly an important centre of trade with Arab and Persian merchants, its chief export is now coffee.

**Manhattan** /mænˈhæt(ə)n/ an island near the mouth of the Hudson River, forming part of the city of New York. The site of the original Dutch settlement of New Amsterdam, it is now a borough containing the cultural and commercial centre of New York City and is famous for its skyscrapers. Among its most notable buildings are the World Trade Center, the Empire State Building, and the UN Headquarters. It takes its name from the Algonquian tribe from whom the Dutch settlers claimed to have bought the island in 1626 for $24 of merchandise.

**Manicaland** /məˈniːkəˌlænd/ a gold-mining province of eastern Zimbabwe; area 35,219 sq. km. (13,603 sq. miles); pop. (1982) 1,099,200; capital, Mutare (formerly Umtali).

**Manichee** /ˈmænɪkɪ/ an adherent of a religious system with Christian, Gnostic, and pagan elements, found in Persia in the 3rd c. by Manes (c. 216–c. 276) and spread widely in the Roman Empire and in Asia, surviving in Chinese Turkestan until the 13th c. The system was based on a supposed primeval conflict between light and darkness, teaching that matter is evil but within each person's brain is imprisoned a particle of the divine 'light' which can be released by the practice of religion, and that Christ, Buddha, the Prophets, and Manes had been sent to help in this task. Severe asceticism was practised within the sect, with the 'elect' living a more rigorous life than the 'hearers' who supported them.
**Manichaean** *adj. & n.*

**Manich Depression** /məˈnɪtʃ/ (also **Manych**) a valley with salt lakes in southern Russia, stretching between the Kuma and Don rivers to the west of Astrakhan.

**Manila** /məˈnɪlə/ the capital and chief port, financial, and industrial centre of the Philippines, on the south-west coast of the island of Luzon at the mouth of the Pasig River; pop. (1990) 1,599,000. Founded in 1571, it was an important trade centre of the Spanish until taken by the USA in 1898.
**Metro Manila**, with a population of c. 6 million, extends over 17 communities and towns including Quezon City and Caloocan. Its many industries include automobile assembly, metallurgical, chemical, and textile manufactures, as well as light industries such as food processing and pharmaceuticals.

**Manipur** /ˌmænɪˈpʊə(r)/ a small state in the north-east of India, east of Assam and south of Nagaland; area 22,327 sq. km. (8,624 sq. miles); pop. (1991) 1,826,710; capital, Imphal. Rice, grain, pulses, fruit, and timber are the chief products.

**Manisa** /məˈnɪsə/ **1.** a province in western Turkey; area 13,237 sq. km. (5,113 sq. miles); pop. (1990) 1,154,420. **2.** its capital; pop. (1990) 158,930.

**Man, Isle of** see ISLE OF MAN.

**Manitoba** /ˌmænɪˈtəʊbə/ a province of central Canada, with a coastline on Hudson Bay; area 649,950 sq. km. (250,947 sq. miles); pop. (1991) 1,091,940; capital, Winnipeg. Its largest settlements are Winnipeg, Brandon, Thompson, Portage La Prairie, and Flin Flon and its highest point is Baldy Mountain (832 m., 2,730 ft.). Ceded to Canada by the Hudson's Bay Company in 1869 and created a province of Canada in 1870, its boundaries were extended in 1881, 1884, and 1912 from the original Red River Settlement. Its economy is dependent on food processing, distilling, the manufacture of agricultural machinery, the generation of hydroelectric power and the production of wheat, sunflowers, sugar-beets, nickel, and copper.

**Manitoba, Lake** a lake in southern Manitoba, Canada, north-west of Winnipeg, linked to Lake Winnipeg by the Dauphin River; area 4,704 sq. km. (1,817 sq. miles).

**Manizales** /ˌmæniːˈsɑːleɪs/ a city in the Andes of central Colombia, situated at an altitude of 2,153 m. (7,064 ft.) in the Central Cordillera; pop. (1985) 308,780. It lies at the centre of a coffee-growing region and is capital of the department of Caldas.

**Mannar** /mæˈnɑː(r)/ **1.** an island off the north-west coast of Sri Lanka, linked to India by the chain of coral islands known as Adam's Bridge. **2.** a town on this island; pop. (1981) 14,000.

**Mannar, Gulf of** an inlet of the Indian Ocean lying between north-west Sri Lanka and the southern tip of India. It lies to the south of Adam's Bridge, which separates it from the Palk Strait.

**Mannheim** /ˈmænhaɪm/ an industrial port at the confluence of the Rhine and the Neckar in the state of Baden-Württemberg, south-west Germany; pop. (1991) 314,685. Industries include engineering, oil refining, and the production of chemicals, motor cars, and machinery.

**Mano** /ˈmɑːnəʊ/ a river of West Africa. It rises in north-west Liberia and flows to the Atlantic, forming for part of its length the boundary between Liberia and Sierra Leone. The **Mano River Union** was an economic alliance created in 1981 by Guinea, Liberia, and Sierra Leone.

**Mans, Le** see LE MANS.

**Manta** /ˈmæntə/ a city in western Ecuador, a port on the Pacific coast north-west of Guayaquil; pop. (1990) 126,000.

**Mantua** /ˈmæntjʊə/ (Italian **Mantova**) a town in Lombardy, northern Italy, on the River Mincio; pop. (1990) 54,230. The Roman poet Virgil (70–19 BC) was born nearby in the village of Andes (Pietole Virgilio) and under the Gonzaga family Mantua became an important political and artistic centre of Europe during the 14th–17th c. The artist Andrea Mantegna (1431–1516) is buried in the Church of Sant'Andrea. Now an agricultural, industrial, and tourist centre.

**Manx** /mæŋks/ **1.** of or relating to the Isle of Man or its people. **2.** the Celtic language of the Isle of Man, a dialect of Gaelic. There are no native speakers alive now but it is still in use for ceremonial purposes.

**Manzhouli** /mɑːndʒəʊˈliː/ a city in Inner Mongolia, north-eastern China, near the frontiers with Russia and Mongolia; pop. (1986) 119,000.

**Manzini** /mænˈziːniː/ a town in central Swaziland, capital of the country until 1902; pop. (1986) 18,080. The University of Swaziland and the country's international airport are located at nearby Matsaya.

**Maoming** /maʊˈmɪŋ/ a city in Guangdong province, southern China, south-west of Guangzhou (Canton); pop. (1986) 450,000.

**Maori** /ˈmaʊri/ a member of the aboriginal people of New Zealand. Having arrived there first as part of a wave of migration from Tahiti, probably in the 9th c., by 1200 they had established settlements in various parts of the islands. The Maoris ceded all their rights and powers of sovereignty to the British Crown in 1840 with the signing of the Treaty of Waitangi. Maori Wars were fought intermittently in 1845–8 and 1860–72 between Maoris and the colonial government of New Zealand over the enforced sale of Maori lands to Europeans. In 1986 the Maoris numbered 404,775.

**map** /mæp/ a flat representation of the earth's surface, or part of it, showing physical features, cities, etc. The earliest evidence of map-making stems from Babylonia, where a cadastral survey for the purpose of taxing property was used in the time of Sargon of Akkad (c. 2300 BC).

**Maputo** /məˈpuːtəʊ/ the capital and chief port of Mozambique; pop. (1991) 1,098,000. Founded as a Portuguese fortress in the late 18th c., it became the capital of Portuguese East Africa in 1907. It was known as Lourenço Marques until 1976. Maputo stands on a large natural harbour and its development was based on its transit trade with the Johannesburg area of South Africa. It is Mozambique's leading manufacturing centre.

**Maracaibo** /ˌmærəˈkaɪbəʊ/ a commercial and industrial city and port in north-west Venezuela, situated on the channel linking the Gulf of Venezuela with Lake Maracaibo; pop. (1991) 1,400,640. It is capital of the state of Zulia, the second-largest city in the country, and the 'oil capital' of South America.

**Maracaibo, Lake** (Spanish **Lago de Maracaibo**) a large lake in north-west Venezuela, linked by a narrow channel to the Gulf of Venezuela and the Caribbean; area 13,261 sq. km. (5,120 sq. miles). It is the largest lake in South America. Discovered in 1917, over 70 per cent of Venezuela's oil output comes from the lake area.

**Maracá Island** /mærəˈkɑː/ one of the world's largest riverine islands, situated in the Amazon Basin of northern Brazil and formed by the dividing and rejoining 60 km. (37 miles) downstream of the Uraricoera River, a northern headwater of the Rio Branco. It is roughly triangular in shape, measuring 25 km. (16 miles) at its widest and has an area of c. 100,000 hectares. It lies on two bio-geographical boundaries, the one between the Amazon Basin and the Guiana Shield, the other between tropical forest and savanna, and was the subject of a Royal Geographical Society research expedition during 1987–8. The Maracá Rainforest Project, involving 148 scientists and 55 technicians, was the largest multidisciplinary research effort ever organized in Amazonia by any European country.

**Maracay** /ˌmærəˈkaɪ/ the capital of the state of Aragua in northern Venezuela, at the east end of Lake Valencia; pop. (1991) 354,430 (956,660 metropolitan area). It has several grandiose buildings started by General Gómez, the Venezuelan dictator, including an unfinished opera house, bull ring, and Gómez mausoleum.

**Maradi** /məˈrɑːdiː/ an industrial and commercial town in southern Niger, between Niamey and Lake Chad and on the route to Kano in Nigeria; pop. (1988) 113,000. It takes its name from the *maradi*

(= chief of the fetishers), a title given to the regional governor of the former Katsina territory.

**Marajó** /mærə'ʒəʊ/ a large flat island at the mouth of the Amazon River, separating the Amazon from the Pará River.

**Maramba** /mə'ræmbə/ a tourist city in southern Zambia, situated about 5 km. (3 miles) from the Zambezi River and the Victoria Falls; pop. (1987) 94,640. Formerly called Livingstone in honour of the explorer David Livingstone, it was the capital of Northern Rhodesia from 1911 until Lusaka became capital in 1935. It has a Livingstone museum, and is the centre of Southern Province of which it is the capital.

**Maranhão** /ˌmærən'jɑːəʊ/ a state of north-eastern Brazil, on the Atlantic coast; area 328,663 sq. km. (126,946 sq. miles); pop. (1991) 4,929,030; capital, São Luis.

**Marañón** /ˌmæræn'jəʊn/ a river in Peru that rises in the Andes and forms one of the principal headwaters of the Amazon. Flowing north and east for *c.* 1,600 km. (1,000 miles), it joins the River Ucayali south-west of Iquitos.

**Maratha** /mə'rɑːtə, -'rætə/ (also **Mahratta**) a member of a warrior people native to the modern Indian state of Maharashtra.

**Marathi** /mə'rɑːtɪ, -'rætɪ/ (also **Mahratti**) the language of the Marathas.

**Marathon** /'mærə,θɒn/ a plain in eastern Attica, Greece, scene of a battle in 490 BC in which the Greeks under Miltiades defeated a much larger Persian army. The non-stop run of a courier named Pheidippides bringing the news to Athens has given the name to the road race.

**Marbella** /mɑː'beɪə/ a resort town in Andalusia, southern Spain, situated to the west of Málaga on the Costa del Sol; pop. (1991) 80,645.

**Marble Arch** an arch with three gateways erected in 1827 in front of Buckingham Palace, London, and moved in 1851 to its present site at the north-east corner of Hyde Park.

**Marburg** the German name for MARIBOR.

**Marche** /'mɑːkeɪ/ (English **the Marches** /'mɑːtʃɪz/) a region of east-central Italy, between the Apennines and the Adriatic Sea, comprising the provinces of Ancona, Ascoli Piceno, Macerata, and Pesaro-Urbino; area 9,692 sq. km. (3,743 sq. miles); pop. (1990) 1,435,570; capital, Ancona. Its name is derived from a word (march = boundary line) used in the early Middle Ages to denote the imperial regions of the Marca di Camerino and the Marca di Fermo, which were buffers against invasion.

**Marches, the 1.** the English name for the Italian region of MARCHE. **2.** the parts of England along the borders with Wales and (formerly) Scotland.

**Mar del Plata** /mɑː del 'plɑːtə/ a very popular resort and fishing port on the Atlantic coast of central Argentina; pop. (1991) 520,000.

**Marengo** /mə'reŋgəʊ/ a village near Turin, scene of a decisive French victory of Napoleon's campaign in Italy in 1800. After military reverses had all but destroyed French power in Italy, Napoleon crossed the Alps to defeat and capture an Austrian army, returning Italy to French possession.

**Margarita** /ˌmɑːgə'riːtə/ an island in the Caribbean Sea, off the coast of Venezuela. Visited by Columbus in 1498, it was used as a base by Simón Bolívar in 1816 in the struggle for independence from Spanish rule. The island has been a centre of pearl fishing for several hundred years and is a popular tourist resort.

**Margherita Peak** the highest of the two peaks of Mount Stanley rising to 5,109 m. (16,765 ft.) in the Ruwenzori Range on the Uganda-Zaire border west of Lake Edward.

**Mari** /'mɑːrɪ/ an ancient city on the west bank of the Euphrates in Syria. Its strategic position commanding major trade routes ensured rapid growth, and by *c.* 2500 BC it was a thriving city, influenced by Sumerian culture. Its period of greatest importance was from the late 19th to the mid-18th c. BC, when it was a kingdom with hegemony over the middle Euphrates valley. The vast palace of the last king, Zimrilim, has yielded an archive of 25,000 cuneiform tablets, which are the principal source for the history of northern Syria and Mesopotamia at that time. The city was sacked by Hammurabi of Babylon in 1759 BC.

**Mariana Islands** /ˌmærɪ'ɑːnə/ (also **Marianas**) a group of islands in the north-west Pacific, visited by Magellan in 1521 and named Las Marianas in 1668 in honour of Maria Anna (Mariana), widow of Philip IV of Spain. They comprise Guam (see entry) and the islands and atolls of the Northern Marianas. Acquired from Spain by the US in 1898, the whole group became, in 1947, part of the Trust Territory of the Pacific Islands, administered by the US; in 1975 the islanders of the Northern Marianas voted to establish a commonwealth (self-governing in 1978) in union with the US and in 1986 they became part of the United States. The three most populated islands of the Northern Marianas are Saipan, Rota, and Tinian; pop. (1990) 43,345; capital, Saipan; the official language is English, but Carolinian and Chamorro are widely spoken. In addition to tourism, the production of coffee, tobacco, fruit, coconuts, and cattle is important.

**Mariana Trench** an ocean trench in the Pacific to the south-east of the Mariana Islands, with the greatest known ocean depth (11,034 m., 36,200 ft.); its bottom was reached in 1960 by the US bathyscape *Trieste*.

**Mariánské Lázně** /mær'jænskeɪ 'lɑːʒnɪ/ (German **Marienbad** /'mærɪən,bæd/) a spa town in the West Bohemia region of the Czech Republic; pop. (1991) 15,380. Founded in the 19th c., it was a favourite resort of writers such as Gogol, Kafka, Ibsen, and Goethe.

**Marib** /'mærəb/ a ruined city 140 km. (87 miles) east of Sana'a, capital of Yemen and of the ancient Kingdom of Sheba *c.*1000 BC. The nearby dam built in the 6th c. BC was 550 m. (1,800 ft.) in length and reckoned to be one of the great engineering feats of antiquity.

**Maribor** /'mærɪbɔ:/ (German **Marburg**) an industrial city in northern Slovenia, on the River Drava near the border with Austria; pop. (1991) 103,900. It produces chemicals, armaments, and textiles.

**Marie Byrd Land** a region of Antarctica lying between Ellsworth Land and the Ross Ice Shelf, claimed for the US by Richard E. Byrd in 1929.

**Marie-Galante** /mə,ri: gæ'lǽt/ a French island in the West Indies administered as a dependency of Guadeloupe; area 158 sq. km. (61 sq. miles); pop. (1990) 13,460; capital, Grand-Bourg. It was originally named in Spanish by Christopher Columbus after his ship the *Maria Graciosa*.

**Mariehamn** /mə'rɪə,hæm(ə)n/ (Finnish **Maarianhamina**) the seaport capital of the Åland Islands in the Gulf of Bothnia; pop. (1990) 10,260. Although part of Finland, the people are predominantly Swedish-speaking.

**Mari El** /'mɑ:ri: el/, **Republic of** a republic in European Russia, 640 km. (400 miles) east of Moscow; area 23,200 sq. km. (8,955 sq. miles); pop. (1990) 754,000; capital, Yoshkar-Ola. Over 40 per cent of its population are Mari people who speak a Finnish dialect. The region was annexed by Russia in 1552 and became an autonomous region (1920) then an autonomous republic (1936) of the Soviet Union. In 1991 it became a republic of the Russian Federation. It produces timber, fruit, and vegetables.

**Marienbad** the German name for MARIÁNSKÉ LÁZNĚ in the Czech Republic.

**Marigot** /'mæri:gəʊ/ the capital of French Saint Martin in the West Indies, situated between Simpson's Bay Lagoon and the Caribbean Sea.

**Maritime Provinces** (also **Maritimes**) the Canadian provinces of New Brunswick, Nova Scotia, and Prince Edward Island, with coastlines on the Gulf of St. Lawrence and the Atlantic. These provinces, with Newfoundland and Labrador, are also known as the Atlantic Provinces.

**Maritsa** /mə'rɪtsə/ (Greek **Evros**, Turkish **Meriç**) a river of southern Europe, which rises in the Rila Mountains of south-west Bulgaria and flows 480 km. (300 miles) south to the Aegean Sea. It forms, for a small part of its length, the border between Bulgaria and Greece and then, for about 185 km. (115 miles), that between Greece and Turkey. Its ancient name is the Hebros or Hebrus.

**Mariupol** /,mæri'u:pɒl/ an industrial port on the south coast of Ukraine, on the Azov Sea; pop.

(1989) 517,000. Between 1948 and 1989 it was named Zhdanov after the Soviet Politburo official Andrei Zhdanov (1896–1948), the defender of Leningrad during the siege of 1941–4.

**Markham** /'mɑ:k(ə)m/, **Mount** a peak of the Transantarctic Mountains in Antarctica, rising to 4,351 m. (14,275 ft.).

**Marmara** /'mɑ:mərə/, **Sea of** (Turkish **Marmara Denizi**) a small sea in north-west Turkey. Connected by the Bosporus to the Black Sea and by the Dardanelles to the Aegean, it separates European Turkey from Asian Turkey. In ancient times it was known as the Propontis.

**Marmore Falls** /'mɑ:mɔ:,reɪ/ (Italian **Cascata delle Marmore**) a dramatic waterfall on the River Velino near Terni in Umbria, central Italy. It falls 165 m. (540 ft.) in three cascades and is the highest waterfall in Italy. Created artificially in 271 BC by the Romans in order to drain the Rieti marshes, its water is rich in calcium salts. Marmore is an old Italian word for marble.

**Marne** /mɑ:n/ **1.** a river of east-central France, which rises in the Langres Plateau north of Dijon and flows 525 km. (328 miles) north and west to join the Seine near Paris. Its valley was the scene of two important battles in World War I. The first battle (September 1914) halted and repelled the German advance on Paris; the second (July 1918) ended the final German offensive. **2.** a department in the Champagne-Ardenne region of north-east France; area 8,162 sq. km. (3,152 sq. miles); pop. (1990) 558,220; capital, Châlons-sur-Marne.

**Maronite** /'mærə,naɪt/ a member of a Christian sect of Syrian origin, living chiefly in Lebanon. They claim to have been founded by St. Maro, a friend of Chrysostom (d. 407), but it seems certain that their origin does not go back beyond the 7th c. Since 1181 they have been in communion with the Roman Catholic Church.

**Maroochydore** /mə'rʊtʃɪ,dəʊ(r)/ a resort town with surfing beaches and yachting facilities on the Sunshine Coast of Queensland, Australia, on the Maroochy River 112 km. (70 miles) north of Brisbane; pop. (1991) 28,510 (with Mooloolaba).

**Maroon** /mə'ru:n/ a person descended from fugitive slaves in the remoter parts of Surinam and the West Indies. The name is derived from the Spanish *cimarrón* (= untamed ones). In Jamaica the Maroons of the Cockpit Country and the Blue Mountains (Windward Maroons) waged war against the British in 1690 and 1795 (the Maroon Wars).

**Maroua** /mə'rʊə/ the chief town of northern Cameroon, situated at the junction of the Kalliao and Tsanaga rivers; pop. (1991) 143,000.

**Marquesas Islands** /mɑ:'keɪsəs/ a group of volcanic islands in the South Pacific, forming part of the overseas territory of French Polynesia; area 1,049 sq. km. (405 sq. miles); pop. (1988) 7,540; its chief settlement is Taiohae on the island of Nuku

Hiva. The islands were annexed by France in 1842. They are described by the American writer Herman Melville in his novel *Typee*, written after he visited them in 1842. The largest island is Hiva Oa, on which the French painter Paul Gaugin spent the last two years of his life (1901–3).

**Marrakesh** /ˌmærəˈkeʃ/ (also **Marrakech**) a town in western Morocco, in the northern foothills of the High Atlas Mountains, one of the four imperial cities of Morocco; pop. (1982) 439,700. It was founded in 1062 by Yusuf ibn Tashfin as capital of the Almoravides, a Moorish people whose dynasty spread from North Africa to Spain in the 11th and 12th centuries. It is a centre of tourism and winter sports and has leather and textile industries.

**Marsala** /mɑːˈsɑːlə/ a fishing port and wine-making town at the western tip of Sicily that gives its name to a dark, sweet fortified dessert wine that was originally made here; pop. (1990) 80,760. Founded by the Carthaginians in 397 BC, the town was originally known as Lilybeum before its name was changed to Marsa Allah by Arabs in the Middle Ages. In 1860 Garibaldi landed here with his 'thousand' to liberate Sicily during the Italian War of Independence.

**Marseilles** /mɑːˈseɪ, -ˈseɪlz/ (French **Marseille**) a major industrial city and port on the Mediterranean coast of southern France, to the east of the Rhône estuary; pop. (1990) 807,725. It was settled as a Greek colony, called Massilia, in about 600 BC and became an ally of the Romans in their campaigns in Gaul in the first century BC. It was an important embarkation point during the Crusades of the 11th to the 14th centuries AD and in the 19th c. served as a major port for French Algeria. It is capital of the department of Bouches-du-Rhône, the largest port and the second-largest city in France. Marseilles gives its name to the national anthem of France, the Marseillaise, which was composed by Rouget de Lisle in 1792, on the declaration of war with Austria. The city's industrialization was accelerated by the French conquest of Algeria and the opening of the Suez Canal in the 19th c. Its industries include the processing of primary products, chemicals, and ship-building.

**Marshall Islands** /ˈmɑːʃ(ə)l/ (also **Marshalls**) official name **The Republic of the Marshall Islands** a group of 34 low-lying coral islands to the east of the Carolines in the north-west

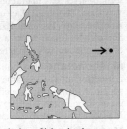

Pacific, comprising two chains of islands, the western Ralik (= sunset) group which includes Bikini, Eniwetok, Jaluit, Kwajalein, and Wotho, and the eastern Ratak (= sunrise) group which includes

Likiep, Majiro, Maloelap, Mili, and Wotje; area 181 sq. km. (70 sq. miles); pop. (1990) 43,420; official languages, English and Marshallese (a Malayo-Polynesian language); capital Darap-Uliga-Darrit on Majuro. Visited by the Spanish in 1529 and by the English adventurer John Marshall in 1788, the Marshalls were not colonized until 1885, when a German protectorate was declared. After being under Japanese mandate following World War I, they were administered by the US as part of the Pacific Islands Trust Territory from 1947 until 1986, when they became a republic in free association with the US. UN trusteeship was terminated in 1990 and the islands were admitted to the UN in 1991. Between 1946 and 1962 the territory was used for testing US atomic and hydrogen bombs (on Bikini and Enewetak atolls), and in 1982 a missile range was constructed at Kwajalein. Tourism and the production of copra are the chief economic activities. The islands are administered by an executive president, a consultative Council of Chiefs (*Iroij*), and a legislative assembly (*Nitijela*).

**Marston Moor** /ˈmɑːstən/ a moor about 11 km. (7 miles) west of York, site of the largest battle (1644) of the English Civil War, in which the combined Royalist armies of Prince Rupert and the Duke of Newcastle were defeated by the English and Scottish Parliamentary armies. The defeat destroyed Royalist power in the north of England and fatally weakened Charles's cause.

**Martaban** /ˌmɑːtəˈbɑːn/**, Gulf of** an inlet of the Andaman Sea, a part of the Indian Ocean, on the coast of south-east Burma east of Rangoon. It receives the Sittang River.

**Martha's Vineyard** /ˌmɑːθəz ˈvɪnjɑːd/ a resort island off the south-east coast of Massachusetts, USA, to the south of Cape Cod; area 280 sq. km. (108 sq miles). Its chief settlement is Edgartown. Settled in 1642 by the English who are said to have found wild grapes here, it was an important fishing and whaling centre during the 18th–19th centuries.

**Martinique** /ˌmɑːtɪˈniːk/ a volcanic Caribbean island in the Lesser Antilles between Dominica and St. Lucia, administered by France as an overseas department; area 1,079 sq. km.

(417 sq. miles); pop. (1990) 359,570; capital, Fort-de-France. Colonized by France in 1635, its former capital St. Pierre was completely destroyed by an eruption of Mount Pelée in 1902. Tourism, oil refining, and the production of fruit and rum are the chief economic activities.

**Maryborough** /ˈmeərɪˌbʌrə/ an industrial port in eastern Queensland, Australia, situated at the mouth of the Mary River between Rockhampton and Brisbane; pop. (1991) 20,790. Founded in the mid-19th c. as a port handling wool, it now lies at the centre of an area producing sugar, grain, timber, fruit, and vegetables.

**Maryland** /'meərɪ,lænd/ a state of the eastern US on the Atlantic coast, surrounding Chesapeake Bay; area 27,092 sq. km. (10,460 sq. miles); pop. (1990) 4,781,470; capital, Annapolis. Also known as the Free State or Old Line State, its largest city is Baltimore. Colonized from England in the 17th c. and named after Queen Henrietta Maria, wife of Charles I, it was one of the original 13 states of the US (1788). Vegetable canning and the manufacture of aircraft, clothing, and chemicals are important industries. Landmarks include Harpers Ferry National Historical Park, Chesapeake and Ohio Canal National Historical Park, Catoctin Mountain Park, Greenbelt Park, Fort Washington Park, Piscataway Park, and the Goddard Space Flight Center. Maryland is divided administratively into one independent city (Baltimore) and 23 counties:

| County | Area (sq. km.) | Pop. (1990) | County Seat |
|---|---|---|---|
| Allegany | 1,095 | 74,950 | Cumberland |
| Anne Arundel | 1,087 | 427,240 | Annapolis |
| Baltimore | 1,555 | 692,130 | Towson |
| Calvert | 554 | 51,370 | Prince Frederick |
| Caroline | 835 | 27,035 | Denton |
| Carroll | 1,175 | 123,370 | Westminster |
| Cecil | 936 | 71,350 | Elkton |
| Charles | 1,175 | 101,150 | La Plata |
| Dorchester | 1,542 | 30,240 | Cambridge |
| Frederick | 1,724 | 150,210 | Frederick |
| Garrett | 1,708 | 28,140 | Oakland |
| Harford | 1,165 | 182,130 | Bel Air |
| Howard | 653 | 187,330 | Ellicott City |
| Kent | 723 | 17,840 | Chestertown |
| Montgomery | 1,287 | 757,030 | Rockville |
| Prince George's | 1,266 | 729,630 | Upper Marlboro |
| Queen Anne's | 967 | 33,950 | Centreville |
| Somerset | 879 | 75,970 | Leonardtown |
| St. Mary's | 970 | 23,440 | Princess Anne |
| Talbot | 673 | 30,550 | Easton |
| Washington | 1,183 | 121,390 | Hagerstown |
| Wicomico | 985 | 74,340 | Salisbury |
| Worcester | 1,235 | 736,010 | Snow Hill |
| Talbot | 673 | 30,550 | Easton |
| Washington | 1,183 | 121,390 | Hagerstown |
| Wicomico | 985 | 74,340 | Salisbury |
| Worcester | 1,235 | 736,010 | Snow Hill |

**Masada** /mə'sɑːdə/ the site, on a steep rocky hill on the south-west shore of the Dead Sea, of the ruins of a palace and fortification built by Herod the Great in the 1st c. BC. It was a Jewish stronghold in the Zealots' revolt against the Romans (AD 66–73) and was the scene in AD 73 of a mass suicide by the Jewish defenders when the Romans breached the citadel after a siege of nearly two years.

**Masai** /'mɑːsaɪ/ (also **Maasai**) a pastoral people of mixed Hamitic stock, speaking a language of the Nilotic language group. Inhabiting some of the best grazing lands in Kenya and Tanzania, much of which has been taken up by national parks, their life and livelihood revolve around their cattle herds.

**Masai Mara** /,mɑːsaɪ 'mɑːrə/ a game reserve on the Serengeti Plains of East Africa, on the border between Kenya and Tanzania. Its open rolling grassland is noted for its abundance of wildlife which includes lion, cheetah, leopard, elephant, buffalo, giraffe, antelope, wildebeest, and zebra.

**Masan** /'mɑːsɑːn/ a port on the south coast of Korea, in South Kyonsang province; pop. (1990) 496,640. Centre of a free-trade zone set up to promote exports. Industries include textiles, flour milling, and electrical goods.

**Masaya** /mə'sɑːjə/ the chief town of the department of Masaya in western Nicaragua, situated 30 km. (19 miles) south-east of Managua in a fertile agricultural area growing tobacco; pop. (1985) 74,950.

**Masbate** /mæs'bɑːtɪ/ an island in the Visayan Islands of central Philippines, to the south of Luzon; area 4,047 sq. km. (1,563 sq. miles); pop. (1990) 599,355. Its chief town is Masbate. Formerly noted for its gold-fields, it now produces copper and cattle.

**Mascara** /'mɑːskərə/ a town in the Atlas Mountains of north-west Algeria. Built on the site of a Roman settlement, it was developed as a garrison town in a region producing tobacco, grain, and wine.

**Mascarene Islands** /,mæskə'riːn/ (also **Mascarenes**) a group of three islands in the western Indian Ocean, east of Madagascar, comprising Réunion, Mauritius, and Rodriguez. The group was named after the 16th-c. Portuguese navigator, Pedro de Mascarenhas.

**Maseru** /,mæsə'ruː/ the capital of Lesotho, a transportation centre on the Caledon River near the country's western frontier with South Africa; pop. (1986) 109,380. It was the capital of Basutoland from 1869 to 1871 and from 1884 to 1966.

**Mashhad** /mæʃ'hæd/ (also **Meshed** /mə'ʃed/) a city in north-east Iran, close to the border with Turkmenistan, capital of Korasan province and second-largest city in the country; pop. (1991) 1,759,000. The burial place in AD 809 of the Abbasid caliph Harun al-Rashid and in 818 of the Shiite leader Imam Ali Riza. It is a famous centre of carpet manufacture and textiles.

**Mashonaland** /mə'ʃəʊnə,lænd/ an area of northern Zimbabwe, occupied by the Shona people. A former province of Southern Rhodesia, it is now divided into the three provinces of Mashonaland East, West, and Central.

**Mason-Dixon Line** /,meɪs(ə)n'dɪks(ə)n/ (also **Mason and Dixon Line**) the boundary line between Pennsylvania and Maryland, which was laid out in 1763–7 by the English surveyors Charles

Mason and Jeremiah Dixon. The name was later applied to the entire southern boundary of Pennsylvania, and in the years before the American Civil War it represented the division between the Northern states and the slave-owning states of the South. (See also Dixie.)

**Massa** /ˈmɑːsə/ a town on the slopes of the Apuan Alps in Tuscany, north-western Italy, capital of the province of Massa-Carrara; pop. (1990) 67,780. It became the seat of the Cybo-Malaspina dukes in the 16th c. Local industries include marble quarrying and chemicals.

**Massachusetts** /ˌmæsəˈtʃuːsɪts/ a state of New England in the north-eastern US, on the Atlantic coast; area 21,456 sq. km. (8,284 sq. miles); pop. (1990) 6,016,425; capital, Boston. The largest cities are Boston, Worcester, Springfield, and Lowell. Massachusetts is also known as the Bay State or Old Colony State. Settled by the Pilgrim Fathers in 1620, it was a centre of resistance to the British before and during the War of American Independence. It became one of the original 13 states of the US in 1788. The state produces vegetables, fruit, garden produce and the largest crop of cranberries in the US but it is an overwhelmingly industrial state with a predominantly urban population. Landmarks include the Boston, Lowell, and Minute Man National Historical Parks. Massachusetts is divided into 14 counties:

| County | Area (sq. km.) | Pop. (1990) | County Seat |
|---|---|---|---|
| Barnstable | 1,040 | 186,605 | Barnstable |
| Berkshire | 2,415 | 139,350 | Pittsfield |
| Bristol | 1,448 | 506,325 | Taunton |
| Dukes | 265 | 11,640 | Edgartown |
| Essex | 1,287 | 670,080 | Salem |
| Franklin | 1,825 | 70,090 | Greenfield |
| Hampden | 1,607 | 456,310 | Springfield |
| Hampshire | 1,373 | 146,570 | Northampton |
| Middlesex | 2,137 | 1,398,470 | Cambridge |
| Nantucket | 122 | 6,010 | Nantucket |
| Norfolk | 1,040 | 616,090 | Dedham |
| Plymouth | 1,703 | 435,280 | Plymouth |
| Suffolk | 148 | 663,910 | Boston |
| Worcester | 3,934 | 709,705 | Worcester |

**Massawa** the chief port of Eritrea, on the Red Sea; pop. (1984) 27,500. In 1993 Ethiopia negotiated the right to use the port.

**Massif Central** /mæˌsiːf sɑ̃ˈtrɑːl/ a mountainous plateau in south-central France. Covering almost one-sixth of the country, it rises to a height of 1,887 m. (6,188 ft.) at Puy de Nancy in the Auvergne. It is bounded to the south-east by the Cévennes.

**Mastia** /ˈmæstɪə/ see CARTAGENA.

**Masulipatnam** the former name of MACHILIPATNAM.

**Masuria** /məˈsjʊərɪə/ a low-lying and forested lakeland region of north-east Poland. Formerly part of East Prussia, it was assigned to Poland after World War II. Extending from the Vistula to Poland's eastern borders, it contains some 2,700 lakes.

**Masvingo** /mæsˈvɪŋgəʊ/ a town in south-central Zimbabwe, capital of a province of the same name; pop. (1982) 31,000. Founded in 1890 as Fort Victoria, it was the first permanent white settlement in the region. It developed as a mining town and transportation centre on the main road from Harare to South Africa and was for a few months in 1982 named Nyanda. Asbestos, copper, and lithium are mined nearby.

**Matabele** /ˌmætəˈbiːlɪ/ (also **Ndebele**) a people of Zulu stock living in Zimbabwe.

**Matabeleland** /ˌmætəˈbiːlɪˌlænd/ a former province of Southern Rhodesia, lying between the Limpopo and Zambezi rivers and occupied by the Matabele people. The area is now divided into the two provinces of Matabeleland North and South, in southern Zimbabwe.

**Matamoros** /ˌmætəˈmɔʊrɒs/ a city in the state of Tamaulipas, north-east Mexico, a chief port of entry to Mexico on the Río Grande opposite Brownsville, Texas; pop. (1990) 303,390. Settled in the 18th c. and named Congregación de Nuestra Señora del Refugio, it was renamed after Father Mariano Matamoros, a hero of the war of independence. Its chief industries include tanneries, distilleries, and cotton mills.

**Matanzas** /məˈtɑːnzəs/ a deep-water port on the north coast of Cuba, east of Havana; pop. (1989) 105,400. Established as a pirate haven in 1693, it later developed as a sugar-refining centre.

**Matera** /məˈteɪrə/ the capital town of Matera province in the Basilicata region of southern Italy, on a hillside overlooking the River Gravina; pop. (1990) 54,870.

**Mathura** /ˈmətərə/ (also **Muttra**) a city in Uttar Pradesh, northern India, on the Yamuna River north-west of Agra; pop. (1991) 233,235. It is an important centre of art and religion, the alleged birthplace of the Hindu god Krishna.

**Matlock** /ˈmætlɒk/ a resort town in central England, on the River Derwent, the county town of Derbyshire; pop. (1981) 13,870.

**Matmata** /mætˈmɑːtə/ a village in south-east Tunisia, in the Matmata Hills, south of Gabès; pop. (est. 1990) 3,500. In this region for many centuries the people have lived in underground cave dwellings hacked from the tufa. The village and surrounding hills take their name from that of a Berber tribe.

**Mato Grosso** /ˌmætəʊ ˈɡrɒsəʊ/ **1.** a high plateau region of south-west Brazil forming a watershed between the Amazon and Plate river systems. Its Portuguese name means 'dense forest'. The region is divided into the two states of Mato Grosso and Mato Grosso do Sul. **2.** a state of west-central Brazil on the border with Bolivia; area 881,000 sq. km. (340,286 sq. miles); pop. (1991) 2,022,520; capital, Cuiabá.

**Mato Grosso do Sul** /-dəʊ 'suːl/ a state of south-west Brazil on the border with Bolivia and Paraguay; area 350,548 sq. km. (135,400 sq. miles); pop. (1991) 1,778,740; capital, Campo Grande.

**Matsubara** /ˌmætsuːˈbɑːrə/ a city in Osaka prefecture, Honshu Island, Japan; pop. (1990) 135,920.

**Matsudo** /mætˈsuːdəʊ/ a suburb of Tokyo in Chiba prefecture, Honshu Island, Japan; pop. (1990) 456,210.

**Matsue** /ˈmɑːtsəˌweɪ/ the capital city of Shimane prefecture, south-west Honshu Island, Japan; pop. (1990) 142,930.

**Matsumoto** /ˌmætsəˈməʊtəʊ/ a city in Nagano prefecture, central Honshu Island, Japan; pop. (1990) 200,720.

**Matsusaka** /ˌmætsəˈsɑːkə/ (also **Matsuzaka**) a city in Mie prefecture, central Honshu Island; pop. (1990) 118,730.

**Matsuyama** /ˌmætsuːˈjɑːmə/ a city in Japan, the capital and largest city of the island of Shikoku; pop. (1990) 443,320. Its castle, dating from 1603, is one of the best-preserved in Japan. Nearby is the hot spring resort of Dogo-onsen. An important agricultural distribution point and fishing port with diverse industries.

**Matterhorn** /ˈmætəˌhɔːn/ (French **Mont Cervin**, Italian **Monte Cervino**) a spectacular mountain in the Alps, on the border between Switzerland and Italy with a distinctive pyramidal peak. Rising to 4,477 m. (14,690 ft.), it was first climbed in 1865 by the English climber Edward Whymper.

**Maui** /ˈmaʊɪ/ a volcanic island in Hawaii. The second-largest of the group of islands, it lies to the north-west of the island of Hawaii; area 1,885 sq. km. (729 sq. miles). The resort town of Lahaina was the former capital of Hawaii.

**Maun** the chief town of northern Botswana, on the south-eastern edge of the Okavango delta; pop. (1991) 26,770.

**Mauna Kea** /ˌmaʊnə ˈkeɪə/ a massive 'shield' volcano on the island of Hawaii, in the central Pacific. It is situated in the centre of the island, to the north of Mauna Loa. Rising to 4,205 m. (13,796 ft.), it is the highest peak in the Hawaiian islands and the highest island mountain in the world. If measured from the floor of the Pacific Ocean it rises to about 9,760 m. (32,000 ft.) which is higher than Mt. Everest.

**Mauna Loa** /ˌmaʊnə ˈləʊə/ an active volcano on the Pacific island of Hawaii, situated to the south of Mauna Kea. Rising to 4,169 m. (13,678 ft.), it is the second-highest active volcano in the world. Major eruptions took place in 1881, 1942, 1949, and 1984.

**Mauretania** /ˌmɒrɪˈteɪnɪə/ an ancient region of North Africa, corresponding to the northern part of Morocco and western and central Algeria. Originally occupied by the Moors (Latin *Mauri*), it was annexed by Claudius in the mid-1st c. AD and divided into two Roman provinces. It was conquered by the Arabs in the 7th century.
**Mauretanian** *adj. & n.*

**Mauritania**
/ˌmɒrɪˈteɪnɪə/ official name **The Islamic Republic of Mauritania** a country in West Africa with a coastline on the Atlantic Ocean and bounded by Western Sahara, Algeria, Mali, and Senegal; area 1,030,700 sq. km. (398,107 sq. miles); pop. (est. 1991) 2,023,000; official languages, Arabic and French; capital, Nouakchott. The north of the country is desert, while the south lies in the Sahel; Mauritania has a predominantly hot and dry climate. Although some settled agriculture exists in the valley of the Senegal River, the people are largely nomadic pastoralists herding sheep, goats, and cattle. Fish and iron ore are the country's chief exports. Mauritania was a centre of Berber power in the 11th and 12th c., at which time Islam became established in the region. Later nomadic Arab tribes became dominant, while on the coast European nations, especially France, established trading posts. A French protectorate from 1902 and a colony from 1920, Mauritania achieved full independence in 1961. The country was ruled as a single-party state for 18 years by a civilian president and from 1978 until the declaration of the Mauritanian Second Republic in 1992 it was a military dictatorship. Mauritania is now a multiparty democracy with a bicameral legislative National Assembly.
**Mauritanian** *adj. & n.*

**Mauritius**
/məˈrɪʃəs/ official name **The Republic of Mauritius** an island country in the Indian Ocean, about 850 km. (550 miles) east of Madagascar; area 2,040 sq. km. (788 sq. miles); pop. (est. 1991) 1,083,000; official language, English; capital, Port Louis. Previously uninhabited, Mauritius was discovered by the Portuguese in the early 16th c. It was held by the Dutch (who named it in honour of Prince Maurice) from 1598 to 1710 and then by the French until 1810, when it was ceded to Britain. The British abolished slavery, used in the sugar plantations, instead importing mainly Indian and Chinese labour. After 158 years as a Crown colony it became independent as a member of the Commonwealth in 1968 and a republic in 1992. Its government claims sovereignty over the Chagos Archipelago which includes the island of Diego Garcia. The economy is largely

dependent on sugar. Mauritius is governed by a Council of Ministers and a unicameral National Assembly.
**Mauritian** *adj. & n.*

**Maya** /'mɑ:jə/ an American Indian people of Yucatán and Central America who still maintain aspects of their ancient culture which developed over an extensive area and reached its peak in the 4th–8th c., a period distinguished by a spectacular flowering of art and learning. Remains include stone temples built on pyramids and ornamented with sculptures. Among the most striking of the Maya achievements are a system of pictorial writing and a calendar system, more accurate than the Julian, that was still in use at the time of the Spanish conquest in the 16th c. The unexplained collapse of the early Mayan civilization with a population of as many as 16 million took place c.900–1500 but at least four million descendants still speak the Mayan language.
**Mayan** *adj. & n.*

**Mayapan** /ˌmɑ:jə'pɑ:n/ a ruined city of the ancient Maya, situated to the south of Mérida on the Yucatán peninsula, south-east Mexico. From 1200 to 1450, it was the last great city of the Mayan empire.

**Mayenne** /mæ'jen/ **1.** a river of western France that rises in Normandy and flows southwards for 195 km. (122 miles) to Angers where it joins the Sarthe to form the Maine. **2.** a department in the Pays de la Loire region of western France; area 5,175 sq. km. (1,999 sq. miles); pop. (1990) 278,040; capital, Laval.

**Mayerling** /'maɪ3:ˌlɪŋ/ an Austrian village on the River Schwechat in the state of Lower Austria, the site of a former hunting lodge associated with the mysterious death of the Crown Prince Rudolf and Baroness Maria Vetsera in January 1889.

**Maykop** /maɪ'kɒp/ see MAIKOP.

**Maymana** see MEYMANEH.

**Maynooth** /mer'nu:θ/ a village on the Royal Canal in County Kildare, eastern Ireland; pop. (1981) 1,300. St. Patrick's College (1795) is the centre for the training of Catholic diocesan clergy in Ireland and 18th-c. Carton House was the home of the dukes of Leinster.

**Mayo** /'meɪəʊ/ a county in the Republic of Ireland, in the province of Connaught; area 5,398 sq. km. (2,085 sq. miles); pop. (1991) 110,700; capital, Castlebar.

**Mayon** /mɑ:'jəʊn/, **Mount** an active volcano on the island of Luzon in the Philippines rising to a height of 2,462 m. (8,077 ft.).

**Mayotte** the French name for MAHORE.

**Mazatenango** /ˌmɑ:zətə'nɑ:ŋgəʊ/ a town in south-west Guatemala, capital of Suchitepéquez department; pop. (1989) 38,320. Situated on the Pacific Highway, it is the chief town of the Costa Grande region.

**Mazar-e-Sharif** /mæˌzɑ:rɪʃə'ri:f/ the largest city in northern Afghanistan, capital of the province of Balkh; pop. (est. 1988) 131,000. The city, whose name means 'tomb of the saint', is one of the reputed burial places of Ali, son-in-law of the prophet Muhammad. It is the centre of Afghanistan's carpet and rug industry.

**Mazatlán** /ˌmɑ:zət'lɑ:n/ a seaport and resort on the Pacific coast of Sinaloa state, western Mexico; pop. (1990) 314,250. Founded in 1531, it developed as a centre of Spanish colonial trade with the Philippines. It is linked by ferry to the Baja California peninsula and there are docking facilities for cruise ships. Shrimp packing is an important industry.

**Mbabane** /ˌəmbɑ:'bɑ:nɪ/ the capital of Swaziland in the highveld of southern Africa; pop. (1986) 38,290. Noted for its gaming casinos, it replaced Manzini as capital in 1902.

**Mbandaka** /ˌəmbɑ:n'dɑ:kə/ a commercial and industrial city in northern Zaire and port on the Zaïre River; pop. (1984) 125,260. Founded in 1883 and known as Coquilhatville until 1966, it is capital of Equateur region.

**Mbeya** /əm'beɪə/ a town in southern Tanzania, north-west of Lake Malawi; pop. (1984) 93,000. It was founded as a gold-mining town in 1927. After mining was abandoned in 1956 it developed as a road and rail centre.

**Mbini** /em'bi:nɪ/ **1.** a river of Equatorial Guinea that rises in central Río Muni and flows north, west, and south-west to join the Gulf of Guinea at Mbini. **2.** a port in Equatorial Guinea, on the coast of Río Muni south of Bata.

**MD** *abbr.* US Maryland (in official postal use).

**Mdina** /mə'di:nə/ a town at the centre of the island of Malta, formerly the capital of Malta; pop. (1983) 930. It is the site of the National Museum of Natural History and a cathedral built to replace an 11th-c. cathedral destroyed in an earthquake in 1693.

**ME** *abbr.* US Maine (in official postal use).

**Mearns** /mɜ:nz/, **the** the name given to a region of north-east Scotland lying to the east of the Grampians, at one time also synonymous with the former County of Kincardineshire. The name is thought to be derived from Mernas who was given the area by his brother King Kenneth II in the 9th c.

**Meath** /mi:θ/ a county of the Republic of Ireland, in the province of Leinster; area 2,339 sq. km. (903 sq. miles); pop. (1991) 105,540; capital, Navan.

**Mecca** /'mekə/ (Arabic **Makkah** /'mækə, mə'kɑ:/) a city in western Saudi Arabia, an oasis town located in the Red Sea region of Hejaz, east of Jiddah; pop. (est. 1986) 618,000. A trading centre in pre-Islamic times, it was the birthplace in AD 570 of the Prophet Muhammad and was the scene of his early teachings and his expulsion to Medina in

622. On his return to Mecca in 630 it became the centre of the new Muslim faith. Considered by Muslims to be the holiest city of Islam, it is the site of the Great Mosque in whose courtyard is the Kaaba shrine, a centre of Islamic ritual that draws over a million pilgrims to the city each year. Devout Muslims try to make the *haj* (pilgrimage) at least once in their lives. Non-Muslims are forbidden to enter the city.

**Mechelen** /'mexələn/ (French **Malines** /mæ'li:n/) a city in Antwerp province, northern Belgium, 25 km. (15 miles) north of Brussels; pop. (1991) 75,310. It is the metroplitan see of Belgium and is noted for its cathedral, which contains a painting of the crucifixion by the Flemish painter Van Dyck (1599–1641). It was formerly known in English as Mechlin, lending its name to the Mechlin lace made there.

**Mechlin** /'meklɪn/ the former name in English for MECHELEN.

**Mecklenburg** /'meklən,bɜ:g/ a former state of north-east Germany on the Baltic coast, now part of Mecklenburg-West Pomerania. Inhabited originally by Germanic tribes, it was occupied in about AD 600 by Slavonic peoples but was reclaimed by Henry the Lion, Duke of Saxony, in 1160. It was divided in the 16th and 17th c. into two duchies, Mecklenburg-Schwerin and Mecklenburg-Strelitz, which were reunited as the state of Mecklenburg in 1934. The region was part of the German Democratic Republic between 1949 and 1990.

**Mecklenburg-West Pomerania** /,meklən,bɜ:g,west ,pɒmə'remɪə/ a state of north-east Germany, on the coast of the Baltic Sea; area 23,838 sq. km. (9,207 sq. miles); pop. (est. 1990) 2,100,000; capital, Schwerin. The modern state consists of the former state of Mecklenburg and the western part of Pomerania.

**Medan** /mə'dɑ:n/ a city in Indonesia, on the Deli River in north-east Sumatra, capital of North Sumatra province; pop. (1990) 1,730,000. Established as a trading centre in 1682, it became the Dutch capital of the region and leading commercial centre of Sumatra. It trades in oil, rubber, and palm oil.

**Mede** /mi:d/ a member of an ancient Indo-European people whose homeland, Media, lay south-west of the Caspian Sea. In the 7th–6th c. BC they were masters of an empire that included most of modern Iran and extended to Cappadocia and Syria; it passed into Persian control after the defeat of King Astyages by Cyrus in 549 BC.

**Medellín** /,meder'i:n/ a city in eastern Colombia, the second-largest city in the country; pop. (1985) 1,468,000. A major centre of coffee production, it has in recent years gained a reputation as a centre for cocaine production and the hub of the Colombian drug trade.

**Medford** /'medfəd/ a northern suburb of Boston in the US state of Massachusetts, on the Mystic River; pop. (1990) 57,400. Founded in 1630, it was a shipping centre during the 17th–19th c.

**Media** /'mi:dɪə/ an ancient region of Asia to the south-west of the Caspian Sea, corresponding approximately to present-day Azerbaijan, north-west Iran, and north-east Iraq. The region is roughly the same as that inhabited today by the Kurds. Originally inhabited by the Medes, the region was conquered in 550 BC by Cyrus the Great of Persia.

**Medicine Hat** /'medsɪn/ a city in south-east Alberta, Canada, on the South Saskatchewan River; pop. (1991) 47,390. It is an agricultural centre with a petrochemical industry that utilizes local natural gas discovered in 1883.

**medina** /mə'di:nə/ an Arabic word for a town or city.

**Medina** /mə'di:nə/ (Arabic **Al Madinah**) a city in western Saudi Arabia, an oasis some 320 km. (200 miles) north of Mecca; pop. (est. 1981) 500,000. Formerly known as Yathrib and controlled by Jewish settlers, in AD 622 it became the refuge of the Prophet Muhammad's infant Muslim community after its expulsion from Mecca. It was renamed Medina, meaning 'the city', by Muhammad and made the capital of the new Islamic state until it was superseded by Damascus in 661. It was Muhammad's burial place and the site of the first Islamic mosque, constructed around his tomb. It is considered by Muslims to be the second most holy city after Mecca and a visit to the prophet's tomb at Medina forms a frequent sequel to the formal pilgrimage to Mecca. The Islamic University was established in 1962.

**Mediterranean climate** a climate characterized by hot, dry summers and warm, wet winters.

**Mediterranean Sea** /,medɪtə'remɪən/ an almost landlocked sea between southern Europe, the north coast of Africa, and south-west Asia. It is connected with the Atlantic by the Strait of Gibraltar, with the Red Sea by the Suez Canal, and with the Black Sea by the Dardanelles, the Sea of Marmara, and the Bosporus; area *c.* 2,589,000 sq. km. (1,000,000 sq. miles); length *c.* 3,200 km. (2,000 miles).

**Medoc** /mer'dɒk, 'medɒk/ a district of Aquitaine in south-west France, between the Bay of Biscay and the estuary of the Gironde River, noted for its fine red claret. Its chief towns are Pauillac and Lesparre.

**Meerut** /'mɪərət/ a commercial and industrial city in the state of Uttar Pradesh, northern India; pop. (1991) 846,950. It was the scene in May 1857 of the first uprising against the British in the Indian Mutiny. Its industries include textiles, sugar, and chemicals.

**Mégara** /'megərə/ a town in Attica, east-central Greece, on the Gulf of Saronica; pop. (1981) 17,720. It was the birthplace of the elegiac poet

Theognis (*c.* 570–485 BC) and Euklides (450–380 BC), founder of the Megarian School of Philosophy.

**Meghalaya** /ˌmegəˈleɪə/ a small state in the extreme north-east of India, on the northern border of Bangladesh; area 22,429 sq. km. (8,663 sq. miles); pop. (1991) 1,760,630; capital, Shillong. Created in 1970 from parts of Assam, it is a largely agricultural state producing rice, wheat, maize, jute, cotton, and mustard. Meghalaya is also rich in minerals such as sillimanite, felspar, quartz, limestone, coal, and glass sand.

**Megiddo** /məˈgɪdəʊ/ (modern **Tel Megiddo** /tel/) an ancient city of north-west Palestine, situated 32 km. (20 miles) south-east of Haifa in present-day Israel. Founded in the 4th millennium BC, the city controlled an important route linking Syria and Mesopotamia with the Jordan valley, Jerusalem, and Egypt. Its commanding location on the southern edge of the plain of Esdraelon made the city the scene of many early battles, and from its name the word *Armageddon* ('hill of Megiddo') is derived. It was the scene in 1918 of the defeat of Turkish forces by the British under General Allenby.

**Meissen** /ˈmaɪs(ə)n/ a city in Saxony, east Germany, on the River Elbe north-west of Dresden; pop. (1981) 39,280. It is famous for its porcelain, known as Dresden china, which has been made there since 1710.

**Mei Xian** /meɪ ʃiːˈɑːn/ a city in Guangdong province, southern China, west of Xiamen; pop. (1986) 749,000.

**Mejicanos** /mehiːˈkɑːnəʊs/ a town in southern El Salvador, a northern suburb of San Salvador; pop. (1989) 118,000.

**Mekele** /mɪˈkeɪlɪ/ the capital of Tigray province in northern Ethiopia; pop. (est. 1984) 62,000.

**Meknès** /mekˈnes/ a historic city in northern Morocco, in the Middle Atlas mountains west of Fez; pop. (1982) 319,800. Founded in the 10th c., it developed around a citadel of the Moorish Almoravides. In the 17th c. it was the residence of the Moroccan sultan. It is now one of the country's four imperial cities and a rich market centre with traditional industries.

**Mekong** /miːˈkɒŋ/ a river of south-east Asia, which rises in Tibet and flows south-east and south for 4,180 km. (2,600 miles) through southern China, Laos, Cambodia, and Vietnam to its extensive delta on the South China Sea. For part of its course it forms the boundary between Laos and its western neighbours Burma and Thailand. Its source was discovered by a joint Franco-British expedition in 1994.

**Melaka** /məˈlækə/ (formerly **Malacca**) **1.** a state in south-west Malaysia, on the south-west coast of the Malay Peninsula, on the Strait of Malacca; area 1,658 sq. km. (640 sq. miles); pop. (1980) 464,750. **2.** its capital and chief port; pop. (1980)

88,070. It has been an important trading centre since it was founded *c.* 1400 and is now a popular tourist resort.

**Melanesia** /ˌmeləˈniːzɪə, -ˈniːʒə/ a region of the western Pacific to the south of Micronesia and west of Polynesia. Lying south of the equator, it contains the Bismarck Archipelago, the

Solomon Islands, Santa Cruz, Vanuatu, New Caledonia, Fiji, and the intervening islands. It was the region of first human settlement in the Pacific. **Melanesian** *adj. & n.*

**Melbourne** /ˈmelbən, -bɔːn/ the capital of Victoria, south-east Australia, on the Bass Strait opposite Tasmania; pop. (1991) 2,762,000. Founded in 1835 and named after the British Prime Minister William Melbourne, it became state capital in 1851 and was capital of Australia from 1901 until 1927. Situated on Port Philip Bay, it is a major port, financial, commercial, and industrial centre, and the second-largest city in Australia. The Melbourne Cup horse-racing event is held annually in November. Melbourne has two universities: Monash (1958) and La Trobe (1964) and a famous Botanical Gardens (1845).

**Melbourne** a city in Florida, USA, on the Indian River near Cape Canaveral; pop. (1990) 59,650. It is a popular watersports centre, a leading manufacturer of electronics, and home of the Florida Institute of Technology (1958).

**Melilla** /meˈlɪljə/ a Spanish enclave on the Mediterranean coast of Morocco; area 14 sq. km. (5.4 sq. miles); pop. (1991) 56,600. It was taken by Spain in 1497 and was the scene of a revolt of army officers that led to the outbreak of the Spanish Civil War in 1936. It exports iron ore from nearby mines, and fishing is an important industry.

**Melitopol** /ˌmeləˈtɒpəl/ a town in southern Ukraine, on the northern shore of the Sea of Azov; pop. (1990) 176,000.

**Melk** /melk/ a town on the Danube in the state of Lower Austria, north-central Austria. Overlooking the river is an immense Benedictine abbey with a vast library which holds some 70,000 books and 2,000 manuscripts.

**Melos** /ˈmiːlɒs/ (Greek **Mílos**) a Greek island in the Aegean Sea, in the south-west of the Cyclades group, midway between Athens and Crete; area 153 sq. km. (59 sq. miles). It was the centre of a flourishing civilization in the Bronze Age and is the site of the discovery in 1820 of a Hellenistic marble statue of Aphrodite (the Venus de Milo), now in the Louvre in Paris. Minerals including sulphur, alum, kaolin, and barium are mined on the island which was an important source of obsidian in ancient times.

**Melian** *adj. & n.*

**Melton** /'meltən/ a town in south-central Victoria, Australia, situated to the west of Melbourne; pop. (1991) 29,040.

**Melton Mowbray** /,meltən 'məʊbrɪ/ a town in Leicestershire, central England, on the River Wreake, whose name is associated with pork pies and Stilton cheeses; pop. (1981) 23,600.

**Melun** /me'lœ̃/ an industrial town on the River Seine in north-central France, the capital of Seine-et-Marne department; pop. (1990) 36,490. Nearby is the abbey of Lys, founded in the 12th c. by the mother of Louis IX (St. Louis). Local plants produce aero engines and car bodies.

**Melville Island** /'melvɪl/ the fourth-largest of the Queen Elizabeth Islands in the Canadian Arctic; area 42,149 sq. km. (16,280 sq. miles). It was discovered in 1819 by the explorer W. E. Parry who named it after Viscount Melville, First Lord of the Admiralty.

**Memel** /'meɪməl/ **1.** the former name of a district of Lithuania lying on the coast of the Baltic Sea to the north of the Neman (Memel) River. It was part of East Prussia until placed under League of Nations-sponsored French administration in 1919. Between 1924 and 1938 it formed an autonomous region of Lithuania before being taken by Germany. In 1945 it was restored to Lithuania by the Soviet Union. **2.** the former German name for the city of KLAIPEDA in Lithuania (1918–23 and 1941–4). **3.** the former German name for the NEMAN.

**Memphis** /'memfɪs/ an ancient city of Egypt, whose ruins are situated on the Nile about 15 km. (10 miles) south of Cairo. It is thought to have been founded as the capital of the Old Kingdom of Egypt in c. 3100 BC by King Menes, the ruler of the Egyptian dynasty, who united the former kingdoms of Upper and Lower Egypt. Associated with the god Ptah, it remained one of Egypt's principal cities even after Thebes was made capital of the New Kingdom in c. 1570 BC. It is the site of the pyramids of Saqqara and Giza and the great sphinx.

**Memphis** /'memfɪs/ a river port and railway junction on the Mississippi in the extreme south-west of Tennessee, USA; pop. (1990) 610,340. Founded in 1819, it is named after the ancient Egyptian city because of its river location. Memphis is a leading commercial centre trading in cotton and agricultural produce. It was the home in the late 19th c. of blues music, the scene in 1968 of the assassination of the civil rights leader Martin Luther King Jr., and the childhood home and burial place, in 1977, of the rock musician Elvis Presley.

**Menai Strait** /'menaɪ/ a channel separating Anglesey from the mainland of north-west Wales. It is spanned by two bridges, the first built by Thomas Telford between 1819 and 1826, the second (a railway bridge) built on the foundations of the Britannia Tubular Bridge constructed by Robert Stephenson between 1846 and 1850, and burnt down in 1970.

**Mende** /mɑ̃d/ a cathedral town on the River Lot in the Languedoc-Roussillon region of southern France, capital of the department of Lozère; pop. (1982) 12,110.

**Menderes** see MAEANDER.

**Mendips** /'mendɪps/, **the** (also **Mendip Hills**) a range of limestone hills in the counties of Somerset and Avon, south-west England, rising to 325 m. (1,068 ft.) at Black Down. The Cheddar Gorge cuts through the hills and there are many underground caverns such as Wookey Hole.

**Mendoza** /men'dəʊsə/ a city in western Argentina, situated in the foothills of the Andes at the centre of a noted fruit-growing and wine-producing region; pop. (1991) 775,000. Founded in 1561 on the site of an Inca fort by Don Garcia Hurtado de Mendoza, it is capital of a province of the same name.

**Mennonite** /'menə,naɪt/ a member of a Protestant sect originating in Friesland in the 16th c., maintaining principles similar to those of the Anabaptists, being opposed to infant baptism, the taking of oaths, military service, and the holding of civic offices. In the following centuries many emigrated, first to other European countries and to Russia, later to North, Central, and South America, in search of political freedom.

**Menorca** the Spanish name for MINORCA.

**Mercator's Projection** /mɜː'keɪt(ə)r/ a map projection devised by the 16th-c. cartographer Gerhard Kremer (Mercator) (1512–94) in which the lines of longitude are parallel. Principally used by navigators because compass courses appear as straight lines, this projection tends to distort land areas in higher latitudes which appear much larger than they in fact are.

**Merced** /mɜː'sed/ a city in the San Joaquin valley, central California, USA, between Modesto and Fresno; pop. (1990) 56,220. It lies near the entrance to Yosemite National Park.

**Mercia** /'mɜːʃɪə/ a former kingdom of central England. It was established by invading Angles in the 6th c. AD in the border areas between the new Anglo-Saxon settlements in the east and the Celtic regions in the west. Becoming dominant in the 8th c. under Offa, it expanded to cover an area stretching from the Humber to the south coast. Its decline began after Offa's death in 796 and in 926, when Athelstan became king of all England, it finally lost its separate identity. In modern times the name has been revived, for example, in the 'West Mercia Authority', an area of police administration covering the counties of Hereford and Worcester, and Shropshire.

**Mercian** *adj. & n.*

**Mercosur** /'mɜ:kəʊˌsʊə(r)/ a Latin American organization founded by Argentina, Brazil, Paraguay, and Uruguay in March 1991 for the purpose of creating a common market in the region.

**Mer de Glace** /mɜ:(r) də 'glæs/ the largest glacier of the Mont Blanc range, in eastern France close to the Italian and Swiss borders. A famous tourist attraction.

**Meriç** /mə'ri:tʃ/ the Turkish name for the MARITSA.

**Mérida** /'meɪrɪdə/ a commercial city in the tropical lowlands of south-east Mexico, capital of the state of Yucatán; pop. (1990) 557,340. Founded in 1542 on the site of an ancient Mayan city, Mérida developed as a centre of the hemp trade in the 19th c. Today it trades in fruit, vegetables, cattle, timber, tobacco, and chicle.

**Mérida** /'meɪrɪdə/ a city in the province of Badajoz, western Spain, on the River Guadiana; pop. (1991) 49,830. It has a Roman theatre built by Agrippa in 24 BC.

**Mérida** /'meɪrɪdə/ the capital city of the state of Mérida in west Venezuela, situated in the northern Andes at an altitude of 1,640 m. (5,380 ft.); pop. (1991) 167,990 (275,360 metropolitan area).

**Meriden** /'mɜ:rɪd(ə)n/ an industrial town in the central valley of Connecticut, USA, once noted for its manufacture of silver goods; pop. (1990) 59,480. It is named after Meriden Farm in Warwickshire, England.

**meridian** /mə'rɪdɪən/ an imaginary circle of constant longitude, passing through a given place and the north and south poles. It is described by the angle it forms east or west of the **prime meridian** which has a value of 0° and runs through Greenwich in England.

**meridional** /mə'rɪdɪən(ə)l/ **1.** of or in the south **2.** relating to a meridian, as in meridional temperature gradient which is the change in temperature north or south along a meridian.

**Merionethshire** /merɪ'ɒnəθʃaɪr/ a former county of north-west Wales which became part of the county of Gwynedd in 1974. Its county town was Dolgellau.

**Mersa Brega** see BREGA.

**Mersa Matruh** /ˌmɜ:sə mə'tru:/ (also **Marsa Matruh** or **Matruh**) a resort town on the Mediterranean coast of Egypt, 250 km. (156 miles) west of Alexandria; it is situated on a bay near the frontier with Libya. There is a war museum dealing with the battles of 1942.

**Mersey** /'mɜ:zɪ/ a river in north-west England, which rises in the Peak District and flows 112 km. (70 miles) to the Irish Sea near Liverpool.

**Merseyside** /'mɜ:zɪˌsaɪd/ a metropolitan county of north-west England; area 652 sq. km. (252 sq. miles); pop. (1991) 1,376,800. Administered by a separate council until 1986, it is divided into five districts:

| District | Area (sq. km.) | Pop. (1991) |
| --- | --- | --- |
| Knowsley | 97 | 149,100 |
| Liverpool | 113 | 448,300 |
| St. Helens | 133 | 175,300 |
| Sefton | 153 | 282,000 |
| Wirral | 158 | 322,100 |

**Mersin** /mɜ:'si:n/ an industrial port in southern Turkey, on the Mediterranean south-west of Adana; pop. (1990) 422,360. It is capital of the province of İçel. Industries include oil refining and textile production, and there are ferry links with northern Cyprus.

**Merthyr Tydfil** /ˌmɜ:θər 'tɪdvɪl/ an industrial town in Mid Glamorgan, south Wales; pop. (1990) 59,300.

**Merton** /'mɜ:t(ə)n/ an outer borough of Greater London, created in 1965 following the merger of the former boroughs of Wimbledon and Mitcham; pop. (1991) 161,800. Largely residential with some light industries.

**Meru** /'meɪru:/ **1.** a town in central Kenya to the south of Mt. Kenya; pop. (est. 1984) 98,000. It takes its name from a tribe who came to the region in the 14th c. **2.** a national park in the lowland plains to the east of Meru in central Kenya. Situated on the equator and to the north of the Tana River, the park was made famous by Joy and George Adamson who used it as a base for rearing orphaned lion and leopard cubs. **3.** a mountain in northern Tanzania, rising to 4,565 m. (14,977 ft.) south-west of Kilimanjaro.

**mesa** /'meɪsə/ a term used in the United States to describe an isolated flat-topped hill with steep sides, and found in landscapes with horizontal strata.

**Mesa** /'meɪsə/ an industrial city in the valley of the Salt River, south-central Arizona, USA; pop. (1990) 288,090. Manufactures include electronic components, fabricated metals, aircraft, and machine tools.

**Mesa Verde** /'meɪsə 'vɜ:dɪ/ a national park extending over a prominent tableland in south-west Colorado, USA. Established in 1906, the park is honeycombed with deep canyons and ancient cliff dwellings of the Pueblo Indians.

**Meshed** see MASHHAD.

**Meso-America** /'mesəʊ, 'mez-/ the central region of America, from northern Mexico to Nicaragua, especially as a region of ancient civilizations and Native American cultures before the arrival of the Spanish settlers.
**Meso-American** *adj. & n.*

**mesolithic** /ˌmezəʊ'lɪθɪk/ the transitional period between the palaeolithic and neolithic, especially in Europe, where it falls between the end of the last glacial period (mid-9th millennium BC) and the beginnings of agriculture. The period is characterized by the use of microliths and the first domestication of animals (such as the dog).

**Mesolóngion** the Greek name for MISSOLONGHI.

**Mesopotamia** /ˌmesəpəˈteɪmɪə/ an ancient region of south-west Asia in present-day Iraq, lying between the rivers Tigris and Euphrates. Its alluvial plains were the site of the ancient civilizations of Akkad, Sumer, Babylonia, and Assyria, now lying within Iraq.
**Mesopotamian** *adj. & n.*

**mesosphere** /ˈmesəʊˌsfɪə(r)/ the region of the atmosphere extending from the top of the stratosphere to an altitude of about 80 km. (50 miles).

**Mesozoic** /ˌmesəʊˈzəʊɪk/ the geological era between the Palaeozoic and Cenozoic, comprising the Triassic, Jurassic, and Cretaceous periods, and lasting from about 248 to 65 million years ago. It was a time of abundant vegetation and saw the dominance of dinosaurs and other reptiles, although by its close they were being rapidly replaced by mammals.

**Mesquite** /mesˈkiːt/ an eastern suburb of Dallas, north-east Texas; pop. (1990) 101,480.

**Messina** /meˈsiːnə/ a busy seaport and commercial and industrial centre in north-east Sicily, Italy; pop. (1990) 274,850. Founded in 730 BC by the Greeks, it is situated on the Strait of Messina. In December 1908 the city was very badly damaged by an earthquake and tidal wave which killed 60,000 people.

**Messina, Strait of** a channel separating the island of Sicily from the 'toe' of Italy. It forms a link between the Tyrrhenian and Ionian seas. The strait, which is 32 km. (20 miles) in length, is noted for the strength of its currents. It is traditionally identified as the location of the legendary sea monster Scylla and the whirlpool Charybdis.

**mestizo** /meˈstiːzəʊ/ (*pl.* **-os**; *fem.* **mestiza** /-zə/, *pl.* **-as**) a Spaniard or Portuguese of mixed race, especially the offspring of a Spaniard and a Native American.

**Meteora** /ˌmetɪˈɔːrə/ a district of Thessaly in eastern Greece, noted for its group of monasteries which were built between the 12th and 16th c. and are precariously perched on curiously shaped rock formations that rise out of the Pinós Plain.

**Methodist** a member of any of several Protestant religious bodies (now united) originating in an 18th-c. evangelistic movement which grew out of a religious society (nicknamed the 'Holy Club') established within the Church of England (from which it formally separated in 1791) by John and Charles Wesley at Oxford. Its theology is Arminian, and its ordained ministry usually presbyterian; its governing body is the Conference, composed of ministers and laymen.

**Metropolitan Museum of Art** a museum of art and archaeology on 5th Avenue in New York City, USA. Opened in 1880, it is the largest repository of art and antiquities in the Western Hemisphere. There are 18 departments and 248 galleries.

**Metz** /mets/ an industrial city in Lorraine, north-east France on the River Moselle near the German border; pop. (1990) 123,920. Formerly the capital of the medieval Frankish kingdom of Austrasia, the city grew to prosperity in the 13th c. when it was a free town within the Holy Roman Empire, ruled by a virtually independent bishop. Annexed in 1552 by Henry II of France, who defended it against a siege by the Emperor Charles V in the same year, it was formally ceded to France in 1648. It fell to a siege by the Prussians in 1870 and was annexed to the German Empire in 1871. It was restored to France in 1918, after World War I, and is now capital of the department of Moselle. Metz lies at the centre of a fertile agricultural area and the iron and steel region of Lorraine.

**Meurthe** /mɜːt/ a river of north-east France that rises in the Vosges Mts. and flows 170 km. (106 miles) north-westwards to join the Mosel.

**Meurthe-et-Moselle** /ˌmɜːt eɪ məʊˈzel/ a department in the Lorraine region of north-east France; area 5,241 sq. km. (2,024 sq. miles); pop. (1990) 711,820; capital, Nancy.

**Meuse** /mɜːz/ **1.** (Flemish and Dutch **Maas** /mɑːs/) a river of western Europe, which rises in north-east France and flows 950 km. (594 miles) through Belgium and the Netherlands to the North Sea south of Dordrecht. **2.** a department in the Lorraine region of north-east France; area 6,216 sq. km. (2,400 sq. miles); pop. (1990) 196,340; capital, Bar-le-Duc.

**Mexicali** /ˌmeksɪˈkɑːlɪ/ the capital of the state of Baja California (Lower California) in north-west Mexico, a duty-free port on the US frontier opposite Calexico; pop. (1990) 602,400. It is a railway terminus and lies at the centre of an extensive area of irrigated agriculture that produces wheat, cotton, and cantaloupe.

**Mexico** /ˈmeksɪˌkəʊ/ official name **The United Mexican States** a country in North America with extensive coastlines on the Gulf of Mexico and the Pacific Ocean, bordered by the USA  to the north and by Guatemala and Belize to the south; area 1,958,200 sq. km. (756,200 sq. miles); pop. (est. 1990) 81,885,000; official language, Spanish; capital, Mexico City. The largest cities are Mexico City, Guadalajara, Monterrey, and Puebla de Zaragoza. The topography ranges from low desert plains and tropical lowlands to high plateaux which lie in the valleys between the Sierra

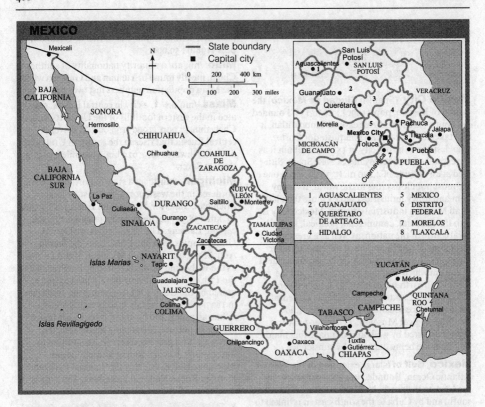

Madre, Sierra Occidental, and Sierra Oriental mountain ranges. Most of Mexico is dry, with temperatures varying with altitude and agriculture is heavily dependent on irrigation. In addition to exporting cotton, coffee, and shrimp, Mexico is a leading producer of oil and petroleum products. The centre of Aztec and Mayan civilization, Mexico was conquered and colonized by the Spanish in the early 16th c. The Aztecs are said to have fulfilled an ancient prophecy when they saw an eagle perched on a cactus eating a snake; on this site they founded a city, and the symbol of the eagle, cactus, and snake is the national emblem of Mexico. Mexico remained under Spanish rule until independence was achieved in 1821; a republic was established three years later. Texas rebelled and broke away in 1836, while all the remaining territory north of the Río Grande was lost to the USA in the Mexican War of 1846–8. Half a century of political instability, including a brief French occupation and imperial rule by Maximilian (1864–7), ended with the establishment of Porfirio Diaz as president in the 1870s. Civil war broke out again in 1910–20, leading to partial political reform. Mexico, which is a federal republic, is governed by an executive president and a bicameral General Congress.

**Mexican** *adj. & n.*

Mexico is administratively divided into 31 states and a federal district:

| State | Area | Pop. (sq. km.) | Capital (1990) |
|---|---|---|---|
| Aguascalientes | 5,471 | 719,650 | Aguascalientes |
| Baja California | 69,921 | 1,657,930 | Mexicali |
| Baja California Sur | 73,475 | 317,330 | La Paz |
| Campeche | 50,812 | 528,820 | Campeche |
| Chiapas | 74,211 | 3,203,915 | Tuxtla Gutiérrez |
| Chihuahua | 244,938 | 2,439,950 | Chihuahua |
| Coahuila | 149,982 | 1,971,340 | Saltillo |
| Colima | 5,191 | 424,660 | Colima |
| Durango | 123,181 | 1,352,160 | Victoria de Durango |
| Guanajuato | 30,491 | 3,980,200 | Guanajuato |
| Guerrero | 64,281 | 2,622,070 | Chilpancingo |
| Hidalgo | 20,813 | 1,880,640 | Pachuca de Soto |
| Jalisco | 80,836 | 5,278,990 | Guadalajara |
| México | 21,355 | 9,815,900 | Toluca de Lerdo |
| Michoacán | 59,928 | 3,534,040 | Morelia |
| Morelos | 4,950 | 1,195,380 | Cuernavaca |
| Nayarit | 26,979 | 816,110 | Tepic |
| Nuevo León | 64,924 | 3,086,470 | Monterrey |
| Oaxaca | 93,952 | 3,021,510 | Oaxaca de Juárez |
| Puebla | 33,902 | 4,118,060 | Puebla de Zaragoza |
| Querétaro | 11,449 | 1,044,230 | Querétaro |
| Quintana Roo | 50,212 | 493,600 | Chetumal |
| San Luis Potosí | 63,068 | 2,001,970 | San Luis Potosí |
| Sinaloa | 58,328 | 2,210,770 | Culiacán Rosales |
| Sonora | 182,052 | 1,822,250 | Hermosillo |
| Tabasco | 25,267 | 1,501,180 | Villahermosa |
| Tamaulipas | 79,384 | 2,244,210 | Ciudad Victoria |

(cont.)

| | | | |
|---|---|---|---|
| Tlaxcala | 4,016 | 763,680 | Tlaxcala |
| Veracruz | 71,699 | 6,215,140 | Jalapa Enríquez |
| Yucatán | 38,402 | 1,363,540 | Mérida |
| Zacatecas | 73,252 | 1,278,280 | Zacatecas |

**Mexico City** (Spanish **Ciudad de México**) the capital of Mexico; pop. (1990) 13,636,130. Founded in about 1300 as the Aztec capital Tenochtitlán, it was taken by the Spanish conquistador Cortez, who destroyed the old city in 1521 and rebuilt it as the capital of the Viceroyalty of New Spain. Situated at an altitude of 2,240 m. (7,350 ft.), it is one of the most populous cities in the world. Its many light and heavy industries employ more than half of all Mexico's industrial workers. Mexico City is also the financial, commercial, political, and cultural centre of the nation, as well as a great tourist attraction. It was the venue of the 1968 summer Olympics, the scene of a major industrial accident in 1984 in which over 450 people died, and the scene of an earthquake in 1985 that killed some 2,000 people. Landmarks include the cathedral, national palace, Castle of Chapultepec, and Anthropological Museum. The water-table has been so lowered by wells and drainage that major buildings are being damaged by subsidence.

**Mexico, Gulf of** a large extension of the western Atlantic Ocean. Bounded in a sweeping curve by the USA to the north, by Mexico to the west and south, and by Cuba to the south-east, it is linked to the Caribbean by the Yucatán Channel and to the Atlantic by the Straits of Florida. Its deepest point is the Sigsbee Deep, which is 3,878 m. (12,723 ft.) below sea-level.

**Meymaneh** /meə'mænə/ (also **Maymana**) a town in north-west Afghanistan, in the northern foothills of the Torkestan Mountains; pop. (est. 1984) 41,930. It is capital of the province of Faryab.

**Mezzogiorno** /ˌmetsəʊ'dʒɔːnəʊ/ the name given to the economically undeveloped and largely agricultural part of southern Italy. Its Italian name, which means 'midday', refers to the intensity of the sun in the middle of the day.

**MI** *abbr.* US Michigan (in official postal use).

**Miami** /maɪˈæmɪ/ a city and port on the coast of south-east Florida, USA; pop. (1990) 358,550. It is an important financial, trading, and industrial centre, and its subtropical climate and miles of beaches make it a year-round holiday resort. Miami is also the prime gateway to Latin America and its port is the largest embarkation point for cruise ships in the world, and the landing-place for immigrants from the Caribbean.

**Miami Beach** a resort town in south-east Florida, USA, on an island opposite Miami from which it is separated by Biscayne Bay; pop. (1990) 92,640. Its elegant Art Deco District is noted for its architecture of the 1920s to 1940s.

**Mianyang** /miːɑːnˈjɑːŋ/ a city in Sichuan province, central China, north-east of Chengdu; pop. (1986) 859,000.

**Miao** /miːˈaʊ/ a minority nationality of southern China, mostly found in Yunnan and Guizhou where the Miao population numbers just over 5 million.

**Miass** /miːˈɑːs/ **1.** a city in central Russia, situated in the eastern foothills of the Ural Mts. west of Chelyabinsk; pop. (1990) 169,000. **2.** a river of central Russia that rises in the southern Urals and flows northwards for *c.* 620 km. (390 miles) to join the Iset River.

**Michigan** /ˈmɪʃɪgən/ a state in northern USA, bordered in the west, north, and east by Lakes Michigan, Superior, Huron, and Erie; area 151,586 sq. km. (58,527 sq. miles); pop. (1990) 9,295,300; capital, Lansing. The largest cities are Detroit, Grand Rapids, Warren, Flint, Lansing, Sterling, Ann Arbor, and Livonia. Michigan is also known as the Wolverine State. Explored by the French in the 17th c., it was ceded to Britain in 1763 and acquired by the US in 1783, becoming the 26th state in 1837. Rich in minerals such as iron, copper, iodine, gypsum, and bromine, its cities are major centres of industry, producing motor vehicles, hardware, and processed cereals. In addition to water sports, its chief tourist attractions are Mackinac Island, Isle Royale National Park, and Pictured Rocks National Lakeshore. The state is divided into 83 counties:

| County | Area (sq. km.) | Pop. (1990) | County Seat |
|---|---|---|---|
| Alcona | 1,765 | 10,145 | Harrisville |
| Alger | 2,371 | 8,970 | Munising |
| Allegan | 2,163 | 90,510 | Allegan |
| Alpena | 1,474 | 30,605 | Alpena |
| Antrim | 1,248 | 18,185 | Bellaire |
| Arenac | 954 | 14,930 | Standish |
| Baraga | 2,343 | 7,950 | L'Anse |
| Barry | 1,456 | 50,060 | Hastings |
| Bay | 1,162 | 111,720 | Bay City |
| Benzie | 837 | 12,200 | Beulah |
| Berrien | 1,498 | 161,380 | Saint Joseph |
| Branch | 1,321 | 41,500 | Coldwater |
| Calhoun | 1,851 | 135,980 | Marshall |
| Cass | 1,290 | 49,480 | Cassopolis |
| Charlevoix | 1,095 | 21,470 | Charlevoix |
| Cheboygan | 1,872 | 21,400 | Cheboygan |
| Chippewa | 4,134 | 34,600 | Sault Sainte Marie |
| Clare | 1,482 | 24,950 | Harrison |
| Clinton | 1,490 | 57,880 | Saint Johns |
| Crawford | 1,453 | 12,260 | Grayling |
| Delta | 3,050 | 37,780 | Escanaba |
| Dickinson | 2,002 | 26,830 | Iron Mountain |
| Eaton | 1,505 | 92,880 | Charlotte |
| Emmet | 1,217 | 25,040 | Petoskey |
| Genesee | 1,669 | 430,460 | Flint |
| Gladwin | 1,313 | 21,900 | Gladwin |
| Gogebic | 2,873 | 18,050 | Bessemer |
| Grand Traverse | 1,212 | 64,270 | Traverse City |
| Gratiot | 1,482 | 38,980 | Ithaca |
| Hillsdale | 1,568 | 44,430 | Hillsdale |

| | | | |
|---|---|---|---|
| Houghton | 2,636 | 35,450 | Houghton |
| Huron | 2,158 | 34,950 | Bad Axe |
| Ingham | 1,456 | 281,910 | Mason |
| Ionia | 1,500 | 57,020 | Ionia |
| Iosco | 1,420 | 30,210 | Tawas City |
| Iron | 3,024 | 13,175 | Crystal Falls |
| Isabella | 1,500 | 54,620 | Mount Pleasant |
| Jackson | 1,833 | 149,760 | Jackson |
| Kalamazoo | 1,461 | 223,410 | Kalamazoo |
| Kalkaska | 1,464 | 13,500 | Kalkaska |
| Kent | 2,241 | 500,630 | Grand Rapids |
| Keweenaw | 1,412 | 1,700 | Eagle River |
| Lake | 1,477 | 8,580 | Baldwin |
| Lapeer | 1,711 | 74,770 | Lapeer |
| Leelanau | 887 | 16,530 | Leland |
| Lenawee | 1,958 | 91,480 | Adrian |
| Livingston | 1,492 | 115,645 | Howell |
| Luce | 2,350 | 5,760 | Newberry |
| Mackinac | 2,665 | 10,670 | Saint Ignace |
| Macomb | 1,253 | 717,400 | Mount Clemens |
| Manistee | 1,412 | 21,265 | Manistee |
| Marquette | 4,735 | 70,890 | Marquette |
| Mason | 1,284 | 25,540 | Ludington |
| Mecosta | 1,456 | 37,310 | Big Rapids |
| Menominee | 2,717 | 24,920 | Menominee |
| Midland | 1,365 | 75,650 | Midland |
| Missaukee | 1,469 | 12,150 | Lake City |
| Monroe | 1,448 | 133,600 | Monroe |
| Montcalm | 1,854 | 53,060 | Stanton |
| Montmorency | 1,430 | 8,940 | Atlanta |
| Muskegon | 1,318 | 158,980 | Muskegon |
| Newaygo | 2,202 | 38,200 | White Cloud |
| Oakland | 2,275 | 1,083,590 | Pontiac |
| Oceana | 1,407 | 22,450 | Hart |
| Ogemaw | 1,482 | 18,680 | West Branch |
| Ontonagon | 3,409 | 8,850 | Ontonagon |
| Osceola | 1,479 | 20,150 | Reed City |
| Oscoda | 1,477 | 7,840 | Mio |
| Otsego | 1,342 | 17,960 | Gaylord |
| Ottawa | 1,474 | 187,770 | Grand Haven |
| Presque Isle | 1,706 | 13,740 | Rogers City |
| Roscommon | 1,373 | 19,780 | Roscommon |
| Saginaw | 2,119 | 211,950 | Saginaw |
| St. Clair | 1,908 | 145,610 | Port Huron |
| St. Joseph | 1,308 | 58,910 | Centreville |
| Sanilac | 2,506 | 39,930 | Sandusky |
| Schoolcraft | 3,050 | 8,300 | Manistique |
| Shiawassee | 1,404 | 69,770 | Corunna |
| Tuscola | 2,111 | 55,500 | Caro |
| Van Buren | 1,589 | 70,060 | Paw Paw |
| Washtenaw | 1,846 | 282,940 | Ann Arbor |
| Wayne | 1,599 | 2,111,690 | Detroit |
| Wexford | 1,472 | 26,360 | Cadillac |

**Michigan, Lake** the third-largest of the five
Great Lakes of North America and the only one to
lie wholly within the USA; area 57,757 sq. km.
(22,300 sq. miles); maximum depth 281 m. (922 ft.).
The cities of Chicago and Milwaukee are on its
shores. It is linked to Lake Huron by the Strait of
Mackinac.

**Michoacán** /ˌmɪtʃwɑːˈkɑːn/ (fully **Michoacán
de Campo**) a mountainous state on the Pacific
west coast of Mexico; area 59,928 sq. km.

(23,147 sq. miles); pop. (1990) 3,534,040; capital,
Morelia.

**Michurinsk** /məˈtʃʊ(ə)rənsk/ an industrial city
and rail junction in western Russia, south-east of
Moscow; pop. (1990) 109,000.

**Mic-Mac** /ˈmɪkmæk/ the name and language of
a North American Indian people of eastern
Canada and New England. Numbering *c.* 10,000,
their language is a subgroup of the eastern
Algonquian language group.

**Micronesia**
/ˌmaɪkrəʊˈniːʒə/ **1.** a
region of the western
Pacific to the north
of Melanesia and
north and west of
Polynesia. It includes
the Mariana,
Caroline, and
Marshall islands

groups and Kiribati. **2.** (official name **Federated
States of Micronesia**) a group of associated
island states comprising the 600 islands of the
Caroline Islands in the western Pacific to the north
of the equator; area 701 sq. km. (271 sq. miles);
pop. (est. 1990) 107,900; official language, English;
capital, Kolonia. The group, which includes the
island states of Yap, Kosrae, Truk, and Pohnpei,
was administered by the US as part of the Pacific
Islands Trust Territory from 1947 until 1986, when
it entered into free association with the US as an independent state.
**Micronesian** *adj. & n.*

**Mid-Atlantic Ridge** see ATLANTIC OCEAN.

**Middle America** a general name for the broad
central region of the Americas that includes
Mexico, Central America, and the West Indies.

**Middle East** a term loosely applied by Europeans to an extensive area of south-west Asia and
northern Africa, stretching from the Mediterranean
to Pakistan, including the Arabian Peninsula, and
having a predominantly Muslim population.
Termed 'South-West Asia' by Americans.

**Middle Passage** the name given to the route
across the Atlantic from Africa to the Americas
formerly taken by slave ships.

**Middle West** (also **Midwest**) that part of the
United States occupying the northern half of the
Mississippi River basin, including the states of
Ohio, Indiana, Illinois, Michigan, Wisconsin,
Iowa, and Minnesota.

**Middlesborough** /ˈmɪd(ə)lzbrə/ the county
town of Cleveland in north-east England, a port on
the estuary of the River Tees; pop. (1991) 141,100.
It was the birthplace of the explorer Captain James
Cook (1728–79). The University of Teesside (formerly Teesside Polytechnic) was established
in 1992.

**Middlesex** /'mɪdlseks/ a former county of south-east England, situated to the north of London. In 1965 it was divided between Hertfordshire, Surrey and the Greater London boroughs of Barnet, Brent, Ealing, Enfield, Haringey, Harrow, Hillingdon, Hounslow, and Richmond upon Thames. The name of the county arose from its location between the lands of the east and west Saxons.

**Midgard** /'mɪdgɑːd/ the name of the earth in Scandinavian mythology, the region encircled by the sea.

**Mid Glamorgan** /glə'mɔːgən/ a county of south Wales; area 1,017 sq. km. (393 sq. miles); pop. (1991) 526,500; administrative centre, Cardiff. It was formed in 1974 from parts of Breconshire, Glamorgan, and Monmouthshire and is divided into six districts:

| District | Area (sq. km.) | Pop. (1991) |
|----------|----------------|-------------|
| Cynon Valley | 176 | 63,600 |
| Merthyr Tydfil | 110 | 59,300 |
| Ogwr | 286 | 130,500 |
| Rhondda | 101 | 76,300 |
| Rhymney Valley | 177 | 101,400 |
| Taff-Ely | 167 | 95,400 |

**Midi** /mi:'di:/, **le** a French term for the hinterland of southern France to the north of the Mediterranean coast. Its name, which means 'midday', refers to the intensity of the sun in the middle of the day.

**Midi-Pyrénées** /mi:di: pire'ni:z/ a region of southern France, centred on Toulouse and lying between the Pyrenees and the Massif Central. It comprises the departments of Ariège, Aveyron, Haute-Garonne, Gers, Lot, Hautes-Pyrénées, Tarn, and Tarn-et-Garonne; area 45,348 sq. km. (17,516 sq. miles); pop. (1990) 2,430,660.

**Midland** /'mɪdlənd/ a city in west Texas, USA, midway between Forth Worth and El Paso; pop. (1990) 89,440. It is the administrative centre of the Permian oil basin.

**Midlands** /'mɪdləndz/, **the** a general name given to the inland counties of central England, including Derbyshire, Leicestershire, Northamptonshire, and Nottinghamshire (East Midlands); Warwickshire, West Midlands, and Staffordshire (West Midlands); and Bedfordshire, Buckinghamshire, and Oxfordshire (South Midlands). For economic planning in a European context the Midlands are divided into East Midlands (Nottinghamshire, Derbyshire, Northamptonshire, Leicestershire, and Lincolnshire) and West Midlands (Hereford and Worcester, West Midlands, Shropshire, Staffordshire, and Warwickshire).

**Midlothian** /mɪd'ləʊðɪən/ a former county in central Scotland. It was a part of Lothian region from 1975 to 1996. Centred on Edinburgh, it was formerly known as Edinburghshire.

**Midway Islands** /'mɪdweɪ/ two small islands (Sand Island and Eastern Island), and a surrounding coral atoll, at the western end of the Hawaiian chain in the central Pacific Ocean; area 5 sq. km. (2 sq. mile). The islands, which lie outside the state of Hawaii, were annexed by the USA in 1867 and remain a US territory and naval base administered by the US Navy. The Midway Islands have been used as a submarine cable station, aircraft stopover, and military base, and were the scene in 1942 of a decisive naval battle, which marked the end of Japanese expansion in the Pacific during World War II.

**Midwest City** /'mɪdwest/ a city in central Oklahoma, USA, forming an eastern suburb of Oklahoma city; pop. (1990) 52,270. It was developed in 1942 in association with the nearby Tinker Air Force Base.

**Mikkeli** /mɪ'keɪlɪ/ (Swedish **Sankt Michel**) a resort town in the Saimaa Lake region of south-central Finland, capital of the province of Mikkeli; pop. (1990) 31,880.

**Míkonos** the Greek name for MYKONOS.

**Milagro** /mi:'lɑːgrəʊ/ a market town to the east of Guayaquil in the tropical lowlands of western Ecuador; pop. (1981) 77,000.

**Milan** /mɪ'læn/ (Italian **Milano** /mɪ'lɑːnəʊ/) a city in north-west Italy, capital of Lombardy region; pop. (1990) 1,432,180. Settled by the Gauls in about 600 BC, it was taken by the Romans in 222 BC, becoming the second city, after Rome, of the Western Empire. Although devastated by Attila the Hun in AD 452, it regained its powerful status, particularly from the 13th to the 15th c. as a duchy under the Visconti and Sforza families. From the 16th c. it was contested by the Habsburgs and the French, finally becoming a part of Italy in 1860. The city is today Italy's leading industrial, financial, and commercial centre. Its industries include motor cars, machinery, chemicals, textiles, clothing, and printing. It has an immense Gothic cathedral and its opera house, La Scala, which was built in 1776–8, is one of the largest in the world. Leonardo da Vinci lived in Milan from 1482 to 1500, during which time he painted the mural of the *Last Supper*, and again from 1506 to 1513. **Milanese** adj. & n.

**Mildura** /mɪl'djuːrə/ a city in north-west Victoria, south-east Australia, on the Murray River 544 km. (342 miles) north of Melbourne; pop. (1991) 23,180. It developed with the irrigation of the surrounding citrus-growing and wine-producing area in the early 19th c.

**Miletus** /maɪ'liːtəs/ an ancient city of the Ionian Greeks in south-west Asia Minor, whose ruins are situated near the present-day village of Yeniköy in the Aegean province of Aydin in western Turkey. In the 7th and 6th centuries BC it was a powerful port, from which more than 60 colonies were founded on the shores of the Black Sea and in Italy and Egypt.

In the same period it was the home of the philo-
sophers Thales, Anaximander, and Anaximenes. It
was conquered by the Persians in 494 BC. By the
6th c. AD its harbours had become silted up by the
alluvial deposits of the Maeander (Menderes) River.

**Milford Haven** /ˌmɪlfɜːd 'heɪv(ə)n/ (Welsh
**Aberdaugleddau**) a port and oil-refining centre in
the county of Dyfed, south-west Wales, on the
northern shore of the tidal estuary of the Cleddau
river; pop. (1981) 13,930.

**Milford Sound** a fiord on the indented south-
western coastline of South Island, New Zealand. It
forms a narrow glacial trough 15 km. (9 miles)
long, surrounded by dramatic mountain landscapes. It was named after the deep-water harbour
of Milford Haven in Wales by the Welsh sailor
Captain John Grono who visited it in the 1820s.

**Milk** /mɪlk/ a river of North America that rises in
the Lewis Range of the Rocky Mountains in northern Montana, USA. It flows 1,006 km. (625 miles)
north and east into southern Alberta, Canada,
before turning south-eastwards back into Montana
where it joins the Missouri River near Glasgow.

**Mílos** the Greek name for MELOS.

**Milpitas** /mɪl'piːtəs/ an industrial city in
California, USA, near San Jose; pop. (1990)
50,690. It lies at the centre of a citrus-growing area.

**Milton Keynes** /ˌmɪlt(ə)n 'kiːnz/ a town in
Buckinghamshire, south-central England, headquarters of the Open University; pop. (1991)
172,300. It was built as a New Town around the village of Milford to a design by Richard Llewelyn-
Davies in 1967, and has become a byword as an
archetypical modern shopping centre.

**Milwaukee** /mɪl'wɔːkiː/ an industrial port and
city in south-east Wisconsin, USA, on the west
shore of Lake Michigan; pop. (1990) 628,090. First
settled in 1822, the city developed from the 1830s,
attracting large numbers of settlers from Germany
in the 1840s and from Poland and Italy later in the
century. It is noted for its brewing industry and is
an important port on the St. Lawrence Seaway.

**Min** /mɪn/ **1.** any of the Chinese dialects spoken in
the Fujian (Fukien) province of south-east China.
**2.** a river in central China that flows c.805 km. (500
miles) southwards across the Chengdu plain to join
the Yangtze River near Yibin. The Dujiangyan
irrigation scheme on the middle reaches of the river
has been in operation for over 2,200 years and is
one of the largest in China.

**Minaean** /mɪ'niːən/ a member of a Semitic-
speaking people who established a kingdom in
southern Arabia c.400 BC, absorbed into the
Sabaean kingdom in the late 1st c. BC.

**Mina Jebel Ali** /ˌmaɪnə ˌdʒebəl 'ɑːlɪ/ a seaport
and industrial complex on the Gulf coast of Dubai
in the United Arab Emirates.

**Minas** /'maɪnəs/ the largest of the tribal groups
of Rajasthan in western India.

**Minas Gerais** /ˌmiːnæs ʒe'ræiːs/ a state of
south-east Brazil, with major deposits of iron ore,
coal, gold, and diamonds; area 587,172 sq. km.
(227,058 sq. miles); pop. (1991) 15,731,960; capital,
Belo Horizonte.

**Minatitlán** /ˌmiːnəti:t'lɑːn/ a city in the state of
Veracruz, south-east Mexico, on the River
Coatzacoalcos; pop. (1980) 145,270. It developed
as a transportation and oil-refining centre during
the 1970s.

**Minch** /mɪntʃ/, **the** (also **the Minches**) a channel of the Atlantic between the mainland of Scotland and the Outer Hebrides. The northern stretch
is called the **North Minch**, the southern stretch,
north-west of Skye, is called the **Little Minch**.

**Mindanao** /ˌmɪndə'naʊ/ the second-largest
island of the Philippines; area 102,000 sq. km.
(39,400 sq. miles); pop. (1990) 14,297,000. Its chief
cities are Davao, Zamboanga, Cagayan de Oro,
Butuan, Iligan, and General Santos. Mindanao
is the centre of a long-standing secessionist
movement.

**Minden** /'mɪnd(ə)n/ an industrial city in North
Rhine-Westphalia, north-west Germany, on the
River Weser; pop. (1985) 80,000. Founded by
Charlemagne c.800, it was the scene of a battle in
1759 during which the French were defeated by a
British and Hanoverian army.

**Mindoro** /mɪn'dɔːrəʊ/ an island in the north-
west-central Philippines, situated to the south-west
of Luzon Island; area 9,732 sq. km. (3,759 sq.
miles). Its chief city is Mamburao and fishing, rice
cultivation, and coconut plantations are the main
economic activities.

**Ming** /mɪŋ/ the name of the Chinese dynasty
founded in 1368 by Chu Yuan-chang after the collapse of Mongol authority in China, and ruling
until succeeded by the Manchus in 1644. It was a
period of expansion and exploration, with lasting
contact made in the 16th c. between China and
Europe, and a culturally productive period in
which the arts flourished. The capital was established at Peking (Beijing) in 1421.

**Minho** /'miːnjəʊ/ (Spanish **Miño**) a river of the
Iberian peninsula which rises in north-west Spain
and flows south to the Portuguese frontier which it
follows before meeting the Atlantic north of Viana
do Castelo.

**Minicoy Islands** see LAKSHADWEEP ISLANDS.

**Minneapolis** /ˌmɪnɪ'æpəlɪs/ an industrial city
and port at the head of navigation on the
Mississippi River in south-east Minnesota; pop.
(1990) 368,380. Settled in 1847, it is a major processing and distribution centre for the grain and
cattle farms of the upper Midwest agricultural
region. Minneapolis is also the home of the world's
most powerful computer, the liquid-cooled Cray-2.

**Minnesota** /ˌmɪnɪ'səʊtə/ a state in the north-
central USA, on the Canadian border; area 218,601

sq. km. (84,402 sq. miles); pop. (1990) 4,375,100; capital, St. Paul. The largest cities are Minneapolis and St. Paul. Minnesota is also known as the North Star or Gopher State. Part of it was ceded to Britain by the French in 1763 and acquired by the US in 1783, the remainder forming part of the Louisiana purchase in 1803. Minnesota was organized as a territory in 1849 and became the 32nd US state in 1858. In addition to producing 75 per cent of the country's iron ore which is mined from the world's largest opencast iron mine, it produces large quantities of grain, vegetables, and livestock. Its principal landmarks include Voyageurs National Park, Mississippi National River and Recreation Area, and the Pipestone and Grand Portage national monuments. The state is divided into 87 counties:

| County | Area (sq. km.) | Pop. (1990) | County Seat |
|---|---|---|---|
| Aitkin | 4,768 | 12,425 | Aitkin |
| Anoka | 1,118 | 243,640 | Anoka |
| Becker | 3,411 | 27,880 | Detroit Lakes |
| Beltrami | 6,518 | 34,380 | Bemidji |
| Benton | 1,061 | 30,185 | Foley |
| Big Stone | 1,292 | 6,285 | Ortonville |
| Blue Earth | 1,947 | 54,040 | Mankato |
| Brown | 1,586 | 26,984 | New Ulm |
| Carlton | 2,246 | 29,260 | Carlton |
| Carver | 913 | 47,915 | Chaska |
| Cass | 5,286 | 21,790 | Walker |
| Chippewa | 1,518 | 13,230 | Montevideo |
| Chisago | 1,084 | 30,520 | Center City |
| Clay | 2,727 | 50,420 | Moorhead |
| Clearwater | 2,597 | 8,310 | Bagley |
| Cook | 3,671 | 3,870 | Grand Marais |
| Cottonwood | 1,664 | 12,690 | Windom |
| Crow Wing | 2,621 | 44,250 | Brainerd |
| Dakota | 1,492 | 275,230 | Hastings |
| Dodge | 1,141 | 15,730 | Mantorville |
| Douglas | 1,672 | 28,670 | Alexandria |
| Fairbault | 1,856 | 16,940 | Blue Earth |
| Fillmore | 2,241 | 20,780 | Preston |
| Freeborn | 1,833 | 33,060 | Albert Lea |
| Goodhue | 1,984 | 40,690 | Red Wind |
| Grant | 1,422 | 6,250 | Elbow Lake |
| Hennepin | 1,407 | 1,032,430 | Minneapolis |
| Houston | 1,466 | 18,500 | Caledonia |
| Hubbard | 2,434 | 14,940 | Park Rapids |
| Isanti | 1,144 | 25,920 | Cambridge |
| Itasca | 6,919 | 40,860 | Grand Rapids |
| Jackson | 1,817 | 11,680 | Jackson |
| Kanabec | 1,370 | 12,800 | Mora |
| Kandiyohi | 2,038 | 38,760 | Willmar |
| Kittson | 2,870 | 5,770 | Hallock |
| Koochiching | 8,081 | 16,300 | International Falls |
| La Sueur | 1,160 | 23,240 | Le Center |
| Lac Qui Parle | 2,007 | 8,920 | Madison |
| Lake | 2,053 | 10,415 | Two Harbors |
| Lake of the Woods | 3,370 | 4,080 | Baudette |
| Lincoln | 1,399 | 6,890 | Ivanhoe |
| Lyon | 1,856 | 24,790 | Marshall |
| Mahnomen | 1,453 | 5,040 | Mahnomen |
| Marshall | 4,576 | 10,990 | Warren |

| | | | |
|---|---|---|---|
| Martin | 1,836 | 22,910 | Fairmont |
| McLeod | 1,271 | 32,030 | Glencoe |
| Meeker | 1,622 | 20,850 | Litchfield |
| Mille Lacs | 1,503 | 18,670 | Milaca |
| Morrison | 2,922 | 29,600 | Falls |
| Mower | 1,847 | 37,385 | Austin |
| Murray | 1,825 | 9,660 | Slayton |
| Nicollet | 1,144 | 28,080 | Saint Peter |
| Nobles | 1,856 | 20,100 | Worthington |
| Norman | 2,280 | 7,975 | Ada |
| Olmsted | 1,703 | 106,470 | Rochester |
| Otter Tail | 5,130 | 50,710 | Fergus Falls |
| Pennington | 1,607 | 13,310 | Thief River Falls |
| Pine | 3,695 | 21,260 | Pine City |
| Pipestone | 1,212 | 10,490 | Pipestone |
| Polk | 5,153 | 32,500 | Crookston |
| Pope | 1,737 | 10,745 | Glenwood |
| Ramsey | 400 | 485,765 | Saint Paul |
| Red Lake | 1,126 | 4,525 | Red Lake Falls |
| Redwood | 2,293 | 17,250 | Redwood Falls |
| Renville | 2,558 | 17,670 | Olivia |
| Rice | 1,303 | 49,180 | Faribault |
| Rock | 1,256 | 9,810 | Luverne |
| Roseau | 4,360 | 15,030 | Roseau |
| Scott | 928 | 57,850 | Shakopee |
| Sherburne | 1,131 | 41,945 | Elk River |
| Sibley | 1,542 | 14,370 | Gaylord |
| St. Louis | 15,925 | 198,210 | Duluth |
| Stearns | 3,479 | 118,790 | Saint Cloud |
| Steele | 1,121 | 30,730 | Owatonna |
| Stevens | 1,456 | 10,630 | Morris |
| Swift | 1,932 | 10,720 | Benson |
| Todd | 2,447 | 23,360 | Long Prairie |
| Traverse | 1,495 | 4,460 | Wheaton |
| Wabasha | 1,396 | 19,740 | Wabasha |
| Wadena | 1,399 | 13,150 | Wadena |
| Waseca | 1,097 | 18,080 | Waseca |
| Washington | 1,014 | 145,900 | Stillwater |
| Watonwan | 1,131 | 11,680 | Saint James |
| Wilkin | 1,953 | 7,520 | Breckenridge |
| Winona | 1,638 | 47,830 | Winona |
| Wright | 1,747 | 68,710 | Buffalo |
| Yellow Medecine | 1,971 | 11,680 | Granite Falls |

**Miño** the Spanish name for the MINHO.

**Minoan** /mɪˈnəʊən/ an ancient civilization centred on Crete (c. 3000–1100 BC). It was the earliest on European soil, and was first revealed by the excavations of Sir Arthur Evans, who gave it its name. It had reached its zenith by the beginning of the late Bronze Age, extending over the islands of the south Aegean while its wares were exported to Cyprus, Syria, and Egypt. Urban centres were dominated by palaces such as those at Knossos, Mallia, Phaistos, and Zakro. Divided into two periods by a devastating earthquake that occurred c. 1700 BC, the Minoan civilization was noted particularly for its Linear A script and distinctive palatial art and architecture. It greatly influenced the later Mycenaeans, whose presence in Crete is attested from the 16th c. BC and who succeeded the Minoans in control of the Aegean c. 1400 BC.

**Minoo** /'mi:nu:/ a city in Osaka prefecture, on the island of Honshu, Japan; pop. (1990) 122,130.

**Minorca** /mɪ'nɔːkə/ (Spanish **Menorca**) the most easterly and second-largest of the Balearic Islands; area 689 sq. km. (266 sq. miles); pop. (1981) 58,700; capital, Mahón.

**Minsk** /mɪnsk/ an industrial and commercial city in eastern Europe, capital of the Republic of Belarus (Belorussia); pop. (1990) 1,612,800. Formerly held by Lithuania and Poland, it passed to Russia in 1793. Its large Jewish population was annihilated in concentration camps during World War II. In 1991 it became capital of the newly independent state of Belorussia. Its factories make motor vehicles, machinery, electronic goods, and textiles.

**Miocene** /'maɪə,siːn/ the fourth epoch of the Tertiary period, following the Oligocene and preceding the Pliocene, lasting from about 24.6 to 5.1 million years ago. It was a period of great earth movements during which the Alps and Himalayas were formed.

**Miquelon** SEE ST. PIERRE AND MIQUELON.

**Mirzapur** /'mɪ(ə)rzə,pʊ(ə)r/ a city in Uttar Pradesh, northern India, on the Ganges south-west of Varanasi; pop. (1991) 169,370. An important grain and cotton market prior to the development of the railway, Mirzapur now includes the Hindu pilgrimage centre of Vindhyachal.

**Mishima** /mɪ'ʃiːmə/ a city on Honshu Island, Japan, north-east of Shizuoka; pop. (1990) 105,320.

**Miskito Indians** /mɪs'kiːtəʊ/ SEE MOSQUITO COAST.

**Miskolc** /'mi:ʃkɒlts/ the third-largest city in Hungary, an industrial city on the Sajó River with iron and steel, engineering, and food-processing plants, 145 km. (90 miles) north-east of Budapest; pop. (1993) 191,000. A Polytechnic University for Heavy Industry was founded in 1949.

**Mission Viejo** /,mɪʃən 'vjeɪhəʊ/ a city in southern California, USA, in the foothills of the Santa Ana Mts.; pop. (1990) 72,820.

**Mississauga** /mɪsɪ'sɔːgə/ a city in southern Ontario, Canada, on the north-western shores of Lake Ontario, a western suburb of Toronto; pop. (1991) 463,400.

**Mississippi** /,mɪsɪ'sɪpɪ/ a major river of North America, which rises near the Canadian border in the US state of Minnesota and flows south for 3,778 km. (2,348 miles) to a delta on the Gulf of Mexico. With its chief tributary, the Missouri (from the source of the Red Rock River), it is 6,019 km. (3,741 miles) long and drains an area of 3.25 million sq. km. (1.25 million sq. miles); Minneapolis, St. Louis, Memphis, and New Orleans lie on the Mississippi. Known to the Indians as the 'Great Water', it provided a route into North America for early explorers such as de Soto (1539), Joliet

(1672), and La Salle (1681). From the 1830s onwards it was famous for the stern-wheeler steamboats which plied between New Orleans, St. Louis, and other northern cities. The river, its traffic, and its people were celebrated in the writings of Mark Twain, who was brought up on its banks in Hannibal, Missouri.

**Mississippi** a state of the southern USA, on the Gulf of Mexico, bounded to the west by the lower Mississippi River; area 123,515 sq. km. (47,689 sq. miles); pop. (1990) 2,573,210; the capital and largest city is Jackson. Mississippi is also known as the Magnolia State. A French colony in the 18th c., it was ceded to Britain in 1763 and to the US in 1783, becoming the 29th state in 1817. Formerly dependent on cotton, its agriculture now produces large quantities of soyabeans, corn, peanuts, pecan, rice, and sugar cane. Landmarks include Vicksburg National Military Park, Tupelo National Battlefield, and the 712-km. (445-mile) long Natchez Trace Parkway. The state is divided into 82 counties:

| County | Area (sq. km.) | Pop. (1990) | County Seat |
|---|---|---|---|
| Adams | 1,186 | 35,360 | Natchez |
| Alcorn | 1,043 | 31,720 | Corinth |
| Amite | 1,903 | 13,330 | Liberty |
| Attala | 1,916 | 18,480 | Kosciusko |
| Benton | 1,058 | 8,050 | Ashland |
| Bolivar | 2,319 | 41,875 | Cleveland and Rosedale |
| Calhoun | 1,490 | 14,910 | Pittsboro |
| Carroll | 1,648 | 9,240 | Carrollton and Valden |
| Chickasaw | 1,308 | 18,085 | Houston and Okolona |
| Choctaw | 1,092 | 9,070 | Ackerman |
| Claiborne | 1,284 | 11,370 | Port Gibson |
| Clarke | 1,799 | 17,310 | Quitman |
| Clay | 1,079 | 21,120 | West Point |
| Coahoma | 1,453 | 31,665 | Clarksdale |
| Copiah | 2,025 | 27,590 | Hazlehurst |
| Covington | 1,082 | 16,530 | Collins |
| De Soto | 1,256 | 67,910 | Hernando |
| Forrest | 1,219 | 68,310 | Hattiesburg |
| Franklin | 1,472 | 8,380 | Meadville |
| George | 1,256 | 16,670 | Lucedale |
| Greene | 1,867 | 10,220 | Leakesville |
| Grenada | 1,095 | 21,555 | Grenada |
| Hancock | 1,243 | 31,760 | Bay Saint Louis |
| Harrison | 1,511 | 165,365 | Gulfport |
| Hinds | 2,275 | 254,440 | Jackson and Raymond |
| Holmes | 1,973 | 21,600 | Lexington |
| Humphreys | 1,118 | 12,130 | Belzoni |
| Issaquena | 1,056 | 1,910 | Mayersville |
| Itawamba | 1,404 | 20,020 | Fulton |
| Jackson | 1,901 | 115,240 | Cascagoula |
| Jasper | 1,763 | 17,110 | Bat Springs and Paulding |
| Jefferson | 1,360 | 8,650 | Fayette |
| Jefferson Davis | 1,063 | 14,050 | Prentiss |

(cont.)

| | | | |
|---|---|---|---|
| Jones | 1,810 | 62,030 | Ellisville and Laurel |
| Kemper | 1,992 | 10,360 | De Kalb |
| Lafayette | 1,739 | 31,830 | Oxford |
| Lamar | 1,297 | 30,420 | Purvis |
| Lauderdale | 1,833 | 75,555 | Meridian |
| Lawrence | 1,131 | 12,460 | Monticello |
| Leake | 1,518 | 18,440 | Carthage |
| Lee | 1,173 | 65,580 | Tupelo |
| Leflore | 1,573 | 37,340 | Greenwood |
| Lincoln | 1,526 | 30,280 | Brookhaven |
| Lowndes | 1,344 | 59,310 | Columbus |
| Madison | 1,867 | 53,790 | Canton |
| Marion | 1,425 | 25,540 | Columbia |
| Marshall | 1,843 | 30,360 | Holly Springs |
| Monroe | 2,007 | 36,580 | Aberdeen |
| Montgomery | 1,061 | 12,390 | Winona |
| Neshoba | 1,487 | 24,800 | Philadelphia |
| Newton | 1,508 | 20,290 | Decatur |
| Noxubee | 1,815 | 12,600 | Macon |
| Octibbeha | 1,193 | 38,375 | Starkville |
| Panola | 1,804 | 30,000 | Batesville and Sardis |
| Pearl River | 2,127 | 38,710 | Poplarville |
| Perry | 1,693 | 10,685 | New Augusta |
| Pike | 1,066 | 36,880 | Magnolia |
| Pontotoc | 1,297 | 22,240 | Pontotoc |
| Prentiss | 1,087 | 23,280 | Booneville |
| Quitman | 1,056 | 10,490 | Marks |
| Rankin | 2,033 | 87,160 | Brandon |
| Scott | 1,586 | 24,140 | Forest |
| Sharkey | 1,131 | 7,070 | Rolling Fork |
| Simpson | 1,537 | 23,950 | Mendenhall |
| Smith | 1,651 | 14,800 | Raleigh |
| Stone | 1,160 | 10,750 | Wiggins |
| Sunflower | 1,836 | 32,870 | Indianola |
| Tallahatchie | 1,693 | 15,210 | Charleston and Sumner |
| Tate | 1,056 | 21,430 | Senatobia |
| Tippah | 1,191 | 19,520 | Ripley |
| Tishomingo | 1,128 | 17,680 | Iuka |
| Tunica | 1,196 | 8,160 | Tunica |
| Union | 1,082 | 22,085 | New Albany |
| Walthall | 1,050 | 14,250 | Tylertown |
| Warren | 1,550 | 47,880 | Vicksburg |
| Washington | 1,906 | 67,935 | Greenville |
| Wayne | 2,114 | 19,520 | Waynesboro |
| Webster | 1,102 | 10,220 | Walthall |
| Wilkinson | 1,763 | 9,680 | Woodville |
| Winston | 1,586 | 19,430 | Louisville |
| Yalobusha | 1,243 | 12,030 | Coffeeville and Water Valley |
| Yazoo | 2,426 | 25,510 | Yazoo City |

**Missolonghi** /ˌmɪsəˈlɒŋgɪ/ (Greek **Mesolóngion** /ˌmesəˈlɒŋgɪ,ɒn/) a city in western Greece, on the north shore of the Gulf of Patras, capital of the department of Aetolia and Acarnania; pop. (1981) 10,150. It resisted the Turkish forces in the War of Greek Independence (1821–9) and is noted as the place where the poet Byron, who had joined the fight, died in 1824.

**Missouri** /mɪˈzʊərɪ/ a major river of North America, one of the main tributaries of the Mississippi. It rises in the Rocky Mountains in Montana and flows 3,725 km. (2,315 miles) to meet the Mississippi just north of St. Louis. Its total length to the head of the Red Rock is 4,125 km. (2,564 miles).

**Missouri** a state of central USA, bounded on the east by the Mississippi River; area 180,516 sq. km. (69,697 sq. miles); pop. (1990) 5,117,070; capital, Jefferson City. The largest cities are Kansas City, St. Louis, Springfield, and Independence. Missouri is also known as the Show-Me State. Acquired from the French as part of the Louisiana Purchase (1803), it became the 24th state in 1821. Grain, cotton, vegetables, and tobacco are produced and important industrial goods include aerospace and transportation equipment. Lead, zinc, coal, and limestone are the principal mineral resources. Notable landmarks include the Ozark National Scenic Riverway, Wilson's Creek National Battlefield, George Washington Carver National Monument, Harry S. Truman National Historic Site, and Ulysses S. Grant National Historic Site. The state is administratively divided into an independent city (St. Louis) and 114 counties:

| County | Area (sq. km.) | Pop. (1990) | County Seat |
|---|---|---|---|
| Adair | 1,474 | 24,580 | Kirksville |
| Andrew | 1,131 | 14,630 | Savannah |
| Atchison | 1,409 | 7,460 | Rockport |
| Audrain | 1,812 | 23,600 | Mexico |
| Barry | 2,010 | 27,550 | Cassville |
| Barton | 1,550 | 11,310 | Lamar |
| Bates | 2,207 | 15,025 | Butler |
| Benton | 1,895 | 13,860 | Warsaw |
| Bollinger | 1,615 | 10,620 | Marble Hill |
| Boone | 1,790 | 112,380 | Columbia |
| Buchanan | 1,063 | 83,080 | Saint Joseph |
| Butler | 1,815 | 38,765 | Poplar Buff |
| Caldwell | 1,118 | 8,380 | Kingston |
| Callaway | 2,189 | 32,810 | Fulton |
| Camden | 1,667 | 27,495 | Camdenton |
| Cape Girardeau | 1,500 | 61,630 | Jackson |
| Carroll | 1,807 | 10,750 | Carrollton |
| Carter | 1,323 | 5,515 | Van Buren |
| Cass | 1,823 | 63,810 | Harrisonville |
| Cedar | 1,222 | 12,090 | Stockton |
| Chariton | 1,971 | 9,200 | Keytesville |
| Christian | 1,466 | 32,640 | Ozark |
| Clark | 1,318 | 7,550 | Kahoka |
| Clay | 1,048 | 153,410 | Liberty |
| Clinton | 1,100 | 16,595 | Plattsburg |
| Cole | 1,019 | 63,580 | Jefferson City |
| Cooper | 1,474 | 14,835 | Boonville |
| Crawford | 1,934 | 19,170 | Steelville |
| Dade | 1,277 | 7,450 | Greenfield |
| Dallas | 1,412 | 12,650 | Buffalo |
| Davies | 1,477 | 7,865 | Gallatin |
| De Kalb | 1,105 | 9,970 | Maysville |
| Dent | 1,963 | 13,700 | Salem |
| Douglas | 2,116 | 11,880 | Ava |
| Dunklin | 1,422 | 33,110 | Kennett |

| Franklin | 2,397 | 80,600 | Union |
|---|---|---|---|
| Gasconade | 1,355 | 14,010 | Hemann |
| Gentry | 1,282 | 6,850 | Albany |
| Greene | 1,760 | 207,950 | Springfield |
| Grundy | 1,136 | 10,540 | Trenton |
| Harrison | 1,885 | 8,470 | Bethany |
| Henry | 1,895 | 20,040 | Clinton |
| Hickory | 985 | 7,335 | Hermitage |
| Holt | 1,188 | 6,030 | Oregon |
| Howard | 1,209 | 9,630 | Fayette |
| Howell | 2,413 | 31,450 | West Plains |
| Iron | 1,435 | 10,730 | Ironton |
| Jackson | 1,589 | 633,230 | Independence |
| Jasper | 1,667 | 90,465 | Carthage |
| Jefferson | 1,719 | 171,380 | Hillsboro |
| Johnson | 2,168 | 42,510 | Warrensburg |
| Knox | 1,318 | 4,480 | Edina |
| Laclede | 1,997 | 27,160 | Lebanon |
| Lafayette | 1,643 | 31,110 | Lexington |
| Lawrence | 1,594 | 30,240 | Mount Vernon |
| Lewis | 1,323 | 10,230 | Monticello |
| Lincoln | 1,630 | 28,890 | Troy |
| Linn | 1,612 | 13,885 | Linneus |
| Livingston | 1,396 | 14,590 | Chillcothe |
| Macon | 2,072 | 15,345 | Macon |
| Madison | 1,292 | 11,127 | Fredericktown |
| Maries | 1,373 | 7,980 | Vienna |
| Marion | 1,139 | 27,680 | Palmyra |
| McDonald | 1,404 | 16,940 | Pineville |
| Mercer | 1,180 | 3,720 | Princeton |
| Miller | 1,542 | 20,700 | Tuscumbia |
| Mississippi | 1,066 | 14,440 | Charleston |
| Moniteau | 1,084 | 12,300 | California |
| Monroe | 1,742 | 9,100 | Paris |
| Montgomery | 1,404 | 11,355 | Montgomery City |
| Morgan | 1,544 | 15,570 | Versailles |
| New Madrid | 1,711 | 20,930 | New Madrid |
| Newton | 1,630 | 44,445 | Neosho |
| Nodaway | 2,275 | 21,710 | Maryville |
| Oregon | 2,059 | 9,470 | Alton |
| Osage | 1,576 | 12,020 | Linn |
| Ozark | 1,901 | 8,600 | Gainesville |
| Pemiscot | 1,344 | 21,920 | Caruthersville |
| Perry | 1,230 | 16,650 | Perryville |
| Pettis | 1,784 | 35,440 | Sedalia |
| Phelps | 1,752 | 35,250 | Rolla |
| Pike | 1,750 | 15,970 | Bowling Green |
| Platte | 1,095 | 57,870 | Platte City |
| Polk | 1,654 | 21,830 | Bolivar |
| Pulaski | 1,430 | 41,310 | Waynesville |
| Putnam | 1,352 | 5,080 | Unionville |
| Ralls | 1,253 | 8,480 | New London |
| Randolph | 1,240 | 24,370 | Huntsville |
| Ray | 1,477 | 21,970 | Richmond |
| Reynolds | 2,103 | 6,660 | Centerville |
| Ripley | 1,641 | 12,300 | Doniphan |
| Saline | 1,963 | 23,520 | Marshall |
| Schuyler | 803 | 4,240 | Lancaster |
| Scotland | 1,139 | 4,820 | Memphis |
| Scott | 1,100 | 39,380 | Benton |
| Shannon | 2,610 | 7,610 | Eminence |
| Shelby | 1,303 | 6,940 | Shelbyville |
| St. Charles | 1,451 | 212,910 | St. Charles |
| St. Clair | 1,817 | 8,460 | Osceola |
| St. Francois | 1,173 | 48,900 | Farmington |

| St. Louis | 1,316 | 993,530 | Clayton |
|---|---|---|---|
| Ste. Genevieve | 1,310 | 16,040 | Ste. Genevieve |
| Stoddard | 2,119 | 28,895 | Bloomfield |
| Stone | 1,173 | 19,080 | Galena |
| Sullivan | 1,693 | 6,330 | Milan |
| Taney | 1,581 | 25,560 | Forsyth |
| Texas | 3,068 | 21,480 | Houston |
| Vernon | 2,176 | 19,040 | Nevada |
| Warren | 1,115 | 19,530 | Warrenton |
| Washington | 1,981 | 20,380 | Potosi |
| Wayne | 1,981 | 11,540 | Greenville |
| Webster | 1,544 | 23,750 | Marshfield |
| Worth | 693 | 2,440 | Grant City |
| Wright | 1,773 | 16,760 | Hartville |

**Misti** see EL MISTI.

**mistral** /'mɪstrɑːl/ a cold, northerly wind that blows down the Rhône valley of southern France into the Mediterranean; in summer it increases the danger of forest fires.

**Misurata** /ˌmɪzəˈrɑːtə/ (Arabic **Misratah**) a city in north-west Libya, on the Mediterranean coast; pop. (1984) 178,295.

**Mitaka** /mɪˈtækə/ a city on Honshu Island, Japan, forming a suburb of Tokyo; pop. (1990) 165,555.

**Mitanni** /mɪˈtænɪ/ a political and geographic term of unknown derivation, first encountered in Egyptian inscriptions dating to Tuthmosis I (c. 1520 BC) in reference to a Late Bronze Age hegemony of north Mesopotamian and Syrian states composed of a predominantly Hurrian-speaking populace and ruled by a succession of Indo-European kings.
**Mitannian** adj. & n.

**Mitilíni** the Greek name for MYTILENE.

**Mitla** /'miːtlə/ an ancient city in southern Mexico, to the east of the city of Oaxaca, now a noted archaeological site. Believed to have been established as a burial site by the Zapotecs some centuries before the arrival of the Spanish, it was eventually overrun by the Mixtecs in about AD 1000. Its Nahuatl name means 'place of the dead'.

**Mito** /'miːtəʊ/ the capital of Ibaraki prefecture in the Kanto region of Honshu Island, Japan; pop. (1990) 234,970.

**Mitsiwa** see MASSAWA.

**Mixtec** /'mɪkstek/ a people of southern Mexico who were outstanding craftsmen in pottery and metallurgy. In the 15th c. they were conquered by the Aztecs.

**Miyakonojo** /miːˌjækəˈnəʊdʒəʊ/ a city on south-east Kyushu Island, Japan; pop. (1990) 130,155.

**Miyazaki** /miːjəˈzɑːkɪ/ an industrial port and resort on the south-east coast of Kyushu Island, Japan, capital of Miyazaki prefecture; pop. (1990) 287,370. Situated on the Miyazaki or 'shrine promontory', its Shinto shrine is dedicated to Jimmu, the first emperor of Japan.

**Mizoram** /mɪˈzɔːrəm/ a state in the far north-east of India, lying between Bangladesh and Burma (Myanmar); area 21,081 sq. km. (8,142 sq. miles); pop. (1991) 686,220; capital, Aizawl. Separated from Assam in 1972, it was administered as a Union Territory of India until 1986, when it became a state.

**Mmabatho** /məˈbɑːtəʊ/ a city in Northern Transvaal, South Africa, the capital of the former independent homeland of Bophuthatswana, situated between Mafikeng and the frontier with Botswana; pop. 28,000.

**MN** *abbr.* US Minnesota (in official postal use).

**MO** *abbr.* US Missouri (in official postal use).

**Moabite** /ˈməʊəˌbaɪt/ a member of a Semitic people traditionally descended from Lot, living in Moab, an ancient region east of the Dead Sea and now part of Jordan.

**Mobile** /məʊˈbiːl/ an industrial city and port in south-west Alabama, USA, at the head of Mobile Bay, an arm of the Gulf of Mexico; pop. (1990) 196,280. Shipbuilding, food processing, and the manufacture of paper, textiles, and petroleum products are its chief industries.

**Mobuto Sese Seko** /məˈbuːtu ˌseɪsɪ ˈseɪkəʊ/, **Lake** the Zairean name for Lake Albert. See ALBERT, LAKE.

**Mocha** /ˈməʊkə/ (Arabic **Al-Makha**) a port on the Red Sea coast of Yemen that gave its name to a type of coffee once exported from here. It was an important centre of trade until the British began to develop the port of Aden in the early 19th c.

**Mochica** /məˈtʃiːkə/ a pre-Inca people living on the coast of Peru AD 100–800. They developed a highly sophisticated agricultural system that was dependent on artificial irrigation, and constructed cities that functioned as ceremonial centres occupied by administrators and members of the ruling dynasty.

**Mochudi** /mɒˈkʊdɪ/ a traditional village in southern Botswana, at the south-eastern edge of the Kalahari Desert 40 km. (25 miles) north of Gaborone; pop. (1991) 25,540.

**Modena** /ˈmɔːdeɪnə/ a city in northern Italy, on the Panaro River north-west of Bologna; pop. (1990) 177,500. An ancient settlement on the Via Emilia, Modena became an independent city-state *c.* 1135 and was the seat of the dukedom of Ferrara. The city was absorbed into Italy in 1860 and is now capital of the province of Modena in the Emilia-Romagna region. The Ferrari racing car was first produced in 1947 in the nearby village of Maranello. It is also a noted centre for the production of balsamic vinegar, agricultural machinery, and machine tools.

**Modesto** /mɒˈdestəʊ/ a city in central California, USA, on the Tuolumne River to the east of San Francisco; pop. (1990) 164,730. It is a processing and marketing centre for the rich farmlands of the central San Joaquin valley and Stanislaus County. The nearby Dom Pedro dam is a major source of power and irrigation water. Modesto was named after a San Francisco banker who was too modest to publicize his own name.

**Mödling** /ˈmɜːdlɪŋ/ a resort town in the state of Lower Austria, north-eastern Austria, situated between Vienna and Baden; pop. (1991) 20,600. It is associated with the composers Beethoven and Schönberg, both of whom lived here for a time.

**Moe** /məʊ/ a residential city in south-east Victoria, Australia, in the Latrobe valley 135 km. (85 miles) east of Melbourne; pop. (1991) 17,990 (with Yallourn).

**Moers** /mɜːz/ (also **Mörs**) an industrial city in North Rhine-Westphalia, western Germany, situated west of the Rhine and north of Düsseldorf; pop. (1991) 105,000.

**Mogadishu** /ˌmɒɡəˈdɪʃuː/ (also **Muqdisho** /mʌkˈdɪʃəʊ/, Italian **Mogadiscio** /mɒɡəˈdɪʃəʊ/) the capital of Somalia, a port on the Indian Ocean; pop. (1982) 377,000. Founded by the Arabs in the 10th c., it was leased to the Italians in 1892 and sold to them in 1905. It was the capital of Italian Somaliland from 1892 to 1960. Following 12 years of civil war in Somalia the city was badly devastated by fighting during 1990–4.

**Mogi das Cruzes** /muːˌʒi dəs ˈkruːziːs/ a city in the state of São Paulo, southern Brazil, to the east of São Paulo; pop. (1990) 262,370.

**Mogilev** /ˈmɒɡələf/ see MAHILYOU.

**Mogpo** see MOKPO.

**Mohács** /məʊˈhɑːtʃ/ a river port and industrial town on the Danube in southern Hungary, 40 km. (25 miles) east of Pécs and close to the borders with Croatia and Serbia; pop. (est. 1984) 21,000. It was the site of a battle in 1526, in which the Hungarians were defeated by a Turkish force under Suleiman I, as a result of which Hungary became part of the Ottoman empire. A site nearby was the scene of a further decisive battle fought in 1687 during the campaign that swept the Turks out of Hungary.

**Mohammerah** /məˈhæmərə/ the former name (until 1924) of KHORRAMSHAHR.

**Mohave Desert** see MOJAVE DESERT.

**Mohawk** /ˈməʊhɔːk/ a subgroup of the North American Iroquois tribe originally found in New York state and Canada.

**Mohawk Trail** an old routeway through the Appalachian Mountains of New York state, USA, used by early settlers travelling from the east coast to the Midwest. It became less important after the building of the transcontinental railroads.

**Mohenjo-Daro** /məˌhendʒəʊ ˈdɑːrəʊ/ an ancient city of the civilization of the Indus Valley (*c.* 2600–1700 BC), now a major archaeological site in Pakistan, south-west of Sukkur. It was first excavated by the Indian Archaeological Survey under Sir John Marshall in 1922 and 1931.

**Mohican** /məʊˈhiːkən/ (also **Mohegan**) an Algonquian-speaking North American Indian tribe formerly occupying the western parts of Connecticut and Massachusetts (not to be confused with the Mahicans of the Hudson River valley in upper New York state). They were made famous in James Fenimore Cooper's book *Last of the Mohicans*.

**Moho discontinuity** /ˈməʊhəʊ/ (also **Mohorovičić discontinuity**) the boundary in the earth's interior between the crust and the upper mantle, occurring at about 35 km. (22 miles) below the continents and at *c.* 10 km. (6 miles) below the oceans.

**Mojave Desert** /məʊˈhɑːvɪ/ (also **Mohave**) a desert in southern California, USA, to the southeast of the Sierra Nevada and north-east of Los Angeles. Edwards Air Force Base, in the Antelope Valley, is a centre of aerospace technology and the small town of Mojave was once a centre of the trade in borax which used to be brought by mule from Death Valley.

**Mokpo** /ˈmɑːkpəʊ/ (also **Mogpo**) a fishing port at the south-western tip of Korea, in South Cholla province; pop. (1990) 253,420. There are ferries to Cheju Island

**Mold** /məʊld/ the county town of Clwyd, north-east Wales, on the River Alyn south-west of Chester; pop. (1981) 8,590. The Clwydian Hills rise to the west. The landscape painter Richard Wilson (1714–82) lies buried here.

**Moldau** /ˈməʊldaʊ/ the German name for the VLTAVA in the Czech Republic.

**Moldavia** /mɒlˈdeɪvɪə/ a former principality of south-east Europe. Formerly part of the Roman province of Dacia, the region became a principality in the 14th c., coming under Turkish rule in the 16th c. The province of Bukovina in the north-west was ceded to Austria in 1777 and Bessarabia, in the north-east, was ceded to Russia in 1812. In 1859 Moldavia united with Wallachia to form the independent kingdom of Romania. Its capital was Iasi (Jassy) and its chief port on the Danube was Galatz (Galați).
**Moldavian** *adj. & n.*

**Moldova** /mɒlˈdeʊvə/ (also **Moldavia** /mɒlˈdeɪvɪə/) official name **The Republic of Moldova** a landlocked country in south-east Europe, between Romania and Ukraine; area  33,700 sq. km. (13,017 sq. miles); pop. (est. 1991) 4,384,000; official language, Moldovan; capital, Chisnau (Kishinev). Lying between the Prut and Dniester rivers, Moldova is a land of hilly plains with a fertile soil that supports the production of fruit, vegetables, grain, and wine. Its climate is warm and dry with relatively mild winters. Formerly part of Romania, Moldova was a constituent republic of the Soviet Union from 1940 to 1991. It comprises a region that was created an Autonomous Soviet Socialist Republic in 1924 and areas of Bessarabia ceded by Romania to the USSR in 1940. Over 60 per cent of the population are Moldovans; the remainder are Russians, Ukrainians, Gagauz and others, some of whom support the separation from Moldova of the Transdniester Moldovian Soviet Socialist Republic (which was first proclaimed in 1990) and the autonomous Gagauz territory. Moldova is governed by an executive president and a Supreme Soviet.
**Moldovan** or **Moldavian** *adj. & n.*

**Moldoveanu** /ˌmɒldəʊvɪˈɑːnuː/ a mountain that rises to 2,544 m. (8,346 ft.) in the Transylvanian Alps south-east of Sibiu, the highest peak in Romania.

**Molepolole** a town on the south-eastern edge of the Kalahari Desert in southern Botswana, chief administrative centre of the Kweng district; pop. (1991) 36,930.

**Molise** /mɒˈliːzɪ/ a region of eastern Italy, on the Adriatic coast, comprising the provinces of Campobasso and Isernia; area 4,437 sq. km. (1,714 sq. miles); pop. (1990) 336,460; capital, Campobasso.

**Mollweide projection** /ˈmɔːlvaɪd/ an equal-area projection on which the central meridian is a straight line at half the scale-length of the equator. All other meridians are ellipses, and all parallels of latitude are straight lines.

**Moluccas** /məˈlʌkəs/ (also **Moluccas Islands** or **Maluku** /məˈluːkuː/) an island group in Indonesia, between Sulawesi (Celebes) and New Guinea; area 74,505 sq. km. (28,777 sq. miles); pop. (est. 1993) 2,001,200; capital, Amboina. Settled by the Portuguese in the early 16th c., the islands were taken a century later by the Dutch, who controlled the lucrative trade in the spices produced on the islands. The islands were formerly known as the Spice Islands.

**Molucca Sea** a stretch of water in south-east Asia separating the northern Moluccas from Sulawesi (Celebes).

**Mombasa** /mɒmˈbæsə/ a seaport and industrial city in south-east Kenya, on the Indian Ocean; pop. (est. 1986) 457,000. Established by the Portuguese as a fortified trading post in 1593, it is the leading port, with a major oil refinery, and second-largest city of Kenya. There are many tourist hotels. It was the capital of the British East Africa Protectorate from 1888 until 1907.

**Monaco** /ˈmɒnəˌkəʊ/ a principality in southern Europe on the Mediterranean coast, forming an enclave within French territory near the Italian frontier; area 1.95 sq. km. (0.75 sq. miles); pop. (1990) 29,880; official language, French; capital, Monaco-Ville. Monaco is divided into the four communes of Monaco-Ville, Monte Carlo, La Condamine, and Fontvieille. Ruled by the Genoese from medieval times, and by the Grimaldi family from 1297, Monaco was under

French occupation from 1793 to 1814 and a protectorate of Sardinia until 1861. It became a constitutional monarchy in 1911, although the constitution was briefly suspended in 1959–62. The smallest sovereign state in the world, apart from the Vatican, Monaco is almost entirely dependent on the tourist trade, with luxurious yachting marinas and famous casinos, and maintains a customs union with France. It is also famous for the Monte Carlo Rally and the Monaco Grand Prix roadrace. The principality is governed by an executive Minister of State and National Council. **Monacan** or **Monégasque** *adj. & n.*

**Monadhliath Mountains** /ˌməʊnəˈlɪə/ a range of mountains in the Scottish Highlands lying between Loch Ness and the River Spey.

**monadnock** /məˈnædnɒk/ a steep-sided isolated hill resistant to erosion and rising above a plain. The term is derived from Mount Monadnock in the US state of New Hampshire.

**Monaghan** /ˈmɒnəhən/ **1.** a county of the Republic of Ireland in the province of Ulster; area 1,290 sq. km. (498 sq. miles); pop. (1991) 51,260. **2.** its county town, a market centre on the Ulster Canal; pop. (1991) 5,750.

**Monastir** /ˌmɒnəˈstɪə(r)/ a resort town with an international airport on the coast of Tunisia, 18 km. (7 miles) south-east of Sousse.

**Monbazillac** a village in the Dordogne department, central France, noted for its sweet white wine which has been produced since monks first planted vines in the 11th c.; pop. (1981) 840.

**Mönchengladbach** /ˌmʊnxənˈɡlædbæx/ a city in the state of North Rhine-Westphalia, northwest Germany, on the River Niers near Düsseldorf; pop. (1991) 262,580. Developed round a Benedictine abbey which now serves as the city hall, it has textiles and machinery industries. It is the site of the NATO headquarters for northern Europe.

**Monclova** /mɒnˈkləʊvə/ a city in the state of Coahuila, north-east Mexico; pop. (1990) 178,020. It is an industrial centre with iron and steel works.

**Moncton** /ˈmʌŋktən/ a town in south-east New Brunswick, Canada, at the head of Chignecto Bay; pop. (1991) 57,000. One of the chief towns of Acadia, it is a road and rail junction with a French-speaking university. It was named after Robert Monckton, the British commander who captured nearby Fort Beauséjour in 1755.

**Monégasque** /ˌmɒneɪˈɡæsk/ a native of Monaco.

**Mongolia** /mɒnˈɡəʊlɪə/ official name **The State of Mongolia** a large and sparsely populated country of eastern Asia, bordered by Russian Siberia and northern China; area 1,565,000 sq.

km. (604,480 sq. miles); pop. (est. 1991) 2,184,000; official languages, Khalka Mongolian and Kazakh; capital, Ulan Bator. To the north of the Gobi Desert, which occupies much of the southern half of the country, lies a fertile tableland at an altitude of 914–1,525 m. (3,000–5,000 ft.). Rainfall is low and winters are long and cold, with a swift transition in April to a warm summer which lasts until October. The economy is largely pastoral although Mongolia is rich in natural resources such as coal, oil, copper, lead, molybdenum, gold, and tungsten. The centre of the medieval Mongol empire, Mongolia subsequently became a Chinese province, achieving *de facto* independence in 1911. In 1924 it became a Communist state after the Soviet model, aligning itself with the former USSR. Free multiparty elections were held in 1990 and a new democratic constitition was introduced in 1992. The country is governed by a unicameral People's Great Hural. It was formerly known as Outer Mongolia to distinguish it from Inner Mongolia, which remains a province of China. **Mongolian** *adj. & n.*

**Mongolian** /mɒnˈɡəʊlɪən/ a racial division occupying regions of east Asia, south-east Asia, and arctic North America, speaking a number of related languages and dialects (including Buryat, Kalmuck, and Khalkha Mongol) which together form the Mongolian group in the Altaic family. During the 13th c. the Mongols under Genghis Khan established a large empire that stretched across northern China and Russia to eastern Europe.

**Mon-Khmer** /məʊnˈkmeə(r)/ a group of Indo-Chinese languages of which the most important are Mon (spoken in eastern Burma and western Thailand), Khmer (= Cambodian), Cham, Khasi, Nicobarese, Sakai, and Samang. Mon (or Talaing) is now a relatively minor language but in the 13th c. it was extremely influential throughout Burma.

**Monklands** /ˈmʌŋkləndz/ an industrial district of Strathclyde Region in central Scotland from 1975 to 1996; area 163 sq. km. (42 sq. miles); pop. (1991) 101,150; administrative centre, Coatbridge.

**Monmouthshire** /ˈmɒnməθˌʃɪə/ a former county of south-east Wales, on the border with England. The major part of it was incorporated into Gwent in 1974.

**Monongahela** /məˌnɒŋgəˈhiːlə/ a river of North America that rises in Virginia and flows 205 km. (128 miles) northwards to Pittsburgh, Pennsylvania, where it joins the Allegheny River to become the Ohio River.

**Monroe** /mənˈrəʊ/ a city in north-east Louisiana, USA, on the Ouachita River; pop. (1990) 54,910. It lies at the centre of one of the world's largest natural gas-fields and nearby forests supply timber for the city's furniture, paper, and chemical industries. Joseph Biedenharn, first bottler of Coca Cola, lived here.

**Monrovia** /mɒnˈrəʊvɪə/ the capital and chief port of the West African state of Liberia; pop. (1985) 500,000. Originally known as Christopolis, but later renamed after US President James Monroe, it was founded in 1822 by the American Colonization Society as a settlement for slaves repatriated from North America.

**Mons** /mɒnz/ (Flemish **Bergen** /ˈbeəxən/) a town in the province of Hainaut, southern Belgium, at the centre of a major coal-mining and industrial region; pop. (1991) 91,730. It was the site of the first British battle on the Continent in World War I, in August 1914.

**monsoon** /mɒnˈsuːn/ a wind in southern and other parts of Asia, especially in the Indian Ocean, blowing from the south-west in summer (**wet monsoon**) and the north-east in winter (**dry monsoon**). The term is also used to describe the heavy rainfall in Ethiopia and West Africa.

**montana** /mɒnˈtɑːnə/ a Spanish word used to describe the equatorial forested slopes of the eastern Andes which have a heavy rainfall.

**Montana** /mɒnˈtænə/ a state in the western US on the Canadian border east of the Rocky Mountains; area 380,848 sq. km. (147,046 sq. miles); pop. (1990) 799,065; capital, Helena. The largest cities are Billings, Great Falls, and Missoula. Montana is also known as the Treasure State. It formed part of the Louisiana Purchase in 1803 and was enlarged in 1846 with land obtained from Britain under the Oregon Treaty. In 1889 it became the 41st state of the Union. Once a leading centre of copper mining, Montana produces grain, vegetables, sheep, and cattle. Major landmarks include Glacier National Park, Yellowstone National Park, and Custer Battlefield National Monument. The state is divided into 56 counties:

| County | Area (sq. km.) | Pop. (1990) | County Seat |
|---|---|---|---|
| Beaverhead | 14,375 | 8,420 | Dillon |
| Big Horn | 12,956 | 11,340 | Hardin |
| Blaine | 11,068 | 6,730 | Chinook |
| Broadwater | 3,091 | 3,320 | Townsend |
| Carbon | 5,346 | 8,080 | Red Lodge |
| Carter | 8,689 | 1,500 | Ekalaka |
| Cascade | 7,017 | 77,690 | Great Falls |
| Chouteau | 10,366 | 5,450 | Fort Benton |
| Custer | 9,818 | 11,700 | Miles City |
| Daniels | 3,710 | 2,270 | Scobey |
| Dawson | 6,172 | 9,505 | Glendive |
| Deer Lodge | 1,924 | 10,280 | Anaconda |
| Fallon | 4,220 | 3,100 | Baker |
| Fergus | 11,284 | 12,080 | Lewistown |
| Flathead | 13,291 | 59,220 | Kalispell |
| Gallatin | 6,526 | 50,460 | Bozeman |
| Garfield | 11,677 | 1,590 | Jordan |
| Glacier | 7,780 | 12,120 | Cut Bank |
| Golden Valley | 3,047 | 910 | Ryegate |
| Granite | 4,495 | 2,550 | Philipsburg |
| Hill | 7,532 | 17,650 | Havre |
| Jefferson | 4,308 | 7,940 | Boulder |
| Judith Basin | 4,865 | 2,280 | Stanford |
| Lake | 3,757 | 21,040 | Polson |
| Lewis and Clark | 8,999 | 47,495 | Helena |
| Liberty | 3,708 | 2,295 | Chester |
| Lincoln | 9,402 | 17,480 | Libby |
| Madison | 9,334 | 5,990 | Virginia City |
| McCone | 6,828 | 2,280 | Circle |
| Meagher | 6,219 | 1,820 | White Sulphur Springs |
| Mineral | 3,162 | 3,315 | Superior |
| Missoula | 6,713 | 78,690 | Missoula |
| Musselshell | 4,865 | 4,110 | Roundup |
| Park | 6,929 | 14,560 | Livingston |
| Petroleum | 4,295 | 520 | Winnett |
| Phillips | 13,338 | 5,160 | Malta |
| Pondera | 4,243 | 6,430 | Conrad |
| Powder River | 8,549 | 2,090 | Broadus |
| Powell | 6,055 | 6,620 | Deer Lodge |
| Prairie | 4,503 | 1,380 | Terry |
| Ravalli | 6,198 | 25,010 | Hamilton |
| Richland | 5,411 | 10,720 | Sidney |
| Roosevelt | 6,128 | 11,000 | Wolf Point |
| Rosebud | 13,049 | 10,505 | Forsyth |
| Sanders | 7,147 | 8,670 | Thompson Falls |
| Sheridan | 4,371 | 4,730 | Plentywood |
| Silver Bow | 1,867 | 33,490 | Butte |
| Stillwater | 4,662 | 6,540 | Columbus |
| Sweet Grass | 4,948 | 3,150 | Big Timber |
| Teton | 5,915 | 6,270 | Choteau |
| Toole | 5,021 | 5,050 | Shelby |
| Treasure | 2,535 | 870 | Hysham |
| Valley | 12,834 | 8,240 | Glasgow |
| Wheatland | 3,689 | 2,250 | Harlowton |
| Wibaux | 2,309 | 1,190 | Wibaux |
| Yellowstone | 6,793 | 113,420 | Billings |

**Montauban** /mɔ̃təʊˈbɑːn/ the capital of Tarn-et-Garonne department in the Midi-Pyrénées region of southern France, situated on the River Tarn; pop. (1990) 53,280. Founded in 1144 by the Count of Toulouse, it is a marketing centre in a fruit and vegetable growing area.

**Mont-aux-Sources** /mɒntəʊˈsʊə(r)s/ a mountain of the Drakensberg Range in southern Africa, rising to 3,299 m. (10,823 ft.) on the border between Lesotho and Natal province, South Africa. It is the source of the Tugela River which falls a total distance of 948 m. (3,110 ft.) over cliffs and cascades, making it the world's second-highest waterfall.

**Montbéliard** /mɔˈbeɪɑː(r)/ an industrial town in the Franche-Comté region of eastern France, in the department of Doubs; pop. (1990) 30,640. It is a centre for the manufacture of the Peugeot motor car and was the birthplace in 1769 of Georges Cuvier, founder of the study of comparative anatomy and palaeontology.

**Mont Blanc** /mɔ̃ blɑ̃/ a peak in the Alps on the border between France and Italy, rising to 4,807 m. (15,771 ft.). It forms part of a massif of 25 peaks over 4,000 m. (13,120 ft.) and is the highest mountain in western Europe. It was first climbed in 1786 by J. Balmat and M. G. Paccard.

**Mont-de-Marsan** /ˌmɔ̃dəˈmɑːsɑ̃/ the capital of the department of Landes in the Aquitaine region of south-west France, at the junction of the Douze and Midou rivers; pop. (1990) 31,860. Situated on the edge of pine forest near a military aircraft testing site, its industries produce timber and resin.

**Mont Cervin** /mɔ̃ seərˈvæ/ the French name for the MATTERHORN.

**Monte Albán** /ˌmɒnteɪ ɑːlˈbɑːn/ an ancient city, now in ruins, in the state of Oaxaca, southern Mexico. Occupied from the 8th c. BC, it became a Zapotec centre from about the 1st c. BC to the 8th c. AD, after which it was occupied by the Mixtecs until the Spanish conquest in the 16th c.

**Montebello** /ˌmɒntɪˈbeləʊ/ a city in the Los Angeles conurbation, southern California, USA, situated to the east of Los Angeles between the Santa Ana and Pomona freeways; pop. (1990) 59,560.

**Monte Carlo** /ˌmɒntɪ ˈkɑːləʊ/ a resort in Monaco, forming one of the four communes of the principality; pop. (1985) 12,000. It is famous as a gambling resort and as the terminus of the annual Monte Carlo Rally. Its casino was built in 1878 by Charles Garnier.

**Monte Cassino** /ˌmɒntɪ kəˈsiːnəʊ/ a hill in west-central Italy near the town of Cassino, midway between Rome and Naples. It is the site of the principal monastery of the Benedictines, founded by St. Benedict c. 529. The monastery, demolished and rebuilt several times in its history, was almost totally destroyed during World War II, but has since been restored. In 1944 Allied forces advancing towards Rome were halted by German defensive positions in which Monte Cassino played a major part. The Allies succeeded in capturing the site only after four months of bitter fighting and the destruction of the town and the monastery. (See also CASSINO.)

**Monte Cervino** /ˈmɒntɪ tʃeəˈviːnəʊ/ the Italian name for the MATTERHORN.

**Montego Bay** a free port and tourist resort on the north coast of Jamaica; pop. (1982) 70,265. It derives its name from the butter or lard (Spanish *mantega*) once exported from here. Its most famous beach, Doctor's Cave Beach, was owned by Dr Alexander McCatty who turned it into a semi-public bathing club in 1906.

**Montélimar** /mɔ̃ˌteɪliːˈmɑː(r)/ a town in the Dauphiné region of south-eastern France, in the department of Drôme; pop. (1990) 31,390. It is noted for the production of nougat.

**Montenegro** /ˌmɒntɪˈnegrəʊ/ (Serbo-Croat **Crna Gora** /ˌsɜːnə ˈɡəʊrə/) a mountainous landlocked republic in the Balkans; area 13,812 sq. km. (5,335 sq. miles); pop. (1988) 632,000; official language, Serbo-Croat; capital, Podgorica (formerly Titograd). Joined with Serbia before the Turkish conquest of 1355, Montenegro became independent in 1851. In 1918 it became part of the federation of Yugoslavia, of which it remains, with Serbia, a nominal constituent.
**Montenegrin** *adj. & n.*

**Monterey** /ˈmɒntəreɪ/ a historic city on the southern shore of Monterey Bay, south of San Francisco, on the Pacific coast of central California, USA; pop. (1990) 31,950. The Mission San Carlos Borromeo del Rio Carmelo was founded here in 1770, and from 1775 until taken by the US in 1846 it was Spanish colonial capital of California. California's first constitution was drawn up here in 1849, and the settlement developed as a whaling and fishing centre. It is the site of the Monterey Jazz Festival, which has been held here annually every September since 1958.

**Monterey Bay** /ˈmɒntəreɪ/ a bay on the Pacific coast of California, to the south of Santa Cruz. Pacific Grove and historic Monterey stand on the Monterey Peninsula at the southern end of the bay. In 1602 the Spanish explorer Sebastian Vizcaino sailed into the bay and named it after the Count of Monte-Ray, Viceroy of Mexico.

**Monterey Park** a city in the Los Angeles conurbation, southern California, USA, to the east of Los Angeles and south of the San Bernardino freeway; pop. (1990) 60,740.

**Monte Rosa** /ˌmɒntɪ ˈrəʊzə/ a group of mountains in the Pennine Alps on the frontier between Switzerland and Italy. Dufourspitze, rising to 4,634 m. (15,203 ft.) east of the Matterhorn, is the highest peak of the group and of Switzerland.

**Monterrey** /ˌmɒnteˈreɪ/ an industrial city in north-east Mexico, capital of the state of Nuevo León; pop. (1990) 2,521,700. It is the third-largest city in Mexico. Founded in 1579, it developed as a steel, iron, and lead-smelting town in the 1880s.

**Montes Claros** /ˌmɒnteʃ ˈklærəs/ a city in the state of Minas Gerais, eastern Brazil, to the north of Belo Horizonte; pop. (1990) 229,180.

**Montevideo** the capital and chief port of Uruguay, on the River Plate; pop. (1985) 1,246,500. Founded in 1726, it has been capital of Uruguay since 1830. It is the commercial and financial centre of Uruguay, the base of a large fishing fleet, and has various light industries.

**Montgomery** /mɒnt'gʌməri, -gɒmərɪ/ the capital of the US state of Alabama, on the Alabama River; pop. (1990) 187,100. Settled in 1819, it was the first capital of the Confederate States of America until its capture by Union troops in July 1861. The capital was subsequently moved to Richmond, Virginia. Martin Luther King, who was a pastor here from 1954 to 1960, directed the bus boycott that initiated the US civil rights movement in the 1960s.

**Montgomeryshire** /mɒnt'gʌmərɪ,ʃɪə(r)/ a former county of central Wales. It became a part of Powys in 1974.

**Montmartre** /mɔ̃'mɑːrtr/ a district in northern Paris, on a hill above the Seine, much frequented by artists in the late 19th and early 20th c. when it was a village separated from Paris. Many of its buildings have artistic associations, e.g. the Moulin de la Galette, which was painted by Renoir, the Bateau-Lavoir occupied successively by Renoir, van Dongen, and Picasso, and various houses associated with Utrillo.

**Montparnasse** /mɔ̃pɑː'næs/ a district of Paris, on the left bank of the River Seine. Noted for its cafés, it was frequented in the late 19th c. by writers and artists and is traditionally associated with Parisian cultural life. The Pasteur Institute and the catacombs are situated in Montparnasse and in its cemetery are buried the composers César Franck (1822–90) and Camille Saint-Saëns (1835–1921), and the writers Charles Baudelaire (1821–67) and Guy de Maupassant (1850–93).

**Montpelier** /mɒnt'peljə(r)/ the capital of the US state of Vermont, situated on the Winooksi River at the centre of a popular vacation area; pop. (1990) 8,250. It was the birthplace of Admiral George Dewey (1837–1917), victor in the battle against the Spanish at Manila Bay in 1898.

**Montpellier** /mɔ̃'pelɪeɪ/ an industrial city (electronic equipment especially) in the Languedoc-Roussillon region of southern France, capital of the department of Hérault; pop. (1990) 210,870. It developed in the 10th c. as a trading centre on the spice route from the Near East, and was a stopover on the pilgrimage to Santiago de Compostela in Spain. A distinguished medical school, world-famous in medieval times, was founded here in 1221 and was confirmed as a university by Pope Nicolas IV in 1289. It was the birthplace of the philosopher Auguste Comte (1798–1857), founder of Positivism.

**Montreal** /,mɒntrɪ'ɔːl/ (French **Montréal** /mɔ̃'reɪɑːl/) a port on the St. Lawrence in southern Quebec, Canada; pop. (1991) 1,017,700; (3,127,240 metropolitan area). It is the second-largest city in Canada and nearly two-thirds of its population are French-speaking. Founded as a missionary outpost in 1642 and named Ville Marie de Montréal, it developed as a trading post under French rule until 1763. Montreal hosted Expo '67, celebrating

Canada's centennial in 1967 and the summer Olympic Games in 1976. In addition to being a commercial and financial centre, its industries produce chemicals, textiles, tobacco, steel, iron, and petroleum. Montreal is the home of the University of Montreal and McGill University.

**Montreux** /mɔ̃'trɜː/ a resort town in Vaud canton, south-west Switzerland, at the east end of Lake Geneva; pop. (1990) 19,850. It is the site of an international jazz festival, which has been held here annually every July since 1967, and an annual television festival which has been held here every spring since 1961.

**Mont-Saint-Michel** /mɔ̃ sæ mi:'ʃel/ a rocky islet off the coast of Normandy, north-west France, in the Gulf of St-Malo. An island only at high tide, it is surrounded by sandbanks and linked to the mainland, since 1875, by a causeway. It is crowned by a magnificent medieval Benedictine abbey-fortress founded in 708.

**Montserrat** /,mɒntsə'ræt/ a mountain in Catalonia, north-east Spain, north-west of Barcelona, site of a famous Benedictine monastery founded in the 11th c. An image of the Virgin is said to have been carved by St. Luke and brought here by St. Peter.

**Montserrat**

/,mɒntsə'ræt/ an island in the West Indies, one of the Leeward Islands; area 102 sq. km. (39 sq. miles); pop. (est. 1988) 12,000; official language, English; capital, Plymouth.

Visited by Columbus in 1493 and named after a Benedictine monastery on the mountain of Montserrat in Spain, it was colonized by Irish settlers in 1632. It was part of the British federal colony of the Leeward Islands from 1871 to 1956 when it became a separate United Kingdom Dependent Territory. In addition to offshore finance, it is a base for the production of light consumer goods, electronic components, and goods made from locally grown cotton. It is governed by a Governor who presides over an Executive Council and a Legislative Council.

**Monywa** /'məʊnjə,wɑː/ a market town in the Sagaing Division of central Burma, situated on the Chindwin River west of Mandalay; pop. (1983) 107,000. Its chief landmark is the well-preserved Thanboddhay Pagoda.

**Monza** /'məʊntsə/ an industrial city in Lombardy, northern Italy, forming part of the Milan conurbation; pop. (1990) 123,190. The cathedral, founded by Queen Theodolinda in the 6th c., contains a 9th-c. iron crown of the kings of Italy, said to have been forged from a nail used in Christ's Crucifixion. Monza was the scene of the assassination of King Umberto I in 1900. The city is noted for its motor-racing events. Textiles and carpets are local industries.

**Moor** /mʊə(r), mɔ:(r)/ a member of a Muslim people of mixed Berber and Arab descent, inhabiting north-west Africa and southern Spain from the 8th to the 15th century. Their name is derived from a Greek word (*Mauros*) for the inhabitants of ancient Mauretania.

**Moose Jaw** /mu:s dʒɔ:/ a town in south-central Saskatchewan, central Canada, at the junction of the Moose Jaw River and Thunder Creek; pop. (1991) 34,640. The town's grain stores and meat-processing industries developed after the building of the Canadian Pacific Railroad in 1881.

**Mopti** a city in central Mali, at the junction of the Niger and Bani rivers; pop. (1976) 53,900. It is a centre of agricultural trade in rice, cotton, peanuts, and cattle.

**Moradabad** /məʊ'rædəbæd/ a city and railway junction in the state of Uttar Pradesh in northern India, on the Ramganga River; pop. (1991) 432,430. It was founded in 1625 by the Mughal general Rustam Khan who named it after Prince Murad Baksh.

**moraine** /mə'reɪn/ an area covered by rocks and debris carried down and deposited at the margin of a glacier.

**Morar** /'mɒrə(r)/, **Loch** a loch in western Scotland. At 310 m. (1,017 ft.), it is the deepest loch in the country.

**Morava** /mə'rɑ:və/ the name of two rivers in central and south-east Europe: **1.** a tributary of the Danube in the Czech Republic; length 385 km. (240 miles). **2.** a tributary of the Danube in Serbia; length 218 km. (136 miles).

**Moravia** a region of the Czech Republic, situated between Bohemia in the west and the Carpathians in the east. Separated from Silesia in the north by the Sudeten Mts. and drained by the Morava River, it is a fertile agricultural region, rich in mineral resources. Its chief town is Brno. Formerly the western part of the medieval Slavonic kingdom of Greater Moravia, it became a province of Bohemia in the 11th c. It was made an Austrian crownland in 1848, becoming a part of Czechoslovakia in 1918.

**Moravian** /mə'reɪvɪən/ a member of a Protestant sect founded in Saxony in 1722 by emigrants from Moravia, holding views derived from the Hussites and a simple unworldly form of Christianity with the Bible as the only source of faith.

**Moray** /'mʌrɪ/ a local government area and former county (Morayshire) of northern Scotland, bordered on the north by the Moray Firth. It was a district of Grampian Region from 1975 to 1996; area 2,224 sq. km. (859 sq. miles); pop. (1991) 82,510; its administrative centre is Elgin.

**Moray Firth** /'mʌrɪ/ a deep inlet of the North Sea on the north-east coast of Scotland. The city of Inverness is near its head.

**Morbihan** /,mɔ:bi:'ɑ̃/ a department of Brittany in western France; area 6,823 sq. km. (2,635 sq. miles); pop. (1990) 619,840; capital, Vannes.

**Mordvinia** /mɔ:'dvɪnɪə/ official name **Mordovan Soviet Socialist Republic** an autonomous republic in western Russia; area 26,200 sq. km. (20,220 sq. miles); pop. (1990) 964,000; capital, Saransk. Absorbed into the Russian empire in the 13th c., the region was constituted as a Mordovian Area in the Middle-Volga Territory of the Soviet Union in 1928. It became an autonomous republic of the USSR in 1934. Over 30 per cent of its population are Finno-Ugric Mordvinians. **Mordovan**, **Mordovian**, **Mordvin** or **Mordvinian** *adj. & n.*

**Morecambe** /'mɔ:(r)kəm/ a resort town and fishing port in Lancashire on the Irish Sea coast of north-west England; pop. (1981) 42,060. The town was known as Poulton-le-Sands until 1870.

**Morecambe Bay** an inlet of the Irish Sea, on the north-west coast of England, between Lancashire and the Furness peninsula of Cumbria. The name was derived in the 18th c. from a reference in a work of the 2nd-c. Greek geographer Ptolemy to *mori kambe*, from the old Celtic name for the Lune estuary, *mori cambo* 'curved bay'.

**Morelia** /mə'reɪlɪə/ a city in west-central Mexico, market town and capital of the state of Michoacán; pop. (1990) 489,760. Founded in 1541 on the site of a Franciscan monastery, it was originally known as Valladolid. Its name was later changed in honour of José María Morelos y Pavón (1765–1815), a key figure in Mexico's independence movement. It has a notable Baroque cathedral.

**Morelos** /mə'reɪlɒs/ a state of central Mexico; area 4,950 sq. km. (1,912 sq. miles); pop. (1990) 1,195,380; capital, Cuernavaca.

**Moresco** see MORISCO.

**Morisco** (also **Moresco**) a term derived from the Spanish word for a 'little Moor' applied especially to the Moors in Spain (or their descendants) who accepted Christian baptism. When the Christians reconquered Muslim Spain in the 11th–15th c. the Islamic religion and customs were at first tolerated, but after the fall of Granada in 1492 Islam was officially prohibited and Muslims were forced to become Christians or go into exile. Many who remained practised their own religion in private, in spite of persecution, but their political loyalty was suspect and in 1609 they were expelled, mainly to Africa.

**Mormon** /'mɔ:mən/ a member of the Church of Jesus Christ of Latter-Day Saints, which was founded in New York in 1830 by Joseph Smith (1805–44). He claimed to have discovered, through divine revelation, the 'Book of Mormon', relating the history of a group of Hebrews who migrated to America c. 600 BC. This work is accepted by Mormons as Scripture along with the Bible. A further revelation led him to institute polygamy, a practice which brought the Mormons into conflict with the Federal Government and was abandoned in 1890. Smith was succeeded as leader by Brigham Young (1801–77), who moved the Mormon headquarters to Salt Lake City, Utah, in 1847. Mormon teaching is strongly adventist; the movement has no professional clergy, self-help is emphasized, and tithing and missionary work are required of its members.

**Moro** /'mɔːrəʊ/ (*pl.* **-os**) the name given to a Muslim living in the Philippines, especially in Mindanao.

**Morogoro** /ˌmɔʊrəʊˈɡəʊrəʊ/ a town in central Tanzania, at the foot of the Uluguru Mountains west of Dar es Salaam; pop. (1984) 72,000. Mikumi National Park and the Selous Game Reserve lie to the south.

### Morocco

/məˈrɒkəʊ/ official name **The Kingdom of Morocco** a country in the north-west corner of Africa, with coastlines on the Mediterranean Sea and Atlantic Ocean; area 458,730 sq. km. (177,184 sq. miles); pop. (est. 1991) 25,731,000; languages, Arabic (official); Berber, Spanish, and French are also widely spoken; capital, Rabat. The largest cities are Casablanca, Rabat, and Marrakesh. A fertile coastal plain on the Atlantic seaboard is separated from the Sahara Desert by the Atlas Mountains which run northeastwards towards the Algerian frontier. The north coast and interior mountains have a Mediterranean climate but the Atlantic coast is exposed to higher rainfall in winter and is cooler in summer. The economy is sustained by a well-developed mining industry, the country being one of the leading exporters of phosphates, but agriculture remains the main occupation of its inhabitants. Tourism and fishing are also important. Conquered by the Arabs in the 7th c., Morocco was penetrated by the Portuguese in the 15th c. and later fell under French and Spanish influence, each country establishing protectorates in the early 20th c. It became a fully fledged independent state after the withdrawal of the colonial powers in 1956. In 1975 Morocco extended its authority over Western Sahara (formerly Spanish Sahara). The country is ruled by a monarch, who appoints a prime minister and cabinet, and by a legislative Chamber of Representatives.

**Moroccan** *adj. & n.*

Morocco is divided into 47 provinces:

| Province | Area (sq. km.) | Pop. (1989) |
| --- | --- | --- |
| Agadir | 5,910 | 751,000 |
| Al Hoceima | 3,550 | 362,000 |
| Azilal | 10,050 | 420,000 |
| Beni Mellal | 7,075 | 873,000 |
| Ben Slimane | 2,760 | 199,000 |
| Boujdour | 100,120 | 10,000 |
| Boulemane | 14,395 | 151,000 |
| Chefchaouen | 4,350 | 880,000 |
| El Aaiún | 39,360 | 135,000 |
| El Jadida | 6,000 | 901,000 |
| El Kelaa Sraghna | 10,070 | 669,000 |
| Errachidia | 59,585 | 490,000 |
| Essaouira | 6,335 | 430,000 |
| Es-Semara | 61,760 | 24,000 |
| Fes | 5,400 | 985,000 |
| Figuig | 55,990 | 111,000 |
| Guelmim | 28,750 | 160,000 |
| Ifrane | 3,310 | 115,000 |
| Kenitra | 4,745 | 356,000 |
| Khemisset | 8,305 | 464,000 |
| Khenifra | 12,320 | 429,000 |
| Khouribga | 4,250 | 526,000 |
| Marrakesh | 14,775 | 1,485,000 |
| Meknes | 3,995 | 734,000 |
| Nador | 6,130 | 750,000 |
| Ouarzazate | 41,550 | 630,000 |
| Oued Eddahab | 50,880 | 25,000 |
| Oujda | 20,700 | 940,000 |
| Safi | 7,285 | 827,000 |
| Settat | 9,750 | 781,000 |
| Sidi Kacem | 4,060 | 590,000 |
| Tanger | 1,195 | 539,000 |
| Tan-Tan | 17,295 | 56,000 |
| Taounate | 5,585 | 597,000 |
| Taroudant | 16,460 | 645,000 |
| Tata | 25,925 | 109,000 |
| Taza | 15,020 | 704,000 |
| Tétouan | 6,025 | 837,000 |
| Tiznit | 6,960 | 370,000 |
| Aïn Chok-Hay Hassani | } 547,000 | 409,000 |
| Aïn Sebaa-Hay Mohammadi | | |
| Ben Msik-Sidi Othmane | } 1,615 | 890,000 |
| Casablanca-Anfa | | 1,054,000 |
| Mohammadia-Znata | | 202,000 |
| Rabat | } 1,275 | 642,000 |
| Salé | | 575,000 |
| Skhirate-Témara | | 188,000 |

**Moroni** /məˈrəʊniː/ the capital of the Comoros Islands, on the island of Grand Comore; pop. (1980) 20,110.

**Morpeth** /'mɔːpəθ/ a town in north-east England, the county town of Northumberland; pop. (1981) 15,000

**Morris Jesup** /ˌmɒrɪs 'dʒesəp/, **Cape** a cape at the northern tip of Greenland, the most northerly point of land in the Arctic, named after an explorer of Arctic and Siberian regions. It is 706 km. (439 miles) from the North Pole.

**Morristown** /'mɒrɪsˌtaʊn/ a town in northern New Jersey, USA, on the Whippany River, associated with the American War of Independence. It was the site of George Washington's military head-quarters in 1779–80 and was the place where S. F. B. Morse devised the Morse Code in the 1830s.

**Mörs** see MOERS.

**Morwell** /'mɔ:wel/ an industrial town in eastern Victoria, Australia, in the Latrobe valley 150 km. (94 miles) east of Melbourne; pop. (1991) 15,420. Brown coal is mined and power is generated in the surrounding area.

**Moscow** /'mɒskəʊ/ (Russian **Moskva** /'mɒskvæ/) the capital and largest city of Russia, situated at the centre of the vast plain of European Russia, on the Moskva River; pop. (1990) 8,801,000. First mentioned in medieval chronicles in 1147, it soon became the chief city of the increasingly powerful Muscovite princes. In the 16th c., when Ivan the Terrible proclaimed himself Tsar of all the Russias, Moscow became the capital of the new empire, its central position giving it supreme military and economic value. Though Peter the Great moved his capital to St. Petersburg in 1712, Moscow remained the heart of Russia and centre of the Russian Orthodox Church. In 1812 it was attacked and occupied by Napoleon and three-quarters of the city was destroyed by fire. By the mid-19th c. Moscow had become a large and growing industrial city. After the Bolshevik Revolution of 1917 it was made the capital of the USSR and seat of the new Soviet government, with its centre in the Kremlin, the ancient citadel of the 15th-c. city. It is a major industrial and cultural centre, with world-famous theatres and museums, and is the home of the Bolshoi Ballet. There are heavy steel, machinery, and vehicle industries, as well as diverse light industries in suburban areas.

**Mosel** /məʊ'zel/ (French **Moselle**) a river of western Europe that rises on the slopes of the Ballon d'Alsace in the Vosges Mountains of north-east France and flows 550 km. (346 miles) north through Lorraine, Luxembourg, and Germany to meet the Rhine at Coblenz. The Mosel valley in Germany is a noted wine-producing region.

**Moselle** /məʊ'zel/ a department of Lorraine in north-east France; area 6,216 sq. km. (2,400 sq. miles); pop. (1990) 1,011,300; capital, Metz.

**Moshi** /'məʊʃi/ a town in northern Tanzania, near Mt. Kilimanjaro; pop. (1984) 62,000. It is the capital of Kilimanjaro region and terminus of the northern railway from Dar es Salaam, and is the centre of a rich coffee-growing area.

**Moslem** see MUSLIM.

**Mosquito Coast** /mə'ski:təʊ/ a sparsely populated strip of swamp, lagoon, and tropical forest along the Caribbean coast of Nicaragua and Honduras, occupied by the Miskito Indians after whose name it is a corruption. The British maintained a protectorate over the area intermittently from the 17th c. until the mid-19th c., granting authority to a series of kings. In 1894 Nicaragua

appropriated the territory and in 1960 the northern part was awarded to Honduras.

**Mossel Bay** /'mɒs(ə)l/ a seaport and resort in Western Cape, South Africa, noted for the mussels from which it derives its name.

**Mossmoran** /mɒs'mɔ:rən/ an industrial location in Fife, east-central Scotland, built on the site of a former peat bog. North Sea gas is converted into liquid products for the chemical industry.

**Mostaganem** /mə‚sta'gə'nem/ (also **Mestghanem**) a fishing and trading port on the Mediterranean coast of north-west Algeria, east of Oran; pop. (1982) 169,520. Founded in the 11th c., it developed as a port under Turkish rule.

**Mostar** /mɒs'ta:(r)/ a largely Muslim city in Bosnia-Herzegovina, on the River Neretva south-west of Sarajevo; pop. (1981) 110,380. It is the chief town of Herzegovina. For many years its chief landmark was the old Turkish bridge over the Neretva, destroyed during a siege in 1993.

**Mosul** /'məʊsʊl/ the third-largest city in Iraq, situated in the north-west of the country on the right bank of the Tigris, opposite the ruins of Nineveh; pop. (est. 1985) 1,250,000. It gives its name to muslin, a cotton fabric first produced here.

**Motala** /məʊ'ta:lə/ an industrial town on the shore of Lake Vättern in south-east Sweden; pop. (1990) 41,990.

**Motherwell** /'mʌðə:‚wel/ **1.** a district in Strathclyde Region, central Scotland from 1975 to 1996; area 171 sq. km. (66 sq. miles); pop. (1990) 140,320. **2.** its administrative centre; pop. (1981) 30,680.

**Motown** /'məʊtaʊn/ a nickname for DETROIT. From an abbreviation of 'motor town'.

**Moulay Idriss** /‚mu:leɪ 'ɪdrɪs/ a Muslim holy town near Meknès in northern Morocco, the burial place of Moulay Idriss I (in the 8th c.), father of the founder of the city of Fez.

**Moulin Rouge** /‚mu:læ̃ 'ru:ʒ/ a cabaret in Montmartre, Paris, a favourite resort of poets and artists around the turn of the century. Toulouse-Lautrec immortalized its dancers in his posters.

**Moulins** /mu:'læ̃/ an industrial town in the Auvergne region of central France, on the River Allier; pop. (1990) 23,350. It is capital of the department of Allier and was once the capital of the duchy of Bourbon.

**Moulmein** /mu:l'meɪn/ (Burmese **Maulamyang**) a seaport in south-east Burma, on the Salween River south-east of Rangoon; pop. (1983) 220,000. It is capital of the state of Mon.

**Moundou** /'mu:ndu:/ a city in southern Chad, capital of the Logone Occidental préfecture; pop. (1993) 281,490.

**Mountains of the Moon** see RUWENZORI, MOUNT.

**Mountain View** a city in California, USA, on San Francisco Bay south-east of Palo Alto; pop. (1990) 67,460.

**Mount Athos** /'æθɒs/ (Greek **Agion Oros**) a semi-autonomous district that forms a peninsula on the Aegean coast of Macedonia in northern Greece; area 336 sq. km. (130 sq. miles); pop. (1991) 1,557. Its chief port is Daphne and its administrative centre is Karyes. Mount Athos, which rises to 1,956 m. (6,417 ft.), is the Holy Mountain of the Greek Orthodox Church and around it are 20 monasteries. Since 1060 women and all female animals have been excluded from the district.

**Mount Gambier** /'gæmbɪeɪ/ a city in south-eastern South Australia, situated beside an extinct volcano 460 km. (290 miles) south of Adelaide; pop. (1991) 21,150. The surrounding area produces, cereals, lambs, and dairy products.

**Mount Isa** /'aɪzə/ a lead- and silver-mining town in Queensland, Australia, on the Leichhardt River; pop. (1991) 23,670. Silver and lead ores were discovered here in 1923 by a prospector named John Miles who named the mining town after his sister Isa.

**Mount Lofty Range** /'lɒftɪ/ a mountain range to the east of Adelaide in south-east South Australia, rising to 934 m. (3,064 ft.) at Mount Bryan. It is crossed by the Barrier Highway.

**Mount Prospect** /'prɒspekt/ a town in north-east Illinois, USA, north-west of Chicago; pop. (1990) 53,170.

**Mount Rushmore** /'rʌʃmɔː(r)/ a granite mountain in the Black Hills of South Dakota, USA, rising to 1,745 m. (5,725 ft.). The colossal heads of US presidents Washington, Jefferson, Lincoln, and Theodore Roosevelt were carved on its face by Gutzon Borglum between 1927 and 1941. The site is a national memorial.

**Mount St. Helens** /sənt 'helənz/ a volcano in Washington state, north-west USA, which erupted in 1980 devastating a huge area of the surrounding countryside and reducing its height from 2,950 m. (9,682 ft.) to 2,560 m. (8,402 ft.).

**Mount Vernon** /'vɜːnən/ **1.** a city in south-east New York state, USA, adjacent to the Bronx; pop. (1990) 67,150. **2.** a property in north-east Virginia, USA, about 24 km. (15 miles) from Washington, DC, on a site overlooking the Potomac River. Built in 1743, it was the home of George Washington from 1747 until his death in 1799.

**Mourne Mountains** /mɔː(r)n/ a range of hills in southern Northern Ireland, in County Down. Slieve Donard (853 m., 2,796 ft.) is the highest peak in northern Ireland.

**Mousalla** see MUSALA.

**Mouscron** /muːˈskrɔ̃/ (Flemish **Moeskroen**) a town in the province of Hainaut, Belgium, near the French frontier; pop. (1991) 53,510.

**Mousterian** /muːˈstɪərɪən/ of or relating to the flint industries of the middle palaeolithic period, named after the type-site, the Moustier cave in the Dordogne region of France, and dated to c. 70,000–30,000 BC. They are attributed to the Neanderthal peoples living in Europe and around the Mediterranean.

**Mozambique** /ˌməʊzæmˈbiːk/ official name **The Republic of Mozambique** a country on the east coast of southern Africa, bordered by the Republic of South Africa,

Swaziland, Zimbabwe, Zambia, Malawi, and Tanzania; area 799,380 sq. km. (308,760 sq. miles); pop. (est. 1991) 16,142,000; official language, Portuguese; capital, Maputo. An extensive coastal plain rises to a plateau bordered by hills in the interior. The climate is mostly tropical, the wettest regions being the highlands on the Malawi and Zimbabwe borders and the south-east coast between Maputo and Beira. Although coal is exploited, the country is largely agricultural, but in relation to its area the export trade is very small. Visited by Arab traders and by Vasco da Gama in the 15th c., Mozambique was colonized by the Portuguese in the early 16th c. and did not gain full independence until 1975 after a 10-year armed struggle by the Frelimo liberation movement. The installation of a Marxist government and the exodus of white settlers was followed by a protracted civil war between the Frelimo government (which abandoned Marxism-Leninism in 1989) and the Renamo rebel movement. A cease-fire was arranged in 1992 to be overseen by the UN.

**Mozambican** *adj. & n.*

Mozambique is divided into 10 provinces:

| Province | Area (sq. km.) | Pop. (est. 1987) | Capital |
| --- | --- | --- | --- |
| Cabo Delgado | 82,625 | 1,109,920 | Pemba |
| Gaza | 75,709 | 1,138,720 | Xaixai |
| Inhambane | 68,615 | 1,167,220 | Inhambane |
| Manica | 61,661 | 756,890 | Chimoio |
| Maputo | 25,756 | 544,690 | Maputo |
| Nampula | 81,606 | 2,837,860 | Nampula |
| Niassa | 129,056 | 607,670 | Lichinga |
| Sofala | 68,018 | 1,257,710 | Beira |
| Tete | 100,724 | 981,320 | Tete |
| Zambézia | 105,008 | 2,952,250 | Quelimane |

**Mozambique Channel** an arm of the Indian Ocean separating the the eastern coast of mainland Africa from the island of Madagascar.

**Mozir** /məˈzɪ(ə)r/ (also **Mozyr**) a city in south-east Belorussia (Belarus), on the Pripyat River south-west of Gomel; pop. (1990) 102,000.

**MS** *abbr.* US Mississippi (in official postal use).

**MT** *abbr.* US Montana (in official postal use).

**Muchinga Mountains** /muːˈtʃɪŋɡə/ a range of mountains in eastern Zambia, north-east of Ndola.

**Muck** /mʌk/ an island in the Inner Hebrides of Scotland, north-west of Ardnamurchan Point.

**Muckle Flugga** /mʌk(ə)l ˈflʌɡə/ an island and lighthouse in the Shetland Islands, the northern-most of the British Isles.

**Mudanjiang** /ˌmʊdɑːnˈdʒæŋ/ a city in Heilongjiang province, north-east China, on the Mudan River south-east of Harbin; pop. (1990) 710,000.

**Mudéjar** /muːˈðeɪhɑː(r)/ **1.** any of the Muslims who were allowed to retain their laws and religion in return for their loyalty to a Christian king after the Christian reconquest of the Spanish peninsula from the Moors (11th–15th c.). After 1492 they were treated with less toleration, dubbed Moriscos (see entry), and forced to accept the Christian faith or leave the country. **2.** a style of architecture and decorative art of the 12th–15th c., combining Islamic and Gothic elements, produced by the Mudéjares. The architecture is characterized especially by the use of the horseshoe arch and the vault; examples can be seen in the churches and palaces of Toledo, Córdoba, and Valencia.

**Mughal** /ˈmuːɡɑːl/ a member of a Mongolian (Muslim) dynasty in India whose empire was consolidated, after the conquests of Tamerlane, by his descendant Babur (who reigned *c.* 1525–30) and greatly extended by Akbar. Gradually broken up by wars and revolts, and faced by European commercial expansion, the Mughal empire disappeared after the Indian Mutiny (1857).

**Mugla** /ˈmuːlə/ **1.** a province of south-west Turkey on the Mediterranean coast; area 12,504 sq. km. (4,830 sq. miles); pop. (1990) 562,810. **2.** its capital; pop. (1990) 33,605.

**Muir Woods** /mjʊə(r)/ a forest of Redwood trees in California, USA, in a mountain valley just north of San Francisco. It was given to the state as a national monument in 1908 by Congressman William Kent and named in honour of the Scottish-born naturalist John Muir.

**Mukalla** /mʊˈkælə/ a port on the south coast of Yemen, on the Gulf of Aden; pop. (1987) 154,360. It is the capital of a governorate (Hadramawt) and an important fishing centre. Founded in 1035, it developed into the leading port of the Hadramawt region in the 17th and 18th c.

**Mukden** a former name for SHENYANG.

**mulatto** /mjuːˈlætəʊ/ a person of mixed White and Black parentage.

**Mulhaçen** /ˌmuːlɑːˈsen/ a mountain in southern Spain, south-east of Granada, in the Sierra Nevada. Rising to 3,482 m. (11,424 ft.) it is the highest mountain in the country.

**Mülheim** /ˈmʊlhaɪm/ (fully **Mülheim an der Ruhr**) an industrial city in the state of North Rhine-Westphalia, western Germany, on the Ruhr south-west of Essen; pop. (1991) 177,040. Heavy industries have given way to light industries such as precision instruments, clothing, and chemicals.

**Mulhouse** /mʊˈluːz/ (German **Mühlhausen**) an industrial city in the Alsace region of north-east France, on the River Ill; pop. (1990) 109,905. Founded in 803, it was a free imperial city until it joined the French in 1798. In 1871, after the Franco-Prussian War, the city became part of the German Empire until it was reunited with France in 1918. Its industries produce textiles, chemicals, machinery, and vehicles.

**Mull** /mʌl/ an island of the Inner Hebrides, off the west coast of Scotland; area 950 sq. km. (367 sq. miles). Its chief town is Tobermory and its highest peak is Ben More (966 m., 3,171 ft.). Its principal landmark is Duart Castle, home of the Chiefs of the Clan Maclean.

**Mullingar** /ˌmʌlɪnˈɡɑː(r)/ the county town of Westmeath, in the Republic of Ireland, on the Brosna River; pop. (1981) 7,470. Its chief landmark is the Cathedral of Christ the King. Mullingar is a cattle-market town and angling centre.

**Mull of Kintyre** /mʌl, kɪnˈtaɪr/ the southern extremity of the Kintyre peninsula on the west coast of Scotland. It is the nearest point to Ireland on the Scottish mainland.

**Multan** /mʊlˈtɑːn/ a commercial city in Punjab province, east-central Pakistan; pop. (est. 1991) 980,000. Before the 8th c., silk from Bukhara was woven here. Today, the city trades in grain, cotton, and fruit.

**Mulu** /ˈmʊluː/ an extensive system of limestone caves in Sarawak, eastern Malaysia. One of the largest cave systems in the world, it was designated a national park in 1975 and explored by a Royal Geographical Society expedition in 1978.

**München** the German name for MUNICH.

**Muncie** /ˈmʌnsɪ/ a city in eastern Indiana, USA, on the White River; pop. (1990) 71,035. Once the home of the Munsee tribe of Delaware Indians, Muncie was settled in 1818 and became an agricultural trading centre. It developed into an industrial city with the arrival of the railroad and the discovery of natural gas nearby.

**Munda** /ˈmuːndə/ an ancient tribal people surviving in north-east India.

**Munich** /ˈmjuːnɪk/ (German **München** /ˈmuːnxen/) an industrial, communications, and commercial city on the River Isar in south-west Germany, capital of Bavaria; pop. (1991) 1,229,050. It is noted for its medieval architecture and as an artistic and cultural centre. It is the home of the Bavarian State Opera Company and Munich Philharmonic. It hosted the Olympic Games in

1972 and is the seat of the European Patent Office. Its industries produce machinery, chemicals, precision instruments, vehicles, and beer. International beer festivals are held each year.

**Munster** /'mʌnstə(r)/ a province of the Republic of Ireland, comprising the south-western counties of Clare, Cork, Kerry, Limerick, Tipperary, and Waterford; area 24,127 sq. km. (9,319 sq. miles); pop. (1991) 1,008,440.

**Münster** /'mʊnstə(r)/ a city and port in North Rhine-Westphalia, north-west Germany, on the River Aa; pop. (1991) 264,180. It has varied industries such as steel, chemicals, and musical instruments. It was formerly the capital of Westphalia; the Treaty of Westphalia, ending the Thirty Years War, was signed simultaneously here and at Osnabrück in 1648.

**Murchison Falls** /'mɜ:tʃɪs(ə)n/ **1.** the former name of the Kabalega Falls on the Victoria Nile in north-west Uganda. **2.** (also **Murchison Rapids**) the former name of a waterfall now known as Kapachira Falls, on the Shire River in southern Malawi.

**Murcia** /'mʊəsɪə/ **1.** an autonomous region in south-east Spain; area 11,313 sq. km. (4,370 sq. miles); pop. (1991) 1,045,600. In the Middle Ages, along with Albacete, it formed an ancient Moorish kingdom. **2.** its capital city on the River Segura; pop. (1991) 328,840. Its industries manufacture pharmaceuticals, textiles, and processed food.

**Mures** /'mu:rəʃ/ (Hungarian **Maros**) a river that rises in the Carpathians of central Romania and flows 755 km. (470 miles) westwards into Hungary to meet the Tisza at Szeged.

**Murmansk** /mʊə'mænsk/ a fishing and trading port in north-west Russia, on the Kola Peninsula, in the Barents Sea; pop. (1990) 472,000. It is the largest city north of the Arctic Circle and its port is ice-free throughout the year. Its industries include shipbuilding, brewing, timber, and food processing.

**Murom** /'mʊərəm/ a city in western Russia, on the Oka River south-west of Nizhniy Novgorod; pop. (1990) 125,000. It is a port and rail junction.

**Murray** /'mʌrɪ/ the principal river of Australia, which rises in the Great Dividing Range in New South Wales and flows 2,590 km. (1,610 miles) generally north-westwards, forming part of the border between the states of Victoria and New South Wales, before turning southwards in South Australia to empty into the Southern Ocean south-east of Adelaide.

**Murrumbidgee** /,mʌrəm'bɪdʒi:/ a river of south-east Australia, in New South Wales. Rising in the Great Dividing Range, it flows 1,759 km. (1,099 miles) westwards to join the Murray, of which it is a major tributary.

**Mururoa** /,mʊərʊ'rəʊə/ a remote South Pacific atoll in the Tuamotu archipelago, in French Polynesia, used as a nuclear testing site since 1966.

**Muş** /mu:ʃ/ **1.** a mountainous province in eastern Turkey; area 8,413 sq. km. (3,249 sq. miles); pop. (1990) 376,540. **2.** its capital city; pop. (1990) 44,020.

**Musala** /mu:'sɑ:lə/ (also **Mousalla**) the highest peak in Bulgaria, rising to a height of 2,925 m. (9,596 ft.) in the Rila Mountains at the north-western extremity of the Rhodope range.

**Muscat** /'mʌskæt/ (Arabic **Masqat**) the capital city of the Sultanate of Oman, a seaport on the south-east coast of the Arabian peninsula adjoining the port of Matrah; pop. (est. 1990) 380,000. Under Portuguese and then Persian rule until 1798 when a treaty was signed giving links with Britain which lasted until the 1960s.

**Muscat and Oman** /'mʌskæt, əʊ'mɑ:n/ the former name (until 1970) of OMAN.

**Muscovite** /'mʌskə,vaɪt/ an inhabitant of Moscow, capital of Russia.

**Muscovy** /'mʌskəvɪ/ a medieval principality in central European Russia, centred on Moscow, which formed the nucleus of modern Russia. It was founded in the late 13th c. by Daniel, son of Alexander Nevski (descendants of the Rurik dynasty), and gradually expanded, despite repeated Tartar depredations, finally overcoming the Tartars in 1380. Princes of Muscovy became the rulers of Russia; in 1472 Ivan III, grand duke of Muscovy completed the unification, overcoming rivalry from the principalities of Novgorod, Tver, and Vladimir and adopting the title 'Ruler of all Russia'. In 1547 Ivan IV, known as 'Ivan the Terrible', became the first tsar of the new empire, with Moscow as its capital.

**muskeg** /'mʌskeg/ a level swamp or bog in the coniferous forests of Canada.

**Muskogean** /,mʌskə'gɪən, -'kəʊgɪən/ a family of Native American languages in south-eastern North America.

**Muslim** /'mʊzlɪm, 'mʌz-/ (also **Moslem** /'mɒzləm/) a follower of the Islamic religion. Of the c.935 million Muslims in the world, about 613 million live in Asia.

**Mussulman** /'mʌs(ə)lmən/ (pl. **-mans** or **men**) of or concerning Muslims.

**Mustique** /mʊ'sti:k/ a small resort island in the northern Grenadines, in the Caribbean Sea to the south of St. Vincent. Taking its name from the French word for mosquito, the island is run as a company.

**Mutare** /mu:'tɑ:rɪ/ an industrial town in the eastern highlands of Zimbabwe, capital of the province of Manicaland; pop. (1982) 69,620. It is the fourth-largest city in Zimbabwe and was known as Umtali until 1982. The city began to develop in 1898 when it became a major railway centre and is today a centre of fuel distribution and industry, producing lumber, paper, furniture, and processed tea and coffee.

**Muzzaffarabad** /mʌz'æfərəbæd/ the chief administrative centre of Azad Kashmir in north-east Pakistan, situated at the junction of the Jhelum and Neelum rivers north-east of Abbottabad.

**Muzzaffarnagar** /mʌz'æfər,nəgər/ a town in Uttar Pradesh, northern India, north of Meerut; pop. (1991) 247,730.

**Muzzaffarpur** /mʌz'æfər,pʊ(ə)r/ a Muslim town in Bihar, north-east India, north of Patna; pop. (1991) 240,450.

**Mwanza** /mə'wænzə/ a town in northern Tanzania, on Lake Victoria; pop. (1984) 111,000. It is an agricultural centre trading in maize, cassava, and cotton grown in the surrounding area.

**Mweru** /'mweɪruː/, **Lake** a lake on the border between Zaire and Zambia in central Africa.

**Myanmar** /,maɪæn'mɑː(r)/, **The Union of** the official name (since 1989) of BURMA.

**Mycenae** /maɪ'siːniː/ an ancient city in Greece, situated near the coast in the north-east Peloponnese, on a site dominating various land and sea routes. The capital of King Agamemnon, it was the centre of the late Bronze Age Mycenaean civilization. Its period of greatest prosperity was c. 1400 to 1200 BC, which saw construction of the palace and massive walls of Cyclopaean masonry, including the 'Lion Gate', the entrance to the citadel (c. 1250 BC). It was destroyed in about 1100 BC by invading Dorians. Systematic excavation of the site began in 1840.

**Mycenaean** /,maɪsɪ'niːən/ of or relating to the late Bronze Age civilization in Greece (c. 1580–1100 BC), depicted in the Homeric poems and represented by finds at Mycenae and other ancient cities of the Peloponnese. The Mycenaeans inherited control of the Aegean after the collapse of the Minoan civilization c. 1400 BC. Their cities, such as those of Mycenae, Tiryns, and Pylos were well populated and prosperous, with fortified citadels enclosing impressive palaces. Artefacts of ivory, gold, and inlaid bronze, of advanced technique and exquisite workmanship, are found in tombs that must have been those of royalty. The language they used was a form of Greek, and transactions were recorded in the script known as Linear B. Trade with other Mediterranean countries flourished, and Mycenaean products are found from southern Italy to Palestine and Syria. The end of Mycenaean power coincided with a period of general upheaval and migrations at the and of the Bronze Age in the Mediterranean.

**Mykolayiv** /,mɪkə'laɪɪf/ an industrial city in Southern Ukraine, on the Southern Bug river near its confluence with the Dnieper and their joint estuaries on the northern shores of the Black Sea; pop. (1990) 507,900. Founded as a fortress town in 1784 near the ancient Greek colony of Olbia, it developed into an important shipbuilding centre. It was known as Nikolayev until the dissolution of the Soviet Union in 1991.

**Mykonos** /'mɪkə,nɒs/ (Greek **Míkonos** /'miːkə,nɒs/) a rocky Greek island in the Aegean Sea, one of the Cyclades; area 85 sq. km. (33 sq. miles); pop. (1981) 4,850. Its chief town and port is Mykonos. Manganese, wine, grain, and figs are produced.

**Mymensingh** /,maɪmən'sɪŋ/ a port on the Brahmaputra River in central Bangladesh; pop. (1991) 186,000. It is capital of Mymensingh region and a centre of trade in rice, sugar-cane, oil seed, jute, and tobacco.

**Mysia** /'mɪsɪə/ an ancient region of north-west Asia Minor, on the Mediterranean coast south of the Hellespont and the Sea of Marmara. **Mysian** adj. & n.

**Mysore** /maɪ'sɔː(r)/ **1.** the former name (until 1973) of the Indian state of Karnataka. **2.** a city in the Indian state of Karnataka, former capital of the princely state of Mysore; pop. (1991) 652,250. It is the second-largest city in the state and is noted for the production of silk, incense, and sandalwood oil.

**Mystic** /'mɪstɪk/ a short river of south-east Connecticut, USA, that flows into Long Island Sound. At its mouth is the Mystic Seaport maritime museum.

**Mytilene** /,mɪtɪ'liːnɪ/ (Greek **Mitilíni**) the chief town and port of the Greek island of Lesbos in the Aegean Sea; pop. (1981) 24,115.

# N *n*

**Naas** /neɪs/ the county town of Kildare in the Republic of Ireland, on the road from Dublin to Cork; pop. (1991) 11,140. It was the seat of the kings of Leinster whose royal palace lay on the North Mote. There are racecourses at Naas and at nearby Punchestown.

**Nabataean** /ˌnæbəˈtiːən/ a member of an ancient Arabian people speaking a form of Aramaic strongly influenced by Arabic. Originally a nomadic Arab tribe, they formed an independent state (312–63 BC), prospering from control of trade routes between southern Arabia and the Mediterranean, which converged at their capital Petra (now in Jordan). Their culture reflects Babylonian, Arab, Greek, and Roman influence in its speech, religion, art, and architecture. From AD 63 they became allies and vassals of Rome, and in AD 106 Trajan transformed their kingdom into the Roman province of Arabia.

**Nabeul** /næˈbɜːl/ a resort town in north-east Tunisia, on the Cape Bon peninsula; pop. (1984) 39,500. It is noted for its pottery, ceramic tiles, and mat-weaving.

**Nablus** /ˈnæbləs/ a town in the Israeli-occupied West Bank, 66 km. (41 miles) north of Jerusalem; pop. (est. 1984) 80,000. It is close to the site of the Canaanite city of Shechem, important in ancient times because of its position at the centre of an east–west route through the mountains of Samaria. The university of Al-Abjah is located here, and oil and soap are manufactured.

**Nacala** /nəˈkɑːlə/ a deep-water port in the province of Nampula on the north-east coast of Mozambique; pop. (1990) 104,300. It is linked by rail with landlocked Malawi.

**NACC** *abbr.* NORTH ATLANTIC COOPERATION COUNCIL.

**Nadiad** /ˌnədiˈɑːd/ a town in Gujarat, western India, south-east of Ahmadabad; pop. (1991) 170,000. It is an agricultural market and metal utensils are manufactured.

**Naestved** /ˈnɛstvəð/ an industrial port and market centre in Storstrøm county, south-west Zealand, Denmark; pop. (1990) 45,175.

**Nafud** /nɑːˈfuːd/ a desert region at the northern end of the Arabian peninsula, occupying a large depression surrounded by sandstone outcrops that have eroded into curious shapes. Noted for its lack of rainfall and its violent sandstorms, its chief oases lie in the foothills of the Hejaz Mts.

**Naga** /ˈnɑːɡə/ a member of a group of tribes living in or near the Naga Hills of Burma and in north-east India. Their language is a member of the Tibetan language group. Nearly half of the population is Christian.

**Naga City** a city on the island of Luzon in the Philippines; pop. (1990) 115,000. Situated on the Naga River, Naga City lies close to the Mt. Isarog National Park, and was one of the earliest Spanish settlements.

**Nagaland** /ˈnɑːɡəˌlænd/ a state in the far north-east of India, on the border with Burma (Myanmar), created in 1962 from the former Naga Hills district of Assam and neighbouring areas; area 16,579 sq. km. (6,404 sq. miles); pop. (1991) 1,215,570; capital, Kohima. There is a strong local separatist movement.

**Nagano** /næˈɡɑːnəʊ/ the capital of Nagano prefecture at the centre of Honshu Island, Japan, on the Tenryu River; pop. (1990) 347,035. The Zenko Buddhist temple houses statues reportedly sent from the King of Korea in 552 (shown every seven years) and pilgrims come to touch the 'key of Paradise' that is supposed to guarantee easy access to heaven. Industries include electrical equipment, foodstuffs, and printing.

**Nagaoka** /nɑːɡəˈəʊkə/ an industrial city in Niigata prefecture at the centre of Honshu Island, Japan; pop. (1990) 185,940. It has an oil refinery, chemicals, and engineering works.

**Nagar Haveli** SEE DADRA AND NAGAR HAVELI.

**Nagasaki** /ˌnæɡəˈsɑːkɪ/ a city and port in south-west Japan, on the west coast of the island of Kyushu; pop. (1990) 444,620. Visited by the Portuguese in 1545, it was the first Japanese port to open up to western trade. During Japan's period of national seclusion (1639–1854), the island of Dejima, built in Nagasaki Bay, was the only port open to foreign trade. On 9 Aug. 1945 it was the target of the second atomic bomb attack on Japan, an event that devastated one-third of the city, killing *c.* 75,000 people immediately and the same number died owing to its after effects. Nagasaki specializes in shipbuilding and heavy engineering.

**Nagercoil** /ˈnɑːɡərˌkɔɪl/ a city and transportation centre in Tamil Nadu, southern India, at the southern tip of the Western Ghats; pop. (1991) 189,480.

**Nagorno-Karabakh** /nəˈɡɔːnəʊˌkærəˈbæx/ a predominantly farming region of Azerbaijan in the southern foothills of the Caucasus; area 4,400 sq. km. (1,700 sq. miles); pop. (1990) 192,400; capital, Stepanakert (Khankendi). Formerly a khanate, it was absorbed into the Russian empire in the 19th c., becoming an autonomous region of the Soviet republic of Azerbaijan in 1923. The desire of the largely Armenian population to be separated from Muslim Azerbaijan and united with Armenia gave rise to ethnic conflict in 1985. After the region declared unilateral independence in 1991 the Azerbaijan government imposed direct rule, abolishing its autonomous status. More recently Nagorno-Karabakh has been virtually independent of Azerbaijan as the fortunes in the war have shifted to the Armenian population. Virtually all Azeris have left the region.

**Nagoya** /nəˈɡɔɪə/ a port and city in central Japan, capital of Aichi prefecture in the Chubu region of Honshu Island; pop. (1990) 2,154,660. It is the fourth-largest city in Japan. Landmarks include Nagoya Castle and the Atsuta Shrine. It has iron and steel works, and aircraft, automobile, and chemical industries.

**Nagpur** /nɑːɡˈpʊə(r)/ a city in the state of Maharashtra, central India, on the Nag River; pop. (1991) 1,661,400. It was a centre of the Chanda dynasty of aboriginal Gonds and capital of the Central provinces. An administrative and commercial centre with textile industries.

**Naha** /ˈnɑːhæ/ a port on the west coast of the Japanese island of Okinawa; pop. (1990) 304,900. It is capital and chief industrial centre of Okinawa prefecture.

**Nahanni National Park** /nəˈhɑːnɪ/ a national park extending over the Mackenzie Mountains in the Northwest Territories of Canada; area 4,700 sq. km. (1,814 sq. miles). Its most dramatic feature is the 90-m. (295-ft.) Virginia Falls on the South Nahanni River.

**Nahe** /ˈnɑːə/ a river of west Germany that flows north-eastwards through Saarland and the Rhineland-Palatinate to meet the River Rhine at Bingen.

**Nahuatl** /nɑːˈwɑːt(l), ˈnɑː-/ an ancient group of peoples native to southern Mexico and Central America including the Aztecs.
**Nahuatlan** *adj.*

**Nahuel Huapi** /nɑːˈwel wɑːˈpiː/ a lake in the Andes of west-central Argentina; area 545 sq. km. (210 sq. miles). The resort town of San Carlos de Bariloche lies on its southern shore. Nahuel Huapi National Park, designated in 1934, was the world's first privately donated national park.

**Nairnshire** /ˈneənʃɪə(r)/ (also **Nairn**) a former county of north-east Scotland, on the Moray Firth. It was a district of Highland Region, from 1975 to 1996 with an administrative centre in the town of Nairn which lies at the mouth of the River Nairn.

**Nairobi** /naɪˈrəʊbɪ/ the capital of Kenya, situated at an altitude of *c.*1,680 m. (5,500 ft.) on the central Kenya plateau; pop. (est. 1987) 1,288,700. Originally a railhead camp on the Ugandan Railway in the 1890s it has been capital since 1905. It is now Kenya's administrative, communications, and economic centre with many light industries and tourist facilities.

**Najaf** /ˈnædʒæf/ (also **An Najaf** /æn/) a city in southern Iraq, on the Euphrates 144 km. south of Baghdad; pop. (est. 1985) 242,600. It contains the shrine of Ali, the prophet Muhammad's son-in-law, and is a holy city of the Shiite Muslims.

**Najd** see NEJD.

**Nakhichevan** /ˌnɑːxɪtʃəˈvɑːn/ **1.** a predominantly Muslim autonomous republic within Azerbaijan, situated on the borders of Turkey and northern Iran and separated from Azerbaijan by a narrow strip of Armenia; area 5,500 sq. km. (2,120 sq. miles); pop. (1990) 300,400. Persian from the 13th to the 19th c., it became part of Russia in 1828 and an autonomous republic of the Soviet Union in 1924. In 1990 it was the first Soviet territory to declare unilateral independence since the 1917 revolution, and along with Nagorno-Karabakh it was subsequently the focal point of conflict between Armenia and Azerbaijan. **2.** the capital city of the republic; pop. (est. 1987) 51,000. It is an ancient settlement, perhaps dating from *c.* 1500 BC, believed in Armenian tradition to have been founded by Noah.

**Nakhodka** /nəˈkɒtkə/ a port and naval base in Far Eastern Russia, on the Sea of Japan east of Vladivostok; pop. (1990) 163,000. The terminal of the Trans-Siberian Railway for passengers and freight going to or from the Far East.

**Nakhon Ratchasima** /nɑːˌkɒn rɑːtʃəˈsiːmə/ (also **Korat**) a city and railway centre in north-east Thailand, on the Takhong River; pop. (1990) 204,120. It is linked to the Mekong River on the Laos frontier by the Friendship Highway which was built with US aid during the Vietnam War when the city was a US air base from where planes set out to bomb the Ho Chi Minh Trail.

**Nakhon Sawan** /nɑːˌkɒn səˈwɑːn/ (also **Paknam Pho**) a port at the junction of the Ping, Wang, Yom, and Nan rivers in central Thailand; pop. (1990) 108,040. It was an important centre of the teak trade until logging was banned in 1989.

**Nakuru** /næˈkuːruː/ an industrial city and regional market with food-processing industries in western Kenya, capital of the Rift Valley province; pop. (1986) 112,000. Nearby is **Lake Nakuru**, a soda lake famous for its spectacular flocks of flamingos.

**Nalchik** /ˈnɑːltʃɪk/ a city in the Caucasus, south-west Russia, capital of Kabardino-Balkaria; pop. (1990) 237,000. Founded as a fortress town by the Russians in 1817, it developed into an industrial centre, tourist resort, and university town in the 20th c.

**Namangan** /ˌnɑːmænˈɡɑːn/ a city in eastern Uzbekistan, situated in the Fergana Basin near the border with Kyrgyzstan; pop. (1990) 312,000. Food processing and cotton production are its chief industries.

**Namaqualand** /nəˈmɑːkwəˌlænd/ the home-land of the Nama people of south-west Namibia and South Africa. **Little Namaqualand** lies immediately to the south of the Orange River in the Cape Province of South Africa, while **Great Namaqualand** lies to the north of the river in Namibia.

**Nam Co** /næm ˈkəʊ/ a lake in Tibet, the second-largest saltwater lake in China; area 1,940 sq. km. (750 sq. miles).

**Namen** the Flemish name for NAMUR.

**Namib Desert** /ˈnɑːmɪb/ a desert of south-west Africa. It extends for 1,900 km. (1,200 miles) along the Atlantic coast, from the Curoca River in south-west Angola through Namibia to the border between Namibia and South Africa. Alluvial diamonds of high quality are mined in the south-ern area.

**Namibe** /næˈmiːbe/ a port on the south-west coast of Angola, formerly known as Moçâmedes; pop. (1981) 100,000.

**Namibia**
/nəˈmɪbɪə/ official name **The Republic of Namibia** a coun-try in south-west Africa, between Angola and the Cape Province of South Africa; area 824,292 sq. km. (318,382 sq. miles); pop. (est. 1991) 1,834,000; languages, Eng-lish (official), Bantu languages, Afrikaans; capital, Windhoek. Namibia is an arid country, with large tracts of desert along the coast and in the east. The principal ethnic groups are Ovambo, Damara, Herero, Nama, Kavango, Caprivians, Basters, and Bushmen. Stock rearing, fishing, and the mining of diamonds and uranium are the chief economic activities. German missionaries explored the area in the 19th c., and it became the German pro-tectorate of Southwest Africa in 1884. In 1919 Southwest Africa was mandated to South Africa by the League of Nations. Despite increasing inter-national insistence, after 1946, that this mandate had ended, South Africa continued to administer the country. Eventually after several years of fight-ing against SWAPO guerrillas, South Africa agreed to withdraw. Free elections were held in 1989, and Namibia became independent in March 1990. In March 1994 South Africa handed over to Namibia the Walvis Bay enclave which had previously been administered as part of the Cape Province. Namibia is a multiparty state governed by an

executive president and a bicameral Constituent Assembly.
**Namibian** *adj. & n.*

**Nampo** /nɑːmˈpəʊ/ (also **Chinnampo**) a city and major port on the west coast of North Korea, on an inlet of Korea Bay south-west of Pyonyang; pop. (1984) 691,000.

**Nampula** a market town in north-eastern Mozambique, capital of a province of the same name; pop. (1990) 202,600.

**Nams** /nɑːms/ (Norwegian **Namsen**) a river of north-central Norway that emerges from Lake Nams and flows 210 km. (131 miles) westwards to the Norwegian Sea.

**Namur** /nəˈmʊə(r)/ (Flemish **Namen** /ˈnɑːmən/) **1.** a province in central Belgium; area 3,666 sq. km. (1,416 sq. miles); pop. (1991) 423,320. It was the scene of the last great German offensive in the Ardennes in 1945. **2.** the capital of this province, at the junction of the Meuse and Sambre rivers; pop. (1991) 103,440. Its strategic position has made it the site of many battles and sieges.

**Nanaimo** /nəˈnaɪməʊ/ a port on the east coast of Vancouver Island in British Columbia, Canada; pop. (1991) 60,100. Originally a trading post of the Hudson's Bay Company, it developed into a pulp and timber-processing centre.

**Nanchang** /nænˈtʃæŋ/ the capital of Jiangxi province in south-east China; pop. (1990) 2,471,000. Dating from the 12th c., it is a major centre of industry (aircraft and diesel trucks) and transportation. In 1927 the first Communist upris-ing against the Kuomintang government took place here.

**Nanchong** /nænˈtʃʊŋ/ a city in Sichuan prov-ince, central China, on the Jialin River east of Chengdu; pop. (1986) 246,000.

**Nancy** /ˈnɑ̃sɪ/ the capital of Meurthe-et-Moselle department in the Lorraine region of north-east France, situated on the Meurthe River; pop. (1990) 102,410. It was the seat of the dukes of Lorraine who are buried in the 15th-c. Eglise des Cordeliers, and is the administrative, economic, and cultural centre of Lorraine. Industries are based on the Lorraine iron fields and include foundry products and boilers. It is nevertheless an elegant city with a large university (1970) and academy.

**Nanded** /ˈnɑːndəd/ a city in the state of Maha-rashtra, central India, on the Godavari River; pop. (1991) 308,850. Guru Gobind Singh, the tenth Sikh guru, was assassinated here in 1708.

**Nanga Parbat** /ˌnəŋɡə ˈpɑːbət/ a mountain massif in the Punjab Himalayas whose highest peak rises to 8,126 m. (26,660 ft.). Known as the 'Naked Mountain', it is the most westerly of the 8,000 m. Himalayan peaks. The mountaineer A. F. Mummery died during an ascent of the north-west Diamir face in 1895.

**Nanjing** /næn'dʒɪŋ/ (formerly **Nanking** /næn'kɪŋ/) a city of eastern China, on the Yangtze River, that has served at times as the country's capital and is now the capital of Jiangsu province; pop. (1990) 3,682,000. It gave its name to a type of yellowish cotton cloth known as *nankeen*, and has a notable college of traditional Chinese medicine. It has an integrated iron and steel works, an oil refinery, and many light industries. There are numerous cultural and educational institutions.

**Nanning** /næn'nɪŋ/ the capital of Guangxi autonomous region in southern China, the southernmost city of China; pop. (1990) 1,070,000. Food processing, sugar refining, and machine building are among its chief industries.

**Nanping** /næn'pɪŋ/ a city in Fujian province, south-east China, on the Min River north-west of Fuzhou; pop. (1986) 427,000.

**Nansei Islands** /næn'seɪ/ see RYUKU ISLANDS.

**Nanshan Islands** /nɑːn'ʃɑːn/ the Chinese name for the SPRATLY ISLANDS in the South China Sea.

**Nanterre** /nã'teə(r)/ a western suburb of Paris on the right bank of the Seine, the capital of the department of Hautes-de-Seine in the Ile-de-France region of central France; pop. (1990) 86,630.

**Nantes** /nãt/ a city and port in western France, capital of the department of Loire-Atlantique in the Pays de la Loire region; pop. (1990) 252,030. Situated at the mouth of the Loire, it was once the leading port of France. It was the scene in 1598 of the signing of the Edict of Nantes by Henry IV of France granting toleration to Protestants, revoked by Louis XIV in 1685. Nantes was the birthplace of Jules Verne (1828–1905). It has numerous light industries including the making of its famous biscuits.

**Nantong** /nɑːn'tuːŋ/ (formerly **Nantung**) a city in the province of Jiangsu, east-central China, near the mouth of the Yangtze River; pop. (1986) 420,000. It is a special economic zone with special emphasis on textiles.

**Nantucket** /næn'tʌkət/ an island off the southeast coast of the US state of Massachusetts, south of Cape Cod from which it is separated by the **Nantucket Sound**. First visited by the English in 1602, the town was settled by the Quakers in 1659. It became an important whaling centre in the 18th and 19th centuries; area 122 sq. km. (47 sq. miles).

**Nanyang** /næn'jæŋ/ a city in Henan province, east-central China, south-west of Zhengzhou; pop. (1986) 304,000.

**Napa** a town in the US state of California, on the Napa River north of San Francisco; pop. (1990) 61,840. The **Napa Valley** is one of the principal wine-producing regions of the USA.

**Naperville** /'neɪpə‚vɪl/ a city in north-east Illinois, USA, on the Du Page River; pop. (1990) 85,350. Founded by Captain Joseph Naper in 1831, Naperville was settled by Pennsylvanians of German descent in the late 1830s. It has expanded rapidly in recent years as a centre of research and high technology.

**Napier** /'neɪpɪə(r)/ a seaport on Hawkes Bay, North Island, New Zealand; pop. (1991) 52,470. Visited seasonally by Australian whalers in the 1830s, but first settled by missionaries in 1844, the town was named after the British military hero Sir Charles Napier (1809–54). Napier and the adjacent town of Hastings were rebuilt after being severely damaged by an earthquake in 1931. Napier is now a major fishing port and food-processing centre.

**Naples** /'neɪpəlz/ (Italian **Napoli** /'næpəlɪ/) a city and port on the west coast of Italy, south of Rome; pop. (1990) 1,206,000. Formerly the capital of the Kingdom of Naples and Sicily (1806–60), it is now capital of the province of Naples and the Campania region. A treasure-house of historic buildings and works of art, it also contains the worst slums in Europe. Industrial areas devoted to steel, chemicals, clothing, leather, and foodstuffs encircle the city. Tourism is also very important, both in the city and surroundings.

**Napo** /'nɑːpəʊ/ a river of South America that rises in the Ecuadorean Andes near Cotopaxi and flows eastwards for 1,120 km. (700 miles) before joining the Amazon in the tropical lowlands of Peru.

**Napoli** the Italian name for NAPLES.

**nappe** /'næpə/ a sheet of rock that has moved sideways over neighbouring strata, usually as a result of overthrust.

**Nara** /'nɑːrɑ/ an ancient cultural and religious city on Honshu Island, central Japan, capital of Nara prefecture; pop. (1990) 349,360. It was the first imperial capital of Japan (710–94) and an important centre of Japanese Buddhism. The East Great Temple (Todai-ji), which houses a bronze statue of the Buddha (the largest in Japan), is said to be one of the largest wooden buildings in the world; the 7th-c. Temple of Horyu complex, some of the oldest in Japan, is reputed to include the oldest wooden buildings in the world.

**Narashino** /‚nɑːrə'ʃiːnəʊ/ an industrial (metals industries) suburb of Tokyo on Tokyo Bay, Chiba prefecture, east Honshu Island, Japan; pop. (1990) 151,470.

**Narayanganj** /nɑː'rɑːjəngəndʒ/ a river port in south-east Bangladesh, on the Lakhya and Dhaleshwari rivers 24 km. east of Dhaka (Dacca); pop. (1991) 406,000. Its chief industry is the production of jute.

**Narbonne** /nɑː'bɒn/ a city in southern France, in Languedoc-Roussillon, just inland from the Mediterranean on the canalized Robine River; pop. (1990) 47,090. It was founded by the Romans in 118 BC, the first Roman colony in Transalpine Gaul. Known as Narbo Martius, it became the

capital of the Roman province of Gallia Narbonensis. It was a prosperous port of medieval France
until its harbour silted up in the early 14th c. Landmarks include a Roman bridge and amphitheatre
and the 13th–14th-c. cathedral of St. Just.

**Narmada** /'nɑːmʌdə/ a river of central India,
sacred to Hindus, that rises in Madhya Pradesh
and flows 1,245 km. (778 miles) westwards to the
Gulf of Cambay.

**Narodnaya** /nɑːˈrɒdnəjə/ a mountain in
Russia, the highest peak of the Urals, rising to
1,894 m. (6,214 ft.) east of Pechora.

**Narragansett** /ˌnærəˈɡɑːnsət/ an Algonquian
Indian tribe of north-east North America, originally living in New England, especially on the western shore of Narragansett Bay, Rhode Island.

**Narrows** /'nærəʊz/, **the** a stretch of water lying
between Long Island and Staten Island, New York
City, USA. Spanned by the Verrazano Bridge, it
links Upper New York Bay with Lower New
York Bay.

**Narvik** /'nɑːvɪk/ an ice-free port on the north-
west coast of Norway opposite the Lofoten
Islands; pop. (1990) 18,640. It lies north of the
Arctic Circle and is linked by rail to the iron-ore
mines of northern Sweden.

**Naryn** /nəˈrɪn/ a river of Central Asia that rises
in the Tien Shan range and flows westwards for
c. 725 km. (450 miles) through the Fergana Valley
before joining the Kara Darya to form the Syr
Darya.

**Naseby** /'neɪzbɪ/ a village in Northamptonshire,
scene of the last major battle (1645) of the main
phase of the English Civil War, in which the last
Royalist army in England, commanded by Prince
Rupert and the King himself, was comprehensively
defeated by the larger and better organized New
Model Army under Fairfax and Oliver Cromwell.
Following the destruction of his army Charles I's
cause collapsed completely; the monarchy was
never so powerful again.

**Nashua** /'næʃuə/ a city in southern New Hampshire, USA, on the Merrimack and Nashua rivers;
pop. (1990) 79,660. Settled in 1656, Nashua developed from a fur-trading post to a textile-mill
town. Modern industries produce a wide range of
goods including computers, tools, and beer.

**Nashik** /'nɑːsɪk/ (also **Nasik**) a city in the state
of Maharashtra, central India, on the Godavari
River north-east of Bombay; pop. (1991) 722,140.
It is a holy city associated with the Hindu god
Rama and his wife Sita.

**Nashville** /'næʃvɪl/ the state capital of Tennessee, USA, a port on the Cumberland River; pop.
(1990) 510,780 (with Davidson). First settled in
1779 and known as Fort Nasborough, its name was
changed to Nashville nearly 50 years later. The city
is noted for its music industry and is the site of
Opryland USA (a family entertainment complex)

and the Country Music Hall of Fame. The Grand
Ole Opry House is the world's largest broadcasting
studio.

**Nassau** /'nɑːsaʊ/ a former duchy of western
Germany, centred on the small town of Nassau on
the Lahn River east of Ems. During the 13th c. the
Nassau dynasty split into two lines descended from
Count Walram II and his younger brother Otto.
The Walramian line ruled Nassau, which eventually united with the electorate of Hesse to form
the Prussian province of Hesse-Nassau in the
1860s, their descendants succeeding in 1890 to the
Grand Duchy of Luxembourg. The Ottonian line
settled in Breda in the Netherlands during the
15th c. where it became known as the House of
Orange.

**Nassau** /'næsɔː/ the capital of the Bahamas in
the West Indies, a port on the island of New
Providence; pop. (1990) 172,000. Once frequented
by pirates, it is now a popular winter tourist resort
and banking centre. Many international companies
have registered offices in Nassau.

**Nasser** /'næsə(r)/, **Lake** a lake to the south of
Aswan in southern Egypt and northern Sudan,
created in the 1960s after the building of the Aswan
High Dam on the River Nile. It is 500 km. (300
miles) long and is named after former Egyptian
president Gamal Abdel Nasser (1918–70).

**Natal** /næ'tɑːl/ a seaport on the Atlantic coast
of north-east Brazil, capital of the state of Rio
Grande do Norte, situated near the mouth of the
Potengi River; pop. (1991) 607,000. The site of a
confrontation between the Portuguese and the
French on Christmas Day 1597, Natal expanded
after the construction of a railway and port in
1892, and during World War II when it was the
take-off point for flights to Africa.

**Natal** /næ'tɑːl/ a former province (until 1994) of
the Republic of South Africa, between the Indian
Ocean and the Drakensberg Mountains, now part
of the province of Kwazulu-Natal; area 91,355
sq. km. (35,286 sq. miles); pop. (1991) 2,074,150;
capital, Pietermaritzburg. It was first settled by
British traders in 1823, then by Boers, becoming a
Boer republic in 1893. Annexed by the British to
Cape Colony in 1845, it became a separate colony
in 1856 and acquired internal self-government in
1893. It became a province of the Union of South
Africa in 1910. It was named *Terra Natalis*—
meaning 'land of the day of birth' in Latin—by
Vasco da Gama in 1497, because he sighted the
entrance to what is now Durban harbour on
Christmas Day. Its chief ports are Durban and
Richards Bay. See KWAZULU-NATAL.

**Natchez** /'nætʃɪz/ a North American Indian
tribe of the Hokan-Natchez linguistic group,
originally living in the lower Mississippi valley.

**Natchez Trace** /'nætʃɪz treɪs/ the name given
to a roadway in the USA linking Natchez, Mississippi, with Nashville, Tennessee. Following old

Indian trails, the Natchez Trace was extensively used by French, English, and Spanish travellers until the coming of steamboat navigation in the 19th c. The 720-km. (450-mile) Natchez Trace Scenic Parkway now follows this routeway.

**National City** a commercial city to the south of San Diego in western California, USA; pop. (1990) 54,250. The first shopping centre in America was opened here in 1953.

**national grid** a rectangular system of lines printed on UK Ordnance Survey maps in order to provide a means of reference using numbered co-ordinates.

**NATO** /ˈneɪtəʊ/ abbr. (also **Nato**) NORTH ATLANTIC TREATY ORGANIZATION.

**Natron** /ˈneɪtrən/**, Lake** a lake in the Rift Valley of northern Tanzania, containing large deposits of salt and soda.

**Natufian** /nɑːˈtuːfɪən/ of a late mesolithic industry of Palestine, which provides evidence for the first settled villages and is characterized by the use of microliths and of bone for implements. It is named after the type-site, a cave at Wadi an-Natuf, 27 km. (17 miles) north of Jerusalem in Israel.

**Nauplia** /ˈnɔːplɪə/ (Greek **Návplion** or **Nauplion** /ˈnæfpliːɒn/) a port on the Gulf of Argolis in the Peloponnese of southern Greece, capital of the department of Argolis; pop. (1981) 10,600. It was the first capital of independent Greece from 1830 to 1834.

**Nauru** /naʊˈruː/ an island country in the south-west Pacific, lying near the equator; area 21 sq. km. (8 sq. miles); pop. (1989) 9,000; official language, English; no official capital. In-habited by Poly-

nesians, Nauru is an oval-shaped tropical island surrounded by a coral reef. Its economy is heavily dependent upon the mining of phosphates, of which it has the world's richest deposits. Discovered by the British in 1798, it was annexed by Germany in 1888, and became a British mandate after World War I. Since 1968 it has been an independent republic with associate membership of the Commonwealth. In 1993 Nauru was awarded compensation for environmental damage caused by the extraction of phosphates by the British Phosphate Commissioners between 1919 and 1968. Nauru is governed by a president and a unicameral parliament.
**Nauruan** adj. & n.

**nautical mile** an international unit of distance used in navigation, equal to one minute of arc on a great circle or 1,852 m. (6,080 ft.).

**Navajo** /ˈnævəˌhəʊ/ (also **Navaho**) (pl. **-os**) a North American Indian people belonging to the Athapaskan linguistic group and native to New Mexico and Arizona. Their name is derived from a Spanish word for 'people with big fields' and their reservation is the largest in the US. They number 220,000 (1990) and are the largest American Indian tribe.

**Navan** /ˈnævən/ the county town of Meath in the Republic of Ireland, situated at the junction of the Boyne and Blackwater rivers; pop. (1991) 3,410. It is one of Ireland's leading centres for the manufacture of furniture.

**Navarino Bay** /ˌnævəˈriːnəʊ/ a bay off Pylos in the Peloponnese of southern Greece, scene of a decisive naval battle in the struggle for Greek independence from the Ottoman empire fought in 1827. Britain, Russia, and France sent a combined fleet which destroyed the Egyptian and Turkish fleet in the last great battle fought by wooden sailing ships.

**Navarre** /nəˈvɑː(r)/ **1.** a former Franco-Spanish kingdom in the Pyrenees, Navarre achieved independence in the 10th c. under Sancho III, but during the Middle Ages fell at various times under French or Spanish domination. The southern part of the country was conquered by Ferdinand V in 1512 while the northern part passed to France in 1589 through inheritance by Henry IV. **2.** (Spanish **Navarra**) an autonomous region of northern Spain; area 10,421 sq. km. (4,025 sq. miles); pop. (1991) 519,230; capital, Pamplona.

**Návpaktos** /ˈnɑːfpɑːktɒs/ (Italian **Lepanto**) a port on the Lepanto Strait in the department of Aetolia and Acarnania, Greece. See LEPANTO.

**Navsari** /nəvˈsɑːrɪ/ (also **Nausari** /ˈnaʊ-/) a town in Gujarat, western India, on the coastal plain north of Bombay; pop. (1991) 190,000.

**Nawabganj** /nəˈwɑːbgəndʒ/ a city in western Bangladesh, on the Mahananda River north-west of Rajshahi; pop. (1991) 121,000.

**Nawabshah** /nəˈwɑːbʃɑː/ a city in the province of Sind in south-east Pakistan, to the north of Hyderabad; pop. (1981) 102,000.

**Naxos** /ˈnæksɒs/ a Greek island in the southern Aegean, the largest of the Cyclades, famous in mythology as the place where Theseus abandoned Ariadne; area 428 sq. km. (165 sq. miles). At the centre of the island is Mt. Zas (Zévs) which rises to 1,004 m. (3,295 ft.) and is the highest peak in the Cyclades. Wine, citrus fruit, olives, figs, pomegranates, and corn are produced, and emery and marble are quarried. Its chief town is Naxos.

**Nayarit** /ˌnaɪəˈriːt/ a state of western Mexico, between the Sierra Madre and the Pacific Ocean; area 26,979 sq. km. (10,420 sq. miles); pop. (1990) 816,110; capital, Tepic.

**Nazaré** /ˈnɑːzəreɪ/ a resort and fishing port on the Atlantic coast of Leiria district, west-central Portugal; pop. (1991) 9,625.

**Nazarene** /ˌnæzəˈriːn, ˈnæ-/ the name given to a native of Nazareth in Israel or, by writers in the 4th c., to Christians of Jewish race in Syria who continued to obey much of the Jewish Law but were otherwise orthodox Christians using a version of the Gospel in Aramaic.

**Nazareth** /ˈnæzərəθ/ (Hebrew **Nazerat**) a historic town in lower Galilee in present-day northern Israel; pop. (1982) 39,000. It was mentioned in the Gospels as the home of Mary and Joseph, is closely associated with the childhood of Jesus, and is a centre of Christian pilrimage.

**Nazca Lines** /ˈnæzkə/ a group of huge drawings of animals, abstract designs, and straight lines on the coastal plain north of Nazca in southern Peru, made by cleaning and aligning the surface stones to expose the underlying sand. They belong to a pre-Inca culture of that region, and their purpose is uncertain; some hold the designs to represent a vast calendar or astronomical information. Virtually indecipherable at ground level, the lines are clearly visible from the air; they have been preserved by the extreme dryness of the region.

**Naze** /neɪz/, **the 1.** a headland to the south of Harwich on the North Sea coast of Essex, southeast England. **2.** (Norwegian **Lindesnes** /ˈlɪndəsˌneɪs/) the southern tip of Norway on the North Sea.

**NC** *abbr.* US North Carolina (in official postal use).

**ND** *abbr.* US North Dakota (in official postal use).

**Ndebele** /ənˌdəˈbiːlɪ/ a Zulu people, branches of which are found in Zimbabwe (where they are better known as Matabele) and in the Transvaal.

**N'Djamena** /ˌəndʒæˈmeɪnə/ the capital and river port of Chad, at the junction of the Chari and Logone rivers; pop. (1993) 529,550. Founded by the French in 1900, it was known as Fort Lamy until 1973. A communications and food-processing centre (groundnuts and meat chilling). There is a university and regional museum.

**Ndola** /ənˈdəʊlə/ a city in central Zambia, capital of the copperbelt-mining province; pop. (1987) 418,140. It is the commercial centre of Zambia, with cobalt and copper refineries and steelworks.

**NE** *abbr.* US Nebraska (in official postal use).

**Neagh** /neɪ/, **Lough** a shallow lake in Northern Ireland, the largest freshwater lake in the British Isles with noted fisheries; area 381.7 sq. km. (147.4 sq. miles). It is fed by several streams, the largest of which is the River Bann.

**Neanderthal** /neɪˈɑːndɜːˌtɑːl/ a valley to the east of Düsseldorf in North Rhine-Westphalia, west Germany, where in 1856 the remains of Neanderthal man, the first fossil hominid to be identified as such, were discovered.

**Neapolitan** /nɪəˈpɒlɪt(ə)n/ a citizen of Naples in Italy.

**Near East** a region comprising the countries of the eastern Mediterranean, sometimes also including those of the Balkan peninsula, south-west Asia, or northern Africa.

**Nearctic** /nɪˈɑːktɪk/ of or relating to the Arctic and the temperate parts of North America as a zoogeographical region.

**Neath** /niːθ/ an industrial town in West Glamorgan, south Wales, on the River Neath near Swansea; pop. (1981) 49,130. The ruins of Neath Abbey date from the 12th c.

**Neblina** /nəˈbliːnə/, **Pico da** a mountain in northern Brazil that rises to 3,014 m. (9,888 ft.) on the frontier with Venezuela. It is the highest mountain in Brazil and the highest mountain in South America outside the Andes.

**Nebraska** /nɪˈbræskə/ a state in the central US to the west of the Missouri River; area 200,350 sq. km. (77,355 sq. miles); pop. (1990) 1,578,385; capital, Lincoln. The largest cities are Omaha and Lincoln. Nebraska is also known as the Cornhusker, Beef, or Tree Planter State. Acquired as part of the Louisiana Purchase in 1803, it became the 37th state of the US in 1867. It is a leading producer of grain, cattle, and pigs and has oil and natural gas resources. Its chief landmarks are Scotts Bluff National Monument, Agate Fossil Beds National Monument, Chimney Rock National Historic Site, and the Homestead National Monument of America. Nebraska is divided into 93 counties:

| County | Area (sq. km.) | Pop. (1990) | County Seat |
|---|---|---|---|
| Adams | 1,466 | 29,625 | Hastings |
| Antelope | 2,233 | 7,965 | Neligh |
| Arthur | 1,849 | 460 | Arthur |
| Banner | 1,942 | 850 | Harrisburg |
| Blaine | 1,856 | 675 | Brewster |
| Boone | 1,786 | 6,670 | Albion |
| Box Butte | 2,800 | 13,130 | Alliance |
| Boyd | 1,383 | 2,835 | Butte |
| Brown | 3,156 | 3,660 | Ainsworth |
| Buffalo | 2,457 | 37,450 | Kearney |
| Burt | 1,264 | 7,870 | Tekamah |
| Butler | 1,518 | 8,600 | David City |
| Cass | 1,448 | 21,320 | Plattsmouth |
| Cedar | 1,924 | 10,130 | Hartington |
| Chase | 2,324 | 4,380 | Imperial |
| Cherry | 15,499 | 6,310 | Valentine |
| Cheyenne | 3,110 | 9,490 | Sidney |
| Clay | 1,492 | 7,120 | Clay Center |
| Colfax | 1,066 | 9,140 | Schuyler |
| Cuming | 1,495 | 10,120 | West Point |
| Custer | 6,685 | 12,270 | Broken Bow |
| Dakota | 671 | 16,740 | Dakota City |
| Dawes | 3,632 | 9,020 | Chadron |
| Dawson | 2,553 | 19,940 | Lexington |
| Deuel | 1,136 | 2,240 | Chappell |
| Dixon | 1,232 | 6,140 | Ponca |
| Dodge | 1,388 | 34,500 | Fremont |
| Douglas | 866 | 416,440 | Omaha |
| Dundy | 2,392 | 2,580 | Benkelman |

(cont.)

| | | | |
|---|---|---|---|
| Fillmore | 1,498 | 7,100 | Geneva |
| Franklin | 1,498 | 3,940 | Franklin |
| Frontier | 2,538 | 3,100 | Stockville |
| Furnas | 1,875 | 5,550 | Beaver City |
| Gage | 2,231 | 22,790 | Beatrice |
| Garden | 4,368 | 2,460 | Oshkosh |
| Garfield | 1,482 | 2,140 | Burwell |
| Gosper | 1,199 | 1,930 | Elwood |
| Grant | 2,015 | 770 | Hyannis |
| Greeley | 1,482 | 3,010 | Greeley |
| Hall | 1,396 | 48,925 | Grand Island |
| Hamilton | 1,412 | 8,860 | Aurora |
| Harlan | 1,443 | 3,810 | Alma |
| Hayes | 1,854 | 1,220 | Hayes Center |
| Hitchcock | 1,843 | 3,750 | Trenton |
| Holt | 6,256 | 12,600 | O'Neill |
| Hooker | 1,875 | 790 | Mullen |
| Howard | 1,466 | 6,055 | Saint Paul |
| Jefferson | 1,495 | 8,760 | Fairbury |
| Johnson | 980 | 4,670 | Tecumseh |
| Kearney | 1,349 | 6,630 | Minden |
| Keith | 2,701 | 8,580 | Ogallala |
| Keya Paha | 1,999 | 1,030 | Springview |
| Kimball | 2,475 | 4,110 | Kimball |
| Knox | 2,873 | 9,530 | Center |
| Lancaster | 2,181 | 213,640 | Lincoln |
| Lincoln | 6,565 | 32,510 | North Platte |
| Logan | 1,485 | 880 | Stapleton |
| Loup | 1,492 | 680 | Taylor |
| Madison | 1,495 | 32,655 | Madison |
| McPherson | 2,233 | 550 | Tryon |
| Merrick | 1,243 | 8,040 | Central City |
| Morrill | 3,653 | f 5,420 | Bridgeport |
| Nance | 1,141 | 4,275 | Fullerton |
| Nemaha | 1,063 | 7,980 | Auburn |
| Nuckolls | 1,498 | 5,790 | Nelson |
| Otoe | 1,599 | 14,250 | Nebraska City |
| Pawnee | 1,126 | 3,320 | Pawnee City |
| Perkins | 2,301 | 3,370 | Grant |
| Phelps | 1,404 | 9,715 | Holdrege |
| Pierce | 1,495 | 7,830 | Pierce |
| Platte | 1,739 | 29,820 | Columbus |
| Polk | 1,136 | 5,675 | Osceola |
| Red Willow | 1,867 | 11,705 | McCook |
| Richardson | 1,438 | 9,940 | Falls City |
| Rock | 2,608 | 2,020 | Bassett |
| Saline | 1,495 | 12,715 | Wilber |
| Sarpy | 619 | 102,580 | Papillion |
| Saunders | 1,958 | 18,285 | Wahoo |
| Scotts Bluff | 1,885 | 36,025 | Gering |
| Seward | 1,495 | 15,450 | Seward |
| Sheridan | 6,378 | 6,750 | Rushville |
| Sherman | 1,466 | 3,720 | Loup City |
| Sioux | 5,382 | 1,550 | Harrison |
| Stanton | 1,121 | 6,240 | Stanton |
| Thayer | 1,495 | 6,635 | Hebron |
| Thomas | 1,854 | 850 | Thedford |
| Thurston | 1,017 | 6,940 | Pender |
| Valley | 1,474 | 5,170 | Ord |
| Washington | 1,004 | 16,610 | Blair |
| Wayne | 1,152 | 9,360 | Wayne |
| Webster | 1,495 | 4,280 | Red Cloud |
| Wheeler | 1,495 | 950 | Bartlett |
| York | 1,498 | 14,250 | York |

**Nechtansmere** /'nektənz‚mɪə(r)/ the site (near Forfar in Tayside, Scotland) of a battle in 685 in which the Northumbrians were decisively defeated by the Picts. Their expansion northwards was permanently thwarted, and they were forced to withdraw south of the Firth of Forth.

**Neckar** /'nek(ə)r/ a river of western Germany, which rises on the eastern edge of the Black Forest and flows 367 km. (228 miles) north and west through Stuttgart to meet the Rhine at Mannheim. Its valley is celebrated for its scenery and vineyards.

**Needles** /'niːdəlz/, **the** a group of rocks in the sea off the west coast of the Isle of Wight, England.

**Negeri Sembilan** /nə‚griː semˈbiːlən/ (also **Negri Sembilan**) a state of Malaysia, on the Malay peninsula; area 6,643 sq. km. (2,566 sq. miles); pop. (1990) 723,800; capital, Seremban.

**Negev** /'negev/, **the** an arid region of strategic importance forming most of southern Israel, between Beersheba and the Gulf of Aqaba, on the Egyptian border. Large-scale irrigation projects have greatly increased the fertility of the region and there are many kibbutz settlements. Mineral resources include natural gas and copper.

**Negoiu** /nə'gɔɪuː/ a mountain that rises to 2,535 m. (8,317 ft.) in the Transylvanian Alps, the second-highest peak in Romania.

**Negombo** /nɪ'gɒmbəʊ/ a port and resort on the west coast of Sri Lanka, to the north of Colombo; pop. (1981) 60,700. It is Sri Lanka's largest tourist complex and chief fishing port.

**Negrillo** /nɪ'grɪləʊ/ a member of a Negroid people native to central and southern Africa.

**Negrito** /nɪ'griːtəʊ/ a member of a Negroid people native to the Malayo-Polynesian region.

**Negro** /'niːgrəʊ/ a term formerly used to refer to a member of the Black or dark-skinned race of people that exist or originated in Africa south of the Sahara.

**Negro** /'neɪgrəʊ/, **Rio** the name of three rivers in South America. **1.** a major river of northern South America which rises as the Guainia in eastern Colombia and flows about 2,255 km. (1,400 miles) through north-west Brazil before joining the Amazon near Manaus. **2.** a river of central Argentina formed in the eastern foothills of the Andes at the junction of the Neuquén and Limay rivers. It flows c. 645 km. (400 miles) eastwards through the province of Rio Negro to empty into the Atlantic near Viedma. **3.** the principal river of Uruguay, rising in southern Brazil and flowing c. 805 km. (500 miles) south-westwards to meet the Uruguay River near Fray Bentos. It passes through the Embalse del Rio Negro, one of the largest manmade lakes in South America.

**Negros** /'neɪgrɒs/ an island in the Visayan group, the fourth-largest island of the Philippines; area 12,710 sq. km. (4,909 sq. miles); pop. (1980)

3,182,180; chief city, Bacolod. It is the principal sugar-producing island of the archipelago.

**Neijiang** /neɪ'dʒæŋ/ a river port and railway centre in Sichuan province, central China, on the Tuo River west of Chongqing; pop. (1986) 310,000.

**Nei Mongol** /neɪ 'mʌŋguː/ the Chinese name for INNER MONGOLIA.

**Neisse** /'naɪsə/ the name of two rivers in Poland. **1.** the **Lausatian Neisse**, which flows c. 225 km. (140 miles) northwards to the Oder from the Sudetes Mts. in the Czech Republic. It forms part of the frontier between Germany and Poland. **2.** the **Glatzer Neisse**, which rises in the Sudetes Mts. in south-west Poland and flows 195 km. (120 miles) north-eastwards to meet the Oder near Brzeg.

**Nejd** /nedʒd/ (also **Najd**) an arid plateau region in central Saudi Arabia, to the east of the Hejaz Mts. and lying between the Nafud desert in the north and the great southern desert or Rub' al Khali. At an altitude of 762–1,525 m. (2,500–5,000 ft.), its oases are frequented by nomadic Bedouins. It was the centre of the Wahabi movement which wrested the Nejd from Turkish rule in the early 20th c.

**Nellore** /nə'lɔː(r)/ a city and river port in the state of Andhra Pradesh, south-east India, on the Penner River north of Madras; pop. (1991) 316,445. Situated close to the river mouth, it is one of the chief ports of the Coromandel coast.

**Nelson** /'nels(ə)n/ a city and port on the north coast of South Island, New Zealand, situated on an inlet at the head of Tasman Bay; pop. (1991) 47,390. It was founded in 1841 by the New Zealand company and named after the British admiral Lord Nelson (1758–1805).

**Nelson** a river in Manitoba, central Canada, that flows 644 km. (400 miles) north-eastwards from the north-east corner of Lake Winnipeg to Hudson Bay. Its length including the South Saskatchewan and Bow rivers is 2,575 km. (1,600 miles).

**Nelson-Marlborough** an administrative region at the north end of South Island, New Zealand, created in 1989 and comprising the districts and cities of Nelson, Marlborough, Kaikoura, and parts of Tasman and Huruni; pop. (1991) 113,490.

**Nelspruit** /'nelsprɔɪt/ the capital of the province of Eastern Transvaal in South Africa, on the Crocodile River east of Johannesburg. It is an agricultural centre and point of departure for the Kruger National Park which lies to the north.

**Neman** /'nemən/ (Lithuanian **Nemunas** /'næmɒnɑːs/) a river of eastern Europe that rises in Belorussia (Belarus) and flows 955 km. (597 miles) west and north to meet the Baltic Sea south of Klaipeda in Lithuania. That part formerly flowing though East Prussia was known as the Memel.

**Nemea** /'niːmɪə/ the site of the ancient Greek Temple of Zeus in the Peloponnese, south-west of Corinth. The Nemean Games, one of the four great Panhellenic festivals, were held here biennially. There are remains of a stadium and the Sanctuary of Zeus.

**Nemi** /'neɪmiː/, **Lake** (Italian **Lago di Nemi**) a crater lake in central Italy, situated at an altitude of 318 m. (1,043 ft.) in the Alban Hills south-east of Rome. Nearby was an ancient temple dedicated to Diana.

**Nenets** /nə'nets/ (formerly **Samoyeds**) a people living in the tundra lands of north-west Russia between the White Sea and the Taimyr Peninsula. Numbering c. 30,000 they speak a Samoyedic language and engage in hunting, fishing, and reindeer farming.

**neocolonialism** /ˌniːəʊkə'ləʊnɪəˌlɪz(ə)m/ the use of economic, political, or other pressures to control or influence other countries. **neocolonialist** adj. & n.

**neolithic** /ˌnɪə'lɪθɪk/ of or relating to the later part of the Stone Age, when ground or polished stone weapons and implements prevailed and which saw the introduction of agriculture and the domestication of animals. Sometimes called the 'Neolithic Revolution', mankind turned during this period from being dependent on nature to controlling it at least partially and indirectly. The change led to the establishment of settled communities, accumulation of food and wealth, and heavier growth of population. In the Old World, agriculture began in the Near East by the 8th millennium BC and had spread to northern Europe by the 4th millennium BC.

**neotropical** /ˌniːəʊ'trɒpɪk(ə)l/ of or relating to tropical America and South America as a biogeographical region.

**Nepal** /nə'pɔːl/ official name **The Kingdom of Nepal** a mountainous landlocked country in southern Asia, bordered by China (Tibet) to the north and India to the south, dominated by  the Himalayas including Mt. Everest; area 147,181 sq. km. (56,849 sq. miles); pop. (est. 1991) 19,406,000; official language, Nepali; capital, Kathmandu. Its chief exports are clothing, carpets, leather goods, and grain. The country was conquered by the Gurkhas in the 18th c. and has maintained its independence despite border defeats by the British in the early 19th c. Nepal has supplied contingents of soldiers to fight in British armies up to the present day. Gautama Buddha was born in Nepal. After 18 years as an absolute monarchy Nepal became a multiparty democracy in 1990 and

elections were held the following year. The country is governed by a bicameral legislature comprising a House of Representatives (*Pratinidhi Sabha*) and a National Council (*Rashtriya Sabha*).
**Nepalese** *adj. & n.*

**Nepali** /nɪˈpɔːlɪ/ the official language of Nepal, spoken also in parts of north-east India. It belongs to the Indic branch of the Indo-European family of languages.

**Nerja** /ˈnɜːxə/ a resort town on the coast of Andalusia, southern Spain, situated 50 km. (31 miles) east of Malaga. There are limestone caves nearby.

**Ness, Loch** see LOCH NESS.

# Netherlands
/ˈneðələndz/, **the**
(Dutch **Nederland**)
official name **The**
**Kingdom of the**
**Netherlands** a
country (often called
**Holland**) in western
Europe bordering on
the North Sea, with

Belgium on its southern frontier; area 37,313 sq. km. (14,412 sq. miles); pop. (1991) 15,010,445; official language, Dutch; capital, Amsterdam; seat of government, The Hague. The largest cities are Amsterdam, Rotterdam, The Hague, Utrecht, and Eindhoven. The most densely populated country in Europe with its population concentrated in the cities of so-called Randstad Holland. A low, flat country with little relief, nearly half of the Netherlands lies below sea-level. Permanent habitation did not become possible over much of the 'Low Netherlands', an area now densely populated, until dikes had been built and land reclaimed. It is calculated that reclamation works in this century have added 2,500 sq. km. (965 sq. miles) to the national area. The canalization of the Lower Rhine, the building of polders in the Zuyder Zee and the construction of dams in the delta of the Scheldt and Meuse (Maas) rivers are the principal water-control schemes that help reduce flooding, aid navigation, and supply water to farms, industry, and domestic users. The area was occupied by Celts and Frisians who came under Roman rule from the 1st c. BC until the 4th c. AD, and was then overrun by German tribes, chief amongst which were the Franks who dominated the region during the 5th–8th c. During the Middle Ages it was divided between numerous principalities. Part of the Habsburg empire in the 16th c., the northern (Dutch) part revolted against Spanish attempts to crush the Protestant faith and won independence in a series of wars lasting into the 17th c., becoming a Protestant republic; meanwhile the southern part passed to the Spanish Habsburgs. Prior to wars with England and France the country enjoyed a great prosperity and became a centre of art and scholarship as well as a leading maritime power. In 1814 north and south were united under a monarchy, but the south revolted in 1830 and became an independent kingdom, Belgium, in 1839; Luxembourg gained its independence in 1867. The Netherlands managed to maintain its neutrality in World War I but was occupied by the Germans in World War II. The post-war period has seen the country turn away from its traditional dependence on agriculture to emerge as an industrial power whose chief exports are food products, chemicals, gas, and textiles. The Netherlands is a constitutional monarchy with a bicameral parliament.
**Netherlander** *n.*
**Netherlandish** *adj.*

The Netherlands is divided into 12 provinces:

| Province | Area (sq. km.) | Pop. (1991) | Capital |
| --- | --- | --- | --- |
| Drenthe | 2,655 | 443,510 | Assen |
| Flevoland | 1,411 | 221,505 | Lelystad |
| Friesland | 3,357 | 600,010 | Leeuwarden |
| Gelderland | 5,015 | 1,816,935 | Arnhem |
| Groningen | 2,347 | 554,600 | Groningen |
| Limburg | 2,169 | 1,109,840 | Maastricht |
| North Brabant | 4,948 | 2,209,050 | 's-Hertogen-bosch |
| North Holland | 2,667 | 2,397,090 | Haarlem |
| Overijssel | 3,340 | 1,036,325 | Zwolle |
| South Holland | 2,871 | 3,245,450 | The Hague |
| Utrecht | 1,359 | 1,026,840 | Utrecht |
| Zeeland | 1,796 | 357,450 | Middelburg |

# Netherlands Antilles
two widely separated groups of Dutch islands in the Caribbean, in the Lesser Antilles. One group comprises the islands of Bonaire and Curaçao which

lie 60 km. (37 miles) north of the Venezuelan coast. The more northerly group, which includes the islands of St. Eustasius, St. Martin, and Saba is situated at the northern end of the Lesser Antilles; area 800 sq. km. (313 sq. miles); pop. (1991) 200,000; capital Willemstad. The islands were originally visited in the 16th c. by the Spanish, who wiped out the native Arawak and Carib Indian population. They were settled by the Dutch between 1634 and 1648 and until 1986 also included Aruba. In 1954 the islands were granted self-government and became an autonomous region. The chief industries are oil refining, tourism, and the production of petroleum products, peanuts, sorghum, and aloes.

**Neubrandenburg** /nɔɪˈbrænd(ə)nbʊə(r)k/ a city in Mecklenburg-West Pomerania, north-east Germany, east of Schwerin; pop. (1991) 87,880.

**Neuchâtel** /ˌnɜːʃæˈtel/, **Lake** the largest lake lying wholly within Switzerland, situated at the foot of the Jura Mountains in western Switzerland; area 218 sq. km. (84 sq. miles).

**Neuchâtel** (German **Neuenburg**) a canton in the Jura Mts. of western Switzerland; area 797 sq. km. (308 sq. miles); pop. (1990) 160,600; capital, Neuchâtel.

**Neumünster** /ˈnɔɪmʊnstə(r)/ an industrial centre in Schleswig-Holstein, north-west Germany, north of Hamburg; pop. (1991) 81,175. Manufactures include machinery and textiles.

**Neuquén** /ˌneɪʊˈkeɪn/ an industrial city and transportation centre in the Andean foothills of western Argentina, capital of Neuquén province; pop. (1991) 183,000. It lies at the centre of an area that produces fruit and oil.

**Neusiedler See** /ˈnɔɪziːdlə(r) ˌzeɪ/ (Hungarian **Fertö Tó** /ˈfɜːtuː təʊ/) a shallow steppe lake straddling the frontier between eastern Austria and north-west Hungary.

**Neuss** /nɔɪs/ an industrial city and canal port in North Rhine-Westphalia, west Germany, on the River Rhine opposite Düsseldorf; pop. (1991) 148,000. Industries include metal goods and machinery.

**Neustadt an der Weinstrasse** /ˈnɔɪstaːt aːn der ˈvaɪnstraːsə/ an industrial city and centre of the wine trade in Rhineland-Palatinate, west Germany, west of the Rhine and south-west of Mannheim; pop. (1991) 52,690.

**Neva** /ˈniːvə/ a river in north-west Russia that links Lake Ladoga with the Gulf of Finland; length 74 km. (46 miles). St. Petersburg stands on the Neva which is connected to the Volga and the White Sea by canals.

**Nevada** /nɪˈvɑːdə/ a state of the western US, between the Rocky Mountains and the Sierra Nevada, much of which comprises dry, sparsely populated sagebrush desert almost totally in the Great Basin area; area 286,352 sq. km. (110,561 sq. miles); pop. (1990) 1,201,830; capital, Carson City. The largest cities are Las Vegas and Reno. Nevada is also known as the Sagebrush, Silver, or Battle-born State. Acquired from Mexico in 1848, it became the 36th state of the US in 1864. Its chief landmarks are the Hoover Dam, Great Basin National Park, Lake Tahoe, and Lake Mead National Recreation Area. In addition to independent Carson City, Nevada is administratively divided into 16 counties:

| County | Area (sq. km.) | Pop. (1990) | County Seat |
|---|---|---|---|
| Churchill | 12,974 | 17,940 | Fallon |
| Clark | 20,491 | 741,460 | Las Vegas |
| Douglas | 1,841 | 27,640 | Minden |
| Elko | 44,551 | 33,530 | Elko |
| Esmeralda | 9,326 | 1,340 | Goldfield |
| Eureka | 10,855 | 1,550 | Eureka |
| Humboldt | 25,215 | 12,840 | Winnemucca |
| Lander | 14,339 | 6,270 | Austin |
| Lincoln | 27,651 | 3,775 | Pioche |
| Lyon | 5,218 | 20,000 | Yerington |
| Mineral | 9,734 | 6,475 | Hawthorne |
| Nye | 47,203 | 17,780 | Tonopah |
| Pershing | 15,694 | 4,340 | Lovelock |
| Storey | 686 | 2,530 | Virginia City |
| Washoe | 16,424 | 254,670 | Reno |
| White Pine | 23,145 | 9,260 | Ely |

**Never-Never Land** /ˌnevəˈnevə(r)/ (or **Country**) a region of Northern Territory, Australia, south-east of Darwin. The chief settlement is Katherine.

**Nevers** /neˈver/ the capital of the department of Nièvre in the Burgundy region of central France, at the junction of the Loire and Nièvre rivers; pop. (1990) 43,890. It was capital of the former province of Nivernais and a noted centre for the manufacture of fine chinaware.

**Nevis** /ˈniːvɪs/ one of the Leeward Islands in the West Indies, forming part of the state of ST. KITTS AND NEVIS; area 93 sq. km. (36 sq. miles); pop. (est. 1989) 9,000; chief settlement, Charlestown; highest peak, Nevis Peak (985 m., 3,232 ft.).

**Nevşehir** /ˈnevʃəhɪə(r)/ **1.** a province of Cappadocia in central Turkey; area 5,540 sq. km. (2,140 sq. miles); pop. (1990) 289,510. **2.** its capital, a market town south-east of Ankara; pop. (1990) 52,720.

**New Amsterdam** the original name given to the capital of the Dutch colony of New Netherland in North America from 1625 to 1664. Situated at the mouth of the Hudson River on Manhattan Island, it was renamed New York by the British.

**Newark** /ˈnjuːək/ a port and industrial city in New Jersey, USA, on the Passaic River; pop. (1990) 275,220. It is the largest city in the state and has an international airport. First settled in 1666, it was the birthplace in 1871 of Stephen Crane, author of *The Red Badge of Courage*. It is a major industrial and commercial centre, and specializes in chemicals, beer, electronic equipment, and paints.

**New Bedford** /ˈbedfə(r)d/ an Atlantic deep-sea fishing port in Massachusetts, USA, at the mouth of the Acushnet River; pop. (1990) 99,920. First settled in 1640, it developed into the world's leading whaling port. The manufacture of cotton textiles was also important until the 1920s.

**New Britain** a mountainous island in the South Pacific, administratively part of Papua New Guinea, lying off the north-east coast of New Guinea; area 37,799 sq. km. (14,600 sq. miles); pop. (1990) 311,955. It is the largest island of the Bismarck archipelago and is divided into the provinces of East and West New Britain whose capitals are Rabaul and Kimbe.

**New Britain** a city in central Connecticut, USA, south-west of Hartford; pop. (1990) 75,490. Its industries manufacture tools, hardware, and machinery.

**New Brunswick** /'brʌnzwɪk/ a maritime province (from 1867) of south-east Canada, joined to Nova Scotia by the narrow Chignecto Isthmus and separated from Prince Edward Island by the Northumberland Strait; area 73,440 sq. km. (28,355 sq. miles); pop. (1991) 723,900; capital, Fredericton. The largest cities are St. John and Moncton. Tourism, fishing, potato farming, dairy farming, forestry, and the mining of potash, zinc, lead, copper, antimony, and bismuth are among its chief industries. Settled by the French and ceded to Britain in 1713, New Brunswick was named by United Empire Loyalists in 1784 after the former German duchy of Brunswick-Lunenburg also ruled by George III.

**Newbury** /'nju:bərɪ/ an industrial town in Berkshire, southern England, on the River Kennet to the west of London; pop. (1981) 31,890. It was one of England's first industrial textile towns and now has a notable racecourse. Paper-making is a local industry.

**New Caledonia**
(French **Nouvelle-Calédonie** /'nuvel ˌkæledəʊ'ni:/) an island in the southwest Pacific Ocean, east of Australia, since 1946 forming, with its dependencies, a French

Overseas Territory; area 18,575 sq. km. (7,172 sq. miles); pop. (1989) 164,170; official language, French; capital, Nouméa. Rising to a height of 1,639 m. (5,377 ft.) at Mt. Paine, the main island is 400 km. (250 miles) long. Also included in the group are the Loyalty Islands, Isles des Pins, Isle Bélep, and the uninhabited Chesterfield and Huon islands. The islands have a mild climate with a wet season from December to March. Coffee, copra, nickel, chrome, and iron ore are the chief exports. It was inhabited for at least 3,000 years before the arrival of Captain James Cook (1774) who named the main island after the Roman name for Scotland. The French annexed the island in 1853, and after the discovery of nickel there (1863) it assumed some economic importance for France. Although there has been a growing separatist movement amongst the minority Kanak people, a referendum in 1987 failed to mobilize enough support for independence from France.

**New Carthage** see CARTAGENA.

**Newcastle** /'nju:kɑ:s(ə)l/ an industrial port on the coast of New South Wales, Australia; pop. (1991) 262,160. Founded as a penal colony, it developed as a port and as a centre for the processing of locally-mined coal, copper, lead, and zinc. It has steel mills, shipyards, and chemical industries. Now the sixth-largest city in Australia, it is known for its fine surfing beaches.

**Newcastle under Lyme** /-laɪm/ an industrial town in Staffordshire, west-central England on the River Lyme; pop. (1991) 117,400. Just to the west of The Potteries, it produces bricks and tiles. The University of Keele was founded in 1962.

**Newcastle upon Tyne** an industrial city on the River Tyne in the county of Tyne and Wear, north-east England; pop. (1991) 263,000. Formerly the county town of Northumberland, it grew up round a strategic site at the east end of Hadrian's Wall and was from Tudor times a major outlet for coal. Once dominated by shipbuilding and heavy engineering, the city is the chief commercial centre of north-east England with large industrial estates. In 1826 George Stephenson opened an ironworks which made the first engine for the Stockton and Darlington Railway. It is the site of the University of Newcastle upon Tyne (1852) and the University of Northumbria (1992).

**New Delhi** see DELHI.

**New England 1.** a district in north-east New South Wales, the largest area of highlands in Australia. Its chief towns are Tamworth, Armidale, Glen Innes, and Inverell and the southern hemisphere's largest granite monolith, Bald Rock, is located near Tenterfield. The district, which has many precious stones, is popular with 'fossickers'. The **New England National Park** preserves one of the largest remaining areas of rainforest in the state. **2.** an area on the north-east coast of the USA, comprising the states of Maine, New Hampshire, Vermont, Massachusetts, Rhode Island, and Connecticut. The name was given to it by the English explorer John Smith in 1614.

**New Forest** an area of heathland with beech and oak woodland in south Hampshire, England, reserved as Crown property since 1079, originally by William I as a royal hunting area. William II was killed by an arrow when hunting there in 1100.

**Newfoundland** /'nju:fənd,lænd, -'faʊndlənd/ **1.** a large island at the mouth of the St. Lawrence River, Canada, visited by Vikings in c. 1000, it was explored in 1497 by John Cabot and named the 'New Isle', 'Terra Nova', or more commonly Newfoundland. A colony (Britain's first) was founded by Sir Humphrey Gilbert and in 1949 it was united with Labrador (as Newfoundland and Labrador) as a province of Canada. **2.** a province of Canada, comprising the island of Newfoundland and the sparsely inhabited coast and interior of Labrador, eastern Canada; area 404,517 sq. km. (156,649 sq. miles); pop. (1991) 586,470; capital, St. John's. South-west Labrador has immense iron deposits and mining and logging are important industries, as are fishing and paper and pulp mills. It gives its name to a large breed of dog with a thick coarse coat.

**Newgate** /'nju:geɪt/ a former London prison, originally the gatehouse of the main west gate to the city, first used as a prison in the early Middle

Ages and rebuilt and enlarged with funds left to the city by Richard Whittington. Its unsanitary conditions became notorious in the 18th c. before the building was burnt down in the anti-Catholic riots of 1780. A new edifice was erected on the same spot soon after but was demolished in 1902 to make way for the Central Criminal Court.

**New Granada** the name of a former Spanish viceroyalty in north-west South America that comprised present-day Colombia, Ecuador, Panama, and Venezuela.

**New Guinea** (Indonesian **Irian** /ˌɪri:ˈɑ:n/) an island of the east Malay archipelago, to the north of Australia, divided between the independent state of Papua New Guinea in the east and the Indonesian province of West Irian in the west. With an area of 789,950 sq. km. (305,000 sq. miles), it is the world's second-largest island.

**Newham** /ˈnju:əm/ an inner borough of Greater London, England, on the River Thames; pop. (1991) 200,200. It was created in 1965 from the former boroughs of East Ham and West Ham and parts of north Woolwich and Barking and is both residential and industrial.

**New Hampshire** a state in the north-eastern US, bordering on the Atlantic; area 24,032 sq. km. (9,279 sq. miles); pop. (1990) 1,109,250; capital, Concord. Its largest cities are Manchester and Nashua. New Hampshire is also known as the Granite State. It was settled from England in the 17th c. and was the first independent colony (1776) before becoming one of the original 13 states of the US in 1788. The chief industries are tourism, the mining of granite, mica, and feldspar, the production of dairy products, garden crops, fruit, and maple syrup, and the manufacture of footwear, plastics, machinery, electrical goods, and electronic products. Landmarks include the White Mountains, Lake Winnipesaukee, and the Saint-Gaudens National Historic Site. New Hampshire is divided into 10 counties:

| County | Area (sq. km.) | Pop. (1990) | County Seat |
| --- | --- | --- | --- |
| Belknap | 1,050 | 49,220 | Laconia |
| Carroll | 2,426 | 35,410 | Ossipee |
| Cheshire | 1,849 | 70,120 | Keene |
| Coos | 4,690 | 34,830 | Lancaster |
| Grafton | 4,469 | 74,930 | Woodsville |
| Hillsborough | 2,278 | 336,070 | Nashua |
| Merrimack | 2,434 | 120,005 | Concord |
| Rockingham | 1,817 | 245,845 | Exeter |
| Strafford | 962 | 104,230 | Dover |
| Sullivan | 1,404 | 38,590 | Newport |

**Newhaven** /ˈnju:heɪv(ə)n/ a port on Long Island Sound, southern Connecticut, USA; pop. (1990) 130,470. It is the home of Yale University which was founded in 1701 and named after Elihu Yale an early patron. Newhaven is associated with the inventor Eli Whitney (1765–1825) and the lexicographer Noah Webster (1758–1843) who compiled his *American Dictionary of the English Language* here in 1828. It was one of the first planned communities in the USA, and later specialized in manufactures such as firearms, coaches, and carriages.

**New Hebrides** the former name (until 1980) of VANUATU.

**New Ireland** an island of Papua New Guinea, lying to the north of New Britain in the Bismarck archipelago; area 9,600 sq. km. (3,708 sq. miles); pop. (1990) 87,190; capital, Kavieng; highest peak, Mt. Gilaut (2,399 m., 7,871 ft.). Copra and tuna fish are the chief products of the island.

**New Jersey** a state in the north-eastern USA, bordering on the Atlantic; area 20,169 sq. km. (7,787 sq. miles); pop. (1990) 7,730,190; capital, Trenton. It has the highest population density of all the United States with more than 95 per cent of its population living in urban areas. The largest cities are Newark, Jersey City, Paterson, and Elizabeth. New Jersey is also known as the Garden State. Colonized by Dutch settlers and ceded to Britain in 1664, it became one of the original 13 states of the US. Among its chief industries are tourism, the production of garden vegetables, and the manufacture of chemicals, pharmaceuticals, clothing, and electrical goods. Its principal landmarks are the Delaware Water Gap, Edison National Historic Site, Morristown National Historic Park, and Pinelands National Reserve. The state is divided into 21 counties:

| County | Area (sq. km.) | Pop. (1990) | County Seat |
| --- | --- | --- | --- |
| Atlantic | 1,477 | 224,330 | Mays Landing |
| Bergen | 616 | 825,380 | Hackensack |
| Burlington | 2,093 | 395,070 | Mount Holly |
| Camden | 580 | 502,820 | Camden |
| Cape May | 684 | 95,090 | Cape May Court House |
| Cumberland | 1,295 | 138,050 | Bridgeton |
| Essex | 330 | 778,210 | Newark |
| Gloucester | 850 | 230,080 | Woodbury |
| Hudson | 120 | 553,100 | Jersey City |
| Hunterdon | 1,108 | 107,780 | Flemington |
| Mercer | 590 | 325,820 | Trenton |
| Middlesex | 822 | 671,780 | New Brunswick |
| Monmouth | 1,227 | 553,120 | Freehold |
| Morris | 1,222 | 420,350 | Morristown |
| Ocean | 1,667 | 433,200 | Toms River |
| Passaic | 486 | 453,060 | Paterson |
| Salem | 879 | 65,290 | Salem |
| Somerset | 793 | 240,280 | Somerville |
| Sussex | 1,368 | 130,940 | Newton |
| Union | 268 | 493,820 | Elizabeth |
| Warren | 933 | 91,610 | Belvidere |

**Newmarket** /ˈnju:mɑ:kɪt/ a town in Suffolk, south-east England, between Cambridge and Bury St. Edmunds; pop. (1981) 16,130. It is a noted horse-racing centre and headquarters of the Jockey Club.

**New Mexico** a state in the south-western USA, to the south of Colorado and bordering on Mexico west of the Rio Grande; area 314,925 sq. km. (121,593 sq. miles); pop. (1990) 1,515,070; capital, Santa Fe. The largest city is Albuquerque. New Mexico is also known as the Sunshine State. It was obtained from Mexico in 1848 and 1853 and became the 47th state of the US in 1912. A major centre of energy research, New Mexico is rich in natural resources which include oil, gas, uranium, potassium salts, copper, zinc, lead, molybdenum, gold, and silver. Its chief landmarks are the Carlsbad Caverns National Park, the Chaco Culture National Historic Park, and El Morro, Bandelier, Picos, Salinas, White Sands, and Gila Cliff Dwellings National Monuments. The state is divided into 32 counties:

| County | Area (sq. km.) | Pop. (1990) | County Seat |
|---|---|---|---|
| Bernalillo | 3,039 | 480,580 | Albuquerque |
| Catron | 18,015 | 2,560 | Reserve |
| Chaves | 15,772 | 57,850 | Roswell |
| Cibola | 11,779 | 23,790 | Grants |
| Colfax | 9,781 | 12,295 | Raton |
| Curry | 3,661 | 42,210 | Clovis |
| De Baca | 6,040 | 2,250 | Fort Sumner |
| Dona Ana | 9,929 | 135,510 | Las Cruces |
| Eddy | 10,878 | 48,605 | Carlsbad |
| Grant | 10,319 | 27,680 | Silver City |
| Guadalupe | 7,883 | 4,160 | Santa Rosa |
| Harding | 5,517 | 990 | Mosquero |
| Hidalgo | 8,957 | 5,960 | Lordsburg |
| Lea | 11,411 | 55,765 | Lovington |
| Lincoln | 12,563 | 12,220 | Carrizozo |
| Los Alamos | 283 | 18,115 | Los Alamos |
| Luna | 7,709 | 18,110 | Deming |
| McKinley | 14,149 | 60,690 | Gallup |
| Mora | 5,018 | 4,260 | Mora |
| Otero | 17,228 | 51,930 | Alamogordo |
| Quay | 7,452 | 10,820 | Tucumcari |
| Rio Arriba | 15,226 | 34,365 | Tierra Amarilla |
| Roosevelt | 6,378 | 16,700 | Portales |
| San Juan | 14,355 | 91,605 | Bernalillo |
| San Miguel | 12,243 | 25,740 | Aztec |
| Sandoval | 9,638 | 63,320 | Las Vegas |
| Santa Fe | 4,953 | 98,930 | Santa Fe |
| Sierra | 10,863 | 9,910 | Truth or Consequences |
| Socorro | 17,225 | 14,760 | Socorro |
| Taos | 5,730 | 23,120 | Taos |
| Torrance | 8,671 | 10,285 | Estancia |
| Union | 9,958 | 4,120 | Clayton |
| Valencia | 14,602 | 45,235 | Los Lunas |

**New Orleans** /ɔːˈlɪənz/ a city and river port in south-east Louisiana, USA, on the Gulf of Mexico and the Mississippi River; pop. (1990) 496,940. Named in honour of the Duc d'Orléans, Regent of France, it was founded by Jean Baptiste Le Moyne in 1718. Steamboats first sailed up river to Natchez in 1812 and the St. Louis Cathedral is the oldest cathedral in the US. The city is noted for its annual Mardi Gras celebrations and for its association with the origins of Jazz. It was the birthplace of the jazz trumpet player and singer Louis Armstrong (1900–71). It has shipbuilding and chemical industries. Tourism is also very important.

**New Plymouth** a town at the western extremity of North Island, New Zealand, a port and commercial centre for offshore oil and gas exploration that also serves an agricultural and pastoral hinterland on the Taranaki plain; pop. (1991) 48,520. Settled by whalers in 1828, a town was laid out in 1841 for the Plymouth Company, a subsidiary of the New Zealand Company, and many of its settlers came from Devon and Cornwall in England.

**Newport** /ˈnjuːpɔːt/ **1.** an industrial town in Gwent, south-east Wales, on the River Usk; pop. (1991) 129,900. The poet W. H. Davies was born here in 1871. **2.** the chief town of the Isle of Wight, off the south coast of England; pop. (1981) 20,320. Parkhurst Prison is situated nearby.

**Newport Beach** a city on the coast of southern California, USA, to the south of Los Angeles; pop. (1990) 66,640. It is a popular resort and yachting centre.

**Newport News** /njuːz/ a city in south-east Virginia, USA, at the mouth of the James River on the Hampton Roads estuary; pop. (1990) 170,045. It is one of the three cities (with Norfolk and Portsmouth) that make up the Port of Hampton Roads and a major shipbuilding centre. Its name is said to be derived from the good 'news' of the arrival of Captain Christopher Newport, who brought additional supplies and settlers to nearby Jamestown.

**New Providence** /ˈprɒvɪdəns/ the principal island of the Bahamas in the West Indies; area 207 sq. km. (80 sq. miles); pop. (1990) 171,540. Its chief settlement is the port of Nassau, capital of the Bahamas.

**Newquay** /ˈnjuːkiː/ a resort town on the north coast of Cornwall, south-west England, to the north of the Gannel estuary; pop. (1981) 15,200.

**New River** a river of the USA that rises in the Blue Ridge Mts. of North Carolina and flows 515 km. (320 miles) through West Virginia before joining the Gauley River to form the Kanawha River.

**New Rochelle** /rɒˈʃel/ a city on Long Island in the US state of New York; pop. (1990) 67,265. Founded by Huguenots in 1688, it initially developed as a boat-building centre. The English radical Thomas Paine (1737–1809) lived here from 1802 until his death.

**Newry** /ˈnjuːrɪ/ an industrial port in County Down, at the head of the Newry River estuary in the south-east of Northern Ireland; pop. (1981) 19,400. From ancient times it occupied a strategic position on the main hill crossing into Ulster from Dublin and the south. The town is intersected by canals built in the 18th c. and St. Patrick's Church (1578) is said to be the oldest Protestant church in Ireland.

**New Siberian Islands** (Russian **Novo-sibirskiye Ostrovo**) a group of uninhabited snow-covered islands in the Arctic Ocean between the Laptev and East Siberian seas; area c. 28,230 sq. km. (10,900 sq. miles). Discovered by Ivan Lyakhov in 1773, they are part of the Yakut (Sakha) region of east Siberia. The northern New Siberian or Anjou islands are separated from the Lyakhov Islands in the south by the Sannikov Strait.

**New South Wales** a state of south-east Australia, first colonized from Britain in 1788 and federated with the other states of Australia in 1901; area 810,428 sq. km. (309,433 sq. miles); pop. (1991) 5,940,800; capital, Sydney. Australia's most populous state, it was originally the name of the entire colony. The plains of the west are semiarid grazing land, but there is richer wheat and grazing country in the central and coastal areas. The main agricultural products are meat, cereals, fruit, wine, dairy products, and wool. There are extensive coal deposits near Newcastle and Wollongong, and silver, lead, and zinc at Broken Hill.

**Newstead** /'nju:sted/ an abbey in Nottingham-shire, central England, founded in the 12th c. and converted to a residence that was the ancestral home of Lord Byron.

**New Territories** that part of the territory of Hong Kong lying to the north of the Kowloon peninsula and including the islands of Lantau, Tsing Yi, and Lamma; area 950 sq. km. (367 sq. miles). Under the 1898 Convention of Peking the New Territories (comprising 92 per cent of the land area of Hong Kong) were leased to Britain by China for a period of 99 years.

**Newton** /'nju:tən/ a city in east Massachusetts, USA, comprising 13 suburban neighbourhoods to the west of Boston; pop. (1990) 82,585.

**Newton Abbot** /'æbət/ a market town in Devon, south-west England, on the River Teign estuary; pop. (1981) 20,740.

**Newton Aycliffe** /-'eɪklɪf/ a town in Durham, north-east England, north of Darlington; pop. (1981) 24,485. It was designated a New Town in 1947.

**Newton St. Boswells** /'bɒzwɪlz/ a town in the Borders Region of Scotland, the administrative centre of Ettrick and Lauderdale district from 1975 to 1996; pop. (1981) 1,095.

**Newtown** /'nju:taʊn/ (Welsh **Drenewydd Y**) a town in Powys, Wales, on the River Severn, 20 km. (12 miles) south-west of Welshpool. It was designated a New Town in 1967.

**Newtownabbey** /ˌnju:tən'æbɪ/ a town in County Antrim, Northern Ireland, situated on the western shore of Belfast Lough and comprising the north Belfast suburbs of Glengormley, Whitewell, Whiteabbey, Jordanstown, Cavehill, Carnmoney, and Whitehouse; pop. (1981) 56,150.

**New York** a state of the USA, bordering on the Atlantic, the second most populous state in the US; area 127,189 sq. km. (49,108 sq. miles); pop. (1990) 17,990,455; capital, Albany. The largest cities are New York, Buffalo, Rochester, Yonkers, Syracuse, and Albany. New York is also known as the Empire State. Settled by the Dutch, it was surrendered to the British in 1664 and in 1788 became one of the original 13 states of the US. Its principal landmarks include the Statue of Liberty, Manhattan Island, the Finger Lakes, the Hudson River, and the Adirondack Forest. New York State is divided into 62 counties:

| County | Area (sq. km.) | Pop. (1990) | County Seat |
|---|---|---|---|
| Albany | 1,362 | 292,590 | Albany |
| Allegany | 2,683 | 50,470 | Belmont |
| Bronx | 109 | 1,203,790 | Bronx |
| Broome | 1,851 | 212,160 | Binghamton |
| Cattaraugus | 3,396 | 84,230 | Little Valley |
| Cayuga | 1,807 | 82,310 | Auburn |
| Chautauqua | 2,766 | 141,895 | Mayville |
| Chemung | 1,069 | 95,195 | Elmira |
| Chenango | 2,332 | 51,770 | Norwich |
| Clinton | 2,712 | 85,970 | Plattsburgh |
| Columbia | 1,659 | 62,980 | Hudson |
| Cortland | 1,300 | 48,960 | Cortland |
| Delaware | 3,744 | 47,225 | Delhi |
| Dutchess | 2,090 | 259,460 | Poughkeepsie |
| Erie | 2,720 | 968,530 | Buffalo |
| Essex | 4,696 | 37,150 | Elizabethtown |
| Franklin | 4,269 | 46,540 | Malone |
| Fulton | 1,292 | 54,190 | Johnstown |
| Genesee | 1,287 | 69,060 | Batavia |
| Greene | 1,685 | 44,740 | Catskill |
| Hamilton | 4,475 | 5,280 | Lake Pleasant |
| Herkimer | 3,682 | 65,800 | Herkimer |
| Jefferson | 3,310 | 110,940 | Watertown |
| Kings | 182 | 2,300,660 | Brooklyn |
| Lewis | 3,336 | 26,800 | Lowville |
| Livingston | 1,646 | 62,370 | Geneseo |
| Madison | 1,706 | 69,120 | Wampsville |
| Monroe | 1,724 | 713,970 | Rochester |
| Montgomery | 1,050 | 51,980 | Fonda |
| Nassau | 746 | 1,287,350 | Mineola |
| New York | 57 | 1,487,540 | New York |
| Niagara | 1,368 | 220,760 | Lockport |
| Oneida | 3,169 | 250,840 | Utica |
| Onondaga | 2,038 | 468,970 | Syracuse |
| Ontario | 1,674 | 95,100 | Canandaigua |
| Orange | 2,148 | 307,650 | Goshen |
| Orleans | 1,017 | 41,850 | Albion |
| Oswego | 2,480 | 121,770 | Oswego |
| Otsego | 2,610 | 60,520 | Cooperstown |
| Putnam | 601 | 83,940 | Carmel |
| Queens | 283 | 1,951,600 | Jamaica |
| Rensselaer | 1,703 | 154,430 | Troy |
| Richmond | 153 | 378,980 | Saint George |
| Rockland | 455 | 265,475 | New City |
| St. Lawrence | 7,093 | 111,970 | Canton |
| Saratoga | 2,106 | 181,280 | Baliston Spa |
| Schenectady | 536 | 149,285 | Schenectady |
| Schoharie | 1,622 | 31,860 | Schoharie |

(cont.)

| | | | |
|---|---|---|---|
| Schuyler | 855 | 18,660 | Watkins Glen |
| Seneca | 850 | 33,680 | Ovid and Waterloo |
| Steuben | 3,630 | 99,090 | Bath |
| Suffolk | 2,369 | 1,321,860 | Riverhead |
| Sullivan | 2,538 | 69,280 | Monticello |
| Tioga | 1,349 | 52,340 | Owego |
| Tompkins | 1,240 | 94,100 | Ithaca |
| Ulster | 2,941 | 165,300 | Kingston |
| Warren | 2,293 | 59,210 | Lake George |
| Washington | 2,174 | 59,330 | Hudson Falls |
| Wayne | 1,573 | 89,120 | Lyons |
| Westchester | 1,139 | 874,870 | White Plains |
| Wyoming | 1,547 | 42,510 | Warsaw |
| Yates | 881 | 22,810 | Penn Yan |

**New York** a city and port in the US state of New York, on the Atlantic Ocean at the mouth of the Hudson River; pop. (1990) 7,322,560. It is the richest and most populous city of the USA, containing the financial centre Wall Street, industries of every kind, several universities, and an opera house, art galleries and museums that are world famous, and the headquarters of the United Nations. Its many famous skyscrapers include the Empire State Building (381 m., 1,250 ft. high) and the twin towers of the World Trade Center (411 m., 1,350 ft. high). The Hudson River and Manhattan Island were discovered in 1609, and in 1626 Dutch colonists purchased Manhattan from the Indians for 24 dollars' worth of trinkets, establishing a settlement there which they called New Amsterdam. In 1664 the English naval officer who received the Dutch surrender renamed it in honour of the Duke of York (later James II), who was at that time Lord High Admiral of England. In 1789 George Washington took his oath as first President of the USA in New York. The city has two international airports (La Guardia and J. F. Kennedy) and is divided into five boroughs (Bronx, Brooklyn, Manhattan, Queens, and Staten Island).

**New Zealand**
/'zi:lənd/ (Maori
**Aotearoa**) an island
country in the South
Pacific, about 1,900
km. (1,200 miles)
east of Australia,
consisting of two
major islands (North
and South Islands)

separated by Cook Strait, and several smaller islands; area 267,844 sq. km. (103,455 sq. miles); pop.(1991) 3,434,950; official language, English; capital, Wellington. The largest cities are Auckland, Wellington, and Christchurch. Active volcanism occurs in the central region of the North Island, with many hot springs and geysers, while South Island is dominated by the Southern Alps which stretch along its western coast and rise to 3,764 m. (12,349 ft.) at Mt. Cook, New Zealand's highest peak. The discoverers and first colonists were Polynesians (see MAORI). It was sighted by the Dutch navigator Tasman in 1642, and named after the Netherlands province of Zeeland. The islands were circumnavigated by Capt. James Cook in 1769–70, and came under reluctant British sovereignty in 1840, having been until then a 'no-man's land' for whalers, escaped convicts, and deserters; colonization led to a series of wars with the Maoris in the 1860s and 1870s. During the late 19th c. New Zealand pioneered social-security systems and universal suffrage. Full dominion status was granted in 1907, and independence in 1931. The economy is heavily agricultural, with meat, wool, and dairy products forming the principal exports. The country has reserves of coal and iron ore, and natural gas is also found. New Zealand is governed by a unicameral parliament.
**New Zealander** n.
New Zealand is divided into 14 local government regions:

| Region | Pop. (1991) |
|---|---|
| North Island | |
| Northland | 131,620 |
| Auckland | 953,980 |
| Waikato | 338,960 |
| Bay of Plenty | 208,160 |
| Gisborne | 44,390 |
| Hawkes Bay | 139,480 |
| Taranaki | 107,220 |
| Manawatu-Wanganui | 226,620 |
| Wellington | 402,890 |
| South Island | |
| Nelson-Marlborough | 113,490 |
| West Coast | 35,380 |
| Canterbury | 442,390 |
| Otago | 186,070 |
| Southland | 103,440 |

**Neyagawa** /ˌneɪjɑ:'gɑ:wə/ a suburb of Osaka, Honshu Island, Japan, on the Shinyodo River; pop. (1990) 256,520.

**Neyshabur** a market town in the province of Khorasan, north-eastern Iran; pop. (1983) 94,670. An important cultural centre under the Seljuk Turks in the 11th–12th c., it was the birthplace of the poet and mathematician Omar Khayyam.

**Nez Percé** /ˌnez pɜ:'seɪ/ (also **Sahaptini**) a North American Indian tribe originally occupying land in Washington, Idaho, and Oregon, but now to be found in the Nez Percé reservation in Idaho. They were named by the French who first encountered members of the tribe wearing pendants attached to their pierced noses.

**Ngamiland** /əŋ'gɑ:mɪˌlænd/ a region in northwest Botswana, north of the Kalahari Desert. It includes the Okavango marshes and Lake Ngami.

**Ngaoundéré** /əŋˌgaʊndeɪ'reɪ/ a town and Islamic centre in north-central Cameroun, capital of the Adamawa region; pop. (1981) 47,500.

Situated at the the northern terminus of Cameroon's main railway line, its chief landmark is Lamidal or chief's house.

**Ngorongoro Crater** /əŋˌgəʊrəŋˈgəʊrəʊ/ a huge extinct volcanic crater in the Great Rift Valley, north-east Tanzania, 326 sq. km. (126 sq. miles) in area. It is the centre of a wildlife conservation area, established in 1959, which includes the Olduvai Gorge.

**NH** *abbr* US New Hampshire (also in official postal use).

**Nhulunbuy** /ˌnjuːlənˈbaɪ/ a bauxite-mining centre in Aboriginal territory on the Gove Peninsula of Arnhem Land, Northern Territory, Australia; pop. (1986) 3,800.

**Niagara** /naɪˈægərə/ a river in North America, which flows northwards for 56 km. (36 miles), joining Lake Erie to Lake Ontario and forming part of the border between Canada and the USA. Niagara Falls is situated halfway along. With a total drop of 99 m. (326 ft.) between lakes, it is a major source of hydroelectric power.

**Niagara Falls 1.** the waterfalls on the Niagara River, one of the most famous spectacles in North America, consisting of two principal parts separated by Goat Island: the Horseshoe Falls adjoining the west (Canadian) bank, which fall 54 m. (176 ft.), and the American Falls adjoining the east (US) bank, which fall 55 m. (182 ft.). The escarpment is being steadily eroded back towards Lake Erie, creating the Niagara Gorge. They are a popular tourist venue and an attraction for various stunts. In 1859 Jean François Gravelet (Blondin) was the first person to cross the falls on a tight-rope and in 1901 Annie Edson Taylor was the first person to go over the falls in a barrel. **2.** a city in southern Ontario, Canada, on the left bank of the Niagara River beside the Falls; pop. (1991) 75,400; (364,550 with St. Catherines). The Seagram Tower, Oneida Tower, and Skylon Observatory overlook the river. **3.** a city in the US state of New York, on the right bank of the Niagara River beside the Falls, opposite Niagara Falls, Canada, to which it is linked by the Rainbow Bridge (1941); pop. (1990) 61,840. One of the world's first hydroelectric power plants was built here by Westinghouse in 1893.

**Niamey** /ˈnjɑːmeɪ/ the capital of the state of Niger in West Africa, on the River Niger; pop. (1988) 398,265. It is a river port and trade centre at an important road junction and was developed by the French who made it capital of the colony of Niger in French West Africa in 1926.

**Nicaea** /naɪˈsiːə/ an ancient city in Asia Minor, on the site of modern Iznik, important in Roman and Byzantine times. It was the site of two ecumenical councils of the Church. The first, the Council of Nicaea in 325, condemned Arianism and produced the Nicene Creed. The second, in 787, condemned the iconoclasts.

**Nicaragua** /ˌnɪkəˈrɑːgjʊə/ official name **The Republic of Nicaragua** the largest country in Central America, with a coastline on both the Atlantic and the Pacific Ocean;

area 120,254 sq. km. (46,448 sq. miles); pop. (est. 1991) 3,975,000; official language, Spanish; capital, Managua. A narrow coastal plain in the west is separated from low rolling uplands and extensive flat plains in the east by a mountain range rising to heights in excess of 2,000 m. (6,500 ft.). The climate is tropical with a wet season from May to November. Nicaragua's chief exports are coffee, cotton, bananas, sugar, and meat. Columbus sighted the eastern coast in 1502, and the country was colonized by the Spaniards in the early 16th c. It broke away in 1821, and after brief membership of the Central American Federation became an independent republic in 1838. Since then its history has been scarred by border disputes, internal disturbances, and resistance to US political and economic domination, as in 1926–33 when Augustino Sandino led a popular revolt. The last major internal conflict witnessed the successful overthrow of the dictator Anastasio Somoza in 1979, an event that was followed by a protracted counter-revolutionary campaign against the new left-wing Sandinista regime. In the 1990 election the Sandanistas were defeated, and Nicaragua had a democratically elected government. Executive power is vested in a President and Cabinet and legislative power is exercised by a unicameral National Assembly.
**Nicaraguan** *adj. & n.*
Nicaragua is divided into 16 administrative departments grouped into three zones:

| Department | Area (sq. km.) | Pop. (1990) | Capital |
| --- | --- | --- | --- |
| **Pacific Zone** | | | |
| Chinandega | 4,789 | 330,500 | Chinandega |
| León | 5,243 | 344,500 | León |
| Managua | 3,368 | 1,026,100 | Managua |
| Masaya | 690 | 230,800 | Masaya |
| Granada | 992 | 162,600 | Granada |
| Carazo | 1,097 | 150,000 | Jinotepe |
| Rivas | 2,190 | 149,800 | Rivas |
| **Central-North Zone** | | | |
| Chontales | 6,324 | 129,600 | Juigalpa |
| Boaco | 4,271 | 117,900 | Boaco |
| Matagalpa | 6,929 | 322,300 | Matagalpa |
| Jinotega | 9,640 | 175,600 | Jinotega |
| Estelí | 2,173 | 169,100 | Estelí |
| Madriz | 1,612 | 88,700 | Somoto |
| Nueva Segovia | 3,594 | 122,100 | Ocotal |
| **Atlantic Zone** | | | |
| Río San Juan | 7,402 | 52,200 | San Carlos |
| Zelaya | 60,035 | 298,900 | Bluefields |

**Nicaragua, Lake** a lake near the west coast of Nicaragua. With an area of 8,029 sq. km. (3,100 sq. miles) it is the largest lake in Central America. The city of Granada lies on its north-western shore.

**Nice** /niːs/ a resort city on the French Riviera, capital of the department of Alpes-Maritimes in the Provence-Alpes-Côte d'Azur region of south-eastern France; pop. (1990) 345,670. Situated on the Baie des Anges, an inlet of the Mediterranean, Nice is the fifth-largest city in France. It was annexed from the kingdom of Sardinia in 1860. Garibaldi (1807–82) was born in Nice.

**Nickerie** /'nɪkəriː/ a river in north-west Surinam, South America, that flows c. 320 km. (200 miles) northwards from the Guiana Highlands to meet the Atlantic near the town of Nieuw Nickerie.

**Nicobar Islands** see ANDAMAN AND NICOBAR ISLANDS.

**Nicomedia** /ˌnɪkə'miːdɪə/ an ancient city of Asia Minor on the site of present-day Izmit in north-west Turkey. Nicomedes I of Bithynia rebuilt the city in 264 BC, replacing Astacus as his capital. It was later chosen by Diocletian as the capital of the Eastern Empire, but was superseded by Byzantium.

**Nicopolis** /nɪ'kɒpəlɪs/ a city of ancient Epirus in north-west Greece, whose ruins stand on a peninsula to the north of Preveza. It was founded by Octavian to celebrate his victory at Actium and became capital of Epirus and Acarnania.

**Nicosia** /ˌnɪkə'siːə/ (Greek **Lefkosia**) the capital of Cyprus, divided since 1974 into Greek and Turkish sectors; pop. (est. 1990) 171,000. Situated on the Pedias River in the centre of the island, Nicosia was known as Ledra in ancient times. Its old walled town centre includes St. Sophia Cathedral, now a mosque. Nicosia has many light industries such as textiles, cigarettes, and footwear.

**Niederösterreich** the German name for LOWER AUSTRIA.

**Niedersachsen** the German name for LOWER SAXONY.

**Nieuwegein** /'njuːwəɡeɪn/ an industrial city in the Randstad conurbation of the Netherlands, south of Utrecht; pop. (1991) 58,910.

**Nièvre** /'njɛvrə/ a department in the Burgundy region of central France; area 6,817 sq. km. (2,633 sq. miles); pop. (1990) 233,280; capital, Nevers.

**Niğde** /'niːdə/ **1.** a mountainous province of south-central Turkey; area 7,831 sq. km. (3,025 sq. miles); pop. (1990) 305,860. **2.** its capital to the north-west of Adana, in the northern foothills of the Taurus Mts.; pop. (1990) 55,035.

**Niger** /'naɪdʒə(r)/ a river in north-west Africa, which rises on the north-east border of Sierra Leone and flows in a great arc for 4,100 km. (2,550 miles) north-east to Mali, then south-east through western Niger and Nigeria, before turning southwards to empty through a great delta into the Gulf of Guinea. It was first explored by Mungo Park in the 1790s and early 1800s. The cities of Bamako and Mopti in Mali lie on the Niger.

**Niger** /'naɪdʒə(r), niː'ʒeə(r)/ official name **The Republic of Niger** a landlocked country of West Africa, lying mainly in the Sahara, taking its name from the river that flows through the south-west part of its territory, and bounded by Mali, Algeria, and Libya on its west and north, by Burkina, Nigeria, and Chad on its south and east; area 1,267,000 sq. km. (489,378 sq. miles); pop. (est. 1991) 7,909,000; languages, French (official), Hausa and other west African languages; capital, Niamey. Occupying a plateau on the southern edge of the Sahara, Niger is arid in the north but has a wet season in the south from June to October. Over 90 per cent of the population are pastoralists or farmers producing cotton, cowpeas, and livestock, and the chief mineral resources of the country are tin ore, iron ore, uranium, and coal. The region was not explored by Europeans until the 18th and 19th centuries. A French colony (part of French West Africa) from 1922, it became an autonomous republic within the French Community in 1958 and fully independent in 1960. Under military rule from 1974, Niger adopted a multiparty constitution in 1992. The country is divided into seven administrative departments:

| Department | Area (sq. km.) | Pop. (1988) | Capital |
|---|---|---|---|
| Agadez | 634,209 | 203,960 | Agadez |
| Diffa | 140,216 | 189,320 | Diffa |
| Dosso | 31,002 | 1,020,000 | Dosso |
| Maradi | 38,581 | 1,389,000 | Maradi |
| Niamey | 670 | 398,265 | Niamey |
| Tahoua | 106,677 | 1,306,650 | Tahoua |
| Tillabéry | 89,623 | 1,332,400 | Tillabéry |
| Zinder | 145,430 | 1,410,800 | Zinder |

**Niger-Congo** a group of languages, the largest in Africa, named after the rivers Niger and Congo. It includes the languages spoken by most of the indigenous peoples of western, central, and southern Africa; the important Bantu group, the Mwande group (West Africa), the Voltaic group (Burkina), and the Kwa group (Nigeria) which includes Yoruba and Ibo.

**Nigeria** /naɪ'dʒɪərɪə/ official name **The Federal Republic of Nigeria** a Commonwealth country on the coast of West Africa, bordered by the River Niger to the north; area 923,768 sq. km. (356,805 sq. miles); pop. (1991) 88,514,500; languages, English (official), Hausa, Ibo, Yoruba, and others; capital, Abuja. The largest cities are Lagos and

Ibadan. North of a narrow coastal plain tropical forest stretches northwards towards a central plateau of open woodland and savanna which lies at the southern edge of the Sahara Desert.

The country was the site of highly developed kingdoms in the Middle Ages, and the coast was explored by the Portuguese during the 15th c. The area of the Niger delta came gradually under British influence in the 18th and 19th c., particularly during the period between the annexation of Lagos in 1861 and the unification of the protectorates of Southern and Northern Nigeria into a single colony in 1914. Independence came in 1960 and the state became a republic in 1963, but since that time it has been troubled by political instability, particularly a civil war with the breakaway eastern area of Biafra (1967–70). The discovery of oil in the 1960s and 1970s resulted in a dramatic expansion of the economy and a shift away from the traditional industries of farming, fishing, and forestry. The most populous country in Africa, Nigeria emerged in the 1970s and 1980s as one of the world's major exporters of oil. However, this linking of the country's economy to the fluctuations of the world oil market has led to the severe recessions of 1981 and 1986. Nigeria is governed by a President and National Council of Ministers and a bicameral National Assembly.

**Nigerian** *adj. & n.*

Nigeria is divided into a Federal Capital Territory and 30 states:

| State | Pop. (1991) | Capital |
|---|---|---|
| Abia | 2,297,980 | Umuahia |
| Adamawa | 2,124,050 | Yola |
| Akwa Ibom | 2,359,740 | Uyo |
| Anabra | 2,767,900 | Awka |
| Bauchi | 4,294,410 | Bauchi |
| Benue | 2,780,400 | Makurdi |
| Borno | 2,596,590 | Maiduguri |
| Cross Rivers | 1,865,600 | Calabar |
| Delta | 2,570,180 | Asaba |
| Edo | 2,159,850 | Benin City |
| Enugu | 3,161,295 | Enugu |
| Imo | 2,485,500 | Owerri |
| Jigawa | 2,829,930 | Dutse |
| Kaduna | 3,969,250 | Kaduna |
| Kano | 5,632,040 | Kano |
| Katsina | 3,878,340 | Katsina |
| Kebbi | 2,062,230 | Birnin Kebbi |
| Kogi | 2,099,050 | Lokoja |
| Kwara | 1,566,470 | Ilorin |
| Lagos | 5,685,780 | Ikeja |
| Niger | 2,482,370 | Minna |
| Ogun | 2,338,570 | Abeokuta |
| Ondo | 3,884,485 | Akure |
| Osun | 2,203,020 | Oshogbo |

| | | |
|---|---|---|
| Oyo | 3,488,790 | Ibadan |
| Plateau | 3,283,700 | Jos |
| Rivers | 3,983,860 | Port Harcourt |
| Sokoto | 4,392,390 | Sokoto |
| Taraba | 1,480,590 | Jalingo |
| Yobe | 1,411,480 | Damaturu |
| Federal Capital Territory | 378,670 | Abuja |

**Niigata** /niːˈɡɑːtə/ an industrial port in the Chubu region of north Honshu Island, central Japan, capital of the prefecture of Niigata; pop. (1990) 486,090. Industries include oil refining and the manufacture of chemicals, textiles, and machinery.

**Niihama** /niːˈhɑːmə/ a fishing port and former mining centre in Ehime prefecture, northern Shikoku, Japan; pop. (1990) 129,150.

**Niiza** /ˈniːzə/ a suburb of Tokyo on the Yonase River, in Saitama prefecture, Honshu Island, central Japan; pop. (1990) 138,920.

**Nijmegen** /ˈnaɪmeɪɡən/ an industrial town in south Gelderland province, the Netherlands, on the River Waal, 20 km. (12 miles) south of Arnhem; pop. (1991) 145,780. Metal products, paper, clothing, and soap are manufactured. Landmarks include the site of Charlemagne's 8th-c. Valkhof Palace.

**Nikko** /ˈniːkəʊ/ a national park in the western Kanto region of Honshu Island, Japan, protecting scenic mountains, forests, and hot springs. Designated in 1934, it extends over 1,407 sq. km. (543 sq. miles).

**Nikolayev** /njɪkəˈleɪef/ see MYKOLAYIV.

**Nikopol** /nɪˈkɒpəl/ an industrial city in the southern Ukraine, on the River Dnieper; pop. (1990) 158,000. Built on the site of a Cossack settlement at a strategic river crossing, Nikopol developed into an industrial city at the centre of a rich manganese-mining region.

**Nile** /naɪl/ a river in eastern Africa, the longest river in the world, which rises in east-central Africa near Lake Victoria and flows 6,673 km. (4,145 miles) northwards through Uganda, Sudan, and Egypt to empty through a large delta into the Mediterranean. It flows from Lake Victoria to Lake Albert, in Uganda, as the **Victoria Nile**. As the **Albert Nile** it flows onwards to the Ugandan-Sudanese border, where it is known as the **White Nile**. It flows through the swampy Sudd region of southern Sudan as the **Bahr el Jabel** until it reaches it confluence with the **Blue Nile** at Khartoum and continues northwards as the Nile. Seasonal flooding in Egypt has been controlled by the construction of a dam at Aswan which also provides hydroelectric power. The Blue Nile contributes more than half of all Nile waters and is the source of floodwaters that reach Egypt in September carrying great quantities of silt from the Ethiopian Highlands. The waters of the Nile support almost all the agriculture of Egypt and much of the Sudan, and are widely used for navigation and hydroelectric power. The flooding of the Nile was the basis of the civilization of ancient Egypt, but the mystery of the great river flowing through desert areas was not solved until the 18th and 19th centuries with the discoveries of Bruce and Speke.

**Nilgiri Hills** /'niːlgərɪ/ a range of hills in the state of Tamil Nadu, southern India, situated to the south of the Deccan plateau and linking the Eastern and Western Ghats. The highest peak is Doda Betta (2,636 m., 8,648 ft.).

**Nilotic** /naɪ'lɒtɪk/ a group of languages spoken in Egypt and the Sudan and further south in Kenya, Uganda, and Tanzania. The western group includes the Luo (Kenya), Dinka (Sudan), and Lango (Uganda); the eastern group includes Masai (Kenya and Tanzania) and Turkana (Kenya).

**nimbostratus** /ˌnɪmbəʊ'strɑːtəs/ a low, thick, dark rain cloud.

**nimbus** /'nɪmbəs/ a general term for a rain cloud.

**Nîmes** /niːm/ a city in southern France, capital of the department of Gard in the Languedoc-Roussillon region; pop. (1990) 133,600. It is noted for its many well-preserved Roman remains. It also gave its name to a type of cloth known as denim which was originally produced there, and the manufacture of textiles and clothing is still the principal local industry.

**Nimrod** /'niːmrɒd/, **Mount** (Turkish **Nemrut Daği**) a mountain rising to 2,000 m. (6,562 ft.) south-east of Malatya in south-eastern Anatolia, Turkey. On its summit are the ruins of colossal statues of Hellenistic and Persian gods built during the 1st century BC by Antiochas I Epiphanes, ruler of a rich principality that lay on the frontier of the Roman and Persian empires.

**Nimrud** the modern name of the ancient city of Kalhu (*Calah* in Genesis), situated on the eastern bank of the Tigris south of Nineveh, near the modern city of Mosul in northern Iraq. Founded in 1250 BC, it was inaugurated as the Assyrian capital in 879 BC by Ashurnasirpal II (883–859 BC). It was later supplanted by Khorsabad with the accession of Sargon II (722–705 BC) and finally destroyed by the Medes in 612 BC. British excavations under Henry A. Layard and later Sir Max Mallowan uncovered palaces of the Assyrian kings with monumental sculptured reliefs, carved ivory furniture inlays, and metalwork.

**Nineveh** /'nɪnɪvə/ an ancient city located on the east bank of the Tigris, opposite the modern city of Mosul in northern Iraq. It was the oldest city of the ancient Assyrian empire and its capital during the reign of Sennacherib (704–681 BC) until it was destroyed by a coalition of Babylonians and Medes in 612 BC. A famous archaeological site, it was first excavated by the French in 1820 and later by the British and is noted for its monumental Neo-

Assyrian palace, library, and statuary as well as for its crucial sequence of prehistoric pottery.

**Ningbo** /nɪŋ'pəʊ/ (formerly **Ningpo** and **Yin-Hsien**) a port and special economic zone in Zhejiang province eastern China, at the junction of the Fenghua, Tong, and Yuyao rivers; pop. (1990) 1,090,000. Its chief industries are oil refining, shipbuilding, and fishing. Landmarks include the 14th-c. Tianfeng Ta Pagoda and the 16th-c. Tianyi Ge Library, the oldest in China.

**Ningxia** /nɪŋ'ʃɪˌɑː/ (formerly **Ningsia**) an autonomous region of northern China, on the Loess Plateau to the south and east of Inner Mongolia; area 66,000 sq. km. (25,492 sq. miles); pop. (1990) 4,655,000; capital, Yinchuan. Separated by mountains from neighbouring provinces to north and south, it is irrigated by the waters of the Yellow River. Landmarks include the Xumi Mountain Grottoes, the King of Xixia's Mausoleum, and over 100 pagodas on the west bank of the Yellow River. It chief products are wheat, rice, millet, fruit, sheep, and coal.

**Niort** /njɔː(r)/ the capital of the department of Deux-Sèvres in the Poitou-Charentes region of western France; pop. (1990) 58,660. Once a cloth and leather town, Niort is now a major centre of the insurance business.

**Nipigon** /'nɪpɪˌgɑːn/, **Lake** a lake in south-west Ontario, Canada, north of Lake Superior to which it is linked by the Nipigon River; area 4,848 sq. km. (1,872 sq. miles).

**Nipissing** /'nɪpəˌsɪŋ/, **Lake** a lake in south-east Ontario, Canada, east of Sudbury and north-east of Georgian Bay to which it is linked by the French River; area 832 sq. km. (321 sq. miles).

**Nipponese** /ˌnɪpə'niːz/ the name formerly given to the people of Japan or Nippon (= land of the rising sun).

**Niš** /niːʃ/ (also **Nish**) an industrial city in south-east-central Serbia, on the River Nišava near its confluence with the Morava; pop. (1981) 230,710. The city, commanding the principal route by river between Europe and the Aegean, was for centuries a strategic stronghold. Dominated by Turks for 500 years, it fell to the Serbs in 1877. It was the birthplace of Constantine the Great c. 274 AD. It is a hub of road and rail routes and a manufacturing centre producing machinery, electrical equipment, ceramics, and foodstuffs.

**Nishinomiya** /ˌniːʃi'nəʊmɪə/ a city in Hyogo prefecture, south Honshu Island, Japan, on Osaka Bay; pop. (1990) 426,920.

**Niterói** /ˌniːtə'rɔɪ/ an industrial port and residential suburb in the state of Rio de Janeiro, south-east Brazil, on the south-eastern shore of Guanabara Bay opposite the city of Rio de Janeiro; pop. (1990) 455,200.

**Nitra** /'njɪtrɑː/ a town in western Slovakia, on the River Nitra; pop. (1991) 89,890. Once an important stronghold, now an agricultural market and religious centre, its 9th-c. bishopric church and castle are the oldest buildings in Slovakia.

**Niue** /'nju:eɪ/ an island territory in the South Pacific to the east of Tonga; area 263 sq. km. (101 sq. miles); pop. (1986) 2,531; capital, Alofi. Sighted by Captain Cook in 1774 and an-  nexed by New Zealand in 1901, the island achieved self-government in free association with New Zealand in 1974. It is the largest coral island in the world. The island's chief export is coconut cream.

**Nivernais** /ˌniːvəˈneɪ/ a former duchy and province of central France. Its capital was the city of Nevers.

**Nizamabad** /nɪˈzɑːməˌbæd/ a market town in Andhra Pradesh, central India, north of Hyderabad; pop. (1991) 240,920.

**Nizhnevartovsk** /ˌnjeʒnjɪˈvɑːrtefsk/ a city in the west Siberian lowland, Russia, that developed from a small village after the discovery nearby of one of the world's largest oilfields in 1965; pop. (1990) 246,000.

**Nizhniy Novgorod** /ˌnɪʒnɪ ˈnɒvgərɒd/ a city and river port in western Russia, at the junction of the Volga and Okra rivers; pop. (1990) 1,443,000. Between 1932 and 1991 it was named Gorky after the revolutionary writer Maxim Gorky. It is a major industrial city making cars, boats, and hydrofoils. Other industries include chemicals, oil refining, aircraft, machinery, and paper. Until recently a 'forbidden city' for foreigners and a place of internal political exile.

**Nizhniy Tagil** /ˌnɪʒnɪ təˈgɪl/ an industrial and mining city of Russia, in the central Ural Mts. north of Yekaterinburg; pop. (1990) 440,000. Its main products are iron, chemicals, and machinery.

**NJ** *abbr.* US New Jersey (in official postal use).

**Nkongsamba** /ˌəŋkɒŋˈsɑːmbə/ a town in the Littoral region of western Cameroon, situated to the north of Mount Nlonako; pop. (1991) 112,000. A major coffee market and tourist town.

**NM** *abbr.* US New Mexico (in official postal use).

**Nobeoka** /ˌnəʊbiːˈəʊkə/ a fishing port and industrial city in Miyazaki prefecture, east Kyushu Island, southern Japan, at the mouth of the Gokase River; pop. (1990) 130,615.

**Noda** /'nəʊdə/ an industrial city in Chiba prefecture, Honshu Island, central Japan, between the Edo and Tone rivers; pop. (1990) 114,480.

**Noginsk** /nəʊˈgɪnsk/ a major textiles city in western Russia, east of Moscow; pop. (1990) 123,000. It was known as Bogorodsk until 1930.

**Nokia** /'nəʊkɪə/ a town in south-west-central Finland, on Lake Pyhä south-west of Tampere; pop. (1990) 26,060. It was known as Pohjois-Pirkkala until 1938.

**Nome** /nəʊm/ the name of a cape and a town on the Seward Peninsula, western Alaska, named in error by the British Admiralty who misread the mark '? Name' on a naval chart. Founded in 1896 as a gold-mining camp, the town became a centre of the Alaskan gold-rush at the turn of the century.

**Non-Aligned Movement** a grouping of 110 countries and liberation movements established in 1961 for the purpose of building closer political, economic, and cultural cooperation in the Third World.

**Nootka** /'nuːtkə/ (also **Aht**) a North American Indian tribe of the Wakashan linguistic group living on the north-west coast of British Columbia, on Vancouver Island. They were traditionally accomplished fishermen and boat builders.

**Nootka Sound** /'nuːtkə/ an inlet of the Pacific Ocean on the west coast of Vancouver Island, British Colombia, Canada. Captain Cook landed here in 1778 and in 1788 a trading post was established by the British explorer John Meares. Settlement claims in the region, which were disputed between Spain and Britain, were finally resolved by the Nootka Convention of 1790.

**Nord** /nɔːd/ a department in the Nord-Pas-de-Calais region of northern France, on the North Sea and the Belgian frontier; area 5,743 sq. km. (2,218 sq. miles); pop. (1990) 2,532,855; capital, Lille.

**Nordic** of or relating to Scandinavia or Finland. The provinces of North and South Trondelag in Norway, Jämtland and Vasternorrland in Sweden, and Vaasa and Central Finland in Finland, with a population of *c.* 1.5 million, are collectively known as the Mid-Nordic Region, a region of economic co-operation.

**Nordkapp** SEE NORTH CAPE.

**Nordkyn** /'nɔːkən/ a promontory on the north coast of Norway, to the east of North Cape. At 71° 8′ N, it is the northernmost point of the European mainland, North Cape being on an island.

**Nord-Pas-de-Calais** /ˌnɔːdpɑːdəkæˈleɪ/ a region of northern France comprising the departments of Nord and Pas-de-Calais; area 12,414 sq. km. (4,795 sq. miles); pop. (1990) 3,965,060.

**Norfolk** /'nɔːfək/ a fertile agricultural county (cereals, sugar-beet, cattle, and poultry) on the east coast of England, with numerous fishing ports and coastal resorts. Area 5,375 sq. km. (2,076 sq. miles); pop. (1991) 736,700; county town, Norwich. The county is divided into seven districts:

| District | Area (sq. km.) | Pop. (1991) |
|---|---|---|
| Breckland | 1,310 | 105,200 |
| Broadland | 552 | 104,500 |
| Great Yarmouth | 174 | 85,900 |

(cont.)

| | | |
|---|---|---|
| Kings Lynn and West Norfolk | 1,427 | 128,400 |
| North Norfolk | 966 | 90,400 |
| Norwich | 39 | 121,000 |
| South Norfolk | 907 | 101,400 |

**Norfolk Broads** /brɔːdz/ see BROADS.

**Norfolk Island** /ˈnɔːfək/ an island in the Pacific Ocean, off the east coast of Australia, adminis-tered since 1913 as an external territory of Australia; area 34.5 sq. km. (13.3 sq. miles); pop. (1986) 1,977. Occupied from 1788 to 1814 as a penal colony, the island was settled by the descendants of the mutineers from the *Bounty* in 1856. Descend-ants of the mutineers are known as 'Islanders' and those of Australian, New Zealand, or UK descent as 'mainlanders'.

**Norilsk** /nəˈrelsk/ a city in northern Siberia within the Arctic Circle, the northernmost city of Russia; pop. (1990) 173,000. Founded in 1935 as a prison settlement, it lies at the centre of a zinc, copper, nickel, cobalt, platinum, and coal mining area. It is reckoned to be the coldest city in the world with a mean annual temperature of $-10.9°C$.

**Norman** /ˈnɔːmən/ a city in central Oklahoma, USA; pop. (1990) 80,070. Settled during the Oklahoma land-rush of 1889, Norman is a centre of tourism, oil production, high technology indus-try, and agriculture. The University of Oklahoma was founded here in 1892.

**Normandy** /ˈnɔːməndɪ/ a former maritime province of north-west France with its coastline on the English Channel, now divided into the two administrative regions of Upper Normandy (Haute-Normandie) and Lower Normandy (Basse-Normandie). It was given by Charles III of France to Rollo, first Duke of Normandy, in 912, and was contested between France and England throughout the Middle Ages until finally con-quered by France in the mid-15th c. It was the site in June 1944 of the D-Day landings and battles which led to the liberation of France. Normandy is noted for its cider and dairy products.

**Norrköping** /ˈnɔːkəpɪŋ/ an industrial city and seaport on an inlet of the Baltic Sea in Ostergöt-land county, south-east Sweden; pop. (1990) 120,520.

**Norse** /nɔː(r)s/ the official language of Norway. **Old Norse** was the Germanic language of Norway and its colonies down to the 14th c. It is the an-cestor of the Scandinavian languages and is most clearly preserved in the saga literature of Iceland.

**Northallerton** /nɔːˈθælət(ə)n/ the county town of North Yorkshire in north-east England; pop. (1981) 13,860.

**North America** the northern half of the American landmass, connected to South America by the Isthmus of Panama, bordered by the At-lantic Ocean to the east and the Pacific Ocean to the west. The southern part of the continent was colonized by the Spanish in the 16th c., while the eastern coast was opened up by the British and French in the 17th c., rivalry between the two end-ing in British victory during the Seven Years War. The American colonies won their independence in the War of American Independence (1775–83), while Canada was granted its own constitution in 1867. The 19th c. saw the gradual development of the western half of the continent, the emergence of Mexico as an independent state, and the growth of the United States as a world power. The USA has progressively dominated the continent, both economically and politically, Canada having a very small population relative to its size and Mexico sharing, albeit to a much lesser extent, the problems of its Central American neighbours to the south. The total population of North America is c. 367 million people.

**Northampton** /nɔːˈθæmptən/ the county town of Northamptonshire in central England, on the River Nene; pop. (1981) 178,200. Shoemaking was for long the principal industry, succeeded by engi-neering; there is also a major cattle-market. North-ampton is increasingly becoming a dormitory town for wealthier London commuters.

**Northamptonshire** /nɔːˈθæmptənʃɪə(r)/ a county of central England; area 2,367 sq. km. (914 sq. miles); pop. (1991) 568,900; county town, Northampton. The county is divided into seven districts:

| District | Area (sq. km.) | Pop. (1991) |
|---|---|---|
| Corby | 80 | 52,300 |
| Daventry | 666 | 61,600 |
| East Northamptonshire | 510 | 66,600 |
| Kettering | 234 | 75,200 |
| Northampton | 81 | 178,200 |
| South Northamptonshire | 633 | 68,800 |
| Wellingborough | 163 | 66,100 |

**Northants** /nɔːˈθænts/ *abbr.* Northamptonshire.

**North Atlantic Cooperation Council** (**NACC**) an international defence and security organization formed in December 1991 at the end of the Cold War. It includes the 16 NATO member-states, the Baltic States, five former Warsaw Pact countries, and Russia.

**North Atlantic Drift** see GULF STREAM.

**North Atlantic Ocean** see ATLANTIC OCEAN.

**North Atlantic Treaty Organization** (**NATO**) an association of European and North

American states, formed in 1949 for the defence of Europe and the North Atlantic against the perceived threat of Soviet aggression. Dominated by the US, it identified in 1991 the disintegration of the USSR and instability in Eastern Europe as new dangers. Its headquarters are in Brussels, Belgium.

**North Bay** a city in Ontario, south-east Canada, on the east shore of Lake Nipissing; pop. (1991) 55,400. Originally a trading post on the fur-trading route from the Ottawa River to Georgian Bay, it is now a popular resort town.

**North Brabant** SEE BRABANT.

**North Cape** (Norwegian **Nordkapp** /ˈnuːkæp/) a promontory on Magerøya Island, off the north coast of Norway. Situated on the edge of the Barents Sea, North Cape is the northernmost accessible point in the world, and as such is popular with mid-summer tourists.

**North Carolina** /ˌkærəˈlaɪnə/ a state of east-central USA, on the Atlantic coast to the south of Virginia; area 136,413 sq. km. (52,669 sq. miles); pop. (1990) 6,628,640; capital, Raleigh. The largest cities are Charlotte, Raleigh, and Greensboro. North Carolina is also known as the Tar Heel State. Settled by the English and named after Charles I, North Carolina was one of the original 13 states of the US (1788). The state is a leading producer of mica and lithium and its chief industrial products include textiles, tobacco, furniture, paper, chemicals, and bricks. Major landmarks include the Great Smoky Mountains National Park, Blue Ridge National Parkway, Fort Raleigh National Historic Site, and Cape Hatteras and Cape Lookout National Seashores. The state is divided into 100 counties:

| County | Area (sq. km.) | Pop. (1990) | County Seat |
|---|---|---|---|
| Alamance | 1,126 | 108,210 | Graham |
| Alexander | 673 | 27,540 | Taylorsville |
| Alleghany | 611 | 9,590 | Sparta |
| Anson | 1,386 | 23,470 | Wadesboro |
| Ashel | 1,108 | 22,210 | Jefferson |
| Avery | 642 | 14,870 | Newland |
| Beaufort | 2,148 | 42,280 | Washington |
| Bertie | 1,823 | 20,290 | Windsor |
| Bladen | 2,285 | 28,660 | Elizabethtown |
| Brunswick | 2,236 | 50,985 | Southport |
| Buncombe | 1,713 | 174,820 | Asheville |
| Burke | 1,310 | 75,740 | Morganton |
| Cabarrus | 946 | 98,935 | Concord |
| Caldwell | 1,225 | 70,710 | Lenoir |
| Camden | 624 | 5,900 | Camden |
| Carteret | 1,368 | 52,560 | Beaufort |
| Caswell | 1,113 | 20,690 | Yanceyville |
| Catawba | 1,030 | 118,410 | Newton |
| Chatham | 1,841 | 38,760 | Pittsboro |
| Cherokee | 1,175 | 20,170 | Murphy |
| Chowan | 473 | 13,510 | Edenton |
| Clay | 556 | 7,155 | Hayesville |
| Cleveland | 1,217 | 84,710 | Shelby |
| Columbus | 2,439 | 49,590 | Whiteville |
| Craven | 1,823 | 81,610 | New Bern |
| Cumberland | 1,708 | 274,570 | Fayetteville |
| Currituck | 666 | 13,740 | Currituck |
| Dare | 1,017 | 22,750 | Manteo |
| Davidson | 1,425 | 126,680 | Lexington |
| Davie | 694 | 27,860 | Mocksville |
| Duplin | 2,129 | 39,995 | Kenansville |
| Durham | 775 | 181,835 | Durham |
| Edgecombe | 1,316 | 56,560 | Tarboro |
| Forsyth | 1,071 | 265,880 | Winston-Salem |
| Franklin | 1,284 | 36,410 | Louisburg |
| Gaston | 928 | 175,090 | Gastonia |
| Gates | 879 | 9,305 | Gatesville |
| Graham | 751 | 7,200 | Robbinsville |
| Granville | 1,388 | 38,345 | Oxford |
| Greene | 692 | 15,380 | Snow Hill |
| Guilford | 1,693 | 347,420 | Greensboro |
| Halifax | 1,882 | 55,520 | Halifax |
| Harnett | 1,563 | 67,820 | Lilington |
| Haywood | 1,443 | 46,940 | Waynesville |
| Henderson | 972 | 69,285 | Hendersonville |
| Hertford | 926 | 22,520 | Winton |
| Hoke | 1,017 | 22,860 | Raeford |
| Hyde | 1,622 | 5,410 | Swanquarter |
| Iredell | 1,492 | 92,930 | Statesville |
| Jackson | 1,277 | 26,850 | Sylva |
| Johnston | 2,067 | 81,310 | Smithfield |
| Jones | 1,222 | 9,410 | Trenton |
| Lee | 673 | 41,370 | Sanford |
| Lenoir | 1,045 | 57,270 | Kinston |
| Lincoln | 775 | 50,320 | Lincolnton |
| McDowell | 1,136 | 35,680 | Marion |
| Macon | 1,344 | 23,500 | Franklin |
| Madison | 1,173 | 16,950 | Marshall |
| Martin | 1,199 | 25,080 | Williamston |
| Mecklenburg | 1,373 | 511,430 | Charlotte |
| Mitchell | 577 | 14,440 | Bakersville |
| Montgomery | 1,274 | 23,350 | Troy |
| Moore | 1,823 | 59,010 | Carthage |
| Nash | 1,404 | 76,680 | Nashville |
| New Hanover | 481 | 120,280 | Wilmington |
| Northampton | 1,399 | 20,800 | Jackson |
| Onslow | 1,984 | 149,840 | Jacksonville |
| Orange | 1,040 | 93,850 | Hillsboro |
| Pamlico | 887 | 11,370 | Bayboro |
| Pasquotank | 593 | 31,300 | Elizabeth City |
| Pender | 2,275 | 28,855 | Burgaw |
| Perquimans | 640 | 10,450 | Hertford |
| Person | 1,035 | 30,180 | Roxboro |
| Pitt | 1,708 | 107,920 | Greenville |
| Polk | 619 | 14,420 | Columbus |
| Randolph | 2,051 | 106,550 | Asheboro |
| Richmond | 1,240 | 44,520 | Rockingham |
| Robeson | 2,467 | 105,180 | Lumberton |
| Rockingham | 1,479 | 86,060 | Wentworth |
| Rowan | 1,349 | 110,605 | Salisbury |
| Rutherford | 1,477 | 56,920 | Rutherfordton |
| Sampson | 2,462 | 47,300 | Clinton |
| Scotland | 829 | 33,750 | Laurinburg |
| Stanly | 1,030 | 51,765 | Albemarle |
| Stokes | 1,175 | 37,220 | Danbury |
| Surry | 1,401 | 61,700 | Dobson |
| Swain | 1,368 | 11,270 | Bryson City |
| Transylvania | 983 | 25,520 | Brevard |

(cont.)

| | | | |
|---|---|---|---|
| Tyrrell | 1,058 | 3,860 | Columbia |
| Union | 1,661 | 84,210 | Monroe |
| Vance | 647 | 38,890 | Henderson |
| Wake | 2,220 | 423,380 | Raleigh |
| Warren | 1,110 | 17,265 | Warrenton |
| Washington | 863 | 14,000 | Plymouth |
| Watauga | 816 | 36,950 | Boone |
| Wayne | 1,440 | 104,670 | Goldsboro |
| Wilkes | 1,955 | 59,390 | Wilkesboro |
| Wilson | 972 | 66,060 | Wilson |
| Yadkin | 874 | 30,490 | Yadkinville |
| Yancey | 816 | 15,420 | Burnsville |

**North Charleston** /'tʃɑːlztən/ a suburb of Charleston, South Carolina, USA, pop. (1990) 70,220.

**North Country, the** a general term given to that part of England north of the Humber.

**North Dakota** /dəˈkəʊtə/ an agricultural state in north-central USA, bordering on Canada; area 183,119 sq. km. (70,702 sq. miles); pop. (1990) 638,800; capital, Bismarck. The largest cities are Fargo and Grand Forks. North Dakota is also known as the Sioux, Flickertail, or Peace Garden State. Acquired partly by the Louisiana Purchase in 1803 and partly from Britain by treaty in 1818, it became the 39th state of the US in 1889. Farms, which cover over 90 per cent of the state, produce grain, sunflowers, beans, and beef cattle, and the state is rich in coal and oil reserves. Its chief landmarks include the Badlands, Fort Union Trading Post National Historic Site, Theodore Roosevelt National Park, and Knife River Indian Villages National Historic Site. The state is divided into 53 counties:

| County | Area (sq. km.) | Pop. (1990) | County Seat |
|---|---|---|---|
| Adams | 2,569 | 3,170 | Hettinger |
| Barnes | 3,895 | 12,545 | Valley City |
| Benson | 3,671 | 7,200 | Minnewaukan |
| Billings | 2,995 | 1,110 | Medora |
| Bottineau | 4,337 | 8,010 | Bottineau |
| Bowman | 3,021 | 3,600 | Bowman |
| Burke | 2,907 | 3,000 | Bowbells |
| Burleigh | 4,207 | 60,130 | Bismarck |
| Cass | 4,594 | 102,870 | Fargo |
| Cavalier | 3,918 | 6,060 | Langdon |
| Dickey | 2,961 | 6,110 | Ellendale |
| Divide | 3,349 | 2,900 | Crosby |
| Dunn | 5,182 | 4,005 | Manning |
| Eddy | 1,648 | 2,950 | New Rockford |
| Emmons | 3,897 | 4,830 | Linton |
| Foster | 1,664 | 3,980 | Carrington |
| Golden Valley | 2,608 | 2,110 | Beach |
| Grand Forks | 3,744 | 70,680 | Grand Forks |
| Grant | 4,316 | 3,550 | Carson |
| Griggs | 1,841 | 3,300 | Cooperstown |
| Hettinger | 2,946 | 3,445 | Mott |
| Kidder | 3,541 | 3,330 | Steele |
| La Moure | 2,990 | 5,380 | La Moure |
| Logan | 2,600 | 2,850 | Napoleon |

| | | | |
|---|---|---|---|
| McHenry | 4,906 | 6,530 | Towner |
| McIntosh | 2,558 | 4,020 | Ashley |
| McKenzie | 7,160 | 6,380 | Watford City |
| McLean | 5,369 | 10,460 | Washburn |
| Mercer | 2,714 | 9,810 | Stanton |
| Morton | 4,995 | 23,700 | Mandan |
| Mountrail | 4,776 | 7,020 | Stanley |
| Nelson | 2,577 | 4,410 | Lakota |
| Oliver | 1,880 | 2,380 | Center |
| Pembina | 2,912 | 9,240 | Cavalier |
| Pierce | 2,696 | 5,050 | Rugby |
| Ramsey | 3,227 | 12,680 | Devils Lake |
| Ransom | 2,241 | 5,920 | Lisbon |
| Renville | 2,272 | 3,160 | Mohall |
| Richland | 3,734 | 18,150 | Wahpeton |
| Rolette | 2,376 | 12,770 | Rolla |
| Sargent | 2,228 | 4,550 | Forman |
| Sheridan | 2,571 | 2,150 | McClusky |
| Sioux | 2,857 | 3,760 | Fort Yates |
| Slope | 3,169 | 910 | Amidon |
| Stark | 3,379 | 22,830 | Dickinson |
| Steele | 1,854 | 2,420 | Finley |
| Stutsman | 5,884 | 22,240 | Jamestown |
| Towner | 2,691 | 3,630 | Cando |
| Traill | 2,239 | 8,750 | Hillsboro |
| Walsh | 3,354 | 13,840 | Grafton |
| Ward | 5,307 | 57,920 | Minot |
| Wells | 3,349 | 5,860 | Fessenden |
| Williams | 5,392 | 21,130 | Williston |

**North Downs Way** a long-distance footpath in the south of England, stretching 227 km. (142 miles) through the North Downs from Farnham to Dover.

**Northeast Passage** a passage for ships eastwards along the northern coast of Europe and Asia, from the Atlantic to the Pacific via the Arctic Ocean, sought for many years as a possible trade route to the East. It was first navigated in 1878–9 by the Swedish Arctic explorer Baron Nordenskjöld (1832–1901).

**northerly** a wind blowing from the north.

**Northern Cape** a province of South Africa created in 1994 from part of the former Cape Province. Its capital is Kimberley.

**Northern Circars** /sɜːˈkɑːz/ a name formerly used of the coastal region of eastern India between the Krishna River and Orissa, now in Andhra Pradesh.

**Northern Ireland** a part of the United Kingdom occupying the north-east part of Ireland and comprising the six Ulster counties of Antrim, Armagh, Londonderry, Down, Fermanagh, and Tyrone, established in 1920 when these withdrew from the newly constituted Irish Free State; area 5,032 sq. km. (1,944 sq. miles); pop. (1991) 1,569,970; capital, Belfast. An agricultural region with few natural resources; industries are concentrated in Belfast and smaller centres. Tourism is important. At first a quasi-autonomous province with its parliament meeting at Stormont in Belfast, it was dominated by the Ulster Unionist Party, opposed by an increasing Roman Catholic minority favouring union with the Irish Republic. Amongst other political problems, discrimination against the latter group in local government, employment, and housing led to violent conflicts and (from 1969) the presence of British army units to keep the peace. Continuing terrorist activities resulted in the suspension of the Stormont assembly and imposition of direct rule from Westminster. After 25 years of sectarian violence, hopes for peace were raised when the Irish Republican Army agreed to a ceasefire in 1994. Northern Ireland is administratively divided into 26 Local Government Districts:

| District | Pop. (1991) |
| --- | --- |
| Antrim | 44,260 |
| Ards | 64,000 |
| Armagh | 51,290 |
| Ballymena | 55,920 |
| Ballymoney | 24,080 |
| Banbridge | 33,140 |
| Belfast | 280,970 |
| Carrickfergus | 32,300 |
| Castlereagh | 60,720 |
| Coleraine | 51,060 |
| Cookstown | 30,880 |
| Craigavon | 74,350 |
| Derry | 94,720 |
| Down | 57,500 |
| Dungannon | 45,410 |
| Fermanagh | 54,290 |
| Larne | 29,280 |
| Limavady | 29,140 |
| Lisburn | 98,830 |
| Magherafelt | 35,880 |
| Moyle | 14,635 |
| Newry and Mourne | 82,240 |
| Newtonabbey | 73,720 |
| North Down | 70,065 |
| Omagh | 45,570 |
| Strabane | 35,710 |

**Northern Marianas** a self-governing territory in the north-west Pacific, comprising the Mariana Islands with the exception of the southernmost, Guam; area 477 sq. km. (184 sq. miles);

pop. (1990) 43,345; languages, English (official), Malayo-Polynesian languages including Chamorro, Woleian, and Filipino; capital, Saipan. The Northern Marianas, which comprise the islands of Saipan, Tinian, Rota, Pagan, Agrihan, Alamagan, and 10 uninhabited islands, are constituted as a self-governing commonwealth in union with the USA. (See also MARIANA ISLANDS.)

**Northern Rhodesia** the former name (until 1964) of ZAMBIA.

**Northern Territory** a territory of north-central Australia; area 1,346,200 sq. km. (519,969 sq. miles); pop. (1991) 167,800; capital, Darwin. Annexed by the state of South Australia in 1863, the administration was taken over by the Commonwealth of Australia in 1911 and in 1978 it became a full self-governing member within the Commonwealth. It is a major source of minerals including uranium, lead, silver, zinc, and bauxite. Cattle-ranching is carried on in the semiarid scrubland. One-third of the territory is Aboriginal land.

**Northern Transvaal** a province of South Africa created in 1994 from part of the former province of Transvaal. Its capital is Pietersburg.

**North Holland** (Dutch **Noord Holland**) a province of north-west Netherlands forming a peninsula between the North Sea and the IJsselmeer; area 2,667 sq. km. (1,030 sq. miles); pop. (1991) 2,397,090; capital, Haarlem.

**North Island** the northernmost and less populated of the two main islands of New Zealand, separated from South Island by Cook Strait; area 114,383 sq. km. (44,180 sq. miles); pop.(1991) 2,553,410.

**North Korea** official name **The Democratic People's Republic of Korea** a country in the Far East occupying the northern part of the peninsula of Korea; area 120,538 sq. km.

(46,558 sq. miles); pop. (est. 1992) 22,227,000; official language, Korean; capital, Pyongyang. Its chief exports are minerals such as iron ore, metal goods, and agricultural products such as corn, rice, and vegetables. North Korea was formed in 1948 when Korea was partitioned along the 38th parallel. In 1950 North Korean forces invaded the south, but were forced back to more or less the previous border. A Communist state which has been dominated by the personality of Kim Il Sung, its leader since 1948, North Korea has always sought Korean unification, latterly by avowed peaceful means. After decades of hostility, North and South Korea signed a series of preliminary peace accords in 1991. (See also KOREA.)

**Northland** an administrative region of North Island, New Zealand created in 1989 and comprising the districts of Far North, Kaipara, and Whangaraei; pop. (1991) 131,620.

**North Little Rock** a town in central Arkansas, USA, on the Arkansas River opposite Little Rock; pop. (1990) 61,740.

**North Minch** see MINCH, THE.

**North Ossetia** see OSSETIA.

**North Platte** /plɑːt/ a river of the USA that rises in northern Colorado and flows 1,094 km. (680 miles) in an arc through Wyoming and Nebraska, joining the South Platte to form the Platte River.

**North Pole** see POLE.

**North Rhine-Westphalia** (German **Nordrhein-Westfalen** /nɔːtˌraɪnvestˈfɑːlən/) a state of western Germany; area 34,070 sq. km. (13,159 sq. miles); pop. (1990) 17,104,000; capital, Düsseldorf.

**North Saskatchewan** see SASKATCHEWAN 2.

**North Sea** (also **German Ocean**) a shallow arm of the Atlantic Ocean lying between the mainland of Europe and the east coast of Britain. Since 1960 it has become important for the exploitation of oil and gas deposits under the seabed. It is a rich fishing ground and major shipping lane.

**North Shields** /ʃiːldz/ a town in Tyne and Wear, north-east England, to the north of the River Tyne and east of Newcastle upon Tyne; pop. (1981) 41,600.

**Northumberland** /nɔːˈθʌmbələnd/ a county in the extreme north-east of England; area 5,031 sq. km. (1,943 sq. miles); pop. (1991) 300,600; county town, Morpeth. The former industries of coal-mining and shipbuilding have declined and the county's economy now depends on tourism and light industry. Northumberland is divided into six districts:

| District | Area (sq. km.) | Pop. (1991) |
|---|---|---|
| Alnwick | 1,080 | 30,000 |
| Berwick-upon-Tweed | 974 | 26,400 |
| Blyth Valley | 70 | 78,000 |
| Castle Morpeth | 619 | 49,700 |
| Tynedale | 2,221 | 56,400 |
| Wansbeck | 66 | 60,100 |

**Northumberland National Park** a national park in north-east England between Hadrian's Wall and the Cheviot Hills. Established in 1956, it extends over 1,031 sq. km. (398 sq. miles) of borderland forest and rolling hills.

**Northumbria** /nɔːˈθʌmbrɪə/ an ancient Anglo-Saxon kingdom of north-east England and southeast Scotland extending from the Humber to the Forth. The name refers to persons living to the north of the Humber and has been revived in modern times by organizations such as the 'Northumbria Authority', an area of police administration in north-east England.
**Northumbrian** adj. & n.

**North Utsire** /ʊtˈsɪərə/ a shipping-forecast area in the North Sea off the south-west coast of Norway. (See also SOUTH UTSIRE.)

**North-West Province** a province of South Africa created in 1994 from part of the former province of Transvaal. Its capital is Klerksdorp.

**North-west Frontier Province** a province of north-west Pakistan; area 74,521 sq. km. (28,784 sq. miles); pop. (est. 1985) 12,290,000; capital, Peshawar. The North-west Frontier is watered by the Indus and is linked to Afghanistan by the Khyber Pass.

**North-west Passage** a sea passage westwards along the north coast of the North American continent, through the Canadian Arctic, Beaufort Sea, and Bering Straits, from the Atlantic to the Pacific. It was formerly sought for centuries as a possible trading route by many explorers, including Sebastian Cabot, John Davis, Henry Hudson, Martin Frobisher, John Ross, David Buchan, William Parry, and John Franklin. In 1853–4 it was first traced on foot by Robert McLure (1807–73). It was finally successfully navigated in 1903–6 by Roald Amundsen. The SS *Manhattan*, an ice-breaking tanker, was the first commercial ship to navigate the passage in 1969.

**Northwest Territories** the part of Canada lying north of the 60th parallel, west of Hudson Bay, and east of the Rocky Mountains; area 3,426,320 sq. km. (1,322,909 sq. miles); pop. (1991) 57,650; capital, Yellowknife. For the most part it consists of vast, inhospitable, and sparsely inhabited forests and tundra. It includes the islands of the Canadian Arctic and is administratively divided into the districts of Fort Smith, Inuvik, Kitikmeot, Keewatin, and Baffin. It was administered by the Hudson's Bay Company from 1670 and transferred by Britain to Canada in 1870. In the past fur-trapping and fishing were the only occupations of the largely Inuit population. Mining of gold, silver, lead, zinc, and cadmium are now important. (See also NUNAVUT.)

**Northwest Territory** (also **Old Northwest**) a region and former territory of the USA lying between the Mississippi and Ohio rivers and the Great Lakes. It was acquired in 1783 after the War of American Independence and now comprises the states of Indiana (1800), Ohio (1803), Michigan (1805), Illinois (1809), and Wisconsin (1836).

**North York Moors National Park** a national park in North Yorkshire and Cleveland, north-east England, comprising open moorland, woodland valleys, and coastal headlands. Established in 1952, it extends over an area of 1,432 sq. km. (553 sq. miles).

**North Yorkshire** a county in north-east England; area 8,312 sq. km. (3,210 sq. miles); pop. (1991) 698,800; administrative centre, Northallerton. It was formed in 1974 from parts of the former North, East, and West Ridings of Yorkshire. It is divided into eight districts:

| District | Area (sq. km.) | Pop. (1991) |
|---|---|---|
| Craven | 1,180 | 49,700 |
| Hambleton | 1,311 | 77,600 |

| | | |
|---|---|---|
| Harrogate | 1,334 | 141,000 |
| Richmondshire | 1,317 | 43,800 |
| Ryedale | 1,598 | 90,000 |
| Scarborough | 817 | 107,800 |
| Selby | 725 | 88,300 |
| York | 29 | 100,600 |

**Norwalk** /'nɔːwɔːk/ **1.** a city in the Los Angeles conurbation of south-west California, USA, situated east of the San Gabriel River to the south-east of Los Angeles; pop. (1990) 94,280. **2.** a city in south-west Connecticut, USA, at the mouth of the Norwalk River; pop. (1990) 78,330. Settled in 1651, it developed as an industrial town producing nails, clocks, and paper. It now manufactures astronoical instruments, chemicals, plastics, electronic components, and aircraft radar equipment.

**Norway** /'nɔːweɪ/ (Norwegian **Norge**) official name **The Kingdom of Norway** a mountainous European country on the northern and western coastline of the Scandinavian peninsula; area 323,878 sq. km. (125,098 sq. miles); pop. (1991) 4,249,830; official language, Norwegian; capital, Oslo. The largest cities are Oslo, Bergen, and Trondheim. Extending some 1,760 km. (1,100 miles) from south to north, Norway's deeply indented coastline stretches north of the Arctic Circle but experiences comparatively mild conditions in winter as a result of the warming influence of the Gulf Stream. Much of the interior is uninhabited forest-covered mountain with glaciers and an Arctic type of climate in the winter. The majority of the population lives in the southern lowland area where summers are dry and warm. There are numerous offshore islands, the northernmost of which are to be found in the barren Svalbard archipelago in the Arctic Ocean. An independent if often divided kingdom in Viking and early medieval times, Norway was united with Denmark and Sweden by the Union of Kalmar in 1397, but after Sweden's withdrawal in 1523 became subject to Denmark. Ceded to Sweden in 1814, Norway emerged as an independent kingdom in 1905. It was occupied by German forces 1940–5. Norway is a leading exporter of fish, ships, paper, pulp, and aluminium, but since the 1960s the opening up of the North Sea oilfields has boosted its economy. It is a parliamentary monarchy with executive power vested in the king and Council of State and legislative power vested in the bicameral Parliament (*Storting*). The country's name means 'north way'.

**Norwegian** *adj. & n.*
Norway is divided into 19 counties:

| County | Area (sq. km.) | Pop. (1991) | Capital |
|---|---|---|---|
| Østfold | 4,183 | 238,345 | Moss |
| Akershus | 4,916 | 418,110 | Oslo |
| Oslo | 454 | 461,640 | |
| Hedmark | 27,388 | 187,310 | Hamar |
| Oppland | 25,260 | 182,590 | Lillehammer |
| Buskerud | 14,927 | 225,260 | Drammen |
| Vestfold | 2,216 | 198,350 | Tønsberg |
| Telemark | 15,315 | 163,870 | Skien |
| Aust-Agder | 9,212 | 97,310 | Arendal |
| Vest-Agder | 7,280 | 145,090 | Kristiansand |
| Rogaland | 9,141 | 337,910 | Stavanger |
| Hordaland | 15,634 | 411,020 | Bergen |
| Sogn og Fjordane | 18,633 | 106,610 | Hermansverk |
| Møre og Romsdal | 15,104 | 238,280 | Molde |
| Sør-Trøndelag | 18,831 | 251,080 | Trondheim |
| Nord-Trøndelag | 22,463 | 127,230 | Steinkjer |
| Nordland | 38,327 | 239,400 | Bodø |
| Troms | 25,954 | 146,820 | Tromsø |
| Finnmark | 48,637 | 74,590 | Vadsø |

**Norwegian** the official language of Norway, spoken by its 4 million inhabitants, which belongs to the Scandinavian language group. During the Middle Ages Danish gradually replaced Norwegian as the language of the upper classes in Norway, the peasants continuing to speak Norwegian, and there are still two separate forms of the modern language, *Bokmål* or *Riksmål*, the more widely used (also called Dan-Norwegian), a modified form of the Danish language used in Norway after its separation from Denmark (1814) following four centuries of union, and *Nynorsk* (= new Norwegian, formerly called *Landsmål*), a literary form devised by the Norwegian philologist Ivar Aasen (d. 1896) from the country dialects most closely descended from Old Norse, and considered to be a purer form of the language than Bokmål.

**Norwegian Sea** that part of the North Atlantic lying to the north-west of Norway.

**Norwich** /'nɒrɪdʒ/ the county town of Norfolk in east England, on the Wesum River near its junction with the Yare; pop. (1991) 121,000. It has many old buildings including a cathedral founded in 1096 and is the home of the University of East Anglia (1963). It is a market and light industry centre. Mustard is a famous local product.

**Notre-Dame** /ˌnɒtrə'dɑːm/ the Gothic cathedral church of Paris, situated on the Ile de la Cité (an island in the Seine). Begun in 1163 and effectively finished by 1250, it is dedicated to the Virgin Mary. It is especially noted for its innovatory flying buttresses, sculptured façade, and great rose windows with 13th-c. stained glass.

**Nottingham** /'nɒtɪŋhəm/ the county town of Nottinghamshire in central England, on the River Trent; pop. (1991) 261,500. Its castle was the headquarters of Richard III before the Battle of Bosworth Field in 1485 and the standard of Charles I was raised here at the outset of the Civil War in

1642. William Booth, founder of the Salvation Army, was born in Nottingham in 1829. The University of Nottingham was founded in 1948. It developed as an industrial town in the 19th c. producing lace, hosiery, tobacco, and bicycles.

**Nottinghamshire** /'nɒtɪŋhəm,ʃɪə(r)/ a county in central England; area 2,161 sq. km. (835 sq. miles); pop. (1991) 980,600; county town, Nottingham. The county is divided into eight districts:

| District | Area (sq. km.) | Pop.(1991) |
|---|---|---|
| Ashfield | 110 | 106,800 |
| Bassetlaw | 637 | 103,000 |
| Broxtowe | 81 | 104,600 |
| Gedling | 120 | 107,600 |
| Mansfield | 77 | 98,800 |
| Newark and Sherwood | 651 | 103,400 |
| Nottingham | 75 | 261,500 |
| Rushcliffe | 409 | 94,900 |

**Notting Hill** /'nɒtɪŋ/ a residential area of north-west-central London, to the north of Holland Park, whose West Indian community holds a popular annual street carnival.

**Notts.** /nɒts/ abbr. Nottinghamshire.

**Nouadhibou** /,nwædɪ'bu:/ the principal port of Mauritania, on the Atlantic coast of West Africa at the border with Western Sahara; pop. (1976) 22,000. Formerly known as Port Étienne, Nouadhibou is linked by rail to the iron-mines of Zouérate on the western edge of the Sahara.

**Nouakchott** /'nwækʃɒt/ the capital of Mauritania, founded on the site of a small village in 1958; pop. (est. 1985) 500,000. It has a power-station, Africa's first desalination plant, and a deep-water harbour for the export of copper ores.

**Nouméa** /nu:'meɪə/ the capital of the island of New Caledonia in the Pacific Ocean; pop. (1989) 65,110. Formerly called Port de France, it became the capital of the French overseas territory of New Caledonia in 1854 and was a penal colony from 1864 to 1897.

**Nouvelle-Calédonie** the French name for NEW CALEDONIA.

**Nova Iguaçu** /,nəʊvə i:'gwɑ:su:/ a city in the state of Rio de Janeiro, south-eastern Brazil, a north-western suburb of Rio de Janeiro; pop. (1990) 1,246,775.

**Nova Lisboa** the former name (until 1978) of HUAMBO.

**Novara** /nəʊ'vɑ:rə/ a town in the Piedmont region of north-west Italy, west of Milan; pop. (1990) 103,350. It is capital of Novara province. It is an agricultural and industrial centre with textiles, chemicals, machinery, and printing, including maps and atlases.

**Nova Scotia** /,nəʊvə 'skəʊʃə/ **1.** a peninsula on the south-east coast of Canada, projecting into the Atlantic Ocean and separating the Bay of Fundy from the Gulf of St. Lawrence. **2.** a province of eastern Canada, comprising the peninsula of Nova Scotia and the adjoining Cape Breton Island; area 55,490 sq. km. (21,425 sq. miles); pop. (1991) 899,940; capital, Halifax. It was settled by the French in the early 18th c., who named it Acadia. It changed hands several times between the French and English before being awarded to Britain in 1713, when it was renamed and the French settlers expelled (mostly to Louisiana). It became a province of Canada in 1867. Iron, coal, steel, lumber, and fish are its chief products.
**Nova Scotian** adj. & n.

**Novaya Zemlya** /'nəʊvəjə ,zemlɪ'ɑ:/ two large uninhabited Russian islands in the Arctic Ocean off the north coast of Siberia; area 81,279 sq. km. (31,394 sq. miles). Covered in tundra vegetation and glaciers, the islands are a geological extension of the Ural Mts. The name means 'new land'.

**Novgorod** /'nɒvgərɒd/ a city in north-west Russia, on the Volkhov River; pop. (1990) 232,000. Claimed as Russia's oldest city, it was first chronicled in 859 and settled by the Varangian chief Rurik in 862, becoming one of the earliest Russian principalities. It was a major commercial and cultural centre of medieval eastern Europe, developing important trade links with Constantinople, the Baltic, Asia, and the rest of Europe. It was ruled by Alexander Nevski between 1238 and 1263. A rival with Moscow for supremacy during the 14th and 15th centuries, it was finally defeated by Ivan the Great in the 1470s. From the 17th c. the city became less prominent. Novgorod today has many light industries including chinaware, furniture, bricks, and food products.

**Novi Sad** /,nɒvi 'sɑ:t/ an industrial city in Serbia, on the River Danube, capital of the nominally autonomous province of Vojvodina; pop. (1991) 178,800. Suburban factories supply textiles, farm machinery, electrical goods, and chemicals.

**Novocherkassk** /,nəʊvətʃ3:'kɑ:sk/ an industrial city in western Russia, on a tributary of the Don north-east of Rostov; pop. (1990) 188,000. It makes locomotives, machine tools and machinery, chemicals, and electrical equipment.

**Novokuznetsk** /,nəʊvəkʊz'netsk/ a steel city in Russia with heavy industries, on the Tom River in the Kuznetz Basin of west Siberia; pop. (1990) 601,000. The original town of Kuznetsk was founded by Cossacks in 1617.

**Novomoskovsk** /,nəʊvəmə'skɒfsk/ an industrial city in western Russia, south of Moscow; pop. (1990) 146,000. It was named Bobriki until 1934 and Stalinogorsk until 1961. It has coal mines and chemical plants.

**Novorossiysk** /,nəʊvərə'si:sk/ a port and naval base founded in 1838 on the Black Sea coast of southern Russia, south-west of Krasnodar with shipyards and cement works; pop. (1990) 188,000.

**Novosibirsk** /ˌnəʊvəsɪ'bɪəsk/ an industrial city, capital of west Siberia, Russia, situated on the River Ob; pop. (1990) 1,443,000. Founded in 1893, it lies on the Trans-Siberian Railway, and grew rapidly during World War II when factories were moved east of the Urals. Today it has many industries and is furthermore a major scientific research centre.

**Nowa Huta** /'nəʊvə ˌhu:tə/ a suburb of Cracow in southern Poland, whose heavy industry was developed after World War II; pop. (1983) 200,000. Steel, iron, and metal products are manufactured. It is Europe's largest New Town.

**Nowra** /'naʊrə/ a tourist resort in eastern New South Wales, south-east Australia, on the south side of the Shoalhaven River to the south of Sydney; pop. (1991) 21,940 (with Bomaderry).

**Nubia** /'nju:bɪə/ an ancient region of southern Egypt and northern Sudan which includes the Nile valley between Aswan and Khartoum. Nubia fell under ancient Egyptian rule from the time of the Middle Kingdom, soon after 2,000 BC, and from about the 15th c. BC was ruled by an Egyptian viceroy. The country was Egyptianized, and trade (especially in gold) flourished. By the 8th c. BC, however, as Egypt's centralized administration disintegrated, an independent Nubian kingdom emerged, and for a brief period extended its power over Egypt. Nubia's capital about 600 BC was Meroe, near Khartoum. Much of Nubia is now drowned by the waters of Lake Nasser, formed by the building of the two dams at Aswan. Nubians constitute an ethnic minority group in Egypt. **Nubian** adj. & n.

**Nubian Desert** /'nju:bɪən/ the eastern part of the Sahara Desert lying between the Nile and the Red Sea in north-east Sudan.

**Nuer** /'nu:ə(r)/ a people of south-eastern Sudan speaking a language of the Nilotic sub-group of the Eastern Sudanic group of Nilo-Saharan languages.

**Nuevo Laredo** /'nweɪvəʊ læ'reɪdəʊ/ a city in the state of Tamaulipas in north-east Mexico, on the US border opposite Laredo; pop. (1990) 217,910. It lies on the Río Grande and is the northern terminus of the Inter-American Highway. It is a centre of international trade.

**Nuevo León** /ˌnweɪvəʊ leɪ'ɒn/ a state of north-east Mexico, on the border with the USA; area 64,924 sq. km. (25,077 sq. miles); pop. (1990) 3,086,470; capital, Monterrey.

**Nuku'alofa** /ˌnu:ku:ə'ləʊfə/ the capital of the Pacific island of Tonga, on the north coast of Tongatabu Island; pop. (1986) 29,020. The main industry is copra processing.

**Nuku Hiva** /ˌnu:kə 'hi:və/ a volcanic island in the South Pacific, the largest of the Marquesas Islands in French Polynesia; area 329 sq. km. (127 sq. miles).

**Nukus** /nu:'ku:s/ the capital of the Karakalpakstan region in the Central Asian republic of Uzbekistan, on the Amu Darya River; pop. (1990) 175,000. It has food-processing and repair industries.

**Nullarbor Plain** /'nʌləˌbɔ:(r)/ a vast arid plain in south-west Australia, comprising a slab of uplifted limestone that stretches inland from the Great Australian Bight. It contains no surface water, with sparse vegetation, and is almost uninhabited. Considered to be the world's largest flat surface in bedrock, its name was coined in 1865 from the Latin *nullus arbor* (= no tree). The Nullarbor Plain is crossed by the Eyre Highway and the Transcontinental Railway which includes the longest section of straight track in the world—500 km. (310 miles).

**Numazu** /nu:'mɑ:tsu:/ a city in Shizuoka prefecture in the Chubu region of central Honshu Island, Japan; pop. (1990) 211,730.

**Numidia** /nju:'mɪdɪə/ an ancient kingdom, later a Roman province, situated in North Africa in an area north of the Sahara corresponding roughly to present-day Algeria.

**nunatak** /'nʌnəˌtæk/ an isolated peak of rock projecting above a surface of land ice or snow, as in Greenland. The word is of Eskimo origin.

**Nunavut** /'nʌnəvu:t/ a semi-autonomous Inuit territory designated in the Northwest Territories of northern Canada in 1993 and scheduled to come into existence on 1 April 1999. It has an area of 46 million sq. km. (18 million sq. miles), equivalent to one-fifth of the Canadian land mass and is occupied by c. 18,000 Inuit who have been given substantial powers to control the exploitation of oil, gas, and mineral resources such as copper, lead, zinc, gold, and silver. Inuit are to own outright some 353,610 sq. km. (136,582 sq. miles) of the territory, the remainder being Crown Land over which they will have joint control with the Federal Government.

**Nuneaton** /nʌn'i:tən/ an industrial town in northern Warwickshire, central England, on the River Anker; pop. (1981) 81,880. The novelist George Eliot was born here in 1819. Local industries include textiles.

**Nuremberg** /'njʊərəmˌbɜ:g/ (German **Nürnberg** /'nʊənˌbeəg/) a city of Bavaria in southern Germany, on the Pegnitz River; pop. (1991) 497,500. It was a leading cultural centre in the 15th and 16th centuries, and was the home of Albrecht Dürer and Hans Sachs, and the setting of Wagner's opera *Die Meistersinger*. In the 1930s the Nazi Party congresses and the annual Nazi Party rallies were held there and in 1945–6 it was the scene of the Nuremberg war trials, in which Nazi war criminals were tried by international military tribunal. After the war the city centre was carefully reconstructed, as its cobbled streets and timbered houses had been reduced to rubble by Allied bombing. It is an important commercial and industrial centre manufacturing electrical equipment, machinery, and food products. It also has major publishing and printing establishments.

**Nuristan** a region of north-east Afghanistan in the Hindu Kush Mountains.

**Nürnberg** the German name for NUREMBERG.

**nusa** /ˈnuːsə/ an Indonesian word for an island.

**Nuuk** /nʊk/ the capital of Greenland, a port on the Davis Strait; pop. (1992) 12,750. It was known by the Danish name Godthåb until 1979 and is the oldest Danish settlement. It has fish canning and freezing plants.

**NY** *abbr.* US New York (in official postal use).

**Nyamlagira** /niːˌɑːmləˈɡɪərə/ an active volcano to the north of Lake Kivu in the Mount Virunga range, eastern Zaire. It rises to a height of 3,058 m. (10,033 ft.) north of Nyiragongo.

**Nyanza** /naɪˈænzə/ a province of north-west Kenya; area 12,526 sq. km. (4,838 sq. miles); pop. (est. 1987) 3,892,600; capital, Kisumu.

**Nyasa** /naɪˈæsə/, **Lake** (in Malawi **Lake Malawi**) a lake in east-central Africa, the third-largest lake in Africa; area 28,879 sq. km. (11,150 miles). About 580 km. (360 miles) long, it forms most of the eastern border of Malawi with Mozambique and Tanzania. Its name means 'lake'

and is due to a misunderstanding by the missionary-explorer David Livingstone who named the lake in 1859.

**Nyasaland** /naɪˈæsəˌlænd/ the former name of Malawi until it gained independence in 1966.

**Nyborg** /ˈnjuːbɔː(r)/ a port on the east coast of Fyn Island, Denmark, at the head of the Nybord Fjord; pop. (1990) 18,200.

**Nyiragongo** /niːˌɪrəˈɡɒŋɡəʊ/ a volcanic peak in the Mount Virunga range, eastern Zaire. Rising to a height of 3,070 m. (10,072 ft.) to the north of Lake Kivu, it is the second-highest active volcano in Africa after Mount Cameroon.

**Nyiregyháza** /ˌnjiːrəˈdʒɑːzəʊ/ a market town in eastern Hungary, capital of Szabolcs-Szátmar-Bereg county; pop. (1993) 115,280.

**Nykøbing** /ˈnjuːkɜːpɪŋ/ a port on the west coast of the Danish island of Falster, capital of Storstrøm county; pop. (1990) 25,210.

**Nyköping** /ˈnjuːtʃɜːpɪŋ/ a port on the Baltic Sea, capital of Södermanland county in south-east Sweden; pop. (1990) 65,900. An atomic research centre is nearby.

**Nyslott** the Swedish name for SAVONLINNA.

**NZ** *abbr.* New Zealand.

# O o

**Oahu** /əʊˈɑːhuː/ an island of Hawaii in the Pacific Ocean, between the islands of Molokai and Kauai; area 1,526 sq. km. (589 sq. miles); pop. (est. 1988) 838,500. Its chief town is Honolulu. Tourism and the production of sugar and pineapples are major industries. It is the third-largest of the Hawaiian islands and chief island of the state. It is the site, at Pearl Harbor, of a US naval base, which suffered a surprise attack by the Japanese in December 1941 which brought the US into World War II.

**Oakland** /ˈəʊklənd/ an industrial port on the east side of San Francisco Bay in western California, USA; pop. (1990) 372,240. It was the birthplace of the American novelist Jack London (1876–1916). Industries include electronics, cars, shipbuilding, and chemicals.

**Oak Lawn** a town in north-east Illinois, USA, a suburb of Chicago; pop. (1990) 56,180. Originally known as Black Oaks Grove, a permanent settlement named Oak Lawn was established in 1882 after the building of the railroad.

**Oak Park** a town in Illinois, USA, a western suburb of Chicago; pop. (1990) 53,650. It was the birthplace of Ernest Hemingway in 1899 and the home of the architect Frank Lloyd Wright from 1889 to 1909.

**Oak Ridge** a city in east Tennessee, USA, on the Black Oak Ridge and the Clinch River, built during World War II to house people working on the production of uranium 235 for the world's first atomic bomb; pop. (1990) 27,310. Derestricted in 1949, it is now the home of the American Museum of Science and Energy.

**Oakville** /ˈəʊkvɪl/ a town in south-east Ontario, Canada, on Lake Ontario south-west of Toronto; pop. (1991) 114,700.

**oasis** /əʊˈeɪsɪs/ (pl. **oases**) a fertile spot in a desert where water is found.

**OAS** *abbr.* ORGANIZATION OF AMERICAN STATES.

**OAU** *abbr.* ORGANIZATION OF AFRICAN UNITY.

**Oaxaca** /wəˈhɑːkə/ **1.** a state of southern Mexico between Chiapas and the Pacific Ocean; area 93,952 sq. km. (36,289 sq. miles); pop. (1990) 3,021,510. **2.** (in full **Oaxaca de Juárez**) its capital, a city in the Sierra Madre del Sur founded by the Aztecs in 1486; pop. (1990) 212,940. It was the home town of Benito Juárez and Porfirio Díaz, former presidents of Mexico and is a commercial and tourist centre. It is known for its jewellery and ceramics.

**Ob** /ɒb/ the principal river of the west Siberian lowlands and one of the largest rivers in Russia. Rising in the Altai Mountains, it flows generally north and west for 3,650 km. (2,287 miles) before entering the **Gulf of Ob** (or Ob Bay), an inlet of the Kara Sea and part of the Arctic Ocean. Its chief tributary is the Irtysh River and its length with that river is 5,411 km. (3,362 miles). The river is frozen for six months of the year but is nevertheless an important trade and transport route. Flooding occurs annually in its middle section.

**Oban** /ˈəʊbən/ a small port and tourist resort on the west coast of Scotland opposite the island of Mull; pop. (1981) 8,110. There are ferry services to the Inner and Outer Hebrides.

**Obed National Scenic River** /ˈəʊbed/ a park on the Cumberland Plateau in the state of Tennessee, established in 1976 to preserve the scenic beauty of the gorges on the Obed River and its tributaries, Clear Creek and Daddy Creek. The rivers are noted for their white-water canoeing in winter.

**Oberammergau** /ˌəʊbəˈræməˌɡaʊ/ a village in the Bavarian Alps of south-west Germany, site of the most famous of the few surviving Passion plays. It has been performed every tenth year (with few exceptions) from 1634 as a result of a vow made during an epidemic of the plague, and remains entirely amateur, the villagers dividing the parts among themselves and being responsible also for the production, music, costumes, and scenery; pop. (1983) 4,800.

**Oberhausen** /ˈəʊbəˌhaʊzən/ a city of western Germany, in the Ruhr valley of North Rhine-Westphalia with heavy industries including iron and steel, machinery, and chemicals; pop. (1991) 224,560.

**Oberland** /ˈəʊbəˌlɑːnt/ **1.** a name used in German-speaking countries to describe mountainous or upland regions as in the Swiss Bernese Oberland. **2.** one of the two districts of Liechtenstein, an upland region separated from the Unterland district by a broad plain. It was formerly a separate Lordship until united with Unterland by the Princes of Liechtenstein in 1719.

**Oberösterreich** the German name for UPPER AUSTRIA.

**Obihiro** /ˌəʊbiːˈhɪərəʊ/ a city on the island of Hokkaido, northern Japan, situated to the south-west of the Daisetsuzan National Park; pop. (1990) 167,390.

**oblast** /'ɒblɑːst/ a first order administrative division in Russia equivalent to a region. There are 49 oblasts and one autonomous oblast in Russia.

**Occident** a literary term used to describe Europe, America, or both, as distinct from the Orient.

**Occitan** /'ɒksɪt(ə)n/ the Provençale language. **Occitanian** *adj. & n.*

**Oceania** /ˌəʊʃɪ'ɑːnɪə/ the islands of the central and south Pacific and adjacent seas lying between the Tropic of Cancer in the north and the southern tip of New Zealand in the south. It includes the islands of Australia, New Zealand, Polynesia (French Polynesia, Line Islands, Pitcairn, Samoa, Tonga, and Tuvalu), Micronesia (Caroline Islands, Guam, Kiribati, the Marianas, and Marshall Islands), and Melanesia (Fiji, New Caledonia, Papua New Guinea, Solomon Islands, Vanuatu); area 8,500,000 sq. km. (3,300,000 sq. miles).

**oceanic ridge** that part of the ocean floor through which magma rises from the centre of the earth. A mid-oceanic ridge stretches the length of the Atlantic Ocean from north to south.

**Ocean Island** see BANABA.

**oceanography** /ˌəʊʃən'ɒgrəfɪ/ the study of the oceans, including their shape, depth, distribution, ecology, water currents, and legal status.

**Oceanside** /ˌəʊʃən'saɪd/ a resort city and agricultural trading centre north of San Diego on the Pacific coast of southern California, USA; pop. (1990) 128,400.

**ocean trench** a deep depression in the ocean floor at a subduction zone where one tectonic plate dives beneath another.

**Odawara** /ˌəʊdə'wɑːrə/ a city to the south-east of Tokyo in Kanagawa prefecture, south-east Honshu Island, central Japan; pop. (1990) 193,415. It is a gateway to the Izu peninsula.

**Odden Feature** /'ɒd(ə)n/ a tongue-shaped sheet of ice at the edge of the Arctic, between the Jan Mayen Islands and Svalbard, capable, along with two other sites in Labrador and Antarctica, of removing up to one-fifth of the earth's carbon dioxide which is dissolved in its surface water. During winter, salt discharged from this surface water sinks to the seabed along with the dissolved carbon dioxide. It was noticed in the 1980s that warmer Arctic water was reducing the capacity of this feature to act as a 'natural plughole' swallowing much of the carbon dioxide caused by air pollution.

**Odense** /əʊ'densə/ a port in eastern Denmark on the island of Fyn, the third-largest city in the country; pop. (1991) 177,640. It was the birthplace of the Danish author Hans Andersen in 1805. It is linked by ship canal to Odense Fjord where there is a major shipyard. It has sugar-refining and food-processing industries.

**Oder** /'əʊdə(r)/ (Czech and Polish **Odra** /'əʊdrə/) a river of central Europe which rises in the Sudetes Mountains in the west of the Czech Republic and flows 907 km. (567 miles) northwards through western Poland to meet the River Neisse where it forms the border between Poland and Germany before emptying into the Baltic Sea. This frontier, known as the Oder–Neisse Line, was adopted at the Potsdam Conference in 1945.

**Odessa** /əʊ'desə/ (Ukrainian **Odesa**) a city and port on the south coast of Ukraine, on the Black Sea; pop. (1990) 1,106,400. It is a resort as well as a commercial and naval port and was the scene of the 1905 workers' revolution led by sailors from the battleship *Potemkin*. It is the home base of the Russian whaling fleet; its industries include steel, shipbuilding, chemicals, and food processing.

**Odessa** /əʊ'desə/ a city in west Texas, USA; pop. (1990) 89,700. An oilfield supply centre for the surrounding Permian Basin, it also has liquefied petroleum, petrochemical, synthetic rubber, and cement plants.

**Odienné** /əʊ'djenei/ a historic town in the northern savanna of the Ivory Coast, formerly capital of the Kabadougou empire. It was founded by Vakaba Touré in the 19th c.

**odometer** /əʊ'dɒmɪtə(r)/ (also **hodometer** /hɒ/) an instrument for measuring the distance travelled by a wheeled vehicle.

**Odra** the Czech and Polish name for the ODER.

**Odra** /'əʊdrə/ an ancient region of eastern India corresponding to the state of Orissa.

**OECD** *abbr.* ORGANIZATION FOR ECONOMIC CO-OPERATION AND DEVELOPMENT.

**Offaly** /'ɒf(ə)lɪ/ a county of the Republic of Ireland, in the province of Leinster, east of the River Shannon; area 1,997 sq. km. (771 sq. miles); pop. (1991) 58,450; capital, Tullamore.

**Offa's Dyke** /'ɒfəz daɪk/ a series of earthworks running the length of the Welsh border from near the mouth of the Wye to near the mouth of the Dee, built or repaired by Offa (king of Mercia 757–96) to mark the boundary established by his wars with the Welsh.

**Offenbach am Main** /'ɒfɪnbɑːx æm maɪn/ an industrial city in the state of Hesse, west Germany, on the River Main; pop. (1991) 115,790. Noted for its leather craft, the city's chief landmark is a 16th-c. Renaissance palace. It is also the headquarters of the German Meteorological Service.

**Ogaden** /ˌɒgə'den, 'ɒg-/ a desert region in south-east Ethiopia, largely inhabited by Somali nomads. Successive governments of neighbouring Somalia have laid claim to the territory which they call Western Somalia.

**Ogaki** /əʊ'gɑːkiː/ a city in Gifu prefecture, west-central Honshu Island, Japan, to the west of Gifu; pop. (1990) 148,280.

**Ogbomosho** /ˌɒgbə'məʊʃəʊ/ a Yoruba city and agricultural market in south-west Nigeria, north of Ibadan; pop. (1983) 527,000.

**Ogden** /'ɒgdən/ a city in northern Utah, USA, at the junction of the Weber and Ogden rivers; pop. (1990) 63,910. Established as a trading post in the 1820s, it was settled by Mormons in 1847. Ogden is now a centre of the aerospace industry.

**Ogooué** /əʊgəʊ'weɪ/ a river of equatorial West Africa that rises in the Batéké plateau in south-west Congo and flows westwards for 900 km. (562 miles) to empty into the Gulf of Guinea near Port Gentil in Gabon.

**OH** *abbr.* US Ohio (in official postal use).

**O'Hare International Airport** an international airport to the north-west of the US city of Chicago. Covering an area of 243 sq. km. (94 sq. miles) and with a take-off or landing every 40 seconds, it is one of the world's busiest airports.

**Ohio** /əʊ'haɪəʊ/ a state in the north-eastern US, bordering on Lake Erie; area 107,044 sq. km. (41,330 sq. miles); pop. (1990) 10,847,115; capital, Columbus. The largest cities are Columbus, Cleveland, Cincinnati, and Toledo. Ohio is also known as the Buckeye State. Acquired by Britain from France in 1763 and by the US in 1783, it became the 17th state of the US in 1803. It is a leading industrial state, producing motor vehicles, steel, rubber, and machinery and is rich in natural resources such as coal, oil, clay, salt, gypsum, and cement. Landmarks include the Cuyahoga Valley National Recreation Area, the Indian burials at Mound Group National Monument, Perry's Victory and International Peace Memorial, and the homes of Presidents Garfield, Grant, Harding, Hayes, and Taft. Ohio is divided into 88 counties:

| County | Area (sq. km.) | Pop. (1990) | County Seat |
| --- | --- | --- | --- |
| Adams | 1,524 | 25,370 | West Union |
| Allen | 1,053 | 109,755 | Lima |
| Ashland | 1,102 | 47,510 | Ashland |
| Ashtabula | 1,828 | 99,820 | Jefferson |
| Athens | 1,321 | 59,550 | Athens |
| Auglaize | 1,035 | 44,585 | Wapakoneta |
| Belmont | 1,396 | 71,070 | Saint Clairsville |
| Brown | 1,282 | 34,970 | Georgetown |
| Butler | 1,222 | 291,480 | Hamilton |
| Carroll | 1,022 | 26,520 | Carrollton |
| Champaign | 1,115 | 36,020 | Urbana |
| Clark | 1,035 | 147,550 | Springfield |
| Clermont | 1,186 | 150,190 | Batavia |
| Clinton | 1,066 | 35,415 | Wilmington |
| Columbiana | 1,388 | 108,280 | Lisbon |
| Coshocton | 1,472 | 35,430 | Coshocton |
| Crawford | 1,048 | 47,870 | Bucyrus |
| Cuyahoga | 1,193 | 1,412,140 | Cleveland |
| Darke | 1,560 | 53,620 | Greenville |
| Defiance | 1,076 | 39,350 | Defiance |
| Delaware | 1,152 | 66,930 | Delaware |
| Erie | 686 | 76,780 | Sandusky |
| Fairfield | 1,316 | 103,460 | Lancaster |
| Fayette | 1,053 | 27,470 | Washington Court House |
| Franklin | 1,412 | 961,440 | Columbus |
| Fulton | 1,058 | 38,500 | Wauseon |
| Gallia | 1,225 | 30,950 | Gallipolis |
| Geauga | 1,061 | 81,130 | Chardon |
| Greene | 1,082 | 136,730 | Xenia |
| Guernsey | 1,357 | 39,020 | Cambridge |
| Hamilton | 1,071 | 866,230 | Cincinnati |
| Hancock | 1,383 | 65,540 | Findlay |
| Hardin | 1,225 | 31,110 | Kenton |
| Harrison | 1,040 | 16,085 | Cadiz |
| Henry | 1,079 | 29,110 | Napoleon |
| Highland | 1,438 | 35,730 | Hillsboro |
| Hocking | 1,100 | 25,530 | Logan |
| Holmes | 1,102 | 32,850 | Millersburg |
| Huron | 1,284 | 56,240 | Norwalk |
| Jackson | 1,092 | 30,230 | Jackson |
| Jefferson | 1,066 | 80,300 | Steubenville |
| Knox | 1,375 | 47,470 | Mount Vernon |
| Lake | 601 | 215,500 | Painesville |
| Lawrence | 1,188 | 61,830 | Ironton |
| Licking | 1,784 | 128,300 | Newark |
| Logan | 1,191 | 42,310 | Bellefontaine |
| Lorain | 1,287 | 271,130 | Elyria |
| Lucas | 887 | 462,360 | Toledo |
| Madison | 1,214 | 37,070 | London |
| Mahoning | 1,084 | 264,810 | Youngstown |
| Marion | 1,048 | 64,270 | Marion |
| Medina | 1,097 | 122,350 | Medina |
| Meigs | 1,123 | 22,990 | Pomeroy |
| Mercer | 1,188 | 39,440 | Celina |
| Miami | 1,066 | 93,180 | Troy |
| Monroe | 1,188 | 15,500 | Woodsfield |
| Montgomery | 1,191 | 573,810 | Dayton |
| Morgan | 1,092 | 14,190 | McConnelsville |
| Morrow | 1,056 | 27,750 | Mount Gilead |
| Muskingum | 1,700 | 82,070 | Zanesville |
| Noble | 1,037 | 11,340 | Caldwell |
| Ottawa | 658 | 40,030 | Port Clinton |
| Paulding | 1,089 | 20,490 | Paulding |
| Perry | 1,071 | 31,560 | New Lexington |
| Pickaway | 1,308 | 48,255 | Circleville |
| Pike | 1,152 | 24,250 | Waverly |
| Portage | 1,282 | 142,585 | Ravenna |
| Preble | 1,108 | 40,110 | Eaton |
| Putnam | 1,258 | 33,820 | Ottawa |
| Richland | 1,292 | 126,140 | Mansfield |
| Ross | 1,799 | 69,330 | Chillicothe |
| Sandusky | 1,063 | 61,960 | Fremont |
| Scioto | 1,594 | 80,240 | Portsmouth |
| Seneca | 1,438 | 59,730 | Tifin |
| Shelby | 1,063 | 44,915 | Sidney |
| Stark | 1,492 | 367,585 | Canton |
| Summit | 1,071 | 514,990 | Akron |
| Trumbull | 1,591 | 227,810 | Warren |
| Tuscarawas | 1,482 | 84,090 | New Philadelphia |
| Union | 1,136 | 31,970 | Marysville |
| Van Wert | 1,066 | 30,460 | Van Wert |
| Vinton | 1,076 | 11,100 | McArthur |
| Warren | 1,048 | 113,910 | Lebanon |
| Washington | 1,664 | 62,250 | Marietta |
| Wayne | 1,448 | 101,460 | Wooster |
| Williams | 1,097 | 36,960 | Bryan |
| Wood | 1,609 | 113,270 | Bowling Green |
| Wyandot | 1,056 | 22,250 | Upper Sandusky |

**Ohio** a major river of east-central USA that is formed at the junction of the Allegheny and Monongahela rivers at Pittsburgh, Pennsylvania. It flows 1,578 km. (981 miles) generally south-westwards past Cincinnati to join the Mississippi at the frontier between the states of Illinois, Kentucky, and Missouri. From its source at the head of the Allegheny River it is 2,101 km. (1,306 miles) long.

**Ohrid** /ˈɒxrɪd/, **Lake** a lake in south-east Europe on the frontier between Albania and the former Yugoslav republic of Macedonia; area 350 sq. km. (135 sq. miles). The Macedonian town of Ohrid lies on its eastern shore.

**Oise** /wɑːz/ **1.** a river in northern France and Belgium that rises in the Ardennes and flows 302 km. (189 miles) south-westwards to meet the Seine near Andresy. **2.** a department in the Picardy region of northern France; area 5,860 sq. km. (2,263 sq. miles); pop. (1990) 725,600; capital, Beauvais.

**Oita** /əʊˈiːtə/ the capital of Oita prefecture on the island of Kyushu, southern Japan, situated on Beppu Bay; pop. (1990) 408,500. It is linked by ferry to Hiroshima, Matsuyama, and Kobe. It is a manufacturing centre and distribution point for agricultural products.

**Ojibwa** /əʊˈdʒɪbweɪ/ see CHIPPEWA.

**Ojos del Salado** /əʊˌhəʊz del səˈlɑːdəʊ/ a volcanic peak rising to 6,908 m. (22,661 ft.) on the frontier between Chile and Argentina, west of San Miguel de Tucumán.

**OK** *abbr.* US Oklahoma (in official postal use).

**Okanagan** /əʊkəˈnɑːgən/, **the** a resort area in the western foothills of the Columbia Mountains of southern British Columbia, western Canada. Dominated by **Lake Okanagan** and drained by the **Okanagan River**, the region is noted for fruit-growing and wine production. Its chief settlements are Oliver, Penticton, Kelowna, and Vernon.

**Okara** /əʊˈkɑːrə/ a commercial city in north-east Pakistan, in Punjab province south-west of Lahore; pop. (1981) 154,000. It produces textiles and trades in cotton, grain, and oilseed.

**Okavango** /ˌəʊkəˈvæŋgəʊ/ (Angolan **Cubango** /kjuːˈbæŋgəʊ/) a river of south-west Africa which rises in central Angola, as the Cubango, and flows *c.* 1,600 km. (1,000 miles) south-eastwards to Namibia, where it turns eastwards to form part of the border between Angola and Namibia before entering Botswana, where it drains into the extensive Okavango marshes of Ngamiland.

**Okayama** /ˌəʊkəˈjɑːmə/ an industrial city and major railway junction on the south-west coast of Honshu Island, south-west Japan, the capital of Okayama prefecture; pop.(1990) 593,740. Its industries include textiles, chemicals, machinery, rubber goods, and traditional *tatami* straw mats.

**Okazaki** /ˌəʊkəˈzɑːkiː/ a city in Aichi prefecture, south Honshu Island, Japan, south-east of Nagoya; pop. (1990) 306,820.

**Okeechobee** /ˌəʊkəˈtʃəʊbiː/, **Lake** a lake in southern Florida, USA; area *c.* 1,815 sq. km. (700 sq. miles). Fed by the Kissimmee river from the north, it drains into the Everglades in the south, this drainage being controlled by embankments and canals. It forms part of the 250-km. (155-mile) Okeechobee Waterway, which crosses the Florida peninsula from west to east, linking the Gulf of Mexico with the Atlantic.

**Okefenokee Swamp** /ˌəʊkəfəˈnəʊkiː/ an area of swampland in south-east Georgia and north-east Florida, USA; area *c.* 1,555 sq. km. (600 sq. miles).

**Okhotsk** /əʊˈxɒtsk/, **Sea of** an inlet of the North Pacific Ocean off the east coast of mainland Russia, bounded to the east by the Kamchatka peninsula and to the south-east by the Kuril Islands which stretch in a long line from Kamchatka to the north-east corner of the Japanese island of Hokkaido. Magadan is the chief port. There is an offshore oilfield but operations are hampered by winter fogs and ice.

**Okinawa** /əʊkˈnɑːwə/ **1.** a region of southern Japan in the southern Ryuku Islands; area 2,246 sq. km. (867 sq. miles); pop. (1990) 1,222,000; capital, Naha. **2.** the largest of the Ryuku (Nansei) Islands, in southern Japan. It was captured from the Japanese in World War II by a US assault in April–June 1945. With its bases commanding the approaches to Japan it was a key objective. After the war it was retained under US administration until 1972.

**Oklahoma** /ˌəʊkləˈhəʊmə/ a state in south-central USA, lying west of Arkansas and north of Texas; area 181,186 sq. km. (69,956 sq. miles); pop. (1990) 3,145,585; capital, Oklahoma City. The largest cities are Oklahoma City and Tulsa. Oklahoma is also known as the Sooner State (so-called from those who entered before April 1889—the set time for legal settlement). It was acquired from the French as part of the Louisiana Purchase in 1803 and during 1834–89 was declared Indian Territory in which Europeans were forbidden to settle. It became the 46th state of the US in 1907. Oklahoma produces large quantities of natural gas, oil, coal, limestone, wheat, cotton, peanuts, and livestock products. Its chief landmarks are the Chickasaw National Recreation Area, the Gibson Stockade near Muskogee, and the Cherokee Cultural Center. Oklahoma is divided into 77 counties:

| County | Area (sq. km.) | Pop. (1990) | County Seat |
| --- | --- | --- | --- |
| Adair | 1,500 | 18,420 | Stillwell |
| Alfalfa | 2,246 | 6,420 | Cherokee |
| Atoka | 2,548 | 12,780 | Atoka |
| Beaver | 4,701 | 6,020 | Beaver |
| Beckham | 2,350 | 18,810 | Sayre |
| Blaine | 2,392 | 11,470 | Watonga |
| Bryan | 2,345 | 32,090 | Durant |

| | | | |
|---|---|---|---|
| Caddo | 3,344 | 29,550 | Anadarko |
| Canadian | 2,343 | 74,410 | El Reno |
| Carter | 2,153 | 42,920 | Ardmore |
| Cherokee | 1,945 | 34,050 | Tahlequah |
| Choctaw | 1,981 | 15,300 | Hugo |
| Cimarron | 4,789 | 3,300 | Boise City |
| Cleveland | 1,375 | 174,250 | Norman |
| Coal | 1,352 | 5,780 | Coalgate |
| Comanche | 2,798 | 111,490 | Lawton |
| Cotton | 1,706 | 6,650 | Walters |
| Craig | 1,984 | 14,100 | Vinita |
| Creek | 2,418 | 60,915 | Sapulpa |
| Custer | 2,551 | 26,900 | Arapaho |
| Delaware | 1,872 | 28,070 | Jay |
| Dewey | 2,618 | 5,550 | Taloga |
| Ellis | 3,203 | 4,500 | Arnett |
| Garfield | 2,756 | 56,735 | Enid |
| Garvin | 2,114 | 26,605 | Pauls Valley |
| Grady | 2,876 | 41,750 | Chickasha |
| Grant | 2,610 | 5,690 | Medford |
| Greer | 1,659 | 6,560 | Mangum |
| Harmon | 1,396 | 3,790 | Hollis |
| Harper | 2,701 | 4,060 | Buffalo |
| Haskell | 1,482 | 10,940 | Stigler |
| Hughes | 2,096 | 13,020 | Holdenville |
| Jackson | 2,124 | 28,760 | Altus |
| Jefferson | 1,999 | 7,010 | Waurika |
| Johnston | 1,661 | 10,030 | Tishomingo |
| Kay | 2,395 | 48,060 | Newkirk |
| Kingfisher | 2,356 | 13,210 | Kingfisher |
| Kiowa | 2,649 | 11,350 | Hobart |
| Latimer | 1,893 | 10,330 | Wilburton |
| Le Flore | 4,121 | 43,270 | Poteau |
| Lincoln | 2,506 | 29,220 | Chandler |
| Logan | 1,945 | 29,010 | Guthrie |
| Love | 1,349 | 8,160 | Marietta |
| Major | 2,491 | 8,055 | Fairview |
| Marshall | 967 | 10,830 | Madill |
| Mayes | 1,674 | 33,370 | Pryor |
| McClain | 1,513 | 22,795 | Purcell |
| McCurtain | 4,748 | 33,430 | Idabel |
| McIntosh | 1,557 | 16,780 | Eufaula |
| Murray | 1,092 | 12,040 | Sulphur |
| Muskogee | 2,119 | 68,080 | Muskogee |
| Noble | 1,914 | 11,045 | Perry |
| Nowata | 1,404 | 9,920 | Nowata |
| Okfuskee | 1,633 | 11,550 | Okemah |
| Oklahoma | 1,841 | 599,610 | Oklahoma City |
| Okmulgee | 1,815 | 36,490 | Okmulgee |
| Osage | 5,889 | 41,645 | Pawhuska |
| Ottawa | 1,209 | 30,560 | Miami |
| Pawnee | 1,433 | 15,575 | Pawnee |
| Payne | 1,797 | 61,510 | Stillwater |
| Pittsburg | 3,253 | 40,580 | McAlester |
| Pontotoc | 1,864 | 34,120 | Ada |
| Pottawatomie | 2,036 | 58,760 | Shawnee |
| Pushmataha | 3,684 | 11,000 | Antlers |
| Roger Mills | 2,980 | 4,150 | Cheyenne |
| Rogers | 1,776 | 55,170 | Claremore |
| Seminole | 1,661 | 25,410 | Wewoka |
| Sequoyah | 1,763 | 33,830 | Sallisaw |
| Stephens | 2,298 | 42,300 | Duncan |
| Texas | 5,304 | 16,420 | Guyman |
| Tillman | 2,350 | 10,380 | Frederick |
| Tulsa | 1,487 | 503,340 | Tulsa |

| | | | |
|---|---|---|---|
| Wagoner | 1,453 | 47,880 | Wagoner |
| Washington | 1,100 | 48,070 | Bartlesville |
| Washita | 2,616 | 11,440 | Cordell |
| Woods | 3,357 | 9,100 | Alva |
| Woodward | 3,229 | 18,480 | Woodward |

**Oklahoma City** the state capital of Oklahoma, USA, on the North Canadian River; pop. (1990) 444,720. First settled during the land rush of 1889, the city is situated on one of the country's largest oilfields, first discovered in 1928. Its chief industries are meat-packing, grain-milling, cotton-processing, and the manufacture of iron, steel, electronics, and oil equipment. Oklahoma City's Metro Concourse is one of the most extensive enclosed pedestrian systems in the US and its stockyards are one of the world's largest cattle markets.

**okrug** /ˈɒkrəg/ an administrative division of Russia subordinate to an autonomous republic, kray (territory), or oblast (region).

**Öland** /ˈɜːlænd/ a narrow island in the Baltic Sea, off the south-east coast of Sweden from which it is separated by the Kalmar Sound. It is the largest Swedish island and lies in the county of Kalmar; area 1,344 sq. km. (519 sq. miles). It is a popular holiday resort and has a fishing fleet, sheep farms, and limestone quarries.

**Olathe** /oʊˈleɪθə/ a city in north-east Kansas, USA, south-west of Kansas City; pop. (1990) 63,352. Manufactures include avionics, batteries, and machinery.

**Old Bailey** the Central Criminal Court, formerly standing in an ancient bailey of London city wall. The present court, trying offences committed in the City and the Greater London Area, and certain other offences, was built in 1903–6 on the site of Newgate Prison.

**Old Delhi** see DELHI.

**Old Dominion** a name adopted by the colony of Virginia after it had been raised to the status of Dominion by Charles II for its prompt recognition of him after his restoration to the throne in 1660.

**Oldenburg** /ˈoʊld(ə)nbʊə(r)k/ a market town and river port in Lower Saxony, north-west Germany, on the River Hunte west of Bremen; pop. (1991) 145,160. It lies on the Coastal Canal and has a university founded in 1970. Oldenburg was formerly the residence of the counts of Ammerland and from 1918 to 1933 was capital of the state of Oldenburg.

**Oldham** /ˈoʊldəm/ an industrial town in Greater Manchester, north-west England, north-east of Manchester; pop. (1991) 100,000. Its industries produce textiles and electronics.

**Old Kent Road, the** a road in the south London borough of Southwark at the traditional beginning of the route to Dover on the south coast of England and then to Europe. Celebrated in song, the street was frequented by Cockney street-traders.

**Ol Doinyo Lengai** /ˈəʊl ˌdɔɪmjəʊ leŋˈgaɪ/ an active volcano in Tanzania, on the eastern edge of the Serengeti Plain to the south of Lake Natron. It rises to 2,856 m. (9,370 ft.) and is the only volcano in the world to emit lava formed of ash and carbonatite (which becomes washing soda on contact with moist air). Its name in Masai means 'Mountain of God'.

**Old Sarum** /ˈseɪrəm/ a hill in Wiltshire, southern England, 3 km. (2 miles) north of Salisbury. It was the site of an ancient Iron Age settlement and hill fort which was later occupied by Romans, Saxons, and Normans who built a castle and a town. It became a bishopric but fell into decline after a dispute in 1220 when the new cathedral and town of Salisbury were established to the south. The site of Old Sarum became deserted and the original cathedral was demolished in 1331. Until the Reform Act of 1832 Old Sarum was a 'rotten borough' with only a handful of electors, returning two Members of Parliament.

**Olduvai Gorge** /ˈɒldʊˌvaɪ/ a gorge in Northern Tanzania, 48 km. (30 miles) long and up to 90 metres (300 ft.) deep. The exposed strata contain numerous fossils spanning the full range of the Pleistocene period. Most importantly, the Gorge has provided the longest sequence of hominid presence and activity yet discovered anywhere in the world, with fossils, stone-tool industries, and other evidence of hominid activities that date from c.2.1—1.7 million years ago for the oldest dated deposits to c.22,000 years ago for the most recent fossil-bearing deposits. The hominids found at individual sites within the gorge include *Australopithecus boisei* (the *Zinjanthropus* fossils), *Homo habilis*, and *Homo erectus*.

**Old Vic** the popular name of a London theatre, opened in 1818 as the Royal Coburg and renamed the Royal Victoria Theatre in honour of Princess (later Queen) Victoria in 1833. Under the management of Lilian Baylis from 1912 it gained an enduring reputation for its Shakespearean productions.

**Old World** a term generally applied to Europe, Asia, and Africa, or that part of the world known by the ancients to exist.

**Olenek** /ˈɒlənˌjək/ (also **Olenyok**) a river of Russia that rises in the central Siberian plateau and flows c.2,175 km. (1,350 miles) generally north-east through Yakutia (Sakha) before joining the Laptev Sea.

**Oléron** /ɒleɪˈrɒn/ a French resort island in the Bay of Biscay, off the coast of the department of Charente-Maritime, opposite the mouth of the River Charente; area 176 sq. km. (68 sq. miles). Noted for its oysters, it is the largest island in the Bay of Biscay. Its chief towns are St.-Pierre d'Oléron and the port of Le Chateau d'Oléron.

**Olgas** /ˈɒlgəs/, **the** a range of mountains in Northern Territory, central Australia, comprising 36 red rock domes made of boulders and pebbles.

The tallest dome is Mount Olga (550 m., 1,800 ft.) which is the highest point in the Uluru National Park.

**Oligocene** /ˈɒlɪgəʊˌsiːn/ a geological period of time equivalent to the third epoch of the Tertiary period, following the Miocene, lasting from about 38 to 24.6 million years ago. It was a time of falling world temperatures and evolution of many mammal species.

**Olinda** /əʊˈlɪndə/ a historic city in the state of Pernambuco, Brazil, situated on the east coast 6 km. (4 miles) north of Recife; pop. (1990) 336,170. It is a cultural centre with many fine old colonial buildings. To the north are the beaches of Praias Maria Farinha, Janga, and Pao Amarelo.

**Olives** /ˈɒlɪvz/, **Mount of** the highest point in the range of hills to the east of Jerusalem. It is a holy place for both Judaism and Christianity and frequently mentioned in the Bible. The Garden of Gethsemane is located nearby and its slopes have been a sacred Jewish burial ground for centuries.

**Olmec** /ˈɒlmek/ **1.** a member of a prehistoric people inhabiting the coast of Veracruz and western Tabasco on the Gulf of Mexico c.1200–100 BC, who established what was probably the first developed civilization of Mesoamerica. They are noted for their sculptures, especially the massive stone-hewn heads with realistic features and round helmets, and small jade carvings featuring a jaguar. **2.** a member of a native American people living in the highlands of Mexico or migrating to the Gulf coast during the 12th c. Their name is derived from a Nahuatl word meaning 'people of the rubber (-tree) country'.

**Olmos** /ˈɒlmɒs/ a small town on the eastern edge of the Sechura Desert in north-west Peru, which gave its name to a major irrigation project initiated in 1926 for the purpose of increasing cotton and sugar production in the arid lowlands of this region.

**Olomouc** /ˌɒlɒˈmaʊts/ an industrial city of North Moravia in the Czech Republic, on the Morava River; pop. (1991) 105,690. Made a royal town in 1253, it was capital of Moravia from 1187 to 1641. Its university was founded in 1566 and it has engineering and food-processing industries.

**Olsztyn** /ˈɔːlˈʃtɪn/ a city in northern Poland, in the lakeland area of Masuria, capital of a county of the same name; pop. (1990) 163,935. Founded in 1348 by the Teutonic knights, it was ceded to Poland in 1466 and became a part of Prussia in 1772. It was returned to Poland in 1945 and is a manufacturing and railway centre.

**Olt** /ɒlt/ a river in southern Romania that rises in the Carpathians and flows southwards for 557 km. (348 miles) to join the Danube near Turnu Măgurele on the Bulgarian frontier.

**Olvera Street** /ɒlˈviːrə/ a historic street at the heart of the original settlement of Los Angeles in the US state of California, restored as a Mexican market place in 1930. Built in 1818, the Avila Adobe is the oldest residential dwelling in Los Angeles.

**Olympia** /ə'lɪmpɪə/ a plain in Greece, in the western Peloponnese. In ancient Greece it was the site of the chief sanctuary of the god Zeus, the venue of the pan-Hellenic Olympic Games (the original Olympic Games), after which the site is named.

**Olympia** /ə'lɪmpɪə/ the capital of the US state of Washington, a port on Puget Sound; pop. (1990) 33,840. Founded in 1850 at the end of the Oregon Trail it became capital of Washington Territory in 1853.

**Olympus** /ə'lɪmpəs/, **Mount 1.** a mountain in Cyprus, in the Troodos range. Rising to 1,951 m. (6,400 ft.), it is the highest peak on the island. **2.** (Greek **Olimbos**) a mountain in north-east Greece at the eastern end of the range dividing Thessaly from Macedonia. In Greek mythology it was the home of the gods and the court of Zeus; height 2,917 m. (9,570 ft.).

**Omagh** /'əʊmɑ:/ the county town of Tyrone, Northern Ireland, situated amidst outlying hills of the Sperrin Mountains where the Drumragh and Camowen rivers join to form the Strule; pop. (1981) 14,630. To the north is the Ulster-American Folk Park.

**Omaha** /'əʊmə,hɑ:/ a name given to part of the Normandy beaches at the mouth of the Vire River in north-west France where American soldiers of the US 1st Division landed on 6 June 1944. There is a US war cemetery nearby (Cemetery of St. Laurence).

**Omaha** /'əʊmə,hɑ:/ a city in eastern Nebraska, USA, on the Missouri River; pop. (1990) 335,795. The largest city in the state, Omaha was settled in 1854 and named after an Indian tribe. It developed into a major livestock and grain market and meat-packing centre after the arrival of the railway in 1865. Omaha is the headquarters of the US Strategic Air Command and was the birthplace in 1913 of Gerald Ford, 38th President of the USA.

**Omaha** a North American Indian Tribe of the Siouan-Dhegiha linguistic group, originally occupying the Mississippi valley near St. Louis and later the plains and prairies of Nebraska.

**Oman** /əʊ'mɑːn/ official name **The Sultanate of Oman** a country in south-west Asia at the eastern corner of the Arabian Peninsula; area 212,458 sq. km. (82,030 sq. miles); pop. (est. 1991)

1,600,000; official language, Arabic; capital, Muscat. Oman, with coastlines on the Arabian Sea and the Gulf of Oman, has a low rainfall except in

the hills of Dhofar in the south and in the Jabal Al-Akhdar mountain range which dominates the northern part of the country. May to September is the hottest season of the year. Formerly known as Muscat and Oman, Oman came under British influence in the mid-19th c., becoming a protectorate in 1891. Despite the general British withdrawal from the area in the postwar years the sultanate still retained links with the UK until independence was gained in 1970. The discovery of oil in 1964 revolutionized the Oman economy, bringing wealth out of all proportion to its size and small population. Oman is an absolute monarchy governed by a sultan assisted by a council of ministers. **Omani** adj. & n.

**Oman, Gulf of** an inlet of the Arabian Sea, connected by the Strait of Hormuz to the Persian Gulf.

**Omdurman** /'ɒmdɜ:mən/ a city in central Sudan, on the White Nile opposite Khartoum and the seat of the National Assembly; pop. (1983) 526,290. It was capital of the Mahdist state of Sudan following the British recapture of Khartoum in 1885 and scene of Kitchener's decisive victory over the Mahdi's successor, the Khalifa, in 1898, which marked the end of the Dervish uprising. It has large markets and specializes in gold and silver jewellery.

**Ome** /'əʊmeɪ/ a city on the island of Honshu, central Japan, to the west of Tokyo; pop. (1990) 125,945. It is the site of the Japanese National Railway Museum Park.

**Omiya** /əʊ'miːə/ a city in Saitama prefecture on the island of Honshu, central Japan, situated to the north of Tokyo; pop. (1990) 403,780.

**Omsk** /ɒmsk/ a city and major river port in west Siberia, Russia, at the junction of the Om and Irtysh rivers; pop. (1990) 1,159,000. Situated on the Trans-Siberian Railway, its industries produce oil, grain, textiles, and machinery.

**Omuta** /əʊ'muːtə/ a city in Fukuoka prefecture on the island of Kyushu, southern Japan; pop. (1990) 150,460. It is a centre of coal-mining and heavy industry.

**Onega** /ə'niːgə/ (Russian **Ozero Onezhskoye**) a lake in north-west Russia, near the border with Finland, the second-largest lake in Europe; area 9,609 sq. km. (3,710 sq. miles).

**Onitsha** /əʊ'niːtʃə/ an industrial town in southern Nigeria, on the River Niger north of Port Harcourt; pop. (1983) 269,000. Brewing and the manufacture of textiles and metal goods are its chief industries.

**Onomichi** /,əʊnə'miːtʃi:/ an industrial city on the island of Honshu, Japan, between Okayama and Hiroshima; pop. (1990) 97,100. It is noted for its old buildings and temples and has a ferry link with Matsuyama and Imabari on Shikoku Island.

**Ontario** /ɒn'teərɪ,əʊ/ a province of eastern Canada, between Hudson Bay and the Great

Lakes; area 1,068,580 sq. km. (412,581 sq. miles); pop. (1991) 10,084,885; capital, Toronto. Its largest cities are Toronto, Hamilton, Ottawa, London, and Windsor. Settled by the French and English in the 17th c., Ontario was ceded to Britain in 1763, and became a province in 1867. It is the second-largest and most populous of the provinces of Canada with a strong economic base rooted in finance, service industries, agriculture, mining, and the manufacture of vehicles, aircraft, transport equipment, and high tech goods.

**Ontario, Lake** the smallest and most easterly of the Great Lakes of North America, lying on the border between Ontario in Canada and New York State; area 19,001 sq. km. (7,336 sq. miles); area on the Canadian side of the border, 10,388 sq. km. (4,010 sq. miles); maximum depth 244 m. (800 ft.). It is linked to Lake Erie in the south by the Niagara River and the Welland Ship Canal and to the Atlantic by the St. Lawrence River. The chief cities on its shores are Hamilton and Toronto in Canada, and Rochester in the USA. Pollution of the lake has reduced commercial fishing.

**Oostende** see OSTEND.

**Ooty** /'uːtɪ/ a shortened English version of Ootacamund which was renamed UDHAGAMANDALAM in 1991.

**OPEC** /'əʊpek/ *abbr.* ORGANIZATION OF THE PETROLEUM EXPORTING COUNTRIES.

**Ophir** /'əʊfə(r)/ (in the Old Testament) an unidentified region, perhaps in south-east Arabia, famous for its fine gold and precious stones.

**opisometer** a wheeled instrument used for measuring distances on a map.

**Opole** /ɒ'pɔːlə/ an industrial city in southern Poland on the River Oder; pop. (1990) 127,650. Capital of the former Prussian province of Upper Silesia (1919–45), it is a river port and railway centre.

**Oporto** /əʊ'pɔːtəʊ/ (Portuguese **Porto**) the principal city of Northern Portugal, near the mouth of the River Douro; pop. (1991) 310,640. A busy port before it was silted up but wine, including port wine which takes its name from the city, is still exported. Oporto is the centre of an industrial region producing chemicals, electrical equipment, tyres and other car parts, textiles, and soap. Prince Henry the Navigator (1394–1460) was born in Oporto.

**OR** *abbr.* US Oregon (in official postal use).

**Oradea** /ɒ'rɑːdɪə/ (Hungarian **Nagyvárad** /'nɑːdʒvɑːræd/) an industrial city in north-western Romania, on the Crişul Repede River near the border with Hungary; pop. (1989) 225,420. It is capital of Bihor county with industries producing aluminium, chemicals, processed food, and machinery. St. Ladislaus founded a Roman Catholic bishopric here *c.* 1080.

**Oral** /əʊ'ræl/ a city in north-west Kazakhstan, on the Ural (Zhayyq) River; pop. (1990) 206,700. It is a market city founded by Cossacks in 1625, dealing in cattle and grain. Under Soviet rule it was known as Uralsk.

**Oran** /ɔ:'rɑːn/ (Arabic **Wahran** /wɑ:'rɑːn/) a port and industrial city on the Mediterranean coast of Algeria; pop. (1989) 664,000. A former provincial capital of the Ottoman Turks and a French naval base, Oran is the second-largest city in Algeria. Its industries include chemicals, textiles, cement, and food processing.

**Orange** /'ɒrɪndʒ/ a town in New South Wales, south-east Australia, situated 264 km. (166 miles) west of Sydney on the slopes of Mount Canobolas; pop. (1991) 29,635. It lies at the centre of a noted fruit-growing area.

**Orange** /ɒ'rɑ̃ʒ/ a tourist and market town in southern France, on the Rhône. It was a small principality in the 16th c. in the possession of the House of Nassau, whose descendants became rulers of the Netherlands.

**Orange 1.** a city in Orange County, south-west California, USA, north of Santa Ana; pop. (1990) 110,660. Founded in 1868 at Richland, it was renamed in 1875. **2.** a county in south-west California, USA, south of Los Angeles County. It is the site of Disneyland and noted for its high tech industries. **3.** a city in Essex County, New Jersey, USA, north-west of Newark; pop. (1990) 29,925. **4.** a deep-water port in eastern Texas, USA, on the Sabine River at its junction with the Intracoastal Waterway; pop. (1980) 23,630. It is connected to the Gulf of Mexico by the Sabine-Neches Waterway.

**Orange Free State** /'ɒrɪndʒ/ (Afrikaans **Oranje-Vrystaat**) a province in central South Africa, situated to the north of the Orange River; area 127,993 sq. km. (49,437 sq. miles); pop. (1991) 1,929,370; capital, Bloemfontein. First settled by Boers after the Great Trek from Cape Colony (1836–8), it was annexed by Britain in 1848 but restored in 1854 to the Boers, who established the Orange Free State Republic. It was re-annexed by Britain in 1900, as the Orange River Colony, was given internal self-government in 1907, and became a province of the Union of South Africa in 1910, as the Orange Free State. It remained a province following local government reorganization in 1994. Grain, livestock, gold, and oil from coal are its chief products.

**Orange River** the longest river in South Africa, which rises in the Drakensberg Mountains in north-east Lesotho and flows generally westward for 2,173 km. (1,350 miles) across almost the whole breadth of the continent before entering the Atlantic on the frontier between Namibia and South Africa. The river is much used for irrigation and the Orange River Scheme for hydroelectric power and irrigation was begun in 1963. There are rich alluvial diamond beds at the mouth of the river.

**Orange Walk** a town in Orange Walk district, northern Belize; pop. (1991) 10,890.

**Oranjestad** /ɒˈrɑːnjəˌstɑːt/ **1.** the capital of the Dutch island of Aruba in the West Indies; pop. (1988) 20,000. Situated on Aruba's principal harbour Paardenbai (Horses Bay), it was named after the Dutch royal family in 1824. **2.** the only settlement on the island of Sint Eustatius in the Netherlands Antilles. Divided into an Upper and Lower Town, it was formerly known as Fort Oranje by the Dutch who, in 1636, built a port on the site of an earlier French fort.

**Orapa** /əʊˈræpə/ a diamond-mining town in the central Kalahari, Botswana; pop. (1991) 8,830. The nearby Orapa diamond mine is one of the richest in the country.

**Oraşul Stalin** a former name for BRAŞOV in Romania.

**Orcadian** /ɔːˈkeɪdɪən/ a native of the Orkney Islands off the north coast of Scotland.

**Ordnance Datum (OD)** /ˌɔːdnəns ˈdeɪtəm/ in the United Kingdom, the mean sea-level at Newlyn, Cornwall, from which all heights on British maps are calculated.

**Ordnance Survey** /ˈɔːdnəns/ **(OS)** an official survey organization in the UK, originally under the control of the Master of the Ordnance, preparing large-scale detailed maps of the whole country. Its headquarters is in Southampton.

**Ordovician** /ˌɔːdəˈvɪsɪən/ the second period of the Palaeozoic era, following the Cambrian and preceeding the Silurian, lasting from about 505 to 438 million years ago. It saw both the diversification of many invertebrate groups and the appearance of the first vertebrates (jawless fish). It takes its name from the Latin name (*Ordovices*) for an ancient British tribe of north Wales.

**Ordu** /ɔːˈduː/ **1.** a province in northern Turkey, on the Black Sea; area 6,142 sq. km. (2,372 sq. miles); pop. (1990) 830,105. **2.** its capital, a port on the Black Sea; pop. (1990) 102,110.

**Ordzhonikidze** /ɑːdʒenɪˈkɪdʒɪ/ the former name (1954–93) for VLADIKAVKAZ.

**Örebro** /ˈɜːrəˌbruː/ an industrial city at the west end of Lake Hielmar (Hjälmaren) in south-central Sweden, capital of a county of the same name and manufacturing paper and shoes; pop. (1990) 120,940.

**Oregon** /ˈɒrɪgən/ a state in north-west USA, on the Pacific coast, to the west of the Snake River; area 251,419 sq. km. (97,073 sq. miles); pop. (1990) 2,842,320; capital, Salem. The largest cities are Portland, Eugene, and Salem. Oregon is also known as the Beaver State. It was occupied jointly by British and Americans until 1846, when it was ceded to the US, and became the 33rd state of the US in 1859. Timber processing, salmon-fishing, and fruit-growing are its leading industries. Notable landmarks include Crater Lake National Park, Oregon Dunes National Recreation Area, John Day Fossil Beds National Monument, and Bonneville Dam on the Columbia River. The state is divided into 36 counties:

| County | Area (sq. km.) | Pop. (1990) | County Seat |
|---|---|---|---|
| Baker | 7,987 | 15,320 | Baker |
| Benton | 1,765 | 70,810 | Corvallis |
| Clackamas | 4,862 | 278,850 | Oregon City |
| Clatsop | 2,093 | 33,300 | Astoria |
| Columbia | 1,693 | 37,560 | Saint Helens |
| Coos | 4,176 | 60,270 | Coquille |
| Crook | 7,758 | 14,110 | Prineville |
| Curry | 4,235 | 19,330 | Gold Beach |
| Deschutes | 7,865 | 74,960 | Bend |
| Douglas | 13,114 | 94,650 | Roseburg |
| Gilliam | 3,154 | 1,720 | Condon |
| Grant | 11,765 | 7,850 | Canyon City |
| Harney | 26,452 | 7,060 | Burns |
| Hood River | 1,355 | 16,900 | Hood River |
| Jackson | 7,246 | 146,390 | Medford |
| Jefferson | 4,651 | 13,680 | Madras |
| Josephine | 4,264 | 62,650 | Grants Pass |
| Klamath | 15,480 | 57,700 | Klamath Falls |
| Lake | 21,453 | 7,190 | Lakeview |
| Lane | 11,861 | 282,910 | Eugene |
| Lincoln | 2,548 | 38,890 | Newport |
| Linn | 5,970 | 91,230 | Albany |
| Malheur | 25,639 | 26,040 | Vale |
| Marion | 3,078 | 228,480 | Salem |
| Morrow | 5,314 | 7,625 | Heppner |
| Multnomah | 1,121 | 583,890 | Portland |
| Polk | 1,927 | 49,540 | Dallas |
| Sherman | 2,150 | 1,920 | Moro |
| Tillamook | 2,863 | 21,570 | Tillamook |
| Umatilla | 8,367 | 59,250 | Pendleton |
| Union | 5,291 | 23,600 | La Grande |
| Wallowa | 8,190 | 6,910 | Enterprise |
| Wasco | 6,198 | 21,680 | The Dalles |
| Washington | 1,885 | 311,550 | Hillsboro |
| Wheeler | 4,454 | 1,400 | Fossil |
| Yamhill | 1,859 | 65,550 | McMinnville |

**Oregon Caves** a national monument in the Siskiyou Mountains in the US state of Oregon, preserving a cave system described by Joaquin Miller, poet of the Sierra, as the 'Marble Halls of Oregon'.

**Oregon Trail** a route across the central US, from the Missouri across to Oregon, some 3,000 km. (2,000 miles) in length and which took the average emigrant train six months to complete. It was used chiefly in the 1840s by settlers moving west.

**Orekhovo Zuyevo** /ˌɒrəˌkɒvə zuːˈjevəʊ/ an industrial (textiles) city in western Russia, on the Klyazma River east of Moscow; pop. (1990) 137,000.

**Orel** /ɑːˈjɔːl/ a communications and agricultural trade centre, and industrial city in south-west Russia, at the junction of the Oka and Orlik rivers, south of Moscow; pop. (1990) 342,000. Founded in the 16th c. as a fortress town to protect the southern frontier of Muscovy from Crimean Tartars, it later served as a place of exile for Polish insurgents.

It was the birthplace of the Russian writer Ivan Turgenev (1818–83). It produces machinery, textiles and clothing, and automobile parts.

**Orem** /'ɔːrəm/ a city in north-central Utah, USA, near Lake Utah; pop. (1990) 67,560. Its industries include steel, electronics, and canned foods.

**Ore Mountains** /ɔː(r)/ (German **Erzgebirge** /'eətsgə͵bɪəgə/) a range of mountains on the frontier between Germany and the Czech Republic where rare metals such as cobalt, bismuth, arsenic, uranium, and antimony are mined. Its highest peaks are Klínovec (1,244 m., 4,081 ft.) and Fichtelberg (1,214 m., 3,983 ft.).

**Orenburg** an industrial city and trading centre in southern Russia, on the Ural River; pop. (1990) 552,000. Founded as a fortress town in 1735, it was known as Chkalov from 1938 to 1957. A major food-processing and agricultural machinery centre.

**Øresund** /'ɜːrə͵sʊnd/ (English **the Sound**) a narrow channel between Sweden and the Danish island of Zealand.

**Organization for Economic Cooperation and Development** (**OECD**) an international organization of western developed countries established in 1961 for the purpose of promoting economic and social welfare and stimulating aid to developing countries. It replaced the Organization for European Economic Cooperation which was established in 1948. There are 25 member-states and the headquarters of the organization is in Paris.

**Organization of African Unity** (**OAU**) an association of African states founded in 1963 for mutual co-operation and the elimination of colonialism. Comprising 51 states in 1991, its headquarters are in Addis Ababa, Ethiopia.

**Organization of American States** (**OAS**) an association of 35 American and Caribbean states. Originally founded in 1890 for largely commercial purposes, it adopted its present name and charter in 1948. Its aims are to work for peace and prosperity in the region and to uphold the sovereignty of member-nations. Its General Secretariat is based in Washington, DC, in the USA.

**Organization of the Petroleum Exporting Countries** (**OPEC**) an association founded in Baghdad in 1960 for the purpose of co-ordinating the policies of petroleum-producing countries and in particular stabilizing prices in the international oil markets. Comprising 13 states, its headquarters are in Vienna, Austria.

**Organ Pipe Cactus** a national Monument in the US state of Arizona, preserving the outwash plains and rocky canyons of part of the Sonoran desert.

**Organ Pipes National Park** a national park in Victoria, Australia, north-west of Melbourne. Hexagonal basalt columns, which rise 20 m. (66 ft.) above Jackson's Creek, were formed when lava cooled in an ancient river bed.

**Orient** /'ɔrɪənt/, **the** a literary name for countries in eastern Asia.
**oriental** adj. & n.

**Orinoco** /͵ɒrɪ'nəʊkəʊ/ a river in northern South America, which rises in south-east Venezuela and flows 2,060 km. (1,280 miles) in a great arc through Venezuela, entering the Atlantic Ocean by a vast delta. For part of its length it forms the border between Colombia and Venezuela.

**Orissa** /ə'rɪsə/ a state in eastern India, on the Bay of Bengal, formerly the ancient region of Odra; area 155,707 sq. km. (60,142 sq. miles); pop. (1991) 31,512,070; capital, Bhubaneswar. Formerly an outlying district of Bengal Presidency and later part of Bihar, Orissa became a separate province in 1936. It merged with Mayurbhanj and became a state in 1949. The state is rich in minerals and is India's leading producer of chromite. Rice, oilseed, sugar-cane, and turmeric are cultivated.

**Oristano** /ɒrɪs'tɑːnəʊ/ the capital town of the Italian province of Oristano on the island of Sardinia; pop. (1990) 32,760. Nearby are the remains of the ancient Carthaginian and Roman town of Tharros.

**Oriya** /ə'riːə/ the Indo-European language of Odra, now the official language of the Indian state of Orissa, which is descended from Sanskrit and closely related to Bengali.

**Orizaba** /ɒrɪ'zɑːbə/ a city in the state of Vera Cruz, east central Mexico; pop. (1980) 114,850. It trades in local agricultural produce, produces textiles, cement, and beer, and its mineral springs attract tourists. Nearby **Mt. Orizaba** (Citlaltépetl), the highest peak in Mexico, rises to 5,699 m. (18,503 ft.).

**Orkney Islands** /'ɔːknɪ/ (also **Orkneys**) a group of over 70 islands off the north-east tip of Scotland (the principal islands are Mainland and Hoy), constituting an Islands Area of Scotland; area 976 sq. km. (377 sq. miles); pop. (1991) 19,450; chief town, Kirkwall. Colonized by the Vikings in the 9th c., they were ruled by Norway and Denmark until 1472 when they came into Scottish possession (together with Shetland) as security against the unpaid dowry of Margaret of Denmark after her marriage to James III. Fishing, livestock, and servicing the North Sea oil industry are the chief occupations.

**Orlando** /ɔː'lændəʊ/ a city in central Florida, USA; pop. (1990) 164,690. It was a camp-ground for soldiers during the Seminole Indian War (1835–42) and then a trading post that developed into a city after the arrival of the railroad in 1880. It trades in citrus fruit and winter vegetables and is a popular winter resort with an international airport. Nearby tourist attractions include the John F. Kennedy Space Center, Sea World, and Disney World.

**Orleans** /ɔː'liːənz/ (French **Orléans**) a city in central France, on the Loire, capital of the department of Loiret; pop. (1990) 107,965. It was conquered by Julius Caesar in 52 BC and by the 10th c. was one of the most important cities in France. In 1429 it was the scene of Joan of Arc's first victory over the English during the Hundred Years War. The city trades in wine, vegetables, and grain. Tourism is also important.

**Orléanais** /ɔːˈleɪəneɪ/ a former province of north-central France in the Loire valley centred on the city of Orleans.

**Orlova** /ɔːˈlɒvə/ a mining town in the North Moravia region of the Czech Republic; pop. (1991) 36,300.

**Orly** /ˈɔːlɪ/ a suburb of Paris, France, in the department of Val-de-Marne, with an international airport located 14 km. (9 miles) south-west of the city centre.

**Ormuz** /ˈɔːmʊz/ a variant of HORMUZ.

**Orne** /ɔːn/ **1.** a river of north-west France that rises in the department of Orne and flows through Calvados to the English channel; length 152 km. (95 miles). **2.** a department in the Basse-Normandie region of north-west France; area 6,103 sq. km. (2,357 sq. miles); pop. (1990) 293,200; capital, Alençon.

**Örnsköldsvik** /ˈɜːnʃəlts̩viːk/ a town in Vasternorrland county, eastern Sweden, on the Gulf of Bothnia; pop. (1990) 59,380. Timber is processed and exported from its deep-water harbour.

**orogeny** /əˈrɒdʒənɪ/ movements on the earth's surface that involve the folding of sediments, faulting, and metamorphism.

**orographic rainfall** /ˌprəˈgræfɪk/ (also **relief rainfall**) rainfall that occurs when moisture-laden air masses are forced to rise over high ground. The air is cooled, water vapour condenses, and rainfall occurs.

**Oronsay** /ˈprənsɪ/ an island to the south of Colonsay in the Inner Hebrides off the west coast of Scotland, named after Oran, a disciple of St. Columba. There are remains of a 14th-c. monastery built by monks who were renowned for their carving of graveslabs.

**Orontes** /əˈrɒntiːz/ a river in south-west Asia, which rises near Baalbek in northern Lebanon and flows 571 km. (355 miles) through western and northern Syria before turning west through southern Turkey to enter the Mediterranean Sea. It is an important source of water for irrigation, especially in Syria where its water wheels (*norias*) have been a feature of the landscape since ancient times.

**Orphism** /ˈɔːfɪz(ə)m/ a mystic religion of ancient Greece, originating in the 7th or 6th c. BC and based in poems (now lost) attributed to Orpheus, emphasizing the mixture of good (or divine) and evil in human nature and the necessity that individuals should rid themselves of the evil part by ritual and moral purification throughout a series of reincarnations. It sank to the level of a superstition

in the 5th c., though the profound thoughts which underlay it were perceived by Pindar and Plato.

**Orsk** /ɔːsk/ a city in southern Russia, in the Urals, at the junction of the Ural and Or' rivers near the border with Kazakhstan; pop. (1990) 271,000. It was founded in 1735 as the fortress of Orenburg, which was moved down river in 1742 and developed as a mining settlement exploiting nearby deposits of iron, copper, nickel, and coal.

**Orthodox Church** /ˈɔːθəˌdɒks/ the Eastern or Greek Church, having the Patriarch of Constantinople as its head, and the national churches of Russia, Romania, etc. in communion with it. Separation from the Western Church came in the 4th c., originally through cultural and political factors, focused from the 5th c. onwards on differences of doctrine and ritual, and took formal effect in 1054 when the Pope and the Patriarch of Constantinople excommunicated each other. In the latter part of the 20th c. the Orthodox Churches have taken an active part in the ecumenical movement; the mutual excommunication of 1054 was abolished in 1965.

**Orumiyeh** /ɒˈruːmjə/ (also **Urumiyeh**) **1.** (English **Lake Urmia**) a shallow salt lake to the west of Tabriz in north-west Iran, formerly known as Lake Rezaiyeh; area 4,700 sq. km. (1,815 sq. miles). **2.** the capital of the province of west Azerbaijan in north-western Iran, formerly known as Rezaiyeh; pop. (1991) 357,000. According to tradition the birthplace of Zoroaster (c. 628–551 BC).

**Oruro** /əˈruərəʊ/ the chief mining city of western Bolivia, capital of the department of Oruro; pop. (1990) 208,700. Tin, silver, antimony, and tungsten are mined.

**Orvieto** /ˌɔːvɪˈeɪtəʊ/ an ancient town in the Paglia valley, Umbria, central Italy; pop. (1990) 21,575. It has been occupied since Etruscan times and lies at the centre of a noted wine-producing area. The principal landmark is a 13th-c. cathedral.

**OS** *abbr.* ORDNANCE SURVEY.

**Osage** /əʊˈseɪdʒ/ a North American Indian tribe of the Siouan-Dhegiha linguistic group, originally occupying the Ohio valley and later the plains and prairies of Missouri and Kansas. The Osage subsequently moved to an Indian reserve in Oklahoma.

**Osaka** /əʊˈsaːkə/ a port, commercial, and cultural city in central Japan, on Honshu Island, chief city of Kinki Region; pop. (1990) 2,642,000. It is the third-largest city in Japan and lies on the northeast shore of Osaka Bay. A great commercial centre during the Edo period, the city was largely destroyed during World War II and later rebuilt. It is a centre of transport with ferry links to Kyushu and Shikoku with many light industries including tourism.

**Osasco** /əʊˈsæskəʊ/ a city in the state of São Paulo, southern Brazil, to the west of São Paulo; pop. (1990) 573,330.

**Oscan** /'ɒskən/ the ancient language of Campania in Italy, related to Latin and surviving only in inscriptions in an alphabet derived from Etruscan.

**Osh** /ɒʃ/ a city in western Kyrgyzstan (Kirghizia), in the Fergana valley near the border with Uzbekistan; pop. (1990) 236,200. It was, until the 15th c., an important post on an ancient trade route to China and India. It is the second-largest city in Kyrgyzstan.

**Oshawa** /'əʊʃəwə/ an industrial city in Ontario, Canada, on the northern shores of Lake Ontario east of Toronto; pop. (1991) 129,300; 240,100 (metropolitan area). It has been a centre of the motor industry since the McLaughlin Buick was produced here in 1907.

**Oshkosh** /'ɒʃkɒʃ/ a city in eastern Wisconsin, USA, on the west shore of Lake Winnebago; pop. (1990) 55,000. Settled in 1836, it was named after a chief of the Menominee Indians. Industries produce transportation equipment, overalls, and candles.

**Oshogbo** /əʊ'ʃɑːgbəʊ/ a city in western Nigeria, north-east of Ibadan, capital of the state of Ogun; pop. (1983) 345,000. Brewing and the manufacture of textiles and metal goods are its chief industries.

**Osijek** /'ɒsɪjek/ a river port and industrial city in eastern Croatia, on the River Drava; pop. (1991) 104,700. Metal manufactures, textiles, and furniture are the principal industries.

**Öskmen** /'ɜːskəmen/ an industrial city in northeast Kazakhstan, on the Irtysh (Ertis) River east of Sewey; pop. (1990) 330,000. Under Soviet rule it was known as Ust-Kamenogosk. It has zinc, lead, and titanium-magnesium smelters.

**Ösling** /'ɜːslɪŋ/ a region of the Ardennes Forest in northern Luxembourg.

**Oslo** /'ɒzləʊ/ the capital, chief port, and largest industrial centre of Norway, on the south coast at the head of Oslofjord; pop. (1990) 458,360. Founded in the 11th c., it was known as Christiania from 1624 to 1924 in honour of Christian IV of Norway and Denmark who rebuilt the city after it had been destroyed by a fire. It became capital of independent Norway in 1905. It is a cultural centre with theatres, museums, and art galleries and exhibitions. Its university was founded in 1811. Oslo's industries include shipbuilding, chemicals, electrical equipment, metal products, machine tools, textiles, and food processing.

**Osnabrück** /'ɒznəˌbrʊk/ an industrial city in Lower Saxony, north-west Germany, on the Hase River; pop. (1991) 165,140. Linked to the Mitelland Canal, its industries manufacture textiles, paper, vehicles, and metal goods. It has a university founded in 1970 and it was the birthplace in 1870 of the writer Erich Maria Remarque.

**Osorno** /əʊ'sɔːnəʊ/ a town in the Los Lagos region of southern Chile, on the Rio Damas; pop.

(1991) 117,440. It is a transport centre *en route* to the Lake District and the Mount Osorno ski area. A Spanish fort was built here in 1793 and many German immigrants came during the latter part of the 19th c.

**Ossa** /'ɒsə/, **Mount 1.** a mountain in Thessaly, north-eastern Greece, south of Mount Olympus, rising to a height of 1,978 m. (6,489 ft.). In Greek mythology the giants were said to have piled Mount Olympus and Mount Ossa onto Mount Pelion in an attempt to reach heaven and destroy the gods. **2.** the highest mountain on the island of Tasmania, Australia, rising to a height of 1,617 m. (5,305 ft.).

**Ossetia** a region of the central Caucasus, divided into **1. North Ossetia**, a republic of the Russian Federation; area 8,000 sq. km. (3,088 sq. miles); pop. (1990) 638,000; capital, Vladikavkaz. Under a new constitution it adopted the name Alania in 1994; and **2. South Ossetia**, a former autonomous region of Georgia; area 3,900 sq. km. (1,506 sq. miles); pop. (1990) 99,000; capital, Tskhinvali. South Ossetia has been the scene of ethnic conflict with the Georgians and is currently (1995) governing itself under a Russian-brokered peace although the Georgian Supreme Soviet voted in 1990 to abolish its former autonomous status.

**Ostend** /ɒ'stend/ (Flemish **Oostende** /əʊ'stendə/, French **Ostende** /ɒ'stɑ̃d/) a port and resort on the North Sea coast of West Flanders in north-west Belgium; pop. (1991) 68,500. It is a major ferry port with links to Dover.

**Ostero** see EYSTUROY.

**Österreich** the German name for AUSTRIA.

**Östersund** /'ɜːstəˌsʊnd/ a commercial and industrial town, the capital of Jämtland county in western Sweden, on the east shore of Lake Storsjön; pop.(1990) 58,320.

**Ostia** /'ɒstɪə/ an ancient city and harbour which was situated on the western coast of Italy at the mouth of the River Tiber. It was the first colony founded by ancient Rome and was a major port and commercial centre. Now located about 6 km. (4 miles) inland, it was buried and its ruins were preserved, by the gradual silting up of the River Tiber.

**Ostrava** /'ɒstrəvə/ an industrial city in the Moravian lowlands of the central Czech Republic; pop. (1991) 327,550. It is capital of the North Moravian region, and is situated in the coal-mining region of Upper Silesia. Founded in 1267, coal was first mined near here in 1767. The city has heavy industries based on steel and a large chemicals industry.

**Ostrogoth** /'ɒstrəˌgɒθ/ a member of the Eastern branch of the Goths, who conquered Italy in the 5th–6th c.

**ostrov** a Russian word for an island.

**Ota** /'əʊtə/ a city in Gumma prefecture, Honshu Island, central Japan; pop. (1990) 139,800.

**Otago** /əʊ'teɪgəʊ/ an administrative region on the east coast of South Island, New Zealand, between Southland and Canterbury. It was created in 1989 and comprises the city of Dunedin and districts of Central Otago, Clutha, Queenstown Lakes, and part of Waitaki; pop.(1991) 186,070. Named after a Maori village, Otago was adopted as the name for the Dunedin settlement by the New Zealand Company in 1848 and later applied to the peninsula and the region. Sheep and fruit farming are the main activities.

**Otaru** /əʊ'tɑːruː/ an industrial city and fishing port in northern Japan, situated on the west coast of the island of Hokkaido, on Ishikari Bay; pop. (1990) 163,215. It is a major coal-exporting port and there are ferry links with several ports on the island of Honshu.

**Otavalo** /ˌəʊtə'vɑːləʊ/ a market town in the Andean province of Imbabura, northern Ecuador; pop. (1982) 17,470.

**Otomi** /ˌəʊtə'miː/ a Nahuatl-speaking Indian people inhabiting parts of central Mexico.

**Otranto** /ɒ'træntəʊ/, **Strait of** a channel linking the Adriatic Sea with the Ionian Sea and separating the 'heel' of Italy from Albania.

**Otsu** /'əʊtsuː/ the capital of Shiga prefecture, central Japan, situated on Honshu Island, on the south-west shore of Lake Biwa, east of Kyoto; pop. (1990) 260,000. It is a tourist centre with textile and precision instrument industries.

**Ottawa** /'ɒtəwə/ the federal capital of Canada, a city in Ontario on the Ottawa River (a tributary of the St. Lawrence) and the Rideau Canal; pop. (1991) 313,990; 920,860 (metropolitan area). Founded in 1827, it was named Bytown in honour of Colonel John By (1779–1836), builder of the Rideau Canal. The city received its present name in 1855 and was chosen as capital (of the United Provinces of Canada) by Queen Victoria in 1857. In 1867 the first Canadian parliament met here after the founding of the Dominion of Canada. The city contains government offices, parliament buildings, national museum and library, and public archives.

**Ottawa** a North American Indian tribe of the Algonquian linguistic group, originally occupying land to the north of the Great Lakes and later to be found in Kansas and Oklahoma. Their chief, Pontiac, was one of the most famous Indian chiefs of the 18th c.

**Ottawa River** a river of eastern Canada that flows 1,271 km. (800 miles) eastwards from south-east Ontario through southern Quebec to join the St. Lawrence near Montreal.

**Ottery St. Mary** /'ɒtərɪ/ a market town in Devon, south-west England, between Exeter and Honiton. It was the birthplace in 1772 of the English poet Samuel Taylor Coleridge.

**Ottoman empire** /'ɒtəmən/ the Muslim empire of the Turks (1299–1922), established in northern Anatolia by Osman I or Othman and expanded by his successors to include all of Asia Minor and much of south-east Europe. Ottoman power received a severe check with the invasion of Tamerlane in 1401, but expansion resumed several decades later, resulting in the capture of Constantinople in 1453. The empire reached its zenith under Suleiman I (1520–66), dominating the eastern Mediterranean and threatening central Europe, but thereafter it began to decline. Still powerful in the 17th c., it had, by the 19th c., become the 'sick man of Europe', eventually collapsing in the early 20th c.

**Ötztal Alps** /'ɜːtstɑːl/ (German **Ötztaler Alpen**) an alpine range in western Austria, rising to 3,774 m. (12,382 ft.) at Wildspitze in the Tyrol.

**Ouachita** /'wɑːʃətɔː/ a river in Arkansas and Louisiana, USA. It rises in headstreams in the Ouachita Mountains south-west Arkansas and flows 973 km. (605 miles) south-eastwards into Louisiana where it receives the Tensas River to become the Black River before joining the Red River.

**Ouagadougou** /ˌwɑːgə'duːguː/ the capital city of Burkina in West Africa; pop. (1985) 442,220. Formerly capital of the Mossi empire, it was taken by the French in 1896. It is linked by rail to the port of Abidjan in the Ivory Coast. Its principal buildings combine African and French architectural styles. There is a large, new sports stadium.

**Ouargla** /'wɑː(r)klə/ (also **Wargla**) a large oasis and oil town to the north of the Grand Erg Oriental in north-eastern Algeria; pop. (1982) 89,470. It is developing as an industrial area.

**Oudenarde** /'uːdənɑːd/ (Flemish **Oudenaarde**, French **Audenarde** /ˌəʊdə'nɑːr/) a town in the province of East Flanders, Belgium, scene of a victory (1708) of allied British and Austrian troops under Marlborough and Prince Eugene over the French; pop. (1991) 27,160.

**Oudh** /aʊd/ a region of northern India. Formerly an independent kingdom until it fell under Muslim rule in the 11th c., it later acquired a measure of independence in the early 18th c. It was the centre of the Indian Mutiny in 1857–8 after annexation by Britain in 1856. In 1877 it joined with Agra and formed the United Provinces of Agra and Oudh in 1902. This was later renamed Uttar Pradesh in 1950.

**oued** /wed/ the Arabic word for a river.

**Ouidah** /'wiːdə/ a port in southern Benin, on the Gulf of Guinea. A centre of the cult of voodoo, it was once a major slave-trading port.

**Oujda** /uːdʒ'dɑː/ a commercial city in north-east Morocco, near the Algerian border; pop. (1982) 260,080. Coal and lead are mined locally and fruit, grain, and wool are traded.

**Oulu** /'aʊlu:/ (Swedish **Uleåborg** /'u:lɪɔ:ˌbɔ:(r)/)
**1.** a province in central Finland; area 61,579 sq.
km. (23,785 sq. miles); pop. (1990) 439,905. **2.** its
capital, a seaport on the Gulf of Bothnia at the
mouth of the Oulu River; pop. (1990) 101,380. It is
the largest city in northern Finland and a centre for
timber processing.

**Ouse** the name of several rivers in England: **1.** a
river in south-east England that rises in the Weald
of West Sussex and flows 48 km. (30 miles) south-
eastwards to the English Channel at Newhaven. **2.** a
river in Yorkshire formed at the junction of the Ure
and Swale. It flows 92 km. (57 miles) south-eastwards through York to join the River Trent which
then becomes the Humber Estuary. **3. (Great
Ouse)** a river that rises in Northamptonshire and
flows 257 km. (160 miles) eastwards through East
Anglia to the Wash near King's Lynn. **4. (Little
Ouse)** a river of East Anglia, which forms a tributary of the Great Ouse. For much of its length it
marks the border between Norfolk and Suffolk.

**Outer Banks** a chain of islands and beaches
forming a barrier reef off the east coast of North
Carolina, USA, stretching some 800 km. (500
miles).

**Outer Mongolia** see MONGOLIA.

**outport** /'aʊtpɔ:t/ a Canadian term for a small
remote fishing village.

**Oval** /'əʊvəl/, **the** a cricket ground in Lambeth,
London, headquarters of the Surrey Cricket Club
and venue for international test matches.

**Ovamboland** /əʊ'væmbəʊˌlænd/ a name generally applied to the homeland of over half a million
Ovambo people in northern Namibia. Although
Namibia has since independence been divided into
26 administrative districts, Ovamboland was in
1967 the first self-governing homeland to be designated in Namibia by the South African government.

**Overijssel** /ˌəʊvər'aɪs(ə)l/ a province of the
east-central Netherlands, north of the Ijssel River
and west of the German border; area 3,340 sq. km.
(1,290 sq. miles); pop. (1991) 1,026,325; capital,
Zwolle.

**Overland Park** /'əʊvərlænd/ a residential town
in north-eastern Kansas, USA, 15 km. (9 miles)
south of Kansas City; pop. (1990) 111,790.

**Oviedo** /ˌɒvɪ'eɪdəʊ/ **1.** a province in northern
Spain co-extensive with the Asturias region; area
10,565 sq. km. (4,080 sq. miles); pop.(1991)
1,093,940. **2.** its capital, a steel-making city in
north-west Spain; pop.(1991) 203,190. It was the
former capital of the kings of Asturias whose
tombs lie in the city's 14th-c. cathedral.

**Owendo** /əʊ'wendəʊ/ a port on the Atlantic
coast of Gabon in equatorial West Africa, principally shipping iron ore and manganese.

**ox-bow lake** /'ɒksbəʊ/ a lake, shaped like a
horseshoe that was once part of a meander of a
river.

**Oxbridge** /'ɒksbrɪdʒ/ Oxford and Cambridge
universities regarded together, especially in contrast to newer institutions.

**Oxford** /'ɒksfəd/ a city in central England, on
the River Thames, the county town of Oxfordshire,
the seat of a major English university organized as
a federation of colleges, and an industrial city; pop.
(1991) 109,000. A university (*studium generale*) was
organized there soon after 1167, perhaps as a result
of a migration of students from Paris. The first colleges were founded in the 13th c.—University
(1249), Balliol (1263), and Merton (1264)—and
Oxford rose to equal status with the great European medieval universities, numbering among its
scholars the philosopher and scientist Roger
Bacon, and Sir Thomas More; Erasmus lectured
there. A centre of Royalism during the 17th c.,
Oxford declined during the 18th c. but was revived
in the 1800s, particularly as a result of a renaissance in religious thought. The University includes
the Bodleian Library (see entry). The first women's
college, Lady Margaret Hall, was founded in 1878.
Other landmarks include the Radcliffe Camera
(1737), the Sheldonian Theatre, and the Ashmolean
Museum. There are many ancient churches and
Christ Church Cathedral is of early 13th c. date.
Apart from its university, Oxford has always been a
market town. Printing and publishing are also
long-established industries but it was the development of the automobile industry in the eastern
part of the city which brought it commercial prosperity.

**Oxfordshire** /'ɒksfəd.ʃɪə(r)/ a county of south-
central England; area 2,608 sq. km. (1,007 sq.
miles); pop. (1991) 553,800; county town, Oxford.
It is divided into five districts:

| District | Area (sq. km.) | Pop. (1991) |
|---|---|---|
| Cherwell | 590 | 115,900 |
| Oxford | 35 | 109,000 |
| South Oxfordshire | 687 | 130,900 |
| Vale of White Horse | 580 | 109,200 |
| West Oxfordshire | 715 | 88,700 |

**Oxnard** /'ɒksnɑ:d/ a city in south-west California, USA, south-east of Ventura; pop. (1990)
142,210. Its chief industries include oil refining,
sugar processing, and trade in fruit and vegetables.

**Oxon.** /'ɒksən/ *abbr.* **1.** Oxfordshire. **2.** of Oxford University or the diocese of Oxford.

**Oxonian** /ɒk'səʊnɪən/ of or relating to Oxford
or Oxford University derived from *Oxonia*, the
Latinized name for *Ox(en)ford*.

**Oxus** /'ɒksəs/ the ancient name for the AMU
DARYA.

**Oyama** /əʊ'jɑ:mə/ **1.** a volcanic peak on the
Japanese island of Miyake-jima in the Izu islands
to the south of Tokyo. It rises to 815 m. (2,674 ft.).
**2.** a city on the island of Honshu, in Toshigi pre-

fecture, central Japan, to the north of Tokyo; pop. (1990) 148,000.

**Oystermouth** /ˈɔɪstərˌmaʊθ/ a village in West Glamorgan, South Wales, 8 km. (5 miles) south-west of Swansea. In its churchyard is the grave of Dr Thomas Bowdler whose expurgated *Family Shakespeare* (1818) gave rise to the word 'bowdlerize'.

**Ozark Mountains** /ˈəʊzɑːk/ (also **Ozarks**) a heavily forested highland plateau in the central USA, dissected by rivers, valleys, and streams, lying between the Missouri and Arkansas rivers and within the states of Missouri, Arkansas, Oklahoma, Kansas, and Illinois.

**Ozark National Scenic Riverways** a park in the US state of Missouri preserving about 225 km. (140 miles) of the Current River and its tributary the Jacks Fork.

**ozero** /ˈɒzərə/ a Russian word for a lake, as in Ladozhskoye Ozero (Lake Ladoga).

**ozone layer** /ˈəʊzəʊn/ a layer of colourless un-stable gas in the upper atmosphere 15–20 km. (9–12 miles) above the earth's surface formed by the interaction of oxygen and ultraviolet radiation. It filters out all forms of incoming ultraviolet short-wave radiation, in particular providing a protective screen against harmful radiation with a wavelength between 290 and 320 nanometers (UV-B) which causes sunburn and can result in skin cancer. Concern over the threat of ozone depletion caused by the extensive use of chlorine-based aerosol pro-pellants, refrigerants, and solvents (CFCs) led to the Vienna Convention for the Protection of the Ozone Layer in 1985 and the signing of the Montreal Protocol in 1987 by major CFC-produc-ing countries. There is evidence, however, that the situation continues to deteriorate.

# P p

**PA** *abbr.* US Pennsylvania (in official postal use).

**Paarl** /pɑːl/ a town in the south-west of Cape Province, South Africa, on the Great Berg River north-east of Cape Town; pop. (1980) 71,300. It is at the centre of a famous tobacco and wine-producing region. The South African President, Nelson Mandela, spent the last years of his imprisonment in the Victor Verster prison near Paarl.

**Pabna** /'pæbnə/ the capital of Pabna region in western Bangladesh, on the north bank of the Ganges; pop. (1991) 109,000.

**Pachuca** /pə'tʃuːkə/ (in full **Pachuca de Soto**) the capital of the state of Hidalgo in central Mexico; pop. (1990) 179,440. An old silver-mining settlement in which the 'patio' process of separating silver from ore by amalgamating it with mercury was invented by Bartolmé de Medina.

**Pacific Ocean** /pə'sɪfɪk/ the world's largest ocean, covering one-third of the earth's surface (181,300,000 sq. km., 70 million sq. miles). It separates Asia and Australia from North and South America and extends from Antarctica in the south to the Bering Strait (which links it to the Arctic Ocean) in the north. It was named by its first European navigator, Magellan, because he experienced calm weather there. It reaches a maximum depth of 11,034 m. (36,200 ft.) in the Challenger Deep in the Mariana Trench.

**Pacific Time** the standard time used in the Pacific region of Canada and the US.

**Padang** /pæ'dæŋ/ a seaport of Indonesia, capital of West Sumatra province, the largest city on Sumatra's west coast; pop. (1990) 631,260. Cement and rubber are produced.

**Paddington** /'pædɪŋtən/ a district of London, south-east England, to the north of Hyde Park and west of Marylebone whose railway station is the terminus for services to the west of England and Wales. The original village green of Paddington lies in the south-east. The poet Robert Browning lived here from 1861 to 1887.

**Paderborn** /'pɑːdəbɔːn/ an industrial city in east North Rhine-Westphalia, north-west Germany; pop. (1991) 126,000. Metal goods and precision instruments are produced.

**Padirac Chasm** /'pædɪræk/ (French **Gouffre de Padirac**) a massive subterranean cave system hollowed out of limestone by a subterranean river, located in the Gramat Causse, in the Corrèze department of Limousin, south-west-central

France. It was first explored by the speleologist E. A. Martel in 1889.

**Padma** /'pædmə/ a river of southern Bangladesh, formed by the meeting of the Ganges and Brahmaputra near Rajbari.

**Padua** /'pædjuːə/ (Italian **Padova** /'pædəvə/) a city in Venetia, north-east Italy, capital of the province of Padua; pop. (1990) 218,190. The city, first mentioned in 302 BC as Patavium, was the birthplace of the Roman historian Livy (59 BC–AD 17) and the artist Mantegna (1431–1506). A leading cultural city from the 11th c., it was ruled by the Cararra family from 1318 until 1405, when it passed to Venice. Dante lived in Padua, St. Antony of Padua is buried there, and from 1592 to 1610 Galileo taught at its university which was founded in 1222. Today the city is an agricultural, commercial, and industrial centre specializing in motorcycles, agricultural machinery, electrical goods, and textiles.

**Pagalu** /ˌpɑːgə'luː/ a former name (1973–9) of ANNOBÓN.

**Pagan** /pə'gɑːn/ a town in Burma, situated on the Irrawaddy south-east of Mandalay. It is the site of an ancient city, founded in about AD 849, which was the capital of a powerful Buddhist dynasty from the 11th to the end of the 13th centuries. Many of the city's numerous pagodas and shrines have been restored and are in use today.

**Pago Pago** /'pɑːŋgəʊ 'pɑːŋgəʊ/ the chief port of American Samoa, on the Pacific island of Tutuila at the west end of Pago Pago Harbour; pop. (1990) 4,000. Acquired by the US in 1872, it originally served as a mid-ocean coaling station. The seat of administration lies further east at Fagatogo on the south side of the harbour.

**Pahang** /pə'hæŋ/ **1.** the longest river on the Malay peninsula, rising in north-west Pahang and flowing 456 km. (285 miles) eastwards to the South China Sea. **2.** a mountainous, forested state of Malaysia, on the Malay peninsula; area 35,960 sq. km. (13,889 sq. miles); pop. (1990) 1,054,800; capital, Kuantan. Ruled by a sultan, its chief products are timber, rubber, tin, and gold.

**Pahlavi** /'pɑːləvɪ/ (also **Pehlevi** /'peɪləvɪ/) the language of Persia spoken from the 3rd c. BC until the 10th c. AD, the official language of the Sassanian empire. It was closely related to Avestan and was written in a version of the Aramaic script. The Pahlavi dynasty was founded by Reza Khan (1878–1944), an army officer who became shah of

Iran 1925–41. He was succeeded by his son who was overthrown in 1979.

**pahoehoe** /pəˈhəʊhəʊ/ a highly fluid volcanic lava which spreads out into sheets whose surface appears like folded rope.

**Pahsien** see CHONGQING.

**Paignton** /ˈpeɪntən/ a seaside resort town on the coast of Devon, in the Torbay urban area, south-west England, overlooking Tor Bay; pop. (1981) 40,820. The 14th-c. Coverdale Tower was part of the palace of the Bishops of Exeter.

**Päijänne** /ˈpeɪjənə/ a lake in central Finland, the largest in the country; area 1,090 sq. km. (421 sq. miles). The towns of Lahti and Jyväskylä lie on its shores.

**Pailin** /ˈpeɪlɪn/ a sapphire- and ruby-mining town in western Cambodia, situated south-west of Battambang close to the frontier with Thailand.

**Paine Towers** /ˈpaɪneɪ/ a group of spectacular granite peaks in southern Chile, rising to a height of 2,668 m. (8,755 ft.).

**Pais Basque** see BASQUE COUNTRY.

**Paisley** /ˈpeɪzlɪ/ a town in central Scotland, to the west of Glasgow; pop. (1981) 84,800. It developed around a Clunaic abbey founded by the Stewarts in 1163. A centre of hand-weaving by the 18th c., it became famous during the 19th c. for its distinctive shawls, woven in imitation of the highly prized shawls imported from Kashmir in India in the late 18th and early 19th centuries. It was the birthplace in 1774 of the weaver-poet Robert Tannahill. The University of Paisley (formerly Paisley College of Technology) was established in 1992.

**Pais Vasco** see BASQUE COUNTRY.

**Paiute** /paɪˈjuːt/ a tribe of North American Indians of the Uto-Aztecan linguistic group, originally occupying the Great Basin of Utah, Nevada, and eastern California and numbering c. 11,000 (1990).

**pakeha** /ˈpɑːkɪˌhɑː/ a term used by the Maori of New Zealand for a White person as opposed to a Maori.

**Pakistan**  /ˌpɑːkɪˈstɑːn, ˌpæk-/ official name **The Islamic Republic of Pakistan** a country in southern Asia, bordered by Afghanistan to the north and India to the east and stretching from the high mountains of the Pamir and Karakoram ranges in the north to the low-lying plains of Punjab and Sind in the valley of the Indus to the south; area 803,943 sq. km. (310,522 sq. miles); pop. (est. 1991) 115,588,000; languages, Urdu (official), Panjabi, Sindhi, Pashto; capital, Islamabad. The largest cities are Karachi, Lahore, Faisalabad, Rawalpindi, and Hyderabad. Part of the Indian subcontinent, Pakistan was created as a separate country following the British withdrawal from India in 1947. It originally comprised two territories, respectively to the north-east and north-west of India, in which the population was predominantly Muslim. The country's history has seen long periods of military rule and an unresolved dispute with India over the territory of Kashmir. Civil war in East Pakistan over local claims for autonomy led to Indian intervention in 1971 and the establishment of the independent state of Bangladesh in 1972. Pakistan withdrew from the Commonwealth as a protest against the decision of Britain, Australia, and New Zealand to recognize Bangladesh, but rejoined in 1989. The economy is predominantly agricultural, wheat, cotton, and rice being the principal crops. Cultivation is made possible in semiarid areas by an extensive contiguous irrigation system that is the largest in the world. Pakistan is a parliamentary democracy with an executive president, prime minister, and cabinet and a bicameral legislature comprising a National Assembly and Senate.
**Pakistani** adj. & n.

Excluding the disputed territory in the Northern Areas and Azad Kashmir, Pakistan is administratively divided into a Federal Capital Territory, Federally Administered Tribal Areas, and four provinces:

| Province | Area (sq. km.) | Pop. (1985) | Capital |
|---|---|---|---|
| Federal Capital Territory | 907 | 379,000 | Islamabad |
| Baluchistan | 347,190 | 4,908,000 | Quetta |
| Federally Administered Tribal Areas | 27,219 | 2,467,000 | Miram Shah |
| North-West Frontier | 74,521 | 12,287,000 | Peshawar |
| Punjab | 205,344 | 53,840,000 | Lahore |
| Sind | 140,914 | 21,682,000 | Karachi |

**Pakse** /ˈpækseɪ/ (also **Pakxe**) the largest town in southern Laos, situated at the junction of the Mekong and Se Don (Xedon) rivers; pop. (est. 1990) 25,000. Capital of the province of Champassak and centre of a former kingdom, Pakse lies at the crossroads of routes to Vietnam and Cambodia. The modern town was developed after it became a French administrative outpost in 1905. The 7th-c. ruins of the ancient Khmer capital of Wat Phou lie to the south.

**Palaearctic** /ˌpælɪˈɑːktɪk/ a biogeographical term for the Arctic and temperate parts of the Old World.

**Palaeocene** /ˈpælɪəˌsiːn/ (US **Paleocene**) the earliest epoch of the Tertiary period, following the Cretaceous period and preceding the Eocene epoch, lasting from about 65 to 54.9 million years ago. The sudden diversification of the mammals is a notable feature of this epoch.

**Palaeolithic** /ˌpælɪəʊˈlɪθɪk/ (US **Paleolithic**) the earlier part of the Stone Age, when primitive stone implements were used; a period, which extends from the first appearance of artefacts, some 2.5 million years ago, to the end of the last ice age *c.*10,000 BC. It has been divided into the *lower palaeolithic*, with the earliest forms of mankind and the presence of hand-axe industries, ending *c.*80,000 BC, *middle palaeolithic* (or Mousterian), the era of Neanderthal man, ending *c.*33,000 BC, and *upper palaeolithic*, which saw the development of *Homo sapiens*.

**Palaeozoic** /ˌpælɪəʊˈzəʊɪk/ (US **Paleozoic**) the geological era between the Precambrian and the Mesozoic. The era comprises the Cambrian, Ordovician, Silurian, Devonian, Carboniferous, and Permian periods. It lasted from about 590 to 248 million years ago, beginning with the first appearance of fossils bearing hard shells and ending with the rise to dominance of the reptiles.

**Palais-Bourbon** /ˌpæleɪˈbʊəbɒn/ a former palace on the Quai d'Orsay in central Paris, seat (since 1827) of the French National Assembly, the lower house of the French Parliament. It was built in 1722–8 for the Duchess Louise-Françoise de Bourbon.

**Palais de Luxembourg** /ˈpæleɪ də ˈlʊksæbʊə(r)/ a former palace in the Rue de Vaugirard, central Paris, seat of the French Senate, the upper house of the French Parliament. It was built between 1615 and 1631 by Marie de Médicis, wife of Henry IV, on property once owned by the Duke of Luxembourg.

**palatinate** /pəˈlætɪneɪt/ a territory formerly under the jurisdiction of a Count Palatine, an official or feudal lord having locally authority that elsewhere only belonged to a sovereign. Palatinates existed in the later Roman empire, in Germany, and in England where the **County Palatine** extended over the earldom of Chester, the duchy of Lancaster, and other territories.

**Palau** /pəˈlaʊ/ see BELAU.

**Palawan** /pəˈlɑːwən/ a long narrow island in the western Philippines, separating the Sulu Sea from the South China Sea; area 11,780 sq. km. (4,550 sq. miles). Its chief town is Puerto Princesa.

**Pale** /peɪl/, **the** (also **the English Pale**) **1.** that part of Ireland over which England exercised jurisdiction, varying in extent from the reign of Henry II until the full conquest of Ireland under Elizabeth I. **2.** the small area round Calais, the only part of France remaining in English hands after the Hundred Years War until its loss in 1588.

**Palembang** /pɑːˈlembæŋ, ˌpɑːləmˈbɑːŋ/ a city in Indonesia, in the south-east part of the island of Sumatra, a river port on the Musi River; pop. (1990) 1,140,900. Formerly the capital of the Buddhist kingdom of Srivijaya, which flourished in Malaya between the 7th and 13th centuries, it became a sultanate in the late 15th c. From 1616 it

was developed as a trading post by the Dutch, who abolished the sultanate in 1825. It is capital of South Sumatra province and a centre of the trade in Sumatran tin, oil, and pepper.

**Palencia** /pæˈlenθjə/ **1.** a province in the Castilla-León region of north-west Spain; area 8,035 sq. km. (3,103 sq. miles); pop. (1991) 185,480. **2.** its capital, on the River Carrión; pop. (1991) 77,125. The first Spanish university was established here in 1208. Textiles, farming machinery, and chemicals are the local industries

**Palenque** /pəˈleŋkeɪ/ the site of a former Mayan city in south-east Mexico, south-east of present-day Villahermosa. The well-preserved ruins of the city, which existed from about AD 300 to 900, include notable examples of Mayan architecture and extensive hieroglyphic texts. The city reached its zenith in the 7th c. during the reign of Pacal the Great whose tomb, opened in 1952, was one of the greatest discoveries of Mayan archaeology. The city's ancient name has been lost and it is now named after a neighbouring village.

**Palermo** /pəˈlɜːməʊ/ the capital of the Italian island of Sicily, a port on the north coast of the island in a bay of the Tyrrhenian Sea; pop. (1990) 734,240. Founded as a trading post by the Phoenicians during the 8th c. BC and later settled by the Carthaginians, it was taken by the Romans in 254 BC. It was conquered by the Arabs in AD 831, becoming in 1072 the capital of Sicily, which was then a Norman kingdom. The city is rich in works of art. Industries include shipbuilding, textiles, cement, and tourism.

**Palestine** /ˈpælɪˌstaɪn/ a territory in the Middle East on the eastern coast of the Mediterranean Sea, also called the 'Holy Land' because of its links with Judaism, Christianity, and Islam. It has seen many changes of frontier and status in the course of history, and contains several places sacred to Christians, Jews, and Muslims. In biblical times Palestine comprised the kingdoms of Israel and Judaea. The land was controlled at various times by the Egyptian, Assyrian, Persian, and Roman empires before being conquered by the Muslims in AD 634. It remained in Muslim hands, except for a brief period during the Crusades (1098–1197), until World War I, being part of the Ottoman empire from 1516 to 1917, when Turkish and German forces were defeated by the British at Megiddo. The name 'Palestine' was used as the official political title for the land west of the Jordan mandated to Britain in 1920. Jewish immigration was encouraged by the Balfour Declaration of 1917, and increased greatly in 1948 when the State of Israel was established. The name Palestine continues to be used, however, to describe a geographical entity, particularly in the context of the struggle for territory and political rights of Palestinian Arabs displaced when Israel was established. In 1993 an accord was reached between the main PLO factions and the government of Israel, and in the fol-

lowing year a Palestine National Authority took over from the Israeli military administration in Gaza and Jericho.
**Palestinian** *adj. & n.*

**Palghat** /ˈpɑːlgɑːt/ (also **Pulicat** or **Palakkad** /ˈpəlɪkət/) a town in the state of Kerala, south-west India, situated in a strategic location commanding one of the most important gaps in the southern part of the Western Ghats; pop. (1991) 179,700.

**Pali** /ˈpɑːlɪ/ an Indic language, closely related to Sanskrit, in which the sacred texts of Theravada Buddhism are written. It was spoken in northern India in the 5th–2nd c. BC. As the language of a large part of the Buddhist scriptures it was brought to Sri Lanka and Burma, and, though not spoken there, became the vehicle of a large literature of commentaries and chronicles.

**Palisades** /ˌpælɪˈseɪdz/, **the** a ridge of high basalt cliffs on the west bank of the Hudson River, in north-east New Jersey, USA.

**Palk Strait** /pɒlk/ an inlet of the Bay of Bengal separating northern Sri Lanka from the coast of Tamil Nadu in India. It lies to the north of Adam's Bridge, which separates it from the Gulf of Mannar.

**Pall Mall** /pæl mæl/ a street in central London that derives it name from the game of pall mall that was played in front of St. James's Palace in the 17th c.

**Palma** /ˈpælmə, ˈpɑːmə/ (in full **Palma de Mallorca**) an industrial port, resort, and capital of the Balearic Islands, chief town of the island of Majorca; pop. (1991) 308,620. It was founded as a Roman colony in 276 BC. Palma exports fruit and wine, and has many light industries.

**Palmas** /ˈpælməs/ the state capital of Tocantins in central Brazil, situated at the southern end of the state at the junction of the Tocantins and Paraná rivers; pop. (1990) 5,750.

**Palm Bay** a city in east Florida, USA, on the Indian River between Daytona Beach and Palm Beach; pop. (1990) 62,630.

**Palm Beach** a resort town on the south-east coast of Florida, USA, situated on an island between Lake Worth and the Atlantic Ocean; pop. (1990) 9,810.

**Palmdale** /ˈpɑːmdeɪl/ a city in south-west California, USA, north of Los Angeles and the San Gabriel Mountains; pop. (1990) 68,840.

**Palmerston North** /ˈpɑːməst(ə)n/ a market town on North Island, New Zealand, on the west bank of the Manawatu River; pop. (1990) 69,300. Founded in 1866 on a site laid out by the Wellington provincial engineer, John Tiffin Stewart, it became an important centre of transport after the arrival of the railway in the 1870s. Originally named Palmerston (after the British Prime Minister Lord Palmerston), the word 'North' was added in 1873 in order to avoid confusion with the town

of Palmerston on South Island. It has a university and an agricultural research centre.

**Palm Springs** a popular desert oasis and fashionable resort city in the desert area of southern California, USA; pop. (1990) 40,180. Occupying an area once inhabited by the Agua Caliente Indians, its mineral springs were discovered by stage-coachers and railroad surveyors, and a spa hotel was eventually built in 1886 by Welwood Murray, a Scottish doctor. By the 1920s Palm Springs had become a popular hideaway for Hollywood film stars. It has a notable racquet club and over 50 golf courses.

**Palmyra** /pælˈmaɪrə/ an ancient city of Syria, an oasis settlement in the Syrian desert, north-east of Damascus on the site of present-day Tadmur. First mentioned in the 19th c. BC, it was an independent state in the 1st c. BC becoming a dependency of Rome between the 1st and 3rd centuries AD. A flourishing city on a trade route between Damascus in the west and the Euphrates in the east, it regained its independence briefly in the second half of the 3rd c. under Zenobia, who became queen of Palmyra in 267, until it was taken by the Emperor Aurelian in 272. The name Palmyra is the Greek form of the city's modern and ancient pre-Semitic name Tadmur or Tadmor, meaning 'city of palms'.

**Palo Alto** a city in western California, USA, to the south of San Francisco; pop. (1990) 55,900. It is a noted centre for electronics and computer technology and nearby is Stanford University (1891).

**Palomar** /ˈpælə,mɑː(r)/, **Mount** a mountain in southern California, USA, north-east of San Diego, which rises to a height of 1,867 m. (6,126 ft.). It is the site of an astronomical observatory, which contains a large telescope developed by the American astronomer George Hale. Its name means 'place of the pigeons' in Spanish.

**Palu** /ˈpɑːluː/ a city on the island of Sulawesi (Celebes), capital of the Indonesian province of Central Sulawesi; pop. (1989) 298,580. Situated in a rain shadow on Palu Bay, an inlet of the Makassar Strait, Palu is one of the driest locations in Indonesia.

**Pamir Mountains** /pəˈmɪə/ (also **Pamirs**) a mountain system of central Asia, centred in Tajikistan and extending into Kyrgyzstan, Afghanistan, Pakistan, and western China. The system's highest peak, in Tajikistan, rises to 7,495 m. (24,590 ft.). Sometimes referred to as the **Pamir Knot**, it is the point at which the Hindu Kush, Karakoram, Tien Shan, and Kunlun Shan mountain ranges meet. This upland region is home to the Wakhi nomads and to the Ismaili Muslims who follow the Aga Khan.

**pampas** /ˈpæmpəs/ large treeless plains in central Argentina and southern Uruguay, South America, dominated by bunch grasses and occasional 'monte' shrub vegetation. Cattle were introduced onto the wide flat grasslands in the 16th c. and in the 19th c. the pampas were settled by immigrant farmers from Europe. The Argentinian pampas are responsible for almost the entire agricultural production—meat and grain—of the country.

**Pamphylia** /pæm'fɪlɪə/ an ancient coastal region of southern Asia Minor, between Lycia and Cilicia, to the east of the modern port of Antalya. It became a Roman province in the reign of Augustus, between 31 BC and AD 14.
**Pamphylian** *adj. & n.*

**Pamplona** /pæm'pləʊnə/ a city in northern Spain, capital of the former kingdom and modern region of Navarre and known in Roman times as Pompaelo (= city of Pompey); pop. (1991) 191,110. Situated on the River Arga, on a routeway over the Pyrenees to France, the city is noted for its fiesta of San Fermin, held there in July, which is celebrated with the running of bulls through the city streets. The city has a Gothic cathedral and its local industries include chemicals and kitchenware.

**Pamporovo** /ˌpæmpə'rəʊvəʊ/ a skiing resort in the Rhodope Mountains of southern Bulgaria, 85 km. (53 miles) south of Plovdiv.

**Panaji** /pəna:dʒɪ/ (also **Panjim** /'pa:nʒɪm/) a city in western India, on the south bank of the Mandovi River, a port on the Arabian sea and capital of the state of Goa; pop. (1991) 85,200. Manganese ore is exported. The Portuguese Viceroys occupied the former palace of Adil Shah in 1759 and moved the capital to Panaji in 1843. The former capital, Old Goa, lies 9 km. (5.5 miles) to the east.

## Panama

/ˌpænə'ma:/ official name **The Republic of Panama** a country in Central America, situated on the isthmus which connects North and South America; area 77,082 sq. km.

(29,773 sq. miles); pop. (1990) 2,329,330; official language, Spanish; capital Panama City. Tropical lowland areas on the Caribbean and Pacific coasts are separated by an interior mountain range that rises to 3,475 m. (11,468 ft.), rainfall being greatest on the Caribbean coast. The majority of the population is of mixed Spanish and Indian stock but there are still indigenous Indian and West Indian ethnic minorities including the Cuna, Guayami, and Choco people. The economy is largely agricultural, Panama's chief exports being bananas, coffee, fish, sugar, and clothing. Reflecting the canal's role as a global transit point, the canal corridor is significantly more developed than the rest of the country. Colonized by Spain in the early 16th c., Panama was freed from imperial control in 1821 and briefly joined the Federation of Gran Colombia before becoming a Colombian province.

It gained full independence in 1903, although the construction of the Panama Canal and the leasing of the zone around it to the US until 1977 split the country in two. In 1989 US troops invaded Panama in a successful attempt to arrest the country's president, General Manuel Noriega, so that he could face trial for drug trafficking. The country is governed by an executive president and a unicameral Legislative Assembly.
**Panamanian** *adj. & n.*
Panama is divided into 10 provinces:

| Province | Area (sq. km.) | Pop. (1990) | Capital |
|---|---|---|---|
| Bocas del Toro | 8,745 | 93,360 | Bocas del Toro |
| Coclé | 4,927 | 173,190 | Penonomé |
| Colón | 4,890 | 168,290 | Colón |
| Chiriquí | 8,653 | 370,230 | David |
| Darién | 16,671 | 43,830 | La Palma |
| Herrera | 2,341 | 93,680 | Chitré |
| Los Santos | 3,805 | 76,950 | Las Tablas |
| Panama | 11,887 | 1,072,130 | Panama City |
| Veraguas | 11,239 | 203,630 | Santiago |
| San Blas | 2,357 | 34,040 | El Porvenir |

**Panama Canal** a canal about 80 km. (50 miles) long and 150 m. (490 ft.) wide, across the isthmus of Panama, connecting the Atlantic and Pacific Oceans. Its construction, begun by Ferdinand de Lesseps in 1881 but abandoned through bankruptcy in 1889, was completed by the US between 1904 and 1914. The surrounding territory, the Panama Canal Zone or Canal Zone, was administered by the US until 1979, when it was returned to the control of Panama. Control of the canal itself remains with the US until 1999, at which date it is due to be ceded to Panama.

**Panama City** the capital of Panama, situated on the shore of the Gulf of Panama near the Pacific end of the Panama Canal; pop. (1990) 584,800. The old city, founded by the Spanish in 1519 on the site of an Amerindian fishing village, was destroyed by the Welsh buccaneer Henry Morgan in 1671. The new city, built in 1674 on a site a little to the west, became capital of Panama in 1903, when the republic gained its independence from Colombia. The city, which developed rapidly after the opening of the Panama Canal in 1914, has industries which produce clothing, chemicals, and plastics.

**Pan-American Highway** a road system in the Americas initiated in the 1920s and stretching a distance of some 25,300 km. (15,700 miles) from Alaska to Chile.

**Panay** /pæ'naɪ/ an island in the western Visayas group of the central Philippines; area 12,295 sq. km. (4,749 sq. miles); chief town Iloilo. Agriculture and the manufacture of textiles are the chief industries.

**Panchevo** /'pa:ntʃəvəʊ/ (also **Pančevo**) a river port on the Danube north-east of Belgrade, in the

Vojvodina autonomous province of Serbia; pop.
(1991) 72,700.

**Pangaea** /pæn'dʒɪə/ a vast continental area or
supercontinent comprising all the continental crust
of the earth which is postulated to have existed in
late Palaeozoic or Mesozoic times before breaking
up into Gondwanaland and Laurasia.

**Pangkor** /pæŋ'kɔ:/ a resort island off the west
coast of Peninsular Malaysia, in the Straits of
Malacca. There is a boat link with Lumut in Perak.

**Panhandle** /'pænhænd(ə)l/ a name given to
several strips of land in the US in the shape of a
panhandle, notably, the Texas Panhandle (north-
west Texas), the Eastern Panhandle (West
Virginia), and the panhandles of northern Idaho,
north-west Oklahoma, and south-east Alaska.

**Panihati** /ˌpænɪ'hɑ:tɪ/ a city in West Bengal,
north-east India, to the north of Calcutta; pop.
(1991) 275,360.

**Panipat** /'pɑ:ni:pət/ a historic market town in
Haryana, north-west India, near the Yamuna
River north of Delhi; pop. (1991) 191,000. It is the
site of a shrine to the Muslim saint Abu Ali
Kalandhar. Famous battles were fought near here
in 1526, 1556, and 1761.

**Panjim** see PANAJI.

**Panjshir** /'pænʃɪə(r)/ a range of mountains in
the Hindu Kush in eastern Afghanistan, to the
north of Kabul.

**Panmunjom** /ˌpænmʊn'dʒɒm/ a village in the
demilitarized zone between North and South
Korea. It was here that the armistice ending the
Korean War was signed on 27 July 1953.

**Pannonia** /pə'nəʊnɪə/ an ancient country of
southern Europe lying south and west of the Danube, in present-day Austria, Hungary, Slovenia,
and Croatia. It was occupied by the Romans from
35 BC, becoming a province in AD 6. It lost its separate identity after the Romans withdrew at the end
of the 4th c.

**Pantanal** /ˌpæntə'næl/ a vast region of tropical
swamp-forest rich in wildlife, lying in the upper
reaches of the Paraguay River, south-west Brazil;
area c. 220,000 sq. km. (84,975 sq. miles).

**Pantelleria** /ˌpæntelə'rɪə/ a small volcanic
Italian island (82.9 sq. km., 32 sq. miles) in the
Mediterranean, situated between Sicily and the
coast of Tunisia. It was used as a place of exile by
the ancient Romans, who called it Cossyra.

**Panthalassa** /ˌpænθə'læsə/ a universal sea or
single ocean, such as would have surrounded
PANGAEA.

**Panthéon** /pæn'teɪɒn/ a building in central
Paris, the burial place of famous Frenchmen in-
cluding Victor Hugo, Jean Jacques Rousseau,
Voltaire, and Emile Zola. Originally built as a
church and completed in 1790 it was turned into a
'Panthéon Français' by the revolutionary National
Assembly in 1791.

**Papal States** a part of central Italy held
between 756 and 1870 by the Catholic Church, corresponding to the modern regions of Emilia-
Romagna, Marche, Umbria, and Latium. Taken
from the Lombards by the Frankish king Pepin III,
the states were given to the papacy as a strategy to
undermine Lombard expansionism. Greatly extended by Pope Innocent III in the early 13th c. and
by Pope Julius II in the 16th c., they were incorporated into the newly unified Italy in 1860 and 1870.
Their annexation to Italy deprived the papacy of its
temporal powers until the Lateran Treaty of 1929
recognized the sovereignty of the Vatican City.

**Papeete** /ˌpɑ:pɪ'eɪtɪ, -pɪ'i:tɪ/ the capital of
French Polynesia, situated on the north-west coast
of the Pacific Island of Tahiti; pop. (1988) 78,800.
The town developed as a tourist centre after the
building of an airport in 1959.

**Paphlagonia** /ˌpæflə'gəʊnɪə/ an ancient region
of northern Asia Minor, on the Black Sea coast be-
tween Bithynia and Pontus, to the north of Galatia.
It was incorporated into Roman Bithynia and
Galatia between 65 and 6 BC.
**Paphlagonian** *adj. & n.*

**Paphos** /'pæfɒs/ a resort town on the Mediterranean coast of south-west Cyprus; pop. (1990)
28,800. It was the legendary birthplace of the goddess Aphrodite. Historic landmarks include the underground 'Tombs of the Kings', the remains of a
7th-c. Byzantine castle, the Roman villa of
Dionysus, and the Chrysopolitiss Basilica.

**Papua** /'pæpjʊə/ the south-eastern part of the
island of New Guinea, now part of the independent
state of Papua New Guinea. Papua was encountered
in 1526–7 by a Portuguese navigator, who named it
from a Malay word meaning 'woolly-haired'.

**Papua New
Guinea** /'pæpjʊə,
'gɪnɪ/ official name
**The Independent
State of Papua
New Guinea** a
country in the Pacific
off the north-east
coast of
Australia; area
462,840 sq. km. (178,772 sq. miles); pop. (1990)
3,529,540; official languages, English, Motu, and
Pidgin (700–800 local languages are also spoken);
capital, Port Moresby. Comprising the eastern half
of the island of New Guinea and island groups to
the east, Papua New Guinea has an equatorial
climate. More than two-thirds of the working population are employed in agriculture, the chief commercial crops being copra, coffee, cocoa, palm oil,
and rubber. Timber is exported and the mining of
copper, gold, and silver is a major source of revenue.
Papua New Guinea was formed from the administrative union, in 1949, of Papua (south-east New
Guinea with adjacent islands), an Australian Territ-

ory since 1906, and the Trust Territory of New Guinea (north-east New Guinea), an Australian trusteeship since 1921. In 1975 the combined territories became an independent state within the Commonwealth. The country is governed by a unicameral National Parliament, an executive prime minister, and a National Executive Council. In recent years a separatist movement on the mineral-rich island of Bougainville has waged an armed struggle against the government. Papua New Guinea is divided into a national capital district and 19 provinces:

| Province | Area (sq. km.) | Pop. (1990) | Capital |
| --- | --- | --- | --- |
| Central | 29,500 | 140,580 | Port Moresby |
| Chimbu | 6,100 | 183,800 | Kundiawa |
| Eastern Highlands | 11,200 | 299,620 | Goroka |
| East New Britain | 15,500 | 184,410 | Rabaul |
| East Sepik | 42,800 | 248,310 | Wewak |
| Enga | 12,800 | 238,360 | Wabag |
| Gulf | 34,500 | 68,060 | Kerema |
| Madang | 29,000 | 270,300 | Madang |
| Manus | 2,100 | 32,830 | Lorengau |
| Milne Bay | 14,000 | 157,290 | Alotau |
| Morobe | 34,500 | 363,535 | Lae |
| New Ireland | 9,600 | 87,190 | Kavieng |
| Northern | 22,800 | 96,760 | Popondetta |
| North Solomons | 9,300 | | Arawa |
| Southern Highlands | 23,800 | 302,720 | Mendi |
| Western | 99,300 | 108,705 | Daru |
| Western Highlands | 8,500 | 291,090 | Mount Hagen |
| West New Britain | 21,000 | 127,550 | Kimbe |
| West Sepik | 36,300 | 135,185 | Vanimo |

**Pará** /pə'rɑː/ a state in northern Brazil, on the Atlantic coast at the delta of the Amazon to the south of Guyana and Surinam; area 1,250,722 sq. km. (483,090 sq. miles); pop. (1991) 5,181,570; capital, Belém. It is a region of dense rainforest.

**Paracas** /pə'rɑːkəs/ an arid peninsula on the Pacific coast of central Peru, c. 250 km. (156 miles) south of Lima. Evidence of a well-developed culture known as the Paracas culture, existing in the area from c. 1300 BC until AD 200, was discovered here in 1925. Paracas Antiguo is the name given to the early centuries of the culture, while the later Paracas culture (500 BC to AD 200) is divided into two periods known as Paracas Cavernas and Paracas Necropolis after the two main burial sites.

**Paracel Islands** /ˌpærə'sel/ (also **Paracels**, Chinese **Xisha**, Vietnamese **Hoang Sa**) a group of about 130 small barren coral islands and reefs in the South China Sea to the south-east of the Chinese island of

Hainan. The islands, which lie close to deposits of oil, are claimed by both China and Vietnam.

**Paraguay** /'pærə,gwaɪ/ official name **The Republic of Paraguay** an inland country in central South America, situated between Argentina, Bolivia, and Brazil; area 406,752 sq. km.

(157,108 sq. miles); pop. (est. 1990) 4,157,290; official language, Spanish; capital, Asunción. North-western Paraguay is part of the flat, desolate, and sparsely populated Chaco region, the south-east being cooler, wetter, and more developed with huge cattle ranches and Mennonite farming communities. Paraguay's main industries are meat packing, vegetable-oil processing, and textiles. Once part of the Spanish viceroyalties of Peru and La Plata, Paraguay achieved its independence in 1811, but was devastated, losing over half of its population, in the megalomaniac dictator Solano Lopez's war against Brazil, Argentina, and Uruguay in 1865–70. It gained land to the west as a result of the Chaco War with Bolivia in 1932–5, but the country has remained largely undeveloped with a low standard of living. Ruled by the military dictator Alfredo Stroessner, from 1954 until his overthrow in 1989, Paraguay is governed by an executive president and Council of Ministers and a bicameral National Congress. The country is divided into the capital city and 19 administrative departments:

| Department | Area (sq. km.) | Pop. (1990) | Capital |
| --- | --- | --- | --- |
| **Oriental** | | | |
| Alto Paraná | 13,498 | 373,300 | Ciudad del Este |
| Amambay | 12,933 | 97,700 | P. J. Caballero |
| Caaguazú | 11,474 | 462,500 | Colonel Oviedo |
| Caazapá | 9,496 | 132,000 | Caazapá |
| Canendiyú | 13,953 | 120,800 | Salto del Guairá |
| Central | 2,652 | 769,100 | Asunción |
| Concepción | 18,051 | 181,500 | Concepción |
| Cordillera | 4,948 | 222,200 | Caacupé |
| Guairá | 3,846 | 179,800 | Villarrica |
| Itapúa | 16,525 | 371,600 | Encarnación |
| Misiones | 7,835 | 97,500 | S. J. Bautista |
| Neembucú | 13,868 | 83,300 | Pilar |
| Paraguarí | 8,255 | 230,700 | Paraguarí |
| San Pedro | 20,002 | 284,000 | San Pedro |
| **Occidental** | | | |
| Alto Paraguay | 45,982 | 10,100 | Puerte Olimpo |
| Boquerón | 46,708 | 16,900 | Pedro P. Peña |
| Chaco | 36,367 | 300 | Mayor P. Lageranza |
| Nueva Asunción | 44,961 | 300 | Colonel Garay |
| Pte. Hayes | 72,907 | 38,200 | Pozo Colorado |

**Paraguay** a river of South America that rises in the Mato Grosso of Western Brazil and flows 2,549 km. (1,584 miles) southwards into Paraguay where it meets the Paraná River.

**Paraíba** /ˌpæræ'iːbə/ a state on the Atlantic coast of eastern Brazil; area 53,958 sq. km. (20,841

sq. miles); pop. (1991) 3,200,680; capital, João Pessoa.

**Paramaribo** /ˌpærəmæˈriːbəʊ/ the capital of Surinam, a port on the Atlantic at the mouth of the Surinam River; pop. (est. 1988) 192,110. Founded by the French in 1540, it became capital of British Surinam in 1650, but was placed under Dutch jurisdiction in 1816. Its port trades in bauxite, coffee, fruit, and timber.

**paramo** /pəˈrɑːməʊ/ a high, treeless plateau in the Andes of South America.

**Paraná** /ˌpærəˈnɑː/ **1.** a river of South America, rising in south-east Brazil and flowing about 3,300 km. (2,060 miles) southwards before meeting the River Plate estuary in Argentina. For part of its length it follows the south-east frontier of Paraguay. **2.** a port and food-processing centre on the Paraná River, capital of Entre Rios province in eastern Argentina; pop. (1991) 277,000. **3.** a state of southern Brazil; area 199,324 sq. km. (76,988 sq. miles); pop. (1991) 8,443,300; capital, Curitiba.

**Parbhani** /ˈpɜːbəniː/ a town in Maharashtra, central India, south-east of Aurangabad; pop. (1991) 190,235.

**Paris** /ˈpærɪs/ the capital and political, commercial, and cultural centre of France, situated on the River Seine; pop. (1990) 2,175,200. An early settlement on the small island in the Seine, known as the Ile de la Cité, was inhabited by a Gallic people called the Parisii. It was taken by the Romans, who called it Lutetia, in 52 BC. In the 5th c. AD it fell to the Frankish king Clovis, who made it his seat of power. It declined under the succeeding Merovingian kings, but was finally established as the capital in 987 under Hugh Capet. The city was extensively developed during the reign of Philippe-Auguste (1180–1223) and organized into three parts; the island of the *cité*, the Right Bank, and the Left Bank. During the reign of Francis I (1515–47) the city expanded again, its architecture showing the influence of the Italian Renaissance. The city's neoclassical architecture characterizes the modernization of the Napoleonic era. This continued under Napoleon III, when the bridges, parks, and boulevards of the modern city were built under the direction of Baron Haussmann. Its chief landmarks are the Eiffel Tower (1889), Hôtel des Invalides (1671–6), the Arc de Triomphe (1806–36), Pompidou Centre (1977), the Louvre (1559–74), and the 12th–13th-c. Notre-Dame Cathedral. Paris is justifiably renowned for its elegance and style which are exemplified in its shops, restuarants, theatres, etc. and which combine with its many cultural attractions to make it probably the world's greatest tourist city. It is also a major intellectual centre with leading universities, academies, and conservatoires, and numerous institutions of higher or technical instruction, and the headquarters of many international organizations, notably UNESCO. Paris, more than most national capitals, has drawn in population both from France and many other countries. Its many workshops manufacture luxury articles of clothing, perfume, and jewellery, whilst heavy industry, such as the making of cars and trucks, is located in the suburban areas. Paris is the transport and communications focus of western Europe with three airports, a large river port, and seven main railway stations.
**Parisian** *adj. & n.*

**Parisian** /pəˈrɪzɪən/ a native of Paris or the kind of French spoken in Paris.

**Paris-Plage** /ˈpæriː plɑːʒ/ a resort town adjacent to Le Touquet in the department of Pas-de-Calais, northern France.

**Park Avenue** an avenue noted for its luxurious apartments and hotels on the East Side of Manhattan Island, New York, USA. It forms part of Fourth Avenue and stretches northwards from Union Square to Harlem. Its chief landmarks are Grand Central Terminal, the Pan Am Building, and the Seagram Building.

**Parma** /ˈpɑːmə/ **1.** a province in the Emilia-Romagna region of northern Italy, south of the Po; area 3,450 sq. km. (1,332 sq. miles); pop. (1981) 400,190. With neighbouring Piacenza, it was detached from the Papal States by Pope Paul III (Alessandro Farnese) in 1545. It was ruled by the Farnese family until 1731, when it passed to the Spanish. It became a part of united Italy in 1861. **2.** its capital, on the River Parma and the Via Emilia, the second city of Emilia-Romagna after Bologna; pop. (1990) 193,990. Founded by the Romans in 183 BC, it became a bishopric in the 9th c. AD and capital of the duchy of Parma and Piacenza in about 1547. Its Teatro Farnese (1618) was one of the first purpose-built theatres in Europe and was for a long time the largest in the world. Parma gives its name to Parmesan, a hard dry type of cheese originally made there, and Parma hams.

**Parma** /ˈpɑːmə/ a residential suburb of southern Cleveland in Ohio, USA; pop. (1990) 87,880.

**Parnassus** /pɑːˈnæsəs/, **Mount** (Greek **Parnassós** /ˌpɑːnæˈsɒs/) a mountain in central Greece, which rises just north of Delphi to a height of 2,457 m. (8,064 ft.). Held to be sacred by the ancient Greeks, as was the spring of Castalia on its southern slopes, it was associated with Apollo and the Muses and regarded as a symbol of poetry.

**Paros** /ˈpeərɒs/ a Greek island in the southern Aegean, in the Cyclades. It is noted for its fine-textured translucent white marble which has been quarried here since the 6th c. BC; area 195 sq. km. (75 sq. miles). Its chief town is Paros (Paríkia).
**Parian** *adj. & n.*

**Parsee** /pɑːˈsiː/ (also **Pahlavi**) an adherent of Zoroastrianism or a descendant of the Persians who fled to India (especially Bombay) from Muslim persecution in the 10th c.

**Parsenn** /pɑːˈsen/ the name given to a skiing area in the Alps lying between the resorts of Davos and Klosters. Its main peak is Weissfluh (2,844 m., 9,330 ft.) and its runs are amongst the longest in the Alps.

**Parthenon** /ˈpɑːθɪnən/ the temple of Athene Parthenos (= the maiden), built on the Acropolis at Athens in 447–432 BC by Pericles to honour the city's patron goddess and to commemorate the recent Greek victory over the Persians. Designed by the architects Ictinus and Callicrates with sculptures by Phidias, including a colossal gold and ivory statue of Athene (known from descriptive accounts) and the 'Elgin marbles' now in the British Museum, the Parthenon was partly financed by tribute from the league of Greek states led by Athens, and housed the treasuries of Athens and the league.

**Parthia** /ˈpɑːθɪə/ an ancient Asian kingdom to the south-east of the Caspian Sea, which from c. 250 BC to c. 230 AD ruled an empire stretching from the Euphrates to the Indus, with Ecbatana as its capital. The Parthian culture contained a mixture of Greek and Iranian elements and the Parthians were superb horsemen, original and competent in warfare. **Parthian** *adj. & n.*

**Pasadena** /ˌpæsəˈdiːnə/ **1.** an industrial city in south-west California, USA, situated in the San Gabriel Mountains north-east of Los Angeles; pop. (1990) 131,590. Its Rose Bowl stadium is the scene of a celebrated American football match held annually on New Year's Day. Its industries include electronics, aerospace components, plastics, and ceramics. **2.** an industrial suburb of east Houston in Texas, USA, a centre of oil, chemical, and steel production; pop. (1990) 119,360.

**Pasay** /ˈpɑːsaɪ/ a city on the island of Luzon in the Philippines, situated on the eastern shore of Manila Bay and part of 'Metro Manila'; pop. (1990) 374,000.

**Pasco** see CERRO DE PASCO 2.

**Pas-de-Calais** /ˌpædəˈkɑːleɪ/ a department in north-west France, on the English Channel; area 6,672 sq. km. (2,577 sq. miles); pop. (1990) 1,433,200; capital, Arras.

**Pashto** /ˈpʌʃtəʊ/ the Iranian language of the Pathans, the official language of Afghanistan, spoken by some 10 million people there and another 6 million in north-west Pakistan. It is an Indo-Iranian language and, like Persian, is written in a form of the Arabic script.

**Pasig** /ˈpɑːsɪɡ/ a market town on the island of Luzon in the Philippines, on the Pasig River east of Manila; pop. (1990) 395,000.

**Passaic** /pəˈseɪɪk/ **1.** a river of New Jersey, USA, that rises near Morristown and flows c. 128 km. (80 miles) south and east before emptying into Newark Bay. At Paterson are the Great Falls. **2.** a city in New Jersey, USA, on the Passaic River; pop. (1990) 58,040. Settled by the Dutch in 1678 and originally known as Acquackanonk, it developed as a textile town and was renamed Passaic in 1854.

**Passau** /ˈpæsaʊ/ a town in Bavaria, southern Germany, situated at the junction of the Danube with the Inn and Ilz rivers on the Austrian frontier; pop. (1991) 50,665. It has an annual Spring Trade Fair and a university founded in 1978.

**Passchendaele** /ˈpæʃ(ə)nˌdeɪl/ (also **Passendale** /ˈpæs(ə)nˌdeɪl/) a village in western Belgium, in West Flanders south of Bruges. During World War I it marked the furthest point of the British advance in the Ypres offensive of 1917 and was the scene of heavy loss of life.

**Pasto** /ˈpɑːstəʊ/ the capital of the department of Nariño in south-west Colombia, in the Atriz valley at the foot of the Galeras Volcano; pop. (1985) 136,650. Founded in 1537 by Sebastián de Belalcázar, it is famous for its decorative coloured varnish known as *barníz de Pasto*.

**Patagonia** /ˌpætəˈɡəʊnɪə/ a region of South America, in southern Argentina and Chile. Consisting largely of a wind-swept arid plateau, it extends from the Colorado River in central Argentina to the Strait of Magellan and from the Andes to the Atlantic coast. The region is barren except in the river valleys where grapes and fruit are farmed. Sheep are raised by the descendants of Welsh settlers who came here in the 19th c. Oil production has become increasingly developed. It takes its name from the *Patagon*, a Native American people alleged by 17th–18th c. travellers to be the tallest known people. **Patagonian** *adj. & n.*

**Pataliputra** /pəˌtælɪˈpuːtrə/ the ancient name for PATNA.

**Patan** /ˈpɑːtən/ **1.** a town in Gujarat, western India, north-west of Ahmadabad; pop. (1991) 120,000. Capital of the Hindu kings of Gujarat in the 8th c., it is noted for its many Jain temples and its silk. **2.** a town in east-central Nepal, adjacent to Kathmandu, formerly known as Lalitpur. It is an important Buddhist centre with many temples and monasteries.

**paternoster lakes** /ˌpætəˈnɒstə(r)/ a series of elongated lakes connected by rivers, all lying within a glacial trough and looking (on a map) like a rosary.

**Paterson** /ˈpætəs(ə)n/ a city in north-east New Jersey, USA, on the Passaic River; pop. (1990) 140,890. First settled in 1771 and named after Governor William Paterson, it became a leading centre of the textile industry using water-power derived from the Great Falls on the Passaic River.

**Pathan** /pəˈtɑːn/ a Pashto-speaking people inhabiting north-west Pakistan and south-east Afghanistan.

**Pathankot** /pəˈtɑːnkəʊt/ a trading centre in Punjab, north-west India, on the main north route to Jammu and Srinagar; pop. (1991) 147,130.

**Patiala** /ˌpætɪəˈɑːlə/ a city in the Punjab state, north-west India; pop. (1991) 268,520. Formerly the capital of an independent Sikh state, its chief landmarks are the 19th-c. Old Motibagh Palace and the 18th-c. Bahadurgarh Fort.

**Patmos** /ˈpætmɒs/ a Greek island in the Aegean Sea, in the Dodecanese. It is believed that St. John was living there in exile (from AD 95) when he had the visions described in Revelations; area 34 sq. km. (13 sq. miles); its chief town is Hora.

**Patna** /ˈpætnə/ the capital of the state of Bihar in northern India, on the south bank of the Ganges; pop. (1991) 1,098,570. Known as Pataliputra, it was the capital between the 5th and 1st centuries BC of the Magadha kingdom and in the 4th c. AD of the Gupta dynasty. After this it declined and had become deserted by the 7th c. It was refounded in 1541 by the Moguls, becoming a prosperous city and viceregal capital. Lying at the centre of a rice-growing region, its chief landmark is the Goghar grain store, built for the British army by Captain John Garstin of the Bengal Engineers in 1786. It has many academic institutions and a library of rare manuscripts and paintings.

**patois** /ˈpætwɑː/ the dialect of the common people in a region, differing fundamentally from the literary language.

**Patos, Lagoa dos** /ləˌgəʊə dəs ˈpætəs/ a lagoon on the east coast of Rio Grande do Sul in southern Brazil. With an area of 10,153 sq. km. (3,920 sq. miles), it is the largest lagoon in the world.

**Patras** /ˈpætrəs/ (Greek **Pátrai** /ˈpætraɪ/) an industrial port in the north-west Peloponnese, on the Gulf of Patras; pop. (1991) 155,000. It is the chief town of Achaia, the largest city in the Peloponnese, and third-largest city in Greece. Patras was rebuilt on a grid plan after the old medieval town was destroyed by the Turks in 1821. There are ferry links with Italy and the Greek islands. The church of Ayios Andreas is said to contain the skull of St. Andrew.

**Pattaya** /pæˈtaɪə/ a beach resort on the coast of southern Thailand, south-east of Bangkok. Its name means 'south-west wind'. Once a small fishing village, it developed into Thailand's leading resort area in the 1970s after being used by US troops for rest and recreation during the Vietnam War.

**Pau** /pəʊ/ a resort and industrial town on the Gave de Pau, capital of the department of Pyrénées-Atlantiques in the Aquitaine region of south-west France; pop. (1990) 83,930. It was capital of the old province of Bearn and birthplace of Henry IV of France and Charles XIV of Sweden. It has metallurgical and textile industries.

**Pauillac** /pəʊˈjɑːk/ a commune in the Médoc district of Aquitaine in south-west France, noted for its wines. It is associated with great claret-producing properties such as Lafite, Latour, and Mouton Rothschild.

**Paulista** /paʊˈliːstə/ a citizen of São Paulo in Brazil.

**Pavia** /pɑːˈvɪə/ a university city of Lombardy in northern Italy, situated at the junction of the Ticino and Po rivers; pop. (1990) 80,070. It is capital of the province of Pavia. Formerly confined within medieval city walls, its industrial development dates from the late 19th c. St. Augustine and the philosopher Severenus Boethius (480–524) are buried here. Light industries include food processing, agricultural machinery, textiles, and sewing machines.

**Pavlodar** /ˌpævləˈdɑː(r)/ a city in north-east Kazakhstan, on the Irtysh River; pop. (1990) 337,000.

**Pavlograd** /ˈpævləˌgræd/ a food-processing town in east-central Ukraine, east of Dnepropetrovsk; pop. (1990) 125,000.

**Pawnee** /ˈpɔːniː/ a tribe of North American Indians of the Hokan-Caddoan linguistic group, originally occupying the plains and prairies of Nebraska.

**Pawtucket** /pɔːˈtʌkɪt/ an industrial city in the US state of Rhode Island; pop. (1990) 72,640. Settled in 1671 by an ironworker who set up a forge on the Blackstone River, Pawtucket became the birthplace of the Industrial Revolution in the USA when Samuel Slater established the country's first water-powered cotton mill here in 1790 (now a museum). Textiles are still important, as are light industries such as jewellery, paper, and tyres.

**pays** /ˈpeɪɪ/ the name given to small regions of France with a distinctive landscape or culture.

**Paysandú** /ˌpaɪsɑːnˈduː/ a port on the Uruguay River in western Uruguay, capital of the department of Paysandú; pop. (1985) 75,080. Situated opposite Colón in Argentina, it is a centre of the meat-packing and livestock trades.

**Pays Basque** SEE BASQUE COUNTRY.

**Pays de la Loire** /ˌpeɪɪ də læ ˈlwɑː(r)/ a region of western France, centred on the Loire valley and comprising the departments of Loire-Atlantique, Maine-et-Loire, Mayenne, Sarthe, and Vendée; area 32,100 sq. km. (12,391 sq. miles); pop. (1990) 3,059,110. Its chief city is Nantes.

**Pazardzhik** /ˌpəzɜːˈdʒiːk/ a spa town in the Plovdiv region of central Bulgaria, situated on the Maritsa River in the northern foothills of the Rhodope Mountains between Plovdiv and Sofia; pop. (1990) 137,930. It was founded by Tartars in 1485.

**Peace** /piːs/ a river in central Canada, that flows 1,923 km. (1,194 miles) from the Rocky Mountains eastwards across Alberta then north, joining the

Athabasca River just north of Lake Athabasca to form the Slave River. Its two main tributaries are the Smoky and Heart rivers.

**Peak District** /pi:k/ a limestone plateau at the southern end of the Pennines in Derbyshire, England, rising to a height of 636 m. (2,088 ft.) at Kinder Scout. A national park was established in 1951 over 1,404 sq. km. (542 sq. miles) of the Peak District.

**Pearl Harbor** /pɜ:l/ a harbour on the Pacific island of Oahu, in Hawaii, the site of a major American naval base, where a surprise attack on 7 December 1941 by Japanese carrier-borne aircraft, inflicted heavy damage and brought the US into World War II.

**Pearl Islands** /pɜ:l/ (Spanish **Archipiélago de las Perlas**) a group of c. 180 islands in the Gulf of Panama, an inlet of the Pacific in Central America. Visited mostly by sea-anglers, the largest islands in the group are San Miguel, San José, and Pedro González. The group also includes the island of Contadora whose name became associated with the Central American peace process during the 1980s.

**Pearl River** (Chinese **Zhu Jiang** /ʒuˈdʒæŋ/) a river of southern China, forming part of the delta of the Xi, Bei, and Dong rivers. Flowing through the city of Canton (Guangzhou), it widens into a bay that forms an inlet of the South China Sea between Hong Kong and Macau.

**Peary Land** /ˈpɪərɪ/ a mountainous region on the Arctic coast of northern Greenland. It is named after the US explorer Robert E. Peary (1856–1920), who explored it in 1892 and 1900.

**Peć** /petʃ/ (also **Pech**) a market town in south-western Serbia, near the Albanian frontier; pop. (1981) 111,070. Its principal landmark is the Patriarchate of Peć, a monastic house occupied by nuns.

**Pechenga** the Russian name for PETSAMO.

**Pechenegs** /ˈpetʃəˌnegz/ a people of the steppes of Central Asia, north of the Aral Sea, who conquered the territory between the Don and the Danube in the 10th c. but were defeated by armies of Kiev Rus in 1036.

**Pech-Merle** /peʃˈmɜ:l/ a cave system in the Périgord district of south-west-central France. Noted for its prehistoric paintings, it was rediscovered in 1922.

**Pechora** /prˈtʃɔ:rə/ a river of north European Russia, which rises in the Urals and flows some 1,809 km. (1,124 miles) north and east to the Barents Sea.

**Pecos** /ˈpi:kɒs/ a river in southern USA that flows 1,490 km. (931 miles) southwards from the Sangre de Cristo Mountains through New Mexico and Texas before joining the Rio Grande.

**Pécs** /peɪtʃ/ an industrial city in Baranya county, south-west Hungary, at the centre of a noted wine-producing region at the foot of the Mecsek Moun-

tains; pop. (1993) 171,560. Formerly the capital of the southern part of the Roman province Pannonia, it was made a bishopric by the first king of Hungary, St. Stephen, in 1009 and Hungary's first university was founded here in 1367. Occupied by Turks between 1543 and 1686, it developed rapidly as a coal-mining centre in the 19th and 20th centuries. The city is noted for its Zsolnay porcelain.

**pedology** /prˈdɒlədʒɪ/ the scientific study of soils: their characteristics, development, and distribution.

**pedometer** /prˈdɒmɪtə(r)/ an instrument for estimating the distance travelled on foot by recording the number of steps taken.

**Peeblesshire** /ˈpi:bl(ə)zʃɪə(r)/ a former county of Scotland, the greater part of which was included in Tweeddale District in the Borders Region from 1975 to 1996. Its county town was Peebles.

**Peenemunde** /ˌpeɪnəˈmʊndə/ a village in the state of Mecklenburg-West Pomerania, north-east Germany. Situated on a small island off the Baltic coast, it was the chief site of German rocket research and testing during World War II.

**Pegu** /pəˈgu:/ a city and river port of southern Burma, on the Pegu River north-east of Rangoon; pop. (1983) 150,400. Founded in 825 as capital of the Mon kingdom, it is a centre of Buddhist culture. Its chief landmark is the Shwemadaw pagoda.

**Peiping** /peɪˈpɪŋ/ the name of Peking (Beijing), capital of China, from 1928 to 1949.

**Peipus, Lake** see CHUDO, LAKE.

**Pekanbaru** /pəˈkɑ:nbəru:/ (also **Pakanbaru**) an oil town and port on the Siak River on the Indonesian island of Sumatra, capital of the province of Riau; pop. (1980) 145,030.

**Peking** /pi:ˈkɪŋ/ (now transliterated as **Beijing**) the capital of China; pop. (1990) 10,819,000. The city, whose name means 'northern capital', developed from Kublai Khan's capital built in the late 13th c. and was the capital of China, except for brief periods, from 1421. At its centre lies the 'Forbidden City', a walled area containing a number of buildings including the imperial palaces of the emperors of China (1421–1911), entry to which was forbidden to all except the imperial family and servants. Tianamen Square outside the Forbidden City was the scene of demonstrations in June 1989 that resulted in the deaths of hundreds of people. Peking is the political, cultural, financial, educational, and transportation centre of China. It is also a major industrial centre with iron and steelworks, textile mills, machine and repair shops, chemical plants and numerous other heavy and light industries.

**pelagian** /prˈleɪdʒɪən/ an inhabitant of the open sea.

**Pelasgian** /prˈlæzgɪən/ an ancient people inhabiting the coasts and islands of the eastern Mediterranean, especially the Aegean Sea, before the arrival of the Greek-speaking peoples in the Bronze Age.

**Pelée** /ˈpeleɪ/, **Mount** an intermittently active volcano on the island of Martinique, in the West Indies. Its eruption in 1902 destroyed the town of St. Pierre, which at that time was the island's capital, killing its population of some 30,000 and rendering a large area a complete wasteland. It rises to a height of 1,397 m. (4,583 ft.).

**Pelion** /ˈpiːlɪən/ a wooded mountain in Greece, near the coast of south-east Thessaly, rising to a height of 1,548 m. (5,079 ft.). It was held in Greek mythology to be the home of the centaurs, and the giants were said to have piled Olympus on Ossa (another Thessalian mountain) and Ossa on Pelion in their attempt to reach heaven and destroy the gods.

**Pella** /ˈpelə/ an ancient city in northern Greece, north-west of Thessalonika (Salonica). It was capital of Macedonia in the 4th c. BC and birthplace of Alexander the Great.

**Peloponnese** /ˈpeləpəˌniːs/, **the** (also **Peloponnesus** /ˌpeləpəˈniːsəs/, Greek **Pelopónnisos** /ˌpeləˈpɒnɪˌsɒs/) the mountainous southern peninsula of Greece, connected to the mainland by the Isthmus of Corinth and comprising the departments of Corinth, Achaia, Elis, Arcadia, Argolid, Messenia, and Laconia; area 21,321 sq. km. (8,235 sq. miles); pop. (1991) 1,077,000. Patras is the largest city. Its Greek name means 'Island of Pelops'.

**Pelotas** /pəˈloʊtəʃ/ an inland port in the state of Rio Grande do Sul, southern Brazil; pop. (1990) 276,835. It is a major centre of the livestock trade.

**Pemba** /ˈpembə/ **1.** a seaport in northern Mozambique, capital of Cabo Delgado province; pop. (1980) 41,200. Under Portuguese rule it was known as Porto Amelia. **2.** an island off the east coast of Tanzania, north of Zanzibar; area 981 sq. km. (379 sq. miles). Settled in the 10th c. by traders from the Persian Gulf, it was taken in 1822 by Sayyid Said who later became Sultan of Zanzibar. Pemba is a major source of cloves.

**Pembroke** /ˈpembrəʊk/ a small port and agricultural market town on the coast of Dyfed, south-west Wales; pop. (1981) 15,600. Its castle was the birthplace of Henry VII in 1457.

**Pembroke Pines** a city in south-east Florida, USA, situated north of Miami; pop. (1990) 65,450.

**Pembrokeshire** /ˈpembrəʊkˌʃɪə(r)/ a former county of south-west Wales which was incorporated into the county of Dyfed in 1974. Its county town was Haverfordwest. The **Pembrokeshire Coast National Park**, established in 1952, includes a 269-km. (168-mile) long-distance footpath along the coast of west Wales.

**Penang** /pɪˈnæŋ/ (also **Pinang**) **1.** a popular resort island off the west coast of the Malay peninsula. In 1786 it was ceded to the East India

Company as a British colony by the sultan of Kedah. Known as Prince of Wales Island until 1867, it united with Malacca and Singapore in a union of 1826, which in 1867 became the British colony called the Straits Settlements. It joined the federation of Malaya in 1948. (Malay = betel nut island.) At 13.5 km. (8.4 miles), the Penang Bridge which links the island to the mainland is the largest in Asia. **2.** a state of Malaysia consisting of this island and a coastal strip on the mainland; area 1,044 sq. km. (403 sq. miles); pop. (1990) 1,142,200; capital, George Town (on Penang Island). The mainland strip, formerly the province of Wellesley, was first united with the island in 1798 as part of a British colony. **3.** see GEORGE TOWN.

**peneplain** /ˈpiːnɪˌpleɪn/ a generally flat area of land produced by erosion.

**Penghu** see PESCADORES.

**peninsula** /pɪˈnɪnsjʊlə/ a piece of land almost surrounded by water or projecting far into a sea or lake, etc.

**Pennines** /ˈpenaɪnz/ (also **Pennine Chain**) a range of hills in northern England extending northwards from the Peak District in Derbyshire to the Scottish border. Described as the 'Backbone of England', its highest peak is Cross Fell (893 m., 2,930 ft.). A long-distance footpath known as the **Pennine Way** stretches for 402 km. (251 miles) along the full length of the Pennines.

**Pennsylvania** /ˌpensɪlˈveɪnɪə/ a state of the north-eastern USA, west of New Jersey and south of New York; area 117,348 sq. km. (45,308 sq. miles); pop. (1990) 11,881,640; capital, Harrisburg. The largest cities are Philadelphia and Pittsburgh. Pennsylvania is also known as the Keystone State. Founded by the Quaker statesman William Penn and named after his father, Admiral Sir William Penn, it was one of the original 13 states of the US (1787). Once dependent on coal, steel, and the railroad industry, the state (though still a major producer of steel and anthracite coal) is now also a leading manufacturer of chemicals, electrical machinery, cement, cigar leaf tobacco, and food products. Its chief landmarks are Gettysburg National Military Park, Valley Forge National Historical Park, and the Delaware Water Gap National Recreation Area.

**Pennsylvanian** *adj. & n.*

The state is divided into 67 counties:

| County | Area (sq. km.) | Pop. (1990) | County Seat |
|---|---|---|---|
| Adams | 1,355 | 78,270 | Gettysburg |
| Allegheny | 1,890 | 1,336,450 | Pittsburgh |
| Armstrong | 1,680 | 73,480 | Kittaning |
| Beaver | 1,134 | 186,090 | Beaver |
| Bedford | 2,644 | 47,920 | Bedford |
| Berks | 2,239 | 336,520 | Reading |
| Blair | 1,370 | 130,540 | Holidaysburg |
| Bradford | 2,995 | 60,970 | Towanda |
| Bucks | 1,586 | 541,170 | Doylestown |

*(cont.)*

| Butler | 2,051 | 152,010 | Butler |
|---|---|---|---|
| Cambria | 1,797 | 163,030 | Ebensburg |
| Cameron | 1,035 | 5,910 | Emporium |
| Carbon | 998 | 56,970 | Jim Thorpe |
| Centre | 2,876 | 124,810 | Bellefonte |
| Chester | 1,971 | 376,400 | West Chester |
| Clarion | 1,578 | 41,700 | Clarion |
| Clearfield | 2,987 | 78,100 | Clearfield |
| Clinton | 2,317 | 37,180 | Lock Haven |
| Columbia | 1,264 | 63,200 | Bloomsburg |
| Crawford | 2,629 | 86,170 | Meadville |
| Cumberland | 1,422 | 195,260 | Carlisle |
| Dauphin | 1,373 | 237,810 | Harrisburg |
| Delaware | 478 | 547,650 | Media |
| Elk | 2,158 | 34,880 | Ridgeway |
| Erie | 2,090 | 275,570 | Erie |
| Fayette | 2,064 | 145,350 | Uniontown |
| Forest | 1,113 | 4,800 | Tionesta |
| Franklin | 2,012 | 121,080 | Chambersburg |
| Fulton | 1,139 | 13,840 | McConnellsburg |
| Greene | 1,500 | 39,550 | Waynesburg |
| Huntingdon | 2,280 | 44,160 | Huntingdon |
| Indiana | 2,155 | 89,990 | Indiana |
| Jefferson | 1,708 | 46,080 | Brookville |
| Juniata | 1,019 | 20,625 | Mifflintown |
| Lackawanna | 1,199 | 219,100 | Scranton |
| Lancaster | 2,475 | 422,820 | Lancaster |
| Lawrence | 944 | 96,250 | New Castle |
| Lebanon | 944 | 113,740 | Lebanon |
| Lehigh | 905 | 291,130 | Allentown |
| Luzerne | 2,317 | 328,150 | Wilkes-Barre |
| Lycoming | 3,216 | 118,710 | Williamsport |
| McKean | 2,545 | 47,130 | Smethport |
| Mercer | 1,747 | 121,000 | Mercer |
| Mifflin | 1,074 | 46,200 | Lewistown |
| Monroe | 1,583 | 95,580 | Stroudsburg |
| Montgomery | 1,264 | 678,110 | Norristown |
| Montour | 341 | 17,735 | Danville |
| Northampton | 978 | 247,105 | Easton |
| Northumberland | 1,199 | 96,770 | Sunbury |
| Perry | 1,448 | 41,170 | New Bloomfield |
| Philadelphia | 354 | 1,585,580 | Philadelphia |
| Pike | 1,430 | 27,970 | Milford |
| Potter | 2,811 | 16,720 | Coudersport |
| Schuylkill | 2,033 | 152,585 | Pottsville |
| Snyder | 855 | 36,680 | Middleburg |
| Somerset | 2,790 | 78,220 | Somerset |
| Sullivan | 1,173 | 6,100 | Laporte |
| Susquehanna | 2,148 | 40,380 | Montrose |
| Tioga | 2,941 | 41,130 | Wellsboro |
| Union | 824 | 36,180 | Lewisburg |
| Venango | 1,765 | 59,380 | Franklin |
| Warren | 2,301 | 45,050 | Warren |
| Washington | 2,231 | 204,580 | Washington |
| Wayne | 1,901 | 39,940 | Honesdale |
| Westmoreland | 2,686 | 370,320 | Greensburg |
| Wyoming | 1,037 | 28,000 | Tunkhannock |
| York | 2,356 | 339,570 | York |

**Pennsylvania Dutch** an area of Pennsylvania, USA, between Philadelphia and the Susquehanna River, largely populated by descendants of 18th-c. migrants from the Rhineland and Palatinate of Germany who retain their original customs and speech. Amish, Mennonites, and Brethren (Dunkards) are among the groups living in this predominantly rural area.

**Pensacola** /ˌpensəˈkəʊlə/ a port in north-west Florida, USA, on Pensacola Bay which is the largest natural landlocked deepwater harbour in Florida; pop. (1990) 58,165. A Naval Air Station was established here in 1914 and its industries produce chemicals, nylon, pulp, paper, and plywood.

**Pentagon** /ˈpentəgən/, **the** the headquarters of the US Department of Defense, near Washington, DC. Built in 1941–3 in the form of five concentric pentagons, it covers 13.8 hectares (34 acres) and is one of the world's largest office buildings. The name is used allusively for the US military leadership.

**Pentland Firth** /ˈpentlənd fɜ:θ/ a channel separating the Orkneys from the northern tip of mainland Scotland. It links the North Sea with the Atlantic.

**Penza** /ˈpjenzə/ an industrial city and transport centre in south-central Russia, situated on the River Sura, a tributary of the Volga and in the middle of a fertile black-earth district; pop. (1990) 548,000. Industries include food processing, paper, and machinery.

**Penzance** /penˈzæns/ a resort town in Cornwall, south-west England; pop. (1981) 19,600. There is a sea link with the Scilly Isles.

**Peoria** /piːˈɔʊrɪə/ **1.** a river port and industrial city in central Illinois, USA, on the Illinois River; pop. (1990) 113,500. The settlement was established in 1691 around a fort (Fort St. Louis II) established by the French in 1680 and named after the Native Americans who occupied the area when the French arrived. It is a centre of information technology, the livestock trade, and the manufacture of steel and earthmoving equipment. **2.** a city in south-west-central Arizona, USA; pop. (1990) 50,170.

**Perak** /ˈpeərə, peˈræk/ a state of Malaysia, on the west side of the Malay peninsula, a major tin-mining region; area 21,005 sq. km. (8,113 sq. miles); pop. (1990) 2,222,200; capital, Ipoh.

**Pereira** /pəˈreərə/ a city in the fertile Cauca valley of central Colombia, capital of the department of Risaralda; pop. (1985) 300,220. It trades in coffee and livestock.

**Père Lachaise** /per ləˈʃez/ a famous cemetery in Paris, France, named after the confessor of Louis XV, Père Lachaise, who enlarged a former Jesuit building on the site. Amongst those buried within its walls are Honoré de Balzac, Frédéric Chopin, Colette, Edith Piaf, Gioacchino Rossini, and Oscar Wilde.

**Pergamum** /ˈpɜːgəməm/ see BERGAMA.

**Périgord** /ˌperɪˈɡɔːr/ an area of south-west France, in the south-western Massif Central. A former countship, it became a part of Navarre in

1470, becoming united with France in 1670. Until the French Revolution it was part of Guyenne. Watered by the Dordogne, Isle, Vézère, and Dronne rivers and covering an area roughly equivalent to the Dordogne department, it is named after the Petrocorii Gauls. It is noted for its gastronomic delights which include foie gras, truffles, mushrooms, chestnuts, walnuts, and wine. The area is divided into four regions: **1.** the **Périgord Vert** (or **Nontronnais**) in the north, with its pastures and chestnut woods; chief town, Nontron; **2.** the **Périgord Blanc** in the valley of the Dordogne River, with its outcrops of chalky limestone; chief town, Périgueux; **3.** the densely wooded **Périgord Noir** in the south-east, to the south of the of the Dordogne River and noted for its prehistoric cave paintings; chief town, Sarlat; and **4.** the wine-producing **Périgord Pourpre** in the south-west; chief town, Bergerac.

**Périgueux** /ˌperɪ'gɜː/ the capital of the Dordogne department of south-west France, on the River Isle; pop. (1990) 32,850. The 12th-c. Cathedral of St.-Front is one of the largest in south-west France. A commercial centre famous for its pâtés.

**Perlis** /'pɜːlɪs/ a state of Peninsular Malaysia on its northern frontier with Thailand; area 818 sq. km. (316 sq miles); pop.(1990) 187,700; capital, Kangar. It is the smallest state of Malaysia.

**Perm** /pɜːm/ an industrial city of Russia, on the Kama River in the western foothills of the Ural Mountains; pop. (1990) 1,094,000. Its industries include steel, paper, timber, textiles, petroleum products, and the manufacture of bicycles.

**permafrost** /'pɜːməˌfrɒst/ subsoil which remains below freezing-point throughout the year, as in Polar regions.

**Permian** /'pɜːmɪən/ the final period of the Palaeozoic era, following the Carboniferous and preceding the Triassic, lasting from about 286 to 248 million years ago. The climate was hot and dry in many parts of the world during this period, which also saw the extinction of many marine animals, including trilobites, and the proliferation of reptiles.

**Pernambuco** /ˌpɜːnəm'buːkuː/ **1.** a state in north-eastern Brazil, on the Atlantic Ocean; area 101,023 sq. km. (39,020 sq. miles); pop. (1991) 7,122,550; capital, Recife. **2.** the former name of RECIFE.

**Pernik** /'peənɪk/ an industrial city in western Bulgaria, south-west of Sofia; pop. (1990) 121,070. The centre of a coal-mining region, it has iron and glass industries.

**Perpignan** /ˌpɜːpiː'njã/ a city of southern France near the Spanish frontier in the north-eastern foothills of the Pyrenees, capital of the department of Pyrénées-Orientales; pop. (1990) 108,050. A centre of food processing and tourism, it was the fortified capital of the old province of Roussillon.

**Perrier** /'perɪˌeɪ/ the name of a spring at Vergèze, south-west of Nîmes in southern France, that gives its name to an effervescent natural mineral water sold throughout the world.

**Persepolis** /pə'sepəlɪs/ a city of ancient Persia, situated to the north-east of Shiraz in modern Iran. It was founded in the late 6th c. BC by Darius I as the ceremonial capital of Persia under the Achaemenids dynasty. It was partially destroyed in 330 BC by Alexander the Great, and though it survived as the capital of Seleucids it began to decline after this date. The city's impressive ruins include functional and ceremonial buildings and cuneiform inscriptions in Old Persian, and are one of the world's greatest archaeological sites.

**Persia** /'pɜːʃə, 'pɜːʒə/ a country of south-west Asia, which is now known as Iran. The ancient kingdom of Persis, corresponding to the modern district of Fars in south-west Iran, became in the 6th c. BC the domain of the Achaemenid dynasty. It was extended under Cyrus the Great into a powerful empire, which included Media, Lydia, and Babylonia and eventually all of western Asia, Egypt, and parts of eastern Europe. The empire, defied by the Greeks in the Persian Wars of the 5th c. BC, was eventually overthrown by Alexander the Great in 330 BC. Persia was subsequently ruled by a succession of dynasties until it was conquered by the Muslim Arabs between AD 633 and 651. Taken by the Mongols in the 13th c., it was ruled by the Kajar dynasty from 1794 until 1925, when Rez Khan Pahlavi became the shah. It was renamed Iran in 1935.
**Persian** adj. & n.

**Persian** /'pɜːʃ(ə)n/ the language of ancient Persia or modern Iran (officially, Farsi), spoken by over 25 million people in Iran and Afghanistan. It belongs to the Indo-Iranian language group and is attested from the 6th c. BC when Old Persian was the language of the Persian Empire, which at one time spread from the Mediterranean to India. Old Persian was written in cuneiform, but in the 2nd c. BC the Persians created their own alphabet (Pahlavi), which remained in use until the Islamic conquest in the 7th c.; since then Persian or Farsi has been written in the Arabic script.

**Persian Gulf** (also called the **Arabian Gulf**, or **the Gulf**) an arm of the Arabian Sea to which it is connected by the Strait of Hormuz and the Gulf of Oman, separating the Arabian peninsula from mainland Asia. It is a major shipping and supply route, linking the oil-producing countries of the Middle East to the outside world.

**Persis** /'pɜːsɪs/ the ancient name of the province of FARS in south-west Iran. (See also PERSIA.)

**Perth** /pɜːθ/ the capital of the state of Western Australia, on the estuary of the River Swan, the leading commercial and transportation centre of west coast Australia; pop. (1991) 1,018,700. Founded in 1829, it developed rapidly after the discovery of gold and the opening of the Fremantle harbour in 1897. The port exports refined oil, wheat, and wool. Perth has two universities: Western Australia (1911) and Murdoch (1975).

**Perth** /pɜ:θ/ a royal burgh at the head of the Tay estuary in eastern Scotland, administrative centre of Perth and Kinross District; pop. (1981) 43,000. The Scottish Reformation was initiated here in 1559 after a sermon by John Knox. It holds an annual arts festival in May and was the birthplace of the author and statesman John Buchan (1875–1940).

**Perthshire** /'pɜ:θʃɪə(r)/ a former county of central Scotland in the Perthshire and Kinross local government area. From 1975 to 1996 it was part of Perth and Kinross District, Tayside Region.

**Peru** /pə'ru:/ official name **The Republic of Peru** a country in South America on the Pacific coast, traversed throughout its length by the Andes and bounded by Ecuador and Colombia to the north, Brazil and Bolivia to the east, and Chile to the south; area 1,285,216 sq. km. (496,414 sq. miles); pop. (est. 1991) 22,135,000; official languages, Spanish and Quechua; capital, Lima. A narrow coastal plain with a dry desert climate is separated from the tropical lowlands of the Amazon basin by the Andes. Agriculture is important, and cattle, sheep, llamas, and alpacas are bred in the mountain districts. Fish-meal is exported, and mineral exports include lead, zinc, copper, iron ore, and silver. The centre of the Inca empire, Peru was conquered by the Spanish conquistador Pizarro in 1532 and remained under Spanish control for nearly three centuries until liberated by Bolivar and San Martín in 1820–4. A democratic republic was then established but it lost territory in the south to Chile in the War of the Pacific (1879–83) and has had border disputes with Colombia and Ecuador. In recent years its fragile democracy has had to contend with guerrilla groups, the most prominent of which is the Marxist Sendero Luminoso ('Shining Path') group, and with a growing trade in drugs produced from the coca plant which is cultivated in the valleys of the Andes. Peru is governed by an executive president and a bicameral National Congress. **Peruvian** adj. & n.

Peru is divided into 24 departments and the constitutional province of Callao:

| Department | Area (sq. km.) | Pop. (1990) | Capital |
|---|---|---|---|
| Amazonas | 39,249 | 335,300 | Chachapoyas |
| Ancash | 35,041 | 983,200 | Huaraz |
| Apurímac | 20,895 | 371,700 | Abancay |
| Arequipa | 63,345 | 965,000 | Arequipa |
| Ayacucho | 43,814 | 566,400 | Ayacucho |
| Cajamarca | 34,023 | 1,270,600 | Cajamarca |
| Callao | 147 | 588,600 | Callao |
| Cuzco | 71,892 | 1,041,800 | Cuzco |
| Huancavelica | 22,131 | 375,700 | Huancavelica |
| Huánuco | 37,722 | 609,200 | Huánuco |
| Ica | 21,328 | 542,900 | Ica |
| Junín | 44,410 | 1,113,600 | Huancayo |
| La Libertad | 24,795 | 1,243,500 | Trujillo |
| Lambayeque | 14,231 | 935,300 | Chiclayo |
| Lima | 34,802 | 6,707,300 | Lima |
| Loreto | 368,852 | 654,100 | Iquitos |
| Madre de Dios | 85,183 | 49,000 | Puerto Maldonado |
| Moquegua | 15,734 | 134,100 | Moquegua |
| Pasco | 25,320 | 282,900 | Pasco |
| Piura | 35,892 | 1,494,300 | Piura |
| Puno | 72,012 | 1,023,500 | Puno |
| San Martín | 51,253 | 460,000 | Moyobamba |
| Tacna | 16,063 | 209,800 | Tacna |
| Tumbes | 4,669 | 144,200 | Tumbes |
| Ucayali | 102,411 | 230,100 | Pucallpa |

**Perugia** /pə'ru:dʒə/ a medieval city in central Italy, on the Tiber, the capital of Perugia province and chief city of Umbria; pop. (1990) 150,580. Founded by the Etruscans, it was occupied by the Romans from 310 BC. Taken by the Lombards in the late 6th c., it was contested over the succeeding centuries by powerful local families. It flourished in the 15th c. as a centre of the Umbrian school of painting. A papal possession from 1540, it became a part of united Italy in 1860. It has many fine medieval buildings and has two universities one the Italian University for Foreigners. The economy is dependent on tourism and confectionery.

**Pervouralsk** /'pɜ:və'rɑ:lsk/ a town in central Russia, in the Ural Mts. west of Yekaterinburg; pop. (1990) 143,000.

**Pesaro** /pə'sɑ:rəʊ/ a port and resort town at the mouth of the River Foglia on the Adriatic coast of the Marches region, east-central Italy, capital of the province of Pesaro and Urbino; pop. (1990) 90,340. It was the birthplace in 1792 of the composer Rossini.

**Pescadores** /peskə'dɔ:reɪz/, **the** (Chinese **Penghu**, English **Fisherman Isles**) a group of 64 small islands (of which 24 are inhabited) in the Taiwan Strait (Formosa Channel) between Taiwan and mainland China; area 127 sq. km. (49 sq. miles); pop. (1991) 120,000. The majority of the population live on Penghu Island whose chief town is Makung. The bridge linking the islands of Paisha (White Sand) and Hsiyu (West Island) is one of the longest in the Far East.

**Pescara** /pes'kɑ:rə/ a tourist resort and seaport at the mouth of the Pescara River on the Adriatic coast of Abruzzi, east-central Italy, capital of Pescara province; pop. (1990) 128,550. It was the birthplace in 1863 of the writer Gabriele D'Annunzio. Industries include shipbuilding and fishing.

**Peshawar** /pə'ʃa:wə(r)/ the capital of North-West Frontier Province, in Pakistan; pop. (1981) 555,000. Mentioned in early Sanskrit literature, it is one of Pakistan's oldest cities. Under Sikh rule from 1834, it was occupied by the British between 1849 and 1947. Situated at a strategic location near the Khyber Pass which leads into Afghanistan, it is a major road, rail, and military centre. Under British rule it was a base for military operations against the Pathan tribesmen and in the 1980s, during the civil war in Afghanistan, it was the headquarters of several mujahedeen rebel groups.

**Petaling Jaya** /pə'ta:lɪŋ/ an industrial city in south-west Malaysia, 6 km. (4 miles) from Kuala Lumpur; pop. (1980) 207,800. Locally known as 'PJ', the city was established during the 1950s as a squatter settlement.

**Petén** /pə'ten/ an administrative department in the sparsely-populated tropical lowlands of north-eastern Guatemala, on the frontier with Belize and Mexico; area 35,854 sq. km. (13,848 sq. miles); pop. (1985) 118,120; capital, Flores. Its most prominent landmark is the ancient Mayan city of Tikal.

**Peter I Island** (Norwegian **Peter I Øy**) an island in the Bellingshausen Sea, to the west of the Antarctic Peninsula, a dependency of Norway; area 180 sq. km. (70 sq. miles). Visited by the *Norvegia* expedition in 1929, the island was placed under the sovereignty of Norway in 1931 at a time when Norwegian whalers dominated the seas of Antarctica.

**Peterborough** /'pi:təbʌrə/ an industrial city in Cambridgeshire, east-central England, on the River Nene; pop. (1991) 148,800. Catherine of Aragon and Mary Queen of Scots were buried in its 12th-c. cathedral (although the latter was later moved to Westminster Abbey). It has been developed as a planned urban centre since the late 1960s. The city has agricultural and brick-making industries.

**Peterhead** /ˌpi:tə'hed/ a fishing port and North Sea oil base on the coast of Banff and Buchan District in Grampian Region, north-east Scotland; pop. (1981) 17,085.

**Peterlee** /ˌpi:tə'li:/ an industrial town on the North Sea coast of Durham, north-east England, 11 km. (7 miles) north-west of Hartlepool; pop. (1981) 31,570. Developed as a New Town from 1948, it was named in honour of Peter Lee, first Labour chairman of the County Council.

**Petra** /'petrə/ an ancient city of south-west Asia, in present-day Jordan. It was the capital of the country of the Nabataeans from 312 BC until 63 BC, when they became subject to Rome. The city, which lies in a hollow surrounded by cliffs, is accessible only through narrow gorges. Its extensive ruins include the temples and tombs hewn from the rose-red sandstone cliffs ('a rose-red city, half as old as Time'); the site was rediscovered in 1812 by the Swiss traveller Burckhardt and is much visited by tourists.

**Petrified Forest National Park** a national park in eastern Arizona, USA, featuring petrified wood and other fossil deposits dating from the Triassic Period and ruins and petroglyphs of the prehistoric Anasazi Indian farmers resident in the area c. AD 900.

**Petrograd** /'petrəʊˌɡræd/ a former name (1914–24) of St. Petersburg.

**Petropavel** /'petrəˌpa:v(ə)l/ (formerly **Petropavlovsk** Kazakh **Petropavl**) a city in northern Kazakhstan, on the Ishim (Esil) River; pop. (1990) 245,000. It originated as a centre for trading between Russia and central Asian kingdoms; its industrial development has come in the last 100 years. It manufactures machinery, leather, felt, and foodstuffs.

**Petropavlovsk** /ˌpetrəpæv'lɒf/ (formerly **Petropavlovsk-Kamchatskiy**) /ˌpetrəpæv'lɒfskkæmˌtʃætskɪ/ a Russian fishing port and naval base on the east coast of the Kamchatka peninsula in eastern Siberia; pop. (1990) 271,000. It is the base for a large fishing and whaling fleet and is ice-free for seven months of the year.

**Petrópolis** /pə'trɒpəlɪs/ a resort city in south-eastern Brazil, north-east of Rio de Janeiro; pop. (1990) 294,185. Founded by Dom Pedro II in 1843, it was for many years the summer capital of the emperor of Brazil. The emperor's former palace contains the Brazilian Crown Jewels.

**Petrozavodsk** /ˌpetrəzə'vɒtsk/ the capital of the republic of Karelia in north-west Russia, a port on the western shore of Lake Onega; pop. (1990) 252,000. It has metal-working, lumbering, and ship-repair industries.

**Pforzheim** /'pfɔ:tshaɪm/ a city in Baden-Württemberg, south-west Germany, on the Enz River at the northern edge of the Black Forest; pop. (1991) 115,550. It developed from an important medieval trade centre into a modern industrial city noted for its watches and jewellery.

**Philadelphia** /ˌfɪlə'delfɪə/ the chief city of Pennsylvania, USA, a deep-water port at the junction of the Delaware and Schuylkill rivers; pop. (1990) 1,585,580. First settled by Swedes in the 1640s, it is now the second-largest city on the east coast and fifth-largest in the US, with industries producing vehicle parts, electrical machinery, clothes, carpets, scientific instruments, and cigars. It was the site in 1776 of the signing of the Declaration of Independence and in 1787 of the adoption of the Constitution of the United States. The city's Independence National Historical Park includes landmarks of the American War of Independence such as Independence Hall and the Liberty Bell. The actors John, Lionel, and Ethel Barrymore were born in Philadelphia and Benjamin Franklin is buried there.

**Philippi** /'fɪlɪpaɪ, fɪ'lɪp-/ (Greek **Fílippoi** /'fɪlɪpeɪ/) a city of ancient Macedonia, the scene in 42 BC of the two battles in which Antony and Octavian defeated Brutus and Cassius. The ruins lie close to the Aegean coast in north-eastern Greece, near the port of Kaválla (ancient Neapolis).

## Philippines

/'fɪlɪˌpiːnz/ official name **The Republic of the Philippines** a country in south-east Asia consisting of a chain of over 7,000 islands of the Malay Archipelago, the chief of which are Luzon in the north and Mindanao in the south, all separated from the Asian mainland by the South China Sea; area 300,000 sq. km. (115,875 sq. miles); pop. (1990) 60,684,890; languages, Filipino (Tagalog), English, Spanish; capital, Manila. The islands are of volcanic origin and have very indented coastlines, the largest being dominated by mountain ranges which rise to a height of 2,954 m. (9,692 ft.) at Mt. Apo on the island of Mindanao. The southern islands have an equatorial climate, and the central and northern islands a tropical monsoon climate with a wet season from July to October. The Philippines have suffered greatly from frequent typhoons and volcanic eruptions such as Mount Pinatubo in 1991. The country's chief exports are timber, copper, nickel, chemicals, and coconut products. The Portuguese navigator Magellan visited the islands in 1521 and was killed there. Conquered by Spain in 1565, and named 'Filipinas' after King Philip, the islands were ceded to the US following the Spanish–American War in 1898. Occupied by the Japanese between 1941 and 1944, the Philippines achieved full independence as a republic in 1946; although it has continued to maintain close links with the US, the last US military bases were eventually closed in 1992. Between 1965 and 1987 the country was governed by Ferdinand Marcos who maintained power through the increasing use of political corruption and coercion. Following the overthrow of Marcos in 1987 a new constitution was approved by referendum. Legislative authority is vested in a bicameral Congress comprising a House of Representatives and a Senate.
**Philippine** adj.
**Filipino** (feminine **Filipina**) adj. & n.
The country is divided into 14 regions:

| Region | Area (sq. km.) | Pop. (1990) |
| --- | --- | --- |
| Bicol | 17,633 | 3,910,000 |
| Cagayan Valley | 26,838 | 2,341,000 |
| Central Luzon | 18,231 | 6,199,000 |
| Central Mindanao | 23,293 | 3,171,000 |
| Central Visayas | 14,952 | 4,593,000 |
| Cordillero Administrative | 18,294 | 1,146,000 |
| Eastern Visayas | 21,432 | 3,055,000 |
| Ilocos | 12,840 | 3,551,000 |
| National Capital | 636 | 7,929,000 |
| Northern Mindanao | 28,328 | 3,510,000 |
| Southern Mindanao | 31,693 | 4,457,000 |
| Southern Tagalog | 46,924 | 8,266,000 |
| Western Mindanao | 18,685 | 3,159,000 |
| Western Visayas | 20,223 | 5,393,000 |

**Philippopolis** /ˌfɪlɪ'pɒpəlɪs/ the ancient Greek name for PLOVDIV in Bulgaria.

**Philistines** /'fɪlɪˌstaɪnz/ a non-Semitic people opposing the Israelites in ancient Palestine. The Philistines ('Peleset' of Egyptian inscriptions from the time of Rameses III, c. 1190 BC), from whom the country of Palestine took its name, were one of the Sea Peoples who, according to the Bible, came from Caphtor/Crete and settled the southern coastal plain of Canaan in the 12th c. BC. Governed by a league of five city-states (Gaza, Ashkelon, Ashdod, Gath, and Ekron), they gained control of the land and sea routes and acquired a monopoly of metal technology. After repeated conflicts with the Israelites they were defeated by David c. 1000 BC and subsequently declined into obscurity after losing control of the sea trade to the Phoenicians.

**Phnom Penh** /nɒm 'pen/ the capital of Cambodia, a port at the junction of the Mekong, Bassac, and Tonlé Sap rivers; pop. (est. 1991) 900,000. Founded by the Khmers in the 14th c., it succeeded Angkor as capital in the mid-15th c. During the 1970s and 1980s its population fluctuated dramatically, first in response to an influx of refugees after the spread of the Vietnam war to Cambodia, and second when the Khmer Rouge took over the city in 1975 and forced its population of 2.5 million into the countryside as part of a radical social programme. The city was repopulated after the arrival of the Vietnamese in 1979.

**Phoenicia** /fə'niːʃə/ an ancient country on the shores of the eastern Mediterranean, corresponding to modern Lebanon and the coastal plains of Syria. It consisted of a number of city-states, including Tyre and Sidon, and was a flourishing centre of Mediterranean trade and colonization during the second millennium BC.

**Phoenician** /fə'niːʃ(ə)n/ a Semitic people of ancient Phoenicia in southern Syria, of unknown origin, but culturally descended from the Canaanites of the 2nd millennium BC, who occupied the coastal plain of modern Lebanon and Syria in the early 1st millennium BC and derived their prosperity from trade and manufacturing industries in textiles, glass, metalware, carved ivory, wood, and jewellery. Their trading contacts extended throughout Asia, and reached westwards as far as Africa (where they founded Carthage), Spain, and possibly Britain. The Phoenicians continued to thrive under Assyrian and then Persian suzerainty until 332 BC when the capital, Tyre, was sacked and the country incorporated in the Greek world by Alexander the Great. The Phoenician alphabet was borrowed by the Greeks and thence passed down into Western cultural tradition.

**Phoenix** /'fi:nɪks/ the capital and largest city of Arizona, USA; pop. (1990) 983,400. Founded in 1870, it became territorial capital in 1889 and remained the capital when Arizona became a state in 1912. Phoenix is now a centre for information technology and the manufacture of computers and aircraft, its dry climate making it a popular winter resort.

**Phoenix Islands** /'fi:nɪks/ a group of eight islands forming part of the Republic of Kiribati in the south-west Pacific and comprising the islands of Birnie, Enderbury, Kanton (Abariringa), Manra (formerly Sydney), McKean, Nikumaroro (formerly Gardner), Orona (formerly Hull), and Rawaki (formerly Phoenix); area 55 sq. km. (21 sq. miles).

**Phrygia** /'frɪdʒɪə/ an ancient region of west-central Asia Minor, to the south of Bithynia. Centred on the city of Gordium west of present-day Ankara, it dominated Asia Minor after the decline of the Hittites in the 12th c. BC., reaching the peak of its power in the 8th c. under King Midas. Conquered by the Cimmerians c.6760 BC, it was eventually absorbed into the kingdom of Lydia in the 6th c. BC.

**Phuket** /pu:'ket/ **1.** the largest island of Thailand, situated at the head of the Strait of Malacca off the west coast of the Malay Peninsula. **2.** a port at the south end of Phuket island, a major resort centre and outlet to the Indian Ocean; pop. (1990) 23,940.

**physical geography** the branch of geography that deals with the natural features of the earth's surface.

**phytogeography** /ˌfaɪtəʊdʒɪˈɒɡrəfɪ/ plant geography or the study of the geographical distribution of plants.

**Piacenza** /pjəˈtʃenzə/ the capital of Piacenza province in the Emilia-Romagna region of northern Italy, situated on the River Po south-west of Milan; pop. (1990) 103,540. As a Roman colony (Colonia Placentia) it protected the Emilia plain against the Gauls and the incursions of Hannibal, its city centre still retaining the plan of a Roman fortified camp. It developed into an important river port in the Middle Ages and became part of the duchy of Parma. Amongst its landmarks are the 16th-c. Palazzo Farnese and the equestrian statues of the Farnese. Piacenza is an industrial and agricultural centre located near oil and natural-gas fields.

**Piatra** /'pjɑːtrə/ (also **Piatra-Neamţ**/-njæmts/) a resort town in north-east Romania, situated in the foothills of the Carpathians on the River Bistriţa pop. (1989) 115,780. It is the capital of Neamţ county and has industries producing textiles, processed food, paper, sawn timber, metal goods, and chemical products.

**Piauí** /pjaʊˈiː/ a state on the Atlantic coast of north-eastern Brazil; area 250,934 sq. km. (96,923 sq. miles); pop. (1991) 2,581,215; capital, Teresina.

**Piave** /'pjɑːvɪ/ a river in Italy that rises in the Carnic Alps and flows southwards for 224 km. (140 miles) to meet the Adriatic east of Venice.

**Picardy** /'pɪkədɪ/ (French **Picardie**) **1.** a former province of northern France between Normandy and Flanders, the scene of heavy fighting in World War I. **2.** a region of northern France centred on Picardy and comprising the departments of Aisne, Oise, and Somme; area 19,399 sq. km. (7,493 sq. miles); pop. (1990) 1,810,690. Its chief town is Amiens.

**Piccadilly** /ˌpɪkəˈdɪlɪ/ a street in central London, south-east England, stretching from Hyde Park eastwards to **Piccadilly Circus**. It is noted for its fashionable shops, hotels, and restaurants. The name was originally applied to a house, Pickadilly Hall, thought to be named from the obsolete word 'piccadil' (= a border of cutwork inserted on the edge of an article of dress), either because piccadils were manufactured here or because houses built here were on the outskirts of the developed area in the 16th c. Its chief landmarks include Burlington House (home of the Royal Academy), the Ritz Hotel, and the celebrated store of Fortnum and Mason. The aluminium statue of Eros or 'Christian Charity' at the centre of Piccadilly Circus was erected in honour of the 7th Earl of Shaftesbury (1801–85) who was responsible for developing much of the property in the area.

**Pic du Midi de Bigorre** /'piːk du: miːdi: də biˈɡɔː(r)/ a mountain peak of the west-central Pyrenees in France. Rising to 2,868 m. (9,409 ft.), it has an observatory on its summit.

**Pichincha** /piːˈtʃiːntʃə/ a volcano in the Andes of northern Ecuador that rises to a height of 4,794 m. (15,728 ft.) west of Quito. The Battle of Pichincha, which secured the independence of Ecuador, was fought on its lower slopes in 1822.

**Pico** /'piːkəʊ/ the southernmost island in the central group of the Azores, dominated by the active volcano, Pico, which rises to 2,351 m. (7,713 ft.) and is the highest peak in the Azores.

**Pico Bolívar** SEE BOLÍVAR.

**Pico da Neblina** SEE NEBLINA.

**Pico de Aneto** /ˌpiːkəʊ dəˈnetəʊ/ (French **Pic d'Aneto**) the highest peak in the Pyrenees, rising to a height of 3,404 m. (11,168 ft.) in northern Spain. It was first climbed in 1842.

**Pico de Orizaba** /ˌpiːkəʊ də ˌɒrɪˈzɑːbə/ the Spanish name for Citlaltépetl.

**Pico Duarte** SEE DUARTE.

**Pico Rivera** /ˌpiːkəʊ rəˈveɪrə/ a city in southern California, USA, on the San Gabriel and Rio Hondo rivers near Los Angeles; pop. (1990) 59,180.

**Pict** /pɪkt/ a member of an ancient people, of disputed origin and ethnological affinities, who formerly inhabited parts of northern Britain. In Roman writings (c. AD 300) the term *Picti*

(= painted people) is applied to the hostile tribes occupying the area north of the Antonine Wall. According to chroniclers the Pictish kingdom was united with the Scottish under Kenneth MacAlpine in 843, and the name of the Picts as a distinct people gradually disappeared.
**Pictish** *adj.*

**Pidurutalagala** /pǝ‚du:ru:tǝ'lɑ:gǝlǝ/ (also **Pedrotalagala**) the highest mountain peak in Sri Lanka, rising to a height of 2,524 m. (8,280 ft.) east of Colombo.

**Piedmont** /'pi:dmɒnt/ (Italian **Piemonte** /pjeɪ'mɒnteɪ/) a region of north-west Italy in the foothills of the Alps, comprising the provinces of Alessandria, Asti, Cuneo, Novara, Torino, and Vercelli; area 25,400 sq. km. (9,810 sq. miles); pop. (1990) 4,357,230; capital, Turin. It is watered by the River Po. Dominated by Savoy from 1400, it became part of the kingdom of Sardinia in 1720 and the kingdom of Italy in 1861. It was the centre of the movement for a united Italy in the 19th c.

**piedmont** /'pi:dmɒnt/ a gentle slope leading from the foot of mountains to a region of flat land.

**Pieria** /paɪ'ɪrɪǝ/ the name in ancient Greece for a coastal plain of Macedonia, the birthplace of the Muses.

**Pierre** /pɪǝr/ the state capital of South Dakota, USA, on the east bank of the Missouri River; pop. (1990) 12,900. It was first settled in 1880 and lies at the geographic centre of the state.

**Pietarsaari** /‚pi:tǝ'sɑ:rɪ/ (Swedish **Jakobstad** /'jækɒbstɑ:t/) a port in Vaasa province, western Finland, on the Gulf of Bothnia; pop. (1990) 19,880. Its chief industry is the manufacture of wood pulp. The national poet of Finland, J. L. Runeberg, was born here in 1804.

**Pietermaritzburg** /‚pi:tǝ'mɑ:rɪts‚bɜ:g/ a city in the province of KwaZulu-Natal, South Africa, situated in the foothills of the Drakensberg Range; pop. (1985) 192,420. Founded in 1838 by Cape Colony Boers, it was named in honour of the Boer leaders Piet Retief and Gert Maritz who were killed by Zulus. It was capital of the former province of Natal from 1843 (when it was annexed by the British) to 1994.

**Pietersburg** /'pi:tǝz‚bɜ:g/ the capital (since 1994) of the province of Northern Transvaal, South Africa, an agricultural and mining centre north-east of Pretoria; pop. (1985) 29,000.

**Pigalle** /pi:'gɑ:l/ a red-light area of central Paris, France, around the Rue Pigalle and Avenue de Clichy.

**Pik Pobedy** /pi:k pǝ'bjedi:/ (also **Victory Peak**) a mountain in Kyrgyzstan, Central Asia, the highest peak in the Tien Shan range; height, 7,439 m. (24,406 ft.).

**Pilcomayo** /‚pi:lkǝʊ'mɑ:jǝʊ/ a river of South America that rises in the Bolivian Andes and flows south-eastwards through the Gran Chaco for

c. 1,125 km. (700 miles) before joining the Paraguay River near Asunción.

**Pilgrim's Way** the route in southern England followed by pilgrims travelling from Southampton to the shrine of Thomas à Becket at Canterbury.

**Pilipino** /‚pɪlɪ'pi:nǝʊ/ an alternative form of Filipino or TAGALOG, a language of the Philippines.

**Pillars of Hercules** the two promontories known in ancient time as Calpe and Abyla and now known as the Rock of Gibraltar and Mount Acho in Ceuta. Situated opposite one another at the eastern end of the Strait of Gibraltar, they were held by legend to have been parted by the arm of Hercules and were regarded as marking the limit of the known world.

**Pilsen** /'pɪls(ǝ)n/ (Czech **Plzeň**/plzenj/) an industrial city of West Bohemia in the Czech Republic, noted for the production of lager beer; pop. (1991) 173,130. It has heavy industries including armaments, locomotives, turbines, and vehicles.

**Piltdown** /'pɪltdaʊn/ a hamlet in East Sussex, southern England, where the prehistoric Piltdown skull (which later proved to be a hoax) was said to have been discovered in 1912.

**Pinang** see PENANG.

**Pinar del Río** /'pi:nɑ:r del 'ri:ǝʊ/ the capital of Pinar del Río province in western Cuba, situated at the centre of a tobacco-growing region 176 km. (110 miles) west of Havana; pop. (est. 1989) 100,900.

**Pinatubo** /‚pɪnǝ'tu:bǝʊ/, **Mount** a volcano on the island of Luzon in the Philippines, 88 km. (55 miles) north of Manila. It erupted in 1991 destroying the homes of over 200,000 people.

**Pindus Mountains** /'pɪndǝs/ (Greek **Pindhos** /'pɪnðɒs/) a mountain range in west-central Greece, stretching from the Gulf of Corinth to the Albanian frontier. The highest peak is Mount Smolikas which rises to 2,637 m. (8,136 ft.).

**Pine Bluff** a city in south-central Arkansas, USA, on the Arkansas River; pop. (1990) 57,140. Founded in 1819 as a trading post, its industries include the processing of cotton, soyabeans, rice, and wood and the manufacture of paper, chemicals, and transformers.

**Pines** /paɪnz/, **Isle of 1.** the former name of the Isle of Youth (Isla de la Juventud), an island off the south-west coast of Cuba; area 2,199 sq. km. (849 sq. miles); pop. (est. 1989) 70,900. **2.** a resort island off the south-east coast of New Caledonia in the South Pacific; area 150 sq. km. (58 sq. miles); pop. (1983) 1,287. Discovered by Captain Cook in 1774, the island was for many years a French penal colony.

**Pingdingshan** /'pɪŋdɪŋ'ʃɑ:n/ a city in Henan province, east-central China, south of Zhengzhou; pop. (1986) 843,000.

**pingo** /'pɪŋgǝʊ/ a conical hill created when water in unfrozen ground below permafrost freezes to form lens-shaped ice blocks that push up the soil into a dome. Most pingos expand and then collapse, leaving a high-rimmed pond that is filled with water in summer.

**Pingxiang** /pɪŋʃiː'æŋ/ a city in Hunan province, south-east-central China, in the foothills of the Luoxiao Shan Mts. south-east of Changsha; pop. (1986) 1,305,000.

**Pinnacles Desert** a part of Nambung National Park, Western Australia, with a flat sandy landscape that is devoid of vegetation and studded with thousands of weathered limestone pinnacles 1–5 m. (3–16 ft.) tall. They cover an area of 4 sq. km. (1.5 sq. miles).

**Pinsk** /'pɪnsk/ a city in south-western Belorussia, at the junction of the Pripyat and Pina rivers in the heart of the Pripyat or Pinsk Marshes; pop. (1990) 122,000. It is a water-transport junction exporting timber. Industries include ship repairing.

**Piracicaba** /pɪrəsə'kæbə/ a city in the state of São Paulo, southern Brazil, north-west of Campinas; pop. (1990) 302,730. It has a famous agricultural institute.

**Piraeus** /paɪ'rɪəs/ the chief port of Athens in ancient and modern Greece, situated on the Saronic Gulf 8 km. (5 miles) south-west of the city; pop. (1981) 196,400. Used as a port by the ancient Athenians, it was connected to the city by the 'long walls', two parallel walls built in the 5th c. BC. It was destroyed by the Roman general Sulla in 86 BC. Extensive development in the 19th c. led to its modern status as the principal seaport of Greece. It has oil refining and shipbuilding industries as well as chemicals and textiles.

**Pírgos** see PYRGOS.

**Pirmasens** /ˌpɪə(r)mə'zents/ a manufacturing town, especially of boots and shoes, in Rhineland-Palatinate, western Germany, south-west of Kaiserslautern; pop. (1991) 47,800.

**Pisa** /'piːzə/ a city in Tuscany, west-central Italy, capital of Pisa province; pop. (1990) 101,500. The city is noted for the 'Leaning Tower of Pisa', an eight-storey circular bell-tower which leans about 5 m. (17 ft.) from the perpendicular over its height of 55 m. (181 ft.), part of this inclination dating from its construction at the end of the 12th c. Formerly situated on the coast, it was an important Etruscan town and a naval base in Roman times, becoming a powerful maritime city-state in the Middle Ages. It now lies about 10 km. (6 miles) inland, as a result of the silting of the Arno on which it stands. Its university dates from the mid-14th c., and it was the birthplace of Galileo in 1564. Pisa's modern industries include engineering, glassware, pharmaceuticals, and clothing.

**Pishpek** /'pɪʃpek/ see BISHKEK.

**Pisidia** /paɪ'sɪdɪə/ an ancient region of Asia Minor, between Pamphylia and Phrygia, north-east of modern Antalya. Traversed by the Taurus Mountains, the region maintained its independence until, on the death of King Amyntas in 25 BC, it was incorporated into the Roman province of Galatia.
**Pisidian** *adj. & n.*

**Pistoia** /pɪs'tɔɪə/ the capital of Pistoia province in Tuscany, north-central Italy, situated at the foot of the Apennines north-west of Florence; pop. (1990) 89,880. Its industries manufacture paper, small arms, and steel.

## Pitcairn Islands

/'pɪtkeən/ a British dependency comprising a group of volcanic islands in the South Pacific, east of French Polynesia; area 4.6 sq. km. (1.75 sq. miles); pop. (1991) 61. The colony's only settlement is Adamstown, on Pitcairn Island, the chief island of the group (which also includes the uninhabited islands of Henderson, Ducie, and Oeno). Pitcairn Island was discovered in 1767 by a British naval officer, Philip Carteret, and named after the midshipman who first sighted it. It remained uninhabited until settled in 1790 by mutineers from HMS *Bounty* and their Tahitian companions, some of whose descendants still live there.

**Pitch Lake** /pɪtʃ/ an upwelling of pitch or natural asphalt in southern Trinidad near the town of La Brea. Derived from the oil sands that lie beneath the area, and perpetually replenished, it is the largest 'lake' of its kind in the world.

**Piteşti** /pi:'teʃt/ an industrial town and rail junction in southern Romania, situated on the Argeş River in the southern foothills of the Transylvanian Alps 112 km. (70 miles) north-west of Bucharest; pop. (1989) 163,395. It is capital of Argeş county and has industries producing chemicals, textiles, shoes, vehicles, machine tools, and processed food. The surrounding area is a major source of Romania's domestic oil supply.

**Pitons** /'pi:tɒnz/, **the** two conical mountains, Gros Piton (798 m., 2,618 ft.) and Petit Piton (750 m., 2,461 ft.), which rise up out of the Caribbean Sea to the south-west of the island of St. Lucia.

**Pitt River Indians** see ACHUMAWI.

**Pitti** /'pɪti/ an art gallery in Florence, Italy, housed in the Pitti Palace which was begun in 1440 but not completed until after 1549. It contains about 500 masterpieces from the Medici collections, a profusion of art treasures including Gobelin tapestries, and a rich collection of plate, goldsmiths' work, ivories, enamels, etc.

**Pittsburgh** /'pɪtsbɜːg/ an industrial city at the junction of the Allegheny and Monongahela rivers in south-west Pennsylvania, USA; pop. (1990) 369,880. The city, originally named Fort Pitt after the British statesman, William Pitt the Elder, was founded in 1758 on the site of a former French settlement. A coal-mining and steel-producing town for many years, it is now a centre of high technology. The city is associated with the industrialists Andrew Carnegie, Thomas Mellon, and Henry Clay Frick, and was the birthplace in 1826 of the composer Stephen Foster.

**Piura** /'pju:rə/ the capital of Piura department in the coastal desert of north-west Peru; pop. (est. 1990) 324,500. The original settlement of San Miguel de Piura, the first Spanish settlement in Peru, was founded in 1532 by Pizarro, but was moved three times before being built on its present site in 1588. It is an agricultural centre for the surrounding irrigated farmland which produces rice, cotton, corn, and plantains.

**Placid** /'plæsɪd/, **Lake** a lake in the Adirondack Mountains of north-east New York State, USA. It is a noted winter sports centre.

**Plains of Abraham** /pleɪnz, 'eɪbrə,hæm/ a plateau in Quebec City, eastern Canada, scene of the decisive battle for North America in 1759. The British Army under General Wolfe surprised the French defenders by scaling the heights above the city under cover of darkness, and the city fell. The battle led to British control over Canada, but both Wolfe and the French commander Montcalm died of their wounds.

**planalto** /plæn'ɑːltəʊ/ a Portuguese word for a plateau.

**Plano** /'pleɪnəʊ/ an agricultural and industrial city in northern Texas, USA, situated to the north of Dallas; pop. (1990) 128,710. It has feed and flour mills and manufactures metal goods, boats, and trailers.

**Plantation** /plæn'teɪʃən/ a city in south-east Florida, USA, west of Fort Lauderdale; pop. (1990) 66,690.

**Plassey** /'plæsɪ/ (also **Palashi**) a village north-west of Calcutta in West Bengal, India, scene of a British victory in 1757, when a very small British army under Robert Clive defeated a much larger force under the Nawab of Bengal, Siraj-ud-Daula, partly because Clive had previously bribed some of the Indian generals. The victory established British supremacy in Bengal.

**Plate** /pleɪt/, **River** (Spanish **Río de la Plata** /'riːəʊ də læ 'plɑːtə/) a wide estuary on the Atlantic coast of South America at the border between Uruguay and Argentina, formed by the confluence of the Rivers Paraná and Uruguay. The cities of Buenos Aires and Montevideo lie on its shores. Its name refers to the export of silver (Spanish *plata*) in the Spanish colonial period. In 1939 it was the scene of a naval battle between British and German warships.

**plateau** /'plætəʊ/ an area of fairly level high ground,

**platteland** /'plɑːtə,lɑːnt/ an Afrikaans term (= flat land) for the remote country districts of southern Africa.

**Plauen** /'plaʊən/ a town in Saxony, east Germany, on the Weisse Elster south of Gera; pop. (1991) 70,860. It is a textile-milling centre.

**playa** /'plɑːjə/ a Spanish word for a beach also used to describe a flat dried-up area, especially a desert basin from which water evaporates quickly.

**Playa Dorada** /'plɑːjə dɒ'rɑːdə/ a beach resort on the northern Atlantic coastline of the Dominican Republic, 4 km. (2.5 miles) east of Puerto Plata.

**Pleasanton** /'plezəntən/ a city in western California, USA, situated to the east of San Francisco; pop. (1990) 50,550. Wine and cheese are local products, and there are publishing and research activities.

**Pleistocene** /'plaɪstə,siːn/ the first period of the two epochs forming the Quaternary period. The Pleistocene epoch followed the Pliocene and preceded the Holocene (Recent); it lasted from about 2,000,000 to 10,000 years ago, is notable for a succession of ice ages, and also saw the evolution of modern mankind. Towards the end of the epoch many animal species, such as woolly mammoths and sabre-toothed tigers, became extinct.

**Pleven** /'plev(ə)n/ an industrial city in the Lovech district of northern Bulgaria, north-east of Sofia; pop. (1990) 168,000. An important fortress town and trading centre of the Ottoman empire, it was taken from the Turks by the Russians in the Russo-Turkish War of 1877, after a siege of 143 days.

**Pliocene** /'plaɪə,siːn/ the last epoch of the Tertiary period, following the Miocene and preceding the Pleistocene, lasting from about 5.1 million to 2 million years ago. It was a time when many modern mountain ranges were being built, world temperatures were falling, and many species of mammals that had flourished earlier in the Tertiary were becoming extinct.

**Płock** /pwɒtsk/ a port on the River Vistula in central Poland, capital of Płock county; pop. (1990) 123,400. A fortified stronghold, Płock was made a bishopric in the 11th c. and a royal residence in the 12th c. During the 1960s oil refining and petrochemical industries were developed.

**Ploieşti** /plɔɪ'eʃt/ an oil-refining city on the Wallachian Plain of central Romania, 59 km. (37 miles) north of Bucharest; pop. (1989) 247,500. It is the capital of Prahova county and leading centre of Romania's petroleum industry, with industries producing petrochemicals, textiles, processed food, and heavy equipment for the mining and oil industries.

**Plovdiv** /'plʌvdɪf/ an industrial and commercial city and market town in central Bulgaria on the River Maritsa, the second-largest city in Bulgaria;

pop. (1990) 379,080. A city of ancient Macedonia from 341 BC, when it was conquered by Philip II of Macedon, it became part of Roman Thrace in AD 46 and was taken by the Turks in 1364. Known to the Greeks as Philippopolis (= Philip's city) and to the Romans as Trimontium, it assumed its present name after World War I. Landmarks include a Roman amphitheatre and medieval buildings. Industries include machinery, textiles, footwear, electrical goods, and foodstuffs.

**Plymouth** /'plɪməθ/ the capital of the island of Montserrat in the West Indies; pop. (1985) 3,500.

**Plymouth** /'plɪməθ/ **1.** a port, naval base, light industry and commercial centre in south-west England, on the Devon coast; pop. (1991) 238,800. It was from here that Sir Francis Drake set sail in 1588 to attack the Spanish Armada, and he and other Elizabethan explorers set out from Plymouth Sound. In 1620 the Pilgrim Fathers sailed from Plymouth to North America in the *Mayflower*. There are many naval monuments and points of interest, and ferry links with Spain and France. Plymouth University (formerly Polytechnic South West) was established in 1992. **2.** a shipping forecast area covering the English Channel roughly between the meridians of the Scilly Isles in the west and Start Point in the east.

**Plymouth** /'plɪməθ/ **1.** a resort town in eastern Massachusetts, USA, on Cape Cod Bay south-east of Boston; pop. (1986) 40,290. Founded by the Pilgrim Fathers in 1620, it was the first permanent setlement by Europeans north of Virginia. The 25-m. (81-ft.) National Monument to the Forefathers, built between 1859 and 1889, is the tallest granite monument in the USA. **2.** an industrial city in south-east Minnesota, USA, situated north-west of Minneapolis; pop. (1990) 50,890. **3.** a village in south-central Vermont, USA, the birthplace in 1872 of Calvin Coolidge, 30th president of the USA.

**Plymouth Rock** a granite boulder at Plymouth in the US state of Massachusetts, on which the Pilgrim Fathers are said to have stepped from the *Mayflower*.

**Plzeň** the Czech name for PILSEN.

**Po** /pəʊ/ a river in northern Italy. Italy's longest river, it rises in the Cottian Alps near the border with France and flows 668 km. (415 miles) eastwards to meet the Adriatic in a wide delta east of Ferrara. Its fertile plain is densely settled and the river is extensively used for irrigation. Many small medieval towns such as Novara and Verona grew up on the spring line or *fontanili* at the margins of the plain.

**Poás** /pəʊ'ɑːs/, **Volcán** a volcanic peak in Costa Rica, rising to 2,704 m. (8,872 ft.) north-west of San José. It has three craters, one of which is still active and contains molten sulphur. It also has the world's most powerful geyser activity.

**Poblano** /pɒb'lɑːnəʊ/ a citizen of Puebla in Mexico.

**Podgorica** /'pɒdgəˌriːtsə/ (also **Podgoritsa**) the capital of the republic of Montenegro in the Balkans; pop. (1981) 132,400. A New Town, from 1948 until 1992 it was named Titograd in honour of Marshall Tito, former president of Yugoslavia. It has tobacco and aluminium industries.

**Podolsk** /pɒ'dɒlsk/ an industrial city in western Russia, on the Pakhra River south of Moscow; pop. (1990) 209,000. It has electro-technical, and heavy machinery and equipment industries.

**P'ohang** /pəʊ'hɑːŋ/ a city in south-east Korea, in North Kyinsang province; pop. (1990) 309,000. It has iron and steel and food-processing industries.

**Pohnpei** /'pəʊnəˌpeɪ/ (formerly **Ponape**) a volcanic island and associated coral atolls forming one of the four states of Micronesia in the North Pacific; area 344 sq. km. (133 sq. miles); pop. (est. 1990) 33,100; capital, Kolonia.

**Point-à-Pitre** /ˌpwæta'piːtr/ the largest town, port, and commercial capital of the French overseas territory of Guadeloupe, on the south-west coast of the island of Grande-Terre; pop. (1988) 25,310.

**Pointe-Noire** /ˌpwæt'nwɑː(r)/ the chief seaport of the Congo, an oil terminal on the Atlantic coast of West Africa; pop. (1990) 387,770. It exports timber, cotton, palm-oil, groundnuts, and coffee, and has shipbuilding, food-processing, and plywood industries.

**Poitiers** /'pwætɪˌeɪ/ a city in west-central France, the capital of the department of Vienne and chief town of the Poitou-Charentes region.; pop. (1990) 82,500. It was capital of the former province of Poitou and the location of a number of important battles; here the Merovingian king Clovis defeated the Visigoths under Alaric in 507, Charles Martel halted the Saracen advance in 732, and Edward the Black Prince defeated the French in 1356.

**Poitou** /pwæ'tuː/ a former province of west-central France now united with Charente to form the region of Poitou-Charentes. Formerly part of Aquitaine, it was held by the French and English in succession until it was finally united with France at the end of the Hundred Years War.

**Poitou-Charentes** /ˌpwætu:ʃæ'rɑ̃t/ a region of western France, on the Bay of Biscay, centred on Poitiers. It comprises the departments of Charente, Charente-Maritime, Deux-Sèvres, and Vienne; area 25,809 sq. km. (9,969 sq. miles); pop. (1990) 1,595,080.

**Pokhara Valley** /'pəʊkərə/ a tropical plain in the mountains of Nepal, accessible by road and air from Kathmandu which lies 200 km. (125 miles) to the south-east. The home of the Gurung people, the valley is a popular area for trekking and fishing.

**Pokrovsk Glazov** /pə'krɒfsk glə'zɒf/ an industrial town in the Caspian lowlands of western Russia, on the Volga opposite Saratov; pop. (1990) 183,000. From 1931 to 1992 it was named Engels in honour of Friedrich Engels (1820–95), the co-founder with Marx of 'Scientific Socialism'. Its industries include chemicals, machinery, railway wagons, and leather goods.

**Poland** /'pəʊlənd/
(Polish **Polska**
/'pɒlskə/) official name
**The Republic of
Poland** a country in
central Europe with a
coastline on the Baltic
Sea, bordered by
Germany, the Czech
Republic, Slovakia,
Ukraine, Belorussia, Russia, and Lithuania; area 304,463 sq. km. (117,599 sq. miles); pop. (1990) 38,183,160; official language, Polish; capital, Warsaw. The largest cities are Warsaw, Łodz, Cracow, Wrocław, and Poznan. Most of Poland is a low-lying rolling plain bounded in the south by the Sudeten Mountains and the Carpathians. The country, whose chief exports are industrial products, has deposits of copper and iron, and some of the largest coalfields in the world. First united in the 11th c., Poland emerged from a period of internal division to become the dominant east European power in the 16th c. Thereafter it suffered severely from the rise of Russian, Swedish, Prussian, and Austrian power, losing territory and eventually its independent identity in three partitions between 1772 and 1795; the country did not regain full independence until (as a republic) after World War I. Its invasion by German forces in 1939 precipitated World War II, and after 1945 it was dominated by the USSR until the late 1980s, when the rise of the independent trade union movement Solidarity, and the eventual introduction of democratic reforms, brought to an end nearly 45 years of Communist rule. Poland chose the path of 'shock therapy' in making the transition to a market economy and de-spite rising unemployment, a fall in average incomes, and a constant regrouping of political parties, industrial production in both the state-owned and private sectors began to grow in the early 1990s. Poland is governed by a bicameral National Assembly comprising the Senate and the *Sejm* (lower house).
**Polish** *adj.*
**Pole** *n.*
The country is divided into 49 counties (*voivod-ships*):

| County | Area (sq. km.) | Pop. (1990) |
|---|---|---|
| Biała Podlaska | 5,348 | 305,340 |
| Białystock | 10,055 | 692,820 |
| Bielsko-Biala | 3,704 | 900,260 |
| Bydgoszcz | 10,349 | 1,110,770 |

| | | |
|---|---|---|
| Chełm | 3,866 | 247,230 |
| Ciechanów | 6,362 | 428,360 |
| Cracow | 3,254 | 1,231,640 |
| Czestochowa | 6,182 | 776,660 |
| Elblag | 6,103 | 478,865 |
| Gdańsk | 7,394 | 1,431,570 |
| Gorzów | 8,484 | 500,670 |
| Jelenia Góra | 4,378 | 517,880 |
| Kalisz | 6,512 | 710,750 |
| Katowice | 6,650 | 3,988,830 |
| Kielce | 9,211 | 1,126,670 |
| Konin | 5,139 | 469,190 |
| Koszalin | 8,470 | 508,170 |
| Krosno | 5,702 | 495,010 |
| Legnica | 4,037 | 515,860 |
| Leszno | 4,154 | 386,840 |
| Łodz | 1,523 | 1,139,500 |
| Łomza | 6,684 | 346,705 |
| Lublin | 6,792 | 1,016,355 |
| Nowy Sacz | 5,576 | 697,875 |
| Olsztyn | 12,327 | 753,030 |
| Opole | 8,535 | 1,018,610 |
| Ostrołeka | 6,498 | 397,280 |
| Piła | 8,205 | 480,745 |
| Piotrków | 6,266 | 642,625 |
| Płock | 5,117 | 516,430 |
| Poznań | 8,151 | 1,334,090 |
| Przemysl | 4,437 | 406,770 |
| Radom | 7,294 | 751,130 |
| Rzeszów | 4,397 | 723,700 |
| Siedlce | 8,499 | 651,430 |
| Sieradz | 4,869 | 408,140 |
| Skierniewice | 3,960 | 419,340 |
| Słupsk | 7,453 | 413,820 |
| Suwałki | 10,490 | 470,620 |
| Szczecin | 9,981 | 972,070 |
| Tarnobrzeg | 6,283 | 599,060 |
| Tarnów | 4,151 | 670,260 |
| Toruń | 5,348 | 659,120 |
| Wałbrzych | 4,168 | 740,900 |
| Warsaw | 3,788 | 2,421,590 |
| Włocław | 4,402 | 429,430 |
| Wrocław | 6,287 | 1,128,790 |
| Zamosc | 6,980 | 490,400 |

**polar circle** each of the circles parallel to the equator at a latitude of 23° 27′ from the North and South Poles.

**polder** /'pəʊldə(r)/ a piece of low-lying land re-claimed from the sea or a river, especially in the Netherlands where *c.* 50 per cent of the total land area consists of polders.

**Pole** /pəʊl/ a citizen of Poland or person of Polish descent.

**pole** /pəʊl/ each of the extremities of the axis of rotation of the earth. The **North Pole** is covered by the Arctic Ocean and the **South Pole** by the con-tinent of Antarctica. The **magnetic poles**, which are the points towards which the needle of a mag-netic compass will point, differ from the geograph-ical poles by an angle known as the *magnetic variation*. The location of the magnetic poles varies with time.

**Polish** /'pəʊlɪʃ/ the language of Poland, which belongs to the Slavonic language group and is spoken by its 38 million inhabitants, by Poles in the Baltic States and Belorussia (Belarus), and by some 2,500,000 people in the USA.

**Polish Corridor** a former region of Poland, which extended northwards to the Baltic coast and separated East Prussia from the rest of Germany. A part of Polish Pomerania in the 18th c., the area had since been subject to German colonization. It was granted to Poland after World War I to ensure Polish access to the coast. Its annexation by Germany in 1939, with the German occupation of the rest of Poland, precipitated World War II. After the war the area was restored to Poland.

**Polonnaruwa** /ˌpɒlənə'ruːvə/ a town in north-east Sri Lanka, on Lake Parakrama Samudra; pop. (1981) 11,600. An ancient capital of Ceylon after the Sinhalese abandoned Anuradhapura, it became an important Buddhist centre in the 12th c. It was subsequently deserted until a modern town was built there in the 20th c.

**Polovtsy** /pə'lɒvtsɪ/ a people of the steppe lands of northern Kazakhstan and southern Siberia who dominated the eastern European steppes between the Volga and the Danube from the mid-11th c. to the mid-13th c. when their state was overcome by the Mongols.

**Poltava** /pəl'taːvə/ a city in east-central Ukraine, on the Vorskla River between Kiev and Kharkov; pop. (1990) 317,000. It was besieged unsuccessfully in 1709 by Charles XII's Swedish forces, who were defeated by the Russians under Peter the Great. A centre of the Ukrainian national movement, it was in the 17th c. the chief town of the Ukrainian Cossack regiment. It is an industrial and agricultural centre with railway works, and vehicle and textile factories.

**Polynesia** /ˌpɒlɪ'niːʒə/ a region of the central Pacific, lying to the east of Micronesia and Melanesia and containing the easternmost of the three great groups of Pacific islands, including New Zealand, Hawaii, the Marquesas Islands, Samoa, the Cook Islands, and French Polynesia.

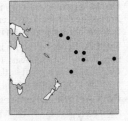

**Polynesian** *adj. & n.*

**Pomerania** /ˌpɒmə'reɪnɪə/ (Polish **Pomorze**, German **Pommern**) a region along the south shore of the Baltic Sea, between the Oder and Vistula rivers. Most of it is now part of Poland, but the western section is in Germany in the state of Mecklenburg-West Pomerania. A former Slavic duchy, Pomerania was divided into the Polish principalities of West Pomerania and East Pomerania

(Pomerelia) in the 12th c., East Pomerania remaining part of Poland until ceded to Prussia in 1772.

**Pomerol** /'pɒmərɔːl/ a wine region of Bordeaux in south-west France, situated north-west of St. Emilion.

**Pomona** /pə'məʊnə/ a residential and industrial city in south-west California, USA, east of Los Angeles; pop. (1990) 131,720. It is a centre of fruit and vegetable canning.

**Pompadour** /'pɒmpəduər/ a village in the Corrèze department of Limousin, south-west-central France, whose 15th-c. chateau was a gift from Louis XV to Madame de Pompadour in 1745. A famous national stud of Anglo-Arab horses was established here in 1761.

**Pompano Beach** /'pɒmpənəʊ/ a resort city on the Atlantic coast of south-east Florida, USA, with a seven-mile-long ocean beach; pop. (1990) 72,410.

**Pompeii** /pɒm'peɪɪ/ an ancient city in western Italy, south-east of Naples. The life of the city came to an abrupt end following an eruption of Mount Vesuvius in AD 79, as described by Pliny the Younger (and in which his uncle, the Elder Pliny, perished). The city lay buried for centuries beneath several metres of volcanic ash until excavations of the site began in 1748. The well-preserved remains of the city include not only buildings and mosaics but wall-paintings, furniture, graffiti, and the personal possessions of the inhabitants, providing an unusually vivid insight into the life, art, and architecture of the period.

**Ponape** see POHNPEI.

**Ponce** /pɒn'seɪ/ the third-largest city on the Caribbean island of Puerto Rico, a port on the south coast named after the Spanish explorer Ponce de León; pop. (1990) 187,750. It exports sugar and its industries include oil refining, distilling, cement, and textiles.

**Pondicherry** /ˌpɒndɪ'tʃerɪ/ **1.** a Union Territory in south-east India, formed from several former French territories incorporated into India in 1954 and comprising the districts of Pondicherry, Karaikal, Mahé, and Yanam; area 492 sq. km. (190 sq. miles); pop. (1991) 789,410. **2.** its capital city on the Tamil Nadu coast; pop. (1991) 401,340. Its industries include cotton textiles.

**Ponferrada** /ˌpɒnfə'raːdə/ an industrial town in the province of León, western Spain; pop. (1991) 59,440.

**Ponta Delgada** /'pɒntə del'gaːdə/ a resort and port on the island of São Miguel in the Portuguese Azores; pop. (1981) 22,200.

**Pont du Gard** /ˌpɒ̃ djuː 'gaː(r)/ an arched structure built by the Romans c. AD 14 over the River Gard or Gardon in southern France as part of an aqueduct carrying water to Nîmes. Three tiers of limestone arches of diminishing span support the covered water-channel at a height of 55 metres

(180 ft.) above the valley. In the 18th c. the lowest tier was widened to form a road bridge that is still in use.

**Pontefract** /'pɒntɪfrækt/ an industrial town in West Yorkshire, England, south-east of Leeds; pop. (1981) 29,050. There are remains of a Norman castle where Richard II died and the town gives its name to liquorice Pontefract cakes.

**Pontevedra** /ˌpɒntɪ'vedrə/ a port of Galicia in north-west Spain, capital of the province of Pontevedra; pop. (1991) 74,850. It has fishing and shipbuilding industries.

**Pontiac** /'pɒnti:æk/ an industrial city in south-east Michigan, USA, on the Clinton River; pop. (1990) 71,170. Once the summer seat of Chief Pontiac of the Ottawa Indians, Pontiac was founded in 1818 as a way station on the wagon-train trail to the west. The manufacture of wagons gave way to the automobile industry and the city became the home of the Pontiac Division of General Motors.

**Pontianak** /ˌpɒntɪ'ɑːnæk/ a seaport of Indonesia, capital of the province of West Kalimantan, situated on the west coast of Borneo at the junction of the Landak and Kapuas rivers; pop. (1990) 397,670. Its name, coined by early hunters who heard strange noises in the jungle, means 'the vampire ghost of a woman who dies in childbirth'. Situated on the equator, the original settlement was founded by an Arab trader, Abdul Rahman, in 1770. It exports the primary products of the surrounding area.

**Pontine Marshes** /'pɒntaɪn/ (Italian **Agro Pontino** /'ægrəʊ pɒn'tiːnəʊ/) an area of reclaimed marshland area in western Italy, on the Tyrrhenian coast south-west of Rome. Uninhabited in ancient times, it became infested with malaria in the later years of the Roman Republic. The area remained unhealthy despite attempts at reclamation, until in 1928 an extensive scheme to drain the marshes was begun. It is now a very productive agricultural area producing grain, fruit, flowers, and dairy produce. In addition to land irrigation, several new towns have been built, including Latina, Sabaudia, Pontinia, and Aprilia.

**Pontus** /'pɒntəs/ an ancient region of northern Asia Minor, on the Black Sea coast north of Cappadocia. Established as an independent kingdom by the end of the 4th c. BC, it reached the height of its powers between 120 and 66 BC under Mithridates VI. At this time it dominated the whole of Asia Minor, but by the end of the 1st c. BC it had been defeated by Rome and absorbed into the Roman Empire.

**Pontoise** /pɔ̃'twɑːz/ the capital of the department of Val d'Oise in the Ile de France region of central France, on the River Oise; pop. (1990) 28,460.

**Pontypool** /'pɒntɪpʊl/ an industrial town in Gwent, south-east Wales; pop. (1981) 36,300.

**Pontypridd** /ˌpɒntɪ'priːθ/ an industrial town in Mid Glamorgan, south Wales, on the River Taff; pop. (1981) 29,800. Glamorgan University (formerly Polytechnic of Wales) was established here in 1992.

**Poole** /puːl/ a port and resort town on the south coast of England, in Dorset just west of Bournemouth; pop. (1991) 130,900. The first Boy Scout camp was held in 1907 on Brownsea Island in Poole Harbour which is a noted yachting centre. There are ferry links with France.

**Poona** see PUNE.

**Popayán** /ˌpɒpə'jɑːn/ a city in south-west Colombia, situated at the foot of Puracé volcano in the Andes; pop. (1985) 164,810. Founded by the Spanish in 1536, it is capital of the coffee-growing department of Cauca.

**Popocatépetl** /ˌpɒpəkæ'teɪpet(ə)l/ a dormant volcano in Mexico, 72 km. (45 miles) south-east of Mexico City, rising to a height of 5,452 m. (17,887 ft.).

**Porbandar** /pɔː'bənər/ a town in Gujarat, western India, a port on the Arabian Sea; pop. (1991) 160,040. It was a former capital of the Jethwa Rajput and the birthplace in 1869 of Mahatma Gandhi. Its industries produce silk, cotton, chemicals, and cement.

**Pordenone** /ˌpɔːdeɪ'nəʊnɪ/ the capital of the province of Pordenone in the Friuli-Venezia-Giulia region of north-eastern Italy; pop. (1990) 50,220. It is a leading producer of 'white goods': washing machines and refrigerators.

**Pori** /'pɔːrɪ/ (Swedish **Björneborg**) an industrial port in south-west Finland at the entrance to the Gulf of Bothnia; pop. (1990) 76,360. Fishing, shipbuilding, the refining of copper and nickel, and trade in coal, oil, and general cargo are its chief industries.

**Portalegre** /pɔːtə'legrɪ/ the capital town of Portalegre district in east-central Portugal, near the Spanish border; pop. (1981) 14,800.

**Port Arthur** /'ɑːθə(r)/ a historic site on the Tasman Peninsula, south-east Tasmania, Australia, once famous as a penal settlement but whose ruins are now a tourist attraction.

**Port Arthur** the former name (1898–1905) of the naval port of LÜSHUN in north-east China, now part of LÜDA.

**Port Arthur** a city in south-east Texas, USA, on Lake Sabine; pop. (1990) 58,720. Once an anchorage for the pirate Jean Lafitte, the area around Port Arthur was settled by French Acadians in the 18th c. In 1895 it was chosen as the Gulf terminus of the Kansas City, Pittsburg and Gulf Railroad and a city was founded. In addition to shipping and chemical industries, Port Arthur is the largest petroleum-refining centre in the US.

**Port Augusta** /ɔː'gʌstə/ an industrial port in South Australia, at the head of Spencer Gulf 317 km. (200 miles) north of Adelaide; pop. (1991) 14,595. It developed as an important shipping centre and supply port for inland pastoralists and is now also a centre of power generation fuelled by coal from the open-cast mines of nearby Leigh Creek.

**Port-au-Prince** /ˌpɔːtəʊˈprɪns/ the capital of Haiti, a port on the west coast of the island of Hispaniola in the West Indies; pop. (1988) 1,143,630. Founded by the French in 1749, it became capital of the new republic in 1806 when it was called Port Republicain. Sugar, rum, and textiles are its chief products.

**Port Bell** a train ferry port in Uganda, situated near Kampala on the north-west coast of Lake Victoria. Opened in 1992, it links the Tanzania Railways terminus at Mwanza.

**Port Blair** /bleə(r)/ a port on the southern tip of South Andaman Island in the Bay of Bengal; pop. (1991) 74,810. It is the capital of the Andaman and Nicobar Islands.

**Port Dickson** /pɔːt ˈdɪksən/ a resort town on the west coast of Peninsular Malaysia, on the Straits of Malacca 32 km. (20 miles) south-west of Seremban. It is a popular weekend retreat from Kuala Lumpur. Originally known as Tanjung Kamuning, the town was renamed in honour of Sir Frederick Dickson, British Colonial Secretary and acting Governor in 1890.

**Porte** /pɔːt/ (in full **the Sublime Porte** or **Ottoman Porte**) the name formerly given to the Ottoman court at Constantinople (now Istanbul).

**Port Elizabeth** /ɪˈlɪzəbəθ/ a seaport and beach resort on the coast of Eastern Cape, South Africa, on Algoa Bay; pop. (1985) 652,000. Settled in 1820 on the site of a British fort (Fort Frederick), it was named after the wife of the acting governor of the province. Largely developed since the creation of the rail link with Kimberley, the city now produces a wide range of goods including steel, textiles, and vehicles.

**Port el Kantaoui** /el kænˈtaʊɪ/ a resort town and yachting centre on the east coast of Tunisia, to the north of Sousse.

**Port Étienne** /pɔːt etˈjen/ the former name (until c. 1965) of NOUADHIBOU.

**Port-Gentil** /ˌpɔːʒɑ̃ˈtiː/ the principal port of Gabon in West Africa, on the Atlantic coast south of Libreville, capital of the province of Ogooué-Maritime; pop. (1983) 123,300. Oil refining and the timber trade are important industries.

**Port Harcourt** /ˈhɑːkɔːt/ the principal seaport of south-east Nigeria, on the River Bonny at the eastern edge of the Niger delta; pop. (1983) 296,200. Established just before World War I as an outlet for coal from the Enugu coalfields, it was named after the British statesman Sir William Harcourt. It has many industries including steel and aluminium products, tyres, paint, and vehicle assembly.

**Port Hedland** /ˈhedlənd/ a seaport on the north-west coast of Western Australia, linked by rail to the iron-ore mines at Newman in the south; pop. (est. 1987) 13,600. Originally an outlet for gold and manganese, an iron-ore boom began in the 1960s. Salt is also exported. It is named in honour of Captain Peter Hedland who discovered the harbour in 1829.

**Port Kelang** /kəˈlæŋ/ (also **Klang** or **Kelang**) a rubber port on the Strait of Malacca in the Malaysian state of Selangor, 30 km. (19 miles) south-west of Kuala Lumpur; pop. (1980) 192,080. Until 1971 it was named Port Sweetenham in honour of British Resident Frank Sweetenham.

**Portland** /ˈpɔːtlənd/ a shipping forecast area covering the English Channel roughly between the meridians of Start Point in the west and Poole in the east, taking its name from the Isle of Portland. (See PORTLAND, ISLE OF.)

**Portland** /ˈpɔːtlənd/ **1.** an industrial port on the Williamette River near its junction with the Columbia River in north-west Oregon, USA; pop. (1990) 437,320. Settled in 1851, it is now the largest city in Oregon and home of the University of Portland (1901), Portland State University (1946), and Lewis and Clark College (1867). It has an international airport and has timber, fishing, and shipbuilding industries. The city hosts an annual rose festival in mid-June. **2.** a city in south-east Maine, USA, on Casco Bay; pop. (1990) 64,360. Settled in 1632, it is the largest city in the state. It is a centre for shipping and North Atlantic fishing and was the boyhood home of the poet Henry Longfellow. **3.** an important naval harbour and base on the coast of Dorset, England. Its 1,829 m.- (6,000 ft.-) long breakwater was built by convicts between 1849 and 1872.

**Portland** /ˈpɔːtlənd/**, Isle of** a rocky limestone peninsula on the Dorset coast of England, south of Weymouth, described by Thomas Hardy as 'the Gibraltar of Wessex'. Its southernmost tip is known as the **Bill of Portland**. Stone from its quarries is a famous building material that was used by Wren for St. Paul's Cathedral.

**Port Laoise** /pɔːtˈliːʃ/ (also **Portlaoighise**) the county town of Laois in the Irish province of Leinster, 80 km. (50 miles) south-west of Dublin; pop. (est. 1990) 9,500. Formerly known as Maryborough, it the site of a top-security prison.

**Port Louis** /ˈluːɪ/ a seaport in the Indian Ocean, capital of the island of Mauritius; pop. (1991) 143,000. Founded in 1735, it developed as a trading port after the construction of the Suez Canal.

**Port Macquarie** a resort town on the Pacific coast of New South Wales, south-east Australia, situated at the mouth of the Hastings River 423 km. (266 miles) north of Sydney; pop. (1991) 26,800. It was founded as a convict settlement in 1821.

**Port Mahon** see MAHÓN.

**Portmeirion** /pɔːtˈmaɪrɪən/ a resort town on Tremadog Bay, Gwynedd, north Wales, created as a 'folly' in Italian style by the Welsh architect Clough Williams-Ellis.

**Port Moresby** /ˈmɔːzbɪ/ the capital of Papua New Guinea, situated on the south coast of the island of New Guinea, on the Coral Sea; pop. (1990) 193,240. Rubber, gold, and copra are exported.

**Porto** the Portuguese name for OPORTO.

**Pôrto Alegre** /ˌpɔːtəʊ əˈlegrə, əˈleɪgreɪ/ a major port and commercial city in south-eastern Brazil, capital of the state of Rio Grande do Sul; pop. (1990) 1,254,640. Situated at the north-western end of the Lagoa dos Patos, a lagoon separated from the Atlantic by a sandy peninsula, it is accessible to ocean-going ships via the port of Rio Grande. It has shipyards, meat-packing plants, and foundries, and many light industries.

**Port-of-Spain** the capital of Trinidad and Tobago, a port on the west coast of the Caribbean island of Trinidad, situated on the Gulf of Paria in the crook of the Charaguaramas peninsula; pop. (1988) 58,400. First visited by Columbus in 1498, it replaced St. Joseph as capital in 1757 and the Savannah roundabout is claimed by Trinidadians to be the largest in the world with a circumference of 4 km. (2.5 miles). It is the commercial and industrial centre of the island.

**portolan charts** /ˈpɔːtəˌlæn/ charts produced for navigators in the Middle Ages. Characteristically they were covered by a series of intersecting rhumb lines radiating from compass roses.

**Porto Novo** /ˌpɔːtəʊ ˈnəʊvəʊ/ the capital of Benin, a port on the Gulf of Guinea close to the border with Nigeria; pop. (1982) 208,260. Formerly a centre of the Portuguese slave-trade, it was for many years, until independence in 1960, a trading port of French West Africa. It is being replaced by Cotonou, which has better links to the sea and with the interior, as the administrative and commercial centre.

**Pôrto Velho** /ˌpɔːtəʊ ˈveləʊ/ the capital of Rondônia in western Brazil, an Amazonian city on the Madeira River; pop. (1991) 286,000. Its chief economic activities are lumbering and the mining of gold, iron, manganese, and casseterite.

**Portoviejo** /ˌpɔːtəʊˈvjeɪhəʊ/ a commercial town in western Ecuador, on the Portoviejo River northwest of Guayaquil, 25 km. (16 miles) from the Pacific coast; pop. (1990) 201,330. It is capital of the province of Manabi.

**Port Petrovsk** /pɪˈtrɒfsk/ a former name (until 1922) of MAKHACHKALA.

**Port Pirie** /ˈpɪrɪ/ a major industrial and commercial port of South Australia, on the Spencer Gulf, north-west of Adelaide; pop. (est. 1987) 15,160. It was established as a wheat-trading port in the 1870s but owes its development to the smelting of ores mined at Broken Hill in New South Wales which began in 1889. Port Pirie is also a vital link in the road and rail routes to Alice Springs, Darwin, and Perth.

**Port Rashid** /raːˈʃiːd/ a port serving Dubai in the United Arab Emirates.

**Port Said** /saɪd/ a duty-free seaport and summer resort of Egypt, at the north end of the Suez Canal; pop. (1991) 449,000. It was founded in 1859 in association with the building of the Suez Canal by the khedive Said Pasha after whom it is named. On the opposite bank is Port Fouad, built in 1926 and named in honour of King Fouad (1868–1936). It was severely damaged in the 1967 war with Israel, but largely reconstructed in 1975. It has chemical, tobacco, and textile industries.

**Port St. Lucie** /ˈluːsɪ/ a city in eastern Florida, USA, situated west of the Inland River south of Fort Pierce; pop. (1990) 55,870.

**Portsmouth** /ˈpɔːtsməθ/ a port, naval base, and tourist city on the south coast of England, in Hampshire; pop. (1991) 174,700. The naval dockyard was established there in 1496. It was the birthplace of Charles Dickens (1812–70) and has associations with the writers Rudyard Kipling, H. G. Wells, and Sir Arthur Conan Doyle. There are ferry links with the Isle of Wight, the Channel Islands, and France; Nelson's flagship HMS *Victory* and the Tudor warship *Mary Rose* rest here. It has several museums, a cathedral dating back to the 12th c., and many engineering industries. Portsmouth University (formerly Portsmouth Polytechnic) was formed in 1992.

**Portsmouth** a city in south-east Virginia, USA, on the Elizabeth River adjacent to Norfolk with which it is connected by toll bridge tunnels and a pedestrian ferry; pop. (1990) 103,910. Founded in 1752, it is part of the great Hampton Roads port and has a naval shipbuilding yard which is the largest in the world.

**Port Stanley** SEE STANLEY.

**Port Sudan** the chief port of Sudan, on the Red Sea; pop.(1983) 206,700. It was founded by the British in 1905 to facilitate the export of cotton, sorghum, sesame, and other commodities.

**Port Sunlight** a town on the south bank of the Mersey in north-west England, built in 1888 as a model village for the employees of Lever Brothers 'Sunlight' soap factory at Birkenhead near Liverpool.

**Port Sweetenham** SEE PORT KELANG.

**Port Talbot** an industrial town on the Bristol Channel in West Glamorgan, south Wales; pop. (1981) 40,260.

**Portugal** /ˈpɔːtjʊg(ə)l/ official name **The Republic of Portugal** a country occupying the western part of the Iberian peninsula in south-west Europe, bordering on the Atlantic Ocean with Spain to the north and east; area 92,072 sq. km.

(35,563 sq. miles); pop. (1991) 9,853,000; official language, Portuguese; capital, Lisbon. Its largest cities are Lisbon and Oporto. Portugal is divided into two distinct geographical regions by the River Tagus which flows into the Atlantic at Lisbon. In the north, the country is mountainous with a rainy, moderately cool climate; the rolling plains of the south are drier and warmer especially in the interior. Portugal also includes the islands of the Azores and Madeira which constitute autonomous regions in the Atlantic off the north-west coast of Africa. In Roman times it constituted the province of Lusitania. The country's history was linked with that of the rest of the peninsula until it became an independent kingdom under Alfonso I in the 12th c. Dynastic disputes with the Spanish kingdoms to the east resulted in the formation of Portugal's long-standing alliance with England in the 14th c., and in the following two hundred years it emerged as one of the leading European colonial powers. Independence was lost to Philip II of Spain in 1580 and not regained until 1688, by which time Portugal had been relegated to a position of secondary importance in European affairs, a state of events exacerbated by domestic political instability which continued into the 20th c. A republic since 1911, Portugal was ruled first by the military and then by the dictators Salazar and Caetano from 1926 until a revolution in 1974 paved the way for a new democratic constitution which came into effect in 1976. The country is governed by an executive president and Council of State and a unicameral Assembly of the Republic. Poor by European standards, its economy is still largely based on agriculture, its chief exports being cork, timber, fish, wine, and textiles. Tourism is also important. Portugal became a member of the European Community on 1 January 1986. **Portuguese** *adj. & n.* Portugal is divided into 18 districts and two autonomous regions:

| District | Area (sq. km.) | Pop. (1991) | Capital |
| --- | --- | --- | --- |
| Aveiro | 2,808 | 656,400 | Aveiro |
| Beja | 10,225 | 167,900 | Beja |
| Braga | 2,673 | 746,100 | Braga |
| Bragança | 6,608 | 158,300 | Bragança |
| Castelo Branco | 6,675 | 214,700 | Castelo Branco |
| Coimbra | 3,947 | 427,600 | Coimbra |
| Evora | 7,393 | 173,500 | Evora |
| Faro | 4,960 | 340,100 | Faro |
| Guarda | 5,518 | 187,800 | Guarda |
| Leiria | 3,515 | 427,800 | Leiria |
| Lisbon | 2,761 | 2,063,800 | Lisbon |
| Portalegre | 6,065 | 134,300 | Portalegre |
| Porto | 2,395 | 1,622,300 | Oporto |
| Santarém | 6,747 | 442,700 | Santarém |
| Setúbal | 5,064 | 713,700 | Setúbal |
| Viana do Castelo | 2,225 | 248,700 | Viana do Castelo |
| Vila Real | 4,328 | 237,100 | Vila Real |
| Viseu | 5,007 | 401,000 | Viseu |
| Autonomous Region | | | |
| Azores | 2,247 | 236,700 | Angra do Heroismo |
| Madeira | 794 | 253,000 | Funchal |

**Portuguese** /ˌpɔːtjʊˈgiːz, ˌpɔːtʃ-/ the official language of Portugal, its territories and former colonies and of Brazil, where it was taken by 15th-c. explorers. It is a Romance language, most closely related to (but clearly distinct from) Spanish, with over 10 million speakers in Portugal and over 150 million in Brazil.

**Portuguese Congo** a former name for CABINDA, an exclave of Angola to the north of the mouth of the Congo River.

**Portuguese East Africa** the former name of MOZAMBIQUE in Africa.

**Portuguese Guinea** the former name of GUINEA-BISSAU in West Africa.

**Portuguese West Africa** the former name of ANGOLA in Africa.

**Posadas** /pəʊˈsædəs/ a city in north-eastern Argentina, on the Paraná river opposite the Paraguayan city of Encarnación; pop. (1991) 220,000. It is capital of the province of Misiones. Founded as a Jesuit mission in the 1650s, it developed in the late 19th c. as a timber and yerba maté trading post. In 1912 it was linked by rail with Buenos Aires. Nearby is the restored mission of San Ignacio-Miní.

**Potenza** /pɒˈtenzə/ a market town in the Basilicata region of southern Italy, capital of Potenza province; pop. (1990) 68,500. Founded by the Romans in the 2nd century BC, it was taken by the Lombards in the 6th c. AD. It has food and clothing industries.

**Potomac** /pəˈtəʊmæk/ a river of the eastern US, which rises in the Appalachian Mountains in West Virginia and flows about 459 km. (285 miles) through Washington, DC, into Chesapeake Bay on the Atlantic coast.

**Potosí** /ˌpɒtəʊˈsiː/ the chief mining city of southern Bolivia, capital of the department of Potosí; pop. (1990) 120,000. Situated at an altitude of about 4,205 m. (13,780 ft.) it is one of the highest cities in the world. Once the largest city in Latin America (with a population of *c.*200,000), it was founded as a silver-mining town in the 1540s by the Spanish who established a mint here to coin the silver. After a period of decline, tin took over as the leading export in the 19th c.

**Potsdam** /'pɒtsdæm/ the capital city of the state of Brandenburg in Germany, situated just west of Berlin on the Havel River; pop. (1991) 139,025. During the 17th and 18th c. it was the summer residence of the electors of Brandenburg and the Prussian royal family. It developed during the reign of Frederick II (1740–86) who built the palace and park of Sans Souci. In August 1945 it was the site of a conference of US, Soviet, and British leaders, following the end of the war in Europe, which established principles for the Allied occupation of Germany. During its session an ultimatum was sent to Japan demanding unconditional surrender. It is an educational and industrial centre with loco-motives, textiles, and food-processing industries.

**Potteries** /'pɒtərɪz/, **the** a district in the upper Trent Valley of north Staffordshire, central Eng-land, where the English pottery industry developed and reached a peak during the life of Josiah Wedgwood (1730–95). It was the setting for many of the novels of Arnold Bennett (1867–1931).

**Poulton-le-Sands** the name (until 1870) of Morecambe. See MORECAMBE BAY.

**Poverty Bay** /'pɒvətɪ beɪ/ an inlet on the east coast of North Island, New Zealand, where Captain James Cook made his first landing in New Zealand in 1769.

**Powys** /'pəʊɪs, 'paʊɪs/ an inland county of Wales, formed in 1974 from the former counties of Montgomeryshire, Radnorshire, and most of Breconshire; area 5,077 sq. km. (1,960 sq. miles); pop. (1991) 116,500; county town, Llandrindod Wells. It is divided into three districts:

| District | Area (sq. km.) | Pop. (1991) |
| --- | --- | --- |
| Brecknock | 1,791 | 41,300 |
| Montgomeryshire | 2,058 | 52,000 |
| Radnorshire | 1,228 | 23,200 |

**Poyang** /pəʊ'jæŋ/ a lake in Jiangxi province south-east-central China, the largest freshwater lake in the country; area 3,583 sq. km. (1,383 sq. miles). It is linked to the Yangtze River for which it acts as an overflow reservoir.

**Poznań** /pɒz'næn/ (German **Posen**) an indus-trial city in western Poland, on the River Warta, capital of the county of Poznań pop. (1990) 590,100. A former capital of Poland, it was settled by German immigrants in 1253 and taken by Prussia in the partition of 1793. The German gen-eral and statesman Hindenburg was born here in 1847. Its many industries include agricultural ma-chinery, marine and railway engines, machine tools, electrical equipment, rubber, and textiles.

**Prado** /'prɑːdəʊ/ the Spanish national art gallery in Madrid. Established in 1818 by Ferdinand VII and Isabella of Braganza, it houses the greatest col-lection in the world of Spanish masters— Velasquez, el Greco, Zurbarán, Ribera, Murillo, Goya—as well as important examples of Flemish

and Venetian art collected as a result of political ties with these countries in the reigns of Charles V, Philip II, and Philip IV. Work produced after 1850 is deemed ineligible for inclusion. The gallery takes its name from the *prado* or meadow that once sur-rounded it.

**Prague** /prɑːg/ (Czech **Praha** /'prɑːhə/) the cap-ital of the Czech Republic and former capital of Czechoslovakia (1918–1992), on the River Vltava; pop. (1991) 1,212,000. The Bohemian king and Holy Roman emperor Charles IV made it the cap-ital of Bohemia in the 14th c. It was the scene of religious conflict in the early 15th c. between the followers of John Huss and the Catholic Church, and again in the 17th c. when, in response to the oppression of the ruling Catholic Habsburgs, the Protestant citizens threw Catholic officials from the windows of Hrdčany Castle. This event, known as the Defenestration of Prague (1618), con-tributed to the outbreak of the Thirty Years War. The city was invaded in 1968 by Soviet troops, an action which crushed the attempts at liberal reform introduced by the government of Alexander Dubček in a period known as the Prague Spring. It is a beautiful town with many elegant streets and buildings which make it a popular tourist destination. Its industries include chemicals, engin-eering, and pharmaceuticals.

**praia** a Portuguese word for a beach.

**Praia** /'praɪə/ the capital of the Cape Verde Islands, a port situated on the south coast of the island of São Tiago; pop. (1990) 62,000.

**prairie** /'preərɪ/ a large area of treeless grassland, especially in North America.

**Prakrit** /'prɑːkrɪt/ any of the (especially ancient or medieval) vernacular dialects of North and Central India existing alongside or derived from Sanskrit.

**Praslin** /'prɑːliːn/ an island of the Seychelles in the Indian Ocean; area 38 sq. km. (15 sq. miles).

**Prato** /'prɑːtəʊ/ a city in Tuscany, northern Italy, north-west of Florence; pop. (1990) 166,690. It has long been a centre of the wool industry.

**Precambrian** /priː'kæmbrɪən/ the earliest era of geological time, preceding the Cambrian period and Palaeozoic era. The Precambrian era includes the whole of the earth's history from its origin about 4,600 million years ago to the beginning of the Cambrian about 590 million years ago. Fossils of animals with hard skeletons are absent from Precambrian rocks, and the era was once con-sidered to be devoid of organic life, but it is now known that a variety of organisms did exist during that time. The oldest known Precambrian rocks on earth are about 3,800 million years old.

**Prešov** /'preʃɒf/ a textile town in east Slovakia, on the River Torysa; pop. (1991) 87,790. Founded in the 13th c., Prešov became a royal town in 1374. Landmarks include the 15th-c. Greek Orthodox Cathedral, the 14th-c. Gothic Church of St.

Nicholas, and the Evangelical Church (1637–42). The short-lived Slovak Republic of the Proletariat was declared here in 1919.

**Pressburg** /ˈpresbʊək/ the German name for BRATISLAVA.

**Preston** /ˈprestən/ the county town of Lancashire, north-west England, on the River Ribble; pop. (1991) 126,200. A spinning and weaving centre since the 15th c., it was the site in the 18th c. of the first English cotton mills and was the birthplace in 1732 of Richard Arkwright, inventor of the cotton spinning-frame. The University of Central England (formerly Lancashire Polytechnic) was established here in 1992. Preston has numerous industries including aircraft, heavy goods vehicles, textiles, and chemicals.

**Prestonpans** /ˌprestənˈpænz/ a village just east of Edinburgh, near which the first major engagement of the Jacobite Rebellion of 1745 took place. A small Hanoverian army under Sir John Cope was routed by the Highlanders of the equally small Jacobite army, leaving the way clear for the Young Pretender's subsequent invasion of England.

**Prestwick** /ˈprestwɪk/ a village and international airport near Ayr on the west coast of Scotland.

**Pretoria** /prɪˈtɔːrɪə/ the administrative capital of the Republic of South Africa, in the province of Pretoria-Witwatersrand-Vereeniging; pop. (1985) 443,000. It was founded in 1855 by Marthinus Pretorius, the first president of the South African Republic, and named after his father, Andries W. J. Pretorius (1799–1853), a South African Boer leader and one of the founders of Transvaal. It was until 1994 capital of the Transvaal. It has iron and steel, car assembly, railway, and machinery industries.

**Pretoria-Witwatersrand-Vereeniging** a province of South Africa, created in 1994 from part of the former Transvaal province. Its capital is Johannesburg.

**Préveza** /ˈpreɪvesə/ the chief town of Préveza department in Epirus, western Greece, situated on a narrow strait opposite Actium at the mouth of the Ambracian Gulf; pop. (1981) 12,660. It occupies the site of ancient Berenikia which was founded c. 290 BC by Pyrrhus and named in honour of his mother Berenice, queen of Ptolemy Soter.

**Pribilof Islands** /ˈprɪbəˌlɒf/ a group of four islands in the Bering Sea off the south-west coast of Alaska, USA, discovered in 1786 by the Russian explorer Gerasim Pribilof. Following the US purchase of Alaska in 1867 the islands became a seal reservation; area 168 sq. km. (65 sq. miles).

**Primorye** /ˈpriːmɔːjə/ (also **Primorskiy Kray** or **Maritime Territory**) a kray (administrative territory) in the far east of Russia, between the Sea of Japan and the Chinese border; pop. (1990) 2,281,000; capital, Vladivostok.

**Prince Albert National Park** a national park in central Saskatchewan, Canada, extending over a region of grassland, lakes, spruce swamp, and wooded uplands on the edge of the Canadian Shield; area 3,875 sq. km. (1,496 sq. miles). The naturalist Grey Owl lived in a log cabin by Ajawaan Lake during the 1930s.

**Prince Charles** /tʃɑːlz/ an island in the Canadian Arctic, the largest island in Foxe Basin to the west of Baffin Island; area 9,521 sq. km. (3,676 sq. miles). Its modern discovery dates from an aerial survey carried out in 1948.

**Prince Edward Island** an island in the Gulf of St. Lawrence, eastern Canada, the country's smallest province; area 5,660 sq. km. (2,185 sq. miles); pop. (1991) 129,765; capital, Charlottetown. Fishing, agriculture, and food processing are its chief industries. Its Inuit name is Abegweit (= cradled on the waves). Explored by Jacques Cartier in 1534 and colonized by the French, it was ceded to the British in 1763. It became a province of Canada in 1873. Potatoes and tobacco are grown in the island's fertile red soil and fishing for lobster and cod is important to the local economy. The island is separated from New Brunswick by the Northumberland Strait.

**Prince George** /dʒɔːdʒ/ a road and railway town on the upper Fraser River in British Columbia, western Canada, situated at the junction of the Yellowhead, John Hart, and Caribou highways; pop. (1991) 69,700. It is also a rail junction on the route from Prince Rupert to Edmonton and the route from Prince Rupert to Vancouver. Simon Fraser of the North West Company founded the trading post of Fort George here in 1806.

**Prince of Wales Island 1.** an island in the Canadian Arctic to the east of Victoria Island from which it is separated by the McClintock Channel; area c. 33,339 sq. km. (12,872 sq. miles). **2.** a heavily forested island in the Alexander Archipelago off the south-east coast of Alaska, USA; area 5,778 sq. km. (2,231 sq. miles). **3.** a former name for the island of PENANG in Malaysia.

**Prince Patrick Island** an island in the Canadian Arctic, in the Queen Elizabeth Islands north-west of Melville Island from which it is separated by the Crozier Channel; area 15,848 sq. km. (6,120 sq. miles). It is named after the Duke of Connaught who was Governor-General of Canada 1911–16.

**Prince Rupert** /ˈruːpə(r)t/ an ice-free port on the Pacific coast of British Columbia, western Canada, situated on Kaien Island in Chatham Sound near the mouth of the Skeena River; pop. (1991) 16,620. Founded in 1906 by the Grand Trunk Pacific Railway as a northern rival to Vancouver, it is a terminus of the Canada National Railway, with ferry links to Vancouver island and the Queen Charlotte Islands. It is an outlet for grain, coal, fish, and timber.

**Princeton** /'prɪnst(ə)n/ a town in west New Jersey, USA, named in 1724 in honour of William III, Prince of Orange-Nassau; pop. (1990) 12,020. From June to November 1783 Princeton was the capital of the USA. It is the site of the fourth-oldest US university, founded in 1756, and was the birthplace of the actor and singer Paul Robeson (1898–1976). Albert Einstein (1879–1955) spent the last years of his life at the Institute for Advanced Study.

**Pripyat** /'pri:pjət/ (also **Pripet** /'pri:pjət/) a river in eastern Europe that rises in north-west Ukraine and flows c. 710 km. (440 miles) eastwards through the Pripyat Marshes of Ukraine and southern Belorussia to meet the River Dnieper north of Kiev.

**Priština** /prɪs'ti:nə/ a city in southern Serbia, capital of the province of Kosovo; pop. (1981) 210,000. A former capital of Serbia, it is situated on the eastern edge of the Kosovo Field where the Serbians attempted but failed to arrest the advance of the Turks in 1389. It remained under Turkish control until 1912. It is an administrative, educational, and communications centre with textile, metal, and electrical industries.

**Privas** /pri:'vɑ:/ the capital town of the department of Ardèche in the Rhône-Alpes region of south-eastern France; pop. (1982) 10,640.

**Prizren** /'pri:zrən/ a market town in the province of Kosovo, southern Serbia, near the Albanian frontier; pop. (1981) 134,530. Built on the site of the Roman town of Theranda, it was capital of Serbia from 1376 to 1389.

**Proddatur** /'prɑ:də͵tʊ(ə)r/ a town in Andhra Pradesh, southern India, on the Penner River in the Eastern Ghats west of Nellore; pop. (1991) 133,860.

**Prokopyevsk** /prə'kɒpjevsk/ a coal-mining city in west Siberia, Russia, on the River Aba in the Kuznetz Basin industrial region to the south of Kemorovo; pop. (1990) 274,000. Founded after the Russian Revolution of 1917, it is a major producer of coal, chemicals, and mining equipment.

**Prome** /prəʊm/ a commercial town and port on the Irrawaddy River, south-west-central Burma, built near the remains of the ancient city of Pyu; pop. (1973) 148,120.

**promontory** /'prɒməntərɪ/ a headland projecting into the sea.

**Propontis** /prə'pɒntɪs/ the ancient name for the Sea of Marmara. See MARMARA, SEA OF.

**Proterozoic** /͵prəʊtərəʊ'zəʊɪk/ the later part of the Precambrian era, characterized by the oldest forms of life.

**Provençal** /͵prɒvɑ̃'sɑ:l, ͵prɒvɑ̃'sæl/ (also **Occitan** or **Langue D'Oc**) a Romance language spoken in Provence, southern France, closely related to French, Italian, and Catalan. In the 12th–14th c. it was the language of the troubadours and cultured speakers of southern France, but the subsequent spread of the northern dialects of French led to its gradual decline despite attempts to revive it.

**Provence** /prɒ'vɑ̃s/ a former province of south-east France, on the Mediterranean coast east of the lower Rhône. Settled by the Greeks in the 6th c. BC, the area around Marseilles became, in the 1st c. BC, part of the Roman colony of Gaul. It was united with France under Louis XI in 1481 and is now part of the region of Provence-Alpes-Côte d'Azur. In Roman times *Provincia* was a name given to southern Gaul which was the first Roman province to be established outside Italy.

**Provence-Alpes-Côte d'Azur**
/prɒ͵vɑ̃sælp͵kəʊtdæ'zjʊə(r)/ a mountainous region of south-east France, on the border with Italy and including the French Riviera. It comprises the departments of Alpes-des-Haute-Provence, Hautes-Alpes, Alpes Maritimes, Bouches-du-Rhône, Var, and Vaucluse; area 31,400 sq. km. (12,128 sq. miles); pop. (1990) 4,257,900. Its chief town is Marseilles.

**Providence** /'prɒvɪd(ə)ns/ the capital of the state of Rhode Island, USA, on the Providence River; pop. (1990) 160,730. The town was founded in 1636 as a haven for religious dissenters by Roger Williams who had been banished for his views from the colony at Plymouth and was grateful that 'God's merciful providence' had led him to this spot. Originally a farming town, it developed as a maritime centre, its clippers sailing to China and the West Indies. Now a centre for jewellery, engineering, and metal manufactures.

**Providencia** /prɒvɪ'densɪə/ (also **Old Providence**) a mountainous resort island of Colombia in the western Caribbean; pop. (est. 1990) 3,000.

**Provo** /'prəʊvəʊ/ a city in central Utah, USA, on the Provo River near Utah Lake; pop. (1990) 86,835. First settled by Mormons in 1849, Provo is an industrial and commercial city at the centre of a mining and irrigated farming region. It is the home of the Brigham Young University (1875).

**Prudhoe Bay** /'prʊdəʊ/ an inlet of the Arctic Ocean on the north coast of Alaska, USA, situated east of the Colville River delta. Since the discovery of oil here in 1968 it has been a major source of petroleum.

**Prusa** /'pru:sə/ an ancient name for BURSA.

**Prussia** /'prʌʃə/ a former kingdom of Germany, which grew from a small country on the south-east shores of the Baltic to an extensive domain covering much of modern north-east Germany and Poland. The forested area to the east of the Vistula, originally inhabited by a Baltic people known as the Prussians, was taken in the 13th c. by the Teutonic Knights, and in the 16th c. it became a duchy of the Hohenzollerns, passing in 1618 to the electors of Brandenburg. The kingdom of Prussia, proclaimed in 1701, with its capital at Berlin, grew in the 18th c. under Frederick the Great to become

a dominant power. After victory in the Franco-Prussian War of 1870–1, Prussia under Wilhelm I became the nucleus of the new German Empire created by Bismarck. With Germany's defeat in World War I, the Prussian monarchy was abolished and Prussia's supremacy came to an end.
**Prussian** *adj. & n.*

**Prut** /pruːt/ (also **Pruth**) a river of south-eastern Europe, which rises in the Carpathian Mountains in southern Ukraine and flows south-east for 850 km. (530 miles), joining the Danube near Galaţi in Romania. For much of its course it forms the border between Romania and Moldova.

**Pskov** /pəˈskɒf/ an ancient city in western Russia, on the Velikaya River south-west of St. Petersburg; pop. (1990) 206,000. It is the centre of a flax-growing region.

**Pucallpa** /puˈkaɪpə/ a town and river port in the tropical lowlands of north-eastern Peru, on the Ucayali River; pop. (1990) 153,000. It is the capital of Ucayali department, with industries that include oil refining, boat building, gold mining, and the export of timber.

**Puebla** /ˈpweblə/ **1.** a state of south-central Mexico; area 33,902 sq. km. (13,095 sq. miles); pop. (1990) 4,118,060. It has a large Indian population dominated by Nahuas and Totonacs. **2.** (in full **Puebla de Zaragoza**) its capital, situated between Veracruz and Mexico City, on the edge of the central Mexican plateau at an altitude of 2,150 m. (7,055 ft.); pop. (1990) 1,054,920. Founded by Spanish settlers as Ciudad de los Angeles in 1532, the city's many old colonial buildings are noted for their hand-painted tiles. Recently the production of cars has been added to tourism as major industries.
**Poblano** (*pl.* **Poblanos**) *adj. & n.*

**Pueblo** /ˈpwebləʊ/ (*pl.* **-os**) a member of certain North American Indian peoples occupying a pueblo settlement. Their prehistoric period is known as the Anasazi (Pueblo) culture. The Chaco Culture National Historical Park in New Mexico, USA, embraces the remains of over 80 prehistoric communities of the Pueblo culture which was centred at Chaco Canyon.

**Pueblo** /ˈpwebləʊ/ a transportation and industrial city in south-central Colorado, USA, on the Arkansas River; pop. (1990) 98,640. Established in 1842 at a crossroads used by Indians and fur traders, Pueblo became the leading centre for steel and coal production west of the Mississippi.

**Puente Alto** /ˌpwenteɪ ˈæltəʊ/ a city in central Chile, situated to the south-east of Santiago; pop. (1991) 187,370.

**Puerto Barrios** /ˌpwɜːtəʊ ˈbaːrjəʊs/ the principal port and city of eastern Guatemala, on the Bay of Amatique, an inlet of the Caribbean; pop. (1989) 338,000. It is capital of Izabal department and an outlet for bananas and citrus. The chief port facilities are located to the south at Santo Tomás de Castilla.

**Puerto Cortés** /ˌpwɜːtəʊ kɔːˈtez/ the principal port and oil-refining centre of Honduras, on the Caribbean coast at the mouth of the Ulúa River; pop. (1986) 40,000.

**Puerto de la Cruz** /ˌpwɜːtəʊ də laː ˈkruːz/ the chief town and resort on Tenerife in the Spanish Canary Islands; pop. (1991) 39,550.

**Puerto Montt** /ˌpwɜːtəʊ ˈmɒnt/ a fishing port in southern Chile, at the head of the Gulf of Ancud; pop. (1991) 106,530. Established by German colonists in 1852, it is capital of the Los Lagos region and a terminus for both road and rail traffic. It was devastated by an earthquake in 1960.

**Puerto Plata** /ˌpwɜːtəʊ ˈplaːtə/ the principal town on the northern Atlantic coastline of the Dominican Republic, with a deep-water harbour for cruise liners; pop. (1986) 96,500. Founded by Christopher Columbus in 1502, its San Felipe Spanish fortress is the oldest in the New World. The mountains behind the town are rich in amber.

**Puerto Presidente Stroessner** the former name (until 1989) of CIUDAD DEL ESTE.

**Puerto Rico**

/ˌpwɜːtəʊ ˈriːkəʊ/ the most easterly island of the Greater Antilles in the West Indies; area 8,959 sq. km. (3,460 sq. miles); pop. (1990) 3,522,040; official language, Spanish; capital, San Juan. The largest cities are San Juan, Bayamón, and Ponce. The island is partly of volcanic origin, rising to a height of 1,325 m. (4,347 ft.) at Cerro de Punta, but in the north is formed of limestone. Visited in 1493 by Christopher Columbus, the island was one of the earliest Spanish settlements in the New World. It was ceded to the US in 1898 after the Spanish–American war, and was established as a Commonwealth in voluntary association with the US with full powers of local government in 1952. In recent decades there has been considerable progress in idustrialization and social welfare, creating a community with one of the highest standards of living in Latin America. Nevertheless many Puerto Ricans have emigrated to the US. The island's chief exports are chemicals, electronic goods, clothing, fish, rum, and tobacco products.
**Puerto Rican** *adj. & n.*

**Puerto Rico Trench** the deepest section of the North Atlantic, forming a submarine trench that extends in an east–west direction to the north of Puerto Rico and the Leeward Islands. It reaches a depth of 9,220 m. (28,397 ft.).

**Puget Sound** /ˈpjuːdʒɪt/ an inlet of the Pacific Ocean in the state of Washington, USA, which receives rivers from the Cascade Range. It was explored by George Vancouver in 1792 and named after his aide Peter Puget. Linked to the Pacific Ocean by the Strait of Juan de Fuca, it is overlooked by the city of Seattle, which is situated on its eastern shore.

**Puglia** the Italian name for APULIA.

**Pula** /'puːlə/ a port and resort town on the Adriatic coast of western Croatia, at the southern tip of the Istrian Peninsula; pop. (1991) 62,300. Landmarks include a Roman amphitheatre, the Roman Temple of Augustus, and a 17th-c. castle.

**pulau** /'pʊlaʊ/ a Malay or Indonesian word for an island.

**puna** /'puːnɑː/ the name given to arid plateau regions of the high Andes in Peru and Bolivia and to the cold wind that blows over them.

**Pune** /'puːnə/ (formerly **Poona**) an industrial city of western India, in Maharashtra state; pop. (1991) 2,485,000. A former capital of the Maharattas, it was a military and administrative centre under British rule from 1817. Its chief products include firearms, pharmaceuticals, machinery, and textiles.

**Punic** /'pjuːnɪk/ of or relating to ancient Carthage in North Africa.

**Punjab** /pʌn'dʒɑːb, 'pʌndʒɑːb/ **1.** (also **the Punjab**) a region of north-west India and Pakistan, a wide fertile plain traversed by the Indus and its five tributaries (Jhelum, Chenab, Ravi, Beas, and Sutlej) which give the region its name (Hindustani *pañj* five *āb* waters). Under Muslim influence from the 11th c., the region became a centre of Sikhism in the 15th c. and, after the capture of Lahore in 1799 by Ranjit Singh, a powerful Sikh kingdom. It was annexed by the British in 1849 and became a part of British India. In the partition of 1947 it was divided between Pakistan and India. The province of Punjab in Pakistan is centred on the former state capital, Lahore. The state of Punjab in India was divided in 1966 into the two states of Punjab and Haryana, both centred on the city of Chandigarh. **2.** a province of Pakistan; area 205,334 sq. km. (79,310 sq. miles); pop. (1981) 47,292,000; capital, Lahore. **3.** a state of India; area 50,362 sq. km. (19,452 sq. miles); pop. (1991) 20,190,795; capital, Chandigarh.
**Punjabi** *adj. & n.*

**Puno** /'puːnəʊ/ a town on the shore of Lake Titicaca, south-eastern Peru; pop. (1990) 99,600. Founded as a silver-mining town by the Spanish in 1688, it is capital of the department of Puno. It is famous for its folk music.

**punta** /'pʊntə/ a Spanish word for a point or cape.

**Punta Arenas** /,pʊntə ə'reɪnəs/ the capital of Magallanes province in southern Chile, on the Straits of Magellan; pop. (1991) 120,030. It is the southernmost city of Chile. It trades in wool, meat, and oil.

**Puntarenas** /,pʊntə'reɪnəs/ a port of western Costa Rica, on the Gulf of Nicoya, an inlet of the Pacific Ocean; pop. (1984) 35,600. It trades in bananas and is capital of the province of Puntarenas.

**Punta Gorda** /,pʊntə 'gɔːdə/ a town on the Caribbean coast of Belize, capital of the southern district of Toledo; pop. (1980) 2,396. There are ferry links with Guatemala.

**Puqi** /pʊ'kiː/ a town in Hubei province, east-central China, on the western shore of Lushui Reservoir south-west of Wuhan; pop. (1986) 413,000.

**Purbeck** /'pɜːbek/, **Isle of** a peninsula on the Dorset coast of southern England extending into the English Channel, with Poole Bay to the north. It is noted for its hard polished limestone used in making pillars, effigies, etc. The **Purbeck Hills** are a range of chalk hills that cross the peninsula from east to west. Britain's first mainland marine reserve protects the kelp beds and coralline seaweeds of the gently shelving Kimmeridge ledges.

**Puri** /'puːrɪ/ a town in the state of Orissa, eastern India, on the Bay of Bengal; pop. (1991) 124,835. The Rath-Yatra Hindu car festival takes place each year in June/July when massive chariots (*raths*) carrying wooden images of Jagannath (Juggernaut), his brother Balabhadra, and his sister Subhadra are pulled through the streets. The chief landmark is the Jagganath Temple of the 'Lord of the Universe'. Toy making and stone carving are local industries.

**Purnia** /'pɜːnɪə/ a town in the state of Bihar, north-east India, situated north of the Ganges; pop. (1991) 136,000.

**Purus** /'pjʊərəs/ a river of South America that rises in the Andes of eastern Peru and flows 3,211 km. (1,995 miles) north-eastwards to join the Amazon in north-west Brazil.

**Pusan** /puː'sɑːn/ a seaport on the south-east coast of the Korean peninsula, the second-largest city and principal port of South Korea; pop. (1990) 3,797,570. It has shipyards, as well as iron and steel, machinery, and textiles industries.

**Putian** /pʊti'ɑːn/ a city in Fujian province, south-east China, south of Fuzhou; pop. (1986) 272,000.

**Putumayo** /,puːtuː'mɑːjəʊ/ a river of South America that rises in the Andes of southern Colombia and flows south-eastwards for *c.* 1,600 km. (1,000 miles) to meet the Amazon in north-western Brazil.

**puy** /pwiː/ the French name for the denuded volcanic cones frequently found in the Auvergne region of the Massif Central, as in the Chaîne des Puys which rise in an unbroken line to the west of Clermont-Ferrand.

**Puy-de-Dôme** /pwiːdə'dəʊm/ a department in the Auvergne region of central France; area 7,955 sq. km. (3,073 sq. miles); pop. (1990) 598,210; capital, Clermont-Ferrand.

**puszta** the grassy steppelands of the Little and Great Plains of eastern Austria and Hungary.

**Puyang** /puˈjæŋ/ a city in Henan province, east-central China, between Anyang and the Yellow River; pop. (1986) 1,125,000.

**PWV** *abbr.* PRETORIA-WITWATERSRAND-VEREENIGING.

**Pyatigorsk** /ˌpyɑːtɪˈɡɔːsk/ an industrial city and spa in the northern Caucasus of Russia, on the Podkumok River; pop. (1990) 130,000. It has electrical and agricultural machinery industries.

**Pyongyang** /pjʌŋˈjɑːŋ/ the capital of North Korea, on the Taedong River; pop. (est. 1984) 2,639,450. The oldest city on the Korean peninsula, it was first mentioned in records of 108 BC. It fell to the Japanese in the late 16th c. and was devastated by the Manchus in the early 17th c. It developed as an industrial city during the years of Japanese occupation, from 1910 to 1945. It is North Korea's principal industrial centre with iron and steel, machinery, railway, and textile industries.

**Pyrenees** /pɪrəˈniːz/ (French **Pyrénées** /piːreɪˈneɪ/, Spanish **Pirineos** /piːriːˈneɪəs/) a range of mountains extending along the border between France and Spain from the Atlantic coast to the Mediterranean. The range is named after the legendary Pyrène who was buried there by Herakles after being killed by wild beasts. Its highest point is the Pico de Aneto in Spain (3,404 m., 11,168 ft.). The Gouffre de la Pierre St. Martin below the Pic d'Arlas is one of the deepest caves in the world and the Grotte Casteret is the highest ice cave in Europe. The glacier on the north side of the Pico de la Maladetta is the largest ice field in the Pyrenees. **Pyrenean** /-ˈniːən/ *adj. & n.*

**Pyrénées-Atlantiques** /ˌpiːreɪˈneɪz ˌætlɑ̃ˈtiːk/ a department of Aquitaine in south-west France, on the frontier with Spain; area 7,633 sq. km. (2,948 sq. miles); pop. (1990) 578,520; capital, Pau.

**Pyrénées-Orientales** /ˌpiːreɪˈneɪz ˌɔːriɑ̃ˈtɑːl/ a department in the Languedoc-Roussillon region of southern France; area 4,087 sq. km. (1,579 sq. miles); pop. (1990) 363,800; capital, Perpignan.

**Pyrgos** /ˈpɪrɡəs/ (Greek **Pírgos**) the capital town of Elis (Ilía), a department in the Peloponnese of south-western Greece; pop. (1981) 21,960. It is a market town trading in currants with a port to the west at Katákolo.

# Q q

**Qabis** see GABÉS.

**Qafsah** see GAFSA.

**Qandahar** see KANDAHAR.

**Qaraghandy** /'kærə,gændɪ/ an industrial city in eastern Kazakhstan, at the centre of a major coal-mining and iron and steel region; pop. (1990) 613,000. Originally founded as a copper-mining settlement in 1552, it developed rapidly in the 1920s with the discovery of large deposits of bituminous soil. It was known as Karaganda until the dissolution of the Soviet Union in 1991.

**Qarshi** the Uzbek name for KARSHI.

**Qatar** /'kæta:(r), 'gæ-/ official name **The State of Qatar** a sheikdom occupying a peninsula on the west coast of the Persian Gulf; area 11,437 sq. km. (4,416 sq. miles); pop. (est.1991) 402,000; 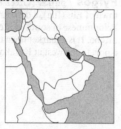 official language, Arabic (English is the language of commerce); capital, Doha. The territory, which has a hot and humid climate, comprises a low barren plateau sloping gently from the western ridge of the Dukhan Heights to the eastern shore, and includes a number of offshore islands. Oil, natural gas, petrochemicals, fertilizer, and steel are the countries chief products. Descended from three Bedouin tribes (Awamir, Manasir, and Bani Hajir), most Qataris are Sunni Muslims. The country was a British protectorate from 1916 until 1971 when it became a sovereign independent state. It is an absolute monarchy with an Emir of the al-Thani dynasty as head of state and no formal constitution. A Basic Law, promulgated in 1970, includes a Bill of Rights and an advisory Council of Ministers.
**Qatari** *adj. & n.*

**Qattara Depression** an extensive, low-lying and largely impassable area of desert in north-east Africa, to the west of Cairo. Falling to 133 m. (436 ft.) below sea-level, it extends over *c.* 18,100 sq. km. (7,000 sq miles).

**Qazvin** /kæz'vi:n/ a market town and transportation centre in northern Iran, north-west of Iran; pop. (1991) 279,000. It makes carpets and textiles.

**Qena** /'keɪnə/ (also **Kena**) a market town in Egypt, on the right bank of the Nile 62 km. (39 miles) north of Luxor; pop. (1991) 137,000. Though largely rebuilt by the Ptolemies and the Romans, the nearby Dendara necropolis includes Early Dynastic tombs. Pottery is a local industry.

**Qilian Mountains** /kɪlɪ'a:n/ (Chinese **Qilian Shan**) a mountain range in northern China, on the frontier between Gansu and Qinghai provinces. It rises to a height of 5,826 m. (19,114 ft.).

**Qin** /tʃɪn/ (also **Ch'in**) the name of a dynasty that ruled China 221–206 BC.

**Qingdao** /tʃɪŋ'daʊ/ a port, naval base, and resort city on the Yellow Sea coast of Shandong province, eastern China; pop. (1990) 4,205,000. The manufacture of Qingdao Beer is one of its industries, together with locomotives and rolling stock.

**Qinghai** /tʃɪŋ'haɪ/ (formerly **Tsinghai**) a mountainous province in north-central China; area 721,000 sq. km. (278,485 sq. miles); pop. (1990) 4,457,000; capital, Xining (Sining).

**Qinghai** /tʃɪŋ'haɪ/ a salt lake in Qinghai province, China, the largest in the country; area 4,583 sq. km. (1,770 sq. miles).

**Qinhuangdao** /,tʃɪŋwæŋ'daʊ/ an industrial port in the province of Hebei, north-eastern China, on the Bohai Gulf; pop. (1990) 448,000. A special economic zone since 1985, it is linked by pipeline to the oilfields of Daqing.

**Qinzhou** /tʃɪn'dʒəʊ/ a city in Guangxi autonomous region, southern China, on an inlet of the Beibu Gulf south of Nanning; pop. (1986) 944,000.

**Qiqihar** /tʃɪtʃɪ'ha:(r)/ (formerly **Tsitsihar**) a port in Heilongjiang province, north-east China, on the River Nen; pop. (1990) 1,380,000.

**Qitaihe** /tʃɪtaɪ'heɪ/ a city in Heilongjiang province, north-east China, east of Harbin; pop. (1986) 327,000.

**Qizilkum** see KYZYL-KUM.

**Qom** see QUM.

**Qonduz** see KUNDUZ.

**Qostanay** /,kɪstə'naʊ/ (also **Kustanay**) a city in northern Kazakhstan, on the River Tobol; pop. (1990) 228,000. It is a centre of gold-mining and agricultural trade.

**Quai d'Orsay** /keɪ dɔː'seɪ/ riverside street on the left bank of the Seine in Paris, France. The name is often used to denote the French ministry of foreign affairs, which has its headquarters there. The French National Assembly is also located here in the Palais-Bourbon.

**Quaker** /'kweɪkə(r)/ a member of the SOCIETY OF FRIENDS.

**Quantock Hills** /'kwɒntɒk/ (also **the Quantocks**) a range of hills north of Taunton in Somerset, south-west England, rising to a height of 385 m. (1,261 ft.).

**Quanzhou** /kwæŋ'dʒəʊ/ a city in Fujian province, south-east China, north-east of Xiamen; pop. (1986) 444,000.

**Quatre Bras** /ˌkætrə 'brɑ:/ a village in Brabant, central Belgium, 32 km. (20 miles) south-east of Brussels, the site of a battle on 16 June 1815 in which Wellington defeated the French under Ney.

**Quebec** /kwɪ'bek/ (French **Québec**) **1.** a heavily forested province in eastern Canada; area 1,667,926 sq. km. (594,860 sq. miles); pop. (1991) 6,895,960; chief cities, Quebec and Montreal. Originally inhabited by the Algonquin and Cree peoples, it was settled by the French from 1608, ceded to the British in 1763, and became one of the original four provinces in the Dominion of Canada in 1867. The majority of its residents are French-speaking and its culture is predominantly French. It has a certain amount of political independence from the rest of Canada, and is a focal point of French–Canadian nationalism, a movement which advocates independence for Quebec. Its chief industries include oil and mineral refining, meat processing, and the manufacture of paper, pulp, iron and steel, motor vehicles, and dairy products. **2.** its capital city, a port on the St. Lawrence River, and industrial, cultural, and tourist centre; pop. (1991) 167,000; 645,550 (metropolitan area). Founded by the French explorer Champlain in 1608, it became capital of the royal province of New France in 1663. The city was eventually captured from the French by a British force under General James Wolfe in 1759 (see ABRAHAM, PLAINS OF) and it became capital of Lower Canada in 1791. Laval University, based on a seminary founded in 1663 by Quebec's first bishop, is the oldest French university in North America and the Basilica of Sainte-Anne-de-Beaupré stands on the oldest pilgrimage site (1658) in North America. The French Canadian Carnaval de Québec with its famous snow sculptures is held every February. Industries include shipbuilding and the manufacture of pulp and paper.
**Québecois** *adj. & n.*

**Quechua** /'ketʃwə/ (also **Quichua** /'kɪ-/) an Amerindian people of Peru and neighbouring parts of Bolivia, Chile, Colombia, and Ecuador whose language (actually a group of related languages) is one of the two official languages of Peru.

**Queen Charlotte Islands** /'ʃɑ:lət/ a group of more than 150 islands off the west coast of Canada, in British Columbia, separated from the mainland by the Hecate Strait and from the islands of Alaska to the north by the Dixon Entrance. The largest islands are Graham Island and Moresby

Island and the chief settlement is the port and military base of Masset. The economy is largely based on timber and fishing, and about 1,300 Haida Indians live on reservations at Skidegate Mission and Haida on Graham Island.

**Queen Maud Land** /mɔ:d/ (Norwegian **Dronning Maud Land**) part of Antarctica bordering the Atlantic Ocean, claimed by Norway since 1939. It is named after Queen Maud of Norway (1869–1938).

**Queens** /kwi:nz/ a residential and industrial borough of New York City, USA, at the west end of Long Island; area 283 sq. km. (109 sq. miles); pop. (1990) 1,951,600.

**Queensland** /'kwi:nzlənd/ a state comprising the north-eastern part of Australia; area *c.* 1,727,000 sq. km. (667,050 sq. miles); pop. (1991) 2,999,900; capital, Brisbane. Originally established in 1824 as a penal settlement, it was constituted a separate colony in 1859, having previously formed part of New South Wales, and was federated with the other states of Australia in 1901. Mainly an agricultural state producing cattle, sugar-cane, wheat, and tropical fruits. There are huge deposits of coal, bauxite, copper, lead, silver, and zinc. Oil and natural gas are also exploited.
**Queenslander** *n.*

**Queluz** /ke'lu:z/ a town in central Portugal, north of Lisbon, with an 18th c. palace that was a residence of the Portuguese royal family; pop. (1991) 43,755.

**Quemoy** /kwɪ'mɔɪ/ an island group of Taiwan situated off the coast of Fujien province, south-east China, and comprising the islands of Quemoy and Little Quemoy, and several islets. A fortress island since the Chinese revolution of 1949, Quemoy has been described as 'a dagger pointed at the heart of Communism'. In 1958 the island experienced a 44-day artillery bombardment from the mainland but in more recent times the Taiwan government has promoted tourism on Quemoy.

**Quercy** /ker'si:/ a historic region of France between the Massif Central and the plains of Aquitaine comprising the limestone plateaux or causses of Haut-Quercy, centred on Cahors; Bas-Quercy, dominated by the valleys of the Garonne, Tarn, and Aveyron rivers; and the Chataîgneraie in the foothills of the Massif Central.

**Querétaro** /ke'reɪtəˌrəʊ/ **1.** a state of central Mexico; area 11,449 sq. km. (4,422 sq. miles); pop. (1990) 1,044,230. **2.** its capital city; pop. (1990) 454,050. The Mexican revolt of 1810 was planned here by Father Miguel Hidalgo, the treaty ending the US–Mexican War was signed here in 1847, Emperor Maximilian was captured and shot here in 1867, and the post-revolutionary Constitution of 1917 was drawn up here. It is an industrial centre with cotton mills and machinery industries. Tourism is also important.

**Quetta** /'kwetə/ the capital of the province of Baluchistan in west Pakistan, a hill station that was for many years a strategic location on the route from Afghanistan to the lower Indus valley; pop. (est.1991) 350,000. Originally known as Shal, it was severely damaged by an earthquake in May 1935.

**Quetzaltenango** /ket₁sɑ:ltə'nɑ:ŋgəʊ/ (also **Xelajú** /₁xeɪlæ'hu:/) a city in south-west Guatemala, capital of a department of the same name; pop. (1989) 246,000. Situated at an altitude of 2,335 m. (7,660 ft.), it is the principal city of western Guatemala. Locally developed hydroelectric power has made it the leading industrial city of Central America.

**Quezon City** /'keɪsɒn/ a city on the island of Luzon in the northern Philippines; pop. (1990) 1,667,000. Situated on the outskirts of Manila, Quezon City was established in 1940 and named after Manuel Luis Quezon, the first President of the republic. From 1948 to 1976 it was the capital of the Philippines. It has a very large university founded in 1908.

**Qufu** /tʃu:'fu:/ a city in Shandong province, eastern China, where Confucious was born in 551 BC and lived for much of his life; pop. (1986) 545,000.

**Quiberon Bay** /'ki:bə₁rɑ̃/ a bay on the east side of the Quiberon Peninsula on the Côte Sauvage (Wild Coast) of the department of Morbihan in Brittany, north-west France. It was the scene of a naval battle, in November 1759 during the Seven Years War, in which the French were defeated by the British under Hawke and Boscawen.

**Quilon** /'kwi:lɒn/ (also **Kollam** /'kɑ:ləm/) a port and market town on the Malabar coast of south-west India, in the state of Kerala; pop. (1991) 362,400. Tiles and electrical equipment are manufactured.

**Quilpué** /kɪl'pweɪ/ a city in central Chile, to the east of Valparaiso; pop. (1991) 107,400.

**Quimper** /'kæpeə(r)/ the capital of the department of Finistère in Brittany, north-west France; pop. (1990) 62,540.

**Quincy** /'kwɪnsɪ/ an industrial and residential city in east Massachusetts, USA, to the south of Boston; pop. (1990) 84,985. It was the birthplace of John Hancock, first signer of the US Declaration of Independence, and of John Adams and his son John Quincy Adams, 2nd and 6th presidents of the USA. George Bush, 41st president, was born at nearby Milton. It has shipbuilding and machinery industries.

**Quintana Roo** /ki:n₁tɑ:nə 'ru:/ a state of south-east Mexico, on the Yucatán Peninsula; area 50,212 sq. km. (19,394 sq. miles); pop. (1990) 493,605; capital, Chetumal. It includes the purpose-built resort of Cancun.

**Quito** /'ki:təʊ/ the capital of Ecuador and its educational, cultural, and political centre, situated just south of the equator at an altitude of 2,850 m. (9,350 ft.) at the foot of Pichincha volcano in the Andes; pop. (1990) 1,387,890. Built on the site of a pre-Columbian settlement taken by the Spanish in 1533, Quito gave its name to a Spanish presidency which became the independent republic of Ecuador in 1830. It has diverse light industries and handicrafts, a historic cathedral, and two universities.

**Qum** /kʊm/ (also **Qom**) a holy city of Shiite Muslims in central Iran; pop. (1986) 551,000. It was the home of Ayatollah Khomeini. Qum manufactures rugs, footwear, and pottery.

**Qumran** /kʊm'rɑ:n/ a region on the north-western shore of the Dead Sea in the Israeli-occupied West Bank, site of caves in which the Dead Sea scrolls were found (1947–56) and of the settlement of an ancient Jewish community (probably the Essenes) to whom these manuscripts belonged.

**Quonset Point** /'kwɒnsɪt/ a peninsula in Rhode Island, USA, that gives its name to a prefabricated metal building with a semicylindrical corrugated roof first made here.

**Qŭqon** the Uzbek name for KOKAND.

**Quzhou** /kʊ'dʒəʊ/ a city in Zhejiang province, eastern China, south-west of Hangzhou; pop. (1986) 981,000.

**Qwaqwa** /'kwækwə/ (also **QwaQwa**) a former homeland established by South Africa for the South Sotho people; pop. (1985) 183,000; capital, Phuthaditjhaba. Situated in the Drakensberg Mountains in Orange Free State, Qwaqwa was designated a self-governing national state in 1974.

**Qyzylorda** /kə₁zɪlɔ:'da/ (also **Kyzyl-Orda**) a town in southern Kazakhstan, on the Syr Darya; pop. (1990) 156,000.

# R r

**Rabat** /rə'bæt/ the capital of Morocco, an industrial port with textile industries on the Atlantic coast on the south bank of the Oued Bou Regreg; pop. (1982) 518,620. It is one of the four Imperial Cities of Morocco and was founded by the Almohad dynasty in the 12th c. when a fortified monastery *ribat* known as Ribat el Fath (Arabic = fort of victory) was built on the site of a Oudaida settlement. The new city was built after 1912 by General Lyautey during the period of the French protectorate. Rabat's chief landmark is the Hassan Tower and the port of Salé lies on the opposite side of the river.

**Rabaul** /rə'baʊl/ the chief town and port of the island of New Britain, Papua New Guinea, situated on Simpson Harbour close to Matupit Volcano; pop. (1990) 17,020. Laid out in a grid system Rabaul was largely rebuilt after its destruction during World War II.

**race** a term used to describe the major divisions of mankind, having distinct physical characteristics. It has been applied to various national or cultural as well as physical groupings (including 'human race' for the entire species of mankind). For centuries geographical races were identified by the most observable physical differences, especially the colour of the skin, hair, and eyes. The reason for human variation has been a subject of interest and speculation since antiquity. Christian tradition of the unity of mankind, descended from a common ancestor, became scientific orthodoxy in medieval Europe, with national genealogies traced to a descendant of Noah, but from the time of Paracelsus onwards a diversity of human origins was argued. In the 19th c. a combination of European overseas migration and the heightening of national consciousness strengthened interest in the differences between human groups, generally with the underlying assumption that the 'races' were once separate and that subsequent obscuring of pure racial types had occurred. In the early 20th c. Franz Boas put forward the theory that racial typing on a purely physical basis was arbitrary and argued the cultural origin of mental differences. His approach became dominant, though the Nazis burned his book. Human variation continues to be studied but the notion of 'race' as a rigid classification or genetic system has largely been abandoned.

**Racine** /rə'siːn/ a city in the US state of Wisconsin, at the mouth of the Root River on Lake Michigan south of Milwaukee; pop. (1990) 84,300. It has the largest population of people of Danish descent in the US and is the centre of an agricultural area with food-processing and lumbering industries.

**Radnorshire** /'rædn(ə)r,ʃɪə(r)/ a former county of eastern Wales. It became part of Powys in 1974.

**Radom** /'rɑːdɒm/ an industrial city in central Poland, to the south of Warsaw; pop. (1990) 228,490. It has engineering, machinery, leather, and food-processing industries.

**Ragusa** /ræ'guːzə/ the Italian name (until 1918) of Dubrovnik. It is probably the source of the word *argosy*, referring to the large and richly-freighted merchant ships of Ragusa in the 16th c.

**Raichur** /'raɪtʃər/ a cotton-market town in the central Deccan, south-central India, in the state of Karnataka; pop. (1991) 170,500. Built in the 14th c., it became the first capital of the Bijapur kingdom in 1489.

**Rainbow Bridge** /'reɪmbəʊ/ **1.** the world's largest bridge of natural rock, situated in semi-desert just north of the Arizona–Utah border, USA. Its span is 86 m. (278 ft.) and it curves upward to a height of 94 m. (309 ft.). **2.** a road bridge across the Niagara River linking the US city of Niagara Falls to the Canadian city of the same name. Replacing earlier bridges (the first of which was built in 1848) the present steel arch construction was completed in 1941.

**Rainier** /'reɪnɪə(r)/, **Mount** the highest volcanic peak in the Cascade Range in south-west Washington, USA, rising to a height of 4,395 m. (14,410 ft.). It was designated a national park in 1899.

**Raipur** /raɪ'pʊə(r)/ a city in south-east Madhya Pradesh, central India; pop. (1991) 461,850. It was the site of a fort built by Raja Bhubaneshwar in 1460. The city is a centre for processing agricultural produce.

**Rajahmundry** /,rɑːdʒə'muːndri:/ a city and centre of pilgrimage in north-east Andhra Pradesh, India, on the Godavari River; pop. (1991) 403,780.

**Rajang** /rɑː'dʒæŋ/ the principal river of Sarawak on the island of Borneo; length, 560 km. (350 miles).

**Rajapalayam** /,rɑːjə'pɑːlɪəm/ a town in Tamil Nadu, southern India, in the foothills of the Western Ghats south-west of Madurai; pop. (1991) 114,000. Engineering and food processing are its chief industries.

**Rajasthan** /ˌrɑːdʒəˈstɑːn/ a state in western India to the east of Pakistan and south of the Punjab; area 342,239 sq. km. (132,190 sq. miles); pop. (1991) 43,880,640; capital, Jaipur. It was formed as the Union of Rajasthan in 1948 from the former region of Rajputana. In 1956 additional territory was added and its name became simply Rajasthan. The western part of the state consists largely of the Thar Desert and is sparsely populated. It is rich in minerals such as gypsum, rock phosphate, silver, asbestos, copper, and felspar. The state is noted for its arts and crafts.
**Rajasthani** *adj. & n.*

**Rajkot** /ˈrɑːdʒkəʊt/ a city in the state of Gujarat, western India; pop. (1991) 651,000. It was the capital of a former Rajput princely state and under British rule was the seat of the British Resident for the Western Indian States. Gandhi was educated at the Alfred High School. Its industries process agricultural products such as groundnuts.

**Rajputana** /ˌrɑːdʒpʊˈtɑːnə/ an ancient region of north-west India largely consisting of a collection of former princely states ruled by dynasties, which came to power between the 9th and 16th centuries. Under British rule they were known as the Rajputana Agency but in 1948 united to form the Union of Rajasthan, now the state of Rajasthan, parts also being incorporated into Gujarat and Madhya Pradesh (= the country of the Rajputs).

**Rajshahi** /ˈrædʒʃəhiː/ a port on the Ganges River in western Bangladesh; pop. (1991) 324,530. Capital of the Pala kings during the 8th c., Rajshahi (= royal territory) is a centre of the silk, cotton, and sugar-cane trade. It was once also a centre of the indigo trade. Nearby is Paharpur an ancient seat of Buddhist learning.

**Raleigh** /ˈrɑːlɪ/ the capital of the US state of North Carolina; pop. (1990) 207,950. Laid out in 1792, the city was named after Sir Walter Raleigh. It is a research centre for the electronic, chemical, and food-processing industries and is home to an annual convention of whistlers. It is at the heart of a major tobacco-growing region.

**Rambouillet** /ˌrɒmbuːˈjeɪ/ a town in the department of Yvelines, northern France, situated in the Forest of Rambouillet; pop. (1990) 25,300. Its former royal chateau is now a summer residence of the French president. Louis XVI established Marie-Antoinette's dairy and an experimental sheep farm that was a forerunner of the modern Bergerie Nationale. The town gives its name to a breed of sheep.

**Ramillies** /ˈræmɪlɪz/ a village north of Namur in Brabant, Belgium, scene of a battle in 1706 at which Marlborough defeated the French under Villeroi.

**Rampur** /ˈrɑːmpʊ(ə)r/ a town in Uttar Pradesh, northern India, on the Kosi River east of Delhi; pop. (1991) 242,750. It was the capital of a princely state ruled by a nawab descended from Roahilla Pathans and holds a fine collection of rare manuscripts and miniature paintings.

**Ramsgate** /ˈræmzgeɪt/ a resort town and fishing port on the coast of Kent, south-east England, made popular in the 19th c. following a visit by George IV; pop. (1981) 39,600. There are ferry links with France and Belgium.

**Rancagua** /rɑːnˈkægwə/ a city and agricultural centre to the south of Santiago in central Chile, capital of the Libertador Bernardo O'Higgins region; pop. (1991) 190,380.

**Rance** /rɑːns/ a river of Brittany, north-west France, that flows into the English Channel near St. Malo. A dam and power station built 1960–7 harness the tidal power of 13-m. (44-ft.) tides at the mouth of the river and was the first in the world to do so.

**Ranchi** /ˈrɑːntʃɪ/ the former summer capital of Bihar State in India, in the Chotanagpur tribal country; pop. (1991) 614,450. It is a resort town and educational centre with heavy engineering industries.

**Rand** /rænd, rɑːnt/, **the** see WITWATERSRAND.

**Randers** /ˈrɑːnəz/ a port and industrial town of Denmark, on the Randers Fjord on the east coast of the Jutland peninsula; pop. (1990) 61,020. Long noted for its craftsmen, its chief manufactures include, shoes, metal goods, and foodstuffs.

**Randstad** /ˈrɔːnstɑːt/ a conurbation in the north-west of the Netherlands that stretches in a horseshoe shape from Dordrecht and Rotterdam round to Utrecht and Amersfoort via the Hague, Leiden, Haarlem, and Amsterdam. The majority of the people of the Netherlands live in this area. Its Dutch name means 'ring of towns'.

**Rangoon** /ræŋˈguːn/ (Burmese **Yangon** /jæŋˈɡɔːn/) the capital of Burma (Myanmar), a seaport on the Rangoon river, one of the mouths of the Irrawaddy; pop. (1983) 2,458,710. The city was named Yangon (= the end of war) in 1755 when King Alaungpaya captured the riverside village of Dagon from the Mons. It was officially renamed Yangon in 1989. Rebuilt by the British on a grid system after the Second Anglo-Burmese War it became the capital in 1885, its chief landmark being the Shwedagon Pagoda, built over 2,500 years ago to house eight sacred hairs of the Buddha. The commercial and industrial centre of Burma, its exports of rice, teak, oil, and rubber have declined since independence.

**Rangpur** /ˈræŋpʊə(r)/ a city in north-west Bangladesh, capital of the Rangpur region; pop. (1991) 220,850. Situated on a tributary of the Jamuna, it produces jute and canvas goods and has a Research Centre for Leprosy.

**Rann of Kutch** /rɑːn, kʌtʃ/ see KUTCH, RANN OF.

**Rapid City** /'ræpɪd/ a mining city in the Black Hills of South Dakota, USA; pop. (1990) 54,520. Settled in 1876 during a gold-rush, it is a popular tourist destination and home of the Ellsworth Air Force Base. Mount Rushmore and the Black Hills Petrified Forest are nearby.

**Rarotonga** /ˌreərə'tɒŋgə/ a mountainous island in the South Pacific, the chief island of the Cook Islands. Its chief town, Avarua, is the capital of the Cook Islands.

**Ras al-Khaimah** /rɑːs æl 'kaɪmə/ **1.** one of the seven member-states of the United Arab Emirates; area 1,690 sq. km. (653 sq. miles); pop. (1985) 116,470. Its name is derived from the Arabic for 'head of the tent', referring to the days when a light was placed at the highest point to guide ships home to port. Fishing and the production of cement, oil, and gas are its chief industries. The ruling sheik is of the Qawasim family. **2.** its capital city on a creek that enters the Persian Gulf; pop. (1980) 42,000. Port Saqr is the principal port facility.

**Ras Dashan** /rɑːs də'saːn/ a mountain in northern Ethiopia, the highest peak in the country and fourth-highest in Africa. It rises to 4,620 m. (15,158 ft.) north-east of Lake Tana.

**Rashid** /ræ'ʃiːd/ (formerly **Rosetta**) an ancient city in northern Egypt, 65 km. (40 miles) east of Alexandria where the western (Rosetta) branch of the Nile empties into the Mediterranean. Founded in the 9th c., it was, after the decline of Alexandria, an important port until the development of Alexandria once again in the 19th c. It is most famous for the Rosetta Stone, an inscribed basalt slab discovered by Napoleon's soldiers in 1799. Dating from the reign of Ptolemy V (c. 196 BC), its combination of Egyptian hieroglyphs, demotic Egyptian, and Greek enabled Jean-François Champollion to decipher the ancient Pharaonic language.

**Rasht** /'rɑːʃt/ a city in northern Iran, near the Caspian Sea and west of the Elburz Mountains; pop. (1991) 341,000. It is capital of Gilan province and a centre of the rice and silk cocoon industries.

**Ras Shamra** SEE UGARIT.

**Rastafarian** /ˌræstə'feɪrɪən/ a sect of Jamaican origin which believes that Blacks are the chosen people, that the late Emperor Haile Selassie of Ethiopia was God Incarnate, and that he will secure their repatriation to their homeland in Africa. Ras Tafari (Amharic, *ras* chief) was the title by which Haile Selassie was known from 1916 until his accession in 1930.

**Rastyapino** /ræ'stjɑːpɪnəʊ/ a former name (1919–29) of DZERZHINSK.

**Rathlin Island** /'ræθlɪn/ an island off the north coast of Antrim, Northern Ireland; area 14.4 sq. km. (5.6 sq. miles); pop. (est.) 100. In ancient times it was a port of call on the journey from Ireland to Scotland and Robert the Bruce is said to have taken refuge in a cave. There is a ferry link with Ballycastle.

**Ratisbon** the French name for the German city of REGENSBURG.

**Ratlam** /rət'laːm/ a market town in Madhya Pradesh, west-central India, north-west of Indore; pop. (1991) 195,750.

**Rauma** /'raʊmə/ (Swedish **Raumo**) a historic town in south-west Finland, on the Gulf of Bothnia north-west of Turku; pop. (1990) 29,755. It is the largest wood-built town preserved in the Nordic countries.

**Raurkela** /rɔː(r)'keɪlə/ (also **Rourkela**) an industrial town in the state of Orissa, east-central India, north-west of Cuttack; pop. (1991) 398,700. Steel and fertilizer are its chief products.

**Ravenna** /rə'venə/ a historic tourist city near the Adriatic coast in the Emilia-Romagna region of north-east-central Italy; pop. (1991) 136,720. An important centre in Roman times, Ravenna became the capital of the Ostrogothic kingdom of Italy in the 5th c. and afterwards served as capital of the Byzantine Empire of Italy. The richest mosaics of the early Christian period are found here. It became an independent republic in the 13th c. and then a papal possession in 1509, remaining in papal hands until 1859. It once lay on the coast surrounded by a lagoon, but is now situated inland as a result of the silting over of the River Po. The philosopher and writer Alighieri Dante was buried here after his death in 1321. The discovery of natural gas nearby in the 1950s has led to the development of refining and petrochemical industries.

**Ravi** /'rɑːvɪ/ a river in the north of the Indian subcontinent, one of the headwaters of the Indus, which rises in the Himalayas in Himachal Pradesh, north-west India, and flows for 725 km. (450 miles) generally south-westwards into Pakistan, where it empties into the Chenab just north of Multan. It is one of the 'five rivers' that gave Punjab its name.

**Rawalpindi** /rɔːl'pɪndɪ/ an industrial city in Punjab province, northern Pakistan, in the foothills of the Himalayas; pop. (1981) 928,000. A former military station controlling the routeways to Kashmir, it was interim capital of Pakistan 1959–67 during the construction of Islamabad. It has an oil refinery and numerous industries.

**Rawson** /'rɔːsən/ a port on the Atlantic coast of Patagonia in southern Argentina, capital of the province of Chubut; pop. (1980) 12,890.

**Reading** /'redɪŋ/ the county town of Berkshire in southern England, on the River Kennet near its junction with the Thames; pop. (1991) 122,600. It has a university (1926) and the remains of a 12th-c Clunaic abbey in which Henry I is buried. Oscar Wilde was imprisoned in Reading gaol (1895–7). A market and residential town with numerous light industries including electronics, engineering, biscuits, and seeds.

**Reading** /'redɪŋ/ an industrial and commercial city in south-east Pennsylvania, USA; on the Schuylkill River; pop. (1990) 78,380. Founded in 1748 on land purchased from the Lenni-Lenape Indians by William Penn, it was named Reading by his sons Thomas and Richard after their former home in England. It was an early iron-production centre making ordnance during both the Revolutionary and Civil Wars. A farmstead near here was the birthplace in 1734 of the frontiersman Daniel Boone.

**Recife** /rə'siːfeɪ/ (formerly **Pernambuco** /ˌpɜːnæm'buːkəʊ/) a port and tourist resort on the Atlantic coast of Pernambuco state, north-east Brazil; pop. (1991) 1,297,000. Situated at the mouth of the River Capibaribe, it is state capital and a leading port of the north-east. It was the original capital of Brazil 1537–49. Recife exports primary products from its hinterland and has sugar refineries and cotton mills.

**Recklinghausen** /ˌreklɪŋ'haʊz(ə)n/ an industrial city in the state of North Rhine-Westphalia, north-west Germany, situated south-west of Münster; pop. (1991) 126,000. It has iron and steel, machinery, chemicals, and textiles industries.

**Redbridge** /'redbrɪdʒ/ a borough of north-east Greater London, England, that includes the suburbs of Chigwell, Ilford, Wanstead, and Woodford; pop. (1991) 220,600. Primarily residential, it is also an important commercial and light industrial centre. It includes much of Epping Forest within its boundaries.

**Redcar** /'redkɑː(r)/ an industrial town in Cleveland, north-east England, north-east of Middlesborough; pop. (1981) 35,400. It has a race-course.

**Red Deer** **1.** a river in western Canada that rises in Banff National Park, Alberta, and flows 724 km. (452 miles) generally eastwards to join the South Saskatchewan River on the border between Alberta and Saskatchewan. **2.** a city in southern Alberta, Canada, to the north of Calgary; pop. (1991) 58,100.

**Redding** /'redɪŋ/ a resort town in northern California, USA, on the Sacramento River; pop. (1990) 66,460.

**Redditch** /'redɪtʃ/ an industrial town in Hereford and Worcester, central England; pop. (1991) 76,900. It developed as a New Town satellite of Birmingham after 1964.

**Redlands** /'redləndz/ a residential city in the San Bernardino Valley, southern California, USA; pop. (1990) 60,390.

**Redonda** /re'dɒndə/ a small uninhabited island in the eastern Caribbean, one of the three islands of Antigua and Barbuda. It was a source of guano in the 19th c. but in 1865 sovereignty was claimed by an Irishman who created for his descendants one of the more curious royal families of the world with a literary aristocracy that later included J. B. Priestley and Rebecca West.

**Redondo Beach** /rɪ'dɑːndəʊ/ a resort town and yachting centre on the Pacific coast of southern California, USA; pop. (1990) 60,170.

**Redoubt** /rə'daʊt/, **Mount** an active volcano in Alaska rising to 3,140 m. (10,197 ft.) in the Aleutian Range west of the Cook Inlet.

**Red River** (Chinese **Yuan Jiang**, Vietnamese **Song Hong**) a river in south-east Asia, which rises in southern China and flows 1,175 km. (730 miles) generally south-eastwards through northern Vietnam to the Gulf of Tonkin north of Haiphong.

**Red River** the name of two rivers in North America named after the reddish soil sediment they carry: **1.** a southern tributary of the Mississippi River that rises in two branches in northern Texas and flows generally south-eastwards for 1,966 km. (1,222 miles) through Shreveport and Alexandria before entering the Mississippi north of Baton Rouge. It is also known as the *Red River of the South*. **2.** a river that rises in North Dakota and flows 877 km. (545 miles) northwards into Manitoba where it empties into Lake Winnipeg. For most of its length before entering Canada it forms the border between North Dakota and Minnesota. It is also known as the *Red River of the North*.

**Red Sea** a long narrow land-locked sea separating Africa from the Arabian Peninsula. It is linked to the Indian Ocean in the south by the Gulf of Aden and to the Mediterranean in the north by the Suez Canal. Its chief ports are Port Sudan, Massawa, Jeddah, and Hodeida.

**Red Square** a large open area at the centre of Moscow below the eastern walls of the Kremlin.

**Redwood National Park** a US national park on the Pacific coast of north-west California established in 1968 to protect coastal redwoods (*Sequoia sempervirens*) which are the world's tallest trees.

**Regensburg** /'reɪɡenzbuː(r)ɡ/ (French **Ratisbon**) a river port, tourist, and industrial city in Bavaria, southern Germany, situated at the northern extremity of the Danube; pop. (1991) 123,000. Founded on the site of the Roman legionary camp of Castra Regina, it became an important commercial centre in early medieval times and was later the seat of the Imperial Diet, Germany's oldest parliament. It was the birthplace of the painter and architect Albrecht Altdorfer (1480–1538) and the poet and writer Georg Britting (1891–1964). It specializes in the manufacture of machines and precision instruments.

**Reggio di Calabria** /'redʒəʊ diː kə'læbrɪə/ a port and tourist resort at the southern tip of the 'toe' of Italy, on the Strait of Messina, capital of Calabria region; pop. (1990) 183,440. The original settlement, named Rhegion in Greek (Latin Rhegium) was founded about 720 BC by Greek colonists. It fell to the Romans in 270 BC and was twice destroyed by an earthquake in 1783 and

1908. From the 13th c. it was included in the kingdom of Sicily and Naples. The bronze statues of Riace, dating from the 5th c. BC, were discovered in the sea near here in 1972. Industries include olive oil and pasta making.

**Reggio nell'Emilia** /'redʒəʊ nel e'mi:ljə/ the capital of a province of the same name in the Emilia-Romagna region of north-central Italy, on the Aemilian Way; pop. (1990) 131,880. In 1797 the tricolour flag, later to become the flag of Italy, was first raised in the Palazzo Comunale by the Congress of the Cities of Emilia. It was the birthplace of the writer and poet Ludovico Ariosto (1474–1533). Industries include electrical equipment, canned meat, and cement.

**Regina** /rɪ'dʒaɪnə/ the capital of the province of Saskatchewan, situated at the centre of the wheat-growing plains of central Canada; pop. (1991) 191,690 (metropolitan area). It was founded on the site of a hunters' camp known as Pile o' Bones and was renamed in 1882 in honour of Queen Victoria; its name means 'queen' in Latin. It was the administrative headquarters of the North West (later Royal Canadian) Mounted Police until 1920. In addition to being Canada's agrarian capital, it has a major oil refinery and steelworks.

**Reigate** /'raɪɡeɪt/ a residential town in Surrey, south-east England, north of Crawley. It forms a district with Banstead; pop. (1991) 114,900.

**Reims** /ri:mz/ see RHEIMS.

**Remscheid** /'remʃaɪt/ an industrial town in North Rhine-Westphalia, north-western Germany, situated east of Düsseldorf; pop. (1991) 123,620. Leading centre of the tool and hardware industry.

**Renfrewshire** /'renfru:ʃaɪr/ a local government area and former county of central Scotland on the south side of the River Clyde, from 1975 to 1996 a district of Strathclyde Region; area 310 sq. km. (120 sq. miles); pop. (1991) 193,620. Its chief town is Renfrew.

**Rennes** /ren/ an industrial city of Brittany in north-west France, capital of the department of Ille-et-Vilaine; pop. (1990) 203,530. It was established as the capital of a Celtic tribe, the Redones, from whom its derives its name, later becoming the capital of the ancient kingdom of Brittany. The city was partially rebuilt after a great fire in 1720. Industries include car assembly, electric and electronic equipment, chemicals, and clothing. It is a cultural and educational centre with two universities, an agricultural college, and a medical school.

**Reno** /'ri:nəʊ/ a city in the US state of Nevada, on the Truckee River; pop. (1990) 133,850. Settled in 1859 and named in honour of General J. L. Reno, it developed after the arrival of the Union and Central Pacific Railroad in 1868 as a centre for trade in livestock, grain, timber, and cement. Reno also has a reputation for gambling and for its liberal laws enabling quick marriages and divorces.

**Repulse Bay** /rə'pʌls/ a bay in northern Canada to the south of the Isthmus between Hudson Bay and the Gulf of Boothia. It lies on the Arctic Circle at the north-eastern extremity of Northwest Territories and was named in 1741 when Captain Middleton arrived here having failed to find the northwest passage to the Pacific.

**Réseau Jean Bernard** /ˌreɪzəʊ ʒã beə'nɑ:(r)/ a cave system in the French Alps near the town of Samoëns in the department of Haute Savoie. Entered at an altitude of 2,264 m. (7,428 ft.) and descending to 1,535 m. (5,036 ft.) on the Lapies de Follis, it is the deepest known cave system in the world. It has a total length of 17 km. (10.5 miles).

**Resistencia** /rezɪs'tensɪə/ the capital of the province of Chaco in northern Argentina, on the River Paraná opposite Corrientes; pop. (1991) 291,000. Founded on the site of an old Quechua Indian settlement, its name refers to an Indian hunting technique of encircling and then closing in on their prey. Its chief products are cotton, cattle, leather, and quebracho which is used in tanning.

**Reşita** /rə'ʃi:tsə/ a city in the foothills of the Transylvanian Alps of western Romania, capital of Caraş-Severin county; pop. (1989) 110,260. Heavy engineering, coal mining, iron mining, and the production of iron and steel are its chief industries.

**Rethymnon** /'reθɪmˌnɒn/ (Greek **Réthimnon**) a port on the north coast of Crete, between Heraklion and Canea; pop. (1981) 17,700. Its chief landmarks are a fortress, a Venetian Loggia, and the Porta Grande Mosque.

**Réunion**
/ˌreɪu:n'jɔ̃/ a volcanically active, subtropical island in the Indian Ocean east of Madagascar, one of the Mascerene Islands; area 2,512 sq. km. (970 sq. miles); pop. (1990)  596,700; capital, Saint-Denis. A French possession since 1638, the island became an overseas department of France in 1946 and an administrative region in 1974. Its chief export is sugar.

**Reus** /'reɪʊs/ an industrial town in Catalonia, eastern Spain, situated north-west of Tarragona; pop. (1991) 87,710. It has an international airport, produces textiles, and trades in flowers, fruit, and vegetables grown in the surrounding area. It was the birthplace of the architect Antonio Gaudi (1852–1926).

**Reutlingen** /'rɔɪtlɪŋ(ə)n/ an industrial (textiles) city in Baden-Württemberg, western Germany, situated south of Stuttgart on the slopes of the Schwabian Hills; pop. (1991) 106,000. An important market town in the Middle Ages, its chief landmark is the 13th-c. Marienkirche.

**Revillagigedo Islands** /rɪˈviːləgəˌgeɪdəʊ/ a group of Mexican islands in the Pacific Ocean, the largest of which is Socorro.

**Reykjavik** /ˈreɪkjəvɪk/ the capital of Iceland, a port on Faxa Bay; pop. (1990) 97,570. It was the first place on Iceland to be settled and is the world's northernmost capital city. It takes its name (Icelandic = smoky bay) from the steam that was seen to rise from nearby geothermal features. It is the base of the fishing fleet and has fish-processing, metal-working, printing, and clothing industries.

**Rhaetia** /ˈriːʃɪə/ (also **Raetia**) an ancient Roman province that lay in the Alps to the south of the Danube and included parts of present-day eastern Switzerland and the Vorarlberg and Tyrol of Austria.

**Rhaeto-Romance** /ˌriːtəʊrəʊˈmæns/ (also **Rhaeto-Romanic** /-ˈmænɪk/) any of the Romance dialects of south-east Switzerland and western Austria, especially Romansh and Ladin.

**Rheims** /riːmz/ (French **Reims** /ræns/) an ancient cathedral city in the department of Marne, north-east France, chief city of the Champagne-Ardenne region; pop. (1990) 185,160. Clovis, king of the Franks, was baptised here in 496 and Charles VII was crowned here in 1429. The building of its famous cathedral began in 1211 and was completed about a century later. Most of the city was destroyed in World War I but has since been rebuilt. It is the centre of the Champagne wine industry.

**Rhein** the German name for the RHINE.

**Rheinland-Pfalz** the German name for the RHINELAND-PALATINATE.

**Rhenish** /ˈriːnɪʃ, ˈren-/ of the Rhine and the regions adjoining it.

**Rhenish Slate Mountains** (German **Rheinisches Schiefergebirge**) a mountainous region of the Rhineland-Palatinate on the western frontier of Germany.

**Rhine** /raɪn/ (German **Rhein**, French **Rhin**, Dutch **Rijn**) a river of Western Europe which rises in the the Rheinwaldhorn glacier in the Swiss Alps and flows for 1,320 km. (820 miles) to the North Sea, first westwards through Lake Constance, forming the German–Swiss border, then turning northwards through Germany, forming the southern part of the German–French border, before flowing westwards again through the Netherlands to empty into the North Sea near Rotterdam. It forms part of an important inland waterway network navigable to Basle and flows through several major cities including Basle, Mannheim, Mainz, Cologne, and Düsseldorf. It carries large loads of freight especially between the Ruhr area and Rotterdam. It is heavily polluted but nevertheless a popular destination for tourists much influenced by its legends and its famous vineyards and castles.

**Rhineland** /ˈraɪnlænd/ the region of western Germany through which the Rhine flows, especially the part to the west of the river. The area was demilitarized as part of the Versailles Treaty in 1919 but was reoccupied by Hitler in 1936.

**Rhineland-Palatinate** /-pəˈlætɪneɪt/ (German **Rheinland-Pfalz** /-fælts/) a state of western Germany; area 19,849 sq. km. (7,666 sq. miles); pop. (est. 1990) 3,702,000; capital, Mainz.

**Rhode Island** /rəʊd/ a state in the northeastern USA, on the Atlantic coast, settled from England in the 17th c.; area 3,140 sq. km. (1,212 sq. miles); pop. (1990) 1,003,460; capital, Providence. The smallest of the 50 states, it is also known as the Ocean State and was one of the original 13 states of the US. The chief landmarks are Samuel Slater's mill in Pawtucket, Roger Williams National Memorial in Providence, and the Touro Synagogue (1763), the oldest in the USA. It is divided into five counties:

| County | Area (sq. km.) | Pop. (1990) | County Seat |
|---|---|---|---|
| Bristol | 68 | 48,860 | Bristol |
| Kent | 447 | 161,135 | East Greenwich |
| Newport | 278 | 87,190 | Newport |
| Providence | 1,082 | 596,270 | Providence |
| Washington | 866 | 110,010 | West Kingston |

**Rhodes** /rəʊdz/ (Greek **Ródhos**) **1.** a Greek island in the south-east Aegean, off the Turkish coast, the largest of the Dodecanese Islands and the most easterly island in the Aegean; area 1,398 sq. km. (540 sq. miles); pop. (1981) 87,800. Rhodes flourished in the late Bronze Age, becoming a significant trading nation and dominating several islands in the Aegean. It came under Byzantine rule in the 5th c. Throughout the 14th and 15th centuries under the Knights of St. John it was a centre for the struggle against Turkish domination, eventually falling under Turkish administration in 1522, which lasted until 1912 when it was ceded to Italy. In 1947, following World War II, it was awarded to Greece. **2.** its capital, a port on the northernmost tip of the island; pop. (1981) 40,390. It was founded c. 408 BC and was the site of the Colossus of Rhodes. It is now a popular tourist resort.

**Rhodesia** /rəʊˈdiːʃə/ **1.** the former name of a large territory in central-southern Africa, divided into Northern Rhodesia (now Zambia) and Southern Rhodesia (now Zimbabwe). The region was developed by and named after Cecil Rhodes, through the British South Africa Company, which administered it until Southern Rhodesia became a self-governing British colony in 1923 and Northern Rhodesia a British protectorate in 1924. From 1953 to 1963 Northern and Southern Rhodesia were united with Nyasaland (now Malawi) to form the federation of Rhodesia and Nyasaland. **2.** the name adopted by Southern Rhodesia when

Northern Rhodesia left the Federation in 1963 to become the independent republic of Zambia.

**Rhodesian** *adj. & n.*

**Rhodope Mountains** /ˈrɒdəpɪ/ (Bulgarian **Rodopi Planina**) a range of mountains on the frontier between Bulgaria and Greece, rising to a height of 2,925 m. (9,596 ft.) at Musala.

**Rhondda** /ˈrɒndə/ a district of Mid Glamorgan, South Wales, which extends along the valleys of the rivers Rhondda Fawr and Rhondda Fach. It was formerly noted as a coal-mining area, and now a centre for light industries.

**Rhône** /rəʊn/ a river in south-west Europe which rises in the Swiss Alps and flows 812 km. (505 miles), at first westwards through Lake Geneva into France, then to Lyon, where it turns southwards, passing Avignon, to the Mediterranean Sea west of Marseilles, where it forms a wide delta that includes the Camargue region. South of Lyon it has been developed for hydroelectric power and irrigation, and in order to improve navigation.

**Rhône** a department in the Rhône-Alpes region of eastern France; area 3,215 sq. km. (1,242 sq. miles); pop. (1990) 1,508,970; capital, Lyon.

**Rhône-Alpes** /rəʊnˈælp/ a region of south-east France, extending from the Rhône valley to the borders with Switzerland and Italy and including much of the former duchy of Savoy. It comprises the departments of Ain, Ardèche, Drôme, Isère, Loire, Rhône, Savoie, and Haute-Savoie; area 43,698 sq. km. (16,878 sq. miles); pop. (1990) 5,350,700.

**Rhum** see RUM.

**RI** *abbr.* US Rhode Island (in official postal use).

**Rialto** /rɪˈæltəʊ/ an island in Venice, containing the old mercantile quarter of medieval Venice. The Rialto Bridge, completed in 1591, crosses the Grand Canal in a single span between Rialto and San Marco islands.

**Rialto** /rɪˈæltəʊ/ a residential city in the San Bernardino Valley, southern California, USA; pop. (1990) 72,388.

**ribat** /riːˈbæt/ a fortified monastery in North Africa.

**Ribatejo** /ˌriːbəˈteɪdʒəʊ/ a fertile region of central Portugal in the lower valley of the Tagus River roughly corresponding to the district of Santarém in the province of Estremadura. The region is celebrated for its horses and fighting-bulls.

**Ribble** /ˈrɪb(ə)l/ a river of northern England that rises in the Pennine Hills and flows south and south-west for 120 km. (75 miles) through Lancashire before meeting the Irish Sea near Preston.

**Ribeirão Prêto** /riːbeɪˈraʊ preɪtəʊ/ a commercial city in the interior of São Paulo state, southern Brazil; pop. (1990) 454,120. Coffee, cotton, grain, rice, and sugar-cane are traded.

**Ricardo Franco Hills** /rɪˈkɑː(r)dəʊ ˈfræŋkəʊ/ a range of flat-topped hills in the Brazilian state of Mato Grosso, between the Verde and Guaporé rivers. Col. Percy Fawcett's description of these hills inspired Arthur Conan Doyle to write *The Lost World*.

**Richardson** /ˈrɪtʃ(ə)rdsən/ a residential city to the north of Dallas in north-east Texas, USA; pop. (1990) 74,840.

**Richland** /ˈrɪtʃlænd/ a city in south-east Washington, USA, on the Columbia River; pop. (1990) 33,300. It was developed after 1943 as an administrative and residential centre for those working at the nearby atomic-energy research station and plutonium production plant.

**Richmond** /ˈrɪtʃmənd/ a town in New South Wales, south-east Australia, to the south of the Hawkesbury river north-east of Sydney; pop. (1991) 18,770 (with Windsor). The University of Western Sydney (1895) lies to the south and Richmond's Air Force base is the oldest in the country.

**Richmond** /ˈrɪtʃmənd/ a town in North Yorkshire, northern England, on the River Swale south-west of Darlington; pop. (1981) 7,730. It has a Norman castle, a large market place, and a Georgian theatre (1788).

**Richmond** /ˈrɪtʃmənd/ **1.** a port in the US state of California, on San Francisco Bay north of Oakland; pop. (1990) 87,425. **2.** the capital of the US state of Virginia, a port on the James River; pop.(1990) 203,060. Patrick Henry made his 'liberty or death' speech in St. John's Church in 1775 and Richmond became state capital in 1780. During the American Civil War it was the Confederate capital from 1861 until its capture in 1865. In additon to producing tobacco products, paper, aluminium, chemicals, textiles, and machinery, it is the seat of the Virginia Commonwealth University and the University of Richmond.

**Richmond Hill** a town in south-east Ontario, Canada, north of Toronto; pop. (1991) 80,100.

**Richmond upon Thames** a residential borough of Greater London, England, on the Thames; pop. (1991) 154,600. Hampton Court Palace and the Royal Botanic Gardens at Kew are located here. There are the remains of a Tudor royal palace where Queen Elizabeth I died in 1603, and White Lodge in Richmond Park is also strongly associated with the British royal family.

**Richter scale** /ˈrɪktə(r), ˈrɪx/ a logarithmic scale of 0 to 10 used to represent the strength of an earthquake. It was developed by the American seismologist C. F. Richter (d. 1985).

**Rideau Canal** /ˈrɪdəʊ/ a canal in eastern Ontario, Canada, linking Ottawa with Kingston on Lake Ontario. Built between 1826 and 1832, it has 24 locks and is 200 km. (124 miles) long.

**Ridgeway Path** /ˈrɪdʒweɪ/ a long-distance footpath following a prehistoric routeway over downland in southern England that stretches for 137 km. (86 miles) from Overton Hill near Avebury in Wiltshire to Ivinghoe Beacon in Buckinghamshire.

**Riding Mountain National Park** /'raɪdɪŋ/ a national park in central Canada, which extends over part of the glacially formed Manitoba Escarpment, north-west of Winnipeg in Western Manitoba. A series of plateaux rise to heights of about 340 m. (1,100 ft.) and there are many lakes, the largest of which is Clear Lake. Buffalo, bears, elk, deer, and wolves are protected over an area of c.3,000 sq. km. (1,158 sq. miles).

**Ridings** /'raɪdɪŋz/, **the** the name given to the three administrative divisions of Yorkshire in England prior to the reorganization of local government in 1974 but still used locally. The **North Riding** extends over the Yorkshire Moors and Dales, the **West Riding** incorporates the industrial towns and cities of Leeds, Bradford, Huddersfield, Doncaster, and Sheffield, and the **East Riding** surrounds the port of Hull. The name is derived from an old Norse word *thrithjungr* (= third part).

**Riegersburg** /'riːgɜːzbʊə(r)k/ a castle in Styria, south-eastern Austria, 55 km. (34 miles) east of Graz. One of the largest castles in Austria, it was never taken by an enemy.

**Rieti** /riː'eɪtɪ/ capital of the province of Rieti in Latium, central Italy, on the River Velino northeast of Rome; pop. (1990) 44,490.

**Rif Mountains** /rɪf/ (also **Er Rif**) a mountain range of northern Morocco, running parallel to the Mediterranean for about 290 km. (180 miles) eastwards from Tangier to near the Algerian frontier. Rising to over 2,250 m. (7,000 ft.), it forms a westward extension of the Atlas Mountains. The retreat of Berber tribesmen who have often been in revolt against occupying authorities.

**rift valley** a valley bounded by two roughly parallel faults formed when the rocks at its base moved downwards. See GREAT RIFT VALLEY.

**Riga** /'riːgə/ the capital of Latvia, a port at the mouth of the Daugava River on the **Gulf of Riga**, an inlet of the Baltic Sea; pop. (1990) 916,500. Founded in c.1190 and becoming a member of the Hanseatic League in 1282, Riga developed as a major Baltic trading centre in the Middle Ages. The medieval old town contains many imposing buildings. Modern industries include shipbuilding and marine engineering, chemicals, textiles, and electronics.

**Rijeka** /riː'ekə/ (Italian **Fiume** /fɪ'uːmeɪ/) a port on the Adriatic coast of Croatia, once the largest port of Yugoslavia; pop. (1991) 167,900. Once a Roman settlement and later occupied by Slavs in the 7th c., Rijeka was the leading naval port of the Austro-Hungarian empire prior to 1918. It has shipyards and oil refineries.

**Rijksmuseum** /'raɪksmʊˌzeɪəm/ the national gallery of the Netherlands, in Amsterdam. Established in the late 19th c. and developed from the collection of the House of Orange, it now contains the most representative collection of Dutch art in the world.

**Rila Mountains** /'riːlə/ (Bulgarian **Rila Planina**) a range of mountains in western Bulgaria, forming the westernmost extent of the Rhodope Mountains. It is the highest range in Bulgaria, rising to a height of 2,925 m. (9,596 ft.) at Mount Musala.

**Rimini** /'rɪmənɪ/ a port, resort, and cultural centre on the Adriatic coast of Emilia-Romagna region, north-east Italy; pop. (1990) 130,900. It is situated at the crossroads of the Via Emilia, the Via Flaminia, and the Via Popilia on the site of the Roman town of Arminum which was founded in 268 BC. It became an independent city-state in the 12th c. and came under the control of the Malatesta family in the 13th c. Rimini passed to the Papal States in 1509 and was annexed to the kingdom of Italy in 1860.

**Ringkøbing** /rɪŋ'køʊpɪŋ/ a picturesque town on the west coast of Jutland, Denmark; pop. (1990) 16,950.

**Ringsted** /'rɪŋsted/ a commercial and food-processing town in central Zealand, Denmark; pop. (1990) 28,400. An important town in the Middle Ages, it was the burial place of Knud Lavard who was canonized in 1169.

**río** /'riːəʊ/ a Spanish word for a river.

**rio** /'riːəʊ/ a Portuguese word for a river.

**Riobamba** /ˌriːəʊ'bæmbə/ a market town in the Andean Sierra of central Ecuador, capital of the province of Chimborazo; pop. (1990) 160,430. Its industries manufacture textiles, carpets, tobacco, and processed food.

**Rio Branco** /ˌriːəʊ 'bræŋkəʊ/ a city in western Brazil, on the River Acre, capital of the state of Acre; pop. (1990) 197,000. Originally known as Empreza, it was founded as a rubber town in 1882.

**Rio Cuarto** /ˌriːəʊ 'kwɑːtəʊ/ a city in central Argentina, situated on the River Cuarto in the province of Córdoba; pop. (1991) 139,000.

**Rio de Janeiro** /ˌriːəʊ də dʒə'nɪəˌrəʊ/ **1.** a state in eastern Brazil, on the Atlantic coast; area 44,268 sq. km. (17,098 sq. miles); pop. (1991) 12,783,760. **2.** the chief port, second-largest city, the cultural, financial, and commercial centre, and former capital of Brazil; pop. (1991) 5,473,000. Situated on Guanabara Bay (an inlet of the Atlantic Ocean), the skyline of the city is dominated by Sugar Loaf Mountain and by Corcovado on which stands the statue of 'Christ the Redeemer'. Copacabana beach and the district of Ipanema are popular resorts. According to tradition, the city was first visited in January 1502 by Portuguese explorers who thought they had arrived at the mouth of a great river. It became a major outlet for gold and replaced Bahía as capital of Brazil in 1763. Its buildings range from beautiful 18th c. churches to famous modern architecture which contrasts with the huge shanty-towns or *favelas* which cling to steep hillsides around the city. The capital was eventually transferred to Brasilia in 1960.

**Río de la Plata** /ˌriːəʊ də lɑː ˈplɑːtə/ the Spanish name for the River Plate. (See PLATE, RIVER)

**Río de Oro** /ˈriːəʊ diː ˈɔːrəʊ/ an arid region on the Atlantic coast of north-west Africa, forming the southern part of Western Sahara; area 189,934 sq. km. (73,362 sq. miles). Occupied by the Spanish in 1884, it was united with Saguia el Hamra in 1958 to form the province of Spanish Sahara. Its chief town is Ad Dakhla.

**Rio Gallegos** /ˌriːəʊ gæˈleɪgəs/ a port near the mouth of the River Gallegos in Patagonia, southern Argentina, capital of the province of Santa Cruz; pop. (1980) 42,000.

**Rio Grande** /ˌriːəʊ ˈgrændɪ/ a port in the state of Rio Grande do Sul, Brazil, at the mouth of the Lagoa dos Patos south of Pôrto Alegre; pop. (1990) 184,040. It is a centre of fishing, oil refining, and the cattle trade.

**Rio Grande** /ˌriːəʊ ˈgrænd, ˈgrændɪ/ a river of North America which rises in the Rocky Mountains of south-west Colorado and flows 3,030 km. (1,880 miles) generally south-eastwards to the Gulf of Mexico. It forms the US–Mexico frontier from El Paso to the sea.

**Rio Grande do Norte** /-də ˈnɔː(r)tɪ/ a state on the Atlantic coast of north-eastern Brazil; area 53,015 sq. km. (20,477 sq. miles); pop. (1991) 2,414,120; capital, Natal. The driest and poorest part of Brazil.

**Rio Grande do Sul** /-də suːl/ the southernmost state of Brazil, to the east of the Uruguay River; area 282,184 sq. km. (108,993 sq. miles); pop. (1991) 9,135,480; capital, Pôrto Alegre.

**Rioja** /riːˈɒxə/, **La** an autonomous region of northern Spain, in the wine-producing valley of the River Ebro; area 5,034 sq. km. (1,944 sq. miles); pop. (1991) 263,430; capital, Logroño.

**Río Muni** /ˌriːəʊ ˈmuːnɪ/ the part of Equatorial Guinea that lies on the mainland of West Africa; area 26,016 sq. km. (10,049 sq. miles). Its chief town is Bata.

**Río Negro** see NEGRO.

**Río Tinto** /ˌriːəʊ ˈtiːntəʊ/ a town in the Andalusian province of Huelva, southern Spain; pop. (1983) 8,400. It lies in a copper-, iron-, and manganese-mining region first exploited by the Phoenicians.

**Ritten Earth Pillars** /ˈrɪtən/ (Italian **Renon**) a series of earth pillars topped with stone that rise up to heights of 40 m. (160 ft.) above the Eisack valley near Bolzano in the southern Tyrol of Italy. The stones were laid down during the Ice Age and subsequent erosion has carried away the earth except where it has been protected by these stones.

**Rivera** /rɪˈveɪrə/ a town in north-eastern Uruguay, on the Brzilian frontier, capital of the department of Rivera; pop. (1985) 56,335.

**Riverina** /ˌrɪvəˈraɪnə/ a rich agricultural region with processing industries in the valley of the Murrumbidgee River, New South Wales, Australia.

**Riverside** /ˈrɪvə(r)saɪd/ a city in southern California, USA, on the Santa Ana River 16 km. (10 miles) south-west of San Bernardino; pop. (1990) 226,505. It lies at the centre of orange groves first planted in the 1870s when the seedless navel orange was introduced. It is the home of the University of California at Riverside (1907).

**Riviera** /ˌrɪvɪˈeərə/, **the** part of the Mediterranean coastal region of southern France and northern Italy, extending from Cannes to La Spezia, famous for its scenic beauty, fertility, and mild climate, and with many fashionable and expensive resorts.

**Rivne** /ˈrɪvnə/ (formerly **Rovno**) an industrial city and transport and nuclear-power centre in western Ukraine, between Kiev and the Polish frontier; pop. (1990) 232,900. It produces electrical apparatus, machinery, and metal goods.

**Riyadh** /riːˈɑːd/ (Arabic **Ar Riyad**) the capital and commercial centre of Saudi Arabia, situated at an oasis on a high plateau in the Central Province (Nejd). The poor central area with its bazaars is surrounded by the modern suburbs built since the 1950s.; pop. (est.1988) 2,000,000.

**Rizhao** /rɪˈʒaʊ/ a city in Shandong province, eastern China, near the Yellow Sea coast south-west of Qingdao; pop. (1986) 988,000.

**Road Town** the capital of the British Virgin Islands, situated on Road Harbour on the island of Tortola; pop. (est.1991) 6,330. It takes its name from the 'road' or open anchorage, a term used in the 17th c.

**Roanoke** /ˈrəʊnəʊk/ a city in west Virginia, USA, between the Blue Ridge and Allegheny mountains; pop. (1990) 96,400. Originally known as Big Lick, the town's name was changed in 1882 when it became a junction of the Norfolk and Western Railway and the Shenandoah Valley Railroad. It is a commercial, medical, and convention centre with industries producing railroad cars, steel, clothes, furniture, plastics, and electronic goods.

**Roanoke Island** an island at the entrance to Albemarle Sound on the Atlantic coast of North Carolina, USA. Fort Raleigh was the site of the first English settlement in North America established by Sir Walter Raleigh in 1585.

**Roaring Forties** the name given to that part of the southern oceans between 40° and 50° south, where strong westerly winds predominate. The seas in similar latitudes to the north of the equator in the North Atlantic are sometimes given the same name.

**Robben Island** an island in Table Bay, Cape Town, South Africa, used by the South African government to house political prisoners including Nelson Mandela.

**Rocamadour** /ˈrɒkæmə͵dʊər/ a holy village built on the side of a cliff in the department of Lot in Quercy, south-central France. Its seven sanctuaries were visited in the Middle Ages by pilgrims on the way to Santiago de Compostela. It is believed that the biblical Zacchaeus was buried here. When sailors in distress pray to Our Lady of Rocamadour a bell is said to ring in the Notre-Dame chapel.

**Rochdale** /ˈrɒtʃdeɪl/ an industrial town in north-west England, north-east of Manchester; pop. (1981) 97,940. Formerly a major centre of the cotton industry it was the birthplace of the British Co-operative Movement in 1844.

**Rochefort-sur-Mer** /ˈrɒʃfɔː suːr mer/ an industrial port in the Poitou-Charentes region of western France, on the Charente south of La Rochelle; pop. (1990) 26,900. An important naval base in the days of sailing ships, Napoleon embarked from here on his journey into exile in 1815.

**roche moutonée** /͵rɒʃ muːˈtɒneɪ/ the geological term for a small bare outcrop of rock shaped by glacial erosion, with one side smooth and gently sloping and the other steep, rough, and irregular.

**Rochester** /ˈrɒtʃəst(ə)r/ a town in Kent, southeast England, on the Medway; pop. (1981) 24,400. It has an 11th-c. castle and 12th-c. cathedral and associations with Charles Dickens who lived at Gadshill nearby for the latter part of his life.

**Rochester** /ˈrɒtʃəst(ə)r/ **1.** a city in south-east Minnesota, USA; pop. (1990) 70,745. It is a noted medical centre and home of the world-famous Mayo clinic founded in 1889 by Charles and William Mayo. **2.** an industrial city in the US state of New York, a port on the Genesee River near its outlet to Lake Ontario; pop. (1990) 231,640. It was the home of George Eastman, inventor of the flexible photographic film, and the birthplace of the musicians Cab Calloway and Mitch Miller. Its industries include photographic, optical, and dental equipment.

**Rockall** /ˈrɒkɔːl/ **1.** a rocky islet in the North Atlantic, about 400 km. (250 miles) north-west of Ireland. Forming part of the Hatton–Rockall bank, the islet and nearby Leonidas Rock were formally annexed by the UK in 1955 but have since become the subject of dispute between Britain, Denmark, Iceland, and Ireland over mineral, oil, and fishing rights. **2.** a shipping forecast area in the north-east Atlantic, containing the islet of Rockall near its northern boundary.

**Rockford** /ˈrɒkf(ə)rd/ a city in the US state of Illinois, on the Rock River; pop. (1990) 139,430. It is named after the river ford once used by the Galena-Chicago stagecoach line. Its industries manufacture screws, fasteners, and machine tools.

**Rockhampton** /rɒkˈhæmpt(ə)n/ a port in Queensland, Australia, situated on the Tropic of Capricorn, nearly 80 km. (50 miles) upstream from the mouth of the Fitzroy River; pop. (1991) 55,790.

In 1858 it was a starting point for the first in a series of gold-rushes, and after the completion of the railway in 1867 it became the centre of Australia's largest beef-producing area.

**Rockingham** /ˈrɒkɪŋhəm/ a resort town on the coast of Western Australia, situated at the southern end of Cockburn Sound 45 km. (28 miles) south of Perth; pop. (1991) 36,675. Established as a port in 1872, it fell into disuse after the opening of the Fremantle inner harbour in 1897.

**Rocky Mountains** (also **Rockies**) the chief mountain system of North America, which extends for c. 4,800 km. (3,000 miles) from the US–Mexico border to the Yukon Territory of northern Canada. It separates the Great Plains from the Pacific Coast and forms the Continental Divide. Several peaks rise to over 4,300 m. (14,000 ft.), the highest being Mount Elbert in Colorado (4,399 m., 14,431 ft.).

**Rodez** /rɒˈdez/ the capital of the department of Aveyron in the Midi-Pyrénées region of southern France, on the Aveyron River; pop. (1990) 26,790. It has a large red-sandstone cathedral built over three centuries (13th–16th).

**Ródhos** the Greek name for RHODES.

**Roedean** /ˈrəʊdiːn/ an independent school for girls to the east of Brighton on the south coast of England. It was founded in 1885.

**Roeselare** /͵ruːsəˈlærə/ (French **Roulers** /ruːˈleə(r)/) a textile-manufacturing town in West Flanders, north-west Belgium, 30 km. (18 miles) south-west of Bruges; pop. (1991) 57,890.

**Rohtak** /ˈrəʊtək/ a market town in the state of Haryana, north-west India, north-west of Delhi; pop. (1991) 215,840.

**Roma** the Italian name for ROME.

**Romaic** /rəʊˈmeɪɪk/ the vernacular language of modern Greece. It is also a term applied to the Eastern Empire of Rome.

**romaji** /ˈrəʊmədʒɪ/ a system of Romanized spelling used to transliterate Japanese.

**Roman** /ˈrəʊmən/ a citizen of the ancient Roman Empire or of modern Rome.

**Roman Catholic Church** that part of the Christian Church which acknowledges the pope as its head, especially that which has developed since the Reformation. It has an elaborately organized hierarchy of bishops and priests, basing its claims on the power entrusted by Christ to his Apostles, particularly to St. Peter, whose successors the popes are traditionally regarded as being. In doctrine, it is characterized by strict adherence to tradition combined with acceptance of the living voice of the Church and belief in its infallibility. The classic definition of its position was made in response to the Reformation at the Council of Trent (1545–63). During the Enlightenment the Church increasingly saw itself as an embattled defender of ancient truth, something that culminated in the proclamation of Papal Infallibility in 1870. The 20th c. has seen a great change as the Church has become more open to the world, a change given effect in the decrees of the 2nd Vatican Council (1963–5).

**Romance** /rəʊˈmæns/ the group of European languages descended from Latin, of which the main languages are French, Spanish, Portuguese, Italian, and Romanian. With the spread of the Roman Empire, Latin was introduced as the language of administration; with its decline the languages of separate areas began to develop in different ways, and the Latin from which they developed seems to have been not the classical Latin of Rome but the informal Latin of the soldiers.

**Roman Empire** the area of the Old World conquered and controlled during the period of Roman history from 27 BC, when Octavian took the power of what was effectively a constitutional monarch with the title of Augustus, until the barbarian invasions of the 4th–5th c., which followed the death of Constantine and ended with the overthrow of the last Roman emperor, Romulus Augustulus, in AD 476. At its greatest extent Roman rule or influence extended from Armenia and Mesopotamia in the east to the Iberian peninsula in the west, and from the Rhine, Danube, and British Isles in the north to Egypt and provinces on the Mediterranean coast of North Africa. The empire was divided by Theodosius (AD 395) into the Western or Latin and Eastern or Greek Empire, of which the Eastern lasted until 1453 and the Western, after lapsing in 476, was revived in 800 by Charlemagne and continued to exist as the Holy Roman Empire until 1806.

## Romania

/rəʊˈmeɪnɪə/ (also **Rumania** /ruːˈ/) a country in southeastern Europe bounded by Ukraine, Moldova, Hungary, Serbia, Bulgaria, and the Black Sea; area 229,027 sq. km. (88,461 sq. miles); pop. (est.1991) 23,276,000; official language, Romanian; capital, Bucharest. Ethnic minorities include 2.5 million Hungarians (mostly in Transylvania), 2.3 million gypsies, and 200,000 Germans. Romania is flat in the south and east, with a short coastline on the Black Sea, and mountainous in the centre and west where the Carpathian Mountains separate Transylvania in the north-west from the rest of the country. The climate is continental, with cold snowy winters and warm summers. The country's chief exports are oil, natural gas, coal, minerals, timber, and machinery. In Roman times Romania formed the imperial province of Dacia, and in the Middle Ages the principalities of Walachia and Moldavia, each of which was swallowed up by the Ottoman empire in the 15th–16th c. The two principalities were unified in 1859 and gained independence in 1878, and

although conquered in 1916 by the Central Powers, Romania emerged from the peace settlement with fresh territorial gains in Bessarabia and Transylvania. The present boundaries are a result of World War II (its oilfields were of vital importance to Germany, which it supported), after which Romania became a Socialist Republic under Soviet influence. After 1974 the country pursued an increasingly independent course under the virtual dictatorship of Nicolae Ceaușescu. His regime collapsed in violent popular unrest in 1989 and a new constitution was approved by referendum in 1991. The country is governed by an executive president and a bicameral legislature which comprises a Chamber of Deputies and a Senate.

**Romanian** *adj. & n.*
Romania is administratively divided into the City of Bucharest and 40 *judet* (districts):

| District | Area (sq. km.) | Pop. (1989) | Capital |
|---|---|---|---|
| Alba | 6,231 | 428,250 | Alba Iulia |
| Arad | 7,652 | 506,680 | Arad |
| Argeş | 6,801 | 676,730 | Piteşti |
| Bacău | 6,606 | 731,050 | Bacău |
| Bihor | 7,535 | 660,256 | Oradea |
| Bistrita-Năsăud | 5,305 | 327,520 | Bistriţa |
| Botoşani | 4,965 | 467,540 | Botoşani |
| Braşov | 5,351 | 694,510 | Braşov |
| Brăila | 4,724 | 404,250 | Brăila |
| Buzău | 6,072 | 524,440 | Buzău |
| Caraş-Severin | 8,503 | 407,940 | Reşita |
| Călăraşi | 5,075 | 351,180 | Călăraşi |
| Cluj | 6,650 | 742,790 | Cluj-Napoca |
| Constanţa | 7,055 | 736,860 | Constanţa |
| Covasna | 3,705 | 237,920 | Sf. Gheorghe |
| Dîmboviţa | 4,036 | 569,740 | Tîrgovişte |
| Dolj | 7,413 | 772,450 | Craiova |
| Galaţi | 4,425 | 642,210 | Galaţi |
| Giurgiu | 3,511 | 324,930 | Giurgiu |
| Gorj | 5,641 | 387,528 | Tîrgu Jiu |
| Harghita | 6,610 | 362,930 | Miercurea-Ciuc |
| Hunedoara | 7,016 | 567,455 | Deva |
| Ialomiţa | 4,449 | 309,190 | Slobozia |
| Iaşi | 5,469 | 809,890 | Iaşi |
| Maramureş | 6,215 | 556,060 | Baia Mare |
| Mehedinţi | 4,900 | 382,665 | Drobeta-Turnu Severin |
| Mureş | 6,696 | 621,250 | Tîrgu Mureş |
| Neamt | 5,890 | 580,240 | Piatra-Neamţ |
| Olt | 5,507 | 534,830 | Slatina |
| Prahova | 4,694 | 877,360 | Ploieşti |
| Satu Mare | 4,405 | 416,720 | Satu Mare |
| Sălaj | 3,850 | 269,090 | Zalău |
| Sibiu | 5,422 | 508,650 | Sibiu |
| Suceava | 8,555 | 698,720 | Suceava |
| Teleorman | 5,760 | 503,770 | Alexandria |
| Timiş | 8,690 | 725,590 | Timişoara |
| Tulcea | 8,430 | 275,080 | Tulcea |
| Vaslui | 5,297 | 469,000 | Vaslui |
| Vîlcea | 5,705 | 430,263 | Rîmnicu Vîlcea |
| Vrancea | 4,863 | 393,710 | Focşani |

**Romanian** /rəʊˈmeɪnɪən/ the official language of Romania, the only Romance language spoken in eastern Europe, which developed from the Latin introduced by Trajan when he conquered the area in the 2nd c. AD and has kept its Latin character, being lightly influenced by the Slavonic languages. It is spoken by over 20 million people in Romania itself and by the majority of the population of Moldavia (Moldova).

**Romansh** /rəʊˈmænʃ, -ˈmɑːnʃ/ (also **Rumansh** /ruː-/) the Rhaeto-Romanic dialects, especially as spoken in the Swiss canton of Grisons.

**Romany** /ˈrɒmənɪ, ˈrəʊ-/ the distinctive language of the gypsies, which shares common features with Sanskrit and the later Indian languages (indicating an origin in the Indian subcontinent), with regional variations reflecting the incorporation of loanwords and other local linguistic features absorbed in their travels.

**Rome** /rəʊm/ (Italian **Roma** /ˈrəʊmə/) the capital of Italy, situated on the River Tiber about 25 km. (16 miles) inland; pop. (1990) 2,791,350. The name is used allusively to refer to the ancient Roman Republic and Empire, and also (as the see of the pope) to the Roman Catholic Church, based in the city at the Vatican. According to tradition, the ancient city was founded by Romulus (after whom it is named) in 753 BC on the Palatine Hill. As it grew it spread to the other six hills of Rome: Aventine, Caelian, Capitoline, Wesquiline, and Quirinal. Rome was ruled by kings until the expulsion of Tarquin the Proud in 510 BC led to the establishment of a republic. By the mid-2nd c. BC Rome had subdued the whole of Italy and had come to dominate the western Mediterranean and the Hellenistic world in the east, acquiring the first of the overseas possessions that became the empire. By the time of the Roman Empire's decline and fall the city was overshadowed politically by Constantinople, but emerged as the seat of the papacy and as the spiritual capital of Western Christianity. In the 14th and 15th centuries Rome became a centre of the Renaissance and a great focus of cultural and artistic activity. It remained under papal control, forming part of the Papal States, until 1871, when it was made the capital of a unified Italy. It has since expanded twelvefold which largely accounts for the congested state of today's traffic. Rome is one of the world's richest cities in history and art, and one of its great cultural, religious, and intellectual centres. Its many famous ruins and buildings include the Forum, the Caracalla Baths, the Colosseum, St. Peter's and many other churches, the Villa Borghese, and countless monuments, academies, and fountains. Its university was founded in 1303 and its music academy in 1584. Not surprisingly its economy depends to a large extent on tourism but it is also a centre of finance, publishing, fashion, and film making. It is the headquarters of the Food and Agriculture Organization (FAO) of the UN and the Treaty of Rome

signed here on 25 March 1957 established the European Economic Community.

**Romney Marsh** /ˈrɒmnɪ/ a level tract of reclaimed land in southern England, on the coast of Kent between Hythe and Rye. Once completely covered by the sea, drainage began in Roman times and the area became known for its pastureland and for the fine quality wool from its sheep.

**Roncesvalles** /ˈrɒnsəˌvæl/ (also **Roncevaux** /-ˌvəʊ/) a mountain pass in the Pyrenees, scene of the defeat of the rearguard of Charlemagne's army in 778 and of the heroic death of one of his nobles, Roland, an event much celebrated in medieval literature.

**Ronda** /ˈrɒndə/ a resort town in the Andalusian province of Malaga, southern Spain; pop. (1991) 35,620. Built on a dramatic site with rock faces on its western side, it overlooks the gorge of the River Guadalevin.

**Rondônia** /rɒnˈdɒnjə/ an Amazonian state of north-western Brazil, on the frontier with Bolivia; area 243,044 sq. km. (93,875 sq. miles); pop. (1991) 1,130,870; capital, Pôrto Velho.

**Roquefort-sur-Soulzon** /ˈrɒkfɔː(r) suː(r) suːlzɔ̃/ a village in the department of Aveyron, in the Midi-Pyrénées region of southern France, in the southern foothills of the Massif Central. It is famous for its cheese which is made from the milk of ewes and matured in the natural limestone caves of the *causse*.

**Roraima** /rɔːˈraɪmə/ **1.** the highest peak of the Guiana Highlands, South America, its flat top rising to a height of 2,774 m. (9,094 ft.) at the junction of the frontiers of Venezuela, Brazil, and Guyana. **2.** a state of northern Brazil on the frontier with Venezuela and Guyana; area 225,017 sq. km. (86,913 sq. miles); pop. (1991) 215,950; capital, Boa Vista.

**Rosario** /rəʊˈsɑːrɪəʊ/ a port on the Paraná River in east-central Argentina; pop. (1991) 1,096,000. It is Argentina's largest inland port and the largest city in the province of Santa Fé. Settled in 1725, it developed as an outlet for agricultural produce from the pampas. Its industrial products include steel and machinery. The Argentine flag was first raised here by General Belgrano.

**Roscoff** /ˈrɒskɒf/ a port and resort in the department of Finistère, northern Brittany, France, with ferry links to the UK; pop. (1982) 4,000. It became a health spa in 1899, and has remained popular as a seaside resort surrounded by market gardens.

**Roscommon** /rɒsˈkɒmən/ **1.** a county in the north-central part of the Republic of Ireland, to the west of the River Shannon in the province of Connaught; area 2,463 sq. km. (951 sq. miles); pop. (1991) 51,880. **2.** its county town; pop. (1991) 17,700. Named after St. Coman who founded a monastery here, it has a 13th-c. castle and an abbey which was established by the King of Connaught in 1253.

**Roseau** /rəʊˈzəʊ/ the capital of Dominica in the West Indies, at the mouth of the Roseau River; pop. (1991) 21,000. It takes its name from the French word for the reeds that used to grow there.

**Rosenheim** /ˈrəʊzənˌhaɪm/ an industrial town in Bavaria, southern Germany, on the River Inn south-east of Munich; pop. (1991) 56,700.

**Rosetta** /rəʊˈzetə/ the former name of the city of RASHID in northern Egypt where the Rosetta Stone was found in 1799.

**Roskilde** /ˈrɒskɪlə/ a port in Denmark, on the island of Zealand; pop. (1990) 49,080. It was the seat of Danish kings from c. 1020 and the capital of Denmark until 1443. Its chief landmarks are the Cathedral of St. Luke and the Viking Ship Museum which has the remains of six ships found nearby.

**Ross and Cromarty** /rɒs, ˈkrɒmɜːtɪ/ a former county of northern Scotland, from 1975 to 1996 a district of Highland Region, stretching from the Moray Firth to the North Minch; area 4,952 sq. km. (1,913 sq. miles); pop. (1991) 49,950. Its chief town is Dingwall.

**Ross Dependency** /rɒs/ part of Antarctica administered by New Zealand. It was explored in 1841 by Sir James Ross (1800–62), after whom it is named, and brought within the jurisdiction of New Zealand in 1923. The territory consists of everything lying to the south of latitude 60° south between longitudes 150° and 160° west. Its land area is estimated at 413,540 sq. km. (159,730 sq. miles) and permanent ice shelf at 336,770 sq. km. (130,077 sq. miles). There are no permanent inhabitants, but in January 1957 the New Zealand Antarctic Expedition established Scott Base on Ross Island.

**Rosslare** /rɒsˈleə(r)/ a ferry port on the south coast of the Republic of Ireland, in county Wexford. It is situated on St. George's Channel south-east of Wexford.

**Ross Sea** /rɒs/ a large arm of the Pacific forming a deep indentation in the coast of Antarctica. It was first explored in January 1841 by an expedition led by Sir James Ross, after whom many features of this area are named. At its head is the Ross Ice Shelf, the world's largest body of floating ice, which is approximately the size of France. On the eastern shores of the Ross Sea lies Ross Island, which is the site of Mount Erebus and of Scott Base, established by New Zealand in 1957.

**Rostock** /ˈrɒstɒk/ an industrial port on the Baltic coast of north-east Germany, at the mouth of the River Warnow in the state of Mecklenburg-West Pomerania; pop. (1991) 244,450. It is a shipbuilding and marine-engineering centre with electrical and textile industries.

**Rostov-on-Don** /ˈrɒstɒf/ an industrial port and cultural, scientific, and transportation centre in southern Russia on the River Don near its point

of entry into the Sea of Azov; pop. (1990) 1,025,000. Built around a fortress erected in the 18th c., it developed as a major centre for the export of grain in the 19th c. before becoming an important manufacturing city. It is a centre of cossack national resurgence. It has ship and locomotive repair yards, and numerous light industries.

**Rosyth** /rɒˈsaɪθ/ a town and naval base with shipyards on the coast of Fife, central Scotland; pop. (est.1988) 11,500.

**Rota** /ˈrəʊtə/ a port and naval base on the Andalusian coast of southern Spain, north-west of Cadiz; pop. (1991) 27,100.

**Rothamsted** /ˈrɒθəmsted/ an agricultural research centre near St. Albans in Hertfordshire, England, founded in 1843 by Sir J. Bennet Lawes on his estate at Rothamsted Park.

**Rotherham** /ˈrɒðərəm/ an industrial town and market centre in South Yorkshire, northern England, on the River Don east of Sheffield; pop. (1991) 247,100. Famous for its steel industries.

**Rotherhithe Tunnel** a road tunnel in southeast England, under the Thames east of Wapping in London. Built in 1904–8 to a design by Maurice Fitzmaurice, it links Rotherhithe on the south side of the river with Shadwell on the north.

**Rothesay** /ˈrɒθsɪ/ a town and royal burgh on the island of Bute in west-central Scotland. Its 13th-c. red-sandstone castle was used by Scottish kings including Robert III, who made his eldest son Duke of Rothesay, a title held today by the Prince of Wales.

**Rotorua** /ˌrəʊtəˈruːə/ a city and tourist town on North Island, New Zealand, on the south-west shore of Lake Rotorua; pop. (1991) 53,700. Situated at the centre of a region of volcanic lakes, thermal springs, and geysers, it became a fashionable spa town in the early 20th c.

**Rottnest Island** /ˈrɒtnest/ a resort island off the south-west coast of Western Australia, 19 km. (12 miles) north-west of Fremantle. In 1696 Commodore Willem de Vlamingh named it Rottnest or Rat's Nest Island after the tiny rat-like marsupial quokkas which he found.

**Rotterdam** /ˈrɒtəˌdæm/ an industrial city and the principal port of the Netherlands, in the province of South Holland at the junction of the Rotte and the Nieuwe Maas rivers; pop. (1991) 582,270. Its expansion dates from the completion in 1890 of the New Waterway linking it with the Hook of Holland, and in 1966 the opening of the Europoort harbour made it one of the world's largest ports. Shipbuilding, engineering, oil refining, and the manufacture of petrochemicals and electronic goods are important industries. It was the birthplace in 1466 of the Dutch humanist Erasmus and is the seat of Erasmus University (1973).

**Rottweil** /ˈrɒtvaɪl/ a town in Baden-Württemberg, south-west Germany, on the River

Neckar south-west of Stuttgart. It has a celebrated carnival (Rottweiller Narrensprung) and gives its name to a breed of dog formerly used by drovers.

**Roubaix** /ruːˈbeɪ/ a textile manufacturing town of northern France, in the department of Nord on the Belgian frontier north-east of Lille; pop. (1990) 98,200.

**Rouen** /ruːˈɑ̃/ a major river port on the Seine in north-west France, the capital of the department of Seine-Maritime in Upper Normandy (Haute-Normandie); pop. (1990) 105,470. Known during Roman times as Rotomagnus, Rouen was in English possession from the time of the Norman Conquest (1066) until captured by the French in 1204, becoming the medieval capital of Normandy. It returned briefly to English rule (1419–49) after its capture by Henry V during the Hundred Years War. In 1431 Joan of Arc was tried and burnt at the stake here. The building of its famous cathedral was begun in the 12th c. It was the birthplace of the French dramatist Pierre Corneille (1606–84) and the novelist Gustave Flaubert (1821–80). Badly damaged during World War II but now restored, it has metal, chemical, drugs, and textile industries, as well as tourism.

**Rouergue** /ruːˈeəg/ a mountainous region and former county of southern France centred on the town of Rodez in the Massif Central. It is watered by the Aveyron and Tarn rivers which form deep gorges.

**Rouffignac** /ˈruːfiːnjæk/ a village in the Dordogne department of south-central France, near to which is a system of limestone caves with 11 km. (7 miles) of galleries and over 200 prehistoric rock carvings.

**Roulers** the French name for ROESELARE.

**Roumelia** /ruːˈmiːliə/ (also **Rumelia**) the territories in Europe which formerly belonged to the Ottoman empire, including Macedonia, Thrace, and Albania. Its name is derived from the Turkish word *Rumeli* 'land of the Romans'.

**Rousse** see RUSE.

**Roussillon** /ruːsiˈɒn/ a former province of southern France, on the border with Spain in the eastern Pyrenees. It united with Languedoc to form the administrative region of Languedoc-Roussillon. For much of its history it was part of Spain until in 1659 it was acquired by Louis XIV for France. Roussillon retains many of its Spanish characteristics and traditions and Catalan is widely spoken.

**Rovaniemi** /ˌrɒvænˈjeɪmɪ/ the principal town of Finnish Lapland, situated at the junction of the Kemi and Ounas rivers 9 km. (5.6 miles) south of the Arctic Circle; pop. (1990) 33,500. Established in 1929, it was destroyed during World War II and later rebuilt to a design by Alvar Aalto, its main streets being laid out in the shape of a reindeer's antlers. Nearby is Sodankylä, home of the Santa

Claus Village where all letters sent to Finland for Santa Claus are answered.

**Rovno** /ˈrɒvnə/ the former name of RIVNE.

**Roxburghshire** /ˈrɒksbərə,ʃɑɪr/ a former county of the Scottish Borders. From 1975 to 1996 Roxburgh has constituted an administrative district of Borders Region; area 1,540 sq. km. (595 sq. miles); pop. (1991) 34,615. Its chief town is Hawick.

**Royal Geographical Society** a learned geographical society whose headquarters are based in Kensington, London, and whose function is to advance exploration and research and promote geographical knowledge. Founded in 1830, it took over the work of the Africa Association. It promotes geographical research and exploration by means of symposia, lectures, the presentation of prestigious awards, and the provision of services which include access to a notable map collection and library and the specialized expertise of an Expedition Advisory Centre. Academic papers are published in the *Geographical Journal* and articles of more popular appeal are published under licence in the *Geographical Magazine*.

**Royal National Park** a national park 35 km. (22 miles) south of Sydney in New South Wales, Australia. Established in 1879, it was the first national park to be designated in Australia and the second to be declared in the world. It extends over 150 sq. km. (58 sq. miles) of heath-covered sandstone plateau.

**Royal Oak** a residential city to the north of Detroit in Michigan, USA; pop. (1990) 65,410.

**Royal Scottish Geographical Society** a scientific society founded in Edinburgh in 1884 at a time when Scotland was pre-eminent in science, and geography was seen as playing an important role in administration both within Great Britain and in the wider context of the Empire. Its inaugural address was given by H. M. Stanley and its first president was Lord Roseberry who was a key figure in the cause for a Scottish dimension, both in government and higher education. Designed to stimulate research and disseminate knowledge, the society continues to promote expeditions, lectures, symposia, and educational activities as well as present prestigious awards for outstanding contributions to geography. Its journal the *Scottish Geographical Magazine*, was first published in February 1885 and the society's office and library are based in Glasgow (since 1993).

**Ruahine** /ˌruːəˈhiːnɪ/ a mountain range on North Island, New Zealand that rises to a maximum height of 1,733 m. (5,686 ft.) at Mangaweka.

**Ruapehu** /ˌruːəˈpeɪhuː/, **Mount** the highest peak on North Island, New Zealand, an active volcano that rises to 2,797 m. (9,175 ft.) south-west of Lake Taupo in the Tongariro National Park. There are ski fields on its slopes, and other tourist activities in the area.

**Rub' al Khali** see GREAT SANDY DESERT.

**Rubicon** /'ru:bɪkɒn/ a small stream in north-east Italy near San Marino that flows into the Adriatic, marking the ancient boundary between Italy and Cisalpine Gaul. By taking his army across it (i.e. outside his own province) in 49 BC Julius Caesar committed himself to war against the Senate and Pompey.

**Rubtsovsk** /'ru:ptsɒfsk/ a city in Altay kray, west Siberian Russia, south-west of Barnaul; pop. (1990) 172,000.

**Rudnyy** /'ru:dni:/ a city in north-west Kazakh-stan, on the Tobol River south-west of Kustanay; pop. (1990) 128,000. Iron-ore is mined in the surrounding area.

**Rudolf** /'ru:dɒlf/, **Lake** the former name of Lake Turkana in north-west Kenya. (See TURKANA, LAKE.)

**Rugby** /'rʌgbɪ/ a cattle-market and engineering town in Warwickshire, central England, on the River Avon 19 km. (12 miles) south-west of Coventry; pop. (1981) 59,720. Rugby School, where the game of Rugby football was developed in the early 19th c., was founded here in 1567. Rupert Brooke, the poet, was born here in 1887.

**Rügen** /'ru:gən/ an island with chalk cliffs in the Baltic Sea to the north of the German port of Rostock, linked to the mainland by a causeway; area 927 sq. km. (358 sq. miles). Part of the state of Mecklenburg-West Pomerania, its chief town is Bergen and its main port is Sassnitz.

**Ruhr** /ruər/ a former major region of coal-mining and heavy industry in North Rhine-Westphalia, western Germany. It is named after the River Ruhr, which rises in the Rothaargebirge Mountains and flows westwards for 233 km. (145 miles) to meet the Rhine near Duisburg. World recession has forced diversification in the eastern area where light industries have developed. Petrochemical industries continue in the west.

**Rum** /rʌm/ (also **Rhum**) an island in the Inner Hebrides of Scotland, separated from the island of Skye to the north by the Cuillin Sound; area 110 sq. km. (42 sq miles). In 1957 the island was designated a nature reserve. Its highest peak is Askival (810 m., 2,659 ft.). Nearly all of its former inhabitants emigrated to America in 1826.

**Rumania** see ROMANIA.

**Rumeila** /ru:'meɪlə/ an oilfield on the frontier between Iraq and Kuwait. The extraction of oil from this field by Kuwait contributed to the Iraqi invasion of 1990 and the subsequent Gulf War.

**Rumelia** see ROUMELIA.

**Rum Jungle** /rʌm 'dʒʌŋgl/ a mining area near Adelaide River south-east of Darwin in the Northern Territory, Australia, where uranium was discovered in 1949. There are also deposits of copper, silver, and lead.

**Runcorn** /'rʌŋkɔːn/ an industrial town in Cheshire, England, on the River Mersey; pop. (est. 1985) 64,600. It was developed as a New Town from 1964.

**Runnymede** /'rʌnɪˌmiːd/ a meadow at Egham on the south bank of the Thames near Windsor, Surrey. It is famous for its association with Magna Carta (which was signed by King John in the meadow or on the island nearby) which is marked by a memorial. There are also memorials to Commonwealth airmen and to John F. Kennedy.

**Rupert's Land** /'ru:pət/ (also **Prince Rupert's Land**) an historic region of northern and western Canada, originally granted in 1670 by Charles II to the Hudson's Bay Company and named after Prince Rupert, the first governor of the Company. It comprised the territory in the drainage basin of Hudson Bay, roughly corresponding to what is now Manitoba, Saskatchewan, Yukon, Alberta, northern Ontario, Quebec, and the southern part of the Northwest Territories. It was purchased from the Hudson's Bay Company by the Dominion of Canada in 1869. Owing to the Red River Rebellion, however, the transfer did not become effective until July 1870. The name is still used for an Anglican diocese.

**Ruse** /'ru:seɪ/ (also **Rustchuk**, **Rousse** /'ru:sə/) a river port and industrial city on the Danube in the Razgrad region of northern Bulgaria; pop. (1990) 209,760. Founded in the 2nd c. BC and known as Prista, it became a Roman port. Later under Turkish rule it was a military base named Rustchuk. It was captured by Russia in 1877 and ceded to Bulgaria. It has shipbuilding, tanning, rubber, plastics, electrical equipment, and agricultural industries.

**Russia** /'rʌʃə/ official name **The Russian Federation** a country in northern Asia and eastern Europe, stretching from the Arctic Ocean in the North to the Black Sea in the south and 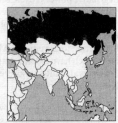 from the Baltic in the west to the Bering Strait in the far east; area 17,075,400 sq. km. (6,595,365 sq. miles); pop. (est.1991) 148,930,000; official language, Russian; capital, Moscow. Its largest cities are Moscow, St. Petersburg, Nizhniy Novgorod, Novosibirsk, and Yekaterinburg. Just over 80 per cent of the population is Russian, the remainder comprising ethnic minorities that include Avars, Bashkirs, Buryats, Chechen, Chuvash, Germans, Jews, Komi, Mari, Mordovs, Tartars, Udmurts, and Yakuts, as well as many of the peoples of the former Soviet republics such as Ukrainians, Belorussians, Kazakhs, etc. The European plain in the west is separated from the west Siberian lowland and the central Siberian plateau by the Ural

Mountains which separate Europe from Asia. Russia includes the greater part of the northern tundra and taiga of Eurasia and large areas of steppeland. Its chief rivers in Europe are the Don, the Volga, and the Pechora and those of Asia include the Ob, Irtysh, Yenisey, Lena, and Amur. The climate is generally continental but varies from extreme winter cold in the north to subtropical on the shores of the Black Sea. Russia has great mineral resources with large deposits of iron ore, gold, platinum, copper, zinc, lead, and tin, and abundant energy resources such as oil, gas, and coal, as well as hydro electric power, and uranium for nuclear power. The country is self-sufficient in all foodstuffs except the tropical varieties, although it is not well distributed. It also has the full range of heavy and light industries. The modern state originated from the expansion of Muscovy under the Rurik and Romanov dynasties, westwards towards Poland and Hungary, southwards to the Black Sea, eastwards to the Pacific Ocean, and southeastwards towards Central Asia. Russia played an increasing role in Europe from the time of Peter the Great in the early 18th c. and pursued imperial ambitions in the east in the second half of the 19th c. Social and economic problems, exacerbated by World War I, led to the overthrow of the Tsar in 1917 and the establishment of a Communist government over the Union of Soviet Socialist Republics (USSR). Following the breakup of the Soviet Union in 1991, what had been the Russian Soviet Federated Socialist Republic (RSFSR) became an independent state and founder member of the Commonwealth of Independent States (CIS). In 1992 18 of the constituent 21 republics of the Russian Federation signed a Federal Treaty. Legislative power is exercised by the bicameral Supreme Soviet. It now faces enormous problems of social, economic, and political reorganization. **Russian** *adj. & n.*
In addition to the cities of Moscow and St. Petersburg which have federal status, the Russian Federation is divided into 21 sovereign republics, six Krays, and 50 oblasts:

| Republic | Area (sq. km.) | Pop. (1990) | Capital |
| --- | --- | --- | --- |
| Adygea | 7,600 | 436,000 | Maikop |
| Bashkortostan | 143,600 | 3,964,000 | Ufa |
| Buryatia | 351,300 | 1,049,000 | Ulan-Ude |
| Chechenya | 16,064 | 1,290,000 | Groznyy |
| Ingushelia | | | Nazran |
| Chuvashia | 18,300 | 1,340,000 | Cheboksary |
| Dagestan | 50,300 | 1,823,000 | Makhachkala |
| Gorno-Altai | 92,600 | 194,000 | Gorno-Altaisk |
| Kabardino-Balkaria | 12,500 | 768,000 | Nalchik |
| Kalmykia | 75,900 | 325,000 | Elista |
| Karachay-Cherkessia | 14,100 | 422,000 | Cherkessk |
| Karelia | 172,400 | 796,000 | Petrozavodsk |
| Khakassia | 61,900 | 573,000 | Abakan |
| Komi | 415,900 | 1,265,000 | Syktyvkar |
| Mari El | 23,200 | 754,000 | Yoshkar-Ola |
| Mordvinia | 26,200 | 964,000 | Saransk |
| North Ossetia | 8,000 | 638,000 | Vladikavkaz |
| Tatarstan | 68,000 | 3,658,000 | Kazan |
| Tuva | 170,500 | 314,000 | Kyzyl |
| Udmurtia | 42,100 | 1,619,000 | Izhevsk |
| Yakutia | 3,103,200 | 1,099,000 | Yakutsk |

| Kray | Area (sq. km.) | Pop. (1990) | Capital |
| --- | --- | --- | --- |
| Altay | 261,700 | 2,835,000 | Barnaul |
| Khabarovsk | 824,600 | 1,840,000 | Khabarovsk |
| Krasnodar | 83,600 | 5,135,000 | Krasnodar |
| Krasnoyarsk | 2,401,600 | 3,612,000 | Krasnoyarsk |
| Maritime | 165,900 | 2,281,000 | Vladivostok |
| Stavropol | 80,600 | 2,855,000 | Stavropol |

| Oblast | Area (sq. km.) | Pop. (1989) | Capital |
| --- | --- | --- | --- |
| Amur | 363,700 | 1,058,000 | Blagoveshchensk |
| Arkhangelsk | 587,400 | 1,570,000 | Archangel |
| Astrakhan | 44,100 | 998,000 | Astrakhan |
| Belgorod | 27,100 | 1,381,000 | Belgorod |
| Bryansk | 34,900 | 1,475,000 | Bryansk |
| Chelyabinsk | 87,900 | 3,626,000 | Chelyabinsk |
| Chita | 431,500 | 1,378,000 | Chita |
| Ivanovo | 23,900 | 1,317,000 | Ivanovo |
| Irkutsk | 767,900 | 2,831,000 | Irkutsk |
| Kaliningrad | 15,100 | 871,000 | Kaliningrad |
| Kaluga | 29,900 | 1,067,000 | Kaluga |
| Kamchatka | 472,300 | 466,000 | Petropavlovsk |
| Kemerovo | 95,500 | 3,175,000 | Kemerovo |
| Kirov | 120,800 | 1,694,000 | Kirov |
| Kostroma | 60,100 | 809,000 | Kostroma |
| Kurgan | 71,000 | 1,105,000 | Kurgan |
| Kursk | 29,800 | 1,339,000 | Kursk |
| Leningrad | 83,900 | 1,659,000 | St Petersburg |
| Lipetsk | 24,100 | 1,231,000 | Lipetsk |
| Magadan | 1,199,100 | 543,000 | Magadan |
| Moscow | 47,000 | 6,686,000 | Moscow |
| Murmansk | 144,900 | 1,146,000 | Murmansk |
| Nizhniy Novgorod | 74,800 | 3,713,000 | Nizhniy Novgorod |
| Novgorod | 55,300 | 753,000 | Novgorod |
| Novosibirsk | 178,200 | 2,782,000 | Novosibirsk |
| Omsk | 139,700 | 2,140,000 | Omsk |
| Orenburg | 124,000 | 2,174,000 | Orenburg |
| Orel | 24,700 | 891,000 | Orel |
| Penza | 43,200 | 1,502,000 | Penza |
| Perm | 160,600 | 3,100,000 | Perm |
| Pskov | 55,300 | 847,000 | Pskov |
| Rostov | 100,800 | 4,304,000 | Rostov-on-Don |
| Ryazan | 39,600 | 1,346,000 | Ryazan |
| Samara | 53,600 | 3,266,000 | Samara |
| Saratov | 100,200 | 2,690,000 | Saratov |
| Sakhalin | 87,100 | 709,000 | Yuzhno-Sakhalinsk |
| Sverdlovsk | 194,800 | 4,731,000 | Yekaterinburg |
| Smolensk | 49,800 | 1,158,000 | Smolensk |
| Tambov | 34,300 | 1,320,000 | Tambov |
| Tomsk | 316,900 | 1,001,000 | Tomsk |
| Tula | 25,700 | 1,868,000 | Tula |

| | | | |
|---|---:|---:|---|
| Tver | 84,100 | 1,670,000 | Tver |
| Tyumen | 1,435,200 | 3,083,000 | Tyumen |
| Ulyanovsk | 37,300 | 1,400,000 | Ultanovsk |
| Vladimir | 29,000 | 1,654,000 | Vladimir |
| Volgograd | 114,100 | 2,593,000 | Volgograd |
| Vologda | 145,700 | 1,354,000 | Vologda |
| Voronezh | 52,400 | 2,470,000 | Voronezh |
| Yaroslavl' | 36,400 | 1,471,000 | Yaroslavl' |

| Autonomous Oblast | Area (sq. km.) | Pop. (1990) | Capital |
|---|---:|---:|---|
| Jewish | 36,000 | 218,000 | Birobijan |

**Russian** /'rʌʃ(ə)n/ the official language of
Russia, the most important of the Slavonic languages, spoken as a first language in Russia and by
people of Russian origin in the former republics of
the Soviet Union. It is written in the Cyrillic alphabet, the invention of which is attributed to St. Cyril
(*c.*827–69).

**Rustavi** /rəs'tɑ:vi:/ an industrial town in the
Republic of Georgia, south-east of Tbilisi; pop.
(1991) 162,000. It has iron and steelworks, and
chemical industries.

**Ruthenia** /ru:'θi:nɪə/ (also **Carpathian
Ukraine**) a region of Ukraine on the southern
slopes of the Carpathian Mountains that takes its
name from the East Slavonic Ruthenes or
Russniaks who live in the area (as well as in
Slovakia, Poland, north-east Romania, and
Vojvodina in Serbia). Formerly part of the Austro-
Hungarian empire, it was divided between Poland,
Czechoslovakia, and Romania in 1918. Gaining
independence for a single day in 1938, it was occu-
pied by Hungary and later taken by the Soviet
Union which incorporated it into the Ukrainian
Republic. In the referendum on Ukrainian inde-
pendence held in 1991, a large proportion of the
people of the region voted for autonomy, but this
was not granted to them by the Ukrainian author-
ities which do not recognize the existence of
Ruthenian nationality.
**Ruthenian** *adj. & n.*

**Rutland** a former county in the East Midlands
of England that became part of Leicestershire in
1974. It was the smallest county in England.

**Ruwenzori** /ˌru:en'zɔ:rɪ/, **Mount** a mountain
range in central Africa, in the Rift Valley between
Lake Edward and Lake Albert and lying on the
border between Uganda and Zaire. Rising to 5,109
m. (16,763 ft.) at Margherita Peak in Mount
Stanley, the range is generally thought to be the
'Mountains of the Moon' mentioned by Ptolemy,
and as such the supposed source of the Nile. A national park was established in 1952 to protect a
wide range of species and habitats including tropical forest, grasslands, savanna, swamp, and the
tundra belt of the Ruwenzori range.

**Rwanda** /ru:'ændə/ official name **The Republic
of Rwanda** a landlocked country in central Africa,

just south of the
equator, bounded by
Zaire, Burundi,
Tanzania, and
Uganda; area 26,338
sq. km. (10,173 sq.
miles); pop.
(est. 1991) 7,403,000;
official languages,
French and Rwanda
(a Bantu language); capital, Kigali. Mainly a country of grassy volcanic uplands and hills, Rwanda is
divided by the Congo and Nile drainage systems
and has many lakes including Lake Kivu. The climate is mild and temperate, with two rainy seasons
during February–May and November–December.
With few natural resources, its chief exports are
agricultural products such as coffee, tea, hides, and
pyrethrum. Its population density is the highest in
sub-Saharan Africa and its ethnic groups include
the pastoral Tutsis, the Twa pygmies, and the farming Hutus who comprise 85 per cent of the population. The area was claimed by Germany from 1890,
and after World War I it became part of a Belgian
trust territory, gaining independence as a republic
in 1962. Prior to independence the ruling Tutsi
monarchy was overthrown in a violent uprising by
the majority Hutu and thousands of Tutsi fled to
neighbouring countries. In 1990 Rwanda was
thrown into conflict when a rebel Tutsi army invaded the country and in 1991 a new multiparty
system was introduced in an attempt to meet rebel
demands for greater democracy. In 1994 international attention focused on Rwanda when civil
war between government forces and Tutsi rebels
resulted in the slaughter of over 500,000 people
and an exodus of large numbers of refugees into
neighbouring countries.
**Rwandan** *adj. & n.*

**Ryazan** /rɪə'zæn/ a river port and industrial city
in western Russia, situated to the south-east of
Moscow on the River Oka; pop. (1990) 522,000.
Industries include oil refining, and the manufacture of agricultural and transport equipment.
The city was founded in 1095 and retains much
medieval architecture.

**Rybinsk** /'rɪbɪnsk/ a city in Yaroslavl' oblast,
north-west Russia, a major port on the River Volga
north-east of Moscow; pop. (1990) 252,000. Between 1984 and 1989 it was known as Andropov in
honour of a former president of the Soviet Union.
It is the site of a hydroelectric power-station and
has shipyards, and timber-machinery, engineering,
and leather industries.

**Rydal** /'raɪd(ə)l/ a village in Cumbria, north-west
England, 3 km. (2 miles) north-west of Ambleside.
**Rydal Mount** was the home of the poet William
Wordsworth from 1813 until his death in 1850.

**Rysy** /'rɪsi:/ a peak in the Tatra Mountains, the
highest mountain in Poland rising to a height of
2,499 m. (8,197 ft.).

**Ryukyu Islands** /riːˈuːkuː/ (also **Nansei Islands** /nænˈseɪ/) a chain of more than seventy islands in the western Pacific, stretching for about 960 km. (600 miles) from the southern tip of Kyushu Island, Japan, to Taiwan. The largest island is Okinawa. Part of China in the 14th c., the archipelago was incorporated into Japan in 1879. The islands were placed under US military control in 1945 and returned to Japan in 1972.

**Rzeszow** /ˈʒeʃuːf/ the capital of Rzeszow county in south-east Poland, on the River Wisłok; pop. (1990) 153,040. Its industries produce machinery and metal products and its chief landmarks are a 17th-c. castle and the 18th-c. palace of the Lubomirski princes.

# S s

**Saale** /ˈsɑːlə/ a river of east-central Germany. Rising in the Fichtelgebirge of northern Bavaria near the border with the Czech Republic, it flows 425 km. (265 miles) north to join the Elbe near Magdeburg.

**Saar** /sɑː(r)/ (French **Sarre** /sær/) a river of western Europe, rising in the Vosges Mountains in eastern France and flowing 240 km. (150 miles) northwards to join the Mosel River in Germany.

**Saarbrücken** /ˈsɑːbruːk(ə)n/ an industrial city in western Germany, the capital of Saarland, on the River Saar close to the border with France; pop. (1991) 361,610. Situated at the centre of a large coal-mining region, its industries produce coke, machinery, rubber, metal goods, and optical equipment.

**Saarland** /ˈsɑːlænd/ a state of western Germany, on the frontiers with France and Luxembourg; area 2,570 sq. km. (1,062 sq. miles); pop. (1991) 1,076,880; capital, Saarbrücken. It is traversed by the River Saar and has rich deposits of coal and iron ore. Between 1684 and 1697 and again between 1792 and 1815 the area belonged to France. After World War I, until 1935, it was administered by the League of Nations. A plebiscite in 1935—and a referendum after World War II—indicated the desire on the part of the population to be part of Germany. The area became the 10th German state in 1959.

**Saba** /ˈsɑːbæ/ the smallest island of the Netherlands Antilles situated in the Caribbean to the north-west of St. Kitts; area 13 sq. km. (5 sq. miles); pop. (est. 1990) 1,119; chief town, The Bottom.

**Sabadell** /sɑːbəˈdel/ a manufacturing city near Barcelona in Catalonia, north-east Spain, on the River Ripoll; pop. (1991) 184,190. Its industries produce textiles, fertilizers, plastics, and electrical goods.

**Sabaean** /səˈbiːn/ a member of a Semitic-speaking people who by the 3rd c. AD had established an elaborate system of government and succeeded in uniting southern Arabia into a single state (the kingdom of Saba) that was eventually overthrown by the Abyssinians in AD 525. Their name is derived from the Hebrew *Sheba*, the people of Yemen.

**Sabah** /ˈsɑːbɑː/ a state of Malaysia, comprising the northern part of Borneo and some offshore islands; area 73,613 sq. km. (28,433 sq. miles); pop. (1990) 1,470,200; capital, Kota Kinabalu. A British Protectorate (North Borneo) from 1888, it gained independence and joined Malaysia in 1963. Mount Kinabalu (4,094 m., 13,431 ft.) is the highest peak in Borneo and south-east Asia.

**Sabellian** /səˈbeɪlɪən/ a member of a group of tribes in ancient Italy (including Sabines, Samnites, Campanians, etc.).

**Sabha** /ˈsæbhɑː/ (also **Sabhah** or **Sebha**) an oasis town in the desert region of central Libya; pop. (1982) 113,000.

**Sabian** /ˈseɪbɪən/ **1.** an adherent of a religious sect mentioned in the Koran and by later Arabian writers. In the Koran, the Sabians are classed with Muslims, Jews, and Christians as believers in the true God. On account of the toleration extended to them by Muslims the name of Sabians was, some centuries after Muhammad, assumed by the half-Christian Mandaeans and other groups. **2.** a member of a group of Syrian pagan star-worshippers.

**Sabine** /ˈsæbaɪn/ a people of ancient Italy of the area north-east of Rome, renowned in antiquity for their frugal and hardy character and their superstitious practices, finally conquered by Rome in 290 BC. The (unhistorical) legend of the Rape of the Sabine Women (said to have been carried off by the Romans at a spectacle to which the Sabines had been invited) reflects the early intermingling of Romans and Sabines; some Roman religious institutions were said to have a Sabine origin.

**Sabratha** /ˈsɑːbrətə/ (also **Sabrata**) the ruins of an ancient city in Libya, North Africa, between Tripoli and the border with Tunisia. It was one of the three cities of Tripolitania.

**Sachsen** see SAXONY.

**Sacramento** /ˌsækrəˈmentəʊ/ **1.** a river of northern California, USA, which rises near the border with Oregon and flows some 611 km. (380 miles) southwards to San Francisco Bay. **2.** the capital of the US state of California, situated 115 km. (72 miles) north-east of San Francisco, on the Sacramento River; pop. (1990) 369,365. Founded during the gold-rush of 1848 on the site of John Sutter's New Helvetia Colony, it became state capital in 1854 and the western terminus of the Pony Express in 1860. It is linked to Suison Bay by a (43-mile) channel and its economy is enhanced by McClellan Air Force Base, Sacramento Army Depot, missile development industries, and market gardening.

**Sadler's Wells Theatre** /ˈsædləz welz/ a London theatre so called because in 1683 Thomas

Sadler discovered a medicinal spring in his garden and established a pleasure-garden which became known as Sadler's Wells. A wooden music room built there in 1685 became a theatre in 1753, whose stone-built successor remained in use until 1906. In 1927 Lilian Baylis took over the derelict building, erecting a new theatre which opened in 1931.

**saeter** /'seɪt(ə)r/ an upland pasture or farm in Norway occupied during the summer.

**Safaqis** see SFAX.

**Safi** /sæfi:/ (originally **Asfi**) an Atlantic port in the province of Tensift, north-west Morocco; pop. (1982) 197,620. During the 17th c. it was the leading city and port of Morocco under the Sa'dian sultans. Today, boat building, sardine fishing and the production of phosphates and fertilizers are its chief industries. The city is a mixture of medieval and modern architecture and is known for its pottery.

**Saga** /'sɑːgɑː/ the capital of Saga prefecture, west Kyushu, Japan; pop. (1990) 169,960. A former feudal castle town, Saga is a transportation centre with textile and ceramic industries.

**Sagamihara** /sə,gɑːmɪˈhɑːrə/ an industrial city in Kanagawa prefecture, central Honshu island, Japan; pop. (1990) 531,560. It has chemical, food-processing, and silk-weaving industries.

**Sagar** /'sɑːgər/ (also **Saugor**) a market town in Madhya Pradesh, north-central India, north-east of Bhopal; pop. (1991) 256,880. It has a university founded in 1946.

**Sagarmatha** /ˌsægəˈmɑːtə/ the Nepalese name for Mount Everest (= Goddess of the Universe).

**Saguia el Hamra** /səˈgiːə el ˈhæmrə/ (also **Sekia el Hamra**) **1.** an intermittent river in the north of Western Sahara. It flows into the Atlantic west of La'youn. **2.** the region through which it flows. A territory of Spain from 1934, it united with Río de Oro in 1958 to form the province of Spanish Sahara.

**Saginaw** /'sægənɔː/ a city in central Michigan, USA, on the Saginaw River; pop. (1990) 69,510. First settled in 1816 as a centre of timber production, its industries now produce vehicle parts, castings, and foodstuffs.

**Saguenay** /ˌsægəˈneɪ/ a river in Quebec, eastern Canada, that flows from Lac St. Jean to the St. Lawrence estuary. Passing through the scenic Saguenay Fiord, it is a source of hydroelectric power. Its total length to the source of the Péribonca is 698 km. (436 miles).

**Sahara** /səˈhɑːrə/ a vast desert in North Africa, the largest in the world, covering an area of about 9,065,000 sq. km. (3,500,000 sq. miles) and extending from the Atlantic in the west to the Red Sea in the east. It is bounded in the north by the Mediterranean Sea and the Atlas Mountains and in recent years it has been increasing its southerly extent into the Sahel.

**Saharanpur** /səˈhɑːrənpʊ(ə)r/ a city in Uttar Pradesh, northern India, north-east of Delhi; pop. (1991) 373,900. Founded in 1340 and named after the Muslim saint Shah Haran Chisti, it was a military base during the British Raj. It is now a furniture and wood products centre.

**Sahel** /sɒˈhel/ a belt of dry savanna on the southern margin of Africa's Sahara Desert. It stretches some 5,000 km. (3,125 miles) from Senegal and Mauritania on the Atlantic coast to the Red Sea coast of Sudan and Eritrea. The area, which covers c. 20 per cent of Africa's land surface, was the first to bring the problem of desertification to world attention. Droughts have caused widespread famine among its pastoral peoples in recent years. Its name is derived from the Arab word meaning 'shore'.

**Saida** the Arabic name for SIDON.

**Saidpur** /'saɪdpʊə(r)/ a city in the Rangpur region of north-west Bangladesh; pop. (1991) 102,000.

**Saigon** the former name of HO CHI MINH CITY.

**Saimaa Canal** /'saɪmɑː/ a 60-km. (37-mile) man-made waterway with eight locks, linking Lake Saimaa in south-east Finland with the Gulf of Finland. The historic spa and garrison town of Lappenranta is its chief port.

**St. Albans** /'ɔːlbənz/ a cathedral city in Hertfordshire, England, on the River Ver; pop. (1981) 55,700. The city developed around the abbey of St. Albans, which was founded in Saxon times on the site of the martyrdom in AD 304 of Alban, a Christian Roman from the nearby Roman city of Verulamium. The ruins of ancient Verulamium lie within the modern city. St Albans was the home of the philospher and statesman Francis Bacon (1561–1626) who was created Viscount St. Albans in 1621. The cathedral, mostly 11th c., incorporates Roman bricks and tiles in its fabric and has medieval wall-paintings. There are several old inns as well as a modern museum and industries including printing and engineering.

**St. Andrews** /'ændruːz/ a university town in east Scotland, on the North Sea coast of Fife; pop. (1981) 11,350. It was the ecclesiastical capital of Scotland until the Reformation. Its university, founded in 1411, is the oldest in Scotland and the Royal and Ancient Golf Club is the ruling authority on the game of golf. There are remains of a castle, cathedral, and medieval town wall.

**St.-Barthélemy** /sæ bɑːˈteɪlˌmiː/ (locally **St. Bart's**) a French island in the West Indies, 230 km. (145 miles) to the north of Guadeloupe of which it is a dependency; area 21 sq. km. (8 sq. miles); pop. (1990) 5,040; capital, Gustavia. Named after the brother of Christopher Columbus, the island was first settled by French colonists from Dieppe in 1645. Between 1784 and 1878 it was held by Sweden. It is a popular resort island and yachting centre.

**St. Bernard Pass** either of two passes across the Alps in southern Europe. The **Great St. Bernard Pass**, on the border with south-west Switzerland and Italy, rises to 2,469 m. (8,100 ft.). The **Little St. Bernard Pass**, on the French–Italian border south-east of Mont Blanc, rises to 2,188 m. (7,178 ft.). Both are named after the hospices founded on their summits in the 11th c. by the French monk St. Bernard.

**St. Catherines** /'kæθərɪnz/ an industrial city in south-east Ontario, Canada, situated to the south of Lake Ontario near Niagara Falls; pop. (1991) 129,300; 364,550 (St. Catherines-Niagara). Industries include shipbuilding, automobile parts, fruit canning, and electrical equipment.

**St. Charles** /tʃɑ:lz/ a town in east Missouri, USA, on the Missouri River, north-west of St. Louis; pop. (1990) 54,555. Settled in 1769, it was the first state capital of Missouri (1821–6). The explorers Lewis and Clark set off from here on their great expedition to the Pacific Ocean (1804–6).

**St. Christopher and Nevis** see ST. KITTS AND NEVIS.

**St.-Cloud** /sæ'klu:/ a western residential suburb of Paris in the French department of Hauts-de-Seine; pop. (1990) 28,670. Its 16th-c. palace (destroyed during the Franco-Prussian War of 1870–1) was the residence of many French rulers including Napoleon I who proclaimed the empire here in 1804. The St.-Cloud porcelain factory (1722–66), managed by Gabriel Trou and under the protection of the duc d'Orleans, was the first of its kind in France.

**St. Croix** /krɔɪ/ an island in the West Indies, the largest of the US Virgin Islands; area 217 sq. km. (84 sq. miles); pop. (1990) 50,140; chief town, Christiansted (formerly the capital of the Danish West Indies). Purchased by Denmark in 1753, it was sold to the US in 1917.
*Cruzan* adj. & n.

**St. David's** /'deɪvɪdz/ (Welsh **Tyddewi**) a village near the Pembrokeshire coast in Dyfed, west Wales, with a 12th-c. cathedral that houses the shrine of St. David, patron saint of Wales. St. David's is the smallest city in Britain.

**Saint-Denis** /sædə'ni:/ **1.** an industrial northern suburb of Paris, France, in Seine-Saint-Denis department manufacturing diesel engines, plastics, and chemicals; pop. (1990) 90,800. Its 12th-c. gothic basilica contains the tombs of French monarchs. **2.** the capital of the French island of Réunion in the Indian Ocean, a port on the north coast; pop. (1990) 121,670.

**Sainte-Foy** /sæ 'fwɑ:/ a city in southern Quebec, eastern Canada, south-west of Quebec; pop. (1991) 71,100.

**St. Elias Mountains** /ɪ'laɪəs/ a range of mountains in north-west North America, straddling the border between Yukon Territory (Canada) and Alaska (USA). It rises to 5,951 m. (19,524 ft.)

at Mt. Logan, the highest peak in Canada. To the south Mount St. Elias rises to 5,589 m. (18,008 ft.).

**St. Émilion** /ˌsæt e'mi:ljɔ̃/ a small town situated in the Gironde department to the north of the Dordogne River in south-west France. It gives its name to one of the best-known groups of Bordeaux wines. The 8th-c. Breton monk Émilion made his hermitage in one of the nearby limestone caves, and later a Benedictine monastery was founded.

**St.-Étienne** /ˌsæt etɪ'en/ an industrial city in south-east-central France, capital of the Loire department; pop. (1990) 201,570. Noted for its 5-km. main street, it developed from the 16th c. into one of the leading steel-manufacturing centres of France. Its industries produce metal goods, arms, electronics, chemicals, and aircraft engines.

**Saint Eustatius** /ju:'steɪʃəs/ (Dutch **Sint Eustatius**, locally **Statia** /'steɪʃə(r)/) a small volcanic island in the Caribbean Sea near St. Kitts, forming part of the Netherlands Antilles; area 21 sq. km. (8 sq. miles); pop. (1990) 1,716; chief town, Oranjestad. Its highest point is the Quill 576 m. (1,890 ft.). Settled by the Dutch West India Company in 1636, it was for many years an important trade and entrepôt centre.

**St. Gall** /sæ 'gæl/ (German **St. Gallen**) **1.** a canton in north-east Switzerland; area 2,016 sq. km. (779 sq. miles); pop. (1990) 420,270. **2.** its capital, a town with a famous abbey founded by St. Gall in the 7th c; pop. (1990) 73,190. Engineering and the production of textiles are its chief industries.

**St. George's** /'dʒɔ:dʒɪz/ the capital of the island of Grenada in the West Indies, situated on a ridge between St. George's Harbour and the Caribbean Sea; pop. (1989) 35,740. The port is named after King George III.

**St. George's Channel** a channel linking the Irish Sea with the Atlantic Ocean and separating Ireland from mainland Britain.

**St. Gotthard Pass** /'gɒtæd/ a high pass rising to an altitude of 2,108 m. (6,916 ft.) in the Lepontine Alps of southern Switzerland, linking Andermatt and Airolo. Beneath it is a 15-km. (9-mile) railway tunnel (constructed in 1872–80) and a road tunnel (opened in 1980). The route is believed to be named after a former chapel and hospice built on the summit and dedicated to St. Godehard or Gotthard (d. 1038), bishop of Hildesheim in Germany.

**St. Helena**
/hɪ'li:nə/ a solitary island of volcanic origin in the South Atlantic, a British dependency, famous as the place of Napoleon's exile (1815–21) and death; area 122 sq. km. (47  sq. miles); pop. (1988) 5,560; chief town, Jamestown. St Helena was discovered by the Portuguese

navigator Joao da Nova Castella who named it after the mother of Constantine the Great whose festival fell on the day it was first visited. Servicing passenger and cargo ships, its chief exports are fish and handicrafts. The island was held by the East India Company from 1659 until 1834 when it became a British colony, and is now administered by a Governor assisted by a Legislative Council.

**St. Helens** /'helenz/ an industrial town north-east of Liverpool in Merseyside, north-west England; pop. (1991) 175,300. Glass-making, chemicals, and soap are the main industries.

**St. Helens** /'helenz/, **Mount** a volcanic peak in the Cascade Range, south-west Washington, USA. A dramatic eruption in May 1980 killed 100 people and reduced the height of the mountain from 2,950 m. (9,578 ft.) to 2,560 m. (8,312 ft.).

**St. Helier** /'helɪə(r)/ a market town and resort on the south coast of the island of Jersey on St. Aubin's Bay; pop. (1981) 25,700. The town, which is the administrative centre of Jersey, is named after a 6th-c. Christian saint who is said to have had a hermitage nearby.

**Saint-Hubert** /sæju:'ber/ a town in Quebec, eastern Canada, east of Montreal; pop. (1991) 74,000.

**St. James's Palace** /'dʒeɪmzɪz/ the old Tudor palace of the monarchs of England in London, built by Henry VIII on the site of an earlier leper hospital dedicated to St. James the Less. The palace was the chief royal residence in London from 1697 (when Whitehall was burnt down) until Queen Victoria made Buckingham Palace the monarch's London residence. The Court of St. James's is the official title of the British court, to which ambassadors from foreign countries are accredited.

**Saint John** /dʒɒn/ **1.** a city in New Brunswick, eastern Canada, a port on the Bay of Fundy at the mouth of the Saint John River; pop. (1991) 75,000. A trading post was established here in the 17th c. by the French and in 1783 Loyalists fleeing the American War of Independence arrived, transforming the small settlement into a town. During the 19th c. it gained prosperity from transatlantic trade and shipbuilding. It is now the largest city and leading industrial centre of the province with oil refining, sugar refining, and paper-making among its chief industries. **2.** a river of North America that rises in Maine, USA, and flows 673 km. (420 miles) south-eastwards through New Brunswick, Canada, before entering the Bay of Fundy at Saint John. For some 100 km. (62 miles) it forms the frontier between the USA and Canada. The river was named by Samuel de Champlain who landed in the estuary on St. John's Day (June 24) 1604.

**St. John** /dʒɒn/ an island in the West Indies, one of the three principal islands of the US Virgin Islands; area 52 sq. km. (20 sq. miles); pop. (1990) 3,500; chief town, Cruz Bay. Formerly dominated

by sugar plantations, the greater part of the island has reverted to forest within the confines of a national park.

**St. John's** /dʒɒnz/ the capital of Antigua and Barbuda, situated on the north-west coast of the island of Antigua; pop. (1986) 36,000. The town, which overlooks a large bay, is dominated by the twin towers of the Cathedral of St. John the Divine (1845).

**St. John's** /dʒɒnz/ the capital of Newfoundland, Canada; pop. (1991) 171,860 (metropolitan area). Named after John the Baptist and claiming to be the oldest 'European' town in North America, the site was allegedly visited by John Cabot in 1497. In 1901 the first transatlantic wireless message transmitted by Marconi was received at St. John's and from here the first successful non-stop transatlantic flight was made in 1919 by Alcock and Brown. The town is noted for its traditional square, flat-roofed, wooden houses painted in different colours. Industries include fish processing, shipbuilding, iron foundries, and paper.

**St. John's Wood** /ˌdʒɒnz 'wʊd/ a residential suburb of north-west London, England, site of Lord's cricket ground, the headquarters of the Marylebone Cricket Club.

**St. Joseph** /'dʒəʊsɪf/ a city in north-west Missouri, USA, on the Missouri River; pop. (1990) 71,850. It was founded in 1826 by Joseph Robidoux, a French fur trader from St. Louis. It was the western terminus of the first railway to cross the state and the eastern terminus of the Pony Express whose riders carried mail to Sacramento, California. The outlaw Jesse James was killed here in 1882. Household equipment and automobile parts are manufactured.

**St. Kilda** /'kɪldə/ a group of five uninhabited islands of the Outer Hebrides group in the North Atlantic Ocean, 64 km. (40 miles) west of Lewis and Harris. Administered as a nature reserve, they are the most westerly group of islands in Scotland. The last inhabitants left the islands in 1930.

**St. Kitts and Nevis** /kɪts, 'niːvɪs/ official name **The Federation of St. Christopher and Nevis** a state in the West Indies consisting of two adjoining islands (St. Kitts and Nevis) of the  Leeward Islands; area 261 sq. km. (101 sq. miles); pop. (est. 1991) 44,000; official language, English; capital, Basseterre (on St. Kitts). St. Kitts was discovered in 1493 by Columbus. He named it after his patron saint, St. Christopher, but the name was shortened by settlers from England who arrived in 1623 and established the first successful English colony in the West Indies. Nevis, which consists

almost entirely of a mountain, gained its name
from the resemblance of the clouds around its peak
to snow (Spanish *las nieves* = the snows). A union
between St. Kitts, Nevis, and Anguilla was created
in 1967, but Anguilla seceded within three months.
St. Kitts and Nevis, whose economy is dependent
on tourism, the manufacture of electronic equipment, and sugar exports, gained self-government in
1967 and became a fully independent member of
the Commonwealth in 1983. Legislative power is
vested in a unicameral National Assembly and the
island of Nevis has its own legislature (the Nevis
Island Assembly).

**Kittitian, Nevisian** *adj. & n.*

**Saint-Laurent** /sæ lə'rɑ̃/ a city in Quebec, eastern Canada, west of Montreal; pop. (1991) 72,400.

**St. Lawrence**  /'lɒrəns/ a river of North America flowing 1,287 km. (800 miles) from Lake
Ontario past Montreal and Quebec City to the
**Gulf of St. Lawrence**, an inlet of the Atlantic
Ocean. The **St. Lawrence Seaway**, which includes a number of artificial sections to bypass
rapids, enables ocean-going vessels to navigate the
entire length of the river and Great Lakes and is
3,768 km. (2,342 miles) long. It is a major transport corridor of North America and was inaugurated by Canada and the USA in 1959. Bypassing
Niagara Falls, the Welland Canal overcomes the
100 m. (326 ft.) difference in levels by means of a
staircase of seven locks. The Lachine rapids between Lake Ontario and Montreal, with a further
75 m. (246 ft.) drop, are bypassed by an additional
series of locks.

**St. Louis** /'luːɪ/ a city and port in Missouri,
USA, a major transportation centre on the Mississippi River; pop. (1990) 396,685. Founded as a fur-
trading post in 1764, the city was dedicated to
Louis XV of France by Pierre Laclede who named
it after his 'name' saint, Louis IX of France. The
first Mississippi steamboat docked at St. Louis in
1817, but after the steamboat era the city developed away from the riverfront. The original city
centre has been redeveloped as the Jefferson National Expansion Memorial. It is one of the world's
largest markets for wool, timber, and pharmaceuticals and its industries produce beer, chemicals and
transportation equipment in addition to processing
iron, lead, zinc, copper, aluminium, and magnesium. St. Louis has a symphony orchestra and is
home to St. Louis University (1818), Washington
University (1857), and the University of Missouri-
St. Louis (1963). The Lambert-St. Louis International Airport lies 28 km. (18 miles) north-west
of the city.

**St. Lucia** /'luːʃə/ an island and independent
state in the West Indies, one of the Windward
Islands of the Lesser Antilles; area 616 sq. km. (238
sq miles); pop. (est. 1991) 152,000; official language, English (French patois is also spoken); capital, Castries. Settled by both French and British in
the 17th c., possession of the island was disputed

until France ceded it
to Britain in 1814.
Self government was
achieved in 1967 and
in 1979 it became an
independent state
within the Common-
wealth. St. Lucia is
governed by a bi-
cameral legislature

comprising a House of Assembly and Senate. Its
chief exports are bananas and cocoa.

**St. Lucian** *adj. & n.*

**St-Malo** /sæ 'mɑːləʊ/ a walled town and port in
the department of Ille-et-Vilaine on the Brittany
coast of western France; pop. (1990) 49,270. It is a
fishing and ferry port, and tourist centre situated at
the mouth of the River Rance whose tidal flow is
used as a source of power. St-Malo was the birthplace of the writer and politician, Chateaubriand
(1768–1848) and Jaques Cartier (1491–1557) who
set sail for Canada from St-Malo in 1534. It was
almost totally destroyed in August 1944 but has
since been exactly restored.

**St-Marcouf Islands** /mɑː'kuːf/ (French **Iles
St-Marcouf**) two small islands (Ile du Large and
Ile de Terre) in the English Channel off the
Cotentin peninsula of France. They are part of the
department of Manche in Normandy.

**St. Mark's Cathedral** /mɑːks/ the church in
Venice, its cathedral church since 1807, built in the
9th c. to house the relics of St. Mark brought from
Alexandria, and rebuilt in the 11th c. It is lavishly
decorated with mosaics (11th–13th c.) and sculptures.

**Saint Martin** /sæ mɑː'tæ/ (Dutch **Sint
Maarten**) a small island in the Caribbean Sea, of
which the southern section forms part of the
Netherlands Antilles and the larger northern section forms part of the French overseas department
of Guadeloupe; area (Dutch sector) 34 sq. km. (13
sq. miles), (French sector) 54 sq. km. (21 sq. miles);
pop. (1990) 31,722 (Dutch sector), 28,520 (French
sector); chief towns, Philipsburg (Dutch sector) and
Marigot (French sector). It is the smallest island in
the world to be shared by two nations. Developed
in the 17th c. as a centre of salt production, the
island was divided between the French and Dutch
in 1648. The production of sugar, cotton and
tobacco was once important but tourism is now the
chief industry.

**St. Michael's Mount** an island in Mount's
Bay on the coast of Cornwall, south-west England.
A castle stands on its 76 m. (250-ft.) summit and
the island is linked to the mainland by a causeway
at low tide.

**St. Moritz** /sæ mɒ'riːts/ a resort and winter-
sports centre in Graubünden canton, south-east
Switzerland, at an altitude of 1,822 m. (5,980 ft.)
between the Albula and Bernina Alps. The village

of **St. Moritz Dorf** lies on the north shore of the small lake of St. Moritz and the spa of **St. Moritz Bad** is situated on the south-west. The chief skiing areas lie on the slopes of Piz Corvatsch (3,303 m., 10,837 ft.), Piz Nair (3,057 m., 10,030 ft.), and Corviglia (2,486 m., 8,156 ft.). The Winter Olympics of 1928 and 1948 were held here.

**St-Nazaire** /sæ næ'zeə(r)/ a seaport and industrial town in the department of Loire-Atlantique, north-west France, at the mouth of the River Loire; pop. (1990) 66,090. Built in the 19th c. for ships too large to enter Nantes, the harbour of St. Nazaire is the leading French naval dockyard and a major commercial port. The oil-port facility to the east at Donges is one of the largest in France.

**Saint Nicolas** /'nɪkələs/ (Flemish **Sint Niklaas** /sɪnt 'nɪklɑːs/) an industrial town in East Flanders, west Belgium, whose market square is the largest in the country; pop. (1991) 68,200. Its industries produce textiles, carpets, tobacco, metal goods, and timber products.

**St. Paul** /pɔːl/ the capital of the US state of Minnesota, on the Mississippi River; pop. (1990) 272,250. Founded in 1840 and originally known as Pig's Eye, it prospered on river trade and became capital of the Minnesota Territory in 1849 and the state in 1858. Today St. Paul is a major manufacturing and distribution centre for north-central USA. Together with its twin city, Minneapolis, it is a centre for printing, publishing and the production of electronics, computers, trucks, and building materials.

**St. Paul's Cathedral** /pɔːlz/ a cathedral on Ludgate Hill, London, England, built between 1675 and 1711 by Sir Christopher Wren to replace a medieval cathedral largely destroyed in the Great Fire of 1666. Its crypt has the tombs of Nelson and Wellington.

**St. Peter Port** the only town on the island of Guernsey in the Channel Islands; pop. (est. 1986) 16,100. A commercial, administrative, and tourist centre with ferry links to other Channel Islands.

**St. Peter's Basilica** /'piːtəz/ the Roman Catholic basilica in the Vatican City, Rome, the largest church in Christendom. The present 16th-c. building replaced a much older basilican structure erected by Constantine on the supposed site of St. Peter's crucifixion. A succession of architects (Bramante, Raphael, Peruzzi, Sangallo) in turn made drastic changes in the design; the dome closely follows a design of Michelangelo. The building was consecrated in 1626.

**St. Petersburg** /'piːtəz,bɜːg/ the second-largest city in Russia, a port near the mouth of the River Neva; pop. (1990) 4,467,000. Founded by Peter the Great in 1703 as a trade outlet to the Baltic, it was capital of Russia from 1712 until 1918 when it was replaced by Moscow, its economic and cultural rival. It was the scene of the revolutions of 1905 and February and October 1917 and was

named Petrograd (1914–24) and Leningrad (1924–91). Its chief landmarks include the 18th-c. Winter Palace, the Fortress of Peter and Paul, the Cathedral of St. Isaac, the Hermitage, and its celebrated main thoroughfare, Nevsky Prospekt. With Moscow, Russia's most important cultural and tourist centre. Also a leading industrial city with engineering, shipbuilding, metal refining, chemicals, and many light industries.

**St. Petersburg** /'piːtəz,bɜːg/ a resort city in west Florida, USA, on the coast of the Gulf of Mexico; pop. (1990) 238,630. Founded in 1876, it is a centre of the aerospace and appliance industries. A museum houses the world's largest collection of paintings by the Spanish artist Salvador Dali.

**St. Pierre and Miquelon** /sæ pɪ'eər, 'miːkə,lɔ̃/ a group of eight small islands in the North Atlantic, south of Newfoundland, which form the last remnants of the once extensive French  possessions in North America; area 242 sq. km. (93 sq. miles); pop. (1990) 6,390; chief town, St. Pierre. Since 1985 the islands, whose chief export is fish, have been a Territorial Collectivity of France.

**St. Pölten** see SANKT PÖLTEN.

**St-Quentin** /sæ kɑ̃'tæ̃/ an industrial town in the department of Aisne, Picardy, northern France, situated on the River Somme; pop. (1990) 62,085. It developed as a textile town in the Middle Ages but now produces chemicals and metal products. It was the birthplace in 1704 of the artist Maurice Quentin de la Tour and its Museum of Entomology houses a unique collection of butterflies.

**St. Sophia** /sə'fiːə, -'faɪə/ (also **Sancta Sophia**, Turkish **Ayasofia** or **Hagia Sophia**) a church at Constantinople (now Istanbul), dedicated to the 'Holy Wisdom' (i.e. the Person of Christ), built by order of Justinian and inaugurated in 537. It replaced an earlier church built by Constantine the Great in 326 and was designed to surpass all other buildings of antiquity. The key monument of Byzantine architecture, its chief feature is the enormous dome, supported by piers, arches, and pendentives and pierced by 40 windows, which crowns the basilica. In 1453, on the day of the Turkish invasion, orders were given for its conversion into a mosque; the mosaics which adorned its interior were covered and partly destroyed, and minarets were added. It was used as a mosque until 1935, when Atatürk converted it into a museum.

**St. Thomas** /'tɒməs/ an island in the West Indies, the second-largest of the US Virgin Islands; area 72.5 sq. km. (28 sq. miles); pop. (1990) 48,170. Its chief settlement is the port of Charlotte Amalie.

One of the most developed islands in the Caribbean, St. Thomas has expanded from a trading centre to a prosperous resort with villas, hotels, and vacation condominiums.

**St. Tropez** /sæ trəʊˈpeɪ/ a fishing port and resort south-west of Cannes on the Côte d'Azur in the department of Var, south-east France; pop. (1985) 6,250. The town was allegedly named after a Roman officer (St. Torpes) who was martyred by the Emperor Nero as a Christian and whose headless body was washed up on the shore. It became a popular retreat for writers and artists such as Matisse, Signac, Colette, and Maupassant.

**St. Vincent** /ˈvɪns(ə)nt/ an island state of the Windward Islands in the West Indies, consisting of the island of St. Vincent and some of the Grenadines; area 389 sq. km. (150 sq. miles); pop.

(est. 1991) 108,000; official language, English; capital, Kingstown. A ridge of mountains divides the island into spurs and valleys, its highest peak rising in the north to 1,234 m. (4,048 ft) at the dormant volcano Soufrière. The French, Dutch, and English all made attempts at settlements in the mid-18th c., and it finally fell to British possession in 1783. It became a self-governing associated state of the UK in 1969 and in 1979 achieved full independence with a limited form of membership of the Commonwealth. In addition to exporting tobacco, coconuts, fruit, and vegetables, it is the world's chief producer of arrowroot. St. Vincent is governed by a unicameral House of Assembly.
**Vincentian** *adj. & n.*

**Saipan** /saɪˈpæn/ the largest of the Northern Marianas Islands in the western Pacific; area 122 sq. km. (47 sq. miles). Its chief town is Chalan Kanoa.

**Sakai** /sɑːˈkaɪ/ an industrial city of Japan, on the east coast of Osaka Bay, Honshu Island; pop. (1990) 807,860. It is an oil and steel centre.

**Sakarya** /səˈkɑː(r)jə/ **1.** a river of north-west Turkey that rises near Afyon and flows 824 km. (510 miles) to join the Black Sea just east of the Bosporus. **2.** a province of north-east Turkey, on the Black Sea; area 4,821 sq. km. (1,862 sq. miles); pop. (1990) 683,060; capital, Adapazari.

**Sakha, Republic of** the official name of YAKUTIA in the Russian Federation.

**Sakhalin** /ˌsɑːxəˈliːn/ an island in the Sea of Okhotsk, separated by the Tatar Strait from the east coast of Russia. Colonized by Russia and Japan in the 18th and 19th c., it passed entirely to Russia in 1875 when it became a place of exile and penal colony. It was divided between 1905 and 1946 into the northern part, held by Russia, and

the southern part, known to the Japanese as Karafuto, which was occupied by Japan. Since 1946 it has been wholly part of Russia and has formed, with the Kurile Islands, the Sakhalin oblast; area 87,100 sq. km. (33,642 sq. miles); pop. (1989) 709,000; its chief settlement is Yuzhno-Sakhalinsk. The island is an important source of coal, oil, iron, and timber. A severe earthquake devastated the northern town of Neftogorsk in 1995.

**Sakura** /səˈkuːrə/ a city in Chiba prefecture, central Honshu, Japan; pop. (1990) 144,690.

**Salamanca** /ˌsæləˈmæŋkə/ a city on the River Tormes in the Castilla-León region of western Spain, capital of Salamanca province; pop. (1991) 185,990. It was the scene of a victory of the British under Wellington over the French in 1812, during the Peninsular War. It is an agricultural centre with industries producing pharmaceuticals, textiles, and rubber goods.

**Salamis** /ˈsæləmɪs/ an island in the Saronic Gulf in Greece. In the straits between it and the western coast of Attica the Greek fleet under Themistocles crushingly defeated the Persian fleet of Xerxes in 480 BC.

**Salang Pass** /ˈsɑːlæŋ/ a high-altitude route across the Hindu Kush mountain range in Afghanistan. Its road and tunnel were built by the Soviet Union during the 1960s in an attempt to improve the supply route from the Soviet frontier to Kabul.

**Salavat** /səˈlɑːvət/ a city in the Russian republic of Bashkortostan, south of Ufa; pop. (1990) 151,000.

**Sale** /seɪl/ an administrative centre in the Gippsland district of south-east Victoria, Australia, situated on the Princes Highway 200 km. (125 miles) east of Melbourne; pop. (1991) 13,860. It services offshore oil development in the nearby Bass Strait.

**Salem** /ˈseɪləm/ an industrial city in the state of Tamil Nadu, southern India, on the River Tirumanimuttar; pop. (1991) 573,685. It is a centre for the production of textiles, iron and steel, and the export of locally-mined iron ore, bauxite, and magnesite. In the surrounding area tapioca is produced on a large scale.

**Salem** /ˈseɪləm/ **1.** a city and port in north-east Massachusetts, USA; pop. (1990) 38,090. First settled in 1626, it became a centre of shipbuilding and was until 1812 a major port of the China trade. It was the scene of a series of celebrated witchcraft trials in 1692, and was the birthplace in 1804 of the American novelist Nathaniel Hawthorne. **2.** the capital of the US state of Oregon, on the Willamette River; pop. (1990) 107,790. Settled by missionaries in 1841, it became state capital in 1859. Its industries produce processed food and high-tech equipment.

**Salerno** /səˈleənəʊ/ a port and centre of light industries on the coast of Campania, south-west Italy, 48 km. (30 miles) south-east of Naples; pop. (1990) 151,370. It is capital of the province of

Salerno and has a noted university and medical school (said to have been the first of its kind). Nearby are the ruins of the ancient Greek city of Paestum.

**Salford** /'sɔːlfəd/ an industrial city in Greater Manchester, England; pop. (1981) 98,340. Engineering and the manufacture of textiles, chemicals, and electrical goods are its chief industries. It has a university (1967) founded in 1896 as the Royal Technical Institute.

**Salii** /'seɪliː/ a 4th-c. Frankish people living near the River IJssel, from which the Merovingians were descended.
**Salian** adj. & n.

**Salinas** /sə'liːnəs/ a town in west-central California, USA, east of Monterey and centre of a fertile fruit and vegetable-growing area; pop. (1990) 108,780. It was the birthplace in 1902 of the novelist John Steinbeck.

**salinization** /ˌsælɪnaɪ'zeɪʃ(ə)n/ the buildup of salts at or near the surface of a soil as a result of waterlogging or in dry climates where surface water evaporates rapidly. Saline soils are often too poor to support plant life. Perennial irrigation schemes, where land is irrigated year after year without ever being left fallow, are a major source of salinization in arid areas.

**Salisbury** /'sɔːlzbəri/ a market town in Wiltshire, southern England, noted for its 13th-c. cathedral whose spire is the highest in England (123 m., 404 ft.) and whose clock is one of the oldest still working. The cathedral library houses one of the four copies of the MAGNA CARTA; pop. (1981) 35,000.

**Salisbury** the former name (until 1980) of HARARE, capital of Zimbabwe.

**Salisbury Plain** a large area of open-undulating chalky downland in Wiltshire, southern England, part of which is a military training area. Stonehenge stands on Salisbury Plain and there are many other minor prehistoric remains.

**Salonica** /sə'lɒnɪkə/ see THESSALONÍKI.

**Salopian** /sə'ləʊpɪən/ a native or inhabitant of Shropshire in England. Salop is an abbreviated form of the county name.

**Salta** /'sæltə/ the capital of the province of Salta in north-west Argentina, on the River Arias; pop. (1991) 370,000. Founded in 1582, it was an important trade centre on the route between Lima and Buenos Aires. General Belgrano inflicted a defeat on Spanish royalists here in 1813. It is the centre of an 'oasis' area rich in oil, sugar, tobacco, and grapes.

**Saltillo** /sɒl'tiːljəʊ/ the capital of the state of Coahuila in north-east Mexico; pop. (1990) 440,845. It has a university (1907) and a reputation for learning that dates back to 1591 when Captain Francisco Urdiñola established a teaching centre for the Northern Plains Indians. Its industries

include engineering and the manufacture of silverware and textiles.

**salting** /'sɒltɪŋ/ a saline marsh that is sometimes used for grazing.

**Salt Lake City** the capital and largest city of the US state of Utah, on the Jordan River near the southern shore of the Great Salt Lake; pop. (1990) 159,940. Founded in 1847 by Brigham Young for the Mormon community, the city is the world headquarters of the Church of Jesus Christ of Latter-Day Saints. Its industries produce processed food, electronic goods, aerospace equipment, agricultural chemicals, and refined minerals.

**Salton Sea** /'sɒltən/ a salt lake in the Colorado Desert of south-eastern California, USA, a popular fishing and boating area; area 958 sq. km. (370 sq. miles). In 1905 the Colorado River flooded through a broken canal gate into the Salton basin, creating a vast new lake.

**Salvador** /ˌsælvə'dɔː(r)/ (also **Bahia** /baː'iːə/) a port on the Atlantic coast of north-east Brazil, capital of the state of Bahia; pop. (1991) 2,072,000. Founded in 1549, Salvador and its surrounding sugar-cane plantations were the economic heartland of colonial Brazil. It was capital until 1763 and after Lisbon, the second city of the Portuguese empire. Salvador is divided into the historic hilltop site of the original settlement (Cidade Alta) and the commercial, financial, and port district (Cidade Baixa). Oil refining and the production of petrochemicals are its chief industries, the bulk of which are located in Brazil's first planned industrial park (Centro Industrial de Aratu) which stretches round the bay of Aratu.

**Salween** /'sæwiːn, sæl'wiːn/ a river of south-east Asia which rises in Tibet and flows 2,849 km. (1,770 miles) south-east and south through Burma to the Gulf of Martaban, an inlet of the Andaman Sea.

**Salzburg** /'sæltsbɜːg/ **1.** a federal state of central Austria that takes its name from the rich deposits of salt that have been mined for centuries in the Salzburg Alps; pop. (1991) 483,880. **2.** its capital city, noted for its music festivals, one of which is dedicated to the composer Mozart who was born in the city in 1756; pop. (1991) 143,970.

**Salzgitter** /'zælts,gɪtə/ an industrial city in Lower Saxony, west Germany, south-east of Hanover; pop. (1991) 115,380. It has iron and steel-works, chemical, textile, and machinery industries.

**Salzkammergut** /zælts'kæməguːt/ the name given to an alpine-resort region of lakes and mountains in the states of Salzburg, Upper Austria, and Styria in western Austria.

**Samar** /'saːmaː(r)/ the third-largest island of the Philippines, situated in the Visayas group south-east of Luzon Island; area 13,424 sq. km. (5,185 sq. miles). It is linked by a bridge to the island of Leyte and its chief towns are Calbayog, Catarman, and Catbalogan. Copra, coconuts, rice, maize, and sweet potatoes are the main agricultural crops and the island's chief natural attractions lie in the Sohoton National Park.

**Samara** /sə'mɑːrə/ a leading industrial city of western Russia, a port on the River Volga; pop. (1990) 1,258,000. From 1935 to 1991 it was known as Kuibyshev. Industries include oil refining. shipbuilding, and the manufacture of textiles, fertilizers, and aircraft.

**Samaria** /sə'meərɪə/ the ancient capital of the northern kingdom of the Hebrews in central Palestine, now occupied by the village of Sabastiyah in the West Bank north-west of Nablus. Built in the 9th c. BC, it was captured in 721 BC by the Assyrians and resettled with people from other parts of their empire (2 Kings 17,18). In New Testament times Samaria was rebuilt and greatly enlarged by Herod the Great. It is the alleged burial place of John the Baptist.

**Samariá Gorge** a deep ravine in the White Mountains (Levká Ori) of south-western Crete. Cut by the River Tarraíos along the line of a fault between the Pachnes massif to the east and the Gíngilos and Volakiás mountains to the west, it is 18 km. (11 miles) long and one of the longest ravines in Europe.

**Samarinda** /ˌsæmə'rɪndə/ the capital of the Indonesian province of East Kalimantan, situated on the island of Borneo near the mouth of the Mahakam River; pop. (1980) 264,720. It trades in timber and is a gateway to the Kutai National Park and to the remote Dayak areas on the frontier with Sarawak.

**Samarkand** /ˌsæmɑː'kænd/ (Uzbek **Samarqand**) a city in the Uzbekistan, Central Asia; pop. (1990) 369,900. One of the oldest cities in Asia, Samarkand was destroyed by Alexander the Great in 329 BC but later rose to fame as the centre of the silk trade, becoming the subject of much legend in the West. It was destroyed again by Genghis Khan in 1221 but later became the capital of Tamerlane's empire. By 1700 it was almost deserted, but in 1868 it was taken by Russia and in 1924 was incorporated into the Uzbek Soviet Socialist Republic, briefly becoming its capital. Its chief industries are the production of cotton and silk.

**Samarra** /sə'mærə/ a city in north-central Iraq, on the River Tigris north of Baghdad; pop. (est. 1985) 62,000. It was founded between the 4th and 7th centuries AD and in 836 it was made the capital of the Abbasid dynasty. Its 17th-c. mosque is a place of Shiite pilgrimage.

**Sambalpur** /'səmbəlˌpʊ(ə)r/ a textile town in Orissa, east-central India, on the Mahanadi River north-west of Cuttack; pop. (1991) 192,920. To the north-west lies the Hirakud Dam which was completed in 1957.

**Sambhal** /'səmbəl/ a town in Uttar Pradesh northern India, east of Delhi; pop. (1991) 150,000.

**Samnites** /'sæmnaɪts/ a people of ancient Italy often at war with republican Rome.

**Samoa** /sə'məʊə/ a group of islands in Polynesia. The group was divided administratively in 1899 into American Samoa in the east and German Samoa in the west. The latter, mandated to New Zealand in 1919, gained independence in 1962 as Western Samoa. See also WESTERN SAMOA and AMERICAN SAMOA.

**Samos** /'seɪmɒs/ a Greek Island in the eastern Aegean Sea, close to the west coast of Turkey; area 476 sq. km. (184 sq. miles); pop. (1991) 41,850; chief town, Vathy. Its chief monument of antiquity is the Heraion or Sanctuary of Hera, and it is said to be the birthplace of the Greek philosopher and mathematician Pythagoras. Wine, tobacco, timber, and olive oil are its chief products.
**Samian** *adj. & n.*

**Samothrace** (Greek **Samothráki** /sæmɒθ'rɑːkiː/) a Greek island in the north-eastern Aegean opposite Alexandroupolis, on which was found the *Victory of Samothrace* sculpture which is now in the Louvre in Paris.

**Samoyed** /'sæməˌjed/ see NENETS.

**Samoyedic** a group of languages spoken in Siberia and the Russian Arctic. They belong to the Uralic group of languages and largely remained unwritten until 1930.

**Samsun** /sæm'suːn/ **1.** a province of Anatolia in northern Turkey, on the Black Sea; area 9,739 sq. km. (3,762 sq. miles); pop. (1990) 1,158,400. **2.** its capital, a Black Sea port and resort at the mouth of the Murat River and site of the ancient city of Amisus which was founded in the 7th c. BC; pop. (1990) 303,980. It is the largest city on the south coast of the Black Sea, with access to the Central Anatolian Plateau through a gap between the eastern and western Pontic Mountains. Kemal Atatürk landed here in May 1919 to begin the struggle against foreign occupying forces that eventually led to the creation of modern Turkey. It is one of the principal sources of Turkish tobacco.

**samun** /sæ'muːn/ a warm, dry wind that blows down from the Zagros Mts. in Iran.

**Sana'a** /sæ'nɑː/ (also **San'a**) the capital of the Republic of Yemen and of the former Yemen Arab Republic (1967–90); pop. (1990) 500,000. It lies inland on a high plateau 2,286 m. (7,500 ft.) above sea-level. It is claimed by the Arabs to be the world's oldest city. Its medina is one of the largest completely preserved walled city centres in the Arab world, many of its decorated tower houses being over 400 years old. It is a noted centre of handicrafts and also has a textile factory and iron foundry.

**Sanaga** /'sɑːnəgə/ the chief river of Cameroon, which rises in headstreams in the the centre of the country and flows c. 515 km. (325 miles) west to meet the Gulf of Guinea south of Douala.

**Sanandaj** /ˌsɑːnənˈdɑːdʒ/ a city in north-western Iran, in the Zagros Mountains west of Tehran; pop. (1991) 244,000. It is capital of Kordestan province and has a large Kurdish population.

**San Andreas fault** /sæn ænˈdreɪəs/ a fault line or fracture of the earth's crust extending for some 965 km. (600 miles) through the length of California, USA. Seismic activity is common along its course and is ascribed to movement of two sections of the earth's crust—the eastern Pacific plate and the North American plate—which abut against each other in this region. The city of San Francisco lies close to the fault, and such movement caused the devastating earthquake of 1906 and further convulsions in 1989 and 1994.

**San Andrés** /sæn ɑːnˈdrez/ a small resort island in the Caribbean, 700 km. (440 miles) north-west of the Colombian mainland and 230 km. (140 miles) east of Nicaragua. It is the largest island in the Colombian archipelago of San Andrés and Providencia with an airport used as a stopover for international flights. It was declared a duty-free zone in 1953; pop. (1985) 33,000; its chief settlement is San Andrés (El Centro).

**San Angelo** /sæn ˈændʒələʊ/ a city in west Texas, USA, at the junction of the North and Middle Concho Rivers; pop. (1990) 84,470. Formerly a staging post on the Goodnight–Loving cattle trail and the Chidester Stage Line, San Angelo is now a commercial centre trading in cattle, mohair, wool, and oil.

**San Antonio** /sæn ænˈtəʊnɪˌəʊ/ an industrial city in south-central Texas, USA, on the San Antonio River; pop. (1990) 935,930. The Mission San Antonio de Valero (the Alamo) was founded here in 1718 and a military post was established by the Spanish Governor of the Province of Texas. The Alamo was defended by Texan heroes during the Mexican siege of 1836. Amongst its most prominent landmarks is the 229-m. (750-ft.) high Tower of the Americas. Its industries produce, beer, aircraft, electronic equipment, textiles, and chemicals.

**San Bernardino** /bɜːnɑːˈdiːnəʊ/ a city in south-east California, USA, in the foothills of the San Bernardino Mts.; pop. (1990) 164,160. It takes its name from the mountains discovered by a group of missionaries in 1810 on the feast of San Bernardine of Siena. The city, which was laid out in 1851 by Mormons, lies at the centre of a vast citrus-growing region.

**San Bernardo** /sæn bɜːˈnɑːdəʊ/ a city in the province of Maipo, central Chile, to the south of Santiago; pop. (1991) 188,160.

**San Carlos de Bariloche** /sæn ˈkɑːlɒs deɪ ˌbærɪˈlɔʊtʃɪ/ the principal Andean skiing resort of Argentina, on the shore of Lake Nahuel Huapi in Río Negro province; pop. (1980) 48,200.

**Sanchi** /ˈsɑːntʃɪ/ the site in Madhya Pradesh, central India, of several well-preserved Buddhist stupas. The largest of these was probably begun by the emperor Asoka in the 3rd c. BC. Sanchi became a seat of Buddhist learning and a place of pilgrimage, and from here Buddhism was taken to Sri Lanka.

**San Cristóbal** /ˌsæn krɪsˈtəʊbæl/ the capital of the state of Táchira in western Venezuela and a commercial and industrial centre, situated in the northern Andes on terraces overlooking the River Torbes; pop. (1991) 220,700; 364,730 (metropolitan area). Textiles, ceramics, leather goods, cement, and tobacco are produced.

**San Cristóbal de las Casas** /ˌsæn krɪsˈtəʊbæl də lɑːs ˈkɑːzəs/ a Spanish colonial town in the Chiapas region of southern Mexico; pop. (est. 1990) 50,000. It was state capital 1824–92.

**Sandakan** /sænˈdɑːkən/ a seaport in the Malaysian state of Sabah, situated on an inlet of the Sulu Sea on the north-east coast of the island of Borneo; pop. (1980) 70,420. Formerly the capital of North Borneo, it trades in timber from the surrounding forests. Nearby is Sepilok Sanctuary, the world's largest orang-utan reserve.

**Sandalwood Island** see SUMBA.

**Sandhurst** /ˈsændhɜːst/ (in full **The Royal Military Academy, Sandhurst**) a training college, now at Camberley, Surrey, for officers for the British Army. It was formed in 1946 from an amalgamation of the Royal Military College at Sandhurst in Berkshire (founded 1799) and the Royal Military Academy at Woolwich, London (founded 1741).

**San Diego** /sæn dɪˈeɪgəʊ/ an industrial city and US naval port on the Pacific coast of southern California; pop. (1990) 1,110,550. The San Diego de Alcalá Mission (1769) was the first to be established in California. It has large aerospace, electronic and shipbuilding industries and is a processing centre for a very productive agricultural area. Its climate, beaches and historical attractions are the basis of its tourist industry. San Diego is also a cultural, educational, and medical centre.

**Sand Island** see MIDWAY ISLANDS.

**Sandringham House** /ˈsændrɪŋəm/ a holiday residence of the British royal family, north-east of King's Lynn in Norfolk. The estate was acquired in 1861 by Edward VII, then Prince of Wales.

**Sandwich Islands** /ˈsænwɪtʃ/ the former name of the Pacific islands of Hawaii.

**San Fernando Valley** /sæn fɜːˈnændəʊ/ the valley of the Los Angeles River to the north and west of Los Angeles, California, USA, surrounded by the Santa Monica, Santa Susana, and San Gabriel mountains. Light industry has expanded over what was formerly a predominantly agricultural area.

**San Francisco** /sæn frænˈsɪskəʊ/ a city and seaport on the Pacific coast of California, USA, with a magnificent land-locked harbour entered by a channel called the Golden Gate; pop. (1990)

723,960. Built on a series of hills, the original settlement dates from the founding of a mission in 1776. Under Mexican rule it was known as Yerba Buena, but after it had been taken by the US Navy in 1846 its name was changed to San Francisco. It grew rapidly after the 1848 gold-rush, and in 1869 it became the western terminus of the first transcontinental railroad. In 1906 it was badly damaged by a severe earthquake and again in 1989. Its chief landmarks are the Golden Gate Bridge (1937), Fisherman's Wharf, Alcatraz Island, Coit Tower, the Transamerica Pyramid, Chinatown (the largest in the US), and Ghirardelli Square. It is a leading US financial and cultural centre, and the beauty of its setting and its climate make it an attractive residential city. It is a major centre of trade with eastern Asia and the Pacific. Industries include shipbuilding, oil refining, metals, chemicals, and foodstuffs.

**Sangli** /'saːŋgli:/ a market town in Maharashtra, western India, on the Krishna River in the Western Ghats south-east of Bombay; pop. (1991) 363,730.

**San José** /sæn xəʊ'zeɪ, həʊ-/ the capital of Costa Rica; pop. (est. 1984) 284,550. Founded in 1737 and made capital of the newly independent state of Costa Rica in 1823, it is laid out in a grid plan. It is a trade centre for coffee, cocoa, and sugar.

**San Jose** /sæn xəʊ'zeɪ, həʊ-/ a city in western California, USA, in the Santa Clara valley at the centre of the vast high-tech area known as 'Silicon Valley'; pop. (1990) 782,250.

**San Juan** /sæn 'xwɑːn, 'hwɑːn/ **1.** the capital of the province of San Juan in western Argentina, situated in the eastern Andes at the centre of a fertile 'oasis' area growing grain, fruit, and vines; pop. (1991) 353,000. Founded in 1562, it was badly damaged by an earthquake in 1944. Wine-making is the chief industry. **2.** the capital and chief port of the island of Puerto Rico; pop. (1990) 437,745. Its main industry is tourism but it also manufactures clothing, cigars, and cigarettes, rum, and refined sugar. It has the oldest church in continuous use in the Americas (San José, founded 1523), and a school of tropical medicine.

**San Juan Capistrano** /sæn ˌxwɑːn kɑːpiːs'trɑːnəʊ/ a town on the Pacific coast of south-west California, USA, built around an old Spanish mission and made popular in songs, short stories, and films; pop. (1990) 26,180.

**Sankt Pölten** /zæŋkt 'pɜːlt(ə)n/ an industrial town in north-eastern Austria, on the River Traisen west of Vienna, capital of Lower Austria; pop. (1991) 49,805. Founded by the Romans, who called it Aelium Cetium, it was the site of the first monastery in Lower Austria, that of St. Hippolytus. Industries include machinery, textiles, and paper.

**San Luis** /sæn luː'iːs/ a city in central Argentina, capital of the province of San Luis; pop. (1991) 110,000. Founded in 1596, it is a trading centre for timber, minerals, and agricultural produce.

**San Luis Potosí** /sæn luː'iːs ˌpɒtəʊ'siː/ **1.** an agricultural and industrial state of north-central Mexico; area 63,068 sq. km. (24,360 sq. miles); pop. (1990) 2,001,970. **2.** its capital, a silver-mining city; pop. (1990) 525,820. It was founded by the Spanish in 1592 but it was an old Chichimecca Indian city before that. Flour, beer, and leather goods are manufactured.

**San Marino** /sæn mæ'riːnəʊ/ official name **The Republic of San Marino** a small, landlocked republic close to the Adriatic near Rimini, Italy, with a capital of the same name; area 61 sq. km. (23.5 sq. miles); pop. (est. 1991) 22,680; official language, Italian. Comprising hill country with Mount Titano at its centre, its economy is based on the production of grain, wine, olive oil, paint, building stones, ceramics, textiles, synthetic rubber, and handicrafts. The state takes its name from the legendary stonecutter Marino who fled from Dalmatia in AD 301 to escape persecution by Emperor Diocletian. It is perhaps Europe's oldest state, claiming to have been independent almost continuously since its foundation in the 4th c. Executive power is in the hands of two Captains Regent and a Congress of State, and legislative power is exercised by a unicameral Great and General Council.

**San Mateo** /sæn mæ'teɪəʊ/ a city on San Francisco Bay, California, USA, situated to the south-east of San Francisco; pop. (1990) 85,490. It is a centre of horse-racing.

**San Miguel** /sæn miː'gel/ an industrial city in eastern El Salvador, on the Pan-American Highway; pop. (1992) 182,800. Founded in 1530 it lies to the east of the volcanoes of San Miguel and Chinameca. It manufactures plastics, textiles, and pharmaceuticals.

**San Miguel de Tucumán** /sæn miː'gel deɪ tuːkuː'mɑːn/ (also **Tucumán**) a city in north-western Argentina, on the Sali River; pop. (1991) 622,000. Founded in 1565, it is the largest city in northern Argentina and capital of the province of Tucumán. The independence of Argentina was proclaimed here in 1816. Its chief industry is the production of sugar.

**Sanming** /sæn'mɪŋ/ a city in Fujian province, south-east China, west of Fuzhou; pop. (1986) 217,000.

**San Nicolas** /sæn niːkəʊ'lɑːs/ a port and rail junction on the Paraná River, central Argentina, situated to the south-east of Rosario; pop. (1991) 115,000.

**San Pedro Sula** /sæn ˌpedrəʊ 'suːlə/ the second-largest city in Honduras, capital of the department of Cortés in the Ulúa valley; pop. (1988) 460,600. It is a trade centre for coffee, bananas, sugar, and timber, and has steel mills, textiles, plastics and many light industries which, together with good communications, make it central America's fastest-growing town.

**San Salvador** /sæn ˈsælvəˌdɔː(r)/ the capital of El Salvador, at an altitude of 680 m. (2,230 ft.) on the Acelhuate River; pop. (1992) 422,520; 1,522,000 (Greater Metropolitan area). The San Salvador volcano rises to 1,885 m. (6,184 ft.) to the north-west. It is principally concerned with processing the locally grown coffee but has many light industries.

**San Salvador de Jujuy** /sæn sælvəˈdɔː deɪ xuːˈxuːɪ/ (also **Jujuy**) a city in the extreme north-west of Argentina, on the Río Grande de Jujuy, capital of the Andean province of Jujuy; pop. (1991) 183,000. Established by the Spanish in the 1590s on routeways linking Argentina with Bolivia and Peru, it later developed as a centre of sugar production in a rich 'oasis' agricultural area.

**San Sebastian** /sæn sɪˈbæstɪən/ a port and resort town in the Basque province of Guipúzcoa, northern Spain, on the Bay of Biscay; pop. (1991) 174,220. It was the former summer residence of the Spanish court. Industries include fishing, tourism, chemicals, cement, and metal goods.

**San Simeon** /sæn ˈsɪmɪən/ an historic old whaling village on the Pacific coast of California, USA, north-west of San Luis Obispo; pop. (1990) 250. Nearby is the Hearst–San Simeon State Historical Monument, a castle that was the home of the newspaper tycoon William Randolph Hearst.

**Sanskrit** /ˈsænskrɪt/ the ancient language of Hindus in India, belonging to a branch of the Indo-European family of languages. It flourished in India as the language of learning for more than three millennia, well into the 19th c., but has been gradually eclipsed by English and the modern Indian languages (e.g. Hindi, Bengali, Gujarati) to which, as a spoken language, it gave rise, and is now used only for religious purposes. It is written in the Devanagari script.

**Santa Ana** /ˌsæntə ˈænə/ **1.** the second-largest city in El Salvador, situated at the centre of a coffee and sugar-cane growing area; pop. (1992) 202,340. **2.** the highest volcano in El Salvador, rising to a height of 2,381 m. (7,730 ft.) south-west of the city of Santa Ana.

**Santa Ana** /ˌsæntə ˈɑːnə/ a city and business centre in the fertile Santa Ana valley of southern California, USA, south-east of Los Angeles; pop. (1990) 293,740. It gives its name to the dry desiccating Santa Ana winds which blow from the mountains across the coastal plain of southern California. It has electronics, nuclear, and aircraft industries.

**Santa Barbara** /ˌsæntə ˈbɑːbrə/ a town on the Pacific coast of western California, USA, north-west of Los Angeles in the foothills of the Santa

Ynez Mts.; pop. (1990) 85,570. It was named by the Spanish explorer Vizcaino who arrived here on Saint Barbara's day, 4 December 1602. A Spanish mission was established here in 1786. A campus of the University of California was founded here in 1891. It is the outlet for a rich agricultural area and has textiles, electronics, and aerospace industries. There are local off-shore oil wells.

**Santa Catarina** /ˌsæntə kætəˈriːnə/ a state of southern Brazil; area 95,318 sq. km. (36,816 sq. miles); pop. (1991) 4,538,250; capital Florianópolis.

**Santa Clara** /ˌsæntə ˈklɑːrə/ a city in the heart of Santa Clara county (also known as 'Silicon Valley'), western California, USA, situated immediately north-west of San José; pop. (1990) 93,610. It was the site of a Spanish mission established in 1777 and is the home of the University of Santa Clara (1851). In addition to high-tech industries Santa Clara is a centre of fruit growing and packing.

**Santa Cruz** /ˌsæntə ˈkruːz/ a leading commercial city in the agricultural central region of Bolivia, capital of the department of Santa Cruz; pop. (1990) 696,000. Founded by the Spanish in 1561 as Santa Cruz de la Sierra, the city proved vulnerable to attack by local Indians and was moved westwards to its current site at the end of the 16th c. It has expanded rapidly since the building of road and rail links in the 1950s and 1960s. Formerly trading in sugar-cane and cattle, it now exports oil and natural gas.

**Santa Cruz de Tenerife** /-tenəˈriːf/ the capital of the Canary Islands and chief city of the island of Tenerife; pop. (1991) 191,970. Admiral Nelson lost his arm in a naval action near here in 1797. The port trades in fruit and acts as a refuelling centre. It is also a popular holiday resort.

**Santa Fe** /ˌsæntə ˈfeɪ/ (also **Santa Fé**) the capital of the US state of New Mexico, at the foot of the Sangre de Cristo (Spanish = blood of Christ) Mountains; pop. (1990) 55,860. Founded in 1610 by Don Pedro de Peralta as the seat of Spanish governors, it claims to be the oldest capital city in the United States. The Palace of the Governors is the oldest public building in continuous use in the US. Santa Fe was the scene of a Pueblo Indian revolt in 1680 and was captured by US troops in 1846. Nearby are the San Ildefonso Pueblo, Santa Fe National Forest, and Pecos National Monument. It is an administrative and tourist centre.

**Santa Fe** /ˌsæntə ˈfeɪ/ the capital of Santa Fe province, central Argentina, and a port on the Salado River; pop. (1991) 395,000. Founded in 1573, it exports timber, cattle, and wool.

**Santa Fe Trail** a trade route established in 1821 by William Becknell, linking Fort Leavenworth in the US state of Kansas to Santa Fe, New Mexico.

**Santa Maria** /ˌsæntə məˈriːə/ a town in west-central California, USA, north of Santa Barbara near the Los Padres National Forest; pop. (1990) 61,280.

**Santa Monica** /ˌsæntə ˈmɒnɪkə/ a beachside resort and industrial city on the Pacific coast of south-west California, USA, situated at the end of Wilshire Boulevard which links it with the centre of Los Angeles to the east; pop. (1990) 86,905. The J. Paul Getty Museum is sited here and there are many industries including aerospace, electronics, chemicals, and ceramics.

**Santander** /ˌsæntænˈdeə(r)/ the principal ferry port of northern Spain, capital of the Cantabria region; pop. (1991) 194,220. For many years a major outlet for Castilian wool and wheat, the city's industries diversified during the 20th c. to include shipbuilding and the production of chemicals and steel. Santander, which was devastated by a tornado and fire in 1941, hosts an annual festival of drama, music, and dance.

**Santarém** /ˌsæntəˈrem/ **1.** a city in the state of Pará, northern Brazil, a port on the River Amazon; pop. (1990) 254,380. A Jesuit mission was founded here at the junction of the Tapajós and Amazon rivers in 1661 and in 1758 the settlement that developed around it was named Santarém. It trades in rubber, timber, peppers, fruit, and bauxite. **2.** a town in central Portugal, situated on the River Tagus north-east of Lisbon; pop. (1981) 15,300. It is capital of a district of the same name and the chief town of the Ribatejo Plain. Known to the Romans as Scalabis, it was later renamed after St. Irene by a Visigoth king converted to Christianity.

**Santa Rosa** /ˌsæntə ˈrəʊzə/ a city in the Sonoma valley north of San Francisco, north-west California, USA; pop. (1990) 113,310. It lies at the centre of extensive vineyards. A museum houses Charles Schulz's original drawings of the *Peanuts* cartoon characters.

**Santiago** /ˌsæntɪˈɑːgəʊ/ the capital of Chile, on the Mapocho River; pop. (1991) 4,385,480. It was founded in 1541 by Pedro de Valdivia and is the country's chief centre of industry, producing chemicals, textiles, and foodstuffs. It has also been the focus of cultural development of Chile since colonial times with libraries, museums, theatres, and three universities. Its cathedral was founded in 1558.

**Santiago de Compostela** /ˌsæntɪˈɑːgəʊ deɪ ˌkɒmpɒsˈtelə/ a city in the province of La Coruña, north-west Spain, capital of Galicia region; pop. (1991) 105,530. It is named after St. James the Great (Spanish *Sant Iago*) whose relics were said to have been brought here. From the 9th c. the city became the centre of the national and Christian movement against Spain's Muslim rulers and during the 10th–16th centuries the tomb of St. James was the principal centre of Christian pilgrimage after Jerusalem and Rome. In Holy Years when the feast day of St. James (25 July) falls on a Sunday the city attracts thousands of pilgrims.

**Santiago de Cuba** /ˌsæntɪˈɑːgəʊ deɪ ˈkjuːbə/ the second-largest city on the island of Cuba, capital of a province of the same name; pop. (1989) 974,100. Founded in 1514, it was moved to its present site in south-east Cuba in 1588 and was for 40 years capital of the island. The town has a strong French heritage that dates back to the influx of 30,000 French planters during the Haitian revolt of 1791. It is a seaport handling iron, manganese, copper, sugar, rum, and tobacco, and has textile mills, distilleries, and an oil refinery.

**Santiago del Estero** /esˈteɪrəʊ/ a city and resort in north-western Argentina, on the Dulce River in the foothills of the Andes; pop. (1991) 264,000. Founded in 1590, it is capital of the province of Santiago del Estero, and a commercial market for cattle.

**Santiago de los Caballeros** /-də lɒs kæbælˈjeɪrəs/ the second-largest city in the Dominican Republic, situated in the northern foothills of the Cordillera Central; pop. (1986) 308,000. It trades in sugar, coffee, and cacao grown in the surrounding area.

**Santo André** /ˌsæntəʊ ænˈdreɪ/ an industrial city in the state of São Paulo, southern Brazil, a suburb of São Paulo; pop. (1990) 610,430. Its industries produce textiles, aircraft, munitions, metal products, rubber goods, porcelain, and furniture.

**Santo Domingo** /ˌsæntəʊ dəˈmɪŋgəʊ/ the capital and chief port of the Dominican Republic, on the River Ozama; pop. (1986) 1,601,000. Founded in 1496, it is the oldest European city in the Americas and was the seat of the Viceroys of the Americas in the early 1500s. From here the Spanish conquistadors departed on their expeditions to explore the mainland of the New World. Devastated by an earthquake in 1562, it was known as Ciudad Trujillo from 1936 to 1961. It has two universities and its 16th c. cathedral has one of the reputed tombs of Christopher Columbus.

**Santo Domingo de los Colorados** /deɪ lɒs kɒləˈrɑːdəs/ a commercial town in north-west Ecuador, in the western foothills of the Andes on the route from Quito to the Pacific port of Esmeraldas; pop. (1990) 114,000. The indigenous Colorados Indians live in villages nearby.

**Santorini** /ˌsæntəˈriːnɪ/ (Greek **Thera** or **Thíra** /ˈθɪərə/) a volcanic Greek island, the most southerly of the Cyclades group in the Aegean Sea; area 75 sq. km. (29 sq. miles); chief town, Thíra (Thera). It is named after St. Irene of Salonica who died here in exile in 304. A volcanic eruption *c.* 1500 BC caused the centre of the island to sink and fill with water from the sea, subsequent seismic activity altering the geography of the island and its neighbouring islets. It has been suggested as the site of Metropolis, the destroyed capital of the lost continent of Atlantis. Sometimes used as a place of exile for political prisoners, the island was once even more notorious for its alleged population of vampires.

**Santos** /'sæntɒs/ a city and port in the state of São Paulo, southern Brazil, on the Atlantic coast to the south of São Paulo; pop. (1990) 546,630. It is one of the largest ports in Brazil handling about half of both exports and imports. It has oil refineries and chemical industries.

**Sanya** /sæn'jɑ:/ (also **Ya Xian**) a city on the south coast of the island of Hainan, southern China; pop. (1986) 324,000.

**São Gonçalo** /sau gən'sɑ:ləu/ a city in the state of Rio de Janeiro, south-eastern Brazil, to the east of Guanabara Bay; pop. (1990) 720,700.

**São Luis** /sau lu'i:s/ the capital of the state of Maranhão in north-east Brazil, situated on an island on San Marcos Bay; pop. (1990) 695,000. First settled in 1612, it was the only city in Brazil to be founded by the French. It developed as a sugar-exporting port and is now a major centre of aluminium processing and an outlet for minerals from the Carajás mines of Amazonia.

**Saône** /səun/ a river rising in the Vosges Mountains in eastern France and flowing 480 km. (300 miles) south-west to join the Rhône near Lyons.

**Saône-et-Loire** /ˌsəunɛɪˈlwɑ:(r)/ a department of Burgundy in east-central France; area 8,565 sq. km. (3,308 sq. miles); pop. (1990) 559,410; capital, Mâcon.

**São José dos Campos** /sau həu'zeɪ dəs ˈkæmpɒs/ a city in the state of São Paulo, southern Brazil, to the north-east of São Paulo; pop. (1990) 387,430.

**São Paulo** /sau 'pauləu/ **1.** a state in south-eastern Brazil; area 248,256 sq. km. (95,890 sq. miles); pop. (1991) 31,546,470. **2.** its capital, the largest city in Brazil and second-largest metropolitan area in South America; pop. (1991) 9,627,000. Founded in 1554 by Jesuits, it developed during the 19th and 20th centuries into the leading commercial city of South America, and the financial, cultural, and industrial centre of Brazil. Its manufactures include motor vehicles, heavy machinery, electrical equipment, pharmaceuticals, chemicals, textiles, and foodstuffs. It has four universities, a medical school, law school, art galleries, and publishing houses.

**São Tomé and Principe** /sau tɒ'meɪ, 'prɪnsɪpɪ/ official name **The Democratic Republic of São Tomé and Principe** a country consisting of two islands and several small islets in

the Gulf of Guinea, formerly an overseas province of Portugal; area 964 sq. km. (372 sq. miles); pop. (est. 1991) 120,000; official language, Portuguese;

capital, São Tomé. First settled by the Portuguese in 1493, the islands became an important port of call for shipping and a producer of cocoa. Full independence from Portugal was achieved in 1975 and a referendum in 1990 approved a new constitution introducing multiparty democracy. The chief exports are cocoa, copra, coffee, and palm kernels.

**São Vicente** /sau vi:'tʃentɪ/ a residential city and beach resort in the state of São Paulo, southern Brazil, on an island off the coast to the south of São Paulo; pop. (1990) 297,975.

**Sapporo** /sə'pɔ:rəu/ a city in northern Japan, the capital of Hokkaido region; pop. (1990) 1,672,000. It became the administrative centre in 1869 and is noted for its winter sports and Snow Festival during which ice sculptures are built on the city's main boulevard. The 1972 Winter Olympics were held here. It has lumbering, woodworking, and printing industries.

**Saqqara** /sə'kɑ:rə/ a vast necropolis of ancient Memphis, Egypt, 24 km. (15 miles) south-west of Cairo. It has monuments dating from the early dynastic period (3rd millennium BC) to the Graeco-Roman age, including the step pyramid of Djoser (c. 2700 BC), the earliest type of pyramid and the first known building entirely of stone.

**Saracen** /'særəs(ə)n/ **1.** an Arab or Muslim at the time of the Crusades. **2.** a nomad of the Syrian and Arabian desert.

**Saragossa** /ˌsærə'gɒsə/ (Spanish **Zaragoza** /ˌθærə'gɒθə/) an industrial city on the River Ebro in northern Spain, the capital of Aragon; pop. (1991) 614,400. A former seat of the kings of Aragon, its chief landmark is the Aljafareria Moorish palace. The heroic exploits during the siege of Saragossa (1808–9) of Maria Augustín, the Maid of Saragossa, are described in Byron's poem *Childe Harold*. It has engineering, sugar-refining, and wine-making industries.

**Sarajevo** /ˌsærə'jeɪvəu/ the capital city of Bosnia-Herzegovina, on the River Miljacka; pop. (est. 1993) 200,000. In this city the Archduke Franz Ferdinand (heir to the Austrian throne) and his wife were assassinated on 28 June 1914, an event which led to the outbreak of World War I. The city was then a centre of Slav opposition to Austrian rule, and connections between Bosnian nationalists and Serbian agents were used by the Austrians as a pretext for war with Serbia. Each side was supported by its European allies, so that within a few weeks most of the continent was at war. The city, which hosted the 1984 Winter Olympics, was badly damaged during the prolonged siege by Bosnian Serbs that took place after the breakup of the former Federal Republic of Yugoslavia in 1991. It has many factories, research centres, a university and over 100 mosques.

**Saransk** /sə'rænsk/ the capital of the republic of Mordvinia in eastern European Russia; pop. (1990)

316,000. Founded as a fortress town in 1680, it is now an industrial and transportation centre specializing in machine building.

**Sarapul** /sə'rɑːpəl/ a city and river port in south-east Udmurtia, east European Russia, on the Kama River; pop. (1990) 111,000. Its industries include steel, aircraft parts, machinery and machine tools. It has major dock facilities and is a railway junction.

**Sarasota** /særə'səʊtə/ a resort town with beach, fishing, and golfing facilities in western Florida, USA, on the Gulf of Mexico; pop. (1990) 50,960. The first golf course in Florida was established here in 1886.

**Saratoga Springs** /ˌsærə'təʊgə/ a city and spa in east New York state, USA; pop. (1990) 25,000. First settled in 1773 around natural geysers and springs, the town became one of the best-known resorts in North America during the 19th c. Near this city two battles, now commemorated in the Saratoga National Historic Park, were fought (1777) in the War of American Independence. The Americans were victorious in both, and in the second battle, the British forces under General Burgoyne, were decisively defeated. The defeat encouraged French support of the Americans and destroyed the best British opportunity to end the rebellion. Today Saratoga Springs is an international centre of thoroughbred racing and polo.

**Saratov** /sə'rætɒf/ an industrial city in western Russia, on the River Volga north of Volgograd; pop. (1990) 909,000. Founded *c.*1590 as a fortress to defend the Volga, the city developed as a centre of river trade especially in cereals, and industries such as oil refining, ship repair, and the manufacture of chemicals and textiles.

**Sarawak** /sə'rɑːwək/ a state of Malaysia on the north-west coast of Borneo; area 124,449 sq. km. (48,068 sq. miles); pop. (1990) 1,669,000; capital, Kuching. Administered by the Brooke dynasty of 'white rajahs' from 1841, Sarawak became a British protectorate in 1888 and a Crown Colony in 1946. In 1963 it became a member of the independent Federation of Malaysia. Its chief exports are timber, oil, and rubber.

**Sardinia** /sɑː'dɪnɪə/ (Italian **Sardegna** /sɑː'deɪnjə/) a large island in the Mediterranean Sea west of Italy, which comprises the Italian provinces of Cagliari, Nuoro, Oristano, and Sassari; area 24,090 sq. km. (9,305 sq. miles); pop. (1990) 1,664,370; capital, Cagliari. Occupied in succession by Phoenicians, Carthaginians, Romans, and Vandals, the island was given to the House of Aragon in 1297 by the pope. It passed to Spain in the 15th c., Austria in the early 18th c., and the House of Savoy in 1720. The kingdom of Sardinia gradually extended over most of Italy and in 1861 Victor Emmanuel II of Sardinia was proclaimed king of Italy. The island is separated from the French island of Corsica to the north by the Strait

of Bonifacio, and its chief products are tobacco, wine, olives, coal, and minerals such as magnesium, zinc, lead, salt, and manganese.

**Sardis** /'sɑːdɪs/ the ruins of an ancient city situated near the village of Sart, north-east of Izmir in the province of Manisa, western Turkey. It was the capital of the Lydian kingdom and a leading cultural centre of Asia Minor during the 7th and 6th centuries BC where gold and silver coins were first minted. Destroyed by Tamerlane in the 14th c., its ruins were only rediscovered in 1958.

**Sargasso Sea** /sɑː'gæsəʊ/ a region of the western Atlantic Ocean between the Azores and the West Indies, around latitude 35°N, so called because of the prevalence in it of floating sargasso seaweed. It is the breeding-place of eels from the rivers of Europe and North America.

**Sargodha** /sɑː'gəʊdə/ a city on the Jhelum Canal in the Punjab province of northern Pakistan; pop. (1981) 294,000. It is an agricultural market centre and railway junction.

**Sarh** /sɑː/ a city in southern Chad, on the Chari River, capital of the Moyen-Chari préfecture; pop. (1993) 198,100. It was known as Fort Archambault until 1973.

**Sark** /sɑːk/ one of the Channel Islands, a small island lying to the east of Guernsey; area 5 sq. km. (2 sq. miles). Divided by an isthmus into Little and Great Sark, it has had its own parliament ruled by a Seigneur/Dame since the reign of Elizabeth I. The island has no towns or motor cars and its residents pay no income tax. It is very popular in the summertime with tourists ferried across from Guernsey.

**Sarmatia** /sɑː'meɪʃə/ the name in ancient times of a region north of the Black Sea inhabited by ancestors of the Slavs, used occasionally by English poets to signify Poland.
**Sarmatian** *adj. & n.*

**Sarnath** /sɑː'nɑːθ/ one of the leading holy shrines of Buddhism, 10 km. east of Varanasi in the state of Uttar Pradesh, northern India. After gaining enlightenment at Bodh Gaya, the Buddha came to Sarnath *c.*528 BC to deliver his first sermon. His relics are displayed each year in May at a festival to mark the birth of the Buddha. The principal monument, the 5th–6th-c. Dhamekh Stupa, lies amidst a complex of religious buildings within a Deer Park which is also a holy place of the Jains.

**Saronic Gulf** /sə'rɒnɪk/ an inlet of the Aegean Sea on the coast of south-east Greece. Athens and the port of Piraeus lie on its northern shores.

**Sarre** see SAAR.

**Sarthe** /sɑːt/ **1.** a river of north-west France that rises in the Perche Hills of the department of Orne and flows 285 km. (178 miles) south past Le Mans to Angers where it is joined by the Mayenne and the Loir. **2.** a department in the Pays de la Loire region of western France; area 6,245 sq. km. (2,412 sq. miles); pop. (1990) 513,650; capital, Le Mans.

**Sarum** /'seərəm/ the ecclesiastical name of Salisbury in Wiltshire, southern England, and its diocese. (see also OLD SARUM). Sarum use is the form of liturgy used in the diocese of Salisbury from the 11th c. to the Reformation.

**Sasebo** /sɑ:'seɪbəʊ/ a city in Nagasaki prefecture, west Kyushu, Japan, a port and naval base on the East China Sea; pop. (1990) 244,690. Shipbuilding is its chief industry.

**Saseno** the Italian name for the Albanian island of SAZAN.

**Saskatchewan** /sə'skætʃɪwən/ **1.** a province of central Canada situated between the 49th and 60th parallels of latitude; area 652,330 sq. km. (251,866 sq. miles); pop. (1991) 988,930; capital, Regina. Its largest settlements are Regina, Saskatoon, and Moose Jaw. and its highest point is in the Cypress Hills (1,392 m., 4,567 ft.). Settled by the Hudson's Bay Company, it became a province of Canada in 1905. It is the largest wheat producer in Canada and also produces rapeseed, oats, rye, barley, copper, zinc, coal, potash, oil, and natural gas. **2.** a river of Canada, flowing eastwards to Lake Winnipeg from two main headsteams (North and South Saskatchewan) that rise in the Rocky Mountains. The **North Saskatchewan** is 1,287 km. long and the **South Saskatchewan** is 1,392 km. long, both rivers meeting to the east of Prince Albert. The total length of the river system to the head of the Bow River, a tributary of the South Saskatchewan, is 1,939 km. (1,220 miles).

**Saskatoon** /ˌsæskə'tu:n/ an industrial city in Saskatchewan, central Canada, on the South Saskatchewan River; pop. (1991) 211,020 (metropolitan area). It was first settled as a temperance colony in 1882 by Ontario Methodists and is now the largest city in the province, the seat of the University of Saskatchewan (1907), and one of Canada's leading mining and high-tech cities.

**Sassanid** /'sæsənɪd/ a dynasty founded by Ardashir I ruling the Persian empire from AD 224 until driven from Mesopotamia by the Arabs (637–51).

**Sassari** /'sæsərɪ/ the capital of the Italian province of Sassari, situated in north-west Sardinia; pop. (1990) 120,010. It is the scene of the great annual Cavalcade of Sardinia on the third Sunday in May and nearby is the prehistoric sanctuary of Monte d'Accoddi.

**Satsuma** /sɑ:'tsu:mɑ:/ (Japanese **Mikan**) a peninsula at the south-west corner of Kyushu Island, Japan, that gives its name to a thin-skinned, seedless type of mandarin orange and to Satsuma ware, a yellowish pottery that was made here from the end of the 16th c.

**Satu Mare** /ˌsɑ:tu: 'mɑ:rɪ/ a city in north-west Romania, on the Someş River near the Hungarian frontier; pop. (1990) 138,000. It is an important crossroads and the capital of the Transylvanian county of Satu Mare. It lies at the centre of an agricultural region producing grain, fruit, vegetables, and livestock.

**Saudi Arabia** /ˌsaʊdɪ ə'reɪbɪə/ official name **The Kingdom of Saudi Arabia** a country in south-west Asia occupying most of the Arabian peninsula; area 2,149,690 sq. km. (829,996 sq.

miles); pop. (est. 1991) 15,431,000; official language, Arabic; capital, Riyadh (royal), Jeddah (administrative). Largely sandy desert or semidesert, Saudi Arabia rises from a coastal plain on the Red Sea to the Asir Highlands before dipping gently towards the oil-rich regions of the north and east. The birthplace of Islam, Saudi Arabia emerged from the Arab revolt against the Turks during World War I to become an independent kingdom in 1932 with the union of Hejaz and Nejd. Since the discovery of oil in the eastern region in 1938 the economy has been revolutionized, the export of oil now accounting for 85 per cent of the government's revenue and making Saudi Arabia the largest oil-producer in the Middle East. Major industries include the manufacture of petrochemicals and fertilizers and the production of grain (although less than 1 per cent of the land is fit for agriculture). Ruled along traditional Islamic lines, the country has exercised a conservative influence over Middle Eastern politics, although the position of the ruling house of Saud was severely threatened by the brief seizure of the Great Mosque in Mecca by Islamic fanatics in 1979 and falling oil prices during the early 1980s. The country, which has no political parties, is governed directly by the King who heads a Council of Ministers.

**Sauer** /saʊə(r)/ a river that rises in the Ardennes of south-east Belgium and flows c. 160 km. (100 miles) eastwards through Luxembourg to join the Moselle River. It is the chief river of Luxembourg.

**Sault Ste. Marie** /'su: seɪnt mə'ri:/ twin ports with the same name on the falls (French *sault*) of the St. Mary's River which links Lake Superior with Lake Huron. One is located in Ontario, Canada, and has a pop. (1991) 81,500 and the other is in the US state of Michigan and has a pop. (1990) 14,700. Both cities attract tourists, particularly for the local fishing and hunting facilities.

**Saumur** /səʊ'mʊə(r)/ a town in the department of Maine-et-Loire, west-central France, on the River Loire south-east of Angers; pop. (1990) 31,890. It is the home of the Cadre Noir cavalry school (1768) and is noted for the wines produced in the surrounding area.

**Sausalito** /sɔ:sə'li:təʊ/ a picturesque town near the Golden Gate Bridge on the north side of San Francisco Bay in the US state of California; pop.

(1990) 1,800. First settled by whalers, it is now a residential suburb with an art colony. For many years its springs were a source of water for San Francisco.

**Sauternais** /ˈsəʊtɜːneɪ/ an area of south-west France, south-east of Bordeaux and south of the Garonne River, noted for its sweet white wines. It lies in the Gironde department.

**Sava** /ˈsɑːvɑː/ a Balkan river that rises in the Julian Alps of western Slovenia and flows south-eastwards for c.930 km. (580 miles) through Croatia and Serbia before joining the Danube at Belgrade.

**Savai'i** /sɑːˈvaɪ/ (also **Savaii**) a mountainous volcanic island in the south-west Pacific, in Western Samoa. It is the largest of the Samoan islands.

**savanna** /səˈvænə/ (also **savannah**) a grassy plain in tropical and subtropical regions, with few or no trees.

**Savannah** /səˈvænə/ a city and port on the Savannah River in the US state of Georgia, noted for its Georgian colonial architecture; pop. (1990) 137,600. Founded in 1733 by General James E. Oglethorpe, it originally prospered on tobacco and cotton. In 1819 the SS *Savannah* sailing from here to Liverpool was the first steamship to cross the Atlantic. It was the birthplace in 1860 of Juliette Gordon Low, founder of the Girl Scouts of America. Chemicals, petroleum, rubber, timber, and plastics are its main industries. Many fine old buildings have survived wars and fires.

**Savannakhet** /ˌsævænəˈket/ a town in southern Laos on the Mekong River, close to the Thailand frontier; pop. (est. 1973) 50,700. It is a leading trade centre between Thailand and Vietnam.

**Savoie** /sæˈvwɑː/ a department in the Rhône-Alpes region of eastern France; area 6,036 sq. km. (2,331 sq. miles); pop. (1990) 348,260; capital, Chambéry.

**Savona** /səˈvəʊnə/ a town and port on the Riviera coast of Liguria in north-west Italy, capital of the province of Savona; pop. (1990) 69,000. A rival to Genoa in the Middle Ages, it is now a ferry port and commercial outlet for coal, oil, and metal goods.

**Savonlinna** /ˌsɑːvɒnˈliːnə/ (Swedish **Nyslott** /ˈniːslɒt/) a town in Mikkeli province, south-east Finland; pop. (1990) 28,560. Once a lakeside resort of the Russian tsars, the town is now famous for its annual opera festival.

**Savoy** /səˈvɔɪ/ a former duchy of south-east France bordering on north-west Italy, ruled by the counts of Savoy from the 11th c. although frequently invaded and fought over by neighbouring states. In 1720 Savoy was formed with Sardinia and Piedmont into the Kingdom of Sardinia. In the mid-19th c. Sardinia served as the nucleus for the formation of a unified Italy, but at the time of unification (1861) Savoy itself was ceded to France. It

now comprises the departments of Haute-Savoie and Savoie.

**Savoyard** /səˈvɔɪɑːd, ˌsævɔɪˈɑːd/ a native of Savoy in south-east France.

**Savu Sea** /ˈsɑːvuː/ (also **Sawu Sea**) part of the Indian Ocean lying to the south of the island of Flores, Indonesia.

**Saxe-Coburg** /sæksˈkəʊbɜːg/ a former duchy of Bavaria in central Germany whose heirs became the ruling dynasty of Belgium and (through Prince Albert, consort of Queen Victoria) of Britain during the 19th c.

**Saxon** /ˈsæks(ə)n/ a north German tribe, originally inhabitants of the area round the mouth of the Elbe, one branch of which, along with the Angles and the Jutes, conquered and colonized much of southern Britain in the 5th and 6th centuries. The language of this people was Old Saxon.

**Saxony** /ˈsæksənɪ/ (German **Sachsen** /ˈzaːks(ə)n/) **1.** a former province of east-central Germany on the upper reaches of the Elbe, earlier part of the large kingdom of Saxony. **2.** a state of the Federal Republic of Germany revived following the reunification of Germany in 1990; area 18,337 sq. km. (7,083 sq. miles); pop. (1991) 4,678,880; capital, Dresden. (See also LOWER SAXONY.)

**Saxony-Anhalt** /ˈɑːnhɑːlt/ (German **Sachsen-Anhalt**) a state of the Federal Republic of Germany, on the plains of the Elbe and the Saale rivers; area 20,445 sq. km. (7,897 sq. miles); pop. (1991) 2,823,320; capital, Magdeburg. Created in 1990, it corresponds to the former duchy of Anhalt and the central part of the former kingdom of Saxony.

**Sayama** /sɑːˈjɑːmə/ a resort town in Saitama prefecture and centre for machine industries, east-central Honshu Island, Japan, on Lake Sayama; pop. (1990) 157,310.

**Sayan** /səˈjɑːn/ a mountain range in East Siberia, in Russia and northern Mongolia, to the west of Lake Baikal. Divided into eastern and western ranges, its highest peak is Munku-Sardyk (3,492 m., 11,457 ft.).

**Sazan** /sɑːˈzɑːn/ (Italian **Saseno** /ˌsəˈzeɪnəʊ/) a small island of Albania in the Strait of Otranto opposite the 'heel' of Italy. Situated at the entrance to the harbour at Vlorë, it was held as an Italian naval base from 1914 to 1947.

**SC** *abbr.* US South Carolina (in official postal use).

**Scafell Pike** /skɔːˈfel/ the highest peak in England, in the Lake District in Cumbria, rising to a height of 978 m. (3,210 ft.).

**Scandinavia** /ˌskændɪˈneɪvɪə/ that part of north-western Europe forming a peninsula bounded by the Arctic Ocean in the north, the Atlantic in the west, the Baltic in the south, and the Gulf of Bothnia in the east. Although the peninsula comprises only Norway and Sweden,

Scandinavia also includes Denmark, Iceland, and Finland in a wider cultural and literary context. **Scandinavian** *adj. & n.*

**Scandinavian** /ˌskændɪˈneɪvɪən/ the North Germanic branch of the Indo-European family of languages, including Danish, Norwegian, Swedish, and Icelandic, all descended from Old Norse.

**Scandinavian Shield** (Finnish **Pohjoiskalotti**, Swedish and Norwegian **Nordkalotten**) the name given to the northernmost parts of Norway, Sweden, Finland, and the Russian Kola peninsula. Its name literally means 'the northern skull-cap'.

**Scapa Flow** /ˌskɑːpə ˈfləʊ/ a stretch of sea encircled by islands in the Orkney Islands, Scotland, an important British naval base in World War I. The entire German High Seas Fleet, which was interned here after its surrender, was scuttled in 1919 as an act of defiance against the terms of the Versailles peace settlement. In October 1939 the defences of Scapa Flow were penetrated when a German U-boat sank HMS *Royal Oak*. In the following year the Churchill Barrier, linking the Orkney Mainland, Burray, and South Ronaldsay, was constructed to protect the eastern approaches to the Scapa Flow. The naval base was closed in 1957 but the anchorage at Flotta at the southern entrance to Scapa Flow became the centre of the oil industry in Orkney.

**Scarborough** /ˈskɑːbərə/ a resort town on the North Sea coast of North Yorkshire that claims to be the oldest spa town in England; pop. (1981) 38,000.

**scarp slope** /skɑːp/ a steep slope or hill face.

**Scarsdale** /ˈskɑːzdeɪl/ a suburb of New York City, USA, in Westchester County, that gives its name to a syndrome observed by psychologists amongst people feeling guilty about living in expensive neighbourhoods.

**Schaffhausen** /ˈʃɑːfhaʊz(ə)n/ (French **Schaffhouse**) a canton in northern Switzerland, to the north of the Rhine, that joined the Swiss Confederation in 1501; area 298 sq. km. (115 sq. miles); pop. (1990) 71,700; capital, Schaffhausen.

**Scheldt** /skelt/ (also **Schelde** /ˈskeldə/, French **Escaut** /esˈkəʊ/) a river that rises in northern France and flows 432 km. (270 miles) through Belgium into the Netherlands where it meets the North Sea. The city of Antwerp lies upon it.

**Schenectady** /skəˈnektədiː/ an industrial city in east New York state, USA, on the Mohawk River north-west of Albany; pop. (1990) 65,570. First settled in 1661, it became a centre of locomotive building in the mid-19th c. Landmarks include the Historic Stockade Area and Nott Memorial (1875) which is the only 16-sided building in the northern hemisphere. Electrical equipment and chemicals are important industries.

**Schiehallion** /ʃɪˈhælj(ə)n/ a conical mountain in Perthshire, Scotland, rising to 1,081 m. (3,547 ft.) to the south-east of Loch Rannoch. In 1774 the English astronomer Nevil Maskelyne measured the earth's density from the deflection of a plumb-line at Schiehallion.

**Schleswig** /ˈʃlesvɪk/ a former duchy of the Danish Crown, acquired by conquest by Prussia in 1864 and incorporated into the province of Schleswig-Holstein. The northern part of this territory was returned to Denmark in 1920 after a plebiscite held in accordance with the Treaty of Versailles.

**Schleswig-Holstein** /-ˈhɒlʃtaɪn/ a state of north-west Germany; area 15,729 sq. km. (6,075 sq. miles); pop. (1991) 2,648,530; capital, Kiel.

**Schönbrunn Palace** /ˈʃɜːnbrʊn/ a Baroque palace in Vienna, Austria, built in the late 17th and early 18th centuries as a summer palace for the rulers of Austria. It replace an earlier house destroyed by the Turks in 1683. The Emperor Francis Joseph (1830–1916) was born and died here.

**Schuylkill** /ˈskuːlkɪl/ a river of North America that rises in east-central Pennsylvania and flows 210 km. (130 miles) south-eastwards to join the Delaware River at Philadelphia.

**Schwabach** /ˈʃvɑːbæx/ an industrial town in Bavaria, southern Germany, south of Nuremberg; pop. (1991) 36,140. Metal industries and chemicals are important.

**Schwarzwald** see BLACK FOREST.

**Schwedt** /ʃveɪt/ (in full **Schwedt an der Oder**) a manufacturing town in Brandenburg, north-east Germany, on the Oder 80 km. (50 miles) north-east of Berlin; pop. (1991) 49,440.

**Schweinfurt** /ˈʃvaɪnfʊət/ an industrial town in Bavaria, southern Germany, on the River Main east of Frankfurt; pop. (1991) 54,520. It manufactures ball-bearings, motors, and chemicals.

**Schwerin** /ʃveˈriːn/ a city on the western shore of Lake Schwerin in north-east Germany, capital of Mecklenburg-West Pomerania since the reunification of Germany in 1990; pop. (1991) 125,960. Commercial and industrial centre manufacturing chemicals, pharmaceuticals, ceramics, and cigarettes.

**Schwyz** /ʃviːts/ the capital of a canton of the same name in central Switzerland; pop. (1990) 12,530. Schwyz was one of the three original districts of the anti-Habsburg league, formed in 1291, that developed into the Swiss Confederation. Because of its leadership in this league its name and its flag were adopted by the whole country.

**Scilly Islands** /ˈsɪlɪ/ (also **Scillies**) a group of about 140 small islands off the western extremity of Cornwall, England, the largest of which are St. Mary's, Tresco, St. Martin's, St. Agnes, and Bryher; pop. (1991) 2,900; capital, Hugh Town (on St.

Mary's). Economy depends on spring flowers, early vegetables, and tourism.

**Scillonian** /sɪˈləʊnɪən/ *adj. & n.*

**Scone** /skuːn/ the name of two villages (**Old Scone** and **New Scone**) in Perthshire, Tayside, Scotland, situated to the north of Perth. The original village of Scone, close to the home of the earls of Mansfield at Scone Palace, was the ancient capital where, on Moot Hill, the kings of Scotland were crowned. The famous Stone of Destiny was allegedly brought here in the 9th c. by Kenneth Macalpine and later taken to Westminster Abbey by Edward I.

**Scoresby Sound** /ˈskɔːzbiː/ a heavily indented inlet of the Greenland Sea on the east coast of Greenland, named after the Arctic explorer William Scoresby (1789–1857).

**Scotch** /skɒtʃ/ a variation of SCOTTISH or SCOTS.

**Scotia** /ˈskəʊʃə/ a Latin name for Scotland frequently used in the Middle Ages and later in a literary context by writers and poets.

**Scotland** /ˈskɒtlənd/ the northern part of Great Britain and of the United Kingdom; area 77,167 sq. km. (29,805 sq. miles); pop. (1991) 4,957,300; capital, Edinburgh. Sparsely populated until Celtic peoples arrived from the Continent during the Bronze and Early Iron Age, the inhabitants of Scotland were named the Picts by the Romans who established a northerly line at Antonine's Wall for about 40 years. An independent country in the Middle Ages, after the unification of various small Dark Age kingdoms of the Picts, Scots, Britons, and Angles between the 9th and 11th c., Scotland successfully resisted English attempts at domination but was amalgamated with her southern neighbour as a result of the union of the crowns in 1603 and of the parliaments in 1707. Broadly divided into Highland and Lowland regions, Scotland has a heavily indented west coast with numerous islands to the west (Inner and Outer Hebrides) and north (Orkney and Shetland Islands). The Highlands to the north and the Southern Uplands north of the English border are sparsely populated, the greater proportion of the Scottish population being concentrated in the Central Lowlands between the Firth of Clyde and the Firth of Forth. Oil and natural gas, agricultural produce, timber, textiles, whisky, paper, and high-tech electronic goods are amongst its chief industrial products. Scotland is divided into nine administrative regions (subdivided into 53 districts) and three Islands Areas (1975–96):

| Region | Area (sq. km.) | Pop. (1991) | Capital |
|---|---|---|---|
| Borders | 4,712 | 102,650 | Newton St. Boswells |
| Central | 2,634 | 267,960 | Stirling |
| Dumfries and Galloway | 6,396 | 147,060 | Dumfries |
| Fife | 1,312 | 339,280 | Glenrothes |
| Grampian | 8,698 | 493,155 | Aberdeen |
| Highland | 25,398 | 209,420 | Inverness |
| Lothian | 1,716 | 723,680 | Edinburgh |
| Strathclyde | 13,503 | 2,218,230 | Glasgow |
| Tayside | 7,492 | 385,270 | Dundee |
| Orkney Islands Area | 976 | 19,450 | Kirkwall |
| Shetland Islands Area | 1,433 | 22,020 | Lerwick |
| Western Isles Islands Area | 2,898 | 29,110 | Stornoway |

From April 1996 Scotland is divided into the following 32 local government areas:

City of Aberdeen
Aberdeenshire
Angus
Argyll and Bute
East Ayrshire
North Ayrshire
South Ayrshire
The Borders
Clackmannan
Dumbarton and Clydebank
Dumfries and Galloway
East Dunbartonshire
City of Dundee
City of Edinburgh
Falkirk
Fife
City of Glasgow
Highland
Inverclyde
North Lanarkshire
South Lanarkshire
East Lothian
Midlothian
West Lothian
Moray
Orkney Islands
Perthshire and Kinross
East Renfrewshire
Renfrewshire
Shetland Islands
Stirling
Western Isles

**Scotland Yard** the headquarters of the London Metropolitan Police, situated from 1829 to 1890 in Great Scotland Yard, a short street off Whitehall in London, from then until 1967 in New Scotland Yard on the Thames Embankment, and from 1967 in New Scotland Yard, Broadway, Westminster.

**Scots** /skɒts/ the dialect or accent of the people of Scotland, especially in the Lowlands.

**Scottish** /ˈskɒtɪʃ/ of or relating to Scotland or its inhabitants.

**Scotts Bluff** a butte in western Nebraska, USA, that was a landmark to travellers on the Oregon and Mormon trails. It rises to a height of 244 m. (800 ft.) above the North Platte river valley and lies within a designated national monument.

**Scottsdale** /ˈskɒtsdeɪl/ a residential suburb of Phoenix in the US state of Arizona; pop. (1990) 130,070.

**scouse** /skaʊs/ the dialect of the people of Liverpool in England.

**Scranton** /ˈskrænt(ə)n/ an city in north-east Pennsylvania, USA; pop. (1990) 81,805. First settled by Europeans in 1771, the manufacture of iron and steel was introduced to the city by George and Seldon Scranton in 1840. Following the depletion of the nearby anthracite mines in the 20th c., Scranton became a trucking terminal with printing and electronics industries.

**Scunthorpe** /ˈskʌnθɔːp/ a town in Humberside, east England, near the River Trent; pop. (1991) 60,500. Engineering and the production of steel, textiles, and electronics are its chief industries.

**Scutari** /ˈskuːtərɪ/ (also **Shkodër** /ˈʃkəʊdə(r)/) **1.** a province of north-west Albania; area 2,528 sq. km. (976 sq. miles); pop. (1990) 241,550. **2.** its capital, at the outlet of Lake Scutari; pop. (1990) 81,900. **3.** a lake on the frontier between north-west Albania and Montenegro. It is the largest lake of the Balkan Peninsula.

**Scutari** the former name of Üsküdar, a suburb of Istanbul on the Asian side of the Bosporus; pop. (1990) 395,620. As one of the earliest Greek settlements on the Bosporus, it was known as Chrysopolis and nearby was the ancient city of Chalcedon, capital of Bithynia. It was the British army base during the Crimean War; a corner of the Selimiye barracks was used by Florence Nightingale as a hospital. It is the terminus of the Anatolian Railway.

**Scylla and Charybdis** /ˈsɪlə, kəˈrɪbdɪs/ the names given since ancient times to a dangerous rock and whirlpool in the narrow Strait of Messina which separates the 'toe' of Italy from Sicily.

**Scythia** /ˈsɪðɪə/ the name given by the ancient Greeks to a country on the north shore of the Black Sea. Its inhabitants were an Indo-European people of Central Asian origin, skilful horsemen and craftsmen, known for their distinctive 'animal style' art. They were eventually absorbed by the Goths and other immigrants during the 3rd and 2nd c. BC. **Scythian** adj. & n.

**SD** abbr. US South Dakota (in official postal use).

**sea** /siː/ the expanse of salt water that covers most (70.98 per cent) of the earth's surface and surrounds its land masses. It covers an estimated 362,033,000 sq. km. (139,835,000 sq. miles). Excluding the major oceans of the world, the largest sea is the South China Sea. The term is also used to designate some large inland salt lakes such as the Caspian Sea, Aral Sea, Dead Sea, and Salton Sea.

**Sealyham** /ˈsiːlɪəm/ a location in Dyfed, south Wales, 9 km. (6 miles) south of Fishguard that gives its name to a wire-haired short-legged breed of terrier.

**Sea Peoples** (also **Peoples of the Sea**) groups of people who encroached on the Levant and Egypt by land and by sea in the late 13th c. Their identity is still being debated. In the Levant they are associated with destruction; the Egyptians were successful in driving them away. Some, including the Philistines, settled in Palestine.

**Sears Tower** /sɪəz/ the tallest office building in the world, a 110-storey building rising to 443 m. (1,454 ft.) in Wacker Drive, Chicago, Illinois, USA. Completed in May 1973, it was built as the headquarters of Sears, Roebuck & Co.

**SEATO** /ˈsiːtəʊ/ abbr. South-East Asia Treaty Organization.

**Seattle** /sɪˈæt(ə)l/ a port and industrial city in the state of Washington, the largest city in the north-western US; pop. (1990) 516,260. Situated on Elliott Bay, between Puget Sound and Lake Washington, its economy is based on tourism, the world's biggest aircraft industry, serving as a provisioner for Alaska, and trading in products from its surrounding forests, farms and waterways. It is named after an Indian chief and was first settled in 1852. The Seattle Center was the site of the 1962 World Fair.

**Sebastapol** /sɪˈbæstəp(ə)l/ (Russian **Sevastopol** /sɪˈvæ-/) a fortress and Black Sea naval base near the southern tip of the Crimea peninsula, southern Ukraine; pop. (1990) 361,000. It was the focal point of military operations during the Crimean War, falling eventually to Anglo-French forces in September 1855 after a year-long siege. It is port to the Black Sea fleet over which Russia and Ukraine have been in dispute.

**Sechuana** a variation of **Setswana**.

**Sedan** /sɪˈdæn/ a town on the River Meuse in the department of Ardennes, north-east France; pop. (1990) 22,400. Its bastions and ramparts date back to the 15th c. It was the site of the decisive battle (1870) in the Franco-Prussian War of 1870–1, in which the Prussian army succeeded in surrounding a smaller French army under Napoleon III and forcing it to surrender, opening the way for a Prussian advance on Paris and marking the end of the Second Empire.

**Sedgemoor** /ˈsedʒmʊə(r)/ a plain in Somerset, scene of a battle (1685) in which Monmouth, who had landed on the Dorset coast as champion of the Protestant party, was defeated by James II's troops. Monmouth himself was captured, and was executed soon afterwards.

**Ségou** /ˈseɪguː/ a port on the Niger River in central Mali; pop. (1976) 64,890. Formerly the capital of the Bambara kingdom, it is the administrative centre of Ségou region and the focal point of a major irrigation project initiated by the French in 1932.

**Segovia** /səˈɡəʊvɪə/ an ancient city in north-central Spain, on the Eresma River in the Sierra Guadarrama; pop. (1991) 58,060. Formerly a favourite residence of the kings of Castile, it is the capital of the province of Segovia in the Castilla-León region. Its chief landmarks are a Roman aqueduct, a Moorish alcazar, and a 16th-c. Gothic cathedral. Its industries of flour milling, tanning, and pottery depend on local products.

**seif dunes** /seɪf/ the Arabic name for long, steep-sided sand dunes aligned across the desert in the direction of the prevailing wind, common in Libya and southern Iran. They range up to 90 m. (295 ft.) in height and up to 100 km. (62 miles) in length.

**Seikan Tunnel** /'seɪkən/ the world's longest underwater tunnel, linking the Japanese islands of Hokkaido and Honshu which are separated by the Tsungaru Strait. Completed in 1988, the tunnel is 51.7 km. (32.3 miles) in length.

**Seinäjoki** /semə'jɒkiː/ a commercial town and railway junction in western Finland, south-east of Vaasa; pop. (1990) 27,765. Developed after the founding of ironworks in 1798, many of its buildings are associated with the architect Alvar Aalto.

**Seine** /sem/ a river of northern France flowing 761 km. (473 miles) from its source on the limestone Plateau de Langres in Burgundy to the English Channel near Le Havre. It drains a region of northern France known as the Paris Basin and the cities of Troyes, Paris, and Rouen lie along its course.

**Seine-et-Marne** /-eɪ mɑːn/ a department to the east of Paris in the Ile-de-France region of northern France; area 5,917 sq. km. (2,285 sq. miles); pop. (1990) 1,078,170; capital, Melun.

**Seine-Maritime** /-mærɪ'tiːm/ a department of Upper Normandy in north-west France; area 6,254 sq. km. (2,416 sq. miles); pop. (1990) 1,223,430; capital, Rouen. It was known as Seine-Inférieure until 1955.

**Seine-Saint-Denis** /-sædə'niː/ a department to the north of Paris in the Ile-de-France region of northern France; area 236 sq. km. (91 sq. miles); pop. (1990) 1,381,200; capital, Bobigny.

**seismology** /saɪz'mɒlədʒɪ/ the scientific study and recording of earthquakes and related phenomena.

**Seixal** /seɪ'ʃɑːl/ an industrial town in Setúbal district, Portugal, situated on the south side of Lisbon Bay; pop. (1991) 2,620.

**Sekondi-Takoradi** /sə,kɒndi: tækə'rɑːdɪ/ a joint urban area, the capital of the Western Province of Ghana, a seaport and naval base on the Gulf of Guinea; pop. (1984) 615,000. See TAKORADI.

**Selangor** /sə'læŋgə(r)/ a state of Malaysia, on the west coast of the Malay peninsula; area 7,956 sq. km. (3,073 sq. miles); pop. (1990) 1,978,000; capital, Shah Alam.

**Selborne** /'selbɔːn/ a village in Hampshire, southern England, the birthplace of Gilbert White, the 18th-c. naturalist and author of the *Natural History of Selbourne*.

**Selby** /'selbɪ/ a town in North Yorkshire, England, situated on the River Ouse; pop. (1981) 12,300. It has a Norman abbey and a wooden toll bridge dating from 1790.

**Selebi-Phikwe** /,seɪleɪbi:'fiːkweɪ/ a mining town in eastern Botswana, to the south of Francistown; pop. (1991) 39,770. Founded after Botswana gained independence in 1966, it is the third-largest town in the country.

**Selenga** /sə'leŋgə/ a river of Asia that is formed in north-west Mongolia by the confluence of the Muren and Ider rivers. It flows 1,568 km. (980 miles) northwards through Ulan-Ude before entering Lake Baikal.

**Seleucid** /sɪ'luːsɪd/ the Hellenistic dynasty founded by Seleucus I Nicator, one of the generals of Alexander the Great, ruling over Syria and a great part of western Asia 312–64 BC. Its capital was at Antioch.

**Seljuk** /'seldʒʊk/ a Turkish dynasty which ruled Asia Minor in the 11th–13th c., successfully invading the Byzantine Empire and defending the Holy Land against the Crusaders.
**Seljukian** *adj. & n.*

**Selkirkshire** /'selkɜːkʃaɪr/ a former county in the Scottish Borders, from 1975 to 1996 included in the Ettrick and Lauderdale District of Borders Region. Its county town was Selkirk.

**Sellafield** /'selə,fiːld/ an industrial site near the coast of Cumbria, north-west England, formerly the site of a Royal Ordnance Factory and now belonging to British Nuclear Fuels. It was the scene in 1957 of a fire which caused a serious escape of radioactivity. The site was known as Windscale between 1947 and 1981.

**selvas** /'selvəs/ a name given to the equatorial rainforest of the Amazon basin in South America.

**Semarang** /sə'mɑːræŋ/ a commercial city and capital of the province of Central Java, Indonesia; pop. (1990) 1,249,200. Ceded to the Dutch in 1677, it was formerly the seat of the Dutch governor of the North-East Provinces. Once the leading port of Indonesia, its harbour gradually silted up. The northern harbour area is the city's commercial centre, while the hillier southern district (called Candi) is a residential quarter. It has shipbuilding and textile industries.

**Semeru** /sə'meru:/ (also **Mahemeru**) a volcanic peak at the eastern end of the Indonesian island of Java. Rising to a height of 3,676 m. (12,060 ft.) from the Bromo-Semeru massif, it is the highest mountain on the island.

**Semey** /sə'meɪ/ (formerly **Semipalatinsk**) a city in Kazakhstan, Central Asia, on the Irtysh River; pop. (1990) 338,800. It is a river port and terminus on the Turkistan-Siberia railway with industries that include food processing, engineering, ship repair, and the manufacture of textiles.

**Seminole** /'semɪnəʊl/ a North American Indian tribe of the Muskogean linguisitic group, originally a branch of the Creek tribe who migrated from Georgia to Florida in the 18th c. Most were resettled in Oklahoma in the 19th c. Today they number *c.* 14,000.

**Semipalatinsk** /sjɪ,miːpəl'jɑːtɪnsk/ the former name of SEMEY .

**Semite** /'siːmaɪt, 'sem-/ any of the peoples supposed to be descended from Shem, son of Noah (Genesis 10: 21 ff.), including especially the Jews, Arabs, Assyrians, and Phoenicians.

**Semitic** /sɪ'mɪtɪk/ a family of languages that includes Hebrew, Arabic, and Aramaic, and certain ancient languages such as Phoenician, Assyrian, and Babylonian. They are closely related both in structure and in vocabulary. Almost all Semitic words are derived from verbs consisting of three consonants.

**Semmering Pass** /'zemərɪŋ/ a mountain pass crossing the eastern Alps on the frontier between the Austrian states of Styria and Lower Austria. Rising to 980 m. (3,215 ft.), the alpine road passes through the winter sports resort of Semmering. The Semmeringbahn (1848–54), the first major mountain railway in Europe, crosses 16 deep gorges and passes through 15 tunnels.

**Sendai** /sen'daɪ/ an industrial city and educational centre of Japan, capital of Tohoku region and largest city of northern Honshu Island; pop. (1990) 918,000. It was founded *c.* 1600 around the Aoba-jo (Green Leaf Castle) built by the feudal lord Masamune Date. It has major oil refining and foodstuffs industries. It has many universities, colleges, institutes, and government offices.

**Seneca** /'senəkæ/ a subgroup of the Iroquois North American Indian people of New York State, USA, one of the Iroquois League or Five Nations of the Iroquois.

**Senegal**
/,senɪ'gɔːl/ official name **The Republic of Senegal** a country on the west coast of Africa, with the River Senegal as its northern boundary and the Gambia forming a narrow  strip within its territory; area 196,722 sq. km. (75,984 sq. miles); pop. (est. 1991) 7,632,000; official language, French; capital, Dakar. Most of the country is savanna or semidesert, but in the southeast plateaus rise to 500 m. (1,640 ft.) to form the foothills of the Fouta Djallon Mountains. The south-west is characterized by marshy swamps interspersed with tropical rainforest. There is a wet season between June and October. Lacking natural resources and vulnerable to droughts, over 70 per cent of the population of Senegal is rural.

Agriculture is concentrated in the Senegal and Casamance river basins where food crops such as rice, millet, sorghum, and corn are grown. The country's chief exports are groundnuts, seafood, and rock phosphate. Part of the Mali empire in the 14th and 15th c., the area was colonized by the French in the second half of the 19th c. Senegal became part of French West Africa in 1895, a member of the French community in 1958, and part of the Federation of Mali in 1959 before becoming an independent republic in 1960. Armed insurrection by a separatist group in the southern Casamance region increased during the early 1990s. Senegal is a multiparty democracy with a unicameral legislative National Assembly and executive power vested in the President who appoints a Council of Ministers. **Senegalese** *adj. & n.*

**Senegal** a river of West Africa, formed in Mali at the junction of the Bafing and Bakoy rivers which rise in the Fouta Djallon massif of northern Guinea. It flows 1,088 km. (680 miles) north and then west along the Senegal–Mauritania frontier before entering the Atlantic Ocean at Saint-Louis. Above Kayes there are numerous rapids and waterfalls, the chief being the Gouina and Felou falls.

**Sensuntepeque** /sensuːntɪ'peɪkeɪ/ a market town in northern El Salvador, the capital of the department of Cabañas; pop. (1980) 50,450.

**Senussi** /se'nuːsɪ/ a Muslim religious fraternity founded in Libya in 1837 by Sidi Mohammad ibn Ali es-Senussi.

**Seoul** /səʊl/ the capital of The Republic of Korea, on the Han River; pop. (1990) 10,627,790. It was the capital of the Korean Yi dynasty from the late 14th c. until 1910, when Korea was annexed by Japan. Extensively developed under Japanese rule, it became capital of South Korea in 1945. Largely rebuilt since its destruction during the Korean War, its chief landmarks are the Namsan Tower, the Royal Ancestral Shrines, the 15th-c. Changdok Palace, and the Kyongbok Palace which houses the National Museum. It was the venue for the 1988 Olympic Games. It accounts for 50 per cent of South Korea's industrial output and is the country's financial and business centre. It has textile manufacturing, agricultural processing, railway repair works, tanneries, and many light industries.

**Sephardi** /sɪ'fɑːdɪ/ (*pl.* **Sephardim**) the name given to a Jew who had settled in Spain or Portugal and, following the expulsions of 1492, made his home in Holland, Greece, and Palestine.

**Sequoia National Park** /sɪ'kwɔɪə/ a national park in the Sierra Nevada, California, USA, established in 1890 to protect groves of giant redwood trees. Located within the park are Mt. Whitney (4,418 m., 14,495 ft.), the highest mountain in the US outside Alaska, and the General Sherman Tree which is the world's largest living tree (83 m., 272 ft. high; 11.2 m., 37 ft. diameter at its greatest girth).

**Seraing** /səˈræ/ an industrial town on the River Meuse in east Belgium, 7 km. (4 miles) south-west of Liège; pop. (1991) 60,840. The first locomotive in Europe was bult here at an ironworks established in 1817 by an Englishman, John Cockerill. The centre of Belgium's steel and heavy engineering industries, with one of the world's leading glass-making centres nearby.

**Serampore** /ˌsɜːrəmˈpɔː(r)/ (also **Serampur** or **Shrirampur**) a town in the state of West Bengal, east-central India, situated on the Hugli River opposite Barrackpore; pop. (1991) 137,090. Founded as a Danish settlement in 1799, it was originally known as Fredricnagore. Serampore College (1818) was the first Christian theological college in India. There is also a College of Textile Technology.

**Seram Sea** see CERAM SEA.

**Serb** /sɜːb/ a native of Serbia or a person of Serbian descent.

**Serbia** /ˈsɜːbɪə/ (Serbo-Croat **Srbija**) a Balkan republic which, with Montenegro, forms the remnant of the former six-member Federal Republic of Yugoslavia; area 88,361 sq. km. (34,129 sq. miles); pop. (1981) 9,313,700; capital, Belgrade. Serbia includes the nominally autonomous provinces of Vojvodina and Kosovo. An independent state as early as the 6th c., it was conquered by the Turks in the 14th c. With the decline of Ottoman power in the 19th c., the Serbs successfully pressed for independence, finally winning nationhood in 1878. Subsequent Serbian ambitions to found a South Slav nation state brought the country into rivalry with the Austro-Hungarian empire and eventually contributed to the outbreak of World War I. Despite early successes against the Austrians, Serbia was occupied by the Central Powers and was, after the end of hostilities, absorbed into the new state of Yugoslavia. With the secession of four out of the six republics from the collective state in 1991–2, Serbia struggled to retain the viability of Yugoslavia and found itself internationally isolated as a result of armed conflict with neighbouring Croatia, involvement in the civil war in Bosnia, and the suppression of Albanian nationalism in Kosovo. **Serbian** adj. & n.

**Serbo-Croat** /ˌsɜːbəʊˈkrəʊæt/ (also **Serbo-Croatian** /-krəʊˈeɪʃ(ə)n/) the language of the Serbs and Croats, generally considered to be one language (the differences between Serbian and Croatian are cultural rather than linguistic). Serbian is spoken by 10 million Serbs who belong to the Eastern Orthodox religion and so use the Cyrillic alphabet; Croat is spoken by five million Croats who are Roman Catholic and use the Roman alphabet.

**Seremban** /seɪrəmˈbɑːn/ the capital of the Malaysian state of Negeri Sembilan, situated at the southern end of the Malay peninsula to the south of Kuala Lumpur; pop. (1980) 132,900. Originally known as Sungei Ujong, it was founded in the early 19th c. by Chinese merchants who exported tin down the Sungei Linggi River to the sea, and is the commercial centre of the rubber-growing and tin-mining area.

**Serengeti** /ˌserənˈgetɪ/ a vast plain lying to the west of the Great Rift Valley in Tanzania. In 1951 a national park was created to protect large numbers of migrating wildebeest, zebra, and Thomson's gazelle.

**Sergipe** /sɜːˈʒiːpeɪ/ a state on the Atlantic coast of north-east Brazil; area 21,994 sq. km. (8,495 sq. miles); pop. (1991) 1,491,870; capital, Aracajú.

**Sergiyev Posad** /ˈsɜːgiːjev pəˈsɑːd/ an industrial town in western Russia, north-east of Moscow; pop. (1990) 115,000. Its 16th-c. Uspenski Cathedral is the burial place of Boris Godunov (1552–1605).

**Seria** /ˈsɜːrɪə/ an oil port on the coast of Brunei with a deep-water tanker terminal; pop. (1988) 23,415. The onshore Seria oilfield was discovered in 1929 but its production is now surpassed by off-shore fields.

**Serowe** /seˈrəʊwɪ/ a market town in eastern Botswana, the largest of the traditional village settlements in the country; pop. (1991) 30,260. It was the birthplace of Sir Seretse Khama, first president of Botswana.

**Serpukhov** /sɜːˈpuːkəf/ an industrial (textiles) city in western Russia, south of Moscow; pop. (1990) 144,000.

**Sérres** /ˈsæreɪs/ (also **Sérrai**, the ancient **Siris**) a leading market town of Macedonia in north-east Greece, capital of Sérres department; pop. (1981) 45,210. It was known to the Turks as Siruz from 1383 to 1913 and was a capital of Serbia in the 14th c.

**sertão** /sɜːˈtaʊn/ the name given to the semiarid interior of north-eastern Brazil, characterized by thorny scrub vegetation.

**Servian Wall** /ˈsɜːvɪən/ the wall said to have been built round Rome by Servius Tullius, the semi-legendary sixth king of ancient Rome (6th c. BC).

**Sesotho** /seˈsuːtuː/ a Bantu language spoken by members of the Sotho people, one of the official languages of Lesotho in southern Africa.

**Sète** /set/ a leading Mediterranean port in the department of Hérault, Languedoc-Roussillon, southern France; pop. (1990) 41,920. It is a major fishing and trading port with oil refineries and industries producing chemicals and textiles. The poet Paul Valéry (1871–1945) is buried here.

**Sétif** /seɪˈtiːf/ a city in north-eastern Algeria, capital of Sétif department; pop. (1989) 187,000. Built on the ruins of Roman Sitifis, it is a commercial centre for textiles, grain, and phosphates. It is one of Algeria's highest places at 1,096 m. (3,595 ft.). In 1959 a rich Roman necropolis was discovered near the town centre.

**Seto** /'seɪtəʊ/ a city in Aichi prefecture, central Honshu Island, Japan, noted for its ceramics since the 13th c.; pop. (1990) 126,340.

**Setswana** a variation of TSWANA (and the preferred form for the language).

**Setúbal** /sə'tu:b(ə)l/ **1.** a district of Estremadura in south-central Portugal to the south of the River Tagus; area 5,064 sq. km. (1,956 sq. miles); pop. (est. 1989) 817,900. The district is noted for the production of sweet white wine. **2.** its capital, a port and industrial town on the Bay of Setúbal at the mouth of the Sado River; pop. (1991) 83,550. Shipbuilding, fish canning, and the manufacture of vehicles and domestic appliances are among its chief industries.

**Sevastopol** see SEBASTOPOL.

**Seven Dials** a district in the West End of London, England, to the east of Soho. It takes its name from a pillar with seven clock faces that once stood at the junction of seven streets. It had a notorious reputation for its poverty and its thieves.

**Sevenoaks** a residential town in the North Downs of Kent, south-east England; pop. (1981) 24,600. The 'seven oaks', after which it was named, were finally blown down during a gale in 1987.

**Seven Wonders of the World** the seven most spectacular man-made structures of the ancient world. The earliest extant list of these dates from the 2nd c.; traditionally they comprise (1) the pyramids of Egypt, especially those at Giza; (2) the Hanging Gardens of Babylon; (3) the Mausoleum of Halicarnassus; (4) the temple of Diana (Artemis) at Ephesus in Asia Minor, rebuilt in 656 BC, measuring 90 × 45 m. (300 × 150 ft.) and with 127 columns; (5) the Colossus of Rhodes; (6) the huge ivory and gold statue of Zeus at Olympia in the Peloponnese, made by Phidias c. 430 BC; (7) the Pharos of Alexandria (or in some lists, the walls of Babylon).

**Severn** /'sevɜ:n/ the longest river of Britain, rising on Mount Plynlimon in eastern Wales and flowing about 320 km. (200 miles) to the Bristol Channel. It is crossed by the Severn Bridge (1966).

**Severnaya Zemlya** /ˌsevərnə'ja: 'zemli:jə/ a group of islands in the Arctic Ocean to the north of the Taymyr peninsula in Siberian Russia. Uninhabited except for weather and radar stations.

**Severodonetsk** /ˌsevərəʊdə'netsk/ a city in south-east Ukraine, north-west of Lugansk; pop. (1990) 132,000.

**Severodvinsk** /ˌsevərɒd'vɪnsk/ a city in northern Russia, situated to the west of Archangel on the White Sea and at the mouth of the Northern Dvina River; pop. (1990) 250,000.

**Seville** /se'vɪl/ (Spanish **Sevilla** /se'vi:ljə/) a port and industrial city in southern Spain, on the Guadalquivir River; pop. (1991) 683,490. It is capital of Andalusia and was the venue in 1992 for the EXPO '92 Universal Exhibition. The artists Murillo (1618–82) and Velasquez (1599–1660) were born in the city and Christopher Columbus is reputedly buried in the 15th-c. Gothic cathedral. Wines, fruit, olives, and cork are exported. Arms and explosives, textiles, machinery, and chemicals are manufactured. Seville is the capital of bullfighting in Spain. It gives its name to a bitter orange used to make marmalade.

**Sèvres** /seɪvr/ a suburb of south-west Paris, France, on the edge of the Saint-Cloud park; pop. (1990) 22,060. It is the site of the French National Ceramics Museum which tells the story of the famous Sèvres porcelain that was first made at a factory founded in 1738 in the Château de Vincennes, east of Paris. This factory moved to Sèvres in 1756 and three years later was purchased by Louis XV to save it from closure; thereafter it became a subsidized royal venture, and its pieces display an opulence matching court life. In 1793 the French Republic took over the factory; it created a sophisticated style at the beginning of the 19th c., but the great designs faded and the factory took to producing copies of the 18th-c. wares.

**Seward Peninsula** /'sju:əd/ a peninsula at the western extremity of Alaska, extending into the Bering Strait and separating Kotzebue Sound in the north from Norton Sound in the south. Its western tip, Cape Prince of Wales, is the westernmost point on the continent of North America. The peninsula is named in honour of US Secretary of State, William H. Seward (1801–72), who negotiated the purchase of Alaska from the Russians in 1867 for the sum of $7.2 million. Largely mountainous or covered in tundra vegetation its chief fur-trading and gold-mining settlements are Nome, Teller, Wales, and Shishmaref.

**Seychelles** /seɪ'ʃelz/ official name **The Republic of Seychelles** a country in the Indian Ocean, a member-state of the Commonwealth, consisting of a group of about 115 islands  scattered over 1,374,000 sq. km. (530,700 sq. miles) of the south-west Indian Ocean; land area 453 sq. km. (175 sq. miles); pop. (est. 1991) 69,000; official language, Creole (English and French are also widely spoken); capital, Victoria (on Mahé Island). The three principal inhabited islands of the Seychelles, which lie within a group of 41 volcanic islands to the north-east, include Mahé, Praslin, and La Digue. To the south-west lie coral islands and atolls including Aldabra. The islands are said to have been named the 'Isles of Gold' by visiting Arab seafarers, perhaps in the 9th c. The Portuguese, who arrived there in the 16th c., called them the 'Seven Sisters', by which name they were known until the French annexed and settled them in the mid-18th c. They formed an excellent hide-out for pirates until these were hunted down by the British and French. The Seychelles were captured by Britain during the Napoleonic Wars and administered from Mauritius before becoming a separate colony in 1903 and finally an independent republic in 1976. Noted for their beauty, the islands have attracted a considerable tourist trade since the opening of an international airport on Mahé in 1971; the economy is also supported by exports of fish, copra, and cinnamon. The country is governed by an executive President and a unicameral People's Assembly which legalized the activities of opposition parties in 1991.

**Seychellois** /ˌseɪʃel'wɑː/ *adj. & n.*

**Seyhan** /seɪ'hɑːn/ a river of southern Turkey that rises in the Anti-Taurus Mountains and flows southwards through Cilicia for 560 km. (350 miles), passing through the city of Adana before entering the Mediterranean Sea east of Mersin.

**Sfax** /sfæks/ (Arabic **Safaqis**) a seaport on the east coast of Tunisia; pop. (1984) 231,900. The city, which is the second-largest in Tunisia, is a major centre of phosphate processing and the production of olive oil.

**s-'Gravenhage** see THE HAGUE.

**Shaanxi** /ʃɑːn'ʃiː/ (formerly **Shensi** /ʃen'siː/) a mountainous province of north-central China to the south of Inner Mongolia; area 195,800 sq. km. (75,628 sq. miles); pop. (1990) 32,882,000; capital, Xian. Dominated by the loess plateau in the north, the south of the province is densely populated and fertile, producing wheat, maize, tea, and sugar cane. It is the site of the earliest settlements of the ancient Chinese civilizations.

**Shaba** /'ʃɑːbə/ a copper-mining region of south-east Zaire; area 496,965 sq. km. (191,952 sq. miles); pop. (1984) 3,874,000; capital, Lubumbashi. It was known as Elizabethville (1935–47) and Katanga (1947–72). In 1993 the province, whose attempted secession had precipitated a civil war in 1960, again declared its autonomy from the rest of Zaire and reverted to its old name, Katanga.

**Shah Alam** /ʃɑː ə'lɑːm/ the capital of the Malaysian state of Selangor, situated on the Malay peninsula between Kuala Lumpur and Port Klang; pop. (1980) 24,140. Its chief landmark is the Sultan Salahuddin Abdul Aziz Shah Mosque (1988), the largest mosque in South-East Asia.

**Shakhty** /'ʃɑːxtiː/ a city in southern Russia, situated northeast of Rostov and north of the River Don; pop. (1990) 227,000. Founded in 1829, it is a major centre of anthracite coal-mining.

**shan** /ʃɑːn/ a Chinese word for a mountain range.

**Shan** /ʃɑːn/ a people of the Shan Plateau in eastern Burma speaking a language closely related to Thai and Lao. The second-largest ethnic minority in Burma, they total about ten per cent of the country's population and are chiefly located in Shan

State where a separatist movement has engaged in guerrilla activities against the central government.

**Shandong** /ʃæn'dʊŋ/ (formerly **Shantung** /ʃæn'tʊŋ/) a province of eastern China on the Yellow Sea; area 153,300 sq. km. (59,212 sq. miles); pop. (1990) 84,893,000; capital, Jinan. A leading industrial and agricultural province, its chief products are maize, wheat, cotton, fruit, vegetables, tobacco, livestock, and silk. The **Shandong Peninsula**, which is the largest peninsula in China, was designated a special economic development zone in 1988. It gives its name to a soft, undressed Chinese silk known as shantung.

**Shang** /ʃæŋ/ the name of a dynasty which ruled China during part of the 2nd millennium BC, probably 16th–11th c. BC. The discovery of inscriptions on more than 100,000 tortoise shells confirmed literary references to the existence of the Shang dynasty, which witnessed the perfection of the wheel, the use of chariots in warfare, bronze casting, and the carving of jade and ivory.

**Shanghai** /ʃæŋ'haɪ/ a port on the estuary of the Yangtze River, the largest city in China; pop. (1990) 7,780,000. Formerly an enclave for western traders, Shanghai is now the country's leading industrial centre and gateway to the great Yangtze basin of central China. Its chief industries include shipbuilding, oil refining and the manufacture of textiles, electronics, bicycles, radios, and televisions. The port of Shanghai handles the major share of China's foreign and coastwise trade. The USA, Great Britain, and France renounced their claims to foreign zones within the city in 1943–6. Shanghai, next to Peking, is China's leading educational centre with universities, learned societies, research institutes, theatres, and an astronomical observatory.

**Shangqiu** /ʃæŋ'kjuː/ a city in north-east Henan province, eastern China, south-east of Zhengzhou; pop. (1986) 205,000.

**Shangrao** /ʃæŋ'graʊ/ a city in Jiangxi province, south-eastern China, east of Nanchang; pop. (1986) 145,000.

**Shangri La** /ˌʃæŋgrɪ 'lɑː/ a Tibetan utopia in James Hilton's novel *Lost Horizon* (1933), often used to describe an earthly paradise, a place of retreat from the worries of modern civilization (Tibetan *la* = mountain pass). Shangri La was the name originally given to the official country home of US presidents in the Appalachian Mountains, later renamed Camp David by President Eisenhower.

**Shankill Road** the main road passing through a Protestant stronghold of Belfast in Northern Ireland. It runs parallel to the predominantly Catholic Falls Road which lies to the north.

**Shannon** /'ʃænən/ the chief river of Ireland, flowing 390 km. (240 miles) southwards through Lough Allen, Lough Ree and Lough Derg to its estuary on the Atlantic coast between Co. Clare and Co. Limerick.

**Shansi** see SHANXI.

**Shantou** /ʃæn'taʊ/ (formerly **Swatow**) a port in Guangdong province, south-east China, situated on the South China Sea at the mouth of the Han River; pop. (1990) 860,000. Designated a special economic zone in 1980, its chief industries include fishing, shipbuilding, and the manufacture of chemicals, textiles, and electronic goods.

**Shantung** see SHANDONG.

**Shanxi** /ʃæn'ʃiː/ (formerly **Shansi** /ʃæn'siː/) a province of north-central China, on the eastern edge of the loess plateau to the south of Inner Mongolia; area 157,100 sq. km. (60,680 sq. miles); pop. (1990) 28,759,000; capital, Taiyuan. Wheat, maize, sorghum, coal, and chemical fertilizers are the chief products.

**Shaoguan** /ʃaʊ'gwaːn/ a city in Guangdong province, southern China, on the Bei River north of Guangzhou (Canton); pop. (1986) 696,000.

**Shaoshan** /ʃaʊ'ʃaːn/ a village in Xiangtan county, Hunan province, China, birthplace in 1894 of the Chinese leader Mao Zedong.

**Shaowu** /ʃaʊ'wuː/ a city in Jiangxi province, south-east China, on the Futun River south-east of Nanchang; pop. (1986) 269,000.

**Shaoxing** /ʃaʊ'ʃɪŋ/ a marketing city in Zhejiang province, eastern China, on the Grand Canal south-east of Hangzhou; pop. (1986) 1,091,000. Silk textiles, handicrafts, and rice wine are local productions.

**Shaoyang** /ʃaʊ'jæŋ/ a city in Hunan province, south-east-central China, south-west of Changsha; pop. (1986) 475,000. It is a centre of coal- and iron-mining.

**Shari** /'ʃaːrɪ/ (also **Chari**) a river in central Africa, formed at the junction of the Gubingui and Bamingui rivers on the border between Chad and the Central African Republic. It flows north-westwards for 944 km. (590 miles) before entering Lake Chad and its total length to the head of the Bamingui is 1,060 km. (660 miles). It is the longest river of interior drainage in Africa.

**Sharjah** /'ʃaːdʒə/ (Arabic **Ash-Shariqah** /ˌæʃaːˈriːkə/) **1.** the third-largest of the member-states of the United Arab Emirates, comprising three enclaves on the Gulf of Oman coast (Khor Fakkan, Dibba Hisn, and Kalba); area 2,600 sq. km. (1,000 sq. miles); pop. (1985) 268,720. It has for centuries been a home base for the trading Qawasim tribe whose fleet was destroyed by the British in 1819. Oil and gas have been exploited since their discovery in the early 1970s and industries also produce petrochemicals, steel products, and cement. **2.** its capital city, a port on the Khaled Lagoon (Port Khaled) and site of the Sharjah Expo Centre; pop. (1984) 125,000.

**Sharon** /'ʃeərən/ a fertile coastal plain in Israel between Haifa and Tel Aviv and between the Mediterranean Sea and the hills of Samaria; area 347 sq. km. (134 sq. miles).

**Sharpeville** /'ʃaːpvɪl/ a South African township near Vereeniging in southern Transvaal, scene of an incident on 21 March 1960 when security forces fired on a crowd demonstrating against apartheid laws, killing 67 Black Africans and wounding about 180.

**Shashi** /ʃaː'ʃiː/ a city in Hubei province, east-central China, on the Yangtze River west of Wuhan; pop. (1986) 558,000. It is an important trade centre.

**Shasta** /'ʃæstə/, **Mount** a dormant volcano rising to 4,317 m. (14,163 ft.) in the Cascade Range in northern California, USA.

**Shatt al-Arab** /ʃæt æl 'ærəb/ (Iranian **Arvand River**) a river of south-east Iraq, formed by the confluence of the Tigris and Euphrates rivers, flowing about 195 km. (120 miles) south-east to the Persian Gulf. It is an important access route to the oil ports of Iran and Iraq between which it forms an international boundary. (Arabic = river of Arabia).

**Shawnee** /'ʃɔːniː/ a North American Indian tribe, the southernmost of the Algonquian speaking peoples, originally living in the Tennessee River valley but later occupying reservations in Oklahoma.

**Shcherbakov** /ʃɜːˈbaːkɒf/ a former name (1946–57) of Rybinsk.

**Sheba** /'ʃiːbə/ the Biblical name of Saba, an ancient country in south-west Arabia, famous for its trade in gold, frankincense, and spices. The Queen of Sheba visited King Solomon in Jerusalem. The Hebrew word is the name of the people (Sabaeans), but was erroneously assumed by Greek and Roman writers to be a place name.

**Sheerness** /ʃɪə'nes/ a town and ferry port on the Isle of Sheppey in Kent, south-east England; pop. (1981) 11,080. A naval dockyard until 1960, it has a ferry link with the Netherlands.

**Sheffield** /'ʃefɪəld/ an industrial city in South Yorkshire, England, on the River Don; pop. (1991) 500,500. From medieval times it was noted for metal-working, and became famous especially for the manufacture of cutlery and silverware and, after the establishment of a works by Henry Bessemer, for the production of steel and steel goods including tools and machinery. It is the site of the University of Sheffield (1905) and Sheffield Hallam University (formerly Sheffield Polytechnic).

**Shelta** /'ʃeltə/ an ancient hybrid secret language used by Irish gypsies and pipers, Irish and Welsh travelling tinkers, etc. It is composed partly of Irish or Gaelic words, mostly disguised by inversion or by arbitrary alteration of initial consonants.

**Shenandoah** /ˌʃenən'dəʊə/ a river of West Virginia and Virginia, USA, which rises in head-streams (the **North Fork** and the **South Fork**) on both sides of the Blue Ridge Mountains and flows about 240 km. (150 miles) to enter the Potomac River at Harpers Ferry. The Shenandoah valley was an important route in the westward pioneer movement. The **Shenandoah National Park**, situated in the Blue Ridge Mountains to the south-east of the Shenandoah River, was established in 1935.

**Shensi** see SHAANXI.

**Shenyang** /ʃenˈjæŋ/ (formerly **Mukden** /ˈmʊkd(ə)n/) the fourth-largest city in China, an important Manchu city between the 17th and early 20th centuries and now the capital of Liaoning province; pop. (1990) 4,500,000. It lies at the hub of the densest railway network in China and is a major industrial centre producing machine tools and mining equipment.

**Shenzhen** /ʃenˈzen/ an industrial city developed as a special economic zone near Canton in Guangdong province, southern China; pop. (1986) 335,000.

**Shepherd's Bush** a residential district of west London, England, to the west of Kensington. The BBC Television Centre has been located here since 1960.

**Shepparton** /ˈʃepɜːtən/ a city in central Victoria, Australia, situated in the fruit-growing and wine-producing Goulburn Valley 180 km. (113 miles) north of Melbourne; pop. (1991) 30,510 (with Mooroopna).

**Sheppey** /ˈʃepɪ/, **Isle of** a fertile island at the mouth of the River Thames in south-east England, separated from the coast of Kent by The Swale, a narrow strait.

**Sherbrooke** /ˈʃɜːbruːk/ an industrial city in southern Quebec, Canada, situated at the junction of the Magog and St. Francis rivers east of Montreal; pop. (1991) 76,400; 139,190 (metropolitan area). It was named in honour of Lord Shelbrooke who was Governor General of Canada (1816–18). It has textile, mining machinery, rubber, and leather industries.

**Sherpa** /ˈʃɜːpə/ a Himalayan people living on the borders of Nepal and Tibet, and skilled in mountaineering.

**'s-Hertogenbosch** /ˌseətʊxenˈbɒs/ (French **Bois-le-Duc** /ˌbwaːləˈduːk/) a city in the Netherlands, at the junction of the Aa and Dommel rivers; pop. (1991) 92,060. It is the capital of North Brabant and was the birthplace (c.1460) of the artist Hieronymus Bosch. Its cathedral dates from the 11th c. and it has the country's largest Catholic church.

**Sherwood Forest** /ˈʃɜːwuːd/ the remnants, near Ollerton, of a once large forest that extended over Nottinghamshire, central England and forever associated with the legends of Robin Hood. Part of the forest is now protected within a country park that contains some of the oldest and largest oaks in Britain.

**Shetland** /ˈʃetlənd/ an Islands Area of Scotland consisting of the Shetland Islands, a group of about

100 islands north-east of the Orkneys (the principal islands are Mainland, Yell, Unst, and Fetlar); area 1,433 sq. km. (553 sq. miles); pop. (1991) 22,020; administrative headquarters, Lerwick. The islands were settled by Norsemen in the 9th c. and became Scottish only in 1472. They are noted for the production of textiles (especially hand knitwear) and have become an important base for the exploitation of oil and gas in the North Sea, the oil terminal at Sullom Voe being the largest in Europe. The islands are linked by ferries, and by sea and air to the mainland of Scotland. Tourism is now an important industry.
**Shetlander** n.

**Shevchenko** /ʃevˈtʃeŋkəʊ/ see AQTAU.

**Shia** /ˈʃiːə/ (also **Shiah**) one of the two main branches of Islam that rejects the first three Sunni Caliphs and regards Ali as Muhammad's first successor. The Shiites followed a succession of imams, whom they believed to possess a Divine Light giving them special wisdom in matters of the faith and community of believers. The more orthodox Sunnis did not recognize Shi'ism as a legitimate school of Islam until 1959. Shia Muslims number c.90 million worldwide and are dominant in Iran, Iraq, Bahrain, and parts of Lebanon.
**Shiite** adj. & n.

**Shibin el Kom** /ʃɪˌbiːn el ˈkɒm/ a market and cotton-processing town in northern Egypt, in the Nile delta, north-west of Cairo; pop. (1991) 153,000.

**shieling** /ˈʃiːlɪŋ/ the name given to the summer pastures at a distance from the farmsteading once occupied in Scotland during the summer months.

**Shihezi** /ʃɪˈheɪzɪ/ a city in Xinjiang autonomous region, north-west China, in the northern foothills of the Tien Shan Mountains west of Urumqi; pop. (1986) 546,000.

**Shijiazhuang** /ˌʃiːdʒɪəˈdʒwæŋ/ (formerly **Shihchiachuang**) a city and transportation centre in north-east-central China, capital of Hebei province; pop. (1990) 1,320,000. Coal, iron ore, limestone and marble are mined nearby and local industries produce textiles and pharmaceuticals. It was known as Shimen (1947–9).

**Shikoku** /ʃɪˈkəʊkuː/ the smallest of the four main islands of Japan, comprising the prefectures of Ehime, Kagawa, Kochi, and Tokushima; area 18,795 sq. km. (7,260 sq. miles); pop. (1990) 4,195,000; chief city, Matsuyama. Its highest peak is Ishizuchi (1,980 m., 6,496 ft.).

**Shillong** /ʃɪˈlɒŋ/ the capital of the state of Meghalaya in north-east India, situated at an altitude of 1,500 m. (4,920 ft.) in the Khasi Hills near the northern border of Bangladesh; pop. (1991) 222,270. Under British rule it was a popular hill station.

**Shiloh** /ˈʃaɪləʊ/ the site of a national military park in the US state of Tennessee, scene of the first major battle of General U. S. Grant's campaign to control the Mississippi River during the American Civil War.

**shima** /ˈʃiːmə/ (also **jima** /ˈdʒiːmə/) a Japanese word for an island.

**Shimbiris** /ʃɪmˈbɪrɪs/ a mountain rising to a height of 2,416 m. (7,926 ft.) in the northern highlands of Somalia, the highest peak in the country.

**Shimizu** /ʃɪˈmiːzuː/ a city in Shizuoka prefecture, east-central Honshu Island, Japan, a port on Suruga Bay; pop. (1990) 241,520. A fishing and canning centre.

**Shimoga** /ʃɪˈməʊɡə/ a city in Karnataka, southern India, in the Western Ghats, north-west of Bangalore; pop. (1991) 192,650. It is the trading centre for local timber and rice.

**Shimonoseki** /ˌʃiːməʊnəʊˈseɪki/ an industrial city in Yamaguchi prefecture, south-west Honshu Island, Japan, a port and fishing centre on the Shimonoseki Strait; pop. (1990) 262,640. The Treaty ending the Sino-Japanese War was signed here in 1895. It has shipyards, engineering works, and metal and chemical plants.

**Shinto** /ˈʃɪntəʊ/ a Japanese religion revering ancestors and nature-spirits and embodying the beliefs and attitudes that are in accordance with this. The name was applied to the indigenous polytheistic religion of Japan of the 6th c. AD to distinguish it from Buddhism. Its oral traditions are recorded in the *Kojiki* (Records of Ancient Matters) and *Nihon Shoki* (Chronicles of Japan), both written c.712–20. Central to the religion is the belief in sacred power (*kami*) in both animate and inanimate things; in its mythology the sun-goddess was the ancestress of the imperial household. Shinto became closely associated with the State, a position that it held until after World War II, when it was disestablished and the Emperor Hirohito disavowed his claim to divine descent. There are over 3 million Shintoists in the world, nearly all in Japan.

**Shiraz** /ʃɪəˈræz/ a city in the Zagros Mountains of south-west-central Iran, capital of Fars province; pop. (1991) 965,800. It was a leading city of the medieval Islamic world and capital of Iran from 1753 to 1794. An important cultural centre since the 4th c. BC, the city is noted for the school of miniature painting based there between the 14th and 16th centuries, and for the manufacture of carpets. The surrounding area is noted for its wine, the city lending its name to a variety of grape.

**Shire** /ˈʃiːreɪ/ a river that flows from Lake Malawi (Nyasa) in Malawi southwards for 400 km. (250 miles) into Mozambique where it joins the Zambezi River. The **Shire Highlands** are a fertile plateau east of the river producing tea, tobacco, and tung oil.

**Shishou** /ʃiːˈʃəʊ/ a city in Hubei province, east-central China, on the Yangtze River east of Jinshi; pop. (1986) 558,000.

**Shiyan** /ʃiːˈjɑːn/ a city in northern Hubei province, east-central China, in the Wudang Shan Mts. west of the Danjiangkou Reservoir; pop. (1986) 338,000.

**Shizuishan** /ʃiːzʊɪˈʃɑːn/ a city in Inner Mongolia, northern China, between the Yellow River and the Helan Shan Mts. north of Yinchuan; pop. (1986) 543,000.

**Shizuoka** /ʃɪˈzuːɒkɑː/ the capital of Shizuoka prefecture, east-central Honshu Island, Japan, a port on Suruga Bay; pop. (1990) 472,200. It is the centre of an industrial zone with shipbuilding, petrochemicals, and fruit-canning industries.

**Shköder** see SCUTARI.

**Sholapur** /ˌʃəʊləˈpʊə(r)/ (also **Solapur**) a city on the Deccan Plateau of western India, a cotton textile town in the state of Maharashtra between Madras and Bombay; pop. (1991) 620,500.

**Shona** /ˈʃəʊnə/ a group of Bantu people living in south-east Africa between the Indian Ocean and Botswana. About three-quarters of the people of Zimbabwe are Shona.

**Shortland Islands** /ˈʃɔːtlənd/ a group of volcanic islands in the Solomon Islands situated to the west of the island of Choiseul.

**Shoshone** /ʃəʊˈʃəʊnɪ/ a North American Indian tribe of the Uto-Aztecan linguistic group, originally occupying the Great Basin from the eastern Oregon desert to southern Colorado.

**Shotts** /ʃɒt/ see CHOTTS.

**Shreveport** /ˈʃriːvpɔːt/ an industrial city in north-west Louisiana, USA, on the Red River; pop. (1990) 198,525. It was founded by the steamboat captain Henry Miller Shreve in 1834. Oil and gas were discovered nearby in 1905 and industries produce timber, oil-field equipment, batteries, telephones, and vehicles.

**Shrewsbury** /ˈʃruːzbəri/ the county town of Shropshire in western England, on the River Severn; pop. (1981) 59,170. A former seat of the princes of Powys, it was absorbed into the kingdom of Mercia in the 8th century. It was the birthplace of Charles Darwin (1809–82) and Admiral John Benbow (1653–1702). It has many medieval buildings and light industries.

**Shropshire** /ˈʃrɒpʃɪə(r)/ a west-midland county of England; area 3,490 sq. km. (1,348 sq. miles); pop. (1991) 401,600; county town, Shrewsbury. Shropshire is divided into six districts:

| District | Area (sq. km.) | Pop. (1991) |
| --- | --- | --- |
| Bridgnorth | 634 | 49,700 |
| North Shropshire | 680 | 52,400 |
| Oswestry | 256 | 33,600 |
| Shrewsbury & Atcham | 602 | 90,900 |
| South Shropshire | 1,028 | 37,800 |
| The Wrekin | 290 | 137,100 |

**Shuangyashan** /ʃwæŋjə'ʃɑːn/ a city in Heilongjiang province, north-east China, north-east of Harbin and south of the Songhua River; pop. (1986) 434,000.

**Shubra el Kheima** /ʃə͵brɑː el 'keɪmə/ a northern suburb of Cairo in Egypt; pop. (1991) 812,000.

**Shumen** /'ʃuːmen/ (also **Shoumen** or **Choumen**) an industrial city in Varna district, north-east Bulgaria; pop. (1990) 126,350. The Romans built a fortress here on the site of a Thracian settlement and in subsequent years it maintained its role as part of the fortified quadrangle of Ruse-Silistra-Shumen-Varna. In the 19th c. it became a centre of Bulgarian national culture and home of Bulgaria's first orchestra and national theatre. The Tombul Mosque is the largest in the country. Shumen was known as Kolarovgrad 1950–65. It manufactures machinery, beer, and furniture.

**Shymkent** /ʃim'kent/ an industrial city in Kazakhstan, 145 km. (91 miles) north of Tashkent; pop. (1990) 438,000. Its industries include lead- and zinc-smelting, machinery, chemicals, and textiles.

**Siachen Glacier** /sɪ'ɑːtʃ(ə)n/ one of the world's longest glaciers, situated at an altitude of c. 5,500 m. (17,800 ft.) in the Karakoram Range of eastern Kashmir in north-west India. The occupation of the glacier by Indian troops in 1984 precipitated a high-altitude armed conflict between India and Pakistan.

**Sialkot** /sɪ'ɑːlkɒt/ an industrial city in Punjab province, Pakistan; pop. (1981) 296,000. Once noted for the manufacture of daggers and swords, its industries now produce sports goods, ceramics, surgical instruments, and rubber and plastic goods.

**Siam** /saɪ'æm/ the name until 1939 of Thailand.

**Siamese** /saɪə'miːz/ the language of Thailand, also called Thai.

**Siam, Gulf of** see THAILAND, GULF OF.

**Sian** see XIAN.

**Siauliai** /saʊ'leɪ/ a manufacturing town in northern Lithuania; pop. (1991) 150,000. It features among its attractions a Cats' Museum and a Museum of Bicycles. To the north is the Hill of Crosses, a Christian memorial kept alive during the years of Communist rule. It has railway repair works and tanneries.

**Šibenik** /ʃiː'benɪk/ (also **Shibenik**) a port and naval base on the Adriatic coast of Croatia, 48 km. (30 miles) north-west of Split; pop. (1991) 41,000.

**Siberia** /saɪ'bɪərɪə/ a region of Russia comprising the northern third of Asia and stretching from the Urals eastwards to the Pacific. It is physiographically divided into (1) the west Siberian lowland, a vast lowland area stretching from the Urals to the Yenisei River and mainly drained by the Ob and its tributaries the Irtysh and Tobol. This region contains some of the worlds largest swamps; (2) the central Siberian plateau, between the Yenisei and

Lena rivers; (3) North-east Siberia, which is thinly settled and comprises a series of mountain ranges to the east of the Lena; (4) Trans-Baikal (Baikalia), a region of high mountains and deep troughs that forms the watershed between the Pacific and the Arctic and includes Lake Baikal, the world's deepest lake; (5) Kamchatka, a peninsula on the Pacific rim dominated by mountain ranges that include nearly 30 volcanic peaks. Siberia is a major source of coal, oil, gas, and hydroelectric power, the Kuzbas coalfields of West Siberia forming one of Russia's largest industrial regions. It is also the major source of Russia's non-ferrous metals and timber. **Siberian** adj. & n.

**Sibiu** /siː'bjuː/ (German **Hermannstadt**) an industrial city in central Romania, capital of Sibiu county; pop. (1990) 188,000. Founded in the 12th c. by German colonists, it lies on the Cibin River in the wine-producing northern foothills of the Transylvanian Alps. Its industries produce textiles, shoes, chemicals, processed food, metal goods, and machinery.

**Sibu** /'siːbuː/ **1.** (Malay **Pulau Sibu**) a small island in the South China Sea, lying off the southeast coast of peninsular Malaysia. **2.** a town in western Sarawak, Malaysia, situated at the junction of the Rejang and Igan rivers 60 km. (38 miles) upstream from the South China Sea; pop. (1980) 85,230. It is the second-largest town in Sarawak, most of its inhabitants being descended from Chinese settlers.

**Sichuan** /sɪtʃ'wɑːn/ (also **Szechuan** /setʃ'wɑːn/) a province of west-central China; area 567,000 sq. km. (219,000 sq. miles); pop. (1990) 107,218,000; capital, Chengdu. Surrounded by mountain ranges, the Chengdu Plain produces rice, wheat, maize, sugar cane, and beans.

**Sicily** /'sɪsɪlɪ/ (Italian **Sicilia** /sɪ'tʃiːljə/) a large triangular island in the Mediterranean Sea, separated from the 'toe' of Italy by the narrow Strait of Messina. It forms, with the neighbouring islands of Lipari, Egadi, Ustica, and Pantelleria, a region of Italy comprising the provinces of Agrigento, Caltanissetta, Catania, Enna, Messina, Palermo, Ragusa, Siracusa, and Trapani; area 25,706 sq. km. (9,929 sq. miles); pop. (1990) 5,196,820; capital, Palermo. Settled successively by Phoenicians, Greeks, and Cartheginians, it became a Roman province in 241 BC after the first Punic War. After various struggles Sicily and southern Italy became a Norman kingdom towards the end of the 11th c. It was conquered by Charles of Anjou in 1266, but the unpopularity of the Angevin regime led to the uprising known as the Sicilian Vespers and the establishment in Sicily of the Spanish House of Aragon in its place; southern Italy remained under Angevin rule until reunited with Sicily in 1442. In 1816 the two areas were officially merged when the Spanish Bourbon Ferdinand styled himself King of the Two Sicilies. The island was liberated by Garibaldi in 1860 and finally incorporated into the

new state of Italy. The Sicilian economy is predominantly agricultural. Tourism is important.
**Sicilian** *adj. & n.*

**Sidi-bel-Abbès** /ˌsɪdɪ bel əˈbez/ a town in
north-west Algeria, situated to the south of Oran
on the Mekerra River; pop. (1989) 186,000. It was
the headquarters of the French Foreign Legion
until Algeria's independence in 1962. An important route junction in a rich agricultural region for
which it acts as market and processing centre.

**Sidlaw Hills** /ˈsɪdlɔː/ a range of hills in east-
central Scotland separating the Carse of Gowrie
from the Strathmore valley and stretching from
Perth to Forfar. Its highest point is Craigowl Hill
(455 m., 1,492 ft.).

**Sidon** /ˈsaɪd(ə)n/ (Arabic **Saida** /ˈsaɪdə/) a city
and ancient seaport of the Phoenicians, now in
Lebanon; pop. (1988) 38,000. It is a centre of oil refining and capital of Al Janub province.

**Sidra** /ˈsɪdrə/, **Gulf of** (also **Gulf of Sirte** /ˈsɜːtɪ/)
a bay on the Mediterranean coast of Libya, be-
tween the towns of Benghazi and Misratah.

**Siebengebirge** /ˈsiːbəŋɡɪˌbɜːɡə/ a range of
hills in western Germany, on the right bank of the
Rhine south-east of Bonn.

**Siedlce** /ˈʃeltzə/ the capital of Siedlce county in
eastern Poland; pop. (1990) 71,960. Food processing, engineering, and the production of clothing
are its chief industries.

**Siegen** /ˈziːɡən/ an iron and steel town on the
River Sieg in the state of North Rhine-Westphalia,
west Germany, the birthplace of the painter Peter
Paul Rubens in 1577; pop. (1991) 110,800.

**Siegfried Line** /ˈsiːɡfriːd/ **1.** an alternative
name for the HINDENBURG LINE. **2.** the line of defence constructed along the western frontier of
Germany before World War II.

**Siena** /siˈenə/ a city of Tuscany in west-central
Italy, noted for its medieval architecture and for its
school of Gothic art, which flourished in the 13th–
14th centuries; pop. (1990) 57,745. It has a university founded in 1240 and a vast cathedral dating
from the 13th c. The city gives its name to sienna, a
ferruginous earth used as a pigment in paint. The
annual *Palio* horse-races take place in July and
August.
**Sienese** /-ˈniːz/ *adj. & n.*

**sierra** /sɪˈerə/ the Spanish word for a range of
high mountains with serrated peaks.

**Sierra Leone** /sɪˌerə lɪˈəʊn/ official name **The
Republic of Sierra Leone** a country on the coast
of West Africa, bounded by Guinea and Liberia;
area 71,740 sq. km. (27,709 sq. miles); pop. (est.
1991) 4,239,000; official language, English; capital,
Freetown. The land rises from a coastal plain towards the Loma and Tingi mountains near the
Guinea frontier. Britain established a refuge for liberated slaves in 1792 in the district around Freetown which became a colony in 1807, but the large

inland territory was
not declared a pro-
tectorate until 1896.
Sierra Leone
achieved inde-
pendence in 1961,
originally as a consti-
tutional monarchy,
but came under mili-
tary rule in 1967

prior to the creation of a republic in 1971. A one-
party state was established in 1978 and the process
of restoring multiparty democracy suffered a set-
back in 1992 when the country was returned to military rule following a coup. Sierra Leone has an
equatorial climate with maximum rainfall in May
to October. Subsistence and small-scale plantation
farming are the main occupations but most of the
country's revenue is from mining and export of iron
ore, bauxite, rutile, and diamonds. Sierra Leone is
governed by a military Supreme Council of State
and is divided into three provinces and the Western
Area:

| Province | Area (sq. km.) | Pop. (1985) | Capital |
|---|---|---|---|
| Northern | 35,936 | 1,262,200 | Makeni |
| Eastern | 15,553 | 960,550 | Kenema |
| Southern | 19,695 | 740,500 | Bo |
| Western Area | 557 | 554,200 | Freetown |

**Sierra Madre** /sɪˌerə ˈmɑːdrɪ/ the chief mountain system of Mexico, stretching from the the US
frontier in the north-west to the Gulf of Tehuan-
tepec in the south-east. It is divided for most of its
length into the **Sierra Madre Occidental** in the
west and the **Sierra Madre Oriental** in the east,
and to the south of Mexico City and west of
Oaxaca the **Sierra Madre del Sur** extends along
the Pacific coast. Rising to 5,699 m. (18,697 ft.)
near Orizaba, Citaltépetl is the highest peak in the
Sierra Madre.

**Sierra Nevada** /sɪˌerə nəˈvɑːdə/ **1.** a mountain range in Andalusia, southern Spain rising to
3,480 m. (11,411 ft.) at Mulhacén. **2.** a mountain
range in California, USA, that rises sharply from
the Great Basin in the west and descends gradually
into the central valley of California. Its highest
point is Mt. Whitney (4,418 m., 14,495 ft.) and
chief amongst its protected areas are Yosemite,
Sequoia, and Kings Canyon national parks.

**Sierra Nevada de Mérida** /-deɪ ˈmeɪriːdə/
an arm of the northern Andes stretching into
north-west Venezuela and rising to a height of
5,005 m. (16,411 ft.) at Pico Bolívar, the highest
point in Venezuela.

**Siirt** /siːrt/ **1.** a province of south-east Turkey,
south-west of Lake Van; area 6,176 sq. km. (2,385
sq. miles); pop. (1990) 243,435. **2.** its capital, situated north-east of the River Tigris; pop. (1990)
68,320.

**Sikasso** /si:'kæsəʊ/ an industrial town and trading centre, the capital of Sikasso region in southern Mali; pop. (1976) 47,000.

**Sikh** /si:k, sɪk/ an adherent of Sikhism. There are over 18 million Sikhs, most of whom live in the Punjab.

**Sikhism** /'si:kɪz(ə)m, 'sɪk-/ a monotheistic religion founded in the Punjab in the 15th c. by Guru Nanak. It combines elements of Hinduism and Islam, accepting the Hindu concepts of karma and reincarnation but rejecting the caste system, and has one sacred scripture, the Adi Granth. The tenth and last of the series of gurus, Gobind Singh, prescribed the distinctive outward forms (the so-called five Ks)—long hair (to be covered by a turban) and uncut beard (*kesh*), comb (*kangha*), short sword (*kirpan*), steel bangle (*kara*), and short trousers for horse-riding (*kaccha*). Originating as a religion, Sikhism became a militant political movement within the Punjab.

**Sikhote Alin** a mountain range in far eastern Russia, stretching southwards from the Amur river to Vladivostok and rising to a height of 2,078 m. (6,817 ft.) at Tardoki Yani.

**Siking** /si:'kɪŋ/ a former name of the Chinese city of XIAN when it was western capital of the Tang dynasty (618–906).

**Sikkim** /'sɪkɪm/ a state of India (since 1975) in the eastern Himalayas, previously an Indian protectorate; area 7,299 sq. km. (2,819 sq. miles); pop. (1991) 405,500; capital, Gangtok. Most of the country is mountainous and dissected by deep valleys. Livestock are grazed on lower slopes and grain, fruit, and vegetable crops grown in the valleys. There are handicraft industries including the weaving of cotton.
**Sikkimese** *adj. & n.*

**Silbury Hill** /'sɪlbərɪ/ an ancient prehistoric earthwork near Avebury in Wiltshire, southern England, 40 m. (130 ft.) high. It is reckoned to be the largest man-made mound in Europe.

**Silchester** /'sɪltʃestə(r)/ a village in Hampshire, southern England, to the east of which lie the remains of the Romano-British town of Calleva Atrebatum.

**Silesia** /saɪ'li:zjə/ (Czech **Slezsko**, Polish **Śląsk**) a region of central Europe (now largely in south-west Poland), an ancient district and duchy, partitioned at various times between the states of Prussia, Austria-Hungary, Poland, and Czechoslovakia. Lying to the north of the Sudeten Mountains and Western Carpathians and drained by the Oder, it is a largely agricultural and forested lowland region with extensive coal and mineral resources.
**Silesian** *adj. & n.*

**Silicon Valley** /'sɪlɪkən/ a name given to the high-tech industrial area between San Jose and Palo Alto in Santa Clara County, California, USA. It is a noted centre for computing and the manufacture

of electronics, and takes its name from the non-metallic element used to make micro-chip circuitry, semiconductors, and transistors.

**Silistra** /sɪ'li:strə/ a port and city in Razgrad district, north-eastern Bulgaria, on the River Danube; pop. (1990) 78,030. Nearby is the Roman city of Novae, founded in the 1st c. AD. It exports grain and manufactures textiles, bricks, and furniture.

**Silkeborg Lakes** /'sɪlkəbʊ(ə)g/ a group of small shallow lakes in eastern Jutland, Denmark, the largest of which is Mossö. Linked by the River Gudenaa, the lake region is a popular resort area.

**Silk Road** (also **Silk Route**) an ancient caravan route linking China with the West, used from Roman times onwards and taking its name from the silk which was a major Chinese export. By this route also Christianity and (from India) Buddhism reached China. A 'North Road' skirted the northern edge of the Taklimakan Desert before heading westwards into Turkestan (and thence to the Levant), while a 'South Road' followed a more southerly route through the high passes of the Kunlun and Pamir mountains into India. A railway (completed in 1963) follows the northern route from Xian to Urumchi and into Kazakhstan.

**Siloam** /saɪ'ləʊəm/ a spring and pool of water near ancient Jerusalem, where the man born blind was bidden to wash (John 9: 7).

**Silurian** /saɪ'ljʊərɪən/ in geological time, the third period of the Palaeozoic era, following the Ordovician and preceding the Devonian, lasting from about 438 to 408 million years ago. The first land plants and the first fish (with jaws) appeared during this period.

**Silver City** a town in New Mexico, USA, west of the San Andres Mountains; pop. (1990) 9,900. Once a centre for gold- and silver-mining, it is now a copper-mining and cattle-ranching town and the site of the Western New Mexico University (1893). It was the birthplace in 1859 of the outlaw William H. Bonney (Billy the Kid).

**Silverstone** /'sɪlvə,stəʊn/ a motor-racing circuit near Towcester in Northamptonshire, England, built on a disused airfield after World War II.

**Silvretta** /si:l'vretə/ a mountain range of the Eastern Alps in Switzerland and Austria. Its highest peaks are Piz Linard (3,411 m., 11,185 ft.) in Switzerland and Piz Buin (3,312 m., 10,866 ft.) in Austria.

**Simbirsk** /sɪm'bɜ:sk/ a city in western Russia, situated on the River Volga north-west of Samara; pop. (1990) 638,000. Between 1924 and 1992 it was called Ulyanovsk after the family name of Lenin who was born here in 1870. Its industries include engineering, machinery, electronics, food processing, distilling and brewing.

**Simferopol** /ˌsjɪmfe'rəʊpəl/ the chief town of the Crimea in southern Ukraine, on the River

Salgir; pop. (1990) 348,900. Now a major marketing and transportation centre with machinery, tools, and many light industries, it lies on the site of an ancient Scythian capital that was later known to the Tartars as Ak-Mechet until taken by Russia in 1784.

**Simi Valley** /sɪˈmiː/ a city in south-west California, USA, situated in a citrus-growing area to the north-west of Los Angeles; pop. (1990) 100,220. It has diverse light industries.

**Simla** /ˈsɪmlə/ (also **Shimla**) a hill station in northern India, capital of the state of Himachal Pradesh; pop. (1991) 109,860. It was the summer capital of British India (1864–1947), and is now a summer resort and army headquarters.

**simoom** /sɪˈmuːm/ (also **simoon** /-ˈmuːn/) a hot, dry dust-laden wind blowing at intervals, especially in the Arabian desert.

**Simplon** /ˈsæplɔ̃/ (Italian **Sempione**) a pass in the Bernese Alps of southern Switzerland linking Brig in the Swiss canton of Valais with Domodosola in Italy. Reaching an altitude of 2,028 m. (6,591 ft.), the road through the pass was built by Napoleon in 1801–5. The nearby railway tunnel (1922) connecting Switzerland and Italy is 19 km. (12 miles) long.

**Simpson Desert** /ˈsɪmps(ə)n/ a desert in central Australia, situated between Alice Springs and the Channel Country to the east. It was named in 1929 after A. A. Simpson, who was President of the Royal Geographical Society of Australia at that time.

**Sinai** /ˈsaɪnaɪ, -nɪaɪ/ a peninsula, mostly desert, at the north end of the Red Sea, now part of Egypt; area 65,000 sq. km. (25,000 sq. miles). In the south is Mount Sinai where according to the Bible (Exodus 19–34) the Ten Commandments and the Tables of the Law were given to Moses. It has been a focus of conflict between Arabs and Jews and was occupied by Israel from 1967 to 1982 when it was returned to Egypt under a treaty signed in 1979. **Sinaitic** /-ˈɪtɪk/ adj.

**Sinaloa** /ˌsiːnəˈləʊə/ a state of western Mexico on the Gulf of California and the Pacific Coast; area 58,328 sq. km. (22,529 sq. miles); pop. (1990) 2,210,770; capital, Culiacán Rosales.

**Sincelejo** /ˌsiːnsəˈleɪxəʊ/ a cattle-marketing town in north-west Colombia, capital of the department of Sucre; pop. (1985) 141,000.

**Sind** /sɪnd/ a province of southern Pakistan, formerly part of British India after its acquisition by Britain in 1843; area 140,914 sq. km. (54,428 sq. miles); pop. (est. 1985) 21,682,000; capital, Karachi.

**Sines** /ˈsiːnɪʃ/ an industrial port with oil refineries south of Setúbal on the Atlantic coast of south-west Portugal; pop. (1980) 10,000. It was the birthplace of the navigator Vasco da Gama c. 1469.

**Singapore** /ˌsɪŋɡəˈpɔː(r)/ official name **The Republic of Singapore** a country in south-east

Asia, a member-state of the Commonwealth, consisting of the island of Singapore and about 54 smaller islands, lying just north of the equator off the southern tip of the Malay peninsula to which it is linked by a causeway carrying a road and railway; area 618 sq. km. (239 sq. miles); pop. (est. 1991) 3,045,000; languages, Malay (national), Chinese (Mandarin), Tamil, and English; capital, Singapore City. Sir Stamford Raffles established a trading post under the East India Company in 1819, and it was incorporated with Penang and Malacca to form the Straits Settlements in 1826; these became a Crown Colony in the following year. Singapore rapidly grew, by virtue of its large protected harbour, to become the most important commercial centre and naval base in south-east Asia. It fell to the Japanese in 1942, and after liberation became first a British Crown Colony in 1946 and then a self-governing state in 1959. Federated with Malaysia in 1963, it regained full independence two years later and remains a world trade and financial centre. Singapore has a unicameral Parliament which elects a Prime Minister.

**Singhalese** see SINHALESE.

**Sing Sing** /sɪŋ ˈsɪŋ/ a New York State Prison, built in 1825–8 at Ossining village on the Hudson River and formerly notorious for its severe discipline. It is now called Ossining Correctional Facility.

**Sinhalese** /ˌsɪnhəˈliːz, ˌsɪnəˈliːz/ (also **Singhalese** /ˌsɪŋɡ-/) an Aryan people deriving from northern India and forming the majority of the population of Sri Lanka. Their language, spoken by 9 million people in Sri Lanka, is descended from Sanskrit and was brought by settlers from northern India in the 5th c. BC; its alphabet resembles that of the Dravidian languages of southern India.

**Sining** see XINING.

**sink hole** a hollow fissure or solution hole in limestone and chalk landscapes down which surface-water drains.

**Sinkiang** see XINJIANG.

**Sinop** /səˈnɒp/ **1.** a Black Sea province of Anatolia in northern Turkey; area 5,657 sq. km. (2,185 sq. miles); pop. (1990) 265,150. **2.** its capital, a Black Sea port to the north-west of Samsun; pop. (1990) 25,540. Founded by colonists from Miletus in the 8th c. BC, it developed a major trade in cinnabar to which the town gave its name. It was the birthplace in 412 BC of the Cynic philosopher Diogenes.

**Sino-Tibetan** /ˌsaɪnəʊtɪˈbet(ə)n/ a language group which includes Chinese, Burmese, Tibetan, Nepalese, and Thai. They are tonal languages, but the exact relationships between them are far from clear.

**Sint Eustatius** see SAINT EUSTATIUS.

**Sint Maarten** see SAINT MARTIN.

**Sint Niklaas** see SAINT NICOLAS.

**Sintra** /'si:ntrə/ (also **Cintra**) a small town in central Portugal, formerly the summer residence of the Portuguese royal family; pop. (1981) 20,000. Its chief landmarks are the National Palace, the gardens of Montserrate, and the hilltop Pena Palace.

**Sinuiju** /'ʃmi:ˌdʒu:/ a city on the Yalu River in western North Korea, capital of North Pyongan province; pop. (est. 1984) 500,000. It is an industrial port which has chemicals and aluminium industries.

**Sion** /sjɔ̃/ the capital of Valais canton in southwest Switzerland, on the River Rhône; pop. (1990) 24,540. It is a historic market town trading in fruit, vegetables, and wine.

**Sioux** /su:/ (Siouan **Dakota**) a group of North American Indian tribes originally occupying the plains and prairies. With a population in the 19th c. of more than 30,000, it was one of the largest tribes in North America.
**Siouan** *adj.*

**Sioux City** a city in west Iowa, USA, on the Missouri River; pop. (1990) 80,505. Described as a cultural and recreational centre of the Great Plains, it is also a major transportation centre for livestock and grain, and has food-processing, fertilizer, and electrical industries.

**Sioux Falls** /su: 'fɒlz/ a city at the falls on the Big Sioux River, south-east South Dakota, USA; pop. (1990) 100,810. First settled in 1848, it has developed as a cattle-shipping town with meat-packing plants. It is also the home of EROS (Earth Resources Observation Systems), an international centre for space and aircraft photography of the earth.

**Siping** /si:'pɪŋ/ a city in Jilin province, northeastern China, south-west of Changchun; pop. (1986) 365,000.

**Siracusa** see SYRACUSE.

**Sirdaryo** see SYR DARYA.

**Siret** /si:'ret/ (German **Sereth**, Romanian **Siretul**) a river of Ukraine and Romania that rises in headwaters on the eastern slopes of the Carpathians and flows 448 km. (280 miles) southwards to join the Danube near Galaţi.

**Siris** see SÉRRES.

**Sirnak** /'si:rnæk/ **1.** a province of south-east Turkey, on the frontiers with Syria and Iraq; area 7,172 sq. km. (2,770 sq. miles); pop. (1990) 262,000. **2.** its capital, east of the River Tigris; pop. (1990) 25,060.

**sirocco** /sɪ'rɒkəʊ/ (also **scirocco**) (*pl.* **-os**) **1.** a hot, dry Saharan wind that blows northwards to the northern shores of the Mediterranean. **2.** a warm, sultry rainy wind in southern Europe.

**Siros** see SYROS.

**Sirte, Gulf of** see SIDRA, GULF OF.

**Sisimiut** see HOLSTEINSBORG.

**Sistine Chapel** /'sɪsti:n, 'sɪstaɪn/ a chapel in the Vatican, built by Pope Sixtus IV, containing Michelangelo's painted ceiling and his fresco of the Last Judgement, and also frescos by Botticelli, Ghirlandaio, and others. It is used for the principal papal ceremonies and also by the cardinals when meeting for the election of a new pope.

**Sitka** /'sɪtkə/ a town and naval base with important fishing and associated processing industries on the west coast of Baranof Island, south-east Alaska. Founded in 1799 by Aleksandr Baranov as New Archangel, the chief town of Russian America. The restored St. Michael's Cathedral was originally built in 1844 and was the first Russian Orthodox cathedral in North America. Sitka National Historic Park centres around the site of a battle in which the Tlingit Indians made their last stand against the Russians in 1804. Sitka gives its name to a fast-growing species of spruce (*Picea sitchensis*) native to this part of North America but now widely grown as a commercial timber crop in the UK.

**Sittang** /'sɪtæŋ/ a river that rises in east-central Burma and flows c. 560 km. (350 miles) south into the Bay of Bengal at the Gulf of Martaban.

**Sittwe** /'sɪtweɪ/ (Burmese **Akyab** /'ækjɑ:b/) a city and port of western Burma, on the Bay of Bengal at the mouth of the Karadan River; pop. (1983) 107,900. It developed as a centre of rice-milling after it was taken by the British in 1826.

**Sivas** /'si:vɑ:s/ **1.** a province of central Turkey; area 28,568 sq. km. (11,034 sq. miles); pop. (1990) 767,480. **2.** its capital, a manufacturing and trading city on the Kizilirmak; pop. (1990) 221,500. It was a leading city of Asia Minor under the Romans, Byzantines, and Turks.

**Siwalik Hills** /sɪ'wɑ:lɪk/ (Nepalese **Churia Range**) the foothills of the Himalayas in northern India and Nepal.

**Six Counties, the** a term used by the Irish to describe the Ulster counties of Antrim, Down, Armagh, Londonderry, Tyrone, and Fermanagh, which since 1922 have comprised the province of Northern Ireland.

**Sjaelland** see ZEALAND.

**Skagerrak** /'skægəˌræk/ a strait separating south Norway from North Denmark and linking the Baltic to the North Sea via the Kattegat. It is crossed by numerous ferry services.

**Skara Brae** /ˌskɑ:rə 'breɪ/ a late neolithic (3rd millennium BC) settlement at the south corner of the Bay of Skaill on the main island (Mainland) of Orkney, consisting of stone-built rooms with slab-shelves, chests, and hearths. Revealed after a great storm in 1850 but not excavated until 1925–30, it is the best preserved prehistoric village in northern Europe.

**Skeena** /'skiːnə/ a river that rises in the Stikine Mts. of British Columbia, Canada, and flows 579 km. (360 miles) south-westwards to the Pacific Ocean near Prince Rupert. It is noted for its salmon fishing.

**Skegness** /skeg'nes/ a resort town on the North Sea coast of Lincolnshire, east England, site of the first Butlin holiday camp; pop. (1981) 16,100.

**Skellefteå** /shə'leftɔː/ a mining town in Vasterbotten county, northern Sweden, on the Gulf of Bothnia at the mouth of the Skellefteå River; pop. (1990) 75,260. The town expanded rapidly after the arrival of the railway and exploitation of the nearby Boliden copper mines in 1912.

**Skeleton Coast** a name given to the arid Atlantic coast of Namibia, south-west Africa.

**Skelmersdale** /'skelmɜːzˌdeɪl/ an industrial town in Lancashire, north-west England, west of Wigan; pop. (1981) 42,600. It was developed as a New Town around an existing mining village in 1961.

**skerry** a reef or rocky offshore island.

**Skerries** /'skerɪz/**, the** a group of island in the Irish Sea off the east coast of Ireland opposite the resort town of Skerries. They include Red Island, Colt Island, and St. Patrick's Island.

**Skiathos** /ski:'æθɒs/ a Greek island in the Northern Sporadhes, the closest of the group to the coast of Thessaly; area 78 sq. km. (30 sq. miles); pop. (1981) 4,129; capital, Skiathos. It was the home of the novelists Alexander Moraitidhis (1851–1929) and Alexander Papadhiamandis (1851–1911).

**Skiddaw** /'skɪdɔː/ a mountain that rises to 931 m. (3,053 ft.) east of Bassenthwaite in the Lake District, Cumbria, north-west England.

**Skien** /'ʃiːən/ the capital of Telemark County, south-east Norway, a port on the Skiensel River south-west of Oslo; pop. (1990) 47,680. It manufactures footwear and foodstuffs.

**Skikda** /'skiːkdə/ a Mediterranean port on the north-east coast of Algeria; pop. (1989) 141,000. Founded by the French in 1838, it was known as Philippeville until 1962. It is an important oil and gas terminal for the Saharan pipelines, and has petrochemical, plastics, and gas-liquefaction plants.

**Skiros** see SKYROS.

**Skokie** /'skəʊki:/ a town in north-east Illinois, USA, north of Chicago; pop. (1990) 59,430. Originally called Niles Center, its name was changed in 1940. Its farmers once supplied Chicago with food, but today it is a headquarters for corporate business.

**Skopelos** /'skɒpəlɒs/ a Greek island of the Northern Sporadhes in the Aegean Sea; area 122 sq. km. (47 sq. miles); pop. (1981) 2,728; capital, Khóra Skopélou. The entire population of the island was slaughtered by Barbaross in 1538.

**Skopje** /'skɒpjeɪ/ the capital of the former Yugoslav Republic of Macedonia, on the River Vardar; pop. (1991) 563,000. An ancient city founded by the Romans, it was under Turkish control from the late 14th until the 20th c. In 1963 it was badly damaged by an earthquake that killed over 1,000 people. It is a communications hub and industrial centre with chemicals, metalwares, glass and steel making, and textiles.

**Skye** /skaɪ/ the largest of the Inner Hebrides in north-west Scotland. It has a heavily indented coastline and much of the island is mountainous, especially the rugged Cuillin Hills. During the 1880s the island crofters were in the forefront of the battle to win rights to land. The chief settlements are Portree and Broadford, and Dunvegan, which is reckoned to be the oldest continuously inhabited castle in Britain, is the seat of the chief of the Clan Macleod. The island gives its name to a small long-bodied short-legged long-haired slate or fawn coloured variety of Scotch terrier. The principal occupations are crofting and sheep farming but tourism is also important.

**Skyros** /'skiːrɒs/ (also **Skiros**) the largest and most easterly of the Greek islands of the Northern Sporadhes in the Aegean Sea; area 209 sq. km. (81 sq. miles); pop. (1981) 2,757; capital, Skyros. It produces wine, wheat, fruit, and honey. Theseus, king of Athens, was killed on the island and the English poet Rupert Brooke (1887–1915) lies buried on the western slope of Mt. Kokhílas (Konchylia).

**Slav** /slɑːv/ a member of a group of peoples in Central and Eastern Europe speaking Slavonic languages including Russian, Ukrainian, Belorussian, Polish, Czech, Slovak, Serbian, Croatian, and Bulgarian. The common Slavonic language from which they are all descended probably broke away from the main Indo-European family before Christian times. They have many characteristics in common: nouns and adjectives are highly inflected (Russian and Polish have as many as seven cases), verbs have few tenses but preserve an ancient distinction (called *aspect*) between actions thought of as finished or limited in time and those regarded as continuous. The two principal alphabets used are the Cyrillic and Latin.
**Slav** or **Slavonic** adj. & n.

**Slave** /sleɪv/ a river in Alberta and Northwest Territories, Canada, that rises in Lake Athabasca and flows northwards to the Great Slave Lake, drawing water from the Peace River. Its length from the Peace River to the Great Slave Lake is 415 km. (259 miles).

**Slave Coast** the name given by Europeans to that part of West Africa along the Guinea coast that was the principal source of slaves between the 16th and 19th centuries.

**Slavonia** /slə'vəʊnɪə/ a historic region of the Balkans in Croatia, lying between the Drava and

Sava rivers. Originally part of the Roman province of Pannonia, it became a Slavic state in the 7th c. and was eventually dominated by the Turks in the 16th c.

**Slavonsky Brod** /slə‚vɒnskɪ 'brɒt/ a town in northern Croatia, on the River Sava; pop. (1991) 55,600.

**Slavyansk** /slɑːˈvjænsk/ an industrial city in the Donets Basin of eastern Ukraine; pop. (1990) 136,000. It has chemical, machine, and ceramic industries.

**Sliema** /ˈsliːmə/ a resort town on the coast of the island of Malta, north-west of Valletta; pop. (1983) 20,120. With the neighbouring St. Julian's–St. George's area it is the largest town in Malta. It has a yacht marina, shopping centre, and 3km.-long sea-front promenade.

**Sligo** /ˈslaɪɡəʊ/ **1.** a county of western Ireland, in Connaught province; area 1,795 sq. km. (693 sq. miles); pop. (1991) 54,740. **2.** its county town, a seaport on **Sligo Bay**, an inlet of the Atlantic; pop. (1991) 17,300. Nearby in Lough Gill is the lake-isle of Innisfree immortalized by the poet W. B. Yeats who lies buried in Drumcliffe churchyard to the north of the town.

**Sliven** /ˈsliːv(ə)n/ (also **Slivno**) a commercial city in Burgas region, east-central Bulgaria, situated in the south-eastern foothills of the Balkan Mountains; pop. (1990) 150,210. To the south-east lies the Sliven Spa used since Roman times for gastro-intestinal cures. It has textiles and woodworking industries.

**Slough** /slaʊ/ an industrial and commercial town in Berkshire, southern England, to the west of London; pop. (1981) 97,400, with many light industries developed during the inter-war period.

### Slovakia

/sləʊˈvɑːkɪə/ (Slovak **Slovensko**) official name **The Slovak Republic** an independent state in central Europe, formerly part of Czechoslovakia; area 49,035 sq. km. (18,940 sq.

miles); pop. (1991) 5,268,935; official language, Slovak; capital, Bratislava. Northern Slovakia is dominated by the Carpathian Mountains which include the Beskid and Tatra ranges and are rich in mineral resources. Formerly a largely agricultural region, Slovakia was heavily industrialized while under post-war Communist rule. Its chief exports are minerals (including iron ore, copper, and mercury), chemicals, machinery, and armaments. Southern Slovakia is part of the fertile Älfold plain which is drained by the Danube. Settled by Slavic tribes in the 5th–6th c., Slovakia was dominated by Hungary until it declared independence in 1918 and united with the Czechs to form Czechoslovakia.

Slovak nationalism led to the creation of a federal republic in 1969 and to eventual separation from the Czech Republic in 1992. The country is governed by a legislative National Council and an executive prime minister and Council of Ministers. **Slovak** adj. & n.

Slovakia is administratively divided into three regions and the capital city of Bratislava:

| Region | Area (sq. km.) | Pop. (1991) | Capital |
|---|---|---|---|
| West Slovakia | 14,492 | 1,712,180 | Bratislava |
| Central Slovakia | 17,982 | 1,609,800 | Banská Bystrica |
| East Slovakia | 16,193 | 1,505,500 | Kosice |

### Slovenia

/sləˈviːnɪə/ (Slovene **Slovenija**) official name **The Republic of Slovenia** an independent state in central Europe to the south of Austria, formerly a constituent republic of Yugo-

slavia; area 20,251 sq. km. (7,822 sq. miles); pop. (est. 1991) 1,962,000; official language, Slovene; capital, Ljubljana. Dominated by the Adriatic Karst plateau, Julian Alps, and eastern foothills of the Dinaric Alps, Slovenia has developed a strong industrial economy based on its mineral resources which include oil, coal, lead, and mercury. Tourism has also been a great source of national revenue. Occupied by Celtic and Illyrian tribes in ancient times, Slovenia was settled by southern Slavs in the 6th c. and later formed part of the Austrian empire. In 1919 the region was ceded to the kingdom of Serbs, Croats, and Slovenes (named Yugoslavia from 1929) and in 1945 it became a constituent republic of Communist-ruled Yugoslavia. With the breakup of the federal republic, Slovenia declared independence from Yugoslavia in 1991. The country is governed by a bicameral National Assembly consisting of a Chamber of Deputies and a State Council.

**Slovene** adj. & n.

**Słupsk** /swuːpsk/ an industrial city of Pomerania on the River Słupia in northern Poland, capital of Słupsk county; pop. (1990) 101,240.

**Smederevo** /ˈsmedərəvəʊ/ an industrial town in Serbia, a port on the River Danube; pop. (1981) 107,370. It has steel and heavy engineering, as well as wine-making industries.

**Smithfield** /ˈsmɪθfɪəld/ a part of London containing the city's principal meat market. Formerly an open area situated just outside the north-west walls of the City of London, it was used as a horse and cattle market, as a fairground, and as a place of execution.

**Smithsonian Institution** /smɪθ'səʊnɪən/ the oldest US foundation for scientific research, established by Congress in 1838 and opened in 1846 in Washington, DC. It originated in a £100,000 bequest in the will of James Smithson (1765–1829), English chemist and mineralogist, for 'an establishment for the increase and diffusion of knowledge among men'.

**Smolensk** /smə'lensk/ an industrial city and transportation centre in western Russia, a port on the River Dnieper; pop. (1990) 346,000. Of strategic importance, the city has been sacked, burned, and devastated in wars from the 13th to the 20th c. Industries include timber, engineering, glass, food, and textiles, especially flax.

**Smyrna** see IZMIR.

**Snake** /sneɪk/ a river in the north-western USA, a tributary of the Columbia River. It rises in Yellowstone Park, Wyoming, and flows 1,609 km. (1,000 miles) through Jackson Lake in Grand Teton National Park before crossing Idaho to meet the Columbia River near Pasco in Washington State. Hell's Canyon on the Idaho–Oregon border is one of the deepest gorges in the world with a maximum depth of c. 2,410 m. (7,900 ft.).

**Sneek** /sneɪk/ a market-town and water-sports centre in the Dutch province of Friesland, with the largest yachting harbour in the country; pop. (1991) 29,280. Its industries produce textiles, paper, chemicals, and dairy produce.

**Snezhnaya** /snez'na:jə/ a cave system in the Bzybsky Massif of the Caucasus Mountains in Georgia. Descending to a depth of 1,370 m. (4,495 ft.), it is one of the deepest in the world. First explored in 1971, its Georgian name is Schachta Towiani (snow cave).

**Snowdon** /'snəʊd(ə)n/ a mountain in Gwynedd, north-west Wales. Rising to 1,085 m. (3,560 ft.) in **Snowdonia National Park** (1951), it is the highest mountain in Wales.

**Sochi** /'sɒtʃɪ/ a Black Sea port and resort in Krasnodar territory, southern Russia, in the western foothills of the Caucasus close to the border with Georgia; pop. (1990) 339,000. It was founded as a spa town in 1910 and now has over 50 sanatoria.

**Society Islands** /sə'saɪətɪ/ a group of Pacific islands in French Polynesia, including Tahiti; area 1,535 sq. km. (593 sq. miles); pop. (1988) 162,570. They were named by Captain Cook (who visited the islands in 1769) in honour of the Royal Society and in 1844 became a French protectorate.

**Socotra** /səʊ'kəʊtrə/ a mountainous island in the Arabian Sea near the mouth of the Gulf of Aden. Its capital is Tamridah and it is administered by Yemen; area 3,582 sq. km. (1,383 sq. miles).

**Södertälje** /,sɜ:də'teljə/ an industrial suburb west of Stockholm, Sweden, situated on the Södertälje Canal and a bay of Lake Mälaren; pop.

(1990) 81,790. It produces machinery, cars, and pharmaceuticals.

**Sodom** /'sɒdəm/ a town of ancient Palestine, probably south of the Dead Sea, destroyed by fire from heaven according to the Bible (Genesis 19: 24), along with Gomorrah, for the wickedness of its inhabitants.

**Sodor** /'səʊdə(r)/ a medieval diocese comprising the Hebrides and the Isle of Man, originally the 'southern isles' (Norse *Sudhreyjar*) of the kingdom of Norway. The Hebrides were separated in 1334, but **Sodor and Man** has been the official name for the Anglican diocese of the Isle of Man since 1684.

**Sofala** see BEIRA.

**Sofia** /'səʊfɪə, sə'fi:ə/ (also **Sophia** or **Sofiya**) the capital of Bulgaria, situated midway between the Adriatic and the Black Sea on a plain to the south of Mt. Vitosha; pop. (1990) 1,220,900. Settled in ancient times by Thracian tribes who used its mineral springs, it was named Serdica by the Romans and Triaditsa by the Byzantines. Held by the Turks between the 14th and late 19th centuries, it became capital of the newly independent Bulgarian state in 1879, and is today Bulgaria's principal industrial, transportation, and cultural centre. Its chief industries are metallurgy, engineering, chemicals, textiles, and food processing. It has an opera house, art galleries and museums, and a university.

**Sogne Fjord** /'sɒŋə fjɔ:/ (Norwegian **Sognefjorden**) a fjord to the north of Eivindvik on the west coast of Norway that extends over 200 km. (125 miles) inland and is the largest fjord in the country.

**Sohag** /səʊ'hæg/ a town in Egypt, situated on the left bank of the River Nile south-east of Asyut; pop. (1991) 152,000.

**Soho** /'səʊhəʊ/ a district centred around Soho Square in the West End of London, England, noted for its clubs, bars, bistros and restaurants. Popular with immigrants since the 17th c., Soho was associated with the avant-garde set after World War II and during the 1960s and 1970s gained a reputation for its sleazy nightlife. It now has a large Chinese community.

**Soka** /'səʊkɑ:/ a city in Saitama prefecture, east-central Honshu Island, Japan, a suburb of Tokyo; pop. (1990) 206,130.

**Sokhumi** see SUKHUMI.

**Sokoto** /sə'kəʊtəʊ/ **1.** a state in north-west Nigeria; area 102,535 sq. km. (39,600 sq. miles); pop. (1991) 4,392,400. Once part of the Fulani empire, it is largely populated by Muslim Hausa and Fulani people. **2.** its capital, an industrial city with a university founded in 1975; pop. (est. 1986) 168,000. The town grew as the southern end of a Saharan caravan route and is a market and distribution centre with cement, pottery, tanning, and dyeing industries.

**Solano** /səʊˈlɑːnəʊ/ see LEVANTER.

**Solapur** see SHOLAPUR.

**Solent** /ˈsəʊlənt/ the west part of the channel between the Isle of Wight and the mainland of England.

**Solfatara** /ˌsɒlfəˈtɑːrə/ a volcanic crater to the west of Naples in the Phlegraean Fields of Campania, southern Italy. It gives its name to the term for a volcanic vent emitting only sulphurous and other vapours.

**Solferino** /ˌsɒlfəˈriːnəʊ/ a village near Mantua in Lombardy, north-west Italy, site of a bloody battle between a combined French and Sardinian army and the forces of Austria in June 1859; pop. (1990) 2,100. The horrors of battle witnessed by the Swiss doctor and philanthropist Henri Dunant (1828–1910) inspired him to found the Red Cross organization.

**solifluction** /ˌsɒlɪˈflʌkʃ(ə)n/ the downhill erosion of water-sodden surface deposits.

**Solihull** /ˈsɒlɪˌhʌl/ an industrial and residential town to the south-east of Birmingham, in West Midlands county, England; pop. (1981) 94,600. The National Exhibition Centre is located nearby.

**Solikamsk** /sɒlɪˈkɑːmsk/ a town in central Russia, on the Usolka River in the western foothills of the Urals; pop. (1990) 110,000.

**Solingen** /ˈsɒlɪŋ(ə)n/ an industrial city in the Ruhr valley of North Rhine-Westphalia, west Germany, situated on the Wupper River opposite Remscheid; pop. (1991) 165,920. The centre of the German cutlery industry.

**Sollentuna** /suːlənˈtuːnə/ a north-western suburb of Stockholm, Sweden; pop. (1990) 51,380.

**Solna** /səʊlˈnɑː/ an industrial northern suburb of Stockholm, Sweden, associated with film-making; pop. (1990) 51,840. It is the seat of the Nobel Institute.

**Solo** /ˈsəʊləʊ/ (also **Sala**) see SURAKARTA.

**Solomon Islands** /ˈsɒləmən/ a country consisting of a group of islands in the South Pacific, south-east of the Bismarck Archipelago; area 27,556 sq. km. (10,643 sq. miles); pop. (est. 1991) 326,000; official language, English (Pidgin English and over 80 local dialects are spoken); capital, Honiara (on Guadalcanal). The principal populated islands, which are volcanic in origin and are clad in equatorial rainforest, include Choiseul, Guadalcanal, Malaita, New Georgia, San Cristobal, and Santa Isabel. There are also many uninhabited coral reefs and atolls. Copra and timber are the main exports. Discovered by the Spanish in 1658, the islands were divided between Britain and

Germany in the late 19th c; the southern islands became a British protectorate in 1893 while the north remained German until mandated to Australia in 1920. The scene of heavy fighting in 1942–3, the Solomons achieved self-government in 1976 and full independence as a member-state of the Commonwealth two years later, with the exception of the northern part of the chain which is now part of Papua New Guinea. Legislative authority is vested in a unicameral National Parliament which appoints an executive prime minister and cabinet. The islands are sparsely populated and the economy is largely one of subsistence agriculture.

**Solothurn** /ˈzəʊlɒˌtʊən/ (French **Soleure**) **1.** a canton in the Jura Mts. of north-west Switzerland that joined the Swiss Confederation in 1481; area 791 sq. km. (305 sq. miles); pop. (1990) 226,655. **2.** its capital, a town on the River Aare; pop. (1990) 15,430.

**solstice** /ˈsɒlstɪs/ the time during the summer and winter when the sun is furthest from the equator. At the **summer solstice** the sun is furthest north from the equator, about 21 June in the northern hemisphere. At the **winter solstice** the sun is furthest south from the equator, about 22 December in the northern hemisphere.

**Solutré Rock** /sɒluːˈtreɪ/ a location near Mâcon in Burgundy, France, with prehistoric remains. It gives its name to the Solutrean Era, characterized by an upper palaeolithic industry, which followed the Aurignacian and preceded the Magdelanian, and is dated to c. 19,000–18,000 BC.

**Solway Firth** /ˈsɒlweɪ/ an inlet of the Irish Sea, formed by the estuary of the Esk and Eden rivers, separating Cumbria (England) from Dumfries and Galloway (Scotland).

**Somali** /səˈmɑːlɪ/ a Hamitic Muslim people of Somalia in north-east Africa, speaking a language that belongs to the Cushitic branch of the Hamito-Semitic family of languages and is the official language of Somalia.

**Somalia** /səˈmɑːlɪə/ official name **The Somali Democratic Republic** a country in north-east Africa with a coastline on the Indian Ocean; area 637,657 sq. km. (246,294 sq. miles); pop. (est. 1991) 8,041,000; official language, Somali; capital, Mogadishu. A dry coastal plain rises to an inland plateau with an average elevation of 1,000 m. (3,280 ft.), the country being watered in the south by the Jubba River and its tributaries. The economy is largely agricultural, dependent upon nomadic stock-raising and (in the southern part of the country) some irrigated plantation-farming. Livestock, skins, and hides form the main

export; the second-largest export is the banana crop, most of which is imported by Italy. The area of the Horn of Africa was divided between British and Italian spheres of influence in the late 19th c., and the modern Somali Republic (which became an independent member of the UN in 1960) is a result of the unification of the former British Somaliland and Italian Somalia. Since independence, Somalia has been involved in border disputes with Kenya and Ethiopia, the latter leading to an intermittent war over the Ogaden Desert. Civil war, which broke out in 1988, eventually led to the overthrow in 1991 of President Mohammed Siyad Barre who had seized power in 1969 and abolished multiparty democracy. Subsequent attempts to install a stable national government were thwarted by factional fighting and the country was reduced to a state of poverty and lawlessness. In 1992 US-led military intervention attempted to restore order and ensure the safe passage of relief supplies to the starving people of Somalia. While fighting continued in the south in and around Mogadishu, a government was established in northern Somalia which declared itself independent as Somaliland in 1991.

**Somali** *adj. & n.*

**Somapuri Monastery** /sʌmə'pʊərɪ/ (also **Somapuri Vihara**) a Buddhist monastery at Paharpur in the Rajshahi region of western Bangladesh. Founded in the 8th c., it is the largest Buddhist monastery south of the Himalayas.

**Somerset** /'sʌmə,set/ a county of south-west England; area 3,452 sq. km. (1,333 sq. miles); pop. (1991) 459,100; county town, Taunton. Somerset is divided into five districts:

| District | Area (sq. km.) | Pop. (1991) |
| --- | --- | --- |
| Mendip | 740 | 95,300 |
| Sedgemoor | 564 | 97,000 |
| South Somerset | 959 | 139,400 |
| Taunton Deane | 462 | 93,300 |
| West Somerset | 727 | 34,100 |

**Somerset Island** an island in the Canadian Arctic, to the north-west of Baffin Island from which it is separated by the Prince Rupert Inlet; area 24,786 sq. km. (9,579 sq. miles). Noted for its caribou, muskoxen, and bird colonies, it was visited by W. E. Parry in 1819 and named after the English county.

**Somerville** /'sʌmɜ:vɪl/ a residential and industrial city in north-east Massachusetts, USA, a north-western suburb of Boston on the Mystic River; pop. (1990) 76,460. Slaughtering and meatpacking are principal industries.

**Somme** /sɒm/ **1.** a river of north-east France that rises in the department of Aisne and flows 245 km. (153 miles) into the English Channel near St. Valéry-sur-Somme. It was the scene of heavy fighting in World War I, especially in July–November 1916. **2.** a department in the Picardy region of

northern France; area 6,175 sq. km. (2,385 sq. miles); pop. (1990) 547,825; capital, Amiens.

**Sondrio** /'sɒndrɪəʊ/ a town on the River Adda in the Valtellina region of Lombardy, north-west Italy; pop. (1990) 22,540. It is capital of the province of Sondrio.

**Song** /sʊŋ/ a dynasty of Chinese emperors ruling from 960 to 1279, between the Tang and Yuan periods. During the Song Dynasty art and literature flourished and paper money was invented.

**Songhai** /'sɒŋhaɪ/ a Muslim empire of West Africa founded by Berbers in the 8th c. and extending its influence over the middle Niger until the 16th c.

**Songnam** /'sʊŋnɑ:m/ (also **Seongnam**) a city in north-west Korea, situated south-east of Seoul; pop. (1990) 540,760.

**Sonoma** /sə'nəʊmə/ a town in Sonoma County, west California, USA, situated north of San Francisco; pop. (1990) 8,120. Mission San Francisco de Solano, most northerly of the 21 Franciscan missions of California, was established here in 1823. The author Jack London (1876–1916) was buried in Sonoma which lies in an area noted for its wine production.

**Sonora** /sə'nɒrə/ a state of north-west Mexico; area 182,052 sq. km. (70,317 sq. miles); pop. (1990) 1,822,250; capital, Hermosillo.

**Sonora Desert** an arid region of North America, comprising south-east California and south-west Arizona in the USA and, in Mexico, much of Baja California and the western part of Sonora.

**Sonsonate** /ˌsɒnsə'nɑ:tɪ/ an agricultural market town on the Río Grande de Sonsonate in western El Salvador, capital of the department of Sonsonate; pop. (1984) 47,490.

**Soochow** see SUZHOU.

**Sophia** see SOFIA.

**Sopron** /ʃɒp'rɔ:n/ (German **Odenburg**) a historic town with many old buildings in Györ-Sopron county, north-west Hungary, situated at the foot of the Lövér Mts. on the frontier with Austria; pop. (1993) 56,090. Its industries produce cotton, wine, and carpets.

**Sorb** see WEND.

**Sorbonne** /sɔ:'bɒn/ originally a theological college founded in Paris by Robert de Sorbon, chaplain to Louis IX c. 1257; later, the faculty of theology in the University of Paris, suppressed in 1792; made a state university by Napoleon, it is now the seat of the faculties of science and letters of the University of Paris. Situated in the Place de la Sorbonne, on the Left Bank, it was one of the centres of student unrest in May 1968 that eventually led to a general strike throughout France.

**Soria** /'sɒrjə/ a market town on the River Duero (Douro) in Castilla-León, central Spain, capital of the province of Soria; pop. (1991) 35,420.

**Sorocaba** /suəru:'kɑ:bə/ a city in the state of São Paulo, southern Brazil, on the Sorocaba River; pop. (1990) 378,500. It is a commercial city trading in citrus fruit, sugar, coffee, textiles, and minerals.

**Sorrento** /sə'rentəu/ a town of Campania in central Italy, situated on a peninsula separating the Bay of Naples, which it faces, from the Gulf of Salerno; pop. (1990) 17,500. It has been a resort since Roman times (Latin *Surrentim*), noted for its climate and the beauty of the surrounding scenery. It was the birthplace in 1544 of the poet Torquato Tasso.

**Sosnowiec** /sɒs'nɒvjets/ an industrial city in the Upper Silesian Katowice region of southern Poland; pop. (1990) 259,350. Coal is mined nearby and its industries manufacture iron, steel, machinery, and chemicals.

**Sotho** /'su:tu:/ a subdivision of the Bantu people which includes tribes living chiefly in Botswana, Lesotho, and the Transvaal.

**Soufrière** /ˌsu:frɪ'eə(r)/ **1.** a dormant volcano on the French island of Guadeloupe in the West Indies. At 1,468 m. (4,813 ft.) it is the highest peak in the Lesser Antilles. **2.** a volcanic peak rising to a

height of 1,234 m. (4,006 ft.) on the island of St. Vincent in the West Indies.

**sound** /saʊnd/ the term for a large inlet of the sea or a wide passage between two land masses.

**Soûr** see TYRE.

**Sousse** /su:s/ a port and major resort on the east coast of Tunisia; pop. (1984) 83,500. Its chief landmarks are the 9th-c. Ribat fortress, and Grand Mosque. There is an international airport at Monastir to the south, and there are local automobile assembly and engineering industries.

**South Africa** a
country occupying
the southernmost
part of the continent
of Africa, bounded
to the north and
north-east by
Namibia, Botswana,
Zimbabwe, Swazi-
land, and Mozam-

bique and enclosing Lesotho; area 1,221,037 sq. km. (471,625 sq. miles); pop. (est. 1991) 36,762,000 (73 per cent are African people of the Zulu, Sotho, Tswana, and Xhosa groups, and 3 per cent are

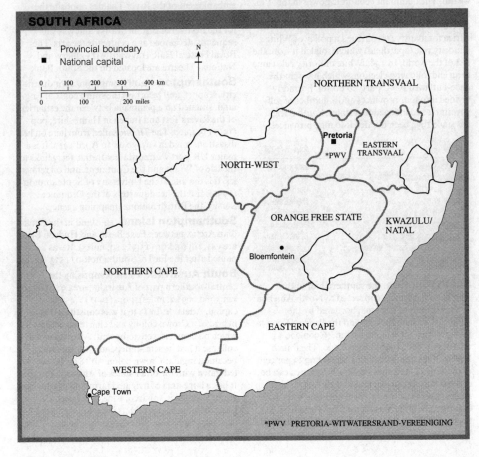

SOUTH AFRICA

— Provincial boundary
■ National capital

0   100   200   300   400 km
0   100        200 miles

N

NORTHERN TRANSVAAL

Pretoria ■
*PWV

EASTERN
TRANSVAAL

NORTH-WEST

ORANGE FREE STATE

KWAZULU/
NATAL

Bloemfontein ●

NORTHERN CAPE

EASTERN CAPE

WESTERN CAPE

Cape Town ●

*PWV  PRETORIA-WITWATERSRAND-VEREENIGING

Asian); official languages, Afrikaans and English; capitals, Pretoria (administrative), Cape Town (legislative), Bloemfontein (judicial). The greater part of South Africa occupies the southern part of the African plateau (including the Kalahari Desert) which is fringed by fold mountains (including the Drakensberg Range in the east) that give way to a narrow coastal margin. It is the world's largest exporter of gold and a major producer of platinum, diamonds, uranium, copper, and agricultural products such as maize, sugar, fruit, wine, and wool. Settled by the Dutch in the 17th c., the Cape area later came under British occupation, setting in motion a series of conflicting political and economic developments leading to inland expansion, confrontation with the indigenous population who were also moving southwards at the time, and finally war between the British and the Boer (Dutch) settlers at the end of the 19th c. The defeated Boer republics of the Transvaal and the Orange Free State were annexed as British Crown Colonies in 1902, but joined with the colonies of Natal and the Cape to form the self-governing Union of South Africa in 1910. After supporting Britain in both World Wars, in 1960–1 South Africa became a republic and left the Commonwealth. The dominant economic power in the southern half of the continent as a result of her well-developed agricultural and economic base, South Africa for many years pursued a policy of White minority rule (apartheid) which isolated it from the rest of the world. In 1994 White minority rule came to an end following elections which brought the once-outlawed ANC party to power. Formerly divided into four provinces and a number of self-governing and independent states, South Africa has since 1994 been divided into nine provinces:

| Province | Capital (1994) |
|---|---|
| Eastern Cape | East London |
| Eastern Transvaal | Nelspruit |
| KwaZulu-Natal | Durban |
| North-West | Klerksdorp |
| Northern Cape | Kimberley |
| Northern Transvaal | Pietersburg |
| Orange Free State | Bloemfontein |
| Pretoria-Witwatersrand-Vereeniging | Johannesburg |
| Western Cape | Cape Town |

**South America** the southern half of the American land mass, connected to North America by the Isthmus of Panama, bordered by the Atlantic Ocean to the east and the Pacific Ocean to the west; area 17,800,000 sq. km. (6,900,000 sq. miles); pop. (est. 1990) 296,716,000. The fourth largest of the continents and occupying 13 per cent of the world's land surface, South America can be divided into six physiographic regions, (1) the Andes, a series of mountain ranges that stretch the entire length of the west coast from Colombia to the tip of Chile; (2) the Guiana and Brazilian Highlands, the uplifted remains of an earlier continental

mass; (3) the Orinoco Basin, a lowland region between the Venezuelan Andes and the Guiana Highlands; (4) the Amazon basin, which stretches from the eastern foothills of the Andes to the Atlantic Ocean; (5) the Pampa-Chaco plain of Argentina, Paraguay, and Bolivia; (6) the Patagonian plateau, a series of rugged terraces that rise up from the Atlantic towards the southern Andes. South America's largest cities are Buenos Aires, São Paulo, Rio de Janeiro, Bogotá, Santiago, Lima, and Caracas. Colonized largely by the Spanish in the 16th c. (although the British, Dutch, and Portuguese were particularly active in the northeast), much of the continent remained part of Spain's overseas empire until liberated under the leadership of Bolívar and San Martín in the 1820s. Both culturally and ethnically the continent is now a mixture of indigenous Indian and imported Hispanic influences, modified slightly by North European and North American penetration in the 19th and 20th centuries. Although many South American countries are still hampered by economic underdevelopment and political instability, a minority have emerged as world industrial powers in their own right.

**South Bank** a name given to the the south embankment of the River Thames opposite the Houses of Parliament in London. It was the venue for the Festival of Britain in 1951 and was subsequently developed as a centre for the arts. The Royal Festival Hall, Hayward Art Gallery, and National Theatre are located on the South Bank.

**Southampton** /saʊθˈhæmpt(ə)n/ an industrial city, seaport, and resort on the south coast of England, situated on a peninsula between the estuaries of the Rivers Test and Itchen in Hampshire; pop. (1991) 194,400. The *Titanic* sailed from here on her disastrous maiden voyage on 10 April 1912. It is a major UK port with container traffic, ferry links to the Isle of Wight and the Continent, and oil refineries. It is the site of the University of Southampton (1952), and the headquarters of the Ordnance Survey, the British national mapping agency.

**Southampton Island** an island in the Canadian Arctic, between Foxe Basin and Hudson Bay; area 41,214 sq. km. (15,912 sq. miles). It was named after the Earl of Southampton (1573–1624).

**South Australia** a state comprising the central-southern part of Australia; area 984,000 sq. km. (380,069 sq. miles); pop. (1991) 1,454,000; capital, Adelaide. In 1836 it was constituted as a hybrid of a Crown colony and chartered colony, to which no convicts were to be sent. After financial collapse it lost its semi-independent status and became a regular Crown colony in 1841. It was federated with the other states of Australia in 1901. It has a large area of irrigated farmland producing grain, vegetables, tobacco, wine, and livestock. Leading industrial products include wood products, paper, processed food, textiles, chemicals, and metal goods.

**South Bend** a city in northern Indiana, USA, on the St. Joseph River; pop. (1990) 105,510. It was first settled in 1820 as a trading post of the American Fur Company. It was the former home of the Studebaker car plant and has numerous light industries.

**South Carolina** /ˌkærəˈlamə/ a state of the US on the Atlantic coast between North Carolina and Georgia; area 80,582 sq. km. (31,113 sq. miles); pop. (1990) 3,486,700; capital, Columbia. Its largest cities are Columbia, Charleston, North Charleston, and Greenville. South Carolina is also known as the Palmetto State. Its industries produce textiles, chemicals, asbestos, wood pulp, and steel products, and agricultural crops include peaches, tobacco, cotton, and peanuts. Settled by the Spanish and English in the 16th–17th c. and named after Charles I, it became one of the original 13 states of the US in 1789. Its chief landmarks are the Fort Sumter and Conagree Swamp National Monuments, the Charles Pinckney and Ninety Six National Historic Sites, Cowpens National Battlefield, and Kings Mountain National Military Park. The state is divided into 46 counties:

| County | Area (sq. km.) | Pop. (1990) | County Seat |
| --- | --- | --- | --- |
| Abbeville | 1,321 | 23,860 | Abbeville |
| Aiken | 2,830 | 120,990 | Aiken |
| Allendale | 1,074 | 11,720 | Allendale |
| Anderson | 1,867 | 145,180 | Anderson |
| Bamberg | 1,027 | 16,900 | Bamberg |
| Barnwell | 1,451 | 20,290 | Barnwell |
| Beaufort | 1,505 | 86,425 | Beaufort |
| Berkeley | 2,881 | 128,780 | Moncks Corner |
| Calhoun | 988 | 12,750 | Saint Matthews |
| Charleston | 2,439 | 295,040 | Charleston |
| Cherokee | 1,030 | 44,510 | Gaffney |
| Chester | 1,508 | 32,170 | Chester |
| Chesterfield | 2,085 | 38,575 | Chesterfield |
| Clarendon | 1,565 | 28,450 | Manning |
| Colleton | 2,735 | 34,380 | Walterboro |
| Darlington | 1,464 | 61,850 | Darlington |
| Dillon | 1,056 | 29,110 | Dillon |
| Dorchester | 1,495 | 83,060 | Saint George |
| Edgefield | 1,274 | 18,360 | Edgefield |
| Fairfield | 1,781 | 22,295 | Winnsboro |
| Florence | 2,090 | 114,340 | Florence |
| Georgetown | 2,137 | 46,300 | Georgetown |
| Greenville | 2,067 | 320,170 | Greenville |
| Greenwood | 1,173 | 59,570 | Greenwood |
| Hampton | 1,459 | 18,190 | Hampton |
| Horry | 2,972 | 144,050 | Conway |
| Jasper | 1,703 | 15,490 | Ridgeland |
| Kershaw | 1,880 | 43,600 | Camden |
| Lancaster | 1,435 | 54,520 | Lancaster |
| Laurens | 1,851 | 58,090 | Laurens |
| Lee | 1,069 | 18,440 | Bishopville |
| Lexington | 1,838 | 167,610 | Lexington |
| Marion | 1,282 | 33,900 | Marion |
| Marlboro | 1,256 | 29,720 | Bennetsville |
| McCormick | 910 | 8,879 | McCormick |
| Newberry | 1,648 | 33,170 | Newberry |

| Oconee | 1,635 | 57,490 | Walhalla |
| --- | --- | --- | --- |
| Orangeburg | 2,889 | 84,800 | Orangeburg |
| Pickens | 1,297 | 93,900 | Pickens |
| Richland | 1,981 | 286,320 | Columbia |
| Saluda | 1,186 | 16,360 | Saluda |
| Spartanburg | 2,116 | 226,790 | Spartanburg |
| Sumter | 1,729 | 102,640 | Sumter |
| Union | 1,339 | 30,340 | Union |
| Williamsburg | 2,428 | 36,815 | Kingstree |
| York | 1,781 | 131,500 | York |

**South China Sea** see CHINA SEA.

**South Dakota** /dəˈkəʊtə/ a state in the north-central US, bounded by North Dakota, Minnesota, Nebraska, Iowa, Wyoming, and Montana; area 199,730 sq. km. (77,355 sq. miles); pop. (1990) 696,000; capital, Pierre. The largest city is Sioux Falls. South Dakota is also known as the Coyote or Sunshine State. Once dominated by Sioux Indians, it was acquired partly by the Louisiana Purchase in 1803. Organized as a territory in 1861 and settled a year latter by those who took up the offer of free land under the Homestead Act, it was the scene of a gold-rush in 1874 and joined the Union as the 40th state in 1889. South Dakota is a leading producer of agricultural crops such as grain, sunflower seed, and livestock, and minerals such as gold, silver, beryllium, uranium, and bentonite. Its principal features are the Missouri River, the Badlands, and the Black Hills which are the highest hills east of the Rockies and include Mt. Rushmore, Jewel Cave National Monument, and Wind Cave National Park. The state is divided into 66 counties:

| County | Area (sq. km.) | Pop. (1990) | County Seat |
| --- | --- | --- | --- |
| Aurora | 1,838 | 3,135 | Plankinton |
| Beadle | 3,273 | 18,250 | Huron |
| Bennett | 3,073 | 3,210 | Martin |
| Bon Homme | 1,435 | 7,090 | Tyndall |
| Brookings | 2,067 | 25,210 | Brookings |
| Brown | 4,477 | 35,580 | Aberdeen |
| Brule | 2,119 | 5,485 | Chamberlain |
| Buffalo | 1,235 | 1,760 | Gannvalley |
| Butte | 5,853 | 7,910 | Belle Fourche |
| Campbell | 1,903 | 1,955 | Mound City |
| Charles Mix | 2,834 | 9,130 | Lake Andes |
| Clark | 2,478 | 4,400 | Clark |
| Clay | 1,063 | 13,180 | Vermillion |
| Codington | 1,804 | 22,700 | Watertown |
| Corson | 6,414 | 4,195 | McIntosh |
| Custer | 4,053 | 6,180 | Custer |
| Davison | 1,134 | 17,500 | Mitchell |
| Day | 2,657 | 6,980 | Webster |
| Deuel | 1,641 | 4,520 | Clear Lake |
| Dewey | 6,006 | 5,520 | Timber Lake |
| Douglas | 1,128 | 3,750 | Armour |
| Edmunds | 2,987 | 4,360 | Ipswich |
| Fall River | 4,524 | 7,350 | Hot Springs |
| Faulk | 2,610 | 2,740 | Faulkton |
| Grant | 1,771 | 8,370 | Milbank |
| Gregory | 2,634 | 5,360 | Burke |
| Haakon | 4,737 | 2,620 | Philip |

(cont.)

| | | | |
|---|---|---|---|
| Hamlin | 1,331 | 4,970 | Hayti |
| Hand | 3,736 | 4,270 | Miller |
| Hanson | 1,126 | 2,990 | Alexandria |
| Harding | 6,963 | 1,670 | Buffalo |
| Hughes | 1,968 | 14,820 | Pierre |
| Hutchinson | 2,122 | 8,260 | Olivet |
| Hyde | 2,236 | 1,700 | Highmore |
| Jackson | | | |
| Washbaugh | 4,867 | 2,810 | Kadoka |
| Jerauld | 1,378 | 2,425 | Wessington |
| | | | Springs |
| Jones | 2,525 | 1,320 | Murdo |
| Kingsbury | 2,142 | 5,925 | De Smet |
| Lake | 1,456 | 10,550 | Madison |
| Lawrence | 2,080 | 20,655 | Deadwood |
| Lincoln | 1,503 | 15,430 | Canton |
| Lyman | 4,365 | 3,640 | Kennebec |
| Marshall | 2,205 | 4,840 | Britton |
| McCook | 1,498 | 5,690 | Salem |
| McPherson | 2,985 | 3,230 | Leola |
| Meade | 9,051 | 21,880 | Sturgis |
| Mellette | 3,409 | 2,140 | White River |
| Miner | 1,482 | 3,270 | Howard |
| Minnehaha | 2,106 | 123,810 | Sioux Falls |
| Moody | 1,352 | 6,510 | Flandreau |
| Pennington | 7,236 | 81,340 | Rapid City |
| Perkins | 7,498 | 3,930 | Bison |
| Potter | 2,259 | 3,190 | Gettysburg |
| Roberts | 2,865 | 9,910 | Sisseton |
| Sanborn | 1,479 | 2,830 | Woonsocket |
| Shannon | 5,444 | 9,900 | (attached to Fall |
| | | | River) |
| Spink | 3,913 | 7,980 | Redfield |
| Stanley | 3,721 | 2,450 | Fort Pierre |
| Sully | 2,527 | 1,590 | Orida |
| Todd | 3,609 | 8,350 | (attached to Tripp) |
| Tripp | 4,207 | 6,920 | Winner |
| Turner | 1,604 | 8,580 | Parker |
| Union | 1,178 | 10,190 | Elk Point |
| Walworth | 1,838 | 6,090 | Selby |
| Yankton | 1,347 | 19,250 | Yankton |
| Ziebach | 5,119 | 2,220 | Dupree |

## South-East Asia Treaty Organization

**(SEATO)** a defence alliance established in 1954 for countries of South-East Asia and part of the southwest Pacific, to further a US policy of containment of Communism. Its members were Australia, Britain, France, New Zealand, Pakistan, the Philippines, Thailand, and the US. The organization was dissolved in 1977.

**South-East Iceland** a shipping-forecast area covering part of the north-east Atlantic between Iceland and the Faeroes.

**Southend-on-Sea** /saʊθ͵endɒnˈsi:/ a resort and commuter town with light industries in Essex, south-east England, on the Thames estuary; pop. (1991) 153,700. The Crow Stone at Westcliff (1836) marks the limit of the Port of London Authority.

**southerly** /ˈsʌðəlɪ/ a wind blowing from the south.

**Southern Alps** the principal mountain range of South Island, New Zealand. Running roughly

parallel to the west coast, it extends for almost the entire length of the island. It rises to 3,764 m. (12,349 ft.) at Mt. Cook, New Zealand's highest peak.

**Southern Ocean** a body of water surrounding the continent of Antarctica.

**Southern Rhodesia** see ZIMBABWE.

**South Georgia** a barren island in the South Atlantic 1,120 km. (700 miles) south-east of the Falkland Islands from where it is administered (with the South Sandwich Islands) by a Commissioner; area 3,754 sq. km. (1,450 sq. miles). There has been no permanent settlement since the whaling port of Leith was abandoned in 1966, but the British Antarctic Survey maintains a research station on Bird Island and since the Falkands War of 1982 a small garrison has been stationed at King Edward Point. First explored by Captain Cook, who named the island after George III in 1775, it was frequented by British and American sealers and later by Norwegian whalers who established a base at Grytviken. It was a dependency of the Falkland Islands until 1985.

**South Glamorgan** /gləˈmɔːgən/ a county of south Wales on the Bristol Channel, bounded by Mid Glamorgan to the north and west and Gwent to the east; area 416 sq. km. (160 sq. miles); pop. (1991) 383,300; county town, Cardiff. It is divided into two districts:

| District | Area (sq. km.) | Pop. (1991) |
|---|---|---|
| Cardiff | 120 | 272,600 |
| Vale of Glamorgan | 296 | 110,700 |

**South Island** the larger of the two principal islands of New Zealand, separated from North Island by the Cook Strait; area 151,215 sq. km. (58,406 sq miles); pop. (1991) 881,540 (25 per cent of the total population of New Zealand). Its chief urban areas are Christchurch, Dunedin, and Invercargill. Dominated by the Southern Alps which extend the entire length of the island and are flanked to the east by the fertile Canterbury Plains, South Island's chief products are grain, sheep, fruit, and timber.

**South Korea** see KOREA, SOUTH.

**South Orkney Islands** a group of uninhabited islands in the South Atlantic, lying to the north-east of the Antarctic Peninsula and including the islands of Coronation, Inaccessible, Laurie, and Signy. Discovered by Captain G. Powell in 1821, they are now administered as part of the British Antarctic Territory; area 620 sq. km. (240 sq. miles).

**South Ossetia** An autonomous region of Georgia. See OSSETIA.

**South Pacific Commission** an agency established in 1947 to promote the economic and social stability of the islands in the South Pacific. There are 27 member-governments and administrations, and the agency provides advice etc. in matters such as marine resources, rural management and technology, and community and education services. Its headquarters are in Noumea, New Caledonia.

**Southport** a resort and commuter town on the Irish Sea coast of Merseyside, north-west England, 25 km. north of Liverpool; pop. (1981) 90,960.

**South Sandwich Islands** a group of uninhabited volcanic islands in the South Atlantic lying 480 km. (300 miles) south-west of South Georgia, with which it is administered from the Falkland Islands. Discovered in 1819 by the British navigator William Smith, the islands were annexed by the UK in 1908 and 1917. The islands include Montagu, Saunders, Bristol, Candlemas, Visokoi, Leskov, Zavodski, and Southern Thule.

**South Saskatchewan** see SASKATCHEWAN 2.

**South Seas** a name once applied to the entire Pacific Ocean but now largely referring to the waters of the central and southern Pacific.

**South Shetland Islands** a group of uninhabited islands in the South Atlantic, lying immediately north of the Antarctic Peninsula. Discovered in 1819 by Captain W. Smith, they are now administered as part of the British Antarctic Territory.

**South Shields** /ˈʃiːldz/ a port and town in Tyne and Wear, north-east England, on the south side of the River Tyne opposite North Shields; pop. (1981) 87,125. It lies at the eastern end of Hadrian's Wall. William Wouldhave, inventor of the modern lifeboat, was born here in 1789. Chemicals, engineering, and paint are the main industries.

**South Uist** see UIST.

**South-West Africa** see NAMIBIA.

**South Yemen** see YEMEN.

**South Yorkshire** a metropolitan county of northern England; area 1,560 sq. km. (602 sq. miles); pop. (1991) 1,249,300. It comprises four districts:

| District | Area (sq. km.) | Pop. (1991) |
|----------|---------------|-------------|
| Barnsley | 329 | 217,300 |
| Doncaster | 581 | 284,300 |
| Rotherham | 283 | 247,100 |
| Sheffield | 368 | 500,500 |

**soviet** /ˈsəʊvɪət, ˈsɒ-/ an elected local, district, or national council in the former member-states of the USSR. Before 1917 the term was applied to a revolutionary council of workers, peasants, and soldiers.

**Soviet Union** (official name **Union of Soviet Socialist Republics**) a former federation of 15 republics occupying the northern half of Asia and part of Eastern Europe, comprising Russia, Belorussia (Belarus), Ukraine, the Baltic States, Georgia, Armenia, Moldova (Moldavia), Azerbaijan, Kazakhstan, Kirghizia, Turkmenistan, Tajikistan, and Uzbekistan; area 22,402,076 sq. km. (865,279 sq. miles); capital, Moscow. Created as a Communist state after the 1917 revolution, the Soviet Union was the largest country in the world. Its agricultural and industrial production were increased, often by brutal means, until the devastation caused by World War II. In the post-war era it emerged as one of the two antagonistic superpowers, rivalling the USA, in the polarization of the Communist and non-Communist worlds. Attempts to reform its centrally planned economy during the 1980s led to a rise in nationalist feeling and unrest in the republics, some of which began to seceded from the Union which was finally dissolved in 1991.

**Soyapango** /sɔɪəˈpæŋgəʊ/ a town in El Salvador, situated between San Salvador and Lake Ilopango; pop. (1989) 104,000.

**Sozopol** /səˈzəʊpəl/ a historic resort town on the Black Sea coast of Bulgaria, south-east of Burgas; pop. (1990) 15,920. The ancient Greek city on this site was known as Apollonia.

**Soweto** /səˈweɪtəʊ/ (abbr. **South West Township**) a large predominantly Black urban area, south-west of Johannesburg (to which many inhabitants commute), that is an amalgamation of several townships, where in June 1976 Black schoolchildren and students demonstrated against legislation proposing to make Afrikaans the compulsory language of instruction. Violence followed, and by the end of the year some 500 Blacks and Coloureds had been killed, many of them children.

**Spa** a small resort town in eastern Belgium, south-east of Liège; pop. (1991) 10,140. It has been celebrated since medieval times for the curative properties of its mineral springs. It has given its name to similar resorts.

**Spain** /speɪn/ (Spanish **España**, /eˈspænjə/) official name **The Kingdom of Spain** a country in south-west Europe, occupying the greater part of the Iberian peninsula to the south of the

Pyrenees and including the Canary Islands in the Atlantic, the Balearic Islands in the Mediterranean, and the exclaves of Ceuta and Melilla on the coast of North Africa; area 504,750 sq. km. (194,959 sq. miles); pop. (est. 1991) 39,045,000; official language, Spanish; capital, Madrid. Much of the interior of Spain is a plateau with an average height of between 450 and 900 m. (1,500 and 3,000 ft.). In the north the Pyrenees and Cantabrian mountains rise to 1,800 m. and 3,000 m. (6,000 ft. and 10,000 ft.) and in the south the valley of the Guadalquivir River forms a wide lowland valley to the south of which lies the Sierra Nevada. Conquered successively by the Carthaginians, Romans, Visigoths, and Arabs, Spain was reunited by the marriage of Ferdinand of Aragon and Isabella of Castile at the end of the 15th c. and emerged under the Habsburg

SPAIN

Region boundary
Province boundary
■ Capital city

kings of the 16th c. to become the dominant European power in both the Old and the New Worlds. Thereafter it declined, suffering as a result of the War of the Spanish Succession and the Napoleonic War, and losing most of its overseas empire in the early 19th c. Endemic political instability finally resulted in the Spanish Civil War (1936–9) and the establishment of a Fascist dictatorship under Franco. Franco's death in 1975 was followed in 1978 by the re-establishment of a constitutional monarchy and a pronounced liberalization of the state. Though predominantly an agricultural country producing grain, citrus fruit, olives, and wine, it has, since it became a member of the European Community in 1986, experienced an accelerated pace of industrial development. The country is governed by a prime minister and Council of Ministers appointed by the king, with legislative authority vested in a bicameral parliament (*Cortes Generales*) comprising a Congress of Deputies and a Senate. **Spanish** *adj. & n.*
Spain is divided into 17 autonomous regions, 50 provinces and the 2 presidios of Ceuta and Melilla:

| Region/ Province | Area (sq. km.) | Pop. (1991) | Capital |
|---|---|---|---|
| **Andalusia** | 87,268 | 6,940,520 | |
| Almeria | 8,774 | 455,500 | Almeria |
| Cadiz | 7,385 | 1,078,400 | Cadiz |
| Córdoba | 13,718 | 754,450 | Córdoba |
| Granada | 12,531 | 790,515 | Granada |
| Huelva | 10,085 | 443,480 | Huelva |
| Jaén | 13,498 | 637,630 | Jaén |
| Malaga | 7,276 | 1,160,840 | Malaga |
| Sevilla | 14,001 | 1,619,700 | Seville |
| **Aragon** | 47,669 | 1,188,820 | |
| Huesca | 15,671 | 207,810 | Huesca |
| Teruel | 14,804 | 143,680 | Teruel |
| Zaragoza | 17,194 | 837,330 | Saragossa |
| **Asturias** | 10,565 | 1,093,940 | Oviedo |
| **Balearic Islands** | 5,014 | 709,140 | Palma |
| **Basque Provinces** | 7,361 | 2,104,040 | |
| Alava | 3,047 | 272,450 | Vitoria |
| Guipúzcoa | 1,997 | 677,490 | San Sebastian |
| Vizcaya | 2,217 | 1,155,100 | Bilbao |
| **Canary Islands** | 7,273 | 1,493,780 | |
| Las Palmas | 4,065 | 767,970 | Las Palmas de Gran Canaria |
| Santa Cruz de Tenerife | 3,208 | 725,815 | Santa Cruz de Tenerife |
| **Cantabria** | 5,289 | 527,330 | |
| Santander | 5,289 | 527,330 | Santander |
| **Castilla-La Mancha** | 79,226 | 1,658,450 | |
| Albacete | 14,858 | 342,680 | Albacete |
| Ciudad Real | 19,749 | 475,435 | Ciudad Real |
| Cuenca | 17,061 | 205,200 | Cuenca |
| Guadalajara | 12,190 | 145,590 | Guadalajara |
| Toledo | 15,368 | 489,540 | Toledo |

| | | | |
|---|---|---|---|
| Castilla-León | 94,147 | 2,545,930 | |
| Avila | 8,048 | 174,380 | Avila |
| Burgos | 14,269 | 352,770 | Burgos |
| León | 15,468 | 525,900 | León |
| Palencia | 8,029 | 185,480 | Palencia |
| Salamanca | 12,336 | 357,800 | Salamanca |
| Segovia | 6,949 | 147,190 | Segovia |
| Soria | 10,287 | 94,540 | Soria |
| Valladolid | 8,202 | 494,210 | Valladolid |
| Zamora | 10,559 | 213,670 | Zamora |
| Catalonia | 31,930 | 6,059,450 | |
| Barcelona | 7,773 | 4,654,400 | Barcelona |
| Gerona | 5,886 | 509,630 | Gerona |
| Lérida | 12,028 | 353,455 | Lérida |
| Tarragona | 6,283 | 542,000 | Tarragona |
| Extremadura | 41,602 | 1,061,850 | |
| Badajoz | 21,657 | 650,390 | Badajoz |
| Cáceres | 19,945 | 411,460 | Cáceres |
| Galicia | 29,434 | 2,731,670 | |
| La Coruña | 7,876 | 1,096,970 | Corunna |
| Lugo | 9,803 | 384,365 | Lugo |
| Orense | 7,278 | 353,490 | Orense |
| Pontevedra | 4,477 | 896,850 | Pontevedra |
| La Rioja | 5,034 | 263,430 | Logroño |
| Madrid | 7,995 | 4,947,555 | Madrid |
| Murcia | 11,317 | 1,045,600 | Murcia |
| Navarre | 10,421 | 519,230 | Pamplona |
| Valencia | 23,305 | 3,857,230 | |
| Alicante | 5,863 | 1,292,560 | Alicante |
| Castellón | 6,679 | 446,740 | Castellón |
| Valencia | 10,763 | 2,117,930 | Valencia |
| Ceuta | 18 | 67,615 | |
| Melilla | 14 | 56,600 | |

**Spaniard** /'spænjəd/ a native of Spain or person of Spanish descent.

**Spanish** /'spænɪʃ/ the language of Spain and Spanish America, the most widely spoken of the Romance languages, with many Arabic words dating from the time when the Moors dominated Spain (8th–15th c.); there are in all about 250 million speakers. It is the official language of Spain, Mexico, and every Central and South American republic except Brazil, Guyana, Surinam, and Belize, and is widely spoken in the islands of the Greater Antilles, the southern states of the USA, and, decreasingly, in the Philippines. In sound it is very like Italian, with a strong 'r' sound and with many masculine words ending in -o and feminine words in -a; the ñ sound /-nj-/ is characteristic. A variety of Spanish known as Ladino is spoken in Turkey and Israel by descendants of Jews expelled from Spain in 1492.

**Spanish America** the parts of America colonized in the 16th c. by the Spanish, including Central and South America and parts of the West Indies.

**Spanish Harlem** /'hɑːləm/ a name given to the sections of Harlem in New York City occupied by immigrants from Puerto Rico and more recently by other Spanish-speaking immigrants.

**Spanish Main** a historic name given to the north-east coast of South America between the Orinoco River and Panama, and adjoining parts of the Caribbean.

**Spanish Sahara** the former name (1958–75) of WESTERN SAHARA.

**Spanish Town** the second-largest town of Jamaica, capital of the parish of St. Catherine in Middlesex county; pop. (1982) 89,100. Situated 19 km. (12 miles) west of Kingston, it was capital of Jamaica until 1872. It is now a centre of sugar and food processing.

**Sparks** /spɑːks/ a mining town on the north-eastern outskirts of Reno, western Nevada, USA; pop. (1990) 53,370. It was named after state governor John Sparks in 1903. There are important distribution and tourism industries.

**Sparta** /'spɑːtə/ (Greek **Spartí** /'spɑːtiː/) a city in the southern Peloponnese in Greece, capital of the department of Lakonia; pop. (1981) 14,390. After enslaving the surrounding populations as helots, in the 5th c. BC Sparta became the chief rival of Athens, whom she defeated in the Peloponnesian War. The ancient Spartans were renowned for the military organization of their state and for their rigorous discipline, courage, and austerity. The modern city of Sparta was laid out in 1834 by King Otto.
**Spartan** *adj. & n.*

**speleology** /ˌspiːlɪ'ɒlədʒɪ/ the exploration or scientific study of caves.

**Spey** /speɪ/ a river that rises near Fort Augustus in the Highlands of Scotland and flows 171 km. (108 miles) north-eastwards past Kingussie, Aviemore, Grantown-on-Spey, and Rothes before emptying into the North Sea at Spey Mouth, north-east of Elgin. Although the River Tay and its headwaters constitute the longest river in Scotland, the Spey is the longest river bearing a single name from its source.

**Speyer** /'ʃpaɪə(r)/ (also **Spires**) an industrial town in Rhineland-Palatinate, west Germany, on the Rhine north of Karlsruhe; pop. (1991) 47,450. The town, which is a noted centre of the wine trade, has a six-towered Romanesque cathedral with imperial tombs.

**Spezia** /lɑː 'spetsɪə/, **La** a naval and commercial seaport on the Mediterranean coast of Liguria, north-west Italy, capital of La Spezia province; pop. (1990) 103,000. It developed after the transfer of the naval dockyard from Genoa and the construction of an arsenal in 1869. There is a ferry link with Corsica. It has shipyards, steel, and petroleum industries.

**Sphinx** /sfɪŋks/, **The** a colossal monument in the desert near Giza in northern Egypt, taking the form of a figure with a couchant lion's body and a man's head. It forms part of the complex of funerary monuments of the pharaoh Chephren (4th dynasty, 3rd millennium BC). It is carved from the natural rock and completed with masonry; the beard and nose have disappeared because the monument was used as a target by the Mameluke sultan. It is believed to be an effigy of Chephren, but it came to be identified with a god whom the Greeks called Harmachis (= Horus in the Horizon), and received its own cult; the Arabs called it *Abu Hol* (= father of terror). It is undergoing urgent restoration.

**Spice Islands** see MOLUCCA ISLANDS.

**spit** /spɪt/ a narrow strip of sand or gravel extending from land to sea or across the mouth of a river.

**Spitsbergen** /ˈspɪtsbɜːɡən/ an island of the Svalbard archipelago in the Arctic Ocean, 657 km. (410 miles) north of Norway, under Norwegian sovereignty; area 39,043 sq. km. (15,080 sq. miles). Its rugged mountain ridges inspired Willem Barents to name the whole archipelago Spitsbergen when he discovered it in 1596. The largest settlement is Longyearbyen and there are rich coal deposits of the Tertiary era mined by Norwegians and Russians. The former mining settlement of Ny-Ålesund has the most northerly post office in the world.

**Split** /splɪt/ a seaport, cultural centre, and resort on the Adriatic coast of Croatia; pop. (1991) 189,300. Founded as a Roman colony in 78 BC, it contains the ruins of the palace of the emperor Diocletian, built in about AD 300, as well as many fine old buildings. Ship repair, engineering, coal-mining, fishing, and tourism are its chief industries.

**Spokane** /spəʊˈkeɪn/ a city in eastern Washington, USA; pop. (1990) 177,200. Founded as a sawmill in 1871, it acts as a transportation centre for minerals, timber, and agricultural produce from the Columbia basin.

**Spoleto** /spəˈleɪtəʊ/ a town of Umbria in Perugia region, central Italy; pop. (1990) 38,030. The site of a settlement from the 7th c. BC, it became a province of Rome in 241 BC. Taken by the Lombards in about AD 570, it was one of Italy's principal cities between the 6th and 8th centuries. An annual summer festival of music, art, and drama (Festival of the Two Worlds) was established in 1958 by the composer Gian Carlo Menotti. It has leather and textile industries.

**Sporades** /ˈspɒrəˌdiːz/ (Greek **Sporadhes** /spɒˈrɑːdiːz/) two separate groups of Greek islands in the Aegean Sea: **1.** The **Northern Sporades**, which lie to the east of mainland Greece, include the islands of Euboea, Skyros, Skiathos, Skópelos, and Iliodhrómia. **2.** The **Southern Sporades**, off the west coast of Turkey, include Rhodes and the Dodecanese Islands.

**Spratly Islands** /ˈsprætlɪ/ (Chinese **Nansha**, Vietnamese **Truong Sa**, Philippino **Kalayaan**) a group of islets and coral reefs in the South China Sea between Vietnam and Borneo. Dispersed over a distance of some 965 km. (600 miles) and commanding the sea route between Singapore and

Japan, the islands are claimed in whole or in part by China, Taiwan, Vietnam, the Philippines, and Malaysia. Oil was discovered beneath its waters in 1976 and in 1988 it was the scene of a brief naval engagement between Chinese and Vietnamese forces.

**Spree** /spriː/ a river that rises in the Lausitz Mts. of east Germany and flows c. 400 km. (250 miles) generally northwards through Cottbus and the Spreewald to join the Havel at Berlin. It is linked to the Oder by the Oder-Spree Canal.

**Springfield** /ˈsprɪŋfiːld/ **1.** an administrative, commercial, medical, and insurance centre, the capital of the US state of Illinois; pop. (1990) 105,230. First settled in 1819, it was named after a spring on the land of Elisha Kelly its first resident. It became state capital in 1837 and was the home and burial place (1865) of Abraham Lincoln. **2.** an industrial city and cultural centre in south-west Massachusetts, USA, on the Connecticut River; pop. (1990) 156,980. It was established in 1636 by William Pynchon of Springfield in England. It has numerous light industries and was once famous for the development and making of rifles. **3.** an industrial city in south-west Missouri, USA, on the northern edge of the Ozark Mountains; pop. (1990) 140,490. 'Wild Bill' Hickok was a scout and spy for Union forces headquartered in Springfield during the Civil War. Nearby is Wilson's Creek National Battlefield. It has many light industries and is the centre of a rich agricultural area. **4.** an industrial town and agricultural centre in the fertile valley of west-central Ohio, USA; pop. (1990) 70,490. It is particularly known for the manufacture of farm machinery.

**spring tide** a tide just after new and full moon when there is the greatest difference between high and low water.

**Sranang Tongo** see TAKI-TAKI.

**Srbija** see SERBIA.

**Sremska Mitrovica** /ˈsremskə ˌmiːtrəʊˈviːtsə/ a town in the province of Vojvodina, north-west Serbia, situated on the River Sava; pop. (1991) 38,900.

**Sri Lanka** /ʃriː ˈlæŋkə, ʃrɪ, srɪ-/ (formerly **Ceylon**) official name **The Democratic Socialist Republic of Sri Lanka** an island and independent state in the Indian Ocean off the

south-east coast of India; area 64,453 sq. km. (24,895 sq. miles); pop. (est. 1991) 17,194,000; official languages, Sinhala, Tamil, English; capital city, Colombo (seat of government is at Srijayawardenepura Kotte). It is a tropical island with a large mountainous interior and extensive coastal

lowlands. The main rainy season is between October and January when the north-east monsoon blows onshore. The economy is largely dependent on exports of tea, rubber, textiles, and coconuts. Attempts are being made to increase tourism. A centre of Buddhist culture from the 3rd c. BC, the island was invaded during the 11th c. by Tamil Hindus who established a strong dynasty in Jaffna. It was successively dominated by the Portuguese, Dutch, and British from the 16th c. and was finally annexed by Britain in 1815. A Commonwealth State from 1948, the country became an independent republic in 1972, taking the name of Sri Lanka (= resplendent island). Its political stability has been continually threatened by conflict between the Sinhalese and Tamil sectors of the population. Sri Lanka has a presidential form of government, the president having the power to appoint or dismiss the prime minister and members of the Cabinet.
**Sri Lankan** *adj. & n.*
Sri Lanka is divided into nine provinces and 25 districts which take the name of their principal towns:

| Province/District | Area (sq. km.) | Pop. (1990) |
| --- | --- | --- |
| **Western** | | |
| Colombo | 657 | 1,935,000 |
| Gampaha | 1,387 | 1,518,000 |
| Kalutara | 1,589 | 934,000 |
| **Central** | | |
| Kandy | 1,916 | 1,236,000 |
| Matale | 1,993 | 414,000 |
| Nuwara-Eliya | 1,741 | 530,000 |
| **Southern** | | |
| Galle | 1,636 | 932,000 |
| Hambantota | 2,579 | 510,000 |
| Matara | 1,283 | 765,000 |
| **Northern** | | |
| Jaffna | 983 | 863,000 |
| Kilinochchi | 1,235 | 99,000 |
| Mannar | 1,985 | 129,000 |
| Mullativu | 2,517 | 91,000 |
| Vavuniya | 1,967 | 114,000 |
| **Eastern** | | |
| Amparai | 4,350 | 474,000 |
| Batticaloa | 2,686 | 409,000 |
| Trincomalee | 2,631 | 311,000 |
| **North Western** | | |
| Kurungela | 4,813 | 1,410,000 |
| Puttalam Chilaar | 3,013 | 589,000 |
| **North Central** | | |
| Anuradhapura | 7,034 | 705,000 |
| Polonnaruwa | 3,248 | 314,000 |
| **Uva** | | |
| Badulla | 2,857 | 701,000 |
| Moneragala | 5,560 | 344,000 |
| **Subaragamuwa** | | |
| Kegalle | 1,693 | 743,000 |
| Ratnapura | 3,275 | 923,000 |

**Srinagar** /'sriːnəgə(r)/ the summer capital of the state of Jammu and Kashmir in north-west India, a crafts, textile-manufacturing, and tourist city on the Jhelum River north-west of the Pir Panjal Range; pop. (1991) 595,000.

**Staffa** /'stæfə/ a small uninhabited island of the Inner Hebrides, west of Mull, noted for its hexagonal basalt columns. It is the site of Fingal's Cave.

**Stafford** /'stæfəd/ the county town of Staffordshire in central England, an industrial town producing footwear, chemicals, and electronics; pop. (1981) 62,240. It was the birthplace in 1593 of Izaak Walton. Staffordshire University (formerly Staffordshire Polytechnic) was established in 1992.

**Staffordshire** /'stæfəd‚ʃɪə(r)/ a county of central England; area 2,716 sq. km. (1,049 sq. miles); pop. (1991) 1,020,300; county town, Stafford. It is divided into nine districts:

| District | Area (sq. km.) | Pop. (1991) |
| --- | --- | --- |
| Cannock Chase | 79 | 87,400 |
| East Staffordshire | 388 | 96,200 |
| Lichfield | 330 | 90,700 |
| Newcastle-under-Lyme | 211 | 117,400 |
| South Staffordshire | 409 | 103,900 |
| Stafford | 599 | 117,000 |
| Staffordshire Moorlands | 576 | 94,000 |
| Stoke-on-Trent | 93 | 244,800 |
| Tamworth | 31 | 68,900 |

**Staines** /steɪnz/ a residential town in Surrey, south-east England, at the junction of the Thames and Colne rivers; pop. (1981) 52,815.

**Stakhanov** /stə'kɒnəv/ a mining city in south-east Ukraine, situated west of Lugansk and south of the Donets River; pop. (1990) 112,300. Named after a miner whose achievements mining coal gave rise to the 'shock-worker' movement in 1930s USSR.

**Stalingrad** see VOLGOGRAD.

**Stamboul** /stæm'buːl/ an obsolete name for Istanbul.

**Stamford** /'stæmfəd/ a market town in Lincolnshire, east-central England, on the River Welland west of Peterborough; pop. (1981) 16,400. Founded by the Danes in the 7th c., it became a prosperous woollen-trading town in the Middle Ages. It retains many fine old streets, squares, and buildings.

**Stamford** /'stæmfəd/ a residential suburb of New York city in the US state of Connecticut; pop. (1990) 108,060. It is a corporate headquarters, and research and manufacturing centre.

**Stanley** /'stænlɪ/ (also **Port Stanley**) the chief port and town of the Falkland Islands, situated on the island of East Falkland; pop. (1991) 1,557. Originally named Port William, Stanley replaced Port Louis as the capital of the Falklands in 1843. During the Argentine occupation of 1982 it was renamed four times in the space of six weeks, being known as Puerto Rivero, Puerto de la Isla Soledad, Puerto de las Islas Malvinas, and Puerto Argentino.

**Stanley, Mount** a mountain in the Ruwenzori Range on the frontier between Zaire and Uganda. Rising to 5,110 m. (16,765 ft.), it is the highest peak in both countries.

**Stanleyville** /'stænlɪ,vɪl/ the former name (1882–1966) of KISANGANI.

**Stann Creek** /stæn kriːk/ a citrus-growing district of southern Belize, between the Maya Mts. and the Caribbean coast; area 2,175 sq. km. (840 sq. miles); pop. (1991) 17,910. Its chief town is Dangriga (formerly Stann Creek Town).

**Stanneries** /'stænərɪz/, **the** a name given to the tin-mining areas of west Devon and east Cornwall in south-west England. Its name is derived from the Latin *stannum* (= tin). Until 1896 the region had its own 'stannary courts' which met in the open air at Crockern Tor on Dartmoor.

**Stanovoy Range** /'stænəʊvɔɪ/ (Russian **Stanovoy Khrebet**) a mountain range to the south of Yakutsk in south-east Siberian Russia that forms the watershed between the Lena and Amur river basins.

**Stansted** /'stænsted/ the site, in north Essex, south-east England, of London's third international airport. Originally a World War II US Airforce base, its £400 million airport complex was designed by Sir Norman Foster and opened in 1991. There is a railway link with Liverpool Street Station in central London.

**Stara Planina** SEE BALKAN MOUNTAINS.

**Stara Zagora** /ˌstɑːrə zəˈɡɔːrə/ a manufacturing city in the Sredna Gora Mountains of Khaskovo district, east-central Bulgaria; pop. (1990) 188,230. Founded by the Thracians as Beroe, it was renamed Augusta Trajana by the Romans and Eski Zagra by the Turks. It was destroyed during the Russo-Turkish war of 1877 but has since been rebuilt as a modern planned city.

**Staryy Oskal** /ˌstɑːrɪ əsˈkɒl/ a city in Belgorod oblast, European Russia, situated to the west of Voronezh; pop. (1989) 174,000.

**Staten Island** /'stɑːt(ə)n/ a borough of New York City, named by early Dutch settlers after the Stahten or States General of the Netherlands; area 153 sq. km. (59 sq. miles); pop. (1990) 378,980. It is linked to Brooklyn by the Verrazano Narrows Bridge, and by ferries to Manhattan. The industrial area is in the north of the island and the residential and resort area in the south-east.

**Stavanger** /stəˈvæŋɡə(r)/ a seaport and county town of Rogaland in south-west Norway; pop. (1991) 98,180. One of the oldest towns in Norway, Stavanger developed as a fishing port following the growth of the herring and sprat fisheries in the late 19th c. It is now an important centre servicing offshore oil fields in the North Sea. Industries also include shipbuilding and fish-canning.

**Stavropol** /'stævrəpɒl/ **1.** an administrative territory (*kray*) of the Russian Federation in the

northern Caucasus, drained by the Kuma and Kuban rivers; area 80,600 sq. km. (31,120 sq. miles); pop. (1989) 2,855,000. Its main products are grain, cotton, oil, and natural gas. **2.** its capital, a city in the the north-western foothills of the Greater Caucasus; pop. (1990) 324,000. It was known as Voroshilovsk 1935–43 and is mainly concerned with food industries. **3.** the former name (until 1964) of TOGLIATTI in western Russia.

**Steiermark** the German name for STYRIA.

**Stellenbosch** /'stelənbɒʃ/ a university town in Cape province, South Africa, on the Eerste River east of Cape Town; pop. (1985) 43,000. Founded in 1679, it is the second-oldest European city in South Africa and a noted centre of wine production.

**Stendal** /'stendɑːl/ a city and rail junction in Saxony-Anhalt, central Germany, on the River Uchte; pop. (1984) 76,500. Founded in the 12th c., the city's name was taken as a pen name (Stendhal) by the French writer Marie Henry Beyle (1783–1842).

**Stepanakert** /ˌstepənəˈkɜːt/ see XAN KÄNDI.

**steppe** /step/ the name given to the vast areas of flat grasslands in eastern Europe and Asia that have been largely altered as a result of cultivation and extensive grazing by livestock. In their natural state they varied from the meadow steppes of the northern forest edge to the semidesert grasslands of central Asia.

**Sterlitamak** /ˌstɜːlɪtəˈmæk/ an industrial city in the republic of Bashkortostan (Bashkiria), in the Russian Federation, a port on the Belaya River; pop. (1990) 250,000.

**Stettin** see SZCZECIN.

**Stevenage** /'stiːvənɪdʒ/ a town in Hertfordshire, south-east England, built as a New Town in 1946; pop. (1981) 74,520. It has light industries including aircraft and electronic equipment.

**Steventon** /'stiːvəntən/ a small village near Basingstoke in Hampshire, southern England, where the novelist Jane Austen was born in 1775.

**Stewart Island** /'stuːət/ an island separated from the south coast of South Island, New Zealand, by the Foveaux Strait; area 1,735 sq. km. (670 sq. miles); chief settlement, Oban. Its highest peak is Mount Anglem (977 m., 3,205 ft.). Named after Captain William Stewart, whaler and sealer, who made a survey of the island in 1809, its economy is based on farming, fishing, and the mining of granite. It is also a summer resort and wildlife refuge.

**Stewartry** /'stuːətrɪ/ a district in Dumfries and Galloway region, south-west Scotland from 1975 to 1996; area 1,671 sq. km. (645 sq. miles); pop. (1991) 23,600. Its chief town is Kirkcudbright. Historically, the name was applied to a border district governed by a steward appointed by the king, a name later applied to the former county of Kirkcudbrightshire.

**Steyr** /ʃtaɪr/ a town in the state of Upper Austria, northern Austria, at the junction of the Ster and Enns rivers south of Linz; pop. (1991) 39,540. Its industries produce iron, steel, and motor vehicles.

**Stilton** /'stɪlt(ə)n/ a village in Cambridgeshire, England, 10 km. (6 miles) south-west of Peter-borough. It gives its name to a strong, rich cheese, often with blue veins, originally made at various places in Leicestershire and formerly sold to travel-lers in Stilton at the Bell Inn, a coaching inn on the Great North Road from London.

**Stirling** /'stɜ:lɪŋ/ a royal burgh to the south of the River Forth in central Scotland, capital of Central Region; pop. (1981) 38,800. The town is dominated by Stirling Castle which stands on a volcanic outcrop and was a regimental depot until 1964. Mary Queen of Scots was crowned in the chapel within the castle and her son James VI was baptized in the parish church. The Revd Ebenezer Erskine, founding father of the Scottish Secession Church (in 1733) is buried here and nearby stands a monument built in 1870 to commemorate the hero of Scottish Independence, Sir William Wallace. It is the site of the University of Stirling founded in 1967.

**Stockholm** /'stɒkhəʊm/ the capital of Sweden, a seaport situated on the mainland and several islands at the outflow of Lake Mälar into the Baltic; pop. (1990) 674,450. The Old Town, situ-ated on the islands of Staden, Helgeandsholmen, and Ryddarholmen, was fortified in the 13th c. Its chief landmarks are the Royal Palace, the Skansen Open-Air Museum, the Wasa Museum (housing the royal flagship which sank on its maiden voyage in 1628), and the home (on the island of Lidingö) of the sculptor Carl Milles (1875–1955). It was the birthplace in 1849 of the Swedish dramatist Johan Strindberg. It is Sweden's economic, administrat-ive, tourist, and cultural centre. It has shipbuilding and port industries as well as machinery, textiles, motor vehicle, and electrical industries. It has two universities, a school of economics, and numerous academies.

**Stockport** /'stɒkpɔ:t/ an industrial town in the metropolitan county of Greater Manchester, England, 10 km. (6 miles) south-east of Man-chester; pop. (1991) 130,000. The Goyt and Tame rivers join here to form the Mersey. Granted a charter in 1220, the town developed as a cotton-spinning centre in the 19th c.

**Stockton** /'stɒkt(ə)n/ a city and inland port in the San Joaquin valley, California, USA; pop. (1990) 210,940. It is connected to the San Francisco Bay by a deepwater channel and is a shipping cen-tre for ore and grain, and a processing centre for agricultural produce.

**Stockton-on-Tees** /ˌstɒkt(ə)nɒn'ti:z/ an industrial town in Cleveland, north-east England, on the River Tees; pop. (1991) 170,200. It developed after the opening of the Stockton–Darlington rail-

way in 1825 (the first passenger rail service in the world) and now has industries engaged in engineer-ing, and the manufacture of chemicals.

**Stoke-on-Trent** /ˌstəʊkɒn'trent/ a pottery-manufacturing city on the River Trent in Stafford-shire, England; pop. (1991) 244,800. It is the home of the University of Keele (1962) and was the birth-place in 1867 of the novelist Arnold Bennett.

**Stonehenge** /stəʊn'hendʒ/ a unique mega-lithic monument on Salisbury Plain in Wiltshire, England. Its alleged connection with the Druids dates from the 17th c., when people's ideas about what constituted 'the past' were very vague. In the 12th c. it was believed to be a monument over King Arthur's grave; other theories have attributed it to the Phoenicians, Romans, Vikings, and visitors from other worlds; modern theory inclines to the view that it was a temple. Scientific study and excavation have identified three main construc-tional phases between c. 3,000 BC and c. 1,500 BC, i.e. it was completed in the Bronze Age. The circular bank and ditch, double circle of 'bluestones' (spotted dolerite), and circle of sarsen stones (some with stone lintels), are concentric, and the main axis is aligned on the midsummer sunrise—an orientation that was probably for ritual rather than scientific purposes. It is believed that the 'blue-stones' were transported from the Prescelly Hills, Dyfed, a distance of 320 km. (200 miles).

**Store Bælt** see GREAT BELT.

**Stormont** /'stɔ:mənt/ a suburb of the east side of Belfast, the seat of the parliament of Northern Ireland (suspended since the imposition of direct rule from London in 1972); pop. (1991) 5,950.

**storm-surge** a rapid rise in sea-level caused by strong on-shore winds.

**Stornoway** /'stɔ:nəweɪ/ a town on the east coast of the island of Lewis in the Outer Hebrides, administrative centre of the Western Isles Islands Area of Scotland; pop. (1981) 8,640.

**Stour** /staʊr/ the name of four English rivers: **1.** a river that rises near Stourhead in Wiltshire and flows south for 88 km. (55 miles) before emptying into the English Channel at Christchurch, Dorset. **2.** a river that flows 75 km. (47 miles) south-east-wards from Cambridge along the Suffolk–Essex border before joining the Orwell and emptying into the North Sea at Harwich. **3.** a river that rises in the West Midlands and flows south-westwards through Stourbridge and Kidderminster to join the Severn at Stourport. **4.** a river that rises in the Cotswold Hills and flows west and north to meet the River Avon near Stratford-upon-Avon, Warwickshire.

**Strabane** /strə'bæn/ an agricultural town in Co. Tyrone, Northern Ireland, on the River Mourne; pop. (1981) 10,300. It was the birthplace in 1747 of John Dunlap, who in 1771 founded the first daily newspaper in the USA, the *Pennsylvania Packet*, and printed the Declaration of Independence.

**strait** the term for a narrow passage of water connecting two seas or larger bodies of water.

**Stralsund** /'ʃtrɑːlzʊnt/ a city on the Baltic coast of Mecklenburg-West Pomerania, north-east Germany, opposite the island of Rügen; pop. (1991) 71,620. It is a fishing and tourist centre.

**Stranraer** /strən'rɑː(r)/ a port at the head of Loch Ryan in Dumfries and Galloway district, south-west Scotland; pop. (1981) 10,870. There is a ferry link with Larne in Northern Ireland.

**Strasbourg** /'stræzbʊəg/ an industrial, and commercial city at the Ill River and Rhine confluence Alsace, north-east France, capital of the department of Bas-Rhin; pop. (1990) 255,940. It is a river port with canal connections. It has an 11th–15th c. Gothic cathedral and many fine 17th c. houses. Its many industries include metal-casting, machinery, and oil and gas refining. Meetings of the Council of Europe and sessions of the European Parliament are held in this city.

**strata** /'strɑːtə/ a term for the layers or beds of sedimentary rock.

### Stratford-upon-Avon

/'strætfədʊˌpɒn'eɪv(ə)n/ a market town on the River Avon in Warwickshire, England, where William Shakespeare was born and is buried; pop. (1981) 20,100. Shakespeare's birthplace, his house, the school he probably attended, and his wife's home are preserved and visited annually by many tourists, as are the church where Shakespeare is buried and the riverside Royal Shakespeare Theatre.

**strath** a broad valley in Scotland, i.e. Strathspey, Strathearn, or Strathmore.

**Strathclyde** /stræθ'klaɪd/ a local government region in western Scotland from 1975 to 1996; area 13,503 sq. km. (5,215 sq. miles); pop. (1991) 2,218,230; capital, Glasgow. It is divided into 19 districts:

| District | Area (sq. km.) | Pop. (1991) |
| --- | --- | --- |
| Argyll and Bute | 6,497 | 66,990 |
| Bearsden and Milngavie | 36 | 39,520 |
| Clydebank | 35 | 44,660 |
| Clydesdale | 1,325 | 57,080 |
| Cumbernauld and Kilsyth | 95 | 61,040 |
| Cumnock and Doon Valley | 801 | 42,000 |
| Cunninghame | 787 | 134,680 |
| Dumbarton | 471 | 75,970 |
| East Kilbride | 285 | 81,400 |
| Eastwood | 116 | 58,320 |
| Glasgow City | 198 | 654,540 |
| Hamilton | 131 | 103,140 |
| Inverclyde | 158 | 88,050 |
| Kilmarnock and Loudon | 373 | 78,560 |
| Kyle and Carrick | 1,296 | 113,570 |
| Monklands | 163 | 101,150 |
| Motherwell | 171 | 140,320 |
| Renfrew | 310 | 193,620 |
| Strathkelvin | 164 | 83,620 |

**Strathmore** /stræθ'mɔː(r)/ a wide and fertile valley to the south of the Grampian Mountains, eastern Scotland, stretching from Perth in the south-west to Brechin in the north-east. J. M. Barrie (1860–1937) was born in Kirriemuir and Glamis Castle, home of the Earl of Strathmore, was the birthplace in 1930 of Princess Margaret.

**Strathspey** /stræθ'speɪ/ an area of the Scottish Highlands in the middle valley of the Spey River, Highland Region. Its chief towns are Aviemore and Grantown-on-Spey. It gives its name to a slow Scottish dance. The area is popular with tourists and anglers and there are several whisky distilleries.

**stratocumulus** /ˌstrætəʊ'kjuːmjʊləs/ a type of cloud combining stratus and cumulus features and forming a uniform grey cloud cover below 2,438 m. (8,000 ft.).

**stratosphere** /'strætəˌsfɪə(r)/ a layer of atmospheric air above the troposphere extending to about 50 km. (31 miles) above the earth's surface, in which the lower part changes little in temperature with height.
**stratospheric** *adj.*

**stratus** /'strætəs/ a continuous horizontal sheet of grey cloud.

**Stretford** /'stretfəd/ an industrial town south-west of Manchester in the metropolitan county of Greater Manchester, England; pop. (1981) 47,770. Old Trafford cricket ground is located here.

**Stromboli** /'strɒmbəlɪ, strɒm'bəʊlɪ/ an active volcano forming one of the Lipari Islands in the Mediterranean, off the north-east coast of Sicily, noted for its perpetual state of mild activity. It rises to 750 m. (2,460 ft.), and on the island's north-east coast lie the villages of Piscità, Ficogrande, and San Vincenzo which are popular with tourists.

**Stroud** /straʊd/ a market town in Gloucestershire, England, on the River Frome; pop. (1981) 38,230.

**Struga** /'struːgæ/ a town in the former Yugoslavian republic of Macedonia, on the shore of Lake Ohrid; pop. (1981) 56,450.

**Struma** /'struːmæ/ (Greek **Strimon**) a river of Bulgaria and Greece that rises in the Vitosha Mts. near Sofia and flows 346 km. (216 miles) southwards to the Aegean Sea east of Thessaloníki.

**Strumica** /'struːmɪtsə/ a market town in the former Yugoslavian republic of Macedonia, on the River Strumica; pop. (1981) 83,350.

**Stubai Alps** /ʃtʊ'baɪ/ (German **Stubaier Alpen**) a range of the Eastern Alps in the Austrian state of Tyrol. Its highest peak is Zuckerhütl (3,507 m., 11,506 ft.).

**Stuttgart** /'ʃtʊtgɑːt/ a motor-manufacturing city and river port in Baden-Württemberg, south Germany, on the Neckar River; pop. (1991) 591,950. It was the capital of the former kingdom of Württemberg and the birthplace in 1770 of the philosopher G. F. W. Hegel. It is an educational, commercial, and tourist centre with several museums (including one in the Daimler-Benz factory, the world's oldest car-plant), a university, the famous Max Planck Research Institute, and a Fine art academy. In addition to vehicles its industries produce textiles, paper, machinery, electronic goods, photographic products, and precision equipment.

**Styria** /'stɪrɪə/ (German **Steiermark** /ʃteɪəˌmɑːk/) a state of south-east Austria on the frontier of Croatia; area 16,387 sq. km. (6,329 sq. miles); pop. (1991) 1,184,600; capital, Graz.

**Styx** /stɪks/ in Greek mythology, one of the nine rivers of the underworld, over which Charon ferried the souls of the dead.

**subcontinent** a term generally used to describe any large subdivision of a continent with a separate character. Until the beginning of the 20th c. it was used in reference to South Africa, but since then has been applied to that part of the Asian landmass to the south of the Himalayas, including India, Pakistan, Bangladesh, Nepal, Bhutan, and Sri Lanka.

**subduction zone** a zone where the rocks of an oceanic plate are forced under a much thicker continental plate. Melting as it descends, it releases magma into the earth's crust creating on the edge of the zone a region of volcanic activity and earthquakes.

**Sublime Porte** /sə'blaɪm pɔːt/, **the** the name given to the Sultan's court in Constantinople (Istanbul) in the days of the Ottoman empire. Mistakenly thought to reflect the city's status as a seaport, it refers to the 'imperial gate' that was probably the entrance to the Sultan's audience chamber.

**Subotica** /ˌsuːbə'tiːtsə/ an industrial city and transportation centre in the Serbian province of Vojvodina; pop. (1991) 100,200. Industries include heavy machinery, farm equipment, foodstuffs, and chemicals. The population are largely Hungarian.

**subtropical** regions with a near-tropical climate or, more precisely, those areas lying between the Tropic of Cancer and 40°N and the Tropic of Capricorn and 40°S.

**Suceava** /suː'tʃɑːvə/ a mining and industrial town in the eastern foothills of the Carpathian mountains, capital of Suceava county, north-east Romania; pop. (1989) 105,920. It was capital of Moldavia (1388–1564). It has numerous light industries.

**Suchou** see SUZHOU.

**Suchow** see XUZHOU.

**Sucre** /'suːkreɪ/ the legal capital and seat of the judiciary of Bolivia, situated at an altitude of 2,700 m. (8,860 ft.) in the Andes; pop. (1990) 101,800. Prior to the arrival of the Spanish it was known as Charcas and was the indigenous capital of the

valley of Choque-Chaca, a name corrupted to Cuquisaca and given to the city by the Spanish. Bolivia's Declaration of Independence was signed in the Legislative Palace in 1825 when the city's name was changed to Sucre in honour of General Antonio José de Sucre, second-in-command to Simon Bolívar and an advocate of independence for the region. It is a major agricultural centre supplying the altiplano mining region, and has an oil refinery.

**Sudan** /suː'dɑːn, suː-/ official name **The Republic of Sudan** a country in north-east Africa, south of Egypt, with a coastline on the Red Sea; area 2,506,000 sq. km. (967,940 sq. miles); 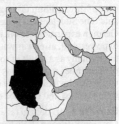 pop. (est. 1991) 25,855,000; official language, Arabic; capital, Khartoum. Its largest cities are Khartoum, Omdurman, and Port Sudan. Sudan is the largest country in Africa and lies astride the Nile entirely within the tropics. The northern part is desert, and south of Khartoum, towards the foothills of the Ethiopian Highlands in the south-east and the Imatong Mts. on the southern frontier with Kenya and Uganda, there is a progressive increase in rainfall which falls largely between April and October. Sudan's chief exports are cotton, peanuts, sorghum, gum arabic, and sesame. The north-east area was part of ancient Nubia. Under Arab rule from the 13th c., the country was conquered by Egypt in 1820–2. The Sudan was separated from its northern neighbour by the Mahdist revolt of 1881–98, and administered after the reconquest of 1898 as an Anglo-Egyptian condominium. It became an independent republic in 1956, but has suffered as a result of political instability and a protracted civil war between the Islamic government in the north and separatist rebels in the south. As a result of war and drought, an estimated 7 million people faced starvation in 1992.

**Sudanese** *adj. & n.*

Sudan is divided into nine regions:

| Region | Area (sq. km.) | Pop. (1983) | Capital |
|---|---|---|---|
| Northern | 183,941 | 1,083,000 | Ed Damer |
| Eastern | 129,086 | 2,208,200 | Kassala |
| Central | 53,716 | 4,012,500 | Wad Medani |
| Kordofan | 146,932 | 3,093,300 | El Obeid |
| Khartoum | 10,883 | 1,802,300 | Khartoum |
| Dafur | 196,555 | 3,093,700 | El Fasher |
| Equatoria | 76,495 | 1,406,200 | Juba |
| Bahr el-Ghazal | 77,625 | 2,265,500 | Wau |
| Upper Nile | 92,269 | 1,599,600 | Malakal |

**Sudbury** /'sʌdbərɪ/ a city in central Ontario, Canada, situated north of Toronto on Ramsey

Lake, at the centre of Canada's largest mining region with nickel, copper, and platinum mines; pop. (1991) 92,900; 157,610 (metropolitan area). The city boasts the highest smokestacks in the world (350 m., 1,150 ft.). It is the home of the bilingual Laurentian University (1960).

**Sudetenland** /sʊˈdeɪtənˌlænd/ an area of Bohemia in the Czech Republic adjacent to the German border, allocated to the new state of Czechoslovakia after World War I despite the presence of three million German-speaking inhabitants. The Sudetenland became the first object of German expansionist policies after the Nazis came to power, and, after war was threatened, was ceded to Germany as a result of the Munich Agreement of September 1938. In 1945 the area was returned to Czechoslovakia, and the German inhabitants were expelled and replaced by Czechs.

**Sudetes** /sʊˈdeɪtiːz/ (also **Sudetic Mountains**, German **Sudeten**, Polish and Czech **Sudety**) a range of mountains with extensive coal and mineral deposits on the frontier between the Czech Republic and Poland and situated between the Carpathians to the east and the Erzgebirge to the west. Its highest peak is Sněka (1,603 m., 5,256 ft.).

**Suez** /ˈsuːɪz/ (Arabic **Suweis**) 1. an isthmus connecting Egypt to the Sinai peninsula. 2. a port in north-eastern Egypt, situated on the Red Sea at the southern end of the Suez Canal; pop. (1991) 376,000. It is the control centre for the Canal with refuelling facilities and two oil refineries.

**Suez Canal** a shipping canal 171 km. (106 miles) long and without locks connecting the Mediterranean (at Port Said) with the Red Sea, constructed in 1859–69 by Ferdinand de Lesseps. The canal, now important for Egypt's economy as providing the shortest route for international sea traffic travelling between Europe and Asia, came under British control after Britain acquired majority shares in it, at Disraeli's instigation, in 1875, and after 1888 Britain acted as guarantor of its neutral status. It was nationalized by Egypt in 1956 and an Anglo-French attempt at intervention was called off after international protest. It has been enlarged to take ships of almost any draught.

**Suffolk** /ˈsʌfək/ a county of eastern England; area 3,797 sq. km. (1,466 sq. miles); pop. (1991) 629,900; county town, Ipswich. The county, which gives its name to a black-faced breed of sheep and a breed of draft horse, is divided into seven districts:

| District | Area (sq. km.) | Pop. (1991) |
|---|---|---|
| Babergh | 595 | 78,500 |
| Forest Heath | 374 | 57,200 |
| Ipswich | 39 | 115,500 |
| Mid Suffolk | 871 | 77,100 |
| St. Edmundsbury | 657 | 89,100 |
| Suffolk Coastal | 891 | 106,800 |
| Waveney | 370 | 105,500 |

**Sugar Loaf Mountain** (Portuguese **Pão de Açucar** /paʊ deɪ æˈʒuːkə(r)/) a rocky peak rising to a height of 2,074 m. (1,296 ft.) north-east of Copacabana Beach, Rio de Janeiro, Brazil.

**Suhl** /ˈzʊəl/ an industrial town in Thuringia, east Germany; pop. (1991) 59,100. It has diverse light industries including precision instruments.

**Sui** /swiː/ a dynasty of emperors ruling China from 589 to 618, between the period of The Three Kingdoms and the Tang Dynasty. Reuniting the country, the Sui emperors built the Grand Canal.

**Suihua** /swiːˈhwɑː/ a city in Heilongjiang province, north-east China, north of Harbin; pop. (1986) 737,000.

**Suita** /suːˈiːtə/ a city in Osaka prefecture, Honshu Island, Japan; pop. (1990) 345,190.

**Suizhou** /swiːˈdʒəʊ/ a city in Hubei province, east-central China, north-west of Wuhan; pop. (1986) 140,000.

**Sukhotai** /ˌsʊkəˈtaɪ/ (also **Sukhothai**) a town in the Northern Region of Thailand; pop. (1990) 22,600. Formerly the capital of an independent state that flourished from the mid-13th to mid-14th c., its Thai name means 'dawn of happiness'. The ruined city, lying in a 70-sq. km. (27-sq. mile) historical park to the west of the modern town, is Thailand's leading historic site.

**Sukhumi** /sʊˈkʊmɪ/ (Georgian **Sokhumi**) the capital of the autonomous republic of Abkhazia in Georgia, a port and resort on the east coast of the Black Sea; pop. (1991) 121,700. In the aftermath of the breakup of the Soviet Union in 1991 it was the focus of armed conflict between Georgian and separatist Abkhazian forces which seized it in September 1993. This led to a mass exodus of Georgians.

**Sukkur** /sʊˈkʊə(r)/ a commercial and industrial city on the Indus River in the province of Sind, south-east Pakistan; pop. (est. 1991) 350,000. Nearby is the Sukkur Barrage, nearly 1.6 km. (1 mile) long, completed in 1932, built across the river and feeding irrigation canals which direct its water to over 12 million hectares (5 million acres) of the Indus valley. It is a centre for trade with Afghanistan and has varied textile industries.

**Sukuma** /səˈkuːmə/ a Bantu people of north-west Tanzania, the largest tribal group in the country. They depend for their livelihood on cattle herding and cotton which is largely sold in the town of Mwanza on Lake Victoria.

**Sula Islands** /ˈsuːlə/ a group of Indonesian islands lying between the Celebes (Sulawesi) and the Moluccas and comprising the islands of Sanana, Mangole, and Taliabu and several small islands. Its chief town is Sanana (on Sanana) and its principal products are rice and timber.

**Sulawesi** /ˌsʊləˈweɪsɪ/ a large island of Indonesia, east of Borneo, formerly called Celebes; area 189,216 sq. km. (73,084 sq. miles); pop. (est. 1993)

13,279,000. It is the third-largest of the Greater Sundas and Ujung Pandang is its chief port and largest city. Beyond a narrow coastal fringe the island has a mountainous interior rising to 3,225 m. (10,580 ft.) at Mount Sonjol. Of the 127 mammal species on the island 79 are endemic. There is a similar degree of endemism amongst birds, insects, reptiles, and amphibians, a fact noted by the Victorian naturalist Alfred Russell Wallace who visited the island and wrote down ideas on evolution that prompted Charles Darwin to write his *Origin of Species*.

**Sullom Voe** /ˌsʌləm ˈvəʊ/ the principal UK North Sea oil terminal, constructed in the 1970s on Sullom Voe, an inlet at the northern end of mainland Shetland.

**Sulu Sea** /ˈsuːluː/ an arm of the Pacific Ocean lying between north-east Borneo and the islands of the Philippines and separating the South China Sea from the Celebes Sea.

**Sumatra** /sʊˈmɑːtrə/ the name given to a blustery wind that blows up quickly in the Malacca Strait during the north-west monsoon.

**Sumatra** /sʊˈmɑːtrə/ (also **Sumatera**) a large island of Indonesia, separated from the Malay peninsula by the Strait of Malacca; area 424,760 sq. km. (164,000 sq. miles); pop. (est. 1993) 39,232,800. Its largest city and port is Medan and its indigenous people include a dozen ethnic groups who speak some 20 dialects. Sumatra's interior is covered by dense rainforest; much of the eastern half of the island is swampland. It produces rubber and timber for export and its oil and other minerals provide three-quarter's of Indonesia's income.

**Šumava** /ˈʃuːmɑːvə/ a range of low forested mountains in the Czech Republic, in south-west Bohemia on the border with Germany.

**Sumba** /ˈsʊmbə/ (also Sandalwood Island) an island of the Lesser Sundas, Indonesia, lying to the south of the islands of Flores and Sumbawa, and noted for its megalith tombs; area 11,148 sq. km. (4,306 sq. miles); pop. (1989) 425,000. Its chief towns are Waikelo in the west and Waingapu in the east and its principal products are sandalwood, copra, cinnamon, and tobacco.

**Sumbawa** /sʊmˈbɑːwə/ an island with popular surfing beaches in the Lesser Sundas, Indonesia, situated to the east of Lombok; area 14,739 sq. km. (5,693 sq. miles). Sumbawa-Besar, Raba, and Bima are the chief towns and its highest peak is Mount Tambora (2,820 m., 9,252 ft.) which erupted in 1815 killing 12,000 people.

**Sumer** /ˈsuːmə(r)/ the name used in antiquity from the 3rd millennium BC for southern Mesopotamia, the region inhabited by Sumerian-speaking people and later known as Babylonia.

**Sumerian** /suːˈmɪərɪən/ a people speaking a non-Semitic language and civilization native to Sumer in the 4th millennium BC. The Sumerians were a hybrid stock speaking an agglutinative language related structurally to Turkish, Hungarian, Finnish, and several Caucasian dialects. As the first historically attested civilization they are credited with the invention of cuneiform writing, the sexagesimal system of mathematics, and the sociopolitical institution of the city-state with bureaucracies, legal codes, division of labour, and a money economy. Their art, literature, and theology had a profound cultural and religious influence on the rest of Mesopotamia and beyond, which continued long after the Sumerian demise c. 2,000 BC, as the prototype of Akkadian, Hurrian, Canaanite, Hittite, and eventually, biblical literature. Two of their main cities were Ur and Lagash.

**Sumqayit** /ˌsʊmgɑˈiːt/ (formerly **Sumgait**) an industrial city of Azerbaijan on the western shore of the Caspian Sea, north of Baku; pop. (1990) 234,600. It has steel, iron, and aluminium works.

**Sumy** /ˈsuːmiː/ an industrial city in north-east Ukraine, north-west of Kharkov; pop. (1990) 296,000.

**sunbelt** /ˈsʌnbelt/ a strip of territory receiving a high amount of sunshine, a term especially applied to **the Sunbelt**, a region in the southern USA stretching from California to Florida experiencing major inward migration. Aerospace and electronics-based industries have developed rapidly.

**Sunbury** /ˈsʌnbɜːrɪ/ a town in south-central Victoria, Australia, situated to the north-west of Melbourne; pop. (1991) 18,530.

**Sun City** a modern resort complex in the Mankwe district of Bophuthatswana, in western North West Province, South Africa, to provide entertainment facilities not generally available in South Africa.

**Sunda Islands** /ˈsʌndə/ islands of the Malay Archipelago, Indonesia, divided into two groups, the **Greater Sunda Islands** which include Borneo, Sumatra, Java, and the islands of Sulawesi, and the **Lesser Sunda Islands** which lie to the east of Java and include Sumbawa, Flores, Sumba, and Timor.

**Sundarbans** /ˈsʌndəbənz/ a low-lying mangrove swamp and jungle region at the mouth of the Ganges Delta in Bangladesh and the Indian state of West Bengal. Much of the jungle is a wildlife sanctuary. The region is liable to devastating floods and cyclones.

**Sunderland** /ˈsʌndələnd/ an industrial city in Tyne and Wear, north-east England, a port at the mouth of the River Wear; pop. (1981) 196,800. Formerly a centre of shipbuilding, its industries now produce chemicals, electronics, furniture, and vehicles. The University of Sunderland (formerly Sunderland Polytechnic) was established in 1992.

**Sundsvall** /ˈsuːnzvɑːl/ a town in Västernorrland county, eastern Sweden, a port on the Gulf of Bothnia; pop. (1990) 93,800. An important trading centre since Viking times, its industries handle oil, paper, and timber products.

**Sung** /sʊŋ/ the name of the dynasty which ruled in China 960–1279.

**Sun Moon Lake** a lake situated at an altitude of 762 m. (2,500 ft.) in Nantou county, central Taiwan. It is a year-round resort.

**Sunni** /'sʌnɪ/ one of the two main branches of Islam regarding Sunna law (based on the words of Muhammad memorized by his disciples) as equal in authority to the Koran. Sunnis comprise the main community in most Muslim countries other than Iran. The split occurred early in the history of Islam over the question of allegiance to the nascent Ummayyad dynasty (supported by the Sunnis) versus the family of Ali, son-in-law of the prophet Muhammad and fourth caliph. After his assassination and that of his son Husayn at the Battle of Kerbala (in present-day Iraq) in 680, one group of Muslims broke away from the main body, declaring their allegiance to the martyred sons, and calling themselves the Shia (= party). What became known as the Sunni Muslims continued to follow the reigning caliph. From the basic split in attitudes to leadership of the community have followed other differences in community organization and legal practice, but doctrinally Sunni and Shiite Muslims adhere to the same body of tenets.
**Sunnite** *adj. & n.*

**Sunset Boulevard** a road which links the centre of Los Angeles with the Pacific Ocean 48 km. (30 miles) to the west. The eastern section of the road between Fairfax Avenue and Beverly Hills is known as Sunset Strip.

**Sunshine Coast** the name given to that part of the Pacific coast of Queensland, Australia, stretching from Bribie Island northwards to Noosa Heads. Noted for its fine beaches, it includes the resorts of Caloundra, Maroochydore, and Coolum Beach.

**Suomi** /'suəumɪ/ the Finnish name for Finland.

**Superior, Lake** one of the five Great Lakes of North America and the largest freshwater lake in the world; maximum depth 405 m. (1,329 ft.); area 84,243 sq. km. (32,526 sq. miles); area on the Canadian side of the border, 29,888 sq. km. (11,540 sq. miles). The cities of Duluth and Thunder Bay lie on its shore and it is linked to Lake Huron by the St. Mary's River.

**Surabaya** /ˌsuərə'baɪə/ a seaport and the principal naval base of Indonesia, capital of the province of East Java and second-largest city in Indonesia; pop. (1990) 2,473,270. It was formerly the largest town and most important port of the Dutch East Indies. Its industries include ship handling and repair, oil refining, automobile assembly, and textiles.

**Surakarta** /ˌsuərə'kɑːtə/ (also **Solo** /'səʊləʊ/ or **Sala**) a city at the centre of the Indonesian island of Java, on the Solo River 65 km. (41 miles) east of Yogyakarta; pop. (1990) 503,830. It was capital of the kingdom of Mataram from the mid-17th to the

mid-18th c. and is today one of Java's oldest cultural centres with a reputation for being the cleanest city in Indonesia. It has a university founded in 1955. It is also a trade centre with light industries including batik cloth and gold articles.

**Surat** /'suərət, su'rɑːt/ a port in the state of Gujarat in west-central India, on the Tapti River; pop. (1991) 1,517,000. Here the East India Company established its first trading post in 1612; Surat was a major city of India in the late 17th–18th c. Amongst its industries are diamond cutting, silk weaving and the production of cotton, saris, and gold and silver thread.

**Surazo** /su'ræzəu/ a cold, winter wind that blows during periods of high pressure in southern Brazil.

**Surgut** /suə'gut/ a city in Tyumen oblast, West Siberia, in the Russian Federation; pop. (1990) 256,000. It lies on the River Ob at the centre of an oil-producing region.

**Surinam**
/ˌsuərɪ'næm/ official
name **The Republic**
**of Suriname** a
country on the
north-east coast of
South America,
bounded by Guyana,
Brazil, French
Guiana, and the

Atlantic Ocean; area 163,265 sq. km. (63,061 sq. miles); pop. (est. 1991) 457,000; official language, Dutch; capital, Paramaribo. A narrow swamp-fringed lowland coastal region rises southwards through an interior plateau towards mountains covered in forest. The climate is subtropical and the population is largely concentrated on the coast. Surinam has large timber resources, but the economy is chiefly dependent on bauxite, which makes up over three-quarters of its exports. Settled by the English in 1650, the country was ceded to the Dutch in 1667 but twice returned to British control before finally reverting to the Netherlands in 1815. Known until 1948 as Dutch Guiana, it attained a measure of autonomy in 1950 and 1954 followed by full independence in 1975. Following a coup in 1980, Surinam was governed by a National Military Council led by Lt.-Col. Désiré Bouterse and the country became isolated internationally as a result of armed conflict between the government and rebel ethnic groups. A new Constitution was approved by referendum in 1987 and the country was restored to peace. Executive authority now rests with the president who is elected by the legislative National Assembly.
**Surinamese** *adj. & n.*

**Surrey** /'sʌrɪ/ a largely residential county of south-east England; area 1,679 sq. km. (648 sq. miles); pop. (1991) 997,000; county town, Guildford. Surrey is divided into 11 districts:

| District | Area (sq. km.) | Pop. (1991) |
| --- | --- | --- |
| Elmbridge | 97 | 109,900 |
| Epsom and Ewell | 34 | 66,000 |
| Guildford | 271 | 121,500 |
| Mole Valley | 258 | 77,400 |
| Reigate and Banstead | 129 | 114,900 |
| Runnymede | 78 | 71,500 |
| Spelthorne | 56 | 87,100 |
| Surrey Heath | 96 | 78,300 |
| Tandridge | 250 | 75,000 |
| Waverley | 345 | 111,000 |
| Woking | 64 | 84,000 |

**Surtsey** /'sɜːtsɪ/ a small island to the south of Iceland, which rose from the sea during a volcanic eruption in 1963. It is named after the Norse god Surtur who was appointed to set fire to the earth the day the gods fall.

**Susa** /'suːsə/ an ancient city near modern Dezful in south-west Iran, the capital of Elam and later of Persia in Achaemenid times.

**Susquehanna** /sʊskwə'haːnə/ a river of the USA that rises in two branches which meet near Sunbury in Pennsylvania. From there it flows 240 km. (150 miles) south through Harrisburg to join Chesapeake Bay. It is named after the Susquehanocks tribe which was exterminated by the Iroquois Indians c. 1675.

**Sussex** /'sʌsɪks/ a former county of southern England, now divided into East and West Sussex and including the chalky South Downs and wooded Weald.

**Sutherland** /'sʌðɜːlənd/ a former county of Scotland, since 1975 a district of Highland Region; area 5,865 sq. km. (2,265 sq. miles); pop. (1991) 13,740. Its administrative centre is Golspie.

**Sutlej** /'sʌtlɪdʒ/ a river that rises in south-west Tibet and flows west through the Indian states of Himachal Pradesh and Punjab before entering Pakistan (Punjab province), where it joins the Chenab River to form the Panjnad. It is one of the 'five rivers' that gave Punjab its name.

**Sutton Courtenay** /ˌsʌt(ə)n' kɔːtnɪ/ a Thames-side village in Oxfordshire, England, between Abingdon and Didcot in whose churchyard are buried Eric Blair (1903–50) who wrote under the pen-name George Orwell, and Herbert Asquith, British prime minister 1908–16.

**Sutton Hoo** /ˌsʌt(ə)n 'huː/ an estate in Suffolk, England, site of a group of barrows, one of which was found (1939) to cover the remains of a Saxon ship burial (or perhaps a cenotaph; no body was discovered) of the 7th c. AD. The timbers had decayed and only their impression was left in the soil, with the iron bolts still in place, and in the centre was a magnificent collection of grave goods, including exotic jewellery, an iron standard, decorated shield, bronze helmet, and Merovingian gold coins.

**Suva** /'suːvə/ the capital of Fiji (since 1882), situated on the Pacific island of Viti Levu; pop. (1986) 71,600. It is a port with a deep-water harbour that receives cargo and cruise ships.

**Suwon** /'suːwən/ (also **Suweon**) an industrial city in Kyonggi province, north-west Korea, south of Seoul; pop. (1990) 644,970. Its chief landmarks are the 18th-c. city wall and the Korean Folk Village. It has large textile mills and chemical industries.

**Suzhou** /su:'dʒəʊ/ **1.** (formerly **Suchou** and **Wuhsien**) a city in Jiangsu province, eastern China, on the Grand Canal; pop. (1990) 84,000. It was capital of the Wu kingdom in the 6th c. BC and became known as a trading centre for silk, and gold. The city today is noted for its ornamental gardens. **2.** a city in Anhui province, eastern China, north of the Huai River; pop. (1986) 225,000.

**Suzuka** /su:'zuːkɑː/ an industrial city in Mie prefecture, central Honshu Island, Japan; pop. (1990) 174,100. It has chemical, textile, and mechanical industries.

### Svalbard

/'svɑːlbɑːd/ a group of islands, comprising Spitsbergen and other groups, in the Arctic Ocean about 640 km. (400 miles) north of Norway, to which country they have belonged since  1925; area 62,000 sq. km. (24,000 sq. miles); pop. (1989) 3,540. There are important coal and mineral deposits.

**Sverdlovsk** /sveəd'lɒfsk/ see YEKATERINBURG.

**Sverdrup Islands** /'sferdrəp/ a group of islands in the Canadian Arctic, in the Queen Elizabeth Islands west of Ellesmere Island. They include Axel Heiberg, Ellef Ringnes, and Amund Ringnes and are named after Otto Sverdrup who led Norwegian expeditions to the islands between 1898 and 1902.

**Swabia** /'sweɪbɪə/ (German **Schwaben**) a former German duchy, now divided between Germany, Switzerland, and France.
**Swabian** adj. & n.

**Swahili** /swə'hiːlɪ, swɑː'hiːlɪ/ **1.** a Bantu people of Zanzibar and the adjacent coast of Africa. **2.** their language, a Bantu language of the Niger-Congo group with a vocabulary heavily influenced by Arabic. It is the most important language in East Africa, spoken also in the central and southern regions and expanding rapidly to the west and north, and while it is the first language of only about a million people it is used as a common language by about twenty million who speak different mother tongues. It is the official language of Kenya and Tanzania.

**Swakopmund** /'sfɑːkəpmənt/ a port and resort town on the Atlantic coast of Namibia, at the
mouth of the Swakop River to the north of Walvis
Bay. It was formerly a leading port of German
Southwest Africa.

**Swansea** /'swɒnzɪ/ (Welsh **Abertawe**) a city in
West Glamorgan, South Wales, at the mouth of the
River Tawe; pop. (1991) 182,100. Swansea developed rapidly in the 19th c. based on the export
of anthracite coal and a major tin-plate and associated steel industry. This has now declined and been
succeeded by light industries and tourism; the popular Gower peninsula is within the city boundaries.
Swansea has one of the University Colleges of
Wales (1982). The UK vehicle-licensing centre is
located here. Swansea was the birthplace in 1914 of
the poet Dylan Thomas.

**Swatow** see SHANTOU.

**Swazi** /'swɑːzɪ/ a people of mixed stock inhabiting Swaziland and parts of eastern Transvaal in the
Republic of South Africa. The Swazi language,
which is of the Niger-Congo group, is one of the
official languages of Swaziland.

## Swaziland

/'swɑːzɪˌlænd/ official
name **The Kingdom
of Swaziland** a
small landlocked
country of southern
Africa, bounded by
Transvaal, Natal,
and Mozambique;
area 17,363 sq. km.
(6,706 sq. miles); pop. (est. 1991) 825,000; official
languages, Swazi and English; capital, Mbabane.
The smallest country in southern Africa, Swaziland takes its name from the Swazis who occupied
it from the mid-18th c. The humid mountainous
high veld in the west descends from an average
elevation of 1,500 m. (5,000 ft.) through a drier
subtropical middle veld to bush-covered low veld at
an elevation of 150–300 m. (500–1,000 ft.). A
largely agricultural country, the chief exports are
sugar, citrus fruit, wood pulp, and asbestos. It was
a South African protectorate from 1894 and came
under British rule in 1902 after the second Boer
War. In 1968 it became a fully independent kingdom within the Commonwealth. There is a bicameral parliament (the *Libandia*) comprising a
Senate and House of Assembly, executive power
being vested in the king and exercised by a Cabinet
appointed by him. Political parties are banned but
members of the House of Assembly were directly
elected for the first time in 1993.

**Swede** /swiːd/ a native of Sweden or person of
Swedish descent.

**Sweden** /'swiːd(ə)n/ (Swedish **Sverige**
/'sværjə/) official name **The Kingdom of Sweden**
a country occupying the eastern part of the
Scandinavian peninsula; area 449,964 sq. km.

(173,798 sq. miles);
pop. (1990)
8,590,630; official
language, Swedish;
capital, Stockholm.
Its largest cities are
Stockholm,
Gothenburg,
Malmö, and
Uppsala. A largely
flat tableland with forests, lakes, and numerous offshore islands in the south-east, Sweden's only upland region lies on the Norwegian frontier where
the Kjölen Mts. rise to peaks in excess of 2,000 m.
(6,560 ft.). Rich in timber and mineral resources,
Sweden exports wood pulp, paper products, motor
vehicles, machinery, and iron and steel goods. Its
Germanic and Gothic inhabitants took part in the
Viking raids. Originally united in the 12th c.,
Sweden formed part of the Union of Kalmar with
Denmark and Norway from 1397 until its re-emer-
gence as an independent state under Gustavus Vasa
in 1523. The following two centuries saw the country's rise and fall as the prominent Baltic power, influence on the European mainland peaking during
the reign of Gustavus Adolphus in the early 17th c.
and collapsing following the defeat of Charles XII
in the Great Northern War at the beginning of the
18th c. Between 1814 and 1905, Sweden was united
with Norway. She maintained her neutrality in the
two World Wars, while her economy prospered
through increasing industrialization, and the political hegemony of the Social Democratic party led
to the creation of an extensive system of social security. Sweden, which joined the European Union
in 1995, is a parliamentary democracy in which the
monarch is retained for ceremonial functions. A
prime minister and Cabinet are responsible to a
unicameral parliament (*Riksdag*).
**Swedish** *adj. & n.*
Sweden is administratively divided into 24 counties
(*Län*):

| County | Area (sq. km.) | Pop. (1990) | Capital |
|---|---|---|---|
| Älvsborg | 11,395 | 441,390 | Vänersborg |
| Blekinge | 2,941 | 150,560 | Karlskrona |
| Gävleborg | 18,191 | 289,290 | Gävle |
| Göteborg and Bohus | 5,141 | 739,945 | Gothenburg |
| Gotland | 3,140 | 57,110 | Visby |
| Halland | 5,454 | 254,725 | Halmstad |
| Jämtland | 49,443 | 134,160 | Östersund |
| Jönköping | 9,944 | 308,290 | Jönköping |
| Kalmar | 11,170 | 241,100 | Kalmar |
| Kopparberg | 28,194 | 289,070 | Falun |
| Kristianstad | 6,089 | 289,280 | Kristianstad |
| Kronoberg | 8,458 | 177,880 | Växjö |
| Malmöhus | 4,938 | 779,310 | Malmö |
| Norrbotten | 98,911 | 263,735 | Luleå |
| Örebro | 8,519 | 272,510 | Örebro |
| Östergötland | 10,562 | 403,010 | Linköping |

| Skaraborg | 7,938 | 276,830 | Mariestad |
| Södermanland | 6,060 | 255,640 | Nyköping |
| Stockholm | 6,488 | 1,641,670 | Stockholm |
| Uppsala | 6,989 | 268,835 | Uppsala |
| Värmland | 17,583 | 283,110 | Karlstad |
| Västerbotten | 55,400 | 251,970 | Umeå |
| Västernorrland | 21,678 | 261,155 | Härnösand |
| Västmanland | 6,302 | 258,487 | Västerås |

**Swedish** /'swiːdɪʃ/ the official language of
Sweden, spoken by its 8.6 million inhabitants, by
another 300,000 in Finland (where it is one of the
two official languages), and by 600,000 in the US.
It belongs to the Scandinavian language group.

**swidden agriculture** /'swɪd(ə)n/ a system of
shifting cultivation used in the tropics.

**Swindon** /'swɪnd(ə)n/ an industrial town in
Wiltshire, southern England; pop. (1991) 100,000.
It is a centre of the high-tech and motor industries
and is a major warehousing and distribution
centre. Swindon developed from a village overnight
into a 'railway town' when it was chosen by Brunel
in 1841 as the site of a major railway works. The
'old' town has a large railway museum.

**Swiss** /swɪs/ a native of Switzerland or a person
of Swiss descent.

**Switzerland** /'swɪtsələnd/ (French **Suisse**
/swiːs/, German **Schweiz** /ʃvaɪts/, Italian **Svizzera**
/'zviːtseɪrə/, Latin **Helvetia** /hel'viːʃə/) official
name **The Swiss Confederation** a small country
in central Europe, dominated by the Alps and Jura
Mountains; area 41,293 sq. km. (15,949 sq. miles);
pop. (1990) 6,673,850; official languages, German,
French, Italian, and
Romansch; capital,
Berne. Its largest
cities are Zürich,
Basle, Geneva,
Berne, and
Lausanne. The popu-
lation is divided lin-
guistically into
French-, German-,

and Italian-speaking areas, while the economy is
centred on precision engineering, chemicals,
pharmaceuticals, dairy products, and tourism, also
benefiting from the country's position as an international financing centre. The area (occupied by a
Celtic people, the Helvetii) was under Roman rule
from the 1st c. BC until the 5th c. AD, and from the
10th c. formed part of the Holy Roman Empire.
Switzerland emerged as an independent country in
the Middle Ages when the local cantons joined in
league to defeat first their Habsburg overlords in
the 14th c. and then their Burgundian neighbours
in the 15th c. The Swiss Confederation maintained
neutrality in international affairs through the 17th
and 18th centuries, and after a period of French
domination (1798–1815), the Confederation's
neutrality was guaranteed by the other European
powers. Neutral in both World Wars, Switzerland
has emerged as the headquarters of such international organizations as the Red Cross, the International Labour Organization, and the World
Council of Churches. Executive power is held by
the Federal Council (*Bundesrat*) and legislative
power resides with the bicameral Federal Assembly

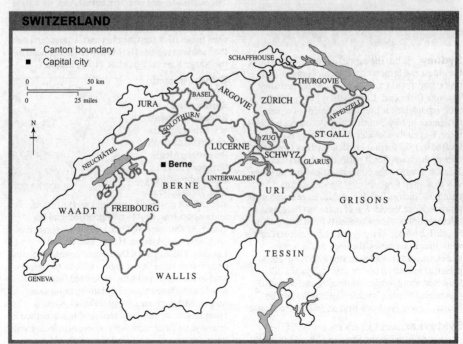

**SWITZERLAND**

— Canton boundary
■ Capital city

(*Bundesversammlung*). Switzerland is federally divided into 20 cantons and six half cantons:

| Canton | Area (sq. km.) | Pop. (1990) | Capital |
|---|---|---|---|
| Argovie (Aargau) | 1,405 | 496,280 | Aarau |
| Berne | 6,049 | 945,570 | Berne |
| Freibourg | 1,670 | 207,750 | Freibourg |
| Geneva | 282 | 375,960 | Geneva |
| Glarus | 685 | 37,650 | Glarus |
| Grisons (Graubünden) | 7,106 | 170,410 | Chur |
| Jura | 837 | 65,700 | Delémont |
| Lucerne | 1,492 | 319,525 | Lucerne |
| Neuchâtel (Neuenburg) | 797 | 160,610 | Neuchâtel |
| Schaffhouse | 298 | 71,700 | Schaffhouse |
| Schwyz | 908 | 110,530 | Schwyz |
| Solothurn | 791 | 226,655 | Solothurn |
| St. Gall(St. Gallen) | 2,014 | 420,270 | St. Gall |
| Tessin (Ticino) | 2,811 | 286,725 | Bellinzona |
| Thurgovie (Thurgau) | 1,013 | 205,950 | Frauenfeld |
| Waadt (Vaud) | 3,218 | 583,625 | Lausanne |
| Wallis (Valais) | 5,226 | 248,310 | Sion |
| Uri | 1,076 | 33,650 | Altdorf |
| Zug | 239 | 84,910 | Zug |
| Zürich | 1,729 | 1,150,550 | Zürich |

| Half Canton | Area (sq. km.) | Pop. (1990) | Capital |
|---|---|---|---|
| Appenzell-Outer Rhoden | 243 | 51,470 | Herisan |
| Appenzell-Inner Rhoden | 172 | 13,570 | Appenzell |
| Basle-Town | 37 | 191,790 | Basle |
| Basle-Country | 428 | 230,110 | Basle |
| Nidwalden | 276 | 32,630 | Stans |
| Obwalden | 491 | 28,810 | Sarnen |

**Sydney** /'sɪdnɪ/ the capital of New South Wales, the oldest and largest city and chief port of Australia; pop. (1991) 3,097,950. It was named after Thomas Townsend, Lord Sydney (1733–1800) who was responsible for the establishment of a penal settlement in New South Wales. A convict settlement, originally considered for Botany Bay, was located in 1788 further north at Sydney Cove, an inlet of the magnificent natural harbour of Port Jackson. By 1820 the convict settlement had given way to a small Regency city. Sydney and its beaches—such as Bondi—attract large numbers of tourists. Since World War II there has been a considerable influx of new residents from Europe and South-East Asia. The city is a major cultural centre with three universities, theatres, opera house, museums, and art galleries. It is also Australia's principal industrial centre with shipyards, oil refineries, automobile, electronics, and chemical plants, and textiles. Its chief landmarks are the Sydney Tower, Harbour Bridge, and Opera House.

**Syktyvkar** /sɪktɪf'kɑ:(r)/ the capital of the republic of Komi in the Russian Federation, a city on the Sysola River; pop. (1990) 235,000. Lumbering and woodworking are the principal industries.

**syncline** /'sɪnklaɪn/ the term given to rock strata folded into a trough.

**synoptic image** /sɪ'nɒptɪk/ an image of part of the earth's surface derived from a remote sensor.

**Syracuse** /'saɪrəˌkju:z/ (Italian **Siracusa** /ˌsɪərə'ku:zə/) a port and tourist centre on the south-east coast of Sicily; pop. (1990) 125,440. Founded by the Corinthians *c.*734 BC, it was a flourishing centre of Greek culture especially in the 5th–4th c. BC under its rulers Dionysius the Elder and Dionysius the Younger. Syracuse was the home of the scientist Archimedes who was put to death by the Romans who laid siege to the city for 13 years. It was subsequently occupied by Romans, Saracens, Genoese, and Pisans. It has petrochemical plants and food-processing industries.

**Syracuse** a city in central New York state, USA, on Onondaga Lake; pop. (1990) 163,860. Founded as a trading post in 1789, it developed as a source of salt and with the completion of the Erie Canal became an industrial town. It is the home of Syracuse University (1870). Its industries include electronics and electrical equipment, ceramics, and pharmaceuticals.

**Syr Darya** /sɪr 'dɑ:rjə/ (also **Syrdaryo**) a river of Central Asia formed from headstreams that rise in the Alay and Tien Shan mountains of eastern Uzbekistan and Kyrgyzstan. It flows 2,212 km. (1,391 miles) west and north-west, skirting the Kyzyl Kum Desert before entering the Aral Sea. The second-largest river in Central Asia, its waters irrigate the Fergana valley, preventing much of its volume from entering Kazakhstan downstream. Its chief tributaries, the Chirchiq and Angren, irrigate the Tashkent region. Its total length to the head of the Naryn River is 2,992 km. (1,859 miles).

**Syria** /'sɪrɪə/ offi-  cial name **The Syrian Arab Republic** a country in south-west Asia with a coastline on the eastern Mediterranean Sea and bounded by Turkey, Iraq, Jordan, Israel, and Lebanon; area 184,050 sq. km. (71,089 sq. miles); pop. (est. 1991) 12,824,000; official language, Arabic; capital, Damascus. Its largest cities are Damascus, Aleppo, Homs, Hama, and Latakia. The largest of the Levant countries, Syria comprises a large desert region with fertile steppeland to the north and west, separated from a narrow Mediterranean coastal plain by mountain ranges. Although largely agricultural, Syria is becoming more industrialized, and has benefited in recent years from increasing oil exports. In ancient times the name was applied to a much wider area, which included also the present countries of Lebanon, Israel, Jordan, and adjacent parts of Iraq and Saudi Arabia. It was the site of various early civilizations, trading with Egypt and Crete; the Phoenicians were settled on the coastal plain. The country was greatly enriched by the transit trade from Babylonia, Arabia, and the Far East. Falling successively within the empires of Persia, Macedon, and Rome it became a centre of Islamic power and civilization from the 7th c. and a province of the Ottoman empire in 1516. After the Turkish defeat in World War I, Syria was mandated to France and achieved independence with the ejection of Vichy troops by the Allies in 1941. After a brief merger with Egypt (1958–61) Syria reestablished itself as an independent state. Since then the ruling socialist Ba'th Party has undertaken a massive land-reform programme and nationalized all major industry and foreign investment. In recent years Syrian history has been dominated by continuing conflict with Israel (which annexed the Golan Heights), involvement in Middle Eastern wars and the internal affairs of the Lebanon (which it helped to stabilize in 1992). The country is governed by an executive president and a legislative People's Assembly.

**Syrian** *adj. & n.*

**Syriac** /'sɪrɪˌæk/ the liturgical language of the Maronite and Syrian Catholic Churches, the Syrian Jacobite Church, and the Nestorian Church. It is descended from the Aramaic spoken near the city of Edessa (now Urfa) in south-east Turkey from shortly before the Christian era, and was extensively used in the early Church owing to the active Christian communities in those parts. After Greek it was the most important language in the eastern Roman Empire until the rise of Islam in the 8th c. The Syriac alphabet developed from a late form of Aramaic used at Palmyra in Syria.

**Syros** /'siːrɒs/ (also **Siros**) a Greek island at the centre of the Cyclades group in the Aegean Sea; area 83.6 sq. km.; pop. (1981) 19,670; capital, Ermoúpolis. It produces wine, barley, figs, and vegetables.

**Syzran** /'sɪzrən/ a city in western Russia, on the River Volga west of Samara; pop. (1990) 175,000. It is a centre of industry and oil-refining.

**Szczecin** /'ʃetsiːn/ (also **Stettin** /ʃteˈtiːn/) a port on the Oder River in the West Pomeranian region of north-west Poland; pop. (1990) 413,440. A Slavonic settlement dating back to the 12th c., Szczecin was formerly capital of the Prussian province of Pomerania. It was the birthplace in 1729 of Catherine the Great. One of Poland's three largest ports and one of the largest in the Baltic, Szczecin is also an industrial centre with shipyards and industries producing chemicals, foodstuffs, and metal products. Its chief landmark is the 14th-c. castle of the Pomeranian dukes.

**Szechwan** SEE SICHUAN.

**Szeged** /'seged/ a port on the River Tisza, in southern Hungary, capital of Csongrád county; pop. (1993) 178,500. Once a Magyar military stronghold and trading centre, it is an important transportation, agricultural, and cultural centre of the Great Plain. Its industries produce foodstuffs, textiles, rubber, and cables, and the city hosts an annual open-air theatre festival.

**Székesfehérvár** /ˌseɪkeʃˈfiːhɜːvɑː(r)/ the capital of Féjer county in western Hungary, an industrial transportation centre situated between Budapest and Lake Balaton; pop. (1993) 109,760. The kings of Hungary were crowned and buried here from the 11th c. to the 16th c.

**Szekszárd** /'sekʃɑːd/ a town in Transdanubia, southern Hungary, on the Sió River; pop. (1993) 37,290. Known to the Romans as Alisca, a Benedictine monastery was later founded here in 1601 by King Béla I. Settled by Germans in the 18th c., it became a centre of wine production and capital of Tolna county. Its industries also produce timber, textiles, machinery, meat, and dairy produce.

**Szolnok** /'sɒlnək/ a town in eastern Hungary between the Tisza and the Danube; pop. (1993) 80,220. It was founded as a fortress town in 1076 and is now the capital of Solnok county. It is a transport and agricultural centre with industries producing chemicals, cellulose, paper, tobacco, and sugar.

**Szombathely** /'sɒmbɒtˌheɪ/ the capital of Vas county in western Hungary, on the Gyöngyös River near the Austrian frontier; pop. (1993) 85,840. Founded as Savaria in AD 43 by the Roman emperor Claudius, it was capital of the Roman province of Upper Pannonia. It developed on intersecting trade routes at the junction between the Great Plain and the mountains. Its industries now produce timber, shoes, textiles, and carpets.

# T t

**Tabasco** /təˈbæskəʊ/ a state of eastern Mexico, on the Gulf of Campeche; area 25,267 sq. km. (9,759 sq. miles); pop. (1990) 1,501,180; capital, Villahermosa. It has tropical plantations but the major oilfields discovered in the 1960s now produce much of Mexico's oil which is refined in the state capital.

**tableland** /ˈteɪb(ə)l‚lænd/ a plateau or extensive elevated region with a level surface.

**Table Mountain** a spectacular flat-topped mountain overlooking **Table Bay** and Cape Town in South Africa, rising to a height of 1,087 m. (3,563 ft.). Its summit is 3 km. (2 miles) long and has served as a beacon to seamen since the Portuguese navigator Bartholomew Diaz sailed this way in 1488.

**Tábor** /ˈteɪbɔː/ a historic city in the South Bohemia region of the Czech Republic; pop. (1991) 36,330. Founded by Hussites in 1420, it was given the name Castle of Mount Tábor after the Biblical Mount Tabor.

**Tabor** /ˈteɪbɔː/, **Mount** (Hebrew **Har Tavor**) a mountain in northern Israel rising to a height of 588 m. (1,938 ft.) above the Plain of Jezreel. It was the site of a Canaanite shrine in the 2nd millennium BC and the alleged site of the Transfiguration of Christ. The Church of Elijah and Tabor Church stand within medieval fortifications on its summit.

**Tabora** /tæˈbəʊrə/ the capital of Tabora region in west-central Tanzania; pop. (1984) 87,000. Founded by Arab traders in 1852, it is now a railway junction and agricutural centre trading in cattle, cotton, and peanuts.

**Tabriz** /təˈbriːz/ the capital of the province of East Azerbaijan, north-west Iran, on the Talkheh River; pop. (1991) 1,089,000. Formerly known as Tauris, it was capital of Armenia in the 3rd c. AD and from the 13th c. was the administrative and commercial centre of the Persian empire. Its industries now produce carpets, metal castings, and cotton and silk textiles.

**Taching** see DAQING.

**Tacoma** /tæˈkəʊmə/ a Pacific coast port in the state of Washington, north-west USA, situated on Puget Sound between Seattle and Olympia; pop. (1990) 176,660. Built near the site of Fort Nisqually, a fur-trading outpost of the Hudson's Bay Company, the city developed after the arrival of the North Pacific Railroad in 1873. In 1940 the Tacoma Bridge, a road bridge over the Narrows,

collapsed. Its industries produce paper, furniture, timber products, chemicals, foodstuffs, and clothing. Mt. Rainier National Park is nearby.

**Tadmur** /ˈtædmʊə(r), -mɔː(r)/ (also **Tadmor**) see PALMYRA.

**Tadzhikistan** see TAJIKISTAN.

**Taegu** /ˈtaɪɡuː/ a city in south-east South Korea, on the Kum River; pop. (1990) 2,228,830. Situated at the centre of an apple-growing region, it is Korea's third-largest city. To the west, in Mt. Kaya National Park, is the Haeinsa temple which was established in AD 802 and contains 80,000 wooden printing-blocks dating from the 13th c., engraved with compilations of Buddhist scriptures. It is a communications and industrial centre with important textile industries.

**Taejon** /taɪˈjɒn/ (also **Daejeon**) the capital of South Chungchong province, central South Korea; pop. (1990) 1,062,080. Nearby stands the largest stone Buddha in Korea, built in 968 during the Koryo Dynasty. It is a manufacturing centre for textiles, ceramics, and furniture.

**Taff** /tæf/ a river of south Wales that rises in two headstreams (the **Taf Fawr** and the **Taf Fechan**) in moorland to the south of the Brecon Beacons in Powys. It flows 64 km. (40 miles) southwards through Mid Glamorgan and South Glamorgan to meet the Bristol Channel at Cardiff.

**Tagalog** /təˈɡɑːlɒɡ/ (also **Filipino** or **Pilipino**) the principal language group of the people of the Philippine Islands, a Malayo-Polynesian language heavily influenced by Spanish with some adaptations from Chinese and Arabic.

**Taganrog** /ˈtɑːɡənrɒɡ/ an industrial port in southern Russia, situated on the north shore of the Gulf of Taganrog, an arm of the Sea of Azov; pop. (1990) 293,000. Settled in turn by Pisans, Mongols, and Turks, the modern city was founded by Peter the Great in 1698 as a fortress and naval base. It has steelworks, shipyards, and a fishing industry. It was the birthplace in 1860 of the Russian writer Anton Chekhov.

**Tagus** /ˈteɪɡəs/ (Spanish **Tajo** /ˈtɑːxəʊ/, Portuguese **Tejo** /ˈteɪʒuː/) a river of the Iberian peninsula that rises in the Sierra de Gudar in eastern Spain and flows westwards into Portugal where it turns south before flowing into the Atlantic near Lisbon; length, c. 1,000 km. (625 miles).

**Tahat** /təˈhæt/ (formerly **Mont Atakor**) the highest peak of the Hoggar Mountains of southern Algeria, rising to a height of 2,918 m. (9,573 ft.).

**Tahiti** /təˈhiːtɪ/ one of the Society Islands of French Polynesia in the South Pacific, administered by France; area 1,042 sq. km. (402 sq. miles); pop. (1988) 115,820; capital, Papeete. Its highest peak is Mt. Orohena (2,237 m., 7,339 ft.). In 1767 Captain Samuel Wallis was the first European to visit Tahiti which was ruled by the Polynesian Pomare dynasty until 1880 when the island became part of a French Colony. It is the largest island in French Polynesia. The French artist Paul Gaugin lived on the island 1891–3 and 1895–1901. It produces tropical fruit and its beauty attracts many tourists.
**Tahitian** /-ˈhiːʃ(ə)n/ adj. & n.

**Tahoe** /ˈtɑːhəʊ/, **Lake** a lake of the USA occupying a basin in the Sierra Nevada, on the frontier between California and Nevada; area 500 sq. km. (193 sq. miles). A popular tourist resort.

**Tahoua** /ˈtɑːʊə/ an agricultural and phosphate-mining town in south-west Niger, capital of the department of Tahoua; pop. (1988) 51,600.

**Tai'an** /taɪˈɑːn/ a city in the province of Shandong, eastern China, to the south of Jinan and the Tai Shan Hills; pop. (1986) 1,370,000.

**Taichung** /taɪˈtʃʊŋ/ a city in west-central Taiwan, the third-largest on the island and chief commercial and cultural city of central Taiwan; pop. (1991) 774,000. Founded in 1721 as Tatun, it was renamed Taichung (= central Taiwan) in the 1890s. In 1976 an international seaport was opened 16 km. (10 miles) to the west. Its chief landmark is the Happy Buddha which, at 26.8 m. (88 ft.), is the tallest Buddha in Taiwan. It is a centre for foreign companies manufacturing goods for export.

**Ta'if** /ˈtɑːɪf/ the unofficial seat of government of Saudi Arabia during the summer, situated in the Asir Mountains to the south-east of Mecca; pop. (est. 1986) 204,850. It is the centre of a fertile area and is noted for its pepper trees and roses.

**taiga** /ˈtaɪɡə/ slow-growing coniferous forest in northern regions, especially in Siberia where it lies between tundra and forest-steppe.

**Taihu** /taɪˈhuː/ a lake in Jiangsu province, eastern China, the third-largest freshwater lake in the country; area 2,425 sq. km. (936 sq. miles).

**Taimyr Peninsula** /taɪˈmɪə(r)/ (also **Taymyr**) a tundra peninsula of Siberia extending into the Arctic Ocean between the Kara Sea and the Laptev Sea, to the west of the estuary of the Yenisey River. Cape Chelyuskin at the tip of the peninsula is the northernmost point of mainland Russia and of Asia. It is underlain by large deposits of natural gas.

**Tainan** /taɪˈnɑːn/ a city on the south-west coast of Taiwan; pop. (1991) 690,000. It is the oldest city on the island and was capital of Taiwan 1684–1887. Its chief landmark is the shrine of Kuo Hsing Yeh

(Koxinga), a Ming Dynasty commander who liberated the island from Dutch rule in 1661 and initiated a cultural renaissance. Now industrialized it produces metals, textiles, and machinery.

**Taipei** /taɪˈpeɪ/ the largest city and capital of Taiwan since the Nationalists under Chiang Kai-shek were forced to flee from the mainland of China in 1949; pop. (1991) 2,718,000. It is a commercial and cultural, as well as administrative centre. Its major industries include metals, engineering, chemicals, wood and paper products, textiles, printing, and foodstuffs.

**Taiping** /taɪˈpɪŋ/ a city in the state of Perak in north-west peninsular Malaysia, in the foothills of the Bintang Mountains; pop. (1980) 146,000. Developed as a tin-mining settlement by Chinese immigrants in the 1840s, its name was later changed from Kelian Pauh to Taiping (= everlasting peace), the only city in Malaysia with a Chinese name.

**Taiwan** /taɪˈwæn/ official name **The Republic of China** an island, mountainous and densely forested on its east side, off the southeast coast of China; area 35,981 sq. km. (14,000 sq. miles);  pop. (est. 1991) 20,454,000; official language, Chinese (Mandarin); capital, Taipei. Settled for centuries by the Chinese, the island was sighted by the Portuguese in 1590; they named it Formosa (= beautiful). It was ceded to Japan by China in 1895 but returned to China after World War II. General Chiang Kai-shek withdrew there in 1949 with 500,000 troops towards the end of the war with the Communist regime, and it became the headquarters of the Chinese Nationalists. Since the 1950s Taiwan has undergone steady economic growth, particularly in its export-oriented industries (electronics, textiles, consumer goods). In 1971 it lost its seat in the United Nations to the People's Republic of China, which regards Taiwan as one of its provinces. The government of Taiwan maintains the structure that ruled the mainland prior to 1949 and claims jurisdiction over China. Executive power is held by the President and legislative power is exercised by a National Assembly.
**Taiwanese** /ˌtaɪwəˈniːz/ adj. & n.

**Taiwan Strait** (also **Formosa Channel**) the stretch of water separating Taiwan from the mainland of China. The Pescadores (Penghu) Islands lie at its southern end.

**Taiyuan** /ˌtaɪʊˈɑːn/ a city in northern China, capital of Shanxi province; pop. (1990) 1,900,000. Its industries manufacture, iron, steel, machinery, chemicals, textiles, and electricity.

**Ta'iz** /tæˈɪz/ a city of Yemen, situated at an altitude of 1,400 m. (4,590 ft.) on the northern slopes of Mt. Sabir; pop. (1987) 178,040. A seat of the Ayyubid and Rasulid dynasties from the 11th to the 15th c., Ta'iz was capital of Yemen from 1948 until the revolution of 1962. It is the centre of a coffee-growing area and has textiles, tanning, and light industries.

**Taizhou** /taɪ'dʒəʊ/ (formerly **Taichow**) a city in Jiangsu province, eastern China, north-east of Nanjing; pop. (1986) 214,000.

**Tajik** /tæ'dʒiːk/ a people of Central Asia descended from Persian-speaking Iranians. They preserved their cultural identity in the face of successive Mongol and Turkic conquests by occupying high mountain valleys to the south of the Syr Darya.

**Tajikistan** /ˌtædʒiːkɪ'stɑːn/ (also **Tadzhikistan**) official name **The Republic of Tajikistan** an independent state in central Asia to the north of Afghanistan, for-

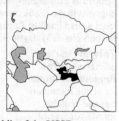

merly a constituent republic of the USSR; area 143,100 sq. km. (55,272 sq. miles); pop. (est. 1991) 5,412,000; official language, Tajik; capital, Dushanbe. Dominated by the Pamirs, it is a mountainous country with little territory below 3,000 m. (10,000 ft.). The climate varies with altitude from continental to subtropical and settlements are chiefly located in the principal river valleys or on the margin between mountain and steppe. A largely agricultural country with livestock and irrigated farms that produce cotton and fruit, Tajikistan is rich in minerals such as brown coal, oil, lead, zinc, and uranium. Its industries include engineering, food processing, and the manufacture of textiles. The Tajiks, an Iranian people of the Sunni Moslem religion, were conquered by the Mongols in the 13th c. and later absorbed into the Russian empire during the 1880s and 1890s. They rebelled against Russian authority after the 1917 revolution and were not brought under control until 1921 when Tajikistan became an autonomous republic within Soviet Uzbekistan. In 1929 it became a constituent republic of the USSR. Following nationalist unrest and the eventual breakup of the Soviet Union, Tajikistan became an independent state in 1991, joining other former republics as a member of the Commonwealth of Independent States. The republican Communist party remained in power until civil war broke out in 1992, an event that prompted Russia and neighbouring Central Asian countries to deploy a peacekeeping force in Tajikistan.
**Tajik** adj. & n.

**Taj Mahal** /tɑːʒ mə'hɑːl/ a mausoleum at Agra in northern India, by the River Jumna. Completed c. 1648, it was built by the Mogul emperor Shah Jahan in memory of his favourite wife who had borne him fourteen children. Set in formal gardens, the domed building in white marble is reflected in a pool flanked by cypresses. It is widely believed to be the world's most beautiful building and has been constituted a world heritage site by UNESCO.

**Tajo** the Spanish name for the TAGUS.

**Takamatsu** /ˌtækə'mætsuː/ a ferry port and industrial centre on the north-east coast of the island of Shikoku, Japan, capital of Kagawa prefecture; pop. (1990) 329,700.

**Takaoka** /ˌtækə'əʊkə/ a city in Toyama prefecture, west-central Honshu Island, Japan, on the Sho River; pop. (1990) 175,470. It is noted for its lacquerware and copper and iron products.

**Takasaki** /ˌtækə'sɑːkɪ/ an industrial city in Gumma prefecture, central Honshu Island, Japan; pop. (1990) 236,460. A transportation and light industrial centre with a renowned 40 m. (130 ft.) high statue of Kannon, the goddess of mercy.

**Takatsuki** /təˈkɑːtsəˌkiː/ a city on Honshu Island, Japan, north-east of Osaka; pop. (1990) 359,870.

**Taki-Taki** the Creole language of Surinam, also known as Sranang Tongo.

**Taklimakan Desert** /ˌtækləmə'kɑːn/ a desert forming the greater part of the Tarim Basin of Xinjiang autonomous region, north-west China.

**Takoradi** /ˌtækə'rɑːdɪ/ a major West African seaport on the Gulf of Guinea, in west Ghana, part of the joint urban area of Sekondi-Takoradi; pop. (1984) 615,000 (with Sekondi). Built in 1923 and since improved, it exports timber, cocoa, and minerals, and has plywood and other light industries.

**Talavera de la Reina** /tælə'veɪrə ðeɪ lɑː 'reɪnə/ a town on the River Tagus (Tajo) in the province of Toledo, Castilla-León, central Spain; pop. (1991) 68,640. There has been a settlement here since Roman times when it was known as Caesarobriga, and since the 15th c. it has been noted for its ceramic tiles and pottery ware. The site of one of Wellington's victories in the Peninsular War (1809).

**Talca** /'tælkə/ the capital of the wine-producing Maule region of central Chile; pop. (1991) 164,490. It has distilleries, foundries, and a tannery.

**Talcahuano** /ˌtælkə'hwɑːnəʊ/ a port and naval base on the Pacific coast of central Chile, in the Bío-Bío region near Concepción; pop. (1991) 246,850. It has a large fishing industry, dry-docks, and oil refineries.

**Taldijqorghan** /ˌtældiː kʊə(r)'gɑːn/ (formerly **Taldykurgan**) a city in east Kazakhstan, to the south-east of Lake Balkhash; pop. (1990) 122,000.

**Tallahassee** /ˌtælə'hæsiː/ the capital of the US state of Florida, situated in the north-west of the state; pop. (1990) 124,770. Settled in 1824, it was the only capital city east of the Mississippi not captured by Union forces during the American Civil

War. It is the seat of Florida State University (1857) with industries that include publishing, printing, food processing, and the manufacture of timber products.

**Tallinn** /'tælɪn/ a commercial and ferry port on the Gulf of Finland, capital of Estonia; pop. (1990) 505,100. It was known as Revel until 1917. The upper town is dominated by Lutheran and Orthodox cathedrals and a lower town surrounded by medieval walls. Industries include shipbuilding, machinery, electrical equipment, textiles, and chemicals.

**Tamale** /tə'mɑːlɪ/ a commercial and market city and capital of Northern Region, Ghana; pop. (1984) 135,950. Nearby are Larabanga, Ghana's oldest mosque, and the Mole Game Reserve.

**Tamanrasset** /ˌtæmənˈræset/ (also **Tamanghasset**) a market town and administrative centre in southern Algeria, at the foot of the Hoggar Mountains, last stop on the southward route across the Sahara to Niger; pop. (1982) 38,000. To the north-east at Asskrem is a Christian hermitage founded in 1910 by Charles de Foucauld. It is the rendezvous of the nomadic Tuaregs and increasingly popular as a tourist destination.

**Tamashek** /'tæməʃek/ a language of the Tuareg of North Africa, a dialect of the Berber Amzirght tongue.

**Tamaulipas** /ˌtæmaʊˈliːpæs/ a state of north-east Mexico; area 79,384 sq. km. (30,662 sq. miles); pop. (1990) 2,244,200; capital, Ciudad Victoria.

**Tambov** /tɑːmˈbɒf/ an industrial city in south-central European Russia; pop. (1990) 307,000. It was founded in the 17th c. as an outpost defending Russia from the Crimean Tartars. Industries include machine tools and chemicals.

**Tamil** /'tæmɪl/ a people inhabiting southern India, Sri Lanka, and Malaysia speaking Tamil, a Dravidian language that is one of the official languages of Sri Lanka.
**Tamilian** *adj.*

**Tamil Nadu** /'tæmɪl 'nɑːduː/ a state in south-east India, bounded by Karnataka, Andhra Pradesh, Kerala, and the Indian Ocean; area 130,058 sq.km. (50,235 sq. miles); pop. (1991) 55,638,320; capital, Madras. Formerly comprising the greater part of Madras State, it was named Tamil Nadu in 1968.

**Tammany Hall** /'tæmənɪ/ any of the successive buildings used as the headquarters of Tammany, a fraternal and benevolent society of New York City, founded in 1789 and developed from an earlier patriotic society. A political organization of the Democratic Party, which identified with this society and was notorious in the 19th c. for corruption, dominated the political life of New York City during the 19th and early 20th c. before being reduced in power by Franklin Roosevelt in 1932. Tammany Hall is named after a late 17th-c. Indian chief who is said to have welcomed William Penn

and was regarded (*c.* 1770–90) as 'patron saint' of Pennsylvania and other northern colonies.

**Tammerfors** the Swedish name for TAMPERE.

**Tampa** /'tæmpə/ a business and vacation centre on the west coast of Florida, USA, the third-largest city and leading industrial port in the state; pop. (1990) 280,015. Situated on Tampa Bay at the mouth of the Hillsboro River, the city was founded at the centre of Seminole Indian territory as Fort Brooke in 1824. Brewing, phosphate mining and the manufacture of cigars are among the many important local industries. It is the home of the University of Tampa (1931) and the University of South Florida (1956).

**Tampere** /'tæmpəˌreɪ/ (Swedish **Tammerfors** /'tɑːməˌfɔːs/) a city in Häme province, south-west Finland, between Lake Pyhäjärvi and Lake Näsijärvi; pop. (1990) 172,560. An important trading centre since the 11th c., it developed during the 18th c. as an industrial town using hydroelectric power generated by the Tammerkoski (= rapids of Tammer). It is now the third-largest city in Finland, and Finland's leading textile centre. It also has railway works, engineering, timber and light industries.

**Tampico** /tæmˈpiːkəʊ/ a principal seaport of the Gulf of Mexico, in Tamaulipas state, east Mexico, on the Pánuco River; pop. (1990) 271,640. It is a major oil port and fish-processing centre, and a popular resort.

**Tamworth** /'tæmwɜːθ/ an agricultural and commercial town in north-eastern New South Wales, Australia, on the Peel River; pop. (1991) 31,720.

**Tamworth** /'tæmwɜːθ/ an industrial town in Staffordshire, central England, on the River Tame north-east of Birmingham; pop. (1981) 64,550.

**Tana** /'tɑːnə/ a river that rises near Mount Kenya in central Kenya and flows *c.* 805 km. (500 miles) north-east, east, then south-east to meet the Indian Ocean north of Malindi. It is the longest river in Kenya.

**Tana** /'tɑːnə/ (Finnish **Tenojoki**) a river of northern Scandinavia that rises in north-east Norway and flows 360 km. (225 miles) along the frontier between Norway and Finland before emptying into the Tanafjord, an inlet of the Barents Sea.

**Tana** /'tɑːnə/, **Lake** a lake in the Gonder and Gojam regions of northern Ethiopia, the source of the Blue Nile; area 3,600 sq. km. (1,390 sq. miles). It is the largest lake in Ethiopia.

**Tanana** /'tɑːnəˌnɔː/ a river of Alaska, USA, that rises in the Wrangell Mountains and flows 1,287 km. (800 miles) north-westwards through Fairbanks to join the Yukon River at Fort Yukon.

**Tananerive** /təˌnænəˈriːv/ the former name (from 1895 to 1976) of ANTANANARIVO, capital of Madagascar.

**Tanezrouft** /'tænezrʊft/ a region of the Sahara Desert to the west of the Hoggar Mountains, on the Mali–Algeria frontier, taking its name from the Tuareg description of this region as 'the land of fear and thirst'.

**Tang** /tæŋ/ the name of the dynasty which ruled in China from 618 to *c.*906, a period noted for territorial conquest and great wealth and regarded as the golden age of Chinese poetry and art.

**Tanga** /'tæŋgə/ the second-largest seaport in Tanzania after Dar es Salaam, situated opposite the island of Pemba; pop. (1984) 121,000. Its chief export is sisal.

**Tangail** /tæn'gaɪl/ a city in central Bangladesh, north-west of Dhaka, capital of Tangail region; pop. (1991) 104,000.

**Tanganyika** /,tæŋgə'niːkə/ see TANZANIA.

**Tanganyika, Lake** a lake in East Africa on the frontier between Tanzania, Zaire, Zambia, and Burundi; area 32,764 sq. km. (12,650 sq. miles). It is the deepest and second-largest lake in Africa. The chief towns on its shores are Bujumbura (capital of Burundi), Kigoma, Ujiji, and Kalémie (formerly Albertville). In 1858 the explorers Richard Burton and John Speke were the first Europeans to encounter it, and the famous meeting between Livingstone and Stanley took place at Ujiji in 1871.

**Tangier** /tæn'dʒɪə(r)/ (also **Tanger**) a seaport of Morocco, situated nearly opposite Gibraltar and commanding the western entrance to the Mediterranean; pop. (1982) 266,300. It had its beginning in the Roman port and town of Tingis, but the present walled city was built in the Middle Ages by the Moors. It was taken by the Portuguese towards the end of the 15th c., and given to Britain as part of the dowry of Princess Catherine of Braganza when she married Charles II in 1662. The diarist Samuel Pepys was king's treasurer in the city which Britain abandoned twenty-two years later to the sultan of Morocco, who retained control of the port and the surrounding countryside until 1904. From then until 1956 (except for five years in World War II) the zone was under international control. In 1956 it passed to the newly independent monarchy of Morocco. It became a free port in 1962 and is today a commercial, cultural, and tourist centre.

**Tangshan** /tæŋ'ʃɑːn/ a coal-mining city in the province of Hebei, northern China; pop. (1990) 1,500,000. It was severely damaged by an earthquake in 1976. It has many light industries.

**Tanimbar Islands** /tɑ:'nɪmbɑ:(r)/ a group of over 60 densely forested islands in the south-east Moluccas, Indonesia, lying between the Aru Islands and Timor in the Banda Sea; pop. (est. 1990) 75,000. The chief towns are Larat (on the island of Larat) and Saumlaki (on Yamdena).

**Tanis** /'tænɪs/ a city of ancient Egypt in the Delta of the Nile, whose ruins lie near the present-day village of San el Hagar. It is thought to be the city in which the Hebrews were persecuted by the Egyptians before fleeing across the Red Sea in search of the Promised Land.

**Tanjore** see THANJAVUR.

**tanjung** /'tændʒʊŋ/ an Indonesian word for a cape or promontory.

**Tanjungkarang** /,tændʒʊŋkə'ræŋ/ see BANDAR LAMPUNG.

**Tannu-Tuva** see TUVA.

**Tanta** /'tæntə/ a city in the Nile Delta, 90 km. (56 miles) north of Cairo, a centre of Sufism; pop. (1991) 372,000. The ruins of Sais, capital of Egypt's 26th dynasty, lie to the north-west on the east bank of the Nile. It processes local cotton and wool.

**Tanzania** /,tænzə'niːə/ official name **The United Republic of Tanzania** a country in East Africa with a coastline on the Indian Ocean, consisting of a mainland area (the former republic of Tanganyika) and the islands of Zanzibar and Pemba; area 939,652 sq. km. (362,940 sq. miles); pop. (est. 1991) 27,270,000; official languages, English and Swahili; capital, Dodoma; chief city and port, Dar es Salaam. A narrow coastal plain rises up to a central plateau with an average elevation of 1,000 m. (3,000 ft.) and extensive grasslands that include the Serengeti Plain. To the east of Lake Victoria and the Serengeti, there are several volcanic peaks including Kilimanjaro (5,895 m., 19,340 ft.), Meru (4,565 m., 14,977 ft.), and the Ngorongoro Crater. Like most of its neighbours Tanzania is largely dependent on agriculture, exporting sisal, cloves, cotton, and coffee. A German colony from the late 19th c., Tanganyika became a British mandate after World War I and a trust territory, administered by Britain after World War II, before achieving independence as a member-state of the Commonwealth in 1961. It was named Tanzania after its union with Zanzibar in 1964 and in 1992 a multiparty system was introduced. The country is governed by an executive president and a legislative National Assembly.
**Tanzanian** *adj. & n.*

Tanzania is divided into 24 administrative regions:

| Region | Area (sq. km.) | Pop. (1988) |
| --- | --- | --- |
| Arusha | 82,306 | 1,351,675 |
| Dar es Salaam | 1,393 | 1,360,850 |
| Dodoma | 41,311 | 1,237,820 |
| Iringa | 56,864 | 1,208,910 |
| Kagera | 28,388 | 1,326,180 |
| Kigoma | 37,037 | 854,820 |
| Kilimanjaro | 13,309 | 1,108,700 |
| Lindi | 66,046 | 646,550 |

| Mara | 19,566 | 970,940 |
|---|---|---|
| Mbeya | 60,350 | 1,476,200 |
| Morogoro | 70,799 | 1,222,740 |
| Mtwara | 16,707 | 889,500 |
| Mwanza | 19,592 | 1,878,270 |
| Pemba North | 574 | 137,400 |
| Pemba South | 332 | 127,640 |
| Pwani | 32,407 | 638,015 |
| Rukwa | 68,635 | 694,970 |
| Ruvuma | 63,498 | 783,330 |
| Shinyanga | 50,781 | 1,772,550 |
| Singida | 49,341 | 791,810 |
| Tabora | 26,808 | 1,283,640 |
| Zanzibar North | 470 | 97,030 |
| Zanzibar South | 854 | 70,180 |
| Zanzibar West | 230 | 208,330 |

**Taoism** /'taʊɪz(ə)m, 'tɑːəʊ-/ (also **Daoism**) one of the two major Chinese religious and philosophical systems (the other is Confucianism), traditionally founded by Lao-tzu in about the 6th c. BC (its texts are slightly later). The central concept and goal is the Tao, an elusive term denoting here the force inherent in nature and, by extension, the code of behaviour that is in harmony with the natural order. Its most sacred scripture is the Tao-te-Ching (also called Lao-tzu), ascribed to its founder.

**Taormina** /ˌtɑːɔːˈmiːnə/ a picturesque medieval resort town on the east coast of Sicily; pop. (1990) 10,905. Built on the side of Mt. Taurus, it was occupied successively by Greeks, Romans, Arabs, and Normans. Its chief landmarks are a Greek amphitheatre and medieval castle.

**Tapachula** /tæpəˈtʃuːlə/ a city in the state of Chiapas, southern Mexico; pop. (1990) 222,280. Situated close to the frontier with Guatemala, it is the southernmost city of Mexico and the centre of the coffee and banana-growing Soconusco coastal plain. Its population increased during the 1970s and 1980s as a result of the influx of refugees from El Salvador and Guatemala.

**Tapajós** /tæpəˈʒɒs/ a southern tributary of the Amazon that is formed by the junction of the Juruena and Arinos rivers in the Mato Grosso of central Brazil. It flows 2,010 km. (1,256 miles) northwards past Itaituba and Aveiro to meet the Amazon west of Santarem.

**Tara** /'tɑːrə/ a hill in County Meath, Ireland, site in early times of the residence of the high kings of Ireland, still marked by ancient earthworks.

**Tarabulus** see TRIPOLI.

**Taranaki** /ˌtærəˈnækɪ/ **1.** a region on the west coast of North Island, New Zealand, comprising the districts of South Taranaki, New Plymouth, and part of Stratford; pop. (1991) 107,220; chief town, New Plymouth. **2.** (formerly **Mount Egmont**) a volcanic peak rising to a height of 2,518 m. (8,260 ft.) at the centre of North Island, New Zealand. Now known by its Maori name, it was in 1770 named Mount Egmont by Captain

Cook in honour of the 2nd Earl of Egmont who was First Lord of the Admiralty 1763–6.

**Taranto** /tə'ræntəʊ/ a seaport, naval base, and fishing centre in the Apulia region of south-east Italy; pop. (1990) 244,030. It is the site of the ancient city of Tarentum, founded by the Greeks in the 8th c. BC and governed by the philosopher Archytas 361–351 BC. Its industries include shipyards, machinery, and chemical works.

**Taranto, Gulf of** (Italian **Golfo di Taranto**) a gulf of the Ionian Sea separating the 'heel' from the 'toe' of Italy.

**Tarawa** /'tærəwə/ the capital of Kiribati, a densely populated Pacific Island, formerly one of the Gilbert Islands; pop. (1990) 28,800. Government offices are mostly located at Bairiki and the international airport at Bonriki.

**Tarbes** /tɑːb/ the capital of the department of Hautes-Pyrénées in the Midi-Pyrénées region of southern France, an industrial centre and agricultural market town on the River Adour; pop. (1990) 50,230. Formerly the capital of the province of Bigorre, it was the birthplace in 1851 of Marshal Foch. The National Stud (1806) is nearby.

**Tardenoisian** /ˌtɑːdɪˈnɔɪzɪən/ a late mesolithic industry of western and central Europe, named after the type-site at Tardenois in north-east France.

**Taree** /tə'riː/ a town in New South Wales, Australia, on the Manning River 320 km. (200 miles) north of Sydney; pop. (1991) 16,300. Established in 1854, it is a local service centre and producer of dairy products and timber goods.

**Tarija** /tə'riːxə/ a town in south-east Bolivia, at an elevation of 1,924 m. (6,312 ft.) in the fertile valley of the Guadalquivir River; pop. (est. 1988) 66,900. Founded by the Spanish in 1574, it is a centre of agricultural trade and sugar-refining. The surrounding area is noted for its fossils.

**Tarim** /tɑːˈrɪm/ a river of north-west China formed by the junction of the Yarkan and Hotan rivers in the west of Xinjiang autonomous region. It flows c. 2,090 km. (1,300 miles) along the northern edge of the **Tarim Basin**, which lies between the Kunlun and Tien Shan mountains and includes the vast Taklimakan Desert and Turfan Depression.

**Tarn** /tɑːn/ **1.** a river of southern France which rises in the Cévennes and flows 380 km. (235 miles) south-west through deep gorges before meeting the Garonne near Moissac. **2.** a department in the Midi-Pyrénées region of southern France; area 5,751 sq. km. (2,221 sq. miles); pop. (1990) 342,720; capital, Albi.

**Tarn-et-Garonne** /tɑːneɪgəˈrɔːn/ a department in the Midi-Pyrénées region of southern France; area 3,716 sq. km. (1,435 sq. miles); pop. (1990) 200,220; capital, Montauban.

**Tarnów** /tɑːˈnʊf/ a city in southern Poland, capital of Tarnów county; pop. (1990) 120,385. Its industries produce chemicals and electrical goods.

**Tarnowskie Góry** /tɑːˌnʊfskjɪ ˈɡuːrɪ/ an industrial mining town of Upper Silesia, situated in Katowice county, southern Poland; pop. (1990) 73,740.

**Taroko Gorge** /təˈrəʊkəʊ/ a ravine flanked by towering cliffs in eastern Taiwan. A 19-km. (12-mile) section of the East–West Highway, which includes 38 tunnels and was completed in 1960, passes through the gorge.

**Taroudant** /tɑːruːˈdɑ̃/ a fortified oasis town in western Morocco, on the Sous River 80 km. (50 miles) east of Agadir; pop. (1982) 35,850.

**Tarpeian Rock** /tɑːˈpiːən/ a cliff, probably at the south-west corner of the Capitoline Hill, over which murderers and traitors were hurled in ancient Rome. Tarpeia, legendary daughter of the commander of the citadel which she betrayed to the Sabines, is said to be buried at the foot of the hill.

**Tarragona** /ˌtærəˈɡɒnə/ the capital of Tarragona province, eastern Spain, a port on the Mediterranean coast of Catalonia; pop. (1991) 112,655. It was a Roman capital (Pontius Pilate was once its governor) and the primacy of Spain until the 11th c. It exports wine and has chemicals and electrical industries.

**Tarrasa** /təˈræsə/ (also **Terrassa**) a manufacturing town of Catalonia in north-eastern Spain, situated north of Barcelona on the Palau River; pop. (1991) 153,520. Its industries produce textiles, glass products, and electrical goods.

**Tarsus** /ˈtɑːsəs/ an ancient city in the province of Içel, southern Turkey, on the River Pamuk, birthplace of St. Paul. Now a market town trading in cotton, it once held a strategic position commanding the southern end of the pass through the Taurus Mountains known as the Cilician Gates.

**Tartar** /ˈtɑːtə(r)/ (also **Tatar**) **1.** a member of any of numerous mostly Muslim and Turkic tribes inhabiting various parts of European and Asiatic Russia, especially parts of Siberia, Crimea, North Caucasus, and districts along the Volga. **2.** a member of the mingled host of Central Asian peoples, including Mongols and Turks, who under the leadership of Genghis Khan overran and devastated much of Asia and eastern Europe in the early 13th c., and under Tamerlane (14th c.) established a large empire in central Europe with its capital at Samarkand.

**Tartar Strait** a stretch of water separating mainland Russia from the island of Sakhalin, linking the Sea of Japan and the Sea of Okhotsk.

**Tartary** /ˈtɑːtərɪ/ the Tartar regions of Asia and eastern Europe, especially the high plateau of Asia and its north-western slopes.

**Tartu** /ˈtɑːtuː/ a city in eastern Estonia, a port on the Ema River; pop. (1990) 115,400. Founded in the 11th c., it has developed into a transportation and cultural centre. Tartu University (1802) was considered the 'Oxford' of the former Soviet Union. It has machinery, footwear, and timber industries.

**Tashauz** /tɑːˈʃaʊz/ see DASHHOWUZ.

**Tashkent** /tæʃˈkent/ the capital of the Central Asian republic of Uzbekistan, in the western foothills of the Tien Shan Mountains; pop. (1990) 2,094,000. The city has been a centre of culture, trade, and transportation since ancient times. Today it is a major industrial centre producing machinery, textiles, chemicals, furniture, and foodstuffs. It suffered a major earthquake in 1966 and had to be rebuilt.

**Tasmania** /tæzˈmeɪnɪə/ the smallest state of the Commonwealth of Australia consisting of one large mountainous island and several smaller islands (including King, Flinders, and Bruny) situated south-east of the continent from which it is separated by the Bass Strait; area 68,331 sq. km. (26,393 sq. miles); pop. (1991) 469,200; capital, Hobart. Like mainland Australia, Tasmania has many unique species of plants and animals, and was inhabited since prehistoric times by Aborigines, most of whom were wiped out by the new settlers. The first European explorer to arrive there (in 1642) was Abel Tasman (1603–59), who called the island Van Dieman's Land, a name which it bore until 1855. Claimed for Britain by Captain Cook and later settled by a British party from New South Wales in 1803, it became a separate colony in 1825 and was federated with the other states of Australia in 1901. In 1869 Tasmania was the first colony in the British Empire to make education compulsory. The islands' chief products are meat, fruit, grain, dairy produce, timber, paper, and minerals such as tin, copper, and zinc.
**Tasmanian** adj. & n.

**Tasman** /ˈtæzm(ə)n/, **Mount** a mountain on South Island, New Zealand, rising to 3,497 m. (11,473 ft.) in the Southern Alps north of Mount Cook. It is the second highest peak in New Zealand.

**Tasman Sea** /ˈtæzm(ə)n/ an arm of the south-west Pacific separating the south-east coast of Australia from New Zealand.

**Tassili-n-Ajjer** /təˈsɪlmæˈdʒɑː/ a plateau in southern Algeria, north-east of the Hoggar Mountains, the site of rock paintings dating from 6,000–10,000 BC. It was designated a national park in 1972.

**Tatabánya** /tætəˈbɑːnjə/ a town in northern Hungary, capital of Komárom-Esztergom county; pop. (1989) 77,000. Situated at the centre of a coalfield 56 km. (35 miles) west of Budapest, it developed during the 20th c. from the three settlements of Alsógalla, Felsögalla, and Bánhida.

The production of brown coal, cement, lime, and aluminium are its chief industries.

**Tatar** see TARTAR.

**Tatarstan** /ˌtætə(r)'stɑːn/ (in full **Republic of Tatarstan**, also **Tataria**) a republic of the Russian Federation, in the middle valley of the Volga and its tributaries; area 68,000 sq. km. (26,265 sq. miles); pop. (1990) 3,658,000; capital, Kazan. Inhabited by Bulgars since the 5th c., the region was conquered by the Mongols, under Genghis Khan, in the 13th c., becoming a Tatar Khanate. In 1552, after a fierce struggle with Ivan the Terrible, it was absorbed into the Russian empire and in 1920 was constituted as an autonomous republic of the USSR. On the breakup of the Soviet Union in 1991 it refused to sign the new Federation Treaty with Russia, voting to become an independent state in 1992. Its chief products are oil, coal, timber, grain, and textiles.

**Tate Gallery** /teɪt/ a national gallery of British art at Millbank, London, which originated in the dissatisfaction felt at the inadequate representation of English schools in the National Gallery. The Tate Gallery, opened in 1897, was built at the expense of (Sir) Henry Tate (1819–99), sugar manufacturer, to house the collection presented by him (in 1890) and other works accumulated by various bequests (including that of Turner) to the nation. In the 20th c. modern foreign paintings and sculpture (both British and foreign) were added. On foundation the gallery was subordinate to the National Gallery, but it was made fully independent in 1955.

**Tatra Mountains** /'tɑːtrə/ (also **Tatras**) the highest range of the Carpathians in east-central Europe. The High Tatra on the frontier between Slovakia and Poland rises to 2,655 m. (8,710 ft.) at Gerlachovsky, the highest peak in Slovakia. The Low Tatra to the south-west rises to 2,043 m. (6,703 ft.) at Dumbier, also in Slovakia.

**Taunggyi** /taʊn'dʒiː/ the capital of Shan state in eastern Burma, a hill station and resort town north-east of Inle Lake at an elevation of 1,430 m. (4,690 ft.); pop. (1983) 107,600.

**Taunton** the county and market town of Somerset, south-west England, on the River Tone; pop. (1981) 48,860. Founded c. 705 as a West Saxon stronghold against the Celts, its castle dates from the 12th c. The Duke of Monmouth was crowned king here in 1685. It has textile and clothing industries as well as cider-making.

**Taupo** /'taʊpəʊ/, **Lake** the largest lake of New Zealand, occupying a volcanic depressions in central North Island; area 619 sq. km. (239 sq. miles). It receives the Tongariro River and its chief outlet is the Waikato River. The townships of the Taupo region are popular resort and fishing centres.

**Taupo** /'taʊpəʊ/ a town in central North Island, New Zealand, on the Waikato River at its outlet from Lake Taupo; pop. (1986) 15,900. Tourism, engineering, boatbuilding, and sawmilling are its chief industries.

**Tauranga** /taʊ'ræŋə/ a seaport and industrial town on the Bay of Plenty, North Island, New Zealand; pop. (1991) 70,800. It is one of the largest export ports of New Zealand, handling timber, pulp, and newsprint.

**Taurus Mountains** /'tɔːrəs/ (Turkish **Toros Dağlari**) a range of mountains in southern Turkey, forming the southern edge of the Anatolian plateau. Its highest peak is Aladağ which rises to 3,734 m. (12,250 ft.) south-east of Niğde and across the Seyhan River the range extends north-eastwards as the Anti-Taurus.

**Tavastehus** the Swedish name for HÄMEEN-LINNA.

**Tavoy** /tə'vɪ/ the capital of Tenasserim Division, south-east Burma, at the mouth of the Tavoy River; pop. (1983) 101,540.

**Taw** /tɔː/ a river that rises in Dartmoor, south-west England, and flows 80 km. (50 miles) north through Devon before emptying into Barnstaple Bay near Appledore.

**Tay** /teɪ/ a river of Scotland that rises on the slopes of Ben Lui as the Fillan and flows 192 km. (120 miles) eastwards through Loch Dochart and Loch Tay before entering the North Sea in a wide estuary known as the **Firth of Tay**. From its source at the head of the Fillan it is the longest river in Scotland. The first railway bridge over the Firth of Tay at Dundee, opened in 1877, was blown down in 1879 while a passenger train was crossing it.

**Taymyr** see TAIMYR.

**Tayside** /'teɪsaɪd/ a local government region in eastern Scotland from 1975 to 1996; area 7,492 sq. km. (2,894 sq. miles); pop. (1991) 385,270; administrative centre, Dundee. Tayside is divided into three districts:

| District | Area (sq. km.) | Pop. (1991) |
| --- | --- | --- |
| Angus | 2,023 | 92,880 |
| Dundee City | 235 | 165,550 |
| Perth and Kinross | 5,234 | 126,840 |

**Taza** /'tɑːzə/ an ancient town in northern Morocco, situated east of Fez between the Middle Atlas and the Rif Mountains; pop. (1982) 77,220. It has an old Islamic college and mosque; its industries include carpets and footwear.

**Tblisi** /təbɪ'liːsɪ/ (formerly **Tiflis** /'tɪflɪs/) the capital of the Republic of Georgia, a city on the Kura River in the Caucasus, between the Caspian and Black Seas; pop. (1991) 1,267,500. It developed in ancient times as a trading centre on the route between Europe and the East and is said to be one of the world's oldest cities. Its industries include chemicals, petroleum products, locomotives, machine tools, and electrical equipment.

**Te Anau** /tiːə'naʊ/ a lake of New Zealand, the largest lake on South Island and second-largest in the country; area 344 sq. km. (133 sq. miles). It is situated at an altitude of 212 m. (695 ft.) on the edge of the forested mountains of Fiordland. Its outlet, the Waiau River, flows into Lake Mana-pouri, feeding one of New Zealand's largest hydro-electric power plants.

**Tees** /tiːz/ a river of north-east England that rises on Cross Fell in Cumbria and flows 128 km. (80 miles) south-eastwards before emptying into the North Sea in a broad estuary. Linked to the River Tyne, it is a major source of water for the industrial towns of north-east England.

**Teesside** an urban area in Cleveland, north-east England, on the estuary of the River Tees; pop. (1991) 363,000. It includes the towns of Stockton-on-Tees, Redcar, Thornaby, and Middlesbrough.

**Tegucigalpa** /teˌguːsɪˈgælpə/ the largest city and capital of Honduras, situated in the highlands of south-central Honduras; pop. (1988) 678,700. It was founded as a gold and silver mining town in the 16th c. by the Spanish and became capital in 1880. It produces textiles, chemicals, and processed foods.

**Tehran** /teəˈrɑːn/ (also **Teheran**) the capital and largest city of Iran, situated in the southern foot-hills of the Elburz Mountains; pop. (1986) 6,042,600. In 1788 it replaced Ispahan (Esfahan) as capital of Persia and in the 20th c. the city was modernized by Reza Shah. It chief landmarks are the Borj-e Azadi monument, built in 1971 to com-memorate the 2,500th anniversary of the Persian Empire, and the tomb of Ayatollah Khomeini whose funeral in 1989 attracted 10 million mourners and was allegedly the largest ever held in the world. Industries include the manufacture of textiles, chemicals, and tobacco.

**Teide** /ˈteɪdɪ/, **Pico de** a volcanic peak on the island of Tenerife in the Canary Islands, which at 3,718 m. (12,198 ft.) is the highest peak in Spain.

**Tejo** the Portuguese name for the TAGUS.

**Tekirdağ 1.** a province of north-west Turkey, on the north side of the Sea of Marmara; area 6,218 sq. km. (2,402 sq. miles); pop. (1990) 468,840. **2.** its capital, a port and agricultural market on the Sea of Marmara; pop. (1990) 80,440.

**Tel Aviv** /tel əˈviːv/ a city on the Mediterranean coast of Israel; pop. (1987) 319,500. Founded in 1909 by Russian Jewish immigrants as a small residential suburb of the port of Jaffa, Tel Aviv was granted the special status of an independent town-ship in 1921 and expanded as the first Hebrew city in British-administered Palestine. Capital of Israel until 1950, its development in the 1920s was strongly influenced by Patrick Geddes. Industries include the manufacture of textiles, sugar, and chemicals.

**Telde** /ˈteldeɪ/ a resort town to the south of Las Palmas on the east coast of Gran Canaria in the Canary Islands; pop. (1991) 75,880.

**Telford** /ˈtelfəd/ a town in Shropshire, west-central England, on the River Severn 52 km. (33 miles) north-west of Birmingham; pop. (1991) 115,000. Designated a New Town in 1963, it com-prises the settlements of Dawley, Oakengates, and Wellington and has diverse light industries. It is named after the engineer Thomas Telford.

**tell** /tel/ an Arabic word for a hill.

**Telugu** /ˈteləˌguː/ (also **Telegu**) a people of south-east India, mainly in the state of Andhra Pradesh, speaking the most widespread of the Dravidian languages of India.

**Tema** /ˈteməˌ/ a seaport and industrial centre of Greater Accra, Ghana, the largest artificial har-bour in Africa; developed from a fishing village and opened in 1961, it specializes in the export of cocoa. It also has aluminium smelting and manu-facturing, an oil refinery, and textiles.

**Teme** /tiːm/ a river that rises in Powys, Wales, and flows 96 km. (60 miles) eastwards through the county of Hereford and Worcester before joining the River Severn at Worcester.

**Temesvár** /ˈtemeʃˈvær/ the Hungarian name for TIMIŞOARA.

**Temirtau** /ˈteɪmərtaʊ/ a coal-mining town in the Kazakh Upland region of north-east Kazakhstan, north-east of Karaganda; pop. (1990) 213,000.

**Tempe** /ˈtempɪ/ a resort city in south-central Arizona, USA, 15 km. (9 miles) east of Phoenix; pop. (1990) 141,865. Founded as a trading post in 1871, it is the seat of Arizona State University (1885).

**Temuco** /teɪˈmʊkəʊ/ a city in the lake district of south-central Chile, capital of Araucania region; pop. (1991) 211,690. Founded in 1881, its chief industries are coal mining and the manufacture of steel and textiles.

**Ténéré Desert** /ˈteɪneɪreɪ/ a desert region of the Sahara in Niger, to the west of the Grand Erg of Bilma and south-east of the Aïr Mountains. It includes the world's highest sand-dune at 244 m. (800 ft.).

**Tenerife** /ˌtenəˈriːf/ a volcanic island in the Atlantic Ocean off the north-west coast of Africa, the largest of the Canary Islands and popular holi-day resort; area 2,059 sq. km. (795 sq. miles); pop. (1986) 759,400. Dominated by the volcanic peak of Mt. Teide (3,718 m., 12,198 ft.), its chief town is Santa Cruz.

**Tennant Creek** /ˈtenənt/ a mining town be-tween Alice Springs and Darwin in Northern Territory, Australia; pop. (1986) 3,300. Originally a station of the Overland Telegraph established in 1872, it developed with the discovery of gold in 1934 and copper in 1955.

**Tennessee** /ˌtenɪˈsiː/ a state in central south-eastern USA, lying to the south of Kentucky between the Mississippi River and the Smoky Mountains; area 109,152 sq. km. (42,144 sq. miles);

pop. (1990) 4,877,185; capital, Nashville. The
largest cities are Memphis, Nashville, Knoxville,
and Chattanooga. It is also known as the Volunteer
State. The floodplain between the Mississippi and
Tennessee rivers is dominated by corn, tobacco,
and cotton fields while central Tennessee is 'bluegrass' country largely given over to livestock
grazing. Its industries produce chemicals, textiles,
electrical goods, and processed food. Ceded by
Britain to the US in 1783, Tennessee became the
16th state of the Union in 1796. Its chief landmarks
are the Great Smoky National Mountains Park,
Cherokee National Forest, Big South Fork National River and Recreation Area, Fort Donelson
and Stones River National Battlefields, and the
Shiloh, Chickamauga, and Chattanooga National
Military Parks. The state is divided into 95
counties:

| County | Area (sq. km.) | Pop. (1990) | County Seat |
| --- | --- | --- | --- |
| Anderson | 881 | 68,250 | Clinton |
| Bedford | 1,235 | 30,410 | Shelbyville |
| Benton | 1,019 | 14,520 | Camden |
| Bledsoe | 1,058 | 9,670 | Pikeville |
| Blount | 1,451 | 85,970 | Maryville |
| Bradley | 850 | 73,710 | Cleveland |
| Campbell | 1,245 | 35,080 | Jacksboro |
| Cannon | 692 | 10,470 | Woodbury |
| Carroll | 1,560 | 27,510 | Huntingdon |
| Carter | 887 | 51,505 | Elizabethton |
| Cheatham | 790 | 27,140 | Ashland City |
| Chester | 751 | 12,820 | Henderson |
| Claiborne | 1,123 | 26,140 | Tazewell |
| Clay | 590 | 7,240 | Celina |
| Cocke | 1,123 | 29,140 | Newport |
| Coffee | 1,113 | 40,340 | Manchester |
| Crockett | 692 | 13,380 | Alamo |
| Cumberland | 1,773 | 34,740 | Crossville |
| Davidson | 1,303 | 510,780 | Nashville |
| Decatur | 858 | 10,470 | Decaturville |
| De Kalb | 757 | 14,360 | Smithville |
| Dickson | 1,277 | 35,060 | Charlotte |
| Dyer | 1,352 | 34,850 | Dyersburg |
| Fayette | 1,833 | 25,560 | Somerville |
| Fentress | 1,295 | 14,670 | Jamestown |
| Franklin | 1,412 | 34,725 | Winchester |
| Gibson | 1,565 | 46,315 | Trenton |
| Giles | 1,586 | 25,740 | Pulaski |
| Grainger | 710 | 17,095 | Rutledge |
| Greene | 1,609 | 55,850 | Greeneville |
| Grundy | 939 | 13,360 | Altamont |
| Hamblen | 406 | 50,480 | Morristown |
| Hamilton | 1,401 | 285,540 | Chattanooga |
| Hancock | 580 | 6,740 | Sneedville |
| Hardeman | 1,742 | 23,380 | Bolivar |
| Hardin | 1,503 | 22,630 | Savannah |
| Hawkins | 1,264 | 44,565 | Rogersville |
| Haywood | 1,388 | 19,440 | Brownsville |
| Henderson | 1,352 | 21,840 | Lexington |
| Henry | 1,456 | 27,890 | Paris |
| Hickman | 1,586 | 16,750 | Centerville |
| Houston | 520 | 7,020 | Erin |
| Humphreys | 1,373 | 15,810 | Waverly |
| Jackson | 801 | 9,300 | Gainesboro |
| Jefferson | 689 | 33,020 | Dandridge |
| Johnson | 772 | 13,770 | Mountain City |
| Knox | 1,316 | 335,750 | Knoxville |
| Lake | 439 | 7,130 | Tiptonville |
| Lauderdale | 1,232 | 23,490 | Ripley |
| Lawrence | 1,604 | 35,300 | Lawrenceburg |
| Lewis | 733 | 9,250 | Hohenwald |
| Lincoln | 1,485 | 28,160 | Fayetteville |
| Loudon | 611 | 31,255 | Loudon |
| McMinn | 1,115 | 42,380 | Athens |
| McNairy | 1,461 | 22,420 | Selmer |
| Macon | 798 | 15,910 | Lafayette |
| Madison | 1,451 | 77,980 | Jackson |
| Marion | 1,331 | 24,860 | Jasper |
| Marshall | 978 | 21,540 | Lewisburg |
| Maury | 1,602 | 54,810 | Columbia |
| Meigs | 491 | 8,030 | Decatur |
| Monroe | 1,685 | 30,540 | Madisonville |
| Montgomery | 1,401 | 100,500 | Clarksville |
| Moore | 335 | 4,720 | Lynchburg |
| Morgan | 1,360 | 17,300 | Wartburg |
| Obion | 1,430 | 31,720 | Union City |
| Overton | 1,126 | 17,640 | Livingston |
| Perry | 1,071 | 6,610 | Linden |
| Pickett | 413 | 4,550 | Byrdstown |
| Polk | 1,139 | 13,640 | Benton |
| Putnam | 1,037 | 51,370 | Cookeville |
| Rhea | 803 | 24,340 | Dayton |
| Rhoane | 928 | 47,230 | Kingston |
| Robertson | 1,238 | 41,490 | Springfield |
| Rutherford | 1,576 | 118,570 | Murfreesboro |
| Scott | 1,373 | 18,360 | Huntsville |
| Sequatchie | 692 | 8,860 | Dunlap |
| Sevier | 1,534 | 51,040 | Sevierville |
| Shelby | 2,007 | 826,330 | Memphis |
| Smith | 814 | 14,140 | Carthage |
| Stewart | 1,180 | 9,480 | Dover |
| Sullivan | 1,079 | 143,600 | Blountville |
| Sumner | 1,375 | 103,280 | Gallatin |
| Tipton | 1,180 | 37,570 | Covington |
| Trousdale | 296 | 5,920 | Hartsville |
| Unicoi | 484 | 16,550 | Erwin |
| Union | 567 | 13,690 | Maynardville |
| Van Burren | 710 | 4,850 | Spencer |
| Warren | 1,121 | 32,990 | McMinnville |
| Washington | 848 | 92,315 | Jonesboro |
| Wayne | 1,908 | 13,935 | Waynesboro |
| Weakley | 1,511 | 31,970 | Dresden |
| White | 970 | 20,090 | Sparta |
| Williamson | 1,518 | 81,020 | Franklin |
| Wilson | 1,482 | 67,675 | Lebanon |

**Tennessee** /ˌtenɪˈsiː/ a river of the USA that
rises in headstreams in eastern Tennessee and flows
1,049 km. (652 miles) south-westwards into
Alabama, then north into Tennessee again before
joining the Ohio River in Kentucky. From the
source of its principal headstream, the French
Broad, it flows a total distance of 1,398 km. (869
miles). The river is used extensively as a source of
irrigation water and hydroelectric power, the
Tennessee Valley Authority (TVA) having converted it into a chain of lakes held back by nine
major dams.

**Teotihuacán** /teɪˌɔʊtɪwəˈkɑːn/ the largest city of pre-Columban America, about 40 km. (25 miles) north-east of Mexico City. Built c. 300 BC it reached its zenith c. AD 300–600, when it was the centre of an influential culture, but by 650 it had declined as a major power and was sacked by the invading Toltec c. 750. Among its monuments are palatial buildings, plazas, and temples, including the pyramids of the Sun and Moon and the temple of Quetzalcóatl. The ruins of the city were rediscovered in the 15th c. by the Aztecs who founded the new city of **Tenochtitlan** nearby on the site of modern Mexico City.

**Tepic** /teˈpiːk/ the capital of the state of Nayarit in western Mexico, situated at the foot of Volcán Sangangüey; pop. (1990) 238,100. It lies in a prosperous agricultural area producing maize, sugar-cane, and cattle, and has sugar-refining and textile industries.

**Teques** /təˈkeɪs/, **Los** the capital of the state of Miranda in northern Venezuela, west of Caracas; pop. (1981) 112,860.

**Teramo** /teɪˈrɑːməʊ/ the capital of Teramo province in the Abruzzi region of east-central Italy, originally situated between the Tordino and Vezzola rivers but now expanded westwards; pop. (1990) 52,490. There are Roman remains and a 12th-c. cathedral.

**Terceira** /tɜːˈseɪrə/ an island of the Azores in the Atlantic Ocean, included in the Portuguese province of Angra do Heroismo. It is the third-largest of the islands of the Azores and third to be discovered and populated by Flemish settlers in the 15th c.; area 397 sq. km. (153 sq. miles). It rises to a height of 1,067 m. (3,500 ft.) at the Caldera de Santa Barbara.

**Terengganu** see TRENGGANU.

**Teresina** /teɪreɪˈsiːnə/ a market town and port on the Parnaíba River, north-eastern Brazil, capital of the state of Piauí; pop. (1991) 598,000. Its industries produce textiles, sugar, soap, and lumber.

**Terni** an industrial town on the Nera River in Umbria, central Italy, capital of Terni province; pop. (1990) 109,800. The Marmore Falls, Italy's highest waterfalls, are nearby and generate power for steel, engineering, and chemical industries.

**Ternopol** /tɜːˈnəʊp(ə)l/ (Ukrainian **Ternopil**) an industrial city in central Ukraine; pop. (1990) 212,400. It produces leather goods, footwear, and processed foods.

**Terra Australis** a name formerly given to the undiscovered southern landmass of Antarctica, later sometimes applied to Australia.

**Terre Haute** /tɜːˈhəʊt/ a city in west Indiana, USA, between Indianapolis and the Illinois frontier; pop. (1990) 57,480. Built on a plateau named *Terre Haute* by the French, the city developed as a trade depot on the lower Wabash River. It later became a railroad, coal-mining, and industrial

centre. The seat of Indiana State University (1865), Terre Haute was the birthplace of the songwriter Paul Dresser.

**Tertiary** /ˈtɜːʃərɪ/ the name given to the first period in the Cenozoic geological era, so-called because it follows the Mesozoic, which was formerly also called *Secondary*. It lasted from about 65 to 2 million years ago, and comprises the Palaeocene, Eocene, Oligocene, Miocene, and Pliocene epochs. World temperatures were generally warm except towards the close of the period, and mammals evolved rapidly, becoming the dominant land vertebrates.

**Teruel** /ˌtevʊˈel/ the capital of the province of Teruel in Aragón, east-central Spain, on the Turia River; pop. (1991) 31,000. It is a market town situated on a plateau at an altitude of 916 m. (3,050 ft.).

**Tessin** the French and German name of TICINO.

**Tete** /ˈteteɪ/ the capital of the province of Tete in western Mozambique, on the River Zambezi; pop. (1980) 45,120. A trade centre that could become an industrial city based on hydroelectric power from the Cabora Bassa dam.

**Tethys** /ˈteθɪs/ an ocean that developed during Palaeozoic and Mesozoic times between southern Spain and South-East Asia.

**Tétouan** /teɪˈtwɑːn/ (also **Tetuán**) a city in the Rif Mountains of northern Morocco, formerly the capital of Spanish Morocco; pop. (1982) 199,600. It has light industries and tourist attractions.

**Tetovo** /ˈtetʔəʊvəʊ/ a market town and ski resort centre in northwest Macedonia, west of Skopje; pop. (1981) 162,410. It has textile and carpet industries.

**Teuton** /ˈtjuːt(ə)n/ a member of a north European tribe mentioned in the 4th c. BC and combining with others to carry out raids on north-eastern and southern France during the Roman period until heavily defeated in 102 BC. The term is often used to describe a member of a Teutonic nation, especially Germany.

**Tevere** the Italian name for the TIBER.

**Tewantin** a resort town on the Noosa River on the Sunshine Coast of Queensland, Australia; pop. (1991) 17,780 (with Noosa). It was first settled in the 1870s by timber-cutters who shipped cedar wood to Brisbane.

**Texas** /ˈteksəs/ a state in the southern USA, bordering on Mexico and the Gulf of Mexico and lying to the south of Oklahoma between New Mexico and Louisiana; area 691,030 sq. km. (266,807 sq. miles); pop. (1990) 16,986,510; capital, Austin. The largest cities are Houston, Dallas, San Antonio, Austin, and Fort Worth. It is also known as the Lone Star State. Mountainous in the southwest, the greater part of northern and western Texas is open range. Plantations of rice, sugar cane and cotton lie to the east and in the valley of the Rio Grande are citrus groves. It is a major producer of cattle, sheep, cotton, oil, gas, and minerals such as sulphur, helium, graphite, and bromine. The area was opened up by Spanish explorers (16th–17th c.) and formed part of Mexico until it became an independent republic in 1836 and the 28th state of the USA in 1845. Amongst its chief landmarks are the Big Bend and Guadalupe National Parks, the Johnson Space Centre at Houston, Padre Island National Seashore, and the Palo Alto Battlefield National Historic Site. Texas is divided into 254 counties:

| County | Area (sq. km.) | Pop. (1990) | County Seat |
|---|---|---|---|
| Anderson | 2,800 | 48,020 | Palestine |
| Andrews | 3,903 | 14,340 | Andrews |
| Angelina | 2,098 | 69,880 | Lufkin |
| Aransas | 728 | 17,890 | Rockport |
| Archer | 2,358 | 7,970 | Archer City |
| Armstrong | 2,363 | 2,020 | Claude |
| Atascosa | 3,167 | 30,530 | Jourdanton |
| Austin | 1,706 | 19,830 | Bellville |
| Bailey | 2,148 | 7,060 | Muleshoe |
| Bandera | 2,062 | 10,560 | Bandera |
| Bastrop | 2,327 | 38,260 | Bastrop |
| Baylor | 2,241 | 4,385 | Seymour |
| Bee | 2,288 | 25,135 | Beeville |
| Bell | 2,743 | 191,090 | Belton |
| Bexar | 3,245 | 1,185,394 | San Antonio |
| Blanco | 1,856 | 5,970 | Johnson City |
| Borden | 2,340 | 800 | Gail |
| Bosque | 2,571 | 15,125 | Meridian |
| Bowie | 2,317 | 81,665 | Boston |
| Brazoria | 3,658 | 191,710 | Angleton |
| Brazos | 1,531 | 121,860 | Bryan |
| Brewster | 16,039 | 8,680 | Alpine |
| Briscoe | 2,306 | 1,970 | Silverton |
| Brooks | 2,449 | 8,200 | Falfurrias |
| Brown | 2,434 | 34,370 | Brownwood |
| Burleson | 1,739 | 13,625 | Caldwell |
| Burnet | 2,584 | 22,680 | Burnet |
| Caldwell | 1,420 | 26,390 | Lockhart |
| Calhoun | 1,404 | 19,050 | Port Lavaca |
| Callahan | 2,337 | 11,860 | Baird |
| Cameron | 2,356 | 260,120 | Brownsville |
| Camp | 528 | 9,900 | Pittsburg |
| Carson | 2,402 | 6,580 | Panhandle |
| Cass | 2,436 | 29,980 | Linden |
| Castro | 2,337 | 9,070 | Dimmitt |
| Chambers | 1,602 | 20,090 | Anahuac |
| Cherokee | 2,735 | 41,050 | Rusk |
| Childress | 1,838 | 5,950 | Childress |
| Clay | 2,824 | 10,020 | Henrietta |
| Cochran | 2,015 | 4,380 | Morton |
| Coke | 2,361 | 3,420 | Robert Lee |
| Coleman | 3,320 | 9,710 | Coleman |
| Collin | 2,213 | 264,040 | McKinney |
| Collingsworth | 2,363 | 3,570 | Wellington |
| Colorado | 2,509 | 18,380 | Columbus |
| Comal | 1,443 | 51,830 | New Braunfels |
| Comanche | 2,418 | 13,380 | Comanche |
| Concho | 2,579 | 3,040 | Paint Rock |
| Cooke | 2,322 | 30,780 | Gainesville |
| Coryell | 2,748 | 64,210 | Gatesville |
| Cottle | 2,327 | 2,250 | Paducah |
| Crane | 2,033 | 4,650 | Crane |
| Crockett | 7,296 | 4,080 | Ozona |
| Crosby | 2,337 | 7,300 | Crosbyton |
| Culberson | 9,919 | 3,410 | Van Horn |
| Dallam | 3,913 | 5,460 | Dalhart |
| Dallas | 2,288 | 1,852,810 | Dallas |
| Dawson | 2,348 | 14,350 | Lamesa |
| Deaf Smith | 3,892 | 19,150 | Hereford |
| Delta | 723 | 4,860 | Cooper |
| Denton | 2,369 | 273,525 | Denton |
| De Witt | 2,366 | 18,840 | Cuero |
| Dickens | 2,358 | 2,570 | Dickens |
| Dimmit | 3,398 | 10,430 | Carrizo Springs |
| Donley | 2,415 | 3,700 | Clarendon |
| Duval | 4,667 | 12,920 | San Diego |
| Eastland | 2,402 | 18,490 | Eastland |
| Ector | 2,348 | 118,930 | Odessa |
| Edwards | 5,515 | 2,270 | Rocksprings |
| Ellis | 2,441 | 85,170 | Waxahachie |
| El Paso | 2,636 | 591,610 | El Paso |
| Erath | 2,808 | 27,990 | Stephenville |
| Falls | 2,002 | 17,710 | Marlin |
| Fannin | 2,327 | 24,800 | Bonham |
| Fayette | 2,470 | 20,095 | La Grange |
| Fisher | 2,332 | 4,840 | Roby |
| Floyd | 2,579 | 8,500 | Floydada |
| Foard | 1,828 | 1,790 | Crowell |
| Fort Bend | 2,278 | 225,420 | Richmond |
| Franklin | 764 | 7,800 | Mount Vernon |
| Freestone | 2,309 | 15,820 | Fairfield |
| Frio | 2,946 | 13,470 | Pearsall |
| Gaines | 3,910 | 14,120 | Seminole |
| Galveston | 1,037 | 217,400 | Galveston |
| Garza | 2,327 | 5,140 | Post |
| Gillespie | 2,759 | 17,200 | Fredericksburg |
| Glasscock | 2,340 | 1,450 | Garden City |
| Goliad | 2,233 | 5,980 | Goliad |
| Gonzales | 2,777 | 17,205 | Gonzales |
| Gray | 2,395 | 23,970 | Pampa |
| Grayson | 2,428 | 95,020 | Sherman |
| Gregg | 710 | 104,950 | Longview |
| Grimes | 2,077 | 18,830 | Anderson |
| Guadalupe | 1,854 | 64,870 | Seguin |
| Hale | 2,613 | 34,670 | Plainview |
| Hall | 2,280 | 3,905 | Memphis |
| Hamilton | 2,174 | 7,730 | Hamilton |
| Hansford | 2,395 | 5,850 | Spearman |
| Hardeman | 1,789 | 5,280 | Quanah |
| Hardin | 2,335 | 41,320 | Kountze |
| Harris | 4,508 | 2,818,200 | Houston |
| Harrison | 2,361 | 57,480 | Marshall |
| Hartley | 3,801 | 3,630 | Channing |
| Haskell | 2,343 | 6,820 | Haskell |
| Hays | 1,763 | 65,610 | San Marcos |
| Hemphill | 2,348 | 3,720 | Canadian |
| Henderson | 2,309 | 58,540 | Athens |
| Hidalgo | 4,079 | 383,545 | Edinburg |
| Hill | 2,517 | 27,150 | Hillsboro |
| Hockley | 2,361 | 24,200 | Levelland |
| Hood | 1,105 | 28,980 | Granbury |
| Hopkins | 2,051 | 28,830 | Sulphur Springs |
| Houston | 3,208 | 21,375 | Crockett |
| Howard | 2,343 | 32,340 | Big Springs |

(cont.)

| | | | | | | | |
|---|---|---|---|---|---|---|---|
| Hudspeth | 11,874 | 2,915 | Sierra Blanca | Ochiltree | 2,389 | 9,130 | Perryton |
| Hunt | 2,184 | 64,340 | Greenville | Oldham | 3,861 | 2,280 | Vega |
| Hutchinson | 2,267 | 25,690 | Stinnett | Orange | 941 | 80,510 | Orange |
| Irion | 2,735 | 1,630 | Mertzon | Palo Pinto | 2,467 | 25,055 | Palo Pinto |
| Jack | 2,392 | 6,980 | Jacksboro | Panola | 2,111 | 22,035 | Carthage |
| Jackson | 2,194 | 13,040 | Edna | Parker | 2,345 | 64,785 | Weatherford |
| Jasper | 2,395 | 31,100 | Jasper | Parmer | 2,301 | 9,860 | Farwell |
| Jeff Davis | 5,868 | 1,950 | Fort Davis | Pecos | 12,420 | 14,675 | Fort Stockton |
| Jefferson | 2,436 | 239,390 | Beaumont | Polk | 2,759 | 30,690 | Livingston |
| Jim Hogg | 2,954 | 5,110 | Hebbronville | Potter | 2,345 | 97,840 | Amarillo |
| Jim Wells | 2,254 | 37,680 | Alice | Presidio | 10,028 | 6,640 | Marfa |
| Johnson | 1,898 | 97,165 | Cleburne | Rains | 632 | 6,715 | Emory |
| Jones | 2,421 | 16,490 | Anson | Randall | 2,384 | 89,670 | Canyon |
| Karnes | 1,958 | 12,455 | Karnes City | Reagan | 3,050 | 4,510 | Big Lake |
| Kaufman | 2,049 | 52,220 | Kaufman | Real | 1,812 | 2,410 | Leakey |
| Kendall | 1,724 | 14,590 | Boerne | Red River | 2,740 | 14,320 | Clarksville |
| Kenedy | 3,611 | 460 | Sarita | Reeves | 6,828 | 15,850 | Pecos |
| Kent | 2,283 | 1,010 | Jayton | Refugio | 2,005 | 7,980 | Refugio |
| Kerr | 2,878 | 36,300 | Kerrville | Roberts | 2,379 | 1,025 | Miami |
| Kimble | 3,250 | 4,120 | Junction | Robertson | 2,246 | 15,510 | Franklin |
| King | 2,376 | 350 | Guthrie | Rockwall | 333 | 25,600 | Rockwall |
| Kinney | 3,533 | 3,120 | Brackettville | Runnels | 2,746 | 11,290 | Ballinger |
| Kleberg | 2,218 | 30,270 | Kingsville | Rusk | 2,423 | 43,735 | Henderson |
| Knox | 2,197 | 4,840 | Benjamin | Sabine | 1,264 | 9,590 | Hemphill |
| La Salle | 3,944 | 5,250 | Cotulla | San Augustine | 1,362 | 8,000 | San Augustine |
| Lamar | 2,389 | 43,950 | Paris | San Jacinto | 1,487 | 16,370 | Coldspring |
| Lamb | 2,634 | 15,070 | Littlefield | San Patricio | 1,802 | 58,750 | Sinton |
| Lampasas | 1,856 | 13,520 | Lampasas | San Saba | 2,954 | 5,400 | San Saba |
| Lavaca | 2,525 | 18,690 | Hallettsville | Schleicher | 3,403 | 2,990 | Eldorado |
| Lee | 1,641 | 12,850 | Giddings | Scurry | 2,340 | 18,630 | Snyder |
| Leon | 2,805 | 12,665 | Centerville | Shackelford | 2,379 | 3,320 | Albany |
| Liberty | 3,052 | 52,730 | Liberty | Shelby | 2,057 | 22,030 | Center |
| Limestone | 2,418 | 20,950 | Groesbeck | Sherman | 23,999 | 2,860 | Stratford |
| Lipscomb | 2,426 | 3,140 | Lipscomb | Smith | 2,423 | 151,310 | Tyler |
| Live Oak | 2,748 | 9,560 | George West | Somervell | 489 | 5,360 | Glen Rose |
| Llano | 2,441 | 11,630 | Llano | Starr | 3,188 | 40,520 | Rio Grande City |
| Loving | 1,742 | 107 | Mentone | Stephens | 2,324 | 9,010 | Breckenridge |
| Lubbock | 2,340 | 222,640 | Lubbock | Sterling | 2,400 | 1,440 | Sterling City |
| Lynn | 2,309 | 6,760 | Tahoka | Stonewall | 2,405 | 2,010 | Aspermont |
| McCulloch | 2,785 | 8,780 | Brady | Sutton | 3,783 | 4,135 | Sonora |
| McLennan | 2,681 | 189,120 | Waco | Swisher | 2,345 | 8,130 | Tulia |
| McMullen | 3,024 | 820 | Tilden | Tarrant | 2,257 | 1,170,100 | Fort Worth |
| Madison | 1,227 | 10,930 | Madisonville | Taylor | 2,384 | 119,655 | Abilene |
| Marion | 1,001 | 9,980 | Jefferson | Terrell | 6,128 | 1,410 | Sanderson |
| Martin | 2,376 | 4,960 | Stanton | Terry | 2,306 | 13,220 | Brownfield |
| Mason | 2,428 | 3,420 | Mason | Throckmorton | 2,371 | 1,880 | Throckmorton |
| Matagorda | 2,930 | 36,930 | Bay City | Titus | 1,071 | 24,010 | Mount Pleasant |
| Maverick | 3,346 | 36,380 | Eagle Pass | Tom Green | 3,939 | 98,460 | San Angelo |
| Medina | 3,461 | 27,310 | Hondo | Travis | 2,571 | 476,410 | Austin |
| Menard | 2,345 | 2,250 | Menard | Trinity | 1,799 | 11,445 | Groveton |
| Midland | 2,345 | 106,610 | Midland | Tyler | 2,397 | 16,650 | Woodville |
| Milam | 2,649 | 22,950 | Cameron | Upshur | 1,526 | 31,370 | Gilmer |
| Mills | 1,945 | 4,530 | Goldthwaite | Upton | 3,232 | 4,450 | Rankin |
| Mitchell | 2,371 | 8,020 | Colorado City | Uvalde | 4,066 | 23,340 | Uvalde |
| Montague | 2,413 | 17,270 | Montague | Val Verde | 8,190 | 38,720 | Del Rio |
| Montgomery | 2,722 | 182,200 | Conroe | Van Zandt | 2,223 | 37,940 | Canton |
| Moore | 2,353 | 17,865 | Dumas | Victoria | 2,306 | 74,360 | Victoria |
| Morris | 666 | 13,200 | Daingerfield | Walker | 2,044 | 50,920 | Huntsville |
| Motley | 2,493 | 1,530 | Matador | Waller | 1,336 | 23,390 | Hempstead |
| Nacogdoches | 2,441 | 54,750 | Nacogdoches | Ward | 2,174 | 13,115 | Monahans |
| Navarro | 2,777 | 39,930 | Corsicana | Washington | 1,586 | 26,150 | Brenham |
| Newton | 2,431 | 13,570 | Newton | Webb | 8,741 | 133,240 | Laredo |
| Nolan | 2,379 | 16,590 | Sweetwater | Wharton | 2,824 | 39,955 | Wharton |
| Nueces | 2,202 | 291,145 | Corpus Christi | Wheeler | 2,350 | 5,880 | Wheeler |
| | | | | Wichita | 1,576 | 122,380 | Wichita Falls |

| Wilbarger | 2,462 | 15,120 | Vernon |
| Willacy | 1,531 | 17,705 | Raymondville |
| Williamson | 2,956 | 139,550 | Georgetown |
| Wilson | 2,098 | 22,650 | Floresville |
| Winkler | 2,184 | 8,630 | Kermit |
| Wise | 2,345 | 34,680 | Decatur |
| Wood | 1,791 | 29,380 | Quitman |
| Yoakum | 2,080 | 8,790 | Plains |
| Young | 2,389 | 18,130 | Graham |
| Zapata | 2,597 | 9,280 | Zapata |
| Zavala | 3,375 | 12,160 | Crystal City |

**Texel** /'teks(ə)l/ (also **Tessel**) the largest and southernmost of the West Frisian Islands in the North Sea, separated from the mainland of the Netherlands by the Wadden Sea; area 185 sq. km. (71 sq. miles). It is part of North Holland province and its chief settlements are Den Burg and the port of Oudeschild. The island gives its name to a breed of large sheep. It is a popular tourist resort, especially with naturists.

**Thabana-Ntlenyana** /tə'bænə ˌentlen'jɑːnə/ a mountain in the Drakensberg Range, southern Africa. Rising to 3,482 m. (11,424 ft.), it is the highest peak in Lesotho and highest in Africa south of Kilimanjaro. Its name means 'nice little mountain'.

**Thai** /taɪ/ the official language of Thailand, a tonal language of the Sino-Tibetan language group. Thai-speaking groups include the Shan, Lue, and Phutai, but it is the language of the Central Thai that is taught in schools and used in government.

## Thailand
/'taɪlænd/ official name **The Kingdom of Thailand** a country in South-East Asia on the Gulf of Thailand; area 513,115 sq. km. (198,190 sq. miles); pop. (1990)  56,303,270; official language, Thai; capital, Bangkok. Mountainous in the north, Thailand has a vast low-lying and thickly populated central plain that stretches southwards into the Malay peninsula. A large plateau in the north-east is bordered in the east by the Mekong River. Thailand is one of the world's largest exporters of rice, but tapioca, tin, tungsten, and textiles are also important products. The country was known as **Siam** until 1939, when it changed its name to Thailand (= land of the free). Having filtered into the region from the 6th c., the Thais established a number of principalities in Thailand and adjacent regions by the 13th c. A powerful kingdom emerged in the 14th c. and engaged in a series of wars with its neighbour Burma before increasing exposure to European powers in the 19th c. resulted in the loss of territory in the east to France and in the south to Britain, though Thailand itself succeeded in retaining its independence. Politically unstable for much of the 20th c., Thailand was occupied by the Japanese in World War II, and supported the USA in the Vietnam campaign; later it experienced a large influx of refugees from Cambodia, Laos, and Vietnam. The system of absolute monarchy abolished in 1932 was replaced by military rule interspersed with short periods of democratic government. The country is governed by a bicameral National Assembly, an executive prime minister and cabinet, and a king as head of state.
**Thai** *adj. & n.*

**Thailand, Gulf of** an inlet of the South China Sea between the Malay peninsula and Thailand–Cambodia.

**Thames** /temz/ a river of southern England, flowing eastwards 338 km. (210 miles) from the Cotswolds in Gloucestershire through London to the North Sea. In Oxfordshire known as the Isis, the Thames is the largest river in England, having a width of c. 700 m. at Gravesend. Oxford, Reading, and London lie on the River, across which a flood barrier to protect London was completed at Woolwich in 1982.

**Thane** /'tɑːnə/ (also **Thana**) an industrial town in the state of Maharashtra, western India, situated 13 km. (21 miles) north of Bombay; pop. (1991) 796, 620. It was an important Portuguese trading centre prior to its capture by the Marathas in 1739 and was the terminus of India's first railway (1856). It has an oil refinery, and chemical and automobile industries.

**Thanet** /'θænɪt/, **Isle of** the easternmost peninsula of Kent, south-east England, including the resort and residential towns of Ramsgate, Broadstairs, and Margate. It was formerly separated from the mainland by the Wantsum Channel.

**Thanjavur** /ˌtəndʒə'vʊ(ə)r/ (also **Tanjore** /tɑːn'dʒɔʊ(ə)r/) a city in the state of Tamil Nadu, southern India, on the Cauvery River north-east of Madurai; pop. (1991) 200,200. A former capital of the Chola empire and the Maratha rulers, noted for its many temples and its music festival. It has libraries of Sanskrit and Tamil manuscripts.

**Thar Desert** /tɑː(r)/ (also **Great Indian Desert**) a desert region to the east of the Indus River in the Rajasthan and Gujarat states of north-west India and the Punjab and Sind regions of south-east Pakistan. It covers c. 259,000 sq. km. (100,000 sq. miles). The 650-km. (400-mile) Indira Gandhi Canal (completed in 1986) brings water from the snow-fed rivers of Himachal Pradesh to the desert regions of Rajasthan.

**Thásos** /'θæsɒs/ an island of Greece in the northern Aegean Sea opposite the mouth of the River Nestos on the frontier between the Greek provinces of Macedonia and Thrace; area 379 sq. km. (146 sq. miles). Its capital is Límen on the site of ancient Thásos.
**Thasian** *adj. & n.*

**Thebes** /θiːbz/ **1.** the Greek name for a city of Upper Egypt, about 675 km. (420 miles) south of modern Cairo, that was the capital of ancient Egypt under the 18th Dynasty (c. 1550–1290 BC). Its monuments (on both banks of the Nile) were the richest in the land, with the town and major temples at Luxor and Karnak on the east bank, and the necropolis, with tombs of royalty and nobles, on the west bank. It was already a tourist attraction in the 2nd c. AD. **2.** (Greek **Thívai** /ˈθiːveɪ/) a city of Greece, in Boetia, about 74 km. (46 miles) north-west of Athens, leader of the whole of Greece for a short period after the defeat of the Spartans at the battle of Leuctra in 371 BC.

**Thera** see SANTORINI.

**Theravada** /ˌθerəˈvɑːdə/ the only surviving ancient school of Buddhism, practised today in Sri Lanka, Burma, Thailand, Cambodia, and Laos.

**Thermopylae** /θəˈmɒpɪˌliː/ a pass in Greece, about 200 km. (120 miles) north-west of Athens, originally narrow but now much widened by the recession of the sea. It was the scene of the heroic defence (480 BC) against the Persian army of Xerxes by 6,000 Greeks including 300 Spartans under their commander Leonidas.

**Thessalonian** /θesəˈləʊnɪən/ a native of ancient Thessalonica (modern Thessaloníki), a city in north-east Greece. The Epistles to the Thessalonians are two books of the New Testament, the earliest letters of St. Paul, written from Corinth to the new church at Thessalonica.

**Thessaloníki** /θesæləˈniːkiː/ (also **Salonica**, Latin **Thessalonica** /θesəˈlɒnɪkə, -ləˈnaɪkə/) a seaport in north-eastern Greece, capital of the modern Greek region of Macedonia; pop. (1991) 378,000. Founded in 316 BC by Cassander, King of Macedon, and named after his wife, it became the capital of the Roman province of Macedonia and an important city of Byzantium. It fell to the Turks in 1430, remaining a part of the Ottoman empire until 1912. It was the scene of a joint Anglo-French campaign in support of Serbia during World War I and is now a major port and the second-largest city in Greece. It is also a university city, a NATO base, and a major industrial centre with oil refineries, engineering, and textile plants.

**Thessaly** /ˈθesəlɪ/ (Greek **Thessalía**) a region of north-eastern Greece comprising the departments of Kardhitsa, Lárisa, Magnesia, and Tríkkala; area 14,037 sq. km. (5,422 sq. miles); pop. (1991) 731,230; capital, Lárisa.

**Thetford** /ˈθetfəd/ a town in Norfolk, east England, at the junction of the Ouse and Thet rivers; pop. (1981) 19,590. A former residence of the kings of East Anglia, it was the birthplace in 1737 of the English radical Thomas Paine.

**Thetford Mines** /ˈθetfəd/ an area of asbestos mining 80 km. (50 miles) south of Quebec in eastern Canada, site of the world's largest asbestos deposits producing some 30 per cent of world supply.

**Thiès** /tjez/ the capital of Thiès region in western Senegal; pop. (est. 1985) 156,200. Located at the centre of the country's railway system, its industries produce cotton, aluminium, phosphates (mined in the Taiba region), asbestos, and crafts such as tapestry.

**Thimphu** /ˈtɪmpuː/ (also **Thimbu**) a town in the Himalayas at an altitude of 2,450 m. (8,000 ft.); pop. (est. 1991) 27,000. It has been the capital of Bhutan since 1952.

**Thingvellir** /tiːŋˈvetlə(r)/ the national shrine of Iceland, site of the founding (in 930) of the Icelandic *Althing*, the oldest parliament in the world.

**Thionville** /ˈtjəʊnviːl/ an industrial town in the department of Moselle, north-east France, on the Moselle River; pop. (1990) 40,835. It is a centre of iron and steel production.

**Thíra** see SANTORINI.

**Third River** a vast drainage canal in Iraq midway between the Tigris and Euphrates rivers. Completed in 1992, it was designed to aid the reclamation of 15,000 sq. km. (5,795 sq. miles) of land made barren by salination. The main canal is 560 km. (359 miles) long and stretches from Mahmudiya to Qorna. Drainage of the southern marshes of Iraq and the destruction of the way of life of the Marsh Arabs became a controversial issue during the construction of the canal.

**Third World** a term derived during the period of the Cold War when the capitalist and Communist blocs were seen to represent the two main ideologies of the world. The name 'Third World', initially given to those other countries with non-aligned status, gradually became synonymous with countries reckoned to be less developed.

**Thiruvananthapuram** see TRIVANDRUM.

**Thívai** the modern Greek name of THEBES.

**Thorshavn** see TÓRSHAVN.

**Thousand Oaks** a residential city with light industries in Ventura county, California, USA, situated in the Conejo Valley between Los Angeles and Santa Barbara; pop. (1990) 104,350.

**Thousand Islands 1.** a group of about 1,500 islands in a widening of the St. Lawrence River, just below Kingston, Ontario. Some of the islands belong to Canada and some to the USA. **2.** (Indonesian **Pulau Seribu**) a group of about 100 small Indonesian islands off the north coast of Java in the south-west Java Sea.

**Thrace** /θreɪs/ (Greek **Thráki** /ˈθrɑːkiː/) **1.** an ancient country lying west of Istanbul and the Black Sea and north of the Aegean, now part of modern Turkey, Greece, and Bulgaria. It extended as far west as the Adriatic but the Thracians retreated eastwards between the 13th and 5th c. BC under pressure from the Illyrians and Macedonians. Conquered by Philip II of Macedon in 342 BC it later became a province of Rome. The region was ruled by the Ottoman Turks from the

15th c. until the end of World War I, but northern Thrace was annexed by Bulgaria in 1885. In 1923 all of Thrace east of the Maritsa River was restored to Turkey. **2.** a region of modern Greece, in the north-east of the country; area 8,578 sq. km. (3,313 sq. miles); pop. (1991) 337,530; capital, Komotiní. **Thracian** *adj. & n.*

**Threadneedle Street** /θred'ni:d(ə)l/ a street in the City of London, England, containing the premises of the Bank of England (the Old Lady of Threadneedle Street). It is possibly named after a tavern with the arms of the Needlemakers.

**Three Mile Island** an island in the Susquehanna River near Harrisburg, Pennsylvania, USA, site of a nuclear power station. In 1979 an accident caused damage to uranium in the reactor core, an incident that provoked strong opposition to the expansion of the nuclear industry in the USA and precipitated a reassessment of safety standards.

**Thrissur** (also **Trichur** /trɪ'tʃʊ(ə)r/) a town in the state of Kerala, southern India, situated at the west end of the Palghat gap between the Nilgiri and Palani hills; pop. (1991) 274,900. It is a leading Hindu religious centre, with shrines dedicated to Vadakkunnatha.

**Thule** /'θju:lɪ/ **1.** a name given by the ancient Greek explorer Pytheas (*c.* 310 BC) to a country described by him as six day's sail north of Britain, and regarded by the ancients as the northernmost point of the world. It has been variously identified as Iceland, one of the Shetland Islands, and part of Scandinavia. **2.** the name given to a prehistoric Inuit culture widely distributed from Alaska to Greenland *c.* AD 500–1400. **3.** (Inuit **Qaanaaq**) a small Eskimo settlement on the north-west coast of Greenland, situated on Hvalsund, an inlet of Baffin Bay extending into Prudoe Land. **4.** the name of a US air base near Dundas (Uummannaq) on the north-west coast of Greenland.

**Thun** /tʊn/ (French **Thoune**) a town in the northern foothills of the Bernese Alps, west-central Switzerland; pop. (1990) 37,700. It is situated on the River Aare (which widens here to form Lake Thun) to the south of Berne and produces watches, clothing, and metal products.

**Thunder Bay** /'θʌndə(r)/ a city on an inlet of Lake Superior in western Ontario, Canada, at the mouth of the Kaministiquia; pop. (1991) 124,430 (metropolitan area). Now one of Canada's major ports, Thunder Bay was created in 1970 by the amalgamation of the twin cities of Fort William and Port Arthur and two adjoining townships. It is the furthermost port on the St. Lawrence Seaway accessible to sea-going vessels and a major outlet for grain from the Canadian prairies.

**Thurgau** /'tʊə(r)gaʊ/ (French **Thurgovie**) a canton of north-east Switzerland to the south of Lake Constance; area 1,013 sq. km. (391 sq. miles); pop. (1990) 205,950; capital, Frauenfeld. It joined the Swiss Confederation in 1803.

**Thuringia** /θjʊə'rɪndʒɪə/ (German **Thüringen**) a densely forested state of the Federal Republic of Germany, lying to the north of the Ore Mountains; area 16,251 sq. km. (6,277 sq. miles); pop. (1991) 2,572,070; capital, Erfurt. From 1946 to 1989 it formed part of East Germany.

**Thurso** /'θɜ:rsəʊ/ a royal burgh and port on the north coast of Scotland, in the Caithness district of Highland Region; pop. (1981) 8,900. Settled since Viking times (Norse = Thor's River), it developed in the Middle Ages as an outlet for grain to Scandinavia. It later thrived on fishing, the trade in Caithness flagstones, and the establishment of an atomic energy establishment at Dounreay. It was the birthplace of Sir William Smith who founded the Boys Brigade in 1883.

**Tiahuanaco** /ˌtjɑ:wɑ:'nɑ:kəʊ/ the ruins of a pre-Inca Indian city in Bolivia, situated to the south of Lake Titicaca in the southern highlands of the Central Andes at an altitude of *c.* 3,965 m. (13,000 ft.). The site is noted for its classic stone architecture and carving which includes the famous Gateway of the Sun, a huge monolith cut from a single block of andesite.

**Tianjin** /ˌtɪən'dʒɪn/ (formerly **Tientsin** /-'tsɪn/) the third-largest city in China, a port on the Hai River; pop. (1990) 7,790,000. It is the leading port of northern China and a special economic zone producing iron, steel, chemicals, motor vehicles, carpets, machinery, and consumer goods such as bicycles and sewing machines. The city preserves much of its 19th-c. colonial architecture.

**Tian Shan** SEE TIEN SHAN.

**Tianshui** /ˌtɪən'ʃwi:/ a city in Shaanxi province, central China, in the northern foothills of the Qin Ling Mts. west of Xi'an; pop. (1986) 1,967,000.

**Tiber** /'taɪbə(r)/ (Italian **Tevere** /'teɪvəreɪ/) a river of central Italy, upon which Rome stands, flowing 405 km. (252 miles) westwards from the Tuscan Apennines to the Tyrrhenian Sea at Ostia.

**Tiberias** /taɪ'bi:rɪəs/ a resort town on the Sea of Galilee (Lake Tiberias), north-east Israel. Built *c.* AD 20, it was named after the Roman emperor Tiberius and following the destruction of Jerusalem in the 2nd c. it became a leading Jewish centre of learning. It is noted for its hot springs and as the site where the Jewish Talmud was edited.

**Tiberias** /taɪ'bi:rɪəs/, **Lake** SEE GALILEE, SEA OF.

**Tibesti Mountains** /tɪ'bestɪ/ a mountain range in north-central Africa, on the frontier between Chad and Libya. The highest peak is Emi Koussi which rises to a height of 3,415 m. (11,208 ft.). Wildlife drawings on rocks indicate that the climate of this region in prehistoric times was much wetter than now.

**Tibet** /tɪ'bet/ (Chinese **Xizang** /ʃi:'zæŋ/) a mountainous region of Asia to the north of the Himalayas, occupying the highest plateau in the world with an average elevation of 4,000 m. (13,123 ft.), an autonomous region of China; area 1,228,000 sq. km. (474,314 sq. miles); pop. (1990) 2,196,000; capital, Lhasa. Ruled by Buddhist lamas since the 7th c., Tibet was conquered by the Mongols in the 13th c. and the Manchus in the 18th c. China extended its authority over Tibet in 1951 but only gained full control after crushing a revolt in 1959 during which the country's spiritual leader the Dalai Lama made his escape into India. Many of Tibet's monasteries and shrines were destroyed in an unsuccessful attempt to change national culture and consciousness. Almost completely surrounded by mountain ranges, Tibet is the source of some of Asia's largest rivers including the Yangtze, Salween, and Mekong.

**Tibetan** /tɪˈbet(ə)n/ the language of Tibet, spoken by about 2 million people there, a similar number in neighbouring provinces of China, and a million people in Nepal. It belongs to the Sino-Tibetan language group and is most closely related to Burmese. Its alphabet is based on that of Sanskrit and dates from the 7th c.

**Ticino** /tiːˈtʃiːnəʊ/ (French and German **Tessin**) a canton in southern Switzerland, on the Italian frontier; area 2,811 sq. km. (1,086 sq. miles); pop. (1990) 286,725; capital, Bellinzona. It joined the Swiss Confederation in 1803.

**Ticonderoga** /ˌtaɪkɒndəˈrəʊgə/ a village in north-east New York State, USA, between Lake George and Lake Champlain. Established in 1755 by the French as Fort Carillon, but renamed Fort Ticonderoga when taken by the British in 1759, it was captured during the American War of Independence by troops under Benedict Arnold.

**Tiefa** /tɪˈefə/ a city in Liaoning province, north-east China, north of Shenyang; pop. (1986) 182,000.

**Tieling** /ˌtiːerˈlɪŋ/ a city in Liaoning province, north-east China, north-east of Shenyang; pop. (1986) 289,000.

**Tien Shan** /ˈtɪen ˈʃæn/ (also **Tian Shan**, English **Heavenly Mountains**) a range of mountains lying to the north of the Tarim Basin in Xinjiang autonomous region, north-west China. Extending westwards into Kyrgyzstan, it rises to a height of 7,439 m. (24,406 ft.) at Pik Pobeda.

**Tientsin** see TIANJIN.

**Tierra del Fuego** /tɪˌerə del ˈfweɪgəʊ/ **1.** an archipelago separated from the southern tip of South America by the Strait of Magellan and the name of its main island. Visited by Magellan in 1520, its name in Spanish meaning 'land of fire', it is now divided between Chile and Argentina. **2.** a province (since 1990) of southern Argentina comprising the eastern half of the archipelago; area 21,263 sq. km. (8,213 sq. miles); pop. (1991) 69,450; capital, Ushuaia. The province's economy is based on oil and sheep farming.

**Tiflis** see TBLISI.

**Tighina** /tɪˈgiːnə/ a market and industrial town in Moldova (Moldavia), on the Dniester River south-east of Chisnau; pop. (1990) 132,000. Prior to the independence of Moldova in 1991 it was known as Bendery. Historically important as the gateway of Bessarabia, the town is a rail and light industry centre.

**Tigray** /ˈtiːgreɪ/ (also **Tigré**) a province in the arid northern highlands of Ethiopia; area 65,900 sq. km. (25,454 sq. miles); pop. (est. 1984) 2,409,700; capital, Mekele. Its predominantly Christian people, who speak a language of the Ethiopic group related to Amharic, were exposed to drought and famine in the 1980s and engaged in a bitter armed conflict with the government of Mengistu Haile Mariam between 1975 and 1991. **Tigrayan** *adj. & n.*

**Tigris** /ˈtaɪgrɪs/ the more easterly of the two rivers of Mesopotamia, 1,900 km. (1,180 miles) long, rising in the mountains of eastern Turkey and flowing through Iraq to join the Euphrates, forming the Shatt al-Arab which flows into the Persian Gulf. The city of Baghdad lies upon it. Its waters have supplied large irrigated areas since earliest times.

**Tihwa** /ˈtiːhwɑː/ the former name (until 1954) of URUMQI.

**Tijuana** /tiˈwɑːnə/ a tourist town in the state of Baja California Norte, north-west Mexico, situated on the Tijuana River just south of the US frontier; pop. (1990) 742,690.

**Tikal** /ˈtiːkæl/ an ancient Maya city in the tropical Petén region of northern Guatemala, with great plazas, pyramids, and palaces. It flourished especially in AD 300–800, reaching its peak towards the end of that period.

**Tilburg** /ˈtɪlbɜːg/ an industrial city in the Dutch province of North Brabant, south-east of Rotterdam; pop. (1991) 158,850. It produces textiles and is the leading city of southern Holland.

**Tilbury** /ˈtɪlbɜːrɪ/ a port on the north bank of the River Thames in Essex, the principal port of London and south-east England.

**Timaru** /ˈtɪməruː/ a seaport and resort in the Canterbury region on the east coast of South Island, New Zealand; pop. (1991) 27,640. Founded in the 1850s, its artificial harbour was completed in 1906. Its port trades in frozen meat, wool, and timber.

**Timbuktu** /ˌtɪmbʌkˈtuː/ (also **Tombouctou**) a town in the Gao region of northern Mali in West Africa, situated to the north of the River Niger; pop. (1976) 20,500. Founded by the Tuareg in the 11th c., it became a centre of Muslim learning and as the southern end of a trans-Saharan caravan route and meeting place for the nomadic people of the Sahara, noted for its market in gold and slaves.

**Timgad** /ˈtɪmgæd/ (ancient **Thamugadis**) a ruined city near Batna in north-east Algeria, founded by Trajan in AD 100. It was abandoned after the Arab invasions of the 7th c.

**Timimoun** /ˌtɪmɪˈmuːn/ a Saharan oasis town at the southern edge of the Grand Erg Occidental in the Adrar department of central Algeria; pop. (1982) 57,440.

**Timişoara** /ˌtɪmɪˈʃwɑːrə/ (Hungarian **Temesvár** /ˈtemesvær/) an industrial city and transportation centre in western Romania, on the Bega River; pop. (1989) 333,365. It is the capital of Timiş county and chief town of the Banat region, with industries that include engineering, food processing, and the manufacture of textiles, chemicals, and metal goods. A centre of science and culture, it has a university founded in 1962. Incidents in this city gave rise to the revolution that brought an end to the Ceauşescu regime and Communist rule in 1989.

**Timor** /ˈtiːmɔː(r)/ the largest of the Lesser Sunda Islands in the southern Malay Archipelago; area 34,190 sq. km. (13,205 sq. miles). The island was formerly divided into Dutch West Timor and Portuguese East Timor. In 1950 West Timor was absorbed into the newly formed Republic of Indonesia, becoming part of the province of Nusa Tenggara Timur (chief town, Kupang). In 1975 East Timor briefly declared itself independent from Portugal but was invaded and occupied by Indonesia. In 1976, against the wishes of the inhabitants, Indonesia formally annexed East Timor and administered it as the province of Timur Timur or Loro Sae (chief town, Dili); area 14,874 sq. km. (5,745 sq. miles); pop. (est. 1993) 808,300. A number of anti-Indonesian resistance movements continue to fight for independence.

**Timor Sea** the part of the Indian Ocean between Timor and north-west Australia.

**Tindouf** /tɪnˈdʊf/ a Saharan oasis town in the Bechar department of western Algeria; pop. (1982) 10,800. It has been a base for refugees and Polisario guerrillas from the Western Sahara since the occupation of that region by Morocco in 1976. Iron ore reserves nearby have been an additional source of conflict between Algeria and Morocco.

**Tinnevelly** see TIRUNELVELI.

**Tin Pan Alley** originally the name given to a district of New York City (28th Street, between 5th Avenue and Broadway) where many songwriters, arrangers, and music publishers were based. The district gave its name to the American popular music industry between the late 1880s and the mid-20th c., particularly to such composers as Irving Berlin, Jerome Kern, George Gershwin, Cole Porter, and Richard Rogers. The term was also applied to Denmark Street in London.

**Tintagel** /tɪnˈtædʒəl/ a village on the coast of northern Cornwall, with ruins of a castle that was a stronghold of the Earls of Cornwall from c. 1145 until the 15th c. It is the traditional birthplace of King Arthur.

**Tintern Abbey** a ruined 12th-c. Cistercian abbey on the River Wye near Chepstow in Gwent, south-east Wales, immortalized in a poem written by William Wordsworth in 1798.

**Tioman** /tiːˈəʊmɑːn/ a resort island in the South China Sea off the south-east coast of Peninsular Malaysia. It is the largest of a group of 64 volcanic islands and islets.

**Tipperary** /ˌtɪpəˈreərɪ/ a county of central Ireland, in the province of Munster; divided into North and South Ridings whose administrative centres are at Nenagh and Clonmel; area 4,254 sq. km. (1,643 sq. miles); pop. (1991) 133,620.

**Tiranë** /tɪˈrɑːnə/ (also **Tirana**) the capital of Albania, situated on the Ishm River in central Albania; pop. (1990) 244,200. Founded by the Turks in the 17th c., it became capital of Albania in 1920. Laid out by Italian architects before World War II, it has been greatly expanded under Communist rule since 1946 with light industries and a hydro-electric power-station.

**Tiraspol** /tɪˈræspəl/ an industrial city in the Republic of Moldova (Moldavia), on the Dniester River; pop. (1990) 183,700. Developed as a Russian fortress town in the 1790s, it is now an agricultural processing centre and chief town of the Trans-Dniester region.

**Tiree** /taɪˈriː/ a flat fertile island in the Inner Hebrides of Scotland, west of Mull. It is said to have more sunshine than anywhere else in the UK. The chief settlement is Scarinish.

**Tîrgovişte** /tɜːˈɡəʊˈviːʃtə/ the capital of Dimboviţa county, south-central Romania, on the Ialomiţa River; pop. (1989) 100,430. Now a centre of Romania's oil industry, it was capital of Walachia 1383–1698. Its Chindia Tower contains a museum to Vlad Tepes ('the impaler') said to be the model for Count Dracula.

**Tîrgu Jiu** /ˈtɜːɡuːˈdʒuː/ the capital of Gorj county in south-west Romania, on the River Jiu; pop. (1989) 93,250.

**Tîrgu Mureş** /ˌtɜːɡuːˈmuːreʃ/ the capital of Mureş county, north-central Romania, on the River Mureş; pop. (1989) 164,780. It is a leading industrial, cultural, and commercial city of Transylvania producing chemicals, textiles, machinery, processed food, and metal goods. It is also the centre of the country's natural gas industry.

**Tir-nan-Og** /ˌtɪənæˈnɒk/ the Gaelic name for the legendary land of perpetual youth equivalent to Elysium.

**Tirol** see TYROL.

**Tiruchchirappalli** /ˌtɪrətʃɪˈrɑːpəlɪ/ (formerly **Trichinopoly**) a city in the state of Tamil Nadu, southern India, at the head of the Cauvery (Kaveri) delta; pop. (1991) 711,120. Known as Trichy or Tiruchi for short, the town developed as a railway junction after 1862. Its industries produce textiles and artificial diamonds.

**Tirunelveli** /ˌtɪruːˈnelvəliː/ (also **Tinnevelly** /tɪnəˈveliː/) a city in Tamil Nadu, southern India, on the Tamramparni River south-west of Madurai; pop. (1991) 365,930. It is a market town and one of the oldest Christian centres in Tamil Nadu. St. Francis Xavier began his ministry in India here and in 1896 it became the head of the Anglican Church of South India. It is now joined with the twin settlement of Palayamkottai.

**Tiruppur** /ˈtɪrəˌpʊ(ə)r/ a commercial town in Tamil Nadu, southern India, east of Coimbatore; pop. (1991) 305,550. It has textile industries.

**Tisza** /ˈtiːsə/ the longest tributary of the Danube in eastern Europe. Rising in the Carpathian Mountains of Ukraine, it flows 962 km. southwards through Romania and Hungary before meeting the Danube in Serbia, south-west of Belgrade.

**Titicaca** /ˌtɪtɪˈkɑːkə/, **Lake** a lake in the Andes of South America, straddling the frontier between Peru and Bolivia. At an altitude of 3,809 m. (12,497 ft.) it is the highest large navigable lake in the world; area 8,288 sq. km. (3,200 sq. miles).

**Titograd** /ˈtiːtəʊˌɡræd/ the name of PODGORICA from 1948 until 1992.

**Tivoli** /ˈtɪvəli/ a city of Latium near Rome in central Italy, noted for its waterfalls formed on the Aniene River and for its villas which include the Villa of Hadrian, the Villa Gregoriana, and the Villa d'Este; pop. (1990) 55,030.

**Tivoli Gardens** /ˈtɪvəli/ an amusement park in central Copenhagen, Denmark, with theatres, concert hall, gardens, boating lake, and fairground attractions.

**Tizi Ouzou** /ˌtiːziː ʊˈzuː/ a commercial and agricultural market town in northern Algeria, to the east of Algiers, capital of Tizi-Ouzou department; pop. (1989) 101,000. It is the chief town of the Kabyle Berbers.

**Tlaxcala** /tlɑːsˈkɑːlə/ **1.** a state of east-central Mexico; area 4,016 sq. km. (1,551 sq. miles); pop. (1990) 763,680. It is the smallest state in Mexico. **2.** (fully **Tlaxcala de Xicohténcatl**) its capital, 30 km. (19 miles) north of Puebla; pop. (est. 1990) 25,000. The San Francisco church is the oldest in the New World.

**Tlemcen** /təlemˈsen/ a city in north-west Algeria, capital of the department of Tlemcen and a road and rail junction; pop. (1989) 146,000. Founded by the Almoravid dynasty, it was capital of the central Maghreb and a trade centre on the trans-Saharan route from Africa to Europe. Nearby are the ruins of the ancient Merenid town of Mansourah and the 14th-c. tomb of the mystic Sidi Bou Mediène. It manufactures carpets, leather goods, brassware, shoes, and furniture.

**Tlingit** /ˈtlɪŋɡɪt/ the northernmost of the north-western Indian tribes of North America, the dominant tribe of the Alaskan panhandle. Once

dependent on subsistence fishing, they numbered some 8,700 in 1985.

**TN** *abbr.* US Tennessee (in official postal use).

**Toamasina** /ˌtəʊəməˈsiːnə/ (formerly **Tamatave** /tæməˈtɑːv/) a seaport on the east coast of Madagascar, the principal Indian Ocean port of that island; pop. (1990) 145,430. Founded by the Portuguese in the 17th c., it is linked to Antananarivo by rail. It has textile, leather, and tobacco industries.

**Toba** /ˈtəʊbɑː/, **Lake** (Indonesian **Danau Toba**) a lake on the island of Sumatra, the largest lake in Indonesia; area 1,160 sq. km. (448 sq. miles). The remains of a volcanic crater rising to a height of 900 m. (2,953 ft.), it is 530 m. (1,740 ft.) deep. At the centre of the lake is the large island of **Samosir**.

**Tobago** see TRINIDAD AND TOBAGO.

**Tobol** /təˈbɒl/ a river of Central Asia that rises in the Mugodzhar Hills of northern Kazakhstan and flows 1,690 km. (1,050 miles) north-eastwards into Russia where it meets the Irtysh River at Tobolsk.

**Tobruk** /təˈbrʊk/ (Arabic **Tubruq**) a port on the Mediterranean coast of north-east Libya; pop. (1984) 94,000. Tobruk was the scene of fierce fighting during the North African campaign in World War II.

**Tocantins** /ˌtəʊkənˈtiːns/ **1.** a river of South America which rises in west-central Brazil and flows 2,699 km. (1,677 miles) north to join the Pará River. **2.** a state of northern Brazil; area 269,911 sq. km. (104,253 sq. miles); pop. (1991) 920,120; capital, Palmas. It was created in 1991 from the northern half of the state of Goias.

**Todd River** /tɒd/ a river of central Australia that rises in the Macdonnell Ranges and flows 320 km. (200 miles) south-eastwards through Alice Springs to the Simpson Desert. It flows only in wet years and its dry bed is the scene of the occasional 'Henley-on-Todd Regatta' in which boats are carried by runners. The river was named in honour of the South Australia Postmaster-General at the time of the installation of the Overland Telegraph in 1870–2.

**Togliatti** /tɒlˈjætɪ/ (also **Tolyatti**) an industrial city and port in western Russia, on the Volga north-east of Samara; pop. (1990) 642,000. Known as Stavropol until 1964, the city was renamed after the sometime leader of the Italian Communist Party and moved to its present location during the construction of the Kuibyshev Reservoir. It is the major car-making centre of Russia.

**Togo** /ˈtəʊɡəʊ/ official name **The Republic of Togo** a country in West Africa between Ghana and Benin with a short coastline on the Gulf of Guinea; area 56,785 sq. km. (21,933 sq. miles); pop. (est. 1991) 3,761,000; official languages, French, Ewe, and Kabye; capital, Lomé. From a narrow coastal strip Togo rises through low-lying plains to the Atakora Mountains which separate the country from semiarid plains in the far north. The climate

varies from tropical in the south to subtropical in the north, most rain occurring between May and October. The majority of the population depends on subsistence agriculture, but coffee, cocoa, and cotton are grown as cash crops for export. Rich in natural resources, Togo has substantial phosphate, marble, and limestone deposits. Annexed by Germany in 1884, the district called Togoland was divided between France and Britain after World War I. The British western section joined Ghana on the latter's independence (1957). The remainder of the area became a United Nations mandate under French administration after World War II and achieved independence, as a republic with the name Togo, in 1960. Political parties were banned following a coup in 1967 and the establishment of military rule. A new multi-party constitution was approved in 1992 but the transition to civilian democracy was marred by civil unrest arising from a power struggle between the president and the transitional government. **Togolese** *adj. & n.*

**Tohoku** /təʊˈhəʊkuː/ the largest of the five regions on Honshu Island, Japan; area 66,942 sq. km. (25,856 sq. miles); pop. (1990) 9,738,000; chief city, Sendai. It is divided into six prefectures:

| Prefecture | Area (sq. km.) | Pop. (1990) | Capital |
| --- | --- | --- | --- |
| Akita | 11,609 | 1,227,000 | Akita |
| Aomori | 9,614 | 1,483,000 | Aomori |
| Fukushima | 13,782 | 2,104,000 | Fukushima |
| Iwate | 15,277 | 1,417,000 | Morioka |
| Miyagi | 7,291 | 2,249,000 | Sendai |
| Yamagata | 9,326 | 1,258,000 | Yamagata |

**Tokaj** /təˈkeɪ/ (also **Tokay**) a town in north-east Hungary on the River Tisza that gives its name to a sweet aromatic wine produced in the region since the 12th c.

**Tokat** /təʊˈkɑːt/ **1.** a province of Anatolia in north-central Turkey; area 9,958 sq. km. (3,846 sq. miles); pop. (1990) 719,250. **2.** its capital, a market town on the Yesilirmak River; pop. (1990) 83,060.

**Tokelau**
/ˌtəʊkəˈlaʊ/ a group of islands between Kiribati and Western Samoa in the western Pacific Ocean, forming an overseas territory of New Zealand; area 10 sq. km. (4 sq. miles); pop. (1986)

1,690. Chief settlement, Nukunonu. It comprises the three low-lying atoll islands of Atafu,

Nukunonu, and Fakaofo. Formerly part of the Gilbert and Ellice Colony, the group was transferred to New Zealand administration in 1926, incorporated as part of New Zealand in 1949, and named Tokelau in 1976.

**Tokushima** /təʊˈkʊʃɪmə/ the capital of Tokushima prefecture, Japan, a port on the east coast of Shikoku Island; pop. (1990) 263,340. Largely destroyed during World War II, it is now a commercial and industrial centre with an important chemical industry.

**Tokyo** /ˈtəʊkjəʊ/ the capital of Japan, situated on the Kanto plain, east-central Honshu Island; pop. (1990) 8,163,000. The city was formerly called Edo and was the centre of the military government under the Shoguns; it was renamed Tokyo in 1868 when it became the imperial capital. One of the largest cities in the world, it is the centre of government, commerce, and industry in Japan. Devastated by an earthquake in 1923 and by bombing during World War II, its chief landmarks are the Imperial Palace and adjoining gardens, and Buddhist temples and shrines. The city is divided into distinct districts. Marunouchi, the country's business centre; Kasumigaseki, the government quarter and political centre; and the Ginza shopping and entertainment area. Tokyo is also Japan's leading educational centre with over 100 universities and colleges, numerous museums, libraries, and art galleries. It has diverse heavy and light industries including steel, chemicals, metals, machinery, transport equipment including automobiles, electronics, optical goods and cameras, and textiles.

**Tolbukhin** the former name (until 1991) of DOBRICH in Bulgaria.

**Toledo** /təˈleɪdəʊ/ an ancient city of Toledo province in the Castilla-La Mancha region, central Spain, situated on the River Tagus; pop. (1991) 63,560. It was the Spanish capital 1087–1560, and was long famous for the manufacture of finely-tempered sword-blades. For many years it was the home of the painter El Greco.

**Toledo** /təˈliːdəʊ/ an industrial city and Great Lakes shipping centre on Lake Erie in north-west Ohio, USA; pop. (1990) 332,940. It is a distribution point for coal, iron ore, steel, grain, and automobile parts, and a noted centre for the manufacture of glass products.

**Tollund** /ˈtɒlənd/ a fen in central Jutland, Denmark, where the well-preserved corpse of an Iron Age man (c. 500 BC–400 AD) was found in a peat bog in 1950. The body was naked save for a leather cap and belt, and round the neck was a plaited leather noose: Tollund Man had met his death by hanging, a victim of murder or ritual slaughter.

**Tolpuddle** /ˈtɒlpʌd(ə)l/ a village in Dorset, England, made famous by the 'Tolpuddle Martyrs', six farm labourers who attempted to form a union to obtain an increase in wages and were sentenced in 1834 to seven years' transportation on a charge of administering unlawful oaths. Their harsh sentences caused widespread protests, and two years later they were pardoned and repatriated from Australia.

**Toltec** /'tɒltek/ a Nahuatl-speaking people who dominated central Mexico *c.* 900–1200. They were a warrior aristocracy whose period of domination was violent and innovative. The Toltec founded or developed cities (their capital was Tula), but were unable to consolidate their hold on the conquered area, which developed into a number of states, mostly independent. In the 12th–13th c. famine and drought (perhaps caused by climatic changes) brought catastrophe, and the disunited area fell to invading tribes from the north.

**Toluca** /tə'luːkə/ (fully **Toluca de Lerdo**) a commercial and industrial city on the central plateau of Mexico, capital of the state of Mexico; pop. (1990) 487,630. It lies at the foot of the extinct volcano Nevado de Toluca and at 2,680 m. (8,793 ft.) is the highest of Mexico's state capitals. Founded in 1530 by Hernan Cortés, its Indian market is said to be the largest in Mexico. It has car, machinery-making, and food-processing industries.

**Tolyatti** see TOGLIATTI.

**Tomakomai** /ˌtəʊmə'kəʊmaɪ/ a port and industrial city on the south coast of Hokkaido Island, Japan; pop. (1990) 160,120.

**tombolo** /tɒm'bəʊləʊ/ a spit that joins an off-shore island to the mainland.

**Tombstone** /'tuːmstəʊn/ a resort town in south-east Arizona, USA, south-east of Tucson; pop. (1990) 1,220. Founded as a silver-mining town in 1879, it gained a reputation for its bawdy saloons and lawlessness which became legendary in 1881 following the shoot-out between the Earps and the Clantons at the O.K. Corral. Tombstone was declared a National Historic Landmark in 1962.

**Tombouctou** see TIMBUKTU.

**Tomor** /'tɒmɔː(r)/, **Mount** a mountain in southern Albania rising to a height of 2,480 m. (8,050 ft.).

**Tomsk** /tɒmsk/ an industrial city, river port and educational centre of Russia on the River Tom in west-central Siberia; pop. (1990) 506,000. It produces machine tools, electrical equipment, machinery, timber, and chemicals.

**Tonga** /'tɒŋə/ (also **Friendly Islands**) official name **The Kingdom of Tonga** a country in the South Pacific to the east of Fiji and south of Western Samoa, consisting of about 170 small volcanic

and coral islands of which 36 are inhabited; area 668 sq. km. (258 sq. miles); pop. (est. 1991)

100,000; official languages, Tongan and English; capital, Nuku'alofa (on Tongatapu). The islands' chief exports are copra, coconut products, fish, vanilla, bananas, and spices. Explored by the Dutch in the early 17th c., the islands were visited in 1773 by Captain Cook who named them the Friendly Islands. The people were converted to Christianity by Methodist missionaries in the early 19th c. and the kingdom became a British protectorate in 1900, gaining independence as a member-state of the Commonwealth in 1970. The constitution, which dates from 1875, provides for a constitutional monarchy with an executive prime minister and cabinet and a unicameral Legislative Assembly. The country's first formal political party was established in 1994.
**Tongan** *adj. & n.*

**Tongariro** /ˌtɒŋə'rɪəˌrəʊ/, **Mount** a mountain in the central volcanic uplands of North Island, New Zealand, rising to 1,968 m. (6,457 ft.) to the south-west of Lake Taupo. It lies at the centre of **Tongariro National Park** which was designated in 1894 and was the first national park of New Zealand. The park incorporates the Ruapehu, Ngauruhoe, and Tongariro peaks. Water rising in this catchment area is channelled through Lake Taupo to the Waikito River where it is used to generate hydroelectric power. Formerly (until 1989) lending its name to an administrative region, Tongariro is a sacred mountain of the Maori.

**Tongariro** a river of North Island, New Zealand, that rises on the east side of Mt. Ruapehu and flows northwards to enter the south end of Lake Taupo. It is noted for its rainbow trout.

**Tongatapu** /ˌtɒŋə'tæpuː/ the main island of Tonga in the South Pacific; area 259 sq. km. (100 sq. miles). Its chief town is Nuku'alofa, capital of Tonga. Tourism and the production of fruit and vegetables are the main economic activities.

**Tongchuan** /tʊŋ'ʃwaːn/ a city in Shaanxi province, central China, north of Xi'an; pop. (1986) 404,000.

**Tonghua** /tʊŋ'hwaː/ a city in Jilin province, north-east China, east of Shenyang; pop. (1986) 373,000.

**Tongliao** /tʊŋ'ljaʊ/ a city in Liaoning province, north-east China, in the valley of the Xiliao River north-west of Shenyang; pop. (1986) 261,000.

**Tongling** /tʊŋ'lɪŋ/ a city in Anhui province, eastern China, in the valley of the Yangtze River north-west of Hangzhou; pop. (1986) 501,000.

**Tonkin** /tɒn'kɪn/, **Gulf of** a north-western arm of the South China Sea between Vietnam and China. It lies to the west of the island of Hainan and its chief port is Haiphong in Vietnam.

**Tonlé Sap** /'tɒnleɪ 'sæp/ a lake in central Cambodia, linked to the Mekong River by the Tonlé Sap River. The area of the lake is tripled during the wet season (June–November). On the north-west shore stand the ruins of the ancient Khmer city of Angkor.

**Toowoomba** /tuːˈwuːmbə/ an agricultural centre to the west of Brisbane on the eastern margin of the Darling Downs region of Queensland, northeast Australia; pop. (1991) 75,960. Its industries produce food products and agricultural machinery.

**Topeka** /təˈpiːkə/ the capital of the US state of Kansas, situated on the Kansas River; pop. (1990) 119,880. Established as a railway town in 1854 and state capital in 1861, it was developed as a terminus and general office of the Atchison, Topeka, and Santa Fe Railroad. Industries include printing, grain milling and the manufacture of tyres, cellophane, and steel products.

**Topkapi Palace** /tɒpˈkɑːpɪ/ the former Seraglio or residence in Istanbul of the sultans of the Ottoman empire, last occupied by Mahmut II (1808–39) and now a museum. Chief among its exhibits are the famous emerald-studded Topkapi Dagger, the eighty-six carat Spoonseller's diamond, and personal belongings of the Prophet Muhammad.

**topography** /təˈpɒɡrəfɪ/ a detailed description or representation on a map, etc., of the surface configuration of the land.

**toponym** /ˈtɒpənɪm/ a descriptive place-name, usually derived from a topographical feature of the place.

**Torbay** /tɔːˈbeɪ/ an urban area on the south coast of Devon, south-west England, comprising the resort towns of Torquay, Paignton, and Brixham; pop. (1991) 121,000.

**Tordesillas** /tɔːdəˈsiːjəs/ a village in the province of Valladolid in Castilla-León, northern Spain, on the Duero (Douro) River. A treaty between Portugal and Spain was signed here in 1494 establishing a line between their respective territories in South America at 46°W.

**Torino** the Italian name for TURIN.

**tornado** /tɔːˈneɪdəʊ/ a destructive rotating wind associated with the meeting of warm moist air from the Gulf of Mexico and cold air from the western USA. They occur most frequently in northern Texas, Oklahoma, Kansas, and Missouri.

**Tornio** /ˈtɔːnɪəʊ/ **1.** (Swedish **Tornea**) a town in the province of Lappi, north-west Finland, situated at the head of the Gulf of Bothnia opposite the Swedish town of Haparanda; pop. (1990) 22,880. The centre of the town is located on the island of Suensaari in the Tornio River. **2.** (Swedish **Torne Älv**, Finnish **Tornionjoki**) a river that rises in north Sweden and flows 566 km. (356 miles) southwards along the border between Sweden and Finland before emptying into the Gulf of Bothnia. The Kukkolankoski Rapids, 15 km. (9 miles) north of Tornio, are the longest free-flowing rapids in Finland.

**Toronto** /təˈrɒntəʊ/ the capital of Ontario and largest city in Canada, situated on the north shore of Lake Ontario at the mouth of the River Don;

pop. (1991) 635,400; 3,893,050 (metropolitan area). Founded in 1793 and laid out in the style of a European city, it was christened York, but in 1834 was renamed Toronto, a name derived from a Huron Indian word meaning 'meeting place'. It developed into a major industrial, financial, and cultural centre on the St. Lawrence Seaway. The University of Toronto (1827) is Canada's largest. The CN Tower (1976), at 553 m. (1,815 ft.), is the tallest building in the world and the University of Toronto (1827) is the largest in Canada. Other landmarks include Ontario Place, Ontario Science Centre, and the New City Hall. Its industries include iron and steel, electrical equipment, farming machinery, and aircraft.

**Torquay** /tɔːˈkiː/ a resort town on the English Channel, in Devon, south-west England; pop. (1981) 57,500. It has associations with Elizabeth Barrett, Charles Kingsley, Edward Bulwer-Lytton, and Benjamin Disraeli who visited the town, and with Sir Richard Burton who was born there in 1821.

**Torrance** /ˈtɒrəns/ a city to the west of Long Beach, California, a suburb of the Los Angeles conurbation; pop. (1990) 133,100.

**Torre del Greco** /ˌtɒrɪ del ˈɡrekəʊ/ a fishing port and resort town on the Bay of Naples in Campania Italy; pop. (1990) 102,650. It lies at the foot of Mount Vesuvius, and has an old coral industry.

**Torrens** /ˈtɒrəns/, **Lake** a lake in Australia, the second-largest of the salt lakes of South Australia, occupying the rift valley to the west of the Flinders Range. It is named in honour of Sir Robert Torrens (1780–1864), chairman of the South Australia Commission to manage land sales and emigration.

**Torreón** /tɒriːˈəʊn/ a city in the state of Coahuila, northern Mexico, west of Monterrey; pop. (1990) 459,800. Founded as a railway town in 1887, it is a shipping point for cotton and wheat at the centre of a vine-growing, dairy farming, and mining region.

**Torres Strait** /ˈtɒrɪs/ a channel linking the Arafura Sea and Coral Sea and separating the north tip of Queensland, Australia, from the island of New Guinea. It is named after Luis Vaez de Torres, captain of one of the ships that sailed under Quiros in 1606 and the first European to sail along the south coast of New Guinea. The Torres Strait Islands, which lie within 96 km. (60 miles) of the coast of Australia, were annexed to Queensland in 1872. Of largely Malaysian descent, the Torres Strait Islanders engage in pearl fishing.

**Tórshavn** /ˈtɔːshaʊn/ the capital of the Faeroe Islands, situated on the island of Strømø; pop. (1992) 14,600. Now a North Atlantic fishing port, it was the site of an Alting (parliament) established here in the 9th c.

**Tortola** /tɔːˈtəʊlə/ the principal island of the British Virgin Islands in the West Indies; area 54 sq. km. (21 sq. miles); chief town, Road Town. The island is mountainous and rises through lush sub-tropical greenery to 366 m. (1,200 ft.) at Mount Sage. Its name means 'turtle dove'.

**Tortuga** /tɔːˈtuːgə/ (also **Ile de la Tortue**) a Caribbean island off the north coast of Haiti, a notorious haunt of pirates in the 17th c.; area 180 sq. km. (70 sq. miles).

**Toruń** /tɔːˈruːnjə/ (German **Thorn**) the capital of Toruń county, northern Poland, a port on the River Vistula north-west of Warsaw; pop. (1990) 200,820. It was the birthplace in 1473 of the astronomer Copernicus. Industries include chemicals, engineering, and timber.

**Toscana** the Italian name for TUSCANY.

**Tottori** /təˈtɒrɪ/ the capital of Tottori prefecture, south Honshu Island, Japan, a port on the Sea of Japan; pop.(1990) 142,480.

**Toubkal** /ˈtuːbkæl/, **Djebel** a mountain in Morocco, in the High Atlas south of Marrakech. Rising to 4,165 m. (13,665 ft.), it is the highest peak in the Atlas Mountains and in North Africa.

**Toulon** /tuːˈlɔ̃/ a port and naval base on the Mediterranean coast of southern France, capital of the department of Var in the Provence-Alpes-Côte d'Azur region; pop. (1990) 170,170. Developed in the 17th c. by Louis XIV and Cardinal Richlieu, it is one of the world's leading naval ports with ship-building and repair industries.

**Toulouse** /tuːˈluːz/ a city of south-west France on the River Garonne, capital of the department of Haute-Garonne in the Midi-Pyrénées region; pop. (1990) 365,930. It was the capital of the Visigoths (419–507), and later the chief town of Aquitaine and of the Languedoc; its university was founded in 1229. Toulouse is now a centre of the aerospace and electronics industries.

**Touraine** /tuːˈreɪn/ a former province of France extending over the valleys of the Loire, Cher, and Vienne in the vicinity of Tours. It is noted for its wines which include those of Vouvray, Chinon, Bourgueil, Montlouis, and St. Nicolas de Bourgueil.

**Tourcoing** /tʊə(r)ˈkwɑ̃/ a textile-manufacturing town in the department of Nord, north-west France, near the Franco-Belgian frontier; pop. (1990) 94,425.

**Tournai** /tʊəˈneɪ/ (Flemish **Doornik** /ˈdɔːniːk/) a textile-manufacturing town in the province of Hainaut, south-west Belgium, on the River Scheldt near the Belgian–French frontier; pop. (1991) 67,730.

**Tours** /tʊə(r)/ an industrial city of Touraine in west-central France, capital of the department of Indre-et-Loire; pop. (1990) 133,400. Situated on the Loire, it is a centre of light industry, data processing, and the wine trade.

**Tower Hamlets** an inner borough of Greater London, England, on the River Thames; pop.

(1990) 153,500. It was created in 1965 from the East End boroughs of Bethnal Green, Poplar, and Stepney which, in medieval times, were hamlets belonging to the Tower of London. Wapping, Millwall, Limehouse, and Bow all lie within the borough.

**Tower of London** a fortress by the River Thames just east of the City of London. The oldest part, the White Tower, was begun in 1078. It was later used as a State prison, and is now a repository of ancient armour and weapons and other objects of public interest, including the Crown jewels (which have been kept there since the time of Henry III).

**Townsend** /ˈtaʊnzend/, **Mount** a mountain rising to 2,214 m. (7,251 ft.) north of Mount Kosciusko in the Australian Alps, New South Wales. It is the second-highest peak in Australia.

**Townsville** /ˈtaʊnzvɪl/ an industrial port and resort town of Queensland, on the north-east coast of Australia; pop. (1991) 101,400 (with Thuringowa). It was founded in 1864 by J. M. Black who was commissioned by the merchant and cotton-grower Robert Towns to develop an outlet for produce from the north. It developed rapidly after the discovery of minerals at Mount Isa in the 1870s and is now a point of access for touring the Great Barrier Reef.

**Toxteth** /ˈtɒkstəθ/ an inner-city district of Liverpool, England, the scene of riots in 1981.

**Toyama** /təʊˈjɑːmə/ the capital of Toyama prefecture, east-central Honshu Island, Japan, an industrial city on Toyama Bay; pop. (1990) 321,260. It has pharmaceutical and textile industries.

**Toyohashi** /ˌtəʊjəˈhɑːʃiː/ a textile-manufacturing city in Aichi prefecture, central Honshu Island, Japan; pop. (1990) 337,990.

**Toyota** /təʊˈjəʊtə/ an industrial city in Aichi prefecture, specializing in textile machinery, east-central Honshu Island, Japan; pop. (1990) 332,340.

**Tozeur** /təʊˈzɜː/ (also **Tawzar**) an oasis and resort town in west Tunisia, on the north-western shore of Chott el Jerid; pop. (1984) 21,600.

**Trâblous** see TRIPOLI, second-largest city of Lebanon.

**Trabzon** /ˈtræbz(ə)n/ (formerly **Trebizond** /ˈtrebɪˌzɒnd/) a commercial city and port of north-east Turkey, on the Black Sea at the mouth of the Degirmen River; pop. (1990) 143,940. Traditionally founded by Greek colonists in 756 BC, its ancient name was Trapezus. From 1204 to 1461 it was the capital of an empire established by Alexis Comnenus. It is now capital of the province of Trabzon, and exports food products and tobacco.

**trade wind** a constant wind blowing towards the equator from the north-east or south-east. The name had in its origin nothing to do with 'trade' in the commercial sense but was originally applied to any wind that 'blows trade', i.e. in a constant direction.

**Trafalgar** /trəˈfælgə(r)/ a cape on the coast of Cadiz province, southern Spain, near which a decisive battle of the Napoleonic Wars was fought on 21 October 1805. The British fleet under Nelson (who was killed in the action) achieved a decisive victory over the combined fleets of France and Spain which were attempting to clear the way for Napoleon's projected invasion of Britain.

**Tralee** /trəˈliː/ the county town of Kerry in the Republic of Ireland, a port at the mouth of the River Lee where it enters Tralee Bay; pop.(1991) 17,200. It was the home of William Mulchinock (1820–64) who wrote the song *The Rose of Tralee*, and the birthplace in 1881 of Roger Bresnahan who became a famous US baseball player and was the inventor of shinguards. St. Brendan the Navigator (484–577), patron saint of Kerry, was born to the west of Tralee near the port of Fenit. Tralee is the headquarters of the Folk Theatre of Ireland.

**tramontana** /træmɒnˈtɑːnə/ the name given to a cold, dry wind that blows southwards from northern Italy and central Spain.

**Transantarctic Mountains** a mountain system extending across the Antarctic continent, separating Greater Antarctica from Lesser Antarctica and the Ross Ice Shelf. Its highest peak is Mount Markham (4,351 m., 14,275 ft.).

**Transcaucasia** /ˌtrænzkɔːˈkeɪzɪə/ that part of Georgia, Armenia, and Azerbaijan lying between the Greater Caucasus Mountains in Russia and the frontiers with Iran and Turkey. Created a republic of the USSR in 1922, Transcaucasia was broken up into its constituent union republics in 1936.

**Transdanubian Highlands** /ˌtrænzdænˈjuːbɪən/ a hilly region to the north of Lake Balaton and west of the Danube in western Hungary, separating the Little Plain from the Great Plain.

**Trans-Dniester** a region of Eastern Moldova (Moldovia) lying between the Dniester River and the border with Ukraine. Its population is Slav-dominated with ethnic Russians and Ukranians together outnumbering ethnic Moldovans. A separatist movement emerged in the 1980s, and in 1994 the region was granted special autonomous status. Its chief city is Tiraspol.

**transhumance** the seasonal movement of people and animals between different grazing grounds.

**Transjordan** /ˌtrænzˈdʒɔːd(ə)n/ the former name of an area of Palestine east of the Jordan River, held under British mandate after the break-up of the Ottoman empire at the end of World War I. It became an independent state in 1946 as the Hashemite Kingdom of Jordan although the name Transjordan was in general use until 1949.

**Transkei** /trænˈskaɪ/ a former independent tribal homeland of the Xhosa people in South Africa, granted self-government in 1963, but united with Eastern Cape province in 1994.

**Trans-Siberian Railway** a railway built in 1891–1904 from Moscow east around the southern end of Lake Baikal to Vladivostok on the Sea of Japan, a distance of 9,311 km. (5,786 miles). It opened up Siberia and advanced Russian interest in east Asia. A major extension to the north of Lake Baikal (the Baikal–Amur Mainline) was completed in 1984 and stretches 3,102-km. (1,952-mile) from Ust-Kut in east Siberia to the Pacific coast.

**Transvaal** /trænzˈvɑːl/ a former province of the Republic of South Africa, lying north of the Orange Free State and separated from it by the River Vaal; area 262,499 sq. km. (101,390 sq. miles); pop. (1991) 8,630,000. Its capital was Pretoria. Inhabited by Ndebele Africans, it was first settled by Europeans c. 1840. In the second half of the 19th c. the right of self-government was lost, regained, and (after defeat in the Second Boer War) lost again, and in 1900 the Transvaal was once more annexed by Britain. Self-government was granted in 1906, and it became a founding province of the Union of South Africa in 1910. In 1994 it was divided into the provinces of Eastern Transvaal, Northern Transvaal, North-West, and Pretoria-Witwatersrand-Vereeniging (PWV).

**Transylvania** /ˌtrænsɪlˈveɪnɪə/ a large tableland region of north-west Romania separated from the rest of the country by the Carpathian Mountains and the Transylvanian Alps. Formerly part of Hungary, Transylvania was annexed by Romania in 1918. Its name means 'beyond the forest' and its chief cities are Brasov, Cluj-Napoca, Timişoara, and Oradea.
**Transylvanian** *adj. & n.*

**Transylvanian Alps** a southern arm of the Carpathians, extending across central Romania. Its highest peak is Moldoveanu (2,543 m., 8,343 ft.).

**Trapani** /trəˈpæniː/ a port on the north-west coast of Sicily, capital of the province of Trapani; pop. (1990) 72,840. Once an important Carthaginian stronghold, it trades in wine, salt, and tuna fish.

**Traralgon** /trəˈrælgən/ a city in south-east Victoria, Australia, in the Latrobe valley 160 km. (100 miles) east of Melbourne; pop. (1991) 19,700. Its chief industries are paper making, cheese processing, and the generation of power.

**Trás-os-Montes** /ˌtræzuːʒˈmɒnteʃ/ a mountainous region of north-east Portugal beyond the Douro River and bounded to the north and east by Spain. Its name means 'beyond the mountains'.

**Traun** /traʊn/ **1.** a town in the state of Upper Austria, northern Austria, between Linz and Wels; pop. (1991) 22,270. **2.** a river of northern Austria that rises in the Totes Gebirge and flows northwards for 153 km. (96 miles) to join the Danube near Linz. **3.** a river in southern Bavaria, Germany, which rises in the Alps west of Salzburg and flows northwards through Traunstein to join the River Alz, a tributary of the Inn.

**Travancore** /'trævənkɔ:/ (also **Tiruvankur**) a former princely state of south-west India, between the Malabar coast and the Western Ghats. It united with the Madras States and Cochin in 1949 to form the state of Travancore-Cochin and in 1956 became part of Kerala state.

**Travnik** /'trævnɪk/a town in Bosnia-Herzegovina, on the Lasva River north-west of Sarajevo; pop. (1981) 64,100. Founded in the 15th c., it was a former Turkish capital of Bosnia.

**Trebizond** see TRABZON.

**Treblinka** /tre'blɪŋkə/ the site of a Nazi concentration camp on the Bug River in Poland, north-east of Warsaw. During World War II the Jews of the Warsaw ghetto were put to death there.

**Tremadoc** /tre'mædək/ a village near Portmadoc in Gwynedd, north-west Wales, birthplace in 1888 of T. E. Lawrence (Lawrence of Arabia). The village was laid out in 1810 by W. A. Madocks.

**Trengganu** /treŋ'gɑ:nu:/ (also **Terrengganu**) a state on the east coast of the Malaysian peninsula; area 12,928 sq. km. (4,993 sq. miles); pop. (1990) 752,000; capital, Kuala Terengganu. It is noted for its silk weaving.

**Trent** /trent/ the anglicized name of TRENTO in northern Italy.

**Trent** /trent/ a river of central England that rises in Staffordshire and flows north-east for 275 km. (170 miles) to join the River Ouse.

**Trentino-Alto Adige** /tren'ti:nəʊ‚æltəʊ'ædɪ‚dʒeɪ/ a region of north-east Italy, comprising the autonomous provinces of Bolzano (in the north) and Trento (in the south); area 13,613 sq. km. (5,258 sq. miles); pop. (1990) 891,420. Bordering on Austria and Switzerland, its alpine mountains and valleys occupy the upper basin of the River Adige and include the Dolomites.

**Trento** /'trentəʊ/ (English **Trent**) a city on the River Adige in northern Italy, capital of the province of Trento in the Trentino-Alto Adige region; pop. (1990) 102,120. Situated on a routeway between the Adriatic and the Baltic used for the amber trade in ancient times, Trento also commanded access from Austria into northern Italy in the days of the Holy Roman and Austro-Hungarian empires. It was the scene of an ecumenical church council meeting from time to time between 1545 and 1563, which defined the doctrines of the Church in opposition to those of the Reformation, reformed discipline, and strengthened the authority of the papacy. Local industries include electrical products, chemicals, silk, pottery, and tourism.

**Trenton** /'trent(ə)n/ the capital (since 1790) of the US state of New Jersey, on the Delaware River; pop. (1990) 88,675. The city, which was named after Chief Justice William Trent, has industries producing metal goods, automobile parts, rubber, pottery, and suspension-bridge cables. It was the site of Washington's famous crossing of the Delaware and victory of 1776.

**Trèves** the French name of TRIER.

**Treviso** /trə'vi:səʊ/ the capital of the province of Treviso in Venetia, north-east Italy, situated on the Sile and Botteniga rivers; pop. (1990) 83,890. It has ceramics and textile industries.

**Trianon** /'tri:ə‚nɔ̃/ either of two small palaces in the great park at Versailles. The larger (**Grand Trianon**) was built by Louis XIV in 1687; the smaller (**Petit Trianon**), built by Louis XV 1762–8, belonged first to Madame du Barry and afterwards to Marie Antoinette.

**Triassic** /traɪ'æsɪk/ the earliest period of the Mesozoic era, following the Permian and preceding the Jurassic, lasting from about 248 to 213 million years ago. Dinosaurs became numerous during this period, which also saw the appearance of the first mammals. The geological strata of this period is divisible into three groups.

**tributary** /'trɪbjuːtərɪ/ a river which flows into another, usually larger one.

**Trichinopoly** see TIRUCHCHIRAPPALLI.

**Trichur** see THRISSUR.

**Trier** /'trɪə(r)/ (French **Trèves** /trev/) a city at the centre of the wine-producing Moselle region of Rhineland-Palatinate in western Germany; pop. (1991) 98,750. Established by a Germanic tribe, the Treveri, c. 400 BC, Trier is one of the oldest cities in Europe. The Roman town of Augusta Treverorum was founded in 15 BC by the Emperor Augustus and it was capital of the Belgic division of Roman Gaul in the 2nd c. AD. Later it became a seat of the Roman emperor. It was a powerful archbishopric from 815 until the 18th c., but fell into decline after the French occupation in 1797. It was the birthplace in 1818 of Karl Marx. Trier, in addition to its vast wine cellars has steel, textile, and precision instruments industries.

**Trieste** /trɪ'est/ a city of north-east Italy, the largest seaport on the Adriatic and capital of Friuli-Venezia Giulia region; pop. (1990) 231,050. Formerly held by Austria, Trieste was annexed by Italy after World War I and retained in 1954 following a failed attempt by the UN to make the area a Free Territory. Oil refining and shipbuilding are amongst its chief industries.

**Triglav** /'tri:glɑ:v/ a mountain rising to 2,863 m. (9,392 ft.) in the Julian Alps, the highest peak in Slovenia and formerly the highest peak in Yugoslavia.

**Trikkala** /'tri:kələ/ the capital of the department of Trikkala in Thessaly, north-central Greece, on the River Lethaios; pop. (1981) 40,860. It is a market town trading in tobacco, cotton, grain, livestock, and textiles, In ancient times it had a noted medical school associated with Aesculapius who is said to have been born there.

**Trim** /trɪm/ a town of County Meath in the Republic of Ireland, situated on the River Boyne 43 km. (27 miles) north-west of Dublin; pop. (1991) 18,120. It is one of the oldest ecclesiastical centres in Ireland with landmarks that include Trim Castle (the largest Anglo-Norman fortress in Ireland), the Yellow Steeple (remains of a 13th-c. Augustinian Abbey), and St. Patrick's Cathedral.

**Trimontium** /traɪ'mɒntiːəm/ the ancient Roman name for PLOVDIV in Bulgaria.

**Trincomalee** /ˌtrɪŋkəmə'liː/ the principal seaport of Sri Lanka, situated on the east coast of the island; pop. (1981) 44,300. Described by Lord Nelson as the 'finest harbour in the world', Trincomalee was the chief British naval base in south-east Asia during World War II after the fall of Singapore.

**Trinidad and Tobago**
/'trɪnɪˌdæd, tə'beɪgəʊ/ official name **The Republic of Trinidad and Tobago** a country in the West Indies consisting of the main island of Trinidad, off

the north-east coast of Venezuela, and the much smaller island of Tobago (further to the north-east); area 5,128 sq. km. (1,981 sq miles); pop. (est. 1991) 1,249,000; official language, English; capital, Port-of-Spain. The population is racially mixed with 43 per cent of African descent and 40 per cent of Asian. The chief settlement of Tobago is Scarborough. Trinidad, which is fringed with mangrove, has a low northern mountain range and flat or undulating plains; a single mountain range dominates Tobago. Both islands have a tropical climate and large areas of forest. A substantial part of national income is generated by the export of petroleum products while the capital Port-of-Spain is a major seaport. Visited by Columbus in 1498, the islands became British during the Napoleonic Wars and were formally amalgamated as a Crown Colony in 1888. After a short period as a member of the West Indies Federation between 1958 and 1962, Trinidad and Tobago became an independent state of the Commonwealth in 1962 and finally a republic in 1976. Trinidad and Tobago is governed by a bicameral parliament and an executive prime minister with a president as head of state. Tobago achieved full self-government in 1987 and has its own House of Assembly.
**Trinidadian** /-'deɪdɪən/, **Tobagan** *adj. & n.*

**Trinity** /'trɪnɪtɪ/ a river of Texas, USA, formed by the junction of the West Fork and Elm Fork rivers north-west of Dallas. It flows 1,150 km. (715 miles) south-eastwards into Trinity Bay, a north-eastern arm of Galveston Bay.

**Tripoli** /'trɪpəlɪ/ (Arabic **Trâblous**) a Mediterranean seaport in north-west Lebanon; pop. (1988) 160,000. It is capital of the province of Ash Shamal and second-largest city in Lebanon. It stands on the site of the Phoenician city of Oea. It was the terminus for the pipeline from the Iraqi oilfields and has an oil refinery.

**Tripoli** /'trɪpəlɪ/ (Arabic **Tarabulus**) the capital, chief port, commercial, industrial, and communications centre of Libya; pop. (1984) 990,700. Founded by Phoenicians in the 7th c. BC, it became the chief city of Tripolitania. It was held successively by Romans, Vandals, Arabs, the Spanish, the Knights of St. John, the Ottoman Turks, and Italians, and was a base of the Barbary pirates in the 18th and early 19th centuries. It was an important base for the Axis powers during World War II. Its manufactures include textiles, tobacco, and processed food.

**Tripolitania** /ˌtrɪpɒlɪ'teɪnɪə/ the coastal region surrounding Tripoli in North Africa in which the Phoenicians established the three colonies of Leptis Magna, Sabratha, and Oea (now Tripoli).
**Tripolitanian** *adj. & n.*

**Tripura** /'trɪpʊrə/ a Hindu state in north-east India, bounded by Assam, Mizoram and Bangladesh; area 10,486 sq. km. (4,050 sq. miles); pop. (1991) 2,744,830; capital, Agartala. It joined the Indian Union in 1949, became a Union Territory in 1957, and was designated a state in 1972. Bengali, Kokbarak, and Manipuri are the chief languages of its people, many of whom practise shifting cultivation in the forests that cover over half the state. The production of tea, jute, and rubber are the chief industries.

**Tristan da Cunha** /ˌtrɪstən də 'kuːnə/ the largest of a small group of volcanic islands in the South Atlantic, 2,112 km. (1,320 miles) south-west of St Helena of which it is a dependency; area 98 sq. km. (38 sq. miles); pop. (1988) 313. Edinburgh is the only settlement. Its original inhabitants were shipwrecked sailors and soldiers who stayed on the island when the St. Helena garrison was withdrawn in 1817. In 1942 the island was commissioned as HMS *Atlantic Isle* and served as a radio and meteorological station. In 1961 the entire population was temporarily evacuated when the island volcano erupted. The people of Tristan da Cunha returned two years later.

**Trivandrum** /trɪ'vændrəm/ (also **Thiruvananthapuram** /ˌθiːruːvəˌnæntəpʊ(ə)'rɑːm/) the capital of the state of Kerala on the Malabar coast of south-west India; pop. (1991) 524,000. Its name is derived from Tiru Anantha Puram, the abode of the sacred serpent Anantha on whose coils a statue of the Hindu god Vishnu lies in the Sri Padmanabhasvami Temple.

**Troad** /'trəʊæd/ an ancient region of north-west Asia Minor of which ancient Troy was the chief city.

**Trois-Rivières** /trwæ rɪv'jer/ a port on the St. Lawrence River, Quebec, Canada; pop. (1991) 136,300 (metropolitan area). It takes its name from the Saint-Maurice River which divides into three channels before entering the St. Lawrence. Founded as a fur-trading post in 1634, it is now a major centre of newsprint production.

**Tromsø** /'trɒmsɜː/ the principal city of Arctic Norway, a seaport on an island just west of the mainland; pop. (1991) 51,330. A base for fishing and expeditions to the Arctic, it is also the administrative centre of Troms County and the seat of a university founded in 1972. In 1944 the German battleship *Tirpitz* was sunk nearby.

**Trondheim** /'trɒndhaɪm/ a fishing port and the second-largest city in Norway, capital of Sør-Trøndelag county; pop. (1991) 138,060. Formerly known as Nidaros, Trondheim is situated on a peninsula in west-central Norway. Founded by Olaf I Tryggvason, it was the capital of Norway during the Viking period, later becoming a pilgrimage centre as the burial place of Olaf II Haraldsson (St. Olaf) who died in battle nearby in 1030. Since 1814 Norwegian monarchs have been proclaimed in Trondheim Cathedral which was built over the tomb of St. Olaf. Trondheim is the headquarters of the Norwegian Royal Society of Sciences.

**Troödos Mountains** /'trɒəθɒs/ the principal mountain range of the island of Cyprus, rising to a height of 1,951 m. (6,400 ft.) at Mt. Olympus. The mountains contain monasteries, copper and asbestos mines, and winter-sports resorts.

**Troon** /truːn/ a resort town on the south-west coast of Scotland, north of Ayr; pop. (1981) 14,230. It has a championship golf course and is a notable centre of boatbuilding.

**tropic** /'trɒpɪk/ the parallel of latitude 23° 27′ north (**tropic of Cancer**) or south (**tropic of Capricorn**) of the equator at which the sun is overhead respectively around 21 June and 22 December. The region between the tropics of Cancer and Capricorn is known as **the Tropics**.

**tropical rainforest** a type of forest that occurs in the tropical lowlands of Asia, Africa, and Latin America where high temperatures and an abundant and well-distributed rainfall results in the luxuriant growth of vegetation. Covering *c.* 9.5 million sq. km. (3.67 million sq. miles) of the earth's surface, it is estimated that tropical forests contain 155,000 of the 250,000 known plant species of the world and 90 per cent of all primates. In the tropical forests of the Malay peninsula there are *c.* 2,500 species of large tree and in the Amazon rainforest one-fifth of all bird species are to be found. Despite the number of tree species encountered in tropical rainforest, only a few, such as mahogany, rosewood, and greenheart, have been highly valued for their timber. The vast majority of the trees of the rainforest are evergreen, many developing buttresses from the lowest few metres of the trunk. In addition to trees there are many lianes (woody climbers) and epiphytes including ferns and orchids. In recent years the destruction of the world's tropical rainforests has been a cause of international concern. Logging, fuelwood cutting, and the felling and burning of forest to create farms and cattle ranches have increased at an alarming rate, estimated in the 1980s to account for the loss of some 100,000 sq. km. (62,000 sq. miles) every year. Scientists have stressed the threat to indigenous tribes and the benefits to be gained from tropical forest plants which produce a wide range of products such as rubber, gum, waxes, rattans, resins, tannins, steroids, lubricants, medicines, pesticides, essential and edible oils, and flavourings and dyestuffs. Soil erosion, a reduction of oxygen in the earth's atmosphere, and a loss of transpiration affecting the global hydrologic cycle are also likely to result from rainforest destruction.

**troposphere** /'trɒpə,sfɪə(r), 'trəʊ-/ a layer of atmospheric air extending from about 6–10 km. upwards from the earth's surface, in which the temperature falls with increasing height.

**Trossachs** /'trɒsəks, **the** a picturesque district in the vicinity of Loch Katrine, central Scotland, made popular as a tourist destination in Victorian times by the novelist Sir Walter Scott.

**trough** /trɒf/ in meteorology, a narrow area of low pressure between highs.

**Trowbridge** /'trəʊbrɪdʒ/ a town in south-west England, the county town of Wiltshire; pop. (1981) 22,980. The birthplace in 1813 of Isaac Pitman, the inventor of modern shorthand writing.

**Troy** /trɔɪ/ (Turkish, **Truva**, ancient **Ilium**) in Homeric legend the city of King Priam that was besieged for ten years by the Greeks in their endeavour to recover Helen, wife of Menalaus, who had been abducted. It was believed to be a figment of Greek legend until a stronghold called by the Turks Hissarlik, in Asiatic Turkey near the Dardanelles, was identified as the site of Troy by the German archaeologist H. Schliemann, who in 1870 began excavations of the mound which proved to be composed of 46 strata, dating from the early Bronze Age to the Roman era. The stratum known as Troy VII, believed to be that of the Homeric city was sacked *c.* 1210 BC. Again destroyed *c.* 1100 BC, the site was resettled by the Greeks *c.* 700 BC and finally abandoned in the Roman period.

**Troy** /trɔɪ/ **1.** a city to the north of Detroit in Michigan, USA; pop. (1990) 72,880. Settled in 1820 it developed in the 19th c. as a trading centre for Detroit and Pontiac before becoming a headquarters for corporate business. **2.** a manufacturing city in the US state of New York, on the Hudson River north-east of Albany; pop. (1990) 54,270. Samuel Wilson, who was meat supplier to the US Army in 1812 and is regarded as the original 'Uncle Sam', is buried in Oakwood Cemetery. Clothing, abrasives, and motor parts are local industries.

**Troyes** /trwæ/ the capital of the department of Aube in the Champagne-Ardenne region of north-eastern France, a town with many fine old buildings on the River Seine; pop. (1990) 60,755. Capital of the former province of Champagne, it has long been noted for its hosiery trade. It gave its name to troy weight, the system of weights and measures which was first used at the medieval fairs which took place in this town. There are many fine churches in and around the town displaying an estimated one-third of the finest stained glass in France. Present industries are electrical goods and textiles.

**Trucial States** /'tru:ʃ(ə)l/ the name applied to seven Arab sheikdoms on the Persian Gulf, which since 1971 have been known as the United Arab Emirates. It refers to the maritime truce made with Britain in 1836 (and subsequently renewed and extended) by which local rulers undertook to abstain from maritime warfare.

**Trujillo** /tru:'hi:ljəʊ/ **1.** a seaport on the Caribbean coast of Honduras, to the east of Puerto Cortés; pop. (est. 1985) 6,970. Founded in 1525, it was the first capital of the Spanish Central American province of Honduras. **2.** the capital of La Libertad department on the north-west coast of Peru; pop. (1990) 532,000. Founded by Pizarro in 1536, the city has retained many of its old colonial buildings despite a severe earthquake in 1970. Nearby is the ancient Chimu capital of Chan Chan. Industries include textiles, leather goods, and drugs. **3.** an agricultural market town in western Venezuela, capital of the state of Trujillo; pop. (1981) 31,770.

**Truk** /trʌk/ (also **Chuuk**) one of the four Federated States of Micronesia in the western Pacific Ocean, comprising 14 volcanic islands and numerous atolls all lying within a reef-fringed lagoon; area 127 sq. km. (49 sq. miles); pop. (est. 1990) 53,700; administrative centre, Moen. The Truk lagoon is one of the largest in the world. **Trukese** adj. & n.

**Truro** /'trʊərəʊ/ a cathedral and tourist city and county town of Cornwall, south-west England, on the River Truro; pop. (1981) 18,560. Its granite-built cathedral was founded in 1879.

**Truth or Consequences** a town in south-west New Mexico, USA, on the Rio Grande; pop. (1990) 6,720. It was known as Hot Springs until 1950 when its citizens voted to adopt the new name offered to them by the host of a radio programme of the same name who promised to feature the town annually in his show.

**Truva** see TROY.

**Tsao-chuang** see ZAOZHUANG.

**Tsaritsyn** a former name (until 1925) of VOLGO-GRAD.

**Tsavo National Park** /'sɑ:vəʊ/ an extensive national park in south-east Kenya, established in 1948 in an area of volcanic hills and plateaus to protect a diversity of woodland and grassland habitats frequented by big game animals such as elephant, black rhino, lion, leopard, cheetah, and hippo.

**Tselinograd** /(t)se'lmə,grɑ:d/ the former name (until 1993) of AQMOLA in Kazakhstan.

**Tsinghai** see QINGHAI.

**Tsitsikamma Forest** /ˌsɪtsɪ'kɑ:mə/ an area of dense natural forest on the south coast of Cape Province, South Africa. Named after the local word for 'clear water', the Tsitsikamma Forest National Park preserves ancient specimens of yellowwood, stinkwood, candlewood, and assegai trees. The Tsitsikamma Coastal National Park (1964) extends 80 km. (50 miles) inland from the mouth of the Groot River near Humansdorp.

**Tskhinvali** /'tskɪnvəli:/ the capital town of the South Ossetian autonomous region in the Republic of Georgia, in the Caucasus north-west of Tbilisi.

**tsunami** /tsu:'nɑ:mɪ/ a long, high sea wave caused by underwater earthquakes of 5.5 or more on the Richter Scale, or by other disturbances such as volcanoes, landslides, or the calving of very large icebergs from glaciers.

**Tsushima** /su:'ʃi:mə/ a Japanese island in the Korean Strait, part of Nagasaki prefecture; area 702 sq. km. (271 sq. miles); chief town, Izuhara. At high tide the northern part of the island is separated from the south. In 1905 the Russian navy was destroyed by a Japanese fleet near here.

**Tsushima Strait** the eastern channel of the Korea Strait between the Japanese islands of Tsushima and Kyushu, linking the Sea of Japan with the East China Sea.

**Tswana** (also **Setswana**) the Bantu language of a people of southern Africa living in Botswana and neighbouring areas.

**Tuamotu Islands** (also **the Tuamotus**, **Dangerous Islands**) a group of 79 coral atolls forming an archipelago in the South Pacific, part of the overseas territory of French Polynesia; area 690 sq. km. (266 sq. miles); pop. (1988) 12,370; chief settlement, Avatoru. The principal islands are Rangiroa, Hao, Turéia, and the Gambier Islands. In the south-east, the atolls of Mururoa and Fangataufa have been used since 1966 as nuclear testing sites. Discovered by the Spanish in 1606, the islands became a French protectorate in 1844 and were annexed by France in 1881. Thor Heyerdahl's raft Kon Tiki was wrecked here in 1947. The islands form the largest group of coral atolls in the world.

**Tuareg** /'twɑ:reg/ a Berber group of nomadic pastoralists of North Africa, the legendary blue-veiled warriors of Timbuktu and the romance of Beau Geste. Known to themselves as Imochagh (= free ones), they were named Tuareg (= forsaken of God) by the Arabs. The main concentrations of

Tuareg population are now in Algeria, Mali, Niger, and western Libya, with smaller groups to be found in Nigeria, the Sudan, etc. In the past they traversed the Sahara in their caravans, trading between the Mediterranean and the Sahel, and subsisting on dates and millet which they traded for their livestock. Their nomadic activity has been threatened in recent years by drought, conflict, and trading restrictions. Their Berber dialect, known as Tamashek, is the only Berber language to have an indigenous written form, its alphabet being related to ancient Phoenician script.

**Tübingen** /'tu:bɪŋən/ a town in Baden-Württemberg, south-west Germany, on the Neckar River; pop. (1983) 74,700. It is a centre of publishing and paper making and has a university founded in 1477.

**Tubruq** see TOBRUK.

**Tubuai Islands** /tu:'baɪ/ (also **Austral Islands**) a 1,300-km. (800-mile) chain of volcanic islands in the southern Pacific Ocean forming part of French Polynesia; area 148 sq. km. (57 sq. miles); pop. (1988) 6,500. The principal islands are Tubuai, Rimatara, Rurutu, Rapa, and Raivavae and the chief settlement and port is Mataura (on Tubuai).

**Tucson** /'tu:sɒn/ a resort city in south-east Arizona, USA, on the Santa Cruz and Rillito rivers; pop. (1990) 405,390. Founded by the Spanish in 1775, the Presidio of Tucson was built to withstand Apache Indian attacks. It is the seat of the University of Arizona (1885). Copper, cotton, and cattle are traded and nearby are the Coronado National Forest and Biosphere 2, a glass-enclosed self-sustaining model of the earth's ecosystems.

**Tucumán** see SAN MIGUEL DE TUCUMÁN.

**Tugela Falls** /tu:'geɪlə/ a series of five waterfalls on the **Tugela River** in KwaZulu-Natal, South Africa. With a total drop of 948 m. (3,110 ft.), they are the highest falls in Africa.

**Tujia** a minority nationality of China, largely located in the provinces of Hunan, Hebei, and Sichuan; pop. (1982) 2.8 million.

**Tula** /'tu:lə/ the ancient capital of the Toltecs in Mexico, usually identified with a site near the town of Tula in Hidalgo state, central Mexico.

**Tula** /'tu:lə/ an industrial city in western Russia to the south of Moscow on the River Upa; pop. (1990) 543,000. A small arms factory was established here in 1712 by Peter the Great. It was principally known for the manufacture of samovars, but today has industries producing chemicals, machinery, iron and steel, musical instruments, and sewing machines.

**Tuli Block** /'tu:lɪ/ a game-farming region in eastern Botswana, between the Kalahari Desert and the Limpopo River.

**Tulle** /tu:l/ the capital of the department of Corrèze in the Limousin region of south-central France; pop. (1982) 20,640. Noted for its

manufacture of crafts, tools, and firearms, it gave its name to the tulle cloth that was first made here.

**Tulsa** /'tʌlsə/ a port on the Arkansas River in north-east Oklahoma, USA, the second-largest city in the state; pop. (1990) 367,300. Settled in 1879, aviation, aerospace and the exploitation of oil and gas are its chief industries. The nearby port of Catoosa is America's westernmost inland river port and the city has an international airport.

**Tumen** /tʊ'men/ a city in Jilin province, north-east China, on the Tumen River where it follows the frontier with North Korea; pop. (1986) 102,000.

**Tumkur** /tʌm'kʊ(ə)r/ a health centre and market town in Karnataka, southern India, north-west of Bangalore; pop. (1991) 179,500.

**Tunb Islands** /'tu:nəb/ two small islands (Greater and Lesser Tunb) in the Persian Gulf, administered by the emirate of Ras al Khaimah until occupied by Iran in 1971.

**Tunbridge Wells** (also **Royal Tunbridge Wells**) a spa and commuter town in Kent, south-east England; pop. (1981) 58,140. Founded in the 1630s after the discovery of iron-rich springs by Lord North in 1606, the town was visited by Queen Victoria and in 1909 given its 'Royal' prefix.

**Tunceli** /tʊndʒə'li:/ **1.** a province of east-central Turkey; area 7,774 sq. km. (3,003 sq. miles); pop. (1990) 133,140. **2.** its capital, at the junction of the Munzur and Pülümür rivers to the south of Erzincan; pop. (1990) 24,510.

**tundra** /'tʌndrə/ a vast, level, treeless Arctic region usually with a marshy surface and underlying permafrost, dominated by low-growing herbaceous plants, dwarf shrubs, grasses, sedges, lichens, and mosses.

**Tungurahua** /tʊngu:'rɑ:wə/ a volcano in the Andes of central Ecuador, rising to a height of 5,016 m. (16,457 ft.) near the town of Baños.

**Tungus** /'tʊŋʌs/ a Mongoloid people of eastern Siberia speaking an Altaic language that was set down in 1931 in an alphabet based on the Russian alphabet.

**Tunguska Basin** /tʊŋ'gu:skə/ that part of eastern Siberia lying between the Yenisei and Lena rivers. It has large reserves of coal.

**Tunis** /'tju:nɪs/ the capital of Tunisia, situated near the Mediterranean coast of North Africa; pop. (1984) 596,650. The ruins of Carthage and the Bardo National Museum are nearby and the city itself contains a large number of ancient monuments. It is linked by a deep-water channel to the new port of La Goulette. Its industries include smelting and railway workshops and there are numerous handicrafts and light industries.

**Tunisia** /tju:'nɪsɪə/ official name **The Tunisian Republic** a country in North Africa on the Mediterranean Sea, bounded by Algeria to the west and Libya to the south-east; area 164,150 sq. km. (63,403 sq. miles); pop. (est. 1991) 8,223,000; official language, Arabic; capital, Tunis. Situated at the eastern end of the Atlas Mountains, the greater part of the country beyond the

fertile north and north-eastern coasts is semiarid or desert. There are numerous salt lakes in central Tunisia. Phoenician settlements on the coast developed into the Carthaginian commercial empire which came into conflict with Rome, and after defeat in the Punic Wars became a Roman province. The area was conquered by the Vandals in the 5th c. AD and subsequently by the Arabs (7th c.); in the 16th c. it became part of the Ottoman empire. Under loose Turkish rule, Tunisia became a centre of piratical activity in the 16th–19th c. before its establishment as a French protectorate in 1886. The rise of nationalist activity after World War II led to independence and the establishment of a republic in 1956–7. The economy is based almost entirely on oil, mining (there are large deposits of phosphates) and agriculture in the better-watered coastal strip, but tourism is of growing importance. Tunisia is governed by an executive president and a unicameral Chamber of Deputies.

**Tunisian** *adj. & n.*

**Tunja** /ˈtuːnhɑː/ the capital of Boyacá department in central Colombia, a market town of the eastern Llanos; pop. (1985) 94,450. It was founded by the Spanish in 1539 on the site of a former royal city of the Chibchas.

**Tunxi** /tʊnˈʃiː/ a city in Anhui province, eastern China, south-west of Hangzhou; pop. (1986) 107,000.

**Tupelo** /ˈtjuːpəˌləʊ/ a city in north-east Mississippi, USA, scene of a Civil War battle in July 1864, when Union forces defeated the Confederates, and birthplace of the singer Elvis Presley (1935–77); pop. (1990) 30,685.

**Tupi** /ˈtuːpɪ/ an American Indian people native to the Amazon valley, South America.

**Turanian** /tjʊˈreɪnɪən/ the group of Asian languages that are neither Semitic nor Indo-European, especially the Ural-Altaic family. The name is derived from the Persian *Turan* meaning 'the region beyond the Oxus'.

**Turcoman** see TURKOMAN.

**Turfan Depression** /ˈtʊəfæn, -ˈfæn/ a deep depression in western China, in the Tarim basin, with an area of 50,000 sq. km. (20,000 sq. miles) and a depth of 154 m. (505 ft.) below sea-level, China's lowest point.

**Turin** /tjʊəˈrɪn/ (Italian **Torino** /tɒˈriːnəʊ/) an industrial city on the River Po in north-west Italy, capital of the Piedmont region; pop. (1990) 991,870. Turin was the capital of the kingdom of Sardinia from 1720. A centre of the Risorgimento in the 19th c., it was the first capital of a unified Italy (1861–4). Its industries produce motor cars, iron and steel, textiles, electrical goods, and food products. Its Romanesque cathedral contains the Turin Shroud, once believed by many to have wrapped Christ's body after the Crucifixion. Turin is a leading centre of publishing, art, fashion, and learning.

**Turkana** /tɜːˈkɑːnə/, **Lake** (formerly **Lake Rudolf** /ˈruːdɒlf/) a salt lake with no outlet set in a barren landscape in north-west Kenya and Ethiopia; area 6,405 sq. km. (2,474 sq. miles). Sometimes known as the Jade Sea, it was explored in 1888 by Count Teleki who named it Lake Rudolf in honour of the Crown Prince of Austria. Hominid remains have been found on its shores.

**Turkey** /ˈtɜːkɪ/ official name **The Republic of Turkey** a country lying partly in Europe but mostly in south-west Asia, comprising the whole of the Anatolian peninsula, extending from the

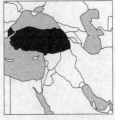

Aegean Sea to the Caucasus; area 779,452 sq. km. (301,063 sq. miles); pop. (1990) 56,473,000; official language, Turkish; capital, Ankara. The largest cities are Istanbul, Ankara, Izmir, Adana, and Bursa. European Turkey (sometimes called Roumelia) is separated from Asian Turkey by the Bosporus, the Sea of Marmara, and the Dardanelles which link the Black Sea with the Mediterranean. Narrow coastal plains surround the Anatolian plateau which becomes more mountainous and less fertile towards the east where the Tigris and Euphrates rivers rise before flowing southwards to the Persian Gulf. Turkey's regional climatic diversity permits the growth of a wide range of agricultural crops including cotton, tobacco, grain, fruit, and vegetables. Modern Turkey is descended from the Ottoman empire, established in the late Middle Ages and largely maintained until its collapse at the end of World War I. The nationalist leader Kemal Ataturk moulded a new westernized state, centred upon Anatolia, from the ruins of the empire, and Turkey successfully avoided involvement in World War II. The Kurds, an ethnic minority (12 per cent of the population) occupying the remote and less developed regions of the east and south-east, have increasingly employed guerrilla tactics in an attempt to gain full Kurdish self-determination in Turkey. Although agriculture employs almost half the total labour force (Turkey was self-sufficient in food during the 1980s), industry has played an increasingly important role in the country's fast-growing economy as does tourism. Turkey is governed by an executive president, prime minister and Council of Ministers and a legislative Grand National Assembly.

**Turkish** *adj. & n.*

Turkey is divided into 73 provinces:

| Province | Area (sq. km.) | Pop. (1990) |
|---|---|---|
| Adana | 17,253 | 1,934,900 |
| Adiyaman | 7,614 | 513,130 |
| Afyon | 14,230 | 739,220 |
| Ağri | 11,376 | 437,090 |
| Aksaray | 7,626 | 326,400 |
| Amasya | 5,520 | 357,190 |
| Ankara | 25,706 | 3,236,630 |
| Antalya | 20,591 | 1,132,210 |
| Artvin | 7,436 | 212,830 |
| Aydin | 8,007 | 824,810 |
| Balikesir | 14,292 | 973,310 |
| Batman | 4,694 | 344,670 |
| Bayburt | 3,652 | 107,330 |
| Bilecik | 4,307 | 175,530 |
| Bingöl | 8,125 | 250,970 |
| Bitlis | 6,707 | 330,115 |
| Bolu | 11,051 | 536,870 |
| Burdur | 6,887 | 254,900 |
| Bursa | 11,043 | 1,603,140 |
| Çanakkale | 9,737 | 432,260 |
| Çankiri | 8,454 | 279,130 |
| Çorum | 12,820 | 609,860 |
| Denizli | 11,868 | 750,880 |
| Diyarbakir | 15,355 | 1,095,000 |
| Edirne | 6,276 | 404,600 |
| Elazığ | 9,153 | 498,225 |
| Erzincan | 11,903 | 299,250 |
| Erzurum | 25,066 | 848,200 |
| Eskişehir | 13,652 | 641,060 |
| Gaziantep | 7,642 | 1,140,590 |
| Giresun | 6,934 | 499,090 |
| Gümüşhane | 6,575 | 169,375 |
| Hakkari | 7,121 | 172,480 |
| Hatay | 5,403 | 1,109,750 |
| Isparta | 8,933 | 434,770 |
| İçel | 15,853 | 1,266,995 |
| Istanbul | 5,712 | 7,309,190 |
| İzmir | 11,973 | 2,694,770 |
| Karaman | 9,163 | 217,540 |
| Kars | 18,557 | 662,155 |
| Kastamonu | 13,108 | 423,610 |
| Kayseri | 16,917 | 943,480 |
| Kirikkale | 4,365 | 349,400 |
| Kirklareli | 6,550 | 309,510 |
| Kirşehir | 6,570 | 256,860 |
| Kocaeli | 3,626 | 936,160 |
| Konya | 38,257 | 1,750,300 |
| Kütahya | 11,875 | 578,020 |
| Malatya | 12,313 | 702,055 |
| Manisa | 13,810 | 1,154,420 |
| K. Maraş | 14,327 | 892,950 |
| Mardin | 8,891 | 557,730 |
| Muğla | 13,338 | 562,810 |
| Muş | 8,196 | 376,540 |
| Neveşehir | 5,467 | 289,510 |
| Niğde | 7,312 | 305,860 |
| Ordu | 6,001 | 830,105 |
| Rize | 3,920 | 348,780 |
| Sakarya | 4,817 | 683,060 |
| Samsun | 9,579 | 1,158,400 |
| Siirt | 5,406 | 243,435 |
| Sinop | 5,862 | 265,150 |
| Sirnak | 7,172 | 262,000 |
| Sivas | 28,488 | 767,480 |
| Tekirdağ | 6,218 | 468,840 |
| Tokat | 9,958 | 719,250 |
| Trabzon | 4,685 | 795,850 |
| Tunceli | 7,774 | 133,140 |
| Sanliurfa | 18,584 | 1,001,455 |
| Uşak | 5,341 | 290,280 |
| Van | 19,069 | 637,430 |
| Yozgat | 14,123 | 579,150 |
| Zonguldak | 8,629 | 1,073,560 |

**Turkic** /'tɜːkɪk/ a group of about 20 Ural-Altaic languages (including Turkish) spoken in Turkey, Iran, and Central Asia.

**Turkish** /'tɜːkɪʃ/ the official language of Turkey spoken by over 50 million people, the most important of the Turkic group. It was originally written in Arabic script but changed over to the Roman alphabet in 1928.

**Turkistan** /tɜːkɪ'stɑːn/ (also **Turkestan**) a region of central Asia east of the Caspian Sea extending over Turkmenistan, Uzbekistan, Kyrgyzstan, Tajikistan, the southern part of Kazakhstan, and the western part of Xinjiang (Sinkiang) province in China. Forming a major geographic frontier between East and West, it includes parts of the Pamir and Tien Shan mountains, the Kyzl-kum and Kara-kum deserts, and the Fergana valley of Uzbekistan. Between 1918 and 1924 there existed in the USSR a Turkistan Autonomous Soviet Republic.

**Turkmen** /'tɜːkmen/ a people of Central Asia speaking Turkoman, a Turkic branch of the Altaic family of languages. For centuries a tribal people, the main groups are the dominant Tekke tribe of central Turkmenistan, the Ersry in the south-east, and the Yomud in the west. They constitute 73 per cent of the population of Turkmenistan.

**Turkmenistan** /tɜːkmenɪ'stɑːn/ (also **Turkmenia**) a republic of Central Asia to the east of the Caspian Sea, bounded to the south by Iran and Afghanistan and to the north by Kazakhstan and  Uzbekistan; area 488,100 sq. km. (188,528 sq. miles); pop. (est. 1991) 3,748,000; official language, Turkoman; capital, Ashgabat (Ashkhabad). Turkmenistan is dominated by a rolling desert lowland, the Karakum Desert, which slopes westward from the Amu Darya and occupies about 90 per cent of the country. Its population, which is predominantly Turkmen, is largely concentrated in the northern foothills of the Kopet Dag Mountains

and along the valleys of the Amu Darya, Tedzhen, and Murgab rivers. Rich in mineral resources, such as oil, gas, coal, sulphur, salt, iodine, bromine, and ozocerite, Turkmenistan has a predominantly agricultural economy based on the production of irrigated crops such as cotton and the grazing of livestock which includes the famous Karakul sheep and Turkoman horses. From 1924 until the breakup of the Soviet Union in 1991 Turkmenistan was a constituent republic of the USSR. It is a member of the Commonwealth of Independent States, governed by an executive president and a People's Council (*Khalk Maslakhaty*).
**Turkmen** *adj. & n.*

**Turkoman** /'tɜ:kəumən/ (also **Turcoman**) the official language of Turkmenistan in Central Asia, spoken by the various Turkic peoples of that country.

## Turks and Caicos Islands

/tɜ:ks, 'keɪkɒs/ a British dependency in the Caribbean, a group of over 30 subtropical islands (of which 6 are inhabited) about 80 km. (50 miles) southeast of the Bahamas; area *c.* 500 sq. km. (193 sq. miles); pop. (1990) 12,350; capital, Cockburn Town (on the island of Grand Turk). Once an important source of salt, the islands' economy is now dependent on tourism, fishing, and the registration of offshore financial companies.

**Turku** /'tuəku:/ (Swedish **Åbo** /'ɔ:bu:/) an industrial port in south-west Finland, capital of Turku-Pori province; pop. (1990) 159,180. Founded in the 11th c., Turku was capital of Finland until 1812. It has ferry links with Sweden and annually hosts a rock festival and classical music festival. Its chief landmarks are the 13th-c. castle and Evangelical-Lutheran cathedral. It has two universities, one Finnish-speaking and one Swedish-speaking. Its industries include shipyards, engineering, textiles, and clothing.

**Turpan** /tuə'pɑ:n/ a Uighur oasis town in Xinjiang autonomous region, north-west China, in the Tien Shan Mts. south-east of Urumqi; pop. (1986) 203,000. Its chief landmarks are the Sugong Mosque and the remains of the ancient city of Gaoshang. Between AD 200 and AD 400 it was the centre of a flourishing civilization.

**Turquino** /tuər'ki:nəu/, **Mount** a mountain in the Sierra Maestra Range, south-east Cuba. Rising to 1,972 m. (6,470 ft.), it is the highest peak on the island.

**Turrialba** /ˌturɪ'ɑ:lbə/ a volcanic peak in central Costa Rica, situated to the north of the town of Turrialba in the department of Cartago. It rises to a height of 3,339 m. (10,955 ft.).

**Tuscaloosa** /ˌtʌskə'lu:sə/ a city in west-central Alabama, USA, situated on the Black Warrior River south-west of Birmingham; pop. (1990) 77,760. Settled in 1809, it was a prosperous cotton-trading town and capital of Alabama 1826–1846. It is now an industrial and agricultural centre and seat of the University of Alabama (1819).

**Tuscany** /'tʌskənɪ/ (Italian **Toscana** /tɒs'kɑ:nə/) a region of west-central Italy comprising the provinces of Arezzo, Firenze, Grosseto, Lucca, Livorno, Massa-Carrara, Pisa, Pistoia, and Siena; area 22,989 sq. km. (8,879 sq. miles); pop. (1990) 3,562,525; capital, Florence. Its many medieval towns and art treasures ensure its popularity with tourists. It is predominantly a farming area with Chianti wine a special product, but there are also important industries: wool at Prato; steel at Piombino; motor scooters at Pontedera; clothing in Arezzo; and marble at Carrara. Modern Tuscany corresponds to the greater part of ancient Etruria.

**Tuticorin** /ˌtu:tɪkə'rɪn/ a town in Tamil Nadu, southern India, a port on the Gulf of Mannar; pop. (1991) 284,190.

**Tutuila** /ˌtu:tu:'i:lɑ/ the largest of the islands of American Samoa in the Pacific Ocean; area 135 sq. km. (52 sq. miles). The island was ceded to the USA in 1900.

**Tuva** /'tu:və/ (in full **Republic of Tuva**) a republic in southern Siberia, in the Russian Federation, on the frontier with Mongolia; area 170,500 sq. km. (65,855 sq. miles); pop. (1990) 314,000; capital, Kyzyl. A mountainous region that includes the upper basin of the Yenisei River, Tuva was formerly part of the Chinese Empire (1757–1911), falling under Tsarist Russia in 1914. As the Tuvinian People's Republic, popularly known as Tannu Tuva, it was independent from 1921 until annexed in 1944 by the USSR which gave it the status of an autonomous oblast and then an autonomous republic (1961). Following the breakup of the Soviet Union in 1991 it maintained its autonomous status within the Russian Federation as the Republic of Tuva. The Tuvans are a Turkic-speaking people and are largely pastoralists. The republic's resources include livestock, gold, cobalt, asbestos, and hydroelectric power.

**Tuvalu** /tu:'vɑ:lu:/ a small country in the south-west Pacific, consisting of a group of nine islands, the former Ellice Islands; area 26 sq. km. (10 sq. miles); pop. (est. 1988) 8,500; official

languages, English and Tuvaluan; capital, Funafuti. The islands formed part of the British colony of the Gilbert and Ellice Islands until they

separated in 1975, becoming independent within the Commonwealth in 1978. Legislative authority is vested in a unicameral parliament and the islands' chief products are coconuts.
**Tuvaluan** *adj. & n.*

**Tuxedo Park** /tʌk'si:dəʊ 'pɑ:k/ a residential area of Orange County, New York, USA, on Tuxedo Lake. It was developed as an exclusive sports resort in 1886 by Pierre Lorillard, giving its name to the Tuxedo dress coat which is said to have originated here.

**Tuxtla Gutiérrez** /'tu:kstlə gu:t'jerez/ the capital of the state of Chiapas in the Chiapas highlands of south-east Mexico; pop. (1990) 295,615. State capital since 1892, it is named in honour of Joaquin Miguel Gutiérrez who campaigned against the state becoming part of Guatemala in the 19th c. Timber and cattle are traded.

**Tuz** /'tu:z/, **Lake** (Turkish **Tuz Gölü**) a salt lake in central Turkey to the south of Ankara.

**Tuzla** /'tu:zlɑ:/ a town in north-eastern Bosnia and Herzegovina, 80 km. (50 miles) north of Sarajevo; pop. (1981) 121,710. Known in ancient times as Salinas, it has for centuries been a source of salt.

**Tver** /tə'vɜ:/ an industrial city in European Russia, a river port at the junction of the Tver and Volga rivers north-west of Moscow; pop. (1990) 454,000. From 1931 until 1991 it was named Kalinin in honour of the Soviet president Mikhail Kalinin (1875–1946). Its industries include engineering, textiles, rolling stock, and rubber.

**Tweed** /twi:d/ a river flowing largely through the Southern Uplands of Scotland for a distance of 155 km. (97 miles) before entering the North Sea at Berwick-upon-Tweed in north-east England. It rises at Tweedswell and passes through the towns of Peebles, Innerleithen, Galashiels, Melrose, and Kelso. It is a famous salmon-fishing river.

**Twente Canal** /'twentə/ a canal in the Netherlands, linking Enschede with the IJssel River; length, 20 km. (32 miles).

**Twi** /twi:/ the chief language spoken in Ghana, consisting of several mutually intelligible dialects.

**Twickenham** /'twɪk(ə)n(ə)m/ a residential district in the Greater London borough of Richmond-upon-Thames, headquarters of the English Rugby Football Union.

**TX** *abbr.* US Texas (in official postal use).

**Tyburn** /'taɪbɜ:n/ a place in London, near the site of Marble Arch, where public hangings were held *c.* 1300–1783.

**Tychy** /'tɪki:/ an industrial town in the province of Katowice, southern Poland, south of Katowice; pop. (1990) 191,720. It is a production centre for Polski Fiat cars.

**Tyler** /'taɪlə(r)/ a city in eastern Texas, USA, between Dallas and the Louisiana frontier; pop.

(1990) 75,450. The headquarters of the East Texas oilfield, Tyler is also at the centre of an area producing livestock, iron ore, forest products, and field-grown roses.

**Tyne** /taɪn/ a river in north-east England that is formed near Hexham from two headstreams that rise in the Cheviot and Pennine hills. It flows eastwards for 50 km. (31 miles) through Tyneside before emptying into the North Sea at Tynemouth.

**Tyne and Wear** /taɪn, wɪə(r)/ a metropolitan county of north-east England; area 540 sq. km. (209 sq. miles); pop. (1991) 1,087,000; county town, Newcastle upon Tyne. It is divided into five districts:

| District | Area (sq. km.) | Pop. (1991) |
| --- | --- | --- |
| Gateshead | 143 | 196,500 |
| Newcastle upon Tyne | 112 | 263,000 |
| North Tyneside | 84 | 188,800 |
| South Tyneside | 64 | 151,900 |
| Sunderland | 138 | 286,800 |

**Tyneside** /'taɪnsaɪd/ a name given to the declining industrial conurbation on either side of the River Tyne in north-east England, stretching from South Shields and Tynemouth to Newcastle upon Tyne.

**typhoon** the English name given to a hurricane in the China Sea.

**Tyre** /taɪə(r)/ (Arabic **Soûr**) a city and Mediterranean seaport in Lebanon, in Al Janub province 80 km. (50 miles) south of Beirut; pop. (1988) 14,000. Once a major commercial centre of the Phoenicians, it was noted for its silk garments, glassware, and purple dye.

**Tyrol** /'tɪr(ə)l, -'rɒl/ (German **Tirol**) an Alpine province of western Austria, the southern part of which was ceded to Italy after World War I; area 12,647 sq. km. (4,885 sq. miles); pop. (1991) 630,350; capital, Innsbruck. The South Tyrol, which remained Italian after 1945, maintains close economic ties with the provinces of Tyrol and Vorarlberg in Austria.
**Tyrolean** *adj. & n.*, **Tyrolese** *n.*

**Tyrone** /tɪ'rəʊn/ a county of Northern Ireland to the west of Lough Neagh; area 3,136 sq. km. (1,211 sq. miles); pop. (1981) 143,880; county town, Omagh.

**Tyrrhenian Sea** /tɪ'ri:nɪən/ a part of the Mediterranean Sea bounded by mainland Italy, Sicily, Sardinia, Corsica, and the Ligurian Sea. The name is an archaic word derived from the Latin *Tyrrhenus* (= Etruscan).

**Tyumen** /tju:'men/ a city in the west Siberian lowlands of Russia, on the Tura River; pop. (1990) 487,000. Regarded as the oldest city in Siberia, it lies on the Trans-Siberian Railway and is a link between rail and river transport. It is the centre of the oil province of Tyumen.

# U u

**Ubaid** /uːˈbaɪd/ a Mesolithic culture in Mesopotamia that flourished during the 5th millennium BC, and was named after Tell Al 'Ubaid near the ancient city of Ur.

**Ubangi** /juːˈbæŋi/ the chief northern tributary of the Congo River in central Africa. It is formed at the junction of the Bomu and Uele rivers and flows 1,060 km. (660 miles) west and south to join the Congo near Mbandaka on the Zaire–Congo frontier.

**Ubangi Shari** a former name (until 1958) of the CENTRAL AFRICAN REPUBLIC.

**Ubatuba** /uːbəˈtuːbə/ a leading beach resort on the São Paulo coast of Brazil, with elegant beach homes and hotels.

**Uberaba** /ˌuːbəˈrɑːbə/ a city in the state of Minas Gerais, eastern Brazil, west of Belo Horizonte; pop. (1990) 241,440.

**Uberlândia** /ˌuːbəˈlɑːndɪə/ a city in the state of Minas Gerais eastern Brazil, on the routeway from São Paulo to Brasilia; pop. (1990) 372,430.

**Ucayali** /ˌuːkæˈjɑːliː/ a river of Peru, one of the principal headstreams of the Amazon. It rises in the Andes as the Apurimac and the Tambo and flows c. 1,600 km. (1,000 miles) northwards through jungle before joining the River Marañón to become the Amazon.

**Udaipur** /uːˈdaɪpʊə(r)/ a city in Rajasthan, north-west India, on Lake Pichola; pop. (1991) 307,680. It was founded in 1586 by Maharana Udai Singh as capital of Mewar, the kingdom of the Udaipur Maharanas. It is popular with tourists who come to see its palaces and Hindu temples.

**Uddevalla** /ˌʌdəˈvælə/ a city in Göteborg och Bohus county, south-west Sweden, a port on the Byfjorden; pop. (1990) 47,345. It has shipyards and light industries.

**Udhagamandalam** /uːˌtækəˈɑːndəlɑːm/ a town in Tamil Nadu, southern India, near the frontiers with Karnataka and Kerala; pop. (1991) 81,730. Until 1991 it was known as Ootacamund, abbreviated in English to Ooty. It lies in rolling hills amidst coffee and tea plantations and was a summer retreat during the British Raj. Amongst its many fine palaces is the Raj Bhavan (1877) which was built in the style of his family home at Stowe by the Duke of Buckingham, Governor of Madras. The Botanical Gardens were developed in the 1840s by the Marquis of Tweeddale.

**Udine** /uːˈdiːneɪ/ an industrial town in the Friuli-Venezia Giulia region of north-east Italy, capital of the province of Udine; pop. (1990) 98,320. Situated in a strategic location on Italy's north-eastern plain, the city has been controlled by the patriarchs of Aquileia, the Venetians, Austria, and Italy, and was the headquarters of the Italian army during World War I. Its industries include chemicals, textiles, and bell-founding.

**Udmurtia** /uːdˈmʊətjə/ (also **Udmurt Republic**) a republic of the Russian Federation, to the north of Tatarstan and north-west of Bashkortostan; area 42,100 sq. km. (16,261 sq. miles); pop. (1990) 1,619,000; capital, Izhevsk. The land of the Udmurts (or Votyaks) was annexed by Russia in the 16th c. and became the Votyak autonomous oblast in 1920 and the Udmurt autonomous oblast in 1932. In 1934 it was designated an autonomous republic of the Soviet Union. The Udmurts, who account for some 30 per cent of the population, speak a language of the Finno-Ugric linguistic group.

**Ufa** /uːˈfɑː/ the capital of the republic of Bashkortostan in the Russian Federation, an industrial city in the Ural Mountains at the junction of the Belaya and Ufa rivers and near the Volga–Urals oilfields; pop. (1990) 1,094,000. It has machinery, chemicals, timber, electric, and electronic industries.

**Uffington** /ˈʌfɪŋtən/ a village in the Vale of the White Horse, Oxfordshire, southern England, the birthplace in 1822 of Thomas Hughes author of *Tom Brown's Schooldays*.

**Uganda**

/juːˈgændə/ official name **The Republic of Uganda** a land-locked country in East Africa, bounded by Sudan, Kenya, Tanzania, Rwanda, and Zaire; area 241,139 sq. km.

(93,140 sq. miles); pop. (est. 1991) 16,876,000; official language, English; capital, Kampala. The greater part of Uganda is savanna or semidesert plateau, bounded in the west by the Rift Valley within which are Lake Edward and Lake Albert (from which the Albert Nile flows northwards). South-east Uganda is dominated by Lake Victoria (source of the Victoria Nile and the largest lake in

Africa). The Ugandan economy is relatively well developed, particularly with respect to the production of coffee, tea, tobacco, and cotton for export. Explored by Europeans in the mid-19th c., Uganda became a British protectorate in 1894 and achieved full independence in 1962, becoming a republic in 1967. Since that time the country has been troubled by political instability and civil conflict (largely owing to tribal divisions), especially during the dictatorship of Idi Amin (1971–9). In 1986 President Yoweri Museveni came to power at the head of the National Resistance Movement which had waged a guerrilla war since 1981. Maintaining a ban on political activity, the government faces rebel activity by the Uganda People's Army. The country is governed by an executive president assisted by a prime minister and cabinet and an interim legislative National Resistance Council.
**Ugandan** *adj. & n.*

**Ugarit** /'uːgærɪt/ (modern **Ras Shamra**) an ancient port in northern Syria, which was occupied from neolithic times until its destruction by the Sea People's in about the 12th c. BC. Ugarit was an important commercial city during the Late Bronze Age, to which period belong a palace, temples, and private residences containing legal, religious, and administrative cuneiform texts in Sumerian, Akkadian, Hurrian, Hittite, and Ugaritic languages. The last of these was written in an early form of the Phoenician alphabet. It was excavated by the French archaeologist Claude Schaeffer in 1929.
**Ugaritic** /ˌuːgəˈrɪtɪk/ *adj. & n.*

**Ugrian** /'uːgrɪən/ (also **Ugric** /'uːgrɪk/) the people and languages of an eastern branch of the Finnic peoples, especially the Finns and Magyars. The name is derived from the Ugry, an early Russian word for a race dwelling east of the Urals.

**Uist** /'juːɪst/ two small islands (**North Uist** and **South Uist**) of the Outer Hebrides of Scotland, lying to the south of Lewis and Harris; separated from each other by Benbecula and from the island of Skye by the Little Minch. The chief settlements and ferry ports are Lochmaddy (on North Uist) and Lochboisdale (on South Uist).

**Uitlander** /'eɪtˌlɒndə(r)/ an Afrikaans name for any of the non-Boer immigrants into the Transvaal, who came after the discovery of gold (1886). To the Boers, these immigrants and particularly British, with foreign capital and different lifestyles, constituted a cultural and economic threat; the Transvaal government of the 19th c. denied them citizenship, taxed them heavily, and excluded them from government, which precipitated the wars of 1880–1, and 1899–1902.

**Ujjain** /uːˈdʒeɪn/ a city of west-central India in the state of Madhya Pradesh, on the River Shipra; pop. (1991) 367,150. It is one of the seven holy cities of Hinduism where the God Siva is said to have triumphed over the demon ruler of Tripuri by changing the name of his capital from Avantika to Ujjaiyini (= one who conquers with pride). It has mosques dating from 13th to 18th c. and ruins of an observatory built by the Maharajah of Jaipur in the 18th c.

**Ujung Pandang** /uːˌdʒʊŋ pænˈdæŋ/ (formerly **Makassar** /məˈkæsə(r)/) the chief seaport of the Sulawesi Islands of Indonesia, situated on the west coast of Sulawesi's southern peninsula; pop. (1990) 944,370. It is capital of the province of South Sulawesi and was formerly a major port of southeast Asia which, as Makassar, gave its name to an oil once used for the hair. Today it is an important commercial centre.

**UK** *abbr.* United Kingdom.

**Ukraine**
/juːˈkreɪn/ formerly the name of a region (**the Ukraine**) north of the Black Sea, now an independent state of eastern Europe; area 603,700 sq. km. (233,179 sq. miles); pop. (est. 1991)

51,999,000; languages, Ukrainian and Russian; capital, Kiev. Its largest cities are Kiev, Kharkov, Dnetropetrovsk, Odessa, and Donetsk. The greater part of Ukraine comprises grain-producing steppeland that stretches east from the Carpathians and is drained by major rivers including the Dniester, Dnieper Southern Bug, and Donets. The Donets Basin in the south-east is a major centre of heavy industry and the mining of coal, iron, and manganese. There are also extensive oil and gas resources. Inhabited by Scythians and Sarmatians in ancient times, the territory now occupied by Ukraine was overrun by Goths, Huns, Avars, and Khazars before the northern part became the powerful Kievan Rus in the 9th c. It later became a borderland divided between Poland, Russia, and the Ottoman empire. After a brief period of independence following the 1917 revolution, it became one of the original constituent Republics of the USSR. In 1991, following the breakup of the Soviet Union, it became an independent state as a member of the Commonwealth of Independent States (CIS). Relations with Russia deteriorated over the status of the Black Sea fleet, nuclear disarmament, the status of the Crimea (which has a largely Russian population), and the future of oil and gas supplies. Ukraine is governed by a legislative Supreme Council.
**Ukrainian** *adj. & n.*

**Ulan Bator** /ʊˌlaːn ˈbaːtɔː(r)/ (also **Ulaanbaatar**) the capital of Mongolia, a city on the River Tola founded in 1639 as a monastery town; pop. (1990) 575,000. It changed its name from Urga to Ulan Bator in 1924, three years after becoming capital of Communist-ruled Mongolia. It has cultural facilities including a university and state circus. Its main industries are food processing, textiles, and the manufacture of building materials.

**Ulanhot** a city in Inner Mongolia, north-eastern China, on the Tao'er River west of Harbin; pop. (1986) 198,000.

**Ulan Ude** /uːˈlɑːn uːˈdeɪ/ an industrial city and transportation centre in south Siberian Russia, capital of the autonomous republic of Buryatia; pop. (1990) 359,000. Founded in 1649 as a Cossack encampment and later developed as a fortress town, it is situated on the Selenga River to the south of Lake Baikal. It was known as Verkhneudinsk until 1934. It has locomotive and rolling stock industries.

**Uleåborg** see OULU.

**Ulhasnagar** /ˌuːlhəsˈnɑːɡə(r)/ a city in Maharashtra state, western India, 40 km. (25 miles) north-east of Bombay; pop. (1991) 368,820.

**Ullapool** /ˈʌləˌpuːl/ a fishing port in Highland Region, north-west Scotland, on the shore of Loch Broom. Founded by the British Fisheries Society in the 18th c., it has a ferry link with Stornoway in the Outer Hebrides.

**Ullswater** /ˈʌlzwɔːtɜː/ a lake in the Lake District of Cumbria, north-west England, the second largest lake in England. It is 12 km. (7.5 miles) long and reaches a depth of 64 m. (210 ft.).

**Ulm** /ʊlm/ an industrial city on the Danube in Baden-Württemberg, southern Germany; pop. (1991) 112,170. Napoleon defeated the Austrians at the Battle of Ulm in 1805 and the city was the birthplace in 1879 of Albert Einstein. Its Gothic cathedral, founded in 1377, has the highest spire in the world (161 m., 528 ft.) Ulm has industries making vehicles, electrical goods, and textiles.

**Ulsan** /uːlˈsɑːn/ an industrial port in South Kyongsang province, south-eastern South Korea; pop. (1990) 682,980. It has oil refineries, chemical plants, and a large sugar refinery.

**Ulster** /ˈʌlstə(r)/ **1.** a name loosely applied as an alternative to Northern Ireland, which comprises six of the former counties of the former Irish province of Ulster. **2.** a province of the Republic of Ireland comprising the counties of Cavan, Donegal, and Monaghan; area 8,012 sq. km. (3,095 sq. miles); pop. (1991) 232,000. It originally also included the 'Six Counties' of Northern Ireland.

**Ulundi** /uːˈluːndɪ/ a town in KwaZulu-Natal, South Africa, north of Durban. It was formerly the capital of Zululand (later KwaZulu).

**Uluru** /uːˈluərʊ/ the Aboriginal name for AYERS ROCK.

**Ulyanovsk** /ʊlˈjɑːnɒfsk/ the former name (1924–92) of SIMBIRSK in Russia.

**Umayyad** /ʊˈmaɪjæd/ a Muslim dynasty, descended from the Quraish tribe to which the prophet Muhammad belonged, that ruled Islam from c. 660 to 750 and later ruled Moorish Spain 756–1031.

**Umbria 1.** a district of ancient central Italy. **2.** a corresponding region of modern Italy; area 8,456 sq. km. (3,266 sq. miles); pop. (1990) 822,765; capital, Perugia. Taking its name from the ancient Umbri, it is the only region of Italy without a coastline. Predominantly agricultural its medieval hill towns are a favourite tourist destination.

**Umeå** /ˌuːməˈəʊ/ a port and the capital of Västerbotten county, north-east Sweden, on an inlet of the Gulf of Bothnia at the mouth of the Ume River; pop. (1990) 91,260. It has Sweden's most northerly university and ferry links with Finland. Timber processing is the main industry.

**Umm al Qaiwain** /ʊm æl kaɪˈwaɪn/ the second-smallest of the seven states of the United Arab Emirates, situated between Dubai and Ras al Khaimah; area 750 sq. km. (290 sq. miles); pop. (1985) 25,230; capital, Umm al Qaiwain. Its economy is based on pearling, trading, fishing, and agriculture (mostly around the oasis of Falaj al-Mualla).

**Umtali** /uːmˈtɑːlɪ/ see MUTARE.

**Umtata** /ʊmˈtɑːtə/ the capital of the state of Transkei in South Africa.

**UN** *abbr.* United Nations.

**Union of Soviet Socialist Republics** see SOVIET UNION.

**Union Territory** any of several territories of India which are administered by the central government.

**United Arab Emirates** an independent state formed in 1971 by the union of seven independent sheikdoms (formerly called the Trucial States and enjoying special treaty rela-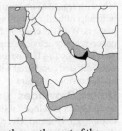tions with Britain) along the south coast of the Persian Gulf westwards from the entrance to the Gulf of Oman. The member states are Abu Dhabi, Ajman, Dubai, Fujairah, Ras al Khaimah (which joined early in 1972), Sharjah, and Umm al Qaiwain; area 77,700 sq. km. (30,010 sq. miles); pop. (est. 1991) 1,630,000; official language, Arabic; capital, Abu Dhabi. The economy is largely based on the production of oil and gas, fishing, entrepôt trade, and the manufacture of aluminium, steel, chemicals, plastics, and clothing. The Emirates are governed by a Supreme Council of Rulers and a Council of Ministers which drafts legislation for submission to a federal National Council.

**United Arab Republic** a political union that existed between Egypt and Syria from 1958 until 1961. It was seen as the first step towards the creation of a pan-Arab union in the Middle East.

**United Kingdom** official name **The United Kingdom of Great Britain and Northern Ireland** the kingdom of Great Britain (Scotland, England, and Wales) and, since

1922, Northern Ireland, including the Channel Isles and the Isle of Man. The term referred to Great Britain and the whole of Ireland from 1801 (when the two countries were united by Act of Parliament) until 1920, when Ireland was partitioned; area 244,129 sq. km. (94,295 sq. miles); pop. (1991) 55,700,000; capital, London.

**United Nations** an international organization of countries set up in 1945, in succession to the League of Nations, to promote international peace, security, and co-operation, with its headquarters in New York. Its members, originally the countries that fought against the Axis in World War II, numbered 186 in 1995 and include most sovereign states of the world. Administration is by the Secretariat, headed by the Secretary-General. The chief deliberative body is the General Assembly, in which each member-state has one vote; recommendations are passed but the UN has no power to impose its will. The Security Council bears the primary responsibility for the maintenance of peace and security; other bodies carry out the functions of the UN with regard to international economic, social, judicial, cultural, educational, health, and other matters. With the close of the Cold War era UN peace-keeping activities expanded rapidly. Between 1987 and 1993 15 UN peace-keeping operations were initiated compared with a total of 13 missions in the previous 40 years.

**United Provinces 1.** the name given to the seven Dutch provinces of Friesland, Gelderland, Groningen, Holland, Overijssel, Utrecht, and Zeeland which formed a union under the Treaty of Utrecht in 1579 following their successful rebellion against Spanish rule, leading to the formation of the Dutch Republic or the Netherlands. **2.** a former administrative division of British India formed by the union of Agra and Oudh. It has been the state of Uttar Pradesh since 1950 when India became a republic.

**United States** official name **The United States of America** a country occupying most of the southern half of North America, situated between Canada to the north and Mexico to the south and including also Alaska in the north-west and Hawaii in the Pacific Ocean; area 9,372,614 sq. km. (3,618,770 sq. miles); pop. (1990) 248,709,870; official language, English; capital, Washington DC. The largest cities in the USA are New York, Los Angeles, Chicago, Houston, Philadelphia, San Diego, Detroit, and Dallas. For the most part the

centre of the US comprises the extensive Great Plains which are drained by the Mississippi, Missouri, Ohio, Red, Arkansas, and Platte rivers; the east coast is separated from the Great Plains by the

Appalachians and the west coast by the Rocky Mountains. A major producer of oil, gas, grain, minerals, and a wide range of industrial goods, the

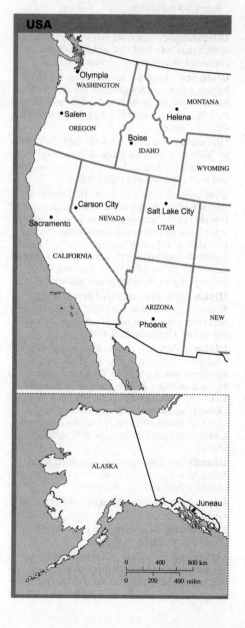

USA

USA is a leading exporter of machinery, aircraft, motor vehicles, cereals, and chemicals. The east coast of North America was colonized by the British in the 17th c., while the south was penetrated by the Spanish from Mexico and the centre taken possession of, but barely colonized by the French. The modern US grew out of the successful rebellion of the east-coast colonies against British rule in 1775–83. The Louisiana Territory was purchased from France in 1803, and the south-west was taken from Mexico after the war of 1846–8. The second half of the 19th c. saw the gradual opening up of the western half of the country after the interruption caused by the Civil War between the northern states and those of the south. In the 20th c. the United States has been the world's principal economic power, participating on the Allied side in both World Wars and becoming one of the two antagonistic superpowers leading the non-Communist world in the Cold War era following World War II. The federal government of the USA comprises an executive president, a bicameral legislature (Congress, which comprises a Senate and House of Representatives), and judiciary headed by the Supreme Court. The USA is divided into 50 states and the District of Columbia which encompasses the federal capital:

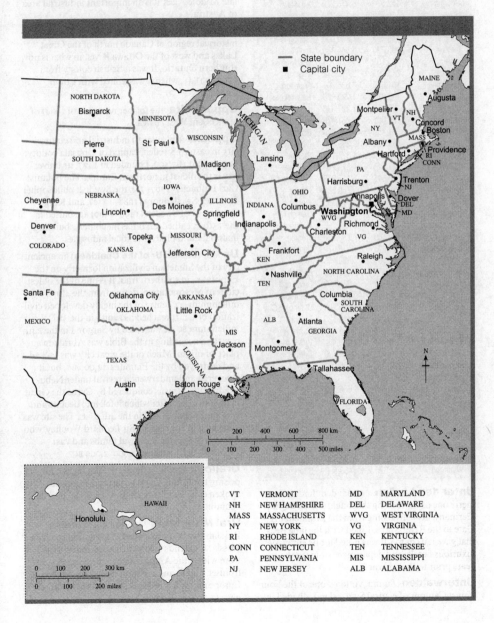

| VT | VERMONT | MD | MARYLAND |
| NH | NEW HAMPSHIRE | DEL | DELAWARE |
| MASS | MASSACHUSETTS | WVG | WEST VIRGINIA |
| NY | NEW YORK | VG | VIRGINIA |
| RI | RHODE ISLAND | KEN | KENTUCKY |
| CONN | CONNECTICUT | TEN | TENNESSEE |
| PA | PENNSYLVANIA | MIS | MISSISSIPPI |
| NJ | NEW JERSEY | ALB | ALABAMA |

| State | Area (sq. km.) | Pop. (1990) | Capital |
|---|---|---|---|
| Alabama | 133,915 | 4,040,590 | Montgomery |
| Alaska | 1,530,700 | 550,400 | Juneau |
| Arizona | 295,260 | 3,665,230 | Phoenix |
| Arkansas | 137,754 | 2,350,725 | Little Rock |
| California | 411,049 | 29,760,020 | Sacramento |
| Colorado | 269,595 | 3,294,390 | Denver |
| Connecticut | 12,997 | 3,287,120 | Hartford |
| Delaware | 5,295 | 666,170 | Dover |
| District of Columbia | 178 | 606,900 | |
| Florida | 151,939 | 12,937,930 | Tallahassee |
| Georgia | 152,576 | 6,478,220 | Atlanta |
| Hawaii | 16,759 | 1,108,230 | Honolulu |
| Idaho | 216,432 | 1,006,750 | Boise |
| Illinois | 145,934 | 11,430,600 | Springfield |
| Indiana | 93,720 | 5,544,160 | Indianapolis |
| Iowa | 145,753 | 2,776,755 | Des Moines |
| Kansas | 213,098 | 2,477,570 | Topeka |
| Kentucky | 104,660 | 3,685,300 | Frankfort |
| Louisiana | 123,677 | 4,219,970 | Baton Rouge |
| Maine | 86,156 | 1,227,930 | Augusta |
| Maryland | 27,092 | 4,781,470 | Annapolis |
| Massachusetts | 21,456 | 6,016,425 | Boston |
| Michigan | 151,586 | 9,295,300 | Lansing |
| Minnesota | 218,601 | 4,375,100 | St. Paul |
| Mississippi | 123,515 | 2,573,220 | Jackson |
| Missouri | 180,516 | 5,117,070 | Jefferson City |
| Montana | 380,848 | 799,065 | Helena |
| Nebraska | 200,350 | 1,578,385 | Lincoln |
| Nevada | 286,352 | 1,201,830 | Carson City |
| New Hampshire | 24,032 | 1,109,250 | Concord |
| New Jersey | 20,169 | 7,730,190 | Trenton |
| New Mexico | 314,925 | 1,515,070 | Santa Fe |
| New York | 127,189 | 17,990,455 | Albany |
| North Carolina | 136,413 | 6,628,640 | Raleigh |
| North Dakota | 183,119 | 638,800 | Bismarck |
| Ohio | 107,044 | 10,847,115 | Columbus |
| Oklahoma | 181,186 | 3,145,585 | Oklahoma City |
| Oregon | 251,419 | 2,842,320 | Salem |
| Pennsylvania | 117,348 | 11,881,640 | Harrisburg |
| Rhode Island | 3,140 | 1,003,460 | Providence |
| South Carolina | 80,582 | 3,486,700 | Columbia |
| South Dakota | 199,730 | 696,000 | Pierre |
| Tennessee | 109,152 | 4,877,185 | Nashville |
| Texas | 691,030 | 16,986,510 | Austin |
| Utah | 219,889 | 1,722,850 | Salt Lake City |
| Vermont | 24,900 | 562,760 | Montpelier |
| Virginia | 105,586 | 6,187,360 | Richmond |
| Washington | 176,479 | 4,866,690 | Olympia |
| West Virginia | 62,759 | 1,793,480 | Charleston |
| Wisconsin | 145,436 | 4,891,770 | Madison |
| Wyoming | 253,326 | 453,590 | Cheyenne |

**Unter den Linden** /ˌuːntɜ den ˈlɪndən/ formerly one of the leading thoroughfares of Berlin, Germany, now stretching from the Brandenburg Gate to the River Spree. Lined with the lime trees that gave it its name, it was noted for its embassies, luxurious hotels, and department stores in the years prior to World War II.

**Unterwalden** /ˈuːntɜːˌvɑːldən/ one of the Four Forest Cantons of central Switzerland, divided into the half-cantons of Obwalden and Nidwalden with their respective capitals at Sarnen and Stans; area 767 sq. km. (296 sq. miles); pop. (1990) 61,440.

**Upolu** /uəˈpəʊluː/ a volcanic island of Western Samoa in the Pacific Ocean, where the Scottish writer Robert Louis Stevenson spent the last years of his life at his home, Vailima, and where he died in 1894.

**Upper Austria** (German **Oberösterreich**) a federal state of northern Austria; area 11,980 sq. km. (4,627 sq. miles); pop. (1991) 1,340,080; capital, Linz. Developed as a separate *Land* in the late Middle Ages, it is an important industrial area of Austria.

**Upper Canada** the mainly English-speaking historical region of Canada north of the Great Lakes and west of the Ottawa River, in what is now southern Ontario. It was a British colony from 1791 to 1841, when it was united with Lower Canada.

**Upper Volta** the former name (until 1984) of BURKINA in West Africa.

**Uppsala** /ʊpˈsɑːlə/ an industrial and cultural city in eastern Sweden, capital of Uppsala county; pop. (1990) 167,500. Founded in 1477, its university is the oldest in northern Europe. The botanist Carl Linnaeus (1707–78), the Swedish philosopher Emanuel Swedenborg (1688–1772), and King Gustavus I of Sweden (1496–1560) are buried in the 15th-c. cathedral. It has machinery, building materials, and pharmaceutical industries.

**Ur** /ɜːr/ (biblical **Ur of the Chaldees**) an ancient city of the Sumerian civilization formerly on the Euphrates, in southern Iraq. It is one of the oldest cities of Mesopotamia, dating from the 4th millennium BC, centre of the highly developed civilization of Ur. It reached its zenith in the 3rd millennium BC. It was ruled by Sargon I in the 24th c. BC and according to the Bible was Abraham's place of origin. Much of the great city was sacked and destroyed by the Elamites c. 2,000 BC, but it recovered and underwent a revival under Nebuchadnezzar. Ur was conquered by Cyrus the Great in the 6th c. BC, after which it fell into decline and was finally abandoned in the 4th c. BC. The site was excavated in 1922–34 by Sir Leonard Woolley, who discovered spectacular royal tombs and vast Ziggurats dating from c. 2,600–2,000 BC.

**Uralic** /jʊəˈrælɪk/ a family of languages comprising the Finno-Ugric group and Samoyed, spoken over a wide area in Europe, Asia, and the Scandinavian countries.

**Ural Mountains** /ˈjʊər(ə)l/ (also **Urals**, Russian **Uralskiy Khrebet**) a mountain range in Russia. It extends 1,600 km. (1,000 miles) south from within the Arctic Circle to the Kazakhstan frontier, and forms a natural boundary between Europe and Asia. Its highest peak is Mt. Narodnaya (1,894 m., 6,214 ft.).

**Uralsk** /juːˈrælsk/ see ORAL.

**Urals Republic** a region of Russia in the Ural Mountains that declared itself independent following the breakup of the Soviet Union in 1991; pop. (1989) 4,731,000; capital, Yekaterinburg. Formerly known as Sverdlovsk, it was the first region to claim a status equivalent to the 21 ethno-territorial republics of the Russian Federation, although it is not officially recognized.

**Urawa** /uːˈrɑːwə/ the capital of Saitama prefecture and a commercial and cultural centre, Honshu Island, Japan; pop. (1990) 418,270.

**Urbino** /ʊəˈbiːnəʊ/ a historic town in the Marches region of central Italy; pop. (1990) 15,410. Ruled by the Montefeltro family from 1213, its ducal palace is a landmark of Rennaissance architecture and houses a collection of fine Italian paintings. Urbino was the birthplace of the painters Raphael (1483–1520) and Bramante (1444–1514).

**Urdu** /ˈʊəduː, ˈɜː-/ an Indic language allied to Hindi, which it resembles in grammar and structure, but with a large admixture of Arabic and Persian words, having been built up from the language of the early Muslim invaders, and usually written in Persian script. It is the language of the Muslim population, spoken as a first language by over 5 million people in Pakistan (where it is an official language), as a second language by another 40 million there, and by about 30 million in India.

**Urfa** /ʊəˈfɑ/ (also **Sanliurfa**) **1.** a rich agricultural province of south-east Turkey, on the frontier with Syria; area 18,584 sq. km. (7,178 sq. miles); pop. (1990) 1,001,055. **2.** its capital, a market town to the east of the Euphrates and south of the Ataturk Barrage; pop. (1990) 276,530. It was known as Edessa before 1637.

**Urga** the former name (until 1924) of ULAN BATOR.

**Urganch** /ʊəˈgentʃ/ (formerly **Urgench**) a city in Uzbekistan, Central Asia, on the Amu Darya near the Turkmenistan frontier; pop. (1990) 128,900. Cotton and food processing are its chief industries. The ancient city of Urgench, which was a major trading centre and capital of the khanate of Khorezm, was destroyed by the Mongols in the 13th c.

**Uruapán** /ʊəruːˈɑːpɑːn/ a city in the mountainous state of Michoacán, western Mexico, on the Cupatitzio River; pop. (1990) 217,140. It was laid out in the 1530s by the Spanish monk Juan de San Miguel. The surrounding area produces coffee, fruit, and vegetables and is noted for the cedar lacquerware handpainted by Tarascan Indians.

**Uruguay** /ˈjʊərə,gwaɪ/ official name **The Oriental Republic of Uruguay** a country in South America lying south of Brazil and north of the River Plate, with a coastline on the Atlantic Ocean; area 176,215 sq. km. (68,063 sq. miles); pop. (est. 1991) 3,110,000; official language,

Spanish; capital, Montevideo. Bounded to the west by the Uruguay River, Uruguay comprises an extensive range of well-watered rolling grassy plains and low hills which, combined with a temperate climate, support stock-raising over much of the country. Uruguay's chief exports are meat, hides, wool, and fish. Not permanently settled by Europeans until the 17th c., Uruguay became an area of long-standing Spanish–Portuguese rivalry. Liberated in 1825, it remained relatively backward and disunited through the 19th c., but in the 20th c., despite its small size (it is one of the smallest of the South American republics) it has emerged as one of the most prosperous and literate nations in the continent, boasting a high rate of economic growth and an extensive social-welfare system. Uruguay is governed by an executive president and a bicameral legislative National Congress comprising a Chamber of Deputies and a Senate.
**Uruguayan** adj. & n.

Uruguay is divided into 19 administrative departments:

| Department | Area (sq. km.) | Pop. (1985) | Capital |
| --- | --- | --- | --- |
| Artigas | 11,928 | 68,400 | Artigas |
| Canelones | 4,536 | 359,700 | Canelones |
| Cerro-Largo | 13,648 | 78,000 | Melo |
| Colonia | 6,106 | 112,100 | Colonia |
| Durazno | 11,643 | 54,700 | Durazno |
| Flores | 5,144 | 24,400 | Trinidad |
| Florida | 10,417 | 65,400 | Florida |
| Lavalleja | 10,016 | 61,700 | Minas |
| Maldonado | 4,793 | 93,000 | Maldonado |
| Montevideo | 530 | 1,309,100 | Montevideo |
| Paysandú | 13,922 | 104,500 | Paysandú |
| Río Negro | 9,282 | 47,500 | Fray Bentos |
| Rivera | 9,370 | 88,400 | Rivera |
| Rocha | 10,551 | 68,500 | Rocha |
| Salto | 14,163 | 107,300 | Salto |
| San José | 4,992 | 91,900 | San José |
| Soriano | 9,008 | 77,500 | Mercedes |
| Tacuarembó | 15,438 | 82,600 | Tacuarembó |
| Treinta y Tres | 9,529 | 45,500 | Treinta y Tres |

**Uruguay** /ˈjʊərə,gwaɪ/ a river of South America that rises in southern Brazil and flows c. 1,610 km. (1,000 miles) west and south along the Brazil–Argentina and Argentina–Uruguay frontiers to join the River Plate opposite Buenos Aires.

**Uruk** /ˈʊərək/ (Arabic **Warka**) an ancient city in southern Mesopotamia, to the north-west of Ur (known also by its biblical name *Erech*). One of the greatest cities of Sumeria, it was built in the 5th millennium BC and was the seat of the legendary hero Gilgamesh. Excavations began in 1928 and revealed ziggurats and temples dedicated to the sky god Anu.

**Urumqi** /ʊˈrʊmtʃɪ/ (also **Urumchi**) the capital of Xinjiang autonomous region in north-west China; pop. (1990) 1,160,000. Known as Tihwa until 1954, it emerged at the junction of several caravan routes and developed during the 20th c. into the main industrial centre of the region. There has been Chinese immigration into the city whose industries include sugar refining and the production of petroleum, iron, steel, and textiles.

**USA** *abbr.* United States of America.

**Uşak** /uːˈʃæk/ **1.** a province of western Turkey; area 5,341 sq. km. (2,063 sq. miles); pop. (1990) 290,280. **2.** its capital to the east of the Gediz River, between Izmir and Afyon; pop. (1990) 105,270.

**Usborne** /ˈʌzbɔːn/ a mountain on the South Atlantic island of East Falkland. Rising to 705 m. (2,312 ft.), it is the highest peak of the Falkland Islands.

**Ushant** /ˈʌʃənt/ (French **Ile d'Ouessant**) an island off the coast of Brittany, part of the French department of Finistère; area 26 sq. km. (10 sq. miles). Naval engagements between French and British fleets took place off Ushant in 1778 and 1794.

**Ushuaia** /uːʃˈwaɪə/ a port on the south coast of the island of Tierra del Fuego, southern Argentina, the most southerly town in the world; pop. (1980) 11,000. Settled by English missionaries in the 1870s, it was taken over by Argentine naval forces in 1884 and used as a penal colony.

**Uspallata Pass** /ˌuːspæˈjɑːtə/ the principal routeway across the Andes of South America, linking Mendoza in Argentina with Santiago, Chile. At its highest point stands a statue of 'Christ of the Andes', erected in 1904 to commemorate the resolution of a boundary dispute.

**Ussuriysk** /uːsuːˈresk/ an industrial coal-mining city in Primorskiy Kray, in the Far East, in Russia, on the Suyfun River north of Vladivostok; pop. (1990) 159,000.

**USSR** *abbr.* Union of Soviet Socialist Republics.

**Ustí nad Labem** /ˌuːstjə næd ləˈbem/ an industrial city in the North Bohemian region of the Czech Republic, on the River Elbe north of Prague; pop. (1991) 99,740. It produces chemicals, textiles, and glass.

**Ustinov** SEE IZHEVSK.

**Ustabakanskoe** /ˌuːstæbəˈkɑːnskəʊjə/ the former name (until 1931) of ABAKAN.

**Ust-Kamenogorsk** /ˌuːstkəmənəˈgɒrsk/ see ÖSKMEN.

**Usumacinta** /uːsuːməˈsiːntə/ a river of Central America that rises in Guatemala as the Chixoy and flows northwards for 965 km. (600 miles) into Mexico before emptying into the Bay of Campeche.

**Usumbura** /ˌuːzəmˈbʊərə/ the former name (until 1962) of BUJUMBARA.

**UT** *abbr.* US Utah (in official postal use).

**Utah** /ˈjuːtɑː/ a name given to the western-most Normandy landing beach where troops of the US 4th Division landed on 6 June 1944.

**Utah** /ˈjuːtɑː:, *US* -tɔː/ a Rocky Mountain state in the western USA, between Nevada to the west and Colorado to the east; area 219,889 sq. km. (84,899 sq. miles); pop. (1990) 1,722,850; capital, Salt Lake City. It is also known as the Beehive State. The area was ceded to the US by Mexico in 1848 and was settled by Mormons; statehood was refused until these abandoned their practice of polygamy—a dispute which led to a brief war (1857) of settlers against US troops. Utah became the 45th state of the Union in 1896. It is rich in oil-shale deposits and minerals such as copper, gold, silver, lead, zinc, and molybdenum, and a leading producer of sheep and irrigated crops such as wheat, beans, and alfalfa. Major landmarks include the Arches, Bryce Canyon, Canyonlands, Capitol Reef, and Zion national parks; and Dinosaur, Natural Bridges, Hovenweep, Timpanogos Cave, Cedar Breaks, and Rainbow Bridge national monuments. The state is divided into 29 counties:

| County | Area (sq. km.) | Pop. (1990) | County Seat |
|---|---|---|---|
| Beaver | 6,724 | 4,765 | Beaver |
| Box Elder | 14,596 | 36,485 | Brigham City |
| Cache | 3,045 | 70,180 | Logan |
| Carbon | 3,845 | 20,230 | Price |
| Daggett | 1,817 | 690 | Manila |
| Davis | 777 | 187,940 | Farmington |
| Duchesne | 8,406 | 12,645 | Duchesne |
| Emery | 11,567 | 10,330 | Castle Dale |
| Garfield | 13,385 | 3,980 | Panguitch |
| Grand | 9,591 | 6,620 | Moab |
| Iron | 8,583 | 20,790 | Parowan |
| Juab | 8,830 | 5,820 | Nephi |
| Kane | 10,135 | 5,170 | Kanab |
| Millard | 17,727 | 11,330 | Fillmore |
| Morgan | 1,568 | 5,530 | Morgan |
| Piute | 1,973 | 1,280 | Junction |
| Rich | 2,688 | 1,725 | Randolph |
| Salt Lake | 1,966 | 725,960 | Salt Lake City |
| San Juan | 20,085 | 12,620 | Monticello |
| Sanpete | 4,126 | 16,260 | Manti |
| Sevier | 4,966 | 15,430 | Richfield |
| Summit | 4,849 | 15,520 | Coalville |
| Tooele | 17,989 | 26,600 | Tooele |
| Uintah | 11,645 | 22,210 | Vernal |
| Utah | 5,247 | 263,590 | Provo |
| Wasatch | 3,097 | 10,090 | Heber City |
| Washington | 6,297 | 48,560 | Saint George |
| Wayne | 6,399 | 2,180 | Loa |
| Weber | 1,472 | 158,330 | Ogden |

**Ute** /juːt/ a North American Indian tribe of the Uto-Aztecan linguistic group which formerly hunted big game in the Great Basin of western Colorado, eastern Utah, and northern New Mexico, and which gave its name to the US state of Utah.

**Utica** /ˈjuːtɪkə/ a city in central New York state, USA, on the Mohawk River; pop. (1990) 68,640.

The first Woolworths store was opened here in 1879.

**Utrecht** /ju:'trext/ a city in the Randstad conurbation of the Netherlands, capital of the province of Utrecht; pop. (1991) 231,230. Situated on a branch of the Lower Rhine, Utrecht is a major transportation, financial, and cultural centre. In 1579 the seven Protestant provinces of the northern Netherlands united under the Union of Utrecht against Spanish rule, and in 1713 the Peace of Utrecht was signed here ending the War of the Spanish Succession.

**Utsire** /ʊt'sɪərə/ a small island off the coast of southern Norway to the north-west of Stavanger. The shipping forecast area **North Utsire** covers Norwegian coastal waters immediately to the north of the island, while **South Utsire** covers the area to the south, as far as the mouth of the Skagerrak.

**Utsunomiya** /ˌu:tsu:'nəʊmɪə/ a city in the Kanto region of eastern Honshu Island, capital of Tochigi prefecture; pop. (1990) 426,800. Industries have relocated from Tokyo to its modern industrial estates and include cars, microchips, and office equipment.

**Uttar Pradesh** /ˌʊtɑ: prə'deʃ/ a state in northern India, bordering on Tibet and Nepal; area 294,413 sq. km. (113,717 sq. miles); pop. (1991) 139,031,130; capital, Lucknow. Prior to it being renamed Uttar Pradesh in 1950 the greater part of the state comprised the United Provinces of Agra and Oudh. A major producer of sugar and grain, it is rich in minerals including bauxite, coal, copper, and limestone.

**Uxbridge** /'ʌksbrɪdʒ/ an industrial and residential district of north-west Greater London, England, on the River Colne. It is the site of Brunel University (1966) and has diverse light industries.

**Uxmal** /'u:ʃmɑ:l/ the remains of an ancient Mayan city to the south of Mérida on the Yucatán peninsula, south-east Mexico. Founded between 600 and 1000 AD and abandoned in the 1440s, it was the largest of the many Classic cities of the Puuc, or hills region of northern Yucatán.

**Uzbek** /'ʌzbek, 'ʊz-/ (also **Uzbeg** /-beg/) a Turkic people of Central Asia mainly living in Uzbekistan and Afghanistan whose language belongs to the Altaic language group. Originally it was written in the Arabic script but that was replaced by the Roman alphabet in 1927 and the Cyrillic in 1940. Turkic Muslim Uzbeks ruled the former khanates of Khiva and Bukhara which were absorbed into the Soviet Union.

**Uzbekistan** /ˌʊzbekɪ'stɑ:n/ official name **The Republic of Uzbekistan** an independent state of Central Asia, lying south and south-east of the Aral Sea; area 447,400 sq. km.

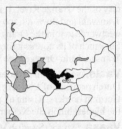

(172,808 sq. miles); pop. (est. 1991) 20,955,000; official language, Uzbek; capital, Tashkent. Largely flat irrigated land to the west and north and mountainous in the east and south, Uzbekistan is rich in pastureland and oil, coal, gas, iron, and other minerals. Its chief products are cotton, textiles, machinery, and heavy equipment. Formerly a constituent republic of the USSR (established in 1924), Uzbekistan gained independence on the breakup of the Soviet Union in 1991 and became a member of the Commonwealth of Independent States. The country is governed by a legislative Supreme Soviet.
**Uzbek** adj. & n.

**Uzhgorod** /'u:ʒgərɒd/ (Ukrainian **Uzhhorod**) an industrial city and transportation centre in the Carpathian foothills of western Ukraine, on the Uzh River; pop. (1990) 119,600. It occupies a strategic location at the southern approach to the Uzhok Pass over the Carpathians.

# V v

**VA** *abbr.* US Virginia (in official postal use).

**Vaal** /vɑːl/ a river of South Africa, the chief tributary of the Orange River. It rises in south-east Transvaal and flows *c.* 1,200 km. (750 miles) south-westwards to join the Orange River near Douglas. For much of its course it forms the border between Transvaal and Orange Free State.

**Vaals** /vɑːls/ a hill in the extreme south of the Dutch province of Limburg near the French and German borders. Rising to 322 m. (1,056 ft.) it is the highest hill in the Netherlands.

**Vaasa** /'vɑːsə/ (Swedish **Vasa**) **1.** a province of western Finland; area 27,319 sq. km. (10,552 sq. miles); pop. (1990) 445,685. **2.** its capital, a port on the Gulf of Bothnia; pop. (1990) 53,430. It is the largest town on the west coast of Finland and the largest bilingual town in the country with some 30 per cent of its inhabitants speaking Swedish. Founded in the 14th c. as Korsholm, it became capital of Ostrobothnia in 1606 when it was renamed after the royal Swedish Wasa family. There is a ferry link with Umeå in Sweden. Its industries include ship repairing and saw milling.

**Vác** /vɑːts/ a port and resort town in Pest county, northern Hungary, on the River Danube; pop. (1993) 33,885. Its industries include ship and crane works, telecommunications, and the manufacture of cement, lime, and photochemicals.

**Vacaville** /'vækə,vɪl/ a food-processing city in central California, USA, between San Francisco and Sacramento near the city of Fairfield; pop. (1990) 71,480.

**Vadodara** /wə'dəʊdərə/ (formerly **Baroda**) a city in the state of Gujarat, western India, on the Vishwamurti River; pop. (1991) 1,115,265. Until 1947 it was the capital of the princely state of Baroda. Its chief landmarks are the 19th-c. Laxmi Vilas and Makarpura palaces and its principal manufactures are textiles, chemicals, metal goods, and silver jewellery.

**Vaduz** /væ'dʊts/ the capital of the Principality of Liechtenstein, on the River Rhine; pop. (1991) 5,000. Dominated by a medieval castle, the town is a tourism and agricultural trade centre with engineering industries, and an international finance centre due to its liberal taxation laws.

**Vail** /veɪl/ a Tyrolean-style skiing resort in the Rocky Mountains west of Denver, Colorado; pop. (1990) 3,660. Situated in the White River National Forest, it is the largest mountain resort in the USA.

**Valais** /'væleɪ/ (French **Wallis**) a canton of southern Switzerland that joined the Swiss Confederation in 1815; area 5,226 sq. km. (2,018 sq. miles); pop. (1990) 248,310; capital, Sion. It includes some of the highest of the Alpine peaks such as the Matterhorn.

**Val-de-Marne** /væl də 'mɑːn/ a department in the Ile-de-France region of northern France, east of Paris; area 244 sq. km. (94 sq. miles) pop. (1990) 1,215,540; capital, Créteil.

**Valdez** /væl'dez/ an ice-free fishing port and oil town in southern Alaska, USA, on Prince William Sound. In 1898 it became a debarkation point for prospectors seeking a duty-free route to the goldfields of the Yukon. In 1964 the town was devastated by an earthquake and in 1989 an oil tanker, the *Exxon Valdez* ran aground in the sound releasing 12 million gallons of crude oil and causing a major environmental disaster.

**Valdivia** /vɑːl'diːvɪə/ the capital of Valdivia province in the Los Lagos region of south-central Chile; pop. (1991) 113,510. Founded by Pedro de Valdivia in 1522, the city expanded with the arrival of German immigrants in the mid-19th c.

**Val-d'Oise** /væl dwɑːs/ a department in the Ile-de-France region of northern France, north of Paris; area 1,249 sq. km. (482 sq. miles); pop. (1990) 1,049,600; capital, Pontoise.

**Valence** /væ'lɑ̃s/ the capital of the department of Drôme in the Rhône-Alpes region of south-east France; pop. (1990) 65,030. It is a market town with electronics industries.

**Valencia** /və'lensɪə/ **1.** a region of eastern Spain, comprising the provinces of Alicante, Castellón, and Valencia; area 23,260 sq. km. (8,940 sq. miles); pop. (1991) 3,857,230. **2.** its capital, a port on the Mediterranean coast at the mouth of the Turia River; pop. (1991) 777,430. There are car ferries to the Balearic and Canary Islands and industries include shipbuilding and the manufacture of chemicals, textiles, motor vehicles, and metal goods.

**Valencia** /və'lensɪə/ an industrial city in northern Venezuela, capital of the state of Carabobo; pop. (1991) 903,080; 1,274,350 (metropolitan area). It is situated on the River Cabriales to the west of **Lake Valencia** which is the second-largest freshwater lake in the country. Its industries include vehicles, brewing, and glass.

**Valenciennes** /væ͵lãsɪˈen/ a town in the Picardy region of northern France, that gave its name to a type of rich lace produced there from the 15th c.; pop. (1990) 39,280. It was the birthplace in 1684 of the artist Jean Watteau and its municipal library holds the *Cantilène de Ste. Eulalie*, one of the first documents written in the French tongue (881).

**Valera** /vəˈleɪrə/ a city in the state of Trujillo, western Venezuela; pop. (1981) 101,980.

**Valhalla** /vælˈhælə/ in Scandinavian mythology, the hall assigned to heroes who have died in battle, in which they feast with Odin.

**Valladolid** /͵vælədəˈliːd/ the capital of Castilla-León region in northern Spain, an industrial city at the junction of the Pisguera and Esguera rivers; pop. (1991) 345,260. It was the principal residence of the kings of Castile in the 15th c. and the scene of the marriage of Ferdinand and Isabella in 1469. Christopher Columbus died here in 1506 and Cervantes wrote part of *Don Quixote* in a house now preserved as a museum. Industries include vehicles, railway engineering, tanning, brewing, chemicals, and textiles.

**Valle d'Aosta** /͵væleɪ dɑːˈɒstə/ a region in the north-west corner of Italy to the south of Mont Blanc; area 3,263 sq. km. (1,260 sq. miles); pop. (1990) 116,000. Its people are largely French-speaking and its chief town is Aosta.

**Valledupar** /͵væljeɪdʊˈpɑː(r)/ a city in northern Colombia, capital of the department of César; pop. (1985) 223,640.

**Vallejo** /væˈleɪhəʊ/ a city in northern California, USA, a port at the mouth of the Napa River northeast of San Francisco; pop. (1990) 109,200. Founded in 1851, it was briefly capital of California during 1852 and 1853. The nearby Mare naval base is the largest on the US Pacific coast.

**Valletta** /vəˈletə/ the capital and chief port of Malta in the Mediterranean; pop. (1987) 9,240, urban harbour area pop. (1992) 102,000. It is named after Jean de Valette, Grand Master of the Knights of St. John, who built the town after the siege of 1565. It is a shipbuilding and yachting centre with an international airport at Luqa, and is a popular tourist destination.

**Valley, The** the capital of the island of Anguilla in the West Indies; pop. (1985) 2,000. Situated at the centre of the island, it is served by Wallblake Airport.

**Valley Forge** the site on the Schuylkill River in Pennsylvania, USA, 32 km. (20 miles) north-west of Philadelphia, where George Washington's Continental Army spent the winter of 1777–8, during the War of American Independence, in conditions of extreme hardship. Log huts of the encampment have been reconstructed in the Valley Forge National Historical Park.

**valley wind** a flow of air moving upslope from a valley floor as it is heated by the sun during the day, and downslope at night as it cools.

**Valois** /ˈvælwɑː/ a medieval duchy of northern France, now part of the departments of Aisne and Oise; the name of the French royal family from the time of Philip VI (1328) to the death of Henry III (1589), when the throne passed to the Bourbons.

**Valona** see VLORË.

**Valparaiso** /͵vælpəˈraɪzəʊ/ the principal port of Chile and one of the chief ports on the Pacific coast of South America; pop. (1991) 276,760. Its industries include ship repairing, foundries, chemicals, and textiles. Founded by the Spanish in 1536, it is the terminus of the trans-Andean railway and seat of the Chilean Naval Academy. It is subject to severe earthquakes: the last was in 1906.

**Van** /væn/ **1.** a province of eastern Turkey; area 19,069 sq. km. (7,365 sq. miles); pop. (1990) 637,430. **2.** its capital, a Kurdish market town on the south-east shore of Lake Van; pop. (1990) 153,110.

**Van** /væn/, **Lake** (Turkish **Van Gölü**) the largest lake in Turkey, a salt lake with no outlet in the mountains of eastern Anatolia; area 3,755 sq. km. (1,450 sq. miles).

**Van Allen belt** /væn ˈælən/ (also **Van Allen layer**) each of two regions of intense radiation partly surrounding the earth at heights of *c.* 3,000 km. and 13,000 km. They were discovered by Explorer I, the first US satellite, and named after the US physicist J. A. Van Allen.

**Vancouver** /vænˈkuːvə(r)/ a city and seaport of British Columbia, Canada; pop. (1991) 471,840; 1,602,500 (metropolitan area). Established in the 1860s, it was named in honour of Captain George Vancouver who explored the waters round Vancouver Island in 1792 and whose boat, the *Discovery*, is berthed at Deadman's Island naval base. The city developed after the arrival of the Canadian Pacific Railway into the largest city on the west coast of Canada and the third-largest metropolitan area of Canada. One of its chief landmarks is the Canada Place convention centre, built for Expo '86. Vancouver's setting and climate make it a popular all-year-round tourist destination. Other industries are shipbuilding, fish processing, oil refining, textiles, and diverse light industries.

**Vancouver Island** an island, off the Pacific coast of British Columbia, Canada, opposite Vancouver; area 31,285 sq. km. (12,080 sq. miles). It is the largest island off the west coast of North America and is separated from the mainland by the Queen Charlotte, Georgia, Johnstone, and Juan de Fuca straits. It was made a crown colony in 1849 and became part of British Columbia in 1866. Its chief city, Victoria, is the capital of British Columbia.

**Vanda** the Swedish name for VANTAA.

**Vanderbijlpark** /'vændəbaɪl,pɑːk/ a city in the province of Pretoria-Witwatersrand-Vereeniging, South Africa, south of Johannesburg; pop. (1985) 540,000 (with Vereeniging). It was laid out and developed as a steel-manufacturing centre in 1946.

**Van Diemen's Land** /væn 'diːmənz/ the former name of Tasmania, Australia. Its name commemorates Anthony van Diemen (1593–1645), Dutch governor of Java, who sent Tasman on his voyage of exploration.

**Vaner** /'vænə(r)/, **Lake** (Swedish **Vänern** /'venən/) the largest lake in Sweden and the third-largest in Europe; area 3,755 sq. km. (1,450 sq. miles).

**Vannes** /vɑːn/ the capital of the department of Morbihan on the south coast of Brittany, north-west France; pop. (1990) 48,450. It was the capital of the kingdom and duchy of Brittany from the 9th to the 16th c. An important agricultural and tourist centre.

**Vantaa** /'væntə/ (Swedish **Vanda**) a city in Uudenmaa province, southern Finland, a northern suburb of Helsinki given separate city status in 1972; pop. (1990) 154,930. A science exhibition centre and international airport are located here.

**Vanua Levu** /və'nuə 'levu:/ (also **Sandalwood Island**) a mountainous volcanic island in the South Pacific, the second-largest of the islands of Fiji; area 5,556 sq. km. (2,146 sq. miles). Its chief town is Labasa.

**Vanuatu** /,vænu:'ɑ:tu:/ official name **The Republic of Vanuatu** a country in the south-west Pacific forming a Y-shaped island chain some 800 km. (500 miles) long; area 14,800 sq. km. (5,716  sq. miles); pop. (est. 1991) 156,000; official languages, English and French (Bislama is the national language); capital, Vila (on Efate). Vanuatu comprises 12 main islands (including Espritu Santo, Malekula, and Efate) and some 60 smaller densely forested islands with an oceanic climate tempered by south-east trade winds from May to October. About 95 per cent of the people are Melanesian. Copra, cocoa, and coffee are the chief exports in addition to fish and manganese. Discovered by the Portuguese in the early 17th c., and later frequented by sandalwood traders, the islands were administered jointly by Britain and France as the condominium of the New Hebrides from 1906 until 1980 when they became an independent republic within the Commonwealth. The country is governed by an executive prime minister and a unicameral Parliament.
**Vanuatuan** *adj. & n.*

**Var** /vɑː(r)/ a department in the Provence-Alpes-Côte d'Azur region of south-east France; area 5,993 sq. km. (2,315 sq. miles); pop. (1990) 815,450; capital, Toulon.

**Varadero** /,værə'deərəʊ/ a leading resort town on the north coast of Cuba, situated on the Hicacos Peninsula north-east of Matanzas.

**Varanasi** /və'rɑːnəsɪ/ (formerly **Benares** /bɪ'nɑːrɪz/) an ancient Hindu holy city on the Ganges in the state of Uttar Pradesh, northern India; pop. (1991) 1,026,470. Because of the Hindu belief that anyone dying in the city goes straight to heaven, many Hindus come here to spend their last days. The dead are cremated at the riverside ghats so that their ashes may be strewn on the sacred waters in which other devotees are bathing. Millions of pilgrims visit the city annually. It has many famous temples and mosques, two Hindu universities, and diverse light industries especially silk and brassware.

**Varaždin** /væ'ræʒdiːn/ a town in northern Croatia, on the River Drava; pop. (1991) 41,800. It is a commercial and textiles centre.

**Varendra** /væ'rendrə/ an ancient kingdom in what is now Bangladesh, described in the Hindu *Mahabharata* epic.

**Varese** /və'reɪzɪ/ a town in Lombardy, northern Italy, capital of Varese province; pop. (1990) 87,970. It lies at the centre of a holiday area between Lake Como and Lake Maggiore. The nearby Sacro Monte is a place of pilgrimage.

**Varna** /'vɑːnə/ a port and resort town on the Black Sea, in the Varna region of eastern Bulgaria; pop. (1990) 320,640. The Greeks established the port of Odessos here in 585 BC and the Romans developed the site as a spa town. It now has naval, textile, and food industries and is the seat of a naval academy. Its museum of history houses finds from the palaeolithic, neolithic, and early Bronze Ages excavated at the golden necropolis of Varna.

**varve** /vɑː(r)v/ a geomorphological term for the annual fluvio-glacial deposits laid down in a lake by streams. Coarse sediments from meltwater streams are deposited during summer months while fine deposits settle in calm water under winter ice forming a thinner layer. The pollen they contain are used for the interpretation of recent climatic history.

**Vaslui** /væs'luːɪ/ a market town on the River Birlad in eastern Romania, capital of Vaslui county; pop. (1989) 73,670.

**Västerås** /'vɑːstərɔːs/ the capital of Västmanland county in eastern Sweden, a manufacturing city and port on the north shore of Lake Mälar; pop. (1990) 119,760. It is a centre of major electrical and engineering industries.

**Vatican** /'vætɪkən/, **the** (also **The Holy See**) **1.** the palace and official residence of the pope in Rome. **2.** the papal government.

**Vatican City** an independent papal state in Rome, the seat of government of the Roman Catholic Church; area 44 hectares (109 acres); pop. (est. 1991) 1,000. The former Papal States, which included Rome and territory in central Italy, became incorporated into a unified Italy between 1861 and 1870, and the temporal power of the pope was in suspense until the Lateran Treaty of 1929, signed by Pope Pius XI and Mussolini, which recognized the full and independent sovereignty of the Holy See in the City of the Vatican. Partly contained within walls on the right bank of the River Tiber, it includes the Apostolic Palace, St. Peter's Basilica, the Vatican Museums and Library, and the Papal Gardens. Extraterritoriality is also extended to some 13 other buildings in Rome as well as the pope's summer residence at nearby Castel Gandolfo. The Vatican has its own police force, diplomatic service, postal service, coinage, and radio station, and citizenship is usually extended to those who reside in the Vatican City by reason of office or employment. The Vatican is visited annually by many thousands of tourists. A major attraction is the recently restored Sistine Chapel decorated by Michelangelo and others, 1508–12.

**Vatnajökull** /'vætnəjə‚ku:l/ the largest icecap of Iceland extending over an area of 8,400 sq. km. (3,245 sq. miles) and up to 1 km. thick.

**Vättern** /'vet(ə)n/ (also **Vetter** or **Wetter**) a lake in southern Sweden, the second-largest lake in the country; area 1,912 sq. km. (738 sq. miles). It is connected to the Baltic Sea and the North Sea (via Lake Väner) by the Göta Canal and at its southern tip lies the city of Jönköping.

**Vaucluse** /vəʊ'klu:z/ a department in the Provence-Alpes-Côte d'Azur region of south-east France; area 3,566 sq. km. (1,377 sq. miles); pop. (1990) 467,075; capital, Avignon.

**Vaud** /vəʊd/ (German **Waadt** /vɑ:t/) a canton on the shores of Lake Geneva in western Switzerland; area 3,218 sq. km. (1,243 sq. miles); pop. (1990) 583,625; capital, Lausanne. Noted for its wines, it joined the Swiss Confederation in 1803. **Vaudois** adj. & n.

**vazante** /və'ʒæntɪ/ a Portuguese word used in Brazil to describe seasonally flooded areas covered in weedy vegetation.

**veld** /velt/ (also **veldt**) an Afrikaans word for treeless open country or grassland in southern Africa, often divided altitudinally into highveld, middleveld, and lowveld.

**Veliko Turnovo** /‚velɪkəʊ 'tɜ:nəvəʊ/ a historic town in the Lovech district of central Bulgaria, situated on the Yantra River in the northern foothills of the Balkan Mountains; pop. (1990) 100,230. It was the scene of a national uprising in 1185 and was capital of the Second Bulgarian State from 1187 to 1396 during which time it was a great cultural centre. The Tsaravets Hill was the site of a Byzantine fortress built by Justinian and partially

restored in the 1930s. It has food, furniture, and textile industries.

**Vellore** /və'lɔ:(r)/ a market town in Tamil Nadu, southern India, in the foothills of the Eastern Ghats west of Madras; pop. (1991) 304,700. It is the site of a 14th-c. fort and a noted Christian Medical College (1900).

**Venda** /'vendə/ a former independent homeland created in northern Transvaal, South Africa, for the Vahvenda people, now part of the province of Northern Transvaal. It was designated a self-governing national state in 1973 and an independent republic in 1979. It united with Northern Transvaal in 1994.

**Vendée** /vɔ̃'deɪ/ a department in the Pays de la Loire region of western France; area 6,721 sq. km. (2,596 sq. miles); pop. (1990) 509,360; capital, La-Roche-sur-Yon.

**Venetia** /vɪ'ni:ʃə/ (Italian **Veneto** /'veɪne‚təʊ/) a region of north-eastern Italy, comprising the provinces of Belluno, Padova, Rovigo, Treviso, Venezia, Verona, and Vicenza; area 18,379 sq. km. (7,099 sq. miles); pop. (1990) 4,398,110; capital, Venice. The region takes its name from the pre-Roman inhabitants, the Veneti.

**Veneto** the Italian name for VENETIA.

**Venezia** the Italian name for VENICE.

**Venezuela**
/‚vene'zweɪlə/ official name **The Republic of Venezuela** a country in northern South America, with a coastline on the Caribbean Sea and bounded by Colombia, Brazil, and Guy-

ana; area 912,050 sq. km. (352,279 sq. miles); pop. (est. 1991) 20,191,000; official language, Spanish; capital, Caracas. Between the Cordillera de Mérida in the north-west and the high plateaus of the Guyana Highlands in the south-east lie the extensive plains or *llanos* of the interior. Most of the population is concentrated in the cities of the Cordillera and Caribbean coast, and the country's chief exports are oil, iron ore, aluminium, steel, coffee, and cocoa. Columbus visited the mouth of the Orinoco in 1498, and in the following year Vespucci explored the coast. It was the early Italian explorers who gave the country its name (= little Venice), when they saw Amerindian houses built on stilts over water and were reminded of the city of Venice. Settled by the Spanish in the 16th c., Venezuela won its independence in 1821 after a ten-year struggle, but did not finally emerge as a separate nation until its secession from the Federation of Gran Colombia in 1830. Its history since then has been characterized by political instability, civil war, dictatorial rule, and the generation of considerable wealth from its well-established oil industry.

Venezuela is governed by an executive president who appoints a Council of Ministers and by a bicameral legislative National Congress comprising a Senate and Chamber of Deputies.
**Venezuelan** *adj. & n.*
Venezuela is divided into 20 states and four federally controlled areas:

| State | Area (sq. km.) | Pop. (1990) | Capital |
|---|---|---|---|
| Anzoátegui | 43,300 | 859,760 | Barcelona |
| Apure | 76,500 | 285,410 | San Fernando |
| Aragua | 7,014 | 1,120,132 | Maracay |
| Barinas | 35,200 | 424,490 | Barinas |
| Bolívar | 238,000 | 900,310 | Ciudad Bolívar |
| Carabobo | 4,650 | 1,453,230 | Valencia |
| Cojedes | 14,800 | 182,070 | San Carlos |
| Falcón | 24,800 | 599,185 | Coro |
| Guárico | 64,986 | 488,620 | San Juan |
| Lara | 19,800 | 1,193,160 | Barquisimeto |
| Mérida | 11,300 | 570,215 | Mérida |
| Miranda | 7,950 | 1,871,090 | Los Teques |
| Monagas | 28,900 | 470,160 | Maturin |
| Nueva Esparta | 1,150 | 263,550 | La Asunción |
| Portuguesa | 15,200 | 576,435 | Guanare |
| Sucre | 11,800 | 679,595 | Cumaná |
| Táchira | 11,100 | 807,710 | San Cristóbal |
| Trujillo | 7,400 | 493,910 | Trujillo |
| Yaracuy | 7,100 | 384,540 | San Felipe |
| Zulia | 63,100 | 2,235,305 | Maracaibo |
| Amazonas Territory | 175,750 | 55,720 | Puerto Ayacucho |
| Delta Amacuro Territory | 40,200 | 84,560 | Tucupita |
| Federal District | 1,930 | 2,103,660 | Caracas |
| Federal Dependencies | 120 | 2,245 | |

**Venice** /'venɪs/ (Italian **Venezia** /ve'netsɪə/) a city of Venetia in north-east Italy, on a lagoon of the Adriatic Sea, built on numerous islands that are separated by canals and linked by bridges; pop. (1990) 317,840. It was a powerful republic in the Middle Ages, and from the 13th to the 16th c. a leading sea-power, controlling trade to the Levant and ruling parts of the eastern Mediterranean. Its commercial importance declined after the Cape route to India was discovered at the end of the 16th c., but it remained an important centre of art and music. After the Napoleonic Wars Venice was placed under Austrian rule; it was incorporated into a unified Italy in 1866. Amongst its many fine buildings are St. Mark's Church, the 15th-c. Doge's Palace, the Bridge of Sighs, and the Grand Canal, all of which make it a prime tourist destination. Venice was the birthplace of many famous artists including Bellini, Giorgione, Titian, Tintoretto, Veronese, Tiepolo, and Canaletto. Many of their works are to be seen in the city. Extraction of water from the subsoil has caused massive sinking and flooding problems which are receiving urgent attention. There is little modern industry: large

petrochemical plants are sited across the lagoon at Mestre and Porto Marghera.
**Venetian** *adj. & n.*

**Vénissieux** /ˌvemi:'sjɜ:/ a town in the Rhône department, eastern France, a south-eastern suburb of Lyons; pop. (1990) 60,740.

**Venlo** /ven'ləʊ/ an industrial city and transportation centre in the province of Limburg, south Netherlands, on the River Meuse (Maas) close to the German border; pop. (1991) 64,390.

**Ventura** /ven'tʊərə/ a city in south-west California, USA, situated on the Pacific coast to the west of Los Angeles; pop. (1990) 93,480. Founded as a Spanish mission in 1782, it now lies at the centre of a farming area growing citrus and avocado. It has boatyard, drydock, and harbour facilities and is the headquarters of the Channel Islands National Park which lies offshore.

**Veracruz** /ˌveərə'kru:z/ **1.** a state of eastern Mexico; area 71,699 sq. km. (27,693 sq. miles); pop. (1990) 6,215,140; capital, Jalapa Enriquez. **2.** a city, port, and resort of Mexico, on the Gulf of Mexico; pop. (1990) 327,520. Now the chief port of Mexico, it was originally founded by Hernán Cortés in 1519 as La Villa Rica de la Veracruz (= the rich town of the true cross). It has important petrochemical industries.

**Vercelli** /vɜ:'tʃelɪ/ a town in the Piedmont region of north-west Italy, capital of the province of Vercelli; pop. (1990) 50,200. It lies at the centre of a major rice-growing area. The Basilica of San Andrea is one of the earliest examples of Italian Gothic architecture.

**Verdon Gorge** /vɜ:'dɔ̃/ a gorge created by the Verdon River in south-east France, the largest chasm in Europe. It is 20 km. (12 miles) long and 700 m. (2,300 ft.) deep and at its broadest is over 1.6 km. (1 mile) wide.

**Verdun** /vɜ:'dʌn/ a fortified town on the River Meuse in north-east France; pop. (1990) 23,430. Of strategic importance, it was the scene of long and severe battles in World War I (1916), where the French and Germans suffered heavy losses. There are huge war cemeteries and monuments.

**Vereeniging** /fə'ri:nɪkɪŋ/ an industrial city in the province of Pretoria-Witwatersrand-Vereeniging, South Africa, on the Vaal River; pop. (1985) 540,100 (with Vanderbjiljpark). A treaty ending the Boer War was signed here in May 1902, and its name means union or reconciliation. It is a coal-mining and steel-making centre.

**Vermont** /vɜ:'mɒnt/ a state of New England in north-eastern USA, bordering on Canada; area 24,900 sq. km. (9,614 sq. miles); pop. (1990) 562,760; capital, Montpelier. Also known as the Green Mountain State, its largest city is Burlington. Explored and settled by the French during the 17th and 18th centuries, it became an independent republic in 1777 and the 14th state of the USA in 1791. Its chief products are granite, marble, asbestos, slate, talc, and maple syrup. In addition to skiing, fishing, and hunting one of Vermont's principal attractions is the Green Mountain National Forest. The state is divided into 14 counties:

| County | Area (sq. km.) | Pop. (1990) | County Town |
|---|---|---|---|
| Addison | 2,010 | 32,950 | Middlebury |
| Bennington | 1,760 | 35,845 | Bennington |
| Caledonia | 1,693 | 27,850 | Saint Johnsbury |
| Chittenden | 1,404 | 131,760 | Burlington |
| Essex | 1,732 | 6,405 | Guildhall |
| Franklin | 1,687 | 39,980 | Saint Albans |
| Grand Isle | 231 | 5,320 | North Hero |
| Lamoille | 1,199 | 19,735 | Hyde Park |
| Orange | 1,794 | 26,150 | Chelsea |
| Orleans | 1,812 | 24,050 | Newport |
| Rutland | 2,423 | 62,140 | Rutland |
| Washington | 1,794 | 54,930 | Montpelier |
| Windham | 2,046 | 41,590 | Newfane |
| Windsor | 2,527 | 55,055 | Woodstock |

**Verona** /vəˈrəʊnə/ a picturesque tourist and market city in Venetia, north-east Italy, on the River Adige; pop. (1990) 258,950. It principal landmarks are the Roman Arena, the medieval Castelvecchio, and the Romanesque San Zeno Maggiore, and among its chief industries are the manufacture of paper, plastics, and furniture.

**Verria** /ˈverɪə/ (Greek **Véroia**) a market town and winter-sports centre in Thessaly, north-eastern Greece, near the eastern foot of Mount Vermion; pop. (1981) 37,090. It is capital of the department of Imathia.

**Versailles** /veəˈsaɪ/ a town south-west of Paris in central France, capital of the department of Yvelines; pop. (1990) 91,030. It is noted for its royal palace, originally built as a hunting lodge for Louis XIII but later extended as a royal seat by Louis XIV. Its architecture is the work of Louis Le Vau, Jules Hardouin-Mansart, and Robert de Cotte. The interiors were designed by Charles Lebrun and the gardens laid out by André Le Nôtre. Versailles was the residence of the French kings until the revolution of 1789. Treaties were signed here ending the War of American Independence (1783) and World War I (1919). Two million tourists a year visit the palace which has been designated a world heritage site by UNESCO.

**Verulamium** see ST. ALBANS.

**Verviers** /ˈveəvɪˌeɪ/ a manufacturing town of Belgium, in the province of Liège; pop. (1991) 53,480. It developed during the 18th c. as a textile town.

**Vesterålen** /ˈvestəˌrɒlən/ an island group off the north-west coast of Norway, to the north of the Lofoten Islands. Its chief islands are Hinnøy, Langøya, Andøya, and Hadseløy.

**Vestmannaeyjar** see WESTMAN ISLANDS.

**Vesuvius** /vɪˈsuːvɪəs/ (Italian **Vesuvio**) an active volcano near Naples in Italy, 1,277 m. (4,190 ft.)

high. It erupted violently in AD 79, burying the towns of Pompeii and Herculaneum.

**Veszprém** /vezˈprem/ a town in the Bakony Mountains of western Hungary, capital of Veszprém county; pop. (1993) 65,380. It is a centre of tourism and chemical research.

**Via Appia** see APPIAN WAY.

**Viana do Castelo** /ˈvjɑːnə duː kæsˈteləʊ/ a resort town and port on the Atlantic coast of northern Portugal, capital of the district of Viana do Castelo; pop. (1991) 8,780.

**Viborg** /ˈviːbɔ:(r)/ a historic and commercial town in northern Denmark, capital of Viborg county; pop. (1990) 29,455. Until 1340 Danish kings were elected here and until 1650 it was the largest town in Jutland. It has a 12th c. cathedral and a 13th c. abbey church.

**Vicenza** /viːˈtʃensə/ a city in the Venetia region of north-east Italy, capital of Vicenza province; pop. (1990) 109,330. Many of its finest buildings are associated with the architect Andrea Palladio and nearby is the Basilica of Monte Bérico where an apparition of the Virgin Mary is said to have appeared in 1426. It has iron and steel, chemicals, machinery, textiles, and glass industries.

**Vichy** /ˈviːʃiː/ a town in the Auvergne region of central France noted for its effervescent mineral waters; pop. (1990) 28,050. During World War II it was the seat of the Vichy government of Marshal Pétain.

**Vicksburg** /ˈvɪksbɜ:g/ a city in west Mississippi, USA, a port on the Mississippi River; pop. (1990) 20,910. It was successfully besieged by Federal forces under General Grant in 1863. It was the last Confederate-held outpost on this river and its loss effectively split the secessionist states in half, bringing the end of the American Civil War much nearer. The event is commemorated in the Vicksburg National Military Park.

**Victoria** /vɪkˈtɔ:rɪə/ a state of south-east Australia; area 227,600 sq. km. (87,910 sq. miles); pop. (1991) 4,439,400; capital, Melbourne. Originally known as the Port Philip district of New South Wales, it became a separate colony in 1851 and was federated with the other states of Australia in 1901. Rich in mineral resources that include brown coal, gold, gypsum, kaolin, bauxite, and offshore oil, the state also produces grain, fruit, wine, wool, and dairy produce.

**Victoria** a port city on the west coast of Canada, provincial capital of British Columbia; pop. (1991) 71,200; 287,900 (metropolitan area). Situated at the southern tip of Vancouver Island, the city was founded in 1843 as a Hudson's Bay Company fort. It was a base for gold prospectors during the gold-rush of 1858 and became provincial capital in 1871. It is a naval and fishing-fleet base with a university. Industries include shipbuilding, timber, paper making, and tourism.

**Victoria** the business centre, port, and capital of Hong Kong, on the north coast of Hong Kong Island. Victoria Harbour is one of the busiest and greatest natural harbours in the world with container terminals and piers for the largest liners and cargo vessels; it is used by more than 20,000 ocean-going ships each year, and has excellent dockyard facilities. The city is connected to Kowloon by ferries and a road tunnel. Central Victoria is Hong Kong's business centre. It is backed by Victoria Peak where crowded tenements give way to the buildings of Government House and the university.

**Victoria** a seaport on the island of Mahé in the Indian Ocean, capital of the Seychelles Islands; pop. (1985) 23,000.

**Victoria** a city in south-east Texas, USA, linked to the Intracoastal Waterway on the coast of the Gulf of Mexico by the 56-km. (35-mile) **Victoria Canal**; pop. (1990) 55,080. Established in 1685 as a fort by the French explorer La Salle, the city was founded in 1824 by Martin DeLeon and named after a Mexican president, Guadalupe Victoria. Lying at the centre of a leading cattle farming area, it has oil and chemical industries.

**Victoria, Lake** (also **Victoria Nyanza** /nɪˈænzə/) the largest lake in Africa (69,464 sq. km., 26,820 sq. miles) and the chief reservoir of the Nile, explored by Speke in 1858. Areas of it lie within the boundaries of Uganda, Tanzania, and Kenya.

**Victoria de Durango** see DURANGO 2.

**Victoria Falls** a spectacular waterfall 109 m. (355 ft.) high on the River Zambezi at the border of Zimbabwe and Zambia, explored by David Livingstone in 1855. Originally known as Mosi-oa-tunya (= the smoke that thunders), it is divided into five main sections: the Eastern Cataract, Rainbow Falls, Devil's Cataract, Horshoe Falls, and Main Falls. The winding gorge below the Falls is crossed by a 198 m. (650 ft.) road and rail bridge 94 m. (310 ft.) above the river.

**Victoria Island** an island in the Canadian Arctic, the third-largest island of Canada; area 217,290 sq. km. (83,928 sq. miles). The surrounding region is administered and supplied from Cambridge Bay on the island's south-east coast.

**Victoria Nile** that part of the upper Nile that emerges from the northern end of Lake Victoria and flows north-westwards through Lake Kyoga to Lake Albert.

**Victoria Peak 1.** the highest peak of the Maya Mountains in Belize, Central America; height, 1,120 m. (3,675 ft.). **2.** a mountain on Hong Kong Island rising to a height of 554 m. (1,818 ft.).

**Victory Peak** see PIK POBEDY.

**Vidin** /ˈviːdɪn/ a river port and market town in the Mikhailovgrad region of northern Bulgaria, on the River Danube opposite Calafat in Romania; pop. (1991) 91,040.

**Viedma** /ˈvjeθmɑː/ a market town in south-central Argentina, capital of the Patagonian province of Río Negro; pop. (1980) 20,000.

**Viedma, Lake** a lake in the Los Glaciares National Park in the Patagonian Andes of southern Argentina.

**Vienna** /vɪˈenə/ (German **Wien** /viːn/) the capital of Austria, situated on the River Danube; pop. (1991) 1,533,180. It was an important military centre (*Vindobona*) under the Romans, and from 1278 to 1918 the seat of the Habsburgs, the rulers of the once-great Austro-Hungarian Empire. It has long been a centre of the arts and especially music, Mozart, Beethoven, Brahms, and Johann Strauss being among the great composers associated with it. The principal landmarks are St. Stephen's Cathedral, the Opera House, Schönbrunn Palace, the Hofburg (the residence of the President of Austria), the Spanish Riding School, and the Giant Wheel in the Prater Park. Vienna's geographical position has made it a natural meeting-place for Eastern and Western Europe. Today it is the headquarters of world agencies such as OPEC and the UN International Atomic Agency. It has numerous light industries but tourists, attracted by Vienna's monumental buildings, theatres, shops, museums, and concert halls, make the biggest contribution to Austria's balance of payments.
**Viennese** *adj. & n.*

**Vienne** /viːˈen/ **1.** a river of central France that rises in the Plateau de Millevaches near Limoges and flows north and west for 350 km. (220 miles) to join the Loire River south-east of Saumur. **2.** a department in the Poitou-Charentes region of west-central France; area 6,984 sq. km. (2,350 sq. miles); pop. (1990) 379,980; capital, Poitiers.

**Vientiane** /vɪˌentɪˈɑːn/ the capital and chief port of Laos, on the Mekong River; pop. (1985) 377,400. It has several Buddhist temples including the Great Sacred Stupa which was allegedly first erected in the 3rd c. BC to enclose a breastbone of the Buddha.

**Vierwaldstätter See** see LAKE LUCERNE.

**Vietnam** /vjetˈnæm/ official name **The Socialist Republic of Vietnam** a country in south-east Asia, with its eastern coastline on the South China Sea; area 329,566 sq. km.  (127,295 sq. miles); pop. (est. 1991) 67,843,000; official language, Vietnamese; capital, Hanoi. The southern part of the country, which is flat and fertile, is dominated by the estuary of the Mekong River, while most of northern Vietnam is mountainous with a thick canopy of tropical forest. In the north-east, the coastal plains and the delta of

the Red River are heavily populated and intensively cultivated. Traditionally dominated by China, Vietnam came under increasing French influence in the second half of the 19th c. The country was occupied by the Japanese during World War II, and post-war hostilities between the French and the Communist Vietminh ended with French defeat and the partition of Vietnam along the 17th parallel in 1954. A prolonged war between North and South Vietnam, fought largely as a guerrilla campaign in the south, ended with the withdrawal of direct American military assistance to South Vietnam and its conquest by Communist forces in 1976, after which a reunited socialist republic was proclaimed. Since then Vietnam has been involved in border disputes with China and military intervention in Cambodia, while its predominantly agricultural economy, now largely collectivized, has been slowly recovering from wartime destruction and dislocation to become a major world producer of rice. A new constitution adopted in 1992 introduced major political and economic reforms (*doi moi*). Vietnam is governed by an executive Council of Ministers and a legislative National Assembly. The Communist Party of Vietnam is the only authorized political party.
**Vietnamese** *adj. & n.*

**Vigo** /ˈviːɡəʊ/ the principal naval and commercial port, and resort on the Atlantic coast of Galicia in north-west Spain; pop. (1991) 276,570. It is the base of tuna and sardine fishing and has shipyards, oil refineries, and canneries.

**Vijayawada** /ˌvɪdʒəjəˈwɑːdə/ a commercial and religious city in the state of Andhra Pradesh, south-east India, at the head of the River Krishna delta; pop. (1991) 845,300. Developed on the route from Madras to Calcutta, the city takes its name from the goddess Vijaya. It is an important Muslim, Buddhist, and Hindu religious centre.

**Vikhren** /ˈviːxren/ (also **Eltepe**) the highest peak of the Pirin Mountains in south-west Bulgaria; height, 2,915 m. (9,564 ft.).

**Viking** /ˈvaɪkɪŋ/ **1.** a member of the Scandinavian traders and pirates who ravaged much of northern Europe, and spread eastwards to Russia and Byzantium, between the 8th and 11th centuries. While their early expeditions were generally little more than raids in search of plunder, in later years they tended to end in conquest and colonization. Much of eastern England was occupied by the Vikings and eventually Cnut, king of Denmark, succeeded to the English throne. **2.** a shipping forecast area covering the central North Sea between southern Norway and the Shetland Islands.

**Vila** /ˈviːlə/ (also **Port Vila**) the capital of Vanuatu, on the south-west coast of the South Pacific island of Efate; pop. (est. 1989) 19,400.

**Vila do Conde** /ˈviːlə du: ˈkɒndɪ/ a resort town on the Atlantic coast of northern Portugal, at the mouth of the River Ave; pop. (1991) 21,755.

**Vilaine** /viːˈlen/ a river of north-west France that rises in the department of Mayenne and flows generally south-westwards for 225 km. (140 miles) to the Bay of Biscay.

**Vila Real** /ˌviːlə reɪˈɑːl/ a town on the River Corgo in northern Portugal, capital of Vila Real district; pop. (1991) 15,480.

**Vila Velha** /ˌviːlə ˈveljə/ a city in the state of Espiritu Santo, eastern Brazil, on the Atlantic coast south of Vitória; pop. (1990) 268,640. There are ruins of the fortified monastery of Nossa Senhora da Penha (1558).

**Villach** /ˈfɪlæx/ an industrial town of Carinthia in southern Austria on the River Drau west of Klagenfurt; pop. (1991) 55,165. There are thermal springs at Warmbad Villach to the south.

**Villa Cisneros** /ˌviːljə sɪsˈneərɒs/ the former name (until 1976) of DAKHLA in Western Sahara.

**Villahermosa** /ˌviːljəhɜːˈməʊzə/ (in full **Villahermosa de San Juan Bautista**) a city in south-east Mexico, capital of the state of Tabasco; pop. (1990) 390,160. Situated between the Grijalva and Carrizal rivers, it was a small river port until the development of agriculture, oil production, and the generation of hydroelectric power during the 1960s.

**Villavicencio** /ˌviːljəviːˈsensjəʊ/ a city in the eastern Andes of central Colombia, capital of the department of Meta; pop. (1985) 191,000. Commercial centre of a cattle, coffee, bananas, rice, and rubber producing region.

**Villeurbanne** /ˌviːlɜːˈbɑːn/ an industrial eastern suburb of Lyons in the Rhône department of eastern France; pop. (1990) 119,850.

**Villmanstrand** the Swedish name for LAPPEENRANTA in Finland.

**Vilnius** /ˈvɪlnɪəs/ the capital of Lithuania, a city on the River Neris; pop. (1991) 593,000. Dating from the 10th c., it became capital of the former grand duchy of Lithuania in 1323. It fell to Russia in 1795 and between 1920 and 1939 was held by Poland. Under Russian control again, it was capital of the Lithuanian Soviet Socialist Republic from 1944 until it once more became capital of an independent Lithuania in 1991. The city's university was founded in 1579 and has a stormy history. Vilnius was a leading centre of Jewish culture until the Nazi extermination of its large Jewish population. Today it has metallurgical and machine industries, as well as chemicals, textiles, and electrical industries.

**Viña del Mar** /ˈviːnjə del ˈmɑː/ a resort town on the Pacific coast of Chile, 9 km. (6 miles) north of Valparaiso; pop. (1991) 281,060. It hosts an annual international song festival.

**Vineland** /ˈvaɪnlænd/ a market city in southern New Jersey, USA, east of the Maurice River; pop. (1990) 54,780. It has large glass and clothing industries.

**Vinland** /'vɪnlənd/ a region of North America, probably on or near the northern tip of Newfoundland, discovered and briefly settled in the 11th c. by Norsemen under Leif Ericsson. It was so named from the report that grapevines were growing there.

**Vinnytsya** /'viːnjɪtsə/ (formerly **Vinnitsya**) a city in the Podolia region of central Ukraine, south-west of Kiev; pop. (1990) 379,000. It has large sugar refineries and makes fertilizers, farm machinery, and clothing.

**Vinson Massif** /'vɪnsən mə'siːf/ a mountain in Ellsworth Land, Lesser Antarctica. Rising to a height of 5,140 m. (16,863 ft.), it is the highest peak in Antarctica.

**Virginia** /və'dʒɪnɪə/ a state on the Atlantic coast of the USA; area 105,586 sq. km. (40,767 sq. miles); pop. (1990) 6,187,360; capital, Richmond. The largest cities are Virginia Beach, Norfolk, Richmond, Newport News, Chesapeake, and Hampton. Virginia is also known as the Old Dominion State or Mother of Presidents. The site of the first permanent European settlement in North America (1607), Virginia was named in honour of Elizabeth I, the 'Virgin Queen'. It was one of the original 13 states of the USA and is now a leading producer of tobacco, peanuts, apples, tomatoes, timber, and coal. Amongst its chief landmarks are the Blue Ridge Mountains, the Shenandoah River, the historic towns of Jamestown, Williamsburg, and Fredericksburg, and the homes of famous statesmen such as George Washington (Mount Vernon), James Monroe (Ashlawn), Thomas Jefferson (Monticello), Robert E. Lee (Arlington House), and Woodrow Wilson (Staunton). Virginia is divided into 41 independent cities and 95 counties:

| County | Area (sq. km.) | Pop. (1990) | County Seat |
| --- | --- | --- | --- |
| Accomack | 1,238 | 31,700 | Accomack |
| Albemarle | 1,885 | 68,170 | Charlottesville |
| Alleghany | 1,160 | 13,180 | Covington |
| Amelia | 928 | 8,790 | Amelia Courthouse |
| Amherst | 1,245 | 28,580 | Amherst |
| Appomattox | 874 | 12,300 | Appomattox |
| Arlington | 68 | 170,890 | Arlington |
| Augusta | 2,571 | 54,680 | Staunton |
| Bath | 1,399 | 4,800 | Warm Springs |
| Bedford | 1,942 | 45,660 | Bedford |
| Bland | 933 | 6,510 | Bland |
| Botetourt | 1,417 | 24,990 | Fincastle |
| Brunswick | 1,464 | 15,990 | Lawrenceville |
| Buchanan | 1,310 | 31,330 | Grundy |
| Buckingham | 1,516 | 12,870 | Buckingham |
| Campbell | 1,313 | 47,570 | Rustburg |
| Caroline | 1,391 | 19,220 | Bowling Green |
| Carroll | 1,243 | 26,590 | Hillsville |
| Charles City | 471 | 6,280 | Charles City |
| Charlotte | 1,240 | 11,690 | Charlotte Courthouse |
| Chesterfield | 1,128 | 209,560 | Chesterfield |
| Clarke | 463 | 12,100 | Berryville |
| Craig | 858 | 4,370 | New Castle |
| Culpeper | 993 | 27,790 | Culpeper |
| Cumberland | 780 | 7,825 | Cumberland |
| Dickenson | 861 | 17,620 | Clintwood |
| Dinwiddie | 1,318 | 22,320 | Dinwiddie |
| Essex | 684 | 8,690 | Tappahannock |
| Fairfax | 1,024 | 818,580 | Fairfax |
| Fauquier | 1,693 | 48,860 | Warrenton |
| Floyd | 991 | 11,965 | Floyd |
| Fluvanna | 754 | 12,430 | Palmyra |
| Franklin | 1,776 | 39,550 | Rocky Mount |
| Frederick | 1,079 | 45,720 | Winchester |
| Giles | 941 | 16,370 | Pearisburg |
| Gloucester | 585 | 30,130 | Gloucester |
| Goochland | 731 | 14,160 | Goochland |
| Grayson | 1,160 | 16,280 | Independence |
| Greene | 408 | 10,300 | Stanardsville |
| Greensville | 780 | 8,630 | Emporia |
| Halifax | 2,122 | 29,030 | Halifax |
| Hanover | 1,215 | 63,310 | Hanover |
| Henrico | 619 | 217,850 | Richmond |
| Henry | 993 | 56,940 | Martinsville |
| Highland | 1,082 | 2,635 | Monterey |
| Isle of Wight | 829 | 25,050 | Isle of Wight |
| James City | 398 | 34,970 | Williamsburg |
| King and Queen | 824 | 6,290 | King and Queen Courthouse |
| King George | 468 | 13,530 | King George |
| King William | 723 | 10,910 | King William |
| Lancaster | 346 | 10,900 | Lancaster |
| Lee | 1,136 | 24,500 | Jonesville |
| Loudoun | 1,355 | 86,130 | Leesburg |
| Louisa | 1,292 | 20,325 | Louisa |
| Lunenburg | 1,123 | 11,420 | Lunenburg |
| Madison | 837 | 11,950 | Madison |
| Mathews | 226 | 8,350 | Mathews |
| Mecklenburg | 1,602 | 29,240 | Boydton |
| Middlesex | 348 | 8,650 | Saluda |
| Montgomery | 1,014 | 73,910 | Christiansburg |
| Nelson | 114 | 12,780 | Lovingston |
| New Kent | 554 | 10,445 | New Kent |
| Northampton | 588 | 13,060 | Eastville |
| Northumberland | 481 | 10,520 | Heathsville |
| Nottoway | 822 | 14,990 | Nottoway |
| Orange | 889 | 21,420 | Orange |
| Page | 814 | 21,690 | Luray |
| Patrick | 1,251 | 17,470 | Stuart |
| Pittsylvania | 2,587 | 55,670 | Chatham |
| Powhatan | 1,764 | 15,330 | Powhatan |
| Prince Edward | 920 | 17,320 | Farmville |
| Prince George | 692 | 27,390 | Prince George |
| Prince William | 881 | 215,680 | Manassas |
| Pulaski | 827 | 34,500 | Pulaski |
| Rappahannock | 694 | 6,620 | Washington |
| Richmond | 502 | 7,270 | Warsaw |
| Roanoke | 653 | 79,330 | Salem |
| Rockbridge | 1,568 | 18,350 | Lexington |
| Rockingham | 2,249 | 57,480 | Harrisonburg |
| Russell | 1,245 | 28,870 | Lebanon |
| Scott | 1,391 | 23,200 | Gate City |
| Shenandoah | 1,331 | 31,640 | Woodstock |
| Smyth | 1,175 | 32,370 | Marion |
| Southampton | 1,568 | 17,550 | Courtland |
| Spotsylvania | 1,050 | 57,400 | Spotsylvania |
| Stafford | 705 | 61,240 | Stafford |

| Surry | 731 | 6,145 | Surry |
|---|---|---|---|
| Sussex | 1,277 | 10,250 | Sussex |
| Tazewell | 1,352 | 45,960 | Tazewell |
| Warren | 564 | 26,140 | Front Royal |
| Washington | 1,461 | 45,890 | Abingdon |
| Westmoreland | 590 | 15,480 | Montross |
| Wise | 1,053 | 39,570 | Wise |
| Wythe | 1,209 | 25,470 | Wytheville |
| York | 294 | 42,430 | Yorktown |

**Virginia Beach** a popular summer resort city
in south-east Virginia, USA; pop. (1990) 393,070.
Its economy is based on tourism, agriculture
(market gardening and livestock), and military
bases.

**Virgin Islands** a
group of Caribbean
islands at the eastern
extremity of the
Greater Antilles, dis-
covered by Colum-
bus in 1493 and now
under divided British
and US administra-
tion: **1. British**

**Virgin Islands** the easternmost group of 40
islands of which the largest are Tortola and Virgin
Gorda; area 153 sq. km. (59 sq. miles); pop. (1991)
16,750; capital, Road Town. Settled by British
planters in 1666, and known as the British Virgin
Islands since 1917, the islands were granted the
status of a self-governing British dependent territory in 1967. **2. The Virgin Islands of the United
States** a group of islands comprising St. Croix,
St. Thomas, St. John and about 50 small islets all
lying to the east of Puerto Rico; area 342 sq. km.
(132 sq. miles); pop. (1990) 101,810; capital, Charlotte Amalie (on St. Thomas). Formerly known as
the Danish West Indies, the islands were purchased
by the USA in 1917 because of their strategic location on the Anegada Passage linking the Atlantic
Ocean to the Caribbean Sea. They have the status
of an unincorporated territory of the USA. Tourism is the largest industry, especially on St. Thomas
which also manufactures watches, textiles, pharmaceuticals, and rum. St. Croix has a large oil refinery
and a bauxite-processing plant. Columbus visited
the islands in 1493 and, because of their number,
named them in honour of St. Ursula and her
11,000 martyred virgins.

**Virunga** /vi:ˈrɒŋgə/ a range of the Mitumbar
Mountains in the Rift Valley of east-central Africa.
Situated to the north of Lake Kivu on the border of
Zaire, Rwanda, and Uganda, its highest peak is
Karisimbe (4,507 m., 14,787 ft.).

**Vis** /vi:s/ an island in the Adriatic Sea off the
Dalmatian coast of Croatia. Its chief towns are Vis
and Komiža.

**Visakhapatnam** /vɪˌʃækəˈpʌtnəm/ a naval
and commercial seaport on the coast of Andhra
Pradesh in south-east India; pop. (1991) 1,051,900.

Its industries include shipbuilding, oil refining,
sugar refining, and the manufacture of jute, steel,
and petrochemicals.

**Visalia** /vɪˈsɑːlɪə/ a city in the San Joaquin valley
of central California, USA; pop. (1990) 75,640. It
manufactures electronic products.

**Visayan Islands** /vɪˈsaɪən/ a group of islands
in the central Philippines, to the south of Luzon
Island. Its chief islands are Cebu, Bohol, Panay,
Leyte, Samar, Negros, and Masbate.

**Visby** /ˈvɪzbɪ/ (also **Gotland**) a Baltic Seaport,
capital of the Swedish island of Gotland; pop.
(1990) 57,110. The town is surrounded by limestone walls built in the 13th c. The miracle play
'Petrus de Dacia' is performed in St. Nicholas's
church.

**Viseu** /viˈseɪu:/ a town on the Pavia River in
north-central Portugal, capital of Viseu district;
pop. (1991) 20,590. It is a centre for the production
of Dão wines and is associated with a 15th–16th c.
school of painting represented by artists such as
Vasco Fernandez (Grão Vasco).

**Visigoth** /ˈvɪzɪˌgɒθ/ a West Goth, a member of
the branch of the Goths who invaded the Roman
Empire between the 3rd and 5th c. and eventually
established in Spain a kingdom that was overthrown by the Moors in 711–12.

**Vistula** /ˈvɪstjʊlə/ (Polish **Wisła** /ˈviːslə/) a river
of central Europe that rises in the Carpathians of
south-west Poland and flows generally northwards
for 940 km. (592 miles) before joining the Baltic at
Gdansk.

**Vitebsk** see VITSYEBSK.

**Viterbo** /viˈtɜːbəʊ/ a tourist town in the Latium
region of central Italy, capital of the province of
Viterbo; pop. (1990) 60,210. It has many historic
buildings and was a papal seat (1257–81).

**Viti Levu** /ˌviːti: ˈleɪvu:/ the largest of the islands
of Fiji in the South Pacific; area 10,429 sq. km.
(4,028 sq. miles). Its chief town is Suva, capital of
Fiji.

**Vitória** /vɪˈtəʊrɪə/ **1.** a port on the east coast of
Brazil, north of Rio de Janeiro, capital of the state
of Espírito Santo; pop. (1990) 276,170. It exports
coffee, timber, and iron ore. **2.** a city in north-east
Spain, capital of the Basque provinces; pop. (1991)
208,570. Here in 1813 the British army under
Wellington defeated a French force under
Napoleon's brother, Joseph Bonaparte, and thus
freed Spain from French domination. It has diverse
light industries.

**Vitoria da Conquista** a city in the state of
Bahia, eastern Brazil, situated to the south-west of
Salvador; pop. (1990) 264,130.

**Vitosha** /ˈviːtɒʃə/ a ski resort, the largest in
Bulgaria, situated in the mountains to the south of
Sofia.

**Vitsyebsk** /ˈviːtsjebsk/ a city in north-east Belorussia (Belarus), on the Western Dvina; pop. (1990)

356,000. It was known as Vitebsk until 1992. Its industries include machine tools, radios, furniture, and clothing.

**Vlaanderen** /'vlændərən/ see FLANDERS.

**Vladikavkaz** /ˌvlædəkæf'kɑːz/ an industrial city on the River Terek in south-west Russia, capital of North Ossetia; pop. (1990) 306,000. Founded as a Caucasus frontier town of the Russian empire in 1784, it was known as Ordzhonikidze from 1954 to 1991. It produces zinc, lead, glass, chemicals, and clothing.

**Vladimir** /'vlædɪmiːr, vlə'diː-/ a tourist and industrial city in western Russia, on the Klyazma River east of Moscow; pop. (1990) 353,000. It was the capital of a principality during the 12th–13th c. Its industries include chemicals, engineering, electrical goods, and textiles.

**Vladivostok** /ˌvlædɪ'vɒstɒk/ the principal seaport, cultural centre, and naval base of Russia on the Pacific east coast; pop. (1990) 643,000. It is an eastern terminus of the Trans-Siberian Railway and a base for fishing and whaling fleets. Its industries include oil refining, timber, machinery, and foodstuffs.

**Vlissingen** the Dutch name for FLUSHING.

**Vlöre** /'vlɔːrə/ (also **Vlonë** or **Vlona** /'vlaʊnə/, Italian **Valona**) a port of south-west Albania, on the Adriatic coast; pop. (1990) 55,800. Known in ancient times as Avlon, it repaced Apollonia and Oricum as the leading port of Illyria during the first century AD. It is now the principal naval base and second port of Albania.

**Vltava** /'vəltəvə/ (German **Moldau** /'məʊldaʊ/) a river of the Czech Republic that rises in the Bohemian Forest and flows c. 435 km. (270 miles) northwards through Prague to join the River Elbe near Melnik.

**Vojvodina** /ˌvɔɪvə'diːnə/ a nominally autonomous province of northern Serbia, on the border with Hungary; area 21,505 sq. km. (8,306 sq. miles); pop. (1981) 2,034,770; official language, Serbo-Croat; capital, Novi Sad.

**volcano** /vɒl'keɪnəʊ/ a mountain or hill having an opening or openings in the earth's crust through which lava, cinders, steam, gases, etc. are or have been expelled. They may be active or dormant. Geologists generally group volcanoes into four main types: **1.** *cinder cones*, created from gas-charged lava ejected from a single vent and falling as cinders to form a circular or oval cone; **2.** *composite volcanoes*, steep-sided symmetrical cones built of alternating layers of lava, ash, and cinders; **3.** *shield volcanoes*, built of fluid basaltic lava that slowly creates a massive gently-sloping cone; **4.** *lava domes*, formed by viscous lava piling up around a vent. The word volcano takes its name from the Mediterranean island of Vulcan near Sicily, thought in ancient times to be the chimney of the forge of Vulcan, blacksmith of the gods. There are nearly 1,350 active volcanoes in the world, the

majority erupting at the boundaries of the earth's crustal plates. About 60 per cent occur around the Pacific Ocean plate in an area known as the 'Ring of Fire'. The largest active volcano is Mauna Loa on the island of Hawaii.

**Volcano Islands** (Japanese **Kazan-retto**) a group of Japanese islands in the western Pacific Ocean to the south of Japan, the largest of which is Iwo Jima. Annexed by Japan in 1891, they were administered by the USA after World War II from 1945 to 1968.

**Volcán Poás** see POÁS, VOLCÁN.

**Volga** /'vɒlgə/ the longest river in Europe, rising in north-west Russia and flowing 3,531 km. (2,194 miles) generally southwards to the Caspian Sea. Navigable for most of its course, it has been linked to the Baltic and the Black Sea to form a major network of trade routes.

**Volgodonsk** /'vɒlgəˌdɒnsk/ a city in western Russia, on the River Don at the south-western end of the Tsimlyansk Reservoir north-east of Rostov; pop. (1990) 178,000.

**Volgograd** /'vɒlgəˌgræd/ an industrial city of Russia, a port on the River Volga at the eastern end of the Volga-Don Canal; pop. (1990) 1,005,000. The city was called Tsaritsyn until 1925, and Stalingrad from then until 1961. During World War II it was the scene of a long and bitterly fought battle in 1942–3, in which the German advance in the Soviet Union was halted. Its industries generate hydroelectric power and produce oil, aluminium, textiles, and footwear.

**Volhynia** /vɒ'lɪnɪə/ (also **Volynia**, Russian **Volyn**) a coal-mining and fertile agricultural area of north-west Ukraine that was a principality during the 10th–14th centuries and later part of Poland. Ceded to Russia at the partition of Poland in 1793 and divided between Russia and Poland after World War I, it eventually found itself entirely within Ukraine after World War II. Lviv is the principal city.

**Vologda** /'vɒləgdə/ a city and transportation centre in northern Russia, on the Vologda River north-east of Moscow; pop. (1990) 286,000. It has shipyards, machine factories, timber mills, and flax-processing plants.

**Volos** /'vɒlɒs/ a port on an inlet of the Aegean Sea in Thessaly, eastern Greece; pop. (1981) 107,400. Built on the site of ancient Iolkos, it is the capital of the department of Magnesia, trading in grain, cotton, sugar, and olive oil produced in the surrounding area. It was badly damaged by earthquakes in 1954–5.

**Volta** /'vəʊltə/ a river of West Africa formed in central Ghana by the junction of the headwaters, the Black Volta (Mouhoun), Red Volta (Nazinon), and White Volta (Nakanbe), which rise in Burkina. At Akosombo in south-east Ghana the river has been dammed, creating **Lake Volta** which is one of the world's largest man-made lakes, completed in

1965. The lake serves for navigation, fishing, irrigation, and the generation of hydroelectric power which serves the large local aluminium industry.

**Voltaic languages** (also **Gur**) a group of Niger–Congo languages spoken in West Africa, chiefly in Benin, northern Togo, northern Ghana, Burkina, and Mali. Mossi, spoken in Burkina, is the most widely spoken of the languages in this group.

**Volta Redonda** /ˌvəʊltə rəˈdɒndə/ a steel-manufacturing city in the state of Rio de Janeiro, south-eastern Brazil, situated to the north-west of Rio de Janeiro; pop. (1990) 230,530.

**Volubilis** /vɒlˈjʊblɪs/ the remains of an ancient Roman town near Meknès in north-west Morocco. It was one of the chief cities of the province of Tingitana.

**Volzhskiy** /ˈvɒlʃki:/ an industrial city in western Russia, on the Volga near Volgograd; pop. (1990) 275,000.

**Vorarlberg** /ˈfɔːrɑːlˌbeək/ an Alpine province of western Austria; area 2,601 sq. km. (1,005 sq. miles); pop. (1991) 333,130; capital, Bregenz.

**Vorkuta** /vɔːˈkʊtə/ a city in the autonomous Russian republic of Komi, on the Vorkuta river in the northern Urals; pop. (1990) 117,000. Located above the Arctic circle it was founded in 1932 as one of the notorious Soviet forced-labour camps.

**Voronezh** /vəˈrɒnjeʒ/ an industrial city in western Russia, on the River Voronezh south-east of Moscow; pop. (1990) 895,000. Founded as a frontier fortress in 1586, its chief landmarks are the Potemkin Palace and the 18th-c. Nikolsk Church. Its industries make machinery, chemicals, electrical and food products.

**Voroshilovgrad** the former name (1935–91) of the Ukrainian city of LUHANSK.

**Vosges** /vəʊʒ/ **1.** a mountain system of eastern France to the west of the Rhine and separated from the Jura in the south by the Belfort Gap. Its highest peak is the Ballon de Guebwiller (Grand Ballon) which rises to 1,423 m. (4,669 ft.). **2.** a department of Lorraine in north-east France; area 5,903 sq. km. (2,280 sq. miles); pop. (1990) 386,260; capital, Épinal.

**Votkinsk** /ˈvɒtkɪnsk/ a city in the autonomous Russian republic of Udmurtia, on the Kama River east of Izhevsk; pop. (1990) 104,000. It was the birthplace in 1840 of the composer Tchaikovsky whose home is now a museum. It has machinery industries, sawmills, and brickyards.

**Vratsa** /ˈvrɑːtsə/ (also **Vraca** or **Vraza**) an industrial city in Mikhailovgrad district, north-west Bulgaria, 55 km. (35 miles) north-east of Sofia; pop. (1990) 102,255. It has textile, metal, and ceramic industries.

**VT** *abbr.* US Vermont (in official postal use).

**Vyatka** /ˈvjætkə/ **1.** a river of western Russia that rises in the Urals and flows west and north for 1,358 km. (850 miles) to join the River Kama near Mamadysh. **2.** a city of western Russia, an industrial port on the Vyatka River; pop. (1990) 487,000. It was known as Kirov (1934–92). It has heavy machinery, chemicals, agricultural equipment, and metal industries.

**Vychegda** /ˈvɪtʃɪgdə/ a river of western Russia that rises in the northern Urals and flows westwards for 1,120 km. (700 miles) to join the Northern Dvina at Kotlas.

# W w

**WA** *abbr.* US Washington State (in official postal use).

**Waal** /wɑːl/ a river of the south-central Netherlands. The most southerly of two major distributaries of the Rhine, it flows for 84 km. (52 miles) from the point where the Rhine forks, just west of the border with Germany, to the Meuse (Maas) on the North Sea.

**Wabash** /ˈwɔːbæʃ/ a river of the USA that rises in the Grand Lake in western Ohio and flows west into Indiana where it turns south to join the Ohio River at the meeting point of the states of Kentucky, Indiana, and Illinois; length, c. 765 km. (475 miles).

**Waco** /ˈweɪkəʊ/ a city in central Texas, USA, on the River Brazos; pop. (1990) 103,590. Founded as a ferry-crossing in 1849, it was named after the Waco (Huaco) Indians. A museum features the history of the Texas Rangers and the Armstrong Browning Library of Baylor University (1845) houses a collection of manuscripts and memorabilia relating to Robert and Elizabeth Barrett Browning. In 1993 a ranch near Waco was the scene of a 51-day armed siege in which four government agents and 72 members of the Branch Davidian religious sect were killed. It is a commercial and industrial centre with tyres, glass, and paper manufactures.

**Waco** /ˈweɪkəʊ/ (also **Huaco**) a North American Indian tribe of the Caddoan linguistic group originally occupying the plains and prairies of Oklahoma where they hunted and cultivated maize. They later migrated to the Brazos River country of eastern Texas. Moved to a reservation in 1859, they only numbered 37 by 1894.

**wadi** /ˈwɒdɪ, ˈwɑːdɪ/ a rocky watercourse in North Africa and south-west Asia, dry except in the rainy season.

**Wadi Halfa** /ˌwɒdɪ ˈhælfə/ a town on the River Nile in the extreme north of Sudan, where the Lake Nasser steamer from Aswan in Egypt meets the railway from Khartoum.

**Wad Medani** /wɒd məˈdænɪ/ the capital of the Central province of Sudan, a market city on the Blue Nile south-east of Khartoum and centre of the El Gezirah cotton-growing area; pop. (1983) 141,065.

**Wagga Wagga** /ˌwægə ˈwægə/ an agricultural centre in New South Wales, south-east Australia, on the Murrumbidgee River west of Canberra;

pop. (1991) 40,875. Its name is sometimes abbreviated to Wagga. Food processing and agricultural trade are among its chief industries.

**Wahabi** /wəˈhɑːbɪ/ (also **Wahhabi**) a sect of Muslim puritans following strictly the original words of the Koran, named after Muhammad ibn Abd al-Wahab (1703–92), a native of Nejd in central Arabia. Dissatisfied with the practices of his contemporaries in the capitals of Islamic learning, Abd al-Wahab called for a return to the earliest doctrines and practices of Islam. Forming an alliance with Muhammad ibn Saud, prince of a small adjacent kingdom, he showed his awareness of the inseparability of spiritual and temporal in Islam. The two leaders forged a state which came to encompass most of the Arabian peninsula, but their expansion and especially their attacks on sites holy to followers of Islam brought a response in the form of a successful campaign undertaken by Muhammad Ali, Viceroy of Egypt, acting for the Ottoman government which was nominal sovereign over the Arabian peninsula. The reconquest of Ottoman territory and dissolution of the Wahabi state was completed in 1919. The term 'Wahabi', however, was appropriated by various movements seeking reform and purification of the faith in the 19th c., and became almost a generic name for such movements.

**Wahran** the Arabic name for ORAN.

**Waialeale** /waɪˌɑːlɪˈɑːlɪ/, **Mount** a volcanic peak rising to a height of 1,548 m. (5,080 ft.) on the island of Kauai in the Hawaiian Islands. The rain falling on its summit averages 12,350 mm. (460 inches) a year, making it one of the rainiest places in the world.

**Waikato** /waɪˈkɑːtəʊ/ **1.** the longest river of New Zealand, flowing north and north-west for 434 km. (270 miles) from Lake Taupo at the centre of North Island to the Tasman Sea. **2.** an administrative region of North Island, New Zealand, comprising Thames Coromandel, Hauraki, Waikato, Waipa, Waitomo, Otorohanga, South Waikato, Matamata-Piako, and parts of Taupo, Rotorua, and Franklin districts; pop. (1991) 338,960. Its chief city is Hamilton.

**Waikiki** /waɪkiˈkiː/ a beach resort forming a suburb of Honolulu on the Hawaiian island of Oahu.

**Wailing Wall** a high wall in Jerusalem, known in Jewish tradition as the 'Western Wall'. Originally part of the Temple structure erected by

Herod the Great, since the 7th c. it has formed the western wall of the sanctuary enclosing the Dome of the Rock and other buildings, the third most holy place to Muslims after Mecca and Medina. Jews have been accustomed, probably since the Middle Ages, to lament at this wall the destruction of the Temple and the Holy City in AD 70 and to pray for its restoration.

**Waitangi** /waɪˈtæŋɡɪ/ the site of a historic house and reserve on the western shore of the Bay of Islands, Northland Region, New Zealand. It was here on 6 February 1840 that the Treaty of Waitangi was signed by Maori chiefs and Captain William Hobson representing Queen Victoria. This treaty formed the basis of British annexation of New Zealand. The Treaty House was originally the home of James Busby a pioneer settler who was appointed British Resident in New Zealand in 1832 and the signing of the treaty is celebrated annually as a national holiday (Waitangi Day).

**Wakayama** /wɑːˈkɑːjəmɑː/ the capital of Wakayama prefecture, central Honshu Island, Japan, a commercial centre on the Inland Sea; pop. (1990) 396,550. It is a former castle town with steel and textile industries and a ferry link with Komatsushima on the island of Shikoku.

**Wakefield** /ˈweɪkfiːld/ the county town of West Yorkshire, England, on the River Calder; pop. (1981) 75,840. A cloth-manufacturing town in medieval times, its modern industrial products include chemicals, textiles, and machinery.

**Wake Island** /weɪk/ an atoll in the central Pacific Ocean between Hawaii and Guam, comprising the three small islets of Wake, Wilkes, and Peale; area 6.5 sq. km. (2.5 sq. miles). Discovered by Captain William Wake in 1796 and later surveyed by Captain Charles Wilkes, Wake Island was annexed by the USA in 1899. It has been used as a commercial and military air base since 1938 and is administered by the US Department of the Air Force.

**Wakhan Salient** /wəˈkɑːn/ a narrow corridor of land forming a 300 km.-long 'panhandle' at the north-east corner of Afghanistan. Demarcated by the Anglo-Russian Pamir Commission in 1895–6, the Salient once formed a buffer between Russian and British spheres of influence in Asia.

**Walachia** see WALLACHIA.

**Wałbrzych** /ˈvɑːlbʒɪk/ (German **Waldenburg** /ˈwɒld(ə)nbɜːɡ/) a coal-mining and industrial city of Lower Silesia in south-west Poland, capital of Wałbrzych county; pop. (1990) 141,000.

**Wales** /weɪlz/ (Welsh **Cymru** /ˈkʊmriː/) a principality extending over the western part of Great Britain and forming a large peninsula bounded by the Irish Sea, St. George's Channel, and the Bristol Channel; area 20,766 sq. km. (8,020 sq. miles); pop. (1991) 2,798,200; capital, Cardiff. Coastal lowlands rise up to high plateaux and mountains which include the Snowdonia, Brecon

Beacons, Black Mountain, and Black Forest ranges. The uplands are deeply dissected by rivers such as the Severn, Wye, Usk, Dee, Towy, Teifi, Taff, Dovey, Taf, and Conway. The Welsh island of Anglesey (Ynys Môn), which lies off the north-west coast of Gwynedd, is linked to the mainland by road and rail bridges. It was overrun by Celts during the Bronze and Iron Ages; the Roman conquest of Wales was completed under Agricola in AD 78. After the Roman withdrawal in the 5th c., the Celtic inhabitants of Wales successfully maintained their independence against the Anglo-Saxons who settled in England and in the 8th c. Offa king of Mercia built an earthwork (see OFFA'S DYKE) marking the frontier established by his struggles against them. Largely isolated from historical developments in the rest of England until the Middle Ages, Wales was eventually conquered by Edward I who, in 1301, created his son Prince of Wales a title subsequently held by the eldest son of each sovereign. Sporadic resistance to English rule, particularly during the 15th c. under Owain Glyndwr, continued until the accession to the English throne in 1485 of Henry VII of the Welsh House of Tudor. In 1536 Wales was finally incorporated into the larger country by Henry VIII. Wales maintains a distinct cultural identity with a language and literature of its own. Nearly 20 per cent of its people speak the Welsh language and a national bardic festival (*Eisteddfod*) has been held annually since it was established in 1176 by Prince Rhys ap Griffith.
**Welsh** *adj.*
Wales is divided into eight counties:

| County | Area (sq. km.) | Pop. (1991) | Administrative Headquarters |
|---|---|---|---|
| Clwyd | 2,430 | 401,500 | Mold |
| Dyfed | 5,766 | 341,600 | Carmarthen |
| Gwent | 1,376 | 432,300 | Cwmbran |
| Gwynedd | 3,863 | 238,600 | Caernarvon |
| Mid Glamorgan | 1,017 | 526,500 | Cathay's Park, Cardiff |
| Powys | 5,077 | 116,500 | Llandrindod Wells |
| South Glamorgan | 416 | 383,300 | Atlantic Wharf, Cardiff |
| West Glamorgan | 820 | 357,800 | Swansea |

**Wallace's Line** a boundary line which may be drawn on a map to distinguish between the distinct flora and fauna of south-east Asia and Australasia. The line was originally determined by the naturalist Alfred Russel Wallace (1823–1913) who noted in his *Malay Archipelago* (1869) that islands to the east of Bali in Indonesia were characterized by an impoverished fauna associated with low rainfall and thorny scrub typical of Australasia while islands to the west had a rich continental fauna associated with high rainfall and tropical vegetation more typical of Asia.

**Wallachia** /wɒˈleɪkɪə/ (also **Walachia**) a former principality of south-eastern Europe, between the

Danube and the Transylvanian Alps, united in 1859 with Moldavia to form Romania.
**Wallachian** *adj. & n.*

**Wallasey** /ˈwɒləsɪ/ a residential town in Merseyside, north-west England, situated at the mouth of the Mersey River on the Wirral peninsula north of Birkenhead; pop. (1981) 62,530.

**Wallis and Futuna Islands** /ˈwɒlɪs, fəˈtuːnə/ an overseas territory of France comprising two groups of islands (the Iles de Hoorn and the Wallis Archipelago) to the west of Samoa in the central Pacific; area 274 sq. km. (106 sq. miles); pop. (1990) 13,700; capital, Mata-Utu (on Uvea).

**Walloonia** /wɒˈluːnɪə/ a French-speaking region of southern Belgium to the south of the Flemish region of Flanders; area 16,841 sq. km. (6,505 sq. miles); pop. (1991) 3,250,000.
**Walloon** *adj. & n.*

**Wallop** /ˈwɒləp/ the name of three villages (Middle, Nether, and Over Wallop) in Hampshire, southern England, to the west of the Test valley.

**Wallsend** /ˈwɒlzend/ an industrial town in Tyneside area of Tyne and Wear, north-east England; pop. (1980) 44,620. It lies on the River Tyne at the eastern end of Hadrian's Wall.

**Wall Street** a street at the south end of Manhattan, New York, where the New York Stock Exchange and other leading American financial institutions are located. The name is used allusively to refer to the American money-market or financial interests. It is named after a wooden stockade that was built in 1653 around the original Dutch settlement of New Amsterdam.

**Walnut Creek** a residential city to the east of Oakland in the San Francisco Bay area of central California, USA; pop. (1990) 60,570.

**Walsall** /ˈwɔːls(ə)l/ an industrial town in the West Midlands of England, north-west of Birmingham; pop. (1991) 171,000. During the 17th c. it became a noted centre for the manufacture of locks and keys. It was the birthplace in 1859 of Jerome K. Jerome, author of *Three Men in a Boat*.

**Walsingham** the name of two villages (Great and Little Walsingham) in Norfolk, east England. Little Walsingham was at one time the most important place of pilgrimage in England, a vision of the Virgin Mary having been seen here during the reign of Edward the Confessor.

**Waltham** /ˈwɒlθ(ə)m/ an industrial city in east Massachusetts, USA, situated to the west of Boston; pop. (1990) 57,880. First settled in 1634, it is named after Waltham Abbey in England. It has varied manufactures including electronics and precision instruments.

**Waltham Abbey** /ˈwɒlθ(ə)m/ an abbey church in Essex, south-east England, burial place of King Harold who was slain at the battle of Hastings in 1066.

**Waltham Forest** /ˈwɒlθ(ə)m/ an outer residential borough of Greater London, south-east England, created in 1965 by the merger of the municipal boroughs of Chingford, Leyton, and Walthamstow; pop. (1991) 203,400.

**Walvis Bay** the principal port and fishing centre of Namibia on the Atlantic coast of south-west Africa; pop. (1980) 25,000. Formerly part of a British enclave in German South West Africa visited by whalers and fishermen, it was later administered by South Africa as part of Cape Province. In 1994 the South African government transferred the port and offshore Penguin Islands to Namibia. Walvis Bay is linked to the interior by rail.

**Wandsworth** /ˈwɒnzwɜːθ/ a largely residential inner borough of Greater London, England, south of the River Thames; pop. (1991) 237,500. It includes the suburbs of Battersea Park, Putney Heath, and Streatham.

**Wanganui** /ˌwɒŋɡəˈnuːɪ/ a seaport on the west coast of North Island, New Zealand, in the Manawatu-Wanganui Region near the mouth of the Wanganui River; pop. (1991) 41,210. Founded in 1840 and originally named Petre (after the 11th Baron Petre, a director of the New Zealand Company), its name was changed to Wanganui in 1854. It serves an area of sheep, cattle, dairy, and poultry farming and is a centre for food processing, sawmilling, engineering, and the manufacture of textiles and chemicals.

**Wangaratta** /ˌwæŋəˈrɑːtə/ a town in the state of Victoria, south-east Australia, at the junction of the Ovens and King rivers; pop. (1991) 15,980. Its industries produce textiles and computer supplies and its air museum (Drage Airworld Museum) houses one of the world's largest collections of flying antique civil aircraft.

**Wankie** the former name (until 1982) of HWANGE.

**Wantage** /ˈwɒntɪdʒ/ a market town in Oxfordshire, southern England, at the foot of the Berkshire Downs, 21 km. (13 miles) south-west of Oxford. A former capital of the Saxon kingdom of Wessex, it was the birthplace in 849 of Alfred the Great. The first steam tramway in England operated here 1873–1948.

**Wanxian** /ˌwænˈʃiːˈɑːn/ a city in Sichuan province, central China, on the Yangtze River ; pop. (1986) 287,000.

**Wapping** /ˈwɒpɪŋ/ a district of London, England, on the north bank of the River Thames in the borough of Tower Hamlets between London

Docks and the Rotherhithe Tunnel. It is a centre of the newspaper industry.

**Warangal** /vəˈrʌŋg(ə)l/ a city on the Deccan plateau to the north-east of Hyderabad in the state of Andhra Pradesh, south-east-central India; pop. (1991) 466,880. Capital of the 12th–13th-c. Hindu Kakatiya empire, it is named after a massive boulder which has religious significance. Warangal is a railway junction trading in cotton, oilseed, grain, and carpets.

**warm front** a meteorological term for the boundary between the warm air at the centre of a depression and the cold air advancing over it. A warm front usually brings an increase in temperature, a change in wind direction, and a change in cloud formation from cirrus to rain-bearing nimbo-stratus.

**Warnham** /ˈwɔːn(ə)m/ a village in West Sussex, southern England, north-west of Horsham. The poet Shelley was born in 1792 at Field Place, one mile to the south.

**Warren** /ˈwɒr(ə)n/ **1.** a northern suburb of Detroit and third-largest city in the US state of Michigan; pop. (1990) 144,860. It developed in the 1930s as a centre of the automobile industry. **2.** an industrial city in north-east Ohio, USA, in the Mahoning valley; pop. (1990) 50,790. Settled in 1799, it developed as a coal- and iron-mining town. Among its chief industries are the manufacture of steel, automobile parts, and electrical goods.

**Warrington** /ˈwɒrɪŋt(ə)n/ an industrial town on the River Mersey in Cheshire, England; pop. (1981) 82,520. It was developed as a new town in 1968. It is noted for soap making and brewing.

**Warrnambool** /ˌwɔːnəmˈbʊl/ a coastal resort and former whaling town in the state of Victoria, south-east Australia, situated on Lady Bay southwest of Melbourne; pop. (1991) 23,950. Its Maritime Village is a leading historic landmark of the state. Between May and October the rare southern right whales make their annual visit to this part of the coast, and in October there is a road race from Melbourne to Warrnambool.

**Warrumbungle National Park** /ˌwɒrəmˈbʌŋg(ə)l/ a national park on the western slopes of the Great Dividing Range in New South Wales, Australia. Situated 490 km. (306 miles) north-west of Sydney, the park protects a diverse scenery stretching from low-lying forest to high peaks covered with snow gums.

**Warsaw** /ˈwɔːsɔː/ (Polish **Warszawa** /vɑːˈʃævə/) the capital of Poland, on the River Vistula, and one of Europe's great historical cities; pop. (1990) 1,655,660. Capital of Poland since 1586, the city was systematically razed to the ground with the loss of 700,000 lives during World War II, but has been painstakingly rebuilt. Warsaw was the birthplace in 1867 of Marie Curie who began her research in the Laboratory of Physical Sciences, and in the Holy Cross Church is buried the heart of the

composer Frédéric Chopin (1810–49) who was born in the village of Zelazowa Wola (58 km., 36 miles west of the city). Warsaw is a major cultural centre; it has a university founded in 1818 and the Polish Academy of Sciences. Amongst its chief industries are the manufacture of steel, vehicles, medicines, scientific instruments, and confectionery.

**Warsaw Pact** a treaty of mutual defence and military aid signed in Warsaw on 14 May 1955 by Communist states of Eastern Europe under Soviet leadership. Established during the era of the Cold War in response to the creation of NATO, it began to break up in 1968 when Albania left and was finally dissolved in February 1991 following the collapse of the Communist system in Russia and Eastern Europe.

**Warta** /ˈvɑː(r)tə/ a river of western Poland that rises north-west of Cracow and flows 808 km. (505 miles) north and west before joining the River Oder on the frontier with Germany.

**Warwick** /ˈwɒrɪk/ the county town of Warwickshire in central England, on the River Avon; pop. (1981) 21,990. Founded in Saxon times, it developed around the great castle of the Earls of Warwick and was largely rebuilt after a fire in 1694. It has a university founded in 1965.

**Warwick** /ˈwɒrɪk/ the second-largest city in Rhode Island, USA, a resort on the Narragansett Bay; pop. (1990) 85,430. It is an industrial and commercial centre with yachting marinas.

**Warwickshire** /ˈwɒrɪkˌʃɪə(r)/ a midland county of England; area 1,980 sq. km. (765 sq. miles); pop. (1991) 477,000; county town, Warwick. Warwickshire is divided into five districts:

| District | Area (sq. km.) | Pop. (1991) |
|---|---|---|
| North Warwickshire | 286 | 59,800 |
| Nuneaton and Bedworth | 79 | 115,300 |
| Rugby | 356 | 83,400 |
| Stratford-on-Avon | 977 | 103,600 |
| Warwick | 282 | 114,900 |

**Wash** /wɒʃ/, **the** an inlet of the North Sea on the east coast of England between Norfolk and Lincolnshire. It receives the Nene, Ouse, Welland, and Witham rivers. Much adjacent land has been reclaimed by dyking and drainage.

**Washington** /ˈwɒʃɪŋt(ə)n/ an industrial town to the west of Sunderland in Tyne and Wear, north-east England, designated a New Town in 1964; pop. (1981) 48,830. Nearby Washington Old Hall was the home of the ancestors of George Washington, first president of the USA.

**Washington** /ˈwɒʃɪŋt(ə)n/ a Pacific state of the USA; area 176,479 sq. km. (68,139 sq. miles); pop. (1990) 4,866,690; capital, Olympia. The largest cities are Seattle, Spokane, and Tacoma. Washington is also known as the Evergreen or Chinook State. Occupied jointly by Britain and the US in the first half of the 19th c., it became the 42nd state of the union in 1889. The state is a major producer of timber, fruit, vegetables, wheat, livestock, fish, and hydroelectric power. Its chief landmarks are Mount Rainier, Mount St. Helens, the Coulee Dam, North Cascades National Park, and the Whitman Mission and Fort Vancouver National Historic Sites. The state is divided into 39 counties:

| County | Area (sq. km.) | Pop. (1990) | County Seat |
|---|---|---|---|
| Adams | 4,995 | 13,600 | Ritzville |
| Asotin | 1,651 | 17,605 | Asotin |
| Benton | 4,459 | 112,560 | Prosser |
| Chelan | 7,582 | 52,250 | Wenatchee |
| Clallam | 4,558 | 56,210 | Port Angeles |
| Clark | 1,630 | 238,050 | Vancouver |
| Columbia | 2,249 | 4,020 | Dayton |
| Cowlitz | 2,964 | 82,120 | Kelso |
| Douglas | 4,724 | 26,205 | Waterville |
| Ferry | 5,720 | 6,295 | Republic |
| Franklin | 3,232 | 37,470 | Pasco |
| Garfield | 1,836 | 2,250 | Pomeroy |
| Grant | 6,916 | 54,800 | Ephrata |
| Grays Harbor | 4,987 | 64,175 | Montesano |
| Island | 551 | 60,195 | Coupville |
| Jefferson | 4,693 | 20,410 | Port Townsend |
| King | 5,533 | 1,507,305 | Seattle |
| Kitsap | 1,022 | 189,730 | Port Orchard |
| Kittitas | 6,001 | 26,725 | Ellensburg |
| Klickitat | 4,888 | 16,620 | Goldendale |
| Lewis | 6,263 | 59,360 | Chehalis |
| Lincoln | 6,006 | 8,860 | Davenport |
| Mason | 2,499 | 38,340 | Shelton |
| Okanogan | 13,731 | 33,350 | Okanogan |
| Pacific | 2,361 | 18,880 | South Bend |
| Pend Orielle | 3,640 | 8,915 | Newport |
| Pierce | 4,355 | 586,200 | Tacoma |
| San Juan | 465 | 10,035 | Friday Harbor |
| Skagit | 4,511 | 79,545 | Mount Vernon |
| Skamania | 4,347 | 8,290 | Stevenson |
| Snohomish | 5,455 | 465,640 | Everett |
| Spokane | 4,581 | 361,330 | Spokane |
| Stevens | 6,422 | 30,950 | Colville |
| Thurston | 1,890 | 161,240 | Olympia |
| Wahkiakum | 679 | 3,330 | Cathlamet |
| Walla Walla | 3,279 | 48,440 | Walla Walla |
| Whatcom | 5,525 | 127,780 | Bellingham |
| Whitman | 5,593 | 38,775 | Colfax |
| Yakima | 11,146 | 188,820 | Yakima |

**Washington, DC** /ˈwɒʃɪŋt(ə)n/ the capital and administrative centre of the USA, coterminous with the District of Columbia; pop. (1990) 606,900. Named after George Washington, in whose presidency it was founded, the city was established in 1790 on land ceded to Congress by Maryland and Virginia. It was planned and partly laid out by a French engineer, Major Pierre Charles L'Enfant, whose work was completed by Major Andrew Ellicott and Benjamin Banneker. Its famous buildings include the Congress building, the Washington Monument and Lincoln Memorial, the Smithsonian Institution, the National Gallery of Art and other museums, the Pentagon, and the White House. Washington is a major cultural centre with five universities and many attractions for the millions of tourists. Its main activity is government service but there are also many business and financial institutions.

**Washita** /ˈwɑːʃətɔː/ a river of south-central USA that rises in north-west Texas and flows eastwards into Texas before turning south-east to join the Red River; length, 1,007 km. (626 miles).

**Waterbury** /ˈwɒtəˌbɜːrɪ/ an industrial town in west Connecticut, USA, on the Naugatuck River south-west of Hartford; pop. (1990) 108,960. Its brass industry, which dates from the 18th c., produces brass goods such as buttons, watches, and clocks.

**waterfall** /ˈwɔːtəˌfɔːl/ a stream or river flowing over a precipice or down a steep hillside, usually occurring where water passes over harder rock to an area of softer rock. The ANGEL FALLS, on a tributary of the Caroni River in Venezuela, is the world's highest waterfall with a total drop of 979 m. (3,212 ft.). The highest waterfall in the UK is EAS COUL AULIN in the Highlands of Scotland (201 m., 658 ft.); the highest in North America is YOSEMITE FALLS (739 m., 2,425 ft.). The Niagara Falls on the USA–Canada frontier has the world's highest mean annual flow of 5,940 cubic metres per second (212,200 cubic feet per second).

**Waterford** /ˈwɑːtəˌfəd/ **1.** a county on the south coast of the Irish Republic, in the province of Munster; area 1,839 sq. km. (710 sq. miles); pop. (1991) 91,600; administrative centre, Dungarvan. **2.** (Gaelic **Port Lairge**) a port in County Waterford at the mouth of the River Suir; pop. (1991) 40,345. Founded by the Danes in 853, it became second in importance to Dublin among Anglo-Norman strongholds. It was the birthplace in 1811 of the actor Charles Keane. Its industries produce processed food, footwear, and its famous colourless flint glass.

**Watergate** /ˈwɔːtəˌɡeɪt/ a building in Washington, DC, housing the offices of the Democratic Party, the scene of a bungled bugging attempt by Republicans during the US election campaign of 1972. The attempted cover-up and subsequent enquiry caused a massive political scandal, gravely weakened the prestige of the government, and finally led to the resignation of President Richard Nixon in August 1974.

**Waterloo** /ˌwɔːtəˈluː/ a village of Brabant in Belgium, situated 18 km. (11 miles) south of Brussels; pop. (1991) 27,860. On 18 June 1815 Napoleon's army was defeated by the British (under the Duke of Wellington) and Prussians. The battlefield can be viewed from the top of the Lion's Mound, a man-made hillock built by the Dutch in 1824–6 with soil obtained when the surrounding land was levelled, and there is a museum in Wellington's former headquarters.

**Waterloo** a town in south-east Ontario, Canada, adjacent to Kitchener; pop. (1991) 71,200. It is the site of the University of Waterloo (1959).

**Waterloo** a city in north-east Iowa, USA, on the Cedar River; pop. (1990) 66,470. Its chief industries are meat packing and the manufacture of farm tractors.

**watershed** the dividing line between drainage basins or river systems. In US parlance it may also be a river basin.

**waterspout** a type of tornado occurring at sea that is made up of a spinning column of water.

## Waterton Lakes National Park
/'wɔ:tət(ə)n/ a national park in the Rocky Mountains of Alberta, Canada. Designated in 1895, it was amalgamated in 1932 with the neighbouring Glacier National Park in the US state of Montana to form the Waterton-Glacier International Peace Park. With a depth of 152 m. (498 ft.) Upper Waterton Lake is the deepest in the Canadian Rockies. The highest peak in the Waterton Lakes National Park is Mount Blakiston (2,940 m., 9,650 ft.).

**Watford** /'wɒtfəd/ an industrial town in Hertfordshire, south-east England, 26 km. (16 miles) north-west of London; pop. (1981) 74,460. Printing and publishing are the chief industries.

**Watling Street** /'wɒtlɪŋ/ a Roman road running north-westwards across England from Richborough in Kent through London and St. Albans to Wroxeter in Shropshire.

**Watts** /wɒts/ an economically depressed residential district of south-central Los Angeles, USA, that gained notoriety in 1965 following a riot that resulted in 34 deaths and extensive damage to property. Its chief landmark is the sculpture known as the Watts Towers, completed in 1954 and built over a period of 35 years by Simon Rodia using old bits of tile and glass.

**Waukegan** /wɒ'ki:g(ə)n/ an industrial city in north-east Illinois, USA, on the shore of Lake Michigan north of Chicago; pop. (1990) 69,390. Established in 1835 on the site of a former French stockade known as the Little Fort, the town's name was changed to Waukegan in 1849. It was the birthplace of the American comedian Jack Benny and the author Ray Bradbury. The Great Lakes Naval Training Center lies to the east.

**Waukesha** /'wɒkəʃɒ/ an industrial city and health resort in south-east Wisconsin, USA, on the Fox River; pop. (1990) 56,960. It bottles spring waters and its industries include engines, bearings, and castings.

**Wave Rock** an unusual 15-metre-high wave-shaped granite rock formation near the town of Hyden in Western Australia.

**Waza National Park** a national park to the south of Lake Chad in the extreme north of Cameroon. Open to tourists during the dry season from November to May, it protects many species of wildlife including lion, elephant, giraffe, hippo, ostrich, gazelle, and antelope.

**Waziristan** /wɑːziːrɪ'stæn/ an arid mountainous region in the North-West Frontier province of Pakistan, on the border with Afghanistan, home of farming Wazir and semi-nomadic Mashud tribes of Pathan descent. When the Durand Line was established as the border between Afghanistan and British India in 1893, Waziristan became an independent territory. It became part of Pakistan in 1947.

**Weald** /'wi:ld/ (also **the Weald**) a formerly wooded district of south-east England including parts of Kent, Surrey, and East and West Sussex. **Wealden** adj. & n.

**Wear** /wɪə(r)/ a river of north-east England that rises in the Pennines and flows c. 100 km. (65 miles) east and north to meet the North Sea at Sunderland.

**Weddell Sea** /'wed(ə)l/ an arm of the South Atlantic Ocean lying adjacent to Antarctica and to the east of the Antarctic Peninsula. It is named after the British navigator, James Weddell (1787–1834) who visited it in 1823.

**Wei** /weɪ/ the name of several dynasties which ruled in China, especially that of 386–535.

**Weifang** /weɪ'fæŋ/ (formerly **Weihsien** /'weɪʃiː,en/) a city to the east of Jinan in the province of Shandong, eastern China; pop. (1986) 310,000.

**Weihai** /weɪ'haɪ/ a city in Shandong province, eastern China, a port on the Yellow Sea; pop. (1986) 226,000.

**Weimar** /'vaɪmɑː(r)/ a town in central Germany; pop. (1991) 59,100. It is famous as the birthplace of the dramatists Goethe (1749–1832) and Schiller (1759–1805) and as the seat of the National Assembly of Germany 1919–33. The **Weimar Republic** of this period was so called because its constitution was drawn up at Weimar.

**Weinan** /weɪ'nɑːn/ a city in Shaanxi province, central China, north-east of Xian; pop. (1986) 709,000.

**Welkom** /'welkəm/ a gold-mining town in central South Africa, in the Orange Free State north-east of Bloemfontein; pop. (1985) 185,500.

**Welland Canal** /'welənd/ a man-made canal on the Great Lakes Waterway in Canada, linking Lake Erie with Lake Ontario. It is 42 km. (26 miles) in length and its eight locks allow ships to bypass the Niagara Falls.

**Wellingborough** /'welɪŋ,bʌrə/ a market and light industrial town in Northamptonshire, central England, at the junction of the Ise and Nene rivers; pop. (1981) 38,770. The parish church of All Hallows is noted for its stained glass.

**Wellington** /'welɪŋt(ə)n/ the capital of New Zealand, situated at the south-western tip of North

Island; pop. (1991) 150,300 (city); 325,680 (urban area). Originally named Port Nicholson when its harbour was first visited by Europeans in 1826, the city was established by the New Zealand Company in 1840 and named after the Duke of Wellington. Many of its major buildings date from the Victorian period. In 1865 the seat of government was moved from Auckland to Wellington. It subsequently developed as a port but being geographically restricted, industrial growth took place in nearby urban areas such as Hutt Valley and the Porirua basin. Its international airport is located at Rangotai, on the narrow isthmus between Evans and Lyall Bays, 6 km. (4 miles) south-east of the city centre. Wellington manufactures vehicles, chemicals, machinery, metal goods, and clothing.

**Wells** /welz/ a city in Somerset, south-west England, the smallest cathedral city in England; pop. (1980) 9,300. Its English Gothic cathedral was built between 1180 and 1340 and its 13th-c. palace of the bishops of Bath and Wells contains the natural wells after which the city is named.

**Wels** /vels/ a market town and light industry centre of Upper Austria in northern Austria, on the River Traun south-west of Linz; pop. (1991) 53,040. In Roman times it was the chief town of the Ovilala district.

**Welsh** /welʃ/ the language of Wales belonging to the Brythonic group of the Celtic languages. It is spoken by about 500,000 people in Wales and has a substantial literature dating from the medieval period. When Wales was united with England in 1536 it seemed likely that Welsh would disappear as a living language, but the publication of a Bible in Welsh in 1588 played an important part in preserving it. Although under great pressure from English, Welsh is widely used and taught in Wales and all official documents are bilingual. It is written phonetically, each letter (except *y*) having one standard sound only.

**Welsh Marches** a name often applied to the countryside on either side of the border between Wales and England.

**Welwyn Garden City** /'welɪn/ an industrial town in Hertfordshire, south-east England, to the north-east of St. Albans; pop. (1981) 41,100. It was founded by Sir Ebenezer Howard in 1920 and designated a New Town in 1948. It is best known for food products.

**Wembley** /'wemblɪ/ a residential district of west London in the outer borough of Brent, south-east England, site of a famous sports stadium.

**Wend** /wend/ (also **Sorb** or **Lusatian**) a member of a Slavic people of western Europe now inhabiting two regions of Germany, the one around Bautzen, the other around Cottbus. They number *c.* 120,000.

**Wensleydale** /'wenzlɪˌdeɪl/ the upper valley of the River Ure above Masham in North Yorkshire,

England. It gives its name to a variety of cheese and a breed of sheep with long wool.

**Wenzhou** /wen'dʒəʊ/ an industrial city in the province of Zhejiang, eastern China, a port on the Qu River; pop. (1986) 519,100. It is a special economic zone trading in agricultural goods.

**Weser** /'veɪzə(r)/ a river of north-west Germany. Formed at the junction of the Werra and Fulda rivers in Lower Saxony, it flows 292 km. (182miles) northwards to meet the North Sea near Bremerhaven.

**Wessex** /'wesɪks/ the kingdom of the West Saxons, established in Hampshire in the early 6th c. and gradually extended by conquest to include much of southern England. Under Alfred the Great and his successors it formed the nucleus for the Anglo-Saxon kingdom of England. The name was revived by Thomas Hardy to designate the south-western counties of England (especially Dorset) in which his novels are set, and is used in the titles of certain present-day regional authorities.

**West Bank** a region west of the River Jordan and north-west of the Dead Sea which became part of Jordan in 1948 and was occupied by Israel in the Six-Day War of 1967; area 5,879 sq. km. (2,270 sq. miles); pop. (1989) 915,000. Its chief town is Jericho and 97 per cent of its people are Palestinian Arabs.

**West Bengal** a state in eastern India to the south of Sikkim and Bhutan, formed in 1947 from the Hindu area of former Bengal; area 87,853 sq. km. (33,933 sq. miles); pop. (1991) 67,982,730; capital, Calcutta. Its chief products are coal, rice, oilseeds, wheat, jute, fish, and tea.

**West Bromwich** /'brɒmɪtʃ/ an industrial town to the north-west of Birmingham in the West Midlands, central England; pop. (1981) 154,530. It has oil refining, chemicals, and light industries.

**West Coast** an administrative region of South Island New Zealand, between the Southern Alps and the Tasman Sea; pop. (1991) 35,380. It comprises the districts of Westland, Grey, Buller, and part of Tasman; chief settlements include Greymouth and Westport.

**West Country** the collective name for the counties of Cornwall, Devon, Somerset, Avon, Wiltshire, and the western half of Dorset in south-west England. Now a popular place for the English to go on vacation, it is historically associated with the West Saxons, who invaded the region at the end of the 5th c., and with the legends of King Arthur.

**West Covina** a city to the west of Pomona in the Los Angeles conurbation, south-west California; pop. (1990) 96,090.

**West End** a name applied to the western part of central London, north of the Thames, associated with department stores, clubs, and theatre entertainment.

**Westerham** /'westɜːˌhəm/ a small town in the North Downs of Kent, south-east England, birthplace in 1727 of General James Wolfe who captured Quebec from the French in 1759. Chartwell, the home of Sir Winston Churchill, is nearby.; pop. (1981) 3,390.

**westerlies** winds blowing from the west, most often occurring in mid-latitudes. In the northern hemisphere they are usually more variable in force and direction than in the southern hemisphere. See ROARING FORTIES.

**Western Australia** a state comprising the western part of Australia; area 2,525,500 sq. km. (975,473 sq. miles); pop. (1991) 1,650,600; capital, Perth. It was first settled by the British in 1826 and 1829, and was federated with the other states of Australia in 1901. Iron ore, nickel, bauxite, and gold are amongst its chief mineral resources. Sheep, wheat, and fruit are the principal agricultural products.

**Western Cape** a province of South Africa created in 1994 from part of the former Cape Province. Its capital is Cape Town.

**Western Desert** that part of the Libyan Desert of North Africa in western and central Egypt. Its name is particularly associated with heavy fighting between Allied forces and the Axis powers during World War II.

**Western Ghats** see GHATS.

**Western Hemisphere** the half of the earth containing the Americas.

**Western Isles** 1. a general name given to the Hebridean islands off the west coast of Scotland; 2. an administrative islands area of Scotland consisting of the Outer Hebrides; area 2,898 sq. km. (1,119 sq. miles); pop. (1991) 29,110; administrative centre, Stornoway.

**Western Sahara** a former Spanish colony (Spanish Sahara) on the Atlantic coast of north-west Africa; area 252,126 sq. km. (97,383 sq. miles); pop. (est. 1989) 186,500 (within the  area controlled by Morocco); capital, La'youn (El Aaiún). It has the world's largest deposits of phosphate rock. Annexed by Morocco and Mauritania in 1976 after it had ceased to become a Spanish province, Mauritania withdrew from the territory in 1979 and Morocco extended its control over the entire region. A liberation movement (*Frente Polisario*), which launched a guerrilla war against the Spanish in 1973, has continued its struggle against Morocco in an attempt to establish an independent Saharawi Arab Democratic Republic.

**Western Samoa** /səˈməʊə/ official name **The State of Western Samoa** a country consisting of a group of islands in the south-west Pacific; area 2,842 sq. km. (1,098 sq miles); pop. (1991) 159,860;  official languages, Samoan and English; capital, Apia. It comprises the volcanic and mountainous islands of Savai'i, Upola, Manono, and Apolima and several small uninhabited islets. They have a tropical marine climate with a wet season from December to April. The chief exports are coconut products, taro, cocoa, fruit juice, beer, and cigarettes. Discovered by the Dutch in the early 18th c., the islands were administered by Germany from 1900. After World War I they were mandated to New Zealand (1920), and became an independent republic in 1962. Robert Louis Stevenson settled there in 1890 and died at Apia in 1894. The head of state (the *O le Ao O le Malo*) acts as a constitutional monarch with the power to dissolve the unicameral legislative assembly (*Fono*) whose members are confined to elected clan leaders (*Matai*).

**Western Somalia** see OGADEN, THE.

**Westerwald** /'vest(ə)r vɑːlt/ a mountain range in west Germany that rises east of the Rhine to an altitude of 656 m. (2,152 ft.) at Fuchskauten.

**West Flanders** (Flemish **West-Vlaanderen** /vest'flɑːndər(ə)n/) a province of western Belgium, on the North Sea coast; area 3,134 sq. km. (1,210 sq. miles); pop. (1991) 1,106,830; capital, Bruges.

**West Glamorgan** a county of South Wales; area 820 sq. km. (317 sq. miles); pop. (1991) 357,800; county town, Swansea. It is divided into four districts:

| District | Area (sq. km.) | Pop. (1991) |
| --- | --- | --- |
| Lliw Valley | 217 | 61,700 |
| Neath | 204 | 64,100 |
| Port Talbot | 152 | 49,900 |
| Swansea | 246 | 182,100 |

**West Ham** a district of east London, south-east England, to the north of the River Thames in the inner borough of Newham. It was the birthplace in 1827 of Joseph Lister who introduced the use of the antiseptic to surgery in 1860.

**West Highland Way** a long-distance footpath in the western highlands of Scotland, stretching 150 km. (95 miles) from Milngavie near Glasgow to Fort William. Opened in 1980, it was the first long-distance footpath to be created in Scotland.

**West Indies** a chain of islands extending from the south coast of Florida in North America to

that of Venezuela in South America, enclosing the Caribbean Sea. Visited by Columbus in 1492 and named in the belief that he had discovered the Asian coast, the islands were opened up by the Spanish in the 16th c. and thereafter were the theatre of rivalry between the European colonial powers. Cultivation of sugar was introduced and the population was transformed by the mass importation of West African slaves to work the agricultural plantations; their descendants form the largest group in the population.
**West Indian** *adj. & n.*

**West Irian** SEE IRIAN JAYA.

**West Malvern** /ˈmɔːlvɜːn/ a village in the Malvern Hills of Hereford and Worcester, England, to the west of Great Malvern. Dr. Roget, author of *The Thesaurus of English Words and Phrases* (1852) is buried in the churchyard.

**Westman Islands** /ˈwestmən/ (Icelandic **Vestmannaeyjar**) a group of 15 volcanic islands to the south of Iceland; pop. (1991) 4,925.

**Westmeath** /westˈmiːθ/ a county of the Irish Republic, in the province of Leinster, north-east of the River Shannon; area 1,764 sq. km. (681 sq. miles); pop. (1991) 61,880; county town, Mullingar.

**West Midlands** a metropolitan county of central England; area 899 sq. km. (347 sq. miles); pop. (1991) 2,500,400; county town, Birmingham. It is divided into seven districts:

| District | Area (sq. km.) | Pop. (1991) |
| --- | --- | --- |
| Birmingham | 266 | 934,900 |
| Coventry | 96 | 292,600 |
| Dudley | 98 | 300,400 |
| Sandwell | 86 | 282,000 |
| Solihull | 179 | 195,100 |
| Walsall | 106 | 255,600 |
| Wolverhampton | 69 | 239,800 |

**Westminster** /ˈwestmɪnstə(r)/ (in full **City of Westminster**) an inner borough of London, England, containing the Houses of Parliament and many government offices, etc. Its name is used allusively to mean British parliamentary life or politics; pop. (1991) 181,500.

**Westminster, Palace of** a palace, supposed to date from Edward the Confessor, on the site now occupied by the Houses of Parliament in London. It was damaged by fire in 1512 and ceased to be a royal residence, but a great part of it remained. The Houses of Lords and Commons for a long time sat in its buildings, until these were destroyed by fire in 1834.

**Westminster Abbey** the collegiate church of St. Peter in Westminster, London, originally the abbey church of a Benedictine monastery. The present building, begun by Henry III in 1245 and altered and added to by successive rulers, replaced an earlier church built by Edward the Confessor.

Nearly all the kings and queens of Britain have been crowned in Westminster Abbey; it is also the burial place of many of Britain's monarchs (up to George II) and of the nation's leading statesmen, poets (in the section called Poet's Corner), and other celebrities, and of the Unknown Warrior.

**Westmorland** /ˈwestmɜːlænd/ a former county of north-west England. In 1974 it was united with Cumberland and northern parts of Lancashire to form the county of Cumbria.

**Weston-super-Mare** /ˌwestən ˌsuːpə ˈmeə(r)/ a resort town on the Bristol Channel in the county of Avon, south-west England; pop. (1981) 62,260. It developed from a fishing village into a spa town during the 19th c. and has a grand pier completed in 1904.

**West Orange** /ˈɔːr(ə)ndʒ/ a town near Newark in the US state of New Jersey, site of a laboratory built in 1887 by Thomas Edison (inventor of the light bulb) and used by him for 44 years; pop. (1990) 39,100.

**West Palm Beach** a city in south-east Florida, USA, a resort on Lake Worth opposite Palm Beach; pop. (1990) 67,640.

**Westphalia** /westˈfeɪlɪə/ a former province of north-west Germany which from 1815 formed part of Prussia, now part of the German state of North Rhine-Westphalia; capital, Düsseldorf. The peace of Westphalia (1648) ended the Thirty Years War.
**Westphalian** *adj. & n.*

**West Point** (in full **West Point Academy**) the US Military Academy, founded in 1802, located on the site of a former strategic fort on the west bank of the Hudson River in New York State.

**Westport** a fashionable community to the east of New York City, USA, on Long Island Sound, Connecticut; pop. (1990) 24,410. Many well-known writers, actors, and executives have their home here.

**West Side** the western part of any of several North American cities or boroughs, especially the island borough of Manhattan, New York.

**West Sussex** /ˈsʌsɪks/ a county of south-east England; area 1,989 sq. km. (768 sq. miles); pop. (1991) 692,800; county town, Chichester. It is divided into seven districts:

| District | Area (sq. km.) | Pop. (1991) |
| --- | --- | --- |
| Adur | 42 | 57,400 |
| Arun | 221 | 127,700 |
| Chichester | 787 | 100,300 |
| Crawley | 44 | 87,100 |
| Horsham | 530 | 107,300 |
| Mid Sussex | 333 | 118,800 |
| Worthing | 33 | 94,100 |

**West Virginia** /vəˈdʒɪnɪə/ a state of the USA, to the west of Virginia; area 62,759 sq. km. (24,231 sq. miles); pop. (1990) 1,793,480; capital, Charleston. It is also known as the Mountain State. It separated from Virginia during the American Civil War (1861), and became the 35th state of the US in 1863. Its industries produce coal, gas, steel, aluminium, glass, timber, and chemicals and amongst its chief landmarks are the New River Gorge and Harpers Ferry. West Virginia is divided into 55 counties:

| County | Area (sq. km.) | Pop. (1990) | County Seat |
|---|---|---|---|
| Barbour | 892 | 15,700 | Philippi |
| Berkeley | 835 | 59,250 | Marlinsburg |
| Boone | 1,308 | 25,870 | Madison |
| Braxton | 1,334 | 13,000 | Sutton |
| Brooke | 234 | 26,990 | Wellsburg |
| Cabell | 733 | 96,830 | Huntington |
| Calhoun | 728 | 7,885 | Grantsville |
| Clay | 900 | 9,980 | Clay |
| Doddridge | 835 | 6,990 | West Union |
| Fayette | 1,734 | 47,950 | Fayetteville |
| Gilmer | 884 | 7,670 | Glenville |
| Grant | 1,248 | 10,430 | Petersburg |
| Greenbrier | 2,665 | 34,690 | Lewisburg |
| Hampshire | 1,674 | 16,500 | Romney |
| Hancock | 218 | 35,230 | New Cumberland |
| Hardy | 1,521 | 10,980 | Moorefield |
| Harrison | 1,084 | 69,370 | Clarksburg |
| Jackson | 1,206 | 25,940 | Ripley |
| Jefferson | 543 | 35,930 | Charles Town |
| Kanawha | 2,343 | 207,620 | Charleston |
| Lewis | 1,011 | 17,220 | Weston |
| Lincoln | 1,141 | 21,380 | Hamlin |
| Logan | 1,186 | 43,030 | Logan |
| McDowell | 1,391 | 35,230 | Welch |
| Marion | 811 | 57,250 | Fairmont |
| Marshall | 793 | 37,360 | Moundsville |
| Mason | 1,126 | 25,180 | Point Pleasant |
| Mercer | 1,092 | 64,980 | Princeton |
| Mineral | 855 | 26,700 | Keyser |
| Mingo | 1,102 | 33,740 | Williamson |
| Monongalia | 944 | 75,510 | Morgantown |
| Monroe | 1,230 | 12,410 | Union |
| Morgan | 598 | 12,130 | Berkeley Springs |
| Nicholas | 1,690 | 26,775 | Summersville |
| Ohio | 276 | 50,870 | Wheeling |
| Pendleton | 1,815 | 8,050 | Franklin |
| Pleasants | 341 | 7,550 | St. Marys |
| Pocahontas | 2,449 | 9,010 | Marlinton |
| Preston | 1,693 | 29,040 | Kingwood |
| Putnam | 900 | 42,835 | Winfield |
| Raleigh | 1,581 | 76,820 | Beckley |
| Randolph | 2,704 | 27,800 | Elkins |
| Ritchie | 1,180 | 10,230 | Harrisville |
| Roane | 1,258 | 15,120 | Spencer |
| Summers | 918 | 14,200 | Hinton |
| Taylor | 452 | 15,140 | Grafton |
| Tucker | 1,095 | 7,730 | Parsons |
| Tyler | 671 | 9,800 | Middlebourne |
| Upshur | 923 | 22,870 | Buckhannon |
| Wayne | 1,321 | 41,640 | Wayne |
| Webster | 1,446 | 10,730 | Webster Springs |
| Wetzel | 933 | 19,260 | New Martinsville |
| Wirt | 611 | 5,190 | Elizabeth |
| Wood | 954 | 86,915 | Parkersburg |
| Wyoming | 1,305 | 28,990 | Pineville |

**Westward Ho** /ˌwestwəd 'həʊ/ a resort village on the north coast of Devon, south-west England, 3 km. (2 miles) north-west of Bideford. It was named after the novel by the Devonshire writer, Charles Kingsley, published in 1855.

**Westwood Village** /'westwuːd/ a district of the Los Angeles conurbation in south-west California, USA, situated to the north of the Santa Monica Boulevard. It is the site of the campus of the University of California at Los Angeles and in its Memorial Cemetery are buried the film stars Marilyn Monroe, Natalie Wood, and Peter Lorre.

**West Yorkshire** a metropolitan county of northern England; area 2,036 sq. km. (786 sq. miles); pop. (1991) 1,984,700; county town, Wakefield. It is divided into five districts:

| District | Area (sq. km.) | Pop. (1991) |
|---|---|---|
| Bradford | 367 | 449,100 |
| Calderdale | 364 | 187,300 |
| Kirklees | 410 | 367,600 |
| Leeds | 562 | 674,400 |
| Wakefield | 333 | 303,300 |

**Wethersfield** /'weðəzˌfiːld/ a town in central Connecticut, USA, to the south of Hartford on the Connecticut River; pop. (1990) 25,650. Settled in 1634, it developed as a commercial centre trading between the American colonies and the West Indies.

**Weymouth** /'weɪməθ/ a seaside resort town in Dorset on the south coast of England; pop. (1981) 38,400. The town became a fashionable resort after it was visited by George III. There are ferry links with France and the Channel Islands.

**Wexford** /'weksfəd/ **1.** a county in south-east Ireland, in the province of Leinster to the south of the Wicklow Mountains; area 2,352 sq. km. (908 sq. miles); pop. (1991) 102,040. **2.** its county town, at the mouth of the River Slaney; pop. (1991) 9,540.

**Whangarei** /ˌwæŋɡə'reɪ/ a port on the east coast of Northland region, North Island, New Zealand, situated at the head of Whangarei Harbour on the Hatea River; pop. (1991) 44,180. Settled by Scots in 1839, it gradually expanded after the building of a shipyard in the 1860s and the completion of rail and road links with Auckland by the 1930s. It is the principal marketing centre of a dairy farming and timber milling region, with industries that include brewing, and the manufacture of glass, fertilizer, and textiles.

**Wharfedale** /'wɔːfdeɪl/ the name given to the middle reaches of the River Wharfe to the north of Bradford and Leeds. The Wharfe rises in Langstrothdale Chase, North Yorkshire and flows south-eastwards to meet the River Ouse south of York.

**Wheaton** /'wiːt(ə)n/ a residential city in north-east Illinois, USA, to the west of Chicago; pop.

(1990) 51,460. It is the headquarters of about two dozen religious publishers and organizations and was the hometown of Elbert Gary, founder of the steel city of Gary in Indiana.

**Whisky Trail** the name given to a tourist route in Grampian Region, north-east Scotland that passes through the towns of Tomintoul, Archiestown, Rothes, Keith, and Dufftown. The six malt whisky distilleries of Glenfiddich, Strathisla, Glen Grant, Tamdhu, Glenfarclas, and The Glenlivet are located on this route.

**Whitby** /'wɪtbɪ/ a resort town and former whaling port on the North Sea coast of North Yorkshire, England, at the mouth of the River Esk; pop. (1981) 13,380. There are remains of a 13th-c. abbey built on the site of a former abbey destroyed by Danes in the 9th c. A conference, known as the Synod of Whitby, held here in 664 chiefly to settle the method of calculating the date of Easter, resulted in England severing its connections with the Irish Church. The explorer Captain James Cook served his apprenticeship in Whitby.

**White** /waɪt/ a river of east-central USA that rises in the Boston Mts. of north-west Arkansas and flows 1,102 km. (685 miles) in a loop north through Beaver Lake into Missouri and then south-east into Arkansas again where it joins the Mississippi River near its junction with the Arkansas River.

**Whitechapel** /'waɪttʃæp(ə)l/ a district in the East End of London, to the east of the Tower of London. During Victorian times it had a notorious reputation as a slum area that came to be associated with Jack the Ripper and the 'Whitechapel murders' of 1888.

**Whitehall** /'waɪthɔːl/ a street in Westminster, London, in which many important government offices are located, whence the allusive use of its name to refer to the British government or its offices or policy. The name is taken from the former royal palace of White Hall, originally a residence of Cardinal Wolsey confiscated by Henry VIII.

**Whitehorse** /'waɪthɔːs/ the capital (since 1953) of Yukon Territory in north-west Canada, situated on the Yukon River at the junction of the Alaska and Klondike highways; pop. (1991) 21,650. Established as a rail terminus by gold prospectors following the 1897 gold-rush, Whitehorse was linked by ore-carrying sternwheelers to the territory's former capital Dawson which lay down river. It was named after the white foaming rapids (which resembled white rearing horses) that used to exist before the damming of the Sunwapta Lakes.

**White House** the official residence of the US President in Washington, DC. It was built in 1792–9 of greyish-white limestone from designs of the Irish-born architect James Hoban (1762–1831) on a site chosen by George Washington; President John Adams took up residence there in 1800. The building was restored in 1814 after being burnt by British troops, the smoke-stained walls being painted white. Although known informally as the White House from the early 19th c., it was not formally so designated until the time of Theodore Roosevelt (1902).

**White Nile** (Arabic **Bahr el Ablad**) that part of the upper Nile River that flows from Uganda through southern Sudan before meeting the Blue Nile at Khartoum.

**White Russia** see BELORUSSIA (Belarus).

**White Sands** a desert in New Mexico, USA, situated in the Tularosa Valley between the San Andres and Sacramento mountains. Designated a national monument in 1933 and extending over 780 sq. km. (300 sq. miles), its white sand is derived from gypsum.

**White Sea** (Russian **Beloye More** /ˌbelərə 'mɔːrə/) an inlet of the Barents Sea on the north-west coast of Russia that receives the Northern Dvina and Onega rivers. Its chief port is Archangel.

**Whitney** /'hwɪtnɪ/, **Mount** a mountain in the Sierra Nevada, California, the highest peak in continental USA. It was named after the Yale-trained geologist Josiah Dwight Whitney, who was appointed first director of the California State Geological Service in 1860. Rising to 4,418 m. (14,495 ft.), its summit can be reached following the John Muir Trail from Yosemite Valley or the Mount Whitney Trail from Whitney Portal.

**Whittier** /'wɪtɪə(r)/ a city in the Los Angeles conurbation, south-west California, at the foot of the Puente Hills; pop. (1990) 77,670. Founded by Quakers in 1887, it was named after the poet John Greenleaf Whittier. It was the birthplace in 1913 of Richard Nixon, 37th president of the USA. It manufactures parts for the aerospace and automobile industries.

**Whyalla** /waɪ'ælə/ a steel-manufacturing town on the Spencer Gulf in South Australia; pop. (1991) 25,525. Founded in the early 1900s as a company town by the Broken Hill Proprietary Co. Ltd., it was developed as an outlet for iron ore from the Middleback Ranges. Between 1939 and 1978 it was also an important centre of shipbuilding, the largest ship ever built in Australia being launched here in 1972.

**WI** *abbr.* US Wisconsin (in official postal use).

**Wichita** /'wɪtʃətɔː/ a commercial and industrial city in southern Kansas, USA, on the Arkansas River; pop. (1990) 304,010. Founded in 1868 on the site of a Wichita Indian village, it developed as a 'cow town' through which cattle were driven on their way to the railhead at Abilene. It further expanded as a centre of the wheat trade and with the discovery of oil to become the largest city in Kansas. It has a large aircraft industry, oil refineries, and meat-packing plants, and manufactures oil-field equipment.

**Wichita** /ˈwɪtʃətɔː/ a North American Indian tribe of the Caddoan linguistic group formerly occupying the plains and prairies of Oklahoma, Arkansas, and Texas.

**Wichita Falls** /ˈwɪtʃətɔː fɔːlz/ an industrial town in northern Texas, USA, on the Witchita River; pop. (1990) 96,259. Founded in 1882, its industries include the manufacture of plate glass, oil field equipment, electronic components. Livestock, wheat, oil, and cotton are traded.

**Wick** /wɪk/ a town on the north-east coast of Scotland, administrative headquarters of Caithness District, Highland Region; pop. (1981) 7,900.

**Wicklow** /ˈwɪkləʊ/ **1.** a county of eastern Ireland, in the province of Leinster; area 2,025 sq. km. (782 sq. miles); pop. (1991) 97,290. **2.** its county town, a resort on the Irish Sea to the south of Dublin; pop. (1991) 5,850.

**Widecombe-in-the-Moor** /ˈwɪdək(ə)m/ a village at the centre of Dartmoor in Devon, south-west England, whose fair was celebrated in a famous song, *Widdecombe Fair*.

**Widnes** /ˈwɪdnɪs/ a town in Cheshire, England, to the east of Liverpool on the River Mersey; pop. (1981) 55,930. It has chemical industries.

**Wien** /viːn/ see VIENNA.

**Wiener Neustadt** /ˈviːnə(r) ˈnɔɪʃtɑːt/ an industrial town of Lower Austria, north-eastern Austria, south of Vienna and west of Eisenstadt; pop. (1991) 35,270. It has heavy machinery, vehicle, and textile industries.

**Wiesbaden** /ˈviːsbɑːd(ə)n/ the capital of the state of Hesse in western Germany, situated on the River Rhine at the foot of the Taunus Mountains; pop. (1991) 264,020. Founded as a Celtic settlement, it became a popular Roman spa known as Aquae Mattiacorum. In 1806 it was made capital of Nassau and in 1866 it passed to Prussia. It is now an important spa and conference centre with industries producing chemicals, textiles, and metal goods.

**Wigan** /ˈwɪg(ə)n/ a town in the Greater Manchester metropolitan county, north-west England; pop. (1981) 88,900. On the site of a Roman fort, it was a market town in medieval times before being transformed by the Industrial Revolution into a textile, engineering, and coal-mining centre. Now a centre of light industries.

**Wight** /waɪt/, **Isle of** see ISLE OF WIGHT.

**Wight** /waɪt/ a shipping forecast area covering the English Channel roughly between the Strait of Dover and the meridian of Pool.

**Wigtownshire** /ˈwɪgtaʊnʃɪə(r)/ a former county of south-west Scotland. It became part of the region of Dumfries and Galloway in 1975.

**Wildspitze** /ˈvɪltʃpɪtsə/ a mountain in the Otztal Alps of Tyrol in western Austria. Rising to 3,774 m. (12,382 ft.), it is the second-highest peak in Austria.

**Wilhelm** /ˈvɪlhelm/, **Mount** a mountain in the Western Highlands of Papua New Guinea, to the south-west of Madang, rising to a height of 4,509 m. (14,793 ft.). Approached from Kegusugl, it is the highest peak in the country.

**Wilhelmshaven** /ˈvɪlhelmzˌhɑːv(ə)n/ a resort, seaport, and naval base to the west of Bremerhaven in Lower Saxony, west Germany; pop. (1991) 91,150. It has important oil-importing and petrochemical industries.

**Wilkes Land** /wɪlks/ an area of Antarctica, bordering the Southern Ocean and lying between Queen Mary Land to the west and Terre Adélie to the east. Claimed by Australia, it is named after the American naval officer Charles Wilkes (1798–1877), who first sighted and surveyed it.

**Willemstad** /ˈvɪləmˌstɑːt/ the capital of the Netherlands Antilles, situated on the south-west coast of the island of Curaçao; pop. (1986) 50,000. It is a port of call for cruise ships and a centre of oil refining. The Mikve Israel-Emanuel synagogue, which dates from 1732, is said to be the oldest in the Western Hemisphere.

**Williamsburg** /ˈwɪliəmzˌbɜːg/ a historic colonial town in south-east Virginia, USA, between the James and York rivers; pop. (1990) 11,530. First settled in 1633 and originally known as Middle Plantation, it was chosen as the site of the William and Mary College in 1693. It was the state capital of Virginia 1699–1779 and was renamed in honour of William III. A large section of the early colonial town has been restored to its 18th-c. appearance.

**Wilmington** /ˈwɪlmɪŋt(ə)n/ **1.** the largest city in the US state of Delaware, situated on the Delaware River; pop. (1990) 71,530. Founded by Swedes in 1631, it was subsequently occupied by Dutch and English settlers who developed the site as a market town and shipping centre. Industrial products include chemicals, automobiles, vulcanized fibre, and dyed cotton. **2.** the chief port of North Carolina, USA, situated on the Cape Fear River c. 48 km. (30 miles) from its mouth; pop. (1990) 55,530. It was the largest town in North Carolina and the principal Atlantic port of the Confederacy during the American Civil War. It is a resort and sports fishing centre with numerous light industries.

**Wilton** /ˈwɪltən/ a town in Wiltshire, south-west England, situated to the west of Salisbury at the junction of the Nadder and Wylye rivers. Noted since the 16th c. for its carpet industry, it was formerly the capital of Wiltshire. Its chief landmark is Wilton House built to a design by Inigo Jones and John Webb in 1653.

**Wiltshire** /ˈwɪltʃɪə(r)/ a county of south-west England; area 3,479 sq. km. (1,344 sq. miles); pop. (1991) 553,300; county town, Trowbridge. It is divided into five districts:

| District | Area (sq. km.) | Pop. (1991) |
|----------|----------------|-------------|
| Kennet | 958 | 67,500 |
| North Wiltshire | 768 | 109,600 |
| Salisbury | 1,005 | 103,200 |
| Thamesdown | 230 | 167,200 |
| West Wiltshire | 517 | 105,900 |

**Wimbledon** /'wɪmb(ə)ld(ə)n/ a residential suburb of London, the most famous of all lawn tennis centres, containing the headquarters of the All England Lawn Tennis and Croquet Club, scene of the 'Lawn Tennis Championships on Grass', the oldest tournament of this kind, since 1877.

**Wimmera** /'wɪmərə/, **the** a wheat-growing area of western Victoria, Australia, that takes its name from an Aboriginal word for spear-thrower. Its chief settlements are Horsham and Warracknabeal.

**Winchester** /'wɪntʃəstə(r)/ the county town of Hampshire in southern England, a city on the River Itchen; pop. (1981) 35,660. Known to the Romans as Venta Belgarum, it became capital of the Anglo-Saxon kingdom of Wessex (519) and later capital of England under Alfred the Great (827). Its 11th-c. cathedral, the second-longest in Europe, is the burial place of Jane Austen and Izaak Walton, and Winchester College, founded by William Wykeham in 1382, is one of the oldest public schools in England. King Arthur's so-called Round Table hangs in the 13th-c. Great Hall of the castle. The reburial of St. Swithin, Bishop of Winchester, in the new cathedral, an event scheduled to take place on 15 July 971, was said to have been delayed by prolonged heavy rain, hence the belief that if it rains on 15 July it will continue to rain for 40 days. The *Domesday Book* was compiled in Winchester.

**Windermere** /'wɪndə,mɪə(r)/ (also **Lake Windermere**) a lake in Cumbria, in the south-east part of the the Lake District of north-west England. At about 17 km. (10 miles) in length, it is the largest lake in England. It is linked to Morecambe Bay by the River Leven and the town of Windermere lies on its eastern shore.

**Windhoek** /'vɪnthuːk/ the capital of Namibia, situated at an altitude of 1,650 m. (5,410 ft.) 300 km. (190 miles) east of Walvis Bay; pop. (1992) 58,600. Originally the seat of a Namaqualand chief, it was made capital of the German colony of South West Africa in 1892 and capital of the independent state of Namibia in 1990. It retains some German influence in its cultural life and buildings. Industries include meat canning, brewing, the making of bone meal, and dressing of lamb skins.

**Windscale** /'wɪndskeɪl/ the name of an industrial site in Cumbria, north-west England, from 1947 to 1981 (known before and after these dates as SELLAFIELD) that became synonymous with the development of nuclear power in Britain, having produced plutonium for weapons and later for the atomic energy programme. In October 1957 a serious fire developed in a reactor there, causing an escape of radioactivity; it was the world's worst nuclear accident until that at Chernobyl in 1986.

**Windsor** /'wɪnsə(r)/ an industrial city in Ontario, Canada, situated on the Detroit River opposite the US city of Detroit; pop. (1991) 191,400; 260,700 (metropolitan area). It is a centre of motor vehicle and pharmaceutical manufacture and a port on the Great Lakes waterway.

**Windsor** /'wɪnsə(r)/ a town in Berkshire, southern England, on the River Thames opposite Eton; pop. (1981) 31,540. Its castle, which is the chief royal residence, was built by William the Conqueror; St. George's Chapel contains the tombs of English kings including Henry VIII, Charles I, and Edward VII, and in the Home Park stands the Frogmore Mausoleum, the burial place of Queen Victoria and Prince Albert.

**Windward Islands** a group of islands in the eastern Caribbean which constitute the southern part of the Lesser Antilles. The largest are Dominica, Martinique, St. Lucia, and Barbados. Their name refers to the fact that they are nearest to the direction of the prevailing winds, which are easterly.

**Winnebago** /wɪnə'beɪgəʊ/ a North American Indian tribe of the Siouan-Chiwere linguistic group formerly occupying territory to the west of Lake Michigan. Between 1828 and 1840 they were moved from Wisconsin to Minnesota but later they were to be found in Nebraska and Wisconsin.

**Winnebago** /wɪnə'beɪgəʊ/ a lake in eastern Wisconsin, USA, on the Fox River; area 557 sq. km. (215 sq. miles).

**Winnetka** /wɪ'netkə/ a residential town in north-east Illinois, USA, on the shore of Lake Michigan north of Chicago; pop. (1990) 12,170. Settled in 1829, it was named in 1854 after an Indian word meaning 'beautiful land'.

**Winnipeg** /'wɪnɪ,peg/ the capital of Manitoba, and the largest city of the prairie provinces of central Canada; pop. (1991) 652,350 (metropolitan area). Established as a trading post in 1821–2 by the Hudson's Bay Company, it is situated at the junction of the Assiniboine and Red rivers which together formed the main routeway followed by early fur traders. In 1882 it became an important stop and outlet for grain on the east–west Canadian Pacific railroad and in the years prior to World War I it attracted large numbers of European immigrants. It has two universities including the University of Manitoba which was founded here in 1877, a ballet company, and symphony orchestra. It is one of the world's largest grain markets and has grain elevators, flour mills, and food-processing plants.

**Winnipeg** /'wɪnɪ,peg/, **Lake** a large lake in Manitoba, Canada, north of the city of Winnipeg; area 24,387 sq. km. (9,416 sq. miles). A remnant of the glacial Lake Agassiz, it is the third-largest lake in Canada. It receives the Red, Saskatchewan, and Winnipeg rivers and is drained by the Nelson River which flows north-eastwards to Hudson Bay.

**Winnipegosis** /ˌwɪnɪpeɡˈəʊsɪs/, **Lake** a lake to the west of Lake Winnipeg in western Manitoba, Canada; area 5,374 sq. km. (2,075 sq. miles). It is fed by the Red Deer and Swan rivers, and drains into Lake Manitoba.

**Winona** /wɪˈnəʊnə/ a town in south-east Minnesota, USA, on the west bank of the Mississippi River; pop. (1990) 25,400. Settled in 1851 by New Englanders and Germans, it developed from a lumbering town into an industrial centre making heavy road equipment.

**Winter Palace** the former Russian imperial residence in St. Petersburg, stormed in the Revolution of 1917, later used as a museum and art gallery.

**Winterthur** /ˈvɪntəˌtʊə(r)/ an industrial and cultural town in Zurich canton, northern Switzerland; pop. (1990) 85,680. It manufactures railway engines, textiles, and clothing.

**Wirral** /ˈwɪrəl/, **the** the name given to the narrow peninsula to the north of Chester, which separates the mouth of the River Dee from the Mersey estuary.

**Wisbech** /ˈwɪzbiːtʃ/ a fenland town in Cambridgeshire, east-central England, on the River Nene south-west of King's Lynn; pop. (1981) 23,190. It lies at the centre of a fruit and bulb growing area and has many Dutch-style buildings. Wisbech was the home of the crime writer Dorothy L. Sayers from 1929 until her death in 1957.

**Wisconsin** /wɪsˈkɒnsɪn/ a state in the northern USA to the east of the Mississippi River, bordering on Lakes Superior and Michigan; area 145,436 sq. km. (56,153 sq. miles); pop. (1990) 4,891,770; capital, Madison. The largest cities are Milwaukee and Madison. It is also known as the Badger State. Dairy farming and the manufacture of automobiles, machinery, paper, and beer are among its chief industries. Ceded to Britain by the French in 1763 and acquired by the USA in 1783, it became the 30th state of the USA in 1848. Its chief landmarks are the Apostle Islands, the Ice Age National Scientific Reserve, and the St. Croix National Scenic Riverway. Wisconsin is divided into 72 counties:

| County | Area (sq. km.) | Pop (1990) | County Seat |
|---|---|---|---|
| Adams | 1,685 | 15,680 | Friendship |
| Ashland | 2,725 | 16,310 | Ashland |
| Barron | 2,249 | 40,750 | Barron |
| Bayfield | 3,801 | 14,010 | Washburn |
| Brown | 1,362 | 194,590 | Green Bay |
| Buffalo | 1,817 | 13,580 | Alma |
| Burnett | 2,127 | 13,080 | Grantsburg |
| Calumet | 848 | 34,290 | Chilton |
| Chippewa | 2,644 | 52,360 | Chippewa Falls |
| Clark | 3,167 | 31,650 | Neillsville |
| Columbia | 2,005 | 45,090 | Portage |
| Crawford | 1,472 | 15,940 | Prairie du Chien |
| Dane | 3,133 | 367,085 | Madison |
| Dodge | 2,306 | 76,560 | Juneau |
| Door | 1,279 | 25,690 | Sturgeon Bay |
| Douglas | 3,393 | 41,760 | Superior |
| Dunn | 2,218 | 35,910 | Menomonie |
| Eau Claire | 1,659 | 85,180 | Eau Claire |
| Florence | 1,264 | 4,590 | Florence |
| Fond du Lac | 1,885 | 90,080 | Fond du Lac |
| Forest | 2,629 | 8,780 | Crandon |
| Grant | 2,974 | 49,270 | Lancaster |
| Green | 1,516 | 30,340 | Monroe |
| Green Lake | 928 | 18,650 | Green Lake |
| Iowa | 1,976 | 20,150 | Dodgeville |
| Iron | 1,953 | 6,150 | Hurley |
| Jackson | 2,595 | 16,590 | Black River Falls |
| Jefferson | 1,461 | 67,780 | Jefferson |
| Juneau | 2,012 | 21,650 | Mauston |
| Kenosha | 710 | 128,180 | Kenosha |
| Kewaunee | 892 | 18,880 | Kewaunee |
| La Crosse | 1,188 | 97,900 | La Crosse |
| Lafayette | 1,648 | 16,070 | Darlington |
| Langlade | 2,270 | 19,505 | Antigo |
| Lincoln | 2,304 | 26,990 | Merrill |
| Manitowoc | 1,544 | 80,420 | Manitowoc |
| Marathon | 4,053 | 115,400 | Wausau |
| Marinette | 3,627 | 40,550 | Marinette |
| Marquette | 1,183 | 12,320 | Montello |
| Menominee | 933 | 3,890 | Keshena |
| Milwaukee | 627 | 959,275 | Milwaukee |
| Monroe | 2,350 | 36,630 | Sparta |
| Oconto | 2,605 | 30,230 | Oconto |
| Oneida | 2,938 | 31,680 | Rhinelander |
| Outagamie | 1,669 | 140,510 | Appleton |
| Ozaukee | 611 | 72,830 | Port Washington |
| Pepin | 610 | 7,110 | Durand |
| Pierce | 1,500 | 32,765 | Ellsworth |
| Polk | 2,389 | 34,770 | Balsam Lake |
| Portage | 2,106 | 61,405 | Stevens Point |
| Price | 3,266 | 15,600 | Phillips |
| Racine | 871 | 175,030 | Racine |
| Richland | 1,521 | 17,520 | Richland Center |
| Rock | 1,880 | 139,510 | Janesville |
| Rusk | 2,374 | 15,080 | Ladysmith |
| St. Croix | 1,880 | 50,250 | Hudson |
| Sauk | 2,179 | 46,975 | Baraboo |
| Sawyer | 3,263 | 14,180 | Hayward |
| Shawano | 2,332 | 37,160 | Shawano |
| Sheboygan | 1,339 | 103,880 | Sheboygan |
| Taylor | 2,535 | 18,900 | Medford |
| Trempealeau | 1,914 | 25,260 | Whitehall |
| Vernon | 2,101 | 25,620 | Viroqua |
| Vilas | 2,254 | 17,710 | Eagle River |
| Walworth | 1,446 | 75,000 | Elkhorn |
| Washburn | 2,119 | 13,770 | Shell Lake |
| Washington | 1,118 | 95,330 | West Bend |
| Waukesha | 1,440 | 304,715 | Waukesha |
| Waupaca | 1,960 | 46,100 | Waupaca |
| Waushara | 1,633 | 19,385 | Wautoma |
| Winnebago | 1,167 | 140,320 | Oshkosh |
| Wood | 2,083 | 73,605 | Wisconsin Rapids |

**Wisła** /'viːslə/ see VISTULA.

**Wismar** /'vɪzmɑː(r)/ a port on the Baltic coast of Mecklenburg-West Pomerania, north-east Germany, between Lübeck and Rostock; pop. (1991) 54,470. It has oil refineries, shipyards, and is also a fishing port.

**Witten** /'vɪtən/ an industrial city on the River Ruhr east of Essen in North Rhine-Westphalia, west Germany; pop. (1991) 105,900. It manufactures iron and steel, glass, and chemicals.

**Wittenberg** /'vɪtən,bɜːg/ an industrial town in Saxony-Anhalt, Germany, on the River Elbe between Halle and Berlin; pop. (1991) 87,000. It is famous as the residence and burial place of Luther and starting-point of the Reformation, with an ancient university (merged with that of Halle in 1817) at which Luther taught. It has machinery, chemicals, rubber, and food industries.

**Witwatersrand** /wɪt'wɔːtəz,rænd/ a series of parallel ridges forming a watershed between the Vaal and Olifant rivers in northern South Africa. The Witwatersrand or Rand area is South Africa's chief centre of gold-mining. Its Afrikaans name means 'ridge of white waters'.

**Włocławek** /vwɒt'swɑːfɪk/ an agricultural market centre and industrial city in central Poland, a port on the Vistula; pop. (1990) 122,140. Its industries manufacture farm machinery, chemicals, metal goods, and paper.

**Woburn** /'wəʊbɜːn/ a village in Berkshire, southern England. Nearby is Woburn Abbey, ancestral home of the dukes of Bedford, built in the 18th c. by Inigo Jones and Henry Flitcroft.

**Wodisław Śląski** /,vɒdʒɪswɑːf 'ʃlɒnskɪ/ an industrial city in southern Poland, in the Rybnik coal basin south-west of Katowice; pop. (1990) 111,740.

**Woking** /'wəʊkɪŋ/ a residential town on the River Wey near Guildford in Surrey, south-east England; pop. (1981) 81,770. It has a large mosque built in 1889.

**Wokingham** /'wəʊkɪŋhəm/ a town in Berkshire, southern England, situated to the south-east of Reading; pop. (1981) 30,770. It has engineering and electronics industries.

**Wolfsberg** /'vɒlfsbɜːk/ an industrial town in Carinthia, southern Austria, between Graz and Klagenfurt; pop. (1991) 28,105.

**Wolfsburg** /'vɒlfsbʊək/ an industrial city in Lower Saxony, north-west Germany, on the Mittelland Canal north-east of Brunswick; pop. (1991) 128,995. It developed as the headquarters of the Volkswagen Company.

**Wollongong** /,wɒlən'gɒŋ/ a port and industrial city to the south of Sydney on the Illawarra Coast of New South Wales, Australia, situated around Port Kembla Harbour; pop. (1991) 211,420. Steel is produced and grain and coal are exported. Since it became the chief port of the southern Wollongong–Lithgow–Newcastle coalfield area in the 1890s, it

has expanded to embrace mining villages such as Thirroul (the 'Mullumimby' of D. H. Lawrence's *Kangaroo*).

**Wolverhampton** /,wʊlvə'hæmpt(ə)n/ an industrial city in the West Midlands of England, north-west of Birmingham; pop. (1991) 239,800. The city is named after Wulfruna, sister of Edgar II, who endowed the first collegiate church here in 994. Engineering and the manufacture of chemicals, aircraft parts, and metal goods are among its chief industries. The University of Wolverhampton (formerly Wolverhampton Polytechnic) was established in 1992.

**Wonsan** /wɒn'sɑːn/ a port and industrial city in eastern North Korea, on the Sea of Japan, east of Pyongyang; pop. (est. 1984) 350,000. It is a centre of heavy industry with shipyards, chemical plants, oil refineries, and railway workshops.

**Woodhenge** a prehistoric site near Amesbury in Wiltshire, southern England. Though little is visible, its former wooden pillars are thought to have been constructed in a style and for a purpose similar to Stonehenge.

**Woodstock** /'wʊdstɒk/ 1. a town in Oxfordshire, England, 13 km. (8 miles) north-west of Oxford. Once the site of a royal palace and noted for its glove-making, it was the birthplace of the Black Prince, the son of Edward III. Blenheim Palace was the birthplace in 1874 of Winston Churchill whose grave is in the nearby village of Bladon. See also BLENHEIM. 2. a town in the south-east of New York state, USA, noted as an artists' colony; pop. (1990) 1,870. In August 1969 a rock festival held at the Woodstock Music and Art Fair near Bethel, 96 km. (60 miles) south-west of Woodstock, drew massive crowds and came to symbolize the youth culture of the period.

**Wookey Hole** /,wuːkɪ 'həʊl/ a complex of caves with spectacular rock formations in the Mendip Hills near Wells in Somerset, south-west England. The River Axe passes underground here.

**Woolwich** /'wuːlɪtʃ/ a district of east London, south-east England, on the south bank of the River Thames in the borough of Greenwich. It was the site of the Royal Dockyard in which famous ships such as Henry VIII's *Great Harry* were built, and of the Royal Arsenal (now being redeveloped) which produced ordnance for the British army from 1716 until the 1960s. The University of Greenwich (formerly Thames Polytechnic) was founded here in 1992.

**Woomera** /'wʊmərə/ a location in central South Australia used as a missile testing site from 1952 to 1957.

**Worcester** /'wʊstə(r)/ a city in the county of Hereford and Worcester, England, on the River Severn; pop. (1991) 81,800. Its cathedral is the burial place of King John and Worcester was the scene of a battle (1651) in which Cromwell defeated a Scottish army under Charles II. The city gives its name to a pungent sauce (Worcester sauce) containing soy, vinegar, and condiments first made here, and to Worcester china (also Royal Worcester), a type of porcelain made here since 1751. The city shares with Hereford and Gloucester the annual Three Choirs Festival.

**Workington** /'wɜ:kɪŋt(ə)n/ a former coal port on the coast of Cumbria, north-west England, at the mouth of the River Derwent; pop. (1981) 26,120.

**Worksop** /'wɜ:ksɒp/ a market town near Sherwood Forest in Nottinghamshire, central England, known as the gateway to the Dukeries; pop. (1980) 36,380.

**World Bank** the popular name of the International Bank for Reconstruction and Development, an agency set up by the United Nations in 1945 to promote the economic development of member-nations by facilitating the investment of capital for productive purposes, encouraging private foreign investment, and if necessary lending money from its own funds. Its headquarters are in Washington, DC.

**World's View** a height in the Matopo Hills in Zimbabwe, south-east of Bulawayo. It is the burial place of the South African statesman Cecil Rhodes (1853–1902).

**Worms** /wɜ:mz, vɔ:mz/ an industrial town on the Rhine in the Rhineland Palatinate of western Germany; pop. (1991) 77,430. At the Diet of Worms (the Imperial Diet of Charles V) in 1521 Martin Luther committed himself to the cause of Protestant reform. On the last day of the Diet his teaching was formally condemned in the Edict of Worms. It is a centre of wine production and the manufacture of chemicals and metal goods.

**Worthing** /'wɜ:ðɪŋ/ a resort town on the south coast of England, in West Sussex at the foot of the South Downs; pop. (1980) 92,050. Formerly a fishing village, it developed after it was visited by royalty in 1798. The writers Richard Jeffries (d. 1887) and W. H. Hudson (d. 1922) are buried here.

**Wounded Knee** the site in South Dakota, USA, of the last major battle (1890) between the US Army and the Sioux Indians, in which over 150 Sioux were massacred. The event was recalled in 1973 when members of the American Indian Movement occupied the site; after a skirmish in which two Indians were killed they agreed to evacuate the area in exchange for negotiations on Indian grievances.

**Wrangel Island** /'ræŋg(ə)l/ (Russian **Ostrov Vrangelya**) an island of eastern Russia in the Arctic Ocean, named after the Russian admiral and explorer Baron Ferdinand Wrangel (1794–1870).

**Wrath, Cape** see CAPE WRATH.

**Wrexham** /'reks(ə)m/ a commercial and industrial town in Clwyd, north-east Wales, on the

Clywedog River to the south-west of Chester; pop. (1981) 40,930. Elihu Yale, benefactor of Yale University, is buried in St. Giles' churchyard. It has developed light industries, including chemicals and textiles.

**Wrocław** /'vrɒtswɑ:f/ (German **Breslau** /'breslaʊ/) a port and industrial city on the Oder River in western Poland; pop. (1990) 643,220. It is the chief town of lower Silesia. It produces electric railway locomotives, machinery, electrical equipment, chemicals, paper, timber, and textiles.

**Wu** /wu:/ a dialect of Chinese spoken in the Jiangsu and Zhejiang provinces of eastern China.

**Wuhai** /wu:'haɪ/ a city in Inner Mongolia, northern China, on the Yellow River north of Yinchuan; pop. (1986) 264,000.

**Wuhan** /wu:'hæn/ (formerly **Hankow**) a port, commercial, and industrial city on the Yangtze River, capital of Hubei province in eastern China; pop. (1990) 3,710,000. Formerly a fishing village, it developed on being designated a treaty port after the 19th-c. Opium Wars, with the arrival of the railway, and with the establishment of China's first modern iron and steel manufacturing complex (1891). It is made up of the cities of Wuchang, Hankow, and Hanyang, and is one of the most important industrial centres in China with iron and steel, paper-making, textiles, and cement industries. The Yangtze is crossed here by a mile-long road and rail bridge. Although 970 km (600 miles) from the sea, the port handles ocean-going ships.

**Wuhsi** see WUXI.

**Wuhsien** see SUZHOU.

**Wuhu** /wu:'hu:/ a deep-water port in Anhui province, eastern China, on the Yangtze River south-west of Nanjing; pop. (1986) 944,000. It is a major rice market and the distribution and processing centre for agricultural produce.

**Wuppertal** /'vʊpə‚tɑ:l/ an industrial city of western Germany, on the River Wupper in North Rhine-Westphalia; pop. (1991) 385,460. It was formed in 1929 by the merger of Barmen, Elberfeld, Vohwinkel, and smaller towns. It is a major textiles centre.

**Würzburg** /'vɜ:tsbʊərk/ an industrial city in north-west Bavaria, southern Germany, on the River Main; pop. (1991) 128,500. It is the cultural and wine-producing centre of the Franconia region.

**Wuxi** /wu:'ʃi:/ (formerly **Wuhsi**) a city in the province of Jiangsu, eastern China, on the Grand Canal; pop. (1990) 930,000. It is a centre of cotton and silk textile industries.

**Wuzhong** /wu:'dʒʊŋ/ a city in Ningxia Hui autonomous region, northern China, in the valley of the Yellow River south of Yinchuan; pop. (1986) 231,000.

**Wuzhou** /wuːˈdʒəʊ/ a city in Guangxi autonomous region, southern China, on the Xun River
west of Guangzhou (Canton); pop. (1986) 267,000.

**WV** *abbr.* US West Virginia (in official postal use).

**WY** *abbr.* US Wyoming (in official postal use).

**Wyandot** /ˈwaɪənˈdɒt/ (also **Wendat**) an
Iroquoian name for the Huron Indians of North
America.

**Wye** /waɪ/ the name of several rivers in England
and Wales: **1.** a river that rises in the Cambrian
Mountains of north-east Dyfed and flows generally south-east for 208 km. (132 miles) to join the
Severn estuary near Chepstow. **2.** a river of central
England that rises in the Chiltern Hills in Buckinghamshire and flows 15 km. (9 miles) south-
eastwards to meet the Thames at Bourne End. **3.** a
river of central England that rises near Buxton in
Derbyshire and flows 32 km. (20 miles) south-
eastwards to join the River Derwent at Rowsley.

**Wyoming** /waɪˈəʊmɪŋ/ a Rocky Mountain state
in the western central USA, the smallest state by
population; area 253,326 sq. km. (97,809 sq. miles);
pop. (1990) 453,590; capital, Cheyenne. It is also
known as the Equality State. Wyoming is a leading
producer of oil, gas, sodium bicarbonate, bentonite, uranium, and wool. Acquired as part of the
Louisiana Purchase in 1803, it became the 44th
state of the USA in 1890. Its chief landmarks are
Yellowstone and Grand Teton national parks,
Fossil Butte National Monument, and Fort
Laramie National Historic Site. Wyoming is
divided into 23 counties:

| County | Area (sq. km.) | Pop (1990) | County Seat |
| --- | --- | --- | --- |
| Albany | 11,097 | 30,800 | Laramie |
| Big Horn | 8,161 | 10,525 | Basin |
| Campbell | 12,470 | 29,370 | Gillette |
| Carbon | 20,480 | 16,660 | Rawlins |
| Converse | 11,105 | 11,130 | Douglas |
| Crook | 7,423 | 5,290 | Sundance |
| Fremont | 23,871 | 33,660 | Lander |
| Goshen | 5,684 | 12,370 | Torrington |
| Hot Springs | 5,213 | 4,810 | Thermopolis |
| Johnson | 10,832 | 6,145 | Buffalo |
| Laramie | 6,978 | 73,140 | Cheyenne |
| Lincoln | 10,582 | 12,625 | Kemmerer |
| Natrona | 13,902 | 61,230 | Casper |
| Niobrara | 6,978 | 2,500 | Lusk |
| Park | 18,034 | 23,180 | Cody |
| Platte | 5,260 | 8,145 | Wheatland |
| Sheridan | 6,583 | 23,560 | Sheridan |
| Sublette | 12,667 | 4,840 | Pinedale |
| Sweetwater | 26,915 | 38,820 | Green River |
| Teton | 10,430 | 11,170 | Jackson |
| Uinta | 5,421 | 18,705 | Evanston |
| Washakie | 5,832 | 8,390 | Worland |
| Weston | 6,245 | 6,520 | Newcastle |

**Wyoming** /waɪˈəʊmɪŋ/ a southern suburb of
Grand Rapids in west-central Michigan, USA;
pop. (1990) 63,890. It manufactures parts for the
aircraft and automobile industries.

# X x

**Xankändi** /kɑ:n ˈkendi:/ (also **Khankendi**) the capital of the Nagorno-Karabakh region of Azerbaijan in Transcaucasia. From the 1930s until 1991 it was named Stepanakert after the Baku communist, Stepan Shaumya.

**Xánthi** /ˈzænθɪ/ a town of Thrace in northern Greece, capital of the department of Xánthi; pop. (1981) 31,540. It is situated at the foot of the Rhodope Mountains in a tobacco-growing region. To the south-east are the ruins of the Ionian colony of Abdera, home town of Democritus in the 5th c. BC.

**Xanthus** /ˈzænθəs/ (also **Xanthos**) the remains of the ancient capital of Lycia in Asia Minor, situated in the valley of the Xanthus River in the province of Muğla, south-west Turkey. The site was discovered in 1838 by Sir Charles Fellows.

**xerophyte** /ˈzɪərəˌfaɪt, ˈze-/ (also **xerophile** /-ˌfaɪl/) a plant able to grow in very dry conditions because it has adapted to restrict water loss by shedding leaves at the begining of the dry season or by growing waxy leaves or dense hairs.

**Xhosa** /ˈkəʊsə, ˈkɔ:-/ a branch of the Bantu people of Cape Province in South Africa. Their language is similar to Zulu.

**Xiamen** /ʃɑ:ˈmen/ (formerly **Amoy** and **Hsia-Men**) a city and port on the coast of Fujian province, south-east China; pop. (1986) 962,000. Situated on an island at the mouth of the Jiulong River opposite Taiwan, it has been a special economic zone since 1981.

**Xian** /ʃi:ˈæn/ (formerly **Changan**, **Siking**, and **Sian**) an industrial city of northern China, capital of Shaanxi province; pop. (1990) 2,911,000. It was the capital of China under several ruling dynasties. The Qin emperor Shi Huangdi (c. 259–210 BC) is buried here in an elaborate tomb complex, guarded by 10,000 life-size pottery soldiers and horses, the 'terracotta army', discovered in 1974. The city was called Siking when it was the western capital of the Tang dynasty, but since the Ming dynasty has been known by its present name. The Chinese leader Chiang Kai-shek was captured here in 1936 (the Xian incident). Its industries manufacture steel, fertilizers, textiles, machine tools, and irrigation equipment.

**Xiangfan** /ʃi:æŋˈfæn/ a city in Hubei province, east-central China, on the Han River north-west of Wuhan; pop. (1986) 442,000.

**Xiangtan** /ʃi:æŋˈtæn/ a city in Hunan province, south-east-central China, on the Xiang River south-west of Changsha; pop. (1986) 616,000.

**Xianning** /ʃi:ænˈnɪŋ/ a city in Hubei province, east-central China, south of Wuhan; pop. (1986) 406,000.

**Xianyang** /ʃi:ænˈjæŋ/ a city in Shaanxi province, central China, to the north of the Wei River north-west of Xian; pop. (1986) 662,000.

**Xiaogan** /ʃi:aʊˈgæn/ a city in Hubei province, east-central China, north-west of Wuhan; pop. (1986) 166,000.

**Xichang** /ʃi:ˈtʃæŋ/ a city in southern Sichuan province, central China, on the Yalong River; pop. (1986) 436,000.

**Xigaze** /ʃi:ˈgæzɪ/ a city in southern Tibet, to the south of the Yarlung Zanbo River south-west of Lhasa. The second-largest city in Tibet, its Tashilhunpo Buddhist monastery was the burial place in 1989 of the 10th Panchen Lama.

**Xilinhot** /ˌsi:lɪnˈhɒt/ a city in Inner Mongolia, north-east China; pop. (1986) 102,000.

**Xingtai** /ʃi:ŋˈtaɪ/ a city in Hebei province, eastern China, north-west of Jinan; pop. (1986) 1,167,000.

**Xingú** /ʃɪŋˈgu:/ a South American river which rises in the Mato Grosso of west Brazil and flows northwards for a distance of 1,979 km. (1,230 miles) to join the Amazon River at the head of the Amazon delta. A proposal to dam the Xingu River and flood adjacent land focused international attention on the plight of the Amerindians of the Brazilian rainforest, over 600 of whom gathered in protest at the town of Altimira in February 1989.

**Xining** /ʃi:ˈnɪŋ/ (formerly **Hsining** or **Sining**) the capital of the province of Qinghai in west-central China; pop. (1986) 927,000. It manufactures iron and steel, farm machinery, and fertilizers.

**Xinjiang** /ˌʃɪntʃiˈæŋ/ (formerly **Sinkiang** /sɪŋˈkjæŋ/) an autonomous region of north-west China; area 1,646,800 sq. km. (636,075 sq. miles); pop. (1990) 15,156,000; capital, Urumqi. Occupying one-sixth of China, the region includes the Tien Shan mountain range, the Taklimakan Desert, and the Turfan Depression. It is rich in mineral resources such as oil, nickel, lead, copper, and manganese which have been exploited since the 1950s. Nomadic herding has been the traditional way of life for non-Chinese ethnic groups, but for reasons of security in this strategic area, and to increase economic development, there has been large-scale compulsory Chinese settlement.

**Xintai** /ʃiːnˈtaɪ/ a city in Shandong province, eastern China, south-east of Jinan; pop. (1986) 1,167,000.

**Xinxiang** /ʃiːnʃɪˈæŋ/ a city in Henan province, east-central China, north-east of Zhengzhou; pop. (1986) 547,000.

**Xinyang** /ʃiːnˈjæŋ/ a city in western Anhui province, eastern China, in the northern foothills of the Tongbai Shan Mts.; pop. (1986) 240,000.

**Xinyu** /ʃiːnˈjuː/ a city in Jiangxi province, south-east-central China, south-west of Nanchang; pop. (1986) 662,000.

**Xinzhou** /ʃiːnˈdʒəʊ/ a city in Shanxi province, eastern China, north of Taiyuan; pop. (1986) 400,000.

**Xizang** /ʃiːˈzæŋ/ the Chinese name for the autonomous region of TIBET.

**Xochicalco** /səʊtʃɪˈkɑːlkəʊ/ an archaeological site south-west of Cuernavaca in the state of Morelos, central Mexico. It is thought that Aztec astronomer-priests met here at the beginning and end of a 52-year cycle to adjust the Aztec calendar.

**Xochimilco** /səʊtʃiːˈmiːlkəʊ/ a town in central Mexico, to the south of Mexico City on the shore of Lake Xochimilco. Its canals, now a tourist attraction known as the 'Floating Gardens of Xochimilco', are the remnants of the 2,000-year-old *chinampa* system of lake shore agriculture.

**Xuchang** /ʃuːˈtʃæŋ/ a city in Henan province, east-central China, south of Zhengzhou; pop. (1986) 254,000.

**Xuzhou** /ʃuːˈdʒəʊ/ (formerly **Tongshan**) an industrial city in north-west Jiangsu province, eastern China, on the Fei Huang River; pop. (1990) 910,000. It was known as Tongshan (1912–45). It is the centre of a rich coal-mining area and has machinery and textiles industries.

# Y y

**Ya'an** /jə'ɑ:n/ (formerly **Yachow**) a city in Sichuan province, central China, south-west of Chengdu; pop. (1986) 282,000. It is a centre of the tea industry.

**Yablonovy Range** /'jɑ:blənə,vi:/ (Russian **Yablonovyy Khrebet**) a mountain range of south-east Siberian Russia, extending north-eastwards from the Mongolian frontier to the east of Lake Baikal. It rises to 2,192 m. (7,192 ft.) at Sokhondo.

**Yakeshi** /jə'keʃɪ/ a city in Inner Mongolia, north-east China; pop. (1986) 393,000.

**Yakima** /'jækəmə/ a city in south-central Washington State, USA, on the Yakima River; pop. (1990) 54,830. It lies at the heart of an area of irrigated farmland producing apples, mint, and hops and is a trade and distribution centre. Settled in 1861, it takes its name from the Yakima Indian Nation whose reservation lies to the south.

**Yakut** /jɑ:'kʊt/ a people of Siberia who speak a Turkic language and who settled in the Lena basin during the 13th–15th c.

**Yakutia** /jɑ:'kʊtɪə/ official name **The Republic of Sakha** a republic of the Russian Federation in north-east Siberia, stretching southwards from the Laptev and East Siberian seas to the Stanovoy Range; area 3,103,200 sq. km. (1,198,610 sq. miles); pop. (1989) 1,081,000; capital, Yakutsk. It is the largest of the republics of Russia, with 40 per cent of its territory lying to the north of the Arctic Circle. Absorbed into the Russian empire during the 17th c., the territory was an autonomous republic of the former Soviet Union from 1922 until 1991 after which it continued as a republic of the Russian Federation. Its principal industries are the production of timber and the mining of diamonds, gold, silver, lead, coal, mica, and tin.

**Yakutsk** /jɑ:'kʊtsk/ the capital of Yakutia (The Republic of Sakha) in Siberian Russia, a port on the River Lena; pop. (1990) 187,000.

**Yale University** /jeɪl/ an American University, now non-sectarian, originally a 'collegiate school' founded in 1701 at Killingworth and Saybrook, Connecticut, by a group of Congregational ministers. In 1716 it moved to its present site at New Haven and soon afterwards was renamed Yale College after Elihu Yale, a notable benefactor. In 1887 it became Yale University.

**Yalta** /'jæltə/ a port and health resort on the Black Sea near the southern tip of the Crimean peninsula, southern Ukraine, site of a conference in February 1945 between the Allied leaders Churchill, Roosevelt, and Stalin, who met to plan the final stages of World War II and to agree the subsequent territorial division of Europe. In spite of the friendship displayed at the time the scene was set for the ensuing Cold War between East and West. Its mild 'Mediterranean' climate has led to the development of Yalta as a health and tourist resort with many sanatoriums and facilities for holiday makers.

**Yalu River** /'jɑ:lu:/ a river of eastern Asia rising in the mountains of Jilin province in north-east China. Flowing about 800 km. (500 miles) south-west to the Gulf of Korea, it forms part of the frontier between China and North Korea. The advance of UN troops towards the Yalu River precipitated the Chinese invasion of North Korea in November 1950.

**Yamagata** /jɑ:mə'gɑ:tə/ a city to the west of Mount Zao on the island of Honshu, Japan, capital of Yamagata prefecture; pop. (1990) 249,500. It specializes in electrical goods and silk textiles.

**Yamaguchi** /jɑ:mə'gʊtʃɪ/ a city near the south-west tip of Honshu Island, Japan, capital of Yamaguchi prefecture; pop. (1990) 129,470. A mission was established here by St. Francis Xavier in 1551.

**Yamato** /jɑ:'mɑ:təʊ/ a city in Kanagawa prefecture, south-east Honshu Island, Japan; pop. (1990) 194,870. The name of an ancient Japanese clan which was given to one of the largest warships ever built (74,000 tonnes).

**Yambol** (also **Jambol**) a port and city in the Burgas region of eastern Bulgaria, on the Tundzha River; pop. (1991) 99,225. Its industries include metal goods, tanning, and textiles.

**Yamoussoukro** / jæmu:'su:krəʊ/ the capital-designate of the Ivory Coast, originally a small village at the heartland of the Baoulé tribe; pop. (1986) 120,000. Designated the new capital in 1983, it was the home of former President Félix Houphouët-Boigny (1905–1993).

**Yamuna** /'jæmʊnə/ (also **Jumna**) a river of northern India that rises in the Himalayas and flows 1,370 km. (860 miles) south and south-east to meet the Ganges at Allahabad. The Hindu shrine at Yamunotri near the source of the river is traditionally the first of the remote Himalayan shrines visited by pilgrims undertaking the *yatra*.

**Yan'an** /jən'ɑ:n/ (formerly **Yenan**) a market and tourist city in the province of Shaanxi, central China; pop. (1986) 268,000. Headquarters of the Communists from 1936 to 1947, and the terminus of the 'Long March', its nine-story Song dynasty pagoda became a national symbol after the 1949 revolution. It was linked to Xian by rail in 1991.

**Yancheng** /jæn'tʃeŋ/ (formerly **Yen-cheng**) a city in Jiangsu province, eastern China, north-east of Nanjing; pop. (1986) 1,265,000.

**Yangchow** see YANGZHOU.

**Yangon** /jæŋ'ɒn/ the Burmese name for RANGOON.

**Yangquan** /jæŋ'kwɑ:n/ a city in Shanxi province, eastern China, east of Taiyuan; pop. (1986) 516,000. A centre of a coal- and iron-mining region.

**Yangshao** /jæŋ'ʃaʊ/ an ancient civilization of northern China during the 3rd millennium BC, characterized by painted pottery with naturalistic designs of fish and human faces, and abstract patterns of triangles, spirals, arcs, and dots.

**Yangtze River** /'jæntsɪ/ (Chinese **Chang Jiang** /tʃæŋ 'dʒæŋ/, formerly also **Yangtse-Kiang**) the principal river of China which rises in Tibet and flows 6,276 km. (3,900 miles) generally eastwards through central China to the East China Sea. On the frontier between the provinces of Sichuan and Hubei it emerges from its upper reaches onto the fertile lowland basin, passing through the **Yangtze Gorges** and hydroelectric schemes that include the immense Gezhouba Dam. A major waterway for many centuries and the third-longest river in the world, its entire length was first navigated in 1986 by a Chinese expedition. In 1994 work began on the Three Gorges Dam, the world's largest hydroelectric power project.

**Yangzhou** /jæŋ'dʒaʊ/ (formerly **Yangchow**) a city in the province of Jiangsu, eastern China, on the Grand Canal; pop. (1988) 400,000. A capital of the Sui dynasty and later an important cultural and religious centre of the Tang dynasty, it was a seat of Nestorian Christianity governed by Marco Polo 1282–5. The site of a major system of water control, it has a long tradition of craftsmanship and story-telling.

**Yanji** /'jændʒɪ/ a city in Jilin province, north-east China, west of Tumen; pop. (1986) 228,000.

**Yanomami** /jænəʊ'mɑ:mɪ/ an Amerindian people of the Amazon rainforest believed to be the world's oldest surving isolated Indian tribe. Numbering 9,000 in 1990, they were the focus of international attention in 1987 when rich mineral deposits were discovered and large numbers of miners (*garimpeiros*) invaded their tribal lands.

**Yantai** /jæn'taɪ/ (formerly **Chefoo** /tʃə'fu:/ and **Yent'ai**) a port on the Yellow Sea in the province of Shandong, eastern China; pop. (1986) 734,000. A convention signed here in 1876 opened many Chinese ports to foreign trade. It is now a special economic zone.

**Yao** /jaʊ/ a minority nationality of southern China, mostly found in Guangxi, Hunan, Yunnan, Guangdong, and Guizhou where the Yao people number *c.* 1.5 million.

**Yao** /jɑ:'aʊ/ a residential suburb of Osaka, Honshu Island, Japan; pop. (1990) 277,720.

**Yaoundé** /jæ'ʊndeɪ/ the capital of Cameroon, situated east of the coastal plain to the south of the Sanaga River; pop. (1991) 750,000. Founded by German traders in 1888, it was made capital of French Cameroon in 1921 and capital of the independent Republic of Cameroon in 1960. The city is an agricultural centre trading in sugar, coffee, and cacao.

**Yap** /jæp/ an island group comprising four islands and 13 coral atolls in the western Pacific, one of the four Federated States of Micronesia; area 119 sq. km. (46 sq. miles); pop. (est. 1990) 13,900; capital, Kolonia (on Pohnpei). Held by Germany from 1899 until World War I, Yap was mandated to Japan from 1920 until its capture by US forces in 1945.
**Yapese** *adj. & n.*

**Yaqui** /'jæki:/ a North American Indian people of the Cahitan (part of the Uto-Aztecan) linguistic group found in south-western states of the USA and in Mexico.

**Yaroslavl** /'jɑ:rəs,lɑ:v(ə)l/ an industrial river port and rail junction of western Russia, on the Volga north-east of Moscow; pop. (1990) 636,000. Formerly the capital of an independent principality, it developed as a textile centre on the trade route between Moscow and Archangel and was Moscow's Volga River port until the building of the Moscow–Volga Canal in 1937.

**Yarrow Water** /'jærəʊ/ a river that flows eastwards from St. Mary's Loch in the Scottish Borders to join the Tweed near Selkirk. Passing through attractive countryside, it has formed the subject of poems by Wordsworth and others.

**Yattenden** /'jætənd(ə)n/ a village in Berkshire, southern England, home from 1882 to 1904 of the poet laureate, Robert Bridges, who was buried there in 1930.

**Ya Xian** see SANYA.

**Yayoi** /jə'jɔɪ/ a neolithic industry of Japan, dating from the 3rd c. BC, named after an area in Tokyo where its characteristic chiefly wheel-made pottery was first discovered in 1884. It is marked by the introduction of rice cultivation to Japan.

**Yazd** /jæzd/ a city in central Iran, capital of Yazd province; pop. (1991) 275,000. It lies on the frontier between the northern salt desert and southern sand desert of Iran at an altitude of 1,230 m. (4,035 ft.).

**Yazoo** /jæ'zu:/ a tributary of the Mississippi River, west-central Mississippi, USA. Formed by the junction of the Tallahatchie and Yalobusha rivers, it flows south-west for 302 km. (189 miles) before joining the Mississippi near Vicksburg. For most of its course it runs parallel to the Mississippi, sharing the same flood plain. The River Yazoo gives its name to a physiographic term (Yazoo type) describing a river system in which the junction of a tributary stream with its main river is delayed by the building up of deposits laid down by the main river as it meanders.

**Yekaterinburg** /jə'kætərɪn,bɜːg/ an industrial city in central Russia, in the eastern foothills of the Urals; pop. (1990) 1,372,000. Founded in 1821 as a military post and trading centre, it was known as Sverdlovsk 1924–91. Tsar Nicholas II and his family were murdered here by Russian revolutionaries in 1918.

**Yelets** /jə'lets/ (also **Elets**) a city in western Russia, on the Sosna River south of Moscow; pop. (1990) 121,000. Famous for its lace, its industries include machinery and hydroelectric equipment.

**Yell** /jel/ the second-largest of the Shetland Islands off the north coast of Scotland, separated from the mainland of Shetland to the south and west by Yell Sound. Crofting, fishing, and the manufacture of knitwear are the chief occupations.

**Yellowhead Highway** a highway across Canada, stretching some 3,000 km. (1,864 miles) from Prince Rupert on the Pacific Coast of British Columbia to Portage la Prairie in Manitoba. Completed in the early 1970s it is the most northerly road link to the Canadian Pacific. It is named after Pierre Hatsination, a Hudson's Bay Company trapper, whose nickname was Yellowhead.

**Yellowknife** /'jeləʊ,naɪf/ the capital of the Northwest Territories of Canada, on the north shore of the Great Slave Lake; pop. (1991) 15,180. Founded in 1935 as a gold-mining town, Yellowknife was named after the copper knives long used by local Indians. It became capital of the Northwest Territories in 1967.

**Yellow Mountain** see HUANG SHAN.

**Yellow River** (Chinese **Huang He** /hwæn 'heɪ/) the second-largest river in China. Rising in the Kunlun Mountains of west Qinghai province in central China, it flows in a great circle for a distance of about 4,630 km. (2,877 miles) before entering the Bo Hai Gulf. The name refers to the large silt content of its waters. Its tendency to frequent disastrous flooding, which gave it the nickname of 'China's Sorrow', has been greatly, reduced by dyking and damming.

**Yellow Sea** (Chinese **Huang Hai** /hwæn 'haɪ/) an inlet of the East China Sea, separating the Korean peninsula from the east coast of China.

**Yellowstone** /'jeləʊ,stəʊn/ **1.** an area of Wyoming, Idaho, and Montana in the USA, reserved as a national park since 1872. It is famous for its scenery, geysers and wildlife and was the first national park to be designated in the USA. **2.** a river which rises in Yellowstone National Park,

north-west Wyoming, USA, and flows 1,080 km. (671 miles) north and east into Montana where it joins the Missouri River. The river passes through **Yellowstone Lake** which lies at an altitude of 2,358 m. (7,735 ft.).

**Yemen** /'jemən/ official name **The Republic of Yemen** a country in the south and south-west of the Arabian peninsula, bounded by Saudi Arabia, Oman, the Gulf of Aden, and the Red Sea; area 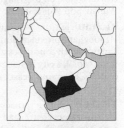 540,000 sq. km. (208,960 sq. miles); pop. (est. 1991) 12,533,000; official language, Arabic; capital, San'a (political), Aden (economic and commercial). Yemen has a flat and sandy coastal plain with a hot, humid climate and a mountainous interior with a temperate climate in the west. Its chief exports are crude oil, refined-oil products, fish, fruits, vegetables, hides, cotton, and coffee. An Islamic country since the mid-7th c., Yemen was part of the Ottoman empire from the 16th. c. In the 19th c. it came under increasing British influence as a result of the strategic importance of Aden at the mouth of the Red Sea. Civil War between royalist and republican forces in the era following World War II ended with the British withdrawal and South Yemen's declaration of independence in 1967. In 1990 the unification of North Yemen (The Yemen Arab Republic) and South Yemen (The People's Democratic Republic of Yemen) was proclaimed, with a 30-month period of implementation. A secessionist rebellion was crushed in 1994 after heavy fighting. **Yemeni** adj. & n.

**Yenan** see YAN'AN.

**Yenisei** /,jenɪ'seɪ/ (also **Yenisey**) a river of Siberian Russia whose headwaters rise in the east Sayan Mountains on the frontier with Mongolia. It flows 3,487 km. (2,195 miles) northwards to join the Yenisei Gulf, an inlet of the Kara Sea, but from the source of its chief headwater, the Angara River, it has a total length of 4,989 km. (3,100 miles). It is navigable for most of its length although frozen in sections throughout much of the year.

**Yeovil** /'jəʊvɪl/ a market town in Somerset, south-west England, on the River Yeo; pop. (1981) 36,600. Industries include engineering and the manufacture of textiles, leather goods, and electronics.

**Yerevan** /'jerɪ,væn/ (also **Erivan**) the capital of the Republic of Armenia, on the Razdan River in the southern Caucasus; pop. (1990) 1,202,000. Its main industries include chemicals, tyres, metals, machinery, electrical equipment, foodstuffs, and wine-making.

**Yi** /jiː/ a minority nationality of southern China, mostly found in Yunnan, Sichuan, Guangxi, and Guizhou where the Yi people number c. 5.5 million.

**Yibin** /jiːˈbɪn/ a city in Sichuan province, central China, on the Min River south of Chengdu; pop. (1986) 664,000.

**Yichang** /jiːˈtʃæŋ/ a city in Hubei province, east-central China, on the Yangtze River west of Wuhan; pop. (1986) 418,000.

**Yichun** /jiːˈtʃʊn/ **1.** (formerly **I-chun**) a city in Heilongjiang province, north-eastern China, on the Tangwang River north-east of Harbin; pop. (1986) 1,167,000. **2.** a city in Jiangxi province, south-east-central China, south-east of Changsha; pop. (1986) 173,000.

**Yiddish** /ˈjɪdɪʃ/ a vernacular language used by Jews in or from central and eastern Europe. Until 1939 it was widely spoken, but since World War II the number of speakers has declined in the face of the rise of Hebrew as a spoken language. It originated in the 9th c. among Jewish emigrants who settled in cities along the Rhine in Germany and adopted the German dialect of the area. Their German was heavily influenced by Hebrew which remained their literary language. In the 14th c. it was carried eastwards where it was again influenced by the Slavonic languages. From this amalgam arose Yiddish. When it was written down, the Hebrew characters were used with the difference that vowels were written with separate signs.

**Yinchuan** /jɪnˈtʃwɑːn/ the capital of the Ningxia autonomous region of north-east China, an industrial city producing textiles, rubber goods, chemicals, and machine tools; pop. (1986) 658,000.

**Yingkou** /jɪŋˈkəʊ/ (formerly **Newchwang**) a city in Liaoning province, north-eastern China, a port on the Hun River near where it meets the Liaodong Bay; pop. (1986) 2,789,000. It has petrochemical, textiles, machinery, vehicle parts, fishing, lumbering, and paper industries.

**Yingtan** /jɪŋˈtæn/ a city in Jiangxi province, south-east-central China, south-east of Nanchang; pop. (1986) 120,000.

**Yining** /jɪˈnɪŋ/ (also **Gulja**) a city in Xinjiang autonomous region, north-west China, in the western Tien Shan Mts.; pop. (1986) 237,000.

**Yiyang** /jɪˈjæŋ/ a city in Hunan province, east-central China, north-west of Changsha; pop. (1986) 372,000.

**Yogyakarta** /ˌjɒɡjəˈkɑːtə/ (also **Jogjakarta**) a city of south-central Java, Indonesia, situated at the foot of Mount Merapi; pop. (1990) 412,000. The modern city was founded in 1755 near the site of the former capital of the Mataram kingdom. Its chief landmarks are the Grand Mosque and the Kraton palace. It is a centre of Javanese culture and its many handicrafts include batik textiles, shadow puppets, and silverware.

**Yoho National Park** /ˈjəʊhəʊ/ a national park in the western Rocky Mountains of British Columbia, Canada, lying adjacent to Banff and Kootenay national parks. The TransCanada Highway passes through the park which was designated in 1930.

**Yokkaichi** /jəʊˈkaɪtʃiː/ an industrial city in the Mie prefecture of central Honshu Island, Japan, a port on Ise Bay south-west of Nagoya; pop. (1990) 274,180. It is a centre of oil refining and the manufacture of chemicals, textiles, and porcelain.

**Yokohama** /ˌjəʊkəʊˈhɑːmə/ a seaport and cultural city to the south of Tokyo on Honshu Island, Japan, capital of Kanagawa prefecture; pop. (1990) 3,220,000. Originally a fishing village, it developed into Japan's second-largest city after 1858 when it became the first port open to foreign trade. It is a centre of shipbuilding, oil refining, engineering, and the manufacture of goods such as glass, textiles, and furniture. It has four universities, Christian churches, Shinto shrines and temples, and many parks and gardens. It was rebuilt after being virtually destroyed by an earthquake in 1923 and bombing during World War II.

**Yokosuka** /jəʊkəˈsuːkə/ a port and naval base in Kanagawa prefecture, east Honshu Island, Japan; pop. (1990) 433,360.

**Yongzhou** /jʊŋˈdʒəʊ/ a city in Hunan province, south-east-central China, south-west of Hengyang; pop. (1986) 517,000.

**Yonkers** /ˈjɒnkəz/ an industrial and cultural city in Westchester County, New York State, USA, on the east bank of the Hudson River to the north of New York City; pop. (1990) 188,082. The trial and acquittal for seditious libel of John Peter Zenger here in 1735 helped establish freedom of the press in America and the St. Paul National Historic Site commemorates the Great Election of 1733 which contributed to the basic freedoms outlined in the US Bill of Rights. It has numerous light industries, colleges, research institutes, and museums.

**Yonne** /jɔːn/ **1.** a river of central France that rises in the Monts du Morvan and flows north-west for 293 km. (184 miles) to join the River Seine near Montereau. **2.** a department in the Burgundy region of north-central France; area 7,425 sq. km. (2,868 sq. miles); pop. (1990) 323,100; capital, Auxerre.

**York** /jɔːk/ a historic walled city in North Yorkshire, England, on the River Ouse; pop. (1991) 100,600. Founded as a Roman provincial capital (Eboracum) in AD 71, it became in turn an Anglo-Saxon capital, a Danish settlement (Jorvik), and seat of the archbishop, Primate of England. It gave its name to the English royal house descended from Edmund of Langley (1341–1402), 5th son of Edward III and (from 1385) 1st Duke of York, which ruled England from 1461 (Edward IV) until the death of Richard III in 1485. Its principal landmarks are the medieval gates, York Minster with its beautiful 15th c. stained-glass windows, and its many old buildings. It has a university founded in 1963, the National Railway Museum, the Castle Museum of Crafts, and Viking Museum. York is a commercial and market centre with a large confectionery industry.

**York, Cape** see CAPE YORK.

**Yorke Peninsula** /jɔːk/ a peninsula in southeast South Australia separating the Spencer Gulf from the Gulf of St. Vincent. Port Victoria on the west coast was once the main port of call for sailing ships transporting grain, and for more than 60 years from the 1850s the Wallaroo–Moonta–Kadina area was an important centre of copper mining.

**Yorkshire** /ˈjɔːkʃɪə(r)/ a former county of northern England, divided administratively into East, West, and North Ridings. In 1974 it was divided into the new counties of North, West, and South Yorkshire, while part of the East Riding went to Humberside and part of the North Riding became Cleveland.

**Yorkshire Dales** **1.** the name generally applied to the valleys or *dales* of the Pennine Chain in the former English county of Yorkshire, most of which are formed by tributaries of the River Ouse. They include Airedale, Nidderdale, Swaledale, Teesdale, Wensleydale, and Wharfedale. **2.** an English national park in North Yorkshire and Cumbria. Designated in 1954, it covers an area of 1,761 sq. km. (680 sq. miles).

**Yorktown** /ˈjɔːktaʊn/ a town in south-east Virginia, USA, on the York River north of Newport News; pop. (est. 1990) 400. Founded in 1690, it became a busy shipping centre but declined along with the tobacco trade. The British general, Lord Cornwallis, surrendered here to George Washington following a siege in 1781 and during the American Civil war the town was besieged again by Union forces.

**Yoruba** /ˈjɒrʊbə/ a people in the coastal region (Yorubaland) of West Africa, especially in Nigeria where they are the largest ethnic group with their own culture, speaking a tonal language of the Niger-Congo language group. Many Yoruba were taken as slaves to Brazil, Hispaniola, and Cuba.

**Yosemite** /jəʊˈsemɪtɪ/ a national park in the Sierra Nevada of eastern California, USA, named after the **Yosemite River** which passes through it. Visited by the naturalist John Muir in 1868 and designated in 1890, its principal features include Half Dome Mountain, the mile-high rock face of El Capitan, and **Yosemite Falls**, the highest waterfall in the United States (739 m., 2,425 ft.).

**Yoshkar-Ola** /jəʃˌkɑːrəˈlɑː/ the capital city of the Republic of Mari El in east-central European Russia, on the Kokshaga River; pop. (1990) 246,000. It manufactures agricultural machinery and pharmaceuticals.

**Youghal** /jɔːl/ a resort town in County Cork on the south coast of Ireland, at the mouth of the Blackwater River; pop. (1991) 5,530. Once a stronghold of the Fitzgeralds, it was the home of Sir Walter Raleigh in later life.

**Yozgat** /jɒzˈgæt/ **1.** a province of central Turkey; area 13,597 sq. km. (5,252 sq. miles); pop. (1990) 579,150. **2.** its capital, situated to the east of Ankara; pop. (1990) 50,335.

**Ypres** /ˈiːprə/ (Flemish **Ieper** /ˈiːprə/) a town in the province of West Flanders, Belgium, on the River Ieper near the French frontier; pop. (1990) 35,235. During the Middle Ages it was a major cloth-making centre. It was the scene of some of the bitterest fighting on the Western Front during World War I, commemorated by the Menin Gate (Menenpoort).

**Yuan** /jʊˈæn/ a Mongol dynasty of emperors in China founded in 1271 by Kublai Khan. Described by Marco Polo, the elaborate court of the Yuan Dynasty lasted until it was overthrown in 1368 and replaced by the Ming Dynasty.

**Yuan Jiang** /juːæn ˈdʒæŋ/ the Chinese name for the RED RIVER 1.

**Yucatán** /ˌjuːkəˈtɑːn/ a state of south-eastern Mexico, at the northern tip of the **Yucatán Peninsula** which is bounded by the Gulf of Mexico and the Caribbean Sea; area 38,402 sq. km. (14,833 sq. miles); pop. (1990) 1,363,540; capital, Mérida.

**Yuci** /juːˈtʃiː/ a city in Shanxi province, eastern China, south-east of Taiyuan; pop. (1986) 425,000.

**Yueyang** /jweɪˈjæŋ/ a city in Hubei province, east-central China, south-west of Wuhan; pop. (1986) 422,000.

## Yugoslavia

/ˌjuːɡəʊˈslɑːvɪə/ official name **The Federal Republic of Yugoslavia** a country in south-east Europe, stretching from the Adriatic coast to the River Danube and com-  prising the federal republics of Serbia and Montenegro; area 102,173 sq. km. (39,464 sq. miles); pop. (est. 1992) 10,500,000; language, Serbo-Croat; capital, Belgrade. The country was formed, as a kingdom, as a result of the peace settlement at the end of World War I from Serbia, Montenegro, Macedonia, and the former Slavic provinces of the Austro-Hungarian empire (Slovenia, Croatia, and Bosnia-Herzegovina), and assumed the name Yugoslavia in 1929. Invaded by the Axis powers during World War II, Yugoslavia emerged from a long guerrilla war as a Communist state but refused to accept Soviet domination. The People's Federal Republic established in 1946, though composed of a mixture of racial and religious groups, was held together under a single-party federal system by its leader, Josip Tito, who granted a degree of autonomy to the six republics of Yugoslavia. Following Tito's death in 1980 and the eventual demise of Communism in Eastern Europe, a rising tide of nationalism brought single-party rule to an end in 1990 and the seces-sion of Slovenia, Croatia, Bosnia-Herzegovina, and Macedonia from the federal republic. A new Federal Republic of Yugoslavia was declared in April 1992 comprising the remaining republics of Serbia (including the nominally autonomous prov-inces of Kosovo and Vojvodina) and Montenegro. Dominated by Serbia, whose involvement in the civil war in Bosnia attracted the imposition of UN sanctions and an EU trade embargo, the new fed-eral republic struggled to remain a viable entity and failed to win widespread international recognition as the sole successor to Yugoslavia.

**Yugoslav** *adj. & n.*, **Yugoslavian** *adj. & n.*

**Yukon** /'juːkɒn/ a river of North America 3,185 km. (2,004 miles) long, rising in Lake Tagish on the northern frontier of British Columbia, Canada. It flows north and north-west through Yukon Territ-ory before entering Alaska where it takes a south-westerly course before entering Norton Sound, an inlet of the Bering Sea. The upper 1,149 km. (723 miles) of the river lies within Canada. It takes its name from an Indian word meaning 'great river' and was the chief migration route followed by the original settlers of North America.

**Yukon Territory** a territory of north-west Canada, largely comprising a subarctic plateau that slopes down towards the Beaufort Sea and is isolated by mountains; area 482,515 sq. km. (186,661 sq. miles); pop. (1991) 27,800. Associated with the Klondike gold-rush of 1896, its economy is based on tourism, fishing, and the mining of gold, zinc, lead, and copper.

**Yulin** /juː'lɪn/ a city in Guangxi autonomous region, southern China, east of Nanning; pop. (1986) 1,255,000.

**Yuma** /'juːmə/ a city in south-west Arizona, USA, on the Colorado River; pop. (1990) 54,920. Settled in 1849, Yuma developed as a military out-post and territorial prison at a crossing point where the river narrows. Now a major trade centre of a fertile farming region and a resort centre.

**Yuma** /'juːmə/ a North American Indian people of the Hokan-Yuman linguistic group, once dominant in the lower Colorado River valley on the frontier between the US states of Arizona and California but also present in Mexico.

**Yuncheng** /jʊn'tʃɛŋ/ a city in Henan province, east-central China, north of the Yellow River and west of Zhengzhou; pop. (1986) 442,000.

**Yunnan** /juː'næn/ a province of southern China on the frontier with Vietnam, Laos, and Burma; area 436,200 sq. km. (168,482 sq. miles); pop. (1990) 36,973,000; capital, Kunming. It is a moun-tainous area, rich in plant species many of which have been introduced into Europe and North America. Agricultural crops include rice, maize, wheat, tobacco, sugar cane, coffee, tea, rubber, and bananas. It has vast mineral resources, especially tin, iron, coal, lead, zinc, copper, mercury, and antimony. Many of China's minority nationalities live in the province.

**Yuxi** /juːʃiː/ a city in Yunnan province, southern China, south of Kunming; pop. (1986) 298,000.

**Yuyao** /juː'jaʊ/ a city in Zhejiang province, east-ern China, north-west of Ningbo; pop. (1986) 778,000.

**Yuzhno-Sakhalinsk** /ˌjuːʒnəskəˈlɪnsk/ (Japanese **Toyohara** /ˌtəʊɪəˈhɑːrɑ/) the chief town of the island of Sakhalin in far eastern Russia; pop. (1990) 159,000.

**Yvelines** /iːvˈliːn/ a department to the west of Paris in the Ile-de-France region of France; area 2,271 sq. km. (877 sq. miles); pop. (1990) 1,307,150; capital, Versailles.

**Yverdon** /iːvɜːˈdɔ̃/ (in full **Yverdon-les-Bains**) a spa town in the Vaud canton, Switzerland, on the south-west shore of Lake Neuchâtel; pop. (1990) 22,400.

# Z z

**Zaanstad** /'zɑːnʃtɑːd/ an industrial town in the Netherlands, north-west of Amsterdam in the province of North Holland; pop. (1991) 130,700. Peter the Great of Russia lived in nearby Zaandam in 1697 while studying shipbuilding. Its industries include machinery, chemicals, and timber.

**Zabrze** /'zæbrəʒə/ an industrial mining city in the upper Silesian coalfields of southern Poland, situated to the west of Katowice; pop. (1990) 205,030. Held by Germany from 1915 to 1945, it was named Hindenburg in honour of the German Field Marshal von Hindenburg. It has steel, coke, chemical, and engineering industries.

**Zacatecas** /ˌzækə'teɪkəs/ **1.** a semiarid state of north-central Mexico, in the Sierra Madre Occidental to the south of Coahuila and Durango; area 73,252 sq. km. (28,293 sq. miles); pop. (1990) 1,278,280. **2.** its capital, a mining city situated at an altitude of 2,500 m. (8,200 ft.) on the Cerro de la Bufa; pop. (1980) 165,000. Built on the site of an Indian settlement, the Spanish began mining great quantities of silver here in 1548.

**Zadar** /'zɑːdɑː/ a port and resort town on the Dalmatian coast of Croatia, north-west of Split; pop. (1991) 76,300.

**Zagazig** /zə'gæziːk/ a town in the Nile Delta of northern Egypt, 80 km. (50 miles) north-east of Cairo; pop. (1991) 279,000. Nearby are the ruins of the ancient city of Bubastis, site of the temple of the cat-goddess Bastet. It is a marketing centre for cotton and grain.

**Zagorsk** /zə'ɡɔːsk/ see SERGIYEV POSAD.

**Zagreb** /'zɑːgreb/ the capital of the Republic of Croatia, on the River Sava; pop. (1991) 706,700. Known as Agram from 1526 to 1918, Zagreb was the birthplace of Josip Tito, president of Yugo-salvia (d. 1980). It has several Gothic and Baroque churches and palaces, numerous museums, which, together with good communications make it an excellent tourist centre. Its industries include electrical machinery and appliances, chemicals, cement, pharmaceuticals, and other light industries.

**Zagros Mountains** /'zægrɒs/ a range of mountains in western Iran comprising a series of ridges separated by fertile valleys that produce tobacco, cotton, and fruit. Most of Iran's oilfields lie along the western foothills of the central Zagros Mountains. There are many peaks over 2,750 m. (9,000 ft.), the highest of which is Zard Kuh which rises to 4,548 m. (14,921 ft.) west of Isfahan.

**Zahedan** /zæhə'dɑːn/ a city in south-east Iran, capital of the province of Sistan and Baluchistan; pop. (1991) 362,000. It was known as Duzdab until the 1930s.

**Zahlé** /'zɑːhəˌleɪ/ (also **Zahlah**) the chief town of the Bekaa valley in central Lebanon; pop. (est. 1988) 200,000.

**Zaire** /zɑː'ɪə(r)/ (also **Zaïre**) official name **The Republic of Zaire** a country in central Africa with a short coastline on the Atlantic Ocean; area 2,343,950 sq. km. (905,350 sq. miles); pop. (est. 1991) 38,473,000; official language, French; capital, Kinshasa.  Straddling the equator and encompassing the greater part of the Zaïre River basin, Zaire comprises a vast low-lying forest-covered central plateau bounded by mountains, savanna, and grassland. It has an equatorial climate that is hot and humid in much of the north and west, and cooler and drier in the south-central area and in the east. The economy is largely based on mineral exports, particularly of copper, of which Zaire is one of the world's major producers. Only gradually opened up by European exploration, the area became a Belgian colony in the late 19th c. and early 20th c., known as the Congo Free State (1885–1908) then as the Belgian Congo (1908–60). Independence (as a republic) in 1960 was followed by civil war and UN intervention and a stable state was some time in emerging. The name Zaire was adopted in 1971 and under President Mobutu (who assumed power in 1965) a highly centralized one-party state was established. In 1991 a national conference on the political future of the country dissolved the country's National Legislative Council, prompting a confrontation between prime minister and president that led to a period of prolonged political instability.

**Zairean** adj. & n.

Zaire is divided into nine regions:

| Region | Area (sq. km.) | Pop. (1984) | Capital |
| --- | --- | --- | --- |
| Bandundu | 295,658 | 3,682,845 | Bandundu |
| Bas-Zaire | 53,920 | 1,971,520 | Matadi |
| Equateur | 403,293 | 3,405,510 | Mbandaka |
| Haut-Zaire | 503,240 | 4,206,070 | Kisangani |

*(cont.)*

| | | | |
|---|---|---|---|
| Kasai Occidental | 156,967 | 2,287,410 | Kananga |
| Kasai Oriental | 168,216 | 2,402,600 | Mbuji-Mayi |
| Kinshasa | 9,965 | 2,653,560 | Kinshasa |
| Kivu | 256,662 | 5,187,865 | Bukavu |
| Shaba | 496,965 | 3,874,020 | Lubumbashi |

**Zaïre** /zɑːˈɪə(r)/ a major river of central Africa. See CONGO.

**Zákinthos** /ˈzækɪnˌθɒs/ (also **Zakynthos** or **Zánte** /ˈzɑːntɪ/) **1.** a volcanic island, the most southerly of the Greek islands in the Ionian Sea; area 406 sq. km. (157 sq. miles); pop. (1991) 32,750. The island was devastated by earthquakes in 1820, 1840, 1893, and 1953. It was the birthplace of the Greek national poet Solomos (1798–1857). **2.** its capital; pop. (1981) 9,760.

**Zakopane** /ˌzækəʊˈpænə/ a winter-sports resort in the High Tatra Mountains of southern Poland; pop. (1990) 28,630.

**Zalaegerszeg** /ˌzɒlɒˈeɪɡɜːseɡ/ a market town in western Hungary, on the River Zala, capital of Zala county; pop. (1993) 62,830. It has been a centre of oil production and refining since the 1930s.

**Zalantun** /zælənˈtʊn/ a city in Inner Mongolia, north-east China, on the Yalu River; pop. (1986) 390,000.

**Zambezi** /zæmˈbiːzɪ/ (also **Zambesi**) an African river that rises in north-west Zambia and flows 2,575 km. (1,600 miles) south through eastern Angola, then generally eastwards along the Zambia–Zimbabwe frontier, and across central Mozambique where it empties into the Mozambique Channel of the Indian Ocean. It is dammed at Cabora Bassa and Kariba where hydroelectric power is generated, and the Victoria Falls are one of Africa's leading landmarks.

**Zambia** /ˈzæmbɪə/ official name **The Republic of Zambia** a land-locked country in central Africa, bounded by Angola, Zaire, Tanzania, Malawi, Mozambique, Zimbabwe,  and Namibia; area 752,613 sq. km. (290,696 sq. miles); pop. (est. 1991) 8,373,000; official languages, English, Tonga, Kaonde, Lunda, and Luvale; capital, Lusaka. The greater part of the country is a savanna plateau with a generally dry and temperate climate. The country's chief exports are minerals including copper, cobalt, lead, and zinc. Explored by David Livingstone in the mid-19th c., the area was administered by the British South Africa Company from 1889 until taken over as a protectorate by the British government in 1924, having been named Northern Rhodesia in

1911. After some nationalist disturbances full independence was gained in 1964 and a single-party state was created under President Kenneth Kaunda. Subsequent economic reconstruction was assisted by Chinese technical and financial aid, including the building of the Tanzam railway to facilitate exports via Tanzania, and the redevelopment of the copper-mining industry and in 1991 a new constitution made provision for multiparty elections. Zambia is governed by an executive president and a unicameral National Assembly.
**Zambian** *adj. & n.*
Zambia is divided into nine provinces:

| Province | Area (sq. km.) | Pop. (1989) | Capital |
|---|---|---|---|
| Central | 94,396 | 722,440 | Kabwe |
| Copperbelt | 31,328 | 1,866,450 | Ndola |
| Eastern | 69,106 | 826,090 | Chipata |
| Luapula | 50,567 | 526,330 | Mansa |
| Lusaka | 21,898 | 1,151,250 | Lusaka |
| Northern | 147,826 | 832,725 | Kasama |
| North-Western | 125,827 | 396,100 | Solwezi |
| Southern | 85,283 | 906,910 | Livingstone |
| Western | 126,386 | 575,460 | Mongu |

**Zamboanga** /ˌsæmbəʊˈæŋɡə/ a port on the west coast of the island of Mindanao in the southern Philippines; pop. (1990) 442,345. It is the hub of a major iron-mining and lumbering area, and is known as the 'city of flowers' from its colourful market.

**Zamora** /səˈmɔːrə/ a city on Duero River in León, north-west Spain, capital of the province of Zamora; pop. (1991) 68,200. Once heavily fortified, it played a key role in the reconquest of Spain from the Moors and in the struggle for the throne of Castile during the Middle Ages. It has a 12th-c. cathedral. It is an agricultural marketing and processing centre.

**Zanjan** /zænˈdʒæn/ a city in north-west Iran, capital of the mountainous province of Zanjan; pop. (1991) 254,000. It is an agricultural marketing centre which manufactures rugs and metalwork.

**Zánte** see ZÁKINTHOS.

**Zanzibar** /ˌzænzɪˈbɑː(r)/ an island off the coast of East Africa, part of Tanzania; area 1,554 sq. km. (600 sq. miles); pop. (1988) 641,000 (with Pemba); capital, Zanzibar. Coming under Omani Arab rule in the 17th c. Zanzibar was developed as a major ivory- and slave-trading port of the Indian Ocean. It became (together with the islands of Pemba and Latham) a sultanate from 1856 before being annexed by Germany in 1885 and then handed over to Britain in exchange for Heligoland in 1890. Zanzibar remained a British protectorate until it gained independence as a member state of the Commonwealth in 1963. In the following year the Sultan's government was overthrown and the country became a republic, uniting with Tanganyika to form the United Republic of Tanzania.

In 1993 there were moves to dissolve the union. In the 19th c. the port of Zanzibar was used by the British navy in its suppression of the slave-trade and as the base for European explorers, traders, and missionaries. Its chief products are cloves and there is a considerable fishing industry.

**Zaozhuang** /zaʊˈdʒwæŋ/ (formerly **Tsao-chuang**) a city in Shandong province, eastern China, to the east of Weishan Lake; pop. (1986) 1,612,000.

**Zaporizhzhya** /ˌzæpəˈrɒʒɪə/ (formerly **Zaporozhye**) an industrial city of south-east Ukraine, on the Dnieper River south of Dnepropetrovsk, site of a dam providing hydroelectric power; pop. (1990) 891,000. Founded as a fortress town in 1770, it was known as Aleksandrovsk until 1921. It has iron and steel, aluminium, vehicles, machinery, and chemical industries.

**Zapotec** /ˈzæpətek/ a Mesoamerican civilization of the Classic Period (AD 300–900) whose culture was centred on the cities of Monte Alban and Mitla in the state of Oaxaca, south-west Mexico.

**Zaragoza** see SARAGOSSA.

**Zaria** /ˈzɑːrɪə/ a walled city in the cotton-growing Kaduna state of northern Nigeria; pop. (1983) 274,000. Originally a Hausa city-state, it was taken by the Fulani in the early 19th c. There is a Regimental Museum of the Nigerian Army and numerous light industries including cigarettes, textiles, palm oil, and bicycles.

**Zarqa** /ˈzɑːrkə/ (also **Az-Zarqa**) an industrial city in north-west Jordan, on the River Zarqa 24 km. (15 miles) north-east of Amman; pop. (1986) 405,000. Founded in the late 19th c. as a Circassian village, it later became the headquarters of the Arab Legion. It is now a centre for tanning and the extraction of phosphate from ore mined in the nearby Ruseifa region.

**Zaysan** /zaɪˈsɑːn/, **Lake** a lake in the Altai Mountains of eastern Kazakhstan. It forms part of the upper course of the Irtysh River.

**Zealand** /ˈziːlənd/ (Danish **Sjælland** /ˈʃelənd/) the principal island of Denmark, situated between the Jutland peninsula and the south tip of Sweden. Its chief city is Copenhagen, capital of Denmark.

**Zeebrugge** /ziːˈbrʊgə/ a seaport on the coast of Belgium, linked by canal to Bruges and by ferry to Hull and Dover in England.

**Zeeland** /ˈziːlənd/ an agricultural province of south-west Netherlands, at the estuary of the Maas, Scheldt, and Rhine rivers; area 1,786 sq. km. (690 sq. miles); pop. (1991) 357,450; capital, Middelburg.

**Zelaya** /zəˈlaɪə/ a department in the tropical lowlands of eastern Nicaragua; area 60,035 sq. km. (23,188 sq. miles); pop. (1990) 298,900; capital, Bluefields.

**Zelazowa Wola** /ʒəˈlɑːzɒvə ˈvɒlɑː/ a village in east-central Poland, 58 km. (36 miles) west of

Warsaw. Its manor house was the birthplace in 1810 of the composer Frédéric Chopin.

**Zemlaya Frantsa-Iosifa** see FRANZ-JOSEF LAND.

**Zen** /zen/ a sect of Japanese Buddhism that teaches the attainment of enlightenment through meditation and intuition rather than through study of the scriptures.

**Zenica** /ˈzenɪtsə/ (also **Zenitsa**) an industrial town in Bosnia-Herzegovina, on the River Bosna north of Sarajevo; pop. (1981) 132,730. It is a coal, steel, and paper industry centre.

**Zermatt** /ˈzɜːmæt/ an Alpine ski resort and mountaineering centre near the Matterhorn in Valais canton, southern Switzerland.

**Zhambyl** /dʒæmˈbuːl/ a city in southern Kazakhstan, on the Talas River between Tashkent and Almaty; pop. (1990) 311,000. Founded in the 7th c., it was known as Auliye-Ata until 1936, Mirzoyan (1936–8) and Dzhambul (1938–92).

**Zhangjiakou** /dʒæŋdʒæˈkəʊ/ (formerly **Changchiakow**) a city in Hebei province, north-eastern China, next to the Great Wall of China north-west of Beijing; pop. (1990) 670,000. It is also known by its Mongolian name, Kalgan. It has grown with the development of the nearby iron-ore fields.

**Zhangye** /dʒæŋˈjeɪ/ a city in Gansu province, northern China, in the northern foothills of the Qilian Shan Mts.; pop. (1986) 400,000.

**Zhangzhou** /dʒæŋˈdʒəʊ/ a city in Fujian province, south-eastern China, west of Xiamen; pop. (1986) 318,000.

**Zhanjiang** /ˈdʒɑːndʒɪˈæŋ/ (formerly **Chanchiang**, French **Fort Bayard**) a port in Guandong province, southern China, situated at the head of the Leizhou peninsula on Leizhou Bay, an inlet of the South China Sea; pop. (1986) 947,000. A centre of shipbuilding, fishing, food processing, and the manufacture of textiles, chemicals, paper, electronics, and machinery, it was designated a special economic zone in 1981. It is a base for offshore oil exploration.

**Zhaodong** /dʒaʊˈdʊŋ/ a city in Heilongjiang province, north-eastern China, north-west of Harbin; pop. (1986) 754,000.

**Zhaotong** /dʒaʊˈtʊŋ/ a city in southern Sichuan province, southern China, east of the Jinsha River; pop. (1986) 560,000.

**Zhdanov** /ʒˈdɑːnɒf/ the name of the Ukrainian city of MARIUPOL from 1948 to 1989.

**Zhejiang** /ˌdʒɜːdʒɪˈæŋ/ (formerly **Chekiang** /ˌtʃekɪˈæŋ/) a mountainous province of eastern China to the south of the Yangtze River; area 101,800 sq. km. (39,320 sq. miles); pop. (1990) 41,446,000; capital, Hangzhou. It is China's smallest mainland province. Chief among its products are rice, rapeseed, silkworm cocoons, bamboo, and tea.

**Zhengzhou** /dʒeŋ'dʒəʊ/ (formerly **Cheng-chow** /tʃeŋ'tʃaʊ/) the capital of Henan province in north-east-central China, situated on the Yellow River; pop. (1990) 1,943,000. It is a major rail centre with textile and food industries.

**Zhenjiang** /dʒendʒɪ'æŋ/ (formerly **Chen-Chiang** or **Chinkiang** /tʃɪn'jæŋ/) a city in Jiangsu province, eastern China, a port at the junction of the Grand Canal with the Yangtze River; pop. (1986) 422,300. Founded in the 6th c. BC, it has many temples and pagodas. It manufactures machinery, chemicals, and paper.

**Zhezqazghan** /dzeskəs'ga:n/ (also **Zhezkazgan**, formerly **Dzezkazgan**) a copper-mining city in central Kazakhstan; pop. (1990) 110,000.

**Zhitomir** see ZHYTOMYR.

**Zhongshan** /dʒʊŋ'ʃæn/ (formerly **Chung-shan**) an industrial city in Guangdong province, southern China, south of Guangzhou (Canton); pop. (1986) 1,073,000. It was the birthplace in 1866 of the Chinese revolutionary Sun Yatsen.

**Zhou** /dʒəʊ/ a dynasty of emperors in early China, ruling territory to the north of the Yangtze River from 1122–221 BC. Their capital moved from Hao to Luoyang c. 700 BC and during the Zhou Dynasty multiplication tables and iron casting were developed.

**Zhoukou** /dʒəʊ'kəʊ/ a city in Henan province, east-central China, south-east of Zhengzhou; pop. (1986) 227,000.

**Zhuang** /dʒwɑ:ŋ/ a minority nationality of southern China, mostly found in Yunnan, Guangxi, and Guizhou. Culturally linked to the Burmese, the Zhuang people number over 13 million and are China's largest minority nationality.

**Zhuhai** /dʒu:'haɪ/ a city in Guangdong province, southern China, near the mouth of the Pearl River north of Macao; pop. (1986) 165,000. It was designated a special economic zone in 1980.

**Zhu Jiang** /dʒu:'dʒæŋ/ see PEARL RIVER.

**Zhumadian** /dʒʊmædi:'ɑ:n/ a city in Henan province, east-central China, south of Zhengzhou; pop. (1986) 216,000.

**Zhuzhou** /dʒu:'dʒəʊ/ a city in Hunan province, south-east-central China, on the Xiang River south of Changsha; pop. (1986) 513,000.

**Zhytomyr** /ʒɪ'tɒmɪə(r)/ (formerly **Zhitomir**) an industrial city and transportation centre in central Ukraine, on the Teterev River west of Kiev; pop. (1960) 226,000. It has grain and timber mills, sugar refineries, and a large brewing industry.

**Zibo** /zi:'bəʊ/ (formerly **Tsu-po**) a city in Shandong province, eastern China, east of Jinan; pop. (1990) 2,460,000.

**Zielona Gora** /ʒə,ləʊnɑ: 'ɡʊərə/ a town in western Poland, capital of Zielona Gora county;

pop. (1990) 114,120. It developed as a commercial town on the trade route between Berlin and Upper Silesia and was known to the Germans as Grüneberg. It has light industries including wine-making.

**Ziggurat** /'zɪɡərət/ a step pyramid of sun-baked brick in ancient Babylonia and Assyria which stood like a shrine.

**Zigong** /zi:'ɡʊŋ/ a city in Sichuan province, central China, south-east of Chengdu; pop. (1986) 1,673,000.

**Ziguinchor** /'zi:ɡ(ə)n,ʃɔ:/ a port on the Casamance River in south-western Senegal; pop. (est. 1985) 79,500. It trades in fish, cotton, rice, and fruit.

**Zillertal Alps** (German **Zillertaler Alpen**) a range of the eastern Alps on the Austro-Italian border. It is separated from the Ötztal Alps to the west by the Brenner Pass and rises to 3,510 m. (11,515 ft.) at Hockfeiler.

**Zimbabwe** /zɪm'bɑ:bwɪ/ official name **The Republic of Zimbabwe** a landlocked country in south-east Africa, south of the River Zambezi, bordered by Zambia, Mozambique, the Transvaal

(South Africa), and Botswana; area 391,090 sq. km. (151,058 sq. miles); pop. (est. 1991) 10,080,000; official language, English; capital, Harare. Mountainous in the east, Zimbabwe is dominated by a high central plateau (middleveld) that is traversed south-west to north-east by a higher plateau (highveld). It has a subtropical climate with temperatures that vary with altitude. In addition to exporting minerals such as gold, asbestos and ferrochrome, Zimbabwe trades agricultural products including tobacco, cotton, and sugar. The country takes its name from the ruins of Great Zimbabwe near Masvingo, centre of an early civilization dating from the 9th to the 13th c. In subsequent centuries successive waves of Bantu peoples from equatorial regions supplanted the original inhabitants and are the ancestors of the country's African population today. In 1888 Cecil Rhodes obtained a concession for mineral rights from local chiefs. Known as Southern Rhodesia and then as Rhodesia, the country was a self-governing British colony from 1923. The ruling White minority sought independence from Britain when Northern Rhodesia became independent (as Zambia) in 1964, but Britain refused to grant this without a guarantee of Black majority rule within a definite period. Led by its prime minister, Ian Smith, Rhodesia issued a unilateral declaration of independence (UDI) in 1965, which was countered by the imposition of economic sanctions by Britain and the UN. These, combined with the growing

activity of nationalist guerrillas, forced Smith eventually to concede the principle of Black majority rule, and after an unsuccessful attempt to introduce this under the moderate Bishop Muzorewa, whose regime failed to come to terms with the guerrilla movement, national elections were held under British supervision in 1980. These resulted in the election of Robert Mugabe as prime minister and were followed by the formal granting of independence to the country as a republic and member-state of the Commonwealth. The country is governed by an executive president and a unicameral legislative House of Assembly.
**Zimbabwean** *adj. & n.*
Zimbabwe is divided into eight provinces:

| Province | Area (sq. km.) | Pop. (1982) |
|---|---|---|
| Manicaland | 35,219 | 1,099,200 |
| Mashonaland Central | 29,482 | 563,400 |
| Mashonaland East | 26,813 | 1,495,980 |
| Mashonaland West | 55,737 | 858,960 |
| Masvingo | 55,777 | 1,031,700 |
| Matabeleland North | 76,813 | 885,340 |
| Matabeleland South | 54,941 | 519,600 |
| Midlands | 55,977 | 1,091,840 |

**Zinder** /'zɪndə(r)/ a walled market town in southern Niger, to the east of Maradi; pop. (1988) 121,000. It was the capital of Niger until replaced by Niamey in 1926, and is the southern end of a trans-Saharan route to Algiers.

**Zion National Park** /'zaɪən/ a national park in the US state of Utah, designated in 1919 to protect canyon lands surrounding the Virgin River.

**Zip code** /zɪp/ a US system of postal codes consisting of five-digit numbers (*abbr.* *z*one *i*mprovement *p*lan).

**Zlatni Pyasutsi** see GOLDEN SANDS.

**Zlatoust** /zlɑ:tə'u:st/ an industrial city in central Russia, in the southern Urals to the west of Chelyabinsk; pop. (1990) 208,000. It specializes in making stainless steel, cutlery, machine tools, clocks, and watches.

**Zlin** /zɑ'li:n/ an industrial town in the Czech Republic, formerly called Gottwaldov after the communist president of Czechoslovakia; pop. (1991) 84,630. It is reputed to have the world's largest shoe factory.

**Zoetermeer** /'zʊtɜ:ˌmɪə(r)/ a town in east Netherlands, situated in the province of South Holland to the east of The Hague; pop. (1991) 99,090.

**Zonguldak** /zɒnɡʊl'dæk/ **1.** a province of northern Turkey on the Black Sea; area 8,560 sq. km. (3,306 sq. miles); pop. (1990) 1,073,560. **2.** its capital, a port and coal-mining town on the Black Sea east of Istanbul; pop. (1990) 116,725.

**Zoroastrianism** /ˌzɒrəʊ'æstrɪəˌnɪz(ə)m/ a monotheistic religion of ancient Iran founded by Zoroaster (or Zarathustra) in the 6th c. BC. According to Zoroastrian mythology the supreme god, Ahura Mazda, created twin spirits, one of which chose truth and light, the other untruth and darkness. Later formulations pit Ahura Mazda (now called Ormazd) against his own evil twin (Ahriman). Zoroastrianism survives today in isolated areas of Iran and in India, where followers are known as Parsees. The Zendavesta are the sacred scriptures of the faith.
**Zoroastrian** *adj. & n.*

**Zouerate** /zuːiːˈræt/ an iron ore-mining town in the Tiris Zemmour region of northern Mauritania, linked by rail to the Atlantic port of Nouadhibou; pop. (1976) 17,500.

**Zrenjanin** /'zrenjənɪm/ a town in the province of Vojvodina, northern Serbia, a port on the River Begej, a tributary of the Tisa; pop. (1991) 81,300. It was known as Veliki Beçkerek until the 1930s and Petrovgrad until 1947.

**Zug** /tsu:g/ **1.** a canton in central Switzerland; area 685 sq. km. (265 sq. miles); pop. (1990) 84,910. It joined the Swiss Confederation in 1352. **2.** its capital, a town on the north-eastern shore of the Lake of Zug (Zuger Zee); pop. (1990) 21,500. It manufactures electrical equipment, metal goods, textiles, and liqueurs.

**Zugspitze** /'tsʊkʃpɪtsə/ an Alpine peak in southern Bavaria, Germany, rising to a height of 2,962 m. (9,718 ft.). It is the highest mountain in Germany.

**Zuider Zee** /ˌzaɪdə 'zi:/ (also **Zuyder Zee**) a large shallow inlet of the North Sea that formerly existed in the Netherlands, large parts of which were reclaimed for agricultural use in a programme started in 1920. A 30-km-long dam (Afsluitdijk) constructed 1927–32 and stretching from the coast of North Holland to the coast of Friesland separated the Zuider Zee from the Wadden Sea, turning the inland sea into Lake IJssel (IJsselmeer). Along the coast of the lake were built five large polders, thereby increasing the area of the Netherlands by about 6 per cent (c. 2,050 sq. km.).

**Zulu** /'zu:lu:/ a South African Bantu people inhabiting the north-eastern part of Natal and speaking a language of the Niger-Congo group of languages.

**Zululand** see KWAZULU.

**Zunyi** /zʊn'ji:/ a city in Guizhou province, southern China, north of Guiyang; pop. (1990) 354,000.

**Zurich** /'zjʊərɪk/ (also **Zürich**) the largest city in Switzerland, situated at the foot of the Alps on Lake Zurich; pop. (1990) 342,860. It is capital of Zurich canton and a major tourist and European financial centre with an international airport (Kloten) to the north of the city. It was a lakeside settlement before the Romans visited the area in the 1st c. BC. Ulrich Zwingli (1484–1531), a priest at the cathedral, founded Swiss Protestantism in 1523 and was killed in consequence in 1531.

**Zwickau** /'tsvɪkaʊ/ a mining and industrial city in the state of Saxony, south-east Germany, on the River Mulde; pop. (1991) 112,565. It was the birthplace in 1810 of the composer Robert Schumann. It manufactures cars and has numerous light industries.

**Zwolle** /'zvɒlə/ a market town on the Zwartewater River, east Netherlands, capital of the province of Overijssel; pop. (1991) 95,570. It has shipbuilding, iron, and chemical industries. Thomas à Kempis lived in a monastery nearby.

# APPENDICES

| | | |
|---|---|---|
| Circumference at the equator | 40,075 km. | 24,902 miles |
| Circumference at the poles | 40,007 km. | 24,860 miles |
| Diameter at the equator | 12,756 km. | 7,926 miles |
| Diameter at the poles | 12,714 km. | 7,900 miles |
| Land surface | 148,941,000 sq. km. | 57,506,000 sq. miles |
| Water surface | 361,132,000 sq. km. | 139,433,000 sq. miles |
| Superficial area | 510,073,000 sq. km. | 196,939,000 sq. miles |
| Mean distance from the Sun | 149,500,000 km. | 92,860,000 miles |
| Average speed around the Sun | 30 km./sec. | 18.5 miles/sec |

## OCEANS AND SEAS

| | Area ('000s) | | Maximum depth | |
|---|---|---|---|---|
| | Sq. km. | Sq. miles | Metres | Feet |
| *Oceans* | | | | |
| Pacific Ocean | 165,250 | 63,800 | 11,034 | 36,200 |
| Atlantic Ocean | 82,440 | 31,830 | 9,219 | 30,246 |
| Indian Ocean | 73,440 | 28,360 | 7,450 | 24,442 |
| Arctic Ocean | 14,090 | 5,400 | 5,450 | 17,881 |
| *Seas* | | | | |
| South China Sea | 3,447 | 1,331 | 5,560 | 18,241 |
| Caribbean Sea | 2,754 | 1,063 | 7,680 | 25,197 |
| Mediterranean Sea | 2,505 | 967 | 5,020 | 16,470 |
| Sea of Okhotsk | 1,580 | 610 | 3,372 | 11,063 |
| Gulf of Mexico | 1,544 | 596 | 4,380 | 14,370 |
| Hudson Bay | 1,230 | 475 | 259 | 850 |
| Sea of Japan | 1,007 | 389 | 3,733 | 12,280 |
| East China Sea | 752 | 290 | 2,782 | 9,126 |
| North Sea | 575 | 222 | 659 | 2,170 |
| Black Sea | 461 | 178 | 2,237 | 7,360 |
| Red Sea | 438 | 169 | 2,240 | 7,370 |
| Baltic Sea | 422 | 163 | 437 | 1,440 |
| Yellow Sea | 417 | 161 | 91 | 300 |

## THE CONTINENTS

| | Area | | Per cent of the world's land |
|---|---|---|---|
| | Sq. km. | Sq. miles | |
| Asia | 44,350,000 | 17,100,000 | 29.6 |
| Africa | 30,300,000 | 11,700,000 | 20.2 |
| North America | 24,250,000 | 9,350,000 | 16.2 |
| South America | 17,800,000 | 6,900,000 | 11.8 |

| | Area | | Per cent of the world's land |
|---|---|---|---|
| | Sq. km. | Sq. miles | |
| Antarctica | 14,250,000 | 5,500,000 | 9.5 |
| Europe | 10,500,000 | 4,050,000 | 7.0 |
| Oceania | 8,500,000 | 3,300,000 | 5.7 |
| World | 149,950,000 | 57,900,000 | |

## POPULATION

| | Pop. (1990) | Pop. density people/sq. km. |
|---|---|---|
| Asia | 3,112,700,000 | 113 |
| Africa | 642,111,000 | 21 |
| Europe | 498,371,000 | 96 |
| North America | 427,226,000 | 13 |
| South America | 296,716,000 | 17 |
| Oceania | 26,481,000 | 3 |
| World | 5,292,200,000 | 39 |

## HIGHEST AND LOWEST ELEVATIONS

| | Highest elevation | Lowest elevation |
|---|---|---|
| Asia | Mt. Everest 8,848 m. (29,028 ft.) | Dead Sea −400 m. (−1,312 ft.) |
| Africa | Kilimanjaro, Tanzania 5,895 m. (19,340 ft.) | Lake Assal, Djibouti −153 m. (−502 ft.) |
| Antarctica | Vinson Massif 5,140 m. (16,864 ft.) | |
| North America | Mt. McKinley 6,194 m. (20,320 ft.) | Death Valley −86 m. (−282 ft.) |
| South America | Aconcagua 6,960 m. (22,834 ft.) | Valdez, Argentina −48 m. (−157 ft.) |
| Europe | Mt. Elbrus, Russia 5,642 m. (18,510 ft.) | Caspian Sea −28 m. (−92 ft.) |
| Oceania | Mt. Wilhelm, Papua New Guinea 4,509 m. (14,793 ft.) | Lake Eyre, Australia −16 m. (−52 ft.) |
| World | Mt. Everest 8,848 m. (29,028 ft.) | Dead Sea −400 m. (−1,312 ft.) |

## THE WORLD'S HIGHEST MOUNTAINS

| Mountain | Location | Height | |
|---|---|---|---|
| | | Metres | Feet |
| *Asia* | | | |
| Everest | Nepal–China | 8,848 | 29,028 |
| K2 | Kashmir | 8,611 | 28,250 |
| Kanchenjunga | Nepal–India | 8,598 | 28,209 |
| Lhotse I | Nepal–China | 8,511 | 27,923 |
| Makalu I | Nepal–China | 8,481 | 27,824 |
| Lhotse Shar | Nepal–China | 8,383 | 27,503 |

| Mountain | Location | Height | |
|----------|----------|--------|------|
| | | Metres | Feet |
| Dhaulagiri | Nepal | 8,172 | 26,810 |
| Manaslu I | Nepal | 8,156 | 26,760 |
| Cho Oyu | Nepal–China | 8,153 | 26,750 |
| Nanga Parbat | Kashmir | 8,126 | 26,660 |
| Annapurna | Nepal | 8,078 | 26,503 |
| Gasherbrum | Kashmir | 8,068 | 26,470 |
| Broad Peak | Kashmir | 8,047 | 26,400 |
| Gosainthan | China | 8,012 | 26,287 |
| *South America* | | | |
| Aconcagua | Argentina–Chile | 6,960 | 22,834 |
| Ojos del Salado | Argentina–Chile | 6,908 | 22,664 |
| Bonete | Argentina | 6,872 | 22,546 |
| Tupungato | Argentina–Chile | 6,800 | 22,310 |
| Pissis | Argentina | 6,779 | 22,241 |
| Mercedario | Argentina | 6,770 | 22,211 |
| Huascaran | Peru | 6,768 | 22,205 |
| Llullaillaco | Argentina–Chile | 6,723 | 22,057 |
| *North America* | | | |
| McKinley | Alsaka, USA | 6,194 | 20,320 |
| Logan | Yukon, Canada | 5,951 | 19,524 |
| Citlaltépetl | Mexico | 5,610 | 18,405 |
| St Elias | Alaska–Yukon | 5,489 | 18,008 |
| Popocatépetl | Mexico | 5,452 | 17,887 |
| Foraker | Alaska, USA | 5,304 | 17,402 |
| Iztaccíhuatl | Mexico | 5,286 | 17,343 |
| Lucania | Yukon, Canada | 5,226 | 17,147 |
| King Peak | Yukon, Canada | 5,173 | 16,971 |
| Steele | Yukon, Canada | 5,067 | 16,624 |
| Bona | Alaska, USA | 5,044 | 16,550 |
| *Africa* | | | |
| Kilimanjaro | Tanzania | 5,895 | 19,340 |
| Kenya | Kenya | 5,200 | 17,060 |
| Margherita Peak | Uganda–Zaïre | 5,109 | 16,763 |
| Ras Dashan | Ethiopia | 4,620 | 15,158 |
| Meru | Tanzania | 4,565 | 14,977 |
| Karisimbe | Zaïre–Rwanda | 4,507 | 14,787 |
| Elgon | Kenya–Uganda | 4,321 | 14,178 |
| Batu | Ethiopia | 4,307 | 14,131 |
| Guna | Ethiopia | 4,231 | 13,881 |
| Gughe | Ethiopia | 4,200 | 13,780 |
| Toubkal | Morocco | 4,165 | 13,664 |
| *Europe* | | | |
| Elbrus | Caucasus, Russia | 5,642 | 18,510 |
| Dykh Tau | Caucasus, Russia | 5,203 | 17,070 |
| Shkara | Caucasus, Russia | 5,201 | 17,064 |
| Kashan Tau | Caucasus, Russia | 5,144 | 16,877 |
| Dzhangi Tau | Caucasus, Russia | 5,049 | 16,565 |

| Mountain | Location | Height | |
|----------|----------|--------|--------|
| | | Metres | Feet |
| Kazbek | Caucasus, Georgia | 5,047 | 16,558 |
| Mont Blanc | France–Italy | 4,807 | 15,771 |
| Dufourspitze | Switzerland | 4,634 | 15,203 |
| Dom | Switzerland | 4,545 | 14,911 |
| Liskamm | Italy–Switzerland | 4,527 | 14,852 |
| Weisshorn | Switzerland | 4,505 | 14,780 |
| Taschhorn | Switzerland | 4,491 | 14,733 |
| Matterhorn | Italy–Switzerland | 4,477 | 14,690 |
| *Oceania* | | | |
| Wilhelm | Papua New Guinea | 4,509 | 14,793 |
| Cook | New Zealand | 3,754 | 12,316 |
| Tasman | New Zealand | 3,497 | 11,473 |
| Dampier | New Zealand | 3,447 | 11,309 |
| Silberhorn | New Zealand | 3,279 | 10,758 |
| Kosciusko | Australia | 2,228 | 7,310 |
| *Antarctica* | | | |
| Vinson Massif | | 5,140 | 16,864 |

## MAJOR NATURAL LAKES OF THE WORLD

| | Area | |
|---|------|------|
| | Sq. km. | Sq. miles |
| Caspian Sea | 370,992 | 143,240 |
| Lake Superior | 84,243 | 32,526 |
| Lake Victoria | 69,464 | 26,820 |
| Aral Sea | 64,501 | 24,904 |
| Lake Huron | 63,096 | 24,361 |
| Lake Michigan | 57,757 | 22,300 |
| Lake Tanganyika | 32,764 | 12,650 |
| Lake Baikal | 31,494 | 12,160 |
| Great Bear Lake | 31,328 | 12,095 |
| Lake Nyasa | 28,879 | 11,150 |
| Great Slave Lake | 28,568 | 11,030 |
| Lake Erie | 25,812 | 9,966 |
| Lake Winnipeg | 24,387 | 9,416 |
| Lake Ontario | 19,001 | 7,336 |
| Lake Balkhash | 18,428 | 7,115 |
| Lake Ladoga | 17,703 | 6,835 |
| Lake Chad* | 16,317 | 6,300 |
| Lake Maracaibo | 13,261 | 5,120 |
| Patos | 10,153 | 3,920 |
| Lake Onega | 9,609 | 3,710 |
| Lake Eyre* | 9,320 | 3,600 |
| Lake Titicaca | 8,288 | 3,200 |
| Lake Nicaragua | 8,029 | 3,100 |
| Lake Mai-Ndombe* | 8,029 | 3,100 |
| Lake Athabasca | 7,935 | 3,064 |

*Note*: * indicates large seasonal variations

## MAJOR RIVERS OF THE WORLD

| River | Length | |
|---|---|---|
| | Km. | Miles |
| Nile | 6,673 | 4,147 |
| Amazon | 6,570 | 4,083 |
| Yangtze | 6,276 | 3,900 |
| Mississippi–Missouri–Red Rock | 6,019 | 3,741 |
| Ob–Irtysh | 5,411 | 3,362 |
| Yenesei–Angara | 4,989 | 3,100 |
| Yellow River | 4,630 | 2,877 |
| Amur–Shilka | 4,416 | 2,744 |
| Lena | 4,400 | 2,734 |
| Congo | 4,374 | 2,178 |
| Mackenzie–Peace–Finlay | 4,241 | 2,635 |
| Mekong | 4,180 | 2,598 |
| Missouri–Red Rock | 4,125 | 2,564 |
| Niger | 4,100 | 2,548 |
| Plate–Paranà | 3,943 | 2,450 |
| Mississippi | 3,778 | 2,348 |
| Murray–Darling | 3,751 | 2,331 |
| Missouri | 3,725 | 2,315 |
| Volga | 3,531 | 2,194 |
| Madeira | 3,241 | 2,014 |
| Purus | 3,211 | 1,995 |
| São Francisco | 3,201 | 1,989 |
| Yukon | 3,185 | 1,979 |
| St Lawrence | 3,058 | 1,900 |
| Rio Grande | 3,030 | 1,883 |
| Tunguska, Lower | 2,995 | 1,861 |
| Indus | 2,897 | 1,800 |
| Danube | 2,857 | 1,775 |
| Salween | 2,849 | 1,770 |
| Brahmaputra | 2,736 | 1,700 |
| Euphrates | 2,736 | 1,700 |
| Para–Tocantins | 2,699 | 1,677 |
| Zambezi | 2,575 | 1,600 |
| Nelson–S. Saskatchewan–Bow | 2,575 | 1,600 |
| Paraguay | 2,549 | 1,584 |
| Amu Darya | 2,541 | 1,579 |
| Kolyma | 2,513 | 1,562 |
| Ganges | 2,494 | 1,550 |
| Ural | 2,428 | 1,509 |
| Japurà | 2,414 | 1,500 |
| Arkansas | 2,333 | 1,450 |
| Colorado | 2,333 | 1,450 |
| Syr Darya | 2,213 | 1,375 |
| Dnieper | 2,202 | 1,368 |
| Orange | 2,173 | 1,350 |

| River | Length | |
|---|---|---|
| | Km. | Miles |
| Kasai | 2,154 | 1,338 |
| Brazos | 2,106 | 1,309 |
| Ohio–Allegheny | 2,101 | 1,306 |
| Irrawaddy | 2,090 | 1,299 |
| Orinoco | 2,060 | 1,280 |
| Red River | 1,966 | 1,222 |
| Columbia | 1,953 | 1,214 |
| Tigris | 1,900 | 1,181 |

## THE WORLD'S LARGEST ISLANDS

| Island | Area | |
|---|---|---|
| | Sq. km. | Sq. miles |
| Greenland | 2,175,600 | 840,325 |
| New Guinea | 789,950 | 305,000 |
| Borneo | 751,100 | 290,000 |
| Madagascar | 587,041 | 226,744 |
| Baffin, Canada | 507,451 | 195,928 |
| Sumatra, Indonesia | 424,760 | 164,000 |
| Honshu, Japan | 227,415 | 89,184 |
| Great Britain | 218,078 | 84,200 |
| Victoria, Canada | 217,290 | 83,928 |
| Ellesmere, Canada | 196,236 | 75,796 |
| Sulawesi, Indonesia | 189,216 | 73,084 |
| South Island, New Zealand | 151,215 | 58,406 |
| Java, Indonesia | 126,501 | 48,842 |
| North Island, New Zealand | 114,383 | 44,180 |
| Newfoundland, Canada | 108,858 | 42,030 |
| Cuba | 104,981 | 40,533 |
| Luzon, Philippines | 104,688 | 40,420 |
| Iceland | 102,820 | 39,714 |

## DESERTS OF THE WORLD

| Desert | Location | Approximate area | |
|---|---|---|---|
| | | Sq. km. | Sq. miles |
| Sahara | North Africa | 9,065,000 | 3,500,000 |
| Gobi Desert | Mongolia–China | 1,295,000 | 500,000 |
| Rub al-Khali | Saudi Arabia | 647,500 | 250,000 |
| Great Sandy Desert | Australia | 338,500 | 150,000 |
| Great Victoria Desert | Australia | 338,500 | 150,000 |
| Gibson Desert | Australia | 310,800 | 120,000 |
| Garagum | Turkmenistan | 310,800 | 120,000 |
| Qizilkum | Uzbekistan | 259,000 | 100,000 |
| Syrian Desert | Middle East | 259,000 | 100,000 |
| Kalahari | Africa | 582,800 | 225,000 |
| Taklimakan | China | 362,600 | 140,000 |

| Desert | Location | Approximate area | |
|---|---|---|---|
| | | Sq. km. | Sq. miles |
| Thar Desert | India–Pakistan | 259,000 | 100,000 |
| Atacama | Chile | 181,300 | 70,000 |
| Sonoran Desert | Mexico–USA | 181,300 | 70,000 |
| Simpson Desert | Australia | 103,600 | 40,000 |
| An Nafud | Saudi Arabia | 103,600 | 40,000 |
| Dasht-e-Lut | Iran | 51,800 | 20,000 |
| Mojave Desert | USA | 38,900 | 15,000 |
| Negev | Israel | 12,200 | 4,700 |
| Death Valley | USA | 7,800 | 3,000 |
| Namib Desert | Namibia | 1,290 | 800 |

## THE WORLD'S HIGHEST WATERFALLS

| Name | Location | Height | |
|---|---|---|---|
| | | Metres | Feet |
| Angel Falls | Venezuela | 979 | 3,212 |
| Yosemite Falls | USA | 739 | 2,425 |
| Mardalsfossen (S) | Norway | 655 | 2,149 |
| Tugela Falls | South Africa | 613 | 2,014 |
| Cuquenan Falls | Venezuela | 610 | 2,000 |
| Sutherland Falls | New Zealand | 580 | 1,904 |
| Ribbon Falls | USA | 491 | 1,612 |
| Great Falls | Guyana | 488 | 1,600 |
| Mardalsfossen (N) | Norway | 468 | 1,535 |
| Della Falls | Canada | 440 | 1,443 |
| Gavarnie Falls | France | 422 | 1,385 |
| Skjeggedal Falls | Norway | 420 | 1,378 |
| Glass Falls | Brazil | 404 | 1,325 |
| Krimml Falls | Austria | 400 | 1,312 |
| Trummelbach Falls | Switzerland | 400 | 1,312 |
| Takakkaw Falls | Canada | 366 | 1,200 |
| Silver Strand Falls | USA | 357 | 1,170 |
| Wallaman Falls | Australia | 347 | 1,137 |
| Wollomombi | Australia | 335 | 1,100 |

## COUNTRIES OF THE WORLD

| Country | Adjectival form | Citizen |
|---|---|---|
| Afghanistan | Afghan | Afghan |
| Albania | Albanian | Albanian |
| Algeria | Algerian | Algerian |
| Andorra | Andorran | Andorran |
| Angola | Angolan | Angolan |
| Antigua and Barbuda | Antiguan, Barbudan | Citizen of Antigua and Barbuda |
| Argentina | Argentine | Argentine |
| Armenia | Armenian | Armenian |

| Country | Adjectival form | Citizen |
|---|---|---|
| Australia | Australian | Australian |
| Austria | Austrian | Austrian |
| Azerbaijan | Azerbaijani | Azerbaijani |
| Bahamas | Bahamian | Bahamian |
| Bahrain | Bahraini, Bahrain | Bahraini |
| Bangladesh | Bangladeshi | Bangladeshi |
| Barbados | Barbadian | Barbadian |
| Belarus | Belarussian, Belarus | Belarus, Belarussian |
| Belau | Belauan, Belau | Belauan |
| Belgium | Belgian | Belgian |
| Belize | Belizean, Belize | Citizen of Belize, Belizean |
| Benin | Beninese | Beninese |
| Bhutan | Bhutanese | Bhutanese |
| Bolivia | Bolivian | Bolivian |
| Bosnia and Herzegovina | Bosnian and Herzegovinian, Bosnian | Citizen of Bosnia and Herzegovina, Bosnian |
| Botswana | Botswana | Citizen of Botswana |
| Brazil | Brazilian | Brazilian |
| Brunei | Bruneian, Brunei | Citizen of Brunei |
| Bulgaria | Bulgarian | Bulgarian |
| Burkina | Burkinan, Burkina | Burkinan |
| Burma | Burmese | Burmese |
| Burundi | Burundi | Citizen of Burundi |
| Cambodia | Cambodian | Cambodia |
| Cameroon | Cameroonian | Cameroonian |
| Canada | Canadian | Canadian |
| Cape Verde | Cape Verdean | Cape Verdean |
| Central African Republic | Central African Republic | Citizen of the Central African Republic |
| Chad | Chadian | Chadian |
| Chile | Chilean | Chilean |
| China | Chinese | Chinese |
| Colombia | Colombian | Colombian |
| Comoros | Comoran | Comoran |
| Congo | Congolese | Congolese |
| Costa Rica | Costa Rican | Costa Rican |
| Croatia | Croatian | Croat |
| Cuba | Cuban | Cuban |
| Cyprus | Cypriot, Cyprus | Cypriot |
| Czech Republic | Czech | Czech |
| Denmark | Danish | Dane |
| Djibouti | Djiboutian | Djiboutian |
| Dominica | Dominican | Dominican |
| Dominican Republic | Dominican Republic | Citizen of the Dominican Republic |
| Ecuador | Ecuadorean | Ecuadorean |
| Egypt | Egyptian | Egyptia |

| Country | Adjectival form | Citizen |
|---|---|---|
| El Salvador | Salvadorean | Salvadorean |
| Equatorial Guinea | of Equatorial Guinea | Equatorial Guinean |
| Eritrea | Eritrean | Eritrean |
| Estonia | Estonian | Estonian |
| Ethiopia | Ethiopia | Ethiopian |
| Fiji | Fiji, of Fiji | Citizen of Fiji |
| [Fijian refers to indigenous Polynesian, Micronesian or Melanesian inhabitants] | | |
| Finland | Finnish | Finn |
| France | French | Frenchman, Frenchwoman |
| Gabon | Gabonese | Gabonese |
| Gambia, The | Gambian | Gambian |
| Georgia | Georgian | Georgian |
| Germany | German | German |
| Ghana | Ghanaian, Ghana | Ghanaian |
| Greece | Greek | Greek |
| Grenada | Grenadian, Grenada | Grenadian |
| Guatemala | Guatemalan | Guatemalan |
| Guinean | Guinean | Guinean |
| Guinea–Bissau | Guinea–Bissau | Citizen of Guinea–Bissau |
| Guyana | Guyanese | Guyanese |
| Haiti | Haitian | Haitian |
| Honduras | Honduran | Honduran |
| Hungary | Hungarian | Hungarian |
| Iceland | Icelandic | Icelander |
| India | Indian | Indian |
| Indonesia | Indonesian | Indonesian |
| Iran | Iranian | Iranian |
| Iraq | Iraqi, Iraq | Iraqi |
| Israel | Israeli, Israel | Israeli |
| Italy | Italian | Italian |
| Ivory Coast | Ivorian, Ivory Coast | Citizen of the Ivory Coast |
| Jamaica | Jamaican | Jamaican |
| Japan | Japanese | Japanese |
| Jordan | Jordanian | Jordanian |
| Kazakhstan | Kazakh | Kazakh |
| Kenya | Kenyan, Kenya | Kenyan |
| Kiribati | Kiribati | Citizen of Kiribati |
| Korea, North | North Korean | North Korean |
| Korea, South | South Korean | South Korean |
| Kuwait | Kuwaiti | Kuwaiti |
| Kyrgyzstan | Kyrgyz | Kyrgyz |
| Laos | Laotian | Laotian |
| Latvia | Latvian | Latvian |
| Lebanon | Lebanese | Lebanese |
| Lesotho | Lesotho | Citizen of Lesotho |
| Liberia | Liberian | Liberian |

| Country | Adjectival form | Citizen |
|---|---|---|
| Libya | Libyan | Libyan |
| Liechtenstein | Liechtenstein | Liechtenstein citizen |
| Lithuania | Lithuanian | Lithuanian |
| Luxembourg | Luxembourg | Luxembourger |
| Macedonia | Macedonian | Macedonian |
| Madagascar | Malagasy | Citizen of Madagascar |
| Malawi | Malawian | Malawian |
| Malaysia | Malaysian | Citizen of Malaysia |
| Maldives | Maldivian | Maldivian |
| Mali | Malian | Malian |
| Malta | Maltese | Maltese |
| Marshall Islands | Marshall Islands | Marshall Islander |
| Mauritania | Mauritanian | Mauritanian |
| Mauritius | Mauritian | Mauritian |
| Mexico | Mexican | Mexican |
| Micronesia | Micronesian | Micronesian |
| Moldova | Moldovan | Moldovan |
| Monaco | Monegasque | Monegasque |
| Mongolia | Mongolian | Mongolian |
| Morocco | Moroccan | Moroccan |
| Mozambique | Mozambican, Mozambique | Mozambican |
| Nauru | Nauruan | Nauruan |
| Nepal | Nepalese | Nepalese |
| Netherlands, The | Dutch, Netherlands | Dutchman, Dutchwoman |
| New Zealand | New Zealand | New Zealander |
| Nicaragua | Nicaraguan | Nicaraguan |
| Niger | Niger | Citizen of Niger |
| Nigeria | Nigerian | Nigerian |
| Norway | Norwegian | Norwegian |
| Oman | Omani, Oman | Omani |
| Pakistan | Pakistan | Pakistani |
| Panama | Panamanian | Panamanian |
| Papua and New Guinea | Papua New Guinean | Papua New Guinean |
| Paraguay | Paraguayan | Paraguayan |
| Peru | Peruvian | Peruvian |
| Philippines | Philippine | Filipino, Filipina |
| Poland | Polish | Pole |
| Portugal | Portuguese | Portuguese |
| Qatar | Qatari, Qatar | Qatari |
| Republic of Ireland | Irish, of the Irish Republic, of the Republic of Ireland | Citizen of the Republic of Ireland, Irish Republic |
| Romania | Romanian | Romanian |
| Russia | Russian | Russian |
| Rwanda | Rwandan | Rwandan |
| St Kitts and Nevis | Kittitian, Nevisian, St Kitts and Nevis | Citizen of St Kitts and Nevis |

| Country | Adjectival form | Citizen |
|---|---|---|
| St Lucia | St Lucian, St Lucia | St Lucian |
| St Vincent | St Vincent | Vincentian |
| San Marino | San Marino | Citizen of San Marino |
| São Tomé and Príncipe | of São Tomé and Príncipe | Citizen of São Tomé and Príncipe |
| Saudi Arabia | Saudi Arabian | Saudi Arabian |
| Senegal | Senegalese | Senegalese |
| Seychelles | Seychelles | Citizen of Seychelles |
| Sierra Leone | Sierra Leone | Sierra Leonean |
| Singapore | Singaporean | Singaporean |
| Slovakia | Slovak | Slovak |
| Slovenia | Slovenian | Slovene |
| Solomon Islands | Solomon Islands | Solomon Islander |
| Somalia | Somali | Somali |
| South Africa | South African | South African |
| Spain | Spanish | Spaniard |
| Sri Lanka | Sri Lankan, Sri Lanka | Citizen of Sri Lanka |
| Sudan | Sudanese | Sudanese |
| Surinam | Surinamese | Surinamer |
| Swaziland | Swazi | Swazi |
| Sweden | Swedish | Swede |
| Switzerland | Swiss | Swiss |
| Syria | Syrian | Syrian |
| Taiwan | Nationalist Chinese | Nationalist Chinese |
| Tajikistan | Tajik | Tajik |
| Tanzania | Tanzanian | Tanzanian |
| Thailand | Thai | Thai |
| Togo | Togolese | Togolese |
| Trinidad and Tobago | Trinidadian, Tobagan, Trinidad and Tobago | Trinidad and Tobago citizen |
| Tunisia | Tunisian | Tunisian |
| Turkey | Turkish | Turk |
| Turkmenistan | Turkmen | Turkmen |
| Tuvalu | Tuvaluan | Tuvaluan |
| Uganda | Ugandan, Uganda | Ugandan |
| Ukraine | Ukrainian | Ukrainian |
| United Arab Emirates | of the United Arab Emirates | Citizen of the United Arab Emirates |
| United States | United States | United States citizen |
| Uruguay | Uruguayan | Uruguayan |
| Uzbekistan | Uzbek | Uzbek |
| Vanuatu | Vanuatu | Citizen of Vanuatu |
| Vatican City | Vatican, Apostolic, Papal | Vatican citizen |
| Venezuela | Venezuelan | Venezuelan |
| Vietnam | Vietnamese | Vietnamese |
| Western Samoa | Western Samoan | Western Samoan |
| Yemen | Yemeni | Yemeni |
| Yugoslavia | Yugoslav | Yugoslav |

| Country | Adjectival form | Citizen |
|---|---|---|
| Zaïre | Zaïrean | Zaïrean |
| Zambia | Zambian | Zambian |
| Zimbabwe | Zimbabwean, Zimbabwe | Zimbabwean |

## THE WORLD'S LARGEST COUNTRIES

| Country | Area | |
|---|---|---|
| | Sq. km. | Sq. miles |
| Russia | 17,075,400 | 6,595,830 |
| Canada | 9,970,610 | 3,849,660 |
| China | 9,571,300 | 3,695,490 |
| United States of America | 9,372,614 | 3,618,777 |
| Brazil | 8,511,965 | 3,286,479 |
| Australia | 7,682,300 | 2,966,145 |
| India | 3,185,019 | 1,229,737 |
| Argentina | 2,780,092 | 1,073,397 |
| Kazakhstan | 2,717,300 | 1,049,153 |
| Sudan | 2,506,000 | 967,569 |
| Algeria | 2,381,741 | 919,593 |
| Zaïre | 2,343,950 | 905,000 |
| Saudi Arabia | 2,149,690 | 829,998 |
| Mexico | 1,958,200 | 756,063 |
| Indonesia | 1,904,569 | 735,356 |
| Libya | 1,775,500 | 685,522 |
| Iran | 1,648,000 | 636,295 |
| Mongolia | 1,565,000 | 604,248 |
| Peru | 1,285,216 | 496,223 |
| Chad | 1,284,000 | 495,752 |

## THE WORLD'S SMALLEST COUNTRIES

| Country | Area | |
|---|---|---|
| | Sq. km. | Sq. miles |
| Vatican City | 0.4 | 0.2 |
| Monaco | 1.9 | 0.7 |
| Nauru | 21 | 8 |
| Tuvalu | 26 | 10 |
| San Marino | 61 | 23.5 |
| Liechtenstein | 160 | 62 |
| Marshall Islands | 181 | 70 |
| St Kitts and Nevis | 261 | 101 |
| Maldives | 298 | 115 |
| Malta | 316 | 122 |
| Grenada | 345 | 133 |
| St Vincent | 389 | 150 |
| Barbados | 431 | 166 |
| Antigua and Barbuda | 442 | 171 |

| Country | Area | |
|---|---|---|
| | Sq. km. | Sq. miles |
| Andorra | 468 | 181 |
| Seychelles | 453 | 175 |
| Belau | 508 | 196 |
| St Lucia | 616 | 238 |
| Singapore | 618 | 239 |
| Bahrain | 620 | 240 |
| Tonga | 668 | 258 |

## THE WORLD'S MOST POPULOUS COUNTRIES

| Country | Population |
|---|---|
| China | 1,188,000,000 |
| India | 879,500,000 |
| United States of America | 255,200,000 |
| Indonesia | 191,200,000 |
| Brazil | 154,100,000 |
| Russia | 149,003,000 |
| Pakistan | 124,800,000 |
| Japan | 124,500,000 |
| Bangladesh | 119,300,000 |
| Nigeria | 115,700,000 |
| Mexico | 88,200,000 |
| Germany | 80,300,000 |
| Vietnam | 69,500,000 |
| Philippines | 65,200,000 |
| Iran | 61,600,000 |
| Turkey | 58,400,000 |
| Italy | 57,800,000 |
| United Kingdom | 57,700,000 |
| France | 57,200,000 |
| Thailand | 56,100,000 |
| Egypt | 54,800,000 |

*Source*: 1991/1992 UNDP estimates

## THE WORLD'S LEAST POPULOUS COUNTRIES

| Country | Population |
|---|---|
| Vatican City | 1,000 |
| Nauru | 9,000 |
| Tuvalu | 9,000 |
| Belau | 15,100 |
| San Marino | 23,000 |
| Monaco | 28,000 |
| Liechtenstein | 29,000 |
| St Kitts and Nevis | 44,000 |
| Marshall Islands | 48,000 |
| Andorra | 58,000 |

| Country | Population |
|---|---|
| Antigua and Barbuda | 64,000 |
| Kiribati | 66,000 |
| Seychelles | 68,000 |
| Dominica | 83,000 |
| Grenada | 84,000 |
| Tonga | 94,000 |
| Micronesia | 101,000 |
| St Vincent | 117,000 |
| São Tomé and Príncipe | 124,000 |
| St Lucia | 153,000 |
| Vanuatu | 163,000 |

*Source*: 1991/1992 UNDP estimates

### THE WORLD'S RICHEST COUNTRIES
(Highest GNP per capita)

| Country | GNP per capita 1991/2 US$ |
|---|---|
| Switzerland | 33,510 |
| Liechtenstein | 33,000 |
| Luxembourg | 31,080 |
| Japan | 26,920 |
| Sweden | 25,490 |
| Finland | 24,400 |
| Norway | 24,160 |
| Denmark | 23,660 |
| Germany | 23,650 |
| Iceland | 22,580 |
| United States of America | 22,560 |
| Canada | 21,260 |
| France | 20,600 |
| Austria | 20,380 |

### THE WORLD'S POOREST COUNTRIES
(Lowest GNP per capita)

| Country | GNP per capita 1991/2 US$ |
|---|---|
| Mozambique | 60 |
| Tanzania | 110 |
| Ethiopia | 110 |
| Somalia | 150 |
| Nepal | 170 |
| Sierra Leone | 170 |
| Uganda | 170 |
| Bhutan | 180 |
| Cambodia | 200 |
| Guinea-Bissau | 210 |
| Burundi | 210 |

| Country | GNP per capita 1991/2 US$ |
|---------|---------------------------|
| Malawi | 210 |
| Bangladesh | 220 |
| Chad | 220 |
| Zaïre | 220 |
| Madagascar | 230 |
| Laos | 250 |
| Rwanda | 250 |

## COUNTRIES WITH THE HIGHEST LIFE EXPECTANCY 1990

| Country | Years | |
|---------|-------|--------|
| | Male | Female |
| Japan | 76 | 82 |
| Iceland | 75 | 81 |
| Sweden | 75 | 81 |
| Switzerland | 75 | 81 |
| Canada | 74 | 81 |
| Norway | 74 | 81 |
| Australia | 74 | 80 |
| Spain | 74 | 80 |
| France | 73 | 81 |
| Italy | 73 | 80 |
| United States of America | 73 | 80 |
| Finland | 72 | 80 |

## COUNTRIES WITH THE LOWEST LIFE EXPECTANCY 1990

| Country | Years | |
|---------|-------|--------|
| | Male | Female |
| Afghanistan | 43 | 44 |
| Guinea-Bissau | 42 | 45 |
| Guinea | 44 | 45 |
| Gambia, The | 43 | 47 |
| Angola | 45 | 48 |
| Niger | 45 | 48 |
| Ethiopia | 45 | 49 |
| Somalia | 45 | 49 |
| Chad | 46 | 49 |
| Benin | 46 | 50 |
| Equatorial Guinea | 46 | 50 |
| Mozambique | 47 | 50 |
| Djibouti | 47 | 51 |
| Malawi | 48 | 50 |
| Senegal | 48 | 50 |
| Burkina | 48 | 51 |
| Burundi | 48 | 51 |
| Bhutan | 51 | 49 |
| Rwanda | 49 | 52 |

## MEMBERS OF THE UNITED NATIONS

| Country | Year of Admission | Country | Year of Admission |
|---|---|---|---|
| Afghanistan | 1946 | Denmark | 1945 |
| Albania | 1955 | Djibouti | 1977 |
| Algeria | 1962 | Dominica | 1978 |
| Andorra | 1993 | Dominican Republic | 1945 |
| Angola | 1976 | Ecuador | 1945 |
| Antigua and Barbuda | 1981 | Egypt | 1945 |
| Argentina | 1945 | El Salvador | 1945 |
| Armenia | 1992 | Equatorial Guinea | 1968 |
| Australia | 1945 | Eritrea | 1993 |
| Austria | 1955 | Estonia | 1991 |
| Azerbaijan | 1992 | Ethiopia | 1945 |
| Bahamas | 1973 | Fiji | 1970 |
| Bahrain | 1971 | Finland | 1955 |
| Bangladesh | 1974 | France | 1945 |
| Barbados | 1966 | Gabon | 1960 |
| Belarus | 1945 | Gambia, The | 1965 |
| Belau | 1994 | Georgia | 1992 |
| Belgium | 1945 | Germany | 1973 |
| Belize | 1981 | Ghana | 1957 |
| Benin | 1960 | Greece | 1945 |
| Bhutan | 1971 | Grenada | 1974 |
| Bolivia | 1945 | Guatemala | 1945 |
| Bosnia and Herzegovina | 1992 | Guinea | 1958 |
| Botswana | 1966 | Guinea-Bissau | 1974 |
| Brazil | 1945 | Guyana | 1966 |
| Brunei | 1984 | Haiti | 1945 |
| Bulgaria | 1955 | Honduras | 1945 |
| Burkina | 1960 | Hungary | 1955 |
| Burma | 1948 | Iceland | 1946 |
| Burundi | 1962 | India | 1945 |
| Cambodia | 1955 | Indonesia | 1950 |
| Cameroon | 1960 | Iran | 1945 |
| Canada | 1945 | Iraq | 1945 |
| Cape Verde | 1975 | Ireland | 1955 |
| Central African Republic | 1960 | Israel | 1949 |
| Chad | 1960 | Italy | 1955 |
| Chile | 1945 | Ivory Coast | 1960 |
| China | 1945 | Jamaica | 1962 |
| Colombia | 1945 | Japan | 1956 |
| Comoros | 1975 | Jordan | 1955 |
| Congo | 1960 | Kazakhstan | 1992 |
| Costa Rica | 1945 | Kenya | 1963 |
| Croatia | 1992 | Korea, North | 1991 |
| Cuba | 1945 | Korea, South | 1991 |
| Cyprus | 1960 | Kuwait | 1963 |
| Czech Republic | 1993 | Kyrgyzstan | 1992 |

| Country | Year of Admission | Country | Year of Admission |
|---|---|---|---|
| Laos | 1955 | St Kitts and Nevis | 1983 |
| Latvia | 1991 | St Lucia | 1979 |
| Lebanon | 1945 | St Vincent | 1980 |
| Lesotho | 1966 | San Marino | 1992 |
| Liberia | 1945 | São Tomé and Príncipe | 1975 |
| Libya | 1955 | Saudi Arabia | 1945 |
| Liechtenstein | 1990 | Senegal | 1960 |
| Lithuania | 1991 | Seychelles | 1976 |
| Luxembourg | 1945 | Sierra Leone | 1961 |
| Macedonia | 1993 | Singapore | 1945 |
| Madagascar | 1960 | Slovakia | 1993 |
| Malawi | 1964 | Slovenia | 1992 |
| Malaysia | 1957 | Solomon Islands | 1978 |
| Maldives | 1965 | Somalia | 1960 |
| Mali | 1960 | South Africa | 1945 |
| Malta | 1964 | Spain | 1955 |
| Marshall Islands | 1991 | Sri Lanka | 1955 |
| Mauritania | 1961 | Sudan | 1956 |
| Mauritius | 1968 | Surinam | 1975 |
| Mexico | 1945 | Swaziland | 1968 |
| Micronesia | 1991 | Sweden | 1946 |
| Moldova | 1992 | Syria | 1945 |
| Monaco | 1993 | Tajikistan | 1992 |
| Mongolia | 1961 | Tanzania | 1961 |
| Morocco | 1956 | Thailand | 1946 |
| Mozambique | 1975 | Togo | 1960 |
| Namibia | 1990 | Trinidad and Tobago | 1962 |
| Nepal | 1955 | Tunisia | 1956 |
| Netherlands, The | 1945 | Turkey | 1945 |
| New Zealand | 1945 | Turkmenistan | 1992 |
| Nicaragua | 1945 | Uganda | 1962 |
| Niger | 1960 | Ukraine | 1945 |
| Nigeria | 1960 | United Arab Emirates | 1971 |
| Norway | 1945 | United Kingdom | 1945 |
| Oman | 1971 | Unites States of America | 1945 |
| Pakistan | 1947 | Uruguay | 1945 |
| Panama | 1945 | Uzbekistan | 1992 |
| Papua New Guinea | 1975 | Vanuatu | 1981 |
| Paraguay | 1945 | Venezuela | 1945 |
| Peru | 1945 | Vietnam | 1977 |
| Philippines | 1945 | Western Samoa | 1976 |
| Poland | 1945 | Yemen | 1947 |
| Portugal | 1955 | Yugoslavia | 1945 |
| Qatar | 1971 | Zaïre | 1960 |
| Romania | 1955 | Zambia | 1964 |
| Russia | 1945 | Zimbabwe | 1980 |
| Rwanda | 1962 | | |

## THE WORLD'S LARGEST URBAN AREAS

| Urban Area | Country | Pop. (1990) in millions |
| --- | --- | --- |
| Mexico City | Mexico | 20.2 |
| Tokyo | Japan | 18.1 |
| São Paulo | Brazil | 17.4 |
| New York | USA | 16.2 |
| Shanghai | China | 13.4 |
| Greater Bombay | India | 12.6 |
| Los Angeles | USA | 11.9 |
| Calcutta | India | 11.8 |
| Buenos Aires | Argentina | 11.5 |
| Seoul | Korea | 11.0 |
| Beijing | China | 10.8 |
| Rio de Janeiro | Brazil | 10.7 |
| Tianjin | China | 9.4 |
| Jakarta | Indonesia | 9.3 |
| Cairo | Egypt | 9.0 |
| Moscow | Russia | 8.8 |
| Delhi | India | 8.8 |
| Metro Manila | Philippines | 8.5 |
| Osaka | Japan | 8.5 |
| Paris | France | 8.5 |

## INTERNATIONAL ORGANIZATIONS

| | |
| --- | --- |
| ACP | African, Caribbean, and Pacific States (EU) |
| ACS | Association of Caribbean States |
| ALADI | Latin American Integration Association |
| AMU | Arab Maghreb Union |
| APEC | Asia–Pacific Economic Co-operation |
| ARPEL | Organization of Latin American State Oil Corporations for Mutual Assistance |
| ASEAN | Association of South East Asian Nations |
| BEAC | Bank of the States of Central Africa |
| BENELUX | Belgium, Netherlands, Luxembourg Economic Union |
| CACM | Central American Common Market |
| CARICOM | Caribbean Common Market |
| CARIFTA | Caribbean Free Trade Association |
| CDB | Caribbean Development Bank |
| CEAO | West African Economic Community |
| CEEAC | Economic Community of Central African States |
| CEPGL | Economic Community of the Great Lakes Countries |
| CIA | US Central Intelligence Agency |
| CIM | Inter-American Commission on Women |
| CIS | Commonwealth of Independent States |
| CSCE | Conference on Security and Co-operation in Europe |
| EBRD | European Bank for Reconstruction and Development |
| EC | European Community |

| ECLAC | Economic Commission for Latin America and the Caribbean |
| ECOWAS | Economic Community of West African States |
| ECSC | European Coal and Steel Community |
| EFTA | European Free Trade Association |
| ETO | European Telecommunications Organization |
| EU | European Union |
| EURATOM | European Atomic Energy Community |
| EUTC | European Trade Union Congress |
| FAO | Food and Agriculture Organization of the UN |
| G-7 | Group of Seven |
| GATT | General Agreement on Tariffs and Trade |
| GCC | Gulf Co-operation Council |
| IACHR | Inter-American Commission on Human Rights |
| IACI | Inter-American Children's Institute |
| IADB | Inter-American Defense Board |
| IAEA | International Atomic Energy Agency |
| IAII | Inter-American Indian Institute |
| IAPA | International Airline Passengers Association |
| ICAO | International Civil Aviation Organization |
| ICRC | International Committee of the Red Cross |
| IDA | International Development Association |
| IDB | Inter-American Development Bank |
| IDB | Islamic Development Bank |
| IFAD | International Development Fund for Agricultural Development |
| IFC | International Finance Corporation |
| IGADD | Inter-governmental Authority on Drought and Development |
| IICA | Inter-American Institute for Co-operation on Agriculture |
| ILO | International Labour Organization |
| IMF | International Monetary Fund |
| IMO | International Maritime Organization |
| INTELSAT | International Telecommunications Satellite Consortium |
| INTERPOL | International Criminal Police Commission |
| IOC | Indian Ocean Commission |
| IPA | International Phonetic Alphabet |
| IPU | Inter-Parliamentary Union |
| ITCZ | Inter-Tropical Convergence Zone |
| ITU | International Telecommunication Union |
| IUCN | International Union for Conservation of Nature and Natural Resources |
| IWC | International Whaling Commission |
| LAFTA | Latin American Free Trade Area |
| LCBC | Lake Chad Basin Commission |
| NACC | North Atlantic Co-operation Council |
| NAFTA | North American Free Trade Area |
| NAM | Non-Aligned Movement |
| NASA | US National Aeronautics and Space Administration |
| NATO | North Atlantic Treaty Organization |
| OAS | Organization of American States |
| OAU | Organization of African Unity |

| | |
|---|---|
| OECD | Organization for Economic Co-operation and Development |
| OECS | Organization of Eastern Caribbean States |
| OLADE | Latin American Energy Organization |
| OMVG | Gambia River Development Organization |
| OMVS | Senegal River Development Organization |
| OPEC | Organization of the Petroleum Exporting Countries |
| PADF | Pan American Development Foundation |
| PAHO | Pan American Health Organization |
| PTA | Preferential Trade Area for Eastern and Southern African States |
| SAARC | South Asian Association for Regional Co-operation |
| SADC | Southern African Development Community |
| SELA | Latin American Economic System |
| SPC | South Pacific Commission |
| SPF | South Pacific Forum |
| UAE | United Arab Emirates |
| UDEAC | Customs and Economic Union of Central Africa |
| UEMOA | West African Economic and Monetary Union |
| UK | United Kingdom |
| UN | United Nations |
| UNCTAD | UN Conference on Trade and Development |
| UNDP | UN Development Programme |
| UNESCO | UN Educational, Scientific, and Cultural Organization |
| UNHCR | UN High Commissioner for Refugees |
| UNICEF | UN Children's Fund |
| UPU | Universal Postal Union |
| USA | United States of America |
| WCL | World Confederation of Labour |
| WEF | World Economic Forum |
| WEU | Western European Union |
| WFC | World Food Council |
| WFTU | World Confederation of Trade Unions |
| WHO | World Health Organization |
| WIPO | World Intellectual Property Organization |
| WMO | World Meteorological Organization |
| WTO | World Tourism Organization |
| WTO | World Trade Organization |

# COLOUR MAPS

# British Isles

**Boundaries**

international

internal

**Communications**

motorway

other major road

railway

**Cities and towns**

major built-up areas

over 1 million inhabitants

more than 100,000 inhabitants

smaller towns

**Land height**

| | metres |
|---|---|
| | 1000 |
| | 500 |
| | 200 |
| | 100 |
| | sea level |
| | land below sea level |

▲ spot height in metres

**Scale 1:6 200 000**

0    50    100 km

Transverse Mercator Projection
Oxford University Press

# 2 Europe

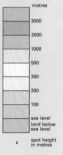

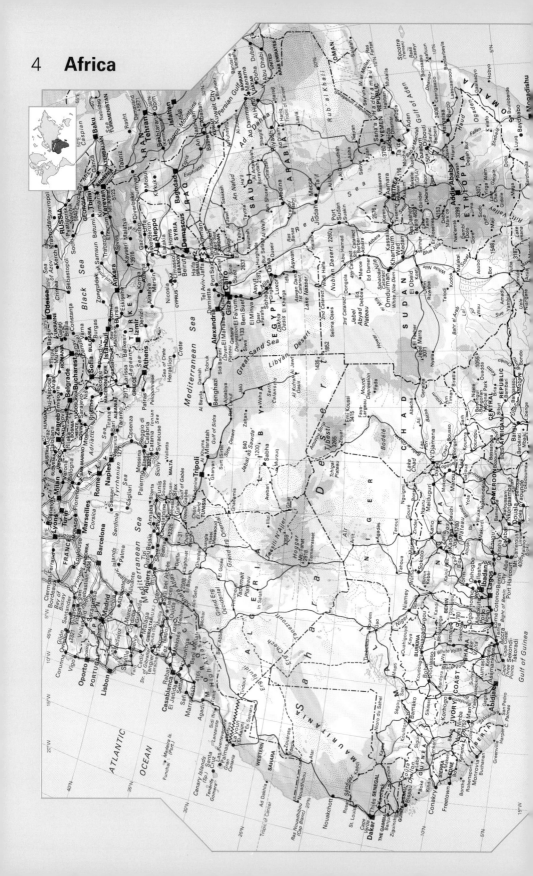

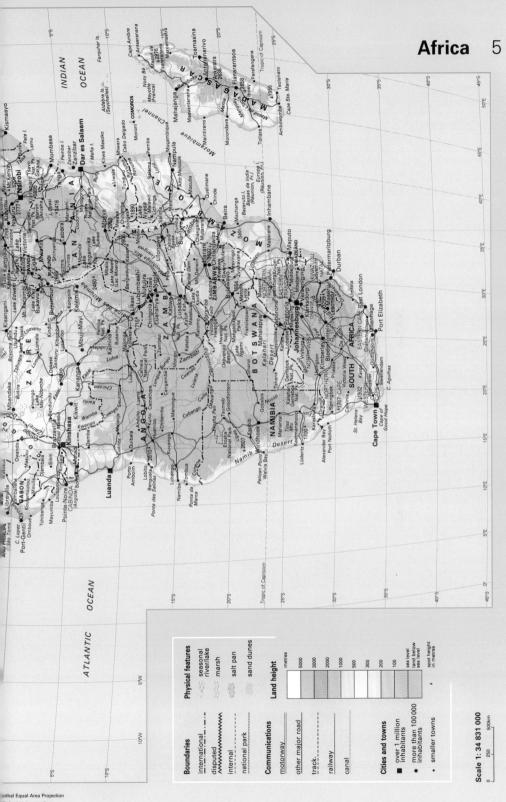

ATLANTIC OCEAN

INDIAN OCEAN

**Boundaries**

international
disputed
internal
national park

**Communications**

motorway
other major road
track
railway
canal

**Cities and towns**

■ over 1 million inhabitants
● more than 100 000 inhabitants
• smaller towns

**Physical features**

seasonal river/lake
marsh
salt pan
sand dunes

**Land height**

| metres |
| 5000 |
| 3000 |
| 2000 |
| 1000 |
| 500 |
| 300 |
| 200 |
| 100 |
| sea level |
| land below sea level |

1996 spot height in metres

**Scale 1: 34 831 000**

0    250    500km

# Northern Asia

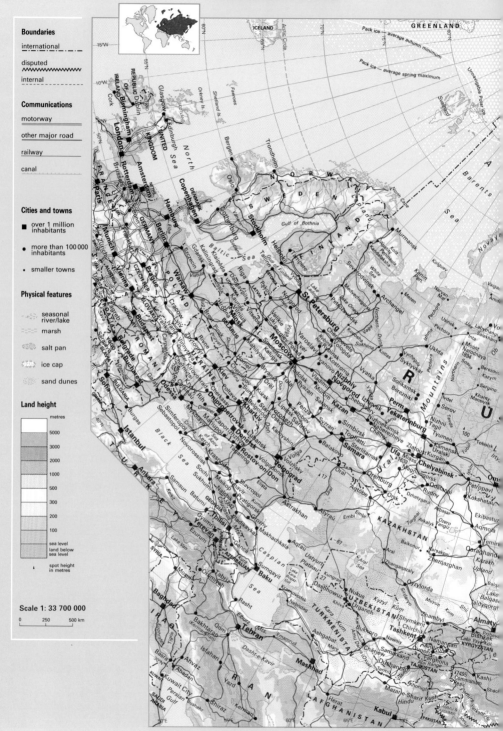

**Boundaries**

international

disputed

internal

**Communications**

motorway

other major road

railway

canal

**Cities and towns**

■ over 1 million
inhabitants

● more than 100 000
inhabitants

· smaller towns

**Physical features**

seasonal
river/lake

marsh

salt pan

ice cap

sand dunes

**Land height**

metres

5000

3000

2000

1000

500

300

200

100

sea level
land below
sea level

▲ spot height
in metres

Scale 1: 33 700 000

0    250    500 km

Conical Orthomorphic Projection

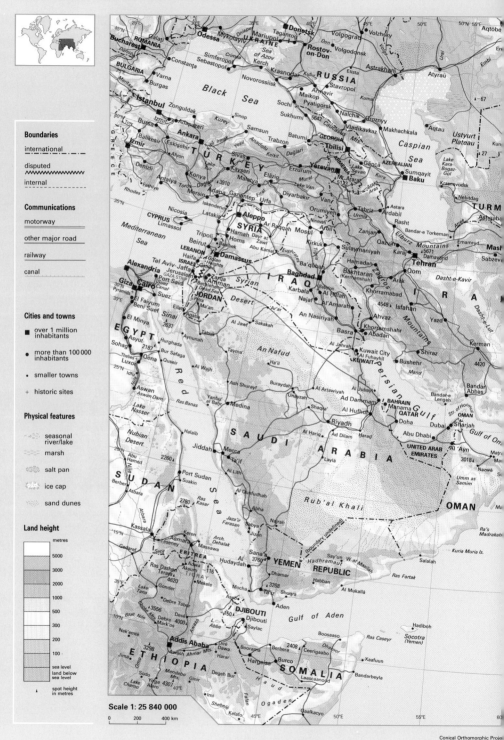

**Boundaries**

international

disputed

internal

**Communications**

motorway

other major road

railway

canal

**Cities and towns**

■ over 1 million
inhabitants

● more than 100 000
inhabitants

• smaller towns

+ historic sites

**Physical features**

seasonal
river/lake

marsh

salt pan

ice cap

sand dunes

**Land height**

metres

5000

3000

2000

1000

500

300

200

100

sea level
land below
sea level

▲ spot height
in metres

Scale 1: 25 840 000

0        200        400 km

Conical Orthomorphic Proje

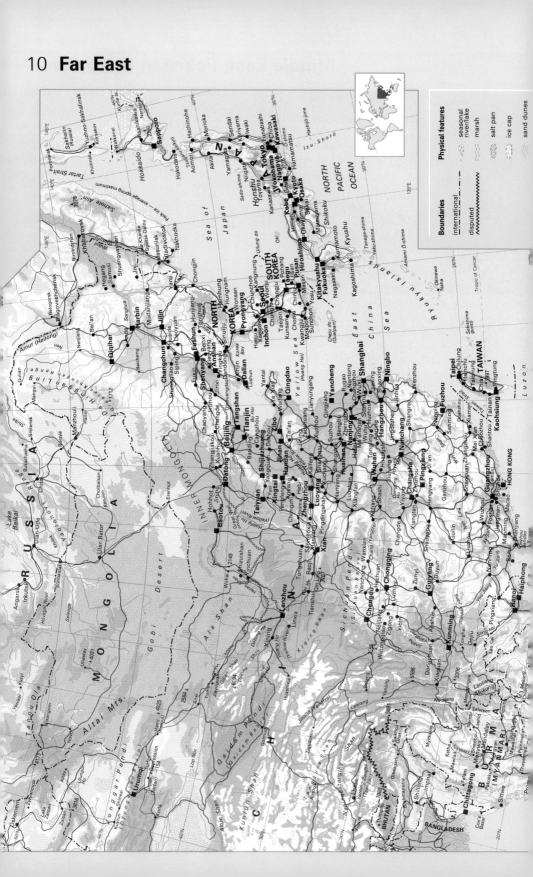

**Boundaries**

international

disputed

**Physical features**

seasonal
river/lake

marsh

salt pan

ice cap

sand dunes

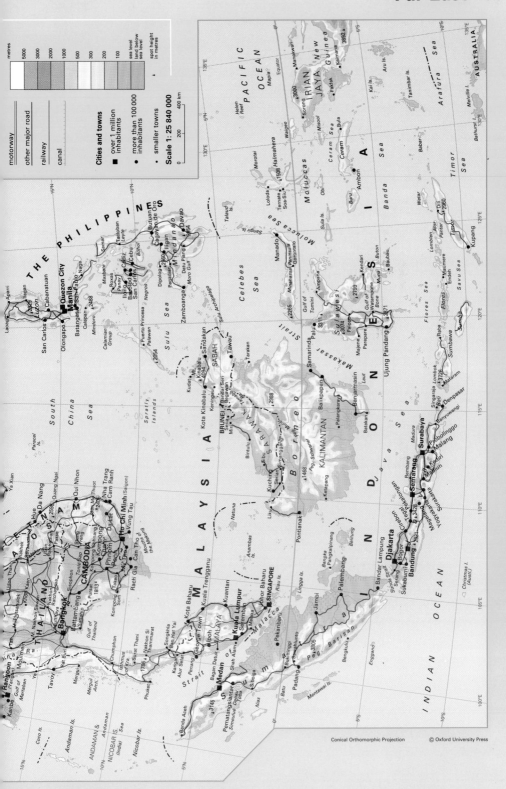

Conical Orthomorphic Projection

Zenithal Equidistant Projec

160°E 165°E 170°E 175°E 180° 175°W 170°W

5°N

Butaritari

Abaiang
• Tarawa
Abemama

**NAURU**    Aranuka  Nonouti   Howland I. (U.S.A.)
Banaba         Beru    Baker I. (U.S.A.)
(Kiribati)  Tabiteuea  Nikunau   Equator
                Onotoa
Tamana  Arorae     Winslow  0°
                    Reef

**K I R I B A T I**

uu Is.  Nukumanu          McKean I.   Kanton I.
Is.                        Birnie I.  Enderbury I.
Otong Java                Nikumaroro   Rāwaki
Atoll                      Orona      Manra
**SOLOMON**    Nanumea
Santa Isabel   • Niutao   Carondelet   **Phoenix
ISLANDS**  Stewart  Nanumanga  Reef     Islands**
Is.                                    (Kiribati)
Honiara  Malaita  Nui
Guadalcanal •2331  Nukufetau  5°S
San      Duff Is.  **TUVALU**   Atafu
Cristobal  Santa Cruz  (Ellice Islands)  **Tokelau  Nukunono
Rennell    Islands    Nukulaelae    Islands   Fakaofo
                              (N.Z.)

**P A C I F I C**

Indispensable   Cherry   Niulakita    Swains I.  Pukapuka
Reefs    Mitre              (U.S.A.)  (N.Z.)
          Banks    Rotuma I.          Nassau
          Islands                     (N.Z.)  10°S
Espiritu Santo  Maéwo           **WESTERN
**VANUATU**  Aoba Pentecost I.  Wallis and  **SAMOA**
Malekula  Ambrym  Futuna Islands  Savai'i  Apia
Vila•  Epi   (Fr.)      Upolu  Manua Is.
Efate   Futuna • Alofi   Tutuila  Pago Pago
Erromango                 •American
Chesterfield Is.  Tanna  Vanua Levu   Samoa
    Loyalty Is.  Lambasa    (U.S.A.)  15°S
New   Lifou  Lautoka  •3324
Caledonia  Maré  Viti Levu• Suva  **FIJI**    Cook
(France)  Nouméa       Kandavu   Islands
    Matthew  Ceva-i-Ra    Vava'u
    Walpole  Hunter    Group   Antiope
              Ha'apai  Reef
              Nuku'alofa  Group  Niue
              **TONGA**  (N.Z.)  Palmerston I.
              Tongatapu      (N.Z.)
              Group    Beveridge
Tropic of Capricorn        Reef

**O C E A N**

20°S
Minerva
Reefs
170°W  165°W

25°S

Norfolk I.
(Aust.)

Lord Howe I.
(Aust.)  Raoul  30°S
                Macauley I.
                Curtis I.

Three
Kings Is.  North Cape
Kaitaia
Dargaville  Whangarei
Auckland  Takapuna  **North
Hamilton  Tauranga  Island**  East Cape
New Plymouth  Rotorua  •754
2518•  Napier  Gisborne  35°S
Wanganui  Hastings
          Palmerston North
Greymouth  Nelson  Porirua
2885  Picton  Lower Hutt
**South  Mt Cook  Wellington
Island**  3754  **NEW ZEALAND**
    Southern  Christchurch
C. Providence  Alps  Timaru  40°S
Stewart I.  •Dunedin  Chatham Is.
  Invercargill  (N.Z.)
              Pitt I.

**t a s m a n**

**S e a**

**Cook Strait**

165°E  170°E  175°E  180°  175°W  45°S  170°W

---

**Boundaries**        **Physical features**

international          seasonal
                      river/lake
internal              marsh

**Communications**     sand dunes

major road            coral reef

railway               **Land height**
                                    metres
                                    3000
**Cities and towns**                2000
                                    1000
■ over 1 million                    500
  inhabitants                       300
                                    200
● more than 100 000                 100
  inhabitants                       sea level
                                    land below
• smaller towns                     sea level

**Scale 1: 29 780 000**        ▲ spot height
                                  in metres
0    250    500 km

Oxford University Press

Land height

| metres | |
| --- | --- |
| | 3000 |
| | 2000 |
| | 1000 |
| | 500 |
| | 300 |
| | 200 |
| | 100 |
| | sea level |
| | spot height in metres |

**Physical features**
- seasonal river/lake
- marsh
- ice cap
- sand dunes

**Cities and towns**
- ■ over 1 million inhabitants
- ■ more than 100 000 inhabitants
- • smaller towns

**Communications**
- motorway
- other major road
- railway
- canal

**Boundaries**
- international
- internal

Scale 1: 33 700 000

0    250    500 km

GREENLAND (Denmark)

ARCTIC OCEAN

Beaufort Sea

NORTHWEST TERRITORIES

Bering Sea

Zenithal Equidistant Projection

Scale 1: 40 450 000

0     500     1000 km

**Boundaries**

international

internal

**Communications**

motorway

other major road

track

railway

canal

**Cities and towns**

■ over 1 million inhabitants

● more than 100 000 inhabitants

· smaller towns

**Physical features**

seasonal river/lake

marsh

salt pan

ice cap

**Land height**

| metres |
| 5000 |
| 3000 |
| 2000 |
| 1000 |
| 500 |
| 300 |
| 200 |
| 100 |
| sea level |

▲ spot height in metres

Transverse Mercator Projection

© Oxford University Press